August 12–16, 2012
Beijing, China

Association for
Computing Machinery

Advancing Computing as a Science & Profession

KDD'12 Vol. 1 of 2

The 18th ACM SIGKDD International Conference on

Knowledge Discovery and DataMining

Sponsored by:

KDD.org and ACM SIGMOD

Supported by:

Huawei, Baidu, Aliyun.com, Facebook, EMC2, Elsevier, PayPal of Ebay, SAS, IBM Research, Opera Solutions, Soso, SAP, Microsoft, Google, Greenplum, Nokia Research Center, Deloitte, Adobe, Media6Degrees, NSF, CityGrid.com, HP, CRC Press, Springer, Zementis, Technicolor, and Morgan & Claypool Publishers

Association for
Computing Machinery

Advancing Computing as a Science & Profession

The Association for Computing Machinery
2 Penn Plaza, Suite 701
New York, New York 10121-0701

Notice to Past Authors of ACM-Published Articles
ACM intends to create a complete electronic archive of all articles and/or other material previously published by ACM. If you have written a work that has been previously published by ACM in any journal or conference proceedings prior to 1978, or any SIG Newsletter at any time, and you do NOT want this work to appear in the ACM Digital Library, please inform permissions@acm.org, stating the title of the work, the author(s), and where and when published.

ISBN: 978-1-4503-1462-6 (Digital)

ISBN: 978-1-4503-1946-1 (Print Vol.1)

Additional copies may be ordered prepaid from:

ACM Order Department
PO Box 30777
New York, NY 10087-0777, USA

Phone: 1-800-342-6626 (USA and Canada)
+1-212-626-0500 (Global)
Fax: +1-212-944-1318
E-mail: acmhelp@acm.org
Hours of Operation: 8:30 am – 4:30 pm ET

ACM Order Number: 618122

Printed in the USA

General Chairs' Welcome Message

KDD-2012, the 18th ACM SIGKDD International Conference on Knowledge Discovery and Data Mining, is being held in Beijing, China, on August 12--16, 2012. KDD is the leading international forum for the exchange of research results and practical experience in the field of knowledge discovery and data mining. As we enter the era of Big Data, there is an increasing need to share our innovative ideas and state-of-the-art solutions on knowledge-discovery and data mining from multiple perspectives, ranging from academic research to industrial applications, from scientific discovery to health services. This volume highlights a snapshot of the developments in this rapidly developing field.

The KDD-2012 technical program features four parallel research tracks, an industrial / government track, and an industry practice expo (IPE), an Asia-pacific Track (APT) and a new KDD Summer School. The APT is specifically designed to take advantage of the fact that this KDD is held in Asia, by inviting a sample of top Asia-pacific researchers to present their data mining projects. We hope this new track will enable the KDD community to learn more on the developments in Asia-pacific region. The KDD Summer School allows students attending the conference to take advantage of availability of the many KDD experts at one location. The courses in the summer school will introduce two of the hot topics in KDD today: `Mining of Complex Data' and `Large Scale Data Mining'.

The KDD 2012 program also features keynotes from leaders of KDD research and practice, 20 workshops, 7 tutorials and one panel. The 2012 KDD Cup competition focuses on microblogging and Web search advertising problems from Tencent, China's Internet and social media giant, which also represent the largest KDD CUP data sets ever. Dozens of technical demonstrations and exhibits from vendors and other organizations underscore the conference's dual role as the leading industry and academic forum to discuss the advances in this field of research and applications.

The call for papers attracted 755 research papers and 113 industrial and government submissions from around the world. Each paper was independently reviewed by three members of the program committee for originality, significance, technical quality, and clarity of presentation. In the end, the program committee accepted 133 papers into the research track, representing an acceptance rate of 17.6%. The industry and government track of the conference accepted 30 papers into the program, representing an acceptance rate of 26.5%.

From the conference, we can see that the KDD community is continuing to be vibrant and growing, and KDD innovations remain very strong and have very high quality. The resulting program is notable for its diversity and vitality. With the exciting program as our backdrop, we certainly hope this conference will become a new starting point, where research and development on data science and data mining, and research and development on Big data analytics, will continue to flourish.

Qiang Yang
KDD2012 General Chair
HKUST, Hong Kong, China

Dou Shen
KDD2012 Associate General Chair
CityGrid Media, Seattle, WA, USA

Research Track Program Chairs' Welcome Message

The KDD conference has seen remarkable growth since its origins as an IJCAI workshop in Detroit in 1989, evolving into a full-fledged research conference in 1995, underscoring the important role data mining as a field has played in extracting knowledge and actionable insights from vast troves of data that is being generated in the digital world around us. This year we received a record 755 submissions to the research program, from which 133 papers were accepted, for an aggregate acceptance rate of 17.6% (quite similar to recent years).

Among the academic conferences, the KDD conference has typically more of an emphasis on research motivated by real-world applications. It is important to keep in mind that it is this synergy of research in areas like algorithms, computational geometry, database, graph theory, machine learning, natural language processing, statistics, visualization and many others when applied to problems arising in diverse fields such as web, medicine, climatology, marketing that drives our field forward, makes it vibrant and fun – who would know that ideas in computational geometry can be adapted to construct fast algorithms to improve online advertising and movie recommendations?

The breadth of topics covered in this year's research program is truly comprehensive, including social networks, privacy, text mining, predictive modeling, time-series forecasting, spatial data analysis, geometry, and more. We are very fortunate to have 4 world-class keynote speakers this year spanning industry and academia, providing inspirational talks on cutting-edge techniques and issues in web mining, information networks, statistical inference for big data, and social computing.

The process of whittling down the initial 734 submissions to the final set of 133 accepted papers required the coordination and time of a large number of willing volunteers. The program committee (PC) consisted of over 350 reviewers (PC members) and 50 senior PC members. In the first phase each submitted paper was automatically assigned to 3 reviewers (after a bidding process). Once the reviews from each of the 3 reviewers were completed, the program chairs rejected papers that did not receive much support from any of the reviewers. We rejected 259 papers at this stage. Special care was taken to minimize the error of rejecting a potentially good paper at this stage. The papers that survived the first phase were assigned to the senior PC members based on their bids, they had the option of initiating a discussion for any of their papers, e.g., if there was significant divergence in scores among reviewers, or if a paper was on the borderline of being accepted. Following the discussion phase, the senior PC members provided a recommendation score and a detailed meta-review for each paper. In the final phase, we (the program chairs) analyzed all of this information, starting with the obvious accept and reject decisions, and then gradually focusing in more detail on the papers near the borderline, seeking additional reviews and input from the PC and senior PC members where appropriate. We also initiated a shepherding phase with 15 papers having the opportunity of fixing mild issues we thought would be possible to address before they can be accepted. 13 of them were accepted after thorough revisions. Finally, it is quite likely that in hindsight some worthy papers may have been rejected as part of this process - these errors are an unfortunate reality of modern computer science conferences, and hard to avoid when a very large number of decisions have to be made over a short time span based on a subjective reviewing process. Nevertheless, we, the PC chairs, are responsible for those unfortunate errors and welcome suggestions on the matter.

We conclude with some well-deserved words of thanks to the large supporting cast. We thank all authors for submitting their research to KDD 2012. We are extremely grateful to the PC members and senior PC members for volunteering their time to help in the reviewing process. Diligent peer review is an essential cornerstone for research progress - we thank you all for the many detailed and conscientious reviews that were generated. Last year's program chairs, Joydeep Ghosh and Padhraic Symth, were generous in providing us with advice and expertise based on lessons learned in 2011. We would also like to convey our sincere thanks to the staff who run the Microsoft CMT system - they were more than willing to answer questions and help us at all times during the submission, reviewing, and decision process. And finally we would like to thank all of our colleagues on the KDD 2012 organization committee who were a pleasure to work with and without whom we would not have such a wonderful conference.

Let the 18th ACM SIGKDD conference begin - we hope you enjoy it!

Deepak Agarwal and Jian Pei
ACM SIGKDD 2012 Program Chairs

Asia Pacific Track Chairs' Welcome

It is our great honor to introduce the ***Asia Pacific Track*** at the 2012 ACM KDD conference. The Asia Pacific track features invited talks from leading data mining research groups located in the Asia Pacific region. We believe that this opportunity for the KDD community to hear directly from these experts will stimulate new research ideas and cross-continent collaborations.

In the last decade, universities and research laboratories in the Asia-Pacific region have made significant progress and contribution to the KDD research. Taking the advantage of the opportunity that KDD 2012 is held in Beijing, China, the conference features a new program of Asia-Pacific Track. The purpose of the Track is to promote KDD research achievements and to elevate the attention and momentum of the KDD research in this region. The program features invited speeches on KDD research results and projects in universities and industrial laboratories in this region. Recommended by a program committee consisting of Tu-Bao Ho, Jianyong Wang, Hiroshi Motoda, and Zhihua Zhou, it is our delight to invite the following 12 distinguished researchers to speak in the Asia Pacific Track.

1. Ming-Syan Chen, National Taiwan University
2. Paul Compton, University of New South Wales
3. Geoff Holmes, University of Waikato
4. Masaru Kitsuregawa, University of Tokyo
5. Cuiping Li, Renmin University
6. Deyi Li, Chinese Academy of Engineering
7. Jianzhong Li, Harbin Institute of Technology
8. Zhongzhi Shi, Chinese Academy of Sciences
9. Gordon Sun, Tencent
10. Naonori Ueda, NTT Communication Lab
11. Bo Zhang, Tsinghua University
12. Aoying Zhou, Eastern Normal University

We would like to thank all of our speakers for accepting our invitation to present their work at the KDD conference. We warmly welcome you to the Asia Pacific Track and hope that you will enjoy it.

David Cheung and Wei Wang
Asia Pacific Track Co- Chairs

Foreword to the KDD 2012 Industry Practice Expo

We warmly welcome you to the second year of the Industry Practice Expo (IPE) track at the KDD 2012 conference. The IPE features invited talks from leading experts who have developed and deployed large-scale data mining applications and systems in their respective fields that generated measurable and meaningful impact. The IPE aspires to bridge the gap between academia and industrial practice by bringing forth key trends, significant insights, and best practices. It complements the two well-established KDD tracks, Research and Industry/Government, which continue to feature the latest advances in the field via peer-reviewed publications. We trust that this opportunity for the KDD community to hear directly from industry pioneers will inspire new advances and broader inter-disciplinary collaboration between the academic researchers and their industry counterparts.

Last year's inaugural IPE was a huge success. The talks were well received and it was fascinating to hear about the numerous discussions between the speakers and attendees during the breaks. An important feedback from the attendees was that IPE should focus on technical talks and avoid talks that are purely marketing or promotional in nature. We have worked hard with our speakers for 2012 to achieve this right balance between business context and technical depth in the IPE talks.

In this year's IPE, we present to you renowned experts from around the world, from whose talks we hope will you will learn and take key ideas back to your respective professional activities. Featured topics at the IPE include large national scale projects on credit scoring and tax compliance, and real-world predictive analytics applications in decision management systems, e-commerce, semantic search, and telecommunications. Social media sites like LinkedIn, Facebook, and Twitter have taken the world by storm. We will hear about the key lessons learned in developing successful recommendation systems that power many interesting applications on these social media sites. Large-scale machine learning algorithms are an integral part of many successful data mining systems. One of the leading developers of industry strength machine learning software will share his experiences in building robust software that is now being used widely across the world. We are fortunate to have such a diverse panel of speakers be part of the IPE and would like to take this opportunity to thank them for their participation.

It has been a great pleasure to work with the IPE advisory comprising of Chid Apte, Usama Fayyad, Gregory Piatetsky-Shapiro, Ted Senator, Ramasamy Uthurusamy, Qiang Yang, and Michael Zeller. We thank them for their advice and support throughout the search for candidate speakers. We would also like to express our heartfelt gratitude to Michelle Chambers who was one of the speakers at the inaugural IPE in 2011. Michelle recommended several speakers and worked closely with us as we discussed the KDD opportunity with them.

We warmly welcome you to the KDD 2012 Industry Practice Expo and hope that you will enjoy it. Your suggestions and comments are very welcome.

Best regards,

Rajesh Parekh and Ying Li
Industry Practice Expo Track co-chairs

Foreword to the Industry & Government Track

The 2012 Industry & Government Track continued the direction that was implemented in 2010 and 2011 by clearly focusing on three areas of applied KDD work that are the sources of value to industrial and government organizations: (1) deployed applications, (2) knowledge discoveries, and (3) emerging applications. These areas build on the results of KDD research by applying the results of such research to enable the construction of novel and useful applications, the discovery of novel, interesting and useful knowledge, and the extension and application of research results to specific real world problems of interest. Papers were solicited and reviewed in these three areas:

- Deployed KDD systems that are providing real value to industry, government, or other organizations or professions. These deployed systems could support ongoing knowledge discovery or could be applications that employ discovered knowledge, or some combination of the two.
- Discoveries of knowledge with demonstrable value to industry, government, or other users (e.g., scientific or medical professionals). This knowledge must be "externally validated" as interesting and useful; it cannot simply be a model that has better performance on some traditional KDD metric such as accuracy or area under the curve.
- Emerging applications and technology that provide insight relevant to the above value propositions. These emerging applications must have clear user interest and support to distinguish them from KDD research papers, or they must provide insight into issues and factors that affect the successful use of KDD technology and methods. Papers that describe infrastructure that enables the large-scale deployment of KDD techniques also are in this area.

Industry & Government Track papers not only document and recognize significant accomplishments in these three areas, but also provide feedback to KDD researchers about needs, constraints, and applicability of KDD algorithms, methods and techniques in the real world. Our emphasis was on papers that advance the understanding of practical, applied, or pragmatic issues related to the use of KDD technologies in industry and government settings and highlight new research challenges arising from attempts to create such real KDD applications. We encouraged potential authors to address these issues and challenges in the Call for Papers and the accompanying Author Instructions http://www.kdd.org/kdd2012/author_instructions_industry.shtml

Our review process began with a validation by the reviewers that the authors correctly classified their paper's area – to ensure that the paper was reviewed according to the applicable criteria for that area – and a check that all required elements for that area were addressed in the paper. These required elements were:

- Deployed KDD case studies describe deployed projects with measurable benefits that include KDD technology. These papers must clearly describe the industry or government problem that is solved, the overall architecture of the deployed system, the data sources used, the reasons for the choices of particular KDD technologies, how KDD technologies solved the problem, the particular KDD process embodied by the deployed application, the use and payoff of the application, the costs to develop the application, the maintenance plan, and the number and types of users.
- Papers that describe discoveries of knowledge must clearly state what data sources and background knowledge were used, what data mining algorithms were tried, what overall KDD process was used, what the new discovered knowledge is, how the new knowledge was

validated, and what the value to the industry or government is of such newly discovered knowledge. Note that this category is intended for significant discoveries of domain knowledge that were enabled by KDD technologies and processes, and not for reporting of KDD research results.

- Emerging application and technology papers discuss prototype applications, tools for focused domains or tasks, useful techniques or methods, useful system architectures, scalability enablers, tool evaluations, or integration of KDD with other technologies. Such papers must clearly explain the requirements arising from the particular industry or government setting for which the application is being developed and from the particular databases on which the application is based. These papers must also identify how the emerging solution is using KDD technologies to address these requirements, the deployment plan, and the evaluation methodology and metrics for the emerging application. Pragmatic issues and considerations include important practical and research considerations, approaches, and architectures that enable successful applications. This category may include comparative evaluations of different KDD technologies for particular application problems. Preferences will be given to papers whose insights may generalize to other domains or problems. Product advertisements will not be accepted.

Specific review criteria included:

- Value/Payoff: What are the measurable benefits of the deployed application, the value of the newly discovered knowledge, or the generalizable insights from the emerging application?
- Cost: What is the cost/effort of the reported project? (To develop and maintain the application or to discover the new knowledge)
- External Significance: Is there clear evidence that the application problem being addressed and the KDD solution matters to an identified external set of users?
- External Validity: Is the knowledge discovered/used by the application externally validated? (This can be demonstrated by its use by a business, government, or profession; by publication in a peer-reviewed domain journal, or other means)
- Does the paper thoroughly describe the data sources and background knowledge used?
- Does the paper thoroughly describe the selection, use, appropriateness and effectiveness of the KDD technologies and/or data mining algorithms?
- Does the paper describe the KDD process enabled by the application or used to discover knowledge?
- Novelty/Originality: Does the work apply KDD technology to a new problem? Does it develop or apply a new type of KDD technology to an existing problem? Does it apply KDD technology to achieve a better result than with previous technology?
- Technical soundness: Does the paper show an accurate understanding of KDD research and technology? Does it identify relevant past work? Does it appropriately match techniques to problem characteristics?
- Evaluation: Is the reported work carefully evaluated? Is it statistically sound? Are the results compared to appropriate baselines? To other approaches and solutions? To previously reported work? Are its claims supported?
- Deployment/Use: Is there clear evidence that the application is deployed or on a path to deployment, or that the discovered knowledge will be used?

- Clarity: Is the paper written clearly? Is it organized logically? Are there sufficient figures and tables to illustrate its main points? Is it accessible to readers without specialized domain knowledge? Is it accessible to readers from different technical specialties and application domains?
- Does the paper contain insights or results that will generalize or apply to other domains or is it specialized to a particular domain?
- Will the paper be accessible to non-specialists in the particular domain?

Overall, the Program Committee reviewed 113 papers, representing an over 50% increase in submissions as compared to 2011 which clearly indicates the increased interest in data mining across Industry and Government. We accepted 30 papers, of which 8 describe deployed applications, 5 knowledge discoveries, and 17 emerging applications. The application areas cover a broad range, including finance, security, internet, text mining, science, public health, retail, mobile computing, and social networks, showing the many different fields to which KDD is being applied and adding value.

We hope you find these papers interesting and look forward to continued improvements in the use of KDD techniques to provide real value to industry and government.

Michael Zeller
Zementis, Inc.

Hui Xiong
Rutgers, the State University of New Jersey

KDD 2012 Industry & Government Track Program Chairs

Table of Contents

Research Session A3: Probabilistic Models

Research Session A4: Supervised Learning

Industry/Govt Track A5: Mobile Computing

Session Chair: Yu Zheng

Asia-Pacific Track A6: Session 1

Research Session B1: Social Opinions

Research Session B2: Time Series

Research Session B3: Matrices and Tensors

Research Session B4: Unsupervised Learning

Industry/Govt Track B5: Social Network Analysis

Session Chair: Amol Ghoting

Industrial Practice Expo B6: Session 1

Research Session C1: Social and Web Mining Applications

Research Session C2: Event Mining

Research Session C3: Matrix Approximation

Research Session C4: Supervised Learning with Multivariate Data

Industry/Govt Track C5: Web Applications

Session Chair: Enhong Chen

Industrial Practice Expo C6: Session 2

Research Session A1: Community Mining

Research Session A2: Sequential and Spatio-temporal Patterns

Research Session A3: Personalization and Recommendation

Research Session A4: Supervised Learning with Auxilliary Information

Industry/Govt Track A5: Computational Advertising

Session Chair: Ron Kohavi

Asia-Pacific Track A6: Session 2

Research Session B1: Review, Discussion, and Q & A

Research Session B2: Outlier and Intrusion Detection

Research Session B3: Feature Selection

Research Session B4: Nearest Neighbors

Industry/Govt Track B5: Business Intelligence

Session Chair: Sreenivas Gollapudi

Industrial Practice Expo B6: Session 3

Research Session C1: Team, Trends, and Social Profiling

Research Session C2: Privacy

Research Session C3: Supervised Learning Applications

Research Session C4: Information Extraction

Research Session A3: Recommendation

Research Session A4: Clustering

Industry/Govt Track A5: Intelligent Systems

Session Chair: Brian Dalessandro

Asia-Pacific Track A6: Session 3

Research Session B1: Keywords and Documents

Research Session B2: Patterns

Research Session B3: Spatial and Pattern Recognition

Demonstration Track

KDD 2012 Conference Organization

General Chair:	Qiang Yang *(Hong Kong University of Science and Technology)*
Honorary Conference Chairs:	Lu Ruqian *(Institute of Mathematics, CAS)* Bo Zhang *(Tsinghua University)*
Advisory Committee Chair:	Deyi Li *(Chinese Academy of Engineering)*
Program Chairs:	Deepak Agarwal *(LinkedIn)* Jian Pei *(Simon Fraser University)*
Associate General Chair:	Dou Shen *(CityGrid Media)*
Industry & Government Track Chairs:	Michael Zeller *(Zementis)* Hui Xiong *(Rutgers)*
Industry Practice Expo Chairs:	Ying Li *(Concurix Corporation)* Rajesh Parekh *(Groupon)*
Asia Pacific Track Chairs:	David Wai-Lok Cheung *(University of Hong Kong)* Wei Wang *(University of North Carolina at Chapel Hill)*
Workshop Chairs:	Zhi-Hua Zhou *(Nanjing University)* Sofus A. Macskassy *(Information Sciences Institute / USC)*
Tutorial Chairs:	Jennifer Neville *(Purdue University)* Yehuda Koren *(Google)*
Local Arrangements Chairs:	Jie Tang *(Tsinghua University)* Lei Zhang *(Web Search & Mining Group Microsoft Research Asia)* Chao Liu *(Tencent Inc.)*
Exhibit and Demo Chairs:	Tie-Yan Liu *(Microsoft Research Asia)* Jian-Tau Sun *(Machine Learning group, Microsoft Research Asia)* Natasha Balac *(University of California, San Diego)*
Industrial Liaison Chairs:	Haixun Wang *(Microsoft Research Asia)* Haifeng Wang *(Baidu)*
KDD Best Paper Awards Chairs:	Ke Wang *(Simon Fraser University)* Rich Caruana *(Microsoft Research)*
SIGKDD 2012 Awards Chair:	Ramasamy Uthurusamy *(General Motors Corp.)*

KDD Cup Chairs: Brian Dalessandro *(Media6Degrees)*
Claudia Perlich *(Media6Degrees)*
Gordon Sun *(Tencent Inc.)*
Yading Yue *(Tencent Inc.)*

KDD Summer School: Maosong Sun *(Tsinghua University)*
Du Xiaoyong *(Renmin University of China)*
Hang Li *(Microsoft Research Asia)*

Media Chairs: Ming Hua *(Facebook Inc.)*
Jianyong Wang *(Tsinghua University)*
Rayid Ghani *(Accenture Technology Labs)*
Emilia Palaveeva *(Yantra PR)*

Panel Chairs: Raghu Ramakrishnan *(Microsoft)*
Charles X. Ling *(University of Western Ontario)*

Poster Chairs: Yan Liu *(University of Southern California)*
Ping Luo *(HP Labs)*

Publications Chairs: Alexandru Niculescu-Mizil *(NEC Laboratories America)*
Jingrui He *(IBM T.J. Watson Research Center)*

Registration Chair: Xingquan Zhu *(University of Technology Sydney)*

Social Network Chairs: Ron Bekkerman *(LinkedIn)*
Qiaozhu Mei *(University of Michigan)*

Sponsorship Chairs: Balaji Krishnapuram *(Siemens Medical Solutions USA)*
Shiqiang Yang *(Tsinghua University)*
Peng Cui *(Tsinghua University)*

Student Awards Chairs: Jimeng Sun *(IBM T.J. Watson Research Center)*
Jennifer G. Dy *(Northeastern University)*

Student Volunteer Chairs: Juanzi Li *(Tsinghua University)*
Min-Ling Zhang *(Southeast University)*

Treasurer: Raymond Chi-Wing Wong *(Hong Kong University of Science and Technology)*

Video Chairs: Steven C.H. Hoi *(Nanyang Technological University)*
Shou-de Lin *(National Taiwan University)*

Web Masters: Weike Pan *(Hong Kong University of Science and Technology)*
Guang-Tong Zhou *(Simon Fraser University)*
Xiao Meng *(Simon Fraser University)*

KDD'12 Senior Program Committee Members

Naoki Abe, *IBM*
Rakesh Agrawal, *Microsoft Research*
James Bailey, *The University of Melbourne*
Soumen Chakrabarti, *IIT Mumbai*
Bee-Chung Chen, *Yahoo! Research*
Diane Cook, *Washington State University*
Ian Davidson, *University of California, Davis*
Inderjit Dhillon, *University of Texas, Austin*
Charles Elkan, *University of California, San Diego*
Martin Ester, *Simon Fraser University*
Johannes Gehrke, *Cornell University*
Lise Getoor, *University of Maryland*
Joydeep Ghosh, *University of Texas, Austin*
Bart Goethals, *University of Antwerp*
Dimitrios Gunopulos, *University of Athens*
Jiawei Han, *University of Illinois at Urbana-Champaign*
David Jensen, *University of Massachussets, Amherst*
Christopher Jermaine, *Rice University*
Benjamin Kao, *The University of Hong Kong*
George Karypis, *University of Minnesota*
Sathiya Keethi, *Yahoo!*
Eamonn Keogh, *University of California, Riverside*
Ravi Kumar, *Yahoo! Research*
Laks Lakshmanan, *The University of British Columbia*
Jure Leskovec, *Stanford University*
Hang Li, *Microsoft Research*
Michael Mahoney, *Stanford University*
Nikos Mamoulis, *The University of Hong Kong*
David Mimno, *Princeton University*
Raymond Ng, *The University of British Columbia*
Zai-qing Nie, *Microsoft Research*
Srinivasan Parthasarathy, *The Ohio State University*
Daryl Pregibon, *Google Research*
Saharon Rosset, *Tel Aviv University*
Joerg Sander, *The University of Alberta*
Sunita Sarawagi, *IIT Bombay*
Alex Smola, *Yahoo! Research*
Ramakrishnan Srikant, *Google*
Dacheng Tao, *University of Technology, Sydney*
Andrew Tomkins, *Google Research*
Suresh Venkatsubramanian, *University of Utah*
Jianyong Wang, *Tsinghua University*
Wei Wang, *University of North Carolina at Chapel*
Ji-rong Wen, *Microsoft Research*
Xifeng Yan, *University of California, Santa Barbara*
Jeffrey Yu, *The Chinese University of Hong Kong*
Philip Yu, *University of Illinois at Chicago*
Mohammed Zaki, *Rensselaer Polytechnic Institute*
Changshui Zhang, *Tsinghua University*
Zhi-Hua Zhou, *Nanjing University*

KDD'12 Research Track Program Committee

James Abello, *DIMACS/Rutgers*
Foto Afrati, *National Technical University of Athens*
Charu Aggarwal, *IBM Research-Watson*
Eugene Agichtein, *Emory University*
Christoforos Anagnostopoulos, *University of Cambridge*
Arthur Asuncion, *Google*
Sitaram Asur, *HP Research Labs*
Vassilis Athitsos, *University of Texas at Arlington*
Gustavo Batista, *University of Sao Paulo - USP*
Roberto Bayardo, *Google*
Tanya Berger-Wolf, *University of Illinois, Chicago*
Michael Berthold, *KNIME*
Kanishka Bhaduri, *NASA*
Mikhail Bilenko, *Microsoft Research*
Francesco Bonchi, *Yahoo! Research*
Gavin Brown, *University Manchester*
Deng Cai, *Zhengjian University, China*
Toon Calders, *Technische Universiteit Eindhoven*
Ricardo Campello, *University of Sao Paulo*
Ed Chang, *Google*
Jonathan Chang, *Facebook*
Kevin Chang, *University of Illinois at Urbana-Champaign*
Nitesh Chawla, *University of Notre Dame*
Sanjay Chawla, *University of Sydney*
Lei Chen, *Hong Kong University of Science and Technology*
Ming-Syan Chen, *NTU*
Weizhu Chen, *Microsoft*
Xuewen Chen, *University of Kansas*
Ye Chen, *Microsoft*
Yixin Chen, *Washington University in St Louis*
Zheng Chen, *Microsoft Research*
Zhiyuan Chen, *UMBC*
Hong Cheng, *Chinese University of Hong Kong*
James Cheng, *Nanyang Technological University*
David Cheung, *University of Hong Kong*
Wei Chu, *Microsoft*
Gao Cong, *Nanyang Technological University*
Alfredo Cuzzocrea, *University of Calabria*
Gautam Das, *University of Texas at Arlington*
Anirban Dasgupta, *Yahoo Research*
Umesh Dayal, *HP Labs*
Laura Dietz, *Max Planck Institute and University of Massachusetts Amherst*
Carlotta Domeniconi, *George Mason University*
Guozhu Dong, *Wright State University*
Zhicheng Dou, *Microsoft Research Asia*
Artur Dubrawski, *Carnegie Mellon University*
Murat Dundar, *Indiana University-Purdue University Indianapolis*
Saso Dzeroski, *Jozef Stefan Institute*
Tina Eliassi-Rad, *Rutgers University*
Andrew Fast, *Elder Research*
Ada Fu, *Chinese University of Hong Kong*
Johannes Furnkranz, *TU, Darmstadt*
Joao Gama, *University of Porto*
Jing Gao, *Univ. of Buffalo*
Rainer Gemulla, *Max-Planck Institute*
Amol Ghoting, *IBM TJ Watson Research Center*
C. Lee Giles, *Penn State University*
Aristides Gionis, *Yahoo! Research*
Aris Gkoulalas-Divanis, *IBM Research - Zurich*
Sharad Goel, *Yahoo! Research*
Michaela Goetz, *Twitter*
Rahul Gupta, *Google Research*
Qi He, *IBM Almaden Research Center*
Tin Kam Ho, *AT&T Bell Labs*
Ming Hua, *Facebook*
Jun Huan, *University of Kansas*
Jian Huang, *Google*
Jimmy Huang, *York University*
Shuiwang Ji, *Old Dominion University*
Yan Jia, *National University of Defense Technology*
Daxin Jiang, *Microsoft*
Rong Jin, *Michigan State University*
Ruoming Jin, *Kent State University*
Xiaoming Jin, *Tsinghua University*
Panos Kalnis, *KAUST*
Anitha Kannan, *Microsoft Research*
Panagiotis Karras, *Rutgers Business School*
Latifur Khan, *University of Texas at Dallas*
Daniel Kifer, *Penn State University*
Irwin King, *The Chinese University of Hong Kong*
George Kollios, *Boston University*
Nick Koudas, *University of Toronto and Sysomos Inc*
Akhil Kumar, *Penn State University*
Diane Lambert, *Google Research*

Thodoros Lappas, *Boston University*
Dongwon Lee, *Penn State University*
Hongrae Lee, *Google Research*
Mong Li Lee, *NUS*
Ronny Lempel, *Yahoo! Research*
Carson Leung, *University of Manitoba*
Guoliang Li, *Tsinghua University*
Jinyan Li, *University of Technology Sydney*
Jiuyong Li, *University of South Australia*
Lihong Li, *Yahoo! Research*
Ee Peng Lim, *Singapore Management University*
Chih Jen Lin, *National Taiwan University*
Jessica Lin, *George Mason University*
Xuemin Lin, *University of New South Wales*
Charles Ling, *University of Western Ontario*
Bing Liu, *University of Illinois at Chicago*
Chao Liu, *Microsoft Research*
Huan Liu, *Arizona State*
Jun Liu, *Siemens Corporate Research at Princeton*
Tie-Yan Liu, *Microsoft Research*
Yan Liu, *University of Southern California*
Eric Lo, *The Hong Kong Polytechnic University*
Stefano Lonardi, *University of California, Riverside*
Aurelie Lozano, *IBM Research*
Chang-Tien Lu, *Virginia Tech*
Jiebo Luo, *University of Rochester*
Shiqian Ma, *Columbia University*
Mohammad Mahdian, *Google*
Cecilia Mascolo, *University of Cambridge*
Prem Melville, *IBM TJ Watson Research Center*
Aditya Menon, *University of California, San Diego*
Donald Metzler, *University of Southern California*
George Michailidis, *University of Michigan*
Abdullah Mueen, *Microsoft Research*
S. Muthu Muthukrishnan, *Rutgers*
Olfa Nasraoui, *University of Louisville*
Jennifer Neville, *Purdue University*
David Newman, *University of California, Irvine*
Siegfried Nijssen, *Katholieke Universiteit Leuven*
Tim Oates, *University of Maryland Baltimore County*
Sandeep Pandey, *Yahoo! Research*
Spiros Papadimitriou, *IBM*
Panagiotis Papapetrou, *Aalto University*
Laurence Park, *University of Western Sydney*
Stott Parker, *UCLA*
Dino Pedreschi, *KDD Lab, University of Pisa, Italy*
Bernhard Pfahringer, *University of Waikato*
Jeff Phillips, *University of Utah*
Claudia Plant, *Florida State University*
John Platt, *Microsoft Research*
Kunal Punera, *Yahoo! Research*
Chedy Raissi, *INRIA*
Daniel Ramage, *Stanford University*
Naren Ramakrishnan, *Virginia Tech*
Louiqa Raschid, *University of Maryland*
Parisa Rashidi, *University of Florida*
Rajeev Rastogi, *Yahoo! Labs*
Chandan Reddy, *Wayne State*
Matthias Renz, *Ludwig-Maximilians-Universitat Munchen*
Matthew Richardson, *Microsoft Research*
Mirek Riedewald, *Northeastern University*
Venu Satuluri, *Ohio State University*
Thomas Seidl, *RWTH Aachen*
Sundararajan Sellamanickam, *Yahoo! Labs, Bangalore*
Jialie Shen, *Singapore Management University*
Kyuseok Shim, *Seoul National University*
Luo Si, *Purdue*
Vikas Sindhwani, *IBM Research-Watson*
Ambuj Singh, *University of California, Santa Barbara*
D. Sivakumar, *Yahoo! Research*
Myra Spiliopoulou, *Otto-von-Guericke-Universitaet Magdeburg*
Rohini Srihari, *University at Buffalo, State University of New York*
Michael Steinbach, *University of Minnesota*
Nick Street, *University of Iowa*
Jimeng Sun, *IBM TJ Watson Research Center*
Pang-Ning Tan, *Michigan State University*
Jie Tang, *Tsinghua University, China*
Yufei Tao, *Chinese University of Hong Kong*
Shirish Tatikonda, *IBM Almaden Research Center*
Manolis Terrovitis, *IMIS, Athena, Greece*
Evimaria Terzi, *Boston University*
Alex Thomo, *University of Victoria*
Hanghang Tong, *IBM Research*
Vincent Tseng, *National Cheng Kung University*
Leong Hou U, *University of Macau*
Duygu Ucar, *Stanford University*
Antti Ukkonen, *Yahoo! Research*
Lyle Ungar, *University of Pennsylvania*
Jaideep Vaidya, *Rutgers Univ.*

Hamed Valizadegan, *University of Pittsburgh*
Michalis Vlachos, *IBM Research*
Chris Volinsky, *AT&T Labs - Research*
Jilles Vreeken, *University of Antwerp, Belgium*
Haixun Wang, *Microsoft Asia*
Ke Wang, *Simon Fraser University*
Xuanhui Wang, *Yahoo! Research*
Markus Weimer, *Yahoo! Research*
Sholom Weiss, *IBM Research*
Tony Wirth, *University of Melbourne*
Ran Wolff, *University of Haifa*
Raymond Chi-Wing Wong, *Hong Kong University of Science and Technology*
Junjie Wu, *Beihang University*
Xindong Wu, *University of Vermont*
Xintao Wu, *University of North Carolina at Charlotte*
Xiaokui Xiao, *Nanyang Technological University*
Hui Xiong, *Rutgers, the State University of New Jersey*
Xiaowei Xu, *University of Arkansas at Little Rock*
Guirong Xue, *Shanghai Jiaotong University*
Kenji Yamanishi, *University of Tokyo*
Rong Yan, *Facebook*
Jieping Ye, *Arizona State University*
Mi-Yen Yeh, *Academia Sinica*
Kevin Yip, *The Chinese University of Hong Kong*
Hwanjo Yu, *Pohang University of Science and Technology*
Lei Yu, *Binghamton University*
Shipeng Yu, *Siemens Medical Solutions*
Bianca Zadrozny, *Fluminense Federal University*
Osmar Zaiane, *University of Alberta*
Carlo Zaniolo, *University of California, Los Angeles*
Hongyuan Zha, *Georgia Tech*
Aidong Zhang, *University at Buffalo*
Dell Zhang, *University of London*
Liang Zhang, *Yahoo! Research*
Nan Zhang, *George Washington University*
Zhongfei Mark Zhang, *SUNY Binghamton*
Wenjun Zhou, *University of Tennessee - Knoxville*
Xingquan Zhu, *University of Technology, Sydney*
Arthur Zimek, *Ludwig-Maximilians-Universitat Munchen*

KDD'12 Industry & Government Track Program Committee Members

KDD'12 Research Track External Reviewers

Mohammad-Ali Abbasi
Jaafar Ben Abdallah
Artur Abdullin
Zubin Abraham
Ferit Akova
Darko Aleksovski
Can Altinigneli
Saeed Amizadeh
Rajul Anand
Sam Anzaroot
Gowtham Atlure
Gowtham Atluri
Anton Bakalov
Lakshika Balasuriya
Honhji Bao
Iyad Batal
Christian Beecks
Gabriel Bender
Thomas Bernecker
Kasturi Bhattacharjee
Jinbo Bi
Hoda Bidkhori
Sam Blasiak
Brigitte Boden
Petko Bogdanov
Ivan Brugere
Fahrettin Cakir
Xin Cao
Lei Cen
Yashu Chamber
Kung-Hua Chang
Xi Chen
Chen Cheng
Si-Chi Chin
Byron Choi
Shumo Chu
Prakash Mandayam Comar
Michele Coscia
Aaron Crandall
Andrew Cron
Bruno Crémilleux
Decheng Dai
Kamalika Das
Mahashweta Das
Ritendra Datta
Elnaz Delpisheh
Sanjoy Dey
Arman Didandeh
Ivica Dimitrovski
Martin Dimkovski
Wenkui Ding
Anton Dries
Lian Duan
Denisa Duma
Narayanan Edakunni
Dora Erdos
Ines Faerber
James Faghmous
S M Faisal
Hadi Fanaee
Lujun Fang
Zheng Fang
Gang Fang
Hongliang Fei
Zhuo Feng
Jing Feng
Carlos Ferreira
Neil Fore
Sergej Fries
Glenn Fung
Stanislav Funiak
Bin Gao
Chuancong Gao
Huiji Gao
Priyanka Garg
Liang Ge
Rossetti Giulio
Rafael Giusti
Olga Gkountouna
Sebastian Goebl
Behzad Golshan
naiyang Guan
Ziyu Guan
Francesco Gullo
Pritam Gundecha
Tias Guns
Fan Guo
Chetan Gupta
Stephan Günnemann
Habiba
MohammadTaghi HajiAghayi
Yue Han
Qian Han
Hyoil Han
Elena Harris
Marwan Hassani
Basheer Hawwash
Xiao He
Di He
Jingrui He
Eric Heim
Minh Hoang
Thanh Lam Hoang
Ryan Hoens
Yuan Hong
Dzung Hong
Xia Hu
Weishu Hu
Yifan Hu
Xin Huang
Dino Ienco
Elena Ikonomovska
Allison Irvine
Anca Ivanescu
Arun Iyer
Ruoyi Jiang
Mehdi Kargar
Shiva Kasiviswanathan
Jaya Kawale
Rohan Khade
Mohammad Khoshneshin
Younghoon Kim
Woo-Cheol Kim
Hyun-Woo Kim
Steffen Kirchhoff
Arno Knobbe
Dragi Kocev
Bettina Konte
Parisa Kordjamshidi
Petr Kosina
NgaiMeng Kou
Philipp Kranen

Hardy Kremer
Georg Krempl
Peer Kröger
Da Kuang
Brian Kulis
Arjun Kumar
Shamanth Kumar
Choudur Lakshminarayan
Diane Lambert
Sean Landman
Nick Larusso
Chao-Hui Lee
Jeonghoon Lee
Victor Lee
Yuhong Lee
Matthijs Van Leeuwen
Jian Li
Ming Li
Wu-Jun Li
Nan Li
Yingming Li
Xiao Li
Fangtao Li
LongJie Li
Baichuan Li
John Liagouris
Shou-de Lin
Guang Ling
Lin Liu
Yi Liu
Haibin Liu
Sitong Liu
Lei Liu
Nathan Liu
Bo Liu
Steven Loscalzo
Grigorios Loukides
Cécile Low-Kam
Eric Hsueh-Chan Lu
Yan Luo
Kathy Macropol
Gjorgji Madjarov
Das Mahashweta
Son T. Mai
Julien Mairal
Charalampos Mavroforakis
Kyle McQuisten
Aranyak Mehta
Iñigo Mendialdua
Jun Miao
Pauli Miettinen
Iris Miliaraki
Darakhshan Mir
Seyed Mirebrahim
Varun Mithal
Samaneh Moghaddam
Anna Monreale
Gianmarco De Francisci Morales
Fred Morstatter
Vinod Nair
Abbas Nayebi
Vincenzo Nicosia
Johannes Niedermayer
Sadegh Nobari
Eirini Ntoutsi
Laurie O'Connor
Omar Odibat
Marcia Oliveira
Jeffrey Junfeng Pan
Pance Panov
Vanja Paunic
Diego Pennacchioli
Marc Plantevit
Michael Plavinski
Yevgeniy Podolyan
Anton Polishko
Miao Qiao
Tao Qin
Lu Qin
Nguyen Quang
Brian Quanz
Alain Rakotomamonjy
Sayan Ranu
Vikas Raykar
Mike Rechenthin
Rabbany K. Reihaneh
Matt Revelle
Elaine Ribeiro
Carlos Rojas
Giulio Rossetti
Senjuti Basu Roy
Yiye Ruan
Brian Ruttenberg
Senay Yasar Saglam
Tanwistha Saha
Ankan Saha
Shaghayegh Sahebi
Esin Saka
Hamman Samuel
Thomas Sandholm
Cicero Nogueira dos Santos
Tamas Sarlos
Christoph Sawade
Hassan Sayyadi
James Schaffer
Leander Schietgat
Johannes Schneider
Erich Schubert
Matthias Schubert
Yu-Keng Shih
Diego Furtado Silva
Michael Simpson
Ayush Singhal
Nick Skapura
Ivica Slavkov
Yangqiu Song
Vinicius Mourao Alves de Souza
Sargur Srihari
Daniela Stojanova
Ja-Hwung Su
Amarnag Subramanya
Fabian Suchanek
Aixin Sun
Khaled Ahsan Talukder
Syed K. Tanbeer
Jiliang Tang
Chayant Tantipathananandh
Vahid Taslimi
Maryam Tavafi
Yasushi Terazonc
Saravanan Thirumuruganathan
Brian Thompson
Ryota Tomioka
Aneta Trajanov
Roberto Trasarti
Pucktada Treeratpituk
Honglei Tu
Vladimir Vacic
Thanasis Vergoulis
Davide Verzotto
Krishnamurthy Viswanathan

Peter Wackersreuther
Jiannan Wang
Qifan Wang
Taifeng Wang
Wenjun Wang
Wen Wang
Ye Wang
Xufei Wang
Jia Wang
Guan Wang
Robert Wright
Huanhuan Wu
Shanchan Wu
Leting Wu
shiming Xiang
Guang Xiang
Chenyan Xiong
Yi Xu
Zhiqiang Xu
Jianpeng Xu
Hui Yan
Haiqin Yang
Tao Yang
Sen Yang
Jaewon Yang
Ming Yang
Yiyang Yang
Chen Yang
Wen Yao
Jihang Ye
Zheng Ye
Beta Chi-Lap Yip
Man Lung Yiu
Shengkang Yu
Xiaofeng Yu
Guoxian Yu
Yintao Yu
Xiao Yu
Jun ZHANG
Zhihua ZHang
Reza Zafarani
Jesin Zakaria
Bernard Zenko
Mingyang Zhang
Yuchen Zhang
Zhihua Zhang
Yang Zhang
Wenjie Zhang
Peng Zhang
Chenyi Zhang
Min-Ling Zhang
Jiashu Zhao
Xueyi Zhao
Kang Zhao
Chao Zhou
Qin Zhou
Zhuojie Zhou
Ke Zhou
Zhe Zhu
Morteza Zihayat
Max Zimmermann
Albrecht Zimmermann
Bo Zong
Haitao Zou
Andreas Züfle

ACM SIGKDD KDD 2012 Sponsors & Supporters

Sponsors:

Supporters

Nine Real Hard Problems We'd Like You to Solve

(Abstract)

Robin Li
Baidu, Inc.
Beijing, China

1. INTRODUCTION

Since 2000, Baidu has set its mission as providing the best way for people to find what they're looking for. Today, the company has become the world's largest Chinese search engine. Everyday, we process billions of search queries and serve hundreds of millions of internet users. The huge volume of online text and multimedia content, as well as user log data, provide us unprecedented opportunities and challenges for further accomplishing our mission. In addition, we have seen several megatrends, cloud computing is becoming a pervasive service infrastructure, mobile internet will surpass traditional internet in user time spend, and social platform has demonstrated its great power. In response to all these opportunities, challenges, and megatrends, we must think ahead on the major technology focuses that may help Baidu to serve our users better. In this talk, I would like to share with the audience the nine areas that are the most important and interesting in my mind. For each of the areas, I will describe the challenges and explain why it is important and interesting. I hope the research community can get excited, and help us provide better services for users.

Categories and Subject Descriptors

H.4.m [**Information Systems**]: Information Systems Applications—*Miscellaneous*

Keywords

search engine, baidu

2. BIO

Robin Li is the co-founder, chairman and chief executive officer of Baidu, Inc., and oversees the company's overall strategy and business operations.

Since co-founding the company in January 2000, Robin has grown Baidu into the largest Chinese search engine. Baidu now has over 75% market share in search in China, and ranks as the third largest independent search engine in the world. In 2005, Baidu completed a successful IPO on NASDAQ, and in 2007 became the first Chinese company to be included in the NASDAQ-100 Index. Today, Baidu is among the most valuable brands in China. The Financial Times named Baidu one of the "Top 10 Chinese Global Brands", making it the youngest and only Internet company on the list.

Robin Li was named "China Economic Figure of the Year 2005" by CCTV and one of "China's Most Powerful Entrepreneurial Thought Leaders" by China Entrepreneurs Forum. He was also named one of the "Best Business Leaders in the World" by Business Week Magazine and one of the "Most Influential Chinese Business Leaders" by Fortune Magazine. In 2010, Robin Li was named by both Forbes and Times magazine as one of the "Most Influential People in the World".

Robin received a Bachelor of Science Degree in Information Management from Peking University in 1991, and a Master of Science Degree in Computer Science from the State University of New York at Buffalo in 1994.

KDD'12, August 12–16, 2012, Beijing, China.
ACM 978-1-4503-1462-6 /12/08.

Mining Heterogeneous Information Networks: The Next Frontier

(Abstract)

Jiawei Han
Department of Computer Science
University of Illinois at Urbana-Champaign
Urbana, IL 61801, U.S.A.
hanj@cs.uiuc.edu

1. INTRODUCTION

Real world physical and abstract data objects are interconnected, forming gigantic, interconnected networks. By structuring these data objects into multiple types, such networks become *semi-structured heterogeneous information networks*. Most real world applications that handle big data, including interconnected social media and social networks, scientific, engineering, or medical information systems, online e-commerce systems, and most database systems, can be structured into heterogeneous information networks. For example, in a medical care network, objects of multiple types, such as patients, doctors, diseases, medication, and links such as visits, diagnosis, and treatments are intertwined together, providing rich information and forming heterogeneous information networks. Effective analysis of large-scale heterogeneous information networks poses an interesting but critical challenge.

In this talk, we present a set of data mining scenarios in heterogeneous information networks and show that mining heterogeneous information networks is a new and promising research frontier in data mining research. Departing from many existing network models that view data as homogeneous graphs or networks, the semi-structured heterogeneous information network model leverages the rich semantics of typed nodes and links in a network and can uncover surprisingly rich knowledge from interconnected data. This heterogeneous network modeling will lead to the discovery of a set of new principles and methodologies for mining interconnected data. The examples to be used in this discussion include (1) meta path-based similarity search, (2) rank-based clustering, (3) rank-based classification, (4) meta path-based link/relationship prediction, (5) relation strength-aware mining, as well as a few other recent developments. We will also point out some promising research directions and provide convincing arguments on that mining heterogeneous information networks is the next frontier in data mining.

Categories and Subject Descriptors

I.2 [**Computing Methodologies**]: Artificial Intelligence

KDD'12, August 12–16, 2012, Beijing, China.
ACM 978-1-4503-1462-6 /12/08.

Keywords

heterogeneous information networks, data mining

2. BIO

Jiawei Han is Abel Bliss Professor in Engineering, in the Department of Computer Science at the University of Illinois. He has been researching into data mining, information network analysis, and database systems, with over 600 publications.

He served as the founding Editor-in-Chief of ACM Transactions on Knowledge Discovery from Data (TKDD) and on the editorial boards of several other journals. Jiawei has received ACM SIGKDD Innovation Award (2004), IEEE Computer Society Technical Achievement Award (2005), and IEEE Computer Society W. Wallace McDowell Award (2009), and Daniel C. Drucker Eminent Faculty Award (2011). He is a Fellow of ACM and IEEE. He is currently the Director of Information Network Academic Research Center (INARC) supported by the Network Science-Collaborative Technology Alliance (NS-CTA) program of U.S. Army Research Lab. His book with Micheline Kamber and Jian Pei, "Data Mining: Concepts and Techniques" (Morgan Kaufmann) has been used worldwide as a textbook.

Acknowledgments

Our work has been supported in part by the U.S. Army Research Laboratory under Cooperative Agreement No. W911NF-09-2-0053 (NS-CTA), U.S. National Science Foundation grants IIS-0905215, CNS-0931975, CCF-0905014, and IIS-1017362, U.S. Air Force Office of Scientific Research MURI award FA9550-08-1-0265, and MIAS, a DHS-IDS Center for Multimodal Information Access and Synthesis at UIUC. The views and conclusions contained in this paper are those of the authors and should not be interpreted as representing any funding agencies.

3. REFERENCES

[1] M. Ji, J. Han, and M. Danilevsky. Ranking-based classification of heterogeneous information networks. In *KDD'11*, San Diego, CA, Aug. 2011.

[2] M. Ji, Y. Sun, M. Danilevsky, J. Han, and J. Gao. Graph regularized transductive classification on heterogeneous information networks. In *ECMLPKDD'10*, Barcelona, Spain, Sept. 2010.

[3] Y. Sun, C. C. Aggarwal, and J. Han. Relation strength-aware clustering of heterogeneous information

networks with incomplete attributes. *PVLDB*, 5:394–405, 2012.

[4] Y. Sun, R. Barber, M. Gupta, C. Aggarwal, and J. Han. Co-author relationship prediction in heterogeneous bibliographic networks. In *ASONAM'11*, Kaohsiung, Taiwan, July 2011.

[5] Y. Sun and J. Han. *Mining Heterogeneous Information Networks: Principles and Methodologies.* Morgan & Claypool Publishers, 2012.

[6] Y. Sun, J. Han, X. Yan, P. S. Yu, and T. Wu. PathSim: Meta path-based top-k similarity search in heterogeneous information networks. In *VLDB'11*, Seattle, WA, Aug. 2011.

[7] Y. Sun, J. Han, P. Zhao, Z. Yin, H. Cheng, and T. Wu. RankClus: Integrating clustering with ranking for heterogeneous information network analysis. In *EDBT'09*, Saint-Petersburg, Russia, Mar. 2009.

[8] Y. Sun, Y. Yu, and J. Han. Ranking-based clustering of heterogeneous information networks with star network schema. In *KDD'09*, Paris, France, June 2009.

[9] C. Wang, J. Han, Y. Jia, J. Tang, D. Zhang, Y. Yu, and J. Guo. Mining advisor-advisee relationships from research publication networks. In *KDD'10*, Washington D.C., July 2010.

Divide-and-Conquer and Statistical Inference for Big Data

(Abstract)

Michael I. Jordan
Department of EECS
Department of Statistics
University of California, Berkeley

1. INTRODUCTION

I present some recent work on statistical inference for Big Data. Divide-and-conquer is a natural computational paradigm for approaching Big Data problems, particularly given recent developments in distributed and parallel computing, but some interesting challenges arise when applying divide-and-conquer algorithms to statistical inference problems. One interesting issue is that of obtaining confidence intervals in massive datasets.

The bootstrap principle suggests resampling data to obtain fluctuations in the values of estimators, and thereby confidence intervals, but this is infeasible with massive data. Subsampling the data yields fluctuations on the wrong scale, which have to be corrected to provide calibrated statistical inferences. I present a new procedure, the "bag of little bootstraps," which circumvents this problem, inheriting the favorable theoretical properties of the bootstrap but also having a much more favorable computational profile. Another issue that I discuss is the problem of large-scale matrix completion. Here divide-and-conquer is a natural heuristic that works well in practice, but new theoretical problems arise when attempting to characterize the statistical performance of divide-and-conquer algorithms. Here the theoretical support is provided by concentration theorems for random matrices, and I present a new approach to this problem based on Stein's method.[1]

Categories and Subject Descriptors

I.2 [**Computing Methodologies**]: Artificial Intelligence

Keywords

big data, divide-and-conquer, confidence intervals, subsampling

2. BIO

Michael I. Jordan is the Pehong Chen Distinguished Professor in the Department of Electrical Engineering and Computer Science and the Department of Statistics at the University of California, Berkeley. He received his Masters in Mathematics from Arizona State University, and earned his PhD in Cognitive Science in 1985 from the University of California, San Diego. He was a professor at MIT from 1988 to 1998. His research in recent years has focused on Bayesian nonparametric analysis, probabilistic graphical models, spectral methods, variational methods, kernel machines and applications to problems in statistical genetics, signal processing, computational biology, information retrieval and natural language processing.

Prof. Jordan is a member of the National Academy of Sciences, a member of the National Academy of Engineering and a member of the American Academy of Arts and Sciences. He is a Fellow of the American Association for the Advancement of Science. He has been named a Neyman Lecturer and a Medallion Lecturer by the Institute of Mathematical Statistics. He is a Fellow of the ACM, the CSS, the IMS, the IEEE, the AAAI and the ASA.

[1]Joint work with Ariel Kleiner, Lester Mackey, Purna Sarkar, Ameet Talwalkar, Richard Chen, Brendan Farrell and Joel Tropp

KDD'12, August 12–16, 2012, Beijing, China.
ACM 978-1-4503-1462-6 /12/08.

Experiments in Social Computation (and the Data They Generate)

(Abstract)

Michael Kearns
Department of Computer and Information Science
University of Pennsylvania

1. INTRODUCTION

For a number of years we have been conducting controlled human-subject experiments in distributed social computation in networks with only limited and local communication. These experiments cast a number of traditional computational, economic and sociological problems (including graph coloring, consensus, independent set, networked bargaining, biased voting and network formation) as games of strategic interaction in which subjects have financial incentives to collectively "compute" global solutions. I will overview and summarize the many behavioral findings from this line of experimentation. I will give particular emphasis to the novel data the experiments have generated, and the analyses this data has permitted, including quantitative studies of subject "personality" traits such as stubbornness, altruism, and patience, and whether those traits seem helpful or harmful to individual and collective performance.

Categories and Subject Descriptors

J.4 [**Computer Applications**]: Social and Behavioral Sciences

Keywords

social network, experiments

2. BIO

Michael Kearns is a professor in the Computer and Information Science Department at the University of Pennsylvania, where he hold the National Center Chair in Resource Management and Technology. He received a Ph.D. in computer science from Harvard University in 1989. Following postdoctoral positions at the Laboratory for Computer Science at MIT and at the International Computer Science Institute (ICSI) in Berkeley, in 1991 he joined the research staff of AT&T Bell Labs, and later in 2002 the Penn faculty.

His research interests include topics in machine learning, algorithmic game theory, social networks, computational finance, and artificial intelligence. He often examines problems in these areas using methods and models from theoretical computer science and related disciplines. While the majority of his work is mathematical in nature, he has also participated in a variety of empirical and experimental projects, including applications of machine learning to finance, spoken dialogue systems, and other areas. Most recently, he has been conducting human-subject experiments on strategic and economic interaction in social networks.

KDD'12, August 12–16, 2012, Beijing, China.
ACM 978-1-4503-1462-6 /12/08.

Rise and Fall Patterns of Information Diffusion: Model and Implications

Yasuko Matsubara
Kyoto University
y.matsubara@
db.soc.i.kyoto-u.ac.jp

Yasushi Sakurai
NTT Communication
Science Labs
yasushi.sakurai@acm.org

B. Aditya Prakash
Carnegie Mellon University
badityap@cs.cmu.edu

Lei Li
University of California, Berkeley
leili@cs.berkeley.edu

Christos Faloutsos
Carnegie Mellon University
christos@cs.cmu.edu

ABSTRACT

The recent explosion in the adoption of search engines and new media such as blogs and Twitter have facilitated faster propagation of news and rumors. How quickly does a piece of news spread over these media? How does its popularity diminish over time? Does the rising and falling pattern follow a simple universal law?

In this paper, we propose SPIKEM, a concise yet flexible analytical model for the rise and fall patterns of influence propagation. Our model has the following advantages: (a) unification power: it generalizes and explains earlier theoretical models and empirical observations; (b) practicality: it matches the observed behavior of diverse sets of real data; (c) parsimony: it requires only a handful of parameters; and (d) usefulness: it enables further analytics tasks such as forecasting, spotting anomalies, and interpretation by reverse-engineering the system parameters of interest (e.g. quality of news, count of interested bloggers, etc.).

Using SPIKEM, we analyzed 7.2GB of real data, most of which were collected from the public domain. We have shown that our SPIKEM model accurately and succinctly describes all the patterns of the rise-and-fall spikes in these real datasets.

Categories and Subject Descriptors: H.2.8 [**Database management**]: Database applications–*Data mining*

General Terms: Algorithms, Experimentation, Theory

Keywords: Information diffusion, Social networks

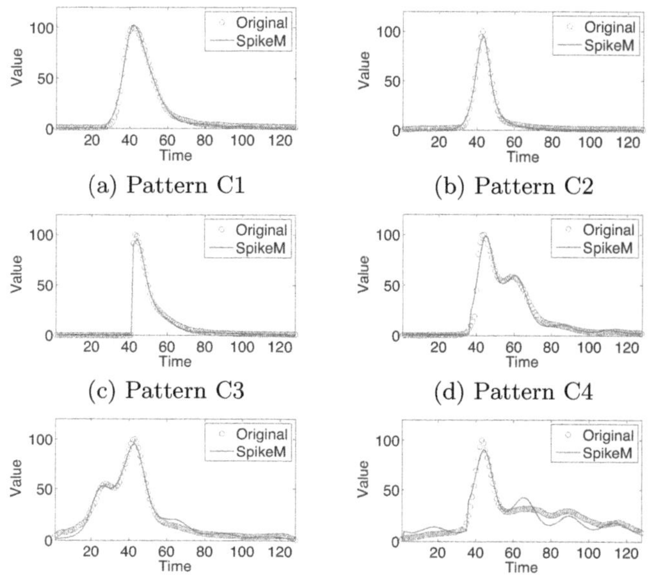

(a) Pattern C1 (b) Pattern C2 (c) Pattern C3 (d) Pattern C4 (e) Pattern C5 (f) Pattern C6

Figure 1: Modeling power of SpikeM: six types of spikes (K-SC from [41]) shown as dots, and our model fit in solid red line. Data sequences span over 120 time-ticks, while SpikeM requires only seven parameters. The fit is so good, that the red line is often invisible, due to occlusion.

1. INTRODUCTION

How do spikes behave in social media? Online social media is spreading news and rumors in new ways and search engines have facilitated such spreading magnificently, creating bursts and spikes. Some rumors (or memes, hashtags) start slowly and linger; others spike early and then decay; others show more complicated behavior, as we show in Figure 1.

Do real rise-and-fall patterns have any qualitative differences? Do they form different classes? If yes, how many? Earlier work on Youtube data claims there are four classes [6]. Empirical work found six classes [41]. How many classes are there after all?

Our answer is: *one.* We provide a unifying model, SPIKEM, that requires only a handful of parameters, and we show that it can generate all patterns found in real data simply by changing the parameter values.

Figure 1 shows six representative spikes of online media (memes) from K-SC [41], as gray circles, as well as our fitted model, as a solid red line. Notice that the fitting is very

KDD'12, August 12–16, 2012, Beijing, China.

	C-S	K-SC	SI	AR	SpikeM
System identification			√		√
Non-linear			√		√
Power law decay	√				√
Periodicity				√	√
Forecasting				√	√

Table 1: Capabilities of approaches. Only our approach meets all specs.

good, despite the fact that our SpikeM model requires only seven parameters, and that the time-sequences span 120 intervals.

Informally, the problem we want to solve is to model/predict an activity (e.g., number of blog postings), as a function of time, given some breaking-news at a given timetick. We will use a blogger example for brevity and clarity, but many other processes could be also modeled (people buying products, computer viruses infecting machines, rumors spreading over Twitter, etc). Thus, we have:

Informal Problem 1 (what-if). **Given** *a network of bloggers (/hosts/buyers), a shock (e.g., event) at time n_b, the interest/quality of the event, the count S_b of bloggers that immediately (= time n_b) blog about the event,* **find** *how the blogging activity will evolve over time.*

A closely related problem is to develop a parsimonious model, that can be made to fit several spikes observed in the past (as we do in Figure 1). That is,

Informal Problem 2 (model design). **Given** *the behavior of several spikes in the past,* **find** *an equation/model that can explain them, with as few parameters as possible.*

It would be good if the parameters had an intuitive explanation (like, 'number of bloggers', 'quality of news', etc, as opposed to, say, a_1, a_2 of an autoregressive model (AR/ARIMA)).

In this paper, we propose SpikeM model to solve both of the aforementioned problems. Our SpikeM has the following advantages:

- **Unification power**: it includes earlier patterns and models as special cases ([41, 21]),
- **Practicality**: it matches the behavior of numerous, diverse, real datasets, including power-law decay
- **Parsimony**: our model requires only a handful of parameters
- **Usefulness**: thanks to the SpikeM model, we can answer 'what-if' questions (see subsection 5.1), spot outliers, reverse-engineer the system parameters (quality of news, count of interested bloggers, time-of-day behavior of bloggers)

Our SpikeM model is enabled by a careful design to incorporate (a) the power-law decay in infectivity, (b) a finite population, and (c) proper periodicities. Earlier models ignored one or more of the above issues.

Thanks to the *practicality* of SpikeM, we can make forecasting, analysis of 'what-if' scenarios, and detection of anomalies, as we show in section 4 and section 5. We should highlight that traditional AR, ARIMA and related linear models are fundamentally unsuitable, because they are *linear* (and can diverge to infinity) and because they lead to exponential decays (as opposed to the power law that reality seems to obey). Table 1 illustrates the relative advantages of our method: the C-S method (Crane and Sornette) [6] assumes an infinite population of bloggers; the clusters in K-SC [41] (repeated in Figure 1) are non-parametric and are incapable of forecasting. The SI model (closely related to the Bass model [3] of the market penetration of new products) leads to exponential decay, as opposed to the power-law decay that we observe in real data.

Outline. The rest of the paper goes as follows: Section 2 presents an overview of the related work and Section 3 the proposed model. Sections 4 and 5 show our experimental results on a variety of datasets. We conclude in section 7.

2. BACKGROUND

In this section, we present the fundamental concepts.

Epidemiology fundamentals. The most basic epidemic model is the so-called 'Susceptible-Infected' (SI) model. Each object/node is in one of two states - Susceptible (S) or Infected (I). Each infected node attempts to infect each of its neighbors independently with probability β, which reflects the strength of the virus. Once infected, each node stays infected forever. If we assume that the underlying network is a clique of N nodes, and use our notation ('B' for blogged = infected) the most basic form of the model is:

$$\frac{dB(t)}{dt} = \beta * (N - B(t)) B(t) \quad (1)$$

where the time t is considered continuous, dB/dt is the derivative, and the initial condition reflects the external shock (say, $B(0) = b$ externally infected people). The justification is as follows: β is the strength of the virus, that is, the probability that an encounter between an infected person ('B') and an uninfected one, will end up in an infection - and we have $B * (N - B)$ such encounters. The solution for $B()$ is the sigmoid, and its derivative is symmetric around the peak, with an exponential rise and an exponential fall (we discuss later in Figure 2). There we also show the weakness of the SI model: real data have a power-law 'fall' pattern.

Self-excited Hawkes process. Crane et al. [6] used a self-excited Hawkes conditional Poisson process [12] to model YouTube views per day, showing that spikes in the activity have a power-law rise pattern, and a power-law fall pattern, depending on the model parameters. Roughly, the Hawkes process is a Poisson process where the instantaneous rate is not constant, but depends on the count of previous events, whose effect drops with the age τ of the event. That is, if there were a lot of events (viewings/bloggings) recently, we will have many such events today.

The base model states that the rate of spread of infection depends on (a) the external source $S(t)$ and (b) self-excitation, that is, on earlier-infected nodes ($i = 1, \ldots$); these nodes spread the infection with decaying virus strength $\phi(\tau)$, their age τ grows, times some constant μ_i. The constant μ_i is equivalent to the degree of the infected node i.

$$\frac{dB(t)}{dt} = S(t) + \sum_{i,t_i \le t} \mu_i \phi(t - t_i) \quad (2)$$

The model typically assumes that the μ_i values are equal, namely that all nodes have the same degree ('homogeneous' graph). It also silently assumes that there are infinite nodes available for infection, and it may actually diverge to infinity.

Next we present our SpikeM model, which avoids the shortcomings of the SI and Hawkes models, and has several more desirable properties.

3. PROPOSED METHOD

In this section we present our proposed method, analyze it, and we provide the reader with several interesting -at least in our opinion- observations.

Our model tries to capture the following behaviors, that we observed with several of our real data

- P1: power-law fall pattern
- P2: periodicities

and at the same time we want to

- P3: avoid the divergence to infinity

that other models may have. To handle P3 (divergence), we force our model to have a finite population, and adjust the equations accordingly. To handle P1 (power-law fall pattern), we assume that the infectivity of a node (= popularity of a blog post) decays with the INFLUENCE EXPONENT, which we set at -1.5. The handling of periodicities is discussed in subsection 3.2.

We describe our model in steps, adding complexity, and we start with the base model.

Preliminaries. We assume there are N bloggers, and none of them is yet blogging about the topic of interest. At time n_b, an event happens (such as the 2004 Indonesian tsunami, or a controversial political speech such as 'lipstick on a pig'), and S_b bloggers immediately blog about it. We refer to this external event as a *shock*, and n_b and S_b are the birth-time and the initial magnitude of the shock.

Our model needs a few more parameters: the first is the quality/interestingness of the news, which we refer to as β, since this is the standard symbol for the infectivity of a virus in epidemiology literature. If β is zero, nobody cares about this specific piece of news; the higher the value, the more bloggers will blog about it.

Finally, we have the decay function $f(n)$, which models how infective/influential a blog posting is, at age n. Standard epidemiology models assume that $f()$ is constant (once sick, you have the same probability of infecting others); recent analysis has shown that the influence drops with age, following a power law.

The above are the parameters of the base model. Before we list the equations, we want to briefly mention a derived quantity, $\beta * N$; this quantity roughly corresponds to the R_0 ('R-naught') found in the epidemiology literature. This tells us the size of the "first burst": if only one person was infected, how many would be infected in the next time-tick?[1]

In summary, the scenario we model is as follows:

- nothing happens, until a news-event appears, at birth-time n_b.
- S_b bloggers immediately blog about it.
- other bloggers visit the initial S_b (or follow-up) bloggers, and occasionally get 'infected' and blog about the event, too.

We also assume that

- each blogger blogs at most once about the event
- no other related event occurs - that is, the shock function $S()$ has only one spike.

[1]yes, it should be $N-1$, but we sacrifice accuracy, for intuition.

Without loss of generality, we also assume that once an uninformed blogger sees an infected/informed blog, he/she always blogs about the event (if he/she blogs with probability $\rho < 1$, we could absorb ρ in the infectivity factor β)

Our goal is to find an equation to describe the number $\Delta B(n)$ of people blogging at time-tick n, as a function of n and of course the system parameters (total number of bloggers N, strength of infection β etc).

3.1 Base model - SPIKEM-BASE

The model we propose has nodes (=bloggers) of two states:

- U: **U**n-informed of the rumor
- B: informed, and **B**logged about it

For those who just got informed at time-tick n, we'll use the symbol $\Delta B(n)$, and we assume that, once informed, a person will blog about the rumor immediately.

Let $U(n)$ be the number of un-informed people at time n, and let $\Delta B(n)$ the number of people that just found out about the rumor at time n, and blogged immediately about it.

MODEL 1 (SPIKEM-BASE). *Our base model is governed by the equations*

$$\Delta B(n+1) = U(n) \cdot \sum_{t=n_b}^{n} \left(\Delta B(t) + S(t)\right) \cdot f(n+1-t) + \epsilon \tag{3}$$

$$U(n+1) = U(n) - \Delta B(n+1) \tag{4}$$

where

$$f(\tau) = \beta * \tau^{-1.5} \tag{5}$$

and initial conditions:

$$\Delta B(0) = 0, \quad U(0) = N$$

In addition, we add an external shock $S(n)$, a spike generated at birth-time n_b. Mathematically, it is defined as follows:

$$S(n) = \begin{cases} 0 & (n \neq n_b) \\ S_b & (n = n_b) \end{cases} \tag{6}$$

Justification of the model. We do it in steps:

- The term $\Delta B(t) + S(t)$ captures the count of bloggers plus external sources, that got activated at time-tick t; their infectivity is modulated by the $f()$ infectivity function, since we assume that the infectivity of a source/blogger decays with time. The summation is over all past time-ticks since the birth-time n_b of the shock.
- The infectivity function $f()$ exactly follows a power law with exponent -1.5 as discovered by earlier work on read data: real bloggers [22], and response to mails by Einstein and Darwin [2].
- The meaning of the summation is the available stimuli at time-tick n; the available targets are the uninformed bloggers $U(n)$, and the product gives the number of new infections.
- We add a noise term ϵ to handle cases such as hashtag 'egypt' on Twitter: some people tweet about Egypt anyway, but a large shock occurred during the events in Tahrir square. Very often, $\epsilon \simeq 0$.

Symbol	Definition
N	total population of available bloggers
n_d	duration of sequence
n	time-tick ($n = 0, \ldots, n_d$)
$U(n)$	count of un-informed bloggers
$B(n)$	count of informed bloggers
$\Delta B(n)$	delta: count of informed bloggers at exactly time n
$f(n)$	infectiveness of a blog-post, at age n
β	strength of infection
$\beta * N$	"first-burst" size of infection
$S(n)$	volume of external shock at time n
n_b	starting time of breaking news
S_b	strength of external shock at birth (time n_b)
ϵ	background noise
P_a	strength of periodicity
P_p	period
P_s	phase shift of periodicity

Table 2: Symbols and definitions

This completes the justification of our base model.

We also mention some facts that our model obeys: by definition

$$B(n) = \sum_{t=0}^{n} \Delta B(t)$$

and of course we have the invariant

$$B(n) + U(n) = N$$

where N is the total number of people/bloggers.

3.2 With periodicity - SpikeM

Bloggers may modulate their activity following a daily cycle (or weekly, or yearly). For example, among the $U(n)$ uninformed bloggers at time n, a fraction of them are not paying attention (say, because they are tired or asleep). How can we reflect this in our equations? We propose an answer below, and then we provide the justification.

Model 2 (SpikeM). *We can capture the periodic behavior of bloggers with the following equations:*

$$\Delta B(n+1) = p(n+1) \cdot \left(U(n) \cdot \sum_{t=n_b}^{n} (\Delta B(t) + S(t)) \cdot f(n+1-t) + \epsilon\right) \quad (7)$$

$$p(n) = 1 - \tfrac{1}{2} P_a \left(sin\left(\tfrac{2\pi}{P_p}(n + P_s)\right) + 1\right) \quad (8)$$

where $U(n)$, $S(t)$ and $f(n)$ are defined in Model 1.

Justification. The model is identical to SpikeM-base, with the addition of the periodicity factor $p(\cdot)$. This captures the fact that bloggers tone down their activity, say, during the night, or even stop it altogether. The idea is that $U(\cdot)$ is the count of victims available for infection, and the summation is the number of attacks. Under normal circumstances, each victim-attack pair would lead to a new victim; however, since the victims are not paying full attention (tired/asleep), the attacks are not so successful, and thus we prorate them by the $p()$ periodic function.

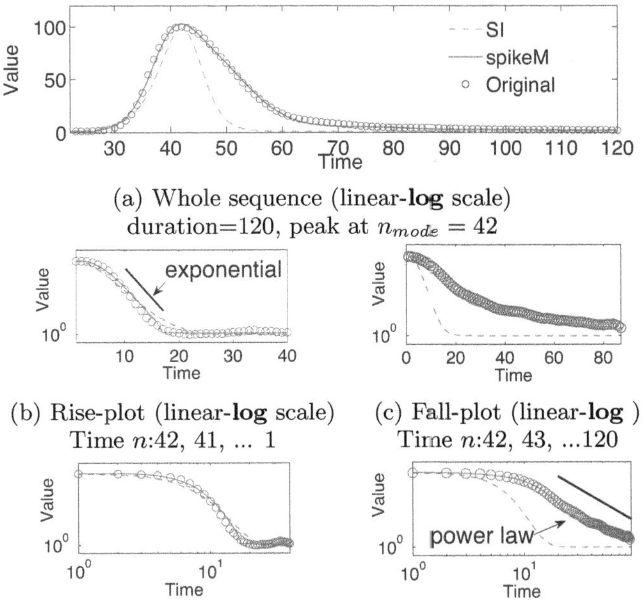

(a) Whole sequence (linear-**log** scale) duration=120, peak at $n_{mode} = 42$

(b) Rise-plot (linear-**log** scale) Time n:42, 41, ... 1

(c) Fall-plot (linear-**log**) Time n:42, 43, ...120

(d) Rise-plot (**log-log** scale) Time n:42, 41, ... 1

(e) Fall-plot (**log-log**) Time n:42, 43, ...120

Figure 2: Fitting results of SpikeM vs. SI for pattern C1 in Figure 1. The original sequence (in gray circles), and our model (red line) have an exponential rise and a power-law drop; the SI model (blue dashed line) is exponential on both and thus unrealistic. Top row: full interval; left column: only the rise part; right column: only the 'fall' part.

- P_p stands for the period of the cycle (say, 24 hours).
- P_s stands for the phase shift: if the peak activity is at noon, and the period is P_p=24 hours, then P_s=18.
- P_a depends on the amplitude of the fluctuation, and specifically it gives the relative value of the off-time (say, midnight), versus peak time (say, noon). Thus, if P_a=0, we have no fluctuation.

3.3 Additional details

Model extensions. We could easily extend our model so that it has several shocks as opposed to just one as considered here. We could also extend it to have multiple cycles (daily, weekly, yearly). We do not elaborate on these extensions for two reasons: (a) for clarity and (b) because the current model fits real data very well, anyway.

Learning the parameters. Our model consists of a set of seven parameters: $\boldsymbol{\theta} = \{N, \beta, n_b, S_b, \epsilon, P_a, P_s\}$. Given a real time sequence $X(n)$ of bloggers at time-tick n ($n = 1, \ldots, n_d$), we use *Levenberg-Marquardt (LM)* [23] to minimize the sum of the errors: $D(X, \boldsymbol{\theta}) = \sum_{n=1}^{n_d}(X(n) - \Delta B(n))^2$.

Analysis - exponential rise, power-law fall. It is not obvious from the equations of our model, but its rise pattern is exponential, while the fall pattern obeys a power law. This is desirable, because this behavior seem to be prevailing in real data, as we show in Figure 2. Let n_{mode} denote the time-tick at which the waveΔ $B()$ reached its maximum volume. By *rise plot* we mean the plot of values from the birth-time n_b until n_{mode} (and reversing time $abs(n - n_{mode})$) The *fall-plot* is defined similarly: activity $\Delta B()$ versus delay from the peak $n - n_{mode}$. Notice that there is a power law for the fall, and an exponential shape for the rise. We also show the traditional 'SI' model, which, as expected, exhibits exponential behavior for both rise and fall.

4. EXPERIMENTS

To evaluate the effectiveness of SpikeM, we carried out experiments on real datasets. The experiments were designed to answer the following questions:

- Q1: Can we explain the cluster centers of K-SC?
- Q2: How well do we match *MemeTracker* data?
- Q3: How does it compare with other data?
- Q4: How well do we forecast future patterns?

Dataset description. We performed experiments on the following three real datasets.

- *MemeTracker*: This dataset covers three months of blog activity from August 1 to October 31 2008[2], It contains short quoted textual phrases ("memes"), each of which consists of the number of mentions over time. We choose 1,000 phrases in blogs with the highest volume in a 7-day window around their peak volume.
- *Twitter*: We used more than 7 million Twitter[3] posts covering an 8-month period from June 2011 to January 2012. We selected the 10,000 most frequently used hashtags.
- *GoogleTrends*: This dataset consists of the volume of searches for various queries (i.e., words) on Google[4]. Each query represents the search volumes that are related to keywords over time.

4.1 Q1: Explaining K-SC clusters

The results on this dataset were already presented in section 1 (see Figure 1). Our model correctly captures the six patterns of K-SC. Table 3 gives a further description of the SpikeM fitting. Our model consists of seven parameters, each of which describes the behavior of spikes. Note that the total populations N are almost the same for all patterns, (around 2,000 to 3,000). This is because these six patterns are scaled on the y-axis so that they all have a peak volume of 100. We can see that $\beta * N$ is between $0.7 - 1.0$ for these six patterns. We also see that Pattern C3 has an extreme shock $S_b = 114$ at time $n_b = 40$, which means that this spike is strongly affected by the external burst of activity (see Figure 1 (c)). On the other hand, Patterns C4-C6 have several peaks about 24 hours apart with a strength $P_a \simeq 0.4$.

We also evaluated our fitting accuracy by using the root mean square error ($RMSE$) between estimated values and real values: $RMSE = \sqrt{\frac{1}{n_d}\sum_n^{n_d}(X(n) - \Delta B(n))^2}$. Table 4 shows the fitting accuracy result for six patterns of K-SC. We compared SpikeM with SI model. As discussed in section 3 (see Figure 2), SI cannot model the tail parts of the spikes. On the other hand, our solution, SpikeM achieves high accuracy for every pattern of K-SC.

[2]http://memetracker.org/
[3]http://twitter.com/
[4]http://www.google.com/insights/search/

	C1	C2	C3	C4	C5	C6
N	2407	1283	1466	3079	4183	3435
$\beta * N$	0.95	1.00	0.86	0.92	0.79	0.69
n_b	26	17	**40**	35	0	34
S_b	4.73	0.06	**114.13**	23.24	2.58	45.58
ϵ	0.36	0.01	0.43	1.48	0.32	13.97
P_a	0.18	0.06	0.22	**0.38**	**0.28**	**0.39**
P_s	12	5	7	**6**	**2**	**2**

Table 3: The model parameters of our SpikeM best fitting on six patterns of K-SC (see Figure 1).

Pattern	C1	C2	C3	C4	C5	C6
SpikeM	**1.84**	**1.61**	**0.97**	**4.08**	**3.33**	**5.89**
SI	15.64	6.78	19.65	25.29	20.36	21.76

Table 4: Fitting accuracy of SI vs. SpikeM on six patterns of K-SC. SpikeM consistently outperforms SI with respect to accuracy ($RMSE$) between the original values and the models.

4.2 Q2: Matching *MemeTracker* patterns

Figure 3 shows the results of model fitting on the *MemeTracker* dataset. We selected six typical sequences according to the K-SC clusters. That is, each sequence corresponds to each pattern (C1-C6). We show the original sequences (black dots) and SpikeM fitting,Δ $B(n)$ (red line) in both linear-linear (top) and log-log (bottom) scales. In the log-log scale, we also show the count of un-informed bloggers, $U(n)$. In Figure 3, the bottom table shows the short phrases (memes) of each sequence. All of the phrases are sourced from U.S. politics in 2008. We obtained several observations for each sequence:

- Patterns C1 and C2: almost the same size of population, $N \simeq 500$, except that C2 has a quicker rise and fall (i.e., stronger infection, $\beta * N = 1.4$) than C1 ($\beta * N = 0.94$).
- Pattern C3: this sequence has a sudden rise and a power law decay. There is a slight daily periodicity.
- Patterns C4 and C5: there are clearly daily periodicities. Pattern C6, "lipstick on a pig" has the largest population of all six sequences (i.e., $N = 6259$).
- Pattern C6: the sequence: "yes we can" consists of huge spikes around $n = 40$, and constant periodic noise. This is because the bloggers mention this phrase as Barack Obama's slogan as well as with more general meanings. We can also find that there are several extreme points (i.e., missing values) around $n = 120$ (see blue circle in log-log scale).

4.3 Q3: Matching other data

We also demonstrate the effectiveness of our model for other types of spikes.

Fitting on Twitter data. Figure 4 describes our fitting results on the *hashtags* of *Twitter* data. In this figure, we can see that *Twitter* data behave similarly to *MemeTracker* data. Due to space limitations, we show only three major hashtags. Note that the top and bottom rows are in linear-linear and log-log scales, respectively. Our model captures the following characteristics: (a) #assange: this is a topic about Julian Assange, the founder of WikiLeaks. There are several mentions before the peak point (December 5, 2011). (b) #stevejobs: there is a sudden peak on Octo-

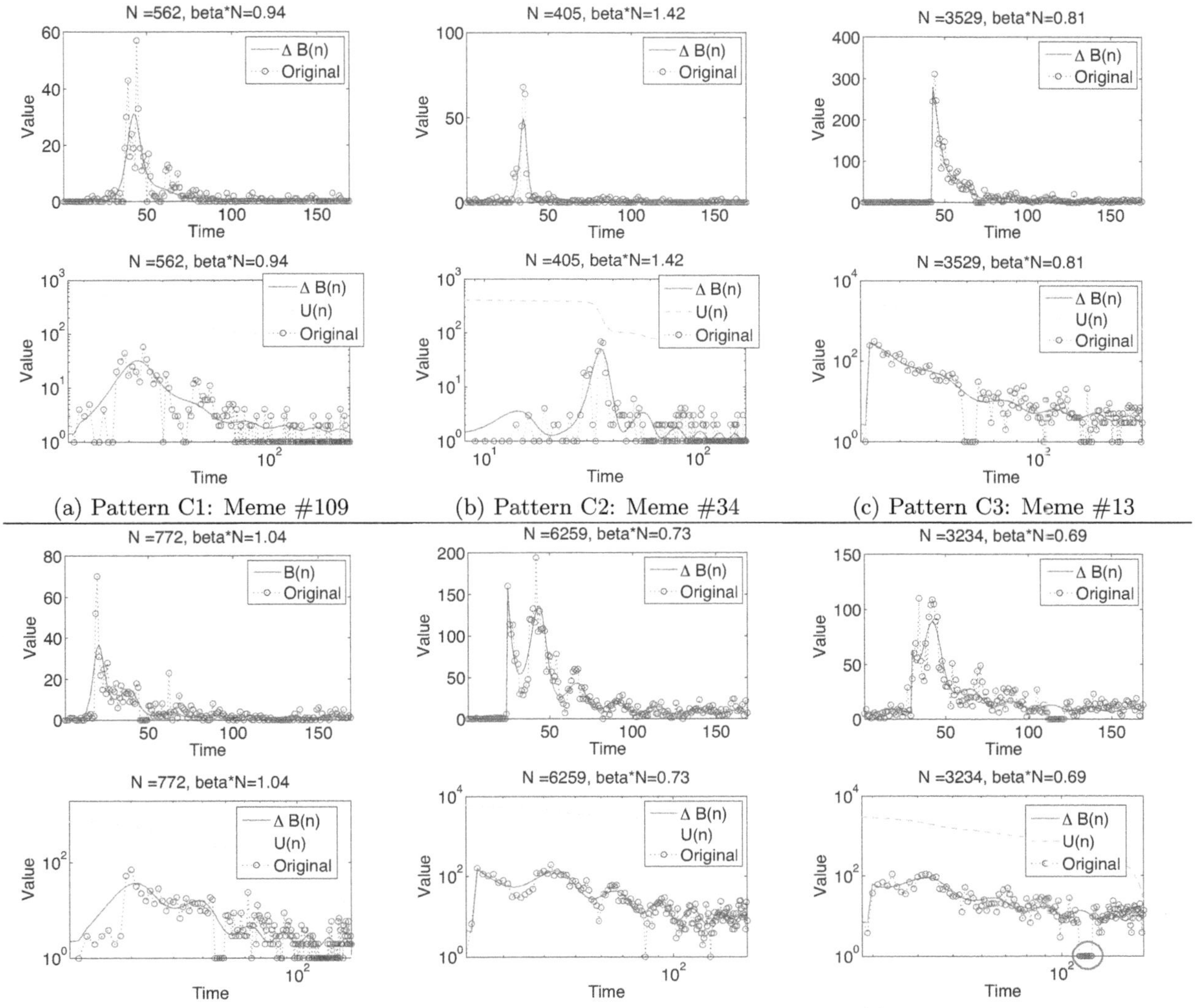

(a) Pattern C1: Meme #109 (b) Pattern C2: Meme #34 (c) Pattern C3: Meme #13

(d) Pattern C4: Meme #87 (e) Pattern C5: Meme #9 (f) Pattern C6: Meme #3

#109	the most serious financial crisis since the great depression	#87	what is required of us now is a new era of responsibility
#34	i love this country too much to let them take over another election	#9	you can put lipstick on a pig
#13	hope over fear, unity of purpose over conflict and discord	#3	yes we can yes we can

Figure 3: Results of SpikeM fitting on six patterns from *MemeTracker* dataset. The figures show in both 'linear-linear'(top) and 'log-log'(bottom) scales. The bottom table lists the phrase ("meme") of each patterns.

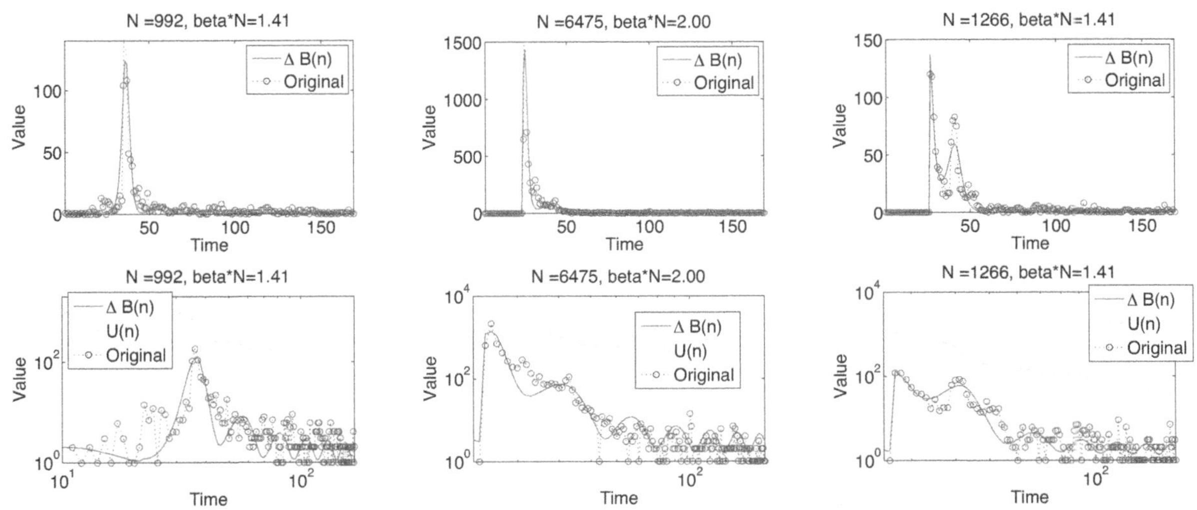

(a) #assange (b) #stevejobs (c) #arresteddevelopment

Figure 4: Results of SpikeM fitting on three hashtags from *Twitter* dataset. The top and bottom rows show in linear-linear scale, and log-log scale, respectively.

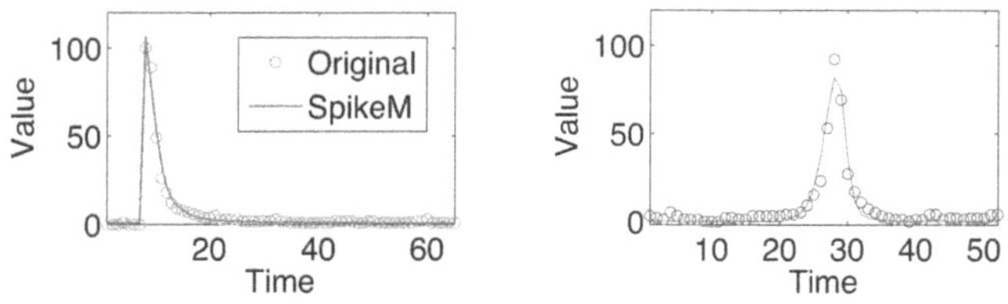

(a) "tsunami" (2005) (b) "Harry Potter" (2007)

Figure 5: SpikeM fitting on *GoogleTrends* dataset: the volume of searches for the keyword (in black dots) and fitting results (in red lines). Note that the window size is per week.

ber 5, 2011, with a long heavy tail (see Figure 4(b) in log-log scale). This was caused by the death of Steve Jobs. (c) #arresteddevelopment: this a topic about the movie "Arrested Development". There is a clear daily periodicity with a peak point.

Fitting on GoogleTrend data. We can also observe influence propagation in queries on internet search engines. Figure 5 shows two different types of spikes on *GoogleTrends*. For an external catastrophic event (a) "tsunami", we see that there is a super quick rise immediately after the Indian Ocean earthquake and tsunami in 2005. In contrast, (b) "harry potter" has a slower rise, which is because this spike was generated by "word-of-mouth" activity surrounding the release of a Harry Potter movie in 2007. SpikeM evidently captures both types of spikes successfully.

4.4 Q4: Tail-part forecasts

So far we have seen how SpikeM captures the pattern dynamics for various spikes. Here, we answer a more practical question: given the first part of the spike, how can we forecast the future behavior of the tail part? Figure 6 shows results of our forecasts on *MemeTracker* data. We selected two the highest population phrases (#9 and #13 in Figure 3). We trained our models by using the values obtained over a period of 54 hours (solid black lines in the figure), and then forecasted the following days (solid red lines, about five days). Note that the vertical axis uses a logarithmic scale. We compared SpikeM with the auto regressive model (AR). For a fair comparison, we used seven regression coefficients, which was the same size as our model parameters.

Our method achieves high forecasting accuracy while AR failed to forecast future patterns. More specifically, the reconstruction errors of SpikeM are $RMSE = 9.26$ and 8.93 for #9 and #13, while AR has errors of 13.98 and 14.19. Similar trends are observed in other phrases, however we omit the results due to space limitations. More importantly, our model can forecast the rise part of spikes as well as the tail part (discussed in Section 5).

5. DISCUSSION - SpikeM AT WORK

Our proposed model, SpikeM is capable of various applications. Here, we describe important applications and show some usefulness examples of our approach.

5.1 "What-if" forecasting

We have discussed tail-part forecasting in subsection 4.4. Ideally, we want to forecast not only the tail-part, but also the rise-part of a spike. This is much more difficult, because we usually have very few points in the rise-part of a spike.

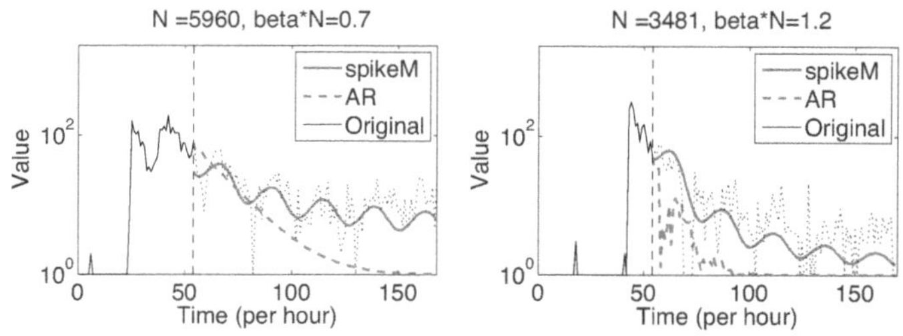

(a) Meme #9 (b) Meme #13

Figure 6: Results of tail-part forecasting on *MemeTracker* data. We train spikes from $n = 0$ to 54, and then, start forecasting at time $n = 54$. Our SpikeM reflects reality better, while AR quickly converges to the zero.

However, if this is a repeating event, like, say, the spikes induced by 'Harry Potter' movies releases, can we forecast future spikes if we know the release date of the next movie? It turns out that our SpikeM model can help with this (difficult) task, too.

Thus, the problem we address in Figure 7 is as follows: we are given (a) the first spike in 2009, "Harry Potter and the Half-Blood Prince" ($n = 185$); (b) the release dates of the two sequel movies (blue text with as arrows pointed at $n = 255$ and 289), and (c) the access volume before the release dates (and specifically from 8 to 2 weeks before). Can we forecast the rise and fall shapes of upcoming spikes and their peak points?

Solution and results. SpikeM can predict the potential population N of users who are interested in "Harry Potter", and the strength of 'word-of-mouth' infection: β. Our solution is to assume that these values are fixed for all of the sequel spikes. The only difference is the strength of the "external shock", i.e., n_b and S_b. Our solution consists of the following three-step process:

1. Train the parameter set $\boldsymbol{\theta}$ by using the first spike (solid black line in the figure).
2. With the fixed parameters $\boldsymbol{\theta}$, infer the new values of $\tilde{n_b}$ and $\tilde{S_b}$ by using the beginning part of the next spike (blue lines between double arrows at $n = 250$ and 280).
3. Generate the spikes using $\boldsymbol{\theta}$ and $\tilde{n_b}$ and $\tilde{S_b}$ (red lines).

In conclusion, Figure 7 shows that our model successfully captures the two sequel spikes and peak points n_{mode}.

5.2 Outlier detection

Since SpikeM has a very high fitting accuracy on real datasets (described in section 4), another natural application would be anomaly detection. Figure 8 shows the fitting result of Figure 5 (a), in a **log-log** scale. Note that the black circles are the original sequence, and the pink line is our model fitting. We can visually observe that there are several points that do not overlap the model. For example, (a) on March 29, there is one spike, since another earthquake occurred on March 28. (b) There is a huge spike on December 26, 2005, which is exactly one year after the Indian Ocean earthquake.

5.3 Reverse engineering

Most importantly, our model can provide an intuitive explanation such as the potential number of interested blog-

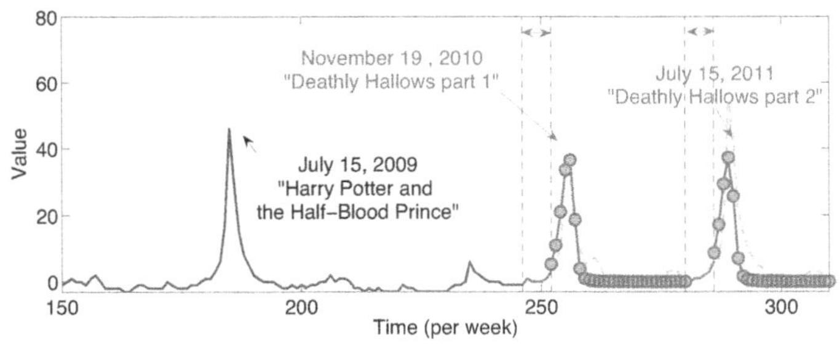

Figure 7: Results of "what-if" forecasting for the Harry Potter series. We trained parameters by using (a) the first spike around July 15, 2009 (black solid line), and (b) access volume two months before the release (blue lines with double arrows around time $n = 250$, 280) and then, forecasted the following two spikes (red lines).

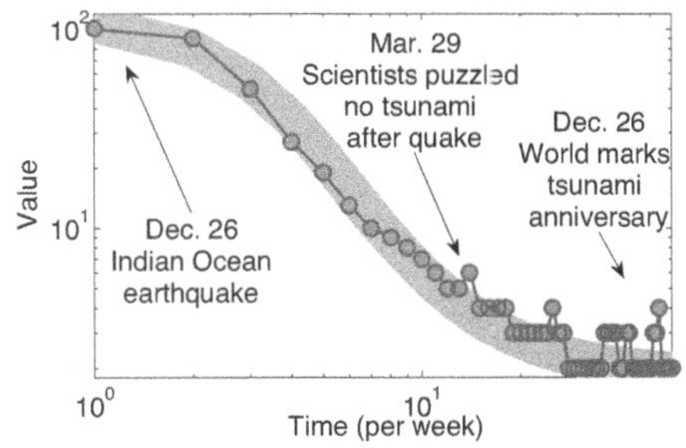

Figure 8: Outlier detection on *GoogleTrends* dataset (in log-log scale). Notice that the biggest spike, "world marks tsunami anniversary" occurred after one year (i.e., 52 weeks later).

gers, and the quality of news. Here we report our discoveries on *MemeTracker* and *Twitter* datasets (see Figure 9).

OBSERVATION 1 (TOTAL POPULATION OF BLOGGERS). *The total populations of potential bloggers/users N are almost same for both datasets (around $N = 1,000 - 2,000$).*

We also note that they are skewed to the right, i.e., there is a long tail of larger values.

OBSERVATION 2 (STRENGTH OF FIRST INFECTION). *The strength of the "first burst" is $\beta * N \simeq 1.0$ for each dataset.*

The above two observations agree with the intuition: we can see common behavior for *MemeTracker* and *Twitter*, which means that they have similar characteristics in terms of social activities.

OBSERVATION 3 (COMMON ACTIVITY AND PERIODICITY). *Typical user behavior is to have a daily periodicity with (a) phase shift $P_s = 0$ (small population during early morning, large population at peak point, 6pm) for MemeTracker, while (b) more spread in P_s.*

Note that more than 90% of all spikes have a daily periodicity in both datasets. The only the difference between the two datasets is that *Twitter* has several P_s values. This is because *Twitter* has multiple time zones (e.g., US, UK, Australia, and India).

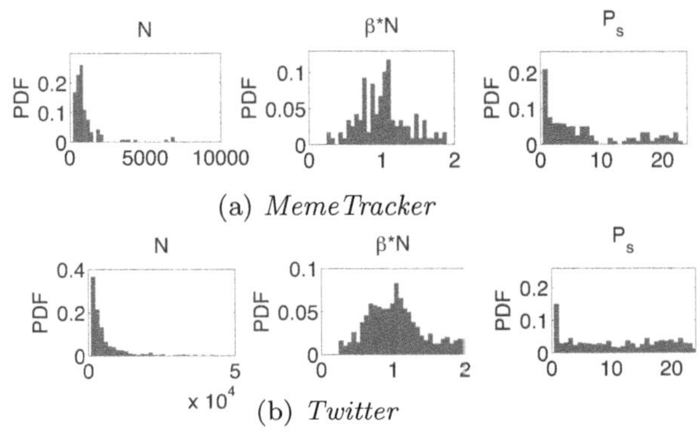

Figure 9: Reverse engineering: pdf of three parameters: $N, \beta * N, P_s$ over 1,000 memes/hashtags. (a) *MemeTracker*: total potential bloggers $N \simeq 1,000$, and strength of "first burst" $\beta * N \simeq 1.0$. More than 90% of the memes have clear daily periodicity with high activities around 6pm (i.e., $P_s \simeq 0$). (b) *Twitter*: similar trends except more spread in P_s, possibly, due to multiple time zone. Also see the text for more observations.

6. RELATED WORK

We present the related work, in three areas: time series analysis, influence propagation, and burst detection.

Time series Analysis. This is an old topic, that has attracted huge interest, and that is dealt with in well-regarded textbooks [4]. Traditional approaches applied to data mining include Auto-Regression (AR) and variations [24], or Linear dynamical systems (LDS), Kalman filters (KF) and variants [13, 25, 26] but they are all linear methods. Nonlinear methods for forecasting tend to be hard to interpret, because they rely on nearest-neighbor search [5], or artificial neural networks [39]. Similarity search, indexing and pattern discovery in time sequences have also attracted huge interest [7, 14, 8, 16, 27, 38, 30, 34, 35, 28], but none of these methods specifically focused on modeling bursts.

Influence propagation. The canonical text-book for epidemiological models like SI is Anderson and May [1]. The power-law decay of influence has been reported in blogs [29], with a exponent of -1.5. Barabasi and his colleagues reported exponents of -1 and -1.5, for the response time in correspondence [2]. Analyses of epidemics, blogs, social media, propagation and the cascades they create have attracted much interest [21, 40, 18, 33, 32, 15, 37, 9, 10, 11, 20], and recently the reverse problem ('find who started it') [19, 36].

Burst detection. Remotely related to our work are the efforts to spot bursts. This includes the work of Kleinberg [17], the algorithm of Zhu and Shasha [42], and the algorithm of Parikh et al. [31]. None of the above gives a parsimonious model for describing the activity in a network.

7. CONCLUSIONS

In this paper, we study the rise-and-fall patterns in information diffusion process through online medias. We presented SPIKEM, a general, accurate and succinct model that explains the rise-and-fall patterns. Our proposed SPIKEM has the following appealing advantages:

- **Unification power**: it includes earlier patterns and models as special cases (K-SC, as well as the SI model);
- **Practicality**: it matches the behavior of numerous, diverse, real datasets, including the power-law decay and much more beyond;
- **Parsimony**: our model requires only a handful of parameters;
- **Usefulness**: we showed how to use our model to do 'short-term' forecasting, to answer what-if scenarios, to spot outliers, and to learn more about the mechanisms of the spikes.

Acknowledgement

This material is based upon work supported by the Army Research Laboratory under Cooperative Agreement No. W911NF-09-2-0053, and the National Science Foundation under Grant No. IIS-1017415. We thank Jaewon Yang and Jure Leskovec for providing the details of the six clusters in Figure 1.

8. REFERENCES

[1] R. M. Anderson and R. M. May. *Infectious Diseases of Humans.* Oxford University Press, 1991.

[2] A. L. Barabasi. The origin of bursts and heavy tails in human dynamics. *Nature*, 435, 2005.

[3] F. M. Bass. A new product growth for model consumer durables. *Management Science*, 15(5):215–227, 1969.

[4] G. E. Box, G. M. Jenkins, and G. C. Reinsel. *Time Series Analysis: Forecasting and Control.* Prentice Hall, Englewood Cliffs, NJ, 3rd edition, 1994.

[5] D. Chakrabarti and C. Faloutsos. F4: Large-scale automated forecasting using fractals. *CIKM*, 2002.

[6] R. Crane and D. Sornette. Robust dynamic classes revealed by measuring the response function of a social system. In *PNAS*, 2008.

[7] C. Faloutsos, M. Ranganathan, and Y. Manolopoulos. Fast subsequence matching in time-series databases. In *SIGMOD*, pages 419–429, 1994.

[8] A. C. Gilbert, Y. Kotidis, S. Muthukrishnan, and M. Strauss. Surfing wavelets on streams: One-pass summaries for approximate aggregate queries. In *VLDB*, pages 79–88, 2001.

[9] M. Goetz, J. Leskovec, M. McGlohon, and C. Faloutsos. Modeling blog dynamics. In *ICWSM*, 2009.

[10] D. Gruhl, D. Liben-Nowell, R. Guha, and A. Tomkins. Information diffusion through blogspace. *SIGKDD Explor. Newsl.*, 6(2):43–52, December 2004.

[11] R. Guha, R. Kumar, P. Raghavan, and A. Tomkins. Propagation of trust and distrust. In *WWW*, pages 403–412, 2004.

[12] A. G. Hawkes and D. Oakes. A cluster representation of a self-exciting process. *J. Appl. Prob.*, 11:493–503, 1974.

[13] A. Jain, E. Y. Chang, and Y.-F. Wang. Adaptive stream resource management using kalman filters. In *SIGMOD*, pages 11–22, 2004.

[14] T. Kahveci and A. K. Singh. An efficient index structure for string databases. In *Proceedings of VLDB*, pages 351–360, September 2001.

[15] D. Kempe, J. Kleinberg, and E. Tardos. Maximizing the spread of influence through a social network. In *KDD*, 2003.

[16] E. J. Keogh, T. Palpanas, V. B. Zordan, D. Gunopulos, and M. Cardle. Indexing large human-motion databases. In *VLDB*, pages 780–791, 2004.

[17] J. M. Kleinberg. Bursty and hierarchical structure in streams. In *KDD*, pages 91–101, 2002.

[18] R. Kumar, M. Mahdian, and M. McGlohon. Dynamics of conversations. In *SIGKDD*, pages 553–562, 2010.

[19] T. Lappas, E. Terzi, D. Gunopulos, and H. Mannila. Finding effectors in social networks. In *KDD*, pages 1059–1068, 2010.

[20] J. Leskovec, L. A. Adamic, and B. A. Huberman. The dynamics of viral marketing. *TWEB*, 1(1), 2007.

[21] J. Leskovec, L. Backstrom, and J. M. Kleinberg. Meme-tracking and the dynamics of the news cycle. In *KDD*, pages 497–506, 2009.

[22] J. Leskovec, M. McGlohon, C. Faloutsos, N. S. Glance, and M. Hurst. Patterns of cascading behavior in large blog graphs. In *SDM*, 2007.

[23] K. Levenberg. A method for the solution of certain non-linear problems in least squares. *Quarterly Journal of Applied Mathmatics*, II(2):164–168, 1944.

[24] L. Li, C.-J. M. Liang, J. Liu, S. Nath, A. Terzis, and C. Faloutsos. Thermocast: A cyber-physical forecasting model for data centers. In *KDD*, 2011.

[25] L. Li, J. McCann, N. Pollard, and C. Faloutsos. Dynammo: Mining and summarization of coevolving sequences with missing values. In *KDD*, 2009.

[26] L. Li and B. A. Prakash. Time series clustering: Complex is simpler! In *ICML*, 2011.

[27] J. Lin, E. J. Keogh, S. Lonardi, J. P. Lankford, and D. M. Nystrom. Visually mining and monitoring massive time series. In *KDD*, pages 460–469, 2004.

[28] Y. Matsubara, Y. Sakurai, and M. Yoshikawa. Scalable algorithms for distribution search. In *ICDM*, pages 347–356, 2009.

[29] M. McGlohon, J. Leskovec, C. Faloutsos, M. Hurst, and N. Glance. Finding patterns in blog shapes and blog evolution. In *International Conference on Weblogs and Social Media*, Boulder, Colo., March 2007.

[30] P. Papapetrou, V. Athitsos, M. Potamias, G. Kollios, and D. Gunopulos. Embedding-based subsequence matching in time-series databases. *ACM Trans. Database Syst.*, 36(3):17, 2011.

[31] N. Parikh and N. Sundaresan. Scalable and near real-time burst detection from ecommerce queries. In *KDD*, pages 972–980, 2008.

[32] B. A. Prakash, A. Beutel, R. Rosenfeld, and C. Faloutsos. Winner takes all: competing viruses or ideas on fair-play networks. In *WWW*, pages 1037–1046, 2012.

[33] B. A. Prakash, D. Chakrabarti, M. Faloutsos, N. Valler, and C. Faloutsos. Threshold conditions for arbitrary cascade models on arbitrary networks. In *ICDM*, 2011.

[34] Y. Sakurai, C. Faloutsos, and M. Yamamuro. Stream monitoring under the time warping distance. In *Proceedings of the 23rd International Conference on Data Engineering, ICDE 2007, April 15-20, 2007, The Marmara Hotel, Istanbul, Turkey*, pages 1046–1055, 2007.

[35] Y. Sakurai, S. Papadimitriou, and C. Faloutsos. BRAID: Stream mining through group lag correlations. In *SIGMOD Conference*, pages 599–610, Baltimore, MD, USA, 2005.

[36] D. Shah and T. Zaman. Rumors in a network: Who's the culprit? *IEEE Transactions on Information Theory*, 57(8):5163–5181, 2011.

[37] H. Tong, B. A. Prakash, C. E. Tsourakakis, T. Eliassi-Rad, C. Faloutsos, and D. H. Chau. On the vulnerability of large graphs. In *ICDM*, 2010.

[38] M. Vlachos, S. S. Kozat, and P. S. Yu. Optimal distance bounds on time-series data. In *SDM*, pages 109–120, 2009.

[39] A. S. Weigend and N. A. Gerschenfeld. *Time Series Prediction: Forecasting the Future and Understanding the Past.* Addison Wesley, 1994.

[40] J. Yang and J. Leskovec. Modeling information diffusion in implicit networks. In *ICDM*, pages 599–608, 2010.

[41] J. Yang and J. Leskovec. Patterns of temporal variation in online media. In *WSDM*, pages 177–186, 2011.

[42] Y. Zhu and D. Shasha. Efficient elastic burst detection in data streams. In *KDD*, pages 336–345, 2003.

Efficient Personalized PageRank with Accuracy Assurance

Yasuhiro Fujiwara[†], Makoto Nakatsuji[‡], Takeshi Yamamuro[†],
Hiroaki Shiokawa[†], Makoto Onizuka[†]
†NTT Software Innovation Center, ‡NTT Service Evolution Laboratories
†3-9-1 Midori-cho Musashino-shi, Tokyo, Japan, ‡1-1 Hikarinooka Yokosuka-shi, Kanagawa, Japan
{fujiwara.yasuhiro, nakatsuji.makoto, yamamuro.takeshi,
shiokawa.hiroaki, onizuka.makoto}@lab.ntt.co.jp

ABSTRACT

Personalize PageRank (PPR) is an effective relevance (proximity) measure in graph mining. The goal of this paper is to efficiently compute single node relevance and top-k/highly relevant nodes without iteratively computing the relevances of all nodes. Based on a "random surfer model", PPR iteratively computes the relevances of all nodes in a graph until convergence for a given user preference distribution. The problem with this iterative approach is that it cannot compute the relevance of just one or a few nodes. The heart of our solution is to compute single node relevance accurately in non-iterative manner based on sparse matrix representation, and to compute top-k/highly relevant nodes exactly by pruning unnecessary relevance computations based on upper/lower relevance estimations. Our experiments show that our approach is up to seven orders of magnitude faster than the existing alternatives.

Categories and Subject Descriptors

H.2.8 [**Database Applications**]: Data mining

General Terms

Algorithms, Theory

Keywords

Personalized PageRank, Relevance computation

1. INTRODUCTION

Graphs arise in a wide range of application domains such as the Internet, social networks, biological networks and more [28]. In these graphs, personalized search has become an increasingly important topic in recent years [18]. One of the most important aspects of personalized search is to measure the relevance (proximity) of nodes according to the user preference distribution[1]. Examples of personalized search are "To what degree is a web page relevant to user's bookmark pages?", "Which books have the top ten relevance scores with a view to being recommended to a user in accordance with his/her shopping logs?", and so on.

Many relevance measures have been reported in the literature [5, 13, 14, 15, 21, 22]. Among the relevance measures, *personalized PageRank (PPR)* [10, 23] has attracted considerable attention due to its effectiveness and solid theoretical foundation. Similar to PageRank [1, 8, 27, 30], PPR is defined with respect to a "random surfer model" and needs to be computed iteratively. Informally speaking, PPR is the stationary distribution of random walks; at each step in a random walk, it randomly selects an outgoing edge from the current node, and, with a certain probability, it jumps to a node in accordance with a given preference distribution.

However, this iterative approach has a serious weakness: it is not effective if the user needs only single node relevance or top-k/highly relevant nodes. This is because its iterative computation approach updates the relevance scores of all nodes that are determined in the previous iteration. If m and t are the number of edges and the number of iteration steps until convergence, respectively, it requires $O(mt)$ time; its computational cost is excessive for large graphs.

1.1 Problem motivation

We address three problems. With our approach, many applications can be processed more efficiently without sacrificing application efficacy. The first problem is to compute the PPR relevance score of a single given node for a preference distribution. This problem is formalized as follows:

Problem 1 (SINGLE-NODE RELEVANCE COMPUTATION).
Given: *Query node x and query distribution* $\mathbf{d}$.
Find: *Relevance score of node x according to query distribution* $\mathbf{d}$.

The second problem is to identify the top-k relevant nodes for a given preference distribution.

Problem 2 (TOP-K NODES IDENTIFICATION).
Given: *The number of required answer nodes, K, and query distribution* $\mathbf{d}$.
Find: *Top K nodes with the highest relevance scores with respect to query distribution* $\mathbf{d}$.

We also solve the problem of finding all nodes whose relevance scores are higher than a given threshold:

Problem 3 (HIGHLY RELEVANT NODE DETECTION).
Given: *The threshold, ϵ, and query distribution* $\mathbf{d}$.
Find: *Nodes whose relevance scores are higher than ϵ with respect to query distribution* $\mathbf{d}$.

These three problems have to be resolved to realize the following applications.

[1] Called as "preference vector" in [23].

KDD'12, August 12–16, 2012, Beijing, China.

Graph analysis (Problem 1). In graph analysis, there is a need for a tool that can analyze the relative importance of each node in a graph with respect to user preferences [22]. This tool reveals the context of interactive exploration of graph data. The PPR-based approach, suggested by White et al., can effectively measure the relative importance of each node in accordance with user preference [36]. By picking up several researchers in a co-authorship network who belong to the same university, this approach reveals that they have low importance scores if they study different research disciplines.

Recommendation (Problem 2). Recommendation systems aim to provide personalized items that are interesting for users. A popular approach is to use the collaborative filtering technique [20]. However, this technique does not directly utilize information about latent user interests in recommendations. PPR-based methods can be used to capture user's possible interest expansion [26]. This method uses PPR to expand the user's latent interests estimated by LDA [6]. And it computes the top-k relevant items for the recommendations. This method outperforms previous approaches such as ItemRank [15] and L^+ [11].

Link prediction (Problem 3). The link prediction problem, attempting to infer which new interactions among social network members are likely to occur in the near future, is an active research topic [37]. The PPR-based approach by Liven-Nowell et al. can answer this problem [25]; the probability of future interactions between members is computed by PPR. If two members have many friends in common, they have high mutual PPR scores, and they are more likely to interact. By identifying those pairs with high PPR scores, this approach provides better link predictions than the random prediction approach.

Our proposed method can also be used in other applications such as person name disambiguation [32], document clustering [2], and protein-protein interaction analysis [35], even though we omit details due to the space limitations.

1.2 Contribution

To the best of our knowledge, our approach is the first solution to comprehensively handle all the three problems that theoretically guarantees exactness unlike previous approximate approaches [3, 4, 10, 17, 23]. To achieve high efficiency, we use a sparse matrix representation and compute single node relevance in a non-iterative manner. Our approach also efficiently identifies the top-k/highly relevant nodes without computing the relevance scores of unnecessary nodes by estimating upper/lower relevance scores. Our approach has the following attractive characteristics:

- **Fast**: The proposed approach, by utilizing the above ideas, is significantly faster than existing approaches.
- **Exact**: Our approach does not sacrifice accuracy; it returns the exact outputs for the three problems.
- **Easy to deploy**: Our approach itself does not require any parameter. Thus it provides the user with a simple solution to PPR-based applications.

While PPR has been used in many applications, it has been difficult to utilize due to its high computational cost. However, by providing exact solutions in a highly efficient manner, the proposed approach will allow many more PPR-based applications to be developed in the future.

The remainder of this paper is organized as follows: Section 2 overviews the background of this paper. Section 3 introduces the details of our approach. Section 4 reviews the experiments conducted and the results gained. Section 5 details case-studies of our approach. Section 6 describes related work. Section 7 provides our brief conclusion.

Table 1: Definition of main symbols.

Symbol	Definition
n	Number of nodes
m	Number of edges
x	Query node for a single node relevance computation
K	Number of answer nodes for top-k identification
ϵ	Threshold in finding highly relevant nodes
c	Restart probability
s_u	Relevance or steady-state probability of node u
$\mathbf{s}$	$n \times 1$ relevance vector
$\mathbf{d}$	$n \times 1$ query distribution vector where $\sum d_i = 1$
$\mathbf{A}$	$n \times n$ column normalized adjacent matrix
$\mathbf{P}$	$n \times n$ permutation matrix
$\mathbf{Q}$	$n \times n$ orthogonal matrix in QR decomposition
$\mathbf{R}$	$n \times n$ upper triangular matrix in QR decomposition
$\lvert\mathbf{R}\rvert$	Number of non-zero elements in matrix $\mathbf{R}$

2. PRELIMINARY

We formally define the notations and introduce the background of this paper. Table 1 lists the main symbols and their definitions. Measuring the relevance scores of nodes according to a preference distribution can be achieved by using PPR. In PPR, starting from one of *seed nodes*[2] whose preference distribution scores are not zero, a random walk is performed by iteratively following an edge to another node at each step. Additionally, at every step, there is a probability, c, of returning to a seed node according to the preference distribution. Let $\mathbf{s}$ be an $n \times 1$ vector where n is the number of nodes, the u-th element s_u denotes the steady-state probability that the random walk is at node u. Let $\mathbf{d}$ be an $n \times 1$ column normalized vector of the preference distribution of seed nodes, i.e. $\sum d_i = 1$, and $\mathbf{A}$ be the $n \times n$ column normalized adjacency matrix of the graph. The steady-state probability for each node can be obtained by recursively applying the following equation until convergence:

$$\mathbf{s} = (1 - c)\mathbf{A}\mathbf{s} + c\mathbf{d} \quad (1)$$

The steady-state probabilities, $\mathbf{s}$, give the long term visit rate of each node given the bias indicated by query distribution $\mathbf{d}$. Therefore, s_u can be considered as the relevance measure of node u with respect to given distribution $\mathbf{d}$.

But this method is not effective to compute the relevance score of a single node or identify the nodes with top-k/high relevance since it recursively updates the relevance scores of all nodes. It needs $O(mt)$ time until convergence. This incurs excessive computational cost for large graphs.

3. PROPOSED METHOD

In this section, we describe the proposed approach. The main advantage of our approach is that it can efficiently compute single node relevance as well as top-k/highly relevant nodes without loss in accuracy.

3.1 Overview

Computing single node relevance. As described in Section 2, exact relevance scores can be obtained by the recursive approach. This approach iteratively updates the relevance scores of all nodes; it cannot compute the relevance of

[2] In the special case of only a single seed node, PPR is equivalent to random walk with restart [13].

just one single node. To avoid iterative processing, we utilize matrix computations and compute single node relevance in non-iterative style. The matrices can be obtained from Equation (1). However, this approach can incur high computational cost if the matrices are dense [31]. We propose an approach to overcome this problem in Section 3.2.

In a precomputation step, we permute nodes of the adjacent matrix, and compute the QR decomposition [19] of the matrix. From the resulting matrices, we then compute the inverse matrices. By properly permuting the nodes, the inverse matrices have a sparse structure. The permutation can be obtained by solving an **NP**-complete problem as described in Section 3.2. Thus, we can compute single node relevance efficiently from the sparse data structure. Since QR decomposition is not an approximate method, we can compute exact relevance scores.

Identifying top-k nodes. When a user queries top-k relevant nodes for a preference distribution, the iterative approach computes the relevance scores of all nodes and finds the answer nodes. However, this approach requires high computational cost. For top-k identification, our approach computes exact relevance scores for just the answer-likely nodes to avoid unnecessary relevance computations as described in Section 3.3.

To find top-k nodes, we estimate the relevance scores of each node at $O(1)$ time. If a node is estimated to be an answer-likely node, we compute its exact relevance. The advantage of this idea is to find top-k nodes exactly although it uses estimations. Exact answer results are obtained by estimating upper bounding relevance scores. This means that we can safely discard unpromising nodes along with their estimated relevance scores at low computational cost.

Finding highly relevant nodes. Although the upper bounding estimation approach can discard most unlikely nodes, it still relies on exact relevance computations to guarantee the exactness of answer results. In section 3.4, we show our approach that reduces the cost of exact computations for finding highly relevant nodes whose scores exceed ϵ.

To find highly relevant nodes, we estimate lower bounding relevance scores as well as upper bounding relevance scores. Our approach to find highly relevant nodes is based on the property that, if the lower bounding relevance of a node is more than ϵ, the exact relevance of the node must be greater than ϵ. Therefore, the node must be an answer node. This idea reinforces the idea of upper bounding estimation by effectively pruning the exact relevance computations. Since the exact relevance computations are limited to a small number, we can efficiently find highly relevant nodes.

3.2 Computing single node relevance

In this section, we describe our approach to efficiently computing the relevance score of a query node for a given distribution. Section 3.2.1 introduces a definition of PPR that allows it to be rewritten as non-iterative matrix computation by using QR decomposition, and then shows our non-iterative approach. In Section 3.2.2, we show that obtaining sparse matrices is an **NP**-complete problem, and we then show our solution for the problem.

3.2.1 Non-iterative relevance computation

We show here how to rewrite Equation (1) into non-iterative matrix form. In our relevance computation, we permute nodes in the graph. That is, let $\mathbf{P}$ be a permutation matrix, the original adjacent matrix $\mathbf{A}$ is transformed into matrix $\mathbf{A}'$ in the form of $\mathbf{A}' = \mathbf{PAP}^T$ where matrix $\mathbf{P}^T$ is the transpose of matrix $\mathbf{P}$ [19]. The $n \times n$ permutation matrix $\mathbf{P}$ is an orthogonal matrix where every row and column contains precisely a single 1 with 0s everywhere else, and $P_{ij} = 1$ indicates that j-th row is permutated into the i-th row. Our approach to obtaining matrix $\mathbf{P}$ is described in Section 3.2.2.

By utilizing matrix $\mathbf{P}$, Equation (1) can be rewritten in the following matrix form since $\mathbf{I} = \mathbf{P}^T\mathbf{IP}$, $\mathbf{P}^{-1} = \mathbf{P}^T$, and $\mathbf{A} = \mathbf{P}^T\mathbf{AP}$ where $\mathbf{P}^{-1}$ is the inverse matrix of $\mathbf{P}$ [19]:

$$\begin{aligned}\mathbf{s} &= c\{\mathbf{I}-(1-c)\mathbf{A}\}^{-1}\mathbf{d} = c\{\mathbf{P}^T\mathbf{IP}-(1-c)\mathbf{P}^T\mathbf{A}'\mathbf{P}\}^{-1}\mathbf{d} \\ &= c\mathbf{P}^T\{\mathbf{I}-(1-c)\mathbf{A}'\}^{-1}\mathbf{Pd}\end{aligned} \quad (2)$$

To compute query node relevance, we perform QR decomposition of the matrix $\mathbf{I}-(1-c)\mathbf{A}'$, i.e., $\mathbf{QR} = \mathbf{I}-(1-c)\mathbf{A}'$ where matrices $\mathbf{Q}$ and $\mathbf{R}$ are an orthogonal matrix and upper triangular matrix, respectively [19]. Formally, we compute the relevance of node x for the given distribution $\mathbf{d}$ from precomputed $\mathbf{Q}^T$ and $\mathbf{R}^{-1}$ as follows:

Definition 1 (RELEVANCE COMPUTATION). *Let $n \times n$ matrix $\mathbf{F} = c\mathbf{P}^T\mathbf{R}^{-1}$, $n \times 1$ vector $\mathbf{g} = \mathbf{Q}^T\mathbf{Pd}$ and $1 \times n$ vector $\mathbf{f}_i$ be the i-th row vector in matrix $\mathbf{F}$ The relevance of node x, s_x, is computed as follows:*

$$s_x = \mathbf{f}_x \cdot \mathbf{g} \quad (3)$$

For Definition 1, we have the following theorem:

Theorem 1 (RELEVANCE COMPUTATION). *Equation (3) outputs exactly the same result as Equation (1).*

Proof From Equation (2), we have the following equation since $\mathbf{Q}^T = \mathbf{Q}^{-1}$ [19]:

$$\mathbf{s} = c\mathbf{P}^T(\mathbf{QR})^{-1}\mathbf{Pd} = c\mathbf{P}^T\mathbf{R}^{-1}\mathbf{Q}^T\mathbf{Pd} = \mathbf{F}\cdot\mathbf{g}$$

Therefore, s_x, x-th element of $n \times 1$ column vector $\mathbf{s}$, can be computed as the inner product of vectors $\mathbf{f}_x$ and $\mathbf{g}$. □

Equation (3) implies that we can compute node relevance as the inner product of vectors $\mathbf{f}_x$ and $\mathbf{g}$ in non-iterative style. Equation (3) also implies that, in the relevance computation, we first compute vector $\mathbf{g} = \mathbf{Q}^T\mathbf{Pd}$ from vector $\mathbf{d}$ since it is given by the user.

We provide the following theorem to describe the time complexity of our relevance computation:

Theorem 2 (RELEVANCE COMPUTATION COST). *Let $|\mathbf{f}_x|$ and $|\mathbf{Q}|$ be the number of non-zero elements in $\mathbf{f}_x$ and $\mathbf{Q}$, respectively, it requires $O(|\mathbf{f}_x| + |\mathbf{Q}|)$ time to compute the relevance score of a single node by our non-iterative approach.*

Proof Our approach computes vector $\mathbf{g}$ to obtain the relevance from the given distribution $\mathbf{d}$. Since vector $\mathbf{Pd}$ is obtained by permutating vector $\mathbf{d}$, it needs $O(|\mathbf{Q}|)$ time to compute vector $\mathbf{g} = \mathbf{Q}^T\mathbf{Pd}$. Since it takes $O(|\mathbf{f}_x| + |\mathbf{Q}|)$ time to compute the inner product of the vectors $\mathbf{f}_x$ and $\mathbf{g}$, it requires $O(|\mathbf{f}_x| + |\mathbf{Q}|)$ time. □

Theorem 2 implies that the numbers of non-zero elements in matrices $\mathbf{R}^{-1}$ and $\mathbf{Q}$ should be reduced to achieve high efficiency since $\mathbf{F} = c\mathbf{P}^T\mathbf{R}^{-1}$ and $\mathbf{g} = \mathbf{Q}^T\mathbf{Pd}$. Note that the number of non-zero elements in $\mathbf{P}$ is trivially n [19]. In particular, the number of non-zero elements in matrix $\mathbf{Q}$ should be reduced since vector $\mathbf{g}$ is computed according to the user's query. In the next section, we show our approach to obtain the sparse matrices $\mathbf{R}^{-1}$ and $\mathbf{Q}$.

3.2.2 *Sparse matrix problem*

As shown in Definition 1, we can compute relevance scores in non-iterative style if we precompute matrices $\mathbf{R}^{-1}$ and $\mathbf{Q}$. However, this approach can incur high computational cost if the matrices have dense structures even if the original graph has sparse structure. In many real graphs, the number of edges is much smaller than the squared number of nodes, i.e. $m \ll n^2$ [29]. In our approach, we permute nodes in the graph to obtain sparse $\mathbf{R}^{-1}$ and $\mathbf{Q}$. Unfortunately, determining the node permutation to yield the sparse matrices is an **NP**-complete problem.

Theorem 3 (SPARSE MATRIX PROBLEM). *Setting the nodes permutation that minimizes non-zero elements in the matrices* $\mathbf{R}^{-1}$ *and* $\mathbf{Q}$ *is* **NP**-*complete.*

Proof We prove the theorem by a reduction from the *minimum fill-in* problem [38]. We transform instances of this problem into instances of the *sparse matrices* problem as follows: For the graph of the *minimum fill-in* problem, we create matrix $\mathbf{A}$. For the node elimination ordering, we create the permutation matrix $\mathbf{P}$, and we create matrix $\mathbf{R}^{-1}$ and $\mathbf{Q}$ for the chordal graph. Thus, it is easy to show that there exists a solution to the *minimum fill-in* problem with the minimum number of edge additions iff there exists a solution to the *sparse matrices* problem with the minimum increase in non-zero elements in the inverse matrices. Thus, the *sparse matrices* problem is trivial in **NP**. □

We introduce an approach for the problem. At the beginning, we show how to compute matrices $\mathbf{Q}$ and $\mathbf{R}^{-1}$ to describe our approach in detail. Let $\mathbf{q}_i$ be the i-th column vector of matrix $\mathbf{Q}$ and $\mathbf{w}_i$ be the i-th column vector of matrix $\mathbf{W} = \mathbf{I} - (1-c)\mathbf{A}'$, matrices $\mathbf{Q}$ and $\mathbf{R}$ can be computed by Gram-Schmidt orthogonalization as follows [19]:

$$\mathbf{q}_i = \mathbf{q}'_i/||\mathbf{q}'_i||,\ \mathbf{q}'_i = \begin{cases} \mathbf{w}_i & (i=1) \\ \mathbf{w}_i - \sum_{j=1}^{i-1}(\mathbf{w}_i \cdot \mathbf{q}_j)\mathbf{q}_j & (i \neq 1) \end{cases} \quad (4)$$

$$R_{ij} = \begin{cases} 0 & (i > j) \\ ||\mathbf{q}'_i|| & (i = j) \\ \mathbf{w}_j \cdot \mathbf{q}_i & (i < j) \end{cases} \quad (5)$$

where $||\mathbf{q}'_i||$ is the norm of $\mathbf{q}'_i$ [19]. Elements in matrix $\mathbf{R}^{-1}$ can be computed as follows by backward substitution [31]:

$$R^{-1}_{ij} = \begin{cases} 0 & (i > j) \\ 1/R_{ij} & (i = j) \\ -1/R_{ii}\sum_{k=i+1}^{j} R_{ik}R^{-1}_{kj} & (i < j) \end{cases} \quad (6)$$

Equation (4) and (5) imply that column vectors of $\mathbf{Q}$ and $\mathbf{R}$ are obtained from left to right by computing orthogonal column vectors and inner products from matrix $\mathbf{W}$. Equation (6) shows that the column vectors of $\mathbf{R}^{-1}$ are obtained from right to left and elements in column vectors from bottom to top. Equations (4), (5), and (6) indicate that matrices $\mathbf{Q}$ and $\mathbf{R}$ are computed from matrix $\mathbf{W}$ which is obtained from matrix $\mathbf{A}'(= \mathbf{PAP}^T)$.

We can obtain sparse matrix $\mathbf{Q}$ based on the following observation: if column vector $\mathbf{w}_i$ has a single non-zero element whose left elements in the matrix $\mathbf{W}$ are all zero, column vector $\mathbf{w}_i$ is orthogonal to all its left column vectors in matrix $\mathbf{Q}$. This is because the column vector $\mathbf{w}_i$ is linearly independent [19], thus matrix $\mathbf{Q}$ has a sparse structure.

We obtain sparse matrix $\mathbf{R}^{-1}$ based on the following two observations: (1) the right/bottom elements of matrix $\mathbf{R}^{-1}$ would be sparse if the corresponding right/bottom elements of matrix $\mathbf{R}$ are sparse, and (2) the right/bottom elements of matrix $\mathbf{R}$ are expected to be zero if the corresponding right/bottom elements of matrix $\mathbf{W}$ are zero.

Algorithm 1 Node permutation

Input: $\mathbf{A}$, adjacent matrix of the graph; n, the number of nodes
Output: $\mathbf{P}$, permutation matrix

```
1: P = 0;
2: 𝒫 = ∅;
3: for i = 1 to n do
4:    𝒰 = argmin(e(u)|u ∈ 𝒱\𝒫);
5:    v = argmax(deg(u)|u ∈ 𝒰);
6:    P_iv = 1;
7:    append node v to 𝒫;
8: end for
9: return P;
```

Algorithm 1 depicts our permutation algorithm for obtaining the sparse matrices. Our algorithm uses the above observations on matrices $\mathbf{Q}$ and $\mathbf{R}^{-1}$. In this algorithm, $\mathcal{V}$ and $\mathcal{P}$ indicate the node set in the graph and the permutated node set, respectively. $deg(u)$ is the number of edges incident to node u, i.e. degree of node u. $e(u)$ is the number of edges that are *not* incident to node set $\mathcal{P}$ from node u. Our algorithm first sets the permutation matrix $\mathbf{P}$ to a zero matrix, and initializes node set $\mathcal{P}$ (lines 1-2). From the unpermutated set of nodes, $\mathcal{V}\backslash\mathcal{P}$, it finds the set of nodes, $\mathcal{U}$, whose numbers of edges are $\min(e(u)|u \in \mathcal{V}\backslash\mathcal{P})$ based on the observation on matrix $\mathbf{Q}$ (line 4). If the right/bottom elements of matrix $\mathbf{A}'$ are zero, matrix $\mathbf{R}^{-1}$ has a sparse structure. Therefore, it identifies node v that has the maximum number of edges to make the left/top elements of matrix $\mathbf{A}'$ dense (line 5). It then sets an element in matrix $\mathbf{P}$ to determine the permutation (lines 6-7). These procedures continue until all nodes are permutated.

This approach can effectively reduce the number of non-zero elements for $\mathbf{R}^{-1}$ and, especially for, $\mathbf{Q}$ as shown in Section 4. Thus, we can efficiently compute a single node relevance score since $\mathbf{F} = c\mathbf{P}^T\mathbf{R}^{-1}$ and $\mathbf{g} = \mathbf{Q}^T\mathbf{Pd}$. This approach has another advantage: we can efficiently precompute matrices $\mathbf{Q}$ and $\mathbf{R}^{-1}$ as demonstrated in Section 4. This is because the efficiency of the precomputation is greatly enhanced by reducing the number of non-zero elements.

3.3 Identifying top-k nodes

We introduce an algorithm that finds top-k nodes by estimating upper bounding scores. We compute the estimations in the process of finding the top-k nodes. Our solution is based on lower bounding estimation which is described in Section 3.3.1. The details of the upper bounding estimation approach are introduced in Section 3.3.2. We show our top-k node identification algorithm in Section 3.3.3.

3.3.1 *Lower bounding estimation*

So as to find the top-k nodes, we estimate lower bounding relevance scores from the numbers of minimum hops from the seed nodes. Let h_u be the number of hops from the seed nodes to node u, and let $\mathcal{H}(i)$ be the set of nodes that are i hops away from the seed nodes; nodes in $\mathcal{H}(i)$ form layer i. $\mathcal{H}(0)$ is equivalent to the set of the seed nodes. We formally estimate the lower bounding relevance scores as follows:

Definition 2 (LOWER BOUND). *The following equation defines the relevance estimation of node* u, $\underline{s}_u$:

$$\underline{s}_u = \begin{cases} cd_u & (u \in \mathcal{H}(0)) \\ (1-c)\sum_{v \in \mathcal{H}(h_u - 1)} A_{uv}\underline{s}_v & (u \notin \mathcal{H}(0)) \end{cases} \quad (7)$$

This equation implies that (1) if node u is a seed node, its estimation is obtained from the restart probability and its preference score, and (2) if node u is not a seed node, its estimation is computed from that of its upper layer nodes, where $\mathcal{H}(0)$ forms the top layer, with their transition probabilities. It requires $O(n+m)$ time to compute the estimations of all nodes. This is because the estimations are yielded from a single breadth-first search that is rooted on the seed nodes, and breadth-first search needs $O(n+m)$ time [9].

We introduce the following lemma to show the property of the above estimation approach:

Lemma 1 (LOWER BOUND). *For any node in $\mathcal{H}(i)$, $\underline{s}_u \le s_u$ holds in the graph.*

Proof We prove that Definition 2 gives lower bounding estimations by using mathematical induction [16].

Initial step: We show the statement holds for any node in $\mathcal{H}(0)$. As described in Section 2, a random walk specifies seed nodes when (1) it jumps to the seed nodes with probability c or (2) outgoing edge of a current node is incident to the seed nodes. In the case of (1), a random walk jumps to node u of the seed nodes with probability cd_u. Therefore, steady-state probability of node u cannot be lower than cd_u. That is, $\underline{s}_u \le s_u$ holds for any node in $\mathcal{H}(0)$.

Inductive step: We assume that $\underline{s}_v \le s_v$ holds for any node in $\mathcal{H}(i-1)$. We prove the statement holds for any node in $\mathcal{H}(i)$. For a node u in $\mathcal{H}(i)$, the following inequality holds from Equation (1) since $\mathcal{H}(i-1)$ is a subset of all node sets in the graph (i.e. $\mathcal{H}(i-1) \subset \mathcal{V}$) and $c, d_u \ge 0$:

$$s_u = (1-c)\sum_{v \in \mathcal{V}} A_{uv}s_v + cd_u \ge (1-c)\sum_{v \in \mathcal{H}(i-1)} A_{uv}\underline{s}_v = \underline{s}_u$$

This completes the inductive step. Therefore, Definition 2 gives lower bounding estimations. □

Therefore, for all nodes in the graph, we can effectively obtain lower bounding estimations by Definition 2.

3.3.2 Upper bounding estimation

In this section, we detail our upper bounding estimation approach which can prune unnecessary exact computations. The upper bounding estimation is based on the lower bounding estimation introduced in Section 3.3.1. To find the top-k nodes, nodes are explored one by one, and we compute the upper bounding estimation and exact relevance score for each node. Let u_i be the i-th explored node, the definition of the upper bounding estimation is as follows:

Definition 3 (UPPER BOUND). *The relevance estimation of i-th explored node u_i, $\overline{s}_{u_i}$, is defined as follows:*

$$\overline{s}_{u_i} = \begin{cases} 1 - \sum_{j=2}^{n} \underline{s}_{u_j} & (i = 1) \\ \underline{s}_{u_i} - s_{u_{i-1}} + \overline{s}_{u_{i-1}} & (i \ne 1) \end{cases} \quad (8)$$

If $i = 1$, it needs $O(n)$ time to compute the estimation of a node from already computed lower bounding estimations. Otherwise, we can incrementally compute the estimation of a node at the cost of $O(1)$ time since $\underline{s}_{u_i}$, $s_{u_{i-1}}$, and $\overline{s}_{u_{i-1}}$ are already computed before computing $\overline{s}_{u_i}$.

In our approach, nodes are explored in descending order of their lower bounding estimations. There are two reasons for this approach. The first is that a node is expected to have high exact relevance score if its lower bounding relevance is high. Thus, we can efficiently find top-k nodes. The second reason is that, if an upper bounding estimation is lower than the K-th highest exact relevance of candidate nodes, our algorithm terminates the process based on the following property of the upper bounding estimation:

Algorithm 2 Top-k node identification

Input: $\mathbf{d}$, query distribution; K, number of answer nodes
Output: $\mathcal{V}_a$, set of answer nodes

```
1: θ = 0;
2: V_e = ∅;
3: V_a = ∅;
4: append K dummy nodes to V_a;
5: compute the lower bounding estimations of all nodes;
6: while V_e ≠ V do
7:    u = argmax(s̲_v | v ∈ V\V_e);
8:    compute the upper bounding estimation of node u;
9:    if s̄_u < θ then
10:      return V_a;
11:   else
12:      compute exact relevance of node u for distribution d;
13:      if s_u > θ then
14:         v = argmin(s_w | w ∈ V_a);
15:         remove node v from V_a;
16:         append node u to V_a;
17:         θ = min(s_w | w ∈ V_a);
18:      end if
19:   end if
20:   append node u to V_e;
21: end while
22: return V_a;
```

Lemma 2 (UPPER BOUND). *$s_{u_i} \le \overline{s}_{u_i} \le \overline{s}_{u_{i-1}}$ holds for i-th explored node u_i if nodes are explored in descending order of their lower bounding estimations.*

Proof We first prove $s_u \le \overline{s}_u$. From Equation (8) and Lemma 1, the following inequality holds since node relevance scores are steady-state probabilities:

$$\overline{s}_u = \underline{s}_{u_i} - s_{u_{i-1}} + \overline{s}_{u_{i-1}} = \underline{s}_{u_i} - s_{u_{i-1}} + \underline{s}_{u_{i-1}} - s_{u_{i-2}} + \ldots + \overline{s}_{u_1}$$
$$= \sum_{j=2}^{i} \underline{s}_{u_j} - \sum_{j=1}^{i-1} s_{u_j} + 1 - \sum_{j=2}^{n} \underline{s}_{u_j} = 1 - \sum_{j=1}^{i-1} s_{u_j} - \sum_{j=i+1}^{n} \underline{s}_{u_j}$$
$$\ge 1 - \sum_{j=1}^{i-1} s_{u_j} - \sum_{j=i+1}^{n} s_{u_j} = 1 - \sum_{j \ne i} s_{u_j} = s_{u_i}$$

We next prove that $\overline{s}_{u_i} \le \overline{s}_{u_{i-1}}$ holds. From Equation (8), we have $\overline{s}_{u_{i-1}} - \overline{s}_{u_i} = s_{u_{i-1}} - \underline{s}_{u_i} \ge \underline{s}_{u_{i-1}} - \underline{s}_{u_i} \ge 0$. This completes the proof. □

Lemma 2 indicates that, if the upper bounding estimation of an explored node is lower than the K-th highest relevance of the candidate nodes, all other unexplored nodes have lower relevance scores than that of the K-th node. Therefore, we can safely terminate the algorithm.

3.3.3 Top-k node algorithm

We show the algorithm that finds the top-k nodes by the estimation approach. In Algorithm 2, θ, $\mathcal{V}_a$, and $\mathcal{V}_e$ indicate the K-th highest relevance among the candidate nodes, the set of candidate/answer nodes, and the set of explored nodes, respectively. The algorithm sets the candidate nodes by appending K dummy nodes whose relevance scores are all 0 (line 4), and computes the lower bounding estimations (line 5). It then finds the node with the highest lower bounding estimation from the unexplored node set, $\mathcal{V}\backslash\mathcal{V}_e$, and computes the upper bounding estimation of the node (lines 7-8). If the upper bounding estimation is lower than θ, the node and all other unexplored nodes cannot be the

Algorithm 3 Finding highly relevant nodes

Input: $\mathbf{d}$, query distribution; ϵ, threshold
Output: $\mathcal{V}_a$, set of answer nodes
1: $\mathcal{V}_e = \emptyset$;
2: $\mathcal{V}_a = \emptyset$;
3: compute the lower bounding estimations of all nodes;
4: **while** $\mathcal{V}_e \neq \mathcal{V}$ **do**
5:   $u = \text{argmax}(\underline{s}_v | v \in \mathcal{V} \backslash \mathcal{V}_e)$;
6:   compute the upper bounding estimation of node u;
7:   **if** $\overline{s}_u \leq \epsilon$ **then**
8:     **return** $\mathcal{V}_a$;
9:   **else if** $\underline{s}_u > \epsilon$ **then**
10:     append node u to $\mathcal{V}_a$;
11:   **else**
12:     compute exact relevance of node u for distribution $\mathbf{d}$;
13:     **if** $s_u > \theta$ **then**
14:       append node u to $\mathcal{V}_a$;
15:     **end if**
16:   **end if**
17:   append node u to $\mathcal{V}_e$;
18: **end while**
19: **return** $\mathcal{V}_a$;

answer nodes (Lemma 2). Therefore, it terminates the process (lines 9-10). Otherwise, the node may be an answer node, so it computes the exact relevance of the node (line 12). If the computed relevance is higher than θ, it updates the candidate set, $\mathcal{V}_a$, and θ (lines 13-18). Finally, it returns the candidate set, $\mathcal{V}_a$, as the answer nodes (line 22).

We introduce the following theorem for Algorithm 2:

Theorem 4 (EXACTNESS IN TOP-K IDENTIFICATION). *Algorithm 2 finds top-k nodes exactly.*

Proof If θ_K are the answer nodes with K-th highest relevance scores, the upper bounding estimations of the answer nodes cannot be lower than θ_K (Lemma 2). The algorithm prunes a node if the upper bounding estimation of the node is lower than θ. Since the K-the highest relevance score of the candidate nodes cannot be more than that of the answer nodes (i.e. $\theta \leq \theta_K$), the answer nodes cannot be pruned by the algorithm. And, if a node have a relevance score less than θ, the node is pruned with its exact/estimated relevance by the algorithm. □

We discuss here the time complexity of Algorithm 2.

Theorem 5 (COMPUTATIONAL COST FOR TOP-K NODES). *Algorithm 2 requires $O(n \log n + m + |\mathbf{F}| + |\mathbf{Q}|)$ time to find top-k nodes.*

Proof The algorithm first computes lower bounding estimations for all nodes by single breadth-first search which takes $O(n + m)$ time. Next, it finds the node of the highest lower bounding estimation and computes the upper bounding estimation of the node. This requires $O(n \log n)$ and $O(n)$ time, respectively, if binomial heap [9] is used and none of the nodes are pruned. It takes $O(|\mathbf{F}| + |\mathbf{Q}|)$ time to compute exact relevance scores of all nodes since $\sum_{i=1}^{n} |\mathbf{f}_i| + |\mathbf{Q}| = |\mathbf{F}| + |\mathbf{Q}|$ (Theorem 2). Therefore, it needs $O(n \log n + m + |\mathbf{F}| + |\mathbf{Q}|)$ time to find the top-k nodes. □

3.4 Finding highly relevant nodes

In this section, we describe our approach to finding nodes whose relevance scores are higher than threshold ϵ. All proofs in this section are omitted due to the space limitations. To find highly relevant nodes, we utilize the lower bounding estimations to avoid unnecessary relevance computations; if the lower bounding estimation of a node is higher than ϵ, the node must be an answer node. Therefore, we prune the exact relevance computation of the node.

Nodes are explored in descending order of their lower bounding estimations. And the upper bounding estimations are utilized to skip unnecessary relevance computations as in top-k search. However, as shown in Definition 3, we cannot compute the upper bounding estimations of node u_i without the exact relevance of node u_{i-1}. In that case, we compute the upper bounding estimation of node u_i as follows:

Definition 4 (UPPER BOUND W/O EXACT RELEVANCES). *The relevance estimation of node u_i, $\overline{s}_{u_i}$, is computed as follows without the exact relevance computation of node u_{i-1}:*

$$\overline{s}_{u_i} = \underline{s}_{u_i} - \underline{s}_{u_{i-1}} + \overline{s}_{u_{i-1}} \tag{9}$$

We introduce the following lemma to show the property of the above estimation approach:

Lemma 3 (UPPER BOUND W/O EXACT RELEVANCES). *For i-th explored node u_i, $s_{u_i} \leq \overline{s}_{u_i} \leq \overline{s}_{u_{i-1}}$ holds, and it requires $O(1)$ time to compute the estimation if $i \neq 1$ in the estimation obtained by Definition 4.*

Algorithm 3 depicts our approach for finding highly relevant nodes. It first computes the lower bounding estimations for all nodes (line 3). It next finds the node with the highest lower bounding estimation and computes the upper bounding relevance of the node (lines 5-6). If the upper bounding estimation is not higher than ϵ, the node and remaining unexplored nodes cannot be answer nodes. Therefore, it terminates the process (lines 7-8). If the lower bounding estimation is higher than ϵ, its exact relevance must be higher than ϵ. So, we add the node to the answer node set (lines 9-10). Otherwise, the node can be answer node, so its exact relevance is computed (lines 11-16).

We have the following theorem for Algorithm 3:

Theorem 6 (FINDING HIGHLY RELEVANT NODES). *Algorithm 3 requires $O(n \log n + m + |\mathbf{F}| + |\mathbf{Q}|)$ time to exactly find highly relevant nodes.*

4. EXPERIMENTAL EVALUATION

We performed experiments to demonstrate the efficiency of the proposed approach against the iterative and approximate approaches. We used following three public datasets for the experiments:

- Social[3]: This is a graph taken from Slashdot.org[4]. The network contains interaction links between the users of Slashdot. There are 82,168 nodes and 948,464 edges.
- Routing[5]: We used routing information of the Internet. This graph was constructed from BGP tables posted by the University of Oregon Route Views Project[6]. This graph has 22,963 nodes and 48,436 edges.
- Web[7]: This dataset was taken from web pages in University of Notre Dame[8]. In this dataset, nodes represent pages from domain nd.edu and edges represent hyperlinks between them. There are 325,729 nodes and 1,497,135 edges.

[3] http://snap.stanford.edu/data/soc-Slashdot0902.html
[4] http://slashdot.org/
[5] http://www-personal.umich.edu/~mejn/netdata/as-22july06.zip
[6] http://routeviews.org/
[7] http://vlado.fmf.uni-lj.si/pub/networks/data/ND/NDnets.htm
[8] http://www.nd.edu/

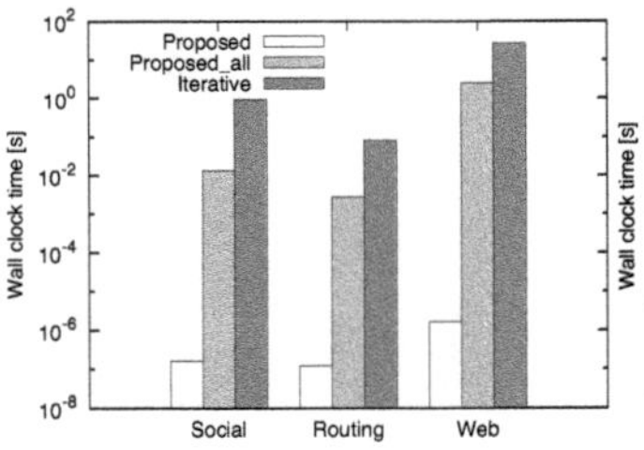

Figure 1: Relevance computation time.

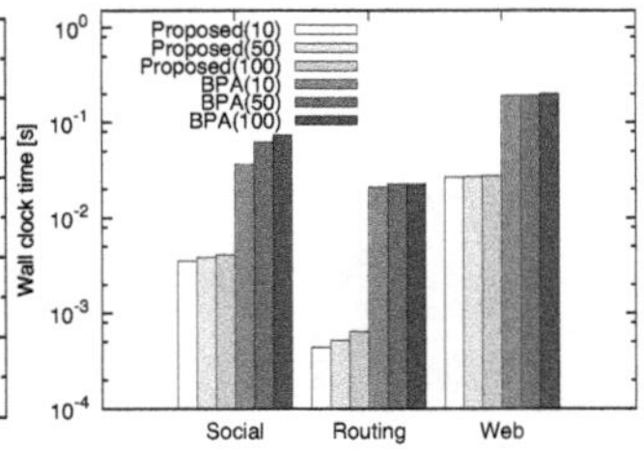

Figure 2: Efficiency of top-k nodes identification.

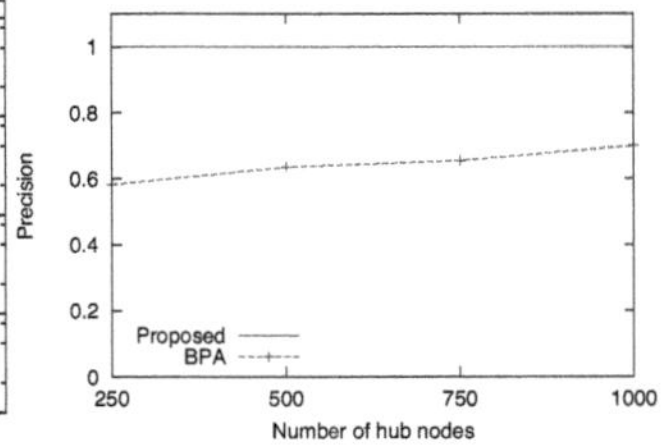

Figure 3: Accuracy versus number of hub nodes.

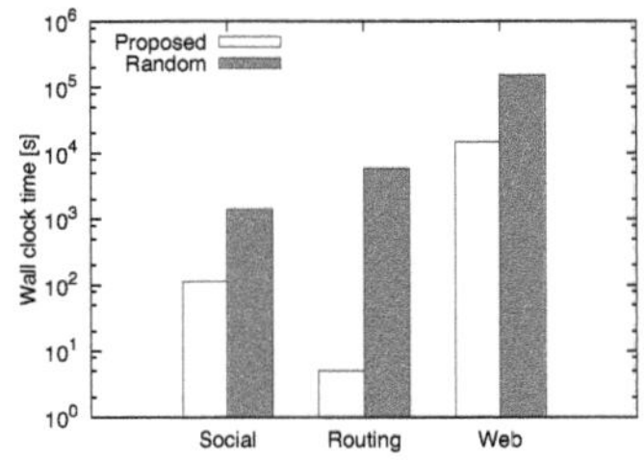

Figure 4: Precomputation time.

Table 2: Ratio of non-zero elements.

	Data set		
	Social	*Routing*	*Web*
$\|\mathbf{Q}\|/n^2$	3.40×10^{-6}	4.88×10^{-6}	2.76×10^{-4}
$\|\mathbf{R}^{-1}\|/n^2$	9.25×10^{-3}	2.40×10^{-3}	1.93×10^{-2}

We set the restart probability $c = 0.9$ as [13] did, and randomly selected ten nodes as seed nodes where the preference scores were equally set to same score. All the experiments were conducted on a Linux 2.26 GHz Intel Xeon server with 144GB of main memory. GCC 4.1.2 was used to implement all approaches.

4.1 Relevance computation time

We assessed relevance computation time for the proposed approach and the iterative approach since the none of previous approximate approaches can compute relevance exactly. To make the comparison fair, we also evaluated the relevance computation time of our approach for all nodes even though our approach can compute just single node relevance.

Figure 1 shows the computation time of the proposed approach for a single node relevance and all nodes relevances, referred to as "Proposed" and "Proposed_all", respectively. "Iterative" indicates the results of the iterative approach. Table 2 shows the ratio of non-zero elements in $\mathbf{Q}$ and $\mathbf{R}^{-1}$ to the squared number of nodes, n^2.

Figure 1 indicates that our approach is up to seven orders of magnitude faster than the iterative approach. The proposed approach is up to 70 times faster even if it computes the relevance scores of all nodes. As shown in Theorem 2, the proposed approach requires $O(|\mathbf{f}_x| + |\mathbf{Q}|)$ time to compute a single node relevance; the number of non-zero elements have an effect on the efficiency of relevance computations in our approach since $\mathbf{F} = c\mathbf{P}^T\mathbf{R}^{-1}$ and $\mathbf{g} = \mathbf{Q}^T\mathbf{Pd}$. Our permutation approach, as described in Section 3.2.2, is designed to obtain sparse matrices $\mathbf{Q}$ and $\mathbf{R}^{-1}$. As shown in Table 2, we can reduce the number of non-zero elements for $\mathbf{R}^{-1}$ and, especially for, $\mathbf{Q}$. That is, $|\mathbf{Q}| \ll |\mathbf{R}^{-1}| \ll n^2$. Therefore, we can compute relevance scores efficiently for the given distribution $\mathbf{d}$ since vector $\mathbf{g}$ is obtained from $\mathbf{d}$. However, as described in Section 2, the iterative approach recursively updates the relevance scores of all nodes until convergence. This leads to high computational cost. Therefore, we can compute relevance more efficiently than the iterative approach.

4.2 Computation time for top-k nodes

We performed experiments to demonstrate the effectiveness of our approach to find top-k nodes in a comparison to Basic Push Algorithm [17]. This algorithm approximately identifies the top-k nodes. It exploits precomputed relevance scores of all nodes from hub nodes to estimate the upper relevance bound. This implies it theoretically guarantees that the recall[9] of its answer results is always 1; all of the answer nodes output by the iterative approach are contained in those output by this algorithm. Other approximate approaches such as [3, 4] do not have this property. This also implies the number of answer nodes yielded by Basic Push Algorithm can be more than K. Hub nodes are selected according to degrees.

Figure 2 shows the efficiency of each approach where the number of hub nodes is set to 1,000. In this figure, the results of the proposed approach and Basic Push Algorithm are referred to as "Proposed(K)" and "BPA(K)", respectively, where K is the number of answer nodes. Figure 3 shows the precision with the various numbers of hub nodes for Social dataset in finding the top ten nodes. Precision is the fraction of answer nodes among top-k results by each approach that match those of the iterative approach. We additionally confirmed similar results for the other datasets even though we omit the results due to space limitations.

As shown in Figure 2, our approach can find the top-k nodes up to 50 times faster than the Basic Push Algorithm. In the worst case, the proposed approach computes the relevance scores of all nodes if none of the nodes are pruned. However, the number of relevance computations is limited to small numbers due to the effectiveness of the estimation approach. It takes $O(n)$ times to compute the estimations for all nodes. Thus our approach can efficiently prune unnecessary relevance computations.

Figure 3 indicates that our approach outputs the same results as the iterative approach. Figure 3 also shows that Basic Push Algorithm can find top-k nodes more accurately as the number of the hub nodes increase since this algorithm computes the upper bounding estimations from the hub nodes[10]. However, this algorithm cannot find the top-k nodes exactly while our approach outputs only exact answers. Moreover, the precomputation time of the Basic Push Algorithm is proportional to the number of hub nodes since the relevance scores of all nodes from all hub nodes must be precomputed by the iterative approach until convergence. Figure 2 and 3 show that our approach is superior to this algorithm in both speed and accuracy.

4.3 Precomputation time

Our approach precomputes the matrices $\mathbf{Q}$ and $\mathbf{R}^{-1}$ to compute node relevance scores. Thus we evaluated the effectiveness of our permutation approach in terms of precom-

[9] Recall is the fraction of answer nodes extracted by the iterative approach that were successfully extracted by this algorithm.

[10] We confirmed that this algorithm more efficiently finds answer nodes as the number of the hub nodes increases for the same reason.

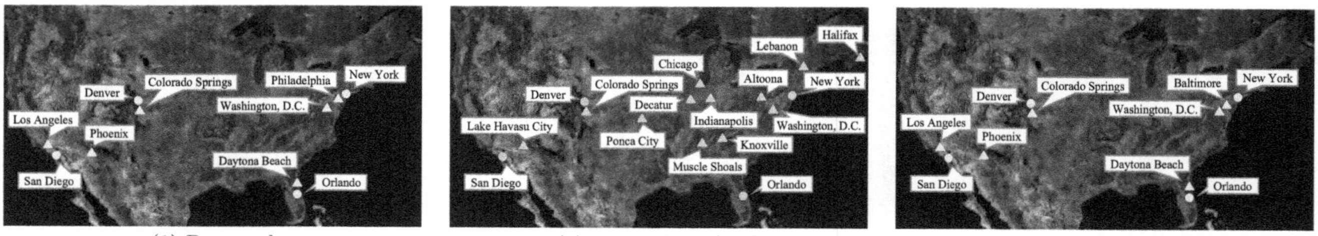

(1) Proposed (2) Monte Carlo(250) (3) Monte Carlo(1,000,000)

Figure 5: Highly relevant cities for San Diego, Denver, Orlando, and New York as detected by each approach.

putation time. In Figure 4, "Random" represents the results achieved when nodes are premutated in random order.

Figure 4 indicates that our permutation approach enhances the precomputation time as well as reducing the number of non-zero elements. Our approach is up to 1,200 times faster than the random permutation approach. Since the matrices $\mathbf{Q}$ and $\mathbf{R}^{-1}$ have sparse data structures in our approach, we can effectively reduce computations of non-zero matrices elements in Equation (4), (5), and (6). Therefore, we can efficiently obtain the matrices $\mathbf{Q}$ and $\mathbf{R}^{-1}$.

5. CASE-STUDIES

Our approach can exactly find nodes whose relevances are higher than ϵ. To show the applicability of our approach, we demonstrate the results of case-studies on a real dataset. Because none of the previous approaches, including Basic Push Algorithm, are designed to find highly relevant nodes, we compared our approach to the state-of-the-art approximate method by Avrachenkov et al. [3]. This approach uses Monte Carlo method to compute approximate relevance scores by performing multiple random walks. The results of case-studies revealed that our approach can obtain reasonable results more efficiently than the Monte Carlo method.

For this evaluation, we used the city dataset[11] consisting of 71,959 direct flights between 456 cities in North America. Flights and cities correspond to edges and nodes. Edge weights in the adjacency matrix are proportional to city proximities. We identified the nodes whose relevance scores exceeded 5×10^{-4}. We set San Diego, Denver, Orlando, and New York as the seed nodes. The preference scores of the seed nodes were equally set to the same score where the restart probability, c, was set to 0.9, the same as in the previous section. Figure 5 shows the results. The number of random walks in the Monte Carlo approach was set to 250 and 1,000,000 in Figure 5-(2) and 5-(3), respectively. In Figure 5, circles and triangles represent seed nodes and highly relevant nodes, respectively.

Figure 5-(1) shows highly relevant cities for San Diego, Denver, Orlando, and New York as determined by the proposed approach. These cities are all large ones in the United States. These cities have big airline hubs from which almost all cities can be directly accessed. Since PPR computes random walks from seed nodes, highly connected nodes from other nodes are expected to be highly relevant nodes if large cities are selected as seed nodes. As expected, relevant cities were Los Angeles, Phoenix, Colorado Springs, Daytona Beach, Philadelphia, and Washington, D.C. which also have big airline hubs. That is, we can detect cities with airline hubs from among large cities. Note that the results of our approach equal those of the iterative approach.

[11] http://www.psi.toronto.edu/index.php?q=affinity propagation

As shown in Figure 5-(2), if the number of random walks is 250, the Monte Carlo approach outputs different results from the proposed approach except for Washington, D.C. and Colorado Springs. The process time of the Monte Carlo approach was 21 microseconds while that of our approach was 20.5 microseconds; they are almost the same. As shown in Figure 5-(3), if the number of random walks is increased, the Monte Carlo approach has the same outputs as the proposed approach except for Baltimore. However, this leads to high computational time since the computational cost of the Monte Carlo approach is proportional to the number of random walks [3]. The Monte Carlo approach took 80.7 milliseconds with this setting; the proposed approach is more than 3,900 times faster.

The result of our approach is reasonable, and is consistent with our intuition. While our approach achieves high efficiency, it is guaranteed to output the same results as the iterative approach. This indicates that our approach can be another option for the research community in utilizing PPR.

6. RELATED WORK

Several approximate approaches have been proposed focusing on efficient computation for PPR. However, none of them guarantees the exact answer result; their outputs can differ from that of the iterative approach. Therefore, it is difficult for these approximate approaches to enhance the quality of real applications. None of them can be taken as a unified scheme that comprehensively solves the three problems described in Section 1.

Jeh et al. suggested a framework that, for nodes that belong to a highly linked subset of hub nodes, provides a scalable solution for PPR [23]. The approach is based on the observation that relevance scores for a given distribution can be approximated as a linear combination of the relevance scores from a single node in hub nodes. They compute approximate relevance scores for a given distribution using the relevance scores precomputed from hub nodes. Fogaras et al. proposed a Monte Carlo algorithm for PPR [10]. To compute approximate relevance scores, they use fingerprints of several nodes; a fingerprint of a node is a random walk starting from the node. They precompute fingerprints by simulating random walks and approximate relevance distributions from the ending nodes of these random walks. They approximate relevance scores by exploiting the linearity property of PPR. Avrachenkov et al. and Bahmani et al. independently improved the realization of the Monte Carlo method [3, 4]. Basic Push Algorithm is an approach that finds top-k nodes approximately but efficiently for PPR [17]. The approach uses precomputed relevance scores of hub nodes to estimate the upper relevance bound. However, their approach outputs ineligible nodes for top-k search, i.e. those that have low relevance scores as shown in Section 4. Basic Push Algorithm, proposed Chakrabarti et al., efficient approximate approach for ER graphs [7].

Random walk with restart (RWR) [13] is a special case of PPR in that it has only a single seed node; many papers have targeted the enhancement of RWR efficiency. Sun et al. proposed an approximate approach for RWR [33]. They used METIS [24] to partition a graph into several disjoint subgraphs, and they performed RWR only on the subgraph that contains the seed node. All nodes outside the subgraph are simply assigned RWR relevance scores of 0. In other words, their approach outputs a local estimation of RWR. Their approach is based on the observation that some of the nodes that are just a few hops away from the seed node have high RWR relevance scores. Based on the same observation, K-dash finds top-k nodes efficiently for RWR [12]. By using upper bounding estimations, it prunes unnecessary relevance computations of nodes that are far from the seed nodes. However, these two approaches do not support the case that there are multiple seed nodes as is true in PPR. Tong et al. showed that eigen-value decomposition [19] can be utilized to approximate RWR relevance scores [34]. They also showed the proof of an error bound of the approach. However, their proof is based on the assumption that the normalized graph Laplacian [39] can be exploited to represent a graph. Furthermore, it is impractical to compute eigen-value decomposition of a large graph since it is extremely time-consuming as they themselves pointed out.

7. CONCLUSIONS

We addressed the problems of computing single node relevance and finding the top-k/highly relevant nodes efficiently and exactly for PPR. Our approach is to compute single node relevance from sparse matrices in a non-iterative style and to prune unnecessary relevance computations by upper/lower relevance estimations. Experiments show that the proposed approach can achieve high efficiency without sacrificing the accuracy of answer results. PPR is fundamental in many applications. The proposed approach allows many applications to be implemented more efficiently, and helps to improve the effectiveness of future applications.

8. REFERENCES

[1] R. Andersen, F. R. K. Chung, and K. J. Lang. Local Graph Partitioning Using PageRank Vectors. In *FOCS*, pages 475–486, 2006.

[2] K. Avrachenkov, V. Dobrynin, D. Nemirovsky, S. K. Pham, and E. Smirnova. PageRank Based Clustering of Hypertext Document Collections. In *SIGIR*, pages 873–874, 2008.

[3] K. Avrachenkov, N. Litvak, D. Nemirovsky, E. Smirnova, and M. Sokol. Quick Detection of Top-k Personalized PageRank Lists. In *WAW*, pages 50–61, 2011.

[4] B. Bahmani, A. Chowdhury, and A. Goel. Fast Incremental and Personalized PageRank. *PVLDB*, 4(3):173–184, 2010.

[5] A. Balmin, V. Hristidis, and Y. Papakonstantinou. ObjectRank: Authority-based Keyword Search in Databases. In *VLDB*, pages 564–575, 2004.

[6] D. M. Blei, A. Y. Ng, and M. I. Jordan. Latent Dirichlet Allocation. *Journal of Machine Learning Research*, 3:993–1022, 2003.

[7] S. Chakrabarti, A. Pathak, and M. Gupta. Index Design and Query Processing for Graph Conductance Search. *VLDB J.*, 20(3):445–470, 2011.

[8] Y.-Y. Chen, Q. Gan, and T. Suel. Local Methods for Estimating PageRank Values. In *CIKM*, pages 381–389, 2004.

[9] T. H. Cormen, C. E. Leiserson, R. L. Rivest, and C. Stein. *Introduction to Algorithms*. The MIT Press, 2009.

[10] D. Fogaras, B. Rácz, K. Csalogány, and T. Sarlós. Towards Scaling Fully Personalized PageRank: Algorithms, Lower Bounds, and Experiments. *Internet Mathematics*, 2(3), 2005.

[11] F. Fouss, A. Pirotte, J.-M. Renders, and M. Saerens. Random-walk Computation of Similarities Between Nodes of a Graph with Application to Collaborative Recommendation. *IEEE Trans. Knowl. Data Eng.*, 19(3):355–369, 2007.

[12] Y. Fujiwara, M. Nakatsuji, M. Onizuka, and M. Kitsuregawa. Fast and Exact Top-k Search for Random Walk with Restart. *PVLDB*, 5(5):442–453, 2012.

[13] B. Gallagher, H. Tong, T. Eliassi-Rad, and C. Faloutsos. Using Ghost Edges for Classification in Sparsely Labeled Networks. In *KDD*, pages 256–264, 2008.

[14] B. Gao, T.-Y. Liu, W. Wei, T. Wang, and H. Li. Semi-supervised Ranking on Very Large Graphs with Rich Metadata. In *KDD*, pages 96–104, 2011.

[15] M. Gori and A. Pucci. Itemrank: A Random-walk Based Scoring Algorithm for Recommender Engines. In *IJCAI*, pages 2766–2771, 2007.

[16] D. S. Gunderson. *Handbook of Mathematical Induction: Theory and Applications*. Chapman and Hall/CRC, 2010.

[17] M. S. Gupta, A. Pathak, and S. Chakrabarti. Fast Algorithms for Top-k Personalized PageRank Queries. In *WWW*, pages 1225–1226, 2008.

[18] A. Harpale, Y. Yang, S. Gopal, D. He, and Z. Yue. Citedata: a New Multi-faceted Dataset for Evaluating Personalized Search Performance. In *CIKM*, pages 549–558, 2010.

[19] D. A. Harville. *Matrix Algebra From a Statistician's Perspective*. Springer, 2008.

[20] J. L. Herlocker, J. A. Konstan, A. Borchers, and J. Riedl. An Algorithmic Framework for Performing Collaborative Filtering. In *SIGIR*, pages 230–237, 1999.

[21] V. Hristidis, L. Raschid, and Y. Wu. Scalable Link-based Personalization for Ranking in Entity-relationship Graphs. In *WebDB*, 2011.

[22] G. Jeh and J. Widom. SimRank: a Measure of Structural-context Similarity. In *KDD*, pages 538–543, 2002.

[23] G. Jeh and J. Widom. Scaling Personalized Web Search. In *WWW*, pages 271–279, 2003.

[24] G. Karypis, V. Kumar, and V. Kumar. Multilevel K-way Partitioning Scheme for Irregular Graphs. *Journal of Parallel and Distributed Computing*, 48:96–129, 1998.

[25] D. Liben-Nowell and J. M. Kleinberg. The Link Prediction Problem for Social Networks. In *CIKM*, pages 556–559, 2003.

[26] Q. Liu, E. Chen, H. Xiong, and C. H. Q. Ding. Exploiting User Interests for Collaborative Filtering: Interests Expansion via Personalized Ranking. In *CIKM*, pages 1697–1700, 2010.

[27] F. McSherry. A Uniform Approach to Accelerated PageRank Computation. In *WWW*, pages 575–582, 2005.

[28] G. Namata, S. Kok, and L. Getoor. Collective Graph Identification. In *KDD*, pages 87–95, 2011.

[29] M. Newman, A.-L. Barabasi, and D. J. Watts. *The Structure And Dynamics of Networks*. Princeton University Press, 2006.

[30] L. Page, S. Brin, R. Motwani, and T. Winograd. The PageRank Citation Ranking: Bringing Order to the Web. Technical Report 1999-66, Stanford InfoLab, November 1999.

[31] W. H. Press, S. A. Teukolsky, W. T. Vetterling, and B. P. Flannery. *Numerical Recipes 3rd Edition*. Cambridge University Press, 2007.

[32] E. Smirnova, K. Avrachenkov, and B. Trousse. Using Web Graph Structure for Person Name Disambiguation. In *CLEF*, 2010.

[33] J. Sun, H. Qu, D. Chakrabarti, and C. Faloutsos. Neighborhood Formation and Anomaly Detection in Bipartite Graphs. In *ICDM*, pages 418–425, 2005.

[34] H. Tong, C. Faloutsos, and J.-Y. Pan. Fast Random Walk with Restart and Its Applications. In *ICDM*, pages 613–622, 2006.

[35] K. Voevodski, S.-H. Teng, and Y. Xia. Spectral Affinity in Protein Networks. *BMC Systems Biology*, 3(1):112, 2009.

[36] S. White and P. Smyth. Algorithms for Estimating Relative Importance in Networks. In *KDD*, pages 266–275, 2003.

[37] J. Yang and J. Leskovec. Patterns of Temporal Variation in Online Media. In *WSDM*, pages 177–186, 2011.

[38] M. Yannakakis. Computing the Minimum Fill-in is NP-complete. *SIAM. J. on Algebraic and Discrete Methods*, 2(1):77–79, 1981.

[39] D. Zhou, O. Bousquet, T. N. Lal, J. Weston, and B. Schölkopf. Learning with Local and Global Consistency. In *NIPS*, 2003.

PageRank on an Evolving Graph

Bahman Bahmani*
Computer Science
Stanford University
Stanford, CA
bahman@stanford.edu

Ravi Kumar
Yahoo! Research
701 First Avenue
Sunnyvale, CA
ravikumar@yahoo-inc.com

Mohammad Mahdian*
Google, Inc.
1600 Amphitheatre Parkway
Mountain View, CA
mahdian@gmail.com

Eli Upfal†
Computer Science
Brown University
Providence, RI
eli@cs.brown.edu

ABSTRACT

One of the most important features of the Web graph and social networks is that they are constantly evolving. The classical computational paradigm, which assumes a fixed data set as an input to an algorithm that terminates, is inadequate for such settings. In this paper we study the problem of computing PageRank on an evolving graph. We propose an algorithm that, at any moment in the time and by crawling a small portion of the graph, provides an estimate of the PageRank that is close to the true PageRank of the graph at that moment. We will also evaluate our algorithm experimentally on real data sets and on randomly generated inputs. Under a stylized model of graph evolution, we show that our algorithm achieves a provable performance guarantee that is significantly better than the naive algorithm that crawls the nodes in a round-robin fashion.

Categories and Subject Descriptors: H.2.8 [**Database Management**]: Database Applications – Data Mining

Keywords: Dynamic graphs, PageRank, Random walks

1. INTRODUCTION

The traditional paradigm in the field of algorithm design assumes that the algorithm reads the input data set, produces a solution for this input, and then terminates. Unfortunately, this simplistic model is inadequate for many of today's data mining applications, particularly applications on the Web and in social networks. Here, the input data is not stationary. Rather, it changes over time and the algorithm, unaware of these changes, needs to probe the input continually and produce solutions at any point in time that are close to the correct solution for the then-current input. A formalization of this framework was introduced by Anagnostopoulos et al., who obtained efficient algorithms for sorting [1] and several classical graph problems [2].

In this work we focus on a problem that is probably the best fit to this framework: computing PageRank on an evolving graph. Since its groundbreaking introduction [23], PageRank has emerged as a very effective measure of reputation for both web graphs and social networks. Despite many advances in the field of web information retrieval, search engines still rely on variants of the notion of PageRank for ranking search results. PageRank is a quantity that is computed based on the graph structure of the web. This graph structure changes over time, and the only way for the search engine to learn about the new changes is to crawl the web, i.e., look up a web page (a node in the graph) to discover all its outgoing links. There is a limit on the crawling capacity, and therefore the search engine often has a stale image of the graph. The objective is to design an algorithm that decides which pages to crawl and computes the PageRank using the obtained information in such a way that the error in the computed PageRank (as compared to the PageRank of the current graph) is bounded at any point in time. PageRank-like measures have applications far beyond search, for example, in computing trust and reputation in online social networks; see [6] for more details.

Several algorithms for updating PageRank values upon changes to the network have been proposed; see Section 2. However, all of these algorithms assume knowledge of *all* the changes in the network. But, this assumption is unrealistic in many modern applications of PageRank. For instance, a web search engine using PageRank in its search rankings can learn about the changes to the web graph only through periodically crawling the web. Similarly, a third-party vendor computing PageRank on a constantly evolving social network such as Twitter or Facebook can only learn about the changes to the network via a rate-limited API.

Our contributions. In this paper we study the problem of computing PageRank in the evolving graph framework. The graph slowly changes over time and the algorithm can

*Part of this work was done while the author was at Yahoo! Research.

†Part of this work was done while the author was visiting Yahoo! Research.

KDD'12, August 12–16, 2012, Beijing, China.

observe the graph by periodically probing its nodes to obtain its current set of outgoing neighbors. The goal is to design a probing algorithm that maintains a good approximation of the true PageRank values of the underlying evolving graph.

We propose two algorithms, one randomized and one deterministic, for solving this problem (Section 4). The randomized algorithm is based on the intuition that nodes with higher PageRank values need to be probed more often since they have more impact on the PageRank values of other nodes; the deterministic algorithm also embodies this intuition, but with additional guarantees. We then evaluate our algorithms empirically on real and randomly generated datasets. We demonstrate that they also perform well in practice when compared to two natural baselines of random probing and round-robin probing (Section 5).

Under a stylized yet arguably natural model of graph evolution, we give a theoretical analysis of the performance of the randomized algorithm and prove that it significantly outperforms the simple algorithm that crawls all pages with equal frequency (Section 6). Finally, we sketch how our theoretical results can be adapted and generalized to variants and extensions of our simple model (Section 6.3).

2. RELATED WORK

Efficient computation of PageRank and its variants on massive graphs has attracted a great amount of interest over time in both academic and industrial settings, and algorithms in different computational models have been proposed; see the survey on PageRank [6]. Broadly speaking, algorithms for PageRank fall into one of two categories: linear algebraic methods [7, 28, 13, 14, 15, 8, 11, 17, 18, 19] and Monte Carlo methods [3, 9, 5, 4]. The simplest linear algebraic method is the basic Power Iteration [23] and typical algorithms in this category aim to speed up the power iteration through a combination of linear algebraic techniques and careful use of the properties of the practical graphs, e.g., the web graph [13, 14, 15]. Monte Carlo methods have the advantage of being very efficient and highly scalable [3]. Hence, they have been adapted to design algorithms for scalable computation of PageRank and its variants in emerging computational models such as data streaming [9] and MapReduce [4].

Algorithms for updating PageRank values upon changes to the network have been proposed in both the broad categories mentioned above. A family of the linear algebraic methods use the "aggregation" idea to efficiently update the PageRank vector [8, 17, 18]. Tong et al. [29] and McSherry [20] also propose algorithms to deal with PageRank updates. Among the Monte Carlo methods, Bahmani et al. [5] proposes an incremental algorithm for computation of PageRank, which is fast enough even for real-time updates. However, all of these algorithms, which belong to either the data streaming [21] or dynamic graph [12] computation models, assume knowledge of all the changes in the network. Our algorithm, on the other hand, must work without being notified of the underlying changes to the network.

The evolving model of computation was introduced and formalized by Anagnostopoulos et al. [1, 2]. In contrast with more traditional computation models such as streaming [21], property testing [26, 27], multi-armed-bandits [16], and dynamic graph models [12], this model captures both of the two essential properties of large evolving data applications: the input is changing over time without notifying the algorithm, and the only way for the algorithm to learn about these changes (to accordingly update its solution) is by periodically probing the input in a limited way. Anagnostopoulos et al. [1, 2] formalize this framework and study sorting, selection, and basic graph connectivity problems in this computation model.

Note that there is a line of research on algorithms for computing optimal crawling schedules on the web [30, 24, 10, 22, 25]. The objective in these papers is generally to put together a crawling schedule that minimizes the staleness of the cached image of the web. This is different from our objective, which is to compute the PageRank with as little error as possible.

3. BACKGROUND

Evolving graph model. We first define the model of computation on evolving graphs that will be used throughout this paper. Our model follows the general framework proposed in [1, 2]. We deliberately do not specify how the graph changes in our model in order to keep the model itself general and to emphasize that our algorithms apply to this level of generality. Later, in Section 6, we will fix a graph change model for the purposes of theoretical analysis.

We assume a discrete notion of time, indexed by nonnegative integers. The directed graph at a point t in time is denoted by G^t. We assume that an upper bound on the total number of nodes of the graph is known ahead of time and is a fixed quantity n. We stress that this assumption is only for the simplicity of analysis and in Section 6.3 we will discuss how this assumption can be relaxed; our algorithms actually do not need this assumption. The sequence $\{G^t \mid t \geq 0\}$ thus defines a graph that changes over time. We assume that the difference between two consecutive graphs in this sequence is small; this assumption is without loss of generality since it can be achieved by choosing a sufficiently fine time granularity.

An algorithm in this model can observe the graph by *probing* its nodes. At each time step the algorithm can probe at most one node,* upon which it will see the current set of outgoing edges of this node. Since the graph is changing and the algorithm can only see a small part of the graph through each probe, it cannot have a completely up-to-date image of the graph. Note that in our model we do not impose constraints on the running time or the storage space of our algorithm. Such constraints, even though interesting and meaningful, lead to completely different aspects of the problem that are well-explored in the literature.[†] Therefore, the focus of our model is on the strategy for deciding which node to probe each time.

PageRank. We now recall the definition of PageRank. Let ϵ be a fixed constant called the *teleport probability* (probability of jumping to a random node). The PageRank of a graph G is a vector π that is the stationary distribution of the following random walk: at any step of the walk, with probability ϵ we move to a node chosen uniformly at random

*This is once again for simplicity of exposition. It will be easy to extend the algorithms and the model to the more general case.

[†]In fact, since the main time-consuming component of our algorithms is the computation of PageRank, they can be made efficient using the previous work on efficient PageRank computation.

and with probability $1-\epsilon$, we choose one of the outgoing edges of the current node uniformly at random and move to the head of that edge.[‡] The vector π is called the *PageRank* vector of G, and π_v is called the PageRank of node v in G. Denote by π_u^t, in_u^t, and out_u^t the PageRank, the in-degree, and the out-degree of node u in G^t.

Recall that our task is to design an algorithm to compute the PageRank of a directed graph that is changing. At the end of each time step, the algorithm should output a PageRank vector ϕ^t for the graph. The goal is to do this in such a way that the difference between π^t and ϕ^t is small.

4. ALGORITHMS

In this section we describe the various algorithms for computing PageRank on an evolving graph. Recall that each algorithm essentially boils down to a probing strategy: in what order the nodes in the graph should be probed to learn the neighborhood of the node. Each of our algorithms will operate by maintaining an image of the graph that it learns according to its probes. It computes PageRank on this maintained image and outputs that as its approximation to the true PageRank. Note that this automatically determines the time and space complexities of the algorithm: it needs to store the entire graph as it sees and can use power iteration to compute the PageRank. The primary quantity of interest is therefore the error caused by a particular probing method. We describe two baseline algorithms where the probe strategy is trivial and two algorithms that use a non-trivial probing strategy. In Section 5, we will experimentally evaluate these algorithms.

Baselines. We start by defining two algorithms that act as baselines used for comparison in Section 5. The first algorithm probes a node chosen uniformly at random at every time step. Based on these probes, at each point t, it has a most recent image H^t of the graph (i.e., the set of out-going edges of v in H^t is the set observed the last time v was probed). The output is the PageRank vector of this image. We call this algorithm *Random Probing*.

Random Probing is based on probing nodes with equal frequencies. An alternative, deterministic, way to implement this is by cycling through the nodes and probing them in this order. Again, the output at any moment is the PageRank vector of the current image of the graph. This algorithm is called *Round-Robin Probing*.

Proportional Probing. To improve over the above baselines, we need to depart from probing nodes with equal frequencies. The intuition is that if the outgoing edges of a node of high PageRank changes, then it affects the PageRank of other nodes by a larger amount. Therefore, such nodes should be probed with higher frequency. This motivates our first algorithm, which we call *Proportional Probing*:

> At each step t, pick a node v to probe with probability proportional to the PageRank of v in the algorithm's current image of the graph. The output, as before, is the PageRank vector of the current image.

For the purpose of the theoretical analysis (in Section 6), we analyze a variant of the Proportional Probing that alternates between probing nodes in a round-robin fashion and probing nodes chosen randomly with probabilities proportional to their PageRank values in the current image. This alternation, while does not necessarily help in practice, makes it easier to analyze the accuracy of the algorithm.

[‡]If the current node has no out-going edge, we jump to a random node with probability 1.

Priority Probing. Finally, we give a deterministic algorithm that probes nodes with frequencies proportional to their current PageRank. The idea is to define a *priority* for each node. Initially, the priority of each node is to zero. In each time step, the node with the highest priority is probed (or if there is more than one, one is arbitrarily chosen). The priority of this node is set to zero, and the priority of other nodes is incremented by their PageRank in the current image of the graph. This pseudo-code is presented in Algorithm 1. We call this algorithm *Priority Probing*.

Algorithm 1 Priority Probing

```
for all nodes u do
  priority_u ← 0
for every time step t do
  v ← arg max_u priority_u
  Probe v
  Let H^t be the current image of the graph
  Output the PageRank vector φ^t of H^t
  priority_v ← 0
  for all nodes u ≠ v do
    priority_u ← priority_u + φ^t_u
```

The main advantage of Priority Probing over Proportional Probing is the following. Proportional Probing picks nodes proportional to their PageRank, but in a stochastic manner. Priority Probing arose out of the following question: is there a (deterministic) probing method such that at each step each node u is picked with the prescribed probability ϕ_u^t and is picked at least once every $O(1/\phi_u^t)$ steps? Note that such a probing strategy will ensure that the algorithm will never miss probing a set of nodes for too long because of the randomness.

It is easy to show using the probabilistic method that such a probing sequence always exists. Priority Probing is a just a simple constructive way of realizing such a sequence. To analyze the guarantee of Priority Probing, for simplicity of analysis, assume that all the ϕ_u^t's are different; therefore, if a node u ever reaches $\text{priority}_u = 1$, then it will be probed in the next step. For any $p \in (0,1]$, there can be no more than $1/p$ nodes with $\phi_u^t \geq p$; this follows since priority_u of each unprobed node u is incremented by ϕ_u^t. Thus, for any node u, by the time priority_u becomes 1, all nodes v such that $\phi_v^t > \phi_u^t$ would have already been probed.

5. EXPERIMENTS

In this section we present the results of our experiments on real-world graphs to study the performance of our algorithms. We start by describing the data set in Section 5.1. Then, in Section 5.2, we will describe the experiments, i.e., the algorithms we run, the parameters we will let vary, and the metrics we will measure. The results are presented in Section 5.3 and the figures therein.

5.1 Data

In this section we describe the data sets used in our experiments. Each data set is comprised of two parts: the initial graph and evolving graph. The initial graph is the graph we use to bootstrap the process. The evolving graph is a sequence of additions and deletions of temporal edges and nodes of the graph. Now, we proceed to describe the data sets. Table 1 shows their statistical characteristics.

AS. The graph of routers comprising the Internet is organized into subgraphs called Autonomous Systems (AS). Each AS exchanges traffic flows with some of its peers and one can construct a communication network from the BGP (Border Gateway Protocol) logs. This data was collected from the University of Oregon Route Views Project and consists of 733 daily instances from November 8, 1997 to January 2, 2000. The dataset is publicly available and can be downloaded from `http://snap.stanford.edu/data/as.html`. We fix the communication graph on November 8, 1997 to be the initial graph and we assume that each link in the communication graph lasts for a day, i.e., if a directed edge is present on the ith day and not on the $(i+1)$st day, we assume that it was deleted on the $(i+1)$st day. Likewise, a directed edge is assumed to be added on the $(i+1)$st day if it was not present on the ith day.

CAIDA. This dataset contains 122 CAIDA Autonomous Systems graphs from January 2004 to November 2007 (see `http://www.caida.org/data/active/as-relationships/`). This dataset is also publicly available from `http://snap.stanford.edu/data/as-caida.html`. As before, this graph denotes the communication patterns of the routers. We take the initial graph to be the communication in January 2004 and we assume that each link exists until the next snapshot. The interpretation of edge addition/deletion is as in AS.

RAND. This is a data set that is randomly generated according to the distribution described in Section 6. We generated the graph with $n = 100$ nodes and out-degrees that form a power law with exponent 0.5 (i.e., the out-degree of the ith node is proportional to $i^{0.5}$). We simulated the model for 500000 changes, i.e., 250000 edge removals and the same number of edge additions.

Dataset	max #nodes (n)	#initial edges	#temporal edges	%edge additions
AS	7,716	10,696	488,986	0.516
CAIDA	31,379	65,911	1,084,388	0.518
RAND	100	715	250,000	0.5

Table 1: Details of the datasets used.

5.2 Experiments

Our goal is to evaluate the four algorithms described in Section 4. Of these four algorithms, Random Probing and Round-Robin Probing serve as baselines, and our goal is to compare Proportional Probing and Priority Probing against these baselines. (As we mentioned earlier, we know of no incremental PageRank algorithm that works in our model, i.e., when the algorithm is not aware of the changes to the graph.) In a sense, Random Probing serves as a baseline for Proportional Probing (as they are both randomized and can select which node to probe in an efficient and parallelizable way), and Round-Robin serves as a baseline for Priority Probing (as they are both deterministic). One can expect the deterministic algorithms to better than the corresponding randomized algorithms, as they avoid some of the "waste" caused by each time flipping a coin independent of the previous steps.

In addition to these algorithms, we run a *hybrid* between Proportional Probing and Round-Robin Probing. The hybrid algorithm is parametrized by a parameter $\beta \in [0,1]$ which controls the ratio of round-robin vs proportional probes made by the algorithm; making $\beta = 1$ will be the same as Round-Robin Probing. This is essentially a generalized version of the algorithm analyzed theoretically in Section 6.

We assume that initially all the algorithms have an image of the graph that is a perturbed version of the graph at that point. This is done to ensure that the simulations reach a steady state quickly. If we initialize the simulation assuming that the algorithms can observe the initial graph, the error will start at zero and will reach the steady state after some time. Similarly, if we start the algorithms without any knowledge of the graph, the error initially will be high, and will decrease to the steady state over time (although this process would take long). At the end, what we are interested in is the error of the algorithms after they stabilize.

For most of our simulations, we assume that the change process and the probing process progress at the same rate, i.e., for each change the algorithm can probe once. More precisely, we will have a *recomputing frequency* K, which indicates that after each K steps, the algorithm gets to do K probes. This is enough for simulations that seek to compare the algorithms. We will also experiment with varying the relative speed of the change and probing frequencies. This will be parameterized by a number α, which indicates the number of probes allowed for the algorithm for every (edge) change; here, an addition or deletion of an edge is considered to be a change. This means that after every K changes to the graph, the algorithm gets to make αK probes.

Metrics. Our main measure of performance is the L_∞ metric, which is defined as $L_\infty(\pi^t, \phi^t) = \max_{u \in V} |\pi^t(u) - \phi^t(u)|$, where π^t is the PageRank vector of the current graph, and ϕ^t is the vector output by the algorithm (both of these vectors are unit vectors in the ℓ_1 norm). To show that our results are "robust" to the choice of performance metric, we also run some of the simulations with the L_1 metric, which is defined as $L_1(\pi^t, \phi^t) = \sum_{u \in V} |\pi^t(u) - \phi^t(u)|$.

5.3 Results

A comparison of the algorithms. As expected intuitively, in both data sets AS and CAIDA and according to both measures L_1 and L_∞, the performance of Proportional Probing is almost always better than Random Probing (i.e., has lower error), and Priority Probing is almost always better than Round-Robin Probing. There is no clear comparison between Proportional Probing and Round-Robin Probing. The results are presented in Figure 1 (for the AS graph) and Figure 2 (for the CAIDA graph). As can be seen, the difference between the algorithms can be significant; for example, Priority and Random Probing have errors that are almost a factor two apart in the CAIDA data set. For RAND the difference is even greater, but this is to be expected given our theoretical analysis in Section 6. Note that the numbers on the y-axis in all these figures are small since the PageRank vector is normalized; the numbers should be viewed with the magnitude of n (from Table 1) in mind.

We also ran the experiments with the probing strategy proportional to the in-degree of a node instead of its PageR-

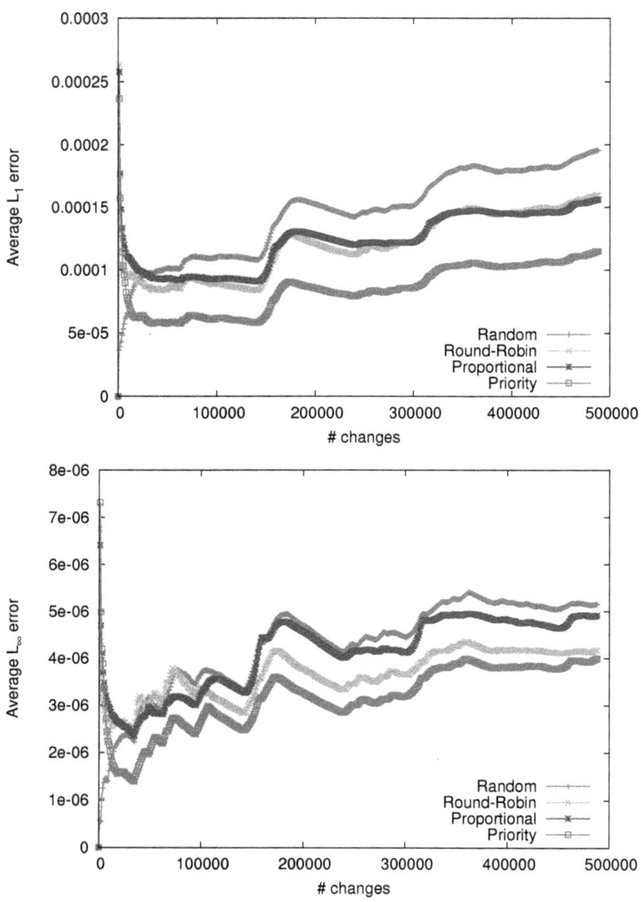

Figure 1: Average L_1 and L_∞ error of various algorithms for the AS graph.

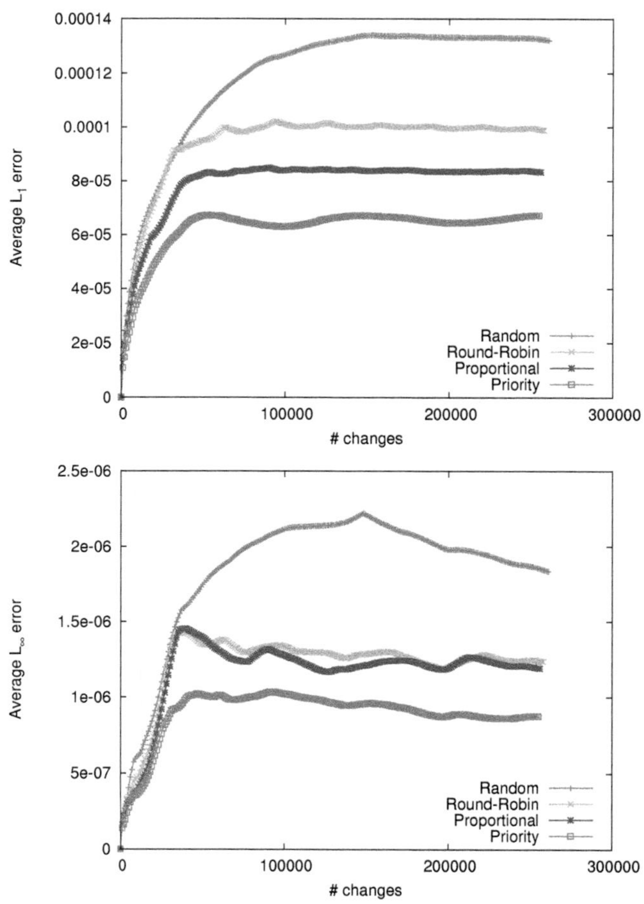

Figure 2: Average L_1 and L_∞ error of various algorithms for the CAIDA graph.

ank value. All of these results were qualitatively identical to the PageRank results and we omit them.

Effect of probing rate α. Figure 4 shows the results of the simulations on the AS graph with $\alpha = 2, 4$. Obviously, the algorithms perform better when they probe more frequently. Furthermore, the choice of α does not seem to affect the comparison between different algorithms, i.e., they are often ordered the same way they were for $\alpha = 1$ (Figure 1).

Algorithm's image vs truth. Another curious question is which of the algorithms has a more "stale" image of the graph. This can be measured by counting the number of edges that are in the image but not in the true graph, and vice versa. The result, for the AS graph, is shown in Figure 5. This figure suggests that there is no clear comparison between the staleness of the images of the four algorithms. This is interesting, since if the changes were happening uniformly at random in the graph, then Random Probing and Round-Robin Probing should have had an advantage in terms of the staleness of their image, whereas we see that quite often this is not the case. This suggests that the change in real-world networks is biased toward nodes with higher importance, and this gives a double advantage to Proportional Probing and Priority Probing.

The hybrid algorithm. We run the hybrid algorithm that interpolates between Round-Robin Probing and Proportional Probing with different parameters to see the effect of the round-robin rate β on the error. As can be seen in Figure 6, the lowest error happens at approximately $\beta = 0.9$. It is curious that this hybrid algorithm performs better than both Round-Robin Probing and Proportional Probing. Perhaps one intuitive reason for this is that the hybrid algorithm assigns more frequency to the more important nodes, while at the same time guaranteeing that each node will be visited at least once during the last $O(n)$ steps. This is precisely the property of the hybrid algorithm that is used in the theoretical analysis.

6. A THEORETICAL ANALYSIS

In this section we provide a theoretical analysis of the hybrid algorithm that alternate between proportional and round robin probing. In order to give a meaningful analysis of the error bound, we need to first fix a model for how the graph changes over time. We do that in the following section by defining a natural stochastic graph process.

6.1 Model and notation

There are many ways to define a model for how G^t changes into G^{t+1}. Intuitively, we want a model that is simple, captures the fact that links on the web change, and that this change happens in a non-uniform way, i.e., popular nodes have higher probabilities of being linked to. At the same

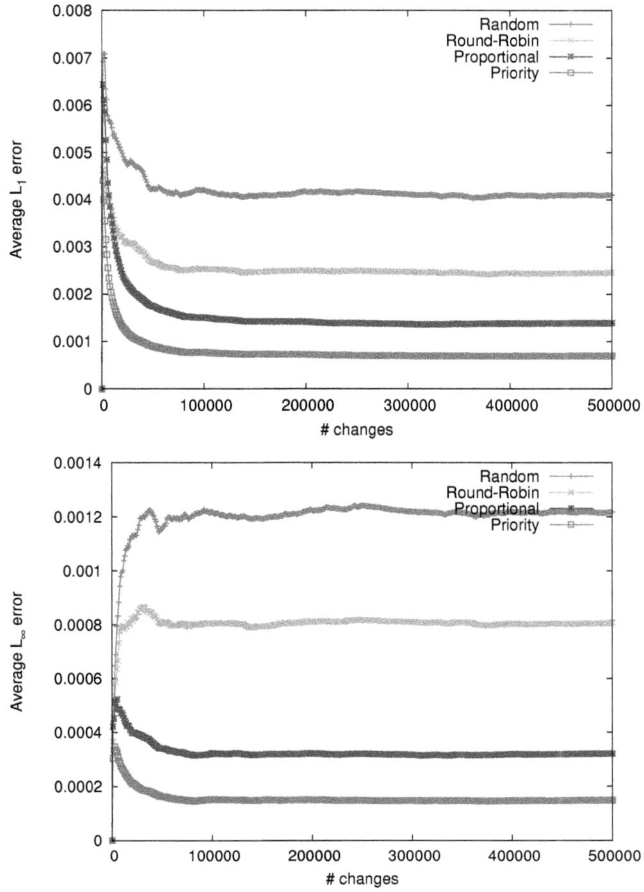

Figure 3: Average L_1 and L_∞ error of various algorithms for the RAND graph.

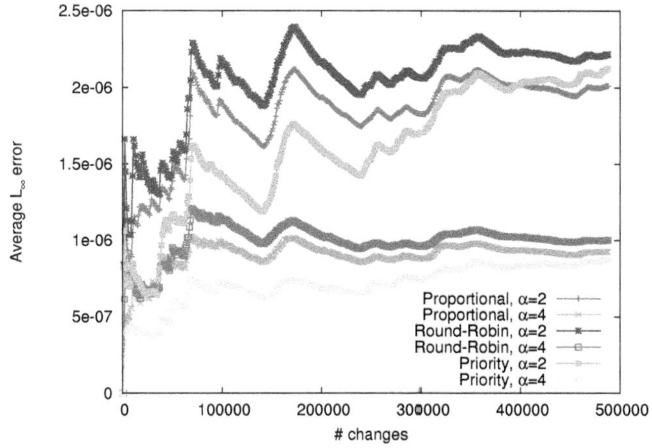

Figure 4: Average L_∞ error of Round-Robin, Proportional, and Priority as a function of the probing rate α for the AS graph.

time, we also want a near-realistic model where we can something formal and rigorous.

As stated before, we assume that the graph does not grow, i.e., the number of nodes of the graph is fixed to be n. Also, we assume that the number of edges does not change in this process. Both these assumptions are for simplicity and we discuss in Section 6.3 how they can be relaxed. At any time instance, we pick one link at random, and change the page it is pointing at to a new page. The new page is picked with probability proportional to its current PageRank, which intuitively captures the importance of this page at that time.

Formally, we define a stochastic directed graph process $\{G^t \mid t \geq 0\}$ where G^0 is an arbitrary directed graph on n nodes and m edges and graph G^{t+1} is obtained from G^t by the following process: an edge (u, v) is chosen uniformly at random from the m edges and its head is moved to a new node v' chosen with probability equal to $\pi^t_{v'}$.

Note that the implicit assumption here is that the rate of probe of our algorithm is the same as the rate of change (since each step corresponds to one probe). This assumption is for simplicity and our analysis carries over to the case that the ratio of the rate of the two processes is any constant, with the appropriate constants modifying the bounds.

Let $P(t)$ be the matrix of a random walk on G^t, where $P(t)_{u,v} = 1/\text{out}^t_u$ if there is a direct edge from u to v, otherwise $P(t)_{u,v} = 0$. Le $\bar{1}$ denote the all-ones vector.

6.2 Analysis

Our analysis is strongly inspired by the Monte Carlo interpretation of the PageRank random walk, even though our algorithms, explained in Section 4, do not depend on this interpretation. Hence, first we give some background about this interpretation. Following [3] one can write the PageRank (row) vector $\bar{\pi}^t$ of G^t as

$$\bar{\pi}^t = \frac{\epsilon}{n}\bar{1}^T\left(I - (1-\epsilon)P(t)\right)^{-1} = \frac{\epsilon}{n}\bar{1}^T\sum_{k\geq 0}(1-\epsilon)^k P(t)^k. \quad (1)$$

To have a random walk interpretation of this formula, as in [5], assume that we start one random walk from each node of G^t. At each step, each walk (independently) terminates with probability ϵ and otherwise follows the transition probabilities in $P(t)$. The sum of the expected lengths of the n walks is n/ϵ. Thus, an interpretation of the right hand of (1) is that π^t_u, the PageRank of node u, equals the expected number of visits of all the n walks to node u divided by the expected sum of lengths of the n walks.

Following this interpretation, for an edge (u, v), let $f^t_{u,v} = (1-\epsilon)\pi^t(u)P(t)_{u,v}$ be the amount of PageRank *flow* through the edge at time t. Then, similar to the relation between the PageRank of a node and the number of random walks visiting a node, $\frac{n}{\epsilon}f^t_{u,v}$ is the expected number of random walks traversing edge (u, v) in that process.

Using this interpretation, we prove our first lemma. We recall that the variation distance is half the L_1 distance.

LEMMA 1. *Let $D(\pi^{t+1}, \pi^t)$ be the total variation distance between π^{t+1} and π^t. Then,*

$$E[D(\pi^{t+1}, \pi^t)] \leq \frac{1-\epsilon}{m\epsilon}.$$

PROOF. Assume that G^{t+1} was obtained from G^t by changing edge (u, v) to edge (u, v'). Only walks that traversed edge (u, v) in G^t are affected by this change. Each such walk has expected length $1/\epsilon$ beyond edge (u, v) (or (u, v')) and the walk removed from one sets of nodes and added to another set of nodes. Thus, the sum of changes of the PageR-

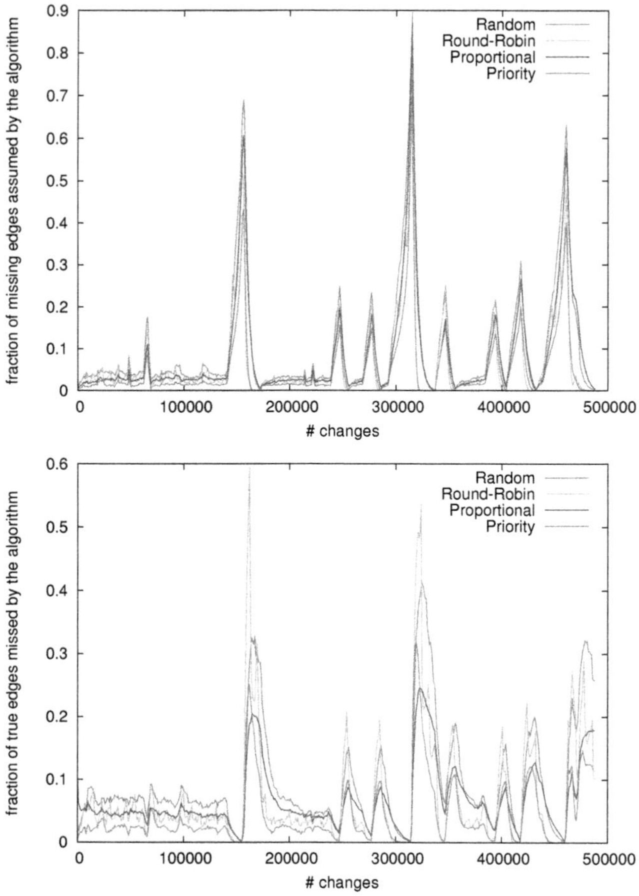

Figure 5: Staleness of the image of algorithms for the AS graph.

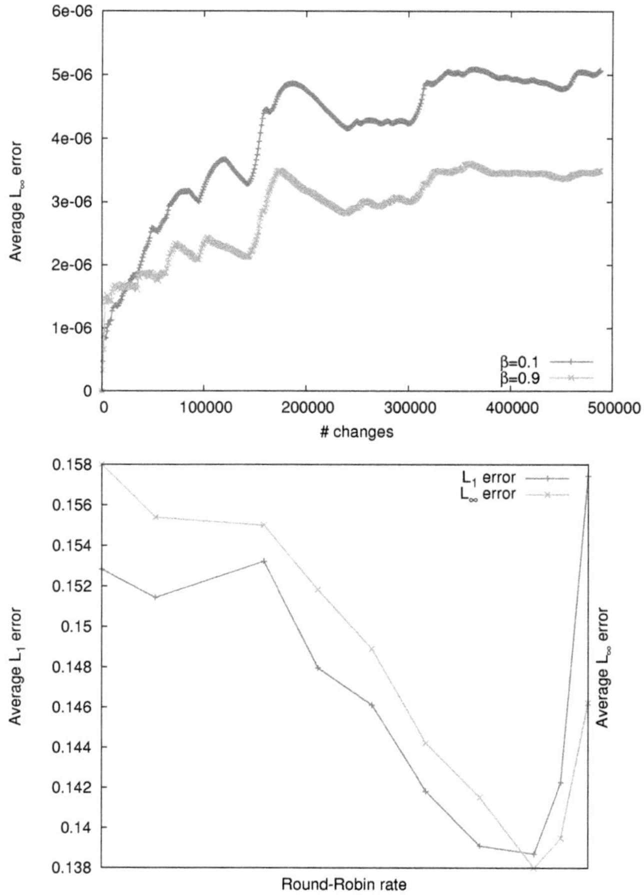

Figure 6: Average L_1 and L_∞ error of the hybrid algorithm as a function of the fraction β of round-robin probes for the AS graph.

ank values of all the nodes from that change is bounded by

$$2f^t_{u,v}\frac{1}{\epsilon} = 2\pi^t_u(1-\epsilon)\frac{1}{\mathrm{out}^t_u}\frac{1}{\epsilon}.$$

Now note that the edge to be removed at time t is chosen uniformly at random, and hence, for any node u, the probability of choosing an outgoing edge from u is out^t_u/m. Summing over all nodes, the expected change is then bounded by

$$2\sum_u \frac{\mathrm{out}^t_u}{m}\pi^t_u(1-\epsilon)\frac{1}{\mathrm{out}^t_u}\frac{1}{\epsilon} \le \frac{2(1-\epsilon)}{m\epsilon},$$

and the total variation distance is by definition half of this quantity. □

The above lemma shows that by probing the nodes in a round-robin fashion we maintain the total variation distance bounded by $\frac{n(1-\epsilon)}{m\epsilon}$. However, the variation distance argument does not give a better bound for the error in the PageRank of individual nodes. So, next we focus on better estimates of the change in the PageRank of individual nodes.

LEMMA 2. *The expected PageRank of any node x at time $t+1$, conditioned on the graph at time t, satisfies*

$$\pi^t_x\left(1-\frac{1}{\epsilon^2 m}\right) \le E[\pi^{t+1}_x \mid G^t] \le \pi^t_x\left(1+\frac{1}{\epsilon^2 m}\right).$$

PROOF. Similarly to the proof of the previous lemma, if G^{t+1} is obtained from G^t by changing edge (u,v) to edge (u,v'), only walks that traversed edge (u,v) are affected by this change, and each such walk has expected length $1/\epsilon$ beyond edge (u,v) or (u,v').

For a node x, we first bound the expected change in the PageRank of x from adding an edge pointing to it (i.e., the case $v'=x$). By our model definition, the probability of the new edge pointing to x is π^t_x, and the flow on that edge is the flow of an edge chosen uniformly at random from all m edges, i.e.,

$$\sum_u (1-\epsilon)\frac{\mathrm{out}^t_u}{m}\pi^t_u\frac{1}{\mathrm{out}^t_u} = \frac{1-\epsilon}{m}.$$

The expected number of times that the flow through the new edge can return to x is at most equal to the expected length of each walk passing through x, i.e., $1/\epsilon$, thus, the expected change in the PageRank of x from adding an edge pointing to it is bounded by $(1-\epsilon)\pi^t_x\frac{1}{m\epsilon}$.

Then, we bound the expected change in the PageRank of x from removing an edge pointing it (i.e., the case $v=x$). The probability of removing an edge pointing to x is in^t_x/m. Since this edge is picked uniformly at random, the flow on it is $\pi^t_x\frac{1}{\mathrm{in}^t_x}$, and again the expected number of times that the flow through this edge could return to x is bounded by

$1/\epsilon$. Thus the expected change in the PageRank of x from deleting an edge pointing to it at step t is bounded by $\pi_x^t \frac{1}{m\epsilon}$.

Hence, from the above two cases, the expected change in the PageRank of a node x from modifying (adding or deleting) an edge directly pointing to x at time t is bounded by $\pi_x^t \frac{1}{m\epsilon}$.

Next, we analyze the effect of modifying an arbitrary edge on the PageRank of x. To do so, we note that since the PageRank vector satisfies the relation

$$\pi^t = \frac{\epsilon}{n}\bar{1}^T + (1-\epsilon)\pi^t P(t),$$

we can write for any $k \geq 1$,

$$\pi_x^t = \frac{\epsilon}{n}\sum_{j=0}^{k-1}(1-\epsilon)^j \sum_w P(t)_{w,x}^j + (1-\epsilon)^k \sum_w \pi_w^t P(t)_{w,x}^k, \quad (2)$$

where $P(t)_{w,x}^j$ is the (w,x)th entry in the jth power of the matrix $P(t)$; thus $P(t)_{w,x}^j > 0$ if and only if there is a path of length j from w to x in G^t. We know that if an edge pointing to a node w is modified, it changes π_w^t by at most $\pi_w^t \frac{1}{m\epsilon}$. So, if w is at distance k from u, we see from Equation (2) that this change affects π_x^t by at most $(1-\epsilon)^k \pi_w^t \frac{1}{m\epsilon} P(t)_{w,x}^k$. Thus, the expected change to the PageRank of x from adding or deleting an edge pointing to a node at distance k from it is bounded by $\pi_x^t (1-\epsilon)^k \frac{1}{m\epsilon}$. Summing over all distances bounds the change in PageRank of x by:

$$\sum_{k\geq 0} \pi_x^t (1-\epsilon)^k \frac{1}{m\epsilon} = \pi_x^t \frac{1}{\epsilon^2 m},$$

which finishes the proof. □

We remark that the above bound is tight only when x has exactly one outgoing edge that is a self-loop. A simple induction, using Lemma 2, then shows:

COROLLARY 3. *For any node x, time t, and time difference $\tau > 0$:*

$$\left(1 - \frac{1}{\epsilon^2 m}\right)^\tau \pi_x^t \leq E[\pi_x^{t+\tau} \mid G^t] \leq \left(1 + \frac{1}{\epsilon^2 m}\right)^\tau \pi_x^t.$$

Next, recalling our notation that H^t is the state of the algorithm's graph at time t and ϕ^t is its PageRank (row) vector, we proceed to our main result.

THEOREM 4. *For a time instance t, assume that there exists an $\alpha > 0$ such that for all nodes $v \in V$ and all $t - 2n \leq \tau \leq t-1$:*

$$(1-\alpha)\phi_v^\tau \leq E[\pi_v^\tau \mid G^{\tau-1}, H^\tau] \leq (1+\alpha)\phi_v^\tau.$$

Then, letting $\beta = (1-\epsilon)\frac{1+\alpha}{m}(1+\frac{1}{\epsilon^2 m})^{2n}$, we have for all $v \in V$:

$$(1-\beta)\phi_v^t \leq E[\pi_v^t \mid G^{t-1}, H^t] \leq (1+\beta)\phi_v^t.$$

PROOF. Since the hybrid algorithm probes each node at least once in each interval of $2n$ steps, any edge in $H^t \setminus G^t$ or in $G^t \setminus H^t$ corresponds to a change in the last $2n$ steps before time t. For each node w let $\tilde{\phi}_w^t = \min_{i=t-2n}^{t-1} \phi_w^i$ denote the minimum value of ϕ_w in the $2n$ steps up to time t.

The head of an outgoing edge from v is changed in each step with probability $1/m$. The probability that the head of edge (v,u) was changed after the last probe of v is bounded by

$$\sum_{k\geq 0} \frac{1}{m}(1-\tilde{\phi}_v^t)^k = \frac{1}{\tilde{\phi}_v^t m}. \quad (3)$$

Let τ^* be the step in which $\phi_v^{\tau^*} = \tilde{\phi}_v^t$. By the theorem's assumption, we have

$$E[\pi_v^{\tau^*} \mid G^{\tau^*-1}, H^{\tau^*}] \leq (1+\alpha)\phi_v^{\tau^*},$$

and by Corollary 3,

$$E[\pi_v^t \mid G^{\tau^*}] \leq (1+\frac{1}{\epsilon^2 m})^{t-\tau^*}\pi_v^{\tau^*} \leq \left(1+\frac{1}{\epsilon^2 m}\right)^{2n} \pi_v^{\tau^*}.$$

Thus,

$$E[\pi_v^t \mid G^{\tau^*}, H^{\tau^*}] \leq (1+\alpha)\left(1+\frac{1}{\epsilon^2 m}\right)^{2n} \tilde{\phi}_v^t. \quad (4)$$

Hence, using Equation (3), we can bound the expected flow out of v not known to the algorithm by

$$E\left[\sum_x \frac{1}{\tilde{\phi}_v^t m} f_{v,x}^t\right] = E\left[\sum_x \frac{1}{\tilde{\phi}_v^t m}(1-\epsilon)\pi_v \frac{1}{\text{out}_v^t}\right] \leq \beta. \quad (5)$$

Applying the random walk interpretation of (1), we can obtain an upper bound for $E[\pi^t \mid G^{t-1}, H^t]$ as follows:

- We start one random walk from each node in H^t.
- For each random walk that traverses an edge in $H^t \setminus G^t$, we remove the part of the walk from that edge to the end of the random walk. Note that the remaining flow is counted both in π^t and ϕ^t.
- Let $\bar{\phi}_v^t$ be the flow through node v after the removal of parts of the random walks, then $E[\pi_v^t \mid G^{t-1}, H^t] \geq E[\bar{\phi}_v^t]$.

By (5) the expected flow removed from H^t can be estimated by applying (1) with a fraction β of a random walk starting at each node. Thus,

$$E[\bar{\phi}_v^t] = (1-\beta)\phi_v^t \leq E[\pi_v^t \mid G^{t-1}, H^t].$$

The other side of the inequality can be proved by applying the same walk fraction removal argument to G^t (instead of H^t). □

This gives us the final result in our analysis.

COROLLARY 5. *In the steady state*

$$\left(1 - O\left(\frac{1}{m}\right)\right)\phi^t \leq E[\pi^t \mid G^{t-1}, H^t] \leq \left(1 + O\left(\frac{1}{m}\right)\right)\phi^t.$$

PROOF. Follows from the observation that for α and β defined in Theorem 4, if $\alpha = \Omega(\frac{1}{m})$, then $\beta < \alpha$. □

This shows that assuming the evolving graph model, the approximate PageRank values returned by our algorithm are very close approximations of the true PageRank values, which finishes our analysis.

6.3 Extensions and variants

Even though we stated and proved our theoretical result in a simplified model, it can be generalized to much more general model using the same set of ideas. First, we note that the assumption that the number of edges of the graph does not change is not necessary, and our proof can be adapted to a model where edges addition and edge removal are two independent processes that add or remove edges at the same rate[§]. The proof is more technical, but the idea is the same, except now when an edge is removed, the paths that were using that edge will be distributed among other outgoing edges of the node (instead of being rerouted to the edge that was just added).

Next, we note that similar results can be proved for a model of graphs with a growing node set. Here we need to be careful about the definition of the model. We assume that at each step, with probability $1-\delta$ an edge is changed according to our edge change model and with probability δ, a new node is added. The new node will have outgoing links but no incoming links. In subsequent steps, the edge change model can add an incoming link to the new node. This is similar to the way networks like the web graph grow: sometimes a new web page is created; the page can contain links to other pages, but only over time it can attract links from other pages. The algorithm does not learn about the new page until it crawls a page that has an incoming link to it. Our theoretical result extends to this model as long as δ is small (hence there are not too many new nodes in the graph at any point), and the expected number of outgoing links from a new page is not large (otherwise the new pages can significantly affect the PageRank of other pages). We will leave the technical details to the full version of the paper.

Finally, we note that even though we proved the analysis for the algorithm that is a hybrid between Proportional Probing and Round Robin, with a little more work (and changes to the constants in the bound) it applies to the pure Proportional Probing method. The reason is that the PageRank of any node in the graph is always at least ϵ/n. Therefore, even without running Round Robin in alternate steps, in expectation each node is guaranteed to have been probed in the last n/ϵ steps.

7. CONCLUSIONS

In this paper we studied the problem of efficiently computing PageRank on an evolving graph. We obtained simple yet effective algorithms and demonstrated that they work well in practice on both real-world and synthetic graphs. We also analyzed the theoretical error bounds of the algorithm, assuming a particular model of graph evolution. While one can complain that the evolution model is specialized, our goal was to showcase the possibility of achieving the best of two worlds: a simple algorithm for a real-world problem and a provable guarantee under a model of the world using a non-trivial analysis. It remains a challenging problem to extend our theoretical analysis to other models of graph evolution. Studying other PageRank-like measures on evolving graphs is an interesting research direction.

8. REFERENCES

[1] A. Anagnostopoulos, R. Kumar, M. Mahdian, and E. Upfal. Sort me if you can: How to sort dynamic data. In *ICALP*, pages 339–350, 2009.

[2] A. Anagnostopoulos, R. Kumar, M. Mahdian, and E. Upfal. Algorithms on evolving graphs. In *ITCS*, pages 149–160, 2012.

[3] K. Avrachenkov, N. Litvak, D. Nemirovsky, and N. Osipova. Monte Carlo methods in Pagerank computation: When one iteration is sufficient. *SIAM J. Numer. Anal.*, 45(2):890–904, 2007.

[§]It is necessary to assume that additions and removals occur at the same rate, since otherwise we will converge to an empty or a complete graph.

[4] B. Bahmani, K. Chakrabarti, and D. Xin. Fast personalized PageRank on MapReduce. In *SIGMOD*, pages 973–984, 2011.

[5] B. Bahmani, A. Chowdhury, and A. Goel. Fast incremental and personalized PageRank. *PVLDB*, 4:173–184, 2010.

[6] P. Berkhin. Survey: A survey on PageRank computing. *Internet Mathematics*, 2(1):73–120, 2005.

[7] Y.-Y. Chen, Q. Gan, and T. Suel. Local methods for estimating PageRank values. In *CIKM*, pages 381–389, 2004.

[8] S. Chien, C. Dwork, S. Kumar, D. Simon, and D. Sivakumar. Link evolution: Analysis and algorithms. *Internet Mathematics*, 1(3):277–304, 2003.

[9] A. Das Sarma, S. Gollapudi, and R. Panigrahy. Estimating PageRank on graph streams. In *PODS*, pages 69–78, 2008.

[10] A. Dasgupta, A. Ghosh, R. Kumar, C. Olston, S. Pandey, and A. Tomkins. The discoverability of the web. In *WWW*, pages 421–430, 2007.

[11] J. V. Davis and I. S. Dhillon. Estimating the global PageRank of web communities. In *KDD*, pages 116–125, 2006.

[12] D. Eppstein, Z. Galil, and G. F. Italiano. Dynamic graph algorithms. In M. J. Atallah, editor, *Algorithms and Theoretical Computing Handbook*. CRC Press, 1999.

[13] S. Kamvar, T. Haveliwala, and G. Golub. Adaptive methods for the computation of PageRank. Technical report, Stanford University, 2003.

[14] S. Kamvar, T. Haveliwala, C. Manning, and G. Golub. Exploiting the block structure of the web for computing PageRank. Technical report, Stanford University, 2003.

[15] S. D. Kamvar, T. H. Haveliwala, C. D. Manning, and G. H. Golub. Extrapolation methods for accelerating PageRank computations. In *WWW*, pages 261–270, 2003.

[16] R. Kleinberg. *Online Decision Problems with Large Strategy Sets*. PhD thesis, MIT, 2005.

[17] A. N. Langville and C. D. Meyer. Updating PageRank using the group inverse and stochastic complementation. Technical report, NCSU, Mathematics Department, 2002.

[18] A. N. Langville and C. D. Meyer. Updating PageRank with iterative aggregation. In *WWW (posters)*, pages 392–393, 2004.

[19] A. N. Langville and C. D. Meyer. Updating Markov Chains with an eye on Google's PageRank. *SIAM J. Matrix Anal. Appl.*, 27(4):968–987, 2006.

[20] F. McSherry. A uniform approach to accelerated PageRank computation. In *WWW*, pages 575–582, 2005.

[21] S. Muthukrishnan. *Data Streams: Algorithms and Applications*. Now Publishers Inc, 2005.

[22] C. Olston and S. Pandey. Recrawl scheduling based on information longevity. In *WWW*, pages 437–446, 2008.

[23] L. Page, S. Brin, R. Motwani, and T. Winograd. The PageRank citation ranking: Bringing order to the web. Technical report, Stanford InfoLab, 1999.

[24] S. Pandey and C. Olston. User-centric web crawling. In *WWW*, pages 401–411, 2005.

[25] S. Pandey and C. Olston. Crawl ordering by search impact. In *WSDM*, pages 3–14, 2008.

[26] D. Ron. Property testing: A learning theory perspective. *Found. Trends Mach. Learn.*, 1:307–402, 2008.

[27] D. Ron. Algorithmic and analysis techniques in property testing. *Found. Trends Theor. Comput. Sci.*, 5:73–205, 2010.

[28] H. H. Song, T. W. Cho, V. Dave, Y. Zhang, and L. Qiu. Scalable proximity estimation and link prediction in online social networks. In *IMC*, pages 322–335, 2009.

[29] H. Tong, S. Papadimitriou, P. S. Yu, and C. Faloutsos. Proximity tracking on time-evolving bipartite graphs. In *SDM*, pages 704–715, 2008.

[30] J. L. Wolf, M. S. Squillante, P. S. Yu, J. Sethuraman, and L. Ozsen. Optimal crawling strategies for web search engines. In *WWW*, pages 136–147, 2002.

Information Diffusion and External Influence in Networks

Seth Myers
Stanford University
samyers@stanford.edu

Chenguang Zhu
Stanford University
cgzhu@stanford.edu

Jure Leskovec
Stanford University
jure@cs.stanford.edu

ABSTRACT

Social networks play a fundamental role in the diffusion of information. However, there are two different ways of how information reaches a person in a network. Information reaches us through connections in our social networks, as well as through the influence external out-of-network sources, like the mainstream media. While most present models of information adoption in networks assume information only passes from a node to node via the edges of the underlying network, the recent availability of massive online social media data allows us to study this process in more detail.

We present a model in which information can reach a node via the links of the social network or through the influence of external sources. We then develop an efficient model parameter fitting technique and apply the model to the emergence of URL mentions in the Twitter network. Using a *complete* one month trace of Twitter we study how information reaches the nodes of the network. We quantify the external influences over time and describe how these influences affect the information adoption. We discover that the information tends to "jump" across the network, which can only be explained as an effect of an unobservable external influence on the network. We find that only about 71% of the information volume in Twitter can be attributed to network diffusion, and the remaining 29% is due to external events and factors outside the network.

Categories and Subject Descriptors: H.2.8 [**Database Management**]: Database Applications – *Data mining*

General Terms: Algorithms, theory, experimentation.

Keywords: Diffusion of innovations, Information cascades, Information diffusion, External influence, Twitter, Social networks.

1. INTRODUCTION

Networks represent a fundamental medium for the emergence and diffusion of information [23]. For example, we often think of information, a rumor, or a piece of content as being passed over the edges of the underlying social network [22, 29]. This way information spreads over the edges of the network like an epidemic [15]. However, due to the emergence of mass media, like newspapers, TV stations and online news sites, the information not only reaches us through the links of our social networks but also through the influence of exogenous out-of-network sources [6]. From the early stages of research on news media and, more generally, information diffusion, there has been the tension between global effects from the mass media and local effects carried by social structure [20].

KDD'12, August 12–16, 2012, Beijing, China.

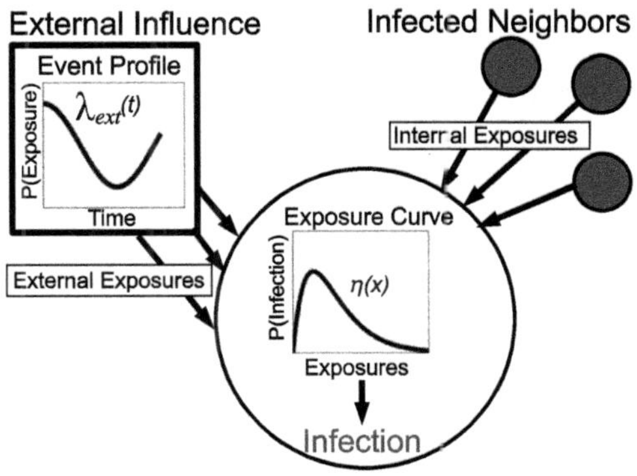

Figure 1: Our model of external influence. A node (denoted by a big circle) is exposed to information through an external source (governed by external activity $\lambda_{ext}(t)$) and by already infected neighbors (governed by the internal hazard function $\lambda_{int}(t)$). With each new exposure x, the probability of infection changes according to the exposure curve $\eta(x)$. We infer both the external activity $\lambda_{ext}(t)$, as well as the exposure curve $\eta(x)$.

Traditionally, it was hard to capture and study the effects of mass media and social networks simultaneously [16]. However, the Web, blogs and social media changed the traditional picture of the dichotomy between the local effects carried by the links of social networks and the global influence from the mass media. Today, mass media as well as the social networks both exist in the same Web "ecosystem," which means that it is possible to collect massive online social media data and at the same time capture the effects of mass media as well as the influence arising from the social networks [21]. This allows us to study processes of information diffusion and emergence in much finer detail than ever before.

In this paper, we ask the question "How does information transmitted by the mass media interact with the personal influence arising from social networks?" Based on the *complete* one month Twitter data we study ways in which information reaches the nodes of the Twitter network. We analyze over 3 *billion* tweets to discover mechanisms by which information appears and spreads through the Twitter network. In particular, we contrast two main ways by which information *emerges* at the nodes of the network: *diffusion* over the edges of the network, and *external influence*, when information "jumps" across the network and appears at a seemingly random node. For example, when information appears at a node that has no connections to nodes that have previously mentioned the information, the emergence of information at that node can only be explained by the influence of some unobserved exogenous source. However, when information appears at a node with a neighbor that already tweeted it, then it is not clear whether the node tweeted the information due to neighbor's influence or due to the influence of the exogenous source. Thus, the effect of internal and external infections get confounded [4] and the goal of the paper is to develop models that will allow us to separate the influence transmitted by social networks from the influence of the exogenous source(s).

Effects of external influence. On Twitter, users often post links to various webpages — most often these are links to news articles, blog posts, funny videos or pictures. Generally there are two fundamental ways how users learn about these URLs and tweet them. One would be due to the exogenous out-of-the-network effects. For example, one can imagine a scenario, where one checks news on CNN.com, finds an interesting article and then posts a tweet with a URL to the article. In this case CNN is the "external influence" that caused that URL to emerge onto a particular Twitter user. At contrast, users can also come across URLs by seeing them posted by other users that they follow. This type of user-to-user exposure is what we refer to as "internal influence," or diffusion. We find that both external and internal influence play significant role in the emergence of URLs in the Twitter network.

Modeling the external influence. In order to accurately model the emergence of content in Twitter we need to consider the activity of the invisible out-of-network sources that also transmit information to the nodes of the Twitter network (via channels, like TV, newspapers, etc.). We present a probabilistic generative model of information emergence in networks, in which information can reach a node via the links of the social network or through the influence of the external source. Developing such a model is important. For example, we simulated a purely non-diffusive process that picks nodes of the Twitter network at random and 'infects' them. After such process infects 10% of the nodes, about 30% of infections (falsely) appear to be a result of diffusion, *i.e.*, the random process picks a node that has (simply by chance) an already infected neighbor. Thus, instead of estimating the amount of internal influence at 0%, naive estimate would be 30%. Due to the confounding of diffusion and external influence, we aim to separate the two factors.

In our model (Figure 1) we distinguish between *exposures* and *infections* [24]. An *exposure event* occurs when a node gets exposed to information I, and an *infection event* occurs when a node posts a tweet with information I. Exposures to information lead to an infection. A node can get exposed to information in two different ways. First, a node U gets exposed to or becomes aware of information I whenever one of his neighbors in the social network posts a tweet containing I (we call this an *internal exposure*). The second way U can be exposed to I is through the activity of the external source (we refer to this as *external exposure*). We refer to the volume of external exposures over time as the *event profile*. In order to establish the connection between exposures and infections, we define the notion of the *exposure curve* that maps the number of times node U has been exposed to I into the probability of U getting infected [24]. Distinguishing between exposures and infections, and explicitly modeling the exposure curve allows us to capture rich effects. For example, during the diffusion of a news story, the story may become stale and less relevant each time a user sees it, so the probability of infection would decrease with each exposure. On the other hand, exposures to a story about new technology may have the opposite effect; with each exposure the user learns more about the technology so the probability of infection would increase. Exposure curves allow us to model such diverse behaviors that our model is able to accurately estimate from the data.

Furthermore, we also develop an efficient parameter estimation technique. We are given a network and a set of node infection times. We then infer the event profile, which quantifies the number of exposures generated by the external source over time. We also infer the exposure curve that models the probability of infection as a function of the number of exposures of a node. Our model accurately distinguishes external influence from network diffusion.

We experiment with our model on Twitter and find that we can accurately detect the occurrence external out-of-network events, and the exposure curve inferred from our model is often 50% more accurate than baseline methods. We find even though we are studying processes intrinsic to the Twitter network, only about 71% of the content that appears in Twitter can be attributed to the diffusion through the edges of the Twitter network. We fit our model to 18,186 different URL's that have appeared across Twitter users, and we use the inferred parameters of the model to provide insights into the mechanics of the emergence of these URLs. Moreover, we also perform per topic analysis and find that topics, like Politics and Sports , are most heavily driven by the external sources, while Entertainment and Technology are driven internally with only $\sim 18\%$ of exposures being external.

2. RELATED WORK

Work on the diffusion of innovations [23] provides a conceptual framework to study the emergence of information in networks. Conceptually, we think of an (often implicit) network where each node is either *active* (infected, influenced) or *inactive*, and active nodes can then spread the *contagion* (information, disease) along the edges of the underlying network. A rich set of models has been developed that all try to describe different mechanisms by which the contagion spreads from the infected to an uninfected node [8, 10, 22, 24, 29]. However, nearly all models only focus on the diffusive part of the contagion adoption process, while neglecting the external influence. In this regard our work introduces an important dimension to the diffusion of innovations framework, where we *explicitly* model the activity and influence of the external source.

External influence in networks has been considered in the case of the popularity of YouTube videos [11]. Authors considered a simple model of information diffusion on an implicit completely connected network and argued that since some videos became popular quicker than their model predicted, the additional popularity must have been a result of external influence. Our approach differs significantly: We directly consider the network and the effect of node-to-node interactions, explicitly infer the activity of external source over time and use a much more realistic model of information adoption that distinguishes between exposures to and the adoption of information. Our model builds on the notion of exposure curves which was proposed and studied by Romero et al. [24]. Recently, it was also argued [26] that it is the shape of exposure curves that stops the information from spreading. We make a step forward by providing an inference method that infers the shape of such exposure curves. Simulations show that our method much more accurately infers the exposure curves than the methods previously proposed [24, 26].

3. PROPOSED MODEL

Here, we develop in detail our novel information diffusion model that incorporates both the spread of information from node to node along edges in the network as well as the external influences acting on the network. Additionally, our model reconciles the gap between a stream of exposures arriving in continuous time and a series of discrete decisions leading to infection.

We refer to the amount of influence external sources have on the network as a function of time as the *event profile*. It is proportional to the probability of any node receiving an external exposure at a particular time. We use the term *contagion* to refer to a particular piece of information emerging in the Twitter network and we say a node is *infected* with a particular contagion when she first mentions/tweets the contagion. We model contagions as independent of each other, which means we consider them one by one.

We illustrate our model in a node-centric context in Fig. 1. Assume a single contagion (i.e., a piece of information). As time progresses, a node receives a stream of varying intensity of external exposures, governed by the event profile $\lambda_{ext}(t)$. Additionally, its neighbors in the network also become infected by the contagion, and each infected neighbor generates an internal exposure. Each exposure has a chance of infecting the node, but with the arrival of each exposure, the probability of infection changes according to the exposure curve $\eta(x)$. Eventually, either the arrival of exposures will cease, or the node will become infected and then expose to its neighbors. Our goal is to infer the number of exposures generated by the external source over time, as well as the shape of the exposure curve $\eta(x)$ that governs the probability of node's infection.

Modeling the internal exposures. Consider a single contagion. In our model, an internal exposure occurs when a neighbor of a node becomes infected, and then an exposure is transmitted after a random interval of time. Imagine a real world scenario in which the social network is the Twitter network and the contagion spreading across the network is a particular URL. If a neighbor writes a tweet involving a particular URL then a user sees their neighbor's tweet, then and only then has the internal exposure propagated along the edge. An infected node will expose each of its outgoing neighbors exactly once, and the time it takes for each exposure to occur is sampled from some distribution universal to all edges in the network. Therefore, a hazard function [12] is appropriate to model this process. Hazard functions were originally developed in actuary sciences, and they describe a distribution of the length of time it takes for an event to occur. Recently, [13] used hazard functions as a basis for disease propagation in continuous time across social networks. They are extremely effective at modeling discrete events that happen over continuous time. In this respect hazard functions represent a principled way of occurrence of discrete events (*i.e.*, exposures) as a function of continuous time.

Specifically, let λ_{int} be the *internal hazard function*, where

$$\lambda_{int}(t)\, dt \equiv P\left(i \text{ exposes } j \in [t, t+dt) \middle|\, i \text{ hasn't exposed } j \text{ yet}\right)$$

for any neighboring nodes i and j, where t is the amount of time that has passed since node i was infected. In our context, λ_{int} effectively models how long it takes a node to notice one of its neighbors becoming infected. It is a function of the frequency with which nodes check-up on each other. For the Twitter network, each time a user logs-in they are updated on all of their neighbors.

The expected number of internal exposures a node i has received by time t, which we will define as $\Lambda_{int}^{(i)}(t)$, is the sum of the cumulative distribution functions of exposures propagating along each of the node's inbound edges and can be derived as follows:

$$\Lambda_{int}^{(i)}(t) = \sum_{j;j \text{ is } i\text{'s inf. neighbor}} P(j \text{ exposed } i \text{ before } t) \quad (1)$$

$$= \sum_{j;j \text{ is } i\text{'s inf. neighbor}} \left[1 - \exp\left(-\int_{\tau_j}^{t} \lambda_{int}(s-\tau_j)ds\right)\right] \quad (2)$$

where τ_j is the infection time of node j.

Modeling the external exposures. The second source of exposures to a particular single contagion for nodes in the network comes from the external source acting on the network. The fundamental property of the problem we are trying to solve is that the external source cannot be observed. The source varies in intensity over time, and this function is called the *event profile*, which we designate as $\lambda_{ext}(t)$. Specifically,

$$\lambda_{ext}(t)\, dt \equiv P(i \text{ receives exposure} \in [t, t+dt))$$

for any node i, where t represents the amount of time since the contagion first appeared in the network. A couple of things should be noted here. First, all nodes have the same probability of receiving an external exposure for any point in time. Second, λ_{ext} is not conditioned upon the node not already having received an external exposure. This means that any node can receive an arbitrary number of external exposures. We call λ_{ext} the event profile because it describes an actual real world event that caused the information to arrive in the network and start spreading. As the event progresses over time, event's efficacy in the network changes. For example, if our contagion is civil unrest in Libya, then every time their ruler Gaddafi gives a speech or the rebels win a battle we would expect a spike in the intensity of the external source and thus the even profile λ_{ext}. As time passes without any new developments or as the event's relevancy fades, we expect λ_{ext} decrease to 0. However, every time there is a new development we expect a spike in the external event profile λ_{ext}. We will infer λ_{ext} non-parametrically, so we can quantify the relevancy of any event over its lifespan.

In order to derive the distribution of exposures a node receives over time as a function of time, we model the arrival of exposures as a binomial distribution. Consider we were to take the entire continuous time interval of the lifetime of the contagion and break it down into smaller but finite time intervals. Then whether an exposure occurred during each such subinterval is a Bernoulli random variable (exposure vs. no exposure) with its own probability. Therefore, the total number of exposures received in a time interval is a sum of Bernoulli random variables, just as a binomial random variable is a sum of Bernoulli random variables. Let's say that λ_{ext} is constant for all time and that time is discretized into finite intervals of length Δt. Then the probability that n external exposures have been received after T time intervals is exactly a binomial distribution:

$$P_{exp}(n; T\cdot\Delta t) = \binom{T}{n} (\lambda_{ext}\cdot\Delta t)^n \cdot (1-\lambda_{ext}\cdot\Delta t)^{T-n}.$$

Set $t = T\cdot\Delta t$. If we take the limit of as $\Delta t \to 0$ and $T \to \infty$ such that t does not change, then this probability approaches

$$P_{exp}(n; t) = \binom{t/dt}{n} (\lambda_{ext}\cdot dt)^n \cdot (1-\lambda_{ext}\cdot dt)^{t/dt-n}.$$

To relax the constraint that λ_{ext} is constant, we use the average of $\lambda_{ext}(t)$ over t:

$$P_{exp}^{(i)}(n; t) \approx \binom{t/dt}{n} \left(\frac{\Lambda_{ext}(t)}{t}\cdot dt\right)^n \cdot \left(1-\frac{\Lambda_{ext}(t)}{t}\cdot dt\right)^{t/dt-n}.$$

where $\Lambda_{ext}(t) \equiv \int_0^t \lambda_{ext}(s)ds$. Finally, users are receiving both external and internal exposures at the same time, so if we need take into account both processes. This would imply taking the convolution of the two probabilities, which would be computationally infeasible. Instead, we use the average of $\lambda_{ext}(t) + \lambda_{int}^{(i)}(t)$:

Symbol	Name	Description	Technical Definition
$\lambda_{ext}(t)$	The Event profile	Proportional to the probability of any node receiving an exposure at time t.	$\lambda_{ext}(t)\,dt = P[\text{ node exposed } \in [t, t+dt)]$
$\lambda_{int}(t)$	Internal Hazard Function	Governs the random amount of time it takes an infected node to expose its neighbors	$\lambda_{int}(t)\,dt =$ $P\,(i \text{ exposes } j \in [t, t+dt] \mid i \text{ hasn't exposed } j \text{ yet})$
$\eta(x)$	The Exposure Curve (parameters ρ_1, ρ_2)	Determines how the probability of infection changes with each exposure.	$\eta(x) = P(\text{ infected right after } x^{th} \text{ exposure})$
$P^{(i)}_{exp}(n;t)$	The Exposure Distribution	The probability that node i has received n exposures by time t	$P^{(i)}_{exp} = \binom{t/\Delta t}{n}\left(\frac{\Lambda^{(i)}_{int}(t)+\Lambda_{ext}(t)}{t}\cdot \Delta t\right)^n$ $\times \left(1 - \frac{\Lambda^{(i)}_{int}(t)+\Lambda_{ext}(t)}{t}\cdot \Delta t\right)^{t/\Delta t - n}$
τ_i	Infection time	The infection time of node i	

Table 1: Definition of symbols used in the model.

$$P^{(i)}_{exp}(n;t) \approx \binom{t/dt}{n}\left(\frac{\Lambda^{(i)}_{int}(t) + \Lambda_{ext}(t)}{t}\cdot dt\right)^n \quad (3)$$

$$\times \left(1 - \frac{\Lambda^{(i)}_{int}(t) + \Lambda_{ext}(t)}{t}\cdot dt\right)^{t/dt-n} \quad (4)$$

Effectively, we approximated the flux of exposures as constant in time such that each interval of time has an equal probability of an exposure arriving, so the sum of the events is a standard binomial random variable.

Modeling the exposure curve. We model the exposure curve as a parameterized equation. Recall that the exposure curve describes the probability of infection as a function of the number of exposures received. More specifically, if x is the current number of exposures the node has received and $\eta(x)$ is the exposure curve, then

$$\eta(x) \equiv P(\text{node } i \text{ is infected immediately after } x^{th} \text{ exposure}).$$

We choose to parameterize $\eta(x)$ as

$$\eta(x) = \frac{\rho_1}{\rho_2}\cdot x \cdot \exp\left(1 - \frac{x}{\rho_2}\right).$$

where $\rho_1 \in (0,1]$ and $\rho_2 > 0$. Parameterizing $\eta(x)$ in this manor allows for several desirable properties. First, $\eta(0) = 0$ so it is impossible to become infected by a contagion before being exposed to it. Secondly, this function is unimodal with an exponential tail, so there is a critical mass of exposures when the contagion is most infectious followed by decay brought on by the idea becoming overexposed/tiresome. Lastly, and most importantly, ρ_1 and ρ_2 have important conceptual meanings: $\rho_1 = \max_x \eta(x)$ and $\rho_2 = \arg\max_x \eta(x)$. Because of this, we can think of ρ_1 as a general measure of how infectious a contagion is in the network and ρ_2 as a measure of the contagion's enduring relevancy. Fig. 2 shows several different forms of $\eta(x)$. This parameterization is expressive, but any other parameterization for $\eta(x)$ is also valid. For the remainder of the paper, we will discuss the model in the context of the $\eta(x)$ parameterization presented above.

From exposures to infections. In order to fit the parameters of the model to observed data, we must now construct the probability functions to describe the model. With the equations given above, building the distribution of the infection time of a node i can be

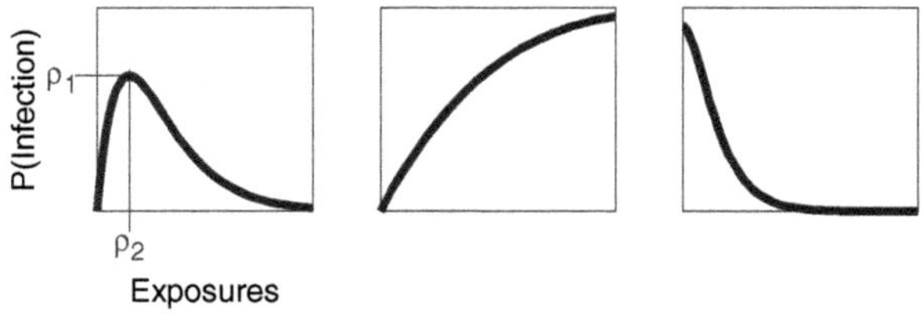

Figure 2: Example exposure curves $\eta(x)$, where $\eta(x)$ is the probability of a node becoming infected upon its xth exposure to the contagion. The parameters of $\eta(x)$ are ρ_1 and ρ_2.

done as follows. Let $F^{(i)}(t) \equiv P(\tau_i \le t)$ be the probability that node i has been infected by time t, where τ_i is the infection time of node i. Making use of the quantity $P^{(i)}_{exp}(n;t)$,

$$F^{(i)}(t) = \sum_{n=1}^{\infty} P[i \text{ has } n \text{ exp. }] \times P[i \text{ inf. } | i \text{ has } n \text{ exp. }] \quad (5)$$

$$= \sum_{n=1}^{\infty} P^{(i)}_{exp}(n;t) \times \left[1 - \prod_{k=1}^{n}[1-\eta(k)]\right]. \quad (6)$$

While $F^{(i)}(t)$ is analogous to the cumulative distribution function of the infection probability, it is important to note that it is not *actually* a distribution; $\lim_{t\to\infty} F(t) < 1$ as a result of $\lim_{x\to\infty}\eta(x) = 0$. This is ideal because it implies that there is a non-zero chance that a node will never become infected, as should be the case.

3.1 Inferring the model parameters

Next we develop a method of inferring the model parameters for a given network and the tract of a single contagion. We fit the model to each contagion separately. We are given the network and the infection times for each node that got infected with the contagion under consideration. We then need to infer the event profile $\lambda_{ext}(t)$ for all t at which at least one node was infected, and parameters of $\eta(x)$, ρ_1 and ρ_2, of the exposure curve. In all, the number of parameters we are inferring is the number of *unique* node infection times plus the two parameters of $\eta(x)$. Our general strategy is to alternate back and forth from inferring $\lambda_{ext}(t)$ to inferring $\eta(x)$, assuming we known one for certain while we infer the other, until both functions converge. Below, we first demonstrate how to infer the event profile when the exposure curve is known. Then, we show

how to infer the exposure curve with a known event profile. Finally, we combine the two steps into a single algorithm.

Inferring the event profile. The following outlines a fast and robust method for inferring $\lambda_{ext}(t)$, given $\eta(x)$. Let $S(t)$ be the number of nodes that are uninfected (by the contagion currently under consideration) at time t. $S(t)$ is a random variable whose expectation value is dependent on $\lambda_{ext}(t)$, $\eta(x)$, and the underlying network. The networks which we are interested in are sufficiently large, so the quantity $S(t) - E[S(t)]$ is usually very small in magnitude. This provides us with a very straight-forward method for inferring $\Lambda_{ext}(t) \equiv \int_0^t \lambda_{ext}(s)ds$. Let t_k be the kth time at which at least one node was infected, then define Λ_k as $\Lambda_{ext}(t_k)$. To calculate $S(t)$,

$$S(t_k) = \sum_{i=1}^{N} P(\text{ node } i \text{ not infected by time } t) \tag{7}$$

$$= \sum_{i=1}^{N}\sum_{n=1}^{\infty} P^{(i)}_{exp}(n; t_k) \prod_{k=1}^{n} [1-\eta(k)] \tag{8}$$

$$\approx \sum_{i=1}^{N}\sum_{n=1}^{\infty} P^{(i)}_{exp}(n; t_k) \exp\left(-\int_{y=0}^{n} \eta(y)dy\right) \tag{9}$$

$$\approx \sum_{i} \exp\left(-\int_{0}^{\Lambda_k+\Lambda^{(i)}_{int}(t_k)} \eta(y)dy\right). \tag{10}$$

The first approximation comes from treating the number of exposures received by a node at any given time as a continuous real number instead of an integer. This provides us with a closed-form expression. The second approximation comes from setting the number of exposures received by each node to be the expected number of exposures.

Since the right-hand side is monotonic (it is strictly decreasing with respect to Λ_k), we can solve for Λ_k using bisection search. Doing this for all t_k gives us $\Lambda_{ext}(t_k)$ for each possible time, and then we can use finite difference to get $\lambda_{ext}(t_k)$.

Once the event profile has been inferred, we must then update the exposure curve accordingly.

Inferring the exposure curve. Now, we assume we know $\Lambda_{ext}(t)$ for all t_k, and we want to infer the exposure curve $\eta(x)$, specifically its parameters ρ_1 and ρ_2. Our strategy in solving for these parameters will be to fix ρ_2, and then solve for a ρ_1 that maximizes the following approximation to the log-likelihood. Making use of Eq. 6, we have

$$\mathcal{L}(\eta, \Lambda_{ext}, \lambda_{int}) = \sum_{i\in\mathcal{I}} \log\left[\frac{d[F^{(i)}(t)]}{dt}\right] + \sum_{i\in\mathcal{I}^c} \log\left[F^{(i)}(t)\right]$$

$$\approx \sum_{i\in\mathcal{I}}\sum_{n=1}^{\infty} P^{(i)}_{exp}(n;\tau_i)\left[\log(\eta(n)) + \sum_{k=1}^{n-1}\log(1-\eta(k))\right]$$

$$+ \sum_{i\in\mathcal{I}^c}\sum_{n=1}^{\infty} P^{(i)}_{exp}(n;\tau_{max}) \cdot \sum_{k=1}^{n}\log(1-\eta(k))$$

where $\mathcal{I}$ is the set of all infected nodes, $\mathcal{I}^c$ is the set of all uninfected nodes, and τ_{max} is the time of the last observed infection. The optimal ρ_1 satisfies $\frac{\partial\mathcal{L}}{\partial\rho_1} = 0$ so

$$0 = \frac{|\mathcal{I}|}{\rho_1} + \sum_{i\in\mathcal{I}}\sum_{n=1}^{\infty} P^{(i)}_{exp}(n;\tau_{max}) \cdot \sum_{k=1}^{n-1}\frac{\eta(k)}{\rho_1\cdot(1-\eta(k))} \tag{11}$$

$$+ \sum_{i\in\mathcal{I}^c}\sum_{n=1}^{\infty} P^{(i)}_{exp}(n;\tau_{max}) \cdot \sum_{k=1}^{n}\frac{\eta(k)}{\rho_1\cdot(1-\eta(k))}. \tag{12}$$

The parameter ρ_1 can be solved iteratively, using and initial value between 0 and 1. Because $P^{(i)}_{exp}$ is independent of ρ_1, they only need to be calculated once. This, along with the iterations converging quickly, makes this entire process very fast.

Now, we combine the event profile inference process with the exposure curve inference process to form a single algorithm that infers the entire model.

Inferring all parameters. If we use the previously mentioned method to infer $\eta(x)$ using the actual ground-truth $\Lambda_{ext}(t)$, it works extremely well. In fact, coming up with contrived instances in which it breaks is difficult. The same thing is true for using the event profile inference method with ground-truth $\eta(x)$. When neither ground-truth function is known and we have to iterate back and forth between both methods, however, the results are not as stable. Both functions' inference methods are sensitive to errors in the other function. Fortunately, all that is needed to correct this is a slight modification. Simply put, we fix ρ_2 to some integer value and then iterate back and forth between the two methods. Then, ρ_1 and $\Lambda_{ext}(t)$ converge to some values dependent on the fixed ρ_2, and we calculate the log-likelihood of the resulting inferred functions. We do this for all reasonable integer values of ρ_2, and we choose the one with the optimal log-likelihood. Algorithm 1 gives the pseudocode.

Algorithm 1 Model Parameter Inference

```
Initialize Λ_ext(t), ρ^1_final, ρ^2_final, L_max
for ρ2 = 1 → ρ_max do
    Initialize ρ1
    while not converged do
        ρ1 ← Solution to Eq. 12 using ρ2, Λ_ext(t)
        Λ_ext(t) ← Solution to Eq. 10 using ρ1, ρ2.
    end while
    L ← Log-Likelihood(Λ_ext(t), ρ1, ρ2)
    if L ≥ L_max then
        L_max ← L
        ρ^1_final ← ρ1
        ρ^2_final ← ρ2
    end if
end for
Λ_ext(t) ← Solution to Eq. 10 using ρ^1_final, ρ^2_final.
```

Practical considerations. Since we infer the event profile $\lambda_{ext}(t)$ in non-parametric form, the number of parameters in the model could potentially scale with the time duration of the contagion (we would have to solve for $\lambda_{ext}(t_i)$ for each node's infection time t_i). This can be prevented, however, by predetermining a set of times $\{\hat{t}_m\}_{m=1}^{M}$ only at which the event profile will be inferred. Then, $\lambda_{ext}(t)$ between these set times can be approximated using linear interpolation. In practice, we used $M = 20$, and we set each $\hat{t}_m$ at the time in which $\frac{m}{M}$ of the infections with the contagion have occurred. Doing this not only makes the runtime constant with respect to the duration of the contagion, it also speeds up the algorithm in general at the price of only a negligible decrease in accuracy.

The algorithm scales linearly with the number of nodes that received at least one exposure. All nodes that received only external exposures and no internal exposures, however, are effectively identical and can be grouped into a single term for both the event profile inference and the exposure curve inference. Therefore, in practice the runtime scales linearly with the number of nodes that received *at least one internal exposure*, i.e. the union of outgoing neighborhoods for all infected nodes. For most real world social networks,

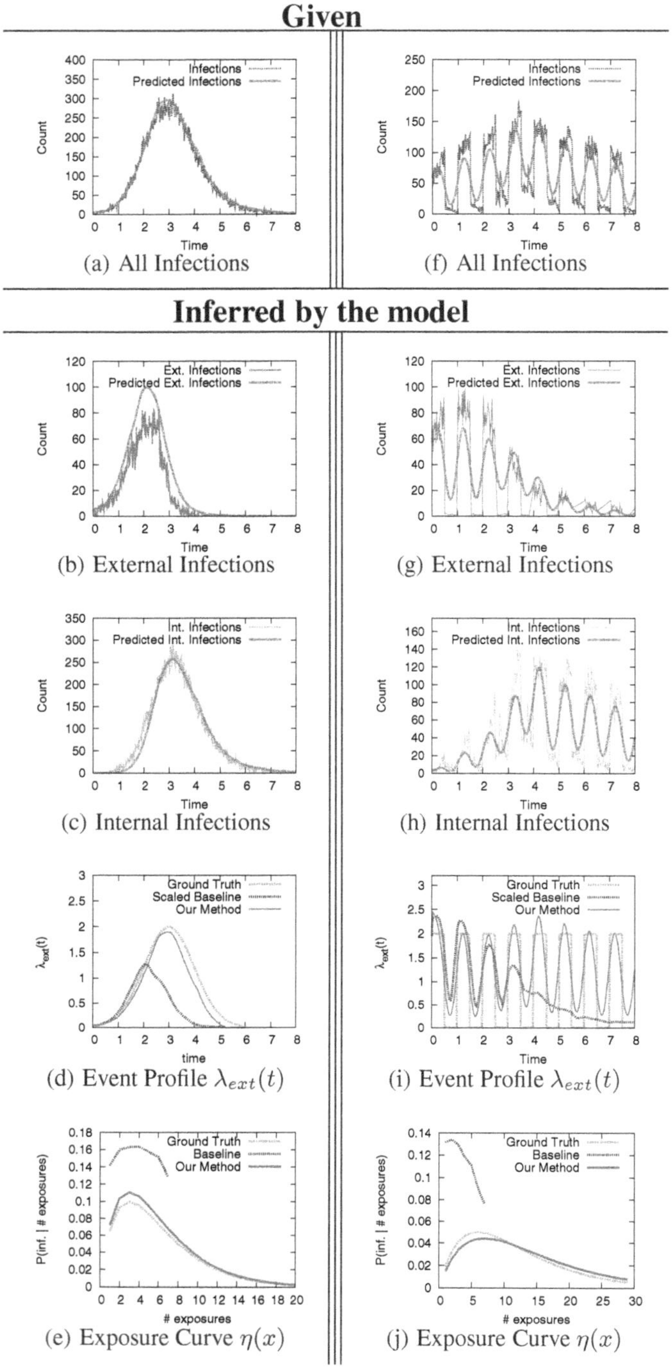

(a) All Infections (f) All Infections

(b) External Infections (g) External Infections

(c) Internal Infections (h) Internal Infections

(d) Event Profile $\lambda_{ext}(t)$ (i) Event Profile $\lambda_{ext}(t)$

(e) Exposure Curve $\eta(x)$ (j) Exposure Curve $\eta(x)$

Figure 3: Experiments on synthetic data. (a)-(e) The model fitted to a synthetic contagion on a scale-free network with 75,879 nodes. The internal hazard function is $\lambda_{int}(t) = t$, which induces a Raleigh (unimodal) distribution for the internal exposure propagation time. Given just the number of infections (a) our model is able to infer all of (b)-(e). (f)-(j) The model fitted to the same network but with the internal hazard function $\lambda_{int}(t) = \frac{1}{t}$, which induces a power law distribution for the internal exposure propagation time.

this implies the runtime scales slightly more than linearly with respect to the number of infections.

We can infer the model parameters for most contagions well inside a minute. A large portion of real-world contagions in our dataset infects about 50-100 nodes, and rarely did the algorithm take more than 10 seconds to converge. For larger contagions, some infecting thousands of nodes, the runtime was 5-10 minutes.

In all, we used the algorithm to fit the model to more than 18,000 real contagions and hundreds of synthetic contagions, and we never encountered convergence issues.

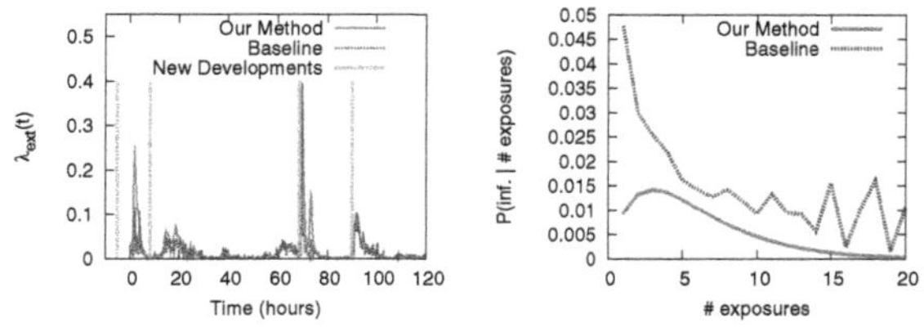

(a) Event Profile $\lambda_{ext}(t)$ (b) Exposure Curve $\eta(x)$

Figure 4: The model fitted to a single contagion representing URLs related to the Tucson, Arizona shootings. The green vertical lines designate when four distinct developments related to the shooting event occurred.

4. EXPERIMENTS

With our model well-defined and with an algorithm for inferring its parameters, we now apply it to real as well as synthetic data. First, to establish the accuracy of the parameter inference algorithm, we fit our model to synthetic data. This allows for direct comparison of ground-truth to inferred parameters. We examine a specific real-world case study to better illustrate the model. Lastly, we run a series of large-scale experiments on the emergence of Twitter URLs. The model reveals the underlying dynamics of information emergence on Twitter.

4.1 Experiments with synthetic data

To test accuracy of the model parameter inference algorithm, we run a series of experiments on simulated data.

For each experiment, we first generate a large synthetic preferential attachment network. We then choose values for $\eta(x)$, $\lambda_{ext}(t)$, and $\lambda_{int}(t)$. At the start of the experiment, all nodes are uninfected. Then, using a small discrete time step Δt we march forward in time, and external exposures are sent to each node with probability $\lambda_{ext}(t) \cdot \Delta t$. If a node becomes infected, it will transmit exactly one exposure to each of its outbound neighbors, and the time each outbound exposure takes to propagate is governed by $\lambda_{int}(t) \cdot \Delta t$. With each exposure a node receives, we sample a binary random variable with bias $\eta(x)$ to determine whether the node will become infected upon that exposure. Once the experiment is complete, the algorithm is given a set of node infection times, the underlying network, and $\lambda_{int}(t)$, and its task is to infer $\eta(x)$ and $\lambda_{ext}(t)$.

Baselines. We compared our algorithm against common sense baselines. For inferring $\eta(x)$, we used the baseline of assuming internal exposures propagate immediately, and that all exposures originate internally. Calculating $\eta(x_k)$ at each exposure count x_k then boils down to counting the fraction of times a node becomes infected immediately after x_k of its neighbors become infected. Note this is exactly the method of inferring $\eta(x)$ used in [24]. The baseline for inferring $\lambda_{ext}(t)$ uses the number of infections that occur for each unit of time in which none of the node's neighbors were previously infected. We refer to these infections as external infections. Since an externally infected node, by definition, has no infected neighbors, we know with certainty that all exposures the node received came from the event profile. Therefore, the arrival of external infections over time should be indicative of the arrival of external exposures over time, *i.e.*, the event profile. This, however, only provides a *shape* (but not the scale) of the event profile, because without knowledge of the exposure curve $\eta(x)$, we do not know how many exposures it takes to typically cause an infection. Thus, the scale of the baseline $\lambda_{ext}(t)$ is usually 1 to 2 orders of magnitude larger.

Experimental results. We ran many different combinations of network topologies, exposure curves, event profiles, and internal hazard functions. Overall, we ran over 100 different combinations on networks of 75k+ nodes, and the algorithm not only performed consistently well but also did significantly better than the baselines. We included the results of two such experiments in Fig. 3.

For the first experiment, our algorithm is given a network and the data on Figure 3(a). Based only on this information, it is able to infer data shown in Figures 3(b) to 3(e). These figures illustrate various aspects of the inferred profile of the external influence, *i.e.*, the event profile, and exposure curve against the ground truth and the baselines. For the event profile, not only is the scale of the baseline off by several orders of magnitude, but it also places the peak of the event profile far too early. On the other hand, the event profile inferred using our algorithm very closely predicts the scale, shape, and the occurrence of the profile peak to the extent that the difference between the ground truth and inferred event profile is negligible. The situation is the same for inferring the exposure curve in Fig. 3(e). The inferred $\eta(x)$ almost exactly fits the ground truth, whereas the baseline overestimates the exposure curve by more than 50%.

For the second experiment (Fig. 3(b)-3(j)), we used a very peculiar zig-zag ground-truth external influence profile (Fig. 3(b)), but the observations are still the same — our model was able to infer all the quantities almost exactly. The event profile inference shown in Fig. 3(i) is very accurate. It resolves each of the 10 peaks, while the baseline, besides being orders of magnitude off in scale, only detects 4 peaks. We infer $\eta(x)$ almost exactly, as shown in Fig. 3(j).

Note that even though we test the algorithm on synthetic data the fact that the model works well is not at all trivial. In particular, from the model fitting point of view the effects of internal and external influence are confounded and the model estimation procedure needs to separate them out. In particular, consider the contrast in the performance of the baseline approaches and the proposed model. Overall, these experiments demonstrate the robustness of the model and allow us to move to the experiments on real data.

4.2 Experiments Using Real Data

We now fit our model to a real data from the Twitter network. We study the emergence of URLs on the Twitter network. URLs emerge by Twitter users mentioning them in their tweets (through tweeting or re-tweeting). Thus, URLs correspond to contagions, posting a tweet mentioning a particular URL corresponds to an infection event.

Twitter dataset. To apply our model to a real-world information diffusion network, we collected *complete* Twitter data for January 2011, which consists of 3 billion tweets. We focus on URLs that have been tweeted by at least 50 users as our contagions of study (we found that contagions smaller than 50 infections did not provide robust enough statistics). For URLs that were shortened, we unshortened them and treated all URLs that point to the same web address as one contagion. We restricted our focus to URLs in which we could classify as written in English. To do this, we extracted natural text from the HTML of the URLs and then used a character sequenced-based classifier to determine their language [7]. We also removed URLs that demonstrated blatant spamming behavior. In all, this resulted in 18,186 different URLs.

We constructed the network over which these URLs propagate as follows. First, we took the union of all users that tweeted at least one of these URLs. Then, for each user in this set we used the Twitter API to extract a list of the users that they follow. When one user follows another, he/she can see all of their tweets, include URLs that they post, and it is through this relationship that contagions spread on Twitter. In all, this created a 1,087,033 node subgraph with 103,112,438 edges. We focus our study on URLs as they clearly emerge due to external events.

For the internal hazard function $\lambda_{int}(t)$, empirical analysis indicates that $\lambda_{int}(t) \equiv \frac{0.14}{t}$, where t is in hours, is a suitable choice. This implies that the distribution of lag time between infections and exposures follows a power law with an exponent of 1.14.

A case study of the influence of external events. We start our investigations on real data with an illustrative case study. Using information diffusion, we aim to detect a sequence of external events that presumably caused bursts of activity on the Twitter network.

We examined the Tucson, Arizona shooting on January 8th in which 6 people were killed and 14 others were injured, and among the injured was U.S. Congresswoman Gabrielle Giffords. There were four key developments related to this event: (1) the shooting occurs (Jan. 8, 10:10am), (2) the Westboro Baptist Church announces plans to protest at the funerals of the victims (Jan. 9, 9:15am), (3) Arizona Governor Jan Brewer signs emergency legislation blocking the protest. (Jan. 11, 9:24am), and (4) an on-line "Get Well Soon" card is formed for Gabrielle Giffords that people can sign (Jan. 12, 6pm).

We collected all URLs that were tweeted at least 50 times that contained the word "Giffords." We then gathered them into a single contagion. Given that we aggregated four separate sub-stories we would expect that when we fit our model to the observed data, the event profile would coincide with developments related to the real-world event. Indeed this is the case as shown in Fig. 4.

The results of the model applied to the contagion are shown in Fig. 4. Additionally, the time of each of the 4 developments listed above is represented as a vertical green line in Fig 4(a). Our model clearly detects all four developments: each of them is followed by a spike in the event profile within 10 hours. For the second two developments, the spikes in the event profile are immediate. Also interesting is how the baseline event profile differs from the model's. For example, immediately after the 3rd development (*i.e.*, when the governor passed a new law) the model infers two spikes in $\lambda_{ext}(t)$ whereas the baseline records only one. In response to the law being passed, many different groups began organizing counter protests to prevent the Westboro Baptist Church from interfering with the funerals. This created a second influx of URLs from sources external to Twitter (Facebook groups, news sites, etc.), which was completely missed by the baseline.

Evaluation using Google Trends. As a global alternative evaluation method we also performed the experiment where we extracted a set of mainstream media articles for which we were able to identify a single keyword W that adequately describes them (*e.g.*, swine flu for a BBC article on "Increase in Northern Ireland swine flu cases"). For each W, we then queried Google Trends to obtain the number of worldwide search traffic of query W over time. This served as a proxy for the activity of the external source. We compared the L2 distance between the inferred event profile and the Google Trends ground-truth. Overall, we found that our model gives 30% relative improvement in the L2 distance of the inferred event profile when compared to the naive event profile estimation.

External influence of different news categories. We now proceed to an aggregate analysis of event profiles and external influence of different category of news. We identified 9 news sites that specify the article's category within the URL. All together, we identified 1,929 URL's belonging to 11 different news categories. We then fit our model each URL and infer the event profile as well as the exposure curve. For each news category, we then calculated the average ρ_1 which is the maximum probability of infection for the exposure curve, ρ_2 which is the number of exposures at which the URL is most infections, the duration or lifetime over which the event profile was inferred, and the number of expected total external exposures each node receives from the URL's event.

The results are displayed in Table 2. The average value of ρ_1 was 0.0013, ρ_2 was 3.21, the average duration of the contagions was 65.69 hours, and the average fraction of external infections was 23.94%. In the first column, we show the maximum probability of infection for the exposure curve. Notice that Entertainment, Business, and Health appear to be the most infectious, where Art, Education, and Travel are the least infectious. This seems reasonable as news articles about topics such as Art or Education would be less likely to be retweeted compared to Entertainment articles. The second column describes upon which exposure the URL is most infectious. World News, which is more time sensitive, reaches maximum infectiousness earlier compared to other topics. After a user has received more than ρ_2 exposures, the probability of infection decreases, so it makes sense that these topics, which become irrelevant as time passes, reach this point sooner. Contrast this with a topic like Art that is naturally less temporally sensitive. Additionally, we learn that topics with a smaller ρ_2 tend to have shorter duration, and topics with a larger ρ_2 tend to have infections appear over a longer interval of time. Intuitively this makes sense as topics related to events (World, Business) get "old" sooner.

Lastly, the last column shows on average what percent of exposures came from external sources versus from within the network. Politics appear to be the most externally driven topic, while Entertainment is the most internally driven. This consistent with the fact that the 22 of the top 30 users followed on Twitter are entertainers.

Global characteristics. The distributions for both the ρ_1 and ρ_2 exposure curve parameters inferred across the entire URL dataset can be found in Figures 6(a), 6(b). Interesting is for how low the values of ρ_1 were inferred, with a mode on the order of .0005. This implies that the people, at least Twitter users, are very selective about the ideas they adopt. Additionally, most of the inferred ρ_2 parameters were small, with $\rho_2 = 1$ being the most common. Recall that a smaller ρ_2 implies that the probability of infection begins to decrease with additional exposures sooner, and from this we see evidence that users quickly fatigue of most diffusing contagions.

Next, for each URL, we went through every user that was infected one by one. For each user, we plotted the order of infection of the user in relation to all other infections versus the fraction of expected exposures the user received from internal sources, and the results can be found in Figure 6(c). This plot demonstrates the interesting time dynamics at play. On average, the first few users are infected almost purely externally, but then there is a surge in internal exposures. As a result, the early infections are largely internally driven, but as the contagion continues to spread the infections are driven more and more by external influences. This initial surge in internally driven infections is also evident in the aggregated exposure curve, shown in Fig. 5. Upon each infection, the expected number of exposures the user has received is recorded and divided by the inferred value of ρ_2. This value shows how far along the node was in the exposure curve when the infection occurred, and the apex of the exposure curve occurs when it is equal to 1. As one might expect, there is a high density of infections occurring at the apex. What is interesting, however, is that there is also a dense group of infections happening early in the exposure curve at low probabilities. This group is almost exclusively populated by internally infected users.

Finally, for each URL we calculated the expected number of exposures each user received during the emergence of the URL and what fraction of these exposures came from an external source. Averaging across all URLs, we found that 71% of all exposures came from internal sources within the network, while the other 29% of the exposures were external. We find this 29% to be significant and clear evidence that external effects cannot be ignored.

5. CONCLUSION

Emergence of information has traditionally been solely modeled as a diffusion process in networks. However, we identified that only around 71% of URL mentions on Twitter can be attributed to network effects, and the remaining 29% of mentions seem to be due to the influence of external out-of-network sources. We then present a model in which information can reach a node via the links of the social network or through the influence of external sources. Applying the model to the emergence of URLs in the Twitter network demonstrated that our model can be used to infer the shape of influence functions as well as the effects of external sources on the information diffusion in networks. We should emphasize that our model does not only reliably capture the external influence but, as a consequence, also leads to a more accurate description of the real network diffusion process.

For future work it would be interesting to relax the assumption of uniform activity of the external source across all nodes of the network. Incorporating our model into methods for identifying "influencers" in networks [18, 5, 9] might be fruitful. Currently, phenomena we are observing are clearly taking place in aggregate. Ultimately, it will be interesting to pursue more fine-grained analyses as well, understanding how patterns of variation at the level of individuals contribute to the overall effects that we observe.

Acknowledgements. This research has been supported in part by NSF CNS-1010921, IIS-1016909, IIS-1149837, IIS-1159679, DARPA SMISC, Albert Yu & Mary Bechmann Foundation, Boeing, Allyes, Samsung, Alfred P. Sloan and the Microsoft Faculty Fellowship.

6. REFERENCES

[1] E. Adar and L. A. Adamic. Tracking information epidemics in blogspace. In *Web Intelligence*, pages 207–214, 2005.

[2] A. Anagnostopoulos, R. Kumar, and M. Mahdian. Influence and correlation in social networks. In *KDD '08*, 2008.

[3] D. Antoniades, I. Polakis, G. Kontaxis, E. Athanasopoulos, S. Ioannidis, E. P. Markatos, and T. Karagiannis. we.b: the web of short urls. In *WWW '11*, 2011.

[4] S. Aral, L. Muchnik, and A. Sundararajan. Distinguishing influence-based contagion from homophily-driven diffusion in dynamic networks. *PNAS*, 106(51):21544–21549, 2009.

[5] E. Bakshy, J. M. Hofman, W. A. Mason, and D. J. Watts. Everyone's an influencer: quantifying influence on twitter. In *WSDM'11*, 2011.

[6] L. Bennett. *News: The Politics of Illusion.* A. B. Longman (Classics in Political Science), seventh edition, 2006.

[7] W. Cavnar and J. Trenkle N-Gram-Based Text Categorization. SDAIR, 94

[8] D. Centola and M. Macy. Complex contagions and the weakness of long ties. *American Journal of Sociology*, 2007.

	ρ_1	ρ_2	Duration (hours)	% Ext. Exposures
Politics (25)	0.0007 +/- 0.0001	4.59 +/- 0.76	51.24 +/- 16.66	47.38 +/- 6.12
World (824)	0.0013 +/- 0.0000	2.97 +/- 0.10	43.54 +/- 2.94	26.07 +/- 1.19
Entertain. (117)	0.0015 +/- 0.0002	3.52 +/- 0.28	89.89 +/- 16.13	17.87 +/- 2.51
Sports (24)	0.0010 +/- 0.0003	4.76 +/- 0.83	87.85 +/- 38.03	43.88 +/- 6.97
Health (81)	0.0016 +/- 0.0002	3.25 +/- 0.30	100.09 +/- 17.57	18.81 +/- 3.33
Tech. (226)	0.0013 +/- 0.0001	3.00 +/- 0.16	83.05 +/- 8 73	18.36 +/- 1.80
Business (298)	0.0015 +/- 0.0001	3.18 +/- 0.16	49.61 +/- 5.14	22.27 +/- 1.79
Science (106)	0.0012 +/- 0.0002	4.06 +/- 0.30	135.28 +/- 16.19	20.53 +/- 2.78
Travel (16)	0.0005 +/- 0.0001	2.33 +/- 0.29	151.73 +/- 39.70	39.99 +/- 6.60
Art (32)	0.0006 +/- 0.0001	5.26 +/- 0.66	188.55 +/- 48.17	27.54 +/- 5.30
Edu. (31)	0.0009 +/- 0.0001	3.77 +/- 0.51	130.53 +/- 38.63	21.45 +/- 6.40

Table 2: External Influence Model fit to news URL's belonging to various categories. The values listed are the percent change that each topic's URLs are from the global average, for each parameter.

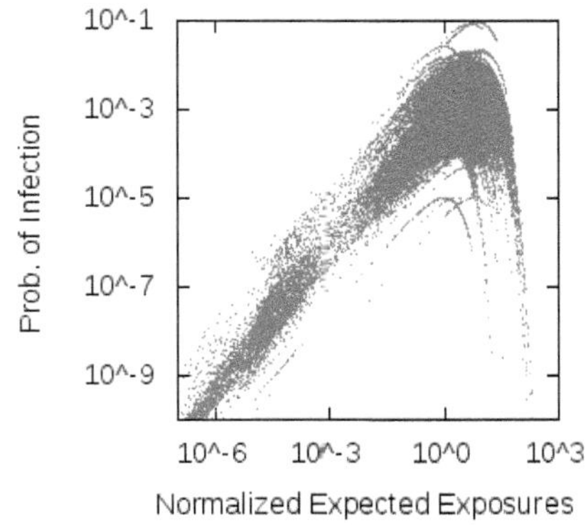

Figure 5: An aggregation of the exposure curves for each URL. Upon the infection of each user, the expected number of exposures received by the user divided by ρ_2 was plotted against inferred infection probability.

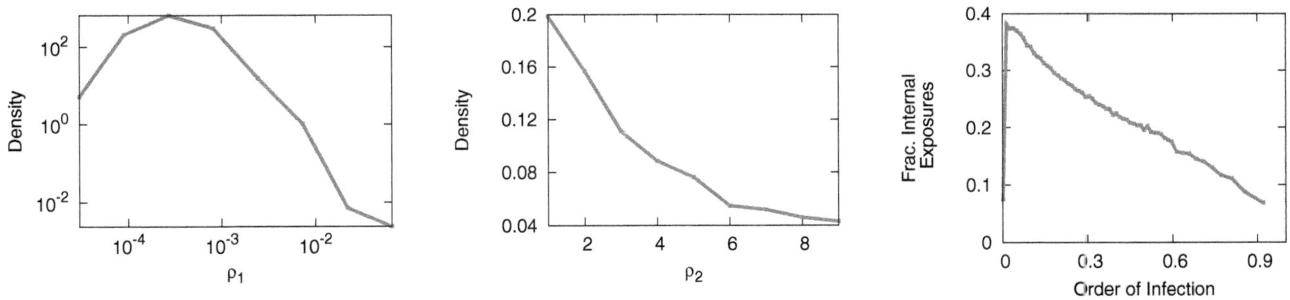

(a) Distribution of ρ_1 (b) Distribution of ρ_2 (c) Fraction of Internal Exposures

Figure 6: (a)The distribution of the inferred ρ_1 (the max. of the exposure curve). (b)The distribution of the ρ_2 (the arg-max. of the exposure curve). (c) For each infection of each URL, the fraction of users already infected was plotted against the inferred fraction of internal exposures the user received.

[9] M. Cha, H. Haddadi, F. Benevenuto, and K. P. Gummadi. Measuring User Influence in Twitter: The Million Follower Fallacy. In *ICWSM '10*, 2010.

[10] D. Cosley, D. P. Huttenlocher, J. M. Kleinberg, X. Lan, and S. Suri. Sequential influence models in social networks. In *ICWSM*, 2010.

[11] R. Crane and D. Sornette. Robust dynamic classes revealed by measuring the response function of a social system. *PNAS*, 105(41):15649–15653, 2008.

[12] R. Elandt-Johnson and N. Johnson. *Survival Models and Data Analysis*. New York: John Wiley and Sons. 1980/1999.

[13] M. G. Rodriguez, D. Balduzzi, and B. Schölkopf. Uncovering the temporal dynamics of diffusion networks. In *ICML '11*, 2011.

[14] M. S. Granovetter. Threshold models of collective behavior. *American Journal of Sociology*, 83(6):1420–1443, 1978.

[15] H. W. Hethcote. The mathematics of infectious diseases. *SIAM Review*, 42(4):599–653, 2000.

[16] E. Katz. The Two-Step flow of communication: An Up-To-date report on an hypothesis. *POQ*,'57.

[17] E. Katz and P. Lazarsfeld. *Personal influence: The part played by people in the flow of mass comm.*. Free Press, '55.

[18] D. Kempe, J. M. Kleinberg, and E. Tardos. Maximizing the spread of influence through a social network. In *KDD '03*.

[19] H. Kwak, C. Lee, H. Park, and S. Moon. What is twitter, a social network or a news media? In *WWW '10*, 2010.

[20] P. F. Lazarsfeld, B. Berelson, and H. Gaudet. *The People's Choice: How the Voter Makes Up His Mind in a Presidential Campaign*. Duell, Sloan, and Pearce. 1944.

[21] J. Leskovec, L. Backstrom, and J. Kleinberg. Meme-tracking and the dynamics of the news cycle. In *KDD '09*, 2009.

[22] J. Leskovec, M. McGlohon, C. Faloutsos, N. Glance, and M. Hurst. Cascading behavior in large blog graphs. *SDM '07*.

[23] E. Rogers. *Diffusion of Innovations*. Free Press, 4th Ed,'95.

[24] D. M. Romero, B. Meeder, and J. M. Kleinberg. Uncovering the Temporal Dynamics of Diffusion Networks *WWW '11*.

[25] C. R. Shalizi and A. C. Thomas. Homophily and contagion are generically confounded in observational social network studies. *Sociological Methods and Research*, 40, 2010.

[26] G. Ver Steeg, R. Ghosh, and K. Lerman. What Stops Social Epidemics? In *ICWSM '11*.

[27] D. Strang and S. A. Soule. Diffusion in organizations and social movements: From hybrid corn to poison pills. *Annual Review of Sociology*, 24:265–290, 1998.

[28] E. Sun, I. Rosenn, C. Marlow, T. Lento. Gesundheit! modeling contagion through facebook. *ICWSM '09*.

[29] D. J. Watts. A simple model of global cascades on random networks. *PNAS*

[30] S. Wu, J. M. Hofman, W. A. Mason, and D. J. Watts. Who says what to whom on twitter. In *WWW '11*

[31] D. J. Watts and P. S. Dodds. Influentials, networks, and public opinion formation. *J. of Consumer Res.*, 34(4), 2007.

The Missing Models: A Data-Driven Approach for Learning How Networks Grow

Rob Patro*
Department of Computer Science
University of Maryland
College Park, MD 20742
rob@cs.umd.edu

Geet Duggal*
Department of Computer Science
University of Maryland
College Park, MD 20742
geet@cs.umd.edu

Emre Sefer
Department of Computer Science
University of Maryland
College Park, MD 20742
esefer@cs.umd.edu

Hao Wang
Department of Electrical and Computer Engineering
University of Maryland
College Park, MD 20742
hwang825@umd.edu

Darya Filippova
Department of Computer Science
University of Maryland
College Park, MD 20742
dfilippo@cs.umd.edu

Carl Kingsford†
Department of Computer Science
University of Maryland
College Park, MD 20742
carlk@cs.umd.edu

ABSTRACT

Probabilistic models of network growth have been extensively studied as idealized representations of network evolution. Models, such as the Kronecker model, duplication-based models, and preferential attachment models, have been used for tasks such as representing null models, detecting anomalies, algorithm testing, and developing an understanding of various mechanistic growth processes. However, developing a new growth model to fit observed properties of a network is a difficult task, and as new networks are studied, new models must constantly be developed. Here, we present a framework, called GrowCode, for the automatic discovery of novel growth models that match user-specified topological features in undirected graphs. GrowCode introduces a set of basic commands that are general enough to encode several previously developed models. Coupling this formal representation with an optimization approach, we show that GrowCode is able to discover models for protein interaction networks, autonomous systems networks, and scientific collaboration networks that closely match properties such as the degree distribution, the clustering coefficient, and assortativity that are observed in real networks of these classes. Additional tests on simulated networks show that the models learned by GrowCode generate distributions of graphs with similar variance as existing models for these classes.

Categories and Subject Descriptors

H.2.8 [**Database Management**]: Database Applications—*Data mining*

*Authors contributed equally.

†To whom correspondence should be addressed.

Keywords

network growth models, algorithms, graph mining

1. INTRODUCTION

The study of the processes by which biological, social, and technological networks have evolved over time has become increasingly central to gaining insight into how these networks function. Of particular importance is understanding the emergence of topological characteristics such as shrinking diameter, assortativity or disassortativity, and modularity as networks grow. One successful approach to understanding how these properties arise is the creation of idealized network models such as the forest fire model [17], the Kronecker model [16], duplication/mutation models [3, 12, 24, 26, 27], preferential attachment models [e.g. 2], and others [6, 9, 14, 15, 23]. These provide a probabilistic and mechanistic way to describe growth of particular classes of networks, generally in terms of combinations of simple operations such as node and edge creation and deletion, node duplication, node expansion (replacing a node by a subgraph), or influence propagation.

In addition to providing an idealized simulation of real-world growth, network models have a number of other uses—some of which do not even require that the programs themselves are interpretable. For example, they can serve as null models for the detection of statistically surprising topological features in a graph, can be used for large-scale performance testing for time-consuming graph algorithms, can aid in reconstructing ancient networks [21], and can help with anonymization [16].

Early theoretical work on network models began in 1960 with the Erdős-Rényi model [10]. Subsequent work identified a scale-free degree distribution [2] and small-world property [28] as common features of real-world networks and produced models that generated them. Later models incorporated other network properties as objectives in various domains, such as shrinking diameter of a growing social network [17] (the forest fire model) and clustering coefficient for biological protein interaction networks [27] (the duplication, mutation, with complementarity or DMC model). Subsequent efforts [e.g. 1, 22] have attempted to manually design models that fit various additional features simultaneously in order to produce more realistic networks. Recently, there has also been work on models that attempt to match not only the topology of real networks, but also richer features such as node attributes [25, 13]. The creation of a parsimonious, plausible, and well-fitting growth model is typically a challenging task, and as more varied, large-scale networks are studied, new important properties will be identified, requiring new models to be developed. However, hand-crafted models can match desired topological properties only as well as the creativity and persistence of the model designer allow.

Here, we introduce a formal representation that can encode many of the most commonly studied growth models, as well as many other models yet to be discovered. We also present an optimization framework that allows for the automatic discovery of new models fitting desired properties within this formal representation. These learned models can be used to generate large classes of exemplar networks that match input features well. They are also interpretable (with some amount of effort). Often, because the framework can generally find many distinct models that match the desired properties, the set of models itself can be minded for motifs that are effective at generating a particular property. Additionally, the ease with which good-fitting models can be found can be used as a measure of the ubiquity of that feature among graph growth mechanisms. Finally, in many cases, the computationally optimized models match real-world properties better than hand-crafted models.

Very little previous work has addressed the challenge of automatic design of network models. Some previous frameworks are capable of adapting known models to new data by re-estimating parameters that govern the network growth process. For example, the Kronecker graph model [16] can be combined with a Markov Chain Monte Carlo method (KronFit [16]) to estimate its parameters in order to fit some properties for very large networks. Similar parameter estimation has been done for other recursive network models [1]. These approaches, however, are limited to parameter estimation only and cannot generate truly novel network growth mechanisms. Middendorf et al. [19, 20] address the model-selection problem of choosing from among a small number of existing models, for example, they found that protein-protein interaction networks were best fit by the DMC [27] model. However, their procedure neither generates new models nor fits parameters for existing models.

The framework we propose, GrowCode, addresses these deficiencies by representing basic random graph operations and other natural building blocks of models as instructions that operate in a register-based virtual machine. The intuitive motivation behind our framework is to provide a general and effective set of atomic operations or building blocks of network growth. A sequence of such operations defines an iteration of the network growth process, and repeated iterations of this sequence of operations evolve a network over time. We show that a small set of instructions — only 4 of which have parameters — are sufficient to describe preferential attachment, a forest-fire-like model, and a duplication model (and intuitively many other models as well). Because, additionally, the instructions operate on a simple machine with only 3 registers, this formal representation limits the search space of possible programs, allowing a genetic algorithm to search the space effectively.

We show that it is possible to quickly and automatically learn network growth models that satisfy key properties of social, technological, and biological networks using the GrowCode framework. The fit of these models to the basic topological properties of degree distribution, assortativity, and clustering coefficient is often superior to hand-crafted models. In particular, we learn a model for yeast protein interaction networks [30] that generates graphs with far better agreement to the observed values of the clustering coefficient and degree distribution than the popular duplication/mutation with complementary (DMC) model often used to simulate these networks. For a recent scientific co-authorship network [5], we are able to better match assortativity and degree distribution than graphs produced by the Kronecker model with optimized parameters [17]. Finally, for an autonomous systems internet graph, we are able to find a model that is simultaneously a much better match than a Kronecker model for clustering coefficient, assortativity, and degree distribution. The models we learn in all these settings produce graphs that are at least as diverse as those produced by the competing hand-crafted models, indicating that we are producing truly random graph models.

Although the framework we present here applies to undirected and unattributed graphs, the GrowCode approach is general, and can be easily extended to other classes of graphs as well. GrowCode also points the way to new techniques for more systematic and automatic study of network growth models themselves.

2. THE GROWCODE FRAMEWORK

We describe a novel framework, GrowCode, in which growth models may be expressed concisely and programmatically. We define a simple register machine and a set of 15 instructions that execute on it. Every sequence of instructions is a syntactically correct program that encodes some network growth model in a compact form. The instruction set contains instructions that represent specific, basic operations affecting the graph topology. There are also few instructions to manage registers and control the program flow. The instructions were selected because they are natural building blocks of growth models capable of representing a variety of extant and unknown models.

As the GrowCode machine executes a program, it modifies the topology of a growing graph. Each pass through a GrowCode program defines a single step of the growth procedure. To grow a network for t steps using the GrowCode program, the program is executed from start to finish t times. Thus, the model described by every GrowCode program is implicitly parameterized on t, which is related to the desired size of the output graph. Between subsequent growth steps (i.e. between subsequent invocations of a program), the registers of the GrowCode machine are populated randomly with nodes from the current graph. In addition to several randomized instructions, this helps GrowCode programs encode non-deterministic growth models, and different runs of the same program nearly always produce different graphs.

2.1 A register machine

GrowCode runs on a virtual machine with three registers `r0`, `r1`, `r2` that can store positive integers. The positive integer values in the registers usually correspond to vertex IDs in the graph, although they sometimes hold implicit parameters used by some instructions. The special value `NIL` in a register means that the register is empty.

The machine maintains a program counter, PC, indicating the currently executing instruction. After an instruction is executed, PC is incremented so that the program is executed sequentially unless one of the instructions responsible for control flow manipulates the PC. Programs can be self-modifying in a very limited way to support looping (see the Rewind instruction below). Program execution terminates once the location of PC has exceeds the length of the program.

Additionally, the machine has a limited memory $\mathtt{L} : V \to V$ that can store a single vertex ID associated with each vertex in V, the set of vertices in the growing graph. The value $\mathtt{L}(v)$ on node v need not be the vertex ID of v, but rather can be the ID of some other node in V. This allows programs to mark nodes with IDs of arbitrary other nodes in the graph, which is how programs can spread the influence

Table 1: Complete GrowCode instruction set

Name	Description
New node	create new node
Create edge	create new edge
Random node	pick random node
Random edge	pick random edge
Influence neighbors(p)	label neighbors with u
Attach to influenced	add edges to neighbors labeled u
Detach from influenced	remove edges to neighbors labeled u
Clear influenced	clear all labels from L
Rewind(r, i)	jump back r positions i times
Skip instruction(p)	skip next instruction
Set(i)	copy node ID to r2
Save	copy r0 to r2
Load	copy r2 to r0
Swap	swap r0 and r1
Clear r2	set r2 to NIL

of a node in the graph (see section 2.2). If $\text{L}(v) = \text{NIL}$, then v is considered to have no label. Other, more sophisticated memories or influence instructions are possible, but the experiments below indicate that this minimal scheme is all that is required to achieve good agreement in several settings.

2.2 An instruction set

Instruction set design.

Design of instruction sets for physical and virtual processors is a difficult, long-standing problem. Operations in the GrowCode instruction set were selected so that they are representative of the basic network operations. Individual instructions are easily interpretable and are similar to those used by the hand-created growth models. Intuitively, combinations of these instructions can produce growth models that can generate networks with the desired properties. The combination of instructions used here is but one example among many possible instruction sets. This set of instructions can be extended to include other instructions to accommodate new growth processes. A good set of instructions makes it much easier to optimize a difficult objective [4]; however, it is out of the scope of this paper to completely resolve the problem of instruction set design. Rather we provide evidence that one instruction set (Table 1) works well for several common classes of graphs.

GrowCode instructions.

The GrowCode instructions (Table 1) can be subdivided into 4 categories: (1) graph operations, (2) influence operations, (3) control flow operations, and (4) register manipulation operations. The first two sets of operations deal with modifying the topology of the growing graph while the 3rd and 4th sets of operations deal with managing the control flow of the GrowCode program and the state of the GrowCode machine. See Table 1 for a complete list of instructions. Below, we describe how each of these affects the state of the GrowCode machine and the graph being generated. In section 3, we show how several network growth models can be expressed with these instructions.

Graph operations. The graph operations perform basic modifications of graph topology. The New node operation creates a new node in the growing graph with a unique ID that is placed in register r0. The Create edge operation is used to introduce a single new edge in the graph. The machine first fetches the nodes from r0 (u)

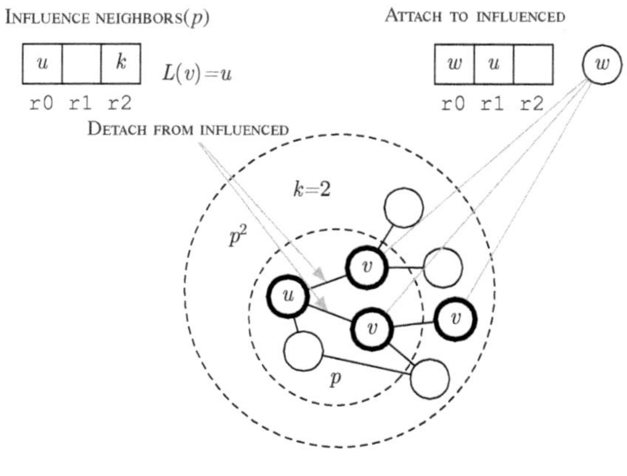

Figure 1: Schematic of the three influence operations. First node u influences its neighbors with probability p, then the influenced neighbors v influence their neighbors with probability p^2. If u were to detach from its influenced neighbors the two edges indicated by the gray arrows would be removed from the graph. Finally, w can attach to all nodes influenced by u.

and r1 (v) and then creates a new edge $\{u, v\}$ in the graph. The state of the registers after a Create edge operation remains unchanged, so if such an edge already exists, the operation has no effect. The Random node operation selects a node uniformly at random from the current graph and places this node into r0. Finally, the Random edge operation selects an edge $\{u, v\}$ uniformly at random from the current graph, and places u in r0 and v in r1.

Influence operations. The influence operations allow nodes to exert an influence on other nodes in the graph. We say that a node v is influenced by u if $\text{L}(v) = u$. This concept of influence is important to produce graphs with properties such as homophily where, to varying degrees, connected nodes share topological neighborhoods. The core influence operation, Influence neighbors(p), allows a node to influence a subset of its neighborhood. To execute the Influence neighbors(p) operation, the machine fetches the node ID from r0; this node, u, becomes the central, or *influential* node. It then assigns the mark u to every neighbor v of u by setting $\text{L}(v) = u$ independently with probability p. Each newly marked node, v, in turn marks its neighbors with the value u with probability $p^{d(u,v)}$, where $d(u, v)$ is the shortest path distance between u and v. If r2 is not NIL, only nodes v such that $d(u, v) < \text{r2}$ can potentially be affected by the influence operation. If $\text{r2} = \text{NIL}$, the influence operation continues until the probabilistic process dies out and no more nodes are marked.

The Influence neighbors(p) operation works in conjunction with three other influence operations. Attach to influenced creates edges between the node in r0, w, and all nodes in the graph marked with the value in $\text{r1} = u$. That is, it creates edges $\{w, v\}$ for all v such that $\text{L}(v) = u$. This provides a general mechanism to make the neighborhoods of two nodes more similar to each other. The Detach from influenced operation fetches a node u from r0 and removes all edges $\{u, v\}$ from the graph where $\text{L}(v) = u$. Finally, the Clear influenced operation erases the contents of L so that future operations can work with a clear memory. Figure 1 illustrates these influence operations.

Control flow operations. The control flow operations alter the order of execution of GrowCode instructions. The Rewind(r, i) instruction allows for loop-like structures in GrowCode programs. The first argument r is a natural number specifying the number of times PC should be decremented when the instruction is executed

Algorithm 1 Barabási-Albert

```
1: NEW NODE                     ▷ Create a new node, u
2: SAVE
3: RANDOM EDGE                  ▷ Choose a random edge, e
4: SKIP INSTRUCTION(0.5)        ▷ Choose random endpoint v of e
5: SWAP
6: LOAD
7: CREATE EDGE                  ▷ Create an edge between v and u
8: REWIND(5, i)                 ▷ Attach it to i random nodes
```

(i.e. how far the PC should jump backwards). The second argument i specifies the number of times the instruction should be executed. Each time the instruction is executed, the instruction is modified by decrementing the value of i by 1. When $i = 0$, the instruction will no longer be executed and the value of PC will not be rewound. The parameters of the rewind instruction are reset between consecutive program executions. The other instruction in this group, SKIP INSTRUCTION(p), advances the PC by a value of 2 with probability p. This allows the next instruction to be conditionally executed with probability $1 - p$.

Register operations. Finally, the register operations allow one to manipulate the 3 registers directly. The SET(i) instruction assigns integer i to `r2`. The SAVE operation copies the contents of `r0` into `r2`. Conversely, LOAD places the contents of `r2` into `r0`. The SWAP operation swaps the contents of `r0` and `r1`. Finally, the CLEAR `r2` sets the contents of `r2` to `NIL`.

3. REPRESENTING EXISTING MODELS

To demonstrate the generality of the GrowCode instruction set, we show how it can be used to express three existing network growth models, Barabási-Albert (B-A) [2], duplication and mutation with complementarity (DMC) [27], and forest fire (FF) [17] by writing hand-coded GrowCode programs that match the properties of these models. These growth models match different classes of real-world networks, and they exhibit different topological qualities. For example, the DMC model (with the appropriate parameters) produces graphs with a range of clustering coefficients that match those observed in protein-protein interaction networks, while the FF model produces graphs that exhibit shrinking diameter and a densification power law property as they grow. Despite significant differences in the mechanisms they model and the graph properties they produce, there are fairly simple GrowCode programs capable of representing each of these models while using the same set of primitive instructions. The instructions are re-used in different models which indicates their overall utility in expressing different network growth behavior.

3.1 Barabási-Albert

In the B-A model, new nodes added to the growing network are more likely to connect to existing high-degree nodes [2]. This process reproduces the scale-free degree distribution often found in real-world networks, where there are relatively few nodes having a very high degree and a long tail of low-degree nodes.

The GrowCode program in Algorithm 1 closely simulates the B-A model. While there are subtle differences between the program and the model, the graphs generated by the program match those produced by B-A closely. The essence of the B-A model is encoded in lines 3–5. The RANDOM EDGE instruction (line 3) picks an edge that is likely to have a high-degree node as one of its endpoints. The probability that a randomly chosen edge e contains the node u is directly proportional to the degree of u: $d(u)/|E| = 2d(u)/\sum_{v \in V} d(v)$. Once e is selected, instructions 4 and 5 choose an endpoint for this edge at random to ensure that there is no bias when selecting a node within the edge. This process selects nodes proportional to their degree as desired with the minor difference that the degrees $d(u)$ are changed as the program executes, in contrast to B-A . The newly added node is then connected to u (line 7) completing the preferential attachment of the new node. The rewind on line 8 iterates this procedure so that we connect the new node to i existing nodes.

Algorithm 2 DMC

```
 1: RANDOM NODE                          ▷ Put a random node v in r0
 2: SET(1)                               ▷ Set r2 (k-hop for influence) to 1
 3: INFLUENCE NEIGHBORS(1.0)             ▷ Influence v's neighbors
 4: SWAP                                 ▷ Swap r0 and r1
 5: NEW NODE                             ▷ Create a new node u and put it in r0
 6: ATTACH TO INFLUENCED                 ▷ Connect u to influenced nodes
 7: CLEAR INFLUENCED
 8: INFLUENCE NEIGHBORS(q_MOD/2)         ▷ Influence u's neighbors
 9: SWAP
10: INFLUENCE NEIGHBORS(q_MOD/2)         ▷ Influence v's neighbors
11: DETACH FROM INFLUENCED               ▷ Actually delete edges from v
12: SWAP
13: DETACH FROM INFLUENCED               ▷ Do the same for u
14: CLEAR INFLUENCED
15: SKIP INSTRUCTION(1.0 − q_CON)        ▷ Skip adding {u, v}
16: CREATE EDGE                          ▷ with probability q_CON
```

3.2 Duplication and Divergence

The duplication and mutation with complementarity model [27] (abbreviated DMC) aims to reproduce the topological characteristics of protein interaction networks. Under the DMC model, the driving mechanism of network growth is the duplication of existing nodes. The model has two parameters, q_{MOD} and q_{CON}, that govern the process as follows. Each new node u chooses an anchor v and attaches to all of v's neighbors. Then, for each node w now adjacent to both u and v, an edge is randomly chosen that connects w either to u or v, and the edge is removed with probability q_{MOD}. Finally, the edge $\{u, v\}$ is added with probability q_{CON}. This mechanism of growth is motivated by the common occurrence of gene duplication, wherein genes, the precursors of proteins, are commonly copied within the genome. Initially, the copied genes are exact duplicates, and therefore the resultant proteins maintain the same set of interactions as the original protein. However, after duplication, evolutionary pressure on genes to maintain the interactions is reduced, and the interaction patterns between the original and copied genes start to diverge. Algorithm 2 gives a close approximation to the DMC model in GrowCode.

The DMC model presented in Algorithm 2 differs slightly from that introduced by Vazquez et al. [27] in that we cannot precisely mimic the procedure of selecting shared neighbors of u and v with probability q_{CON} and then deleting the edge to one or the other. However, to achieve a similar effect, we can influence the shared neighbors of each node with probability $q_{\text{MOD}}/2$ (lines 8 and 10) after we have copied v's neighborhood to u. If the set of influenced neighbors is disjoint, then the influence instruction has exactly the same effect as the traditional DMC operation. It is possible that a neighboring node will be influenced by both u and v. Complementarity (the fact that only the edge to u or v is removed, and not both) is maintained in this case as well since the mark on the shared node will be overwritten, ensuring that only one of $\{u, w\}$ and $\{v, w\}$ can be deleted. This procedure can result in values of q_{MOD} having a

Algorithm 3 FF

1:	RANDOM NODE	▷ Put a random node in `r0`
2:	CLEAR `r2`	▷ Clear `r2` to allow full graph influence
3:	INFLUENCE NEIGHBORS(b)	▷ Breadth-first recursive influence
4:	SWAP	▷ Move the random node into `r1`
5:	NEW NODE	▷ Create a new node, u
6:	CREATE EDGE	
7:	ATTACH TO INFLUENCED	▷ Connect u to influenced nodes

slightly different effect in the GrowCode program as compared to the original DMC model. However, we have verified that graphs generated by GrowCode DMC and the original DMC have similar Zipf plots (through visual inspection) and clustering coefficients (section 5.3), which are the two features on which the authors of the DMC model focused. Further, Algorithm 2 produces graphs with similar Zipf plots and clustering coefficients as those observed in the yeast protein interaction network. Thus, despite the subtle differences, the GrowCode algorithm 2 maintains the essential characteristics of the original growth model.

3.3 Forest fire

The forest fire (FF) model [17] was first introduced to model scale-free degree distributions (of both in-degree and out-degree) as well as shrinking diameter and densification over time (under certain parameter regimes). The FF model is very intuitive and easy to explain from the perspective of network growth. We present a model that has been slightly altered to apply to undirected networks. When a new node u enters the network, it chooses an existing node v uniformly at random to act as an *ambassador*, and the edge $\{u, v\}$ is added to the network. Next, a number n is drawn from a geometric distribution with probability b of success, and n neighbors of v are chosen to be *burned*. An edge is added from u to each of these burned nodes, and the process of selecting a set of neighbors and burning them is repeated recursively.

Algorithm 3 shows a GrowCode program that encodes the forest fire model. We observe that it produces networks with the same essential characteristics as those produced via the forest fire model. In particular, the networks produced by algorithm 3 exhibit (for certain parameter ranges of b) shrinking diameter and densification power law during network growth.

4. LEARNING GROWCODE MODELS

One of the benefits of expressing growth models as a set of instructions is that we can now formalize the problem of learning a growth model as an optimization problem over the space of GrowCode programs. Given a set of graph features, we use genetic programming techniques to learn a GrowCode program that produces graphs closely approximating these features. These graph properties are encoded into the fitness function of an individual GrowCode program. The goal of our learning procedure is not to recover previously proposed growth models, but rather to learn programs that grow graphs that are representative of a particular class of graphs as measured under specific similarity measures.

4.1 Constructing a fitness function

We define a feature collection $\mathbf{x} = [x_1, x_2, \ldots, x_m]$ to be a m-long vector of features where each property x_i may be a scalar (such as clustering coefficient) or a vector (such as a sampling of the graph's effective diameter during its growth process). The goal of the feature collection is to represent the essential graph characteristics that we want our growth model to match. We define a (possibly weighted) similarity measure between any two feature collections $s(\mathbf{x}^i, \mathbf{x}^j)$, which are of the same size, as:

$$s(\mathbf{x}^i, \mathbf{x}^j) = \sum_{\ell=1}^{m} w_\ell s_\ell(x_\ell^i, x_\ell^j), \tag{1}$$

where $s_\ell(\cdot, \cdot)$ is a user-defined measure of similarity between the ℓth features of the collections. This measure of similarity can be as simple as the inverse of the difference between the two features (e.g. for scalar features), or it could be as complex as a measure of the similarity of distributions (for more complex features). The only requirement on $s_\ell(x_\ell^i, x_\ell^j)$ is that it should be a monotonically non-decreasing function of similarity between the two features, and it should achieve its maximum value when $x_\ell^i = x_\ell^j$. The w_ℓ allow one to weight each feature differently, forcing the optimization procedure to prefer some features over the others. In the experiments reported here, $w_\ell = 1$ for all ℓ.

We define the fitness of a GrowCode program based on eq. (1). Let $\mathbf{x}^{\text{T}}$ be a target feature collection and let $\mathbf{x}^{\text{P}}$ be a random variable representing the feature collection for the graph generated by the randomized program P. Then we can define our problem as the search for P* such that:

$$\text{P}^* = \arg\max_{\text{P}} \mathbb{E}[s(\mathbf{x}^{\text{P}}, \mathbf{x}^{\text{T}})], \tag{2}$$

where the expectation is taken over various runs of P. That is, we seek the program P* such that the graph generated by P* are expected to have features most similar to those given by $\mathbf{x}^{\text{T}}$ as measured by the similarity function $s(\cdot, \cdot)$. This optimization problem is difficult given the size of the space of potential programs. To tackle this problem effectively, we adopt genetic programming techniques which have proven effective in similarly difficult optimization scenarios.

4.2 Optimization with genetic algorithms

We use the ECJ package [18] to perform the optimization, and we use its abilities to evaluate individuals within a generation in parallel, customize the selection methods and breeding architecture for multiple sub-populations, perform NSGA-II multi-objective optimization [8], and handle arbitrary representations of fixed and variable length genomes.

Each individual encodes a program. At each generation, we evaluate the fitness for all individuals in the fixed-size population. Each program's fitness is calculated by running it for k iterations, and comparing its feature vector $\mathbf{x}^{\text{P}}$ against the target set of features. This is repeated some number M times, and the results are averaged, so that the fitness of program P is:

$$\mathcal{F}(\text{P}) = \text{avg}\, s(\mathbf{x}^{\text{P}}, \mathbf{x}^{\text{T}}). \tag{3}$$

Alternatively, we can average each $s_\ell(x_\ell^i, x_\ell^j)$ in eq. (1) as a separate objective, and employ a multi-objective optimization strategy (e.g. NSGA-II) [8].

When breeding individual programs, a two-point crossover operation allows the programs to mix with each other thus varying their contents and length. At the end of each generation, individuals compete in a tournament of successive comparisons of two randomly chosen individuals, where winners are chosen deterministically based on the higher fitness value. Winners of the tournament become members of the subsequent population. Individuals are drawn with replacement and can thus be replicated in the subsequent population. More fit individuals are more likely to win tournaments, making "elite" members more likely to survive into the next generation.

5. APPLICATIONS TO SYNTHETIC AND REAL NETWORKS

We demonstrate the use of our framework to learn GrowCode programs that produce networks matching specified properties of both synthetic and real networks. Unless specified otherwise, we use the following parameters in our optimization procedures. All programs in the first generation of an optimization are initialized randomly with 10 instructions. Each generation consists of 100 programs that are evaluated on the basis of a single-objective (section 5.1) or multi-objective (sections 5.2 to 5.4) fitness function. Individuals are chosen to advance to successive generations using tournament-selection. At the start of each generation, the population of individuals is bred from the selected individuals from the previous generation using two-point list crossover breeding. This produces new individuals, potentially with programs of different length, which are then subject to mutation (we use a mutation rate of 0.1). The optimization procedure is carried out for 15 generations, and we select the most fit individual from the final generation as the representative GrowCode program against which we compare other models.

5.1 Learning scale-free graphs

Scale-free distributions are the key network property that motivated the B-A growth model, and we show that GrowCode can learn models that produce scale-free distributions. Given the large space of models defined by the instruction set and their parameters, it is unclear at first if effectively exploring this space is even possible.

We measure the similarity of two degree distributions via a shape function. Although one straightforward option is to choose the goodness of fit to a scale-free distribution as one of our features, this approach is specific to scale-free distributions, and in general, we would like to generate graphs that match the shape of any specified degree distribution, not only scale-free distributions. We define the shape ψ_{shape} of a graph to be the cumulative distribution of node degrees where the support of the distribution (the degrees of the nodes) is normalized between 0 and 1. This normalization allows for the comparison of the degree distribution of graphs of different sizes. We define the similarity metric for the shape feature to be:

$$s_{\text{shape}}(\psi^i_{\text{shape}}, \psi^j_{\text{shape}}) = \frac{1}{\left\|\psi^i_{\text{shape}} - \psi^j_{\text{shape}}\right\|_1 + \epsilon}, \tag{4}$$

where ϵ is a small positive constant to assure that the fitness is defined (as a large value) when the shapes coincide exactly.

The B-A model is parameterized on i, the number of vertices to which a new vertex connects. To get the target degree distribution shape for various i, we generate graphs for $i = 3, 4, 5, 6$ and obtain maximum-likelihood estimates of scale-free exponents of $\alpha = 2.61, 2.71, 2.73, 2.92$, respectively. We then use s_{shape} in eq. (3) to define the fitness of a program as the difference in degree-distribution shape between the graphs produced by the program and the estimated target shape.

With this fitness, GrowCode learns many non-identical programs that are scale free. Algorithm 4 shows one of the effective scale free GrowCode programs learned during the optimization process. To test for the plausibility of a scale-free distribution, we use statistical tests specific to that distribution as described in [7]. We find that even though the α parameter was not directly used in the fitness function, the networks instantiated from the learned models that pass the scale-free test have an average α value of 2.69, which is reasonably close to that of the target graphs.

In fact, we posit that it is quite easy for our optimization procedure to discover a GrowCode program that produces networks with a scale-free degree distribution. Figure 2 shows a trace of one of the optimization runs when attempting to fit a degree-distribution generated from the B-A model with $i = 4$. Scale-free models are discovered in the first generation of the optimization procedure, even before fitness selection has had an opportunity to affect the population. The total fitness of the scale-free individuals grows quickly, and by generation 6, is already substantially greater than the total fitness of the non-scale-free individuals (fig. 2). These observations have two implications. First, the shape function seems to correlate well with the scale-free plausibility of the graph. Second, discovering a scale-free model is not difficult.

Algorithm 4 Example Learned Scale-Free Model

1: NEW NODE
2: RANDOM NODE
3: ATTACH TO INFLUENCED
4: CLEAR r2
5: SET(1)
6: RANDOM EDGE
7: DETACH FROM INFLUENCED
8: RANDOM NODE
9: CREATE EDGE
10: INFLUENCE NEIGHBORS(0.692)

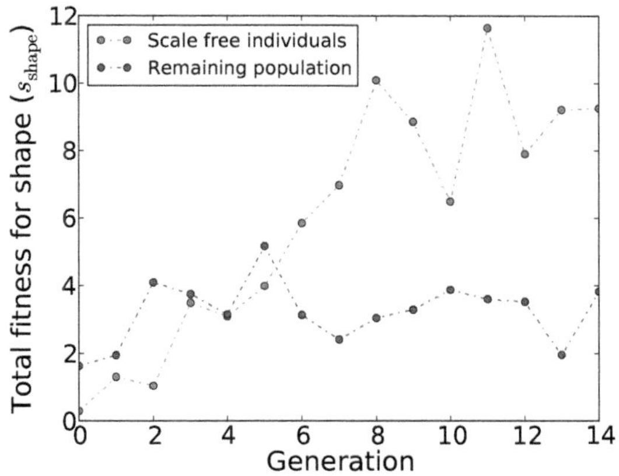

Figure 2: Total fitness for shape (s_{shape}) at each generation. The total fitness for those individuals that pass the scale-free plausibility test is drawn in red, while the total fitness for the rest of the individuals in the generation is drawn in blue. After just the fifth generation, the total fitness of scale-free individuals is approximately twice as large as the remaining population.

5.2 Performance on a social network

We apply GrowCode to a recent network of co-authorship of genome-wide association studies (GWAS) [5]. Specifically, we consider the social network of "repeated co-authorship" where pairs of scientists are linked if they published together more than once. This network is associated with a high assortativity (0.19), which implies that scientists who collaborate prolifically tend to connect with scientists who also collaborate with many other researchers. We simultaneously optimize for the shape distribution feature commonly studied in social networks [7] and assortativity using the multi-objective scheme of section 4.2.

We compare graphs generated by GrowCode programs to graphs

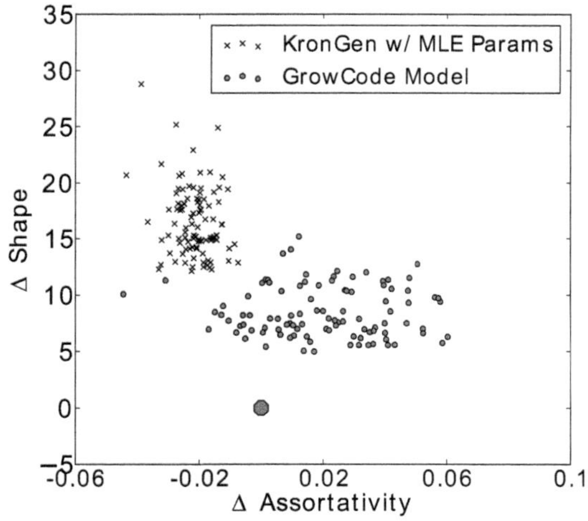

Figure 3: GWAS target network. Each point represents a single generated graph from a model. The x axis represents the difference between the assortativity of a graph and the target co-authorship graph. The y axis represents the difference between the shape of a learned graph and the co-authorship graph. The green dot represents a perfect match to the co-authorship graph.

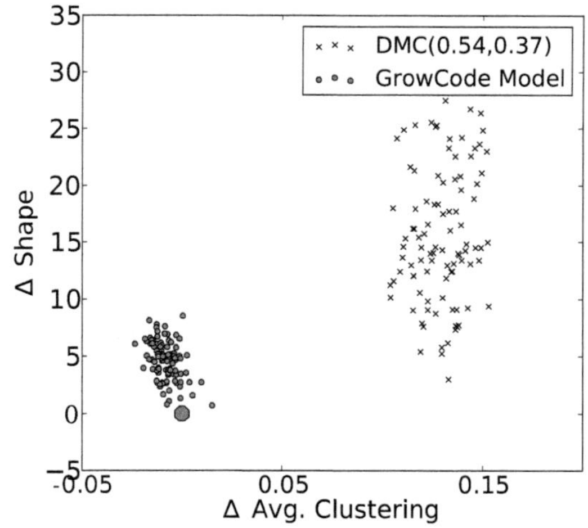

Figure 4: PPI target network. Each point represents a single generated graph. The x axis gives the difference between the average clustering coefficients of a graph and the protein interaction graph. The y axis gives the difference between the shape of a learned graph and the protein interaction graph. The green dot represents the origin and the protein interaction graph.

generated by the Kronecker model [16], a fast, recursive graph generation model that has been shown to reproduce many characteristics of real-world networks. The Kronecker model requires parameters to generate random graphs with the desired properties, and we use the KronFit maximum-likelihood algorithm on the GWAS graph to estimate these parameters. We compare the features of 100 graphs generated by each model to the real GWAS network.

The learned GrowCode model better matches the assortativity of the original graph as well as the shape of the degree distribution (Figure 3) than the best-fit Kronecker model. The average shape difference of the GrowCode model (mean 8.47, std. dev 2.24) is closer to the shape of the co-authorship network than that for the Kronecker model (mean 16.6, std. dev 3.09). The mean assortativity for the GrowCode graphs is 0.206 while the mean for the Kronecker graphs is 0.165. However, in this case, different graphs produced by the GrowCode model are associated with a wider range of assortativity values (std. dev 0.0208) than the Kronecker graphs (std. dev 0.00629).

5.3 Performance on a biological network

We demonstrate the ability of GrowCode to learn a program that generates graphs similar to a high-quality and recent yeast protein interaction network compiled by Gibson et al. [11]. We optimize for both the shape distribution and the clustering coefficient, both shown to be biologically relevant in protein interaction networks [27]. We follow a similar procedure as in section 5.2, but instead of the Kronecker model, we use the DMC model as the baseline comparison. We determined the best parameters for DMC ($q_{\text{mod}} = 0.55$ and $q_{\text{con}} = 0.37$) via a grid search over the parameter space, and we selected the pair of parameters for which the graphs produced by the model closely match the number of edges, clustering coefficient, and diameter of the input PPI network.

The networks generated by the learned GrowCode program match the target characteristics of the real network substantially better than the networks produced by the DMC model (Figure 4). The mean average clustering coefficient produced by the GrowCode program is 0.091 (std. dev 0.006), which matches the average clustering coefficient (0.099) of the protein interaction network very well. Conversely, the mean average clustering coefficient produced by DMC is 0.227 (std. dev 0.013) which is quite far from the true value. The results for the shape distribution yield a similar conclusion (fig. 4). Over the random networks generated by the GrowCode program, the average shape distribution distance is 4.58 (std. dev 1.69) while the average distance among the DMC-generated networks is 15.48 (std. dev 6.29). The GrowCode program not only produces graphs that match the target better but also that exhibit greater parametric stability (i.e. less variance) with regard to these metrics.

5.4 Performance on a technological network

Above, we showed that GrowCode performs well when learning models for pairs of network properties. In each case, the particular pair of properties were chosen because they had been studied in the context of the corresponding class of network. The GrowCode framework is not restricted to only two target features, and here, we provide evidence that it is possible to extend the learning process to more attributes. Using the Autonomous Systems (AS) Route View graph discussed in [16] as a target, we learn a GrowCode program by simultaneously optimizing for all three of the previously considered features (shape, assortativity, and average clustering coefficient). In this case, 150 individuals were evolved for 25 generations. As in Section 5.2, we compare graphs generated by the learned GrowCode program to those generated by the Kronecker model.

The three plots in Figure 5 show that for all pairs of properties, graphs generated by GrowCode are close to the real world network and, in fact, match the AS graph better than those generated by the Kronecker model. Note that the plots show only two dimensions at a time, but a single learned GrowCode program was optimized for

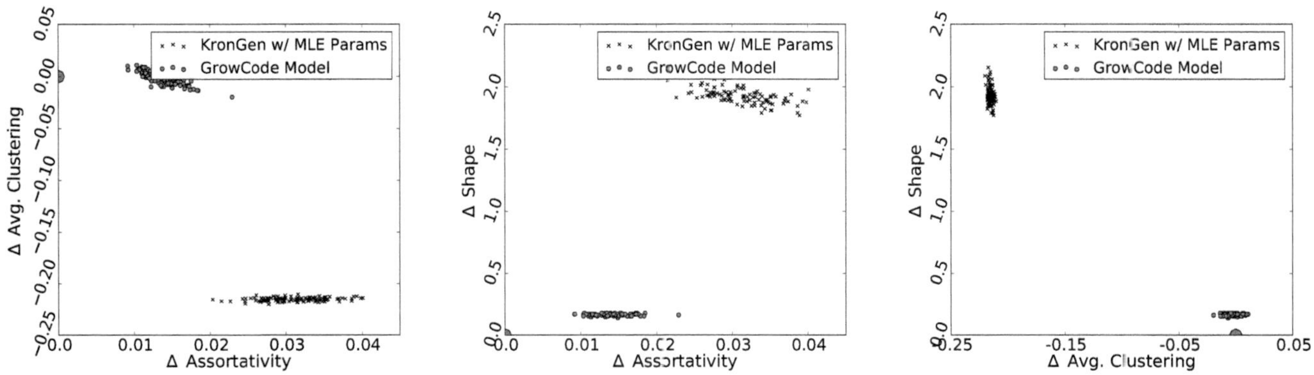

Figure 5: AS target network. Each point represents a single generated graph. The difference between the coefficients of a graph and the AS graph are plotted for three pairs of network properties: average clustering vs. assortativity, shape vs. assortativity, and shape vs. average clustering. The green dot represents the origin and the AS graph.

Table 2: Mean and standard deviation ($\mu \pm \sigma$) of spectral distance between all graphs generated by the B-A model and by GrowCode programs.

i	3	4	5	6
B-A	0.0086 ± 0.0058	0.0034 ± 0.0007	0.0029 ± 0.0006	0.0026 ± 0.0005
GC	0.0141 ± 0.0115	0.0252 ± 0.0206	0.0288 ± 0.0228	0.0182 ± 0.0152

all three features at once. As with the biological network in Section 5.3, the GrowCode program produces graphs that have low variance with respect to the target topological properties.

5.5 GrowCode generates random models

To ensure that the diversity of the graphs produced by GrowCode matches that of those produced by hand-coded models, we computed the mean and standard deviation of the spectral distance between 100 graphs generated by both the traditional B-A model and the GrowCode program that best fit a scale-free graph. The spectral distance is a reasonable, efficiently-computable measure of graph similarity that correlates well with graph edit distance [29]. In order to estimate spectral distances between graphs, we used a discretized histogram of the normalized Laplacian eigenvalue distribution (100 bins). The spectral distance is then the Euclidean distance between such histograms.

As Table 2 shows, GrowCode does not produce deterministic models, and in fact the models learned by GrowCode generate an ensemble of graphs that has higher diversity than the ensemble produced by the B-A model, despite matching the target properties better. Similar diversity is also observed when this experiment is repeated to compare graphs generated by the optimal model learned by GrowCode to fit the yeast PPI network and the graphs generated by DMC (data not shown).

6. CONCLUSIONS AND FUTURE WORK

We have introduced a novel framework, GrowCode, for representing network growth models as programs composed from a short and descriptive set of instructions. We demonstrate that this representation is sufficiently general to reproduce close approximations to several existing growth models. Additionally, this formal encoding allows for an effective search procedure to find models with desired properties. In representative social, biological, and technological networks, a fairly fast optimization procedure (no run took more than 30 minutes for two objectives and no more than 4 hours for three objectives) is able to produce GrowCode programs that are competitive with recent network growth models designed to match properties of graphs in these domains.

We are also able to match scale-free graphs with several different attachment parameters i, and we are able to learn GrowCode programs that pass rigorous statistical tests for scale-free plausibility. Indeed, our optimization procedure comes across scale-free GrowCode programs quickly, and by the end yields a large number of non-identical programs that produce graphs passing the scale-free plausibility test. Additionally, we show that the graphs produced by these GrowCode programs are at least as diverse as graphs generated by the B-A model. This indicates that the scale-free property is quite ubiquitous among possible growth models.

The framework presented here applies to both undirected and unattributed networks, yet we believe it can be extended to handle directed networks and networks with node and edge attributes. Certain generalizations may be achieved by extending the instruction set, for example, by incorporating instructions that create and modify directed edges, allow node attributes to spread throughout the network, or that encode a more complex and general influence mechanism. Others may require enhancements to the machine. For example, handling edge attributes may require the addition of an edge memory akin to the label memory of the current machine. Such modifications, however, are not conceptually difficult, though their careful design is important.

Finally, although the instructions used in GrowCode programs are individually interpretable, the optimization procedure may produce programs whose overall growth mechanisms are sometimes, though not always, opaque. In the future, we plan to explore how ensembles of learned programs can be analyzed to extract from them interpretable mechanisms of growth by finding commonly occurring instruction patterns (motifs). For example, on further analysis of programs like Algorithm 4, we have noticed certain repeated patterns of instructions that are often used to match scale-free networks and to create edges to existing nodes proportional to their degrees. These patterns show up with NEW NODE and CREATE EDGE instructions as well as the influence operations. Mining GrowCode programs for repeated patterns could reveal sets of instructions that are interpretable as a unit.

Acknowledgements

This work was partially supported by the National Science Foundation [CCF-1053918, EF-0849899, and IIS-0812111], the National Institutes of Health [1R21AI085376], and a University of Maryland Institute for Advanced Studies New Frontiers Award. C.K. received support as an Alfred P. Sloan Research Fellow.

References

[1] L. Akoglu and C. Faloutsos. RTG: a recursive realistic graph generator using random typing. *Data Mining and Knowledge Discovery*, 19(2):194–209, 2009.

[2] A. Barabási. Emergence of Scaling in Random Networks. *Science*, 286(5439):509–512, 1999.

[3] A. Bhan, D. Galas, and T. Dewey. A duplication growth model of gene expression networks. *Bioinformatics*, 18:1486–1493, 2002.

[4] M. Brameier. *On linear genetic programming*. PhD thesis, University of Hamburg, 2004.

[5] B. K. Bulik-Sullivan and P. F. Sullivan. The authorship network of genome-wide association studies. *Nature Genetics*, 44(2):113–113, 2012.

[6] D. Callaway, J. E. Hopcroft, J. M. Kleinberg, M. E. Newman, and S. H. Strogatz. Are randomly grown graphs really random? *Phys. Rev. E*, 64:041902–041908, 2001.

[7] A. Clauset, C. R. Shalizi, and M. E. J. Newman. Power-Law Distributions in Empirical Data. *SIAM Review*, 51(4):661, 2009.

[8] K. Deb, A. Pratap, S. Agarwal, and T. Meyarivan. A fast and elitist multiobjective genetic algorithm: NSGA-II. *IEEE Transactions on Evolutionary Computation*, 6(2):182–197, 2002.

[9] S. N. Dorogovtsev, J. F. Mendes, and A. N. Samukhin. Structure of growing networks with preferential linking. *Phys. Rev. Lett.*, 85(21), 2000.

[10] P. Erdős and A. Rényi. On the evolution of random graphs. *Evolution*, 5(1):17–61, 1960.

[11] T. A. Gibson and D. S. Goldberg. Improving evolutionary models of protein interaction networks. *Bioinformatics*, 27(3):376–382, 2011.

[12] I. Ispolatov, P. L. Krapivsky, and A. Yuryev. Duplication-divergence model of protein interaction network. *Phys. Rev. E*, 71(6 Pt 1):061911, 2005.

[13] M. Kim and J. Leskovec. Multiplicative attribute graph model of real-world networks. *Internet Mathematics*, 8(1-2):113–160, 2012.

[14] W. K. Kim and E. M. Marcotte. Age-dependent evolution of the yeast protein interaction network suggests a limited role of gene duplication and divergence. *PLoS Comput. Biol.*, 4(11):e1000232, 2008.

[15] R. Kumar, J. Novak, and A. Tomkins. Structure and evolution of online social networks. In *Proceedings of SIGKDD Conference on Knowledge Discovery and Data Mining*, pages 611–617, 2006.

[16] J. Leskovec, D. Chakrabarti, J. Kleinberg, C. Faloutsos, and Z. Ghahramani. Kronecker Graphs: An Approach to Modeling Networks. *The Journal of Machine Learning Research*, 11:985–1042, 2010.

[17] J. Leskovec, J. Kleinberg, and C. Faloutsos. Graphs over time. In *Proceedings of SIGKDD Conference on Knowledge Discovery and Data Mining*, pages 177–187, New York, USA, 2005.

[18] S. Luke. *Issues in Scaling Genetic Programming: Breeding Strategies, Tree Generation, and Code Bloat*. PhD thesis, University of Maryland, College Park, 2000.

[19] M. Middendorf, E. Ziv, C. Adams, J. Hom, R. Koytcheff, C. Levovitz, G. Woods, L. Chen, and C. Wiggins. Discriminative topological features reveal biological network mechanisms. *BMC Bioinformatics*, 5:181, 2004.

[20] M. Middendorf, E. Ziv, and C. Wiggins. Inferring network mechanisms: The *Drosophila melanogaster* protein interaction network. *Proc. Natl. Acad. Sci. USA*, 102:3192–3197, 2005.

[21] S. Navlakha and C. Kingsford. Network archaeology: Uncovering ancient networks from present-day interactions. *PLoS Comput. Biol.*, 7(4):e1001119, 2011.

[22] G. Palla, L. Lovász, and T. Vicsek. Multifractal network generator. *Proc. Natl. Acad. Sci. USA*, 107:7640–7645, 2010.

[23] N. Przulj, O. Kuchaiev, A. Stevanovic, and W. Hayes. Geometric evolutionary dynamics of protein interaction networks. *Pac. Symp. Biocomput.*, 15:178–189, 2010.

[24] R. Solé, R. Pastor-Satorras, E. Smith, and T. B. Kepler. A model of large-scale proteome evolution. *Adv. Complex Syst.*, 5(1):43–54, 2002.

[25] Y. Sun, Y. Yu, and J. Han. Ranking-based clustering of heterogeneous information networks with star network schema. In *Proceedings of SIGKDD Conference on Knowledge Discovery and Data Mining*, pages 797–806, New York, NY, USA, 2009. ACM.

[26] S. A. Teichmann and M. M. Babu. Gene regulatory network growth by duplication. *Nat. Genet.*, 36:492–496, 2004.

[27] A. Vazquez, A. Flammini, A. Maritan, and A. Vespignani. Modeling of protein interaction networks. *Complexus*, 1(38):9, 2001.

[28] D. Watts and S. Strogatz. Collective dynamics of 'small-world' networks. *Nature*, 363:202–204, 1998.

[29] R. C. Wilson and P. Zhu. A study of graph spectra for comparing graphs and trees. *Pattern Recognition*, 41:2833–2841, 2008.

[30] H. Yu, P. Braun, M. A. Yildirim, I. Lemmens, K. Venkatesan, J. Sahalie, T. Hirozane-Kishikawa, F. Gebreab, N. Li, N. Simonis, T. Hao, J.-F. Rual, A. Dricot, A. Vazquez, R. R. Murray, C. Simon, L. Tardivo, S. Tam, N. Svrzikapa, C. Fan, A.-S. De Smet, A. Motyl, M. E. Hudson, J. Park, X. Xin, M. E. Cusick, T. Moore, C. Boone, M. Snyder, F. P. Roth, A.-L. Barabási, J. Tavernier, D. E. Hill, and M. Vidal. High-quality binary protein interaction map of the yeast interactome network. *Science*, 322(5898):104–110, 2008.

Finding Minimum Representative Pattern Sets

Guimei Liu
School of Computing
National University of Singapore
liugm@comp.nus.edu.sg

Haojun Zhang
School of Computing
National University of Singapore
zhanghao@comp.nus.edu.sg

Limsoon Wong
School of Computing
National University of Singapore
wongls@comp.nus.edu.sg

ABSTRACT

Frequent pattern mining often produces an enormous number of frequent patterns, which imposes a great challenge on understanding and further analysis of the generated patterns. This calls for finding a small number of representative patterns to best approximate all other patterns. An ideal approach should 1) produce a minimum number of representative patterns; 2) restore the support of all patterns with error guarantee; and 3) have good efficiency. Few existing approaches can satisfy all the three requirements. In this paper, we develop two algorithms, MinRPset and FlexRPset, for finding minimum representative pattern sets. Both algorithms provide error guarantee. MinRPset produces the smallest solution that we can possibly have in practice under the given problem setting, and it takes a reasonable amount of time to finish. FlexRPset is developed based on MinRPset. It provides one extra parameter K to allow users to make a trade-off between result size and efficiency. Our experiment results show that MinRPset and FlexRPset produce fewer representative patterns than RPlocal—an efficient algorithm that is developed for solving the same problem. FlexRPset can be slightly faster than RPlocal when K is small.

Categories and Subject Descriptors

H.2.8 [**DATABASE MANAGEMENT**]: Database Applications—*Data Mining*

Keywords

representative patterns, frequent pattern summarization

1. INTRODUCTION

Frequent pattern mining is an important problem in the data mining area. It was first introduced by Agrawal et al. in 1993 [4]. Frequent pattern mining is usually performed on a transaction database $D = \{t_1, t_2, ..., t_n\}$, where t_j is a transaction containing a set of items, $j \in [1, n]$. Let $I = \{i_1, i_2, ..., i_m\}$ be the set of distinct items appearing in D. A pattern X is a set of items in I, that is, $X \subseteq I$. If a transaction $t \in D$ contains all the items of a pattern X, then we say t supports X and t is a supporting transaction of X. Let $T(X)$ be the set of transactions in D supporting pattern X. The support of X, denoted as $supp(X)$, is defined as $|T(X)|$. If the support of a pattern X is larger than a user-specified threshold min_sup, then X is called a frequent pattern. Given a transaction database D and a minimum support threshold min_sup, the task of frequent pattern mining is to find all the frequent patterns in D with respect to min_sup.

Many efficient algorithms have been developed for mining frequent patterns [10]. Now the focus has shifted from how to efficiently mine frequent patterns to how to effectively utilize them. Frequent patterns has the anti-monotone property: if a pattern is frequent, then all of its subsets must be frequent too. On dense datasets and/or when the minimum support is low, long patterns can be frequent. All the subsets of these frequent long patterns are frequent too based on the anti-monotone property. This leads to an explosion in the number of frequent patterns. The huge quantity of patterns can easily become a bottleneck for understanding and further analyzing frequent patterns.

It has been observed that the complete set of frequent patterns often contains a lot of redundancy. Many frequent patterns have similar items and supporting transactions. It is desirable to group similar patterns together and represent them using one single pattern. Frequent closed pattern is proposed for this purpose [16]. Let X be a pattern and S be the set of patterns appearing in the same set of transactions as X, that is, $S = \{Y|T(Y) = T(X)\}$. The longest pattern in S is called a closed pattern, and all the other patterns in S are subsets of it. The closed pattern of S is selected to represent all the patterns in S. The set of frequent closed patterns is a lossless representation of the complete set of frequent patterns. That is, all the frequent patterns and their exact support can be recovered from the set of frequent closed patterns. The number of frequent closed patterns can be much smaller than the total number of frequent patterns, but it can still be tens of thousands or even more.

Frequent closed patterns group patterns supported by exactly the same set of transactions together. This condition is too restrictive. Xin et al. [25] relax this condition to further reduce pattern set size. They propose the concept of δ-covered to generalize the concept of frequent closed pattern. A pattern X_1 is δ-covered by another pattern X_2 if X_1 is a subset of X_2 and $(supp(X_1) - supp(X_2))/supp(X_1) \leq \delta$.

KDD'12, August 12–16, 2012, Beijing, China.

The goal is to find a minimum set of representative patterns that can δ-cover all frequent patterns. When δ=0, the problem corresponds to finding all frequent closed patterns. Xin et al. show that the problem can be mapped to a set cover problem. They develop two algorithms, RPglobal and RPlocal, to solve the problem. RPglobal first generates the set of patterns that can be δ-covered by each pattern, and then employs the well-known greedy algorithm [9] for the set cover problem to find representative patterns. The optimality of RPglobal is determined by the optimality of the greedy algorithm, so the solution produced by RPglobal is almost the best solution we can possibly have in practice. However, RPglobal is very time-consuming and space-consuming. It is feasible only when the number of frequent patterns is not large. RPlocal is developed based on FPClose [11]. It integrates frequent pattern mining with representative pattern finding. RPlocal is very efficient, but it produces much more representative patterns than RPglobal.

In this paper, we analyze the bottlenecks for finding a minimum representative pattern set and develop two algorithms, MinRPset and FlexRPset, to solve the problem. Algorithm MinRPset is similar to RPglobal, but it utilizes several techniques to reduce running time and memory usage. In particular, MinRPset uses a tree structure called CFP-tree [14] to store frequent patterns compactly. The CFP-tree structure also supports efficient retrieval of patterns that are δ-covered by a given pattern. Our experiment results show that MinRPset is only several times slower than RPlocal, while RPglobal is often several orders of magnitude slower than RPlocal. Algorithm FlexRPset is developed based on MinRPset. It provides one extra parameter K which allows users to make a trade-off between efficiency and the number of representative patterns selected. When $K = \infty$, FlexRPset is the same as MinRPset. With the decrease of K, FlexRPset becomes faster, but it produces more representative patterns. When K=1, FlexRPset is slightly faster than RPlocal, and it still produces fewer representative patterns than RPlocal in almost all cases.

The rest of the paper is organized as follows. Section 2 introduces related work. Section 3 gives the formal problem definition. The two algorithms, MinRPset and FlexRPset, are described in Section 4 and Section 5 respectively. Experiment results are reported in Section 6. Finally, Section 7 concludes the paper.

2. RELATED WORK

The number of frequent patterns can be very large. Besides frequent closed patterns, several other concepts, such as generators [5], disjunction-free generators[7], δ-free sets [6], non-derivable patterns[8], maximal patterns [13], top-k frequent closed patterns [21] and redundancy-aware top-k patterns [24], have been proposed to reduce pattern set size. The number of generators is larger than that of closed patterns. Furthermore, the set of generators itself is not lossless. It requires a border to be lossless [7], so does the set of disjunction-free generators and δ-free sets. The number of non-derivable patterns can also be larger than that of closed patterns on some datasets. The number of maximal patterns is much smaller than the number of closed patterns. All frequent patterns can be recovered from maximal patterns, but their support information is lost. Another work that also ignores the support information is [3]. It selects k patterns that best cover a collection of patterns.

Frequent closed patterns preserve the exact support of all frequent patterns. In many applications, knowing the approximate support of frequent patterns is sufficient. Several approaches have been proposed to make a trade-off between pattern set size and the precision of pattern support. The work by Xin et al. [25] described in Section 1 is one such approach. Another approach proposed by Pei et al. [17] uses absolute error bound. It uses heuristic algorithms to mine a minimal condensed pattern-base, which is a superset of the maximal pattern set. All frequent patterns and their support can be restored from a condensed pattern-base with error guarantee.

Yan et al. [26] use profiles to summarize patterns. A profile consists of a master pattern, a support and a probability distribution vector which contains the probability of the items in the master pattern. The set of patterns represented by a profile are subsets of the master pattern, and their support is calculated by multiplying the support of the profile and the probability of the corresponding items. To summarize a collection of patterns using k profiles, Yan et al. partition the patterns into k clusters, and use a profile to describe each cluster. There are several drawbacks with this profile-based approach: 1) It makes contradictory assumptions. On one hand, the patterns represented by the same profile are supposed to be similar in both item composition and supporting transactions, thus the items in the same profile are expected to be strongly correlated. On the other hand, based on how the support of patterns are calculated from a profile, the items in the same profile are expected to be independent. It is hard to make a balance between the two contradicting requirements. 2) There is no error guarantee on the estimated support of patterns. 3) The proposed algorithm for generating profiles is very slow because it needs to scan the original dataset repeatedly. 4) The boundary between frequent patterns and infrequent patterns cannot be determined using profiles.

Several improvements have been made to the profile-based approach. Jin et al. [12] develop a regression-based approach to minimize restoration error. They cluster patterns based on restoration errors instead of similarity between patterns, thus their approach can achieve lower restoration error. However, there is still no error guarantee on the restored support. CP-summary [18] uses conditional independence to reduce restoration error. It adds one more component to each profile: a pattern base, and the new profile is called c-profile. The items in a c-profile are expected to be independent with respect to the pattern base. CP-summary provides error guarantee on estimated support. However, patterns of a c-profile often share little similarity, so a c-profile is not representative of its patterns any more.

Profiles can be considered as generalizations of closed patterns. Wang et al.[20] make generalization on another concise representation of frequent patterns—non-derivable patterns. They use Markov Random Field (MRF) to summarize frequent patterns. The support of a pattern is estimated from its subsets, which is similar to non-derivable patterns. Markov Random Field model is not as intuitive as profiles, and it is also expensive to learn. It does not provide error guarantee on estimated support either.

The above approaches aim to summarize frequent patterns. Mampaey et al. [15] aim to summarize data instead with a collection of non-redundant patterns. A probabilistic maximum entropy model is used in their approach.

3. PROBLEM STATEMENT

We follow the problem definition in [25]. The distance between two patterns is defined based on their supporting transaction sets.

DEFINITION 1 $(D(X_1, X_2))$. *Given two patterns X_1 and X_2, the distance between them is defined as* $D(X_1, X_2) = 1 - \frac{|T(X_1) \cap T(X_2)|}{|T(X_1) \cup T(X_2)|}$.

DEFINITION 2 (ϵ-COVERED). *Given a real number $\epsilon \in [0,1]$ and two patterns X_1 and X_2, we say X_1 is ϵ-covered by X_2 if $X_1 \subseteq X_2$ and $D(X_1, X_2) \leq \epsilon$.*

In the above definition, condition $X_1 \subseteq X_2$ ensures that the two patterns have similar items, and condition $D(X_1, X_2) \leq \epsilon$ ensures that the two patterns have similar supporting transaction sets and similar support. Based on the definition, a pattern ϵ-covers itself.

LEMMA 1. *Given two patterns X_1 and X_2, if pattern X_1 is ϵ-covered by pattern X_2 and we use $supp(X_2)$ to approximate $supp(X_1)$, then the relative error $\frac{supp(X_1)-supp(X_2)}{supp(X_1)}$ is no larger than ϵ.*

PROOF. $\frac{supp(X_1)-supp(X_2)}{supp(X_1)} = 1 - \frac{supp(X_2)}{supp(X_1)} = 1 - \frac{|T(X_2)|}{|T(X_1)|} \leq 1 - \frac{|T(X_1) \cap T(X_2)|}{|T(X_1) \cup T(X_2)|} \leq \epsilon$. □

LEMMA 2. *If a frequent pattern X_1 is ϵ-covered by pattern X_2, then $supp(X_2) \geq min\_sup \cdot (1-\epsilon)$.*

PROOF. Based on Lemma 1, $1 - \frac{supp(X_2)}{supp(X_1)} \leq \epsilon$, so we have $supp(X_2) \geq supp(X_1) \cdot (1-\epsilon) \geq min\_sup \cdot (1-\epsilon)$. □

Our goal here is to select a minimum set of patterns that can ϵ-cover all the frequent patterns. The selected patterns are called representative patterns. Based on Lemma 1, the restoration error of all frequent patterns is bounded by ϵ. We do not require representative patterns to be frequent. Based on Lemma 2, the support of representative patterns must be no less than $min\_sup \cdot (1-\epsilon)$. The problem is how to find a minimum representative pattern set? In the next two sections, we describe two algorithms to solve the problem.

4. THE MINRPSET ALGORITHM

Let $\mathcal{F}$ be the set of frequent patterns in a dataset D with respect to threshold min_sup, and $\hat{\mathcal{F}}$ be the set of patterns with support no less than $min\_sup \cdot (1-\epsilon)$ in D. Obviously, $\mathcal{F} \subseteq \hat{\mathcal{F}}$. Given a pattern $X \in \hat{\mathcal{F}}$, we use $C(X)$ to denote the set of frequent patterns that can be ϵ-covered by X. We have $C(X) \subseteq F$. If X is frequent, we have $X \in C(X)$.

A straightforward algorithm for finding a minimum representative pattern set is as follows. First we generate $C(X)$ for every pattern $X \in \hat{\mathcal{F}}$, and we get $|\hat{\mathcal{F}}|$ sets. The elements of these sets are frequent patterns in $\mathcal{F}$. Let $S = \{C(X) | X \in \hat{\mathcal{F}}\}$. Finding a minimum representative pattern set is now equivalent to finding a minimum number of sets in S that can cover all the frequent patterns in $\mathcal{F}$. This is a set cover problem, and it is NP-hard. We use the well-known greedy algorithm [9] to solve the problem, which achieves an approximation ratio of $\sum_{i=1}^{k} \frac{1}{i}$, where k is the maximal size of the sets in S. We call this simple algorithm MinRPset.

The greedy algorithm is essentially the best-possible polynomial time approximation algorithm for the set cover problem. Our experiment results have shown that it usually takes little time to finish. Generating $C(X)$s is the main bottleneck of the MinRPset algorithm when $\mathcal{F}$ and $\hat{\mathcal{F}}$ are large because we need to find $C(X)$s over a large $\mathcal{F}$ for a large number of patterns in $\hat{\mathcal{F}}$. We use the following techniques to improve the efficiency of MinRPset: 1) consider closed patterns only; 2) use a structure called CFP-tree to find $C(X)$s efficiently; and 3) use a light-weight compression technique to compress $C(X)$s.

4.1 Considering closed patterns only

A pattern is closed if it is more frequent than all of its supersets. If a pattern X_1 is non-closed, then there exists another pattern X_2 such that $X_1 \subset X_2$ and $supp(X_2) = supp(X_1)$.

LEMMA 3. *Given two patterns X_1 and X_2 such that $X_1 \subseteq X_2$ and $supp(X_1) = supp(X_2)$, if X_2 is ϵ-covered by a pattern X, then X_1 must be ϵ-covered by X too.*

The above lemma directly follows from Definition 2. It implies that instead of covering all frequent patterns, we can cover frequent closed patterns only, which leads to the following lemma.

LEMMA 4. *Let $\mathcal{F}$ be the set of frequent patterns in a dataset D with respect to a threshold min_sup. If a set of patterns R ϵ-covers all the frequent closed patterns in $\mathcal{F}$, then R ϵ-covers all the frequent patterns in $\mathcal{F}$.*

LEMMA 5. *Given two patterns X_1 and X_2 such that $X_1 \subseteq X_2$ and $supp(X_1) = supp(X_2)$, if a pattern X is ϵ-covered by X_1, then X must be ϵ-covered by X_2 too.*

This lemma also directly follows from Definition 2. It suggests that we can use closed patterns only to cover all frequent patterns.

The number of frequent closed patterns can be orders of magnitude smaller than the total number of frequent patterns. Consider only closed patterns improves the efficiency of the MinRPset algorithm in two aspects. On one hand, it reduces the size of individual $C(X)$s since now they contain only frequent closed patterns. On the other hand, it reduces the number of patterns whose $C(X)$ needs to be generated as now we need to generate $C(X)$s for closed patterns only.

4.2 Using CFP-tree to find $C(X)$s efficiently

The CFP-tree structure is specially designed for storing and querying frequent patterns [14]. It resembles a set-enumeration tree [19]. We use an example dataset D in Table 1 to illuminate its structure. Table 2 shows all the frequent patterns in D when $min\_sup = 3$. The CFP-tree constructed from these frequent patterns is shown in Figure 1. The CFP-tree is constructed using a pattern-growth approach. The root node contains all frequent items sorted in ascending frequency order. Each item i in the root node points to a subtree, and this subtree stores all the frequent patterns discovered from item i's conditional database.

Each node in a CFP-tree is a variable-length array. If a node contains multiple entries, then each entry contains exactly one item. If a node has only one entry, then it is called a *singleton node*. Singleton nodes can contain more than one item. For example, node 2 in Figure 1 is a singleton node with two items m and a. An entry E stores several pieces of information: (1) m items ($m \geq 1$), (2) the support

Table 1: An example dataset D

TID	Transactions
1	a, c, e, f, m, p
2	b, e, v
3	a, b, f, m, p
4	d, e, f, h, p
5	a, c, d, m, v
6	a, c, h, m, s
7	a, f, m, p, u
8	a, b, d, f, g

Table 2: Frequent patterns (min_sup=3)

ID	Itemsets	ID	itemsets	ID	itemsets
1	a:6	9	ac:3	17	acm:3
2	b:3	10	af:4	18	afm:3
3	c:3	11	am:5	19	afp:3
4	d:3	12	ap:3	20	amp:3
5	e:3	13	cm:3	21	fmp:3
6	f:5	14	fm:3	22	afmp:3
7	m:5	15	fp:4		
8	p:4	16	mp:3		

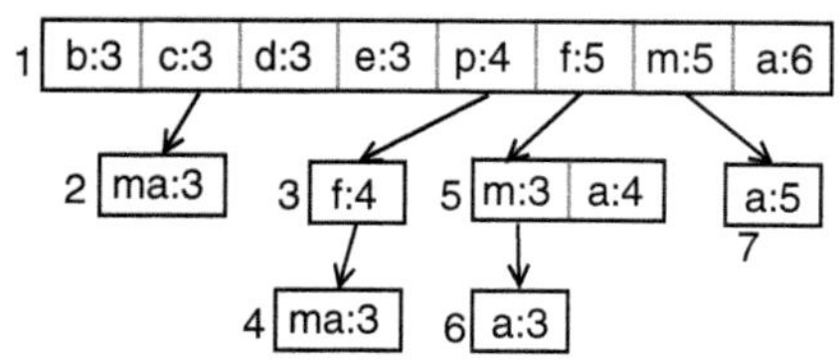

Figure 1: CFP-tree constructed on the frequent patterns in Table 2

of E, (3) a pointer pointing to the child node of E and (4) the id of the entry which is assigned using preordering. In the rest of this paper, we use $E.items$, $E.support$, $E.child$ and $E.preorder$ to denote the above fields.

The CFP-tree structure allows different patterns to share the storage of their prefixes as well as suffixes. Prefix sharing is easy to understand. For example, patterns $\{f, m\}$ and $\{f, a\}$ share the same prefix $\{f\}$ in Figure 1. In a multi-entry CFP-tree node, only the items after an entry E can appear in the subtree pointed by E, and these items are called *candidate extensions* of E. Suffix sharing occurs when a candidate extension of an entry E occurs in the same set of transactions as the pattern represented by E. Let i be a candidate extension of E and X be a pattern represented by E. If $supp(X) = supp(X \cup \{i\})$, then for any pattern Z, we must have $supp(X \cup Z) = supp(X \cup \{i\} \cup Z)$. In other words, X and $X \cup \{i\}$ have the same extensions. In CFP-tree, a singleton node containing item i is created to enable the sharing between X and $X \cup \{i\}$. In Figure 1, patterns $\{p\}$ and $\{p, f\}$ have the same support, so a singleton node containing item f is created, which is node 3, to allow $\{p\}$ and $\{p, f\}$ to share the same subtree.

Every entry in a CFP-tree represents one or more patterns with the same support, and these patterns contain the items on the path from the root to the entry. Items contained in singleton nodes are optional. Let E be an entry, X_m be the set of items in the multiple-entry nodes and X_s be the set of items in the singleton nodes on the path from the root to the parent of E respectively. The set of patterns represented by E is $\{X_m \cup Y \cup Z | Y \subseteq X_s, Z \subseteq E.items, Z \neq \emptyset\}$. The longest pattern represented by E is $X_m \cup X_s \cup E.items$. Let us look at an example. Node 4 contains only one entry. For this entry, we have $X_m = \{p\}$, $X_s = \{f\}$ and $E.items = \{m, a\}$. Hence node 4 represents 6 patterns: $\{p, m\}$, $\{p, a\}$, $\{p, m, a\}$, $\{p, f, m\}$, $\{p, f, a\}$ and $\{p, f, m, a\}$. We use $E.pattern$ to denote the longest pattern represented by E.

The above feature makes CFP-tree a very compact structure for storing frequent patterns. The number of entries in a CFP-tree is much smaller than the total number of patterns stored in the tree. For each entry, we consider its longest pattern only based on Lemma 3 and Lemma 5. For an entry E, only its longest pattern can be closed. Other patterns of E that are shorter than the longest pattern cannot be closed based on the definition of closed patterns. If the longest pattern of an entry is not closed, then we call the entry a *non-closed entry*.

The CFP-tree structure has the following property.

PROPERTY 1. *In a multiple-entry node, the item of an entry E can appear in the subtrees pointed by entries before E, but it cannot appear in the subtrees pointed by entries after E.*

For example, in the root node of Figure 1, item p is allowed to appear in the subtrees pointed by entries b, c, d and e, but it is not allowed to appear in the subtrees pointed by entries f, m and a. This property implies the following lemma.

LEMMA 6. *In a CFP-tree, the supersets of a pattern cannot appear on the right of the pattern. They appear either on the left of the pattern or in the subtree pointed by the pattern.*

4.2.1 Finding one $C(X)$

Given a pattern X, $C(X)$ contains the subsets of X that can be ϵ-covered by X. CFP-tree supports efficient retrieval of subsets of patterns. To find the subsets of a pattern X, we simply traverse the CFP-tree and match the items of the entries against X. For an entry E in a multiple-entry node, if its item appears in X, then entry E represents some subsets of X and the search is continued on its subtree. Otherwise, entry E and its subtree is skipped because all the patterns in the subtree of E contain $E.items \notin X$, and these patterns cannot be subsets of X. An entry E in a singleton node can contain items not in X, and these items are simply ignored.

Algorithm 1 shows the pseudo-codes for retrieving $C(X)$. Initially, *cnode* is the root node of the CFP-tree. Parameter Y contains the set of items to be searched in *cnode*. It is set to X initially. Once an entry E is visited, the item of E is removed from Y when Y is passed to the subtree of E (line 8, 18). The item of E is also excluded when Y is passed to the entries after E (line 21). This is because the item of E cannot appear in the subtrees pointed by entries after E based on Property 1.

During the search of $C(X)$s, we also mark non-closed patterns. If the longest pattern of E is a proper subset of X and $E.support$=$supp(X)$, then E is marked as non-closed (line 2-3, 12-13), and it is skipped in subsequent search.

The *early termination* technique. If a pattern is ϵ-covered by X, then its support must be no larger than $\frac{supp(X)}{(1-\epsilon)}$ based on Definition 2. We use this requirement to further improve the efficiency of Algorithm 1. Given an entry E in a multiple-entry node, after we visit the subtree of E, if we find $supp(E.pattern \cup Y) > \frac{supp(X)}{(1-\epsilon)}$, where Y is the set of items that is passed to E, then there is no need

Algorithm 1 Search_CX Algorithm

Input:
cnode is a CFP-tree node; //*cnode* is the root node initially.
Y is the set of items to be searched in *cnode*; //Y=X initially.
supp(X) is the support of X;
Output:
$C(X)$;
Description:
1: **if** *cnode* contains only one entry E **then**
2: **if** $E.support == supp(X)$ AND $E.pattern \subset X$ **then**
3: Mark E as non-closed;
4: **if** E is not marked as non-closed AND E is frequent **then**
5: **if** $E.items \bigcap Y \neq \emptyset$ AND $E.support \leq \frac{supp(X)}{(1-\epsilon)}$ **then**
6: Put $E.preorder$ into $C(X)$;
7: **if** $E.child \neq NULL$ AND $Y - E.items \neq \emptyset$ **then**
8: Search_CX($E.child$, $Y - E.items$, $supp(X)$);
9: **else if** *cnode* contains multiple entries **then**
10: **for** each entry $E \in cnode$ from left to right **do**
11: **if** $E.items \in Y$ AND E is frequent **then**
12: **if** $E.support == supp(X)$ AND $E.pattern \subset X$ **then**
13: Mark E as non-closed;
14: **if** E is not marked as non-closed **then**
15: **if** $E.support \leq \frac{supp(X)}{(1-\epsilon)}$ **then**
16: Put $E.preorder$ into $C(X)$;
17: **if** $E.child \neq NULL$ AND $Y - E.items \neq \emptyset$ **then**
18: Search_CX($E.child$, $Y - E.items$, $supp(X)$);
19: **if** $supp(E.pattern \cup Y) > \frac{supp(X)}{(1-\epsilon)}$ **then**
20: **return** ;
21: Y=$Y - E.items$;

to visit the subtrees pointed by entries after E (line 19-20). The reason being that all the subsets of X in these subtrees must be subsets of ($E.pattern \cup Y$), and their support must be larger than $\frac{supp(X)}{(1-\epsilon)}$ too based on the anti-monotone property. We call this pruning technique *early termination*.

4.2.2 *Finding $C(X)$s of all closed patterns*

Algorithm 2 shows the pseudo-codes for generating all $C(X)$s. It traverses the CFP-tree in depth-first order from left to right. Using this traversal order, the supersets of a pattern X that are on the left of X are visited before X. If the support of X is the same as one of these supersets, then X should be marked as non-closed when *Search_CX* is called for that superset. If X is not marked as non-closed when X is visited, it means that X is more frequent than all its supersets on its left. Based on Lemma 6, the supersets of a pattern appear either on the left of the pattern or in the subtree pointed by the pattern. If X is also more frequent than its child entries, then X must be closed. The conditions listed at line 2 and line 3 ensure that Algorithm 2 generates $C(X)$s for only closed patterns.

In Algorithm 2, if an entry E is marked as non-closed because it has the same support as one of its supersets on its left, then all the patterns in the subtree pointed by E are non-closed. We can safely skip E and its subtree in subsequent traversal (line 2). The same pruning is done in Algorithm 1 (line 4, 14). This pruning technique has been used in almost all frequent closed pattern mining algorithms to prune non-closed patterns [11, 22].

4.3 Compressing $C(X)$s

In a CFP-tree, each entry E has an id, which is denoted as $E.preorder$. In Algorithm 1, we put the id of entry E into $C(X)$ if E is ϵ-covered by X (line 6, 16). Each id takes 4 bytes. The total number of $C(X)$s generated by Algorithm 2 grows with the number of frequent (closed) patterns. When the number of frequent closed patterns is large, the total size of $C(X)$s can be very large. If the main memory cannot accommodate all $C(X)$s, the greedy set cover algorithm becomes very slow.

Algorithm 2 DFS_Search_CXs Algorithm

Input:
cnode is a CFP-tree node; //*cnode* is the root node initially.
Output:
$C(X)$s;
Description:
1: **for** each entry $E \in cnode$ from left to right **do**
2: **if** E is not marked as non-closed **then**
3: **if** E is more frequent than its child entries **then**
4: X=$E.pattern$;
5: $C(X)$ = Search_CX($root$, X, $E.support$);
6: **if** $E.child \neq NULL$ **then**
7: DFS_Search_CXs($E.child$);

To alleviate this problem, we compress $C(X)$s using a light-weight compression technique [23]. Each entry id occupies one or more bytes depending on its value. To reduce the number of bytes needed for storing entries ids, we sort the entry ids in ascending order and store the differences between consecutive ids instead. Our experiment results show that this compression technique can reduce the space needed for storing $C(X)$s by about three quarters in many cases.

Algorithm 3 MinRPset Algorithm

Description:
1: Mine patterns with support $\geq min\_sup \cdot (1-\epsilon)$ and store them in a CFP-tree; let *root* be the root node of the tree;
2: DFS_Search_CXs(*root*);
3: Remove non-closed entries from $C(X)$s;
4: Apply the greedy set cover algorithm on $C(X)$s to find representative patterns;
5: Output representative patterns;

Algorithm 3 shows the pseudo-codes of MinRPset, and it calls Algorithm 2 to find $C(X)$s. Note that we store all patterns, including non-closed patterns, with support no less than $min\_sup \cdot (1-\epsilon)$ in a CFP-tree (line 1). Non-closed patterns are identified during the search of $C(X)$s. Hence it is possible that some $C(X)$s contains some non-closed entries. These non-closed entries are removed from $C(X)$s (line 3) before the greedy set cover algorithm is applied.

5. THE FLEXRPSET ALGORITHM

When the number of frequent patterns is large on a dataset, the MinRPset algorithm may become very slow since it needs to search subsets over a large CFP-tree for a large number of patterns. Furthermore, the set of $C(X)$s may become too large to fit into the main memory. To solve this problem, instead of searching $C(X)$s for all closed patterns, we can selectively generate $C(X)$s such that every frequent pattern is covered a sufficient number of times, in the hope that the greedy set cover algorithm can still find a near-optimal solution. Intuitively, the fewer the number of $C(X)$s generated, the more efficient the algorithm is. This is the basic idea of the FlexRPset algorithm.

The FlexRPset algorithm uses a parameter K to control the minimum number of times that a frequent pattern needs

Algorithm 4 Flex_Search_CXs Algorithm

Input:

cnode is a CFP-tree node; //*cnode* is the root node initially.
K is the minimum number of times that a frequent closed pattern needs to be covered;

Output:

$C(X)$s;

Description:

1: **for** each entry $E \in$ *cnode* from left to right **do**
2:   **if** E is not marked as non-closed **then**
3:     **if** $E.child \neq NULL$ **then**
4:       Flex_Search_CXs($E.child$);
5:     **if** E is more frequent than its child entries **then**
6:       **if** (E is frequent AND E is covered less than K times) OR ($\exists$ an ancestor entry E' of E such that E' is frequent, E' can be ϵ-covered by E and E' is covered less than K times) **then**
7:         X=$E.pattern$;
8:         $C(X)$ = Search_CX($root$, X, $E.support$);

to be covered. Algorithm 4 shows how FlexRPset selectively generates $C(X)s$. The other steps of FlexRPset are the same as those of MinRPset.

Algorithm 4 still uses the depth-first order to traverse a CFP-tree from left to right. It traverses the subtree of an entry E first (line 3-4) before it processes E (line 5-8), which means that when E is processed, all the supersets of E have been processed already based on Lemma 6, and E cannot be covered any more except by itself. If E is frequent and it is covered less than K times, then we generate $C(E.patterns)$ to cover E (the first condition at line 6). If E has already be covered at least K times when E is visited, then we look at the ancestor entries of E. For an ancestor entry E' of E, most of its supersets are already processed too when E is visited, hence not many remaining entries can cover E'. If E' is frequent, E' can be ϵ-covered by E and E' is covered less than K times, then we also generate $C(E.patterns)$ to cover E' (the second condition at line 6).

With the increase of parameter K, more information are gathered, hence less representative patterns are generated. However, the running time of FlexRPset becomes longer. How can users make a trade-off between running time and result size conveniently? We observe that the $C(X)$s generated at a smaller K value can be re-used at a larger K value. This leads to the incremental FlexRPset algorithm. It starts from K=1 and works like FlexRPset. If the user is happy with the number of representative patterns generated at K=1, then it stops. Otherwise, it increases K to 10 and generates $C(X)$s in a way similar to Algorithm 4. The only difference is that the set of $C(X)$s generated at K=1 are taken into consideration. During the traversal of the CFP-tree, the times that an entry E is covered is decided not only by the $C(X)$s generated in the current traversal of the CFP-tree, but also by the $C(X)$s generated in previous traversal. This process is repeated until either users are happy with the number of representative patterns, or K has reached a certain limit. In every iteration, we increase K by 10 times.

6. EXPERIMENTS

In this section, we study the performance of our algorithms. The experiments were conducted on a PC with 2.33Ghz Intel Duo Core CPU and 3.25GB memory. Our algorithms were implemented using C++. We downloaded the source codes of RPlocal from the IlliMine system package [2]. All source codes were compiled using Microsoft Visual Studio 2005.

6.1 Datasets

The datasets used in the experiments are shown in Table 3. They are obtained from the FIMI repository [1]. Table 3 shows the number of transactions (#trans) and items (#items), the maximal and average length of transactions (MaxTL, AvgTL) on the datasets.

Table 3: Datasets

dataset	#trans	#items	MaxTL	AvgTL
accidents	340183	468	52	33.81
chess	3196	75	37	37.00
connect	67557	129	43	43.00
mushroom	8124	119	23	23.00
pumsb	49046	2113	74	74.00
pumsb_star	49046	2088	63	50.48

6.2 Comparison with RPlocal

The first experiment compares MinRPset and FlexRPset with RPlocal. Let N be the number of representative patterns generated by an algorithm. Figure 2 shows the ratio of N to the number of representative patterns generated by RPlocal when *min_sup* is varied. Obviously, the ratio is always 1 for RPlocal. ϵ is set to 0.2 on mushroom and to 0.1 on other datasets. In [25], the authors have shown that the number of representative patterns selected by RPlocal can be orders of magnitude smaller than the number of frequent closed patterns. MinRPset further reduces the number of representative patterns by 5%-65%. The FlexRPset algorithm generates a similar number of representative patterns with MinRPset when K is large. When K gets smaller, the number of representative patterns generated by FlexRPset increases. When K=1, FlexRPset still generates less representative patterns than RPlocal in most of the cases.

Figure 3 shows the running time of the several algorithms when *min_sup* is varied. The running time of MinRPset and FlexRPset includes the time for mining frequent patterns. The running time of all algorithms increases with the descrease of *min_sup*. MinRPset has similar running time with RPlocal on mushroom. On accidents and pumsb_star, when *min_sup* is relatively high, the running time of MinRPset and RPlocal is similar too. In other cases except for dataset pumsb, MinRPset is several times slower than RPlocal. RPglobal is often hundreds of times slower than RPlocal as shown in [25]. This indicates the techniques used in MinRPset is very effective in reducing running time. On pumsb, MinRPset is more than 10 times slower than RPlocal when $min\_sup \leq 0.7$, but it achieves the greatest reduction in the number of representative patterns on this dataset.

FlexRPset has similar running time with RPlocal when K is small. When K increases, FlexRPset becomes slower. For the incremental FlexRPset algorithm, we set the maximum value of K to 1000. The incremental algorithm tries 4 values of K incrementally: 1, 10, 100 and 1000. Figure 3 shows that the running time of the incremental algorithm (denoted as "incremental" in the figures) is slightly longer than that of FlexRPset with K=1000. The reason being that the most costly steps in FlexRPset are constructing the CFP-tree and generating $C(X)$s, and these two steps are shared among different K values in the incremental algorithm.

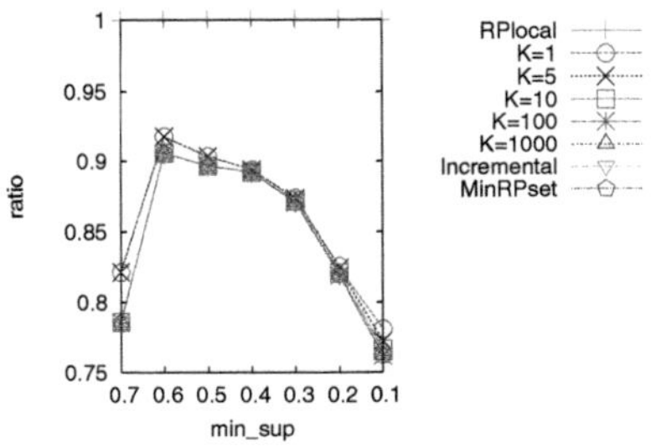

(a) accidents, ϵ=0.1

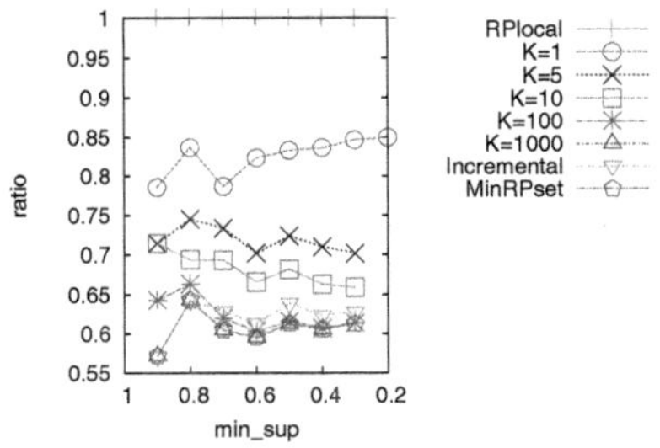

(b) chess, ϵ=0.1

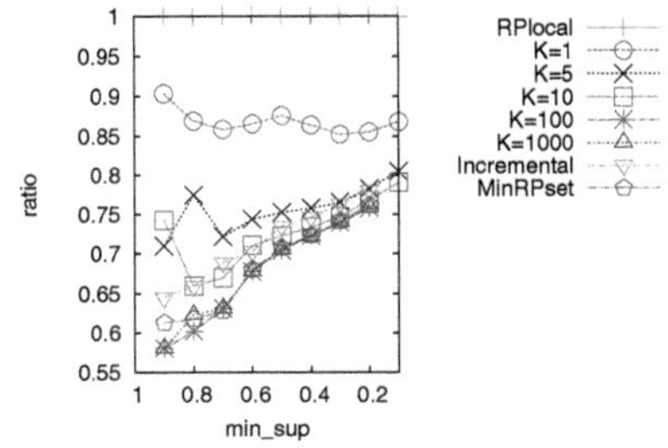

(c) connect, ϵ=0.1

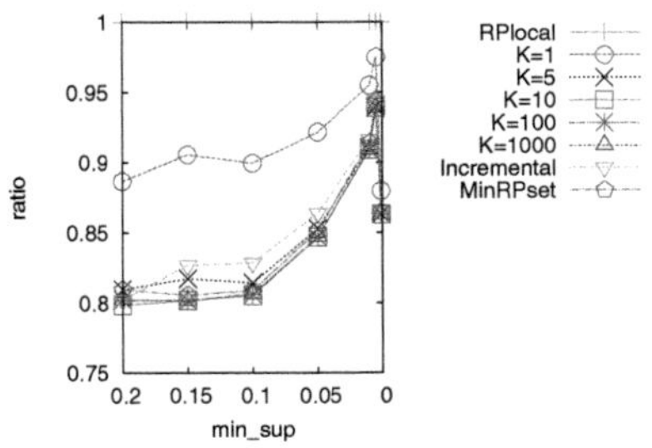

(d) mushroom, ϵ=0.2

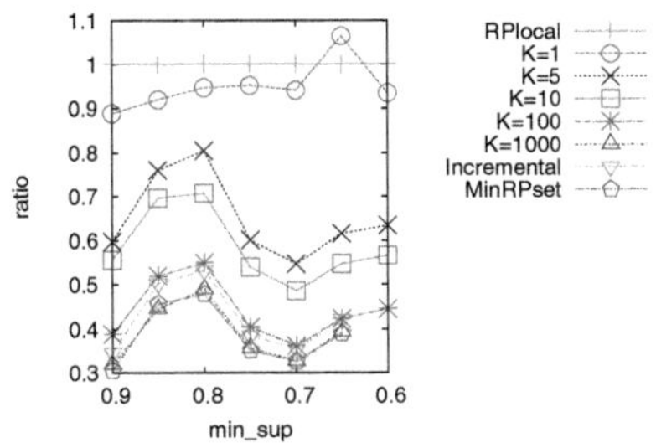

(e) pumsb, ϵ=0.1

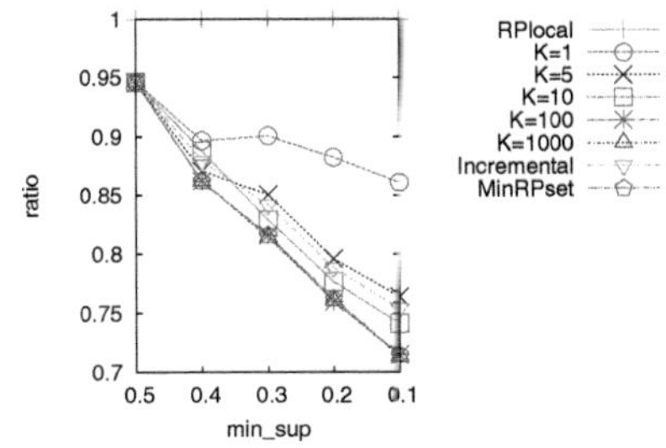

(f) pumsb_star, ϵ=0.1

Figure 2: Number of representative patterns when varying *min_sup*

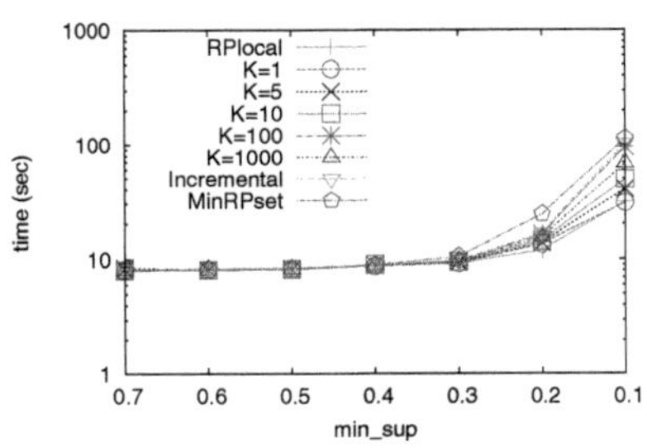

(a) accidents, ϵ=0.1

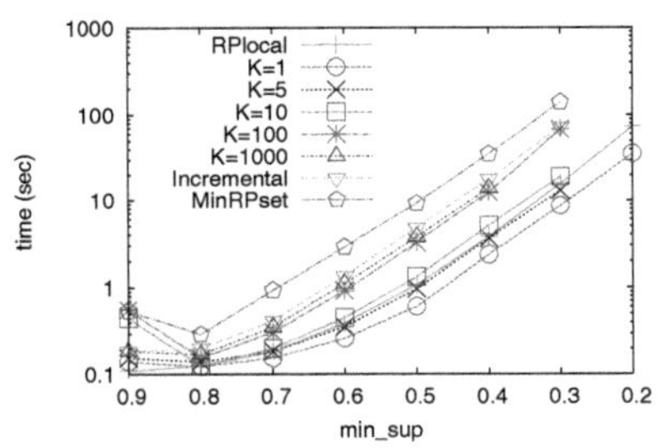

(b) chess, ϵ=0.1

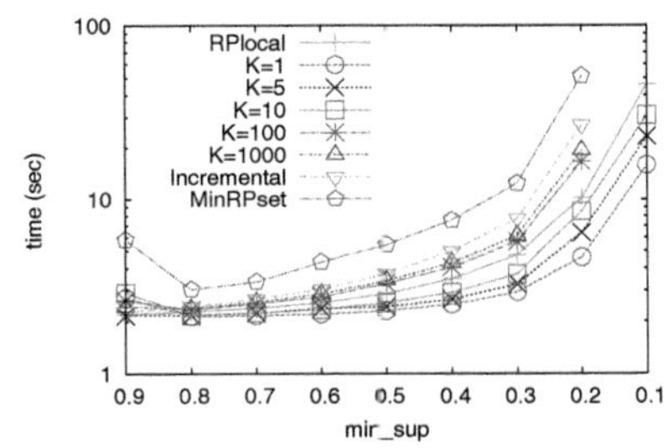

(c) connect, ϵ=0.1

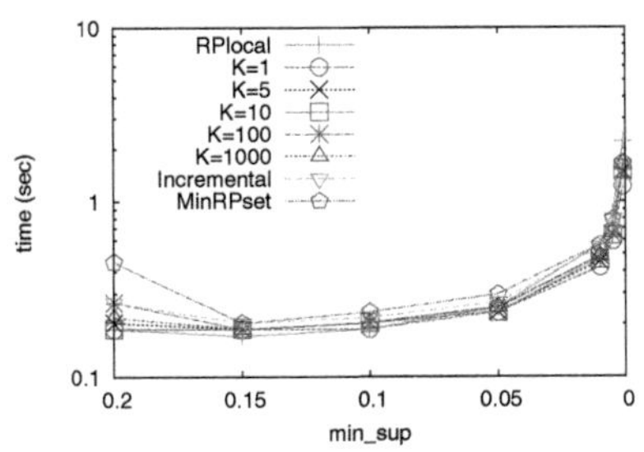

(d) mushroom, ϵ=0.2

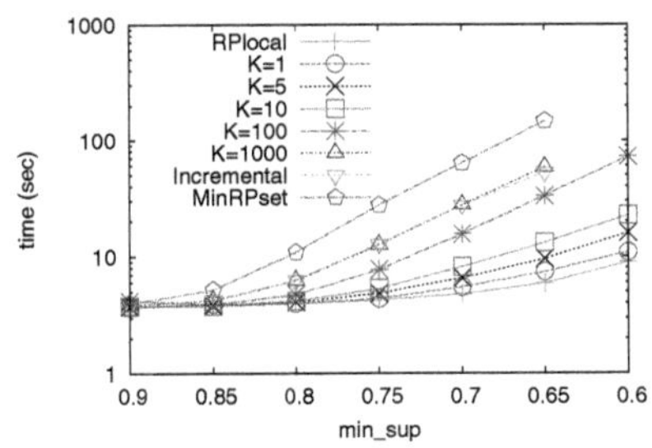

(e) pumsb, ϵ=0.1

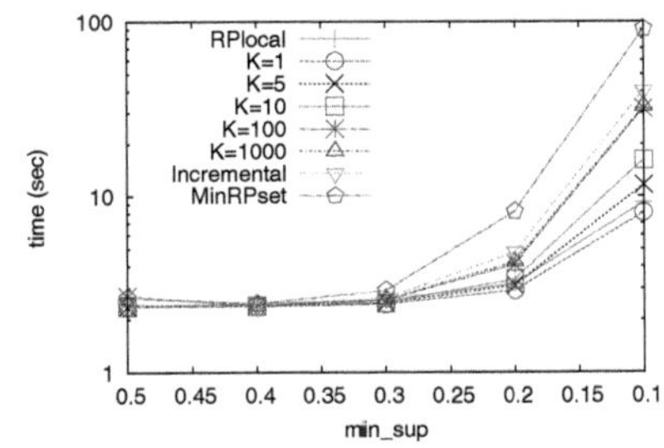

(f) pumsb_star, ϵ=0.1

Figure 3: Running time when varying *min_sup*

Figure 4 compares the number of representative patterns generated by the several algorithms when ϵ is varied. When ϵ increases, MinRPset achieves greater reduction in the number of representative patterns. However, its running time increases quickly too as shown in Figure 5. The running time of RPlocal is relatively stable with respect to ϵ, so is the running time of FlexRPset when $K \leq 10$. When $K \geq 100$, the running time of FlexRPset increases more obviously with ϵ.

6.3 Effect of the early termination technique

In Algorithm 1, we use an early termination technique (described at the end of Section 4.2.1) to improve the efficiency of Algorithm 1. Table 4 shows the effect of the early termination technique on the running time of MinRPset. Columns "W/O (sec)" and "With (sec)" are the running time of MinRPset without and with the early termination technique respectively. The last column is the ratio of "With (sec)" to

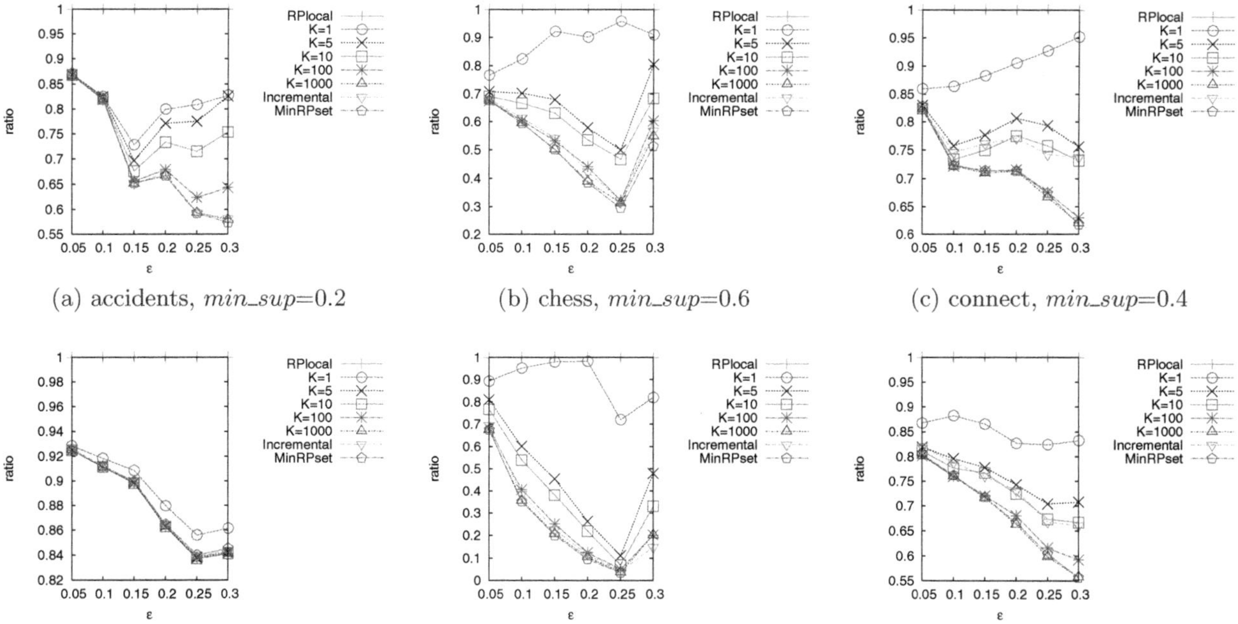

(a) accidents, *min_sup*=0.2 (b) chess, *min_sup*=0.6 (c) connect, *min_sup*=0.4

(d) mushroom, *min_sup*=0.001 (e) pumsb, *min_sup*=0.75 (f) pumsb_star, *min_sup*=0.2

Figure 4: Number of representative patterns when varying ϵ

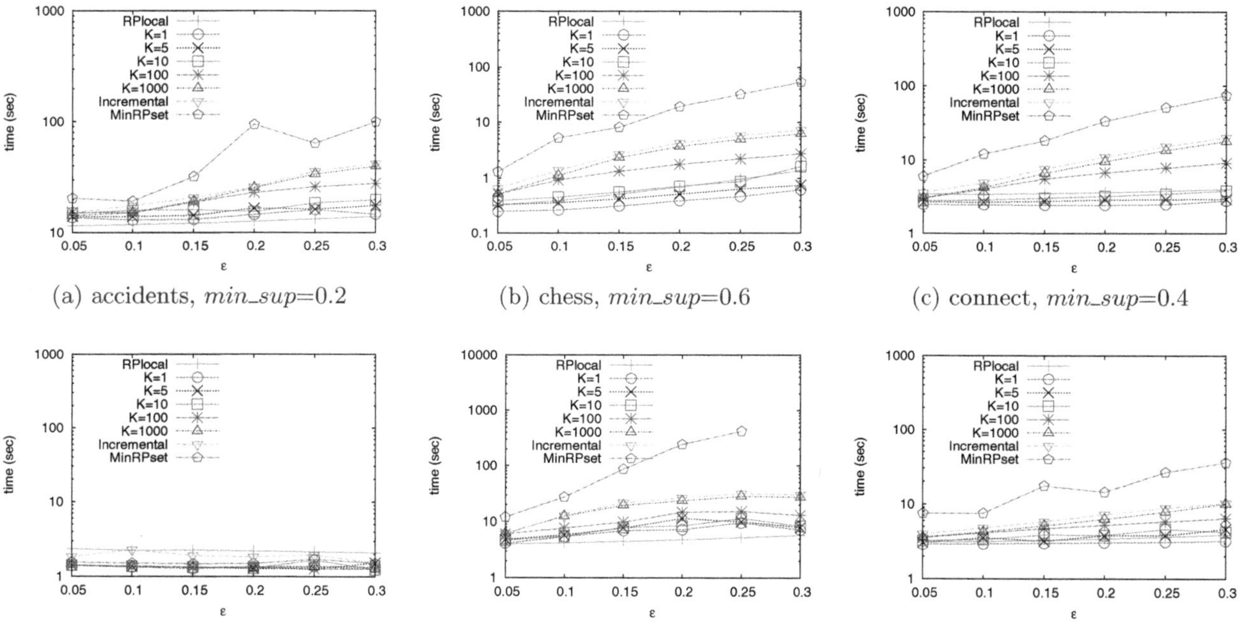

(a) accidents, *min_sup*=0.2 (b) chess, *min_sup*=0.6 (c) connect, *min_sup*=0.4

(d) mushroom, *min_sup*=0.001 (e) pumsb, *min_sup*=0.75 (f) pumsb_star, *min_sup*=0.2

Figure 5: Running time when varying ϵ

"W/O (sec)". On dataset pumsb, the early termination technique achieves the lowest reduction in running time. This is one reason why MinRPset is more than 10 times slower than RPlocal on pumsb. On other datasets, the early termination technique can reduce the running time by 5-15 times. Similar results are observed for FlexRPset.

The early termination technique is more effective when ϵ is smaller. This is because when ϵ is smaller, fewer subsets of X can be ϵ-covered by X, and more subsets of X that do not satisfy the support constraint are pruned by the early termination technique.

7. DISCUSSION AND CONCLUSION

In this paper, we have described two algorithms, MinRPset and FlexRPset, for finding minimum representative pattern sets. Both algorithms generate less representative

Table 4: Running time of MinRPset with and without the early termination technique.

dataset	*min_sup*	ϵ	W/O(sec)	With(sec)	ratio
accidents	0.2	0.1	12.139	2.406	19.8%
accidents	0.2	0.05	10.280	1.640	16.0%
chess	0.3	0.1	323.964	48.107	14.8%
chess	0.3	0.05	240.312	22.392	9.3%
connect	0.2	0.1	104.444	15.014	14.4%
connect	0.2	0.05	88.492	5.625	6.4%
mushroom	0.001	0.2	3.312	0.312	9.4%
mushroom	0.001	0.1	0.281	3.266	8.6%
mushroom	0.001	0.05	0.265	3.266	8.1%
pumsb	0.6	0.1	160.670	242.33	66.3%
pumsb	0.6	0.05	34.687	106.388	32.6%
pumsb_star	0.1	0.1	109.796	24.904	22.7%
pumsb_star	0.1	0.05	88.148	13.934	15.8%

patterns than previous work RPlocal. FlexRPset takes one extra parameter K, which allows users to make a trade-off between result size and efficiency. With the increase of K, FlexRPset produces less representative patterns, but its running time increases. When K is small, FlexRPset can be slightly faster than RPlocal even though RPlocal integrates frequent pattern mining with representative pattern finding, while FlexRPset first mines frequent patterns and then finds representative patterns in a post-processing step.

Definition 2 allows a pattern to cover its subsets only. This condition allows users to restore the support of a pattern by searching the supersets of the pattern in the representative pattern set, and then using the highest support of the supersets to approximate the support of the pattern. Without this condition, it is impossible to estimate the support of a pattern as we do not know which representative pattern covers it. In MinRPset and FlexRPset, all frequent patterns are stored in a CFP-tree compactly. Users can retrieve the support of patterns from the CFP-tree directly. The set of representative patterns merely provides a concise view of all patterns. In this situation, the subset condition becomes unnecessary. We can relax Definition 2 by removing condition $X_1 \subseteq X_2$ to further reduce the number of representative patterns. This will be our future work.

8. ACKNOWLEDGMENT

This work is supported in part by Singapore Agency for Science, Technology and Research grant SERC 102 101 0030.

9. REFERENCES

[1] Frequent itemset mining dataset repository. http://fimi.ua.ac.be/data/.

[2] Illimine system package. http://illimine.cs.uiuc.edu/download/.

[3] F. N. Afrati, A. Gionis, and H. Mannila. Approximating a collection of frequent sets. In *KDD*, pages 12–19, 2004.

[4] R. Agrawal, T. Imielinski, and A. N. Swami. Mining association rules between sets of items in large databases. In *SIGMOD Conference*, pages 207–216, 1993.

[5] Y. Bastide, N. Pasquier, R. Taouil, G. Stumme, and L. Lakhal. Mining minimal non-redundant association rules using frequent closed itemsets. In *Proc. of Computational Logic Conference*, pages 972–986, 2000.

[6] J.-F. Boulicaut, A. Bykowski, and C. Rigotti. Free-sets: A condensed representation of boolean data for the approximation of frequency queries. *Data Mining and Knowledge Discovery*, 7(1):5–22, 2003.

[7] A. Bykowski and C. Rigotti. A condensed representation to find frequent patterns. In *PODS*, 2001.

[8] T. Calders and B. Goethals. Mining all non-derivable frequent itemsets. In *PKDD*, pages 74–85, 2002.

[9] V. Chvatal. A greedy heuristic for the set-covering problem. *Mathematics of Operations Research*, 4(3):233–235, 1979.

[10] B. Goethals and M. J. Zaki. Advances in frequent itemset mining implementations: Introduction to fimi03. In *Proc. of the ICDM 2003 Workshop on Frequent Itemset Mining Implementations*, 2003.

[11] G. Grahne and J. Zhu. Efficiently using prefix-trees in mining frequent itemsets. In *FIMI*. 2003.

[12] R. Jin, M. Abu-Ata, Y. Xiang, and N. Ruan. Effective and efficient itemset pattern summarization: regression-based approaches. In *KDD*, pages 399–407, 2008.

[13] R. J. B. Jr. Efficiently mining long patterns from databases. In *SIGMOD Conference*, pages 85–93, 1998.

[14] G. Liu, H. Lu, and J. X. Yu. Cfp-tree: A compact disk-based structure for storing and querying frequent itemsets. *Inf. Syst.*, 32(2):295–319, 2007.

[15] M. Mampaey, N. Tatti, and J. Vreeken. Tell me what i need to know: succinctly summarizing data with itemsets. In *KDD*, pages 573–581, 2011.

[16] N. Pasquier, Y. Bastide, R. Taouil, and L. Lakhal. Discovering frequent closed itemsets for association rules. In *ICDT*, pages 398–416, 1999.

[17] J. Pei, G. Dong, W. Zou, and J. Han. Mining condensed frequent-pattern bases *Knowledge and Information Systems*, 6(5):570–594, 2004.

[18] A. K. Poernomo and V. Gopalkrishnan. Cp-summary: a concise representation for browsing frequent itemsets. In *KDD*, pages 687–696, 2009.

[19] R. Rymon. Search through systematic set enumeration. In *KR*, pages 539–550, 1992.

[20] C. Wang and S. Parthasarathy. Summarizing itemset patterns using probabilistic models. In *KDD*, pages 730–735, 2006.

[21] J. Wang, J. Han, Y. Lu, and P. Tzvetkov. Tfp: An efficient algorithm for mining top-k frequent closed itemsets. *IEEE Trans. Knowl. Data Eng.*, 17(5):652–664, 2005.

[22] J. Wang, J. Han, and J. Pei. Closet+: searching for the best strategies for mining frequent closed itemsets. In *KDD*, pages 236–245, 2003.

[23] T. Westmann, D. Kossmann, S. Helmer, and G. Moerkotte. The implementation and performance of compressed databases. *SIGMOD Record*, 29(3):55–67, 2000.

[24] D. Xin, H. Cheng, X. Yan, and J. Han. Extracting redundancy-aware top-k patterns. In *KDD*, pages 444–453, 2006.

[25] D. Xin, J. Han, X. Yan, and H. Cheng. Mining compressed frequent-pattern sets. In *VLDB*, pages 709–720, 2005.

[26] X. Yan, H. Cheng, J. Han, and D. Xin. Summarizing itemset patterns: a profile-based approach. In *KDD*, pages 314–323, 2005.

Mining Emerging Patterns by Streaming Feature Selection

Kui Yu[1, 2], Wei Ding[2], Dan A. Simovici[2], and Xindong Wu ✉ [1,3]

[1]Department of Computer Science, Hefei University of Technology, Hefei, 230009, China

[2]Department of Computer Science, University of Massachusetts Boston, Boston, 02125, USA

[3]Department of Computer Science, University of Vermont, Burlington, 05405, USA

{ykui,ding,dsim}@cs.umb.edu, xwu@uvm.edu (✉ corresponding author)

ABSTRACT

Building an accurate emerging pattern classifier with a high-dimensional dataset is a challenging issue. The problem becomes even more difficult if the whole feature space is unavailable before learning starts. This paper presents a new technique on mining emerging patterns using streaming feature selection. We model high feature dimensions with streaming features, that is, features arrive and are processed one at a time. As features flow in one by one, we online evaluate each coming feature to determine whether it is useful for mining predictive emerging patterns (EPs) by exploiting the relationship between feature relevance and EP discriminability (the predictive ability of an EP). We employ this relationship to guide an online EP mining process. This new approach can mine EPs from a high-dimensional dataset, even when its entire feature set is unavailable before learning. The experiments on a broad range of datasets validate the effectiveness of the proposed approach against other well-established methods, in terms of predictive accuracy, pattern numbers and running time.

Categories and Subject Descriptors

I.5.2 [**Computing Methodologies**]: Design Methodology-classifier design and evaluation, feature evaluation and selection

General Terms

Algorithms, Experimentation

Keywords

Emerging patterns, Feature relevance, Streaming features

1. INTRODUCTION

An emerging pattern (EP for short) is a pattern whose support value changes significantly from one class to another [9]. Highly accurate classifiers can be built by aggregating the differentiating power of EPs [7, 10].

Mining EPs is still a daunting problem when the number of feature dimensions can be in the thousands, as it is difficult to store, retrieve, prune, and sort them efficiently for classification with a huge number of candidate EPs. With the advent of emerging massive datasets involved with hundreds of thousands of features, such as in image processing, gene expression data, text data, and so on, this pattern search space is rather huge and even smoothing the full feature space sometimes becomes very costly or simply impossible. Therefore, mining EPs from such a space has to face two challenging research issues: (1) how to efficiently mine a small set of strongly predictive EPs from a high-dimensional dataset; and (2) how to mine strongly predictive EPs from a large feature space as exhaustive search over it is either very time-consuming or simply infeasible.

In this paper, we propose a new approach to battle these two challenging issues. A novel contribution of our approach is that it uses streaming features to model a high-dimensional feature space, and then integrates streaming feature selection into the EP mining process to help efficient and effective discovery of a small set of strongly predictive EPs in a large feature space yet to get promising performances.

The concept of streaming features has been proposed to handle feature selection in a changing feature space over time [19, 24]. Unlike data streams, with streaming features, feature dimensions are modeled as a feature stream, and features flow in one by one and each feature is processed upon its arrival. Recent research has shown that streaming feature selection is effective and efficient with not only a huge feature space but also an unknown full feature space before learning [19]. However, if we consider streaming feature selection and EP mining as a whole, aggregating all features and samples to mine EPs is a hard research problem:

(1) Online data processing. Since feature dimensions flow in one by one, it is required to online transform, map and partition arriving features. Firstly, converting a real-world dataset into a desired encoded dataset of all items is infeasible before mining starts. Secondly, the mapping between the item numbers and real-world features needs to be constructed and updated as features flow in one by one over time. Thirdly, as a feature is available, we must online divide the data of each class accordingly instead of dividing all data with all features in advance.

(2) Dynamical EP mining. With streaming features, one solution to mine EPs is to employ streaming feature selection to dynamically control the EP mining process. The problem is how to integrate streaming feature selection into this EP mining process to get an accurate EP classifier.

In this paper, we propose *EPSF* (mining ***E****merging* ***P****atterns by* ***S****treaming* ***F****eature selection*). More specifically, *EPSF* assumes that features arrive one at a time, and each feature is online processed upon its arrival. With the online processing, a two-level framework is proposed to handle dynamical EP mining. In the first level, by exploiting the relations between feature relevance and EP discriminability (the predictive ability of an EP), *EPSF* online builds an influential feature pool by evaluating each arriving feature whether it is useful for mining strongly predictive EPs. In the second level, *EPSF* online builds a candidate EP pool by using this feature pool to online guide EP mining. As features flow in one by one, by interleaving the two levels, *EPSF* provides a natural way to integrate streaming feature selection and EP mining for the high feature dimension challenge in EP mining.

The rest of this paper is organized as follows. Section 2 reviews related work. Section 3 gives the preliminary and Section 4 presents our approach. Section 5 reports our experimental results. Finally, Section 6 provides our conclusion and future work.

KDD'12, August 12–16, 2012, Beijing, China.

2. RELATED WORK

Dong and Li [9] introduced EPs to represent strong contrasts between different classes of data. In addition, a Jump Emerging Pattern (JEP for short) is a special type of EPs whose support increases from zero in one class to non-zero in the other class [12]. Like other patterns composed of conjunctive combinations of elements, EPs can be easily understood and used directly in a wide range of applications, such as failure detection [16] and discovering knowledge in gene expression data [8, 18].

One of the biggest challenges of mining EPs is the high computational cost due to an exponential number of candidate patterns [17]. A number of interestingness measures are defined to reduce the number of discovered EPs without sacrificing their discriminative power. Dong and Li [9] first proposed a border-based approach inspired by the Max-Miner algorithm [2]. In their approach, borders are used to represent candidates and subsets of EPs and the border differentiation operation is used to discover EPs. The ConsEPMiner algorithm follows a level-wise, candidate generation-and-test approach to mine EPs [23]. Bailey et al. [3] proposed a fast algorithm for mining JEPs, which is much faster than the border-based approach. Later Bailey et al. [4] presented a new algorithm for efficiently mining EPs by computing minimal hypergraph transversals. Inspired by the FP-tree, a CP-Tree miner based on the CP-tree data structure was presented to improve EP mining performance [6]. Despite the significant improvement on EP mining, [17] demonstrated that those previous techniques were unable to handle more than sixty dimensions. They proposed a ZBDD EP-miner using Zero-Suppressed Binary Decision Diagrams (ZBDDs) for mining EPs from high-dimensional data.

Much research on EPs has largely focused on classification. Dong et al. [10] proposed the first EP classifier, called CAEP (***C**lassification by **A**ggregating **E**merging **P**atterns*). Based on CAEP, Li et al. proposed a JEP-classifier which is distinct from the CAEP classifier [12].The JEP-classifier uses JEPs exclusively because JEPs discriminate between different classes more strongly than any other type of EPs. Both of these classifiers mine EPs by a border-based approach. Meanwhile, Li et al. [13] also presented a lazy EP classifier based on an instance-based EP discovery, called DeEPs, to improve the efficiency and accuracy of CAEP and JEP-classifier. In addition, Fan and Ramamohanarao [7] proposed a robust EP-classifier, called SJEP-classifier, using a strong jumping emerging pattern that is a special JEP whose support is zero in one class but non-zero and satisfying a minimal support threshold in the other class. The SJEP-classifier integrates the CP-tree miner into the EP classifier, and uses many fewer JEPs than the JEP-classifier.

Limited to the EP mining techniques, existing EP classifiers still cannot handle a dataset with more than sixty dimensions. Although the ZBDD EP-miner can deal with a high-dimensional dataset, like previous approaches, it still suffers from an explosive number of EPs, even with a rather high support threshold. It is still a challenging research issue to mine a small but strongly predictive EPs from a huge number of candidate EPs. In a recent study, Yu et al. addressed the concept of causal associative classification using Bayesian networks to help construct EP classifiers [21]. The study has shown that integrating causal-structure learning into EP mining can efficiently extract a minimal set of strongly predictive patterns from high-dimensional data and get highly accurate EP classifiers. In comparison to [21], we propose a new approach on mining emerging patterns by streaming feature selection. The method is capable of dealing with an unknown or very large full feature space, while exhaustive search is either very time-consuming or simply infeasible.

3. PRELIMINARY KNOWLEDGE

Assume we have a dataset D defined upon a set of N features $F=(F_1, F_2, \dots, F_N)$ and the class attribute C. For every feature F_i, $i = 1, \dots, N$, we assume it is in a discrete domain $dom(F_i)$. Let I be the set of all items, $I = \cup_{i=1}^{N} dom(F_i)$. An itemset X is a subset of I and its $support_D = count_D(X)/|D|$, where $count_D(X)$ is the number of instances in D containing X and $|D|$ is the number of instances in D. Let $C = \{C_1, C_2, \dots, C_K\}$ be a finite set of K distinct class labels. The dataset D can be partitioned into $D_1, D_2, \dots, D_K$,where D_j consists of instances with class label C_j, $j = 1, \dots, K$. The ***G**rowth **R**ate* (GR for short) of X from D_l to D_m, $l, m = 1, \dots, K$ and $l \neq m$, is defined as follows.

Definition 1. (GR: Growth Rate) [9] $GR_{D_l \to D_m}(X) = \frac{support_{D_m}(X)}{support_{D_l}(X)}$. If $support_{D_m}(X) = 0$ and $support_{D_l}(X) = 0$, then $GR_{D_l \to D_m}(X) = 0$; if $support_{D_m}(X) \neq 0$ but $support_{D_l}(X) = 0$, then $GR_{D_l \to D_m}(X) = \infty$.

Definition 2. (EP: Emerging Pattern) [9] Given a threshold $\rho > 1$, an EP from D_l to D_m is an itemset X where $GR_{D_l \to D_m}(X) \geq \rho$.

An EP e from D_l to D_m is also called an EP of D_m. If $GR(e) = \infty$, e is called a Jumping EP (JEP). The goal of EP mining is to extract the EP set E_i for each class C_i which consists of EPs from $D - D_i$ to D_i , given a minimum growth rate threshold and a minimum support threshold.

Definition 3. (Growth Rate Improvement) [23] Given an EP e, the growth rate improvement of e, Rateimp(e), is defined as the minimum difference between its growth rate and the growth rates of all of its subsets,

$$Rateimp(e) = \min(\forall e' \subset e, GR(e) - GR(e')).$$

A positive growth rate improvement threshold ensures a concise and representative set of EPs which are not subsumed by one another and consist of items that are strong contributors to their predictive power. The growth rate improvement can also help to reduce the search space by eliminating EPs that are uninteresting or redundant.

An illustrating example is given in Tables 1 and 2 using the Balloon dataset from the UCI machine learning repository [5]. Assuming the minimum support threshold is 0.2 and the growth rate threshold $\rho > 1$, the candidate EPs are of two classes T (the inflated class) and F (the not inflated class) with 20 samples and 4 features: *color*, *size*, *act* and *age*.

Table 1 The candidate EPs from class T to class F

Candidate EP	Support (class T)	Support (class F)	$GR_{T \to F}(e)$
{act=dip}	0.33	1	3
{age=child}	0.33	1	3
{act=dip, age=child}	0	1	∞

Table 2 The candidate EPs from class F to class T

Candidate EP	Support (class F)	Support (class T)	$GR_{F \to T}(e)$
{act=stretch}	0	0.67	∞
{age=adult}	0	0.7	∞

From Definition 2, in Table 2, both {act=stretch} and {age=adult} are EPs of class T. In Table 1, by Definition 3, we can see that {act=dip, age=child} is the EP of class F since both {act=dip} and {age=child} are subsumed by it.

When applying EPs to classification, we get all the EPs of each class C_i in a training set that are subsets of a test instance t to contribute to the final decision as to whether t should be labeled as C_i. More specifically, we derive k scores for t, one score per class, by feeding the EPs of each class into a scoring function. Then $\text{label}(t) = \text{argmax}_{C_i \in C} \text{score}(t, C_i)$. The following definition provides the scoring function of the EP-Classifier [10].

Definition 4 (Aggregate Score). Given an instance t and a set E_i of EPs of class $C_i \in C$ mined from the training data, the aggregate score of t for C_i is defined as

$$\text{score}(t, C_i) = \sum_{e \subseteq t, e \in E_i} \frac{GR_{D-D_{C_i} \to D_{C_i}}(e)}{GR_{D-D_{C_i} \to D_{C_i}}(e)+1} * \text{support}_{C_i}(e)$$

A potential problem in Definition 4 is that the number of EPs from different classes is likely unbalanced. If a class C_i contains more EPs than another class C_j, a test instance tends to obtain a higher score for C_i than for C_j, even when the test actually belongs to C_j. To solve this problem, Dong et al. [10] presented the concept of a base score for each class C_i named $\text{baseScore}(C_i)$, which is first calculated from the training instances of the class. With the base score, the new score of an instance t for C_i, named $\text{normScore}(t, C_i)$, is defined as the ratio of the score calculated by Definition 4 and the base score of C_i,

$$\text{normScore}(t, C_i) = \frac{\text{score}(t, C_i)}{\text{baseScore}(C_i)}.$$

The class with the highest normScore wins, and ties are broken by choosing the largest class as the winner.

4. EMERGING PATTERN MINING BY STREAMING FEATURE SELECTION

4.1 Feature Relevance and EP Discriminability

It is infeasible to examine a search space covering all possible item combinations for a large high-dimensional dataset. The question is whether some feature values could be pruned before mining EPs. As illustrated in Tables 1 to 2, the final set of EPs does not contain features *size* and *color*, since they have no impact on the predictive ability of their corresponding EPs. We propose to integrate streaming feature selection to significantly improve EP mining in high-dimensional data to produce an accurate EP classifier, which otherwise would be impossible due to the large search space. In this section, we first analyze on the relationships between feature relevance and EP discriminability, and then evaluate the degree of features relevance with the discriminative power of EPs as the features flow over time.

An input feature can be in one of three disjoint categories, namely, strongly relevant, weakly relevant, and irrelevant, with respect to its relevance to the class attribute [11]. Weakly relevant features can be further divided into redundant features and non-redundant features, and then an optimal feature subset should contain weakly relevant but non-redundant features and strongly relevant features [22]. In the following definitions, let F be a full set of features, F_i denote the ith input feature, C be the class attribute and P(C|S) is the probability distribution of different classes given a feature subset $S \subseteq F$.

Definition 5 (Strong Relevance) A feature F_i is strongly relevant to C iff $\forall S \subseteq F - \{F_i\}$ s.t. $P(C|S) \neq P(C|S, F_i)$.

Definition 6 (Weak Relevance) A feature F_i is weakly relevant to C iff it is not strongly relevant, and

$$\exists S \subset F - \{F_i\} \text{ s.t. } P(C|S) \neq P(C|S, F_i).$$

Definition 7 (Irrelevance) A feature F_i is irrelevant to C iff it is neither strongly nor weakly relevant, and

$$\forall S \subseteq F - \{F_i\} \text{ s.t. } P(C|S, F_i) = P(C|S).$$

As defined in Definitions 1 and 2, the discriminability of an EP is determined by its support value and growth rate. Proposition 1 below establishes the relations between non-EPs and irrelevant features.

Proposition 1 For $\forall F_i \in F$, $\forall f \in dom(F_i)$, and $\forall C_i \in dom(C)$, $GR_{D-D_{C_i} \to D_{C_i}}(F_i = f) = 1$ holds iff F_i is irrelevant to C.

Proof: Assume a dataset D has two classes $C = \{C_p, C_n\}$, D_p represents C_p class data, D_n represents C_n class data, $\text{supp}_{D_p}(F_i = f)$ is the support value of the itemset $\{F_i = f\}$ in D_p, and $\text{supp}_{D_n}(F_i = f)$ is its support value in D_n. Then $GR(F_i = f)$ from D_n to D_p is calculated as follows.

$$\begin{aligned} GR_{D_n \to D_p}(F_i = f) &= \text{supp}_{D_p}(F_i = f) / \text{supp}_{D_n}(F_i = f) \\ &= P(F_i = f|C = C_p) / P(F_i = f|C = C_n) \\ &= \frac{P(F_i = f, C = C_p)}{P(C = C_p)} \Big/ \frac{P(F_i = f, C = C_n)}{P(C = C_n)} \\ &= \frac{P(C = C_p \mid F_i = f)P(F_i = f)}{P(C = C_p)} \Big/ \frac{P(C = C_n \mid F_i = f)P(F_i = f)}{P(C = C_n)} \\ &= \frac{P(C = C_n)}{P(C = C_p)} * \frac{P(C = C_p \mid F_i = f)}{P(C = C_n \mid F_i = f)} \end{aligned}$$

On the one hand, if the term $GR_{D_n \to D_p}(F_i = f) = 1$ holds, then

$$\frac{P(C = C_p)}{P(C = C_n)} = \frac{P(C = C_p|F_i = f)}{P(C = C_n|F_i = f)}$$

As $P(C = C_p) + P(C = C_n) = 1$ and $P(C = C_p|F_i = f) + P(C = C_n|F_i = f) = 1$, we get $P(C = C_p|F_i = f) = P(C = C_p)$ (with $\frac{a}{b} = \frac{c}{d}$ equivalent to $\frac{a}{b+a} = \frac{c}{d+c}$), as well as $P(C = C_n|F_i = f) = P(C = C_n)$.

According to Definition 7, for any assignments $f \in dom(F_i)$ and $c \in dom(C)$ to F and C, $P(C = c|F_i = f) = P(C = c)$ holds, therefore F_i is irrelevant to C. Clearly, from D_p to D_n, if $GR(F_i = f) = 1$, we can also prove that F_i is irrelevant to C. On the other hand, if F_i is irrelevant to C, we get

$$\begin{aligned} GR_{D_n \to D_p}(F_i = f) &= \frac{P(C = C_n)}{P(C = C_p)} * \frac{P(C = C_p|F_i = f)}{P(C = C_n|F_i = f)} \\ &= \frac{1 - P(C = C_p)}{P(C = C_p)} * \frac{P(C = C_p \mid F_i = f)}{1 - P(C = C_p \mid F_i = f)} \\ &= 1 \end{aligned}$$

Thus, Proposition 1 is proven. □

Definition 8 (Markov Blanket) [11] Let $M_i \subset F - \{F_i\}$ be a subset of features. If F_i is conditionally independent of $F - M_i - \{F_i\}$ given M_i, then M_i is a Markov blanket for F_i.

Definition 9 (Redundant Feature) [22] A feature is redundant hence should be removed from F, if and only if it is weakly relevant and has a Markov blanket M within F.

From Definition 3, as for an EP e, if we can find an $e' \subset e$ to make $\text{rateimp}(e) \leq 0$, then e is an uninteresting or redundant EP, and might be replaced by a subset. Thus, avoiding generation of those redundant EPs in advance will improve search efficiency. Proposition 2 below explains the relationship between feature redundancy and EP redundancy.

Proposition 2 For $\exists F_i \in F$, $\exists S \subset F$, $\forall f \in dom(F_i)$, $\forall s \subset \cup_{i=1}^{|S|} dom(S_i)$, and $\forall C_i \in dom(C)$, $GR_{D-D_{C_i} \to D_{C_i}}(F_i = f, S = s) = GR_{D-D_{C_i} \to D_{C_i}}(S = s)$ holds iff F_i is redundant to C conditioning on the subset S.

Proof: $GR(F_i = f, S = s)$ from D_n to D_p is calculated as follows.

$$GR_{D_n \to D_p}(F_i = f, S = s) = \sup_{D_p}(F_i = f, S = s) / \sup_{D_n}(F_i = f, S = s)$$

$$= P(F_i = f, S = s|C = C_p) / P(F_i = f, S = s|C = C_n)$$

$$= \frac{P(F_i = f, S = s, C = C_p)}{P(C = C_p)} \Big/ \frac{P(F_i = f, S = s, C = C_n)}{P(C = C_n)}$$

$$= \frac{P(C = C_p | F_i = f, S = s) P(F_i = f, S = s)}{P(C = C_p)} \Big/ \frac{P(C = C_n | F_i = f, S = s) P(F_i = f, S = s)}{P(C = C_n)}$$

$$= \frac{P(C = C_p | F_i = f, S = s)}{P(C = C_n | F_i = f, S = s)} * \frac{P(C = C_n)}{P(C = C_p)}$$

From D_n to D_p, $GR(S = s) = P(S = s|C = C_p)/P(S = s|C = C_n)$

$$\frac{P(C = C_p | F_i = f, S = s)}{P(C = C_n | F_i = f, S = s)} * \frac{P(C = C_n)}{P(C = C_p)} = \frac{P(S = s | C = C_p)}{P(S = s | C = C_n)}$$

$$\frac{P(C = C_p | F_i = f, S = s)}{P(C = C_n | F_i = f, S = s)} = \frac{P(S = s | C = C_p) P(C = C_p)}{P(S = s | C = C_n) P(C = C_n)}$$

$$\frac{P(C = C_p | F_i = f, S = s)}{P(C = C_n | F_i = f, S = s)} = \frac{P(C = C_p | S = s)}{P(C = C_n | S = s)}$$

Using the same reasoning in proving Proposition 1, we can get two equations: $P(C = C_p | F_i = f, S = s) = P(C = C_p | S = s)$ and $P(C = C_n | F_i = f, S = s) = P(C = C_n | S = s)$. By Definitions 8 and 9, we can find a subset $S \subset F$ as a Markov blanket of F_i, and for any assignments $f \in dom(F_i)$, $s \in dom(S)$ and $c \in dom(C)$ to F_i, S and C, $P(C = c|F_i = f, S = s) = P(C = c|S = s)$ holds, and so F_i is redundant to C given S.

On the other hand, if F_i is redundant to C, from D_n to D_p, then

$$GR_{D_n \to D_p}(F_i = f, S = s) = \frac{P(C = C_p | F_i = f, S = s)}{P(C = C_n | F_i = f, S = s)} * \frac{P(C = C_n)}{P(C = C_p)}$$

$$= \frac{1 - P(C = C_n | F_i = f, S = s)}{P(C = C_n | F_i = f, S = s)} * \frac{P(C = C_n)}{P(C = C_p)}$$

$$= \frac{1 - P(C = C_n | S = s)}{P(C = C_n | S = s)} * \frac{P(C = C_n)}{P(C = C_p)}$$

$$= \frac{P(C = C_p | S = s)}{P(C = C_n | S = s)} * \frac{P(C = C_n)}{P(C = C_p)}$$

$$= \frac{P(S = s | C = C_p)}{P(S = s | C = C_n)} = GR_{D_n \to D_p}(S = s)$$

Thus, we have proven Proposition 2. □

Proposition 2 shows that if F_i is redundant to C given a subset S, then an itemset $\forall f \in dom(F_i)$ together with itemsets $\forall s \in \cup_{i=1}^{|S|} dom(S_i)$ contains the same predictive information as the itemsets $\forall s \in \cup_{i=1}^{|S|} dom(S_i)$.

According to Propositions 1 and 2, we can extract EPs without considering irrelevant and redundant features. We thus integrate streaming feature selection into the EP mining process to avoid generating non-EPs and redundant EPs.

Since the irrelevant features can be easily identified, we face two challenges here: (1) how to identify redundant features when the features stream in; and (2) how to online extract EPs from the current feature pool. We give two more propositions below to handle redundant features. From Definition 3, since the Markov blanket of C subsumes the information that all of the other features have about C, we set a Markov blanket of C (MB(C) for short) as an empty set initially, and gradually build the MB(C) as features flow in one by one over time. Clearly, by Definition 9, we can get Proposition 3 to identify whether a new arriving feature is redundant for the time being.

Proposition 3 As the features flow in one by one, a current Markov blanket of C at time t is denoted as $CMB(C)_t$. Assume an arriving feature F_i at time t+1 is weakly relevant to C. If $\exists S \subseteq CMB(C)_t$ such that $P(C|F_i, S) = P(C|S)$, then F_i can be removed.

With Proposition 3, if the new feature F_i is added into CMB(C), we can get Proposition 4 to determine which of the features in CMB(C) become redundant as F_i is added.

Proposition 4 With $CMB(C)_t$ at time t, as a new feature F_i arrives at time t+1, we suppose there does not exist any $MB(F_i)$ within $CMB(C)_t$. If $\exists Y \in CMB(C)_t$ and $\exists S \subseteq \{CMB(C)_t \cup F_i\} - \{Y\}\ s.t.\ P(C|Y, S) = P(C|S)$, then Y can be removed from $CMB(C)_t$.

4.2 Mining Emerging Patterns with Streaming Feature Selection

With the theoretical analysis in Section 4.1, we propose an algorithm *EPSF* (mining ***E****merging* ***P****atterns* by ***S****treaming* ***F****eature* selection) in Fig. 1.

```
1. Initialization of the minimum support threshold α, growth rate threshold ρ, CMB(C) = {}, and setting C as the class attribute
2. Input a new feature F_i
3. //Identify and remove irrelevant features
4. If P(C|F_i) = P(C), discard F_i and goto step 2;
5. //Identify redundant features by Proposition 3
6. If ∃S ⊆ CMB(C) s.t. P(C|F_i, S) = P(C|S), go to step 2
7. //Add F_i into the current feature pool CMB(C)
8.  CMB(C) = CMB(C) ∪ F_i;
9. //Convert feature F_i into a set of itemsets
10.  I_Fi = convert(F_i), I_Fi ∈ dom(F_i)
11. //Map between I_Fi and F_i
12. map_form = mapping(F_i, I_Fi)
13. For i=1: |C| // |C| denotes the number of classes
14. //Mine 1-itemset EPs for each class with the thresholds α, ρ
15.        EP_i = mineEP(I_Fi, α, ρ)
16. //Add EP_i to the current EP pool CEP
17.        CEP = CEP ∪ EP_i
18. Endfor
19. //Update CMB(C) by Proposition 4
20.  For each feature Y within CMB(C) excluding F_i
21.      If ∃S ⊆ CMB(C) s.t. P(C|Y, S) = P(C|S)
22.            CMB(C) = CMB(C) − Y
23. //Update CEP by removing EPs generated from feature Y
24.              For each y ∈ I_y
25.                  if y ∈ CEP, then CEP = CEP − y endif
26.              Endfor
27.            map_form = map_form−I_y //Update map_form
28.      Endif
29. Endfor
30. Repeat steps 2 to 29 until all features have arrived
31. Find all EPs from CEP with map_form
32. Classify unlabeled instances by the mined EPs
```

Fig. 1. The *EPSF* algorithm

EPSF online builds two pools: a feature pool and an EP pool. The feature pool stores the influential features which are useful for mining predictive EPs and dynamically changes as the features flow in one by one, while the EP pool keeps candidate EPs which are mined from the feature pool and online updates as the feature pool changes over time. As a feature arrives, if it is a strongly relevant or non-redundant feature, *EPSF* adds it into the feature pool, online transforms it into a set of itemsets, and online mines EPs which are added into the EP pool. With the features flowing over time, the current EP pool online updates with the changing feature pool. In order to fast respond to this change, we only online mine 1-itemset EPs as features arrive one by one, and then mine all EPs with these 1-itemset EPs as all features have arrived. More specifically, *EPSF* consists of the following key stages:

- Online mining 1-itemset EPs (steps 2 to 18). As a new feature F_i arrives, *EPSF* first assesses whether it is an irrelevant one; and if so, it is discarded. Otherwise, we evaluate whether it is redundant to C by Proposition 3; and if so, it is also discarded. If not, it is added to the feature pool CMB(C). And then, *EPSF* converts feature F_i into a set of itemsets I_{F_i} and has a mapping between I_{F_i} and F_i. This mapping can guarantee that itemsets contain items mapped from the same feature, and their supersets should be pruned. With I_{F_i} and the mapping, *EPSF* divides each class data, mines EPs for each class and stores the EPs in a candidate EP pool named CEP.
- Online updating CEP and the map_form (steps 19 to 30). Due to F_i inclusion, *EPSF* updates the feature pool CMB(C) by removing redundant features. If some features are removed from CMB(C), then we update CEP and map_form.

The *EPSF* algorithm is relevant for large datasets with high feature dimensions, as it does not need to store the whole data in the memory to check whether a new feature is redundant and to update CMB(C) when a new feature is added. As a novel contribution, *EPSF* can mine EPs from a high dimensional dataset without knowing its entire feature set in advance. When the features flow in one by one, each feature is processed upon its arrival. Feature redundancy checking (step 6) and CMB(C) updating (steps 20-22) are both conducted within the current CMB(C), not in the whole feature set.

5. EXPERIMENTAL RESULTS

5.1 Experimental Setup

In order to thoroughly evaluate the proposed *EPSF* algorithm, thirty six datasets in Table 3 are selected from the UCI machine learning repository (the first 24 datasets), very high-dimensional biomedical datasets (*hiva*, *ovarian-cancer*, *lymphoma*, and *breast-cancer*), NIPS 2003 feature selection challenge datasets (*madelon*, *arcene*, *dorothea*, and *dexter*), and four frequently studied public microarray datasets (the last 4 datasets), respectively.

Our comparative study involves three types of comparisons, using ten-fold cross-validation on all datasets.

- Comparing against state-of-the-art EP classifiers, CAEP [10] and CE-EP [21].
- Comparing *EPSF* with three well-known associative classifiers: CBA [15], CMAR [14] and CPAR [20].
- Comparing the predictive accuracy of *EPSF* with state-of-the-art non-associative classifiers, including Decision Tree J48, SVM, and AdaBoost using their Weka implementations with default parameters.

We use the method proposed by Aliferis et al. [1] to discretize continuous features for continuous datasets. In the experiments, we set the minimum confidence threshold to 0.8 for CBA and CMAR, and set the growth rate to 20 for *EPSF*, CAPE and CE-EP. To test the impact of the minimum support threshold, we set seven minimum supports for *EPSF*, CE-EP, CAEP, CBA and CMAR, including 0.005, 0.01, 0.05, 0.1, 0.2, 0.3, and 0.4, respectively. The parameters for CPAR are set the same as those reported in [20]. CBA, CMAR, and CPAR are implemented in LUCS KDD Software Library, while *EPSF*, CAEP and CE-EP are implemented in C++. The experiments are performed on a Window 7 DELL workstation with an Intel Xeon 2.93 GHz processor and 12.0GB RAM.

Table 3 Summary of 36 Datasets.
#: number of features, SIZE: number of instances

Dataset	#	SIZE	Dataset	#	SIZE
australian	14	690	promoters	57	106
breast-w	9	3,146	spect	22	267
crx	15	690	spectf	44	267
cleve	13	303	tictactoe	9	958
diabetes	8	768	vote	16	435
german	20	1,000	wdbc	30	569
house-votes	16	230	madelon	500	2,000
hepatitis	19	155	hiva	1,617	4,229
horse-colic	22	368	ovarian-cancer	2,190	216
hypothyroid	25	3,163	lymphoma	7,399	227
heart	13	270	dexter	20,000	300
infant	86	5,337	breast-cancer	17,816	286
ionosphere	34	351	arcene	10,000	100
kr-vs-kp	36	3,196	dorothea	100,000	800
labor	16	57	colon	2,000	62
liver	6	345	leukemia	7,129	72
mushroom	22	8,124	lung-cancer	12,533	181
pima	8	768	prostate	6,033	102

5.2 Comparison of Predictive Accuracy

Tables 4 to 6 report detailed results in terms of predictive accuracy of the proposed *EPSF* classifier and the other eight classifiers, including two EP, three associative and three non-associative classifiers on the thirty six benchmark datasets. We select the best predictive accuracy under the seven minimum supports as the results for our comparative study. In Table 6, CBA, CMAR and CPAR only have results on the twenty four low dimensional datasets as they fail to deal with a high feature space. The best result is highlighted in bold face for each dataset and the symbol "/" denotes a classifier runs out of memory due to a huge number of candidate patterns.

To further investigate the classification results, we conduct paired t-tests at a 95% significance level and summarize the win/tie/loss counts of *EPSF* against the other algorithms in Table 7 (note: if a classifier fails to run on a dataset while *EPSF* works, then *EPSF* wins).

In Table 7, *EPSF* generally outperforms CAEP on all thirty six datasets and CBA, CMAR and CPAR on twenty four low dimensional datasets. *EPSF* is also superior to CE-EP which is a state-of-the-art EP classifier for handling high feature dimensions. Meanwhile, in comparison with the well-known non-associative classifiers, *EPSF* is significantly superior to J48 and AdaBoost and also very competitive with SVM as shown in Table 7. We have demonstrated in the experiments that the integration of streaming feature selection into EP mining can avoid generating non-EPs and redundant EPs. This enables *EPSF* to not only handle high-dimensional datasets such as the last twelve datasets in Table 3, but also produce very promising predictive accuracy.

Table 4 Comparison of predictive accuracy (%): *EPSF*, CAEP and CE-EP

Dataset	*EPSF*	CAEP	CE-EP	Dataset	*EPSF*	CAEP	CE-EP
australian	**87.50**	84.71	83.97	promoters	71.00	/	**72.00**
breast-w	**96.88**	**96.88**	**96.88**	spect	**72.69**	66.92	**72.69**
crx	**85.29**	84.85	82.21	spectf	**86.92**	/	83.85
cleve	82.76	**85.52**	84.83	tictactoe	72.11	**82.95**	69.58
diabetes	**72.11**	68.95	**72.11**	vote	95.48	90.00	**95.95**
german	69.10	**72.80**	71.50	wdbc	**83.39**	81.96	81.79
house-votes	**96.82**	90.91	**96.82**	madelon	**61.20**	/	59.00
hepatitis	82.67	**86.00**	85.33	hiva	**95.17**	/	93.70
horse-colic	85.28	79.72	**85.83**	ovarian-cancer	**93.81**	/	92.86
hypothyroid	**73.03**	67.78	72.82	lymphoma	76.82	/	**77.73**
heart	85.56	**85.93**	83.70	dexter	**89.67**	/	88.33
infant	91.46	/	**94.92**	arcene	80.00	/	**86.67**
ionosphere	**93.24**	90.29	92.94	breast-cancer	**92.96**	/	92.22
kr-vs-kp	**92.42**	83.49	92.23	dorothea	94.94	/	**95.06**
labor	92.00	94.00	**96.00**	colon	91.67	/	**95.00**
liver	**61.76**	57.65	**61.76**	leukemia	**100.00**	/	**100.00**
mushroom	**97.30**	96.18	96.18	lung-cancer	98.89	/	**99.44**
pima	**72.11**	68.95	**72.11**	prostate	**95.00**	/	94.00

Table 5 Comparison of predictive accuracy (%): *EPSF*, J48, SVM and AdaBoost

Dataset	*EPSF*	J48	SVM	AdaBoost	Dataset	*EPSF*	J48	SVM	AdaBoost
australian	**87.50**	85.79	85.36	86.38	promoters	71.00	63.21	**79.25**	66.04
breast-w	96.88	94.56	**97.00**	94.85	spect	**72.69**	65.54	70.04	69.66
crx	85.29	84.20	**85.51**	85.36	spectf	**86.92**	62.57	81.25	75.40
cleve	82.76	75.91	82.51	**84.82**	tictactoe	72.11	85.70	**98.33**	72.31
diabetes	72.11	72.00	**73.18**	**73.18**	vote	**95.48**	94.01	94.93	82.87
german	69.10	74.00	**76.20**	71.60	wdbc	**83.39**	75.92	79.61	76.27
heart	**85.56**	77.03	83.33	81.11	madelon	**61.20**	57.50	56.35	60.50
hepatitis	82.67	80.65	**84.52**	80.65	hiva	95.17	96.39	94.70	**96.47**
horse-colic	**85.28**	81.79	81.79	83.70	lymphoma	76.82	70.93	**77.53**	60.79
hypothyroid	73.03	**95.64**	95.57	95.23	breast-cancer	**92.96**	80.77	92.31	83.57
house-votes	96.82	96.52	**96.96**	**96.96**	ovarian-cancer	**93.81**	89.35	93.52	90.74
infant	91.46	95.39	95.41	**95.43**	dorothea	**94.94**	/	/	/
ionosphere	**93.24**	92.02	91.74	89.46	arcene	80.00	56.00	**81.00**	71.00
kr-vs-kp	92.42	**99.31**	94.99	93.84	dexter	89.67	82.67	**91.33**	81.33
labor	92.00	**92.98**	85.96	87.72	colon	**91.67**	79.03	85.48	85.48
liver	**61.76**	60.00	60.29	60.87	leukemia	**100**	90.28	98.61	**100**
mushroom	97.30	**100**	99.11	98.44	lung-cancer	98.89	90.61	**100**	96.69
pima	72.11	72.01	**73.18**	**73.18**	prostate	**95.00**	88.24	94.12	91.18

Table 6 Comparison of predictive accuracy (%): *EPSF*, CBA, CMAR and CPAR

Dataset	*EPSF*	CBA	CMAR	CPAR	Dataset	*EPSF*	CBA	CMAR	CPAR
australian	**87.50**	86.96	86.96	85.51	ionosphere	**93.24**	88.88	90.58	88.88
breast-w	**96.88**	94.09	90.82	92.95	kr-vs-kp	92.42	**93.56**	89.41	88.71
crx	85.29	**86.52**	85.51	85.51	labor	**92.00**	54.33	89.17	80.33
cleve	82.76	83.12	**85.82**	78.61	liver	**61.76**	60.90	4.12	58.14
diabetes	72.11	73.18	64.24	**73.31**	mushroom	97.30	78.67	**99.37**	98.66
german	69.10	**74.50**	71.00	65.70	pima	72.11	**73.45**	63.94	67.97
house-votes	96.82	**96.96**	**96.96**	**96.96**	promoters	**71.00**	28.13	42.50	63.00
hepatitis	82.67	49.50	**83.33**	72.34	spect	**72.69**	64.42	62.66	64.42
horse-colic	**85.28**	83.69	83.91	82.02	spectf	**86.92**	55.84	80.07	54.74
hypothyroid	73.03	**94.78**	90.00	89.56	tictactoe	72.11	**100**	99.26	71.43
heart	**85.56**	84.07	84.07	77.41	vote	**95.48**	95.40	95.40	94.01
infant	**91.46**	63.72	90.00	84.30	wdbc	83.39	**95.79**	95.61	92.91

Table 7 Win/tie/loss counts of *EPSF* vs. the other 8 classifiers (pairwise t-test at 95% significance level)

	CAEP	CE-EP	CBA	CMAR	CPAR	J48	SVM	AdaBoost
EPSF	28/3/5	13/15/8	13/3/8	13/6/5	17/3/4	24/5/7	14/9/13	20/7/9

Table 8 Comparison of running time (in seconds): *EPSF*, CAEP and CE-EP

Dataset	*EPSF*	CAEP	CE-EP	Dataset	*EPSF*	CAEP	CE-EP	Dataset	*EPSF*	CAEP	CE-EP
australian	16	50	43	ionosphere	30	146	43	madelon	23	/	32
breast-w	38	51	51	kr-vs-kp	43	481	48	hiva	163	/	36
crx	17	42	31	labor	17	42	31	ovarian-cancer	68	/	34
cleve	26	53	31	liver	10	10	10	lymphoma	44	/	32
diabetes	26	48	31	mushroom	44	100	64	dexter	387	/	38
german	28	129	31	pima	27	46	45	arcene	30	/	34
house-votes	27	54	27	promoters	16	/	30	breast-cancer	958	/	47
hepatitis	21	43	37	spect	16	87	30	dorothea	440	/	164
horse-colic	20	51	31	spectf	17	/	31	colon	18	/	32
hypothyroid	30	107	32	tictactoe	16	33	31	leukemia	22	/	50
heart	26	50	45	vote	17	47	30	lung-cancer	117	/	42
infant	41	/	50	wdbc	24	85	31	prostate	27	/	34

5.3 Comparison of Numbers of Patterns

Figures 2 to 4 compare the numbers of patterns mined by *EPSF* against CBA, CMAR, CAEP and CE-EP, since these five classifiers all focus on generating patterns with the support-confidence framework. We report the average numbers of mined patterns over all seven minimum support thresholds. Since on *wdbc*, *kr-vs-kp*, *ionosphere*, *horse-colic* and *german*, CAEP cannot run using all the support thresholds due to huge numbers of patterns, the number of patterns on those datasets is averaged over the available support thresholds.

Fig.2 only plots 21 low-dimensional datasets since CAEP cannot run on the datasets of *infant*, *promoters* and *spectf*. In Fig.3, the X-axis denotes the twenty four datasets corresponding to the first twenty four datasets in Table 3 while in Fig.4 the X-axis denotes all of thirty six datasets corresponding to Table 3. It is clear that *EPSF* selects many fewer patterns than CAEP, CBA, and CMAR on all low-dimensional datasets.

In Fig. 4, *EPSF* also selects fewer patterns than CE-EP on most of the thirty six datasets. These results illustrate that both *EPSF* and CE-EP can select a small set of strongly predictive EPs from a very high dimensional dataset. In Fig.4, numbers 25 to 36 correspond to the last twelve high-dimensional datasets in Table 3. We can see that even with very high feature dimensions, the numbers of patterns selected by CE-EP and *EPSF* do not change much in comparison with those on the twenty four low-dimensional datasets.

5.4 Comparison of Running Time

The running time (in seconds) of *EPSF*, CAEP and CE-EP contains all learning time, including importing datasets, ten-fold cross validation learning and testing. Table 8 shows the running time of *EPSF* against CAEP and CE-EP, respectively. In Table 8, we can see that *EPSF* is faster than CAEP on all the datasets. Compared to CE-EP, on the first twenty four low-dimensional datasets, *EPSF* is faster than CE-EP. But on the last twelve high dimensional datasets, *EPSF* is not faster than CE-EP on some datasets. This is because at each fold cross-validation, *EPSF* takes all features into account to mine EPs while CE-EP discovers the direct causes and direct effects of the class attribute before EP mining, and then mines EPs in this reduced feature space at each fold cross-validation instead of all features. Thus, in Figures 5 to 6, we only plot the running time of EP mining (not including the time of training and testing classifiers) in one fold with the support threshold up to 0.2.

In Fig.5, the X-axis denotes the same twenty one datasets as Fig. 2. In Fig.6, on the X-axis, numbers 1 to 3 denote the datasets of *infant*, *promoters* and *spectf* respectively and numbers 4 to 15 denote the last twelve high-dimensional datasets in Table 3. From Fig.5, we can see that *EPSF* is still faster than CAEP and CE-EP on all twenty one low-dimensional datasets.

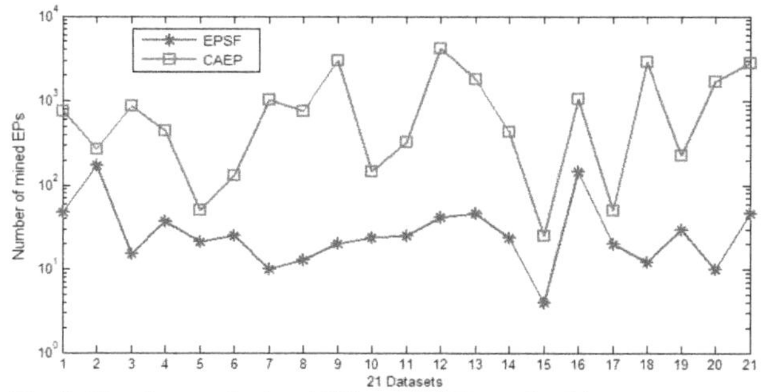

Fig.2. Numbers of mined EPs: *EPSF* vs. CAEP (the 21 datasets on the X-axis are: 1.australian, 2. breast-w, 3.crx, 4.cleve, 5.diabetes, 6.german,7. house-votes, 8.hepatitis, 9.horse-colic,10. hypothyroid, 11.heart, 12.ionosphere, 13.kr-vs-kp, 14.labor, 15. liver, 16.mushroom, 17. pima, 18.spect, 19.tictactoe, 20. vote, 21. wdbc).

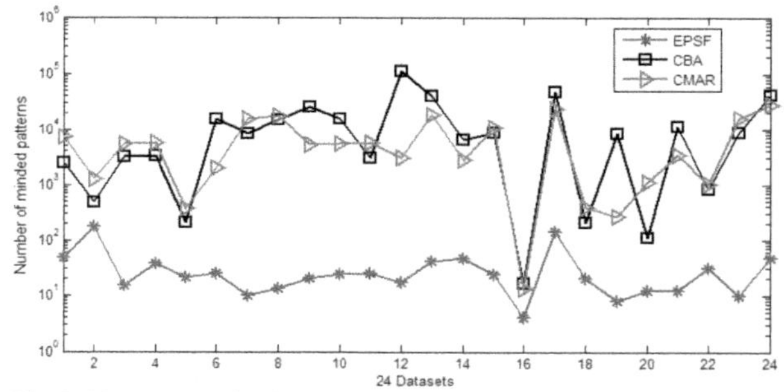

Fig.3. Numbers of mined patterns: *EPSF*, CBA and CMAR

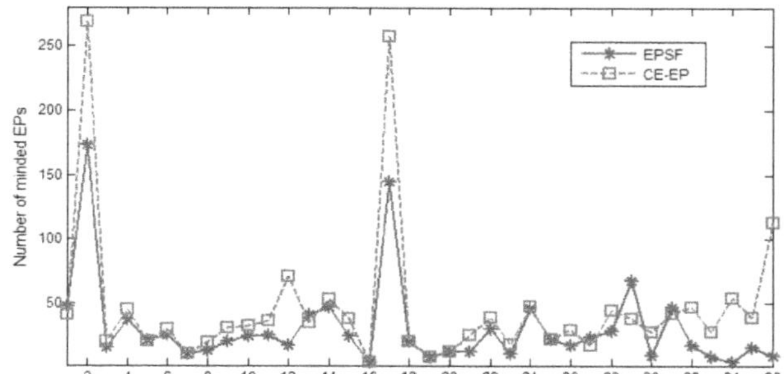

Fig.4. Numbers of mined EPs: *EPSF* against CE-EP

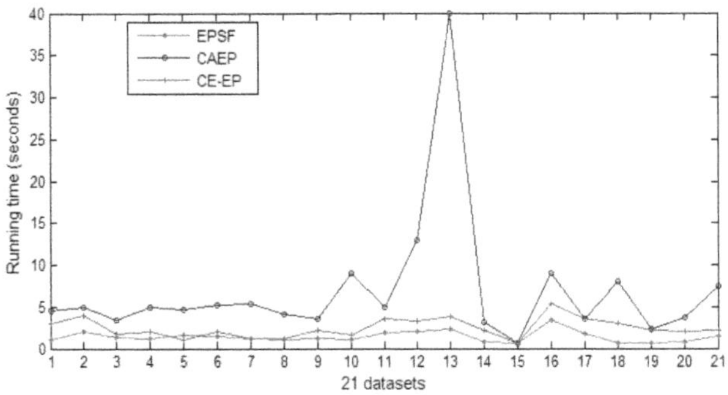

Fig.5. EP mining time: *EPSF* against CAEP and CE-EP

In Fig.6, *EPSF* is only slower than CE-EP on 3 datasets: *hiva*, *dexter* and *breast-cancer*. In summary, *EPSF* is faster than CE-EP on thirty three out of the thirty six datasets.

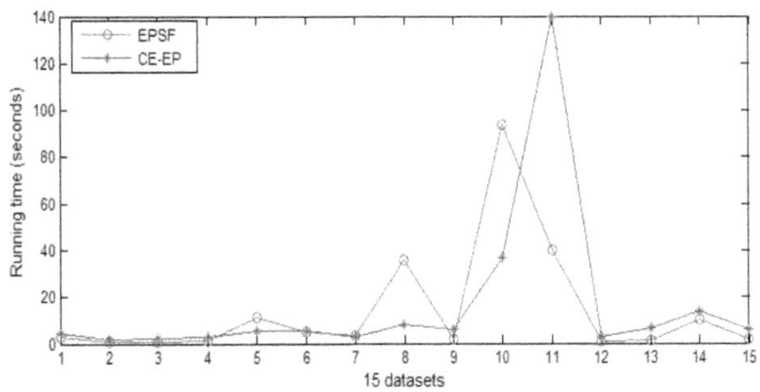

Fig.6. EP mining time: *EPSF* against CE-EP

5.5 Analysis on the Predictive Accuracy under Different Growth Rate Thresholds

To further explore the performance of *EPSF*, CE-EP, and CAEP, we conduct an analysis on the predictive accuracy of *EPSF*, CE-EP, and CAEP under seven minimum growth rate thresholds, as shown in Figures 7 to 9, where GR stands for ***G**rowth **R**ate* thresholds and the minimum support threshold is fixed at 0.1. Since on *infant*, *ionosphere*, *promoters* and *spectf*, CAEP cannot run under all seven growth rate thresholds, Fig.7 plots the predictive accuracy of the remaining 20 low-dimensional datasets under seven growth rate thresholds. In Figures 8 and 9, the X-axis denotes all of the thirty six datasets corresponding to Table 3. From Figures 7 to 9, we can see that CAEP, CE-EP and *EPSF* are not sensitive to the minimum growth rate thresholds at all, especially for CE-EP and *EPSF*.

5.6 Mining EPs without Smoothing through the Whole Feature Space

In comparison with CE-EP, *EPSF* can handle not only a large feature space, but also a high-dimensional dataset without knowing its entire feature set in advance. Sometimes, if a feature space is so large that exhaustive search over this whole feature space is either very time-consuming or simply infeasible. *EPSF* provides a solution to this problem, by processing features one by one upon its arrival and stopping this process using the EPs seen so far with a user-specified criterion. CE-EP cannot deal with this situation since it needs all features in advance to identify the causes and effects of the class attribute. We evaluate this performance of *EPSF* on only four gene datasets in Fig. 10 due to the page limit. For each dataset, we randomly select ten samples as the testing instances (five positive and five negative) and the rest for training. SVM and AdaBoost are used as baselines on the training and testing sets with all features. Without the knowledge of the whole feature space in advance, *EPSF* mines EPs on the training samples as the features flow in one by one and evaluates the current EPs on the testing samples.

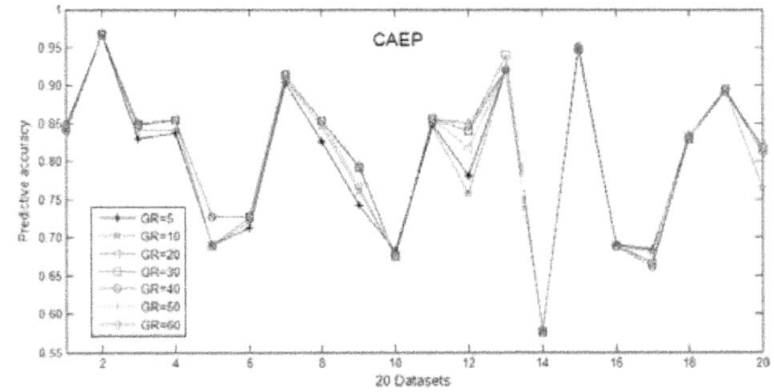

Fig.7. The impact of growth rate thresholds on CAEP (the 20 datasets on the X-axis are: 1.australian, 2. breast-w, 3.crx, 4.cleve, 5.diabetes, 6.german, 7. house-votes, 8.hepatitis, 9.horse-colic, 10. hypothyroid, 11.heart, 12.kr-vs-kp, 13.labor, 14. liver, 15.mushroom, 16. pima, 17.spect, 18.tictactoe, 19. vote, 20. wdbc)

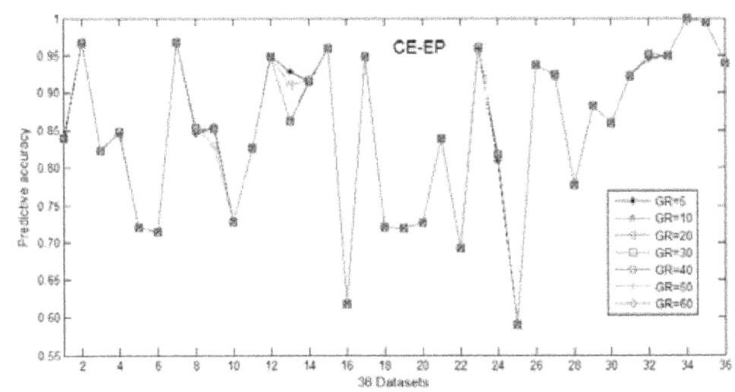

Fig.8. The impact of growth rate thresholds on CE-EP

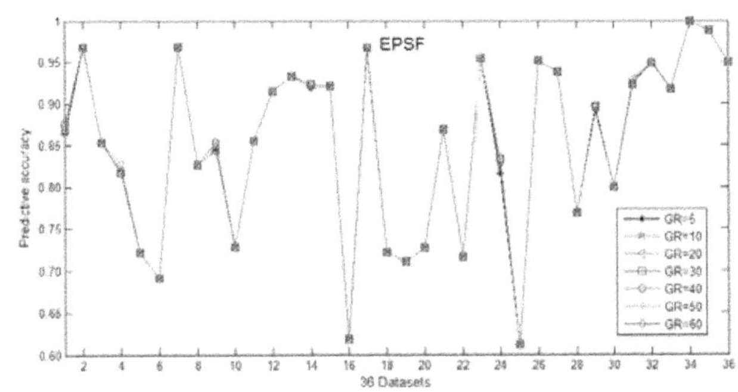

Fig.9. The impact of growth rate thresholds on *EPSF*

On the colon dataset, when the percentage of arrived features is up to 20% or 50%, the predictive accuracy of *EPSF* is the same as SVM. And when all features arrive, the accuracy of *EPSF* is up to 100%, and is better than SVM. For the remaining datasets, *EPSF* is never worse than AdaBoost and is also up to the accuracy of SVM without exhaustive search over the full feature space. This demonstrates that *EPSF* provides an effective and efficient solution to the EP mining problem when smoothing through the whole feature space is expensive or simply impossible.

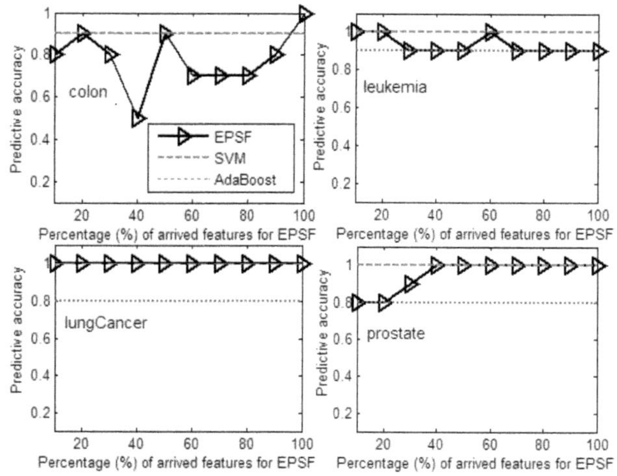

Fig.10. Comparative performance of *EPSF* without knowing the entire feature set before learning starts

5.7 A Summary of Experimental Results

Based on the comparative study in Sections 5.2 to 5.6, we have the following observations:

(1) On all datasets, *EPSF* produces significantly smaller numbers of patterns. It is more accurate than the four associative classifiers (CAEP, CBA, CMAR, and CPAR) and the two state-of-the-art non-associative classifiers (J48 and AdaBoost), and is very competitive with SVM. Moreover, as associative classifiers, CAEP, CBA, CMAR and CPAR cannot deal with high-dimensional datasets. As for the running time, *EPSF* is faster than CAEP on all datasets.

(2) *EPSF* vs. CE-EP. Both *EPSF* and CE-EP can handle very high feature dimensions yet get promising predictive accuracy. When the entire feature set is known in advance, on three evaluation metrics, accuracy, number of patterns and running time, *EPSF* is superior to CE-EP, although they are quite close. This empirically verifies the relationships between feature relevance and EP discriminability. In addition, with streaming feature selection, compared to CE-EP, *EPSF* deals well with not only a high feature dimension, but also an unknown full feature space before learning. It is possible that *EPSF* can avoid an exhaustive search over the full feature space.

6. CONCLUSION AND FUTURE WORK

In this paper, we explored the relationships between feature relevance and EP discriminability. By employing the relationships, we integrated streaming feature selection to guide a dynamic EP mining process. This new approach can handle not only a large feature space, but also a high-dimensional dataset without knowing its entire feature set in advance. Experimental results have demonstrated the effectiveness and efficiency of our approach. We plan to apply our new approach to real planetary images that can generate infinite texture-based features.

ACKNOWLEDGMENTS

This work is supported by the National 863 Program of China (2012AA011005), the National Natural Science Foundation of China (61070131, 61175051 and 61005007), the US National Science Foundation (CCF-0905337), and the US NASA Research Award (NNX09AK86G).

REFERENCES

[1] C. F. Aliferis, I. Tsamardinos, A. Statnikov & L.E. Brown. (2003) Causal Explorer: a causal probabilistic network learning toolkit for biomedical discovery. METMBS'03.

[2] Roberto J. Bayardo. (1998) Efficiently mining long patterns from databases. SIGMOD'98, 85-93.

[3] J. Bailey, T. Manoukian & K. Ramamohanarao. (2002) Fast algorithms for mining emerging patterns. PKDD'02, 39-50.

[4] J. Bailey, T. Manoukian & K. Ramamohanarao. (2003) A fast algorithm for computing hypergraph transversals and its application in mining emerging patterns. ICDM'03, 485-488.

[5] C.L. Blake & C.J. Merz. (1998) UCI Repository of Machine Learning Databases.

[6] H. Fan & K. Ramamohanarao. (2002) An efficient single-scan algorithm for mining essential jumping emerging patterns for classification. PAKDD'02, 456-462.

[7] H. Fan & K. Ramamohanarao. (2006) Fast discovery and the generalization of strong jumping emerging patterns for building compact and accurate classifiers. IEEE Transactions on Knowledge and Data Engineering, 18(6), 721-737.

[8] G. Fang, G. Pandey, W. Wang, M. Gupta, M. Steinbach, & V. Kumar. (2012) Mining low-support discriminative patterns from dense and high-dimensional data. IEEE Transactions on Knowledge and Data Engineering, 24(2), 279 - 294.

[9] G. Dong & J. Li. (1999) Efficient mining of emerging patterns: discovering trends and differences. KDD'99, 43-52.

[10] G. Dong, X. Zhang, L. Wong, & J. Li. (1999) CAEP: Classification by Aggregating Emerging Patterns. DS'99, 30-42.

[11] R. Kohavi & G. H. John. (1997) Wrappers for feature subset selection. Artificial Intelligence, 97, 273-324.

[12] J. Li, G. Dong, & K. Ramamohanarao. (2000) Making use of the most expressive jumping emerging patterns for classification. PAKDD'00, 220-232.

[13] J. Li, G. Dong & K. Ramamohanarao (2000). Instance-based classification by emerging patterns. PKDD'00, 191-200.

[14] W. Li, J. Han, & J. Pei. (2001) CMAR: accurate and efficient classification based on multiple-class association rule. ICDM'01, 369–376.

[15] B. Liu, W. Hsu, & Y. Ma. (1998) Integrating classification and association rule mining. KDD'98, 80-86.

[16] D. Lo, H. Cheng, J. Han, S. Khoo, & C. Sun. (2009) Classification of software behaviors for failure detection: a discriminative pattern mining approach. KDD'09, 557-566.

[17] E. Loekito & J. Bailey. (2006) Fast mining of high dimensional expressive contrast patterns using zero suppressed binary decision diagrams. KDD'06, 307–316.

[18] S.Mao & G.Dong. (2005) Discovery of highly differentiative gene groups from microarray gene expression data using the gene club approach. J. Bioinformatics and Computational Biology, 3(6):1263-1280.

[19] X. Wu, K.Yu, H. Wang & W. Ding. (2010) Online streaming feature selection. ICML'10, 1159-1166.

[20] X. Yin & J. Han. (2003) CPAR: classification based on predictive association rule. SDM'03, 369-376.

[21] K. Yu, X. Wu, W. Ding, H. Wang & H. Yao. (2011) Causal associative classification. ICDM'11, 914-923.

[22] L.Yu & H. Liu. (2004) Efficient feature selection via analysis of relevance and redundancy. J. of Machine Learning Research, 5, 1205-1224.

[23] X. Zhang, G. Dong & K. Ramamohanarao. (2000) Exploring constraints to efficiently mine emerging patterns from large high-dimensional datasets. KDD'00, 310-314.

[24] J. Zhou, D. Foster, R.A. Stine & L.H. Ungar. (2006) Streamwise feature selection. J. of Machine Learning Research, 7, 1861-1885.

Linear Space Direct Pattern Sampling using Coupling From The Past

Mario Boley
Fraunhofer IAIS and
University of Bonn
mario.boley@iais.fhg.de

Sandy Moens
University of Antwerp
sandy.moens@ua.ac.be

Thomas Gärtner
Fraunhofer IAIS and
University of Bonn
thomas.gaertner@iais.fhg.de

ABSTRACT

This paper shows how coupling from the past (CFTP) can be used to avoid time and memory bottlenecks in direct local pattern sampling procedures. Such procedures draw controlled amounts of suitably biased samples directly from the pattern space of a given dataset in polynomial time. Previous direct pattern sampling methods can produce patterns in rapid succession after some initial preprocessing phase. This preprocessing phase, however, turns out to be prohibitive in terms of time and memory for many datasets. We show how CFTP can be used to avoid any super-linear preprocessing and memory requirements. This allows to simulate more complex distributions, which previously were intractable. We show for a large number of public real-world datasets that these new algorithms are fast to execute and their pattern collections outperform previous approaches both in unsupervised as well as supervised contexts.

Categories and Subject Descriptors: H.2.8 [Database Management]: Database Applications—*Data Mining*

Keywords: Local patterns, Sampling, CFTP, Frequent sets

1. INTRODUCTION

This paper presents a unified sampling algorithm for efficiently drawing local patterns [11] directly from the pattern space of a given input dataset. Traditionally, local pattern discovery problems are often addressed by branch-and-bound search algorithms (e.g., for association discovery [16] or subgroup discovery [10]). These methods allow to exhaustively inspect a high-frequency fraction of the pattern space that is limited by the available computation time and sometimes memory (e.g., for best-first-search priority queues or candidate pruning). This can be problematic for two reasons: 1) Although it is reasonable to prune patterns of very low frequency, for the remaining patterns, frequency is not generally a good ranking criterion. 2) There is a high level of redundancy among the contained patterns, i.e., all local phenomena are approximately described by many alternative descriptions. While both factors seem to make the discovery task very hard, in particular the redundancy allows *random pattern collections* to perform robustly and well in many applications. For instance, suppose we are interested in combinations of low-frequency singletons (items) that have a relatively high conjunctive frequency. Then, instead of exhaustively listing a huge part of the pattern space, it can be much more efficient to just draw a small number of patterns according to a distribution $\mathcal{F}$ with, e.g.,

$$\mathcal{F}(F) = \mathsf{frq}^2(F) \prod_{e \in F} (1 - \mathsf{frq}(\{e\})) \ . \tag{1}$$

Direct pattern sampling refers to the idea of drawing such random collections directly from the pattern space—in polynomial time without physically materializing auxiliary parts of the space (see Figure 1(a)).

1.1 Two-step Direct Pattern Sampling

Many instances of direct pattern sampling can be realized by a simple two-step random procedure, which is a generalization of several previous algorithms for specific distributions [4]. The procedure is applicable if the desired distribution can be expressed as a product of singleton prior weights and a small number of factors based on variants of frequency. For the example given in Eq. (1) this holds because it consists of two frq-factors and multiplicative singletons weights $b(e) = 1 - \mathsf{frq}(\{e\})$. Many other variants are possible, including products of area, lift, disjunctive frequency, various discriminativity measures, and additive singleton weights (see Section 3). The two-step approach can be outlined as follows (see also Figure 1(b)):

Step 1 draw from the input data a tuple of data records of dimensionality equal to the number of frequency factors (with probability proportional to the total prior weight of all patterns it contains); and

Step 2 draw a pattern contained in that tuple according to the prior weights.

For the example of Eq. (1), Step 1 corresponds to drawing a pair of data records (D_1, D_2) according to the total multiplicative pattern weight

$$w(D_1, D_2) = \sum_{F \subseteq (D_1 \cap D_2)} \prod_{e \in F} (1 - \mathsf{frq}(\{e\})) \ .$$

Step 2 corresponds to drawing a pattern F supported by both, D_1 and D_2, according to $\prod_{e \in F}(1 - \mathsf{frq}(\{e\}))$.

In contrast to the cited branch-and-bound algorithms or earlier approaches to pattern sampling based on Markov

KDD'12, August 12–16, 2012, Beijing, China.

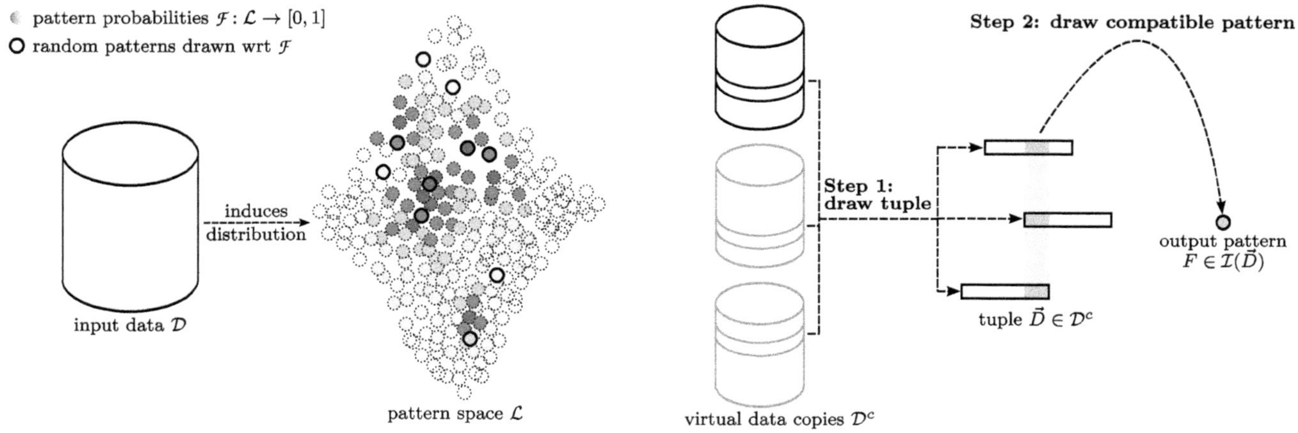

(a) direct pattern sampling (b) two-step sampling framework

Figure 1: Direct pattern sampling (a) means to directly materialize a set of random patterns from input data wrt to a distribution that favors useful patterns. Two-step sampling (b) is an approach to direct pattern sampling for distributions that are a product of c (negative) frequency factors: in Step 1 a tuple of c data records is drawn and in Step 2 a pattern is generated that is (not) supported by all elements of that tuple.

chain Monte Carlo [1, 3, 5], this two-step sampling framework can be implemented as a proper polynomial time algorithm. However, the direct (enumerative) implementation of Step 1 requires the availability of the weights w of all tuples of data records. Generally, for c frequency factors this corresponds to a data structure of size $|\mathcal{D}|^c$, which has to be constructed in a pre-processing phase. Depending on the available hardware, this renders distributions with two factors already infeasible for datasets with between 10^4 and 10^5 data records. Distributions with three factors are only feasible for very small datasets of at most a few 100 records.

1.2 Outline and Contributions

In this paper we substantially push the limits of the distributions one can practically simulate by replacing the enumerative implementation of Step 1 by an indirect approach based on coupling from the past[1] (CFTP [13, 18]; Sections 2 and 4). This allows to omit any super-linear preprocessing and memory requirements. Without this bottleneck a much wider range of datasets becomes accessible for simulating distributions with two factors and even with three and four factors. This is demonstrated empirically with 47 public real-world datasets. For many distributions we also show a theoretical polynomial upper bound on the expected running time. To fully utilize the power of this new algorithm, we lift the two-step sampling idea to a general framework and instantiate it with 17 different distributions based on pattern frequency, area, rare singletons, and label discriminativity (Section 3). We evaluate these distributions in both, an unsupervised context based on the compression-based pattern selector Krimp [19] and a supervised context based on a selection measure used in pattern-based classification (e.g., [6]). Our experiments show that the distributions that are enabled by the techniques of this paper, are indeed valuable for discovering patterns of greater utility: they outperform previously available distributions as well as top-k frequent closed set mining by a wide margin.

[1]See http://www-kd.iai.uni-bonn.de/index.php?page=software.

2. PRELIMINARIES

Before we present the technical contributions of the paper, we give a comprehensive summary of local pattern discovery and CFTP. Also we fix some basic notational conventions. We denote random variables by boldface letters, e.g., $\boldsymbol{r}$, and distributions by stylized letters, e.g., $d: \Omega \to [0,1]$. The **uniform distribution** on Ω is denoted $u[\Omega]$. For the most part we are interested in finite domains Ω. In this case, we are identifying distributions with row vectors, and, as a convention, for a set of positive weights $w: \Omega \to \mathbb{R}_+$ we denote by w the distribution on Ω resulting from normalizing the weights w, i.e., $w(x) = w(x)/\sum_{x' \in \Omega} w(x')$. For two distributions d, d' on finite Ω we denote by $\|d, d'\|_{\text{tv}} = 1/2 \sum_{x \in \Omega} |d(x) - d'(x)|$ the **total variation distance** between d and d'. When extending real-valued functions—in particular weight and probability functions—to sets, we interpret them additively, i.e., $w(\Omega') = \sum_{x \in \Omega'} w(x)$ for $\Omega' \subseteq \Omega$. For the **image set** of arbitrary functions f with domain X we write $\text{img}(f) = \{f(x) \colon x \in X\}$. The **power set** of a set X is denoted $\mathcal{P}(X)$.

2.1 Local Pattern Discovery

A binary **dataset** $\mathcal{D}$ over some finite set E of **singletons** (items) is a bag (multiset) of sets, called **data records**, $D_1, \ldots, D_m$ each of which is a subset of E. The **size** of $\mathcal{D}$, denoted by $\|\mathcal{D}\|$, is defined as the sum of all its data record sizes $\sum_{D \in \mathcal{D}} = |D|$. For a given dataset $\mathcal{D}$ over E, the **pattern space** (or pattern *language*) $\mathcal{L}(\mathcal{D})$ considered in this paper is the family of non-empty non-singleton subsets of E, i.e., $\mathcal{L}(\mathcal{D}) = \{F \subseteq E \colon |F| \geq 2\}$. The elements of $\mathcal{L}$ are interpreted conjunctively. That is, the *local* data portion described by a set $F \subseteq E$, called the **support (set)** of F in $\mathcal{D}$ and denoted $\mathcal{D}[F]$, is defined as the multiset of all data records from $\mathcal{D}$ that contain *all* elements of F, i.e., $\mathcal{D}[F] = \{D \in \mathcal{D} \colon D \supseteq F\}$.

We recap some basic measures of pattern utility that we use in this paper. The most fundamental measures for set patterns are the **support (count)**, i.e., the size of its support set $\mathsf{supp}(\mathcal{D}, F) = |\mathcal{D}[F]|$, and the **frequency**, i.e., the relative size of its support with respect to the total number of data records $\mathsf{frq}(\mathcal{D}, F) = |\mathcal{D}[F]| / |\mathcal{D}|$. Correspondingly, we define the **negative support** and the **negative frequency** as $\overline{\mathsf{supp}}(\mathcal{D}, F) = |\overline{\mathcal{D}}[F]|$ and $\overline{\mathsf{frq}}(\mathcal{D}, F) = |\overline{\mathcal{D}}[F]| / |\mathcal{D}|$, respectively, where $\overline{\mathcal{D}}[F] = \mathcal{D} \setminus \mathcal{D}[F]$ denotes the complement of the support set of F. A further measure considered here is the **area function** [9] $\mathsf{area}(\mathcal{D}, F) = |F|\,|\mathcal{D}[F]|$. In some application contexts, e.g., subgroup discovery or emerging pattern mining [7], each data record $D \in \mathcal{D}$ has an associated **class label** $l(D) \in \{\oplus, \ominus\}$. We denote by $\mathcal{D}_l \in \{\oplus, \ominus\}$ the data portion labeled l, i.e., $\mathcal{D}_l = \{D \in \mathcal{D} \colon l(D) = l\}$. For such datasets we consider as a representative utility measure the **information gain**, which is defined by

$$\mathsf{ig}(\mathcal{D}, F) = H(\mathcal{D}) - \mathsf{frq}(\mathcal{D}, F) H(\mathcal{D}[F]) - \overline{\mathsf{frq}}(\mathcal{D}, F) H(\overline{\mathcal{D}}[F])$$

where for a data portion $\mathcal{D}' \subseteq \mathcal{D}$

$$H(\mathcal{D}') = - \sum_{l \in \{\oplus, \ominus\}} |\mathcal{D}'_l| / |\mathcal{D}'| \log |\mathcal{D}'_l| / |\mathcal{D}'|$$

is the entropy of the label distribution associated with $\mathcal{D}'$. Note that all concepts discussed here can be easily extended to the case of more than two classes.

2.2 Coupling From The Past

Coupling from the past is a technique to acquire a sample from a distribution $\mathcal{d}$ on some domain Ω without explicitly constructing it. It is based on an indirect simulation of a Markov chain on Ω with a state distribution that converges to $\mathcal{d}$. Within the two-step sampling framework of this paper, it is used to efficiently implement Step 1.

A (time-homogeneous) Markov chain on finite state space Ω is a discrete time random process that can be specified by a stochastic **state transition matrix** $P \in [0, 1]^{\Omega \times \Omega}$. The chain is called **ergodic** if for all $x, y \in \Omega$ there is a number $t_0 \in \mathbb{N}$ of steps such that for all $t > t_0$ it holds that $P^t_{x,y} > 0$ ($P^t_{x,y}$ is equal to the probability of going from x to y in t steps). An ergodic Markov chain has a **stationary distribution**, i.e., a distribution $\mathcal{d} \colon \Omega \to [0, 1]$ with $\mathcal{d}P = \mathcal{d}$, that it converges to, i.e., for all distributions $\mathcal{d}'$ $\lim_{t \to \infty} \|\mathcal{d}' P^t, \mathcal{d}\|_{\text{tv}} = 0$. Given a desired target distribution $\mathcal{d}$ on Ω, a Markov chain with stationary distribution $\mathcal{d}$ can be constructed by using as transition procedure the **Metropolis-Hastings algorithm** [12]: in a current state x propose a successor state y with some proposal distribution $q_x \colon \Omega \to [0, 1]$ and then accept the proposal y as the new current state if $\boldsymbol{u} \leq (\mathcal{d}(y) q_y(x)) / (\mathcal{d}(x) q_x(y))$ with uniform $\boldsymbol{u} \sim u[[0, 1)]$ and otherwise keep x as current. The resulting transition probabilities are

$$P_{x,y} = q_x(y) \min \left(\frac{\mathcal{d}(y) q_y(x)}{\mathcal{d}(x) q_x(y)}, 1 \right) \tag{2}$$

if $q_x(y) > 0$ and 0 otherwise. If the Markov chain described by P is ergodic the stationary distribution is the desired $\mathcal{d}$.

In order to acquire a sample of the stationary distribution one needs an efficient single step simulation algorithm that computes a **random transition map** $\phi(\cdot, \boldsymbol{r}) \colon \Omega \to \Omega$ with a suitable random variable $\boldsymbol{r}$ such that

$$\forall x, y \in \Omega,\ \mathbb{P}[\phi(x, \boldsymbol{r}) = y] = P_{x,y} \ . \tag{3}$$

One way of sampling is then to run a **forward simulation** for t time steps from some starting state x_0, i.e., to compute $(\phi(\cdot, \boldsymbol{r}_t) \circ \cdots \circ \phi(\cdot, \boldsymbol{r}_1))(x_0)$ where the $\boldsymbol{r}_i$ are i.i.d. copies of $\boldsymbol{r}$. This is what is commonly referred to as Markov chain Monte Carlo method. Disadvantages of this approach are that it yields only approximate samples of $\mathcal{d}$ and that it is hard to come up with good a priori bounds for the required number of steps t. **Coupling from the past** (CFTP) is an alternative method that avoids these drawbacks. It is based on **backward simulations** defined by $\Phi_i = \Phi_{i-1} \circ \phi(\cdot, \boldsymbol{r}_i)$ for $i > 0$ and $\Phi_0(x) = x$. The crucial insight is: if for some $t > 0$ it holds that Φ_t is a constant function, i.e.,

$$\text{img}(\Phi_t) = \{\boldsymbol{x}\} \tag{4}$$

then $\boldsymbol{x}$ must be an observation of the stationary distribution ($\mathbb{P}[\boldsymbol{x} = x] = \mathcal{d}(x)$). This event is referred to as **coalescence**. Intuitively we can consider the backward simulation to be running already since infinitely far in the past, hence the current state is distributed according to $\mathcal{d}$, but for determining the current state no information beyond the **time horizon** t is required. This is because Eq. (4) corresponds to the event that all possible realizations of the Markov chain agree in their current state (using all possible starting states but fixing the source of randomness for state transition). The CFTP protocol checks Eq. (4) for Φ_t in exponentially increasing **epochs**, i.e., $t = 2^i$ for $i = 1, 2, \ldots$. The challenge is how to efficiently compute $\text{img}(\Phi_t)$. Naively keeping track of all realizations would diminish any advantage over enumerative sampling (explicitly constructing Ω). Sec. 4 shows how this can be achieved for our specific sampling task.

3. TWO-STEP DIRECT SAMPLING

In this section we present a general form of the two-step sampling framework and show how it can be instantiated to simulate various distributions relevant to local pattern discovery.

3.1 Distributions

Given an input dataset $\mathcal{D}$ over E, the framework can be used to sample according to distributions $\mathcal{F} \colon \mathcal{L}(\mathcal{D}) \to [0, 1]$ that can be expressed in the following product form:

$$\mathcal{F}(F) = b_\star(F) \prod_{i=1}^{c} q_i(\mathcal{D}_i, F) / Z \tag{5}$$

where Z is a normalizing constant, $\varsigma_i \in \{\mathsf{supp}, \overline{\mathsf{supp}}\}$ are support resp. negative support measures for some specific portions of the input data $\mathcal{D}_i \subseteq \mathcal{D}$, and $b_\star \colon \mathcal{P}(E) \to \mathbb{R}_+$ is a weight function based on positive singleton prior weights $b \colon E \to \mathbb{R}_+$ that are interpreted either multiplicative or additive, i.e., $b_\star(F) = \bigstar_{e \in F} b(e)$ with $\bigstar \in \{\Pi, \Sigma\}$.

Out of the many possible distributions that can be represented with Eq. (5), in this paper, we consider 17 representative examples with between one and four factors. The distributions can be categorized into four groups, each of which has a base-case with one or two factors, respectively. Distributions with a greater number of factors result then from multiplying the base-case with more frequency-factors. The groups are:

Frequency with base-case $\mathcal{F}_{\mathsf{frq}}(F) = \mathsf{frq}(\mathcal{D}, F)/Z$ by setting $q_1 = \mathsf{supp}$, $\mathcal{D}_1 = \mathcal{D}$, $b(e) = 1$, and $\star = \Pi$ (creating uniform priors $b_\star(\cdot) = 1$); and distributions $\mathcal{F}_{\mathsf{fq}^2}$, $\mathcal{F}_{\mathsf{fq}^3}$, $\mathcal{F}_{\mathsf{fq}^4}$ by setting factors accordingly.

Area with base-case $\mathcal{F}_{\mathsf{area}}(F) = \mathsf{area}(\mathcal{D}, F)/Z$ by setting $q_1 = \mathsf{supp}$, $\mathcal{D}_1 = \mathcal{D}$, $b(e) = 1$, and $\star = \Sigma$; and distributions $\mathcal{F}_{\mathsf{ar\text{-}fq}}$, $\mathcal{F}_{\mathsf{ar\text{-}fq}^2}$, $\mathcal{F}_{\mathsf{ar\text{-}fq}^3}$.

Algorithm 1 Two-Step Sampling Framework

Require: data portions $\mathcal{D}_1, \ldots, \mathcal{D}_c$ of input data $\mathcal{D}$ over E, measures $q_1, \ldots, q_c \in \{\mathsf{supp}, \overline{\mathsf{supp}}\}$, singleton weights $b\colon E \to \mathbb{R}_+$ and $\star \in \{\Pi, \Sigma\}$
Returns: random pattern $\boldsymbol{F} \sim \mathcal{F}$ as in Eq. (5)

1. **draw** tuple $\vec{\boldsymbol{D}} \sim w\colon \mathfrak{D} \to [0,1]$ with weights
$$w(\vec{D}) = b_\star(\mathcal{I}(\vec{D})) - b_\star(\overline{\mathcal{L}}(\vec{D}))$$
2. **draw** result pattern $\boldsymbol{F} \sim b'_\star\colon \mathcal{L} \to [0,1]$ with
$$b'_\star(F) = \begin{cases} b_\star(F) & \text{, if } F \in \mathcal{I}(\vec{\boldsymbol{D}}) \text{ and } |F| \geq 2 \\ 0 & \text{, otherwise} \end{cases}$$

Rare containing the example from the introduction with base-case $\mathcal{F}_{\mathsf{rare}}(F) = \mathsf{frq}(\mathcal{D}, F)\prod_{e \in F} \overline{\mathsf{frq}}(\mathcal{D}, \{e\})/Z$ by setting $q_1 = \mathsf{supp}$, $\mathcal{D}_1 = \mathcal{D}$, $b(e) = \overline{\mathsf{frq}}(\mathcal{D}, \{e\})$ and $\star = \Pi$; and distributions $\mathcal{F}_{\mathsf{rr}\cdot\mathsf{fq}}$, $\mathcal{F}_{\mathsf{rr}\cdot\mathsf{fq}^2}$, $\mathcal{F}_{\mathsf{rr}\cdot\mathsf{fq}^3}$.

Discriminativity containing distributions biased towards patterns with a high label discriminativity with base-case $\mathcal{F}_{\mathsf{dscr}}(F) = \mathsf{frq}(\mathcal{D}_\oplus, F)\overline{\mathsf{frq}}(\mathcal{D}_\ominus, F)$ by $q_1 = \mathsf{supp}$, $q_2 = \overline{\mathsf{supp}}$, $\mathcal{D}_1 = \mathcal{D}_\oplus$, $\mathcal{D}_2 = \mathcal{D}_\ominus$; and distributions $\mathcal{F}_{\mathsf{dr}\cdot\mathsf{fq}}$ and $\mathcal{F}_{\mathsf{dr}\cdot\mathsf{fq}^2}$ as well as distributions resulting from multiplying with frequency within the positively labeled data, i.e., $\mathcal{F}_{\mathsf{dr}\cdot\mathsf{fq}_+}$ and $\mathcal{F}_{\mathsf{dr}\cdot\mathsf{fq}_+^2}$.

Note that, while enumerating patterns in descending order of utility is NP-hard for the underlying measures of the area and the discriminativity group, using them as a bias for random pattern collections is possible in polynomial time using the sampling framework presented below.

3.2 Algorithm

The underlying idea of the algorithm follows a simple intuition: a pattern (not) supported by a random data record is likely to be (not) supported by many data records altogether. This principle can be further extended by considering patterns that are simultaneously (not) supported by independent data records drawn from the respective data portions. Algorithmically this can be realized in two steps: Step 1 is to draw a tuple of data records from the Cartesian product of the c data portions and then Step 2 is to draw a pattern compatible with the complete tuple according to its weight $b_\star$. Note that in Step 1 the tuple must be sampled according to the total weight of patterns compatible with it.

In order to precisely formalize this approach, let us introduce some further notation. We denote by $\mathfrak{D} = \times_{i=1}^{c} \mathcal{D}_i$ the **data product**, i.e., the set of all tuples that can be drawn in Step 1. Moreover, let $P \subseteq \{1, \ldots, c\}$ be the set of **positive indices**, i.e., $i \in \{1, \ldots, c\}$ with $q_i = \mathsf{supp}$ and correspondingly N the set of **negative indices**, i.e., $j \in \{1, \ldots, c\}$ with $q_j = \overline{\mathsf{supp}}$. Then a pattern $F \in \mathcal{L}$ is **compatible** with a tuple $\vec{D} \in \mathfrak{D}$ if it satisfies all support requirements, i.e., $F \subseteq \vec{D}(i)$ for all $i \in P$ and $F \not\subseteq \vec{D}(j)$ for all $j \in N$. We refer to the family of all patterns compatible with a tuple $\vec{D}$ as the patterns **induced** by $\vec{D}$ and denote it $\mathcal{I}(\vec{D})$

$$= \{F \subseteq E\colon (\forall i \in P, F \subseteq \vec{D}(i)) \wedge (\forall j \in N, F \not\subseteq \vec{D}(j))\} \ .$$

Finally let us denote the **induced non-pattern sets** by a $\vec{D} \in \mathfrak{D}$ as $\overline{\mathcal{L}}(\vec{D}) = \{F \in \mathcal{I}(\vec{D}) : |F| \leq 1\}$. With this we can express the weights $w\colon \mathfrak{D} \to R_+$ according to which the tuples must be sampled in Step 1 as

$$w(\vec{D}) = b_\star(\mathcal{I}(\vec{D})) - b_\star(\overline{\mathcal{L}}(\vec{D})) \ .$$

The complete sampling procedure is summarized in the formal pseudo-code given in Alg. 1. Before we turn to the efficiency of the algorithm we first note its correctness.

Proposition 1. *Given data portions $\mathcal{D}_1, \ldots, \mathcal{D}_c \subseteq \mathcal{D}$, $q_1, \ldots, q_c \in \{\mathsf{supp}, \overline{\mathsf{supp}}\}$, singleton weights $b\colon E \to \mathbb{R}_+$ and $\star \in \{\Pi, \Sigma\}$, Algorithm 1 returns a random pattern $\boldsymbol{F} \in \mathcal{L}(\mathcal{D})$ according to $\mathcal{F}$ as specified in Equation* (5).

Proof. We show that every pattern $F \in \mathcal{L}$ has the correct marginal probability with respect to the joint distribution of all pairs of inducing tuples and patterns drawn in line 1 and 2 of the algorithm, respectively. Let us denote by $\mathcal{I}^-(F) = \{\vec{D} \in \mathfrak{D}\colon F \in \mathcal{I}(\vec{D})\}$ the inverse induces-relation. Then we have

$$\begin{aligned}\mathbb{P}[\boldsymbol{F} = F] &= \sum_{\vec{D} \in \mathfrak{D}} \mathbb{P}[\vec{\boldsymbol{D}} = \vec{D}, \boldsymbol{F} = F] \\ &= \sum_{\vec{D} \in \mathcal{I}^-(F)} \frac{w(\vec{D})}{Z} \frac{b_\star(F)}{w(\vec{D})} \\ &= \left|\{\vec{D} \in \mathfrak{D}\colon F \in \mathcal{I}(\vec{D})\}\right| b_\star(F)/Z \\ &= b_\star(F) \prod_{i=1}^{c} q_i(\mathcal{D}_i, F)/Z = \mathcal{F}(F)\end{aligned}$$

with $Z = \sum_{\vec{D} \in \mathfrak{D}} b'_\star(\mathcal{I}(\vec{D}))$ being the sum of all prior weights of patterns among all inducing tuples. □

3.3 Implementation

We now describe how Algorithm 1 can be implemented efficiently. Step 1 requires to sample a tuple according to its weight. Since there are at most $|\mathcal{D}|^c$ inducing tuples, for some datasets this can be done enumeratively, i.e., by constructing a list of all weights $w(\vec{D}_1), \ldots, w(\vec{D}_{m^c})$, draw a random real $\boldsymbol{u} \sim u[[0,1)]$ and then return the unique $\vec{D}_i \in \mathfrak{D}$ with $\sum_{i=1}^{k-1} w(\vec{D}_i) \leq \boldsymbol{u} < \sum_{i=1}^{k} w(\vec{D}_i)$. This is what we refer to as the **enumerative baseline** for Step 1 [4]. In Section 4 we present a much more effective realization based on CFTP. However, both approaches require a method to efficiently compute the weights w. By the inclusion-exclusion formula

$$b_\star(\mathcal{I}(\vec{D})) = b_\star(\mathcal{P}(\bigcap_{i \in P} \vec{D}(i))) + \sum_{\emptyset \neq I \subseteq N} (-1)^{|I|} b_\star(\mathcal{P}(\bigcap_{j \in I \cup P} \vec{D}(j))) \quad (6)$$

the total weight of the family of patterns induced by some tuple $\vec{D}$ can be reduced to computing the total weights of power sets $\mathcal{P}(S)$ with $S \subseteq E$. This is independent of the choices of $\star$. Computing the total weight of all subsets of a set $S \subseteq E$ differs based on whether we have multiplicative or additive weights. For multiplicative weights we can use

$$b_\Pi(\mathcal{P}(S)) = \prod_{s \in S}(1 + b(e)) \quad (7)$$

and for additive weights the formula is

$$b_\Sigma(\mathcal{P}(S)) = b_\Sigma(S)2^{|S|-1} \ . \quad (8)$$

Both can be shown straightforwardly by induction on $|S|$. Note that although the evaluation of Equation 6 requires

Algorithm 2 Sequential Step 2

Require: tuple $\vec{D} \in \mathfrak{D}$,
Returns: random pattern $\boldsymbol{F} \sim b'_\star$ as in Step 2 of Alg. 1

1. $X \leftarrow \{\}, Y \leftarrow \{\}$
2. **for** $e \in E$ **do**
3.   with prob. $\mathbb{P}_{\boldsymbol{F}\sim b'_\star}[e \in \boldsymbol{F} \mid X \subseteq \boldsymbol{F}, Y \cap \boldsymbol{F} = \emptyset]$ **set** $X \leftarrow X \cup \{e\}$; otherwise **set** $Y \leftarrow Y \cup \{e\}$
4. **return** X

Algorithm 3 CFTP Step 1

Require: i.i.d. $\vec{\boldsymbol{C}}_t, \boldsymbol{u}_t \sim \overline{w} \times u[[0,1)]$ with w as in (11),
Returns: tuple $\vec{\boldsymbol{D}} \sim w$ as in Step 1 of Alg. 1

1. $i \leftarrow 1$, $\vec{D} \leftarrow \perp$
2. **while** $\vec{D} = \perp$ **do**
3. $i \leftarrow i + 1$
4.   **for** $t = 2^i, \ldots, 0$ **do**
5.   **if** $\boldsymbol{u}_t \le \frac{\overline{w}(\vec{D})}{w(\vec{D})} \frac{w(\vec{\boldsymbol{C}}_t)}{\overline{w}(\vec{\boldsymbol{C}}_t)}$ **then** $\vec{D} \leftarrow \vec{\boldsymbol{C}}_t$ //*with* $\frac{\overline{w}(\perp)}{w(\perp)} = 1$
6. **return** $\vec{D}$

the evaluation of $2^{|N|}$ terms, this does not pose a problem for the small values of $c \ge |N|$ we are usually interested in.

For the implementation of Step 2 we need to sample a pattern according to $b'_\star$, i.e., a pattern F according to $b_\star(F)$ that is compatible with $\vec{\boldsymbol{D}}$ drawn in Step 1. As a single tuple can induce $2^{|E|}$ patterns, enumerative sampling is not an option for this step even for small datasets. Instead one can use the following sequential selection process on the singletons $e \in E$ that keeps track of the set X of already selected and the set Y of already considered but discarded singletons (see Alg. 2): As long as one can find a singleton $e \notin (X \cup Y)$, add it to the current solution X with probability

$$\mathbb{P}_{\boldsymbol{F}\sim b'_\star}[e \in \boldsymbol{F} \mid X \subseteq \boldsymbol{F}, Y \cap \boldsymbol{F} = \emptyset] \tag{9}$$

or add it to Y otherwise. In order to compute these probabilities, let $\mathcal{I}_{X,Y}(\vec{D}) = \{F \in \mathcal{I}(\vec{D}) \colon X \subseteq F \wedge Y \cap F = \emptyset\}$ denote all sets induced by a tuple $\vec{D}$ that contain X and are disjoint with Y. With this we can express Eq. (9) as $b_\star(\mathcal{I}_{X+e,Y}(\vec{D}))/b_\star(\mathcal{I}_{X,Y}(\vec{D}))$ for the case that $|X| \ge 2$. For the cases when the current solution X contains only one or no element the expression has to be modified slightly: in order to avoid generating singletons or the empty set, their $b_\star$-values have to be subtracted from the above expression.

Finally, it remains to compute the expression $b_\star(\mathcal{I}_{X,Y}(\vec{D}))$. This can be reduced to Equations (7) and (8) for the weight computation by constructing record tuples $\vec{D}_{X,Y}$ such that $\mathcal{I}_{X,Y}(\vec{D}) = \{F \cup X \colon F \in \mathcal{I}(\vec{D}_{X,Y})\}$:

$$\vec{D}_{X,Y}(i) = \begin{cases} \emptyset & \text{, if } i \in N \text{ and } X \not\subseteq \vec{D}(i) \\ \vec{D}(i) \setminus (X \cup Y) & \text{, otherwise} \end{cases} .$$

Then we can re-write $b_\star(\mathcal{I}_{X,Y}(\vec{D}))$ based on the choice of $\star$ as either $b_\Pi(\mathcal{I}_{X,Y}(\vec{D})) = b_\Pi(X) b_\Pi(\vec{D}_{X,Y})$ or $b_\Sigma(\mathcal{I}_{X,Y}(\vec{D})) = \left|\mathcal{I}(\vec{D}_{X,Y})\right| b_\Sigma(X) + b_\Sigma(\vec{D}_{X,Y})$.

4. LINEAR SPACE SAMPLING

In this section we present a CFTP-based implementation of Step 1 of the two-step sampling framework. After developing the algorithm, we show that it is applicable to a wide range of real-world datasets for pattern distributions based on 2, 3, and even 4 factors.

4.1 CFTP Algorithm

In order to design a CFTP algorithm for sampling tuples $\vec{\boldsymbol{D}} \sim w$ we have to construct a Markov chain on the data product $\mathfrak{D}$ with stationary distribution w. Moreover, this chain must have a corresponding random transition function that allows us to efficiently compute backward simulations and to detect coalescence (Eq. (4)). The right stationary distribution can be achieved by using the Metropolis-Hastings construction (Eq. (2)) where on has the freedom of choosing a state proposal function. For this choice, we construct an upper bound of the weight function w, which results in a Markov chain that can be used efficiently within CFTP.

We start with the following state-transition specification (which is a simplified form of Eq. (2)): from a current state $\vec{D} \in \mathfrak{D}$ propose a new state $\vec{C} \in \mathfrak{D}$ based on some suitable proposal probability potential $q \colon \mathfrak{D} \to \mathbb{R}_+$ and accept this proposal if

$$\boldsymbol{u} \le \frac{w(\vec{C}) q(\vec{D})}{w(\vec{D}) q(\vec{C})}$$

where $\boldsymbol{u} \sim u[[0,1)]$. That is, independently of the current state, we have a single probability function $q \colon \mathfrak{D} \to [0,1]$ for proposing the next state. Moreover, we will construct q such that it is strictly positive, i.e., $q(\vec{C}) > 0$ for all $\vec{C} \in \mathfrak{D}$. Besides guaranteeing ergodicity of the Markov chain, this allows efficient coalescence monitoring. In order to discuss this, consider the representation of the chain by a random transition function $\phi(\cdot, \boldsymbol{r})$—as specified in Eq. (3). With the above construction this is given naturally by letting $\boldsymbol{r} = (\vec{\boldsymbol{C}}, \boldsymbol{u})$ be a pair of a proposed state and a unit random real for checking acceptance. Suppose one knows a lower bound l on $\min_{\vec{D} \in \mathfrak{D}} q(\vec{D})/w(\vec{D})$. Then detecting coalescence, i.e., checking $|\mathrm{img}(\Phi_t)| = 1$, can be done by the implication

$$\boldsymbol{u}_i \le l \frac{w(\vec{\boldsymbol{C}}_i)}{q(\vec{\boldsymbol{C}}_i)} \Rightarrow \left|\mathrm{img}(\phi(\cdot, (\vec{\boldsymbol{C}}_i, \boldsymbol{u}_i)))\right| = 1 \tag{10}$$

for $i \in \{t, \ldots, 1\}$, because the left-hand side implies that after applying $\phi(\vec{D}, (\vec{\boldsymbol{C}}_i, \boldsymbol{u}_i))$ all possible chain realizations coalesce to $\vec{\boldsymbol{C}}_i$ independent of their current state $\vec{D}$. A natural choice to achieve this is using the uniform distribution for proposal, i.e., to set $q = u[\mathfrak{D}]$. It can be efficiently simulated and finding the lower bound l then boils down to finding an upper bound to $\max_{\vec{D} \in \mathfrak{D}} w(\vec{D})$, which can be done efficiently for many relevant choices of the final pattern distribution $\mathcal{F}$.

However, one can improve this choice of the proposal probabilities in a way that—besides allowing efficient backward simulation and coalescence monitoring—also improves the expected coalescence time substantially. Suppose an upper bound to the weight function w is used for proposing new tuples in the CFTP algorithm, i.e., setting $q(\cdot) = \overline{w}(\cdot)$ with $\overline{w}(\vec{D}) \ge w(\vec{D})$ for all $\vec{D} \in \mathfrak{D}$. Then the lower bound l that is used in Eq. (10) becomes 1 by construction. On the one hand, we want an upper bound that is as tight as possible in order to maximize the coalescence probability—and consequently to minimize the computation time. On the other hand, we need a proposal function that we can efficiently compute and use for sampling. The following def-

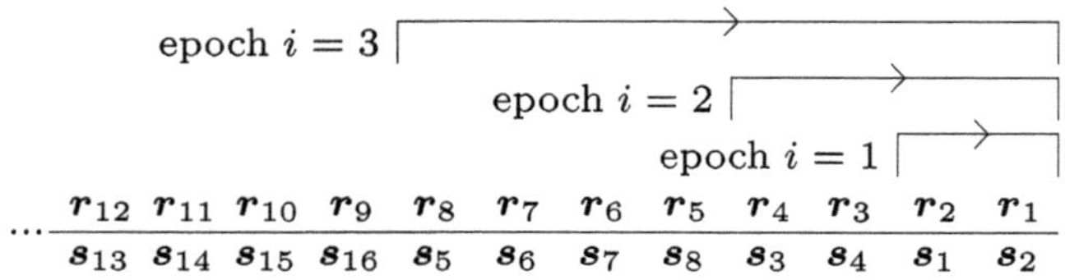

Figure 2: Order in which the elements of the infinite random string $(r_i)_{i\in\mathbb{N}}$ are materialized by Alg. 3. The time horizon is doubled in every epoch. Only seed of random sequence $(s_i)_{i\in\mathbb{N}}$ has to be stored to efficiently re-construct earlier materialized r_i.

inition achieves the latter while at the same time provides good coalescence probabilities in theory and in practice (see Section 4.2):

$$\overline{w}(\vec{D}) = \prod_{i=1}^{c} \sqrt[c]{w_i(\vec{D}(i))} \tag{11}$$

where $w_i \colon \mathcal{D}_i \to \mathbb{R}_+$ defined by

$$w_i(D) = \begin{cases} b_\star(\mathcal{P}(D)) - b_\star(\overline{\mathcal{L}}(D)) & ,\text{for } i \in P \\ b_\star(\mathcal{P}(E) \setminus \mathcal{P}(D)) - b_\star(\overline{\mathcal{L}}(D)) & ,\text{for } i \in N \end{cases}$$

are component-wise weight functions. The w_i upper bound w in the following sense: for all tuples $\vec{D}$ with $\vec{D}(i) = D$ we have $w_i(D) \geq w(\vec{D})$. This follows from $b_\star$ being positive and $\mathcal{P}(\vec{D}(i)) \supseteq \mathcal{I}(\vec{D})$ for $i \in P$ as well as $\mathcal{P}(E) \setminus \mathcal{P}(\vec{D}(j)) \supseteq \mathcal{I}(\vec{D})$ for $j \in N$. Hence, we also have for their geometric mean $\overline{w}(\vec{D}) \geq w(\vec{D})$ as desired. Also, simulating $\vec{C} \sim \overline{w}$ can be done efficiently by drawing $\vec{C}(i)$ according to w_i independently per component. Implementing this enumeratively is not a problem, because the number of required weights are linear in the input and have to be computed only once.

This concludes the specification of our instantiation of CFTP. All ideas are summarized in the pseudo-code of Alg. 3 and in the proof of the following correctness statement.

PROPOSITION 2. *With probability 1 Algorithm 3 terminates and returns a tuple drawn according to w.*

PROOF. Suppose the algorithm terminates with final values of i and $\vec{D}$ equal to i^* and $\vec{D}^*$, respectively. In this case the if-condition in line 5 was true for some value t^* of t when $\vec{D} = \perp$. Then

$$u_{t^*} \leq 1 \cdot \frac{w(\vec{C}_{t^*})}{\overline{w}(\vec{C}_{t^*})} \leq \frac{\overline{w}(\vec{B})}{w(\vec{B})} \frac{w(\vec{C}_{t^*})}{\overline{w}(\vec{C}_{t^*})}$$

for all $\vec{B} \in \mathfrak{D}$ because $\overline{w}$ is an upper bound to w, hence, $\overline{w}(\vec{B})/w(\vec{B}) \geq 1$. It follows that in this iteration Alg. 3 correctly computes $\mathrm{img}(\phi(\mathfrak{D}, (\vec{C}_{t^*}, u_{t^*})) = \{\vec{C}_{t^*}\}$. For $t < t^*$ the inner loop correctly computes $\phi(\vec{D}, (\vec{C}_t, u_t))$. Thus, when the algorithm terminates it has correctly computed

$$\begin{aligned} &\mathrm{img}(\Phi_{2^{i^*}}) = \\ &\mathrm{img}(\phi(\cdot, (\vec{C}_1, u_1)) \circ \cdots \circ \phi(\cdot, (\vec{C}_{t^*}, u_{t^*}))) = \{\vec{D}^*\} \end{aligned}$$

and by Eq. (4) we know that the output $\vec{D}^* \sim w$ as required. That termination has a probability of 1 can be verified by checking that there is a tuple $\vec{B} \in \mathfrak{D}$ with $w(\vec{B}) > 0$ and consequently also $\overline{w}(\vec{B}) > 0$ (assuming $\mathcal{F}$ is a distribution). It follows that for every t there is a strictly positive probability of coalescence, hence, the probability of non-coalescence ($\vec{D} = \perp$) converges to zero for increasing t. □

Before we investigate the time requirements of Algorithm 3, we end this subsection with a remark clarifying that it can be implemented memory efficient. That is, it indeed leads to a linear space pattern sampling algorithm.

Remark 1. Regarding the *memory requirements*, it might seem that Algorithm 3 uses unbounded space because the realizations of the $r_t = (\vec{C}_t, u_t)$ have to be reused in every epoch. However, assuming a standard model of randomness, this can be achieved with constant memory and without asymptotic time overhead. Assume the random sequence can be enumerated with unit delay between any two elements and constant memory from a single seed. The problem is that the random sequence is accessed in a reverse non-consecutive order: in epoch i the random variables r_{2^i} down through $r_{2^{i-1}+1}$ are realized and then the realizations of the first 2^{i-1} variables are reused. Let $(s_i)_{i\in\mathbb{N}}$ be the sequence we can generate consecutively. Applying a reordering scheme (see Fig. 2) we generate r_t based on $s_{t'}$ with

$$t' = 3 \cdot 2^{\lceil \log_2 t \rceil - 1} - t + 1$$

and reconstruct s_t from s_1 for t with $\lceil \log_2 t \rceil \neq \lceil \log_2 t - 1 \rceil$. The total reconstruction cost within a complete inner loop is $2t$—not effecting the asymptotic time complexity.

dataset	irreg	$\mathcal{F}_{\mathsf{frq}^3}$	$\mathcal{F}_{\mathsf{rr}\cdot\mathsf{fq}^2}$
pumsb	0	1	> 40.6
ionosphere	0	1	2.1
anneal	0	1	8.3
krvskp	0	1	53.4
hypothyroid	0.03	1.3	13.3
sick	0.03	1.4	15.4
censusincome2000	0.05	3.2	243.3
vote	0.06	1.8	2.6
icdmabstracts	0.23	> 8947848.9	> 8347048.2
mammals	0.28	> 53938.7	8716

Table 1: Reduction factor of simulation steps when using proposals w.r.t. $\overline{w}$ instead of uniform; higher irregularity (irreg) of dataset increases gain.

4.2 Time Complexity

For a theoretical analysis of the time complexity of Algorithm 3, note that the expected computation time is proportional to the expected time of the event that a complete coupling coalesces in one step. This time is geometrically distributed with a success probability

$$p_c = \mathbb{P}[w(\vec{C})/\overline{w}(\vec{C}) \geq u] \ ,$$

hence the expected time is $1/p_c$. This probability, in turn, depends on how close $\overline{w}$ is to w, and, unfortunately, in general this can be exponentially small in the input size. However, in the special case of $\mathcal{D}_i = \mathcal{D}$ and $q_i = \mathsf{supp}$ for $i \in \{1, \ldots, c\}$, the worse case situation is much better; namely at most proportional to the inverse of the state space size $|\mathcal{D}|^c$. This setting is for instance met in all the distributions we consider in this paper except the discriminativity variants (but as we will see below, in practice the behavior of discrimininativity does not differ much from the theoretically good cases). The bound can be seen as follows: p_c is bounded from below by the probability that a tuple is proposed for which $\overline{w}$ is a sharp estimation of w, i.e., $\mathbb{P}[\overline{w}(\vec{C}) = w(\vec{C})] \leq p_c$. In particular this holds for the tuples $\vec{D}$ with $\vec{D}(1) = \cdots = \vec{D}(c)$. Let $\vec{D}^*$ be one of these tuples maximizing w. Then $\vec{D}^*$ is proposed with probability

$$\begin{aligned}\overline{w}(\vec{D}^*) &= \prod_{i=1}^{c} w_i(\vec{D}^*(i)) \qquad (12)\\ &= \prod_{i=1}^{c} \frac{\max_{D \in \mathcal{D}} b_\star(\mathcal{P}(D))}{\sum_{D \in \mathcal{D}} b_\star(\mathcal{P}(D))} \geq \prod_{i=1}^{c} \frac{1}{|\mathcal{D}|} = \frac{1}{|\mathcal{D}|^c}\end{aligned}$$

as required. Thus, the order of the expected time is upper bounded by the pre-processing time $|\mathcal{D}|^c$ of the enumerative algorithm for drawing tuples—in other words: the CFTP variant can asymptotically not be worse than the straightforward implementation. It can, however, be much better. In contrast to the enumerative algorithm, CFTP is not bound to its worse case behavior. Instead it is adaptive to the hardness of the input dataset, which is why it is sometimes referred to as a "true algorithm" (e.g., [13]). Thus, ultimately the computation time "in practice" is the relevant quantity.

In order to assess the practical performance, we report the empirical[2] time requirements for 47 real-world datasets taken from the UCI machine learning repository [8] and from the FIMI repository [2] for adding some larger datasets. We test the CFTP algorithm against the enumerative solution for all distributions defined in Section 3.1 with $c \geq 2$ (for $c = 1$ the two algorithms are essentially identical). For having a realistic settings, we impose some memory constraint as well as some time constraint. The specific choices (here we use a 2GB memory cap and 10 minute time cap) carry relatively little significance for the baseline method: due to the preprocessing bottleneck, the enumerative baseline method has a fixed behavior in terms of both, time and space, that grows exponentially in c and is determined by the number of data records m. Hence, qualitatively we end up with the same results if we, e.g., double the limits (note that for the given settings it always hits the memory limit before it hits the time limit). The CFTP algorithm, on the other hand, is not affected by memory limits at all (as long as the dataset itself fits into main memory), and, although also affected by c and m can potentially behave much better than its worst case (m^c). What is more important is to fix a realistic number of patterns, because the enumerative method for Step 1 has to go through the preprocessing bottleneck only once, and then—given that it does not run out of memory—patterns are produced rapidly in time $\log^c m$ per pattern. Although the expected time of CFTP can be even smaller than $\log^c m$, the pattern number is still a sensitive quantity because it directly influences the baseline method's relative time per pattern—in contrast, for CFTP it is constant on expectation. For this purpose we use function (13) from the empirical evaluation of the pattern collections in application contexts (Section 5).

Table 2 contains a list of all datasets along with the number of data records, patterns, and the detailed results for the frequency distributions. The first observation is that, indeed, CFTP shows the anticipated good behavior: although the theoretical bound grows exponentially in the number of factors, even for $\mathcal{F}_{\mathsf{fq}^4}$ with $c = 4$ the computation can be performed within 1 seconds for 21 datasets, and for all but 3 datasets it can at least be performed within the 10 minute time limit. In contrast, the enumerative implementation of Step 1 runs out of memory already for small datasets as determined by m and c. The time requirements for the area variants, $\mathcal{F}_{\mathsf{area}}$ through $\mathcal{F}_{\mathsf{ar}\cdot\mathsf{fq}^3}$, are essentially identical to the frequency variants. The reason for this is that they share the characteristic that the proposal weights $\overline{w}_i$ are only a function of the data record size. In case the dataset is (close to) being regular, this improves the coalescence time bound because all of the tuples of the form $\vec{D}(1) = \cdots = \vec{D}(c)$ contribute to the bound of Eq. 12. In contrast, the variants of $\mathcal{F}_{\mathsf{rare}}$ do not have this property, and, consequently for some datasets the behavior deviates upwards. All three groups, however, have the same abort statistics: while the enumerative baseline fails on 9 of the 47 datasets for 2-factor distributions, on 38 for $c = 3$, and on 46 for $c = 4$, the CFTP implementation fails on no dataset for $c = 2$, on 2 for $c = 3$, and on 3 for $c = 4$. Finally, although, not polynomially bounded, the variants of $\mathcal{F}_{\mathsf{dscr}}$ typically are even the least demanding. This is because $\mathfrak{D}$ is smaller for these distributions because

[2]Test system is Intel Core i5, 2.4GHz with Java 7 (Win7).

			$\mathcal{F}_{\mathsf{fq}^2}$		$\mathcal{F}_{\mathsf{fq}^3}$		$\mathcal{F}_{\mathsf{fq}^4}$	
dataset	#m	#pat	em	cp	em	cp	em	cp
labor	57	64	0	0	0	0	12	1
zoo	101	119	0	0	1	0	-	0
lymph	148	136	0	0	4	0	-	1
iris	150	36	0	0	3	0	-	0
hepatitis	155	130	0	0	5	1	-	2
wine	178	104	0	0	6	1	-	20
autos	205	191	0	0	12	5	-	214
glass	214	77	0	0	11	0	-	0
audiology	226	531	0	0	17	1	-	6
heartstatlog	270	113	0	0	-	0	-	1
breastcancer	286	73	0	0	-	0	-	0
hearth	294	90	0	0	-	0	-	0
heartc	303	107	0	0	-	0	-	2
primarytumor	339	142	0	0	-	0	-	1
ionosphere	351	295	0	0	-	26	-	-
colic	366	144	0	0	-	7	-	82
vote	435	140	0	0	-	0	-	0
balancescale	625	46	0	0	-	0	-	0
soybean	683	301	1	0	-	4	-	44
credita	690	141	1	0	-	1	-	4
breastw	699	85	0	0	-	0	-	0
diabetes	768	86	1	0	-	0	-	1
vehicle	846	184	1	0	-	5	-	135
icdmabstracts	859	477	1	0	-	0	-	0
annealsmall	898	137	1	0	-	0	-	1
anneal	898	382	1	0	-	1	-	2
tictactoe	958	99	1	0	-	0	-	1
vowel	990	139	1	0	-	2	-	32
creditg	1000	209	1	0	-	4	-	22
germanstatlog	1000	209	1	0	-	4	-	21
pokerh2000	2000	120	5	0	-	1	-	10
censusinc2000	2000	427	5	0	-	6	-	98
mammals [15]	2183	266	6	0	-	1	-	16
segment	2310	223	7	0	-	3	-	37
krvskp	3196	430	15	0	-	2	-	26
hypothyroid	3772	332	19	0	-	1	-	1
sick	3772	332	19	0	-	1	-	1
abalone	4177	108	22	0	-	0	-	0
mushroom	8124	285	-	0	-	3	-	25
censusinc10K	10K	518	-	1	-	9	-	141
pendigits	11K	228	-	1	-	6	-	90
nursery	13K	122	-	0	-	0	-	1
letter	20K	242	-	1	-	29	-	421
adult	49K	218	-	1	-	1	-	1
pumsb	49K	1153	-	28	-	-	-	-
connect	68K	689	-	3	-	36	-	256
accidents	340K	606	-	43	-	-	-	-

Table 2: Datasets along with detailed computation time for the frequency distributions; "-" corresponds to out of time (>10 minutes) for CFTP or out of memory (>2GB) for enumerative; in case of CFTP the median of five repetitions is reported.

the $\mathcal{D}_l$ are proper subsets of $\mathcal{D}$, hence, the individual factors are smaller. The corresponding CFTP abort statistics are 0, 1, and 4 for 2, 3, and 4 factors, respectively; as opposed to 5, 28, and 46 for the enumerative baseline. In summary, the CFTP technique substantially increases the set of distributions and datasets for which two-step sampling is applicable.

We close this investigation with a note on the effectiveness of choosing $\overline{w}$ over uniform as proposal probabilities. Table 1 contains the reduction factor of simulated time steps for a few representative datasets. Again, the behavior differs between the $\mathcal{F}_{\mathsf{rare}}$ variants and, e.g., the $\mathcal{F}_{\mathsf{frq}}$ variants. Here the reason is that the closer the dataset is to being regular (i.e., $|D| = |D'|$ all $D, D' \in \mathcal{D}$) the closer is $\overline{w}$ to u for those distributions where $\overline{w}_i$ is a function of the record size. Consequently, while the gain of $\overline{w}$ over u is substantial throughout all datasets for rare, for the other distributions this depends on the degree of regularity. Irregularity is measured here by $\|D| - \text{avg}_{D\in\mathcal{D}} |D|| / \|\mathcal{D}\|$.

5. EVALUATION OF DISTRIBUTIONS

In the previous sections we developed an algorithm that can be used to efficiently perform pattern sampling based on three or even four factor distributions. Now we show that using such distributions brings indeed a substantial boost in pattern quality.

5.1 Unsupervised Performance

In order to assess the unsupervised descriptive performance of a pattern collection we use the pattern-based compressor Krimp [19]. Krimp selects a sub-collection of the extracted patterns and builds a code table from them along with a compressed version of the input dataset. The code table assigns code symbols to the patterns it contains, and occurrences of the patterns are replaced by their respective code symbols in the compressed database. Krimp approximates a minimum description length code table, i.e., one that minimizes the combined length of the code table and the compressed dataset. Note that this principle factors in redundancy—a pattern is not selected for the code table if it does not achieve sufficient additional compression (over the other selected patterns) that compensates for its own size. The size reduction achieved this way can be regarded as a measure of the information about the dataset that is contained in a pattern collection.

	c	avg r	r1	rq	rh	avg s
area · frq^2	3	3.70	9	23	37	0.767
frq^3	3	4.48	2	16	38	0.768
rare · frq^3	4	4.52	15	22	29	0.768
area · frq^3	4	4.77	1	17	34	0.767
frq^4	4	5.32	2	17	29	0.768
rare · frq^2	3	6.14	6	13	25	0.797
frq^2	2	7.05	1	4	16	0.785
frq	1	7.45	2	4	14	0.787
rare · frq	2	7.48	0	4	14	0.800
area · frq	2	7.75	2	6	15	0.790
top-k closed	–	8.61	4	5	11	0.824
area	1	11.50	0	1	1	0.859
rare	1	11.95	0	1	1	0.890

Table 3: Pattern extraction methods ordered by average rank (avg r) in Krimp experiments; number of factors (c), number of datasets with top rank (r1), upper quarter rank (rq), upper half rank (rh), and average score, i.e., relative size reduction (avg s).

In our experiment we use all datasets from Table 2, and for each we consider pattern collections consisting of size

$$k(\mathcal{D}) = \log |\mathcal{D}| \operatorname*{avg}_{D\in\mathcal{D}} |D| \ . \tag{13}$$

We include all distributions from Section 3.1 that do not rely on label information. In addition we include top-k frequent closed set extraction as a deterministic pattern collection that can be extracted efficiently (see [17]), i.e., in polynomial time of the combined size of the input dataset and the output pattern collection. The same could be done with the top-k frequent patterns (including non-closed), but closed patterns are a stronger baseline for moderate values of k. Thus, all methods considered here are true polynomial (expected) time algorithms.

The results are summarized in Table 3 where all methods are listed ordered according to the average rank they achieved on all datasets. It stands out firmly that the distribution with $c = 3$ and $c = 4$ are dominating the ranking. A notable difference between the family of distributions based on rare singletons to the others is that it stills receives a substantial gain in the $c = 4$ variant over the $c = 3$ variant. In contrast, for the families based on plain frequency and area, the fourth factor does not improve the average rank anymore. For some datasets it is even counter-productive. It is not surprising that the effectiveness of adding powers of frequency to the distributions has a natural limit, because at a certain point this will degenerate the pattern collections again to sets of high frequency and high redundancy patterns. Finally, it can be observed that already the distributions with $c = 2$ outperform the deterministic baseline of the top-k closed frequent sets.

5.2 Supervised Performance

	c	avg r	r1	rq	rh	avg s
dscr · frq_+^2	4	4.38	19	28	34	2.118
rare · frq^2	3	4.63	6	19	36	1.734
dscr · frq_+	3	4.8	5	23	36	1.966
frq^3	3	7	0	8	30	1.772
rare · frq	2	7.15	2	11	26	1.546
rare · frq^3	4	7.33	3	15	27	1.589
dscr · frq	3	7.58	1	11	27	1.771
dscr · frq^2	4	7.7	0	12	30	1.844
area · frq^2	3	8.53	0	6	22	1.663
frq^4	4	8.98	0	6	20	1.689
area · frq^3	4	8.98	0	6	20	1.644
frq^2	2	10.18	0	3	13	1.406
area · frq	2	11.68	0	0	8	1.298
top-k closed	–	12.2	3	5	12	1.024
dscr	2	13.95	0	0	3	0.829
rare	1	14.1	0	1	4	0.788
frq	1	15.7	0	1	1	0.667
area	1	16.18	1	1	2	0.646

Table 4: Pattern extraction methods ordered by their average rank (avg r) in the information gain experiments with all attributes as in Table 3.

In a second experiment, we evaluate the supervised performance of the random pattern collections. Patterns that help distinguish between different classes, are needed in a variety of application contexts, ranging from exploratory data analysis to pattern-based-classification. In exploratory data analysis a domain expert considers the patterns in their own right, e.g., for finding malfunctioning or high-value subgroups of a population. In pattern-based-classification the patterns are human-readable building blocks of a compound prediction model [14]. In both cases, redundant information about the target label, i.e., information that is already contained in other result patterns, is useless or even counterproductive. Therefore, we settle here for an evaluation measure that is based on the pattern's information gain, down-weighted by its similarity to more informative patterns. The score of a pattern collection $\mathcal{F} = \{F_1, \ldots, F_k\}$, where the F_i are in descending order of information gain, is defined as

$$s(\mathcal{F}) = \mathsf{ig}(F_1) + \sum_{i=2}^{k} \mathsf{ig}(F_i) \min_{j \in \{1,\ldots,i\}} \delta(F_j, F_i)$$

where $\delta(F_i, F_j)$ is the Jaccard distance between the extension of the patterns

$$\delta(F_i, F_j) = 1 - |\mathcal{D}[F_i] \cap \mathcal{D}[F_j]| \,/\, |\mathcal{D}[F_i] \cup \mathcal{D}[F_j]| \ .$$

When used for feature selection, this measure leads to high accuracy pattern-based classifiers [6].

The results are summarized in Table 4; this time also including the distributions from the discriminativity group. Again, all methods are ordered according to the average rank achieved on all datasets. Similarly to the unsupervised performance, also in terms of supervised performance, distributions with $c = 3$ and $c = 4$ dominate the ranking with the only exception of $\mathsf{rare} \cdot \mathsf{frq}$. A further similarity is that variants with four factors do not necessarily improve over their three factor counterparts. An important exception is the overall best method $\mathsf{dscr} \cdot \mathsf{frq}_+^2$. In this case, the additional factor further emphasizes the difference in the support of the patterns per class, hence it is chosen sensitively to the supervised evaluation scenario. Finally, note that top-k frequent closed sets are again outperformed by most of the random collections.

6. DISCUSSION

The CFTP-based variant of the two-step sampling framework that is developed in this paper avoids the super-linear space requirement of the previous enumerative version of Step 1. In addition, the expected running time of CFTP is usually much smaller than the previously fixed pre-processing time, and for many pattern distributions it is also theoretically upper bounded by the complexity of the enumerative Step 1. Consequently, the new algorithm allows to efficiently draw samples for previously intractable distributions containing up to four factors. The experimental evaluation of these distributions shows that going up from two to three or four factors, indeed, boosts the pattern quality substantially.

At the same time one can also observe a satiation effect in the sense that the step from three to four factors does not provide as much gain as the step from two to three. Therefore, for future research it appears to be of higher priority to identify the distributions best suited for specific application tasks than to further boost the number of possible factors. In particular, stratified random pattern collections that are drawn from a mixture of distributions (and possible deterministic methods) appear to be worth investigating. Also, a currently unused potential lies in post-processing the random pattern collections by applying fast local optimization procedures. Finally, it is open how to lift the two-step sampling framework to large scale inputs that do not fit into main memory.

Acknowledgment. This work was supported by the DFG (GA 1615/2-1 and GA 1615/1-1), the EC (ICT-FP7-LIFT-255951) and Research Foundation Flanders (FWO).

7. REFERENCES

[1] M. Al Hasan and M. J. Zaki. Output space sampling for graph patterns. *PVLDB*, 2(1):730–741, 2009.

[2] R. Bayardo, B. Goethals, and M. J. Zaki, editors. *IEEE ICDM Workshop on Frequent Itemset Mining Implementations, 2004*, volume 126 of *CEUR Workshop Proceedings*. CEUR-WS org, 2004.

[3] M. Boley, T. Gärtner, and H. Grosskreutz. Formal concept sampling for counting and threshold-free local pattern mining. In *SDM*, pages 177–188, 2010.

[4] M. Boley, C. Lucchese, D. Paurat, and T. Gärtner. Direct local pattern sampling by efficient two-step random procedures. In *KDD*, pages 582–590, 2011.

[5] V. Chaoji, M. A. Hasan, S. Salem, J. Besson, and M. J. Zaki. Origami: A novel and effective approach for mining representative orthogonal graph patterns. *Stat. Anal. and Data Min.*, 1(2):67–84, 2008.

[6] H. Cheng, X. Yan, J. Han, and C.-W. Hsu. Discriminative frequent pattern analysis for effective classification. In *ICDE*, pages 716–725, 2007.

[7] G. Dong and J. Li. Efficient mining of emerging patterns: Discovering trends and differences. In *KDD*, pages 43–52. ACM, 1999.

[8] A. Frank and A. Asuncion. UCI machine learning repository, 2010.

[9] F. Geerts, B. Goethals, and T. Mielikäinen. Tiling databases. In *DS*, pages 278–289. Springer, 2004.

[10] H. Grosskreutz, S. Rüping, and S Wrobel. Tight optimistic estimates for fast subgroup discovery. In *ECML/PKDD, Part I*, pages 440–456, 2008.

[11] D. J. Hand. Pattern detection and discovery. In *ESF Exploratory Workshop on Pattern Detection and Discovery*, pages 1–12. Springer, 2002.

[12] W. Hastings. Monte carlo sampling methods using markov chains and their applications. *Biometrika*, 57(1):97–109, 1970.

[13] M. Huber. Perfect sampling using bounding chains. *Annals of App. Prob.*, 14(2):734–753, 2004.

[14] A. J. Knobbe, B. Crémilleux, J. Fürnkranz, and M. Scholz. From local patterns to global models: the lego approach to data mining. In *From Local Patterns to Global Models: Proceedings of the ECML/PKDD 2008 Workshop*, 2008.

[15] A. Mitchell-Jones. *The Atlas of European Mammals*. Poyser Natural History. T & AD Poyser.

[16] S. Morishita and J. Sese. Traversing itemset lattice with statistical metric pruning. In *PODS*, pages 226–236, 2000.

[17] A. Pietracaprina and F. Vandin. Efficient incremental mining of top-k frequent closed itemsets. In *DS*, pages 275–280, 2007.

[18] J. G. Propp and D. B. Wilson. Exact sampling with coupled markov chains and applications to statistical mechanics. *Rand. Struct. Alg.*, 9(1-2):223–252, 1996.

[19] J. Vreeken, M. van Leeuwen, and A. Siebes. Krimp: mining itemsets that compress. *Data Min. Knowl. Discov.*, 23(1):169–214, 2011.

Mining Top-K High Utility Itemsets

Cheng Wei Wu[1], Bai-En Shie[1], Philip S. Yu[2], Vincent S. Tseng[1]

[1]Department of Computer Science and Information Engineering, National Cheng Kung University, Taiwan, ROC

[2]Department of Computer Science, University of Illinois at Chicago, Chicago, Illinois, USA

{silvemoonfox, brianshie}@gmail.com, psyu@cs.uic.edu, tsengsm@mail.ncku.edu.tw

ABSTRACT

Mining high utility itemsets from databases is an emerging topic in data mining, which refers to the discovery of itemsets with utilities higher than a user-specified minimum utility threshold *min_util*. Although several studies have been carried out on this topic, setting an appropriate minimum utility threshold is a difficult problem for users. If *min_util* is set too low, too many high utility itemsets will be generated, which may cause the mining algorithms to become inefficient or even run out of memory. On the other hand, if *min_util* is set too high, no high utility itemset will be found. Setting appropriate minimum utility thresholds by trial and error is a tedious process for users. In this paper, we address this problem by proposing a new framework named *top-k high utility itemset mining*, where *k* is the desired number of high utility itemsets to be mined. An efficient algorithm named *TKU* (*Top-K Utility itemsets mining*) is proposed for mining such itemsets without setting *min_util*. Several features were designed in *TKU* to solve the new challenges raised in this problem, like the absence of anti-monotone property and the requirement of lossless results. Moreover, *TKU* incorporates several novel strategies for pruning the search space to achieve high efficiency. Results on real and synthetic datasets show that *TKU* has excellent performance and scalability.

Categories and Subject Descriptors

H.2.8 [**Database Management**]: Database Applications — Data Mining

General Terms: Algorithms, Performance

Keywords: Utility mining, high utility itemset, top-k pattern mining

1. INTRODUCTION

Frequent itemset mining (abbreviated as FIM) [1, 8] is a fundamental research topic in data mining. However, the traditional model of FIM may discover a large amount of frequent but low revenue itemsets and lose the information on valuable itemsets having low selling frequencies. Hence, FIM cannot satisfy the requirement of users who desire to discover itemsets with high utilities such as high profits. To address these issues, utility mining [2, 3, 6, 11, 12, 13, 18, 19, 20, 21, 23, 24, 25] emerges as an important topic in data mining. In utility mining, each item has a weight (e.g. unit profit) and can appear more than once in each transaction (e.g. purchase quantity). The utility of an itemset represents its importance, which can be measured in terms of weight, profit, cost, quantity or other information depending on the user preference. An itemset is called a *high utility itemset* (abbreviated as HUI) if its utility is no less than a user-specified *minimum utility threshold*. Utility mining is an important task and has a wide range of applications such as website click stream analysis [2, 11, 18, 20, 24], cross-marketing in retail stores [6, 12, 13, 19, 21, 23, 25] and biomedical applications [3].

Although this framework is essential to many applications, mining high utility itemsets is not an easy task because the *downward closure property* [1] does not hold. To facilitate the task of high utility itemset mining, most approaches [2, 11, 12, 21] utilize the *TWU* model and *TWDC* property to prune the search space. In this model, an itemset is called *HTWUI* if its *TWU* is no less than *min_util*, where the *TWU* of an itemset represents the upper bound of its utility. The TWDC property states that for any itemset that is not an HTWUI, all its supersets are low utility itemsets. The TWU-model consists of two phases named *phase I* and *phase II*. In *phase I*, all the HTWUIs are found. In phase II, the exact utilities of HTWUIs are calculated by scanning the database.

Although many studies have devoted to HUI mining, it is difficult for users to choose an appropriate minimum utility threshold in practice. Depending on the threshold, the output size can be very small or very large. Besides, the choice of the threshold also greatly influences the performance of the algorithms. If the threshold is set too low, too many high utility itemsets will be presented to the users. It is difficult for the users to comprehend the results. A large number of high utility itemsets also causes the mining algorithms to become inefficient or even run out of memory, because the more high utility itemsets the algorithms generate, the more resources they consume. On the contrary, if the threshold is set too high, no high utility itemset will be found. In this case, users need to try different thresholds by guessing and re-executing the algorithms over and over until being satisfied with the results. This process is both inconvenient and time-consuming.

We illustrate the problem of setting the minimum utility threshold with a real shopping transaction database named *Chainstore*. Figure 1 shows the runtime and the number of high utility itemsets in Chainstore dataset of the state-of-the-art utility mining algorithm UP-Growth [19]. As it can be seen, the choice of *min_util* has a major impact on the output size even if it is just changed slightly. For example, consider the case of a user who is interested in finding the top 1000 itemsets that contribute the highest profits in the Chainstore dataset. If the user does not possess the background knowledge about the database for setting *min_util* (he needs to make a guess to choose the threshold), he has only a very small chance of selecting a *min_util* that will satisfy his requirements (he would need to set *min_util* between 0.02% and 0.03%). Moreover, if the threshold is set below 0.02%, the algorithm can take up to one hour before terminating on a typical desktop computer.

KDD'12, August 12–16, 2012, Beijing, China.

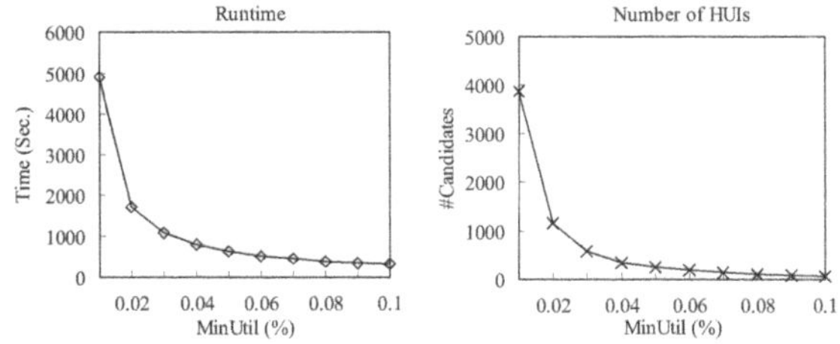

(a) Runtime (b) Number of high utility itemsets

Figure 1. Runtime and number of high utility itemsets in Chainstore dataset under varied minimum utility thresholds

A similar problem occurring in FIM is how to determine an appropriate *minimum support threshold* to mine enough but not too many itemsets for the users. To precisely control the output size and discover the most frequent patterns without setting the threshold, a good solution is to change the task of mining frequent patterns to the task of mining the top-*k* frequent patterns [4, 5, 7, 9, 10, 14, 16, 17, 22]. The idea is to let the users specify *k*, i.e., the number of desired patterns, instead of specifying the minimum support threshold. Setting *k* is more intuitive than setting the threshold because *k* represents the number of itemsets that the user wants to find whereas choosing the threshold depends solely on database's characteristics, which are often unknown to users.

Although using a parameter *k* instead of a threshold would also be desirable in utility mining, developing an efficient algorithm for mining top-*k* high utility itemsets is not an easy task. It poses four major challenges as discussed below.

First, the utility of an itemset is neither monotone nor anti-monotone. In other words, the utility of an itemset may be equal to, higher or lower than that of its supersets and subsets. Therefore, many techniques [5, 7, 9, 10, 14, 16, 17, 22] developed in top-*k* frequent pattern mining that rely on anti-monotonicity to prune the search space cannot be directly applied to top-*k* high utility itemset mining.

The second challenge is how to incorporate the concept of top-*k* pattern mining with the TWU-model. Although the TWU-model is widely used in utility mining, it is difficult to adapt this model to top-*k* high utility itemset mining because the exact utilities of itemsets are unknown in phase I. When an HTWUI is generated in phase I, we cannot guarantee that its utility is higher than other HTWUIs and it is a top-*k* high utility itemset before performing phase II. To guarantee that all the top-*k* high utility itemsets can be captured in the set of HTWUIs, a naive approach is to run the algorithm with *min_util* = 0. However, this approach may encounter the large search space problem.

The third challenge is that *min_util* is not given in advance in top-*k* high utility itemset mining. In the traditional high utility itemset mining, the search space can be efficiently pruned by the algorithms with a given *min_util*. However, in the scenario of top-*k* high utility mining, the threshold is not provided. Therefore, the minimum utility threshold is initially set to 0. The mining task has to gradually raise the threshold to prune the search space. Thus the challenge is to design an algorithm that can raise the threshold as high as possible and make the number of candidates produced in phase I as small as possible.

The last challenge is how to effectively raise the threshold without missing any top-*k* high utility itemsets. A good algorithm is one that can effectively raise the threshold during the mining process. However, if an incorrect method for raising the threshold is used, it may result in some top-*k* high utility itemsets being pruned. Thus, how to effectively raise the threshold without missing any top-*k* high utility itemsets is a crucial challenge for this work.

In this paper, we address all of the above challenges by proposing an efficient algorithm named *TKU* for *T*op-*K* *U*tility itemset mining. This work has three major contributions.

First, we propose a novel framework for mining top-*k* high utility itemsets. An algorithm named *TKU* is proposed for efficiently mining the complete set of top-*k* high utility itemsets in the database without specifying *min_util* threshold.

Second, five new strategies are proposed for effectively raising the threshold at different stage of the mining process. The first four strategies effectively raise the threshold during the mining process to prune the search space and reduce the number of candidates in phase I. The last strategy effectively reduces the number of candidates that need to be checked in phase II. It improves the runtime of phase II and the overall performance.

Third, we conducted different kinds of experiments with real datasets. The results show that the performance of the proposed algorithm TKU is close to that of the optimal case of the state-of-the-art utility mining algorithm UP-Growth [19]. Moreover, it is over 100 times faster than the compared baseline algorithm.

The remainder of this paper is organized as follows. In Section 2, we introduce the background for utility mining and top-*k* pattern mining. Section 3 presents the proposed methods. Experiments are shown in Section 4 and conclusions are given in Section 5.

Table 1. An example database

TID	Transaction	TU
T_1	(A,1) (C,1) (D,1)	8
T_2	(A,2) (C,6) (E,2) (G,5)	27
T_3	(A,1) (B,2) (C,1) (D,6) (E,1) (F,5)	30
T_4	(B,4) (C,3) (D,3) (E,1)	20
T_5	(B,2) (C,2) (E,1) (G,2)	11

Table 2. Profit table

Item	A	B	C	D	E	F	G
Profit	5	2	1	2	3	1	1

2. BACKGROUND

This section introduces the preliminaries related to utility mining, and then defines the problem statement of top-*k* high utility itemset mining. We adopt the notations used in [19]. For more details about high utility itemsets, readers can refer to [19].

2.1 Problem definition

Given a finite set of distinct *items* $I = \{i_1, i_2, \ldots, i_m\}$. Each item $i_j \in I$ is associated with a positive number $p(i_j, D)$, called its *external utility*. A *transactional database* $D = \{T_1, T_2, \ldots, T_n\}$ is a set of transactions, where each transaction $T_c \in D$, $(1 \le c \le n)$ is a subset of I and has an unique identifier c, called *Tid*. In transaction T_c, each item i_j is associated with a positive number $q(i_j, T_c)$, called its *internal utility* in T_c. An itemset $X = \{i_1, i_2, \ldots, i_l\}$ is a set of l distinct items, where $i_j \in I$, $1 \le j \le l$, and l is the length of X. A l-itemset is an itemset of length l. An itemset X is said to be *contained* in a transaction T_c if $X \subseteq T_c$.

Definition 1. The *support count* of an itemset X is the number of transactions containing X in D and denoted as $SC(X)$. The *support of X* is defined as the ratio of $SC(X)$ to $|D|$.

Definition 2. The *utility of an item* i_p *in a transaction* T_c is denoted as $u(i_j, T_c)$ and defined as $p(i_j, D) \times q(i_j, T_c)$.

Definition 3. The *utility of an itemset X in a transaction* T_c is denoted and defined as $u(X, T_c) = \sum_{i_j \in X} u(i_j, T_c)$.

Definition 4. The *utility of an itemset X in D* is denoted and defined as $u(X) = \sum_{X \subseteq T_c \wedge T_c \in D} u(X, T_c)$.

Definition 5. An itemset *X* is called *high utility itemset* if $u(X)$ is no less than a user-specified *minimum utility threshold min_util*.

Definition 6. Let *min_util* be the minimum utility threshold, the complete set of high utility itemsets in *D* is denoted as $f_H(D, min\_util)$. The goal of high utility itemset mining is to discover $f_H(D, min\_util)$.

Example 1. Let Table 1 be an example database containing five transactions. Each row in Table 1 represents a transaction, in which each letter represents an item and has a purchase quantity (internal utility). The unit profit of each item is shown in Table 2 (external utility). Suppose *min_util* is set to 30, the set of high utility itemsets in Table 1 is {{BD}:30, {ACE}:31, {BCD}:34, {BCE}:31, {BDE}:36, {BCDE}:40, {ABCDEF}:30}, where the number beside each itemset is its utility.

Note that the utility constraint is neither *monotone* nor *anti-monotone*. In other words, the utility of an itemset may be equal to, higher or lower than that of its supersets and subsets. Therefore, we cannot directly use the anti-monotone property (also known as downward closure property) to prune the search space. To facilitate the mining task, Liu et al. introduced the concept of *transaction-weighted downward closure* [12], which is based on the following definitions.

Definition 7. The *transaction utility* of a transaction T_R is denoted as $TU(T_R)$ and defined as $u(T_R, T_R)$.

Definition 8. The *transaction-weighted utilization* of an itemset *X* is the sum of the transaction utilities of all the transactions containing *X*, which is denoted as $TWU(X)$ and defined as $TWU(X) = \sum_{X \subseteq T_R \wedge T_R \in D} TU(T_R)$.

Definition 9. An itemset *X* is a *high transaction-weighted utilization itemset* (abbreviated as HTWUI) if $TWU(X) \geq min\_util$.

Property 1. (TWDC property) The *transaction-weighted downward closure* property states that for any itemset *X* that is not a HTWUI, all its supersets are low utility itemsets [12].

Definition 10. (Top-*k* high utility itemset) An itemset *X* is called a *top-k high utility itemset* in a database *D* if there are less than *k* itemsets whose utilities are larger than $u(X)$ in $f_H(D, 0)$.

Property 2. Let *H* be the complete set of top-*k* high utility itemsets in *D*. *H* may contain less than *k* high utility itemsets when $|f_H(D, 0)| \leq k$. Besides, *H* may contain more than *k* high utility itemsets when some itemsets have the same utility.

Definition 11. (Optimal minimum utility threshold) Let *H* be the complete set of top-*k* high utility itemsets in *D*. A minimum utility threshold δ^* is called *optimal minimum utility threshold* if there does not exist another threshold δ such that $\delta \geq \delta^*$ and $|f_H(D, \delta)| \geq k$. If $|H| \geq k$, $\delta^* = min\{u(X) | X \in H\}$.

Problem Statement. Given a transaction database *D* and the desired number of high utility itemsets *k*, the problem of finding the complete set of top-*k* high utility itemsets in *D* is to discover *k* itemsets with the highest utilities in *D*. An equivalent problem statement is to discover all the itemsets whose utilities are no less than δ^* in *D*.

Example 2. Suppose the desired number of high utility itemset *k* is set to 3, the top-3 high utility itemsets in Table 1 is *H* = {{BCDE}:40, {BDE}:36, {BCD}:34}. The optimal minimum utility threshold δ^* to retrieve *H* is equal to *min*{40, 36, 34} = 34.

2.2 Related work

2.2.1 High Utility Itemset Mining

Many studies have been proposed for mining HUIs, including *Two-Phase* [12], *IHUP* [2], *IIDS* [13] and *UP-Growth* [19]. *Two-Phase* and *IHUP* utilize *transaction-weighted downward closure* property to find high utility itemsets. They consist of two phases. In phase I, they find all HTWUIs from the database. In phase II, high utility itemsets are identified from the set of HTWUIs by scanning the original database. Although these methods capture the complete set of HUIs, they may generate too many candidates in phase I, i.e. HTWUIs, which degrades the performance of phase II and the overall performance (in terms of time and space). To reduce the number of candidates in phase I, various methods have been proposed (e.g. [13, 19]). Recently, Tseng et al. proposed *UP-Growth* [19] with four effective strategies *DGU*, *DGN*, *DLU* and *DLN*, for mining HUIs. Experiments showed that the number of candidates generated by UP-Growth in phase I can be order of magnitudes smaller than that of HTWUIs. To the best of our knowledge, UP-Growth is the state-of-the-art method for mining high utility itemsets. Although many studies addressed the topic of mining high utility itemset from transaction databases, few of them showed the flexibility of mining top-*k* high utility itemsets. Although the concept of top-k high utility itemset mining was first introduced in [3], the definition of high utility itemset in [3] is different from [2, 13, 15, 20] and our work.

2.2.2 Top-k Frequent Itemset Mining

In frequent pattern mining, several top-*k* pattern mining algorithms have been proposed [4, 5, 7, 9, 10, 14, 16, 17, 22]. Most of them (e.g. [5, 9, 10, 22]) follow a same general process for finding top-*k* patterns, although they also have several differences. We describe this general process below and then highlight the challenges for top-k high utility itemset mining.

The general process for mining top-*k* patterns from a database is the following. Initially, a top-*k* pattern mining algorithm sets minimum support threshold *minsup* to 0 to ensure that all the top-*k* patterns will be found. Then, the algorithm starts searching for patterns by using a search strategy. As soon as a pattern is found, it is added to a list of patterns *L* ordered by the support of patterns. The list *L* is used to maintain the top-*k* patterns found until now. Once *k* patterns are found, the value of *minsup* is raised to the support of the least interesting pattern in *L*. Raising *minsup* is used to prune the search space when searching for more patterns. Thereafter, each time a pattern is found that meets the minimum support threshold, the pattern is inserted into *L*, the patterns in *L* not respecting the threshold anymore are removed from *L*, and the threshold is raised to the support of the least frequent patterns in *L*. The algorithm continues searching for more patterns until no pattern is found by the search strategy.

What distinguish each top-*k* pattern mining algorithm are the data structures and search strategies to discover patterns. Top-*k* pattern mining algorithm needs to use appropriate data structure and search strategies to be efficient in both memory and execution time. Besides, the efficiency of a top-*k* algorithm depends largely on how fast it can raise the minimum interestingness criterion (*minsup*) to prune the search space. To raise the threshold quickly, it is desirable that a top-*k* pattern mining algorithm uses a search strategy that will find the most interesting patterns as early as possible. Although several efficient top-*k* pattern mining algorithms [5, 9, 10, 22] have been designed based on this idea, it is not possible to simply adapt this idea to HUI mining. The reason is that the HUI mining is performed in two phases and that the exact utility of itemsets is only known during phase II. Therefore, mining the top-*k* HTWUIs during phase I would not necessarily result in finding the top-*k* HUIs in phase II. Another challenge is how to integrate effective strategies for raising *min-_util* given that the exact utility is only known in phase II.

By the above literature reviews, although there are many studies about utility mining and top-*k* pattern mining, fewer of them focus on the integration of mining top-*k* high utility itemsets. This paper addresses this topic to find top-*k* high utility itemsets.

Table 3. Items and their TWUs

Item	A	B	C	D	E	F	G
TWU	65	61	96	58	88	30	38

Table 4. Reorganized transactions and their RTUs

TID	**Reorganized transaction**	**RTU**
T_1'	(C,1) (A,1) (D,1)	8
T_2'	(C,6) (E,2) (A,2)	27
T_3'	(C,1) (E,1) (A,1) (B,2) (D,6)	30
T_4'	(C,3) (E,1) (B,4) (D,3)	20
T_5'	(C,2) (E,1) (B,2)	11

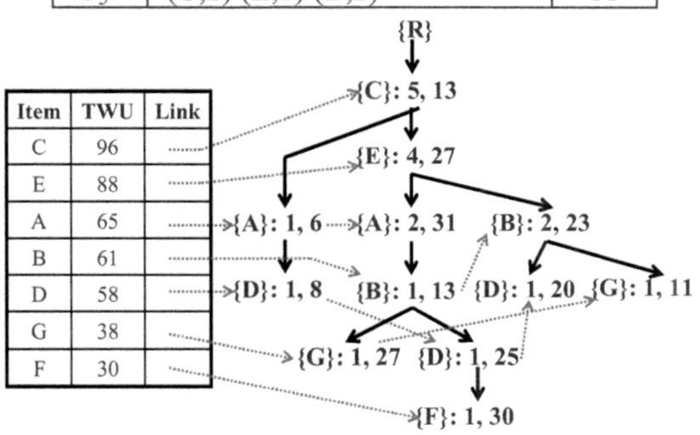

Figure 2. An UP-Tree when *min_util* = 0.

3. MINING TOP-K HIGH UTILITY ITEMSETS

In this section, we propose an efficient algorithm named *TKU* (*mining Top-K Utility itemsets*) for discovering top-*k* high utility itemsets without specifying *min_util*. We first present a baseline named TKU_{Base} approach and then introduce effective strategies to enhance its performance.

3.1 The baseline approach

The baseline approach TKU_{Base} takes *k* as parameter and outputs the *k* itemsets with the highest utilities. It is an extension of UP-Growth, the current best method for mining high utility itemsets, and it adopts the idea of *UP-Tree* [19] to maintain the information of transactions and top-*k* high utility itemsets. The framework of TKU_{Base} consists of three parts: (1) construction of *UP-Tree*, (2) generation of potential top-*k* high utility itemsets (abbreviated as *PKHUIs*) from the UP-Tree, and (3) identifying top-*k* high utility itemsets from the set of *PKHUIs*.

3.1.1 UP-Tree Structure

In this subsection, we briefly introduce the structure of UP-Tree. For the details about the UP-Tree, readers can refer to [19].

In UP-Tree, each node *N* consists of the following elements: *N.name* is the item name of *N*; *N.count* is the support count of *N*; *N.nu* is the node utility of *N*; *N.parent* records the parent node of *N*; *N.hlink* is a node link which points to a node whose item name is the same as *N.name*. *Header table* is employed to facilitate the traversal of UP-Tree. In the header table, each entry is composed of an *item name*, an *estimate utility value*, and a *link*. The link points to the last occurrence of the node having the same item name as the entry in the UP-Tree. The nodes whose item names are the same can be traversed efficiently by following the links in header table and the nodes in UP-Tree.

3.1.2 Construction of UP-Tree

A UP-Tree can be constructed with only two scans of the original database. In the first scan, the transaction utility of each transaction and TWU of each single item are computed. Thus, items and their TWUs are obtained. Subsequently, items are inserted into the header table in descending order of their TWUs. During the second database scan, transactions are reorganized and then inserted into the UP-Tree. Initially, the tree is created with a root *R*. When a transaction is retrieved, items in the transaction are sorted in descending order of TWU. A transaction after the above reorganization is called *reorganized transaction* and its transaction utility is called *RTU* (*reorganized transaction utility*). The RTU of a reorganized transaction T_d' is denoted as $RTU(T_d')$. When a reorganized transaction $T_d' = \{i_1, i_2, \ldots, i_m\}$ ($i_j \in I$, $1 \le j \le m$) is retrieved, TKU_{Base} applies the strategy *DGN* (*D*iscarding *G*lobal *N*ode utilities) [19] and calls the function ***Insert_Reorganized_Transaction***(R, i_1) to insert t_d'.

The function ***Insert_Reorganized_Transaction***(N, i_x) takes a node *N* in the UP-Tree and an item i_x ($i_x \in T_d'$, $1 \le x \le m$) in the reorganized transaction T_d' as inputs. The function is performed as follows:

Line 1: If *N* has a child *S* such that $S.item = i_x$, then increment *S.count* by 1; otherwise, create a new child node *S* with $S.item = i_x$, $S.count = 1$, $S.parent = N$ and $S.nu = 0$.

Line 2: Increase *S.nu* by $(RTU(T_d') - \sum_{p=(x+1)}^{m} u(i_p, T_d'))$, where $i_p \in T_d'$ and $1 \le p \le m$.

Line 3: Call ***Insert_Reorganized_Transaction***(S, i_{x+1}) if $p \neq m$.

After inserting all reorganized transactions, the construction of the UP-Tree is completed. Figure 2 shows an UP-Tree for Table 1 when *min_util* = 0.

3.1.3 Generating PKHUIs from the UP-Tree

The proposed algorithm uses an internal variable named *border minimum utility threshold* (denoted as *border_min_util*) which is initially set to 0 and raised dynamically after a sufficient number of itemsets with higher utilities has been captured during the generation of PKHUIs. The development of the proposed method is based on the following definitions and lemmas.

Lemma 1. Let $P = \langle X_1, X_2, \ldots, X_m \rangle$ be a set of itemsets ($m \ge k$), where X_i is the *i*-th itemset in *P* and $u(X_i) \ge u(X_j), \forall\, i < j$. (In other words, X_i is the itemset with the *i*-th highest utility in *P*). For any itemset *Y*, if $u(Y) < u(X_k)$, *Y* is not a top-*k* high utility itemset.

Rationale. According to Definition 10, if there exist k itemsets whose utilities are higher than the utility of Y, Y is not a top-k high utility itemset.

Lemma 2. Let P=<$X_1, X_2, ..., X_m$> be a set of itemsets ($m \geq k$), where X_i is the i-th itemset in P and $u(X_i) \geq u(X_j), \forall\ i < j$. If $\delta_P = u(X_k)$, $f_H(D, \delta^*) \subseteq f_H(D, \delta_P)$.
Rationale. Let H be the complete set of top-k high utility itemsets. If $|H| \geq k$, $\delta^* = min\{u(X)|\ X \in H\}$ (by Definition 11). Because $\delta^* = min\{u(X)|\ X \in H\} \geq min\{u(X_i)|\ X_i \in P,\ 1 \leq i \leq k\} = u(X_k) = \delta_P$, $\delta^* \geq \delta_P$ and $f_H(D, \delta^*) \subseteq f_H(D, \delta_P)$.

Example 3. Suppose $k = 4$ and *border_min_util* = 0 initially. Let P be the set of 1-items in D. Then P = {{A}:20, {D}:20, {B}:16, {E}:15, {C}:13, {G}:7, {F}:5}, where the number beside each item is its exact utility. By Lemma 1, items {C}, {G}, {F} are unpromising to be the top-4 high utility itemsets. Therefore *border_min_util* can be raised to 15, the 4th highest utility value in P, and no top-k high utility itemset will be missed.

After raising *border_min_util*, the algorithm performs the *UP-Growth* search procedure with *min_util* = *border_min_util* to generate PKHUIs. Although Lemma 1 provides a way to raise *border_min_util*, it cannot be applied during the generation of PKHUIs in phase I. This is because the exact utilities of the PKHUIs are unknown during phase I. One of the solutions to this problem is to use *lower bound of the utility* of PKHUI to raise the *border_min_util*. A lower bound of the utility of an itemset can be estimated by the following definitions.

Definition 12. The *minimum item utility* of an item a is denoted as $miu(a)$ and defined as the value $u(a, T_r)$ for which $\neg\exists\ T_s \in D$ such that $u(a, T_s) < u(a, T_r)$.

Definition 13. The *minimum item utility of an itemset* $X=\{a_1, a_2,..., a_m\}$ is defined as $MIU(X) = \sum_{i=1}^{m} miu(a_i) \times SC(X)$.

Lemma 3. Let C = <$X_1, X_2, ..., X_m$> be a set of itemsets ($m \geq k$), where X_i is the i-th itemset in C and $MIU(X_i) \geq MIU(X_j), \forall\ i < j$. For any itemset Y, if $TWU(Y) < \delta_C = min\{MIU(X_i)\ |\ X_i \in C,\ 1 \leq i \leq k\}$, Y is not a top-k high utility itemset.
Rationale. According to Definition 8, $u(Y) \leq TWU(Y)$. If $TWU(Y) < \delta_C$, $u(Y) < \delta_C$. Besides, $u(Y) < MIU(X_i) \leq u(X_i)$, $X_i \in C$, $1 \leq i \leq k$. According to Definition 10, if there exist k itemsets whose utilities are higher than the utility of Y, Y is not a top-k high utility itemset.

Lemma 4. Let C =<$X_1, X_2, ..., X_m$> be a set of itemsets ($m \geq k$), where X_i is the i-th itemset in C and $MIU(X_i) \geq MIU(X_j), \forall\ i < j$. If $\delta_C = MIU(X_k)$, $f_H(D, \delta^*) \subseteq f_H(D, \delta_C)$.
Rationale. Let H be the complete set of top-k high utility itemsets. If $|H| \geq k$, $\delta^* = min\{u(X)|\ X \in H\}$ (by Definition 10). Because $\delta^* = min\{u(X)|\ X \in H\} \geq min\{u(X_i)|\ X_i \in C,\ 1 \leq i \leq k\} \geq min\{MIU(X_i)\ |\ X_i \in C,\ 1 \leq i \leq k\} = MIU(X_k)$, we have $\delta^* \geq \delta_C$ and $f_H(D, \delta^*) \subseteq f_H(D, \delta_C)$.

Lemma 5. For any itemset X, if $TWU(X)$ < *border_min_util* $\leq \delta^*$, X and all its supersets are not top-k high utility itemsets.

Definition 14. The *maximum item utility* of an item a is denoted as $mau(a)$ and defined as the value $u(a, T_r)$ for which $\neg\exists\ T_s \in D$ such that $u(a, T_s) > u(a, T_r)$.

Table 5. Items and their mius and maus

Item	A	B	C	D	E	F	G
miu	5	4	1	2	3	5	2
mau	5	8	3	6	6	5	5

Definition 15. The *maximum utility of an itemset* $X=\{a_1, a_2,..., a_m\}$ is defined as $MAU(X) = \sum_{i=1}^{m} mau(a_i) \times SC(X)$.

Lemma 6. For any itemset X, if $MAU(X)$ < *border_min_util* < δ^*, X is not a top-k high utility itemset.
Rationale. According to Definition 15, we have $u(X) \leq MAU(X)$. If $MAU(X)$ < *border_min_util*, $u(X)$ < *border_min_util*. According to Definition 10, X is not a top-k high utility itemset.

Lemma 7. For any itemset X, the relationships between $MAU(X)$ $TWU(X)$, $u(X)$ and $MIU(X)$ is $MIU(X) \leq u(X) \leq min\{MAU(X), TWU(X)\}$.

Definition 16. An itemset is called a *PKHUI* (*P*otential top-*K* *H*igh *U*tility *I*temset) if its estimated utility (i.e., TWU) and MAU are no less than the *border_min_util*.

Based on the above lemmas and definitions, we have the following ideas to raise *border_min_util* during the generation of PKHUIs. As soon as a candidate X is found by the UP-Growth search procedure, we check whether its estimated utility (i.e, $TWU(X)$) is higher than *border_min_util*. If $TWU(X)$ < *border_min_util*, X and all its supersets are not top-k high utility itemsets (Lemma 5). Otherwise, we check whether its MAU is higher than *border_min_util*. If MAU(X) < *border_min_util*, X is not a top-k high utility itemset (Lemma 6). Otherwise, X is considered as a candidate for phase II and it is outputted with its estimated utility value according to Lemma 7. If X is a valid PKHUI and $MIU(X) \geq$ *border_min_util*, $MIU(X)$ can be used to raise the *border_min_util* (Lemma 3). To efficiently update *border_min_util*, we use a min-heap structure L to maintain the k highest MIUs of the PKHUIs until now. Once k *MIUs* are found, *border_min_util* is raised to the k-th MIU in L according to Lemma 3. Each time a PKHUI X is found and its MIU is higher than *border_min_util*, X is added into L and the lowest MIU in L is removed. After that, *border_min_util* is raised to the k-th MIU in L. The algorithm continues searching for more PKHUIs until no candidate is found by the UP-Growth search procedure. Figure 3 gives the pseudo code for the above processes.

```
If(TWU(X) ≥ border_min_util and MAU(X) ≥ border_min_util)
{   Output X and min{TWU(X), MAU(X)}
    If (MIU(X) ≥ border_min_util)
    { Add X to L and raise border_min_util by MIU(X)}
}
else
    {   X is not a valid PKHUI   }
```

Figure 3. The pseudo code for the strategy *MC*

Strategy 1. Raising the threshold by *M*UI of *C*andidate (MC)
For any newly mined PKHUI X, if its MIU, TWU and MAU are no less than the current *border_min_util*, then it is safe to use $MIU(X)$ to raise *border_min_util*.

3.1.4 Identifying top-k HUIs from PKHUIs

In this part, we propose a basic method for identifying top-k high utility itemsets from the set of PKHUIs. Exact utilities of PKHUIs are identified and top-k high utility itemsets are examined by scanning the original database. Main method of this part is similar to that of phase II in [12, 19]. However, in previous work [12, 19], all candidates should be checked. Therefore, we only check the candidate itemset X whose estimated utility is larger than or equal to the *border_min_util* finally reached after phase I, i.e., $min(TWU(X), MAU(X)) \geq$ *border_min_util*.

3.2 Effective strategies

In this subsection, we introduce four effective strategies to effectively raise *border_min_util* during different stage of the mining process.

3.2.1 Pre-evaluation Step

Although TKU_{Base} provides a way to mine top-*k* HUIs, *border_min_util* is set to 0 before the construction of the UP-Tree. This results in the construction of a full UP-Tree in memory, which degrades the performance of the mining task. If we could raise *border_min_util* before the construction of the UP-Tree and prune unpromising items in the transactions, the number of nodes maintained in memory could be reduced and the mining algorithm could achieve better performance. To solve this problem, we propose a strategy named *PE* (*P*re-*E*valuation) to raise *border_min_util* during the first scan of the database. A structure named *pre-evaluation matrix* (*PEM*) is used to store lower bounds for the utility of certain 2-itemsets. Each entry in *PEM* is denoted as *PEM*[*x*][*y*] and corresponds to a lower bound of $u(xy)$, where x, $y \in I$. Initially, each value in the matrix is set to 0. When a transaction $T_d = \{i_1, i_2, \ldots, i_m\}$ ($i_j \in I$, $1 \leq j \leq m$) is retrieved during the first scan of the database, the utility of the itemset $\{i_1\, i_j\}$ ($1 < j \leq m$) in T_d is added to the value of the corresponding entry of $PEM[i_1][i_j]$. For example, when $T_1 = \{(A,1), (C,1), (D,1)\}$ is retrieved, the corresponding entries *PEM*[A][C], *PEM*[A][D] are accumulated with $u(\{AC\}, T_1) = 6$ and $u(\{AD\}, T_1) = 7$. After scanning the database, *border_min_util* is set to the *k*-th highest value in *PEM*. Figure 4 shows the value of each entry in *PEM* after scanning Table 1. When $k = 4$, the 4th highest value in *PEM* is 18. Therefore, *border_min_util* can be raised to 18.

Strategy 2. Pre-Evaluation (PE) PE is applied during the first scan of the database. When a transaction $T_d = \{i_1, i_2, \ldots, i_m\}$ ($i_j \in I$, $1 < j \leq m$) is retrieved, the utility of $u(i_1\, i_j, T_d)$ is added to the corresponding entry $PEM[i_1][i_j]$ in the pre-evaluation matrix, $1 < j \leq m$. Then, *border_min_util* can be raised to the *k*-th highest values in *PEM*. The space complexity is $O(|I|/2)$, where $|I|$ is the number of distinct items in the database.

Notice that in TKU_{Base}, the strategy DGU in [19] cannot be applied, because *border_min_util* is 0 before the construction of UP-Tree. However, if we raise *border_min_util* at pre-evaluation step, the strategy DGU can be applied to prune those items whose TWUs are less than *border_min_util*, which further reduces the size of UP-Tree and the number of candidates produced in phase I.

	B	C	D	E	F	G
A	9	28	24	24	10	15
B		17	14	18	0	6
C			0	0	0	0
D				0	0	0
E					0	0
F						0

Figure 4. Pre-evaluation matrix

3.2.2 Raising the threshold by node utilities

The next proposed strategy is called *NU* (Raising the threshold by *N*ode *U*tilities), which is applied during the construction of UP-Tree. The strategy *NU* is developed based on the following lemmas.

Lemma 8. Let $PA = \{N_1, N_2, \ldots, N_m, R\}$ be a path from a node N_1 to the root R in the UP-Tree and i_j be an item in N_j, $1 \leq j \leq m$. The node utility of N_1 is a lower bound for the utility of the itemset $\{i_1, i_2 \ldots, i_m\}$, $1 \leq j \leq m$.

Rationale. The UP-Tree is constructed by applying the strategy DGN [19]. According to the rationale described in [19], the utility of the itemset $\{i_1, i_2 \ldots, i_m\}$ is guaranteed to be higher than the node utility of N_1. Therefore, $N_1.nu \leq u(\{i_1, i_2 \ldots, i_m\})$.

Lemma 9. Let $S = <N_1, N_2, \ldots, N_m>$ be an ordered set of nodes in UP-Tree ($m \geq k$), where N_i is the *i*-th node in *S* and $N_i.nu \geq N_j.nu, \forall\, i < j$. If $\delta_{NU} = N_k.nu$, then $f_H(D, \delta^*) \subseteq f_H(D, \delta_{NU})$.

Rationale. Each node N_j to the root *R* represents an unique itemset X_j, $1 \leq j \leq m$ (Lemma 8). Let $S' = <X_1, X_2, \ldots, X_m>$ be an ordered set of itemsets, where $N_j.nu \leq u(X_j)$ and $1 \leq j \leq m$. If $|H| \geq k$, then $\delta^* = min\{u(X) | X \in H\}$ (Definition 10). Because $min\{u(X) | X \in H\} \geq min\{u(X_j) | X_j \in S, 1 \leq j \leq k\} \geq min\{N_j.nu \mid N_j \in S', 1 \leq j \leq k\}$, we have $\delta^* \geq \delta_{NU}$ and $f_H(D, \delta^*) \subseteq f_H(D, \delta_{NU})$.

By Lemma 8 and 9, if there are more than *k* nodes in the UP-Tree during its construction and this value is higher than the current *border_min_util*, we can raise *border_min_util* to the *k*-th highest node utility in the UP-Tree. For example, suppose $k = 4$, when the first reorganized transaction $T_1' = \{(C,1), (A,1), (D,1)\}$ is inserted into the UP-Tee, the nodes {C}, {A} and {D} are created with node utilities 1, 6 and 8, which represent lower bounds for the utilities of itemsets {C}, {AC} and {DAC}. When the second reorganized transaction is inserted into the tree, there are more than four nodes in the UP-Tree. Therefore, we can apply Lemma 9 to raise *border_min_util* to the *4*-th highest node utility in the UP-Tree.

Strategy 3. Raising the threshold by Node Utilities (NU) *NU* is applied during the construction of the UP-Tree (the second scan of the database). If there are more than *k* nodes in the current UP-Tree and *k*-th highest node utility is no less than the current *border_min_util*, *border_min_util* can be raised to the *k*-th highest node utility in the current UP-Tree.

3.2.3 Raising the threshold by MIU of Descendents

The third strategy that we propose is called *MD* (Raising the threshold by *MIU* of *D*escendents). It is applied after the construction of the UP-Tree and before the generation of PKHUIs. For each node N_α under the root in the UP-Tree, we traverse the sub-tree under N_α once to calculate the MIU of $N_\alpha N_\beta$ for each descendent node N_β of N_α. If there are more than *k* such values, *border_min_util* can be raised to the *k*-th highest value. For example, consider the UP-Tree in Figure 2 and suppose $k = 4$. The node under the root is {C}. We traverse the sub-tree under the node {C} once and calculate the MIUs of its descendents. For the descendent {A}, the total support count of {A} in the sub-tree of {C} is $(1 + 2) = 3$. Therefore, the MIU of {AC} is $(miu(\{A\}) + miu(\{C\})) \times SC(\{AC\}) = (5 + 4) \times 3 = 27$.

Strategy 4. Raising the threshold by *MIU* of Descendents (MD) *MD* is applied after the construction of UP-Tree and before the generation of PKHUIs. For each node N_α under the root in the UP-Tree, the support count of $N_\alpha N_\beta$ is calculated by traversing every its descendent node N_β. For each pair $N_\alpha N_\beta$, we calculate the MIU of $N_\alpha N_\beta$. If there are more than *k* MIUs larger than *border_min_util*, the *border_min_util* can be raised to *k*-th highest value.

Table 6. MIUs of descendents

Descendent	E	A	B	D	G	F
MIU	16	18	15	9	3	1

3.2.4 Raising the threshold during Phase II

In this part, top-*k* high utility itemsets are identified by checking the real utilities of PKHUIs in the database. The purpose of this part is the same as the basic method (in Section 3.1.4). Although the basic method can skip checking some candidates, the number of checked PKHUIs is still too large. Scanning database for checking the large amount of PKHUIs is very time-consuming.

In view of this, we propose an additional strategy for cooperating with the candidate skipping mechanism in Section 3.1.4. There are two main steps in this strategy. First, the candidates are sorted by the descendent order of estimated utilities, i.e., *min*(*TWU*(*X*), *MAU*(*X*)). Thus, the candidates with larger estimated utility values will be first checked; in other words, those having lower values will be checked later.

After *k* PKHUIs whose exact utilities are larger than *border_min_util* are found, a mechanism for raising *border_min_util* is applied. If the exact utility of a new HUI *Y* is larger than *border_min_util*, *Y* and *u*(*Y*) is inserted into a *top-k HUI list E* (All HUIs in *E* are ordered by their exact utilities), and the HUI with the lowest utility value is removed from *E*. Then *border_min_util* is raised to the utility of *k*-th HUI in *E*. If the estimated utility of the current candidate *Z*, i.e., *min*(*TWU*(*Z*), *MAU*(*Z*)), is less than the new border minimum utility threshold, all of the remaining candidates do not need to be checked. This is because that their upper bounds of exact utilities are not larger than *border_min_util*. Finally, *E* is the set of top-*k* high utility itemsets of the database. By this mechanism, the candidates with lower estimated utility values may not be checked since the *border_min_util* is raised. The I/O cost and execution time for phase II can be further reduced. This technique works well especially when *k* is small.

Strategy 5. Sorting candidates & raising threshold by the exact utility of candidates. (SE) *SE* is applied during phase II of TKU. Let CI be the set of candidates produced in phase I. Candidates in *CI* are sorted in the descendent order of their estimated utilities. Next, if there are more than *k* HUIs whose exact utilities are larger than *border_min_util*, *border_min_util* can be raised to the *k*-th highest exact utility. For any candidate *Z*, if *min*(*TWU*(*Z*), *MAU*(*Z*)) is less than *border_min_util*, *Z* and the remaining candidates do not need to be checked anymore.

4. EXPERIMENTAL EVALUATION

In this section, we evaluate the performance of the proposed algorithm. Experiments were performed on computer with a 3.40 GHz Intel Core Processor with 4 gigabyte memory, and running on Windows 7. All of the algorithms are implemented in Java. Different types of real world datasets were used in the experiments. *Foodmart*, a sparse dataset, was acquired from Microsoft foodmart 2000 database [27]; *Mushroom*, a dense dataset, was obtained from the FIMI Repository [26]; *Chainstore*, a large dataset, was obtained from NU-MineBench 2.0 [15]. The two datasets Foodmart and Chainstore already contain unit profits and purchased quantities. For Mushroom dataset, unit profits for items are generated between 1 and 1000 by using a log-normal distribution and quantities of items are generated randomly between 1 and 5, as the settings of [19]. Table 7 shows the characteristics of the datasets used in the experiments. To evaluate the performance of the proposed strategies, we prepared three versions of TKU and gave them the names TKU, TKU_{noSE} and TKU_{Base} as shown in Table 8. These three versions are compared with the state-of-the-art utility mining algorithm UP-Growth [19].

Table 7. Datasets' characteristics

Dataset	#Transactions	Avg. length	#Items	Type
Foodmart	4,141	4.4	1,559	Sparse
Mushroom	8,124	23.0	119	Dense
Chainstore	1,112,949	7.2	46,086	Sparse Large

Table 8. Strategies used by the algorithms

Algorithm	Phase I				Phase II
	PE	NU	MD	MC	SE
TKU	Y	Y	Y	Y	Y
TKU_{noSE}	Y	Y	Y	Y	
TKU_{Base}				Y	Y

Because UP-Growth is not developed for mining top-*k* HUIs, it cannot be compared directly with TKU. To compare their performance, we considered the scenario where the users choose the optimal parameters for UP-Growth to produce the same amount of patterns as TKU (denoted as $UP_{Optimal}$ in the following experiments).

We first show the performance of the algorithms on the Foodmart dataset. The results are shown in Figure 5 and Table 9. In Figure 5 (a), it can be observed that the runtime for phase I of TKU approaches that of $UP_{Optimal}$. On the contrary, the performance of TKU_{Base} is the worst among all the algorithms. Its runtime is about 100 times slower than that of TKU. The reason is shown in Figure 5 (b). This figure shows the thresholds that the TKU and TKU_{Base} reached after phase I. Since UP-Growth does not raise the thresholds during the mining process, we show its initial thresholds (the optimal thresholds). In this figure, it can be observed that the thresholds reached by TKU are closer to the optimal thresholds than those of TKU_{Base}. On the other hand, TKU_{Base} does not apply the strategies PE, NU and MD. Therefore, it constructs a full UP-Tree with *min_util* = 0. Since raising the threshold for TKU_{Base} strictly depends on the MC strategy, it cannot be raised effectively. Thus its search space is the largest and its runtime is the longest.

The ineffectiveness of raising the threshold for TKU_{Base} also influences the number of candidates generated in phase I. The number of candidates generates by each algorithm is shown in Table 9. In this table, it can be observed that the number of candidates for TKU_{Base} is over 1000 times larger than TKU when *k* is less than 1000. The reason is that the strategies PE, NU and MD effectively raise the threshold at different stages of the mining process. Thus the number of patterns generated by TKU is much smaller than that of TKU_{Base}.

The runtime of each algorithm for phase II is shown in Figure 5 (c). Because each candidate needs to be checked in phase II and TKU_{Base} has the largest number of candidates, its performance for phase II is the worst. The performance of TKU_{noSE} is worse than TKU because the latter uses the strategy SE, which reduces the number of candidates need to be checked in phase II. Overall runtime of the algorithms is shown in Figure 5 (d). We can see that the runtime of TKU is over 100 times faster than TKU_{Base}, and only about twice less than that of $UP_{Optimal}$. Therefore, it can be concluded that TKU is an efficient algorithm since it can exactly find the top-*k* HUIs within a reasonable time.

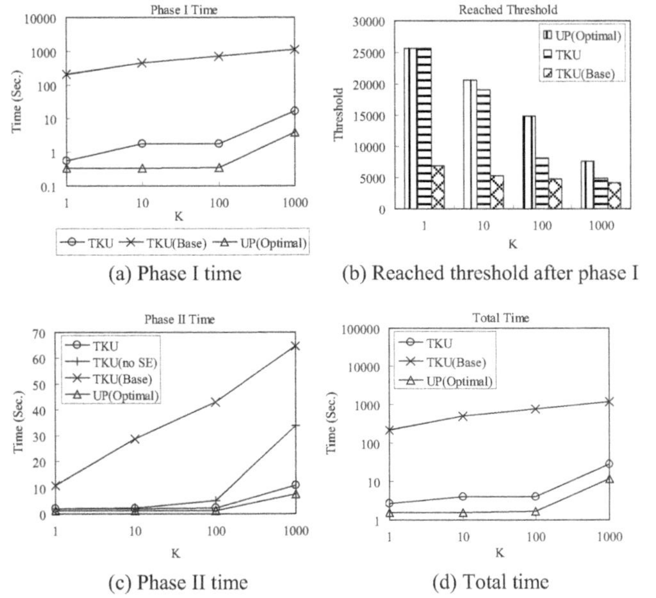

(a) Phase I time (b) Reached threshold after phase I

(c) Phase II time (d) Total time

Figure 5. Performance of the algorithms on Foodmart

Table 9. Number of candidates after Phase I

K	TKU	TKU_{Base}	Reduction ratio
1	1,379	2,466,459	1788.59
10	1,503	2,494,446	1659.65
100	2,456	2,537,225	1033.07
1,000	39,289	2,585,300	65.80

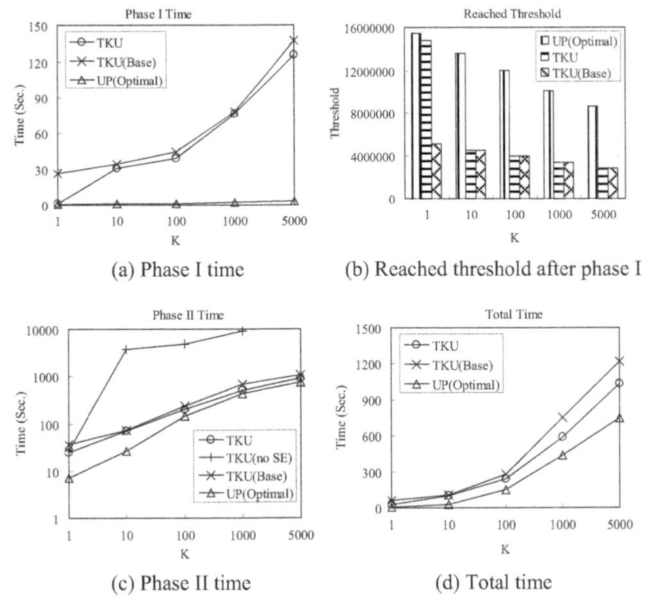

(a) Phase I time (b) Reached threshold after phase I

(c) Phase II time (d) Total time

Figure 6. Performance of the algorithms on Mushroom

Table 10. Number of candidates after Phase I

K	TKU	TKU_{Base}	Reduction ratio
1	427	508,462	1190.78
10	597,301	713,793	1.20
100	803,377	920,040	1.14
1,000	1,540,583	1,657,403	1.08
5,000	2,594,337	2,711,248	1.05

Next, we show the performance on the Mushroom dataset. The results are shown in Figure 6 and Table 10. Figure 6 (a) shows the runtime for phase I of the algorithms. It can be observed that the runtime for phase I of TKU is close to that of TKU_{Base}. This is because Mushroom is a dense dataset. The estimated utility values, i.e., TWU values, of itemsets are much larger than their exact utilities. Thus the thresholds cannot be raised effectively in phase I. The thresholds reached by the algorithms are shown in Figure 6 (b). It can be seen that if k is larger than 1, the threshold reached by TKU is close to TKU_{Base}.

Table 10 shows the number of candidates generated by the algorithms during phase I. In this table, it can be seen that when k is larger than 1, the reduction ratio is slightly larger than 1. The reduction ratio decreases when k increases. Figure 6 (c) shows the runtime for phase II of the algorithms. The runtime for phase II of TKU_{noSE} is the worst among the algorithms. This is because, without the SE strategy, TKU_{noSE} needs to check all the candidates to determine which itemsets are top-k HUIs. When k is set to 5,000, the runtime of TKU_{noSE} is too long to be executed (over 10,000 seconds). Finally, Figure 5 (d) shows the total runtime of the algorithms. We can conclude that although TKU is not as efficient as for the Foodmart dataset, it is still more efficient than TKU_{Base}.

Finally, we show the performance of the algorithms on Chainstore, a large dataset with over 1 million transactions. Because the runtime of TKU_{Base} for this dataset is too long to be executed (over 20 hours when $k = 1$), we instead use UP-Growth with a low minimum utility threshold (0.01%) as the baseline (denoted as UP_{Low} in the following experiments). The number of HUIs generated with *min_util* = 0.01% is about 3800. The results are shown in Figure 7 and Table 11. Figure 7 (a) shows the runtime for phase I of the algorithms. Since the threshold of UP_{Low} is fixed, its runtime remains the same. It can be seen that the runtime of TKU is worse than UP_{Low} when k is larger than 200. The reasons are that TKU needs to perform more computation for the strategies and it raises the threshold by the strategies step by step.

Figure 7 (b) shows the runtime for phase II of the algorithms. Although the runtime for phase I of TKU is slightly worse than UP_{Low}, the runtime for phase II of TKU is much faster than that of UP_{Low}. The total runtimes (the sum of the runtimes of phase I and phase II) are shown in Figure 7 (c). TKU is much faster than UP_{Low}. Generally, overall runtime of TKU is close to $UP_{Optimal}$. This is because UP_{Low} needs to check all candidates in phase II; on the other hand, TKU only needs to check some of them because it uses the SE strategy.

Figure 7 (d) shows the number of candidates checked in phase II by each algorithm. It can be observed that although TKU generates much more candidates in phase I, the number of candidates that need to be checked by TKU is close to $UP_{optimal}$ in phase II. This is because using the SE strategy, TKU avoids checking some candidates that do not need to be checked. In contrary, since all candidates are checked by TKU_{noSE}, its performance is worse than TKU and $UP_{Optimal}$.

Finally, we show the threshold changes after applying the strategies in phase I. The results are shown in Table 11. In this table, it can be observed that the thresholds are raised higher when the strategies are applied. On the other hand, it can also be seen that the thresholds decrease when k increases. This is reasonable because the larger k is, the lower the thresholds are.

Overall, Table 11 shows the effectiveness of all proposed strategies in phase I.

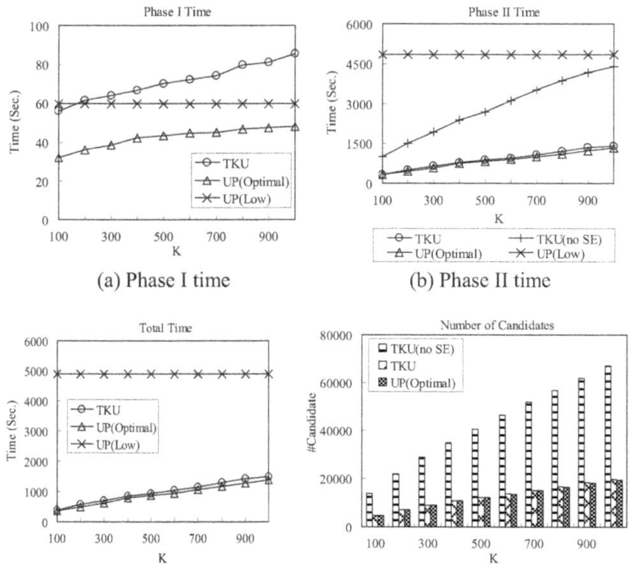

(a) Phase I time (b) Phase II time

(c) Total time (d)Number of candidates checked in Phase II

Figure 7. Performance of the algorithms on Chainstore

Table 11. Reached thresholds after each step in Phase I

K	PE	NU	MD	MC
100	2254.35	7509.38	7509.38	7509.38
200	1578.67	3929.84	3929.84	5324.16
300	1307.68	2728.92	2804.48	4346.16
400	1116.25	2158.83	2382.52	3803.76
500	988.49	1739.42	2050.96	3438.30
600	899.52	1457.85	1820.28	3145.21
700	826.38	1270.27	1650.04	2899.80
800	758.63	1117.47	1515.24	2734.67
900	712.97	1015.57	1412.70	2588.88
1,000	677.37	915.22	1334.82	2469.60

In general, the experimental results show that TKU outperforms TKU_{Base} and UP_{Low}. Moreover, the performance of TKU is close to $UP_{Optimal}$. The reasons are listed as follows. First, strategies PE, NU, MD and MC in phase I effectively raise the threshold step by step in phase I. Thus the number of candidates that need to be checked in phase II is less and the search space in phase I is successfully reduced. Second, the SE strategy in phase II effectively reduces the number of candidates that need to be checked in phase II. Therefore, TKU is shown to be efficient with a performance that is close to that of the optimal case of the state-of-the-art utility mining algorithm UP-Growth.

5. CONCLUSION

In this paper, we have proposed an efficient algorithm named *TKU* for mining top-*k* high utility itemsets from transaction databases. TKU guarantees there is no pattern missing during the mining process. We develop four strategies for phase I to raise the border minimum utility threshold and reduce the search space and number of generated candidates. Moreover, a strategy is designed for phase II to decrease the number of checked candidates. The mining performance is enhanced significantly since both the search space and the number of candidates are effectively reduced by the proposed strategies. In the experiments, different types of real datasets are used to evaluate the performance of our algorithm. The experimental results show that TKU outperforms the baseline algorithms substantially and the performance of TKU is close to the optimal case of the state-of-the-art utility mining algorithm.

ACKNOWLEDGMENTS

This research was supported in part by National Science Council, Taiwan, R.O.C. under grant no. NSC100-2631-H-006-002, US NSF through grants DBI-0960443 and OISE-1129076, and Google Mobile 2014 Program.

REFERENCES

[1] R. Agrawal and R. Srikant. Fast algorithms for mining association rules. In *Proc. of the 20th Int'l Conf. on Very Large Data Bases*, pp. 487-499, 1994.

[2] C. F. Ahmed, S. K. Tanbeer, B.-S. Jeong and Y.-K. Lee. Efficient Tree Structures for High-utility Pattern Mining in Incremental Databases. In *IEEE Transactions on Knowledge and Data Engineering*, Vol. 21, Issue 12, pp. 1708-1721, 2009.

[3] R. Chan, Q. Yang and Y. Shen. Mining high-utility itemsets. In *Proc. of Third IEEE Int'l Conf. on Data Mining*, pp. 19-26, Nov., 2003.

[4] Y. L. Cheung, A. W. Fu, Mining frequent itemsets without support threshold: with and without item constraints. *IEEE Transactions on Knowledge and Data Engineering*, Vol. 16, No. 6, pp. 1052-1069, 2004.

[5] K. Chuang, J. Huang, M. Chen, Mining Top-K Frequent Patterns in the Presence of the Memory Constraint, *The VLDB Journal*, Vol. 17, pp. 1321-1344, 2008.

[6] A. Erwin, R. P. Gopalan and N. R. Achuthan. Efficient Mining of High-utility Itemsets from Large Datasets. In *PAKDD 2008, LNAI 5012*, pp. 554-561, 2008.

[7] A. W. Fu, R. W. Kwong and J. Tang, Mining N-Most Interesting Itemsets, In *Proc. of ISMIS'00*, 2000.

[8] J. Han, J. Pei and Y. Yin. Mining frequent patterns without candidate generation. In *Proc. of the ACM-SIGMOD Int'l Conf. on Management of Data*, pp. 1-12, 2000.

[9] J. Han, J. Wang, Y. Lu and P. Tzvetkov, "Mining Top-k Frequent Closed Patterns without Minimum Support," *In Proc. of ICDM*, 2002.

[10] Y. Hirate, E. Iwahashi and H. Yamana, TF^2P-Growth: An Efficient Algorithm for Mining Frequent patterns without any Thresholds, In *Proc. of ICDM* 2004.

[11] H.-F. Li, H.-Y. Huang, Y.-C. Chen, Y.-J. Liu, S.-Y. Lee. Fast and Memory Efficient Mining of High Utility Itemsets in Data Streams. In *Proc. of the 8th IEEE Int'l Conf. on Data Mining*, pp. 881-886, 2008.

[12] Y. Liu, W. Liao, and A. Choudhary. A fast high-utility itemsets mining algorithm. In *Proc. of the Utility-Based Data Mining Workshop*, 2005.

[13] Y.-C. Li, J.-S. Yeh and C.-C. Chang. Isolated Items Discarding Strategy for Discovering High-utility Itemsets. In *Data & Knowledge Engineering*, Vol. 64, Issue 1, pp. 198-217, 2008.

[14] S. Ngan, T. Lam, R. C. Wong and A. W. Fu, Mining N-most Interesting Itemsets without Support Threshold by the COFI-Tree, Int. J. Business Intelligence & Data Mining, Vol. 1, No. 1, pp. 88-106, 2005.

[15] J. Pisharath, Y. Liu, B. Ozisikyilmaz, R. Narayanan, W. K. Liao, A. Choudhary and G. Memik, NU-MineBench version 2.0 dataset and technical report, http://cucis.ece.northwestern.edu/projects/DMS/MineBench.html

[16] T. M. Quang, S. Oyanagi, and K. Yamazaki, ExMiner: An Efficient Algorithm for Mining Top-K Frequent Patterns, *ADMA 2006, LNAI 4093*, pp. 436 – 447, 2006.

[17] L. Shen, H. Shen, P. Pritchard and R. Topor, Finding the N Largest Itemsets, in Proc. *Int'l Conf. on Data Mining*, pp. 211-222, 1998.

[18] B.-E. Shie, V. S. Tseng, and P. S. Yu. Online Mining of Temporal Maximal Utility Itemsets from Data Streams. In *Proc. of the 25th Annual ACM Symposium on Applied Computing (ACM SAC 2010)*, 2010.

[19] V. S. Tseng, C.-W. Wu, B.-E. Shie, and P. S. Yu. UP-Growth: an efficient algorithm for high utility itemset mining. In *Proc. of Int'l Conf. on ACM SIGKDD*, pp. 253–262, 2010.

[20] V. S. Tseng, C. J. Chu, and T. Liang. Efficient mining of temporal high-utility itemsets from data streams. In *ACM KDD Workshop on Utility-Based Data Mining Workshop*, 2006.

[21] B. Vo, H. Nguyen, T. B. Ho, and B. Le. Parallel Method for Mining High-utility Itemsets from Vertically Partitioned Distributed Databases. In *KES 2009, Part I, LNAI 5711*, pp. 251-260, 2009.

[22] J. Wang and J. Han, TFP: An Efficient Algorithm for Mining Top-K Frequent Closed Itemsets, *IEEE Transactions on Knowledge and Data Engineering*, Vol. 17, No. 5, pp. 652-664, May 2005.

[23] H. Yao, H. J. Hamilton, L. Geng, A unified framework for utility-based measures for mining itemsets. In *Proc. of ACM SIGKDD 2nd Workshop on Utility-Based Data Mining*, pp. 28-37, 2006.

[24] J.-S. Yeh, C.-Y. Chang and Y.-T. Wang. Efficient Algorithms for Incremental Utility Mining. In *Proc. of the 2nd Int'l Conf. on Ubiquitous information management and communication*, pp. 212-217, 2008.

[25] S.-J. Yen and Y.-S. Lee. Mining High-utility Quantitative Association Rules. In *Proc. of 9th Int'l Conf. on Data Warehousing and Knowledge Discovery (DaWaK'2007)*, *Lecture Notes in Computer Science (LNCS) 4654*, pp. 283-292, 2007.

[26] Frequent itemset mining implementations repository, http://fimi.cs.helsinki.fi/

[27] FoodMart2000, Microsoft Developer Network (MSDN), http://msdn.microsoft.com/en-us/library/aa217032(v=sql.80).asp

Sampling Minimal Frequent Boolean (DNF) Patterns

Geng Li and Mohammed J. Zaki
Rensselaer Polytechnic Institute, Troy, NY
{lig2, zaki}@cs.rpi.edu

ABSTRACT

We tackle the challenging problem of mining the simplest Boolean patterns from categorical datasets. Instead of complete enumeration, which is typically infeasible for this class of patterns, we develop effective sampling methods to extract a representative subset of the minimal Boolean patterns (in disjunctive normal form – DNF). We make both theoretical and practical contributions, which allow us to prune the search space based on provable properties. Our approach can provide a near-uniform sample of the minimal DNF patterns. We also show that the mined minimal DNF patterns are very effective when used as features for classification.

Categories and Subject Descriptors: H.2.8 [Database Management]: Database Applications - Data Mining

Keywords: Minimal Generator, Boolean Expression Patterns, Sampling, Pattern-based Classification

1. INTRODUCTION

Frequent pattern mining, long a mainstay of data mining, is moving away from complete enumeration methods to approaches that can effectively sample the pattern space for the most interesting patterns. This shifting trend is in keeping with the growing complexity of the data as well as the types of patterns sought. Whereas much research in the past has focused on itemset mining, i.e., conjunctive patterns, our focus is on the entire class of Boolean patterns in the disjunctive normal form (DNF), i.e., disjunctions over conjunctive patterns. Such Boolean patterns can help discover interesting relationships among attributes (e.g., gene expression mining [22]).

Complete enumeration of all frequent Boolean patterns is prohibitive in most real-world datasets, and thus the main issue is how to effectively sample a representative subset, which can in turn be used as features to build classification models. Furthermore, we focus on the problem of mining only the most simple Boolean patterns that completely characterize a subset of the data, i.e., the minimal DNF expressions. Our work makes number of novel contributions:

i) We propose the first approach to generate a near-uniform sample of the minimal Boolean expressions. Our method, based on Markov Chain Monte Carlo (MCMC) sampling, yields a succinct subset of the simplest frequent Boolean patterns.

ii) We propose a novel theoretical characterization of the minimal DNF expressions, which allows us to prune the pattern search space effectively. When combined with other optimization techniques, our approach is also practically effective. For instance, we are able to sample interesting "support-less" patterns, i.e., where the minimum frequency threshold is set to one. The pruning techniques can be applied by any method (even a complete one) for mining Boolean expressions.

iii) We perform an extensive set of experiments to demonstrate the effectiveness of our method. In particular, we classify a variety of datasets from the UCI Machine Learning Repository [13], and show that minimal DNF patterns make very effective features for classification; more so than purely conjunctive features. We also study the sample quality of our approach, as well as its scalability.

1.1 Preliminaries

Dataset: Let $\mathcal{Z} = \{z_1, z_2, \ldots, z_m\}$ be a set of binary-valued attributes or *items*, and let $\mathcal{T} = \{t_1, t_2, \ldots, t_n\}$ be a set of transactions identifiers or *tids*. A dataset $\mathcal{D}$ is a binary relation $\mathcal{D} \subseteq \mathcal{Z} \times \mathcal{T}$. $\mathcal{D}$ can also be considered as a set of tuples of the form $(t, t.X)$ where $t \in \mathcal{T}$ and $t.X \subseteq \mathcal{Z}$. Note that any categorical dataset can easily be converted into this format by assigning an item for each attribute-value pair.

Given dataset $\mathcal{D}$, we call $\mathcal{D}^T$ the *vertical* or transposed dataset comprising tuples of the form $(z, z.Y)$ where $z \in \mathcal{Z}$ and $z.Y \subseteq \mathcal{T}$. Table 1 shows an example dataset $\mathcal{D}$ and its transpose $\mathcal{D}^T$. The dataset has six items $\mathcal{Z} = \{A, B, C, D, E, F\}$ and five transactions $\mathcal{T} = \{1, 2, 3, 4, 5\}$. For example, the tuple $(2, ACDF) \in \mathcal{D}$ denotes the fact that tid 2 has four items A, C, D, F, whereas the tuple $(E, 134) \in \mathcal{D}^T$ denotes the fact that item E is contained in transactions $1, 3, 4$. For convenience, we write subsets without commas. Thus $\{A, C, D, F\}$ is written as ACDF, and so on.

tid	set of items
1	ABE
2	ACDF
3	BEF
4	ADE
5	BF

(a)

item	tidset
A	124
B	135
C	2
D	24
E	134
F	235

(b)

Table 1: Dataset $\mathcal{D}$ (a) and its transpose $\mathcal{D}^T$ (b)

Boolean Expressions: Let AND, OR, and NOT denote the logical operators. We denote a negated item (NOT z)

KDD'12, August 12–16, 2012, Beijing, China.

as $\bar{z}$. We also call $\bar{z}$ the complement of z. We use the symbols $\wedge$ and $\vee$ to denote AND and OR, respectively. For example, $A \vee B$ and $A \wedge B$ denote logical expressions A OR B, A AND B, respectively. For conciseness we also use $|$ in place of $\vee$ and we usually omit the $\wedge$ operator. For example, $A|BC|D$ denotes the Boolean expression A OR (B AND C) OR D.

A *literal* is either an item z or its complement $\bar{z}$. A clause is either the logical AND or the logical OR of a set of literals. An AND-clause contains only the AND operator over all its literals, e.g., BCD. Likewise, an OR-clause contains only the OR operator over all its literals, e.g., $C|E|F$. We assume that a clause does not contain both a literal and its complement – e.g., $A \wedge \bar{A}$ leads to contradiction, and $\bar{A} \vee A$, to a tautology.

We adopt the disjunctive normal form (DNF) to represent Boolean expressions. A Boolean expression Z is said to be in DNF if it consists of OR of AND-clauses, with the NOT operator (if any) directly preceding only literals, written as:

$$Z = \bigvee_{i=1}^{k} Z_i = \bigvee_{i=1}^{k} (z_{i1} \wedge z_{i2} \wedge \cdots \wedge z_{im_i})$$

Here each z_{ik} is a literal and each $Z_i = (z_{i1} \wedge \ldots \wedge z_{im_i})$ is an AND-clause. The size or length of a Boolean expression Z is the number of literals in Z, denoted $|Z| = \sum_{i=1}^{k} m_i$.

Tidset and Support: Given a tuple $(t, t.X) \in \mathcal{D}$, and a literal l, the *truth value* of l in t is 1 if $l \in t.X$, and 0 otherwise. Likewise, the truth value of $\bar{l}$ is 1 if $l \notin t.X$, and 0 otherwise. We say t *satisfies* a Boolean expression Z, if after replacing every literal in the Boolean expression with its truth value, the Boolean expression evaluates to true. The set of all satisfying transactions is called the *tidset* of Z, and is denoted as

$$T(Z) = \{t \in \mathcal{T} | t \text{ satisfies } Z\}$$

The number of satisfying transactions is called the *support* of Z in $\mathcal{D}$, denoted $sup(Z) = |T(Z)|$.

Minimal Boolean Expressions: Given DNF expressions $X = \bigvee_{i=1}^{m} X_i$ and $Y = \bigvee_{j=1}^{n} Y_j$, where X_i and Y_j are AND-clauses, we say that X is a *subset* of Y, denoted $X \subseteq Y$, iff there exists an injective (or into) mapping $\phi : X \to Y$, that maps each clause X_i to $\phi(X_i) = Y_{j_i}$, such that $X_i \subseteq Y_{j_i}$. If $X \subset Y$ and $|X| = |Y| - 1$, we say that X is a parent of Y, and Y is a child of X.

Definition 1. *A DNF expression Z is said to be* minimal *or* minDNF *(with respect to support) if there does not exist any expression $Y \subset Z$, such that $T(Y) = T(Z)$. A minimal AND-clause is called minAND for short. A minimal Boolean expression is also called a* minimal generator.

A minDNF expression Z is thus the simplest DNF expression with tidset $T(Z)$. Given a user-specified minimum support threshold $\sigma_{\min}$, we say that a DNF expression Z is frequent if $sup(Z) \geq \sigma_{\min}$. However, note that the support of a minDNF expression is not monotonic, since the addition of an item to a clause causes the support to drop, whereas, the addition of an item as a new clause causes the support to increase. For example, $sup(A) = 3$, since $T(A) = 124$, but $sup(AB) = 1$ (since $T(AB) = 1$) and $sup(A|E) = 4$ (since $T(A|E) = 1234$). Thus, the support of Z's children can be higher or lower. Further, any infrequent clause can be made frequent by adding additional clauses. For example, if $\sigma_{\min} = 2$, then C is infrequent, but $C|F$ is frequent. To prevent such "trivial" clauses, we also impose a minimum support threshold $\sigma_{\min}^{c}$ on the clauses. For any DNF expression $Z = \bigvee_{i=1}^{m} Z_i$, we say that Z is *frequent* if $sup(Z) \geq \sigma_{\min}$, and $\sup(Z_i) \geq \sigma_{\min}^{c}$ for all $i = 1, \ldots, m$. Since a clauses' support cannot exceed the support of the whole DNF expression, we have the condition that $\sigma_{\min}^{c} \leq \sigma_{\min}$ (usually, we just set them equal).

Given $\sigma_{\min}$ and $\sigma_{\min}^{c}$, the *complete minDNF mining task* is to enumerate all frequent minDNF expressions. However, given the huge search space, it is typically not feasible to mine the complete set of minDNF expressions. Instead, we will focus on sampling a representative subset.

Markov Chain Monte Carlo (MCMC) Methods: A *Markov chain* is a mathematical model for stochastic systems with discrete or continuous states controlled by transition probabilities. A Markov chain satisfies the property that the current state depends only on the previous state, i.e., $P(X_{t+1} = s_{t+1}|X_t = s_t, X_{t-1} = s_{t-1}, \ldots, X_0 = s_0) = P(X_{t+1} = s_{t+1}|X_t = s_t)$ for all $t \in \mathcal{N}$ and $s_t \in \mathcal{S}$, where $\mathcal{N}$ and $\mathcal{S}$ denote the time space and state space, respectively. Let $p^t(i,j)$ denote the t-step transition probability, i.e., $p^t(i,j) = P(X_{n+t} = s_{n+t}|X_n = s_n)$. If for all states $s_i, s_j \in \mathcal{S}, i \neq j$, there $\exists\ t' \in \mathcal{N}$, s.t. $P^t(i,j) > 0$ is satisfied for all $t > t'$, we call the Markov chain *aperiodic*. Given two states s_i and s_j, we say s_j is *reachable* from s_i, if $\exists\ t, s.t.\ P^t(i,j) > 0$, and we denote it as $s_i \to s_j$. If all state pairs are mutually reachable, we call the Markov chain *irreducible*. A Markov chain that is aperiodic and irreducible is called *ergodic*. An ergodic Markov chain has a stationary distribution $\pi = (\pi_i | s_i \in \mathcal{S})$, that satisfies three properties: (1) $\pi_i > 0$. (2) $\sum_{s_i \in \mathcal{S}} \pi_i = 1$. (3) $\pi P = \pi, i.e., \sum_{s_i \in \mathcal{S}} \pi_i P(i,j) = \pi_j$. The stationary distribution for an ergodic Markov chain is unique. A Markov chain is *time reversible* iff it has a stationary distribution π that satisfies the balance condition $\forall s_i, s_j \in \mathcal{S}, \pi_i P(i,j) = \pi_j P(j,i)$.

In the context of minDNF mining, each Markov state can be taken to be a Boolean expression, with transitions allowed, for example, only between parent and child expressions. Starting from the empty expression, we can then use Monte Carlo methods to perform random walks in the expression space to sample the minimal expressions. The main challenges include efficiency, and guaranteeing sampling quality. We address these questions below.

1.2 Related Work

Mining frequent AND-clauses has been extensively studied within the context of itemset mining [14]. The notion of minimal AND-clauses (called minimal itemset generators) was proposed in [3]. Methods that can mine minAND expressions include [11] (that focuses on finding the succinct minimal generators), CHARM-L [20] and Blosom [22]. The task of mining minimal monotone DNF expressions was proposed in [19], whereas Blosom [22] proposed a complete framework to extract the minimal DNF and pure AND-clauses, as well as the minimal CNF (conjunctive normal form – AND of OR-clauses) and pure OR-clauses. Blosom uses a two-step process to mine the minDNFs. It first mines all minimal AND-clauses, treats them as new items, as then extracts minimal OR-clauses over these composite AND-items. Disjunctive association rules have also been considered in [18]; they first mine all frequent AND-clauses, and then greedily select good OR combinations. The notion of disjunctive emerging patterns (EPs) for classification was proposed in [17]. Disjunctive EPs are Boolean expressions in CNF form, such that their support is high for the positive class and low for the negative class. However, they consider restricted CNF expressions that must contain a clause for each attribute. We mine general DNF expressions, without any constraints.

As we shall see, complete mining is infeasible for all but

very high support values. Thus, the focus in recent work has shifted to sampling based approaches. One of the earliest use of sampling was for mining maximal itemsets via randomization [15]. In the context of frequent graph mining, [8] proposed a randomized sampling method to generate a small representative set of frequent maximal graph patterns; the method did not provide any sampling guarantee. The first method to sample maximal graph patterns with uniform sampling via MCMC was presented in [16]. In [2], the authors introduced a generic sampling framework to sample the output space of frequent subgraphs, which is based on MCMC algorithm as well. In the context of itemset mining, [5] proposed a randomized approximation method for counting the number of frequent itemsets. In [4] a Metropolis-Hastings algorithm for sampling closed itemsets is given. More recently, [6] presented a direct sampling approach for mining AND-clauses. Unfortunately, direct sampling cannot be used for sampling minDNFs since the pattern space of minDNFs is not connected, as it is for closed AND-clauses. We thus focus on MCMC sampling, designing an appropriate transition probability matrix that ensures near-uniform sampling of the set of minDNF patterns.

2. MINIMAL BOOLEAN EXPRESSIONS

In this section we prove some properties of minDNF expressions, which will allows us to design effective pruning strategies while sampling.

LEMMA 1. *Any subset of a minimal AND-clause must also be a minimal AND-clause.*

PROOF. Let X be a minAND expression, and let $Y \subset X$. Assume that Y is not minimal. Then there exists a minAND expression $Z \subset Y$, such that $t(Z) = t(Y)$. However, in this case, $t((X \setminus Y) \cup Z) = t(X)$, which contradicts the fact that X is minimal. Thus, Y must be a minAND expression. □

THEOREM 1. *A DNF expression $Z = \bigvee_{i=1}^{n} Z_i$ is minDNF iff it satisfies the following two properties:*

a) For any Z_i, $(i = 1, \dots, n)$, we have $T(Z_i) \nsubseteq \bigcup_{j \neq i} T(Z_j)$. In other words, for any tidset of a clause, it is cannot be a subset of the unions of tidsets over the other clauses.

b) If we delete any item z_{ja} from a clause Z_j to yield a new clause $Z'_j = Z_j \setminus z_{ja}$, then for the resulting DNF expression $Z' = (\bigvee_{i \neq j} Z_i) \vee Z'_j$, we have $T(Z') \neq T(Z)$.

PROOF. If (a) is violated, we can simply delete Z_i without changing support, which would contradict the fact that Z is minimal. Likewise, if (b) is violated, it would contradict Z's minimality. For the reverse direction, suppose a DNF expression $Z = \bigvee_{i=1}^{n} Z_i$ satisfies properties (a) and (b). We have to show that Z is a minDNF. Assume that Z is not minimal. Then there exists a minDNF $Y = \bigvee_{j=1}^{m} Y_j$, such that $Y \subset Z$ and $T(Y) = T(Z)$, which implies that there exists an injective mapping ϕ that maps each $Y_j \in Y$ to $\phi(Y_j) = Z_i \in Z$, such that $Y_j \subseteq Z_i$ and $T(Y_j) \supseteq T(Z_i)$. There are two cases to consider: (1) If ϕ is a bijection, then $m = n$, and there exist a clause $Y_j \in Y$, such that $Y_j \subseteq \phi(Y_j) = Z_i \in Z$. However, in this case property (b) of Z is violated, since we can delete some item from $(Z_i \setminus Y_j)$, and the resulting expression will still have the same support at Z. (2) If ϕ is not a bijection, then $m < n$, and there exists a clause $Z_k \in Z$, such that $\phi^{-1}(Z_k) \notin Y$. However, in this case property (a) of Z violated, since $T(Y) = T(Z)$ implies that $T(Z_k) \subseteq \bigcup_{i \neq k} T(Z_i)$. Therefore, Z must be a minimal DNF expression. □

LEMMA 2. *A minDNF consists of OR of minAND expressions, i.e., if $Z = \bigvee_{i=1}^{n} Z_i$ is minDNF, then each Z_i must be a minimal AND-clause.*

PROOF. Assume some Z_i is not a minimal AND-clause. Then there exists a literal $l \in Z_i$, such that $T(Z_i \setminus l) = T(Z)$. In this case we can delete l from Z_i without affecting $T(Z)$, which violates property (b) in Theorem 1. □

LEMMA 3. *If $Z = \bigvee_{i=1}^{n} Z_i$ is minDNF, for any $Z_i, Z_j \in Z$, we have $Z_i \nsubseteq Z_j$. In other words, no clause is a subset of another clause.*

PROOF. Suppose $Z_i \subseteq Z_j$. Thus $T(Z_i) \supseteq T(Z_j)$ and property (a) in Theorem 1 is violated. □

Please note that Theorem 1 is a sufficient condition for Lemmas 2 and 3 but not a necessary condition. As such a DNF expression that satisfies Lemmas 2 and 3, need not be a minimal generator. We use this observation to reduce the random walk state space.

COROLLARY 1. *Any clause-wise subset (obtained by deleting an entire clause) of a minDNF expression Z is also minDNF.*

PROOF. The proof is similar to Lemma 1. Suppose a clause-wise subset $Z_s \subset Z$ is not minDNF. Then we can replace Z_s with its equivalent minDNF, say Z'_s, in Z, without affecting the tidset of Z. This would contradict the minimality of Z. □

For example, for the example in Table 1, $B|DF|E$ is a minimal DNF generator, with tidset $T(B|DF|E) = 12345$. Thus all clause-wise subsets, namely B, DF, E, $B|DF$, $B|E$, $DF|E$ are minDNF expressions.

COROLLARY 2. *Disallowing the empty pattern $\emptyset$ as a valid minDNF, then a single item is always a minimal AND-clause and thus a minDNF as well.*

In our running example in Table 1, items A, B, C, D, E and F are all minDNFs.

3. MINDNF SAMPLING ALGORITHM

The state space for the Markov chain for the minDNF mining consists of DNF expressions linked by immediate subset-superset or parent-child relationships. The DNF partial order is generated via the following four operations: a) Add_As_Clause (AAC): add a new clause comprising a single item into the DNF. b) Add_To_Clause (ATC): add an item to an existing clause. c) Delete_The_Clause (DTC): Delete a single item clause from the DNF. d) Delete_From_Clause (DFC): Delete an item from a clause (with at least two items) in the DNF. The added or deleted item can be either an item or its complement.

LEMMA 4. *The partial order graph of minimal DNF generators is disconnected.*

Consider the example in Table 1. We ignore negated items for now. $AB|AF|EF$ is a minDNF with $T(AB|AF|EF) = 123$. However, all its parents are not minimal DNFs. Take its parent $B|AF|EF$ as an example, $T(B) = 135$, $T(AF) = 2$, $T(EF) = 3$, thus property (a) in Theorem 1 is violated. Similarly, all its children are not minimal DNF generators. For instance, $AB|ACF|EF$ is not a minimal DNF generator since property (b) in Theorem 1 is violated. So, if we only keep minDNF expressions in the partial order graph, $AB|AF|EF$ would become an isolated point, and would never be reached! We provide two sampling solutions below.

3.1 Sampling in Clause-wise State Space

The first, rather naive, solution is to sample in the clause-wise state space. In particular, rather than adding or deleting an item by AAC, ATC, DTC or DFC each time, we add or delete a clause instead. From Lemma 2, every minDNF consists of only minimal AND-clauses. Also by Corollary 1, any clause-wise subset is also a a minDNF. Thus, the partial order graph is connected and all parents of the nodes in the graph will be minDNFs as shown in Figure 1(a). The solid ovals represent nodes which are minDNFs. However, this naive idea requires that we first mine the complete set of minimal AND-clauses from the dataset. As we shall see in the experiments, for reasonable support values mining all possible minimal AND-clauses is very expensive or intractable.

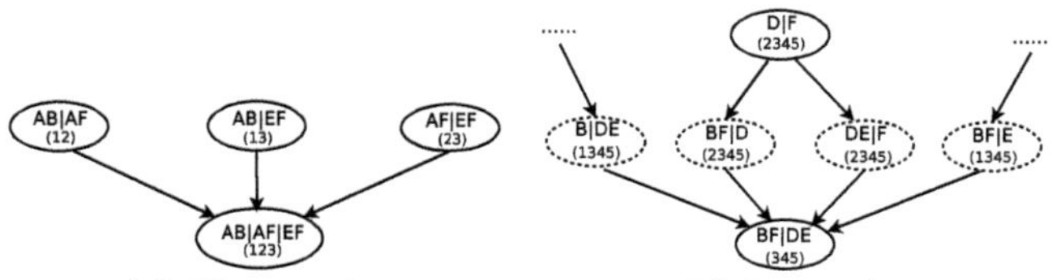

(a) Clause-wise (b) Item-wise

Figure 1: Clause- and Item-wise State Space

3.2 Sampling in Item-wise State Space

Given that the item-wise state space is disconnected, in order to guarantee all minDNFs are reachable, we also need to keep non-minimal DNFs in the graph. However, the goal is to reduce the number of non-minimal DNF in the graph to as few as possible while retaining all possible minDNFs. The following two lemmas help in this direction.

LEMMA 5. *Let Z be a DNF that violates Lemma 2. No extension of Z (by AAC or ATC operations) can result in a minDNF.*

PROOF. At least one of the clauses in Z is not a minimal AND-clause. Any future extension by adding a literal to Z cannot be a minDNF, since all its minimal AND-clause subsets must also be minimal by Lemma 1. □

This lemma states that any DNF that violates Lemma 2 should be removed from the graph, which can greatly reduce the size of the search space. Furthermore, we also remove any DNF node that violates Lemma 3. Note that this pruning still keeps the graph connected since it is always possible to find other paths. As an example, for the data in Table 1, $DE|E$ should be removed since one of its parents $DE|EF$, which is a minimal generator, can be reached by another path, namely from $DE|F$. As mentioned earlier, Definition 1 is a sufficient condition for Lemma 2 and Lemma 3, but not a necessary condition. There still exist DNFs that satisfy Lemma 2 and Lemma 3 but are not minimal generators.

Transition Probability Matrix: It is well known that a regular random walk on the partial order graph favors the nodes with higher degree [16]. In fact, if the edges are weighted, and the graph is undirected (i.e., symmetric weights: $w(u,v) = w(v,u)$ for all connected node pairs), then nodes are sampled proportional to the total weight of a node $s(u) = \sum_v w(u,v)$. We state without proof from [16]: In an ergodic random walk with an associated weighted connected (undirected) graph, the stationary distribution of a vertex is directly proportional to the sum of the edge weight incident to that vertex.

Consider a random walk on the partial order graph where there are both minimal and non-minimal DNF generators, with the transition probability matrix P given as:

$$P(u,v) = \begin{cases} \frac{w(u,v)}{\sum_{x \in N_u} w(u,x)} & \text{if } v \in N_u \\ 0 & \text{otherwise} \end{cases} \tag{1}$$

Here N_u denotes the *neighbors* of u, i.e., the set of nodes adjacent to u. Further, let $N_u^m = \{v \in N_u | v \text{ is a minDNF}\}$ and $N_u^n = \{v \in N_u | v \text{ is not a minDNF}\}$ denote set of u's neighbors that are minDNF and not minDNF, respectively. Also, let $d_u^m = |N_u^m|$ and $d_u^n = |N_u^n|$ be the minDNF degree and non-minDNF degree of expression u. Clearly the degree of u is given as $d_u = |N_u| = d_u^m + d_u^n$. We define the weight $w(u,v)$ on each edge (u,v) as follows:

$$w(u,v) = \begin{cases} \frac{(1-\alpha)c}{\max\{d_u^m, d_v^m\}} & \text{if } u \text{ and } v \text{ are minDNFs} \\ \frac{\alpha c}{d_v^n} & \text{if } v \text{ is minDNF but } u \text{ is not} \\ \frac{\alpha c}{d_u^n} & \text{if } u \text{ is minDNF but } v \text{ is not} \\ 1 & \text{if } u \text{ and } v \text{ are not minDNFs} \end{cases} \tag{2}$$

Here $0 < \alpha < 1$ is a weighting term, and $c > 0$ is a scaling constant. We shall see that α controls the degree of non-uniformity in the sampling, and along with c also affects the convergence rate of the sampling method (it has no impact on the correctness). From the definition, one can verify that the edge weights in the graph are symmetric and the transition probability matrix is stochastic. Moreover, the weights favor transitions to minDNF nodes. We prove that the defined random walk converges to a stationary distribution.

THEOREM 2. *An ergodic random walk on the weighted graph where the transition matrix P is defined via Eq. (1), using the weight function in Eq. (2) is reversible. Further, the random walk converges to a stationary distribution.*

PROOF. Essentially, we can show that P satisfies the detailed balance condition: $\forall s_i, s_j \in \mathcal{S}$, $\pi_i P(i,j) = \pi_j P(j,i)$. Furthermore, the walk is finite, irreducible, and can be made aperiodic with minor tweaking [16]. Details omitted due to lack of space. □

DEFINITION 2. *Let π denote the stationary distribution for a Markov chain, where $\pi(u)$ denotes the probability of visiting node u. The* non-uniformity *of a random walk is defined as the ratio of the maximum to the minimum probability of visiting a minDNF node.*

THEOREM 3. *The non-uniformity of minDNF sampling defined by Eq. (2) is bounded by the ratio $1/\alpha$.*

PROOF. The stationary distribution for any node v is given as $\pi(v) = \frac{s(v)}{W}$, where $s(v) = \sum_{y \in N_v} w(v,y)$ is the total weight for node v, and $W = \sum_v s(v)$ is the sum of the weights over all nodes in the Markov chain [16]. W is a constant for a given graph, thus $\pi(u) \propto s(u)$. Let u be a minDNF expression, with minDNF degree d_u^m and non-minDNF degree d_u^n. The total weight for u is given as

$$s(u) = \sum_{v \in N_u} w(u,v) = d_u^n \cdot \frac{\alpha c}{d_u^n} + (1-\alpha)c \sum_{y \in N_u^m} \frac{1}{\max(d_u^m, d_y^m)}.$$

Note that $\sum_{y \in N_u^m} \frac{1}{\max(d_u^m, d_y^m)} \leq d_u^m \cdot \frac{1}{d_u^m} = 1$. Equality is achieved only if $d_u^m \geq d_y^m$ for all $y \in N_u^m$, in which case $s(u) = \alpha c + (1-\alpha)c = c$. On the other hand, in the worst case we may assume that $d_y^m \gg d_u^m$ so that the second term vanishes in the limit, in which case we have $s(u) = \alpha c$. Thus the worst-case non-uniformity in sampling is $\frac{c}{\alpha c} = \frac{1}{\alpha}$. □

The pseudo-code for the minDNF sampling algorithm is outlined in Figure 2. The method always starts by picking a

minDNF Sampling Algorithm
Input: $\mathcal{D}, \sigma_{\min}, \sigma^c_{\min}, k$
Output: k minimal DNF generators
1. B= select a frequent item randomly
2. IF **is_minimal**(B)
3.   Output B, insert B in $\mathcal{B}$
4. IF $|\mathcal{B}| == k$ THEN return //k minDNFs sampled
5. $\mathcal{F}$ = **Compute-Local-Neighborhood**(B)
6. $\mathbf{P}$ = **Local-Transition-Matrix**(B, $\mathcal{F}$) //Eq. (1), (2)
7. Select a DNF B_{next} from $\mathcal{F}$ proportional to $\mathbf{P}$
8. Set $B = B_{next}$, and go to Line 2

Compute-Local-Neighborhood(B)
9. For each Boolean expression f in neighborhood of B
10.   IF $sup(f)$ satisfies $\sigma^c_{\min}$ and $\sigma_{\min}$
11.   If Lemma 2 and Lemma 3 are satisfied
12.   Insert f in $\mathcal{F}$
13.   If conditions (a), (b) in Theorem 1 satisfied
14.   Set f.min = True;

Figure 2: minDNF Sampling Algorithm

random frequent item (or its negation; we omit that here). Given the current node B, we first check if it minimal, and if so add it to the sampled set of patterns $\mathcal{B}$. If k steps have been performed, we stop (line 4). Otherwise, in line 5, determine all the immediate parents and children of the current node B that satisfy support constraints, as given in the function **Compute-Local-Neighborhood** in lines 9-14. To get all possible parents and children of the current node B, the four operations AAC, ATC, DTC, DFC are used in line 9. In Line 10 we test the support and prune out those patterns that do not satisfied the conditions. In line 11, we use Lemmas 2 and Lemma 3 to determine whether f is qualified to be remain in the partial order graph. We further test property (a) and (b) in Theorem 1 for f to determine its minimality. Returning back to line 6, we compute the transition probability $\mathbf{P}$ according to Equation 1, 2. Then we select a DNF expression B_{next} proportional to P to continue the walk in lines 7-8. Note that ideally, we should have a burn-in period for the random walk before patterns are output. We can start counting patterns after a sufficient number of steps (for line 4 check). We omit these details here, for clarity.

3.3 Optimizations

Transition Probability Matrix: Whereas Eq. (2) gives a good guarantee on the sampling quality, it can be expensive to compute, since we have to determine the minDNF and non-minDNF degree for a node, as well as for all of its neighbors N_u. Instead, we propose another weighting scheme that leads to much faster sampling, without sacrificing the sampling quality too much:

$$w(u,v) = \begin{cases} 1 & \text{if } u \text{ and } v \text{ are minDNFs} \\ \frac{c}{d_v} & \text{if } v \text{ is minDNF but } u \text{ is not} \\ \frac{c}{d_u} & \text{if } u \text{ is minDNF but } v \text{ is not} \\ 0.5 & \text{if } u \text{ and } v \text{ are not minDNFs} \end{cases} \quad (3)$$

We note that if the nodes u and v are both either minDNFs or non-minDNFs then we do not need to compute their degrees. Only if one of the nodes is a minDNF, we have to compute its degree (d_u or d_v), but we do not have to determine its minDNF or non-minDNF degrees. The theorem below, shows that sampling quality is still good:

THEOREM 4. *The sampling non-uniformity of weighting scheme in Eq. (3) is bounded by $1+d^m/c$, where d^m is maximum minDNF degree of a node.*

PROOF. Let u be a minDNF node, with minDNF degree d^m_u and non-minDNF degree d^n_u. The total weight for u is given as $s(u) = \sum_{v \in N_u} w(u,v) = d^n_u \cdot \frac{c}{d_u} + d^m_u \leq c + d^m_u$. The last step holds since $d^n_u \leq d_u$. The least weight at any node occurs when $d^m_u = 0$, and the most weight is when $d^m_u = \max_u \{d^m_u\} = d^m$. Thus, the non-uniformity is given as $\frac{c+d^m}{c} = 1 + d^m/c$. □

In practice, this weighting scheme works well. One reason for this is that the expected minDNF degree of a node is much better than the worst-case d^m given above.

Random Walks with Jumps and Restarts: Even after pruning, the partial order graph of sampling minimal DNF generators is large. The walker may be thus get trapped in local regions of the graph which consists of non-minimal DNFs. If this happens, our algorithm will not output minimal DNFs even after a long run, although the samples are guaranteed to be uniform. To avoid avoid getting stuck in local parts, we use the following two strategies: i) Random Walks with Random Jumps (RWRJ): In case the algorithm outputs no minimal DNF generators even after r consecutive steps, we abort the current path, and randomly jump to any earlier minimal DNF generator in the history as its new start. Any such node is then deleted, so that it will not again be chosen as a jump point. ii) Random Walks with Restart (RWR): At each step in the random walk, we enable a certain probability r that the walker jumps back to the root node (empty itemset). We confirm empirically that RWRJ is the better strategy.

AND- and OR-Clause Cache: To further improve execution time, we pre-compute the frequent AND-clauses and OR-Clauses of length 2, and store them in a hash table, so that they can be used to quickly test for the valid ATC and AAC operations. For example, when we apply ATC operations on a clause Z_i in DNF Z, we first get all frequent candidate items I_{ij} to be added for each literal $z_{ij} \in Z_i$. Then the candidate items to be added by ATC for the clause Z_i are $\{ \bigcap_j I_{ij} | z_{ij} \in Z_i \}$. We can do so quickly by looking up the candidate items in the hash table. This step avoids searching the whole $\mathcal{Z}$ space when we apply ATC operations and thus improves the efficiency.

Fast Minimality Determination: Since we perform random walks on a partial order graph that consists of both minimal and non-minimal DNFs, Lemma 6 and Lemma 7 mentioned below can help to quickly determine the minimality of a DNF when performing random walks without explicitly testing properties (a), (b) in Theorem 1, which can save a lot of computational overhead.

LEMMA 6. *Let $Z = \bigvee_{i=1}^m Z_i$, with $m \geq 2$, be a general DNF expression that violates property (a) in Theorem 1. Let $T(Z_k) \subseteq \bigcup_{j \neq k} T(Z_j)$. By adding an item to clause Z_k in Z, the resulting DNF cannot be minDNF.*

PROOF. The tidset of a clause is anti-monotonic. By adding an item x to clause Z_k, resulting in clause Z_k', i.e., $Z_k' = Z_k \wedge x$, we still have $T(Z_k') \subseteq \bigcup_{j \neq k} T(Z_j)$. Hence property (a) is violated. □

However, note that adding an item to other clauses rather than Z_1 in Z can result in a minDNF node.

LEMMA 7. *Let $Z = \bigvee_{i=1}^m Z_i$ be a general DNF expression, with $m \geq 2$, and let clause $Z_k \in Z$ violate property (b) in Theorem 1. Adding an item to clause Z_k cannot result in a minimal DNF expression.*

PROOF. Since Z_k violates property (b) in Theorem 1, there exists item $x \in Z_k$, such that $T(Z_k) \cup (\bigcup_{j \neq k} T(Z_j)) = T(Z_k^{'}) \cup (\bigcup_{j \neq k} T(Z_j))$, where $Z_k = Z_k^{'} \wedge x$. Let $Z_k^{''} = Z_k \wedge y = Z_k^{'} \wedge x \wedge y$ and consider the DNF expression $Z'' = Z_k^{''} \vee (\bigvee_{j \neq k} Z_j)$. Assume that Z'' is minDNF, which implies that $(Z_k^{'} \wedge x \wedge y)$ is minAND by Lemma 1. This in turn implies that the difference set $D_y = T(Z_k^{'} \wedge y) - T(Z_k^{'} \wedge x \wedge y)$ is non-empty. We consider three cases: (1) If $D_y \subseteq \bigcup_{j \neq k} T(Z_j)$, then $T(Z_k^{'} \wedge x \wedge y) \cup (\bigcup_{j \neq k} T(Z_j)) = T(Z_k^{'} \wedge y) \cup (\bigcup_{j \neq k} T(Z_j))$, which contradicts the assumption that Z'' is a minDNF. (2) If $D_y \cap \bigcup_{j \neq k} T(Z_j) = \emptyset$, then we have $D_y \subseteq T(Z_k^{'}) \subseteq T(Z_k^{'}) \cup (\bigcup_{j \neq k} T(Z_j)) = T(Z_k) \cup (\bigcup_{j \neq k} T(Z_j))$, which implies that $D_y \subseteq T(Z_k) = T(Z_k^{'} \wedge x)$. However, by definition, $D_y \subseteq T(Z_k^{'} \wedge y)$. Hence $D_y \subseteq T(Z_k^{'} \wedge x) \cap T(Z_k^{'} \wedge y) = T(Z_k^{'} \wedge x \wedge y)$. But thus implies that $D_y = \emptyset$, which contradicts the assumption that $Z_k^{'} \wedge x \wedge y$ is minAND. (3) If $D_y \nsubseteq \bigcup_{j \neq k} T(Z_j)$ and $D \cap \bigcup_{j \neq k} T(Z_j) \neq \emptyset$ then we can divide D_y into two parts $D_y = D_y' \cup D_y''$, such that $D_y' \subseteq \bigcup_{j \neq k} T(Z_j)$, $D_y'' \cap \bigcup_{j \neq k} T(Z_j) = \emptyset$, and $D_y' \neq \emptyset, D_y'' \neq \emptyset$. Similar to step (2), $D_y'' \subseteq T(Z_k^{'} \wedge x \wedge y)$, which implies that $D_y = D_y' \cup D_y'' = T(Z_k' \wedge y) - T(Z_k' \wedge x \wedge y) = D_y'$. However, this implies that $D_y'' = \emptyset$, which is a contradiction. From the three cases above, we conclude that Z'' is not minDNF. □

Once again, note that adding an item to $Z_j, j \neq k$, may possibly generate a minimal DNF. Consider an example from Table 1 again, with DNF $D|BF$. It violates property (*b*) in Theorem 1 since $T(D|BF) = T(D|F)$ and $D|F$ is a minimal DNF generator. However, one extension of this DNF is $BF|DE$, which is a minimal DNF generator. Figure 1(b) shows this example. The solid ovals in the figure are minimal DNF generators, and dashed ovals represent non-minimal DNFs.

3.4 Sampling Minimal AND-clauses

LEMMA 8. *The partial order graph on minimal AND-clause is connected.*

PROOF. According to Lemma 1, any subset of a minimal AND-clause generator is also the minimal AND-clause. Thus, in the partial order graph a node is connected to to all its immediate subsets/parents. □

For example, if ABC is a minAND then ABC has three parents, AB, AC and BC, which are all minANDs. Given this connected state-space, a simple symmetric transition probability matrix suffices to sample minAND expressions:

$$P(u,v) = \begin{cases} \frac{1}{max(d_u,d_v)} & \text{if } v \in N_u \\ 1 - \sum_{x \in N_u} P(u,x) & \text{if } u = v \end{cases} \quad (4)$$

We can use this matrix in the algorithm in Figure 2 to mine all minAND clauses.

4. EXPERIMENTS

We evaluate the benefits of mining minDNF expressions by using them as features for categorical data classification task. We also evaluate the sampling quality. We compare our results with Blosom [22], which is the only current algorithm that can mine minDNF patterns (although it is a complete method). For pure-AND clauses, we also compare with CHARM-L [21], a state-of-the-art method for mining minimal AND-clauses (i.e., minimal generators.) All experiments are performed on a quad-core Intel i7 3.5GHz CPU, with 16GB memory, and 2TB disk, running Linux (Ubuntu 11.10). The minDNF sampling code was implemented in C++. All datasets and source code are available at: `http://www.cs.rpi.edu/~zaki/www-new/pmwiki.php/Software`.

4.1 Classification Performance

We experimented with a wide range of datasets from the UCI repository [13] as shown in Table 2. First, each of the 34 datasets was converted into a categorical one using entropy-based discretization [12], as implemented in the Orange data mining suite [10]. The total number of transactions and items in each dataset, and the number of classes (ranging from 2 to 24) are shown in the table. Next we ran a linear SVM, on the original (non-discretized) dataset, as well as on the discretized dataset, using 5-fold cross-validation. For a given run of minDNF sampling, we converted each of the mined minDNF patterns into a binary attribute, that takes on the value 1 if a transaction satisfies the minDNF formula, and 0 otherwise. This binary-valued dataset is then classified using linear SVM with 5-fold cross-validation, again using the Orange library (which in turn uses LIBSVM [7]). Since the sampling is randomized, we repeat the sampling 10 times, and report the averages.

For minDNF and minAND sampling the default parameters are as follows: We use the random walks with random jump approach, with $j = 3$. We use $\alpha = 0.9$ and set c to the average transaction length. The minimum support for the DNF and clause were both set to 1, i.e., $\sigma_{\min} = \sigma^c_{\min} = 1$. Finally, we sampled $k = 100$ minDNF patterns. Thus, for minDNF and minAND the number of "items" or features is at most k for all datasets (it can be less after removing duplicates). Note also that we do not perform any feature selection (it may be possible to further improve the performance if this is done).

Table 2 shows the 5-fold cross-validation classification accuracy and standard-error for each algorithm, over each of the datasets, averaged over 10 runs. The best results are shown in bold. In the table, results for minDNF sampling using the weight matrix in Eq. (2) are denoted as minDNF, whereas results using the faster weight computation in Eq. (3) are denoted as minDNF*. SVM-orig and SVMd denote the performance of SVM on the original and discretized dataset, respectively. Finally, non-default parameters are indicated in the table (third row), when we compare minAND with $k = 500$, and minDNF/minAND with $\sigma_{\min} = 5\%$.

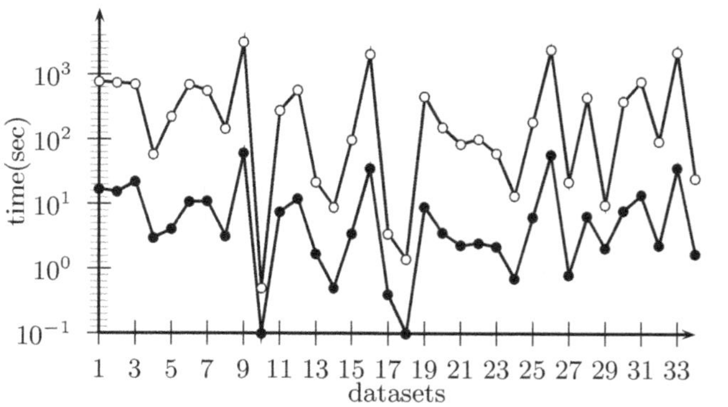

Figure 3: Time (in sec) for minDNF (white dots) and minDNF* (black dots)

minDNF Time: The total time for minDNF and minDNF* is shown in Figure 3. The datasets are numbered in the order they appear in Table 2. The running time is affected by the number of items, since the more the items, the more

dataset	description			SVM		minDNF Sampling			minAND Sampling		
	cls	trans	items	SVM-orig	SVMd	minDNF	minDNF $\sigma_{\min} = 5\%$	minDNF*	minAND	minAND $k = 500$	minAND $\sigma_{\min} = 5\%$
adultsample	3	977	113	59.5±11.7	36.6±0.7	79.8±0.9	**81.8±1.3**	57.1±1.6	48.6±1.4	45.[illegible]±0.5	75.2±0.9
anneal	5	898	73	33.6±5.0	43.7±3.5	**97.6±0.4**	97.2±0.4	92.0±0.6	80.0±0.6	91.7±0.7	82.5±0.6
audiology	24	226	154	33.2±2.8	33.2±2.8	**79.7±3.0**	75.1±2.3	48.3±3.3	43.8±2.0	33.4±1.4	37.5±1.5
balancescale	3	625	20	**87.8±1.0**	**87.8±1.0**	71.7±1.4	74.1±1.3	72.0±1.4	46.8±3.9	74.0±1.2	15.7±7.7
breastwisc1	2	683	30	86.7±0.8	60.8±1.6	95.4±0.5	**95.5±0.6**	95.0±0.6	75.6±1.1	93.2±0.8	77.2±0.5
breastwisc2	2	699	90	88.0±1.1	88.0±1.1	**94.4±0.6**	91.9±0.9	89.4±1.0	61.5±1.0	72.2±1.3	86.6±0.9
breastwisc3	2	683	89	84.2±1.5	84.0±1.5	**93.8±0.6**	**93.8±0.9**	87.1±1.1	45.8±1.0	93.5±0.8	52.1±0.3
breastcancer	2	286	41	71.3±1.3	**72.0±1.0**	67.8±3.0	68.5±2.3	64.7±2.1	54.8±2.3	60.3±2.1	68.5±2.4
brownselected	3	186	182	89.8±1.5	39.2±2.1	**99.5±0.4**	99.0±0.6	88.3±2.1	50.4±1.8	64.4±2.5	67.9±2.9
bupa	2	345	7	50.1±3.5	54.8±3.2	**63.2±2.7**	**63.2±2.7**	**63.2±2.7**	54.8±3.2	54.8±3.2	54.8±3.2
car	4	1728	21	64.0±0.8	64.0±0.8	**81.0±0.4**	77.2±0.6	76.7±0.8	71.2±0.4	79.1±0.8	87.2±0.7
crx	2	690	53	74.8±2.5	**85.4±1.1**	83.6±1.5	83.7±1.5	74.1±1.5	62.1±1.5	76.4±1.3	71.9±1.2
glass	6	214	22	48.1±4.7	23.3±3.9	75.7±1.0	**77.2±1.1**	75.2±1.4	62.5±1.6	50.5±0.7	70.0±1.6
hayesroth	3	132	15	46.1±4.6	46.1±4.6	73.5±3.5	**76.8±2.8**	72.3±4.0	68.4±3.2	78.7±3.3	58.9±4.0
heartdisease	2	303	29	70.3±5.5	65.7±2.8	78.5±2.2	**78.9±2.2**	76.0±2.7	67.2±3.5	62.0±1.7	71.6±3.1
ionosphere	2	351	142	83.8±0.7	84.6±1.6	**89.5±1.5**	88.8±1.3	86.3±1.6	49.3±0.8	80.8±1.2	46.5±0.9
iris	3	150	12	93.3±2.4	68.7±2.0	94.9±1.3	**95.5±1.4**	94.9±1.8	95.2±1.4	95.4±1.3	94.7±1.8
lenses	3	24	9	83.0±7.7	83.0±7.7	80.3±6.8	72.5±7.9	61.6±11.1	78.2±6.2	**87.0±8.3**	86.2±8.2
lungcancer	3	32	157	**52.9±10.3**	**52.9±10.3**	52.1±7.5	44.6±7.5	39.3±8.2	33.2±6.1	31.7±4.3	34.4±6.8
lymphography	4	148	50	**82.4±4.1**	81.1±3.0	80.0±3.6	79.1±2.4	70.9±3.3	63.6±3.1	75.9±2.9	68.0±2.6
monks1	2	556	17	67.6±2.6	67.6±2.6	84.3±1.4	83.7±1.4	77.5±1.6	65.4±1.8	**92.7±0.9**	66.6±1.6
monks2	2	601	17	64.2±1.1	64.2±1.1	66.3±1.1	71.9±1.7	62.6±1.4	53.8±1.6	**74.7±1.6**	68.2±1.7
monks3	2	554	17	74.4±0.6	74.4±0.6	93.4±1.1	**96.4±0.9**	89.2±1.2	69.7±1.4	93.6±1.1	84.5±1.0
postoperative	3	90	20	66.7±1.8	**67.8±2.1**	57.4±4.3	55.1±3.8	56.3±3.1	58.4±4.7	58.2±4.2	61.6±3.4
primarytumor	21	339	37	28.6±0.6	28.6±0.6	**40.2±2.0**	38.6±2.1	32.6±2.1	30.0±1.7	36.2±2.5	33.9±2.3
promoters	2	106	228	72.5±6.5	72.5±6.5	**74.2±3.0**	65.2±3.8	62.5±3.9	57.6±3.2	65.5±4.3	66.1±4.6
shuttle	2	253	16	96.5±0.7	96.8±1.0	**97.1±0.9**	94.4±1.2	90.5±1.8	81.2±2.3	96.4±1.1	95.0±1.5
tictactoe	2	958	27	67.8±1.0	67.7±0.9	**78.7±1.2**	76.9±1.3	70.2±1.3	47.4±1.0	68.8±1.6	76.1±1.4
titanic	2	2201	8	76.8±1.1	76.8±1.1	79.0±0.9	77.9±1.0	79.0±0.9	78.9±1.0	**79.1±0.9**	79.0±0.9
voting	2	435	32	91.0±0.7	91.3±0.8	**94.6±1.1**	93.9±0.8	91.8±1.0	71.9±1.1	83.1±1.4	78.3±1.1
wdbc	2	569	64	88.9±4.3	75.9±3.8	95.3±0.8	**95.5±0.8**	92.9±1.0	69.6±1.0	84.8±0.9	85.2±0.8
wine	3	178	37	85.9±4.8	96.7±2.0	**97.9±0.5**	97.6±1.1	94.4±1.3	76.3±2.6	95.9±1.3	74.7±1.9
yeastRPR	3	186	182	89.8±1.5	39.2±2.1	99.3±0.7	**99.7±0.2**	87.6±2.0	59.7±2.2	73.7±1.8	43.6±2.0
zoo	7	101	36	95.1±1.5	95.1±1.5	**96.3±1.6**	96.2±1.5	89.5±2.1	82.5±3.5	95.5±1.9	83.2±3.7

Table 2: Classification Performance: Accuracy ± Standard Error: cls denotes #classes

the number of neighbors, which affects the weight/transition probability computation time. However, note that these results are with support one, and substantial speedup is possible for higher support values. We can observe that minDNF* is typically over an order of magnitude faster than minDNF, though this comes at some penalty in classification performance, as we describe next.

minDNF versus SVMd: Our minDNF sampling algorithm yields a near-uniform sample and we can see from the classification accuracies in columns 7 & 8 that the sampled minDNF patterns make excellent features. In 24 out of the 34 datasets, they yield the best accuracy among all methods, including SVM-orig (on the original) and SVMd (on the discretized datasets). On three datasets, the differences between minDNF and best method is not significant. On two datasets SVMs substantially outperform minDNF (namely, balancescale and postoperative, where the difference is more than 10%).

minDNF versus minAND: Comparing the Boolean expression features comprising minDNF patterns versus minAND patterns (both with $k = 100$), we find that minDNF substantially outperforms minAND (see columns 7 and 10). Although initially unexpected, it is perhaps not that surprising, given the fact that minDNFs can be considered as disjunctive rules, and are much more informative than simple conjunctive rules. Over all the 34 datasets, minDNF sampling yields on average 2.69 clauses per DNF expression, with a standard deviation of 1. For fairness, we also compared minDNF (with $k = 100$) to minAND with $k = 500$ features (see column 11). The larger number of features improves minAND in most cases. However, minDNF (with $k = 100$) is still substantially better than minAND ($k = 500$); only on three datasets (lenses, monks1, and monks2) does minAND outperform minDNF. These results indicate that overall minDNF patterns are more effective than minAND patterns.

minDNF* Sampling: Since minDNF sampling using Eq. (2) does take more time, we also compared with minDNF* that uses the faster weight computation in Eq. (3). We can see that minDNF* sampling suffers in performance compared to minDNF. However, minDNF* still outperforms SVMd on 22, SVM-orig on 21, minAND patterns (with $k = 100$) on 31, and minAND (with $k = 500$) on 18 out of the 34 datasets.

Effect of Support: To see the effect of minimum support on classification accuracy, we ran minDNF and minAND sampling with the minimum support set to 5% of the number of transactions (see columns 8 & 12). Overall, we find that adding the frequency constraint is not that beneficial to for minDNF sampling, since mining frequent minDNFs improves the accuracy only slightly in 13 datasets, when compared to the minDNFs with support one. On the other hand, frequent minANDs are better than support-one minANDs on 26 datasets. Mining frequent expressions obviously lowers running times.

Negated Items: We also experimented with minDNF expressions containing negated items. However, in this case the accuracy was slightly better for the negated items in only 5 out of the 34 datasets, which unfortunately came at the expense of a significant increase in the runtime (sometimes by orders of magnitude). We conclude that negated items do not confer significant advantages in terms of classification (at least for the UCI datasets tested).

Our results above clearly demonstrate the value of mining/sampling minDNF patterns, especially in support-less mode (i.e., $\sigma_{\min} = 1$).

4.2 Sampling Evaluation

Having shown the effectiveness of minDNF sampling for classification, we now study the sampling quality provided by minDNF and the sensitivity to various parameters. We use both small (first three) and large (last three) datasets shown in Table 3 for these experiments. The last four are taken from the FIMI repository [14]. The Gene dataset is from [22], and IBM100 is a synthetic dataset generated using the IBM itemset generator [1].

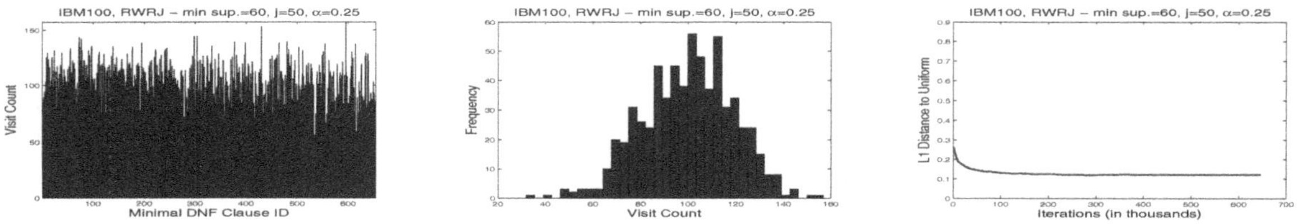

(a) Visit Counts (b) Count Histogram (c) Variation Distance

Figure 4: Sampling Quality (RWRJ): IBM100

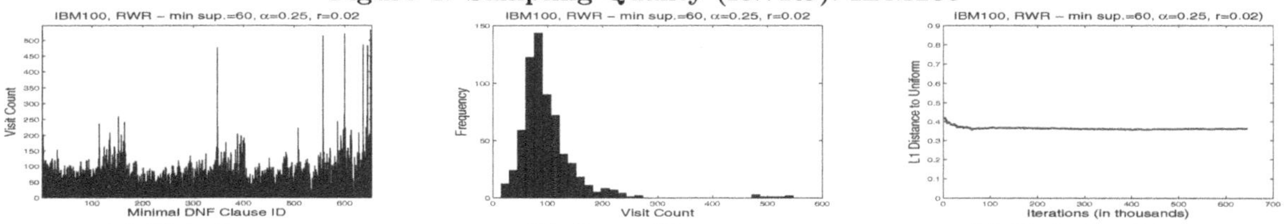

(a) Visit Counts (b) Count Histogram (c) Variation Distance

Figure 5: Sampling Quality (RWR): IBM100

Dataset	trans	items	avg. trans len
IBM100	100	20	9.3
Gene	74	824	86.1
Chess	3196	75	37
Connect	67557	129	43
Retail	88162	16470	10.3
Kosarak	990002	41270	8.1

Table 3: Datasets

Random Walk Type: We first show the effect of the type of random walk, i.e., random walk with random jumps (RWRJ, $j = 50$) versus random walks with restart (RWR, $r = 0.02$), as shown in Figures 4 and 5. With $\sigma_{\min} = 60$, on the IBM100 dataset, there are 654 distinct minDNF patterns (found using Blosom). We ran minDNF sampling for $k = 654 \times 100$ iterations. We use $\alpha = 0.25$ and c is set to the avg. transaction length.

If the dataset has f minDNF patterns and we perform the uniform sampling for $k = f \times t$ steps, the number of times m a specific pattern will be sampled is described by the binomial distribution, $\mathcal{B}(m|k,p)$, where $p = \frac{1}{f}$. The expected number of times a minDNF pattern is visited is given as $kp = f \cdot t \cdot \frac{1}{f} = t$, and the standard deviation is $\sqrt{kp(1-p)} = \sqrt{\frac{t(f-1)}{f}}$. For the IBM100 dataset, we have $f = 654$ and $t = 100$, and thus in the ideal case we expect to see each pattern 100 times, with standard deviation of $\sqrt{100 \cdot 653/654} = 9.99$. Figures 4 and 5 plot the number of times each pattern is visited (a), and the count histogram (b). The sampling statistics, namely the maximum, minimum, median, and standard deviation of visits counts for RWRJ and RWR are shown in Table 4. It is very clear that RWRJ is much superior to the RWR strategy; its median is closer to the ideal case, and the standard deviation is smaller. Whereas the RWRJ strategy jumps to a node in its history, RWR always restarts from the empty pattern. As such RWR is biased towards sampling patterns close to the origin, and this is reflected in the sampling quality.

	Maximum	Minimum	Median	Std
RWRJ	157	32	101	19.0
RWR	547	15	89	60.5

Table 4: Sampling Statistics: IBM100

Convergence Rate: One important issue in using MCMC sampling is to determine when the initial distribution converges to the stationary distribution and how fast the convergence rate is. It is well known that the mixing time is closely related to the spectral gap, $\gamma = |\lambda_1 - \lambda_2| = |1 - \lambda_2|$, which is defined as the absolute difference between the largest $\lambda_1 = 1$ and the second largest eigenvalue λ_2 of the transition matrix P [9]. The larger the spectral gap, the faster the walk converges. Unfortunately, we cannot compute the entire transition matrix P; the whole point of sampling is to avoid enumerating all the minDNF patterns. An alternative strategy to measure the convergence rate is to compute the total variation distance, defined as $vd(P^t(s,.),\pi) = 0.5\sum_{q\in\mathcal{S}} |P^t(s,q) - \pi(q)|$, where s is the initial state, P^t is the transition matrix at time t, and π is the desired stationary distribution.

Figures 4(c) and 5(c) plot the variation distance for the RWRJ and RWR sampling methods. Here we compute the variation distance empirically. To be more specific, we estimate $P^t(s,q)$ at time t via the count histogram, converted into a probability distribution of visitations, to each pattern q from the initial empty pattern $s = \emptyset$. We compute the variation distance after every 1000 steps. We can see that the distance converges to slightly around 0.12 for RWRJ and to 0.36 for RWR, indicating that RWRJ is the better strategy. We also ran experiments on the Gene and Chess datasets, and obtained similar results (figures omitted due to space constraints).

α, c, j	npats	mean	std	max	min	med	time
$j = 3$	636.2	15.7	10.0	60.2	1	14	98.8s
$j = 5$	635.2	15.7	8.9	48.0	1	15.8	100.2s
$j = 10$	636	15.7	8.1	45.2	1	16.4	100.2s
$j = 50$	629	15.9	7.6	38.2	1	16	100.2s
$j = 100$	637.4	15.7	7.6	39.6	1	16.2	101.6s
$\alpha = 0.1$	654	15.3	5.4	34	1.6	15	74.8s
$\alpha = 0.25$	654	15.3	5.3	34.2	2.6	15	80s
$\alpha = 0.5$	654	15.3	5.6	35.4	2.2	15	89.4s
$\alpha = 0.75$	651.8	15.3	7.0	39.4	1	16	96.8s
$\alpha = 0.9$	634.8	15.8	7.6	37.8	1	16.4	101.7s
$c = 5$	633.2	15.8	7.3	35.8	1	16.4	125.6s
$c = avg(9.3)$	632.8	15.8	7.5	45.4	1	16	100.0s
$c = max(17)$	639	15.7	7.9	47.2	1	16.2	88.8s
$c = 50$	633.2	15.8	8.8	50.6	1	15.8	79.1s

Table 5: Effect of Parameters: IBM100

Effect of α, c, j: Table 5 shows the effect of these three parameters on the sampling quality on IBM100 with $\sigma_{\min} = 60$. We set $k = 10000$ iterations. We run each experiment 5 times, and report the average number of distinct minDNFs sampled (npats), mean, standard deviation (std), maximum, minimum, and median (med) of the visit counts, and the average total time. Ideal sampling should yield a mean visit count of $k/f = 15.3$, and a standard deviation of $\sqrt{k/f(1-1/f)} = 3.9$, since IBM100 has $f = 654$ minDNF patterns for $\sigma_{\min} = 60$. First, we look at the effect of j, fixing $c = avg$ and $\alpha = 0.9$. Larger j results in a smaller standard deviation, and ideally j should not be constrained. However, for many of the classification datasets the random walk could get trapped in a local region, and therefore, we set $j = 3$ in our earlier experiments. Next, we look at the effect of α, setting $j = 50$ and $c = avg$. We find that larger α takes more time, with a slight increase in std, most likely due to the constraint on j. Lastly, we fix $j = 50$, $\alpha = 0.9$ and vary c. Larger c values take lesser time, but also result in higher deviation. The average c value (9.3 for IBM100) offers an acceptable choice.

Dataset	1%	5%	10%	20%
IBM100	1m50s	45.5s	40.2s	20.9s
*	17.5s	1.6s	14.5s	9.9s
Gene	3h45m12s	46m13s	31m1s	3m45s
*	19m11s	6m52s	5m23s	3m36s
Chess	11h26m11s	6h41m34s	5h23m29s	4h28m33s
*	1h6m8s	59m22s	42m15s	28m33s
Connect	15h52m47s	8h23m18s	7h59m22s	6h31m39s
*	4h44m2s	2h19m22s	1h58m53s	1h34m48s
Retail	50m4s	1m6s	35.0s	3.1s
*	59m25s	21.5s	12.8s	4.7s
Kosarak	27h58m43s	2h24m39s	9m55s	3m41s
*	8h31m4s	20m3s	2m14s	1m40s

Table 6: Running Time: minDNF and minDNF*

Scalability: Table 6 shows the time to sample the small (with $k = 1000$) and large datasets (with $k = 100$) for various support thresholds using minDNF and minDNF*. Blosom was unfortunately not able to mine the complete set of patterns for any of these datasets for the support levels shown even after 24hours for the smaller datasets, and 48hrs for the large ones. We note that whereas minDNF provides better theoretical guarantee, minDNF* is significantly faster (by as much as an order of magnitude). We also compared minAND sampling time with Blosom-MA and CHARM-L, both of which can mine minimal AND-clauses. For example, for the Gene dataset with 10% support, minAND took 0.7s to sample 1000 patterns, whereas CHARM-L took 40m54s and Blosom-MA took 2h58m56s. For lower support values, neither of these methods could finish within 24hours, whereas for 1% support minAND finished in 1.3s. These results confirm that complete mining is practically infeasible, whereas sampling provides a viable alternative.

5. CONCLUSIONS

In this paper we presented the first approach to mine the simplest Boolean patterns, namely the minimal DNF expressions. We propose a novel weighting scheme to compute the transition probability matrix for the Markov chain Monte Carlo sampling algorithm, which bounds the amount of non-uniformity in the sampling. Since the method can be slow in practice, we also suggest a faster alternative, that yields effective sampling quality as well. We perform an extensive set of experiments to test various design parameters, and justify our choices. Finally, somewhat surprisingly, we found that the minimal DNF patterns make very effective features for classification. Via an extensive set of experiments on UCI datasets, we show that our method outperforms simple AND-clause based features, as well as the SVM method, typically by a wide margin, though it does suffer in the runtime comparison. However, the faster weight computation approach yields significantly faster running times, with some loss in the classification accuracy. The minDNF features still remain the effective across the different classifiers. Perhaps the most interesting aspect of the classification study is that we use support-less patterns (with minimum support one), and do not perform any feature selection. Our future work will target more effective feature selection by considering other interestingness criteria for the patterns while sampling, such as their discrimination power. Efficiency still remains an issue, which may be tackled by implementing the approach on multi-core processors, as well and utilizing graphics computing units (GPUs), since the MCMC methods are inherently parallel.

Acknowledgments

This work was supported in part by NSF grant EMT-0829835.

6. REFERENCES

[1] R. Agrawal, H. Mannila, R. Srikant, E. Toivonen, A. Verkamo, et al. Fast discovery of association rules. *Advances in knowledge discovery and data mining*, 12:307–328, 1996.

[2] M. Al Hasan and M. Zaki. Output space sampling for graph patterns. *Proceedings of the VLDB Endowment*, 2(1):730–741, 2009.

[3] Y. Bastide, R. Taouil, N. Pasquier, G Stumme, and L. Lakhal. Mining frequent patterns with counting inference. *SIGKDD Explorations*, 2(2), Dec. 2000.

[4] M. Boley, T. Gärtner, H. Grosskreutz, and I. Fraunhofer. Formal concept sampling for counting and threshold-free local pattern mining. In *SIAM Data Mining Conf.*, 2010.

[5] M. Boley and H. Grosskreutz. Approximating the number of frequent sets in dense data. *Knowledge and Information Systems*, 21(1):65–89, 2009.

[6] M. Boley, C. Lucchese, D. Paurat, and T. Gärtner. Direct local pattern sampling by efficient two-step random procedures. In *ACM SIGKDD Conference*, 2011.

[7] C.-C. Chang and C.-J. Lin. LIBSVM: A library for support vector machines. *ACM Transactions on Intelligent Systems and Technology*, 2:27:1–27:27, 2011. Software available at `http://www.csie.ntu.edu.tw/~cjlin/libsvm`.

[8] V. Chaoji, M. A. Hasan, S. Salem, J. Besson, and M. J. Zaki. ORIGAMI: A Novel and Effective Approach for Mining Representative Orthogonal Graph Patterns. *Statistical Analysis and Data Mining*, 1(2):67–84, June 2008.

[9] M. Cowles and B. Carlin. Markov chain monte carlo convergence diagnostics: a comparative review. *J. American Statistical Association*, 91(434):883–904, 1996.

[10] T. Curk, J. Demsar, Q. Xu, G. Leban, U. Petrovic, I. Bratko, G. Shaulsky, and B. Zupan. Microarray data mining with visual programming. *Bioinformatics*, 21:396–398, Feb. 2005.

[11] G. Dong, C. Jiang, J. Pei, J. Li, and L. Wong. Mining succinct systems of minimal generators of formal concepts. In *Int'l Conf. Database Systems for Advanced Applications*, 2005.

[12] U. Fayyad and K. Irani. Multi-interval discretization of continuous-valued attributes for classification learning. In *Int'l Joint Conf. on AI*, 1993.

[13] A. Frank and A. Asuncion. UCI machine learning repository (http://archive.ics.uci.edu/ml), 2010.

[14] B. Goethals and M. J. Zaki. Advances in frequent itemset mining implementations: report on FIMI'03. *SIGKDD Explorations*, 6(1):109–117, June 2004.

[15] D. Gunopulos, H. Mannila, and S. Saluja. Discovering all Most Specific Sentences by Randomized Algorithm. In *6th Int'l Conf. on Database Theory*, 1997.

[16] M. A. Hasan and M. J. Zaki. Musk Uniform sampling of k maximal patterns. In *9th SIAM Data Mining Conf.*, Apr. 2009.

[17] E. Loekito and J. Bailey. Fast mining of high dimensional expressive contrast patterns using zero-suppressed binary decision diagrams. In *ACM SIGKDD Conf.* ACM, 2006.

[18] A. A. Nanavati, K. P. Chitrapura, S. Joshi, and R. Krishnapuram. Mining generalised disjunctive association rules. In *ACM CIKM Conference*, 2001.

[19] Y. Shima, S. Mitsuishi, K. Hirata, and M. Harao. Extracting minimal and closed monotone dnf formulas. In *Int'l Conf. on Discovery Science*, 2004.

[20] M. Zaki and N. Ramakrishnan. Reasoning about sets using redescription mining. In *ACM SIGKDD Conference*, 2005.

[21] M. J. Zaki and C.-J. Hsiao. Efficient algorithms for mining closed itemsets and their lattice structure. *IEEE Transactions on Knowledge and Data Engineering*, 17(4):462–478, Apr. 2005.

[22] L. Zhao, M. J. Zaki, and N. Ramakrishnan. Blosom: A framework for mining arbitrary boolean expressions. In *12th ACM SIGKDD Conference*, Aug. 2006.

The Contextual Focused Topic Model

Xu Chen
Department of Electrical and Computer Engineering
Duke University
Durham, NC 27708
xu.chen@duke.edu

Mingyuan Zhou
Department of Electrical and Computer Engineering
Duke University
Durham, NC 27708
mz1@ee.duke.edu

Lawrence Carin
Department of Electrical and Computer Engineering
Duke University
Durham, NC 27708
lcarin@ee.duke.edu

ABSTRACT

A nonparametric Bayesian contextual focused topic model (cFTM) is proposed. The cFTM infers a sparse ("focused") set of topics for each document, while also leveraging contextual information about the author(s) and document venue. The hierarchical beta process, coupled with a Bernoulli process, is employed to infer the focused set of topics associated with each author and venue; the same construction is also employed to infer those topics associated with a given document that are unusual (termed "random effects"), relative to topics that are inferred as probable for the associated author(s) and venue. To leverage statistical strength and infer latent interrelationships between authors and venues, the Dirichlet process is utilized to cluster authors and venues. The cFTM automatically infers the number of topics needed to represent the corpus, the number of author and venue clusters, and the probabilistic importance of the author, venue and random-effect information on word assignment for a given document. Efficient MCMC inference is presented. Example results and interpretations are presented for two real datasets, demonstrating promising performance, with comparison to other state-of-the-art methods.

Categories and Subject Descriptors

H.3.3 [**Information Storage and Retrieval**]: Information Search and Retrieval-Clustering; H.2.8 [**Information Systems Applications**]: Database Applications-Data mining

General Terms

Algorithm, Experimentation

Keywords

Topic modeling, Bayesian nonparametric, clustering, Dirichlet process, hierarchical beta process

1. INTRODUCTION

With the popularization of Web applications and other digital media, frequently one is interested in analyzing a large corpus [14, 1, 11, 13, 26], and it is desirable to place the analysis of such data within the context of other readily available associated information [22, 19, 6, 18, 5]. For example, with a large corpus, many documents may be written by the same authors or groups of authors, and it is desirable to account for this information when analyzing the documents [22]. It is likely that a given author may concentrate on a subset of topics, and utilization of this information may help infer the topics associated with each of the documents in the corpus. Further, each document is typically published in a venue (*e.g.*, magazine, newspaper, website, conference proceedings, etc.), and the network of venue information also carries significant information [6] (the inference of topics associated with any single document is influenced by other documents published at the same or similar venues). It is therefore of interest to learn interrelationships between venues, and between the authors, to allow an appropriate sharing of information from multiple documents.

In the specific examples considered in this paper, the corpus of documents consists of technical papers and proposals, and we leverage information from the associated author names and publication venues. We propose a novel nonparametric Bayesian approach that extends the recently developed focused topic model (FTM) [28]. We refer to the proposed model as a *contextual* FTM, or cFTM, as it is capable of accounting for an arbitrary set of relational contextual information; while here we focus on two forms of context, author names and publication venues, the basic approach may be extended to arbitrary types and numbers of context. The model is nonparametric in the sense that it infers the number of topics characteristic of the corpus automatically, and it also infers a clustering of the authors and venues (such that documents from similar authors and venues influence the topics associated with any given document). In addition to increasing the power of the model by appropriate sharing of data, the clustering of venues and authors is of interest in its own right, for inferring relational information. The Dirichlet process [9, 10, 21, 25] is employed to perform the clustering nonparametrically (the number of clusters required of the data is inferred, and additional clusters may be added as new data warrants).

The proposed cFTM has three principal advantages compared to related models: (1) It automatically infers the number of topics by combining properties from the Dirichlet process [25] and hierarchical beta process [27], allowing

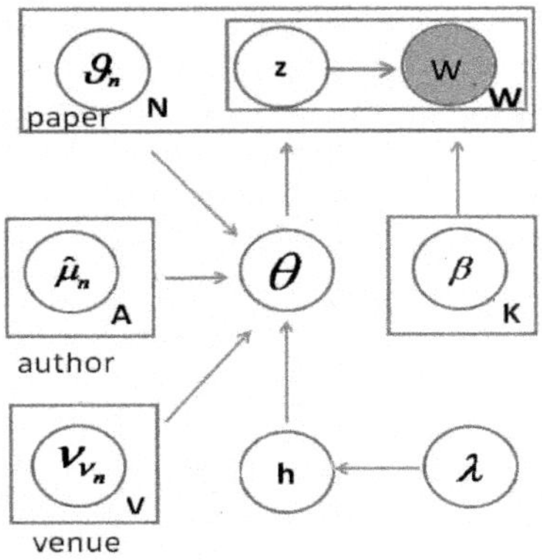

Figure 1: The graphical model for the proposed contextual focused topic model (cFTM), where A is the total set of authors, V is the total set of venues. The shaded variable is the observable variable and the hyper-parameters are omitted.

an unbounded number of topics for the entire corpus, while inferring a focused (sparse) set of topics for each individual document. (2) The cFTM nonparametrically clusters the authors and venues, thereby increasing statistical strength while also inferring useful relational information. (3) Instead of pre-specifying the importance of author/venue information (as was done in [6]), the cFTM automatically infers the document-dependent, probabilistic importance of the author/venue information on word assignment.

2. CONTEXTUAL FOCUSED TOPIC MODEL

Consider a corpus of N documents with W unique words in the vocabulary, A unique authors, and V unique venues. The corpus is represented as $\{\boldsymbol{d}_n, \boldsymbol{a}_n, v_n\}_{n=1,\dots,N}$, where $\boldsymbol{d}_n$ denotes the set of words in document n (the order of the words is exchangeable, *i.e.*, a bag-of-words model), $\boldsymbol{a}_n$ consists of a subset of authors from the set $\{1, \cdots, A\}$, and $v_n \in \{1, \cdots, V\}$ is the venue index. Each document appears in one venue and has one or multiple authors.

2.1 Word Assignment

In a topic model, document n is typically characterized by a distribution over topics, $\boldsymbol{\theta}_n$, and topic k by a distribution over words, $\boldsymbol{\beta}_k$. Let $w_{ni} \in \{1, \dots, V\}$ denote word i in document n. Each w_{ni} is assumed constituted by first drawing a single topic index $z_{ni} \in \{1, \dots, K\}$ from a multinomial distribution with probability vector $\boldsymbol{\theta}_n$; then w_{ni} is drawn from a multinomial distribution with probability vector $\boldsymbol{\beta}_{z_{ni}}$. Different topic models are distinguished by how $\{\boldsymbol{\theta}_n\}_{n=1,N}$ are constituted. For example, in latent Dirichlet allocation (LDA) [1], an early topic model, the words are generated as

$$w_{ni} \sim \text{Discrete}(\boldsymbol{\beta}_{z_{ni}}), \; z_{ni} \sim \text{Discrete}(\boldsymbol{\theta}_n) \quad (1)$$

$$\boldsymbol{\beta}_k \sim \text{Dir}(\eta, \cdots, \eta), \; \boldsymbol{\theta}_n \sim \text{Dir}(\alpha_\theta, \cdots, \alpha_\theta) \quad (2)$$

where Discrete($\boldsymbol{\beta}_{z_{ni}}$) is a distribution over indices, from which a *single* index is drawn from a multinomial distribution, with probability vector $\boldsymbol{\beta}_{z_{ni}}$ defining the probabilities of selecting the indices; η and α_θ are hyperparameters. In this simple model the $\boldsymbol{\theta}_n$ are drawn *independently*, not leveraging information from across the corpus, and not leveraging contextual information. We first discuss how this is generalized such that the distribution over topics for document n accounts for author and venue information, while also allowing a document-dependent "random effect" that accounts for idiosyncratic characteristics of a given document (*e.g.*, an outlier among papers by particular authors, published in a particular venue).

Let $\boldsymbol{\mu}_j$ represent a distribution over topics for author $j \in \{1, \dots, A\}$, and let $\boldsymbol{\mu}_v$ represent a distribution over topics for venue $v \in \{1, \dots, V\}$. Finally, let $\boldsymbol{\vartheta}_n$ represent a distribution over topics for document n, with this term constituting a "random effect" term, meaning that it captures unique aspects of document n that are not captured by the distribution over topics associated with the corresponding author(s) and venue. Recalling that $\boldsymbol{a}_n$ denotes the authors associated with document n, the averaged author distribution over topics for document n is

$$\hat{\boldsymbol{\mu}}_n = \frac{1}{|\boldsymbol{a}_n|} \sum_{j \in \boldsymbol{a}_n} \boldsymbol{\mu}_j \quad (3)$$

where $|\boldsymbol{a}_n|$ is the number of authors in document n. In (3) each of the $|\boldsymbol{a}_n|$ authors is assumed to contribute topics equally (uniformly) to document n; the model may be extended to infer the relative importance of the individual authors to multi-author documents (this may be done in a manner analogous to that discussed below, where we infer the importance of the author(s), venue and random effects to topic generation).

In the proposed model, word w_{ni} is drawn either from $\boldsymbol{\vartheta}_n$, $\hat{\boldsymbol{\mu}}_n$ or $\boldsymbol{\nu}_{v_n}$, where v_n is the venue of document n. The probability of selecting from these is respectively λ_{n1}, λ_{n2} and λ_{n3}, with $\sum_{j=1}^{3} \lambda_{nj} = 1$ and $\lambda_{nj} \geq 0$. Assuming $\{\boldsymbol{\vartheta}_n\}$, $\{\boldsymbol{\mu}_j\}$ and $\{\boldsymbol{\nu}_v\}$ are given/specified, the generative model is

$$w_{ni} \sim \text{Discrete}(\boldsymbol{\beta}_{z_{ni}}), z_{ni} \sim \text{Discrete}(\boldsymbol{\theta}_{ni}) \quad (4)$$

$$\boldsymbol{\beta}_k \sim \text{Dir}(\eta, \cdots, \eta) \quad (5)$$

$$\boldsymbol{\theta}_{ni} = h_{ni1}\boldsymbol{\vartheta}_n + h_{ni2}\hat{\boldsymbol{\mu}}_n + h_{ni3}\boldsymbol{\nu}_{v_n} \quad (6)$$

$$(h_{ni1}, h_{ni2}, h_{ni3}) \sim \text{Mult}(\lambda_{n1}, \lambda_{n2}, \lambda_{n3}) \quad (7)$$

$$(\lambda_{n1}, \lambda_{n2}, \lambda_{n3}) \sim \text{Dir}(\alpha, \alpha, \alpha) \quad (8)$$

where $(h_{ni1}, h_{ni2}, h_{ni3}) \in \{(1,0,0), (0,1,0), (0,0,1)\}$ is a three dimensional binary vector indicating which of the three terms the word w_{ni} belongs to.

The construction in (4)-(8) will prove convenient for inference; however, to connect it to more-conventional models like (1), (4)-(8) is equivalent to specifying $\boldsymbol{\theta}_n = \lambda_{n1}\boldsymbol{\vartheta}_n + \lambda_{n2}\hat{\boldsymbol{\mu}}_n + \lambda_{n3}\boldsymbol{\nu}_{v_n}$, where λ_{n1} represents the probability that w_{ni} is drawn from a topic unanticipated from the authors and venue, λ_{n2} represents the probability that the associated topic is characteristic of the author(s), and λ_{n3} quantifies the probability that the topic is characteristic of the venue.

This decomposition suggests developing *focused* (sparse) topic distributions for $\{\boldsymbol{\vartheta}_n\}$, $\{\boldsymbol{\mu}_j\}$ and $\{\boldsymbol{\nu}_v\}$, such that each of these distributions over topics focuses on the characteristics of authors and venues, while also identifying random-effect topics not anticipated by either; the construction of focused distributions for $\{\boldsymbol{\vartheta}_n\}$, $\{\boldsymbol{\mu}_j\}$ and $\{\boldsymbol{\nu}_v\}$ is detailed in Section 2.3. We first discuss how we may cluster the authors and venues, with the clustering manifested in terms of the probabilities over topics, $\{\boldsymbol{\mu}_j\}$ and $\{\boldsymbol{\nu}_v\}$; within each author/venue cluster, topic usage is similar.

2.2 Author and Venue Clustering

It is expected that authors working in the same area tend to write documents addressing similar topics. It is also anticipated that publication venues that are closely related to one other (*e.g.*, KDD and SDM), tend to publish documents on similar topics. So motivated, we seek to cluster authors and venues based on their usage of topics. This clustering is performed nonparametrically through use of the Dirichlet process (DP) [10].

The probability vectors $\{\boldsymbol{\mu}_j\}$ are drawn from a DP as $\boldsymbol{\mu}_j \sim \hat{G}_\mu$ with $\hat{G}_\mu \sim \mathrm{DP}(\lambda_\mu, G_\mu)$, and a stick-breaking construction is employed [21]. Hence, $\boldsymbol{\mu}_j$ is drawn

$$\boldsymbol{\mu}_j \sim \sum_{m=1}^{\infty} c_m \delta_{\boldsymbol{\mu}_m^*} \tag{9}$$

$$c_m = c_m' \prod_{l<m} (1 - c_l'), \; c_l' \sim \mathrm{Beta}(1, \lambda_\mu) \tag{10}$$

$$\lambda_\mu \sim \mathrm{Gamma}(g, h), \tag{11}$$

where each $\boldsymbol{\mu}_m^*$ is drawn i.i.d. from the "base" probability measure G_μ, and $\delta_{\boldsymbol{\mu}_m^*}$ is a unit point measure concentrated at $\boldsymbol{\mu}_m^*$. The form of G_μ is discussed in Section 2.3. Letting $\boldsymbol{c}$ represent the vector of probabilities $\boldsymbol{c} = (c_1, \dots)^T$, we denote the above process as $\boldsymbol{c} \sim \mathrm{Stick}(\lambda_\mu)$. In practice, the number of "sticks" is truncated as $\boldsymbol{\mu}_j \sim \sum_{m=1}^{M} c_m \delta_{\boldsymbol{\mu}_m^*}$, with $c_M' = 1$. We similarly draw the $\{\boldsymbol{\nu}_v\}$ as $\boldsymbol{\nu}_v \sim \hat{G}_\nu$ with $\hat{G}_\nu \sim \mathrm{DP}(\lambda_\nu, G_\nu)$.

In (9), c_m represents the probability that a given $\boldsymbol{\mu}_j$ is associated with cluster m; cluster m has a corresponding probability vector over topics defined by $\boldsymbol{\mu}_m^*$. Therefore, the number of components in the vector $\boldsymbol{c}$ with significant weight plays an important role in defining the number of clusters the vectors $\{\boldsymbol{\mu}_j\}$ are associated with. In this context parameter λ_μ is important, with only one cluster manifested as $\lambda_\mu \to 0$ (in this case all probability vectors in the set $\{\boldsymbol{\mu}_j\}$ are the same), and when $\lambda_\mu \to \infty$ all of the components in $\boldsymbol{c}$ have infinitesimal weight (in this case all probability vectors in the set $\{\boldsymbol{\mu}_j\}$ are unique, with probability one). Since λ_μ and λ_ν are important parameters, each is inferred, with gamma priors placed on each.

What remains is to define G_μ and G_ν, as well as the distribution on $\{\boldsymbol{\vartheta}_n\}$. These probability distributions are defined in a hierarchical manner, through a generalization of the focused topic model [28].

2.3 Hierarchical Beta Process

A direct extension of the LDA framework in (1) is to let the document-dependent random effects be drawn $\boldsymbol{\vartheta}_n \sim \mathrm{Dir}(\alpha_\vartheta, \cdots, \alpha_\vartheta)$, and similarly to define $G_\mu = \mathrm{Dir}(\alpha_\mu, \cdots, \alpha_\mu)$ and $G_\nu = \mathrm{Dir}(\alpha_\nu, \cdots, \alpha_\nu)$. However, in this setting the number of topics needs to be set *a priori*. Further, by the construction in (6) it is desirable that the probability vector $\boldsymbol{\mu}_j$ "focus" on the topics typically associated with author j, with $\boldsymbol{\nu}_v$ focusing on the topics typically associated with venue v. The probability vector $\boldsymbol{\vartheta}_n$ may then focus on those topics associated with document n that are unique to that document, and not addressed by the probabilities over topics associated with the corresponding author(s) and venue. These objectives motivate extending the focused topic model [28] for the purposes of the proposed model. In [28, 32] a beta-Bernoulli construction was employed to infer focused topics. Here we extend this setting to a *hierarchical* beta process (HBP) setting, coupled with the Bernoulli process; the hierarchical construction is motivated by our use of relational information, which was not considered in [28, 32].

The hierarchical beta process (HBP) was first studied in [27] and applied to dictionary learning for image reconstruction [33]. Reviewing, a draw $B \sim \mathrm{BP}(c_0, B_0)$ is defined by a real constant $c_0 > 0$ and a probability measure B_0. The measure B may be expressed in the form

$$B = \sum_{k=1}^{\infty} \pi_k \delta_{\boldsymbol{\beta}_k} \tag{12}$$

where each $\boldsymbol{\beta}_k$ is drawn i.i.d. from B_0. If B_0 is a continuous (non-atomic) probability measure, then each $\pi_k \in [0,1]$ is drawn i.i.d. from the "degenerate" beta distribution $c_0\pi^{-1}(1-\pi)^{c_0-1}$, which has a singularity at $\pi = 0$, encouraging that only a minority of the $\{\pi_k\}$ will have significant values, away from $\pi = 0$. For an atomic base measure $B_0 = \sum_k q_k \delta_{\omega_k}$, with $q_k \in [0,1]$, the draw B is of the same form as in (12), but now $\pi_k \sim \mathrm{Beta}(c_0 q_k, c_0(1-q_k))$. A draw B from a beta process is often linked with a Bernoulli process, where $X \sim \mathrm{Bernoulli}(B)$ is of the form $X = \sum_{k=1}^{\infty} b_k \delta_{\omega_k}$, with $b_k \in \{0,1\}$ and $b_k \sim \mathrm{Bernoulli}(\pi_k)$.

While the form of B_0 is general, here $B_0 = \mathrm{Dir}(\eta, \dots, \eta)$, and therefore each draw $\boldsymbol{\beta}_k \sim B_0$ corresponds to a topic, reflected in a distribution over the W words in the vocabulary; this is the same $\boldsymbol{\beta}_k$ as considered in the above discussion (*e.g.*, in (1)), but now the π_k in $B = \sum_{k=1}^{\infty} \pi_k \delta_{\boldsymbol{\beta}_k}$ reflects (through the Bernoulli process) the probability of whether topic k is utilized. The proposed HBP construction is defined by drawing $B \sim \mathrm{BP}(c_0, B_0)$, and

$$B^{(\vartheta)} \sim \mathrm{BP}(c_1, B), \quad B^{(\mu)} \sim \mathrm{BP}(c_1, B), \quad B^{(\nu)} \sim \mathrm{BP}(c_1, B)$$

The measure $B^{(\mu)} = \sum_{k=1}^{\infty} \pi_k^{\mu} \delta_{\boldsymbol{\beta}_k}$ defines the probability π_k^{μ} that topic k is utilized by the authors, while similarly $B^{(\nu)} = \sum_{k=1}^{\infty} \pi_k^{\nu} \delta_{\boldsymbol{\beta}_k}$ defines the probability π_k^{ν} that topic k is utilized across the venues, and $B^{(\theta)} = \sum_{k=1}^{\infty} \pi_k^{\theta} \delta_{\boldsymbol{\beta}_k}$ defines the probability π_k^{θ} that topic k is utilized across the document-dependent random effects. Since B is shared across the draws for $B^{(\vartheta)}$, $B^{(\mu)}$ and $B^{(\nu)}$, the topics reflected by $\{\boldsymbol{\beta}_k\}$ are also shared, but each has a unique set of probabilities $\{\pi_k^{\theta}\}$, $\{\pi_k^{\mu}\}$ and $\{\pi_k^{\nu}\}$ that the topics are utilized.

Note that for convenient implementation, one often employs a finite approximation for BP draws [32], with a truncation to $K_{\max}$ topics. In this setting we have

$$\pi_k \sim \mathrm{Beta}(c_0\epsilon, c_0(1-\epsilon)), \pi_k^{\vartheta} \sim \mathrm{Beta}(c_1\pi_k, c_1(1-\pi_k))$$
$$\pi_k^{\mu} \sim \mathrm{Beta}(c_1\pi_k, c_1(1-\pi_k)), \pi_k^{\nu} \sim \mathrm{Beta}(c_1\pi_k, c_1(1-\pi_k))$$

where $\epsilon = 1/K_{\max}$.

For document n, cluster m for the authors, and cluster m' for the venues, we employ the Bernoulli process (BeP), yielding $X_n^{(\vartheta)} \sim \mathrm{BeP}(B^{(\vartheta)})$, $X_m^{(\mu)} \sim \mathrm{BeP}(B^{(\mu)})$ and $X_{m'}^{(\nu)} \sim \mathrm{BeP}(B^{(\nu)})$, which can be expressed as

$$X_n^{(\vartheta)} = \sum_{k=1}^{K_{\max}} b_{nk}^{(\vartheta)} \delta_{\boldsymbol{\beta}_k}, \; b_{nk}^{(\vartheta)} \sim \mathrm{Bernoulli}(\pi_k^{(\vartheta)}) \tag{13}$$

$$X_m^{(\mu)} = \sum_{k=1}^{K_{\max}} b_{mk}^{(\mu)} \delta_{\boldsymbol{\beta}_k}, \; b_{mk}^{(\mu)} \sim \mathrm{Bernoulli}(\pi_k^{(\mu)}) \tag{14}$$

$$X_{m'}^{(\nu)} = \sum_{k=1}^{K_{\max}} b_{m'k}^{(\nu)} \delta_{\boldsymbol{\beta}_k}, \; b_{m'k}^{(\nu)} \sim \mathrm{Bernoulli}(\pi_k^{(\nu)}). \tag{15}$$

The binary vector $\boldsymbol{b}_n^{(\vartheta)} = (b_{n1}^{(\vartheta)}, \ldots, b_{nK_{\max}}^{(\vartheta)})^T$ defines which of the $K_{\max}$ topics are "on" (those for which $b_{nk} = 1$). Since the beta-Bernoulli process leads to a sparse set of non-zero b_{nk}^{ϑ}, the vector $\boldsymbol{b}_n^{(\vartheta)}$ defines which topics the random effects associated with document n focuses on. The binary vectors $\boldsymbol{b}_m^{(\mu)}$ and $\boldsymbol{b}_{m'}^{(\nu)}$ similarly define which topics are focused on by cluster m of the authors and cluster m' of the venues respectively. Completing the model, we have

$$\boldsymbol{\vartheta}_n \sim \text{Dir}(\boldsymbol{b}_n^{(\vartheta)} \circ \boldsymbol{r}^{(\vartheta)}),\ r_k^{(\vartheta)} \sim \text{Gamma}(\gamma_1, 1) \tag{16}$$

$$\boldsymbol{\mu}_m^* \sim \text{Dir}(\boldsymbol{b}_m^{(\mu)} \circ \boldsymbol{r}^{(\mu)}),\ r_k^{(\mu)} \sim \text{Gamma}(\gamma_2, 1) \tag{17}$$

$$\boldsymbol{\nu}_m^* \sim \text{Dir}(\boldsymbol{b}_m^{(\nu)} \circ \boldsymbol{r}^{(\nu)}),\ r_k^{(\nu)} \sim \text{Gamma}(\gamma_3, 1) \tag{18}$$

where γ_1, γ_2 and γ_3 are hyperparameters and $\circ$ represents the Hadamard (element-wise) product. Note, for example, that $\boldsymbol{\vartheta}_n$ will only have non-zero components for the topic indices k for which the components of $\boldsymbol{b}_n^{(\vartheta)}$ are non-zero, yielding the desired focused set of topics.

Relating the above discussion to the DP base measures G_μ and G_ν discussed in Section 2.2, G_μ is defined by the hierarchical combination of the HBP, Bernoulli process, and the construction in (17), with G_ν defined similarly. Further, the $\boldsymbol{\vartheta}_n$ in (6) is defined by the hierarchy of HBP, the Bernoulli process, and the construction in (16).

Denote $\Omega_{nk}^{(\vartheta)}$ as the number of words associated with the kth topic and assigned to the nth document's random effect term $\boldsymbol{\vartheta}_n$, denote $\Omega_{mk}^{(\mu)}$ as the number of words associated with the kth topic and assigned to the mth author cluster $\boldsymbol{\mu}_m^*$, and denote $\Omega_{mk}^{(\nu)}$ as the number of words associated with the kth topic and assigned to the mth venue cluster $\boldsymbol{\nu}_m^*$. Following [28] and the derivations in [32],

$$\Omega_{nk}^{(\vartheta)} \sim \text{NB}(b_{nk}^{(\vartheta)} r_k^{(\vartheta)}, 0.5) \tag{19}$$

$$\Omega_{mk}^{(\mu)} \sim \text{NB}(b_{mk}^{(\mu)} r_k^{(\mu)}, 0.5) \tag{20}$$

$$\Omega_{mk}^{(\nu)} \sim \text{NB}(b_{mk}^{(\nu)} r_k^{(\nu)}, 0.5) \tag{21}$$

where NB denotes the negative binomial distribution. The above equations together with (16)-(18) can be used to infer the posterior distributions of $r_k^{(\vartheta)}$, $r_k^{(\mu)}$ and $r_k^{(\nu)}$.

3. MCMC INFERENCE

We utilize MCMC inference to sample latent variables from their conditional posterior distributions. The inputs for cFTM include the text information $\{\boldsymbol{d}_n\}_{n=1,N}$, author information $\{\boldsymbol{a}_n\}_{n=1,N}$, venue information $\{v_n\}_{n=1,N}$, the hyperparameters $\eta, \alpha, \gamma_1, \gamma_2, \gamma_3, g, h$ and the number of sticks M (the setting of these parameters is discussed when presenting results).

I). For $k = 1, 2, \ldots, K$,

(a) Sample π_k, $\pi_k^{(\vartheta)}, \pi_k^{(\mu)}, \pi_k^{(\nu)}$. We sample π_k with slice sampling utilized in [33]. The rejection sampling proposed in [27] may also be used to sample π_k.

$$p(\pi_k^{(\vartheta)}|-) \sim \text{Beta}(c_1\pi_k + \sum_{n=1}^{N} b_{nk}^{(\vartheta)}, N + c_1(1-\pi_k) - \sum_{n=1}^{N} b_{nk}^{(\vartheta)})$$

$$p(\pi_k^{(\mu)}|-) \sim \text{Beta}(c_1\pi_k + \sum_{m=1}^{M} b_{mk}^{(\mu)}, M + c_1(1-\pi_k) - \sum_{m=1}^{M} b_{mk}^{(\mu)})$$

$$p(\pi_k^{(\nu)}|-) \sim \text{Beta}(c_1\pi_k + \sum_{m=1}^{V} b_{mk}^{(\nu)}, V + c_1(1-\pi_k) - \sum_{m=1}^{V} b_{mk}^{(\nu)}).$$

(b) Sample $r_k^{(\vartheta)}$, $r_k^{(\mu)}$, $r_k^{(\nu)}$, γ_1, γ_2, γ_3.

$$p(r_k^{(\vartheta)}|-) \propto \text{Gamma}(r_k^{(\vartheta)}; \gamma_1, 1) \prod_{n:b_{nk}^{(\vartheta)}=1} \text{NB}\left(\Omega_{nk}^{(\vartheta)}; r_k^{(\vartheta)}, 0.5\right)$$

$$p(r_k^{(\mu)}|-) \propto \text{Gamma}(r_k^{(\mu)}; \gamma_2, 1) \prod_{m:b_{mk}^{(\mu)}=1} \text{NB}\left(\Omega_{mk}^{(\mu)}; r_k^{(\mu)}, 0.5\right)$$

$$p(r_k^{(\nu)}|-) \propto \text{Gamma}(r_k^{(\nu)}; \gamma_3, 1) \prod_{m:b_{mk}^{(\nu)}=1} \text{NB}\left(\Omega_{mk}^{(\nu)}; r_k^{(\nu)}, 0.5\right).$$

The above equations are log differentiable with respect to $r_k^{(\vartheta)}$, $r_k^{(\mu)}$, $r_k^{(\nu)}$, γ_1, γ_2 and γ_3. Therefore, the Hybrid Monte Carlo [17, 28] is utilized to sample them from their conditional posteriors. We may also use the Metropolis-Hastings algorithm to sample these values [32].

II). For $m = 1, \ldots, M$, $n = 1, \ldots, N$, sample the binary vector for the documents $(b_{n1}^{(\vartheta)}, \ldots, b_{nK_{\max}}^{(\vartheta)})$, the author $(b_{m1}^{(\mu)}, \ldots, b_{mK_{\max}}^{(\mu)})$ and the venue $(b_{m1}^{(\nu)}, \ldots, b_{mK_{\max}}^{(\nu)})$. When $\Omega_{nk}^{(\vartheta)} > 0$, we have $b_{nk}^{(\vartheta)} \equiv 1$. When $\Omega_{nk}^{(\vartheta)} = 0$, we have

$$p(b_{nk}^{(\vartheta)} = 1|-) \propto \pi_k^{(\vartheta)} \text{NB}(0; r_k^{(\vartheta)}, 0.5) = \frac{\pi_k^{(\vartheta)}}{2^{r_k^{(\vartheta)}}} \tag{22}$$

$$p(b_{nk}^{(\vartheta)} = 0|-) \propto (1 - \pi_k^{(\vartheta)}). \tag{23}$$

Similar formulations can be derived for b_{mk}^{μ} and b_{mk}^{ν}.

III). Sample the variables z: when $h_{ni1} = 1$

$$p(z_{ni} = k|\gamma_{n1}, \boldsymbol{\vartheta}_{nk}, w, \boldsymbol{z}_{-ni}, \gamma_1, \pi_k^{(\vartheta)}, r_k^{(\vartheta)}) \propto p(w_{ni}|\boldsymbol{\beta}_k)$$
$$\int d\boldsymbol{\vartheta}_{nk} p(z_{ni}|\boldsymbol{\vartheta}_{nk}) p(\boldsymbol{\vartheta}_{nk}|\boldsymbol{z}_{-ni}, \gamma_1, \pi_k^{(\vartheta)}, r_k^{(\vartheta)}), \tag{24}$$

where $\boldsymbol{z}_{-ni}$ defines all $\boldsymbol{z}$ but z_{ni} conditioned on the sparse binary vector $\boldsymbol{b}_n^{(\vartheta)}$ and the gamma random variables $\boldsymbol{r}^{(\vartheta)}$, the topic proportion vector $\boldsymbol{\vartheta}_n$ is distributed according to a Dirichlet distribution. The sparse vector $\boldsymbol{b}_n^{(\vartheta)}$ determines the subset of topics over which the Dirichlet distribution is defined and $\boldsymbol{r}^{(\vartheta)}$ determines the values of the Dirichlet parameters at these points.

$$p(\boldsymbol{\vartheta}_n|\boldsymbol{z}_{-ni}, \pi_k^{(\vartheta)}, \gamma_1, r_k^{(\vartheta)}) \propto \int dr_k^{(\vartheta)}$$
$$\sum_{b_n^{(\vartheta)}} \text{Dir}(\boldsymbol{\vartheta}_n|(Q_{-i}^n + r^{(\vartheta)}) \circ \mathbf{b}_n^{(\vartheta)}) p(\boldsymbol{b}_n^{(\vartheta)}, r_k^{(\vartheta)}|\gamma_1, \pi_k^{(\vartheta)}),$$

where Q_{-i}^n is the topic assignment statistic excluding word w_{ni}. When $h_{ni2} = 1$ or $h_{ni3} = 1$, similar derivations are constituted.

IV). Sample λ_{n1}, λ_{n2}, λ_{n3}:

$$p((\lambda_{n1}, \lambda_{n2}, \lambda_{n3})|-) \sim$$
$$\text{Dir}\left(\alpha + \sum_{i=1}^{|\boldsymbol{d}_n|} h_{ni1}, \alpha + \sum_{i=1}^{|\boldsymbol{d}_n|} h_{ni2}, \alpha + \sum_{i=1}^{|\boldsymbol{d}_n|} h_{ni3}\right). \tag{25}$$

V). Sample $h_{ni1}, h_{ni2}, h_{ni3}$:

$$p(h_{ni1}|-) \propto \lambda_1 \text{Discrete}(w_{ni}; \boldsymbol{\Phi}\boldsymbol{\vartheta}_n) \tag{26}$$

$$p(h_{ni2}|-) \propto \lambda_2 \text{Discrete}(w_{ni}, \boldsymbol{\Phi}\hat{\boldsymbol{\mu}}_n) \tag{27}$$

$$p(h_{ni3}|-) \propto \lambda_3 \text{Discrete}(w_{ni}; \boldsymbol{\Phi}\boldsymbol{\nu}_{v_n}) \tag{28}$$

where $\boldsymbol{\Phi} = [\boldsymbol{\beta}_1, \cdots, \boldsymbol{\beta}_K] \in \mathbb{R}^{W \times K}$.

VI). Sample the stick lengths c_l':

$$p(c_l'|-) \sim \text{Beta}(1 + N_l, \lambda_\mu + \sum_{m=l+1}^{M} N_m) \quad (29)$$

where N_m is the number of authors assigned to the mth stick. The parameter λ_μ is inferred as in [20] and we similarly sample the stick lengths for venue clustering.

4. RELATED MODELS

A topic model with biased propagation (TMBP) [6] was recently proposed to discover latent semantic topics, while leveraging contextual information such as the authors and venue. However, in TMBP the number of topics and the importance weights of the author and venue information on word assignment have to be predefined, with cross-validation often necessary.

A FTM using the Indian buffet process (IBP) compound DP prior [28] is proposed as a nonparametric Bayesian topic model to automatically determine the number of topics. The FTM employs an IBP [12] to place binary weights on the topics used within a given document, and therefore only a subset of topics are used within a given document. This imposes that the model focuses on representing a document in terms of a concise set of topics, which should be contrasted with previous hierarchical Dirichlet process (HDP) [26] models for a document corpus, in which each topic is manifested in general with non-zero probability within a given document. The FTM decouples the across-document popularity and within-document prevalence of topic usages, leading to improved performance compared to the HDP [26]. However, the FTM does not utilize contextual information such as the authors and venue.

A key contribution of this paper concerns extending the FTM to the class of problems considered by TMBP, thereby developing a novel nonparametric model for a document corpus that infers a focused set of topics, while also leveraging author/venue contextual information. Our cFTM model can readily handle multiple types of context in a nonparametric Bayesian framework. We demonstrated in the experiments that such flexibility provides significantly better performance in the analysis of documents.

Concerning other related work, the author topic model (ATM) [22] constitutes a representation in which topic distributions are tied to authors. The proposed cFTM extends ATM by considering venue information in addition to author identity, by inferring clusters of authors and venues, and by doing so with focused topics (via use of HBP). Additionally, the proposed cFTM has a "random effects" term ϑ_n that accounts for situations in which a given document has topic usage that is inconsistent with the expectations of a given author or venue, increasing model flexibility, and allowing detection of outlier documents. Other related work includes NetPLSA [18], Laplacian PLSI [3], locally-consistent topic model [4], and citation and social network analysis [19][24][5] have been proposed for combining topic modelling and network structure. Graph-based semi-supervised learning [34] [30] [31] and link analysis [2][29][15] have also been applied to data mining [7][8]. However, these models did not explore contextual information.

5. EXPERIMENTAL RESULTS

We evaluate the proposed cFTM on the Digital Bibliography and Library Project (DBLP) dataset[1]and the NSF Research Awards Abstracts (NSF) dataset[2], as considered in [6]. The DBLP dataset is a collection of bibliographic information on major computer science journals and proceedings. We use a DBLP subset[3] containing the titles and abstracts of $N = 28569$ documents, with $W = 11771$ words in the vocabulary, $A = 28702$ authors and $V = 20$ conferences. Each conference is labeled with one of the four research areas: data mining, information retrieval, database, and artificial intelligence; each document is given the same label as the conference it appears in, and each author is labeled with the research area where he publishes the most number of documents [23].

The NSF dataset is made up of $N = 129000$ abstracts describing NSF awards for research from 1990 to 2003. We consider a subset, containing $N = 16405$ documents and $A = 9989$ investigators. These documents belong to the largest 10 research programs, such as applied mathematics, economics and geophysics. There are in total 20,717 links between the documents and investigators and $W = 18674$ unique words. Note that there are no venue information for this dataset.

We use both the accuracy (AC) and normalized mutual information (NMI) described in [6] for performance evaluations. The AC is defined as $AC = \frac{\sum_{i=1}^{n} \delta(a_i, map(l_i))}{n}$, where n denotes the total number of objects to be labeled, $\delta(x, y)$ equals one if $x = y$ and equals zero if $x \neq y$. The mapping function $map(l_i)$ maps each class label l_i to the corresponding label from the dataset. The mutual information $\text{MI}(C, C')$ between the labeled cluster C and the learned cluster C' is defined as

$$\text{MI}(C, C') = \sum_{c_i \in C, c_j' \in C'} p(c_i, c_j') \log_2 \frac{p(c_i, c_j')}{p(c_i)p(c_j')} \quad (30)$$

where $p(c_i)$ and $p(c_j')$ denote the probabilities that a document arbitrarily selected from the corpus belongs to the clusters c_i and c_j', respectively, and $p(c_i, c_j')$ denotes the joint probability that an arbitrarily selected document belongs to the clusters c_i as well as c_j' at the same time. The NMI is defined as $\text{MI}(C, C')/\text{MI}(C, C)$.

We compare the proposed cFTM with nine algorithms: nonnegative matrix factorization (NMF) [16], probabilistic latent semantic analysis (PLSA) [14], laplacian probabilistic semantic indexing (Lap-PLSI) [3], latent Dirichlet allocation (LDA) [1], author-topic model (ATM) [22], ranking-based clustering (NetClus) [23], topic modeling with biased propagation including the biased random walk framework (TMBP-RW) and biased regularization framework (TMBP-Regu) [6], and focused topic model (FTM) [28]. Note that in the special case that $\lambda_{n1} = 1$, $\lambda_{n2} = 0$ and $\lambda_{n3} = 0$, the cFTM reduces to the FTM in which the contextual information is not utilized.

The parameter settings for the algorithms that are compared to are described in [6]. In cFTM, we set the parameters as $\alpha = 1/3$, $g = h = 10^{-6}$, $\eta = 0.05$, $c_1 = 1$, $c_0 = 1$, $M = 20$ and $K_{\max} = 50$. The gamma shape parameters

[1]http://www.informatik.uni-trier.de/~ley/db/
[2]http://kdd.ics.uci.edu/databases/nsfabs/nsfawards.data.html
[3]http://www.cs.uiuc.edu/~hbdeng/data/kdd2011.htm

$\gamma_1, \gamma_2, \gamma_3$ are given the prior of Gamma(5, 0.1) and they are sampled with the Hybrid Monte Carlo algorithm [28]. The model proved insensitive to these parameter settings, and many other related settings give similar results. For the FTM and cFTM, we consider 6000 MCMC iterations, with the first 3000 samples discarded as burn-in and the remaining ones collected.

5.1 Classification Performance Comparison

For the DPLP dataset, the cFTM infers 12 frequently used topics, 10 author clusters (discarding clusters with less than 5 authors), and 4 venue clusters, according to the MCMC sample with the maximum likelihood. With the topic proportion vector for each document learned by the cFTM, we use the K-means to cluster these vectors into 4 and 10 classes for the DBLP and NSF datasets, respectively, equal to the number of labels in these two datasets (this is done only to quantify performance relative to "truth," allowing quantitative comparisons to other models; this is not a necessary step in our actual model). Based on these classes, we calculate the AC and NMI with the provided class labels.

As shown in Table 1, the proposed cFTM achieves the best overall performance on the DBLP data, notably outperforming the state-of-the-art TMBP algorithm [6] in both the document and author classifications, and having comparable results in venue classification. A characteristic distinguishing the cFTM from the TMBP algorithm [6] is that the cFTM automatically learns the importance weights of the author and venue information on word assignment, in a document dependent manner, while the TMBP algorithm fixes these weights to be the same for all the documents and uses cross-validation to tune the values. Furthermore, in the cFTM, the number of topics is automatically inferred with the HBP prior and the author and venues are automatically clustered with the DP, while in the TMBP algorithm [6], the number of topics is tied to the number of class labels and the author and venue clusterings are not considered. In addition, the cFTM is able to decouple the across document popularity and within document prevalence of the usages of topics under the FTM framework, while the TMBP algorithm, building on the PLSA framework, does not have this property. These differences may explain the performance gain achieved by the cFTM.

We also report in Table 2 the document classification performance of different methods on the NSF data, where the cFTM infers 35 topics and 26 investigator clusters. Among these methods, the ATM, TMBP and cFTM have comparable performance, outperforming all the other methods. Since in the NSF data, there is no venue information, the improvement of cFTM method over other methods is less significant compared to the results in the DBLP dataset. Another reason is that the heterogeneous information network of NSF is much sparser than that of DBLP: there are only 1.26 links per document for the NSF, while there are 3.61 links per document for the DBLP (here a "link" is defined as the connection between a investigator and a document) [6].

5.2 Inferred Author/Venue Relationships

We examine in detail the topic modeling and author and venue clustering results of the cFTM, concentrating on the DBLP data. Shown in Table 4 are typical topics characterized by their most-probable words, where Topics 4, 10, 6 and 11 correspond well to the research areas of database, data mining, information retrieval and artificial intelligence, respectively. For example, the top three key words of Topic 4 (database) are "data", "query" and "database" and the top three key words of Topic 11 (artificial intelligence) are "learning", "methods" and "knowledge". It is interesting to notice that the top key words of Topic 7, such as "mining", "learning" and "retrieval", appear frequently in both the data mining and information retrieval research areas. We also notice several topics frequently used across the documents are devoted to general terminology commonly found in all the four research areas, e.g., the top key words of Topic 5 are "method", "developed" and "applied". Compared to the top words from the topics extracted from TMBP [6], the cFTM method has the advantage that it absorbs the common words across different areas into several globally popular topics, while other topics focus on specific aspects of the corpus, which are only used by a subset of the documents.

Shown in Figure 2 are the author clustering results on

Table 2: Classification performance comparison of different algorithms on the NSF dataset. Except for the results of the FTM and cFTM, all the other results were reported in [6].

Metric	AC (Paper)	NMI (Paper)
NMF	45.97	40.02 [6]
PLSA	63.00	64.48 [6]
LapPLSI	63.65	64.58 [6]
LDA	65.06	63.36 [6]
ATM	**65.69**	69.58 [6]
NetClus	63.51	66.11 [6]
TMBP-RW	64.84	68.74 [6]
TMBP-Regu	65.15	69.83 [6]
FTM	63.75	64.60
cFTM	65.49± 0.57	**70.07 ±0.26**

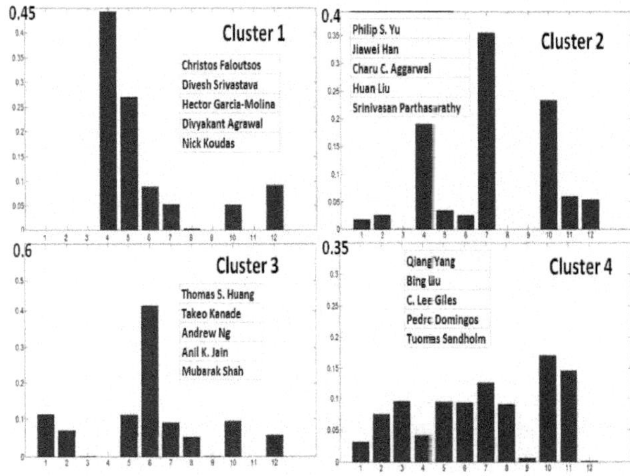

Figure 2: The topic usage probabilities of author clusters inferred by the cFTM on the DBLP dataset. Ten author clusters are inferred. We also show in each cluster the names of the authors who have the most number of publications. The horizontal axis represents topic indices (see Table 3), and the vertical axis reflects the probability of each topic appearing in a author cluster.

Table 1: **Classification performance comparison of different algorithms on the DBLP dataset. Except for the results of the FTM and cFTM, all the other results were reported in [6].**

Object	Paper	Paper	Author	Author	Venue	Venue	Average	Average
Metric (%)	AC	NMI	AC	NMI	AC	NMI	AC	NMI
NMF	44.55	22.92	-	-	-	-	44.55	22.92
PLSA	59.45	32.75	65.0	37.97	80.0	74.74	68.15	48.49
LapPLSI	61.35	33.93	-	-	-	-	60.70	33.37
LDA	47.00	20.48	-	-	-	-	47.00	20.48
ATM	77.00	52.21	74.13	40.67	-	-	75.57	46.44
NetClus	65.00	40.96	70.82	47.43	79.75	76.69	71.86	55.03
TMBP-RW	73.10	53.13	82.59	67.76	81.75	**77.53**	79.15	66.14
TMBP-Regu	79.15	59.16	89.81	74.25	**82.75**	76.56	83.90	69.99
FTM	69.37	43.51	-	-	-	-	69.37	43.51
cFTM	**82.73 ±0.65**	**62.91 ±0.51**	**92.51 ±0.71**	**76.20 ±0.39**	81.97 ±0.36	76.05 ±0.43	**85.73 ±0.57**	**71.72 ±0.45**

the DBLP dataset. Based on the MCMC sample with the maximum likelihood, the cFTM infers 10 author clusters in total, with the first four largest clusters and their representative authors shown in Figure 2. The largest cluster (Cluster 1) contains about 4,700 authors and the smallest cluster contains about 30 authors. As shown in Figure 2, Cluster 1 consists of researchers in database, such as Christos Faloutsos, Divesh Srivestava and Hector Garcia-Molina. The authors in Cluster 3 are experts focusing on information retrieval, such as Thomas Huang, Takeo Kanade and Andrew Ng. Cluster 4 consists of authors who have publications in both data mining and artificial intelligence, such as Qiang Yang, B. Liu and C.Lee Giles. Authors in Cluster 4 typically have frequently published papers not only in artificial intelligence venues such as CIKM and WWW but also in data mining venues such as KDD and SDM.

The author topic usage probability vector for each cluster is also intuitive. Taking Cluster 1 for example, the topic usage probability vector has a large weight on Topic 4, which is characterized by words in database as shown in Table 4. The topic usage probability vector of Cluster 3 has a large weight in Topic 6, which is characterized by words in information retrieval. It is also not surprising that the usage probabilities of Topic 5 across clusters have a low variance, since Topic 5 contains common words frequently used in all documents regardless their research areas.

The venue clustering results on the DBLP data with the cFTM is investigated in Figure 4. We find that the venue clustering results are also quite intuitive. For example, the data mining conferences KDD, PKDD and PAKDD always stay in the same cluster in all the 3000 collected MCMC samples. Similarly, the database conferences ICDE, EDBT and PODS share the same cluster in all the collection samples. Note that in 83% of the collection samples AAAI and CVPR are in the same cluster, likely because AAAI consists of papers from both information retrieval and artificial intelligence.

6. CONCLUSIONS

Employing nonparametric Bayesian priors, including the Dirichlet process and hierarchical beta process, we propose a new contextual focused topic model (cFTM). The cFTM utilizes both the text and contextual information to model a document corpus. It infers a set of semantically meaningful topics to summarize the corpus, as well as the relational information between the authors and venues. It automatically infers the number of topics, the number of author and venue clusters, and the probabilistic importance of the author and venue information on word assignment in a document dependent manner. Efficient MCMC inference is presented. Example results on the DBLP and NSF datasets are used to demonstrate the consistent and promising performance of the proposed cFTM, with quantitative comparison to other state-of-the-art methods and intuitive qualitative analysis. The computational expense of the proposed model is comparable to that of related topic models [28]. In non-optimized Matlab, running on a 2.26GHz CPU computer, each MCMC sample required approximately 2.3 seconds to compute, when considering the DBLP data.

Acknowledgements

The research reported here was supported by ARO, NGA, ONR and DARPA (MSEE program).

7. REFERENCES

[1] D. M. Blei, A. Y. Ng, and M. I. Jordan. Latent Dirichlet allocation. *Journal of Machine Learning Research*, 3:993–1022, 2003.

[2] S. Brin and L. Page. The anatomy of a large-scale hypertextual web search engine. In *Computer Networks*, volume 30, 1998.

[3] D. Cai, Q. Mei, J. Han, and C. Zhai. Modeling hidden topics on document manifold. In *CIKM*, 2008.

[4] D. Cai, X. Wang, and X. He. Probabilistic dyadic data analysis with local and global consistency. In *ICML*, 2009.

[5] D. A. Cohn and T. Hofmann. The missing link - a probabilistic model of document content and hypertext connectivity. In *NIPS*, 2000.

[6] H. Deng, J. Han, B. Zhao, Y. Yu, and C. Lin. Probabilistic topic models with biased propagation on heterogeneous information networks. In *KDD*, 2011.

[7] H. Deng, M. R. Lyu, and I. King. Effective latent space graph-based re-ranking model with global consistency. In *WSDM*, 2009.

	AAAI	CIKM	CVPR	ECIR	ECML	EDBT	ICDE	ICML	ICDM	IJCAI	KDD	PAKDD	PKDD	PODS	SDM	SIGIR	SIGMOD	VLDB	WWW	WSDM
AAAI	1	0.34	0.83	0.34	0.83	0	0	0.34	0.83	1	0.34	0.34	0.34	0	0.34	0.17	0	0	0.17	0
CIKM	0.34	1	0.34	0.83	0.17	0	0	0.66	0.83	0.34	0.66	0.66	0.66	0	0.66	0.17	0	0	0.83	0.83
CVPR	0.83	0.34	1	0.17	1	0	0	0.17	0.83	0.83	0.17	0.17	0.17	0	0.17	0.34	0	0	0.17	0
ECIR	0.34	0.83	0.17	1	0.17	0	0	0	0	0.17	0	0	0	0	0	0.34	0	0	1	1
ECML	0.83	0.17	1	0.17	1	0	0	0.83	0.83	0.83	0.66	0.66	0.66	0	0.66	0.17	0.17	0	0	0
EDBT	0	0	0	0	0	1	1	0	0	0	0	0	0	1	0	0	1	1	0	0
ICDE	0	0	0	0	0	1	1	0	0	0	0	0	0	1	0	0	1	1	0	0
ICML	0.34	0.66	0.17	0	0.83	0	0	1	0.66	0.17	1	1	1	0	1	0.34	0	0	0	0
ICDM	0.83	0.83	0.83	0	0.83	0	0	0.66	1	0.83	0.66	0.66	0.66	0	0.66	0	0	0	0	0
IJCAI	1	0.34	0.83	0.17	0.83	0	0	0.17	0.83	1	0.17	0.17	0.17	0	0.17	0.34	0	0	0.17	0
KDD	0.34	0.66	0.17	0	0.66	0	0	1	0.66	0.17	1	1	1	0	1	0	0	0	0	0
PAKDD	0.34	0.66	0.17	0	0.66	0	0	1	0.66	0.17	1	1	1	0	1	0	0	0	0	0
PKDD	0.34	0.66	0.17	0	0.66	0	0	1	0.66	0.17	1	1	1	0	1	0	0	0	0	0
PODS	0	0	0	0	0	1	1	0	0	0	0	0	0	1	0	0	1	1	0	0
SDM	0.34	0.66	0.17	0	0.66	0	0	1	0.66	0.17	1	1	1	0	1	0	0	0	[illegible]	0
SIGIR	0.17	0.17	0.34	0.34	0.17	0	0	0.34	0	0.34	0	0	0	0	0	1	0	0	0.83	0.83
SIGMOD	0	0	0	0	0.17	1	1	0	0	0	0	0	0	1	0	0	1	1	[illegible]	0
VLDB	0	0	0	0	0	0	1	1	0	0	0	0	0	0	1	0	1	1	[illegible]	0
WWW	0.17	0.83	0.17	1	0	0	0	0	0	0.17	0	0	0	0	0	0.83	0	0	[illegible]	0.83
WSDM	0	0.83	0	1	0	0	0	0	0	0	0	0	0	0	0	0.83	0	0	0.83	1

Figure 3: The venue clustering results of the proposed cFTM algorithm on the DBLP dataset. The (i, j)th element of the matrix represents the fraction of samples among the 3000 collected MCMC samples in which the ith and jth venues are in the same cluster.

Table 3: Most probable words of eight representative topics inferred by the cFTM model on the DBLP dataset. The top key words shown in each topic are ranked based on their probabilities to be used.

Topic 4	Prob	**Topic 10**	Prob	**Topic 6**	Prob	**Topic 11**	Prob
data	0.12374	data	0.14957	information	0.159	learning	0.22921
query	0.10022	mining	0.12614	retrieval	0.143	methods	0.19101
database	0.09728	information	0.10091	web	0.09	knowledge	0.06013
system	0.05506	clustering	0.05262	search	0.05	systems	0.05637
algorithm	0.05452	classification	0.04902	text	0.046	reasoning	0.05011
distributed	0.04651	algorithm	0.04469	model	0.045	model	0.04886
queries	0.0417	based	0.04037	user	0.039	algorithm	0.02882
algorithms	0.0302	analysis	0.02884	document	0.024	logic	0.01817
performance	0.02753	experimental	0.02343	semantic	0.015	representation	0.01091
Topic 3	Prob	**Topic 5**	Prob	**Topic 7**	Prob	**Topic 8**	Prob
show	0.21758	method	0.14874	mining	0.17164	query	0.17989
results	0.17505	methods	0.1235	learning	0.14517	structure	0.15442
system	0.14233	developed	0.0929	algorithm	0.13634	database	0.08111
systems	0.13524	applied	0.06015	clustering	0.09355	language	0.04784
propose	0.02891	based	0.05961	discovery	0.03972	computer	0.03692
set	0.018	results	0.04511	retrieval	0.03575	specific	0.0338
large	0.01528	experimental	0.04296	detection	0.03266	information	0.02341
analysis	0.01091	research	0.02095	image	0.01722	space	0.01457
efficient	0.01076	analysis	0.0129	search	0.0106	order	0.01353

Table 4: The author clustering results on the DBLP dataset. Within each cluster, the five authors with the most number of publications are displayed.

Cluster 1	**Cluster 2**	**Cluster 3**	**Cluster 4**	**Cluster 5**
C. Faloutsos	P. S. Yu	T. S. Huang	Q. Yang	H. P. Kriegel
D. Srivastava	J. Han	T. Kanade	B. Liu	E. J. Keogh
H. G. Molina	C. C. Aggarwal	A. Ng	C. L.Giles	S. B. Zdonik
D. Agrawal	H. Liu	A. K. Jain	P. Domingos	T. Li
N. Koudas	S. Parthasarathy	M. Shah	T. Sandholm	C. Zaniolo
Cluster 6	**Cluster 7**	**Cluster 8**	**Cluster 9**	**Cluster 10**
S. Chaudhuri	G. Weikum	H. Mannila	W. B.Croft	C. T.Yu
R. Ramakrishnan	J. F. Naughton	K. Wang	Z. Chen	W. Y.Ma
W. Wang	E. A.Rundensteiner	V. Kumar	C. Zhai	R. Rastogi
J. Pei	H. Pirahesh	R. Jin	J. Allan	J. Gehrke
H. Wang	D. Gunopulos	R. J. Mooney	R. Kumar	J. X. Yu

[8] H. Deng, M. R. Lyu, and I. King. A generalized co-hits algorithm and its application to bipartite graphs. In *KDD*, 2009.

[9] T. Ferguson. Bayesian analysis of some nonparametric problems. *Annals of Statistics*, 1973.

[10] S. Ghosal. Dirichlet process, related priors and posterior asymptotics. *Bayesian Nonparametrics*, pages 35–79, 2010.

[11] T. Griffiths and M. Steyvers. Finding scientific topics. *PNAS*, 2004.

[12] T. L. Griffiths and Z. Ghahramani. Infinite latent feature models and the Indian buffet process. In *NIPS*, 2005.

[13] M. Hoffman, D. Blei, and F. Bach. Online learning for latent Dirichlet allocation. In *NIPS*, 2010.

[14] T. Hofmann. Probabilistic semantic indexing. *SIGIR*, pages 50–57, June 1999.

[15] J. M. Kleinberg. Authoritative sources in a hyperlinked environment. In *Journal of the ACM (JACM)*, 1999.

[16] D. D. Lee and H. S. Seung. Algorithms for non-negative matrix factorization. In *NIPS*, 2000.

[17] D. J. C. MacKay. *Information Theory, Inference and Learning Algorithms*. Cambridge University Press, 2002.

[18] Q. Mei, D. Cai, D. Zhang, and C. Zhai. Topic modeling with network regularization. In *WWW*, 2008.

[19] R. Nallapati, A. Ahmed, E. P. Xing, and W. Cohen. Joint latent topic models for text and citations. In *KDD*, 2008.

[20] L. Ren, L. Du, L. Carin, and D. Dunson. Logistic stick-breaking process. In *The Journal of Machine Learning Research*, volume 12, 2011.

[21] J. Sethuraman. A constructive definition of Dirichlet priors. *Statistica Sinica*, 1994.

[22] M. Steyvers, P. Smyth, M. Rosen-Zvi, and T. Griffiths. Probabilistic author-topic models for information discovery. In *KDD*, 2004.

[23] Y. Sun, Y. Yu, and J. Han. Ranking-based clustering of heterogeneous information networks with star network schema. In *KDD*, 2009.

[24] J. Tang, J. Zhang, L. Yao, J. Li, L. Zhang, and Z. Su. Arnetminer: extraction and mining of academic social networks. In *KDD*, 2008.

[25] Y. W. Teh. Dirichlet processes. In *Encyclopedia of Machine Learning*. Springer, 2010.

[26] Y. W. Teh, M. I. Jordan, M. J.Beal, and D. M. Blei. Hierarchical Dirichlet processes. *Journal of the American Statistical Association*, 101(476):1566–1581, 2006.

[27] R. J. Thibaux and M. I. Jordan. Hierarchical beta processes and the Indian buffet process. In *AISTATS*, 2007.

[28] S. Williamson, C. Wang, K. A. Heller, and D. M. Blei. The IBP compound Dirichlet process and its application to focused topic modeling. In *ICML*, 2010.

[29] B. Zhang, H. Li, Y. Liu, L. Ji, W. Xi, W. Fan, Z. Chen, and W.-Y. Ma. Improving web search results using affinity graph. In *SIGIR*, 2005.

[30] D. Zhou, O. Bousquet, T. N. Lal, J. Weston, and B. Scholkopf. Learning with local and global consistency. In *NIPS*, 2003.

[31] D. Zhou, B. Scholkopf, and T. Hofmann. Semisupervised learning on directed graphs. In *NIPS*, 2004.

[32] M. Zhou, L. Hannah, D. Dunson, and L. Carin. Beta-negative binomial process and Poisson factor analysis. In *AISTATS*, 2012.

[33] M. Zhou, H. Yang, G. Sapiro, D. Dunson, and L. Carin. Dependent hierarchical beta process for image interpolation and denoising. In *AISTATS*, 2011.

[34] X. Zhu, Z. Ghahramani, and J. D. Lafferty. Semi-supervised learning using gaussian fields and harmonic functions. In *ICML*, 2003.

Practical Collapsed Variational Bayes Inference for Hierarchical Dirichlet Process

Issei Sato
The University of Tokyo, Japan
sato@r.dl.itc.u-tokyo.ac.jp

Kenichi Kurihara
Google
kenichi.kurihara@gmail.com

Hiroshi Nakagawa
The University of Tokyo, Japan
n3@dl.itc.u-tokyo.ac.jp

ABSTRACT

We propose a novel collapsed variational Bayes (CVB) inference for the hierarchical Dirichlet process (HDP). While the existing CVB inference for the HDP variant of latent Dirichlet allocation (LDA) is more complicated and harder to implement than that for LDA, the proposed algorithm is simple to implement, does not require variance counts to be maintained, does not need to set hyperparameters, and has good predictive performance.

Categories and Subject Descriptors

G.3 [**Probability and Statistics**]: Nonparametric statistics

General Terms

Algorithms

Keywords

Latent Dirichlet Allocation, Nonparametric Bayes, Hierarchical Dirichlet Process, Collapsed Variational Bayes Inference

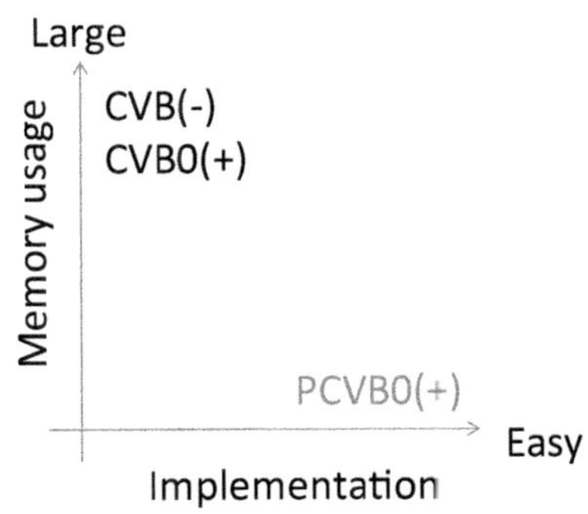

Figure 1: Overview of proposed and related inferences for HDP-LDA. CVB and CVB0 indicates second order and zero order approximation of the CVB inference. PCVB0 indicates the proposed (practical CVB0) inference. $(+)$ and $(-)$ mean that the predictive performance of $(+)$ is better than that of $(-)$ in terms of perplexity.

1. INTRODUCTION

Probabilistic models with latent variables have attracted attention in knowledge discovery and data mining because of their power and flexibility in modeling real world phenomena. The goals of such probabilistic modeling are to capture the underlying generation mechanism and the statistical relationships of data and to make predictions yet to be observed.

Latent Dirichlet allocation (LDA) [1] has been one of the most studied probabilistic latent variable models in the last decade. LDA was originally used to model the co-occurrence of words by using latent variables called topics where a document is represented as a "bag of words," meaning that the order of words is ignored. Now we have a wide variety of topic models in many fields: modeling authors and topics [2, 3], entities and topics [4], document and citations [5], hypertext and topics [6], annotated biological figures and topics [7], the dynamics of documents and topics [8, 9, 10, 11, 12], power-law and topics[13], and a partially labeled data [14]. A non-probabilistic formulation also have been proposed called a conditional topical model [15]. Topic modeling has also been applied to information retrieval [16, 17], measuring redundancy by LDA-based submodular function[18], augmenting social networks [19], measuring scholarly impact [20], predicting legislative roll calls [21], and recommendationing scientific article [22].

An important LDA extension is a nonparametric one using the hierarchical Dirichlet process (HDP) [23]. In actual applications, we do not know the number of topics a priori and HDP-LDA can determine this automatically. The purpose of this paper is to explore an efficient deterministic inference for HDP-LDA.

There are two common inferences for HDP-LDA: collapsed Gibbs sampler [23] and collapsed variational Bayes (CVB) inference [24]. The CVB inference is a deterministic algorithm for learning HDP-LDA that was originally developed for LDA [25]. The CVB inference is a variational approximation improved by collapsing parameters, which indicates integrating out the parameters as in a collapsed Gibbs sampler. The CVB inference was proposed for solving some problems of a sampling method; for example, sampling often requires many iterations and its averaging of topic-dependent quantities on the basis of samples is inefficient for estimating test data.

Teh et al. proposed the CVB inference for LDA [25] and HDP-LDA[24] by using a second-order Taylor expansion. Asuncion et al. [26, 27] proposed another approximation by using only the zero-order information, called the CVB0 inference. The CVB0 inference for LDA [26] is computationally faster and requires a smaller memory than the CVB inferences for LDA [25] since it does not require calculating and holding variance counts, and converges more quickly than the collapsed Gibbs sampler since it is deterministic.. Furthermore, their empirical results suggest that the CVB0 inference learns models that are as good or better (predictively) than those learned by the collapsed Gibbs sampler.

Problems: It is easy to apply the CVB0 inference to HDP-LDA. However, the naive CVB0 inference for HDP-LDA does not provide the same efficiency as LDA because variance counts are used for estimating other statistics, e.g. $\mathbb{G}[\alpha_0\pi_k]$ and $\mathbb{G}[\beta_0\tau_{w_{d,i}}]$ in Eq.(19) (see the work of Teh et al.[24] for details). Calculating these statistics is extremely complicated and so requires large computational cost. Moreover, we needed to set hyper parameters for each dataset; however, we do not wish to tune them for each dataset in practice.

Contributions: We developed a novel CVB0 inference for HDP-LDA. We intended that the proposed algorithm be as simple and easy to implement as the previous algorithm for LDA [25, 26], and outperform the previous CVB inference for HDP-LDA [24]. The proposed algorithm has the following properties:

1. The proposed CVB0 inference for HDP-LDA does not require the variance counts.
2. Our algorithm does not require the setting of hyper-parameters.

These properties lead to a simple algorithm for learning HDP-LDA that will be useful to researchers in many scientific fields when they apply HDP-LDA to their problems. An overview of the proposed and related algorithms of HDP-LDA is shown in Fig.1. We define the notation symbols used in this paper in Table 1.

The remainder of this paper is organized as follows. Sections 2 and 3 overview LDA and HDP-LDA, respectively. Section 4 explains the CVB / CVB0 inference for HDP-LDA. Section 5 proposes the proposed algorithm. Section 6 evaluates algorithms in three kinds of experiments: document modeling, nearest neighbor search, and social network analysis.

2. OVERVIEW OF LDA

The following generative process is assumed with LDA.

First, document-topic distribution $\boldsymbol{\theta}_d$ and topic-word distribution $\boldsymbol{\phi}_k$ are generated by

$$\boldsymbol{\theta}_d \sim \text{Dir}(\boldsymbol{\alpha})\ (d = 1, \cdots, N), \quad \boldsymbol{\phi}_k \sim \text{Dir}(\boldsymbol{\beta})\ (k = 1, \cdots, K), \tag{1}$$

where $\boldsymbol{\alpha} = (\alpha_1, \cdots, \alpha_K)$ is a K-dimensional vector and $\boldsymbol{\beta} = (\beta_1, \cdots, \beta_V)$ is a V-dimensional vector.

For each document d, generate the i-th topic $z_{d,i}$ and word $w_{d,i}$:

$$z_{d,i} \sim \text{Multi}(\boldsymbol{\theta}_d), \quad w_{d,i} \sim \text{Multi}(\boldsymbol{\phi}_{z_{d,i}}). \tag{2}$$

Wallach et al. [28] explored the effects of choosing $\boldsymbol{\alpha}$ and $\boldsymbol{\beta}$ in LDA. The symmetric Dirichlet priors indicate $\alpha_k = \alpha_0/K$ for all k and $\beta_v = \beta_0/V$ for all v. In the asymmetric Dirichlet priors, they used a nonuniform base measure $\boldsymbol{\pi} = (\pi_1, \cdots, \pi_K)$ and $\boldsymbol{\tau} = (\tau_1, \cdots, \tau_V)$ instead of $1/K$ and $1/V$, i.e., $\alpha_k = \alpha_0\pi_k$ and $\beta_v = \beta_0\tau_v$. They found in Markov chain Monte Carlo (MCMC) simulations that using asymmetric $\boldsymbol{\alpha}$ and symmetric $\boldsymbol{\beta}$ results in better predictive performance of held-out documents. We investigate the effects of the choice of prior over the topic-word distributions in the CVB/CVB0 inference.

Table 1: Notation Table

Symbol	Definition
N	Total number of documents
V	Vocabulary size
K	Total number of topics
T	Truncation level of stick-breaking process
d	Document index, i.e., $d = 1, \cdots, N$
v	Vocabulary index, i.e., $v = 1, \cdots, V$
n_d	Number of words in documents d
$n_{d,k}$	Number of times topic k appears in document d
$n_{k,v}$	Number of times word v appears in topic k
$w_{d,i}$	i-th word in document d
$\boldsymbol{w}$	Set of all words, i.e., $\{\boldsymbol{w}_d\}_{d=1}^N$
$z_{d,i}$	Assigned topic at i-th word in document d
$\boldsymbol{z}$	Set of all latent topic variables, i.e., $\{\boldsymbol{z}_d\}_{d=1}^N$
$\theta_{d,k}$	Probability of topic k appearing in document d
$\boldsymbol{\theta}_d$	K-dimensional probability vector
$\phi_{k,v}$	Probability of word v appearing in topic k
$\boldsymbol{\phi}_k$	V-dimensional probability vector
$\boldsymbol{\alpha}$	K-dimensional vector
α_0	$= \sum_k \alpha_k$, or concentration parameter of DP
γ_0	concentration parameter of DP or SBP
$\boldsymbol{\beta}$	V-dimensional vector
β_0	$= \sum_v \beta_v$
$\mathbb{E}[x]$	Expectation of x
$\mathbb{G}[x]$	Geometric expectation $\exp(\mathbb{E}[\log x])$
$\mathbb{V}[x]$	Variance $\mathbb{E}[x^2] - \mathbb{E}[x]^2$
$\Gamma(x)$	Gamma function
$\Psi(x)$	Digamma function.
Beta$(\cdot)$	Beta distribution
Multi$(\cdot)$	Multinomial distribution
Dir$(\cdot)$	Dirichlet distribution
DP$(\cdot)$	Dirichlet process
SBP$(\cdot)$	Stick-breaking process formulated as Eq.(9)
TSBP$(\cdot)$	Truncated SBP formulated as Eq.(12)
KL$[\cdot\|\cdot]$	Kullback-Leibler divergence

3. OVERVIEW OF HDP-LDA

We have a nonparametric Bayes model of LDA by using the HDP, called HDP-LDA [23]. The generation process of HDP-LDA is

$$G_0 \sim DP(\gamma_0, Dir(\boldsymbol{\beta})), \tag{3}$$
$$G_d \sim DP(\alpha_0, G_0), \tag{4}$$
$$\phi_{z_{d,i}} \sim G_d, \tag{5}$$
$$w_{d,i} \sim Mult(\phi_{z_{d,i}}). \tag{6}$$

Using a stick-breaking process (SBP), G_0 and G_d are represented as sums of point masses given by

$$G_0 = \sum_{k=1}^{\infty} \pi_k \delta_{\boldsymbol{\phi}_k}, \; G_d = \sum_{k=1}^{\infty} \boldsymbol{\theta}_{d,k} \delta_{\boldsymbol{\phi}_k}, \tag{7}$$

$$\boldsymbol{\theta}_d \sim \text{DP}(\alpha_0, \boldsymbol{\pi}), \; \boldsymbol{\phi}_k \sim \text{Dir}(\boldsymbol{\beta}), \tag{8}$$

$$\pi_k = \tilde{\pi}_k \prod_{l=1}^{k-1} (1 - \tilde{\pi}_l), \; \tilde{\pi}_k \sim \text{Beta}(1, \gamma_0). \tag{9}$$

The construction of $\boldsymbol{\pi}$ in Eq.(9) is called the stick-breaking construction and is denoted by $\boldsymbol{\pi} \sim \text{SBP}(\gamma_0)$.

We describe a truncated stick-breaking process (TSBP) construction of HDP-LDA because we truncate an infinite number of components to apply the CVB inference to HDP. The TSBP has the advantage of being able to estimate running time per iteration, which is a useful property in actual applications. Using the TSB representation, G_0 and G_j are represented as sums of point masses given by

$$G_0 = \sum_{k=1}^{T} \pi_k \delta_{\phi_k}, \; G_j = \sum_{k=1}^{T} \boldsymbol{\theta}_{j,k} \delta_{\phi_k}, \tag{10}$$

$$\boldsymbol{\theta}_d \sim Dir(\alpha_0 \boldsymbol{\pi}), \; \phi_k \sim \mathrm{Dir}(\boldsymbol{\beta}), \tag{11}$$

$$\pi_k = \tilde{\pi}_k \prod_{l=1}^{k-1} (1 - \tilde{\pi}_l), \; \tilde{\pi}_k \sim Beta(1, \gamma_0), \; \tilde{\pi}_T = 1. \tag{12}$$

Note that since T is not the number of topics but the truncation level in HDP-LDA, we can estimate the effective number of topics K if we set $T > K$. The mixing proportions $\boldsymbol{\pi}$ distributed according to the TSBP, denoted by $\boldsymbol{\pi} \sim \mathrm{TSBP}(\gamma_0)$, decreases exponentially fast at the tail of the distribution. This motivates the use of the TSBP, which is easier to handle than the infinite case. Ishwaran and James [29] give a bound for the error introduced by truncating the SBP; they showed that truncating the number of mixture components to a moderate level is sufficient to successfully approximate the DP.

In the collapsed Gibbs sampler for HDP-LDA, the topic assignment of the i-th word in document d using α_0 and $\boldsymbol{\pi}$ is given by

$$p(z_{d,i} = k | w_{d,i} = v, \boldsymbol{z}^{-d,i}, \boldsymbol{w}^{-d,i}) = \frac{n_{d,k}^{-d,i} + \alpha_0 \pi_k}{n_d^{-d,i} + \alpha_0} \frac{n_{k,v}^{-d,i} + \beta_v}{n_{k,\cdot}^{-d,i} + \beta_0}, \tag{13}$$

where the superscription "$-d, i$" denotes the corresponding variables or counts with $w_{d,i}$ and $z_{d,i}$ excluded, e.g., $\boldsymbol{w}^{-d,i} = \boldsymbol{w} \backslash \{w_{d,i}\}$, $\boldsymbol{z}^{-d,i} = \boldsymbol{z} \backslash \{z_{d,i}\}$, and $n_{k,v}^{-d,i}$ is the number of observations of word v assigned to topic k leaving out $z_{d,i}$.

We need to use the Chinese restaurant process (CRP) procedure for sampling α_0 and $\boldsymbol{\pi}$, where a document, word, and topic represent respectively a restaurant, a customer, and a dish served at a table. The procedure in which the i-th word in document d is assigned to topic k indicates that the i-th customer sits at a table serving dish k in restaurant d. However, sampling the seating arrangements in this CRP procedure is time consuming. Fortunately, we only need the table numbers serving topic k at restaurant d, denoted by $m_{d,k}$, not the seating arrangements of customers. Therefore, we have alternates consisting of three sampling stages: (1) sampling the topic assignments $z_{d,i}$, (2) sampling the number of tables $m_{d,k}$, and (3) sampling α_0 and $\boldsymbol{\pi}$.

The number of tables serving topic k in document d, i.e., $m_{d,k}$, is sampled using the Stirling numbers of the first kind denoted by $str(\cdot)$ [23]:

$$p(m_{d,k} = m | n_{d,k}, \alpha_0, \pi_k) = str(n_{d,k}, m)(\alpha_0 \pi_k)^m \frac{\Gamma(\alpha_0 \pi_k)}{\alpha_0 \pi_k + n_{d,k}}. \tag{14}$$

The conditional posterior for the mixing proportions $\boldsymbol{\pi}$ is also given as a stick-breaking construction as follows.

$$\tilde{\pi}_k \sim Beta(1 + m_{\cdot,k}, \gamma_0 + \sum_{l=k+1}^{T} m_{\cdot,l}), \; \tilde{\pi}_T = 1, \tag{15}$$

$$\pi_1 = \tilde{\pi}_1, \; \pi_k = \tilde{\pi}_k \prod_{l=1}^{k-1} (1 - \tilde{\pi}_l). \tag{16}$$

Algorithm 1 PCVB0 inference for HDP-LDA

```
for each iteration do
    for each document d do
        for each word w_{d,i} do
            Update q(z_{d,i}) by using Eq.(35).
        end for
    end for
    Update q(π̃_k) by using Eq.(24)
    Update α_0 by using Eq.(29).
    Update γ_0 by using Eq.(33).
    Update β0 and τ_v by using Eqs.(30) and Eqs.(32).
end for
```

The concentration parameter, α_0, can be estimated by auxiliary variable sampling [23, 30].

4. CVB/CVB0 INFERENCE FOR HDP-LDA

Teh et al. [24] proposed the CVB inference for HDP-LDA. They marginalize over $\boldsymbol{\theta}$ and $\boldsymbol{\phi}$ in the CVB inference as in a collapsed Gibbs sampler. They assumed an asymmetric Dirichlet prior over the topic-word distributions, i.e., $\boldsymbol{\beta} = \beta_0 \boldsymbol{\tau}$. By integrating out $\boldsymbol{\theta}_d$ and $\boldsymbol{\phi}_k$, a join distribution over $\boldsymbol{w}$ and $\boldsymbol{z}$ is given by

$$p(\boldsymbol{z}, \boldsymbol{w} | \alpha_0, \beta_0, \boldsymbol{\pi}, \boldsymbol{\tau}) = \left[\prod_{d=1}^{N} \frac{\Gamma(\alpha_0)}{\Gamma(\alpha_0 + n_d)} \prod_{k=1}^{T} \frac{\Gamma(\alpha_0 \pi_k + n_{d,k})}{\Gamma(\alpha_0 \pi_k)} \right] \left[\prod_{k=1}^{T} \frac{\Gamma(\beta_0)}{\Gamma(\beta_0 + n_{k,\cdot})} \prod_{v=1}^{V} \frac{\Gamma(\beta_0 \tau_v + n_{k,v})}{\Gamma(\beta_0 \tau_v)} \right]. \tag{17}$$

The CVB inference for $q(z_{d,i} = k)$ is given by

$$q(z_{d,i} = k) \propto \frac{\mathbb{E}[n_{k,w_{d,i}}^{-d,i}] + \mathbb{G}[\beta_0 \tau_{w_{d,i}}]}{\mathbb{E}[n_{k,\cdot}^{-d,i}] + \mathbb{G}[\beta_0]} \frac{\mathbb{E}[n_{d,k}^{-d,i}] + \mathbb{G}[\alpha_0 \pi_k]}{n_d^{-d,i} + \mathbb{G}[\alpha_0]}$$
$$\exp\left(- \frac{\mathbb{V}[n_{k,w_{d,i}}^{-d,i}]}{2(\mathbb{E}[n_{k,w_{d,i}}^{-d,i}] + \mathbb{G}[\beta_0 \tau_{w_{d,i}}])^2} + \frac{\mathbb{V}[n_{k,\cdot}^{-d,i}]}{2(\mathbb{E}[n_{k,\cdot}^{-d,i}] + \mathbb{G}[\beta_0])^2} \right)$$
$$\exp\left(- \frac{\mathbb{V}[n_{d,k}^{-d,i}]}{2(\mathbb{E}[n_{d,k}^{-d,i}] + \mathbb{G}[\alpha_0 \pi_k])^2} \right), \tag{18}$$

where "-d,i" denotes subtracting $q(z_{d,i} = k)$ and $q(z_{d,i} = k)(1 - q(z_{d,i} = k))$. The calculations of $\mathbb{G}[\alpha_0 \pi_k]$ and $\mathbb{G}[\beta_0 \tau_{w_{d,i}}]$ are extremely complicated and so require large computational cost (see the work of Teh et al. [24] for details).

Asuncion et al. [26, 27] showed the usefulness of an approximation using only zero-order information, called the CVB0 inference, in LDA. It is easy to apply the CVB0 inference to HDP-LDA. The update using only zero-order information for HDP-LDA is given by

$$q(z_{d,i} = k) \propto \frac{\mathbb{E}[n_{k,w_{d,i}}^{-d,i}] + \mathbb{G}[\beta_0 \tau_{w_{d,i}}]}{\mathbb{E}[n_{k,\cdot}^{-d,i}] \mathbb{G}[\beta_0]} \frac{\mathbb{E}[n_{d,k}^{-d,i}] + \mathbb{G}[\alpha_0 \pi_k]}{n_d^{-d,i} + \mathbb{G}[\alpha_0]}. \tag{19}$$

However, the problem is that this CVB0 inference also requires the calculations of $\mathbb{G}[\alpha_0 \pi_k]$ and $\mathbb{G}[\beta_0 \tau_{w_{d,i}}]$, i.e., it requires complicated calculations and must keep variance counts for them. Consequently, in using it, we cannot avoid the computational drawbacks of the CVB inference. We solve this problem in the next section.

5. PROPOSED INFERENCE

This section explains our inference which is an approximation of the existing CVB inference[24]. First, we describe our motivation for developing this approximation and then explain the derivation.

The proposed inference can be summarized as follows. We marginalize over $\boldsymbol{\theta}_d$ and $\boldsymbol{\phi}_k$ and estimate a factorized variational posterior over $\boldsymbol{z}$ and $\boldsymbol{\pi}$, i.e., $q(\boldsymbol{z},\boldsymbol{\pi}) = \prod_{j,i} q(z_{j,i}) \prod_k q(\tilde{\pi}_k)$. We use the point estimation for $\alpha_0, \beta_0, \gamma_0$ and $\boldsymbol{\tau}$ because we do not wish to set any hyper parameters. The proposed update algorithms are given in Algorithm 1.

5.1 Motivation

We were strongly motivated by David Sontag and Daniel Roy, who in [31] theoretically showed that small parameters of Dirichlet distribution over document-topic distribution, i.e. $\boldsymbol{\alpha}$, encourage sparsity. The meaning of "sparsity" here is that the topic distribution will be large on as few topics as necessary to explain every word of a document and otherwise will be close to zero. They reported that when they applied LDA to a NIPS corpus with 200 topics, the parameters found range from 0.0009 to 0.135 with the median being 0.01. We think HDP-LDA also has this property because HDP-LDA, actually a stick-breaking process, induces sparsity of the topic distributions. We surveyed the parameters $\{\mathbb{G}[\alpha_0\pi_k]\}_{k=1}^{T}$ of HDP-LDA with the existing CVB inference [24] on several datasets and found that the parameters took small values (shown in Sec.6). We utilize this property for deriving an approximation of the CVB inference.

5.2 Derivation

Note that $\boldsymbol{\pi}$ in the Dirichlet distribution $\text{Dir}(\alpha_0\boldsymbol{\pi})$ is generated from the TSBP, i.e., $\boldsymbol{\pi} \sim \text{TSBP}(\gamma_0)$. The difficulty in the derivation of variational inference, in fact the estimation for $q(\boldsymbol{\pi})$, is that the Dirichlet distribution $\text{Dir}(\alpha_0\boldsymbol{\pi})$ does not conjugate to the stick-breaking process $\text{TSBP}(\gamma_0)$. Therefore, we use the following approximation for calculating the Gamma function to estimate $q(\boldsymbol{\pi})$.

Suppose $\alpha < 1$ and $n \geq 1$. We can use the approximations

$$\Gamma(\alpha+n) \approx \Gamma(n),\ \Gamma(\alpha) \approx \frac{1}{\alpha}. \tag{20}$$

These approximations are obtained as follows. By using $\Gamma(\alpha+1) = \alpha\Gamma(\alpha)$, we have $\Gamma(\alpha) = \frac{\Gamma(\alpha+1)}{\alpha}$. Thus, when $\alpha < 1$, in particular, $\Gamma(\alpha+1) \approx \Gamma(1) = 1$, we have $\Gamma(\alpha) \approx \frac{1}{\alpha}$. Furthermore, $\Gamma(\alpha+n) = (\alpha+n-1)\cdots(\alpha+1)\alpha\Gamma(\alpha) \approx (n-1)\cdots 1\alpha\frac{1}{\alpha} = \Gamma(n)$. Note that in fact $\Gamma(\alpha) \leq \frac{1}{\alpha}\ (\alpha \leq 1), \Gamma(n+\alpha) \geq \Gamma(n)\ (\alpha \leq 1, n \geq 2), \Gamma(\alpha+1) \leq \Gamma(1) = 1\ (\alpha \leq 1)$. These approximations are also described in [32, 33]

These approximations enable us to obtain a closed form update for $q(\tilde{\boldsymbol{\pi}})$ in Eq.(24). In the experimental section, we look into $\mathbb{E}[\alpha_0\pi_k]$ of the CVB inference in HDP-LDA to verify these approximations. Although we use the same approximation for β_v as α_k, we can also use Minka's fixed point iterations for estimating β_v used in [26].

Using Eq.(20), Eq.(17) is approximated by

$$\tilde{p}(\boldsymbol{z},\boldsymbol{w}|\alpha_0,\beta_0,\boldsymbol{\pi},\boldsymbol{\tau}) = \left[\prod_{d=1}^{N} \frac{\Gamma(\alpha_0)}{\Gamma(\alpha_0+n_d)} \prod_{k=1}^{T} [\Gamma(n_{d,k})\alpha_0\pi_k]^{I(n_{d,k}>0)}\right] \left[\prod_{k=1}^{T} \frac{\Gamma(\beta_0)}{\Gamma(\beta_0+n_{k,\cdot})} \prod_{v=1}^{V} [\Gamma(n_{k,v})\beta_0\tau_v]^{I(n_{k,v}>0)}\right]. \tag{21}$$

The variational lower bound on log likelihood is approximately given by

$$\begin{aligned}
&\log p(\boldsymbol{w}|\alpha_0,\beta_0,\gamma_0,\boldsymbol{\tau}) \\
&\geq \mathbb{E}[\log p(\boldsymbol{z},\boldsymbol{w}|\alpha_0,\beta_0,\boldsymbol{\pi},\boldsymbol{\tau}) - \log q(\boldsymbol{z})] - \text{KL}[q(\boldsymbol{\pi})||p(\boldsymbol{\pi}|\gamma_0)], \quad (22)\\
&\approx \mathbb{E}[\log \tilde{p}(\boldsymbol{z},\boldsymbol{w}|\alpha_0,\beta_0,\boldsymbol{\pi},\boldsymbol{\tau}) - \log q(\boldsymbol{z})] - \text{KL}[q(\boldsymbol{\pi})||p(\boldsymbol{\pi}|\gamma_0)]. \quad (23)
\end{aligned}$$

Taking the functional derivative of the lower bound Eq.(23) with respect to $q(\tilde{\boldsymbol{\pi}}_k)$ and equating them to zero, we have

$$q(\tilde{\boldsymbol{\pi}}_k) = Beta(a_k,b_k)\ (k=1,\cdots,T-1),\ q(\tilde{\pi}_T=1)=1, \tag{24}$$

$$a_k = 1 + \sum_d \mathbb{E}[I(n_{d,k} \geq 1)], \tag{25}$$

$$b_k = \gamma_0 + \sum_{l=k+1}^{T} \sum_d \mathbb{E}[I(n_{d,l} \geq 1)], \tag{26}$$

$$\mathbb{E}[I(n_{d,k} \geq 1] = q(n_{d,k} \geq 1) = 1 - q(n_{d,k}=0) = 1 - \prod_i q(z_{d,i} \neq k) = 1 - \exp\left(\sum_i \log(1-q(z_{d,i}=k))\right). \tag{27}$$

Note that

$$\mathbb{E}[\pi_1] = \mathbb{E}[\tilde{\pi}_1],\ \mathbb{E}[\pi_k] = \mathbb{E}[\tilde{\pi}_k \prod_{l=1}^{k-1}(1-\tilde{\pi}_l)] = \frac{a_k}{a_k+b_k}\prod_{l=1}^{k-1}\frac{b_l}{a_l+b_l}. \tag{28}$$

Moreover, taking derivatives of $\mathbb{E}[\log \tilde{p}(\boldsymbol{z},\boldsymbol{w}|\alpha_0,\beta_0,\boldsymbol{\pi},\boldsymbol{\tau})]$ in Eq.(23) with respect to α_0, β_0 and τ_v and equating them to zero, we obtain the following fixed point iteration equations

$$\alpha_0^{\text{new}} = \frac{\sum_{d,k}\mathbb{E}[I(n_{d,k} \geq 1)]}{\sum_d [\Psi(n_d+\alpha_0^{\text{old}}) - \Psi(\alpha_0^{\text{old}})]}, \tag{29}$$

$$\beta_0^{\text{new}} = \frac{\sum_{k,v}\mathbb{E}[I(n_{k,v} \geq 1)]}{\sum_k [\Psi(\mathbb{E}[n_{k,\cdot}]+\beta_0^{\text{old}}) - \Psi(\beta_0^{\text{old}})]}, \tag{30}$$

$$\tau_v \propto \sum_k \mathbb{E}[I(n_{k,v} \geq 1)], \tag{31}$$

$$\mathbb{E}[I(n_{k,v} \geq 1)] = 1 - \exp\left(\sum_{d,i} I(w_{d,i}=v)\log(1-q(z_{d,i}=k))\right). \tag{32}$$

We update γ_0 by taking derivatives of $\text{KL}[q(\tilde{\boldsymbol{\pi}}_k)||p(\tilde{\boldsymbol{\pi}}_k|\gamma_0)]$ in Eq.(23) with respect to γ_0 and equating them to zero.

$$\gamma_0 = \frac{T-1}{-\sum_{k=1}^{T-1}\mathbb{E}[\log(1-\tilde{\pi}_k)]} = \frac{T-1}{\sum_{k=1}^{T-1}\Psi(a_k+b_k)-\Psi(b_k)}. \tag{33}$$

By using a second-order Taylor expansion as an approximation, we have the CVB inference for $q(z_{d,i})$ given by

$$
\begin{aligned}
q(z_{d,i}=k) \propto & \frac{\mathbb{E}[n_{k,w_{d,i}}^{-d,i}] + \beta_0 \tau_{w_{d,i}}}{\mathbb{E}[n_{k,\cdot}^{-d,i}] + \beta_0} \frac{\mathbb{E}[n_{d,k}^{-d,i}] + \alpha_0 \mathbb{E}[\pi_k]}{n_d^{-d,i} + \alpha_0} \\
& \exp\left(-\frac{\mathbb{V}[n_{k,w_{d,i}}^{-d,i}]}{2(\mathbb{E}[n_{k,v_{d,i}}^{-d,i}] + \beta_0 \tau_{w_{d,i}})^2} + \frac{\mathbb{V}[n_{k,\cdot}^{-d,i}]}{2(\mathbb{E}[n_{k,\cdot}^{-d,i}] + \beta_0)^2} \right) \\
& \exp\left(-\frac{\mathbb{V}[n_{d,k}^{-d,i}]}{2(\mathbb{E}[n_{d,k}^{-d,i}] + \alpha_0 \mathbb{E}[\pi_k])^2} \right),
\end{aligned}
\tag{34}
$$

The CVB0 inference for $q(z_{d,i})$ can be made by using only the zero-order information as follows.

$$
q(z_{d,i}=k) \propto \frac{\mathbb{E}[n_{k,w_{d,i}}^{-d,i}] + \beta_0 \tau_{w_{d,i}}}{\mathbb{E}[n_{k,\cdot}^{-d,i}] + \beta_0} (\mathbb{E}[n_{d,k}^{-d,i}] + \alpha_0 \mathbb{E}[\pi_k]).
\tag{35}
$$

Note that this CVB0 inference for HDP-LDA does not require the maintenance of variance counts, the same as the CVB0 inference for LDA [26]. As previously mentioned, although the CVB0 inference described in Sec.4 does not use variance counts for estimating $q(\boldsymbol{z})$, it needs to estimate other parameters ($\mathbb{G}[\alpha_0\pi_k]$ and $\mathbb{G}[\beta_0\tau_v]$ using variance counts), which negatively affects its good properties of the CVB0 inference. We clarify the relationship between our CVB0 inference and the collapsed Gibbs sampler Eq.(13) in the next section.

5.3 Interpretation

The differences between Eq.(13) and Eq.(35) can be interpreted as the difference between the calculations for the number of tables in the CRP representation, although Eq.(13) is stochastic while Eq.(35) is deterministic. From the analogy to $m_{\cdot,k}$ of Eq.(15), $\sum_{d=1}^{N} \mathbb{E}[I(n_{d,k} \geq 1)]$ in Eq.(24), (25), and (26) indicates the number of tables where $\mathbb{E}[I(n_{d,k} \geq 1)]$ means the number of tables at which dish k is served is limited to one in a restaurant(document), i.e., $\sum_{d=1}^{N} \mathbb{E}[I(n_{d,k} \geq 1)] \leq m_{\cdot,k}$. In other words, it can be said that we approximate the number of tables $m_{\cdot,k}$ by using lower bound $\sum_{d=1}^{N} \mathbb{E}[I(n_{d,k} \geq 1)]$ in our inference. This limitation seems to be a good approximation throughout a whole corpus.

Equation (35) also helps us understand the sparsity of topics. Intuitively , a topic with low document frequency is eliminated because $\sum_{d=1}^{N} \mathbb{E}[I(n_{d,k} \geq 1)]$ also indicates the document frequency of topic k, i.e., the number of unique documents in which topic k occurs. The constraint $\sum_k q(z_{j,i}=k) = 1, \forall k$ will lead to some topics with small assignment probabilities, which makes $\mathbb{E}[n_{d,k} \geq 1]$ and $\mathbb{E}[n_{d,k}]$ small for some topics $\{k\}$. Moreover, $\mathbb{E}[\pi_k]$ will take very small value for some topics due to the constraint $\sum_k \mathbb{E}[\pi_k] = 1$. As a result, $\mathbb{E}[n_{d,k}] + \alpha_0 \mathbb{E}[\pi_k]$ will also become smaller for some topics, which makes $q(z_{j,i}=k)$ more sharply distributed and gives topics almost no chance to become bigger $q(z_{j,i}=k)$ in the future. In this way, we obtain only a smaller number of effective topics than a truncation level.

6. EXPERIMENTS

We evaluated the proposed inferences on three tasks: (1) document modeling in terms of perplexity, (2) a nearest neighbor search on the topic simplex, and (3) a link prediction in a social network. All results are averaged values from five experimental runs with random initialization. We initialized $\alpha_0\pi_k = 0.1/T$, $\beta_0\tau_v = 0.1/T$ and $q(z_{d,i}=k) \propto 0.1 + u$ where u is generated from the uniform distribution over $[0,1]$. We set the number of iterations to 100 for each inference. First, we give preliminaries for reading experimental results, next describe datasets, and then discuss the experimental results. In this section, we empirically show that the results of our inference algorithms are similar to those of the existing algorithms, which means our approximation works well.

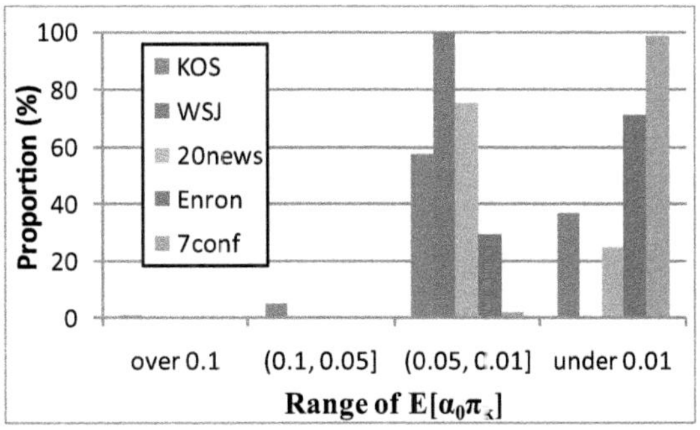

Figure 2: The proportion of $\mathbb{E}[\alpha_0\pi_k]$ ($k = 1, \cdots, T = 300$) of CVB-AA estimated from five datasets.
For example, almost 99% of $\mathbb{E}[\alpha_0\pi_k]$ ($k = 1, \cdots, T = 300$) are in the range $(0.05, 0.01]$ in WSJ. For the lack of space, we eliminated the results of $\mathbb{E}[\beta_v]$. Almost $\mathbb{E}[\beta_v]$ ($v = 1, \cdots, V$) of CVB-AA also takes small value as in $\mathbb{E}[\alpha_k]$. Maximum values of $\mathbb{E}[\alpha_k]$ is 0.1532 in KOS, 0.0610 in WSJ, 0.0309 in 20news, 0.0176 in Enron, and 0.0122 in 7conf. Note that $\Gamma(1) = 1, \Gamma(1+0.05) = 0.9735, \Gamma(0.05) = 19.47$, and $1/0.05 = 20$.

6.1 Preliminaries

The purpose of the experiments is to investigate the performance of our approximation and the effect of the choice of prior over the topic-word distributions in HDP-LDA with the (practical) CVB / CVB0 inferences. In this section's figures, "CVB" and "CVB0" indicates second order and zero order approximation of the CVB inference for HDP, while "PCVB" and "PCVB0" indicate the proposed (practical CVB and CVB0) inferences where we use the second order Taylor approximation in PCVB as in CVB.

Wallach et al.[28] explored the effects of the choice of prior (symmetric versus asymmetric Dirichlets) over the document-topic distributions, denoted by $\boldsymbol{\theta}$, and topic-word distributions, denoted by $\boldsymbol{\phi}$, in LDA. They introduced notations, SS, AS and AA, as the choice of prior over $\boldsymbol{\theta}$ and $\boldsymbol{\phi}$. SS uses symmetric priors over $\boldsymbol{\theta}$ and $\boldsymbol{\phi}$. AS uses asymmetric priors over $\boldsymbol{\theta}$, and symmetric prior over $\boldsymbol{\phi}$. AA uses asymmetric priors over $\boldsymbol{\theta}$ and $\boldsymbol{\phi}$. It is assumed with HDP-LDA that a prior over the document-topic distributions is asymmetric, i.e., we consider AS and AA models. Using these notations, CVB-AA was proposed in Teh et al. [24].

Wallach et al.[28] found in MCMC simulations that the AS model results in better predictive performance of held-out documents. Asuncion et al. showed in [26] that using the appropriate the Dirichlet parameters plays a large role in learning accurate topic models in the SS model. Asuncion also showed in [27] that the predictive performance of the CVB0 inference clearly outperformed that of the CVB inference when they used the AA model. We investigated the AS model in our experiments because this choice performed well in MCMC simulations reported by Wallach et al.[28].

6.2 Datasets

We used five sets of text data with different properties. The first was 'KOS blog corpus (KOS)" where the number of documents was $N = 3,430$ and the vocabulary size was $V = 6,906$. The second was "The Wall Street Journal (WSJ)" where we randomly chose $N = 3,000$ ($V = 30,576$) documents. The third was "Enron email corpus (Enron)" made by Frank and Asuncion [34] where we randomly chose $N = 10,000$ ($V = 15,258$) documents. The fourth was "20 news group corpus (20news)[1]" where we randomly chose $N = 10,000$ ($V = 13,178$). The fifth was "7 Conference paper corpus (7conf)" where we used seven conference abstracts (KDD ($N = 1252$), ICDM (N=867), SIGMOD ($N = 2155$), SIGIR ($N = 2074$, WWW ($N = 1064$), ICML ($N = 1525$), and CVPR ($N = 1411$)) collected by Deng et al. [35]. In total, we obtained $N = 10,311$ ($V = 4,950$) documents. Stop words were eliminated.

As previously mentioned, we were strongly motivated by David Sontag and Daniel Roy, who in [31] showed that small parameters of Dirichlet distribution over document-topic distribution $\boldsymbol{\theta}_d$ encourage sparsity. We looked into $\mathbb{E}[\alpha_0\pi_k]$ of the existing CVB inference proposed by Teh et al. [24] with $T = 300$, noting that a large truncation level makes the TSBP approach the SBP. Figure 2 shows that $\mathbb{E}[\alpha_0\pi_k]$ takes small values in datasets. This is because in HDP-LDA even if a whole corpus contains many topics, a document usually does not, which means the document-topic distribution has sparsity. What we found from Fig. 2 inspired us to assume $\alpha_k (= \alpha_0\pi_k) < 1$ to derive our practical inference.

6.3 Document modeling

The comparison metric we used for document modeling was the perplexity that indicates the prediction performance for held-out words that was used by Teh et al. [25, 24]. We randomly split the words in a document into training words $\boldsymbol{w}_d^{train}$ (80%) and test words $\boldsymbol{w}_d^{test}$ (20%). The perplexity of $\{\boldsymbol{w}_d^{test}\}$ is given by

$$\exp\left[-\frac{1}{\sum_{d=1}^{N} n_d^{test}} \sum_{d=1}^{N} \sum_{i=1}^{n_d^{test}} \log p(w_{d,i}^{test} | \boldsymbol{w}_d^{train})\right]. \quad (36)$$

The predictive distributions of our inferences are given by

$$p(w^* | \boldsymbol{w}_d) = \sum_{k=1}^{K} \frac{\beta_0\tau_v + \mathbb{E}[n_{k,w^*}]}{\beta_0 + \mathbb{E}[n_{k,\cdot}]} \frac{\alpha_0\mathbb{E}[\pi_k] + \mathbb{E}[n_{d,k}]}{\alpha_0 + n_d}. \quad (37)$$

Figure 3 shows the experimental results we obtained for perplexity. The left line indicates the results for test set perplexity in terms of the truncation level ($T = 100, 200, 300$) in each corpus where the number of iterations is 100. The right line shows the relationships between test set perplexity and the number of iterations where the truncation level was $T = 300$. We show CVB-AA,CVB0-AA, and PCVB0-AA in figure because the AS and AA models and the CVB and PCVB inferences were almost the same and it became difficult to distinguish their respective lines. We show 50 iterations to clarify the differences among algorithms, although we ran 100 iterations.

CVB0 and PCVB0 basically outperformed CVB and PCVB in terms of perplexity. In the experiments, the convergence rate of CVB0 and PCVB0 were respectively slower than those of CVB and PCVB. The performance of PCVB and PCVB0 were respectively similar to those of CVB and CVB0. The difference between AS and AA was small in our experiments.

[1]http://www.csie.ntu.edu.tw/~cjlin/libsvmtools/datasets/multiclass.html\#news20

6.4 Nearest Neighbor Search on Topic Simplex

The purpose of this experiment was to evaluate the estimation performance of topic distributions for test documents. We estimated a topic distribution $\boldsymbol{\theta}^{\text{test}}$ of a test document and searched for the nearest neighbor of a test document in the training documents by using the distance between $\boldsymbol{\theta}^{\text{test}}$ and $\boldsymbol{\theta}_d$ for each training document d.

LDA can be regarded as a tool for reducing the dimensions of a document from a word space to a topic space. One application of LDA as a dimension reduction tool is to perform the nearest neighbor search in the topic simplex. Generally, the nearest neighbor search is fast as the dimension of a data point is low.

We used the Hellinger distance as the distance metric of topic distributions. The Hellinger distance is a symmetric measure and that is often used in statistics to quantify the similarity between two probability distributions given by

$$H^2(\boldsymbol{\theta}_d, \boldsymbol{\theta}^{\text{test}}) = \sum_{k=1}^{T} (\sqrt{\theta_{d,k}} - \sqrt{\theta_k^{\text{test}}})^2, \quad (38)$$

in which we actually used the expectation of $\theta_{d,k}$, e.g., $E[\theta_{d,k}] = \frac{\mathbb{E}[\alpha_0\pi_k] + \mathbb{E}[n_{d,k}]}{\sum_k \mathbb{E}[\alpha_0\pi_k] + \mathbb{E}[n_{d,k}]}$.

Using the 7conf and 20news corpora, we randomly split both data sets into training documents (90%) and test documents (10%). We evaluated the estimation performance of topic distributions for test documents with the nearest neighbor classification task. We categorized test documents into the same category to which the nearest neighbor document is labeled. We had seven labels in 7conf and 20 labels in 20news. Figure 4 shows the accuracy of the models, from which it can be seen that (P)CVB0 outperformed (P)CVB and the accuracy of PCVB and PCVB0 were respectively similar to those of CVB and CVB0. It is important to note that the performance of our approximation algorithms was similar to that of the existing ones, which means that the estimated topic distributions were similar and that our approximation does not negatively affects the performance of the existing algorithms.

6.5 Link Prediction in Social Networks

We used two social network datasets. The first one was a collaboration network of the Arxiv Astro Physics category (AstroPh) used in [36, 37], where nodes represent scientists, edges represent collaborations (co-authoring a paper), and there were 18,772 nodes and 396,160 links. The second one is the Enron email network (EnronNet) used in [36], where an link indicated that email was exchanged, and there are 36,692 nodes and 367,662 links. In network modeling by LDA, we assumed that a node indicates a document and that a link to other node indicates a word, i.e., we represented a node as a "bag of links." We evaluated the algorithms with a recommendation task that ranks link-nodes with high link probability for each query-node using its link history. We ranked link-nodes for each query-node with a predictive distribution used in evaluating the perplexity in the previous section, i.e.,

$$p(\text{query-node } j \text{ links link-node } l | \text{link history of query-node } j). \quad (39)$$

We performed an information retrieval based evaluation to compare the algorithms. We used the mean average precision (MAP), which is often used in information retrieval. The MAP reflects the overall retrieval accuracy. To calculate the MAP, we need query sets, candidate item sets for ranking, and relevance judgments lists. We constructed the test collection as follows. We used nodes with over 20 links as query sets. We split the link data of each query into

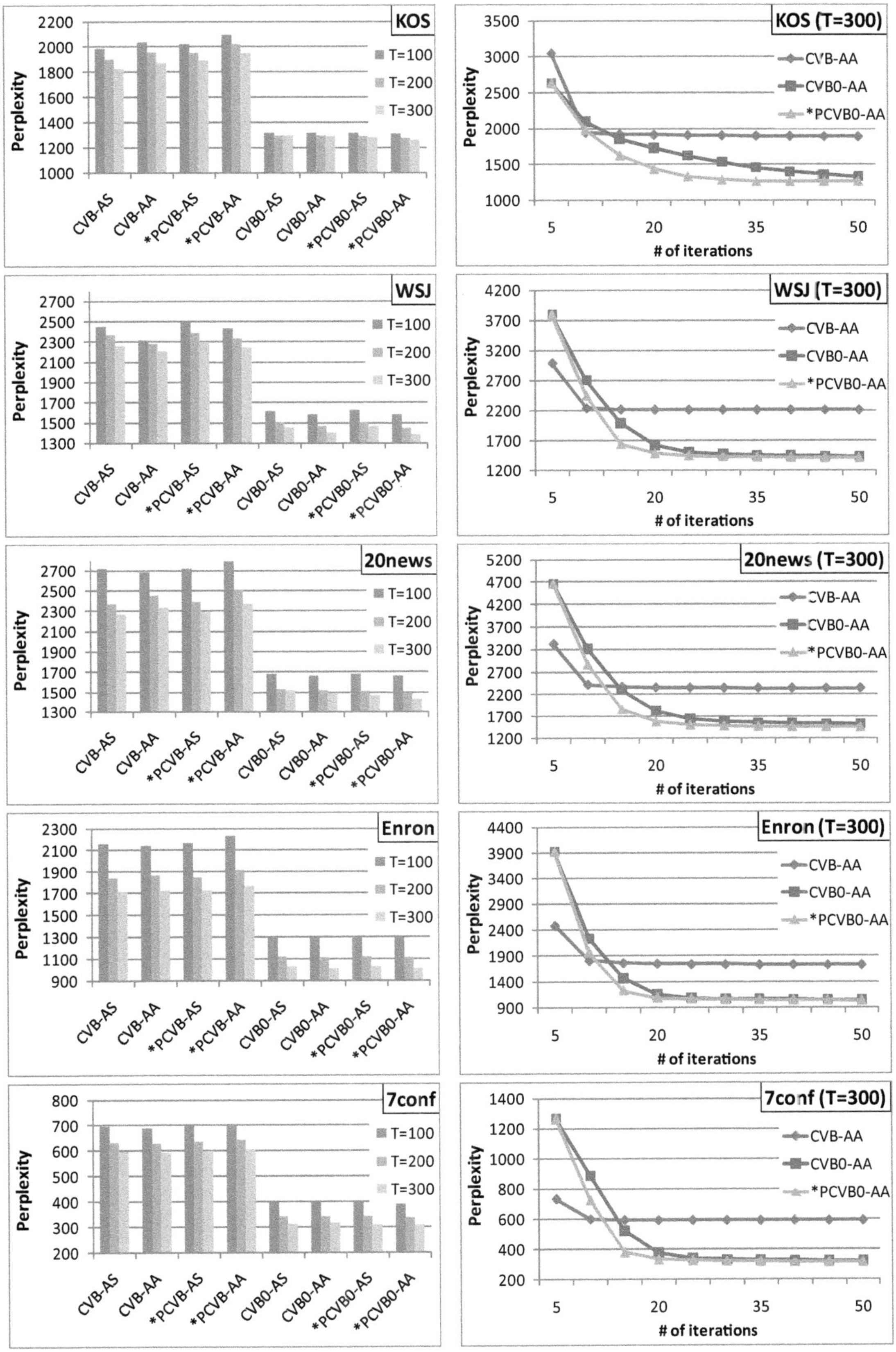

Figure 3: Experiment results for document modeling in five datasets where * indicates our inferences. T denotes the truncation level of TSBP. Lower perplexity indicates better performance.

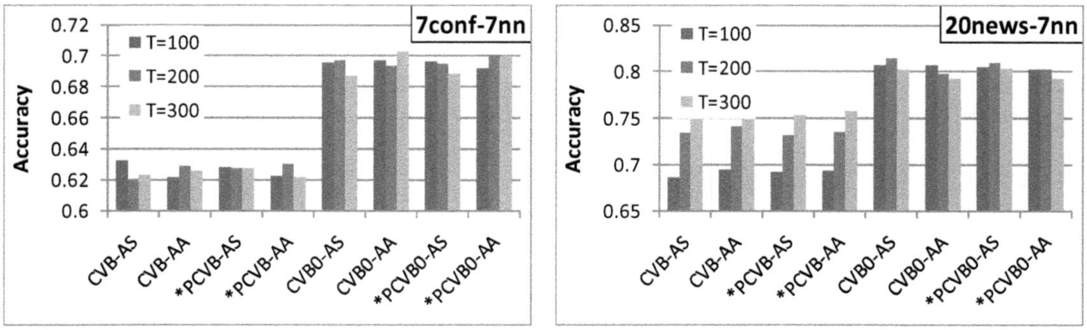

Figure 4: Evaluations for Nearest Neighbor Search.
Results for accuracy among inference algorithms by changing the number of topics in 7-nearest neighbors in the 7conf and 20news corpus. Higher accuracy indicates better classification performance.

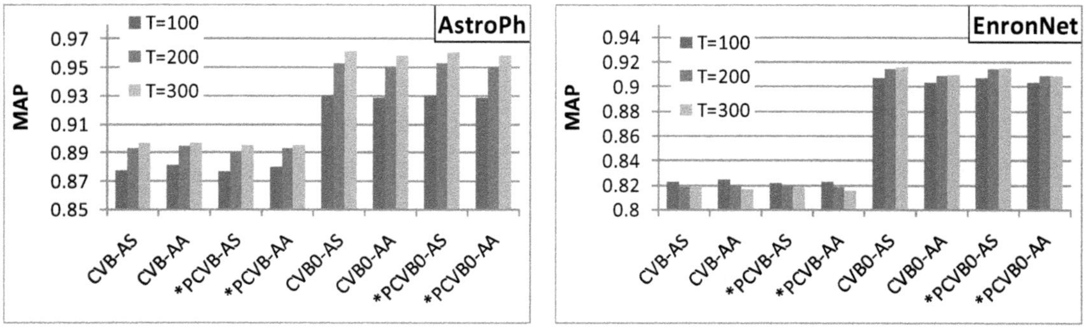

Figure 5: Evaluations for Link Prediction in Social Networks.
Results for MAP among inference algorithms by changing the number of topics in the co-author network in Astro Physics (AstroPh) and the Enron communication networks (EnronNet). Higher MAP indicates better recommendation (ranking) performance.

80% training links and 20% test links. We used the 20% test links for positive examples and labeled those link-nodes "relevance". We constructed negative examples by using randomly selected nodes that were not linked from a query node and labeled those nodes "non-relevance". The number of negative examples was equal to that of the 80% training sets. This is because the MAP does not depend on the number of links for each query-node. The MAP results for various methods are shown in Fig.5. The performance of the link prediction is similar to that of perplexity.

6.6 Discussion

Asunction [27] described the interest relationships between the CVB0 inference and other inferences, e.g., belief propagation, to explain the performance of the CVB0 inference. Here, we explain the (P)CVB0 performance from another aspect. From the results shown on the right side of Fig.3, we see that the convergence of CVB is faster than that of (P)CVB0. This rapid convergence seems to be the reason that the performance of CVB is worse than that of (P)CVB0, i.e., CVB seems to rapidly stuck in poor local optima. This is because for estimating $q(z_{d,i})$, CVB uses the exponential function $\exp(-\mathbb{V}/x^2)$ which makes $q(z_{d,i})$ a sharper distribution when variance $\mathbb{V}$ takes a larger value (note that variance is large in initial iterations). This is similar to the inverse temperature of simulated annealing, which induces the rapid convergence of stochastic inference. We think that the poor local optima can negatively affects the performance of the HDP modeling, which means the HDP model will not work well even if we use a high truncation level.

7. CONCLUSION

We proposed a practical deterministic inference for HDP-LDA. Moreover, we investigated the effects of the choice of prior (symmetric versus asymmetric Dirichlets) over the topic-word distributions in the CVB/CVB0 inference. Although the choice of a symmetric Dirichlet prior over the topic-word distribution model performed well in MCMC simulations reported by Wallach et al.[28], the choice of prior has a small difference in our variational settings. The purpose of this study was to explore a simple learning algorithm for HDP-LDA because the CVB inference of HDP-LDA [24] is more complicated and harder to implement than the variational inference for LDA. The PCVB0 inference is particularly simple to implement, does not require variance counts to be maintained, does not need to set hyper-parameters, and has good predictive performance. Consequently, we recommend the PCVB0 inference in practice and hope that the proposed inference will alleviate researchers' difficulties in using HDP-LDA in a wide range of fields. For future work, we extend the PCVB0 inference into an online algorithm such as [38, 39, 40].

8. REFERENCES

[1] D. M. Blei, A. Y. Ng, and M. I. Jordan. Latent Dirichlet Allocation. *Journal of Machine Learning Research*, 3:993–1022, 2003.

[2] M. Rosen-Zvi, T. Griffiths, M. Steyvers, and P. Smyth. The author-topic model for authors and documents. In *Proceedings of the 20th conference on Uncertainty in artificial intelligence*, pages 487–494. AUAI Press, 2004.

[3] M. Steyvers, P. Smyth, M. Rosen-Zvi, and T. Griffiths. Probabilistic author-topic models for information discovery. In *Proceedings of the tenth ACM SIGKDD international conference on Knowledge discovery and data mining*, pages 306–315. ACM Press, 2004.

[4] D. Newman, C. Chemudugunta, and P. Smyth. Statistical entity-topic models. In *Proceedings of the 12th ACM SIGKDD international conference on Knowledge discovery and data mining*, pages 680–686. ACM Press, 2006.

[5] R. M. Nallapati, A. Ahmed, E. P. Xing, and W. W. Cohen. Joint latent topic models for text and citations. In *Proceeding of the 14th ACM SIGKDD international conference on Knowledge discovery and data mining*, pages 542–550. ACM, 2008.

[6] A. Gruber, M. Rosen-Zvi, and Y. Weiss. Latent Topic Models for Hypertext. In *UAI*, pages 230–239, 2008.

[7] A. Ahmed, E. P. Xing, W. W. Cohen, and R. F. Murphy. Structured correspondence topic models for mining captioned figures in biological literature. In *Proceedings of the 15th ACM SIGKDD international conference on Knowledge discovery and data mining*, KDD '09, pages 39–48. ACM, 2009.

[8] D. M. Blei and J. D. Lafferty. Dynamic topic models. In *Proceedings of the 23rd international conference on Machine learning*, pages 113–120. ACM, 2006.

[9] C. Wang, D. M. Blei, and D. Heckerman. Continuous Time Dynamic Topic Models. In *UAI*, pages 579–586, 2008.

[10] L. Yao, D. Mimno, and A. McCallum. Efficient methods for topic model inference on streaming document collections. In *Proceedings of the 15th ACM SIGKDD international conference on Knowledge discovery and data mining*, KDD '09, pages 937–946. ACM, 2009.

[11] T. Iwata, T. Yamada, Y. Sakurai, and N. Ueda. Online multiscale dynamic topic models. In *Proceedings of the 16th ACM SIGKDD international conference on Knowledge discovery and data mining*, pages 663–672. ACM, 2010.

[12] L. Hong, D. Yin, J. Guo, and B. D. Davison. Tracking trends: incorporating term volume into temporal topic models. In *Proceedings of the 17th ACM SIGKDD international conference on Knowledge discovery and data mining*, KDD '11, pages 484–492. ACM, 2011.

[13] I. Sato and H. Nakagawa. Topic Models with Power-Law Using Pitman-Yor Process. In *Proceedings of 16th ACM SIGKDD International Conference on Knowledge Discovery and Data Mining*, 2010.

[14] D. Ramage, C. D. Manning, and S. Dumais. Partially labeled topic models for interpretable text mining. In *Proceedings of the 17th ACM SIGKDD international conference on Knowledge discovery and data mining*, KDD '11, pages 457–465. ACM, 2011.

[15] J. Zhu, N. Lao, N. Chen, and E. P. Xing. Conditional topical coding: an efficient topic model conditioned on rich features. In *Proceedings of the 17th ACM SIGKDD international conference on Knowledge discovery and data mining*, KDD '11, pages 475–483. ACM, 2011.

[16] X. Wei and W. B. Croft. LDA-based document models for ad-hoc retrieval. In *Proceedings of the 29th annual international ACM SIGIR conference on Research and development in information retrieval*, SIGIR '06, pages 178–185. ACM, 2006.

[17] D. Andrzejewski and D. Buttler. Latent topic feedback for information retrieval. In *Proceedings of the 17th ACM SIGKDD international conference on Knowledge discovery and data mining*, KDD '11, pages 600–608. ACM, 2011.

[18] K. El-Arini, G. Veda, D. Shahaf, and C. Guestrin. Turning down the noise in the blogosphere. In *Proceedings of the 15th ACM SIGKDD international conference on Knowledge discovery and data mining*, KDD '09, pages 289–298. ACM, 2009.

[19] J. Chang, J. L. Boyd-Graber, and D. M. Blei. Connections between the lines: augmenting social networks with text. In *Proceedings of the 15th ACM SIGKDD International Conference on Knowledge Discovery and Data Mining, Paris, France, June 28 - July 1, 2009*, pages 169–178. ACM, 2009.

[20] S. Gerrish and D. M. Blei. A Language-based Approach to Measuring Scholarly Impact. In *Proceedings of the 27th International Conference on Machine Learning (ICML2010), year = 2010, pages = 375-382*.

[21] S. Gerrish and D. M. Blei. Predicting Legislative Roll Calls from Text. In *Proceedings of the 28th International Conference on Machine Learning, ICML 2011*, pages 489–496, 2011.

[22] C. Wang and D. M. Blei. Collaborative topic modeling for recommending scientific articles. In *Proceedings of the 17th ACM SIGKDD International Conference on Knowledge Discovery and Data Mining*, pages 448–456, 2011.

[23] Y. W. Teh, M. I. Jordan, M. J. Beal, and D. M. Blei. Hierarchical Dirichlet Processes. *Journal of the American Statistical Association*, 101(476):1566–1581, 2006.

[24] Y. W. Teh, K. Kurihara, and M. Welling. Collapsed Variational Inference for HDP. In *Advances in Neural Information Processing Systems 20*, 2008.

[25] Y. W. Teh, D. Newman, and M. Welling. A Collapsed Variational Bayesian Inference Algorithm for Latent Dirichlet Allocation. In *Advances in Neural Information Processing Systems 19*, 2007.

[26] A. Asuncion, M. Welling, P. Smyth, and Y. W. Teh. On Smoothing and Inference for Topic Models. In *Proceedings of the International Conference on Uncertainty in Artificial Intelligence*, 2009.

[27] A. Asuncion. Approximate Mean Field for Dirichlet-Based Models. In *Topic Models Workshop, ICML*.

[28] H. Wallach, D. Mimno, and A. McCallum. Rethinking LDA: Why Priors Matter. In *Advances in Neural Information Processing Systems 22*, pages 1973–1981. 2009.

[29] H. Ishwaran and L. F. James. Gibbs Sampling Methods for Stick Breaking Priors. *Journal of the American Statistical Association*, 96(453):161–173, 2001.

[30] Escobar and West. Bayesian Density Estimation and Inference using Mixtures. *Journal of the American Statistical Association*, 90, 1995.

[31] D. Sontag and D. Roy. Complexity of Inference in Latent Dirichlet Allocation. In *Advances in Neural Information Processing Systems 24*, pages 1008–1016. 2011.

[32] T. P. Minka. Estimating a Dirichlet distribution. Technical report, Microsoft, 2000.

[33] C. Elkan. Clustering documents with an exponential-family approximation of the Dirichlet compound multinomial distribution. In *Proceedings of the 23rd international conference on Machine learning*, pages 289–296, 2006.

[34] A. Frank and A. Asuncion. UCI Machine Learning Repository, 2010.

[35] H. Deng, J. Han, B. Zhao, Y. Yu, and C. X. Lin. Probabilistic topic models with biased propagation on heterogeneous information networks. In *Proceedings of the 17th ACM SIGKDD international conference on Knowledge discovery and data mining*, pages 1271–1279, 2011.

[36] J. Leskovec, J. Kleinberg, and C. Faloutsos. Graphs over time: densification laws, shrinking diameters and possible explanations. In *Proceedings of the 11th ACM SIGKDD international conference on Knowledge discovery in data mining*, KDD '05, pages 177–187. ACM, 2005.

[37] J. Leskovec, J. Kleinberg, and C. Faloutsos. Graph evolution: Densification and shrinking diameters. *ACM Transactions on Knowledge Discovery from Data (ACM TKDD)*, 1(1), 2007.

[38] M. D. Hoffman, D. M. Blei, and F. R. Bach. Online Learning for Latent Dirichlet Allocation. In *Advances in Neural Information Processing Systems 23: 24th Annual Conference on Neural Information Processing Systems 2010*, pages 856–864, 2010.

[39] I. Sato, K. Kurihara, and H. Nakagawa. Deterministic Single-Pass Algorithm for LDA. In J. Lafferty, C. K. I. Williams, R. Zemel, J. Shawe-Taylor, and A. Culotta, editors, *Advances in Neural Information Processing Systems 23*, pages 2074–2082. 2010.

[40] C. Wang, J. W. Paisley, and D. M. Blei. Online Variational Inference for the Hierarchical Dirichlet Process. *Journal of Machine Learning Research - Proceedings Track*, 15:752–760, 2011.

Overlapping Decomposition for Causal Graphical Modeling

Lei Han[†], Guojie Song[†*], Gao Cong[‡], Kunqing Xie[†]
[†]Key Laboratory of Machine Perception (Ministry of Education), EECS, Peking University, China
{hanlei, gjsong, xkq}@cis.pku.edu.cn
[‡]School of Computer Engineering, Nanyang Technological University, Singapore
gaocong@ntu.edu.sg

ABSTRACT

Causal graphical models are developed to detect the dependence relationships between random variables and provide intuitive explanations for the relationships in complex systems. Most of existing work focuses on learning a single graphical model for all the variables. However, a single graphical model cannot accurately characterize the complicated causal relationships for a relatively large graph. In this paper, we propose the problem of estimating an overlapping decomposition for Gaussian graphical models of a large scale to generate overlapping sub-graphical models. Specifically, we formulate an objective function for the overlapping decomposition problem and propose an approximate algorithm for it. A key theory of the algorithm is that the problem of solving a $k+1$ node graphical model can be reduced to the problem of solving a one-step regularization based on a solved k node graphical model. Based on this theory, a greedy expansion algorithm is proposed to generate the overlapping subgraphs. We evaluate the effectiveness of our model on both synthetic datasets and real traffic dataset, and the experimental results show the superiority of our method.

Categories and Subject Descriptors

G.3 [**Mathematics of Computing**]: Probability and Statistics

Keywords

Causality, Graphical Model, Overlapping Decomposition

1. INTRODUCTION

Causal graphical models are established to meaningfully characterize causal or statistical relationships that exist among variables of interest and quantify them. The problem of characterizing the causal relationships between variables in complex systems, such as economics, biological systems, traffic systems, climate change, etc., is important and fundamental. For example, economists want to know whether *burning natural gas* is a causal factor for the *global warming*.

*Corresponding author. Email: gjsong@cis.pku.edu.cn

The Gaussian graphical model [7], which learns the causalities between variables through their covariance, is one of the most promising causal modeling methods. It has been successfully employed in many applications, such as mining the causalities of climate attributes [2], gene regulatory network discovery [5], etc. In addition, several causal models on temporal evolving graphs have been proposed with applications in cross-species gene expression analysis [11], oil-production equipment stage capture [10] and climate research [12].

These methods construct a single graphical model to capture all the causalities between variables, treating all the variables together. They are typically developed for a small number of variables (usually in the order of tens). We will discuss theoretically in Section 4.2 that learning causalities through a single Gaussian graphical model by the variable covariance will be inaccurate, when large number of variables are considered and small number of observations are available. As a matter of fact, a causality model with only 20 variables can be overwhelming and difficult to interpret at a global level [1, 15]. Worse still, it is much more challenging to understand and construct causal relationships using causal graphical models for a relatively large graph (e.g., with hundreds of variables), although many applications need to deal with large graphs with heterogenous and complicated relationships. For instance, a highway network in traffic systems often contains hundreds of sample nodes, whose observations are counts of passing vehicles collected by sensors. In such traffic networks, complicated causalities exist between the vehicle counts.

Therefore, it is essential to develop techniques to discover such causalities in a large network. To cope with the challenging problem, we propose to decompose a large graphical model into multiple overlapping sub-graphical models. For decomposing a graphical model, it is important to consider both the heterogeneity and homogeneity, where heterogeneity means the local causalities and homogeneity refers to the overlaps between sub-graphical models. For example in traffic systems, some crucial traffic nodes may highly correlate with several different local regions, and thus these important nodes should be considered as overlap (homogeneity) by these local regions; meanwhile, we also need to find the causalities within a region (heterogeneity).

Unfortunately, decomposing graphical models is NP-hard [15] even if overlaps are not allowed. When we allow overlaps, the decomposition problem becomes more challenging because the search space becomes larger, which is due to more combinations of subgraph structures than those in the non-overlapping case.

In this paper, we address the challenging problem of estimating an overlapping decomposition for Gaussian graphical models of a large scale. We propose a novel approximation algorithm with performance guarantee, which is based on a local subgraph expansion strategy. Specifically, we first formulate the optimization problem with an objective function comprising the negative log-likelihood of the observations of Gaussian sub-graphical models and some penalized items to constrain the structure of the subgraphs. Unfortunately, the penalized log-likelihood methods [4, 19] in Gaussian graphical model cannot be used to solve the approximation problem. Instead, we propose an algorithm that starts with the initial small subgraphs and incrementally computes the new Gaussian graphical model when a new node is involved.

One key technique is that we prove that the problem of solving a $k+1$ node graphical model can be reduced to the problem of solving a one-step regularization based on a solved k node graphical model, referred to as additive expanding property. We study the correctness and accuracy of this technique with detailed analysis. Based on the technique, we propose a greedy expansion algorithm for generating the overlapping sub-graphical models.

We evaluate the proposed method with two sets of experiments: First we empirically verify the properties of the proposed overlapping decomposition method on synthetic networks, and compare with the single graphical model [4, 19] and the non-overlapping decomposition method (which is a special case of the proposed overlapping decomposition method). The experimental results demonstrate the advantages of our techniques. Second, we evaluate the proposed techniques on real-life traffic data by learning the causalities between traffic observation points (e.g., a on-ramp) and detecting the traffic regularity in large traffic networks, which is essential for traffic analysis.

In summary, our main contributions are four-fold:

1. We formulate an objective function for the problem of overlapping decomposition of graphical model, and reduce the problem to a local subgraph expansion problem.
2. We extend the penalized log-likelihood in Gaussian graphical model to satisfy an additive expanding property and demonstrate its correctness and accuracy with detailed asymptotic analysis.
3. We propose a constrained greedy subgraph expansion algorithm for generating the overlapping subgraphs.
4. We evaluate our method on both synthetic and real-life traffic data. Experimental results show the effectiveness and superiority of our overlapping decomposition theory.

The rest of this paper is organized as follows. In Section 2, we briefly review closely related work. Section 3 presents the preliminaries and the problem statement. In Section 4, we present the proposed method including two core techniques and a demonstration. Experimental studies are reported in Section 5. We conclude this paper and present future directions in Section 6.

2. RELATED WORK

Most of existing work on causal graphical models builds a single graphical model. This renders them impractical to relatively large graphs (with more than hundreds of nodes). To cope with larger set of time series variables, Ruan et al. [15] propose to cluster time series variables into groups such that strong causal relations appear only between time series within a group while the causal relation between inter-group variables is weak. The clustering problem is formulated as a regression coefficient sparsification problem for graphical model decomposition. However, the approach [15] only considers non-overlapping decompositions while ignoring the overlap between subgraphs, which exists in many real-world applications. Moreover, the approach [15] is developed for time series variables, and is based on the Vector Autoregressive model, a type of temporal graphical model, rather than Gaussian graphical model as we use.

Our work is closely related to the joint estimation methods for multiple graphical models that share common structures [3,6]. The joint estimation methods [3,6] are proposed to learn multiple graphical models on the data from different categories but with the same set of features (variables), considering both the underlying homogeneity and heterogeneity of networks. They estimate multiple graphical models for different categories of the features, but not decomposing the features themselves. We proceed to use the example application scenario [3] to illustrate these methods. Consider a set of webpages collected from computer science departments of universities, and we want to find the causalities between selected keywords (e.g., "book", "model", "problem", etc.) appearing in the collection. These keywords can be treated as features, and appear in webpages of different categories, such as "student", "faculty", "project", etc. These features may display different dependence structures for different categories while sharing some common causalities across categories. The joint estimation methods cannot be applied to solve our problem, and they cannot be employed to discover the complicated causal relationships in large feature networks. First, these methods do not consider the decomposition on features of a large graph. Second, these methods are developed for graphs with a small number of features (in the order of tens).

Our proposed approach is also related to detecting overlapped community structures [9]. Community structure detection aims to group similar nodes together based on known distance measurements of nodes or correlations among nodes themselves. In contrast, in our problem we aim to uncover the causalities among correlated nodes, and furthermore find subgraphs based on the discovered causalities but not the known properties of nodes themselves. Thus, our problem is essentially different from community structure detection.

3. PRELIMINARY AND PROBLEM STATEMENT

3.1 Preliminary: Gaussian graphical model

As a member of the causal graphical model, Gaussian graphical model(GGM) assumes the joint distribution of the variables to be Gaussian. In GGM, the dependence structure (or causality) is determined from the covariance matrix of the variables, and a natural way to evaluate the causalities is to estimate the inverse of the covariance matrix [7, 8, 18]. Consider p random variables $\boldsymbol{X} = (\boldsymbol{x}_1, ..., \boldsymbol{x}_p)$, each variable $\boldsymbol{x}_i$ having n observations $\boldsymbol{x}_i = (x_i^1, ..., x_i^n)^T$, where we usually have $n \gg p$. Without loss of generality, we assume $\boldsymbol{X}$ follows a multivariate Gaussian distribution $N(\boldsymbol{\mu}, \Sigma)$, where the mean vector $\boldsymbol{\mu}$ is p-dimensional and each element in covariance matrix Σ is the expected value $\Sigma_{ij} = E[(X_i - \mu_i)(X_j - \mu_j)]$. The causality matrix Ω is the inverse of the covariance matrix, i.e., $\Omega = \Sigma^{-1}$. There exists a causal relationship between variables x_i and x_j iff $\Omega_{ij} \neq 0$ [7,18]. Therefore, the key problem is to calculate Ω. The estimation of Ω can be obtained by minimizing the penalized log-likelihood criterion [4, 19],

$$\widehat{\Omega} = \arg\min_{\Omega} \quad tr(\widehat{\Sigma}\Omega) - \log|\Omega| + \lambda \sum_{i \neq j} |\theta_{ij}| \qquad (1)$$

where θ_{ij} is the element in Ω; $\widehat{\Sigma}$ is the sample covariance matrix estimated on input X; $|\cdot|$ and $tr(\cdot)$ are the determinant and the trace in matrix calculus, respectively; λ is a tuning parameter.

The part $tr(\widehat{\Sigma}\Omega) - \log|\Omega|$ of Equation 1 corresponds to the negative log-likelihood of the observations of a Gaussian graphical model. The part $\lambda\sum_{i\neq j}|\theta_{ij}|$ is called a ℓ_1 penalty, which is to shrink some of the off-diagonal elements in $\widehat{\Omega}$ to zero. The tuning parameter λ controls the sparsity of $\widehat{\Omega}$. This minimization problem can be solved efficiently by the graphical lasso algorithms proposed in [4, 19].

3.2 Problem Definition

Problem Definition: Given p random variables $\boldsymbol{X} = (\boldsymbol{x}_1, ..., \boldsymbol{x}_p)$, where p is large and each variable $\boldsymbol{x}_i$ has n observations, $\boldsymbol{x}_i = (x_i^1, ..., x_i^n)^T$, we aim to learn the causal relationships between these variables.

In other words, we aim to encode the structure of $\boldsymbol{X}$ with an undirected graph $G = (V, E)$, where each node v in $V = \{v_1, \cdots, v_p\}$ corresponds to a variable in $\boldsymbol{X}$. The edge set E indicates the causalities between any two variables. More precisely, if $\boldsymbol{x}_i$ is correlated to $\boldsymbol{x}_j$, then edge e_{ij} is included in E. Thus, our objective is to obtain E. As introduced in Section 3.1, E can be constructed by estimating the causality matrix Ω of $\boldsymbol{X}$. We add an edge e_{ij} to E iff $\Omega_{ij} \neq 0$.

Instead of creating a single Gaussian graphical model for G, we propose to construct K Gaussian sub-graphical models with overlaps to discover the causalities between variables. Each subgraph, corresponding to a Gaussian sub-graphical model, is denoted as $g_i = (SV_i, SE_i), 1 \leq i \leq K$. The causal relationships reflected in E, $E = \bigcup_i SE_i$, are the output.

The challenge is to generate the K sub-graphical models and estimate Ω_i for each SE_i. To achieve this, we proceed to define a new objective function, which helps to formulate the decomposition problem clearly. We first introduce some notations: K vectors $\{\Gamma_1, \cdots, \Gamma_K\}$, where each $1 \times p$ vector Γ_i represents the component of a subgraph g_i. Element γ_{ij} in Γ_i is 1 if node j appears in subgraph g_i, and 0 otherwise. In addition, we set $\sum_{i=1}^{K}\sum_{j=1}^{p}\gamma_{ij} \geq p$, because we allow overlaps and we do not restrict that every node has to be included in at least one subgraph. This is reasonable because if a node is independent from all others, it should be left alone.

Objective function: We formulate the overlapping decomposition for a graphical model into the problem of estimating a set of Ω_i by minimizing

$$\{\widehat{\Omega}_i\}_{i=1}^K = \arg\min_{\{\Omega_1,\cdots,\Omega_K\}} \sum_{i=1}^{K}\{tr(\widehat{\Sigma}_i\Omega_i) - \log|\Omega_i|\} + \lambda_1\sum_{i=1}^{K}\sum_{j\neq k}|\theta_{i,jk}| + \lambda_2\sum_{i=1}^{K}\|\Gamma_i\|_1^2 + \lambda_3\sum_{i<i'}\|\Gamma_i \circ \Gamma_{i'}\|_1^2,$$
$$s.t. \sum_{i=1}^{K}\|\Gamma_i\|_1 \geq p, \qquad (2)$$

where $\theta_{i,jk}$ is the element in Ω_i; $\|\cdot\|_1$ is the ℓ_1 norm; $\circ$ means the Hadamard product; λ_1, λ_2 and λ_3 are tuning parameters.

In Equation 2, $tr(\widehat{\Sigma}_i\Omega_i) - \log|\Omega_i|$ represents the negative log-likelihood of the observations of Gaussian sub-graphic model g_i. The equation includes three penalized items:

- penalty $\lambda_1\sum_{i=1}^{K}\sum_{j\neq k}|\theta_{i,jk}|$ controls the sparsity of the causalities in each subgraph;
- penalty $\lambda_2\sum_{i=1}^{K}\|\Gamma_i\|_1^2$ is a constraint on the size of each subgraph and balances them, because the sum of the square is small when the subgraphs have the similar size;
- penalty $\lambda_3\sum_{i<i'}\|\Gamma_i \circ \Gamma_{i'}\|_1^2$ gives a constraint on the sizes of overlaps and balances the sizes of overlaps, because the Hadamard product between any two Γ_i and $\Gamma_{i'}$ denotes the common nodes they share.

Given p random variables $\boldsymbol{X} = (\boldsymbol{x}_1, ..., \boldsymbol{x}_p)$, and assume $\boldsymbol{X}$ is encoded with a large graph G, our problem of discovering the causality structures in G is formulated as finding a set of overlapped subgraphs based on Equation 2.

Challenge and Solution Overview: The overlapping decomposition problem is a combinational optimization problem and it is NP-hard even if the penalty factors are not considered [15] . The problem involves $Kp+Kp^2$ unknown variables in the worst case, where $\{\Gamma_1, \cdots, \Gamma_K\}$ needs Kp variables, and $\{\Omega_1, \cdots, \Omega_K\}$ needs at most Kp^2 variables. Note that $\{\Omega_1, \cdots, \Omega_K\}$ needs fewer variables if we do not allow overlaps. Such a large number of unknown variables makes this problem computationally challenging. Moreover, we even do not know how to select a best K for this problem.

Hence, instead of finding the optimal solution to the complicated function, we propose a novel approximation algorithm for solving the overlapping decomposition problem, called *local subgraph expansion*. Our algorithms adopt a bottom-up strategy that expand the initial subgraphs by adding selected nodes gradually until the structure of overlapped subgraphs will reach convergence.

During this process, a key operation is to choose whether to include a new node in a subgraph. This operation is invoked many times, and calls for efficient techniques. Specifically, assume that there is a k-node subgraph whose inner causal relationships have been detected. We want to know whether a node v_{k+1} should be added to it. A straightforward method is creating a new Gaussian graphical model on all the $k+1$ nodes. However, this ignores the known causal relationships in the k-node subgraph and is computationally expensive. Thus, a natural question is whether we can reuse the known causal relationships in a subgraph to detect the causal relationships between a new node and the subgraph. In the next section, we present the proposed approximation method with performance guarantees for the operation.

4. PROPOSED METHOD

In this section, we propose two techniques. The first technique is generalized by a theorem in Section 4.1. This technique is used to check whether a new variable (node) should be included in a subgraph. The technique extends the penalized log-likelihood criterion in Equation 1 so that it can be incrementally expanded to accommodate new nodes. We call it Additive Penalized Log-likelihood Expansion (APLE). In Section 4.2, we also show the correctness and accuracy for APLE, which also motivate the necessity to decompose a large graphical model into sub-graphical models from a theoretical view.

The second technique is a local greedy approach presented in Section 4.3. We define a fitness function based on APLE approach. Moreover, taking into account the constraints (penalties in Equation 2) on the subgraph structures, we develop the Constraint Greedy Subgraph Expansion (CGSE) algorithm, which can achieve the *local subgraph expansion* process.

4.1 Additive Penalized Log-likelihood Expansion

Suppose that $\ell(\Omega^{(k+1)})$ is a new penalized log-likelihood criterion computed by Equation 1, which is from adding a new variable x_{k+1} into a solved penalized log-likelihood criterion $\ell(\Omega^{(k)})$, where

$$\Omega^{(k+1)} = \begin{bmatrix} \Omega^{(k)} & \boldsymbol{\theta} \\ \boldsymbol{\theta}^T & \theta_{k+1} \end{bmatrix}$$

and $\boldsymbol{\theta}$ is a $k \times 1$ causality vector between x_{k+1} and $\{x_1, ..., x_k\}$ which we want to get. Since $\Omega^{(k)}$ is already solved (we assume it is solved by graphical lasso), it is positive definite [4, 19]. Thus, θ_{k+1} controls whether $\Omega^{(k+1)}$ is positive definite, and determines the $k+1$ th eigenvalue of $\Omega^{(k+1)}$. Also we select θ_{k+1} to guarantee $\Omega^{(k+1)}$ positive definite.

Theorem 1: Suppose $\widehat{\Omega}^{(k)}$ is a local minimizer of $\ell(\Omega^{(k)})$, then there exists a local minimizer of $\ell(\Omega^{(k+1)})$, $\widehat{\Omega}^{(k+1)}$, such that $\widehat{\Omega}^{(k+1)} = (\widehat{\Omega}^{(k)}, \widehat{\boldsymbol{\theta}}^{(k)})$, where $\widehat{\boldsymbol{\theta}}^{(k)}$ is a local minimizer of

$$\begin{aligned} min \quad & 2\widehat{\boldsymbol{\varepsilon}}^T\boldsymbol{\theta} + \widehat{\varepsilon}_{k+1}\theta_{k+1} \\ & -log(\theta_{k+1} - \boldsymbol{\theta}^T \cdot \widehat{\boldsymbol{\Sigma}}^{(k)} \cdot \boldsymbol{\theta}) + 2\lambda_\theta\|\boldsymbol{\theta}\|_1 \end{aligned} \tag{3}$$

where $(\widehat{\boldsymbol{\varepsilon}}, \widehat{\varepsilon}_{k+1})$ is the sample covariance vector between x_{k+1} and $\{x_1, ..., x_{k+1}\}$.

Proof: The new penalized log-likelihood criterion $\ell(\Omega^{(k+1)})$ is

$$\ell(\Omega^{(k+1)}) = tr(\widehat{\Sigma}^{(k+1)}\Omega^{(k+1)}) - \log|\Omega^{(k+1)}| + \lambda\sum_{i\neq j}^{k+1}|\theta_{ij}|$$

Compactly, we introduce three symbols to denote the items

$$I_1^{(k+1)} = tr(\widehat{\Sigma}^{(k+1)}\Omega^{(k+1)})$$

$$I_2^{(k+1)} = \log|\Omega^{(k+1)}|$$

$$I_3^{(k+1)} = \lambda\textstyle\sum_{i\neq j}^{k+1}|\theta_{ij}|$$

We unfold $\widehat{\Sigma}^{(k+1)}$ and $\Omega^{(k+1)}$ into block matrices to detect the relationship between $\ell(\Omega^{(k+1)})$ and $\ell(\Omega^{(k)})$. The unfolded matrices are derived as

$$\begin{aligned} I_1^{(k+1)} &= tr(\begin{bmatrix} \widehat{\Sigma}^{(k)} & \widehat{\boldsymbol{\varepsilon}} \\ \widehat{\boldsymbol{\varepsilon}}^T & \widehat{\varepsilon}_{k+1} \end{bmatrix} \cdot \begin{bmatrix} \Omega^{(k)} & \boldsymbol{\theta} \\ \boldsymbol{\theta}^T & \theta_{k+1} \end{bmatrix}) \\ &= tr(\begin{bmatrix} \widehat{\Sigma}^{(k)}\Omega^{(k)} + \widehat{\boldsymbol{\varepsilon}}\boldsymbol{\theta}^T & \widehat{\Sigma}^{(k)}\boldsymbol{\theta} + \theta_{k+1}\widehat{\boldsymbol{\varepsilon}} \\ \widehat{\boldsymbol{\varepsilon}}^T\Omega^{(k)} + \widehat{\varepsilon}_{k+1}\boldsymbol{\theta}^T & \widehat{\boldsymbol{\varepsilon}}^T\boldsymbol{\theta} + \widehat{\varepsilon}_{k+1}\theta_{k+1} \end{bmatrix}) \\ &= tr(\widehat{\Sigma}^{(k)}\Omega^{(k)}) + tr(\widehat{\boldsymbol{\varepsilon}}\boldsymbol{\theta}^T) + \widehat{\boldsymbol{\varepsilon}}^T\boldsymbol{\theta} + \widehat{\varepsilon}_{k+1}\theta_{k+1} \\ &= I_1^{(k)} + 2\widehat{\boldsymbol{\varepsilon}}^T\boldsymbol{\theta} + \widehat{\varepsilon}_{k+1}\theta_{k+1} \end{aligned}$$

$$\begin{aligned} I_2^{(k+1)} &= \log\begin{vmatrix} \Omega^{(k)} & \boldsymbol{\theta} \\ \boldsymbol{\theta}^T & \theta_{k+1} \end{vmatrix} \\ &= \log(|\Omega^{(k)}| \cdot |\theta_{k+1} - \boldsymbol{\theta}^T(\Omega^{(k)})^{-1}\boldsymbol{\theta}|) \\ &= I_2^{(k)} + \log(\theta_{k+1} - \boldsymbol{\theta}^T\widehat{\Sigma}^{(k)}\boldsymbol{\theta}) \end{aligned}$$

$$I_3^{(k+1)} = \lambda\sum_{i\neq j}^{k+1}|\theta_{ij}| = I_3^{(k)} + 2\lambda\|\boldsymbol{\theta}\|_1$$

where $\widehat{\boldsymbol{\varepsilon}}$ and $\boldsymbol{\theta}$ are $k\times 1$ vectors; the derivation of $I_2^{(k+1)}$ is obtained by Leibniz formula. Finally, we can get

$$\begin{aligned} \ell(\Omega^{(k+1)}) = \ell(\Omega^{(k)}) + \\ 2\widehat{\boldsymbol{\varepsilon}}^T\boldsymbol{\theta} + \widehat{\varepsilon}_{k+1}\theta_{k+1} - \log(\theta_{k+1} - \boldsymbol{\theta}^T\widehat{\Sigma}^{(k)}\boldsymbol{\theta}) + 2\lambda\|\boldsymbol{\theta}\|_1 \end{aligned} \tag{4}$$

□

Similarly, we use $\ell(\boldsymbol{\theta}^{(k)})$ to represent Equation 4, then we have

$$\ell(\Omega^{(k+1)}) = \ell(\Omega^{(k)}) + \ell(\boldsymbol{\theta}^{(k)}) \tag{5}$$

Thus, it is understandable that to solve $\ell(\Omega^{(k+1)})$ based on a solved $\ell(\Omega^{(k)})$, we just need to solve $\ell(\boldsymbol{\theta}^{(k)})$ for an additional problem. Note that Equation 3 is exactly a ℓ_1 regularization problem which can be solved efficiently using the algorithms in [16,17].

One should be noted that the correctness and accuracy of $\widehat{\Omega}^{(k+1)} = (\widehat{\Omega}^{(k)}, \widehat{\boldsymbol{\theta}}^{(k)})$ has not been completely guaranteed by the above proof, because parameter λ_θ must be selected appropriately to make sure $(\widehat{\Omega}^{(k)}, \widehat{\boldsymbol{\theta}}^{(k)})$ equals the local minimizer $\widehat{\Omega}^{(k+1)}$. In other words, λ_θ has to be adapted corresponding to k as the expansion continues (until subgraphs converge). Since λ_θ controls the sparsity of $\widehat{\boldsymbol{\theta}}^{(k)}$, if λ_θ stays unchangeable, when the subgraph expands, constraint on $\|\widehat{\boldsymbol{\theta}}^k\|_1$ will become inappropriate which leads to the uncertainty of $\widehat{\Omega}^{(k+1)} = (\widehat{\Omega}^{(k)}, \widehat{\boldsymbol{\theta}}^{(k)})$.

Thus, a new question raises that how to adapt λ_θ to make the evaluation accurate when the subgraph expands. In next subsection, we will discuss the asymptotic behavior of APLE and show how to select λ_θ to ensure the correctness and accuracy of *Theorem 1*.

4.2 Asymptotic Analysis of APLE

Asymptotic property is crucial for APLE which makes sure that $\widehat{\Omega}^{(k+1)}$ can be obtained by $\widehat{\Omega}^{(k)}$ and $\widehat{\boldsymbol{\theta}}^{(k)}$ separately under an appropriate λ_θ. A detailed asymptotic analysis of Equation 1 has been discussed in [14]. Inspired by it, we establish the analysis to our APLE approach as follows.

Let the true causality matrix of $\ell(\Omega)$ be Ω_0, the true covariance matrix be Σ_0, $\Omega_0 = (\Sigma_0)^{-1}$, as well as true causality vector $\boldsymbol{\theta}_0$ and true covariance vector $\boldsymbol{\varepsilon}_0$. Let $\|\cdot\|_F$ be the Frobenius norm. We make the following assumptions.

A1: There exists a constant η such that $0 < \varphi_{max}(\Omega_0^{(k)}) \leq \eta$, where $\varphi_{max}(\cdot)$ denotes the maximum eigenvalue.

A2: There exist constants σ_1 and σ_2 such that $\sigma_1 \leq \theta_{k+1} \leq \sigma_2$ will guarantee $\Omega^{(k+1)}$ positive definite and $\varphi_{max}(\Omega_0^{(k+1)}) \leq \eta$. (Note that θ_{k+1} determines the $k+1$ th eigenvalue of $\Omega^{(k+1)}$).

Theorem 2: Let $\widehat{\boldsymbol{\theta}}^{(k)}$ be the local minimizer in Equation 3. Under A1 and A2, if $\lambda_\theta = C_0\sqrt{\frac{\log k}{n}}$, C_0 is a positive constant, then

$$\|\widehat{\boldsymbol{\theta}}^{(k)} - \boldsymbol{\theta}_0^{(k)}\|_F = O_P\left(\sqrt{\frac{k\log k}{n}}\right) \tag{6}$$

where $O_P(\cdot)$ is the order in probability.

Proof Let $G(\Delta_\theta) = \ell(\boldsymbol{\theta}_0 + \Delta_\theta) - \ell(\boldsymbol{\theta}_0)$. Assume that there exists a bounded convex set

$$\mathcal{G} = \{\Delta_\theta : \|\Delta_\theta\|_F \leq Mr_n\},$$

where M is a positive constant and

$$r_n = \sqrt{\frac{k\log k}{n}} \to 0 \quad (n \gg k)$$

Note that $G(\Delta_\theta)$ is a convex function, if we demonstrate that G is strictly positive everywhere on the boundary $\partial\mathcal{G}$ ($\|\Delta_\theta\|_F = Mr_n$), then G has a local minimum inside $\mathcal{G}$. Actually,

$$G(\Delta_\theta) = \ell(\boldsymbol{\theta_0} + \Delta_\theta) - \ell(\boldsymbol{\theta_0})$$
$$= 2\widehat{\boldsymbol{\varepsilon}}^T\Delta_\theta - (\log(\theta_{k+1} - (\boldsymbol{\theta}_0^T + \Delta_\theta)\widehat{\Sigma}^{(k)}(\boldsymbol{\theta}_0 + \Delta_\theta)) \quad (7)$$
$$- \log(\theta_{k+1} - \boldsymbol{\theta}_0^T\widehat{\Sigma}^{(k)}\boldsymbol{\theta}_0)) + 2\lambda_\theta(\|\boldsymbol{\theta}_0 + \Delta_\theta\|_1 - \|\boldsymbol{\theta}_0\|_1)$$

For the subtraction of the logarithm terms in Equation 7, assume that $f(\boldsymbol{\theta}) = \log(\theta_{k+1} - \boldsymbol{\theta}^T\widehat{\boldsymbol{\Sigma}}^{(k)}\boldsymbol{\theta})$, we can get from the derivation in proof of *Theorem 1* that $f(\boldsymbol{\theta}) = I_2^{(k+1)} - I_2^{(k)}$, therefore

$$f(\boldsymbol{\theta}_0 + \Delta_\theta) - f(\boldsymbol{\theta}_0) = (\log|\Omega_0^{(k+1)} + \Delta^{(k+1)}| - \log|\Omega_0^{(k+1)}|) - (\log|\Omega_0^{(k)} + \Delta^{(k)}| - \log|\Omega_0^{(k)}|)$$

As has been proved by [14], for Ω_0 we have

$$\log|\Omega_0 + \Delta| - \log|\Omega_0|$$
$$= tr(\Sigma_0\Delta) - \widetilde{\Delta}^T[\int_0^1 (1-v)(\Omega_0 + v\Delta)^{-1} \otimes (\Omega_0 + v\Delta)^{-1}dv]\widetilde{\Delta}$$

where

$$F = \widetilde{\Delta}^T[\int_0^1 (1-v)(\Omega_0 + v\Delta)^{-1} \otimes (\Omega_0 + v\Delta)^{-1}dv]\widetilde{\Delta}$$
$$\geq \frac{1}{4\eta^2}\|\Delta\|_F^2$$

Thus we have

$$f(\boldsymbol{\theta}_0 + \Delta_\theta) - f(\boldsymbol{\theta}_0)$$
$$= (tr(\Sigma_0^{(k+1)}\Delta^{(k+1)}) - tr(\Sigma_0^{(k)}\Delta^{(k)})) - (F^{(k+1)} - F^{(k)})$$
$$\approx 2\boldsymbol{\varepsilon}_0^T\Delta_\theta - (F^{(k+1)} - F^{(k)})$$

Thus, we get

$$G(\Delta_\theta) = 2(\widehat{\boldsymbol{\varepsilon}}^T - \boldsymbol{\varepsilon}_0^T)\Delta_\theta + (F^{(k+1)} - F^{(k)})$$
$$+ 2\lambda_\theta(\|\boldsymbol{\theta}_0 + \Delta_\theta\|_1 - \|\boldsymbol{\theta}_0\|_1)$$

For each item in $G(\Delta_\theta)$ we have the following boundaries

$$B1: |(\widehat{\boldsymbol{\varepsilon}}^T - \boldsymbol{\varepsilon}_0^T)\Delta_\theta| \leq C_1\sqrt{\frac{\log k}{n}}\|\Delta_\theta\|_1 \leq C_1\sqrt{\frac{k\log k}{n}}\|\Delta_\theta\|_F$$

$$B2: F^{(k+1)} - F^{(k)} \geq \frac{1}{4\eta^2}(\|\Delta^{(k+1)}\|_F^2 - \|\Delta^{(k)}\|_F^2) \geq \frac{1}{2\eta^2}\|\Delta_\theta\|_F^2$$

$$B3: \lambda_\theta(\|\boldsymbol{\theta}_0 + \Delta_\theta\|_1 - \|\boldsymbol{\theta}_0\|_1) \leq \lambda_\theta\|\Delta_\theta\|_1 \leq \lambda_\theta\sqrt{k}\|\Delta_\theta\|_F$$

where B1 is a boundary from [14], and B3 can be obtained by mean inequalities. Combine all the above items and finally we can get

$$G(\Delta_\theta) \geq \frac{1}{2\eta^2}\|\Delta_\theta\|_F^2 - 2C_1\sqrt{\frac{k\log k}{n}}\|\Delta_\theta\|_F - 2\lambda_\theta\sqrt{k}\|\Delta_\theta\|_F$$
$$= \|\Delta_\theta\|_F^2(\frac{1}{2\eta^2} - (2C_1\sqrt{\frac{k\log k}{n}} + 2\sqrt{k}\lambda_\theta)\|\Delta_\theta\|_F^{-1})$$

Take $\lambda_\theta = C_0\sqrt{\frac{\log k}{n}}$,

$$G(\Delta_\theta) \geq \|\Delta_\theta\|_F^2(\frac{1}{2\eta^2} - \frac{2C_1 + 2C_0}{M})$$

for M sufficiently large we can get $G(\Delta_\theta) > 0$.

□

According to the theorem in [3, 14], under certain assumptions, local minimizer $\widehat{\Omega}^{(k)}$ of Equation 1 satisfies

$$\|\widehat{\Omega}^{(k)} - \Omega_0^{(k)}\|_F = O_P(\sqrt{\frac{(k+s_k)\log k}{n}}) \quad (8)$$

where s_k is the count of non-zero off-diagonal elements in $\Omega_0^{(k)}$ ($s_k = \frac{k(k-1)}{2}$ would give a full matrix). For a local minimizer $\widehat{\Omega}^{(k+1)}$, we have

$$\|\widehat{\Omega}^{(k+1)} - \Omega_0^{(k+1)}\|_F^2 \approx \|\widehat{\Omega}^{(k)} - \Omega_0^{(k)}\|_F^2 + 2\|\widehat{\boldsymbol{\theta}}^{(k)} - \boldsymbol{\theta}_0^{(k)}\|_F^2$$

Thus, combined with our *Theorem 2*, it can be easily found

$$O_P(\frac{(k+s_k)\log k}{n}) + O_P(\frac{2k\log k}{n})$$
$$\approx O_P(\frac{(k+1+s_{k+1})\log(k+1)}{n})$$

since $0 \leq s_{k+1} - s_k \leq 2k$.

So, if $\widehat{\boldsymbol{\theta}}^{(k)}$ is a local minimizer of Equation 3, we know that there exists a local minimizer $\widehat{\Omega}^{(k+1)}$ of $\ell(\Omega^{(k+1)})$ that ensures $\widehat{\Omega}^{(k+1)} = (\widehat{\Omega}^{(k)}, \widehat{\boldsymbol{\theta}}^{(k)})$. So far, the correctness and accuracy of *Theorem 1* has been guaranteed completely under *Theorem 2*.

It is worth mentioning that both Equation 8 and our *Theorem 2* are in line with the motivation of the decomposition on large scale graphical model. Note that both of them show that when the number of variables k is relatively large or exceeds the number of observations n of each variable, the error on the estimation will increase dramatically.

This suggests that, when we consider only a single graphical model on a large network, the result will be inaccurate especially when there are not enough observations to establish such a large graphical model. An example is that traffic systems often contain hundreds of ramps (variables), and the number of the observations for each ramp is limited by the sampling quantity. The periodicity of traffic behaviors is often measured by days. Thus, if we want to know the causalities between observations at a specific time period in a day, we can just get one value for each ramp one day. Therefore, the decomposition of a large graphical model is necessary.

4.3 Constraint Greedy Subgraph Expansion

We present the algorithm for the *local subgraph expansion* process based on our APLE approach. We consider the constraints corresponding to the penalized items in Equation 2, and apply them to the *local subgraph expansion* process in this subsection.

Add Constraints: When there is a new node (variable) x_{new} joint in a solved k-node subgraph g to do expansion, based on APLE we can obtain a new causality vector $\widehat{\boldsymbol{\theta}}_{new} = APLE(g, x_{new}, \lambda_\theta)$. Let $E_{\widehat{\theta}} = \{i : \widehat{\theta}_i \neq 0, 1 \leq i \leq k\}$, we define the fitness as

$$Fitness(\widehat{\boldsymbol{\theta}}_{new}) = e^{-\gamma o}\frac{|E_{\widehat{\theta}}|}{k} \quad (9)$$

where o is the number of subgraphs to which node v_{new} has been mapped, and thus γ controls the degree of overlaps, which can be regarded as a constraint. With γ, we have that the causality contributions of v_{new} to other subgraphs reduce as the number of subgraphs to which v_{new} has already been mapped increases.

Because the fitness in Equation 9 is always nonnegative, a threshold ϵ_f should be given as the minimum accepted fitness, which is actually a constraint on the size of each subgraph.

After each iteration of expansion, we check whether there are near-duplicated subgraphs based on the following equation.

$$max\{\frac{|SV_i \cap SV_j|}{|SV_i|}, \frac{|SV_i \cap SV_j|}{|SV_j|}\} > \epsilon_o, \quad (10)$$

where SV_i is the set of edges in subgraph g_i and SV_j is for g_j; ϵ_o is the combination threshold.

We combine subgraphs g_i and g_j into a new subgraph if the above equation is satisfied. Here ϵ_o balances the sizes of overlaps.

Adaption of λ_θ: It has been mentioned above that as the subgraph expands, λ_θ has to be adapted to make APLE correct and accurate. According to *Theorem 2*, we know that $\lambda_\theta^{(k)} = C_0\sqrt{\frac{\log k}{n}}$, and thus when k expands to $k+1$, we have

$$\lambda_\theta^{(k+1)} = C_0\sqrt{\frac{\log{(k+1)}}{n}} = \sqrt{\log_k{(k+1)}}\lambda_\theta^{(k)} \quad (11)$$

In the following algorithm we will update λ_θ based on Equation 11.

The proposed Constraint Greedy Subgraph Expansion(CGSE) algorithm is outlined in *Algorithm 1*.

Algorithm 1 CGSE Algorithm

Input: (1)p random variables $X = \{x_1, ..., x_p\}$ where x_i contains n observations; (2)$\mathcal{K}$ initial seeds $S = \{S_1, ..., S_\mathcal{K}\}$ where $|S_1| = ... = |S_\mathcal{K}|$;
Parameters: (1)fitness threshold ϵ_f; (2)combination threshold ϵ_O; (3)initial tuning parameter λ_O;
Output: Correlations among p variables and the overlapping subgraphs;

1: $g = S$;
2: $K = \mathcal{K}$;
3: **for** $i = 1$ to K **do**
4: $\quad \lambda_i = \lambda_O$;
5: **end for**
6: **repeat**
7: $\quad$ **for** $i = 1$ to K **do**
8: $\quad\quad$ Find an unvisited variable x_j from the nodes that are not in subgraph g_i;
9: $\quad\quad$ $k = |g_i|$;
10: $\quad\quad$ $\lambda_i = (\log_{(k-1)} k)^{1/2}\lambda_i$;
11: $\quad\quad$ $\boldsymbol{\theta}_{new} = APLE(g_i, x_j, \lambda_i)$;
12: $\quad\quad$ **if** $Fitness(\boldsymbol{\theta}_{new}) > \epsilon_f$ **then**
13: $\quad\quad\quad$ Add x_j into g_i;
14: $\quad\quad$ **end if**
15: $\quad$ **end for**
16: $\quad$ **for** each g_i in g **do**
17: $\quad\quad$ **for** each g_j in g $(j \neq i)$ **do**
18: $\quad\quad\quad$ **if** $|g_i \cap g_j|/|g_i| > \epsilon_o$ **or** $|g_i \cap g_j|/|g_j| > \epsilon_o$ **then**
19: $\quad\quad\quad\quad$ Combine g_j into g_i;
20: $\quad\quad\quad$ **end if**
21: $\quad\quad$ **end for**
22: $\quad$ **end for**
23: $\quad$ $K = |g|$;
24: **until** Each subgraph stays unchangeable
25: Output g;

Algorithm Explanation: Without loss of generality, S can be selected randomly as long as the seeds in S are disjoint with each other. Lines 3–5 initialize the tuning parameter λ_0 for each seed. Lines 7–15 give one step expansion for each subgraph. We expand all the subgraphs together, which can achieve a balance for the size of each subgraph. Lines 16–22 check if two subgraphs should be combined.

Complexity Analysis: Assume that the final average subgraph size is R, lines 7-15 can be computed in $O(\mathcal{K} \cdot L(R))$ time. Lines 16–22 take at most $O(\mathcal{K}^2 p)$ time with auxiliary $O(p)$ space. The number of iteration of line 6 reaches p at most. Thus our CGSE algorithm takes $O(\mathcal{K}^2 p^2 + \mathcal{K}p \cdot L(R))$ time in the worst case. Where $L(R)$ is the complexity of ℓ_1 regularization method in [16], which is logarithmic complexity with R [16].

5. EXPERIMENTAL STUDY

We evaluate the proposed overlapping decomposition of graphical model (ODGM). We compare with the single graphical model(SGM), which is solved by the graphical lasso [4]. To further study the advantage of the overlapping decomposition, we adapt the proposed CGSE algorithm to support the non-overlapping decomposition of graphical model (NODGM) by setting $\gamma = +\infty$ in Equation 9 to forbid overlaps.

We report results on synthetic datasets in Section 5.1. In Section 5.2, we report the performance study on real-life traffic dataset, and show the usefulness of the results for traffic analysis.

5.1 Synthetic Data

5.1.1 Setting

Since we focus on graphical models of a relatively large scale, we generate a set of networks whose number of nodes, p, ranges from 100 to 900. Note that previous work normally uses networks containing tens of nodes. We set the number of observations $n = 800$. We follow the approach [6] to generate the synthetic data. To simulate the heterogeneity in large networks, we generate local centered network by K local Erdös-Rényi random graphs $\{g_1, g_2, ..., g_K\}$, $g_i = (SV_i, SE_i)$; for homogeneity we add edges between any g_i and g_j randomly. Specifically,

1. We generate K Erdös-Rényi graphs, each with a random size in $[20, 80]$, such that $\sum_i^K |SV_i| = p$. Let E_{cross} be the set of cross links between the K graphs, and let $E_{inner} = \bigcup_i^K SE_i$ be the set of total inner links. Let $\rho = |E_{cross}|/|E_{inner}|$ be a factor to control the homogeneity. We randomly add $\rho|E_{inner}|$ cross edges. Finally, we can get a network $G = (V, E)$, where $V = \bigcup_i^K SV_i$ and $E = E_{inner} \bigcup E_{cross}$.

2. Based on the above network, we create a covariance matrix following [13]. Define a $p \times p$ matrix A as

$$A_{ij} = \begin{cases} 1, & i = j \\ U([-1, -0.5] \cup [0.5, 1]), & (i, j) \in E \\ 0, & Else \end{cases}$$

where $U(\cdot)$ represents uniform distribution. We scale the diagonal elements to ensure positive definiteness and average the matrix with its transpose to get a symmetric A. Then the covariance matrix Σ is calculated as

$$\Sigma_{ij} = (A^{-1})_{ij}/\sqrt{(A^{-1})_{ii}(A^{-1})_{jj}}$$

3. We generate p dimensional samples from N(0,Σ).

We define Precision, Recall and F1-score to measure the effectiveness of different models in finding the causal relationships. Note that the true causal relationships in E are known in the generated data. Given an estimated $\widehat{E}$ returned by a method, we define these metrics as follows.

$$Pre = \frac{|\{(i,j) : (i,j) \in E, (i,j) \in \widehat{E}\}|}{|\{(i,j) : (i,j) \in \widehat{E}\}|}$$

$$Rec = \frac{|\{(i,j) : (i,j) \in E, (i,j) \in \widehat{E}\}|}{|\{(i,j) : (i,j) \in E\}|}$$

$$F1 = \frac{2 \cdot Pre \cdot Rec}{Pre + Rec}$$

Moreover, we set the fitness threshold $\epsilon_f = 0.1$, combination threshold $\epsilon_o = 0.6$, $\gamma = 0.1$ and $\lambda_0 = 0.2$. We set the number of seeds at $|S| = K$ and each S_i is selected randomly from the K Erdös-Rényi graphs with size $|S_i| = 3$.

5.1.2 Results

Varying p To evaluate these methods on networks of various sizes, we vary p from 100 to 900. We set $\rho = 0.3$. The performances of all the methods are shown in Figure 1. We can see that when p is small, SGM performs as well as ODGM, because a single graphical model can work well. However, as p increases, the accuracy of SGM falls dramatically. As explained in Section 4.2, such a large p makes it infeasible to derive a single graphical model from n observations. However, both decomposition methods still work well with the increase of p. ODGM achieves a high accuracy and outperforms NODGM consistently, because non-overlapping decomposition cannot capture the overlap information.

Varying ρ The parameter ρ plays an important role on controlling the homogeneity of the network. When $\rho = 0$, it means the network is essentially heterogeneous and is actually composed of several separate sub-networks, while a large ρ indicates that the edges in the network tend to distribute homogeneously. Figure 2 shows the F1-score of ODGM and NODGM while ρ is varied, where we set $p = 500$. As expected, when ρ approaches zero, NODGM performs as well as ODGM because the network can be divided completely into sub-networks. But as ρ increases, the disparity between ODGM and NODGM becomes larger since ODGM can discover the overlaps while NODGM losses more information.

We do not report the results for varying the parameters ϵ_f, ϵ_o and γ due to space limitation. Instead, we will study and visualize the effect of these parameters on a real-life traffic network in an intuitive way in the next section.

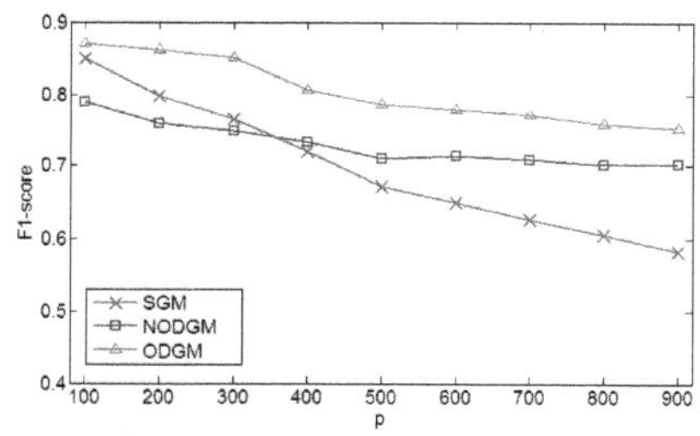

Figure 1: F1-score with p varying.

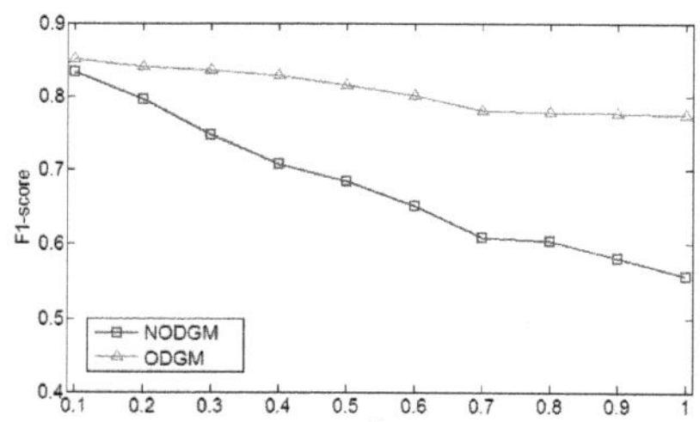

Figure 2: F1-score with ρ varying.

5.2 Traffic Data

5.2.1 Description and setting

We evaluate our methods on real-life traffic data. The features in this traffic dataset are observations collected from sensors located

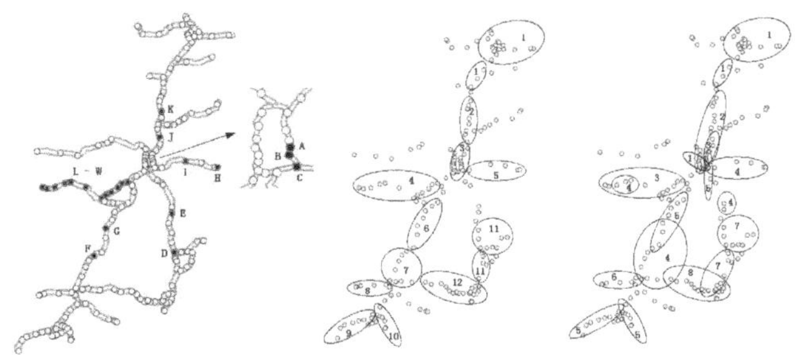

(a) (b) (c)

Figure 3: (a)Real traffic network; (b)the non-overlapping decomposition structure(NODGM); (c)the overlapping decomposition structure(ODGM).

on ramps in a highway traffic network. Each observation is the vehicle count during a time interval. Figure 3(a) gives the structure of the highway traffic network from a province in China, in which each circle represents a traffic station consisting of an on-ramp and an off-ramp, and the line between any connected traffic stations is the bidirectional highway. There is an important ring in the network which is amplified on the right hand—the city in the center of this ring is a big city and plays a central role in the entire traffic network.

There are total 180 traffic stations(circles), which correspond to 360 ramps, i.e., $p = 360$. The observations are collected at time interval 9:00-9:15 AM from 2011/1/1 to 2011/2/28 (59 days). Therefore, $n = 59$ for each feature. Due to the stability and periodicity of traffic behaviors, the observations follow a Gaussian distribution.

We set $\epsilon_f = 0.1$, $\epsilon_o = 0.6$, $\gamma = 0.1$ and $\lambda_0 = 50$. We set the number of seeds $|S| = 12$, and each $|S_i| = 6$.

Because there is no ground truth for causality matrix in real traffic data, F1-score cannot be measured. Nevertheless, the causal information detected is the most important for traffic research, and our domain experts can help with their knowledge on the causal relationship in the traffic network we use. Next, we compare the results returned from the different methods and discuss how the parameters in CGSE influence the causality structures.

5.2.2 Results and Analysis

Figure 3(b) and Figure 3(c) give the subgraph structures returned by NODGM and ODGM, respectively. For clear representation, we draw the results based on the initial traffic network with 180 traffic stations instead of 360 features, and a subgraph contains a traffic station node iff at least one feature (ramp) of this traffic station belongs to it. In the figures, the ellipses with the same label denote a subgraph. Since non-overlapping subgraphs have no intersections, the subgraphs cannot be combined together, and thus the number of final subgraphs equals to the number of seeds in Figure 3(b). For overlapping structure, when two subgraphs overlap at a certain rate ϵ_o, they are combined together. Thus, we end up with 8 subgraphs in Figure 3(c).

From the two figures, we observe: (1)Both NODGM and ODGM show that the causalities between vehicle flows follow the spatial distribution in general— the nearer are two features spatially in traffic network, the more correlated they tend to be; (2)ODGM highlights some crucial traffic nodes with highly overlaps, such as the nodes on the central ring. As mentioned earlier, the central ring is around the central city and plays an important role in the the entire traffic network. Additionally, traffic station C on the ring is the passageway connecting the unique airport of the entire network; and traffic stations A and B are the top 2 highest vehicle flow traffic stations on both on-ramp and off-ramp. These domain information

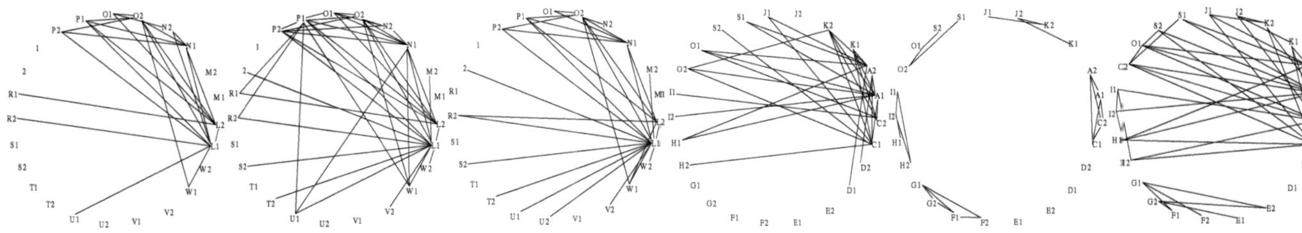

(a) SGM (b) NODGM (c) ODGM (d) SGM (e) NODGM (f) ODGM

Figure 4: Detail causalities among the selected features: (a), (b) and (c) are causalities by SGM, NODGM and ODGM under local concentrated features; (d), (e) and (f) are causalities by SGM, NODGM and ODGM under scattered features.

matches well with our ODGM result and gives an reasonable explanation. (3)ODGM is able to detect long distance causalities in addition to the local causalities within distances. For example, the components(ellipses) of subgraph 1, 3, 4 and 5 are distributed spatially, but they are highly correlated within the vehicle flow. In other words, there also exists long distance origin-destination demand in the traffic network. However, NODGM cannot mine such information described in both (2) and (3). (4) The sparsely located traffic stations are not included in any subgraphs in both the figures. We find that the vehicle flows in most of these traffic station ramps are nearly 0 during the observation periods, and almost 80% of the ramps and their located highways are newly built. Thus they are seldom used and have no causal relationship with other ramps.

Figure 4 gives the detailed causalities among a set of selected features. For each selected traffic station i, $i1$ and $i2$ denote the on-ramp and off-ramp features, respectively. In Figures 4(a), 4(b) and 4(c), the features are selected from traffic station L-W in Figure 3(a), and these traffic stations are selected locally concentrated. We can see that SGM detects fewer causal information than do NODGM and ODGM because a single graphical model treats the entire network globally, and can only detect the causalities from a global view. In this setting, NODGM detects more causal relationships than do ODGM, which also demonstrates that NODGM focuses more on a local view while ODGM is a nice compromise of SGM and NODGM.

While Figures 4(d), 4(e) and 4(f) provide the detailed causalities among the features selected from A, C-K, O and S, which are scattered in the network. As can be observed from the results, ODGM discovers more meaningful causal information than do SGM and NODGM, e.g., the causalities among $\{E1, E2, F1, F2, G1, G2\}$. Both ODGM and SGM are able to discover the important long distance causalities for the key traffic station A and C. However, NODGM is restrained by its non-overlapping structure and only detects the inner relationship within subgraphs, even if A and C are highly correlated with others.

These results obtained by ODGM are essentially important for the analysis of traffic systems for the following reasons. First, the traffic stations in the same subgraph are highly correlated and should be considered together by traffic systems. For example, it is possible that vehicle flows rush into each other within the same subgraph. Second, the causalities are very helpful for traffic flow prediction and anomaly detection which are hot concerns of traffic operators and managers. Third, it is important to find the highly overlapped traffic stations. These crucial traffic stations are correlated with a number of regions, based on which the regions with heavy traffic can be detected. On the other hand, the regions with light traffic can also be reflected by independent traffic stations. These information can be used by highway construction planners to design new roads.

5.2.3 Varying parameters

We study the effect of parameters γ, ϵ_f, ϵ_o and λ_0 for CGSE. Figure 5 shows the decomposition results of varying parameters. When varying each parameter, we use the aforementioned default values for the other parameters.

Parameter ϵ_f controls the minimum fitness, and restricts the size of each subgraph. As shown in Figure 5(a), when ϵ_f decreases, more features are added into subgraphs and the size of each subgraph becomes larger. Figure 5(b) shows the effect of ϵ_o. When ϵ_o is reduced, the subgraphs are more likely to be combined together under ϵ_o. Figure 5(c) shows the effect of γ, which controls overlaps, on the number of features with different overlap degrees. We observe that when γ increases, fewer overlaps exist in the decomposition structure, thus the number of overlapped features.

Figure 6 visualizes the generated subgraphs for selected parameter values to show the details. From these figures, we can see that the property of each parameters is in line with the results in Figure 5, and these figures give a more intuitive and understandable description for our method.

Due to space limitation and as λ_0 works similarly as ϵ_f, we do not give the results of varying λ_0, which controls the sparsity of the causalities in the penalize estimation problem in Equation 3. When λ_0 increases with ϵ_f fixed, the constraint on the sparsity becomes tighter and fewer causalities are detected, and thus smaller subgraphs generated. Conversely, when λ_0 decreases, more causalities will be discovered and the size of each subgraph will increase.

6. CONCLUSION AND FUTURE WORK

In this paper, we propose an overlapping decomposition technique for large scale graphical models. The techniques enables the penalized log-likelihood in Gaussian Graphical Model to satisfy an additive expanding property. We demonstrate its asymptotic stability. Based on this property, we develop a constraint greedy subgraph expansion algorithm to generate overlapped subgraphs. We demonstrate on both synthetic data and real-life traffic data that the overlapping decomposition method is more powerful than the single graphical model and its non-overlapping decomposition counterpart. In the application of traffic data analysis, the meaningful results show that our model can provide rich information for traffic analysis.

For future work, it is interesting to extend the static overlapping decomposition technique to deal with time-varying observations so that we can follow the evolvement of the causalities in a network.

7. ACKNOWLEDGMENTS

This work is supported by the National Natural Science Foundation of China (60703066, 60874082), and Beijing municipal natural science foundation (4102026).

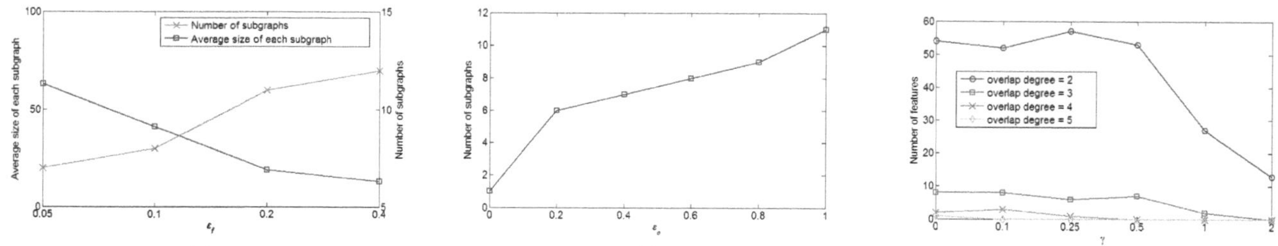

(a) (b) (c)

Figure 5: (a)relationship among average subgraph size, the number of subgraphs and ϵ_f; (b) relationship between the number of subgraphs and ϵ_o; (c)relationship between overlap degree and γ.

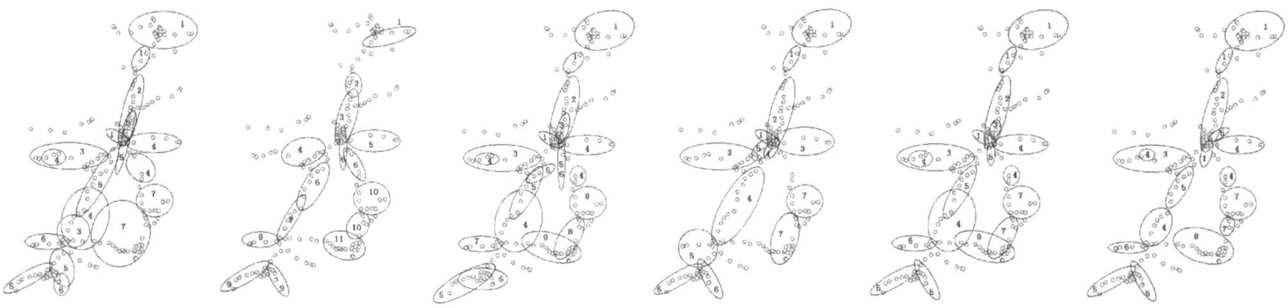

(a) $\epsilon_f = 0.05$ (b) $\epsilon_f = 0.2$ (c) $\epsilon_o = 0.8$ (d) $\epsilon_o = 0.4$ (e) $\gamma = 0.5$ (f) $\gamma = 2$

Figure 6: Decomposition structures when varying each parameter while keeps others stable. Default setting: $\epsilon_f = 0.1$, $\epsilon_o = 0.6$ and $\gamma = 0.1$.

8. REFERENCES

[1] A. Arnold, Y. Liu, and N. Abe. Temporal causal modeling with graphical granger methods. In *Proceedings of the 13th ACM SIGKDD international conference on Knowledge discovery and data mining*, pages 66–75. ACM, 2007.

[2] X. Chen, Y. Liu, H. Liu, and J. Carbonell. Learning spatial-temporal varying graphs with applications to climate data analysis. In *Twenty-Fourth AAAI Conference on Artificial Intelligence*, 2010.

[3] P. Danaher, P. Wang, and D. Witten. The joint graphical lasso for inverse covariance estimation across multiple classes. *Arxiv preprint arXiv:1111.0324*, 2011.

[4] J. Friedman, T. Hastie, and R. Tibshirani. Sparse inverse covariance estimation with the graphical lasso. *Biostatistics*, 9(3):432–441, 2008.

[5] N. Friedman. Inferring cellular networks using probabilistic graphical models. *Science's STKE*, 303(5659):799, 2004.

[6] J. Guo, E. Levina, G. Michailidis, and J. Zhu. Joint estimation of multiple graphical models. *Biometrika*, 98(1):1–15, 2011.

[7] D. Koller and N. Friedman. *Probabilistic graphical models: principles and techniques*. The MIT Press, 2009.

[8] S. Lauritzen. *Graphical Models*. Oxford University Press, 1996.

[9] C. Lee, F. Reid, A. McDaid, and N. Hurley. Detecting highly overlapping community structure by greedy clique expansion. *Arxiv preprint arXiv:1002.1827*, 2010.

[10] Y. Liu, J. Kalagnanam, and O. Johnsen. Learning dynamic temporal graphs for oil-production equipment monitoring system. In *Proceedings of the 15th ACM SIGKDD international conference on Knowledge discovery and data mining*, pages 1225–1234. ACM, 2009.

[11] Y. Liu, A. Niculescu-Mizil, A. Lozano, and Y. Lu. Temporal graphical models for cross-species gene regulatory network discovery. In *Proceedings of the 9th annual international conference on Computational Systems Bioinformatics*, 2010.

[12] A. Lozano, H. Li, A. Niculescu-Mizil, Y. Liu, C. Perlich, J. Hosking, and N. Abe. Spatial-temporal causal modeling for climate change attribution. In *Proceedings of the 15th ACM SIGKDD international conference on Knowledge discovery and data mining*, pages 587–596. ACM, 2009.

[13] J. Peng, P. Wang, N. Zhou, and J. Zhu. Partial correlation estimation by joint sparse regression models. *Journal of the American Statistical Association*, 104(486):735–746, 2009.

[14] A. Rothman, P. Bickel, E. Levina, and J. Zhu. Sparse permutation invariant covariance estimation. *Electronic Journal of Statistics*, 2:494–515, 2008.

[15] N. Ruan, R. Jin, V. Lee, and K. Huang. A sparsification approach for temporal graphical model decomposition. In *Data Mining, 2009. ICDM'09. Ninth IEEE International Conference on*, pages 447–456. IEEE, 2009.

[16] M. Schmidt, G. Fung, and R. Rosales. Fast optimization methods for l1 regularization: A comparative study and two new approaches. *Machine Learning: ECML 2007*, pages 286–297, 2007.

[17] M. Schmidt, G. Fung, and R. Rosales. Optimization methods for l1-regularization. *University of British Columbia, Technical Report TR-2009-19*, 2009.

[18] R. Thompson. Graphical models in applied multivariate statistics. *Journal of Classification*, 9(1):159–160, 1992.

[19] M. Yuan and Y. Lin. Model selection and estimation in the gaussian graphical model. *Biometrika*, 94(1):19–35, 2007.

TM-LDA: Efficient Online Modeling of Latent Topic Transitions in Social Media

Yu Wang
Emory University
yu.wang@emory.edu

Eugene Agichtein
Emory University
eugene@mathcs.emory.edu

Michele Benzi
Emory University
benzi@mathcs.emory.edu

ABSTRACT

Latent topic analysis has emerged as one of the most effective methods for classifying, clustering and retrieving textual data. However, existing models such as Latent Dirichlet Allocation (LDA) were developed for static corpora of relatively large documents. In contrast, much of the textual content on the web, and especially social media, is temporally sequenced, and comes in short fragments, including microblog posts on sites such as Twitter and Weibo, status updates on social networking sites such as Facebook and LinkedIn, or comments on content sharing sites such as YouTube. In this paper we propose a novel topic model, Temporal-LDA or TM-LDA, for efficiently mining text streams such as a sequence of posts from the same author, by modeling the topic transitions that naturally arise in these data. TM-LDA learns the transition parameters among topics by minimizing the prediction error on topic distribution in subsequent postings. After training, TM-LDA is thus able to accurately predict the expected topic distribution in future posts. To make these predictions more efficient for a realistic online setting, we develop an efficient updating algorithm to adjust the topic transition parameters, as new documents stream in. Our empirical results, over a corpus of over 30 million microblog posts, show that TM-LDA significantly outperforms state-of-the-art static LDA models for estimating the topic distribution of new documents over time. We also demonstrate that TM-LDA is able to highlight interesting variations of common topic transitions, such as the differences in the work-life rhythm of cities, and factors associated with area-specific problems and complaints.

Categories and Subject Descriptors

H.2.8 [**Database Applications**]: Data mining

General Terms

Algorithm, Experimentation

Keywords

topic transition modeling, temporal language models, mining social media data

KDD'12, August 12–16, 2012, Beijing, China.

1. INTRODUCTION

Latent semantic topic analysis has emerged as one of the most effective methods for classifying, clustering, and retrieving textual data. Many latent topic modeling methods have been developed and intensively studied, such as probabilistic Latent Semantic Analysis (pLSA) and Latent Dirichlet Allocation (LDA). These models are designed to analyze static collections of documents. The recent proliferation of social media textual data, such as microblog posts, Facebook status updates, or comments on YouTube, brings new challenges to these models: (1) to model and analyze latent topics in social textual data; (2) to adaptively update the models as massive amounts of social content stream in; (3) to facilitate temporal-aware applications of social media, such as predicting future trends and learning social behavioral patterns.

Semantic analysis of social content has been intensively investigated in recent years. It has been shown that information derived from social media, such as Twitter, can help event detection [17], news recommendation [1] and public health applications [14]. Yet, the models can be significantly enriched by directly considering the *temporal sequence* of the topics in the microblog post stream, instead of treating it as a "static" corpus.

Consider a microblog post stream of an author. The timestamp of each post determines the order of it along the timeline. Since microblog posts reflect activities or status of the author, the temporal order of posts reflects the time dimension of the author's behavioral patterns. Thus the temporal sequence of an author's post stream is a factor connecting post content and one's real life activities. Users' posts include a variety of topics and rich information, such as breaking news, their comments on popular events, daily life events and social interaction. Clearly, the topics of post streams will not be static, but change over time. In other words, users tend to post about different topics instead of simply repeat previous posts. This observation implies that to better model the dynamic semantics of microblog post streams, we need a temporally-sensitive model that can capture the changing pattern among topics. The implications of better modeling topic dynamics reach far beyond microblogging sites such as Twitter and Weibo, as most social textual data are naturally sequenced by time. Better understanding and modeling of the temporal dynamics of social content can benefit not only these applications, but also provide powerful analytical tools for researchers and analysts.

In this paper, we propose *Temporal Latent Dirichlet Allocation* (TM-LDA) to model topic transitions in temporally-sequenced documents. In the case of microblog post streams, we claim that topic transitions of an author's posts follow certain social behavioral patterns. For example, people tend to talk about the topic "Drink" after "Food", which implies a certain dietary and social manner. In some cities, users complain about "Traffic" mostly after they post about "Places", which reflects poor traffic condition in those areas. Understanding these topic transition could be meaningful in several ways:

- Dynamically predicting future trends of a microblog post stream based on the previous posts.
- Providing a tool for researchers and analysts to get a more in-depth view of temporal relationships among social phenomena reflected by popular topics in microblog posts.
- Providing a signal of unusual events when topics fail to follow expected transitions.

TM-LDA is designed to learn the topic transition parameters from historical temporally-sequenced documents to predict future topic distributions of new documents over time. TM-LDA takes pairs of consecutive documents as input and finds the optimal transition parameters, which minimize the least square error between predicted topic distribution and the actual topic distribution of the new documents. Additionally, transition parameters among topics can vary over time because of the changing popularity of certain topics and external events. To adaptively update the transition parameters as new documents stream in, we propose an efficient algorithm to adjust the transition parameters by replacing outdated document pairs with new ones.

The main contribution of this paper are:

- We propose a novel temporally-aware topic language model, TM-LDA, which captures the latent topic transitions in temporally-sequenced documents. (Section 2).
- We design an efficient algorithm to update TM-LDA which enables it to operate over large-scale data. Section 3 illustrates the details of the updating algorithm, and provides the complexity analysis.
- Our evaluation of TM-LDA against the static topic modeling method (LDA) on 30 million microblog posts shows that TM-LDA consistently outperforms LDA in predicting the topic distribution of future posts. (Section 4).

2. TM-LDA MODEL AND ALGORITHMS

In this section, we mathematically define TM-LDA, and discuss the way to build TM-LDA from document streams in practice.

2.1 TM-LDA Algorithm

We design TM-LDA as a system which generates topic distributions of new documents by taking previous documents as input. More precisely, if we define the space of topic distributions as $X = \{x \in \mathbb{R}^n_+ : ||x||_1 = 1\}$, TM-LDA can be considered as a function $f : X \to X$. Notice that n is the dimension of the space X, in other words, n is the number of topics; $||\cdot||_1$ is the ℓ^1 norm of vector x. Given the topic distribution vector of a historical document x, the estimated topic distribution of a new document $\hat{y}$ is given by $\hat{y} = f(x)$. Once we know the real topic distribution of the new document y, the prediction error of the TM-LDA system would be:

$$err_f = ||\hat{y} - y||_2^2 = ||f(x) - y||_2^2.$$

Function err_f uses the ℓ^2 norm to measure the prediction error because the minimization of err_f can thus be reduced to a least squares problem, which can be efficiently solved (Section 2.1.3). The training stage of TM-LDA is to find the function f which minimizes err_f.

In our work, the function f is designed as a non-linear mapping:

$$f(x) = \frac{xT}{||xT||_1}, \tag{1}$$

where x is a row vector, $T \in \mathbb{R}^{n\times n}$. The product of x and T is also a row vector, which is the estimated new topic weighting vector (before normalization). After xT is normalized by its ℓ^1 norm, it becomes a topic distribution vector.

In our system settings, x and y are topic distribution vectors of two consecutive posts of a user, where x represents the "old" post, and y corresponds to the "new" post. TM-LDA predicts the topic distribution of y by taking historical post x as input and applies function f on it to obtain $\hat{y}$. Therefore the prediction error of TM-LDA is the difference between $\hat{y}$ and y.

2.1.1 *Error Function of TM-LDA*

Function (1) defines the prediction function for a single document x. The error function is therefore:

$$err_f = \left|\left| \frac{xT}{||xT||_1} - y \right|\right|_2^2. \tag{2}$$

Intuitively, this function measures the prediction error for a single pair of documents, x and y, where x represents the "old" document and y is the "new" document. Now we generalize it and define the error function for a collection of documents. Suppose we have a collection of sequenced documents D, where the number of documents is $|D| = m + 1$; the topic distribution of the i-th document is d_i, where d_i is a row vector and i indicates the temporal order of d_i. Next, we construct two matrices $D^{(1,m)}$ and $D^{(2,m+1)}$ as follows:

$$D^{(1,m)} = \begin{bmatrix} d_1 \\ d_2 \\ \vdots \\ d_m \end{bmatrix}, \quad D^{(2,m+1)} = \begin{bmatrix} d_2 \\ d_3 \\ \vdots \\ d_{m+1} \end{bmatrix}.$$

Notice that both $D^{(1,m)}$ and $D^{(2,m+1)}$ are $m \times n$ matrices. The i-th rows of these two matrices are d_i and d_{i+1}, and they are sequentially adjacent in the collection D. In other words, $D^{(1,m)}$ represents the topic distribution matrix of "old" documents and $D^{(2,m+1)}$ is the matrix of "new" documents. According to the error function for a single document pair (Function (2)), the prediction error for the sequenced document collection D is defined as:

$$err_f = ||LD^{(1,m)}T - D^{(2,m+1)}||_F^2. \tag{3}$$

where $||\cdot||_F$ is the Frobenius matrix norm. L is a $m \times m$ diagonal matrix which normalizes each row of $D^{(1,m)}T$. The i-th diagonal entry of L is the reciprocal of the ℓ^1-norm of the i-th row in $D^{(1,m)}T$:

$$L = \begin{bmatrix} \frac{1}{||d_1 T||_1} & & & \\ & \frac{1}{||d_2 T||_1} & & \\ & & \ddots & \\ & & & \frac{1}{||d_m T||_1} \end{bmatrix}.$$

2.1.2 *Iterative Minimization of the Error Function*

The function err_f is a non-linear function. Numerical experiments show that function err_f is convex, which suggests using iterative methods to approach the optimal T that minimizes err_f. Each iteration updates the solution T as below:

$$T^{(j)} = (L^{(j-1)}D^{(1,m)})^{\dagger}D^{(2,m+1)},$$

where

$$L^{(j-1)} = \begin{bmatrix} \frac{1}{||d_1 T^{(j-1)}||_1} & & \\ & \ddots & \\ & & \frac{1}{||d_m T^{(j-1)}||_1} \end{bmatrix}.$$

Such iterative method can be initialized by

$$T^{(0)} = D^{(1,m)\dagger}D^{(2,m+1)},$$

where $D^{(1,m)\dagger}$ is the pseudo-inverse of $D^{(1,m)}$.

2.1.3 *Direct Minimization of the Error Function*

Iterative methods may be slow to converge and only give an approximate solution. Ideally, we would like to have a direct solution procedure for TM-LDA which could be efficiently and accurately implemented. By noticing an important property of the error function (3), we use Theorem 1 to derive a least squares characterization of the TM-LDA solution and to render an explicit form of the exact solution.

HEORE 1. *Let* $\mathbf{e}$ *denote the* $n \times 1$ *matrix of all ones. For any* $A \in \mathbb{R}_+^{m\times n}$ *and* $B \in \mathbb{R}_+^{m\times n}$ *such that* $A\mathbf{e} = \mathbf{e}$ *and* $B\mathbf{e} = \mathbf{e}$*, it holds*

$$AA^{\dagger}B\mathbf{e} = \mathbf{e},$$

where $A^{\dagger}$ *is the pseudo-inverse of* A.

PROOF Because $B\mathbf{e} = \mathbf{e}$,

$$AA^{\dagger}B\mathbf{e} = AA^{\dagger}\mathbf{e}.$$

$AA^{\dagger}\mathbf{e}$ is the orthogonal projection of $\mathbf{e}$ onto *Range*(A). Since $A\mathbf{e} = \mathbf{e}$, $\mathbf{e} \in$ *Range*(A). Therefore $AA^{\dagger}\mathbf{e} = \mathbf{e}$. □

The matrices $D^{(1,m-1)}$ and $D^{(2,m)}$ satisfy the properties $D^{(1,m-1)}\mathbf{e} = \mathbf{e}$ and $D^{(2,m)}\mathbf{e} = \mathbf{e}$ since each row of these two matrices is a topic distribution vector of a document and the row sum is naturally 1. By adapting the result of Theorem 1 to TM-LDA, we obtain the following result:

$$D^{(1,m)}T^{(0)}\mathbf{e} = D^{(1,m)}D^{(1,m)\dagger}D^{(2,m+1)}\mathbf{e} = \mathbf{e}.$$

In other words, $||d_i T^{(0)}||_1 = 1$ for any $i \in \{1, 2, \ldots, m\}$. Therefore $L^{(0)} = I$, the $m \times m$ identity matrix. Hence, $T^{(1)}$ can be written as

$$T^{(1)} = (L^{(0)}D^{(1,m)})^{\dagger}D^{(2,m+1)} = T^{(0)}.$$

This indicates that

$$T = D^{(1,m)\dagger}D^{(2,m+1)}$$

gives the optimal solution for minimizing err_f. Hence, computing the TM-LDA solution amounts to solving a matrix least squares problem:

$$\min_T ||D^{(1,m)}T - D^{(2,m+1)}||_F^2.$$

2.2 TM-LDA for a Document Stream

A document stream of an author consists of temporally sequenced posts. After we train LDA on the collection of documents, the topic distribution vector of each post is obtained. We can therefore construct the matrices $D^{(1,m)}$ and $D^{(2,m+1)}$. Suppose we collect 20 consecutive posts per user and the number of users is p, then the training stage of TM-LDA on such stream is illustrated in Figure 1. The left matrix is $D^{(1,m)}$ and the right matrix is $D^{(2,m+1)}$, where $m = 19 \times p$ in this case. For each user, 20 consecutive posts makes 19 pairs, they are (post 1, post 2), (post 2, post 3), ..., (post 19, post 20). Each pair is one training sample, and forms one row of the matrix $D^{(1,m)}$ and $D^{(2,m+1)}$. By multiplying the "old" post matrix $D^{(1,m-1)}$ with the transition parameter matrix T, the predicted topic distribution of "new" posts is obtained.

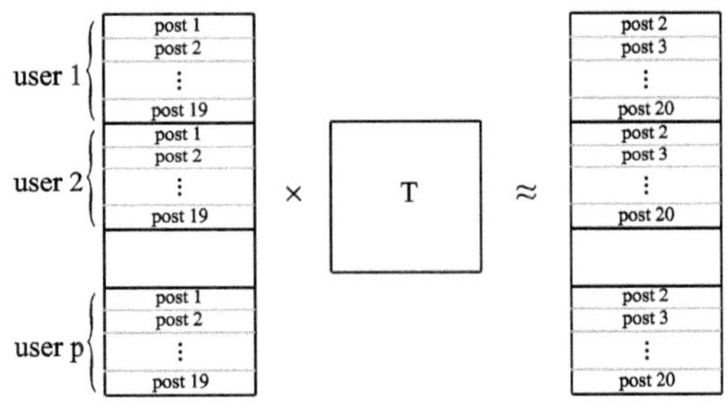

Figure 1: Constructing TM-LDA for document streams.

To simplify the notations, let $A = D^{(1,m)}$ and $B = D^{(2,m+1)}$. According to Theorem 1, TM-LDA is reduced to the following problem:

$$\min_T ||AT - B||_F^2. \tag{4}$$

Again, A is the topic distribution matrix of "old" posts and B is the topic distribution matrix of "new" posts. The training phase of TM-LDA becomes a least squares problem. When the condition number of A, $\kappa(A)$, is small and the system is overdetermined, we can effectively obtain T as:

$$T = A^{\dagger}B = (A'A)^{-1}A'B, \tag{5}$$

where A' denotes the transpose of A. In practice, multiplication by $(A'A)^{-1}$ is accomplished by Cholesky factorization of $A'A$ followed by forward and backward substitutions. We also observe that from Theorem 1 and the fact that $A\mathbf{e} = \mathbf{e}$ it readily follows that it is also $T\mathbf{e} = \mathbf{e}$, since A has full column rank.

3. UPDATING TOPIC TRANSITION PARAMETERS

Not only the topics of a user's posts are likely to change, but the transition weights from one topic to another could also vary over time. Both the changing popularity of certain topics and external events will affect the transition parameters of related topics. In other words, the transition parameters have to be updated and adjusted by using recently-generated posts as training samples. One way to solve this updating problem is to compute the transition parameter matrix as the new documents emerge each time. However, re-computing transition parameters may result in lower efficiency and a less smooth parameter adjustment process. In this section, we present an efficient algorithm which can gradually and smoothly adjust transition parameters as the new posts emerge, with significantly less computation than re-computing TM-LDA from scratch.

3.1 Updating Transition Parameters

We now introduce the algorithm for updating the transition parameter matrix T. Suppose we append k rows of new document pairs, U_k and V_k, to the bottom of A and B and form $\hat{A}$ and $\hat{B}$ as below:

$$\hat{A} = \begin{bmatrix} A \\ U_k \end{bmatrix}, \quad \hat{B} = \begin{bmatrix} B \\ V_k \end{bmatrix}.$$

According to Equation (5), the new transition parameter matrix, $\hat{T}$ is:

$$\hat{T} = (\hat{A}'\hat{A})^{-1}\hat{A}'\hat{B}.$$

We apply the Sherman-Morrison-Woodbury formula [7] to $(\hat{A}'\hat{A})^{-1}$ and obtain the following result:

$$(\hat{A}'\hat{A})^{-1} = (A'A + U_k'U_k)^{-1}$$

$$= (A'A)^{-1} - (A'A)^{-1}U_k'(I + U_k(A'A)^{-1}U_k')^{-1}U_k(A'A)^{-1}.$$

Let $C = (A'A)^{-1}U_k'$, then the updated transition parameter matrix $\hat{T}$ is:

$$\hat{T} = (\hat{A}'\hat{A})^{-1}(A'B + U_k'V_k)$$

$$= T + CV_k - C(I + U_kC)^{-1}C'(A'B + U_k'V_k). \quad (6)$$

Notice that $A'A$ and $A'B$ have been computed and stored when computing T. In other words, to compute $\hat{T}$, we just need $U_k'V_k$ and C. The only possibly time-consuming part is to obtain $(I + U_kC)^{-1}C'$, which requires no more than $O(k^3)$, as shown in reference [7]. The remaining components of computing $\hat{T}$ have the complexity of $O(k)$, and even less when U_k and V_k are sparse. Therefore the overall cost for updating the transition parameter matrix is at most $O(k^3)$.

3.2 Updating Transition Parameters with QR-factorization

The least squares problem can also be solved by QR-factorization [7]. Suppose the QR-factorization of matrix A is $A = QR$, where $Q'Q = I$ and R is an upper triangular matrix. The solution of Formula (4) can be written as:

$$RT = Q'B.$$

Since R is upper triangular, T can be easily found.

When a new pair of documents, u and v, is added on the top of A and B, we have the updated topic distribution matrices as below:

$$\hat{A} = \begin{bmatrix} u \\ A \end{bmatrix}, \quad \hat{B} = \begin{bmatrix} v \\ B \end{bmatrix}.$$

The QR-factorization of $\hat{A}$ can be written as:

$$\hat{A} = \hat{Q}\hat{R},$$

$$\hat{R} = J_1 \ldots J_n \begin{bmatrix} u \\ R \end{bmatrix},$$

$$\hat{Q} = \begin{bmatrix} 1 & \\ & Q \end{bmatrix} J_n' \ldots J_1',$$

where $J_1, \ldots, J_n$ are rotation matrices which make $\hat{R}$ upper triangular, and n is the number of columns in both A and B. Therefore, the updated transition parameter matrix $\hat{T}$ can be computed as follows:

$$\hat{R}\hat{T} = \hat{Q}'\hat{B} = J_1 \ldots J_n \begin{bmatrix} 1 & \\ & Q \end{bmatrix} \begin{bmatrix} v \\ B \end{bmatrix}$$

$$= J_1 \ldots J_n \begin{bmatrix} v \\ Q'B \end{bmatrix}. \quad (7)$$

In practice, we use the Sherman-Morrison-Woodbury formula to update the transition parameter matrix because the condition number of A is typically small, which means the document topic distribution matrix is well-conditioned. Hence, it will not easily become singular or ill-conditioned during the updating process. Also, the Sherman-Morrison-Woodbury formula provides a way to control the speed of updating by tuning the parameter k. When k is small, each update will take less time and a more fine-grained matrix changing process can be obtained. On the other hand, the updating algorithm will have similar complexity as re-computing the transition parameter matrix when k gets larger. Therefore if k is greater than the "balanced" complexity point, it is preferable to re-compute the matrix.

4. EXPERIMENTS

In this section, TM-LDA is evaluated empirically over a large crawl of Twitter data. By measuring perplexity (Section 4.2), we show that TM-LDA significantly outperforms static topic models on predicting actual word distributions of future Twitter posts (Section 4.3). Additionally, the efficiency of the algorithm for updating transition weights is assessed in Section 4.4.

4.1 Dataset

To validate TM-LDA, we collect Twitter posts (henceforth, Tweets) from more than 260,000 public user accounts, over a period of one month. The public user accounts are selected from the TREC 2011 microblog track[1] and we only keep the users with valid geo-location information. A list of 89 candidate cities are generated by taking the union of top 50 U.S. cities (in population) and the capital cities of the 50 U.S. states. After that, the users whose claimed geo-locations are one of the candidate cities will be selected.

All selected user accounts are tracked daily, generating an average of around 1.1 million new Tweets per day. However, Tweets are usually short and informal, which makes

[1] http://trec.nist.gov/data/tweets/

the quality of Tweets vary a lot from each other. To attempt to filter low-quality Tweets, we first filter out stopwords and the words with less than 5 occurrences in our dataset, and then keep only the Tweets with more than 3 terms after filtering. As a result, one third of the raw Tweets are excluded, with more than 20 million "high quality" Tweets remaining for analysis.

Dates	From 12-15-2011 To 1-15-2012
Number of Raw Tweets	34,150,390
Number of Valid Tweets	23,096,894
Average Length of Valid Tweets (words)	5.12
Number of Users	264,628
Number of Cities	89
Number of Valid Tweet Pairs	13,273,707

Table 1: Description of Tweet Stream Data.

4.2 Using Perplexity as Evaluation Metric

TM-LDA is designed to predict the topic distribution of future Tweets based on historical Tweets. Therefore we employ the measurement of *Perplexity* to evaluate TM-LDA against the actual word occurrences in future Tweets. Usually, perplexity is used to measure how well a language model fits the word distribution of a corpus. It is defined as:

$$Perplexity_l = 2^{-\sum_{i=1}^{N} \log_2 p_l(x_i)}. \quad (8)$$

Formula (8) dictates the perplexity of the language model l, where $p_l(x_i)$ is the probability of the occurrence of word x_i estimated by the language model l and N is the number of words in the document. Intuitively, if the language model yields higher probability for the occurrences of words in the document than words that are not in the document, the language model is more accurate and the perplexity will be lower.

4.3 Predicting Topics of Future Tweets

TM-LDA predicts the topic distribution of future Tweets by taking the "previous" Tweets as input (Formula (1)). Basically, TM-LDA will multiply the topic distribution vector by the transition parameter matrix and normalize it to form the topic distribution of a "future" Tweet. There are two key components in this process: (1) the transition parameter matrix, and (2) the topic distribution of the "previous" Tweets.

The transition parameter matrix is trained according to the algorithm introduced in Section 2. In practice, TM-LDA will use 7-day (one week) historical Tweets to train the transition parameter matrix, and then predict the Tweets generated on the 8th day. For example, if we want to predict the Tweets on the date Dec. 22, 2011, we will collect all the Tweets generated from Dec. 15, 2011 to Dec. 21, 2011 and train LDA on this one-week Tweet collection to obtain the topic distribution vectors for each single Tweet. During the training of LDA, each Tweet is treated as a document and the number of topics is set to 200. After that, we build two topic distribution matrices, "old" Tweet matrix and "future" Tweet matrix, as in Figure 1 and compute the transition parameter matrix according to Formula (5).

For the Tweets generated on the 8th day (which we want to predict), we cannot have their topic distributions from LDA directly. Figure 2 illustrates this situation: LDA is trained on one-week Tweets but not on the Tweets a and b, which means we need to map them to the topics through the results of LDA. The topic distribution of "previous" Tweets a is inferred from the LDA model. Given the words appearing in the Tweet t, the topic distribution is inferred as:

$$p(z|t) = \sum_{w} p(z|w)p(w|t) = \sum_{w} \frac{p(w|z)p(z)}{\sum_{z'} p(w|z')p(z')} p(w|t), \quad (9)$$

where $p(w|t)$ is the normalized frequency of word w in Tweet t. Both $p(w|z)$ and $p(z)$ are the results of LDA model.

In summary, TM-LDA first trains LDA on 7-day historical Tweets and compute the transition parameter matrix accordingly. Then for each new Tweet generated on the 8th day, it predicts the topic distribution of the following Tweet. When the actual "future" Tweet b (in Figure 2) becomes available, we can measure the perplexity of TM-LDA.

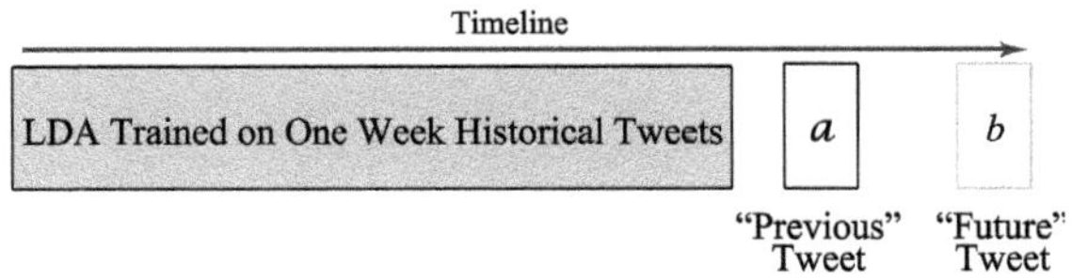

Figure 2: The Scheme for Predicting "Future" Tweets.

Figure 2 illustrates the prediction scheme of TM-LDA and other methods. All methods build LDA on one-week historical Tweet data, and for each new Tweet a, they predict the topic distribution of the "following" Tweet b. Although many dynamic topic modeling algorithms have been developed [4] [20] [16] [9], they are mainly designed to model topic trends and dynamic word distributions over time. In [4], it shows that the predictive power of static LDA and Dynamic Topic Model are very close. Therefore, we compare TM-LDA with the following methods:

1. **Estimated Topic Distributions of "Future" Tweets**: the topic distribution of the Tweet b. This is computed based on the actual words in the "future" Tweets according to Formula (9). This system approximately reflects the optimal perplexity of LDA-based models.

2. **LDA Topic Distributions of "Future" Tweets**: the inferred topic distribution of the Tweet b. They are inferred from the LDA model which is trained on the one-week historical Tweets. The inferring algorithm is introduced by Blei et al. [5]. This system knows the words appearing in the "future" Tweets, so that it shows the optimal perplexity of the original LDA [5].

3. **LDA Topic Distributions of "Previous" Tweets**: the inferred topic distribution [5] of the Tweet a. They are also inferred from the LDA trained on one-week historical Tweets. This system uses the topic distributions of "previous" Tweets as the topic distributions of the "Future" Tweets. It shows the perplexity of static prediction model built on LDA.

We test these three methods above along with our model, TM-LDA, on the Twitter corpus described in Section 4.1. In Figure 3, we can see that TM-LDA consistently provides lower perplexity than the static prediction model, reducing

Topics	*Weather*	*Social Media*	*U.S. Deficit*	*Traffic*	*Job Hunting*	*Reading Media*	*Weight Loss*	*Presidential Election*
5 Top Words	cold	social	bill	traffic	sales	daily	weight	romney
	winter	media	house	accident	hiring	news	loss	paul
	snow	marketing	budget	bridge	jobs	digest	healthy	iowa
	weather	network	cut	lane	project	newspaper	fitness	republican
	warm	internet	obama	blocked	position	headlines	diet	debate

Table 2: LDA Sample Topics with 5 Top Representative Words.

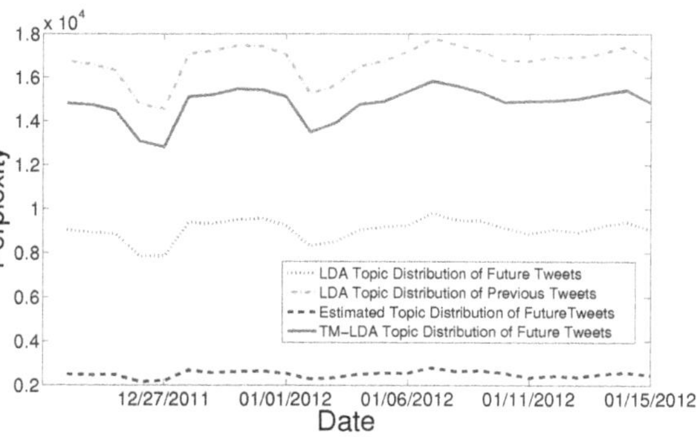

Figure 3: Perplexity of Different Models.

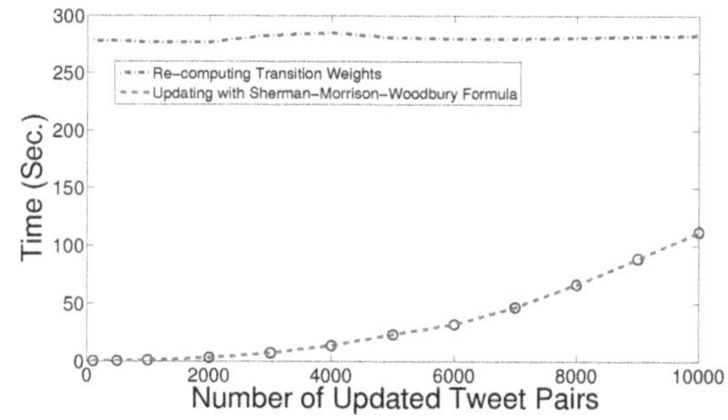

Figure 4: Time Complexity of Updating Transition Parameter Matrix based on One-Week Tweet Data.

it by 11.4% compared to the static LDA models. The improvements are statistically significant with the significance level $\alpha < 0.001$. It turns out that the performance of TM-LDA could be affected by the topic estimation of "previous" Tweets, which TM-LDA uses as input arguments.

Interestingly, we find that Tweets are easier to predict on holidays than other days. We can see that the perplexity drops on the dates of Christmas and New Year, which suggests that the topics discussed during holiday seasons are more predictable. Also note that we use the ℓ^2 norm to define the error function for TM-LDA, which enables us to efficiently optimize it by solving a least squares problem. In future work, we plan to test the use of the ℓ^1 norm of the error, which may give better results due to its being less sensitive to the presence of outliers.

4.4 Efficiency of Updating Transition Parameters

In Section 3, we introduced the Sherman-Morrison-Woodbury formula to update the transition parameter matrix. We now empirically evaluate the runtime costs of this algorithm for different values of k. Suppose we have computed a transition parameter matrix T based on one-week historical Tweet data, which consists of more than 3 million Tweet pairs. Given k new pairs of Tweets, we measure the time needed to update matrix T for different values of k.

We test the time complexity by running the Matlab implementation of our updating algorithm on a machine with 24 *AMD Opteron(tm) 6174* processors and 128 Gigabytes of RAM. Figure 4 shows that our updating algorithm can efficiently find T when k is not too large. Compared with re-computing T, which usually takes around 280 seconds for one-week historical Tweets in our corpus (about 7.7 million posts), our updating algorithm consumes 61.4% less time when k is 10,000, while resulting in a more smooth T.

4.5 Properties of Transition Parameters

The transition parameter matrix T is the key result of TM-LDA. It enables us to adjust the topic weights based on historical Tweets and make more precise prediction. The empirical results indicate several consistent properties of matrix T.

First, T is a square matrix where the size of T is determined by the number of topics trained in LDA. Each entry in T reflects the weight that a certain topic will propagate to another topic in future Tweets. More precisely, entry t_{ij} of T shows the degree that topic i will contribute to topic j in the following Tweet. The algorithm in Section 2.1 does not enforce non-negativity of T, but it turns out that T has very few negative entries and all the negative entries in T are close to zero. Second, as already observed at the end of section 2 the row sums of T are all 1, which means that the overall weight emitted from a topic is 1, and this ensures topics will not amplify themselves and make the system unstable. Note that T is close to a row-stochastic matrix, which can be regarded as the transition matrix of a Markov chain. We can make T into a Markov chain transition matrix by making small adjustments that enforce nonnegativity in T while preserving the unit row sums property. In practice, we have not found these adjustments to be necessary.

5. APPLYING TM-LDA FOR TWITTER TREND ANALYSIS AND SENSEMAKING

The previous section shows that TM-LDA can consistently and significantly improve the prediction quality of future Tweets compared to the static model. Additionally, TM-LDA can provide a more in-depth view of temporal relationships among topics and public opinion of popular events. We now turn to discuss the analytical power of TM-LDA.

As previously mentioned, LDA is trained on the Tweet stream dataset and the number of topics is set to 200. We show the words with top weights for several topics as in Table 2. The "names" of the topics are manually labeled based on the words in each topic with highest probabilities.

5.1 Global Topic Transition Patterns

To analyze the global topic transition patterns, TM-LDA is trained on all the valid Tweet pairs. The topic transition parameter matrix T has the size of 200×200 and the average transition weight of all 40,000 entries in T is 0.005. We visualize the matrix T in Figure 5; however, from the initial visualization it could be challenging to locate interesting topic transition patterns. We therefore pre-select "interesting points" from the raw transition matrix using a procedure described by Formula (10), and then do a case study on those "interesting transition points".

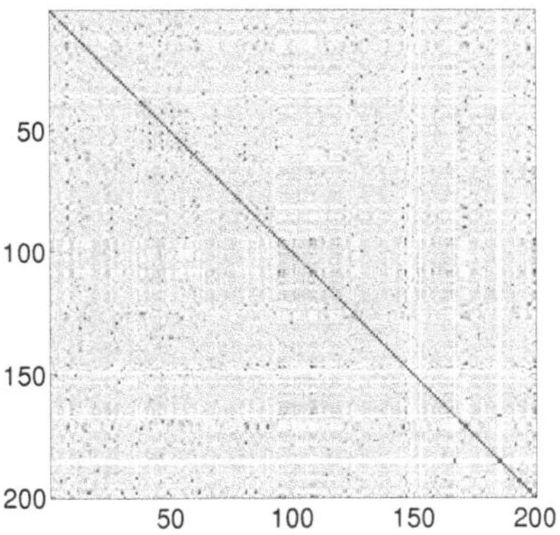

Figure 5: Visualization of Global Topic Transitions.

In Figure 5, it's clear that matrix T has relatively large diagonal entries. This provides the evidence that topics of historical Tweets do not randomly transition from one to another, but follow certain statistical rules. However, the diagonal entries of T are always less than 1. Meanwhile, the empirical average value of diagonal entries in T, $\bar{t}$ is 0.095, which shows that new Tweets usually do not simply repeat the topics of historical Tweets. The standard deviation of non-diagonal (non-self-transition) entries, σ, is 0.003. We define the threshold to be the average plus five times the standard deviation:

$$Threshold = \bar{t} + 5 \times \sigma, \quad (10)$$

which is $0.005 + 0.003 \times 5 = 0.02$, as the bar of "interesting" points. After filtered by this threshold, a clearer transition pattern is obtained and shown in Figure 6.

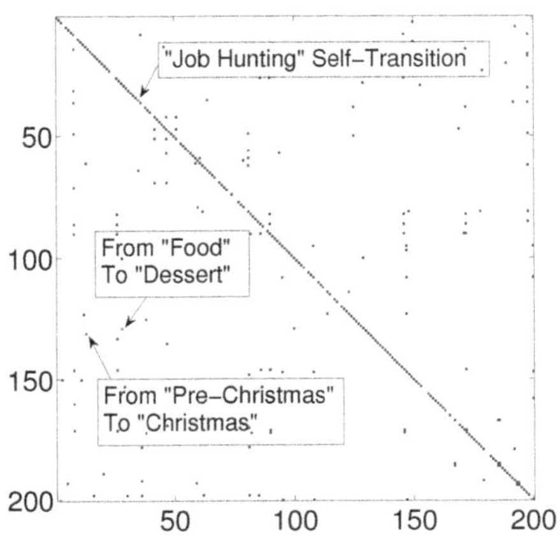

Figure 6: Interesting Transition Points.

Figure 6 shows three types of "interesting" transition points: (1) diagonal points: these points have high self-transition weights and they are the topics people tend to keep discussing about; (2) symmetric points: both t_{ij} and t_{ji} are interesting points. These topics are highly correlated and they are usually mentioned in consecutive Tweets; (3) non-symmetric points: one and only one of t_{ij} and t_{ji} is an interesting point. These topics usually reflect strongly time-sensitive properties of certain events and scenarios. We rank the points in Figure 6 by their values and list the most representative ones in Table 3.

	From Topic	*To Topic*	*Weight*
(1)	Job Hunting	Job Hunting	0.448
	Weather	Weather	0.304
	Reading Media	Reading Media	0.286
	Weight Loss	Weight Loss	0.282
(2)	Internet Company	Social Media	0.045
	U.S. Deficit	Presidential Election	0.044
	Food	Dessert	0.041
	Security and Crime	Military Action	0.039
(3)	Traffic and Accident	Rescue and Police	0.044
	Restaurant	Food	0.040
	Pre-Christmas	Christmas	0.032
	Startup Business	Social Media	0.030

Table 3: Three Kinds of Topic Transitions: (1) Self-Transition (2) Symmetric Transition (3) Non-Symmetric Transition.

Table 3 shows the general topic transition patterns in our Twitter data. We can tell that certain topics are very popular according to their high self-transition weights, such topics include "Job hunting" and "Weight loss". The topic popularity provided by TM-LDA not only shows the amount of related Tweets, but also reflect the persistence of certain topics. Additionally, transition weights can also be indicators of relatedness among topics. For example, the topic "Internet company" and the topic "Social media" are very close to each other and therefore one topic could trigger users' interest in the other topic. Additionally, we can also find some "one way" transitions, which may suggest strong temporal orders or cause-effect relationships among topics. For instance, the topic "Pre-Christmas" is about the ideas and preparation of Christmas gifts; this topic always appears before the topic "Celebration of Christmas". This information could be potentially useful not only for predicting future Tweets, but also for personalization, content recommendation, and advertising.

5.2 Changing Topic Transitions Weights

Topic transitions could help dynamically model the Twitter data. We now show that topic transition parameters are also dynamic and will change over time. Figure 7 shows the changing topic transition weights for three example topics. For instance, the self-transition weight of the topic "U.S. troops withdrawal" increases before the holiday season and becomes flat after that. As another example, the transition probability between topic "Obama Government" and topic "Republican Debate" increases as the presidential election is approaching. Again, all these topics are time-sensitive and the changing transition parameters can describe how they progress over time. Figure 7 also shows how transition weights change for out-dated topics The topic "Christmas decoration" rapidly gains popularity before the holiday, but the weights start dropping right after Christmas, which implies that users lose interest after the Christmas holiday.

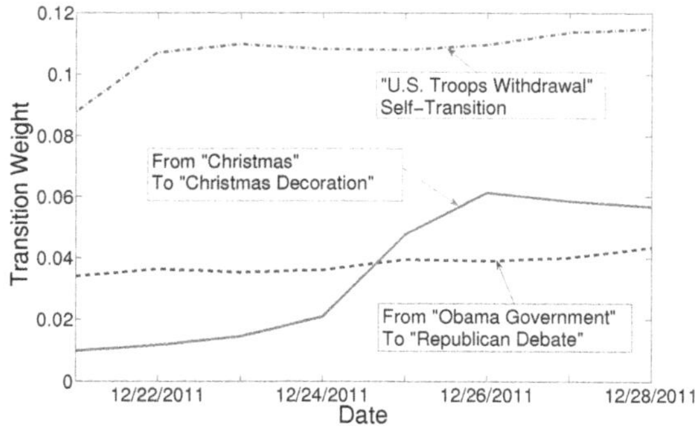

Figure 7: Topic Transition Weights Change over Time.

5.3 Varying Topic Transition Patterns by Cities

Topic transition patterns can help reveal potential social issues and identify interesting behavioral patterns in various cities. As an example, we compare the transition parameter matrices for nine major cities in the United States. Empirical results show that these cities have very different topic transition weights from each other.

The topic transitions of cities could be studied in two ways: (1) for a particular t, what topics tend to *precede* t (Table 4); and (2) what topics tend to *follow* t (Table 5). The former could indicate potential causes of a topic; the latter could help understand aftermath and potential consequences of an event.

	Traffic	*Complaints*	*Compliments*
Atlanta, GA	Airport	Smoke/Drug	Holidays
Boston, MA	Trip	Music	Love
Chicago, IL	Weather	Work Life	Pray
Los Angeles, CA	Church	Break-up	Basketball
Miami, FL	Party	Alcohol	Holidays
New York, NY	Manhattan	Break-up	Movies
San Francisco, CA	Japan/Sushi	Hate	Love
Seattle, WA	Weather	Party	Planning
Washington, D.C.	Plaza	Sleep	Dress

Table 4: Top Topics Preceding the Topics "Traffic", "Complaints" and "Compliments" (columns) for 9 U.S. Major Cities (rows).

Table 4 reports the sample topic transitions of nine major U.S. cities, and it reflects the different characteristics and problems. For example, the topics occurring before "Compliments" could potentially be pleasing, and the topics before "Complaints" might be related to social problems. The result of TM-LDA can also benefit targeted analysis. In Table 4, we show the top topics occurring *before* the topic "Traffic", which may imply the potential traffic issues in various cities. It turns out that the results align with the actual traffic conditions quite well, such as the airport in Atlanta (the busiest airport in the world), Manhattan (a busy area in New York) and Japan-town in San Francisco.

Table 5 shows the topics mentioned after "Work life" and "Dining". It provides the observation of what people tend to do or discuss after work and dinner. This can potentially be applied to advertisement and marketing to target consumers. For example, the users in Los Angeles and Boston areas tend to discuss "Beauty" topics (e.g., make-up and spas) after "Dining", which suggests a better advertising strategy in these cities. These results could also be used to better understand the common lifestyle and culture in these cities.

	Work Life	*Dining*
Atlanta, GA	Complaint	Party
Boston, MA	Book	Beauty
Chicago, IL	Celebration	Weight Loss
Los Angeles, CA	E-shopping	Beauty
Miami, FL	Music	Shopping
New York, NY	Social Media	Weight Loss
San Francisco, CA	Weight Loss	Entertainment
Seattle, WA	Job Hunting	Weight Loss
Washington, D.C.	Presidential Election	Reading Media

Table 5: Top Topics Following "Work Life" and "Dining".

6. RELATED WORK

Topic modeling of temporally-sequenced documents has been studied extensively over the last decade. Blei et al. [4] model the topic evolution over time as a discrete chain-style process and each slice is modeled by LDA. Wang et al. [20] try to model the topics continuously over time. Kawamae [10] models topic evolution by treating temporal words differently from other words. However, TM-LDA differs from these previously proposed dynamic topic models in three ways. First, TM-LDA is designed to learn the topic transition patterns from temporally-ordered documents, while dynamic topic models focus on changing word distributions of topics over time. Second, the efficient optimization algorithm of TM-LDA enables it to be applied on large scale data. Third, TM-LDA can be updated effectively as the new documents stream in.

Meanwhile, the proliferation of social media content makes large-scale temporally ordered data increasingly available. Lin et al. [12] use the social network structure to learn how topics temporally evolve within the social community. Saha and Sindhwani [16] adapt Non-negative Factorization to learn the trending topics in social media. Yang and Leskovec [21] analyze the common "shape" of popularity-time curve in social media via a time-aware clustering algorithm. TM-LDA also takes advantage of temporal information in social media data, but works differently. Rather than learning the dynamic word distributions or trends of topics over time, TM-LDA learns the *relationships* or *transitions* among topics. This allows TM-LDA to compare not only topic popularity in isolation, but also common sequences of topics over time. Additionally, TM-LDA provides trend prediction algorithm for an individual thread of documents, such as the Tweet thread of a particular user, where most of the models only focus on topic evolution over entire corpora.

Social media applications also bring challenges, such as the requirement to efficiently process large-scale data and to support online learning from social data streams, for example, Tweet streams. There has been some previous work on efficient learning from data streams [11]. Ramage et. al [15] attempt to facilitate Twitter content representation by incorporating labeled topic models. Bulut and Singh [6] provide a framework to monitor streaming data. Zhu et. al [22] propose a wavelet-tree based data structure to efficiently detect bursts in data streams. Our model, TM-LDA, is able to efficiently process Tweet stream data and dynamically update the connections among topics in real time.

Semantic analysis and topic modeling in social media can facilitate many applications, such as event tracking [13], trend detection [3] and popularity prediction [19]. Additionally, previous work demonstrated that understanding social media content could benefit applications in many other fields. For example, Asur and Huberman [2] show that Tweets can help predict movie revenues. More recently, Paul and Dredze[14] show that Twitter data could be useful for tracking and analyzing public health information. Similarly, TM-LDA could be potentially applied to public health or even advertising domains, for example by anticipating the future activities of a user based on common topic transition patterns.

7. CONCLUSIONS

We presented and evaluated a temporally-aware language model, TM-LDA, for efficiently modeling the topics and topic transitions that naturally arise in document streams. We have shown that our method is able to more faithfully model the word distribution of a large collection of real microblogging messages, compared to previous state-of-the-art methods. Furthermore, we introduced an efficient model updating algorithm for TM-LDA that dramatically reduces the training time needed to update the model, making our method appropriate for online operation. In a series of experiments, we demonstrated ways in which TM-LDA can be naturally applied for mining, analyzing, and exploring temporal patterns in microblogging data.

Our promising results in this paper suggest applying TM-LDA to other datasets and domains. One such natural application, to be explored in future work, is modeling topic transitions within threads on Community Questions Answering forums or social comment streams, to better analyze the evolution of the discussions and to identify valuable contributions. Additionally, TM-LDA provides a general framework of modeling topic transitions that could be applied to other probabilistic topic modeling algorithms, such as probabilistic Latent Semantic Analysis (pLSA) [8] and author-topic models such as [18]. Together, TM-LDA and the associated algorithms provide a valuable tool to improve upon and complement previous approaches to mining social media data.

ACKNOWLEDGMENTS The work of Yu Wang and Eugene Agichtein was supported in part by DARPA grants N11AP20012 and D11AP00269, and by the Google Research Award; Michele Benzi's work has been supported in part by National Science Foundation Grant DMS1115692.

8. REFERENCES

[1] F. Abel, Q. Gao, Houben, G.J., and K. Tao. Analyzing user modeling on Twitter for personalized news recommendations. In *Proceedings of the International Conference on User Modeling, Adaptation and Personalization (UMAP)*, 2011.

[2] S. Asur and B. A. Huberman. Predicting the future with social media. In *Web Intelligence*, 2010.

[3] S. Asur, B. A. Huberman, G. Szabó, and C. Wang. Trends in social media: Persistence and decay. In *Proceedings of the 5th International AAAI Conference on Weblogs and Social Media (ICWSM)*, 2011.

[4] D. M. Blei and J. D. Lafferty. Dynamic topic models. In *Proceedings of the 23rd International Conference on Machine learning (ICML)*, 2006.

[5] D. M. Blei, A. Y. Ng, and M. I. Jordan. Latent dirichlet allocation. In *Journal of Machine Learning Research*, 2003.

[6] A. Bulut and A. K. Singh. A unified framework for monitoring data streams in real time. In *Proceedings of the 21st International Conference on Data Engineering (ICDE)*, 2005.

[7] G. H. Golub and C. F. V. Loan. *Matrix Computations*. The Johns Hopkins University Press, 3rd edition, 1996.

[8] T. Hofmann. Probabilistic latent semantic analysis. In *Proceedings of the 15th Conference on Uncertainty in Artificial Intelligence*, 1999.

[9] S. P. Kasiviswanathan, P. Melville, A. Banerjee, and V. Sindhwani. Emerging topic detection using dictionary learning. In *Proceedings of the 20th ACM International Conference on Information and Knowledge Management (CIKM)*, 2011.

[10] N. Kawamae. Trend analysis model: trend consists of temporal words, topics, and timestamps. In *Proceedings of the 4th ACM International Conference on Web Search and Data Mining (WSDM)*, 2011.

[11] J. Kleinberg. Temporal dynamics of on-line information streams. *In Data Stream Management: Processing High-Speed Data*, 2006.

[12] C. X. Lin, Q. Mei, J. Han, Y. Jiang, and M. Danilevsky. The joint inference of topic diffusion and evolution in social communities. In *Proceedings of the 11th IEEE International Conference on Data Mining (ICDM)*, 2011.

[13] C. X. Lin, B. Zhao, Q. Mei, and J. Han. PET: a statistical model for popular events tracking in social communities. In *Proceedings of the 16th ACM SIGKDD International Conference on Knowledge Discovery and Data Mining (KDD)*, 2010.

[14] M. Paul and M. Dredze. You are what you tweet: Analyzing Twitter for public health. In *Proceedings of the 5th International AAAI Conference on Weblogs and Social Media (ICWSM)*, 2011.

[15] D. Ramage, S. T. Dumais, and D. J. Liebling. Characterizing microblogs with topic models. In *Proceedings of the 4th International AAAI Conference on Weblogs and Social Media (ICWSM)*, 2010.

[16] A. Saha and V. Sindhwani. Learning evolving and emerging topics in social media: A dynamic NMF approach with temporal regularization. In *Proceedings of the 5th International Conference on Web Search and Data Mining (WSDM)*, 2012.

[17] T. Sakaki, M. Okazaki, and Y. Matsuo. Earthquake shakes Twitter users: real-time event detection by social sensors. In *Proceedings of the 19th International Conference on World wide web (WWW)*, 2010.

[18] M. Steyvers, P. Smyth, M. Rosen-Zvi, and T. Griffiths. Probabilistic author-topic models for information discovery. In *Proceedings of the 10th ACM SIGKDD International Conference on Knowledge Discovery and Data Mining (KDD)*, 2004.

[19] G. Szabo and B. A. Huberman. Predicting the popularity of online content. *Commun. ACM*, 53:80–88, Aug. 2010.

[20] X. Wang and A. McCallum. Topics over time: a non-Markov continuous-time model of topical trends. In *Proceedings of the 12th ACM SIGKDD International Conference on Knowledge Discovery and Data Mining (KDD)*, 2006.

[21] J. Yang and J. Leskovec. Patterns of temporal variation in online media. In *Proceedings of the 4th ACM International Conference on Web Search and Data Mining (WSDM)*, 2011.

[22] Y. Zhu and D. Shasha. Efficient elastic burst detection in data streams. In *Proceedings of the 9th ACM SIGKDD International Conference on Knowledge Discovery and Data Mining (KDD)*, 2003.

Multi-View Clustering Using Mixture Models in Subspace Projections

Stephan Günnemann, Ines Färber, and Thomas Seidl
RWTH Aachen University, Germany
{guennemann, faerber, seidl}@cs.rwth-aachen.de

ABSTRACT

Detecting multiple clustering solutions is an emerging research field. While data is often multi-faceted in its very nature, traditional clustering methods are restricted to find just a single grouping. To overcome this limitation, methods aiming at the detection of alternative and multiple clustering solutions have been proposed. In this work, we present a Bayesian framework to tackle the problem of multi-view clustering. We provide multiple generalizations of the data by using *multiple mixture models*. Each mixture describes a specific view on the data by using a mixture of Beta distributions in *subspace projections*. Since a mixture summarizes the clusters located in similar subspace projections, each view highlights specific aspects of the data. In addition, our model handles *overlapping views*, where the mixture components compete against each other in the data generation process. For efficiently learning the distributions, we propose the algorithm MVGen that exploits the ICM principle and uses Bayesian model selection to trade-off the cluster model's complexity against its goodness of fit. With experiments on various real-world data sets, we demonstrate the high potential of MVGen to detect multiple, overlapping clustering views in subspace projections of the data.

Categories and Subject Descriptors: H.2.8 Database management: Database applications [Data mining]

Keywords: model-based clustering, generative model

1. INTRODUCTION

Mixture models have proven to be well suited for adequately modeling and learning the characteristics of complex probability distributions of given observations in various applications [16]. In particular in the presence of an underlying clustering structure, multivariate mixture models are widely used as a compact representation of the data's distribution. Given a parametric family $\mathcal{K}$, e.g. the set of all Gaussian distributions, a mixture model describes the data by a set of components (each selected from $\mathcal{K}$) and a set of mixture weights. Intuitively, each component represents a cluster (more precisely: its distribution of the attribute values) and the mixture weight represents the number of objects belonging to this cluster.

KDD'12, August 12–16, 2012, Beijing, China.

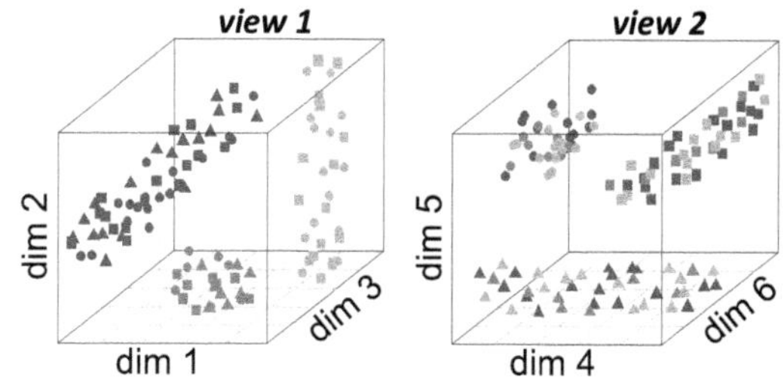

Fig. 1: Example for the multi-view scenario

Key to a reasonable data representation is an appropriate modeling of the underlying data structure. Traditional mixture models work with only a single mixture distribution, i.e. each observation is assumed to follow a single component's distribution. However, as the research areas of subspace clustering [15] and multi-view clustering [17] have taught us, for many data collections multiple, differing aspects of the observations are captured. This aspect has already been touched by approaches like [22, 11, 3] that allow for a mixed membership in different components. Thus, they realize an overlapping clustering and, e.g., allow for a movie to participate in the 'humor' as well as in the 'action' genre [3]. These approaches still only realize a single clustering (i.e. one mixture model) and, therefore, are able to present only one view on the data, e.g. the view 'genre' for the movie example. For many scenarios, however, a more complex clustering structure, where different views on the data (i.e. considering different characteristics of the observations) reveal different clustering structures, has to be expected [18, 8, 20]. Movies cannot only be clustered according to their 'genre' but also based on 'location', 'cast', 'budget', or other characteristics. Since data is rarely collected pursuing only one defined goal, the multi-view hypothesis is very likely for various databases, e.g. customer data, sensor data, biological records but also for data with various heterogeneous characteristics like images or multimedia in general.

Just summarizing the data by a single global view, which considers all characteristics simultaneously, does not do such data justice. Instead, a generalization of the data by a mixture model *for each view* and its specific characteristics, reveals more insight in the data. Given the toy example in Fig. 1, we can easily identify two different but valuable clusterings: characterizing the observations' color (first view: subspace $\{1, 2, 3\}$) and the observations' shape (second view: subspace $\{4, 5, 6\}$). If a single partitioning of this data in the full-space $\{1, \ldots, 6\}$ is enforced, the result will be very small, specialized clusters, e.g. 'blue rectangles'. For the purpose of generalization, 3 clusters in 2 views are preferable over 9 clusters considering all attributes. Especially for data with

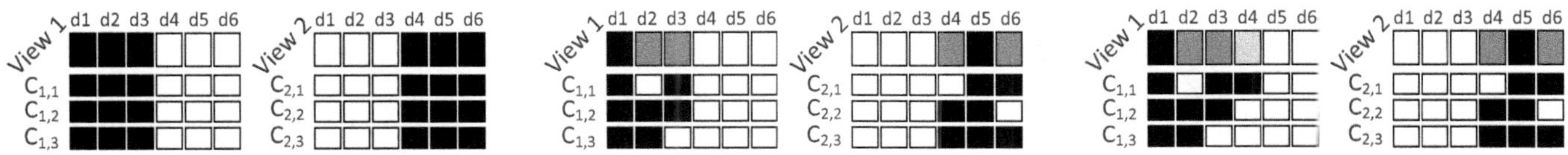

(a) Disjoint views

(b) Disjoint views & subspace clusters

(c) View overlaps & subspace clusters

Fig. 2: Different scenarios of multi-view data (black: relevant dimensions; white: irrelevant dimensions)

many attributes a mixture distribution in the full-space does not generalize the data well.

Taking a generative perspective, we can assume each object to be generated by *multiple mixture distributions*, each referring to a different view of the data. Consequentially, each object follows *multiple* components, each in a different mixture model, each defining a distribution only for a certain view (i.e. subspace) of the data, and each representing a different role of the object. This poses several challenges:

Challenge 1: Multiple Groupings. In the most simple scenario of multi-view data, the views do not share any characteristics (disjoint subspaces). A schematic representation of this case for a database with 6 dimensions, 2 views, each with 3 clusters, is given in Fig. 2(a). Intuitively, we can model this scenario by 'concatenating' several traditional mixture models. The question remains, how to appropriately model the relevant dimensions of each view.

Challenge 2: Subspace Clusters. Usually, the solution via traditional mixture models discussed above is too restrictive for the characteristics of real world data. While for a certain view a set of attributes is relevant in general, we cannot expect that each cluster covers exactly the same set of dimensions as its view (subspace cluster w.r.t. the view). While the dimension 'viewers age' might be relevant for the view 'genre' in general (e.g. 'Horror' movies target only adults), some genres like, e.g., '3D Animations' show no certain characteristic in this dimension. This scenario corresponds to Fig. 1 and is illustrated in Fig. 2(b). Subspace clusters cannot be represented by traditional mixture models. While in the relevant dimensions of a subspace cluster, the attribute values are distributed according to, e.g., a Gaussian distribution, irrelevant dimensions follow a completely different model, e.g. a uniform distribution. That is, depending on the dimension's relevance a different parametric family is used. Thus, to model data containing subspace clusters, we encounter the challenge of model selection, i.e. before we can estimate the actual mixture model parameters, we first have to determine the parametric families that are used for each cluster.

Challenge 3: Overlapping Views. So far, we just discussed non-overlapping views. In general, however, dimensions can occur in multiple views (Fig. 2(c)). E.g., the dimensions 'gender' and 'age' might be characteristic for the two views 'hobby' and 'profession' of a customer data base. This scenario is particularly challenging as several components might compete with each other for generating an object in one or more dimensions (e.g. clusters $C_{1,1}$ and $C_{2,3}$ in dimension four). Obviously, the *dominant* view (and hence dominant distribution) might vary for each dimension and each object: while in dimension 'gender' some objects rate the view 'hobby' as dominant, other objects use the view 'profession' in this dimension; in the dimension 'age' completely different views might be considered as dominant. This observation is even intensified by considering subspace clusters: some clusters might not be relevant in the overlapping dimensions. Accordingly, it is not sufficient to consider only the views, but we need to consider the actual subspace clusters to determine the dominant view. Since each object might be located in different subspace clusters, different overlap scenarios can occur.

To tackle all these challenges, we propose a Bayesian framework modeling data with an inherent multi-view clustering structure. Our model:

- provides multiple generalizations of the data by modeling individual mixture models, each representing a distinct view
- handles individual sets of relevant dimensions for each cluster by performing Bayesian model selection
- tackles the ambiguity of the objects' memberships regarding multiple, competing components

2. GENERATIVE MULTI-VIEW MODEL

In this section, we introduce a Bayesian framework modeling the process of generating data containing multiple clustering views. An overview of our framework is given by the graphical model depicted in Fig. 3. We start in Section 2.1 by describing our model from a generative perspective, i.e. we show how our model generates data containing multiple views. The inverse process where a set of observations is *given* and the model's components are learned, is introduced in Section 2.2. Following convention, we do not distinguish between a random variable X and its realization $X = \mathbf{X}$ if it is clear from the context. As an abbreviation, we denote sets of random variables with the index $*$, e.g. $Y_{*,d}$ is the set of random variables $\{Y_{i,d}\}$ with i in the corresponding index domain, and Y is an abbreviation for the set $Y_{*,*}$.

2.1 Generating Multi-View Data

In our model we explicitly differentiate between the relevant dimensions of the clusters and the relevant dimensions of the views. The relevant dimensions of a view provide a concise description for the relevant dimensions for a *set* of clusters. That is, the clusters belonging to the same view are located in similar subspace projections. Since the clusters' relevant dimensions might slightly vary, the relevance of dimensions for the view can also vary. In Figure 2(b), for example, dimension 1 has a high relevance for view 1 since all of its represented clusters use this dimension; dimension 1 is a good descriptor for the whole set of clusters. Dimension 3, in contrast, has a slightly smaller relevance since one of the clusters does not require this dimension. Thus, to reflect the differing relevances of dimensions $d \in D = \{1, \ldots, d_{max}\}$ for each view $m \in M = \{1, \ldots, m_{max}\}$, our model includes the (continuous) latent variables $V_{m,d}$ on $(0, 1)$.

Based on this relevance information, the actual relevant dimensions of each subspace cluster can be generated. We model this aspect by the (discrete) random variable $S_{m,k,d}$

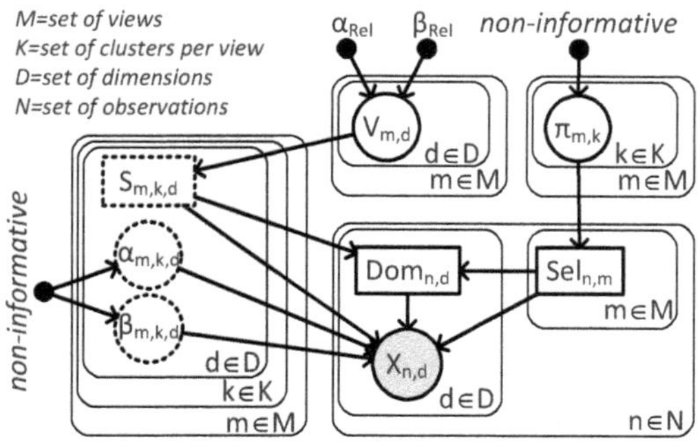

Fig. 3: Graphical model of our method. Rectangles denote discrete random variables, circles continuous random variables, and black dots (deterministic) hyperparameters of the prior distributions.

on $\{0,1\}$ for $d \in D$, $k \in K$ and $m \in M$.[1] The latent variable is 1 if the dimension d is relevant for the k-th cluster of view m, and 0 otherwise. The higher the relevance of a view's dimension, the more likely is the dimension relevant for the cluster. This property can be realized by a Bernoulli process. With probability $V_{m,d}$ the dimension d is relevant for the cluster, while with probability $1 - V_{m,d}$ it is not. Formally, the distribution of the latent variable $S_{m,k,d}$ is given by

$$\begin{aligned} p(S_{m,k,d} = 1 \mid V_{m,d} = r) &= r \\ p(S_{m,k,d} = 0 \mid V_{m,d} = r) &= (1-r) \end{aligned} \tag{1}$$

If the value of $V_{m,d}$ is either close to 1 or close to 0, then the subspaces of each cluster in the same view are very similar. If $V_{m,d}$ is close to 0.5, we do not have a clear decision, and thus the subspaces of the clusters may differ stronger.

Prior distributions. To allow a fully Bayesian approach, we specify prior distributions for the variables $V_{m,d}$. We select the prior according to a Beta distribution, i.e.

$$V_{m,d} \sim Beta(\alpha_{Rel}, \beta_{Rel})$$

with hyperparameters $\alpha_{Rel} \in \mathbb{R}_{>0}$ and $\beta_{Rel} \in \mathbb{R}_{>0}$. A Beta distribution is suited due to the following reasons: First, since $V_{m,d}$ simulates a Bernoulli process, the Beta distribution corresponds to its conjugate prior. Second, based on the hyperparameters, the user can control the views' purity. That is, one can control the similarity between the clusters' subspaces originating from the same view. As mentioned above, high similarity between the subspaces can be realized by choosing $V_{m,d}$ close to 1 or close to 0. This issue can be modeled by selecting $\alpha_{Rel} = \beta_{Rel} < 1$. If no knowledge about the views' purity is given, we can simply choose $\alpha_{Rel} = \beta_{Rel} = 1$, leading to a non-informative prior.

Generating the membership information. After generating the relevant dimensions of each cluster, we now aim at generating observations that follow multiple overlapping views. More precisely, in each of the views each object shall belong to a single cluster; thereby, we realize a single grouping within a single view and multiple overlapping groupings among different views.

This idea can be modeled by the latent variable $Sel_{n,m}$ on $K = \{1, \ldots, k_{max}\}$ that models which of the k_{max} clusters an object n follows in view m. The distribution of Sel is governed by the (relative) weights $\pi_{m,k}$ of the clusters, i.e.

$$p(Sel_{n,m} = k \mid \pi_{m,*}) = \pi_{m,k}$$

As for usual mixture models, the larger the weight of a cluster, the more objects belong (in expectation) to the cluster. Please note that in contrast to traditional mixture models, in our model each view represents a certain grouping of *all* objects. Thus, in our model we have $\sum_{k \in K} \pi_{m,k} = 1$ for each view $m \in M$, while in traditional mixture models the overall weight of all clusters is normalized to 1.

As discussed in challenge 3 (and illustrated in Fig. 2(c)), different views compete with each other. An object might belong to two clusters which both are marked as relevant in a specific dimension d. To solve the ambiguity about the object's membership in this dimension, we specify one of the views as dominant (for this object and dimension). This aspect is modeled by the latent variable $Dom_{n,d}$ on $M = \{1, \ldots, m_{max}\}$. Here, a view $m \in M$ can only be dominant in d if the selected cluster is also relevant in d. Thus, let $M'_{n,d} = \{m' \in M \mid S_{m',Sel_{n,m'},d} = 1\}$ be the set of views that are potentially dominant for object n in dimension d, the distribution of $Dom_{n,d}$ is modeled by

$$p(Dom_{n,d} = m \mid Sel_{n,*}, S_{*,*,d}) = \begin{cases} 1/|M'_{n,d}| & \text{if } m \in M'_{n,d} \\ 0 & \text{if } m \notin M'_{n,d} \wedge M'_{n,d} \neq \emptyset \\ 1/|M| & \text{else} \end{cases}$$

That is, we randomly select a view from the potentially dominant views (case 1), while the remaining views cannot be selected (case 2). The third case just occurs, if none of the selected clusters of an object is relevant in this dimension. In this case, an arbitrary view can be selected as dominant since any cluster represents just noise in this dimension.

Generating Observations. Finally, we specify the distributions from which the attribute values of a cluster are sampled, i.e. we model the actual components of the multiple mixture models. However, keep in mind that for subspace clustering we have two different parametric families: $\mathcal{K}_1$ for the relevant dimensions and $\mathcal{K}_0$ for irrelevant ones.

In our model we select the parametric family $\mathcal{K}_1$ according to the set of Beta distributions, i.e. we consider a mixture of Beta distributions. This is advantageous compared to the frequently used Gaussian distributions since Gaussian distributions have an infinite support, which usually does not match the observed data. In many applications, we have a finite attribute domain that can be normalized to the range $(0,1)$; this is exactly captured by the Beta distribution. Additionally, the Beta distribution is able to model distributions near the border of the data space. These Beta distributions are modeled by the two random variables $\alpha_{m,k,d}$ and $\beta_{m,k,d}$ on $\mathbb{R}_{>0}$ providing the necessary shape parameters of each distribution (for each view m, each cluster k, and each dimension d). For the parametric family $\mathcal{K}_0$, we simply use the uniform distribution on $(0,1)$ since this corresponds to a noisy dimension. Thus, $|\mathcal{K}_0| = 1$ holds.

Which parametric family a mixture component in dimension d belongs to was modeled by the latent variable S. Thus, finally, the attribute values of each object can be modeled by the random variable $X_{n,d}$ with distribution:

$$X_{n,d} \mid Dom_{n,d}, Sel_{n,*}, S_{*,*,d}, \alpha_{*,*,d}, \beta_{*,*,d} \sim \begin{cases} Beta(\alpha_{i,j,d}, \beta_{i,j,d}) & \text{if } S_{i,j,d} = 1 \\ Uni(0,1) & \text{else} \end{cases}$$

where $Dom_{n,d}{=}i$ and $Sel_{n,i}{=}j$. Thus, for each dimension d

[1]To simplify our model description, we assume that each view $m \in M$ describes k_{max} clusters, i.e. $K = \{1, \ldots, k_{max}\}$.

an object follows the distribution given by the *selected* cluster in the *dominant* view.

Prior distributions. Again, we choose appropriate prior distributions to enable inference. We select non-informative priors since usually no further knowledge is provided about the data's clustering structure. A non-informative prior for the cluster weights $\pi_{m,k}$ is simply realized by choosing $p(\pi_{m,1}, \ldots, \pi_{m,k_{max}}) = const$ for each view m.

For the variables $\alpha_{m,k,d}$ and $\beta_{m,k,d}$ we suggest a non-informative prior $p(\alpha, \beta)$ that ensures a uniform distribution over the mean and variance of the resulting Beta distributions $Beta(\alpha, \beta)$. Intuitively, this way the cluster centers are uniformly selected from the domain $(0, 1)$ and the variance from the domain $(0, \frac{1}{12})$. Thus, the prior fulfills

$$\int_\alpha \int_\beta p(\alpha, \beta) \cdot \mathbf{1}(\mathbb{E}(Beta(\alpha, \beta)) = x) \; d\alpha d\beta \sim Uni(0, 1)$$

regarding the mean x of the resulting Beta distribution (same for the variance with $Uni(0, \frac{1}{12})$). We can approximately[2] achieve these properties by selecting the priors according to exponential distributions with rate parameter 0.1, i.e.

$$\alpha_{m,k,d} \sim Exp(0.1) \quad , \quad \beta_{m,k,d} \sim Exp(0.1)$$

2.2 Learning Objective

In the following, we describe our learning objective if a set of observed data points $\mathbf{X}$ is given. Usually, the learning objective would be to maximize the a posteriori probability $p(V, S, \alpha, \beta, Dom, Sel, \pi \mid X = \mathbf{X})$.

For our model, however, this idea is not meaningful since in this case usually all dimensions of a cluster are relevant: the data's likelihood is always higher when selecting a (certain) Beta distribution in contrast to selecting a uniform distribution. This is obvious since a uniform distribution is a special case of a Beta distribution with shape parameters $\alpha = \beta = 1$ and, hence, $\mathcal{K}_0 \subset \mathcal{K}_1$. Thus, simply determining the maximum a posteriori (MAP) estimate as given above leads to the problem of overfitting since a complex model obviously fits the data better than a simple one[3]; one would only choose relevant dimensions.

To overcome this problem, we first perform a model selection before learning the subspaces S and the shape parameters of the Beta distributions. That is, we balance the models' goodness of fit and their simplicity[4]. Thus, our learning objective is separated in two phases:

First, we perform Bayesian model selection [6] by finding the best realization for V, Dom, Sel, and π. That is, we determine the MAP estimate

$$(\mathbf{V}^*, \mathbf{Dom}^*, \mathbf{Sel}^*, \boldsymbol{\pi}^*) = \arg \max_{(\mathbf{V}, \mathbf{Dom}, \mathbf{Sel}, \boldsymbol{\pi})} p(V = \mathbf{V}, Dom = \mathbf{Dom}, Sel = \mathbf{Sel}, \pi = \boldsymbol{\pi} \mid X = \mathbf{X})$$

These variables are illustrated in our graphical model with solid lines. Since learning these variables involves a marginalization over S, α, and β we realize the balancing of the model's complexity and its goodness of fit. Thus, due to this model selection step, some dimensions might be irrelevant for certain views, corresponding to a more simple model.

Since after the first phase the cluster model is determined, we can estimate in the second phase the actual mixture components and the clusters' subspaces. That is, we can now determine the MAP estimate for the variables S, α and β:

$$(\mathbf{S}^*, \boldsymbol{\alpha}^*, \boldsymbol{\beta}^*) = \arg \max_{(\mathbf{S}, \boldsymbol{\alpha}, \boldsymbol{\beta})} p(S = \mathbf{S}, \alpha = \boldsymbol{\alpha}, \beta = \boldsymbol{\beta} \mid X = \mathbf{X}, V = \mathbf{V}^*, Dom = \mathbf{Dom}^*, Sel = \mathbf{Sel}^*, \pi = \boldsymbol{\pi}^*)$$

Overall, our model allows to learn the clustering structure of data containing multiple overlapping views by using multiple mixture models. Clusters, i.e. mixture components, are located in individual subspace projections and views summarize these clusters by a concise description of their relevant dimensions. We discuss advantages of our method in comparison to existing techniques in Section 4.

3. THE MVGen ALGORITHM

In this section we introduce our MVGen (Multi-View Generative Model) algorithm that learns the multi-view clustering structure given a set of observed data points. Since exactly computing the MAP estimate $p(V, Dom, Sel, \pi \mid X)$ is intractable, we compute approximations that can be efficiently determined. In general, we exploit the principle of iterated conditional modes (ICM [5]), which can be regarded as a greedy variant of the Gibbs sampling method [6]. That is, instead of considering a complex joint distribution $p(A_1, \ldots, A_n)$, we iteratively maximize a set of conditional probabilities $p(A_i \mid A_1, \ldots, A_{i-1}, A_{i+1}, \ldots, A_n)$ until the process converges. This way, the random variables A_i are updated sequentially. The traditional k-means processing scheme can be seen as an instance of the ICM principle with just two easily computable update steps: recomputation of means and reassignment of points to clusters.

3.1 Update Equations

We briefly present the update equations required in our algorithm; they are summarized in Equation (U1)-(U4).

Updating the views V. We start with the variable $V_{m,d}$, i.e. for each $m \in M, d \in D$ we aim at maximizing

$$p(V_{m,d} \mid V \backslash \{V_{m,d}\}, Dom, Sel, \pi, X) \propto \sum_S \int_\alpha \int_\beta p(V, Dom, Sel, \pi, S, \alpha, \beta, X) \; d\alpha d\beta \tag{2}$$

The most important aspect here is that we have to marginalize over the variable S, α and β, as stated in Section 2.2. Only if the model selection step is performed, we can estimate α, β and S.

We proved[5] that the optimal realization of $V_{m,d}$ can be computed based on the equation

$$V_{m,d} = \arg \max_{x \in (0,1)} c_a \cdot \log x + c_b \cdot \log(1 - x) + c_c \cdot \log(x + c_d) + \sum_{k \in K} \log(c_k \cdot x + 1) \tag{U1}$$

where the c_* are constant values given by

$c_a = \alpha_{Rel} - 1 + |N_{m,d}|$ $\quad c_b = \beta_{Rel} - 1$ $\quad c_c = -|N|$

$c_d = \sum_{m' \in M, m' \neq m} V_{m',d}$ $\quad c_k = Beta_d(N_{m,k,d}) - 1$

[2]Indeed, the distribution of the mean is exactly captured since the Beta distribution's mean is given by $\frac{\alpha}{\alpha+\beta}$, and for any λ it holds: $X, Y \sim Exp(\lambda) \Rightarrow \frac{X}{X+Y} \sim Uni(0, 1)$

[3]A similar example is polynomial interpolation: since the set of polynomials with degree x is a subset of the ones with degree $x + 1$, the interpolation error decreases with increasing degree.

[4]In the example of polynomial interpolation, one balances the degree of the polynomial against its regression error.

[5]The detailed derivation of this equation can be found on our website http://dme.rwth-aachen.de/mvgen

Here, $N_{m,d} = \{n \in N \mid Dom_{n,d} = m\}$ is the set of all observations that choose the view m in dimension d as *dominant* and $N_{m,k,d} = \{n \in N_{m,d} \mid Sel_{n,m} = k\}$ are those observations which additionally *select* the cluster k. The term $Beta_d(N_{m,k,d})$ is computed based on the following equation

$$Beta_d(I) := \Big[\prod_{n\in I} Beta(X_{n,d}; \alpha_{MAP}, \beta_{MAP})\Big] \;/\; |I| \quad (3)$$

where I is an index set denoting which observations are considered and α_{MAP} and β_{MAP} are the MAP estimates of the Beta distribution's shape parameters using the set I of observations. The function $Beta_d(I)$ approximates the term

$$\int_\alpha \int_\beta p(\alpha)p(\beta) \prod_{n\in I} Beta(X_{n,d}; \alpha, \beta)\; d\alpha d\beta$$

which has to be solved during the derivation of our update equations. $Beta_d(I)$ exploits the Bayesian Information Criterion (BIC, or Schwarz criterion [21, 6]) in combination with the observation that in our case the Beta distribution is controlled by two free parameters.

Overall, Equation (U1) describes a simple univariate function in the variable x whose optimization can, for example, be done by Brent's algorithm [7].

Updating π. We perform a block update for the variables $\pi_{m,*}$. Since we use a non-informative prior, maximizing $p(\pi_{m,*} \mid V, Dom, Sel, \pi\backslash\{\pi_{m,*}\}, X)$ is simply obtained by

$$\pi_{m,k} = |\{n \in N \mid Sel_{n,m} = k\}| \cdot |N|^{-1} \quad \forall k \in K \quad (U2)$$

Updating ***Dom*** ***and*** ***Sel.*** Finally, we derive the update equations for the variables *Dom* and *Sel*. We perform a block update of the variables $Sel_{n,m}$ and $Dom_{n,*}$, i.e. for each observation n we simultaneously update its selected cluster in view m and its dominant views over all dimension. Formally, we aim at maximizing:

$$p(Sel_{n,m}, Dom_{n,*} \mid V, Dom\backslash\{Dom_{n,*}\}, Sel\backslash\{Sel_{n,m}\}, \pi, X)$$

$$\propto \sum_S \int_\alpha \int_\beta p(S \mid V)p(Sel_{n,m} \mid \pi) \prod_{d\in D} \Big[p(Dom_{n,d} \mid S, Sel)$$

$$p(\alpha)p(\beta) \prod_{n'\in N} p(X_{n',d} \mid Dom, Sel, S, \alpha, \beta)\Big]\; d\alpha d\beta \quad (4)$$

We first resolve the integral over α and β by again using the BIC approximation (cf. Eq. 3). We assume that the MAP estimates α^{MAP} and β^{MAP} derivable from the current grouping change only marginally when reassigning a single point n to a different cluster. Similarly, the cluster sizes change only marginally, i.e. the sets $N_{m,k,d}$ differ by at most one element when reassigning observation n to a different cluster. Using this idea, we can substitute the part $p(\alpha)p(\beta)\prod_{n'\in N} p(X_{n',d} \mid Dom, Sel, S, \alpha, \beta)$ by $Beta(X_{n,d}; \alpha^{MAP}_{i,j,d}, \beta^{MAP}_{i,j,d})$ if $S_{i,j,d} = 1$ and by 1 (uniform distribution) if $S_{i,j,d} = 0$.[6] This simplification stems from the fact that with given, constant MAP estimates also the densities $p(X_{n',d} \mid ...)$ for $n' \neq n$ are constant. Thus, Eq. 4 simplifies to:

$$\propto \sum_S p(S \mid V)p(Sel_{n,m} \mid \pi) \prod_{d\in D} \Big[p(Dom_{n,d} \mid S, Sel)$$

$$\begin{cases} Beta(X_{n,d}; \alpha^{MAP}_{i,j,d}, \beta^{MAP}_{i,j,d}) & \text{if } S_{i,j,d} = 1 \\ 1 & else \end{cases}\Big] \quad (5)$$

[6]We use the abbreviations $i{:=}Dom_{n,d}$ and $j{:=}Sel_{n,Dom_{n,d}}$

Due to the integration over all possible realizations of S, the term $p(Dom_{n,d} \mid S, Sel)$ can well be approximated by the expected dominance of a view m in dimension d. The expected dominance is given by

$$ED_d(m) := \frac{V_{m,d}}{\sum_{m'\in M} V_{m',d}}$$

Thus, the above equation simplifies to

$$\propto \sum_S p(S \mid V)p(Sel_{n,m} \mid \pi) \prod_{d\in D} \Big[ED_d(Dom_{n,d})$$

$$\begin{cases} Beta(X_{n,d}; \alpha^{MAP}_{i,j,d}, \beta^{MAP}_{i,j,d}) & \text{if } S_{i,j,d} = 1 \\ 1 & else \end{cases}\Big] \quad (6)$$

Since the $S_{m,k,d}$ are independent given V, the summation over S is effective only for the variable $S_{i,j,d}$. Thus, the summation vanishes when making the two cases of $S_{i,j,d}$ explicit. That is, we introduce the term

$$AD_d(m,k) := p(S_{m,k,d} = 1 \mid V) \cdot Beta(X_{n,d}; \alpha^{MAP}_{m,k,d}, \beta^{MAP}_{m,k,d}) + p(S_{m,k,d} = 0 \mid V) \cdot 1$$

and Equation 6 simplifies to

$$p(Sel_{n,m} \mid \pi) \cdot \prod_{d\in D} ED_d(Dom_{n,d}) AD_d(Dom_{n,d}, Sel_{n,Dom_{n,d}})$$

Please note that the functions ED_d and AD_d are independent of *Sel* and *Dom* and fully specified by the values of V, α^{MAP}, and β^{MAP} (which are given!). Thus, while updating the values of *Dom* and *Sel*, we do *not* have to recompute the functions ED_d and AD_d.

Based on the above equation it becomes apparent that $Dom_{n,*}$ can be optimized for each dimension individually. Especially, if the variable *Sel* is *given*, we can efficiently compute the optimal realization of $Dom_{n,d}$ by

$$Dom_{n,d} = \arg\max_{m\in M} ED_d(m) AD_d(m, Sel_{n,m}) \quad (U3)$$

As shown, the optimal realization of *Dom* depends on *Sel* in a simple way. Thus, we can focus on finding a good solution for $Sel_{n,m}$. The optimal solution of $Sel_{n,m}$ can efficiently be computed by

$$Sel_{n,m} = \arg\max_{k\in K} \Big\{\pi_{m,k} \prod_{d\in D} \max\{ED_d(m) \cdot AD_d(m,k), c_{m,d}\}\Big\} \quad (U4)$$

where $c_{m,d} = \max_{m'\in M, m'\neq m} ED_d(m') \cdot AD_d(m', Sel_{n,m'})$. The value of $c_{m,d}$ is constant since it neither depends on $Sel_{n,m}$ nor on $Dom_{n,*}$. Please note that the update of $Sel_{n,m}$ directly uses the best solution for $Dom_{n,*}$. Thus, we do not have to optimize $Dom_{n,*}$ separately but the optimal values are computed while updating $Sel_{n,m}$.

3.2 Recommended Update Sequence

Given the derived update equations, any sequence that recurrently invokes each of these equations is possible to determine a desired clustering solutions. However, based on the dependencies as given by our graphical model and the particular role of the model selection phase, we recommend the following update sequence for the random variables:

1. We sequentially update the variables $V_{m,d}$ for each $m \in M, d \in D$ until the views are stable. [Eq. (U1)]
2. For each object $n \in N$, we sequentially update the variables $Sel_{n,*}$ and $Dom_{n,*}$ until *Sel* and *Dom* are stable.
   (a) To update $Sel_{n,*}$ and $Dom_{n,*}$ we sequentially update $Sel_{n,m}$ for each $m \in M$ until $Sel_{n,*}$ is stable. [Eq. (U3) & (U4)]

3. Update of $\pi_{m,*}$ for each $m \in M$ [Eq. (U2)]; goto step (2) until the process has converged.

4. goto step (1) until the process has converged.

Thus, overall, we exploit the ICM principle in a nested fashion. The outer loop iterating over steps 1 and 2/3 represents the alternation between learning the views and learning the groupings. For the inner loop, iterating over 2 and 3, the views are given and we try to optimize the cluster assignments as good as possible. Note that implicitly also the mixture components α and β are optimized since based on the BIC approximation their MAP estimates are considered.

Initialization. To complete the above algorithm, we describe a straight-forward initialization. We simply initialize Sel by the following method: For each dimension $d \in D$ we apply the k-means method with $k = |K|$. Thus, leading to $|D|$ many clusterings. Since, however, Sel requires just $|M|$ different views, we follow an approach inspired by traditional agglomerative clustering methods: To reduce the number of clusterings, we successively determine those clusterings that are most similar to each other, and we merge these clusterings to a single one. Thus, in each step the number of clusterings is reduced by one until the required number $|M|$ is reached. To merge two clusterings, we simply union the corresponding sets of dimensions and we recompute the k-means result in the novel space. As similarity measure between the clusterings we use the F-measure [23].

After initializing Sel, the variable π is determined based on Equation U2. Furthermore, Dom is initialized randomly since no information about the views is given. The variable V is also initialized randomly based on its prior distribution.

3.3 Determining Components and Subspaces

According to Section 2.2, the second phase of our learning objective is to determine the MAP estimate of $p(S, \alpha, \beta \mid X, V, Dom, Sel, \pi)$.

Since the variables Dom and Sel are given, the set of observations that contribute to the Beta distribution of cluster k in dimension d and view m is known, and was denoted by the set $N_{m,k,d} = \{n \in N_{m,d} \mid Sel_{n,m} = k\}$. Thus, the shape parameters $\alpha_{m,k,d}$ and $\beta_{m,k,d}$ of each mixture component simply correspond to their MAP estimate given the set of observations $N_{m,k,d}$.

In general, however, determining the MAP estimate for the shape parameters of a Beta distribution is not possible in closed form; one has to iteratively solve systems of equations [4]. Since this is highly inefficient, we refer to the commonly used approach of moment matching: the shape parameters are computed based on the mean and variance values of the observations. This approach is in line with the non-informative prior distributions of α and β, which do not favor certain means or variance values. Thus, we get:

$$\alpha_{m,k,d} = \frac{(1-\mu)\mu^2 - \mu \cdot \sigma^2}{\sigma^2} \text{ and } \beta_{m,k,d} = \frac{\mu(\mu-1)^2}{\sigma^2} + \mu - 1$$

where μ denotes the mean of the observations $\{X_{n,d} \mid n \in N_{m,k,d}\}$, and σ^2 the variance, respectively. Note that these equations are also used for the MAP estimates required in Section 3.1. Thus, the estimates for α^{MAP} and β^{MAP} can be efficiently computed in these steps.

Finally, an estimate for the random variables S can be obtained by testing which of the models – relevant or irrelevant dimension – is more likely. That is, if

$$p(S_{m,k,d} = 1 \mid V) \cdot \prod_{n \in N_{m,k,d}} Beta(X_{n,d}; \alpha_{m,k,d}, \beta_{m,k,d}) > p(S_{m,k,d} = 0 \mid V) \cdot 1$$

, the dimension d of cluster k in view m will be relevant. Here, we do not have to refer to the BIC approximation but can use the likelihood of the Beta distribution. Since the view V is already learned, i.e. the model selection is done, the trade-off between the models' complexities and their goodness of fit is already reflected in the term $p(S_{m,k,d} \mid V)$.

4. RELATED WORK

Our MVGen exploits a Bayesian framework to model the generation of data with an underlying multi-view clustering structure. We discuss three paradigms related to this topic:

Subspace clustering: In contrast to traditional full-space clustering, subspace clustering (co-clustering/bi-clustering) [15] assumes that for each cluster an individual subset of attributes might be irrelevant. These locally irrelevant attributes cause an obfuscation of the clustering structure in the full-space, which makes full-space approaches futile. The consideration of attribute subsets is highly related to our multi-view scenario, where different views of the data are most likely reflected by different attributes. However, subspace clustering does neither realize a grouping of clusters to reflect partitionings under several views nor is it aware of the varying competition and dominance of multiple clusters concerning the attribute values of the data. Therefore it does not meet the requirements for multi-view clustering.

Multi-view clustering: The paradigm of multi-view or alternative clustering meets our goal of revealing the cluster structure of multi-faceted data. In [17] three different categories are identified. The first category's representatives, e.g. [14, 2, 10], operate in the full-space and, therefore, suffer from similar problems as traditional clustering. Furthermore, they are usually focused on determining just two alternative clusterings, whereas for complex datasets multiple views can be expected. Approaches from the second category detect clusters in subspace projections [18, 13]. However, [18] cannot handle overlapping views and does not allow individual subspaces per clusters, and [13] does not provide a grouping into views, i.e. the views remain unknown. Approaches of the last category iteratively determine an alternative clustering based on the previous one via space transformations such as PCA [8] or distortion of the distance function [20]. Distortions of the original space like this, usually hinder an intuitive interpretation of the clustering result. Contrarily, axis-parallel projections of the data as for our approach, directly refers to the originating attributes for each cluster.

Model-based clustering: This general paradigm assumes the considered data to be sampled from a statistical model. Several approaches for estimating the parameters of the underlying probability distributions, e.g., to maximize the log-likelihood of the data, were proposed including the EM algorithm and ICM [6, 5]. Model-based clustering is very flexible as the modeled distributions can be arbitrarily complex. Traditionally, such approaches use a *single* mixture distribution (which spans across all dimensions of the data space). Even though each observation might be associated with a membership degree (e.g. the likelihood of belonging to a cluster), such a principle of *soft clustering* does not support the idea of generating objects through multiple components as for the multi-view scenario.

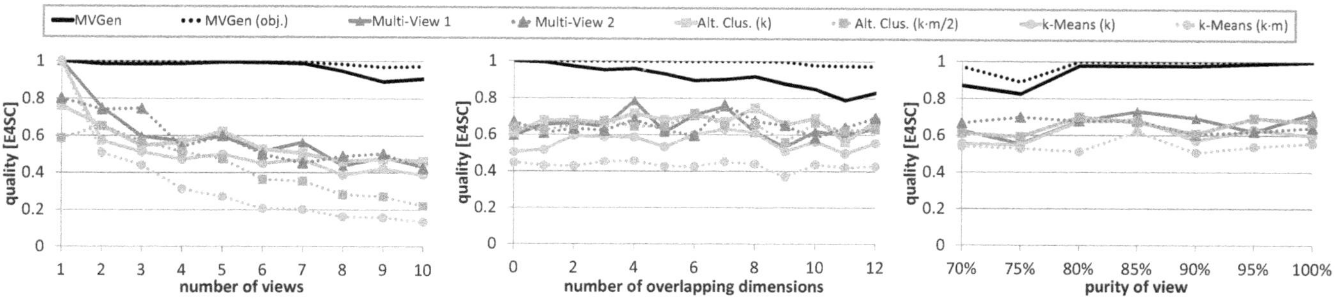

Fig. 4: Varying number of views Fig. 5: Effects of overlapping views Fig. 6: Effects of the views' purity

To overcome this issue, a few models [22, 11, 3] try to represent such multi-component membership (i.e. overlapping clusters). However, they are still not suited for multi-view clustering: They do not consider a grouping of clusters into views, i.e. they do not model that an object takes a single role within a single view but different roles among different views. Instead, these models lead to results where an object might take multiple roles within a single view. Note that global dimensionality reduction and feature selection [19] also do not solve our task: First, we consider multiple views in multiple different subspaces. Second, in our model each cluster is associated with an individual subspace projection.

Overall, none of the existing methods is able to handle multiple views that compete against each other in overlapping dimensions and containing clusters with individual sets of relevant dimensions. Our novel statistical model handles all these aspects.

5. EXPERIMENTAL ANALYSIS

Setup. We compare MVGen with the multi-view clustering techniques *Multi-View 1* and *Multi-View 2* proposed in [8] and with two variants of the *Alternative Clustering* method proposed in [20]. These approaches best reflect the demands for multi-view clustering as discussed in Sec. 4. Additionally, we use two variants of the k-means method.

For case studies on real world data we use the CMUFaces, liver disorders, diabetes, iris and vowel data (all from the UCI repository [1]), and Escher images. Synthetic data containing multiple views is generated based on our generative model. The default data set contains 2 disjoint views, each with 5 clusters, 10 dimensions, 1000 objects, and the clusters' subspaces deviate to the views' dimensions by 5%.

The methods of [8] and MVGen are provided with the number m_{max} of views and the number k_{max} of clusters per view. Since [20] just detects two groupings, we use two variants: 1) The true number of clusters per view is set. In this case the method detects $2 \cdot k_{max}$ clusters. 2) We parametrize the method with $k_{max} \cdot m_{max}/2$. In this case, $k_{max} \cdot m_{max}$ clusters are detected, which matches the overall number of clusters hidden in the data. Similarly, we use for k-means $k{=}k_{max}$ as well as $k = k_{max} \cdot m_{max}$. Runtime is measured on 2.33GHz Intel XEON CPU with 8 GB main memory. Quality is assessed based on the *E4SC* measure [12] used in evaluation of subspace clustering. Since MVGen is the only method performing multi-view *subspace* clustering, we do not evaluate the subspaces of the competing methods but just concentrate on their detected object groupings. To enable a direct comparison of MVGen with these approaches, we also include the results of MVGen if we ignore the subspaces in its evaluation, denoted with 'MVGen (obj.)'.

5.1 Evaluation on Synthetic Data

In Fig. 4 we vary the number of hidden views in the data. The overall dimensionality of the data is 30. As depicted, MVGen is the only approach able to detect the clustering structure in the case of a large number of views. The clustering quality is very high, even if we incorporate the detected subspaces in our evaluation (solid line of MVGen). Obviously, the quality is even higher if we evaluate the object groupings only (dashed line). The competing methods behave differently: while for single-view data the quality is relatively high, their quality heavily decreases with an increasing number of views. Interestingly, for a high number of views, the quality of the two multi-view techniques (depicted by triangles) is not much larger than the quality of the k-means method with $k = k_{max}$. These methods are not well suited to analyze data containing multiple views.

Next, we analyze the potential of our method to detect overlapping views. In Fig. 5 we use a dataset with 12 dimensions containing 3 views. We vary the number of overlapping dimensions, i.e. dimensions that occur in more than one view, until each dimension occurs in two views. As shown, the methods are nearly not influenced by overlapping dimensions. The reason might be that none of the views is completely contained in another one. One is still able to detect the clusters of each view. MVGen detects the object groupings almost perfectly; some of the clusters' relevant dimensions are missed for high overlapping degrees. Note: The good quality of the competing methods is only observed because we just have 3 views in this experiment.

In Fig. 6 we show that MVGen is able to find subspace clusters (located in subspace views). In our model we allow a certain deviation of the clusters' subspaces to the relevant dimensions of their views; here, denoted as the purity. In this experiment, we vary the purity from 70% to 100%. Since each view covers 5 dimensions, a purity of 70% leads to subspace clusters covering now only 3 relevant dimensions. As shown, MVGen succesfully detects the relevant dimensions of each cluster. Since we use a model selection approach, we trade-off the simplicity of the model against its goodness of

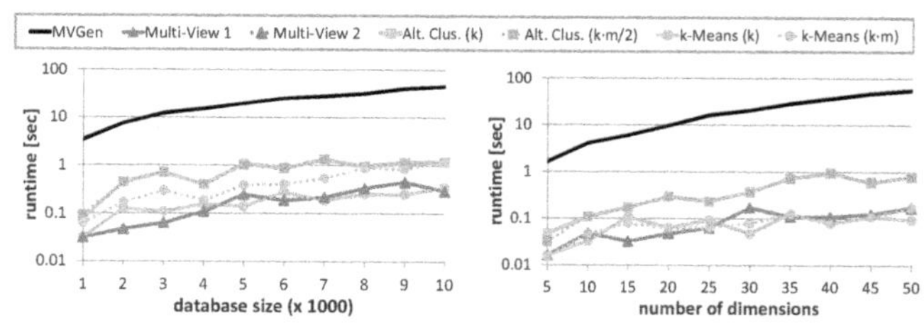

Fig. 7: Runtime vs. database size & dimensionality

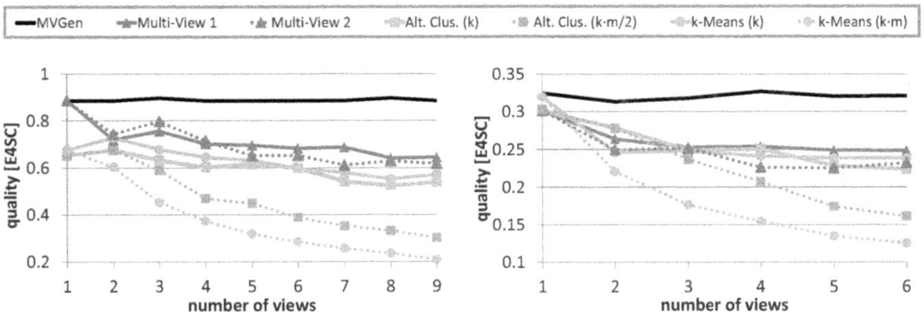

Fig. 8: Quality on iris data

Fig. 9: Quality on vowel data

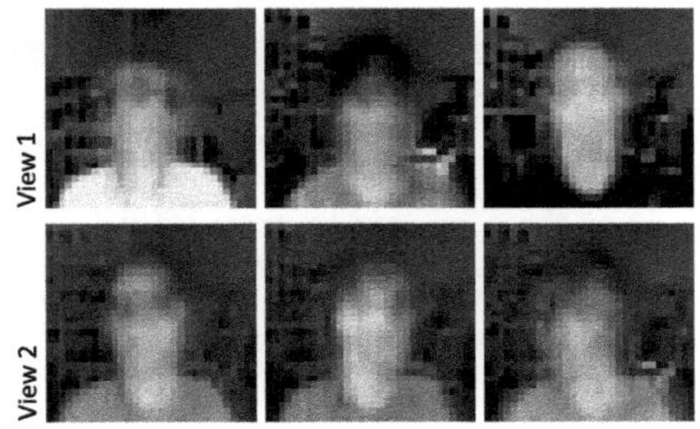

Fig. 10: MVGen on face data

fit. For the competing method no conclusion can be drawn since for their evalution we do not consider subspaces.

Scalability. Even though our focus is on clustering quality, we briefly analyze MVGen's efficiency. In Fig. 7 (left) we increase the number of objects in the database. All methods show increasing runtime and the slopes of the curves are in a similar range. Please note that the two approaches Multi-View 1 & 2 have almost identical runtimes, and, since we use 2 views, the two Alt. Clus. approaches are also identical in their runtimes. Apparently, the absolute runtime of our method is the highest due to the complex model selection phase that trades off relevant and irrelevant dimensions. However, the absolute runtime of MVGen is still low. Furthermore, as we believe, the higher runtime is compensated by the significantly higher clustering quality of MVGen. In Fig. 7 (right) we increase the dimensionality of the data set. We observe a similar behavior as in the previous experiment.

Overall, MVGen shows good scalability and it is the only method simultaneously achieving high clustering qualities.

5.2 Evaluation on Real World Data

For evaluation on real world data we use different evaluation principles, all focusing on the aspect of detecting multiple views. In our first experiment, we extend the datasets iris and vowel to data containing multiple views: for this, we randomly concatenate the attribute values of different objects to a higher dimensional space. The original data sets have dimensionalities of 4 and 10, respectively, while the extension to multi-view data leads to dimensionalities up to $9 \cdot 4 = 36$ (iris) and $6 \cdot 10 = 60$ (vowel), respectively. Figures 8 & 9 show the results: For a small number of views, the quality of some competing approaches is similar to the one of MVGen. However, increasing the number of views leads to decreasing clustering quality for all competing approaches. In contrast, MVGen shows constant quality values; MVGen is not affected by an increasing number of views but detects the different object groupings even for a high number of views. These results for real world data are consistent with the observations made for the synthetic data.

In the next experiment we analyze the clustering result of MVGen on the CMUFace data. This data is interesting for multi-view clustering since it consists of images taken from persons showing varying characteristics as their facial expressions (neutral, happy, sad, angry), head positions (left, right, straight), and eye states (open, sunglasses). As also done in [9], we randomly select 3 persons with all their images and applied PCA retaining at least 90% of the data's variance as a pre-processing. The result of MVGen for two views each with three clusters is illustrated in Fig. 10. The images correspond to the means of each detected cluster. By visual inspection, we can easily find the reason for detecting these two views: The first view, describes the grouping based on the different persons, while the second view, corresponds to a grouping based on their head positions.

Next, we perform an experiment as introduced in [20]. They propose to perform image segmentation on Escher images, which are known to have multiple interpretations to the human eye. For clustering, each pixel is regarded as an object with RGB and HSV values as features. In Fig. 11 (left), such an image is depicted (followed by the three views detected by MVGen). Focusing on the dark regions, there is a segmentation of the image as given by the first view of MVGen. This segmentation is dominant since the dark parts clearly deviate from the orange/yellow parts. However, MVGen is also able to discover the more subtle view where the yellow parts are decoupled from the others. Most interesting is the third view detected by MVGen: it corresponds to only the background of the image. Due to space limitations, we do not show the resulting images of the other methods; though, we observed the following: The work of [20] was only able to detect groupings similar to MVGen's first and second view (as also shown in [20]). Interestingly, the work of [8], which is designed to detect more than 2 views, was only able to find view 1. The detected 'alternative' groupings were all similar. None of the competing methods was able to detect the third, background view.

In our last case study, we want to highlight the benefit of explicitly modeling the relevant subspace for each view as done by MVGen. Knowing the relevant attributes enables us to reason about the views context and to explain the clusters. Table 1 depicts for the liver disorders and diabetes data the detected subspaces of each view. The number of clusters per view was chosen as 2. As shown for the liver disorders data, the two views/clusterings clearly differ from each other (small rand index), and the views do not correspond to the full-dimensional space, i.e. for each view some dimensions are irrelevant. For liver, we observe disjoint views. The first view clearly describes the relation between alcohol consumption and the mean corpuscular volume, while the second view represents the weaker indicators. On the dia-

Liver Disorders Data (rand index between views: 0.25)	
V1	mean corpuscular volume, number of half-pint equivalents of alcoholic beverages drunk per day
V2	alkaline phosphotase, alamine aminotransferase, aspartate aminotransferase, gamma-glutamyl transpeptidase
Diabetes Data (rand index between views: 0.51)	
V1	body mass index, diabetes pedigree function, triceps skin fold thickness, 2-hour serum insulin; (for one cluster: plasma glucose concentration)
V2	age, diastolic blood pressure, # of times pregnant, plasma glucose concentration; (for one cluster: body mass index)

Table 1: Subspace views on liver and diabetes

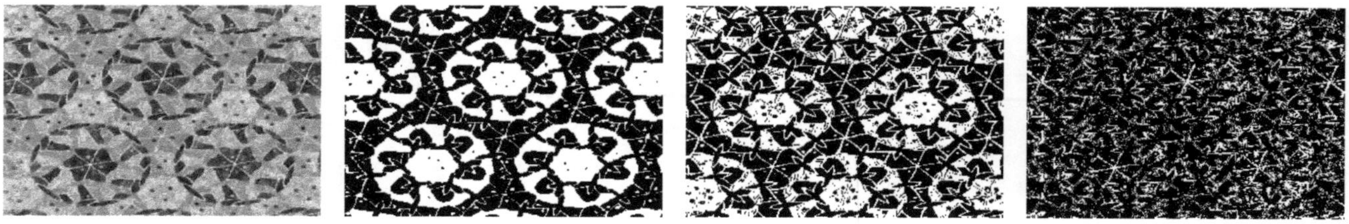

Original image View 1 View 2 View 3

Fig. 11: Result of MVGen on an Escher image

betes data, the detected views match well to some factors causing diabetes of type 1 or type 2 (adult-onset diabetes; also caused by high blood glucose levels during pregnancy). Here, a further interesting observation can be made: Besides finding dissimilar groupings in subspace projections, we now also get slightly overlapping views. E.g., the dimension 'body mass index' is relevant for both clusters in view 1 and for a single cluster in view 2. This result also confirms our hypothesis that the clusters of the *same* view may slightly differ in their relevant dimensions.

Overall, our experiments show that MVGen successfully detects the multi-view clustering structure on a variety of real world data sets.

6. CONCLUSION

Our MVGen approach successfully exploits the model-based clustering paradigm for the multi-view context. Our Bayesian framework accounts for the challenges of multiple, overlapping, and competing mixture distributions for differing views. Since each view reflects specific characteristics of the data, each mixture component is defined in an individual subspace. The comparison of MVGen with competing approaches demonstrated the strengths of detecting views in multiple subspace projections. Our MVGen approach was able to discover multiple clustering views for various real world data sets. Especially the explicit modeling of the views' relevant subspaces has proven to be very valuable for interpreting the final clustering results.

As future work, we plan to extend our method to handle outliers that might occur only in some of the views. Furthermore, we want to address the still open research question how to estimate the number of views hidden in the data.

Acknowledgment. This work has been partly funded by the UMIC Research Centre, RWTH Aachen University, Germany and the DFG grant SE1039/6-1.

7. REFERENCES

[1] A. Asuncion and D. Newman. UCI machine learning repository, http://archive.ics.uci.edu/ml, 2010.

[2] E. Bae and J. Bailey. Coala: A novel approach for the extraction of an alternate clustering of high quality and high dissimilarity. In *ICDM*, pages 53–62, 2006.

[3] A. Banerjee, C. Krumpelman, J. Ghosh, S. Basu, and R. J. Mooney. Model-based overlapping clustering. In *KDD*, pages 532–537, 2005.

[4] R. J. Beckman and G. L. Tietjen. Maximum likelihood estimation for the beta distribution. *Journal of Statistical Computation and Simulation*, 7(3-4):253–258, 1978.

[5] J. Besag. On the statistical analysis of dirty pictures. *Journal of the Royal Statistical Society. Series B (Methodological)*, 48(3):259–302, 1986.

[6] C. Bishop. *Pattern recognition and machine learning*, volume 4. Springer, 2006.

[7] R. Brent. *Algorithms for Minimization Without Derivatives.* Dover, 2002.

[8] Y. Cui, X. Z. Fern, and J. G. Dy. Non-redundant multi-view clustering via orthogonalization. In *ICDM*, pages 133–142, 2007.

[9] X. H. Dang and J. Bailey. Generation of alternative clusterings using the cami approach. In *SDM*, pages 118–129, 2010.

[10] X. H. Dang and J. Bailey. A hierarchical information theoretic technique for the discovery of non linear alternative clusterings. In *KDD*, pages 573–582, 2010.

[11] Q. Fu and A. Banerjee. Multiplicative mixture models for overlapping clustering. In *ICDM*, pages 791–796, 2008.

[12] S. Günnemann, I. Färber, E. Müller, I. Assent, and T. Seidl. External evaluation measures for subspace clustering. In *CIKM*, pages 1363–1372, 2011.

[13] S. Günnemann, E. Müller, I. Färber, and T. Seidl. Detection of orthogonal concepts in subspaces of high dimensional data. In *CIKM*, pages 1317–1326, 2009.

[14] P. Jain, R. Meka, and I. S. Dhillon. Simultaneous unsupervised learning of disparate clusterings. *SADM*, 1(3):195–210, 2008.

[15] H.-P. Kriegel, P. Kröger, and A. Zimek. Clustering high-dimensional data: A survey on subspace clustering, pattern-based clustering, and correlation clustering. *TKDD*, 3(1), 2009.

[16] G. J. McLachlan and T. Krishnan. *The EM algorithm and extensions.* Wiley, 1996.

[17] E. Müller, S. Günnemann, I. Färber, and T. Seidl. Discovering multiple clustering solutions: Grouping objects in different views of the data. In *ICDM*, 2010.

[18] D. Niu, J. G. Dy, and M. I. Jordan. Multiple non-redundant spectral clustering views. In *ICML*, pages 831–838, 2010.

[19] L. K. M. Poon, N. L. Zhang, T. Chen, and Y. Wang. Variable selection in model-based clustering: To do or to facilitate. In *ICML*, pages 887–894, 2010.

[20] Z. Qi and I. Davidson. A principled and flexible framework for finding alternative clusterings. In *KDD*, pages 717–726, 2009.

[21] G. Schwarz. Estimating the dimension of a model. *The annals of statistics*, 6(2):461–464, 1978.

[22] M. Somaiya, C. M. Jermaine, and S. Ranka. Mixture models for learning low-dimensional roles in high-dimensional data. In *KDD*, pages 909–918, 2010.

[23] J. Wu, H. Xiong, and J. Chen. Adapting the right measures for k-means clustering. In *KDD*, pages 877–886, 2009.

A Simple Methodology for Soft Cost-sensitive Classification

Te-Kang Jan
Institute of Information Science, Academia Sinica, Taipei, Taiwan
tekang@iis.sinica.edu.tw

Da-Wei Wang
Institute of Information Science, Academia Sinica, Taipei, Taiwan
wdw@iis.sinica.edu.tw

Chi-Hung Lin
Institute of Microbiology and Immunology, National Yang-Ming University, Taipei, Taiwan
linch@ym.edu.tw

Hsuan-Tien Lin
Department of Computer Science and Information Engineering, National Taiwan University, Taipei, Taiwan
htlin@csie.ntu.edu.tw

ABSTRACT

Many real-world data mining applications need varying cost for different types of classification errors and thus call for cost-sensitive classification algorithms. Existing algorithms for cost-sensitive classification are successful in terms of minimizing the cost, but can result in a high error rate as the trade-off. The high error rate holds back the practical use of those algorithms. In this paper, we propose a novel cost-sensitive classification methodology that takes both the cost and the error rate into account. The methodology, called soft cost-sensitive classification, is established from a multicriteria optimization problem of the cost and the error rate, and can be viewed as regularizing cost-sensitive classification with the error rate. The simple methodology allows immediate improvements of existing cost-sensitive classification algorithms. Experiments on the benchmark and the real-world data sets show that our proposed methodology indeed achieves lower test error rates and similar (sometimes lower) test costs than existing cost-sensitive classification algorithms.

Categories and Subject Descriptors

I.2.6 [**Artificial Intelligence**]: Learning; H.2.8 [**Database Management**]: Database Applications—*Data mining*

Keywords

Classification, Cost-sensitive learning, Multicriteria optimization, Regularization

1. INTRODUCTION

Classification is important for machine learning and data mining [16,17]. Traditionally, the regular classification problem aims at minimizing the rate of misclassification errors. In many real-world applications, however, different types of errors are often charged with different costs. For instance, in bacteria classification, mis-classifying a Gram-positive species as a Gram-negative one leads to totally ineffective treatments and is hence more serious than misclassifying a Gram-positive species as another Gram-positive one [24,31]. Similar application needs are shared by targeted marketing, information retrieval, medical decision making, object recognition and intrusion detection [1, 14, 15, 26, 33, 34], and can be formalized as the cost-sensitive classification problem. In fact, cost-sensitive classification can be used to express any finite-choice and bounded-loss supervised learning problems [5]. Thus, it has been attracting much research attention in recent years, in terms of both new algorithms and new applications [4, 6, 23, 24, 27, 34, 36].

Studies in cost-sensitive classification often reveal a trade-off between costs and error rates [23, 27, 36]. Mature regular classification algorithms can achieve significantly lower error rates than their cost-sensitive counterparts, but result in higher expected costs; state-of-the-art cost-sensitive classification algorithms can reach significantly lower expected cost than their regular classification counterparts, but are often at the expense of higher error rates. In addition, cost-sensitive classification algorithms are "sensitive" to large cost components and can thus be conservative or even "paranoid" in order to avoid making any big mistakes. The sensitivity makes cost-sensitive classification algorithms prone to overfitting the data or the costs. In fact, it has been observed that for some simpler classification tasks, cost-sensitive classification algorithms are inferior to regular classification ones in terms of even the expected test cost because of the overfitting [27, 36].

The expense of high error rates and the potential risk of overfitting holds back the practical use of cost-sensitive classification algorithms. Arguably, applications call for classifiers that can reach low costs *and* low error rates. The task of obtaining such a classifier has been studied for binary cost-sensitive classifier [30], but the more general task for multi-class cost-sensitive classification is yet to be tackled.

In this paper, we propose a methodology to tackle the task. The methodology takes both the costs and the error rates into account and matches the realistic needs better. We name the methodology *soft cost-sensitive classification* to distinguish it from existing *hard cost-sensitive classification* algorithms that focus on only the costs. The methodology is designed by formulating the associated problem as a multicriteria optimization task [19]: one criterion being the cost and the other being the error rate. Then, the methodology solves the task by the weighted sum approach for multicriteria optimization [38]. The simplicity of the weighted sum approach allows immediate reuse of modern cost-sensitive classification algorithms as the core tool. In other words, with our proposed methodology, promising (hard) cost-sensitive classification algorithms can be immediately improved via soft cost-sensitive classification, with performance guarantees on costs and error rates supported by the theory behind multicriteria optimization.

We conduct experiments to validate the performance of the proposed methodology on the benchmark and the real-world data sets. Experimental results suggest that soft cost-sensitive classification can indeed achieve both low costs and low error rates. In particular, soft cost-sensitive classification algorithms out-perform regular ones in terms of the test costs on most of the data sets. In addition, soft cost-sensitive classification algorithms reach significantly lower test error rates than their hard siblings, while achieving similar (sometimes better) test costs. The observations are consistent across four different sets of tasks: the traditional benchmark tasks in cost-sensitive classification for balancing class influences [12], new benchmark tasks designed for examining the effect of using large cost components, the real-world medical task for classifying bacteria [24], and the real-world task for intrusion detection in KDD Cup 1999 [3].

The paper is organized as follows. We formally introduce the regular and the cost-sensitive classification problems in Section 2, and discuss related works on cost-sensitive classification. Then, we present the proposed methodology of soft cost-sensitive classification in Section 3. We discuss the empirical performance of the proposed methodology on the benchmark and the real-world data sets in Section 4. Finally, we conclude in Section 5.

2. COST-SENSITIVE CLASSIFICATION

We shall start by defining the regular classification problem and extend it to the cost-sensitive one. Then, we briefly review existing works on cost-sensitive classification.

In the regular classification problem, we are given a training set $\mathcal{S} = \{(\mathbf{x}_n, y_n)\}_{n=1}^N$, where the input vector $\mathbf{x}_n$ belongs to some domain $\mathcal{X} \subseteq \mathbb{R}^D$, the label y_n comes from the set $\mathcal{Y} = \{1, \ldots, K\}$ and each example $(\mathbf{x}_n, y_n)$ is drawn independently from an unknown distribution $\mathcal{D}$ on $\mathcal{X} \times \mathcal{Y}$. The task of regular classification is to use the training set $\mathcal{S}$ to find a classifier $g \colon \mathcal{X} \to \mathcal{Y}$ such that the expected error rate $E(g) = \mathop{\mathcal{E}}\limits_{(\mathbf{x},y)\sim\mathcal{D}} [\![y \neq g(\mathbf{x})]\!]$ is small,[1] where the expected error rate $E(g)$ penalizes every type of mis-classification error equally.

[1]The Boolean operation $[\![\cdot]\!]$ is 1 when the argument is true and 0 otherwise.

Cost-sensitive classification extends regular classification by charging different costs for different types of classification errors. We adopt the example-dependent setting of cost-sensitive classification, which is rather general and can be used to express other popular settings [6, 23, 25, 27, 36]. The example-dependent setting couples each example $(\mathbf{x}, y)$ with a cost vector $\mathbf{c} \in [0, \infty)^K$, where the k-th component of $\mathbf{c}$ quantifies the cost for predicting the example $\mathbf{x}$ as class k. The cost $\mathbf{c}[y]$ of the intended class y is naturally assumed to be 0, the minimum cost. Consider a cost-sensitive training set $\mathcal{S}_c = \{(\mathbf{x}_n, y_n, \mathbf{c}_n)\}_{n=1}^N$, where each cost-sensitive training example $(\mathbf{x}_n, y_n, \mathbf{c}_n)$ is drawn independently from an unknown cost-sensitive distribution $\mathcal{D}_c$ on $\mathcal{X} \times \mathcal{Y} \times [0, \infty)^K$, the task of cost-sensitive classification is to use $\mathcal{S}_c$ to find a classifier $g \colon \mathcal{X} \to \mathcal{Y}$ such that the expected cost $E_c(g) = \mathop{\mathcal{E}}\limits_{(\mathbf{x},y,\mathbf{c})\sim\mathcal{D}_c} \mathbf{c}[g(\mathbf{x})]$ is small.

One special case of the example-dependent setting is the class-dependent setting, in which the cost vectors $\mathbf{c}$ are taken from the y-th row of a cost matrix $\mathbf{C} \colon \mathcal{Y} \times \mathcal{Y} \to [0, \infty)^K$. Each entry $\mathbf{C}(y, k)$ of the cost matrix represents the cost for predicting a class-y example as class k. The special case is commonly used in some applications and some benchmark experiments [23, 24, 27].

Regular classification can be viewed as a special case of the class-dependent setting, which is in term a special case of the example-dependent setting. In particular, take a cost matrix that contains 0 in the diagonals and 1 elsewhere, which equivalently corresponds to the regular cost vectors $\bar{\mathbf{c}}_y$ with entries $\bar{\mathbf{c}}_y[k] = [\![y \neq k]\!]$. Then, the expected cost $E_c(g)$ with respect to $\{\bar{\mathbf{c}}_y\}$ is the same as the expected error rate $E(g)$. In other words, regular classification algorithms can be viewed as "wiping out" the given cost information and replacing it with a naïve cost matrix. Intuitively, such algorithms may not work well for cost-sensitive classification because of the wiping out.

The intuition leads to the past decade of studying cost-sensitive classification algorithms that respect the cost information during training and/or prediction. The cost-sensitive classification algorithms can be grouped into two categories: the binary ($K = 2$) cases and the multiclass ($K > 2$) cases. Binary cost-sensitive classification is well-understood in theory and in practice. In particular, every binary cost-sensitive classification problem can be reduced to a binary regular classification one by re-weighting the examples based on the costs [13, 39]. Multiclass cost-sensitive classification, however, is more difficult than the binary one, and is an ongoing research topic.

MetaCost [12] is one of the earliest multiclass cost-sensitive classification algorithms. It makes any regular classification algorithm cost-sensitive by re-labeling the training examples. Somehow the re-labeling procedure depends on an overly-ideal assumption, which makes it hard to rigorously analyze the performance of MetaCost in theory. Many other early approaches suffer from similar shortcomings [29].

In order to design multiclass cost-sensitive classification algorithms with stronger theoretical guarantees, modern cost-sensitive classification algorithms are mostly reduction-based, which allows not only reusing mature existing algorithms for cost-sensitive classification, but also extending existing theoretical results to the area of cost-sensitive classification. For instance, [1] reduces the multiclass cost-sensitive classification problem into several multiclass regular classification

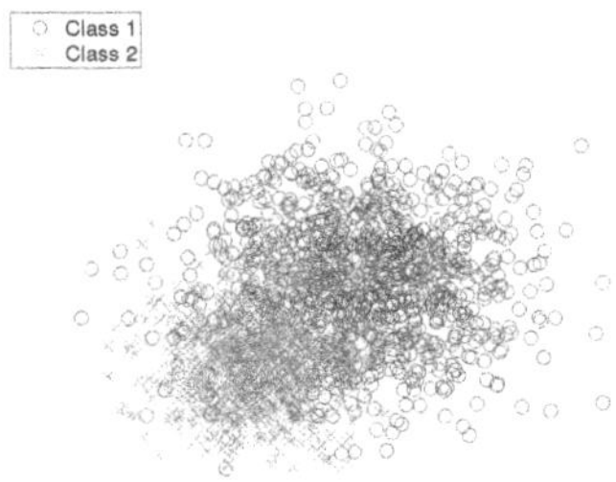

Figure 1: a two-dimensional artificial data set

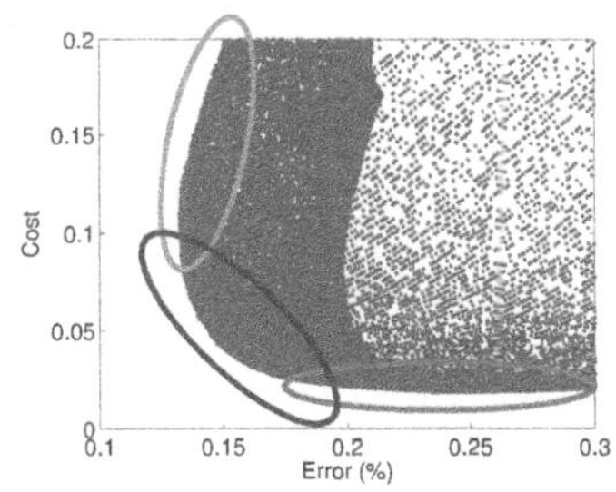

Figure 2: the different goals of regular (green), cost-sensitive (red) and soft cost-sensitive (blue) classification algorithms

problems using a boosting-style method and some intermediate traditional classifiers. The reduction is somehow too sophisticated for practical use. [40] derives another reduction approach from multiclass cost-sensitive classification to multiclass regular classification based on re-weighting with the solution to a linear system. The proposed reduction approach works with sound theoretical guarantees when the linear system attains a non-trivial solution; otherwise the approach decomposes the multiclass cost-sensitive classification problem to several binary classification problems to get an approximate solution [40].

There are many more studies on reducing multiclass cost-sensitive classification to binary cost-sensitive classification by decomposing the multiclass problem with a suitable structure and embedding the cost vectors into the weights for the re-weighted binary classification problems. For instance, cost-sensitive one-versus-one (CSOVO; [27]) and weighted all-pair (WAP; [5]) are based on pairwise comparisons of the classes. Another leading approach within the family is cost-sensitive filter tree (CSFT; [6]), which is based on a single-elimination tournament of competing classes.

Yet another family of approaches reduce the multiclass cost-sensitive classification problem into regression ones by embedding the cost vectors in the real-valued labels instead of the weights [35]. A promising representative of the family is to reduce to one-sided regression (OSR; [36]). Based on some earlier comparisons on general benchmark data sets [23,36], OSR, CSOVO and CSFT are some of the leading algorithms that can reach state-of-the-art performance. Each algorithm corresponds to a popular sibling for regular classification. In particular, the common one-versus-all decomposition (OVA) [21] is the special case of OSR, the one-versus-one decomposition (OVO) [21] is the special case of CSOVO, and the modern filter tree decomposition (FT) [6] is the special case of CSFT. The regular classification algorithms, OVA, OVO and FT, do not consider any costs during their training. On the other hand, the cost-sensitive ones, OSR, CSOVO and CSFT, respect the costs faithfully during their training.

3. SOFT COST-SENSITIVE CLASSIFICATION

The difference between regular and cost-sensitive classification is illustrated with a binary and two-dimensional artificial data set shown in Figure 1. Class 1 is generated from a Gaussian distribution of standard deviation $\frac{4}{5}$; class 2 is generated from a Gaussian distribution of standard deviation $\frac{1}{2}$; the centers of the two classes are of $\sqrt{2}$ apart. We consider a cost matrix of $\begin{bmatrix} 0 & 1 \\ 30 & 0 \end{bmatrix}$. Then, we enumerate many linear classifiers in $\mathbb{R}^2$ and evaluate their average errors and average costs. The results are plotted in Figure 2. Each black point represents the achieved (error, cost) of one linear classifier.[2] We can see that there is a region of low-cost linear classifiers, as circled in red. There is also a region of low-error linear classifiers, as circled in green. Modern cost-sensitive classification algorithms are designed to seek for *something* in the red region, which contains classifiers with a wide range of different errors Traditional regular classification algorithms, on the other hand, are designed to locate something in the green region (without using the cost information), which is far from the lowest achievable cost. In other words, there is a trade-off between the cost and the error, while cost-sensitive and regular classification each takes the trade-off to the extreme.

Figure 2 motivates us to study the methodology for aiming at the blue region instead. The region does not take the trade-off between the cost and the error to the extreme, and contains classifiers that are of low cost *and* low error. Those classifiers match the real-world application needs better, with the cost being the subjective measure of performance and the error being the objective safety-check. The blue region improves the green one (regular) by taking the cost into account; the blue region also improves the red one (cost-sensitive) by keeping the error under control. The three regions, as depicted, are not meant to be disjoint. The blue region may contain the better cost-sensitive classifiers in its intersection with the green region, and the better regular classifiers in its intersection with the red region.

Figure 2 results from a simple artificial data set for the illustrative purpose. When applying more sophisticated classifiers on real-world data sets, the set of achievable (error, cost) may be of a more complicated shape—possibly non-convex, for instance. Somehow the essence of the problem remains the same: cost-sensitive classification only knocks down the cost and results in a red region at the bottom; regular classification only considers the error and lands on a green region at the left; our proposed methodology focuses on a blue region at the left-bottom, hopefully achieving the better for both criteria.

Formally speaking, regular classification algorithm is a process from $\mathcal{S}$ to g such that $E(g)$ is small. Cost-sensitive classification algorithm, on the other hand, is a process from $\mathcal{S}_c$ to g such that $E_c(g)$ is small. We now want a process

[2]Ideally, the points should be dense. The uncrowded part comes from simulating with a finite enumeration process.

from $\mathcal{S}_c$ to g such that both $E(g)$ and $E_c(g)$ are small, which can be written as

$$\min_g \mathbf{E}(g) = [E_c(g), E(g)] \text{ subject to all feasible } g. \quad (1)$$

The vector $\mathbf{E}$ represents the two criteria of interest.

Such a problem belongs to multicriteria optimization [19], which deals with multiple objective functions. The general form of multicriteria optimization is

$$\min_g \mathbf{F}(g) = [F_1(g), F_2(g), \ldots, F_M(g)] \quad \text{subject to all feasible } g, \quad (2)$$

where M is the number of criteria. For a multicriteria optimization problem (2), often there is no global optimal solution g^* that is the best in terms of every dimension (criterion) within $\mathbf{F}$. Instead, the goal of (2) is to seek for the set of "better" solutions, usually referred to as the Pareto-optimal front [20]. Formally speaking, consider two feasible candidates g_1 and g_2. The candidate g_1 is said to *dominate* g_2 if $F_m(g_1) \leq F_m(g_2)$ for all m while $F_i(g_1) < F_i(g_2)$ for some i. The Pareto-optimal front is the set of all non-dominated solutions [19].

Solving the multicriteria optimization problem is not an easy task, and there are many sophisticated techniques, including evolutionary algorithms like Non-dominated Sorting Genetic Algorithms [11] and Strength Pareto Evolutionary [9]. One important family of techniques is to transform the problem to a single-criterion optimization one that we are more familiar with. A simple yet popular approach of the family considers a non-negative linear combination of all the criteria F_m, which is called the weighted sum approach [38]. In particular, the weighted sum approach solves the following optimization problem:

$$\min_g \sum_{m=1}^{M} \alpha_m F_m(g) \text{ subject to all feasible } g, \quad (3)$$

where $\alpha_m \geq 0$ is the weight (importance) of the m-th criterion. By varying the values of α_m, the weighted sum approach identifies *some* of the solutions that are on the tangential of the Pareto-optimal front [19]. The drawback of the approach [10] is that *not all* the solutions within the Pareto-optimal front can be found when the achievable set of $\mathbf{F}(g)$ is non-convex.

We can reach the goal of getting a low-cost and low-error classifier by formulating a multicriteria optimization problem with $M = 2$, $F_1(g) = E_c(g)$ and $F_2(g) = E(g)$. Without loss of generality, let $\alpha_1 = 1 - \alpha$ and $\alpha_2 = \alpha$ for $\alpha \in [0, 1]$, the weighted sum approach solves

$$\min_g (1-\alpha)E_c(g) + \alpha E(g), \quad (4)$$

which is the same as

$$\min_g \mathop{\mathcal{E}}_{(\mathbf{x},y,\mathbf{c})\sim\mathcal{D}_c} (1-\alpha)\Big(\mathbf{c}[g(\mathbf{x})]\Big) + \alpha\Big(\bar{\mathbf{c}}_y[g(\mathbf{x})]\Big) \quad (5)$$

with the regular cost vectors $\bar{\mathbf{c}}_y$ defined in Section 2. For any given α, such an optimization problem is exactly a cost-sensitive classification one with modified cost vectors $\tilde{\mathbf{c}} = (1-\alpha)\mathbf{c} + \alpha\bar{\mathbf{c}}_y$. Then, modern cost-sensitive classification algorithms can be applied to locate a decent g, which would belong to the Pareto-optimal front with respect to $E_c(g)$ and $E(g)$.

The weighted sum approach has also been implicitly taken by other algorithms in machine learning. For instance, [32] combines the pairwise ranking criterion and squared regression criterion and shows that the resulting algorithm achieves the best performance on both criteria. Our proposed methodology similarly utilizes the simplicity of the weighted sum approach to allow seamless reuse of modern cost-sensitive classification algorithms. If other techniques for multicriteria optimization (such as evolutionary computation) are taken instead, new algorithms need to be designed to accompany the techniques. Given the prevalence of promising cost-sensitive classification algorithms (see Section 2), we thus choose to study only the weighted sum approach.

The parameter α in (4) can be intuitively explained as a soft control of the trade-off between costs and errors, with $\alpha = 0$ and $\alpha = 1$ being the two extremes. The traditional (hard) cost-sensitive classification problem is a special case of soft cost-sensitive classification with $\alpha = 0$. On the other hand, the regular classification problem is a special case of soft cost-sensitive classification with $\alpha = 1$.

Another explanation behind (4) is regularization. From Figure 2, there are many low-cost classifiers in the red region. When picking one classifier using only the limited information in the training set $\mathcal{S}_c$, the classifier can be overfitting. The added term $\alpha E(g)$ can be viewed as restricting the number of low-cost classifiers by only favoring those with lower error rates. This similar explanation can be found from [30], which considers cost-sensitive classification in the binary case. Furthermore, the restriction is similar to common regularization schemes, where a penalty term on complexity is used to limit the number of candidate classifiers [2].

We illustrate the regularization property of soft-sensitive classification with the data set vowel as an example. The details of the experimental procedures will be introduced in Section 4. The test cost of soft cost-sensitive classification with various α when coupled with the one-sided regression (OSR) algorithm is shown in Figure 3. For this data set, the lowest test cost does not happen at $\alpha = 0$ (hard cost-sensitive) nor $\alpha = 1$ (non cost-sensitive). By choosing the regularization parameter α appropriately, some intermediate, non-zero values of α (soft cost-sensitive) could lead to better test performance. The figure reveals the potential of soft cost-sensitive classification not only to improve the test error with the added $\alpha E(g)$ term during optimization, but also to possibly improve the test cost with the effect of regularization.

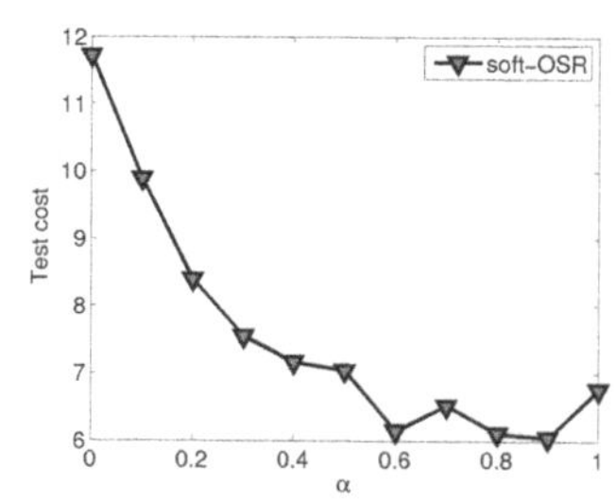

Figure 3: the effect of the regularization parameter α on soft cost-sensitive classification

4. EXPERIMENTS

In this section, we set up experiments to validate the usefulness of the proposed methodology of soft cost-sensitive classification in various scenarios. We take three state-of-the-art multiclass cost-sensitive classification algorithms (see Section 2). Then we examine if the proposed methodology can improve them. The three algorithms are one-sided regression (OSR), cost-sensitive one-versus-one (CSOVO) and cost-sensitive filter tree (CSFT). We also include their regular classification siblings, one-versus-all (OVA), one-versus-one (OVO), and filter tree (FT) for comparisons. The other state-of-the-art multiclass cost-sensitive classification algorithms would also be compared in the longer version of this paper.

We couple all the algorithms with the support vector machine (SVM) [37] with the perceptron kernel [28] as the internal learner for the reduced problem, and take LIBSVM [8] as the SVM solver.[3] The regularization parameter λ of SVM is chosen within $\{2^{10}, 2^{7}, \ldots, 2^{-2}\}$ and the parameter α for soft cost-sensitive classification is chosen within $\{0, 0.1, \ldots, 1\}$. For the hard or soft cost-sensitive classification algorithms, the best parameter setting is chosen by minimizing the 5-fold cross-validation cost. For the regular classification algorithms, which are not supposed to access any cost information in training or in validation, the best parameter λ is chosen by minimizing the 5-fold cross-validation error.

We consider four sets of tasks: the traditional benchmark tasks for balancing the influence of each class, new benchmark tasks for emphasizing some of the classes, a real-world biomedical task for classifying bacteria (see Section 1) and the KDD Cup 1999 task for the intrusion detection. The four sets of broad tasks will demonstrate that soft cost-sensitive classification is useful both as a general algorithmic methodology and as specific application tools.

4.1 Comparison on Benchmark Tasks

Twenty-two real-world data sets (iris, wine, glass, vehicle, vowel, segment, dna, satimage, usps, zoo ,yeast, pageblock, anneal, solar, splice, ecoli, nursery, soybean, arrhythmia, optdigits, mfeat, pendigit) are used in our experiment. To the best of our knowledge, our experiment is the most extensive empirical study on cost-sensitive classification in terms of the number of data sets taken. All data sets come from the UCI Machine Learning Repository [18] except usps [22]. In each run of the experiment, we randomly separate each data set with 75% of the examples for training and the rest 25% for testing. All the input vectors in the training set are linearly scaled to $[0, 1]$ and then the input vectors in the test set are scaled accordingly.

The data sets do not contain any cost information and we make them cost-sensitive by adopting the randomized proportional benchmark that was similarly used by [5, 27, 36]. In particular, the benchmark is class-dependent and is based on a cost matrix $\mathbf{C}(y, k)$, where the diagonal entries $\mathbf{C}(y, y)$ are 0, and the other entries $\mathbf{C}(y, k)$ are uniformly sampled from $\left[0, \frac{|\{n: y_n = k\}|}{|\{n: y_n = y\}|}\right]$. This means that mis-classifying a rare class as a frequent one is of a high cost in expectation. In other words, the benchmark can be used to balance the influence of each class. We further scale every $\mathbf{C}(y, k)$ to $[0, 1]$ by dividing it with the largest component in $\mathbf{C}$. We then record the average test costs and their standard errors for all algorithms over 20 random runs in Table 1. We also report the average test errors in Table 2.

From Table 1, soft-OSR and soft-CSOVO usually result in the lowest test cost. Most importantly, soft-OSR is among the best algorithms (bold) on 17 of the 22 data sets, and achieves the lowest cost on 8 of them. The follow-ups, OSR and CSOVO, were the state-of-the-art algorithms in cost-sensitive classification and reach promising performance often. Filter-tree-based algorithms (FT, CSFT, soft-CSFT) are generally falling behind, and so are the regular classification algorithms (OVA, OVO, FT). The results justify that soft cost-sensitive classification can lead to similar and sometimes even better performance when compared with state-of-art cost-sensitive classification algorithms.

On the other hand, when we move to Table 2, regular classification algorithms like OVA and OVO generally achieve the lowest test errors. The hard cost-sensitive classification ones result in the highest test errors; soft ones lie in between.

Overall, soft cost-sensitive classification is better than the regular sibling in terms of the cost, the major criterion. It is similar to (sometimes better than) the hard sibling in terms of the cost, but usually better in terms of the error. We further justify the claims above by comparing the average test cost between soft cost-sensitive classification algorithms with their corresponding siblings for regular classification and hard cost-sensitive classification using a pairwise one-tailed t-test of significance level 0.1, as shown in Table 3. For each family of algorithms (OVA, OVO or FT), soft cost-sensitive classification algorithms are generally among the best of the three, and are significantly better than their regular siblings.

Table 4 shows the same t-test for comparing the test errors between soft cost-sensitive classification algorithms and their hard siblings. We see that soft-OSR improves OSR on 16 of the 22 data sets in terms of the test error; soft-CSOVO improves CSOVO on 13 of the 22; soft-CSFT improves CSFT on 14 of the 22. Given the similar test costs between soft and hard cost-sensitive classification algorithms in Table 3, the significant improvements on the test error justify that soft cost-sensitive classification algorithms are better choices for practical applications.

4.2 Comparison on New Benchmark Tasks: Emphasizing Cost

Next, we explore the usefulness of the algorithms with a different benchmark for generating the costs. Consider a situation where one hopes to indicate some of the classes is important. Traditionally, this task is done with re-weighting the examples of those classes, which corresponds to scaling the rows of the cost matrix. As discussed in Section 2, cost-sensitive classification is more sophisticated than re-weighting. In particular, it allows us to mark important classes by scaling up some *columns* of the cost matrix. In our benchmark, we scale up one random column of the regular cost matrix (that contains $\bar{\mathbf{c}}_y$) by an emphasis parameter w, and we call the benchmark *emphasizing cost*.

We vary the the emphasis parameter w between $\{10^2, 10^3, \ldots, 10^6\}$ to examine the stability of the algorithms when using large cost components. The results are shown in Figure 4. Due to the page limits, we only report the results of OSR and soft-OSR on iris, vehicle, and segment. Results on other data sets are similar and will be reported in a longer

[3]We use the cost-sensitive SVM implementation at http://www.csie.ntu.edu.tw/~htlin/program/cssvm/

Table 1: average test cost ($\cdot 10^{-3}$) on benchmark data sets

data set	OVA	OSR	soft-OSR	OVO	CSOVO	soft-CSOVO	FT	CSFT	soft-CSFT
iris	**18.34±4.48**	**17.21±3.84**	**18.79±3.72**	21.93±4.99	20.74±4.32	19.89±4.24	23.80±5.21	19.54±4.67	**15.94±3.26***
wine	**12.98±3.37**	**13.42±2.55**	**14.34±2.76**	15.04±4.05	**11.45±3.53***	**12.95±4.15**	15.21±3.49	**11.87±3.09**	**13.66±4.14**
glass	159.19±10.37	**126.84±9.71***	**129.42±9.51**	145.90±10.36	**128.56±9.77**	**132.69±9.62**	151.06±10.20	143.78±8.66	143.22±9.85
vehicle	114.14±9.08	**95.33±10.29***	**97.81±10.85**	112.31±8.82	**103.63±11.17**	**97.34±11.16**	112.48±7.71	**105.58±10.90**	106.74±11.27
vowel	**6.76±0.93**	11.72±1.44	**6.43±1.11**	**6.29±0.94***	9.58±1.08	**6.82±0.90**	9.53±1.31	13.71±1.58	11.87±1.47
segment	**14.02±1.17**	**13.84±0.94**	**13.03±1.08***	14.15±1.18	**14.00±1.11**	**14.10±1.31**	15.01±1.33	14.17±1.15	15.36±1.26
dna	24.43±1.26	24.40±1.55	**22.76±1.47***	24.51±1.37	28.26±2.04	24.51±1.52	27.94±2.34	31.49±2.09	29.23±2.28
satimage	40.20±2.08	**35.04±2.16**	**34.86±2.11***	40.43±1.92	**36.49±2.27**	**36.46±2.31**	41.98±2.08	40.16±2.10	39.63±2.23
usps	6.87±0.28	7.32±0.23	**6.58±0.27***	7.08±0.27	7.20±0.26	6.98±0.25	9.05±0.29	8.97±0.40	8.59±0.27
zoo	8.59±1.81	10.14±1.29	7.22±1.16	9.35±1.87	**5.91±1.15**	**6.56±1.37**	8.68±1.77	**6.56±1.27**	8.70±1.71
yeast	36.66±3.37	**0.58±0.07**	**0.58±0.07**	39.71±3.62	**0.55±0.08***	**0.55±0.08**	38.97±3.88	**0.62±0.09**	0.64±0.09
pageblock	2.80±0.48	0.18±0.04	0.19±0.04	2.59±0.45	**0.16±0.03**	**0.16±0.03**	2.78±0.48	**0.16±0.03**	**0.16±0.03***
anneal	0.85±0.23	**0.35±0.12***	**0.38±0.13**	0.83±0.23	0.61±0.16	0.67±0.17	0.85±0.23	0.58±0.16	0.65±0.16
solar	46.08±6.53	25.35±4.06	25.32±4.05	44.51±6.31	**18.04±1.94**	**17.89±1.95***	47.18±7.14	20.54±2.64	20.43±2.06
splice	14.01±0.84	**12.59±1.11***	**12.85±0.71**	13.97±0.76	17.06±1.26	**13.28±0.88**	16.64±0.79	18.19±1.62	16.06±1.17
ecoli	17.11±2.85	1.27±0.31	**0.92±0.18**	19.93±2.61	1.35±0.49	1.11±0.41	20.43±4.49	**0.85±0.14***	1.96±1.13
nursery	0.62±0.20	**0.00±0.00**	**0.00±0.00***	0.07±0.06	0.00±0.00	0.00±0.00	1.42±0.45	0.00±0.00	0.39±0.34
soybean	9.84±1.60	2.78±0.36	2.99±0.43	11.41±1.85	**2.13±0.29**	**2.08±0.30***	9.61±1.57	3.07±0.52	3.97±0.55
arrhythmia	6.46±1.23	0.55±0.08	0.63±0.08	7.32±1.48	**0.36±0.05***	**0.37±0.05**	8.69±1.78	0.57±0.19	0.55±0.17
optdigits	5.33±0.34	5.64±0.26	**4.90±0.35***	**4.98±0.26**	6.12±0.32	**5.23±0.31**	6.23±0.34	7.67±0.43	6.57±0.35
mfeat	**7.99±0.55**	9.27±0.74	**7.56±0.55***	8.74±0.59	8.36±0.61	8.70±0.64	11.74±0.76	11.23±0.89	10.87±0.83
pendigit	1.99±0.11	2.46±0.12	**1.88±0.09***	**1.88±0.10**	**1.95±0.08**	**1.95±0.08**	2.12±0.11	2.36±0.11	2.43±0.19
# bold	5	10	17	3	12	15	0	6	3

(those with the lowest mean are marked with *; those within one standard error of the lowest one are in bold)

Table 2: average test error (%) on benchmark data sets

data set	OVA	OSR	soft-OSR	OVO	CSOVO	soft-CSOVO	FT	CSFT	soft-CSFT
iris	**4.21±0.78***	6.71±0.98	**4.74±0.73**	**4.74±0.80**	10.66±2.32	5.26±0.70	**4.61±0.79**	7.11±1.24	**4.47±0.77**
wine	**1.78±0.43**	4.00±0.62	2.44±0.38	**2.11±0.51**	**1.78±0.51**	**1.67±0.52***	2.22±0.47	**1.67±0.44**	**2.00±0.49**
glass	**28.52±0.82***	32.22±1.11	31.94±1.21	**28.89±0.84**	44.26±2.73	45.28±2.52	29.81±0.96	39.17±2.35	36.02±2.52
vehicle	**20.66±0.62**	24.15±0.83	22.78±0.73	**20.31±0.67***	28.73±2.19	25.14±1.57	**20.75±0.64**	29.88±2.92	30.40±3.04
vowel	**1.27±0.17***	5.38±0.47	1.88±0.27	**1.29±0.18**	5.93±0.63	**1.43±0.17**	1.94±0.24	6.25±1.43	2.74±0.39
segment	**2.60±0.16***	3.69±0.27	**2.76±0.15**	**2.60±0.15**	5.57±0.95	4.11±0.59	2.78±0.15	4.30±0.62	3.43±0.35
dna	**4.20±0.14**	6.96±0.65	4.87±0.27	**4.19±0.13***	7.90±0.80	5.81±0.85	4.81±0.24	9.14±1.52	5.32±0.30
satimage	**7.19±0.10***	9.52±0.30	9.01±0.34	**7.24±0.09**	12.55±0.66	12.51±0.68	7.55±0.11	10.58±0.63	9.85±0.75
usps	**2.19±0.07***	3.82±0.13	2.66±0.11	2.28±0.06	5.27±0.70	3.53±0.17	2.79±0.06	6.26±0.86	3.50±0.10
zoo	**5.19±0.83**	15.38±1.61	13.08±1.52	6.15±1.03	10.77±1.71	8.27±1.77	**4.81±0.81***	12.69±2.54	6.35±1.47
yeast	40.38±0.64	73.76±0.55	73.68±0.55	**39.27±0.56***	76.58±0.68	76.70±0.67	40.20±0.52	77.02±0.92	76.70±0.81
pageblock	3.22±0.09	39.25±4.36	38.54±4.74	**3.06±0.08***	76.75±6.18	76.75±6.18	**3.10±0.10**	78.25±6.10	81.82±5.81
anneal	**1.40±0.15***	8.78±0.94	6.98±1.13	**1.51±0.15**	19.02±4.24	10.60±4.53	**1.47±0.17**	11.31±1.94	9.47±4.40
solar	27.27±0.42	34.83±1.16	35.22±1.75	**26.61±0.43***	47.49±3.30	47.83±3.12	27.27±0.46	46.15±3.12	43.48±2.85
splice	**3.86±0.15***	7.68±1.16	5.21±0.56	**3.92±0.12**	13.34±2.69	8.13±2.60	4.62±0.18	9.59±1.46	6.52±0.74
ecoli	15.12±0.99	32.68±1.67	33.63±1.61	**14.05±0.75***	37.80±3.30	38.45±3.19	16.85±1.14	36.73±2.72	40.89±3.85
nursery	0.11±0.02	33.33±0.17	31.02±1.54	**0.02±0.01***	37.62±2.17	3.31±2.21	0.32±0.08	33.89±0.44	20.04±3.61
soybean	**6.55±0.32***	24.53±0.82	21.67±1.42	7.46±0.34	39.06±3.51	40.12±3.76	7.13±0.38	35.41±2.48	28.48±3.40
arrhythmia	**28.41±0.93**	66.37±2.25	66.42±2.11	**27.92±0.74***	85.18±2.49	83.05±3.37	30.40±0.62	88.81±2.47	86.15±3.12
optdigits	1.09±0.06	1.85±0.06	1.15±0.07	**1.04±0.05***	2.25±0.09	1.36±0.12	1.35±0.05	2.14±0.24	1.55±0.05
mfeat	**1.69±0.09***	3.10±0.18	1.84±0.11	1.86±0.08	4.32±0.53	2.50±0.22	2.45±0.10	3.89±0.37	2.99±0.38
pendigit	**0.40±0.02**	0.85±0.04	**0.39±0.02**	**0.38±0.02***	0.65±0.03	0.42±0.02	0.45±0.02	0.62±0.04	0.52±0.03

(those with the lowest mean are marked with *; those within one standard error of the lowest one are in bold)

version of this paper. The figures plot the scaled test cost E_c/w on different values of $\log_{10} w$. From the three figures, we see that soft-OSR is better than OSR across all w. When the emphasis is very high (like 10^6), OSR can be conservative and "paranoid." It avoids classifying any of the test examples as the emphasized class, which results in the worse performance. On the other hand, the curves of soft-OSR remain mostly flat, which demonstrate that soft cost-sensitive classification is less sensitive (paranoid) to large cost components. The results again justify the superiority of soft-OSR, a promising representative of soft cost-sensitive classification, over its hard sibling.

4.3 Comparison on a Real-world Biomedical Task

To test the validity of our proposed soft cost-sensitive classification methodology on true applications, we use two real-world data sets for our experiments. The first one is a biomedical task [24], and the other one to be introduced later is from KDDCup 1999 [3]. Both data sets go through similar splitting and scaling procedures, as we did for the benchmark data sets.

The biomedical task is on classifying the bacterial meningitis, which is a serious and often life-threatening form of the meningitis infection. The inputs are the spectra of bacterial pathogens extracted by the Surface Enhanced Raman Scattering (SERS) platform [7]. In this paper, we call the task SERS, which contains 79 clinical samples of ten meningitis-causing bacteria species collected in the National Taiwan University Hospital and 17 standard bacteria samples from American Type Culture Collection. The cost matrix of SERS is shown in Table 5, which is specified by two human physicians who are specialized in infectious diseases.

The results are shown in Table 6. Among the nine algorithms, soft-CSOVO gets the lowest cost. If we compare the other eight algorithms with soft-CSOVO using a pairwise one-tailed t-test of significance level 0.1, we see that soft-CSOVO is significantly better than all other algorithms. The results confirm the usefulness of soft cost-sensitive classification for this real-world task.

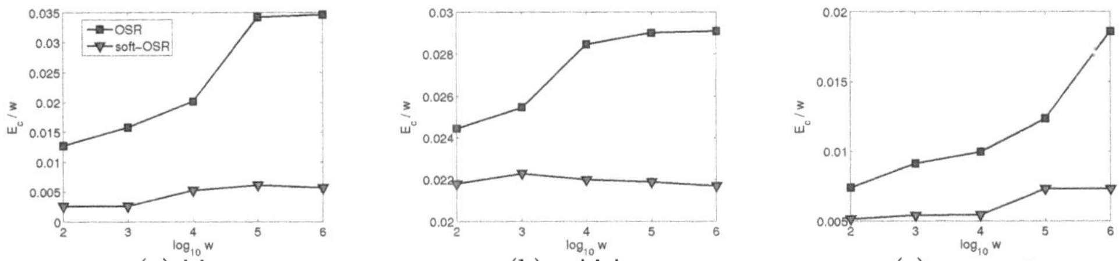

(a) iris (b) vehicle (c) segment

Figure 4: test E_c/w of OSR and soft-OSR with the emphasizing cost for different emphasis parameter w

Table 3: comparisons on the test costs between the algorithms and their soft cost-sensitive classification sibling using a pairwise one-tailed t-test of significance level 0.1

data set	OVA	OSR	OVO	CSOVO	FT	CSFT
iris	≈	≈	≈	≈	○	≈
wine	≈	≈	≈	≈	≈	≈
glass	○	≈	≈	≈	≈	≈
vehicle	○	≈	○	○	≈	≈
vowel	≈	○	≈	○	≈	○
segment	○	○	≈	≈	≈	≈
dna	○	○	≈	○	≈	○
satimage	○	≈	○	≈	○	≈
usps	≈	○	≈	≈	○	≈
zoo	≈	○	○	≈	≈	≈
yeast	○	≈	○	≈	○	≈
pagblock	○	≈	○	≈	○	≈
anneal	○	≈	≈	≈	≈	≈
solar	○	≈	○	≈	○	≈
splice	○	≈	≈	○	≈	○
ecoli	○	≈	○	○	○	≈
nursery	○	≈	≈	≈	≈	≈
soybean	○	≈	○	≈	○	≈
arrhythmia	○	≈	○	≈	○	≈
optdigits	○	○	≈	○	≈	○
mfeat	≈	○	≈	≈	≈	≈
pendigit	≈	○	≈	≈	×	≈

○: soft cost-sensitive algorithms significantly better
×: soft cost-sensitive algorithms significantly worse
≈: otherwise

Table 4: comparison on the test errors between the hard cost-sensitive classification algorithms and their soft sibling using a pairwise one-tailed t-test of significance level 0.1

data set	OSR	CSOVC	CSFT
iris	○	○	○
wine	○	≈	≈
glass	○	≈	≈
vehicle	○	○	≈
vowel	○	○	○
segment	○	○	○
dna	○	○	○
satimage	○	○	○
usps	○	○	○
zoo	○	○	○
yeast	≈	≈	≈
pagblock	≈	≈	≈
anneal	≈	○	○
solar	≈	≈	≈
splice	○	≈	○
ecoli	○	≈	≈
nursery	≈	○	○
soybean	○	≈	○
arrhythmia	≈	≈	≈
optdigits	○	○	○
mfeat	○	○	○
pendigit	○	○	○

○: soft cost-sensitive algorithms significantly better
×: soft cost-sensitive algorithms significantly worse
≈: otherwise

SERS is an interesting data set in which regular classification algorithms like OVO or FT can perform better than their hard cost-sensitive classification siblings like CSOVO or CSFT. Given the small number of examples in SERS, the phenomenon can be attributed to overfitting with respect to the cost—i.e. over-using the cost information. Soft cost-sensitive classification provides a balanced alternative between over-using (hard) or not using (regular) the cost. The balancing can lead to significantly lower test cost, as demonstrated by the promising performance of soft-CSOVO on this biomedical task.

4.4 Comparison on the KDD Cup 1999 Task

The KDDCup 1999 data set (kdd99) is another real-world cost-sensitive classification task [3]. The task contains an intrusion detection problem for distinguishing the "good" and "bad" connections. Following the usual procedure in literature [1], we extract a random 40% of the 10%-training set for our experiments. The test set accompanied is not used because of the known mismatch between training and test distributions [1]. We take the given cost matrix in the competition for our experiments.[4]

The results are listed in Table 7. While the cost-sensitive classification algorithm OSR achieves the lowest test cost, other algorithms (soft, hard, or regular) all result in similar performance. The reason of the similar performance is because all the algorithms are of error rate less than 1% and are thus of low costs. That is, the data set is easy to classify, and there is almost no room for improvements. The easiness is partly because the data set is highly imbalanced. In particular, the size of the majority class is over 8000 times more than the size of the minority class.

To further compare the performance of the algorithms, we consider a more challenging version of the real-world task. The version is called kdd99-balanced, which is generated by

[4]http://www.kdd.org/kddcup/site/1999/files/awkscript.htm

Table 5: cost matrix on SERS

real class \ classify to	Ab	Ecoli	HI	KP	LM	Nm	Psa	Spn	Sa	GBS
Ab	0	1	10	7	9	9	5	8	9	1
Ecoli	3	0	10	8	10	10	5	10	10	2
HI	10	10	0	3	2	2	10	1	2	10
KP	7	7	3	0	4	4	6	3	3	8
LM	8	8	2	4	0	5	8	2	1	8
Nm	3	10	9	8	6	0	8	3	6	7
Psa	7	8	10	9	9	7	0	8	9	5
Spn	6	10	7	7	4	4	9	0	4	7
Sa	7	10	6	5	1	3	9	2	0	7
Gbs	2	5	10	9	8	6	5	6	8	0

Table 6: experiment results on SERS, with t-test for cost

	error (%)	cost ($\cdot 10^0$)	t-test
OVA	23.0 ± 2.51	1.056 ± 0.097	○
OSR	27.6 ± 2.27	0.986 ± 0.092	○
soft-OSR	25.8 ± 2.80	1.024 ± 0.095	○
OVO	23.2 ± 2.55	0.970 ± 0.106	○
CSOVO	27.4 ± 1.53	1.150 ± 0.109	○
soft-CSOVO	26.6 ± 2.55	0.906 ± 0.069	$*$
FT	23.0 ± 2.51	0.986 ± 0.092	○
CSFT	27.6 ± 1.40	1.118 ± 0.090	○
soft-CSFT	31.4 ± 4.09	1.054 ± 0.040	○

$*$: best entry of cost
○: best entry significantly better in cost
$\approx$: otherwise

scaling down the y-th row of the cost matrix by the size of the y-th class. The results on kdd99-balanced are shown in Table 8. OSR remains to be the best algorithm, with comparable test cost to soft-OSR. Nevertheless, when comparing the errors of OSR and soft-OSR, we see that soft-OSR can reach lower test error. Similar results hold (even more significantly) between CSOVO and soft-CSOVO, and between CSFT and soft-CSFT. The results again demonstrate the usefulness of soft cost-sensitive classification in reaching low cost *and* low error on this real-world task.

5. CONCLUSIONS

We have explored the trade-off between the cost and the error rate in cost-sensitive classification tasks, and have identified the practical needs to reach both low cost and low error rate. Based on the trade-off, we have proposed a simple and novel methodology between traditional regular classification and modern cost-sensitive classification. The proposed methodology, soft cost-sensitive classification, takes both the cost and the error into account by a multicriteria optimization problem. By using the weighted sum approach to solving the optimization problem, the proposed methodology allows immediate improvements of existing cost-sensitive classification algorithms in terms of similar or sometimes lower costs, and of lower errors. The significant improvements have been observed on a broad range of benchmark and real-world tasks in our extensive experimental study.

An immediate future work is to take more state-of-art algorithms for comparison. Furthermore, instead of treating the cost and error symmetrically in the methodology, an

Table 7: average test results on kdd99, with t-test for cost

	error (%)	cost ($\cdot 10^{-3}$)	t-test
OVA	0.11 ± 0.003	1.84 ± 0.179	$\approx$
OSR	0.11 ± 0.003	1.80 ± 0.171	$*$
soft-OSR	0.11 ± 0.003	1.92 ± 0.178	$\approx$
OVO	0.10 ± 0.002	1.85 ± 0.174	$\approx$
CSOVO	0.11 ± 0.003	1.81 ± 0.169	$\approx$
soft-CSOVO	0.11 ± 0.003	1.82 ± 0.169	$\approx$
FT	0.10 ± 0.002	1.84 ± 0.170	$\approx$
CSFT	0.11 ± 0.003	1.83 ± 0.171	$\approx$
soft-CSFT	0.11 ± 0.003	1.83 ± 0.171	$\approx$

$*$: best entry of cost
○: best entry significantly better in cost
$\approx$: otherwise

Table 8: average test results on kdd99-balanced, with t-test for cost

	error (%)	cost ($\cdot 10^{-6}$)	t-test
OVA	0.11 ± 0.00	2.35 ± 0.167	○
OSR	2.96 ± 0.63	1.80 ± 0.157	$*$
soft-OSR	2.51 ± 0.53	1.85 ± 0.160	$\approx$
OVO	0.10 ± 0.00	2.49 ± 0.176	○
CSOVO	3.12 ± 0.64	1.81 ± 0.128	$\approx$
soft-CSOVO	2.28 ± 0.40	1.82 ± 0.140	$\approx$
FT	0.10 ± 0.00	2.46 ± 0.178	○
CSFT	2.70 ± 0.58	1.90 ± 0.148	$\approx$
soft-CSFT	1.46 ± 0.46	2.11 ± 0.183	$\approx$

$*$: best entry of cost
○: best entry significantly better in cost
$\approx$: otherwise

interesting future research direction is to consider them in an asymmetric way that treats the cost as the major criterion and the error as the minor one.

Our work reveals a new insight for cost-sensitive classification in machine learning and data mining: Feeding in the exact cost information for the machines to learn may not be the best approach, much like how fitting the provided data faithfully without regularization may lead to overfitting. Our work takes the error rates to "regularize" the cost information and leads to better performance. Another interesting direction for future research is to consider other types of regularization on the cost information.

6. ACKNOWLEDGMENTS

The authors thank Yao-Nan Chen, Ku-Chun Chou, Chih-Han Yu and the anonymous reviewers for valuable comments. This work was supported by the National Science Council (NSC 100-2628-E-002-010 and NSC 100-2120-M-001-003-CC1) of Taiwan.

7. REFERENCES

[1] N. Abe, B. Zadrozny, and J. Langford. An iterative method for multi-class cost-sensitive learning. In *Proc. SIGKDD*, pages 3–11, 2004.

[2] Y. S. Abu-Mostafa, M. Magdon-Ismail, and H.-T. Lin. *Learning from Data: A Short Course*. AMLBook, 2012.

[3] S. D. Bay. UCI KDD archive. Department of Information and Computer Sciences, University of California, Irvine, 2000. Downloaded from `http://kdd.ics.uci.edu/`.

[4] A. Bernstein, F. Provost, and S. Hill. Toward intelligent assistance for a data mining process: An ontology-based approach for cost-sensitive classification. *IEEE TKDE*, 17(4):503–518, 2005.

[5] A. Beygelzimer, V. Daniand, T. Hayes, J. Langford, and B. Zadrozny. Error limiting reductions between classification tasks. In *Proc. ICML*, pages 49–56, 2005.

[6] A. Beygelzimer, J. Langford, and P. Ravikumar. Multiclass classification with filter trees. Downloaded from `http://hunch.net/~jl`, 2007.

[7] A. Campion and P. Kambhampati. Surface enhanced Raman scattering. *Chem. Soc. Rev.*, 27(4):241–250, 1998.

[8] C.-C. Chang and C.-J. Lin. LIBSVM: A library for support vector machines. *ACM TIST*, 2:27:1–27:27, 2011. Software available at `http://www.csie.ntu.edu.tw/~cjlin/libsvm`.

[9] D. Corne, N. Jerram, J. Knowles, and M. Oates. PESA-II: Region-based selection in evolutionary multiobjective optimization. In *Proc. GECCO*, 2001.

[10] I. Das and J. E. Dennis. A closer look at drawbacks of minimizing weighted sums of objectives for Pareto set generation in multicriteria optimization problems. *Struct. Multidiscip. Opti.*, 14(1):63–69, 1996.

[11] K. Deb, A. Pratap, S. Agarwal, and T. Meyarivan. A fast and elitist multiobjective genetic algorithm: NSGA-II. *IEEE TEC*, 6(2):182–197, 2002.

[12] P. Domingos. MetaCost: A general method for making classifiers cost-sensitive. In *Proc. SIGKDD*, pages 155–164, 1999.

[13] C. Elkan. The foundations of cost-sensitive learning. In *Proc. IJCAI*, pages 973–978, 2001.

[14] W. Fan, W. Lee, S. Stolfo, and M. Miller. A multiple model cost-sensitive approach for intrusion detection. In *Proc. ECML*, pages 142–154, 2000.

[15] A. Freitas. Building cost-sensitive decision trees for medical applications. *AI Comm.*, 24(3):285–287, 2011.

[16] M. Hall, E. Frank, G. Holmes, B. Pfahringer, P. Reutemann, and I. Witten. The WEKA data mining software: an update. *SIGKDD Explor. Newsl.*, 11(1):10–18, 2009.

[17] J. Han, M. Kamber, and J. Pei. *Data mining: concepts and techniques*. Morgan Kaufmann, 2011.

[18] S. Hettich, C. L. Blake, and C. J. Merz. UCI repository of machine learning databases, 1998.

[19] C. Hillermeier. *Nonlinear multiobjective optimization*. Birkhauser, 2001.

[20] J. Horn, N. Nafpliotis, and D. Goldberg. A niched Pareto genetic algorithm for multiobjective optimization. In *Proc. IEEE WCCI*, pages 82–87, 1994.

[21] C.-W. Hsu and C.-J. Lin. A comparison of methods for multi-class support vector machines. *IEEE TNN*, 13(2):415–425, 2002.

[22] J. J. Hull. A database for handwritten text recognition research. *IEEE TPAMI*, 16(5):550–554, 1994.

[23] T.-K. Jan. A comparison of methods for cost-sensitive support vector machines. Master's thesis, National Taiwan University, 2010.

[24] T.-K. Jan, H.-T. Lin, H.-P. Chen, T.-C. Chern, C.-Y. Huang, C.-Y. Huang, C.-W. Chung, Y.-J. Li, Y.-C. Chuang, L.-L. Li, Y.-J. Chan, J.-K. Wang, Y.-L. Wang, C.-H. Lin, and D.-W. Wang. Cost-sensitive classification on pathogen species of bacterial meningitis by surface enhanced Raman scattering. In *Proc. IEEE BIBM*, pages 406–409, 2011.

[25] J. Langford and A. Beygelzimer. Sensitive error correcting output codes. In *Proc. COLT*, pages 158–172, 2005.

[26] W. Lee, W. Fan, M. Miller, S. Stolfo, and E. Zadok. Toward cost-sensitive modeling for intrusion detection and response. *JCS*, 10(1/2):5–22, 2002.

[27] H.-T. Lin. A simple cost-sensitive multiclass classification algorithm using one-versus-one comparisons. Downloaded from `http://www.csie.ntu.edu.tw/~htlin/paper/doc/csovo.pdf`, 2010.

[28] H.-T. Lin and L. Li. Support vector machinery for infinite ensemble learning. *JMLR*, 9(2):285–312, 2008.

[29] D. D. Margineantu. *Methods for cost-sensitive learning*. PhD thesis, Oregon State University, 2001.

[30] S. Rosset. Value weighted analysis: Building prediction models for data with observation. Downloaded from `http://www.tau.ac.il/~saharon/`, 2002.

[31] K. Schleifer. Classification of bacteria and archaea: past, present and future. *Syst. Appl. Microbiol.*, 32(8):533–542, 2009.

[32] D. Sculley. Combined regression and ranking. In *Proc. SIGKDD*, pages 979–988, 2010.

[33] Y. Sun, M. Kamel, A. Wong, and Y. Wang. Cost-sensitive boosting for classification of imbalanced data. *PR*, 40(12):3358–3378, 2007.

[34] M. Tan. Cost-sensitive learning of classification knowledge and its applications in robotics. *ML*, 13(1):7–33, 1993.

[35] H.-H. Tu. Regression approaches for multi-class cost-sensitive classification. Master's thesis, National Taiwan University, 2009.

[36] H.-H. Tu and H.-T. Lin. One-sided support vector regression for multiclass cost-sensitive classification. In *Proc. ICML*, pages 1095–1102, 2010.

[37] V. N. Vapnik. *Statistical Learning Theory*. Wiley, 1998.

[38] L. Zadeh. Optimality and non-scalar-valued performance criteria. *IEEE TAC*, 8(1):59–60, 1963.

[39] B. Zadrozny, J. Langford, and N. Abe. Cost-sensitive learning by cost-proportionate example weighting. In *Proc. ICDM*, pages 435–442, 2003.

[40] Z.-H. Zhou and X.-Y. Liu. On multi-class cost-sensitive learning. In *Proc. AAAI*, pages 567–572, 2006.

Intelligible Models for Classification and Regression

Yin Lou
Dept. of Computer Science
Cornell University
yinlou@cs.cornell.edu

Rich Caruana
Microsoft Research
Microsoft Corporation
rcaruana@microsoft.com

Johannes Gehrke
Dept. of Computer Science
Cornell University
johannes@cs.cornell.edu

ABSTRACT

Complex models for regression and classification have high accuracy, but are unfortunately no longer interpretable by users. We study the performance of generalized additive models (GAMs), which combine single-feature models called *shape functions* through a linear function. Since the shape functions can be arbitrarily complex, GAMs are more accurate than simple linear models. But since they do not contain any interactions between features, they can be easily interpreted by users.

We present the first large-scale empirical comparison of existing methods for learning GAMs. Our study includes existing spline and tree-based methods for shape functions and penalized least squares, gradient boosting, and backfitting for learning GAMs. We also present a new method based on tree ensembles with an adaptive number of leaves that consistently outperforms previous work. We complement our experimental results with a bias-variance analysis that explains how different shape models influence the additive model. Our experiments show that shallow bagged trees with gradient boosting distinguish itself as the best method on low- to medium-dimensional datasets.

Categories and Subject Descriptors

I.2.6 [**Computing Methodologies**]: Learning—*Induction*

Keywords

intelligible models, classification, regression

1. INTRODUCTION

Everything should be made as simple as possible, but not simpler.
— Albert Einstein.

Classification and regression are two of the most important data mining tasks. Currently, the most accurate methods on many datasets are complex models such as boosted trees, SVMs, or deep neural nets. However, in many applications *what* is learned is just as important as the accuracy of the predictions. Unfortunately, the high accuracy of complex models comes at the expense of interpretability; e.g., even the contribution of individual features to the predictions of a complex model are difficult to understand.

KDD'12, August 12–16, 2012, Beijing, China.

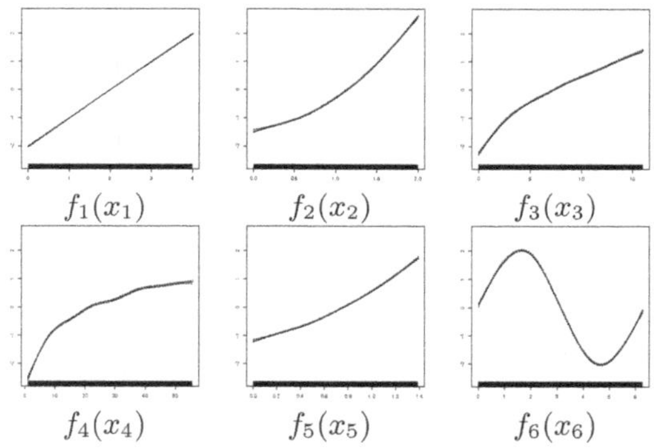

Figure 1: Shape Functions for Synthetic Dataset in Example 1.

The goal of this work is to construct accurate models that are interpretible. By interpretibility we mean that users can understand the contribution of individual features in the model; e.g., we want models that can quantify the impact of each predictor. This desiderata permits arbitrary complex relationships between individual features and the target, but excludes models with complex interactions between features. Thus in this paper we fit models of the form:

$$g(y) = f_1(x_1) + ... + f_n(x_n), \tag{1}$$

which are known as *generalized additive models* in the literature [15, 22]. The function $g(\cdot)$ is called the *link function* and we call the f_is *shape functions*. If the link function is the identity, Equation 1 describes an additive model (e.g., a regression model); if the link function is the logistic function, Equation 1 describes a generalized additive model (e.g., a classification model).

EXAMPLE 1. *Assume we are given a dataset with 10,000 points generated from the model* $y = x_1 + x_2^2 + \sqrt{x_3} + \log(x_4) + \exp(x_5) + 2\sin(x_6) + \epsilon$, *where* $\epsilon \sim \mathcal{N}(0, 1)$. *After fitting an additive model to the data of the form shown in Equation 1, we can visualize the contribution of* x_i*s as shown in Figure 1: Because predictions are a linear function of the* $f_i(x_i)$, *scatterplots of* $f_i(x_i)$ *on the y-axis vs.* x_i *on the x-axis allow us to visualize the shape function that relates the* $f_i(x_i)$ *to the* x_i, *thus we can easily understand the contribution of* x_i *to the prediction.*

Because the data in Example 1 was drawn from a model with no interactions between features, a model of the form in Equation 1 is able to fit the data perfectly (modulo noise). However, data are not always so simple in practice. As a second example, consider a real dataset where there may be interactions between features.

Model	Form	Intelligibility	Accuracy
Linear Model	$y = \beta_0 + \beta_1 x_1 + ... + \beta_n x_n$	+++	+
Generalized Linear Model	$g(y) = \beta_0 + \beta_1 x_1 + ... + \beta_n x_n$	+++	+
Additive Model	$y = f_1(x_1) + ... + f_n(x_n)$	++	++
Generalized Additive Model	$g(y) = f_1(x_1) + ... + f_n(x_n)$	++	++
Full Complexity Model	$y = f(x_1, ..., x_n)$	+	+++

Table 1: From Linear to Additive Models.

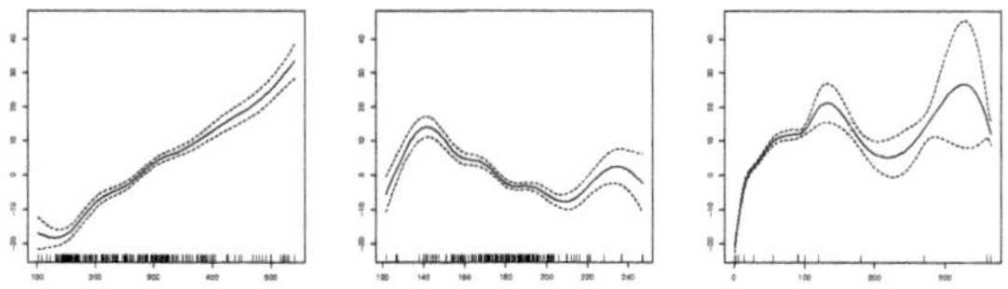

Cement Water Age

Figure 2: Shape Functions for Concrete Dataset in Example 2.

EXAMPLE 2. *The "Concrete" dataset relates the compressive strength of concrete to its age and ingredients. The dataset contains 1030 points with eight numerical features. We again fit an additive model of the form in Equation 1. Figure 2 shows scatterplots of the shape functions learned for three of the eight features. As we can see from the figure, the compressibility of concrete depends nearly linearly on the Cement feature, but it is a complex non-linear function of the Water and Age features; we say that the model has* shaped *these features. A linear model without the ability to shape features would have worse fit because it cannot capture these non-linearities. Moreover, an attempt to interpret the contribution of features by examining the slopes of a simple linear model would be misleading; the additive model yields much better fit to the data while still remaining intelligible.*[1]

As we saw in the examples, additive models explicitly decompose a complex function into one-dimensional components, its shape functions. Note, however, that the shape functions themselves may be non-linear: Each feature x_i can have a complex non-linear shape $f_i(x_i)$, and thus the accuracy of additive models can be significantly higher than the accuracy of simple linear models. Table 1 summarizes the differences between models of different complexity that we consider in this paper. Linear models, and generalized linear models (GLMs) are the most intelligible, but often the least accurate. Additive models, and generalized additive models (GAMs) are more accurate than GLMs on many data sets because they capture non-linear relationships between (individual) features and the response, but retain much of the intelligibility of linear models. Full complexity models such as ensembles of trees are more accurate on many datasets because they model both non-linearity and interaction, but are so complex that it is nearly impossible to interpret them.

In this paper we present the results of (to the best of our knowledge) the largest experimental study of GAMs. We consider shape functions based on splines [14, 22] and boosted stumps [13], as well as novel shape functions based on bagged and boosted ensembles of trees that choose the number of leaves adaptively. We experiment with (iteratively re-weighted) least squares, gradient boosting, and backfitting to both iteratively refine the shape functions and construct the linear model of the shaped features. We apply these methods to six classification and six regression tasks. For comparison, we fit simple linear models as a baseline. We also fit unrestricted ensembles of trees as full complexity models to get an idea of what accuracy is achievable.

Model	Regression	Classification	Mean
Linear/Logistic	1.68	1.22	1.45
P-LS/P-IRLS	1.00	1.00	1.00
BST-SP	1.03	1.00	1.02
BF-SP	1.00	1.00	1.00
BST-bagTR2	0.96	0.96	0.96
BST-bagTR3	0.97	0.94	0.96
BST-bagTR4	0.99	0.95	0.97
BST-bagTRX	0.95	0.94	0.95
Random Forest	0.88	0.80	0.84

Table 2: Preview of Empirical Results.

Table 2 summarizes the key findings of our study. Entries in the table are the average accuracies on the regression and classification datasets, normalized by the accuracy of Penalized (Iteratively Re-weighted) Least Squares with Splines (P-LS/P-IRLS). As expected, the accuracy of GAMs falls between that of linear/logistic regression without feature shaping and full-complexity models such as random forests. However, surprisingly, the best GAM models have accuracy much closer to the full-complexity models than to the linear models. Our results show that bagged trees with 2-4 leaves as shape functions in combination with gradient boosting as learning method (Methods BST-bag-TR2 to BST-bag-TR4) outperform all other methods on most datasets. Our novel method of adaptively selecting the right number of leaves (Method BST-bagTRX) is almost always even better, and thus we recommend it as the method of choice. On average, this method reduces loss by about 5% over previous GAM models, a significant improvement in practice.

The rest of the paper is structured as follows. Section 2 presents algorithms for fitting generalized additive models with various shape functions and learning methods. Section 3 describes our experimental setup, Section 4 presents the results and their interpretation, followed by a discussion in Section 5 and an overview of related work in Section 6. We conclude in Section 7.

2. METHODOLOGY

Let $\mathcal{D} = \{(\boldsymbol{x}_i, y_i)\}_1^N$ denote a training dataset of size N, where $\boldsymbol{x}_i = (x_{i1}, ..., x_{in})$ is a feature vector with n features and y_i is the target. In this paper, we consider both regression problems where $y_i \in \mathbb{R}$ and binary classification problems where $y_i \in \{1, -1\}$. Given a model F, let $F(\boldsymbol{x}_i)$ denote the prediction of the model for data point $\boldsymbol{x}_i$. Our goal in both classification and regression is to minimize the expected value of some loss function $L(y, F(\boldsymbol{x}))$.

We are working with generalized additive models of the form in Equation 1. To train such models we have to select (i) the shape functions for individual features and (ii) the learning method used to train the overall model. We discuss these two choices next.

[1]See Section 4 for the fit of different models to this dataset.

2.1 Shape Functions

In our study we consider two classes of shape functions: regression splines and trees or ensembles of trees. Note that all shape functions relate a single attribute to the target.

Regression Splines. We consider regression splines of degree d of the form $y = \sum_{k=1}^{d} \beta_k b_k(x)$.

Trees and Ensembles of Trees. We also use binary trees and ensembles of binary trees with largest variance reduction as split selection method. We control tree complexity by either fixing the number of leaves or by disallowing leaves that have fewer than an α-fraction of the number of training examples.

We consider the following ensemble variants:

- Single Tree. We use a single regression tree as a shape function.
- Bagged Trees. We use the well-known technique of bagging to reducing variance [6].
- Boosted Trees. We use gradient boosting, where each successive tree tries to predict the overall residual from all preceding trees [12].
- Boosted Bagged Trees. We use a bagged ensemble in each step of stochastic gradient boosting [13], resulting in a boosted ensemble of bagged trees.

2.2 Generalized Additive Models

We consider three different methods for fitting additive models in our study: Least squares fitting for learning regression spline shape functions, and gradient boosting and backfitting for learning tree and tree ensemble shape functions. We review them here briefly for completeness although we would like to emphasize that these methods are not a contribution of this paper.

2.2.1 *Least Squares*

Fitting a spline reduces to learning the weights $\beta_k(x)$ for the basis functions $b_k(x)$. Learning the weights can be reduced to fitting a linear model $y = \boldsymbol{X}\boldsymbol{\beta}$, where $\boldsymbol{X}_i = [b_1(x_{i1}), ..., b_k(x_{in})]$; the coefficients of the linear model can be computed exactly using the least squares method [22]. To control smoothness, there is a "wiggliness" penalty: we minimize $\|y - \boldsymbol{X}\boldsymbol{\beta}\| + \lambda \sum_i \int [f_i''(x_i)]^2 dx$ with the smoothing parameter λ. Large values of λ lead to a straight line for f_i while low values of λ allow the spline to fit closely to the data. We use thin plate regression splines from the R package "mgcv" [22] that automatically selects the best values for the parameters of the splines [21]. We call this method penalized least-squares (P-LS) in our experiments.

The fitting of an additive logistic regression model using splines is similarly reduced to fitting a logistic regression with a different basis, which can be solved using penalized-iteratively reweighted least squares (P-IRLS) [22].

2.2.2 *Gradient Boosting*

We use standard gradient boosting [12, 13] with one difference: Since we want to learn shape functions for all features, in each iteration of boosting we cycle sequentially through all features. For completeness, we include pseudo-code in Algorithms 1 and 2. In Algorithm 1, we first set all shape functions to zero (Line 1). Then we loop over M iterations (Line 2) and over all features (Line 3) and then calculate the residuals (Line 4). We then learn then one-dimensional function to predict the residuals (Line 5) and add it to the shape function (Line 6).

2.2.3 *Backfitting*

A popular algorithm for learning additive models is the backfitting algorithm [15]. The algorithm starts with an initial guess of all shape functions (such as setting them all to zero). The first shape function f_1 is then learned using the training set with the goal to predict y. Then we learn the second shape function f_2 on the residuals $y - f_1(x_1)$, i.e., using training set $\{(x_{i2}, y - f_1(x_{i1}))\}_1^N$. The third shape function is trained on the residuals $y - f_1(x_1) - f_2(x_2)$, and so on. After we have trained n shape functions, the first shape function is *discarded* and retrained on the residuals of the other $n-1$ shape functions. Note that backfitting is a form of the "Gauss-Seidel" algorithm and its convergence is usually guaranteed [15]. Its pseudocode looks identical to Algorithm 1 except that Line 6 is replaced by $f_j \leftarrow S$.

To fit an additive logistic regression model, we can use a generalized version of the backfitting algorithm called the "Local Scoring Algorithm" [15], which is a general method for fitting generalized additive models. We form the response

$$\tilde{y}_i = F(\boldsymbol{x}_i) + \frac{\mathbf{1}(y_i = 1) - p(\boldsymbol{x}_i)}{p(\boldsymbol{x}_i)(1 - p(\boldsymbol{x}_i))},$$

where $p(\boldsymbol{x}_i) = \frac{1}{1+\exp(-F(\boldsymbol{x}_i))}$. We then apply the weighted backfitting algorithm to the response $\tilde{y}_i$ with observation weights $p(\boldsymbol{x}_i)(1 - p(\boldsymbol{x}_i))$ [15].

Algorithm 1 Gradient Boosting for Regression

1: $f_j \leftarrow 0$
2: **for** $m = 1$ to M **do**
3:   **for** $j = 1$ to n **do**
4:     $\mathcal{R} \leftarrow \{x_{ij}, y_i - \sum_k f_k\}_1^N$
5:     Learn shaping function $S : x_j \rightarrow y$ using $\mathcal{R}$ as training dataset
6:     $f_j \leftarrow f_j + S$

Algorithm 2 Gradient Boosting for Classification

1: $f_j \leftarrow 0$
2: **for** $m = 1$ to M **do**
3:   **for** $j = 1$ to n **do**
4:     $\tilde{y}_i \leftarrow \frac{2y_i}{1+\exp(2y_i F(\boldsymbol{x}_i))}, i = 1, ..., N$
5:     Learn $\{R_{km}\}_1^K \leftarrow$, a tree with K leaf nodes using $(\{x_{ij}, \tilde{y}_i\}_1^N)$ as training dataset
6:     $\gamma_{km} = \frac{\sum_{x_{ij} \in R_{km}} \tilde{y}_i}{\sum_{x_{ij} \in R_{km}} |\tilde{y}_i|(2 - |\tilde{y}_i|)}, k = 1, ..., K$
7:     $f_j \leftarrow f_j + \sum_{k=1}^{K} \gamma_{km} \mathbf{1}(x_{ij} \in R_{km})$

3. EXPERIMENTAL SETUP

In this section we describe the experimental design.

3.1 Datasets

We selected datasets of low-to-medium dimensionality with at least 1000 points. Table 3 summarizes the characteristics of the 12 datasets. One of the regression datasets is a synthetic problem used to illustrate feature shaping (but we do not use the results on this dataset when comparing the accuracy of the methods).

The "Concrete," "Wine," and "Music" regression datasets are from the UCI repository [1]; "Delta" is the task of controlling the ailerons of a F16 aircraft [2]; "CompAct" is a regression dataset from the Delve repository that describes the state of multiuser computers [3]. The synthetic dataset was described in Example 1.

Dataset	Size	Attributes	%Pos
Concrete	1030	9	-
Wine	4898	12	-
Delta	7192	6	-
CompAct	8192	22	-
Music	50000	90	-
Synthetic	10000	6	-
Spambase	4601	58	39.40
Insurance	9823	86	5.97
Magic	19020	11	64.84
Letter	20000	17	49.70
Adult	46033	9/43	16.62
Physics	50000	79	49.72

Table 3: Datasets.

Shape Function	Least Squares	Gradient Boosting	Backfitting
Splines	P-LS/P-IRLS	BST-SP	BF-SP
Single Tree	N/A	BST-TRx	BF-TR
Bagged Trees	N/A	BST-bagTRx	BF-bagTR
Boosted Trees	N/A	BST-TRx	BF-bstTRx
Boosted Bagged Trees	N/A	BST-bagTRx	BF-bbTRx

Table 4: Notation for learning methods and shape functions.

The "Spambase," "Insurance," "Magic," "Letter" and "Adult" classification datasets are from the UCI repository. "Adult" contains nominal attributes that we transformed to boolean attributes (one boolean per value). "Letter" has been converted to a binary problem by using A-M as positives and the rest as negatives. The "Physics" dataset is from the KDD Cup 2004 [4].

3.2 Methods

Recall from Section 2 that we have two different types of shape functions and three different methods of learning generalized additive models; see Table 4 for an overview of these methods and their names. While penalized least squares for regression (P-LS) and penalized iteratively re-weighted least squares for classification (P-IRLS) only work with splines, gradient boosting and backfitting can be applied to both splines and ensembles of trees.

In gradient boosting, we vary the number of leaves in the bagged or boosted trees: $2, 3, 4, 8, 12$ to 16 (indicated by appending this number to the method names). Trained models will contain M such trees for each shape function after M iterations. In backfitting, we re-build the shape function for each feature from scratch in each round, so the shape function needs to have enough expressive power to capture a complex function. Thus we control the complexity of the tree not by the number of leaves, but by adaptively choosing a parameter α that stops splitting nodes smaller than an α fraction of the size of the training data; we vary $\alpha \in \{0.00125, 0.025, 0.05, 0.1, 0.15, 0.2, 0.25, 0.3, 0.35, 0.4, 0.45, 0.5\}$. A summary of the combinations of shape functions and learning methods can be found in Table 4.

Beyond the parameters that we already discussed, P-LS and P-IRLS have a parameter λ, which is estimated using generalized cross validation as discussed in Section 2. We do not fix the number of iterations for gradient boosting and backfitting but instead run these methods until convergence as follows: We divide the training set into five partitions. We then set aside one of the partitions as a validation set, train the model on the remaining four partitions, and use the validation set to check for convergence. We repeat this process five times and then compute M, the average number of iterations until convergence across the five iterations. We then retrain the model using the whole training set for M iterations. We follow a similar procedure for backfitting where we pick the best α for each partition and average them to train the final model using the whole training dataset.

3.3 Metrics

For regression problems, we report the root mean squared error (RMSE) for linear regression (no feature shaping), additive models with shaping with splines or trees (penalized least squares, gradient boosting and backfitting), and unrestricted full-complexity models (random forest regression trees and Additive Groves [5, 19]).

For classification problems, we report the error rates for logistic regression, generalized additive models with splines or trees (penalized iteratively re-weighted least squares, gradient boosting and backfitting), and full-complexity unrestricted models (random forests [8]).[2]

In all experiments we use 100 trees for bagging. We do not notice significant improvements by using more iterations of bagging. For Additive Groves, the number of trees is automatically selected by the algorithm on the validation set. For P-LS and P-IRLS, we use an R package called "mgcv" [22]. We perform 5-fold cross validation for all experiments.[3]

4. RESULTS

The regression and classification results are presented in Table 5 and Table 6, respectively. We report means and standard deviations on the 5-fold cross validation test-sets. To facilitate comparison across multiple datasets, we compute normalized scores that average the performance of each method across the datasets, normalized by the accuracy of P-LS/P-IRLS on each dataset.

Table 5 and Table 6 are laid out as follows: The top of each table shows results for linear/logistic regression (no feature shaping) and the traditional spline-based GAM models P-LS/P-IRLS, BST-SP, and BF-SP. The middle of the tables present results for new methods that do feature shaping with trees instead of splines such as boosted size-limited trees (e.g., BST-TR3), boosted-bagged size-limited trees (e.g., BST-bagTR3), backfitting of boosted trees (e.g., BF-bstTR3), and backfitting of boosted-bagged trees (e.g., BF-bbTR3). The bottom of each table presents results for unrestricted full-complexity models such as random forests and additive groves. Our goal is to devise more powerful GAM models that are as close in accuracy as possible to the full-complexity models, while preserving the intelligibility of linear models.

Several clear patterns emerge in both tables.

(1) There is a large gap in accuracy between linear methods that do not do feature shaping (linear or logistic regression) and most methods that perform feature shaping. For example, on average the spline-based P-LS GAM model has 60% lower normalized RMSE than vanilla linear regression. Similarly, on average, P-IRLS is about 20% more accurate than logistic regression.

(2) The new tree-based shaping methods are more accurate than the spline-based methods as long as model complexity (and variance — see Section 5.1) is controlled. In both tables, the most accurate tree-based GAM models use boosted-bagged trees that are size-limited to 2-4 leaves.

[2]Random forests is a very competitive full complexity model [10].
[3]We use 5-fold instead of 10-fold cross validation because some of the experiments are very expensive.

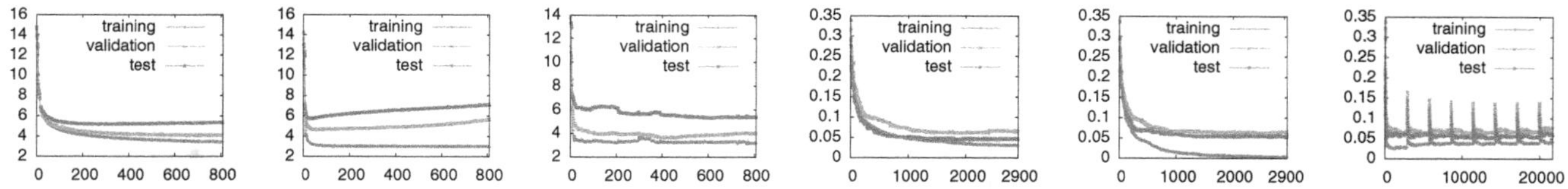

(a) BST-bagTR2 (b) BST-bagTR16 (c) BF-bagTR (d) BST-bagTR2 (e) BST-bagTR16 (f) BF-bagTR

Figure 3: Training curves for gradient boosting and backfitting. Figure (a), (b) and (c) show the behavior of BST-bagTR2, BST-bagTR16 and BF-bagTR on the "Concrete" regression problem, respectively. Figure (d), (e) and (f) illustrate behavior of BST-bagTR2, BST-bagTR16 and BF-bagTR on the "Spambase" classification, respectively.

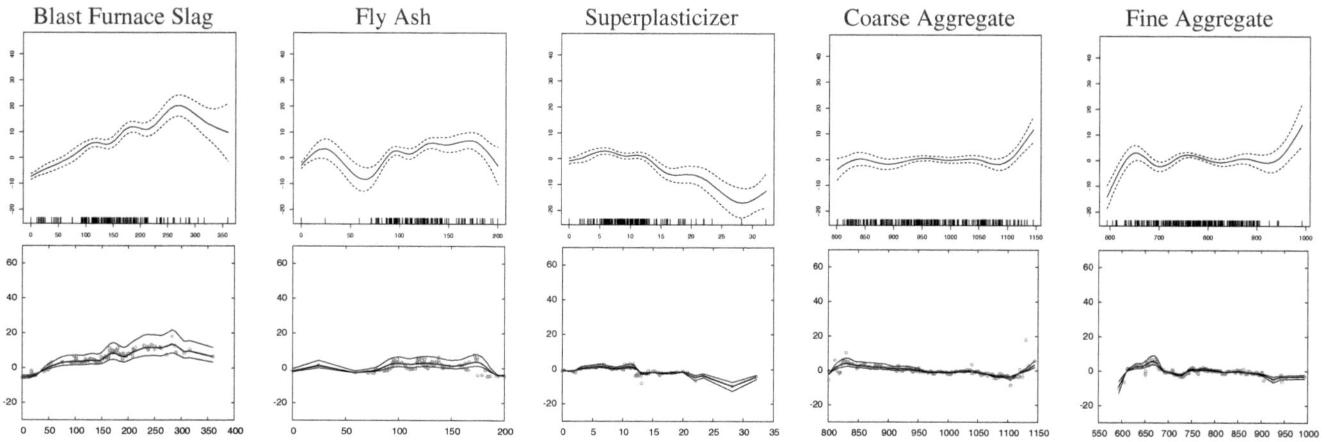

0.14 0.06 0.04 0.05 0.06

Figure 4: Shapes of features for the "Concrete" dataset produced by P-LS (top) and BST-bagTR3 (bottom).

(3) Unrestricted full-complexity models such as random forests and additive groves are more accurate than any of the GAM models because they are able to model feature interactions, which linear models of shaped features cannot capture. Our goal is to push the accuracy of linear shaped models as close as possible to the accuracy of these unrestricted full-complexity models.

Looking more closely at the results for models that shape features with trees, the most accurate model on average is BST-bagTR2 for regression, and BST-bagTR3 for classification. Models that use more leaves are consistently less accurate than comparable models with 2-4 leaves. It is critical to control tree complexity when boosting trees for feature shaping. Moreover, the most accurate methods used bagging inside of boosting to reduce variance. (More on model variance in Section 5.1.) Finally, on the regression problems, methods based on gradient boosting of residuals slightly edged out the methods based on backfitting, though the difference is not statistically significant. On the classification problems, however, where backfitting is performed on pseudo-residuals, there were stability problems that caused some runs to diverge or fail to terminate. Overall, tree-based shaping methods based on gradient-boosting appear to be preferable to tree-based methods based on backfitting because the gradient boosting methods may be a little more accurate, are often faster, and on some problems are more robust.

Although tree-based feature shaping yields significant improvements in accuracy for GAMs, on most problems they are not able to close the gap with unrestricted full-complexity models such as random forests. For example, all linear methods have much worse RMSE on the wine regression problem than the unrestricted random forest model. On problems where feature interaction is important, linear models without interaction terms must be less accurate.

4.1 Model Selection

There is a risk when comparing many parameterizations of a new method against a small number of baseline methods, that the new method will appear to be better because selecting the best model on the test set leads to overfitting to the test sets. To avoid this, the table includes results for a method called "BST-bagTRX" that uses the cross-validation validation sets (*not* the CV test sets) to pick the best parameters from the BST-bagTRx models for each dataset. This method is not biased by looking at results on test sets, is fully automatic and thus does not depend on human judgement, and is able to select different parameters for each problem. The results in Table 5 and Table 6 suggest that BST-bagTRX is more accurate than any single fixed parameterization. Looking at the models selected by BST-bagTRX, we see that BST-bagTRX usually picks models with 2, 3 or 4 leaves, and that the model it selects often is the one with the best test-set performance. On both the regression and classification datasets, BF-bagTRX is significantly more accurate than any of the models that use splines for feature shaping.

5. DISCUSSION

5.1 Bias-Variance Analysis

The results in Tables 5 and 6 show that adding feature shaping to linear models significantly improves accuracy on problems of small-medium dimensionality, and feature shaping with tree-based models significantly improves accuracy compared to feature shaping with splines. But why are tree-based methods more accurate for feature shaping than spline-based methods? In this section we show that splines tend to underfit, i.e., have very low variance at the expense of higher bias, but tree-based shaping models can have both low bias and low variance if tree complexity is controlled.

To show why spline models do not perform as well as tree mod-

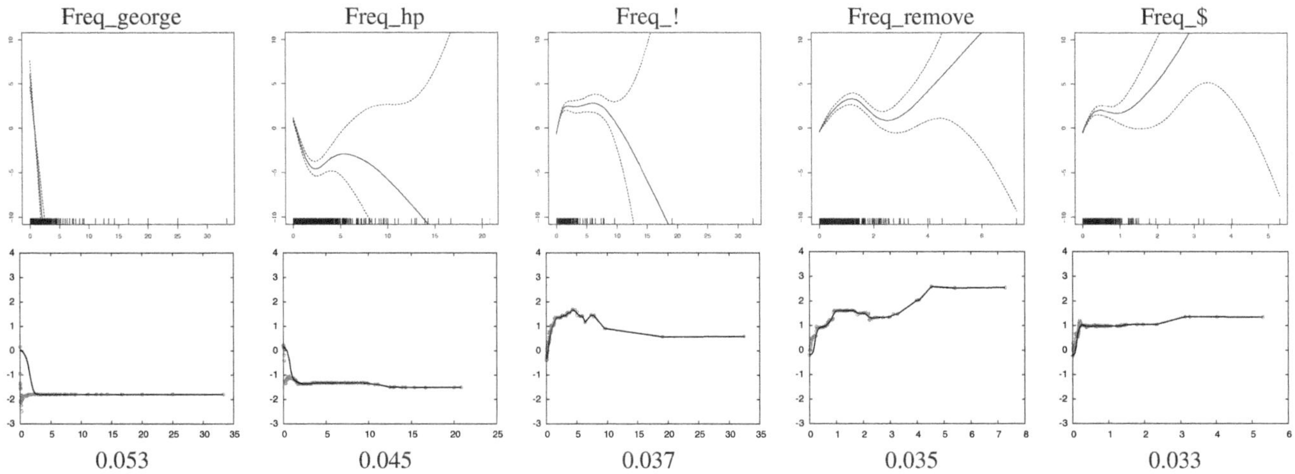

Figure 5: Shapes of features for the "Spambase" dataset produced by P-IRLS (top) and BST-bagTR3 (bottom).

els, and why controlling complexity is so critical with trees, we perform a bias-variance analysis on the regression datasets.[4] As in previous experiments, we randomly select 20% of the points as test sets. We then draw L samples of size $M = 0.64N$ points from the remaining points to keep the training sample size the same as with 5-fold cross validation in previous experiments. We use $L = 10$ trials. The bias-variance decomposition is calculated as follows:

$$Expected\ Loss = (bias)^2 + variance + noise$$

Define the average prediction on L samples for each point $(\boldsymbol{x}_i, y_i)$ in test set as $\bar{y}_i = \frac{1}{L}\sum_{l=1}^{L} \hat{y}_i^l$, where $\hat{y}_i^l$ is the predicted value for $\boldsymbol{x}_i$ using sample l. The squared bias $(bias)^2 = \frac{1}{N'}\sum_{i=1}^{N'}[\bar{y}_i - y_i]^2$, where y_i is the known target in the test set and $N' = 0.2N$ is the size of test set. The variance is calculated as $variance = \frac{1}{N'}\sum_{i=1}^{N'} \frac{1}{L}\sum_{l=1}^{L}[\hat{y}_i^l - \bar{y}_i]^2$.

The bias-variance results for the six regression datasets are shown in Figure 6. We can see that methods based on regression splines have very low variance, but sometimes at the expense of increased bias, while the best tree-based methods consistently have lower bias combined with low-enough variance to yield better overall RMSE. If tree complexity is not carefully controlled, however, variance explodes and hurts total RMSE. As expected, adding bagging inside boosting further reduces variance, making tree-based feature shaping methods based on gradient-boosting of residuals with internal bagging the most accurate method overall. (We do not expect bagging would help regression splines because the variance of regression splines is so low to begin with.) But even bagging will not prevent overfitting if the trees are too complex. Figure 3 shows training curves on the train, validation and test sets for gradient boosting with bagging and backfitting with bagging on a regression and classification problem. BST-bagTR2 is more resistant to overfitting than BST-bagTR16 which easily overfits.

The training curves for backfitting are not monotonic, and have distinct peaks on the classification problem. Each peak corresponds to a new backfitting iteration when pseudo residuals are updated. In our experience, backfitting on classification problems is consistently inferior to other methods, in part because it is harder for the local scoring algorithm to find a "good" set of pseudo residuals, which ultimately leads to instability and poor fit. Interestingly, in the bias-variance analysis of backfitting, both bias and variance often increase as the trees become larger, and the worst performing models on the five non-synthetic datasets are backfit models with large trees. We suspect backfitting can get stuck in inferior local minima when shaping with larger trees, hurting both bias and variance, which may explain the instability and convergence problems observed with backfitting on some classification problems.

[4]We do not perform bias-variance analysis on the classification problems because the bias-variance decomposition for classification is not as well defined.

5.2 Underfitting, Intelligibility, and Fidelity

One of the main reasons to use GAMs (linear models of nonlinearly shaped features) is intelligibility. Figure 1 in Section 1 showed shape models for features in the synthetic dataset. In this section we show shape models learned for features from real regression and classification problems.

Figure 4 shows feature shape plots for the "Concrete" regression problem. Figure 5 show shape plots for the "Spambase" clasification problem. In each figure, the top row of plots are from the P-LS spline method, and the bottom row of plots are from BST-bagTR3. Confidence intervals for the least squres method can be computed analytically. Confidence intervals for BST-bagTR3 are generated by running BST-bagTR3 multiple times on bootstrap samples. As expected, the spline-based approach produces smooth plots. The cost of this smoothness, however, is poorer fit that results in higher RMSE or lower accuracy. Moreover, not all phenomena are smooth. Freezing and boiling occur at distinct temperatures, the onset of instability occurs abruptly as fluid flow increases relative to Reynolds Number, and many human decision making processes such as loans, admission to school, or administering medical procedures use discrete thresholds.

On the "Concrete" dataset, all features in Figure 4 are clearly non-linear. On this dataset P-LS is sacrificing accuracy for smoothness — the tree-based fitting methods have significantly lower RMSE than P-LS. The smoother P-LS models may appear more appealing and easier to interpret, but there is structure in the BST-bagTR3 models that is less apparent or missing in the P-LS plots that might be informative or important. As just one example, the P-LS and BST-bagTR3 models do not agree on the slopes of parts of the models for the Coarse and Fine Aggregate features.

On the "Spambase" dataset, the shape functions are nonlinear with sharp turns. Again, the BST-bagTR3 model is significantly more accurate than P-IRLS. Interestingly, the spline models for features Freq_hp, Freq_!, Freq_remove and Freq_$ show strong positive or negative slope in the right-hand side of the shape plots

Model	Concrete	Wine	Delta	CompAct	Music	Synthetic	Mean
Linear Regression	10.43±0.49	7.55±0.13	5.68±0.14	9.72±0.55	9.61±0.09	1.01±0.00	1.68±0.98
P-LS	5.67±0.41	7.25±0.21	5.67±0.16	2.81±0.13	9.27±0.07	0.04±0.00	1.00±0.00
BST-SP	5.79±0.37	7.27±0.18	5.68±0.18	3.19±0.37	9.29±0.08	0.04±0.00	1.03±0.06
BF-SP	5.66±0.42	7.25±0.21	5.67±0.17	2.77±0.06	9.27±0.08	0.04±0.00	1.00±0.01
BST-TR2	5.19±0.39	7.17±0.10	5.75±0.18	2.68±0.33	9.55±0.08	0.11±0.00	0.98±0.08
BST-TR3	5.13±0.37	7.20±0.16	5.82±0.19	3.18±0.45	9.77±0.07	0.05±0.01	1.02±0.11
BST-TR4	5.24±0.39	7.24±0.15	5.83±0.21	3.70±0.52	9.88±0.09	0.07±0.01	1.07±0.15
BST-TR8	5.57±0.61	7.35±0.17	5.97±0.22	5.07±0.54	10.03±0.10	0.19±0.02	1.19±0.33
BST-TR12	5.92±0.63	7.39±0.13	6.03±0.19	6.59±0.71	10.15±0.07	0.26±0.02	1.31±0.54
BST-TR16	6.08±0.37	7.41±0.23	6.09±0.19	7.07±1.01	10.23±0.08	0.33±0.03	1.36±0.60
BST-bagTR2	5.06±0.39	7.05±0.11	5.67±0.20	**2.59±0.34**	**9.42±0.08**	0.07±0.00	0.96±0.08
BST-bagTR3	4.93±0.41	7.01±0.10	5.67±0.20	2.82±0.35	9.45±0.07	**0.03±0.00**	0.97±0.09
BST-bagTR4	4.99±0.43	7.01±0.12	5.70±0.20	2.95±0.35	9.46±0.08	**0.03±0.00**	0.99±0.09
BST-bagTR8	5.04±0.43	7.04±0.13	5.79±0.18	3.40±0.34	9.48±0.08	0.06±0.00	1.02±0.13
BST-bagTR12	5.11±0.44	7.07±0.15	5.85±0.18	3.76±0.33	9.50±0.07	0.07±0.00	1.05±0.16
BST-bagTR16	5.18±0.49	7.10±0.18	5.91±0.20	4.16±0.39	9.52±0.09	0.09±0.00	1.09±0.21
BST-bagTRX	**4.89±0.37**	**7.00±0.10**	5.65±0.20	**2.59±0.34**	**9.42±0.08**	**0.03±0.00**	**0.95±0.09**
BF-TR	5.80±0.60	7.19±0.09	5.67±0.21	2.81±0.25	9.88±0.08	0.06±0.03	1.02±0.07
BF-bagTR	5.10±0.49	7.02±0.13	**5.61±0.21**	2.69±0.31	9.43±0.07	0.04±0.00	0.97±0.07
BF-bstTR2	5.11±0.37	7.14±0.11	5.73±0.20	2.66±0.35	9.62±0.07	0.13±0.01	0.98±0.08
BF-bstTR3	5.21±0.38	7.29±0.19	5.84±0.21	4.38±0.24	10.77±0.10	0.04±0.01	1.14±0.24
BF-bstTR4	5.49±0.72	7.44±0.20	5.94±0.21	4.97±0.73	11.24±0.07	0.06±0.03	1.21±0.33
BF-bstTR8	6.74±0.76	7.93±0.32	6.08±0.24	9.18±0.77	12.08±0.07	0.04±0.01	1.59±0.87
BF-bstTR12	7.13±0.68	8.10±0.27	6.15±0.24	11.20±0.72	12.31±0.15	0.08±0.03	1.76±1.16
BF-bstTR16	7.22±0.73	8.33±0.35	6.18±0.24	11.41±0.29	12.59±0.10	0.11±0.08	1.79±1.17
BF-bbTR2	5.13±0.41	7.05±0.12	5.66±0.19	2.59±0.37	9.50±0.07	0.12±0.00	0.97±0.08
BF-bbTR3	5.15±0.44	7.07±0.17	5.74±0.20	2.85±0.33	9.80±0.07	0.04±0.00	0.99±0.09
BF-bbTR4	6.20±0.86	7.12±0.22	5.80±0.23	3.01±0.23	9.83±0.08	0.04±0.00	1.05±0.09
BF-bbTR8	6.33±0.46	7.30±0.21	5.95±0.23	3.72±0.84	9.86±0.11	0.04±0.00	1.11±0.16
BF-bbTR12	6.52±0.56	7.52±0.30	6.01±0.20	4.32±0.94	9.89±0.06	0.04±0.00	1.17±0.23
BF-bbTR16	6.37±0.48	7.63±0.26	6.07±0.24	4.85±0.76	9.91±0.07	0.05±0.01	1.21±0.29
Random Forests	4.98±0.44	6.05±0.23	5.34±0.13	2.45±0.09	9.70±0.07	0.55±0.00	0.88±0.06
Additive Groves	4.25±0.47	6.21±0.20	5.35±0.14	2.23±0.15	9.03±0.05	0.02±0.00	0.86±0.10

Table 5: RMSE for regression datasets. Each cell contains the mean RMSE ± one standard deviation. Average normalized score on five datasets (excludes synthetic) is shown in the last column, where the score is calculated as relative improvement over P-LS.

where data is sparse (albeit with very wide confidence intervals) while the BST-bagTR3 shape plots appear to be better behaved.

Below each shape plot in Figures 4 and 5 is the weight of each shape term in the linear model. These weights tell users how important each term is to the model. Terms can be sorted by weight, and if necessary terms with low weight can be removed from the model and the retained features reshaped.

In both figures there is coarse similarity between the feature shape plots learned by the spline and tree-based methods, but in many plots the tree-based methods appear to have caught structure that is missing or more difficult to see in the spline plots. The spline models may be more appealing to the eye, but they are clearly less accurate and appear to miss some of details of the shape functions.

5.3 Computational Cost

In our experiments, P-LS and P-IRLS are very fast on small datasets, but on the larger datasets they are slower than the BST-TRx. Due to the extra cost of bagging, BST-bagTRx, BF-bagTR and BF-bbTRx are much slower than P-LS/P-IRLS or BST-TRx. The slowest method we tested is backfitting, which is expensive because at each iteration the previous shape functions are discarded and a new fit for each feature must be learned. Gradient boosting converges faster because in each iteration the algorithm adds a patch to the existing pool of predictors, thus building on previous efforts rather than discarding them.

Gradient boosting is easier to parallelize [17] than backfitting (Gauss-Seidel). The Jacobi method is sometimes used as an alternative to Gauss-Seidel because it is easier to parallelize, however, in our experience, Jacobi-based backfitting converges to suboptimal solutions that can be much worse.

5.4 Limitations and Extensions

The experiments in this paper are on datasets of low-to-medium dimensionality (less than 100 dimensions). Our next step is to scale the algorithm to datasets with more dimensions (and more training points). Even linear models lose intelligibility when there are hundreds of terms in the model. To help retain intelligibility in high dimensional spaces, we have begun developing an extension to BST-bagTRX that incorporates feature selection in the feature shaping process to retain only those features that, after shaping, make the largest contributions to the model. We do not present results for feature selection in this paper because of space limitations, and because it is important to focus first on the foundational issue of what algorithm(s) train the best models.

In this paper we focus exclusively on shape functions of individual features; feature interaction is not allowed. Because of this, the models will not be able to achieve the same accuracy as unre-

Model	Spambase	Insurance	Magic	Letter	Adult	Physics	Mean
Logistic Regression	7.67±1.03	6.11±0.29	20.99±0.46	27.54±0.27	16.04±0.46	29.24±0.36	1.22±0.23
P-IRLS	6.43±0.77	6.11±0.30	14.53±0.41	17.47±0.24	15.00±0.28	29.04±0.49	1.00±0.00
BST-SP	6.24±0.65	6.07±0.31	14.54±0.31	17.61±0.23	15.02±0.25	28.98±0.43	1.00±0.03
BF-SP	6.37±0.29	6.11±0.29	14.58±0.32	17.52±0.17	15.01±0.28	28.98±0.46	1.00±0.03
BST-TR2	5.22±0.77	5.97±0.38	14.63±0.36	17.40±0.22	14.90±0.26	29.58±0.53	0.97±0.08
BST-TR3	5.09±0.79	5.97±0.38	14.54±0.14	17.29±0.25	14.58±0.33	28.81±0.52	0.95±0.08
BST-TR4	5.11±0.70	5.97±0.38	14.60±0.25	17.44±0.26	14.65±0.35	28.72±0.48	0.96±0.08
BST-TR8	5.39±1.06	5.97±0.38	14.64±0.23	17.44±0.27	14.61±0.34	28.77±0.55	0.96±0.08
BST-TR12	5.61±0.76	5.97±0.38	14.57±0.41	17.45±0.24	14.57±0.36	28.63±0.60	0.97±0.08
BST-TR16	5.93±0.96	5.97±0.38	14.83±0.38	17.47±0.23	14.62±0.32	28.63±0.51	0.98±0.05
BST-bagTR2	5.00±0.65	5.97±0.38	14.47±0.20	17.25±0.22	14.95±0.35	29.32±0.67	0.96±0.09
BST-bagTR3	4.89±1.01	5.97±0.38	14.39±0.13	17.22±0.24	**14.57±0.29**	28.65±0.47	0.94±0.09
BST-bagTR4	4.98±1.07	5.98±0.35	14.40±0.28	17.31±0.23	14.63±0.30	29.05±0.50	0.95±0.09
BST-bagTR8	5.22±1.05	5.99±0.36	14.43±0.33	17.42±0.15	14.68±0.35	28.73±0.64	0.96±0.08
BST-bagTR12	5.48±1.09	6.00±0.36	14.44±0.35	17.45±0.19	14.67±0.39	29.06±0.77	0.97±0.07
BST-bagTR16	5.52±1.01	5.99±0.36	14.45±0.29	17.47±0.23	14.69±0.34	28.77±0.65	0.97±0.07
BST-bagTRX	**4.78±0.82**	**5.95±0.37**	**14.31±0.21**	**17.21±0.23**	14.58±0.28	**28.62±0.49**	**0.94±0.09**
BF-TR	6.41±0.37	6.34±0.27	16.81±0.35	17.36±0.26	14.96±0.28	31.64±0.57	1.05±0.07
BF-bagTR	5.63±0.47	6.34±0.22	15.09±0.48	17.41±0.23	14.95±0.34	29.51±0.46	0.99±0.06
BF-bstTR2	5.39±0.68	6.28±0.18	14.43±0.37	17.44±0.35	14.87±0.21	29.70±0.66	0.98±0.35
BF-bstTR3	6.85±1.48	6.31±0.54	15.11±0.24	17.53±0.18	14.64±0.32	29.90±0.34	1.02±0.06
BF-bstTR4	7.63±0.85	6.40±0.48	15.47±0.26	17.46±0.29	14.66±0.27	29.67±0.80	1.05±0.09
BF-bstTR8	10.20±1.30	6.52±0.54	16.26±0.36	17.47±0.25	14.60±0.36	30.32±0.41	1.13±0.24
BF-bstTR12	12.39±1.04	6.53±0.54	16.95±0.40	17.50±0.25	14.76±0.32	31.08±0.43	1.21±0.35
BF-bstTR16	13.11±1.32	6.55±0.58	17.68±0.56	17.52±0.24	14.79±0.33	31.97±0.37	1.24±0.40
BF-bbTR2	5.48±0.59	6.20±0.26	15.26±0.43	17.86±0.30	14.90±0.31	29.36±0.56	0.99±0.08
BF-bbTR3	5.83±0.76	6.42±0.24	14.64±0.18	17.43±0.34	14.77±0.34	28.64±0.56	0.99±0.06
BF-bbTR4	6.13±0.90	6.48±0.20	14.68±0.24	17.43±0.26	14.74±0.35	28.64±0.50	1.00±0.07
BF-bbTR8	6.48±0.97	6.59±0.26	14.79±0.20	17.51±0.27	14.64±0.33	28.65±0.50	1.01±0.07
BF-bbTR12	7.35±1.24	6.56±0.21	14.90±0.22	17.53±0.18	14.58±0.33	28.88±0.29	1.04±0.10
BF-bbTR16	7.72±1.36	6.56±0.20	15.02±0.40	17.52±0.24	14.58±0.28	29.16±0.38	1.05±0.11
Random Forests	4.48±0.64	5.97±0.41	11.99±0.50	6.23±0.27	14.85±0.25	28.55±0.56	0.80±0.23

Table 6: Error rate for classification datasets. Each cell contains the classification error ± one standard deviation. Averaged normalized score on all datasets is shown in the last column, where the score is calculated as relative improvement over P-IRLS.

stricted full-complexity models on many datasets. The addition of a few carefully selected interaction terms would further close this gap [16]. Because 3-D plots can be visualized, we may be able to allow pairwise interactions in our models while preserving some of the intelligibility.

Our empirical results suggest that bagging small trees of only 2-4 leaves yields the best accuracy. These are very small trees trained for one feature at a time and thus they divide the number line into 2-4 subintervals. We could imagine replacing bagged decision trees with some type of dynamic programming algorithm that directly works on (possibly smoothed) subintervals of the number line.

6. RELATED WORK

Generalized additive models were introduced by the statistics community [14, 15, 22] and have been extended to include LASSO feature selection [18] and to incorporate interaction terms [16]. Binder and Tutz performed a comprehensive comparison of methods for fitting GAMs with regression splines [7]. They compared backfitting, boosting, and penalized iteratively re-weighted least squares on simulated datasets. Our work differs from theirs in that we examine both regression splines and regression trees, most of our experiments are with real datasets, we look at both regression and classification, and we introduce a new method that is more accurate than splines.

Methods have been proposed for fitting GAMs with arbitrary link functions where the link function also is unknown and must be fitted. ACE [9] is probably the most well-known method for fitting these kind of GAMs. We do not evaluate ACE in this work because learned link functions can be complex, making it difficult to interpret the feature shape models. We focus on the identity and logit link functions because these are the link functions appropriate for regression and classification.

Forman *et al.* proposed feature shaping for linear SVM classifiers [11]. Their focus is on estimating the posterior probability $P(y = 1|\boldsymbol{x}_i = v)$.

Recently there have been efforts to scale GAMs. [17] uses MapReduce to parallelize gradient boosting and large tree construction. [20] parallelizes growing regression trees via gradient boosting using a master-worker paradigm where data are partitioned among workers. The algorithm carefully orchestrates overlap between communication and computation to achieve good performance.

7. CONCLUSIONS

We present a comprehensive empirical study of algorithms for fitting generalized additive models (GAMs) with spline and tree-based shape functions. Our bias-variance analysis shows that spline-based methods tend to underfit and thus may miss important non-smooth structure in the shape models. As expected, the bias-variance analysis also shows that tree-based methods are prone to overfitting and require careful regularization. We also introduce a new GAM

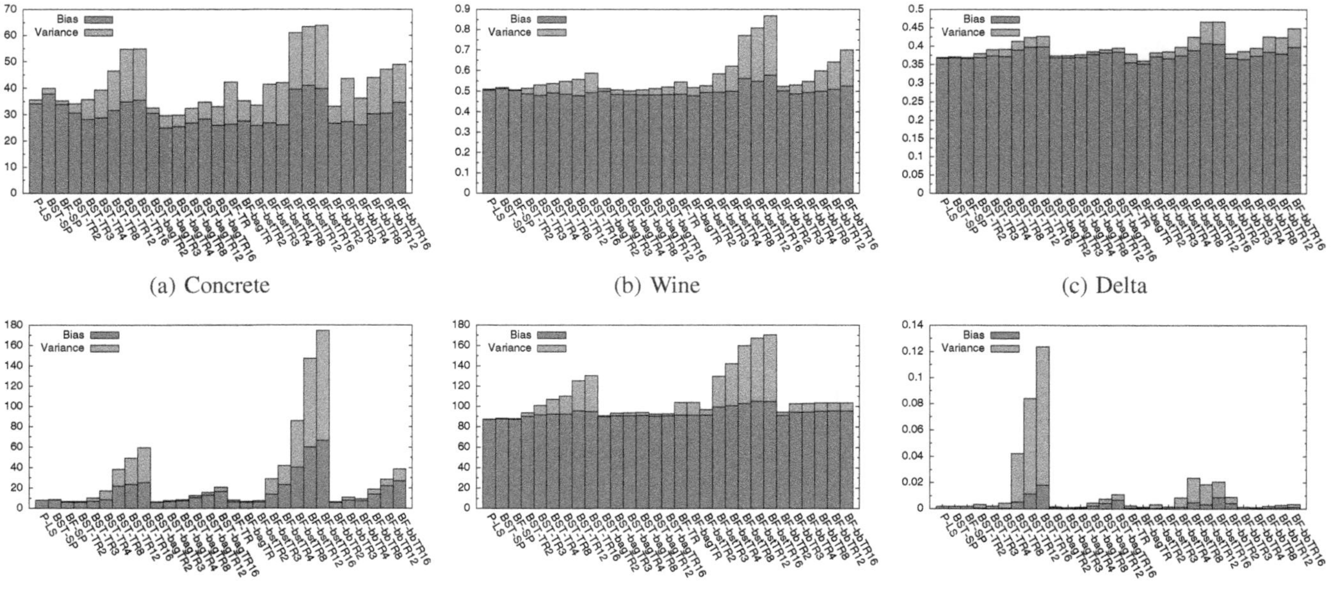

(a) Concrete (b) Wine (c) Delta

(d) CompAct (e) Music (f) Synthetic

Figure 6: Bias-variance analysis for the six regression problems (bias = red at bottom of bars; variance = green at top of bars).

method based on gradient boosting of size-limited bagged trees that yields significantly more accuracy than previous algorithms on both regression and classification problems while retaining the intelligibility of GAM models.

Acknowledgments. We thank the anonymous reviewers and Daria Sorokina for their valuable comments. This research has been supported by the NSF under Grants IIS-0911036 and IIS-1012593 and by a gift from NEC. Any opinions, findings, conclusions or recommendations expressed are those of the authors and do not necessarily reflect the views of the sponsors.

8. REFERENCES

[1] `http://archive.ics.uci.edu/ml/`.

[2] `http://www.liaad.up.pt/~ltorgo/Regression/DataSets.html`.

[3] `http://www.cs.toronto.edu/~delve/data/datasets.html`.

[4] `http://osmot.cs.cornell.edu/kddcup/`.

[5] `http://additivegroves.net`.

[6] E. Bauer and R. Kohavi. An empirical comparison of voting classification algorithms: Bagging, boosting, and variants. *Machine learning*, 36(1):105–139, 1999.

[7] H. Binder and G. Tutz. A comparison of methods for the fitting of generalized additive models. *Statistics and Computing*, 18(1):87–99, 2008.

[8] L. Breiman. Random forests. *Machine learning*, 45(1):5–32, 2001.

[9] L. Breiman and J. Friedman. Estimating optimal transformations for multiple regression and correlation. *Journal of the American Statistical Association*, pages 580–598, 1985.

[10] R. Caruana and A. Niculescu-Mizil. An empirical comparison of supervised learning algorithms. In *ICML*, 2006.

[11] G. Forman, M. Scholz, and S. Rajaram. Feature shaping for linear svm classifiers. In *KDD*, 2009.

[12] J. Friedman. Greedy function approximation: a gradient boosting machine. *Annals of Statistics*, 29:1189–1232, 2001.

[13] J. Friedman. Stochastic gradient boosting. *Computational Statistics and Data Analysis*, 38:367–378, 2002.

[14] T. Hastie and R. Tibshirani. Generalized additive models (with discussion). *Statistical Science*, 1:297–318, 1986.

[15] T. Hastie and R. Tibshirani. *Generalized additive models*. Chapman & Hall/CRC, 1990.

[16] G. Hooker. Generalized functional anova diagnostics for high-dimensional functions of dependent variables. *Journal of Computational and Graphical Statistics*, 16(3):709–732, 2007.

[17] B. Panda, J. Herbach, S. Basu, and R. Bayardo. Planet: massively parallel learning of tree ensembles with mapreduce. *PVLDB*, 2009.

[18] P. Ravikumar, H. Liu, J. Lafferty, and L. Wasserman. Sparse additive models. *Journal of the Royal Statistical Society: Series B (Statistical Methodology)*, 71(5):1009–1030, 2009.

[19] D. Sorokina, R. Caruana, and M. Riedewald. Additive groves of regression trees. In *ECML*, 2007.

[20] S. Tyree, K. Weinberger, K. Agrawal, and J. Paykin. Parallel boosted regression trees for web search ranking. In *WWW*, 2011.

[21] S. Wood. Thin plate regression splines. *Journal of the Royal Statistical Society: Series B (Statistical Methodology)*, 65(1):95–114, 2003.

[22] S. Wood. *Generalized additive models: an introduction with R*. CRC Press, 2006.

NASA: Achieving Lower Regrets and Faster Rates via Adaptive Stepsizes

Hua Ouyang
Computational Science and Engineering
Georgia Institute of Technology
houyang@cc.gatech.edu

Alexander Gray
Computational Science and Engineering
Georgia Institute of Technology
agray@cc.gatech.edu

ABSTRACT

The classic Stochastic Approximation (SA) method achieves optimal rates under the black-box model. This optimality does not rule out better algorithms when more information about functions and data is available.

We present a family of *Noise Adaptive Stochastic Approximation* (*NASA*) algorithms for online convex optimization and stochastic convex optimization. NASA is an adaptive variant of Mirror Descent Stochastic Approximation. It is novel in its practical variation-dependent stepsizes and better theoretical guarantees. We show that comparing with state-of-the-art adaptive and non-adaptive SA methods, lower regrets and faster rates can be achieved under low-variation assumptions.

Categories and Subject Descriptors

F.1.2 [**Theory of Computation**]: Modes of Computation—*Online computation*; I.2.6 [**Artificial Intelligence**]: Learning—*Parameter learning*; G.1.6 [**Numerical Analysis**]: Optimization—*Gradient methods*

General Terms

Algorithms

Keywords

online learning, online convex optimization, adaptive learning, stochastic optimization

1. INTRODUCTION

Stochastic Approximation (*SA*) method originally proposed by [12] for solving root finding problems is a recursive first-order algorithm:

$$\mathbf{x}_{t+1} \leftarrow \mathbf{x}_t + \eta_t \mathbf{Y}_t, \tag{1}$$

where $\eta_t \geq 0$ are called *stepsizes*. This simple paradigm has since then thrived in many fields such as adaptive signal processing, adaptive control, scientific computing and machine learning [6, 2]. In this paper we study SA in two specific and closely-related backgrounds: *online learning* and *stochastic optimization*.

SA is one of the main tools for stochastic optimization [14] which can expressed as:

$$\min_{\mathbf{x}\in\mathcal{X}} \Phi(\mathbf{x}) := \mathbb{E}_{\boldsymbol{\xi}}[f(\mathbf{x}, \boldsymbol{\xi})], \tag{2}$$

where $\boldsymbol{\xi}$ is a random vector with a fixed (and possibly unknown) probability distribution P. Taking $\mathbf{Y}_t$ in (1) as noisy first order information of Φ leads to the popular Stochastic Gradient Descent (SGD). Under the convexity assumption over f, SA's $O(1/\epsilon^2)$ iteration complexity (or equivalent, $O(1/\sqrt{T})$ rate of convergence for $\Phi(\mathbf{x})$) was shown to be optimal under the black-box (oracle) model [10]. With a strong convexity assumption over f, the $O(1/\sqrt{T})$ rate of convergence can be improved to $O(1/T)$ [9].

As an application of SA to online learning (specifically, online convex optimization), where no i.i.d. assumptions are made upon the sequential functions $\{f_t\}$, the Online Gradient Descent (OGD) algorithm proposed in [17] attains a $O(\sqrt{T})$ regret bound for minimizing general convex functions. When $\{f_t\}$ are H-strongly convex, logarithmic regrets can be attained using $1/Ht$ stepsizes [4].

SA is very sensitive to the selection of stepsizes which are crucial to its convergence. Classic analysis of SA relies on the assumptions that $\sum_{t\to\infty} \eta_t = \infty$ and $\sum_{t\to\infty} \eta_t^2 < \infty$ [6]. Despite the black-box-optimalities of SA, there is no unified theory that guides the selection of optimal stepsizes when more information is provided. Our motivation of this paper is that: a successful SA algorithm must explore the structures and properties of functions and data based on reasonable assumptions.

In a recent work [15], smoothness is considered as an important property for minimizing online nonnegative functions. The authors utilize properties of self-bounded functions termed in [13], and show that the regret of minimizing general convex functions is upper bounded by $O\big(\sqrt{\sum_{t=1}^{T} f_t(\mathbf{x}^*)}\big)$. This bound equals SA's $O(\sqrt{T})$ bound only in worst cases, and is much benign in low-noise (e.g. separable classification) applications. The underlying intuition is that, when functions are smooth, the gradient vanishes and the function value decreases as $\mathbf{x}_t$ is approaching the optimum $\mathbf{x}^*$. Hence instead of using a data-independent diminishing stepsize scheme (e.g. $1/\sqrt{t} \to 0$), it is preferable to adapt the current stepsize to the sum of (nonnegative) function values over previous iterations. In this paper we generalize this idea to nonsmooth and strongly convex functions and show that even faster rates and lower regret bounds can be attained using stepsizes .

We propose a Noise Adaptive Stochastic Approximation (NASA) scheme for online convex optimization (OCO) and stochastic convex optimization (SCO). It is an adaptive variant of Mirror Descent Stochastic Approximation (MDSA) [9]. NASA is novel in

KDD'12, August 12–16, 2012, Beijing, China.

its variation-dependent stepsizes and better theoretical guarantees. We show that for OCO and SCO, very low regrets and fast rates can be achieved under low-variation assumptions.

In contrast to previous adaptive online learning works by [8] and [3], where the authors proposed to use constant stepsizes and data-dependent Mahalanobis distance $\psi(\mathbf{z},\mathbf{x}_t) = (\mathbf{z}-\mathbf{x}_t)^T Q_t(\mathbf{z}-\mathbf{x}_t)$ as regulators (prox-functions), NASA's prox-function follows that of MDSA that is much more general than the Mahalanobis distance. Moreover, as we show in Section 4.1, NASA's regret bound is lower than AdaGrad [3] in most circumstances.

2. NOTATIONS AND ASSUMPTIONS

The subgradient of a function f is denoted as g. When f differentiable at $\mathbf{x}$, we also use ∇f to denote its gradient and $\nabla f(\mathbf{x}) = g(\mathbf{x})$. In OCO, we use subscripts t to denote the function and its (sub)gradients in round t. In SCO (2), we denote the (sub)gradient of Φ as $\Phi'(\mathbf{x}) := \mathbb{E}_{\boldsymbol{\xi}} g(\mathbf{x},\boldsymbol{\xi})$. To unify some analysis which applies for both stochastic and online settings, we use $f_t(\mathbf{x})$ and $g_t(\mathbf{x})$ interchangeably with $f(\mathbf{x},\boldsymbol{\xi}_t)$ and $g(\mathbf{x},\boldsymbol{\xi}_t)$.

In the proposed noise-adaptive algorithms, *variations* play important roles in the analysis and results, and hence deserve their own notations. In OCO, we denote

$$\bar{g}_{1:t} := \frac{1}{t}\sum_{i=1}^{t} g_i(\mathbf{x}_i), \tag{3}$$

$$\bar{\delta}_t := g_t(\mathbf{x}_t) - \bar{g}_{1:t} \quad \text{and} \quad \gamma_t := \bar{g}_{1:t} - \bar{g}_{1:t-1}; \tag{4}$$

while in SCO with i.i.d. assumptions, we use

$$\Phi'(\mathbf{x}) := \mathbb{E}_{\boldsymbol{\xi}} g(\mathbf{x},\boldsymbol{\xi}) \text{ and } \delta_t := g_t(\mathbf{x}) - \Phi'(\mathbf{x}). \tag{5}$$

A norm $\|\cdot\|$ is endowed with an inner product $\langle\cdot,\cdot\rangle$. We denote the corresponding dual norm as $\|\cdot\|_*$. A function f is *H-strongly convex* in $\mathcal{X}$ w.r.t. $\|\cdot\|$ iff for any $\mathbf{a},\mathbf{b}\in\mathcal{X}$, there is a constant $H>0$ such that

$$f(\mathbf{a}) - f(\mathbf{b}) \geq \langle g(\mathbf{b}), \mathbf{a}-\mathbf{b}\rangle + \frac{H}{2}\|\mathbf{a}-\mathbf{b}\|^2. \tag{6}$$

A *distance generating function* ω is differentiable and α-strongly convex w.r.t. $\|\cdot\|$. The corresponding *Bregman divergence* ψ is defined as

$$\psi(\mathbf{a},\mathbf{b}) := \omega(\mathbf{a}) - \omega(\mathbf{b}) - \langle\nabla\omega(\mathbf{b}), \mathbf{a}-\mathbf{b}\rangle. \tag{7}$$

Due to convexity of ω, Bregman divergence is always nonnegative.

In OCO, the *regret* is defined as $R(T) := \sum_{t=1}^{T} f_t(\mathbf{x}_t) - f_t(\mathbf{x}^*)$, where $\mathbf{x}^* := \arg\min_{\mathbf{z}\in\mathcal{X}} \sum_{t=1}^{T} f_t(\mathbf{z})$. In SCO, $\mathbf{x}^* := \arg\min_{\mathbf{z}\in\mathcal{X}} \Phi(\mathbf{z})$.

The following notations appear frequently in our analysis and results:

$$\Delta_t := \max_{1\leq i\leq t} \|\bar{\delta}_i\|_*, \quad \Gamma_t := \max_{1\leq i\leq t} \|\gamma_i\|_*. \tag{8}$$

The convexity assumption is made throughout the paper:

ASSUMPTION 2.1. *Function $f:\mathbb{R}^d\to\mathbb{R}$ is proper and convex, and $\mathcal{X}\subseteq\mathbb{R}^d$ is a convex closed set. Moreover, f is M-Lipschitz continuous in $\mathcal{X}$:*

$$|f(\mathbf{a}) - f(\mathbf{b})| \leq M\|\mathbf{a}-\mathbf{b}\| \;\; \forall \mathbf{a},\mathbf{b}\in\mathcal{X}, \text{ where } M>0.$$

We list three more assumptions that will be used either independently or jointly with others in the analysis.

ASSUMPTION 2.2. *Function $f:\mathbb{R}^d\to\mathbb{R}$ is continuously differentiable with L-Lipschitz continuous gradient ∇f w.r.t. $\|\cdot\|_*$:*

$$\|\nabla f(\mathbf{a}) - \nabla f(\mathbf{b})\|_* \leq L\|\mathbf{a}-\mathbf{b}\|, \;\; \forall\mathbf{a},\mathbf{b}\in\mathbb{R}^d, \text{ where } L>0.$$

Functions satisfy this assumption are also called *L-Lipschitz smooth*.

ASSUMPTION 2.3. *Function $f:\mathbb{R}^d\to\mathbb{R}$ is H-strongly convex in $\mathcal{X}$ w.r.t. $\|\cdot\|_*$, where $H>0$.*

ASSUMPTION 2.4. *Bregman divergence $\psi(\cdot,\cdot)$ grows Q-quadratically w.r.t. $\|\cdot\|_*$:*

$$\psi(\mathbf{a},\mathbf{b}) \leq \frac{Q}{2}\|\mathbf{a}-\mathbf{b}\|_*^2, \;\; \forall\mathbf{a},\mathbf{b}\in\mathbb{R}^d, \;\; \text{where } Q>0.$$

3. NOISE ADAPTIVE STOCHASTIC APPROXIMATION (NASA)

Mirror Descent Stochastic Approximation (MDSA) is a non-Euclidean generalization of the classic SA. It is employed as our basis algorithm for both OCO and SCO due to its universality [16]. MDSA's updating rule can be expressed as minimizing a regularized first order approximation of f at the current solution:

$$\mathbf{x}_{t+1} \leftarrow \arg\min_{\mathbf{z}\in\mathcal{X}} \eta_t \langle g_t(\mathbf{x}_t), \mathbf{z}-\mathbf{x}_t\rangle + \psi(\mathbf{z},\mathbf{x}_t), \tag{9}$$

where $\eta_t \geq 0$ is a stepsize which plays an important role in the convergence analysis. Classic SA and MDSA typically use a data-independent stepsize or a constant stepsize for all iterations. In all variations of NASA, we propose to use adaptive stepsizes $\eta_t(\delta_t)$, which is a function of variations δ_t of (sub)gradients over previous samples.

Section 4 is devoted to online learning, where we propose two variants of NASA for convex and strongly convex functions. The same adaptation idea is extended to stochastic optimization in Section 5.

4. NASA FOR ONLINE LEARNING

4.1 General Convex Functions

For general functions where we know nothing other than their convexities[1] (Assumption 2.1), Noise Adaptive Stochastic Approximation (NASA) uses MDSA's update scheme (9) together with the following stepsizes:

$$\eta_t = \frac{\sqrt{\alpha}D_{\psi,\mathcal{X}}}{\sqrt{\sum_{i=1}^{t}\|\bar{\delta}_i\|_*^2}}, \tag{10}$$

where we denote the upper bound of Bregman divergence:

$$D_{\psi,\mathcal{X}} := \max_t \sqrt{\psi(\mathbf{x}_t,\mathbf{x}^*)}. \tag{11}$$

Using updating scheme (9) and optimality conditions, we have the following key lemma that relates three vectors: $\mathbf{w}$, $\mathbf{w}^+$ and $\mathbf{v}$.

LEMMA 4.1. *Denote $\mathbf{w}^+ := \arg\min_{\mathbf{z}\in\mathcal{X}} \langle\mathbf{u},\mathbf{z}-\mathbf{w}\rangle + \psi(\mathbf{z},\mathbf{w})$, where ψ is defined in (7). For any $\mathbf{v},\mathbf{w}\in\mathcal{X}$ and $\mathbf{u},\bar{\mathbf{u}}\in\mathbb{R}^d$:*

$$\begin{aligned}\langle\mathbf{u},\mathbf{w}-\mathbf{v}\rangle &\leq \psi(\mathbf{v},\mathbf{w}) - \psi(\mathbf{v},\mathbf{w}^+) \\ &+ \frac{\|\mathbf{u}-\bar{\mathbf{u}}\|_*^2}{2\alpha} + \langle\bar{\mathbf{u}},\mathbf{w}-\mathbf{w}^+\rangle.\end{aligned} \tag{12}$$

PROOF. Since $\langle\mathbf{u},\mathbf{z}-\mathbf{w}\rangle + \psi(\mathbf{z})$ is convex and differentiable and $\mathcal{X}$ is convex, the necessary and sufficient optimality condition for $\mathbf{w}^+$ is

$$\langle\mathbf{u}+\nabla\psi(\mathbf{w}^+,\mathbf{w}), \mathbf{v}-\mathbf{w}^+\rangle \geq 0, \;\; \forall\mathbf{v}\in\mathcal{X}.$$

[1]Even if we know that a function is strongly convex, the algorithms and analysis in this section still apply, and they are robust to the overestimation of strong-convexity constants.

Recalling the definition of ψ, we have $\nabla\psi(\mathbf{z},\mathbf{w}) = \nabla\omega(\mathbf{z}) - \nabla\omega(\mathbf{w})$ and the above can be written as

$$\langle \nabla\omega(\mathbf{w}^+) - \nabla\omega(\mathbf{w}) + \mathbf{u}, \mathbf{w}^+ - \mathbf{v}\rangle \le 0. \tag{13}$$

It follows that: $\psi(\mathbf{v},\mathbf{w}^+) - \psi(\mathbf{v},\mathbf{w})$

$$\begin{aligned}
&= \left[\omega(\mathbf{v}) - \omega(\mathbf{w}^+) - \langle\nabla\omega(\mathbf{w}^+), \mathbf{v} - \mathbf{w}^+\rangle\right] \\
&- \left[\omega(\mathbf{v}) - \omega(\mathbf{w}) - \langle\nabla\omega(\mathbf{w}), \mathbf{v} - \mathbf{w}\rangle\right] \\
&= \langle \nabla\omega(\mathbf{w}^+) - \nabla\omega(\mathbf{w}) + \mathbf{u}, \mathbf{w}^+ - \mathbf{v}\rangle + \langle \mathbf{u}, \mathbf{v} - \mathbf{w}^+\rangle \\
&- \left[\omega(\mathbf{w}^+) - \omega(\mathbf{w}) - \langle\nabla\omega(\mathbf{w}), \mathbf{w}^+ - \mathbf{w}\rangle\right] \qquad (14) \\
&\overset{(13)}{\le} \langle \mathbf{u}, \mathbf{v} - \mathbf{w}^+\rangle - \psi(\mathbf{w}^+,\mathbf{w}) \\
&= \langle \mathbf{u} - \bar{\mathbf{u}}, \mathbf{w} - \mathbf{w}^+\rangle - \psi(\mathbf{w}^+,\mathbf{w}) \\
&+ \langle \mathbf{u}, \mathbf{v} - \mathbf{w}\rangle + \langle \bar{\mathbf{u}}, \mathbf{w} - \mathbf{w}^+\rangle
\end{aligned}$$

By Hölder's Inequality,

$$\begin{aligned}
&\langle \mathbf{u} - \bar{\mathbf{u}}, \mathbf{w} - \mathbf{w}^+\rangle \le \|\mathbf{u} - \bar{\mathbf{u}}\|_*\|\mathbf{w} - \mathbf{w}^+\| \\
&\le \frac{\|\mathbf{u} - \bar{\mathbf{u}}\|_*^2}{2\alpha} + \frac{\alpha}{2}\|\mathbf{w} - \mathbf{w}^+\|^2 \le \frac{\|\mathbf{u} - \bar{\mathbf{u}}\|_*^2}{2\alpha} + \psi(\mathbf{w}^+,\mathbf{w}),
\end{aligned} \tag{15}$$

where the last inequality is due to the α-strong convexity of $\omega()$ and definition (7). Combining (14) and (15) and rearranging our claim follows. □

We now apply this lemma to online MDSA.

LEMMA 4.2. *Under Assumption 2.1, we have* $\forall \mathbf{v} \in \mathcal{X}$:

$$\begin{aligned}
&\sum_{t=1}^{T} [f_t(\mathbf{x}_t) - f_t(\mathbf{v})] \le \frac{D^2_{\psi,\mathcal{X}}}{\eta_T} \\
&+ \sum_{t=1}^{T} \left[\frac{\eta_t}{2\alpha}\|\bar{\delta}_t\|_*^2 + \langle \bar{g}_{1:t}, \mathbf{x}_t - \mathbf{x}_{t+1}\rangle\right].
\end{aligned} \tag{16}$$

PROOF. By convexity and letting $\mathbf{u} = \eta_t g_t(\mathbf{x}_t)$, $\bar{\mathbf{u}} = \eta_t \bar{g}_{1:t}$, $\mathbf{w} = \mathbf{x}_t$ and $\mathbf{w}^+ = \mathbf{x}_{t+1}$ in Lemma 4.1 we have $\forall \mathbf{v} \in \mathcal{X}$: $f_t(\mathbf{x}_t) - f_t(\mathbf{v}) \le$

$$\begin{aligned}
&\langle g_t(\mathbf{x}_t), \mathbf{x}_t - \mathbf{v}\rangle \le \eta_t^{-1}\left[\psi(\mathbf{v},\mathbf{x}_t) - \psi(\mathbf{v},\mathbf{x}_{t+1})\right] \\
&+ \frac{\eta_t}{2\alpha}\|\bar{\delta}_t\|_*^2 + \langle \bar{g}_{1:t}, \mathbf{x}_t - \mathbf{x}_{t+1}\rangle.
\end{aligned} \tag{17}$$

Summing up (17) over $t = 1, \ldots, T$ and using (11) the result follows. □

Note that this lemma differs from Theorem 1 of [17] in two places One is that the squared magnitude of subgradient g is now replaced by $\|\bar{\delta}_t\|_*^2$; the other difference is the additional term $\langle \bar{g}_{1:t}, \mathbf{x}_t - \mathbf{x}_{t+1}\rangle$. Before proceeding, we present a lemma that will help bounding this additional term.

LEMMA 4.3. *For any* $t \ge 1$,

$$\bar{g}_{1:t} - \bar{g}_{1:t-1} = \frac{\bar{\delta}_t}{t} + \frac{\gamma_t}{t}, \tag{18}$$

where $\bar{\delta}_t$ *and* γ_t *are defined in (4) and we let* $\bar{g}_{1:0} = 0$.

PROOF. For any $t \ge 1$ we have

$$\begin{aligned}
\bar{g}_{1:t+1} - \bar{g}_{1:t} &= \frac{1}{t+1}\sum_{i=1}^{t+1} g_i(\mathbf{x}_i) - \frac{1}{t}\sum_{i=1}^{t} g_i(\mathbf{x}_i) \\
&= \frac{1}{t(t+1)}\left[t g_{t+1}(\mathbf{x}_{t+1}) - \sum_{i=1}^{t} g_i(\mathbf{x}_i)\right] \\
&= \frac{1}{t+1}\left[g_{t+1}(\mathbf{x}_{t+1}) - \bar{g}_{1:t}\right] \\
&= \frac{1}{t+1}\left\{\left[g_{t+1}(\mathbf{x}_{t+1}) - \bar{g}_{1:t+1}\right] + \left[\bar{g}_{1:t+1} - \bar{g}_{1:t}\right]\right\}.
\end{aligned}$$

Combing with $\bar{g}_{1:1} = \frac{\bar{\delta}_1}{1} + \frac{\gamma_1}{1}$ our claim is proved. □

Rearranging (18) we have:

COROLLARY 4.4. *For any* $t \ge 2$, $\gamma_t = \frac{\bar{\delta}_t}{t-1}$.

This corollary is not used to obtain regret bounds, yet it helps to understand the physical meanings of our bounds. If we regard $\|\bar{\delta}_t\|_*$ as the *magnitude* of variations, then $\|\gamma_t\|_*$ can be regarded as the *rate* of variations.

We are now ready to present the very low regret bound.

THEOREM 4.5. *Under Assumption 2.1 NASA's regret has the following upper bound:*

$$\begin{aligned}
R(T) \le &\frac{2D_{\psi,\mathcal{X}}}{\sqrt{\alpha}}\sqrt{\sum_{t=1}^{T}\|\bar{\delta}_t\|_*^2 - C} \\
&+ B_{\mathcal{X}}\left[\Delta_T\left(1 + \log\sum_{t=s_1}^{T}\frac{\|\bar{\delta}_t\|_*}{\Delta_T}\right)\right. \\
&\left. + \Gamma_T\left(1 + \log\sum_{t=t_1}^{T}\frac{\|\gamma_t\|_*}{\Gamma_T}\right)\right]
\end{aligned} \tag{19}$$

where Δ_T *and* Γ_T *are defined in (8),* $D_{\psi,\mathcal{X}}$ *is defined in (11),* $B_{\mathcal{X}} := \max_t\|\mathbf{x}_t\|$, $C := \langle \bar{g}_{1:T}, \mathbf{x}_{T+1}\rangle$ *and we denote* $s_1 := \min\{\tau : \sum_{i=1}^{\tau}\|\bar{\delta}_i\|_*/\Delta_T \ge 1\}$ *and* $t_1 := \min\{\tau : \sum_{i=1}^{\tau}\|\gamma_i\|_*/\Gamma_T \ge 1\}$.

PROOF. Replacing η_t in (16) with NASA's stepsize (10) and letting $\mathbf{v} = \mathbf{x}^*$ we have

$$\begin{aligned}
R(T) \le &\frac{D_{\psi,\mathcal{X}}}{\sqrt{\alpha}}\sqrt{\sum_{t=1}^{T}\|\bar{\delta}_t\|_*^2} + \frac{D_{\psi,\mathcal{X}}}{2\sqrt{\alpha}}\sum_{t=1}^{T}\frac{\|\bar{\delta}_t\|_*^2}{\sqrt{\sum_{i=1}^{t}\|\bar{\delta}_i\|_*^2}} \\
&+ \sum_{t=1}^{T}\langle \bar{g}_{1:t}, \mathbf{x}_t - \mathbf{x}_{t+1}\rangle.
\end{aligned} \tag{20}$$

By Lemma A.1 in the appendix we can bound the second term on the RHS of above as

$$\frac{D_{\psi,\mathcal{X}}}{2\sqrt{\alpha}}\sum_{t=1}^{T}\frac{\|\bar{\delta}_t\|_*^2}{\sqrt{\sum_{i=1}^{t}\|\bar{\delta}_i\|_*^2}} \le \frac{D_{\psi,\mathcal{X}}}{\sqrt{\alpha}}\sqrt{\sum_{t=1}^{T}\|\bar{\delta}_t\|_*^2}. \tag{21}$$

By Lemma 4.3 we can bound the third term on the RHS of (20) as below.

$$
\begin{aligned}
&\sum_{t=1}^{T}\langle \bar{g}_{1:t}, \mathbf{x}_t - \mathbf{x}_{t+1}\rangle + C = \sum_{t=1}^{T}\langle \bar{g}_{1:t} - \bar{g}_{1:t-1}, \mathbf{x}_t\rangle \\
&\le \sum_{t=1}^{T} \|\bar{g}_{1:t} - \bar{g}_{1:t-1}\|_* \|\mathbf{x}_t\| \overset{(18)}{\le} B_{\mathcal{X}} \sum_{t=1}^{T} \left\| \frac{\bar{\delta}_t + \gamma_t}{t} \right\|_* \\
&\le B_{\mathcal{X}} \sum_{t=1}^{T} \left(\left\| \frac{\bar{\delta}_t}{t} \right\|_* + \left\| \frac{\gamma_t}{t} \right\|_* \right) \\
&\le B_{\mathcal{X}} \left[\Delta_T \sum_{t=1}^{T} \frac{\|\bar{\delta}_t\|_*/\Delta_T}{t} + \Gamma_T \sum_{t=1}^{T} \frac{\|\gamma_t\|_*/\Gamma_T}{t} \right] \\
&\le B_{\mathcal{X}} \Delta_T \left(1 + \sum_{t=s_1}^{T} \frac{\|\bar{\delta}_t\|_*/\Delta_T}{\sum_{i=1}^{t} \|\bar{\delta}_i\|_*/\Delta_T} \right) \\
&+ B_{\mathcal{X}} \Gamma_T \left(1 + \sum_{t=t_1}^{T} \frac{\|\gamma_t\|_*/\Gamma_T}{\sum_{i=1}^{t} \|\gamma_i\|_*/\Gamma_T} \right)
\end{aligned} \tag{22}
$$

Applying Lemma A.3 in the appendix to the last inequality our claim follows. Note that in (19), if $T < s_1$ or $T < t_1$, then the corresponding logarithmic term vanishes. □

REMARK 4.6. We can compare NASA with Online Gradient Descent (OGD, [17]) and Online Adaptive Subgradient Method (AdaGrad, [3]). In OGD, $O(1/\sqrt{t})$ data-independent stepsizes are suggested. Denote $G_T := \max_{1\le t\le T} \|g_t(\mathbf{x}_t)\|_*$. Taking the optimal stepsize

$$
\eta_t = \frac{\sqrt{\alpha} D_{\psi,\mathcal{X}}}{G_T \sqrt{t}} \tag{23}
$$

we have

$$
R_{\text{OGD}}(T) \le \frac{2 D_{\psi,\mathcal{X}} G_T \sqrt{T}}{\sqrt{\alpha}}. \tag{24}
$$

In AdaGrad, if we take an adaptive diagonal scaling matrix in its Mahalanobis distance prox-function [8], the equivalent stepsize can be written as:

$$
\eta_t = \frac{\sqrt{\alpha} D_{\psi,\mathcal{X}}}{\sqrt{\sum_{i=1}^{t} \|g_i(\mathbf{x}_i)\|_*^2}} \tag{25}
$$

and we have

$$
R_{\text{AdaGrad}}(T) \le \frac{2 D_{\psi,\mathcal{X}}}{\sqrt{\alpha}} \sqrt{\sum_{t=1}^{T} \|g_t(\mathbf{x}_t)\|_*^2}. \tag{26}
$$

In an adversarial situation, e.g. the adversary has access to any mixed strategy such that $\|g_t(\mathbf{x}_t)\|_* = G \; \forall t = \{1 : t\}$, both OGD (24) and AdaGrad (26) retain $D_{\psi,\mathcal{X}} G\sqrt{T}$ bounds, while NASA's bound (19) becomes a constant. In benign cases, for example when $g_t(\mathbf{x}_t)$ are constants for all iterations except the kth iteration: $\|g_t(\mathbf{x}_t)\|_*^2 = T^{1/p-1} \; \forall t = \{1 : t\}\backslash k$ for some $p \ge 1$ and $\|g_k(\mathbf{x}_k)\|_*^2 = G^2$, then $R_{\text{OGD}}(T)$ is $O(T^{1/2})$, $R_{\text{AdaGrad}}(T)$ is $O(T^{1/(2p)})$, while NASA still retains a constant bound, providing that T is large enough to averaging out $\|\bar{\delta}_k\|_*$.

Besides, NASA's stepsize (10) is more practical than OGD's (23) where one needs to estimate G in addition to $D_{\psi,\mathcal{X}}$. A bad estimation of G, either too small or too large, will results in a even larger regret for OGD. In practice, even if one knows the form of function f_t and its subgradient, it is almost impossible to estimate G appropriately without seeing any data.

In contrast to AdaGrad, NASA is more flexible and it can be applied to any prox-function of a Bregman divergence style, while AdaGrad only applies to Mahalanobis distance prox-functions.

4.2 Strongly Convex Functions

In this section, we assume that the functions are strongly convex (Assumption 2.3) and the Bregman divergence $\psi()$ in MDSA grows Q-quadratically (Assumption 2.4).

For strongly convex functions, NASA uses MDSA's update scheme (9) together with the following stepsizes:

$$
\eta_t = \begin{cases} \frac{Q}{H} & \text{if } t < r_1, \\ \frac{Q\Delta_t^2}{H\sum_{i=1}^{t} \|\bar{\delta}_i\|_*^2} & \text{otherwise,} \end{cases} \tag{27}
$$

$$
\text{where} \quad r_1 := \min \left\{ \tau : \sum_{i=1}^{\tau} \|\bar{\delta}_i\|_*^2 \ge 1 \right\}. \tag{28}
$$

We can bound the cumulative function value reductions as follows.

LEMMA 4.7. *Under Assumption 2.1, 2.3 and 2.4, for any nonnegative stepsizes that satisfy* $\frac{1}{\eta_1} \le \frac{H}{Q}$ *and* $\frac{1}{\eta_t} - \frac{1}{\eta_{t-1}} \le \frac{H}{Q} \; \forall t \ge 2$, *we have* $\forall \mathbf{v} \in \mathcal{X}$:

$$
\sum_{t=1}^{T} [f_t(\mathbf{x}_t) - f_t(\mathbf{v})] \le \sum_{t=1}^{T} \left[\frac{\eta_t}{2\alpha} \|\bar{\delta}_t\|_*^2 + \langle \bar{g}_{1:t}, \mathbf{x}_t - \mathbf{x}_{t+1}\rangle \right]. \tag{29}
$$

PROOF. By the definition of strong-convexity (6), Lemma 4.1 and Assumption 2.4 we have $\forall \mathbf{v} \in \mathcal{X}$:

$$
\begin{aligned}
&f_t(\mathbf{x}_t) - f_t(\mathbf{v}) \le \langle g_t(\mathbf{x}_t), \mathbf{x}_t - \mathbf{v}\rangle - \frac{H}{2}\|\mathbf{x}_t, \mathbf{v}\|_*^2 \\
&\le \frac{1}{\eta_t}[\psi(\mathbf{x}_t, \mathbf{v}) - \psi(\mathbf{x}_{t+1}, \mathbf{v})] - \frac{H}{Q}\psi(\mathbf{x}_t, \mathbf{v}) \\
&+ \frac{\eta_t}{2\alpha}\|\bar{\delta}_t\|_*^2 + \langle \bar{g}_{1:t}, \mathbf{x}_t - \mathbf{x}_{t+1}\rangle.
\end{aligned} \tag{30}
$$

Summing up the first two terms of RHS over $t = 1, \ldots, T$ we have:

$$
\begin{aligned}
&\sum_{t=1}^{T} \left[\frac{1}{\eta_t}[\psi(\mathbf{x}_t, \mathbf{v}) - \psi(\mathbf{x}_{t+1}, \mathbf{v})] - \frac{H}{Q}\psi(\mathbf{x}_t, \mathbf{v}) \right] \\
&\le \sum_{t=2}^{T} \left[\psi(\mathbf{x}_t, \mathbf{v}) \left(\frac{1}{\eta_t} - \frac{1}{\eta_{t-1}} - \frac{H}{Q} \right) \right] \\
&- \frac{\psi(\mathbf{x}_{T+1}, \mathbf{v})}{\eta_T} + \frac{\psi(\mathbf{x}_1, \mathbf{v})}{\eta_1} - \frac{H}{Q}\psi(\mathbf{x}_1, \mathbf{v}) \le 0,
\end{aligned} \tag{31}
$$

where the last inequality is due to the nonnegativity of Bregman divergences. Thus the claim is proved. □

We are now ready to present the low regret result for strongly convex OCO problems.

THEOREM 4.8. *Under Assumption 2.1, 2.3 and 2.4, NASA's regret has the following upper bound:*

$$
\begin{aligned}
R(T) \le &\frac{Q}{2\alpha H}\left[1 + \Delta_T^2 \log \sum_{t=r_1}^{T} \|\bar{\delta}_t\|_*^2 \right] - C \\
&+ B_{\mathcal{X}} \left[\Delta_T \left(1 + \log \sum_{t=s_1}^{T} \frac{\|\bar{\delta}_t\|_*}{\Delta_T} \right) \right. \\
&\left. + \Gamma_T \left(1 + \log \sum_{t=t_1}^{T} \frac{\|\gamma_t\|_*}{\Gamma_T} \right) \right]
\end{aligned} \tag{32}
$$

where r_1 *is defined in (28), and* s_1, t_1, C *are defined in Theorem 4.5.*

PROOF. We first show that in the nontrivial case where $t \geq r_1$, NASA's stepsizes (27) satisfy the condition $\frac{1}{\eta_t} - \frac{1}{\eta_{t-1}} \leq \frac{H}{Q}$ in Lemma 4.7. For any fixed $t \geq 2$, if $\|\bar{\delta}_t\|_*^2 \geq \Delta_{t-1}^2$, then

$$\frac{Q}{H}\left(\frac{1}{\eta_t} - \frac{1}{\eta_{t-1}}\right) = \frac{\sum_{i=1}^t \|\bar{\delta}_i\|_*^2}{\|\bar{\delta}_t\|_*^2} - \frac{\sum_{i=1}^{t-1} \|\bar{\delta}_i\|_*^2}{\Delta_{t-1}^2}$$
$$\leq \frac{\sum_{i=1}^t \|\bar{\delta}_i\|_*^2}{\|\bar{\delta}_t\|_*^2} - \frac{\sum_{i=1}^{t-1} \|g_i(\mathbf{x}_i)\|_*^2}{\|\bar{\delta}_t\|_*^2} = 1.$$

If $\|\bar{\delta}_t\|_*^2 < \Delta_{t-1}^2$, then

$$\frac{Q}{H}\left(\frac{1}{\eta_t} - \frac{1}{\eta_{t-1}}\right) = \frac{\sum_{i=1}^t \|\bar{\delta}_i\|_*^2}{\Delta_{t-1}^2} - \frac{\sum_{i=1}^{t-1} \|\bar{\delta}_i\|_*^2}{\Delta_{t-1}^2}$$
$$= \frac{\|\bar{\delta}_t\|_*^2}{\Delta_{t-1}^2} < 1.$$

The regret bound follows immediately. Replacing $\mathbf{v}$ with $\mathbf{x}_*$ in (29) we have:

$$R(T) \leq \frac{Q}{2\alpha H}\sum_{t=1}^T \frac{\Delta_t^2 \|\bar{\delta}_t\|_*^2}{\sum_{i=1}^t \|\bar{\delta}_i\|_*^2} + \sum_{t=1}^T \langle \bar{g}_{1:t}, \mathbf{x}_t - \mathbf{x}_{t+1}\rangle$$
$$\leq \frac{Q}{2\alpha H}\left(\sum_{t=1}^{r_1 - 1} \|\bar{\delta}_t\|_*^2 + \sum_{t=r_1}^T \frac{\Delta_t^2 \|\bar{\delta}_t\|_*^2}{\sum_{i=1}^t \|\bar{\delta}_i\|_*^2}\right) \tag{33}$$
$$+ \sum_{t=1}^T \langle \bar{g}_{1:t}, \mathbf{x}_t - \mathbf{x}_{t+1}\rangle$$

Due to the fact that $\Delta_t \leq \Delta_T$ and combine Lemma A.3 and (22) the claim is proved. As in Theorem 4.5, if $T < r_1$ or $T < s_1$ or $T < t_1$, the corresponding logarithmic term vanishes. □

REMARK 4.9. Although [8] and [3] are only proposed for general convex functions and there is no strongly convex counterparts, we can have an analogy to NASA (27) and let

$$\eta_t = \frac{QG_t^2}{H\sum_{i=1}^t \|g_i(\mathbf{x}_i)\|_*^2}, \tag{34}$$

where $G_t := \max_{1 \leq i \leq t} \|g_i(\mathbf{x}_i)\|_*$. Let us call it SAdaGrad, and its regret bound is

$$R_{\text{SAdaGrad}}(T) \leq \frac{Q}{2\alpha H}\left[1 + G_T^2 \log \sum_{t=1}^T \|g_t(\mathbf{x}_t)\|_*^2\right]. \tag{35}$$

We can compare NASA with SAdaGrad and strongly convex OGD [4] where logarithmic regret

$$R_{\text{OGD}}(T) \leq \frac{QG_T^2}{2\alpha H}(1 + \log T), \tag{36}$$

is attained by taking the data-independent stepsize $\eta_t = \frac{Q}{Ht}$. In an adversarial case where $\|g_t(\mathbf{x}_t)\|_*^2 = G,\ \forall t = 1, \ldots, T$, NASA's bound (33) becomes a constant since $\|\bar{\delta}_t\|_* = 0$, while both R_{OGD} and R_{SAdaGrad} are of $O(\log T)$. In benign cases, for example when $g_t(\mathbf{x}_t)$ are constants for all iterations except the kth iteration: $\|g_t(\mathbf{x}_t)\|_*^2 = T^{1/p-1}\ \forall t = \{1 : t\}\backslash k$ for some $p \geq 1$ and $\|g_k(\mathbf{x}_k)\|_*^2 = G^2$, then $R_{\text{OGD}}(T)$ is $O(\log T)$, $R_{\text{SAdaGrad}}(T)$ is $O(\log T^{1/p})$, while NASA still remains a constant bound, providing that T is large enough to averaging out $\|\bar{\delta}_k\|_*$.

5. NASA FOR STOCHASTIC OPTIMIZATION

The idea of noise-adaptive SA can be naturally extended to stochastic convex optimization problems (SCO), where $\{f_t\}$ are i.i.d. We first quickly review two recent progresses in solving SCO.

RMDSA [9] is a stochastic counterpart of mirror descent for SCO. Taking time-varying stepsize policy $\eta_t = \frac{\sqrt{\alpha}D_{\psi,\mathcal{X}}}{G\sqrt{t}}$, RMDSA's rate of convergence for minimizing general convex functions is

$$\mathbb{E}[\Phi(\tilde{\mathbf{x}}_T) - \Phi(\mathbf{x}^*)] \leq \frac{D_{\psi,\mathcal{X}}G}{\sqrt{\alpha}} \cdot \frac{3 + \ln T}{4(\sqrt{T+1} - 1)}, \tag{37}$$

where $\tilde{\mathbf{x}}_T := \left(\sum_{t=1}^T \eta_t\right)^{-1} \sum_{t=1}^T \eta_t \mathbf{x}_t$ and $G := \sup_{\mathbf{x}} \mathbb{E}[\|g(\mathbf{x}, \boldsymbol{\xi})\|_*]$. This bound can be improved when smoothness assumptions are made. With Lipschitz gradients, Nesterov's accelerated gradient descent (AGD) is proved to be optimal for convex programming [11]. Stochastic versions of AGD [7], [5] are proposed and shown to outperform RMDSA. In following we show that when applying NASA to stochastic AGD, even faster rates can be attained for optimizing smooth or nonsmooth functions.

Algorithm 1 lists the accelerated MDSA (aka AC-SA) proposed in [7]. To unify the analysis for both smooth and nonsmooth functions we adopt the "composite" setting: $f_t(\mathbf{x}) = p_t(\mathbf{x}) + q_t(\mathbf{x})$, where p_t is a convex function satisfying Assumption 2.1, and q_t is a smooth function satisfying Assumption 2.2

Algorithm 1 Accelerated MDSA (AC-SA)

1: Initialize $\mathbf{x}_0^{\text{ag}} = \mathbf{x}_0 \in \mathcal{X}$
2: **for** $t = 1, \ldots, T$ **do**
3: $\quad \mathbf{x}_t^{\text{md}} \leftarrow \beta_t^{-1}\mathbf{x}_{t-1} + (1 - \beta_t^{-1})\mathbf{x}_{t-1}^{\text{ag}}$
4: $\quad \mathbf{x}_t \leftarrow \arg\min_{\mathbf{z}\in\mathcal{X}} \{\eta_t \langle g_t(\mathbf{x}_t^{\text{md}}), \mathbf{z}\rangle + \psi(\mathbf{z}, \mathbf{x}_{t-1})\}$
5: $\quad \mathbf{x}_t^{\text{ag}} \leftarrow \beta_t^{-1}\mathbf{x}_t + (1 - \beta_t^{-1})\mathbf{x}_{t-1}^{\text{ag}}$
6: **end for**

Two series of stepsizes β_t and η_t need to be specified to complete this algorithm. With the notation $\delta_t := g_t(\mathbf{x}_t^{\text{md}}) - \nabla\Phi(\mathbf{x}_t^{\text{md}})$, we propose the following stepsize policy for NASA:

$$\beta_t = \frac{t+1}{2}, \quad \eta_t = \frac{t+1}{2}\min\left\{\frac{\alpha}{2L}, \frac{\Lambda_t}{t+1}\right\}, \tag{38}$$

where

$$\Lambda_t := \begin{cases} \sqrt{\alpha}D_{\psi,\mathcal{X}} & \text{if } t < s_1, \\ \frac{\sqrt{\alpha}D_{\psi,\mathcal{X}}}{\sqrt{\sum_{i=1}^t (2M + \|\delta_i\|_*)^2}} & \text{otherwise,} \end{cases}$$

$$s_1 := \min\left\{\tau : \sum_{i=1}^\tau (2M + \|\delta_i\|_*)^2 \geq 1\right\}. \tag{39}$$

and

$$D_{\psi,\mathcal{X}} := \max_t \sqrt{\psi(\mathbf{x}_t, \mathbf{x}^*)}. \tag{40}$$

We firstly present the key lemma of AC-SA, which is due to [7].

LEMMA 5.1. *[7] Assume that the stepsizes β_t and η_t satisfy $\beta_t \geq 1$ and $\alpha\beta_t > L\eta_t$. Under Assumption 2.1, 2.2 and 2.4, using AC-SA (Alg. 1), we have $\forall \mathbf{v} \in \mathcal{X}$:*

$$\beta_t\eta_t\left[\Phi(\mathbf{x}_t^{ag}) - \Phi(\mathbf{v})\right] \leq (\beta_t - 1)\eta_t\left[\Phi(\mathbf{x}_{t-1}^{ag}) - \Phi(\mathbf{v})\right]$$
$$+ \psi(\mathbf{x}_{t-1}, \mathbf{v}) - \psi(\mathbf{x}_t, \mathbf{v}) - \eta_t\langle \delta_t, \mathbf{x}_{t-1} - \mathbf{v}\rangle + U_t \tag{41}$$

$$\textit{where} \quad U_t := \frac{\beta_t\eta_t^2(2M + \|\delta_t\|_*)^2}{2(\alpha\beta_t - L\eta_t)}. \tag{42}$$

NASA's convergence rate follows immediately.

THEOREM 5.2. *Under Assumption 2.1, 2.2, 2.4, taking NASA's stepsizes (38) we have:* $\mathbb{E}\left[\Phi(\mathbf{x}_T^{ag}) - \Phi(\mathbf{x}^*)\right] \le$

$$\left[\frac{2LD^2_{\psi,\mathcal{X}}}{\alpha T(T+2)} + \frac{D_{\psi,\mathcal{X}}}{\sqrt{\alpha(T+2)}}\sqrt{\frac{\sum_{t=1}^{T+1}\sigma_t^2}{T+1}}\right]\left(5+\log\sum_{t=1}^{T}\sigma_t^2\right) \quad (43)$$

where $\sigma_t^2 := \mathbb{E}[(2M + \|\delta_t\|_*)^2]$ *and* s_1 *is defined in (39).*

PROOF. See Appendix B. □

6. EXPERIMENTAL RESULTS

6.1 Environment-Changing Ridge Regression

To demonstrate the adaptive capacity of NASA , we make a simulated dataset and perform experiments with it on the ridge regression problem: $f_t(\mathbf{x}) = (y_t - \mathbf{x}^T\mathbf{s}_t)^2 + \lambda\|\mathbf{x}\|_2^2$. Here $(\mathbf{s}_t, y_t)$ represents a data sample and its target response variable at round t. We let $\lambda = 0.0001$ in all the experiments. The data simulation is as follows. Instead of using a linear regressor with a fixed set of coefficients, we have two sets of "true" regression coefficients: $\mathbf{c}_1 = [0.31, -0.45, 0.92, 0.03, -0.75, -0.39]^T$ and $\mathbf{c}_2 = 2\mathbf{c}_1$. We generate $4,000$ data samples $\mathbf{s}_t \in \mathbb{R}^6$ where each dimension is drawn from the normal distribution $\mathcal{N}(2, 10)$. These samples are evenly divided into two subsets. For the first $2,000$ samples, $y_t = \mathbf{c}_1^T\mathbf{s}_t + n_t$, and for $t = 2,001 \sim 4,000$, $y_t = \mathbf{c}_2^T\mathbf{s}_t + n_t$, where $n_t \sim \mathcal{N}(0, 0.01)$ are noises.

We perform two sets of experiments. In the first set we assume a black-box model, hence the general convex NASA (10) is adopted. Strong-convexities are assumed in the second set of experiments, and (27) is adopted. It has been observed that the estimation of the strong-convexity constant H is crucial in the convergence of SA algorithms [1, 9]. Without tackling this drawback, in our experiments, H is searched within $\{1, 10, 10^2, 10^3, 10^4, 10^5, 10^6\}$, and the one with the lowest $\sum_t f_t$ is reported.

The results are depicted in Fig.1. We can see that in both general and strongly convex settings, when $t > 2000$, NASA can very quickly adapt to the changes of the adversary's behavior. OGD can slowly recover from the changes and converges after a much longer time (Fig.1 Left). Comparing with NASA, OGD's total sum of function values for $T = 4000$ is 5-times higher. Strongly convex OGD even fails to converge due to the improperly estimated H.

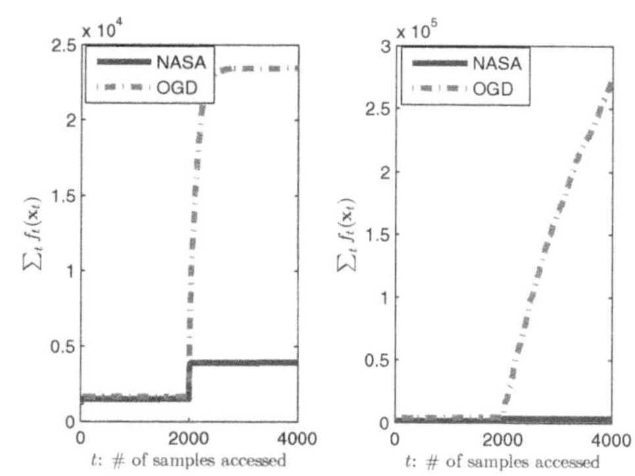

Figure 1: Online ridge regression. Left: convex; Right: strongly convex.

6.2 Real World Data

To evaluate the efficiency of NASA in real world applications, we take three datasets from `www.csie.ntu.edu.tw/~cjlin/libsvmtools/datasets/`. **abalone** is for regression, while **svmguide1** and **covtype** are for binary classification. The ridge regression and SVM cost functions $f_t(\mathbf{x}) = [1 - y_t\mathbf{x}^T\mathbf{s}_t]_+ + \lambda\|\mathbf{x}\|_2^2$ are adopted. Both convex and strongly convex algorithms are tested, and as in Section 6.1, best H is searched within a fixed set.

The results are shown in Fig.2, 3 and 4. We can see that in all settings NASA outperforms OGD. Since the cost functions are strongly convex, the cumulated function values are slightly lower than when we use strongly convex OGD/NASA. This difference is not as prominent as that in Fig. 1. The reason might be that the loss function weakens the strong-convexity of the squared l_2 norm.

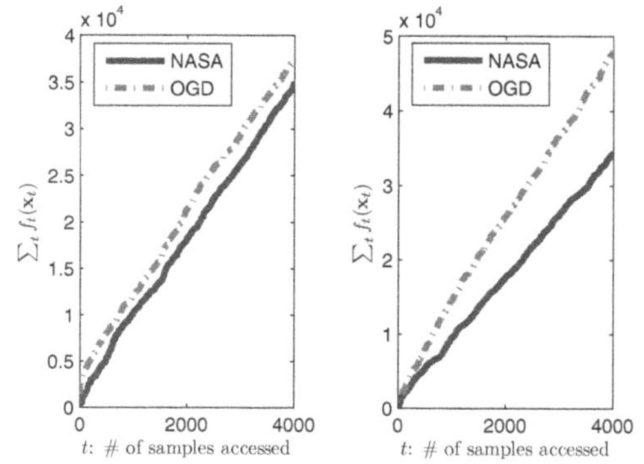

Figure 2: abalone. Left: convex; Right: strongly convex.

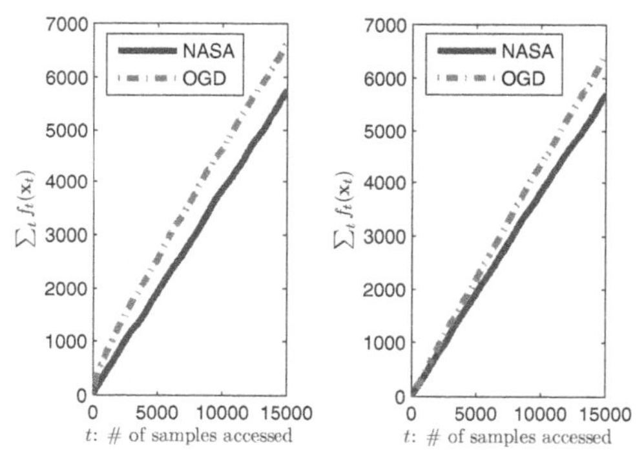

Figure 3: svmguide1. Left: convex; Right: strongly convex.

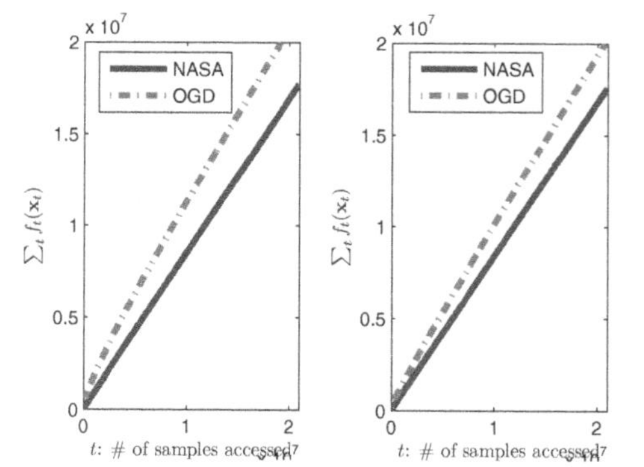

Figure 4: covtype. Left: convex; Right: strongly convex.

6.3 Comparisons to AdaGrad

6.3.1 *Simulated Gradients*

As discussed in the Remark 4.6, AdaGrad [3] is another way to adaptively take the advantage of previous gradient history, begging the question of whether it has similar behavior as NASA.

In the comparisons of upper bounds for OGD, AdaGrad and NASA presented in Remark 4.6 and 4.9, our statements are supported by extreme cases. In this section we use three sets of simulated experiments to further explore the advantages of NASA vs AdaGrad. Indeed, the comparison depends on the statistical properties of gradients. In these experiments, we assume that gradient vectors are from certain classes of statistical distributions. We observe that in most cases, NASA achieves a lower regret bound than AdaGrad.

In the first set of experiments, we focus on the general convex functions. We assume that each dimension of gradients $g_t(\mathbf{x}_t)$ are from a normal distribution $\mathcal{N}(\mu, \sigma)$. We let the dimension of our data to be 500, and plot the regret bounds for 1000 iterations.

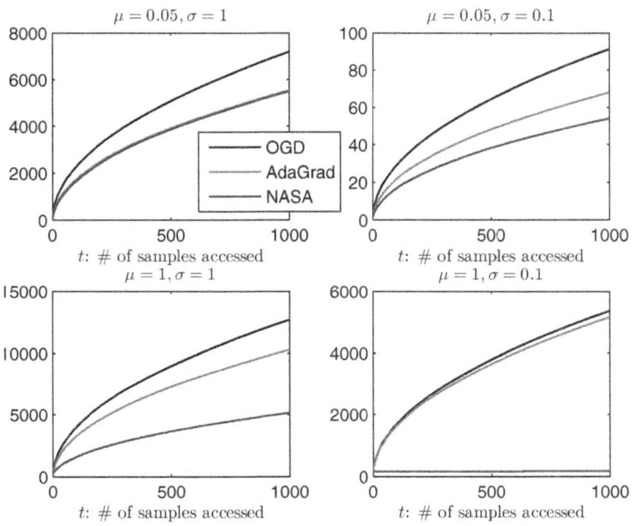

Figure 5: Comparing regret bounds.

Form Fig.5 we can observe that in all the 4 combinations of μ and σ, NASA outperforms both OGD and AdaGrad. When μ is relatively large (lower two figures), NASA achieves a significantly lower regret bound. This corresponds to difficult problems where the noise level is high. Moreover, when σ is relatively small (lower right), AdaGrad's performance is close to OGD, while NASA significantly outperforms its competitors. When μ is small (upper two figures), NASA's advantage is not as significant as that of large μ. This corresponds to the situations where the problem is relatively easy to solve. Moreover, for large σ (upper left), NASA's bound is very close to AdaGrad, but still lower.

In the second set of experiments we assume that each dimension of the gradient vectors has a uniform distribution, which corresponds to a stationary process. The simulation results are illustrated in Fig.6. We can observe that NASA's bound is significantly lower than the other two algorithms, while AdaGrad is marginally better than OGD.

In the third set of experiments we assume that each dimension of the gradient vectors is monotonically approaching 0 at the rate of $\frac{1}{t^p}$, where $p > 0$. In Fig.7 we plot regret bounds for $p = 0.1,\ 0.5, 1$

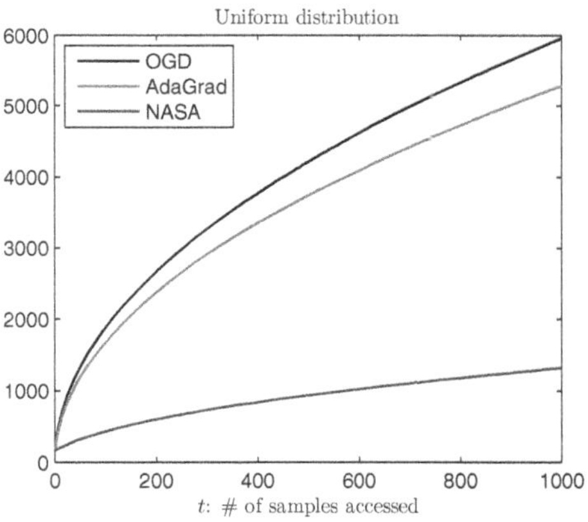

Figure 6: Comparing regret bounds.

and 2. When $p = 0.5,\ 1$ and 2, we omit the result for OGD to magnify the differences between NASA and AdaGrad. We can observe that NASA's bound is lower than AdaGrad when $p <= 1$. For extremely easy problems where gradient vectors approaches 0 at a fast rate of $\frac{1}{t^2}$, AdaGrad achieves a slightly lower regret.

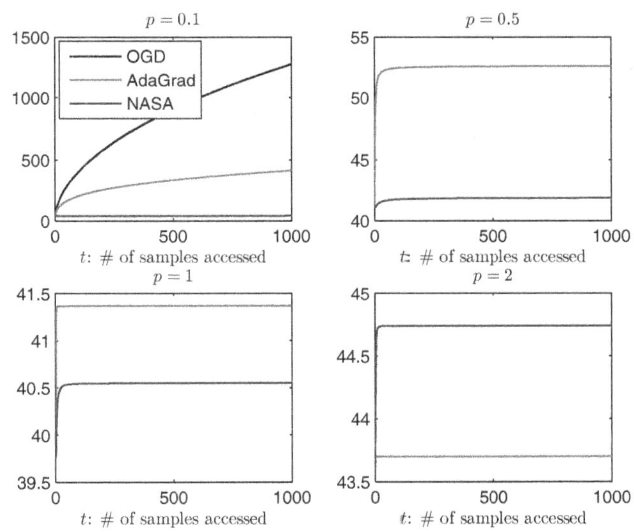

Figure 7: Comparing regret bounds.

6.3.2 *Real World Data*

To empirically compare the performance of NASA vs AdaGrad, we use a real-world text dataset RCV1 collected from Reuters news stories. We use unregularized hinge loss as our objective function, and do not assume strong convexity. The means and standard deviations of cumulated function values are shown in Table 1. Each value is calculated from 10 experiments under the same setting.

We can see that in all the settings, NASA's cumulated function values are lower than OGD and AdaGrad. When the number of iterations increases, the differences between NASA and AdaGrad

Table 1: Comparing $\sum_t f_t(\mathbf{x}_t)$

	OGD	AdaGrad	NASA
1 epoch	3461.9 ± 48.1	3260.5 ± 40.3	$\mathbf{3253.0 \pm 30.2}$
2 epochs	5268.7 ± 59.3	4688.5 ± 51.2	$\mathbf{4590.2 \pm 33.1}$
3 epochs	6814.1 ± 53.9	5809.5 ± 53.6	$\mathbf{5624.6 \pm 34.9}$
4 epochs	8050.0 ± 43.4	6722.1 ± 69.4	$\mathbf{6426.7 \pm 33.7}$

increases accordingly, which give the empirical evidence of the regret bound simulations presented in Section 6.3.1.

7. CONCLUSIONS

We propose a family of adaptive stochastic approximation algorithms, named NASA, for online convex optimization (both convex and strongly convex assumptions) and stochastic optimization. Their stepsizes are adaptive to the previous-seen data. These algorithms achieve lower regret bounds or faster rates of convergence, provided that the variations of (sub)gradients is low. NASA is under the mirror descent framework, hence is very flexible to various prox-functions. Experiments show that NASA is adaptive to the behaviors of the adversary. They outperform OGD and AdaGrad in both convex and strongly convex minimizations.

8. REFERENCES

[1] P. Bartlett, E. Hazan, and A. Rakhlin. Adaptive online gradient descent. In *Proceedings of NIPS*, 2007.

[2] L. Bottou and N. Murata. Stochastic approximations and efficent learning. In M. A. Arbib, editor, *The Handbook of Brain Theory and Neural Networks*. Cambridge University Press, 2nd edition, 2002.

[3] J. Duchi, E. Hazan, and Y. Singer. Adaptive subgradient methods for online learning and stochastic optimization. In *Proceedings of COLT*, 2010.

[4] E. Hazan, A. Agarwal, A. Kalai, and S. Kale. Logarithmic regret algorithms for online convex optimization. In *COLT*, 2006.

[5] C. Hu, J. Kwok, and W. Pan. Accelerated gradient methods for stochastic optimization and online learning. In *NIPS*, 2009.

[6] H. J. Kushner and G. G. Yin. *Stochastic Approximation and Recursive Algorithms and Applications*. Springer, 2nd edition, 2003.

[7] G. Lan. Efficient methods for stochastic composite optimization. Technical report, Georgia Institute of Technology, August 2008.

[8] H. B. McMahan and M. Streeter. Adaptive bound optimization for online convex optimization. In *Proceedings of COLT*, 2010.

[9] A. S. Nemirovski, A. Juditsky, G. Lan, and A. Shapiro. Robust stochastic approximation approach to stochastic programming. *SIAM Journal on Optimization*, 19(4):1574–1609, 2009.

[10] A. S. Nemirovsky and D. B. Yudin. *Problem Complexity and Method Efficiency in Optimization*. John Wiley & Sons, 1983.

[11] Y. Nesterov. *Introductory Lectures on Convex Optimization*. Kluwer Academic Publishers, 2004.

[12] H. Robbins and S. Monro. A stochastic approximation method. *Annals of Mathematical Statistics*, 22(3):400–407, 1951.

[13] S. Shalev-Shwartz. *Online Learning: Theory, Algorithms, and Applications*. PhD thesis, The Hebrew University of Jerusalem, 2007.

[14] A. Shapiro, D. Dentcheva, and A. Ruszczynski. *Lectures on Stochastic Programming: Modeling and Theory*. SIAM, 2009.

[15] N. Srebro, K. Sridharan, and A. Tewari. Smoothness, low-noise and fast rates. In *NIPS*, 2010.

[16] K. Sridharan, N. Srebro, and A. Tewari. On the universality of online mirror descent. In *Proceedings of NIPS 24*, 2011.

[17] M. Zinkevich. Online convex programming and generalized infinitesimal gradient ascent. In *ICML*, 2003.

APPENDIX

A. TECHNICAL LEMMAS

LEMMA A.1. *For any $\delta_i \geq 0, i = 1, 2, \ldots$ and integers $t \geq s \geq 1$ one has*

$$\sum_{i=s}^{t} \frac{\delta_i}{\sqrt{\sum_{j=1}^{i} \delta_j}} \leq 2\left(\sqrt{\sum_{i=1}^{t} \delta_i} - \sqrt{\sum_{i=1}^{s-1} \delta_i}\right).$$

PROOF.

$$\sum_{i=s}^{t} \frac{\delta_i}{\sqrt{\sum_{j=1}^{i} \delta_j}} \leq \int_{\sum_{i=1}^{s-1} \delta_i}^{\sum_{i=1}^{t} \delta_i} \frac{1}{\sqrt{m}} dm$$

$$= 2\left(\sqrt{\sum_{i=1}^{t} \delta_i} - \sqrt{\sum_{i=1}^{s-1} \delta_i}\right).$$

□

COROLLARY A.2. *For any integers $t \geq i \geq s \geq 1$ one has*

$$2\left(\sqrt{t+1} - \sqrt{s}\right) \leq \sum_{i=s}^{t} \frac{1}{\sqrt{i}} \leq 2\left(\sqrt{t} - \sqrt{s-1}\right).$$

PROOF. For the LHS:

$$\sum_{i=s}^{t} \frac{1}{\sqrt{i}} \geq \int_{s-1}^{t} \frac{1}{\sqrt{m+1}} dm = 2\left(\sqrt{t+1} - \sqrt{s}\right).$$

The RHS follows immediately from Lemma A.1. □

LEMMA A.3. *For any $\delta_i \geq 0, i = 1, 2, \ldots$ and integers $t \geq s \geq 1$ such that $\sum_{i=1}^{s-1} \delta_i \geq 1$ one has*

$$\sum_{i=s}^{t} \frac{\delta_i}{\sum_{j=1}^{i} \delta_j} \leq \ln\left(\sum_{i=1}^{t} \delta_i\right) - \ln\left(\sum_{i=1}^{s-1} \delta_i\right).$$

PROOF. Since $\sum_{i=1}^{s-1} \delta_i \geq 1$,

$$\sum_{i=s}^{t} \frac{\delta_i}{\sum_{j=1}^{i} \delta_j}$$

$$\leq \int_{\sum_{i=1}^{s-1} \delta_i}^{\sum_{i=1}^{t} \delta_i} \frac{1}{m} dm = \ln\left(\sum_{i=1}^{t} \delta_i\right) - \ln\left(\sum_{i=1}^{s-1} \delta_i\right).$$

□

COROLLARY A.4. *For any integers $t \geq i \geq s \geq 2$ one has*

$$\ln(t+1) - \ln(s) \leq \sum_{i=s}^{t} \frac{1}{i} \leq \ln t - \ln(s-1).$$

PROOF. For the LHS:

$$\sum_{i=s}^{t} \frac{1}{i} \geq \int_{s-1}^{t} \frac{1}{m+1} dm = \ln(t+1) - \ln(s).$$

The RHS follows immediately from Lemma A.3. □

B. PROOF OF THEOREM 5.2

PROOF. We firstly show that (38) satisfies conditions in Lemma 5.1:

$$\alpha\beta_t = \frac{\alpha(t+1)}{2} \geq 2L\frac{t+1}{2}\frac{\alpha}{2L} \geq 2L\eta_t. \tag{44}$$

Next we show that

$$(\beta_{t+1} - 1)\eta_{t+1} \leq \beta_t\eta_t. \tag{45}$$

It is easy to check that $\frac{\Lambda_{t+1}}{t+2} \leq \frac{\Lambda_t}{t+1}$ using the fact that $\|\delta_t\|_* \geq 0$. If $\frac{\Lambda_{t+1}}{t+2} \geq \frac{\alpha}{2L}$, then $\frac{\Lambda_t}{t+1} \geq \frac{\alpha}{2L}$, hence

$$(\beta_{t+1} - 1)\eta_{t+1} = \frac{t^2+2t}{4}\frac{\alpha}{2L} \leq \frac{t^2+2t+1}{4}\frac{\alpha}{2L} = \beta_t\eta_t.$$

If $\frac{\Lambda_{t+1}}{t+2} < \frac{\alpha}{2L}$ and $\frac{\Lambda_t}{t+1} \geq \frac{\alpha}{2L}$, then

$$(\beta_{t+1} - 1)\eta_{t+1} = \frac{t^2+2t}{4}\frac{\Lambda_{t+1}}{t+2} \leq \frac{t^2+2t+1}{4}\frac{\alpha}{2L} = \beta_t\eta_t.$$

If $\frac{\Lambda_{t+1}}{t+2} < \frac{\alpha}{2L}$ and $\frac{\Lambda_t}{t+1} < \frac{\alpha}{2L}$, then

$$(\beta_{t+1} - 1)\eta_{t+1} = \frac{t^2+2t}{4}\frac{\Lambda_{t+1}}{t+2} \leq \frac{t^2+2t+1}{4}\frac{\Lambda_t}{t+1} = \beta_t\eta_t.$$

Hence (45) holds. Combine (41) and (45) we have the following:

$$\begin{aligned}
&(\beta_{t+1} - 1)\eta_{t+1}\left[\Phi(\mathbf{x}_t^{ag}) - \Phi(\mathbf{x}^*)\right] \\
&\leq \beta_t\eta_t\left[\Phi(\mathbf{x}_t^{ag}) - \Phi(\mathbf{x}^*)\right] \\
&\leq (\beta_t - 1)\eta_t\left[\Phi(\mathbf{x}_{t-1}^{ag}) - \Phi(\mathbf{x}^*)\right] \\
&+ \psi(\mathbf{x}_{t-1}, \mathbf{x}^*) - \psi(\mathbf{x}_t, \mathbf{x}^*) - \eta_t\langle\delta_t, \mathbf{x}_{t-1} - \mathbf{x}^*\rangle + U_t.
\end{aligned}$$

By induction we have:

$$\Phi(\mathbf{x}_T^{ag}) - \Phi(\mathbf{x}^*) \leq \frac{1}{(\beta_{T+1} - 1)\eta_{T+1}} \left(D_{\psi,\mathcal{X}}^2 - \sum_{t=1}^{T}\eta_t\langle\delta_t, \mathbf{x}_{t-1} - \mathbf{x}^*\rangle + \sum_{t=1}^{T} U_t\right) \tag{46}$$

Using Lemma A.3, $\sum_{t=1}^{T} U_t$ can be bounded as

$$\begin{aligned}
\sum_{t=1}^{T} U_t &= \sum_{t=1}^{T} \frac{\beta_t\eta_t^2(2M + \|\delta_t\|_*)^2}{2(\alpha\beta_t - L\eta_t)} \\
&\overset{(44)}{\leq} \sum_{t=1}^{T} \frac{\eta_t^2(2M + \|\delta_t\|_*)^2}{\alpha} \leq \frac{D_{\psi,\mathcal{X}}^2}{4}\left[\sum_{t=1}^{s_1-1}(2M + \|\delta_t\|_*)^2 \right. \\
&\left. + \sum_{t=s_1}^{T} \frac{(2M + \|\delta_t\|_*)^2}{\sum_{i=s_1}^{t}(2M + \|\delta_i\|_*)^2}\right] \\
&\leq \frac{D_{\psi,\mathcal{X}}^2}{4}\left[1 + \log\sum_{t=s_1}^{T}(2M + \|\delta_t\|_*)^2\right]
\end{aligned} \tag{47}$$

Conditioned on $\{\boldsymbol{\xi}_1, \ldots \boldsymbol{\xi}_{t-1}\}$, $\mathbf{x}_t$ is deterministic and the expectation of $\langle\delta_t, \mathbf{x}_t - \mathbf{x}^*\rangle$ is 0.

According to (38), if $\frac{\alpha}{2L} \leq \frac{\Lambda_t}{t+1}$, one will take $\eta_t = \frac{\alpha(t+1)}{4L}$. Substituting this stepsize into (46) we have

$$\begin{aligned}
\mathbb{E}\left[\Phi(\mathbf{x}_T^{ag}) - \Phi(\mathbf{x}^*)\right] &\leq \frac{D_{\psi,\mathcal{X}}^2 + \mathbb{E}[\sum_{t=1}^{T} U_t]}{\left(\frac{T+2}{2} - 1\right)\frac{\alpha(T+2)}{4L}} \\
&\overset{(47)}{\leq} \frac{2LD_{\psi,\mathcal{X}}^2}{\alpha T(T+2)}\left[5 + \mathbb{E}\log\sum_{t=s_1}^{T}(2M + \|\delta_t\|_*)^2\right] \\
&\leq \frac{2LD_{\psi,\mathcal{X}}^2}{\alpha T(T+2)}\left(5 + \log\sum_{t=1}^{T}\sigma_t^2\right),
\end{aligned} \tag{48}$$

where we use Jensen's Inequality in the last step. If $\frac{\alpha}{2L} > \frac{\Lambda_t}{t+1}$, one will take $\eta_t = \frac{\Lambda_t}{2}$ and we have

$$\begin{aligned}
&\mathbb{E}\left[\Phi(\mathbf{x}_T^{ag}) - \Phi(\mathbf{x}^*)\right] \leq \mathbb{E}\left[\frac{1}{\left(\frac{T+2}{2}\frac{\Lambda_{T+1}}{2}\right)}\left(D_{\psi,\mathcal{X}}^2 + \sum_{t=1}^{T} U_t\right)\right] \\
&\leq \frac{4\mathbb{E}\left[\sqrt{\frac{\sum_{t=1}^{T+1}(2M+\|\delta_t\|_*^2)}{T+1}}\left(D_{\psi,\mathcal{X}}^2 + \sum_{t=1}^{T} U_t\right)\right]}{D_{\psi,\mathcal{X}}\sqrt{\alpha(T+2)}} \\
&\overset{(47)}{\leq} \frac{D_{\psi,\mathcal{X}}}{\sqrt{\alpha(T+2)}}\mathbb{E}\left[\sqrt{\frac{\sum_{t=1}^{T+1}(2M + \|\delta_t\|_*)^2}{T+1}}\left(5 + \log\sum_{t=s_1}^{T}(2M + \|\delta_t\|_*)^2\right)\right] \\
&\leq \frac{D_{\psi,\mathcal{X}}}{\sqrt{\alpha(T+2)}}\sqrt{\frac{\sum_{t=1}^{T+1}\sigma_t^2}{T+1}}\left(5 + \log\sum_{t=1}^{T}\sigma_t^2\right),
\end{aligned} \tag{49}$$

where again the last step is due to Jensen's Inequality. Combining (48) and (49) our claim follows. If $T < s_1$, the logarithmic term vanishes. □

Learning in Non-stationary Environments with Class Imbalance

T. Ryan Hoens
Department of Computer Science and Engineering
University of Notre Dame
Notre Dame, Indiana 46556
thoens@cse.nd.edu

Nitesh V. Chawla
Department of Computer Science and Engineering
University of Notre Dame
Notre Dame, Indiana 46556
nchawla@cse.nd.edu

ABSTRACT

Learning in non-stationary environments is an increasingly important problem in a wide variety of real-world applications. In non-stationary environments data arrives incrementally, however the underlying generating function may change over time. In addition to the environments being non-stationary, they also often exhibit class imbalance. That is one class (the majority class) vastly outnumbers the other class (the minority class). This combination of class imbalance with non-stationary environments poses significant and interesting practical problems for classification. To overcome these issues, we introduce a novel instance selection mechanism, as well as provide a modification to the Heuristic Updatable Weighted Random Subspaces (HUWRS) method for the class imbalance problem. We then compare our modifications of HUWRS (called HUWRS.IP) to other state of the art algorithms, concluding that HUWRS.IP often achieves vastly superior performance.

Categories and Subject Descriptors

I.2.6 [**Artificial Intelligence**]: Learning

General Terms

Algorithms

Keywords

concept drift, class imbalance, non-stationary learning

1. INTRODUCTION

Two of the most common problems faced in data mining and machine learning research are the class imbalance problem and learning in non-stationary data streams. In spite of being well studied individually, the combination of the two problems has received considerably less attention. In this paper we discuss the confluence of the non-stationary data streams with class imbalance, and the complications that arise. We then provide a novel solution which we compare to the state of the art methods.

In traditional data mining classification contexts, algorithms have been developed such that given a training set, they are able to classify new instances into their appropriate classes. Recently, however, more and more problems have gone *online*, i.e., data arrives incrementally over time, and is therefore not all available at once. In order to solve this problem, various classifiers have been developed which adapt over time as more data becomes available.

One limitation of the naïve online model is that it assumes that the class boundary remains constant over time. In general, however, this assumption need not be true, and the underlying data generation function f from which the data is assumed to be drawn from may change over time. When a data stream experiences such a change (or *drift*), it is known as a *non-stationary environment* and is said to exhibit *concept drift*. In this paper when a sudden change in the underlying generation function f occurs, we say that the data stream has experienced concept drift. Alternatively, if the drift is occurring gradually over time, we say the data stream is experiencing concept drift.

When learning from non-stationary environments, a classifier must be able to respond to concept drift while ensuring that it retains all (relevant) past knowledge. These two goals bring rise to what is known as the stability-plasticity dilemma [9]. The problem becomes more pronounced if data cannot be stored due to space constraints, and thus all forgetting results in irretrievable loss of information.

While data in streams arrive over time, there are multiple different models for when and how they arrive. One popular model is to assume that instances first arrive without labels for testing, and then, once a prediction is given, a label is made available to update the classifier. While this assumes that instances arrive one at a time in this manner, another possible alternative is that the data may arrive in batches. That is, the data may arrive as a non-empty set of instances which are initially unlabeled for testing. Once predictions have been given for all instances in the batch, the labels for each of the instances are made available in order to update the classifier. For the sake of this paper, we only consider data streams for which instances arrive in batches.

While concept drift is a phenomenon only relevant in data streams, the class imbalance problem has a rich history of research in the traditional data mining literature [5, 4]. In the class imbalance problem one class (the positive class) is severely under represented in the dataset. This causes issues for traditional data mining algorithms, as under certain metrics it becomes optimal to merely predict the majority class, ignoring the minority class entirely. For instance, if the majority class makes up 99% of the dataset, the naïve classifier which always predicts the majority class will achieve 99% accuracy on testing data.

The problem of class imbalance is further exacerbated when learning from non-stationary data streams. This is for two main reasons. First, the distance — not only in time but also in distributional divergence — between observing positive class examples can become arbitrarily large. That is, there can be an arbitrarily long time — hours, days, or even months — between seeing successive minority class instances. Additionally, successive minority class instances may be drawn from arbitrarily different distributions. Such differences, however, can have very different meanings depending on the contexts.

For example, in one context the difference in minority class instances may indicate a drift in the minority class definition. Alternatively, the current minority class concept may merely define both instances as minority instances, even if there is no similarity between them (e.g., minority instances may be located in two pockets in the feature space, with no discernible similarity between the two types of minority class instances; such differences can be found in spam emails, where there are many different types of "categories" of minority class instances). Finally, the new minority class instance may just be the result of noise in the data, and not indicative of a more general trend.

While all three of the above alternatives are possible, it is impossible to know a priori the current scenario in any non-stationary data stream. This is due to the fact that the speed, type, and time of drift are assumed arbitrary and unknown. Therefore any algorithm developed for non-stationary data streams must be robust to any and all situations which may arise.

As a concrete example, consider the recent mortgage crisis. Models were built based on historical data which suggested certain properties in the rate of defaults (and therefore foreclosures) for various populations. Based on these models, loan recommendations were made which seemed sound. Due to a variety of factors outside of the model, however, the entire housing climate changed drastically, very quickly. As a result, the predictions of the models became based on faulty assumptions, and lead to a disaster.

By combining the class imbalance and non-stationary data problems, we see that the two problems together provide confounding effects. That is, in an imbalanced data stream undergoing concept drift, the time until the concept drift is detected can be arbitrarily long. This is due to the fact that since there are so few positive examples present in the stream, it is difficult to infer the source of the error for the positive class. In such instances, the misclassified positive class instance can merely be a result of noise in the data stream. In other cases, however, such a misclassification can signify a drift in concept which must be handled by the algorithm. Any algorithm designed to handle concept drift with class imbalance must account for this fact.

1.1 Contributions

In summary, the key **contributions** of this paper are:

1. A novel, non-temporal, instance selection method for the minority class in concept drifting data streams which exhibit class imbalance.
2. HUWRS with Instance Propagation HUWRS.IP as a method for overcoming class imbalance and concept-drift in data streams which perform well when compared against the state of the art on a variety of streaming datasets.

2. MOTIVATION

One prevailing unstated assumption of current state of the art non-stationary learning methods is that any detected feature drift requires model relearning. Specifically, if drift is detected in a feature, the entire model is often relearned, and past data discarded as belonging to a past concept [13]. There is no reason to believe, however, that this is necessarily true in practice. Thus while such a coarse grained approach to learning in non-stationary streams has proven effective, it may discard important information that can be used to improve performance.

Consider, for instance, a situation where certain features are drifting, while other features remain constant. This is a common case in concept drift injection mechanisms, and is most likely applicable in real world datasets. In such streams discarding past data about the stationary features, and forcing the model to be relearned, is unnecessary, and sacrifices performance while new instances are gathered. A more sophisticated approach may be able to still use the information available in the non-drifting features while also discarding the data from drifting features.

This observation provides the impetus for questioning the assumption of whether drift in one feature requires the model to change if the remainder of the features remain constant. This is especially true when the stream suffers from class imbalance, as discarding old instances can be costly, since it may require a lot of time (and potentially money) to observe new minority class instances. In addition to requiring more instances before the model can be retrained, one must also include the cost of rebuilding/retraining/modifying the classification algorithms once the data becomes available, and the opportunity cost associated with all instances which are misclassified before the model can be updated.

Currently there are very few methods available to overcome both the class imbalance and non-stationary problems in the literature. The most well known framework is due to Gao et. al. [8], which advocates propagating minority class examples from recent batches to the current batch in order to promote class balance. This attempts to overcome the previously mentioned issue of unnecessarily forgetting minority class instances by merely saving them all, and using them when necessary. The main drawback of this approach is that even if a change in the posterior distribution is detected, old instances are still used in order to increase the number of minority class instances. In the context of class imbalance in non-stationary data streams, however, these instances are likely drawn from a different concept than the current minority class concept, and may therefore inject improper bias into the classifier.

As a result, a more general approach to propagating past instances is required. The more general approach should be able to select only those instances which are relevant to the current minority class context. More specifically, only instances which are drawn from the same generating function as the current generating function should be selected. In this way, only the current concept defined by the minority class is strengthened, and the old, out of date concepts are forgotten.

While the novel instance selection mechanism will aid in not unnecessarily eliminating minority class instances, it is also advantageous to not unnecessarily eliminate majority class instances as well. In order to do this, we employ the Heuristic Updatable Weighted Random Subspaces method (HUWRS) [13] to build models only on a subset of the features. By combining HUWRS with the aforementioned instance selection mechanisms for propagating minority class instances when necessary, we retain the majority class benefits of HUWRS, and the minority class benefits of the propagation methods. The use of the novel instance selection method provides further benefit over the naïve instance propagation method, as depending on which features a classifier is built on, the selected instances may vary. That is, if there is a cyclic nature in which features drift, the method will be able to more accurately choose the instances relevant for each base learner.

With this goal in mind, we now introduce our instance selection technique. We then demonstrate how to incorporate it into the HUWRS framework to create HUWRS.IP for non-stationary environments which exhibit class imbalance.

3. METHOD

In this section we begin by describing the instance selection method. We then describe how to incorporate this method into the HUWRS framework to create HUWRS.IP.

3.1 Instance Propagation Method

In the framework proposed by Gao et. al [8], the most recent instances were selected to reinforce class balance when updating the ensemble on the current batch. The main drawback of the approach due to Gao et. al. is that it only selects a specific number of recently seen minority class instances. This inflexibility ignores the similarity of the minority class instance to the current concept, relying only on its similarity in time.

Selecting instances based on their temporal similarity to the current batch can pose serious drawbacks in practice. For instance, in data streams where concept drift occurs often and suddenly it will result in the selection of instances which used to be minority class instances, however after concept drift represent majority class instances. In order to combat this, we must devise a method that does not use temporal data about an instance to determine its similarity to the current concept.

We therefore define an instance selection strategy based on the probability that old instances are drawn from the same distribution as the new minority class concept. That is, let B_t (M_t) for $0 \leq t \leq T$ be the set of all instances (minority instances only) observed at time t, and B (M) be the set of all instances (minority instances, respectively) observed. Instead of merely selecting the last k instances observed, we can instead build a generative model on the most recent minority class instances.

We choose to use a generative model in our instance selection strategy as they, by definition, attempt to model $P(X|Y)$, i.e., they attempt to model the likelihood of a given feature vector X, given that the instance is class Y. This is valuable in our instance selection approach, as we are attempting to select only instances drawn from the same distribution as the current concept.

Another advantage of generative models is the fact that they are applicable in datasets which exhibit class imbalance, since the probability that instance X belongs to class Y is $P(Y|X) = P(X|Y) \cdot P(Y)$. This normalization by the class prior, $P(Y)$, allows the generative model to provide useful predictions in the face of class imbalance.

Therefore, we train a Naïve Bayes classifier C on the current batch of instances B_T. One important thing to note is that if B_T contains no minority class instances (which is not unusual in highly imbalanced environments), building C is not possible. As a result, for any batches B_i for which there are no minority class instances, we propagate the most recent set of minority class instances M_j (where j is $\arg\max_j |M_j| > 0$), to create the hybrid batch H_i. The classifier C can then be trained on this hybrid batch H_i in order to learn the distribution of the most recent batch of minority class instances. Note that this is the most naïve way of attempting to determine the instances which belong to the most recent batch. In general a more sophisticated approach can be employed in order to ensure that the hybrid batch contains the most recent concept.

We can then use C to classify all minority instances in M, and only use those for which the probability is above a threshold. An alternative approach is to use the same classifier C, but instead of choosing only those instances which score above a certain threshold, we can instead choose the k most likely instances.

The main advantage of this instance selection approach over the naïve approach in general is that it avoids the problem of determining where the boundary is between the old concept and the new concept. This allows it to more accurately accrue only instances which are drawn from the same concept as the current concept, and therefore provide better classification accuracy. This is the reason why we do not apply the approach of choosing the k most likely instances, since it, like the naïve approach, assumes that at least k instances are available from the new concept. Since this need not be the case in the case of a sudden change in the features, only selecting instances which are above a threshold should allow for better performance in the face of sudden concept drift.

One problem with the pure instance selection approach, however, is that it relies on finding instances which are similar to the current minority class context. In some cases of rapid drift, however, such instances may not be available. As a result, we allow our instance selection strategy to default to the naïve strategy if no previously seen minority class instances are propagated. In this way the instance selection strategy is able to remain robust in the face of rapid, non-reoccurring, concept drift.

As a result, we propose Algorithm 1. In Algorithm 1, instances are classified based on the probability they belong to the minority class as defined by the current batch of minority class instances. This is accomplished via the use of a Naïve Bayes classifier, which is a generative model that attempts to model $P(X|Y)$. To do this, it assumes each of the features are independent, and computes $P(X|Y) = \prod_{i \in features} P(X_i|Y)$, where $P(X_i|Y)$ is the probability of observing feature value X_i for feature i, given the class is Y. By using Bayes' theorem, the model can then use this to compute $P(Y|X) = P(X|Y) \cdot P(Y)$, where $P(Y)$ is the class prior, or the probability of observing class Y. If no instances are above the threshold, then the instance selection mechanism reverts to the naïve approach.

The use of the hybrid approach allows us to leverage the instance selection method when there are a sufficient number of instances available, but otherwise balances the class distribution with the recently available instances. This enables our hybrid approach to be robust to a wide variety of non-stationary data streams. In particular, the instance selection mechanism will be especially beneficial in environments in which contexts reoccur (e.g., seasonally, yearly, etc.). In such scenarios the instance selection mechanism can select the instances from the "correct" time period to augment the current batch. In rapidly changing environments where the instance selection mechanism is not applicable, the simple propagation method can aid in balancing out the class distributions.

Algorithm 1 *Instance_Select*

Require: Training batch B_T, minority batches to test M_t for $0 \leq t < T$, and threshold *threshold*.
Ensure: $M_{threshold}$ are the selected instances to add to the base learner.
  Train a Naïve Bayes classifier C on B_T.
  $numAdded \leftarrow 0$
  for $i = 0$ to $T - 1$ **do**
    for Each instance $instance \in B_i$ **do**
      Let p be the probability that *instance* is a minority instance according to C.
      if $p > threshold$ **then**
        Let $M_{threshold} \leftarrow M_{threshold} \bigcup \{instance\}$
        $numAdded \leftarrow numAdded + 1$
      end if
    end for
    if $numAdded = 0$ **then**
      Add the last $k = 0.2 \cdot |B_t|$ instances to $M_{threshold}$.
    end if
  end for
  Return $M_{threshold}$.

As a result, this method enables us to more accurately determine which instances are relevant to the current batch. This should lead to better performing base learners, and therefore better overall performance.

3.2 HUWRS for Non-stationary Learning and Class Imbalance

In the previous section we introduced a new instance selection mechanism for class imbalance in non-stationary environments. In this section we describe how to incorporate it into the Heuristic Updatable Weighted Random Subspaces (HUWRS) method [13] to produce a robust ensemble framework for concept drift and class imbalance.

3.2.1 Combining Instance Propagation and HUWRS

For completeness, before introducing HUWRS.IP, we first define the *Random_Subspace_Method* in Algorithm 2 as it is used in HUWRS. The important thing to note about the method is it generates an ensemble of classifiers, each built on a different (potentially differently sized) set of features.

The combination of the instance selection method defined above with HUWRS results in the Heuristic Updatable Weighted Random Subspaces with Instance Propagation (HUWRS.IP) (Algorithms 3 and 4). There are two main facets to HUWRS.IP. First, Algorithm 3 updates the classifier when labeled instances become available. Second, Algorithm 4 updates the classifier as new testing (i.e., unlabeled) instances become available. For the sake of space, we omit some of the details of HUWRS, and limit the discussion to the impact of class imbalance on the classifier weighting function, since it is the major change for HUWRS.IP. For more details on HUWRS, the reader can consult [13].

Algorithm 2 *Random_Subspace_Method*

Require: Training set X, a range of number of features to consider P, and number of classifiers to train $n > 0$.
Ensure: CLASSIFIER is the model trained on training set X, consisting of n classifiers.
  for $i = 1$ to n **do**
    Select F, a random subset of the features such that $|F| \in P$.
    Let $Y \leftarrow X$.
    for all a such that a is a feature of Y **do**
      if $a \notin F$ **then**
        Remove feature a from Y
      end if
    end for
    Train CLASSIFIER$_i$ on dataset Y.
  end for

3.2.2 Hellinger Distance

One of the most important part of the HUWRS algorithm is the drift detection mechanism based on Hellinger distance [12]. The use of Hellinger distance as a method of detecting concept drift has been previously explored [7, 16].

Fundamentally, Hellinger distance is a distributional divergence measure [14, 20]. Let (P,B,ν) be a measure space [11], where P is the set of all probability measures on B that are absolutely continuous with respect to ν. Consider two probability measures $P_1, P_2 \in P$. The Bhattacharyya coefficient between P_1 and P_2 is defined as:

$$p(P_1, P_2) = \int_\Omega \sqrt{\frac{dP_1}{d\nu} \cdot \frac{dP_2}{d\nu}} d\nu. \quad (1)$$

The Hellinger distance is derived using the Bhattacharyya coefficient as:

$$d_H(P_1, P_2) = 2\left[1 - \int_\Omega \sqrt{\frac{dP_1}{d\nu} \cdot \frac{dP_2}{d\nu}} d\nu\right] = \sqrt{\int_\Omega \left(\sqrt{\frac{dP_1}{d\nu}} - \sqrt{\frac{dP_2}{d\nu}}\right)^2 d\nu}. \quad (2)$$

3.2.3 Hellinger Weight

In HUWRS, the Hellinger weight of a classifier was defined as follows. Let D_1 and D_2 be two separate sets of probability distributions over a set of features. That is, let $D_{1,f}$ denote the probability distribution for dataset D_1 and feature f. We can convert Hellinger distance into a Hellinger weight as:

$$Classless\_HW(D_1, D_2) = \frac{1}{n} \sum_{f=1}^{n} \frac{\sqrt{2} - d_H(D_{1,f}, D_{2,f})}{\sqrt{2}} \quad (3)$$

Algorithm 3 *Train_HUWRS.IP*

Require: Training batches B, previously seen minority instances M, range of number of features p, retraining threshold $threshold_{retrain}$, instance selection threshold $threshold_{select}$, number of bins b, and ensemble size $n > 0$.

Ensure: CLASSIFIER is the model trained on training set B consisting of n classifiers, FEATURES_i is a vector consisting of the features used to train CLASSIFIER_i, CLASS_WEIGHT is a length n vector containing the weights given to each base classifier, and M is a set of batches of minority class instances.

```
CLASSIFIER, FEATURES ← Random_Subspace_Method(B_0)
for c = 1 to n do
  BINS_c ← BIN(B_0, FEATURES_c, b)
end for
CLASS_WEIGHT ← →1
while New time step i is available do
  Let M_i be the set of minority instances in batch B_i.
  CLASSLESS_WEIGHT ← →0
  for c = 1 to n do
    temp ← BIN(B_i, FEATURES_c, b)
    CLASS_WEIGHT_c ← Class_HW(temp, BINS_c)
    CLASSLESS_WEIGHT_c ← 0
    if CLASS_WEIGHT_c < threshold then
      Let X be the current batch B_i with only features
      from FEATURES_c.
      toAdd ← Instance_Select(X, M, threshold_select)
      Train CLASSIFIER_i on dataset B_i ⋃ toAdd using
      features in FEATURES_c.
      CLASS_WEIGHT_c ← 1
      BINS_c ← BIN(B_i, FEATURES_c, b)
    end if
  end for
end while
```

Algorithm 4 *Test_HUWRS.IP*

Require: CLASSIFIER as learned using *Train_HUWRS.IP*, testing instance x, set of previously seen testing instances X, intra-batch update frequency u, and *Test* returns a probability vector associated with testing x on a classifier.

Ensure: $prob_i$ contains the probability that x is class i, and CLASSLESS_WEIGHTupdated if $|X| \geq u$.

```
prob = →0
num_classes ← the number of classes in the dataset.
X ← X ⋃ {x}
for c = 1 to n do
  if |X| ≥ u then
    tmp_bins ← BIN(X, FEATURES_c, b)
    CLASSLESS_WEIGHT_c ← Classless_HW(tmp_bins, BINS_c)
  end if
  w ← CLASS_WEIGHT_c + CLASSLESS_WEIGHT_c
  prob ← prob + (w · Test(CLASSIFIER_c, x)/n)
end for
```

where n is the number of features to consider, D_1 (D_2) the distribution of positive (negative, respectively) class instances, and d_H is the Hellinger distance between distributions $D_{1,f}$ and $D_{2,f}$.

Thus when classes are available, the Hellinger weight is calculated as the average of the minority class and majority class Hellinger distance between the two feature distributions. In this way we are giving equal weight to the Hellinger distance between the minority class distribution, and majority class distribution. By balancing the weight in this way, implicitly more weight is given to a shift in the minority class. In future work the combining function can be optimized for use in non-stationary data streams with class imbalance, however in practice this simple heuristic is very effective.

One final observation is that when classes are not available, the Hellinger weight is computed as the average of the Hellinger weights of each of the features, and thus the relative frequency of each class is not relevant.

3.2.4 *Benefits of HUWRS*

The value of using HUWRS in addition to the instance selection method is that we maintain all of the benefits HUWRS gives for non-stationary environments. That is, we retain the advantages of building classifiers which are robust in the face of a subset of features drifting, as well as high latency in obtaining class labels (since we can use the testing set to re-weight the ensemble, see [13] for details).

In addition to obtaining robustness from concept drift by using a subset of the features for each classifier, we also obtain robustness from class imbalance by using the instance selection method. The instance selection method is also further enhanced, as each member of the ensemble can individually determine which instances are most relevant in its feature space, and therefore obtain better overall performance.

4. MEMORY USAGE

One of the important factors when developing an algorithm that handles concept drift in data streams is to ensure that the algorithm does not use an unreasonable amount of memory. We now demonstrate that the memory usage of HUWRS.IP is reasonable, and can be easily controlled.

From our previous work [13], we know that memory usage of HUWRS is finite and bounded. Since the instance selection method requires a number of previously seen minority instances, we note that as the number of batches goes to infinity, the number of instances saved by the algorithm also goes to infinity. Since the only instances saved, however, are from the minority class, we note that this is not a substantial burden in general, as the minority class instances will only represent a manageable number of instances.

Therefore, we propose to allow the algorithm to maintain all minority class instances seen by the algorithm (as in the framework due to Gao et. al.[8]). If this limitation is not possible in practice, then two simple forgetting mechanisms can be employed. First, we can merely forget the oldest instances until we have dropped under the quota. Since this runs counter to the motivation of the method, however, an alternative approach is to instead keep a count of the number of times each instance has been reused by a classifier, dropping the instances with the smallest count. In order to ensure that older batches are not more likely to be kept than newer batches, a reweighting scheme can be used to ensure the selection method is not biased.

Thus, we can either assume that saving all minority instances is possible, and thereby satisfy the memory constraints trivially. If this assumption is not applicable in practice, we can instead use either of the two forgetting techniques to ensure that HUWRS.IP maintains a finite and bounded memory footprint.

5. EXPERIMENTAL DESIGN

We begin with a description of the implementation details of the methods used, defining relevant parameters for each of the algorithms. We then describe each of the datasets used.

5.1 Implementation Details

We implemented HUWRS.IP as an extension to HUWRS in MOA [1], a stream mining suite based off of Weka [10]. For our comparative analysis, we compare against the framework of Gao et. al [8]. We also present the results of two state of the art learners for non-stationary environments, namely: Adaptive Hoeffding Option Trees (AHOT) [2], and Dynamic Weighted Majority (DWM) [15] (further information about these methods can be found in Section 8). As HUWRS.IP is an ensemble applicable to any traditional base classifier, we chose C4.4 [18] decision trees, i.e., unpruned, uncollapsed C4.5 decision trees [19] with Laplace smoothing applied at the leaves. As outlined by Kolter and Maloof [15], the base learner used used for DWM was standard Naïve Bayes.

In addition to a base learner, HUWRS.IP requires several other parameters. As recommended for many ensembles, we set the ensemble size for HUWRS.IP to $n = 100$. As in HUWRS [13] we set $threshold_{retrain} = 0.7$, and $b = 30$, and the minority class instance propagation threshold was set to $threshold_{select} = 0.9$. For Gao, we use the recommended parameters of propagating all minority instances, and undersampling the majority class by 40%.

By setting the weights once, and not optimizing them for each dataset, we set a general guideline, and provides results which are not susceptible to random noise. In addition to these parameters, we also define a frequency for updating the weights of the classifier based on test instances. Due to the varying sizes of the training datasets, we chose to update the classless weights every 10% of the window size, or 30 instances, whichever is larger. We can hence ensure a minimum number of instances to consider, while still allowing for multiple weight updates.

Finally, while HUWRS (and thus HUWRS.IP) relies on using a subset of features to train each base learner, a comprehensive search through different subspace size may lead to dramatic overfitting and overstated performance. Therefore, instead of choosing a fixed subspace size for each classifier, every time a classifier is initially trained we choose a random subset size between 10% and 90% of the number of features. Thus we can test not only the effectiveness of the algorithm, but also its robustness to various subspace sizes.

When testing the algorithms, we considered a batch learning framework. That is, we partitioned the dataset into multiple equal sized chunks, testing each instance in a chunk without labels first. Once all instances in a chunk were tested, we computed the area under the ROC curve (AUROC) of the classifier over the chunk, introduced labels for all of the instances, finally presenting them to the classifier for updating. The AUROC presented for each algorithm is computed as the average chunk performance of the classifier on the dataset.

Note that we use AUROC as it is the de facto standard for performance in the class imbalance literature. One important thing to note is that for some chunks no positive class instances are available. In such cases, the AUROC for that chunk is not considered when computing the average performance of the classifiers.

5.2 Datasets

To ensure a fair comparison, we tested the algorithms on multiple real world datasets, as well as a synthetic dataset. The details of the datasets are available in Table 1. The choice to use a combination of real and synthetic datasets is motivated by the fact that while concept drift is assumed in real datasets, it is difficult to identify. For this reason, synthetic datasets are often considered when learning in the presence of concept drift, as the drift type and properties can be precisely controlled. We now describe the datasets in brief detail.

Dataset	# Ftrs	# Insts	% Minority	WS
Can	9	443,872	1.88	4,439
Compustat	20	16,956	3.86	1,131
Ozone_1h	72	2,536	2.88	363
Ozone_8h	72	2,534	6.31	363
Stagger	3	12,000	44.19	1,000
Text	11,466	11,162	6.35	1,117
Wrds	41	99,200	49.22	3,307

Table 1: Statistics for the datasets used. # Ftrs is the number of features, # Insts is the number of instances, % Minority represents the percent of instances in the dataset that are minority class, and WS denotes the window size used for the dataset.

can: *Can* is a real world dataset derived from crunching a can over time. Domain experts then marked certain instances as salient or based on their expertise. Due to the nature of the problem, the vast majority of regions are not-salient, and thus salient regions represent the minority class.

compustat: *Compustat* contains information about the fiscal health of firms over time. The class represents the default status of the firm at the current time step.

ozone_1h: The *Ozone_1h* dataset was built from hourly ozone readings over the Houston, Galveston, and Brazoria area. The class value is whether or not the current readings represent an "ozone day", i.e., they have a higher concentration of ozone than normal.

ozone_8h: *Ozone_8h* is analogous to the *Ozone_1h* dataset, however readings were taken every eight hours.

STAGGER: *STAGGER* is a non-stationary data stream generator developed by Schlimmer and Granger [21] where each instance has three nominal features. The generator then simulates concept drift by changing the meaning of each of the features over time.

text: *Text* is a text document recognition dataset, where each feature is a word. The dataset represents medical documents, where the minority class is defined as documents pertaining to carcinoma.

wrds: *Wrds* contains customer buying history for 100,000 customers over time. The positive class represents customers who respond to a marketing campaign.

6. RESULTS

In this section we discuss the performance of HUWRS.IP against various other state of the art machine learning algorithms. In particular, we compare it to the method of Gao et. al. [8], which is the state of the art learning algorithm for non-stationary environments and class imbalance. In addition, we also include three non-stationary learning algorithms which don't compensate for class imbalance, namely: HUWRS, Adaptive Hoeffding Option Trees (AHOT), and Dynamic Weighted Majority (DWM).

From the results in Table 2 there are a few interesting observations. First, we note that HUWRS does extremely poorly on *Can*. This is due to the fact that in *Can*, there are multiple consecutive batches in a row which don't have any minority class instances. Consequently if any of these batches are determined to be drifting by the classifier, there may be no minority class instances in the retraining batch. This has a severe negative impact on the performance of the ensemble, as demonstrated by its very poor performance.

In HUWRS.IP, we avoid this issue by always propagating the last batch of minority class instances to be used for instance selection. Therefore if the current batch is batch B_i, but the last batch with minority instances was batch B_{i-5}, the minority instances from batch B_{i-5} (i.e., M_{i-5}) are added to the current batch, and the instance selection classifier is built using the new hybrid batch $H_i = B_i \bigcup M_{i-5}$. In this way the classifier is able to overcome long time periods of no minority class instances.

The efficacy of this approach is borne out in the results, as we see that HUWRS.IP always outperforms HUWRS, even on the datasets which are reasonably balanced, i.e., *STAGGER* and *Wrds*. This performance increase can be explained as HUWRS.IP are able to add more diversity to the ensemble by selecting relevant instances from the past to use to train new classifiers. This diversity allows the ensemble to obtain better performance.

When comparing HUWRS.IP to Gao, we see in Table 2 that HUWRS.IP (often drastically) outperforms Gao in average AUROC. On the *Can*, *Ozone_1h*, *Ozone_8h*, *STAGGER*, and, *Text* datasets, HUWRS.IP achieves significant improvements in performance over Gao (although only minor improvements over HUWRS on *STAGGER*). On *Compustat*, HUWRS.IP shows improvements over Gao, however they are much more modest. The only dataset on which HUWRS.IP is outperformed by another method is on the *Wrds* dataset, where Gao achieves the best performance. While Gao achieves the best performance, its improvement over HUWRS.IP is rather minor.

Such a drastic improvement in performance indicates that HUWRS, combined with our instance selection mechanism, is a valuable tool for combating class imbalance and non-stationary environments.

7. ANALYSIS OF THE INSTANCE PROPAGATION TECHNIQUE

In Section 6 we presented the results of HUWRS.IP as compared against a variety of other non-stationary learning algorithms. From the results, we observed that HUWRS.IP performed very well compared to the other state of the art learning algorithms, often providing drastic performance increases. Given its effectiveness, we now compare HUWRS.IP against its constituent instance propagation mechanisms in order to determine the effectiveness of the instance selection algorithm described in Section 3.1. In particular, we compare the instance propagation method to the naïve instance propagation method due to Gao, and to a modification of Algorithm 1 with the naïve instance propagation removed.

In Table 3, we present the results of each of the methods: HUWRS.IP, HUWRS.Prop (i.e., HUWRS with naïve instance propagation), and HUWRS.IS (i.e., HUWRS with the simple instance selection). From the table, we see that HUWRS.IP generally outperforms both HUWRS.Prop and HUWRS.IS. In fact, on the *Can*, and *Ozone_1h* datasets, HUWRS.IP provides significant performance improvements over the two other methods. This indicates that for certain datasets, the instance propagation method described leverages both of the constituent parts to provide much improved performance.

There are two datasets for which HUWRS.IP performs worse than one of the other methods, namely *Compustat*, and *STAGGER*. The decreased performance on *Compustat* is due to the fact that the minority class changes drastically over time. As a result, for most ensemble members on most of the batches, the naïve instance selection mechanism selects only a few instances to add to the current batch. Since the majority of the batches have less than 5 instances propagated, the class imbalance problem remains unaddressed, and performance suffers (as seen in the performance of HUWRS.IS on *Compustat*). HUWRS.Prop, on the other hand, consistently propagates the most recent minority class instances, and thereby demonstrates superior performance. HUWRS.IP, therefore, achieves performance gains over HUWRS.IS (since there are no batches for which no instances are propagated), however fails to meet the performance of HUWRS.Prop (since there are numerous classifiers for which only 1 or 2 instances are propagated).

While on *Compustat* HUWRS.Prop provides superior performance than both HUWRS.IP and HUWRS.IS, on *STAGGER* HUWRS.IS outperforms both other methods. This is due to the fact that *STAGGER* is a reasonably balanced dataset, and therefore does not require much rebalancing. Therefore HUWRS.IS is able to correctly and accurately choose only those instances which are relevant to the current classifier on the current batch, and ignore any others. HUWRS.Prop, on the other hand, continues to propagate instances, even if they're no longer relevant. HUWRS.IP, however, is unable to realize the same performance, as it cannot be as selective as HUWRS.IP, and therefore sees a drop in performance.

From these results, we see that our novel instance propagation mechanism is effective for most datasets. There are, however, some datasets on which the naïve method provides superior performance, and others where the instance selection approach achieves superior performance. Since, however, the performance gains of using any of the naïve approaches is small compared to that of using the instance propagation method, we recommend the use of the:instance propagation method defined in Algorithm 1.

One final thing to note is that while HUWRS.IP achieves better performance, in general than Gao, HUWRS.Prop, and HUWRS.IS, generally outperform Gao as well. This

Dataset	HUWRS	HUWRS.IP	AHOT	DWM	Gao
Can	0.50306	**0.88671**	0.55544	0.78939	0.81203
Compustat	0.75660	**0.79769**	0.53347	0.75360	0.79078
Ozone_1h	0.79009	**0.87032**	0.50000	0.81463	0.77199
Ozone_8h	0.84414	**0.88243**	0.50000	0.82924	0.79160
STAGGER	0.88122	**0.89762**	0.83462	0.86972	0.68460
Text	0.91606	**0.97134**	0.61539	0.73009	0.93835
Wrds	0.90154	0.97000	0.76189	0.89973	**0.97267**

Table 2: Average AUROC results for each of the datasets and methods.

Dataset	HUWRS.IP	HUWRS.Prop	HUWRS.IS
Can	**0.88671**	0.83349	0.83335
Compustat	0.79769	**0.80572**	0.78452
Ozone_1h	**0.87032**	0.81715	0.81642
Ozone_8h	**0.88243**	0.85727	0.88180
STAGGER	0.89762	0.89875	**0.89949**
Text	**0.97134**	**0.97134**	**0.97134**
Wrds	**0.97000**	0.96686	0.96983

Table 3: AUROC results for each of the datasets for the two different instance selection methods. HUWRS.Prop represents propagating the last 20% of instances, while HUWRS.IP represents selecting instances based on the instance selection criteria.

indicates that HUWRS building classifiers on only a subset of the features is a very powerful method for overcoming concept drift.

8. RELATED WORK

Developing classifiers to overcome concept drift and class imbalance is a relatively new field of study. As a result, there are not many techniques in the literature which are designed for to work in that environment. In this section we will give an overview of the current techniques which combat concept drift and class imbalance, as well as a brief overview of the state of the art in non-stationary learners.

8.1 Non-Stationary Learners

As an extension to the standard C4.5 decision tree due to Quinlan [19], Buntine introduced option trees [3]. In standard decision trees, there is only one possible path from the root to a leaf node, where predictions are made. In option trees, however, a new type of node — known as an option node — is added to the tree, which splits the path along multiple split nodes. Pfahringer, Holmes, and Kirby combined the concept of Hoeffding trees and option trees to create Hoeffding Option Trees [17]. They combine these two methods by beginning with a standard Hoeffding tree and, as data arrives, if a new split is found to be better than the current split at a point in the tree, an option node is added and both splits are kept. Further extending Hoeffding Option Trees are Bifet et. al. [2]. In their extension, called Adaptive Hoeffding Option Trees, each leaf is provided with an exponential weighted moving average estimator, where the decay is fixed at 0.2. The weight of each leaf is then proportional to the square of the inverse of the error.

Dynamic Weighted Majority (DWM) [15] is an alternative to building decision trees that creates an ensemble of classifiers. In order to test an instance, the ensemble combines the prediction of each base classifier using a weighted vote. In order to train DWM the ensemble begins by attempting to classify each training instance. Each base classifier that misclassifies the instance has its weight reduced by a multiplicative constant β. If the entire ensemble misclassifies the instance, the ensemble adds a new classifier with a weight of 1 after rescaling the weights of the ensemble (in order to prevent new classifiers from dominating the voting process). The ensemble then removes each classifier with a weight lower than some threshold θ, and then trains each base classifier on the new instance.

8.2 Non-Stationary Learners for Class Imbalance

The first technique developed which attempted to learn in non-stationary environments which also exhibit class imbalance is due to Gao et. al. [8]. Gao et. al. proposed a framework based on collecting positive class examples. In their ensemble algorithm, they break each incoming chunk into a set of positive (P) and negative (Q) class instances. One then selects all seen positive class instances (AP), and a subset of the negative class instances (O) which is determined randomly based on a distribution ratio. These two sets are then combined to form a complete dataset to train the new ensemble classifier C_i. By accumulating all positive class instances, this approach implicitly assumes, however, that the minority class is not drifting.

Building on this concept, Chen and He propose SERA [6], which is similar to the proposal of Gao et. al., however instead of using all past instances, the algorithm selects the "best" n minority class instances as defined by the Mahalanobis distance. Given these instances, the algorithm then uses all majority class instances and uses bagging to build an ensemble of classifiers. Thus SERA suffers from a similar, albeit less severe, concern as the method proposed by Gao et. al., as the algorithm may not be able to track drift in minority instances depending on the parameter n.

9. DISCUSSION AND FUTURE WORK

We introduced Heuristic Updatable Weighted Random Subspaces with Instance Propagation (HUWRS.IP) as a new method for dealing with concept drift in data streams which also suffer from class imbalance. In this method an ensemble of classifiers is built as in HUWRS, however when trained each classifier selects certain minority instances to be propagated. In HUWRS.IP, the instances selected to be propagated are based on their similarity to the current minority class instances when possible, and otherwise are those instances most temporally similar to the current batch.

In order to demonstrate the effectiveness of HUWRS.IP, we compared them to a variety state of the art methods in both the concept drifting environment (HUWRS, Adaptive Hoeffding Option Trees, and Dynamic Weighted Majority), and the concept drifting environment with class imbalance (Gao). For a majority of the datasets HUWRS.IP outperforms the other methods. This indicates that HUWRS, when combined with a method for propagating minority class instances, is very effective at overcoming class imbalance and concept drift.

In addition to comparing HUWRS.IP to other state of the art methods, we also compared it to HUWRS.Prop and HUWRS.IS, where HUWRS.Prop is HUWRS augmented with the simple instance propagation technique of Gao, and HUWRS.IS is HUWRS augmented with a naïve version of the instance selection technique in Algorithm 1. This comparison demonstrated that while the instance propagation technique defined in Algorithm 1 is, in general, a significantly more effective instance propagation technique than both the naïve instance propagation mechanism and the naïve instance selection mechanism.

One current shortcoming of HUWRS (and by extension HUWRS.IP) is its dependence on observing batches of instances. Since this is a common situation in practice, it is not a major limitation, however in future work this limitation can be overcome, resulting in a more robust method which is applicable in a wider range of environments.

Two other areas of future work relate to the instance propagation mechanism, and the classifier weighting mechanism. Currently, the instance propagation mechanism merely uses the previous batch of minority instances to build the Naïve Bayes classifier. In general, however, it might be possible to more accurately select instances corresponding to the current concept. This would allow the classifier to be trained on more instances, and thus more accurately learn the current minority class concept.

Additionally, the classifier weighting mechanism assumes concept drift in the minority class and majority class are equally as important. This may prove an unreasonable assumption in some cases, and various weighting strategies can be employed so remove this assumption.

Given all of these considerations, in scenarios where data arrives in batches and is subject to either gradual concept drift or sudden concept change, as well as class imbalance, we recommend using Heuristic Updatable Weighted Random Subspaces with Instance Propagation, as it makes less assumptions about the underlying data stream, and in general achieves better performance.

Acknowledgments

Work is supported in part by the NSF Grant ECCS-0926170, and the Notebaert Premier Fellowship.

10. REFERENCES

[1] A. Bifet, G. Holmes, R. Kirkby, and B. Pfahringer. Moa: Massive online analysis. *JMLR*, 11:1601–1604, 2010.

[2] A. Bifet, G. Holmes, B. Pfahringer, R. Kirkby, and R. Gavaldà. New ensemble methods for evolving data streams. In *KDD*, pages 139–148. ACM, 2009.

[3] W. Buntine. Learning classification trees. *Statistics and Computing*, 2(2):63–73, 1992.

[4] N. Chawla. Data mining for imbalanced datasets: An overview. *Data Mining and Knowledge Discovery Handbook*, pages 853–867, 2005.

[5] N. Chawla, N. Japkowicz, and A. Kotcz. Editorial: special issue on learning from imbalanced data sets. *ACM SIGKDD Explorations Newsletter*, 6(1):1–6, 2004.

[6] S. Chen and H. He. SERA: Selectively recursive approach towards nonstationary imbalanced stream data mining. In *Neural Networks, 2009. IJCNN 2009. International Joint Conference on*, pages 522–529. IEEE, 2009.

[7] D. Cieslak and N. Chawla. A framework for monitoring classifiers' performance: when and why failure occurs? *KAIS*, 18(1):83–108, 2009.

[8] J. Gao, W. Fan, J. Han, and P. Yu. A general framework for mining concept-drifting data streams with skewed distributions. In *SDM*, pages 3–14. Citeseer, 2007.

[9] S. Grossberg. Nonlinear neural networks: Principles, mechanisms, and architectures. *Neural Networks*, 1(1):17–61, 1988.

[10] M. Hall, E. Frank, G. Holmes, B. Pfahringer, P. Reutemann, and I. H. Witten. The weka data mining software: an update. *SIGKDD Explorations Newsletter*, 11(1):10–18, 2009.

[11] P. Halmos. *Measure theory*. Van Nostrand and Co., 1950.

[12] E. Hellinger. Neue begründung der theorie quadratischer formen von unendlichvielen veränderlichen (german). *Journal fur die Reine und Angewandte Mathematik*, 136:210–271, 1909.

[13] T. R. Hoens, N. V. Chawla, and R. Polikar. Heuristic updatable weighted random subspaces for non-stationary environments. In *ICDM*, pages 241–250. IEEE, 2011.

[14] T. Kailath. The divergence and bhattacharyya distance measures in signal selection. *IEEE Transactions on Communication Technology*, 15(1):52–60, 1967.

[15] J. Kolter and M. Maloof. Dynamic weighted majority: A new ensemble method for tracking concept drift. In *ICDM*, pages 123–130. IEEE, 2003.

[16] R. Lichtenwalter and N. V. Chawla. Adaptive methods for classification in arbitrarily imbalanced and drifting data streams. In *New Frontiers in Applied Data Mining*, volume 5669 of *Lecture Notes in Computer Science*, pages 53–75. Springer, 2010.

[17] B. Pfahringer, G. Holmes, and R. Kirkby. New options for hoeffding trees. *AAI*, pages 90–99, 2007.

[18] F. Provost and P. Domingos. Tree induction for probability-based ranking. *Machine Learning*, 52(3):199–215, September 2003.

[19] J. Quinlan. *C4.5: programs for machine learning*. 1993.

[20] C. Rao. A review of canonical coordinates and an alternative to correspondence analysis using hellinger distance. *Questiio (Quaderns d'Estadistica i Investigacio Operativa)*, 19:23–63, 1995.

[21] J. Schlimmer and R. Granger. Incremental learning from noisy data. *Machine learning*, 1(3):317–354, 1986.

Linear Support Vector Machines via Dual Cached Loops

Shin Matsushima[*]
Information Science
and Technology
The University of Tokyo, Tokyo
masin@r.dl.itc.u-tokyo.ac.jp

S.V. N. Vishwanathan
Statistics & Computer Science
Purdue, West Lafayette IN
vishy@stat.purdue.edu

Alexander J. Smola
Yahoo! Research
Santa Clara CA
alex@smola.org

ABSTRACT

Modern computer hardware offers an elaborate hierarchy of storage subsystems with different speeds, capacities, and costs associated with them. Furthermore, processors are now inherently parallel offering the execution of several diverse threads simultaneously. This paper proposes StreamSVM, the first algorithm for training linear Support Vector Machines (SVMs) which takes advantage of these properties by integrating caching with optimization. StreamSVM works by performing updates in the dual, thus obviating the need to rebalance frequently visited examples. Furthermore we trade off file I/O with data expansion on the fly by generating features on demand. This significantly increases throughput. Experiments show that StreamSVM outperforms other linear SVM solvers, including the award winning work of [38], by orders of magnitude and produces more accurate solutions within a shorter amount of time.

Categories and Subject Descriptors

I.5.2 [**Pattern Recognition**]: Design Methodlogy—*Classifier design and evaluation*

General Terms

Algorithm, Experimentation, Performance

Keywords

Support Vector Machines, Optimizatation, Coordinate Descent

1. INTRODUCTION

In this paper we propose StreamSVM an efficient method for large scale *single machine* linear Support Vector estimation, yielding the fastest currently available solver which runs on general purpose hardware by over an order of magnitude. To the best of our knowledge, this is the first work on training linear Support Vector Machines (SVMs) which takes explicit advantage of different storage subsystems on a computer to achieve very high data throughput. In particular, our optimization algorithm is co-designed to take advantage of the fact that memory access is much faster than disk access. Our approach is entirely generic and can be extended to a more fine-grained storage hierarchy and a larger class of convex optimization problems.

1.1 Solvers for Training SVMs

Support Vector Machines (SVMs) have arguably revolutionized machine learning over the past decade. Fueled by their impressive performance in a number of real-world applications, there have been numerous efforts to scale SVMs to large data sets. Some notable contributions include Sequential Minimal Optimization (SMO) [28, 10], SVMLight [19], LaSVM [4], and gradient projection based solvers [39].

Much of the initial success of SVMs was attributed to the so-called *kernel trick* wherein training data is implicitly mapped to a high dimensional feature space, and a margin maximizing linear classifier is learned in this mapped space. In contrast, *linear* SVMs do not employ the kernel trick explicitly.[1] As massive, high-dimensional data sets are becoming commonplace, there is a recent surge of interest in linear SVMs. Some recent papers [20, 18, 17, 35] tackle this problem with great success, and provide algorithms with convergence guarantees. The above solvers either assume that the data resides in memory or that a cluster of machines with appropriate communication and synchronization facilities are available.

In an award winning paper [38] revisited the problem of training linear SVMs when the data does not fit into memory [29, 27, 19]. In a nutshell, the key idea is to split the data into manageable blocks, compress and store each block on disk, and perform dual coordinate descent by loading each block sequentially. This basic idea was improved upon by [11] who observed that the block minimization (BM) algorithm of [38] does not retain important points before discarding each block. They therefore, propose to retain some important points from the previous blocks in the RAM. This simple idea leads to significant speed-ups, and [11] demonstrate that their selective block minimization (SBM) algorithm outperforms BM. Here we propose a new algorithm StreamSVM, and show that it outperforms both BM and SBM on a number of publicly available datasets.

[*]The research was performed when visiting Purdue.

[1]They may, however, use the kernel trick implicitly by hashing and direct feature expansion as described in [31].

1.2 Exploiting the Storage Hierarchy

StreamSVM takes advantage of the different characteristics inherent in the storage hierarchy of modern computers. That is, while hard disks excel at storing large amounts of data, they have typically mediocre data transfer rates and are outright slow at random access operations. Compared to that, main memory comes at a hundredfold premium in terms of space but offers two to three orders of magnitude faster data transfer rates. CPU caches are yet faster again. Similar considerations hold for solid state drives, PCI interconnects, and graphics subsystems.

This suggests that algorithms which require streaming through data from disk should take advantage of the data they already have in main memory while waiting for more data to arrive from disk. Obviously, the same rationale applies to a sequence of storage systems with different capacity/bandwidth characteristics. To make things somewhat more explicit we list a range of such systems below:

System	Capacity	Bandwidth	IOPs
Disk	3TB	150MB/s	10^2
SSD	256GB	500MB/s	$5 \cdot 10^4$
RAM	16GB	30GB/s	10^8
Cache	16MB	100GB/s	10^9

In the present paper we focus on two parts of this hierarchy — disk and memory (see Figure 1). This already affords quite dramatic improvements in terms of speed relative to sequential algorithms. In a nutshell our algorithm does the following:

> *Iterate over the data in main memory while streaming data from disk. Evict primarily examples from main memory that are "uninformative".*

A naive approach which takes, e.g. stochastic gradient descent steps based on the importance of examples would likely run afoul of data weighting problems — informative examples need not have extended statistical weight but rather only a higher influence on the choice of objective function. One way of dealing with this issue is to resort to dual updates. That is, we consider the dual optimization problem to SVMs (and related problems) and judiciously update the associated Lagrange multipliers. This leads to the following algorithm:

Reader
while not converged **do**
  read example (x, y) from disk
  if buffer full **then** evict random (x', y') from memory
  insert new (x, y) into ring buffer in memory
end while

Trainer
while not converged **do**
  randomly pick example (x, y) from memory
  update dual parameter α
  update weight vector w
  if deemed to be uninformative **then** evict (x, y) from memory
end while

1.3 Enterprise Scale Solvers

To place our research in perspective note that industrial datasets regularly exceed the capacities offered by single computers in terms of both storage and computation. This means that distributed inference techniques are required. Unfortunately, large server centers often come with rather severe restrictions on reliability, inter-machine latency, communication trees, delays, etc. such that it is desirable to find algorithms which compute estimates using a bare minimum of communication. Note that not all estimation problems are amenable to efficient high-latency scenarios. For instance, latent variable models typically require excellent communication and great care needs to be taken to obtain fast estimates [2, 32]. A common attribute of these models is that they have a large degree of symmetry and non-convexity in their parametrization.

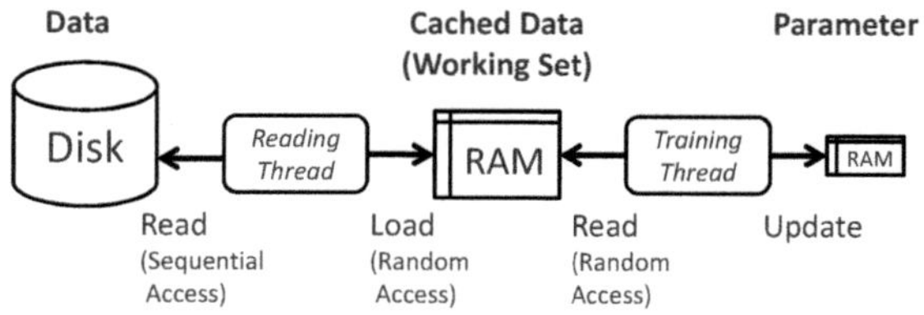

Figure 1: Basic data flow diagram of the optimization algorithm. A reader keeps on filling the main memory from disk while the optimization thread(s) perform updates on the data available in RAM. Both threads operate asynchronously.

Fortunately much of what is commonly known as generalized linear models can be addressed with convex solvers. That is, the estimation problems can be decomposed efficiently into parts which are guaranteed to yield very similar solutions. In statistical learning terminology this is known as *stability* of the solution space and there exists a rich body of research [7, 36, 9, 16] extolling the desirable theoretical properties of convexly penalized estimation problems. It is therefore natural to take advantage of these properties in terms of implementations. For instance, [40] show that it is possible to perform stochastic gradient descent on individual processors *independently*, using random sub-samples of the data and to average the parameter estimates afterwards and *simultaneously* reaping the benefits of parallelization. Note that in previous work [25] suggested a similar averaging strategy, however their theoretical analysis only showed that averaging does not hurt, rather than actually accelerate convergence. It is in the spirit of [40] that we approach the problem of estimation:

1. Decompose (possibly with oversampling) the data for several machines.
2. *Solve the estimation problem per machine as efficiently as possible.*
3. Average the solutions between machines to obtain a final estimate.

Much work in the analysis of [40] was invested into proving that the stochastic gradient descent solutions on subsets are sufficiently independent for averaging to be actually beneficial. If we treat the optimization step as a standard batch problem this obstacle disappears. In this case we can appeal directly to the asymptotic analysis of [26] to see that averaging is beneficial: in particular, [26] show that the parameter distribution of a penalized empirical risk minimizer $w^*|X, Y$ conditioned on some data X, Y is asymptotically normal. This means that if we obtain such estimates based on various subsets of data via $w^*|X_i, Y_i$, we will be able to aggregate this to an improved joint estimate via $\frac{1}{n}\sum_{i=1}^{n} w^*|X_i, Y_i$.

Consequently, in the present paper we are primarily concerned with step 2 of the above approach — to find the most efficient way of solving a convex optimization problem on a single machine. While we primarily focus on linear SVMs in this paper, our ideas are fairly generic and can be applied to other convex losses including losses used in structured prediction [3].

Outline. We will briefly review dual descent algorithms for linear Support Vector Machines in Section 2. Subsequently Section 3 gives a detailed description of the nested loop used in traversing through data in core memory and streaming from disk. Experimental results are provided in Section 4 and we conclude with a discussion in Section 5.

2. DUAL COORDINATE DESCENT

2.1 Support Vector Classification

In the following we assume that we are given n examples $x_i \in \mathcal{X}$ and labels $y_i \in \{\pm 1\}$ drawn independently and identically from some distribution $(x_i, y_i) \sim p(x, y)$. It is our goal to find some function $f : \mathcal{X} \to \mathbb{R}$ which minimizes the misclassification error, e.g. by minimizing the probability that $yf(x) \leq 0$. This constitutes the most basic of all estimation problems, namely that of binary classification. We simplify things further by assuming that $\mathcal{X} = \mathbb{R}^d$. This assumption will be relaxed subsequently when we discuss how to expand features on the fly. The primal formulation of a linear SVM can be written as follows[2] [13]:

$$\underset{w \in \mathbb{R}^d}{\text{minimize}} \ \frac{1}{2}\|w\|^2 + C\sum_{i=1}^{n} \max\{0, 1 - w^\top y_i x_i\} \qquad (1)$$

Using standard convex optimization tools [8] the above problem can be rewritten in its dual form

$$\underset{\alpha}{\text{minimize}} \ D(\alpha) := \frac{1}{2}\alpha^\top Q\alpha - \alpha^\top \mathbf{1} \qquad (2a)$$

$$\text{subject to } \mathbf{0} \leq \alpha \leq C\mathbf{1}. \qquad (2b)$$

Here, Q is an $n \times n$ matrix whose entries are given by $Q_{ij} = y_i y_j x_i^\top x_j$, and $\mathbf{1}$ is the vector of all ones. The minimizer w^* of (1) and the minimizer α^* of (2) are related by the primal dual connection: $w^* = \sum_{i=1}^{n} \alpha_i^* y_i x_i$. The dual problem (2) is a Quadratic Programming (QP) with box constraints, and the i-th coordinate α_i corresponds to the i-th example (x_i, y_i).

2.2 Dual Updates

The following coordinate descent scheme can be used to minimize the dual [18]:

- Initialize $\alpha^1 = \mathbf{0}$.
- At iteration t select coordinate i_t
- Update α^t to α^{t+1} via

$$\alpha_{i_t}^{t+1} = \underset{0 \leq \alpha_{i_t} \leq C}{\text{argmin}} \ D(\alpha^t + (\alpha_{i_t} - \alpha_{i_t}^t)\mathbf{e}_{i_t}) \qquad (3a)$$

$$\alpha_i^{t+1} = \alpha_i^t \qquad \text{if } i \neq i_t \qquad (3b)$$

[2]We omit an explicit bias term since this greatly simplifies the dual problem while remaining entirely general since the bias can be introduced easily as an additional coordinate in the data.

Here, $\mathbf{e}_i$ denotes the i-th standard basis vector. Since $D(\alpha)$ is a QP, the one-variable subproblem (3a) can be solved exactly (see [18] for details):

$$\alpha_{i_t}^{t+1} = \min\left\{\max\left\{0, \alpha_{i_t}^t - \frac{\nabla_{i_t} D(\alpha^t)}{Q_{i_t i_t}}\right\}, C\right\}. \qquad (4)$$

Here, $\nabla_i D(\alpha)$ denotes the i-th coordinate of the gradient. The above updates are also closely related to implicit updates of [21, 22, 12] and the passive aggressive updates of [14]. If we maintain $w^t := \sum_{i=1}^{n} \alpha_i^t y_i x_i$, then the gradient $\nabla_{i_t} D(\alpha)$ can be computed efficiently using

$$\nabla_{i_t} D(\alpha) = \mathbf{e}_{i_t}^\top (Q\alpha - \mathbf{1}) = w^{t\top} y_{i_t} x_{i_t} - 1. \qquad (5)$$

w^{t+1} is kept related to α^{t+1} by computing

$$w^{t+1} = w^t + (\alpha_{i_t}^{t+1} - \alpha_{i_t}^t) y_{i_t} x_{i_t}. \qquad (6)$$

A naive choice for i_t is to traverse examples periodically, which means that $i_t = t \bmod n$. We call an iteration from α^{nk} to $\alpha^{n(k+1)}$ an *outer iteration*, contrasted with an *inner iteration* from α^t to α^{t+1}. An alternative is to randomly permute the index and to access examples in arbitrary order. In that case, $i_t = \sigma^k(t \bmod n)$ where $\sigma^k \in \mathfrak{S}_n$ is a permutation.

3. PROPOSED METHOD

We assume that the entire dataset cannot fit in RAM, therefore there must exist an $\Omega < n$, which is an upper bound for the number of training data which can be stored in the RAM. Our algorithm, StreamSVM, maintains a set of indices A cotaining the indices of the data points in memory and ensures that $|A| \leq \Omega$ at all times. The major challenge is to select the working set carefully. Towards this end, we use a strategy that is inspired by shrinking[19, 18].

A remarkable property of the dual problem is that we can potentially reduce the size of optimization problem by carefully choosing the subset of the data. This property was first observed by [19] and is widely used in popular solvers such as SVMLight[19], LibSVM [10], and Liblinear [17]. We also aim to utilize the property and solve the entire problem efficiently. First we look at the following fact:

FACT 1. *Let α^* be the optimal solution of* (2). *Define A^{in} and A^{bo} as $\{i|\alpha_i^* = 0\}$ and $\{i\ \alpha_i^* = C\}$ respectively. Any optimal solution of*

$$\underset{\alpha}{\text{minimize}} \ D(\alpha)$$

$$\text{subject to } \alpha_i = \begin{cases} 0 & \text{if } i \in A^{\text{in}} \\ C & \text{if } i \in A^{\text{bo}} \end{cases}$$

is also an optimal solution of (2).

A^{in} is called the *inactive set*, A^{bo} the *bound set*, and $A^{\text{ac}} := \{i|0 < \alpha_i^* < C\}$ the *active set*. If w^* denotes the optimal primal solution corresponding to α^*, then using the KKT conditions [8] it follows that [29] $i \in A^{\text{in}}$ implies that $w^{*\top} y_i x_i > 1$. Similarly, $w^{*\top} y_i x_i < 1$ for all $i \in A^{\text{bo}}$. Intuitively, what this means is that data which is in the inactive set are well classified and the points in the bound set are not. If these sets are known beforehand, the solver can concentrate on data in the active set by setting the other coordinates to 0 or C accordingly and freezing them. Usually A^{ac} is a small fraction of the original dataset, and therefore it is advantageous to focus most of the attention of the solver on identifying the coordinates in A^{ac} and optimizing them.

One way to identify the active set is to use projected gradients. For the bound constrained optimization problem (2) the i-th component of the projected gradient $\nabla_i^\pi D(\alpha)$ can be computed via

$$\nabla_i^\pi D(\alpha) := \begin{cases} 0 & \text{if } \alpha_i = 0 \text{ and } \nabla_i D(\alpha) > 0 \\ 0 & \text{if } \alpha_i = C \text{ and } \nabla_i D(\alpha) < 0 \\ \nabla_i D(\alpha) & \text{otherwise .} \end{cases} \quad (8)$$

The shrinking heuristic then works as follows: At the end of each outer iteration we compute $M_+ = \max_i \nabla_i^\pi D(\alpha)$ and $M_- = \min_i \nabla_i^\pi D(\alpha)$. During the inner iteration, if a point is found to satisfy $\alpha_i = 0$ and $\nabla_i D(\alpha) > M_+$ or $\alpha_i = C$ and $\nabla_i D(\alpha) < M_-$ then it is shrunk, that is, the corresponding α_i is frozen. If needed, the shrunk variables are visited at a later stage of the optimization process.

Maintaining the Working Set.

Just like in shrinking, points which are very well classified or very badly classified with respect to the current solution are eliminated. However, unlike shrinking our criterion is adaptive and also takes into account the size of the RAM. Let $\alpha^1, \ldots, \alpha^n$ denote the intermediate solutions produced by the trainer in the last n steps. We compute

$$\varepsilon := \max_{t=1,\ldots,n} |\nabla_{i_t}^\pi D(\alpha^t)|. \quad (9)$$

During the next n updates, a point is evicted from the RAM if $\alpha_i = 0$ and $\nabla_i D(\alpha) > \varepsilon$ or $\alpha_i = C$ and $\nabla_i D(\alpha) < -\varepsilon$. Furthermore, if the RAM is deemed to be full, that is, if $|A| > 0.9\Omega$ then we set $\varepsilon = \beta\varepsilon$ for some $\beta < 1$. We find that $\beta = 0.9$ works well in practice. In general, our criterion is more aggressive than shrinking, but this is not a problem; even if a point is evicted, it will subsequently be reloaded by the reader into the RAM, and the trainer will get a chance to update the corresponding α_i.

Synchronization Issues.

Detailed pseudo-codes of our scheme are shown in Algorithms 1 and 2. Our algorithm utilizes two threads namely the **reader** and **trainer**. The reader thread, as the name implies, is tasked with reading the data from disk and storing it into the RAM. If the RAM is full then the reader randomly replaces a cached point with the new data. The trainer thread randomly selects training points in the RAM and performs updates.

A major advantage of our method is that there is very little need for synchronization between the readervand the trainer. The only process which needs to be accessed mutually exclusively is the manimuplation of the working set. In order to process the eviction and addition of data efficiently with the thread safety, we can utilize a widely used database manegement library. Then the only shared object we have to manage explicitly is the set of indices, A. This also means that our framework is fairly modular. For instance, the reader can read data from the disk, and perform pre-processing such as computing a feature vector $\phi(x)$ without affecting the trainer.

Stopping Criterion.

If the data resides in main memory then one can use the infinity norm of the projected gradient as an effective stopping criterion. However, in our case this is not possible. Therefore, we use the following approximate scheme: Suppose the trainer performs T updates in the time that it takes the reader to perform one scan through the data. With some abuse of notation let $\alpha^1, \ldots, \alpha^T$ denote the intermediate solutions produced by the trainer. Then we compute

$$M_+ := \max_{t=1,\ldots,T} \nabla_{i_t}^\pi D(\alpha^t),\ M_- := \min_{t=1,\ldots,T} \nabla_{i_t}^\pi D(\alpha^t), \quad (10)$$

and stop when the gap $M_+ - M_-$ falls below a pre-specified threshold, which is set to a default value of 0.0001. Note that since T is usually much larger than n the gap computed here is usually a more stringent stopping criterion than that used by either LibLinear, BM, or SBM. In our implementation, the trainer is responsible for computing the gap. When the gap is lower than the tolerance threshold or the number of iterations exceeds the maximum, then both the threads exit.

Algorithm 1 Reader

```
for k = 1, ..., max_iter do
  for i = 1, ..., n do
    read y_i, x_i from the Disk
    calculate Q_ii = x_i^T x_i
    if |A| = Ω then
      randomly select i' ∈ A
      lock mutex
      A = A \ {i'}
      unlock mutex
      delete y_i', Q_i'i', x_i' from the RAM
    end if
    store y_i, Q_ii, x_i in the RAM
    lock mutex
    A = A ∪ {i}
    unlock mutex
  end for
  if stopping criterion is met then
    exit
  end if
end for
```

3.1 Proof of Convergence (sketch)

Our analysis builds upon the results of [24] and [18].

Definition 1 (Luo and Tseng Problem). *Consider the following minimization problem*

$$\underset{\alpha}{\text{minimize}} \quad g(E\alpha) + b^\top \alpha \quad (11)$$

$$\text{subject to} \quad L_i \le \alpha_i \le U_i \quad (12)$$

where α and b are n-dimensional vectors, E is a $d \times n$ dimensional fixed matrix, $L_i \in [-\infty, \infty)$ and $U_i \in (-\infty, \infty]$ are upper and lower bounds respectively. The above optimization problem is a Luo and Tseng problem if the following conditions hold:

1. *E has no zero columns*
2. *the set of optimal solutions $\mathcal{A}$ is non-empty*
3. *the function g is strictly convex and twice continuously differentiable*
4. *for all optimal solutions $\alpha^* \in \mathcal{A}$, $\nabla^2 g(E\alpha^*)$ is positive definite.*

The following result was implicitly shown in the proof of Theorem 1 in [18].

Algorithm 2 Trainer

$\alpha^1 = \mathbf{0}, w^1 = \mathbf{0}, \varepsilon = 9, \varepsilon^{\text{new}} = 0, \beta = 0.9$
while stopping criterion is not met **do**
  for $t = 1, \ldots, n$ **do**
    while $|A| = 0$ **do**
      sleep
    end while
    if $|A| > 0.9 \times \Omega$ **then**
      $\varepsilon = \beta\varepsilon$ // aggressively shrink ε
    end if
    randomly select $i \in A$
    read y_i, Q_{ii}, x_i from the RAM
    compute $\nabla_i D := {w^t}^\top y_i x_i - 1$
    if ($\alpha_i^t = 0$ and $\nabla_i D > \varepsilon$) or ($\alpha_i^t = C$ and $\nabla_i D < -\varepsilon$) **then**
      lock **mutex**
      $A = A \setminus \{i\}$
      unlock **mutex**
      delete y_i, Q_{ii}, x_i from the RAM
      continue
    end if
    $\alpha_i^{t+1} = \min\{\max\{0, \alpha_i^t - \frac{\nabla_i D}{Q_{ii}}\}, C\}$
    $w^{t+1} = w^t + (\alpha_i^{t+1} - \alpha_i^t) y_i x_i$
    if $\varepsilon^{\text{new}} < |\nabla_i D|$ **then**
      $\varepsilon^{\text{new}} = |\nabla_i D|$
    end if
  end for
  Update stopping criterion
  $\varepsilon = \varepsilon^{\text{new}}$
end while

LEMMA 1. *If no data $x_i = \mathbf{0}$, then the SVM dual (2) is a Luo and Tseng problem.*

PROOF. Set $E_{ij} = y_i x_i^\top \mathbf{e}_j, b = \mathbf{1}, L_i = 0, U_i = C$ and $g(\cdot) = \frac{1}{2}\|\cdot\|^2$. E has no zero columns because of our assumption that $x_i \neq \mathbf{0}$. Since the constraint set is bounded, and g is a strictly convex function, the set of optimal solutions $\mathcal{A}$ is non-empty. Since g is twice differentiable and strongly convex, $\nabla^2 g$ is positive definite everywhere. □

DEFINITION 2 (ALMOST CYCLIC RULE). *There exists an integer $B \geq n$ such that every coordinate is iterated upon at least once every B successive iterations.*

THEOREM 2 (THEOREM 2.1 OF [24]). *Let $\{\alpha^t\}$ be a sequence of iterates generated by a coordinate descent method (3) using the almost cyclic rule. The α^t converges linearly to an element of $\mathcal{A}$.*

All that remains to establish the convergence our coordinate descent scheme is to show it satisfies the almost cyclic rule. If the trainer accesses the cached training data sequentially, and the following conditions hold:

- The trainer is at most $\kappa \geq 1$ times faster than the reading thread, that is, the trainer performs at most κ coordinate updates in the time that it takes the reader to read one training data from disk.
- A point is never evicted from the RAM unless the α_i corresponding to that point has not been updated.

Then it is easy to see that this corresponds to the almost cyclic rule with $B = \kappa n$. In practice, the trainer randomly accesses training points from the RAM, and if the RAM is full then the reader evicts a random point. Therefore, there is a very small probability that a point is evicted before the corresponding α_i is updated. However, in practice we find that this does not affect convergence.

4. EXPERIMENTS

We performed experiments on some of the largest publicly available data sets for binary classification to evaluate the performance of our algorithm, and to compare it with two existing methods namely SBM and BM. Since SBM was shown to be competitive with other methods such as Vowpal Wabbit (VW), Stochastic Gradient Descent (SGD), or Pegasos we do not explicitly compare against them here.

Datasets.

Table 1 summarizes the datasets used in our experiments. The webspam trigram dataset `webspam-t`[3], as well as the the KDD cup 2010 dataset `kddb`[4] are from the LibSVM binary data collection[5]. The `dna` and `ocr` datasets were obtained from the Pascal Large Scale Learning Workshop website [34]. For all the datasets we randomly selected 80% of the labeled data for training and the remaining 20% for testing. Besides being massive, note that our datasets cover a variety of real-life scenarios. The `dna` dataset is dense, but is heavily imbalanced in terms of the number of positive vs negative examples. The `ocr` dataset is dense and balanced while both `kddb` and `webspam-t` are very sparse but very high dimensional.

Implementation Details.

Our code is implemented in portable C++ and uses `POSIX` threads (pthreads) for multi-threaded programming. In order to cache the data efficiently we use a thread safe in-memory hash table (StashDB) provided by Kyoto Cabinet[6]. We empirically find that the use of Kyoto Cabinet reduces our memory footprint by approximately 25% compared to SBM and BM. Open-source code as well as all the scripts needed to reproduce our experimental results will be made available for download from `http://www.stat.purdue.edu/~vishy`.

Hardware.

All experiments were conducted on the `Rossmann` computing cluster at Purdue University[7], where each node has two 2.1 GHz 12-core AMD 6172 processors with 48 GB physical memory per node.

Experimental Setup.

We focused our study on the following two aspects: How does StreamSVM compare with SBM and BM for different values of C? How does the size of RAM Ω affect the performance of StreamSVM? We also conducted an experiment

[3] Originally from `http://www.cc.gatech.edu/projects/doi/WebbSpamCorpus.html`.
[4] This dataset was derived from KDD CUP 2010 second problem bridge_to_algebra_2008_2009.
[5] `http://www.csie.ntu.edu.tw/~cjlin/libsvmtools/datasets/binary.html`.
[6] `http://fallabs.com/kyotocabinet/`
[7] `http://www.rcac.purdue.edu/userinfo/resources/rossmann`.

Table 1: Summary of the datasets used in our experiments. n is the total # of examples, d is the # of features, s is the feature density (% of features that are non-zero), $n_+ : n_-$ is the ratio of the number of positive vs negative examples, Datasize is the size of the data file on disk, Ω is the number of points in the RAM, and each Blocks is the data split used for the corresponding method. M denotes a million.

dataset	n	d	$s(\%)$	$n_+ : n_-$	Datasize	Ω	SBM Blocks	BM Blocks
ocr	3.5 M	1156	100	0.96	45.28 GB	150,000	40	20
dna	50 M	800	25	3e−3	63.04 GB	700,000	60	30
webspam-t	0.35 M	16.61 M	0.022	1.54	20.03 GB	15,000	20	10
kddb	20.01 M	29.89 M	1e-4	6.18	4.75 GB	2,000,000	6	3

where we expanded the features on the fly to demonstrate the scalability and flexibility of our framework. Since the objective functions we are minimizing are strongly convex, all optimizers will converge the same solution (within numerical precision) and produce the same generalization performance eventually. Therefore, what we are specifically interested in is the rate at which the objective function decreases.

4.1 Results

Varying C.

As C increases the effect of the regularizer decreases and the non-smooth hinge loss dominates the primal objective. Intuitively, this means that the problem becomes harder to solve for large values of C. Therefore, it is important to test an optimization algorithm across a range of C values.

We used $C \in \{0.0001, 0.001, \ldots, 1000.0\}$ to test the performance of StreamSVM and contrast it with SBM and BM. For this experiment we set the maximum number of iterations for all algorithms to be 100; for StreamSVM an iteration is defined as one complete pass through the data by the reader thread. The stopping tolerance was set to be 10^{-3}. A job is killed by the queue manager on the cluster if it does not finish within 48hrs. Besides the space required to store the weight vector w and the coefficients α, both algorithms were allowed to use up to 2GB of extra RAM.

In Figure 2 we used the dna dataset and plot the relative function value difference as function of wall clock time for SBM, BM, and StreamSVM[8] The relative function value difference is defined as $(D^* - D^t)/D^*$ where D^t is the dual objective function output by the optimizer at the t-th iteration, and D^* is the largest dual objective function value produced by either SBM, BM, or StreamSVM for the same parameter settings. Note that since we are plotting the y-axis on a log scale some points with relative function value difference of 0 are not displayed.

In the top three plots in Figure 3 we used the same value of $C = 1.0$, and plot the convergence behavior of SBM, BM, and StreamSVM on kddb, ocr, and webspam-t datasets respectively.

Note that in almost all cases, StreamSVM outperforms SBM and BM comprehensively. In particular, on the dna, ocr and webspam-t datasets, StreamSVM has converged to a high accuracy solution even before BM and SBM have managed to read and compress the data during the first pass. Also, both SBM and BM do not converge for large values of C on the dna dataset.

[8]Due to lack of space we plot only a subset of our results here. Detailed results including the generalization error and evolution of the gap can be found at http://www.r.dl.itc.u-tokyo.ac.jp/~masin/Appendix.pdf.

On the kddb dataset, StreamSVM does not exhibit any particular advantage over SBM. We investigated this further and found that the major bottleneck here is the need to frequently access random elements of w (29.89 million entries) and α (20.01 million entries), both of which are stored as dense vectors. This causes a number of cache misses and consequently slows down the trainer. On the other hand, since the data is very sparse (maximum 200 nonzero entries per training example) the reader thread is very fast. Consequently StreamSVM is not faster than SBM, although it is very competitive as compared to BM.

Varying Ω.

Next we study the effect of varying the RAM size Ω on the performance of StreamSVM. The same setup as the previous experiment was used here but with two notable changes. First, we fixed the value of C to be 1.0 for all datasets. Second, we set the RAM size to 256MB, 1GB, 4GB, and 16GB respectively.

On all datasets, the performance with 256MB RAM was inferior compared to higher RAM sizes. However, increasing the RAM size beyond 4GB does not help much. In fact, on the kddb dataset, increasing the size of RAM actually reduces performance. The reasons are as the same as above. Even though we can cache a large number of training points, the bottleneck here is in updating w and α. Therefore, the increase in Ω does not significantly improve convergence speed. For the ocr and webspam-t datasets there is marginal improvement when moving from 4GB to 16GB. This could potentially be explained by the fact that at the final solution there were relatively few training examples in the active set (675 for ocr and 1509 for webspam-t). We conjecture that large RAM sizes help only if the number of non-zero entries per training example are large, or of the dataset is very high dimensional and noisy because of which a large number of training examples are in the active set.

Expanding Features on the Fly.

In our final experiment, our aim is to show that explicit feature expansion can be easily incorporated into our framework. We computed an expanded feature $\phi(x)$ before the reader stores an example in RAM. Following the work of [33], we used dna dataset at http://sonnenburgs.de/soeren/projects/coffin/splice_data.tar.xz and computed the same feature corresponding to the feature referred to as "WD $d = 8$ explicit". This results in a sparse feature vector of 12,495,240 dimensions. We examined the performances with RAM size of 16GB and 32GB.

We plot the relative function value difference vs wall clock time in the bottom plot of Figure 3. The same figure also shows how the gap is decreasing as a function of wall clock

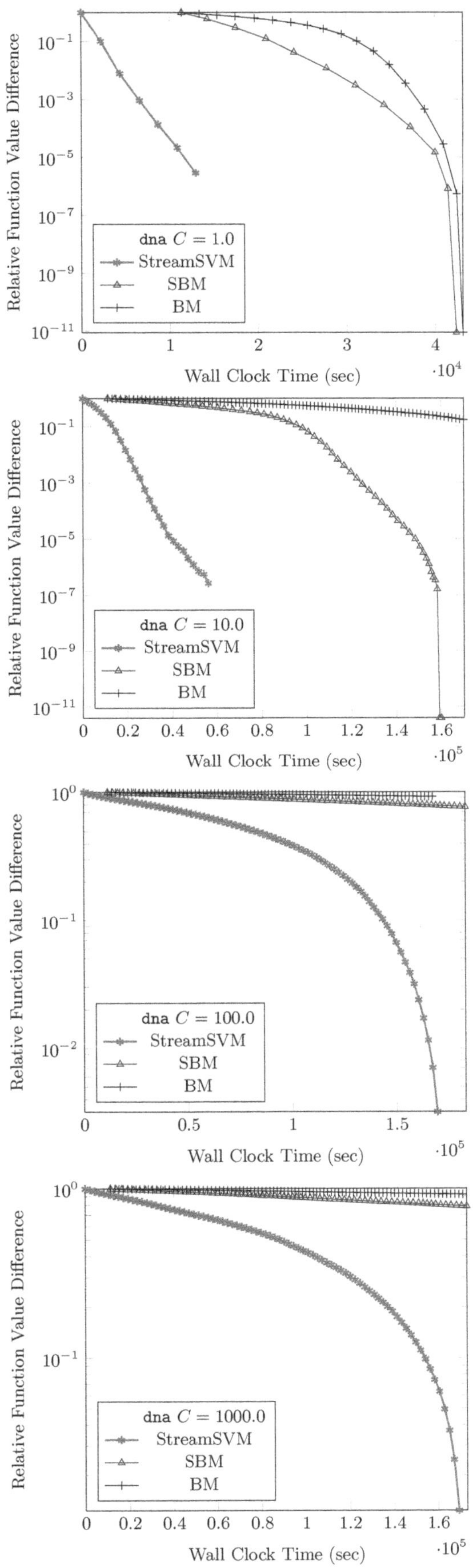

Figure 2: Relative function value difference vs wall clock time on the dna dataset for various values of C

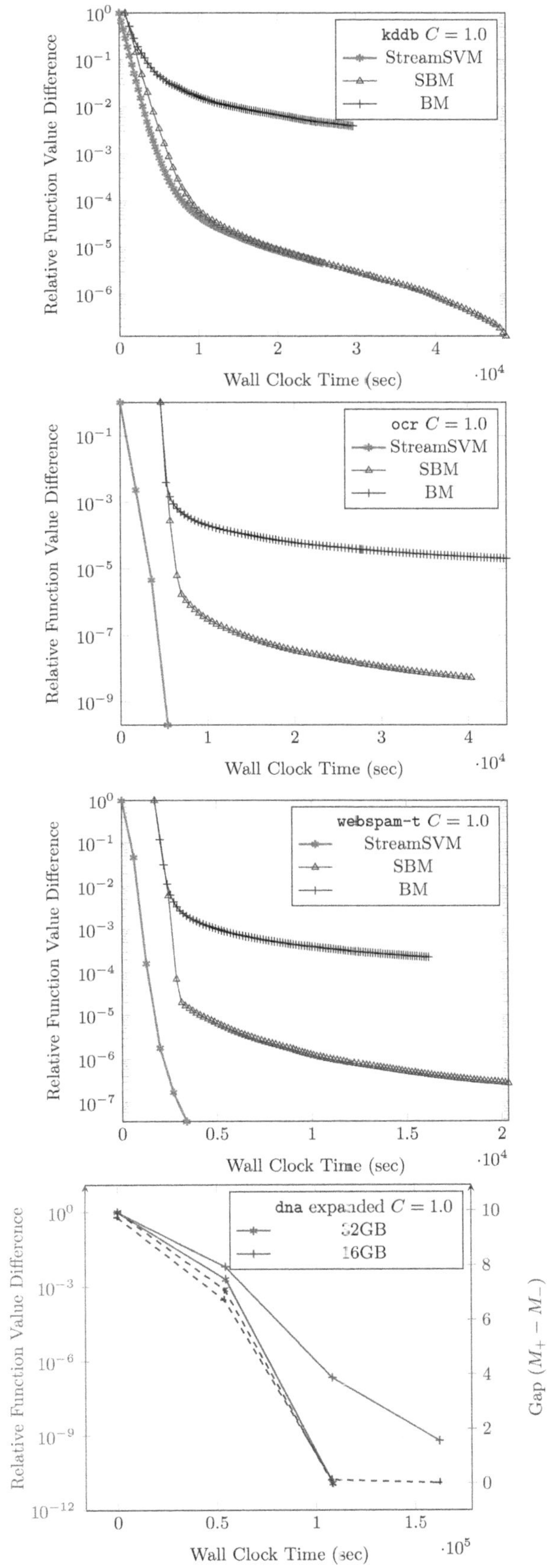

Figure 3: Top three figures: Relative function value vs wall clock time on the kddb, ocr, and webspam-t datasets for $C = 1.0$. The bottom figure: The red solid curve is the relative function value vs wall clock time and the blue dashed curve is the gap vs wall clock time on the dna dataset expanded using the "WD $d = 8$ explicit" feature with $C = 1.0$.

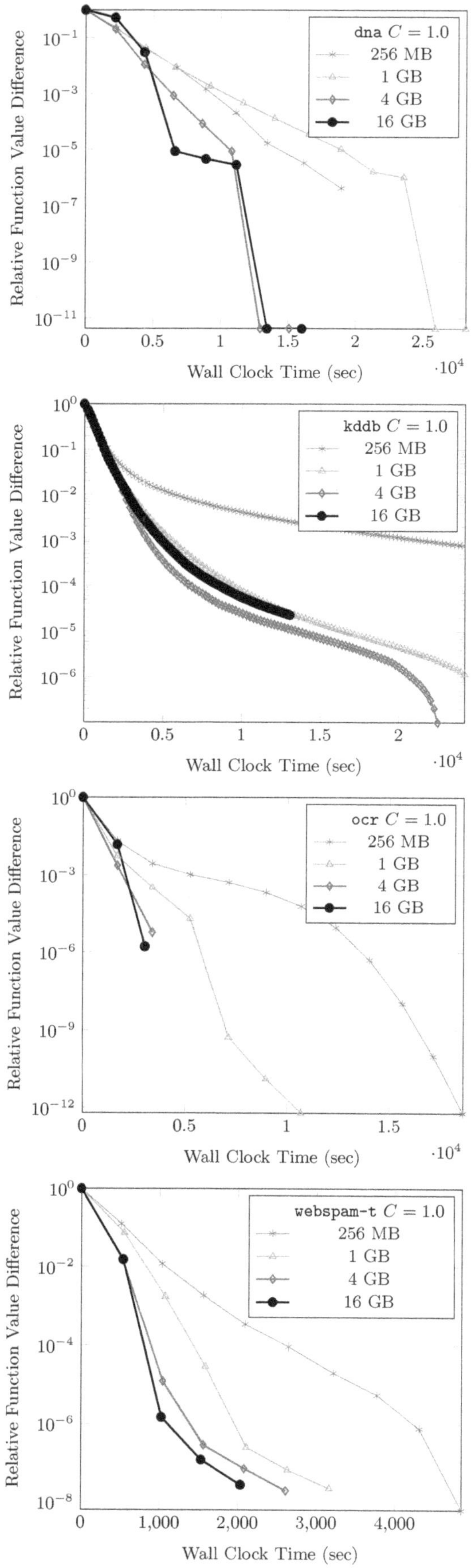

Figure 4: Relative objective function value as a function of wall clock time for various datasets as the RAM size Ω is varied.

time. In less than 10 hours StreamSVM could finish the optimization in both cases. To put our results in perspective, contrast this which the recent work of [1] who use a very similar feature representation as ours and train using LBFGS. Their algorithm requires around 30 iterations with each iteration requiring approximately 1 hour when distributed across 100 machines (total of 3000 CPU hours).

5. DISCUSSION

To conclude we would like to discuss some related work and place our contributions in perspective. Perhaps the closest in spirit to our work is the online version of SBM described by [11]. Here, data is assumed to arrive in a streaming fashion, and a dual coordinate descent procedure is used on blocks of data. However, there are some important differences between the two methods. First, online SBM only looks at the data once, while our algorithm StreamSVM performs multiple passes through the data. Second, the reading and the training in SBM happen in a synchronous fashion, while our reader thread asynchronously reads and caches data. In our experiments, StreamSVM also achieves near-optimal generalization performance after just one or two passes through the data.

In order to speed up linear SVMs where the feature mapping can be computed explicitly, [33] introduced a computational framework for linear SVMs (COFFIN). Along the same lines, one can use hash functions to map sparse high-dimensional features into dense low-dimensional features. This idea, first described in [31] and improved upon in [37] is one of the important reasons why the Vowpal Wabbit learning frameworkis fast. These techniques are very naturally incorporated into our framework as demonstrated in our experiments.

A closely related alternative to dual coordinate descent is stochastic gradient descent (SGD). Recently there have been numerous variants of which have been studied both theoretically [6, 30] as well as empirically [5]. However, SGD in its most basic form is inherently serial, and therefore there is a recent flurry of activity on developing parallel stochastic gradient descent solvers [23, 40, 15]. As explained in Section 1.3 we view our research as complimentary.

Our long term research goal is to design, analyze, and implement novel optimization algorithms that take advantage of modern hardware to enable learning on and mining of massive datasets. With the increasing availability of many-core processors, general-purpose graphics processing units, and solid-state drives, we are witnessing a hardware revolution. The next generation of systems-aware, efficient, scalable machine learning algorithms need to take advantage of these emerging computing paradigms. We view this paper as a step towards that direction.

6. REFERENCES

[1] A. Agarwal, O. Chapelle, M. Dudík, and J. Langford. A reliable effective terascale linear learning system. Technical report, 2011. http://arxiv.org/abs/1110.4198.

[2] A. Ahmed, M. Aly, J. Gonzalez, S. Narayanamurthy, and A. J. Smola. Scalable inference in latent variable models. In *WSDM*, 2012.

[3] G. Bakir, T. Hofmann, B. Schölkopf, A. Smola, B. Taskar, and S. V. N. Vishwanathan. *Predicting Structured Data*. 2007.

[4] A. Bordes, S. Ertekin, J. Weston, and L. Bottou. Fast kernel classifiers with online and active learning. *JMLR*, 6:1579–1619, September 2005.

[5] L. Bottou. Stochastic gradient SVMs. `http://leon.bottou.org/projects/sgd`, 2008.

[6] L. Bottou and O. Bousquet. The tradeoffs of large scale learning. In *NIPS 20*, 2007.

[7] O. Bousquet and A. Elisseeff. Algorithmic stability and generalization performance. In *NIPS 12*, pages 196–202, 2001.

[8] S. Boyd and L. Vandenberghe. *Convex Optimization*. Cambridge University Press, 2004.

[9] E. Candes and T. Tao. Decoding by linear programming. *IEEE Trans. Information Theory*, 51(12):4203–4215, 2005.

[10] C. C. Chang and C. J. Lin. *LIBSVM: a library for support vector machines*, 2001. `http://www.csie.ntu.edu.tw/~cjlin/libsvm`.

[11] K. W. Chang and D. Roth. Selective block minimization for faster convergence of limited memory large-scale linear models. In *KDD*, pages 699–707, 2011.

[12] L. Cheng, S. V. N. Vishwanathan, D. Schuurmans, S. Wang, and T. Caelli. Implicit online learning with kernels. In *NIPS 19*, 2006.

[13] C. Cortes and V. Vapnik. Support vector networks. *Machine Learning*, 20(3):273–297, 1995.

[14] K. Crammer, Ofer Dekel, Joseph Keshet, Shai Shalev-Shwartz, and Y. Singer. Online passive-aggressive algorithms. *JMLR*, 7:551–585, March 2006.

[15] O. Dekel, R. Gilad-Bachrach, O. Shamir, and L. Xiao. Optimal distributed online prediction using mini-batches. Technical report, 2010. `http://arxiv.org/abs/1012.1367`.

[16] D. L. Donoho, A. Maleki, and A. Montanari. Message-passing algorithms for compressed sensing. *PNAS*, 106, 2009.

[17] R.-E. Fan, J.-W. Chang, C.-J. Hsieh, X.-R. Wang, and C.-J. Lin. LIBLINEAR: A library for large linear classification. *JMLR*, 9:1871–1874, August 2008.

[18] C. J. Hsieh, K. W. Chang, C. J. Lin, S. S. Keerthi, and S. Sundararajan. A dual coordinate descent method for large-scale linear SVM. In *ICML*, pages 408–415, 2008.

[19] T. Joachims. Making large-scale SVM learning practical. In B. Schölkopf, C. J. C. Burges, and A. J. Smola, editors, *Advances in Kernel Methods — Support Vector Learning*, pages 169–184, 1999.

[20] T. Joachims. Training linear SVMs in linear time. In *KDD*, 2006.

[21] J. Kivinen and M. K. Warmuth. Exponentiated gradient versus gradient descent for linear predictors. *Information and Computation*, 132(1):1–64, January 1997.

[22] J. Kivinen, M. K. Warmuth, and B. Hassibi. The p-norm generaliziation of the LMS algorithm for adaptive filtering. *IEEE Trans. Signal Processing*, 54(5):1782–1793, May 2006.

[23] J. Langford, A. J. Smola, and M. Zinkevich. Slow learners are fast. `http://arxiv.org/abs/0911.0491`, 2009.

[24] Z. Q. Luo and P. Tseng. On the convergence of coordinate descent method for convex differentiable minimization. *Journal of Optimization Theory and Applications*, 72(1):7–35, 1992.

[25] G. Mann, R. McDonald, M. Mohri, N. Silberman, and D. Walker. Efficient large-scale distributed training of conditional maximum entropy models. In *NIPS 22*, pages 1231–1239, 2009.

[26] N. Murata, S. Yoshizawa, and S. Amari. Network information criterion — determining the number of hidden units for artificial neural network models. *IEEE Trans. Neural Networks*, 5:865–872, 1994.

[27] E. Osuna and F. Girosi. Reducing the run-time complexity in support vector regression. In B. Schölkopf, C. J. C. Burges, and A. J. Smola, editors, *Advances in Kernel Methods — Support Vector Learning*, pages 271–284, 1999.

[28] J. Platt. Fast training of support vector machines using sequential minimal optimization. In B. Schölkopf, C. J. C. Burges, and A. J. Smola, editors, *Advances in Kernel Methods — Support Vector Learning*, pages 185–208, 1999.

[29] B. Schölkopf and A. J. Smola. *Learning with Kernels*. MIT Press, 2002.

[30] S. Shalev-Shwartz, Y. Singer, and N. Srebro. Pegasos: Primal estimated sub-gradient solver for SVM. In *ICML*, 2007.

[31] Q. Shi, J. Petterson, G. Dror, J. Langford, A. Smola, A. Strehl, and S. V. N. Vishwanathan. Hash kernels. In *AISTATS*, 2009.

[32] A. J. Smola and S. Narayanamurthy. An architecture for parallel topic models. In *VLDB*, 2010.

[33] S. Sonnenburg and V. Franc. COFFIN: A computational framework for linear SVMs. In *ICML*, 2010.

[34] S. Sonnenburg, V. Franc, E. Yom-Tov, and M. Sebag. Pascal large scale learning challenge. 2008. `http://largescale.ml.tu-berlin.de/workshop/`.

[35] C. H. Teo, S. V. N. Vishwanthan, A. J. Smola, and Q. V. Le. Bundle methods for regularized risk minimization. *JMLR*, 11:311–365, January 2010.

[36] M. Wainwright. Sharp thresholds for noisy and high-dimensional recovery of sparsity. Technical report, Department of Statistics, UC Berkeley, 2006.

[37] K. Weinberger, A. Dasgupta, J. Attenberg, J. Langford, and A. J. Smola. Feature hashing for large scale multitask learning. In *ICML*, 2009.

[38] H. F. Yu, C. J. Hsieh, K. W. Chang, and C. J. Lin. Large linear classification when data cannot fit in memory. In *KDD*, pages 833–842, 2010.

[39] L. Zanni, T. Serafini, and G. Zanghirati. Parallel software for training large scale support vector machines on multiprocessor systems. *JMLR*, 7:1467–1492, July 2006.

[40] M. Zinkevich, A. Smola, M. Weimer, and L. Li. Parallelized stochastic gradient descent. In *NIPS 23*, pages 2595–2603, 2010.

Discovering Regions of Different Functions in a City Using Human Mobility and POIs

Jing Yuan
Microsoft Research Asia
v-jinyua@microsoft.com

Yu Zheng
Microsoft Research Asia
yuzheng@microsoft.com

Xing Xie
Microsoft Research Asia
xing.xie@microsoft.com

ABSTRACT

The development of a city gradually fosters different functional regions, such as educational areas and business districts. In this paper, we propose a framework (titled DRoF) that **D**iscovers **R**egions **o**f different **F**unctions in a city using both human mobility among regions and points of interests (POIs) located in a region. Specifically, we segment a city into disjointed regions according to major roads, such as highways and urban express ways. We infer the functions of each region using a topic-based inference model, which regards a region as a document, a function as a topic, categories of POIs (e.g., restaurants and shopping malls) as metadata (like authors, affiliations, and key words), and human mobility patterns (when people reach/leave a region and where people come from and leave for) as words. As a result, a region is represented by a distribution of functions, and a function is featured by a distribution of mobility patterns. We further identify the intensity of each function in different locations. The results generated by our framework can benefit a variety of applications, including urban planning, location choosing for a business, and social recommendations. We evaluated our method using large-scale and real-world datasets, consisting of two POI datasets of Beijing (in 2010 and 2011) and two 3-month GPS trajectory datasets (representing human mobility) generated by over 12,000 taxicabs in Beijing in 2010 and 2011 respectively. The results justify the advantages of our approach over baseline methods solely using POIs or human mobility.

Categories and Subject Descriptors

H.2.8 [**Database Management**]: data mining, spatial databases and GIS.

General Terms

Algorithms, Design, Experimentation, Performance

Keywords

functional regions, urban computing, taxi trajectories, human mobility

1. INTRODUCTION

The step of urbanization and modern civilization leads to different functional regions in a city, e.g., residential areas, business districts, and educational areas, which support different needs of people's urban lives and serve as a valuable organizing technique for framing detailed knowledge of a metropolitan. These regions may be artificially designed by urban planners, or naturally formulated according to people's actual lifestyle, and would change functions and territories with the development of a city.

In this paper, we aim to discover regions of different functions in urban areas using human mobility and points of interests (POIs). Here, a city is partitioned into individual regions by major roads, like high way and ring roads (refer to Figure 1(a)). Human mobility is represented by people's movement trajectories, which can be cell-tower traces in a cellular network, or trajectories of driving routes, or a sequence of posts (like geo-tweets, geo-tagged photos, or check-ins) in location-based services [22]. A POI is associated with a coordinate and a category like restaurants and shopping malls. Specifically, we fill regions that could have similar functions with the same color in Figure 1(a) and identify the functionality intensity of each function in different locations. For example, Figure 1(b) shows the functionality intensity of developed commercial/entertainment (a kind of function) areas in Beijing, where the darker part suggests a higher intensity. This step is motivated by the following observations. Sometimes, only a part of a region contributes to a function. On the other hand, a function could be formulated across several individual regions (e.g., a shopping street). Finally, each function is titled with some tags in a semi-manual way based on the output of our method.

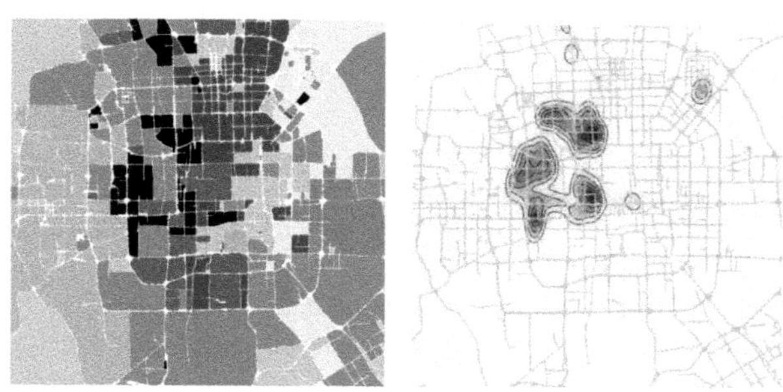

(a) (b)

Figure 1: The objectives of this paper: a) functional regions; b) intensity of a function

Discovering regions of different functions can enable a variety of valuable applications. First, it can provide people with a quick understanding of a complex city (like New York City, Tokyo, and Paris) and social recommendations. For example, tourists can easily differentiate some scenic areas from business districts given these functional regions, thereby reducing effort for trip planning. Local people can also expand their knowledge about a city by finding regions that have similar functions (e.g., entertainment areas). It is very common that local people may not well understand each part of a metropolitan even if they have been in the metropolitan for a few years. Second, these functional regions can calibrate the urban planning of a city and contribute to the future planning to some extent. It is not surprising that a city did not evolve as its original planning, given the complexity of urban planning itself and the difficulty in predicting the development of a city. Third, these functional regions would also benefit location choosing for a business and advertisement. For instance, when building a supermarket we need to consider the distance to the residential areas, and the advertisement for a training course could be better put considering the geospatial intensity of the educational function.

To identify the functions of a region, we need to take into account both POIs located in a region and human mobility among these regions due to the following two aspects:
1) *POI data*: On the one hand, POIs feature the function of a region. For example, a region containing a number of universities and schools has a high probability to be an educational area. On the other hand, a region usually contains a variety of POIs, thereby having compound functions instead of a single function. Some regions may serve as both business districts and entertainment areas in a city. In addition, the information from POI data cannot differentiate the quality of different venues and reflect the interactions between functional regions. For instance, restaurants are everywhere in a city, however, they could denote different functions. Some small restaurants were built just for satisfying local residences' daily needs, while a few famous restaurants attracting many people might be regarded as a feature of an entertainment area. As a result, sometimes two regions sharing a similar distribution of POIs could still have different functions.
2) *Human mobility*: The functions of a region have a strong correlation with the traveling behavior of people who visit the region. The knowledge that human mobility contributes to reveal the functions of a region mainly lies in two folds. One is when people arrive at and leave a region. The other is where people come from and leave for. Intuitively, in a workday people usually leave a residential area in the morning and return in the evening. The major time when people visit an entertainment area, however, is the evening of workdays or the whole day of non-workdays. Furthermore, regions of different functions are correlated in the context of human mobility. For instance, people reaching an entertainment area have a high probability from a working area (in a workday) and a residential area (in non-workdays). As a result, two regions are more likely to have similar functions, if people travel to the two regions from similar functional regions or leave for similar ones.

The research reported in this paper is a step towards urban computing which enables smart cities by understanding urban dynamics. The contribution of this paper consists of three points:

- We propose a topic model-based method to identify the functions of individual regions, which are obtained using morphological image segmentation approach. The proposed method regards a region as a document, deems a function as a topic, uses human mobility related to the region as words, and treats POIs located in a region as metadata (like titles, authors, affiliations, and key words). As a result, a region is represented by a distribution of topics (functions), and each topic is a denoted by a distribution of words. This model fits the research intuitively and reduces the data sparseness problem.
- We infer the territory of these functions by clustering regions into groups according to the topic distribution of each region. Regions from the same cluster have similar functions, and different clusters represent different functions. Then, for each cluster of regions, we identify the functionality intensity in the regions (belonging to the cluster), using Kernel Density Estimation which employs human mobility as samples.
- We evaluated our method using large-scale and real-world datasets, consisting of two POI datasets of Beijing (in year 2010 and 2011) and two 3-month GPS trajectory datasets (representing human mobility) generated by over 12,000 taxicabs in Beijing in 2010 and 2011 respectively. The results justify the advantages of our approach over baseline methods solely using POI or human mobility. In addition, these powerful datasets allow us to study not only the functional regions in a city but also the evolving of the city across years.

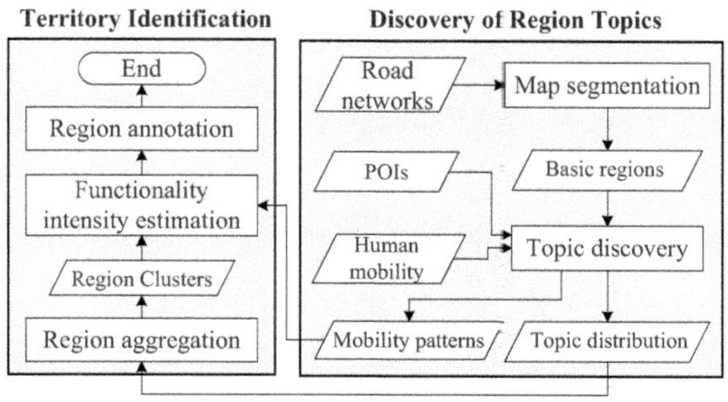

Figure 2: Framework for discovering the functional regions

In accordance with the framework of our work presented in Figure 2, the rest of this paper is organized as follows: Section 2 discovers the distributions of functions for each region, which consists of a map segmentation and an analogy from topic model of documents. Section 3 identifies the aggregated functional regions based on the discovered distribution of functions pertaining to each region and estimates the intensity of each function. Evaluation results are reported in Section 4 and related works are categorized in Section 5. Finally, we briefly conclude the paper in Section 6.

2. DISCOVERY OF REGION TOPICS

In this section we first segment the urban area of a city into region units in terms of major road networks, and then infer the distribution of functions in each region unit using a topic-model-based method.

2.1 Map Segmentation

A road network is usually comprised of some major roads like highways and ring roads, which naturally partition a city into regions. For example, as shown in Figure 4, the red segments denote freeways and city expressways in Beijing, and blue segments represent urban arterial roads. The three kinds of roads are associated with a road level 0, 1, and 2 respectively (in a road network database), forming a natural segmentation of the urban area of Beijing. We term each segmented region as a "formal region" in the rest of this paper, following the definition proposed in [2]. Intrinsically, a formal region is a basic unit carrying social-economic functions due to the following reasons. First, people live in formal regions and POIs fall in regions. Second, formal regions as the origin and destination of a trip are the root cause of human mobility. In short, people travel among formal regions.

In our method, we choose the raster-based model to represent the road network and utilize morphological image processing tech-

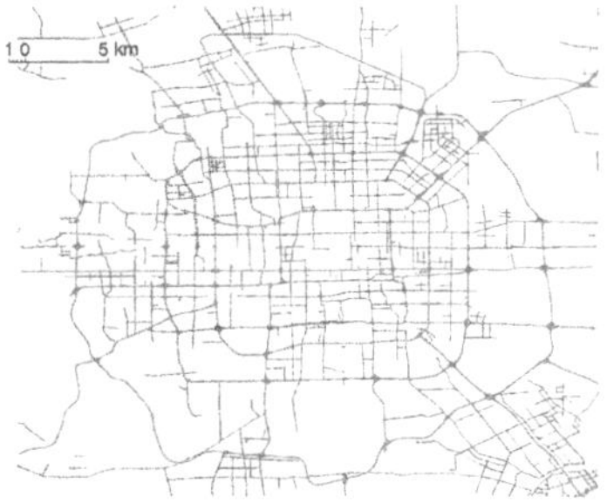

Figure 4: Beijing road network. red: level-0/1; blue: level-2

niques to address the task of map segmentation. Typically, in a Geographical Information System (GIS), there are two models to represent spatial data: *vector*-based model and *raster*-based model. Vector-based model uses geometric primitives such as points, lines and polygons to represent spatial objects referenced by Cartesian coordinates, while raster-based model quantizes an area into small discrete grid-cells. Both of the two models have advantages and disadvantages depending on the specific applications. For instance, vector-based method is more powerful for precisely finding shortest-paths, whereas it requires intensive computation when performing topological analysis, such as the problem of map simplification[5], which is proved to be NP-complete [5]. On the other hand, raster-based model is more computational efficient and succinct for territorial analysis, but the accuracy is limited by the number of cells used for discretizing the road networks.

Specifically, a raster-based map is a binary image (e.g., 0 stands for road segments and 1 stands for blank space). In order to remove the unnecessary details, such as the lanes of a road and the overpasses (see Figure 3(a)), we first perform a *dilation* operation to thicken the roads. As a result,we can fill the small holes and smooth out the unnecessary details, as shown in Figure 3(b). Second, we obtain the skeleton of the road networks by performing a *thinning* operation based on the algorithm proposed in [9], as depicted in Figure 3(c). This operation recovers the size of a region which was reduced by the dilation operation, while keeping the connectivity between regions. The last step is to perform a connected component labeling (CCL) that finds individual regions by clustering "1"-labeled grids, using the method proposed in [15]. Figure 3(d) presents the results.

2.2 Topic Discovery

2.2.1 Preliminary

DEFINITION 1 (TRANSITION). A *transition* Tr is a quaternion containing the following four items: origin region ($Tr.r_O$), leaving time ($Tr.t_L$), destination region ($Tr.r_D$) and arrival time ($Tr.t_A$). Here, $Tr.r_O$ and $Tr.r_D$ are spatial features while the others are temporal features. □

DEFINITION 2 (MOBILITY PATTERN). A *mobility pattern* M is a triple extracted from a transition. Given a transiton $Tr = (Tr.r_O, Tr.r_D, Tr.t_L, Tr.t_A)$, we obtain two mobility patterns: the *leaving mobility pattern* $M_L = (Tr.r_O, Tr.r_D, Tr.t_L)$, and the *arriving mobility pattern* $M_A = (Tr.r_O, Tr.r_D, Tr.t_A)$. □

DEFINITION 3 (TRANSITION CUBOIDS). A *transition cuboid* C is an $R \times R \times T$ cuboid, where R is the number of regions and T is the number of time bins. Since there exist two types of mobility patterns, we define two types of transition cuboids: *leaving cuboid* C_L and *arriving cuboid* C_A. The cell with index (i, j, k) of the leaving cuboid records the number of mobility patterns that leave r_i for r_j at time t_k, i.e.,

$$C_L(i, j, k) = \|\{M_L = (x, y, z) | x = r_i, y = r_j, z = t_k\}\|.$$

Similarly,

$$C_A(i, j, k) = \|\{M_A = (x, y, z) | x = r_i, y = r_j, z = t_k\}\|. \quad \square$$

We project each trajectory representing human mobility on the segmented region units, turning a trajectory into a transition. Then, we discretize time of day into time bins in each of which we deposit the transitions and formulate mobility patterns. Here, we do not differentiate different weekdays but differ the time bins in weekdays from those in weekends. For example, setting 2 hours as a bin, we will have 24 bins (12 for weekdays and 12 for weekends) in total. Later, two transition cuboids are built using the mobility patterns.

Concepts of Topic Models. Probabilistic topic models have been successfully used for extracting the hidden thematic structure in large archives of documents[3]. In this model, each *document* of a *corpus* exhibits multiple *topics* and each *word* of a document supports a certain topic. Given all the words of each document in a corpus as observations, a topic model is trained to infer the hidden thematic structure behind the observations. Latent Dirichlet Allocation (LDA) is a generative model that includes hidden variables. The intuition behind this model is that documents are represented as random mixtures over latent topics, where each topic is characterized by a distribution over words [4]. Let α and η be the prior parameters for the Dirichlet document-topic distribution and topic-word distribution respectively. Assume there are K topics and β is a $K \times V$ matrix where V is the number of words in the vocabulary (all the words in the corpus D). Each β_k is a distribution over the vocabulary. The topic proportions for the dth document are θ_d, where $\theta_{d,k}$ is the topic proportion for topic k in the dth document. The topic assignments for the dth document are z_d, where $z_{d,n}$ is the topic assignment for the nth word in the dth document. Finally, the observed words for document d are w_d, where $w_{d,n}$ is the nth word in document d, which is an element from the fixed vocabulary.

Using the above notations, as presented in Figure 5, the generative process can be described as follows:

1. For each topic k, draw $\beta_k \sim Dir(\eta)$.

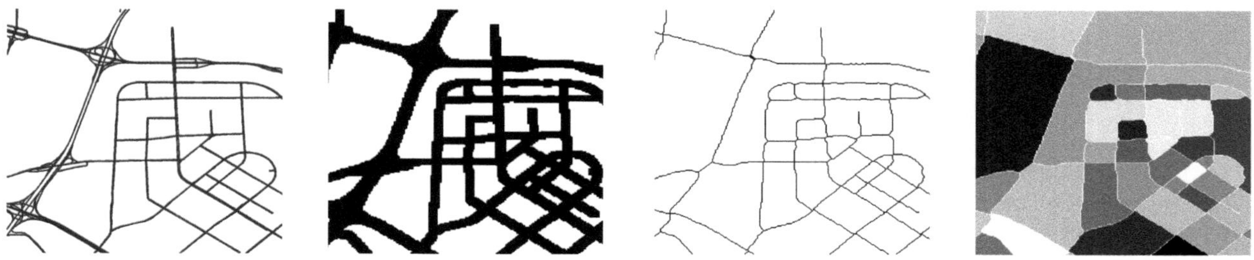

(a) Original (b) Step 1: dilation (c) Step 2: thinning (d) Step 3: CCL

Figure 3: Map Segmentation

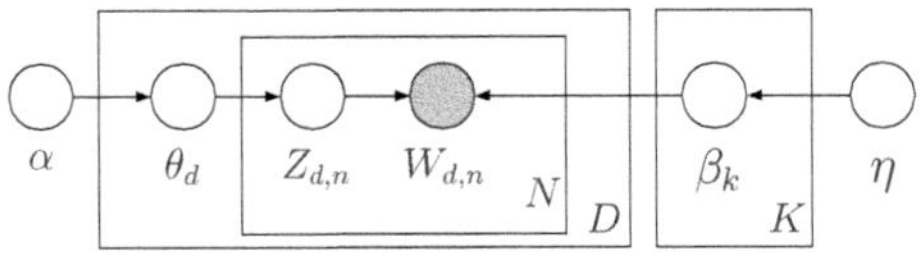

Figure 5: Graphic model of LDA

2. Given the dth document d in corpus D, draw $\theta_d \sim Dir(\alpha)$.
3. For the nth word in the dth document $w_{d,n}$,
   (a) draw $z_{d,n} \sim Mult(\theta_d)$;
   (b) draw $w_{d,n} \sim Mult(\beta_{z_{d,n}})$.

Here, $Dir(\cdot)$ is the Dirichlet distribution and $Mult(\cdot)$ is the multinomial distribution. The estimation of LDA can be implemented using the EM algorithm and the most commonly used inference method of LDA is Gibbs sampling. See [4] for a variational inference method and detailed discussions of LDA.

2.2.2 *Topic Modeling*

As shown in Table 1, we draw an analogy between discovering functions of a region and the topic discovery of a document. Specifically, we regard a formal region as a document and a function as a topic. In other words, a region having multiple functions is just like a document containing a variety of topics. Meanwhile, we deem the mobility patterns associated with a region as words and POIs as metadata of a document, as a functional region is characterized by its agglomeration of activities, its intraregional transport infrastructure, mobility of people, and inputs within its interaction borders [8].

Table 1: Analogy from region-functions to document-topics

transition cuboids	$\longrightarrow$ vocabulary
formal regions	$\longrightarrow$ documents
function of a region	$\longrightarrow$ topic of a document
mobility patterns	$\longrightarrow$ words
POI feature vector	$\longrightarrow$ metadata of a document

Figure 6 further details the analogy using an example. In our method, given the mobility dataset, we build the arriving and leaving cuboids respectively according to Definition 3. For a specific region r_i, the mobility patterns associated with r_i are counted by $C_A(1{:}R, i, 1{:}T)$ and $C_L(i, 1{:}R, 1{:}T)$, which are two "slices" extracted from arriving cuboid and leaving cuboid (termed as arriving matrix and leaving matrix respectively). The right part of Figure 6 shows a "document" we compose for region r_1, where a cell (in the matrices) represents a specific mobility pattern and the numbers in the cell denote the occurrences of the pattern. For example, in the right most column of the arriving matrix, the cell containing "5" means on average the mobility that went to r_1 from r_j in time bin t_k occurred 5 times per day. A POI is recorded with a tuple (in a POI database) consisting of a POI category (as listed in Table 2), name and a geo-position (latitude, longitude). For each formal region r, the number of POIs in each POI category can be counted. The *frequency density* v_i of the ith POI category in r is calculated by:

$$v_i = \frac{\text{Number of the POIs of the } i\text{th POI category}}{\text{Area of region } r \text{ (measured by grid-cells)}},$$

and the POI *feature vector* of r is denoted by $x_r = (v_1, v_2, \ldots, v_F, 1)$ where F is the number of POI categories and the last "1" is a default feature to account for the mean value of each topic, as explained in

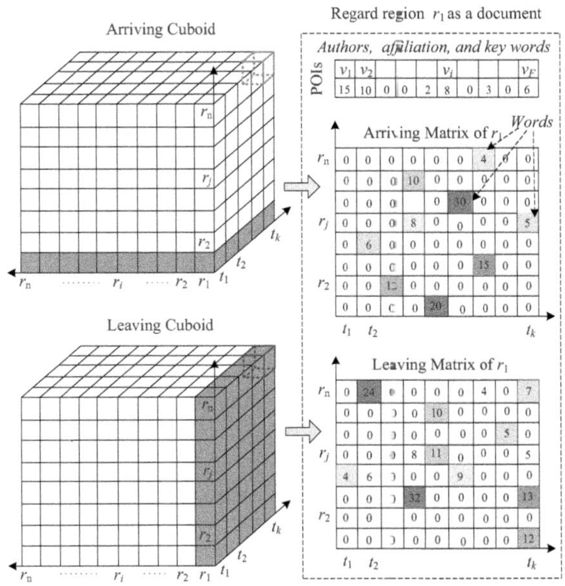

Figure 6: Analogy between mobility patterns and words based on transition cuboids

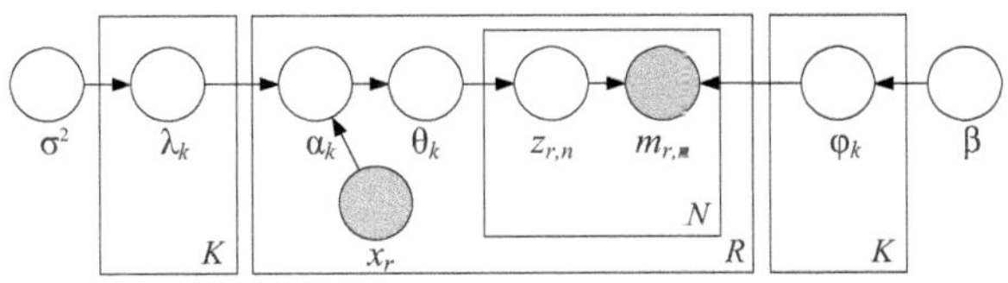

Figure 7: DMR-based topic model

[11]. The POI feature vector is regarded as the metadata of each region, which is an analogue of the observed features such as author/email/institution of a document.

Using the basic LDA model, region topics can be discovered using the mobility patterns. However, as stated in Section 1, the region topics are products of both the POIs and mobility patterns. In order to combine the information from both of them, we utilize a more advanced topic model based on LDA and Dirichlet Multinomial Regression (DMR) [11].

The DMR-based topic model (for simplicity, DMR in the rest of the paper) takes into account the influence of the observable metadata in a document by using a flexible framework, which supports arbitrary features [11]. Compared to other models designed for specific data such as Author-Topic model and Topic-Over-Time model (a member in the supervised-LDA family of topic models), DMR achieves similar or improved performance while is more computational efficient and succinct in implementation [11].

As presented in Figure 7, the generative process of the DMR model is:

1. For each region topic k,
   (a) draw $\lambda_k \sim \mathcal{N}(0, \sigma^2 I)$;
   (b) draw $\beta_k \sim Dir(\eta)$.
2. Given the rth region,
   (a) for each region topic k, let $\alpha_{r,k} = \exp(x_r^T \lambda_k)$;
   (b) draw $\theta_r \sim Dir(\alpha_r)$;
   (c) for the nth mobility pattern in the rth region $m_{r,n}$,
      i. draw $z_{r,n} \sim Mult(\theta_r)$;
      ii. draw $m_{r,n} \sim Mult(\beta_{z_{r,n}})$.

Here, $\mathcal{N}$ is the Gaussian distribution with σ as a hyper parameter, and λ_k is a vector with the same length as the POI feature vector.

Table 2: POI category taxonomy

code	POI category	code	POI category
1	car service	16	banking and insurance service
2	car sales	17	corporate business
3	car repair	18	street furniture
4	motorcycle service	19	entrance/bridge
5	Café/Tea Bar	20	public utilities
6	sports/stationery shop	21	Chinese restaurant
7	living service	22	foreign restaurant
8	sports	23	fastfood restaurant
9	hospital	24	shopping mall
10	hotel	25	convenience store
11	scenic spot	26	electronic products store
12	residence	27	supermarket
13	governmental agencies and public organizations	28	furniture building materials market
14	science and education	29	pub/bar
15	transportation facilities	30	theaters

The nth observed mobility pattern of region r is denoted as $m_{r,n}$. Other notations are similar to the previous LDA model. This model can also be estimated using EM and inferred using Gibbs sampling. Different from the basic LDA model, here, the Dirichlet prior α is now specified to individual regions (α_r) based on the observed POI features of each region. Therefore, for different combination of POI category distributions, the resulting α values are distinct. Thus the thematic region topic distributions extracted from the data are induced by both the POI features and mobility patterns. As a result, by applying DMR, given the mobility patterns and POI features, we obtain the topic assignment for each region and the mobility pattern distribution of each topic.

3. TERRITORY IDENTIFICATION

3.1 Region Aggregation

This step aggregates similar formal regions in terms of region topic distributions by performing a clustering algorithm. Regions from the same cluster have similar functions, and different clusters represent different functions. For region r, after parameter estimations based on the DMR model, the topic distribution is a K dimensional vector $\theta_r = (\theta_{r,1}, \theta_{r,2}, \ldots, \theta_{r,K})$, where $\theta_{r,k}$ is the proportion of topic k for region r. We perform the k-means clustering method on the K-dimensional points θ_r, $r \in 1, 2, \ldots, R$. The number of clusters can be predefined according to the needs of an application or determined using the average *silhouette* value as the criterion [14]. The silhouette value of a point i in the dataset, denoted by $s(i)$ is in the range of $[-1, 1]$, where $s(i)$ close to 1 means that the point is appropriately clustered and very distant from its neighboring clusters; $s(i)$ close to 0 indicates that the point is not distinctly in one cluster or another; $s(i)$ close to -1 means the point is probably assigned to the wrong cluster. The average silhouette value of a cluster measures how tightly the data in this cluster are grouped, and the average silhouette of the entire dataset reflects how appropriately all the data has been clustered. In practice, we perform cross validation on the dataset for different k multiple times and choose an appropriate k with the maximum overall silhouette value. Consequently, we aggregate the formal regions into k clusters, each of which is termed as a *functional region*.

3.2 Functionality Intensity Estimation

On the one hand, the functionality of a functional region is generally not uniformly distributed within the entire region. On the other hand, sometimes, the core functional area may span multiple formal regions and may have an irregular shape, e.g., a hot shopping street crossing several formal regions. In order to reveal the degree of functionality and glean the essential territory of a functional region, we estimate the *functionality intensity* for each aggregated functional region (a cluster of formal regions).

Intuitively, the number of visits implicitly reflects the popularity of a certain functional region. In other words, people's mobility patterns imply the functionality intensity. As a result, we feed the origin and destination of each mobility (represented by latitude and longitude) into a Kernel Density Estimation (KDE) model to infer the functionality intensity in a functional region. Note that the real place that an individual visited may not be the destination that we can obtain from a mobility dataset. For example, the drop-off points of taxi trajectories may not be people's final destinations like a shopping mall. However, the pick-up/drop-off points should not be too far from the really-visited locations according to common-sense knowledge. The farther distance a location to the drop-off point, the lower probability that people would visit the location.

Given n points $x_1, x_2, \ldots, x_n$ located in a 2D spatial space, KDE estimates the intensity at location s by a kernel density estimator, defined as:

$$\lambda(s) = \sum_{i=1}^{n} \frac{1}{nr^2} K\left(\frac{d_{i,s}}{r}\right), \tag{1}$$

where $d_{i,s}$ is the distance from x_i to s, r is the bandwidth and $K(\cdot)$ is the kernel function whose value decays with the increasing of $d_{i,r}$, such as the Gaussian function, Quartic function, Conic and negative exponential. The choice of the bandwidth usually determines the smoothness of the estimated density – a large r achieves smoother estimation while a small r reveals more detailed peaks and valleys. In our case, we choose the Gaussian function as the kernel function, i.e.,

$$K\left(\frac{d_{i,s}}{r}\right) = \frac{1}{\sqrt{2\pi}} \exp\left(-\frac{d_{i,s}^2}{2r^2}\right). \tag{2}$$

and the bandwidth r is determined according to MISE criterion [17].

3.3 Region Annotation

In this step, given the results we obtained, we try to annotate each cluster of regions with some semantic terms, which could contribute to the understanding of its real functions. Note that region annotation is a very challenging problem in both traditional urban planning and document processing. Essentially, this annotation problem is the visualization problem of topic model, which is listed as a future direction of topic modeling in the recent survey paper by Blei [3]. A compromised method so far is to use the most frequent words in a discovered topic to annotate a document. But in our case, listing the frequent mobility patterns (analogue to words) is far from enough to name a functional region.

In our method, we annotate a functional region by considering the following 4 aspects: 1) The POI configuration in a functional region. We compute an average POI feature vector across the regions in functional region. According to the average frequency density in the calculated POI feature vector, we rank each POI category in a functional region (termed as internal ranking) and rank all the functional regions for each POI category (termed as external ranking). We will give an example in the experiment as shown in Table 4. 2) The most frequent mobility patterns of each functional region. 3) The functionality intensity. We study the representative POIs located in each functionality kernel, e.g., a function region could be an educational area if its kernel is full of universities and schools. 4) The human-labeled regions. People may know the functions of

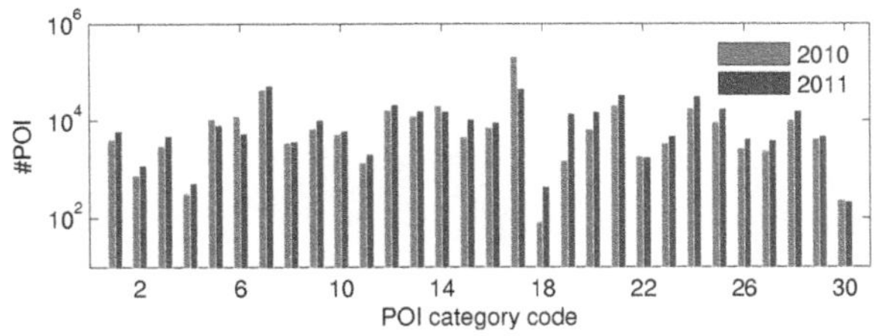

Figure 8: POI counts for each category in 2010 and 2011

a few well-known regions, e.g., the region contains the Forbidden City is an area of historic interests. After clustering, the human labeled regions will help us understand other regions in a cluster. Refer to the experiments for the detailed results and analysis.

4. EVALUATION

4.1 Settings

We use the following datasets for the evaluation:

a) *POI Data*: Two Beijing POI datasets in year 2010 and 2011. The count of each POI category (see Table 2) is presented in Figure 8.

b) *Mobility Data*: Two GPS trajectory datasets generated by Beijing taxis in 2010 and 2011, with the statistics shown in Table 3. We only choose the occupied trips (identified by the information of a taxi meter) from the data. Actually, there are over 30 cities in this world having over 10,000 taxicabs, e.g., Beijing has over 67,000 taxis. The taxi trips represent a significant portion of people's urban mobility. According to the report of Beijing Transportation Bureau, the taxi trips occupy over 12 percent of traffic flows on road surfaces[20]. Of course, other mobility datasets such as mobile phone traces can be used in our framework.

c) *Road Networks*: We have the road networks of Beijing in 2010 and 2011, with statistics shown in Table 3.

Table 3: Statistics of taxi trajectories and road networks

	year	2010	2011
Trajectories	#taxis	12,726	13,597
	#occupied trips	21,678,203	8,202,012
	#effective days	112	92
	average trip distance(km)	7.22	7.47
	average trip duration(min)	15.98	16.1
	average sampling interval(sec)	74.46	70.45
Roads	#road segments	150,357	162,246
	percentage of major roads	18.9%	17.1%
	#segmented formal regions	565	554
	size of "vocabulary" (non-0 items)	3,318,331	3,244,901

We implement our method on a 64-bit server with a Quad-Core 2.67G CPU and 16GB RAM. We train our model with 10 topics for 1000 iterations, optimize the parameters every 50 iterations. For k-means clustering, we incorporate the average silhouette value to determine the k and use the average results based on a 5-fold cross-validation. The efficiency (on average) is presented in Table 4.

Table 4: Overall efficiency of DRoF

operation	time(min)
map segmentation	0.325
building transition cuboids	40.1
estimate topic model(1000 iterations)	1353
region aggregation	0.124
total	1394

We compare our method with two baselines: a) the *TF-IDF-based Clustering*, which solely uses the POI data. This method employs the *term frequency-inverse document frequency* (tf-idf) to measure the importance of a POI in a formal region. Specifically, for a given formal region, we formulate a POI vector, $\langle v_1, v_2, \ldots, v_F\rangle$ where v_i is the tf-idf value of the i-th POI category, given by:

$$v_i = \frac{n_i}{N} \times \log \frac{R}{\|\{r|\text{the } i\text{-th POI category} \in r\}\|},$$

where n_i is the number of POIs belonging to the i-th category and N is the number of POIs located in this region. The idf term is calculated by computing the quotient of the number of regions divided by the number of regions which have the i-th POI category, and taking the logarithm of that quotient. Later, a k-means clustering is used to cluster the formal regions into k functional regions. b) *LDA-based Topic Model*, which uses only the mobility data. Similar to our analogy from regions to documents, this method feeds the mobility patterns (the analogue to words) into an LDA model. Later, we perform the k-means clustering, similar to the method we used when grouping all the formal regions based on their topic distributions learned from LDA. The parameters such as number of iterations, number of topics are set in accordance with our DRoF. As the number of POI categories usually has the same scale with that of the topics, applying the LDA model solely to POIs (as words) will not reduce the dimension of words.

We carry out the following three studies to evaluate the effectiveness of our framework though it is very difficult. 1) We invite some local people (who have been in Beijing for over 6 years) and request them to label two representative regions for each kind of function. We check whether the regions having the same labels are assigned into the same functional region and whether the regions with different labels are improperly clustered into one functional region. 2) We find the evolving of Beijing by comparing the results of 2010 and 2011, and identify whether the differences make sense. 3) We match our results against the land use planning of Beijing.

4.2 Results

4.2.1 Discovered Functional Regions

Figure 9 shows the aggregated functional regions discovered by different methods, where different colors indicate different functions. Note that in different figures, the same color may stand for different functions. As a result, tf-idf-based method forms 7 clusters (c_0–c_6) while LDA-based method and our method (DRoF) form 9 functional regions.

The TF-IDF method performs the worst among the three approaches. For example, as shown in Figure 9(a), region B is an university, which should be clustered with region A (another university) and region D (a high school). Meanwhile, region F (the Forbidden City) is not distinguished from other commercial areas like region E (Xidan). Another example is the Wangjing area (C), which is an emerging residential area with some companies and many living services, like apartments, shopping malls and restaurants. Unfortunately, the TF-IDF method improperly divides this area into many small functional regions as this method only considers POI distributions.

Basically, the LDA-based method and DRoF have a similar output of functional regions. However, there still exist several exemplary regions where DRoF outperforms LDA obviously. For example, region F in Figure 9(b) is a developing commercial/entertainment area in Wangjing area. But LDA aggregates it with the Forbidden City (Region F in Figure 9(a)), which is a region of historical interests; Area B (China Agricultural University) and Area E (Tsinghua University) are typical science and education areas where LDA fails to correctly cluster them together; Area A around Sanlitun is a well-known diplomatic district of Beijing, which is mixed with a developing commercial area C; Region D is a park where

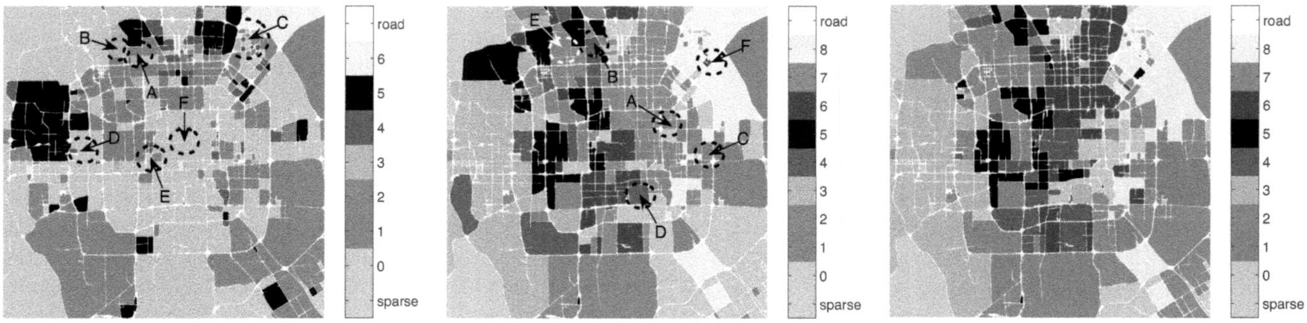

(a) TF-IDF (b) LDA (c) DRoF

Figure 9: Functional regions discovered by different methods

Table 5: Overall POI feature vector and ranking of functional regions by DRoF. FD: frequency density, IR: internal ranking

	c0		c1		c2		c3		c4		c5		c6		c7		c8	
POI	FD	IR	FD	IR	FD	IR	FD	IR	FD	IR	FD	IR	FD	IR	FD	IR	FD	IR
CarServ	0.046	25	0.016	23	0.052	26	0.044	18	0.060	17	0.028	25	0.056	24	0.091	13	0.053	21
CarSale	0.009	28	0.005	27	0.061	24	0.006	27	0.009	27	0.005	28	0.021	27	0.015	26	0.006	27
CarRepa	0.021	26	0.011	24	0.062	23	0.042	19	0.051	20	0.023	27	0.062	23	0.057	18	0.039	25
MotServ	0.002	30	0.003	28	0.004	28	0.001	28	0.002	29	0.004	29	0.001	29	0.001	29	0.003	28
Caf/Tea	0.226	14	0.121	9	0.226	12	0.066	15	0.113	13	0.252	6	0.237	13	0.052	19	0.153	10
StaStor	0.135	17	0.037	20	0.127	17	0.037	20	0.058	18	0.080	19	0.100	19	0.073	15	0.072	17
LivServ	1.289	1	0.581	2	1.322	2	0.399	1	0.698	1	0.780	2	1.345	2	0.430	2	0.886	2
Sports	0.054	23	0.035	21	0.092	21	0.030	22	0.041	22	0.033	23	0.080	20	0.035	20	0.093	16
Hospital	0.244	13	0.088	13	0.222	13	0.069	14	0.137	12	0.144	15	0.246	12	0.070	16	0.194	8
Hotel	0.202	15	0.063	16	0.115	18	0.058	16	0.071	16	0.086	18	0.211	15	0.059	17	0.049	22
SceSpo	0.048	24	0.007	26	0.032	27	0.012	25	0.016	25	0.029	24	0.044	25	0.012	27	0.031	26
Residen	0.795	3	0.230	5	0.638	6	0.203	5	0.323	5	0.398	5	0.797	4	0.221	4	0.440	3
Gov/Pub	0.442	7	0.103	11	0.276	11	0.094	10	0.188	9	0.169	12	0.375	7	0.177	6	0.150	11
Sci/Edu	0.315	11	0.139	7	1.084	3	0.109	9	0.323	6	0.251	8	0.530	6	0.124	9	0.266	6
TrasFac	0.459	6	0.115	10	0.397	7	0.091	11	0.150	11	0.191	11	0.364	8	0.113	10	0.257	7
Bank/Fina	0.376	9	0.128	8	0.383	8	0.078	13	0.107	14	0.197	10	0.320	10	0.083	14	0.135	12
CopBusi	1.128	2	0.593	1	1.947	1	0.334	2	0.348	4	0.548	4	1.738	1	0.475	1	0.977	1
StrFur	0.002	29	0.000	30	0.001	30	0.001	30	0.000	30	0.001	30	0.000	30	0.001	30	0.000	30
Entr/Bri	0.296	12	0.065	14	0.210	14	0.081	12	0.160	10	0.160	14	0.228	14	0.133	7	0.097	15
PubUti	0.405	8	0.101	12	0.285	9	0.112	8	0.238	7	0.209	9	0.314	11	0.132	8	0.132	13
ChiRes	0.692	5	0.252	4	0.926	5	0.294	3	0.399	3	0.813	1	0.829	3	0.235	3	0.370	4
ForRes	0.098	18	0.050	17	0.054	25	0.010	26	0.009	26	0.163	13	0.063	21	0.018	25	0.101	14
FasRes	0.095	19	0.046	18	0.141	16	0.034	21	0.050	21	0.126	16	0.132	17	0.026	22	0.057	20
ShopMal	0.724	4	0.268	3	0.929	4	0.242	4	0.476	2	0.559	3	0.734	5	0.203	5	0.306	5
ConvStor	0.370	10	0.157	6	0.281	10	0.128	7	0.234	8	0.251	7	0.362	9	0.108	11	0.160	9
E-Stor	0.056	21	0.017	22	0.107	20	0.029	23	0.037	23	0.037	22	0.063	22	0.018	24	0.040	23
SupMar	0.055	22	0.008	25	0.065	22	0.020	24	0.025	24	0.042	21	0.040	26	0.021	23	0.040	24
FurBuil	0.086	20	0.065	15	0.151	15	0.192	6	0.093	15	0.088	17	0.142	16	0.099	12	0.064	19
Pub/Bar	0.179	16	0.043	19	0.114	19	0.044	17	0.053	19	0.060	20	0.120	18	0.031	21	0.071	18
Theater	0.011	27	0.001	29	0.002	29	0.001	29	0.006	28	0.025	26	0.007	28	0.002	28	0.002	29

LDA fails to put it with other park/mountain areas (the green regions shown in Figure 9(b)). The LDA method only using human mobility overlooks the feature of POIs, thereby drops behind the DRoF (shown in Figure 9(c)).

4.2.2 Region Annotation

Table 5 shows the average POI feature vector of each region cluster (c_0–c_8, remember that DRoF generated 9 clusters) and the corresponding internal and external rankings, where the external rank is represented by the depth of the color (1 darkest, 4 lightest). Clearly, region cluster c_0, c_2, c_5, c_6, c_8 are more mature and more developed areas as compared to other clusters, since they have more high ranked POI categories, which are annotated as follows:

Diplomatic and embassy areas[c_0]. The most characteristic POI category in this functional region is the governmental agencies and public organizations, with a significant higher frequency density than other functional regions. Actually, most of the embassies are located in these areas, which are well configured for the diplomatic function, e.g., they have the highest external rank of Pub/Bars and transportation facilities, and the second highest rank of residential buildings, hospitals, and hotels, among all the clusters.

Education and science areas[c_2]. This region cluster contains the maximum number of science and education POIs (e.g., Tsinghua university and Beijing university). In addition, the biggest electronic market in China "ZhongguanCun", known as the Silicon Valley in China, is located in this functional region.

Developed residential areas[c_6]. This region cluster is clearly a mature residential area with the most residential building, living services, hospitals, hotels. In this kind of areas, an adequate number of services supports the people's living, such as the restaurants, shopping malls, banking services, schools, sports centers.

Emerging residential areas[c_8]. This area is annotated as the emerging residential area since it has a balanced POI configuration, such as living services, residential buildings, sports centers, hospitals and some companies etc.

Figure 10 compares the arriving/leaving transitions of (region clusters) c_6 and c_8 with that of other clusters respectively, where the x-axes are time of day (by hour) and y-axes are the functional regions that come from (left subfigures) and leave for (right subfigures). Both c_6 and c_8 follow the trend that most leaving transitions in the morning (8-9am, go to work) and most arriving transitions in the early evening (5-6pm, go back home), which is a typical pattern for the residential area. However, in terms of the absolute quantity, c_8 is much lower than c_6, which shows that there are more people living in c_6.

Developed commercial/entertainment areas[c_5]. They are typical entertainment areas with the highest external rank of theaters, foreign restaurants and café/tea bars. Moreover, there are a great many shopping malls, Chinese restaurant and convenience stores. Figure 12 shows the difference of arriving transitions of c_5 (developed commercial areas) on weekdays and weekends. It's clear that the people reach this kind of areas from the residential regions(c_6) much earlier on weekends (about 9am-11am) than on weekdays (7pm-9pm).

With regard to the other region clusters, since the frequency densities of POIs are much lower than the above functional regions, we identify their semantic functions with more consideration on the functionality intensity and frequent mobility patterns derived for each functional region in addition to the POI configurations.

Developing commercial/business/entertainment areas [c_1]. The POI configuration of this cluster is similar to cluster c_5 and c_7, but in terms of the absolute quantity, c_1 is less than c_5 while more than c_7. A certain number of shopping malls, restaurants and banking services feature this cluster as a developing commercial/ business/ entertainment functional region (either of them is possible). In the meantime, the functionality intensity provides another corroboration for this annotation. As depicted in Figure 13(a), the core of this functional regions is the new CBD of Beijing.

Regions under construction[c_7]. As analyzed above for region c_1, this region will potentially become regions 1 or 8 since the POI configuration produces a rudiment of the commercial/residential area with related supporting services. Figure 14 validates the degree of development with respect to c_5, c_1 and c_7.

Areas of historic interests[c_4]. If we only consider the POI config-

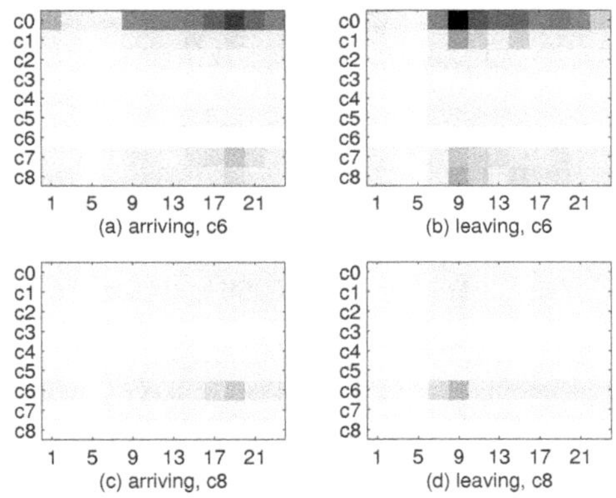

(a) arriving, c6 (b) leaving, c6 (c) arriving, c8 (d) leaving, c8

Figure 10: Transitions of c_6 and c_8

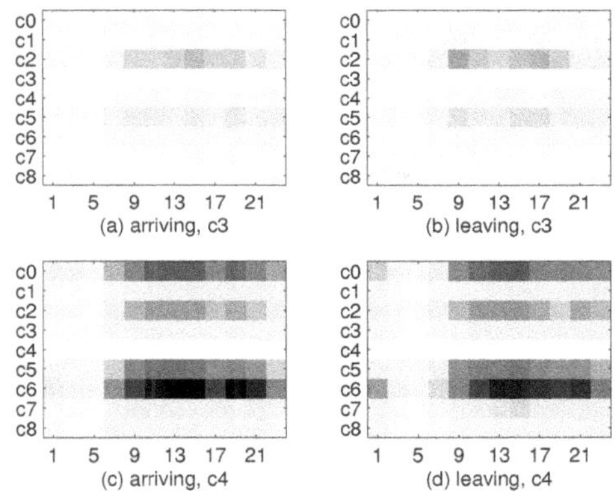

(a) arriving, c3 (b) leaving, c3 (c) arriving, c4 (d) leaving, c4

Figure 11: Transitions of c_3 and c_4

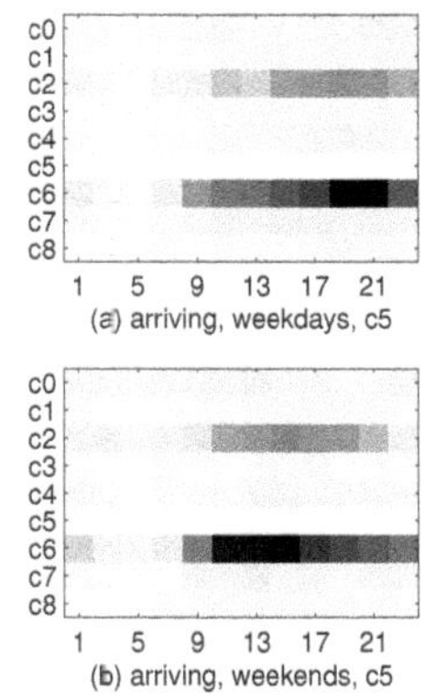

(a) arriving, weekdays, c5 (b) arriving, weekends, c5

Figure 12: Transitions of c_5

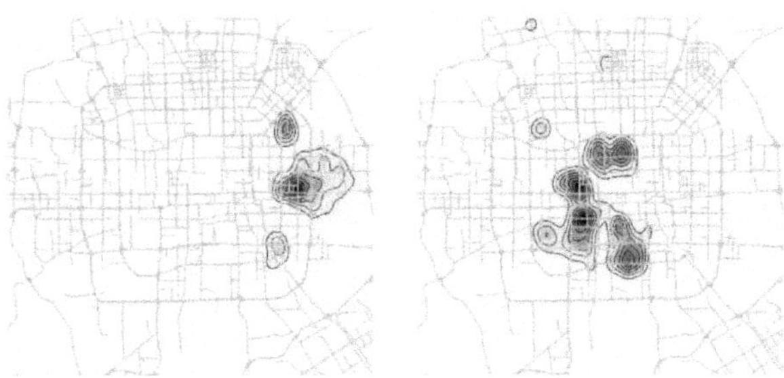

(a) functional region c_1 (b) functional region c_4

Figure 13: Functionality intensity of functional regions

uration, the characteristic of this cluster does not reveal obviously, which contains some public utilities, entrance/bridges, government organizations, science and education spots. However, by considering the functionality intensity estimated by the mobility patterns, we are easy to find that they are places of historic interests in Beijing. As shown in Figure 13(b), the famous historical places like Forbidden City and Temple of Heaven are located in these areas.

Nature and parks[c_3]. These areas have the fewest POIs in most of the POI categories. Actually, a lot of forests and mountains cover this cluster, e.g., the Xishan Forest Park, Century Forest Park, Baiwang Moutain etc. Figure 11 shows that people come to this functional region following the similar temporal patterns with c_4 (the historical areas), but the diversity and quantity are reasonably weaker than c_4, since many POIs in c_4 are very famous scenic spots.

4.2.3 Results in Different Years

We apply our method to the data (road network, POI and mobility) of 2010 and 2011 respectively. The discovered functional regions in 2010 are similar with 2011, while is slightly different in some regions. Figure 15 shows the detailed comparison around the east areas of the Forbidden City. For example, region A (Qianmen Street) becomes a developed commercial area from a nature/park area. The reason is that this region was developing in 2010 after a major repair since 2009. Similar to region A, region B (close to the new CBD of Beijing) becomes a developing commercial area from an under construction area. Intriguingly, region C becomes an under construction area in 2011 from an developing commercial area! We later found the truth that the tallest building of Beijing will rise up in this region in 2015 leading to a relocation work in 2011.

4.2.4 Calibration for Urban Planning

The discovered functional regions provide calibration and reference for urban planning. For example, Figure 16 presents the comparison between the governmental land use planning (2002-2010)

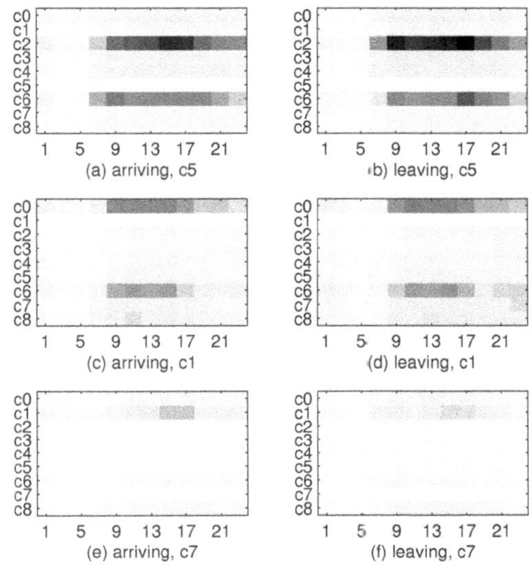

(a) arriving, c5 (b) leaving, c5 (c) arriving, c1 (d) leaving, c1 (e) arriving, c7 (f) leaving, c7

Figure 14: Transitions of c_1, c_5 and c_7

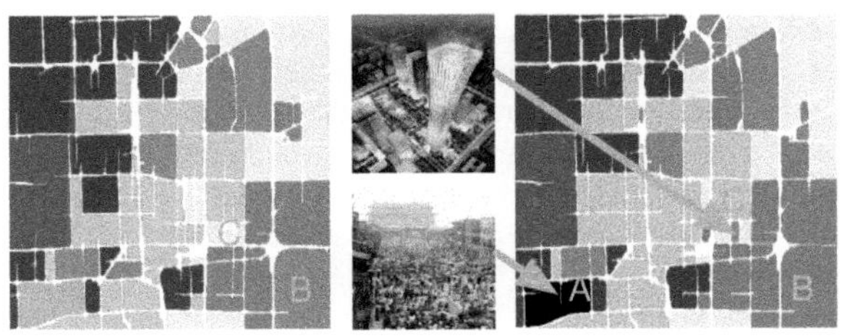

Figure 15: The east area of Forbidden City in 2010 and 2011

and the results of DRoF in 2011. This area forms an emerging residential area as planned by the government, while some small regions become developing commercial areas, such as A, B and C after 2 years' development.

5. RELATED WORK

Urban computing with taxicabs: Urban computing is emerging as a concept where every sensor, device, person, vehicle, building, and street in urban areas can be used as a component to probe city dynamics and further enable a city-wide computing for serving people and their cities. The increasing availability of GPS-embedded taxicabs provides us with an unprecedented wealth to understand human mobility in a city, thereby enabling a variety of novel urban computing research recently. For example, Ge et al. [7][6] and Yuan et al. [20] respectively study the strategies for improving

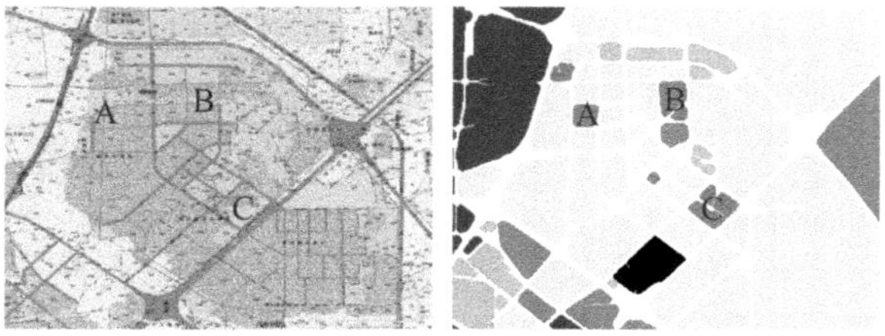

(a) (b)

Figure 16: (a) governmental land use planning (2002-2010) (b) discovered functional regions in 2011

taxi drivers' income by analyzing the pick-up and drop-off behavior of taxicabs in different locations. [19] aims to find the practically fastest driving route to a destination according to a large number of taxi trajectories, and Zheng et al. [21] glean the problematic urban planning in a city using the corresponding taxi trajectories. Based on the traffic flow represented by taxi trajectories, the technology for detecting anomalies in urban areas has been reported in [10].

The work presented in this paper is also a step towards urban computing. Different from the above-mentioned research, however, we focus on the discovery of functional regions in a city, which we have never seen before in this research theme.

Discovery of functional regions: Functional regions [1] have been studied in traditional fields of GIS and urban planning for years, as the discovery of them can benefit policy making, resource allocation, and the related research. [8] gives a good survey on the related literatures which are mainly based on clustering algorithms. Some algorithms classify regions in urban area based on remote-sensor data, as thoroughly compared in [16]. Other network-based clustering algorithms (e.g., spectral clustering), however, employ interaction data, such as the economic transactions and people's movement between regions.

Recently, a brunch of work aims to study the geographic distribution of some topic in terms of user-generated social media. For example, Yin et al. [18] study the distributions of some geographical topics (like beach, hiking, and sunset) in USA using geo-tagged photos acquired from Flickr. Pozdnoukhov et al. [12] explore the space-time structure of topical content from a large number of geo-tweets. The social media generated in a geo-region is still used as static features to feature a region. On the other hand, a few literatures have reported that human mobility can describe the functions of regions. For instance, Qi et al. [13] observe that the getting on/off amount of taxi passengers in a region can depict the social activity dynamics in the region.

Our work is different from the research mentioned above in the following aspects. First, to the best of our knowledge, our method is the first one that simultaneously considers static features (POIs) of a region and interactions (human mobility) between regions when identifying functional regions. Second, rather than directly using some clustering algorithm, we propose a topic-model-based solution which represents a region with a distribution of functions. The function distribution is more practical than a single function for a region. Moreover, it reduces the data sparseness problem before clustering regions. We justify the advantage of our method over just using clustering approach in the experiments.

6. CONCLUSION

This paper proposes a framework (titled DRoF) for discovering regions of different functions (e.g., educational areas, entertainment areas, and regions of historic interests) in a city using both human mobility and POIs. The discovered functional regions help people easily understand a complex metropolitan, benefiting a variety of applications, such as urban planning, location choosing for a business, advertisement casting, and social recommendations. We evaluated this framework with a two-year Beijing POI dataset (2010 and 2011) and GPS trajectory datasets generated by over 12,000 taxis in year 2010 and 2011. According to the extensive studies, DRoF outperforms two baselines solely using POIs or mobility data in effectively finding functional regions. We also compared the results of DRoF in 2010 with that of 2011, discovering the evolving of Beijing. In addition, by matching the discovered functional regions against Beijing land use planning (2002-2010), we do not only validate our framework but also find interesting results.

In the future, we will further study the effectiveness of our method changing over the scale of the data we use. At the same time, we are going to employ or add other mobility data sources, such as cell-tower traces and check-ins in location-based services.

7. REFERENCES

[1] J. Antikainen. The concept of functional urban area. *Findings of the Espon project*, 1(1), 2005.

[2] S. Bednarz et al. *Geography for Life: National Geography Standards.* 1994.

[3] D. Blei. Introduction to probabilistic topic models. *Communications of the ACM*, 2011.

[4] D. Blei, A. Ng, and M. Jordan. Latent dirichlet allocation. *The Journal of Machine Learning Research*, 3:993–1022, 2003.

[5] R. Estkowski. No Steiner point subdivision simplification is NP-Complete. In *Proc. 10th Canadian Conf. Computational Geometry*. Citeseer, 1998.

[6] Y. Ge, C. Liu, H. Xiong, and J. Chen. A taxi business intelligence system. In *Proc. KDD '11*, pages 735–738, 2011.

[7] Y. Ge, H. Xiong, A. Tuzhilin, K. Xiao, M. Gruteser, and M. Pazzani. An energy-efficient mobile recommender system. In *Proc. KDD '10*, pages 899–908, 2010.

[8] C. Karlsson. Clusters, functional regions and cluster policies. *JIBS and CESIS Electronic Working Paper Series (84)*, 2007.

[9] L. Lam, S. Lee, and C. Suen. Thinning methodologies-a comprehensive survey. *IEEE Transactions on pattern analysis and machine intelligence*, 14(9):869–885, 1992.

[10] W. Liu, Y. Zheng, S. Chawla, J. Yuan, and X. Xing. Discovering spatio-temporal causal interactions in traffic data streams. In *Proc. KDD '11*, pages 1010–1018, 2011.

[11] D. Mimno and A. McCallum. Topic models conditioned on arbitrary features with dirichlet-multinomial regression. In *Uncertainty in Artificial Intelligence*, pages 411–418, 2008.

[12] A. Pozdnoukhov and C. Kaiser. Space-time dynamics of topics in streaming text. In *Proc. LBSN '11*, pages 8:1–8:8, 2011.

[13] G. Qi, X. Li, S. Li, G. Pan, Z. Wang, and D. Zhang. Measuring social functions of city regions from large-scale taxi behaviors. In *IEEE PERCOM Workshops*, pages 384–388, 2011.

[14] P. Rousseeuw. Silhouettes: a graphical aid to the interpretation and validation of cluster analysis. *Journal of computational and applied mathematics*, 20:53–65, 1987.

[15] L. Shapiro and G. Stockman. *Computer Vision.* Prentice Hall, 2001.

[16] R. R. Vatsavai, E. Bright, C. Varun, B. Budhendra, A. Cheriyadat, and J. Grasser. Machine learning approaches for high-resolution urban land cover classification: a comparative study. In *Proc COM.Geo '11*, pages 11:1–11:10, 2011.

[17] M. Wand and M. Jones. *Kernel smoothing*, volume 60. Chapman & Hall/CRC, 1995.

[18] Z. Yin, L. Cao, J. Han, C. Zhai, and T. Huang. Geographical topic discovery and comparison. In *Proc. WWW '11*, pages 247–256, 2011.

[19] J. Yuan, Y. Zheng, X. Xie, and G. Sun. Driving with knowledge from the physical world. In *Proc. KDD '11*, pages 316–324, 2011.

[20] J. Yuan, Y. Zheng, L. Zhang, X. Xie, and G. Sun. Where to find my next passenger. In *Proc. Ubicomp '11*, pages 109–118, 2011.

[21] Y. Zheng, Y. Liu, J. Yuan, and X. Xie. Urban computing with taxicabs. In *Proc. Ubicomp '11*, pages 89–98, 2011.

[22] Y. Zheng and X. Zhou. *Computing with spatial trajectories.* Springer-Verlag New York Inc, 2011.

Constructing Popular Routes from Uncertain Trajectories

Ling-Yin Wei
National Chiao Tung University
Hsinchu, Taiwan
lywei.cs95g@nctu.edu.tw

Yu Zheng
Microsoft Research Asia
Beijing, China
yuzheng@microsoft.com

Wen-Chih Peng
National Chiao Tung University
Hsinchu, Taiwan
wcpeng@cs.nctu.edu.tw

ABSTRACT

The advances in location-acquisition technologies have led to a myriad of spatial trajectories. These trajectories are usually generated at a low or an irregular frequency due to applications' characteristics or energy saving, leaving the routes between two consecutive points of a single trajectory uncertain (called an uncertain trajectory). In this paper, we present a Route Inference framework based on Collective Knowledge (abbreviated as RICK) to construct the popular routes from uncertain trajectories. Explicitly, given a location sequence and a time span, the RICK is able to construct the top-*k* routes which sequentially pass through the locations within the specified time span, by aggregating such uncertain trajectories in a mutual reinforcement way (i.e., uncertain + uncertain → certain). Our work can benefit trip planning, traffic management, and animal movement studies. The RICK comprises two components: *routable graph construction* and *route inference*. First, we explore the spatial and temporal characteristics of uncertain trajectories and construct a routable graph by collaborative learning among the uncertain trajectories. Second, in light of the routable graph, we propose a routing algorithm to construct the top-*k* routes according to a user-specified query. We have conducted extensive experiments on two real datasets, consisting of Foursquare check-in datasets and taxi trajectories. The results show that RICK is both effective and efficient.

Categories and Subject Descriptors

H.2.8 [**Database Management**]: Database Applications – *data mining, spatial databases and GIS.*

General Terms

Algorithms, Design, Experimentation.

Keywords

Collaborative learning, trajectory data mining, route inference, social media.

1. INTRODUCTION

The increasing availability of location-acquisition technology (e.g., GPS), has led to a huge volume of spatial trajectories that represent the movement routes of humans, animals, hurricanes, and vehicles. Without loss of generality, a trajectory is a sequence of data points where each data point records location information and a time-stamp [18]. For example, the driving routes of vehicles and migratory routes of animals are usually recorded by GPS trajectories. Meanwhile, users could perform check-in services (e.g., Foursquare) to note their locations via a mobile phone and share their photos and activities. The time-ordered check-in records of a user are able to be expressed by trajectories. Moreover, on a photo sharing website (e.g., Flickr), people share geotagged photos whose time-stamps and geolocations can be represented as trajectories as well. However, these trajectories are usually generated at a low frequency due to energy saving and features of applications, resulting in the uncertainty of a moving object's mobility in a trajectory.

Figure 1 shows statistic information from Foursquare datasets in Manhattan. As shown in Figure 1(a), most check-in time intervals vary from 1 to 180 minutes. Moreover, we further investigate the distances among these check-in records. The medians of the distances between two check-in records are less than two kilometers in Figure 1(b). The above two observations show that even in Manhattan, which has a lot of tourists, the uncertain routes apparently exist between two check-in records.

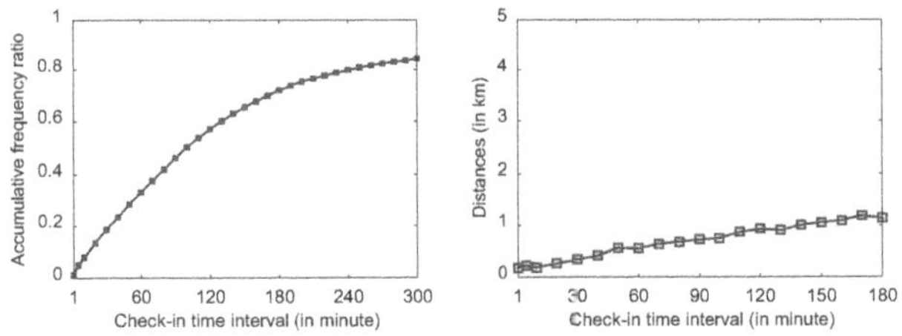

(a) (b)

Figure 1. Observations from Foursquare datasets.

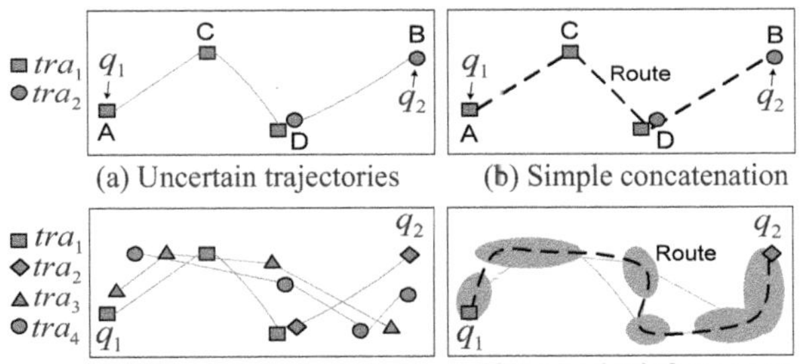

(a) Uncertain trajectories (b) Simple concatenation

(c) Uncertain trajectories (d) Mutual reinforcement

Figure 2. Examples of uncertain trajectories.

These low sampled trajectories do not detail the routes, and raise uncertain routes between two consecutive sampled points in the trajectories. In this paper, we call such trajectories uncertain trajectories. Examples of uncertain trajectories are illustrated in Figure 2. Figure 2(a) shows two check-in trajectories, tra_1: A → C → D and tra_2: D → B, in a rural space (i.e., road network information is not available). If a tourist would like to travel from q_1 to q_2, he/she may have no idea of how to travel without the aid of road networks or by referring to a trajectory (e.g., tra_1 or tra_2). In addition, given one migratory trajectory of a bird, we do not know where the bird flew between two sampled points which are several miles away from each other. Due to the uncertainty of low sampled trajectories, how to derive detailed routes from uncertain trajectories is an important task.

The prior work [16] proposed a framework to discover the routes from historical trajectories. Explicitly, given a set of historical trajectories, an underlying road network, and a location sequence, the work aims to suggest the top-*k* possible routes sequentially passing the queried locations. Note that by the aid of the given road network, the work explores possible routes derived from road networks. However, for some applications (e.g., animal migration routes or hurricane routes), road network information is not available. As for check-in datasets and geo-photo datasets, the service providers may not have road network information either. Without road network information, the work [16] cannot derive the top-*k* routes.

In this paper, without road network information, we propose a Route Inference framework based on Collective Knowledge (abbreviated as RICK) to construct the popular routes from uncertain trajectories. Explicitly, given a location sequence and a time span, RICK constructs the top-*k* routes, sequentially passing the locations within the specified time span. The RICK is beneficial for many practical applications. Examples of applications are trip planning [2,5,7,8,15,17], animal movement behavior studies [9] and traffic flow analysis [14]. For example, a user plans to take a tour that consists of three attractions (e.g., the Temple of Heaven, the Palace Museum and the Houhai Bar Street in Figure 3(a)) in Beijing, while having no idea of how to travel around them. At this moment, the RICK can recommend the popular travel route, inferred from check-in records (or geo-tagged photos) generated by other tourists. Another example in Figure 3(b) is to help biologists discover birds' moving behaviors from uncertain trajectories.

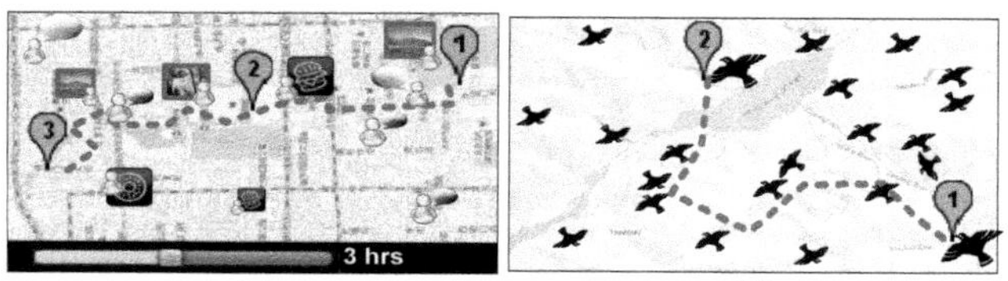

(a) (b)

Figure 3. Scenarios of applications.

To infer routes from uncertain trajectories, in many cases, we need to construct a route based on segments from multiple uncertain trajectories as there is no historical trajectory passing all the queried locations. For instance, in Figure 2(a), tra_1 and tra_2 do not pass through both q_1 and q_2. If a tourist would like to travel from q_1 to q_2, existing trip planning [1,7,15,17] could explore the sequential relations among these places and derive A → C → D → B by concatenation in Figure 2(b). However, the distances between two consecutive locations are still far away and a travel route still cannot be derived according to the users' trajectory. In addition, one could extract the trajectories that capture similar movements. However, due to the sparseness of data points in uncertain trajectories, two uncertain trajectories usually have totally different geospatial representations even though the two trajectories follow the same route or have the same subroutes (i.e., are correlated). As such, the similarity between two uncertain trajectories is hard to measure.

In this paper, given a set of uncertain trajectories (e.g., Figure 2(c)), a routable graph (e.g., the blue part in Figure 2(d)) is generated for indicating routing information in a free space by exploring spatio-temporally correlated uncertain trajectories. In light of the routable graph, we have designed a route score function and proposed a routing algorithm to construct the top-*k* routes (e.g., the dashed curve in Figure 2(d)) satisfying the query. We have conducted extensive experiments on two real datasets and the results show the effectiveness and efficiency of the RICK.

The contributions of this paper are summarized as follows:

- Without the aid of road networks, we develop a route inference framework to infer routes from uncertain trajectories.
- We propose a routable graph with routing information, generated by exploring spatio-temporal correlations among uncertain trajectories.
- In light of the routable graph, we define a route score function and develop a routing algorithm to construct the top-*k* routes.
- We have conducted extensive experiments using real datasets of 15,000 driving trajectories and 6,600 check-in sequences. The results indicate the RICK is effective and efficient.

The remainder of the paper is organized as follows. Section 2 gives the preliminary of our work. Section 3 illustrates the routable graph construction. Section 4 details the route inference. Section 5 presents the experimental results. Section 6 reviews related work. Section 7 concludes the paper.

2. PRELIMINARY

We present some terms and the problem addressed in this paper, and then overview the proposed framework.

Definition 1 (*Trajectory*): A *trajectory* tra_i is a time-ordered sequence of sampled points, i.e., $tra_i: p_1^i \to p_2^i \to \cdots \to p_n^i$. Each point $p_k^i \in tra_i$ is represented by $(p_k^i.l, p_k^i.t)$ where $p_k^i.l$ is a geographic coordinate (a location for short) at a time-stamp $p_k^i.t$.

As discussed before, trajectories are usually generated at a low sampling rate, leading to the real route between two consecutive points of a trajectory being uncertain. If a time interval between two consecutive sampled points is large, the uncertainty of the route between the two points would increase. In this paper, we further claim that road networks are not always available for inferring routes between two locations. For animal trace data and outdoor activities in urban areas, the movements are not along road networks. Thus, our problem is defined as follows:

Problem: Given an uncertain trajectory dataset D and a user-specified query consisting of a time span Δt and a location sequence $q: q_1 \to q_2 \to \cdots \to q_m$, we infer the top-*k* popular routes in a free space such that each route sequentially traverses the given locations, and the travel time of the route between any two consecutive query locations is within Δt.

Figure 4 overviews our framework RICK, which consists of two components: routable graph construction and route inference.

Routable graph construction: This offline component builds up a routable graph from an uncertain trajectory dataset. To generate a routable graph, there are two stages: region construction and edge inference. First, we partition the space into disjoint cells and then index the given uncertain trajectories in the gridded space. By exploring the spatio-temporal characteristics of the uncertain trajectories passing these cells, we merge these individual cells to form some geographical regions. Here, each cell forms a vertex in the routable graph that we are going to build up. Second, we infer the edges between the cells with the uncertain trajectories. These edges can be categorized into two types: they are inside a region or they are between regions. The information inferred for an edge comprises a moving direction, a transition support, and a travel time, indicating the transition relationship between two cells.

Route inference: This component, consisting of the route generation and the route refinement, is responsible for on-line queries. In the route generation stage, given a query, we propose a routing algorithm to infer the top-*k* rough routes, each of which is represented by a sequence of cells, with the constructed graph. The routing algorithm first finds out the qualified subroutes between any two consecutive query locations, and then concatenates these subroutes into completed routes in a branch-and-bound manner. In addition, we define a score function based on historical movements for ranking these routes. In the route refinement stage, we further refine each rough route to derive a detailed route represented by a sequence of consecutive segments from historical data points of uncertain trajectories.

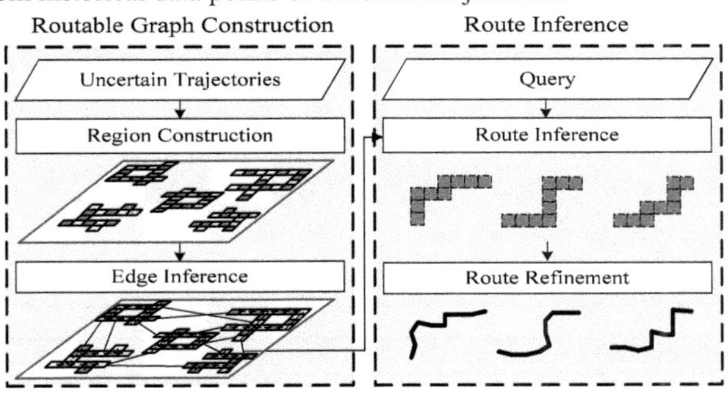

Figure 4. Overview of RICK.

Table 1. Notations

Symbol	Description
p_j^i	The *j*th point in trajectory *i*
p.g	The cell that *p* locates in
(x,y)	A cell id
c(x,y)	The number of distinct trajectories traversing (x,y)
θ	A temporal constraint
C	A minimum connection support
$\mathcal{T}(g \rightarrow g', tra)$	A set of the travel times from *g* to *g'* by *tra*

3. ROUTABLE GRAPH CONSTRUCTION

3.1 Region Construction

To construct a routable graph, we discover connected geographical areas by collaborative learning among historical uncertain trajectories. We first observe the spatial and temporal characteristics of the uncertain trajectories. For instance, Figure 5(a) shows three trajectories, $tra_1: p_1^1 \xrightarrow[10\,mins]{} p_2^1 \xrightarrow[20\,mins]{} p_3^1$, $tra_2: p_1^2 \xrightarrow[13\,mins]{} p_2^2 \xrightarrow[10\,mins]{} p_3^2$, and $tra_3: p_1^3 \xrightarrow[30\,mins]{} p_2^3$, where times are travel times between two consecutive points. The locations of data points of tra_1 and tra_2 are different even if the two trajectories follow the same route (e.g., the black solid line). We observe that 1) $p_2^1.l$ and $p_2^2.l$ are at the same place; 2) tra_1 and tra_2 have similar travel times from their first points (e.g., p_1^1, p_1^2) to the place; 3) $p_1^1.l$ and $p_1^2.l$ are spatially close. The observations indicate that the route of tra_1 from p_1^1 to p_2^1 and the route of tra_2 from p_1^2 to p_2^2 may be the same. We say that the two subtrajectories $p_1^1 \rightarrow p_2^1$ and $p_1^2 \rightarrow p_2^2$ are *spatio-temporally correlated (st-correlated)*. Moreover, if p_1^1 and p_1^2 are sampled on the same route, $p_1^1.l$ and $p_1^2.l$ could be connected. Specifically, this means that there exists at least one route between $p_1^1.l$ and $p_1^2.l$. On the other hand, in Figure 5(a), although $p_2^1.l$ and $p_2^3.l$ are at the same place and p_1^1 and p_1^3 are spatially close, tra_3 may be sampled from the other route (e.g, the green dotted line). The reason is that tra_3 has a longer travel time from p_2^3 to p_1^3.

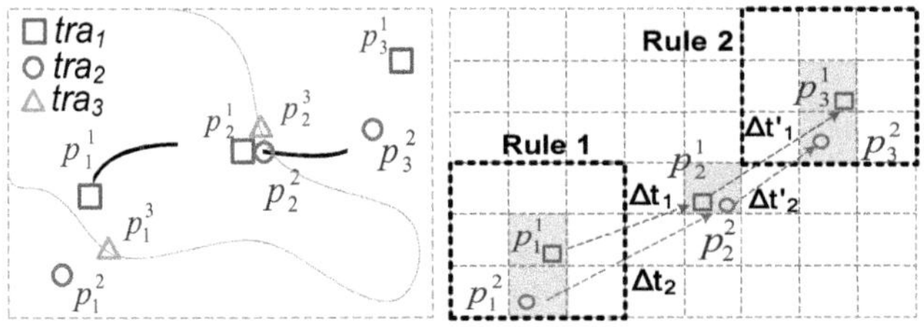

(a) (b)

Figure 5. Spatio-temporally correlated uncertain trajectories.

Based on the aforementioned observations, we define some terms for constructing connected geographical areas. Table 1 summarizes the notations used in this paper. To clearly describe spatial relations among data points of uncertain trajectories, we adopt a gridded space. First, we divide a geographical range into disjoint cells by a given cell length *l*. The set of the cells is denoted as $\mathcal{G}$, and the GID of a cell g is represented by (x, y). Moreover, each point of an uncertain trajectory can be mapped into a cell, and an uncertain trajectory can be transformed into a sequence of cells. As such, given an uncertain trajectory $tra_i: p_1^i \rightarrow p_2^i \rightarrow \cdots \rightarrow p_n^i$, the trajectory can be transformed into $p_1^i.g \rightarrow p_2^i.g \rightarrow \cdots \rightarrow p_n^i.g$, where $p_k^i.g$ represents the cell that $p_k^i.l$ locates in. Given two cells $g = (x, y)$ and $g' = (x', y')$, the cells g and g' are called *spatially close* if $|x - x'| \le 1$ and $|y - y'| \le 1$.

To explore connected geographical areas, we formally define st-correlated relations among uncertain trajectories. Given a cell *g*, if $g = p_k^i.g$ for some $p_k^i \in tra_i$, we say that tra_i traverses cell *g*, denoted $g \in tra_i$. If tra_i traverses from cell g to cell g', we say $g \rightarrow g' \in tra_i$. The set of the travel times of $g \rightarrow g'$ by tra_i is denoted by $\mathcal{T}(g \rightarrow g', tra_i)$. If $g \rightarrow g' \in tra_i$, $\mathcal{T}(g \rightarrow g', tra_i) \neq \emptyset$.

Definition 2 (*Spatio-temporally correlated relation*): Given two uncertain trajectories $tra_i: p_1^i \rightarrow \cdots \rightarrow p_n^i$ and $tra_j: p_1^j \rightarrow \cdots \rightarrow p_m^j$, and *a temporal constraint* θ, tra_i's subtrajectory $p_k^i \rightarrow \cdots \rightarrow p_{k'}^i$ and tra_j's subtrajectory $p_h^j \rightarrow \cdots \rightarrow p_{h'}^j$ are st-correlated if

1) $\exists\, \Delta t_1 \in \mathcal{T}(p_k^i.g \rightarrow p_{k'}^i.g, tra_i), \Delta t_2 \in \mathcal{T}(p_h^j.g \rightarrow p_{h'}^j.g, tra_j)$ s.t. $\frac{|\Delta t_1 - \Delta t_2|}{\max\{\Delta t_1, \Delta t_2\}} \le \theta$;

2) one of the two rules is satisfied:

Rule1: $p_k^i.g$ and $p_h^j.g$ are spatially close, and $p_{k'}^i.g = p_{h'}^j.g$.

Rule2: $p_k^i.g = p_h^j.g$, and $p_{k'}^i.g$ and $p_{h'}^j.g$ are spatially close.

Note that if a trajectory tra' is a subtrajectory of a trajectory *tra*, we denote it as $tra' \subseteq tra$.

Given trajectories in Figure 5(a), Figure 5(b) depicts the st-correlated relation between tra_1 and tra_2. Let $\Delta t_1 \in \mathcal{T}(p_1^1.g \rightarrow p_2^1.g, tra_1)$ and $\Delta t_2 \in \mathcal{T}(p_1^2.g \rightarrow p_2^2.g, tra_2)$ and assume Δt_1 and Δt_2 satisfy a given temporal constraint. According to Rule 1 in Definition 2, $p_1^1 \rightarrow p_2^1$ and $p_1^2 \rightarrow p_2^2$ are st-correlated, because $p_1^1.g$ and $p_1^2.g$ are spatially close and $p_2^1.g = p_2^2.g$. Similarly, let $\Delta t'_1 \in \mathcal{T}(p_2^1.g \rightarrow p_3^1.g, tra_1)$ and $\Delta t'_2 \in \mathcal{T}(p_2^2.g \rightarrow p_3^2.g, tra_2)$ and assume $\Delta t'_1$ and $\Delta t'_2$ satisfy a given temporal constraint. According to Rule 2 in Definition 2, $p_2^1 \rightarrow p_3^1$ and $p_2^2 \rightarrow p_3^2$ are st-correlated since $p_2^1.g = p_2^2.g$ and $p_3^1.g$ and $p_3^2.g$ are spatially close.

Definition 3 (*Connection support*): Given an uncertain trajectory dataset *D*, a set of cells $\mathcal{G}$, a temporal constraint θ, and two cells $g, g' \in \mathcal{G}$, where g and g' are spatially close, *the connection support of the cell pair* (g, g') is defined as $|T_1 \cup T_2|$ where $T_1 = \{(tra_i, tra_j) | tra_i'$ and tra_j' are st-correlated, $g \rightarrow g'' \in tra_i'$, and $g' \rightarrow g'' \in tra_j'$ for some $g'' \in \mathcal{G} - \{g, g'\}$, $tra_i' \subseteq tra_i, tra_j' \subseteq tra_j$, and $T_2 = \{(tra_i, tra_j) | tra_i'$ and tra_j' are st-correlated, $g'' \rightarrow g \in tra_i'$, and $g'' \rightarrow g' \in tra_j'$ for some $g'' \in \mathcal{G} - \{g, g'\}, tra_i' \subseteq tra_i, tra_j' \subseteq tra_j\}$.

For example, in Figure 5(b), given $p_1^1.g$ and $p_1^2.g$, which are spatially close, the support of the cell pair $(p_1^1.g, p_1^2.g) = |T_1 \cup T_2| = 1$ because $T_1 = \{(tra_1, tra_2)\}$ and $T_2 = \emptyset$. Similarly, given $p_2^1.g$ and $p_3^2.g$, which are spatially close, the support of the cell pair $(p_3^1.g, p_3^2.g) = |T_1 \cup T_2| = 1$ because $T_1 = \emptyset$ and $T_2 = \{(tra_1, tra_2)\}$.

Definition 4 (*Neighbor*): Given an uncertain trajectory dataset D, a set of cells $\mathcal{G}$, two cells $g, g' \in \mathcal{G}$, a temporal constraint θ, and a *minimum connection support* C, if the connection support of the cell pair (g , g') is greater than or equal to C, g and g' are *neighbors*, denoted as gNg'.

We define a *region* as a connected geographical area as follows:

Definition 5 (*Region*): Given a set of cells $\mathcal{G}'$, $\mathcal{G}'$ forms *a* region if for any two cells $g, g' \in \mathcal{G}'$, there exists a chain of cells $(g =) g_1 = g_2 = \cdots = g_k (= g')$ s.t. $g_i N g_{i+1}$ for each $g_i \in \mathcal{G}'$ and $i \in [1, k)$.

To construct regions, a naïve method is that we generate all cell pairs from the set of cells $\mathcal{G}$ and then compute the connection support of each cell pair by checking other cells in $\mathcal{G}$. We then verify whether the connection supports of cell pairs satisfy the given minimum connection support C to construct regions. However, the time complexity of the method is costly. In this paper, we propose an efficient algorithm to construct regions.

The proposed algorithm utilizes an index structure presented as follows. Given a cell length and an uncertain trajectory dataset D, we build up a *grid index* in which each cell g has a unique GID, a value $c(g)$, and a corresponding trajectory list. Note that $c(g) = |\{tra | g \in tra, tra \in D\}|$. In the grid index, each GID indexes a list of trajectories that records which uncertain trajectories traverse the cell and which points of these uncertain trajectories locate in the cell by TIDs and PIDs, respectively. To improve the efficiency of the region construction, the trajectories in a cell's corresponding trajectory list are sorted by m_{tra}, where m_{tra} is the median of $\{c(p.g) | p \in tra\}$ with given tra.

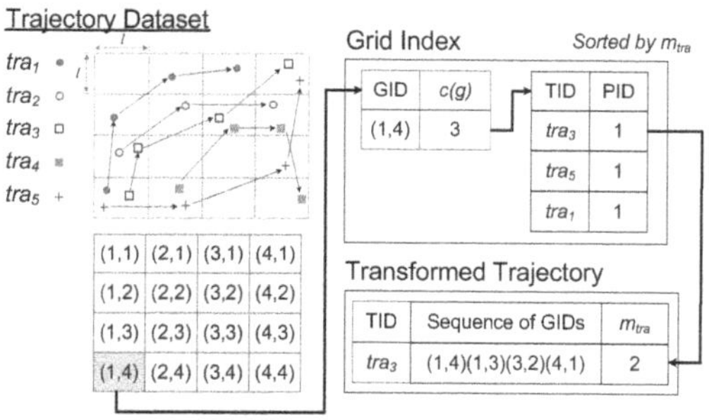

Figure 6. An example of an index structure.

For instance, given a cell length l and an uncertain trajectory dataset $D = \{tra_1, tra_2, tra_3, tra_4, tra_5\}$, Figure 6 shows an example of an index structure. Given a cell (1,4), $c(1,4)$=3 since three distinct uncertain trajectories (i.e., tra_1, tra_3, tra_5) traverse cell (1,4). The trajectory list of cell (1,4) records these TIDs (i.e., tra_1, tra_3, tra_5) and the corresponding PID of each trajectory. The corresponding PID of tra_1 is 1 since the point of tra_1 that locates in cell (1,4) is the first point of tra_1. As shown in Figure 6, tra_3 traverses four cells (i.e., (1,4), (1,3), (3,2), and (4,1)), and we can calculate that $c(1,4)$=3, $c(1,3)$=2, $c(3,2)$=2, and $c(4,1)$=2. The median among {2, 2, 2, 3} is 2 and thus m_{tra_3}=2.

Before constructing regions, we let $\mathcal{G} = \mathcal{G} - \mathcal{G}'$, where $\mathcal{G}' = \{g | c(g) = 0, g \in \mathcal{G}\}$. The algorithm of region construction is detailed in Algorithm 1. Note that the term *enclosed* is defined as follows.

Algorithm 1: Region Construction

Input: An uncertain trajectory dataset D, a set of cells $\mathcal{G}$, a temporal constraint θ, and a minimum connection support C.
Output: A set of regions R.

1. $\mathcal{G}' \leftarrow$ Sort cells in $\mathcal{G}$ in a decreasing order of $c(g)$;
2. **Do**
3. $g \leftarrow$ Pop the cell from $\mathcal{G}'$;
4. **Foreach** *tra* traversing g by the order stored in the grid index
5. $\tau(g) \leftarrow \{p | p.g = g \; and \; p \in tra\}$;
6. **Foreach** $p \in tra - \tau(g)$ and $p.g$ is not enclosed
7. **If** $p.g$ is contained in some region
8. $r \leftarrow$ The region contains $p.g$;
9. **Else**
10. $r \leftarrow \emptyset$;
11. **If** p is before p' for all $p' \in \tau(g)$
12. $r \leftarrow CM(r, p.g, g, \theta, C, Rule1)$;
13. **ElseIf** p is after p' for all $p' \in \tau(g)$
14. $r \leftarrow CM(r, p.g, g, \theta, C, Rule2)$;
15. **Else**
16. $r \leftarrow CM(r, p.g, g, \theta, C, Rule1)$;
17. $r \leftarrow CM(r, p.g, g, \theta, C, Rule2)$;
18. $R \leftarrow R \cup \{r\}$;
19. **Until** $\mathcal{G}'$ is empty or each cell in $\mathcal{G}$ is in some $r \in R$;
20. **Return** R;

Algorithm 2: Cell Merging (CM)

Input: A region r, a cell $p.g$, a cell g, a temporal constraint θ, a minimum connection support C, and an indicator I
Output: A region r

1. Let $p.g = (x, y)$;
2. **Foreach** cell $g' = (x', y') \in \mathcal{G} - r$ where $|x' - x| \leq 1$ and $|y' - y| \leq 1$
3. **If** I is Rule1
4. Verify whether $p.gNg'$ is held with given g by rule 1;
5. **Else**
6. Verify whether $p.gNg'$ is held with given g by rule 2;
7. **If** $p.gNg'$
8. **If** $r = \emptyset$
9. $r \leftarrow \{p.g\}$;
10. **If** g' is contained in some region
11. $r' \leftarrow$ The region contains g';
12. **Else**
13. $r' \leftarrow \emptyset$
14. $r' \leftarrow CM(r', g', g, \theta, C, I)$;
15. $r \leftarrow r \cup r'$;
16. **Return** r;

Definition 6 (*Enclosed*): Given a set of cells $\mathcal{G}$ and a cell $g \in \mathcal{G}$, the cell g is *enclosed* if there exists a region $r \subseteq \mathcal{G}$ s.t. $g, g' \in r$, $\forall g' \in \{g' | \; g'$ and g are spatially close, $g' \in \mathcal{G}\}$.

In Algorithm 1, we iteratively merge cells to form regions by calculating the connection supports of cell pairs. To efficiently construct regions, we determine an order for the calculation of connection supports of cell pairs according to $c(g)$. Once a cell is chosen, we iteratively pick a trajectory from the cell's trajectory list in Step 4. We then calculate the connection supports of the cell pairs around the points of the trajectory and merge qualified cells from Step 5 to Step 18. An example of this procedure is illustrated in Figure 7. Let a chosen cell be g. Assume the trajectory tra_1 traversed it and $p_2^1.g = p_4^1.g = g$ (i.e., $\tau(g) = \{p_2^1, p_4^1\}$). In Step 6, we pick a point (e.g., p_1^1) from tra_1 but not the point is not in $\tau(g)$. If the cell that the point locates in is not enclosed, the cell would be possibly merged with other cells. The connection supports of the cell pairs of $p_1^1.g$ and each cell around $p_1^1.g$ are calculated and the qualified cell pairs will be merged. Based on $p_1^1.g$, a region (e.g., the blue cells in Figure 7) is generated in the first round and more cells (e.g., the red cells in Figure 7) are merged into the region around $p_1^1.g$ in the second round (i.e., Step

14 in Algorithm 2). Similarly, for $p_1^1.g$, a merging process will be stopped if no cell can be merged around $p_1^1.g$. We then chose other points (e.g., p_3^1, p_5^1) to construct regions around these points in the same way.

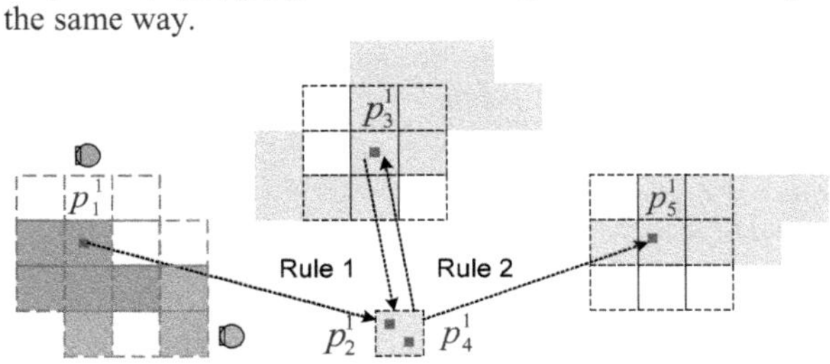

Figure 7. Region construction process.

Time complexity analysis: Given an uncertain trajectory dataset D and a set of cells $\mathcal{G}$, the time complexity of the naïve method is $O(mn^3)$ where $|\mathcal{G}| = n$ and $|D| = m$. Similarly, the time complexity of Algorithm 1 is $O(n(logn + cm^2))$, where c is the minimal number of the first loop. For Step 1 in Algorithm 1, it costs $O(nlogn)$ to sort cells in decreasing order of $c(g)$. In addition, the time complexity of Algorithm 2 is $O(m)$ because there are at most m uncertain trajectories for counting the connection support of a cell pair. Thus the time complexity of the remaining steps in Algorithm 1 is $O(cnm^2)$.

3.2 Edge Inference

Once the regions are generated, we then infer edges and derive edge information including moving directions, transition supports, and travel times from historical uncertain trajectories. To generate the edges of a routable graph, we infer the edges within each region, and then infer the edges among regions.

A routable graph is a directed graph $G = (V, E)$, where V is a set of vertices and E is a set of edges. Each vertex represents a geographical area, i.e., a cell. Each directed edge e indicates a transition relationship and has two attributes, *the transition support* $e.s$ and *the travel time* $e.t$. To derive the transition support of an edge, we record which distinct uncertain trajectories traverse the edge. In other words, an edge has an uncertain trajectory list to record which distinct uncertain trajectories traverse it.

According to the definition of a region, a region is composed of connected cells, and thus we first generate virtual bidirected edges between cells if the cells are neighbors in a region, To infer edges' realistic directions, transition supports, and travel times, we propose *a shortest path based inference approach.*

Given a region and an uncertain trajectory dataset, we utilize the uncertain trajectories traversing the region to derive edge information in the region. For each trajectory traversing the region, we infer the shortest path between any two consecutive points of the trajectory by virtual bidirected edges in the region. We illustrate edge inference in a region in Figure 8. As shown in Figure 8(a), four uncertain trajectories pass through the region. For instance, in Figure 8(b), an uncertain trajectory $p_1 \to p_2 \to p_3$ (blue squares) traverses the region, and we infer the shortest paths from p_1 to p_2 and the shortest paths from p_2 to p_3. As shown in Figure 8(b), we find one shortest path from p_1 to p_2, and two shortest paths from p_2 to p_3. After finding the shortest path between two consecutive locations, we divide the travel time evenly and add it to the travel time list of each edge in the shortest path. In addition, each edge of the shortest path adds the trajectory ID into its corresponding trajectory list, and the transition support of each edge in the shortest path is accumulated one. If there are multiple shortest paths between two consecutive locations, we similarly update the information of each edge in these paths.

By using historical uncertain trajectories to infer edge information in a region, we further eliminate the redundant edges in the region and the edges whose transition supports are 0. Given an edge e_1 from the cell g and the cell g', where g and g' are spatially close, the edge e_1 is *redundant* in a region if there exist an edge e_2 from g to g'' and an edge e_3 from g'' to g', such that 1) g and g'' are spatially close and g' and g'' are spatially close, 2) $\frac{e_2.s+e_3.s}{2} < e_1.s$, and 3) $\frac{|e_2.t+e_3.t-e_1.t|}{\max\{(e_2.t+e_3.t),e_1.t\}} \le \theta$ where θ is a given temporal constraint. Figure 8(c) shows the inferred edges in the region after reducing edges. The travel time of each edge is estimated by the median of all the travel times of the edge.

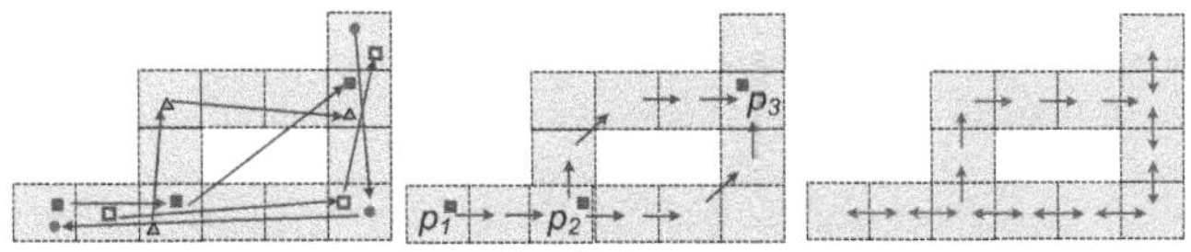

(a) (b) (c)

Figure 8. Edge inference in a region.

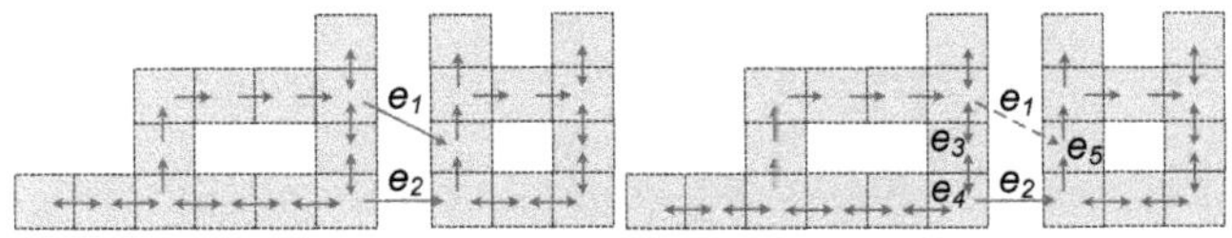

(a) (b)

Figure 9. Edge inference between regions.

In the following, we construct edges between regions. Similarly, we generate edges between regions by using historical uncertain trajectories first. This means that if an uncertain trajectory traverses a cell of one region to a cell of another region, an edge is constructed between the two cells. Next, we eliminate the redundant edges between regions. Given an edge e_1 from the cell g to the cell g', where g and g' are in different regions, the edge e is a *redundant* edge between the two regions if there exists an alternative route $e_i \to \cdots \to e_j$ from the cell g to the cell g' such that 1) $\frac{1}{j-i+1}\sum_{k=i}^{j} e_k.s < e.s$, and 2) $\frac{\left|\sum_{k=i}^{j} e_k.t-e.t\right|}{\max\left\{\sum_{k=i}^{j} e_k.t,e.t\right\}} \le \theta$ where θ is a given temporal constraint. Figure 9 shows an example of edge inference between two regions. As shown in Figure 9(a), edge e_1 and edge e_2 are generated between the two regions by historical uncertain trajectories. For instance, in Figure 9(b), edge e_1 is a redundant edge if 1) $\frac{1}{4}\sum_{k=2}^{5} e_k.s < e_1.s$, and 2) $\frac{|\sum_{k=2}^{5} e_k.t-e_1.t|}{\max\{\sum_{k=2}^{5} e_k.t,e_1.t\}} \le \theta$ with a given θ.

Note that the transition information of an eliminated edge is propagated to alternative routes. The travel time of an eliminated edge is evenly propagated to the edges of each alternative route. The trajectory list of an eliminated edge is updated to each edge's corresponding trajectory list in alternative routes.

4. ROUTE INFERENCE

Given a location sequence and a time span, we generate the top-*k* popular routes by two phases: route generation and route refinement. In the first phase, we propose routing algorithms to search for the top-*k* coarse routes with the routable graph. We further refine the discovered the top-*k* routes to effectively derive specific routes in the second phase.

In the route generation phase: we first generate possible routes between each two consecutive queried locations (called *local routes*) and then search for the top-k routes (called *global routes*) from the generated local routes.

A *route* derived in this phase is represented by a sequence of vertices with a given graph $G = (V, E)$. Note that a vertex in the graph represents a cell; thus a route here is regarded as a sequence of cells, denoted as $\wp: g_1 \longrightarrow g_2 \longrightarrow \cdots \longrightarrow g_k$. Given a sequence of query locations and a time span, we search for qualified routes between any two consecutive query locations with the constructed graph. Before searching for routes with the graph, we need to specify the corresponding vertices of query locations. Since a vertex represents a geographical area of a cell, a query location can be mapped to the vertex whose corresponding geographical area overlaps the location. However, it is possible that a query location cannot be mapped to any vertex in the graph. We further select the vertices whose corresponding cells are close to the query location. We adopt the minimum distance (MINDIST) [12] to formulate the distance between a query location and a cell. According to the distance measurement, we specify the cells that are close to such query locations. Thus, a given location sequence is transformed into a sequence of sets of cells. Moreover, we transform a location sequence into cell sequences by combining these cells. After query transformation, we search for the top-k routes according to each cell sequence.

For instance, given a location sequence $q: q_1 \rightarrow q_2 \rightarrow q_3$ in Figure 10(a), the locations q_1 and q_2 are mapped to cells g_1 and g_2, respectively. By the minimum distance measurement, the set of cells $\{g_3, g_4\}$ is used to represent the location q_3. Then, the location sequence $q_1 \rightarrow q_2 \rightarrow q_3$ is transformed into two cell sequences, i.e., $g_1 \rightarrow g_2 \rightarrow g_3$ and $g_1 \rightarrow g_2 \rightarrow g_4$.

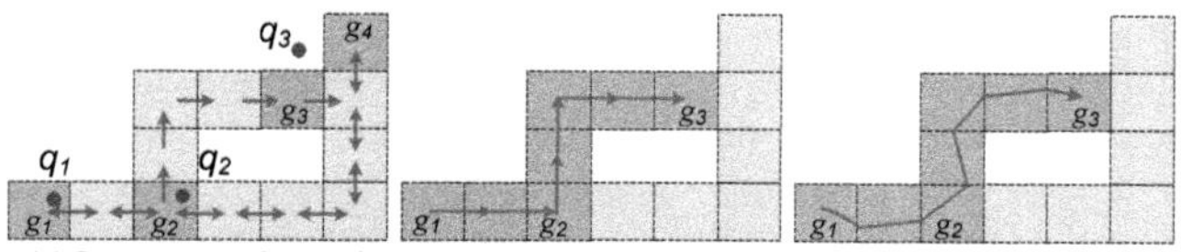

(a)Query transformation. (b)Route generation. (c)Route refinement

Figure 10. Route inference.

We generate routes with respect to each cell sequence. Before introducing the routing algorithm, we define the score function for the routes as follows.

Definition *7* (*Route score*): Given a graph $G = (V, E)$, a route $\wp: \wp_1 \rightarrow \wp_2 \rightarrow \cdots \rightarrow \wp_m$, where $\wp_i: g_{i_1} \longrightarrow g_{i_2} \longrightarrow \cdots \longrightarrow g_{i_j}$, the score of the route is defined as $f(\wp) = \sum_{i=1}^{m} \rho(\wp_i)$, where $\rho(\wp_i) = \frac{1}{j-1} | \bigcup_{k=1}^{j-1} \{tra | g_{i_k} \rightarrow g_{i_{k+1}} \in tra\} |$.

For each cell sequence, we first search for the top-k local routes between any two consecutive cells in the cell sequence (e.g., g and g') by an A*-like routing algorithm. However, a possible maximum speed could be derived from historical uncertain trajectories or be determined by difference applications. Given a maximum speed, possible positions between any two consecutive query locations can be restricted in a range if a time interval between the two locations is specified [11]. That is, the possible routes are restricted in the cells overlapping the range. For the A*-like routing algorithm, an estimated score of a route from a cell g to a cell g' is represented as follows.

Given two cells g and g', a current visited cell g'', and a specified range r, an estimated score of a route $\wp: \wp_c \longrightarrow \wp_f$ from a cell g to a cell g' in a specified range r is $\hat{f}(\wp) = \rho(\wp_c) + h(\wp_f)$, where $\wp_c$ is a known route from cell g to cell g'', and $h(\wp_f)$ is the score of an estimated route $\wp_f$ from cell g'' to cell g'.

Definition *8* (*Optimal score*): Given a graph $G = (V, E)$, an uncertain trajectory dataset D, a specified range r, and two cells g and g', the optimal score of the routes from a cell g to a cell g' in r is defined as

$$\hat{h}(\wp) = |\{tra | tra \text{ passes through the range } r, tra \in D\}|$$

for some estimated route $\wp$ from a cell g to a cell g'.

Once a local route is generated from the cell g to the cell g' and satisfies the given time span, the score of the local route is calculated. If there are more than k local routes constructed from the cell g to the cell g', the k-th maximum score of these local routes is recorded and incrementally updated. Based on the estimated optimal score function, a branch of searching routes will be stopped if the optimal score of routes generated from the branch is less than the updated k-th maximum score.

Based on the top-k local routes between any two consecutive cells of each cell sequence, we search for the top-k global routes by a branch-and-bound search approach. For instance, given a cell sequence $g_1 \rightarrow g_2 \rightarrow g_3$ in Figure 10(a), a global route is derived as a sequence of cells (dark grey) in Figure 10(b). To derive a specific route, a route is further transformed into a line by concatenating the centers of any two consecutive cells in the route. Figure 10(b) shows an example of such a route by a blue line.

However, it is possible that we search for local routes between two cells belonging to different regions. In the A*-like algorithm, although we search for local routes between two given cells in a restricted range of a graph, the search space is still large if the distance between two given cells is far and they are in different regions. It induces that a route between the two cells would possibly pass through several other regions. On the other hand, a lower bound of transition times between any two regions can be estimated by edge information. It helps us stop searching for routes between two regions if the lower bound of transition time between the two regions exceeds the time span. Hence, to improve the efficiency of route generation, we modify the proposed A*-like routing algorithm and introduce a two-layer routing algorithm.

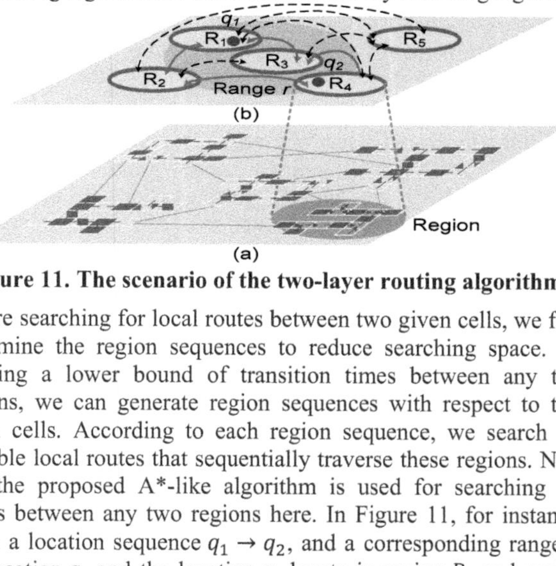

Figure 11. The scenario of the two-layer routing algorithm.

Before searching for local routes between two given cells, we first determine the region sequences to reduce searching space. By utilizing a lower bound of transition times between any two regions, we can generate region sequences with respect to two given cells. According to each region sequence, we search for possible local routes that sequentially traverse these regions. Note that the proposed A*-like algorithm is used for searching for routes between any two regions here. In Figure 11, for instance, given a location sequence $q_1 \rightarrow q_2$, and a corresponding range r, the location q_1 and the location q_2 locate in region R_1 and region R_2, respectively. There are multiple possible region combinations for searching for routes between the two locations. Although the searching space of route generation is restricted to the range r (e.g., the red part), the routes from q_1 to q_2 would possibly traverse the regions in different orders. In Figure 11, there are many possible region sequences from q_1 to q_2 (e.g., $R_1 \rightarrow R_4$,

$R_1 \rightarrow R_2 \rightarrow R_4$, $R_1 \rightarrow R_3 \rightarrow R_4$, $R_1 \rightarrow R_2 \rightarrow R_3 \rightarrow R_4$ etc.). With utilizing lower bounds of transition times between regions, the possible region sequences would be reduced to satisfy the given time span. For instance, the qualified region sequences are marked by red edges in Figure 11 (i.e., $R_1 \rightarrow R_2 \rightarrow R_4$, $R_1 \rightarrow R_3 \rightarrow R_4$). After deriving region sequences, we search for possible routes which traverse each region sequence.

After route generation, the top-*k* routes are inferred, and we further refine each route using historical data points. Route refinement has three steps: data point selection, segment formulation, and segment concatenation. First, given an inferred rough route represented by a sequence of cells, we select the historical uncertain trajectories that traverse the cells in the same order as the route. Next, we extract the data points that locate in cells of the rough route from these selected uncertain trajectories, and thus derive a set of points for each cell of the route. To formulate a specific route from selected points, we adopt linear regression for the set of points of each cell to derive a segment. We then concatenate the segments in the same order as an original inferred route. Figure 10(c) shows an example of a refined route.

5. PERFORMANCE EVALUATION

In this section, we evaluate the performance of the proposed RICK using real datasets, including check-in records from Foursquare and taxi trajectories. The datasets and experimental setting is presented in Section 5.1. In the experiments, we first demonstrate the results using check-in records in Manhattan. To evaluate the effectiveness of our proposed RICK, we use the dataset of taxi trajectories. In the experiments of the performance study, we compare our proposed RICK with the existing method in terms of effectiveness and efficiency. Furthermore, the experiments demonstrate the improvements of routable graph construction and route inference.

5.1 Datasets and Settings

5.1.1 Real Datasets

In this paper, we use two real datasets to conduct the extensive experiments. One is the check-in dataset from Foursquare. We collected check-in records in Manhattan, and for each user, a series of check-in records recorded in one day is regarded as a trajectory. We pruned the trajectories that contained less than three check-in records. There are totally 6,600 trajectories. The other real dataset contained 15,000 taxi trajectories in Beijing. The average sampling rate of the raw trajectories is less than one minute. To simulate uncertain trajectories, we resampled each raw trajectory such that the time interval between two consecutive resampled points of the trajectory at least exceeded a given sampling rate *S*. In the experiments, the sampling rate *S* is set from one minute to five minutes and the default *S* is five minutes. For example, given *S*=5, the time interval between two consecutive resampled points is at least five minutes or even more.

5.1.2 Metrics

To evaluate the effectiveness of our RICK, we introduce an approach to generate the ground-truth from the raw trajectories to evaluate the effectiveness of the inferred routes. For each query, the raw trajectories that satisfy the query are selected and ranked. To rank these trajectories, a raw trajectory is transformed into a sequence of road segments and the frequency of a road segment is defined as the number of distinct trajectories that traverse it. The score of a transformed trajectory $tra: r_1 \rightarrow r_2 \rightarrow \cdots \rightarrow r_n$ is defined by $(\sum_{i=1}^{n} \mathrm{d}(r_i))/tra.length$, where r_i is a road segment and $\mathrm{d}(r_i)$ is the frequency of the road segment r_i. Hence, the selected trajectories can be ranked by their scores.

To evaluate the difference between an inferred trajectory and a raw trajectory of the ground-truth, we first apply the length-normalized dynamic time warping distance (NDTW). Given an inferred route p and a raw trajectory tra, we define the NDTW between two trajectories as $\mathrm{NDTW}(p, tra) = \mathrm{DTW}(p, tra)/p.length$ for an optimal alignment path. To further reflect the quality of inferred routes, we utilize a maximum distance (MD) between an inferred route and a raw trajectory of the ground-truth according to the discovered NDTW. MD is defined as the maximum value of the distances measured by the optimal alignment path. Therefore, the two measurements for evaluating the inferred top-*k* routes are defined as follows:

$\mathrm{NDTW}(\mathrm{T}, \mathrm{T}')= \mathrm{Avg}_{p_k \in \mathrm{T}} \min_{tra \in \mathrm{T}'} \mathrm{NDTW}(p_k, tra)$, and

$\mathrm{MD}(\mathrm{T}, \mathrm{T}')=\mathrm{Avg}_{p_k \in \mathrm{T}} \mathrm{MD}(p_k, tra')$,

where T is the set of inferred top-*k* routes, T′ is the set of top-*k* raw trajectories, and $tra'=\mathrm{Arg}\min_{tra \in \mathrm{T}'} \mathrm{NDTW}(p_k, tra)$.

In the experiments, the default rank threshold *k* is 3.

5.2 Visualization of Results

In this subsection, we use the check-in dataset in Manhattan to visualize the results derived by RICK. We first demonstrate the constructed routable graph in Figure 12 with given cell length *l*=500 (meters), temporal constraint θ =0.2 and minimum connection support *C*=3. In Figure 12, the regions are represented by different colors in Figure 12(a), and Figure 12(b) shows the edges between cells. Note that the edges within a region are drawn by blue lines, and the edges between regions are drawn by black lines. Based on the routable graph, we perform one query and let the span time be one hour for each query. Given a query as "Central Park → The Museum of Modern Art → Times Square → Empire State Building → SoHo", the top-1 route inferred by RICK is depicted in Figure 12(c). As shown in Figure 12(c), the route does not simply connect the query locations, but passes through other attractions. For example, for the partial route from "The Museum of Modern Art" to "Times Square", RICK constructs this partial route to pass by the "Rockefeller Center" based on users' historical check-in records.

(a) Regions (b) Routable graph (c) Top-1 route

Figure 12. Visualization of results in Manhattan.

5.3 Performance Study

In this section, we evaluate the performance of RICK by taxi trajectories. First, to analyze the effect of queries, the length of query location sequence $|q|$ is set from 2 to 4. In addition, a query location sequence is generated by considering a given distance between any two consecutive query locations, denoted as Δd. For a query, Δt is determined according to Δd. In the experiments, Δd is varied from 1 to 5 (in kilometers), and the corresponding Δt is set from 4 to 20 (in minutes). For each experiment, we perform almost 100 queries and averaged the results.

5.3.1 *Evaluation of Route Inference*

We compare our framework with a baseline and analyze the effectiveness of our inferred routes in different aspects.

Baseline: To evaluate the effectiveness of the discovered routes, we compare the proposed RICK with the existing approach (MPR) in [3]. In [3], given two locations (i.e., $|q|$=2), the most popular rout, which connects the two query locations, is derived. In the experiments, the parameters of MPR are set as α=2, β=2, the coherence threshold τ=0.8, and the cluster size threshold φ=20. For RICK, the settings are l=300 (meter) and k=1. Figure 13 shows the experimental results of MPR and RICK under the Taxi dataset with S and Δd varied. As shown in Figure 13(a), the error of MPR increases as S or Δd increases. It is worth mentioning that the error of RICK slightly increases as S or Δd increases, showing that RICK is able to derive the routes from uncertain trajectories. Figure 13(a) shows that RICK is more effective than MPR, although Figure 13(b) demonstrates that the query time of RICK is slightly higher than the query time of MPR.

Effect on route refinement: In the route inference of the proposed RICK, the top-k routes are derived after route generation and are further refined by route refinement. In this subsection, we compare the effectiveness of the route inference without route refinement (w/o RR) and that of the route inference with route refinement. We set k=1 and $|q|$=2 in the experiments. Figure 14 shows the error of top-1 routes by NDTW and MD. As shown in Figure 14, the errors of inferred routes increase as Δd increases. In addition, a larger l increases the error of routes discovered without route refinement. In Figure 14, with route refinement, the error of the inferred routes is obviously reduced as l increases.

Impact of data sparseness: To study the effect of the data sparseness, we calculate the number of GPS points per km^2 and derive different data sparseness by setting different S. The number of GPS points per km^2 is increased from 77 to 275 while S is decreased from five minutes to one minute. Figure 15 shows that the errors (both NDTW and MD) slightly decrease as the data sparseness increases. When the data sparseness is 275 GPS points per km^2, the errors of the inferred routes of at least 4 km (i.e., $|q|$=2 and Δd=4) are less than 500 meters and the errors of the inferred routes of at least 12 km (i.e., $|q|$=4 and Δd=4) are less than 800 meters. However, NDTW is less than 300 meters even though the data sparseness is 77 GPS points per km^2. The proposed framework is effective for inferring the top-k routes.

Efficiency: We investigated the query time of RICK and show the results in Figure 16. In the experiments, l=300 (meters), $\theta = 0.1$, C=8, S=5 (minutes), and k=3. In the route inference, we improve the efficiency of the route generation by a two-layer routing algorithm. To demonstrate the effectiveness of the two-layer routing algorithm, we compare the query time of RICK and the query time of RICK without using the two-layer routing algorithm (denoted by RICK-) in Figure 16(a) with varied $|q|$ and Δd. As shown in Figure 16(a), RICK outperforms RICK-, and the query time is obviously reduced while $|q|$ or Δd is larger. In Figure 16(b), the query time of RICK gradually increases as $|q|$ or Δd increases. However, the query time is less than one second.

5.3.2 *Evaluation of Routable Graph*

In the routable graph construction of RICK, we construct the regions referring to the connected areas and further infer and refine the moving directions within the regions. To investigate the impact of exploring shortest path on refining the routable graph, we evaluate the graph built without refinement (denoted as RG), and the graph refined by shortest path based edge inference (denoted as RG+).

To evaluate the correctness of the connectivity in a routable graph, given a raw trajectory dataset D and a graph $G = \langle V, E \rangle$, the precision of connectivity in G is measured as follows:

$$|\{e|e \text{ is traversed by some } tra \in D \text{ and } e \in E\}|/|E|.$$

The temporal constraint θ and the minimum connection support C are used for constructing a routable graph. Hence, we analyze the precision of connectivity in the graph with varying θ and C.

In Figure 17, S is set as 5 minutes in the experiments. In Figure 17(a), C is varied from 8 to 12 and $\theta = 0.1$. Figure 17(a) shows

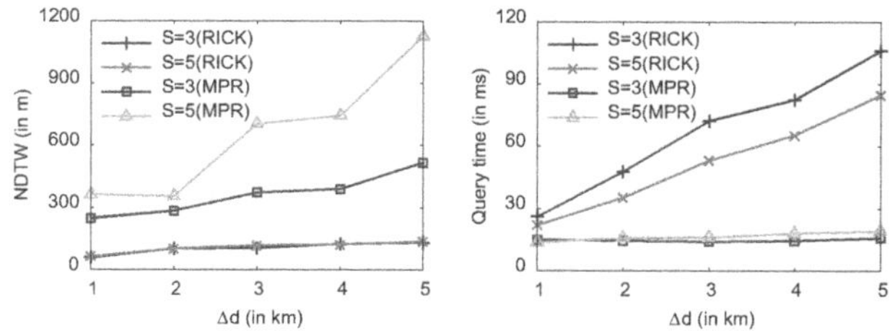

(a) (b)

Figure 13. Performance comparison of RICK and MPR.

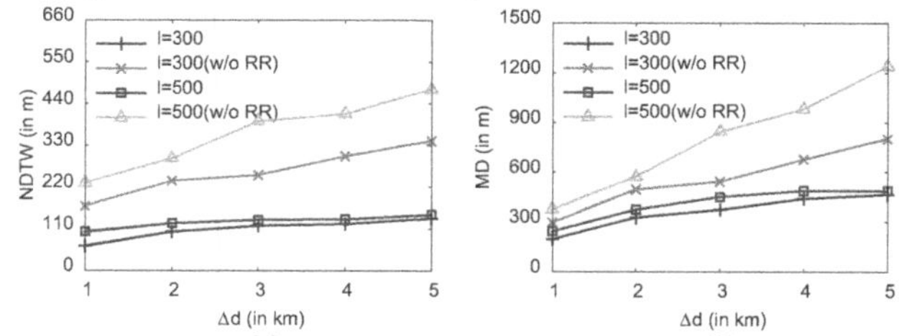

(a) (b)

Figure 14. Effect on route refinement.

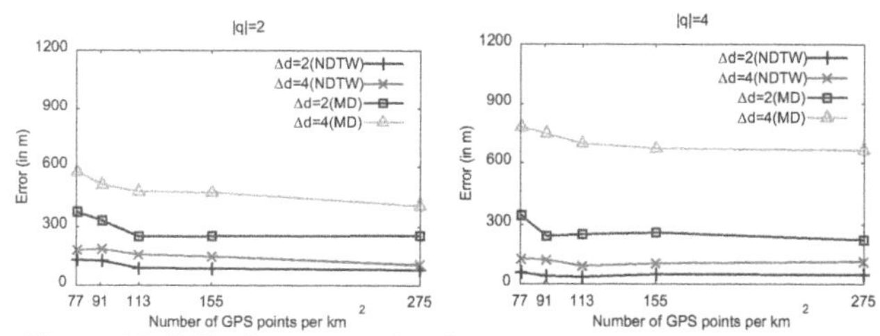

Figure 15. Effectiveness evaluation with data sparseness varied.

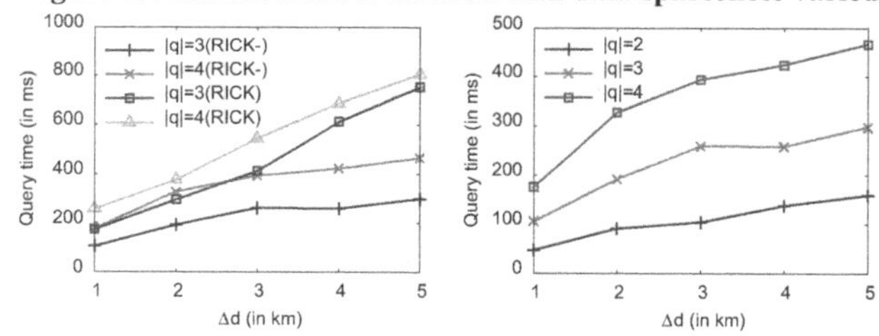

(a) (b)

Figure 16. Efficiency evaluation.

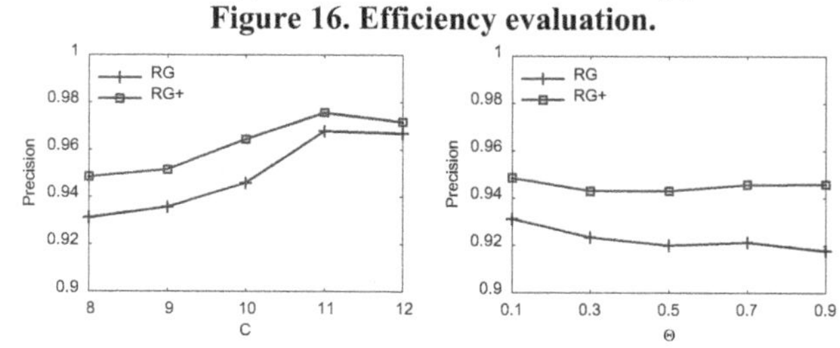

(a) (b)

Figure 17. Connectivity evaluation.

that the precision of RG and the precision of RG+ increase as C increases. This is because a stricter constraint induces a higher precision (i.e., a higher C). In Figure 17(b), C=8 and θ is varied from 0.1 to 0.9. As shown in Figure 17(b), the precision of RG and the precision of RG+ decrease as θ increases. The reason is that the precision is reduced as the constraint is loosened (i.e., a higher θ). Figure 17 depicts that the precision of RG+ is higher than that of RG, and it demonstrates that the shortest path based edge inference improves the correctness of the explored connectivity in a geographic space.

6. RELATED WORK

Route planning based on GPS trajectories: Route planning is widely investigated in [14,13,4,3] with GPS trajectories. The work [14] mainly inferred fastest routes from historical trajectories. In [13], the authors study travel route planning based on searching GPS trajectories. In [4], given a set/a sequence of locations, the top-k trajectories that best connect the given locations are retrieved from existing GPS trajectories. In [3], the authors investigated the problem of popular route planning without road network information. They introduced a transfer network model by exploiting intersections from historical GPS trajectories, and inferred the most popular route between two given locations by the turning probability of each intersection. However, these works were carried out using high sampled GPS trajectories. Given uncertain trajectories, the results obtained by [13,4] are historical uncertain trajectories and these uncertain trajectories still reveal rough routes. In addition, the trajectories derived by [4] may be far away from the query locations because these trajectories are low sampled. Using a dataset of uncertain trajectories, the accuracy of a transfer network model in [3] would be destroyed and then the effectiveness of inferred routes would be decreased.

Trip Planning based on geo-tagged social media: In recent years, mobile social applications have become popular, generating a huge volume of social media data, such as check-in records or geo-tagged photos. Such social media data can be regarded as sequences of visited locations, thereby revealing users' travel experience in terms of travel routes that link points-of-interest (POIs). Using geo-tagged photos, several studies [1,7,15] have investigated the problem of trip planning. However, the recommended trips are represented by a sequence of POIs, and the detailed route between two consecutive POIs is not specified. Different from these works, our method aims to construct the detailed route that is most likely to be taken by people by learning from the uncertain POI sequences in a mutual reinforcement way (e.g., Figure 2).

Uncertain trajectories: The research topics of trajectory uncertainty are studied in [6,10,11,16]. The work [10] introduces the problem of uncertain trajectory clustering, and focuses on the trajectory uncertainty caused by measurement errors. To reduce the uncertainty of an uncertain trajectory, the work [11] formulates an uncertain trajectory in a free space by a given maximum moving speed. However, the indistinct parts of an uncertain trajectory are enclosed in a spatio-temporal range without pointing out specific routes. In addition, the study [6] applies the techniques developed in a free space to model an uncertain trajectory in a road network. The possible routes between two sampled locations of an uncertain trajectory are restricted in a set of road segments by road network information and speed limits. Although the work [16] investigated the problem of discovering the top-k possible routes sequentially passing the queried locations from uncertain trajectories, they use road network information to reduce the uncertainty of low sampled trajectories. These works cannot derive routes from uncertain trajectories without road network information.

7. CONCLUSIONS

In this paper, we proposed RICK to infer the top-k routes traversing a given location sequence within a specified travel time from uncertain trajectories. The proposed RICK consists of the routable graph construction and the route inference. We have evaluated the proposed RICK in terms of both effectiveness and efficiency using two real datasets, check-in datasets and driving trajectories. The experiments show three aspects: 1) the inferred routes not only connect user-specified locations but also indicate detailed routes; 2) the proposed routable graph provides a good model of the uncertain trajectory dataset with an accuracy of 0.9; 3) on average, our routing algorithm can find the top-3 routes within 0.5 seconds, with a distance error smaller than 300 meters compared to its corresponding ground-truth. Meanwhile, RICK clearly outperforms the baseline by generating routes 300-700 meters closer (than those of the baseline) to the ground-truth. The experiments demonstrate the effectiveness and the efficiency of RICK. In the future, we will plan routes considering different start times and different user preferences. In addition, we will evaluate RICK by given other uncertain trajectory datasets, e.g., geo-tagged photo trips.

8. REFERENCES

[1] S. Basu Roy, S. Amer-Yahia, G. Das, and C. Yu. Interactive Itinerary Planning. In *IEEE ICDE*, pages 15-26, 2011.

[2] X. Cao, G. Cong, and C. S. Jensen. Mining Significant Semantic Locations from GPS Data. In *VLDB*, 3(1): 1009-1020, 2010.

[3] Z. Chen, H. T. Shen, and X. Zhou. Discovering Popular Routes from Trajectories. In *IEEE ICDE*, pages 900-911, 2011.

[4] Z. Chen, H. T. Shen, H. T., X. Zhou, Y. Zheng, and X. Xie. Searching Trajectories by Locations: An Efficiency Study. In *ACM SIGMOD*, pages 255-266, 2010.

[5] F. Giannotti, M. Nanni, D. Pedreschi, and F. Pinelli. Trajectory Pattern Mining. In *ACM SIGKDD*, pages 330-339, 2007.

[6] B. Kuijpers, B. Moelans, W. Othman, and A. Vaisman. Analyzing Trajectories Using Uncertainty and Background Information. In *SSDT*, pages 135-152, 2009.

[7] T. Kurashima, T. Iwata, G. Irie, and K. Fujimura. Travel route recommendation using geotags in photo sharing sites. In *ACM CIKM*, pages 579-588, 2010.

[8] Q. Liu, Y. Ge, Z. Li, E. Chen, and H. Xiong. Personalized Travel Package Recommendation. In *IEEE ICDM*, pages 407-416, 2011.

[9] Z. Li, B. Ding, J. Han, R. Kays, and P. Nye. Mining Periodic Behaviors for Moving Objects. In *ACM SIGKDD*, pages 1099-1108, 2010.

[10] N. Pelekis, I. Kopanakis, E. E. Kotsifakos, E. Frentzos, and Y. Theodoridis. Clustering Trajectories of Moving Objects in an Uncertain World. In *IEEE ICDM*, pages 417-427, 2009.

[11] R. Praing and M. Schneider. Modeling Historical and Future Movements of Spatio-temporal Objects in Moving Objects Databases. In *ACM CIKM*, pages 183-192, 2007.

[12] N. Roussopoulos, S. Kelley, and F. Vincent. Nearest Neighbor Queries. In *ACM SIGMOD*, pages 71-79, 1995.

[13] L.-Y. Wei, W.-C. Peng, B.-C. Chen, and T.-W. Lin. PATS: A Framework of Pattern-Aware Trajectory Search. In *UMMM*, pages 372-377, 2010.

[14] J. Yuan, Y. Zheng, C. Zhang, W. Xie, X. Xie, G. Sun, and Y. Huang. T-drive: Driving Directions Based on Taxi Trajectories. In *ACM SIGSPATIAL GIS*, pages 99-108, 2010.

[15] Z. Yin, L. Cao, J. Han, J. Luo, and T. S. Huang. Diversified Trajectory Pattern Ranking in Geo-tagged Social Media. In *SDM*, pages 980-991, 2011.

[16] K. Zheng, Y. Zheng, X. Xie, and X. Zhou. Reducing Uncertainty of Low-Sampling-Rate trajectories. In *IEEE ICDE*, 2012.

[17] Y. Zheng, L. Zhang, X. Xie, and W.-Y Ma, Mining Interesting Locations and Travel Sequences from GPS Trajectories. In *WWW*, pages 791-800, 2009.

[18] Y. Zheng and X. Zhou. *Computing with Spatial Trajectories*. Springer-Verlag New York Inc, 2011.

GetJar Mobile Application Recommendations with Very Sparse Datasets

Kent Shi
GetJar Inc.
San Mateo, CA, USA
kent@getjar.com

Kamal Ali
GetJar Inc.
San Mateo, CA, USA
kamal@getjar.com

ABSTRACT

The Netflix competition of 2006 [2] has spurred significant activity in the recommendations field, particularly in approaches using latent factor models [3, 5, 8, 12]. However, the near ubiquity of the Netflix and the similar MovieLens datasets[1] may be narrowing the generality of lessons learned in this field. At GetJar, our goal is to make appealing recommendations of mobile applications (apps). For app usage, we observe a distribution that has higher kurtosis (heavier head and longer tail) than that for the aforementioned movie datasets. This happens primarily because of the large disparity in resources available to app developers and the low cost of app publication relative to movies.

In this paper we compare a latent factor (PureSVD) and a memory-based model with our novel PCA-based model, which we call Eigenapp. We use both accuracy and variety as evaluation metrics. PureSVD did not perform well due to its reliance on explicit feedback such as ratings, which we do not have. Memory-based approaches that perform vector operations in the original high dimensional space overpredict popular apps because they fail to capture the neighborhood of less popular apps. They have high accuracy due to the concentration of mass in the head, but did poorly in terms of variety of apps exposed. Eigenapp, which exploits neighborhood information in low dimensional spaces, did well both on precision and variety, underscoring the importance of dimensionality reduction to form quality neighborhoods in high kurtosis distributions.

Categories and Subject Descriptors

H.2.8 [**Database Management**]: Database Applications—*Data mining*; H.3.3 [**Information Storage and Retrieval**]: Information Search and Retrieval—*Information filtering*

General Terms

Algorithms, Experimentation, Performance

[1] http://www.grouplens.org/node/73

KDD'12, August 12–16, 2012, Beijing, China.

Keywords

Recommender system, mobile application, evaluation, sparse data, PCA

1. INTRODUCTION

In the last few years, there has been a tremendous amount of growth in the mobile app space, particularly in the Android platform. As of January 2012, there are more than 400,000 apps hosted on Google's app store:[2] Google Play (formerly known as Android Market). However, Google Play provides little personalization beyond location-based tailoring of catalogs. That means all users from a given country will see the same list of apps regardless of their tastes and preferences.

Since most users typically navigate no more than a few pages when browsing the store, lack of personalization limits exposure for the majority of the apps. By analyzing the usage of apps on a sample of devices, we find that this space is dominated by a few apps, which unsurprisingly are ones that have been "featured" recently on the front page of Google Play.

GetJar, founded in 2004, is the largest free app store in the world. It provides mobile apps to users of all mobile platforms. We have recently begun to focus on the Android platform due to its openness and surging market share. Our goal is to become an attractive destination for Android apps by providing high quality personalization as a means to app discovery.

1.1 Challenges

While recommendations techniques, especially those using collaborative filtering, have been common since the early 1990s [6] and have been deployed on a number of e-commerce websites such as Amazon.com [9], recommendation in the emerging app domain is a task beset by unique challenges mainly due to the greater kurtosis in the distribution of app usage data.

From anonymous usage data collected at GetJar, we find that there are a few well-known apps popular among a large number of users, but the vast majority of apps are rarely used by most users. Figure 1(a) shows a comparison of the data distribution between the movie (Netflix) and app (GetJar) domains. Note the plot only includes apps that have been recently used by GetJar users. This constitutes approximately 55,000 apps, or about 14% of all apps. The movie

[2] http://www.distimo.com/blog/2012_01_google-android-market-tops-400000-applications

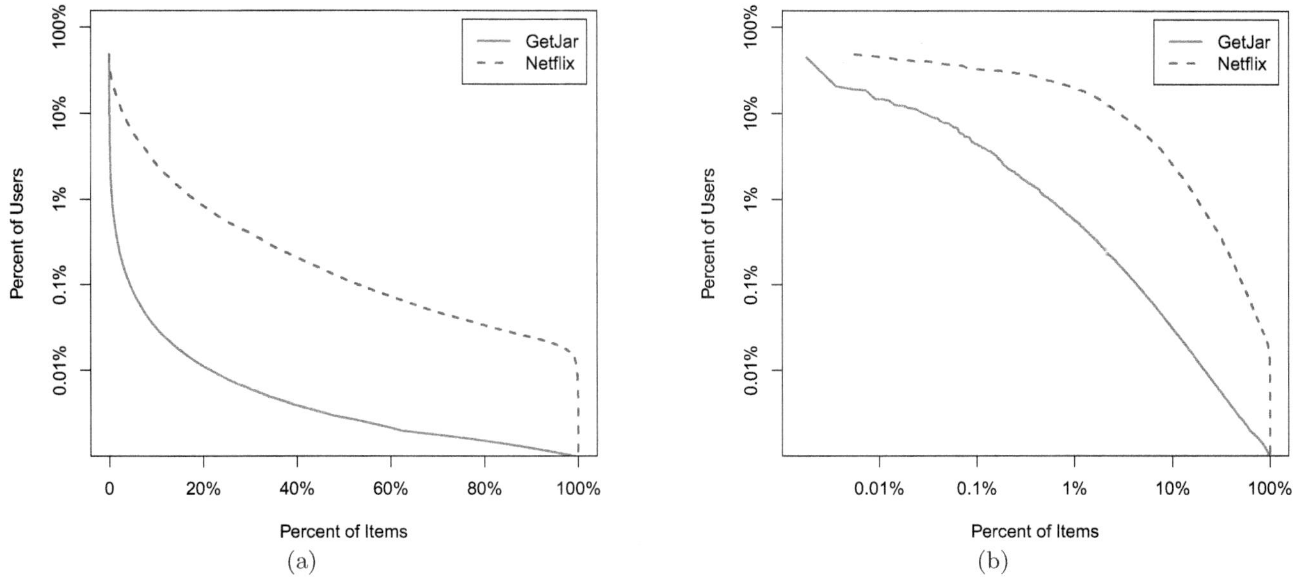

Figure 1: (a) Distribution of items (GetJar apps or Netflix movies) in terms of percentage of total users, with items sorted by popularity. (b) Distributions of items plotted in log-log scale.

at the first percentile (rank 177) is rated by 20% of Netflix users. In contrast, the app at the first percentile (rank 550) is used only by 0.6% of GetJar users. Furthermore, the movie at the first percentile has 42% as many users as the most popular movie, but app at the first percentile has only 1.3% as many users as the most popular app. Therefore, even though there are over 400,000 available apps, in reality only a few thousand of them are being used in any significant sense.

The same data is plotted in Figure 1(b), this time using a log scale for both axes. We can see that the GetJar curve is almost a straight line in log-log space, indicating that the frequencies can be approximated by a Zipf distribution[17]. This figure definitively shows the *qualitative* difference in distribution: App distribution is linear in log-log space whereas movie distribution isn't. Traditional collaborative filtering techniques [9, 14] or even the newer latent factor models [3, 5, 8, 12, 13] were not designed to handle this level of sparsity.

There are at least three reasons for this difference. First, the disparity in available resources among the app developers is larger than that of movie producers. This is mainly due to the cost (time and money) of publishing apps being much lower than that for releasing movies. Second, due to the less mature nature of the smart phone space, most casual users are unaware of the full capabilities of their device or what apps are available for it. This is in contrast to other domains such as movies, where there are numerous outlets dedicated to reviewing or promoting those products. Third, discovery mechanisms in the app space are less effective and mature compared to those of other domains.

Today, most app stores offer three ways for users to discover apps: (1) Listings of apps sorted by the number of downloads or a similar trending metric, (2) Category-based browsing and (3) Keyword-based searching. We know that the number of apps that can be exposed using listings is limited, and that methods 2 and 3 are not as effective as we would like. Browsing by category is only useful if the ontology of categories is rich, as in the case of Amazon. But most app stores rely on developers to categorize their own apps using a fixed inventory of labels. This leads to a small number of categories and a large number of apps within each, causing only the top few apps in each category to ever have significant visibility. Search is also ineffective because we find that most users don't know what to search for. About 90% of search queries at GetJar are titles (or close variants) of popular apps, which means search currently is not being used as an effective vehicle to discover new apps.

1.2 Goal and evaluation criteria

Users visit GetJar hoping to find interesting and useful apps. But as we have seen, common strategies such as browsing and searching, which have worked well for other e-commerce sites don't work as well in domains where many items remain under-publicized. Our goal is to use personalization to help users find a greater variety of appealing apps. Our prototype recommendation system recommends a *top-N* list of apps to each user based on her recent app usage. We judge the quality of the recommendations primarily by accuracy, which represents the ability of the recommender to predict the presence of an app on the user's device. To increase the exposure of under-publicized apps, the recommender is also evaluated on its ability to recommend tail apps as well as the variety of the apps it recommend.

A number of app stores currently offer personalized app recommendations, most notably the Apple App Store and the Amazon Appstore. However, little is known about how they generate their recommendations. Furthermore, we are unaware of any publications on mobile app recommendations.

The rest of the paper is organized as follows: Section 2 will review how the data was collected and some of its properties; Section 3 will provide details of the algorithms that we considered; Section 4 will provide the experimental setup and results; and finally Sections 5 and 6 provide discussion and conclusions.

2. THE GETJAR DATA

The data we report upon in this paper comes from server log files at GetJar where all personally identifying information had been stripped, but information pertaining to a single source can be uniquely identified up to a common anonymous identifier. The apps we report here include those hosted on GetJar as well as those on Google Play.

For the purposes of this study, we rely upon app usage data rather than installation data. The reason we choose not to use installation data is that it is a poor indicator of interest since many app installations are *experimental* from a user's perspective. A significant fraction of our users are found to uninstall an app on the same day as they installed it. Also, there is another significant fraction of users that have a vast number of installed apps that never get used.

Many users are new to the mobile app space and thus are likely experimenting with a variety of apps. We restrict our data to *recent* app usage to account for this fact, that users' tastes for apps can change more rapidly than for traditional domains such as movies and music. We are only interested in recommending apps that reflect their current tastes or interests.

The observation period for data used for this study is from November 7 to November 21, 2011. We find that varying length of the observation period by a few days makes almost no difference in the number of apps used by the users.[3] In an effort to reduce noise in the data from apps that were being trialed by users, we filtered out apps that were not used other than on the day of installation. We further cleaned the data by removing users that joined or left midway during the observation period and those that were not associated with a pre-determined list of legitimate devices. The resultant dataset contains 101,106 users. For each user we used the list of apps and the number of days each app was used during the observation period. The total number of unique apps used by all users during the interval satisfying our constraints was 55,020.

2.1 Data sparsity and long tail

As we have already illustrated in Figure 1, our data is extremely sparse and that the vast majority of apps have low usage. While it is well known that sparsity and a long tail [1] are two characteristics of all e-commerce data, these are especially pronounced in our dataset.

Figure 2 plots the cumulative distribution of the items in terms of the total amount of usage. We can see that the GetJar dataset is far more head-heavy compared to the Netflix dataset, with the top 1% of apps accounting for 58% of usage in contrast to Netflix where the top 1% of movies contribute to 22% of all ratings. An even more selective subset - the 100 most popular apps - account for 30% of total app usage. For the GetJar dataset, we define *the head* to be the top 100 apps and the remaining apps to be *the tail.*

One major reason for this difference is that many apps are used every day, but movies are seldom watched more than once or twice. Thus Netflix users may be more likely to explore new items relative to GetJar users. Another reason is that the Netflix data was collected over a much longer period of time. The reason for the longer tail in the GetJar dataset, as previously alluded to, is primarily due to the low cost of publishing apps compared to the cost of releasing a movie. This encourages developers to release as many apps as possible to increase the chances of their apps being discovered by search. This strategy often leads to apps being published multiple times with different titles but similar functionalities. This also encourages the proliferation of a large number of apps tailored for very specific needs (e.g. ringtone apps dedicated to music by specific artists) as opposed to general apps (e.g. a single ringtone app containing music by all artists).

Given that we have little or no usage information on the bulk of the tail apps, it makes recommending them a very difficult task. In order to ensure that the recommended apps will have certain amount of support, for this study, we limited our app population by only including apps with more than 20 users. This reduces the number of apps from 55,030 to 7,304. Even though this pruning process removed 87% of apps (or 98% if we include apps with no usage), it is noteworthy that only 9% of the total usage was thus eliminated from our modeling. Table 1 shows the size and density of the user-item matrices before and after our pruning. It shows that even after rejecting the bottom 87% of the apps, the GetJar* dataset is still much sparser relative to Netflix.

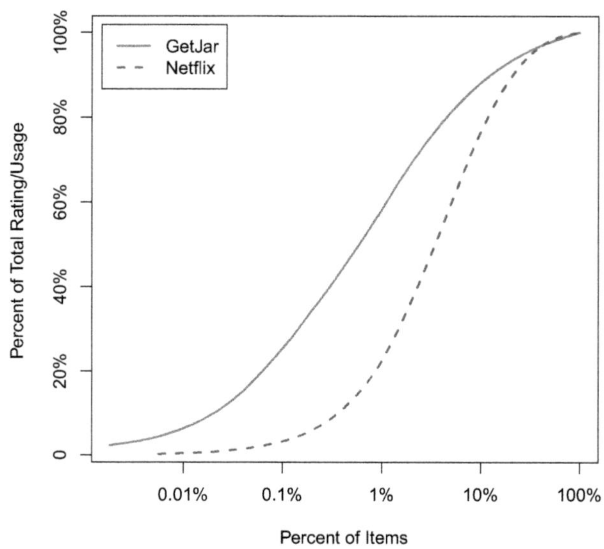

Figure 2: Cumulative distribution of items in terms of percentage of total usage, the curves can be viewed as the integral of the curves in Figure 1.

Dataset	Users	Items	Usages/Ratings	Density
GetJar	101,106	55,020	1.99M	0.04%
GetJar*	101,031	7,304	1.82M	0.25%
Netflix	480,189	17,770	100M	1.18%

Table 1: Size of user-item matrices for Netflix and GetJar dataset. GetJar* denotes the GetJar dataset including only apps that have been used by more than 20 users.

2.2 Usage versus ratings

Another difference between the GetJar dataset and the

[3]We use the more convenient word *users* to denote their anonymized identifiers.

Netflix dataset is that movie ratings is an *explicit* feedback for interest whereas days of usage is *implicit* [11]. The benefit of an explicit rating system is that it is well-defined and standardized, thus generating a more accurate measurement of interest compared to implicit feedbacks such as days of usage. The latter can be influenced by a number of factors such as mood, unforeseen events, or logging errors. Furthermore, there is also correlation between usage and category - we find that "social" apps are consistently the most heavily used apps among nearly all users. This is because "social" apps need to be used often in order to serve their purpose, but apps in categories such as "productivity" are seldom needed on a continuous basis. So while it is safe to assume that a user enjoyed a movie that she rated highly relatively to one rated lowly, the same cannot be said for a user that used a "social" app more than a "productivity" app.

We choose not to use ratings because it has a number of drawbacks in the mobile app domain. Most importantly, it is very difficult to collect for a large number of users without forceful intervention. Furthermore, since users' taste in apps may change and many app developers frequently update their apps with new features or functionalities, ratings may become obsolete in as little as one month. Finally, observing ratings on Google Play, we find they are polarized, with the vast majority of ratings being either 1 or 5. This is likely due to fragmentation of the Android platform,[4] resulting in most ratings being given based on whether the app worked (5) or not (1) for the user.

Due to the influence of the Netflix competition, most research in the recommendations community has been geared toward rating *prediction* by means of minimizing root mean square error (RMSE). However, Cremonesi et. al [3] reported that improving RMSE does not translate into improvement in accuracy for the top-N task. On the Netflix and MovieLens datasets, the predictive accuracy of a naive most popular list is comparable to those by sophisticated algorithms optimized for RMSE. We tried the same using the GetJar dataset but substituting days of usage for ratings, and found that algorithms optimized for RMSE actually performed far worse than a simple most popular list.

With that said, days of usage can still be used for neighborhood approaches, provided that there still exists some correlation between it and interest. A part of this study is to evaluate the usefulness of this metric. Thus, for our experiments, we used two versions of the user-item matrix. In the first version, each cell represents the number of days the app was used, and in the second, each cell is a binary indicator of usage during the observation period. We'd like to see if the additional granularity provided by the days of usage will generate better recommendations than when using a binary indicator.

3. MODELS

Two common recommendation approaches in use today are those using memory-based models and latent factor models. Memory-based models leverage the neighborhood of items in user space or that of users in item space. A user-user or item-item similarity matrix is computed for pairs and recommendations are generated based on these similarities. Latent factor models are more sophisticated approaches where the user-item matrix is decomposed via matrix factorization techniques such as Singular Value Decomposition (SVD). Latent factors are then extracted and used to generate predictions.

We evaluated both the above approaches using our data. In addition, we developed a hybrid system using Principal Components Analysis (PCA) which we call Eigenapp. These three algorithms were also compared against a non-personalized baseline recommendation system that serves the most popular items.

Dataset	Number of Common Users				
	0	1	2-10	11-20	> 20
GetJar*	83.2%	9.1%	6.6%	0.6%	0.6%
Netflix	0.2%	0.4%	33.8%	22.2%	43.3%

Table 2: Breakdown of number of common users for the GetJar and Netflix datasets. For n items, the total number of item pairs is $\frac{n^2-n}{2}$.

3.1 Non-personalized models

Non-personalized models are those that serve the same list of items to all users. They commonly sort items by the number of purchases, profit margin, click-through rate (CTR), or other similar metrics. In this paper, our non-personalized baseline algorithm sorts items by popularity, where popularity is defined as the number of distinct users that have used the item during the observation period.

3.2 Memory-based models

There are two types of memory-based models: Item-based and user-based. Item-based models find similarities between items, and for a given user they recommend items that are similar to items she already owns. User-based models find similarities between users, and for a given user they recommend items owned by her most similar users.

Computationally, item-based models are more scalable because there are usually far fewer items than users, as is the case in the mobile app space. In addition, there is research showing that item-based algorithms generally perform better than user-based algorithms [9, 14]. Hence, our memory-based model uses the item-based approach.

Two of the most common neighborhood similarity metrics in current use are the Pearson correlation coefficient and cosine similarity. The Pearson correlation coefficient is computed for a pair of items based on the set of users that have used both. Since the vast majority of our items reside in the long tail, many of those items are unlikely to share common users with most other items.

Table 2 presents the distribution of number of common users in the GetJar and Netflix datasets. The table shows that 83.2% of item pairs in the GetJar dataset have zero users in common, whereas that same percentage for Netflix is 0.2%. For GetJar, more than 90% of item pairs have one or no common users. Thus it is impossible to compute correlations for these item pairs. In addition, the vast majority of the remaining item pairs share 10 or fewer users,

[4]There are many manufacturers that produce Android devices with various hardware specifications and tweaks of the operating system. This makes it difficult for developers to to test their apps on all devices, resulting in apps not working as intended on many devices.

meaning that the sample correlation estimate is likely to be inaccurate due to poor support. In contrast, the published Netflix dataset has less than 1% of movie pairs sharing 1 or fewer common users and about 65% of movie pairs share more than 10 common users. Since the Pearson correlation coefficient is undefined for 90% of our item pairs, we will use cosine similarity.

Let $\mathbf{R}$ denote the $m \times n$ user-item matrix where m is the number of users and n is the number of items. From $\mathbf{R}$, we compute an item-item similarity matrix $\mathbf{S}$, whose (i, j) entry is:

$$s_{i,j} = \frac{r_{*,i} \cdot r_{*,j}}{\|r_{*,i}\|_2 \cdot \|r_{*,j}\|_2} \tag{1}$$

where $r_{*,i}$ and $r_{*,j}$ are the ith and jth columns respectively of $\mathbf{R}$. Cosine similarity does not require items to share common users. In such case it will simply produce a similarity of 0. However, it still suffers from low overlap support. The closest neighbors for a less popular item will often occur by coincidence simply because they are the only ones that produced non-zero similarity scores.

Using $\mathbf{S}$, the affinity $t_{u,i}$ between user u and item i is the sum of similarities between i and items used by u:

$$t_{u,i} = \sum_{j \in \mathbf{I}_u} s_{i,j} \tag{2}$$

where $\mathbf{I}_u$ is the set of items used by u. For a given user, all items are sorted by their affinity score in order to produce a top-N list.[5]

We made two slight modifications to the above method that produced better results. First, the item-item similarity scores $s_{i,j}$ were normalized before being used in equation (2). Deshpande et al. [4] suggested using a normalization such that the sum of the similarities add up to 1. However, we found that normalizing using z-score worked much better for the GetJar dataset, producing the asymmetric similarity:

$$s'_{i,j} = \frac{s_{i,j} - \overline{s_{*,j}}}{\sigma_{s_{*,j}}} \tag{3}$$

where $\overline{s_{*,j}}$ is the average similarity to item j and $\sigma_{s_{*,j}}$ is the standard deviation of similarities to item j. Second, for each item candidate i, instead of summing over all items in $\mathbf{I}_u$, we only considered the l *nearest* items, which are those with the greatest normalized similarly scores to i. This has the effect of noise reduction by discarding weakly related items to the given i. For the GetJar dataset, we find that setting $l = 5$ seemed to work the best.

3.3 Latent factor models

Latent factor models work by factorizing the user-item matrix $\mathbf{R}$ into two lower rank matrices: user factors and item factors. These models are often used for rating predictions, where a rating $r_{u,i}$ for user u on item i can be predicted by taking the inner product of their respective vectors in the user factors and item factors. User bias and item bias are commonly removed by subtracting the row and column means from $\mathbf{R}$ prior to the factorization step. The biases are added back on to the inner product to generate the final prediction.

[5]In equation (2), users that use a greater number of items will have more summands, but since we're only interested in the relative order of items for a given user, the varying number of summands does not pose a problem.

Examples of this approach include [5, 8, 12, 13]. We tried [5] and [13] by substituting days of usage for ratings, and then sorting the predictions to generate a top-N recommended list. The results were by far the worst of all algorithms, for reasons explained in Section 2.2. We expect similar results for other rating prediction based algorithms.

The only latent factor top-N algorithm we are aware of is PureSVD [3]. The algorithm works by replacing all missing values (those with no ratings) in $\mathbf{R}$ with 0, and then factorizing $\mathbf{R}$ via SVD:

$$\mathbf{R} = \mathbf{U} \cdot \mathbf{\Sigma} \cdot \mathbf{V}^T \tag{4}$$

Then affinity between user u and item i can be computed by:

$$t_{u,i} = r_{u,*} \cdot \mathbf{Q} \cdot \mathbf{q}_i^T \tag{5}$$

where $\mathbf{Q}$ stands for the top k singular vectors extracted from $\mathbf{V}$ and $\mathbf{q}_i$ is the row in $\mathbf{Q}$ corresponding to item i. Note that $t_{u,i}$ is simply an association measure and not a predicted rating. A top-N list can then be made for user u by selecting the N items with the highest affinity score to u.

PureSVD is the only latent factor algorithm we evaluated that was able to generate reasonable recommendations. The main reason for this is that, unlike the other algorithms, PureSVD is not optimized for RMSE based rating prediction but rather the relative ordering of items produced by the association scores.

3.4 Eigenapp model

Of the two previously mentioned approaches, memory-based models yielded far better results despite only having neighborhoods for popular items. We want to improve the result of memory-based models by borrowing ideas from the latent factor models. Along these lines, we used dimensionality reduction techniques to extract meaningful features from the items and then applied memory-based techniques to generate recommendations in this reduced space.

Our neighborhood is still item-based, but items are now represented using *features* instead of *users*. Similar to [3], we also replace all missing values in $\mathbf{R}$ with 0. Given the large disparity in app frequencies, we normalized the item vectors to prevent the features from being based on only popular items. This is done by normalizing each column in $\mathbf{R}$ to have zero mean and length of one: $\sum_u r'_{u,i} = 0$ and $\sum_u {r'_{u,i}}^2 = 1$. We denote this new normalized user-item matrix as $\mathbf{R}'$ and apply PCA to $\mathbf{R}'$ for feature extraction.

PCA is performed via eigen decomposition of the covariance matrix $\mathbf{C}$. $\mathbf{C}$ is computed by first calculating the mean item vector $\mathbf{b}$ with $b_u = \frac{1}{n}\sum_i r'_{u,i}$. Then remove the mean by forming matrix $\mathbf{A}$ where each cell $a_{u,i} = r'_{u,i} - b_u$ and finally compute $\mathbf{C} = \mathbf{A}\mathbf{A}^T$. Note that $\mathbf{C}$ is an $m \times m$ matrix with the number of users m likely to be a very large number. This makes eigen decomposition practically impossible in time and space. Observing that the number of items n is likely to be much lower, we used the same procedure as in Eigenface [16] to optimize the process. The procedure works by first conducting eigen decomposition on the $n \times n$ matrix $\mathbf{A}^T\mathbf{A}$ obtaining eigenvectors $\mathbf{v}^*$ and eigenvalues λ^* such that for each j:

$$\mathbf{A}^T\mathbf{A}\mathbf{v}_j^* = \lambda_j^*\mathbf{v}_j^* \tag{6}$$

Multiplying both sides by $\mathbf{A}$, we get:

$$\mathbf{A}\mathbf{A}^T(\mathbf{A}\mathbf{v}_j^*) = \lambda_j^*(\mathbf{A}\mathbf{v}_j^*) \tag{7}$$

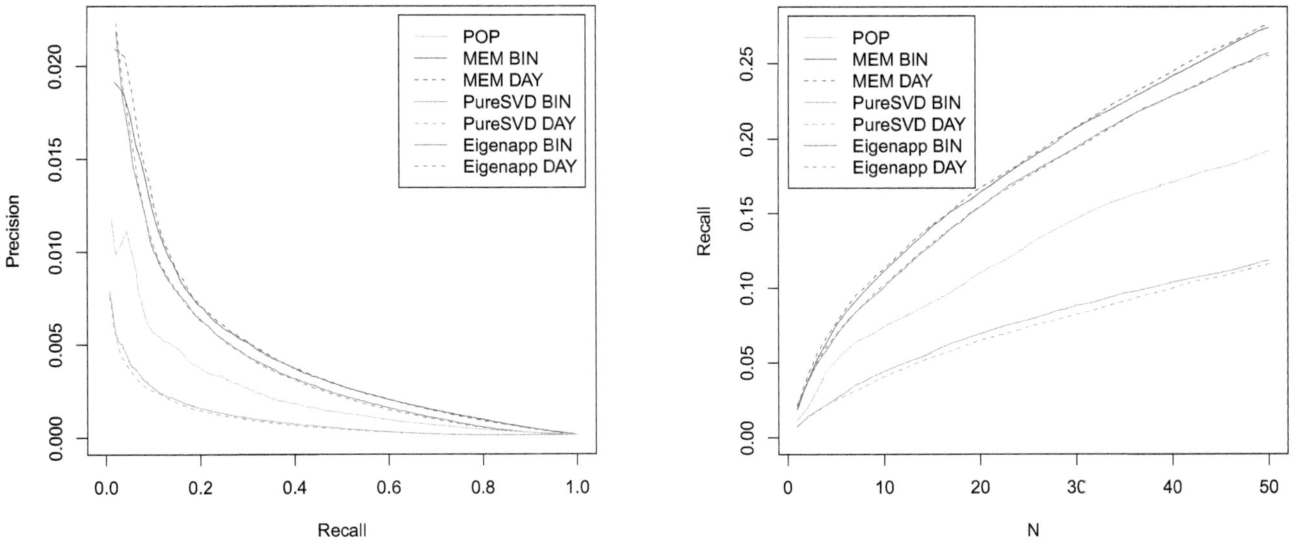

(a) Precision-Recall

(b) Recall at N

Figure 3: (a) Precision-recall curves and (b) Recall at N curves using all users in the test set.

We see that vectors $\mathbf{v}_j = \mathbf{A}\mathbf{v}_j^*$ are the eigenvectors for $\mathbf{C}$. From there, we normalize each $\mathbf{v}_j$ to length one and keep only the k eigenvectors with the highest corresponding eigenvalues. The eigenvectors represent the dimensions with the largest variances, or the dimensions that can best differentiate the items. Alternatively, these eigenvectors can also be viewed as item features, items with similar projected values on a particular eigenvector are likely to be similar in certain attributes. We will denote these eigenvectors as *eigenapps*. Finally, we can project all the items onto the reduced eigenspace by $\mathbf{D} = \mathbf{v}\mathbf{A}$. $\mathbf{D}$ is a $k \times n$ matrix, where each column contains the projected values of the item onto each of the eigenapps. The values can be viewed as the coefficients or weights of the eigenapp for the items. By observing several rows in $\mathbf{D}$, apps with high projected values in these eigenapps are often similar types of apps. This was useful in preliminary validation showing that the Eigenapp approach indeed captured latent item features.

Item-item similarities can be computed using equation (1) except that we use $\mathbf{D}$ instead of $\mathbf{R}$. Since $\mathbf{D}$ is dense, similarity scores will likely be non-zero for all item pairs. Once the item-item similarity matrix $\mathbf{S}$ has been computed, the remainder of the algorithm is identical to the memory-based algorithm described in Section 3.2. We find that the computed neighborhood in the reduced eigenspace is of much better quality compared to the one computed using the memory-based methods in the non-reduced space. However, neighborhood quality is still better for popular items than for less popular items, likely due to better support. We also find that the quality of neighborhood improves when we increase the number of eigenapps used, and that the neighborhood becomes relatively stable after $k = 200$.

The computation complexity of this algorithm, up to generating $\mathbf{S}$, is $O(mn^2)$. Using the current GetJar dataset, that process took about 11 minutes on an Intel Core i7 machine using the Eigen library.[6] However, since the computation of $\mathbf{S}$ is the offline phase of the recommender system, and the number of apps with some minimum amount of usage is unlikely to increase significantly with more users, we do not believe this will pose a problem.

Eigenapp is similar to another PCA based algorithm Eigentaste [7]. The main difference is that Eigentaste, which was evaluated on the Jester joke dataset,[7] requires a gauge item set where every user must have rated every item in the gauge set. Coming up with such a gauge set is impossible for our application, much less one that is representative. In addition, Eigentaste uses a user-based neighborhood approach to generate recommendations, whereas Eigenapp utilizes item-based neighborhoods.

4. EVALUATION

We evaluated the four types of models from Section 3: Non-personalized (POP), Memory-based (MEM), PureSVD and Eigenapp, using the GetJar dataset. The experiment is set up by randomly dividing the users into five equal sized groups. Four of the groups are used for training, and the remaining one for evaluation. Using the training set, we compute the item-item similarity matrix $\mathbf{S}$ for MEM and Eigenapp, item factor matrix $\mathbf{Q}$ for PureSVD, and the list of most popular items for POP. The number of eigenvectors used for Eigenapp and number of singular vectors used for PureSVD are both 300. For each user in the test set, we sort the apps by install time. We feed the first $M-1$ apps to the model to generate its recommendation list of N apps. Then we check if the left out app is in the recommended list (all algorithms make sure to exclude from their recommendation list the $M-1$ apps known to already be installed for the given user). This procedure is repeated on all 5 possible ways of dividing the user groups, allowing every group to be used as the evaluation group once, and thus a recommendation list for every user exists.

Two forms of user-item matrix $\mathbf{R}$ were considered for the experiments, as described in Section 2.2. The first version

[6] `http://eigen.tuxfamily.org`

[7] `http://eigentaste.berkeley.edu/dataset`

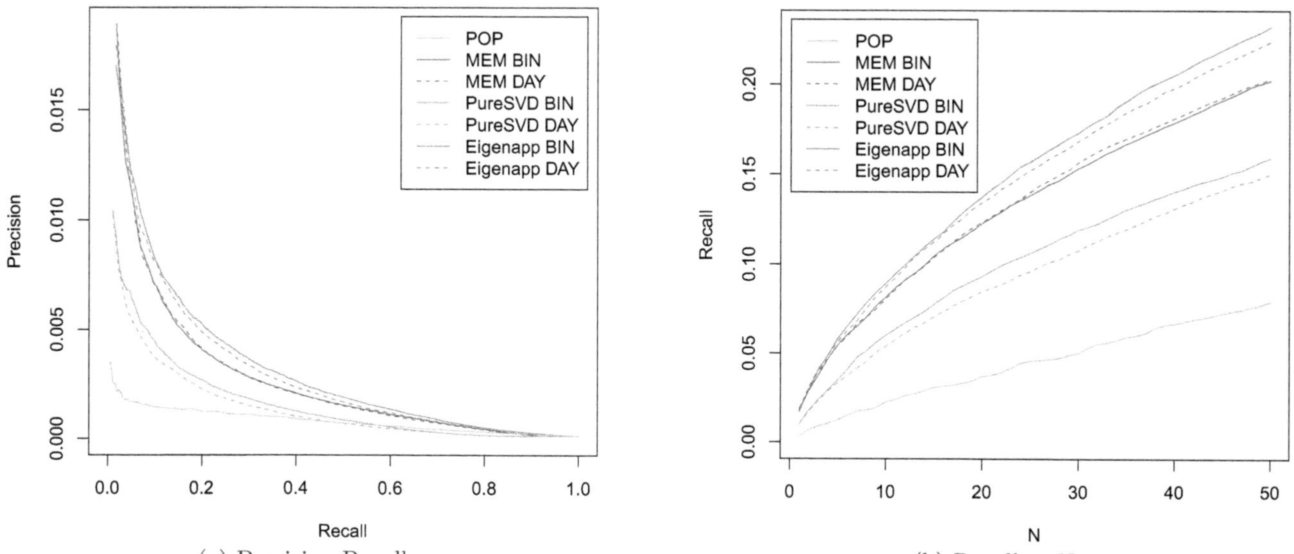

(a) Precision-Recall

(b) Recall at N

Figure 4: (a) Precision-recall curves and (b) Recall at N curves after removing the 100 most popular items.

using days of usage will be denoted as DAY, and the binarized version will be denoted as BIN.

Accuracy is the first evaluation criterion we used because we want our recommendations to be relevant to user's interest and preferences. However, user satisfaction is not solely dependent on accuracy [10]. In particular, given the dominance of the popular apps in this domain, it is important to expose apps in the tail. With that in mind, we also evaluated the accuracy of the models in recommending tail apps, and the variety of the apps recommended.

4.1 Accuracy

The accuracies of the models were evaluated by the standard precision-recall methodology. Since we have only one relevant item to be predicted for each user (the left out app), we set h_u equal to 1 if the relevant item is in the top-N list for user u and 0 otherwise. Precision and recall at each N is computed by:

$$precision(N) = \frac{\sum_{u=1}^{m} h_u}{m \cdot N} \quad (8)$$

$$recall(N) = \frac{\sum_{u=1}^{m} h_u}{m} \quad (9)$$

where m is the number of users.

Figure 3(a) illustrates the precision-recall curves for the algorithms . As we can see, the best performer was MEM despite using an item-item similarity matrix consisting mostly of zeros. A close second was Eigenapp, followed by POP and PureSVD. Figure 3(b) illustrates the recall at each N, up to $N = 50$. This figure shows the percentage of users whose missing app was identified in the top-N. When N is 10, MEM identified the missing app for about 11% of users, Eigenapp identified the missing app for about 10% of users, and POP and PureSVD identified the missing app for about 7% and 4% of users respectively.

The two types of user-item matrix (BIN and DAY) made little difference in the global accuracy of any of the three algorithms. Indicating that the additional signals contributed by number of days of usage do not outweigh its inaccuracies.

4.2 Accuracy of less popular items

Given the overwhelming exposure popular apps receive today in the Android ecosystem, many users will use them simply because those are the only apps they know. Thus using a popular app may not be a strong indicator of interest relative to less popular apps. In order to measure precision and recall on the "tail", we redrew the precision-recall curves by excluding the 100 most popular apps from the recommended list of each user. Note therefore, that h_u will always be 0 for users whose relevant items are among the 100 most popular apps. Thus those users were removed for this experiment.

Figure 4(a) shows the precision-recall curves after removing the 100 most popular items. The figure shows that Eigenapp has the highest accuracy for this tail subset. MEM is now second, followed by PureSVD and POP. Recall at N shown in Figure 4(b) shows a similar picture, but it is worth noting that relative to Figure 3(b), recall dropped for every algorithm with the exception of PureSVD. This shows it is more difficult to recommend relevant tail apps than head apps.

Using the two types of user-item matrix (BIN and DAY) still achieved similar performance for all three algorithms, but it appears Eigenapp and PureSVD yielded slightly better results using BIN compared to DAY.

4.3 Presentation

The impression that the recommended list makes to the user is also important to their satisfaction [10]. An artifact of our methodology for predicting the left-out item means that we penalize algorithms for predicting items that the user may have liked had she known about them. Since it is impossible for us to know which of the "irrelevant" items (those that do not correspond to the left out item) in the top-N are potentially interesting ones, we can only judge the diversity of items that are presented. In this study, we are interested in recommending a diverse list of apps from all popularity spectrums.

Algorithm	Popularity Rank				
	1-50	51-100	101-500	501-1000	>1000
POP	100%	0	0	0	0
MM BIN	85%	5%	6%	2%	2%
MM DAY	80%	6%	8%	3%	4%
PS BIN	<1%	<1%	74%	22%	5%
PS DAY	1%	5%	54%	29%	11%
EA BIN	34%	18%	27%	8%	14%
EA DAY	34%	18%	23%	7%	18%

Table 3: Distribution of recommended apps in terms of app popularity for the different algorithms (MM stands for Memory, PS stands for PureSVD, and EA stands for Eigenapp) with N set to 10. The frequencies are computed by collecting all $m \cdot N$ recommended apps, where m is the number of users, and find the percentage of apps that lies in each of the stated popularity ranges.

Table 3 shows the popularity ranking of the recommended apps when N is set to 10. As expected, all recommended apps by POP are from the 50 most popular apps. Of the remaining algorithms, more than 80% of apps recommended by MEM are from the 50 most popular. This is due to less popular apps not having many non-zero similarities in the high dimensional neighborhood used by MEM. We also see that PureSVD recommends almost no apps from the 100 most popular, particularly when using BIN, which explains why its accuracy increased significantly when we only considered the less popular items.

From a presentation perspective, it is better to show a good mixture of items from the head and the tail. Only recommending items at the head is poor for discovery because they are items that users most likely already know. Only recommending items at the tail may not be good because users will not recognize any of the recommended items and so may lose trust in the recommender [15]. With that said, it appears that the Eigenapp performed the best under this measurement as it recommends items across all popularity levels.

4.4 Variety

In addition to higher exposure of less popular items, we also like the exposure to be more spread out rather than concentrated on a few items. We measure variety by calculating the entropy of the recommended results, which can be computed as follows:

$$H = -\sum_i p(i) \cdot \log p(i) \qquad (10)$$

where $p(i)$ is the relative frequency of item i among the top-N recommended items for all users ($m \cdot N$ total items).

Figure 5 plots the entropy of the recommendations for the different models with N ranging from 1 to 50. We see that Eigenapp and PureSVD have the largest entropy meaning that the top of their recommendation lists are comprised of a wider variety of items. MEM has a far lower entropy, which we can expect since it largely only recommend the popular items. And as expected, POP has the smallest entropy. It is also worth noting that as N increases from 1 to 5, there is a large increase in variety for MEM, indicating its variety

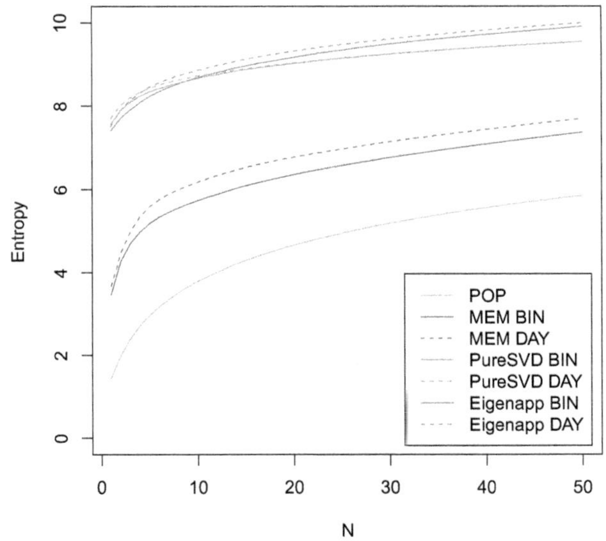

Figure 5: Entropy of the recommended list for all users with N ranging from 1 to 50.

is particularly poor in the top 5 of the recommendation list - exactly the region to which users pay the most attention. We verified this by finding that for MEM, the most popular app is the first item recommended to approximately 40% of users (or 80% of users that don't already have that item).

This finding is expected given the result presented in Section 4.3. Algorithms that recommend tail apps are expected to have a larger variety because the tail is where the vast majority of apps reside. However, Eigenapp actually recommended fewer tail apps than PureSVD, and yet it had slightly higher entropy, indicating that the exposure of tail apps by Eigenapp is more evenly distributed relative to that of PureSVD.

5. DISCUSSION

The recent Netflix competition has significantly influenced the recommendation community towards usage of RMSE-based evaluation metrics. We were unable to find many algorithms expressly tailored for the top-N items task with the exception of [3]. In addition, we find most recent research to be focused on the movie domain using Netflix or Movielens datasets where interest is explicitly expressed through ratings. It is questionable how well these models would translate into other domains, particularly to those where explicit feedback is not available.

Among the models we evaluated, neighborhood approaches are found to generate accurate recommendations. In particular, traditional memory based models operating in high dimensional user space performed surprisingly well when evaluated using precision-recall. However, further analysis showed that this was due to the presentation of a small set of popular items to almost every user, albeit in different orders. The high kurtosis of app usage distribution benefits algorithms that concentrate on a small set of popular items when evaluated under precision-recall, although such recommenders are unlikely to generate a pleasing experience for the users.

The Eigenapp model performed very well on the GetJar dataset, particularly in its ability to recommend a diverse list of apps. This is because all item vectors are normalized prior to applying PCA, thus usage of less popular apps can be captured by the top eigenvectors. That makes it possible for the less popular apps to be among the closest neighbors of the popular apps. This is particularly important for exposure of the less popular apps, because given the dominance of the popular apps, only apps that are close to one of the popular apps can make frequent appearances at the top of the recommended lists. Using traditional memory-based models, the popular apps form a tight cluster (relative to the less popular apps) in its neighborhood, thus making it difficult for less popular apps to surface to the top of the recommended lists for many users.

6. CONCLUSION

With increasing numbers of people switching to smart phones, the mobile application space is an emerging domain for recommendation systems. Due to the wide disparity in resources among app publishers, the apps that large companies develop receive far more exposure than those developed by individual developers. This results in app usage being dominated by a few popular apps. The problem is further exacerbated by existing apps stores using non-personalized ranking mechanisms. While that approach may help most users find high quality and essential apps quickly, it is less effective in recommending apps to users who are in an exploratory mode

In this study, we used app-usage as our metric. Given the characteristics of this data, we found that traditional memory-based approaches heavily favor popular apps contrary to our mission. On the other hand, latent factor models that were developed based on the Netflix data performed quite poorly accuracy-wise. We find that the Eigenapp model performed the best in accuracy and in promotion of less well known apps in the tail of our dataset.

A system using the Eigenapp model is currently in internal trials at GetJar. It presents a personalized app list to users along with a non-personalized most popular list. The first list is elicited when users are in an exploratory mode and the second when they are looking for the most sought-after apps. We plan to open this system for general use in the second half of 2012. Simultaneously, we are also working continuously to improve our system.

A limitation of the current model is that it includes only apps with certain minimum of usage, a condition that most apps do not satisfy. While the set of apps included probably contains most of the potentially interesting ones, it is possible that we removed some interesting niche apps, or high quality apps by individual developers that were not exposed due to lack of marketing. The latter case is particularly important to us. We are currently exploring content-based models that extract useful features from app metadata and plan to combine the results of the collaborative and content-based approaches in future work.

7. ACKNOWLEDGEMENTS

The authors would like to thank Anand Venkataraman for guidance, edits and help with revisions. Chris Dury provided valuable feedback and Sunil Yarram helped during various stages of data preparation.

8. REFERENCES

[1] C. Anderson. *The Long Tail: Why the Future of Business Is Selling Less of More.* Hyperion, 2006.

[2] J. Bennett and S. Lanning. The netflix prize. In *Proceedings of KDD Cup and Workshop*, pages 3–6, 2007.

[3] P. Cremonesi, Y. Koren, and R. Turrin. Performance of recommender algorithms on top-n recommendation tasks. In *Proceedings of the fourth ACM conference on Recommender systems*, RecSys '10, pages 39–46, New York, NY, USA, 2010. ACM.

[4] M. Deshpande and G. Karypis. Item-based top-n recommendation algorithms. *ACM Trans. Inf. Syst.*, 22(1):143–177, Jan. 2004.

[5] S. Funk. Netflix update: Try this at home. http://sifter.org/˜simon/journal/20061211.html, 2006.

[6] D. Goldberg, D. Nichols, B. M. Oki, and D. Terry. Using collaborative filtering to weave an information tapestry. *Commun. ACM*, 35(12):61–70, Dec. 1992.

[7] K. Goldberg, T. Roeder, D. Gupta, and C. Perkins. Eigentaste: A constant time collaborative filtering algorithm. *Inf. Retr.*, 4(2):133–151, July 2001.

[8] Y. Koren. Factorization meets the neighborhood: a multifaceted collaborative filtering model. In *Proceedings of the 14th ACM SIGKDD international conference on Knowledge discovery and data mining*, KDD '08, pages 426–434, New York, NY, USA, 2008. ACM.

[9] G. Linden, B. Smith, and J. York. Amazon.com recommendations: Item-to-item collaborative filtering. *IEEE Internet Computing*, 7:76–80, 2003.

[10] S. M. McNee, J. Riedl, and J. A. Konstan. Being accurate is not enough: how accuracy metrics have hurt recommender systems. In *CHI '06 extended abstracts on Human factors in computing systems*, CHI EA '06, pages 1097–1101, New York, NY, USA, 2006. ACM.

[11] D. W. Oard and J. Kim. Implicit feedback for recommender systems. In *Proceedings of the AAAI Workshop on Recommender Systems*, pages 81–83, 1998.

[12] A. Paterek. Improving regularized singular value decomposition for collaborative filtering. In *Proceedings of KDD Cup and Workshop*, pages 39–42, 2007.

[13] B. Sarwar, G. Karypis, J. Konstan, and J. Riedl. Application of dimensionality reduction in recommender system – a case study. In *Proceedings of the ACM WebKDD Workshop*, 2000.

[14] B. Sarwar, G. Karypis, J. Konstan, and J. Riedl. Item-based collaborative filtering recommendation algorithms. In *Proceedings of the 10th international conference on World Wide Web*, WWW '01, pages 285–295, New York, NY, USA, 2001. ACM.

[15] G. Shani and A. Gunawardana. Evaluating recommendation systems. *Recommender Systems Handbook*, pages 257–297, 2011.

[16] M. Turk and A. Pentland. Eigenfaces for recognition. *J. Cognitive Neuroscience*, 3(1):71–86, Jan. 1991.

[17] G. K. Zipf. *Human Behavior and the Principle of Least Effort.* Addison-Wesley, 1949.

Differentially Private Transit Data Publication: A Case Study on the Montreal Transportation System

Rui Chen
Concordia University
Montreal, QC, Canada
ru_che@encs.concordia.ca

Benjamin C. M. Fung
Concordia University
Montreal, QC, Canada
Benjamin.Fung@concordia.ca

Bipin C. Desai
Concordia University
Montreal, QC, Canada
BipinC.Desai@concordia.ca

Nériah M. Sossou
Société de transport de Montréal
Montreal, QC, Canada
Neriah.Sossou@stm.info

ABSTRACT

With the wide deployment of smart card automated fare collection (SCAFC) systems, public transit agencies have been benefiting from huge volume of transit data, a kind of sequential data, collected every day. Yet, improper publishing and use of transit data could jeopardize passengers' privacy. In this paper, we present our solution to transit data publication under the rigorous *differential privacy* model for the *Société de transport de Montréal* (STM). We propose an efficient *data-dependent* yet differentially private transit data sanitization approach based on a *hybrid-granularity* prefix tree structure. Moreover, as a post-processing step, we make use of the inherent consistency constraints of a prefix tree to conduct constrained inferences, which lead to better utility. Our solution not only applies to general sequential data, but also can be seamlessly extended to trajectory data. To our best knowledge, this is the first paper to introduce a practical solution for publishing large volume of sequential data under differential privacy. We examine data utility in terms of two popular data analysis tasks conducted at the STM, namely count queries and frequent sequential pattern mining. Extensive experiments on real-life STM datasets confirm that our approach maintains high utility and is scalable to large datasets.

Categories and Subject Descriptors

H.2.7 [**Database Administration**]: [Security, integrity, and protection]; H.2.8 [**Database Applications**]: [Data mining]

General Terms

Algorithms, Performance, Security

Keywords

Differential privacy, transit data, non-interactive release, data mining

1. INTRODUCTION

Over the last few years, smart card automated fare collection (SCAFC) systems have been increasingly deployed in transportation systems as a secure method of user validation and fare collection. These systems generate and collect passengers' transit data every day, which, after being anonymized, needs to be shared for various reasons, such as administrative regulations, profit sharing and data analysis. Transit data usually contains individual-specific sensitive information, and publishing raw data would directly violate passengers' privacy. In this paper, we study the real-life transit data publishing scenario at the *Société de transport de Montréal* (STM, http://www.stm.info), the public transport agency in Montréal area, and propose an efficient solution to publishing transit data under the rigorous *differential privacy* model [10] while satisfying the data utility requirements specified by the STM.

The STM deployed SCAFC systems in its transportation network in 2008. Transit information, such as smart card number and station ID, is collected when a passenger swipes his smart card at a SCAFC terminal, and is then stored in a central database management system, where the transit information of a passenger is organized as a sequence of stations in time order, a kind of *sequential data* (see a formal definition in Section 3). The deployment of SCAFC systems allows the seamless integration with other transit networks of neighboring cities, for example, the *Agence métropolitaine de transport* (AMT), which consequently requires data sharing among several collaborating parties. In addition, periodically, the IT department of the STM shares transit data with other departments, e.g., the marketing department, for basic data analysis, and publishes its transit data to external research institutions for more complex data analysis tasks, such as marketing analysis [28], customer behavior analysis [4], and demand forecasting [28].

According to its preliminary research [4], [20], [5], the STM can substantially benefit from transit data analysis at strategic, tactical, and operational levels. Yet, it has also realized that the nature of transit data is raising major privacy concerns on the part of card users in information sharing [20]. This fact has been an obstacle to conducting further data analysis much less performing regular commercial operations. In this paper, we aim to provide a practical solution to such a real-life transit data sharing scenario. We point out that our solution also benefits many other sectors, for example cell phone communication and credit card payment, which have been facing a similar dilemma in sequential data publishing and individual privacy protection.

Previous efforts have been made in addressing the problem of transit data publication at the STM. Chen et al. [6] propose local suppression techniques based on the $(K, C)_L$-privacy model (a composition of k-anonymity [26] and confidence bounding [27]). However, recent works have shown that *partition-based* privacy models, for example k-anonymity and confidence bounding, are vulnerable to many types of privacy attacks, such as *composition attack* [14], *deFinetti attack* [18] and *foreground knowledge attack* [29], demonstrating their vulnerability to an adversary's background knowledge. Due to their deterministic nature, it is foreseeable that more types of privacy attacks could be discovered on these privacy models in the future. For this reason, we employ *differential privacy* [10], one of the strongest privacy models. Differential privacy provides provable privacy guarantees independent of an adversary's background knowledge and computational power (this claim may not be valid in some special cases [19], but is still correct for the STM case, as discussed in Section 4.3).

Traditional differentially private *non-interactive* approaches [3], [11], [31] are *data-independent* in the sense that all possible entries in the output domain need to be *explicitly* considered no matter what the underlying database is. For high-dimensional data, such as transit data, this is computationally infeasible. Consider a transit database $\mathcal{D}$ with all stations drawn from a universe of size m. Suppose the maximum length of a record (the number of stations in a record) in $\mathcal{D}$ is l. These approaches need to generate $\sum_{i=1}^{l} m^i = \frac{m^{l+1}-m}{m-1}$ output entries. For a STM transit database with $m = 1,000$ and $l = 20$, it requires to generate 10^{60} entries. Hence, these approaches are not computationally applicable with today's systems to real-life transit databases.

To tackle the challenge, we develop a *data-dependent* solution by extending the ideas proposed in two very recent papers [23], [7]. The general idea of a data-dependent solution is to adaptively narrow down the output domain by using *noisy* answers obtained from the underlying database. However, the methods in [23], [7] cannot be directly applied to sequential data for two reasons. First, the inherent sequentiality of sequential data is not considered in [23], [7]. Second, the methods only work for *sets*, yet a record in a sequential database may contain a *bag* of locations. Therefore, non-trivial efforts are needed to develop a differentially private data publishing approach for sequential data.

Protecting individual privacy is one aspect of sanitizing data. Another equally important aspect is preserving utility in sanitized data for data analysis. In this paper, we consider two important data mining tasks conducted at the STM, namely *count queries* (see a formal definition in Section 3.3) and *frequent sequential pattern mining* [2]. Count queries, as a general data analysis task, are the building block of many advanced data mining tasks. In the STM case, with accurate answers to count queries, data recipients can answer questions, such as "how many passengers have visited both stations *Guy-Concordia* and *McGill* [1]". Frequent sequential pattern mining, as a concrete data mining task, helps, for example, the STM better understand passengers' transit patterns and consequently allows the STM to adjust its network geometry and schedules in order to better utilize its existing resources.

Contribution. This is the first paper that introduces a practical solution for publishing large volume of real-life sequential data via differential privacy in the *non-interactive* setting. We summarize the major contributions of the paper as follows. First, we study the real-life transit data sharing scenario at the STM and propose an efficient sanitization algorithm to generate a differentially private sequential data release by making use of a *hybrid-granularity* prefix tree. We design a statistical process for efficiently constructing such a noisy prefix tree under Laplace mechanism, which is vital to the scalability of our solution. We emphasize that our approach can be seamlessly extended to trajectory data (see Section 4.4). Second, we make use of two sets of inherent constraints of a prefix tree to conduct constrained inferences, which helps generate a more accurate release. Third, we conduct an extensive experimental study over different real-life STM datasets. We examine utility of sanitized data for two different data mining tasks performed by the STM, namely count queries (a generic data analysis task) and frequent sequential pattern mining (a concrete data mining task). Experimental results demonstrate that our approach maintains high utility and is scalable to large volume of real-life sequential data.

[1] *Guy-Concordia* and *McGill* are two metro stations on the green line of the STM metro network.

2. RELATED WORK

More broadly, sequential data can be considered as a special kind of trajectory data. There have been some recent works [1], [27], [32], [17], [13], [6], [24] on privacy-preserving sequential (trajectory) data publishing based on partition-based privacy models. Abul et al. [1] propose the (k, δ)-anonymity model based on the inherent imprecision of sampling and positioning systems, where δ represents possible location imprecision. Terrovitis and Mamoulis [27] model an adversary's background knowledge as a set of projections of sequences in a sequential database, and consequently propose a data suppression technique that limits the confidence of inferring the presence of a location in a sequence to a pre-defined probability threshold. Yarovoy et al. [32] propose to k-anonymize a moving object database (MOD) by considering timestamps as the quasi-identifiers (QIDs). Adversaries are assumed to launch privacy attacks based on *attack graphs*. Monreale et al. [24] present an approach based on spatial generalization in order to achieve k-anonymity. The novelty of their approach lies in a generalization scheme that depends on the underlying trajectory dataset rather than a fixed grid hierarchy.

Hu et al. [17] present the problem of k-anonymizing a trajectory database with respect to a sensitive event database. The goal is to make sure that every event is shared by at least k users. Specifically, they develop a new generalization mechanism known as *local enlargement*. Fung et al. [13] propose the $(K, C)_L$-privacy model that thwarts both identity linkages on trajectory data and attribute linkages via trajectory data. Based on the $(K, C)_L$-privacy model, Chen et al. [6] develop a generic solution for various data utility metrics by use of *local suppression*. Compared to all these approaches [1], [27], [32], [17], [13], [6], [24], the major contribution of our paper is the use of differential privacy, which provides significantly stronger privacy guarantees.

In the last few years, differential privacy has emerged as the de facto successor to partition-based privacy models. Currently most of the research on differential privacy concentrates on the *interactive setting*. Dwork [9] provides an overview of recent works on differential privacy in the interactive setting.

The works closest to ours are by Blum et al. [3], Dwork et al. [11], Xiao et al. [31], Mohammed et al. [23], and Chen et al. [7]. All these works consider *non-interactive* data publishing under differential privacy. Blum et al. [3] demonstrate that it is possible to release *synthetic* private databases that are useful for all queries over a discretized domain from a concept class with polynomial Vapnik-Chervonenkis dimension. However, their mechanism is not efficient, taking runtime complexity of $superpoly(|\mathcal{C}|, |I|)$, where $|\mathcal{C}|$ is the size of a concept class and $|I|$ the size of the universe. Dwork et al. [11] propose a recursive algorithm of generating a *synthetic* database with runtime complexity of $poly(|\mathcal{C}|, |I|)$. This improvement, however, is still insufficient to handle real-life sequential

Table 1: Sample sequential database

Rec. #	Path
1	$L_1 \to L_2 \to L_3$
2	$L_1 \to L_2$
3	$L_3 \to L_2 \to L_1$
4	$L_1 \to L_2 \to L_4$
5	$L_1 \to L_2 \to L_3$
6	$L_3 \to L_2$
7	$L_1 \to L_2 \to L_4 \to L_1$
8	$L_3 \to L_1$

datasets due to the exponential size of $|\mathcal{C}|$. Xiao et al. [31] propose a wavelet-transformation based approach for *relational data* to lower the magnitude of noise, rather than adding independent Laplace noise.

Two very recent papers [23], [7] point out that data-dependent approaches are more efficient and more effective for generating a differentially private release. Mohammed et al. [23] propose a generalization-based sanitization algorithm for *relational data* with the goal of classification analysis. Chen et al. [7] propose a probabilistic top-down partitioning algorithm for *set-valued data*. Due to the reasons mentioned in Section 1, they cannot be directly applied to sequential data.

3. PRELIMINARIES

Let $\mathcal{L} = \{L_1, L_2, \cdots, L_{|\mathcal{L}|}\}$ be the universe of locations, where $|\mathcal{L}|$ is the size of the universe. Without loss of generality, we consider locations as discrete spatial areas in a map. For STM transit data, $\mathcal{L}$ represents all stations in the STM transportation network. Each record in a sequential database consists of a *sequence* of time-ordered locations drawn from this universe. Formally, a sequence S of length $|S|$ is an ordered list of locations $S = L_1 \to L_2 \to \cdots \to L_{|S|}$, where $\forall 1 \le i \le |S|$, $L_i \in \mathcal{L}$. A location may occur multiple times in S, and may occur consecutively in S.

A sequential database $\mathcal{D}$ of size $|\mathcal{D}|$ is composed of a multiset of sequences $\mathcal{D} = \{S_1, S_2, \cdots, S_{|\mathcal{D}|}\}$. Each sequence represents the movement history of a record owner. Table 1 presents a sample sequential database with $\mathcal{L} = \{L_1, L_2, L_3, L_4\}$.

3.1 Prefix Tree

A sequential database can be represented in a more compact way in terms of a *prefix tree*. A prefix tree groups sequences with the same prefix into the same branch. A sequence $S' = L'_1 \to L'_2 \to \cdots \to L'_{|S'|}$ is a prefix of a sequence $S = L_1 \to L_2 \to \cdots \to L_{|S|}$, denoted by $S' \preceq S$, if and only if $|S'| \le |S|$ and $\forall 1 \le i \le |S'|$, $L'_i = L_i$. For example, $L_1 \to L_2$ is a prefix of $L_1 \to L_2 \to L_4 \to L_3$, but $L_1 \to L_4$ is *not*. We formally define a prefix tree below.

DEFINITION 3.1 (PREFIX TREE). A prefix tree $\mathcal{PT}$ of a sequential database $\mathcal{D}$ is a triplet $\mathcal{PT} = (V, E, Root)$, where V is the set of nodes labeled with locations, each corresponding to a unique prefix in $\mathcal{D}$; E is the set of edges, representing transitions between nodes; $Root \in V$ is the virtual root of $\mathcal{PT}$. The unique prefix represented by a node $v \in V$, denoted by $prefix(v, \mathcal{PT})$, is a sequence of locations starting from $Root$ to v. ■

Each node $v \in V$ keeps a doublet in the form of $\langle tr(v), c(v)\rangle$, where $tr(v)$ is the set of sequences in $\mathcal{D}$ having $prefix(v, \mathcal{PT})$, that is, $\{S \in \mathcal{D} : prefix(v, \mathcal{PT}) \preceq S\}$, and $c(v)$ is a noisy version of $|tr(v)|$ (e.g., $|tr(v)|$ plus Laplace noise). $tr(Root)$ contains

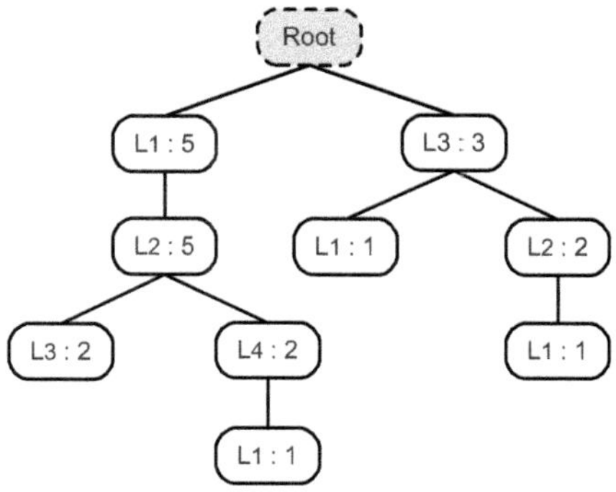

Figure 1: The prefix tree of the sample data

all sequences in $\mathcal{D}$. We call the set of all nodes of $\mathcal{PT}$ at a given depth i a *level* of $\mathcal{PT}$, denoted by $level(i, \mathcal{PT})$. $Root$ is at depth zero. When $\mathcal{PT}$ is clear in the context, it is omitted in the notation. Figure 1 illustrates the prefix tree of the sample database in Table 1, where each node v is labeled with its location and $|tr(v)|$.

3.2 Differential Privacy

Differential privacy, in general, requires that the removal or addition of a single database record does not significantly affect the outcome of any analysis based on the database. Therefore, for a record owner, any privacy breach will not be a result of participating in the database since anything that can be learned from the database with his record can also be learned from the one without his record. We formally define differential privacy in the *non-interactive* setting [3] as follow.

DEFINITION 3.2 (DIFFERENTIAL PRIVACY). A privacy mechanism $\mathcal{A}$ gives ϵ-differential privacy if for any database $\mathcal{D}_1$ and $\mathcal{D}_2$ differing on at most one record, and for any possible sanitized database $\widetilde{\mathcal{D}} \in Range(\mathcal{A})$,

$$Pr[\mathcal{A}(\mathcal{D}_1) = \widetilde{\mathcal{D}}] \le e^{\epsilon} \times Pr[\mathcal{A}(\mathcal{D}_2) = \widetilde{\mathcal{D}}] \quad (1)$$

where the probability is taken over the randomness of $\mathcal{A}$. ■

Two principal techniques for achieving differential privacy are *Laplace mechanism* [10] and *exponential mechanism* [22]. A fundamental concept of both techniques is the *global sensitivity* of a function [10] mapping underlying databases to (vectors of) reals.

DEFINITION 3.3 (GLOBAL SENSITIVITY). For any function $f : \mathcal{D} \to \mathbb{R}^d$, the sensitivity of f is

$$\Delta f = \max_{\mathcal{D}_1, \mathcal{D}_2} ||f(\mathcal{D}_1) - f(\mathcal{D}_2)||_1 \quad (2)$$

for all $\mathcal{D}_1, \mathcal{D}_2$ differing in at most one record. ■

Laplace Mechanism. For the analysis whose outputs are real, a standard mechanism to achieve differential privacy is to add Laplace noise to the true output of a function. Dwork et al. [10] propose the Laplace mechanism which takes as inputs a database $\mathcal{D}$, a function f, and the privacy parameter ϵ. The noise is generated according to a Laplace distribution with the probability density function (pdf) $p(x|\lambda) = \frac{1}{2\lambda} e^{-|x|/\lambda}$, where λ is determined by both Δf and the desired privacy parameter ϵ.

THEOREM 3.1. *For any function $f : \mathcal{D} \to \mathbb{R}^d$, the mechanism $\mathcal{A}$*

$$\mathcal{A}(\mathcal{D}) = f(\mathcal{D}) + Laplace(\Delta f/\epsilon) \quad (3)$$

gives ϵ-differential privacy. ■

Exponential Mechanism. For the analysis whose outputs are not real or make no sense after adding noise, McSherry and Talwar [22] propose the exponential mechanism that selects an output from the output domain, $r \in \mathcal{R}$, by taking into consideration its score of a given utility function q in a differentially private manner. The exponential mechanism assigns exponentially greater probabilities of being selected to outputs of higher scores so that the final output would be close to the optimum with respect to q. The chosen utility function q should be insensitive to changes of any particular record, that is, has a low sensitivity. Let the sensitivity of q be $\Delta q = \max_{\forall r, \mathcal{D}_1, \mathcal{D}_2} |q(\mathcal{D}_1, r) - q(\mathcal{D}_2, r)|$.

THEOREM 3.2. *Given a utility function $q : (\mathcal{D} \times \mathcal{R}) \rightarrow \mathbb{R}$ for a database $\mathcal{D}$, the mechanism $\mathcal{A}$,*

$$\mathcal{A}(\mathcal{D}, q) = \left\{ return\ r\ with\ probability \propto exp(\frac{\epsilon q(\mathcal{D}, r)}{2\Delta q}) \right\} \tag{4}$$

gives ϵ-differential privacy. ■

3.3 Utility Requirements

In the STM case, sanitized data is mainly used to perform two data mining tasks, namely *count query* and *frequent sequential pattern mining* [2]. Count queries, as a general data analysis task, are the building block of many data mining tasks.

DEFINITION 3.4 (COUNT QUERY). For a given set of locations $\mathbb{L}$ drawn from the universe $\mathcal{L}$, a count query Q over a database $\mathcal{D}$ is defined to be $Q(\mathcal{D}) = |\{S \in \mathcal{D} : \mathbb{L} \subseteq ls(S)\}|$, where $ls(S)$ returns the set of locations in S. ■

Note that sequentiality among locations is not considered in count queries, because the major users of count queries are, for example, the personnel of the marketing department of the STM, who are merely interested in users' presence in certain stations for marketing analysis, known as *passenger counting*, but *not* the sequentiality of visiting. Instead, the preservation of sequentiality in sanitized data is examined by frequent sequential pattern mining. We measure the utility of a count query Q over the sanitized database $\widetilde{\mathcal{D}}$ by its *relative error* [31], [30], [7] with respect to the true result over the original database $\mathcal{D}$, which is computed as:

$$error(Q(\widetilde{\mathcal{D}})) = \frac{|Q(\widetilde{\mathcal{D}}) - Q(\mathcal{D})|}{max\{Q(\mathcal{D}), s\}},$$

where s is a *sanity bound* used to mitigate the influences of queries with extremely small *selectivities* [31], [30], [7].

For frequent sequential pattern mining, we measure the utility of sanitized data in terms of *true positive* (TP), *false positive* (FP) and *false drop* (FD) [12]. Given a positive number k, we denote the set of top k most frequent sequential patterns with size greater than 1 [2] on the original database $\mathcal{D}$ by $\mathcal{F}_k(\mathcal{D})$ and the set of frequent sequential patterns on the sanitized database $\widetilde{\mathcal{D}}$ by $\mathcal{F}_k(\widetilde{\mathcal{D}})$. True positive is the number of frequent sequential patterns in $\mathcal{F}_k(\mathcal{D})$ that are correctly identified in $\mathcal{F}_k(\widetilde{\mathcal{D}})$, that is, $|\mathcal{F}_k(\mathcal{D}) \cap \mathcal{F}_k(\widetilde{\mathcal{D}})|$. False positive is the number of infrequent sequential patterns in $\mathcal{D}$ that are mistakenly included in $\mathcal{F}_k(\widetilde{\mathcal{D}})$, that is, $|\mathcal{F}_k(\widetilde{\mathcal{D}}) - \mathcal{F}_k(\mathcal{D}) \cap \mathcal{F}_k(\widetilde{\mathcal{D}})|$. False drop is the number of frequent sequential patterns in $\mathcal{F}_k(\mathcal{D})$ that are wrongly omitted in $\mathcal{F}_k(\widetilde{\mathcal{D}})$, that is, $|\mathcal{F}_k(\mathcal{D}) \cup \mathcal{F}_k(\widetilde{\mathcal{D}}) - \mathcal{F}_k(\widetilde{\mathcal{D}})|$. Since in our setting $|\mathcal{F}_k(\mathcal{D})| = |\mathcal{F}_k(\widetilde{\mathcal{D}})| = k$, false positives always equal false drops.

[2]Nearly every single location forms a size-1 frequent sequential pattern.

Algorithm 1 Sequential Data Sanitization Algorithm

Input: Raw sequential dataset $\mathcal{D}$
Input: Privacy budget ϵ
Input: Height of the prefix tree h
Input: Location taxonomy tree $\mathcal{T}$
Output: Sanitized dataset $\widetilde{\mathcal{D}}$
1: Noisy prefix tree $\mathcal{PT} \leftarrow BuildNoisyPrefixTree(\mathcal{D}, \epsilon, h, \mathcal{T})$;
2: Sanitized dataset $\widetilde{\mathcal{D}} \leftarrow GeneratePrivateRelease(\mathcal{PT})$;
3: **return** $\widetilde{\mathcal{D}}$;

4. SANITIZATION ALGORITHM

We first provide an overview of our two-step sanitization algorithm in Algorithm 1. Given a raw sequential dataset $\mathcal{D}$, a privacy budget ϵ, a user specified height of the prefix tree h and a location taxonomy tree $\mathcal{T}$, it returns a sanitized dataset $\widetilde{\mathcal{D}}$ satisfying ϵ-differential privacy. *BuildNoisyPrefixTree* constructs a *noisy hybrid-granularity* prefix tree $\mathcal{PT}$ of $\mathcal{D}$ using a set of count queries based on the given taxonomy tree $\mathcal{T}$, which defines multiple levels of granularities over the location universe. It can be either public knowledge or generated from the location universe on-the-fly by specifying a fan-out value. In the STM case, we use a two-level taxonomy tree where each station can be generalized to the metro/bus line on which it locates. For the simplicity of illustration, we give our algorithm based on a two-level taxonomy tree. The extension to a multiple-level taxonomy tree is straightforward. *GeneratePrivateRelease* employs utility boosting techniques on $\mathcal{PT}$ based on two sets of consistency constraints, and then generates a differentially private release.

4.1 Noisy Prefix Tree Construction

Our strategy for *BuildNoisyPrefixTree* is to recursively group sequences in $\mathcal{D}$ into *disjoint* sub-datasets based on their prefixes. Procedure 1 presents the details of *BuildNoisyPrefixTree*. We first create a prefix tree $\mathcal{PT}$ with a virtual root *Root* (Lines 2-3). To build $\mathcal{PT}$, we employ a *uniform* privacy budget allocation scheme, that is, divide the total privacy budget ϵ into equal portions $\bar{\epsilon} = \frac{\epsilon}{h}$, each is used for constructing a level of $\mathcal{PT}$ (Line 4). In Lines 6-20, we iteratively construct each level of $\mathcal{PT}$ in a noisy way.

To satisfy differential privacy, we need to guarantee that every sequence that can be derived from the location universe (either in or not in $\mathcal{D}$) has a non-zero probability to appear in the noisy prefix tree. Therefore, at each level, for each node, we need to consider *every* possible location as its potential child. Our goal is to identify the children that are associated with non-zero number of sequences (referred to as *non-empty node*) so that we can continue to expand them. Here decisions have to be made based on noisy counts.

In order to achieve good utility, it is critical to prune out nodes associated with zero number of sequences (*empty node*) reliably as early as possible. For this reason, instead of using a simple prefix tree, we divide a level of $\mathcal{PT}$ into two sub-levels with different location granularities. The first sub-level consists of nodes associated with *generalized* location information (*generalized node*), and then, depending on noisy counts of these nodes, we decide whether to further expand them to create the second sub-level in which nodes are associated with non-generalized locations (e.g., ask the noisy count of passengers in a metro line and then decide whether to ask the count of each station on this line). $\bar{\epsilon}$ is then allocated to the two sub-levels as a function of the fan-out f of the location taxonomy tree $\mathcal{T}$: the first sub-level receives $\bar{\epsilon}_1 = \frac{2\bar{\epsilon}}{f}$ and the second receives $\bar{\epsilon}_2 = \frac{(f-2)\bar{\epsilon}}{f}$. One important observation is that all nodes on the same sub-level are associated with *disjoint* sequence subsets, and

Procedure 1 $BuildNoisyPrefixTree$ Procedure

Input: Raw sequential dataset $\mathcal{D}$
Input: Privacy budget ϵ
Input: Height of the prefix tree h
Input: Location taxonomy tree $\mathcal{T}$
Output: Noisy prefix tree $\mathcal{PT}$

$i = 0$;
Create a prefix tree $\mathcal{PT}$ with a virtual root $Root$;
Add all sequences in $\mathcal{D}$ to $tr(Root)$;
$\bar{\epsilon} = \frac{\epsilon}{h}$;
Calculate $\bar{\epsilon}_1$ and $\bar{\epsilon}_2$ s.t. $\bar{\epsilon}_1 + \bar{\epsilon}_2 = \bar{\epsilon}$;
while $i < h$ **do**
  for each non-generalized node $v \in level(i)$ **do**
    $\mathcal{U}_g \leftarrow$ the set of generalized nodes from $\mathcal{T}$;
    for each node $u \in \mathcal{U}_g$ **do**
      Add sequences S with $prefix(u) \preceq S$ to $tr(u)$;
      $c(u) = NoisyCount(|tr(u)|, \bar{\epsilon}_1)$;
      if $c(u) \geq \theta_g$ **then**
        Add u to $\mathcal{PT}$;
        $\mathcal{U}_{ng} \leftarrow u$'s non-generalized children in $\mathcal{T}$;
        for each node $w \in \mathcal{U}_{ng}$ **do**
          Add sequences S with $prefix(w) \preceq S$ to $tr(w)$;
          $c(w) = NoisyCount(|tr(w)|, \bar{\epsilon}_2)$;
          if $c(w) \geq \theta_{ng}$ **then**
            Add w to $\mathcal{PT}$;
  $i{+}{+}$;
return $\mathcal{PT}$;

therefore the privacy budget allocated to a sub-level can be used *in full* for each node in it. We provide formal analysis on utility improvement of a hybrid-granularity prefix tree after presenting Theorem 4.1.

For a dataset with a very large location universe $\mathcal{L}$, processing all locations explicitly may be slow. We provide an efficient implementation by *separately* handling potential non-empty and empty nodes. For a non-empty node u, we add Laplace noise to $|tr(u)|$ and use the noisy answer $c(u)$ to decide if it is non-empty. If $c(u)$ is greater than or equal to the pre-defined threshold θ, we deem that u is non-empty and insert u to $\mathcal{PT}$. In the STM case, the threshold of a non-generalized node $\theta_{ng} = \frac{2\sqrt{2}}{\bar{\epsilon}_2}$ (two times of the standard deviation of noise) while the threshold of a generalized node $\theta_g = \frac{4\sqrt{2}}{\bar{\epsilon}_1}$. Intuitively, this setting more reliably eliminates empty nodes while having very limited effect on non-empty nodes. Since non-empty nodes are typically of a small number, this process can be done efficiently.

For empty nodes, we need to conduct a series of *independent* boolean tests, each calculates $NoisyCount(0, \bar{\epsilon}')$ to check if it passes θ, where $\bar{\epsilon}'$ is the privacy budget assigned to a node (either $\bar{\epsilon}_1$ or $\bar{\epsilon}_2$). The number of empty nodes that pass θ, k, follows the *binomial distribution* $B(m, p_\theta)$, where m is the total number of empty nodes we need to check and p_θ is the probability for a single experiment to succeed. We design a statistical process for Laplace mechanism to directly extract k empty nodes without explicitly processing every empty node. This is inspired by [8], in which a statistical process is designed for *geometric mechanism* [15].

THEOREM 4.1. *Independently conducting m pass/not pass experiments based on Laplace mechanism with privacy budget $\bar{\epsilon}'$ and threshold θ is equivalent to the following steps: 1) generate a value k from the binomial distribution $B(m, p_\theta)$, where $p_\theta = \frac{exp(-\bar{\epsilon}'\theta)}{2}$; 2) select k uniformly random empty nodes without replacement with noisy counts sampled from the distribution*

$$P(x) = \begin{cases} 0 & \forall x < \theta \\ 1 - exp(\bar{\epsilon}'\theta - \bar{\epsilon}'x) & \forall x \geq \theta \end{cases} \blacksquare$$

Proof. The probability of a single experiment passing the threshold θ is

$$Pr[PASS] = \int_\theta^\infty \frac{\bar{\epsilon}'}{2} exp(-\bar{\epsilon}'x)dx = \frac{exp(-\bar{\epsilon}'\theta)}{2}.$$

Since the experiments are independent, the number of successful experiments, k, follows the binomial distribution $B(m, \frac{exp(-\bar{\epsilon}'\theta)}{2})$. Once k is determined, we can uniformly at random select k empty nodes. The probability density function of the noisy counts x for the k empty nodes, conditional on $x \geq \theta$, is:

$$p(x|x \geq \theta) = \begin{cases} 0 & \forall x < \theta \\ \frac{\frac{\bar{\epsilon}'}{2} exp(-\bar{\epsilon}'x)}{p_\theta} = \bar{\epsilon}' exp(\bar{\epsilon}'\theta - \bar{\epsilon}'x) & \forall x \geq \theta \end{cases}$$

The corresponding cumulative distribution function is:

$$P(x) = \begin{cases} 0 & \forall x < \theta \\ \int_\theta^x \bar{\epsilon}' exp(\bar{\epsilon}'\theta - \bar{\epsilon}'x)dx = 1 - exp(\bar{\epsilon}'\theta - \bar{\epsilon}'x) & \forall x \geq \theta \end{cases} \blacksquare$$

Now we give a theoretical analysis on the utility improvement due to a hybrid-granularity prefix tree in terms of reduction of number of empty non-generalized nodes that are mistakenly generated. This number directly reflects the level of noise in sanitized data.

THEOREM 4.2. *For an empty node v at level i, a noisy hybrid-granularity prefix tree of height h reduces the number of empty non-generalized nodes mistakenly generated due to identifying v as non-empty by a factor of $O(2^{h-i} exp(4\sqrt{2}(h-i)))$.* $\blacksquare$

Proof. From Theorem 4.1, we learn that $p_{\theta_{ng}} = \frac{exp(-2\sqrt{2})}{2}$ and $p_{\theta_g} = \frac{exp(-4\sqrt{2})}{2}$. Consider an empty node v at level i. In a simple noisy prefix tree, if v is mistakenly considered as non-empty, the expected value of number of descendants of v, which are all empty nodes, is $\mathbb{E}_1 = (|\mathcal{L}| p_{\theta_{ng}})^{h-i}$. In a hybrid-granularity prefix tree, the expected value of number of descendants of v is

$$\mathbb{E}_2 = (f p_{\theta_{ng}})(\frac{|\mathcal{L}|}{f} p_{\theta_g} \cdot f p_{\theta_{ng}})^{h-i} = (f p_{\theta_{ng}})(|\mathcal{L}| p_{\theta_g} p_{\theta_{ng}})^{h-i}.$$

where f is the fan-out of the location taxonomy tree. This implies a reduction of

$$\frac{\mathbb{E}_1}{\mathbb{E}_2} = \frac{1}{f p_{\theta_{ng}} p_{\theta_g}^{h-i}} = O(2^{h-i} exp(4\sqrt{2}(h-i))). \blacksquare$$

EXAMPLE 4.1. Consider the sequential database $\mathcal{D}$ in Table 1, the height $h = 2$, and the calculated threshold $\theta = 3$. Suppose that L_1 and L_2 can be generalized to $L_{\{1,2\}}$ and L_3 and L_4 can be generalized to $L_{\{3,4\}}$. The construction of a possible noisy hybrid-granularity prefix tree $\mathcal{PT}$ is illustrated in Figure 2. A path of $\mathcal{PT}$ may be of a length shorter than h if it has been considered "empty" before h is reached. $\blacksquare$

4.2 Private Release Generation

We can generate the sanitized database by traversing $\mathcal{PT}$ once in *postorder* (ignore generalized nodes), calculating the number n of sequences terminated at each non-generalized node v and appending n copies of $prefix(v, \mathcal{PT})$ to the output. However, due to the noise added to ensure differential privacy, we may not be able to obtain a meaningful and consistent release. If we leave such inconsistencies unsolved, the resulting release may not be meaningful and therefore provides poor utility.

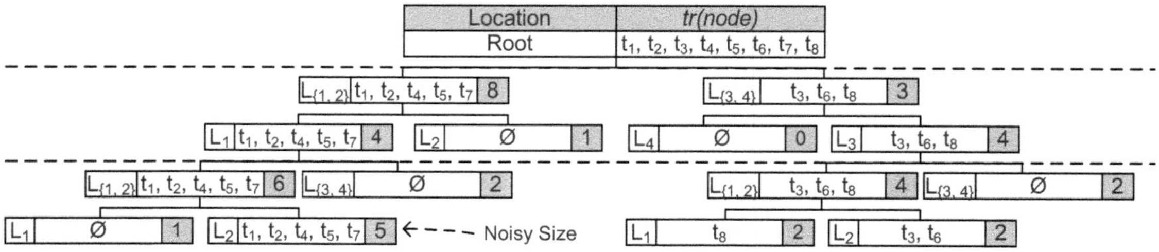

Figure 2: The noisy hybrid-granularity prefix tree of the sample data

DEFINITION 4.1 (CONSISTENCY CONSTRAINT). In a prefix tree, there exist two sets of consistency constraints:

1. For any root-to-leaf path p, $\forall v_i \in p, |tr(v_i)| \leq |tr(v_{i+1})|$, where v_i is a child of v_{i+1};
2. For each node v, $|tr(v)| \geq \sum_{u \in children(v)} |tr(u)|$. ■

Our goal is to enforce such consistency constraints on the noisy prefix tree (with all generalized nodes removed [3]) in order to produce a consistent and more accurate private release. We adapt the constrained inference technique proposed in [16] to adjust the noisy counts of nodes in the noisy prefix tree so that the constraints defined in Definition 4.1 are respected. Note that the technique proposed in [16] cannot be directly applied to our case because: 1) the noisy prefix tree has an irregular structure (rather than a complete tree with a fixed degree); 2) the noisy prefix tree has different constraints $|tr(v)| \geq \sum_{u \in children(v)} |tr(u)|$ (rather than $|tr(v)| = \sum_{u \in children(v)} |tr(u)|$). Consequently, we propose a two-phase procedure to obtain a *consistent* estimate with respect to Definition 4.1 for each node (except the virtual root) in the noisy prefix tree $\mathcal{PT}$.

We first generate an intermediate estimate for the noisy count of each node v (except the virtual root) in $\mathcal{PT}$. Consider a root-to-leaf path p of $\mathcal{PT}$. Let us organize the noisy counts of nodes $v_i \in p$ into a sequence $\mathcal{S} = \langle c(v_1), c(v_2), \cdots, c(v_{|p|})\rangle$, where v_i is a child of v_{i+1}. Let $mean[i,j]$ denote the mean of a subsequence of $\mathcal{S}$, $\langle c(v_i), c(v_{i+1}), ..., c(v_j)\rangle$, that is, $mean[i,j] = \frac{\sum_{m=i}^{j} c(v_m)}{j-i+1}$. We compute the intermediate estimate $\widetilde{\mathcal{S}}$ by Theorem 4.3 [16].

THEOREM 4.3. *Let* $I_m = min_{j \in [m,|p|]} max_{i \in [1,j]} mean[i,j]$ *and* $U_m = max_{i \in [1,m]} min_{j \in [i,|p|]} mean[i,j]$. *The minimum* L_2 *solution* $\widetilde{\mathcal{S}} = \langle I_1, I_2, ..., I_{|p|}\rangle = \langle U_1, U_2, ..., U_{|p|}\rangle$. ■

The result of Theorem 4.3 satisfies the first type of constraints in Definition 4.1. However, a node v in $\mathcal{PT}$ appears in $|leaves(v)|$ root-to-leaf paths, where $leaves(v)$ denotes the leaves of the subtree of $\mathcal{PT}$ rooted at v, and therefore, has $|leaves(v)|$ intermediate estimates, each being an independent observation of the true count $|tr(v)|$. We compute the *consolidated* intermediate estimate of v as the mean of the estimates, normally the best estimate for $|tr(v)|$. We denote the consolidated intermediate estimate of v by $\widetilde{c}(v)$.

After obtaining $\widetilde{c}(v)$ for each node v, we compute its consistent estimate $\bar{c}(v)$ in a top-down fashion as follows:

$$\bar{c}(v) = \begin{cases} \widetilde{c}(v) & if v \in level(1, \mathcal{PT}) \\ \widetilde{c}(v) + min(0, \frac{\bar{c}(w) - \sum_{u \in children(w)} \widetilde{c}(u)}{|children(w)|}) & otherwise \end{cases}$$

where w is the parent of v. It follows the intuition that the observation $\sum_{u \in children(w)} \widetilde{c}(u) > \bar{c}(w)$ is strong evidence that excessive noise is added to the children. Since the variance of noise in $\bar{c}(w)$ is approximately $|children(w)|$ times smaller than $\sum_{u \in children(w)} \widetilde{c}(u)$, it is reasonable to decrease the children's counts according to $\bar{c}(w)$. However, we never increase the children's counts based on $\bar{c}(w)$ because a large $\bar{c}(w)$ simply indicates that many sequences actually terminate at w. It is easy to see that the consistency constraints in Definition 4.1 are respected among consistent estimates, and therefore the proof is omitted here.

[3]The utility improvements of constrained inferences on a prefix tree with and without generalized nodes are almost identical.

4.3 Analysis

Privacy Analysis. Kifer and Machanavajjhala [19] point out that differential privacy must be applied with caution. The privacy protection provided by differential privacy relates to the data generating mechanism and deterministic aggregate-level background knowledge. In the STM case, transit data is independent of each other and no deterministic statistics of the raw database will ever be released. Hence differential privacy is appropriate for our problem. We now show that Algorithm 1 satisfies ϵ-differential privacy.

THEOREM 4.4. *Given the total privacy budget* ϵ, *Algorithm 1 ensures* ϵ*-differential privacy.* ■

Proof. Algorithm 1 consists of two steps, namely *BuildNoisyPrefixTree* and *GeneratePrivateRelease*. In the procedure *BuildNoisyPrefixTree*, our approach appeals to the well-understood query model to construct the noisy prefix tree $\mathcal{PT}$. Consider a level of $\mathcal{PT}$, which is composed of two sub-levels. Since all nodes on the same sub-level contain *disjoint* sets of sequences. According to the *parallel composition* (Theorem 4.5 [21]), the entire privacy budget needed for a sub-level is bounded by the worst case, that is, $\frac{2\bar{\epsilon}}{f}$ for the first sub-level and $\frac{(f-2)\bar{\epsilon}}{f}$ for the second sub-level.

THEOREM 4.5. *Let* $\mathcal{A}_i$ *each provide* ϵ_i*-differential privacy. A sequence of* $\mathcal{A}_i(\mathcal{D}_i)$ *over a set of disjoint datasets* $\mathcal{D}_i$ *provides* $max(\epsilon_i)$*-differential privacy.* ■

The use of privacy budget on different sub-levels follows *sequential composition* (Theorem 4.6 [21]).

THEOREM 4.6. *Let* $\mathcal{A}_i$ *each provide* ϵ_i*-differential privacy. A sequence of* $\mathcal{A}_i(\mathcal{D})$ *over the database* $\mathcal{D}$ *provides* $(\sum_i \epsilon_i)$*-differential privacy.* ■

Since there are at most h levels, the total privacy budget needed to build the noisy prefix tree $\leq h \times (\frac{2\bar{\epsilon}}{f} + \frac{(f-2)\bar{\epsilon}}{f}) = \epsilon$.

For the procedure *GeneratePrivateRelease*, we make use of the inherent constraints of a prefix tree to boost utility. The procedure only accesses a differentially private noisy prefix tree, not the underlying database. As proven by Hay et al. [16], a post-processing of differentially private results remains differentially private. Therefore, Algorithm 1 as a whole maintains ϵ-differential privacy. ■

Complexity Analysis. Algorithm 1 is of runtime complexity $O(|\mathcal{D}| \cdot |\mathcal{L}|)$, where $|\mathcal{D}|$ is the number of sequences in the input database $\mathcal{D}$ and $|\mathcal{L}|$ is the size of the location universe. For *BuildNoisyPrefixTree*, the major computational cost is node generation and sequence distribution. For each level of the noisy prefix tree, the number of

Table 2: Experimental dataset statistics.

Datasets	$\|\mathcal{D}\|$	$\|\mathcal{L}\|$	$max\|S\|$	$avg\|S\|$
Metro	847,668	68	90	4.21
Bus	778,724	944	121	5.67

nodes to generate approximates $k(1+\frac{1}{f})|\mathcal{D}|$, where $k \ll |\mathcal{L}|$ is a number depending on $|\mathcal{L}|$. For each level, we need to distribute *at most* $2|\mathcal{D}|$ sequences to the newly generated nodes. Hence, the complexity of constructing a single level is $O(|\mathcal{D}| \cdot |\mathcal{L}|)$. Therefore, the total runtime complexity of *BuildNoisyPrefixTree* for constructing a noisy prefix tree of height h is $O(h|\mathcal{D}| \cdot |\mathcal{L}|)$. In *GeneratePrivateRelease*, the complexity of calculating the intermediate estimates for a single root-to-leaf path is $O(h)$. Since there can be at most $|\mathcal{D}|$ distinct root-to-leaf paths, the complexity of computing all intermediate estimates is $O(h|\mathcal{D}|)$. To compute consistent estimates, we need to visit every node exactly twice, which is of complexity $O(|\mathcal{D}| \cdot |\mathcal{L}|)$. Similarly, the computational cost of generating the private release by traversing the noisy prefix tree once in postorder is $O(|\mathcal{D}| \cdot |\mathcal{L}|)$. Since h is a very small constant compared to $|\mathcal{D}|$ and $|\mathcal{L}|$, the total complexity of Algorithm 1 is $O(|\mathcal{D}| \cdot |\mathcal{L}|)$.

4.4 Extensions

Our solution can be seamlessly applied to trajectory data. A trajectory is composed of a sequence of *location-timestamp* pairs in the form of $loc_1t_1 \rightarrow loc_2t_2 \rightarrow \cdots \rightarrow loc_nt_n$, where $t_1 \leq t_2 \leq \cdots \leq t_n$. The time factor is often discretized into intervals at different levels of granularity, e.g., hour, which is typically determined by the data publisher. All timestamps of a trajectory database form a timestamp universe.

In this case, we can label each node in the prefix tree by both a location and a timestamp. Therefore, two trajectories with the same sequence of locations but different timestamps are considered different. Consequently, when constructing the noisy prefix tree, in order to expand a node loc_it_i, we have to consider the combinations of all locations and the timestamps in the time universe that are greater than t_i (because the timestamps in a trajectory are non-decreasing), resulting in a larger candidate set. Due to the efficient implementation we propose in Section 4.1, the computational cost will remain moderate.

5. EXPERIMENTAL EVALUATION

In this section, we examine the utility of sanitized data in terms of count queries and frequent sequential pattern mining, and evaluate the scalability of our approach for processing large-scale real-life data. In particular, we compare the utility improvements of the method using a hybrid-granularity prefix tree (referred to as *Hybrid*) over the method using a simple prefix tree (referred to as *Simple*). Our implementation was done in C++, and all experiments were performed on an Intel Core 2 Duo 2.26GHz PC with 2GB RAM. Extensive experiments were conducted on two real-life STM transit datasets, *Metro* and *Bus*, which record the transit history of passengers in the STM metro and bus networks, respectively. The characteristics of the datasets are summarized in Table 2, where $max|S|$ is the maximum sequence length and $avg|S|$ the average length.

5.1 Utility

Count Query. In our first set of experiments, we examine relative errors of count queries with respect to two different parameters, namely the privacy budget ϵ and the noisy prefix tree height h. We follow the evaluation scheme from previous works [31], [7]. For each privacy budget, we generate 40,000 random count queries

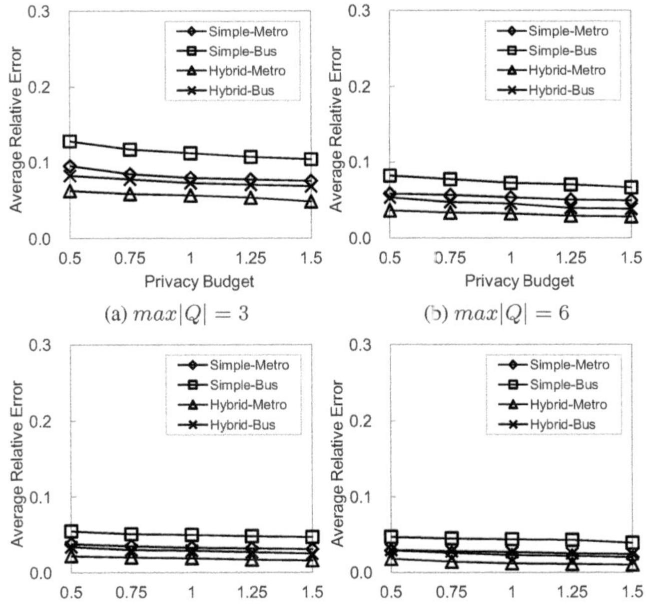

(a) $max|Q| = 3$ (b) $max|Q| = 6$ (c) $max|Q| = 9$ (d) $max|Q| = 12$

Figure 3: Average relative error vs. privacy budget.

with varying numbers of locations. We call the number of locations in a query the *length* of the query. We divide the query set into 4 subsets such that the query length of the i-th subset is uniformly distributed in $[1, \frac{ih}{4}]$ and each location is randomly drawn from the location universe $\mathcal{L}$. The sanity bound s is set to 0.1% of the dataset size, the same as [31], [7].

Figure 3 examines average relative errors under varying privacy budgets from 0.5 to 1.5 with $h = 12$. The X-axes represent the different query subsets by their maximum length $max|Q|$. As expected, the average relative errors decrease when ϵ increases because less noise is added and the construction process is more precise. In general, our approach maintains high utility for count queries. Even in the worst case ($\epsilon = 0.5$ and $max|Q| = 3$), the average relative error of *Hybrid* is still less than 8.2% on both datasets. Such level of relative errors is acceptable for data analysis at the STM. We can also observe that a hybrid-granularity structure can substantially reduce average relative errors (with 33%-48% improvement), especially on *Bus*, which is more sparse.

Figure 4 studies how average relative errors vary under different h values with maximum query length fixed to 6. We can observe that with the increase of h, the relative errors do not decrease monotonically. Initially, the relative errors decrease when h increases because the increment of h allows to retain more information from the underlying database. However, after a certain threshold, the relative errors become larger with the increase of h, because when h gets larger, the noise added to each level grows quickly. It is interesting to see that the hybrid-granularity structure indeed better eliminates noise, and makes relative errors less sensitive to varying h values. This allows a wider range of h values (e.g., 10-16) to be used in order to obtain desirable relative errors.

Frequent Sequential Pattern Mining. In the second set of experiments, we demonstrate the utility of sanitized data by frequent sequential pattern mining. Specifically, we employ PrefixSpan to mine frequent sequential patterns [4].

[4]An implementation of the PrefixSpan algorithm proposed in [25], available at http://code.google.com/p/prefixspan/.

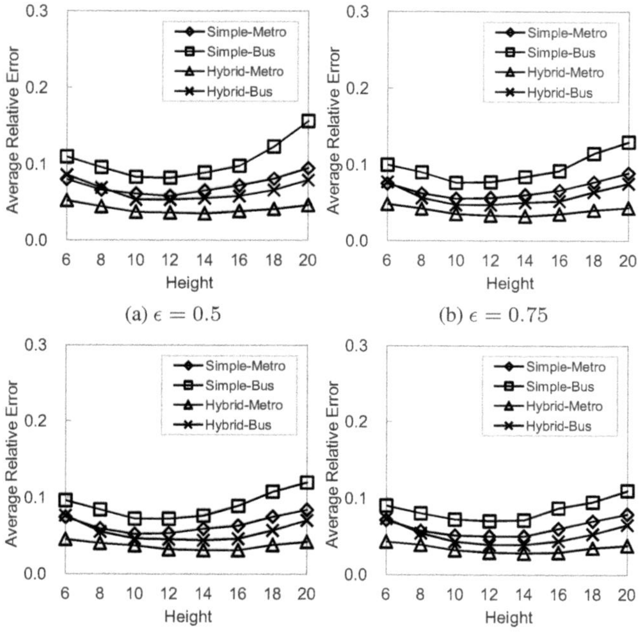

(a) $\epsilon = 0.5$ (b) $\epsilon = 0.75$

(c) $\epsilon = 1.0$ (d) $\epsilon = 1.25$

Figure 4: Average relative error vs. prefix tree height.

Table 3: Utility for frequent sequential pattern mining vs. k

k	TP (M/B) *Simple*	FP(FD) (M/B) *Simple*	TP (M/B) *Hybrid*	FP(FD) (M/B) *Hybrid*
100	99/97	1/3	100/100	0/0
150	143/139	7/11	149/144	1/6
200	178/168	22/32	185/177	15/23
250	209/195	41/55	220/209	30/41
300	241/212	59/88	257/233	43/67

Table 3 shows how the utility changes with different top k values while fixing $\epsilon = 1.0$ and $h = 12$. When $k = 100$, the sanitized data generated by *Hybrid* is able to give the exact top 100 most frequent patterns that are of size greater than 1. With the increase of k values, the *accuracy* (the ratio of true positive to k) decreases. However, even when $k = 300$, the accuracy of *Hybrid* is still as high as $257/300 = 85.7\%$ on *Metro* and $233/300 = 77.7\%$ on *Bus*. Again we can observe that $Hybrid$ always outperforms $Simple$ on both datasets under all k values. When $k = 300$, the improvement due to the hybrid-granularity structure is 6.6% on *Metro* and 9.9% on *Bus*.

Table 4 presents the utility for frequent sequential pattern mining under different ϵ values while fixing $h = 12$ and $k = 300$. Generally, larger privacy budgets lead to more true positives and fewer false positives (false drops). This conforms to the theoretical analysis that a larger privacy budget results in less noise and therefore a more accurate result. Since the most frequent sequential patterns are of small length, they have large supports from the underlying database. As a result, the utility is relatively insensitive to varying privacy budgets, and the accuracy is high even when the privacy budget is small.

Table 5 studies how the utility varies under different h values with $\epsilon = 1.0$ and $k = 300$. It is interesting to see that in general frequent sequential pattern mining is also insensitive to varying h values. This can be similarly explained by the large supports of frequent sequential patterns, which make them more resistant to noise. In addition, we can observe that good performance for frequent sequential pattern mining can be obtained by a h value between 10 and 16, the same range as that for count queries.

Table 4: Utility for frequent sequential pattern mining vs. ϵ

ϵ	TP (M/B) *Simple*	FP(FD) (M/B) *Simple*	TP (M/B) *Hybrid*	FP(FD) (M/B) *Hybrid*
0.5	227/194	73/106	244/215	56/85
0.75	239/206	61/94	253/224	47/76
1.0	241/212	59/88	257/233	43/67
1.25	243/216	57/84	259/238	41/62
1.5	248/224	52/76	261/242	39/58

Table 5: Utility for frequent sequential pattern mining vs. h

h	TP (M/B) *Simple*	FP(FD) (M/B) *Simple*	TP (M/B) *Hybrid*	FP(FD) (M/B) *Hybrid*
6	234/212	66/88	241/221	59/79
8	240/217	60/83	254/232	46/68
10	241/215	58/85	255/236	45/64
12	241/212	59/88	257/233	43/67
14	241/212	59/88	258/233	42/67
16	240/210	60/90	258/231	42/69
18	240/209	60/91	255/230	45/70
20	238/206	62/94	254/228	46/72

5.2 Scalability

In the last set of experiments, we examine the scalability of our approach. Recall that the runtime complexity of our approach is dominated by the database size $|\mathcal{D}|$ and the location universe size $|\mathcal{L}|$. Therefore, we study the runtime under different database sizes and different location universe sizes. Figure 5.a presents the runtime under different database sizes with $\epsilon = 1.0$ and $h = 20$ for both *Simple* and *Hybrid*. The test sets are generated by randomly extracting records from *Metro* and *Bus*. We can observe that the runtime is linear to the database size. Moreover, it can be seen that the computational cost of a hybrid-granularity prefix tree structure is negligible. This further confirms the benefit of employing a hybrid-granularity prefix tree.

Figure 5.b shows how runtime varies under different location universe sizes. Since *Metro* is of a small universe size, we only study the effect of universe sizes on *Bus*. For each universe size, we remove all locations falling out of the universe from *Bus*. This results in a smaller database size. Consequently, we fix the database size for all test sets to 600,000. Again, it can be observed that the runtime scales linearly with the location universe size and that the computational cost of *Hybrid* is comparable to that of *Simple* under different location universe sizes. As a summary, our approach is scalable to large sequential datasets. It takes less than 22 seconds to sanitize both datasets in all previous experiments.

6. CONCLUSION AND LESSON LEARNED

In this paper, we have studied the problem of publishing transit data at the STM in the framework of differential privacy. For the first time, we present a practical solution for sanitizing large-scale sequential data, which can also be seamlessly applied to trajectory data. Our solution has been tested on real-life STM transit data for two fundamental data analysis tasks performed at the STM and exhibits satisfactory effectiveness and efficiency. We believe that our solution could benefit many other sectors that are facing the dilemma between the demands of sequential data publishing and privacy protection.

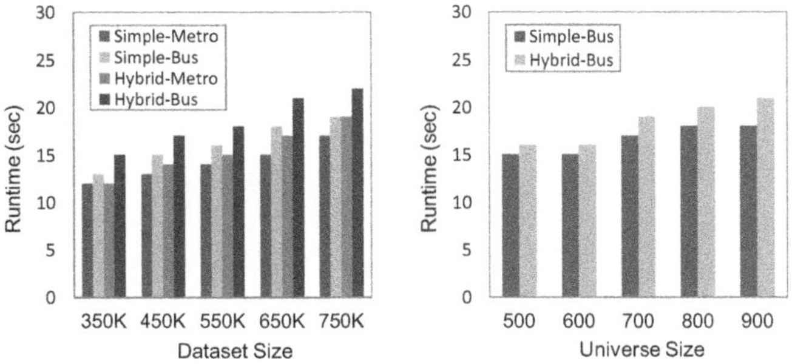

(a) Runtime vs. $|\mathcal{D}|$ (b) Runtime vs. $|\mathcal{L}|$

Figure 5: Runtime vs. different parameters.

Finally, we would like to share our collaborative experience with the public transport sector. Transit data is useful for many data analysis tasks. So far, we have focused on two most fundamental ones. Though many data analysis tasks can be done based on accurate count queries, it is still worth exploring the utility of differentially private release for more complex data analysis. Besides the technical aspect, it is equally important to educate transport service practitioners about the latest privacy-preserving technology. This is especially important for a solution based on differential privacy because any accidental release of *deterministic* aggregate-level information may expose previously sanitized data to privacy threats [19].

7. ACKNOWLEDGMENT

The research is supported in part by the Discovery Grants (356065-2008) and Canada Graduate Scholarship from the Natural Sciences and Engineering Research Council of Canada (NSERC).

8. REFERENCES

[1] O. Abul, F. Bonchi, and M. Nanni. Never walk alone: Uncertainty for anonymity in moving objects databases. In *ICDE*, 2008.

[2] R. Agrawal and R. Srikant. Mining sequential patterns. In *ICDE*, 1995.

[3] A. Blum, K. Ligett, and A. Roth. A learning theory approach to non-interactive database privacy. In *STOC*, 2008.

[4] A. Bruno, M. Catherine, and T. Martin. Mining public transport user behaviour from smart card data. In *IFAC SICPM*, 2006.

[5] M. Catherine, T. Martin, and A. Bruno. Measuring transit performance using smart card data. In *World Conference on Transportation Research*, 2007.

[6] R. Chen, B. C. M. Fung, N. Mohammed, and B. C. Desai. Privacy-preserving trajectory data publishing by local suppression. *Information Sciences*, in press.

[7] R. Chen, N. Mohammed, B. C. M. Fung, B. C. Desai, and L. Xiong. Publishing set-valued data via differential privacy. *PVLDB*, 2011.

[8] G. Cormode, M. Procopiuc, and D. Srivastava. Differentially private summaries for sparse data. In *ICDT*, 2012.

[9] C. Dwork. A firm foundation for private data analysis. *Communications of the ACM*, 54(1):86–95, 2011.

[10] C. Dwork, F. McSherry, K. Nissim, and A. Smith. Calibrating noise to sensitivity in private data analysis. In *TCC*, 2006.

[11] C. Dwork, M. Naor, O. Reingold, G. N. Rothblum, and S. Vadhan. On the complexity of differentially private data release: Efficient algorithms and hardness results. In *STOC*, 2009.

[12] A. V. Evfinievski, R. Srikant, R. Agrawal, and J. Gehrke. Privacy preserving mining of association rules. *Information Systems*, 29(4):343–364, 2004.

[13] B. C. M. Fung, M. Cao, B. C. Desai, and H. Xu. Privacy protection for RFID data. In *SAC*, 2009.

[14] S. R. Ganta, S. P. Kasiviswanathan, and A. Smith. Composition attacks and auxiliary information in data privacy. In *SIGKDD*, 2008.

[15] A. Ghosh, T. Roughgarden, and M. Sundararajan. Universally utility-maximizing privacy mechanisms. In *STOC*, 2009.

[16] M. Hay, V. Rastogi, G. Miklau, and D. Suciu. Boosting the accuracy of differentially private histograms through consistency. *PVLDB*, 2010.

[17] H. Hu, J. Xu, S. T. On, J. Du, and J. K.-Y. Ng. Privacy-aware location data publishing. *ACM TODS*, 35(3):17, 2010.

[18] D. Kifer. Attacks on privacy and definetti's theorem. In *SIGMOD*, 2009.

[19] D. Kifer and A. Machanavajjhala. No free lunch in data privacy. In *SIGMOD*, 2011.

[20] P. Marie-Pierre, T. M., and M. Catherine. Smart card data use in public transit: A literature review. *Transportation Research C: Emerging Technologies*, 19(4):557–568, 2011.

[21] F. McSherry. Privacy integrated queries: An extensible platform for privacy-preserving data analysis. In *SIGMOD*, 2009.

[22] F. McSherry and K. Talwar. Mechanism design via differential privacy. In *FOCS*, 2007.

[23] N. Mohammed, R. Chen, B. C. M. Fung, and P. S. Yu. Differentially private data release for data mining. In *SIGKDD*, 2011.

[24] A. Monreale, G. Andrienko, N. Andrienko, F. Giannotti, D. Pedreschi, S. Rinzivillo, and S. Wrobel. Movement data anonymity through generalization. *Transactions on Data Privacy*, 3(2):91–121, 2010.

[25] J. Pei, J. Han, B. Mortazavi-Asl, H. Pinto, Q. Chen, U. Dayal, and M. Hsu:. Prefixspan: Mining sequential patterns by prefix-projected growth. In *ICDE*, 2001.

[26] L. Sweeney. k-anonymity: A model for protecting privacy. *International Journal on Uncertainty, Fuzziness and Knowledge-based Systems*, 10(5):557–570, 2002.

[27] M. Terrovitis and N. Mamoulis. Privacy preservation in the publication of trajectories. In *MDM*, 2008.

[28] M. Utsunomiya, J. Attanucci, and N. Wilson. Potential uses of transit smart card registration and transaction data to improve transit planning. *Transportation Research Record: Journal of the Transportation Research Board*, (1971):119–126, 2006.

[29] R. C. W. Wong, A. Fu, K. Wang, P. S. Yu, and J. Pei. Can the utility of anonymized data be used for privacy breaches. *ACM TKDD*, 5(3):16, 2011.

[30] X. Xiao, G. Bender, M. Hay, and J. Gehrke. ireduct: Differential privacy with reduced relative errors. In *SIGMOD*, 2011.

[31] X. Xiao, G. Wang, and J. Gehrke. Differential privacy via wavelet transforms. In *ICDE*, 2010

[32] R. Yarovoy, F. Bonchi, L. V. S. Lakshmanan, and W. H. Wang. Anonymizing moving objects: How to hide a MOB in a crowd? In *EDBT*, 2009.

Interaction and Collective Intelligence in Internet Computing

Deyi Li
Chinese Academy of Engineering
China
leedeyi@nlsde.buaa.edu.cn

Abstract

Network interconnection, information interoperability, and crowds interaction on the Internet could inspire better computation models than Turing machine, since that human plays an important factor in Internet computing, so that the human-machine and machine-machine interactions have evolved to be the kernel of Internet computing. Internet has not been simply equivalent to a virtual huge computer, or a set of computers. On the Internet, human's behaviors are uncertain, the interactions and influence among people are also uncertain. These uncertainties cannot be described by Turing machine and traditional interaction machine. As a new computation platform, Internet computing requires new theories and methods. By combining topology in mathematics with the field theory in physics, we propose the topological potential approach, which set up a virtual field by the topological space to reflect individual activities, local effects and preferential attachment. This approach can be used to research the emergence of collective intelligence. Here, we introduce three case studies to illustrate the analysis on the collective intelligence on the Internet and discuss some potential applications of the topological potential approach.

Categories & Subject Descriptors: H. Information Systems: H.2 DATABASE MANAGEMENT: H.2.8 Database applications: Subjects: Data mining

Author Keywords: Collaborative Intelligence; Crowd Computing

Bio

Deyi Li is a member of the Chinese Academy of Engineering and the International Academy of Sciences for Europe and Asia. He is the Chairman of the Chinese Artificial Intelligence Society (http://caai.cn/). He is a professor of software engineering at Tsinghua University, China, and heads the Information Science Directorate of the Natural Science Foundation of China. His current research interests include networked data mining, artificial intelligence with uncertainty, and cloud computing.

KDD '12, August 12-16, 2012, Beijing, China.
ACM 978-1-4503-1462-6 /12/08.

Building an Engine for Big Data

Masaru Kitsuregawa
University of Tokyo
Japan
kitsure@tkl.iis.u-tokyo.ac.jp

Abstract

IT program in Japan to build powerful engine for big data was launched. Quite recently the initial version is commercialized. This presentation will give a brief overview of the project. Also some of the potential applications will be introduced.

Categories & Subject Descriptors: H.2.8 Database applications: Subjects: Data mining

Author Keywords: Big Data; Search Engine

Bio

Masaru Kitsuregawa is the recipient of the 2009 SIGMOD Edgar F. Codd Innovations Award for contributions to high-performance database technology. Kitsuregawa made major contributions to the development of hash-join algorithms, which significantly improved the performance of join operations in relational database systems. That work has influenced related research in areas such as query execution, plan optimization and dynamic query-workload balancing, as well as the development of commercial database products. He implemented the hash-based approach on a variety of platforms, including the Functional Disk System and multi-node PC clusters, demonstrating its substantial advantages through detailed evaluations. He has also applied hash-based strategies to parallel association mining and showed its effectiveness there. His contributions in the hardware area include a high-speed sorting system with a sophisticated memory management algorithm. That work was eventually commercialized in collaboration with colleagues, and won the Datamation sort benchmark in 2000.

KDD'12, August 12-16, 2012, Beijing, China.
ACM 978-1-4503-1462-6 /12/08.

A New Challenge of Information Processing under the 21st Century

Bo Zhang
Tsinghua University
China
dcszb@tsinghua.edu.cn

Abstract

In web era, we are confronted with a huge amount of raw data and a tremendous change of man-machine interaction modes. We have to deal with the content (semantics) of data rather than their form alone. Traditional information processing approaches face a new challenge since they cannot deal with the semantic meaning or content of information. But humans can handle such a problem easily. So it's needed a new information processing strategy that correlated with the content of information by learning some mechanisms from human beings. Therefore, we need (1) a set of robust detectors for detecting semantically meaningful features such as boundaries, shapes, etc. in images, words, sentences, etc. in text, and (2) a set of methods that can effectively analyze and exploit the information structures that encode the content of information. During the past 40 years the probability theory has made a great progress. It has provided a set of mathematical tools for representing and analyzing information structures. In the talk we will discuss what difficulty we face, what we can do, and how we should do in the content-based information processing.

Categories & Subject Descriptors: H. Information Systems: H.2 DATABASE MANAGEMENT: H.2.8 Database applications: Subjects: Data mining

Author Keywords: Semantic Web; Content-based Information Processing

Bio

Bo Zhang is now a professor of Computer Science and Technology Department of Tsinghua University, the fellow of Chinese Academy of Sciences. In 1958 he graduated from Automatic Control Department of Tsinghua University, and became a faculty member since then. From 1980/02 to 1982/02 he visited University of Illinois at Urbana-Champaign, USA as a scholar. He is now the chairman of steering committee of Research Institute of Information Technology, Tsinghua University, the technical advisor of Fujian government, and the member of Technical Advisory Board of Microsoft Research Asia. He was the founding director of the State Key Lab of Intelligent Technology and Systems from 1991 to 1996. From 1987 to 1994 he served as a member of specialist group of Intelligent Robots theme of National '863' High-Tech Program. He won an ICL European Artificial Intelligence Prize, a third award of National Natural Science Prize, a third award of National Science and Technology Progress Prize, a first and second award of Science and Technology Progress Prize from the State Educational Commission, a first award of Science & Technology Progress Prize from Electronic Industry Ministry and a first award of Science & Technology Progress Prize from Committee of National Defense.

KDD'12, August 12-16, 2012, Beijing, China.
ACM 978-1-4503-1462-6 /12/08.

Developing Data Mining Applications

Geoff Holmes
University of Waikato
New Zealand
geoff@waikato.ac.nz

Abstract

In this talk I will review several real-world applications developed at the University of Waikato over the past 15 years. These include the use of near infrared spectroscopy coupled with data mining as an alternate laboratory technique for predicting compound concentrations in soil and plant samples, and the analysis of gas chromatography mass spectrometry (GCMS) data, a technique used to determine in environmental applications, for example, the petroleum content in soil and water samples. I will then briefly discuss how experience with these applications has led to the development of an open-source framework for application development.

Categories & Subject Descriptors: H. Information Systems: H.2 DATABASE MANAGEMENT: H.2.8 Database applications: Subjects: Data mining

Author Keywords: Data Mining Application; Environmental Science

Bio

Geoffrey Holmes is Dean of the Faculty of Computing and Mathematical Sciences at the University of Waikato, Hamilton, New Zealand. He received a Ph.D. in mathematics from Southampton University in 1986. Following a research position at the engineering Department, Cambridge University, UK, he joined the Computer Science Department at Waikato. His research interests include topics in machine learning, data stream mining, open-source machine learning and application development. He is a senior member of the Waikato machine learning group that have provided open-source solutions to the community such as WEKA and MOA. He has been actively involved in promoting open-source for machine learning and is an action editor for JMLR MLOSS. He has extensive experience of application development and the provision frameworks for data mining and data stream mining application development. Most recently, he has been working on instance-incremental methods for data streams across a wide range of tasks.

KDD'12, August 12-16, 2012, Beijing, China.
ACM 978-1-4503-1462-6 /12/08.

Learning from Crowds in the Presence of Schools of Thought

Yuandong Tian
School of Computer Science
Carnegie Mellon University
Pittsburgh, PA 15213, USA
yuandong@andrew.cmu.edu

Jun Zhu
Department of Comp. Sci. & Tech.
Tsinghua University
Beijing, 10084, China
dcszj@mail.tsinghua.edu.cn

ABSTRACT

Crowdsourcing has recently become popular among machine learning researchers and social scientists as an effective way to collect large-scale experimental data from distributed workers. To extract useful information from the cheap but potentially unreliable answers to tasks, a key problem is to identify reliable workers as well as unambiguous tasks. Although for objective tasks that have one correct answer per task, previous works can estimate worker reliability and task clarity based on the single gold standard assumption, for tasks that are subjective and accept multiple reasonable answers that workers may be grouped into, a phenomenon called *schools of thought*, existing models cannot be trivially applied. In this work, we present a statistical model to estimate worker reliability and task clarity without resorting to the single gold standard assumption. This is instantiated by explicitly characterizing the grouping behavior to form schools of thought with a rank-1 factorization of a worker-task groupsize matrix. Instead of performing an intermediate inference step, which can be expensive and unstable, we present an algorithm to analytically compute the sizes of different groups. We perform extensive empirical studies on real data collected from Amazon Mechanical Turk. Our method discovers the schools of thought, shows reasonable estimation of worker reliability and task clarity, and is robust to hyperparameter changes. Furthermore, our estimated worker reliability can be used to improve the gold standard prediction for objective tasks.

Categories and Subject Descriptors

I.5.1 [**Pattern Recognition**]: Models - Statistical

General Terms

Algorithms, Experimentation

Keywords

Crowdsourcing, Schools of Thought, Pattern Analysis

KDD'12, August 12–16, 2012, Beijing, China.

1. INTRODUCTION

Crowdsourcing has emerged as an effective way to collect large-scale data to help solve challenging scientific and engineering problems. In web services such as Amazon Mechanical Turk (M-Turk)[1], human intelligence tasks (HITs) (e.g., "Does the image contain a car?") are distributed from the requestor to an *unknown* set of workers, called *crowds*, who are paid with a low cost to fulfill them. There are two kinds of applications for crowdsourcing. One application is to obtain correct labels of a dataset, used in computer vision [21], natural language processing [19], etc. In such a scenario, task is objective with one correct answer, called *gold standard*. The goal is to recover it from the noisy worker responses. The other application is to use crowdsourcing for qualitative user studies [11], demographic survey [16] or solving a hard problem [1]. In this case, each task may have multiple valid answers, called *schools of thought*, since the tasks are subjective or can be misinterpreted, and the workers come from a variety of cultural and educational background [16].

Due to the open and anonymous nature of crowdsourcing, the quality of the collected data is not guaranteed. In order to use these data well, in both scenarios we need to address two common key problems – "how to identify a small number of unreliable workers whose answers may be random or even adversary" and "how to identify tasks that may cause confusion to workers". Formally, we call these two factors worker *reliability* and task *clarity*. In crowdsourcing applications that aim to obtain ground truth labels of a dataset, only the labels from reliable workers should be trusted, and ambiguous tasks should be redesigned to remove any misunderstanding in the future. In applications that aim for user study or look for multiple opinions, one needs to distinguish whether a worker has a reasonable opinion, or just puts random answers that may ruin the data distribution.

In the former case, many previous works [15, 23, 19, 14, 10] have been presented and shown promising results compared to the "majority voting" heuristic. The worker reliability is defined either as the degree of concentration (precision) [15, 23, 22] or confusion matrix [9, 18, 5] referencing the estimated gold standard, whose existence is an essential assumption in these works. Some works also model task difficulty [22], again based on the existence of gold standard. Computationally, an iterative approach is usually adopted to estimate the gold standard and worker reliability simultaneously. The rationale is that knowing the gold standard helps to identify reliable workers and workers' reliability is useful to weigh their answers to recover the gold standard.

[1]https://www.mturk.com

However, in the latter case where *more than one* answers could be valid and reasonable, defining worker reliability on top of a single gold standard is no longer a good idea. For some workers, their reliability can be underestimated only because they support a reasonable idea that is not the estimated single gold standard, yet in fact they may follow a unique but reasonable thinking and should be respected. On the other hand, an unambiguous task that is supposed to have alternative answers may also be estimated as confusing.

To deal with this problem, in this paper, we directly model worker *reliability* and task *clarity* without the help of gold standard. As a result, this model works in both scenarios of crowdsourcing applications. Our model is built on the following two mild assumptions on the grouping behavior that happens in schools of thought: 1) reliable workers tend to agree with other workers in many tasks; and 2) the answers to a clear task tend to form tight clusters. Following this idea, we develop a low-rank computational model to explicitly relate the grouping behavior of schools of thought, characterized by *group sizes*, to worker reliability and task clarity. To bypass the hard model selection problem of determining the unknown number of clusters (i.e., schools), we apply nonparametric Bayesian clustering techniques, which have shown great promise in statistics and machine learning [3, 6, 24]. Moreover, instead of performing a potentially expensive and unstable intermediate inference step, which is necessary for all the previous works [15, 23, 21, 22], we derive an analytical form to estimate the expected group sizes. The analytic form only depends on pairwise distances between answers, making it generalizable to different answer types. Interestingly, our model could provide a generative interpretation of latent distance model for social networks [8]. The worker reliability and task clarity are thus obtained via the rank-1 factorization of the expected group size matrix.

Different from most previous works that focus on gold standard estimation, recent work [21] also models the schools of thought for binary queries by assigning each worker a (different) linear classifier on hidden multidimensional representations of tasks, with Gaussian priors on both representations and classifiers. The worker reliability is thus defined as the precision of the linear model. However, it remains a question whether such linear representations and Gaussian priors for both tasks and workers are faithful to the data, and whether heterogeneous tasks can be represented in the same space. Our work avoids such representation issues by explicitly modeling the grouping structure of the data. This leads to fewer assumptions and parameters. Moreover, our method allows an analytic solution, while [21] uses a coordinate descent procedure to obtain a local optimum.

Finally, we apply our method to both simulation data and the real data collected from M-Turk. In the real data, we discover the group structure of schools of thought (Fig. 1), and show estimated worker reliability and task clarity, as well as a comparison with several benchmarks and sensitivity analysis. For objective tasks, we use the estimated worker reliability to select high quality workers for recovering gold standard, which outperforms previous works [15, 21].

The paper is structured as follows. Section 2 introduces our statistical model for crowdsourcing data analysis in the presence of schools of thought, together with a simple algorithm. Section 3 presents synthetic validation, and Section 4 presents analytical results on M-Turk. Finally, Section 5 concludes with future directions discussed.

2. A LOW-RANK SCHOOLS OF THOUGHT MODEL

In this section, we present a computational model to estimate worker reliability and task clarity for crowdsourcing data in the presence of schools of thought.

2.1 Basic Assumptions

In crowdsourcing, let N be the number of workers and K be the number of tasks. Each worker is required to finish all the K tasks (See the experimental design for more details). We use a scalar $\lambda_i > 0$ to model the *constant* reliability of worker i among different tasks, and a scalar $\mu_k > 0$ to model the *constant* degree of clarity of task k that holds for all workers[2].

Like any useful statistical models, we need to make appropriate assumptions in order to perform meaningful estimation and discover useful patterns. Specifically, for our problem of estimating worker reliability and task clarity in the presence of schools of thought, it suffices to make the following two mild assumptions on the behavior of workers and tasks:

1. *A worker i who is consistent with many other workers in most of the tasks is reliable, i.e. λ_i is large.*

2. *A task k whose answers form a few tight clusters is easy, well-addressed and objective (large μ_k); while a task whose answers form lots of small clusters is complicated, confusing and subjective (small μ_k).*

We argue that the above two assumptions are reasonable for characterizing crowdsourcing data. The first assumption may fail if all the workers collaborate to cheat, or the task is too hard so that most of the workers are misled towards the same wrong answer. However, since the basic idea of crowdsourcing is to ask the crowds for useful information, it is not restrictive to trust the behavior of the majority of workers. Furthermore, most previous works (e.g., majority voting, [15] and [22]) in crowdsourcing assuming the existence of gold standards implicitly make the first assumption, which is shown in both their initialization steps and their model designs.

The second assumption can be interpreted as "sense-making" that people make efforts to find interpretations from "experience" (their answers) [17]. Reliable workers are expected to use more mental resource to obtain a reasonable answer, while unreliable workers may give random nonsense answers. A sensible task only contain a few reasonable answers but random answers could be many. Thus reliable workers will form large groups, while unreliable ones are discordant. This assumption may fail if only a few candidate choices are available for a confusing task that has many potential answers. This can be avoided by concatenating multiple questions into one task, which expands the answer space to reveal the true clustering structure (See the experiment section).

Note that K tasks and N workers have to be considered jointly. A single task cannot identify whether a worker is of high quality or not. Similarly, a single worker cannot identify the ambiguity of tasks.

[2]A worker's reliability can be possibly different in various tasks and time-evolving; a task may be clear to a certain subgroup of workers but not to others. A systematic study of this more complicated phenomenon is beyond the scope of this paper. We leave it for future work.

Figure 1: Depict of schools of thought in our experiment that asks 402 unique workers to categorize an object in images (*sky, building, computer*) and pick beautiful images (*beauty1, beauty2*). First row: As shown in the posterior link probability matrix computed from our model (Eqn. (7)), workers give a variety of responses that tend to cluster together, i.e., the *schools of thought*. Moreover, the scale (number) of schools of thought is task-specific. Second row: Example images in each task. *Sky:* Only positive and negative images. *Building:* Positive, ambiguous and negative images. *Computer:* Positive, ambiguous and negative images that contains elusive objects. *Image aesthetics:* Beautiful/ordinary-looking images. See Section 4 for experiment design.

2.2 The Low-rank Model

Given the two assumptions, a quantitative relation follows. Suppose we have somehow clustered the worker responses of task k into M_k clusters (the cluster model will be presented in Section 2.3), where M_k is an unknown parameter. Let z_{ik} denote the group index that worker i corresponds to in task k, and $\#z_{ik}$ be the *size* of that group. In this paper, $\#z_{ik}$ is regarded as a way to represent the scale of schools of thought. The larger $\#z_{ik}$ is, the smaller the scale is. We thus formally define our computational model by relating $\#z_{ik}$ to λ_i and μ_k as follows:

$$\#z_{ik} = \lambda_i \mu_k + \epsilon_{ik}. \quad (1)$$

where ϵ_{ik} is a zero-mean random noise (its distribution is determined by our clustering model). In matrix form,

$$\#\mathbf{Z} = \boldsymbol{\lambda}\boldsymbol{\mu}^T + \epsilon. \quad (2)$$

Under expectation, we have $\#\tilde{\mathbf{Z}} = \boldsymbol{\lambda}\boldsymbol{\mu}^\top$, which is a rank-1 factorization of the $N \times K$ *worker-task* groupsize matrix $\#\tilde{\mathbf{Z}}$. The resulting μ_k and λ_i can thus be used to rank tasks or workers. The intuition underlying the low-rank factorization is that according to the assumptions, reliable workers working on clear and well-defined tasks will give unanimous answers, yielding large group sizes in expectation. Note that we treat $\#z_{ik}$ as a continuous variable rather than an integer. Section 2.4 discusses how to estimate its expected value.

Given the assumptions, rank-1 factorization is the most straightforward way to formulate the relationship between $\#z_{ik}$, λ_i and μ_k. More complicated modeling may help, e.g. assuming a nonlinear relationship or enforcing $\#Z$ to be rank-m rather than rank-1 to find multiple factors for both workers and tasks that are related to the grouping behavior. However, we leave these extensions for future work.

2.3 The Clustering Model

To obtain worker reliability and task clarity, a key step is to estimate the expected group sizes. Although many clustering methods, such as spectral clustering [13], Kmeans and etc., can be applied to first infer the group assignment of each worker in each task and then calculate the group sizes, most of them have a difficult time in determining the unknown cluster number M_k. To bypass the hard model selection problem and also to allow the model to adaptively grow as more data are provided[3], we resort to nonparametric Bayesian techniques, which have shown great promise in machine learning, statistics, and many application areas [3, 6, 24]. More specifically, we propose to use the Dirichlet process (DP) mixture model [3], which is a nonparametric Bayesian model that can automatically resolve the unknown number of clusters M_k. Moreover, as we shall see, for our DP mixture model, we can analytically compute the expected group sizes without an intermediate inference step, which can be expensive and unstable.

Formally, let $\mathbf{x}_{ik}$ be the d-dimensional observed answers of worker i to task k. Typically, $\mathbf{x}_{ik}$ is a vector encoding the worker i's answers to a sequence of questions in task k (e.g., a worker gives answers to d questions of a survey). For a task k, answers of workers form M_k clusters. Let $\mathbf{c}_{ik}$ denote the center of the cluster that worker i belongs to. For different workers i and j, $\mathbf{c}_{ik} = \mathbf{c}_{jk}$ if they are in the same group. For each task $k = 1 \dots K$, the DP mixture with a Gaussian likelihood model can thus be written as:

$$\begin{aligned} G_k | \{\alpha_k, G_0^k\} &\sim \mathcal{DP}(\alpha_k, G_0^k) \\ \mathbf{c}_{ik} | G_k &\sim G_k \\ \mathbf{x}_{ik} | \{\mathbf{c}_{ik}, \sigma^2\} &\sim \mathcal{N}(\mathbf{x}_{ik} | \mathbf{c}_{ik}, \sigma^2 \mathbf{I}), \end{aligned} \quad (3)$$

Although in principle, we could use a separate variance σ_{ik}^2 for each worker i and each task k, here we treat them as one single hyperparameter σ for simplicity and will provide sensitivity analysis of our model with respect to σ^2. Due to the fact that the distributions G_k sampled from a DP are discrete almost surely [4], there is a non-zero probability that two workers belong to the same cluster. Thus, we will have a partition of $\mathbf{x}_{ik}$ according to the sampled values $\mathbf{c}_{ik}$ and automatically infer the cluster number M_k. Alternatively, the mixture model can be equivalently represented using Chinese restaurant process (CRP)[4] prior, which is:

$$\begin{aligned} z_{ik} &\sim \mathcal{CRP}(\cdot | \alpha_k) \\ \mathbf{c}_{mk} &\sim G_0^k \\ \mathbf{x}_{ik} | \{z_{ik}, \mathbf{c}, \sigma^2\} &\sim \mathcal{N}(\cdot | \mathbf{c}_{z_{ik},k}, \sigma^2 \mathbf{I}), \end{aligned} \quad (4)$$

where $\mathbf{c}_{mk}$ is the cluster center for cluster m at task k. In

[3]For example, the number of clusters can grow for a DP mixture model when more data are provided. In other words, DP mixture can have an unbounded number of clusters.

[4]A CRP is a marginalized version of a DP [6].

this work, we set the base distribution G_0^k as $\mathcal{N}(\mathbf{0}, \sigma_{k0}^2\mathbf{I})$, where σ_{k0}^2 are the task-specific variances that characterize how much the means of clusters are scattered around the origin. We will present a procedure to automatically estimate them. On the other hand, the hyperparameter σ characterizes the variance within each cluster and need to be specified. A sensitivity analysis is shown in the experiment.

For the DP mixture, exact inference of the group assignment z_{ik} is intractable. Typical solutions resort to variational or sampling [12] methods. However, these approximate inference methods often lead to local optimum solutions and can be expensive and sensitive to initialization. Thus, we need to estimate the expected group sizes in a more efficient and robust way. Here we derive an analytic solution to the expected group sizes for the clustering model, without intermediate inference. Our approach can be expected to be faster and more stable compared to those using approximate inference, analogous to what people have popularly done in collapsed sampling [7] or collapsed variational inference [20] in probabilistic latent variable models.

2.4 Expected Group Size

For each task k, we use $\mathbf{X}_k = \{\mathbf{x}_{ik}\}_{i=1}^N$ to denote all its worker responses. Let W_{ij}^k be a binary random variable that equals to 1 if workers i and j are in the same group of thought in task k ($W_{ii}^k = 1$). From W_{ij}^k, the group size $\#z_{ik}$ for worker i can be computed as $\#z_{ik} = \sum_{j=1}^N W_{ij}^k$. Thus, by linearity of expectation, the expected group size conditioned on $\mathbf{X}_k$ is:

$$\begin{aligned} \#\tilde{z}_{ik} &\equiv \mathbb{E}\left[\#z_{ik}|\mathbf{X}_k\right] = \mathbb{E}\left[\sum_{j=1}^N W_{ij}^k \middle| \mathbf{X}_k\right] \\ &= \sum_{j=1}^N \mathbb{E}\left[W_{ij}^k|\mathbf{X}_k\right] = \sum_{j=1}^N \mathbb{P}\left(W_{ij}^k|\mathbf{X}_k\right), \end{aligned} \quad (5)$$

where the last equality holds because W_{ij}^k is binary. Note that the linearity of expectation still applies even if W_{ij}^k are not independent variables (e.g., for $i \neq i'$, W_{ij}^k and $W_{i'j}^k$ may be dependent because they share the same worker j).

To compute the posterior distribution of W_{ij}^k, we make the following approximation:

$$\mathbb{P}\left(W_{ij}^k|\mathbf{X}_k\right) \approx \mathbb{P}\left(W_{ij}^k|D_{ij}^k\right), \quad (6)$$

where $D_{ij}^k = \|\mathbf{x}_{ik} - \mathbf{x}_{jk}\|^2$ is the squared Euclidean distance[5] between responses of workers i and j. The intuition is that two workers i and j being in the same group is largely due to their affinity, but is *almost* independent of other workers' responses. Our synthetic experiments verify that this approximation is very accurate (See Section 3 for details). In practice, this approximation is also reasonable in crowdsourcing services like M-Turk, where the onsite communication between workers is not allowed. After computing the likelihood $\mathbb{P}\left(D_{ij}^k|W_{ij}^k\right)$ and prior $\mathbb{P}\left(W_{ij}^k = 1\right)$, with Bayes' rule we obtain the posterior link probability:

$$\mathbb{P}\left(W_{ij}^k = 1|D_{ij}^k\right) = \frac{1}{1 + \exp\left(\beta_k D_{ij}^k + \beta_{k0}\right)} \quad (7)$$

where $\beta_k \equiv \frac{\sigma_{k0}^2}{4\sigma^2(\sigma_{k0}^2+\sigma^2)}$ and $\beta_{k0} \equiv \log \alpha_k + \frac{d}{2}\log\frac{\sigma^2}{\sigma_{k0}^2+\sigma^2}$.

[5]The same result follows when using Euclidean distance.

Please see Appendix for detailed derivation. In this work, we derive the prior from the exchangeability property of CRP.

Note that the posterior distribution in Eqn. (7) is not restricted to the CRP-Gaussian cluster model proposed in Eqn. (4). In general, we can apply other priors or explicitly define $\mathbb{P}\left(W_{ij}^k\right)$. Besides Gaussian, each cluster's noise model can follow any other unimodal distribution and Eqn. (7) still hold with D_{ij}^k with a different distance metric. The metric could also be redefined and generalized to arbitrary type of answers (e.g. binary, categorical).

Interestingly, our link distribution model in Eqn. (7) for two workers being in the same group has the same logistic form as the latent distance model for social network analysis [8], where the link distribution model is directly defined.

2.5 Worker Reliability and Task Clarity

Once we have obtained the expected group size $\#\tilde{z}_{ik}$ for each worker i and each task k, the worker reliability $\boldsymbol{\lambda}$ and task clarity $\boldsymbol{\mu}$ can be estimated as the first left and right singular vector corresponding to the largest singular value of the expected group size matrix $\#\tilde{\mathbf{Z}} \equiv \{\#\tilde{z}_{ik}\}$ (Eqn. (1)). The entire algorithm is summarized in Alg. 1. Note we do not need to impose positive constraints for $\boldsymbol{\lambda}$ and $\boldsymbol{\mu}$, since the first left and right singular vector of a matrix with positive entries is always positive by Perron-Frobenius theorem.

Algorithm 1 Estimation worker reliability and task clarity in the presence of schools of thought.

1: **(Input)** The worker responses $\{\mathbf{X}_k\}_{k=1}^K$ for K tasks.
2: **(Output)** Worker reliability $\boldsymbol{\lambda}$ and task clarity $\boldsymbol{\mu}$.
3: **for** k = 1:K **do**
4: Compute the posterior $\mathbb{P}\left(W_{ij}^k|D_{ij}^k\right)$ that worker i and j are in the same group (Eqn. (7)).
5: Computer the expected group size $\#\tilde{z}_{ik}$ (Eqn. (5)).
6: **end for**
7: Run SVD on expected *worker-task* groupsize matrix $\#\tilde{\mathbf{Z}}$: $\#\tilde{\mathbf{Z}} = U\Lambda V^\top$
8: Set $\boldsymbol{\lambda} = U_{.1}\sqrt{\Lambda_{11}}$ and $\boldsymbol{\mu} = V_{.1}\sqrt{\Lambda_{11}}$, where $U_{.1}$ is the first column of U, alike for $V_{.1}$.

2.6 Hyperparameters

Before ending this section, we introduce a simple procedure to estimate the hyperparameters α_k and σ_{k0}, with the assumption that σ is given. As we shall see, our model is insensitive to the only tunable hyperparameter σ. Thus, although the procedure does not estimate all hyperparameters, it is good enough for our use.

Specifically, after marginalizing cluster partition, we can obtain $\mathbb{P}\left(D_{ij}^k\right)$, a distribution of the observable pairwise squared distances parameterized by the hyperparameters α_k, σ_{k0} and σ. Similarly we compute $\mathbb{P}\left(\|\mathbf{x}_{ik}\|^2\right)$. Given σ, we can estimate α_k and σ_{k0} from the equations:

$$\mathbb{E}\left[D_{ij}^k\right] = 2d\left(\sigma^2 + \sigma_{k0}^2\frac{\alpha_k}{1+\alpha_k}\right) \quad (8)$$

$$\mathbb{E}\left[\|\mathbf{x}_{ik}\|^2\right] = d(\sigma^2 + \sigma_{k0}^2). \quad (9)$$

The derivation is simple by noticing that $\mathbb{E}\left[D_{ij}^k\right] = \sum_{l=0,1}\mathbb{E}\left[D_{ij}^k|W_{ij}^k = l\right]\mathbb{P}\left(W_{ij}^k = l\right)$. Similarly for $\mathbb{P}\left(\|\mathbf{x}_{ik}\|^2\right)$.

3. SYNTHETIC VALIDATION

Before presenting the experiments on real data, we first conduct synthetic experiments to show empirically that our

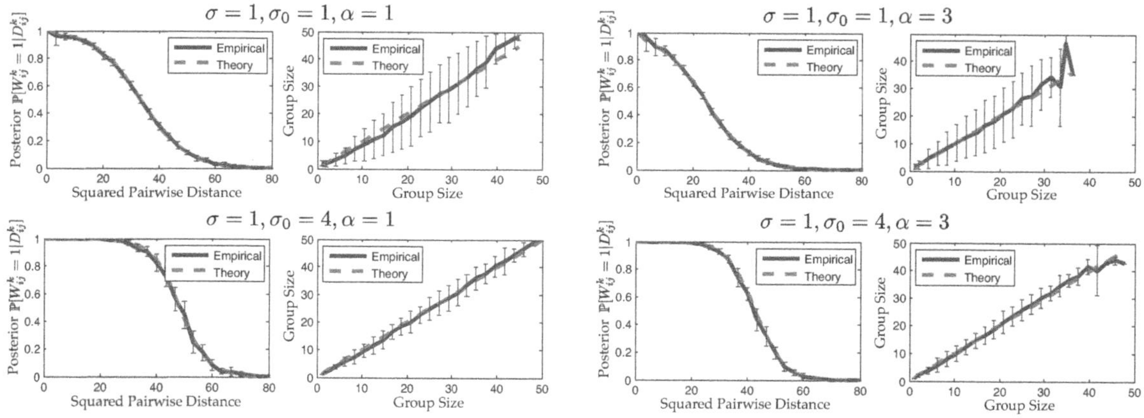

Figure 2: Validation of posterior link probability (Eqn. (7)) and expected group size (Eqn. (5)). Our theoretical estimation matches well with the simulation under different parameter settings.

approximation (Eqn. (6)) is valid and our estimation of expected group sizes is reasonably accurate for the clustering model. We investigate the performance with four sets of parameters $(\alpha, \sigma_0, \sigma)$ as shown in Fig. 2. For each set of parameters, we set $d = 12$ and generate $K = 500$ independent tasks according to Eqn. (4), each with $N = 50$ workers and $\sigma_{k0} = \sigma_0, \alpha_k = \alpha$. We compare our estimated group sizes using Eqn. (5) and posterior link probability using Eqn. (7) with those empirically computed from the simulation. We can see that our theoretical estimation is very accurate, especially when the clusters are well-separated (i.e., $\sigma_0 \gg \sigma$).

4. EXPERIMENTS ON M-TURK

Now, we present empirical studies on the real data collected from Amazon Mechanical Turk (M-Turk). Since our main focus is to characterize the schools of thought phenomenon in crowdsourcing, most of the experiments are qualitative. At the end, we also present some quantitative results to demonstrate the potential usefulness of our statistical analysis for predicting gold standard (if exists).

4.1 Experimental setup

For each HIT (i.e., Human Intelligence Task), we design three missions, each containing several tasks with different levels of clarity listed as follows. Each worker is required to finish all the tasks only once. Following [21], all tasks are vision-related. We expect to see workers of various reliability, task-specific schools of thought due to diversity of clarity, and give insights to possible confusions in human-aided vision tasks. We emphasize that our analysis is not restricted to vision tasks and our techniques can be applied to analyze crowdsourcing data collected in other fields, including text mining, natural language processing, etc.

Mission 1: Object Categorization. In this mission, we provide three tasks. In each task, workers are asked to decide which of the 12 images contain a certain object category, namely *sky*, *building* and *computer*. Each task is designed to have a different level of clarity. For task *sky*, there are simply 6 images with sky and 6 without sky. For the less clear task *building*, there are 4 images with a typical building, 4 images without a building, and 4 images that contain a building-like structure. The task *computer* is the most confusing one, in which 6 out of 12 images are equally divided into three subsets, each containing a typical computer, a

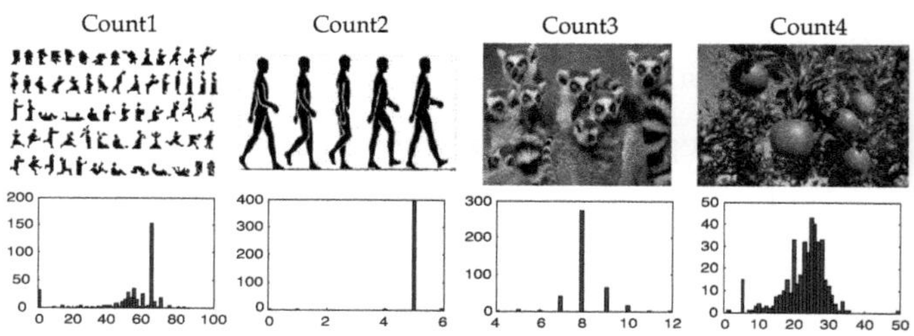

Figure 3: Object counting task. A counting histogram is shown as well as the image. In all tasks, the cluster structures of worker responses are clear. For *Count3*, an outlier response 725 is not shown.

typical object that is not a computer, and a computer-like electrical appliance (e.g., Apple iPad or Amazon Kindle); and the other 6 images follow the same strategy of three-way-division but the objects in the images are elusive and require some efforts to find.

Mission 2: Object Counting. In this objective mission, workers are asked to count the number of objects in 4 images. We regard each image as one task. Among the 4 images, the simplest one contains 5 humans, one contains 65 small human-shaped objects that are laborious to count, one contains 8 animals huddling together and requires efforts to count, and the most confusing one contains 27 apples that are of various sizes and partially hidden in tree branches. All the 4 images have gold standards counted by authors.

Mission 3: Images Aesthetics. In this subjective mission, there are two tasks with comparably low clarity. In each task, workers are asked to pick 6 most beautiful images from 12 images. Among the 12 images, 3 are considered ordinary-looking, 3 are beautiful, 3 are impressively beautiful, and 3 are of astonishing beauty, according to authors' criterion.

Fig. 1 and Fig. 3 show example images. All images are manually picked online. The images are randomly shuffled when presented to workers to avoid any order bias ("Donkey vote"). Once we have obtained the responses of workers, we remove incomplete and duplicate responses from the same worker and construct a dataset that contains the responses of 402 unique workers to the 9 tasks. For each worker, the response includes a 12 dimensional binary vector for each task in object categorization and image aesthetics missions, and a 1 dimensional integer for each object counting task.

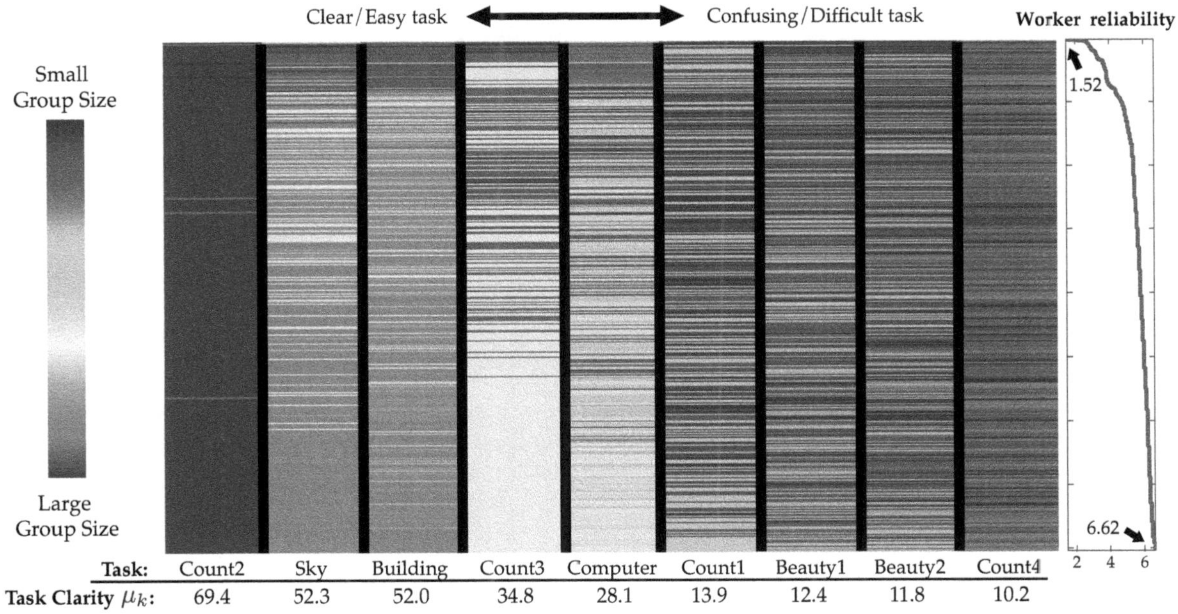

Figure 4: Expected *worker-task* groupsize matrix with rows sorted by worker reliability $\boldsymbol{\lambda}$ and columns sorted by task clarity $\boldsymbol{\mu}$. The matrix shows a strong factorizable structure. Workers: Reliable workers (the bottom part of the matrix) show their consistency across different tasks. Coinciding with our assumption, they always stay with large groups. In addition, from the distribution of reliability, a small portion of the workers can be identified as low quality (the top part of the matrix). Tasks: Tasks in object categorization mission are generally clear while tasks in image aesthetics mission are in general ambiguous. Tasks in counting missions show mixed clarity. *Count2* (Counting five humans) is the clearest task, while *Count4* (Counting apples) is the most confusing one. (This figure is best viewed in color.)

Unless explicitly mentioned, in all tasks we set the hyperparameter $\sigma = 0.2$ and estimate α and σ_0 from empirical expectation (Eqn. (8) and Eqn. (9)). We will also provide a sensitivity analysis on the hyperparameter σ.

4.2 Characterization of Schools of Thought

We apply our low-rank model to all the 9 tasks. The rank-1 residual error $\|\#\tilde{\mathbf{Z}} - \boldsymbol{\lambda}\boldsymbol{\mu}^T\|_F / \|\#\tilde{\mathbf{Z}}\|_F$ is 0.27, which means 73% of the energy in $\#\tilde{\mathbf{Z}}$ has been explained away by $\boldsymbol{\lambda}$ and $\boldsymbol{\mu}$. This shows that our model can fit the data well. Although we do not jointly model the interaction between clustering and factorization, the cluster size matrix $\#\tilde{\mathbf{Z}}$ *naturally* follow the rank-1 factorization, which verifies our low-rank assumption. It may be theoretically intriguing to formulate a joint model and design an iterative procedure for model fitting. However, this may result in an improper bias on the data.

Below, we first examine the existence of schools of thought and its two major latent factors – worker reliability and task clarity, and then provide detailed analysis on worker reliability.

Visualization of schools of thought. We show the patterns of schools of thought for the tasks in object categorization and image aesthetics missions as the posterior link probability matrix (Fig. 1) computed from Eqn. (7). For better visualization, we set $\alpha = 750$, $\sigma = 0.6$ and $\sigma_0 = 1$. Rather than posterior link probability matrix, histograms are shown separately for each of the 4 counting tasks (Fig. 3). Different visualization is used because each counting task is done separately, while for the other missions, workers' responses are based on 12 images at a time.

Task-specific schools of thought. From Fig. 1 and Fig. 3 we can clearly see the task-dependent schools of thought. Even for the simplest task (e.g., *sky*) and tasks with ground truth (e.g., object counting), there are still substantially diverse answers. For task *sky*, a large group of people think the outer space looking from the Moon is not sky, or a glowing bluish icy ceiling in a cave is sky. For counting, some workers think the image with 65 human-like drawings does not contain humans and give zero answer. For more complicated and confusing tasks, the number of clusters goes up, and each cluster size goes down. In subjective tasks, almost everyone has their own responses and the cluster structure is almost invisible.

Distribution of worker reliability. Fig. 4 shows the structure of the expected *worker-task* groupsize matrix $\#\tilde{\mathbf{Z}}$ as well as the estimated worker reliability $\boldsymbol{\lambda}$ and task clarity $\boldsymbol{\mu}$. From the worker reliability plot, most of the workers are comparably reliable and they tend to stay consistently in larger groups in different tasks. A small portion of workers did a very poor job, consistent with the observation in [19]. Among the three types of missions, object categorization is relatively clear, image aesthetics is in general very subjective and vague. Counting mission shows mixed results. Nearly all workers are correct in task *Count2*, making it the clearest one. One the other hand, counting apples of varied size with background clutters (task *Count4*) is extremely confusing.

4.3 Closer Examination of Worker Reliability

In this subsection, we present a closer examination of the estimated worker reliability and compare it with baselines. Besides, we also show how to use it for improving prediction of gold standard for objective tasks.

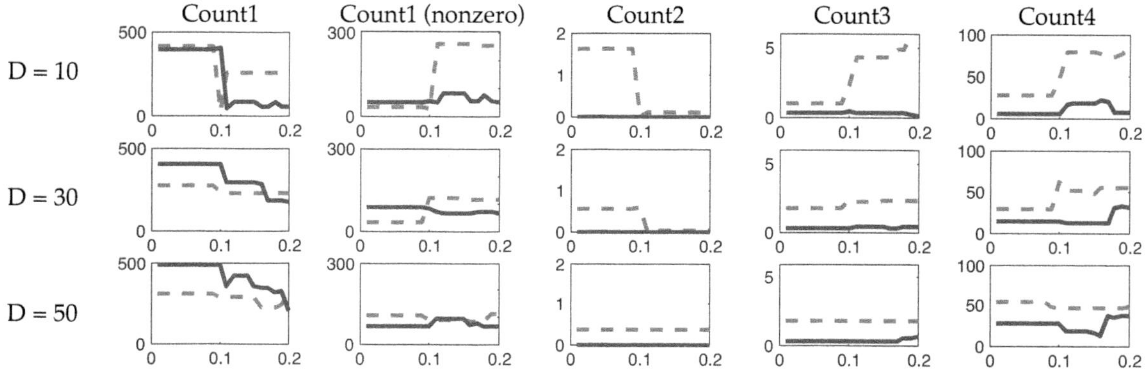

Figure 5: The variance $\bar{\sigma}_T^2$ of the responses of D most reliable workers (blue solid lines) versus the variance $\bar{\sigma}_{UT}^2$ of D most unreliable workers (red dashed lines) averaged on the 4 counting tasks. Ideally $\bar{\sigma}_T^2 \ll \bar{\sigma}_{UT}^2$ (i.e., blue solid lines are below red dashed lines). In all plots, x-axis shows hyperparameter σ ranging from 0.01 to 0.2.

Ranking workers. To verify the computed worker reliability $\boldsymbol{\lambda}$, we first estimate $\boldsymbol{\lambda}$ on the 5 tasks (*sky, building, computer, beauty1, beauty2*), then check if the estimation makes sense in the remaining four objective tasks. For checking, we rank the workers according to $\boldsymbol{\lambda}$, compute the answer variance $\bar{\sigma}_T^2$ for reliable workers, and the answer variance $\bar{\sigma}_{UT}^2$ for unreliable workers, and then compare the two variances. If $\bar{\sigma}_{UT}^2 \gg \bar{\sigma}_T^2$, which means workers labeled as "unreliable" give inconsistent answers compared to those labeled as "reliable", then the ranking is meaningful and can be generalized to other unseen tasks. Specifically, $\bar{\sigma}_T^2$ is computed from D most reliable workers, and is averaged over 4 remaining counting tasks. Similarly for $\bar{\sigma}_{UT}^2$. The result is shown in Fig. 5. We vary D from 10 to 50, and vary σ from 0.01 to 0.2 for sensitivity analysis. A subset of workers give zero responses to task *Count1*, (presumably thinking those drawings are not humans). In the second column, we also show the results after excluding zeros from ranking.

It is clear that in most of the cases, the reliable workers estimated on one set of tasks give answers that are much more consistent (i.e., with a lower variance) than the unreliable ones in a different set of tasks. This suggests that the worker reliability is generalizable from one task to another task, which is consistent with what we have observed in Fig. 4. From the results, we can also see that our approach is relatively insensitive to the change of hyperparameter σ and parameter D.

Comparison with baseline clustering models. As we have stated in Section 2.3, we can use alternative methods to perform the clustering on worker responses. Now, we compare the performance of our method ($\sigma = 0.2$) with spectral clustering [13], PCA-Kmeans and Gibbs sampling on the DP mixture model in Eqn. (3). Note that all these baselines require inference on the cluster assignment of each worker in order to compute the group sizes, while our method does not. For spectral clustering, we take the $L = 5$ to 70 smallest eigenvectors of normalized graph Laplacian and normalize them to be unit vectors as the low-dimensional embedding, on which Kmeans are performed with L clusters. For PCA-Kmeans, we first reduce the dimension of the workers' response to 5 using PCA, and run Kmeans with $L = 5$ to 70 clusters. For Gibbs sampling, we use the Algorithm 8 in [12] with the same set of hyperparameters as estimated in Eqn. (9) with $\sigma = 0.2$.

Table 1: Time cost comparison between the methods using various baseline clustering algorithms and ours.

Methods	Time (sec)
Ours	1.41 ± 0.05
Spectral Clustering	3.90 ± 0.36
PCA-Kmeans	0.19 ± 0.06
Gibbs Sampling	53.63 ± 0.19

Fig. 6 shows the performances of different methods. All the baselines are repeated for 500 times with random initialization. We present their best average performances and its associated standard deviations, achieved by tuning the hyperparameter (i.e., the number of clusters). We can see that our approach is comparable with baselines but is much more stable because it does not require initialization. Tbl. 1 shows the average time cost over 50 runs. Ours is faster than spectral clustering and Gibbs sampling. PCA-Kmeans is the fastest since it does not compute pairwise distance, but its performance is worse than ours.

Table 2: Performance comparison on predicting the gold standard counts for the four counting tasks.

	Cnt1	Cnt2	Cnt3	Cnt4
Ours. $D = 5$	65	5	8	26
Ours. $D = 10$	65	5	8	26
Ours. $D = 20$	65	5	8	25.6
MV	53.7	5.0	9.9	22.9
MV(median)	60	5	8	24
LFC [15]	56	5	8	24
MDW [21] ($c = 1$) (top-10 pred., 50 init.)	63.7	5	8	25.96
MDW [21] ($c = 3$) (top-10 pred., 50 init.)	65.01	5	8	25.48
Gold Standard	65	5	8	27

Prediction of gold standard. As a specific case of schools of thought, our approach can also be applied for those tasks having one unanimous answer (e.g., the counting tasks) and predict the gold standard. Here, we provide one example that uses selective "majority voting", namely, we first select D most reliable workers based on the estimated worker reliability $\boldsymbol{\lambda}$, and then apply majority voting for

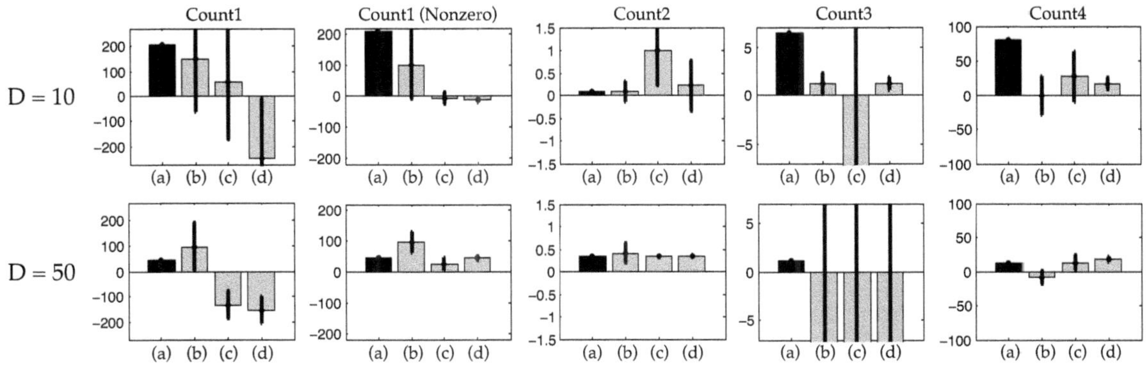

Figure 6: Comparison between (a) our method (with $\sigma = 0.2$), (b) spectral clustering, (c) PCA+Kmeans, and (d) Gibbs sampling, on the difference $\bar{\sigma}^2_{UT} - \bar{\sigma}^2_T$, where $\bar{\sigma}^2_{UT}$ is the variance of the answers of D most unreliable workers and $\bar{\sigma}^2_T$ is the variance of D most reliable workers averaged on 4 counting tasks. Ideally $\bar{\sigma}^2_{UT} \gg \bar{\sigma}^2_T$, and thus the bar should be a large positive number. The first row shows $D = 10$, and the second shows $D = 50$.

prediction. An alternative method would be weighing the responses of workers with their reliability. Yet we obtain the same performance.

Tbl. 2 shows the comparison of our method to three very competitive baseline methods on predicting the count numbers for 4 counting tasks. The baselines include the classic inclusive "majority voting" (MV) heuristic, which performs over all the 402 workers, the "learning from crowds" (LFC) method [15], which iteratively estimates workers' precisions and tasks' gold standard using an EM procedure, and the "multidimensional wisdom of crowds" (MDW) method [21] as we have discussed in the introduction. For LFC, we follow Eqn.(10)-(11) in [15] and use MV as the initial guess of gold standard as suggested in the paper. For MDW, since it does not handle the case that the gold standard is in the continuous domain, we first find maximum a posteriori estimation of the workers' precisions, treat them as workers' reliability, and estimate the gold standard by averaging the answers of top-10 reliable workers. In MDW, each task k is a hidden c-dimensional vector $\mathbf{v}_k$ and each worker is represented as a set of weights in the same dimension. Both need to be estimated from the data. In the experiment, we choose $c = 1$ and $c = 3$.

We can see that our selective MV outperforms all the three baselines, especially on *Count1* and *Count4*, and our prediction matches the gold standard very well. MDW has comparable performance yet it is quite sensitive to the initialization. When $d = 1$, MDW gives the same prediction as ours (i.e. $(65, 5, 8, 26)$) in most random initializations, however, it also gives $(0, 5, 8, 24.05)$ if not initialized properly. The reason is that, although most workers vote for 65 (called "65-voters"), there is a small group voting for 0s ("0-voters") on *Count1*. If MDW falls into this small cluster and regards 0-voters as more reliable than 65-voters, the gold standard estimation of *Count4* will also change. In contrast, ours always rate 65-voters over 0-voters since 65-voters form a larger cluster than 0-voters. Thus, ours gives a deterministic answer to worker reliability. Besides, on the four counting tasks, using the stopping criterion

$$\sqrt{\sum_k \|\mathbf{v}_k^{t+1} - \mathbf{v}_k^t\|^2} / \sqrt{\sum_k \|\mathbf{v}_k^t\|^2} \leq 10^{-4}$$

(where $\mathbf{v}_k$ is the hidden representation of task k in iteration t), MDW spends 3.25 ± 3.34 seconds for $c = 1$, and 4.26 ± 3.70 seconds for $c = 3$, averaged over 50 random initializations. The large variation in the rate of convergence is due to different initialization. In comparison, our method runs for 0.68 seconds, is insensitive to the parameter D and the value of the hyperparameter σ, and has no initialization.

5. CONCLUSIONS AND FUTURE WORK

This paper formally analyzes the schools of thought phenomenon and its two key underlying factors, worker reliability and task clarity, in crowdsourcing by presenting a computational model based on a low-rank assumption, which characterizes the relationships between the group sizes of worker responses and the two key factors. Furthermore, the expected group sizes can be estimated analytically instead of performing an expensive and unstable inference step. We report real experiments on Amazon Mechanical Turk.

In terms of time cost, the major bottleneck of our work is to compute the groupsize matrix $\#\mathbf{Z}$, which has time complexity of $O(KN^2)$ (K is the number of tasks and N is the number of workers). However, if N is large, given worker i, we can sample a few other workers to obtain an unbiased estimate of $\#z_{ik}$, yielding approximately $O(KN)$ complexity. Another interesting future direction is to handle the case of missing data that some workers may not give answer to some tasks. In such a case, how to estimate the group size for observed answers and how to factorize the group size matrix $\#\mathbf{Z}$ in the presence of missing entries deserve more exploration.

From a learning point of view, our analysis could provide insights for developing better predictive tools in several ways. For example, we have shown that high quality labels can be selected from the answers of workers who enjoy top ranking in worker reliability for building better predictive models. For future work, we can acquire new labels from those workers that have higher reliability in the context of active learning [14]. Finally, our analysis could help the market price "high-reputation" workers [2].

Acknowledgements Yuandong Tian is supported by Microsoft Research PhD Fellowship (2011-2013) and an ONR grant N00014-11-1-0295.

6. REFERENCES

[1] J. Abernethy and R.M. Frongillo. A collaborative mechanism for crowdsourcing prediction problems. In *NIPS*, 2011.

[2] E. Adar. Why I hate Mechanical Turk research (and workshops). In *CHI*, 2011.

[3] C.E. Antoniak. Mixtures of Dirichlet processes with applications to Bayesian nonparametric problems. *Annals of statistics*, 2(6):1152–1174, 1974.

[4] D. Blackwell and J.B. MacQueen. Ferguson distributions via Pólya urn schemes. *Annals of statistics*, 1(2):353–355, 1973.

[5] AP Dawid and AM Skene. Maximum likelihood estimation of observer error-rates using the EM algorithm. *Journal of the Royal Statistical Society. Series C (Applied Statistics)*, 28(1):20–28, 1979.

[6] S.J. Gershman and D. Blei. A tutorial on bayesian nonparametric models. *Journal of Mathematical Psychology (in press)*, 2011.

[7] T.L. Griffiths and M. Steyvers. Finding scientific topics. *National Academy of Sciences of the United States of America*, 101(Suppl 1):5228, 2004.

[8] P.D. Hoff, A.E. Raftery, and M.S. Handcock. Latent space approaches to social network analysis. *Journal of the American Statistical Association*, 97(460):1090–1098, 2002.

[9] P.G. Ipeirotis, F. Provost, and J. Wang. Quality management on Amazon Mechanical Turk. In *ACM SIGKDD workshop on human computation*, 2010.

[10] D.R. Karger, S. Oh, and D. Shah. Iterative learning for reliable crowdsourcing systems. In *NIPS*, 2011.

[11] A. Kittur, E. Chi, and B. Suh. Crowdsourcing user studies with Mechanical Turk. In *CHI*, 2008.

[12] R.M. Neal. Markov chain sampling methods for Dirichlet process mixture models. *Journal of computational and graphical statistics*, 9(2):249–265, 2000.

[13] A. Ng, M. Jordan, and Y. Weiss. On spectral clustering: Analysis and an algorithm. In *NIPS*, 2001.

[14] D. Pinar, J. Carbonell, and J. Schneider. Efficiently learning the accuracy of labeling sources for selective sampling. In *SIGKDD*, 2009.

[15] V.C. Raykar, S. Yu, L.H. Zhao, G.H. Valadez, C. Florin, L. Bogoni, and L. Moy. Learning from crowds. *Journal of Machine Learning Research*, 99:1297–1322, 2010.

[16] J. Ross, L. Irani, M. Silberman, A. Zaldivar, and B. Tomlinson. Who are the crowdworkers? Shifting demographics in Mechanical Turk. In *CHI*, 2010.

[17] D.M. Russell, M.J. Stefik, P. Pirolli, and S.K. Card. The cost structure of sensemaking. In *CHI*, 1993.

[18] P. Smyth, U. Fayyad, M. Burl, P. Perona, and P. Baldi. Inferring ground truth from subjective labelling of venus images. In *NIPS*, 1995.

[19] R. Snow, B. O'Connor, D. Jurafsky, and A. Ng. Cheap and fast – but is it good? evaluating non-expert annotations for natural language tasks. In *EMNLP*, 2008.

[20] Y.W. Teh, D. Newman, and M. Welling. A collapsed variational Bayesian inference algorithm for latent Dirichlet allocation. In *NIPS*, 2006.

[21] P. Welinder, S. Branson, S. Belongie, and P. Perona. The multidimensional wisdom of crowds. In *NIPS*, 2010.

[22] J. Whitehill, P. Ruvolo, T. Wu, J. Bergsma, and J. Movellan. Whose vote should count more: Optimal integration of labels from labelers of unknown expertise. In *NIPS*, 2009.

[23] Y. Yan, R. Rosales, G. Fung, M. Schmidt, G. Hermosillo, L. Bogoni, L. Moy, J.G. Dy, and PA Malvern. Modeling annotator expertise: Learning when everybody knows a bit of something. In *AISTATS*, 2010.

[24] J. Zhu, N. Chen, and E. Xing. Infinite Latent SVM for Classification and Multi-task Learning. In *NIPS*, 2011.

Appendix: Derivation of posterior distribution $\mathbb{P}\left(W_{ij}^k = 1 | D_{ij}^k\right)$

By the Bayes' rule, we have

$$\mathbb{P}\left(W_{ij}^k = 1 | D_{ij}^k\right) = \frac{\mathbb{P}\left(D_{ij}^k | W_{ij}^k = 1\right)\mathbb{P}\left(W_{ij}^k = 1\right)}{\mathbb{P}\left(D_{ij}^k | W_{ij}^k = 0\right)\mathbb{P}\left(W_{ij}^k = 0\right) + \mathbb{P}\left(D_{ij}^k | W_{ij}^k = 1\right)\mathbb{P}\left(W_{ij}^k = 1\right)},$$

where the likelihood term $\mathbb{P}\left(D_{ij}^k | W_{ij}^k\right)$ and the prior term $\mathbb{P}\left(W_{ij}^k = 1\right)$ are computed as follows.

The likelihood term $\mathbb{P}\left(D_{ij}^k | W_{ij}^k\right)$. For $W_{ij}^k = 1$, both $\mathbf{x}_{ik}$ and $\mathbf{x}_{jk}$ are generated independently from the same cluster center with variance σ^2, thus we have $\mathbf{x}_{ik} - \mathbf{x}_{jk} \sim \mathcal{N}(\cdot|\mathbf{0}, 2\sigma^2)$. Therefore, $D_{ij}^k = \|\mathbf{x}_{ik} - \mathbf{x}_{jk}\|^2$ satisfies χ^2 distribution with the following pdf:

$$\begin{aligned}\mathbb{P}\left(D_{ij}^k | W_{ij}^k = 1\right) &= \phi(D_{ij}^k; d, \sigma^2) \\ &= \frac{1}{2^{d/2}\Gamma(d/2)} \frac{1}{(\sigma^2)^{d/2}} (D_{ij}^k)^{d/2-1} \exp\left(-\frac{D_{ij}^k}{4\sigma^2}\right)\end{aligned}$$

where d is the dimension of the workers' responses. Similarly, for $W_{ij}^k = 0$, by integrating their cluster centers out, we can show $\mathbf{x}_{ik}, \mathbf{x}_{ik}$ are independently generated from $\mathcal{N}(\cdot|\mathbf{0}, \sigma_0^2 + \sigma^2)$. Thus we have $\mathbb{P}\left(D_{ij}^k | W_{ij}^k = 0\right) = \phi(D_{ij}^k; d, \sigma^2 + \sigma_0^2)$.

The prior term $\mathbb{P}\left(W_{ij}^k = 1\right)$. By the exchangeability property of Chinese restaurant process, all workers are equal. Thus

$$\begin{aligned}\mathbb{P}\left(W_{ij}^k = 1\right) &= \mathbb{P}\left(W_{12} = 1\right) \\ &= \mathbb{P}\left(z_1 = 1\right)\mathbb{P}\left(z_2 = 1 | z_1 = 1\right) \\ &= \frac{1}{1+\alpha}\end{aligned}$$

Combining the two parts, we thus obtain the posterior distribution $\mathbb{P}\left(W_{ij}^k = 1 | D_{ij}^k\right)$:

$$\mathbb{P}\left(W_{ij}^k = 1 | D_{ij}^k\right) = \frac{1}{1 + \exp\left(\beta_k D_{ij}^k + \beta_{k0}\right)}$$

where $\beta_k \equiv \frac{\sigma_{k0}^2}{4\sigma^2(\sigma_{k0}^2 + \sigma^2)}$ and $\beta_{k0} \equiv \log \alpha_k + \frac{d}{2}\log\frac{\sigma^2}{\sigma_{k0}^2 + \sigma^2}$.

Note the same derivation follows if we use Euclidean distance $l_{ij,k} = \|\mathbf{x}_{ij} - \mathbf{x}_{ik}\|$ and

$$\begin{aligned}\mathbb{P}\left(W_{ij}^k = 1 | l_{ij,k}\right) &= \mathbb{P}\left(W_{ij}^k = 1 | D_{ij}^k\right) \\ &= \frac{1}{1 + \exp\left(\beta_k l_{ij,k}^2 + \beta_{k0}\right)},\end{aligned}$$

where is exactly the same as the one using squared Euclidean distance.

Social Sampling

Anirban Dasgupta Ravi Kumar D. Sivakumar
Yahoo! Research, 701 First Avenue, Sunnyvale, CA 94089.
{anirban,ravikumar,dsiva}@yahoo-inc.com

ABSTRACT

We investigate a class of methods that we call "social sampling," where participants in a poll respond with a summary of their friends' putative responses to the poll. Social sampling leads to a novel trade-off question: the savings in the number of samples (roughly the average degree of the network of participants) vs. the systematic bias in the poll due to the network structure.

We provide precise analyses of estimators that result from this idea. With non-uniform sampling of nodes and non-uniform weighting of neighbors' responses, we devise an ideal unbiased estimator. We show that the variance of this estimator is controlled by the second eigenvalue of the normalized Laplacian of the network (the network structure penalty) and the correlation between node degrees and the property being measured (the effective savings factor). In addition, we present a sequence of approximate estimators that are simpler or more realistic or both, and analyze their performance.

Experiments on large real-world networks show that social sampling is a powerful paradigm in obtaining accurate estimates with very few samples. At the same time, our results urge caution in interpreting recent results about "expectation vs. intent polling".

Categories and Subject Descriptors: H.2.8 [**Database Management**]: Database Applications – Data Mining

Keywords: Polling, Social networks

1. INTRODUCTION

Polling is a method commonly employed to estimate the fraction of a population that possesses some property of interest (e.g., supporters of a political party, alcoholics, consumers of organic food, living on minimum wages, smartphone owners, gun owners, people who understand compound interest, etc.). The fundamental quantities of interest in polling are the number of samples and the error rate, and their trade-off is understood well from a statistical viewpoint: if we wish to approximate a fraction to within an additive error of ϵ, roughly $1/\epsilon^2$ samples are both necessary and sufficient.

Small subpopulations constrain the error ϵ to be small, and thus in reality the sampling cost often becomes a significant burden to deal with. In practice, researchers resort to multiple alternatives in trying to reduce this burden. For example, one could sample members of the population not uniformly but with some built-in biases that make the estimates more reliable with fewer samples; in the absence of proper normalization such schemes could often be prone to a systematic bias. In a specific instance, while estimating the fraction of schools that implement a particular program, educationalists often resort sampling schools with probability proportional to the square root of the teachers or students.*

Yet another sampling approach, and one that has found recent interest in polling research, is to inquire a respondent about how prevalent the property of interest is among the respondent's circle of friends, family, or their neighborhood, and aggregate these responses in some meaningful way. A particular example is given by economists Rothschild and Wolfers who in [14] propound the benefits of using "expectation polling" (where voters are asked about who they expect will win the election) over "intent polling" (where they are asked about their voting intent). While different such sampling methods often produce reasonable estimates in practice, few come with any kind of theoretical guarantees on either the *sampling bias* or on the *sampling error*, equivalently the number of samples required to have an ϵ-error estimate.

The framework. In this work, we investigate a class of methods we call "social sampling." The broad idea is that there is a social network underlying the population of interest, and members of the social network often have knowledge of their neighbors' predilections — social, political, as well as in other aspects of life — and will be able to summarize them meaningfully, when asked the right questions. By doing so, one could expect a savings in the number of samples required by a factor roughly equal to the d, the average degree of the social network of the participants, since a randomly chosen respondent is summarizing the results from d of his friends in order to give an answer. On the other hand, this sampling strategy now depends intimately on the network and so the analysis of the sampling bias† and error would have to incorporate the systematic effects introduced by the network structure. Our main contribution is to design the sampling strategy such that such sampling bias is overcome, and to precisely characterize the sampling error, and hence the number of samples sufficient for an ϵ-error estimate,

*See the DoE report at `http://nces.ed.gov/pubs92/92082.pdf`. In doing so, the statistical estimate one obtains is not a measure of the prevalence of the program itself, but of the number of students impacted by the program; we address this specific type of skew momentarily via volume estimates.

†This is different from the subtle bias arising from the fact that participants often tailor their notion of "friends" while answering a question, which leads to overestimation; for example, when asked how many of a respondent's friends drive a hybrid car, their notion of friendship might expand to include any acquaintance who drives a hybrid car.

in terms of both the spectral property of the network, and the correlation of the attribute and the network degree distribution.

Formally, the social sampling framework models the sampling problem as follows: $G = (V, E)$ is a social network, $f : V \to \{0, 1\}$ is a binary function that tells us whether each node in V satisfies some property, and our goal is to estimate the fraction of nodes $v \in V$ such that $f(v) = 1$. We derive several *unbiased* estimators of this fraction based on the idea of social sampling outlined above, and provide a precise analysis of the resulting estimators.

Network-induced biases. Before we describe our actual estimators in more detail, we outline the difficulties alluded to above: how does the network structure play a role in saving number of samples vs. in introducing statistical errors. Consider, for example, the network in Figure 1(a), where there is only one RED node that is connected to all the remaining $n - 1$ nodes, which are all colored BLUE. The fraction of RED nodes is vanishingly small, and yet, every node that is sampled reports having a RED node in the neighborhood; thus unless we tune the sampling method to account for network structure, we will end up with a very biased estimate.

The interplay of the *sampling error* and network structure is even more subtle. As the example in Figure1(b) shows, we might have a subpopulation of RED nodes that, although significant in overall size, is barely connected to the BLUE nodes. Furthermore, even the interconnection between the RED nodes could very well be sparse (none in Figure 1(b)). In this case, any sampling method that asks users to only proffer a summary from their neighbor's information is doomed to have a higher variance than the naive estimator, since exactly one high degree node in this graph reports a very large number of RED neighbors. Thus, the variance analysis needs to encode some characterization of the network structure, and it is not a priori obvious what could be that characterization.

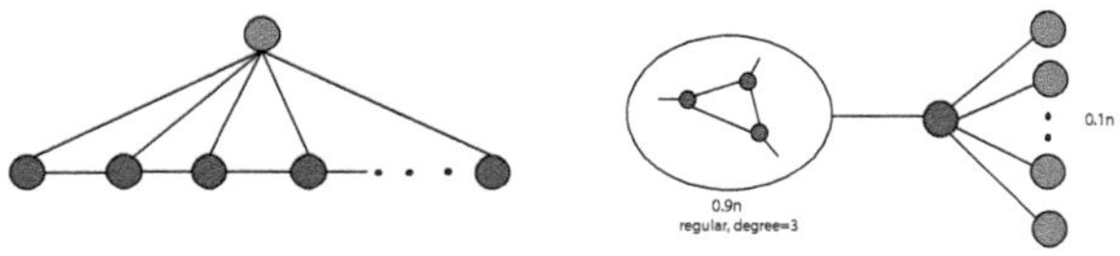

Figure 1: (a) Need to scale neighbor contributions by their degree. (b) Need for expansion: in this case neighbor querying has high variance.

Main results. We first introduce an 'ideal' unbiased estimator where nodes are sampled from the social network according a non-uniform distribution and where the function values of the nodes' neighbors are weighted in a non-uniform way (the function value at a neighbor is weighted by the reciprocal of its degree). This is intuitive since weighting the neighbors' values by the reciprocal of the degree undoes the bias introduced by large degree nodes (that will appear as neighbors of several nodes), and picking high-degree nodes as respondents of the poll naturally gives us large savings, and helps us 'reach deeper' into the network. Our main result is that the variance of this estimator is controlled by two factors: the second eigenvalue $(1 - \lambda_2)$ of the normalized Laplacian of the network, and the correlation between node degrees and the property being measured. The first factor captures the penalty to be paid because of correlation in the samples caused by the network structure, and the second factor captures the savings resulting from having a larger number of 'effective samples.' Specifically, the first factor is $m\lambda_2^2/n$, which always lies in the range $[O(1), d_{\text{avg}}]$ (d_{avg} being the average degree). The smaller λ_2 is than 1, the better connected is the network; for random regular graphs and well-connected regular expanders with degree d, λ_2^2 is roughly $1/d$, so this factor is only a constant. The second factor is $\|D^{-1/2}f\|_2^2$, where D is the diagonal matrix of the node degrees, and f is the vector representation of the function whose average is being estimated. This factor captures the correlation of f with the node degrees; again, for regular graphs, this is $\bar{f}/d$, where $\bar{f}$ is the (true) estimate and the factor d represents the savings from social sampling.

The ideal estimator assumes significant knowledge of the network, specifically about the degrees of nodes. Since this information may not be available in severely restricted contexts, we present a sequence of approximate estimators and analyze their performance (both rigorously and empirically). One simple and natural variant is when the pollster picks the nodes uniformly at random (thus eliminating the need for the knowledge of the node degrees), and the respondents incorporate their knowledge of the (putative) responses as well as the degrees of their neighbors. Another variant of interest is one where the pollster (e.g., a social networking site) has perfect knowledge of the network structure (except for the function values), but it is unrealistic to expect nodes to have perfect information about their neighbors' degrees. In this case, the pollster picks nodes according to the ideal estimator, but for each chosen node, samples a small number of its neighbors, and asks the chosen node a query of the form "among your friends A, B, and C, how many exercise regularly?" In both of these highlighted cases, we derive unbiased estimators and analyze their variances.

A third variant attempts to formally model "expectation polling," a subject of interest in polling research [14]. The authors presented empirical analysis to conclude that expectation polling is often significantly more accurate than intent polling. As an explanation, they suggested that when polled about their expectations, respondents implicitly summarize the intents of their friends and family. Our analysis shows that if this is carried out on a social network, the result will incorporate each person's intent with a weight proportional to its degree in the social network; thus, well-connected nodes might end up skewing the poll result significantly. However, it is incorrect to assume that in an expectation poll, the respondents include all of their acquaintances with equal importance; it is natural for a respondent to "discount" one of their neighbors if the neighbor is an exceptionally popular person (unless they are truly close to the respondent). We model this in the following probabilistic way. When polled, each person implicitly creates an "effective set" of their friends to which each of their neighbors belongs with probability inversely proportional to its (the neighbor's) degree. The polled person then tosses a coin with probability of heads equal to the fraction of this effective set that is RED, and reports either RED or BLUE depending on the outcome, and also announces the size of the effective set. We show that this model, too, enjoys the savings in the number of samples similar to the ideal estimator; our analysis of this model complements [14] and offers a way to rigorously analyze the success of expectation polls.

Another variant of the estimators touches upon the difference between two useful ways to reason about the popularity of a concept within a society. One way, of course, is the *prevalence* of the concept, measured as the fraction of the set of members to whom the concept applies; another way is to measure the *pervasiveness* of the concept, measured as the fraction of the pairwise relations such that at least one of members involved subscribes to the concept. Often, the prevalence and pervasiveness of a concept are wildly different, depending on how influential its adopters are. We show that pervasiveness can be modeled by the *volume* of the set of nodes[‡] with the given property, and show how to estimate this quantity efficiently (by a much simpler variant of the ideal estimator).

[‡]Formally, volume of a set $S \subseteq V$ of nodes in a network is the total degree of the nodes in S.

Finally, we apply the estimators to several large real-world graphs, and report experimental results. One of the networks is a snapshot of around 4M nodes from the LiveJournal social network, where we estimate the prevalence of various natural properties — users from geographic locations of various magnitudes (cities, states, countries), users of various age groups, users interested in a variety of topics, etc. The other network we study is the coauthorship network among roughly 1M authors whose papers are included in the DBLP database; here we estimate the prevalence of various publishing outlets (conferences and journals). Our experiments show that social sampling is a powerful paradigm in obtaining accurate estimates from significantly fewer samples than standard sampling. At the same time, they also highlight how the performance of the estimators are sensitive to the structure of the network, and how prevalent and pervasive the properties are.

2. RELATED WORK

Sampling to estimate hidden subpopulation is classical. The fact that an ϵ-additive error can be achieved with constant probability using $O(\frac{1}{\epsilon^2})$ samples can be shown using a variety of tail inequalities and is folklore. Lower bounds on the number of samples, on the other hand, is more recent [4, 2]. Sampling algorithms have been studied in large networks, from a perspective of estimating different network properties. Leskovec and Faloutsos [12] defined the problem of creating a representative sample of the network that approximates multiple properties of the original network such as average shortest path, centrality, etc; see also [5, 13]. An intriguing variant of the network sampling question was posed by Backstrom and Kleinberg [1] in the context of creating buckets of social network users for A/B testing of features that require social interactions. There is an implicit trade-off of independence in sampling and correlation (due to ties to chosen samples) that they study; see also [11]. Voting on social networks has been considered by Boldi et al. [3] who studied different vote delegation mechanisms.

Katzir, Liberty, and Somekh [10] presented a method to estimate the size of online social networks using degree-biased sampling and counting collisions in the samples collected; their method can also be used to estimate subpopulations. Their technique is more geared for settings where the sampling is restricted to using the public API provided by the social networks; for instance, choosing an uniformly random node is expensive in their model since it requires rejection sampling.

In the theoretical domain, Goldreich's survey [7, 8] provides a nice elucidation of the trade-off between the number of random bits utilized, the number of samples, and the computational complexity in sampling to estimate a function within an ϵ-additive error. In fact, our guarantees in Theorem 4 and Theorem 12 are generalizations of a result [8] on regular (large degree) expanders, and show the same order of improvement in sample size. Our model, though is different, in that we are not interested in saving randomness and we consider neighbor queries by sampled nodes to be free.

As mentioned before, the question inspiring our work is closest to the one studied by Rothschild and Wolfers [14], where they study the value of asking "who is expected to win" as opposed to "whom do you expect to vote for" and show empirical evidence that the former often leads to better estimates; they do not investigate the question in the context of explicit social networks or present theoretical quantification of when such a gain could be expected.

The presence of social connections among the sampled population has also been exploited in the *snowball sampling* class of techniques of which *respondent driven sampling* (RDS) [9] is probably the best known. RDS has proven to be useful in practice, having being used in over 120 studies. RDS, however, has not yet been amenable to theoretical analysis, except under assumptions of random graph models [6]. Our technique is orthogonal to RDS (and in principle composable) since the purpose there is to use the network to recruit the next respondent, not reduce the number of samples by using people's knowledge of their neighbors' predilections.

There have also been numerous studies on the interaction of network structure and node attributes. One theory that deserves a mention in our setting is that of *homophily* or *assortativity*: the tendency of nodes that are alike to link to each other. The network structure in fact has a much more subtle effect on the sampling error than a simple homophily metric can measure. The effect of increasing homophily on our estimates is obtained through the second eigenvalue characterization: if increasing homophily makes the network more partitioned, our estimates will degrade In Section 4, we show some experiments with attributes that have different homophilies.

3. ALGORITHMS

3.1 Notation

The network is represented by an undirected graph $G = (V, E)$, where V denotes the set of nodes and E denotes the set of edges. Let $n = |V|$ and $m = |E|$. Frequently, the variables u, v will denote the nodes of G. For any node u, the set of neighbors of u is denoted by $N(u)$. The *degree* of node u is denoted $d_u = |N(u)|$. We will assume that $d_u \geq 1$ for all nodes. Let $f : V \to \{0, 1\}$ denote the function of interest, i.e., we wish to estimate the fraction $\bar{f} = \frac{1}{n}|\{u \mid f(u) = 1\}|$. We will also consider f as the indicator (column) vector of the set $\{u \mid f(u) = 1\}$ i.e., $f_u = f(u)$. Let A denote the adjacency matrix of the graph, i e., $A_{uv} = 1$ if and only if $(u, v) \in E$. Let D be a diagonal matrix such that $D_{uu} = d_u$. For any vector $p \in \mathbb{R}^n$ such that $\sum_u p_u = 1$ we define the diagonal matrix P by $P_{uu} = p_u$. Finally, let $\mathbb{1}$ denote the n-element vector of all 1's, i.e., $\mathbb{1}_u = 1$ for all u.

3.2 Estimating size

The most basic algorithm for estimating $|\{u \mid f(u) = 1\}|$, or equivalently the fraction $\bar{f}$, is the standard estimator (Algorithm 1) that samples a set of nodes and polls each sampled node u to check if $f(u) = 1$, and reports the fraction of the nodes that satisfy this. The following guarantee on the Naive estimator is well-known [7].

Algorithm 1 Naive size estimator.

Require: Graph G, function $f : V \to \{0, 1\}$, sample size r.
Choose a random sample $S \subseteq V$ of r nodes with replacement by including node u with probability $\frac{1}{n}$.
Return $\hat{f} = \frac{1}{r}\sum_{u \in S} f(u)$.

FACT 1. *If we pick* $r = 2/(\epsilon^2\delta)$ *samples, with probability* $1-\delta$, *the* Naive *estimator will give an estimate* $\hat{f}$ *such that* $|\hat{f} - \bar{f}| < \epsilon$.

The intuition behind "social sampling" is that if we poll a node u to obtain some estimate of $\{f(v) \mid v \in N(u)\}$, we could use fewer samples than we need with the naive estimator. As the example in Figure 1 showed, we need to normalize by the degree of the node in order to get an unbiased estimator. The next sampler we present, the ideal size estimator (Algorithm 2), corrects precisely for this bias, by scaling $f(v)$ by $1/d_v$.

We now proceed to analyze the quality of the ideal estimator for different distributions p. We do this by establishing a lemma that bounds the variance of the above estimator; first, of course, we note that the ideal estimator is an unbiased estimator of $\bar{f}$.

Algorithm 2 Ideal size estimator(p).

Require: Graph G, function $f : V \to \{0,1\}$, probability distribution p on V, and sample size r.
Choose a random sample $S \subseteq V$ of r nodes with replacement by including node u with probability p_u.
Return $\hat{f} = \frac{1}{nr}\sum_{u\in S}\frac{1}{p_u}\sum_{v\in N(u)} f(v)/d_v$.

Define $e_u \in \mathbb{R}^n$ to be the vector with only $e_u(u) = 1$ and $e_u(v) = 0$ for $v \neq u$. Define the random variable F as follows: pick $u \in V$ with probability p_u, and let $F = \frac{e_u^T AD^{-1}f}{np_u}$, which is well defined since by assumption $d_v \geq 1$ for all v. To help the analysis, note that the vth component of the vector $D^{-1}f$ is precisely $f(v)/d_v$, and the uth component of the vector $AD^{-1}f$ is precisely $\sum_{v\in N(u)} f(v)/d_v$. Recall that P is a diagonal matrix such that $P_{uu} = p_u$. The following establishes the unbiasedness property, independent of p, and characterizes the variance in terms of a quantity that we will later bound.

LEMMA 2. *The random variable F satisfies* $\mathrm{E}[F] = \bar{f}$ *and* $\mathrm{E}[F^2] = \frac{1}{n^2} f^T D^{-1}AP^{-1}AD^{-1}f$.

PROOF. The expectation can be simply computed as

$$\mathrm{E}[F] = \sum_u p_u \frac{e_u^T AD^{-1}f}{np_u} = \sum_u e_u^T AD^{-1}f/n$$
$$= \mathbb{1}^T AD^{-1}f/n = DD^{-1}f/n = \bar{f}.$$

For $\mathrm{E}[F^2]$, we have

$$n^2\mathrm{E}[F^2] = \sum_u p_u \left(\frac{e_u^T AD^{-1}f}{p_u}\right)^2$$
$$= \sum_u \frac{(e_u^T AD^{-1}f)^2}{p_u}$$
$$= \sum_u f^T D^{-1}Ae_u e_u^T AD^{-1}f/p_u$$
$$= f^T D^{-1}A\left(\sum_u e_u e_u^T/p_u\right)AD^{-1}f = f^T D^{-1}AP^{-1}AD^{-1}f. \quad \square$$

Next, we bound its variance for the special case when respondents are sampled with probability proportional to their degree.

LEMMA 3. *Let the sampling probability* $p_u = \frac{d_u}{2m}$. *Define the matrix L by* $L = D^{-1/2}AD^{-1/2}$ *and let λ_2 denote the second largest eigenvalue of L.*[§] *Then* $\mathrm{var}(F) \leq (2m/n^2)\lambda_2^2\|D^{-1/2}f\|^2$.

PROOF. When the sampling probability p_u satisfies $p_u = d_u/2m$, we have $P = D/2m$.

$$\mathrm{var}(F) = f^T D^{-1}AP^{-1}AD^{-1}f/n^2 - \bar{f}^2$$
$$= f^T D^{-1}A(2mD^{-1})AD^{-1}f/n^2 - \bar{f}^2$$
$$= \frac{2m}{n^2} f^T D^{-1}AD^{-1}AD^{-1}f - \bar{f}^2$$
$$= \frac{2m}{n^2} f^T D^{-1/2}L^2D^{-1/2}f - f^T\mathbb{1}\mathbb{1}^T f/n^2$$
$$= \frac{2m}{n^2} f^T D^{-1/2}\left(L^2 - \frac{D^{1/2}\mathbb{1}\mathbb{1}^T D^{1/2}}{2m}\right)D^{-1/2}f$$
$$\leq \frac{2m}{n^2}\left\|L^2 - \frac{D^{1/2}\mathbb{1}\mathbb{1}^T D^{1/2}}{2m}\right\|\left\|D^{-1/2}f\right\|^2.$$

[§] $I - L$ is called the *normalized Laplacian* and thus $1 - \lambda_2$ is the second smallest eigenvalue of the normalized Laplacian.

Now, it can be verified by basic manipulations that the first eigenvector of L^2 is $\frac{D^{1/2}\mathbb{1}}{\sqrt{2m}}$ with eigenvalue 1. Thus we have $\|L^2 - \frac{D^{1/2}\mathbb{1}\mathbb{1}^T D^{1/2}}{2m}\| = \lambda_2(L^2) = \lambda_2^2$. The proof follows. $\square$

Using this variance bound, we can easily obtain a bound on the number of samples sufficient in order to get an ϵ-error estimate.

THEOREM 4. *With* $p_u = \frac{d_u}{2m}$ *and sample size* $r = \lceil\frac{4m\lambda_2^2\|D^{-1/2}f\|^2}{n^2\epsilon^2\delta}\rceil$ *the* Ideal *size estimator produces $\hat{f}$ such that* $|\bar{f} - \hat{f}| < \epsilon$ *with probability* $1-\delta$.

PROOF. If we take r samples and denote the corresponding estimators by $F_1, \ldots F_r$, then, $\hat{f} = \sum_i F_i/r$. Applying the Chebyshev inequality, we have

$$\Pr[|\hat{f} - \bar{f}| > \epsilon] \leq \frac{2\mathrm{var}(\hat{f})}{\epsilon^2} \leq \frac{2\mathrm{var}(F)}{r\epsilon^2}.$$

Choosing $r = \frac{2\mathrm{var}(F)}{\epsilon^2\delta} = \frac{4m\lambda_2^2\|D^{-1/2}f\|^2}{n^2\epsilon^2\delta}$, the proof follows. $\square$

If the initial sampling probabilities are changed from being proportional to degree to being proportional to the square roots of degrees, we obtain a similar bound. Instead of presenting a very similar proof again, we summarize the result below.

COROLLARY 5. *Let* $m_s = \sum_u \sqrt{d_u}$. *If we take* $p_u = \frac{\sqrt{d_u}}{m_s}$ *and* $r = \lceil d_{\max}^{1/2}\frac{2m_s\lambda_2^2\|D^{-1/2}f\|^2}{n^2\epsilon^2\delta}\rceil$ *samples, the* Ideal *estimator satisfies* $|\hat{f} - \bar{f}| < \epsilon$ *with probability* $1-\delta$.

The number of samples required for uniform sampling can be bound similarly as follows. Its proof follows from the proofs of Corollary 5 and Theorem 4, by plugging in the suitable probabilities.

COROLLARY 6. *For sampling probabilities* $p_u = \frac{1}{n}$, *the variance of the sampler can be bounded by* $\mathrm{var}(F) \leq \frac{1}{n} f^T D^{-1}A^2D^{-1}f - \bar{f}^2$. *In order to get an ϵ-error estimate with probability $1-\delta$, it suffices to take* $r = \lceil d_{\max}\frac{2\lambda_2^2\|D^{-1/2}f\|^2}{n\epsilon^2\delta}\rceil$ *samples.*

The actual gain obtained by using the degree-based sampler instead of the Naive estimator can be clearly seen if the graph is regular, and more specifically, an expander. Recall that $\lambda_2 < 1$ always.

COROLLARY 7. *Suppose G is a d-regular graph. Then the* Ideal *estimator with probability distribution* $p_u = \frac{1}{n}$ *requires* $\lceil\frac{\lambda_2^2}{\epsilon^2\delta}\rceil$ *samples to produce an ϵ-error estimate of $\bar{f}$ with probability $1-\delta$. If in addition G is also an expander, with* $\lambda_2 = cd^{-1/2}$, *then the* Ideal *estimator requires* $\lceil\frac{c^2}{d\epsilon^2\delta}\rceil$ *samples.*

From the preceding analyses, it follows that the correlation between the function f on V and the degrees of the nodes in V is one source of variance. We consider an interesting special case, where there is no such correlation, i.e., when f is obtained by tossing independent coins with probability $\bar{f}$ for each $u \in V$. In this case, we can actually compute the optimal strategy for sampling the nodes. It is obtained by minimizing the resulting variance.

THEOREM 8. *If for each node u $f_u = 1$ as a result of a i.i.d. coin toss with probability $\bar{f}$, then the optimal strategy to include node u in the sample with probability p_u proportional* $\sum_{v\in N(u)}\frac{1}{d_v}$.

PROOF. Under a sampling strategy given by distribution p, the variance is given by

$$\mathrm{var}_p(F) = \sum_u \frac{1}{p_u}\left(e_u^T AD^{-1}f\right)^2 - \bar{f}^2.$$

Thus

$$\mathrm{E}_f[\mathrm{var}_p(F)] + \bar{f}^2 = \sum_u \frac{1}{p_u}\mathrm{E}_f[(e_u^T AD^{-1}f)^2]$$

$$= \sum_u \frac{1}{p_u}\mathrm{E}_f\left[\sum_{v\in N(u)} f_v/d_v\right]^2 = \sum_u \frac{1}{p_u}\mathrm{E}_f\left[\sum_{v,v'\in N(u)} f_v f_{v'}/d_v d_{v'}\right]$$

$$= \sum_u \frac{1}{p_u}\sum_{v,v'\in N(u)} \bar{f}^2/d_v d_{v'} = \bar{f}^2 \sum_u \frac{1}{p_u}\left(\sum_{v\in N(u)} \frac{1}{d_v}\right)^2.$$

Thus, we need to find the optimal set of probabilities p_u such that the above expression is minimized under the constraint $\sum_u p_u = 1$. By using a Lagrangian it is possible to show that $p_u \propto \sum_{v\in N(u)} \frac{1}{d_v}$ minimizes the above expression. □

3.3 Approximating the Ideal estimator

The Ideal estimator and its variants incorporate the idea that a sampled node u has enough knowledge about its neighbors v to give the pollster responses based on $f(v)$ and d_v (for all its neighbors v). Next we introduce a variant that we motivate in two ways. The common outcome in both cases is that each node u only includes a small number of its neighbors in producing its response to the poll. The first setting is where the pollster has complete knowledge of the network (e.g., an online social network like Facebook), including the neighborhood structure and the degrees of all nodes. The only unknown is f. What is expensive in this model is asking a node u about too many of its neighbors; it would be desirable to poll a node u about $f(v)$ for a small number (say five) of carefully chosen neighbors v of u.¶ The second motivation for this style of sampling is that it serves as a model for polls of the form "Think of three of your best friends, and then tell us how many of them are left-handed." The hypothesis is that when a person is asked a question of this form, they will tend not to pick their highly popular neighbors, so the distribution that picks neighbors with probability inversely proportional to their degrees may be thought of as a good model for the distribution with which they pick their friends.

Algorithm 3 Sparse size estimator(p).

Require: Graph G, function $f : V \to \{0,1\}$, probability distribution p on V, and sample size r.
Choose a random sample S of r nodes with replacement by including node u with probability p_u.
For each node $u \in S$, create a set $T_u \subseteq N(u)$ by picking each neighbor $v \in N(u)$ with probability $1/d_v$.
For each node $u \in S$, create a set $T'_u \subseteq T_u$ by picking k of its neighbors from T_u (without replacement).
For $u \in S$, compute $H_u = (|T_u|/k)\sum_{v\in T'_u} f(v)$.
Return $\hat{f} = \frac{1}{nr}\sum_{u\in S}\frac{1}{p_u}H_u$.

Deriving a variance bound on the error of this sampler is harder. We just claim that this is an unbiased estimator. The proof is a simple application of the linearity of expectation.

LEMMA 9. *Algorithm 3 obtains an unbiased estimate of* $\bar{f}$.

3.4 A model of expectation polling

Next we present a model of "expectation" polling, a type of polling used for predicting elections, where the participants are asked not about their voting *intent*, but about who they *expect* will win the election. Rothschild and Wolfers [14] have recently argued that expectation polling is more powerful than intent polling, and have suggested that the power of expectation polling comes from the fact that the respondents often give an aggregate view of their friends and family (i.e., neighbors in a social network).

We propose a model of how respondents in expectation polls summarize the intent of their neighbors in a social network (Algorithm 4). The idea is that the polled node, instead of giving just a 0/1 vote, gives a weighted vote: either zero or an estimate of the neighborhood belonging to $f = 1$. We can show a similar bound

Algorithm 4 Expec: winner estimator(p).

Require: Graph A, function $f : V \to \{0,1\}$. Probability of sampling node u is p_u and size of sample is r.
Choose a random sample S of r nodes with replacement by including node u with probability p_u.
Node u when picked, computes $q_u = \sum_{v\in N_u}\frac{f_v}{d_v}$ and $r_u = \sum_{v\in N_u}\frac{1}{d_v}$ and returns G_u where $G_u = r_u$ with probability $\frac{q_u}{r_u}$ and 0 else.
Return $\hat{f} = \frac{1}{nr}\sum_{u\in S}\frac{1}{p_u}G_u$.

to Theorem 4, using a similar variance computation.

LEMMA 10. *For* $p_u = \frac{d_u}{2m}$, *if we use* $\lceil \frac{4n\lambda_2^2\|D^{-1/2}f\|\|D^{-1/2}(1-f)\|}{n^2\epsilon^2\delta}\rceil$ *samples, the resulting estimate* $\hat{f}$ *satisfies* $|\bar{f} - \hat{f}| < \epsilon$ *with probability* $1-\delta$.

3.5 Estimating volume

The fraction of nodes that satisfy some property $f : V \to \{0,1\}$ is an estimate of the prevalence of a property within the nodes of a social network. However, the participants modeled as nodes in a social network interact with each other, and often have knowledge of their neighbors. This motivates the problem of measuring the *pervasiveness* of a property, measured not just as the fraction of nodes that possess that property, but taking into account all the pairwise interactions in which at least one node has $f = 1$. The intuition here is that this represents the amount of "mindshare" this property has in the social network, assuming interactions happen only over, and uniformly across, the existing edges. To capture this, we invoke the concept of the *volume* of the function $f : V \to \{0,1\}$, defined by $d_f = \sum_{u:f(u)=1} d_u$; in order to estimate volume, we use the same set of analysis and methods. The main difference is that now each sampled node u only needs to return $\sum_{v\in N(u)} f(v)$ instead of the degree-normalized sum as in Algorithm 2. The lemma corresponding to Lemma 2 is the following. Define again the random variable G as $G_u = e_u^T Af/2mp_u$ with probability p_u.

Algorithm 5 Ideal volume estimator(p).

Require: Graph A, function $f : V \to \{0,1\}$. Probability of sampling node u is p_u and size of sample is r.
Choose a random sample S of r nodes with replacement by including node u with probability p_u.
Return $\widehat{d_f} = \frac{1}{2mr}\sum_{u\in S}\frac{1}{p_u}\sum_{v\in N(u)} f(v)$.

LEMMA 11. *For the random variable* G, $\mathrm{E}[G] = d_f/2m$, *and* $\mathrm{var}[G] = (1/4m^2)(f^T AP^{-1}Af - d_f^2)$.

The proof follows by calculation similar to Lemma 2. And thus, we obtain the following result for degree-based sampling.

¶In fact, the pollster only needs to ask how many of the five chosen neighbors have $f(v) = 1$.

THEOREM 12. *With $p_u = d_u/2m$, if we use $\lceil \lambda_2^2/(\epsilon^2\delta) \rceil$ samples, then the resulting estimate $\widehat{d}_f$ satisfies $|\frac{d_f}{2m} - \frac{\widehat{d}_f}{2m}| \le \epsilon$ with probability at least $1-\delta$.*

PROOF. (Sketch) First, choosing $p_u = d_u/2m$, the variance of the estimator is

$$\begin{aligned}\mathrm{var}(G) &= \frac{1}{4m^2} f^T A P^{-1} A f - \frac{d_f^2}{4m^2} \\ &= \frac{1}{2m} f^T A D^{-1} A f - \frac{D\mathbb{1}\mathbb{1}^T D}{4m^2} \\ &= \frac{1}{2m} f^T D^{1/2} \left(D^{-1/2} A D^{-1} A D^{-1/2} f - \frac{D^{1/2}\mathbb{1}\mathbb{1}^T D^{1/2}}{2m} \right) D^{1/2} f \\ &= \frac{1}{2m} f^T D^{1/2} \left(L^2 - \frac{D^{1/2}\mathbb{1}\mathbb{1}^T D^{1/2}}{2m} \right) D^{1/2} f \\ &\le \frac{1}{2m} \| f^T D^{1/2} \|^2 \| L^2 - \frac{D^{1/2}\mathbb{1}\mathbb{1}^T D^{1/2}}{2m} \| \text{ using Cauchy–Schwarz.}\end{aligned}$$

Note that $\|f^T D^{1/2}\|^2 = d_f$ and that $\|L^2 - \frac{D^{1/2}\mathbb{1}\mathbb{1}^T D^{1/2}}{2m}\|$ equals $\lambda_2(L^2) = \lambda_2^2$. Thus $\mathrm{var}(G) \le \frac{1}{2m} d_f \lambda_2^2$. Recall $\widehat{d}(f) = \sum_i G_i$ where G_i is an independent copy of G. Using the Chebyshev inequality, we have

$$\Pr\left[\left|\frac{\widehat{d}_f}{2m} - \frac{d_f}{2m}\right| > \epsilon\right] \le \frac{\mathrm{var}(G)}{r\epsilon^2} \le \frac{d_f \lambda_2^2}{2mr\epsilon^2}.$$

Since $d_f \le 2m$, choosing $r = \frac{\lambda_2^2}{\epsilon^2\delta}$, we have the result. □

Similarly, when f is the result of a random coin toss, the optimal set of sampling probabilities are now obtained by sampling each node proportional to its degree.

THEOREM 13. *If for each node u, $f_u = 1$ as a result of an i.i.d. coin toss with probability $\bar{f}$, then the optimal strategy to sample in order to estimate d_f is to sample node u with probability proportional to d_v.*

Again, the proof works by writing down the expression for the $\mathrm{var}(F_p)$ from Algorithm 5 and choosing the appropriate probability distribution to minimize this quantity for a random f.

4. EXPERIMENTAL SETUP

Data. Our dataset consists of large networks where each node in the network is associated with one or more attributes. Specifically, we consider the following two networks.

The LIVEJOURNAL network is built from the social network LiveJournal (`livejournal.com`). The network consists of about 5.36M nodes and about 160M directed edges and is a version of the social network crawled in March 2008 (the entire data is available through a public API). For our purposes, we treat the network as an undirected network by dropping the edge directions. In addition to the network, we also extract the following attributes (if available) for each of the users from their public profiles: age, location, and a list of interests expressed as free text (e.g., cricket, tennis). The locations were parsed using Yahoo! geolocation API to filter out invalid ones and extract the city, state, country information. Note that not all the nodes have all the attributes. About 58% of the users have a valid location, 40% of the users of have a valid age, and 60% of the users have at least one interest.

The DBLP network is built from the DBLP database (`http://www.informatik.uni-trier.de/~ley/db/`). This data is also available publicly. The network consists of 968K nodes and about 8M undirected edges, where the nodes correspond to authors and the edges corresponding to coauthorship on some publication. We extract all the publication venues of an author and these (free text, abbreviations) form the node attributes. By construction, every node has at least one attribute and there are over a million distinct attributes. We sampled 100 of these attributes with probability proportional to their popularity and used these in our experiments.

Error. In all our experiments, we measure the absolute error of our estimator with respect to the true value, i.e., if the output of our estimator is $\tilde{z}$ and the true value is z, we measure the error as $|z - \tilde{z}|$; in all our experiments, $z \in [0,1]$. Recall that our estimators are designed to output an additive $\pm\epsilon$-approximation to the truth and hence measuring the absolute error is valid. Estimators that work with relative accuracy will require a lot more samples: to measure the bias p of a coin to within $(1 \pm \epsilon)$ error requires $\Omega(\frac{1}{p\epsilon^2})$ samples.

Sampling. We chose a set of number of samples, from a minimum of 100 samples to a maximum of 50000 samples. For a specified number k of samples, we will sample k nodes from the network according to various distributions. We consider the following distributions: uniform at random (unif), proportional to the degree of the node (deg), proportional to the square root of the degree of the node (sqrtdeg), and proportional to the reciprocal of the sum of the degree of the neighbors of the node (recdeg).

Given a set A of k samples and an estimator g, we proceed in the following way. Let $L = \{1, 3, 5, 7, 9\}$. For each $\ell \in L$, we first chop A into ℓ partitions $A_1, \ldots, A_\ell$, apply the estimator $g(\cdot)$ on each of the partitions, and then output the median of the results, i.e., we output $g'_\ell(A) = \mathrm{med}\{g(A_1), \ldots, g(A_\ell)\}$. We then output both $\min_{\ell \in L} g'_\ell(A)$ as well as $\mathrm{mean}_{\ell \in L} g'_\ell(A)$. For simplicity, we report all our results with respect to the latter; in Section 5.6, we show that using the min vs mean does not affect the results/trends.

Estimators. We called the basic estimator Naive: recall that this estimator samples nodes uniformly at random (unif) and outputs an estimate based on how many of the sampled nodes have the attribute. We refer to the ideal estimator as Ideal, the estimator that is meant to capture the social expectation of a user as Expec, and the estimator based on a sampling of close friends as Sparse.

5. RESULTS

We summarize the results of our experiments on the two datasets. Recall than in LIVEJOURNAL, the attributes of interest were the geo (each of five cities, states, and countries), a set of ages, a set of age-buckets and a set of interests (various sports). In each of the cases, the typical size of the attribute set ranged from 0.4% to 4%, with the maximum country size being 38% and the maximum age-bucket size being 30% of the entire network. In each of the cases, the additive errors plotted are typically smaller than the average size of the attribute in that category. In each of the cases, in order to generate the curves, after computing the grouping described above, we plot the mean error over multiple groupings. To simplify presentation, we aggregated the results of the geo attributes, those of the age attributes, and the age-bucket attributes.

In DBLP, the set of attributes corresponded to venues of publication, and the set of 100 selected ranged in size from 0.01% to 3% in size, with a median of 0.5%. Again, each of our curves is obtained by averaging over all these attributes.

To clarify the trend better, we also smoothed the curves using Bezier smoothing in `gnuplot`; this lets us compare the trends without being too concerned about the variance issues that are bothersome at this small scale. For larger scale experiments, the corresponding sample sizes would be larger and variance would be less.

5.1 Performance on LIVEJOURNAL

The results for the LIVEJOURNAL dataset for the geo attributes are summarized in Figure 2. They show the performance of the sampling algorithms on the city, state, and country attributes. The algorithms considered are the Naive estimator with uniform bias, the Ideal estimator with degree and square-root degree biases, the Sparse and Expec both with degree biases. Any other biases would only increase the variance of the Naive estimator. The performance of the estimator that has sampling bias of sum of inverse-degrees of neighbors is almost always subsumed by the degree-biased and square-root biased estimators, and furthermore, is computationally more expensive. Thus, we leave out this inverse-degree-sum estimator in most experiments except for one in Figure 5.

The x-axis is the sample size and the y-axis is the additive error. From the plot, it is clear that the performance of Ideal for the degree and square-root-degree biases are the same. The performance curves all exhibit similar trends; as expected, the error decreases faster than linearly with an increase in the number of samples.

For the city attributes, the performance of Naive is comparable to that of Expec and is significantly worse than that of Ideal. In the sample size range up to 10k, the error incurred by Naive is about 200% that of the Ideal sampler. In terms of the absolute error size, this corresponds to about 0.1% of the network even near sample size 1k. For the smaller attributes that we have, this difference is essentially one between detecting or not detecting its presence at all. If we fix the error, Naive requires at least twice as many or more samples to achieve the same error as Ideal does. Note that at 10k samples, we are already at 2% of the entire network, a significant sample size. The performance of Sparse (with sparsity parameter = 5) is similar to that of Naive. Also, Expec seems to have a non-monotone behavior near sample size 200, that is again caused by the variance due to small sample sizes: for a fixed sample size Expec has a higher variance than the other estimators due to the discretization of the value returned by each node.

For the state and country attributes, the performance of the samplers are very much similar: Naive performs comparably with degree and square-root biases, and these three perform slightly better than both Expec and Sparse. For states, square-root performs marginally better than every one else, and performs better than degree in both. This is interesting as the theoretical bound we have for the variance of square-root bias is strictly worse than the theoretical bound for the degree bias. Different factors could be contributing to the disparity of the theoretical and empirical performance: the variance bound given is only a crude bound that does not capture the real interaction of f with the structure of G (upper bounds the interaction using a heavy-handed Cauchy–Schwarz inequality). Furthermore, even though the bound given is in terms of λ_2, this quantity itself is not small for these networks since these networks are not known to be expanders at the small scales ($\lesssim$ 10k), which in fact are the attribute sizes that we mostly have.

Figure 3 summarizes the results for the age- and interest-related attributes. Five age attributes (20, 25, 30, 35, and 40) and five age buckets ($[20, 29), \ldots,$) were considered. Once again, the performance of Ideal with degree and square-root degree are much better than that of Naive, offering the same error bound at about half the number of samples. Expec performs worse than Naive in these cases. Together with the results of Figure 2, the indifferent performance of Expec suggests that our model of expectation polling leads to high-variance estimators; to the extent that our model reflects the reality of expectation polling, this is a caveat in interpreting the recent excitement about expectation polling. The final set of attributes for LIVEJOURNAL are a set of sports-related interests, tennis, cricket, etc. Here the performance of the estimators converge sooner, and after sample size 2k, they are virtually identical.

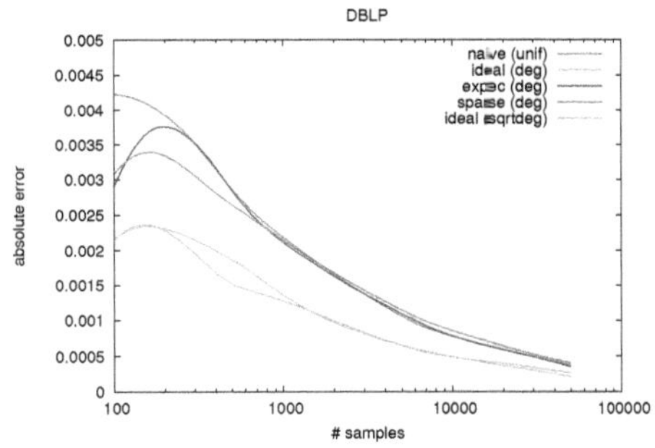

Figure 4: Performance of various algorithms on DBLP.

5.2 Performance on DBLP

For the DBLP network, the attributes refer to publication venues, as described above. We randomly selected 100 such attributes from the set of million attributes with probability proportional to their popularity. The parameter settings for grouping to compute the median are similar as in Section 5.1.

In the DBLP network, the improvement offered by the Ideal set of samplers is starker. For the sample size, the error by the Naive sampler is again 200-300% of the error by the ideal sampler, and Naive requires at least 3-5 times the samples that Ideal uses to achieve the same error. In fact, for the DBLP network, the performance samplers do not converge even at 20k samples, which is about 4% of the entire set of nodes, a pretty big sample size.

5.3 Effect of the initial node selection bias

We now investigate, in Figure 5, the effect of the initial node selection bias in more details, in the context of the cities attribute in LIVEJOURNAL, and for two sampling strategies, Ideal and Expec. We first consider the Ideal algorithm and investigate the different node selection biases — uniform, degree, square-root of degree, and sum of reciprocal-degrees of neighborhood. It is interesting to see that the performances quickly converge, even at sample size 500, with the reciprocal-sum degree and the square-root performing only marginally than the others till sample size 10k. For the Expec sampler, we observe the same phenomenon, but here the uniform strategy is slightly worse, and the reciprocal-sum slightly better than the all the rest.

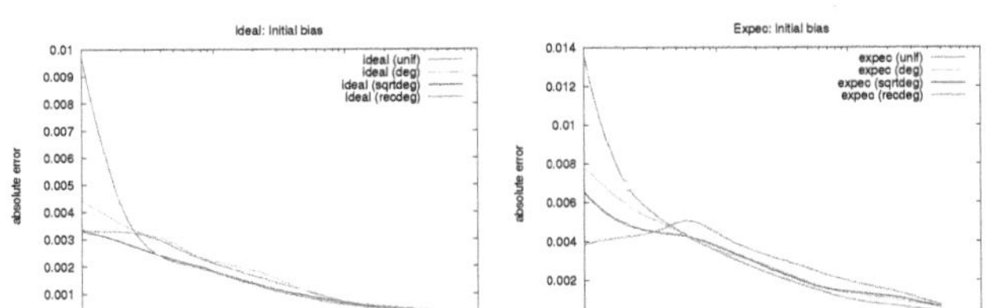

Figure 5: Performance of Ideal and Expec algorithms on the LIVEJOURNAL data for different initial node selection bias.

5.4 Homophily vs. Homogeneity

A natural question to ask is whether the sampling error is correlated with the homophily of the attribute f. In this section, we show that a better way of characterizing the error is not in terms of

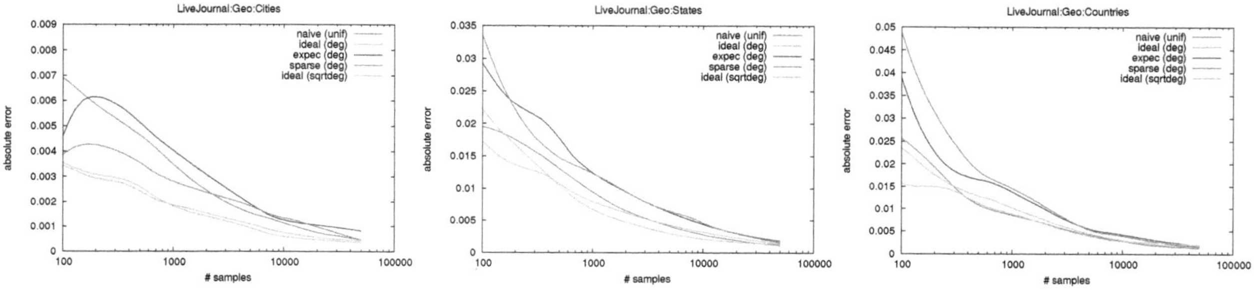

Figure 2: Performance of various algorithms on the LIVEJOURNAL data for random cities, states, and countries.

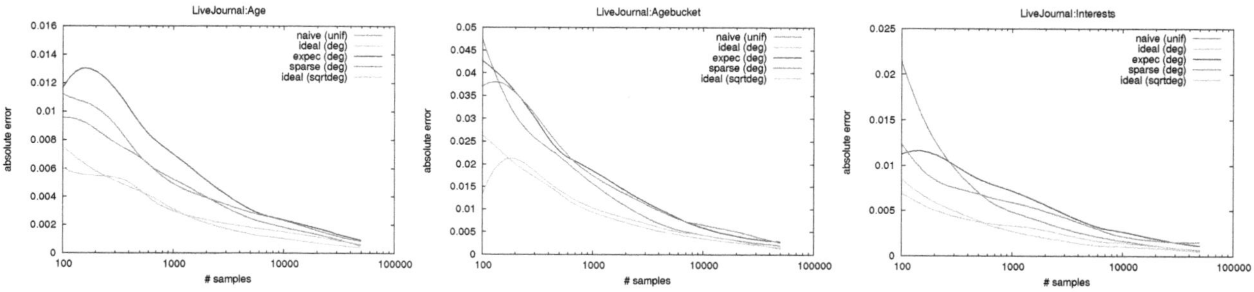

Figure 3: Performance of various algorithms on the LIVEJOURNAL data for random ages, age buckets, and interests.

	f	Naive	Ideal
spearman	0.223	0.126	0.212
pearson	0.086	0.087	0.121

Table 1: Correlation of CH with attribute size, Naive and Ideal errors using both rank (spearman) and a moment (pearson) methods.

homophily, but rather in terms of a weighted measure of "homogeneity" of neighbors — whether neighbors of a node are of same color. In investigating the effect of homophily on error, we measure homophily by the following metric, commonly known as the *Coleman homophily index.*

$$H_f = \frac{\sum_{u,v \in f} 2A_{uv}}{\sum_{u,v \in f} 2A_{uv} + \sum_{u \in f, v \in V \setminus f} A_{uv}}, \qquad \mathrm{CH}_f = \frac{H_f - \bar{f}}{1 - \bar{f}}.$$

Note that $\mathrm{CH}_f \in [0, 1]$ and is zero if f is the result of a random coin toss for every node. Table 1 shows the correlation between the homophily index of 241 cities with the size of the city and with the Naive and Ideal errors. If there was a homophily effect independent of size, then we would see the correlation between Ideal and CH to be higher than the correlation of CH with both Naive-error and $\bar{f}$. From Table 1, the effect of attribute homophily on the sampling error does not seem to be significant.

The sampling error, on, the other hand, depends on the variance of the estimator, as expressed in Lemma 2. In Figure 6 we investigate relation of the variance and the actual error using the same 241 cities. For the variance bound, we use the expression in Lemma 2, that is, $\mathrm{E}[F^2] - \bar{f}^2$. In order to generate this plot, we grouped the 241 attributes into 10 buckets based on the variance quantiles — then the average in each bucket error was plotted against the average variance in each bucket. This was done for both the uniform and the degree bias. In both case, the error has mostly a linear relation with the variance, showing that to a reasonable degree of

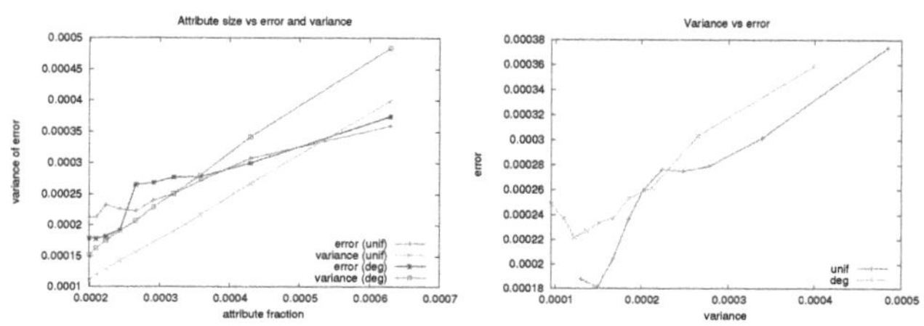

Figure 6: Relation of error and variance for uniform and degree-biased selection and for different attribute sizes.

approximation, bounding the variance is the right strategy in order to minimize the error. Furthermore, the network structure interpretation that the variance encodes is one that is different from homophily. The worst case bound (over all f) on the variance is in terms of the second eigenvalue, which is a measure of the uniform conductance over the entire network. A different nuanced interpretation of a network property from the variance becomes clearer when we consider the regular graph case. We can then rewrite the variance in terms of a measure of *homogeneity of neighbors*, as follows.

FACT 14. *For a function $f : V \to \{0, 1\}$, and a d-regular graph G, define the* neighbor homogeneity *of f in G to be*

$$H(G, f) = \frac{1}{n} \sum_{w} |\{(u, v) \mid u, v \in N(w) \cap f\}| / d^2.$$

Then, the variance of Ideal *is given by* $\mathrm{var}(F) = H(G, f) - \bar{f}^2$.

For non-regular graphs, the corresponding homogeneity measure would weigh the nodes with the corresponding degrees.

5.5 Effect of rarity of truth

We then investigate the effect of the rarity (i.e., the quantity $\bar{f}$) on the error and the variance of the Ideal sampling strategy for the

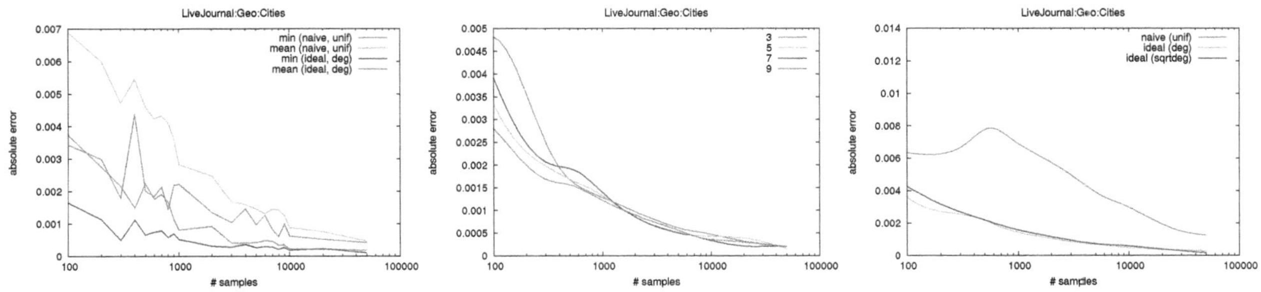

Figure 7: (a) Min vs mean in the partitioning of samples. (b) Effect of the sparsity parameter in Sparse on LIVEJOURNAL data. (c) Volume estimation.

uniform and degree bias. We bucket the cities based on the size of the attribute ($\bar{f}$). For each of these buckets, we computed the average error and the average variance for both the uniform and degree bias. The uniform has mostly a lower variance than the degree-biased samples, but the errors are comparable. The likely explanation is that the degree-biased sampling generates a few outliers, and the median operation helps reduce the error in spite of these outliers.

5.6 Minimum vs mean error of groupings

In order to construct the error values, we employed a median of means approach that we described earlier. Although this is commonly used in practice, there is no rule of thumb for deciding the right way to partition into groups in order to compute this median of means. We thus tried a number of combinations and reported the mean error over these partitions, which corresponds to the error if one chooses one of these partitions at random. Instead, we investigate how the error would look if we were to explicitly find out the partition with the minimum error and use that. Figure 7(a) shows the relation between the mean and the minimum computed over the partitions considered for each sample size, for the uniform and degree-biased Ideal strategy. Note that although the trends are similar for mean and minimum, there is a significant difference between the mean and minimum errors for each sample size. Our results have been reported using the mean aggregation: using the minimum prevents us from making statements such as "sampler X is better than sampler Y," since we would need to specify the partitioning strategy too. However, this leaves open the interesting question of how to define the optimal aggregation strategy when given a fixed number of samples.

5.7 Effect of the sparsity parameter

Figure 7(b) shows the effect of the sparsity parameter in the strategy Sparse, using the LIVEJOURNAL data. Interestingly sampling three neighbors is almost as good as sampling nine neighbors, indicating that a big savings is possible in terms of how many neighbors information we expect the respondents of the poll to summarize. A plausible explanation is that the expander properties of the network when sampling three neighbors on average are qualitatively equivalent to the properties arising from sampling nine neighbors.

5.8 Volume

Finally, we show (Figure 7(c) how our results also translate when we are trying to estimate volume of the attribute set, i.e., the fraction $d_f/2m$. For estimating volume, the Ideal strategies are orders of magnitude better than the Naive one.

6. CONCLUSIONS

We have analyzed a novel trade-off question: what are the benefits and difficulties that arise from sampling nodes of a social network and querying them about their neighbors' properties? We presented variance bounds of a variety of samplers that account for the network structure; our experiments strongly affirm the hypothesis that we started with, namely when done correctly (and incorporating a significant amount of knowledge about the network), the resulting estimators are considerably more efficient than standard polling. We believe that this work joins the exciting body of research at the intersection of statistics and social network theory.

7. REFERENCES

[1] L. Backstrom and J. M. Kleinberg. Network bucket testing. In *WWW*, pages 615–624, 2011.

[2] Z. Bar-Yossef, R. Kumar, and D. Sivakumar. Sampling algorithms: Lower bounds and applications. In *STOC*, pages 266–275, 2001.

[3] P. Boldi, F. Bonchi, C. Castillo, and S. Vigna. Voting in social networks. In *CIKM*, pages 777–786, 2009

[4] R. Canetti, G. Even, and O. Goldreich. Lower bounds for sampling algorithms for estimating the average. *IPL*, 53(1):17–25, 1995.

[5] M. Gjoka, M. Kurant, C. Butts, and A. Markopoulou. Walking in Facebook: A case study of unbiased sampling of OSNs. In *INFOCOM*, pages 1–9, 2010.

[6] S. Goel and M. Salganik. Respondent-driven sampling as Markov chain Monte Carlo. *Statistics in Medicine*, 28(17):2202–2229, 2009.

[7] O. Goldreich. A sample of samplers: A computational perspective on sampling. In O. Goldreich, editor, *Studies in Complexity and Cryptography*, volume 6650, pages 302–332. Springer, 2011.

[8] O. Goldreich and A. Wigderson. Tiny families of functions with random properties: A quality-size trade-off for hashing. *Random Struct. Algorithms*, 11(4):315–343, 1997.

[9] D. Heckathorn. Respondent-driven sampling: A new approach to the study of hidden populations. *Social Problems*, pages 174–199, 1997.

[10] L. Katzir, E. Liberty, and O. Somekh. Estimating sizes of social networks via biased sampling. In *WWW*, pages 597–606, 2011.

[11] L. Katzir, E. Liberty, and O. Somekh. Framework and algorithms for network bucket testing. In *WWW*, pages 1029–1036, 2012.

[12] J. Leskovec and C. Faloutsos. Sampling from large graphs. In *KDD*, pages 631–636, 2006.

[13] B. Ribeiro and D. Towsley. Estimating and sampling graphs with multidimensional random walks. In *IMC*, pages 390–403, 2010.

[14] D. Rothschild and J. Wolfers. Forecasting elections: Voter intentions versus expectations, 2011. Manuscript, `http://researchdmr.com/RothschildExpectations`.

From User Comments to On-line Conversations

Chunyan Wang
Department of Applied Physics
Stanford University
California, USA
chunyan@stanford.edu

Mao Ye
Social Computing Group
HP Labs
California, USA
mxy177@cse.psu.edu

Bernardo A. Huberman
Social Computing Group
HP Labs
California, USA
bernardo.huberman@hp.com

ABSTRACT

We present an analysis of user conversations in on-line social media and their evolution over time. We propose a dynamic model that predicts the growth dynamics and structural properties of conversation threads. The model reconciles the differing observations that have been reported in existing studies. By separating artificial factors from user behavior, we show that there are actually underlying rules in common for on-line conversations in different social media websites. Results of our model are supported by empirical measurements throughout a number of different social media websites.

Categories and Subject Descriptors

J.4 [**Computer Applications**]: Social and Behavior Sciences; G.3 [**Mathematics of Computing**]: Probability and Statistics

General Terms

Human Factors, Theory, Measurement

Keywords

conversation dynamics, social networks

1. INTRODUCTION

The rapid development of social media websites has dramatically changed the way that people communicate with each other. A particularly interesting phenomenon is the prominent role of users as a leading information source within these websites. For example, various on-line media and review sites provide commenting facilities for users to exchange opinions and express sentiments about news, stories and products. These user-generated comments link together and form a conversation thread, which is essentially a distinctive kind of information network that has a life span significantly shorter than other information networks.

KDD'12, August 12–16, 2012, Beijing, China.

As pointed out in [1], despite the significant research efforts made on information networks, dynamics of conversation threads have not received enough attention so far. As a matter of fact, the dynamics of such linked information plays a fundamental role in opinion spread and formation [2, 3], word-of-mouth effects [4] and collective problem solving [5,6]. Existing empirical studies on on-line conversations seem to yield conflicting results about the basic statistical properties: while some results demonstrate that the size distribution of posts and reviews follow a heavy-tailed distribution such as Zipf's law [1,7] or lognormal distribution [8,9], another portion of the literature suggest a light-tailed one, such as negative binomial [10, 11]. A fundamental question is how can two apparently different categories of distributions describe the same type of information network? And what are the dominating factors that are responsible for the observed differences? In this paper, we focus on addressing these problems by proposing a dynamic model for on-line conversations. The contributions of our study can be summarized in three complementary dimensions:

- **User Attention on New Items.** We examine the dynamics of user attention on new items. We analyze the duration of new topics displayed to users, and also the non-Poisson nature of user commenting behavior.
- **Model of On-line Conversations.** We propose a dynamic model for conversation growth based on a number of different factors, including the exposure duration of topics on the website, patterns of users' commenting behavior, and also the impacts of social propagation and social influence. The model successfully reconciles existing discrepancies in reported studies, and also explains the structural properties within a conversation thread.
- **Size and Structure of Conversations.** We compare results from our model with empirical measurements using datasets from Digg[1], Reddit[2] and Epinions[3].

The rest of this paper is organized as follows. Section 2 reviews the related work. Section 3 introduces the datasets used in our empirical studies. Section 4 introduces key observations on user behavior and the impact of featuring mechanisms on user attention. Based on these observations, Section 5 introduces the dynamic model for user conversation.

[1]http://digg.com
[2]http://reddit.com
[3]http://epinions.com

Section 6 compares predictions of the model with empirical measurements. Section 7 concludes the paper with a discussion.

2. RELATED WORK

In this section, we discuss some of the relevant studies categorized in three sub-areas.

2.1 Information Spread and Conversations

In the field of information dissemination, the pioneering work of Liben-Nowell and Kleinberg [12] modeled information spread as a propagation of chain letter. Golub and Jackson [13] extended this work with a branching process model combined with the selection bias of observation. In social media, Leskovec et al. [14] investigated the propagation of memes across the Web. The main concern of these studies is to understand information spread in the context of social network. Other relevant studies focused on properties of information networks that are formed in the process of information spread. Mishne et al. [7] investigated weblog comments for identifying blog post controversy, Duarte et al. [15] engaged in describing blogsphere access patterns from the blog server point, Kaltenbrunner et al. [8] measured community response time in terms of comment activity on Slashdot stories, Choudhury et al. [16] characterize conversations through their interestingness, and finally, Kumar et al. [1] modeled the dynamics of conversations with a branching process incorporating recency. Along with the increasing results in on-line conversations, one emerging problem is the seemingly conflicting observations even about the most basic statistical properties of conversation threads. As mentioned earlier, some studies suggest that the size follows a heavy-tailed distribution[4] such as Zipf's law [1, 7] or lognormal distribution [8, 9]. Other measurements point to a Poisson family [10, 11]. One main focus of this paper is to provide an explanation for these differing observations.

2.2 Dynamics of User Attention

Another set of studies related to our work is the dynamics of user attention. In the information age, posts on websites compete with each other for the scarce attention of users [17, 18]. To help users find high quality content, social media websites usually place information in a "featured column" for popular items, such as the "popular" page on Youtube, the "trending" column on Twitter, the "what's hot" column on Reddit. Existing studies show that this featuring mechanism has significant impact on user attention [19]. To enter the featured column, posts need to reach a threshold of critical mass. Studies on Digg [20, 21], Youtube [22], Wikipedia [23] and Twitter [4, 24] successfully explain the attention dynamics of topics after the critical mass threshold. However, it is still unclear about the attention dynamics of the vast majority of topics and stories before reaching the critical mass. As such, it has remained an open question about the attention dynamics and the initial growth of these items. We attempt to propose dynamics of the user attention, measured in the number of user comments, for these general items on social media websites.

[4]In this paper, we use the term heavy-tailed to denote the probability distributions whose tails are not exponentially bounded, i.e. $\lim_{x\to\infty} e^{\lambda x}P(X > x) = \infty, \lambda > 0$.

2.3 Dynamics of Human Behavior

Traditionally, the dynamics of human behavior is described by a series of Poisson process events under the context of Internet [31]. Recent advances in human behavior suggest that the waiting time between two consecutive events follows power law scaling, ranging from email exchanges [25–27] to web browsing [22, 28–30]. Various new models have been proposed to interpret the observed scaling of waiting times [25, 30, 32]. While most existing studies emphasize on explaining the nature and origin of the observation, the implications of this power law scaling on information spread and attention dynamics has not been exploited thus far. In this paper, we examine the waiting time of human comments and more importantly, we use the power law scaling of human behavior to understand the dynamics of on-line conversation.

3. DATA

Three datasets from Digg, Reddit and Epinions are used in our empirical measurements. To collect these datasets, we monitored the website for newly created items or topics. We kept track of these topics' user comments for a time span of at least three months since the topics' creation, to make sure that the growth saturates. We also recorded related information such as the time stamp when the topic is removed from the column for displaying new items. In our empirical studies, we perform the same treatments on these datasets whenever possible.

Digg is an interactive social media website, which allows its users to share and comment on news and stories. Users of the website select and direct attention to a few items from a very large pool of submissions. They can read, Digg, Bury, and leave comments on the topic or other users' comments. In our study, we monitored the website for a total number of 17, 322 topics containing 158, 782 comments. Each comment was labeled by its posting time. To obtain information about individual user's commenting behavior, we also monitored a number of 8, 616 users on Digg and collected all these users' comments.

Another dataset used in our study was from the social news website Reddit. Users on Reddit submit content in the form of either a link or a text post. Other users reading the post can express their opinions by commenting on the original post. Similar to Digg, comments on Reddit can also be directed to existing comments. In our study, we collected over 78, 312 comments from 8, 428 conversation threads. For each comment, we recorded the user-id and timestamps of the comments. We also recorded to which comment or post that comment is referring.

To ensure that our observations are not limited to news media sites, we included a dataset of consumer review from Epinions. Epinions is a who-trust-whom consumer review site, and users write their personal reviews on a wide variety of products, ranging from automobiles to media (music, books, movies and etc.). Members of the site can decide whether to trust other members based on their reviews. Again, every user on the website can comment on the reviews or on the existing comments. We collected 88, 859 unique users' comments from the website. We also collected 286, 317 topics from different categories containing a total of 722, 475 user comments.

4. USER ATTENTION TO NEW ITEMS

To understand the underlying mechanisms governing user attention and on-line conversations, we first look at the growth of attention on newly generated items in social media. Figure 1 (a) shows the growth of cumulative user attention measured in Digg count of four typical topics from Digg. Results from Reddit and Epinions are similar to the one in Digg. One general observation for topics from different categories and different websites is that the cumulative count saturates to a point where a sharp drop of the growth rate is apparent. We explain this observation with the following reasoning. To help users explore new topics, typical social media websites place newly generated topics in the "upcoming" and "new" columns since their creation time. Users visit the website regularly and discover these newly generated stories. After a period of time, the old topics are replaced with newly generated contents. While these replaced items can still be accessed through search queries, it has significantly less chance to be exposed to general users. So it explains why the growth of attention eventually saturates. To confirm this explanation, we kept track of the time when the topics are removed from the front page of "upcoming" column on Digg. We find that the saturation point has a high correlation with the time point when the topic is removed. The black arrow in Figure 1 (a) identifies the time point of removal, which is very close to the saturation point. Figure 1 (b) compares the number of user comments happened before and after the inflection point. The averaged percentages of comments happened before the inflection points are 0.8616, 0.9509, 0.9215 and 0.8548 respectively for categories of entertainment, technology, offbeat, and lifestyle. Different colors in the plot represent different sub-categories. Error bars in the plot indicate one standard deviation of the data in the sub-category. As expected, most of the comments are generated before removing from the "upcoming" column. In

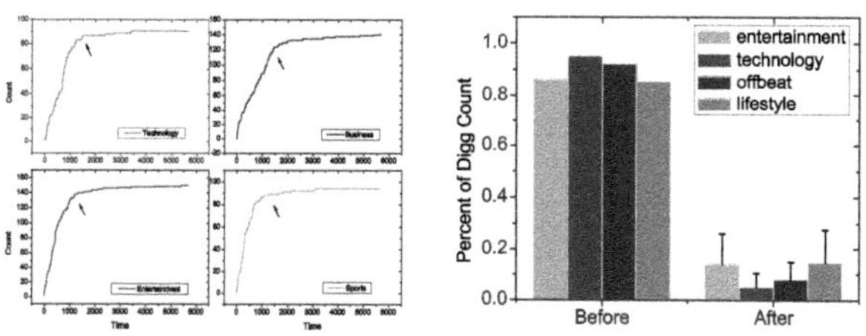

(a) Cumulative Size (b) Ratio

Figure 1: (a) User attention as a function of time (minutes) for four typical topics on Digg. The black arrow in each plot shows the inflection point where the topic is removed from the "upcoming" column. (b) Percentage of user comments happened before and after the inflection point.

the rest of this paper, we name the point, when a topic is replaced from "new" or "upcoming" column, as "inflection point". We name the duration that a topic stays in the column as "exposure duration". The exposure duration varies from topic to topic, which is largely determined by the speed of generating new items and the hidden algorithms used by the website to remove old ones. There are two important factors that are dominating the conversation growth before saturation: (i) the length of exposure duration and (ii) the patterns of user commenting behavior. Next, we investigate these two factors in detail separately.

4.1 Distribution of Exposure Durations

The duration of items placed in the "new" column since creation plays a fundamental role in the initial growth of attention dynamics and comment counts. Here, we empirically measure the distribution of this exposure duration from three mainstream social media websites Digg, Reddit and Epinions.

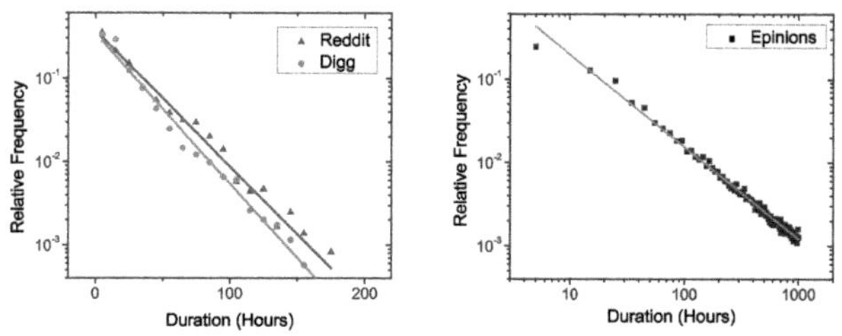

(a) Digg & Reddit (b) Epinions

Figure 2: Density plot of exposure duration for new topics. (a) Digg and Reddit, (b) Epinions.

On Digg, there is a specific column named "upcoming news" for newly generated items. Topics in this column are sorted by creation time, with the newest item ranking on the top of the page. When new topic comes, all of the existing items move downwards on the web page. In doing so, topics of the website would fade away from users' attention gradually. Here we measure the duration that the item maintains on the first top 50 items in the "upcoming news' column. Similar results are observed when we change this threshold limit. On Reddit and Epinions, we use similar gathering methodologies and treatments. In Figure 2 (a), an exponential distribution can be observed from the semi-log plot for both of Digg and Reddit. And for Epinions in Figure 2 (b), a Pareto distribution for the exposure duration is observed from the straight line in log-log plot. Since the exposure duration is determined by various specific factors such as the speed of item generation and the hidden algorithms used, different distribution of exposure durations are expected for websites with similar appearances. For instance, if items in the column are removed with a fixed probability at each time step, the duration is expected to be geometrically or exponentially distributed [24]. If items are pushed down a fixed-size list until falling off, the duration would follow Erlang distribution, which is the sum of exponentials. Various other optimizing strategies can result in a power law distribution or a lognormal distributed durations [33]. For this reasoning, one could not presume the distribution of exposure duration without knowledge about the hidden algorithms or empirical measurements. The impact of this observed differences is later discussed in the model section.

4.2 Patterns of User Commenting Behavior

In last sub-section, we focus on the side of websites, looking at the distribution of for how long a new item is exposed to general users. Now, we turn our attention to users'

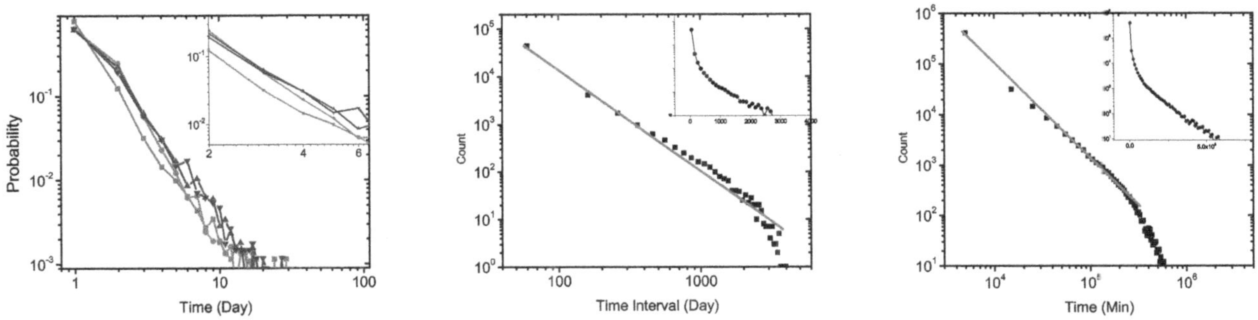

(a) Individuals (b) Epinions (c) Digg

Figure 3: Density plot of waiting times between two consecutive comments from a user, (a) time intervals of four users with largest comment count on Digg, (b) intervals from all users in Epinions dataset and (c) intervals from all users in Digg dataset. The upper-right plot in (a) shows a zoomed-in view of density plot. The red straight line in (b) and (c) suggests a power-law family of distribution. The plot on the upper right corner in (b) and (c) demonstrates data in a semi-log scale.

commenting behavior, i.e. the distribution of waiting times between two comments from the same user.

First, we look at the distribution of two consecutive comments from single users. Figure 3 (a) demonstrates the distribution of waiting times for four typical users on Digg in a log-log scale. The upper right plot in the figure shows the scaling region ranging from 2 to 6 days. One interesting observation from the plot is that the four colored lines, despite coming from different users, show similar scaling relationship. And the slope of the line also varies little in the four samples with the largest comment count in our dataset. Similar scaling is observed for other users of the website. This observation suggests that different users share similar patterns of commenting behaviors. So we turn our attention to study the behavior of aggregated users on a whole, by treating users as identical. We empirically measure the distribution of waiting times by collecting the time series data of all comments from users. The density plot of waiting times between two consecutive comments in a log-log scale is shown in Figure 3 (b) and (c). The red straight line in the plot suggests a power-law scaling of waiting times distribution. The plots on the upper right corner demonstrate the same data but in a semi-log scale. From these two plots, the distribution clearly deviates from an exponential distribution. The cutoff for (b) and (c) can be explained by the finite-size effect. The above observations suggest that the commenting behavior of human can not be described by a Poisson process as assumed in prior studies [31]. We find that the density plot is best fitted with an upper-truncated Pareto distribution. Based on the maximum-likelihood estimation (MLE) approach [34] for upper-truncated Pareto distribution, the exponent for Epinions is estimated to be -1.5670, when the lower bound is set to equal one unit and the upper bound is set to be equal to the largest observation in our records. Similarly for the MLE of Digg dataset, the exponent is estimated to be -1.1262. This result implies that, for each user, frequent comments may follow by a significantly long period of inactivity. In the following, we explore the implications of this non-Poisson nature of human behavior.

5. MODEL OF ON-LINE CONVERSATIONS

We introduced basic properties about the duration of new topics getting displayed to users and the patterns of user behavior. In this section, based on these properties, we propose a model for the growth dynamics of on-line conversations. We show that the basic scaling relationship deduced from our model is a robust one, in that the scenario discussed can arise under very simple assumptions.

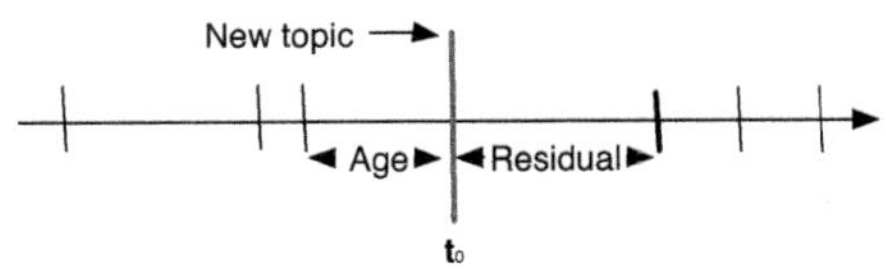

Figure 4: The arrival pattern of comments from one user. Every short vertical line in the figure represents the time of a comment from the user. The blue thick vertical bar represents the time point when a new topic is released.

Based on results form Section 4, we assume that users check the websites' "new" columns regularly to discover topics. In our model, we use t_0 to denote the time point when the topic is created. We use t to denote the time passed since the creation of the topic, and T to denote the exposure duration for a topic. We use $N(t)$ to denote the cumulative count of user comments on a topic, or the size of conversation. The waiting time of two consecutive comments from a user follows a upper truncated Pareto distribution. Here, we simplify the problem by assuming that users share the same microscopic behaviors, i.e. the waiting time for different users comes from the same distribution. In doing so, we are able to model the process of M users as M independent concurrent counting process, so it is sufficient to consider the case of one individual user. For that user, the waiting time between two comments is an independent and identical variable. The counting process of that specific user forms a renewal process, as depicted in Figure 4. Here, we let x_i denote the inter-arrival time of the ith comment from the user, $Y(t_0)$ denote the time from t_0 until the next renewal,

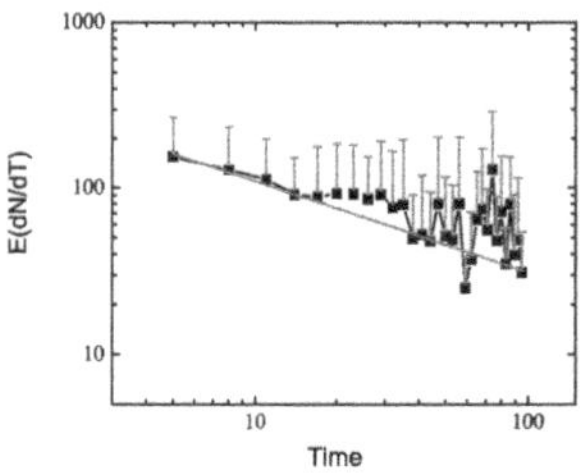

(a) Digg dN-dT

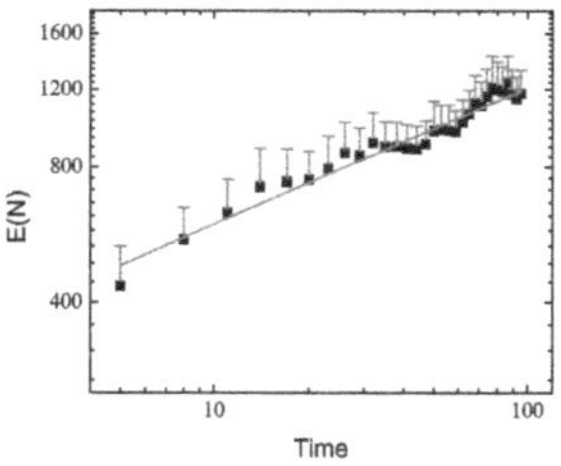

(b) Digg N-dT

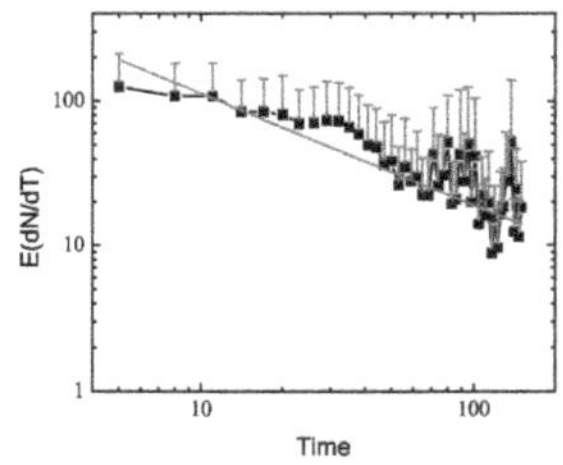

(c) Reddit dN-dT

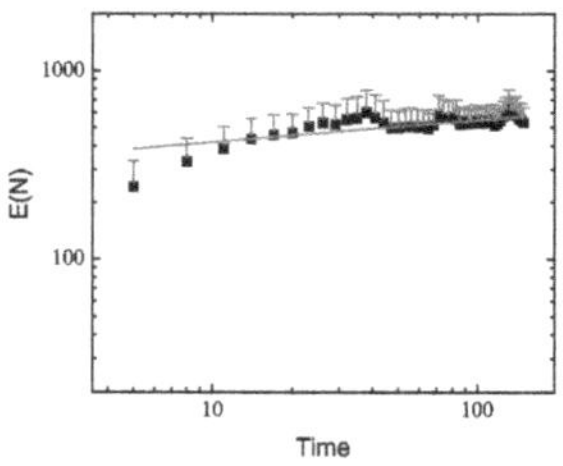

(d) Reddit N-dT

Figure 5: Comment growth dynamics on Digg in log-log scale. (a) dN/dT as a function of T, the red line in the figure shows the linear fit of data in log-log scale, with a slope of -0.5483 and a standard error of 0.3809. (b) N as a function of T, the red line in the figure shows the linear fit of data in log-log scale, with a slope of 0.3066 and a standard error of 0.046. Comment growth dynamics on Reddit in log-log scale. (c) dN/dT as a function of T, the red line in the figure shows the linear fit of data in log-log scale, with a slope of -0.7720 and a standard error of 0.2454. (d) N as a function of T, the red line in the figure shows the linear fit of data in log-log scale, with a slope of 0.1172 and a standard error of 0.0057.

$A(t_0)$ denote the time from t_0 since the last renewal. If the waiting time of each user's comments follows an independent and identical upper-truncated Pareto distribution, the distribution of the interval can be written as

$$f(x) = \frac{c}{a^{-c} - b^{-c}} x^{-c-1}. \qquad (1)$$

Here, a is the lower bound of the time interval required for a user to post another comment. b is the upper bound of the Pareto distribution stemming from its finite size effect. The cumulative distribution of the truncated power-law takes form of $F(x) = \frac{a^{-c}-x^{-c}}{a^{-c}-b^{-c}}$, for $a \le x \le b$. We have

$$\overline{F(x)} = 1 - F(x) = \begin{cases} 1, & x < a \\ \frac{x^{-c}-b^{-c}}{a^{-c}-b^{-c}}, & a \le x \le b \\ 0, & x \ge b \end{cases} \qquad (2)$$

For an individual user, the quantity of interest is the probability that a comment happens at $Y(t_0)$ on the specified topic, as $t_0 \to \infty$. To derive this, we begin with the probability of the user commenting on any of the existing topics in the column at time $Y(t_0)$. Since the inter-arrival time is independent and identically distributed, $Y(t_0)$ and $A(t_0)$ form an alternating renewal process. From results of the key renewal theorem [35], we have

$$\lim_{t_0 \to \infty} P\{Y(t_0) \le y\} = \frac{1}{\mu} \int_0^y \overline{F(x)} dx, \qquad (0 \le y \le b). \quad (3)$$

In this equation, $\mu = \frac{c}{c-1} \frac{a^{-c+1}-b^{-c+1}}{a^{-c}-b^{-c}}$ is the expectation of random variable x. $A(t_0)$ and $Y(t_0)$ do not have to share the same distribution, due to the impact of the lower bound a. By taking Equation 2 back to Equation 3, we obtain the probability of user comment on any of the items at $Y(t_0)$,

$$P\{Y(t_0) = y\} = \frac{\partial P(Y(t_0) \le y)}{\partial y} \sim y^{-c}. \qquad (4)$$

Based on our assumptions, users can choose to comment on one topic from the column at a time. So at t_0, the user may choose to comment on any of the existing topics that are still in the column. Neglecting all other factors, if we assign a fixed probability α for the user to choose the specified topic from all topics in the column, the size of conversation scales with $N(t) \sim \alpha t^{-c+1}$. One insight of this equation is that the probability of one more additional comment adding to the topic inversely scales with time. The interestingness measurement α can be assigned different values to different topics. To derive the most common properties of conversation growth dynamics, we fix α over topics in our model.

Thus far, we have derived the growth of conversation size without considering the resonating nature of on-line conversations. Now we take these important characteristics into consideration by writing α as $\alpha(N(t))$. The reason that α is a function of $N(t)$ comes from existing works in information cascades and social influence. The intuitive understanding is that the more popular a topic is, the more likely that a user comment on it or come back to comment again. Given that N scales with t, we assume $\alpha = \gamma t^{c_0}$, γ is a constant factor. c_0 is a positive exponent measuring the combined impacts of factors such as resonance and social influence. In the extreme of $c_0 = 0$, α would be a constant, when there is no other impacts such as social influence. Now we combine existing two parts together to derive the dynamics of conversation size growth. Noting that the expected number of increment of comments at time point t would be proportional to $\gamma t^{c_0} M t^{-c}$. The total number of comments for a given topic, N, grows like

$$\frac{dN(t)}{dt} = \gamma M t^{-c+c_0}. \qquad (5)$$

Thus, $N(t) \sim t^{-c+c_0+1}$, i.e. $ln(N(t))$ scales linearly with $ln(t)$. To confirm this derivation, we compare this result with the empirically measured growth of conversation size. As shown in Figure 5, the plot in log-log scale shows the expected scaling relationship between time and number of increments. In the figures, the red line in the figure shows the linear fit of data in log-log scale. For Digg, linear fitting gives a slope of -0.5483 and a standard error of 0.3809 as shown in Figure 5 (a) and a slope of 0.3066 with a standard error of 0.046 for Figure 5 (b). For Reddit, linear fitting yields a slope of -0.7720 and a standard error of 0.2454 for Figure 5 (c) and a slope of 0.1172 with a standard error of 0.0057 for Figure 5 (d). The two estimated exponent values obtained from two fittings have a difference around one for both Digg and Reddit, which result agrees well with the relationship of $N(t) \sim t^{-c+c_0+1}$ and $\frac{dN(t)}{dt} \sim t^{-c+c_0}$ from our model. One point worth mentioning here is that, in some of existing works about attention dynamics, the above derived relationship is used as an assumption upon which the model is built [20, 21].

Now, we turn our attention to the distribution of conversation sizes when topics reaches inflection points, i.e. $N(T)$, based on the observed distribution of T. For simplicity, we use $c' = -c + c_0 + 1$, and $\gamma' = \gamma M$ in our derivations, so that $N(T) = \gamma' T^{c'}$. We then have

$$P(N(T) \leq n) = P(\gamma' T^{c'} \leq n) = \mathrm{P}(T \leq (\frac{n}{\gamma'})^{\frac{1}{c'}}). \quad (6)$$

The actual form of the cumulative distribution depends on the distribution of exposure durations, which is website specific as discussed earlier. We now discussed in more detail the impact that different exposure duration distributions have on the empirically measured conversation size distributions. We look at two general cases of exposure duration: (i) exponential distribution and (ii) Pareto distribution.

5.1 Exponential Exposure Duration

For an exponentially distributed T with rate parameter λ as measured in Digg and Reddit, its cumulative distribution has a form of $P(T \leq x) = 1 - e^{-\lambda x}$. Replacing this back to Equation 6, we have

$$\mathrm{P}(N(T) \leq n) = 1 - e^{-\lambda(\frac{n}{\gamma'})^{\frac{1}{c'}}}. \quad (7)$$

By taking the derivative of this equation, we arrive at the distribution of $N(T)$, which takes the form:

$$\mathrm{P}(N(T) = n) = \frac{\lambda}{c'\gamma'}(\frac{n}{\gamma'})^{\frac{1}{c'}-1} e^{-\lambda(\frac{n}{\gamma'})^{\frac{1}{c'}}}. \quad (8)$$

This is actually a Weibull distribution with its shape parameter k' equals $\frac{1}{c'}$ and scale parameter λ' equals $\frac{\gamma'}{\lambda^{c'}}$. Interestingly, the tail of the distribution scales as $e^{-\lambda(\frac{n}{\gamma'})^{\frac{1}{c'}}}$. So the distribution has following properties:

- **Case 1:** ($k' = \frac{1}{c'} < 1$) In this case, when the social influence factor has a stronger impact than the decay factor, $c' > 1$, the shape factor is smaller than one. So
$$\lim_{n \to \infty} e^{n} P(N > n) = \infty, \quad (9)$$
which results in a heavy tailed distribution of conversation size.
- **Case 2:** ($k' = \frac{1}{c'} > 1$) In this case, the tail decays faster than an exponential distribution. The distribution would appear to be light-tailed.
- **Case 3:** ($k' = \frac{1}{c'} = 1$) This is the case when the size distribution has an exponential distribution, which is corresponding to the red line in Figure 6 (a) and (b)

Thus for the case of exponentially distributed exposure duration, both heavy tailed and non-heavy tailed distributions can appear. The actual form of the distributions is determined by the factor c_0. If social propagation dominates, there is a good chance that one would observe extremely large comment threads. Figure 6 (a) demonstrates the simulated density plot under the three cases of heavy-tailed, exponential and light-tailed size distribution. And Figure 6 (b) shows the complementary cumulative distribution function(CCDF) Plot in a semi-log scale of above three cases. If the tail is not exponentially bounded, the CCDF curve will lie above the straight lin,e as seen in the blue one in Figure 6 (b).

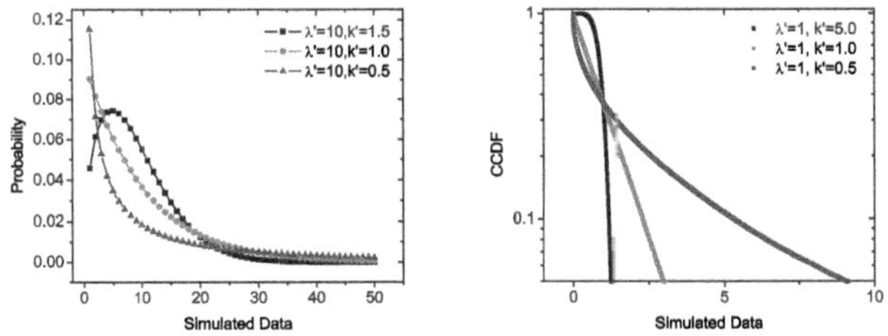

(a) Density Plot

(b) CCDF Plot

Figure 6: (a) Density plot of simulated size for the situation of exponentially distributed exposure duration, when $\lambda' = 10$ and (i)$k' = 1.5$, (ii)$k' = 1.0$, (iii) $k' = 0.5$. (b) CCDF plot of simulated size, when $\lambda' = 1$ and (i)$k' = 5.0$, (ii)$k' = 1.0$, (iii) $k' = 0.5$.

5.2 Pareto Exposure Duration

Next, we investigate the situation when the exposure duration follows a Pareto distribution, as measured in Epinions. We have

$$P(T < x) = 1 - (\frac{x}{T_{\min}})^{-\alpha}, x > T_{\min}. \quad (10)$$

By taking this back to Equation 6, we have

$$P(N(T) \leq n) = P(\gamma' T^{c'} \leq n) = 1 - T_{\min}^{-\alpha}(\frac{n}{\gamma'})^{-\frac{\alpha}{c'}}. \quad (11)$$

Taking the derivative on n, the size distribution has the form of:

$$P(N(T) = n) \sim \frac{\alpha}{c'}(\frac{n}{\gamma'})^{-\frac{\alpha}{c'}-1}, \quad (12)$$

which is a Pareto distribution. Thus the conversation size of topics with a Pareto exposure duration has a heavy-tail.

From the above analysis of conversation size distribution under different exposure durations, we can see that the discrepancies in the reported size distributions stem from the hidden algorithms that websites employ for deciding which new topics to display on their websites. By separating these artificial factors from user behavior, we show that there are actually underlying mechanisms in common for different social media websites. This explains why different categories of distributions (heavy tailed and non-heavy tailed) are observed in existing studies [1, 7–11]. The model can be adapted to other empirically measured exposure durations. For instance, for a lognormal distribution of exposure duration, a lognormal size distribution is expected from our model. Due to the space limitations, we omit the derivations here. We compare the predictions of this model with empirical measurements in Section 6.

5.3 Structure of Conversation

Another interesting characteristics of on-line conversations is the interactive nature of comments. For example, when a new comment is added to the thread, it is following either the original post or one of the existing comments, so that the comments form a directed graph with each comment as a node. Figure 7 shows one such example based on a sample thread of comments from Digg. The node 0 is the original post of topic, and the others nodes represent the following comments. Node 2 has a in-degree of 2 in this graph. Within

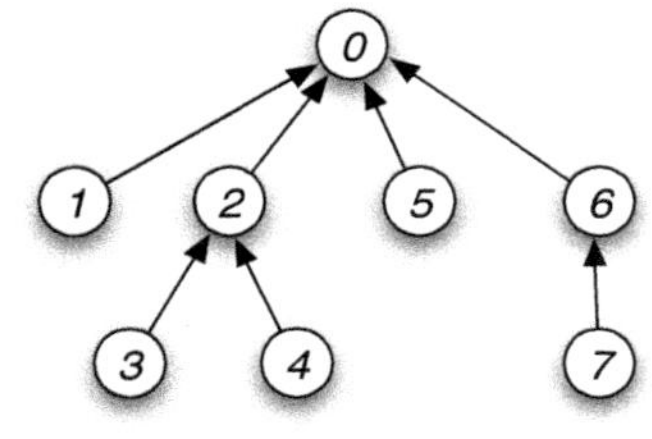

Figure 7: **Structure of a sample conversation thread from Digg. Node 0 is the initial post of the topic.**

such an information network formed by user comments, one of the most important properties is the in-degree distribution of the associated directed graph. We now show that by adding to our dynamic model for conversations a Yule process [14,36], one can derive the in-degree distribution of the network. The Yule process assumes that each new comment added into the thread follows one simple rule: it is added to one of the existing comments with a probability proportional to their existing in-degree. Notice that there is also a probability to comment on one with zero in-degree, denoted by δ_0. We use $k_j(t)$ to denote the in-degree at time t for comments that are created at time point j. Based on our model, the number of new comments added into the thread at time t is proportional to $t^{c'-1}$. The cumulative count of comments up to time t is proportional to $t^{c'}$. The sum of in-degree would thus be equal to $(1+\delta_0)\gamma' t^{c'}$. Based on our assumptions on Yule process, the probability of a new comment attaching to an existing comment with k_i in-degree would be $\frac{(k_i(t)+\delta_0)}{(1+\delta_0)\gamma' t^{c'}}$. Since there are $c'\gamma' t^{c'-1}$ new comments added at t, the growth dynamics of $k_j(t)$ can be written as

$$\frac{\partial k_i(t)}{\partial t} = \frac{(k_i(t)+\delta_0)c'\gamma' t^{c'-1}}{(1+\delta_0)\gamma' t^{c'}}. \tag{13}$$

After integrating this equation and taking into account the initial condition $k_i(i) = 0$, we have

$$\ln(\frac{k_i(t)+\delta_0}{\delta_0}) = \frac{c'}{1+\delta_0}\ln(\frac{t}{t_i}). \tag{14}$$

The in-degree of node i at the inflection point equals to

$$k_i(T) = \delta_0[(\frac{T}{t_i})^{\frac{c'}{1+\delta_0}} - 1]. \tag{15}$$

So now we have

$$P(k_i(T) < l) = P(\delta_0[(\frac{T}{t_i})^{\frac{c'}{1+\delta_0}} - 1] < l) = P(t_i > T[1+\frac{l}{\delta_0}]^{-\frac{1+\delta_0}{c'}}) \tag{16}$$

For a randomly chosen node, $P(t_i > t) = 1 - \frac{t^{c'}}{T^{c'}}$, so Equation 16 becomes

$$P(k_i(T) < l) = 1 - [\frac{l}{\delta_0} + 1]^{-1-\delta_0}. \tag{17}$$

By taking the derivative of this equation we see that the distribution of in-degrees scales with $[\frac{l}{\delta_0}+1]^{-2-\delta_0}$, which amounts to a Pareto scaling. An interesting consequence from the above derivation is that the in-degree distribution within a conversation network is independent of the distribution of exposure durations. That is to say, despite of the different hidden algorithms used by websites, the structure within a conversation thread is universal. This result explains why existing studies observe the same Pareto scaling of in-degree distribution within conversation threads in different social media sites [1,7–11].

6. EMPIRICAL OBSERVATIONS

In the last section we modeled the process of conversation growth and predicted that the distribution of conversation sizes is determined by several factors including the exposure duration, the users' commenting behavior, the social propagation and resonating factors. We also demonstrated that a universal Pareto in-degree distribution is expected for each comment. In this section, we compare these results with empirical observations.

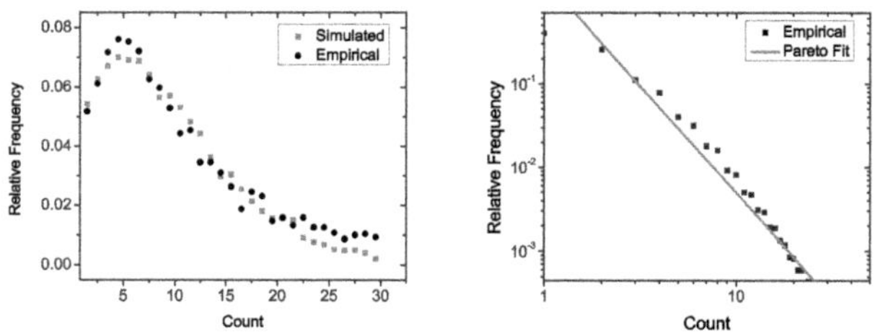

(a) Digg (b) Epinions

Figure 9: The density plot of conversation size on (a) Digg and (b) Epinions.

First, we compare the size distribution of Digg conversation size with our model. Since the exposure duration within Digg is observed to follow an exponential duration (Figure 2(a)), and c' is less than one (Figure 5), the size distribution of conversation is expected to be described by the second case in Section 5.1, which is a light tailed Weibull distribution. To exclude the impact of stories promoted to front page in the popular column, we filtered out topics with extreme large comment size. We fit the empirically measured conversation size with Weibull distribution using MLE and estimate that the scale factor equals 10.834 and the shape factor equals 1.439. We use the estimated parameters to simulate the conversation size distribution. The density plot of empirical observation and simulated data is as shown in Figure 9 (a). In Figure 10 (a), we plot the empirically measured size in a Weibull Plot. And in Figure 10 (b), we plot the simulated and empirically measured data in a QQ Plot. The straight lines in both plots demonstrate that the empirically observed conversation size fits well with the predicted size distribution. From the CCDF Plot in semi-log scale as in Figure 8 (a), we can see that the distribution has a light-tail. Similarly on Reddit, the size distribution is expected to follow a lighted-tailed Weibull distribution, as shown in Figure 8 (b). We also measure the size distribution using dataset from Epinions. Based on Figure 2 (b), the size distribution of Epinions is expected to follow a Pareto distribution from results in Section 5.2. The density plot of size in log-log scale is as shown in Figure 9 (b). The Pareto scaling agrees with our model. The distribution is not exponentially bounded as shown in Figure 8 (c). A summary of the tail properties in different social media is shown in Figure 8 (d). The size distributions from Digg and Reddit have a light-tail and that from Epinions a heavy-tail. The

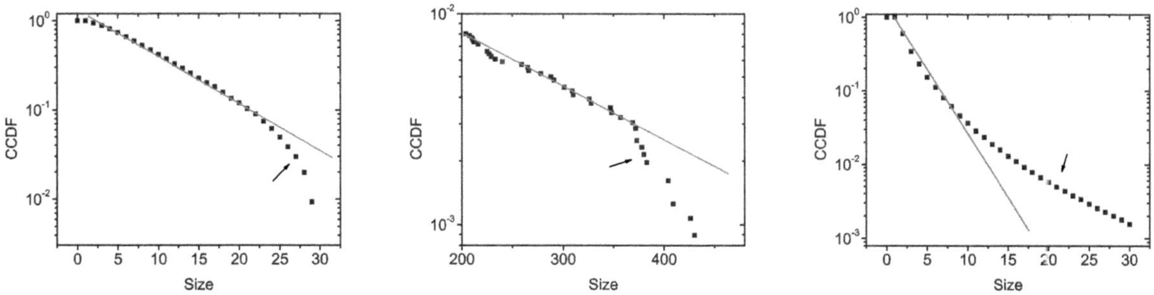

(a) Digg (b) Reddit (c) Epinions

	Digg	Reddit	Epinions
Topic Exposure Duration Distribution	Exponential	Exponential	Pareto
Predicted Size Distribution	Weibull (Light Tailed)	Weibull (Light Tailed)	Pareto
Observed Size Distribution	Weibull (Light Tailed)	Light Tailed	Pareto

(d) Summarization of the size distribution in different websites.

Figure 8: (a) Digg, (b) Reddit and (c) Epinions, the CCDF Plot in semi-log scale for three social media websites. If the density tail (black squares in the plot) is above the red exponential line, then it is a heavy-tailed distribution, otherwise not. (d) Summarization of predicted and measured tail properties in different websites.

derived size distribution from model agrees well with empirical measurements.

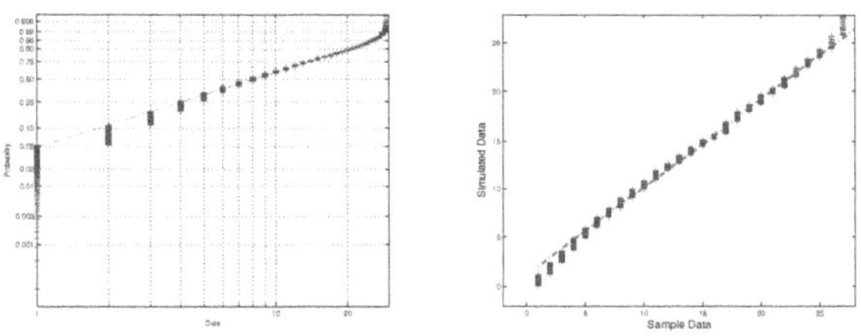

(a) Weibull Plot (b) QQ-Plot

Figure 10: (a) Weibull Plot of empirically observed conversation size. (b) QQ-Plot of empirically measured and simulated conversation size.

In addition, we compare the derived Pareto scaling of in-degree size distribution for different datasets. Figure 11 shows the density plot of in-degree in a log-log scale of Digg and Reddit. We observed the same scaling in Epinions dataset. The straight line in the figure confirms that the in-degree size follows a Pareto distribution. From the above comparisons, our model quantitatively explains the observed discrepancies of size distribution in different social media, as well as the in-degree size distribution in the information network formed by user comments.

7. CONCLUSION AND FUTURE WORK

In this paper, we investigated properties of user conversations in on-line social media. We started from the commenting behavior of individual users and the distribution of exposure duration during which the new topics are displayed to users. Based on these observations, we proposed a general

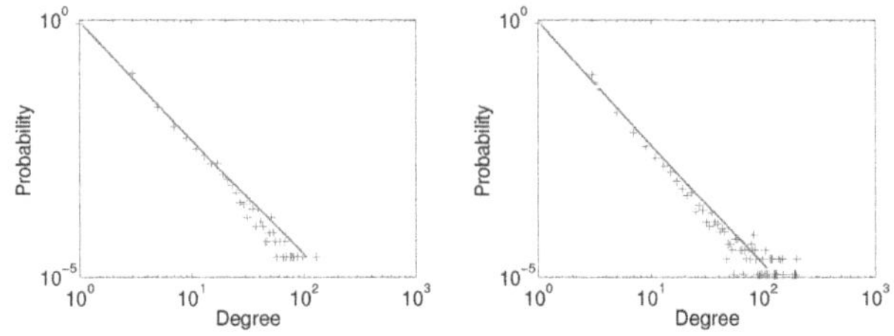

(a) Digg (b) Reddit

Figure 11: In-degree size distribution of comments in log-log scale (a) Digg and (b) Reddit. The red straight line in the plots suggests a Pareto distribution.

dynamic model for conversation growth. The model successfully explains the reported difference in existing studies from different social media websites. We further extended our model with a Yule process to derive the structure of conversations. The results of our model were compared with various empirical measurements, such as the scaling relationship between time and size, the tail properties of size distribution and also the in-degree distribution from different social media sites. Our model provides a powerful framework that can be easily modified and applied to various specific scenarios for studying on-line conversations. We also noticed that for the model to be suitable for the most general cases, we make some simplified assumptions such as the similarities of users and the introduction of inflection point. Possible refinements of the model may take into considerations of the differences between users, the interestingness of topics, and also the impacts of other featuring mechanisms used by the website. In closing, we note that although the focus in this paper has been on user comments and on-line conversations, the framework of our growth model may be suitable to a wide category of attention dynamics related studies. The wide applicability and the relatively simple assumptions make our model an extremely general one and therefore should provide ample opportunities for future work.

8. ACKNOWLEDGMENTS

C. W. would like to thank HP Labs for financial support.

9. REFERENCES

[1] R. Kumar, M. Mahdian, and M. McGlohon. Dynamics of conversations. In *KDD*, 2010.

[2] Guimer Roger, Uzz Brian, Spiro Jarrett, and Amaral Lus A. Nunes. Team assembly mechanisms determine collaboration network structure and team performance. *Science*, 308(5722), 2005.

[3] Wuchty Stefan, Jones Benjamin, and Uzzi Brian. The increasing dominance of teams in production of knowledge. *Science*, 316(5827), 2007.

[4] B. J. Jansen, M. Zhang, K. Sobel, and A. Chowdhury. Twitter power: Tweets as electronic word of mouth. *J. Am. Soc. Inf. Sci.*, 60(11), 2009.

[5] D. Gruhl, R.Guha, R. Kumar, J. Novak, and A. Tomkins. The predictive power of online chatter. In *KDD*, 2005.

[6] M. Kearns, S. Suri, and N. Monfort. An experimental study of the coloring problem on human subject networks. *Science*, 313, 2006.

[7] G. Mishne and N. Glance. Leave a reply: An analysis of weblog comments. In *Third Annual Workshop on the Weblogging Ecosystem: Aggregation, Analysis and Dynamics.*, 2006.

[8] V. Gomez, H. Kappen, and A. Kaltenbrunner. Modeling the structure and evolution of discussion cascades. In *HT*, 2011.

[9] V. Gomez, A. Kaltenbrunner, and V. Lopez. Statistical analysis of the social network and discussion threads in slashdot. In *WWW*, 2008.

[10] P. Ogilvie. Modeling blog post comment counts. In *http://livewebir.com/blog/page/2/*, 2008.

[11] M. Tsagkias, W. Weerkamp, and M. de Rijke. Predicting the volume of comments on online news stories. In *CIKM*, 2009.

[12] David Liben-Nowell and Jon Kleinberg. Tracing information flow on a global scale using internet chain-letter data. *Proc. Natl. Acad. Sci.*, 105(12), 2008.

[13] Benjamin Goluba and Matthew O. Jackson. Using selection bias to explain the observed structure of internet diffusions. *Proc. Natl. Acad. Sci.*, 107(24), 2010.

[14] J. Leskovec, L. Backstrom, and J. Kleinberg. Meme-tracking and the dynamics of the news cycle. In *KDD*, 2009.

[15] F. Duarte, B. Mattos, A. Bestravras, V. Almedia, and J. Almedia. Traffic characteristics and communication patterns in blogosphere. In *ICWSM*, 2007.

[16] M. De Choudhury, H. Sundaram, A. John, and D. Duncan Seligmann. What makes conversations interesting? themes, participants and consequences of conversations in online social media. In *WWW*, 2009.

[17] B. A. Huberman. The laws of the web: Patterns in the ecology of information. *The MIT Press*, 2001.

[18] Josef Falkinger. Limited attention as a scarce resource in information-rich economies. *Economic Journal*, 118(532), 2008.

[19] Eugene Agichtein, Carlos Castillo, Debora Donato, Aristides Gionis, and Gilad Mishne. Finding high-quality content in social media. In *WSDM*, 2008.

[20] Fang Wu and B. A. Huberman. Novelty and collective attention. *Proc. Natl. Acad. Sci.*, 105(17599), 2007.

[21] Kristina Lerman and Tad Hogg. Using a model of social dynamics to predict popularity of news. In *WWW*, 2010.

[22] R. Crane and D. Sornette. Robust dynamic classes revealed by measuring the response function of a social system. *Proc. Natl. Acad. Sci.*, 105(15649), 2008.

[23] Jacob Ratkiewicz, Santo Fortunato, Alessandro Flammini, Filippo Menczer, and Alessandro Vespignani. Characterizing and modeling the dynamics of online popularity. *Phys. Rev. Lett.*, 105(158701), 2010.

[24] Sitaram Asur, B. A. Huberman, Gabor Szabo, and Chunyan Wang. Predicting the volume of comments on online news stories. In *ICWSM*, 2011.

[25] A.L. Barabasi. The origin of bursts and heavy tails in human dynamics. *Nature*, 435, 2005.

[26] J.P. Eckmann, E. Moses, and D. Sergi. Entropy of dialogues creates coherent structures in e-mail traffic. *Proc. Natl. Acad. Sci.*, 101(14333), 2004.

[27] D. Rybski, S. Buldyrev, S. Havlin, F. Liljeros, and H. Makse. Scaling laws of human interaction activity. *Proc. Natl. Acad. Sci.*, 106(12640), 2009.

[28] B. A. Huberman, P. L. T. Pirolli, J. E. Pitkow, and R. M. Lukose. Social attention in the age of the web. *Science*, 280(95), 1998.

[29] Eytan Adar, Jaime Teevan, and Susan Dumais. Resonance on the web: Web dynamics and revisitation patterns. In *CHI*, 2009.

[30] Anna Chmiel, Kamila Kowalska, and Janusz A. Holyst. Scaling of human behavior during portal browsing. *Phys. Rev. E*, 80(066122), 2010.

[31] S. L. Scott and P. Smyth. The markov modulated poisson process and markov poisson cascade with applications to web traffic data. *Bayesian Statistics*, 7, 2003.

[32] Juliette Stehle, Alain Barrat, and Ginestra Bianconi. Dynamical and bursty interactions in social networks. *Phys. Rev. E*, 81(035101), 2010.

[33] D. Helbing and B. Tilch. A power law for the duration of high-flow states and its interpretation from a heterogeneous traffic flow perspective. *The European Physical Journal B*, 68(4), 2009.

[34] A. Clauset, C.R. Shalizi, and M.E.J. Newman. Power-law distributions in empirical data. *SIAM Review*, 51(4), 2009.

[35] Erhan Ćinlar. *Introduction to stochastic processes.* Prentice-Hall, Englewood Cliffs, NJ, 1975.

[36] G. Yule. A mathematical theory of evolution based on the conclusions of dr. j.c. willis f.r.s. *Philosophical Transactions of the Royal Society London*, 213(21-87), 1924.

eTrust: Understanding Trust Evolution in an Online World

Jiliang Tang, Huiji Gao and Huan Liu
Computer Science & Engineering
Arizona State University
Tempe, AZ 85281
{Jiliang.Tang, Huiji.Gao, Huan.Liu}@asu.edu

Atish Das Sarma
eBay Research Labs
eBay Inc.
San Jose, CA, USA
{atish.dassarma}@gmail.com

ABSTRACT

Most existing research about online trust assumes static trust relations between users. As we are informed by social sciences, trust evolves as humans interact. Little work exists studying trust evolution in an online world. Researching online trust evolution faces unique challenges because more often than not, available data is from passive observation. In this paper, we leverage social science theories to develop a methodology that enables the study of online trust evolution. In particular, we propose a framework of evolution trust, eTrust, which exploits the dynamics of user preferences in the context of online product review. We present technical details about modeling trust evolution, and perform experiments to show how the exploitation of trust evolution can help improve the performance of online applications such as rating and trust prediction.

Categories and Subject Descriptors

H3.3 [**Information Storage and Retrieval**]: Information Search and Retrieval—*Information filtering*

General Terms

Algorithms, Design, Experimentation

Keywords

Multi-faceted Trust, Trust Evolution, User Preference

1. INTRODUCTION

The notion of online trust has attracted increasing attention from the computer science community in recent years [8, 22, 15]. Trust plays a central role in helping users overcome perceptions of risk and insecurity [6], especially for online users who seek advice from trusted sources to make decisions. The trustworthiness of the users is often tantamount to the reliability of the information they provide. Trust is widely exploited to help online users collect reliable information in applications such as high-quality reviews detection [19] and product recommendation [10].

Most existing work on online trust assumes static trust relationships between users [27, 8, 7]. However, trust evolves as humans interact based on the findings from social sciences [11, 30, 12]. Sociologists investigate the evolution of trust in a physical world [30, 29]. Recent years witness many trust related online applications such as intelligent recommender systems [21, 7], collaborative filtering [10, 2], review quality prediction [19] and viral marketing [26], but little work is on online trust evolution due to some unique challenges. For example, in an online world, most of the information that a sociologist collects for trust evolution may not be available. In a physical world, sociologists first invite a group of participants, usually a small group, and then record their sociometric information on interpersonal trust and conditions or situations for the change [30]. In an online world, users are distributed all over the world. Even if one could find a study group, it would be difficult to gather sociometrics on trust. In other worlds, passive observation is the modus operandi for studying trust evolution. Since it is important to study trust evolution, we ask whether we can study online trust evolution and how we can gather online information to model trust evolution.

An important characteristic of product review sites such as Epinions[1] is that there exist trust networks among users. Such sites provide a sensible platform to study trust in an online world [8, 24, 18, 20]. Figure 1 shows a simple online rating system from Epinions at two different time points, denoted as T_1 and T_2. There are two types of objects: users (u_1 to u_5) and items (I_1 to I_5), and two types of actions: establishing trust relations among users and creating ratings from users to items. The rating system evolves over time, highlighted in Figure 1(b), when (1) new users (e.g.,u_5) and new items (e.g.,I_5) are added; and (2) new trust relations (e.g.,$u_2 \rightarrow u_1$) and new ratings (e.g.,$u_5 \rightarrow I_4$) are created. The dynamic online rating system on product review sites serves an observable environment to investigate online trust evolution. First, trust networks with temporal information from product review sites are available, including time points when users entered and the trust relations established. Second, sources, reflecting the changing of user preferences, are available from product review sites. The dynamics of user preferences can be captured by their rating information, widely exploited for collaborative filtering [4, 14, 16]. The evolution of people's trust can be witnessed

[1]http://www.epinions.com

KDD'12, August 12–16, 2012, Beijing, China.

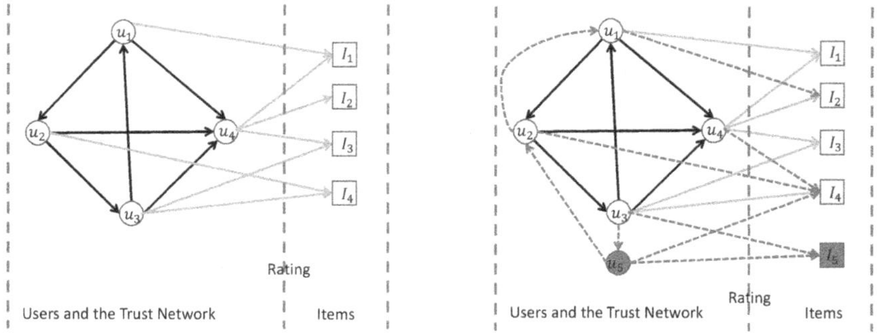

(a) Rating System at T_1 (b) Rating System at T_2

Figure 1: A Simple Example of Rating System at Time T_1 and T_2

via the changes of their preferences [11]. For example, when people are interested in "Electronics" at time t, they trust experts in "Electronics" while people shift their preferences to "Sports" at time $t+1$, they trust experts in this facet. Ziegler et al. [32] pointed out that there is a strong and significant correlation between trust and user preference similarity. The more similar two persons are, the greater the trust between them exists. In other words, trust relationships will evolve with the drifting of user preferences.

In this paper, we make a first attempt to study online trust evolution by exploiting the dynamics of user preferences in the context of online product review. Main contributions of this work include:

- Providing a methodology to study the evolution of trust in an online world;
- Proposing a framework, eTrust, to understand trust evolution by exploiting the dynamics of user preferences of online product review;
- Presenting findings from this eTrust study about the change of user preferences w.r.t. users or items, and trust relations; and
- Evaluating eTrust via online applications such as rating and trust prediction using real-world data.

The rest of paper is organized as follows. The problem of trust evolution is formally stated in Section 2. Section 3 introduces the details about our proposed framework, eTrust. Section 4 discusses applications of eTrust. Section 5 presents experimental results and findings about eTrust. Section 6 briefly reviews related work. Finally, Section 7 concludes this study with future work.

2. PROBLEM STATEMENT

A rating system of product review sites consists of two types of objects with two different actions, as shown in Figure 1(a). Let $\mathcal{U}_t = \{u_1, u_2, \ldots, u_{n_t}\}$ be the set of users at time t (e.g., $\mathcal{U}_{T_1} = \{u_1, u_2, u_3, u_4\}$) where n_t is the number of users at time t. $\mathcal{I}_t = \{I_1, I_2, \ldots, I_{m_t}\}$ is the set of items at time t (e.g., $\mathcal{I}_{T_1} = \{I_1, I_2, I_3, I_4\}$) where m_t is the number of items at time t. Note that new users or new items may be added [2] thus $\mathcal{U}_t \subseteq \mathcal{U}_{t+1}$ and $\mathcal{I}_t \subseteq \mathcal{I}_{t+1}$. Users can perform two types of actions in the rating system: establishing new trust relations and creating new ratings. Let $\mathbf{X}_t \in \mathbb{R}^{n_t \times n_t}$ denote the trust network at time t where $\mathbf{X}_t(i,j) = 1$ if u_i is trusted by u_j at time t and zero otherwise. Let $\mathbf{R}_t \in \mathbb{R}^{n_t \times m_t}$ represent the ratings at time t and r_{ij}^t is used to represent the entity at i-th row and j-th column, i.e., the rating of I_j given by u_i at time t.

Users may have quite different preferences over items from different facets. We assume that there are K latent facets for items and a user has similar preferences over items of the same latent facet. Let $\mathbf{p}_i^t \in \mathbb{R}_+^K$ denote the u_i's preference vector at time t and each element of $\mathbf{p}_i^t$, $\mathbf{p}_i^t(k)$, represent the u_i's preference over the k-th facet at time t. Let $\mathbf{q}_j \in \mathbb{R}_+^K$ be the characteristic vector of the item I_j and $\mathbf{q}_j(k)$ denote the characteristic of I_j in the k-th latent facet. Let $\mathcal{W}_t \in \mathbb{R}^{n_t \times n_t \times K}$ denote the multi-faceted trust relations at time t and w_{ivk}^t is used to denote the strength of trust relation from u_i to u_v in the k-th facet at time t.

With above notations, the trust evolution problem with the dynamics of user preferences can be stated below.

Given T time slices, $\{\mathcal{U}_t\}_{t=1}^T$, $\{\mathcal{I}_t\}_{t=1}^T$, $\{\mathbf{X}_t\}_{t=1}^T$ and $\{\mathbf{R}_t\}_{t=1}^T$, understand the evolution of trust (eTrust), i.e., $\{\mathcal{W}_t\}_{t=1}^T$, by exploiting the changing of user preferences, $\{\{\mathbf{p}_i^t\}_{u_i \in \mathcal{U}_T}\}_{t=1}^T$, which is formally defined as,

$$\text{eTrust}: \{\mathcal{U}_t, \mathcal{I}_t, \mathbf{X}_t, \mathbf{R}_t\}_{t=1}^T \xrightarrow{\{\{\mathbf{p}_i^t\}_{u_i \in \mathcal{U}_T}\}_{t=1}^T} \{\mathcal{W}_t\}_{t=1}^T \tag{1}$$

3. A TRUST EVOLUTION FRAMEWORK

One challenge to studying online trust evolution is lack of conventional sociological data, and passive observation is a common approach to data collection. The dynamic rating system on product review sites provides a new means to the study of online trust evolution. In the next subsections, we introduce a framework of trust evolution, eTrust, with details on modeling and parameter estimation.

3.1 eTrust - Modeling Trust Evolution

It is observed [32] that trust has a strong correlation with user preference similarity in rating systems, reflected in their rating information. Thus most existing work about trust is studied in the context of rating prediction [2, 27]. In this work, we explore the dynamics of user preferences to model trust evolution for rating prediction. The user-item pairs, (i,j), and their known ratings at time t, r_{ij}^t, are stored in $\mathcal{O}_t = \{(i,j) | r_{ij}^t \text{ is known}\}$. We use $\hat{r}_{ij}^t$ to distinguish the predicted rating from the known rating r_{ij}^t. A baseline model for rating prediction is the latent factor model [13] based on

[2] We do not consider the deletion of existing users or items in this work.

user preferences $\mathbf{p}_i^t$ and item characteristics $\mathbf{q}_j$,

$$\hat{r}_{ij}^t = \mathbf{q}_j^\top \mathbf{p}_i^t = \sum_{k=1}^{K} \mathbf{q}_j(k)\mathbf{p}_i^t(k), \tag{2}$$

Another approach for rating prediction is based on the trust network, a variant of the nearest-neighborhood model [13] by considering multi-faceted trust relationships between users,

$$\hat{r}_{ij}^t = \frac{\sum_{v\in N_i^t}\sum_{k=1}^K w_{ivk}^t \mathbf{q}_j(k) r_{vj}}{\sum_{v\in N_i^t}\sum_{k=1}^K w_{ivk}^t \mathbf{q}_j(k)} \tag{3}$$

where N_i^t represents the set of people trusted by u_i at time t. Assume that $r_{vj}^{t_{vj}}(t_{vj} < t)$ is the rating given by u_v to I_j at time t_{vj}. The influence of u_v to u_i on the rating given to I_j at time t, or the impact of $r_{vj}^{t_{vj}}$ on r_{ij}^t, is related to the distance between t_{vj} and t. The earlier ratings reflect users' previous preferences and should have less influence on the current ratings [4]. The closer t_{vj} and t, the more strongly $r_{vj}^{t_{vj}}$ influences r_{ij}^t. Thus we choose an exponential time function to allow the influence of past ratings to decay gradually, which is widely adopted in such applications [4, 14]. Thus r_{vj} in Eq. (3) can be stated as,

$$r_{vj} = e^{-\eta_i(t-t_{vj})} r_{vj}^{t_{vj}}, \tag{4}$$

$\eta_i \geq 0$ controls the user specific decay rate for u_i and should be learnt from the data. w_{ivk}^t in Eq. (3) is the trust strength between u_i and u_v in the k-th facet at time t. There is a strong and significant correlation between trust and user preference similarity [32]. Thus we define $\mathbf{s}_{ivk}^t \in \mathbb{R}^L$ as the preference similarity vector between u_i and u_v in the k-th facet at time t, based on their preferences in k-th facet at time t, i.e., $\mathbf{p}_i^t(k)$ and $\mathbf{p}_v^t(k)$, where L is the number of metrics to measure their preference similarity. We further assume a linear relation between trust strength w_{ijk}^t and $\mathbf{s}_{ijk}^t$ [31], formally stated as,

$$w_{ivk}^t = f(\mathbf{w}^\top \mathbf{s}_{ivk}^t + b_i), \tag{5}$$

where $f : \mathbb{R} \to [0, 1]$ is an active function to control the trust strength, $0 \leq w_{ivk} \leq 1$ and b_i is a user specific bias of u_i.

The latent factor model does not incorporate the influence from the trust network while the neighborhood model does not consider the user preferences and item characteristics. Earlier work [13, 2, 27] indicated that a proper combination of these two models would help rating prediction. Therefore, we estimate the rating of u_i about I_j at time t as,

$$\hat{r}_{ij}^t = \alpha \sum_{k=1}^{K} \mathbf{q}_j(k)\mathbf{p}_i^t(k) + (1-\alpha)\frac{\sum_{v\in N_i^t}\sum_{k=1}^K w_{ivk}^t \mathbf{q}_j(k) r_{vj}}{\sum_{v\in N_i^t}\sum_{k=1}^K w_{ivk}^t \mathbf{q}_j(k)} \tag{6}$$

In this formulation, the rating of u_i on I_j at time t is determined by two factors. One captures the preferences of u_i at time t and the characteristics of I_j, and the other is about user's trusted people. $\hat{r}_{ij}^t$ should be influenced by u_i's trusted people. w_{ivk}^t indicates their trust strength in the k-th facet. The stronger u_i trusts u_v, the more similar $\hat{r}_{ij}^t$ is to r_{vj}. The second part models the influence from their trusted people. The parameter $\alpha \in [0, 1]$ adjusts the contributions from these two parts. Then the trust evolution problem, embedded in rating prediction, can be formulated as the following minimization problem,

$$\begin{aligned}
\min_{\mathbf{p}_i^t\geq 0,\ \mathbf{q}_j\geq 0,\ \eta_i\geq 0} & \sum_{t=1}^{T}\sum_{(i,j)\in\mathcal{O}_t}\Big(r_{ij}^t - \alpha\sum_{k=1}^{K}\mathbf{q}_j(k)\mathbf{p}_i^t(k) - \\
&(1-\alpha)\frac{\sum_{v\in N_i^t}\sum_{k=1}^K f(\mathbf{w}^\top\mathbf{s}_{ivk}^t + b_i)\mathbf{q}_j(k) r_{vj}}{\sum_{v\in N_i^t}\sum_{k=1}^K f(\mathbf{w}^\top\mathbf{s}_{ivk}^t + b_i)\mathbf{q}_j(k)}\Big)^2 \\
&+\beta\Big(\sum_{u_i\in\mathcal{U}_T}\sum_{t=t_{u_i}}^{T}\|\mathbf{p}_i^t\|_2^2 + \sum_{I_j\in\mathcal{I}_T}\|\mathbf{q}_j\|_2^2 \\
&+\|\mathbf{w}\|_2^2 + \sum_{u_i\in\mathcal{U}_T}\|b_i\|_2^2 + \sum_{u_i\in\mathcal{U}_T}\|\eta_i\|_2^2\Big) \\
&+\lambda\sum_{u_i\in\mathcal{U}_T}\sum_{t=t_{u_i}+1}^{T}\sum_{k=1}^{K} c\Big(\mathbf{p}_i^t(k) - \mathbf{p}_i^{t-1}(k)\Big)
\end{aligned} \tag{7}$$

where the parameter β controls the quadratic regularized term to avoid overfitting, $c(\cdot)$ a function to model how user preferences change, and λ for the speed of change. When $\lambda \to 0$, we do not consider any relations of user preferences at different time points. When $\lambda \to +\infty$, the user preference vectors at different time points are restricted to be the same.

3.2 Estimating Parameters for eTrust

eTrust requires the following parameters: $\mathbf{w}$, b_i, η_i, the characteristics vector for each item I_j, $\mathbf{q}_j$, the user preference vector for each user u_i at each time slice t, $\mathbf{p}_i^t$. Different users enter the rating system at different time points, t_{u_i} for user u_i . Thus, for each u_i, we need to estimate his preferences from t_{u_i} to T, $\{\mathbf{p}_i^t\}_{t=t_{u_i}}^T$.

In our implementation, we use a projected gradient method to solve Eq. (7) and parameters can be updated as,

$$\begin{aligned}
&\mathbf{w} \leftarrow \mathbf{w} - \gamma_{\mathbf{w}}\nabla_{\mathbf{w}}, \\
&\forall u_i \in \mathcal{U}_T \\
&\quad b_i \leftarrow b_i - \gamma_{b_i}\nabla_{b_i}, \\
&\forall u_i \in \mathcal{U}_T \\
&\quad \eta_i \leftarrow \max(0, \eta_i - \gamma_{\eta_i}\nabla_{\eta_i}) \\
&\forall I_j \in \mathcal{I}_T,\ k \in [1, K] \\
&\quad \mathbf{q}_j(k) \leftarrow \max(0, \mathbf{q}_j(k) - \gamma_{\mathbf{q}_j(k)}\nabla_{\mathbf{q}_j(k)}), \\
&\forall u_i \in \mathcal{U}_T,\ t \in [t_{u_i}, T],\ k \in [1, K] \\
&\quad \mathbf{p}_i^t(k) \leftarrow \max(0, \mathbf{p}_i^t(k) - \gamma_{\mathbf{p}_i^t(k)}\nabla_{\mathbf{p}_i^t(k)}),
\end{aligned}$$

where $\gamma_{\mathbf{w}}$, γ_{b_i}, γ_{η_i}, $\gamma_{\mathbf{q}_j(k)}$ and $\gamma_{\mathbf{p}_i^t(k)}$ are learning step sizes, which are chosen to satisfy Goldstein Conditions [25]. $\nabla_{\mathbf{w}}$, ∇_{b_i}, ∇_{η_i}, $\nabla_{\mathbf{q}_j(k)}$ and $\nabla_{\mathbf{p}_i^t(k)}$ are the partial derivatives of the objective function in Eq. (7) with respect to $\mathbf{w}$, b_i, η_i, $\mathbf{q}_j(k)$ and $\mathbf{p}_i^t(k)$, respectively,

$$\nabla_{\mathbf{w}} = 2\beta\mathbf{w} - 2(1-\alpha)\sum_{t=1}^{T}\sum_{(i,j)\in\mathcal{O}_t} E_{ij}^t \frac{1}{(Q_{ij}^t)^2}$$

$$\Big(Q_{ij}^t \sum_{v\in N_i^t}\sum_{k=1}^{K} f'_{\mathbf{w}}\mathbf{q}_j(k) r_{vj} - P_{ij}^t \sum_{v\in N_i^t}\sum_{k=1}^{K} f'_{\mathbf{w}}\mathbf{q}_j(k)\Big),$$

$$\nabla_{b_i} = 2\beta b_i - 2(1-\alpha)\sum_{t=1}^{T}\sum_{(i,j)\in\mathcal{O}_t} E_{ij}^t \frac{1}{(Q_{ij}^t)^2}$$

$$\Big(Q_{ij}^t \sum_{v\in N_i^t}\sum_{k=1}^{K} f'_{b_i}\mathbf{q}_j(k) r_{vj} - P_{ij}^t \sum_{v\in N_i^t}\sum_{k=1}^{K} f'_{b_i}\mathbf{q}_j(k)\Big)$$

$$\nabla_{\eta_i} = 2\beta\eta_i + 2(1-\alpha)\sum_{t=1}^{T}\sum_{(i,j)\in\mathcal{O}_t}\frac{E_{ij}^t}{Q_{ij}^t}\sum_{v\in N_i^t}\sum_{k=1}^{K} f\mathbf{q}_j(k) r_{vj}(t-t_{vj})$$

$$\nabla_{\mathbf{q}_j(k)} = 2\beta\mathbf{q}_j(k) - 2\sum_{t=1}^{T}\sum_{(i,j)\in\mathcal{O}_t} E_{ij}^t\Big(\alpha\mathbf{p}_i^t(k) + (1-\alpha)\frac{1}{(Q_{ij}^t)^2}$$

$$(Q_{ij}^t \sum_{v\in N_i^t} f r_{vj} - P_{ij}^t \sum_{v\in N_i^t} f)\Big),$$

$$\nabla_{\mathbf{p}_i^t(k)} = 2\beta\mathbf{p}_i^t(k) - 2\sum_{(i,j)\in\mathcal{O}_t} E_{ij}^t\Big(\alpha\mathbf{q}_j(k) + (1-\alpha)$$

$$\frac{1}{(Q_{ij}^t)^2}(Q_{ij}^t \sum_{v\in N_i^t} f'_{\mathbf{p}_i^t(k)}\mathbf{q}_j(k) r_{vj} - P_{ij}^t \sum_{v\in N_i^t} f'_{\mathbf{p}_i^t(k)}\mathbf{q}_j(k)\Big)$$

$$-2(1-\alpha)\sum_{z\in T_i^t}\sum_{(z,j)\in\mathcal{O}_t}\frac{1}{(Q_{zj}^t)^2}\Big(Q_{zj}^t f'_{\mathbf{p}_i^t(k)}\mathbf{q}_j(k) r_{ij}$$

$$-P_{zj}^t f'_{\mathbf{p}_i(k)}\mathbf{q}_j(k)\Big) + H_i^t \tag{8}$$

where $f'_{\mathbf{w}}$, f'_{b_i} and $f'_{\mathbf{p}_i^t(k)}$ are the partial derivatives of f with respect to $\mathbf{w}$, b_i and $\mathbf{p}_i^t(k)$, respectively. T_i^t denotes the users who trust u_i at time t. E_{ij}^t, P_{ij}^t, Q_{ij}^t and H_i^t are defined as,

$$E_{ij}^t = r_{ij}^t - \alpha\sum_{k=1}^{K}\mathbf{q}_j(k)\mathbf{p}_i^t(k) -$$

$$(1-\alpha)\frac{\sum_{v\in N_i^t}\sum_{k=1}^{K} f(\mathbf{w}^\top\mathbf{s}_{ivk}^t + b_i)\mathbf{q}_j(k) r_{vj}}{\sum_{v\in N_i^t}\sum_{k=1}^{K} f(\mathbf{w}^\top\mathbf{s}_{ivk}^t + b_i)\mathbf{q}_j(k)},$$

$$P_{ij}^t = \sum_{v\in N_i^t}\sum_{k=1}^{K} f(\mathbf{w}^\top\mathbf{s}_{ivk}^t + b_i)\mathbf{q}_j(k) r_{vj},$$

$$Q_{ij}^t = \sum_{v\in N_i^t}\sum_{k=1}^{K} f(\mathbf{w}^\top\mathbf{s}_{ivk}^t + b_i)\mathbf{q}_j(k),$$

$$H_i^t = \begin{cases} -\lambda c'_{\mathbf{p}_i^t k}(\mathbf{p}_i^{t+1}(k) - \mathbf{p}_i^t(k)), & t = t_{u_i} \\ \lambda c'_{\mathbf{p}_i^t k}(\mathbf{p}_i^t(k) - \mathbf{p}_i^{t-1}(k)), & t = T \\ \lambda\Big(c'_{\mathbf{p}_i^t k}(\mathbf{p}_i^t(k) - \mathbf{p}_i^{t-1}(k)) - c'_{\mathbf{p}_i^t k}(\mathbf{p}_i^{t+1}(k) - \mathbf{p}_i^t(k))\Big), \\ \quad t_{u_i} < t < T \end{cases}$$

Next we discuss our choice of $f(\cdot)$ and $c(\cdot)$ for eTrust. $f(\cdot)$ is an active function to control the estimated trust strength in $[0,1]$. It should be real-valued and differentiable function and the range of this function is limited in $[0,1]$. However, we still lack the detailed description about this function. In this case, a sigmoid function is often used [1]. It exhibits a progression from small beginnings that accelerates and approaches a climax over the domain, formulated as,

$$f(\mathbf{w}^\top\mathbf{s}_{ivk}^t + b_i) = \frac{1}{1 + exp(-(\mathbf{w}^\top\mathbf{s}_{ivk}^t + b_i))}. \tag{9}$$

Then $f'_{\mathbf{w}}$, f'_{b_i} and $f'_{\mathbf{p}_i^t(k)}$ are formally stated as,

$$f'_{\mathbf{w}} = f(1-f)\mathbf{s}_{ivk}^t,$$
$$f'_{b_i} = f(1-f),$$
$$f'_{\mathbf{p}_i^t(k)} = f(1-f)\mathbf{w}^\top(\mathbf{s}_{ivk}^t)'_{\mathbf{p}_i^t(k)}. \tag{10}$$

$c(\cdot)$ is used to capture how user preferences change over time. User preferences are usually assumed to change smoothly over time [16]. Under this assumption, $c(\cdot)$, $c'_{\mathbf{p}_i^{t-1}k}$ and $c'_{\mathbf{p}_i^t k}$ are defined as follows:

$$c\Big(\mathbf{p}_i^t(k) - \mathbf{p}_i^{t-1}(k)\Big) = \|\mathbf{p}_i^t(k) - \mathbf{p}_i^{t-1}(k)\|_2^2,$$
$$c'_{\mathbf{p}_i^{t-1}k} = -2\Big(\mathbf{p}_i^t(k) - \mathbf{p}_i^{t-1}(k)\Big),$$
$$c'_{\mathbf{p}_i^t k} = 2\Big(\mathbf{p}_i^t(k) - \mathbf{p}_i^{t-1}(k)\Big). \tag{11}$$

4. APPLICATIONS OF eTrust

We discuss the role of eTrust in product review applications to help improve the performance of rating and trust prediction.

4.1 Rating Prediction

Rating prediction is the task of predicting a given user's ratings for a given item based on past ratings or other information, regarded as one of the most important algorithms for recommendation system. People tend to seek advices from their trusted friends thus trust networks are widely exploited to improve the task of rating prediction. Most existing trust network based methods assume single and static trust relations. However, rating systems in product review sites are highly dynamic and user preferences are drifting over time, indicating the evolution of trust relations. Thus eTrust, modeling the trust evolution, can be used to further improve the performance of prediction.

Given the previous ratings $\{\mathcal{O}_t\}_{t=1}^T$, the task of trust prediction aims to predict the ratings at time $T+1$, $\mathcal{O}_{T+1}$. The rating from u_i to I_j at time $T+1$ can be predicted as,

$$\hat{r}_{ij}^{T+1} = \alpha\mathbf{q}_j^\top\mathbf{p}_i^{T+1}$$
$$+(1-\alpha)\frac{\sum_{v\in N_i^{T+1}}\sum_{k=1}^{K} f(\mathbf{w}^\top\mathbf{s}_{ivk}^{T+1} + b_i)\mathbf{q}_j(k) r_{vj}}{\sum_{v\in N_i^{T+1}}\sum_{k=1}^{K} f(\mathbf{w}^\top\mathbf{s}_{ivk}^{T+1} + b_i)\mathbf{q}_j(k)}, \tag{12}$$

where $\mathbf{w}$ is learnt from testing data. For the existing item, I_j, its characteristics vector, $\mathbf{q}_j$, is not evolved. For the existing user, u_i, b_i and η_i are independent on time slices, directly applied to $T+1$. We define the change speed of u_i's preference in the k-facet, Z_{ik}, as,

$$Z_{ik} = \frac{1}{T - t_{u_i} - 1}\sum_{t=t_{u_i}+1}^{T} |\mathbf{p}_i^t(k) - \mathbf{p}_i^{t-1}(k)|, \tag{13}$$

then user preference at $T+1$, i.e., $\mathbf{p}_i^{T+1}(k)$, can be estimated from that at T by considering the change speed of the user preference as,

$$\mathbf{p}_i^{T+1}(k) = \mathbf{p}_i^T(k) + Z_{ik}. \tag{14}$$

At time $T+1$, new users and new items might be introduced; and a challenge for eTrust is how to address the cold-start problem where no historical ratings on items or users are available. Homophily [23] is employed to deal with the cold-start problem: similar users are more likely to trust each other. Therefore, for a new user, we first find his top-ℓ similar users based on their profiles to establish his trust network and then use the average user preferences from his trust network to estimate his preferences. A similar strategy is adopted for each new item: the characteristics of a new item are estimated from its top similar items.

4.2 Trust Prediction

Trust between users is widely exploited by search and recommendation systems. Inferring unknown trust between users attracts more and more attention recently [8, 18, 3]. Trust propagation model is a popular model to derive trust relationships based on known trust relationships [8]. However, users' trust relationships usually follow a pow-law distribution and 80% of users are in the long tail. Thus in practical, there is not enough information to apply this technique. Furthermore, the propagation model is not directly applicable to the new users who have little information. Previous work suggests that models, combining rating similarity with trust networks, can achieve better performance than trust propagation model [18, 3]. eTrust can be applied to the task of trust prediction.

Given trust networks and ratings before time T, we want to recommend trust relationships at time $T+1$. eTrust learns its parameters by solving the problem in Eq. (7) based on the trust networks and rating information before T. Then the trust strength between u_i and u_v in the k-th facet can be calculated by Eq. (5). For a new user, we use the average user preferences of his top-ℓ similar users in terms of profiles to represent his preferences. After obtaining trust strengths for each facet, the overall strength can be computed as,

$$w_{iv}^{T+1} = \frac{1}{\|\mathbf{p}_i^{T+1}\|_2} \sum_{k=1}^{K} \mathbf{p}_i^{T+1}(k) w_{ivk}^{T+1}, \tag{15}$$

5. EXPERIMENTS

In this section, we conduct experiments to evaluate the proposed framework, eTrust. We first introduce the details about the dataset used in the experiments; next describe the findings and results of applying eTrust to online applications, i.e., rating prediction and trust prediction.

5.1 Dataset and Experiment Setting

To study the evolution of trust, we collect a dataset from a popular product review site, Epinions, in the month of May, 2011. In Epinions, people can rate various products and add members to their trust networks or "Circle of Trust". We started with a set of most active users and then did breadth-first search until no new users could be found. For each user, we collected their profiles (user name, location, real name, registration time, self-description, and favorite websites), product rating entries and trust relations. For each product rating entry, we collected the time point of the entry, product name, category and the rating. For each trust relation, we collected trustee, trustor and the time point when the trust relation established.

We compute the trustors and trustees for each user and the distributions are shown in Figure 2(a) and Figure 2(b). Most people have few trustors and trustees, while a few users have an extremely high number of trustees or trustors: suggesting a power-law distribution that is typical in social networks. We check the distributions of new actions and new objects w.r.t. the current number of actions and objects. The results for new actions and new objects are shown in Figure 2(c) and Figure 2(d), respectively: also suggesting power-law-like distributions. Some other statistics of the dataset are shown in Table 1.

The earliest rating was published on Jul 05, 1999 and the latest one was on May 08, 2011. However, the temporal information about the trust relations established before

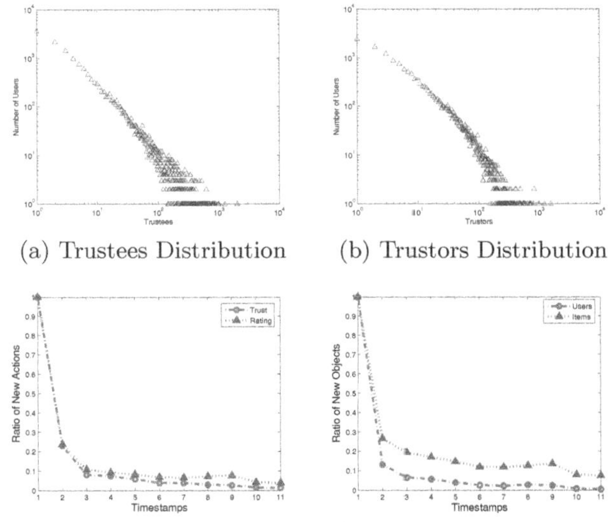

(a) Trustees Distribution (b) Trustors Distribution

(c) New Actions Distribution (d) New Objects Distribution

Figure 2: Distributions in Epinions

Table 1: Statistics of the Dataset

# of Users	22,166
# of Items	296,277
# of Categories	27
# of Ratings	922,267
# of Links	355,813
First Rating on	Jul 05 1999
Last Rating on	May 08 2011
Trust Network Density	0.0014
Clustering Coefficient	0.1518

11th January, 2001 is not available from Epinions. Therefore we split the whole dataset into 11 timestamps, i.e., $\mathcal{T} = \{T_1, \ldots, T_{11}\}$, where T_1 covers the data before 11th January, 2001, T_{11} contains data after 11th January, 2010 and for T_2 to T_{10}, each of them contains one-year data. For example, T_2 contains data from 12th January, 2001 to 11th January, 2002. In the following experiments, we choose T_1 to T_{10} as the training set to estimate the parameters of eTrust.

In Eq. (7), $\mathbf{s}_{ivk}^t$ is the preference similarity vector for u_i and u_v in the k-th facet at time t and in this work, we define the following 9 metrics of preference similarity as,

$$\mathbf{s}_{ijk}^t = [\mathbf{p}_i^t(k), \mathbf{p}_j^t(k), \mathbf{p}_i^t(k) + \mathbf{p}_j^t(k), \mathbf{p}_i^t(k) - \mathbf{p}_j^t(k),$$
$$\mathbf{p}_j^t(k) - \mathbf{p}_i^t(k), (\mathbf{p}_i^t(k) - \mathbf{p}_j^t(k))^2, \mathbf{p}_j^t(k)\mathbf{p}_i^t(k), \frac{\mathbf{p}_i^t(k)}{\mathbf{p}_j^t(k)}, \frac{\mathbf{p}_j^t(k)}{\mathbf{p}_i^t(k)}].$$

5.2 Findings about eTrust

Some interesting findings are summarized below.

- For each trust relation, x_{iv}, the evolution speed of this relation in the k-th facet (facet speed), f_{ivk}, is defined as,

$$f_{ivk} = \frac{1}{T - t_{iv} - 1} \sum_{t=t_{iv}+1}^{T} |w_{ivk}^t - w_{ivk}^{t-1}| \tag{16}$$

  where t_{iv} is the time point when x_{iv} established and the overall evolution speed, F_{iv}, is defined as the sum of all K facet speed, $F_{iv} = \sum_{k=1}^{K} f_{ivk}$. We find that the evolution speed varies with facets and trust relations within an open triad, shown as the left subgraph in Figure 3, are more likely to evolve than those within a closed triad, demonstrated in the right subgraph in Figure 3. On average, the evolution speed of trust relations within an open triad is 6.12 times of the speed of those within a closed triad.

- Users with similar preferences are more likely to trust each other, demonstrating the homophily [23] in the trust network. For example, the average preference similarity between trusted users is 3.44 times as that of users without trust relations at T_{10} and we have similar observations in other time slices.

- User preferences drift over time which can be observed in Figure 4, depicting user preferences from 2001 to 2009, i.e., $\{\{\mathbf{p}_i^t\}_{u_i \in \mathcal{U}_T}\}_{t=1}^{9}$. The change of user preference from t to $t+1$, Y_t^{t+1}, is defined as,

$$Y_t^{t+1} = \frac{1}{n_{t+1}} \sum_{u_i \in \mathcal{U}_{t+1}} \|\mathbf{p}_i^{t+1} - \mathbf{p}_i^t\| \quad (17)$$

we find that the change of user preferences varies in different years. For example, the changes of user preferences from 2003 to 2004 and from 2005 to 2006 are 2.96 and 1.79 times of the average, respectively. This might be related to two big events happened in Epinions: Epinions was acquired by Shopping.com [3] in 2003 and in turn was acquired by Ebay [4] in 2005 [5].

- The speed of change, defined in Eq. (13), varies with people and facets. Figure 5 shows the average speed of change from 2001 to 2009 w.r.t. different facets. Different people have different speeds of change while user preferences change much faster for some facets than others. For example, the average changing speed for the 13-th latent facet is almost 60 times of that for 2-th latent facet.

- People have multiple and heterogeneous trust relations with others. For each facet, people only trust a part of their networks strongly. For example, on average, people trust only 15.8% of their trust networks for a specific facet when the number of latent facets are 20 at T_{10}. We also observe heterogeneous trust relations including heterogeneous pairs of reciprocal trust relations, transitive relations and co-citation relations. These observations are very consistent with the findings of our previous multi-faceted trust research [27].

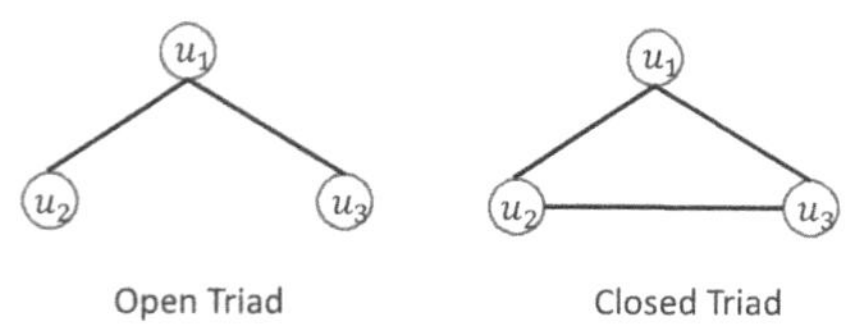

Figure 3: Open Triad vs Closed Triad

[3]http://www.shopping.com/
[4]http://www.ebay.com/
[5]http://en.wikipedia.org/wiki/Epinions

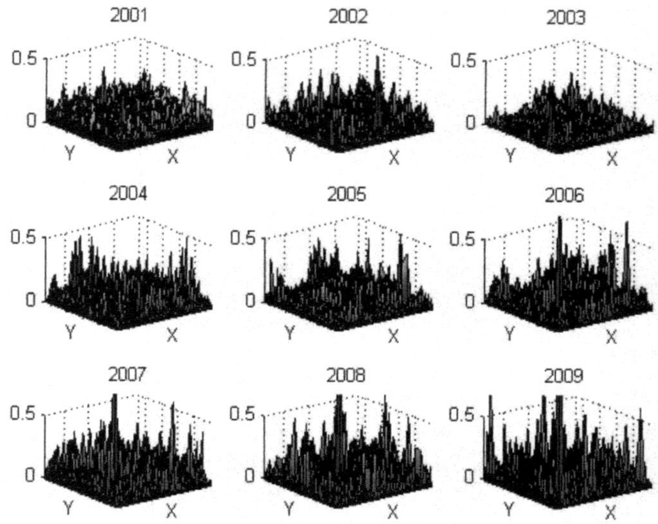

Figure 4: User Preference Evolution. Note that x-axis, y-axis and z-axis denote the facet ID, user ID and user preference, respectively.

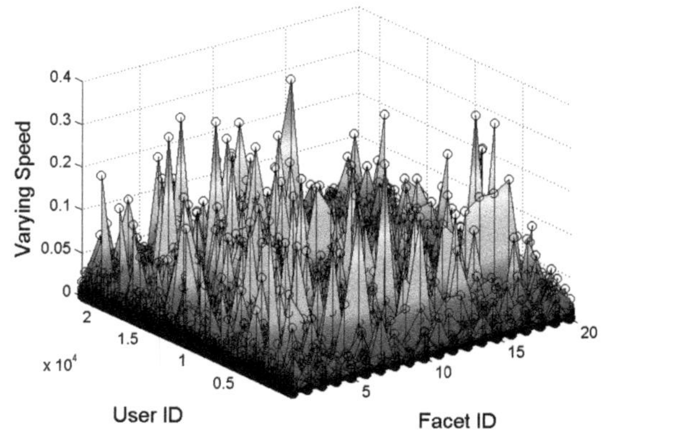

Figure 5: Speed of Changes w.r.t. Users and Facets

5.3 Rating Prediction

eTrust can be naturally applied to the online application of rating prediction, as discuss in Section 4.1. T_{11} is the testing set in this experiment and we further divide it into two parts: the ratings involved in new items or new users(cold-start problem), denoted as $\mathcal{N}$; the remaining ratings from T_{11} denoted as $\mathcal{K}$. We closely examine T_{11} and find that $\mathcal{N}$ contains 10.06% of the ratings at T_{11}.

We use Root Mean Squared Error (RMSE), a common metric, to evaluate prediction accuracy [13].

$$RMSE(\mathcal{M}) = \sqrt{\frac{\sum_{(i,j)\in\mathcal{M}} (r_{ij} - \hat{r}_{ij})^2}{|\mathcal{M}|}} \quad (18)$$

where $|\mathcal{M}|$ is the size of the testing set, $\mathcal{M}$. Note that eTrust can be easily applied to other rating prediction methods thus we aim to investigate whether considering dynamics of trust relations and user preferences allows us to improve the prediction performance, instead of comparing different rating prediction methods.

Table 2: RMSE of Rating Prediction in Epinions

	$\mathcal{K}$	$\mathcal{N}$	$\mathcal{K}+\mathcal{N}$
Mean	1.1054	1.1562	1.1106
NN	1.1092	1.1566	1.1148
MF	1.0804	1.1472	1.0872
MF+NN	1.0675	1.1392	1.0747
mTrust	1.0566	1.1375	1.0646
eTrust	1.0299	1.0783	1.0347

The prediction results are shown in the Table 2 and the methods listed in the table are defined as follows:

- *Mean*: the rating of an item is predicted by the mean of known ratings of the product;
- *MF*: this method is based on user preferences and item characteristics, however it assumes that user preferences do not evolve over time [13];
- *NN*: this model is a simple nearest-neighbor algorithm, assuming that a user has the similar rating as his trust network for the same item [13];
- *MF+NN*: this model is a combination of *NN* and *MF*, however, it considers heterogeneous strengths of trust relations [2];
- *mTrust*: this model considers the multi-faceted trust relations between users and assumes people place trust differently on different people [27];
- *eTrust*: our proposed method, considering the dynamics of both trust relations and user preferences.

Note that all baseline methods cannot tackle the cold-start problem thus we adopt the similar strategy as eTrust by considering their top-ℓ similar existing users (items) based on their profiles. For example, for *Mean*, the rating of a new item is predicted by the average rating of its top-ℓ similar items. The parameters of all methods are determined through cross-validation. For eTrust, the parameters are set as: $K = 20$, $\alpha = 0.3$, $\beta = 0.05$ and $\gamma = 0.1$.

We notice that RMSE values for all methods are very close to each other. However, small improvement in RMSE terms can have a significant impact on the quality of the top few recommendation [13]. As reported in [13], when the performance improved from 0.9025 to 0.8870 w.r.t. RMSE, it gains more than 50% relative improvement in terms of top few recommendation. *Mean* obtains better performance than *NN*. There are two main reasons. First, most of the time, the majority of users actual ratings are close to the average and by closely examining the dataset, we find that more than 70% users give a score of 4 or 5. Second, *NN* treats all trust relations equally, however, people may trust a part of their trust networks more strongly than others. When considering heterogeneous trust strengths, *MF+NN* outperforms both *MF* and *NN*, further demonstrating that people trust their friends differently while only give similar ratings with their strongly trusted friends.

NN and *MF+NN* assume single and homogeneous trust relations, however, people with multi-faceted interests and experts of different types suggest multiple and heterogeneous trust relations [27]. *mTrust* considers multi-faceted trust relations and obtains better performance than *MF+NN*. *eTrust* consistently outperforms all other methods and we believe that this improvement is contributed by exploiting the dynamics of both trust relations and user preferences.

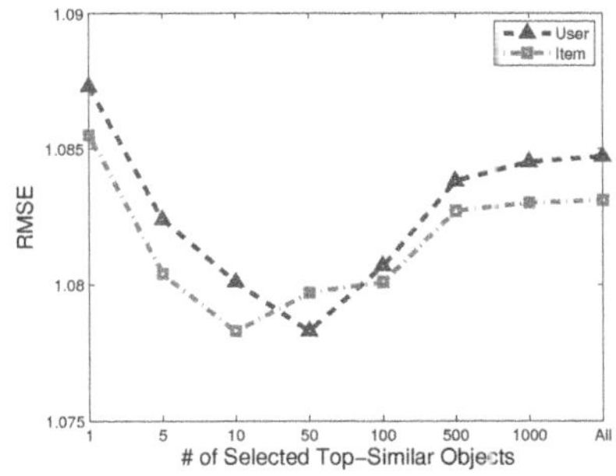

Figure 6: RMSE w.r.t. the Number of Selected Top Similar Users

The performance of all methods degrades in $\mathcal{N}$. However, eTrust obtains much better performance than other methods, gaining 0.0592 absolute improvement in terms of RMSE. These results demonstrate that eTrust is more robust to the cold-start problem. We also investigate how the performance of eTrust varies with the number of selected top-similar users or items, ℓ, and the results are shown in Figure 6. The performance with $\ell = 1$ is always worst, even worse than that with all users or items. It suggests that users (items) with most similar profiles do not necessarily have most similar user preferences (item characteristics).

5.4 Trust Prediction

Trust plays an important role in helping collect reliable information for users in online communities. If trust relations can be predicted accurately, users can use these relations to make decisions on the reliability of information. For eTrust, trust relations can be inferred by user preferences with estimated $\mathbf{w}$ and user specific bias $\{b_i\}$ by Eq. (5).

Data from T_{11} are treated as the testing set, separated into two parts: $\mathcal{E}$: trust relations established among existing users and $\mathcal{N}$: trust relations involved in new users, covering 23.51% of the whole trust relations at T_{11}. We follow the metric used in [17] to evaluate the performance of trust prediction. Let A be the set of pairs of users, having no relations at time T_{10}, and B denote the set of pairs of users, establishing trust relations at time T_{11}. Each trust predictor ranks pairs in A in decreasing order of confidence and we take the first $|B|$ pairs as the set of predicted trust relations, denoting as C. Then the prediction accuracy (PA) can be calculated as,

$$PA = \frac{|B \cap C|}{|B|} \tag{19}$$

where $|\cdot|$ denotes the size of a set.

The PA results are shown in Table 3 and the trust predictors mentioned in the table are defined as follows:

- *Simi*: it ranks the pairs according to their rating similarity (if available) and profile similarity, which only considers profile information or rating information.
- *TP*: the trust relations are inferred through trust propagation, only considering the existing trust network information [8].

Table 3: Accuracy of Trust Prediction in Epinions

	$\mathcal{E}(\%)$	$\mathcal{N}(\%)$	$\mathcal{E}+\mathcal{N}(\%)$
Simi	48.41	28.94	43.93
TP	45.47	N.A.	35.01
Simi+TP	50.19	28.94	45.31
eTrust	55.07	33.83	50.18

- *TP + Simi*: a combination of *Simi* and *TP*, integrating both the existing trust network and rating or profile similarity [3].
- *eTrust*: trust relations are predicted by eTrust through Eq. (5) and details are shown in the subsection 4.2.

Trust propagation always obtains the worst performance. *TP* predicts trust relationship between two users when there are existing trust relationships connecting them indirectly. However, connectivity information is not always enough for correct trust prediction, especially when trust connectivity is not high enough for applying propagation techniques. For example, *TP* cannot be applied to the dataset $\mathcal{N}$. *Simi* obtains better performance than *TP*, demonstrating that users with similar ratings or profiles are likely to trust each other. When considering both existing trust networks and similarity, *Simi+TP* outperforms both *TP* and *Simi*, indicating similarity information and existing trust networks are complementary with each other for trust prediction.

eTrust performs consistently best. For example, eTrust gains 9.72% and 14.45% relative improvement in $\mathcal{E}$ and $\mathcal{N}$, respectively. There are two main reasons: (1) eTrust performs trust prediction facet by facet, overcoming the problem of the heterogeneous trust relations [27]; and (2) trust relations are inferred based on user current preferences. We observe that the performance of all predictors decreases in $\mathcal{N}$. However, based on profile similarity, *Simi* still obtains 28.94% in terms of prediction accuracy, much larger than a random predictor whose accuracy is less than 1%. This observation demonstrates the existence of homophily in trust networks: similar users are more likely to trust each other.

6. RELATED WORK

Trust has attracted more and more attention from computer science community [20, 5]. In recent years, many trust related online applications are proposed and we next briefly review some of them related to our work.

Rating Prediction. People are likely to seek advices from their trust networks thus trust networks are widely exploited in the task of rating prediction. In [20], several methods for incorporating trust networks are proposed to improve the performance of rating prediction. [22] studied and modeled the bidirectional effects between trust relations and product rating. Koren introduced some innovations to both latent factor models and neighborhood models. The factor and neighborhood models can now be smoothly merged, thereby building a more accurate combined model [13]. It reported that a proper combination of these two models can significantly improve the prediction performance. All these methods do not consider the changes of user purchase interest. However, customer preferences for products are drifting over time [14]. Ding et al. presented a novel algorithm to compute the time weights for different items by assigning a decreasing weight to old data [4]. Koren proposed a methodology and specific techniques for modeling the dynamics of user preferences in recommender systems [14]. It claimed that temporal dynamics in the data can have more significant impacts on accuracy than designing more complex learning algorithms.

Trust Prediction. Trust plays an important role in helping online people collect reliable information. If trust relations can be predicted accurately, users can use these relations to make decisions on the reliability of information. Guha et al. developed a formal framework of trust propagation schemes [8]. It first separates trust and distrust matrix and then performs operations on them to obtain the transitive trust between two nodes. The connection between trust and user similarity was studied in [32], and a strong and significant correlation is found between trust and similarity. The more similar two people are, the greater the trust between them is. In [3], rating similarity is exploited to enrich traditional trust propagation methods. This work demonstrated that predicting trust is more successful for pairs of users that are similar to each other if we combine the topology of the trust network with rating similarity.

Trust Strength Prediction is another direction of related research, which differs from trust prediction. The former focuses on modeling the strength of existed links rather than link existence. In [31] a latent variable model is developed to estimate relationship strength from various interaction activities and user similarities. In this model, relationship strength is modeled as the hidden effect of user similarities and it also impacts the nature and frequency of online interactions. Au et al. show heterogeneous trust strengths of trust relations in product review sites and a modified matrix factorization technique is proposed to estimate strengths of trust relations. Trust, as a social concept, naturally has multiple facets, indicating multiple and heterogeneous trust relations between users. Our previous work, mTrust, investigated multi-faceted trust relations between users. People place trust differently on different people and the work of mTrust demonstrates that trust strength can be inferred under the context of rating prediction [27].

7. CONCLUSIONS

In this paper, we study online trust evolution in the context of product review. By exploiting the correlation between user preferences and trust relations, we propose a framework, eTrust, to understand the evolution of trust in an online world and apply eTrust to various online applications such as rating prediction and trust prediction. Interesting findings are observed in our experiments using real-world data, Epinions; and eTrust can be applied to improve the performance of rating prediction and trust prediction. In our future work, we will continue our research on eTrust and investigate trust evolution in areas such as ranking evolution, useful message recommendation [9] and linked feature selection [28].

Acknowledgments

The work is, in part, supported by ARO (#025071) and NSF (#0812551).

8. REFERENCES

[1] J. Anderson, R. Michalski, R. Michalski, J. Carbonell, and T. Mitchell. *Machine learning: An artificial*

intelligence approach, volume 2. Morgan Kaufmann, 1986.

[2] C. Au Yeung and T. Iwata. Strength of social influence in trust networks in product review sites. In *Proceedings of the fourth ACM international conference on Web search and data mining*, pages 495–504. ACM, 2011.

[3] P. Borzymek, M. Sydow, and A. Wierzbicki. Enriching trust prediction model in social network with user rating similarity. In *International Conference on Computational Aspects of Social Networks*, pages 40–47. IEEE, 2009.

[4] Y. Ding and X. Li. Time weight collaborative filtering. In *Proceedings of the 14th ACM international conference on Information and knowledge management*, pages 485–492. ACM, 2005.

[5] H. Gao, G. Barbier, and R. Goolsby. Harnessing the crowdsourcing power of social media for disaster relief. *Intelligent Systems, IEEE*, 2011.

[6] D. Gefen, E. Karahanna, and D. Straub. Trust and tam in online shopping: An integrated model. *Mis Quarterly*, pages 51–90, 2003.

[7] J. Golbeck. Trust and nuanced profile similarity in online social networks. *ACM Transactions on the Web*, 3(4):1–33, 2009.

[8] R. Guha, R. Kumar, P. Raghavan, and A. Tomkins. Propagation of trust and distrust. In *Proceedings of the 13th international conference on World Wide Web*, pages 403–412. ACM, 2004.

[9] X. Hu, N. Sun, C. Zhang, and T. Chua. Exploiting internal and external semantics for the clustering of short texts using world knowledge. In *CIKM*, 2009.

[10] M. Jamali and M. Ester. Trustwalker: a random walk model for combining trust-based and item-based recommendation. In *Proceedings of the 15th ACM SIGKDD international conference on Knowledge discovery and data mining*, pages 397–406. ACM, 2009.

[11] G. Jones and J. George. The experience and evolution of trust: Implications for cooperation and teamwork. *Academy of management review*, pages 531–546, 1998.

[12] P. Karmakar and R. Roy. Evolution of trust and formation of preference clusters in distributed networked structure. *International Journal of Virtual Communities and Social Networking*, 3(2):17–50, 2011.

[13] Y. Koren. Factorization meets the neighborhood: a multifaceted collaborative filtering model. In *Proceeding of the 14th ACM SIGKDD international conference on Knowledge discovery and data mining*, pages 426–434. ACM, 2008.

[14] Y. Koren. Collaborative filtering with temporal dynamics. In *Proceedings of the 15th ACM SIGKDD international conference on Knowledge discovery and data mining*, pages 447–456. ACM, 2009.

[15] J. Leskovec, D. Huttenlocher, and J. Kleinberg. Predicting positive and negative links in online social networks. In *Proceedings of the 19th international conference on World wide web*, 2010.

[16] R. Li, B. Li, C. Jin, X. Xue, and X. Zhu. Tracking user-preference varying speed in collaborative filtering. In *Twenty-Fifth AAAI Conference on Artificial Intelligence*, 2011.

[17] D. Liben-Nowell and J. Kleinberg. The link-prediction problem for social networks. *Journal of the American society for information science and technology*, 58(7):1019–1031, 2007.

[18] H. Liu, E. Lim, H. Lauw, M. Le, A. Sun, J. Srivastava, and Y. Kim. Predicting trusts among users of online communities: an epinions case study. In *Proceedings of the 9th ACM Conference on Electronic Commerce*, pages 310–319. ACM, 2008.

[19] Y. Lu, P. Tsaparas, A. Ntoulas, and L. Polanyi. Exploiting social context for review quality prediction. In *Proceedings of the 19th international conference on World wide web*, pages 691–700. ACM, 2010.

[20] H. Ma, H. Yang, M. Lyu, and I. King. Sorec: social recommendation using probabilistic matrix factorization. In *Proceeding of the 17th ACM conference on Information and knowledge management*, pages 931–940. ACM, 2008.

[21] P. Massa and P. Avesani. Trust-aware recommender systems. In *Proceedings of the 2007 ACM conference on Recommender systems*, pages 17–24. ACM, 2007.

[22] Y. Matsuo and H. Yamamoto. Community gravity: measuring bidirectional effects by trust and rating on online social networks. In *Proceedings of the 18th international conference on World wide web*, pages 751–760. ACM, 2009.

[23] M. McPherson, L. Smith-Lovin, and J. Cook. Birds of a feather: Homophily in social networks. *Annual review of sociology*, pages 415–444, 2001.

[24] A. Mishra and A. Bhattacharya. Finding the bias and prestige of nodes in networks based on trust scores. In *Proceedings of the 20th international conference on World wide web*, pages 567–576. ACM, 2011.

[25] J. Nocedal and S. Wright. *Numerical optimization.* Springer verlag, 1999.

[26] M. Richardson and P. Domingos. Mining knowledge-sharing sites for viral marketing. In *Proceedings of the eighth ACM SIGKDD international conference on Knowledge discovery and data mining*, pages 61–70. ACM, 2002.

[27] J. Tang, H. Gao, and H. Liu. mtrust: Discerning multi-faceted trust in a connected world. In *the 5th ACM International Conference on Web Search and Data Mining*, 2012.

[28] J. Tang and H. Liu. Feature selection with linked data in social media. In *SDM*, 2012.

[29] S. Tang. The social evolutionary psychology of fear (and trust): Or why is international cooperation difficult? In *annual meeting of the ISA's 49th Annual Convention, Bridging Multiple Divides, Hilton San Francisco, San Francisco, CA, USA*, 2010.

[30] G. Van de Bunt, R. Wittek, and M. de Klepper. The evolution of intra-organizational trust networks. *International sociology*, 20(3):339–369, 2005.

[31] R. Xiang, J. Neville, and M. Rogati. Modeling relationship strength in online social networks. In *Proceedings of the 19th international conference on World wide web*, 2010.

[32] C. Ziegler and J. Golbeck. Investigating interactions of trust and interest similarity. *Decision Support Systems*, 43(2):460–475, 2007.

Searching and Mining Trillions of Time Series Subsequences under Dynamic Time Warping

Thanawin Rakthanmanon, Bilson Campana, Abdullah Mueen, Gustavo Batista[2], Brandon Westover[1], Qiang Zhu, Jesin Zakaria, Eamonn Keogh
UC Riverside, [1]Brigham and Women's Hospital, [2]University of São Paulo
{rakthant, bcampana, mueen, qzhu, jzaka, eamonn}@cs.ucr.edu, gbatista@icmc.usp.br, mwestover@partners.org

ABSTRACT

Most time series data mining algorithms use similarity search as a core subroutine, and thus the time taken for similarity search is *the* bottleneck for virtually all time series data mining algorithms. The difficulty of scaling search to large datasets largely explains why most academic work on time series data mining has plateaued at considering a few millions of time series objects, while much of industry and science sits on billions of time series objects waiting to be explored. In this work we show that by using a combination of four novel ideas we can search and mine truly massive time series for the first time. We demonstrate the following extremely unintuitive fact; in large datasets we can exactly search under DTW much more quickly than the current state-of-the-art *Euclidean distance* search algorithms. We demonstrate our work on the largest set of time series experiments ever attempted. In particular, the largest dataset we consider is larger than the combined size of all of the time series datasets considered in all data mining papers ever published. We show that our ideas allow us to solve higher-level time series data mining problem such as motif discovery and clustering at scales that would otherwise be untenable. In addition to mining massive datasets, we will show that our ideas also have implications for real-time monitoring of data streams, allowing us to handle much faster arrival rates and/or use cheaper and lower powered devices than are currently possible.

Categories and Subject Descriptors

H.2.8 [**Information Systems**]: Database Application — *Data Mining*

General Terms

Algorithm, Experimentation

Keywords

Time series, Similarity Search, Lower Bounds

1. INTRODUCTION

Time series data is pervasive across almost all human endeavors, including medicine, finance, science and entertainment. As such, it is hardly surprising that time series data mining has attracted significant attention and research effort. Most time series data mining algorithms require similarity comparisons as a subroutine, and in spite of the consideration of dozens of alternatives, there is increasing evidence that the classic Dynamic Time Warping (DTW) measure is the best measure in most domains [6].

KDD'12, August 12–16, 2012, Beijing, China.

It is difficult to overstate the ubiquity of DTW. It has been used in robotics, medicine [5], biometrics, music/speech processing [1][27][41], climatology, aviation, gesture recognition [3][38], user interfaces [16][22][29][38], industrial processing, cryptanalysis [7], mining of historical manuscripts [15], geology, astronomy [20][31], space exploration, wildlife monitoring, etc.

As ubiquitous as DTW is, we believe that there are thousands of research efforts that would like to use DTW, but find it too computationally expensive. For example, consider the following: "*Ideally, dynamic time warping would be used to achieve this, but due to time constraints…*" [5]. Likewise, [3] bemoans DTW is "*still too slow for gesture recognition systems*", and [1] notes, even "*a 30 fold speed increase may not be sufficient for scaling DTW methods to truly massive databases.*" As we shall show, our subsequence search suite of four novel ideas (called the *UCR suite*) removes all of these objections. We can reproduce all the experiments in all these papers in well under a second.

We make an additional claim for our UCR suite which is almost certainly true, but hard to prove, given the variability in how search results are presented in the literature. We believe our exact DTW sequential search is much faster than any current *approximate* search or exact *indexed* search. In a handful of papers the authors *are* explicit enough with their experiments to see this is true. Consider [28], which says it can answer queries of length 1,000 under DTW with 95% accuracy, in a random walk dataset of one million objects in 5.65 seconds. We can *exactly* search this dataset in 3.8 seconds (on a very similar machine). Likewise, a recent paper that introduced a novel inner product based DTW lower bound greatly speeds up exact subsequence search for a wordspotting task in speech. The authors state: "*the new DTW-KNN method takes approximately 2 minutes*" [41]; however, we can reproduce their results in less than a second. An influential paper on gesture recognition on multi-touch screens laments that "*DTW took 128.26 minutes to run the 14,400 tests for a given subject's 160 gestures*" [38]. However, we can reproduce these results in under 3 seconds.

1.1 A Brief Discussion of a Trillion

Since we use the word "trillion" in this work and to our knowledge, it has never appeared in a data mining/database paper, we will take the time to briefly discuss this number. By a trillion, we mean the short scale version of the word [14], one million million, or 10^{12}, or 1,000,000,000,000.

If we have a single time series T of length one trillion, and we assume it takes eight bytes to store each value, it will require 7.2 terabytes to store. If we sample a electrocardiogram at 256Hz, a trillion data points would allow us to record 123 years of data, every single heartbeat of the longest lived human [37].

A time series of length one trillion is a very large data object. In fact, it is more than all of the time series data considered in all papers ever published in all data mining conferences *combined.* This is easy to see with a quick back-of-the-envelope calculation.

Up to 2011 there have been 1,709 KDD/SIGKDD papers (including industrial papers, posters, tutorial/keynote abstracts, etc. [9]). If *every* such paper was on time series, and *each* had looked at five hundred million objects, this would still not add up to the size of the data we consider here). However, the largest time series data considered in a SIGKDD paper was a "mere" one hundred million objects [35].

As large as a trillion is, there are thousands of research labs and commercial enterprises that have this much data. For example, many research hospitals have trillions of data points of EEG data, NASA Ames has tens of trillions of datapoints of telemetry of domestic flights, the Tennessee Valley Authority (a power company) records a trillion data points every four months, etc.

1.2 Explicit Statement of our Assumptions

Our work is predicated on several assumptions that we will now enumerate and justify.

1.2.1 Time Series Subsequences must be Normalized

In order to make meaningful comparisons between two time series, both must be normalized. While this may seem intuitive, and was explicitly empirically demonstrated a decade ago in a widely cited paper [19], many research efforts do not seem to realize this. This is critical because some speedup techniques *only* work on the un-normalized data; thus, the contributions of these research efforts may be largely nullified [8][28].

To make this clearer, let us consider the classic Gun/NoGun classification problem which has been in the public domain for nearly a decade. The data, which as shown in Figure 1.*center* is extracted from a video sequence, *was* Z-normalized. The problem has a 50/150 train/test split and a DTW one-nearest-neighbor classifier achieves an error rate of 0.087.

Suppose the data had *not* been normalized. As shown in Figure 1.*left* and Figure 1.*right*, we can simulate this by adding a tiny amount of scaling/offset to the original video. In the first case we randomly change the *offset* of each time series by ± 10%, and in the second case we randomly change the *scale* (amplitude) by ± 10%. The new one-nearest-neighbor classifier error rates, averaged over 1,000 runs, are 0.326 and 0.193, respectively, significantly worse than the normalized case.

Figure 1: Screen captures from the original video from which the Gun/NoGun data was culled. The center frame is the original size; the left and right frames have been scaled by 110% and 90% respectively. While these changes are barely perceptible, they double the error rate if normalization is not used. (Video courtesy of Dr. Ratanamahatana)

It is important to recognize that these tiny changes we made are completely dwarfed by changes we might expect to see in a real world deployment. The apparent *scale* can be changed by the camera zooming, by the actor standing a little closer to the camera, or by an actor of a different height. The apparent *offset* can be changed by this much by the camera tilt angle, or even by the actor wearing different shoes.

While we did this experiment on a visually intuitive example, all forty-five datasets in the UCR archive increase their error rate by at least 50% if we vary the offset and scale by just ± 5%.

It is critical to avoid a common misunderstanding. We must normalize *each* subsequence before making a comparison, it is not sufficient to normalize the entire dataset.

1.2.2 Dynamic Time Warping is the Best Measure

It has been suggested many times in the literature that the problem of time series data mining scalability is only due to DTW's oft-touted lethargy, and that we could solve this problem by using some other distance measure. As we shall later show, this is not the case. In fact, as we shall demonstrate, our optimized DTW search is much faster than all current *Euclidean* distance searches. Nevertheless, the question remains, is DTW the right measure to speed up? Dozens of alternative measures have been suggested. However, recent empirical evidence strongly suggests that none of these alternatives routinely beats DTW. When put to the test on a collection of forty datasets, the very *best* of these measures are sometimes a little better than DTW and sometimes a little worse [6]. In general, the results are consistent with these measures being minor variants or "flavors" of DTW (although they are not typically presented this way). In summary, after an exhaustive literature search of more than 800 papers [6], we are not aware of any distance measure that has been shown to outperform DTW by a statistically significant amount on reproducible experiments [6][19]. Thus, DTW is *the* measure to optimize (recall that DTW subsumes Euclidean distance as a special case).

1.2.3 Arbitrary Query Lengths cannot be Indexed

If we know the length of queries ahead of time we can mitigate at least some of the intractability of search by indexing the data [2][11][35]. Although to our knowledge no one has built an index for a trillion real-valued objects (Google only indexed a trillion webpages as recently as 2008), perhaps this could be done.

However, what if we do not know the length of the queries in advance? At least two groups have suggested techniques to index arbitrary length queries [18][23]. Both methods essentially build multiple indexes of various lengths, and at query time search the shorter and longer indexes, "interpolating" the results to produce the nearest neighbor produced by a virtual index of the correct length. This is an interesting idea, but it is hard to imagine it is the answer to our problem. Suppose we want to support queries in the range of, say, 16 to 4096. We must build indexes that are not too different in size, say MULTINDEX-LENGTHS = {16, 32, 64, .., 1024, 2048, 4096}[1]. However, for time series data the index is typically about one-tenth the size of the data [6][18]. Thus, we have doubled the amount of disk space we need. Moreover, if we are interested in tackling a trillion data objects we clearly cannot fit *any* index in the main memory, much less all of them, or any two of them.

There is an underappreciated reason why this problem is so hard; it is an implication of the need for normalization discussed above. Suppose we have a query Q of length 65, and an index that supports queries of length 64. We search the index for $Q_{[1:64]}$ and find that the best match for it has a distance of, say, 5.17. What can we say about the best match for the full Q? The answer is surprisingly little: 5.17 is neither an upper bound nor a lower bound to the best match for Q. This is because we must renormalize the subsequence when moving from $Q_{[1:64]}$ to the full Q. If we do not normalize any data, the results are meaningless (cf. Section 1.2.1), and the idea *might* be faster than sequential search. However, if we normalize the data we get so little information from indexes of the wrong length that we are no better off than sequential search.

In summary, there are no known techniques to support similarity search of arbitrary lengths once we have datasets in the billions.

[1] This collection of sizes is very optimistic. The step size should be at most 100, creating two orders of magnitude space overhead.

1.2.4 *There Exists Data Mining Problems that we are Willing to Wait Some Hours to Answer*

This point is almost self-evident. If a team of entomologists has spent three years gathering 0.2 trillion datapoints [35], or astronomers have spent billions dollars to launch a satellite to collect one trillion datapoints of star-light curve data per day [20], or a hospital charges $34,000 for a daylong EEG session to collect 0.3 trillion datapoints (c.f. Section 5.2) [26], then it is not unreasonable to expect that these groups would be willing to spend hours of CPU time to glean knowledge from their data.

2. RELATED WORK

Our review of related work on time series indexing is necessarily superficial, given the vast amount of work on the topic and page limits. Instead, we refer the interested reader to two recent papers [6][28], which have comprehensive reviews of existing work. It has now become common (although not yet *routine*) to see papers indexing/mining datasets with millions of objects. For example, Jegou et al. have demonstrated very fast approximate main memory search of 10 million images [17]. However, this work and much of the current work that addresses multi-million object datasets focus on *approximate* search, whereas we are only considering *exact* search here. Moreover, we are interested in datasets which are five to six orders of magnitude larger than anything else considered in the literature [6]. Thus, comparisons to related work are very difficult to do meaningfully.

3. BACKGROUND AND NOTATIONS

3.1 Definitions and Notations

We begin by defining the data type of interest, time series:

Definition 1: A *Time Series T* is an ordered list: $T=t_1,t_2,\ldots,t_m$.

While the source data is one long time series, we ultimately wish to compare it to shorter regions called *subsequences*:

Definition 2: A *subsequence* $T_{i,k}$ of a time series T is a shorter time series of length k which starts from position i. Formally, $T_{i,k} = t_i,t_{i+1},\ldots,t_{i+k-1}$, $1 \leq i \leq m-k+1$.

Where there is no ambiguity, we may refer to subsequence $T_{i,k}$ as C, as in a Candidate match to a query Q . We denote $|Q|$ as n.

Definition 3: The Euclidean distance (ED) between Q and C, where $|Q| =|C|$, is defined as:

$$ED(Q,C) = \sqrt{\sum_{i=1}^{n} (q_i - c_i)^2}$$

We illustrate these definitions in Figure 2.

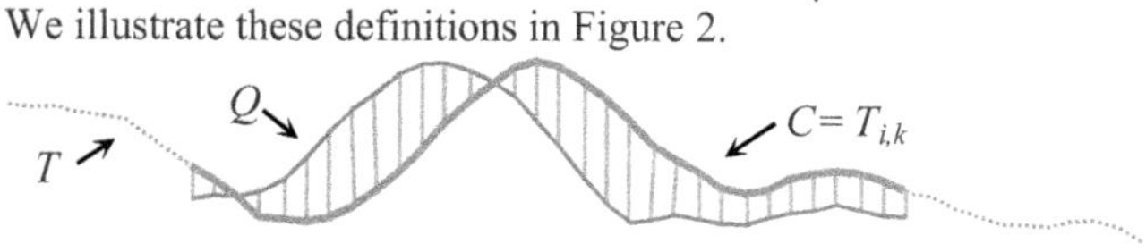

Figure 2: A long time series T can have a subsequence $T_{i,k}$ extracted and compared to a query Q under the Euclidean distance, which is simply the square root of the sum of the squared hatch line lengths

The Euclidean distance, which is a one-to-one mapping of the two sequences, can be seen as a special case of DTW, which allows a one-to-many alignment, as illustrated in Figure 3.

To align two sequences using DTW, an n-by-n matrix is constructed, with the (i^{th}, j^{th}) element of the matrix being the Euclidean distance $d(q_i, c_j)$ between the points q_i and c_j.

A warping path P is a contiguous set of matrix elements that defines a mapping between Q and C. The tth element of P is defined as $p_t = (i, j)_t$ so we have:

$$P = p_1, p_2, \ldots, p_t, \ldots, p_T \quad n \leq T \leq 2n\text{-}1$$

The warping path that defines the alignment between the two time series is subject to several constraints. For example, the warping path must start and finish in diagonally opposite corner cells of the matrix, the steps in the warping path are restricted to adjacent cells, and the points in the warping path must be monotonically spaced in time. In addition, virtually all practitioners using DTW also constrain the warping path in a global sense by limiting how far it may stray from the diagonal [6][28]. A typical constraint is the Sakoe-Chiba Band which states that the warping path cannot deviate more than R cells from the diagonal [6][28][32].

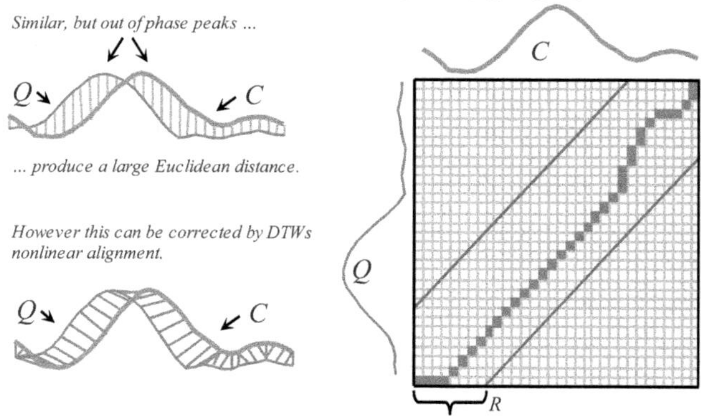

Figure 3: *left*) Two time series which are similar but out of phase. *right*) To align the sequences we construct a warping matrix, and search for the optimal warping path (red/solid squares). Note that Sakoe-Chiba Band with width R is used to constrain the warping path

4. ALGORITHMS

4.1 Known Optimizations

We begin by discussing previously known optimizations of sequential search under ED and/or DTW.

4.1.1 *Using the Squared Distance*

Both DTW and ED have a square root calculation. However, if we omit this step, it does not change the relative rankings of nearest neighbors, since both functions are monotonic and concave. Moreover, the absence of the square root function will make later optimizations possible and easier to explain. Note that this is only an internal change in the code; the user can still issue range queries with the original units, as the code simply internally squares the desired value, does the search, and after finding the qualifying objects, takes the square root of the distances for the qualifying objects and presents the answers to the user.

Where there is no ambiguity below, we will still use 'DTW' and 'ED'; however, the reader may assume we mean the squared versions of them.

4.1.2 *Lower Bounding*

A classic trick to speed up sequential search with an expensive distance measure such as DTW is to use a cheap-to-compute lower bound to prune off unpromising candidates [6][20]. Figure 4 shows two such lower bounds, one of which we have modified.

Figure 4: *left*) The LB_KimFL lower bound is $O(1)$ and uses the distances between the First (Last) pair of points from C and Q as a lower bound. It is a simplification of the original LB_Kim [21]. *right*) The LB_Keogh lower bound is $O(n)$ and uses the Euclidean distance between the candidate sequence C and the closer of {U,L} as a lower bound

The original definition of LB_Kim also uses the distances between the maximum values from both time series and the minimum values between both time series in the lower bound, making it $O(n)$. However, for *normalized* time series these two extra values tend to be tiny and it does not pay to compute them, and ignoring them allows the bound to be $O(1)$, a fact we will exploit below. The LB_Keogh bound is well-documented elsewhere, for brevity we ask the unfamiliar reader to refer to [11][20][6] for a review.

4.1.3 Early Abandoning of ED and LB_Keogh

During the computation of the Euclidean distance or the LB_Keogh lower bound, if we note that the current sum of the squared differences between each pair of corresponding datapoints exceeds the *best-so-far*, then we can stop the calculation, secure in the knowledge that the exact distance or lower bound, had we calculated it, would have exceeded the *best-so-far*, as in Figure 5.

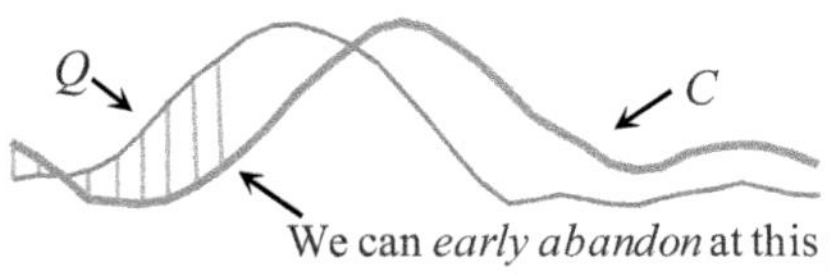

Figure 5: An illustration of ED *early abandoning*. We have a *best-so-far* value of *b*. After incrementally summing the first nine (of thirty-two) individual contributions to the ED we have exceeded *b*, thus it is pointless to continue the calculation [20]

4.1.4 Early Abandoning of DTW

If we have computed a full LB_Keogh lower bound, but we find that we must calculate the full DTW, there is still one trick left up our sleeves. We can incrementally compute the DTW from left to right, and as we incrementally calculate from 1 to K, we can sum the *partial* DTW accumulation with the LB_Keogh contribution from K+1 to *n*. Figure 6 illustrates this idea.

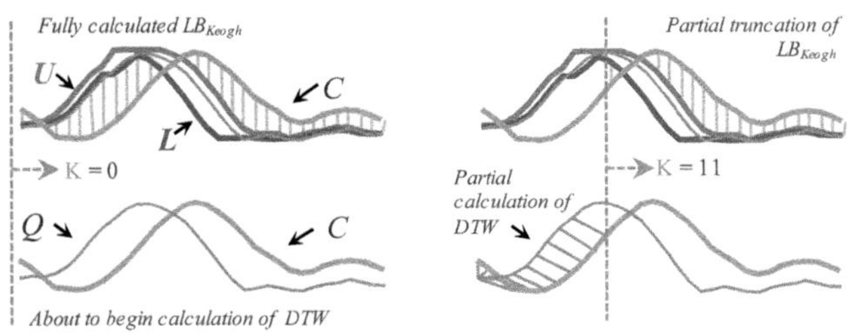

Figure 6: *left*) At the top we see a completed LB_Keogh calculation, and below it we are about to begin a full DTW calculation. *right*) We can imagine the orange/dashed line moving from left to right. If we sum the LB_Keogh contribution from the right of dashed line (*top*) and the partial (incrementally calculated) DTW contribution from the left side of the dashed line (*bottom*), this is will be a lower bound to DTW(*Q*,*C*)

This sum of $DTW(Q_{1:K},C_{1:K}) + LB\_Keogh(Q_{K+1:n},C_{K+1:n})$ is a lower bound to the true DTW distance (i.e., $DTW(Q_{1:n},C_{1:n})$). Moreover, with careful implementation the overhead costs are negligible. If at any time this lower bound exceeds the *best-so-far* distance we can admissibly stop the calculation and prune this *C*.

4.1.5 Exploiting Multicores

It is important to note that while we can get essentially linear speedup using multicores, the *software* improvements we will present in the next section completely dwarf the improvements gained by multicores. As a concrete example, a recent paper shows that a search of a time series of length 421,322 under DTW takes "*3 hours and 2 minutes on a single core. The* (8-core version) *was able to complete the computation in 23 minutes*" [34]. However, using our ideas, we can search a dataset of this size in just under one second on a single core. Nevertheless, as it is simple to port to the now ubiquitous multicores, we consider them below.

4.2 Novel Optimizations: The UCR Suite

We are finally in a position to introduce our four original optimizations of search under ED and/or DTW.

4.2.1 Early Abandoning Z-Normalization

To the best of our knowledge, no one has ever considered optimizing the *normalization* step. This is surprising, since it takes slightly longer than computing the Euclidean distance itself.

Our insight here is that we can interleave the early abandoning calculations of Euclidean distance (or LB_Keogh) with the online Z-normalization. In other words, as we are incrementally computing the Z-normalization, we can also incrementally compute the Euclidean distance (or LB_Keogh) of the same datapoint. Thus, if we can early abandon, we are pruning not just distance calculation steps as in Section 4.1.3, but also *normalization* steps.

Recall that the mean and standard deviation of a sample can be computed from the sums of the values and their squares. Therefore, it takes only one scan through the sample to compute the mean and standard deviation, using the equations below.

$$\mu = \frac{1}{m}\sum x_i \qquad \sigma^2 = \frac{1}{m}\sum x_i^2 - \mu^2$$

In similarity search, every subsequence needs to be normalized before it is compared to the query (c.f. Section 1.2.1). The mean of the subsequence can be obtained by keeping two running sums of the long time series which have a lag of exactly *m* values. The sum of squares of the subsequence can be similarly computed. The formulas are given below for clarity.

$$\mu = \frac{1}{m}\left(\sum_{i=1}^{k} x_i - \sum_{i=1}^{k-m} x_i\right) \qquad \sigma^2 = \frac{1}{m}\left(\sum_{i=1}^{k} x_i^2 - \sum_{i=1}^{k-m} x_i^2\right) - \mu^2$$

The high-level outline of the algorithm is presented in Table 1.

Table 1: Subsequence search with online Z-normalization

Algorithm	Similarity Search
Procedure	[*nn*] = *SimilaritySearch* (T,*Q*)
1	*best-so-far* ← ∞, *count*← 0
2	*Q* ← *z-normalize*(*Q*)
3	**while** !*next*(T)
4	*i*← *mod*(*count*,*m*)
5	X[*i*] ←*next*(T)
6	*ex*← *ex*+X[*i*], *ex2*← *ex2*+X[*i*]^2
7	**if** *count* ≥ *m*-1
8	*μ*← *ex*/*m*, σ← *sqrt*(*ex2*/*m* - *μ*^{2})
9	*j*← 0, *dist*← 0
10	**while** *j* < *m* **and** *dist* < *best-so-far*
11	*dist*← *dist* + (*Q*[*j*]-(X[*mod*(*i*+1+*j*,*m*)]-*μ*)/σ)^2
12	*j*← *j*+1
13	**if** *dist* < *best-so-far*
14	*best-so-far* ←*dist*, *nn*← *count*
15	*ex*← *ex*-X[*mod*(*i*+1,*m*)]
16	*ex2*← *ex2*-X[*mod*(*i*+1,*m*)]^2
17	*count* ← *count*+1

Note the online normalization in line 11 of the algorithm, which allows the early abandoning of the distance computation in addition to the normalization.

In the above algorithm, we use a circular buffer (X) to store the current subsequence being compared with the query *Q*.

One potential problem of this method of maintaining the statistics is the accumulation of the floating-point error [13]. The effect of such error accumulation is more profound if all of the numbers are positive, as in our case with sum of squares. With the "mere" millions of datapoints the rest of the community has dealt with this effect is negligible, however when dealing with billions of datapoints it *will* affect the answer. Our simple solution is that once every one million subsequences, we force a complete Z-normalization to "flush out" any accumulated error.

4.2.2 *Reordering Early Abandoning*

In the previous section, we saw that the idea of early abandoning discussed in Section 4.1.3 can be generalized to the Z-normalization step. In both cases, we assumed that we incrementally compute the distance/normalization from left to right. Is there a better ordering?

Consider Figure 7.*left*, which shows the normal left-to-right ordering in which the early abandoning calculation proceeds. In this case *nine* of the thirty-two calculations were performed before the accumulated distance exceeded *b* and we could abandon. In contrast, Figure 7.*right* uses a different ordering and was able to abandon earlier, with just *five* of the thirty-two calculations.

Figure 7: *left*) ED *early abandoning*. We have a *best-so-far* value of *b*. After incrementally summing the first *nine* individual contributions to the ED, we have exceeded *b*; thus, we abandon the calculation. *right*) A different ordering allows us to abandon after just *five* calculations

This example shows what is obvious: on a query-by-query basis, different orderings produce different speedups. However, we want to know if there is a *universal* optimal ordering that we can compute *in advance*. This seems like a difficult question because there are *n*! possible orderings to consider.

We conjecture that the universal optimal ordering is to sort the indices based on the absolute values of the Z-normalized *Q*. The intuition behind this idea is that the value at Q_i will be compared to many C_i's during a search. However, for subsequence search, with Z-normalized candidates, the distribution of many C_i's will be Gaussian, with a mean of zero. Thus, the sections of the query that are farthest from the mean, zero, will *on average* have the largest contributions to the distance measure.

To see if our conjecture is true we took the heartbeat discussed in Section 5.4 and computed its full Euclidean distance to a million other randomly chosen ECG sequences. With the conceit of hindsight we computed what the best ordering *would* have been. For this we simply take each C_i and sort them, largest first, by their sum of their contributions to the Euclidean distance. We compared this *empirically* optimal ordering with our predicted ordering (sorting the indices on the absolute values of *Q*) and found the rank correlation is 0.999. Note that we can use this trick for both ED and LB_{Keogh}, and we can use it in conjunction with the early abandoning Z-normalization technique (Section 4.2.1).

4.2.3 *Reversing the Query/Data Role in* LB_{Keogh}

Normally the LB_{Keogh} lower bound discussed in Section 4.1.2 builds the envelope around the *query*, a situation we denote $LB\_{Keogh}EQ$ for concreteness, and illustrate in Figure 8.*left*. This only needs to be done once, and thus saves the time and space overhead that we would need if we built the envelope around each *candidate* instead, a situation we denote $LB\_{Keogh}EC$.

Figure 8: *left*) Normally the LB_{Keogh} envelope is built around the query (see also Figure 4.*right*), and the distance between *C* and the closer of {*U*,*L*} acts as a lower bound. *right*) However, we can reverse the roles such that the envelope is built around *C* and the distance between *Q* and the closer of {*U*,*L*} is the lower bound

However, as we show in the next section, we can selectively calculate $LB\_{Keogh}EC$ in a "just-in-time" fashion, *only* if all other lower bounds fail to prune. This removes *space* overhead, and as we will see, the *time* overhead pays for itself by pruning more full DTW calculations. Note that in general, $LB\_{Keogh}EQ \neq LB\_{Keogh}EC$ and that on average each one is larger about half the time.

4.2.4 *Cascading Lower Bounds*

One of the most useful ways to speed up time series similarity search is the use of lower bounds to admissibly prune off unpromising candidates [6][11]. This has led to a flurry of research on lower bounds, with at least eighteen proposed for DTW [1][6][20][21][33][40][41][42]. In general, it is difficult to state definitively which is the best bound to use, since there is a tradeoff between the tightness of the lower bound and how fast it is to compute. Moreover, different datasets and even different queries can produce slightly different results. However, as a starting point, we implemented all published lower bounds and tested them on fifty different datasets from the UCR archive, plotting the (slightly idealized for visual clarity) results in Figure 9. Following the literature [20], we measured the *tightness* of each lower bound as *LB*(A,B)/*DTW*(A,B) over 100,000 randomly sampled subsequences A and B of length 256.

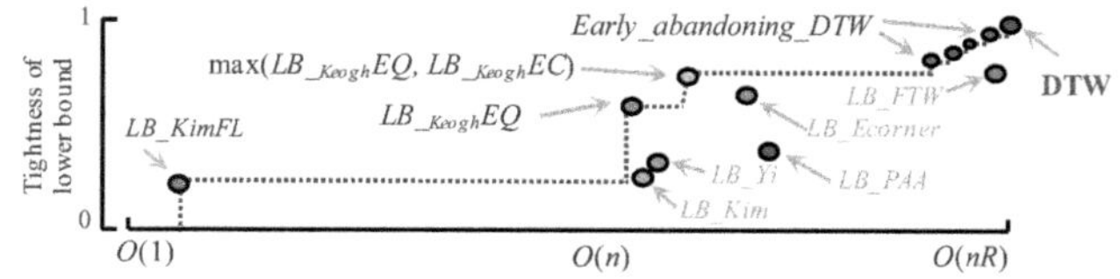

Figure 9: The mean tightness of selected lower bounds from the literature plotted against the time taken to compute them

The reader will appreciate that a *necessary* condition for a lower bound to be useful is for it to appear on the "skyline" shown with a dashed line; otherwise there exists a faster-to-compute bound that is at least as tight, and we should use that instead. Note that the early abandoning DTW discussed in Section 4.1.4 is a special case in that it produces a spectrum of bounds, as at every stage of computation it is incrementally computing the DTW until the last computation gives the final true DTW distance.

Which of the lower bounds on the skyline should we use? Our insight is that we should use *all* of them in a cascade. We first use the *O*(1) $LB\_{Kim}FL$, which while a very weak lower bound prunes many objects. If a candidate is not pruned at this stage we compute the $LB\_{Keogh}EQ$. Note that as discussed in Sections 4.1.3, 4.2.1 and 4.2.2, we can incrementally compute this; thus, we may be able to abandon anywhere between *O*(1) and *O*(*n*) time. If we complete this lower bound without exceeding the *best-so-far*, we reverse the query/data role and compute $LB\_{Keogh}EC$ (cf. Section 4.2.3). If this bound does not allow us to prune, we then start the early abandoning calculation of DTW (cf. Section 4.1.4).

Space limits preclude detailed analysis of which lower bounds prune how many candidates. Moreover, the ratios depend on the query, data and size of the dataset. However, we note the following: Detailed analysis *is* available at [43], lesion studies tell us that *all* bounds do contribute to speedup; removing any lower bound makes search at least twice as slow; and finally, using this technique we can prune more than 99.9999% of DTW calculations for a large-scale search.

5. EXPERIMENTAL RESULTS

We begin by noting that we have taken extraordinary measures to ensure our experiments are reproducible. In particular, all data and code will be available in perpetuity, archived at [43]. Moreover, the site contains several videos which visualize some of the experiments in real time. We consider the following methods:

- **Naive**: Each subsequence is Z-normalized from scratch. The full Euclidean distance or the DTW is used at each step.

Approximately 2/3 of the papers in the literature do (some minor variant of) this.

- **State-of-the-art (SOTA)**: Each sequence is Z-normalized from scratch, early abandoning is used, and the LB_{Keogh} lower bound is used for DTW. Approximately 1/3 of the papers in the literature do (some minor variant of) this.
- **UCR Suite**: We use all of our applicable speedup techniques.

DTW uses $R = 5\%$ unless otherwise noted. For experiments where Naive or SOTA takes more than 24 hours to finish, we terminate the experiments and present the interpolated values, shown in gray. Where appropriate we also compare to an oracle algorithm:

- **GOd's ALgorithm** (GOAL) is an algorithm that only *maintains* the mean and standard deviation using the online $O(1)$ incremental calculations.

It is easy to see that, short of an algorithm that precomputes and stores a *massive* amount of data (quadratic in m), GOAL is a lower bound on the fastest possible algorithm for either ED or DTW subsequence search with unconstrained and unknown length queries. The acronym reminds us that we would like to be as close to this *goal* value as possible.

It is critical to note that our implementations of Naive, SOTA and GOAL are incredibly efficient and tightly optimized, and they are not "crippled" in any way. For example, had we wanted to claim spurious speedup, we could implement SOTA recursively rather than iteratively, and that would make SOTA at least an order of magnitude slower. In particular, the code for Naive, SOTA and GOAL is exactly the same code as the UCR suite, except the relevant speedup techniques have been commented out.

While very detailed spreadsheets of all of our results are archived in perpetuity at [43], we present subsets of our results below. We consider wall clock time on a 2 Intel Xeon Quad-Core E5620 2.40GHz with 12GB 1333MHz DDR3 ECC Unbuffered RAM (using just one core unless otherwise explicitly stated).

5.1 Baseline Tests on Random Walk

We begin with experiments on random walk data. Random walks model financial data very well and are often used to test similarity search schemes. More importantly for us, they allow us to do reproducible experiments on massive datasets without the need to ship large hard drives to interested parties. We have simply archived the random number generator and the seeds used. We *have* made sure to use a very high-quality random number generator that has a period longer than the longest dataset we consider. In Table 2 we show the length of time it takes to search increasingly large datasets with queries of length 128. The numbers are averaged over 1000, 100 and 10 queries, respectively.

Table 2: Time taken to search a random walk dataset with $|Q|$ =128

	Million (*Seconds*)	Billion (*Minutes*)	Trillion (*Hours*)
UCR-ED	0.034	0.22	3.16
SOTA-ED	0.243	2.40	39.80
UCR-DTW	0.159	1.83	34.09
SOTA-DTW	2.447	38.14	472.80

These results show a significant difference between SOTA and UCR suite. However, this is for a very short query; what happens if we consider longer queries? As we show in Figure 10, the ratio of SOTA-DTW over UCR-DTW *improves* for longer queries.

To reduce visual clutter we have only placed one Euclidean distance value on the figure, for queries of length 4,096. Remarkably, UCR-DTW is even faster than SOTA *Euclidean* distance. As we shall see in our EEG and DNA examples below, even though 4,096 is longer than any published query lengths in the literature, there is a need for even *longer* queries.

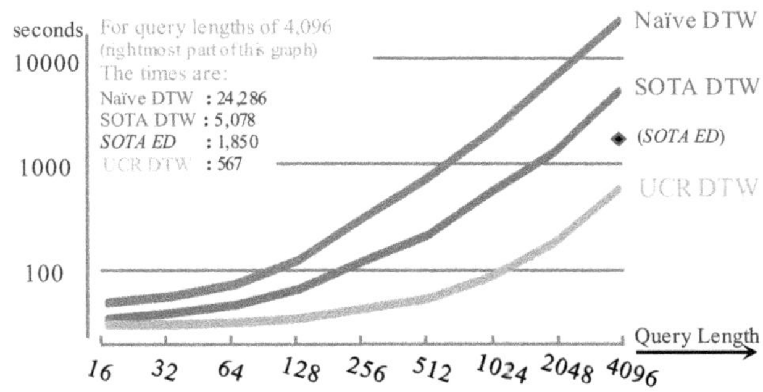

Figure 10: The time taken to search random walks of length 20 million with increasingly long queries, for three variants of DTW. In addition, we include just length 4,096 with SOTA-ED for reference

It is also interesting to consider the results of the 128-length DTW queries as a ratio over GOAL. Recall that the cost for GOAL is independent of query length, and this experiment is just 23.57 seconds. The ratios for Naive, SOTA and UCR suite are 5.27, 2.74 and 1.41, respectively. This suggests that we are asymptomatically closing in on the fastest possible subsequence search algorithm for DTW. Another interesting ratio to consider is the time for UCR-DTW over UCR-ED, which is just 1.18. Thus, the time for DTW is not significantly different than that for ED, an idea which contradicts an assumption made by almost all papers on time series in the last decade (including papers by the current authors).

5.2 Supporting Long Queries: EEG

The previous section shows that we gain the greatest speedup for long queries, and here we show that such long queries are really needed. The first user of the UCR suite was Dr. Sydney Cash, who together with author B.W. wants to search massive archives of EEG data for examples of epileptic spikes, as shown Figure 11.

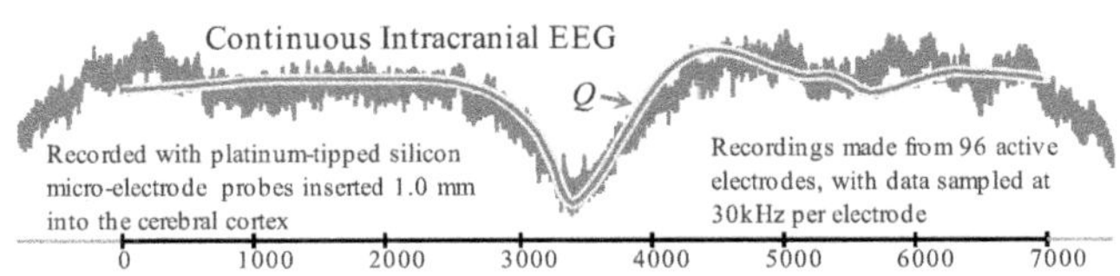

Figure 11: Query Q shown with a match from the 0.3 trillion EEG dataset

From a single patient S.C. gathered 0.3 trillion datapoints and asked us to search for a prototypical epileptic spike Q he created by averaging spikes from other patients. The query length was 7,000 points (0.23 seconds). Table 3 shows the results.

Table 3: Time to search 303,523,721,928 EEG datapoints, $|Q|$ = 7000

Note that only ED is considered here because DTW may produce false positives caused by eye blinks		UCR-ED	SOTA-ED
	EEG	3.4 hours	494.3 hours

This data took multiple sessions over seven days to collect, at a cost of approximately \$34,000 [43], so the few hours of CPU time we required to search the data are dwarfed in comparison.

5.3 Supporting Very Long Queries: DNA

Most work on time series similarity search (and *all* work on time series *indexing*) has focused on relatively short queries, less than or equal to 1,024 data points in length. Here we show that we can efficiently support queries that are two orders of magnitude longer.

Table 4: An algorithm to convert DNA to time series

$T_1 = 0$,	**for** i = 1 **to** |DNAstring|		
		if $DNAstring_i$ = A,	**then** $T_{i+1} = T_i + 2$
		if $DNAstring_i$ = G,	**then** $T_{i+1} = T_i + 1$
		if $DNAstring_i$ = C,	**then** $T_{i+1} = T_i - 1$
		if $DNAstring_i$ = T,	**then** $T_{i+1} = T_i - 2$

We consider experiments with DNA that has been converted to time series. However, it is important to note that we are not claiming any particular bioinformatics utility for our work; it is simply the case that DNA data is massive, and the ground truth can be obtained through other means. As in [35], we use the algorithm in Table 4 to convert DNA to time series[2].

We chose a section of Human chromosome 2 (H2) to experiment with. We took a subsequence beginning at 5,709,500 and found its nearest neighbor in the genomes of five other primates, clustering the six sequences with single linkage to produce the dendrogram shown in Figure 12.

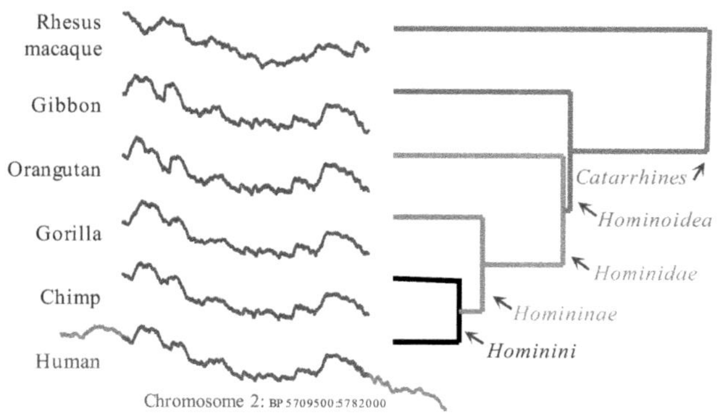

Figure 12: A subsequence of DNA from Human chromosome 2, of length 72,500 beginning at 5,709,500 is clustered using single linkage with its Euclidean distance nearest neighbors from five other primates

Pleasingly, the clustering *is* the correct grouping for these primates [24]. Moreover, because Human chromosome 2 is widely accepted to be a result of an end-to-end fusion of two progenitor ancestral chromosomes 2 and 3 [24], we should expect that the nearest neighbors for the non-human apes come from one of these two chromosomes, and that is exactly what we found.

Our query is of length 72,500, and the genome chimp is 2,900,629,179 base pairs in length. The single-core nearest neighbor search in the entire chimp genome took 38.7 days using Naive, 34.6 days using SOTA, but only 14.6 hours using the UCR suite. As impressive as this is, as we shall show in the next section, we can do *even better*.

5.3.1 Can we do better than UCR Suite?

We claim that for the problem of exact similarity search with arbitrary length queries, our UCR suite is close to optimal. However, it is instructive to consider an apparent counterexample and its simple "patch."

Consider the search for a query of length 64 considered in Section 5.1. Using GOAL took 9.18 seconds, but UCR suite took only a little longer, just 10.64 seconds. Assume that the original query was:

Q = [2.34, 2.01, 1.99,...]

But we make it three times longer by padding it like this:

QP = [2.34, 2.34, 2.34, 2.01, 2.01, 2.01, 1.99, 1.99, 1.99,...]

Further assume that we do the same to database T, to get TP, which is three times longer. What can we now say about the time taken for the algorithms? GOAL will take exactly three times longer, and Naive takes exactly nine times longer, because each ED calculation takes three times longer and there are three times as many calculations to do. Our UCR suite does not take nine times longer, as it can partly exploit the "smoothness" of the data; however, its overhead *is* greater than three. Clearly, if we had known that the data was contrived in this manner, we could have simply made a one-in-three downsampled version of the data and query, done the search on this data, and reported the location and distance back in the TP space by multiplying each by three.

Of course, this type of pathological contrived data does not occur in nature. However, some datasets are richly *oversampled*, and this has a *very* similar effect. For example, a decade ago, most ECGs were sampled at 256Hz, and that seems to be adequate for virtually all data analysis applications [4]. However, current machines typically sample at 2,048 Hz which, given the above reasoning, would take up to sixty-four times longer to search ($(2{,}048/256)^2$) with almost certainly identical results.

We believe that oversampled data can be searched more quickly by exploiting a provisional search in a downsampled version of the data that can quickly provide a low *best-so-far*, which, when projected back into the original space can be used to "prime" the search by setting a low *best-so-far* at the beginning of the search, thus allowing the early abandoning techniques to be more efficient.

To test this idea, we repeated the experiment in the previous section, with a one-in-ten downsampled version of the chimp genome / human query. The search took just 475 seconds. We denoted the best matching subsequence distance rD. We reran the full resolution search after initializing the *best-so-far* to rD*10. This time the search fell from 14.64 hours to 4.17 hours, and we found the same answer, as we logically must.

Similar ideas have been proposed under the name of Iterative Deepening DTW [1] or Multi Scale DTW [27][42]; thus, we will not further develop this idea here. We simply caution the reader that oversampled (i.e., "smooth") data may allow more speedup than a direct application of the UCR suite may initially suggest.

5.4 Realtime Medical and Gesture Data

The proliferation of inexpensive low-powered sensors has produced an explosion of interest in monitoring real time streams of medical telemetry and/or Body Area Network (BAN) data [22]. There are dozens of research efforts in this domain that explicitly state that while monitoring under DTW is *desirable*, it is impossible [38]. Thus, approximations of, or alternatives to DTW are used. Dozens of suggested workarounds have been suggested. For example, [16] resorts to only "*dealing with shorter test and class templates, as this is more efficient*"; many research efforts including [36] resort to a low cardinality version of DTW using integers, or DTW approximations that operate on piecewise linear approximations of the signals [20][29], or drastically downsampled versions of the data [12][30]. In spite of some progress from existing ideas such as lower bounding, [3] bemoans DTW is "*still too slow for gesture recognition systems*", [29] laments that the "*problem of searching with DTW (is) intractable*", [12] says "*Clearly (DTW) is unusable for real-time recognition purposes*" and [34] notes "*Processing of one hour of speech using DTW takes a few hours.*"

We believe that the UCR suite makes all of these objections moot. DTW *can* be used to spot gestures/brainwaves/musical patterns/anomalous heartbeats in *real-time*, even on low-powered devices, even with multiple channels of data, and even with multiple simultaneous queries.

To see this, we created a dataset of one year of electrocardiograms (ECGs) sampled at 256Hz. We created this data by concatenating the ECGs of more than two hundred people, and thus we have a highly diverse dataset, with 8,518,554,188 datapoints. We created a query by asking USC cardiologist Dr. Helga Van Herle to

---

[2] To preserve the reversible one-to-one mapping between time series and DNA we normalize the offset by subtracting *round(mean)* and we do not divide by the STD.

produce a query she searches for on a regular basis, she created an idealized Premature Ventricular Contraction (PVC). The results are shown in Table 5. While this was on our multi-core desktop machine, the fact that our results are 29,219 times faster than real-time (256Hz) suggests that real-time DTW is tenable even on low-power devices.

Table 5: Time taken to search one year of ECG data with $|Q| = 421$

	UCR-ED	SOTA-ED	UCR-DTW	SOTA-DTW
ECG	4.1 minutes	66.6 minutes	18.0 minutes	49.2 hours

5.5 Speeding up Existing Mining Algorithms

In this section, we demonstrate that we can speed up much of the code in the time series data mining literature with minimal effort, simply by replacing their distance calculation subroutines with the UCR suite. In many cases, the difference is small, because the algorithms in question already typically try to prune as many distance calculations as possible. As an aside, in at least some cases we believe that the authors could benefit from redesigning the code in light of the drastically reduced cost for similarity search that UCR suite offers. Nevertheless, even though the speedups are relatively small (1.5X to 16X), they are "free", requiring just minutes of cut-and-paste code editing.

Time Series Shapelets have garnered significant interest since their introduction in 2009 [39]. We obtained the original code and tested it on the Face (four) dataset, finding it took 18.9 minutes to finish. After replacing the similarity search routine with UCR suite, it took 12.5 minutes to finish.

Online Time Series Motifs generalize the idea of mining repeated patterns in a batch time series to the streaming case [25]. We obtained the original code and tested it on the EEG dataset used in the original paper. The fastest running time for the code assuming linear space is 436 seconds. After replacing the distance function with UCR suite, it took just 156 seconds.

Classification of Historical Musical Scores [10]. This dataset has 4,027 images of musical notes converted to time series. We used the UCR suite to compute the rotation-invariant DTW leave-one-out classification. It took 720.6 minutes. SOTA takes 142.4 hours. Thus, we have a speedup factor of 11.8.

Classification of Ancient Coins [15]. 2,400 irregularly shaped coins are converted to time series of length 256, and rotation-invariant DTW is used to search the database, taking 12.8 seconds per query. Using the UCR suite, this takes 0.8 seconds per query.

Clustering of Star Light Curves is an important problem in astronomy [20], as it can be a preprocessing step in outlier detection [31]. We consider a dataset with 1,000 (purportedly) phase-aligned light curves of length 1,024, whose class has been determined by an expert [31]. Doing spectral clustering on this data with DTW (R = 5%) takes about 23 minutes for all algorithms, and averaged over 100 runs we find the Rand-Index is 0.62. While this time may seem slow, recall that we must do 499,500 DTW calculations with relatively long sequences. As we do not trust the original claim of phase alignment, we further do *rotation-invariant* DTW that dramatically increases Rand-Index to 0.76. Using SOTA, this takes 16.57 days, but if we use the UCR suite, this time falls by an order of magnitude, to just 1.47 days on a single core.

6. DICUSSION AND CONCLUSIONS

While our work has focused on fast *sequential search*, we believe that for DTW, our work is faster than all known *indexing* efforts. Consider [2], which indexes a random walk time series of length 250,000 to support queries of length 256. They built various indexes to support DTW queries, noting that the fastest of the four carefully tuned approaches requires approximately 15,000 pages accesses to answer a query. These disk accesses are necessarily *random* accesses. While they did not give wall clock time, if we assume an HDD spindle speed of 7,200 rpm (average rotational latency = 4.17*ms*), then just the disk I/O time to answer this query must be at least 62.55 seconds. However, as we have shown, we can load all of the data into the main memory with more efficient sequential disk accesses and answer these queries in 0.4 seconds, *including* disk I/O time, on a single core machine.

Note that *all* experiments in this paper include the time taken to read the data from disk. However, for more than a few million objects this time is inconsequential thus we did not report it separately.

We have made a strong and unintuitive claim in the abstract. We said that our UCR-*DTW* is faster than all current *Euclidean* distance searches. In Table 5, for example, we show that DTW can be three times faster than state-of-the-art ED searching. How is this possible? Recall that all Euclidean searches in the literature require an $O(n)$ data normalizing step to be performed for each subsequence. Thus, no matter how effective the pruning/search strategy used, the amortized time for a single sequence must be at least $O(n)$. In contrast, using the ideas developed in this work, the vast majority of potential DTW calculations are pruned with $O(1)$ work, while some require up to $O(n)$ work, and only a vanishingly small fraction require $O(nR)$ work. The weighted average of these possibilities is less than $O(n)$.

To put our results in perspective, we compare them with a very recent state-of-the art embedding-based DTW search technique, called EBSM (*including* the variant called BSE) [28]. This is an excellent paper to use as a benchmark, as it exhaustively compares to almost all other methods in the literature, and it tests its contributions over different datasets, query lengths, warping widths, etc. In contrast to EBSM:

- Our method is *exact*; EBSM is *approximate*.
- EBSM requires setting some parameters (number of reference sequences, dimensionality, number of split points, etc.). Our method requires *zero* parameters.
- EBSM requires offline preprocessing that takes over 3 hours for just 1 million objects. We have *zero* preprocessing time.
- The EBSM method does not, and cannot, Z-normalize. As noted in Section 1.2.1, we believe that Z-normalizing is critical, and we have shown that failure to do it hurts on 45 out of 45 of the UCR time series classification datasets.
- EBSM can support queries in a predetermined range, which must be predetermined and limited for efficiently. In contrast, we have no minimum/maximum query length.
- We can also handle exact queries under uniform scaling [11].
- Finally, we are simply much faster! (c.f. Section 1)

Note, however, that there *can* be great utility in fast approximate search. There exist data mining algorithms that can use a combination of (hopefully few) exact distance measures and (hopefully much faster) approximate searches to produce overall exact results [35]. However an approximate search method being faster than our approach is a very high threshold to meet.

We have shown our suite of ideas is 2 to 164 times faster than the *true* state-of-the-art, depending on the query/data. However, based on the quotes from papers that we have sprinkled throughout this work, we are sometimes more than 100,000 times faster than recent papers; how is this possible? The answer seems to be that it is possible to produce very naive implementations of DTW. For example, the *recursive* version of DTW can be one to three orders of magnitude slower than the *iterative* version, depending on the computer language and query length. Thus, the contributions of this paper are twofold. First, we have shown that much of the recent pessimism about using DTW for real-time problems was simply unwarranted [6]. *Existing* techniques, especially lower bounding, if carefully implemented can make DTW tractable for many problems. Our second contribution is the introduction of the UCR suite of techniques that make DTW and Euclidean distance subsequence search significantly faster than current state-of-the-art techniques.

We regret that the page limitations preclude full pseudo-code; however, full pseudo-code (and source-code) *is* available at [43].

In future work we plan to revisit algorithms for time series motif discovery [25][26], anomaly detection [35][31], time series summarization, shapelet extraction [39], clustering, and classification [6] in light of the results presented in this work.

7. ACKNOWLEDGEMENTS

We thank all the donors of code and data. We would like to acknowledge the financial support for our research provided by NSF grants 0803410 and 0808770, FAPESP award 2009/06349-0, and Royal Thai Government scholarship.

8. REFERENCES

[1] N. Adams, D. Marquez, and G. Wakefield. 2005. Iterative deepening for melody alignment and retrieval. *ISMIR*, 199-206.

[2] I. Assent, R. Krieger, F. Afschari, and T. Seidl. 2008. The TS-Tree: efficient time series search and retrieval. *EDBT*, 252-63.

[3] J. Alon, V. Athitsos, Q. Yuan, and S. Sclaroff. 2009. A unified framework for gesture recognition and spatiotemporal gesture segmentation. *IEEE PAMI* 31, 9, 1685-1699.

[4] T. Bragge, M.P. Tarvainen, and P. A. Karjalainen. 2004. *High-Resolution QRS Detection Algorithm for Sparsely Sampled ECG Recordings.* Univ. of Kuopio, Dept. of Applied Physics Report.

[5] N. Chadwick, D. McMeekin, and T. Tan. 2011. Classifying eye and head movement artifacts in EEG Signals. *DEST.*

[6] H. Ding, G. Trajcevski, P. Scheuermann, X. Wang, and E. J. Keogh. 2008. Querying and mining of time series data: experimental comparison of representations and distance measures. *PVLDB* 1, 2, 1542-52.

[7] B. Dupasquier and S. Burschka. 2011. Data mining for hackers – encrypted traffic mining. *The 28th Chaos Comm' Congress.*

[8] Y. Chen, G. Chen, K. Chen, and B. C. Ooi. 2009. Efficient processing of warping time series join of motion capture data. *ICDE*, 1048-1059.

[9] Faceted DBLP. 2011. *http://dblp.l3s.de*

[10] A. Fornés, J. Lladós, and G. Sanchez. 2007. Old handwritten musical symbol classification by a dynamic time warping based method. *Graphics Recognition* 5046, 51-60.

[11] A. Fu, E. Keogh, L. Lau, C. Ratanamahatana, and R. Wong. 2008. Scaling and time warping in time series querying. *VLDB J.* 17, 4, 899-921.

[12] N. Gillian, R. Knapp, and S. O'Modhrain. 2011. Recognition of multivariate temporal musical gestures using n-dimensional dynamic time warping. *Proc of the 11th Int'l conference on New Interfaces for Musical Expression.*

[13] D. Goldberg. 1991. What every computer scientist should know about floating-point arithmetic. *ACM Computing Surveys* 23, 1.

[14] G. Guitel. 1975. *Histoire comparée des numérations écrites.* Chapter: "Les grands nombres en numération parlée," Paris: Flammarion, 566–574.

[15] R. Huber-Mörk, S. Zambanini, M. Zaharieva, and M. Kampel. 2011. Identification of ancient coins based on fusion of shape and local features. *Mach. Vis. Appl.* 22, 6, 983-994.

[16] M. Hsiao, K. West, and G. Vedatesh. 2005. Online context recognition in multisensor system using dynamic time warping. *ISSNIP*, 283-288.

[17] H. Jegou, M. Douze, C. Schmid, and P. Perez. 2010. Aggregating local descriptors into a compact image representation. *IEEE CVPR*, San Francisco, CA, USA.

[18] T. Kahveci and A. K. Singh. 2004. Optimizing similarity search for arbitrary length time series queries. *IEEE Trans. Knowl. Data Eng.* 16, 4, 418-433.

[19] E. Keogh and S. Kasetty. 2003. On the need for time series data mining benchmarks: a survey and empirical demonstration. *Data Mining and Knowledge. Discovery* 7, 4, 349-371.

[20] E. Keogh, L. Wei, X. Xi, M. Vlachos, S.H. Lee, and P. Protopapas. 2009. Supporting exact indexing of arbitrarily rotated shapes and periodic time series under Euclidean and warping distance measures. *VLDB J.* 18, 3, 611-630.

[21] S. Kim, S Park, and W. Chu. 2001. An index-based approach for similarity search supporting time warping in large sequence databases. *ICDE*, 607–61.

[22] K. Laerhoven, E. Berlin, and B. Schiele. 2009. Enabling efficient time series analysis for wearable activity data. *ICMLA*, 392-397.

[23] S. H. Lim, H. Park, and S. W. Kim. 2007. Using multiple indexes for efficient subsequence matching in time-series databases. *Inf. Sci.* 177, 24, 5691-5706.

[24] D. P. Locke, L. W. Hillier, W. C. Warren, et al. 2011. Comparative and demographic analysis of orangutan genomes. *Nature* 469, 529-533.

[25] A. Mueen and E. Keogh. 2010. Online discovery and maintenance of time series motifs. *KDD*, 1089-1098.

[26] A. Mueen, E. Keogh, Q. Zhu, S. Cash, M. B. Westover, and N. Shamlo. 2011. A disk-aware algorithm for time series motif discovery. *Data Min. Knowl. Discov.* 22, 1-2, 73-105.

[27] M. Muller. 2009. Analysis and retrieval techniques for motion and music data. *EUROGRAPHICS tutorial.*

[28] P. Papapetrou, V. Athitsos, M. Potamias, G. Kollios, and D. Gunopulos. 2011. Embedding-based subsequence matching in time-series databases. *ACM TODS* 36, 3, 17*.

[29] W. Pressly. 2008. TSPad: a Tablet-PC based application for annotation and collaboration on time series data. *ACM Southeast Regional Conference*, 527-52.

[30] B. Raghavendra, D. Bera, A. Bopardikar, and R. Narayanan. 2011. Cardiac arrhythmia detection using dynamic time warping of ECG beats in e-healthcare systems. *WOWMOM*, 1-6.

[31] U. Rebbapragada, P. Protopapas, C. Brodley, and C. Alcock. 2009. Finding anomalous periodic time series. *Machine Learning* 74, 3, 281-313.

[32] Y. Sakurai, C. Faloutsos, and M. Yamamuro. 2007. Stream monitoring under the time warping distance. *ICDE*, 1046-55.

[33] Y. Sakurai, M. Yoshikawa, and C. Faloutsos. 2005. FTW: fast similarity search under the time warping distance. *PODS'05.*

[34] S. Srikanthan, A.Kumar, and R. Gupta. 2011. Implementing the dynamic time warping algorithm in multithreaded environments for real time and unsupervised pattern discovery. *IEEE ICCCT*, 394-398.

[35] J. Shieh and E. J. Keogh. 2008. *i*SAX: indexing and mining terabyte sized time series. *KDD*, 623-631.

[36] T. Stiefmeier, D. Roggen, and G. Tröster. 2007. Gestures are strings: efficient online gesture spotting and classification using string matching. *Proceedings of the ICST 2nd international conference on Body area networks.*

[37] C. R. Whitney. 1997. Jeanne Calment, World's elder, dies at 122. *New York Times* (August 5th, 1997).

[38] J. O. Wobbrock, A. D. Wilson, and Y. Li. 2007. Gestures without libraries, toolkits or training: a $1 recognizer for user interface prototypes. *ACM UIST*, 159-168.

[39] L. Ye and E. Keogh. 2009. Time series shapelets: a new primitive for data mining. *KDD*, 947-956.

[40] B. Yi, H. Jagadish, and C. Faloutsos. 1998. Efficient retrieval of similar time sequences under time warping. *ICDE*, 201-208.

[41] Y. Zhang and J. Glass. 2011. An inner-product lower-bound estimate for dynamic time warping. *ICASSP*, 5660-5663.

[42] A. Zinke and D. Mayer. 2006. *Iterative Multi Scale Dynamic Time Warping.* Universität Bonn, Tech Report # CG-2006-1.

[43] Project Website: *www.cs.ucr.edu/~eamonn/UCRsuite.html*

*The paper [28] omits to mention the length of the test data we mention in the Introduction Section. The first author was kind enough to give us the one million figures by email on 11/16/2011.

Fast Mining and Forecasting of Complex Time-Stamped Events

Yasuko Matsubara
Kyoto University
y.matsubara@
db.soc.i.kyoto-u.ac.jp

Yasushi Sakurai
NTT Communication
Science Labs
yasushi.sakurai@acm.org

Christos Faloutsos
Carnegie Mellon University
christos@cs.cmu.edu

Tomoharu Iwata
NTT Communication
Science Labs
iwata.tomoharu@lab.ntt.co.jp

Masatoshi Yoshikawa
Kyoto University
yoshikawa@i.kyoto-u.ac.jp

ABSTRACT

Given huge collections of time-evolving events such as web-click logs, which consist of multiple attributes (e.g., URL, userID, timestamp), how do we find patterns and trends? How do we go about capturing daily patterns and forecastsing future events? We need two properties: (a) effectiveness, that is, the patterns should help us understand the data, discover groups, and enable forecasting, and (b) scalability, that is, the method should be linear with the data size.

We introduce *TriMine*, which performs three-way mining for all three attributes, namely, URLs, users, and time. Specifically *TriMine* discovers hidden topics, groups of URLs, and groups of users, simultaneously. Thanks to its concise but effective summarization, it makes it possible to accomplish the most challenging and important task, namely, to forecast future events. Extensive experiments on real datasets demonstrate that *TriMine* discovers meaningful topics and makes long-range forecasts, which are notoriously difficult to achieve. In fact, *TriMine* consistently outperforms the best state-of-the-art existing methods in terms of accuracy and execution speed (up to *74x faster*).

Categories and Subject Descriptors: H.2.8 [**Database management**]: Database applications–*Data mining*

General Terms: Algorithms, Experimentation, Performance

Keywords: Time-stamped events, Tensor analysis, Topic model, Forecasting

1. INTRODUCTION

Our motivating application is to find patterns and trends in a large set of clicks, consisting of multiple attributes (URL, user ID, timestamp, access devices, http/document referrer, etc). Are there emerging topics? Can we group URLs (and users), accordingly? How many clicks should we expect from user 'Smith', tomorrow?

KDD'12, August 12–16, 2012, Beijing, China.

We shall refer to such settings as a sequence of *complex events*. Each event has a timestamp, and has multiple categorical attributes associated with it - in our example, a URL, which we shall refer to as an '*object*', and a userID as an '*actor*'. Such settings naturally appear in countless domains including click logs on web sites [1], social network services, location-based services [15], social tagging, and many more. Informally, if each event has a time stamp and two attributes, the problem we want to solve is that described below.

INFORMAL PROBLEM 1 (COMPLEX EVENT MINING). *Given a sequence of millions of triplets (object, actor, time stamp),*

- *find the major topics and their trends*
- *make traffic forecasts*

We can generalize for an arbitrary number of attributes (i.e., more than three attributes) and we describe this later. The ideal method should be (a) *effective* in finding patterns, (b) *accurate* in forecasting, and (c) *scalable*; it should help us understand what are the major trends, it should provide an easy-to-understand summary, it should help spot anomalies (with respect to *all three* aspects - URLs, users, time); and to visualize the results; and of course, the processing should be fast, and ideally, linear with the input size.

We present a novel method, *TriMine*, which automatically finds patterns in huge collections of complex events. Specifically, it finds three-way patterns (hence the prefix): It finds hidden topics (such as, 'sports', 'news'), and correlates each topic with all three aspects.

Preview of our results. Figure 1 shows the results we obtained with *TriMine* on real web-click logs, where each click is of the form $(URL, userID, timestamp)$. We will see this collection of plots so often that we have given it a name, "*TriMine*-plot". This plot consists of two *ternary* plots, and a time plot, as described later.

In general, each web site may cover one or more topic(s), and each user would be associated with a few topics. Thus, we could expect both finance news and stock market sites to attract roughly the same users, with similar temporal patterns, and so those sites should be grouped under the same topic, say, 'business'.

Figure 1 shows a *TriMine*-plot with some of our findings, namely it detects/reveals the hidden topics of web click events. More specifically, the figure shows the three major topics, and how they related to each of the three aspects, namely (a) to each web site (URL), expressed in the **O** matrix, (b) to each user (in the **A** matrix), and (c)

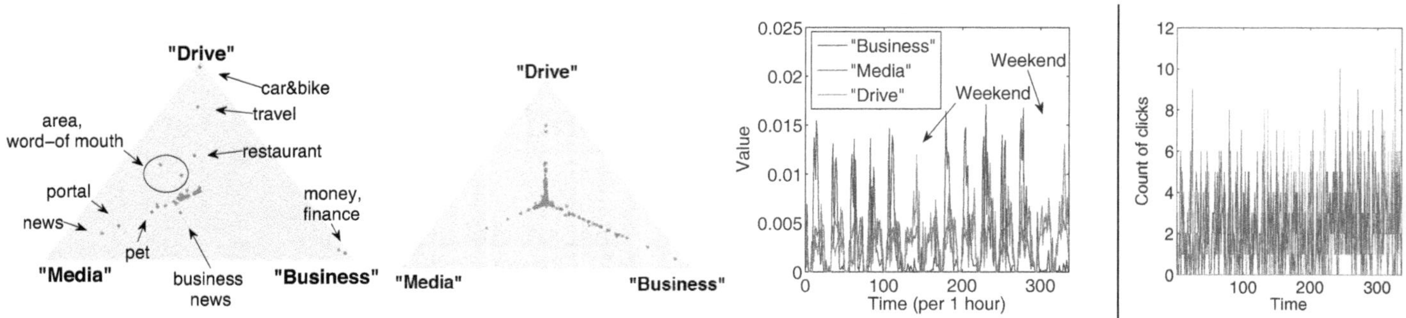

(a) URLs in topic space (object matrix **O**)
(b) Users in topic space (actor matrix **A**)
(c) Time evolution in topic space (time matrix **C**)
(d) Original sequence of 100 random users

Figure 1: *TriMine* is effective in spotting three-way patterns. Results for web-click data (URL, userID, timestamp), with three hidden topics, manually labeled as shown. (a) Ternary plot for URLs - notice the three groups along the center-vertex spokes, (b) ditto for users - showing very clear groups along the spokes, (c) temporal evolution of the three topics: 'business' traffic (in blue) drops during weekends; 'drive/travel' traffic (in red) *spikes* during weekends; and 'media/news' traffic (in green) remains the same. All show daily periodicity. (d) original counts of "money" site, 100 randomly selected users, appears bursty and noisy.

to each time-tick (**C** matrix). The first two are represented as triangular plots (also known as 'ternary plots'), where each 3-d point is represented as a point in a triangle (since the sum of the 3 coordinates is less than 1).

TriMine successfully detects some of the hidden topics in the web click logs, and we have manually named them 'business', 'media' and 'drive'. The first ternary plot shows the URLs; notice that several of them focus almost exclusively on the topic 'drive', several others on 'media/news', a few focus exclusively on 'business'. The ternary plot of the users shows an even clearer separation: most dots (= users) are on the spokes from the center to the vertices, indicating a very clear clustering of users, along the three hidden topics. Neither of the two ternary plots exhibits any striking outliers.

The third plot (Figure 1 (c)), shows the evolution of each topic over time (red, green, blue, for 'drive', 'media', 'business' respectively). Notice a clear daily periodicity for all the topics (unsurprising), but also notice (1) the decline in 'blue' (='business') during weekends, and (2) the spiking of 'red' (='drive/traveling') during weekends. In retrospect, both make sense. Also notice that 'green' (= 'media/news') does *not* have a weekly periodicity, apparently because our users are constantly interested in news.

In contrast, Figure 1 (d) shows the original raw sequences of 100 randomly selected users (at a "money" site). Notice that the raw data exhibits no obvious patterns, neither periodicities nor clusters of users.

Our main point is that the two 'ternary plots' and a simple time-plot can give a clear, concise summary of both '*actors*' (users) and '*objects*' (URLs), as well as of the major temporal patterns. Thanks to these three building blocks, we can extend this approach to complex event forecasting, which is notoriously difficult to achieve.

Contrast with competitors. Table 1 compares *TriMine* and its forecasting method, *TriMine-F*, with existing methods. We illustrate their strengths and shortcomings: a check mark (√) indicates that the corresponding method (column) fulfills the corresponding requirement (row). Only our approach has checks against all entries, while,

- Wavelet transforms can identify multi-scale trends in a *"single"* sequence as regards objects or actors, but find it hard to determine the *"relationship"* between all these objects/actors.
- Complex events can be turned into a tensor. Higher-order SVD (HOSVD) [12] and alternating least squares (ALS) [23] capture the hidden components from tensors, but they cannot handle categorical/non-Gaussian data or perform forecasting.
- Topic models (e.g., latent Dirichlet allocation (LDA) [4]) are probabilistic models for sparse vectors of count data, and they can find hidden topics and perform clustering. However, they are not intended to capture cyclic time-evolving patterns, or undertake forecasting.
- Auto regression (AR) and *PLiF* [13] have the ability to forecast sequences, however, they cannot handle multi-scale sequences, and so cannot perform long-term forecasting, because they converge quickly to the mean (see Figures 7 and 8).

Table 1: Capabilities of approaches. Only our approach meets all specifications.

	DWT	HOSVD /ALS	LDA	*AR /PLiF*	*TriMine /TriMine-F*
Multi-scale	√				√
Tensor		√			√
Categorical			√		√
Short-term forecasting				√	√
Long-term forecasting					√

Contributions. The proposed method has the following advantages:

1. *Effectiveness: TriMine* operates on large collections of complex events, summarizes them succinctly, gives three-way patterns (i.e., with respect to *objects*, *actors*, and time stamps), and enables forecasting, clustering and anomaly detection.
2. *Accuracy:* as we will show, our approach is accurate in forecasting complex time-stamped events.
3. *Scalability: TriMine* is linear with the input size, and thus scales up very well.

The rest of the paper is organized in a typical way: Next we describe related work, followed by definitions, the proposed method, experiments and conclusions.

2. RELATED WORK

Recently significant progress has been made on understanding the theoretical issues surrounding learning mixture distributions in theoretical computing and machine learning [9, 28, 22]. Latent Dirichlet allocation (LDA) [4] and probabilistic latent semantic analysis (PLSA) [5] are well-known latent variable models for analyzing large sets of categorical data, such as bags of words for text, and bags of features for images. A number of methods have been proposed for analyzing the time evolution of topics in document collections, such as the dynamic topic model (DTM) [3], topics over time (TOT) [24], and more [25, 2, 27, 7, 8, 6]. For example, DTM employs a fixed length of window size, and takes account of capturing only the current epoch distribution. Similarly, TOT handles a single window size, and it uses Beta distributions to capture time-evolving topics. Very recently, Hong et al. presented a new topic model for predicting the volume of terms in documents (i.e., aggregate count of each keyword). These models do not focus on finding multiscale and/or periodical trends, which means that it is difficult to employ them for the long-term forecasting of complex time-stamped events. On the other hand, as shown in the introduction section (see Table 1), our method finds cyclic patterns with different timescales, which allows it to predict future events effectively and efficiently.

For web-click analysis, Agarwal et al. [1] exploit the Gamma-Poisson model to estimate click-through rates (number of clicks per display) in the context of content recommendation, which does not focus on trend discovery of time-stamped events.

The work on tensors is also related. Kolda et al. [10] provide a powerful tool for tensor analysis on a web link structure. Rendle et al. [19] propose a method for tag recommendation based on tensor factorization. Unlike our method, these methods are not intended to predict future events.

Remotely related is the work on large-scale time-series mining. Similarity search and pattern discovery in time sequences have also attracted huge interest [20, 14]. Papadimitriou et al. [17] propose an algorithm for discovering multi-scale local patterns, which concisely describes the main trends in data streams. Skewed stream problems have been studied in the context of summarization and modeling [11]. Sakurai et al. [21] proposed BRAID, which efficiently detects lag correlations between data streams. AWSOM [16] is one of the first streaming methods for forecasting and is designed to discover arbitrary periodicities in single time sequences.

3. PROBLEM FORMULATION

In this section, we formally define related concepts and the task of event forecasting. Consider that we receive time-stamped event entries of the form *(object, actor, timestamp)*. We then have a collection of entries with u unique objects and v unique actors. Assume that we are given time intervals t $(= 1, 2, \ldots, n)$ of length l (e.g., one hour). It is convenient to treat our complex-event sequence as a 3rd-order tensor, i.e., $\mathcal{X} \in \mathbb{N}^{u \times v \times n}$, where n is the duration of events.

DEFINITION 1 (COMPLEX EVENT TENSOR). *Let $\mathcal{X}$ be a 3rd-order tensor of complex time-stamped events. The element $x_{i,j,t}$ of $\mathcal{X}$ shows the total number of event entries of the i-th object and the j-th actor at time interval t.*

After we decide on some time granularity (say, one hour) then we have (actor, object, time-stamp; count), for example, ('Smith', 'cnn.com', '3am June 1, 2003'; 23). Unless otherwise specified, our time granularity is one hour. Thus, the example tuple above means that 'smith' visited 'cnn.com' 23 times, between 3am-4am on June 1, 2003.

For a particular event collection, we assume that an event entry has a certain "*latent topic*". We model such hidden topics in terms of three aspects, namely, "*object*", "*actor*", and "time". In that case, the original tensor will be decomposed in three matrices $\mathbf{O}$, $\mathbf{A}$, $\mathbf{C}$ with the following definitions and properties:

Table 2: Symbols and definitions.

Symbol	Definition
u	Number of unique objects
v	Number of unique actors
n	Duration: number of time-ticks
$\mathcal{X}$	3rd-order tensor of complex time-stamped events ($\mathcal{X} \in \mathbb{N}^{u \times v \times n}$)
k	Number of hidden topics
$\mathbf{O}$	Object matrix, $u \times k$
$\mathbf{A}$	Actor matrix, $k \times v$
$\mathbf{C}$	Time matrix, $k \times n$

DEFINITION 2 (OBJECT MATRIX $\mathbf{O}$ ($u \times k$)). *Each entry $o_{i,j}$ shows the participation strength of object i for topic j.*

Our upcoming *TriMine* forces that the participation weights $o_{i,j}$ to be non-negative, and they sum up to 1, for each object ($\sum_j o_{i,j} = 1$). The definitions of $\mathbf{A}$ and $\mathbf{C}$ are analogous, and omitted for brevity. We shall refer to $\mathbf{O}$, $\mathbf{A}$ and $\mathbf{C}$ as *participation matrices*, exactly because they show how strongly each *actor*, *object*, time stamp participates in topics #1, #2, ..., #k, respectively. Figure 1 plots the visualization of the three matrices for a real dataset (we show three major topics).

We also consider a case where every event has more than three attributes (i.e., $M > 3$). We provide an Mth-order tensor, which is decomposed in M matrices, $\mathbf{O}$, $\mathbf{A}^{(1)}, \ldots, \mathbf{A}^{(M-2)}$, and $\mathbf{C}$. We mainly focus on a 3rd-order tensor for simplicity throughout this paper, our method however can be applied to higher order tensors. Table 2 summarizes the notation correspondences for the time-stamped events.

3.1 Problem definition

Our goal is to extract the main trends and hidden patterns of an event tensor $\mathcal{X}$, and forecast future events. Specifically, the sub-problem that we want to solve is as follows:

PROBLEM 1 (PATTERN DISCOVERY IN COMPLEX EVENTS). **Given** *a tensor $\mathcal{X}$ of complex events of (actor, object, time stamp) triplets,* **Find** *the hidden topics that best summarize the events in $\mathcal{X}$, and the corresponding actor- and object- groupings.*

Once we have the main trends from $\mathcal{X}$, we can proceed to solve the forecasting problem:

PROBLEM 2 (TRAFFIC FORECASTING). **Given** *a tensor $\mathcal{X}$ of complex events,* **Forecast** *future traffic.*

More specifically, we want to forecast, e.g., how many clicks user 'Smith' will generate tomorrow; or how many clicks 'www.cnn.com' will attract over the next seven days; or we want to generate a realistic-looking set of clicks, for, say, next Sunday.

As mentioned in the introduction, the ideal method should be *effective* (capturing trends that make sense), *accurate* in its forecasts, and *scalable*, to handle millions or billions of events.

3.2 Running examples

There are many applications for time-stamped events. Here, we briefly describe application domains and provide some illustrative, intuitive examples of the usefulness of our approach.

Access analysis. Web content such as blogs, on-line news, web mail and SNS has been attracting considerable interest for business purposes as well as personal use. Consider a large number of clicks on web sites, where each click has a list of attributes, e.g., *access (url_id, user_id, time)*. Suppose that we can record all these attributes on an hourly basis for all users of the web sites. For this huge collection of web-click logs, we would like to find patterns of user behavior to allow us to perform a sociological and behavioral analysis. For example, web masters and web-site owners could find daily access patterns and forecast the subsequent week to aid the design of advertisements.

E-commerce. Let us assume an online service such as ondemand TV, which records the TV programs viewed by every user; each record is an online viewing event of form *view (channel_id, user_id, time)*. Discovering groups in such data and forecasting future viewing events would assist with tasks such as content targeting.

4. PROPOSED METHOD

In this section we describe our method, *TriMine*, for dealing with the pattern discovery problem (Problem 1). In the next section we show how to employ *TriMine* results for forecasting (Problem 2).

4.1 Intuition behind our method

There are two main ideas behind *TriMine*:

- *M-way analysis*: For a single time granularity (say, l_0=1 hour), we perform an M-way topic analysis, which discovers k topics and shows the relationship between these topics and the M matrices. As an example of a 3-way case, we show how the topics relate to the *objects* (*object* matrix $\mathbf{O}$, $u \times k$), to the *actors* (*actor* matrix $\mathbf{A}$, $k \times v$), and to time-ticks (time matrix $\mathbf{C}$, $k \times n$).
- *Multi-scale analysis*: To achieve better forecasting (see Figures 7 and 8), and to capture longer-period trends, we repeat the analysis, for several time granularities $\{\mathbf{C}^{(0)}, \mathbf{C}^{(1)}, \dots\}$ (say, hours, days, etc), insisting on *fixed object* and *actor* matrices $\mathbf{O}, \mathbf{A}$.

Figure 1(a)-(c) illustrates the $\mathbf{O}$, $\mathbf{A}$ and $\mathbf{C}$ matrices, respectively, for the *WebClick* dataset. *objects* and *actors* are categorical, and the $\mathbf{O}$ and $\mathbf{A}$ matrices are visualized as ternary plots, where each dot is an *object / actor*. The three columns of the time matrix are plotted in (c), illustrating the temporal evolution of the three discovered topics.

Single-level analysis - ***TriMine-single*****.** Figure 2 (dotted-line rectangle) gives a pictorial description of the 3-way analysis. The object matrix $\mathbf{O}$ takes account of all the objects over the entire time range, which produces an accurate summary of the object-topic relationship. The actor matrix $\mathbf{A}$ shows the frequency of entries over actors for the i-th topic ($i = 1, \dots, k$). The time matrix $\mathbf{C}$ describes the degree to which the time stamp is associated with the i-th topic.

Multiple-level analysis - ***TriMine*****.** Figure 2 (solid-boundary rectangle) also shows an example to explain how to perform the multi-level analysis. Instead of handling only a single window size, we introduce a multiple time window approach to capture the main trends of multiple scales. Starting with the window size l_0 on the first level $h = 0$, we compute the time matrix $\mathbf{C}^{(0)}$, then increase the window size l_h, and repeatedly obtain $\mathbf{C}^{(h)}$ for various sizes. This enables the forecasting method (discussed later in Section 5) to exploit the relationship between $\mathbf{C}^{(h)}$ across different scales.

4.2 Proposed solution - TriMine

Given an Mth-order complex event tensor $\mathcal{X}$, our goal is to find a meaningful summary with k hidden topics that best describes $\mathcal{X}$.

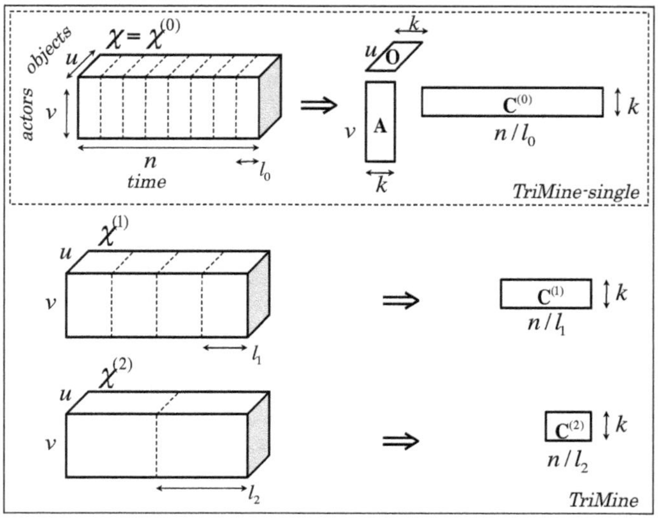

Figure 2: Illustration of *TriMine*. *TriMine-single* (dotted-line rectangle): We extract k topics from an event tensor $\mathcal{X}$ with respect to three aspects, i.e., objects O, actors A, and time C. *TriMine* (full, solid-boundary rectangle): We perform a 3-way analysis for multiple window sizes l_0, l_1, l_2, ... to capture the multi-scale dynamics of $\mathcal{X}$. Note that we reuse the O and A matrices for all scale levels to provide an efficient solution.

More specifically, we want to compute the "interpretable features" with respect to all M aspects. We propose using the concept of topic modeling to extract the major factors automatically. *TriMine* infers the M matrices, i.e., the *object* matrix $\mathbf{O}$, the *actor* matrices $\mathbf{A}^{(1)}, \dots, \mathbf{A}^{(M-2)}$, and the time matrix $\mathbf{C}$, and then identifies the relationship between the properties of these matrices. It can also discard many redundancies (e.g., noise) from the events, and focus on what really matters.

4.2.1 *Single level inference*

The task is to infer the M matrices over the hidden topics. We assume that each event entry has its own "latent topic", and thus we propose using collapsed Gibbs sampling [18] to assign a latent topic for each event entry. The generative process for a set of event entries is as follows:

1. For each topic $r = 1, \dots, k$:
   (a) For each tensor mode $m = 1, \dots, M-2$:
      i. Draw $\mathbf{A}_r^{(m)} \sim$ Dirichlet($\beta^{(m)}$).
   (b) Draw $\mathbf{C}_r \sim$ Dirichlet(γ).
2. For each object $i = 1, \dots, u$:
   (a) Draw $\mathbf{O}_i \sim$ Dirichlet(α).
   (b) For each entry $j = 1, \dots, N_i$:
      i. Draw a latent variable $z_{i,j} \sim$ Multinomial($\mathbf{O}_i$).
      ii. For each tensor mode $m = 1, \dots, M-2$:
         A. Draw an actor $e_{i,j}^{(m)} \sim$ Multinomial($\mathbf{A}_{z_{i,j}}^{(m)}$).
      iii. Draw a timestamp $t_{i,j} \sim$ Multinomial($\mathbf{C}_{z_{i,j}}$).

Here, α, $\beta^{(m)}$ and γ are the hyperparameters for $\mathbf{O}$, $\mathbf{A}^{(m)}$ and $\mathbf{C}$, respectively.

For simplicity, hereafter we focus on a 3rd-order tensor (i.e., $M = 3$). For each non-zero element $x_{i,j,t}$ in $\mathcal{X}$, we draw $x_{i,j,t}$ latent variables with probability p (Equation 1), and decide the latent variable for every event entry. The latent variable $z_{i,j,t}$ is assigned for element $x_{i,j,t}$ in the following manner:

$$\begin{aligned} p(z_{i,j,t} &= r|\mathcal{X}, \mathbf{O}', \mathbf{A}', \mathbf{C}', \alpha, \beta, \gamma) \quad (1)\\ &\propto \frac{o'_{i,r}+\alpha}{\sum_r o'_{i,r}+\alpha k} \cdot \frac{a'_{r,j}+\beta}{\sum_j a'_{r,j}+\beta v} \cdot \frac{c'_{r,t}+\gamma}{\sum_t c'_{r,t}+\gamma n} \end{aligned}$$

where $o'_{i,r}$, $a'_{r,j}$, and $c'_{r,t}$ are the total counts that topic r is assigned to the i-th *object*, j-th *actor*, and time-tick t, respectively. Note that the prime (e.g., $o'_{i,r}$) indicates that the current datum has been excluded from the count summations, that is, it indicates the count with the entry of the i-th object and the j-th entry at time t removed. Here, α, β, and γ are the parameters of the Dirichlet priors for $\mathbf{O}$, $\mathbf{A}$, and $\mathbf{C}$, respectively. After the sampler has burned-in, we can produce estimates of $\tilde{\mathbf{O}}$, $\tilde{\mathbf{A}}$, and $\tilde{\mathbf{C}}$ as follows:

$$\tilde{o}_{i,r} \propto \frac{o_{i,r}+\alpha}{\sum_r o_{i,r}+\alpha k}, \quad \tilde{a}_{r,j} \propto \frac{a_{r,j}+\beta}{\sum_j a_{r,j}+\beta v}, \quad \tilde{c}_{r,t} \propto \frac{c_{r,t}+\gamma}{\sum_t c_{r,t}+\gamma n}. \quad (2)$$

The time complexity of each sampling iteration is $O(N)$, where N is the total number of event entries in $\mathcal{X}$ (i.e., $\sum_{i,j,t} x_{i,j,t}$).

4.2.2 *Full TriMine: multiple levels*

Until now, we have assumed that the window size (say, l) was given. In reality, it is up to us to choose it. What is the right value for it? minute? hour? day? This is a difficult choice - our approach is to *not* make a choice, and use all of the above. More specifically, we use several window sizes. Our approach makes the algorithm slightly more complicated, but it pays off significantly in terms of long-term forecasting accuracy, as our experiments show (see Figures 7 and 8).

In short, as a typical choice, we use a set of all such window sizes, i.e., an hour, a day, a week, a month. Another reasonable idea is that we use a geometric progression of window sizes, that is $l_h := l_0 \cdot L^h$ for $h = 0, 1, 2, ..., \lceil \log n \rceil$, where l_0 is the shortest window, and L is the growth factor, typically $L = 2$. Thus, in either case, the count of the window set $\mathcal{L}$ that we need to examine is greatly reduced, as compared, say, to an arithmetic progression.

Here, we explain how to perform the necessary computations for multi-scale trend discovery. The straightforward solution is that we consider a set of tensors $\{\mathcal{X}^{(0)}, \mathcal{X}^{(1)} \dots\}$ for all window sizes, and compute *TriMine-single*, for each level. We refer to this approach as *TriMine* (naive). Still, this is computationally expensive because we need an inference for each window.

Efficient solution. We propose reusing the inference results of the first level to approximate the inference for the other levels. We show how our method performs the computations in Figure 2. For level $h = 0$, we compute the matrices, $\mathbf{O}$, $\mathbf{A}$, and $\mathbf{C}^{(0)}$ with the tensor $\mathcal{X}^{(0)}$ (= $\mathcal{X}$). For the other levels ($h \geq 1$), we reuse the results of the sampling in the first level, and compute the current matrices, i.e., (a) we share $\mathbf{O}$ and $\mathbf{A}$ for all levels, and (b) compute the time matrix $\mathbf{C}^{(h)}$ by using the set of sampling results for the first level, as follows:

$$c^{(h)}_{r,t} \propto \sum_{i=1}^{l_h} c^{(0)}_{r,t-l_h+i} \quad (3)$$

where l_h denotes the window size at level h. The justification is that the assignment for each event entry is probabilistically equivalent for all levels, which means that the latent topics of every level are computed by the same procedure. Compared with *TriMine* (naive), which needs $O(N \log n)$ time to update the parameters for all levels of the structure, the efficient version of *TriMine* is linear with the input size, i.e, $O(N)$.

The overall procedure of *TriMine* is given by Algorithm 1. For each entry in $\mathcal{X}^{(0)}$ at the first level, we assign a hidden variable z according to Equation (1). After the sampling, we compute the triplet matrices $\mathbf{O}$, $\mathbf{A}$, and $\mathbf{C}^{(0)}$ given a set of hidden variables. For each window size level, we approximate the matrices from their first level. Our method maintains the multi-scale window structure, which allows us to provide the output of an arbitrary window scale.

Algorithm 1 TriMine($\mathcal{X}^{(0)}$)

```
/* compute the triplet matrices at level h = 0 */
for each iteration do
  for each non-zero element x in X^(0) do
    for each entry for x do
      Draw hidden variable z by Equation (1)
    end for
  end for
end for
Compute O, A, C^(0) by Equation (2)
/* compute the multi-scale matrices */
for h = 1 to ⌈log n⌉ do
  Compute C^(h) by Equation (3)
end for
return O, A, {C^(0), ..., C^(h)}
```

5. TRIMINE-F: FORECASTING

We have already presented some of our meaningful features (see Figure 1, ternary plots of $\mathbf{O}$, $\mathbf{A}$, time-topic sequences $\mathbf{C}$), both visually and numerically, extracted from complex time-stamped events. While clustering, visualization and anomaly detection are provided straightforwardly by our output, we focus on the most challenging problem of *TriMine*, namely, complex event forecasting (Problem 2). We refer to this extension of *TriMine* for forecasting as *TriMine-F*.

Individual-sequence forecasting. Once we decide a time-window length l, we can turn the problem into $u \times v$ forecasting problems, one for each (*actor*, *object*) time sequence. Then we can use any forecasting method. This approach requires at least $O(u\, v)$ space and $O(u\, v\, n)$ time, to predict the future event counts of all sequences. Here, one subtle, but important issue is that most of the (*object*, *actor*) pairs have very sparse sequences, which derails all typical forecasting methods because they look like noise (e.g., $\{0, 0, 0, 1, 0, 0, 2, 0, 0, 0, 1, \dots\}$), and thus are hard to predict. So how can we avoid this issue? We propose using the "*hidden topics*" to achieve much better forecasting. Our proposed *TriMine-F* method can avoid the sparsity problem, because "topics" have non-trivial activities, even if some of the actors (or objects) of these topics have sparse activity.

5.1 Forecasting topic activity

Given the results of *TriMine*, we can forecast the dynamics of activities $\mathbf{C}$ for each topic r ($r = 1, \dots k$), and then translate it to URL (*object*), or user (*actor*) activity, using the participation matrices $\mathbf{O}$ and $\mathbf{A}$, respectively.

Preliminary: single-level equation. If we had a single time granularity (say, window width l_0), then we would do auto regression (AR), and we could forecast the activity $c_{r,t}$ for topic r at time t as a function of the w previous activity levels $c_{r,t-1}, \dots c_{r,t-w}$, plus, (filtered) noise ϵ_t:

$$c_{r,t} = \lambda_1 c_{r,t-1} + \dots + \lambda_w c_{r,t-w} + \epsilon_t, \quad (4)$$

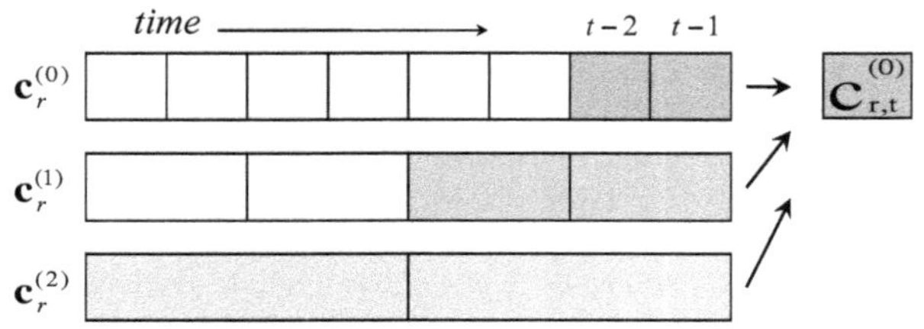

Figure 3: Illustration of multi-scale forecasting (here, $l_0 = 1, l = 2$). The gray cells indicate the variables we use to forecast $c_{r,t}$. Note that we use w variables ($w = 2$ in this example) from each level.

where λ is a regression coefficient.

Multi-scale dynamics. How should we operate multi-scale proportions for event forecasting? Real time-stamped events typically include bursty patterns, noise, spikes, and dips, as well as the event trends of multi-scale periods, all of which are unknown in advance. Long-term patterns are included in the time matrix at the top level while short and sharp fluctuations appear at the first level. Thus, instead of using a single level of window size, we fit a model to the time matrices of multiple levels, (i.e., $\mathbf{C}^{(0)}, \mathbf{C}^{(1)}, \ldots$). In a multi-level case, our forecasting method uses $\lceil \log n \rceil$ additional levels (see Figure 3). Thus, we try to fit models of the following form:

$$c_{r,t}^{(0)} = \sum_{h=0}^{\lceil \log n \rceil} \sum_{i=1}^{w} \lambda_{i,r}^{(h)} c_{r,t-i}^{(h)} + \epsilon_t. \quad (5)$$

5.2 Complex event forecasting

Here we answer two questions:

- **Count estimate:** How many clicks $x_{i,j,t}$ should we expect to see from user/*actor* j, to URL/*object* i, at the next time-tick t (e.g., the next hour)?
- **Event-set forecast:** How can we generate a realistic set of event entries of form $\{object, actor\}$ for time-tick t.

Clearly, the second question is more general. if we can answer that, we can easily give the count estimate for the first question (and also the variance etc, since we can generate many event samples).

A few clarifications, first: (a) without loss of generality, we assume that we have agreed on the aggregation length l, and each time-tick is l seconds long. (b) We can easily extend our solutions to long-term forecasting such as *estimate the number of clicks from user 'Smith' to URL 'CNN.com', for the next 30 days*, i.e., $x_{i,j,t}$, $(t = 1, 2, ..., 30)$. (c) We can easily extend our answers to marginals (or "don't cares"), for example, *estimate the number of clicks from user 'Smith', to* any *URL, for tomorrow*, i.e., estimate $x_{*,j,t}$ where we follow the Unix convention and '*' means "don't care".

Count estimation. The 'count' question can be answered easily by using following steps: (a) forecasting the strength $c_{r,t}$ for every topic $r = 1, \ldots, k$ at time-tick t, and (b) using the *participation* matrices $\mathbf{O}$ and $\mathbf{A}$ to translate from topic activity to URL-and-user activity (= clicks). We can then estimate the count of an element ($x_{i,j,t}$) of the i-th *object* and the j-th *actor* at time t:

$$\hat{x}_{i,j,t} = n\bar{x}_i \sum_{r=1}^{k} o_{i,r} \cdot a_{r,j} \cdot \hat{c}_{r,t}, \quad (6)$$

where n is the duration of forecasted events, and $\bar{x}_i$ is the average number of events per time-tick for the i-th *object*.

Complex event generation. For the event-generation problem, the answer is more elaborate, and is illustrated by Algorithm 2. The idea is again to forecast the future activity $\hat{c}_{t,r}$ and then draw multinomial samples using the participation matrices $\mathbf{O}$, $\mathbf{A}$, and $\hat{\mathbf{C}}$. To generate a set of event entries, our sampling-based approach obtains an appropriate number of independent samples of the statistic directly from the underlying generative model. The samples can then be organized into a set of entries of form $\{object, actor, time\}$, simply by gathering all the event entries together.

Algorithm 2 EventGeneration ($\bar{x_1}, \ldots, \bar{x_u}, n, \mathbf{O}, \mathbf{A}, \hat{\mathbf{C}}$)

```
/* Ê is a set of generated entries of form {object, actor, time} */
Ê ← ∅
for each object i = 1, ..., u do
  for each entry j = 1, ..., n x̄_i do
    Draw a hidden variable z_{i,j} ~ Multinomial(O_i)
    Draw an actor e ~ Multinomial(A_{z_{i,j}})
    Draw a timestamp t ~ Multinomial(Ĉ_{z_{i,j}})
    Ê = Ê_t ∪ {i, e, t}
  end for
end for
Return Ê
```

6. EXPERIMENTS

To evaluate the effectiveness of *TriMine*, we carried out experiments on real datasets. Our experiments were conducted on an Intel Core 2 Duo 1.86GHz with 4GB of memory, running Linux. The experiments were designed to answer the following questions:

1. Effectiveness: How successful is *TriMine* in capturing time-stamped events, and spotting meaningful patterns?
2. Forecasting accuracy: How well does our method forecast future event entries?
3. Scalability: How does our method scale with the dataset size in terms of computational time?

Datasets. We performed experiments on two real datasets:

- *WebClick*: This dataset consists of web-click records, obtained over one month, (from 1st to 30th Apr. 2007). It contains one billion records, each of which has three attributes: URL ID (1,797 URLs), user ID (10,000 heavy users), and the time stamp of the click. There are various types of URLs, such as "blog", "news", "money", and "diet".
- *Ondemand TV*: This consists of 13,231 TV programs that 100,000 users viewed in a 6-month time frame (from 14th May to 15th Nov. 2007), and there are many genres of TV programs including "cartoons", "sports", "movies", and "music". This dataset contains a list of attributes (e.g., channel ID (*object*), user/viewer ID (*actor*), the date the user watched the program). We selected 100 TV programs from the dataset.

6.1 Effectiveness - patterns and visualization

WebClick **dataset.** For a few users (or URLs), human could eyeball them, and derive meaningful patterns. But, how can we accomplish this automatically for thousands of users? Some of the results obtained with for our method for the *WebClick* dataset have already been presented in Section 1 (see Figure 1), which shows that *TriMine* effectively and efficiently discovers the three-way patterns (i.e., *TriMine*-plot). Figure 4 also shows a *TriMine*-plot on *WebClick* in relation to three different topics, 'communication', 'blog', and 'food'.

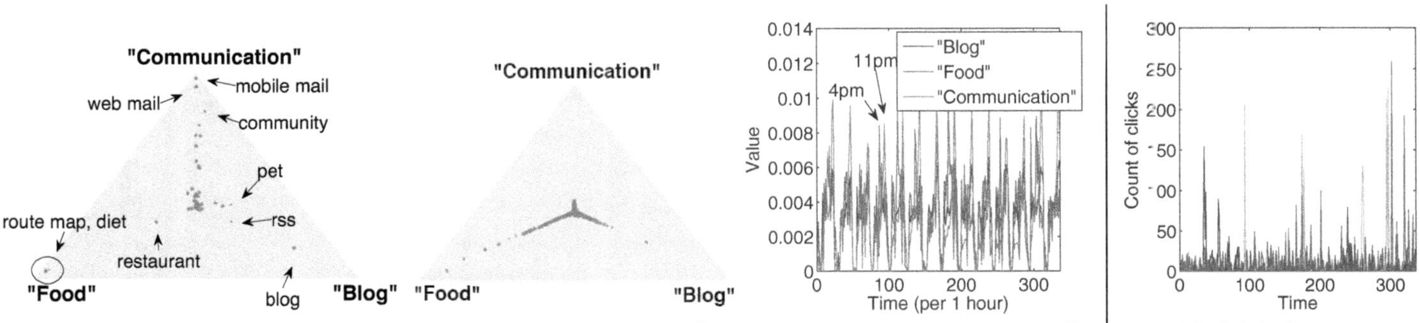

(a) URLs in topic space (**O**) (b) Users in topic space (**A**) (c) Time evolution of topics (**C**) (d) Original sequence

Figure 4: ***TriMine*** **finds patterns (see (a-c)), when raw data seem noisy (part (d)).** ***WebClick*** **dataset and its** ***TriMine*****-plot (a-c); number of clicks for 100 random users (d).** ***TriMine*****-plot shows clear groups ('food', 'communication' etc), and clear temporal trends (daily periodicity etc, see (c)). Raw data (d), appears bursty and noisy.**

- *Membership Clusters*: Most *objects* (URLs) fall along the center-to-vertex spokes. The route map and restaurant sites are related as a food topic (see Figure 4 (a)), and the diet site also falls into the same topic. From the figure, we can recognize that the users carefully check out restaurants, the route map in their area, and also the calories of their meals.
- *Temporal Trends*: In Figure 4 (c), we observed that the food-related URLs are visited in the early evening before the users go out. We consider the communication sites (web mail, SNS, etc.) to be used heavily in the late evening for private purposes. Figure 4 (d) shows the original sequence of the "blog" site for randomly selected users. Unlike Figure 4 (c), Figure 4 (d) does not exhibit any daily periodicity or any relationship between users.

Ondemand TV **dataset.** Figure 5 shows the major topics, 'sports', 'action', and 'romance' (namely, 'soap operas').

- *Membership Outliers*: The ternary plot of the URLs shows clear clustering of the URLs with only one exception, the 2007 French Open men's tennis final. Soap operas and romances (like the series 'Desperate Housewives') probably attract a female audience, who do not seem to be interested in sports, except, apparently, for the men's tennis final of the French Open. We think perhaps that they are interested in one or both of the players in that match (i.e., Rafael Nadal and/or Roger Federer).
- *Temporal Trends*: The time-evolution pattern of the sports topic agrees with our intuition – daily periodicity for all three topics; 'action' and 'sports' show high peaks on weekends, but there is no weekly periodicity for the 'soap opera' topic.

6.2 Accuracy - forecasting

We demonstrate how our forecasting method, *TriMine-F*, works well for time-stamped events, specifically, we evaluate our method using a real dataset, *WebClick*, in terms of long-term forecasting, which is a challenging task. We should note that generating more than, say, 10 steps ahead is very rare: most reported methods [26] generate one step ahead, obtain the correct value of time-tick t, and only then try to generate $t+1$. Nevertheless, our goal is to capture long-term behavior, and we will show that our method achieves this, unlike the alternative methods.

Experimental setup. In our setting, we first trained our models by using the click entries of the first two weeks, and then forecasted the following weeks. We selected the window size $l_0 = 2$, that is,

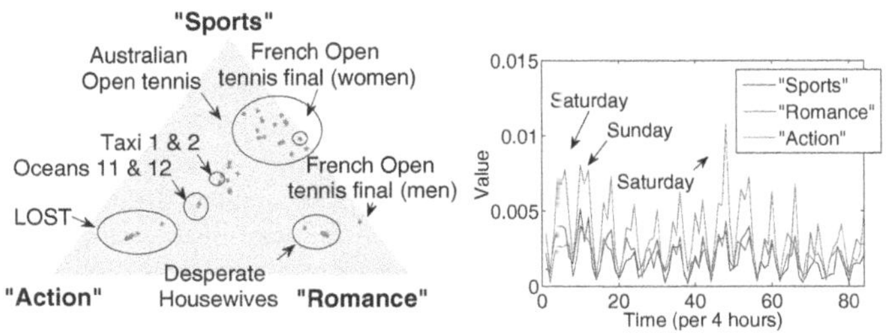

(a) URL ternary plot (*object*-topic) (b) time evolution of topics

Figure 5: Effectiveness of ***TriMine*** **on the** ***Ondemand TV*** **dataset. Rather clear separation of URLs into 'action', 'sports' and 'romance' (see (a)); clear daily periodicity for all topics (see (b)), with weekly periodicity for 'sports' and 'action', but** ***not*** **for 'romance'.**

the length of the training set $\mathcal{X}^{(0)}$ was $n = 168$. We chose the total forecasting coefficients as 40, and the hidden topics $k = 30$.

We compared our algorithm with state-of-the-art methods with respect to forecasting the number of "future" clicks for all possible URL and user combinations. (a) **AR**: This is a straightforward solution to the forecasting problem. We turned the event tensor $\mathcal{X}$ into a set of $u \times v$ sequences for each URL and user. After obtaining the sequence set, we applied standard *AR* modeling for each sequence individually. For a fair comparison, we used 40 regression coefficients. (b) **PLiF**: We compared our algorithm with *PLiF* [13], which is based on Linear Dynamical Systems (also known as Kalman filters). It captures the correlations between multiple sequences, and has the ability to forecast sequences. The original signals are bursty, thus we take their logarithm according to [13]. (c) **T2**: Very recently, Hong et al. present a new topic model for tracking trends [6]. We refer to it as *T2* in this paper. We used the model parameters of *T2*, which can capture the evolution of topics in data collections. In our setting, we inferred the model parameters using entries of duration n. At time-tick n, we stopped the inference, and the latest model parameters were used to predict all of the future events.

6.2.1 *Forecast accuracy*

Temporal perplexity. We first evaluate the forecasting accuracy of our method in terms of perplexity. Here, we compare *TriMine-F* with *T2*. A lower perplexity indicates a higher predictive accuracy. The perplexities per time-tick are shown in Figure 6. *TriMine-F* captures the general periodic trend, with a desirable slight confu-

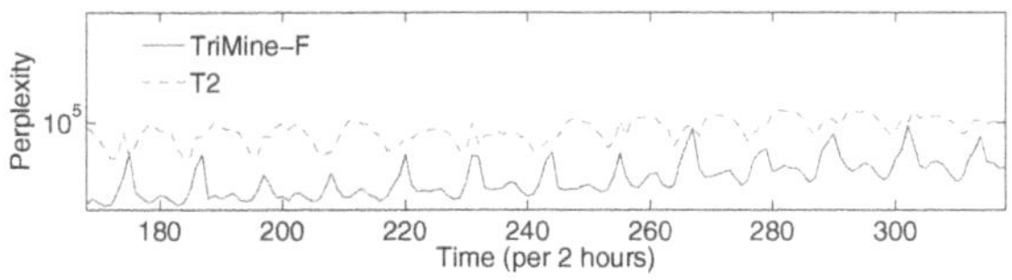

(a) *WebClick*

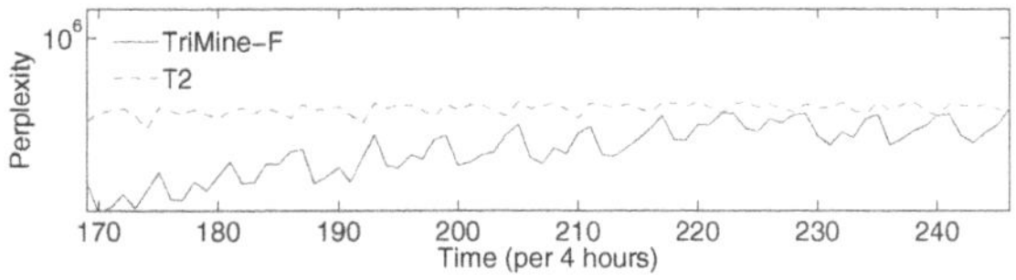

(b) *Ondemand TV*

Figure 6: Perplexity at each time-tick. ***TriMine*** **achieves the lower perplexity; we can appropriately forecast the dynamics of hidden patterns.**

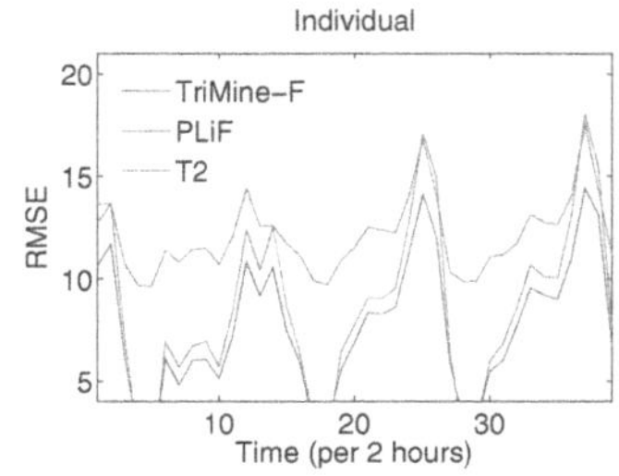

(a) Individual (hourly)

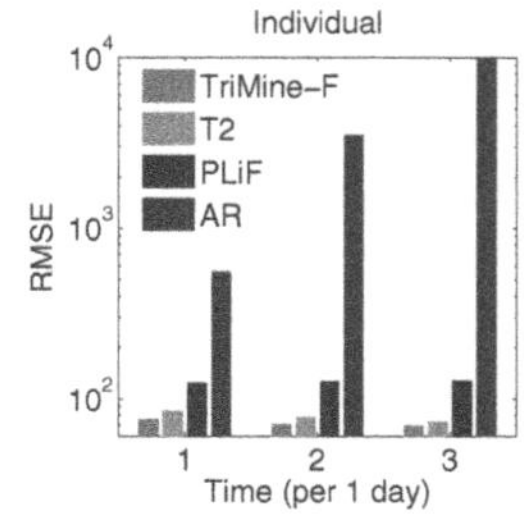

(b) Individual (daily)

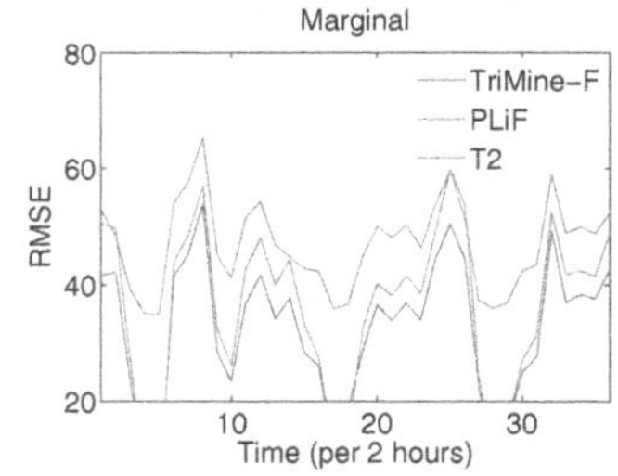

(c) Marginal (hourly)

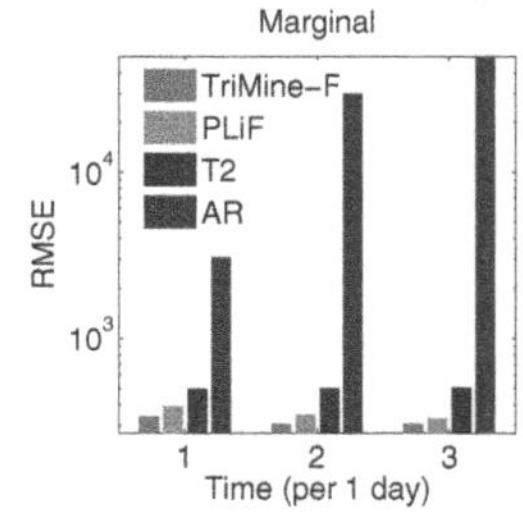

(d) Marginal (daily)

Figure 7: Forecasting accuracy for individual $x_{i,j,t}$ (top) and marginal $x_{*,j,t}$ (bottom): ***TriMine-F*** **consistently outperforms the state-of-the-art methods with respect to accuracy (root mean square error ($RMSE$) between real values and forecasts).** ***WebClick*** **dataset, long-term forecasts starting at t=168 (i.e., after two weeks) (also see Figure 8). Lower is better. We omit the** ***AR*** **results for hourly error (a) and (c), due to high error values. Notice that** ***TriMine-F*** **gives the lowest error. Also see the text for more observations.**

sion about the period in both datasets (i.e., *WebClick* and *Ondemand TV*). *T2*, on the other hand, is not intended to capture long-term trends. The figure shows that *T2* fails to predict the future events.

Accuracy of event forecasting. We also compared our algorithm with the standard *AR* method and the state-of-the-art methods, *PLiF* and *T2*, with respect to forecasting a number of "future" events. Figure 7 (a)-(b) shows the root mean square error ($RMSE$) between the original and the forecasted event sets of each URL and each user (we call it "individual forecasts: $x_{i,j,t}$"). Similarly, Figure 7 (c)-(d) describes the results of "marginal" forecasts: $x_{*,j,t}$, that is we forecast the aggregated counts of each user j at every time-tick t. A lower value indicates a better forecasting accuracy. Note that cyclic dips occur in the middle of the night, because we have only a few click entries at this time interval. *T2* was partially successful in generating the future clicks, however, it frequently failed to forecast future event entries. The alternative forecasting methods, *AR* and *PLiF* also failed to forecast the entries, because each sequence was too sparse to capture the cyclic patterns. Unlike the alternative methods, our method achieves high forecasting accuracy for every time-tick. *TriMine-F* outperforms the state-of-the-art methods in terms of forecasting accuracy, and similar trends were observed with the other dataset. We omit the results due to space limitations.

6.2.2 *Benefit of multi-scale approach*

In this subsection, we discuss how *TriMine-F* captures the pattern dynamics. To evaluate the effort from the properties of multiple time scales in our model, we implement a special version of *TriMine-F* by removing this property. Specifically, we use only a single regression coefficient set, (i.e., Equation (4)). We refer to it as *TriMine-F* (single). We used the same coefficients ($= 40$) for a fair comparison. Figure 8 shows the temporal evolution of two major topics for the *WebClick* dataset. We trained our models with click events over a period of two weeks (dotted lines in the figure), and then forecasted the following two weeks. The top, middle and bottom rows of this figure show the output of *TriMine*, *TriMine-F* (single), and *TriMine-F*, respectively. In this figure, *TriMine* does not undertake forecasting, it simply shows the current topic weights at each time. *TriMine-F* is our full solution for event forecasting, which includes multi-scale analysis. The figure shows that our forecasting method, *TriMine-F*, successfully forecasts the subsequent weeks. Specifically, *TriMine-F* (single) failed to capture the dynamics and moved towards convergence. On the other hand, our full solution successfully captured cyclic patterns and periodicity. Consequently, using multi-scale analysis has a significant advantage, which leads to high forecasting accuracy.

6.3 Scalability

We now evaluate the efficiency of *TriMine-F* for event forecasting. Figure 9 compares our method with the AR method in terms of wall clock time when duration n is varied. We use the *WebClick* dataset for this experiment, where the numbers of URLs and users are $u = 1,000$, and $v = 10,000$. The wall clock time is the processing time needed to compute statistics/coefficients and provide the output (i.e., forecasts). Note that *T2* and *PLiF* are based on the Kalman filter and are not scalable for large datasets. These methods need more than 10^6 seconds to compute even at $n = 100$, thus we omit the results. We present our efficient approach for multi-scale analysis in Section 4.2.2. To evaluate the efficiency of this approach, we also show the basic approach, which we call *TriMine-F* (naive). The empirical results in these figures fully substantiate the superiority of *TriMine-F* (i.e., our full solution). We observed that *TriMine-F* achieved a dramatic reduction in computation time that can be up to 7 times faster than *TriMine-F* (naive), and 74 times faster than AR.

7. CONCLUSIONS

We addressed the problem of finding patterns and trends, for "complex" events of the form ($URL, userID, timestamp$), and, in general (*object*, *actor*, time).

We presented *TriMine*, which has all of the following properties:

- Effective: *TriMine* finds meaningful patterns in several real datasets. It thus enables visualization (*TriMine*-plots), anomaly detection, summarization and 'sense-making' (see Figures 1, 4, 5).

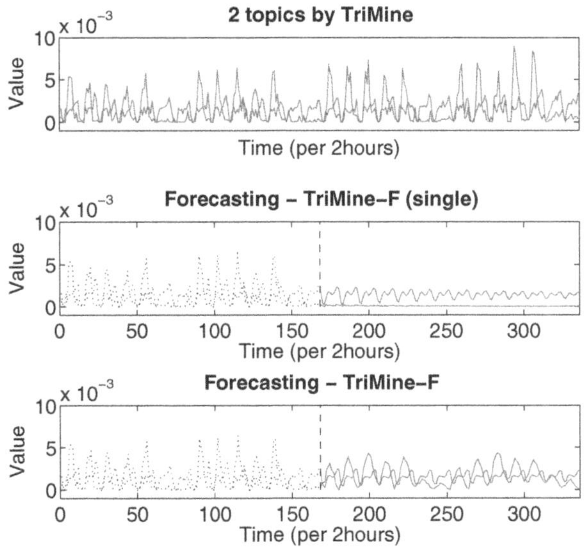

Figure 8: Benefit of multiple time scales. Top: the two main trends of the *WebClick* dataset, namely, 'business' (blue) and 'media' (red). Middle and bottom: *TriMine-F* clearly outperforms *TriMine-F* (single). Both methods start long-term forecasting at t=168 (i.e., after two weeks). Our multi-scale *TriMine-F* reflects reality better, while *TriMine-F* (single) quickly converges to the mean (red), and even worse, predicts near-zero for (blue), blinded by the low activity during weekends.

- Accurate *TriMine* enables forecasting, and specifically, our multi-scale *TriMine-F* is significantly faster and consistently more accurate than state-of-the-art methods.
- Scalable: *TriMine* scales very well, being linear on the database size, and several times faster than its competitors (7x, 74x).

We also demonstrated the practicality of *TriMine*, by applying it to several real datasets, both for pattern discovery and forecasting.

8. REFERENCES

[1] D. Agarwal, B.-C. Chen, and P. Elango. Spatio-temporal models for estimating click-through rate. In *WWW Conference*, pages 21–30, Madrid, Spain, April 2009.

[2] L. AlSumait, D. Barbará, and C. Domeniconi. On-line lda: Adaptive topic models for mining text streams with applications to topic detection and tracking. In *ICDM*, pages 3–12, 2008.

[3] D. M. Blei and J. D. Lafferty. Dynamic topic models. In *ICML*, pages 113–120, 2006.

[4] D. M. Blei, A. Y. Ng, and M. I. Jordan. Latent dirichlet allocation. *Journal of Machine Learning Research*, 3:993–1022, 2003.

[5] T. Hofmann. Probabilistic latent semantic indexing. In *SIGIR*, pages 50–57, 1999.

[6] L. Hong, D. Yin, J. Guo, and B. D. Davison. Tracking trends: incorporating term volume into temporal topic models. In *KDD*, pages 484–492, 2011.

[7] T. Iwata, S. Watanabe, T. Yamada, and N. Ueda. Topic tracking model for analyzing consumer purchase behavior. In *IJCAI*, pages 1427–1432, 2009.

[8] T. Iwata, T. Yamada, Y. Sakurai, and N. Ueda. Online multiscale dynamic topic models. In *KDD*, pages 663–672, 2010.

[9] R. Kannan, H. Salmasian, and S. Vempala. The spectral method for general mixture models. In *18th Annual Conference on Learning Theory (COLT)*, pages 444–457, 2005.

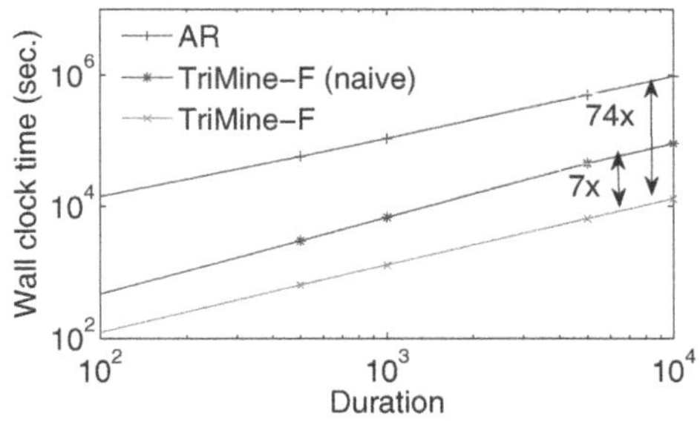

Figure 9: Scalability of event forecasting: wall clock time vs. dataset size (= duration n). Our methods are linear (i.e, slope 1, in log log). *TriMine-F* is 7x times faster than *TriMine-F* (naive), and 74x faster than *AR*. We omit the *T2* and *PLiF* results due to the high computation cost.

[10] T. G. Kolda, B. W. Bader, and J. P. Kenny. Higher-order web link analysis using multilinear algebra. In *ICDM*, pages 242–249, 2005.

[11] F. Korn, S. Muthukrishnan, and Y. Wu. Modeling skew in data streams. In *SIGMOD '06: Proceedings of the 2006 ACM SIGMOD international conference on Management of data*, pages 181–192, New York, NY, USA, 2006. ACM.

[12] L. D. Lathauwer, B. D. Moor, and J. Vandewalle. A multilinear singular value decomposition. *SIAM J. Matrix Anal. Appl.*, 21(4):1253–1278, 2000.

[13] L. Li, B. A. Prakash, and C. Faloutsos. Parsimonious linear fingerprinting for time series. *PVLDB*, 3(1):385–396, 2010.

[14] Y. Matsubara, Y. Sakurai, and M. Yoshikawa. Scalable algorithms for distribution search. In *ICDM*, pages 347–356, 2009.

[15] R. V. Nehme, E. A. Rundensteiner, and E. Bertino. Tagging stream data for rich real-time services. *PVLDB*, 2(1):73–84, 2009.

[16] S. Papadimitriou, A. Brockwell, and C. Faloutsos. Adaptive, hands-off stream mining. In *Proceedings of VLDB*, pages 560–571, Berlin, Germany, Sept. 2003.

[17] S. Papadimitriou and P. S. Yu. Optimal multi-scale patterns in time series streams. In *SIGMOD Conference*, pages 647–658, 2006.

[18] I. Porteous, D. Newman, A. T. Ihler, A. Asuncion, P. Smyth, and M. Welling. Fast collapsed gibbs sampling for latent dirichlet allocation. In *KDD*, pages 569–577, 2008.

[19] S. Rendle, L. B. Marinho, A. Nanopoulos, and L. Schmidt-Thieme. Learning optimal ranking with tensor factorization for tag recommendation. In *KDD*, pages 727–736, 2009.

[20] Y. Sakurai, C. Faloutsos, and M. Yamamuro. Stream monitoring under the time warping distance. In *Proceedings of ICDE*, pages 1046–1055, Istanbul, Turkey, April 2007.

[21] Y. Sakurai, S. Papadimitriou, and C. Faloutsos. Braid: Stream mining through group lag correlations. In *Proceedings of ACM SIGMOD*, pages 599–610, Baltimore, Maryland, June 2005.

[22] T. Shi, M. Belkin, and B. Yu. Data spectroscopy: learning mixture models using eigenspaces of convolution operators. In *ICML*, pages 936–943, 2008.

[23] G. Tomasi and R. Bro. Parafac and missing values. *Chemometrics and Intelligent Laboratory Systems*, 75(2):163–180, 2005.

[24] X. Wang and A. McCallum. Topics over time: a non-markov continuous-time model of topical trends. In *KDD*, pages 424–433, 2006.

[25] X. Wei, J. Sun, and X. Wang. Dynamic mixture models for multiple time-series. In *IJCAI*, pages 2909–2914, 2007.

[26] A. Weigend and N. Gershenfeld. *Time Series Prediction: Forecasting the Future and Understanding the Past*. Addison-Wesley, 1993.

[27] L. Yao, D. M. Mimno, and A. McCallum. Efficient methods for topic model inference on streaming document collections. In *KDD*, pages 937–946, 2009.

[28] Z. Zhang, B. T. Dai, and A. K. H. Tung. Estimating local optimums in em algorithm over gaussian mixture model. In *ICML*, pages 1240–1247, 2008.

Mining Recent Temporal Patterns for Event Detection in Multivariate Time Series Data

Iyad Batal
Dept. of Computer Science
University of Pittsburgh
iyad@cs.pitt.edu

Dmitriy Fradkin
Siemens Corporate Research
dmitriy.fradkin@siemens.com

James Harrison
Dept. of Public Health Sciences
University of Virginia
james.harrison@virginia.edu

Fabian Moerchen
Siemens Corporate Research
fabian.moerchen@siemens.com

Milos Hauskrecht
Dept. of Computer Science
University of Pittsburgh
milos@cs.pitt.edu

ABSTRACT

Improving the performance of classifiers using pattern mining techniques has been an active topic of data mining research. In this work we introduce the recent temporal pattern mining framework for finding predictive patterns for monitoring and event detection problems in complex multivariate time series data. This framework first converts time series into time-interval sequences of temporal abstractions. It then constructs more complex temporal patterns backwards in time using temporal operators. We apply our framework to health care data of 13,558 diabetic patients and show its benefits by efficiently finding useful patterns for detecting and diagnosing adverse medical conditions that are associated with diabetes.

Categories and Subject Descriptors

I.2.6 [**LEARNING**]: General

Keywords

Temporal Pattern Mining, Temporal Abstractions, Time-interval Patterns, Event Detection, Patient Classification.

1. INTRODUCTION

Advances in data collection and data storage technologies led to emergence of complex temporal datasets, where the data instances are traces of complex behaviors characterized by time series of multiple variables. Designing algorithms capable of learning classification models from such data is one of the most challenging topics of data mining research.

The majority of existing classification methods that work with temporal data [12, 6, 4, 24, 8, 28] assume that each data instance (represented by a single or multiple time series) is associated with a single class label that affects its *entire* behavior. That is, they assume that all temporal observations are equally useful for classification.

KDD'12, August 12–16, 2012, Beijing, China.

However, the above assumption is not the best when considering monitoring and event detection problems. In this case, the class label denotes an event that is associated with a specific time point (or a time interval) in the instance, not necessarily in the entire instance. The goal is to learn a model that can accurately identify the occurrence of events in unlabeled instances (a monitoring task). Examples of such problems are the detection of adverse medical events (e.g. drug toxicity) in clinical data [10], detection of the equipment malfunction [9], fraud detection [23], environmental monitoring [16], intrusion detection [7] and others.

Given that class labels are associated with specific time points (or time intervals), each instance can be annotated with multiple labels[1]. Consequently, the context in which the classification is made is often local and affected by the most *recent* behavior of the monitored instances.

The focus of this paper is to develop a pattern mining technique that takes into account the local nature of decisions for monitoring and event detection problems. We propose the ***Recent Temporal Pattern (RTP)*** mining framework, which mines frequent temporal patterns backward in time, starting from patterns related to the most recent observations. Applying this technique, temporal patterns that extend far into the past are likely to have low support in the data and hence would not be considered for classification. Incorporating the concept of recency in temporal pattern mining is a new research direction that, to the best of our knowledge, has not been previously explored in the pattern mining literature.

We study our *RTP* mining approach by analyzing temporal data encountered in Electronic Health Record (EHR) systems. In EHR data, each record (data instance) consists of multiple time series of clinical variables collected for a specific patient, such as laboratory test results and medication orders. The record may also provide information about patient's diseases and adverse medical events over time. Our objective is to learn classification models that can accurately detect adverse events and apply it to monitor future patients.

The task of temporal modeling for EHR data is challenging because the data are *multivariate* and the time series for clinical variables are *irregularly sampled in time* (measured asynchronously at different time moments). Therefore, most existing times series classification methods [6, 24], time series similarity measures [29, 20] and time series feature extraction methods [4, 13] cannot be directly applied on the raw EHR data.

This paper proposes a temporal pattern mining approach that can

[1]In the clinical domain, a patient may be healthy at first, then develop an adverse medical condition, then be cured and so on.

handle complex data such as EHR. The key step for this approach is defining a language that can adequately represent the temporal dimension of the data. Our approach relies on 1) temporal abstractions [21] to convert numeric time series variables to *time-interval* sequences and 2) temporal relations [3] to represent temporal interactions among the variables. For example, this allows us to define complex *temporal patterns* (time-interval patterns) such as "the administration of heparin precedes a decreasing trend in platelet counts".

After defining patterns from temporally abstracted data, we need to design an efficient mining algorithm for finding patterns that are useful for event detection. Mining time-interval data is a relatively young research field that extends sequential pattern mining [2, 31, 18, 30] to the more complex case of time-interval pattern mining[2]. Most existing methods mine frequent patterns in an unsupervised way in order to find temporal association rules [22, 11, 17, 14, 26, 27, 15]. Our objective is different because we are interested in mining temporal patterns that are potentially important for the event detection task. To address this, we present an efficient algorithm for mining *RTPs* (see above) from time-interval data.

We test and demonstrate the usefulness of our framework on real-world EHR data collected for 13,558 diabetes patients. Our task is to learn classification models that can correctly diagnose disorders associated with diabetes, such as cardiological, renal or neurological disorders. We first show that incorporating the temporal dimension is beneficial for this task. In addition, we show the following advantages of our framework:

1. *RTP* mining focuses the search on temporal patterns that are potentially more useful for classification.
2. The number of frequent *RTPs* is much smaller than the number of frequent temporal patterns. This can facilitate the process of reviewing and validating the mined patterns by human experts.
3. Our mining algorithm is much more efficient than other temporal pattern mining approaches and it can scale up much better to large datasets.

2. PROBLEM DEFINITION

Let $D = \{<\boldsymbol{x}_i, y_i>\}_{i=1}^n$ be a training dataset such that $\boldsymbol{x}_i \in X$ is a multivariate temporal instance up to some time t_i and $y_i \in Y$ is a class label associated with $\boldsymbol{x}_i$ at time t_i. The objective is to learn a function $f : X \rightarrow Y$ that can label unlabeled instances. This general setting is applicable to different monitoring and event detection problems, such as the ones described in [23, 7, 9, 16].

In this work, we test our method on data from electronic health records (EHR), hence we will use the EHR application as example throughout the paper. For this task, every data instance x_i is a record for a specific patient up to time t_i and the class label y_i denotes whether or not this patient is diagnosed with an adverse medical condition (e.g., renal failure) at t_i. Figure 1 shows a graphical illustration of an EHR instance with 3 clinical temporal variables. The objective is to learn a classifier that can predict well the studied medical condition and apply it to monitor future patients.

Learning the classifier directly from EHR data is very difficult because the instances consist of multiple irregularly sampled time series of different length. Therefore, we want to apply a space transformation $\psi : X \rightarrow X'$ that maps each instance $\boldsymbol{x}_i$ to a fixed-size feature vector $\boldsymbol{x}'_i$, while preserving the predictive temporal characteristics of $\boldsymbol{x}_i$ as much as possible.

[2]Sequential pattern mining is a special case of time-interval pattern mining, in which all intervals are instantaneous (with zero durations).

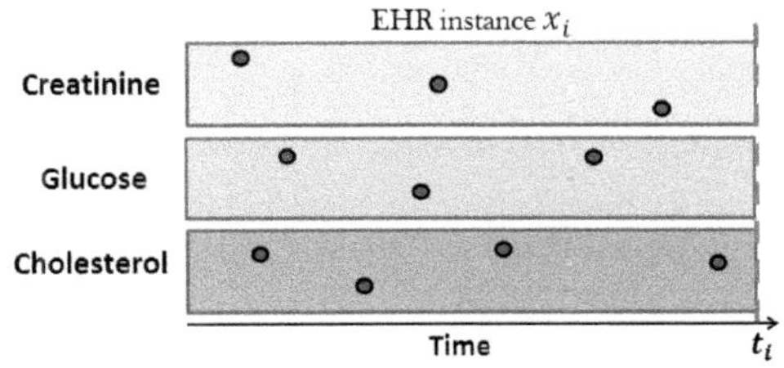

Figure 1: An example of an EHR data instance with three temporal variables. The black dots represent their values over time.

One approach to define ψ is to represent the data using a *predefined* set of features and their values (a *static transformation*) as in [10]. Examples of such features are "most recent platelet measurement", "most recent platelet trend", "maximum hemoglobin measurement", etc. Our approach is different and we *learn* transformation ψ from the data using temporal pattern mining (a *dynamic transformation*). This is done by applying the following steps:

1. Convert the numeric time series variables into time interval sequences using temporal abstraction.
2. Mine recent temporal patterns from the time interval data.
3. Transform each instance $\boldsymbol{x}_i$ into a binary indictor vector $\boldsymbol{x}'_i$ using the patterns obtained in step 2.

After applying transformation ψ, we can use a standard machine learning method (e.g. support vector machines, decision tree, or logistic regression) on $\{<\boldsymbol{x}'_i, y_i>\}_{i=1}^n$ to learn function f.

In the following, we explain in details each of these steps.

3. TEMPORAL ABSTRACTION PATTERNS

3.1 Temporal Abstraction

The goal of **temporal abstraction** [21] is to transform the numeric time series variables to a high-level qualitative form. More specifically, each clinical variable (e.g., series of white blood cell counts) is transformed into an *interval-based* representation $\langle v_1[s_1, e_1], ..., v_n[s_n, e_n]\rangle$, where $v_i \in \Sigma$ is an abstraction that holds from time s_i to time e_i and Σ is the **abstraction alphabet** that represents a finite set of permitted abstractions.

For the EHR data, we segment all laboratory variables based on their values into the following abstract states: *Very Low (VL)*, *low (L)*, *Normal (N)*, *High (H)* and *Very High (VH)*, i.e., Σ = {*VL, L, N, H, VH*}. We use the 10th, 25th, 75th and 90th percentiles of the lab values to define these 5 states: a value below the 10th percentile is *very low (VL)*, a value between the 10th and 25th percentiles is *low (L)*, and so on.

3.2 Multivariate State Sequences

Let a **state** be an *abstraction for a specific variable*. We denote a state S by a pair (F, V), where F is a temporal variable and $V \in \Sigma$ is an abstraction value. Let a **state interval** be a *state that holds during an interval*. We denote a state interval E by a 4-tuple (F, V, s, e), where F is a temporal variable, $V \in \Sigma$ is an abstraction value, and s and e are the start time and end time (respectively) of the state interval ($E.s \leq E.e$)[3]. For example, assuming the time granularity is days, $(glucose, H, 5, 10)$ represents high glucose values from day 5 to day 10.

After abstracting all time series variables, we represent every instance $\boldsymbol{x}_i$ in the database D as a **Multivariate State Sequence (MSS)** Z_i. Let $\boldsymbol{Z_i.end}$ denote the end time of the instance.

[3]If $E.s = E.e$, state interval E corresponds to a time point.

For notational convenience, we represent an MSS Z_i as a series of state intervals that are sorted according to their start times[4]:

$$Z_i = \langle\, E_1, E_2, ..., E_l \,\rangle \;\; : E_j.s \leq E_{j+1}.s : j \in \{1, ..., l-1\}$$

Note that we do not require $E_j.e$ to be less than $E_{j+1}.s$ because the state intervals are obtained from different temporal variables and their intervals may overlap.

EXAMPLE 1. *Figure 2 shows an MSS Z_i with two temporal variables: creatinine (C) and glucose (G). Assuming the time granularity is days, this MSS represents 24 days of the patient's record ($Z_i.end = 24$). For instance, we can see that the creatinine values are normal from day 2 until day 14, then become high from day 15 until day 24. We represent Z_i as: $\langle\, E_1 = (G, H, 1, 5)$, $E_2 = (C, N, 2, 14)$, $E_3 = (G, N, 6, 9)$, $E_4 = (G, H, 10, 13)$, $E_5 = (C, H, 15, 24)$, $E_6 = (G, VH, 16, 23) \,\rangle$.*

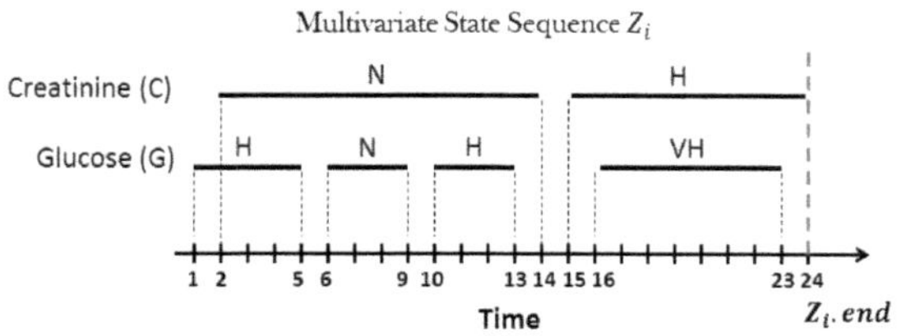

Figure 2: An MSS representing 24 days of a patient record. In this example, there are two temporal variables (creatinine and glucose).

3.3 Temporal Relations

The temporal relation between two instantaneous events (time points) can be easily described using three relations: *before*, *at the same time* and *after*. However, when the events have time durations (state intervals), the relations become more complex. Allen [3] described the temporal relation between two state intervals using 13 possible relations (Figure 3). But it suffices to use the following 7 relations: *before*, *meets*, *overlaps*, *is-finished-by*, *contains*, *starts* and *equals* because the other relations are simply their inverses. Allen's relations have been introduced in artificial intelligence for temporal reasoning and have been used later in the fairly young research of time interval data mining [22, 11, 17, 26, 15].

E_1 E_2	E_1 before E_2	E_2 after E_1
E_1 E_2	E_1 meets E_2	E_2 is-met-by E_1
E_1 E_2	E_1 overlaps E_2	E_2 is-overlapped-by E_1
E_1 E_2	E_1 is-finished-by E_2	E_2 finishes E_1
E_1 E_2	E_1 contains E_2	E_2 during E_1
E_1 E_2	E_1 starts E_2	E_2 is-started-by E_1
E_1 E_2	E_1 equals E_2	E_2 equals E_1

Figure 3: Allen's temporal relations.

As we can see, most of these relations require equality of one or two of the intervals' end points. That is, there is only a slight difference between *overlaps*, *is-finished-by*, *contains*, *starts* and *equals* relations. When the time information in the data is noisy, which is the case for EHR data, using Allen's relations may cause the problem of pattern fragmentation[5] [14] .

[4]If two state intervals have the same start time, we sort them by their end time. If they also have the same end time, we sort them by lexical order (see [11]).

[5]Having many different temporal patterns that describe a very similar situation in the data.

Therefore, we opt to use only two temporal relations: ***before* (*b*)** and ***co-occurs* (*c*)**, which we define as follows:
Given two state intervals E_i and E_j:

- E_i is ***before*** E_j, denoted as $\boldsymbol{b(E_i, E_j)}$, if $E_i.e < E_j.s$ (same as Allen's *before*).
- E_i ***co-occurs*** with E_j, denoted as $\boldsymbol{c(E_i, E_j)}$, if $E_i.s \leq E_j.s \leq E_i.e$. That is, E_i starts before E_j and there is a nonempty time period where both E_i and E_j occur. Note that this relation covers the following Allen's relations: *meets*, *overlaps*, *is-finished-by*, *contains*, *starts* and *equals*.

3.4 Temporal Patterns

In order to obtain temporal descriptions of the data, basic states are combined using temporal relations to form temporal patterns (time interval patterns). In the previous section, we defined the relation between two states to be either *before* (*b*) or *co-occurs* (*c*). In order to define relations between k states, we use Höppner's representation of temporal patterns [11].

DEFINITION 1. ***(Temporal Pattern)*** *A temporal pattern is defined as $P = (\langle S_1, ..., S_k \rangle, R)$ where S_i is the ith state of the pattern and R is an upper triangular matrix that defines the temporal relations between each state and all of its following states: $i \in \{1, ..., k-1\} \wedge j \in \{i+1, ..., k\} : R_{i,j} \in \{b, c\}$ specifies the relation between S_i and S_j.*

The size of a temporal pattern P is the number of states it contains. If P contains k states, we say that P is a *k-pattern*. Hence, a single state is a *1-pattern* (a singleton). We also denote the space of all temporal patterns of arbitrary size by ***TP***.

Figure 4 shows a graphical representation of a *4-pattern* $\langle S_1 = (C, H), S_2 = (G, N), S_3 = (B, H), S_4 = (G, H) \rangle$, where the states are abstractions of temporal variables creatinine (C), glucose (G) and BUN (Blood Urea Nitrogen) (B). The half matrix on the right represents the temporal relations between every state and the states that follow it. For example, the first state S_1 *co-occurs* with the third state S_3: $R_{1,3} = c$.

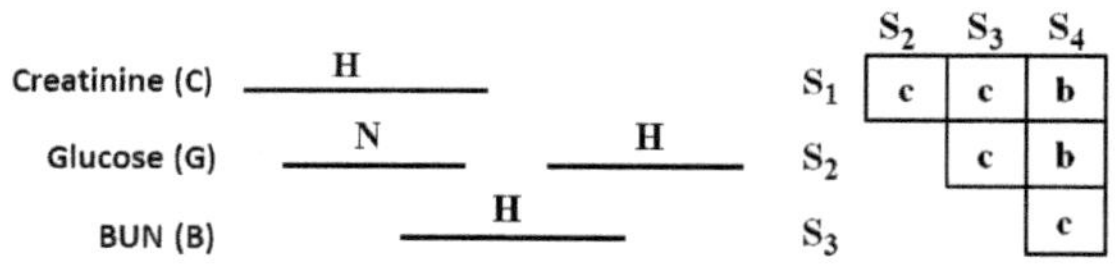

Figure 4: A temporal pattern with states $\langle (C, H), (G, N), (B, H), (G, H) \rangle$ and temporal relations $R_{1,2} = c$, $R_{1,3} = c$, $R_{1,4} = b$, $R_{2,3} = c$, $R_{2,4} = b$ and $R_{3,4} = c$.

DEFINITION 2. *Given an MSS $Z = \langle\, E_1, E_2, ..., E_l \,\rangle$ and a temporal pattern $P = (\langle S_1, ..., S_k \rangle, R)$, we say that Z **contains** P, denoted as $\boldsymbol{P \in Z}$, if there is an injective mapping π from the states of P to the state intervals of Z such that:*

$$\forall i \in \{1, ..., k\} : \; S_i.F = E_{\pi(i)}.F \;\wedge\; S_i.V = E_{\pi(i)}.V$$

$$\forall i \in \{1, ..., k-1\} \wedge j \in \{i+1, ..., k\} : \; R_{i,j}\left(E_{\pi(i)}, E_{\pi(j)}\right)$$

The definition says that checking whether an MSS contains a *k-pattern* requires: 1) matching all k states of the pattern and 2) checking that all $k(k-1)/2$ temporal relations are satisfied. As an example, the MSS in Figure 2 contains the temporal pattern $P = (\langle\, (C, N), (G, N) \,\rangle, R_{1,2} = c)$ (normal creatinine *co-occurs* with normal glucose). To improve readability, we usually write *2-patterns* of the form $(\langle S_1, S_2 \rangle, R_{1,2})$ simply as $S_1\ R_{1,2}\ S_2$. That is, we can write $P = (C, N)\ c\ (G, N)$.

4. MINING RECENT TEMPORAL PATTERNS

4.1 Recent Temporal Patterns

In the event detection setting, each training temporal instance x_i (e.g. an electronic health record) is associated with class label y_i at time t_i (e.g. whether or not a medical condition is detected). Consequently, recent measurements of the variables of x_i (close to t_i) are usually more predictive than distant measurements, as was shown in [25] for clinical data. In the following, we present the definitions of recent state intervals and recent temporal patterns.

DEFINITION 3. *Given an MSS $Z = \langle E_1, E_2, ..., E_l \rangle$ and a maximum gap parameter g, we say that $E_j \in Z$ is a* ***recent state interval*** *in Z, denoted as $\boldsymbol{r_g(E_j, Z)}$, if* ***any*** *of the following two conditions are satisfied:*

- $\nexists E_k \in Z : E_k.F = E_j.F \wedge k > j$
- $Z.end - E_j.e \leq g$

The first condition is satisfied if E_j is the most recent state interval in its variable ($E_j.F$) and the second condition is satisfied if E_j is less than g time units away from the end of the MSS ($Z.end$). Note that if $g = \infty$, any $E_j \in Z$ is considered to be recent.

DEFINITION 4. ***(RTP)*** *Given an MSS $Z = \langle E_1, E_2, ..., E_l \rangle$ and a maximum gap parameter g, we say that temporal pattern $P = (\langle S_1, ..., S_k \rangle, R)$ is a* ***Recent Temporal Pattern (RTP)*** *in Z, denoted as $\boldsymbol{R_g(P, Z)}$, if* ***all*** *the following conditions are satisfied:*

1. *$P \in Z$ with a mapping π from the states of P to the state intervals of Z*
2. *S_k matches a recent state interval in Z: $r_g(E_{\pi(k)}, Z)$*
3. *$\forall i \in \{1, ..., k-1\}$, S_i and S_{i+1} match state intervals not more than g away from each other: $E_{\pi(i+1)}.s - E_{\pi(i)}.e \leq g$*

The definition says that in order for temporal pattern P to be an *RTP* in MSS Z, 1) P should be contained in Z (Definition 2), 2) the last state of P should map to a recent state interval in Z (Definition 3), and 3) any pair of consecutive states in P should map to state intervals that are "close to each other". This forces the pattern to be close to the end of Z and to have a limited temporal extension in the past. Note that g is a parameter that specifies the restrictiveness of the *RTP* definition. If $g = \infty$, any pattern $P \in Z$ would be considered to be an *RTP* in Z. When an *RTP* contains k states, we call it a *k-RTP*.

EXAMPLE 2. *Let Z_i be the MSS in Figure 2 and let the maximum gap parameter be $g = 5$ days. Temporal pattern $P_1 = (C, N)\ b\ (G, VH)$ is an RTP in Z_i because $P_1 \in Z_i$, $(G, VH, 16, 23)$ is a recent state interval in Z_i, and $(C, N, 2, 14)$ is "close to" $(G, VH, 16, 23)$ $(16-14 \leq g)$. On the other hand, $P_2 = (G, H)\ b\ (G, N)$ is not an RTP in Z_i because $(G, N, 6, 9)$ is not a recent state interval.*

DEFINITION 5. ***(Suffix)*** *Given temporal patterns $P = (\langle S_1, ..., S_{k_1} \rangle, R)$ and $P' = (\langle S'_1, ..., S'_{k_2} \rangle, R')$ with $k_1 \leq k_2$, we say that P is a* ***suffix subpattern*** *of P', denoted as* ***Suffix(P, P')***, *if:*

$$\forall i \in \{1, ..., k_1\} \wedge j \in \{i+1, ..., k_1\} :$$
$$S_i = S'_{i+k2-k1} \wedge R_{i,j} = R'_{i+k2-k1, j+k2-k1}$$

If P is a suffix subpattern of P', we say that P' is a **backward-extension superpattern** of P.

PROPOSITION 1. *Given an MSS Z and temporal patterns P and P', $R_g(P', Z) \wedge Suffix(P, P') \Rightarrow R_g(P, Z)$*

The proof directly follows from Definition 4.

EXAMPLE 3. *Assume that $P = (\langle S_1, S_2\ S_3 \rangle, R_{1,2}, R_{1,3}, R_{2,3})$ is an RTP in Z. Proposition 1 says that its suffix subpattern $(\langle S_2, S_3 \rangle, R_{2,3})$ must also be an RTP in Z. However, this does not imply that $(\langle S_1, S_2 \rangle, R_{1,2})$ must be an RTP (the second condition of Definition 4 may be violated) nor that $(\langle S_1, S_3 \rangle, R_{1,3})$ must be an RTP (the third condition of Definition 4 may be violated).*

DEFINITION 6. ***(Frequent RTP)*** *Given a dataset D of MSS, a maximum gap parameter g and a minimum support threshold σ, we define the support of an RTP P as* ***RTP-sup$_g$(P, D)*** $= |\{Z_i : Z_i \in D \wedge R_g(P, Z_i)\}|$. *We say that P is a* ***frequent RTP*** *in D given σ if RTP-sup$_g(P, D) \geq \sigma$.*

Note that Proposition 1 implies the following property of *RTP-sup*, which we will use in our algorithm for mining frequent *RTPs*.

$$\forall P, P' \in TP, Suffix(P, P') \Rightarrow RTP\text{-}sup_g(P, D) \geq RTP\text{-}sup_g(P', D)$$

4.2 The Mining Algorithm

In this section, we present the algorithm for mining frequent *RTPs*. We chose to utilize the class information and *mine frequent RTPs from each class label separately using local minimum supports* as opposed to mining frequent *RTPs* from the entire data using a single global minimum support. The approach is reasonable when pattern mining is applied in the supervised setting because 1) for unbalanced data, mining frequent patterns using a global minimum support threshold may result in missing many important patterns in the rare classes and 2) mining patterns that are frequent in one of the classes (hence potentially predictive for that class) is more efficient than mining patterns that are globally frequent.

The algorithm takes as input D_y: the MSS from class y, g: the maximum gap parameter and σ_y: the local minimum support threshold for class y. It outputs all temporal patterns that satisfy:

$$\{P \in TP : RTP\text{-}sup_g(P, D_y) \geq \sigma_y\}$$

The mining algorithm performs a level-wise search. It first scans the database to find all frequent *1-RTPs* (recent states). Then it extends the patterns ***backward in time*** to find more complex temporal patterns. For each level k, the algorithm performs the following two phases to obtain the frequent *(k+1)-RTPs*:

1. **The candidate generation phase:** Generate candidate *(k+1)-patterns* by extending frequent *k-RTPs* backward in time.
2. **The counting phase:** Obtain the frequent *(k+1)-RTPs* by removing the candidates with *RTP-sup* less than σ_y.

This process repeats until no more frequent *RTPs* can be found.

In the following, we describe in details the candidate generation algorithm. Then we proposed techniques to improve the efficiency of candidate generation and counting.

4.2.1 Backward Candidate Generation

We generate a candidate *(k+1)-pattern* by appending a new state (*1-pattern*) to the beginning of a frequent *k-RTP*. Let us assume that we are backward extending pattern $P = (\langle S_1, ..., S_k \rangle, R)$ with state S_{new} to generate candidates of the form $(\langle S'_1, ..., S'_{k+1} \rangle, R')$. First of all, we set $S'_1 = S_{new}$, $S'_{i+1} = S_i$ for $i \in \{1, ..., k\}$ and $R'_{i+1, j+1} = R_{i,j}$ for $i \in \{1, ..., k-1\} \wedge j \in \{i+1, ..., k\}$. This way, we know that every candidate P' of this form is a *backward-extension superpattern* of P: *Suffix(P, P')*.

In order to fully define a candidate, we still need to specify the temporal relations between the new state S'_1 and states $S'_2, ..., S'_{k+1}$, i.e., we should define $R'_{1,i}$ for $i \in \{2, ..., k+1\}$. Since we have two possible temporal relations (*before* and *co-occurs*), there are 2^k possible ways to specify the missing relations, resulting in 2^k different candidates. Let L denote all possible states and let F_k denote all frequent *k-RTPs*, generating the *(k+1)-candidates* **naively** in this fashion results in $2^k \times |L| \times |F_k|$ different candidates.

This large number of candidates makes the mining algorithm computationally very expensive and limits its scalability. Below, we describe the concept of incoherent patterns and introduce a method that generates fewer candidates without missing any real pattern from the mining results.

4.2.2 *Improving the Efficiency of Candidate Generation*

DEFINITION 7. *A temporal pattern P is* ***incoherent*** *if there does not exist any valid MSS that contains P.*

Clearly, we do not have to generate and count incoherent candidates because we know that they will have zero support in the data. We introduce the following two lemmas to avoid generating incoherent candidates when specifying the relations $R'_{1,i} : i \in \{2, ..., k+1\}$ in candidates of the form $P' = (\langle S'_1, ..., S'_{k+1}\rangle, R')$.

LEMMA 1. *$P' = (\langle S'_1, ..., S'_{k+1}\rangle, R')$ is incoherent if $\exists i \in \{2, ..., k+1\} : R'_{1,i} = c$ and $S'_1.F = S'_i.F$.*

Two state intervals from the same temporal variable cannot co-occur because temporal abstraction segments each variable into non-overlapping state intervals.

LEMMA 2. *$P' = (\langle S'_1, ..., S'_{k+1}\rangle, R')$ is incoherent if $\exists i \in \{2, ..., k+1\} : R'_{1,i} = c \wedge \exists j \in \{2, ..., i-1\} : R'_{1,j} = b$.*

PROOF. Let us assume that there exists an MSS $Z = \langle E_1, ..., E_l\rangle$ where $P' \in Z$. Let π be the mapping from the states of P' to the state intervals of Z. The definition of temporal patterns and the fact that state intervals in Z are ordered by their start values implies that the matching state intervals $\langle E_{\pi(1)}, ..., E_{\pi(k+1)}\rangle$ are also ordered by their start times: $E_{\pi(1)}.s \leq ... \leq E_{\pi(k+1)}.s$. Hence, $E_{\pi(j)}.s \leq E_{\pi(i)}.s$ since $j < i$. We also know that $E_{\pi(1)}.e < E_{\pi(j)}.s$ because $R'_{1,j} = b$. Therefore, $E_{\pi(1)}.e < E_{\pi(i)}.s$. However, since $R'_{1,i} = c$, then $E_{\pi(1)}.e \geq E_{\pi(i)}.s$, which is a contradiction. Therefore, there is no MSS that contains P'. □

EXAMPLE 4. *Assume we want to extend $P = (\langle S_1 = (C, H), S_2 = (G, N), S_3 = (B, H), S_4 = (G, H)\rangle, R)$ in Figure 4 with state $S_{new} = (G, H)$ to generate candidates of the form $(\langle S'_1 = (G, H), S'_2 = (C, H), S'_3 = (G, N), S'_4 = (B, H), S'_5 = (G, H)\rangle, R')$. The relation between S'_1 and S'_2 is allowed to be either before or co-occurs: $R'_{1,2} = b$ or $R'_{1,2} = c$. However, according to Lemma 1, $R'_{1,3} \neq c$ because both S'_1 and S'_3 belong to the same temporal variable (G), which in turn implies that $R'_{1,4} \neq c$ and $R'_{1,5} \neq c$ according to Lemma 2. By removing incoherent patterns, we reduce the number of candidates that result from adding (G, H) to 4-RTP P from $2^4 = 16$ to only 2.*

THEOREM 1. *There are at most $k+1$ coherent candidates that result from backward extending a single k-RTP with a new state.*

PROOF. We know that every candidate $P' = (\langle S'_1, ..., S'_{k+1}\rangle, R')$ corresponds to a specific assignment of $R'_{1,i} \in \{b, c\}$ for $i \in \{2, ...k+1\}$. When we assign the temporal relations, once a relation becomes *before*, all the following relations have to be *before* as well according to Lemma 2. We can see that the relations can be *co-occurs* in the beginning of the pattern, but once we see a *before* relation at point $q \in \{2, ..., k+1\}$ in the pattern, all subsequent relations $(i > q)$ should be *before* as well:

$$R'_{1,i} = c : i \in \{2, ..., q-1\}; \quad R'_{1,i} = b : i \in \{q, ..., k+1\}$$

Therefore, the total number of coherent candidates cannot be more than $k+1$, which is the total number of different combinations of consecutive *co-occurs* relations followed by consecutive *before* relations. □

In some cases, the number of coherent candidates is less than $k+1$. Assume that there are some states in P' that belong to the same variable as state S'_1. Let S'_j be the first such state $(j \leq k+1)$. According to Lemma 1, $R'_{1,j} \neq c$. In this case, the number of coherent candidates is $j-1 < k+1$.

Algorithm 1 illustrates how to extend a *k-RTP P* with a new state S_{new} to generate coherent candidates (without violating Lemmas 1 and 2).

ALGORITHM 1: Extend backward a *k-RTP* P with a state S_{new}.

Input: A *k-RTP*: $P = (\langle S_1, ..., S_k\rangle, R)$; a new state: S_{new}
Output: Coherent candidates: C

$S'_1 = S_{new}$; $S'_{i+1} = S_i : i \in \{1, ..., k\}$;
$R'_{i+1,j+1} = R_{i,j} : i \in \{1, ..., k-1\}, j \in \{i+1, ..., k\}$;
$R'_{1,i} = b : i \in \{2, ..., k+1\}$; $P' = (\langle S'_1, ..., S'_{k+1}\rangle, R')$;
$C = \{P'\}$;
for *i=2* **to** *k+1* **do**
  if $(S'_1.F = S'_i.F)$ **then**
    break;
  else
    $R'_{1,i} = c$; $P' = (\langle S'_1, ..., S'_{k+1}\rangle, R')$;
    $C = C \cup \{P'\}$;
  end
end
return C

COROLLARY 1. *Let L denote all possible states and let F_k denote all frequent k-RTPs. The number of coherent (k+1)-candidates is always less or equal to $(k+1) \times |L| \times |F_k|$.*

4.2.3 *Improving the Efficiency of Counting*

Even after eliminating incoherent patterns, the mining algorithm is still computationally expensive because for every candidate, we need to scan the *entire database* in the counting phase to determine its *RTP-sup*. The question we try to answer in this section is whether we can omit portions of the database that are guaranteed not to contain the candidate we want to count. The proposed solution is inspired by [32] that introduced the *vertical format* for itemset mining and later applied it for sequential pattern mining [31].

Let us associate every frequent *RTP P* with a list of identifiers for all MSS that have P as an *RTP* (Definition 4):

$$P.RTP\text{-}list = \langle i_1, i_2, ..., i_n\rangle : Z_{i_j} \in D_y \wedge R_g(P, Z_{i_j})$$

Clearly, $RTP\text{-}sup_g(P, D_y) = |P.RTP\text{-}list|$.

Let us also associate every state S with a list of identifiers for all MSS that contain S (Definition 2):

$$S.list = \langle q_1, q_2, ..., q_m\rangle : Z_{q_j} \in D_y \wedge S \in Z_{q_j}$$

Now, when we generate candidate P' by backward extending *RTP P* with state S, we define the potential list (***p-RTP-list***) of P' as follows:

$$P'.p\text{-}RTP\text{-}list = P.RTP\text{-}list \cap S.list$$

PROPOSITION 2. *Let P' be a backward-extension of RTP P with state S: P'.RTP-list $\subseteq$ P'.p-RTP-list*

PROOF. Assume Z_i is an MSS such that $R_g(P', Z_i)$. By definition, $i \in P'.RTP\text{-}list$. We know that $R_g(P', Z_i) \Rightarrow P' \in Z_i \Rightarrow S \in Z_i \Rightarrow i \in S.list$. Also, we know that *Suffix*(P, P') (Definition 5) $\Rightarrow R_g(P, Z_i)$ (Proposition 1) $\Rightarrow i \in P.RTP\text{-}list$. Therefore, $i \in P.RTP\text{-}list \cap S.list = P'.p\text{-}RTP\text{-}list$ □

Putting it all together, we compute the *RTP-lists* in the counting phase (based on the true matches) and the *p-RTP-lists* in the candidate generation phase. The key idea is that when we count candidate P', we only need to check the instances in its *p-RTP-list* because according to Proposition 2: $i \notin P'.p\text{-}RTP\text{-}list \Rightarrow i \notin P'.RTP\text{-}list \Rightarrow P'$ is not an *RTP* in Z_i. This offers a lot of computational savings because the *p-RTP-lists* get smaller as the size of the patterns increases, making the counting phase much faster.

Algorithm 2 outlines the candidate generation. Line 4 generates coherent candidates using Algorithm 1. Line 6 computes the *p-RTP-list* for each candidate. Note that the cost of the intersection is *linear* because the lists are always sorted according to the order of the instances in the database. Line 7 applies an *additional pruning* to remove candidates that are guaranteed not to be frequent according to the following implication of Proposition 2:

$$|P'.p\text{-}RTP\text{-}list| < \sigma_y \Longrightarrow |P'.RTP\text{-}list| = RTP\text{-}sup_g(P, D_y) < \sigma_y$$

ALGORITHM 2: A high-level description of candidate generation.

Input: All frequent *k-RTPs*: F_k; all frequent states: L
Output: Candidate *(k+1)-patterns*: $Cand$, with their *p-RTP-lists*

```
1  Cand = Φ;
2  foreach P ∈ F_k do
3  |  foreach S ∈ L do
4  |  |  C = extend_backward(P, S);     (Algorithm 1)
5  |  |  for q = 1 to | C | do
6  |  |  |  C[q].p-RTP-list = P.RTP-list ∩ S.list;
7  |  |  |  if ( | C[q].p-RTP-list | ≥ σ_y ) then
8  |  |  |  |  Cand = Cand ∪ {C[q]};
9  |  |  |  end
10 |  |  end
11 |  end
12 end
13 return Cand
```

4.3 Learning the Classifier

In this section, we summarize our approach for learning classification models for event detection problems. Given a training dataset $\{<\boldsymbol{x}_i, y_i>\}_{i=1}^n$, where x_i is a multivariate time series instance up to time t_i and y_i is a class label at t_i, apply the following steps:

1. Convert every instance x_i to an MSS Z_i using temporal abstraction.
2. Mine the frequent *RTPs* from the MSS of each class label separately and combine the class-specific *RTPs* to obtain the final result Ω.
3. Convert every MSS Z_i into a binary vector x'_i of size equal to $|\Omega|$, where $x'_{i,j}$ corresponds to a specific pattern $P_j \in \Omega$ and its value is 1 if $R_g(P_j, Z_i)$; and 0 otherwise.
4. Learn the classification model on the transformed binary representation of the training data $\{<\boldsymbol{x}'_i, y_i>\}_{i=1}^n$.

5. EXPERIMENTAL EVALUATION

In this section, we present our experiments on large-scale electronic health record (EHR) data collected for diabetic patients. We test our approach on the problem of detecting various types of disorders that are frequently associated with diabetes.

5.1 Dataset

The diabetes dataset consists of 13,558 records of adult diabetic patients (both type I and type II diabetes). Each patient's record consists of time series of 19 different lab values, including blood glucose, creatinine, glycosylated hemoglobin, blood urea nitrogen, liver function tests, cholesterol, etc. In addition, we have access to time series of ICD-9 diagnosis codes reflecting the diagnoses made for the patient over time. Overall, the database contains 602 different ICD-9 codes. These codes were grouped by our medical expert into nine major categories: cardiovascular disease, renal disease, peripheral vascular disease, neurological disease, metabolic disease, inflammatory disease, ocular disease, cerebrovascular disease and hypertension. These disease categories are frequently associated with diabetes. Our objective is to learn models that are able to accurately diagnose these diseases More specifically, at any point in time, we are interested in assigning a label for the disorder the patient with the diabetes suffers from. We omit the hypertension category from the analysis because it occurred in almost all patients, making it difficult to find negative examples.

5.2 Experimental Setup

The experiments are performed separately for each of the 8 major diagnosis categories (diseases). For each category, we divide the data into cases (positives) and controls (negatives) as follows:

- The *cases* are records of patients with the target disease that include clinical variables up to the time the disease was *first* diagnosed.
- The *controls* are selected randomly from the remaining patients (without the target disease) and they include clinical variables up to a randomly selected time point in the patient's record.

To avoid having uninformative training data, we discard instances that contain less than 10 lab measurements or that span less than 3 months (short instances). We choose the same number of controls as the number of cases for each category to make the datasets balanced. Table 1 shows the number of cases for each diagnosis category (the number of controls is the same).

To construct the features, we consider both the laboratory tests and the diagnosis codes. Note that the diagnosis of one or more disease categories may be predictive of the (first) occurrence of another disease, so it is important to include them as features. Laboratory tests are represented as numeric time series. We abstract them using value abstraction (see Section 3.1). Diagnosis categories, when used as features, are represented as intervals that start at the time of the diagnosis and extend until the end of the record.

5.3 Classification Performance

In this section, we test the ability of our *RTP* mining framework to represent and capture temporal patterns important for the prediction task. In particular, we compare the classification performance of the following feature construction methods:

1. ***Last_values:*** The features are formed from the most recent values of each clinical variable[6].

[6]The features are numeric for the laboratory variables (e.g., last creatinine value is 2.2) and binary for the disease categories (whether or not the disease was diagnosed).

Dx code	Description	# cases
CARDI	Cardiovascular disease	2,743
RENAL	Renal disease	3,355
PERIP	Peripheral vascular disease	3,370
NEURO	Neurological disease	2,193
METAB	Metabolic disease	968
INFLM	Inflammatory (infectious) disease	2,394
OCULR	Ocular (ophthalmologic) disease	2,245
CEREB	Cerebrovascular disease	2,824

Table 1: The eight major diagnosis categories (diseases) used in the diabetes study and the number of cases for each category. The number of controls is set to be the same as the number of cases.

2. ***TP:*** The features correspond to all frequent temporal patterns.
3. ***TP_sparse:*** The features correspond to the top 50 discriminative temporal patterns that are selected using a sparse linear model. These features are obtained by adjusting the cost parameter of an L_1 regularized support vector machine (SVM) classifier until at most 50 patterns are used for classification (features corresponding to other patterns are zeroed out).
4. ***RTP:*** The features correspond to all frequent *RTPs*.
5. ***RTP_sparse:*** The features correspond to the top 50 discriminative *RTPs* that are selected using a sparse linear model (similar to 3).

The first method is atemporal and only considers the most recent values for defining the classification features (a static transformation). On the other hand, methods (2-5) use temporal patterns (built using temporal abstractions and temporal relations) as their features (a dynamic transformation). For *TP* (*TP_sparse*), the feature value is one if the corresponding temporal pattern occurs anywhere in the instance (Definition 2), and zero otherwise. For *RTP* (*RTP_sparse*), the feature value is one if the corresponding temporal pattern occurs recently in the instance (Definition 3), and zero otherwise.

For methods (2-5), we set the local minimum supports (σ_y) to 15% of the number of instances in the class. For the *RTP* mining methods (4-5), we set the maximum gap parameter (g) to 6 months. The reason for including methods 3 and 5 is to test the ability of *TP* and *RTP* to represent the target disease using only a limited number of temporal patterns (50 patterns in our case).

We judged the quality of the different feature representations in terms of their induced classification performance. More specifically, we use the features extracted by each method to build a linear **SVM** classifier and evaluate its performance using the classification accuracy and the area under the ROC curve (AUC). We did not compare against other time series classification methods because most methods [24, 6, 28, 4] cannot be directly applied on multivariate irregularly sampled time series data.

Below, we show the classification accuracy (Table 2) and the AUC (Table 3) for each feature representation method on each classification task (major disease). All classification results are reported using averages obtained via *10-folds cross validation*.

The results show that features based on temporal patterns are beneficial for the classification task, since they outperform features based on most recent values (see for example the *NEURO*, *OCLUR* and *CARDI* datasets). The results also show that *RTP* and *RTP_sparse* mostly outperform *TP* and *TP_sparse*. It is important to note that although patterns generated by *TP* subsume the ones generated by *RTP* (by definition, every frequent *RTP* is also a frequent *TP*), the induced binary features are often different. For

Dataset	*Last_values*	*TP*	*TP_sparse*	*RTP*	*RTP_sparse*
CARDI	67.41	71.82	71.62	71.82	**71.98**
RENAL	77.71	76.38	76.66	78.08	**78.33**
PERIP	66.82	68.55	68.38	**70.01**	69.91
NEURO	64.66	68.95	68.33	69.18	**69.68**
METAB	72.83	**74.64**	73.61	73.3	73.09
INFLM	64.6	66.73	66.69	67.5	**67.94**
OCULR	65.83	**70.8**	70.71	68.82	69.22
CEREB	65.21	66.64	66.7	**67.93**	66.98

Table 2: The classification accuracy for the different feature representation methods (SVM is used for classification).

Dataset	*Last_values*	*TP*	*TP_sparse*	*RTP*	*RTP_sparse*
CARDI	75.1	80.13	79.61	80.18	**80.52**
RENAL	85.45	84.8	84.97	86.13	**86.23**
PERIP	74.38	76.08	75.95	77.88	**78.31**
NEURO	72.25	76.43	75.81	**77.34**	76.98
METAB	80.64	82.67	81.66	82.52	**82.97**
INFLM	71.04	73.62	73.43	74.39	**74.92**
OCULR	72.12	**78.34**	78.28	76.11	76.85
CEREB	72.23	73.46	74.42	**75.37**	75.18

Table 3: The area under the ROC curve (AUC) for the different feature representation methods (SVM is used for classification).

instance, a pattern that is not discriminative when considered in the entire records may become more discriminative when considered as a recent pattern. This can be seen clearly for the *RENAL* dataset, where *TP* and *TP_sparse* perform poorly because the discriminative signal is mostly contained in the recent values.

5.4 Knowledge Discovery

Figure 5 compares the number of temporal patterns that are extracted by frequent temporal pattern mining (*TP*) and by frequent *RTP* mining (*RTP*). Similar to the previous setting, we set the local minimum supports for both methods to 15% and we set the maximum gap parameter for *RTP* to 6 months.

The results show that the number of temporal patterns mined by *RTP* is at least an order of magnitude smaller than the number of patterns mined by *TP* for all datasets. This can facilitate the process of reviewing and validating the patterns by human experts.

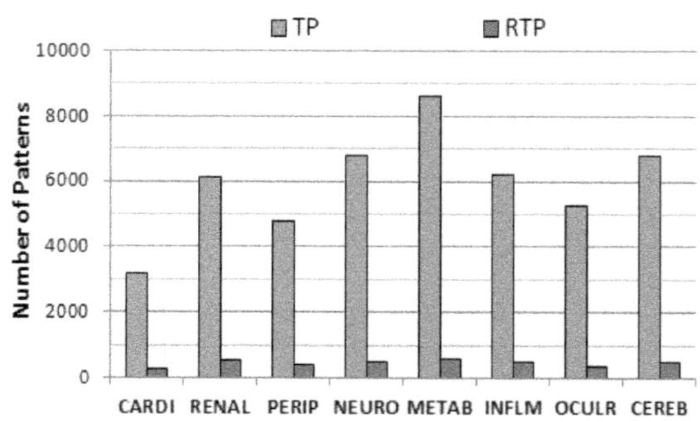

Figure 5: The number of temporal patterns of *TP* and *RTP* on all major diagnosis datasets (minimum support is 15%).

Table 4 shows some of the top predictive *RTPs* according to their precision (confidence)[7]. The first three *RTPs* (P_1, P_2 and P_3) are predicting renal (kidney) disease. These patterns relate the risk of renal problems with very high values of the BUN test (P_1), an increase in creatinine levels from normal to high (P_2), and high values of BUN co-occurring with high values of creatinine (P_3). P_4 shows that an increase in glucose levels from high to very high may indicate a metabolic disease. Finally, P_5 indicates that patients who were previously diagnosed with cardiovascular disease and exhibit an increase in glucose levels are prone to develop a cerebrovascular disease. These patterns, extracted automatically from data without incorporating prior clinical knowledge, are in accordance with the medical diagnosis guidelines.

RTP	*prec*	*recall*
P_1: *BUN=VH* ⇒ *Dx=RENAL*	0.97	0.17
P_2: *Creat=N before Creat=H* ⇒ *Dx=RENAL*	0.96	0.21
P_3: *BUN=H co-occurs Creat=H* ⇒ *Dx=RENAL*	0.95	0.21
P_4: *Gluc=H before Gluc=VH* ⇒ *Dx=METAB*	0.79	0.24
P_5: *Dx=CARDI co-occurs (Gluc=N before Gluc=H)* ⇒ *Dx=CEREB*	0.71	0.22

Table 4: Predictive *RTPs* with their precision (*prec*) and recall. Abbreviations: *Dx*: diagnosis code (one of the 8 major categories in Table 1); *BUN*: Blood Urea Nitrogen; *Creat*: creatinine; *Gluc*: blood glucose. Abstractions: *BUN=VH*: $>$ 49 mg/dl; *BUN=H*: $>$ 34 mg/dl; *Creat=H*: $>$ 1.8 mg/dl; *Creat=N*: [0.8-1.8] mg/dl; *Gluc=VH*: $>$ 243 mg/dl; *Gluc=H*: $>$ 191 mg/dl.

5.5 Mining Efficiency

In this section, we study the efficiency of different temporal pattern mining methods. In particular, we compare the running time of the following methods:

1. ***TP_Apriori:*** Mine frequent temporal patterns by extending the Apriori algorithm [1, 2] to the time interval domain. This method applies the Apriori pruning in the candidate generation phase to prune any candidate *k-pattern* if it contains an infrequent *(k-1)-patterns*.

2. ***RTP_no-lists:*** Mine frequent *RTPs* backward in time as described in this paper. However, this method does not apply the technique we propose in Section 4.2.3 to speed up the counting phase. This means that it scans the entire dataset for each candidate in order to compute its *RTP-sup* .

3. ***TP_lists:*** Mine frequent temporal patterns by extending the vertical format [32, 31] to the time interval domain as described in [5]. This method applies the Apriori pruning [1] in candidate generation and use id-lists to speed up the counting.

4. ***RTP_lists:*** Our proposed method for mining frequent *RTPs*.

To make the comparison fair, all methods apply the techniques we propose in Section 4.2.2 to avoid generating incoherent candidates. Note that if we do not remove incoherent candidates, the execution time for all methods greatly increases.

The experiments are conducted on a Dell PowerEdge R610 server with an Intel Xeon 3.3GHz CPU and 96GB of RAM. Similar to the previous settings, we set the local minimum supports to 15% and the maximum gap parameter to 6 months (unless stated otherwise).

[7]Most of the highest precision *RTPs* are predicting the RENAL category because it is the easiest prediction task. So to diversify the patterns, we show the top 3 predictive *RTPs* for RENAL and the top 2 predictive *RTPs* for other categories.

Figure 6 shows the execution time (in seconds) of the above methods on all major diagnosis datasets. We can see that our proposed *RTP_lists* method is much more efficient the other methods. For instance, on the *INFLM* dataset, *RTP_lists* is around 5 times faster than *TP_lists*, 10 times faster than *RTP_no-lists* and 30 times faster than *TP_Apriori*.

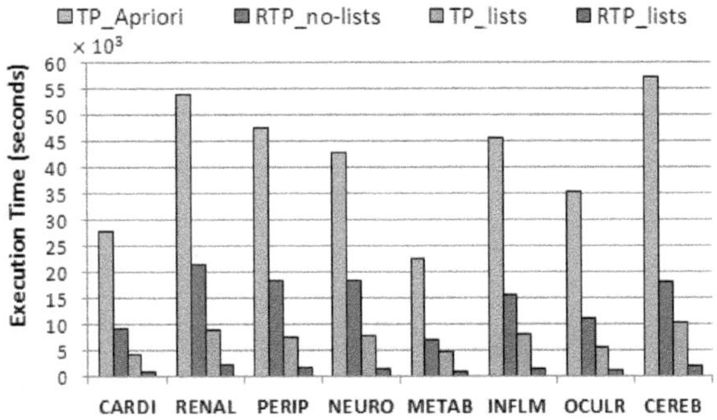

Figure 6: The mining time (in seconds) of *TP_Apriori*, *RTP_no-lists*, *TP_lists* and *RTP_lists* on all major diagnosis datasets (minimum support is 15%).

Figure 7 compares the execution time (in seconds) of the methods on the *CARDI* dataset for different minimum support thresholds. Note that the difference in the execution time between *RTP_lists* and the other methods becomes larger when the minimum support is low (10%).

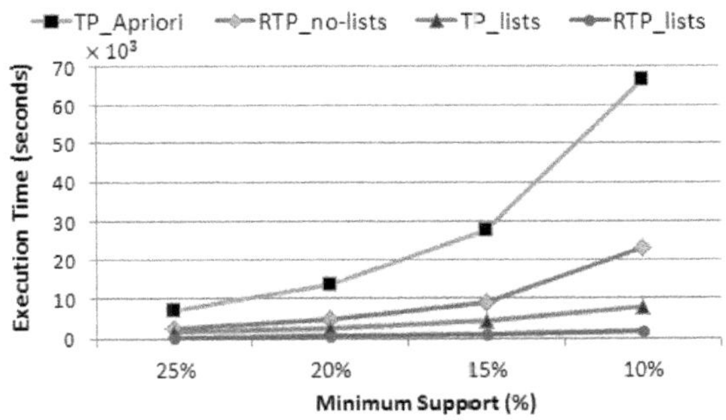

Figure 7: The mining time (in seconds) of *TP_Apriori*, *RTP_no-lists*, *TP_lists* and *RTP_lists* on the *CARDI* dataset for different minimum support values.

Finally, let us examine the effect of the maximum gap parameter (g) on the efficiency of recent temporal pattern mining. Figure 8 shows the execution time (in seconds) of all methods on the *CARDI* dataset for different values of g (the execution time of *TP_Apriori* and *TP_lists* does not depend of g).

Clearly, the execution time of both *RTP_no-lists* and *RTP_lists* increases with g because the search space becomes larger (more temporal patterns become *RTPs*). The figure shows that when the maximum gap is 21 months, *RTP_no-lists* becomes slower than *TP_Apriori*. The reason is that for large values of g, applying the Apriori pruning [1] in candidate generation becomes more efficient (generates less candidates) than the backward extension of temporal patterns (see Example 3). On the other hand, *RTP_lists* increases much slower with g and maintains its efficiency advantage over *TP_lists* for larger values of g.

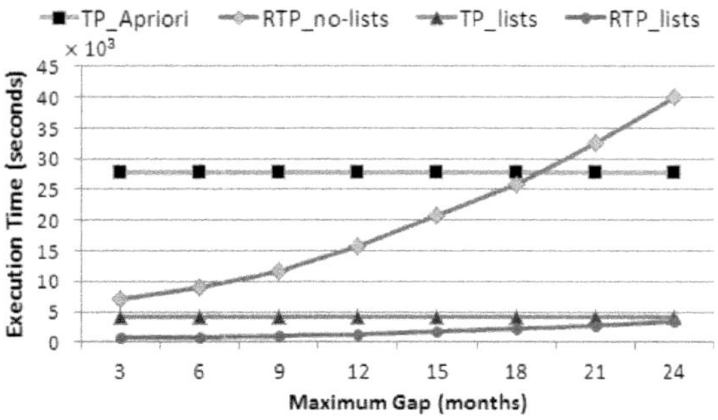

Figure 8: The mining time (in seconds) of *TP_Apriori*, *RTP_no-list*, *TP_lists* and *RTP_lists* on the *CARDI* dataset for different maximum gap values (in months). The minimum support is 15%.

6. CONCLUSION

The increasing availability of large temporal datasets prompts the development of scalable and more efficient temporal pattern mining techniques. Methods for mining sequential (time-point) data were first introduced in the literature starting in the mid-1990 [2, 31, 18, 30]. Since then, these methods have been extended to mining time interval data [22, 11, 17, 14, 26, 27, 15]. Unfortunately, mining the entire set of temporal patterns (sequential patterns or time-interval patterns) from large-scale datasets is inherently a computationally expensive task. To alleviate this problem, temporal constraints (e.g., restricting the total pattern duration or restricting the permitted gap between consecutive events in a pattern) have been proposed to scale up the mining [19].

In this paper, we proposed a new class of temporal constraints for finding Recent Temporal Patterns (*RTPs*), which are particularly important for monitoring and event detection problems. We presented an efficient algorithm that mines time-interval patterns backward in time, starting from patterns related to the most recent observations. Our experimental evaluation on EHRs for diabetes patients showed that the *RTP* framework is very useful to efficiently find patterns that are important for predicting various types of disorders associated with diabetes.

7. ACKNOWLEDGMENTS

This work was supported by grants 1R21LM009102-01A1, 1R01LM010019-01A1, 1R01GM088224-01 and T15LM007059-24 from the NIH. Its content is solely the responsibility of the authors and does not necessarily represent the official views of the NIH.

8. REFERENCES

[1] R. Agrawal and R. Srikant. Fast algorithms for mining association rules in large databases. In *Proceedings of VLDB*, 1994.

[2] R. Agrawal and R. Srikant. Mining sequential patterns. In *Proceedings of ICDE*, 1995.

[3] F. Allen. Towards a general theory of action and time. *Artificial Intelligence, 23:123-154*, 1984.

[4] I. Batal and M. Hauskrecht. A supervised time series feature extraction technique using dct and dwt. In *Proceedings of ICMLA*, 2009.

[5] I. Batal, H. Valizadegan, G. F. Cooper, and M. Hauskrecht. A pattern mining approach for classifying multivariate temporal data. In *Proceedings of the IEEE international conference on bioinformatics and biomedicine (BIBM)*, 2011.

[6] S. Blasiak and H. Rangwala. A hidden markov model variant for sequence classification. In *Proceedings of the International Joint Conferences on Artificial Intelligence (IJCAI)*, 2011.

[7] V. Chandola, E. Eilertson, L. Ertoz, G. Simon, and V. Kumar. *Data Warehousing and Data Mining Techniques for Computer Security*, chapter :Data Mining for Cyber Security. Springer, 2006.

[8] T. P. Exarchos, M. G. Tsipouras, C. Papaloukas, and D. I. Fotiadis. A two-stage methodology for sequence classification based on sequential pattern mining and optimization. *Data and Knowledge Engineering*, 66:467–487, 2008.

[9] S. Guttormsson, I. Marks, R.J., M. El-Sharkawi, and I. Kerszenbaum. Elliptical novelty grouping for on-line short-turn detection of excited running rotors. *IEEE Transactions on Energy Conversion*, 1999.

[10] M. Hauskrecht, M. Valko, I. Batal, G. Clermont, S. Visweswaram, and G. Cooper. Conditional outlier detection for clinical alerting. In *Proceedings of AMIA*, 2010.

[11] F. Höppner. *Knowledge Discovery from Sequential Data*. PhD thesis, Technical University Braunschweig, Germany, 2003.

[12] G. Ifrim and C. Wiuf. Bounded coordinate-descent for biological sequence classification in high dimensional predictor space. In *Proceedings of the international conference on Knowledge Discovery and Data mining (SIGKDD)*, 2011.

[13] L. Li, B. A. Prakash, and C. Faloutsos. Parsimonious linear fingerprinting for time series. *PVLDB*, 3:385–396, 2010.

[14] F. Moerchen. Algorithms for time series knowledge mining. In *Proceedings of SIGKDD*, pages 668–673, 2006.

[15] R. Moskovitch and Y. Shahar. Medical temporal-knowledge discovery via temporal abstraction. In *Proceedings of AMIA*, 2009.

[16] S. Papadimitriou, J. Sun, and C. Faloutsos. Streaming pattern discovery in multiple time-series. In *Proceedings of VLDB*, 2005.

[17] P. Papapetrou, G. Kollios, and S. Sclaroff. Discovering frequent arrangements of temporal intervals. In *Proceedings of ICDM*, 2005.

[18] J. Pei, J. Han, B. Mortazavi-asl, H. Pinto, Q. Chen, U. Dayal, and M. chun Hsu. Prefixspan: Mining sequential patterns efficiently by prefix-projected pattern growth. In *Proceedings of the 17th International Conference on Data Engineering (ICDE)*, 2001.

[19] J. Pei, J. Han, and W. Wang. Constraint-based sequential pattern mining: the pattern-growth methods. *Journal of Intelligent Information Systems*, 28:133–160, 2007.

[20] C. Ratanamahatana and E. J. Keogh. Three myths about dynamic time warping data mining. In *Proceedings of the SIAM International Conference on Data Mining (SDM)*, 2005.

[21] Y. Shahar. A Framework for Knowledge-Based Temporal Abstraction. *Artificial Intelligence, 90:79-133*, 1997.

[22] P. shan Kam and A. W. chee Fu. Discovering temporal patterns for interval-based events. In *Proceedings of the DaWaK*, 2000.

[23] A. Srivastava, A. Kundu, S. Sural, and A. Majumdar. Credit card fraud detection using hidden markov model. *IEEE Transactions on Dependable and Secure Computing*, 2008.

[24] D. L. Vail, M. M. Veloso, and J. D. Lafferty. Conditional random fields for activity recognition. In *Proceedings of the international joint conference on Autonomous agents and multiagent systems (AAMAS)*, 2007.

[25] M. Valko and M. Hauskrecht. Feature importance analysis for patient management decisions. In *Proceedings of MedInfo*, 2010.

[26] E. Winarko and J. F. Roddick. Armada - an algorithm for discovering richer relative temporal association rules from interval-based data. *Data and Knowledge Engineering*, 63:76–90, 2007.

[27] S.-Y. Wu and Y.-L. Chen. Mining nonambiguous temporal patterns for interval-based events. *IEEE Transactions on Knowledge and Data Engineering*, 19:742–758, 2007.

[28] X. Xi, E. Keogh, C. Shelton, L. Wei, and C. A. Ratanamahatana. Fast time series classification using numerosity reduction. In *Proceedings of the International Conference on Machine Learning (ICML)*, 2006.

[29] K. Yang and C. Shahabi. A pca-based similarity measure for multivariate time series. In *Proceedings of the international workshop on Multimedia databases*, 2004.

[30] M. yen Lin and S. yin Lee. Fast discovery of sequential patterns through memory indexing and database partitioning. *Journal Information Science and Engineering*, 21:109–128, 2005.

[31] M. Zaki. Spade: An efficient algorithm for mining frequent sequences. *Machine Learning*, 42:31–60, 2001.

[32] M. J. Zaki. Scalable algorithms for association mining. *IEEE Transactions on Knowledge and Data Engineering*, 2000.

A Shapelet Transform for Time Series Classification

Jason Lines
University of East Anglia
Norwich, Norfolk
United Kingdom
j.lines@uea.ac.uk

Luke M. Davis
University of East Anglia
Norwich, Norfolk
United Kingdom
luke.davis@uea.ac.uk

Jon Hills
University of East Anglia
Norwich, Norfolk
United Kingdom
j.hills@uea.ac.uk

Anthony Bagnall
University of East Anglia
Norwich, Norfolk
United Kingdom
anthony.bagnall@uea.ac.uk

ABSTRACT

The problem of time series classification (TSC), where we consider any real-valued ordered data a time series, presents a specific machine learning challenge as the ordering of variables is often crucial in finding the best discriminating features. One of the most promising recent approaches is to find shapelets within a data set. A shapelet is a time series subsequence that is identified as being representative of class membership. The original research in this field embedded the procedure of finding shapelets within a decision tree. We propose disconnecting the process of finding shapelets from the classification algorithm by proposing a shapelet transformation. We describe a means of extracting the k best shapelets from a data set in a single pass, and then use these shapelets to transform data by calculating the distances from a series to each shapelet. We demonstrate that transformation into this new data space can improve classification accuracy, whilst retaining the explanatory power provided by shapelets.

Categories and Subject Descriptors

H.2.8 [**Database Management**]: Database Applications—*Data Mining*

Keywords

time series, shapelet, filter, transformation

1. INTRODUCTION

The problem of time series classification (TSC), in which we consider any real-valued ordered data a time series, presents a specific machine learning challenge as the ordering of variables is often crucial in finding the best discriminating features. Until recently, the vast majority of data mining TSC research has focused on alternative distance measures for 1-Nearest Neighbour (1-NN) classifiers based on either the raw data, or on compressions or smoothing of the raw data (see [7] for a comprehensive summary). Despite the evidence in favour of 1-NN classifiers with Euclidean or Dynamic Time Warping (DTW) distance, there has been a spate of recent research proposing alternative approaches. These include shapelets [13, 20, 19], weighted dynamic time warping [10], support vector machines built on variable intervals [16], tree based ensembles constructed on summary statistics [6], fusion of alternative distance measures [2], and transform-based ensembles [1]. We consider the shapelet approach one of the most promising of these new methods.

A shapelet is a time series subsequence that is representative of class membership. The initial shapelet-based classification algorithm is proposed in [19]. The algorithm constructs a decision tree classifier by recursively searching for a discriminatory shapelet on data split via an information gain measure, calculated on the distance to the branching shapelet. The distance between a shapelet and a full series is defined as the closest subsequence in the series to the shapelet, as measured by the normalised Euclidean distance. This was extended by the research presented in [13], where they describe a form of oblique/multi-variate decision tree that uses a branching condition based on conjunctions or disjunctions of shapelets. Shapelets have also been used in futher applications, such as early classification [18] and gesture recognition [8].

Classification with shapelets offers several benefits over competing approaches. Firstly, shapelets are directly interpretable and can offer explanatory insights into the problem domain. Secondly, the shapelet classifier is more compact than many of the alternatives, and hence classifying new instances is faster. Thirdly, shapelets allow for the detection of phase-independent shape-based similarity of subsequences. This type of similarity is often hard to detect with algorithms based on whole series.

In both [20] and [13], the shapelet algorithm is embedded within the decision tree classifier. Whilst decision trees are highly interpretable, they are often outperformed by other classifiers and have a tendency to overfit unless post-pruned or used with a conservative stopping condition. Furthermore, the recursive nature of the decision tree algorithm means that the relatively time-consuming shapelet detection method is called repeatedly. Techniques that significantly speed up the

KDD'12, August 12–16, 2012, Beijing, China.

shapelet search are described in [13], but it is still a costly operation, especially with multi-class problems.

In [1] we show that transforming a TSC problem into an alternative data space prior to classification can provide a greater level of improvement than developing classifier refinements. Hence, we propose a shapelet transform that creates a new classification data set independently of the classifier. By doing so, we wish to increase classification accuracy while reducing training time and maintaining the interpretability of the model. The essence of the technique is to find the best k shapelets and then derive a new attribute for each shapelet, where the attribute value represents the distance from each case to a shapelet. In doing so, we have introduced several alterations to the shapelet algorithm. Our contributions can be summarised as follows:

1. We introduce a caching algorithm to store the k best shapelets from a data set in a single pass.
2. We propose an alternative shapelet evaluation method that is easier to use with multi-class problems.
3. We evaluate our proposed algorithms and compare them with the tree-based shapelet algorithm.

The paper is structured as follows. Section 2 provides background into time series classification and summarises the shapelet algorithms proposed in [19, 20]. In Section 3, we describe the changes we have made to the shapelet algorithm and propose a way of generating a shapelet transform. In Section 4, we describe our experimental design, and in Section 5, we evaluate the proposed algorithms. Finally, in Section 6, we form our conclusions and discuss future work.

2. BACKGROUND

2.1 Time Series Classification

A time series is a sequence of data that is typically recorded in temporal order at fixed intervals of time. For the problem of time series classification, suppose we have a set of n time series, $\mathbf{T} = \{T_1, T_2, ..., T_n\}$, where each time series has m ordered real-valued observations $T_i =< t_{i1}, t_{i2}, ..., t_{im} >$ and a class value c_i. The objective is to find a function that maps from the space of possible time series to the space of possible class values. Note, we assume for simplicity that all series are the same length.

Classification is a widely explored problem in machine learning and, to some extent, all classification problems rely on a measure of similarity between data. What makes time series classification a distinct and interesting area of investigation is that similarity between series is often embedded within the autocorrelation structure of the data. There are three general approaches to measuring similarity between time series: similarity in time (i.e. correlation-based), similarity in shape (shape-based) and similarity in change (autocorrelation-based). A fuller discussion can be found in the literature [11, 12]. The majority of research has focused on similarity in time or shape. For shape-based similarity, it is common to use elastic measures such as DTW in conjunction with an instance based classifier. Whilst this approach has been shown to work well in a wide variety of domains, using an elastic measure on the whole series means the discriminatory shape can be masked by noise. Shapelets offer a mechanism for detecting phase-independent shape-based similarity of subsequences, and hence represent a better solution to a class of shape-based similarity problems than global elastic measures.

2.2 Shapelets

Shapelets are a time series data mining primitive that can be used to determine similarity based on small common shapes occurring at any point in a series. Finding a shapelet requires generating a set of candidates, defining a distance measure between a shapelet and each time series, and defining a measure of the discriminatory power of a shapelet.

2.2.1 *Generating Candidates*

A subsequence S of length l of a time series T of length m is a contiguous sequence of l points in T, where $l \leq m$. Any time series of length m contains $(m - l) + 1$ distinct subsequences of length l. We denote the set of all subsequences of length l for series T_i to be $W_{i,l}$ and the set of all subsequences of length l for data set T to be

$$W_l = \{W_{1,l}, \ldots, W_{n,l}\}.$$

The set of all candidate shapelets for data set T is

$$W = \{W_{min}, W_{min+1}, \ldots, W_{max}\},$$

where $min \geq 3$ and $max \leq m$. Note that W is very large, with $O(m^3)$ candidate shapelets. The majority of the research in [19, 20, 13] relates to the efficient pruning of W to improve the time complexity of the exhaustive search. Our main focus, as described in Section 3, is using shapelets more effectively for classification. The generic shapelet finding algorithm is defined in Algorithm 1.

Algorithm 1 ShapeletSelection (T, min,max)

$best = 0$;
$bestShapelet = \emptyset$;
$C = classLabels(T)$;
$W = generateCandidates(T, min, max)$;
for $l = min$ to max **do**
  for all subsequence S in W_l **do**
    $D_S = findDistances(S, W_l)$;
    $quality = assessCandidate(S, D_S)$;
    if $quality > best$ **then**
      $best = quality$;
      $bestShapelet = S$;
    end if
  end for
end for
return $bestShapelet$;

Note that we independently normalise all elements of W. This is justified because we are interested in detecting localised shape similarity, and wish to be invariant to scale and offset. Although there is no reference to normalisation in [19, 20], an amortised constant time normalisation method based on maintaining updated statistics is proposed in [13]. We have separated the procedures *findDistances* and *assessCandidate* for clarity, but for the implementation they may be combined to take advantage of speed-up techniques.

2.2.2 Measuring Distances

We denote the Euclidean distance between two subsequences S and R of length l as

$$dist(S, R) = \sum_{i=1}^{l} (s_i - r_i)^2.$$

The distance between a subsequence S of length l and time series T_i is the minimum distance between S and all normalised subsequences of T_i of length l, i.e.

$$d_{i,S} = \min_{R \in W_{i,l}} dist(S, R).$$

We generate all distances between a candidate shapelet S and all series in T to generate a list of n distances,

$$D_S = < d_{1,S}, d_{2,S}, \ldots, d_{n,s} > .$$

Note that since $d_{i,S}$ is a minima, [20] propose speeding up the calculation of $d_{i,S}$ with an early abandon.

2.2.3 Measuring The Quality of a Shapelet

The original shapelet papers use information gain to determine the quality of a shapelet [19, 20, 13]. This involves sorting the distance list D_S, then evaluating the information gain on the class values for each possible split value. [20] propose an early abandon on calculating D_S through maintaining an upper bound on the *quality* of the candidate whilst generating D_S. If this upper bound falls below the *best* found so far, the calculation of D_S can be abandoned. After each $d_{i,S}$ is found, the current best information gain split is calculated and the upper bound is found by assuming the most optimistic division of the remaining distances.

3. SHAPELET TRANSFORM

The transformation we propose handles shapelets in three distinct stages, Firstly, the algorithm conducts a single scan of the data to extract the best k shapelets. Note that whilst k is a parameter to set, it is simply a cut-off value for the maximum number of shapelets to store and has no effect on the quality of the individual shapelets that are extracted. Secondly, an appropriate value for the number of shapelets to use in the final transformed data set is estimated using a simple cross-validation approach. Finally, a new transformed data set is created where each attribute represents a shapelet, and the value of each attribute is the distance from the shapelet to the original series. The key motivation for transforming the data in this way is that we can disassociate shapelet finding from building a classifier, allowing the transformed data set to be used in conjunction with any classifier.

3.1 Alternative Quality Measure

As discussed in Section 2.2, the original shapelet decision tree uses information gain to assess the quality of a candidate. The motivation for this is two-fold; firstly, information gain is suitable for identifying how to produce a partition of the data, which is essential when it is necessary to recursively divide the data. Secondly, it is possible to use information gain in conjunction with the upper bounding/early abandon technique described in [20]. We use an alternative to information gain for the following reasons.

Firstly, since we are trying to generate a set of shapelets from the entire data set, our concern is not necessarily how well a candidate splits the data. Rather, we are concerned with how the distribution of the distances of the alternative classes differ. To elaborate, if we have the list of distances D_S, rather than find the best way of partitioning D_S we address the issue of how different are the lists $D_S^1, D_S^2, \ldots, D_S^c$, where D_S^j contains all the distances from the candidate to time series of class j.

Secondly, the upper bounding technique for information gain relies on identifying the ideal partition of a number of unevaluated distances. However, the utility of this approach degrades with multi-class problems, as a simple binary split is impossible with 3 or more class values. In the most pessimistic cases, all possible optimistic combinations of unevaluated distances must be considered and can quickly become untenable.

There are several alternative approaches we could adopt to assess the difference in distributions between the class distances. The simplest approach, which we adopt, is to use the F-statistic used for the difference of means in an ANOVA. Whilst a non-parametric test, such as multiple-sample Mann-Whitney, would possibly be more robust, the fact that we are not actually performing a hypothesis test (but instead using the test statistic as a comparative metric) means the reduced power of the F-statistic in the face of outliers is less of a problem. Hence the *assessCandidate* method we use is simply the F-statistic of a fixed effects ANOVA.

3.2 Shapelet Generation

The process of extracting the k best shapelets is defined in Algorithm 2.

Algorithm 2 ShapeletCachedSelection(T, min, max, k)

1: $kShapelets = \emptyset$;
2: $C = classLabels(T)$;
3: **for all** time series T_i in T **do**
4:   $shapelets = \emptyset$;
5:   **for** $l = min$ to max **do**
6:     $W_{i,l} = generateCandidates(T_i, min, max)$;
7:     **for all** subsequence S in $W_{i\,l}$ **do**
8:       $D_S = findDistances(S, W_{i,l})$;
9:       $quality = assessCandidate(S, D_S)$;
10:       $shapelets.add(S, quality)$;
11:     **end for**
12:   **end for**
13:   $sortByQuality(shapelets)$;
14:   $removeSelfSimilar(shapelets)$;
15:   $kShapelets = merge(k, kShapelets, shapelets)$;
16: **end for**
17: **return** $kShapelets$;

The algorithm begins by processing the data in a very similar manner to the original shapelet selection algorithm of [20], defined earlier in Algorithm 1. For each series in the data set, all subsequences of all possible lengths according to the min and max length parameters are visited. However, unlike Algorithm 1, where all candidates are assessed and only the best is stored, the caching algorithm stores all candidates for a given time series along with their associated quality measures (line 10). Once all candidates of a series have been assessed, the candidates are sorted in order of fitness and self-similar shapelets are removed. We define two shapelets as being self-similar if they are taken from the same series and have any overlapping indices. Once we have the set of non self-similar shapelets for a series, we merge these with the current best shapelets and retain the top k, and continue to iterate through the data until all series have been processed. Note that we do not store all candidates indefinitely; after processing each series, we simply retain those that belong to the best k so far overall, and discard all other shapelets. This means that we can avoid the large space overhead that would be caused by retaining all possible candidates.

We choose to store shapelets from a series separately and merge them later, rather than keeping the best k on the fly, to ensure that we are left with the best shapelets after removing self-similar candidates. For example, if we have a set of the best k shapelets at a given point in the series, the next candidate that is processed could potentially overlap two or perhaps more shapelets in the store. If this current shapelet is deemed to be better, all overlapping self-similar candidates must be removed from the store. A problem would then arise if a better shapelet is found later in the series that overlaps the one currently being stored, but isn't self-similar to at least one of the previously removed candidates. As each subsequence is only ever visited once, it would be impossible to get back the previously removed candidates, even if they ultimately should be amongst the best k shapelets. Therefore to avoid this problem, we initially extract all possible shapelets from a series, sort them by their quality and then remove those that are self similar in order. This gives priority to the best shapelets and ensures that no candidates are prematurely removed. We can then safely merge these with the existing k best shapelets before moving on to processes the next series. At this point it is safe to discard all other shapelets from the current series as they are not in the top k and cannot be self-similar to shapelets from another series.

3.2.1 Length Parameter Approximation

Similarly to the original shapelet finding algorithm of [20], the algorithm that we define in Algorithm 2 requires two length parameters to be set: min and max. These values define the range of possible candidate shapelet lengths, which provides scope to the search and can help make the algorithm more efficient. However, setting the parameters incorrectly can be detrimental to the outcome of the shapelet transformation if they prevent the most informative subsequences from being considered. To accommodate running the shapelet filter on a range of data sets without any specialised knowledge of the data, we define a simple algorithm for estimating the min and max parameters.

Algorithm 3 EstimateMinAndMax(T)

$shapelets = \emptyset$;
$length = T_1.length$;
for $i = 1$ to 10 **do**
  $randomiseOrder(T)$;
  $T' = [T_1, T_2, ..., T_{10}]$;
  $currentShapelets = ShapeletCachedSelection(T', 1, length, 10)$;
  $shapelets.add(currentShapelets)$;
end for
$orderByLength(shapelets)$;
$min = shapelets_{25}.length$;
$max = shapelets_{75}.length$;
return min, max;

The procedure outlined in Algorithm 3 takes 10 random series from the dataset T and uses Algorithm 2 to find the 10 best shapelets within this small subset of data. The search parameters here are set from 1 to the length of a whole series in T, meaning no constraints are placed on the length of shapelets in this search. This is repeated 10 times in total, producing a set of 100 shapelets. The shapelets are sorted in order of their length and the lengths of the 25th and 75th shapelets are extracted and returned as min and max respectively. Note that this will not necessarily result in the optimal solution for parameter finding. However, it was important that we could adopt an automatic approach to approximate min and max parameters across a number of datasets to allow us to compare our filter fairly against the original tree implementation of shapelets. Therefore we use this approach to approximate min and max for each data set and build all shapelet trees and filters using these values.

3.3 Data Transformation

One of the main motivations of the proposed transformation is to allow shapelets to be used with a diverse range of classification algorithms. Rather than restricting them to classification through decision tree structures, our algorithm uses shapelets to transform instances of data into a number of features that can then be treated as a generic classification problem. The transformation process is defined in Algorithm 4.

Algorithm 4 FilterData(Shapelets S, Dataset D)

$output = \emptyset$;
for all time series ts in D **do**
  $transformed = \emptyset$;
  for all shapelets s in S **do**
    $dist = subsequenceDist(ts, s)$;
    $transformed.add(dist)$;
  end for
  $output.add(transformed)$;
end for
return $output$;

The transformation process is carried out using the subsequence distance calculation described in Section 2.2.2. Firstly, a set of k shapelets, S, is generated from the training data T, as seen in the previous section. For each instance of data T_i, the subsequence distance is computed between T_i and S_j, where $j = 1, 2, \ldots, k$. The resulting k distances are used to form a new instance of transformed data, where each attribute corresponds to the distance from each shapelet to the original time series. When using data split into training and test partitions, the shapelet extraction is carried out on only the training data to avoid bias; these shapelets are then used to transform each instance of the training and test data to create transformed data sets, which can then be used with any traditional classification algorithm.

3.4 Shapelet Selection

Using k shapelets in the filter will not necessarily yield the best data for classification. Using too few shapelets would not provide enough information to make informed classification decisions, whilst using too many could overfit classifiers trained with the transformed data and dilute the influence of important shapelets. In the experiments contained in this paper, we use two strategies for selecting the number of shapelets to use in the filter for a given set of data; firstly, as a benchmark we use $\frac{n}{2}$ shapelets in the filter, where n is the number of readings in a single series of the data. The second approach automatically selects the number of shapelets to use based on the results of a 5-fold cross-validation experiment.

This is performed by firstly partitioning the training data into five equal parts. For each fold, we use the data as a testing set and combine the four other folds to form a set of training data. We then pass the training data into our filtering algorithm and produce n shapelets. These shapelets are used to create n different sets of transformed training data, where the first set is the original training data transformed by one shapelet, the second is transformed by two, and so on until the final set consists of n transformed features. This same procedure is applied to the testing data, creating n sets of transformed test data. Given the class of the classifier that we wish to use the final shapelet with, we train a range of new classifiers using the n sets of transformed training data and classify the appropriate set of transformed test data. Therefore, for each of the five folds we obtain n classification accuracies, each corresponding to the number of shapelets used to transform the data.

The value of n with the best overall accuracy across all five folds of the data is selected as the number of shapelets to use in the final filter. In cases where multiple values obtain the best results, we evaluated three strategies for selecting a single value from the set of best values: pick the smallest, middle or largest value. We found that picking the maximum marginally outperformed using the middle value, whilst both approaches performed better than selecting the smallest value. For brevity, we do not include the experiments for this here, but they can be found at [15].

4. EXPERIMENTAL DESIGN

To evaluate the shapelet transform, we selected 18 data sets from the UCR time series repository (listed in Table 1) and 8 new data sets provided by us. We selected these particular data sets because they have relatively few cases; even with optimisation, the shapelet algorithm is time consuming. At the time of writing, we have not evaluated the transform on any other data sets. We use a simple train/test split and all reported results are testing accuracy. All shapelet selection, model selection, and classifier construction is done exclusively on the training set, whilst the test set is only used once with the final trained classifier. All algorithms and experiments were implemented in Java within the Weka framework, and the shapelet transform is implemented as a Weka batch filter to allow easy integration into existing classification code. All the code to generate our results is available at [15].

4.1 New Data Sets

We provide 8 new data sets that contain data taken from hand x-rays, originally from [9]. The data consists of images focusing on eight specific bones of the hand, where each data set contains 1045 cases of a single type of bone. The eight bones in the data are the proximal phalanges of the thumb, little and middle fingers; the middle phalanges of the little and middle fingers; and the distal phalanges of the thumb, middle and little fingers. Each instance of data has a class label that is either infant (0-6 years), junior (7-12 years) or teen (13-18) years. This approach is similar to the system proposed in [17].

For each of the 8 bones, the data is partitioned into 200 instances of training and 845 instances of test data. The images were converted to 1-d series by initially calculating the outlines of the 1045 hand x-ray images using the algorithm described in [4]. The locations of the tips and webs of the hand were extracted from these outlines using the algorithm presented in [3]. From these positions, the axes of the thumb, middle and little fingers were calculated by finding the midpoint between adjacent webs in the hand. In the cases of the thumb and little finger where there is only one adjacent web for each, the axes were approximated by extending the line from the previous finger and calculating where this intersects the hand outline. Once provided with these axes, region-of-interest boxes were calculated for each of the eight bones (as shown in Figure 1). Each box was warped into a rectanglular-shaped mesh (500 × 150 pixels) using a piecewise affine warp to create a new image for each of the 8 bones. Each image was converted into 1-d series, creating 1045 instances of data for each of the 8 bone types.

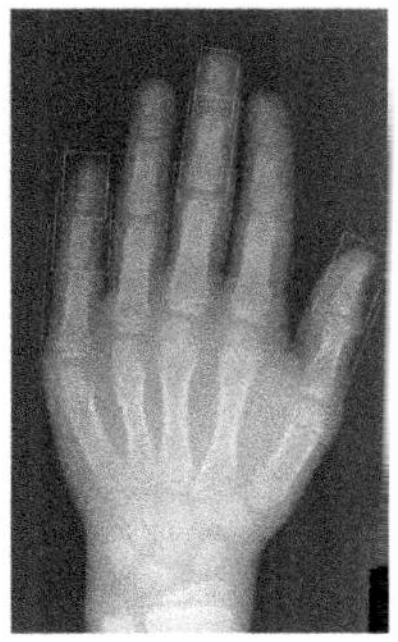

Figure 1: A hand x-ray with the eight bones boxed: proximal (purple, bottom), middle (green, middle), and distal (blue, top) phalanges. Note, the thumb does not have a middle phalange.

A common method for converting an image into a 1-d series is to calculate a histogram of the image [14]. However, this approach doesn't incorporate any location information from the original image. To preserve this contextual information, we convert images to 1-d series by resizing them to 30 × 9 pixels, which is represented as a vector of length 270. This allows us to retain location information in the data, whilst converting the images into 1-d series that can be posed as a TSC problem.

5. RESULTS

We have proposed several changes to the way shapelets can be used for classification and present a range of experiments to test these changes.

5.1 Shapelets: Embedded vs. Transformed

Our first objective is to establish that separating shapelets from the classifier does not reduce classification accuracy. We implemented a shapelet decision tree classifier as described in [20], and compared results to a C4.5 decision tree trained and tested on shapelet transformed data (using information gain as the quality measure and $\frac{n}{2}$ shapelets). Table 1 shows the results for the 26 data sets used. The Shapelet tree was best on 13, C4.5 best on 12 and they were tied on one. There is no significant difference detected by a paired t-test or a Wilcoxon signed rank test. There is no evidence that performing the shapelet extraction prior to constructing the decision tree makes the classifier less accurate.

Table 1: Shapelet tree classification vs. C4.5 classification with $\frac{n}{2}$ shapelet filtered features

Data	Shapelet Tree	C4.5
Adiac	29.92%	24.30%
Beef	50.00%	60.00%
ChlorineConcentration	58.80%	56.48%
Coffee	96.43%	85.71%
DiatomSizeReduction	72.22%	75.16%
ECGFiveDays	77.47%	96.17%
ElectricDevices	54.90%	53.45%
FaceFour	84.09%	76.14%
GunPoint	89.33%	90.67%
ItalyPowerDemand	89.21%	90.96%
Lighting7	49.32%	53.42%
MedicalImages	48.82%	44.87%
MoteStrain	82.51%	84.42%
SonyAIBORobotSurface	84.53%	84.53%
Symbols	77.99%	47.14%
SyntheticControl	94.33%	90.33%
Trace	98.00%	98.00%
TwoLeadECG	85.07%	85.25%
DP_Little	65.44%	65.92%
DP_Middle	70.53%	71.24%
DP_Thumb	58.11%	57.99%
MP_Little	66.39%	63.43%
MP_Middle	71.01%	73.25%
PP_Little	59.64%	57.40%
PP_Middle	61.42%	62.49%
PP_Thumb	60.83%	59.53%

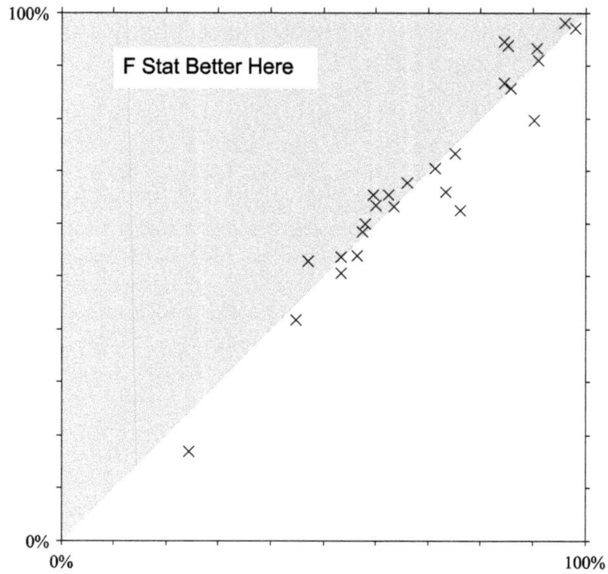

Figure 2: A comparison of using the F-stat quality criteria against information gain for the shapelet transform. Accuracy results were obtained with a C4.5 classifier built on the transformed data set.

5.2 Information Gain vs F-Statistic

Our second experiment is designed to compare the F-statistic to information gain for shapelet selection. Figure 2 compares the accuracy of a C4.5 classifier built on a shapelet transform using information gain and the F-statistic in the style presented in [7]. Information gain slightly outperforms the F-statistic, winning 15 of the 26 comparisons. Whilst this single experiment is not significant, further experiments with other classifiers indicated that this pattern was repeated. Qualitatively at least, we think information gain may produce more discriminatory shapelet features. Table 2 compares the build time for the shapelet tree, the information gain shapelet transform and the F-statistic shapelet transform. The F-statistic filter is faster on all but one of the data sets. However, there is an important caveat to these results; our shapelet tree implementation does not employ the information gain upper bound. We found that for problems with multiple classes, it was somewhat counter productive, with the requirement to recalculate split points offsetting any early abandon gains. However, we recognize this may be due to our implementation, and acknowledge a potential source of implementation bias. We conclude that whilst there is a case for using the F-statistic over information gain on performance grounds, particularly on large multi-class problems, the marginal accuracy differential means that we continue with information gain.

Table 2: Build times of shapelet tree, information gain shapelet transform and F-stat transform (time in seconds)

Data	Shapelet Tree	Info Gain Transform	F-Stat Transform
Adiac	31403.17	20896.47	**5321.30**
Beef	2501.50	1492.31	**1458.21**
ChlorineConcentration	121019.15	31723.73	**18595.21**
Coffee	305.17	**295.07**	298.51
DiatomSizeReduction	100.88	68.65	**66.27**
ECGFiveDays	189.52	192.56	**187.30**
ElectricDevices	5524.90	3040.93	**2187.11**
FaceFour	8653.46	5821.65	**5757.35**
GunPoint	743.69	731.84	**708.59**
ItalyPowerDemand	5.09	4.17	**1.94**
Lighting7	35877.14	20279.77	**19748.46**
MedicalImages	36227.04	19877.87	**9693.09**
MoteStrain	11.13	11.39	**10.22**
SonyAIBORobotSurface	9.36	9.61	**8.08**
Symbols	17539.63	10833.19	**10790.84**
SyntheticControl	4312.67	2801.06	**1180.79**
Trace	108658.88	72401.39	**71566.33**
TwoLeadECG	5.35	5.41	**4.46**
DP_Little	13447.14	5941.87	**4854.11**
DP_Middle	16426.07	8414.13	**7261.95**
DP_Thumb	24074.84	12798.50	**10868.34**
MP_Little	33585.39	19364.60	**17456.99**
MP_Middle	20049.11	8370.00	**7176.03**
PP_Little	44027.99	23555.03	**20518.56**
PP_Middle	32190.56	15115.02	**13513.17**
PP_Thumb	22505.93	11749.81	**10130.71**

5.3 Shapelet Transformation Classifiers

The main contribution of this paper is to demonstrate how moving the shapelet discovery outside of the classification algorithm can improve the overall accuracy. Table 3 shows the classification test accuracy of the shapelet tree, C4.5, 1-NN, Naive Bayes, a Bayesian Network, Random Forest,

Table 3: Testing accuracy and ranks of 8 classifiers constructed on the shapelet transform with $n/2$ shapelets.

Data	Shapelet Tree		C4.5		1NN		Naïve Bayes		Bayesian Network		Random Forest		Rotation Forest		SVM (linear)	
Adiac	29.92%	(3)	24.30%	(7)	25.32%	(5)	28.13%	(4)	25.06%	(6)	30.43%	(2)	**30.69%**	**(1)**	23.79%	(8)
Beef	50.00%	(8)	60.00%	(6.5)	83.33%	(3)	73.33%	(4)	**90.00%**	**(1)**	60.00%	(6.5)	70.00%	(5)	86.67%	(2)
ChlorineConcentration	58.80%	(2)	56.48%	(6)	56.93%	(5)	45.96%	(8)	57.08%	(4)	57.58%	(3)	**63.52%**	**(1)**	56.15%	(7)
Coffee	96.43%	(4.5)	85.71%	(8)	**100.00%**	**(1.3)**	92.86%	(6)	96.43%	(4.5)	**100.00%**	**(1.3)**	89.29%	(7)	**100.00%**	**(1.3)**
DiatomSizeReduction	72.22%	(8	75.16%	(7)	**93.46%**	**(1)**	78.76%	(6)	90.20%	(3)	80.39%	(5)	83.01%	(4)	92.16%	(2)
ECGFiveDays	77.47%	(8)	96.17%	(6)	98.37%	(4)	96.40%	(5)	**99.54%**	**(1)**	93.26%	(7)	98.61%	(3)	98.95%	(2)
ElectricDevices	54.90%	(2)	53.45%	(4)	24.25%	(7)	25.37%	(5)	53.63%	(3)	**55.98%**	**(1)**	24.25%	(7)	24.25%	(7)
FaceFour	84.09%	(7)	76.14%	(8)	**100.00%**	**(1.5)**	97.73%	(4.5)	**100.00%**	**(1.5)**	87.50%	(6)	98.86%	(3)	97.73%	(4.5)
GunPoint	89.33%	(8)	90.67%	(7)	98.00%	(4)	92.00%	(6)	99.33%	(2)	96.00%	(5)	98.67%	(3)	**100.00%**	**(1)**
ItalyPowerDemand	89.21%	(8)	90.96%	(7)	92.13%	(4.5)	92.52%	(2)	92.42%	(3)	**93.00%**	**(1)**	92.03%	(6)	92.13%	(4.5)
Lighting7	49.32%	(7.5)	53.42%	(6)	49.32%	(7.5)	57.53%	(5)	65.75%	(2.5)	64.38%	(4)	65.75%	(2.5)	**69.86%**	**(1)**
MedicalImages	48.82%	(4)	44.87%	(6)	45.66%	(5)	17.37%	(8)	28.16%	(7)	50.79%	(3)	51.45%	(2)	**52.50%**	**(1)**
MoteStrain	82.51%	(8)	84.42%	(7)	**90.34%**	**(1)**	88.82%	(3)	89.06%	(2)	84.58%	(6)	86.98%	(5)	88.66%	(4)
SonyAIBORobotSurface	84.53%	(6)	84.53%	(5)	84.03%	(7)	79.03%	(8)	**89.68%**	**(1)**	85.19%	(4)	89.02%	(2)	86.69%	(3)
Symbols	77.99%	(6)	47.14%	(8)	85.63%	(2)	77.99%	(7)	**92.26%**	**(1)**	84.62%	(3.5)	84.42%	(5)	84.62%	(3.5)
SyntheticControl	**94.33%**	**(1)**	90.33%	(4)	93.00%	(2)	78.00%	(7)	76.67%	(8)	89.00%	(5)	92.00%	(3)	87.33%	(6)
Trace	98.00%	(5)	98.00%	(5)	98.00%	(5)	98.00%	(5)	**100.00%**	**(1)**	98.00%	(5)	98.00%	(5)	98.00%	(5)
TwoLeadECG	85.07%	(8)	85.25%	(7)	**99.47%**	**(1)**	99.12%	(3)	98.77%	(4)	96.14%	(6)	97.98%	(5)	99.30%	(2)
DP_Little	65.44%	(8)	65.92%	(7)	72.78%	(6)	73.49%	(3)	72.90%	(5)	73.02%	(4)	74.67%	(2)	**75.15%**	**(1)**
DP_Middle	70.53%	(8)	71.24%	(7)	73.73%	(6)	73.96%	(5)	74.67%	(4)	75.50%	(3)	76.80%	(2)	**79.64%**	**(1)**
DP_Thumb	58.11%	(7)	57.99%	(8)	60.71%	(6)	62.96%	(5)	63.91%	(4)	64.14%	(3)	67.10%	(2)	**69.82%**	**(1)**
MP_Little	66.39%	(7)	63.43%	(8)	68.52%	(6)	68.76%	(5)	69.47%	(4)	71.36%	(3)	**75.15%**	**(1)**	75.03%	(2)
MP_Middle	71.01%	(7)	73.25%	(4)	70.89%	(8)	71.95%	(5)	71.12%	(6)	75.15%	(2)	74.67%	(3)	**76.92%**	**(1)**
PP_Little	59.64%	(7)	57.40%	(8)	67.22%	(5)	69.23%	(4)	70.06%	(2)	66.63%	(6)	69.82%	(3)	**72.07%**	**(1)**
PP_Middle	61.42%	(8)	62.49%	(7)	68.52%	(6)	69.82%	(5)	71.36%	(3)	70.53%	(4)	75.38%	(2)	**75.86%**	**(1)**
PP_Thumb	60.83%	(7)	59.53%	(8)	67.69%	(6)	69.35%	(4)	69.47%	(3)	67.81%	(5)	72.78%	(2)	**75.50%**	**(1)**
Average Rank	6.27		6.60		4.48		5.10		3.33		4.04		3.33		2.8	

Rotation Forest and a Support Vector Machine, all with default Weka settings. The support vector machine is the best performing classifier, with an average rank of 2.86 and best performance in 10 out of 26 problems. Figure 3 shows a critical difference diagram as described in [5]. This diagram is derived from the overall test of significance in mean ranks, and groups classifiers together into *cliques*, illustrated by the bars. There is a clear division in performance between the simpler classifiers (shapelet tree, C4.5, Naive Bayes and 1-NN) and the more complex classifiers (Rotation forest, Random Forest, Bayesian Networks and SVM). Whilst there may be a trade off between interpretability and accuracy (a tree is easier to understand than a SVM), our point is that by separating the shapelet discovery, there is greater potential to explore possible solutions.

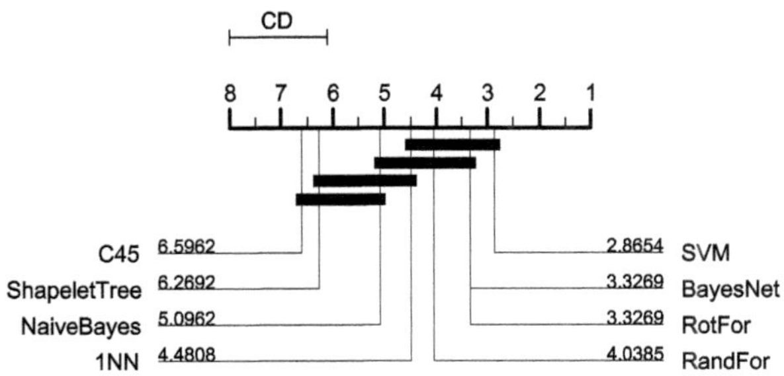

Figure 3: Critical difference plot for eight shapelet based classifiers derived from the results in Table 3

5.4 Shapelets Selection

In Section 3.4, we defined a method for shapelet selection through cross validation. To demonstrate the utility of this technique, we calculated the number of shapelets to use for each data set and repeated the classification experiments from Table 3. The results presented in Table 4 show the relative performance change of these classifiers against simply training the classifiers with $n/2$ shapelets, as in Table 3. The results show that using an automatically selected number of shapelets set through cross-validation improves the average

Table 5: Accuracy of the SVM built on a shapelet transform, Dynamic Time Warping with 1-NN on the raw data and an ensemble of 1-NN classifiers built on alternative transformations (see [1])

	Shapelet SVM	DTW 1-NN	Ensemble
Adiac	31.20%	61.13%	64.45%
Beef	83.33%	63.33%	60.00%
Coffee	100.00%	92.86%	82.14%
ElectricDevices	24.25%	65.00%	62.21%
FaceFour	98.86%	81.82%	86.36%
GunPoint	100.00%	91.33%	95.33%
Lighting7	71.23%	71.23%	69.86%
SyntheticControl	90.67%	97.67%	91.00%
Trace	98.00%	99.00%	81.00%

classification accuracy of 7 out of the 8 classifiers. In all cases, the classifiers achieve equal or better results on over half of the data sets, with the Random Forest classifier improving the most overall.

5.5 Other Classifiers

Our final accuracy results are used to demonstrate that there are problems where a shapelet approach will outperform others. Table 5 shows the accuracy of three classifiers trained with 9 of the 26 datasets. The classifiers are: an SVM built on selected shapelets (results comparable with Table 4), Dynamic Time Warping with 1-NN on the raw data and an ensemble of 1-NN classifiers built on transformations into the power spectrum, autocorrelation function and principle component space (described in [1]). These data sets were selected as they are common to both papers.

The comparison is provided for information only; we have obviously introduced some selection bias by choosing the best classifier (SVM) from out experiments. Nevertheless, it is interesting to note that the shapelet approach is clearly the best on some data sets (Beef, Coffee and FaceFour), and yet fails dramatically on others (Adiac and ElectricDevices). This offers promising support for shapelet-based approaches, suggesting that they fill a classification niche that has not been covered in the literature.

Table 4: Relative accuracies of the classifiers when trained with an automatically selected number of shapelets through cross-validation vs. using $n/2$ shapelets (as in Table 3)

Data	C4.5	1NN	Naïve Bayes	Bayesian Network	Random Forest	Rotation Forest	SVM (linear)
Adiac	2.30%	0.00%	3.58%	5.37%	4.86%	7.16%	7.42%
Beef	-10.00%	-13.33%	0.00%	-6.67%	20.00%	0.00%	-3.33%
ChlorineConcentration	-1.09%	-2.63%	4.32%	0.36%	0.05%	0.83%	0.03%
Coffee	0.00%	0.00%	3.57%	0.00%	0.00%	3.57%	0.00%
DiatomSizeReduction	0.00%	-0.65%	-21.24%	-2.94%	1.96%	-1.63%	1.96%
ECGFiveDays	0.00%	-1.63%	1.74%	0.00%	5.92%	0.46%	-0.46%
ElectricDevices	0.00%	0.00%	0.00%	1.01%	0.37%	0.00%	0.00%
FaceFour	0.00%	0.00%	2.27%	0.00%	6.82%	-9.09%	1.14%
GunPoint	0.00%	0.00%	0.67%	0.00%	2.00%	0.00%	0.00%
ItalyPowerDemand	0.00%	3.89%	-3.89%	0.10%	0.68%	2.92%	3.21%
Lighting7	0.00%	-2.74%	2.74%	9.59%	-4.11%	2.74%	1.37%
MedicalImages	0.00%	3.03%	33.16%	23.29%	-0.79%	0.00%	3.16%
MoteStrain	0.00%	-0.08%	0.48%	-3.83%	1.12%	0.00%	0.56%
SonyAIBORobotSurface	0.00%	0.17%	0.00%	0.00%	-0.50%	0.00%	0.00%
Symbols	2.41%	-2.21%	-4.32%	1.31%	-2.71%	0.70%	-8.74%
SyntheticControl	-1.67%	0.67%	0.33%	0.33%	-2.00%	0.00%	3.33%
Trace	0.00%	0.00%	0.00%	-2.00%	0.00%	2.00%	0.00%
TwoLeadECG	0.00%	0.00%	-0.44%	0.70%	-3.16%	-1.76%	0.26%
DP_Little	-1.54%	1.54%	2.25%	2.37%	-2.49%	0.59%	1.42%
DP_Middle	1.07%	-1.89%	-1.07%	-0.83%	1.42%	0.83%	-0.12%
DP_Thumb	4.26%	0.36%	-0.95%	-1.42%	0.83%	0.59%	0.95%
MP_Little	1.18%	0.12%	1.89%	0.59%	0.36%	-1.54%	-1.78%
MP_Middle	1.42%	1.30%	-0.12%	0.47%	0.36%	3.43%	-0.12%
PP_Little	8.17%	0.83%	0.95%	0.59%	0.95%	-2.84%	-1.66%
PP_Middle	1.30%	1.18%	1.42%	1.42%	3.79%	-0.24%	-2.37%
PP_Thumb	1.18%	0.71%	1.30%	0.36%	-0.36%	-3.43%	0.36%
Average Improvement	0.35%	-0.44%	1.10%	1.16%	1.36%	0.20%	0.25%
Data Sets Improved	9	11	15	15	16	12	13

5.6 Exploratory Data Analysis

The results we have reported show that using shapelets as a filter can provide some very promising classification results. However, one of the strengths of using shapelets as a classification tool is that they allow a level of interpretation that other classification approaches simply do not. The original work on shapelets in [19] demonstrated this, with a number of examples where they show the decision trees that they train on datasets and the associated shapelets.

One of the key motivations behind our work using shapelets for TSC is to produce accurate and reliable classification decisions that are interpretable. To demonstrate that our filter retains this desirable trait of the original shapelet implementation, we briefly analyse one of our previous experiments using the GunPoint data set. The GunPoint data contains time series of an actor carrying out the motion of drawing a gun, and the classification problem is to determine whether or not they were holding a prop or just miming the action (the *Gun/NoGun* problem). In [19], they identified that the most important shapelet for classification was when the actor lowered their arm; if they had no gun, a phenomenon called overshoot occurred and caused a dip in the data. This is summarised in Figure 4, originally presented in [19].

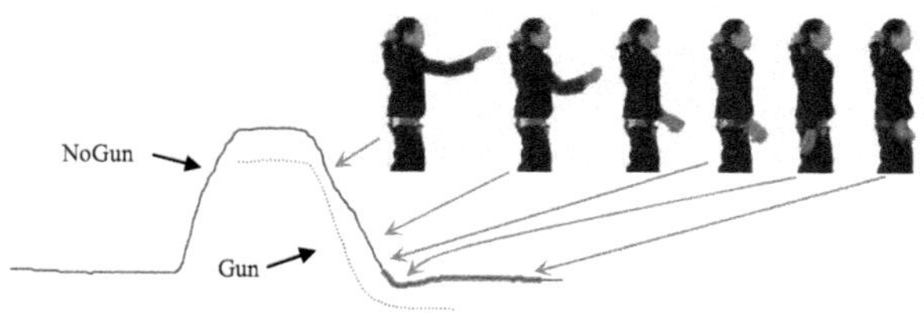

Figure 4: An illustration of the *Gun/NoGun* problem taken from [19]. The shapelet that they extract is highlighted at the end of the series.

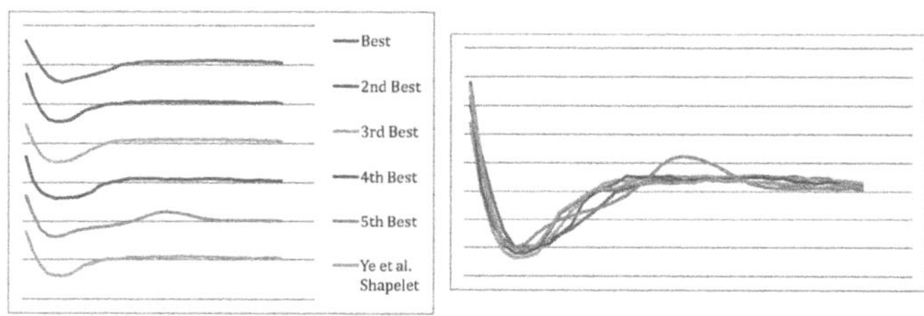

Figure 5: An illustration of the five best shapelets extracted by our filter. The graph to the right shows how closely matched they are when place on top of one another.

The shapelet decision tree trained by [19] contains a single shapelet corresponding to the arm being lowered back into position at the end of the series. To demonstrate that our filter agrees with this and extracts the important information from the data, we filtered the GunPoint data set using the length parameters specified in the original paper to allow for a fair comparison between the two methods. The top five shapelets that we extracted are presented in Figure 5, along with the shapelet reported by [19].

The graphs in Figure 5 show that each of the top five shapelets from our filter were very closely matched with the shapelet from [19], reinforcing the notion that our filter produces interpretable results. Furthermore, if we extract the top ten shapelets from the filter we can gain even further insight. Figure 6 shows that the top ten shapelets form two distinct clusters. Interestingly, the shapelets to the left of the figure correspond to the moments where the arm is lifted and are instances where there is a gun. These shapelets could correspond to the subtle extra movements required to lift the prop, aiding classification by providing more information.

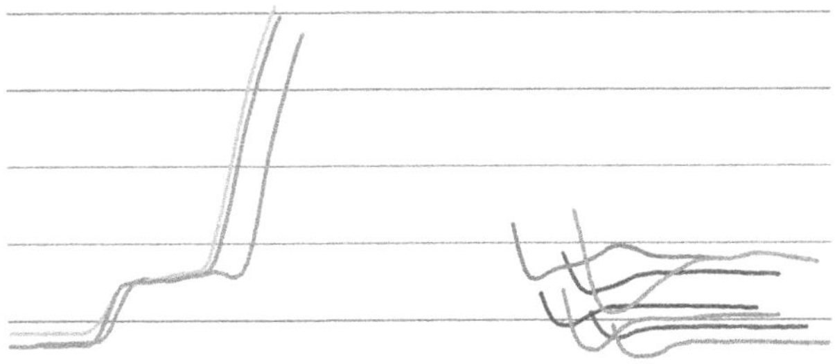

Figure 6: The 10 best shapelets for the *Gun/NoGun* problem as extracted by our filter. The shapelets form two distinct clusters, the first where the arm is raised and the second when the arm is lowered.

6. CONCLUSIONS AND FUTURE WORK

In this paper, we have proposed a shapelet transform for TSC that extracts the k best shapelets from a dataset in a single pass. We implement this using a novel caching algorithm to store shapelets, and apply a simple, parameter-free cross-validation approach for extracting the most significant shapelets. We transform a total of 26 data sets with our filter and demonstrate that a C4.5 decision tree classifier trained with transformed data is competitive with an implementation of the original shapelet decision tree of [19]. We show that our filtered data can be applied to further, non-tree based classifiers to achieve improved classification performance, whilst still maintaining the interpretability of shapelets. We provide two implementations of the filter using different quality measures for discriminating between shapelets; we use information gain as proposed by [19] in the first, and introduce the application of the F-statistic as an evaluation method for shapelets in the second. We show that classifiers trained using features derived from an F-statistic filter are competitive with classifiers trained with the information gain approach, whilst being easier to apply to multi-class classification problems. Finally, we provide exploratory data analysis of the shapelets extracted by our filter on the *Gun/NoGun* problem and compare them with the output of [20]. We show that the shapelets we find are consistent with the discriminatory shapelet in the original work, and show that our approach can lead to further insight into the problem by looking at a number of the top shapelets.

Future direction of our work could involve investigating how we handle extracted shapelets. We have shown that using a number of shapelets to transform data can lead to strong classification results, but it is obvious that some shapelets produced across a data set may be very similar. An interesting extension of our work would be to perform a cluster analysis on the shapelets produced by our filter, and then train classifiers using data transformed by single shapelets of distinct clusters, rather than the top k shapelets.

7. REFERENCES

[1] A. Bagnall, L. Davis, J. Hills, and J. Lines. Transformation based ensembles for time series classification. In *Proc. 12th SDM*, 2012.

[2] K. Buza. *Fusion Methods for Time-Series Classification.* PhD thesis, University of Hildesheim, Germany, 2011.

[3] L. Davis, B. Theobald, J. Lines, A. Toms, and A. Bagnall. On the segmentation and classification of hand outlines (under review). *International Journal of Neural System*, 2012.

[4] L. Davis, B. J. Theobald, A. Toms, and A. Bagnall. On the extraction and classification of hand outlines. In *Proc. of the 12th IDEAL*, 2011.

[5] J. Demšar. Statistical comparisons of classifiers over multiple data sets. *JMLR*, 7:1–30, 2006.

[6] H. Deng, G. Runger, E. Tuv, and M. Vladimir. A time series forest for classification and feature extraction. Technical report, Arizona State University, 2011.

[7] H. Ding, G. Trajcevski, P. Scheuermann, X. Wang, and E. Keogh. Querying and mining of time series data: Experimental comparison of representations and distance measures. In *Proc. 34th VLDB*, 2008.

[8] B. Hartmann and N. Link. Gesture recognition with inertial sensors and optimized DTW prototypes. In *Proc. IEEE International Conference on Systems Man and Cybernetics (SMC)*, 2010.

[9] Image Processing and Informatics Lab, University of Southern California. The digital hand atlas database system. `http://www.ipilab.org/BAAweb/`.

[10] Y. Jeong, M. Jeong, and O. Omitaomu. Weighted dynamic time warping for time series classification. *Pattern Recognition*, 44:2231–2240, 2010.

[11] E. Keogh and S. Kasetty. On the need for time series data mining benchmarks: A survey and empirical demonstration. *Data Mining and Knowledge Discovery*, 7(4):349–371, 2003.

[12] F. Mörchen, I. Mierswa, and A. Ultsch. Understandable models of music collections based on exhaustive feature generation with temporal statistics. In *12th International Conference on Knowledge Discovery in Data and Data Mining (ACM SIGKDD 2006)*, pages 882–891, 2006.

[13] A. Mueen, E. Keogh, and N. Young. Logical-shapelets: An expressive primitive for time series classification. In *Proc. 17th ACM SIGKDD*, 2011.

[14] A. Mueen, E. Keogh, Q. Zhu, S. Cash, and M. Westover. Exact discovery of time series motifs. In *Proc. 9th SDM*, 2009.

[15] paper authors. Accompanying information for this paper. `https://sites.google.com/site/shapelettransform/`.

[16] J. Rodriguez and C. Alonso. Support vector machines of interval-based features for time series classification. *Knowledge-Based Systems*, 18, 2005.

[17] H. Thodberg, S. Kreiborg, A. Juul, and K. Pedersen. The bonexpert method for automated determination of skeletal maturity. *IEEE Trans. Med. Imaging*, 28(1):52–66, 2009.

[18] Z. Xing, J. Pei, P. Yu, and K. Wang. Extracting interpretable features for early classification on time series. In *Proc. 11th SDM*, 2011.

[19] L. Ye and E. Keogh. Time series shapelets: A new primitive for data mining. In *Proc. 15th ACM SIGKDD*, 2009.

[20] L. Ye and E. Keogh. Time series shapelets: a novel technique that allows accurate, interpretable and fast classification. *Data Min. Knowl. Discov.*, 22(1-2):149–182, 2011.

Accelerated Singular Value Thresholding for Matrix Completion

Yao Hu[1] Debing Zhang[1] Jun Liu[3] Jieping Ye[2] Xiaofei He[1]

[1]Zhejiang University, HangZhou, China
[2]Arizona State University, Tempe, AZ 85287
[3]Imaging and Computer Vision Department, Siemens Corporate Research, Princeton, NJ 08540
{huyao001, debingzhangchina, junliu.nt, jieping, xiaofeihe}@gmail.com

ABSTRACT

Recovering a large matrix from a small subset of its entries is a challenging problem arising in many real world applications, such as recommender system and image inpainting. These problems can be formulated as a general matrix completion problem. The Singular Value Thresholding (SVT) algorithm is a simple and efficient first-order matrix completion method to recover the missing values when the original data matrix is of low rank. SVT has been applied successfully in many applications. However, SVT is computationally expensive when the size of the data matrix is large, which significantly limits its applicability. In this paper, we propose an Accelerated Singular Value Thresholding (ASVT) algorithm which improves the convergence rate from $O(\frac{1}{N})$ for SVT to $O(\frac{1}{N^2})$, where N is the number of iterations during optimization. Specifically, the dual problem of the nuclear norm minimization problem is derived and an adaptive line search scheme is introduced to solve this dual problem. Consequently, the optimal solution of the primary problem can be readily obtained from that of the dual problem. We have conducted a series of experiments on a synthetic dataset, a distance matrix dataset and a large movie rating dataset. The experimental results have demonstrated the efficiency and effectiveness of the proposed algorithm.

Categories and Subject Descriptors

H.2.8 [**Database Management**]: Database Applications-Data Mining

General Terms

Algorithms

Keywords

Matrix Completion, Singular Value Thresholding, Nesterov's Method, Adaptive Line Search Scheme

KDD'12, August 12–16, 2012, Beijing, China.

1. INTRODUCTION

Estimating missing values from very limited information of an unknown matrix has received considerable attention recently. This problem occurs in both theoretical studies [4, 5, 7], and real world applications such as recommender system [13, 14, 22] and image/video analysis [17, 11]. Since the completion of arbitrary matrices is an ill-posed problem, it is usually assumed that the underlying matrix comes from a restricted class. One of the most natural assumption is that the matrix has a low-rank or approximately low-rank structure. Specifically, given the incomplete data matrix $M \in \mathbb{R}^{m\times n}$, the matrix completion problem can be formulated as follows:

$$\begin{aligned} \min_{X} \quad & rank(X) \\ s.t. \quad & X_{ij} = M_{ij}, (i,j) \in \Omega, \end{aligned} \tag{1}$$

where Ω is the set of locations corresponding to the observed entries.

However, the rank minimization problem (1) is NP-hard in general due to the non-convexity and discontinuous nature of the rank function. The existing algorithms can not directly solve the rank minimization problem efficiently. It is known that the nuclear norm is the tightest convex lower bound of the rank function of matrices on the unit ball $\{X \in \mathbb{R}^{m\times n} | \|X\|_2 \leq 1\}$ [20], where the spectral norm, $\|\cdot\|_2$, of a matrix is equal to the largest singular value of the matrix. Therefore, a widely used approach is to apply the nuclear norm $\|\cdot\|_*$ (i.e., the summation of all the singular values) as a convex surrogate of the non-convex matrix rank function. Thus, the rank minimization problem can be approximated by the nuclear norm minimization problem as its convex relaxation:

$$\begin{aligned} \min_{X} \quad & \|X\|_* \\ s.t. \quad & X_{ij} = M_{ij}, (i,j) \in \Omega. \end{aligned} \tag{2}$$

Recent theoretical breakthrough in matrix completion [4, 5] shows that, under some general constraints, the solution of nuclear norm minimization problems is unique and, with a high probability, is equal to the solution of rank minimization problems if the number of observed entries is large enough.

Many algorithms have been proposed to solve nuclear norm minimization problems (2). Fazel [8] firstly shows that problem (2) can be expressed as a Semi-Definite Programming (SDP) problem, which can be solved by conventional SDP solvers such as SDPT3 and SeDuMi [28, 23]. However, such solvers are usually based on interior point methods, and do not scale to large matrices. This limits the usage of the matrix completion technique in real world applications. Recently, to solve the rank minimization problem for large scale matrices, Toh et al. apply an accelerated proximal gradient optimization technique (NNLS) [27] for solving nuclear regularized least squares problems. It has been shown theoretically that NNLS can terminate within $O(\frac{1}{\sqrt{\epsilon}})$ iterations with an ϵ-optimal solution. Keshavan et al. [12] consider the matrix completion problem by formulating it in a matrix factorization view. Their theoretical analysis shows that one could reconstruct a low-rank matrix by observing a set of entries of size at most a polylogarithmic factor larger than the intrinsic dimension of the variety of rank r matrices. The Singular Value Thresholding algorithm (SVT) [3] is a simple and efficient algorithm for nuclear norm minimization problems proposed by Cai et al., which has been shown to achieve superior performance in practice. However, as a special case of gradient method, SVT has a global convergence rate of $O(\frac{1}{N})$, where N is the number of iterations during optimization. This is too slow especially when dealing with large scale datasets.

In this paper, we propose a novel matrix completion algorithm called Accelerated Singular Value Thresholding (ASVT) for speeding up the standard SVT algorithm. Our basic idea is to obtain the solution of the nuclear norm minimization problem in SVT by solving its dual problem whose objective function can be shown to be continuously differentiable with Lipschitz continuous gradient. Specifically, we exploit the relationship between the optimal solution of the primal problem and that of its dual problem, based on which, the optimal solution of the primary problem can be readily obtained from the optimal solution of the dual problem. We show that the dual problem can be efficiently solved by using an adaptive line search algorithm with a convergence rate of $O(\frac{1}{N^2})$. Moreover, compared with the standard SVT algorithm, our approach can tune the step size adaptively for each iteration. This can further improve the efficiency of the proposed algorithm.

The rest of the paper is organized as follows. We provide a brief review of the standard SVT algorithm in Section 2. In Section 3, we detail our proposed approach and provide some theoretical analysis. We propose an adaptive line search algorithm to solve the optimization problem in Section 4. Experimental results on both synthetic and real world datasets are presented in Section 5. Finally, we provide some concluding remarks and suggestions for future work in Section 6.

Notions: Let $X = (\mathbf{x}_1, \cdots, \mathbf{x}_n)$ be an $m \times n$ matrix, $\Omega \subset \{1, ..., m\} \times \{1, ..., n\}$ denote the indices of the observed entries of X, and let Ω^c denote the indices of the missing entries. The Frobenius norm of X is defined as $\|X\|_F^2 = \sqrt{\Sigma_{(i,j)} X_{ij}^2}$. Let $\mathcal{P}_\Omega$ be the orthogonal projection operator onto the span of matrices vanishing outside of Ω so that the (i,j)-th component of $\mathcal{P}_\Omega(X)$ is equal to X_{ij} when $(i,j) \in \Omega$ and zero otherwise. Let $X = U\Sigma V^T$ be the singular value decomposition for X, where $\Sigma = diag(\sigma_i), 1 \le i \le \min\{m,n\}$ and σ_i is the i-th largest singular value of X. The "shrinkage" operator $D_\tau(X)$ is defined as [3]:

$$D_\tau(X) = U\Sigma_\tau V^T,$$

where $\Sigma_\tau = diag(\max\{\sigma_i - \tau, 0\}), 1 \le i \le \min\{m,n\}$.

Let $S_{\mu,L}^{1,1}(\mathbb{R}^{m\times n})$ be the class of convex functions with Lipschitz gradient [19]. A continuous differentiable function $f(Y)$ belongs to $S_{\mu,L}^{1,1}(\mathbb{R}^{m\times n})$ for some $L \ge \mu \ge 0$ if for any $X, Y \in \mathbb{R}^{m\times n}$ we have both of the following:

$$\|f'(X) - f'(Y)\|_F \le L\|X - Y\|_F, \tag{3}$$

$$\langle f'(X) - f'(Y), X - Y\rangle \ge \mu\|X - Y\|_F^2. \tag{4}$$

2. A BRIEF REVIEW OF SVT

The Singular Value Thresholding (SVT) algorithm solves the following problem:

$$\begin{aligned} \min_X \quad & \tau\|X\|_* + \tfrac{1}{2}\|X\|_F^2 \\ s.t. \quad & \mathcal{P}_\Omega(X) = \mathcal{P}_\Omega(M). \end{aligned} \tag{5}$$

Cai et al. [3] give a theoretical analysis that when $\tau \to \infty$, the optimal solution of problem (5) converges to that of problem (2).

With a given $\tau > 0$ and starting with $Y_0 \in \mathbb{R}^{m\times n}$, the SVT algorithm operates as follows

$$\begin{cases} X^k = D_\tau(Y^{k-1}) \\ Y^k = Y^{k-1} + \delta_k \mathcal{P}_\Omega(M - X^k), \end{cases} \tag{6}$$

until a stopping criterion is reached, where $\{\delta_k\}$ is a positive step size sequence. It has been shown that, when the step sequence obeys $0 < \inf \delta_k \le \sup \delta_k < 2$, the sequence $\{X^k\}$ obtained via (6) exactly converges to the unique solution of the problem in (5).

Actually the iteration scheme (6) is the linearized Bregman iteration, which is a special instance of Uzawa's algorithm [3]. Furthermore, by defining the Lagrangian function of problem (5) as

$$\mathcal{L}(X,Y) = \tau\|X\|_* + \frac{1}{2}\|X\|_F^2 + \langle Y, \mathcal{P}_\Omega(M - X)\rangle, \tag{7}$$

where Y is the Lagrangian dual variable, we can derive its dual function as

$$f(Y) = \inf_X \mathcal{L}(X,Y). \tag{8}$$

Cai et al. show that SVT indeed optimizes the dual function $f(Y)$ via the gradient ascent method.

The SVT algorithm is shown to be an efficient algorithm for matrix completion, especially for large low rank matrices. However, SVT has a global convergence rate of $O(\frac{1}{N})$, which is still too slow for real world applications such as recommender systems.

3. THE OBJECTIVE FUNCTION

In this section we first examine the properties of the dual function $f(Y)$. We then analyze the relationship between the optimal solution of the problem (5) and that of its dual problem. Based on these results, we show how to achieve the optimal solution of the problem (5) from its dual optimum directly.

As the nuclear norm $\|\cdot\|_*$ is not differentiable, it is difficult to optimize the dual function $f(Y)$ directly. However, by using the Moreau-Yosida regularization technique [10], we can obtain some interesting and useful properties of the dual function $f(Y)$.

In the SVT method, the shrinkage operator plays a critical role in the whole iteration scheme. We have the following result about the nuclear norm minimization problem (5).

THEOREM 1. *[3] For each $\tau \geq 0$ and $Y \in \mathbb{R}^{m\times n}$, we have*

$$\mathcal{D}_\tau(Y) = \arg\min_X \tau\|X\|_* + \frac{1}{2}\|X - Y\|_F^2. \quad (9)$$

Theorem 1 tells us that the shrinkage operator is the proximal point mapping associated with the nuclear norm. Based on the properties of Moreau-Yosida regularization (see the Theorem 4.1.4 of [10]), we obtain the following results:

LEMMA 2. *For any $X, Y \in \mathbb{R}^{m\times n}$, we have*

$$\langle \mathcal{D}_\tau(X) - \mathcal{D}_\tau(Y), X - Y\rangle \geq \|\mathcal{D}_\tau(X) - \mathcal{D}_\tau(Y)\|_F^2. \quad (10)$$

It follows that $\mathcal{D}_\tau(Y)$ is globally Lipschitz continuous with modulus 1.

The main result of this section is summarized in the following theorem:

THEOREM 3. *$\forall \tau \geq 0$, the dual function $f(Y)$ in (8) is continuously differentiable with Lipschitz continuous gradient at most 1. Furthermore, when the dual optimal Y^* of the problem (5) is obtained, the primal optimal X^* of the problem (5) is given by:*

$$X^* = \mathcal{D}_\tau(\mathcal{P}_\Omega(Y^*)). \quad (11)$$

PROOF.

$$\begin{aligned}
& f(Y) & (12)\\
= \; & \inf_X \mathcal{L}(X, Y) & (13)\\
= \; & \inf_X (\tau\|X\|_* + \frac{1}{2}\|X\|_F^2 + \langle Y, \mathcal{P}_\Omega(M - X)\rangle) & (14)\\
= \; & \inf_X (\tau\|X\|_* + \frac{1}{2}\|X - \mathcal{P}_\Omega(Y)\|_F^2 + \langle Y, \mathcal{P}_\Omega(M)\rangle & (15)\\
& -\frac{1}{2}\|\mathcal{P}_\Omega(Y)\|_F^2) & (16)\\
= \; & \inf_X (\tau\|X\|_* + \frac{1}{2}\|X - \mathcal{P}_\Omega(Y)\|_F^2) + \langle Y, \mathcal{P}_\Omega(M)\rangle & (17)\\
& -\frac{1}{2}\|\mathcal{P}_\Omega(Y)\|_F^2 & (18)\\
= \; & g(Y) + \langle Y, \mathcal{P}_\Omega(M)\rangle - \frac{1}{2}\|\mathcal{P}_\Omega(Y)\|_F^2, & (19)
\end{aligned}$$

where the first part of (19), i.e. $g(Y)$, is the Moreau-Yosida Regularization of the nuclear norm $\|\cdot\|_*$ [10]. Using the well known properties of Moreau-Yosida Regularization [10] and Theorem 1, we get the following results

- $g(Y)$ is a globally continuously differentiable convex function,
- $g'(Y) = \mathcal{P}_\Omega(Y - \mathcal{D}_\tau(\mathcal{P}_\Omega(Y)))$,
- $g'(Y)$ is continuously differentiable with Lipschitz continuous gradient 1. That is, for any $Y_1, Y_2 \in \mathbb{R}^{m\times n}$,

$$\|g'(Y_1) - g'(Y_2)\|_F \leq \|Y_1 - Y_2\|_F.$$

Then the gradient of $f(Y)$ can be obtained as follows:

$$\begin{aligned}
f'(Y) &= g'(Y) + \mathcal{P}_\Omega(M) - \mathcal{P}_\Omega(Y)\\
&= \mathcal{P}_\Omega(Y) - \mathcal{P}_\Omega(\mathcal{D}_\tau(\mathcal{P}_\Omega(Y))) + \mathcal{P}_\Omega(M) - \mathcal{P}_\Omega(Y)\\
&= \mathcal{P}_\Omega(M - \mathcal{D}_\tau(\mathcal{P}_\Omega(Y))).
\end{aligned} \quad (20)$$

It follows that for any $Y_1, Y_2 \in \mathbb{R}^{m\times n}$, we have

$$\begin{aligned}
&\|f'(Y_1) - f'(Y_2)\|_F\\
=&\|\mathcal{P}_\Omega(\mathcal{D}_\tau(\mathcal{P}_\Omega(Y_1))) - \mathcal{P}_\Omega(\mathcal{D}_\tau(\mathcal{P}_\Omega(Y_2)))\|_F\\
\leq&\|\mathcal{D}_\tau(\mathcal{P}_\Omega(Y_1)) - \mathcal{D}_\tau(\mathcal{P}_\Omega(Y_2))\|_F\\
\leq&\|\mathcal{P}_\Omega(Y_1) - \mathcal{P}_\Omega(Y_2)\|_F\\
\leq&\|Y_1 - Y_2\|_F,
\end{aligned} \quad (21)$$

where the second inequality follows from Lemma 2. Therefore, $f(Y)$ is continuously differentiable with Lipschitz continuous gradient at most 1.

When the dual optimal Y^* is obtained, by using the result of (19), we can get

$$\begin{aligned}
X^* &= \arg\min_X \mathcal{L}(X, Y^*)\\
&= \arg\min_X \tau\|X\|_* + \frac{1}{2}\|X - \mathcal{P}_\Omega(Y^*)\|_F^2 \quad (22)\\
&= \mathcal{D}_\tau(\mathcal{P}_\Omega(Y^*)),
\end{aligned}$$

where the third equality follows from Theorem 1. □

Since $f(Y)$ is the dual function of the objective function (5), $f(Y)$ is concave. Define

$$\begin{aligned}
h(Y) &= -f(Y)\\
&= -(\tau\|\mathcal{D}_\tau(\mathcal{P}_\Omega(Y))\|_* + \frac{1}{2}\|\mathcal{D}_\tau(\mathcal{P}_\Omega(Y))\|_F^2 \quad (23)\\
&+ \langle Y, \mathcal{P}_\Omega(M - \mathcal{D}_\tau(\mathcal{P}_\Omega(Y)))\rangle),
\end{aligned}$$

which is convex. Thus, the following holds for any $Y_1, Y_2 \in \mathbb{R}^{m\times n}$:

$$\langle h(Y_1) - h(Y_2), Y_1 - Y_2\rangle \geq 0. \quad (24)$$

From (20) and (21), it is easy to see $h(Y)$ belongs to the class $S_{0,1}^{1,1}(\mathbb{R}^{m\times n})$ and

$$h'(Y) = -\mathcal{P}_\Omega(M - \mathcal{D}_\tau(\mathcal{P}_\Omega(Y))). \quad (25)$$

Furthermore, in view of the relationship between the primal and dual optimal solutions of problem (5), we can solve problem (5) by firstly minimizing the objective function $h(Y)$, i.e.,

$$\min_{Y\in\mathbb{R}^{m\times n}} h(Y). \quad (26)$$

4. OPTIMIZATION METHOD

The key step in our proposed algorithm is to solve the dual problem (26). In this section, we develop an efficient optimization algorithm to solve this problem. Because the objective function $h(Y)$ is continuously differentiable with Lipschitz continuous gradient 1, in the following we propose to solve the smooth convex optimization problem (26) using the Nesterov's method.

It has been shown that Nesterov's method is a very powerful optimization technique for class $S_{\mu,L}^{1,1}(\mathbb{R}^{m\times n})$ [19]. However, how to choose the step size in each iteration is a critical issue in the Nesterov's method. To overcome this problem, we propose an Accelerated Singular Value Thresholding (ASVT) method with an adaptive line search scheme to solve problem (26).

The Nesterov's method attempts to find the optimal solution of (26) by utilizing two sequence $\{Y_k\}$ and $\{S_k\}$, where $\{Y_k\}$ is the sequence of approximate solutions, and $\{S_k\}$ is the sequence of searching points. The searching point S_k is the affine combination of Y_k and Y_{k-1} as

$$S_k = Y_k + \beta_k(Y_k - Y_{k-1}), \tag{27}$$

where β_k is a tuning parameter. The approximate solution Y_{k+1} can be computed as a gradient step of S_k as

$$Y_{k+1} = S_k - \frac{1}{L_k}h'(S_k), \tag{28}$$

where $1/L_k$ is the step size. Starting from an initial point Y_0, we compute S_k and Y_{k+1} according to (27) and (28), and arrive at the optimal solution Y^*.

In the Nesterov's method, β_k and L_k are two key parameters. When they are set properly, the sequence $\{Y_k\}$ can converge to the optimal Y^* at a certain convergence rate. The Nesterov's constant scheme [19] and Nemirovski's line search scheme [18] usually need to set β_k and L_k. However, the Nesterov's constant scheme assumes L_k and β_k to be constant, while in Nemirovski's line search scheme, L_k is required to monotonically increase, $L_k \leq L_{k+1}$ and β_k is independent on L_k [18], resulting in slow convergence.

In the following, we assume that $\tilde{\mu}$ is the lower bound of μ, and $\tilde{\mu}$ is known in advance. This assumption is reasonable, since 0 is always a lower-bound for μ in (4). With this assumption, we adopt an adaptive line search scheme proposed by Liu et al. [16] for the Nesterov's method. This adaptive line search scheme is built upon the estimate sequence [19], which is defined as follows:

Definition 1. [19] A pair of sequences $\{\phi_k(Y)\}$ and $\{\lambda_k \geq 0\}$ is called an *estimate sequence* of function $h(Y)$ if the following two conditions hold:

1. $\lim_{k\to\infty} \lambda_k = 0$.
2. $\phi_k(Y) \leq (1-\lambda_k)h(Y) + \lambda_k\phi_0(Y), \forall Y \in \mathbb{R}^{m\times n}$.

The following theorem provides a systematic way for constructing the estimate sequence:

THEOREM 4. *[19] Let us assume that:*

1. *$h(Y)$ is smooth and strongly convex with Lipschitz gradient L. Moreover we know the value of $\tilde{\mu}$, which satisfies $\mu \geq \tilde{\mu} \geq 0$.*
2. *$\phi_0(Y)$ is an arbitrary function on $\mathbb{R}^{m\times n}$.*
3. *S_k is an arbitrary searching sequence on $\mathbb{R}^{m\times n}$.*
4. *α_k satisfies: $\alpha_k \in (0,1)$ and $\sum_{k=0}^{\infty}\alpha_k = \infty$.*
5. *$\lambda_0 = 1$.*

Then $\{\phi_k(Y), \lambda_k\}$ can be defined as follows:

$$\begin{aligned} \lambda_{k+1} &= (1-\alpha_k)\lambda_k, & (29)\\ \phi_{k+1}(Y) &= (1-\alpha_k)\phi_k(Y) + \alpha_k[h(S_k) + \\ &\quad \langle h'(S_k), Y - S_k\rangle + \frac{\tilde{\mu}}{2}\|Y - S_k\|_F^2]. & (30)\end{aligned}$$

If we choose a simple quadratic function for $\phi_0(Y)$ as

$$\phi_0(Y) = \phi_0^* + \frac{\gamma_0}{2}\|Y - V_0\|_F^2, \tag{31}$$

Algorithm 1 The Adaptive Line Search Scheme

1: **Input:** $\tilde{\mu}, \alpha_{-1} = 0.5, Y_{-1} = Y_0, L_{-1} = L_0, \gamma_0 \geq \tilde{\mu}, \lambda_0 = 1$.
2: **Output:** Y_N
3: **for** $k = 0, 1, 2, \cdots, N$ **do**
4:   **while** 1 **do**
5:     compute $\alpha_k \in (0,1)$ as the root of $L_k\alpha_k^2 = (1-\alpha_k)\gamma_k + \alpha_k\tilde{\mu}, \gamma_{k+1} = (1-\alpha_k)\gamma_k + \alpha_k\tilde{\mu}, \beta_k = \frac{\gamma_k(1-\alpha_{k-1})}{\alpha_{k-1}(\gamma_k + L_k\alpha_k)}$;
6:     compute $S_k = Y_k + \beta_k(Y_k - Y_{k-1})$
7:     compute $Y_{k+1} = S_k - \frac{1}{L_k}h'(S_k)$
8:     **if** $h(Y_{k+1}) \leq h(S_k) - \frac{1}{2L_k}\|h'(S_k)\|_F^2$ **then**
9:       goto Step 14
10:     **else**
11:       $L_k = 2L_k$
12:     **end if**
13:   **end while**
14:   set $\omega = 2L_k\frac{h(S_k) - h(Y_{k+1})}{\|h'(S_k)\|_F^2}$, $L_{k+1} = h(\omega)L_k$
15:   set $\lambda_{k+1} = (1-\alpha_k)\lambda_k$
16: **end for**

then we can specify the estimation sequence defined in Theorem 4 as [19]:

$$\phi_k(Y) = \phi_k^* + \frac{\gamma_k}{2}\|Y - V_k\|_F^2, \tag{32}$$

where the sequences γ_k, V_k and ϕ_k^* satisfy:

$$\begin{aligned} V_{k+1} &= \frac{1}{\gamma_{k+1}}[(1-\alpha_k)\gamma_k V_k + \tilde{\mu}\alpha_k S_k - \alpha_k h'(S_k)], & (33)\\ \gamma_{k+1} &= (1-\alpha_k)\gamma_k + \alpha_k\tilde{\mu}, & (34)\\ \phi_{k+1}^* &= \frac{\alpha_k(1-\alpha_k)\gamma_k}{\gamma_{k+1}}(\langle h'(S_k), V_k - S_k\rangle + \frac{\tilde{\mu}}{2}\|S_k - V_k\|_F^2) \\ &\quad +(1-\alpha_k)\phi_k^* + \alpha_k h(S_k) - \frac{\alpha_k^2}{2\gamma_{k+1}}\|h'(S_k)\|_F^2. & (35)\end{aligned}$$

The estimate sequence defined in Definition 1 has the following important property:

THEOREM 5. *[19] Let $\{\phi_k(Y)\}$ and $\{\lambda_k \geq 0\}$ be an estimate sequence. For any sequence $\{Y_k\}$, if*

$$h(Y_k) \leq \phi_k^* \equiv \min_{Y\in\mathbb{R}^{m\times n}} \phi_k(Y), \tag{36}$$

we have

$$h(Y_k) - h^* \leq \lambda_k[\phi_0(Y^*) - h^*] \to 0. \tag{37}$$

Based on Theorem 5, we propose an Accelerated Singular Value Thresholding (ASVT) algorithm based on Nesterov's method with an adaptive line search scheme. The complete procedure is summarized in Algorithm 1. In this scheme, the proper adaptive step size $1/L_k$ is designed to look for the approximate solution sequence $\{Y_k\}$ satisfying the condition (36). Then according to Theorem 5, the convergence rate of the solution sequence can be analyzed using the sequence $\{\lambda_k\}$.

In Algorithm 1, the while loop from Step 4 to Step 13 is designed to choose a proper step size to satisfy step 8. As the Lipschitz gradient of $h(Y)$ is 1, just like the Nemirovski's line search scheme, L_k is upper-bounded by 2, since the step 8 always holds when $L_k \geq 1$ [18]. Recall the fact that the iteration of L_k in Nemirovski's line search scheme is

Iteration	20	40	60	80
SVT	2.25e-04	7.36e-07	3.14e-09	1.52e-11
ASVT	**2.50e-06**	**5.94e-12**	**2.11e-14**	**2.40e-14**

Table 1: Relative error comparison between SVT and ASVT on solving the synthetic low rank matrix problem ($m = 1,000, n = 500$, $r = 15$, $p = 0.7$ and $\tau = 2\sqrt{mn}$). As can be seen, our proposed ASVT can accelerate the convergence by 2-5 orders of magnitude.

required to monotonically increase, in step 14 we adopt a more flexible iteration scheme of L_k [16] as

$$L_{k+1} = L_k \cdot h(\omega), h(\omega) = \begin{cases} 1, & 1 \leq \omega \leq 5 \\ 0.8, & \omega > 5 \end{cases} \quad (38)$$

where the parameter ω is computed as

$$\omega = 2L_k \frac{h(S_k) - h(Y_{k+1})}{\|h'(S_k)\|_F^2} \geq 1 \quad (39)$$

due to the condition in Step 8. When ω is too large, L_{k+1} is reduced to $0.8L_k$ to avoid the step size $\frac{1}{L_k}$ used in Step 7 becoming too small, which may slow down the convergence rate. Our experimental results show this particular choice of $h(\cdot)$ works well.

Although the step size $\frac{1}{L_k}$ does not monotonically decrease any more in our adaptive line search scheme, the proposed line search scheme preserves the convergence property, as summarized in the following theorem:

THEOREM 6. *[16] For Algorithm 1, we have*

$$\lambda_N \leq \min \left\{ \prod_{k=1}^{N} (1 - \sqrt{\frac{\tilde{\mu}}{L_k}}), \frac{1}{(1 + \sum_{k=1}^{N} \frac{1}{2}\sqrt{\frac{\gamma_0}{L_k}})^2} \right\}, \quad (40)$$

and

$$h(Y_N) - h^* \leq \lambda_N \left[h(Y_0) - h^* + \frac{\gamma_0}{2}\|Y_0 - Y^*\|_F^2 \right]. \quad (41)$$

Recall that $h(Y)$ is continuously differentiable with Lipschitz continuous gradient 1 and L_k is upper bounded by 2. When we set r_0 larger than 2, ASVT can get a global convergence rate $O(\frac{1}{N^2})$ from Theorem 6, which is significantly better than the original SVT algorithm.

5. EXPERIMENTS

In this section, we evaluate the performance of ASVT in comparison with SVT on both synthetic and real world datasets.

5.1 Experiments on Synthetic Data

We generate matrices $M \in \mathbb{R}^{m \times n}$ of rank r by sampling two matrices of $M_L \in \mathbb{R}^{m \times r}$ and $M_R \in \mathbb{R}^{r \times n}$, each having i.i.d. Gaussian entries, and setting $M = M_L M_R$. Suppose M_Ω is the observed part of M, and the set of observed indices Ω is sampled uniformly at random. Let p be the ratio between the observed entries and all $m \times n$ entries. Then different algorithms will be used to recover the missing entries from the partially observed information by solving the optimization problem in (5) with a given parameter τ. As suggested in [3], τ can be set to $t\sqrt{mn}$, where $2 \leq t \leq 5$.

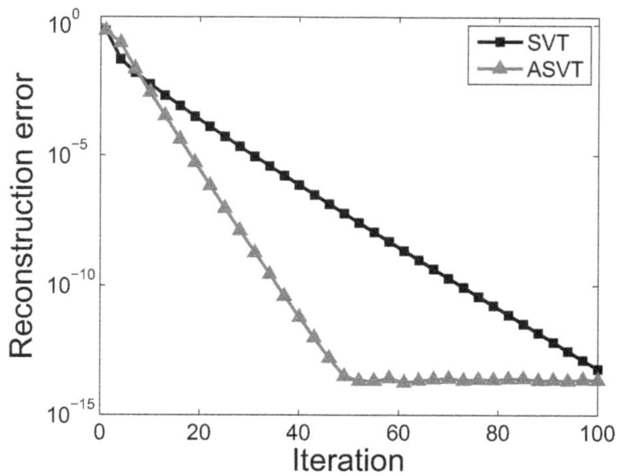

Figure 1: Convergence rate of SVT and ASVT on synthetic data ($m = 1,000, n = 500$, $r = 15$, $p = 0.7$ and $\tau = 2\sqrt{mn}$).

We evaluate the quality of the computed solution X of an algorithm by the relative reconstruction error defined by:

$$error = \|X - M\|_F / \|M\|_F, \quad (42)$$

which is a very commonly used criterion to evaluate the performance of a matrix completion algorithm [27]. For the parameter setting of SVT, we choose the constant step size as $\delta = 1.2/p$ which is recommended in [3]. For ASVT we set the initial L and $\tilde{\mu}$ as $L = p/1.2, \tilde{\mu} = 0.1$.

Firstly we conduct a simulation study with the following parameters: $m = 1,000, n = 500$, $r = 15$, $p = 0.7$ and $\tau = 2\sqrt{mn} \approx 1,414$. So 70% entries are observed. We will recover the other 30% entries by running SVT and ASVT separately. Fig. 1 illustrates the fast convergence rate of ASVT compared with SVT. Table 1 reports the relative reconstruction error of different methods after 20, 40, 60 and 80 iterations. We can observe that the convergence rate of ASVT is at least two orders of magnitude faster than that of SVT, which is consistent with our analysis.

To check how the performance of both algorithms changes with different settings, we test SVT and ASVT on the following different low rank matrix completion problems:

- Fix the matrix size (m, n), the rank r and the ratio of the observed entries p. Then test the performance with respect to different choices of the parameter τ. We fix $m = 1,000$, $n = 500$, $r = 15$, $p = 0.7$, and let τ change from $2\sqrt{mn}$ to $5\sqrt{mn}$.

- Fix the matrix size (m, n), the ratio of observed entries p and the parameter τ. Then test the performance with respect to different choices of the rank r. We fix $m = 1,000$, $n = 500$, $r = 15$, $\tau = 2\sqrt{mn}$, and let p change from 0.4 to 0.9.

- Fix the matrix size (m, n), the matrix rank r and the parameter τ. Then test the performance with respect to different choices of the ratio of observed entries p. We fix $m = 1,000$, $n = 500$, $p = 0.7$, $\tau = 2\sqrt{mn}$, and let r change from 5 to 50.

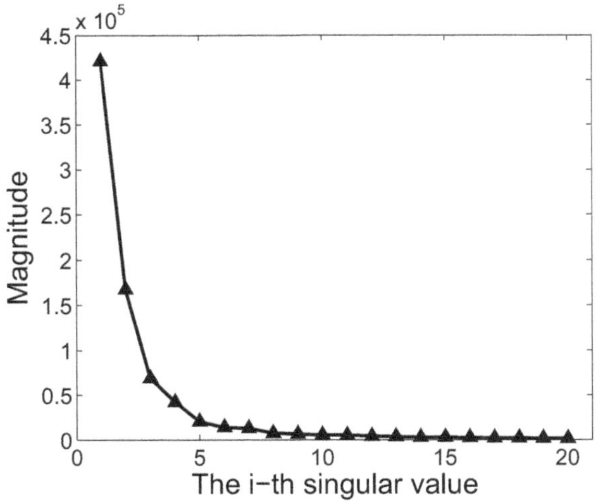

Figure 2: The largest 20 singular values of the distance matrix data.

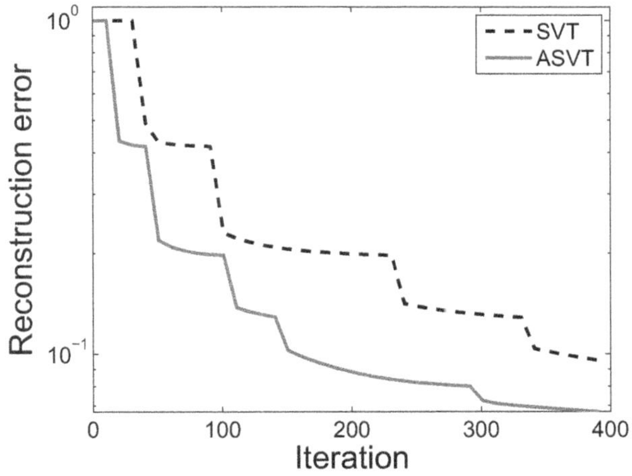

Figure 4: Convergence rates of SVT and ASVT on the real world distance matrix.

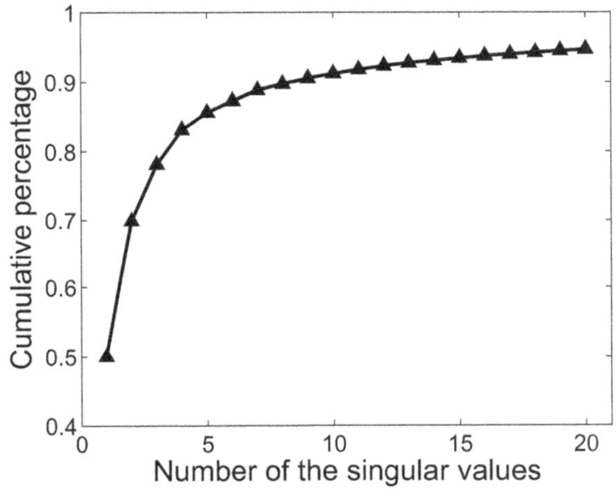

Figure 3: The normalized cumulative sums of the singular values of the distance matrix data.

- Fix the matrix rank r, the ratio of the observed entries p and the parameter τ. Then test the performance with respect to different choices of the matrix size (m, n). We fix $r = 15$, $p = 0.7$, $\tau = 2\sqrt{mn}$, and let (m, n) change from $(m = 400, n = 200)$ to $(m = 5,000, n = 2,500)$.

Table 2 reports the comparative results of randomly generated matrix completion problems. We can observe that ASVT converges much faster than SVT in all cases. ASVT's performance after 50 iterations surpasses SVT by several orders of magnitude. In average ASVT only needs 60% of the iterations required by SVT to achieve a given relative reconstruction error.

5.2 Experiments on Distance Matrix Data

In this experiment, we compare the performance of SVT and ASVT on a real world distance matrix dataset [2]. We consider the problem of recovering the real world distance matrix M of 312 cities in the United States and Canada. The element M_{ij} of M measures the geodesic distance between the city i and the city j. Suppose some locations of M are unknown, we can recover the missing information by using the known part of the pairwise distance matrix. As mentioned in [3], the squared Euclidean distance matrix is a low rank matrix. With geodesic distances, the distance matrix M can also be well approximated by low rank matrices (the top several singular values of M are actually dominant as shown in Fig. 2 and Fig. 3). It is thus reasonable to recover the missing information using matrix completion algorithms.

Suppose the recovered matrix after k iterations is X^k. The rank of X^k has been shown empirically to be nondecreasing in the SVT algorithm [3]; we observe that ASVT has the same property. Since the complete data matrix is known, as suggested in [3], we also use the relative reconstruction error $\|X^k - M\|_F / \|M\|_F$ to measure the effectiveness of SVT and ASVT after the k-th iteration.

The reconstruction error of SVT and ASVT after each iteration is shown in Fig. 4. To achieve the same level of accuracy (measured by the reconstruction error), ASVT needs much fewer iterations than SVT. Fig. 5 shows the change of the rank with the iteration of SVT and ASVT. To reach a certain rank, ASVT needs much fewer iterations than SVT too. The iterations and computational times needed to reach the i-th rank are shown in Table 3. Moreover, we can see that the computational costs in one iteration of SVT and ASVT are similar (time/number of iterations). Note that, the last column of Table 3 ($\|M - M_r\|_F / \|M\|_F$) is the minimum relative error that we can achieve, where M_r is the best rank r approximation of M by computing the SVD of M.

5.3 Experiments on Recommendation Data

We now focus on the application of the proposed algorithm on the recommendation problem. We show the results of SVT and ASVT on the MovieLens data which is a widely used recommendation dataset [27, 29] and can be downloaded from [9]. The dataset is collected by the Grou-

	Settings					iteration (1e-8)		error after 50 iterations	
	m	n	r	p	τ	SVT	ASVT	SVT	ASVT
τ	1,000	500	15	0.7	$5\sqrt{mn}$	121	**61**	8.18e-05	**1.22e-07**
	1,000	500	15	0.7	$4\sqrt{mn}$	99	**47**	1.97e-05	**3.70e-09**
	1,000	500	15	0.7	$3\sqrt{mn}$	77	**30**	1.96e-06	**1.94e-13**
	1,000	500	15	0.7	$2\sqrt{mn}$	56	**30**	4.11e-08	**2.81e-14**
p	1,000	500	15	0.4	$2\sqrt{mn}$	94	**62**	1.04e-05	**1.40e-07**
	1,000	500	15	0.5	$2\sqrt{mn}$	77	**43**	1.91e-06	**8.85e-10**
	1,000	500	15	0.6	$2\sqrt{mn}$	64	**30**	2.36e-07	**2.41e-14**
	1,000	500	15	0.8	$2\sqrt{mn}$	49	**29**	7.23e-09	**3.56e-14**
	1,000	500	15	0.9	$2\sqrt{mn}$	44	**29**	9.29e-10	**3.67e-14**
r	1,000	500	5	0.7	$2\sqrt{mn}$	46	**27**	2.43e-09	**1.61e-14**
	1,000	500	10	0.7	$2\sqrt{mn}$	53	**28**	1.85e-08	**2.37e-14**
	1,000	500	20	0.7	$2\sqrt{mn}$	61	**30**	1.43e-07	**3.72e-14**
	1,000	500	50	0.7	$2\sqrt{mn}$	95	**44**	1.43e-05	**1.19e-09**
m, n	400	200	15	0.7	$2\sqrt{mn}$	91	**41**	9.64e-06	**3.42e-10**
	700	350	15	0.7	$2\sqrt{mn}$	66	**31**	3.64e-07	**6.05e-14**
	1,500	750	15	0.7	$2\sqrt{mn}$	49	**28**	6.96e-09	**2.04e-14**
	2,000	1,000	15	0.7	$2\sqrt{mn}$	46	**27**	2.11e-09	**2.26e-14**
	5,000	2,500	15	0.7	$2\sqrt{mn}$	38	**26**	7.28e-11	**2.68e-14**

Table 2: Comparisons between SVT and ASVT on the synthetic dataset with different settings (matrix size (m, n), rank r, observed ratio p and parameter τ). As can be seen, our proposed ASVT can accelerate the convergence by 2-7 orders of magnitude.

Rank(r)	iteration(k)		time(second)		$\|M - X^k\|_F/\|M\|_F$		$\|M - M_r\|_F/\|M\|_F$
	SVT	ASVT	SVT	ASVT	SVT	ASVT	
0	39	**17**	1.96	**0.87**	1.0000	1.0000	1.0000
1	96	**42**	5.06	**2.23**	0.4173	0.4173	0.4091
2	231	**101**	12.40	**5.46**	0.1977	0.1976	0.1895
3	334	**145**	18.51	**7.88**	0.1284	0.1284	0.1159
4	692	**300**	38.39	**16.89**	0.0797	0.0797	0.0706

Table 3: Comparisons between SVT and ASVT on recovering the distance matrix data. $\|M - X^k\|_F/\|M\|_F$ is the relative reconstruction error after the k-th iteration. Note that, the last column ($\|M - M_r\|_F/\|M\|_F$) is the minimum relative error that we can achieve, where M_r is the best rank r approximation of M by computing the SVD of M.

pLens Research Project at the University of Minnesota and contains 100,000 rating information from 943 users on 1,682 movies. The data has been cleaned up such that users who had less than 20 ratings were removed. So each user in the data has rated at least 20 movies. The ratings are from 1 (strongly unsatisfactory) to 5 (strongly satisfactory). In the recommendation situation, the data matrix is highly sparse (only about 6.3% entries are known). In order to test SVT and ASVT, we split the ratings into training and test sets. In our experiment, 80,000 ratings (80%) are randomly chosen to be the training set and the test set contains the remaining 20,000 ratings (20%).

Evaluation of recommendation algorithms has long been divided between accuracy metrics (e.g. precision/recall) and error metrics (notably, RMSE and MAE). The mathematical convenience and fitness with formal optimization methods have made error matrics like RMSE more popular [6]. Suppose all the existing rating locations of the test set are denoted as Ω. Like many recent research papers [29, 1], we also take the Root Mean Squared Error (RMSE) to measure the effectiveness of an algorithm on solving recommendation problems:

$$RMSE = \sqrt{\frac{\Sigma_{(i,j)\in\Omega}(X_{ij} - M_{ij})^2}{\#|\Omega|}}, \tag{43}$$

where X_{ij} is the recovered value and M_{ij} is the ground truth, and $\#|\Omega|$ is exactly the number of test ratings, i.e. 20,000. So the setting here is $m = 943, n =1{,}682, p = 80{,}000/(mn) \approx 0.05$, and $\#|\Omega| =20{,}000$. We empirically choose $\tau = 10^4$. Both SVT and ASVT automatically recover the rating matrix by estimating the rank from a small to a large value.

As expected, the RMSE value decreases very fast with the iterations of both SVT and ASVT at first. And when the estimated rank is large enough, RMSE value becomes stable. The comparison result in terms of RMSE is shown in Fig. 6. It is clear that ASVT has a much faster convergence rate than SVT on the MovieLens dataset. Fig. 7 shows the change of the rank after each iteration of SVT and ASVT. Similar to Fig. 5, less time is needed for ASVT to reach a certain rank. More detailed numerical results are listed in Table 4. For the MovieLens dataset, it costs ASVT only about half of the time to get a similar RMSE value compared with SVT.

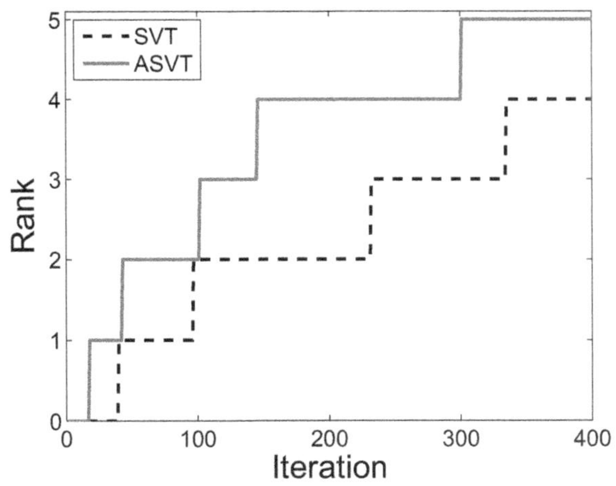

Figure 5: Rank vs. number of iterations of SVT and ASVT on the real world distance matrix.

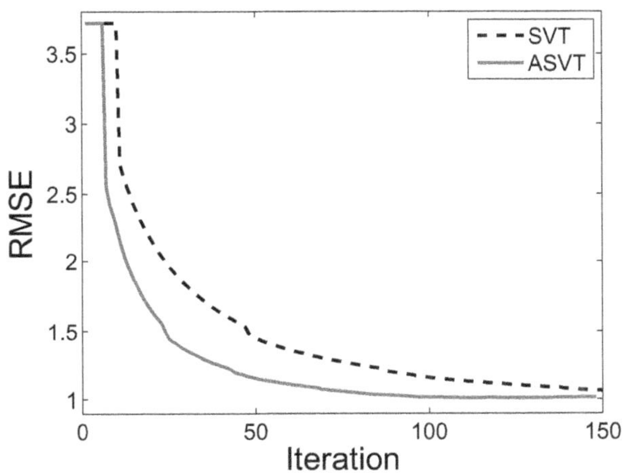

Figure 6: Convergence rates of SVT and ASVT on MovieLens dataset.

6. CONCLUSIONS

In this paper, we present an Accelerated Singular Value Thresholding method (ASVT) for estimating missing values for large scale matrix completion problems. The original SVT method solves the problem (5) with a global convergence rate $O(\frac{1}{N})$. We show how to speed up the original SVT algorithm using the Nesterov's method, which is an optimal first-order black-box method for the smooth convex optimization with a global convergence rate $O(\frac{1}{N^2})$. To further improve the efficiency, we adopt an adaptive line search scheme to tune the step size adaptively and in the meantime preserve the optimal convergence rate. We have conducted a series of experiments on synthetic and real world datasets. Experimental results show that ASVT is more efficient than the original SVT algorithm.

Recovering the missing values from limited information has been well studied for matrices. However, there is not much work on tensors, which are higher dimensional extensions of matrices. In many fields such as computer vision and biomedical signal progressing, it is more natural to represent the data as a tensor. Based on the recent development of tensor techniques [26, 25, 24, 17, 21, 15], it is promising to extend our work from matrix completion to tensor completion.

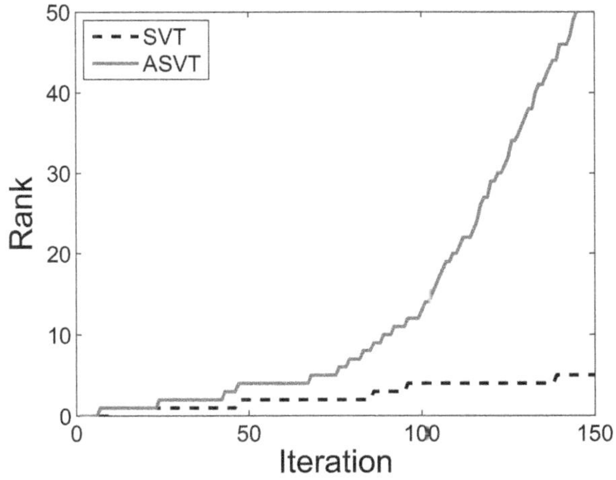

Figure 7: Rank vs. number of iterations of SVT and ASVT on MovieLens dataset.

7. ACKNOWLEDGMENTS

This work was supported by the National Natural Science Foundation of China (Grant No: 61125203).

8. REFERENCES

[1] D. Agarwal, B.-C. Chen, and B. Long. Localized factor models for multi-context recommendation. In *Proceedings of the 17th ACM SIGKDD international conference on Knowledge discovery and data mining*, San Diego, California, USA, 2011.

[2] J. Burkardt. Cities – city distance datasets. `http://www.csit.fsu.edu/~burkardt/datasets/cities/cities.html`.

[3] J. F. Cai, E. J. Candès, and Z. Shen. A singular value thresholding algorithm for matrix completion. *SIAM Journal on Optimization*, 20(4):1956–1982, 2010.

[4] E. J. Candès and B. Recht. Exact matrix completion via convex optimization. *Foundations on Computational Mathematics*, 9(6):717–772, 2009.

[5] E. J. Candès and T. Tao. The power of convex relaxation: Near-optimal matrix completion. *IEEE Transduction on Information Theory*, 56(5):2053–2080, 2009.

[6] P. Cremonesi, Y. Koren, and R. Turrin. Performance of recommender algorithms on top-n recommendation tasks. In *Proceedings of the fourth ACM conference on Recommender systems*, Barcelona, Spain, 2010.

[7] A. Eriksson and A. van den Hengel. Efficient computation of robust low-rank matrix approximations in the presence of missing data using the l1 norm. In *IEEE Conference on Computer Vision*

Rank	iteration		time(second)		RMSE	
	SVT	ASVT	SVT	ASVT	SVT	ASVT
1	46	**23**	24.37	**11.80**	1.5503	1.5574
2	85	**42**	47.40	**22.83**	1.2283	1.2273
3	95	**46**	53.54	**25.14**	1.1775	1.1818
4	138	**67**	80.45	**37.77**	1.0834	1.0841
5	152	**75**	89.28	**42.53**	1.0588	1.0564

Table 4: Comparisons between SVT and ASVT on the MovieLens dataset. We can see that ASVT only needs half of the time to get a similar RMSE value compared with SVT.

and Pattern Recognition, San Francisco, CA, USA, 2010.

[8] M. Fazel. Matrix rank minimization with applications. *PhD thesis, Stanford University*, 2002.

[9] GroupLens. Movielens. `http://www.grouplens.org/taxonomy/term/14`, 2009.

[10] J.-B. Hiriart-Urruty and C. Lemaréchal. *Convex Analysis and Minimization Algorithms*. Springer Verlag, Heidelberg, 1996. Two volumes - 2nd printing.

[11] H. Ji, C. Liu, Z. Shen, and Y. Xu. Robust video denoising using low rank matrix completion. In *IEEE Conference on Computer Vision and Pattern Recognition*, San Francisco, CA, USA, 2010.

[12] R. H. Keshavan, A. Montanari, and S. Oh. Matrix completion from a few entries. *IEEE Transactions on Information Theory*, 56(6):2980–2998, 2010.

[13] Y. Koren. Factorization meets the neighborhood: a multifaceted collaborative filtering model. In *Proceedings of the 14th ACM SIGKDD international conference on Knowledge discovery and data mining*, Las Vegas, Nevada, USA, 2008.

[14] Y. Koren. Collaborative filtering with temporal dynamics. In *Proceedings of the 15th ACM SIGKDD international conference on Knowledge discovery and data mining*, Paris, France, 2009.

[15] N. Li and B. Li. Tensor completion for on-board compression of hyperspectral images. In *Proceedings of the International Conference on Image Processing*, Hong Kong, China, 2010.

[16] J. Liu, J. Chen, and J. Ye. Large-scale sparse logistic regression. In *Proceedings of the 15th ACM SIGKDD international conference on Knowledge discovery and data mining*, Paris, France, 2009.

[17] J. Liu, P. Musialski, P. Wonka, and J. Ye. Tensor completion for estimating missing values in visual data. In *International Conference on Computer Vision*, pages 2114–2121, Kyoto, Japan, 2009.

[18] A. Nemirovski. *Efficient Methods in Convex Programming*. Lecture Notes, 1994.

[19] Y. Nesterov. *Introductory Lectures on Convex Optimization: A Basic Course*. Kluwer Academic Publishers, 2003.

[20] B. Recht, M. Fazel, and P. A. Parrilo. Guaranteed minimum-rank solutions of linear matrix equations via nuclear norm minimization. *SIAM Review*, 52(3):471–501, 2010.

[21] B. R. Silvia Gandy and I. Yamada. Tensor completion and low-n-rank tensor recovery via convex optimization. *Inverse Problems*, 2011.

[22] H. Steck. Training and testing of recommender systems on data missing not at random. In *Proceedings of the 16th ACM SIGKDD international conference on Knowledge discovery and data mining*, Washington, DC, USA, 2010.

[23] J. F. Sturm. Using sedumi 1.02, a matlab toolbox for optimization over symmetric cones, 1998.

[24] D. Tao, X. Li, X. Wu, W. Hu, and S. J. Maybank. Supervised tensor learning. *Knowledge and Information Systems*, 13(1):1–42, 2007.

[25] D. Tao, X. Li, X. Wu, and S. J. Maybank. General tensor discriminant analysis and gabor features for gait recognition. *IEEE Transactions on Pattern Analysis and Machine Intelligence*, 29(10):1700–1715, 2007.

[26] D. Tao, M. Song, X. Li, J. Shen, J. Sun, X. Wu, C. Faloutsos, and S. J. Maybank. Bayesian tensor approach for 3-d face modeling. *IEEE Transactions on Circuits and Systems for Video Technology*, 18(10):1397–1410, 2008.

[27] K.-C. Toh and S. Yun. An accelerated proximal gradient algorithm for nuclear norm regularized least squares problems. *Pacific Journal of Optimization*, 6:615–640, 2010.

[28] R. H. Tutuncu, K. C. Toh, and M. J. Todd. Sdpt3 – a matlab software package for semidefinite quadratic linear programming, version 3.0, 2001.

[29] Y. Zhang and J. Koren. Efficient bayesian hierarchical user modeling for recommendation system. In *Proceedings of the 30th annual international ACM SIGIR conference on Research and development in information retrieval*, Amsterdam, The Netherlands, 2007.

Fast Bregman Divergence NMF using Taylor Expansion and Coordinate Descent

Liangda Li, Guy Lebanon, Haesun Park
School of Computational Science and Engineering
Georgia Institute of Technology
Atlanta, GA 30032
{ldli, lebanon, hpark}@cc.gatech.edu

ABSTRACT

Non-negative matrix factorization (NMF) provides a lower rank approximation of a matrix. Due to nonnegativity imposed on the factors, it gives a latent structure that is often more physically meaningful than other lower rank approximations such as singular value decomposition (SVD). Most of the algorithms proposed in literature for NMF have been based on minimizing the Frobenius norm. This is partly due to the fact that the minimization problem based on the Frobenius norm provides much more flexibility in algebraic manipulation than other divergences. In this paper we propose a fast NMF algorithm that is applicable to general Bregman divergences. Through Taylor series expansion of the Bregman divergences, we reveal a relationship between Bregman divergences and Euclidean distance. This key relationship provides a new direction for NMF algorithms with general Bregman divergences when combined with the scalar block coordinate descent method. The proposed algorithm generalizes several recently proposed methods for computation of NMF with Bregman divergences and is computationally faster than existing alternatives. We demonstrate the effectiveness of our approach with experiments conducted on artificial as well as real world data.

Categories and Subject Descriptors

I.2.6 [**Artificial Intelligence**]: Learning; G.1.6 [**Numerical Analysis**]: Optimization

General Terms

Algorithms, Experimentation, Performance

Keywords

Non-negative Matrix Factorization, Bregman Divergences, Euclidean distance, Taylor Series Expansion

1. INTRODUCTION

Non-negative matrix factorization (NMF) is a dimensionality reduction method that has attracted great attention over a decade. It approximates a matrix $\mathbf{A}$ by a product of two lower rank matrices $\mathbf{W}$ and $\mathbf{H}$ with non-negative entries minimizing the divergence between $\mathbf{A}$ and $\mathbf{W}\mathbf{H}^T$. Using Bregman divergences, our problem is to find

$$\underset{\mathbf{W}\geq 0,\mathbf{H}\geq 0}{\arg\min}\ D_\phi(\mathbf{A}\|\mathbf{W}\mathbf{H}^T),$$

where $D_\phi(\mathbf{A}\|\mathbf{W}\mathbf{H}^T)$ denotes a Bregman divergence between $\mathbf{A}$ and $\mathbf{W}\mathbf{H}^T$. The decomposition discovers a latent structure in the data and is useful in signal processing, collaborative filtering, clustering, and other data-mining tasks. Due to the non-negativity constraint on $\mathbf{W}$ and $\mathbf{H}$, NMF discovers a latent structure that is often more interpretable than SVD based factorizations.

Various Bregman divergences, such as Frobenius norm and KL divergence, have been used in a wide range of applications, including text clustering, signal processing, image processing, and music analysis. A general NMF algorithm for various Bregman divergences not only offers a general solution for different applications, but also enables the knowledge share across different domains. Recent years have seen a surge of interest in NMF [25, 7, 22, 20]. The earliest NMF algorithms aimed at directly optimizing the divergence, resulting in higher scale computational costs. Moreover, most algorithms have been developed for Frobenius norm(which becomes the Euclidean distance for scalars) minimization, a popular special case of the Bregman divergence.

Lee and Seung's simple multiplicative update rule [25] has been one of the most utilized method for NMF over a decade, for both Frobenius norm and KL(Kullback-Leibler) divergence. Dhillon et al. [8] extended it to solve NMF with general Bregman divergences. By using an auxiliary function, Fevotte et al. [11] discussed the updating rule under the IS divergence, and applied it to music analysis. An alternative updating rule is also provided based on the statistical interpretation of the properties of the IS divergence. Nevertheless, the above algorithms generally suffer from high computational cost and slow convergence [23].

Cichocki et al. [5] introduced an alternative algorithm with improved local updating rules, achieving high efficiency in solving NMF problems. The resulting algorithm applies to the Frobenius norm. Similar algorithms have been proposed for a few other divergences, but these algorithms show a relatively slow convergence.

Other NMF algorithms are proposed by Lin et al. [27] using projected gradient with Armijo rule to build the updating rule. Kim and Park [19, 20] proposed an NMF algorithm based on alternating non-negative least squares (ANLS) and an active set based algorithm. This algorithm was further

KDD'12, August 12–16, 2012, Beijing, China.

Table 1: Notations used in the paper

$\mathbb{R}$	real number
$\mathbb{R}_+$	nonegative real number
$\mathbb{R}^{M\times N}$	vector space of matrice of size $M \times N$
$\mathbb{R}^K$	vector space of vectors of size K
$\odot$	element-wise product or Hadamard product
$\oslash$	element-wise division
$\mathbf{a}_j$	j-th column vector of matrix $\mathbf{A}$
a_{ij}	element in the i-th row and j-th column of $\mathbf{A}$
$\lVert\cdot\rVert_2$	Euclidean distance(Frobenius norm)
D_ϕ	Bregman divergences
$\nabla^t\phi(x)$	a element-wise t-order derivative operator of ϕ at x
$\text{sgn}(x)$	sign function or signum function

improved by block principal pivoting in ANLS. An extensive comparison of these algorithms appears in [22, 23]. For a survey of NMF algorithms, see [21].

In this paper, we propose a fast NMF algorithm for a general class of Bregman divergences. Using Taylor series we relate Bregman divergences to the Euclidean distance and show that the Bregman divergence optimization problem can be expressed in terms of the Euclidean distance. The discovered relationship between Bregman divergence and the Euclidean distance leads to local updating rules, and provides one efficient algorithmic framework which is applicable to NMF formulated in Bregman divergences, and solutions for a wide range of applications.

We investigate the performance of the new algorithm on both artificial and real world data sets, including Xspectra [6], AT&T Laboratory Face Image data set [1], Movielens, and Netflix. We conduct a series of experiments comparing our proposed methods to previously proposed algorithms. Our experiments show that for a wide range of Bregman divergences our new algorithm is substantially faster.

Our main contributions in this paper include

1. a new relationship connecting Bregman divergences and the Euclidean distance via Taylor series expansion, and
2. an NMF algorithm applicable for all Bregman divergences that is substantially faster.

Note that by relating all Bregman divergences to the Euclidean distance, we propose one united highly efficient algorithm applicable for all NMF formulated in any Bregman divergences. In contrast, most other existing algorithms are designed for one or only a subset of Bregman divergences.

Table 1 summarizes the notations used in this paper.

2. NMF WITH BREGMAN DIVERGENCES

In NMF, given a matrix $\mathbf{A} = [a_{ij}] \in \mathbb{R}_+^{M\times N}$, and an integer $K \leq \min(M, N)$, we are to find $\mathbf{W} = [\mathbf{w}_1, \mathbf{w}_2, \ldots, \mathbf{w}_K] \in \mathbb{R}_+^{M\times K}$ whose columns represent basis vectors in a K-dimensional space, and $\mathbf{H} = [\mathbf{h}_1, \mathbf{h}_2, \ldots, \mathbf{h}_K] \in \mathbb{R}_+^{N\times K}$ whose columns represent mixing proportions, such that

$$\mathbf{A} \approx \mathbf{A}' = \mathbf{W}\mathbf{H}^T. \tag{1}$$

The quality of this approximation can be measured using Bregman divergences,

$$\begin{aligned} D_\phi(\mathbf{A}\|\mathbf{A}') &= \sum_{i,j} D_\phi(a_{ij}\|a'_{ij}) \\ &= \sum_{i,j} (\phi(a_{ij}) - \phi(a'_{ij}) - \nabla\phi(a'_{ij})(a_{ij} - a'_{ij})) \end{aligned}$$

where ϕ is a univariate convex smooth function.

Bregman divergences are not symmetric in general, and the solution for $\min D_\phi(\mathbf{W}\mathbf{H}^T\|\mathbf{A})$ will be different from that of $\min D_\phi(\mathbf{A}\|\mathbf{W}\mathbf{H}^T)$. In this paper, we focus on $D_\phi(\mathbf{A}\|\mathbf{W}\mathbf{H}^T)$ which is more widely used in applications. For instance, Probabilistic Latent Semantic Analysis (PLSI) [16], a statistical technique for data analysis, optimizes the same objective function as NMF with Kullback-Leibler divergence [9]. Other examples are signal analysis using $D_{KL}(\mathbf{A}\|\mathbf{W}\mathbf{H}^T)$ and music analysis using Itakura-Saito divergence $D_{IS}(\mathbf{A}\|\mathbf{W}\mathbf{H}^T)$. From a theoretical perspective, maximum likelihood estimation and information theory indicate that $D_{KL}(\mathbf{A}\|\mathbf{W}\mathbf{H}^T)$ is better motivated than $D_{KL}(\mathbf{W}\mathbf{H}^T\|\mathbf{A})$, at least when the two arguments are probability vectors.

The choice of $\phi(x) = x^2/2$ reduces D_ϕ to the squared Frobenius norm of $\mathbf{E} = \mathbf{A} - \mathbf{W}\mathbf{H}^T$, which is the sum of squared entries of the residual matrix $\mathbf{E}$ (Notice that the Frobenius norm of a matrix can be viewed as the Euclidean distance of the corresponding vectorized matrix). Other choices for ϕ result in the non-negative Kullback-Leibler (KL) divergence or Itakura-Saito (IS) divergence. The specific choice of ϕ depends on the application. For example, the Frobenius norm has been used successfully in text clustering [3]. KL divergence is well suited for many problems in signal processing [5] while IS divergence has been shown to perform well in music recommendation [11]. For other choices of ϕ and areas where these divergences are ultilized, see [7].

In [2], Bregman divergences have been used to derive an exact characterization of the difference between the two sides of Jensen's inequality. Banerjee et al. [3] discussed a clustering algorithm for general Bregman divergences. They also showed that there exists a bijection between regular exponential families and large classes of Bregman divergences. Singh and Gordon [31] showed that methods such as NMF, Weighted SVD, pLSI can be viewed in a general framework of matrix factorization with Bregman divergences. Pietra et al. [30] derived and proved convergence of iterative algorithms to minimize Bregman divergence subject to linear constraints based on auxiliary functions. Wang and Schuurmans [32] proposed a novel algorithm that extracts hidden latent structure by minimizing Bregman divergences. Lebanon [24] used Taylor series approximation to show a relationship between KL divergences and the Fisher geometry which enjoys certain axiomatic properties.

Some examples of Bregman divergences and the corresponding ϕ functions are listed in Table 2.

3. FAST ALGORITHM FOR NMF

Many existing NMF algorithms can be explained using the block coordinate descent framework [21]. Different partitions of variables $\mathbf{W}$ and $\mathbf{H}$ lead to different NMF algorithms. One natural way of partition [8, 19, 22] is the two blocks representing $\mathbf{W}$ and $\mathbf{H}$, with which the subproblems result in a nonnegativity constrained least square (NLS) problem. Another way of partition [5, 14] is $K(M + N)$ blocks where each represents a single element in $\mathbf{W}$ or $\mathbf{H}$.

Coordinate descent is also employed to solve many other problems. Wu et al. [33] came up with coordinate descent algorithm for l_1 regularized regression, Lasso. A greedy coordinate descent method was proposed in [26] to solve the Basis Pursuit problem, and can be applied to tasks such as compressed sensing and image denoising. Yun and Toh [34] proposed a block coordinate gradient descent method for general l_1-regularized convex minimization problems. Recently, a fast coordinate descent algorithm was developed in [13] to estimate generalized linear models with convex penalties. Coordinate descent was also used for solving non-convex penalty functions, such as smoothly clipped absolute deviation (SCAD) penalty and the minimax concave penalty (MCP) in [4].

We denote the residual term in the NMF approximation (1) as $\mathbf{A}-\mathbf{W}\mathbf{H}^T = \mathbf{A}^{(k)} - \mathbf{w}_k\mathbf{h}_k^T$, where the k-residual $\mathbf{A}^{(k)}$ is define as

$$\mathbf{A}^{(k)} = \mathbf{A} - \sum_{p\neq k} \mathbf{w}_p\mathbf{h}_p^T = \mathbf{A} - \mathbf{W}\mathbf{H}^T + \mathbf{w}_k\mathbf{h}_k^T,$$

for $k = 1,\ldots,K$. In the case of $\phi(x) = \frac{1}{2}x^2$, D_ϕ leads to the squared Frobenius norm

$$\begin{aligned} D_\phi(\mathbf{A}\|\mathbf{A}') &= D_\phi(\mathbf{A}\|\mathbf{W}\mathbf{H}^T) = \frac{1}{2}\|\mathbf{A}-\mathbf{W}\mathbf{H}^T\|_F^2 \\ &= \frac{1}{2}\|\mathbf{A}^{(k)} - \mathbf{w}_k\mathbf{h}_k^T\|_F^2 = D_\phi(\mathbf{A}^{(k)}\|\mathbf{w}_k\mathbf{h}_k^T). \end{aligned} \quad (2)$$

Let us define

$$E_t(\mathbf{A}\|\mathbf{A}') = \sum_{ij} |a_{ij} - a'_{ij}|^t, \quad t \in \{1,2,\ldots\}$$

which is the t-th power of t-norm distance between vectorized matrices $\mathbf{A}$ and $\mathbf{A}'$. Then we have

$$\begin{aligned} E_t(\mathbf{A}\|\mathbf{A}') &= E_t(\mathbf{A}^{(k)}\|\mathbf{w}_k\mathbf{h}_k^T) \quad \text{or} \\ E_t(a_{ij}\|a'_{ij}) &= E_t(a_{ij}^{(k)}\|w_{ik}h_{jk}). \end{aligned} \quad (3)$$

Cichocki et al. [5] proposed an algorithm called Hierarchical Alternating Least Squares (HALS) for NMF with Frobenius norm. They designed local updating rules based on the relationship in Eqn (2), leading to a fast algorithm. Each updating step solves a sub-optimization problem with a closed form solution, and the algorithm converges much faster than the multiplicative updating rule in [25, 8]. Although similar algorithms for Alpha divergence and Beta divergence have been proposed, they aimed at minimizing $D_\phi(\mathbf{A}^{(k)}\|\mathbf{w}_k\mathbf{h}_k^T)$ instead of $D_\phi(\mathbf{A}\|\mathbf{W}\mathbf{H}^T)$, which are two different functions for most Bregman divergences other than the Frobenius norm.

In this paper, using the relationship in Eqn (3), the optimization goal changes from the approximation between the given matrix and the multiplication of two low-rank matrices to the approximation between the k-residual matrix and the multiplication of two vectors. Since elements in $\mathbf{w}_k$(or $\mathbf{h}_k$) can be computed independently, we actually focus on the approximation between $a_{ij}^{(k)}$(single element in k-residual matrix) and the multiplication of w_{ik} and h_{jk}. Based on this observation, a novel scalar coordinate descent algorithm with $k(m+n)$ scalar blocks can be designed. In the rest of this section, we will

- Derive a new relationship between general Bregman divergences and the Euclidean distance;
- Use the above relationship to replace the minimization goal from the Bregman divergences $D_\phi(\mathbf{A}\|\mathbf{W}\mathbf{H}^T)$ with an expression of $E_t(a_{ij}^{(k)}\|w_{ik}h_{jk})$;
- Design coordinate descent algorithm to optimize $E_t(a_{ij}^{(k)}\|w_{ik}h_{jk})$.

3.1 A Taylor Series Expansion of Bregman Divergences

The following proposition shows a new relationship between Bregman divergences and the Euclidean distance, which plays a key role in our fast algorithm development.

PROPOSITION 3.1.

$$D_\phi(\mathbf{A}\|\mathbf{A}') = \sum_{i,j}\sum_{t=2}^{\infty} \frac{\nabla^t\phi(a'_{ij})}{t!}(-\text{sgn}(a'_{ij}-a_{ij}))^t E_t(a_{ij}\|a'_{ij}).$$

PROOF. The Taylor expansion of $D_\phi(a_{ij}\|a'_{ij})$ leads to

$$\begin{aligned} D_\phi(a_{ij}\|a'_{ij}) &= \phi(a_{ij}) - \phi(a'_{ij}) - \nabla\phi(a'_{ij})(a_{ij}-a'_{ij}) \\ &= \nabla\phi(a'_{ij})(a_{ij}-a'_{ij}) + \sum_{t=2}^{\infty}\frac{\nabla^t\phi(a'_{ij})}{t!}(a_{ij}-a'_{ij})^t \\ &\quad - \nabla\phi(a'_{ij})(a_{ij}-a'_{ij}) \\ &= \sum_{t=2}^{\infty}\frac{\nabla^t\phi(a'_{ij})}{t!}(a_{ij}-a'_{ij})^t \\ &= \sum_{t=2}^{\infty}\frac{\nabla^t\phi(a'_{ij})}{t!}(-\text{sgn}(a'_{ij}-a_{ij}))^t E_t(a_{ij}\|a'_{ij}) \end{aligned} \quad (4)$$

where $\nabla^t\phi(a'_{ij})$ is the t-order derivative of ϕ at a'_{ij}. □

The above relationship is then employed to replace our objective function $D_\phi(\mathbf{A}\|\mathbf{W}\mathbf{H}^T)$ with an expression that involves $E_t(a_{ij}^{(k)}\|w_{ik}h_{jk})$. In the following subsection, we show how this relationship allows us to recast the problem in a form that is easier to solve and leads to a novel and efficient algorithm. Notice that this relationship is an equality rather than an approximation.

Taylor expansion has been utilized in numerical problems including a quadratic approximation of the objective or loss function. For instance, to solve a regularized log-determinant program, Hsieh et al. [18] proposed a novel algorithm which is based on Newton's method and employs a quadratic approximation. For the l_1-regularized linear least squares problem, a gradient projection method was proposed in [12] to solve the bound constrained quadratic programming reformulation. Yun. et al [34] went a step further by using quadratic approximation to solve the general l_1-regularized convex minimization problem. In each iteration, the objective is replaced by a strictly convex quadratic approximation, then block coordinate descent is used to obtain a feasible descent direction. Taylor explansion was also employed to approximate non-convex penalties, such as SCAD [10] and MCP [29].

3.2 A New Algorithm for NMF with Bregman Divergences

Based on Eqns (3) and (4) , the Bregman divergences $D_\phi(\mathbf{A}\|\mathbf{W}\mathbf{H}^T)$ can be expressed in terms $E_t(a_{ij}^{(k)}\|w_{ik}h_{jk})$ as

$$D_\phi(\mathbf{A}\|\mathbf{W}\mathbf{H}^T) = \sum_{i,j}\sum_{t=2}^{\infty}\frac{\nabla^t\phi(a'_{ij})}{t!}(-\text{sgn}(a'_{ij}-a_{ij}))^t E_t(a_{ij}^{(k)}\|w_{ik}h_{jk}).$$

Instead of calculating the partial derivatives of $D_\phi(\mathbf{A}\|\mathbf{W}\mathbf{H}^T)$ with respect to $\mathbf{W}$ and $\mathbf{H}$, we turn to the partial derivative of $E_t(a_{ij}^{(k)}\|w_{ik}h_{jk})$ with respect to smaller blocks, w_{ik} and h_{jk}. Using this and the scalar block coordinate descent framework in constrained optimization where each block consists of a single unknown element in $\mathbf{W}$ or $\mathbf{H}$ (assuming other elements are fixed), a novel fast algorithm can be derived.

From

$$\frac{\partial}{\partial h_{jk}}\left(\frac{\nabla^t \phi(a'_{ij})}{t!}(-\mathrm{sgn}(w_{ik}h_{jk} - a_{ij}^{(k)}))^t E_t(a_{ij}^{(k)} \| w_{ik}h_{jk})\right)$$
$$= w_{ik}\frac{\nabla^{t+1}\phi(a'_{ij})}{t!}(a_{ij}^{(k)} - w_{ik}h_{jk})^t - w_{ik}\frac{\nabla^t \phi(a'_{ij})}{(t-1)!}(a_{ij}^{(k)} - w_{ik}h_{jk})^{t-1}$$

and Eqn (4), we obtain

$$\begin{aligned}\frac{\partial D_\phi(a_{ij}\|a'_{ij})}{\partial h_{jk}} &= w_{ik}\nabla^2\phi(a'_{ij})(w_{ik}h_{jk} - a_{ij}^{(k)}) \\ &+ \sum_{t=2}^{\infty}\Big(- w_{ik}\frac{\nabla^{t+1}\phi(a'_{ij})}{t!}(a_{ij}^{(k)} - w_{ik}h_{jk})^t \\ &+ w_{ik}\frac{\nabla^{t+1}\phi(a'_{ij})}{t!}(a_{ij}^{(k)} - w_{ik}h_{jk})^t\Big) \\ &= w_{ik}\nabla^2\phi(a'_{ij})(w_{ik}h_{jk} - a_{ij}^{(k)}).\end{aligned}$$

Summing over the matrix rows and columns, we have[1]

$$\begin{aligned}\frac{\partial D_\phi(\mathbf{A}\|\mathbf{W}\mathbf{H}^T)}{\partial h_{jk}} &= \sum_{i=1}^{M} w_{ik}\nabla^2\phi(a'_{ij})(w_{ik}h_{jk} - a_{ij}^{(k)}) \\ &= [\mathbf{W}^T(\nabla^2\phi(\mathbf{W}\mathbf{H}^T)\odot(\mathbf{w}_k\mathbf{h}_k^T - \mathbf{A}^{(k)}))]_{kj}. \quad (5)\end{aligned}$$

The solution for the scalar block h_{jk} can be obtained by solving:

$$0 = \frac{\partial D_\phi(\mathbf{A}\|\mathbf{W}\mathbf{H}^T)}{\partial h_{jk}} = \sum_{i=1}^{M} w_{ik}\nabla^2\phi(a'_{ij})w_{ik}h_{jk} - \sum_{i=1}^{M} w_{ik}\nabla^2\phi(a'_{ij})a_{ij}^{(k)}$$

which leads to the element-wise updating rule:

$$h_{jk} = \frac{\sum_{i=1}^{M}\nabla^2\phi(a'_{ij})a_{ij}^{(k)}w_{ik}}{\sum_{i=1}^{M}\nabla^2\phi(a'_{ij})w_{ik}w_{ik}}. \quad (6)$$

Similarly, we can derive an updating rule for w_{ik}.

The summary of the algorithm, which we refer to as `sBCD` (Scalar Block Coordinate Descent) is shown in Algorithm 1[2]. Note that the algorithm follows the block coordinate descent framework where each element in $\mathbf{W}$ and $\mathbf{H}$ is considered as a scalar block that we update in each step.

The algorithm above is expressed in a general form for all Bregman divergences. Replacing $\phi(x)$ with the corresponding expression provides the specific algorithm for each specific Bregman divergence. Interestingly, for squared Frobenius norm, the updating rule is precisely the same as `HALS` algorithm proposed in [5]. Some specific updating rules are listed in Table 2.

The following rearrangements of expressions show an interesting relationship between `sBCD` and two other NMF algorithms, `Multiplcative Updating` and `Gradient Descent` methods. According to Eqns (5) and (6), we have

$$\begin{aligned}h_{jk} &= \left[\frac{\sum_{i=1}^{M}\nabla^2\phi(a'_{ij})(a_{ij} - a'_{ij} + w_{ik}h_{jk})w_{ik}}{\sum_{i=1}^{M}\nabla^2\phi(a'_{ij})w_{ik}w_{ik}}\right]_+ \\ &= \left[h_{jk} + \frac{[\mathbf{W}^T(\nabla^2\phi(\mathbf{W}\mathbf{H}^T)\odot(\mathbf{A} - \mathbf{W}\mathbf{H}^T))]_{kj}}{[(\mathbf{W}\odot\mathbf{W})^T\nabla^2\phi(\mathbf{W}\mathbf{H}^T)]_{kj}}\right]_+ \\ &= \left[h_{jk} + \frac{1}{[(\mathbf{W}\odot\mathbf{W})^T\nabla^2\phi(\mathbf{W}\mathbf{H}^T)]_{kj}}\left(-\frac{\partial D_\phi(\mathbf{A}\|\mathbf{W}\mathbf{H}^T)}{\partial h_{kj}}\right)\right]_+\end{aligned}$$

[1]definition of $\odot$ can be found in Table 1.

[2]$[x]_+ = \max\{x, 0\}$.

Algorithm 1 `sBCD` Algorithm

Given $\mathbf{A} \in \mathbb{R}^{M\times N}$, a reduced dimension K, and function ϕ for a Bregman divergence, initialize values for $\mathbf{W}$ and $\mathbf{H}$.
$\mathbf{A}' = \mathbf{W}\mathbf{H}^T$
$\mathbf{E} = \mathbf{A} - \mathbf{A}'$
repeat
  $\mathbf{B} = \nabla^2\phi(\mathbf{A}')$
  for $k = 1, 2, \ldots, K$ **do**
    $\mathbf{A}^{(k)} = \mathbf{E} + \mathbf{w}_k\mathbf{h}_k^T$
    for $j = 1, 2, \ldots, N$ **do**
      $h_{jk} = \left[\frac{\sum_{i=1}^{M} b_{ij}a_{ij}^{(k)}w_{ik}}{\sum_{i=1}^{M} b_{ij}w_{ik}w_{ik}}\right]_+$
    end for
    for $i = 1, 2, \ldots, M$ **do**
      $w_{ik} = \left[\frac{\sum_{j=1}^{N} b_{ij}a_{ij}^{(k)}h_{jk}}{\sum_{j=1}^{N} b_{ij}h_{jk}h_{jk}}\right]_+$
    end for
    $\mathbf{E} = \mathbf{A}^{(k)} - \mathbf{w}_k\mathbf{h}_k^T$
  end for
  $\mathbf{A}' = \mathbf{W}\mathbf{H}^T$
until stopping criterion is reached

where we can view $-\frac{\partial D_\phi(\mathbf{A}\|\mathbf{W}\mathbf{H}^T)}{\partial h_{jk}}$ as the gradient direction, $\frac{1}{[(\mathbf{W}\odot\mathbf{W})^T\nabla^2\phi(\mathbf{W}\mathbf{H}^T)]_{kj}}$ as the step size. Notice that a hard constraint is enforced to ensure h_{jk} to be nonnegative.

On the other hand, multiplicative updating rule proposed in [25] can be written as:

$$\begin{aligned}h_{jk} &= h_{jk}\frac{[\mathbf{W}^T(\nabla^2(\mathbf{W}\mathbf{H}^T)\odot\mathbf{A})]_{kj}}{[\mathbf{W}^T(\nabla^2(\mathbf{W}\mathbf{H}^T)\odot\mathbf{W}\mathbf{H}^T)]_{kj}} \\ &= h_{jk} + \frac{h_{jk}}{[\mathbf{W}^T(\nabla^2\phi(\mathbf{W}\mathbf{H}^T)\odot\mathbf{W}\mathbf{H}^T)]_{kj}}\left(-\frac{\partial D_\phi(\mathbf{A}\|\mathbf{W}\mathbf{H}^T)}{\partial h_{jk}}\right).\end{aligned}$$

A gradient descent algorithm for NMF is also proposed in [25], which uses a fixed step size. With the above rearrangements of expressions, we can see that the difference between `sBCD`, `Multiplicative Updating` and `Gradient Descent` is the step sizes only. The advantage of `sBCD` and `Multiplicative Updating` over `Gradient Descent` is that they choose step sizes according to the result of previous iteration. Further comparsion of step sizes of `sBCD` and `Multiplicative Updating` shows that

$$\frac{1}{[(\mathbf{W}\odot\mathbf{W})^T\nabla^2\phi(\mathbf{W}\mathbf{H}^T)]_{kj}} \geq \frac{h_{jk}}{[\mathbf{W}^T(\nabla^2\phi(\mathbf{W}\mathbf{H}^T)\odot\mathbf{W}\mathbf{H}^T)]_{kj}}.$$

The above equation illustrates that `Multiplicative Updating` uses a conservative step size in order to keep the update result nonnegative, while a longer step is used by `sBCD` to make each updating more efficient.

3.3 Fast NMF algorithm with Sparsity Constraints

An important variation of NMF is the NMF subject to sparsity constraints [19] on one or both factors. For imposing sparsity on $\mathbf{H}$, the objective function is replaced with the following penalized version:[3]

$$L(\mathbf{A}\|\mathbf{W}\mathbf{H}^T) = D_\phi(\mathbf{A}\|\mathbf{W}\mathbf{H}^T) + \alpha\sum_{k=1}^{K}\|\mathbf{h}_k\|_1,$$

[3]Notice in implementation, regularization term $\|\mathbf{W}\|_F$ is added to prevent it from growing too large.

Table 2: Updating rules for specific Bregman Divergences

Description	Function $\phi(x)$	$\nabla^2\phi(x)$	$D_\phi(a\|a')$	updating rule
Frobenius norm	$\frac{x^2}{2}$	1	$(a-a')^2/2$	$h_{jk} = \frac{\sum_{i=1}^M a_{ij}^{(k)} w_{ik}}{\sum_{i=1}^M w_{ik}w_{ik}}$
KL-divergence	$x \log x$	$1/x$	$a \log \frac{a}{a'} - a + a'$	$h_{jk} = \frac{\sum_{i=1}^M a_{ij}^{(k)} w_{ik}/a'_{ij}}{\sum_{i=1}^M w_{ik}w_{ik}/a'_{ij}}$
Itakura-Saito divergence	$-\log x$	$1/x^2$	$\frac{a}{a'} - \log \frac{a}{a'}$	$h_{jk} = \frac{\sum_{i=1}^M a_{ij}^{(k)} w_{ik}/{a'_{ij}}^2}{\sum_{i=1}^M w_{ik}w_{ik}/{a'_{ij}}^2}$
Beta divergence	$\frac{1}{\beta(\beta+1)}(x^{\beta+1} - (\beta+1)x + \beta)$	$x^{\beta-1}$	$\frac{1}{\beta(\beta+1)}(a^{\beta+1} - a'^{\beta+1} - (\beta+1)a'^{\beta}(a-a'))$	$h_{jk} = \frac{\sum_{i=1}^M {a'_{ij}}^{\beta-1} a_{ij}^{(k)} w_{ik}}{\sum_{i=1}^M {a'_{ij}}^{\beta-1} w_{ik}w_{ik}}$

where α is regularization paramter. Although $\|\cdot\|_1$ is not differentiable in general, in NMF it is differentiable in the specific domain due to the condition that $\mathbf{H}$ is non-negative.

The corresponding sBCD updating rule is

$$h_{jk} = \frac{\alpha + \sum_{i=1}^M \nabla^2\phi(a'_{ij}) a_{ij}^{(k)} w_{ik}}{\sum_{i=1}^M \nabla^2\phi(a'_{ij}) w_{ik} w_{ik}},$$

$$w_{ik} = \frac{\sum_{j=1}^N \nabla^2\phi(a'_{ij}) a_{ij}^{(k)} h_{jk}}{\sum_{i=1}^N \nabla^2\phi(a'_{ij}) h_{jk} h_{jk}}.$$

Sparsity on $\mathbf{W}$ can be imposed in an analogous way.

4. EXPERIMENTAL RESULTS

4.1 Data Set and Performance Evaluation

The experiments are conducted on artificial and real world data sets. The randomly generated data sets have problem sizes $(M, N, K) = (2000, 1000, 30)$, $(2000, 1000, 60)$, and $(3000, 2000, 30)$. The initial matrices for $\mathbf{W}$ and $\mathbf{H}$ were generated with uniform random values in $[0.5, 1.5]$. To remove sampling noise we average results using 5 different initial values. Our first real world data set follows the Xspectra setup in [6]. A matrix of size 1000×10 is formed by using ten noisy mixtures of five smooth sources. Mixed signals are corrupted by additive Guassian noise. For this data set, the ground-truth factors are provided, enabling the testing of algorithms' accuracy in recovering factors. A larger real world data set is the AT&T face image data set [1]. This data set contains 400 facial images (10 images of each of 40 different people) with a single facial image containing 92×112 pixels in 8-bit grey level. The resulting data matrix is of size 10304×400. Movielens data set with rating matrix of size 71567×65133 is also used, The largest data set is Netflix with a sparse rating matrix of size 480189×17770.

We employ two types of metrics, Bregman divergences $D_\phi(\mathbf{A}\|\mathbf{W}\mathbf{H}^T)$ and Signal to Interference Ratio(SIR) [5]. SIR is a commonly used metric in signal processing. We employ it here to judge how well the computed factors $\mathbf{W}$ and $\mathbf{H}$ match the ground-truth. Denoting the ground-truth as $\hat{\mathbf{W}}$ and $\hat{\mathbf{H}}$, the values of SIR for $\mathbf{W}$ is calculated as:

$$\mathrm{SIR}(\mathbf{W}, \hat{\mathbf{W}}) = \frac{10}{K}\sum_{k=1}^{K} \log\left(\frac{\|\hat{\mathbf{w}}_k\|_2^2}{\|\mathbf{w}_k - \hat{\mathbf{w}}_k\|_2^2}\right)$$

where $\mathbf{w}_k$ and $\hat{\mathbf{w}}_k$ are normalized to have unit L_2 norm. SIR for $\mathbf{H}$ is computed analogously.

4.2 Performance with Various Bregman Divergences

In our experiments we use four Bregman divergences: Frobenius, KL, IS and Beta ($\beta = 2$) divergences. Our algorithm is compared to the following three methods for NMF using specific subset of Bregman divergences:

Conjugate gradient(CG): This approach is based on the alternating nonnegative least squares (ANLS) framework, and solves the nonnegative least square subproblems efficiently by conjugate gradient method [15] for the numerical solution of particular systems of linear equations.

BlockPivot: This algorithm [22] is also based on the alternating nonnegative least squares (ANLS) framework and solves the nonnegative least square subproblems efficiently by using an active set like method called block principal pivoting.

GCD/CCD: A coordinate descent algorithm called Greedy Coordinate Descent (GCD) described in [17] to solve the NMF with Frobenius norm. It takes a greedy step of maximum decrease in objective function, and select important variables to update more often.

A Cyclic Coordinate Descent (CCD) algorithm is also proposed for the NMF with KL divergence. It differs from GCD by that the number of update for each variable is exactly the same, thus may conduct some unnecessary updates on unimportant variables. Newton's method is employed to solve each one-variable sub-problem.

and the following methods which are designed for NMF formulating using general Bregman divergences:

Multiplicative updating: This approach uses the multiplicative updating rule in [25, 8].

Gradient descent: This algorithm [25] calculates the first derivative of divergence based objective function, and uses a fixed step size in each iteration.

sBCD: Our proposed approach. The code is available at http://www.cc.gatech.edu/grads/l/lli86/sbcd.zip.

Table 3 shows above approaches' applicability to different divergences. For each specific divergence, not all listed approaches are compared since some of them may be not applicable. Therefore, for each case we conduct a separate series of experiments.

Figure 1 and 3 compare the performance of our approach with others measured by $D_\phi(\mathbf{A}\|\mathbf{W}\mathbf{H}^T)$. In general, Multiplicative updating converges relatively slow compared to others, but often find a good solution. For real world data, Gradient descent performs poorly. Multiplicative updating performs better than Gradient descent.

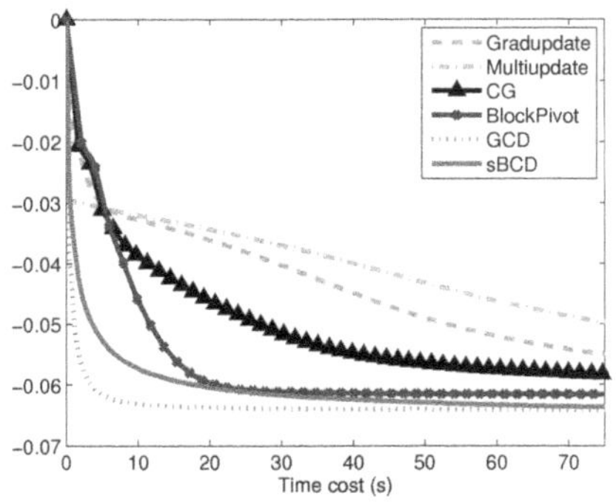

(a) Frobenius, RD1

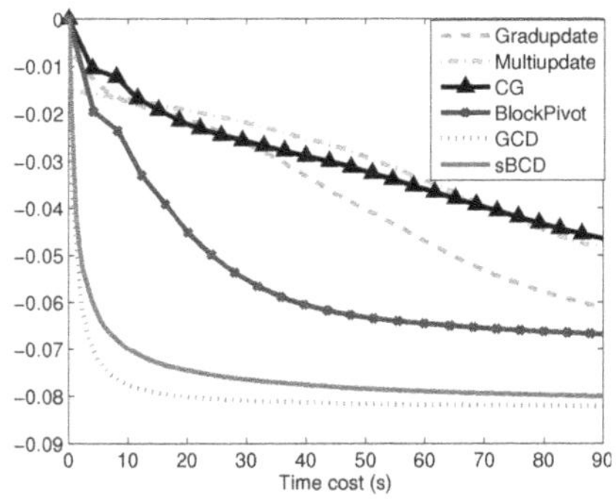

(b) Frobenius, RD2

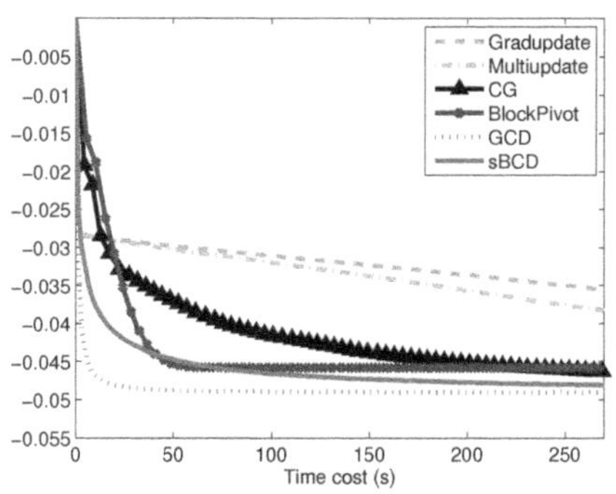

(c) Frobenius, RD3

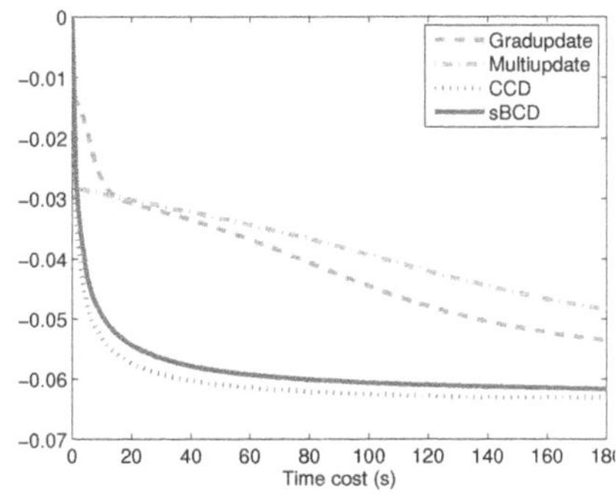

(d) KL, RD1

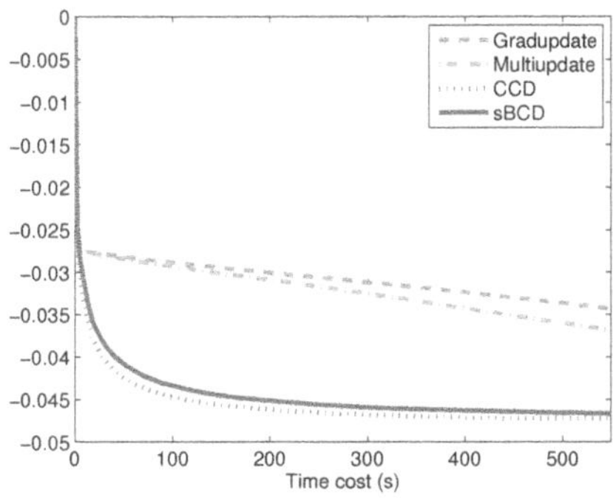

(e) KL, RD2

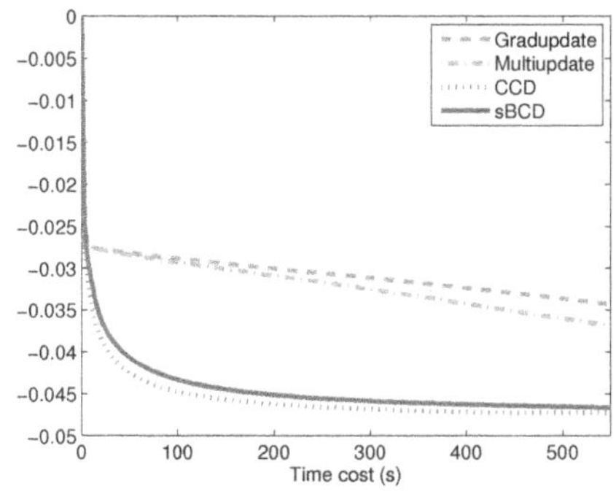

(f) KL, RD3

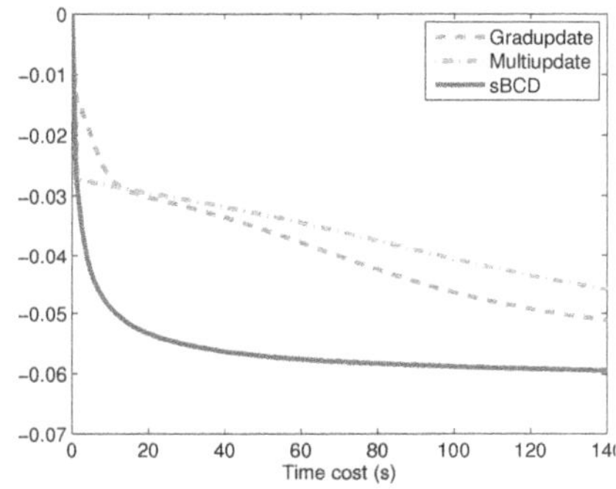

(g) IS, RD1

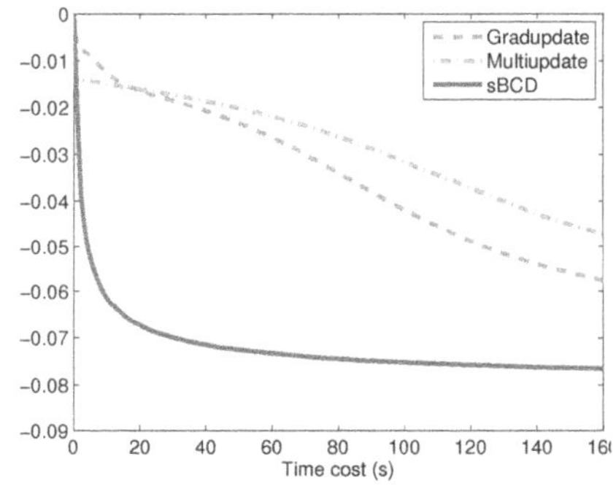

(h) IS, RD2

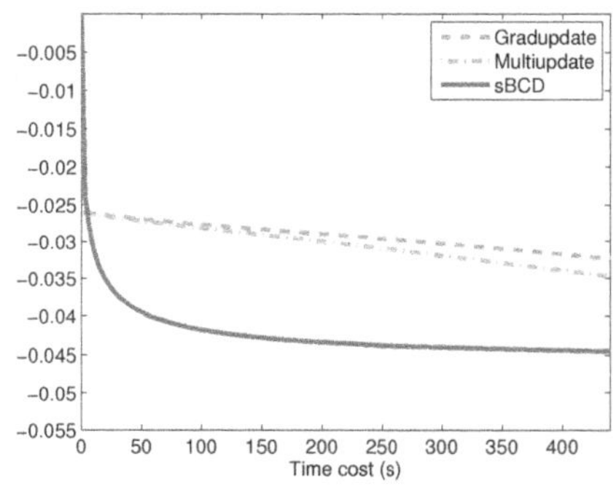

(i) IS, RD3

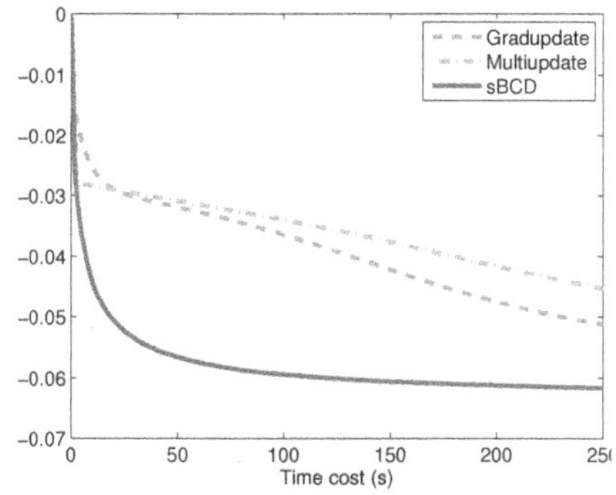

(j) Beta, RD1

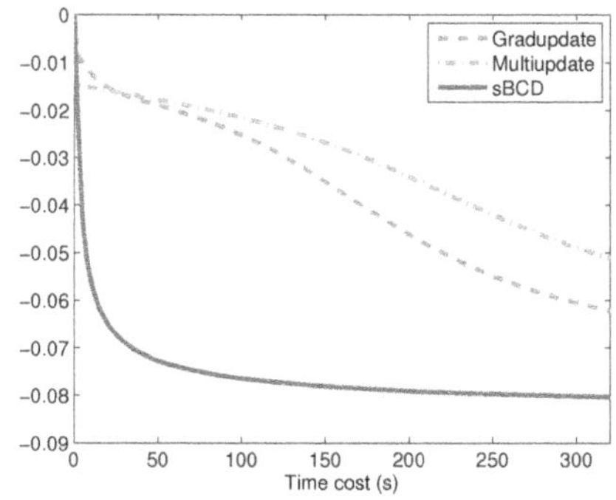

(k) Beta, RD2

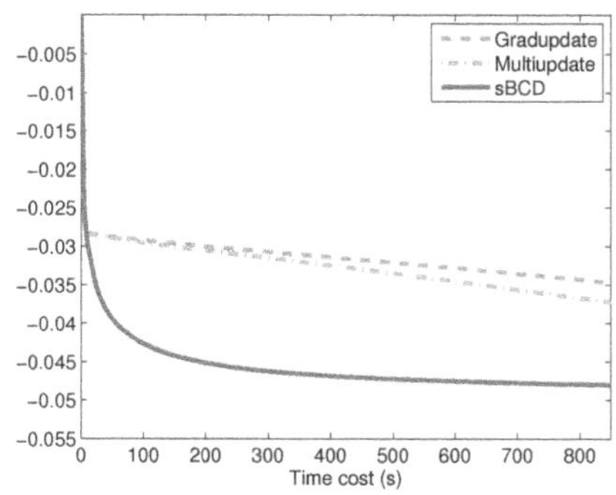

(l) Beta, RD3

Figure 1: Performance of NMF with various Bregman Divergences

`CG`: dash triangle line, `BlockPivot`: dash cross line, **`Multiplicative updating`**: dash dot line, **`Gradient descent`**: dash line, **`sBCD`**: solid line. y axis: relative residual value $log_{10} \frac{D_\phi(\mathbf{A}\|\mathbf{W}\mathbf{H}^T)}{D_\phi(\mathbf{A}\|\mathbf{W}_0\mathbf{H}_0^T)}$, where $\mathbf{W}_0$ and $\mathbf{H}_0$ are initial values for $\mathbf{W}$ and $\mathbf{H}$. (M, N, K) values are `RD1`: $(2000, 1000, 30)$, `RD2`: $(2000, 1000, 60)$, `RD2`: $(3000, 2000, 30)$.

Table 3: Applicability of Compared Methods

	Frobenius	KL	IS	Beta
CG	√	×	×	×
BlockPivot	√	×	×	×
GCD	√	×	×	×
CCD	×	√	×	×
Multiupdate	√	√	√	√
Gradupdate	√	√	√	√
sBCD	√	√	√	√

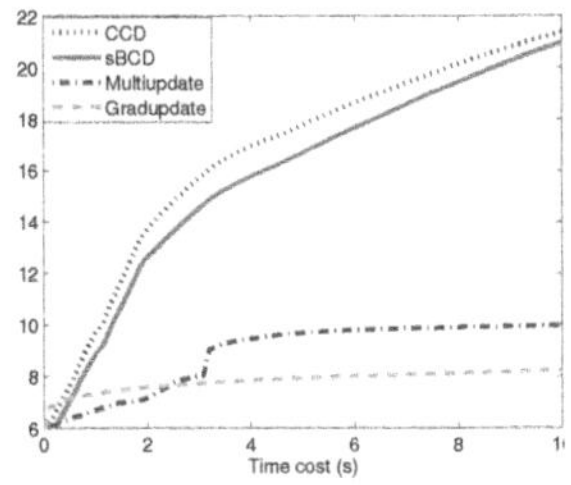

(a) KL, SIR($\mathbf{H}, \hat{\mathbf{H}}$)

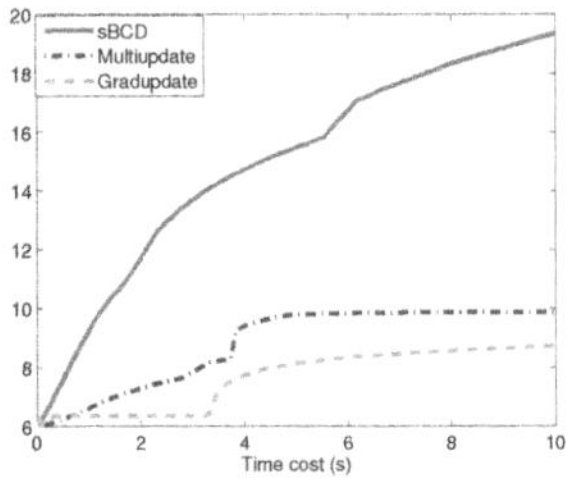

(b) IS, SIR($\mathbf{H}, \hat{\mathbf{H}}$)

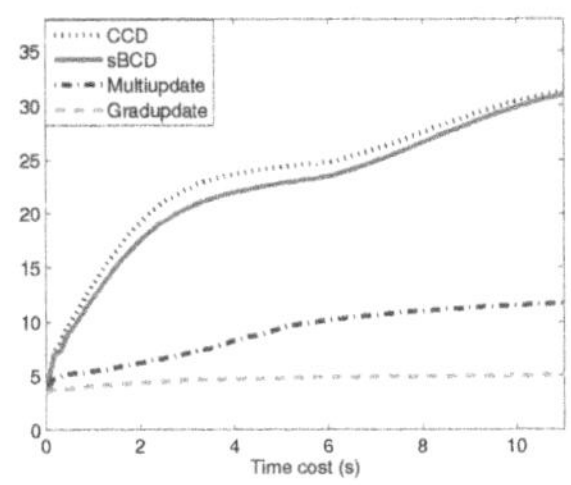

(c) KL, SIR($\mathbf{W}, \hat{\mathbf{W}}$)

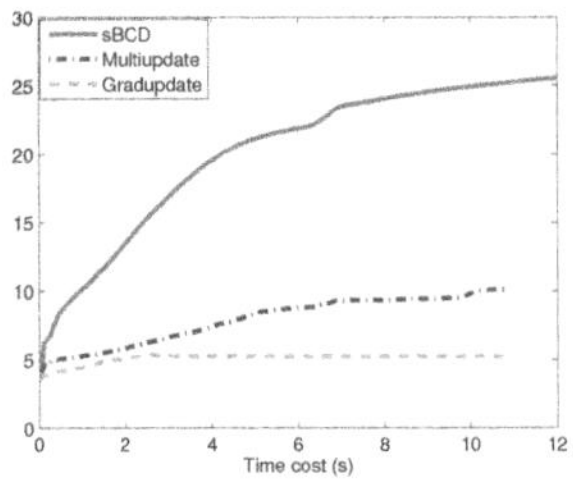

(d) IS, SIR($\mathbf{W}, \hat{\mathbf{W}}$)

Figure 2: Performance of NMF with various Bregman Divergences
This experiment is conducted on 5 `smooth` data set where the problem size is $(M, N, K) = (1000, 10, 5)$. In the figures of the first row, the y axis measures SIR($\mathbf{W}, \hat{\mathbf{W}}$); in the figures of the second row, the y axis measures SIR($\mathbf{H}, \hat{\mathbf{H}}$).

For Frobenius norm, `CG` can reach better solutions than the above two, but requires huge computational cost. `BlockPivot` performs better than `CG`, significantly reducing the computational cost by using block pvioting scheme to speed up the process of finding optimal solution. Our approach performs better than all others expect `GCD`. For KL divergence, `CCD` is only slightly better than `sBCD`. The difference is much smaller than the difference between `GCD` and `sBCD` under Frobenius norm. Although our approach does not outperform `GCD` and `CCD`, we must notice that `GCD` targets at solving NMF with Frobenius norm only, while `CCD` targets at KL divergence only. On the other hand, our approach provides a general solution to NMF with Bregman divergences.

For IS and Beta divergences, our approach performs better than all other compared approaches, in both artificial and real world data. Its convergence behavior and the solution to the factorization is the best among all the approaches.

When handling large real world data sets, we notice that the performance curve of the above algorithms was not necessarily so smooth. However, the advantage of `sBCD` and `CCD` over `Multiplicative updating` and `Gradient descent` is still very significant, especially at the first several iterations. The more sparse $\mathbf{A}$ is, the greater improvement `sBCD` can obtain over the others.

Table 4: Performance for various reduced ranks
The table shows the time and iteration numbers needed for convergences under both IS and Beta divergence. The input matrix is of size 2000×1500 and the convergence criterion $\frac{\Delta D_\phi(\mathbf{A}\|\mathbf{W}\mathbf{H}^T)}{D_\phi(\mathbf{A}\|\mathbf{W}_0\mathbf{H}_0^T)} = 10^{-0.4}$ is set to measure the relative decrease in residual values, where $\Delta D_\phi(\mathbf{A}\|\mathbf{W}\mathbf{H}^T)$ is the absolute difference of $D_\phi(\mathbf{A}\|\mathbf{W}\mathbf{H}^T)$ between two consecutive iterations.

		IS			Beta		
	K	Grad	Multi	sBCD	Grad	Multi	sBCD
time	5	466.97	353.43	150.61	1109.56	803.84	346.51
(s)	10	632.48	525.91	200.17	1498.8	1198.62	461.98
	20	1082.11	905.42	236.77	2392.99	2009.69	550.89
	30	1318.35	1089.61	310.01	3241.07	2550.13	711.39
	40	2032.49	1634.5	325.22	4337.59	3838.38	829.43
	60	2474.16	2196.3	393.08	5103.28	4715.99	973.78
	80	3293.67	2769.9	446.3	7157.01	5591.19	1042.86
iter	5	171.1	85.74	30.4	174.3	91.2	26.1
	10	268.4	147.4	41.1	277	180.4	42.4
	20	320	221.6	45	378	213.1	46.6
	30	435.4	338.2	50.1	536	381.9	56.3
	40	588.3	416.8	53.3	620	466.5	63
	60	718.1	595.7	62.8	840.9	686.4	72.4
	80	891.5	784.6	71.7	1057.7	865.3	81.3

Figure 2 compares the performance of our approach with the other algorithms and the performance is measured by `SIR`. It illustrates that `sBCD` and `CCD` can recover the ground-truth factors $\hat{\mathbf{W}}$ and $\hat{\mathbf{H}}$ much better than `Multiplicative updating` and `Gradient descent`. The results from Figure 2 $\hat{\mathbf{H}}$ can be recovered much better than $\hat{\mathbf{W}}$. This may due to the fact that $\hat{\mathbf{H}}$ is given signal matrix while $\hat{\mathbf{W}}$ is generated randomly.

The following experiments evaluate how the variation of K influences the performance. From Table 4 we can see that our algorithm has a significant advantage in convergence behavior over the other two approaches. The advantage becomes greater with the increase of K. For `sBCD`, the number of iterations needed for convergence increases very slowly, while there is a sharp increase in the case of `Multiplicative updating` and `Gradient descent`.

4.3 Other Variations

In `sBCD`, the computation of the term $\nabla^2\phi(a'_{ij})$ may be costly, since a'_{ij} varies in each iteration. To address this issue, we also consider the following two alternative updating rules which can, in some cases, provide additional computational savings. Performance comparison of `sBCD` and those two variations is shown in Figure 4.

sBCD-AL-A	sBCD-AL-B
$h_{jk} = \frac{\sum_{i=1}^{M} \nabla^2\phi(a_{ij}) a_{ij}^{(k)} w_{ik}}{\sum_{i=1}^{M} \nabla^2\phi(a_{ij}) w_{ik} w_{ik}}$	$h_{jk} = \frac{\sum_{i=1}^{M} a_{ij}^{(k)} w_{ik}}{\sum_{i=1}^{M} w_{ik} w_{ik}}$

As shown in Figure 4, in most cases, `sBCD-AL-A` gives the slowest convergence and the worst solution. `sBCD` converges faster and obtains a better solution than `sBCD-AL-B`. `sBCD` also performs better consistently. The nature of $\mathbf{A}$ and the ϕ may decide how well the alternative updating rules approximate `sBCD`. For example, in IS divergence, `sBCD` gains an impressive advantage over the other two algorithms. However, in a few cases(especially the signal data), the difference among the three algorithms is not significant. This indicates that the two alternative algorithms may be more suitable for certain real world applications due to their simplicity in implementation and relatively lower storage cost.

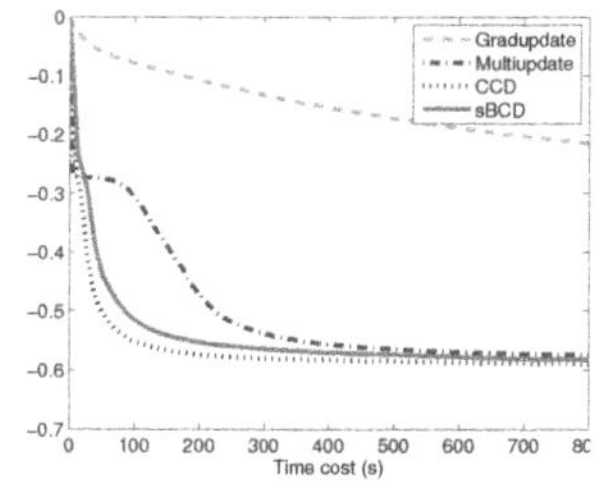

(a) KL, Face Image

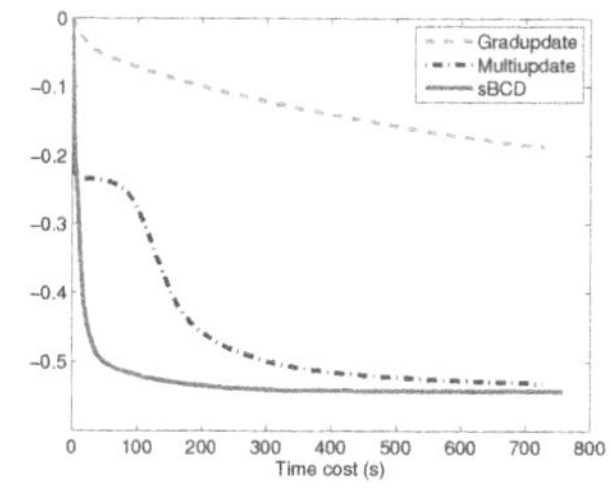

(b) IS, Face Image

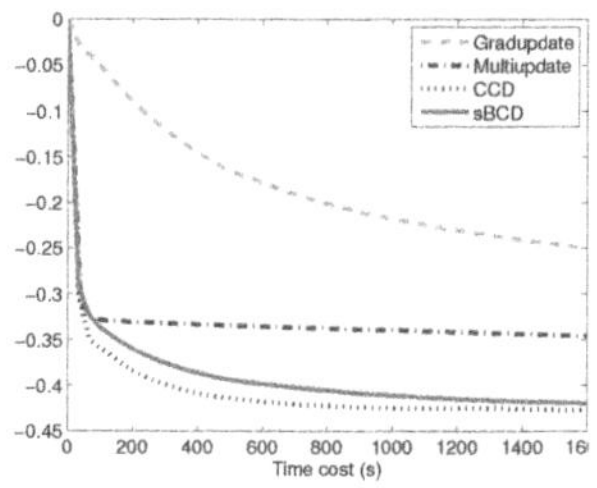

(c) KL, Movielens

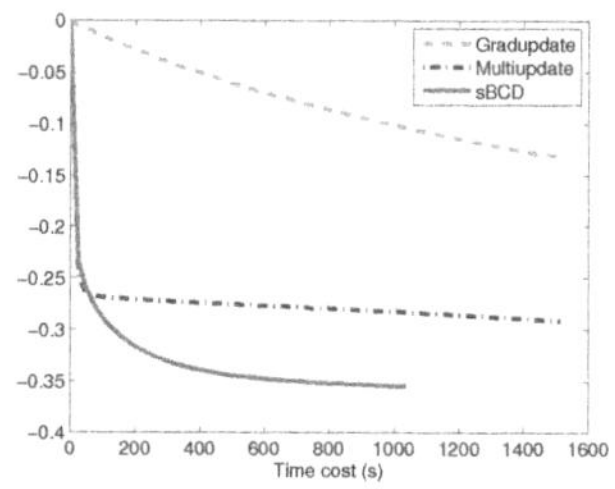

(d) IS, Movielens

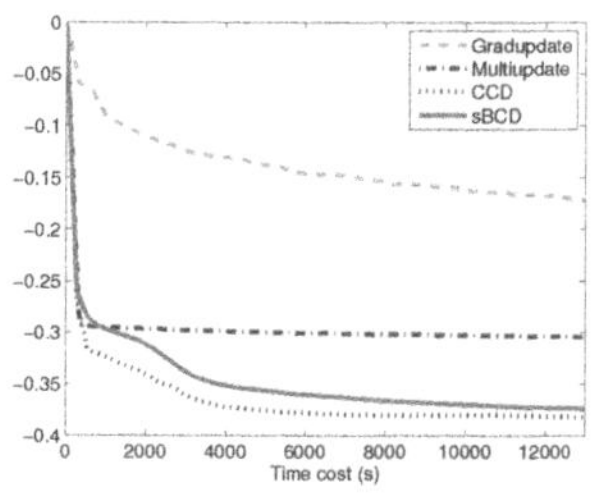

(e) KL, Netflix

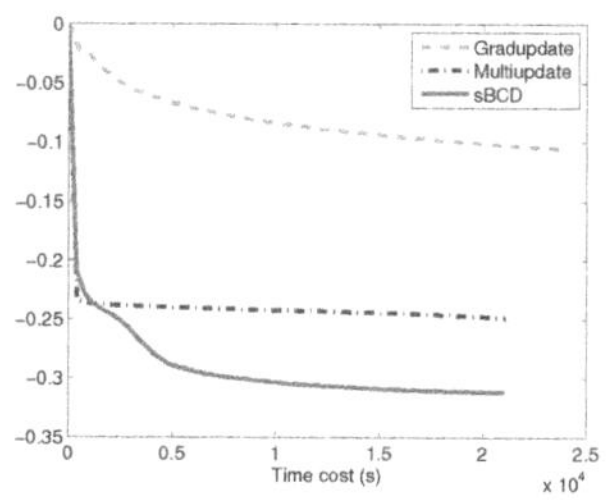

(f) IS, Netflix

Figure 3: Performance of NMF with various Bregman Divergences on Large Scale Data

The y axis measures the logarithm of the relative residual value. (M, N, K) values are Face Image: $(10304, 400, 20)$, Movielens: $(71567, 65133, 20)$, Netflix: $(480189, 17770, 20)$. Matrices in Movielens and Netflix are very sparse.

For NMF with additional constraints, due to lack of space we only report here the result for the KL-divergence case when imposing sparsity constraint on $\mathbf{H}$ only. Figure 5 shows that with even with constraints added, the relative trends of our three proposed algorithms remain the same.

Here we choose text summarization as the application task, and conduct experiments to explore how different divergences can affect the topic generation. In this application, a document-text matrix is first built to describe the corpus. The matrix is then factorized by our proposed NMF algorithms to analyze the topic distribution over the corpus. Finally, the obtained document-topic matrix is used as features in model training for text summarization. We expect stronger features obtained from this NMF process.

The DUC2001 data set is used for evaluation in this series of experiments. It contains around 147 summary-document pairs. The respective ground-truth summaries are generated by manually extracting a certain number of sentences from each single document. A 10-fold cross validation process is employed in the experiments. Structural SVM algorithm is used for model training and prediction. For evaluation, we employ the ROUGE metric[4] [28].

[4]For details, see http://berouge.com/default.aspx.

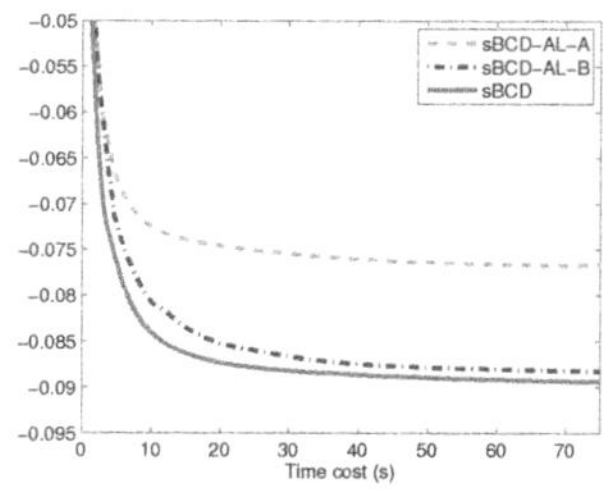

(a) KL, 1500*1000, K=30

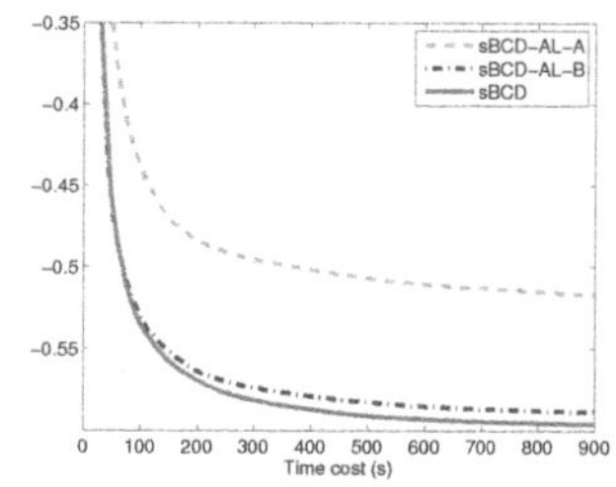

(b) KL, Face image

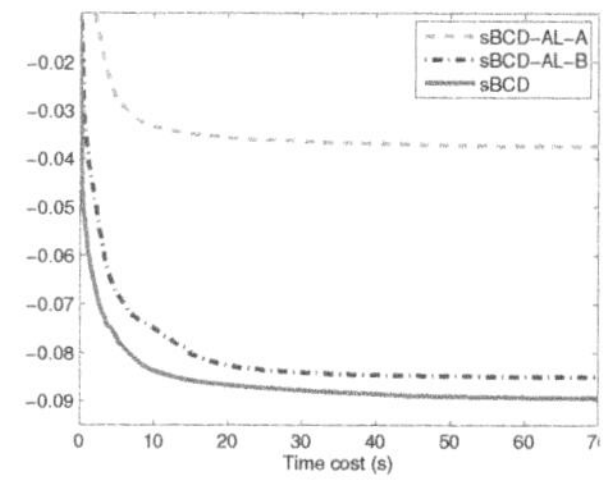

(c) IS, 1500*1000, K=30

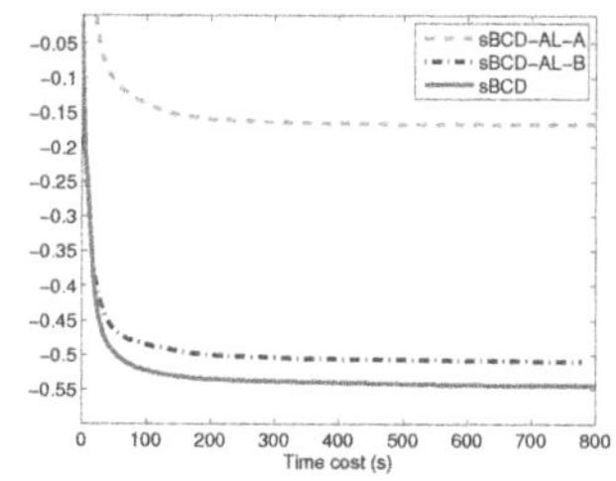

(d) IS, Face image

Figure 4: Comparison of Our Three Proposed Algorithms

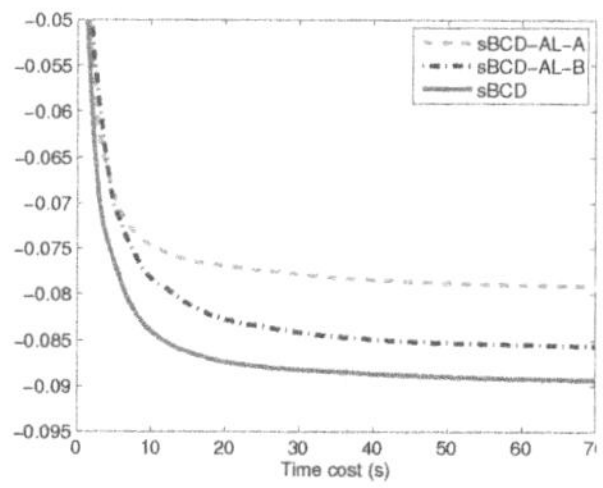

(a) KL, 1500*1000, K=30

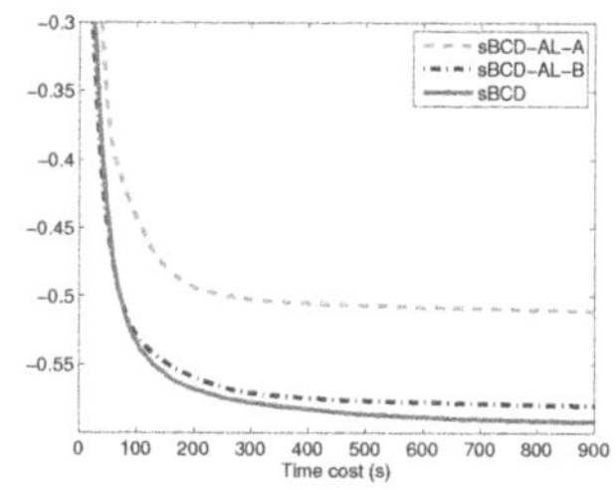

(b) KL, Face image

Figure 5: NMF with Additional Constraints

Table 5 shows that when divergence is KL, a best summarization model can be trained. Using Frobenius norm also leads to a comparable result. When divergence is IS or Beta, the summary prediction is relatively inaccurate. Thus, we can conclude that, in text topic analysis, using the NMF with Frobenius norm and KL divergence is more suitable than IS divergence and Beta divergence. The above results also illustrate that stronger features extracted from NMF contribute to a better summarization model.

5. CONCLUSIONS AND FUTURE WORK

In this paper, a novel fast algorithm named `sBCD` is proposed to solve the NMF with Bregman divergences. The algorithm is designed by deriving an equivalent optimization problem involving the Euclidean distance. A local updating rule is obtained by setting the gradient of the new objective function to zero with respect to each element of the two matrix factors. Experimental results demonstrate the effectiveness of our approach.

The relationship that we derive between Bregman divergences and the Euclidean distance is new. In addition to leading to our updating rule, this connection may be used in other data mining algorithms based on Bregman divergences, such as K-means, SVM.

Table 5: **Performance of Text Summarization Using NMF with Different Divergences**

Divergence	Frobenius	KL	IS	Beta
ROUGE-1-R	0.58215	0.58342	0.57931	0.57826
ROUGE-1-P	0.45734	0.46137	0.45432	0.45391
ROUGE-1-F	0.51001	0.52043	0.50043	0.49422
ROUGE-2-R	0.44123	0.45231	0.43921	0.43491
ROUGE-2-P	0.35342	0.36031	0.34232	0.34412
ROUGE-2-F	0.38634	0.39872	0.38123	0.38092
ROUGE-W-R	0.24107	0.24532	0.23726	0.23581
ROUGE-W-P	0.32313	0.33342	0.30523	0.30343
ROUGE-W-F	0.27132	0.28023	0.26932	0.26808

6. ACKNOWLEDGMENTS

We are very grateful to the editor and anonymous reviewers for valuable comments and suggestions based on which we were able to improve the manuscript substantially. The work of the first and third authors were supported in part by the National Science Foundation grants CCF-0732318 and CCF-0808863.

7. REFERENCES

[1] http://www.cl.cam.ac.uk/research/dtg/attarchive/facedatabase.html.

[2] A. Banerjee. Optimal bregman prediction and jensenąŕs equality. In *In Proc. International Symposium on Information Theory (ISIT)*, page 2004, 2004.

[3] A. Banerjee, S. Merugu, I. S. Dhillon, and J. Ghosh. Clustering with bregman divergences. *J. Mach. Learn. Res.*, 6:1705–1749, December 2005.

[4] P. Breheny and J. Huang. Coordinate descent algorithms for nonconvex penalized regression, with applications to biological feature selection. *Annals of Applied Statistics*, 5(1):232–253, 2011.

[5] A. Cichocki and A.-H. Phan. Fast local algorithms for large scale nonnegative matrix and tensor factorizations. *IEICE Transactions on Fundamentals of Electronics*, 92:708–721, 2009.

[6] A. Cichocki and R. Zdunek. Nmflab for signal and image processing. In *tech. rep, Laboratory for Advanced Brain Signal Processing*, Saitama, Japan, 2006. BSI, RIKEN.

[7] A. Cichocki, R. Zdunek, and S. A. A.-H. Phan. Nonnegative matrix and tensor factorizations: Applications to exploratory multi-way data analysis and blind source separation. New York, USA, 2009. Wiley.

[8] I. S. Dhillon and S. Sra. Generalized nonnegative matrix approximations with bregman divergences. In *Neural Information Proc. Systems*, pages 283–290, 2005.

[9] C. Ding, T. Li, and W. Peng. On the equivalence between non-negative matrix factorization and probabilistic latent semantic indexing. *Comput. Stat. Data Anal.*, 52:3913–3927, April 2008.

[10] J. Fan and R. Li. Variable selection via nonconcave penalized likelihood and its oracle properties. *Journal of the American Statistical Association*, 96(456).

[11] C. Fevotte, N. Bertin, and J.-L. Durrieu. Nonnegative matrix factorization with the itakura-saito divergence: With application to music analysis. *Neural Comput.*, 21:793–830, March 2009.

[12] M. Figueiredo, R. Nowak, and S. J. Wright. Gradient projection for sparse reconstruction: Application to compressed sensing and other inverse problems. *IEEE J. of Selected Topics in Signal Proc*, 1:586–598, 2007.

[13] J. Friedman, T. Hastie, and R. Tibshirani. Regularization paths for generalized linear models via coordinate descent. *Journal of Statistical Software*, 33(1), 1 2010.

[14] N. Gillis and F. Glineur. Accelerated multiplicative updates and hierarchical als algorithms for nonnegative matrix factorization. *Neural Comput.*, 24(4):1085–1105, 4 2012.

[15] M. R. Hestenes and E. Stiefel. Methods of conjugate gradients for solving linear systems. *Journal of Research of the National Bureau of Standards*, 49(6), 1952.

[16] T. Hofmann. Probabilistic latent semantic indexing. In *SIGIR '99*, pages 50–57, New York, NY, USA, 1999. ACM.

[17] C.-J. Hsieh and I. S. Dhillon. Fast coordinate descent methods with variable selection for non-negative matrix factorization. In *Proceedings of the 17th ACM SIGKDD international conference on Knowledge discovery and data mining*, KDD '11, pages 1064–1072, New York, NY, USA, 2011. ACM.

[18] C.-J. Hsieh, M. A. Sustik, I. S. Dhillon, and P. Ravikumar. Sparse inverse covariance matrix estimation using quadratic approximation. In *Advances in Neural Information Processing Systems 24*, pages 2330–2338, 2011.

[19] H. Kim and H. Park. Sparse non-negative matrix factorizations via alternating non-negativity-constrained least squares for microarray data analysis. *Bioinformatics*, 23:1495–1502, June 2007.

[20] H. Kim and H. Park. Nonnegative matrix factorization based on alternating nonnegativity constrained least squares and active set method. *SIAM J. Matrix Anal. Appl.*, 30:713–730, July 2008.

[21] J. Kim, Y. He, and H. Park. Algorithms for nonnegative matrix and tensor factorizations: A unified view based on block coordinate descent framework. Under review.

[22] J. Kim and H. Park. Toward faster nonnegative matrix factorization: A new algorithm and comparisons. *IEEE International Conference on Data Mining*, 0:353–362, 2008.

[23] J. Kim and H. Park. Fast nonnegative matrix factorization: An active-set-like method and comparisons. In *SIAM Journal on Scientific Computing*, 2011.

[24] G. Lebanon. Axiomatic geometry of conditional models. *Information Theory, IEEE Transactions*, 51:1283–1294, April 2005.

[25] D. D. Lee and H. S. Seung. Algorithms for non-negative matrix factorization. In *NIPS*, pages 556–562. MIT Press, 2000.

[26] Y. Li and S. Osher. Coordinate descent optimization for l1 minimization with application to compressed sensing; a greedy algorithm. *Inverse Probl. Imaging*, 3(3).

[27] C.-J. Lin. Projected gradient methods for non-negative matrix factorization. *Neural Computation*, 19:2756–2779, October 2007.

[28] C. Y. Lin and E. Hovy. Automatic evaluation of summaries using n-gram co-occurrence statistics. In *NAACL*, pages 71–78, Morristown, NJ, USA, 2003. Association for Computational Linguistics.

[29] R. Mazumder, J. Friedman, and T. Hastie. Variable selection via nonconcave penalized likelihood and its oracle properties. *Journal of the American Statistical Association*, 106(495).

[30] S. D. Pietra, V. D. Pietra, and J. Lafferty. Duality and auxiliary functions for bregman distances. Technical report, School of Computer Science, Carnegie Mellon University, 2002.

[31] A. P. Singh and G. J. Gordon. A unified view of matrix factorization models. In *Proceedings of the European conference on Machine Learning and Knowledge Discovery in Databases - Part II*, ECML PKDD '08, pages 358–373, Berlin, Heidelberg, 2008. Springer-Verlag.

[32] S. Wang and D. Schuurmans. Learning continuous latent variable models with bregman divergences. In *In Proc. IEEE International Conference on Algorithmic Learning Theory*, page 2004, 2003.

[33] T. Wu and K. Lange. Coordinate descent algorithms for lasso penalized regression. *The Annals of Applied Statistics*, 2(1):224–244, 2008.

[34] S. Yun and K.-C. Toh. A coordinate gradient descent method for l1-regularized convex minimization. *Computational Optimization and Applications*, 48(2).

GigaTensor: Scaling Tensor Analysis Up By 100 Times - Algorithms and Discoveries

U Kang, Evangelos Papalexakis, Abhay Harpale, Christos Faloutsos
Carnegie Mellon University
{ukang, epapalex, aharpale, christos}@cs.cmu.edu

ABSTRACT

Many data are modeled as tensors, or multi dimensional arrays. Examples include the predicates (subject, verb, object) in knowledge bases, hyperlinks and anchor texts in the Web graphs, sensor streams (time, location, and type), social networks over time, and DBLP conference-author-keyword relations. Tensor decomposition is an important data mining tool with various applications including clustering, trend detection, and anomaly detection. However, current tensor decomposition algorithms are not scalable for large tensors with billions of sizes and hundreds millions of nonzeros: the largest tensor in the literature remains thousands of sizes and hundreds thousands of nonzeros.

Consider a knowledge base tensor consisting of about 26 million noun-phrases. The intermediate data explosion problem, associated with naive implementations of tensor decomposition algorithms, would require the materialization and the storage of a matrix whose largest dimension would be $\approx 7 \cdot 10^{14}$; this amounts to ~ 10 Petabytes, or equivalently a few data centers worth of storage, thereby rendering the tensor analysis of this knowledge base, in the naive way, practically impossible. In this paper, we propose GIGATENSOR, a scalable distributed algorithm for large scale tensor decomposition. GIGATENSOR exploits the sparseness of the real world tensors, and avoids the intermediate data explosion problem by carefully redesigning the tensor decomposition algorithm.

Extensive experiments show that our proposed GIGATENSOR solves 100× bigger problems than existing methods. Furthermore, we employ GIGATENSOR in order to analyze a very large real world, knowledge base tensor and present our astounding findings which include discovery of potential synonyms among millions of noun-phrases (e.g. the noun 'pollutant' and the noun-phrase 'greenhouse gases').

Categories and Subject Descriptors

H.2.8 [**Database Management**]: Database Applications—*Data Mining*

General Terms

Algorithms, Design, Experimentation

KDD'12, August 12–16, 2012, Beijing, China.

Keywords

Tensor, Distributed Computing, Big Data, MapReduce, Hadoop

1. INTRODUCTION

Tensors, or multi-dimensional arrays appear in numerous applications: predicates (subject, verb, object) in knowledge bases [9], hyperlinks and anchor texts in the Web graphs [20], sensor streams (time, location, and type) [30], and DBLP conference-author-keyword relations [22], to name a few. Analysis of multi-dimensional arrays by tensor decompositions, as shown in Figure 1, is a basis for many interesting applications including clustering, trend detection, anomaly detection [22], correlation analysis [30], network forensic [25], and latent concept discovery [20].

There exist two, widely used, toolboxes that handle tensors and tensor decompositions: the Tensor Toolbox for Matlab [6], and the N-way Toolbox for Matlab [3]. Both toolboxes are considered the state of the art; especially, the Tensor Toolbox is probably the fastest existing implementation of tensor decompositions for sparse tensors (having attracted best paper awards, e.g. see [22]). However, the toolboxes have critical restrictions: 1) they operate strictly on data that can fit in the main memory, and 2) their scalability is limited by the scalability of Matlab. In [4, 22], efficient ways of computing tensor decompositions, when the tensor is very sparse, are introduced and are implemented in the Tensor Toolbox. However, these methods still operate in main memory and therefore cannot scale to Gigabytes or Terabytes of tensor data. The need for large scale tensor computations is ever increasing, and there is a huge gap that needs to be filled. In Table 1, we present an indicative sample of tensor sizes that have been analyzed so far; we can see that these sizes are nowhere near as adequate as needed, in order to satisfy current real data needs, which call for tensors with billions of sizes and hundreds of millions of nonzero elements.

In this paper, we propose GIGATENSOR, a scalable distributed algorithm for large scale tensor decomposition. GIGATENSOR can handle Tera-scale tensors using the MAPREDUCE [11] framework, and more specifically its open source implementation, HADOOP [1]. To the best of our knowledge, this paper is the first approach of deploying tensor decompositions in the MAPREDUCE framework. The main contributions of this paper are the following.

- **Algorithm.** We propose GIGATENSOR, a large scale tensor decomposition algorithm on MAPREDUCE. GIGATENSOR is carefully designed to minimize the intermediate data size and the number of floating point operations.
- **Scalability.** GIGATENSOR decomposes 100× larger tensors compared to existing methods, as shown in Figure 4. Furthermore, GIGATENSOR enjoys near linear scalability on the number of machines.

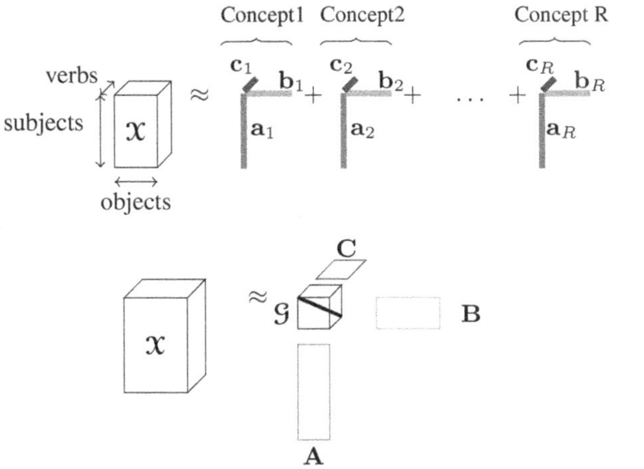

Figure 1: PARAFAC decomposition of three-way tensor as sum of R outer products (rank-one tensors), reminiscing of the rank-R SVD of a matrix (top), and as product of matrices **A**, **B**, **C**, and a super-diagonal core tensor $\mathcal{G}$ (bottom).

Work	Tensor Size	Non-zeros
Kolda et al. [20]	$787 \times 787 \times 533$	3583
Acar et al. [2]	$3.4\text{ K} \times 100 \times 18$	(dense)
Maruhashi et al. [25]	$2\text{ K} \times 2\text{ K} \times 6\text{ K} \times 4\text{ K}$	281 K
GIGATENSOR (**This work**)	$26\text{ M} \times 26\text{ M} \times 48\text{ M}$	144 M

Table 1: Indicative sizes of tensors analyzed in the data mining literature. Our proposed GIGATENSOR analyzes tensors with $\approx 1000\times$ larger sizes and $\approx 500\times$ larger nonzero elements.

- **Discovery.** We discover patterns in a very large knowledge-base tensor dataset from the 'Read the Web' project [9], which until now, was unable to be analyzed using tensor tools. Our findings include potential synonyms of noun-phrases, which were discovered after decomposing the knowledge base tensor; these findings are shown in Table 2 and a detailed description of the discovery procedure is covered on Section 4.

The rest of paper is organized as follows. Section 2 presents the preliminaries of the tensor decomposition. Sections 3 describes our proposed algorithm for large scale tensor analysis. Section 4 presents the experimental results. After reviewing related works in Section 5, we conclude in Section 6.

2. PRELIMINARIES; TENSOR DECOMPOSITION

In this section, we describe the preliminaries on the tensor decomposition whose fast algorithm will be proposed in Section 3. Table 3 lists the symbols used in this paper. For vector/matrix/tensor indexing, we use the Matlab-like notation: $\mathbf{A}(i,j)$ denotes the (i,j)-th element of matrix $\mathbf{A}$, whereas $\mathbf{A}(:,j)$ spans the j-th column of that matrix.

Matrices and the bilinear decomposition. Let $\mathbf{X}$ be an $I \times J$ matrix. The rank of $\mathbf{X}$ is the minimum number of rank one matrices that are required to compose $\mathbf{X}$. A rank one matrix is simply an *outer product* of two vectors, say $\mathbf{ab}^T$, where $\mathbf{a}$ and $\mathbf{b}$ are vectors. The (i,j)-th element of $\mathbf{ab}^T$ is simply $\mathbf{a}(i)\mathbf{b}(j)$. If rank($\mathbf{X}$) = R,

(Given) Noun Phrase	(Discovered) Potential Contextual Synonyms
pollutants	dioxin, sulfur dioxide, greenhouse gases, particulates, nitrogen oxide, air pollutants, cholesterol
disabilities	infections, dizziness, injuries, diseases, drowsiness, stiffness, injuries
vodafone	verizon, comcast
Christian history	European history, American history, Islamic history, history
disbelief	dismay, disgust, astonishment
cyberpunk	online-gaming
soul	body

Table 2: (Left:) Given noun-phrases; (right:) their potential *contextual* synonyms (i.e., terms with similar roles). They were automatically discovered using tensor decomposition of the NELL-1 knowledge base dataset (see Section 4 for details).

Symbol	Definition
$\mathcal{X}$	a tensor
$\mathbf{X}_{(\mathbf{n})}$	mode-n matricization of a tensor
m	number of nonzero elements in a tensor
a	a scalar (lowercase, italic letter)
$\mathbf{a}$	a column vector (lowercase, bold letter)
$\mathbf{A}$	a matrix (uppercase, bold letter)
R	number of components
$\circ$	outer product
$\odot$	Khatri-Rao product
$\otimes$	Kronecker product
$*$	Hadamard product
$\cdot$	standard product
$\mathbf{A}^T$	transpose of $\mathbf{A}$
$\mathbf{M}^\dagger$	pseudoinverse of $\mathbf{M}$
$\|\mathbf{M}\|_F$	Frobenius norm of $\mathbf{M}$
$bin(\mathbf{M})$	function that converts non-zero elements of $\mathbf{M}$ to 1

Table 3: Table of symbols.

then we can write

$$\mathbf{X} = \mathbf{a}_1\mathbf{b}_1^T + \mathbf{a}_2\mathbf{b}_2^T + \cdots + \mathbf{a}_R\mathbf{b}_R^T,$$

which is called the *bilinear decomposition* of $\mathbf{X}$. The bilinear decomposition is compactly written as $\mathbf{X} = \mathbf{AB}^T$, where the columns of $\mathbf{A}$ and $\mathbf{B}$ are $\mathbf{a}_r$ and $\mathbf{b}_r$, respectively, for $1 \le r \le R$. Usually, one may truncate this decomposition for $R \ll$ rank($\mathbf{X}$), in which case we have a low rank approximation of $\mathbf{X}$.

One of the most popular matrix decompositions is the Singular Value Decomposition (SVD):

$$\mathbf{X} = \mathbf{U\Sigma V}^T,$$

where $\mathbf{U}, \mathbf{V}$ are unitary $I \times I$ and $J \times J$ matrices, respectively, and $\mathbf{\Sigma}$ is a rectangular diagonal matrix, containing the (non-negative) singular values of $\mathbf{X}$. If we pick $\mathbf{A} = \mathbf{U\Sigma}$ and $\mathbf{B} = \mathbf{V}$, and pick $R <$ rank($\mathbf{X}$), then we obtain the optimal low rank approximation of $\mathbf{X}$ in the least squares sense [13]. The SVD is also a very powerful tool used in computing the so called Moore-Penrose pseudoinverse [28], which lies in the heart of the PARAFAC tensor decomposition which we will describe soon. The Moore-Penrose pseudoinverse $\mathbf{X}^\dagger$ of $\mathbf{X}$ is given by

$$\mathbf{X}^\dagger = \mathbf{V}\boldsymbol{\Sigma}^{-1}\mathbf{U}^T.$$

We now provide a brief introduction to tensors and the PARAFAC decomposition. For a more detailed treatment of the subject, we refer the interested reader to [21].

Introduction to PARAFAC. Consider a three way tensor $\mathcal{X}$ of dimensions $I \times J \times K$; for the purposes of this initial analysis, we restrict ourselves to the study of three way tensors. The generalization to higher ways is trivial, provided that a robust implementation for three way decompositions exists.

DEFINITION 1 (THREE WAY OUTER PRODUCT). *The three way outer product of vectors* $\mathbf{a}, \mathbf{b}, \mathbf{c}$ *is defined as*

$$[\mathbf{a} \circ \mathbf{b} \circ \mathbf{c}](i, j, k) = \mathbf{a}(i)\mathbf{b}(j)\mathbf{c}(k).$$

DEFINITION 2 (PARAFAC DECOMPOSITION). *The PARAFAC [14, 8] (also known as CP or trilinear) tensor decomposition of* $\mathcal{X}$ *in* R *components is*

$$\mathcal{X} \approx \sum_{r=1}^{R} \mathbf{a}_r \circ \mathbf{b}_r \circ \mathbf{c}_r.$$

The PARAFAC decomposition is a generalization of the matrix bilinear decomposition in three and higher ways. More compactly, we can write the PARAFAC decomposition as a triplet of matrices $\mathbf{A}, \mathbf{B}$, and $\mathbf{C}$, i.e. the r-th column of which contains $\mathbf{a}_r$, $\mathbf{b}_r$ and $\mathbf{c}_r$, respectively.

Furthermore, one may normalize each column of the three factor matrices, and introduce a scalar term λ_r, one for each rank-one factor of the decomposition (comprising a $R \times 1$ vector $\boldsymbol{\lambda}$), which forces the factor vectors to be of unit norm. Hence, the PARAFAC model we are computing is:

$$\mathcal{X} \approx \sum_{r=1}^{R} \lambda_r \mathbf{a}_r \circ \mathbf{b}_r \circ \mathbf{c}_r.$$

DEFINITION 3 (TENSOR UNFOLDING/MATRICIZATION). *We may unfold/matricize the tensor* $\mathcal{X}$ *in the following three ways:* $\mathbf{X}_{(1)}$ *of size* $(I \times JK)$, $\mathbf{X}_{(2)}$ *of size* $(J \times IK)$ *and* $\mathbf{X}_{(3)}$ *of size* $(K \times IJ)$. *The tensor* $\mathcal{X}$ *and the matricizations are mapped in the following way.*

$$\mathcal{X}(i, j, k) \rightarrow \mathbf{X}_{(1)}(i, j + (k-1)J). \quad (1)$$

$$\mathcal{X}(i, j, k) \rightarrow \mathbf{X}_{(2)}(j, i + (k-1)I). \quad (2)$$

$$\mathcal{X}(i, j, k) \rightarrow \mathbf{X}_{(3)}(k, i + (j-1)I). \quad (3)$$

We now set off to introduce some notions that play a key role in the computation of the PARAFAC decomposition.

DEFINITION 4 (KRONECKER PRODUCT). *The Kronecker product of* $\mathbf{A}$ *and* $\mathbf{B}$ *is:*

$$\mathbf{A} \otimes \mathbf{B} := \begin{bmatrix} \mathbf{B}\mathbf{A}(1,1) & \cdots & \mathbf{B}\mathbf{A}(1,J_1) \\ \vdots & \ddots & \vdots \\ \mathbf{B}\mathbf{A}(I_1,1) & \cdots & \mathbf{B}\mathbf{A}(I_1,J_1) \end{bmatrix}$$

If $\mathbf{A}$ *is of size* $I_1 \times J_1$ *and* $\mathbf{B}$ *of size* $I_2 \times J_2$, *then* $\mathbf{A} \otimes \mathbf{B}$ *is of size* $I_1 I_2 \times J_1 J_2$.

DEFINITION 5 (KHATRI-RAO PRODUCT). *The Khatri-Rao product (or column-wise Kronecker product)* $(\mathbf{A} \odot \mathbf{B})$, *where* $\mathbf{A}, \mathbf{B}$ *have the same number of columns, say* R, *is defined as:*

$$\mathbf{A} \odot \mathbf{B} = \left[\mathbf{A}(:,1) \otimes \mathbf{B}(:,1) \cdots \mathbf{A}(:,R) \otimes \mathbf{B}(:,R)\right]$$

If $\mathbf{A}$ *is of size* $I \times R$ *and* $\mathbf{B}$ *is of size* $J \times R$ *then* $(\mathbf{A} \odot \mathbf{B})$ *is of size* $IJ \times R$.

The Alternating Least Squares Algorithm for PARAFAC. The most popular algorithm for fitting the PARAFAC decomposition is the Alternating Least Squares (ALS). The ALS algorithm consists of three steps, each one being a conditional update of one of the three factor matrices, given the other two. The version of the algorithm we are using is the one outlined in Algorithm 1; for a detailed overview of the ALS algorithm, see [21, 14, 8].

Algorithm 1: Alternating Least Squares for the PARAFAC decomposition.

Input: Tensor $\mathcal{X} \in \mathbb{R}^{I \times J \times K}$, rank R, maximum iterations T.
Output: PARAFAC decomposition $\boldsymbol{\lambda} \in \mathbb{R}^{R \times 1}$, $\mathbf{A} \in \mathbb{R}^{I \times R}$, $\mathbf{B} \in \mathbb{R}^{J \times R}$, $\mathbf{C} \in \mathbb{R}^{K \times R}$.

Initialize $\mathbf{A}, \mathbf{B}, \mathbf{C}$;
for $t = 1, \ldots, T$ **do**
  $\mathbf{A} \leftarrow \mathbf{X}_{(1)}(\mathbf{C} \odot \mathbf{B})(\mathbf{C}^T\mathbf{C} * \mathbf{B}^T\mathbf{B})^\dagger$;
  Normalize columns of $\mathbf{A}$ (storing norms in vector $\boldsymbol{\lambda}$);
  $\mathbf{B} \leftarrow \mathbf{X}_{(2)}(\mathbf{C} \odot \mathbf{A})(\mathbf{C}^T\mathbf{C} * \mathbf{A}^T\mathbf{A})^\dagger$;
  Normalize columns of $\mathbf{B}$ (storing norms in vector $\boldsymbol{\lambda}$);
  $\mathbf{C} \leftarrow \mathbf{X}_{(3)}(\mathbf{B} \odot \mathbf{A})(\mathbf{B}^T\mathbf{B} * \mathbf{A}^T\mathbf{A})^\dagger$;
  Normalize columns of $\mathbf{C}$ (storing norms in vector $\boldsymbol{\lambda}$);
  if convergence criterion is met **then**
    break for loop;
  end if
end for
return $\boldsymbol{\lambda}, \mathbf{A}, \mathbf{B}, \mathbf{C}$;

The stopping criterion for Algorithm 1 is either one of the following: 1) the maximum number of iterations is reached, or 2) the cost of the model for two consecutive iterations stops changing significantly (i.e. the difference between the two costs is within a small number ϵ, usually in the order of 10^{-6}). The cost of the model is simply the least squares cost.

The most important issue pertaining to the scalability of Algorithm 1 is the 'intermediate data explosion' problem. During the life of Algorithm 1, a naive implementation thereof will have to materialize matrices $(\mathbf{C} \odot \mathbf{B})$, $(\mathbf{C} \odot \mathbf{A})$, and $(\mathbf{B} \odot \mathbf{A})$, which are very large in sizes.

PROBLEM 1 (INTERMEDIATE DATA EXPLOSION). *The problem of having to materialize* $(\mathbf{C} \odot \mathbf{B}), (\mathbf{C} \odot \mathbf{A}), (\mathbf{B} \odot \mathbf{A})$ *is defined as the intermediate data explosion.*

In order to give an idea of how devastating this intermediate data explosion problem is, consider the NELL-1 knowledge base dataset, described in Section 4, that we are using in this work; this dataset consists of about $26 \cdot 10^6$ noun-phrases (and for a moment, ignore the number of the "context" phrases, which account for the third mode). Then, one of the intermediate matrices will have an explosive dimension of $\approx 7 \cdot 10^{14}$, or equivalently a few data centers worth of storage, rendering any practical way of materializing and storing it, virtually impossible.

In [4], Bader et al. introduce a way to alleviate the above problem, when the tensor is represented in a sparse form, in Matlab. This approach is however, as we mentioned earlier, bound by the memory limitations of Matlab. In Section 3, we describe our proposed method which effectively tackles intermediate data explosion, especially for sparse tensors, and is able to scale to very large tensors, because it operates on a distributed system.

3. PROPOSED METHOD

In this section, we describe GIGATENSOR, our proposed MAPREDUCE algorithm for large scale tensor analysis.

3.1 Overview

GIGATENSOR provides an efficient distributed algorithm for the PARAFAC tensor decomposition on MAPREDUCE. The major challenge is to design an efficient algorithm for updating factors (line 3, 5, and 7 of Algorithm 1). Since the update rules are similar, we focus on updating the $\mathbf{A}$ matrix. As shown in the line 3 of Algorithm 1, the update rule for A is

$$\hat{\mathbf{A}} \leftarrow \mathbf{X}_{(1)}(\mathbf{C} \odot \mathbf{B})(\mathbf{C}^T\mathbf{C} * \mathbf{B}^T\mathbf{B})^{\dagger}, \tag{4}$$

where $\mathbf{X}_{(1)} \in \mathbb{R}^{I \times JK}$, $\mathbf{B} \in \mathbb{R}^{J \times R}$, $\mathbf{C} \in \mathbb{R}^{K \times R}$, $(\mathbf{C} \odot \mathbf{B}) \in \mathbb{R}^{JK \times R}$, and $(\mathbf{C}^T\mathbf{C} * \mathbf{B}^T\mathbf{B})^{\dagger} \in \mathbb{R}^{R \times R}$. $\mathbf{X}_{(1)}$ is very sparse, especially in real world tensors, while $\mathbf{A}$, $\mathbf{B}$, and $\mathbf{C}$ are dense.

There are several challenges in designing an efficient MAPREDUCE algorithm for Equation (4) in GIGATENSOR:

1. **Minimize flops.** How to minimize the number of floating point operations (flops) for computing Equation (4)?
2. **Minimize intermediate data.** How to minimize the intermediate data size, i.e. the amount of network traffic in the shuffling stage of MAPREDUCE?
3. **Exploit data characteristics.** How to exploit the data characteristics including the sparsity of the real world tensor and the skewness in matrix multiplications to design an efficient MAPREDUCE algorithm?

We have the following main ideas to address the above challenges which we describe in detail in later subsections.

1. **Careful choice of order of computations** in order to minimize flops (Section 3.2).
2. **Avoiding intermediate data explosion** by exploiting the sparsity of real world tensors (Section 3.3 and 3.4.1).
3. **Parallel outer products** to minimize intermediate data (Section 3.4.2).
4. **Distributed cache multiplication** to minimize intermediate data by exploiting the skewness in matrix multiplications (Section 3.4.3).

3.2 Ordering of Computations

Equation (4) entails three matrix-matrix multiplications, assuming that we have already computed $(\mathbf{C} \odot \mathbf{B})$ and $(\mathbf{C}^T\mathbf{C} * \mathbf{B}^T\mathbf{B})^{\dagger}$. Since matrix multiplication is commutative, Equation (4) can be computed by either multiplying the first two matrices, and multiplying the result with the third matrix:

$$[\mathbf{X}_{(1)}(\mathbf{C} \odot \mathbf{B})](\mathbf{C}^T\mathbf{C} * \mathbf{B}^T\mathbf{B})^{\dagger}, \tag{5}$$

or multiplying the last two matrices, and multiplying the first matrix with the result:

$$\mathbf{X}_{(1)}[(\mathbf{C} \odot \mathbf{B})(\mathbf{C}^T\mathbf{C} * \mathbf{B}^T\mathbf{B})^{\dagger}]. \tag{6}$$

The question is, which equation is better between (5) and (6)? From a standard result of numerical linear algebra (e.g. [7]), the Equation (5) requires $2mR + 2IR^2$ flops, where m is the number of nonzeros in the tensor $\mathcal{X}$, while the Equation (6) requires $2mR + 2JKR^2$ flops. Given that the product of the two dimension sizes (JK) is larger than the other dimension size (I) in most practical cases, Equation (5) results in smaller flops. For example, referring to the NELL-1 dataset of Table 7, Equation (5) requires $\approx 8 \cdot 10^9$ flops while Equation (6) requires $\approx 2.5 \cdot 10^{17}$ flops. For the reason, we choose the Equation (5) ordering for updating factor matrices. That is, we perform the following three matrix-matrix multiplications for Equation (4):

$$\texttt{Step 1:} \quad \mathbf{M}_1 \leftarrow \mathbf{X}_{(1)}(\mathbf{C} \odot \mathbf{B}) \tag{7}$$

$$\texttt{Step 2:} \quad \mathbf{M}_2 \leftarrow (\mathbf{C}^T\mathbf{C} * \mathbf{B}^T\mathbf{B})^{\dagger} \tag{8}$$

$$\texttt{Step 3:} \quad \mathbf{M}_3 \leftarrow \mathbf{M}_1\mathbf{M}_2 \tag{9}$$

3.3 Avoiding the Intermediate Data Explosion Problem

As introduced at the end of Section 2, one of the most important issue for scaling up the tensor decomposition is the intermediate data explosion problem. In this subsection we describe the problem in detail, and propose our solution.

Problem. A naive algorithm to compute $\mathbf{X}_{(1)}(\mathbf{C} \odot \mathbf{B})$ is to first construct $\mathbf{C} \odot \mathbf{B}$, and multiply $\mathbf{X}_{(1)}$ with $\mathbf{C} \odot \mathbf{B}$, as illustrated in Figure 2. The problem ("intermediate data explosion ") of this algorithm is that although the matricized tensor $\mathbf{X}_{(1)}$ is sparse, the matrix $\mathbf{C} \odot \mathbf{B}$ is very large and dense; thus, $\mathbf{C} \odot \mathbf{B}$ cannot be stored even in multiple disks in a typical HADOOP cluster.

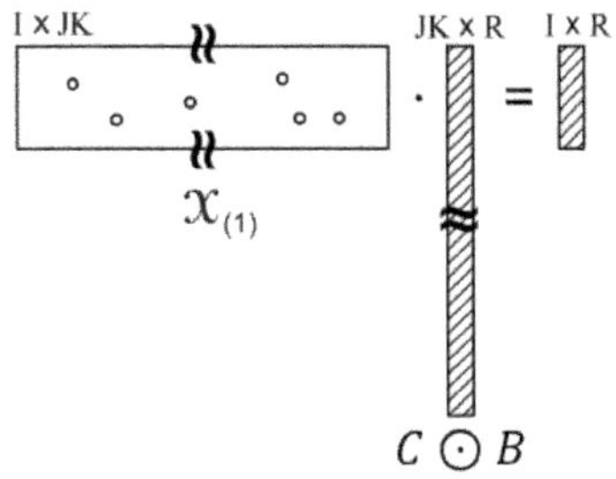

Figure 2: The "intermediate data explosion " problem in computing $\mathbf{X}_{(1)}(\mathbf{C} \odot \mathbf{B})$. Although $\mathbf{X}_{(1)}$ is sparse, the matrix $\mathbf{C} \odot \mathbf{B}$ is very dense and long. Materializing $\mathbf{C} \odot \mathbf{B}$ requires too much storage: e.g., for $J = K \approx 26$ million as in the NELL-1 data of Table 7, $\mathbf{C} \odot \mathbf{B}$ explodes to *676 trillion* rows.

Our Solution. Our crucial observation is that $\mathbf{X}_{(1)}(\mathbf{C} \odot \mathbf{B})$ can be computed without explicitly constructing $\mathbf{C} \odot \mathbf{B}$. [1] Our main idea is to decouple the two terms in the Khatri-Rao product, and perform algebraic operations involving $\mathbf{X}_{(1)}$ and $\mathbf{C}$, then $\mathbf{X}_{(1)}$ and $\mathbf{B}$, and then combine the result. Our main idea is described in Algorithm 2 as well as in Figure 3. In line 7 of Algorithm 2, the Hadamard product of $\mathbf{X}_{(1)}$ and a matrix derived from $\mathbf{C}$ is performed. In line 8, the Hadamard product of $\mathbf{X}_{(1)}$ and a matrix derived from $\mathbf{B}$ is performed, where the $bin()$ function converts any nonzero value into 1, preserving sparsity. In line 9, the Hadamard product of the two result matrices from lines 7 and 8 is performed, and the elements of each row of the resulting matrix are summed up to get the final result vector $\mathbf{M}_1(:, r)$ in line 10. The following Theorem demonstrates the correctness of Algorithm 2.

THEOREM 1. *Computing $\mathbf{X}_{(1)}(\mathbf{C} \odot \mathbf{B})$ is equivalent to computing $(\mathbf{N}_1 * \mathbf{N}_2) \cdot \mathbf{1}_{JK}$, where $\mathbf{N}_1 = \mathbf{X}_{(1)} * (\mathbf{1}_I \circ (\mathbf{C}(:, r)^T \otimes \mathbf{1}_J^T))$, $\mathbf{N}_2 = bin(\mathbf{X}_{(1)}) * (\mathbf{1}_I \circ (\mathbf{1}_K^T \otimes \mathbf{B}(:, r)^T))$, and $\mathbf{1_{JK}}$ is an all-1 vector of size JK.*

[1] Bader et al. [4] has an alternative way to avoid the intermediate data explosion.

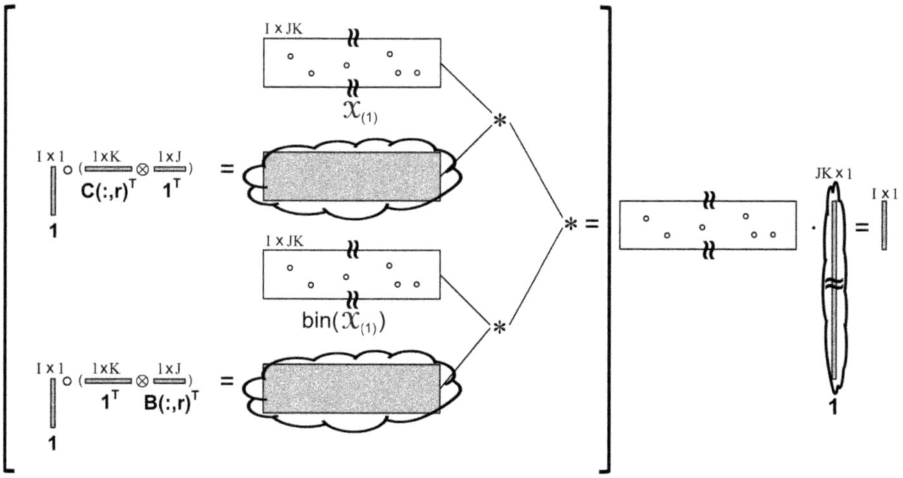

Figure 3: Our solution to avoid the intermediate data explosion. The main idea is to decouple the two terms in the Khatri-Rao product, and perform algebraic operations using $\mathbf{X}_{(1)}$ and $\mathbf{C}$, and then $\mathbf{X}_{(1)}$ with $\mathbf{B}$, and combine the result. The symbols $\circ, \otimes, *$, and $\cdot$ represents the outer, Kronecker, Hadamard, and the standard product, respectively. Shaded matrices are dense, and empty matrices with several circles are sparse. The clouds surrounding matrices represent that the matrices are <u>not</u> materialized. Note that the matrix $\mathbf{C} \odot \mathbf{B}$ is never constructed, and the largest dense matrix is either the $\mathbf{B}$ or the $\mathbf{C}$ matrix.

Algorithm 2: Multiplying $\mathbf{X}_{(1)}$ and $\mathbf{C} \odot \mathbf{B}$ in GIGATENSOR.

Input: Tensor $\mathbf{X}_{(1)} \in \mathbb{R}^{I \times JK}, \mathbf{C} \in \mathbb{R}^{K \times R}, \mathbf{B} \in \mathbb{R}^{J \times R}$.
Output: $\mathbf{M}_1 \leftarrow \mathbf{X}_{(1)}(\mathbf{C} \odot \mathbf{B})$.

```
M1 ← 0;
1I ← all 1 vector of size I;
1J ← all 1 vector of size J;
1K ← all 1 vector of size K;
1JK ← all 1 vector of size JK;
for r = 1, ..., R do
    N1 ← X(1) * (1I ∘ (C(:, r)^T ⊗ 1J^T));
    N2 ← bin(X(1)) * (1I ∘ (1K^T ⊗ B(:, r)^T));
    N3 ← N1 * N2;
    M1(:, r) ← N3 · 1JK;
end for
return M1;
```

PROOF. The (i, y)-th element of $\mathbf{N}_1$ is given by

$$\mathbf{N}_1(i, y) = \mathbf{X}_{(1)}(i, y)\mathbf{C}(\lceil \frac{y}{J} \rceil, r).$$

The (i, y)-th element of $\mathbf{N}_2$ is given by

$$\mathbf{N}_2(i, y) = \mathbf{B}(1 + (y - 1)\%J, r).$$

The (i, y)-th element of $\mathbf{N}_3 = \mathbf{N}_1 * \mathbf{N}_2$ is

$$\mathbf{N}_3(i, y) = \mathbf{X}_{(1)}(i, y)\mathbf{C}(\lceil \frac{y}{J} \rceil, r)\mathbf{B}(1 + (y - 1)\%J, r).$$

Multiplying $\mathbf{N}_3$ with $\mathbf{1}_{JK}$, which essentially sums up each row of $\mathbf{N}_3$, sets the i-th element $\mathbf{M}_1(i, r)$ of the $\mathbf{M}_1(:, r)$ vector equal to the following:

$$\mathbf{M}_1(i, r) = \sum_{y=1}^{JK} \mathbf{X}_{(1)}(i, y)\mathbf{C}(\lceil \frac{y}{J} \rceil, r)\mathbf{B}(1 + (y - 1)\%J, r),$$

which is exactly the equation that we want from the definition of $\mathbf{X}_{(1)}(\mathbf{C} \odot \mathbf{B})$. □

Notice that in Algorithm 2, the largest dense matrix required is either $\mathbf{B}$ or $\mathbf{C}$ (not $\mathbf{C} \odot \mathbf{B}$ as in the naive case), and therefore we have effectively avoided the intermediate data explosion problem.

Discussion. Table 4 compares the cost of the naive algorithm and GIGATENSOR for computing $\mathbf{X}_{(1)}(\mathbf{C} \odot \mathbf{B})$. The naive algorithm requires total $JKR + 2mR$ flops (JKR for constructing $(\mathbf{C} \odot \mathbf{B})$, and $2mR$ for multiplying $\mathbf{X}_{(1)}$ and $(\mathbf{C} \odot \mathbf{B})$), and $JKR + m$ intermediate data size (JKR for $(\mathbf{C} \odot \mathbf{B})$, and m for $\mathbf{X}_{(1)}$). On the other hand, GIGATENSOR requires only $5mR$ flops ($3mR$ for three Hadamard products, and $2mR$ for the final multiplication), and $max(J + m, K + m)$ intermediate data size. The dependence on the term JK of the naive method makes it inappropriate for real world tensors which are sparse and the sizes of dimensions are much larger compared to the number m of nonzeros ($JK \gg m$). On the other hand, GIGATENSOR depends on $max(J+m, K+m)$ which is $O(m)$ for most practical cases, and thus fully exploits the sparsity of real world tensors.

Algorithm	**Flops**	**Intermediate Data**
Naive	$JKR + 2mR$	$JKR + m$
GIGATENSOR	$5mR$	$max(J + m, K + m)$

Table 4: Cost comparison of the naive and GIGATENSOR for computing $\mathbf{X}_{(1)}(\mathbf{C} \odot \mathbf{B})$. J and K are the sizes of the second and the third dimensions, respectively, m is the number of nonzeros in the tensor, and R is the desired rank for the tensor decomposition (typically, $R \sim 10$). GIGATENSOR does not suffer from the intermediate data explosion problem, and is much more efficient than the naive algorithm in terms of both flops and intermediate data sizes. An arithmetic example, referring to the NELL-1 dataset of Table 7, for 8 bytes per value, and $R = 10$ is: $1.25 \cdot 10^{16}$ flops, 100 PB for the naive algorithm and $8.6 \cdot 10^9$ flops, 1.5GB for GIGATENSOR.

3.4 Our Optimizations for MapReduce

In this subsection, we describe MAPREDUCE algorithms for computing the three steps in Equations (7), (8), and (9).

3.4.1 Avoiding the Intermediate Data Explosion

The first step is to compute $\mathbf{M}_1 \leftarrow \mathbf{X}_{(1)}(\mathbf{C} \odot \mathbf{B})$ (Equation (7)). The factors $\mathbf{C}$ and $\mathbf{B}$ are given in the form of $< j, r, \mathbf{C}(j,r) >$ and $< j, r, \mathbf{B}(j,r) >$, respectively. The tensor $\mathcal{X}$ is stored in the format of $< i, j, k, \mathcal{X}(i,j,k) >$, but we assume the tensor data is given in the form of mode-1 matricization ($< i, j, \mathbf{X}_{(1)}(i,j) >$) by using the mapping in Equation (1). We use Q_i and Q^j to denote the set of nonzero indices in $\mathbf{X}_{(1)}(i,:)$ and $\mathbf{X}_{(1)}(:,j)$, respectively: i.e., $Q_i = \{j | \mathbf{X}_{(1)}(i,j) > 0\}$ and $Q^j = \{i | \mathbf{X}_{(1)}(i,j) > 0\}$.

We first describe the MAPREDUCE algorithm for line 7 of Algorithm 2. Here, the tensor data and the factor data are joined for the Hadamard product. Notice that only the tensor $\mathcal{X}$ and the factor $\mathbf{C}$ are transferred in the shuffling stage.

- MAP-1: map $< i, j, \mathbf{X}_{(1)}(i,j) >$ on $\lceil \frac{j}{J} \rceil$, and $< j, r, \mathbf{C}(j,r) >$ on j such that tuples with the same key are shuffled to the same reducer in the form of $< j, (\mathbf{C}(j,r), \{(i, \mathbf{X}_{(1)}(i,j)) | \forall i \in Q^j\}) >$.
- REDUCE-1: take $< j, (\mathbf{C}(j,r), \{(i, X_{(1)}(i,j)) | \forall i \in Q^j\}) >$ and emit $< i, j, \mathbf{X}_{(1)}(i,j)\mathbf{C}(j,r) >$ for each $i \in Q^j$.

In the second MAPREDUCE algorithm for line 8 of Algorithm 2, we perform the similar task as the first MAPREDUCE algorithm but we do not multiply the value of the tensor, since line 8 uses the binary function. Again, only the tensor $\mathcal{X}$ and the factor $\mathbf{B}$ are transferred in the shuffling stage.

- MAP-2: map $< i, j, \mathbf{X}_{(1)}(i,j) >$ on $\lceil \frac{j}{J} \rceil$, and $< j, r, \mathbf{B}(j,r) >$ on j such that tuples with the same key are shuffled to the same reducer in the form of $< j, (\mathbf{B}(j,r), \{i | \forall i \in Q^j\}) >$.
- REDUCE-2: take $< j, (\mathbf{B}(j,r), \{i | \forall i \in Q^j\}) >$ and emit $< i, j, \mathbf{B}(j,r) >$ for each $i \in Q^j$.

Finally, in the third MAPREDUCE algorithm for lines 9 and 10, we combine the results from the first and the second steps using Hadamard product, and sums up each row to get the final result.

- MAP-3: map $< i, j, \mathbf{X}_{(1)}(i,j)\mathbf{C}(j,r) >$ and $< i, j, \mathbf{B}(j,r) >$ on i such that tuples with the same i are shuffled to the same reducer in the form of $< i, \{(j, \mathbf{X}_{(1)}(i,j)\mathbf{C}(j,r), \mathbf{B}(j,r))\} | \forall j \in Q_i >$.
- REDUCE-3: take $< i, \{(j, \mathbf{X}_{(1)}(i,j)\mathbf{C}(j,r), \mathbf{B}(j,r))\} | \forall j \in Q_i >$ and emit $< i, \sum_j \mathbf{X}_{(1)}(i,j)\mathbf{C}(j,r)\mathbf{B}(j,r) >$.

Note that the amount of data traffic in the shuffling stage is small (2 times the nonzeros of the tensor $\mathcal{X}$), considering that $\mathcal{X}$ is sparse.

3.4.2 *Parallel Outer Products*

The next step is to compute $(\mathbf{C}^T\mathbf{C} * \mathbf{B}^T\mathbf{B})^\dagger$ (Equation (8)). Here, the challenge is to compute $\mathbf{C^T C} * \mathbf{B^T B}$ efficiently, since once the $\mathbf{C}^T\mathbf{C} * \mathbf{B}^T\mathbf{B}$ is computed, the pseudo-inverse is trivial to compute because matrix $\mathbf{C}^T\mathbf{C} * \mathbf{B}^T\mathbf{B}$ is very small ($R \times R$ where R is very small; e.g. $R \sim 10$). The question is, how to compute $\mathbf{C^T C} * \mathbf{B^T B}$ efficiently? Our idea is to first compute $\mathbf{C}^T\mathbf{C}$, then $\mathbf{B}^T\mathbf{B}$, and performs the Hadamard product of the two $R \times R$ matrices. To compute $\mathbf{C}^T\mathbf{C}$, we express $\mathbf{C}^T\mathbf{C}$ as the sum of outer products of the rows:

$$\mathbf{C}^T\mathbf{C} = \sum_{k=1}^{K} \mathbf{C}(k,:)^T \circ \mathbf{C}(k,:), \tag{10}$$

where $\mathbf{C}(k,:)$ is the kth row of the $\mathbf{C}$ matrix. To implement the Equation (10) efficiently in MAPREDUCE, we partition the factor matrices row-wise [24]: we store each row of $\mathbf{C}$ into a line in the HADOOP File System (HDFS). The advantage of this approach compared to the column-wise partition is that each unit of data is self-joined with itself, and thus can be independently processed; column-wise partition would require each column to be joined with other columns which is prohibitively expensive.

The MAPREDUCE algorithm for Equation (10) is as follows.

- MAP: map $< j, \mathbf{C}(j,:) >$ on 0 so that all the output is shuffled to the only reducer in the form of $< 0, \{\mathbf{C}(j,:)^T \circ \mathbf{C}(j,:)\} \forall j >$.
- COMBINE, REDUCE: take $< 0, \{\mathbf{C}(j,:)^T \circ \mathbf{C}(j,:)\} \forall j >$ and emit $< 0, \sum_j \mathbf{C}(j,:)^T \circ \mathbf{C}(j,:) >$.

Since we use the combiner as well as the reducer, each mapper computes the local sum of the outer product. The result is that the size of the intermediate data, i.e. the number of input tuples to the reducer, is very small ($d \cdot R^2$ where d is the number of mappers) in GIGATENSOR. On the other hand, the naive column-wise partition method requires KR (the size of $\mathbf{C}^T$) + K (the size of a column of $\mathbf{C}$) intermediate data for 1 iteration, and thereby requires $K(R^2 + R)$ intermediate data for R iterations, which is much larger than the intermediate data size $d \cdot R^2$ of GIGATENSOR, as summarized in Table 5.

Algorithm	Flops	Intermediate Data	Example
Naive	KR^2	$K(R^2 + R)$	40 GB
GIGATENSOR	KR^2	$d \cdot R^2$	40 KB

Table 5: Cost comparison of the naive (column-wise partition) method and GIGATENSOR for computing $\mathbf{C}^T\mathbf{C}$. K is the size of the third dimension, d is the number of mappers used, and R is the desired rank for the tensor decomposition (typically, $R \sim 10$). Notice that although the flops are the same for both methods, GIGATENSOR has much smaller intermediate data size compared to the naive method, considering $K \gg d$. The example refers to the intermediate data size for NELL-1 dataset of Table 7, for 8 bytes per value, $R = 10$ and $d = 50$.

3.4.3 *Distributed Cache Multiplication*

The final step is to multiply $\mathbf{X}_{(1)}(\mathbf{C} \odot \mathbf{B}) \in \mathbb{R}^{I \times R}$ and $(\mathbf{C}^T\mathbf{C} * \mathbf{B}^T\mathbf{B})^\dagger \in \mathbb{R}^{R \times R}$ (Equation (9)). We note the skewness of data sizes: the first matrix $\mathbf{X}_{(1)}(\mathbf{C} \odot \mathbf{B})$ is large and does not fit in the memory of a single machine, while the second matrix $(\mathbf{C}^T\mathbf{C} * \mathbf{B}^T\mathbf{B})^\dagger$ is very small to fit in the memory. To exploit this into better performance, we propose to use the distributed cache multiplication [16] to broadcast the second matrix to all the mappers that process the first matrix, and perform join in the first matrix. The result is that our method requires only one MAPREDUCE job with smaller intermediate data size (IR^2). On the other hand, the standard naive matrix-matrix multiplication requires two MAPREDUCE jobs: the first job for grouping the data by the column id of $\mathbf{X}_{(1)}(\mathbf{C} \odot \mathbf{B})$ and the row id of $(\mathbf{C}^T\mathbf{C} * \mathbf{B}^T\mathbf{B})^\dagger$, and the second job for aggregation. Our proposed method is more efficient than the naive method since in the naive method the intermediate data size increases to $I(R + R^2) + R^2$ (the first job: $IR + R^2$, and the second job: IR^2), and the first job's output of size IR^2 should be written to and read from discs for the second job, as summarized in Table 6.

4. EXPERIMENTS

To evaluate our system, we perform experiments to answer the following questions:

Algorithm	Flops	Intermediate Data	Example
Naive	IR^2	$I(R + R^2) + R^2$	23 GB
GIGATENSOR	IR^2	IR^2	20 GB

Table 6: Cost comparison of the naive (column-wise partition) method and GIGATENSOR for multiplying $\mathbf{X}_{(1)}(\mathbf{C} \odot \mathbf{B})$ and $(\mathbf{C}^T\mathbf{C} * \mathbf{B}^T\mathbf{B})^\dagger$. I is the size of the first dimension, and R is the desired rank for the tensor decomposition (typically, $R \sim 10$). Although the flops are the same for both methods, GIGATENSOR has smaller intermediate data size compared to the naive method. The example refers to the intermediate data size for NELL-1 dataset of Table 7, for 8 bytes per value and $R = 10$.

Q1 What is the scalability of GIGATENSOR compared to other methods with regard to the sizes of tensors?
Q2 What is the scalability of GIGATENSOR compared to other methods with regard to the number of nonzero elements?
Q3 How does GIGATENSOR scale with regard to the number of machines?
Q4 What are the discoveries on real world tensors?

The tensor data in our experiments are summarized in Table 7, with the following details.

- NELL: real world knowledge base data containing (noun phrase 1, context, noun phrase 2) triples (e.g. 'George Harrison' 'plays' 'guitars') from the 'Read the Web' project [9]. NELL-1 data is the full data, and NELL-2 data is the filtered data from NELL-1 by removing entries whose values are below a threshold.
- Random: synthetic random tensor of size $I \times I \times I$. The size I varies from 10^4 to 10^9, and the number of nonzeros varies from 10^2 to $2 \cdot 10^7$.

Data	I	J	K	Nonzeros
NELL-1	26 M	26 M	48 M	144 M
NELL-2	15 K	15 K	29 K	77 M
Random	10 K~1 B	10 K~1 B	10 K~1 B	100~20 M

Table 7: Summary of the tensor data used. B: billion, M: million, K: thousand.

4.1 Scalability

We compare the scalability of GIGATENSOR and the Tensor Toolbox for Matlab [6] which is the current state of the art in terms of handling fast and effectively sparse tensors. The Tensor Toolbox is executed in a machine with a quad-core AMD 2.8 GHz CPU, 32 GB RAM, and 2.3 Terabytes disk. To run GIGATENSOR, we use CMU's OpenCloud HADOOP cluster where each machine has 2 quad-core Intel 2.83 GHz CPU, 16 GB RAM, and 4 Terabytes disk.

Scalability on the Size of Tensors. Figure 4 (a) shows the scalability of GIGATENSOR with regard to the sizes of tensors. We fix the number of nonzero elements to 10^4 on the synthetic data while increasing the tensor sizes $I = J = K$. We use 35 machines, and report the running time for 1 iteration of the algorithm. Notice that for smaller data the Tensor Toolbox runs faster than GIGATENSOR due to the overhead of running an algorithm on distributed systems, including reading/writing the data from/to disks, JVM loading type, and synchronization time. However as the data size grows beyond 10^7, the Tensor Toolbox runs out of memory while GIGATENSOR continues to run, eventually solving at least 100× larger problem than the competitor. We performed the same experiment while fixing the nonzero elements to 10^7, and we get similar results. We note that the Tensor Toolbox at its current implementation cannot run in distributed systems, thus we were unable to compare GIGATENSOR with a distributed Tensor Toolbox. We note that extending the Tensor Toolbox to run in a distributed setting is highly non-trivial; and even more complicated to make it handle data that don't fit in memory. On the contrary, our GIGATENSOR can handle such tensors.

Scalability on the Number of Nonzero Elements. Figure 4 (b) shows the scalability of GIGATENSOR compared to the Tensor Toolbox with regard to the number of nonzeros and tensor sizes on the synthetic data. We set the tensor size to be $I \times I \times I$, and the number of nonzero elements to be $I/50$. As in the previous experiment, we use 35 machines, and report the running time required for 1 iteration of the algorithm. Notice that GIGATENSOR decomposes tensors of sizes at least 10^9, while the Tensor Toolbox implementation runs out of memory on tensors of sizes beyond 10^7.

Scalability on the Number of Machines. Figure 5 shows the scalability of GIGATENSOR with regard to the number of machines. The Y-axis shows T_{25}/T_M where T_M is the running time for 1 iteration with M machines. Notice that the running time scales up near linearly.

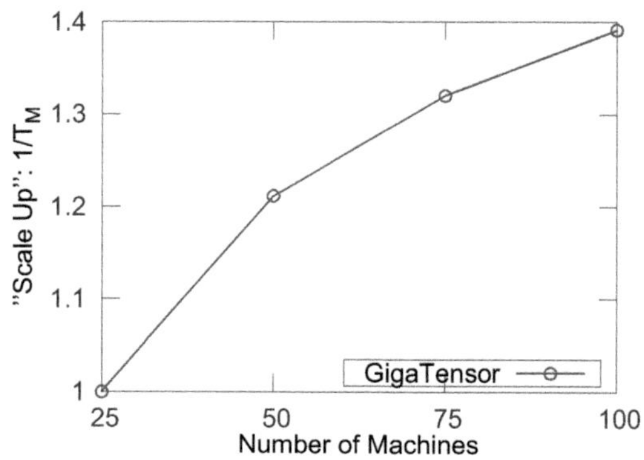

Figure 5: The scalability of GIGATENSOR with regard to the number of machines on the NELL-1 data. Notice that the running time scales up near linearly.

4.2 Discovery

In this section, we present discoveries on the NELL dataset that was previously introduced; we are mostly interested in demonstrating the power of our approach, as opposed to the current state of the art which was unable to handle a dataset of this magnitude. We perform two tasks: concept discovery, and (contextual) synonym detection.

Concept Discovery. With GIGATENSOR, we decompose the NELL-2 dataset in $R = 10$ components, and obtained λ_i, $\mathbf{A}, \mathbf{B}, \mathbf{C}$ (see Figure 1). Each one of the R columns of $\mathbf{A}, \mathbf{B}, \mathbf{C}$ represents a grouping of similar (noun-phrase np1, noun-phrase np2, context words) triplets. The r-th column of $\mathbf{A}$ encodes with high values the noun-phrases in position np1, for the r-th group of triplets, the r-th column of $\mathbf{B}$ does so for the noun-phrases in position np2 and the r-th column of $\mathbf{C}$ contains the corresponding context words. In order to select the most representative noun-phrases and contexts for each group, we choose the k highest valued coefficients for each column. Table 8 shows 4 notable groups out of 10, and within each group the 3 most outstanding noun-phrases and contexts. Notice that each concept group contains relevant noun phrases and contexts.

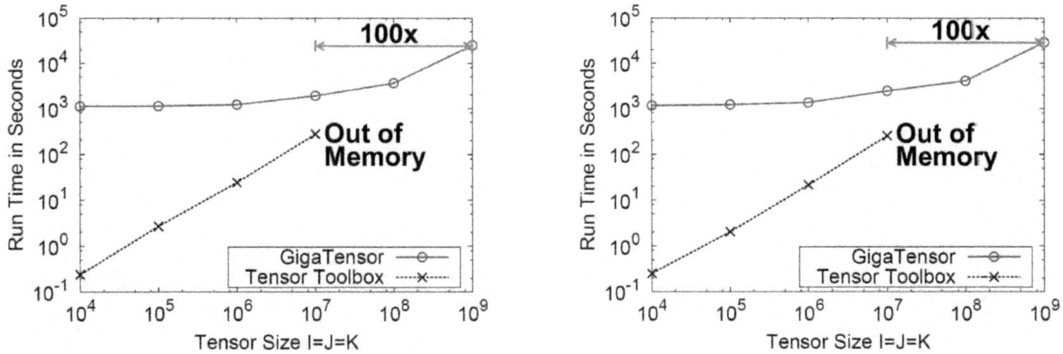

(a) Number of nonzeros = 10^4.

(b) Number of nonzeros = $I/50$.

Figure 4: The scalability of GIGATENSOR compared to the Tensor Toolbox. (a) The number of nonzero elements is set to 10^4. (b) For a tensor of size $I \times I \times I$, the number of nonzero elements is set to $I/50$. In both cases, GIGATENSOR solves at least $100\times$ larger problem than the Tensor Toolbox which runs out of memory on tensors of sizes beyond 10^7.

Noun Phrase 1	Noun Phrase 2	Context
Concept 1: "Web Protocol"		
internet	protocol	'np1' 'stream' 'np2'
file	software	'np1' 'marketing' 'np2'
data	suite	'np1' 'dating' 'np2'
Concept 2: "Credit Cards"		
credit	information	'np1' 'card' 'np2'
Credit	debt	'np1' 'report' 'np2'
library	number	'np1' 'cards' 'np2'
Concept 3: "Health System"		
health	provider	'np1' 'care' 'np2'
child	providers	'np' 'insurance' 'np2'
home	system	'np1' 'service' 'np2'
Concept 4: "Family Life"		
life	rest	'np2' 'of' 'my' 'np1'
family	part	'np2' 'of' 'his' 'np1'
body	years	'np2' 'of' 'her' 'np1'

Table 8: Four notable groups that emerge from analyzing the NELL dataset.

Contextual Synonym Detection. The lower dimensional embedding of the noun phrases also permits a scalable and robust strategy for synonym detection. We are interested in discovering noun-phrases that occur in similar contexts, i.e. *contextual synonyms*. Using a similarity metric, such as Cosine Similarity, between the lower dimensional embeddings of the Noun-phrases (such as in the factor matrix **A**), we can identify similar noun-phrases that can be used alternatively in sentence templates such as *np1 context np2*. Using the embeddings in the factor matrix **A** (appropriately column-weighted by λ), we get the synonyms that might be used in position *np1*, using **B** leads to synonyms for position *np2*, and using **C** leads to contexts that accept similar *np1* and *np2* arguments. In Table 2, which is located in Section 1, we show some exemplary synonyms for position *np1* that were discovered by this approach on NELL-1 dataset. Note that these are not synonyms in the traditional definition, but they are phrases that may occur in similar semantic roles in a sentence.

5. RELATED WORK

In this section, we review related works on tensor analysis (emphasizing on data mining applications), and MAPREDUCE/HADOOP.

Tensor Analysis. Tensors have a very long list of applications, pertaining to many fields additionally to data mining. For instance, tensors have been used extensively in Chemometrics [8] and Signal Processing [29]. Not very long ago, the data mining community has turned its attention to tensors and tensor decompositions. Some of the data mining applications that employ tensors are the following: in [20], Kolda et al. extend the famous HITS algorithm [19] by Kleinberg et al. in order to incorporate topical information in the links between the Web pages. In [2], Acar et al. analyze epilepsy data using tensor decompositions. In [5], Bader et al. employ tensors in order perform social network analysis, using the Enron dataset for evaluation. In [31], Sun et al. formulate click data on the Web pages as a tensor, in order to improve the Web search by incorporating user interests in the results. In [10], Chew et al. extend the Latent Semantic Indexing [12] paradigm for cross-language information retrieval, using tensors. In [33], Tao et al. employ tensors for 3D face modelling and in [32], a supervised learning framework, based on tensors is proposed. In [25], Maruhashi et al. present a framework for discovering bipartite graph like patterns in heterogeneous networks using tensors.

MAPREDUCE and HADOOP. MAPREDUCE is a distributed computing framework [11] for processing Web-scale data. MAPREDUCE has two advantages: (a) the data distribution, replication, fault-tolerance, and load balancing is handled automatically; and furthermore (b) it uses the familiar concept of functional programming. The programmer needs to define only two functions, a *map* and a *reduce*. The general framework is as follows [23]: (a) the *map* stage reads the input file and outputs (key, value) pairs; (b) the *shuffling* stage sorts the output and distributes them to reducers; (c) the *reduce* stage processes the values with the same key and outputs another (key, value) pairs which become the final result.

HADOOP [1] is the open source version of MAPREDUCE. HADOOP uses its own distributed file system HDFS, and provides a high-level language called PIG [26]. Due to its excellent scalability, ease of use, cost advantage, HADOOP has been used for many graph mining tasks (see [18, 15, 16, 17]).

6. CONCLUSION

In this paper, we propose GIGATENSOR, a tensor decomposition algorithm which scales to billion size tensors, and present interesting discoveries from real world tensors. Our major contributions include:

- **Algorithm.** We propose GIGATENSOR, a carefully designed large scale tensor decomposition algorithm on MAPREDUCE.
- **Scalability.** GIGATENSOR decomposes 100× larger tensors compared to previous methods, and GIGATENSOR scales near linearly to the number of machines.
- **Discovery.** We discover patterns of synonyms and concept groups in a very large knowledge base tensor which could not be analyzed before.

Future work could focus on related tensor decompositions, such as PARAFAC with sparse latent factors [27], as well as the TUCKER3 [34] decomposition.

Acknowledgement

Funding was provided by the U.S. ARO and DARPA under Contract Number W911NF-11-C-0088, by DTRA under contract No. HDTRA1-10-1-0120, and by ARL under Cooperative Agreement Number W911NF-09-2-0053, The views and conclusions are those of the authors and should not be interpreted as representing the official policies, of the U.S. Government, or other funding parties, and no official endorsement should be inferred. The U.S. Government is authorized to reproduce and distribute reprints for Government purposes notwithstanding any copyright notation here on.

7. REFERENCES

[1] Hadoop information. http://hadoop.apache.org/.

[2] E. Acar, C. Aykut-Bingol, H. Bingol, R. Bro, and B. Yener. Multiway analysis of epilepsy tensors. *Bioinformatics*, 23(13):i10–i18, 2007.

[3] C.A. Andersson and R. Bro. The n-way toolbox for matlab. *Chemometrics and Intelligent Laboratory Systems*, 52(1):1–4, 2000.

[4] B. W. Bader and T. G. Kolda. Efficient MATLAB computations with sparse and factored tensors. *SIAM Journal on Scientific Computing*, 30(1):205–231, December 2007.

[5] B.W. Bader, R.A. Harshman, and T.G. Kolda. Temporal analysis of social networks using three-way dedicom. *Sandia National Laboratories TR SAND2006-2161*, 2006.

[6] B.W. Bader and T.G. Kolda. Matlab tensor toolbox version 2.2. *Albuquerque, NM, USA: Sandia National Laboratories*, 2007.

[7] S. Boyd and L. Vandenberghe. *Convex Optimization*. Cambridge University Press, New York, NY, USA, 2004.

[8] R. Bro. Parafac. tutorial and applications. *Chemometrics and intelligent laboratory systems*, 38(2):149–171, 1997.

[9] A. Carlson, J. Betteridge, B. Kisiel, B. Settles, E. R. Hruschka Jr., and T. M. Mitchell. Toward an architecture for never-ending language learning. In *AAAI*, 2010.

[10] P.A. Chew, B.W. Bader, T.G. Kolda, and A. Abdelali. Cross-language information retrieval using parafac2. In *KDD*, 2007.

[11] J. Dean and S. Ghemawat. Mapreduce: Simplified data processing on large clusters. In *OSDI*, pages 137–150, 2004.

[12] S. Deerwester, S. T. Dumais, G. W. Furnas, T. K. Landauer, and R. Harshman. Indexing by latent semantic analysis. *Journal of the American Society for Information Science*, 41(6):391–407, September 1990.

[13] C. Eckart and G. Young. The approximation of one matrix by another of lower rank. *Psychometrika*, 1(3):211–218, 1936.

[14] R.A. Harshman. Foundations of the parafac procedure: Models and conditions for an" explanatory" multimodal factor analysis. 1970.

[15] U. Kang, D. H. Chau, and C. Faloutsos. Mining large graphs: Algorithms, inference, and discoveries. In *ICDE*, pages 243–254, 2011.

[16] U. Kang, B. Meeder, and C. Faloutsos. Spectral analysis for billion-scale graphs: Discoveries and implementation. In *PAKDD (2)*, pages 13–25, 2011.

[17] U. Kang, H. Tong, J. Sun, C.-Y. Lin, and C. Faloutsos. Gbase: a scalable and general graph management system. In *KDD*, pages 1091–1099, 2011.

[18] U. Kang, C. E. Tsourakakis, and C. Faloutsos. Pegasus: A peta-scale graph mining system. In *ICDM*, pages 229–238, 2009.

[19] J.M. Kleinberg. Authoritative sources in a hyperlinked environment. *Journal of the ACM*, 46(5):604–632, 1999.

[20] T.G. Kolda and B.W. Bader. The tophits model for higher-order web link analysis. In *Workshop on Link Analysis, Counterterrorism and Security*, volume 7, pages 26–29, 2006.

[21] T.G. Kolda and B.W. Bader. Tensor decompositions and applications. *SIAM review*, 51(3), 2009.

[22] T.G. Kolda and J. Sun. Scalable tensor decompositions for multi-aspect data mining. In *ICDM*, 2008.

[23] R. Lämmel. Google's mapreduce programming model – revisited. *Science of Computer Programming*, 70:1–30, 2008.

[24] C. Liu, H. c. Yang, J. Fan, L.-W. He, and Y.-M. Wang. Distributed nonnegative matrix factorization for web-scale dyadic data analysis on mapreduce. In *WWW*, pages 681–690, 2010.

[25] K. Maruhashi, F. Guo, and C. Faloutsos. Multiaspectforensics: Pattern mining on large-scale heterogeneous networks with tensor analysis. In *ASONAM*, 2011.

[26] C. Olston, B. Reed, U. Srivastava, R. Kumar, and A. Tomkins. Pig latin: a not-so-foreign language for data processing. In *SIGMOD '08*, pages 1099–1110, 2008.

[27] E.E. Papalexakis and N.D. Sidiropoulos. Co-clustering as multilinear decomposition with sparse latent factors. In *ICASSP*, 2011.

[28] R. Penrose. A generalized inverse for matrices. In *Proc. Cambridge Philos. Soc*, volume 51, pages 406–413. Cambridge Univ Press, 1955.

[29] N.D. Sidiropoulos, G.B. Giannakis, and R. Bro. Blind parafac receivers for ds-cdma systems. *Signal Processing, IEEE Transactions on*, 48(3):810–823, 2000.

[30] J. Sun, S. Papadimitriou, and P. S. Yu. Window-based tensor analysis on high-dimensional and multi-aspect streams. In *ICDM*, pages 1076–1080, 2006.

[31] J.T. Sun, H.J. Zeng, H. Liu, Y. Lu, and Z. Chen. Cubesvd: a novel approach to personalized web search. In *WWW*, 2005.

[32] D. Tao, X. Li, X. Wu, W. Hu, and S.J. Maybank. Supervised tensor learning. *KAIS*, 13(1):1–42, 2007.

[33] D. Tao, M. Song, X. Li, J. Shen, J. Sun, X. Wu, C. Faloutsos, and S.J. Maybank. Bayesian tensor approach for 3-d face modeling. *IEEE TCSVT*, 18(10):1397–1410, 2008.

[34] L.R. Tucker. Some mathematical notes on three-mode factor analysis. *Psychometrika*, 31(3):279–311, 1966.

Active Learning for Online Bayesian Matrix Factorization

Jorge Silva
Dept. of Electrical and Computer Engineering
Duke University
Durham, NC
jg.silva@duke.edu

Lawrence Carin
Dept. of Electrical and Computer Engineering
Duke University
Durham, NC
lcarin@duke.edu

ABSTRACT

The problem of large-scale online matrix completion is addressed via a Bayesian approach. The proposed method learns a factor analysis (FA) model for large matrices, based on a small number of observed matrix elements, and leverages the statistical model to actively select which new matrix entries/observations would be most informative if they could be acquired, to improve the model; the model inference and active learning are performed in an online setting. In the context of online learning, a greedy, fast and provably near-optimal algorithm is employed to sequentially maximize the mutual information between past and future observations, taking advantage of submodularity properties. Additionally, a simpler procedure, which directly uses the posterior parameters learned by the Bayesian approach, is shown to achieve slightly lower estimation quality, with far less computational effort. Inference is performed using a computationally efficient online variational Bayes (VB) procedure. Competitive results are obtained in a very large collaborative filtering problem, namely the Yahoo! Music ratings dataset.

Categories and Subject Descriptors

H.2.8 [**Database management**]: Database applications-Data mining

Keywords

Online learning, matrix factorization

1. INTRODUCTION

There has been growing interest in the problem of matrix completion, *i.e.*, estimating unknown elements in matrices based on a subset of observed entries (with the observed entries usually assumed observed at random). Concretely, assume that $\mathbf{X} \in \mathbb{R}^{N_u \times N_v}$ is a matrix, for which we know only the values of the elements x_{ij} at locations given by the set $\Omega = \{(i,j) : x_{ij} \text{ is observed}\}$. In a collaborative filtering/recommender system setting, N_u is often the number of users, while N_v is the number of items.

The matrix $\mathbf{X}$ can be very large; also, the number of observations can be very small relative to $N_u \times N_v$, but large in absolute terms, which poses computational and statistical challenges. For example, in the Netflix challenge [2] there are $N_u = 480189$ users, $N_v = 17770$ movies and the number of observed ratings is $|\Omega| = 100480507$, which corresponds to less than 1.18 percent of $\mathbf{X}$. More recently, the even larger Yahoo! Music dataset [4] has been released. It contains $|\Omega| = 262810175$ ratings (integers between 0 and 100) pertaining to $N_u = 1000990$ users and $N_v = 624961$ items (music tracks, albums, artists and genres).

For many such real problems, the matrices of interest can be assumed to be approximately low-rank, in which case it is appropriate to consider a matrix factorization model of the form

$$\mathbf{X} \approx \mathbf{U}^T \mathbf{V}, \tag{1}$$

with $\mathbf{U} \in \mathbb{R}^{K \times N_u}$, $\mathbf{V} \in \mathbb{R}^{K \times N_v}$ and $K \ll N_u, N_v$. Recent advances in matrix completion theory [3] provide bounds on the number of observations needed for successfully recovering low-rank matrices using convex optimization (and assuming the observed entries are selected at random). However, existing convex optimization algorithms are incapable of handling the very large matrix sizes typical of real collaborative filtering problems.

Hence, the most popular approaches for large-scale problems are based on solving (1), or some variant thereof, for $\mathbf{U}, \mathbf{V}$ through minimization of the ℓ_2 norm of the residual computed for the known locations Ω (see, *e.g.*, [7]). Regularization is often employed, typically using the ℓ_2 or ℓ_∞ norm [9] of the parameters (these regularizers are imposed on the columns of $\mathbf{U}$ and $\mathbf{V}$; the ℓ_1 or ℓ_0 sparseness regularizers characteristic of convex optimization solutions [3] are not used here, because we explicitly set the rank to K, with $K \ll N_u, N_v$). Due to memory and speed considerations, the minimization is often performed through stochastic gradient descent. Stochastic gradient descent is an online learning method, in which the training examples are presented sequentially, obviating the need to store the entire dataset in memory. Typically, the order of presentation is random. Stochastic gradient descent has also been used successfully in other large-scale problems such as image inpainting [11] and topic modeling [5]. It enjoys local convergence guarantees, as shown in [17].

Alternative methods for solving (1) include Bayesian probabilistic matrix factorization [16], which achieves state-of-

KDD'12, August 12–16, 2012, Beijing, China.

the-art performance on the Netflix dataset. However, since this is a batch method, scalability to even larger problems such as the Yahoo! Music dataset is less straightforward than with stochastic gradient descent. Additionally, [16] uses Markov chain Monte Carlo inference, for which it is harder to assess convergence.

In our work, we propose a statistical factor analysis (FA) model that extends the basic low-rank factorization shown in (1), and we develop an associated variational Bayesian (VB) [1] online inference algorithm, which incorporates the scalability of stochastic gradient descent while providing approximate posterior estimates of all model parameters. Other VB methods that have been applied to collaborative filtering, such as [10, 14], are based on batch learning. Our method is an online extension of the batch VB principal component analysis (PCA) approach proposed in [14, 15, 12].

Another contribution of our paper is that we leverage the statistical model to *actively* select the best subset of observations at each step of the online learning process, instead of assuming that the training examples follow a random order of presentation as in stochastic gradient descent. This active learning procedure is motivated by the fact that each measurement x_{ij} is often obtained sequentially and requires user interaction, which may be expensive and time-consuming. Therefore, by prioritizing the most informative users and items, we can potentially guide the data acquisition process in a more efficient way. In general, the problem of finding the m best locations of $\mathbf{X}$ to measure is NP-complete. We avoid this difficulty by developing two types of greedy algorithms: (i) a near-optimal method based on [8], relying on the submodularity properties of mutual information; (ii) a simpler algorithm based on the estimated variance of the user and item factors returned by the VB inference. A non-Bayesian active algorithm is also used for comparison.

The remainder of the paper is organized as follows. Section 2 describes our proposed factor analysis model, as well as the associated VB inference. This section also briefly discusses how to incorporate time information in the model. The active learning algorithms are presented in Section 3, which also contains an explanation of the submodularity property. Experimental results with online VB and active learning on the Yahoo! Music dataset are shown in Section 4. Concluding remarks are presented in Section 5.

2. FACTOR ANALYSIS MODEL

The matrix factorization problem expressed in (1) can be cast as factor analysis (FA) with $x_{ij} = \boldsymbol{u}_i^T \boldsymbol{v}_j + \epsilon_{ij}$, where ϵ_{ij} is a residual term, assumed small, $\boldsymbol{u}_i \in \mathbb{R}^K$ is the ith column of $\mathbf{U}$, and $\boldsymbol{v}_j \in \mathbb{R}^K$ is the jth column of $\mathbf{V}$. Previous work on collaborative filtering [7, 6] shows that it is advantageous to also incorporate user and item biases, leading to the complete FA model

$$x_{ij} = \alpha_i + \beta_j + \boldsymbol{u}_i^T \boldsymbol{v}_j + \epsilon_{ij}. \tag{2}$$

The scalars α_i and β_j allow the model to adapt to phenomena such as anomalous user behavior or different item popularities. A particular item j may be popular among all users, and therefore this item does not provide as much information about individual preferences, which are captured in the feature vectors $\boldsymbol{u}_i$; if this is the case for item j, the model should infer the associated β_j as being large. Likewise, a given individual i may rate all items as being poor/good, and this individual therefore does not provide as useful information about the features of the items $\boldsymbol{v}_j$; in this case α_i would be correspondingly small/large. In the statistical literature, these inferred biases are often called random effects.

Defining the independent priors

$$p(\alpha_i) = \mathcal{N}(0, \tau_\alpha^2) \tag{3}$$

$$p(\beta_j) = \mathcal{N}(0, \tau_\beta^2) \tag{4}$$

$$p(\mathbf{U}) = \prod_{k=1}^{K} \prod_{i=1}^{N_U} \mathcal{N}(u_{ki}; 0, 1) \tag{5}$$

$$p(\mathbf{V}) = \prod_{k=1}^{K} \prod_{j=1}^{N_V} \mathcal{N}(v_{kj}; 0, \rho_k^2) \tag{6}$$

$$p(\rho_k^2) = \mathrm{InvGamma}(\kappa_1, \kappa_2) \tag{7}$$

$$p(\epsilon_{ij}) = \mathcal{N}(0, \sigma_\epsilon^2) \tag{8}$$

with hyperparameters $\sigma_\epsilon^2, \tau_\alpha^2, \tau_\beta^2, \kappa_1, \kappa_2$, and the likelihood

$$p(x_{ij}|\boldsymbol{\alpha}, \boldsymbol{\beta}, \mathbf{U}, \mathbf{V}, \boldsymbol{\rho}) = \mathcal{N}(x_{ij}; \alpha_i + \beta_j + \boldsymbol{u}_i^T \boldsymbol{v}_j, \sigma_\epsilon^2) \tag{9}$$

completes the model specification. In the above expressions, InvGamma denotes the inverse gamma distribution, and the notation u_{ki}, v_{kj} refers to the (k,i)th and (k,j)th elements of $\mathbf{U}$ and $\mathbf{V}$, respectively. For simplicity, we set the value of σ_ϵ, although it would also be possible to define a corresponding inverse gamma prior. Note that we choose a unit-variance prior for $\boldsymbol{u}_i$; otherwise, the product of the variances of $\boldsymbol{u}_i$ and $\boldsymbol{v}_j$ would not be identifiable.

Our goal is to estimate posteriors for the model parameters $\boldsymbol{\lambda} = \{\boldsymbol{\alpha}, \boldsymbol{\beta}, \mathbf{U}, \mathbf{V}, \boldsymbol{\rho}\}$ given the observed data $\mathbf{D} = \{x_{ij} : (i,j) \in \Omega\}$ at locations Ω.

2.1 Variational Bayes inference

The posterior distribution of the model parameters satisfies

$$\begin{aligned} p(\boldsymbol{\alpha}, \boldsymbol{\beta}, \mathbf{U}, \mathbf{V}, \boldsymbol{\rho}|\mathbf{D}) \propto & p(\mathbf{D}|\boldsymbol{\alpha}, \boldsymbol{\beta}, \mathbf{U}, \mathbf{V}, \boldsymbol{\rho}) \\ & p(\boldsymbol{\alpha})p(\boldsymbol{\beta})p(\mathbf{U})p(\mathbf{V})p(\boldsymbol{\rho}), \end{aligned} \tag{10}$$

while the negative logarithm of the posterior is, up to constant terms, given by

$$\sum_{ij} \frac{1}{2\sigma_x^2}(x_{ij} - \alpha_i - \beta_j - \boldsymbol{u}_i^T \boldsymbol{v}_j)^2 + \sum_{k=1}^{K} \frac{1}{2}(\|\boldsymbol{u}_k\|_2^2 + \frac{1}{\rho_k^2}\|\boldsymbol{v}_k\|_2^2), \tag{11}$$

where $\boldsymbol{u}_k$ and $\boldsymbol{v}_k$ are the kth rows of $\mathbf{U}$ and $\mathbf{V}$, respectively. Hence, the statistical model is closely related to optimization-based approaches with ℓ_2 regularization on the model components [7]. An important advantage of the statistical model is that it does not require cross-validation for regularization terms (Lagrange multipliers in optimization-based methods). Moreover, it yields an approximate posterior on all model parameters, instead of maximum *a posteriori* (MAP) point estimates.

As the true posterior $p(\boldsymbol{\alpha}, \boldsymbol{\beta}, \mathbf{U}, \mathbf{V}, \boldsymbol{\rho}|\mathbf{D})$ is not tractable, we employ a variational approximation [1]. In general, assume that $\boldsymbol{\lambda}$ denotes parameters to be inferred, and $\mathbf{D}$ represents observed data. The likelihood of the data is $p(\mathbf{D}|\boldsymbol{\lambda})$ and the prior on the parameters is $p(\boldsymbol{\lambda})$. It follows that the posterior on the model parameters is

$$p(\boldsymbol{\lambda}|\mathbf{D}) = \frac{p(\mathbf{D}|\boldsymbol{\lambda})p(\boldsymbol{\lambda})}{\int d\boldsymbol{\lambda} p(\mathbf{D}|\boldsymbol{\lambda})p(\boldsymbol{\lambda})} \tag{12}$$

Let $q(\boldsymbol{\lambda};\boldsymbol{\theta})$ be a parametric distribution with parameters $\boldsymbol{\theta}$, and consider the variational expression

$$\begin{aligned} F(\boldsymbol{\theta}) &= \int d\boldsymbol{\lambda} q(\boldsymbol{\lambda};\boldsymbol{\theta}) \log \frac{q(\boldsymbol{\lambda};\boldsymbol{\theta})}{p(\mathbf{D}|\boldsymbol{\lambda})p(\boldsymbol{\lambda})} \\ &= D_{\mathrm{KL}}[q(\boldsymbol{\lambda};\boldsymbol{\theta})\|p(\boldsymbol{\lambda}|\mathbf{D})] - \log p(\mathbf{D}). \end{aligned} \tag{13}$$

Minimization of $F(\boldsymbol{\theta})$ in (13) with respect to $\boldsymbol{\theta}$ corresponds to minimization of the Kullback-Leibler divergence between $q(\boldsymbol{\lambda};\boldsymbol{\theta})$ and the true posterior $p(\boldsymbol{\lambda}|\mathbf{D})$.

For the parametric distribution, we use a fully factorized form $q(\boldsymbol{\lambda};\boldsymbol{\theta}) = \prod_l q(\lambda_l;\theta_l)$. If $q(\lambda_i;\theta_i)$ and the prior for λ_i are selected in the conjugate-exponential family, then we obtain closed-form expressions for the θ_i, based on gradient descent of $F(\theta_i)$ [1]. This procedure is guaranteed to converge to a local optimum, and it extends MAP estimation of $\boldsymbol{\theta}$, yielding an approximate posterior.

The term *variational* comes from calculus of variations; we choose a class $\mathcal{Q}$ such that $q(\boldsymbol{\lambda};\boldsymbol{\theta}) \in \mathcal{Q}$ and then minimize a functional over $\mathcal{Q}$. As discussed above, minimization of the functional $F(\boldsymbol{\theta})$ is equivalent to minimization of the Kullback-Leibler (KL) divergence between q and the true $p(\lambda|\mathbf{D})$. We choose $\mathcal{Q}$ to be fully factorized distributions; for the problem at hand, we write

$$\begin{aligned} q(\boldsymbol{\alpha},\boldsymbol{\beta},\mathbf{U},\mathbf{V},\boldsymbol{\rho};\boldsymbol{\theta}) = &\prod_i q(\alpha_i)\prod_j q(\beta_j)\prod_{k,i} q(u_{ki})\prod_{k,j} q(v_{kj}) \\ &\prod_k q(\rho_k), \end{aligned} \tag{14}$$

where

$$q(u_{ik}) = \mathcal{N}(\mu_{u_{ki}}, \sigma^2_{u_{ki}}) \tag{15}$$
$$q(v_{kj}) = \mathcal{N}(\mu_{v_{kj}}, \sigma^2_{v_{kj}}) \tag{16}$$
$$q(\alpha_i) = \mathcal{N}(\mu_{\alpha_i}, \sigma^2_{\alpha_i}) \tag{17}$$
$$q(\beta_j) = \mathcal{N}(\mu_{\beta_j}, \sigma^2_{\beta_j}) \tag{18}$$
$$q(\rho_k^2) = \mathrm{InvGamma}(\xi_{1k}, \xi_{2k}). \tag{19}$$

The posterior parameters are $\boldsymbol{\theta} = \{\{\mu_{\alpha_i}\}, \{\mu_{\beta_j}\}, \{\sigma_{\alpha_i}\}, \{\sigma_{\beta_j}\}, \{\rho_k^2\}, \{\xi_{1k}\}, \{\xi_{2k}\}, \{\mu_{u_{ki}}\}, \{\mu_{v_{kj}}\}, \{\sigma^2_{u_{ki}}\}, \{\sigma^2_{v_{kj}}\}\}$.

Defining the cost function $C_{KL} \triangleq F(\boldsymbol{\theta})$, we build on [14], where the gradients w.r.t. the components of $\boldsymbol{\theta}$ are derived. We depart from [14] in the following way: the dataset $\mathbf{D}$ is partitioned into smaller subsets $\mathcal{S}^{(t)}$, called *mini-batches*, which change for each iteration t. The standard stochastic gradient approach [9] is to draw each mini-batch $\mathcal{S}^{(t)}$ uniformly at random from the (fixed) training set $\mathbf{D}$. Then, in the sums over i and j below, only the indices in the current $\mathcal{S}^{(t)}$ are considered. All mini-batches have the same size m, which is chosen to yield the best trade-off between computational speed and robustness to local minima.

Example components of the gradient so computed are

$$\frac{\partial C_{KL}}{\partial \mu_{u_{ki}}} = \mu_{u_{ki}} + \sum_{j:(i,j)\in\mathcal{S}} \frac{-(x_{ij} - \alpha_i - \beta_j - \sum_{m=1}^K \mu_{u_{mi}}\mu_{v_{mj}})\mu_{v_{kj}} + \mu_{u_{ki}}\sigma^2_{v_{kj}}}{\sigma^2_\epsilon} \tag{20}$$

$$\frac{\partial C_{KL}}{\partial \mu_{v_{kj}}} = \frac{\mu_{v_{kj}}}{\rho_k^2} + \sum_{i:(i,j)\in\mathcal{S}} \frac{-(x_{ij} - \alpha_i - \beta_j - \sum_{m=1}^K \mu_{u_{mi}}\mu_{v_{mj}})\mu_{u_{ki}} + \mu_{v_{kj}}\sigma^2_{u_{ki}}}{\sigma^2_\epsilon} \tag{21}$$

$$\frac{\partial C_{KL}}{\partial \mu_{\alpha_i}} = \frac{\mu_{\alpha_i}}{\tau_\alpha^2} + \sum_{j:(i,j)\in\mathcal{S}} \frac{-(x_{ij} - \alpha_i - \beta_j - \sum_{m=1}^K \mu_{mi}\mu_{mj})}{\sigma^2_\epsilon} \tag{22}$$

$$\frac{\partial C_{KL}}{\partial \mu_{\beta_j}} = \frac{\mu_{\beta_j}}{\tau_\beta^2} + \sum_{i:(i,j)\in\mathcal{S}} \frac{-(x_{ij} - \alpha_i - \beta_j - \sum_{m=1}^K \mu_{mi}\mu_{mj})}{\sigma^2_\epsilon}. \tag{23}$$

Once we have the gradients, it is then possible to sequentially update $\mu_{u_{ki}}, \mu_{v_{kj}}, \mu_{\alpha_i}$ and μ_{β_j} according to

$$\mu^{(t)}_{u_{ki}} \leftarrow \mu^{(t-1)}_{u_{ki}} + \eta^{(t)} \sum_{i:(i,j)\in\mathcal{S}^{(t)}} \frac{\partial C_{KL}}{\partial \mu^{(t)}_{u_{ki}}} \tag{24}$$

$$\mu^{(t)}_{v_{kj}} \leftarrow \mu^{(t-1)}_{v_{kj}} + \eta^{(t)} \sum_{i:(i,j)\in\mathcal{S}^{(t)}} \frac{\partial C_{KL}}{\partial \mu^{(t)}_{v_{kj}}} \tag{25}$$

$$\mu^{(t)}_{\alpha_i} \leftarrow \mu^{(t-1)}_{\alpha_i} + \eta^{(t)} \sum_{i:(i,j)\in\mathcal{S}^{(t)}} \frac{\partial C_{KL}}{\partial \mu^{(t)}_{\alpha_i}} \tag{26}$$

$$\mu^{(t)}_{\beta_j} \leftarrow \mu^{(t-1)}_{\beta_j} + \eta^{(t)} \sum_{i:(i,j)\in\mathcal{S}^{(t)}} \frac{\partial C_{KL}}{\partial \mu^{(t)}_{\beta_j}} \tag{27}$$

where $\eta^{(t)}$ is the learning step for the gradient descent procedure. The learning step follows the schedule $\eta^{(t)} = \tau\eta^{(t-1)}$, where $\tau \in (0.5, 1]$ controls the rate of decay of the contribution of old mini-batches.

The variances can be updated according to

$$\sigma^2_{u_{ki}} \leftarrow (1-\eta^{(t)})\sigma^2_{u_{ki}} + \eta^{(t)} \left(1 + \sum_{j:(i,j)\in\mathcal{S}^{(t)}} \frac{\mu^2_{v_{kj}} + \sigma^2_{v_{kj}}}{\sigma^2_\epsilon}\right)^{-1} \tag{28}$$

$$\sigma^2_{v_{kj}} \leftarrow (1-\eta^{(t)})\sigma^2_{v_{kj}} + \eta^{(t)} \left(\frac{1}{\rho_k^2} + \sum_{i:(i,j)\in\mathcal{S}^{(t)}} \frac{\mu^2_{u_{ki}} + \sigma^2_{u_{ki}}}{\sigma^2_\epsilon}\right)^{-1} \tag{29}$$

$$\sigma^2_{\alpha_i} \leftarrow (1-\eta^{(t)})\sigma^2_{\alpha_i} + \eta^{(t)} \left(\frac{1}{\tau_\alpha} + \sum_{j:(i,j)\in\mathcal{S}^{(t)}} \frac{1}{\sigma^2_\epsilon}\right)^{-1} \tag{30}$$

$$\sigma^2_{\beta_j} \leftarrow (1-\eta^{(t)})\sigma^2_{\beta_j} + \eta^{(t)} \left(\frac{1}{\tau_\beta} + \sum_{i:(i,j)\in\mathcal{S}^{(t)}} \frac{1}{\sigma^2_\epsilon}\right)^{-1}. \tag{31}$$

Finally, the parameters of $q(\rho_k^2)$ obey

$$\xi_{1k} \leftarrow (1-\eta^{(t)})\xi_{1k} + \eta^{(t)}(\kappa_1 + \sum_{j:(i,j)\in\mathcal{S}^{(t)}} \frac{K}{2}) \tag{32}$$

$$\xi_{2k} \leftarrow (1-\eta^{(t)})\xi_{2k} + \eta^{(t)}(\kappa_2 + \frac{1}{2} \sum_{j:(i,j)\in\mathcal{S}^{(t)}} \mu^2_{v_{kj}}). \tag{33}$$

2.2 Using time information

Each rating in the Yahoo! Music dataset includes a time stamp. This is the case both for the training set and for each (i, j) pair in the test set, which means that it is possible to improve the predictions by incorporating temporal information into the factor model. The following approach is based on [6], who obtained one of the best single-model results on the Yahoo! dataset. The FA model in (2) is changed to

$$x_{ij} = \alpha_i + \beta_j + (\boldsymbol{u}_i + \boldsymbol{u}_{it_m} + \boldsymbol{u}_{it_h} + \boldsymbol{u}_{it_d})^T(\boldsymbol{v}_j + \boldsymbol{v}_{jt_h} + \boldsymbol{u}_{it_d}), \tag{34}$$

where t_m, t_h and t_d are indices over the total number of minutes, hours and days in the dataset, respectively. The large number of user/time factors (particularly $\boldsymbol{u}_{it_m}$) vectors poses computational challenges; however, each user only has ratings for very few minutes on average, which makes the storage requirements feasible.

The priors for the new factors that depend on t_d are

$$p(\boldsymbol{u}_{it_d}) = \prod_{k=1}^{K} \mathcal{N}(u_{kit_d}; 0, 1) \tag{35}$$

$$p(\boldsymbol{v}_{jt_d}) = \prod_{k=1}^{K} \mathcal{N}(v_{kjt_d}; 0, \rho_k^2) \tag{36}$$

and similarly for those factors that depend on t_h and t_m. We apply the VB algorithm to (34) in much the same way as in the original formulation, with new variational posteriors $q(\boldsymbol{u}_{it_d})$, $q(\boldsymbol{v}_{jt_d}), \ldots$, of the same form as in Section 2.1. Writing out (34) as a sum of cross-products, we have

$$x_{ij} = \alpha_i + \beta_j + \boldsymbol{u}_i^T\boldsymbol{v}_j + \boldsymbol{u}_i^T\boldsymbol{v}_{jt_h} + \boldsymbol{u}_i^T\boldsymbol{u}_{it_d} + \boldsymbol{u}_i^T\boldsymbol{v}_{jt_m} + \ldots \tag{37}$$

which means that the gradient updates for $\alpha_i, \beta_j, \boldsymbol{u}_i$ and $\boldsymbol{v}_j$ are changed only slightly from Section 2.1. For example, defining

$$e_{ij} = x_{ij} - \alpha_i - \beta_j - (\boldsymbol{\mu}_{\boldsymbol{u}_i} + \boldsymbol{\mu}_{\boldsymbol{u}_{itm}} + \boldsymbol{\mu}_{\boldsymbol{u}_{ith}} + \boldsymbol{\mu}_{\boldsymbol{u}_{itd}})^T (\boldsymbol{\mu}_{\boldsymbol{v}_j} + \boldsymbol{\mu}_{\boldsymbol{v}_{jth}} + \boldsymbol{\mu}_{\boldsymbol{v}_{itd}}),$$

we now have

$$\frac{\partial C_{KL}}{\partial \mu_{u_{ki}}} = \mu_{u_{ki}} + \sum_{j:(i,j)\in\mathcal{S}} \frac{-e_{ij}(\mu_{v_{kj}} + \mu_{v_{kjt_h}} + \mu_{v_{kjt_d}})}{\sigma_\epsilon^2} + \sum_{j:(i,j)\in\mathcal{S}} \frac{\mu_{u_{ki}}(\sigma^2_{v_{kj}} + \sigma^2_{v_{kjt_h}} + \sigma^2_{v_{kjt_d}})}{\sigma_\epsilon^2} \tag{38}$$

$$\frac{\partial C_{KL}}{\partial \mu_{v_{kj}}} = \frac{\mu_{v_{kj}}}{\rho_k^2} + \sum_{j:(i,j)\in\mathcal{S}} \frac{-e_{ij}(\mu_{u_{ki}} + \mu_{u_{kit_h}} + \mu_{u_{kit_d}} + \mu_{u_{kit_m}})}{\sigma_\epsilon^2} + \sum_{j:(i,j)\in\mathcal{S}} \frac{\mu_{v_{kj}}(\sigma^2_{v_{kj}} + \sigma^2_{u_{kit_h}} + \sigma^2_{u_{kit_d}} + \sigma^2_{u_{kit_m}})}{\sigma_\epsilon^2}. \tag{39}$$

The gradients for the new time-related factors are computed similarly to those for $\boldsymbol{u}_i$ and $\boldsymbol{v}_j$.

3. ACTIVE LEARNING

In the following, we address the problem of finding the best mini-batch $\mathcal{S}^{(t)} = \{(i, j) : x_{ij}$ is observed at step $t\}$ of size m, thereby extending standard gradient descent. Instead of having a fixed training set $\mathbf{D}$ as before, the goal is now to incrementally construct a set of observed locations $\mathcal{A}$ by starting with $\mathcal{A} = \emptyset$ and sequentially appending $\mathcal{A} \leftarrow \mathcal{A} \cup \mathcal{S}^{(t)}$. Define $\mathcal{V} = \{(i, j), \forall_{i,j}\}$ to be the set of all entries of $\mathbf{X}$, whether observed or not. Hence, $\mathcal{V}\backslash\mathcal{A}$ is the set of missing locations. It is known [8] that finding the best $\mathcal{S}^{(t)}$ among $\mathcal{V}\backslash\mathcal{A}$ is, in general, an NP-hard problem.

The active selection of mini-batches $\mathcal{S}^{(t)}$ may be constituted in at least two forms. In one case, all of the (sparsely sampled) data may be available *a priori*, and rather than selecting $\mathcal{S}^{(t)}$ from that data in a random manner, one may use active learning to select the most-informative samples. In a second case, we may actually seek entries (acquire the database) actively and sequentially, based on the results of active learning. This may be done by asking selected customers to rate selected items. There may be other settings that are a combination of the above two cases.

We wish to leverage the current posterior estimate of $\boldsymbol{\theta}$ for selecting the m most informative observations in $\mathcal{V}\backslash\mathcal{A}$. One possible strategy is to select the observations x_{ij} for which the posterior implies the greatest variance, and thus uncertainty. This method, while simple, does not account for correlations between similar samples, *i.e.*, the fact that many high variance users/items may be very similar to each other, and therefore redundant. Moreover, selecting high variance users/items tends to unduly emphasize outliers.

A better alternative is to select the observations that are most informative about $\mathcal{V}\backslash\mathcal{A}$. Toward this end, we build on [8], where near-optimal, polynomial-time greedy algorithms are proposed. These algorithms exploit *submodularity* properties of mutual information, under a Gaussian process formulation.

3.1 Gaussian process formulation

In general, assume that each observation $x_s \in \mathbb{R}$, where s is an index over elements of $\mathcal{V}$, has an associated covariate $\boldsymbol{r}_s \in \mathbb{R}^d$. We wish to impose that, when $\boldsymbol{r}_s$ and $\boldsymbol{r}_{s'}$ are similar, then x_s and $x_{s'}$ are correlated. If we have a vector $\boldsymbol{x} = (x_1, \ldots, x_N)$ drawn from a Gaussian process (GP), with covariance function given by a Mercer kernel $\mathcal{K}(\cdot,\cdot)$, then $\boldsymbol{x} \sim \mathcal{N}(\boldsymbol{\mu}, \boldsymbol{\Sigma})$, with

$$\boldsymbol{\Sigma}_{s,s'} = \mathcal{K}(\boldsymbol{r}_s, \boldsymbol{r}_{s'}). \tag{40}$$

A frequent choice for $\mathcal{K}(\cdot,\cdot)$ is the radial basis function (RBF) kernel

$$\mathcal{K}(\boldsymbol{r}_s, \boldsymbol{r}_{s'}) = \exp(-\frac{1}{\sigma^2}\|\boldsymbol{r}_s - \boldsymbol{r}_{s'}\|^2). \tag{41}$$

A key property of GPs is that, given a vector $\boldsymbol{x} = (x_1, \ldots, x_N)$ with associated covariates $(\boldsymbol{r}_1, \ldots, \boldsymbol{r}_N)$, one may readily draw x_{N+1} for any new covariate $\boldsymbol{r}_{N+1}$. This property facilitates active learning in the following way. Assume that the set $\mathcal{V}$ defines a set of covariates and the associated data vector is $\boldsymbol{x} \sim \mathrm{GP}(\boldsymbol{\mu}, \boldsymbol{\Sigma}_{\mathcal{V}\mathcal{V}})$. The active learning problem now becomes one of choosing a subset $\mathcal{A} \subset \mathcal{V}$ of covariates at which to sample data.

To connect the GP formulation with our matrix factorization problem, it is appropriate to consider the user and item factors, $\boldsymbol{u}_i$ and $\boldsymbol{v}_j$, as covariates. The ratings x_{ij} are considered to be drawn from a GP where the covariance matrix is related to the $\boldsymbol{u}_i$ and $\boldsymbol{v}_j$ covariates, which are *latent*, *i.e.*, non-observed. The online VB procedure is employed to provide approximate posteriors for these latent covariates.

Accordingly, we wish to define kernels which make use of the estimated posterior distributions $q(\boldsymbol{u}_i)$ and $q(\boldsymbol{v}_i)$. A natural choice consists of the symmetrized KL divergence kernel, which for user factors $\boldsymbol{u}_i$ is defined as

$$\mathcal{K}(\boldsymbol{u}_i, \boldsymbol{u}_{i'}) = \exp\{D_{\mathrm{KL}}(q(\boldsymbol{u}_i)||q(\boldsymbol{u}_{i'})) + D_{\mathrm{KL}}(q(\boldsymbol{u}_{i'})||q(\boldsymbol{u}_i))\} \tag{42}$$

$$D_{\mathrm{KL}}(q(\boldsymbol{u}_i)||q(\boldsymbol{u}_{i'})) = \frac{1}{2}[\mathrm{tr}(\boldsymbol{\Phi}_{i'}^{-1}\boldsymbol{\Phi}_i) + \|\boldsymbol{\mu}_{\boldsymbol{u}_i'} - \boldsymbol{\mu}_{\boldsymbol{u}_i}\|^T\boldsymbol{\Phi}_{i'}^{-1}\|\boldsymbol{\mu}_{\boldsymbol{u}_i'} - \boldsymbol{\mu}_{\boldsymbol{u}_i}\| + \log\frac{|\boldsymbol{\Phi}_i|}{|\boldsymbol{\Phi}_{i'}|} - K], \tag{43}$$

where $\boldsymbol{\Phi}_i \triangleq \mathrm{diag}(\sigma^2_{u_{1i}}, \ldots, \sigma^2_{u_{Ki}})$. Item factors $\boldsymbol{v}_j$ are treated similarly, substituting $\boldsymbol{v}_j$ for $\boldsymbol{u}_i$ and $\boldsymbol{\Psi}_j \triangleq \mathrm{diag}(\sigma^2_{v_{1j}}, \ldots, \sigma^2_{v_{Kj}})$ for $\boldsymbol{\Phi}_i$. Note that the matrices $\boldsymbol{\Phi}_i$ and $\boldsymbol{\Psi}_j$ are diagonal, which simplifies inversions and determinants. An attractive feature of the symmetrized KL divergence kernel is the absence of tuning parameters such as kernel bandwidths.

3.2 Submodularity and mutual information

An appropriate criterion for choosing $\mathcal{A}$ is to seek to maximize the mutual information $\mathrm{MI}(\mathcal{A}) \triangleq \mathrm{I}(\mathcal{A}; \mathcal{V}\backslash\mathcal{A}) = h(\boldsymbol{x}_{\mathcal{A}}) - h(\boldsymbol{x}_{\mathcal{A}}|\boldsymbol{x}_{\mathcal{V}\backslash\mathcal{A}})$, with $h(\cdot)$ denoting the differential entropy. Given $\mathcal{A}$, it is straightforward to compute $\mathrm{MI}(\mathcal{A})$ within the GP model. However, when $|\mathcal{A}| > 1$ the computation to select the set $\mathcal{A}$ that maximizes this mutual information is NP-complete. This difficulty can be overcome by using the fact that $\mathrm{MI}(\mathcal{A})$ is *submodular*.

Definition of submodularity [13]: A set function $F : \mathcal{A} \to F(\mathcal{A})$ is submodular if, for all $\mathcal{A} \subseteq \mathcal{B} \subseteq \mathcal{V}$, and $y \in \mathcal{V}\backslash\mathcal{B}$, it holds that $F(\mathcal{A} \cup y) - F(\mathcal{A}) \geq F(\mathcal{B} \cup y) - F(\mathcal{B})$.

Intuitively, F is submodular if it has a "diminishing returns" property, *i.e.*, a new datum y has more impact when the set $\mathcal{A}$ is smaller. The following theorem ensures that choosing $\mathcal{A}$ to maximize $F(\mathcal{A})$ can be done in a near-optimal manner by a greedy algorithm.

Theorem [13]: Let F be a monotone submodular set function over a finite ground set $\mathcal{V}$ with $F(\emptyset) = 0$. Let $\mathcal{A}$ be the set of the first m elements chosen to maximize $F(\cdot)$ by a greedy algorithm, and let OPT= $\max_{\mathcal{A}\subset\mathcal{V};|\mathcal{A}|=m} F(\mathcal{A})$. Then

$$F(\mathcal{A}) \geq (1 - \frac{1}{e})\mathrm{OPT}. \tag{44}$$

Importantly, the mutual information $\mathrm{MI}(\mathcal{A}) \triangleq \mathrm{I}(\mathcal{A}; \mathcal{V}\backslash\mathcal{A})$ is submodular [8], and $\mathrm{MI}(\emptyset)$=0. There are conditions of practical relevance for which the mutual information metric is a monotone function, namely when $|\mathcal{A}|$ is small relative to the total number of entries that may searched over, which is certainly the case for the massive matrices of interest here; see [8] for a related discussion, although that work did not consider the matrix-completion problem. Therefore, there exist polynomial-time greedy algorithms for finding $\widehat{\mathcal{A}}$ such that

$$\mathrm{MI}(\widehat{\mathcal{A}}) > (1 - 1/e) \max_{\mathcal{A}\subset\mathcal{V},|\mathcal{A}|=m} \mathrm{MI}(\mathcal{A}) - m\epsilon \tag{45}$$

for some small ϵ. The mutual information metric discourages acquisition of samples that are anticipated to be correlated to each other based upon the GP covariance $\mathcal{K}(\cdot, \cdot)$.

Specifically, Algorithm 1 in [8] finds candidate $y \in \mathcal{V}\backslash\mathcal{A}$ to maximize the increase in mutual information

$$\mathrm{MI}(\mathcal{A} \cup y) - \mathrm{MI}(\mathcal{A}) = h(\boldsymbol{x}_y|\boldsymbol{x}_{\mathcal{A}}) - h(\boldsymbol{x}_y|\boldsymbol{x}_{\bar{\mathcal{A}}}), \tag{46}$$

where $\bar{\mathcal{A}}$ denotes $\mathcal{V}\backslash(\mathcal{A} \cup y)$. The conditional distributions needed to compute the conditional differential entropies in (46) are readily manifested by leveraging the ability of GP to compute such densities, as discussed above. This property is a key reason for imposing the GP representation for matrix values, with associated covariates defined by the inferred feature vectors $\boldsymbol{u}_i$ and $\boldsymbol{v}_j$. In the GP model, the maximization is done by computing

$$\max_y \delta_y = \frac{\mathcal{K}(y,y) - \boldsymbol{\Sigma}_{y\mathcal{A}}\boldsymbol{\Sigma}_{\mathcal{A}\mathcal{A}}^{-1}\boldsymbol{\Sigma}_{\mathcal{A}y}}{\mathcal{K}(y,y) - \boldsymbol{\Sigma}_{y\bar{\mathcal{A}}}\boldsymbol{\Sigma}_{\bar{\mathcal{A}}\bar{\mathcal{A}}}^{-1}\boldsymbol{\Sigma}_{\bar{\mathcal{A}}y}}. \tag{47}$$

Equation (47) is a ratio of conditional covariances of the form $\sigma^2_{y|\mathcal{A}} = \mathcal{K}(y,y) - \boldsymbol{\Sigma}_{y\mathcal{A}}\boldsymbol{\Sigma}_{\mathcal{A}\mathcal{A}}^{-1}\boldsymbol{\Sigma}_{\mathcal{A}y}$, which due to the GP properties can be computed without first measuring x at location y.

Unfortunately, the aforementioned algorithm requires $O(|\mathcal{V}\backslash\mathcal{A}|^4)$ operations, which is indeed polynomial-time but infeasible in many situations of interest. For instance, in the case of the Yahoo! dataset, we have $N_u \approx 10^6$ and $N_v \approx 6 \times 10^5$, leading to $|\mathcal{V}\backslash\mathcal{A}| \approx 6 \times 10^{11}$. This problem can be mitigated by employing Algorithm 3 in [8] which uses *local kernels*, *i.e.*, only a small neighborhood around each y is considered. More specifically, in expression (46) the approximation $h(y|\tilde{\mathcal{A}}) \approx h(y|\mathcal{A})$ is used, where $\tilde{\mathcal{A}}$ results from removing all but the k-nearest neighbors of y from $\mathcal{A}$. This approximation drastically reduces the size of all $\boldsymbol{\Sigma}_{(\cdot,\cdot)}$ matrices in (47), to a maximum of $k \times k$, at a small cost in the objective function [8]. The overall complexity is thus reduced to $O(|\mathcal{V}\backslash\mathcal{A}|)$, which nevertheless remains impractical for our purposes.

Our proposed approach circumvents these limitations by exploiting the structure of the matrix factorization problem. Instead of exploring all possible pairs (i, j), of which there are approximately N_uN_v, our main idea is to choose the best row and the best column *separately*. The resulting computations are now $O(N_u) + O(N_v)$, which is feasible.

The objective function for rows of $\mathbf{X}$ is, therefore,

$$\delta_i = \frac{\sigma_i^2 - \boldsymbol{\Sigma}_{i\mathcal{A}_u}\boldsymbol{\Sigma}_{\mathcal{A}_u\mathcal{A}_u}^{-1}\boldsymbol{\Sigma}_{\mathcal{A}_u i}}{\sigma_i^2 - \boldsymbol{\Sigma}_{i\bar{\mathcal{A}}_u}\boldsymbol{\Sigma}_{\bar{\mathcal{A}}_u\bar{\mathcal{A}}_u}^{-1}\boldsymbol{\Sigma}_{\bar{\mathcal{A}}_u i}}, \tag{48}$$

where $\bar{\mathcal{A}}_u$ denotes $\{1, \ldots, N_u\}\backslash(\mathcal{A}_u \cup y)$, with y the candidate ith row. An identical objective function is defined for the columns of $\mathbf{X}$, substituting j for i and v for u.

The goal is now to find optimum sets $\mathcal{S}_u = \{i_1, \ldots, i_m\}$, $\mathcal{S}_v = \{j_1, \ldots, j_m\}$ sorted by δ_i and δ_j, respectively. Then, we form $\mathcal{S}$ based on $\mathcal{S}_u$ and $\mathcal{S}_v$. There are multiple possibilities for combining $\mathcal{S}_u$ and $\mathcal{S}_v$. We choose to construct $\mathcal{S} = \{(i_1, j_1), \ldots, (i_m, j_m)\}$. We then sequentially build $\mathcal{A} \leftarrow \mathcal{A} \cup \mathcal{S}$, as prescribed initially. The entire procedure is summarized in Algorithm 1, which we call VB-MI.

Algorithm 1 Active learning for matrix factorization with VB-MI

1: Initialize $q(\mathbf{U}) : \mu, \phi$, and $q(\mathbf{V}) : \nu, \psi$
2: Initialize active set $\mathcal{A} \leftarrow \emptyset$
3: **while** Stopping criterion is not met **do**
4:     **for** $i \in \{1, \dots, N_u\} \backslash \{i : i \in \mathcal{A}\}$ **do**
5:         Compute δ_i based on $\mu, \phi, \mathcal{A}$ and kernel $\mathcal{K}$
6:     **end for**
7:     Repeat steps 4–6 for $j \in \{1, \dots, N_v\} \backslash \{j : j \in \mathcal{A}\}$, substitute δ_j, ν, ψ
8:     $\mathcal{S}_u = \{i_1, \dots, i_m\}$ sorted in descending order of δ_i
9:     $\mathcal{S}_v = \{j_1, \dots, j_m\}$ sorted in descending order of δ_j
10:     $\mathcal{S} = \{(i_1, j_1), \dots, (i_m, j_m)\}$
11:     Collect observations $x_{ij}, \forall (i,j) \in \mathcal{S}$
12:     $\mathcal{A} \leftarrow \mathcal{A} \cup \mathcal{S}$
13:     Update μ, ϕ and ν, ψ via online VB
14: **end while**

3.3 Simplified active learning

A simpler alternative to the aforementioned submodularity approach consists of finding $\mathcal{S}_u$ and $\mathcal{S}_v$ by sorting the user and item factors in decreasing order of the posterior trace-covariance, given by $\mathrm{tr}(\mathbf{\Phi}_i)$ and $\mathrm{tr}(\mathbf{\Psi}_j)$, respectively. The mini-batch $\mathcal{S}$ is then constructed as in VB-MI and appended to $\mathcal{A}$. The resulting algorithm makes direct use of $q(\boldsymbol{u}_i)$ and $q(\boldsymbol{v}_j)$ without necessitating any GP formulation or kernel, and the only overhead over online VB consists of two sorting steps per mini-batch, which is negligible.

As discussed above, a limitation of this approach is that it does not account for correlations, and therefore many high-variance items may also have high correlation, and consequently it is redundant to sample all of them. Nevertheless, as discussed below, this has been found to work well in practice, at low computational expense, for the large-scale examples considered. This approach explicitly exploits the products (parameter variance) from the VB analysis, and it is referred to below as VB-Variance.

3.4 Non-Bayesian method

For the purpose of comparison, and also to isolate the contribution of the active learning method towards performance from that of the VB algorithm, we have implemented an active learning method capable of utilizing products from a non-Bayesian matrix analysis; in that analysis, the RMSE is directly minimized w.r.t. $\{\alpha_i, \beta_i, \boldsymbol{u}_i, \boldsymbol{v}_j\}$ by traditional gradient descent (we learn a "point" estimate for these parameters, rather than estimating a full posterior). This is distinct from the VB method, which minimizes the KL divergence between $q(\boldsymbol{\alpha}, \boldsymbol{\beta}, \mathbf{U}, \mathbf{V}, \rho; \boldsymbol{\theta})$ and the posterior $p(\boldsymbol{\alpha}, \boldsymbol{\beta}, \mathbf{U}, \mathbf{V}, \rho | \mathbf{X})$ w.r.t. the posterior parameters $\boldsymbol{\theta}$.

We follow an approach similar to [9] and estimate the parameters $\alpha_i, \beta_j, \boldsymbol{u}_i, \boldsymbol{v}_j$ by solving the optimization problem

$$\begin{aligned} \min_{\alpha_i, \beta_j, \boldsymbol{u}_i, \boldsymbol{v}_j} \quad & \sum_{(i,j) \in \mathcal{A}} (x_{ij} - \alpha_i - \beta_j - \boldsymbol{u}_i^T \boldsymbol{v}_j)^2 \\ \text{subject to} \quad & \max\{\|\boldsymbol{u}_i\|_2^2, \|\boldsymbol{v}_j\|_2^2\} \le B, \forall_{ij} \\ & |\alpha_i|^2 \le B, \forall i, \quad |\beta_j|^2 \le B, \forall j \end{aligned} \tag{49}$$

where the constraint on the norms of the factors $\boldsymbol{u}_i$, $\boldsymbol{v}_j$ is equivalent to max-norm regularization of $\mathbf{U}^T\mathbf{V}$, controlled by the parameter B. The max-norm of a matrix $\mathbf{Z}$ is defined as $\|\mathbf{Z}\|_{\max} = \max\{|z_{ij}|\}$. The bias vectors $\boldsymbol{\alpha}$ and $\boldsymbol{\beta}$ are regularized in the same way.

Problem (49) can be solved by slightly modifying the simple projected gradient method proposed in [9] to take α_i and β_j into account. Given one training example x_{ij}, the following updates are computed for $\boldsymbol{u}_i$ and $\boldsymbol{v}_j$:

$$\boldsymbol{u}_i \leftarrow P_B[\boldsymbol{u}_i - \eta(x_{ij} - \alpha_i - \beta_j - \boldsymbol{u}_i^T \boldsymbol{v}_j)\boldsymbol{v}_j] \tag{50}$$

$$\boldsymbol{v}_j \leftarrow P_B[\boldsymbol{v}_j - \eta(x_{ij} - \alpha_i - \beta_j - \boldsymbol{u}_i^T \boldsymbol{v}_j)\boldsymbol{u}_i], \tag{51}$$

with $P_B(\cdot)$ a projection operator defined by

$$P_B(\boldsymbol{z}) = \begin{cases} \boldsymbol{z} & \|\boldsymbol{z}\|_2^2 \le B \\ \frac{\boldsymbol{z}}{\sqrt{B}} & \|\boldsymbol{z}\|_2^2 > B \end{cases}. \tag{52}$$

Note how the gradient term $-(x_{ij} - \alpha_i - \beta_j - \boldsymbol{u}_i^T \boldsymbol{v}_j)\boldsymbol{v}_j$ is also present in the VB update equation (20), where it is weighted by the noise level $1/\sigma_\epsilon^2$ and combined with other terms that depend on the model variances. The updates for α_i and β_j are given by

$$\alpha_i \leftarrow P_B[\alpha_i + \eta(x_{ij} - \alpha_i - \beta_j - \boldsymbol{u}_i^T \boldsymbol{v}_j)] \tag{53}$$

$$\beta_j \leftarrow P_B[\beta_j + \eta(x_{ij} - \alpha_i - \beta_j - \boldsymbol{u}_i^T \boldsymbol{v}_j)], \tag{54}$$

which also resemble the corresponding VB updates.

To perform active learning with this model, the user and item submodular objective functions δ_i and δ_j are computed as before, with the difference that we can no longer use the KL divergence kernel. Instead, we define standard RBF kernels

$$\mathcal{K}(\boldsymbol{u}_i, \boldsymbol{u}_{i'}) = \exp(-\frac{1}{\sigma^2}\|\boldsymbol{u}_i - \boldsymbol{u}_{i'}\|_2^2) \tag{55}$$

$$\mathcal{K}(\boldsymbol{v}_j, \boldsymbol{v}_{j'}) = \exp(-\frac{1}{\sigma^2}\|\boldsymbol{v}_j - \boldsymbol{v}_{j'}\|_2^2) \tag{56}$$

where σ^2 is the bandwidth parameter. Typically, σ^2 is set via cross-validation (which we emphasize is avoided with the VB inference).

4. RESULTS

We first present results for the online VB algorithm applied to the dataset of Yahoo! Music ratings provided for the KDD Cup 2011 challenge [4]. The purpose of this analysis is to examine the performance of the online VB solution on such large-scale data. In that analysis the mini-batches in the online analysis are selected randomly, as done in most previous related research (although virtually none of that work was done with a VB analysis). We then compare results in which the mini-batches for the online method are selected randomly versus actively, via the method discussed in Section 3.

4.1 Results of online VB on Yahoo! dataset

We consider the FA model and online VB inference from Section 2.1 on the Yahoo! Music dataset. We set the number of factors to $K = 20$ and choose the learning step size to follow the rule $\eta^{(t)} = \tau\eta^{(t-1)}$, with $\eta^{(0)} = 2.5 \times 10^{-7}$ and $\tau = 0.9$. The mini-batch size was set to $m = |\mathcal{S}^{(t)}| = 100000$. Hyperparameter values were set to $\sigma_\epsilon^2 = 10^{-6}, \tau_\alpha^2 = \tau_\beta^2 = 1, \kappa_1 = \kappa_2 = 10^{-6}$, which yield standard "flat" (nearly non-informative) priors. The variational posterior parameters $\boldsymbol{\theta}$ were initialized at random, and the algorithm was executed for 40 epochs. Each epoch consists of a full pass through the training set, *i.e.*, approximately 252 million ratings. A further 6 million ratings is used for validation (these validation ratings were supplied to the users), while the test set consists of 4 million ratings whose scores were withheld at the time of the KDD Cup 2011 challenge. These scores

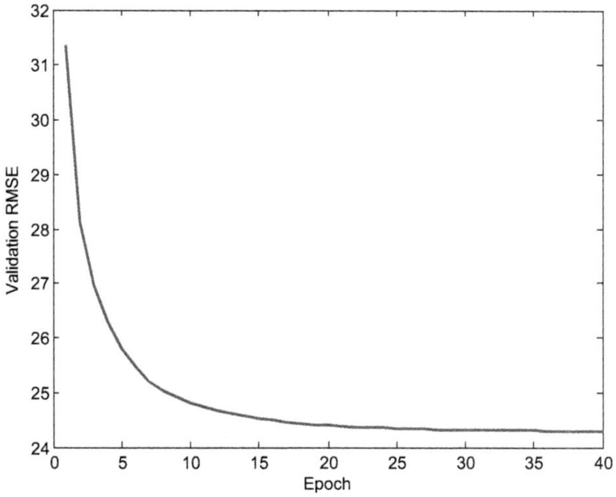

Figure 1: RMSE on the validation set for 40 epochs. Each epoch is a full pass over approximately 252M ratings. The total running time is slightly less than 10 hours.

have been released after the competition. The performance measure is the root mean square error (RMSE) over the test dataset, defined as

$$\text{RMSE} = \sqrt{\frac{1}{|\mathbf{D}_{\text{test}}|} \sum_{x_{ij} \in \mathbf{D}_{\text{test}}} (x_{ij} - \mu_{\alpha_i} - \mu_{\beta_j} - \boldsymbol{\mu}_{\boldsymbol{u}_i}^T \boldsymbol{\mu}_{\boldsymbol{v}_j})^2}, \tag{57}$$

where the posterior means of $\boldsymbol{\theta}$ are used to provide point estimates.

We show the RMSE and computation time per epoch on both the validation and test sets for our VB method in Table 4.1. For comparison, we also show the RMSE and time achieved by the baseline model supplied by Yahoo!, which models the ratings as

$$x_{ij} \approx a_i + b_j + c, \tag{58}$$

with a_i, b_j and c learned by standard stochastic gradient descent. The performance gain over the baseline is over 10%, which is considered quite significant and places the method near the top 100 in the competition. Note that the initialization is random and that there are no separate learning steps for the various parameters. Moreover, this is a single model (the best competitors employed a blend of dozens of different models) and it has relatively few parameters.

The convergence behavior is illustrated in Figure 4.1. While it takes slightly less than 10 hours to execute 40 epochs (we have used MATLAB code, non-optimized, on a 2.4 GHz CPU), it is apparent that the algorithm has essentially converged after approximately 25 epochs.

Additionally, we have implemented the time-dependent FA model described in Section 2.2, and achieved a further RMSE drop from 25.94 to 24.8. The most demanding aspect of the time-dependent model is the large number of user/minute factors $\boldsymbol{u}_{t_m}$, since $t_m \in \{0, \ldots 5726101\}$, although the fact that, on average, each user only has ratings for104 minutes in the dataset makes the storage requirements feasible. Currently, we are pursuing the implementation of active learning methods with this model (with time dependence), which will likely require extensive parallelization in order to overcome the large computational requirements.

4.2 Results with active learning

We have applied the three active learning procedures described in Section 3 (VB-MI, VB-Variance and Non-Bayesian) to the Yahoo! Music problem, and compared to online VB with random sampling. In this analysis we consider the model in (2), without time dependence. These experiments differ from using online VB as in Section 4.1. Here we synthesize all ratings, in order to be able to measure any desired x_{ij}, and not limit ourselves to the fixed training dataset $\mathbf{D}$ supplied by Yahoo!. We first use online VB to learn a factor model of the form (2) using all available data from $\mathbf{D}$, as in Section 4.1. The resulting posterior parameters $\boldsymbol{\theta}^*$ are withheld. Then, we discard the data supplied by Yahoo! and use the posterior mean components of $\boldsymbol{\theta}^*$ to synthesize any observation x_{ij} on demand, by computing

$$x_{ij} = \mu^*_{\alpha_i} + \mu^*_{\beta_j} + (\mu^*_{\boldsymbol{u}_i})^T (\mu^*_{\boldsymbol{v}_j}). \tag{59}$$

We report the RMSE on a test set of size 4 million, separately drawn at random from the factor model and withheld from the algorithms.

In all cases, the algorithms were initialized with one single mini-batch of online VB and then executed for 40 epochs. The mini-batch size is $m = 100000$. In this setting, since there no longer exists a dataset $\mathbf{D}$ over which to perform a full pass, we define an epoch as the number of steps necessary for the set $\mathcal{A}$ to have the same size as $\mathbf{D}$. Once this happens, we reset $\mathcal{A} \leftarrow \emptyset$ and begin a new epoch. The factor model parameters carry over between successive epochs.

As seen in Figure 2, all active methods outperform random sampling by a significant margin. The differences in RMSE between the three active methods are less pronounced, with the mutual-information-based VB-MI algorithm slightly outperforming the others. It is particularly notable that the simpler VB-Variance method is competitive with the submodularity based approaches, at a fraction of the computational cost. The running times, per epoch, of VB-MI, Non-Bayesian and VB-Variance are 5100 seconds, 4700 seconds and 1100 seconds, respectively. Thus, the VB-Variance method is only slightly more demanding than online VB.

Figure 3 shows histograms of the (scalar) components of the user and item factors, respectively $\boldsymbol{u}_i$ and $\boldsymbol{v}_j$. The model assigns low variance to most components, which can be seen as an indicator of good model fit.

The plot in Figure 3 depicts the trace-covariance of the item factors $\boldsymbol{v}_j$, as returned by the online VB algorithm. There exists a clear relationship with the number of item ratings. As anticipated, rarely rated items tend to have higher variance, although a few spikes in the variance for relatively highly rated items may warrant further investigation. We do not show an equivalent plot for user factors due to the fact that the relationship with the number of ratings is much less evident.

5. CONCLUSIONS

We have presented an online variational Bayesian approach to the problem of large-scale matrix completion, with applications in collaborative filtering. Unlike standard matrix factorization approaches, the developed statistical model enables sequential selection of near-optimal subsets of users

Table 1: Online VB method with random mini-batches vs. Yahoo! baseline model

Model	Validation RMSE	Test RMSE	Time/Epoch
Yahoo!	26.68	28.98	$\sim$ 0.5 min.
Online VB	24.34	25.94	$\sim$ 15 min.

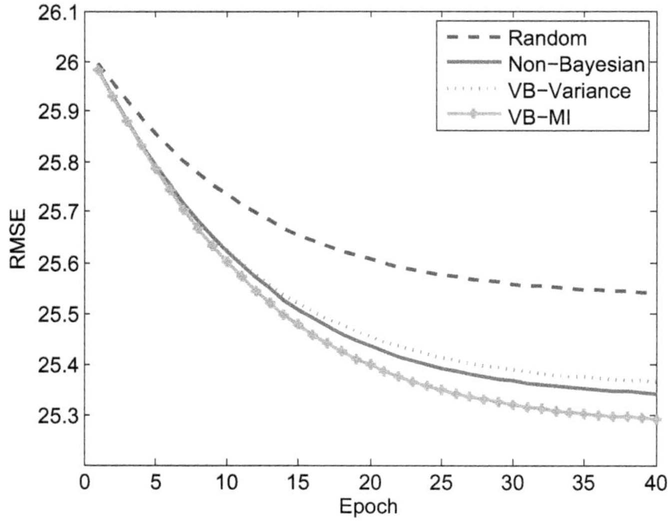

Figure 2: RMSE over 40 epochs. The VB-MI algorithm is based on mutual information with the KL divergence kernel, VB-Variance is based on sampling the users and items with highest variance and the Non-Bayesian method uses mutual information with the RBF kernel.

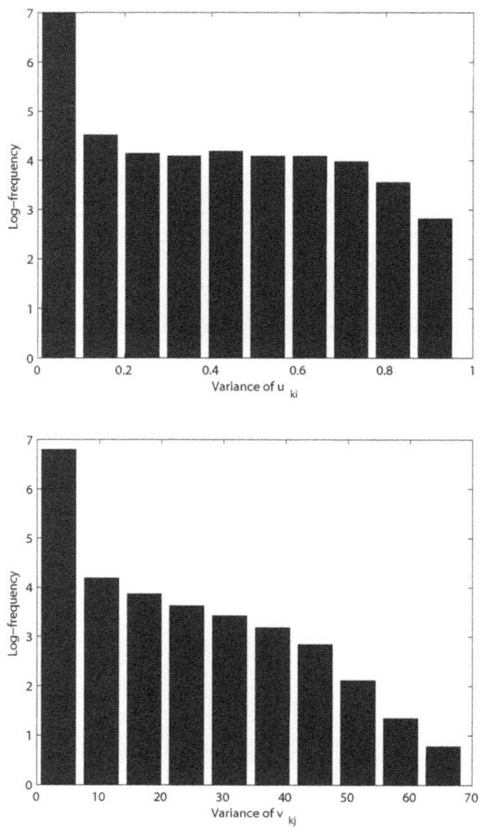

Figure 3: Histograms of the variance of u_{ki} (top) and v_{kj} (bottom), where i, j, k are indices over users, items and factors, respectively. Shown in logarithmic scale. The majority of the components have low variance.

and items through active learning. This can be done using efficient greedy algorithms which rely on submodularity.

We have also described an alternative method based directly on the inferred variance of the factors, which relaxes the near-optimality guarantees and requires much lower computational effort, at the cost of a small performance penalty. The aforementioned methods have been compared with random sampling and with a non-Bayesian submodularity-based algorithm.

We have demonstrated the proposed framework using the challenging Yahoo! Music dataset, with promising results. Notably, all proposed active learning algorithms outperform random sampling. Comparison with the non-Bayesian method shows comparable performance. However, the RBF kernel in non-Bayesian method requires tuning of the bandwidth parameter, while the KL divergence kernel used in the Bayesian approaches is parameter-free. Moreover, the computational overhead of the submodular methods far outweighs the difference in computations between the Bayesian and non-Bayesian algorithms. Importantly, neither the KL divergence kernel nor the fast variance-based active learning algorithm would be possible without the (approximate) posterior estimate provided by the Bayesian method.

Future research will focus on incorporating temporal information into the active learning algorithms. This should be possible via developments in parallel computation.

Acknowledgements

The research reported here was supported by ARO, NGA, ONR and DARPA (MSEE program).

6. REFERENCES

[1] H. Attias. A variational bayesian framework for graphical models. *Advances in Neural Information Processing Systems (NIPS)*, 12(1-2):209–215, 2000.

[2] R. Bell and Y. Koren. Lessons from the Netflix prize challenge. *ACM SIGKDD Explorations Newsletter*, 9(2):75–79, 2007.

[3] E. Candès and T. Tao. The power of convex relaxation: Near-optimal matrix completion. *Information Theory, IEEE Transactions on*, 56(5):2053–2080, 2010.

[4] G. Dror, N. Koenigstein, Y. Koren, and M. Weimer. The Yahoo! Music Dataset and KDD-Cup'11. In *ACM*

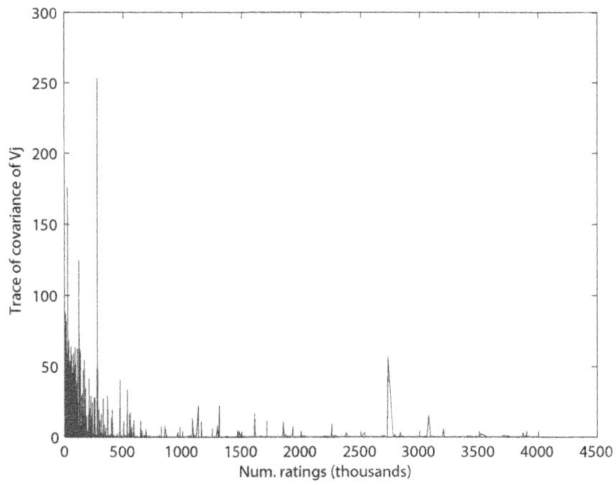

Figure 4: Trace of covariance of v_j (item factors) as a function of number of ratings. Rarely rated items tend to have higher variance.

International Conference on Knowledge Discovery and Data Mining (KDD), KDD Cup Workshop, 2011.

[5] M. Hoffman, D. Blei, and F. Bach. Online learning for latent Dirichlet allocation. *Advances in Neural Information Processing Systems (NIPS)*, 23:856–864, 2010.

[6] M. Jahrer and A. Töscher. Collaborative filtering ensemble. In *ACM International Conference on Knowledge Discovery and Data Mining (KDD), KDD Cup Workshop*, 2011.

[7] Y. Koren. Factorization meets the neighborhood: a multifaceted collaborative filtering model. In *ACM International Conference on Knowledge Discovery and Data Mining (KDD)*, pages 426–434, 2008.

[8] A. Krause, A. Singh, and C. Guestrin. Near-optimal sensor placements in Gaussian processes: Theory, efficient algorithms and empirical studies. *Journal of Machine Learning Research*, 9:235–284, 2008.

[9] J. Lee, B. Recht, R. Salakhutdinov, N. Srebro, and J. Tropp. Practical large-scale optimization for max-norm regularization. *Advances in Neural Information Processing Systems (NIPS)*, 23:1297–1305, 2010.

[10] Y. Lim and Y. Teh. Variational bayesian approach to movie rating prediction. In *ACM International Conference on Knowledge Discovery and Data Mining (KDD), KDD Cup Workshop*, pages 15–21, 2007.

[11] J. Mairal, F. Bach, J. Ponce, and G. Sapiro. Online learning for matrix factorization and sparse coding. *Journal of Machine Learning Research*, 11:19–60, 2010.

[12] S. Nakajima and M. Sugiyama. Implicit regularization in variational Bayesian matrix factorization. In *27th International Conference on Machine Learning (ICML)*, 2010.

[13] G. Nemhauser, L. Wolsey, and M. Fisher. An analysis of approximations for maximizing submodular set functions. *Mathematical Programming*, 14(1):265–294, 1978.

[14] T. Raiko, A. Ilin, and J. Karhunen. Principal component analysis for large scale problems with lots of missing values. *Machine Learning: ECML 2007*, pages 691–698, 2007.

[15] T. Raiko, H. Valpola, M. Harva, and J. Karhunen. Building blocks for variational Bayesian learning of latent variable models. *Journal of Machine Learning Research*, 8:155–201, 2007.

[16] R. Salakhutdinov and A. Mnih. Bayesian probabilistic matrix factorization using Markov chain Monte Carlo. In *Proceedings of the 25th International Conference on Machine Learning (ICML)*, 2008.

[17] M. Sato. Online model selection based on the variational Bayes. *Neural Computation*, 13(7):1649–1681, 2001.

A Sparsity-Inducing Formulation for Evolutionary Co-Clustering

Shuiwang Ji
Old Dominion University
Norfolk, VA 23529
sji@cs.odu.edu

Wenlu Zhang
Old Dominion University
Norfolk, VA 23529
wzhang@cs.odu.edu

Jun Liu
Siemens Corporate Research
Princeton, NJ 08540
jun-liu@siemens.com

ABSTRACT

Traditional co-clustering methods identify block structures from static data matrices. However, the data matrices in many applications are dynamic; that is, they evolve smoothly over time. Consequently, the hidden block structures embedded into the matrices are also expected to vary smoothly along the temporal dimension. It is therefore desirable to encourage smoothness between the block structures identified from temporally adjacent data matrices. In this paper, we propose an evolutionary co-clustering formulation for identifying co-cluster structures from time-varying data. The proposed formulation encourages smoothness between temporally adjacent blocks by employing the fused Lasso type of regularization. Our formulation is very flexible and allows for imposing smoothness constraints over only one dimension of the data matrices, thereby enabling its applicability to a large variety of settings. The optimization problem for the proposed formulation is non-convex, non-smooth, and non-separable. We develop an iterative procedure to compute the solution. Each step of the iterative procedure involves a convex, but non-smooth and non-separable problem. We propose to solve this problem in its dual form, which is convex and smooth. This leads to a simple gradient descent algorithm for computing the dual optimal solution. We evaluate the proposed formulation using the Allen Developing Mouse Brain Atlas data. Results show that our formulation consistently outperforms methods without the temporal smoothness constraints.

Categories and Subject Descriptors

H.2.8 [**Database Management**]: Database Applications - Data Mining

General Terms

Algorithms

Keywords

Sparsity learning, evolutionary co-clustering, optimization, bioinformatics, neuroscience

1. INTRODUCTION

Clustering is one of the major techniques for unsupervised discovery of hidden structures from complex data sets. Common clustering methods include the K-means algorithm, the spectral methods, and the hierarchical clustering techniques. These approaches treat the two dimensions of the data matrix as instances and features, respectively, and group the instances into clusters based on all the features. When the data matrix is re-ordered according to the clustering results, the re-ordered matrix usually assumes a banded structure along the instance dimension, since instances in the same cluster are assumed to be similar, while those in different cluster are assumed to be dissimilar.

The classical clustering paradigm assumes that all the features are equally relevant to all instances. In many applications, certain group of instances are only similar to each other with respect to a subset of features. That is, the hidden structure of the data matrix can be more accurately described by a "checkerboard" structure in which a subset of the rows and a subset of the columns form a block. Co-clustering, also known as bi-clustering, aims at identifying the block structures of the data matrix by clustering the rows and columns of the data matrix simultaneously into co-clusters [17, 6, 9, 10, 28]. Currently, co-clustering finds applications in many areas, including biological data analysis [25, 20], text mining [10, 9], and social studies [14].

As a class of powerful methods for unsupervised pattern mining, existing co-clustering methods invariably assume that the data matrices are static; that is, they do not evolve over time. However, in many real-world domains, the processes that generated the data are time-evolving. Hence, the observed data are usually dynamic. As a consequence, the block structures embedded into the time-varying data should also evolve smoothly over time. Therefore, it is desirable to incorporate the temporal smoothness constraint into the co-clustering formalism.

In this paper, we propose an evolutionary co-clustering formulation for identifying co-clusters from time-varying data. The proposed formulation employs sparsity-inducing regularization [29] to identify block structures from the time-varying data matrices. Meanwhile, it applies fused Lasso type of regularization [30] to encourage temporal smoothness over the block structures identified from contiguous time points. The proposed formulation is very flexible and can be applied to encourage temporal smoothness over either one or both dimensions of the data matrices. The optimization problem for the proposed formulation is non-convex, non-smooth, and non-separable. We propose an iterative procedure to compute the solution, and each of the iterative step involves a convex, but non-smooth and non-separable problem. To enable efficient optimization, we derive the dual form of this problem and employ a gradient descent algorithm to solve the smooth dual problem. We evaluate the proposed formulation using the Allen Developing Mouse Brain Atlas data [22, 19]. Results show that the proposed method consistently outperforms other methods by identifying blocks that are consistent with classical neuroanatomy.

The rest of this paper is organized as follows: We introduce the sparse singular value decomposition method for co-clustering in Section 2. In Section 3, we describe the proposed evolutionary co-clustering formulation. We discuss related work in Section 4 and report the experimental evaluation in Section 5. This paper concludes with conclusions and future work in Section 6.

Notations: We use boldface lower-case letters, e.g., $\mathbf{u}$, to denote vectors and upper-case letters, e.g., A, to denote matrices. $\mathbf{e}_n$ denotes a vector of all ones of length n. For a vector $\mathbf{u}$, its ℓ_1-norm, defined as the summation of the absolute values of its components, is denoted as $\|\mathbf{u}\|_1$. For a matrix A, its Frobenius norm is denoted as $\|A\|_F$. $\odot$ denotes component-wise multiplication, and $\otimes$ denotes the Kronecker product. The soft-thresholding operator $\mathcal{T}_\lambda$, acting on a vector $\mathbf{x}$, is defined component-wise as:

$$(\mathcal{T}_\lambda(\mathbf{x}))_i = \begin{cases} x_i - \lambda & \text{if } x_i > \lambda \\ x_i + \lambda & \text{if } x_i < -\lambda \\ 0 & \text{if } |x_i| \leq \lambda. \end{cases} \quad (1)$$

2. SPARSE SINGULAR VALUE DECOMPOSITION FOR CO-CLUSTERING

The problem of co-clustering is closely related to the singular value decomposition (SVD) of the data matrices [9, 36, 21]. In [9, 36], the spectral clustering formalism is extended to derive a spectral formulation for co-clustering. In these spectral co-clustering formulations, the data are projected onto the left and the right singular vector spaces before they are concatenated and clustered to identify the co-clusters. Motivated by the relationship between SVD and co-clustering, a sparse SVD formulation is proposed in [21] for co-clustering. Formally, let $B \in \mathbb{R}^{m \times n}$ be a data matrix. The first singular value and the corresponding left and right singular vectors of B can be computed as

$$\min_{s,\mathbf{p},\mathbf{q}} \|B - s\mathbf{p}\mathbf{q}^T\|_F^2, \quad (2)$$

where $s \in \mathbb{R}$ is the first singular value, and $\mathbf{p} \in \mathbb{R}^m$ and $\mathbf{q} \in \mathbb{R}^n$ are the corresponding left and right singular vectors, respectively, and $\|\cdot\|_F$ denotes the matrix Frobenius norm. It is well known that the matrix $s\mathbf{p}\mathbf{q}^T$ is the optimal rank one approximation to the matrix B [12]. Note that $\mathbf{p}$ and $\mathbf{q}$ lie in the row space and column space, respectively, of B. In addition, the singular vectors $\mathbf{p}$ and $\mathbf{q}$ are usually not sparse; that is, most of their components are nonzero.

Motivated by the optimal rank one approximation property of the SVD, a sparse SVD formulation is proposed in [21]. Furthermore, it is shown that this sparse SVD formulation can be employed for solving co-clustering problems. Specifically, the following sparsity-inducing formulation is involved in sparse SVD:

$$\min_{s,\mathbf{p},\mathbf{q}} \frac{1}{2}\|B - s\mathbf{p}\mathbf{q}^T\|_F^2 + \lambda\|s\mathbf{p}\|_1 + \gamma\|s\mathbf{q}\|_1, \quad (3)$$

where $\|\cdot\|$ denotes the vector ℓ_1-norm, and λ and γ are the regularization parameters. It is well known that the ℓ_1-norm regularization on $\mathbf{p}$ and $\mathbf{q}$ encourages sparse solutions [29]. Thus, when λ and γ are set to large values, many entries of $\mathbf{p}$ and $\mathbf{q}$ will be set of zero. The regularization parameters λ and γ control the tradeoff between the quality of the rank one approximation and the sparsity of $\mathbf{p}$ and $\mathbf{q}$, respectively.

It is shown in [21] that the sparse SVD formulation can be readily employed to solve co-clustering problems. Specifically, the rows and columns of B corresponding to nonzero entries of $\mathbf{p}$ and $\mathbf{q}$, respectively, can be naturally interpreted to form a co-cluster. If multiple co-clusters are desired, subsequent co-clusters can be identified by removing the rank one approximation from the data matrix and solving the optimization problem in Eq. (3) using the residual matrix. It is shown that this sparse SVD method outperforms prior co-clustering methods by identifying distinctive gene expression profiles corresponding to various pathological conditions from a microarray gene expression data set.

The optimization problem in Eq. (3) is non-convex and non-smooth. An iterative procedure has been developed in [21] to compute the solution. In this procedure, one of the vector variables is fixed while the other one is optimized, and this process is alternated between the two vector variables until it converges to a locally optimal solution. Specifically, when $\mathbf{p}$ is fixed, $\mathbf{q}$ can be computed by solving

$$\min_{\tilde{\mathbf{q}}} F(\tilde{\mathbf{q}}) \equiv \frac{1}{2}\|B - \mathbf{p}\tilde{\mathbf{q}}^T\|_F^2 + \gamma\|\tilde{\mathbf{q}}\|_1, \quad (4)$$

where $\tilde{\mathbf{q}} = s\mathbf{q}$. After $\tilde{\mathbf{q}}$ is obtained, we have $s = \|\tilde{\mathbf{q}}\|$ and $\mathbf{q} = \tilde{\mathbf{q}}/s$. Similarly, when $\mathbf{q}$ is fixed, the following problem is involved:

$$\min_{\tilde{\mathbf{p}}} G(\tilde{\mathbf{p}}) \equiv \frac{1}{2}\|B - \tilde{\mathbf{p}}\mathbf{q}^T\|_F^2 + \lambda\|\tilde{\mathbf{p}}\|_1, \quad (5)$$

and $\mathbf{p} = \tilde{\mathbf{p}}/s$ where $s = \|\tilde{\mathbf{p}}\|$. It can be shown that the problems in Eqs. (4) and (5) are convex and can be solved analytically.

The objective function in Eq. (4) can be written as

$$\begin{aligned} F(\tilde{\mathbf{q}}) &= \frac{1}{2}\|B - \mathbf{p}\tilde{\mathbf{q}}^T\|_F^2 + \gamma\|\tilde{\mathbf{q}}\|_1 \\ &= \frac{1}{2}\operatorname{Tr}(B^TB) - \mathbf{p}^TB\tilde{\mathbf{q}} + \frac{1}{2}\tilde{\mathbf{q}}^T\tilde{\mathbf{q}} + \gamma\|\tilde{\mathbf{q}}\|_1. \quad (6) \end{aligned}$$

Taking the subdifferential of Eq. (6) with respect to $\tilde{\mathbf{q}}$, we have

$$\partial F(\tilde{\mathbf{q}}) = -B^T\mathbf{p} + \tilde{\mathbf{q}} + \gamma\,\mathrm{SGN}(\tilde{\mathbf{q}}), \quad (7)$$

where $\mathrm{SGN}(\cdot)$ is defined component-wise as

$$(\mathrm{SGN}(\tilde{\mathbf{q}}))_i = \begin{cases} \{1\} & \text{if } (\tilde{\mathbf{q}})_i > 0 \\ \{-1\} & \text{if } (\tilde{\mathbf{q}})_i < 0 \\ [-1, 1] & \text{if } (\tilde{\mathbf{q}})_i = 0. \end{cases} \quad (8)$$

Note that the subdifferential of a function is a set, and when the function is differentiable, the set is a singleton containing the derivative [27]. It follows from the optimality condition for unconstrained problems [27] that $\tilde{\mathbf{q}}^*$ is an optimal solution to Eq. (4) if and only if $\mathbf{0} \in \partial F(\tilde{\mathbf{q}}^*)$. Hence, it can be

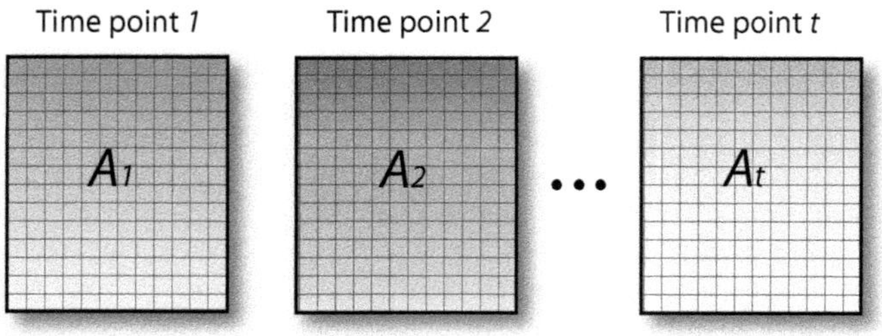

Figure 1: Illustration of the evolutionary co-clustering problem.

easily verified that the optimal $\tilde{\mathbf{q}}^*$ is given by

$$(\tilde{\mathbf{q}}^*)_i = \begin{cases} (B^T\mathbf{p} - \gamma)_i & \text{if } (B^T\mathbf{p})_i > \gamma \\ (B^T\mathbf{p} + \gamma)_i & \text{if } (B^T\mathbf{p})_i < -\gamma \\ 0 & \text{if } |(B^T\mathbf{p})_i| \leq \gamma. \end{cases} \quad (9)$$

Similarly, the optimal $\tilde{\mathbf{p}}^*$ for the optimization problem in Eq. (5) is given by

$$(\tilde{\mathbf{p}}^*)_i = \begin{cases} (B\mathbf{q} - \lambda)_i & \text{if } (B\mathbf{q})_i > \lambda \\ (B\mathbf{q} + \lambda)_i & \text{if } (B\mathbf{q})_i < -\lambda \\ 0 & \text{if } |(B\mathbf{q})_i| \leq \lambda. \end{cases} \quad (10)$$

The iterative procedure in [21] applies Eqs. (9) and (10) alternately until a locally optimal solution is reached.

3. EVOLUTIONARY CO-CLUSTERING

In the traditional co-clustering framework [17, 6, 9, 20, 28, 25], we assume that the data matrix is time-invariant; that is, it does not evolve along the temporal dimension. In many application domains, each data matrix is usually associated with a particular time point, and it evolves smoothly over time as shown in Figure 1. For example, in the developing mouse brain gene expression analysis, the spatial gene expression patterns at a particular developing time point is captured by a data matrix in which one dimension corresponds to the genes and the other dimension corresponds to the spatial locations. Since gene regulation acts sequentially, the expression patterns usually evolves smoothly over time, thereby resulting a series of time-stamped data matrices, one for each sampled developing time point. A simple approach for mining these time-evolving data matrices is to treat the data matrices at different time points separately. This approach, however, ignores the time-dependent nature of the underlying process, thereby yielding results that are not amenable to domain interpretation. In this paper, we propose an evolutionary co-clustering formulation for uncovering patterns from time-evolving data matrices. The proposed formulation encourages smooth changes in the row and/or column patterns over time, thereby capturing the time-evolving nature of the underlying process faithfully. The proposed framework is very flexible and can be applied to applications in which only one dimension of the data matrices evolves.

Given a set of time-evolving data matrices $A_i \in \mathbb{R}^{m\times n}$ for $i = 1, \cdots, t$, where t is the number of sampled time points, we are interested in identifying block structures from each of the data matrices. A simple approach is to compute the sparse SVD for each data matrix separately, leading to the following optimization problem:

$$\min_{s_i,\mathbf{u}_i,\mathbf{v}_i} \sum_{i=1}^{t} \left\{ \frac{1}{2}\|A_i - s_i\mathbf{u}_i\mathbf{v}_i^T\|_F^2 + \lambda\|s_i\mathbf{u}_i\|_1 + \gamma\|s_i\mathbf{v}_i\|_1 \right\}$$

where $\mathbf{u}_i \in \mathbb{R}^m$ and $\mathbf{v}_i \in \mathbb{R}^n$ are associated with the rows and columns, respectively, of A_i, and s_i is the corresponding singular value. However, this approach decouples the data matrices for contiguous time points and ignores the temporal evolving nature of the underlying process that generated the data matrices.

3.1 The Proposed Formulation

To incorporate the temporal smoothness constraints into the co-clustering framework, we propose the following sparsity-inducing evolutionary co-clustering formulation:

$$\min_{s_i,\mathbf{u}_i,\mathbf{v}_i} \sum_{i=1}^{t} \left\{ \frac{1}{2}\|A_i - s_i\mathbf{u}_i\mathbf{v}_i^T\|_F^2 + \lambda\|s_i\mathbf{u}_i\|_1 + \gamma\|s_i\mathbf{v}_i\|_1 \right\} \quad (11)$$
$$+ \sum_{i=1}^{t-1} \left\{ \eta\|s_{i+1}\mathbf{u}_{i+1} - s_i\mathbf{u}_i\|_1 + \xi\|s_{i+1}\mathbf{v}_{i+1} - s_i\mathbf{v}_i\|_1 \right\},$$

where η and ξ and tunable parameters. In this formulation, the last two regularization terms are fused Lasso type of regularization [30], and they encourage the $\mathbf{u}_i$ and $\mathbf{v}_i$ for contiguous time points to be similar. Specifically, these regularization terms encourage the differences of contiguous $\mathbf{u}_i$ and $\mathbf{v}_i$ to be zero, thus enforcing many entries of contiguous $\mathbf{u}_i$ and $\mathbf{v}_i$ to be identical. These fused Lasso type of regularization naturally incorporates the time-evolving nature of the data matrices by encouraging the block structures for contiguous time points to be similar. Note that we can also encourage only the rows or the columns of the block structures to be similar by setting either ξ or η to zero.

The objective function in Eq. (11) can be expressed equivalently as

$$\sum_{i=1}^{t} \frac{1}{2}\|A_i - s_i\mathbf{u}_i\mathbf{v}_i^T\|_F^2 + \lambda\|\tilde{\mathbf{u}}\|_1 + \gamma\|\tilde{\mathbf{v}}\|_1 + \eta\|E\tilde{\mathbf{u}}\|_1 + \xi\|F\tilde{\mathbf{v}}\|_1,$$

where $\tilde{\mathbf{u}} = (\mathbf{s}\otimes\mathbf{e}_m)\odot\mathbf{u}$, $\mathbf{s} = [s_1, s_2, \cdots, s_t]^T$, $\tilde{\mathbf{v}} = (\mathbf{s}\otimes\mathbf{e}_n)\odot\mathbf{v}$, $\mathbf{u} = [\mathbf{u}_1^T, \mathbf{u}_2^T, \cdots, \mathbf{u}_t^T]^T \in \mathbb{R}^{mt}$, $\mathbf{v} = [\mathbf{v}_1^T, \mathbf{v}_2^T, \cdots, \mathbf{v}_t^T]^T \in \mathbb{R}^{nt}$, $E \in \mathbb{R}^{m(t-1)\times mt}$ and $F \in \mathbb{R}^{n(t-1)\times nt}$ are defined as

$$(E)_{ij} = \begin{cases} -1 & \text{if } j = i, \;\; i = 1, \cdots, m(t-1) \\ 1 & j = i + m, \;\; i = 1, \cdots, m(t-1) \\ 0 & \text{otherwise,} \end{cases} \quad (12)$$

$$(F)_{ij} = \begin{cases} -1 & \text{if } j = i, \;\; i = 1, \cdots, n(t-1) \\ 1 & j = i + n, \;\; i = 1, \cdots, n(t-1) \\ 0 & \text{otherwise.} \end{cases} \quad (13)$$

The objective function in Eq. (11) is non-convex and non-smooth. In addition, the fused Lasso regularization terms are non-separable [33, 13]. We propose an iterative procedure to compute $\mathbf{u}$ and $\mathbf{v}$. Specifically, we optimize $\mathbf{u}$ by fixing $\mathbf{v}$ and then optimize $\mathbf{v}$ by fixing $\mathbf{u}$. This iterative process is repeated until convergence. In the following, we discuss the detailed procedure of computing $\mathbf{v}$ when $\mathbf{u}$ are fixed. The other case can be derived in a similar way. Specifically, when $\mathbf{u}$ are fixed, $\tilde{\mathbf{v}}$ can be computed by solving the following optimization problem:

$$\min_{\tilde{\mathbf{v}}} f_\xi^\gamma(\tilde{\mathbf{v}}) \equiv \sum_{i=1}^{t} \frac{1}{2}\|A_i - \mathbf{u}_i\tilde{\mathbf{v}}_i^T\|_F^2 + \gamma\|\tilde{\mathbf{v}}\|_1 + \xi\|F\tilde{\mathbf{v}}\|_1. \quad (14)$$

The objective function in Eq. (14) is convex, but non-smooth and non-separable. In the following, we develop an efficient algorithm to compute the optimal $\tilde{\mathbf{v}}^*$.

3.2 A Two-Step Procedure

A central challenge for solving the optimization problem in Eq. (14) is the ℓ_1-norm and the fused Lasso regularization terms, which are non-smooth and non-separable. A key property that leads to an efficient algorithm to this problem is that the ℓ_1-norm term and the fused Lasso term can be solved sequentially in two steps, giving rise to a two-step procedure. This result is originally given in [13, 24] and is summarized in the following theorem:

THEOREM 3.1. *Define*

$$\pi_\xi^\gamma(\mathbf{u}) = \arg\min_{\tilde{\mathbf{v}}} f_\xi^\gamma(\tilde{\mathbf{v}}). \quad (15)$$

Then for any $\gamma, \xi \geq 0$, we have

$$\pi_\xi^\gamma(\mathbf{u}) = \mathcal{T}_\gamma\left(\pi_\xi^0(\mathbf{u})\right). \quad (16)$$

PROOF. We consider the case when $\gamma = 0$:

$$\pi_\xi^0(\mathbf{u}) = \arg\min f_\xi(\tilde{\mathbf{v}}), \quad (17)$$

where

$$f_\xi(\tilde{\mathbf{v}}) \equiv f_\xi^0(\tilde{\mathbf{v}}) = \sum_{i=1}^{t} \frac{1}{2}\|A_i - \mathbf{u}_i\tilde{\mathbf{v}}_i^T\|_F^2 + \xi\|F\tilde{\mathbf{v}}\|_1. \quad (18)$$

The subdifferentials of $f_\xi^\gamma(\tilde{\mathbf{v}})$ and $f_\xi(\tilde{\mathbf{v}})$ can be computed as

$$\begin{aligned} \partial f_\xi^\gamma(\tilde{\mathbf{v}}) &= \tilde{\mathbf{v}} - A^T\mathbf{u} + \gamma\,\mathrm{SGN}(\tilde{\mathbf{v}}) + \xi F^T\,\mathrm{SGN}(F\tilde{\mathbf{v}}), \quad (19)\\ \partial f_\xi(\tilde{\mathbf{v}}) &= \tilde{\mathbf{v}} - A^T\mathbf{u} + \xi F^T\,\mathrm{SGN}(F\tilde{\mathbf{v}}), \quad (20) \end{aligned}$$

where

$$A = \begin{pmatrix} A_1 & & & 0 \\ & A_2 & & \\ & & \ddots & \\ 0 & & & A_t \end{pmatrix} \in \mathbb{R}^{mt\times nt}. \quad (21)$$

It follows from the optimality condition for unconstrained problems [27] that

$$\mathbf{0} \in \partial f_\xi\left(\pi_\xi^0(\mathbf{u})\right).$$

Hence, there exists

$$\mathbf{y}^* \in \xi\,\mathrm{SGN}(F\pi_\xi^0(\mathbf{u})) \quad (22)$$

such that $\pi_\xi^0(\mathbf{u}) = A^T\mathbf{u} - F^T\mathbf{y}^*$. Define

$$\begin{aligned} \mathbf{a} &= \mathcal{T}_\gamma(\pi_\xi^0(\mathbf{u})), \\ \mathbf{b} &= \mathrm{sgn}(\pi_\xi^0(\mathbf{u})) \odot \min(|\pi_\xi^0(\mathbf{u})|, \gamma), \end{aligned}$$

where $\mathrm{sgn}(\mathbf{x})$ is defined component-wise as $(\mathrm{sgn}(\mathbf{x}))_i = 1$ if $x_i > 0$, $(\mathrm{sgn}(\mathbf{x}))_i = -1$ if $x_i < 0$, and 0 otherwise. It can be verified that $\mathbf{a} - A^T\mathbf{u} + \mathbf{b} + F^T\mathbf{y}^* = \mathbf{0}$ and $\mathbf{b} \in \gamma\,\mathrm{SGN}(\mathbf{a})$. It follows from the definition of $\mathbf{a}$, the fact that each row of F consisting of two nonzero elements 1 and -1, and Eq. (22) that $\mathbf{y}^* \in \xi\,\mathrm{SGN}(F\mathbf{a})$. Therefore, we have

$$\mathbf{0} = \mathbf{a} - A^T\mathbf{u} + \mathbf{b} + F^T\mathbf{y}^* \in \partial f_\xi^\gamma(\mathbf{a}).$$

This completes the proof of this theorem. □

Theorem 3.1 shows that we can solve the optimization problem in two sequential steps. Specifically, we can first solve the problem in Eq. (14) with $\gamma = 0$ to obtain the intermediate solution $\pi_\xi^0(\mathbf{u})$. Then the final optimal solution $\pi_\xi^\gamma(\mathbf{u})$ can be obtained by applying the soft thresholding operator to the intermediate solution as in Eq. (16). We now discuss how the $\gamma = 0$ case can be solved efficiently in its dual form.

3.3 The Dual Formulation

A key to the two-step procedure in Section 3.2 is to solve the optimization problem in Eq. (17), which can be rewritten in its full form as

$$\min_{\tilde{\mathbf{v}}} f_\xi(\tilde{\mathbf{v}}) \equiv \sum_{i=1}^{t} \frac{1}{2}\|A_i - \mathbf{u}_i\tilde{\mathbf{v}}_i^T\|_F^2 + \xi\|F\tilde{\mathbf{v}}\|_1. \quad (23)$$

We propose to solve this problem in its dual form. To this end, we introduce the dual variable

$$\mathbf{w} = [\mathbf{w}_1^T, \mathbf{w}_2^T, \cdots, \mathbf{w}_{t-1}^T]^T \in \mathbb{R}^{n(t-1)}$$

and obtain the following equivalent min-max problem:

$$\min_{\tilde{\mathbf{v}}} \max_{\|\mathbf{w}\|_\infty \leq \xi} \phi(\tilde{\mathbf{v}}, \mathbf{w}) \equiv \sum_{i=1}^{t} \frac{1}{2}\|A_i - \mathbf{u}_i\tilde{\mathbf{v}}_i^T\|_F^2 + \langle F\tilde{\mathbf{v}}, \mathbf{w}\rangle. \quad (24)$$

The existence of the saddle point to this min-max problem is guaranteed by the Von Neumann Lemma [26], because $\phi(\cdot,\cdot)$ is differentiable, convex in $\tilde{\mathbf{v}}$, and concave in $\mathbf{w}$. Exchanging the min and max and setting the derivative of $\phi(\tilde{\mathbf{v}}, \mathbf{w})$ with respect to $\tilde{\mathbf{v}}$ to zero, we obtain

$$\tilde{\mathbf{v}} = A^T\mathbf{u} - F^T\mathbf{w}. \quad (25)$$

Substituting Eq. (25) into Eq. (24), we obtain the following dual problem:

$$\min_{\mathbf{w}:\|\mathbf{w}\|_\infty \leq \xi} \psi(\mathbf{w}) \equiv \frac{1}{2}\|F^T\mathbf{w}\|^2 - \left\langle A^T\mathbf{u}, F^T\mathbf{w}\right\rangle - c, \quad (26)$$

where $c = \frac{1}{2}\sum_{i=1}^{t} \mathrm{Tr}\left((A_i - \mathbf{u}_i\mathbf{u}_i^T A_i)(A_i - \mathbf{u}_i\mathbf{u}_i^T A_i)^T\right)$. Note that we have changed max to min in Eq. (26) by negating the objective function for ease of presentation. The dual formulation in Eq. (26) is convex and smooth. Hence, it can be solved by gradient descent algorithms.

3.4 A Gradient Descent Algorithm

The dual problem in Eq. (26) is a constrained quadratic program (QP) and can be solved by general QP solvers. However, direct application of general QP solvers would ignore the special structure of this problem, incurring excessive computational cost. In this paper, we propose to solve this dual formulation by a gradient descent algorithm, since the objective function is differentiable. Note that the Hessian of $\psi(\mathbf{w})$ is a $n(t-1)\times n(t-1)$ matrix and can be express as

$$FF^T = \begin{pmatrix} 2 & \overbrace{\cdots}^{(n-1)\,0s} & -1 & \cdots & \cdots & 0 \\ \vdots & 2 & \cdots & -1 & \cdots & 0 \\ -1 & \vdots & \ddots & \cdots & \ddots & \vdots \\ \vdots & -1 & \vdots & \ddots & \cdots & -1 \\ \vdots & \vdots & \ddots & \vdots & \ddots & \vdots \\ 0 & 0 & \cdots & -1 & \cdots & 2 \end{pmatrix}. \quad (27)$$

Since F is a full rank matrix, the Hessian matrix FF^T is positive definite. Thus a unique solution exists for the optimization problem in Eq. (26).

In this gradient descent algorithm, we have the following iterative update in each iteration:

$$\mathbf{w}_{k+1} = P_{\|\cdot\|_\infty \le \xi}\left(\mathbf{w}_k - \frac{1}{\lambda_{\max}}\mathbf{g}_k\right), \tag{28}$$

where $\mathbf{g}_k = \psi'(\mathbf{w}_k) = FF^T\mathbf{w}_k - FA^T\mathbf{u}$ is the gradient of the objective function at $\mathbf{w}_k$, $\lambda_{\max}$ is the largest eigenvalue of the Hessian matrix FF^T, and

$$\left(P_{\|\cdot\|_\infty \le \xi}(\mathbf{x})\right)_i = \begin{cases} x_i & \text{if } |x_i| \le \xi \\ \text{sgn}(x_i)\xi & \text{if } |x_i| > \xi \end{cases} \tag{29}$$

is the projection onto the feasible region. It follows from the analysis in [27] that this algorithm has a linear convergence rate as

$$\|\mathbf{w}_k - \mathbf{w}^*\|^2 \le \left(1 - \frac{\lambda_{\min}}{\lambda_{\max}}\right)^k \|\mathbf{w}_0 - \mathbf{w}^*\|^2, \tag{30}$$

where $\mathbf{w}_0$ is the initial starting point, and $\lambda_{\min}$ denotes the smallest eigenvalue of the Hessian matrix. This algorithm can also be accelerated by the Nesterov's method [27].

3.5 Duality Gap and Convergence

The gradient descent algorithm is an iterative procedure, and thus a criterion is required to assess the convergence of the algorithm. Following [24], we define a duality gap for the min-max problem in Eq. (24) and derive a simple equation for computing the duality gap in each iteration. We use this duality gap as the stopping criterion in our experiments, and the gradient descent algorithm returns when the duality gap is smaller than 10^{-8}.

Let $\bar{\mathbf{w}}$ be an appropriate solution computed by the gradient descent algorithm. Note that $\|\bar{\mathbf{w}}\|_\infty \le \xi$, as it has been projected onto the feasible region in each step. Let $\bar{\mathbf{v}} = A^T\mathbf{u} - F^T\bar{\mathbf{w}}$ be the corresponding solution for the primal formulation. We can define the duality gap for Eq. (24) at $(\bar{\mathbf{v}}, \bar{\mathbf{w}})$ as

$$\text{dg}(\bar{\mathbf{v}}, \bar{\mathbf{w}}) = \max_{\mathbf{w}:\|\mathbf{w}\|_\infty \le \xi} \phi(\bar{\mathbf{v}}, \mathbf{w}) - \min_{\tilde{\mathbf{v}}} \phi(\tilde{\mathbf{v}}, \bar{\mathbf{w}}). \tag{31}$$

The following results show that the duality gap in Eq. (31) is an upper bound for the errors in both the primal and the dual formulations. In addition, it can be computed easily by a simple equation.

THEOREM 3.2. *The duality gap defined in Eq. (31) can be computed as*

$$dg(\bar{\mathbf{v}}, \bar{\mathbf{w}}) = \xi\|\psi'(\bar{\mathbf{w}})\|_1 + \langle \bar{\mathbf{w}}, \psi'(\bar{\mathbf{w}})\rangle. \tag{32}$$

In addition, we have the following results:

$$\psi(\bar{\mathbf{w}}) - \psi(\mathbf{w}^*) \le dg(\bar{\mathbf{v}}, \bar{\mathbf{w}}), \tag{33}$$

$$f_\xi(\bar{\mathbf{v}}) - f_\xi(\mathbf{v}^*) \le dg(\bar{\mathbf{v}}, \bar{\mathbf{w}}). \tag{34}$$

The proof of this theorem is similar to that of Theorem 3 in [24] and is thus omitted.

3.6 Regularization Parameter Interval

The regularization parameter ξ controls the temporal smoothness over $\mathbf{v}_i$. That is, when ξ is larger than a certain value $\xi_{\max}$, $\mathbf{v}_i$ and $\mathbf{v}_{i+1}$, for $i = 1, 2, \cdots, t-1$, will be enforced to be identical. We show that such a $\xi_{\max}$ can be computed via solving a linear system of equations. To this end, we need to state the optimality condition for the problem in Eq. (26).

It follows from the optimality condition for constrained problems [27] that $\mathbf{w}^*$ ($\|\mathbf{w}^*\|_\infty \le \xi$) is a minimizer of Eq. (26) if and only if

$$\langle \psi'(\mathbf{w}^*), \mathbf{w} - \mathbf{w}^*\rangle \ge 0, \ \forall \mathbf{w} : \|\mathbf{w}\|_\infty \le \xi. \tag{35}$$

This is the well-known variational inequality, and it gives the optimality condition for constrained optimization problems.

Based on the above result, we show that $\xi_{\max}$ can be computed via solving a linear system of equations with a special structure.

THEOREM 3.3. *Let $\hat{\mathbf{w}}$ denote the unique solution of the linear system*

$$FF^T\mathbf{w} = FA^T\mathbf{u}, \tag{36}$$

and let

$$\xi_{max} = \|\hat{\mathbf{w}}\|_\infty. \tag{37}$$

Then for any $\xi \ge \xi_{max}$, we have $\tilde{\mathbf{v}}_i = \tilde{\mathbf{v}}_j$, $\forall i, j$.

PROOF. Since the Hessian of $\psi(\cdot)$ is positive definite, the linear system in Eq. (36) has a unique solution $\hat{\mathbf{w}}$. For any $\xi \ge \xi_{\max}$, it can be easily verified that $\|\hat{\mathbf{w}}\|_\infty = \xi_{\max} \le \xi$ and $\psi'(\hat{\mathbf{w}}) = FF^T\hat{\mathbf{w}} - FA^T\mathbf{u} = \mathbf{0}$. It follows from the optimality condition in Eq. (35) that $\hat{\mathbf{w}}$ is the optimal solution to Eq. (26) when $\xi \ge \xi_{\max}$. In addition, when $\xi \ge \xi_{\max}$, we have $\pi_\xi(\mathbf{u}) = A^T\mathbf{u} - F^T\hat{\mathbf{w}}$ from Eq. (25). It follows that

$$F\pi_\xi(\mathbf{u}) = F(A^T\mathbf{u} - F^T\hat{\mathbf{w}}) = \mathbf{0}.$$

Therefore, we have $\tilde{\mathbf{v}}_i = \tilde{\mathbf{v}}_j$, $\forall i, j$. □

The value of $\xi_{\max}$ can be used to guide the selection of an appropriate value for ξ in practice. We evaluate the effectiveness of ξ in the experiments and observe that the best performance is achieved when $\xi = \xi_{\max}$ on the biological data sets.

4. RELATED WORK

Simultaneous row and column clustering for identifying block structures from matrix data has been initially studied in [17]. Recent surge of interests in co-clustering is motivated by biological applications, which aim at identifying subset of genes co-expressed in a subset of samples from microarray gene expression data [6]. Co-clustering has also been applied in many other applications, including simultaneous clustering of words and documents [10, 9], authors and conference [32], etc. Early work on co-clustering focuses on defining an error measure and then identifying blocks that minimize this measure using heuristic search algorithms [17, 6]. These early work has recently been reformulated using matrix and optimization techniques [8]. Following the spectral clustering formalism, it has been shown recently that co-clustering is closely related to the singular value decomposition (SVD) of the data matrix [4]. In [9, 36], co-clustering is formulated as a bipartite graph cut problem, and the data are projected onto the left and right singular vector spaces before they are concatenated and clustered to identify row and column co-clusters. It is shown in [21] that sparsity-inducing regularization can be employed to compute sparse singular vectors, which in turn can be used to form co-clusters.

Figure 2: Sample slices of the 3D expression patterns for the gene *Neurog1* across seven developmental ages shown in the coronal view.

Table 1: Statistics of the Allen Developing Mouse Brain Atlas data used in the experiments. For each developing age, the data consist of a matrix in which one dimension corresponds to the brain voxels while the other dimension corresponds to the genes. This data set contains 7 developing ages, 4 of them are embryonic ages (denoted as E followed by the age in terms of days) and three are postnatal ages (denoted as P followed by the age). In addition, each voxel is annotated to a brain region manually. The number of genes, voxels, and brain regions for each age are summarized in this table.

Ages	E11.5	E13.5	E15.5	E18.5	P4	P14	P28
# of genes	1798	1798	1798	1798	1798	1798	1798
# of voxels	12949	17351	13454	12394	22170	25048	28333
# of regions	159	242	262	89	90	94	222

This work is also related to recent studies on mining from time-evolving data, which is becoming an increasingly important topic. Chakrabarti *et al.* [5] first proposed the concept of evolutionary clustering and extended the K-means and the hierarchical clustering algorithms for uncovering smooth patterns from time-evolving data matrices. In [7], the spectral clustering formalism is systematically extended to the evolutionary setting by incorporating a temporal cost into the objective function, leading to a suite of formulations for evolutionary spectral clustering. In [23], the nonnegative matrix factorization is employed for soft clustering, and a temporal cost is included for mining from time-evolving data. Evolutionary nonnegative matrix factorization is also studied in [34].

The fused Lasso penalty was originally proposed in [30] for encouraging smoothness over related coefficients in regression problems. This type of penalty is very attractive and has been applied for encouraging smoothness over spatial and temporal smoothness in many applications, including biological data analysis [31] and social studies [1]. A critical challenge in employing the fused Lasso formalism is that this class of penalty is non-smooth and non-separable and thus is very challenging to optimize. In [13], a modified coordinate descent algorithm is developed to solve the fused Lasso formulation. However, this algorithm is not guaranteed to give the exact solution. In [18], a path algorithm is proposed to solve the fused Lasso signal approximator. Instead of solving the original primal problem, Liu *et al.* developed a dual formulation for the fused Lasso signal approximator and devised a gradient descent algorithm for computing the dual solution [24].

The formulation proposed in this work is radically different from the evolutionary clustering and matrix factorization formalisms studied in the literature [5, 7, 23, 34]. The differences lie in both the studied problems and in the adopted approaches. Specifically, the existing evolutionary methods deal with clustering problems while our work is concerned with co-clustering problem. Indeed, to the best of our knowledge, our work is the first systematic study of co-clustering on time-varying data. In addition, our work is based on the optimization framework of sparsity-inducing formulations, while the current evolutionary clustering methods is mostly motivated by matrix decomposition techniques.

5. EXPERIMENTAL EVALUATION

5.1 Experimental Setup

We evaluate the proposed evolutionary co-clustering formulation using the Allen Developing Mouse Brain Atlas data, which are publicly available[1]. This data set contains *in situ* hybridization gene expression pattern images in the developing mouse brain across 7 developmental ages (see Figure 2). The 3D images are registered to a reference atlas separately for each age, and a regular grid is applied to partition the 3D brain space into voxels. The expression energy within each voxel is given as a numerical value. The statistics of the data are summarized in Table 1. There is one data matrix associated with each of the 7 developing ages. The rows of the matrices correspond to brain voxels while the columns correspond to genes. Note that the brain voxels are not registered across ages, and the data for each age contain different number of voxels. Hence, we only apply the fused Lasso regularization over the columns (genes); that is, we set $\eta = 0$. This is one of the unique advantages of the proposed formulation in which the smoothness constraint can be applied to either or both dimensions. We use the duality gap as the stopping criterion for the gradient descent algorithm and the error tolerance is set to 10^{-8} in the experiments.

To measure the co-clustering performance, we consider the annotated brain region of each voxel as its class and compare the clustering results with the region labels of voxels, since it has been shown that the results of gene expression data clustering are largely consistent with classi-

[1] `http://developingmouse.brain-map.org/`

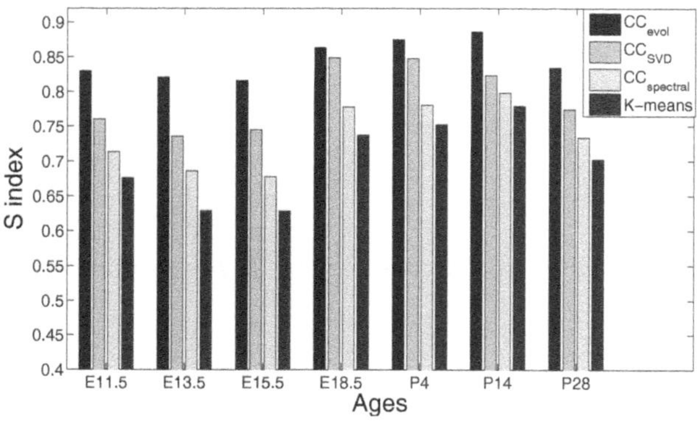

Figure 3: Performance of the proposed method ($\xi = \xi_{\max}$), denoted as CC_{evol}, in comparison with three other methods measured using the S index. CC_{SVD} denotes the co-clustering method based on SVD proposed in [21]; $\text{CC}_{\text{spectral}}$ denotes the spectral co-clustering method proposed in [9]; K-means denotes the K-means method applied to gene expression vectors of each voxel.

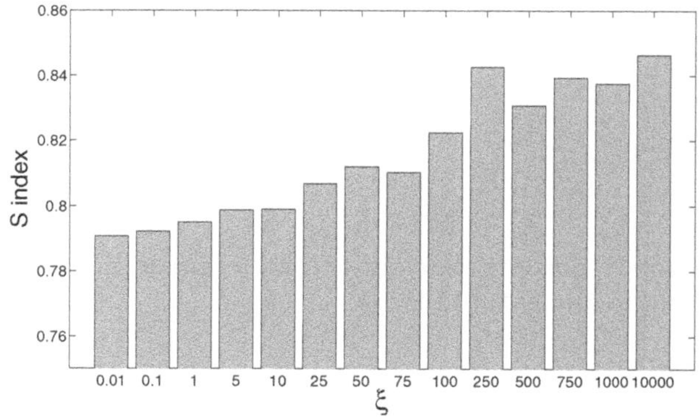

Figure 4: Performance of the proposed method as the value of the fused Lasso regularization parameter ξ increases. The performance is measured using the S index and is averaged across the 7 data sets.

cal neuroanatomy [3]. Following [2, 3], the S index is used to quantitatively measure the correspondence of the clustering results with the classical neuroanatomy reflected in the region annotations. Specifically, let $R = \{r_1, \cdots, r_N\}$ be a partition of the set of brain voxels in which each r_i comprises the set of indices of the voxels that map to that cluster (or anatomical label). The spatial overlap between a region from the annotation and the clustering result is defined as: $P_{ij} = |r_i \cap r_j|/|r_j|$. From the P_{ij} values that are computed over all pairs of brain regions and cluster result, we can then derive a global scalar index of similarity between the two partitions. Since $P_{ij} \neq P_{ji}$, X_{ij} is defined as $X_{ij} = \max\{P_{ij}, P_{ji}\}$ along with $W_{ij} = U_{ij}/\sum U_{ij}$, where $U_{ij} = \min\{|r_i|, |r_j|\}$ if $X_{ij} > 0$ and 0 otherwise. Finally, the S index is defined as $S = 1 - 4\sum_{ij} W_{ij}X_{ij}(1 - X_{ij})$. The S index lies in [0,1], and larger value indicates higher consistency between the clustering results and the annotated regions.

5.2 Co-Clustering Performance Evaluation

To evaluate the performance of the proposed evolutionary co-clustering method, we compare the proposed method with two other co-clustering methods and one clustering method. The two co-clustering methods are the one based on sparse SVD in [21] and the spectral co-clustering method proposed in [9, 36]. We also compare our method with the K-means algorithm when it is applied to cluster the voxels of the data set for each age separately. Note that the evolutionary clustering methods [5, 7, 23] cannot be applied to this data set, since the brain voxels are not registered across ages.

The performance of the four methods on the seven data sets is reported in Figure 3. We observed that the best performance is achieved when $\xi = \xi_{\max}$ and report the results under this parameter setting. Detailed studies on parameter sensitivity are reported in Section 5.3. It can be observed from Figure 3 that the proposed evolutionary co-clustering method outperforms other compared methods consistently across all seven data sets, demonstrating that incorporation of the smoothness constraints between contiguous age data yield improved performance. We can also observe that co-clustering based methods consistently outperform clustering based method. This result is in accordance with the common observation that co-clustering of gene expression data usually leads to improved performance. In addition, the co-clustering method based on sparse SVD outperforms the spectral co-clustering method on all seven data sets.

5.3 Parameter Sensitivity Evaluation

In order to fully understand how the fused Lasso regularization parameter ξ affects the performance, we conduct a series of experiments and report the results in the following. We first investigate how the performance changes as the value for ξ changes. To this end, we vary the value for ξ from 0.01 to $\xi_{\max} = 10^4$ and report the performance on each data set in Table 2 and summarize the average performance across data sets in Figure 4. We can observe that the performance improves in general as the value for ξ increases. Indeed, the proposed formulation achieves the highest performance when $\xi = \xi_{\max}$. This demonstrate that incorporation of the fused Lasso regularization is very effective in boosting the performance.

To evaluate the effectiveness of the fused Lasso regularization in encouraging smoothness over the temporal dimension, we again vary ξ from 0.01 to 10^4 and report the ℓ_1-norm differences between temporally adjacent variable vectors in Figure 5. We can observe that, as ξ increases, the values for the fused Lasso regularization terms decrease monotonically until they reach zero, where the adjacent variables are forced to be identical.

We also evaluate the effectiveness of the defined duality gap in determining the convergence of the gradient descent algorithm. To this end, we plot the values of the duality gap in the first 50 iterations of the gradient descent algorithm under multiple ξ values in Figure 6. We can observe that the duality gap decreases monotonically in all cases. In addition, as the value of ξ increases, the duality gap approaches zero at a slower speed. This is because more computations are required to fuse adjacent variables when the value for ξ increases. We use the duality gap as the stopping criterion in all experiments, and the error tolerance is set to 10^{-8}.

Table 2: **Performance of the proposed method (measured using the S index) on the seven data sets as ξ increases from 0.01 to $\xi_{max} = 10^4$. The data are publicly available at http://developingmouse.brain-map.org and the statistics are given in Table 1**

ages\ξ	10^{-2}	10^{-1}	1	5	10	25	50	75	100	250	500	750	10^3	10^4
E11.5	0.769	0.766	0.775	0.765	0.772	0.781	0.791	0.801	0.801	0.824	0.814	0.823	0.818	0.829
E13.5	0.736	0.738	0.730	0.730	0.735	0.754	0.757	0.779	0.797	0.815	0.805	0.816	0.818	0.820
E15.5	0.729	0.717	0.730	0.745	0.748	0.760	0.776	0.773	0.784	0.812	0.796	0.812	0.798	0.815
E18.5	0.840	0.843	0.835	0.842	0.848	0.845	0.854	0.839	0.847	0.866	0.842	0.857	0.856	0.863
P4	0.855	0.852	0.843	0.843	0.848	0.863	0.864	0.863	0.868	0.872	0.865	0.871	0.862	0.875
P14	0.807	0.830	0.850	0.838	0.834	0.842	0.837	0.831	0.846	0.873	0.867	0.869	0.877	0.886
P28	0.796	0.797	0.799	0.824	0.804	0.800	0.801	0.782	0.810	0.833	0.823	0.823	0.831	0.834

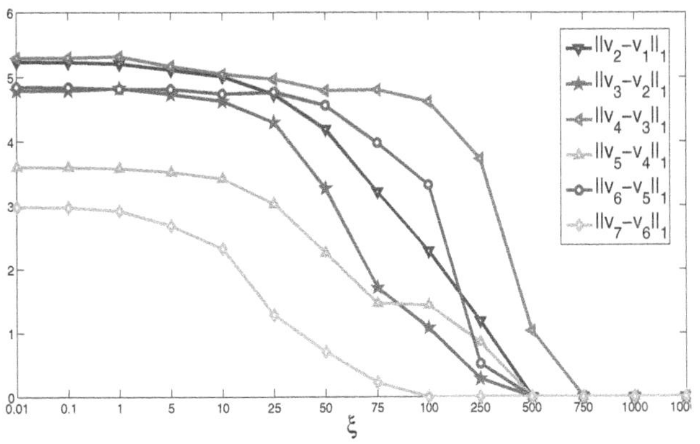

Figure 5: The values of the fused Lasso regularization terms as ξ increases.

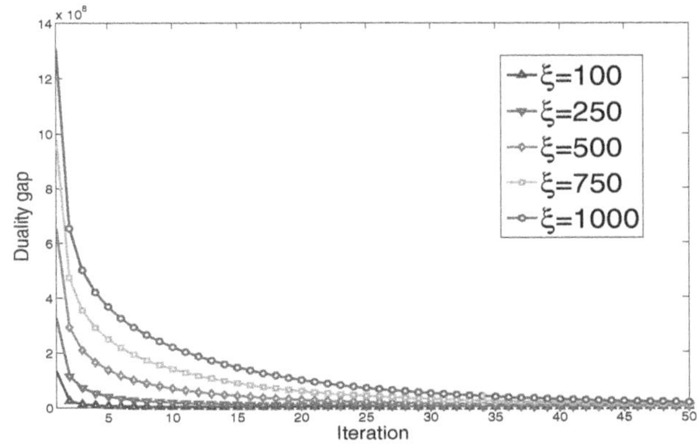

Figure 6: The duality gap in the first 50 iterations for different ξ values.

In all cases, the duality gap is reduced below the tolerance level within a relatively small number of iterations.

6. CONCLUSIONS AND DISCUSSIONS

In this paper, we propose an evolutionary co-clustering method for identifying block structures from time-evolving data. The proposed formulation employs the fused Lasso type of regularization to encourage the smoothness of the block structures, and it is applicable to scenarios in which only one sides of the blocks are required to be temporally smooth. The resulting optimization problem is non-convex, non-smooth, and non-separable, and we employ an iterative procedure to compute the solution. Each step of the iterative procedure involves a convex problem. We derive the dual form of this problem and employ a gradient descent algorithm to compute the dual optimal solution. Experimental results on the Allen Developing Mouse Brain Atlas data show that the proposed method yields consistently higher performance in comparison to other methods.

It has been shown that nonnegative matrix factorization (NMF) can be used for clustering [11] and co-clustering [35]. However, to the best of our knowledge, NMF has not been employed to perform evolutionary co-clustering. We plan to investigate how NMF [15, 16] can be adapted for co-clustering on time-evolving data. In this paper, we solve the dual form of the convex problem in each iteration. In the literature, coordinate descent and path algorithms have been developed to solve the fused Lasso signal approximator. We will explore and compare other alternative methods for solving this convex problem. This paper focuses on evaluating the proposed method on the mouse brain gene expression data, but this method can be applied to many other domains. We plan to apply our method to other data sets in the future.

7. ACKNOWLEDGMENTS

We thank the Allen Institute for Brain Science for making the developing mouse brain data available to us. This research is supported by NSF DBI-1147134, NSFC 60905035, and by Old Dominion University.

8. REFERENCES

[1] A. Ahmed and E. P. Xing. Recovering time-varying networks of dependencies in social and biological studies. *Proceedings of the National Academy of Sciences*, 106(29):11878–11883, 2009.

[2] J. W. Bohland, H. Bokil, C. B. Allen, and P. P. Mitra. The brain atlas concordance problem: Quantitative comparison of anatomical parcellations. *PLoS ONE*, 4(9):e7200, 09 2009.

[3] J. W. Bohland *et al.* Clustering of spatial gene expression patterns in the mouse brain and comparison with classical neuroanatomy. *Methods*, 50(2):105–112, 2010.

[4] S. Busygin, O. Prokopyev, and P. M. Pardalos. Biclustering in data mining. *Computers and Operations Research*, 35:2964–2987, September 2008.

[5] D. Chakrabarti, R. Kumar, and A. Tomkins. Evolutionary clustering. In *Proceedings of the 12th*

ACM SIGKDD International Conference on Knowledge Discovery and Data Mining, pages 554–560, 2006.

[6] Y. Cheng and G. M. Church. Biclustering of expression data. In *Proceedings of the Eighth International Conference on Intelligent Systems for Molecular Biology*, pages 93–103, 2000.

[7] Y. Chi, X. Song, D. Zhou, K. Hino, and B. L. Tseng. On evolutionary spectral clustering. *ACM Transactions on Knowledge Discovery from Data*, 3:17:1–17:30, December 2009.

[8] H. Cho, I. S. Dhillon, Y. Guan, and S. Sra. Minimum sum-squared residue co-clustering of gene expression data. In *Proceedings of the Fourth SIAM International Conference on Data Mining*, 2004.

[9] I. S. Dhillon. Co-clustering documents and words using bipartite spectral graph partitioning. In *Proceedings of the seventh ACM SIGKDD International Conference on Knowledge Discovery and Data Mining*, pages 269–274, 2001.

[10] I. S. Dhillon, S. Mallela, and D. S. Modha. Information-theoretic co-clustering. In *Proceedings of the ninth ACM SIGKDD International Conference on Knowledge Discovery and Data Mining*, pages 89–98, 2003.

[11] C. Ding, T. Li, W. Peng, and H. Park. Orthogonal nonnegative matrix t-factorizations for clustering. In *Proceedings of the 12th ACM SIGKDD International Conference on Knowledge Discovery and Data Mining*, pages 126–135, 2006.

[12] C. Eckart and G. Young. The approximation of one matrix by another of lower rank. *Psychometrika*, 1(3):211–218, 1936.

[13] J. Friedman, T. Hastie, H. Höfling, and R. Tibshirani. Pathwise coordinate optimization. *Annals of Applied Statistics*, 1(2):302–332, 2007.

[14] E. Giannakidou, V. Koutsonikola, A. Vakali, and Y. Kompatsiaris. Co-clustering tags and social data sources. In *Proceedings of the 2008 The Ninth International Conference on Web-Age Information Management*, pages 317–324, 2008.

[15] N. Guan, D. Tao, Z. Luo, and B. Yuan. Non-negative patch alignment framework. *IEEE Transactions on Neural Networks*, 22(8):1218–1230, 2011.

[16] N. Guan, D. Tao, Z. Luo, and B. Yuan. NeNMF: An optimal gradient method for nonnegative matrix factorization. *IEEE Transactions on Signal Processing*, 60(6):2882–2898, 2012.

[17] J. A. Hartigan. Direct clustering of a data matrix. *Journal of the American Statistical Association*, 67(337):123–129, 1972.

[18] H. Höfling. A path algorithm for the fused Lasso signal approximator. *Journal of Computational and Graphical Statistics*, 19(4):984–1006, 2010.

[19] S. Ji. Computational network analysis of the anatomical and genetic organizations in the mouse brain. *Bioinformatics*, 27(23):3293–3299, 2011.

[20] Y. Kluger, R. Basri, J. T. Chang, and M. Gerstein. Spectral biclustering of microarray data: Coclustering genes and conditions. *Genome Research*, 13(4):703–716, 2003.

[21] M. Lee, H. Shen, J. Z. Huang, and J. S. Marron. Biclustering via sparse singular value decomposition. *Biometrics*, 66:1087–1095, 2010.

[22] E. S. Lein *et al.* Genome-wide atlas of gene expression in the adult mouse brain. *Nature*, 445(7124):168–176, 2007.

[23] Y.-R. Lin, Y. Chi, S. Zhu, H. Sundaram, and B. L. Tseng. Analyzing communities and their evolutions in dynamic social networks. *ACM Transactions on Knowledge Discovery from Data*, 3:8:1–8:31, April 2009.

[24] J. Liu, L. Yuan, and J. Ye. An efficient algorithm for a class of fused Lasso problems. In *Proceedings of the 16th ACM SIGKDD International Conference on Knowledge Discovery and Data Mining*, pages 323–332, 2010.

[25] S. C. Madeira and A. L. Oliveira. Biclustering algorithms for biological data analysis: A survey. *IEEE/ACM Transactions on Computational Biology and Bioinformatics*, 1:24–45, January 2004.

[26] A. Nemirovski. Efficient methods in convex programming, 1994. Lecture Notes.

[27] Y. Nesterov. *Introductory Lectures on Convex Optimization: A Basic Course.* Kluwer Academic Publishers, 2003.

[28] C. Soneson and M. Fontes. A method for visual identification of small sample subgroups and potential biomarkers. *Annals of Applied Statistics*, 5(3):2131–2149, 2011.

[29] R. Tibshirani. Regression shrinkage and selection via the lasso. *Journal of the Royal Statistical Society: Series B*, 58(1):267–288, 1996.

[30] R. Tibshirani, M. Saunders, S. Rosset, J. Zhu, and K. Knight. Sparsity and smoothness via the fused lasso. *Journal of the Royal Statistical Society: Series B (Statistical Methodology)*, 67(1):91–108, 2005.

[31] R. Tibshirani and P. Wang. Spatial smoothing and hot spot detection for CGH data using the fused lasso. *Biostatistics*, 9(1):18–29, 2008.

[32] H. Tong, S. Papadimitriou, P. S. Yu, and C. Faloutsos. Proximity tracking on time-evolving bipartite graphs. In *Proceedings of the SIAM International Conference on Data Mining*, pages 704–715, 2008.

[33] P. Tseng. Convergence of a block coordinate descent method for nondifferentiable minimization. *Journal of Optimization Theory and Applications*, 109:475–494, June 2001.

[34] F. Wang, H. Tong, and C.-Y. Lin. Towards evolutionary nonnegative matrix factorization. In *Proceedings of the Twenty-Fifth AAAI Conference on Artificial Intelligence*, 2011.

[35] J. Yoo and S. Choi. Orthogonal nonnegative matrix tri-factorization for co-clustering: Multiplicative updates on Stiefel manifolds. *Information Processing and Management*, 46(5):559–570, 2010.

[36] H. Zha, X. He, C. Ding, H. Simon, and M. Gu. Bipartite graph partitioning and data clustering. In *Proceedings of the tenth International Conference on Information and Knowledge Management*, pages 25–32, 2001.

Detecting Changes of Clustering Structures Using Normalized Maximum Likelihood Coding

So Hirai
Graduate School of Information Science and Technology, The University of Tokyo
7-3-1 Hongo, Bunkyo-ku
Tokyo, Japan
So_Hirai@mist.i.u-tokyo.ac.jp

Kenji Yamanishi
Graduate School of Information Science and Technology, The University of Tokyo
7-3-1 Hongo, Bunkyo-ku
Tokyo, Japan
yamanishi@mist.i.u-tokyo.ac.jp

ABSTRACT

We are concerned with the issue of detecting changes of clustering structures from multivariate time series. From the viewpoint of the minimum description length (MDL) principle, we propose an algorithm that tracks changes of clustering structures so that the sum of the code-length for data and that for clustering changes is minimum. Here we employ a Gaussian mixture model (GMM) as representation of clustering, and compute the code-length for data sequences using the normalized maximum likelihood (NML) coding. The proposed algorithm enables us to deal with clustering dynamics including merging, splitting, emergence, disappearance of clusters from a unifying view of the MDL principle. We empirically demonstrate using artificial data sets that our proposed method is able to detect cluster changes significantly more accurately than an existing statistical-test based method and AIC/BIC-based methods. We further use real customers' transaction data sets to demonstrate the validity of our algorithm in market analysis. We show that it is able to detect changes of customer groups, which correspond to changes of real market environments.

Categories and Subject Descriptors

H.2.8 [**Database Applications**]: Data mining

Keywords

Minimum Description Length principle, Normalized Maximum Likelihood, Dynamic Model Selection, Clustering

1. INTRODUCTION

1.1 Motivation and Purpose of This Paper

We are concerned with the issue of clustering multi-variate data sequences. Suppose that the nature of data changes over time. We are then specifically interested in tracking changes of clustering structures, which we call *clustering change detection* (see also evolutionary clustering [2]). This is an important issue, for example, in marketing. Suppose that each customer may be specified by her/his purchase history for a number of products, i.e., each feature shows how large each product was bought by the customer in a day. One may conduct clustering of these data to obtain a number of clusters, each of which shows a group of customers having similar purchase behaviors. The customers' data may change day by day. Tracking changes of such a time-varying clustering structure will lead to the understanding of how the organization of customer group changes over time. It is expected to give an important insight to marketing research. Figure 1.1 and 1.2 show an example of clustering change detection. Figure 1.1 shows that customers C and F change their patterns to create a new cluster. Figure 1.2 shows that new customers α and β emerge to create a new cluster.

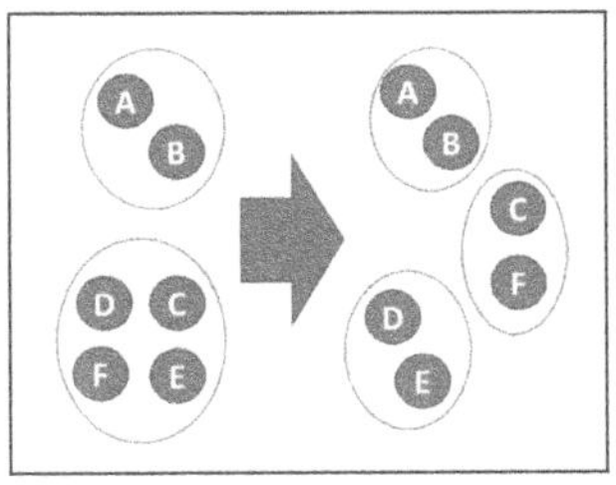

Figure 1.1: The Customers Change Their Purchase

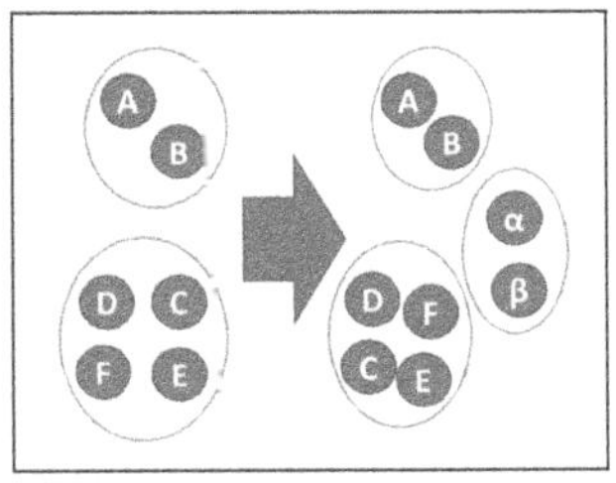

Figure 1.2: The New Customers Emerge

The purpose of this paper is twofold. One is to propose a new algorithm that tracks changes of clustering structures in the sequential setting where time series data are sequentially given and the clustering must be conducted in a sequential fashion. Although changes of clustering structures do not always imply changes of the number of clusters in general, we specifically focus on clustering changes which accompny changes of the number of clusters. We employ a Gaussian mixture model (GMM) as a representation of clustering and design the algorithm on the basis of the minimum description length (MDL) principle [10]. That is, it tracks changes of clustering structures so that the sum of the code-length for data and that for clustering changes is minimum. Here we calculate the code-length using the normalized maximum likelihood (NML) coding (see e.g.[7]). This is because the NML code-length has optimality in the sense that it achieves Shatarkov's minimax criterion [13].

The other purpose is to empirically demonstrate the va-

KDD'12, August 12–16, 2012, Beijing, China.

lidity of our proposed algorithm using both artificial and real data sets. As for the artificial data sets, we evaluate how well our algorithm works in comparison with clustering change detection algorithms using other criteria and an existing statistical-test based algorithm [14]. As for the real data sets, we employ real customers' transactions for a number of kinds of beers to conduct clustering of customers, where each cluster is a group of customers having similar purchase patterns. We investigate how well our algorithm can detect changes of customers' purchase patterns.

1.2 Previous Works

There exist a number of methods for tracking changes of clustering structures from non-stationary data sequences. Song and Wang [14] proposed a statistical-test based algorithm for dynamic clustering. It is an algorithm that estimates a GMM in an on-line manner and then conducts a statistical test to determine whether a new cluster is identical to an old one or not. If it is, the new cluster is merged into the older one, otherwise it is recognized as a cluster which has newly emerged. Sato [11] proposed an algorithm for merging and splitting of clusters in a GMM based on the variational Bayes method. Note that changes of clusters are not necessarily classified into merging or splitting. Actually some members in a number of clusters may move to generate a new cluster. Sato's algorithm cannot deal with the case.

Krempl et.al.[8] proposed a method of tracking clutering changes using the EM algorithm and Kalman filters. Our work is different from Krempl's one in that the former is concerned with changes of the number of clusters while the latter is concerned with parameter trajectories keeping the number of clusters fixed.

Yamanishi and Maruyama [16, 17] developed a theory of dynamic model selection (DMS) for tracking changes of statistical models from non-stationary data. Although this theory has been developed in a general setting for statistical model sequence selection, it can be applied to tracking of changes of clustering structures. The theory of DMS is based on the MDL principle and offers a strategy for selecting a model sequence so that the total sum of the code-length for the model sequence plus that for the data sequence relative to it is minimum. Sun et. al. [15] proposed a graph clustering algorithm called GraphScope, in which a change point for clustering was detected when the sum of code-lengths before and after it was significantly smaller than the code-length calculated without assuming that change-point. It was also designed based on the MDL principle.

1.3 Novelty and Significance of This Paper

The novelty and significance of this paper are summarized as follows:

1)*An extension of DMS into a sequential clustering setting:* In [16, 17], the theory of DMS for estimating model sequences has been explored in the batch scenario where the whole data set is given at once, and the model sequence must be detected in a retrospective way. It has remained open how to extend the DMS algorithm into the sequential scenario where data are sequentially input and the model must be selected in a sequential fashion. In this paper we extend DMS to the sequential setting and newly propose a *sequential DMS algorithm.* Every time data is input, it sequentially detects changes of clustering structures on the basis of the MDL principle so that the sum of the code-length for the data and that for the clustering change is minimum. This algorithm enables us to deal with the dynamics of clustering structures, including "merging", "splitting", "emergence", "disappearance", etc. within a unified framework from the viewpoint of the MDL principle.

2)*A new application of the RNML code-length to sequential DMS:* In the sequential DMS algorithm, the code-length for the data sequence relative to a GMM must be calculated. It is crucial how to choose a method for coding. The best choice may be the NML coding, which turns out to be the optimal code-length in the sense of minimax criterion [10]. However, it is analytically and computationally difficult to compute the NML code-length for a GMM exactly. Hirai and Yamanishi gave a method for efficiently computing an approximate variant of the NML code-length for a GMM [5]. They have recently modified it using the renormalizing technique to develop the *renormalized maximum likelihood (RNML) coding* [6]. We employ the RNML coding for the calculation of a code-length. Although it has turned out in [6] that RNML is more effective than NML in estimating the number of clusters in the batch clustering scenario, this is the first work on the application of the RNML coding to the scenario of sequential clustering change detection.

3)*Empirical demonstration of the superiority of the sequential DMS with the RNML code-length over the existing methods:* There exist a number of methods for tracking changes of clustering structures, we employ both artificial and real data sets to empirically demonstrate that our method–the sequential DMS with the RNML code-length–outperforms other methods including Song and Wang's method, AIC (Akaike's information criteria) / BIC (Bayesian information criteria)-based tracking methods etc.

4)*A novel application of clustering change detection into market research:* This paper presents a new application scenario of clustering change detection into market research. We employ a real data set consisting of customers' purchase records for a number of kinds of beers. Tracking changes of clusters of customers leads to the understanding of how customers' purchase patterns change over time and how customers move from clusters to clusters. This analysis gives a new methodology to market research.

The rest of this paper is organized as follows: Sec.2 introduces the sequential DMS algorithm. Sec.3 gives experimental results using artificial data sets. Sec.4 gives an application to market analysis. Sec.5 gives concluding remarks.

2. CLUSTERING CHANGE DETECTION

2.1 Sequential DMS Algorithm

We give a formal setting of clustering change detection. Suppose that we are sequentially given data. At each time t, we observe an n_t tuple of d-dimensional data: $X_t = (\mathbf{x}_{1t}, \dots, \mathbf{x}_{n_t t})$ $(t = 1, \dots, T)$, where $\mathbf{x}_{it} \in \mathbb{R}^d$ $(i = 1, \dots, n_t)$. Let $K_t \in \mathbb{N}$ be the number of clusters at t, which we call a *model*. Let $\mathcal{Z}_t = \{1, 2, \dots, K_t\}$. Let $Z_t = (z_{1t}, \dots, z_{n_t t}) \in \mathcal{Z}_t^{n_t}$ $(t = 1, \dots, T)$, where $z_{it} \in \mathcal{Z}_t$ $(i = 1, \dots, n_t)$. We think of z_{it} as a cluster index which data $\mathbf{x}_{it}$ comes from.

For example, we may consider the case where $\mathbf{x}_{it}$ is data of the i-th customer at time t, specified by d-dimensional features (e.g., the j-th feature indicates how large the customer consumed the j-th brand beer). The cluster to which the i-th customer belongs is specified by an index z_{it}.

Dynamic model selection (DMS) is a process of estimating a model sequence $K_1 \cdots K_T$ on the basis of the MDL principle. We first give the original form of DMS that was designed for the batch scenario. Let $X^{t-1} = X_1 \cdots X_{t-1}$, $Z^{t-1} = Z_1 \cdots Z_{t-1}$ and $K^{t-1} = K_1 \cdots K_{t-1}$. Note that Z_t is supposed to be determined for X_t once K_t is given. Let $\ell(X_t, Z_t|X^{t-1}, Z^{t-1} : K_t \cdot K^{t-1})$ be the code-length for X_t and Z_t given X^{t-1},Z^{t-1}, and $K_t \cdot K^{t-1}$. Suppose that K_t is probabilistically determined by K^{t-1}. We write the code-length for K_t given K^{t-1} as $\ell(K_t|K^{t-1})$.

When a sequence X_t $(t = 1, \ldots, T)$ is given, we select an optimal sequence of models $Z^T = Z_1 \cdots Z_T$, $K^T = K_1 \cdots K_T$ so that the following criterion is minimum:

$$\sum_{t=1}^{T} \ell(X_t, Z_t|X^{t-1}, Z^{t-1} : K_t \cdot K^{t-1}) + \sum_{t=1}^{T} \ell(K_t|K^{t-1}), \quad (1)$$

where X_0, Z_0, and K_0 are initially given.

Eq.(1), which we call the DMS criterion, is the total code-length required for the encoding X^T, Z^T and K^T. Hence the process for the minimizing Eq.(1) with respect to Z^T and K^T is considered as a strategy based on the MDL principle. Note that the minimization of Eq.(1) is a batch process in the sense that Z^T and K^T must be determined in a retrospective way after the whole data X^T is observed. We are rather concerned with sequential estimation of the number of clusters K_t, i.e., every time X_t is observed, we are to choose an optimal value of K_t in a sequential fashion.

For the purpose of sequential estimation of Z_t and K_t, we approximate the minimum of Eq.(1) by locally minimizing it with respect to Z_t and K_t. That is, at each time t, letting $\hat{Z}^{t-1} = \hat{Z}_1 \cdots \hat{Z}_{t-1}$ and $\hat{K}^{t-1} = \hat{K}_1 \cdots \hat{K}_{t-1}$ be the sequence of cluster indices and the numbers of clusters obtained until $t-1$, respectively. We select an optimal model Z_t, K_t so that the following criterion is minimum:

$$\ell(X_t, Z_t|X^{t-1}, \hat{Z}^{t-1} : K_t \cdot \hat{K}^{t-1}) + \ell(K_t|\hat{K}^{t-1}). \quad (2)$$

We call this criterion the *sequential DMS criterion*. The sequential DMS algorithm is an algorithm that at each time t, takes X_t as input and outputs K_t and the resulting clustering result that minimize the criterion (2), and conducts this estimation sequentially with respect to t.

Let $\hat{Z}^T = \hat{Z}_1 \cdots \hat{Z}_T$ and $\hat{K}^T = \hat{K}_1 \cdots \hat{K}_T$ be the sequence of $\hat{Z}_t$ and $\hat{K}_t$ so that Eq.(2) is minimum at each t. Then the sum of the minimum value of Eq.(2) is given by

$$\sum_{t=1}^{T} \ell(X_t, \hat{Z}_t|X^{t-1}, \hat{Z}^{t-1} : \hat{K}_t \cdot \hat{K}^{t-1}) + \sum_{t=1}^{T} \ell(\hat{K}_t|\hat{K}^{t-1}). \quad (3)$$

This quantity is considered as an approximation of the minimum of Eq.(1) with respect to Z^T and K^T.

We employ a Gaussian mixture model (GMM) as a representation of a clustering structure. Let $f(X_t, Z_t|\theta)$ be a joint probability distribution of X_t and Z_t with parameter θ. Then the likelihood for X_t, Z_t is given as follows:

$$f(X_t, Z_t|\theta) = \prod_{j=1}^{K_t} \pi_j^{n_{tj}} \prod_{i:z_{it}=j} f(\mathbf{x}_{it}|\mu_j, \Sigma_j),$$

where we set $\theta = (\pi_j, \mu_j, \Sigma_j)$ $(j = 1, \ldots, K_t)$; π_j is the probability that $z = j$, μ_j is the mean of cluster $z = j$, and Σ_j is the variance-covariance matrix of cluster $z = j$. n_{tj} is the number of data in X_t which fall into the cluster $z = j$ $(j = 1, \ldots, K_t)$, and $f(\mathbf{x}_{it}|\mu_j, \Sigma_j)$ is a Gaussian distribution with mean μ_j and variance-covariance matrix Σ_j.

Let $\hat{\theta}(X_t, Z_t)$ be an estimator of θ from X_t and Z_t. Notice that we would like to employ the maximum likelihood estimator (MLE), but it is analytically intractable to compute it. Hence $\hat{\theta}$ may be obtained using the EM algorithm [3]. An initial value of θ in the EM algorithm is determined by $X^{t-1}, \hat{Z}^{t-1}$, and $\hat{K}^{t-1}$. We employ the renormalized maximum likelihood (RNML) code-length [6] for X_t and Z_t for the calculation of $\ell(X_t, Z_t|X^{t-1}, \hat{Z}^{t-1} : K_t \cdot \hat{K}^{t-1})$. It is defined as follows:

$$\ell_{\mathrm{RNML}}(X_t, Z_t|X^{t-1}, \hat{Z}^{t-1} : K_t \cdot \hat{K}^{t-1}; \gamma) = -\log \frac{f_{\mathrm{NML}}(X_t, Z_t; \hat{\eta}(X_t, Z_t), K_t)}{\sum_Z \int_{X \in Y'(\gamma)} f_{\mathrm{NML}}(X, Z; \hat{\eta}(X, Z), K_t) \mathrm{d}X}, \quad (4)$$

where f_{NML} is the NML distribution defined by

$$f_{\mathrm{NML}}(X_t, Z_t; \eta) = \frac{f(X_t, Z_t; \hat{\theta}(X_t, Z_t), K_t)}{\int_{X \in Y(\eta)} f(X, Z_t; \hat{\theta}(X, Z_t), K_t) \mathrm{d}X},$$

where γ is a hyper parameter, η is a parameter, and $Y(\eta)$ and $Y'(\gamma)$ denote the ranges of X for which the integrals are taken. See Sec.2.2 for details of the RNML code-length.

Below we give an algorithm for computing $\hat{\theta}(X_t, Z_t)$ and Z_t. For the sake of notational simplicity, we denote $\hat{\theta}(X_t, Z_t)$ as $\hat{\theta}^{(t)}$. Note that the number of possible changes of clustering is $O(K^n)$. Hence we restrict possible changes of the number of clusters into $\{-1, 0, 1\}$. In more details, we consider the following three cases:

Case 1: $K_t = K_{t-1}$; *the number of clusters does not change.* We set $Z_t = Z_{t-1}$ and estimate $\hat{\theta}^{(t)}$ by using the EM algorithm for which the initial values of θ are set to be $\hat{\theta}^{(t-1)}$.

Case 2: $K_t = K_{t-1} - 1$; *the number of clusters decreases.* First keep the cluster indices for data in $K_{t-1} - 1$ clusters and assign the data of $z_{it-1} = K_{t-1}$ $(i = 1, \ldots, n)$ to other clusters randomly. Then run the EM algorithm with the above indices as initial values to obtain new cluster indices Z_t.

Case 3: $K_t = K_{t-1} + 1$; *the number of clusters increases.* First keep the cluster indices for data in K_{t-1} clusters and generate indices $i_1, \ldots, i_m$ $(m < n)$ randomly and set $z_{jt} = K_{t-1} + 1$ $(j = i_1, \ldots, i_m)$. Then run the EM algorithm with the above indices as initial values of Z_t to obtain a new cluster indices Z_t.

Next we consider the probability of transition from K_{t-1} to K_t. Let α be a 1-dimensional parameter. Let $K_{\max}$ be the upper bound on K_t for any t. We set the model transition probability distribution as follows:

$$P(K_1|K_0 : \alpha) = 1/K_{\max},$$

$$P(K_t|K_{t-1} : \alpha) = \begin{cases} 1-\alpha, & \text{if } K_t = K_{t-1} \text{ and } K_{t-1} \neq 1, K_{\max}, \\ 1-\alpha/2, & \text{if } K_t = K_{t-1} \text{ and } K_{t-1} = 1, K_{\max} \\ \alpha/2, & \text{if } K_t = K_{t-1} \pm 1 \end{cases} \quad (5)$$

We set K_{max} from a practical reason why an optimal K should be computed in finite memories from all possible Ks. We do not simply input K_{max} for the number of clusters because we are concerned with selecting the minimal number of clusters from among those which explain the same clustering structures. Hence we require that any clusters to which no instance contributes do not exist.

Here α should be estimated. We employ Krichevsky-Trofimov (KT) estimate [9] of α defined by

$$\hat{\alpha}_t = (N_t + 1/2)/t, \quad (6)$$

where N_t shows how many times the number of clusters has changed until time $t-1$.

For a Gaussian mixture, a single Gaussian distribution corresponds to a cluster. The increase of mixture size means that new clusters emerge and some members whose latent variables z correspond to other existing clusters move to the new ones. It includes as a special case "splitting," which means that a single Gaussian distribution is replaced with two ones. The decrease of mixture size means that an existing cluster disappears and whose z correspond to that cluster move to others. It includes as a special case "merging," which means that two Gaussian distributions are no longer discriminated and are unified into a single one. Although the change of number of clusters is restricted to $\{-1, 0, +1\}$, it would easily be extended into the case where the number of changes ranges over $\{-M, ... -1, 0, +1, ..., +M\}$ for $M > 1$.

Once we have estimated the model transition probability, then we can compute the code-length for K_t given $\hat{K}^{t-1}$ by

$$\ell(K_t|\hat{K}^{t-1}) = -\log P(K_t|\hat{K}^{t-1} : \hat{\alpha}_t). \quad (7)$$

Plugging Eq.(4) and Eq.(7) into Eq.(2) yields the following form of the sequential DMS criterion:

$$\begin{aligned} & L(X_t, Z_t, K_t|X^{t-1}, \hat{Z}^{t-1}, \hat{K}^{t-1}) \\ = \ & \ell_{\mathrm{RNML}}(X_t, Z_t|X^{t-1}, \hat{Z}^{t-1} : K_t \cdot \hat{K}^{t-1}; \gamma) + \ell(K_t|\hat{K}^{t-1}) \\ = \ & -\log \frac{f_{\mathrm{NML}}(X_t, Z_t; \hat{\eta}(X_t, Z_t), K_t)}{\sum_Z \int_{X \in Y'(\gamma)} f_{\mathrm{NML}}(X, Z; \hat{\eta}(X, Z) K_t) \mathrm{d}X} \\ & - \log P(K_t|\hat{K}^{t-1}; \hat{\alpha}_t). \quad (8) \end{aligned}$$

The sequential DMS algorithm outputs K_t and Z_t that minimize (8) at each time t. It is given in Algorithm 1.

Algorithm 1 The sequential DMS algorithm

STEP 1. At time $t = 1$, compute $\hat{Z}_1$ and $\hat{K}_1$ from X_1.
STEP 2. At time $t = 2, \ldots,$, compute $\hat{Z}_t$ and $\hat{K}_t$ as follows:
for $t \in \{2, 3, \ldots\}$ **do**
  Consider the three cases of cluster changes: $\{-1, 0, +1\}$.
  if $K_t^0 = \hat{K}_{t-1}$ **then**
    · $Z_0 \leftarrow \hat{Z}_{t-1}$
    · Run the EM algorithm with Z_0 being initial values to obtain Z_t^0.
    · $L_{-1} \leftarrow L(X_t, Z_t^0, \hat{K}_{t-1}|X^{t-1}, \hat{Z}^{t-1}, \hat{K}^{t-1})$
  else if $K_t^{-1} = \hat{K}_{t-1} - 1$ **then**
    · $Z_0 \leftarrow \hat{Z}_{t-1}$
    · From Z_0, pick up all the data such that $z_{i0} = K_{t-1}$ $(i = 1, \ldots, n)$ and assign them to other clusters randomly.
    · Run the EM algorithm with Z_0 being initial values to obtain Z_t^{-1}.
    · $L_0 \leftarrow L(X_t, Z_t^{-1}, \hat{K}_{t-1} - 1|X^{t-1}, \hat{Z}^{t-1}, \hat{K}^{t-1})$
  else if $K_t^1 = \hat{K}_{t-1} + 1$ **then**
    · $Z_0 \leftarrow \hat{Z}_{t-1}$
    · Generate indices $i_1, \ldots, i_p$ $(p < n)$ randomly.
    · $z_{j0} \leftarrow \hat{K}_{t-1} + 1$ $(j = i_1, \ldots, i_p)$
    · Run the EM algorithm with Z_0 being initial values to obtain Z_t^1.
    · $L_1 \leftarrow L(X_t, Z_t^1, \hat{K}_{t-1} + 1|X^{t-1}, \hat{Z}^{t-1}, \hat{K}^{t-1})$
  end if
  Compute $\hat{Z}_t$ and $\hat{K}_t$–the values after the change as follows:
  · $change = \arg\min_c L_c$ $(c = -1, 0, 1)$
  · $\hat{Z}_t \leftarrow Z_t^{change}$
  · $\hat{K}_t \leftarrow K_t^{change}$
end for

2.2 Re-normalized Maximum Likelihood Code-length

Next, we show how to compute the RNML code-length (4) for a GMM as in the sequential DMS criterion (8).

Let $\mathbf{x}^n = (\mathbf{x}_1, \ldots, \mathbf{x}_n)$, $\mathbf{x}_i = (x_{i1}, \ldots, x_{im})^\top$ $(i = 1, \ldots, n)$ be a given sequence where $\mathbf{x}_i$ is distributed according to a Gaussian distribution with the mean $\mu \in \mathbb{R}^m$ and the variance-covariance matrix $\Sigma \in \mathbb{R}^{m \times m}$ for a some positive integer m with density:

$$f(\mathbf{x}; \mu, \Sigma) = \frac{1}{(2\pi)^{\frac{m}{2}} |\Sigma|^{\frac{1}{2}}} \exp\Big\{ -\frac{1}{2}(\mathbf{x} - \mu)^\top \Sigma^{-1} (\mathbf{x} - \mu) \Big\}.$$

The NML distribution for a Gaussian distribution is given by

$$f_{\mathrm{NML}}(\mathbf{x}^n) \stackrel{\mathrm{def}}{=} \frac{f(\mathbf{x}^n; \hat{\mu}(\mathbf{x}^n), \hat{\Sigma}(\mathbf{x}^n))}{\int f(\mathbf{y}^n; \hat{\mu}(\mathbf{y}^n), \hat{\Sigma}(\mathbf{y}^n)) \mathrm{d}\mathbf{y}^n}. \quad (9)$$

The reason why we employ this code-length is that it is optimal in the sense that it attains Shtarkov's minimax criterion [13]. Notice here that the normalization term in Eq.(9) diverges. According to [5], we restrict the range of data so that the MLE lies in a bounded range specified by a parameter. Then the NML distribution is given as follows:

$$f_{\mathrm{NML}}(\mathbf{x}^n; R, \lambda_{\min}) \stackrel{\mathrm{def}}{=} \frac{f(\mathbf{x}^n; \hat{\mu}(\mathbf{x}^n), \hat{\Sigma}(\mathbf{x}^n))}{\mathcal{C}(R, \lambda_{\min})},$$

where

$$\begin{aligned} \mathcal{C}(R, \lambda_{\min}) &= \int_{Y(R, \lambda_{\min})} f(\mathbf{y}^n; \hat{\mu}(\mathbf{y}^n), \hat{\Sigma}(\mathbf{y}^n)) \mathrm{d}\mathbf{y}^n, \\ Y(R, \lambda_{\min}) &\stackrel{\mathrm{def}}{=} \{\mathbf{y}^n | \ ||\hat{\mu}(\mathbf{y}^n)||^2 \leq R, \ \lambda_{\min}^{(j)} \leq \hat{\lambda}_j(\mathbf{y}^n) \\ & \qquad (j = 1, \ldots, m), \ \mathbf{y}^n \in \mathcal{X}^n\}, \quad (10) \end{aligned}$$

where R and $\lambda_{\min} = (\lambda_{\min}^{(1)}, \ldots, \lambda_{\min}^{(m)})$ are parameters, and $\hat{\lambda}_j(\mathbf{y}^n)$ is the j-th largest eigenvalue of $\hat{\Sigma}(\mathbf{y}^n)$. If we let R and $\lambda_{\min}$ bounded, then the normalization term is also bounded.

Note here that the normalization term depends on the choice of the parameters R and $\lambda_{\min}$. Next, we consider the optimization of the NML code-length with respect to R and $\lambda_{\min}$. The terms including R and $\lambda_{\min}$ in the NML code-length are given by:

$$\frac{m}{2} \log R - \frac{m}{2} \sum_{j=1}^{m} \log \lambda_{\min}^{(j)}.$$

Considering the range of parameters (10), the MLE of R and $\lambda_{\min}$ are given as follows:

$$\begin{aligned} \hat{R}(\mathbf{y}^n) &= ||\hat{\mu}(\mathbf{y}^n)||^2, \\ \hat{\lambda}_{\min}^{(j)}(\mathbf{y}^n) &= \hat{\lambda}_j(\mathbf{y}^n) \ (j = 1, \ldots, m). \end{aligned}$$

We then introduce the hyper parameters $\gamma = (\lambda_1, \lambda_2, R_1, R_2)$ and define the renormalized maximum likelihood (RNML) distribution by

$$f_{\mathrm{RNML}}(\mathbf{x}^n; \gamma) = \frac{f_{\mathrm{NML}}(\mathbf{x}^n; \hat{R}(\mathbf{x}^n), \hat{\lambda}_{\min}(\mathbf{x}^n))}{\mathcal{C}(\gamma)},$$

where the normalization term is expanded as follows:

$$\begin{aligned} \mathcal{C}(\gamma) &= \int_{Y'(\gamma)} f_{\mathrm{NML}}(\mathbf{y}^n; \hat{R}(\mathbf{y}^n), \hat{\lambda}_{\min}(\mathbf{y}^n)) \mathrm{d}\mathbf{y}^n, \\ Y'(\gamma) &= \{\mathbf{y}^n | \ V(\sqrt{R_1}) \leq V(\sqrt{\hat{R}(\mathbf{y}^n)}) \leq V(\sqrt{R_2}), \end{aligned}$$

$$\lambda_1 \leq \hat{\lambda}^{(j)}_{\min}(\mathbf{y}^n) \leq \lambda_2 \ (j=1,\ldots,m),\ \mathbf{y}^n \in \mathcal{X}^n\},$$

where $V(r) = 2\pi^{\frac{m}{2}} r^m/(m\Gamma(\frac{m}{2}))$, which denotes the volume of the m-dimensional ball with radius r.

Hirai and Yamanishi [6] proved that the RNML code-length for a GMM was further expanded as follows:

THEOREM 2.1. *[6] The RNML code-length of* $\mathbf{x}^n$ *relative to a GMM is expanded as follows:*

$$\ell_{\mathrm{RNML}}(\mathbf{x}^n, z^n; \gamma, K) = -\log f(\mathbf{x}^n, z^n; K, \hat{\mu}(\mathbf{x}^n, z^n), \hat{\Sigma}(\mathbf{x}^n, z^n)) + \log \mathcal{C}_1(K,n) + \log \mathcal{C}_2(K,n) + \log B(\mathbf{x}^n, z^n) + K \log I(m,\gamma), \quad (11)$$

where

$$\mathcal{C}_1(K,n) = \sum_{h_1+\cdots+h_K=n} \frac{n!}{h_1!\cdots h_K!} \prod_{k=1}^{K} \left(\frac{h_k}{n}\right)^{h_k}, \quad (12)$$

$$\mathcal{C}_2(K,n) = \sum_{h_1+\cdots+h_K=n} \frac{n!}{h_1!\cdots h_K!} \prod_{k=1}^{K} \left(\frac{h_k}{n}\right)^{h_k} \cdot J(h_k), \quad (13)$$

$$B(\mathbf{x}^n, z^n) = \prod_{p=1}^{K} \frac{2^{m+1} \cdot ||\hat{\mu}_p(\mathbf{x}^n, z^n)||^m \cdot |\hat{\Sigma}_p(\mathbf{x}^n, z^n)|^{-\frac{m}{2}}}{m^{m+1}\Gamma(\frac{m}{2})},$$

$$I(m,\gamma) = \mathcal{C}(\gamma) = \left(\frac{m}{2}\right)^{m+1} \cdot \log \frac{R_2}{R_1} \cdot \left(\log \frac{\lambda_2}{\lambda_1}\right)^m,$$

$$J(h_k) = \left(\frac{h_k}{2e}\right)^{mh_k} \cdot \frac{1}{\Gamma_m(\frac{h_k - 1}{2})}. \quad (14)$$

Here h_k *denotes the number of data belonging to the* k*-th cluster, and* $\hat{\mu}_p$ *and* $\hat{\Sigma}_p$ *denote the MLE of the mean and the variance-covariance matrix of the* p*-th cluster.*

Note that a straightforward computation of $\mathcal{C}_1(K,n)$ and $\mathcal{C}_2(K,n)$ as in Eq.(12) and Eq.(13) requires $O(n^K)$ time. Below we give methods for efficient computation of $\mathcal{C}_1(K,n)$ and $\mathcal{C}_2(K,n)$. As for the computation of $\mathcal{C}_1(K,n)$, Kontkanen and Myllymäki [7] proved the following theorem:

THEOREM 2.2. *[7]* $\mathcal{C}_1(K,n)$ *satisfies the following recursive formula:*

$$\mathcal{C}_1(K+2,n) = \mathcal{C}_1(K+1,n) + \frac{n}{K}\mathcal{C}_1(K,n).$$

Hence $\mathcal{C}_1(K,n)$ *is computed in* $O(n+K)$ *time.*

As for the computation of $\mathcal{C}_2(K,n)$, Hirai and Yamanishi [6] gave the following result:

THEOREM 2.3. *[6]* $\mathcal{C}_2(K,n)$ *satisfies the following recursive formula:*

$$\mathcal{C}_2(K+1,n) = \sum_{r_1+r_2=n} {}_nC_{r_1} \left(\frac{r_1}{n}\right)^{r_1} \left(\frac{r_2}{n}\right)^{r_2} \mathcal{C}_2(K,r_1)J(r_2),$$

where $J(r_2)$ *is as in Eq.(14). Hence* $\mathcal{C}_2(K,n)$ *is computed in* $O(n^2K)$ *time.*

Combining all of the theorems as above, the RNML code-length of $\mathbf{x}^n$ relative to a GMM is computed in $O(n^2K)$ time. We employ Eq.(11) as the RNML code-length in Eq.(8).

3. EXPERIMENTAL RESULTS

We give results on empirical comparison of the sequential DMS algorithm with other methods using artificial data sets.

3.1 Comparison Methods

First we consider variants of the sequential DMS algorithm in which the RNML code-length, Schwarz's Bayesian information criterion (BIC) [12], and Akaike's information criterion (AIC) [1] are employed as criteria for selecting the optimal number of clusters, which we call these methods RNML, BIC, and AIC, respectively.

For the RNML code-length, the sequential DMS criterion is given by Eq.(8). If the RNML code-length is replaced with BIC, the sequential DMS criterion is given as follows:

$$L_{\mathrm{BIC}}(X_t, Z_t, K_t | X^{t-1}, \hat{Z}^{t-1}, \hat{K}^{t-1}) = -\log f(X_t, Z_t; \hat{\theta}(X_t, Z_t), K_t) + \frac{1}{2}K_t \log n + \frac{m(m+3)K_t}{4} \sum_{k=1}^{K_t} \log h_k - \log P(K_t | \hat{K}^{t-1}),$$

where m is the dimension of each data. If the RNML code-length is replaced with AIC, the sequential DMS criterion is given as follows:

$$AIC(X_t, Z_t, K_t | X^{t-1}, \hat{Z}^{t-1}, \hat{K}^{t-1}) = -\log f(X_t, Z_t; \hat{\theta}(X_t, Z_t), K_t) + \frac{1}{2}m(m+3)K + \frac{1}{2}K,$$

where the code-length for a model change is not added to AIC because AIC has no interpretation of a code-length. All of RNML, AIC, and BIC are obtained by changing criteria in Algorithm 1. We compared these algorithms.

We introduce three criteria to evaluate the algorithms

1. **AR** (accuracy rate): It is defined as the average rate of correctly estimating the true number of clusters over all time where the average is taken over all 100 trials. See Figure 3.2 for the illustration of the estimation of the number of clusters.
2. **IR** (identification rate): It is defined as the probability of correctly estimating the locations of change-points and the number of clusters before and after change-points over all 100 trials.
3. **FAR** (false alarm rate): It is defined as the rate of the number of false alarms over all detected change-points where the average is taken over all 100 trials.

3.2 Comparison of Criteria

We prepared two artificial data sets to compare RNML, AIC, and BIC in terms of the three indices as above.

3.2.1 Data Set 1

We generated Data Set 1 so that the number of clusters changed as follows:

$$K_t = \begin{cases} 3 & \text{if } 1 \leq t \leq 50, \\ 4 & \text{if } 51 \leq t \leq 100. \end{cases}$$

Algorithm 2 is the one which generated this data set. It created a new cluster at time 51.

For this data set, we conducted experiments 100 times by taking 100 different initial values. Figure 3.1 shows the average numbers of clusters and standard deviation per time for RNML, AIC, and BIC. Figure 3.2 shows **AR**s for RNML, AIC, and BIC. We observe that RNML was able to track changes of the number of clusters in a more stable way than AIC and BIC. Figure 3.3 shows **AR**s, **IR**s, and **FAR**s for RNML, AIC, and BIC. We observe that RNML was able to detect true change-points, and achieved significantly higher **AR** and **IR** and significantly less **FAR** than AIC and BIC.

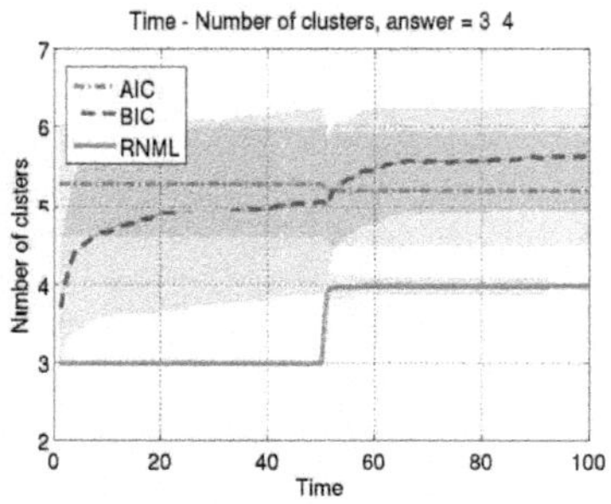

Figure 3.1: Data Set 1: Average Number of Clusters Over Time

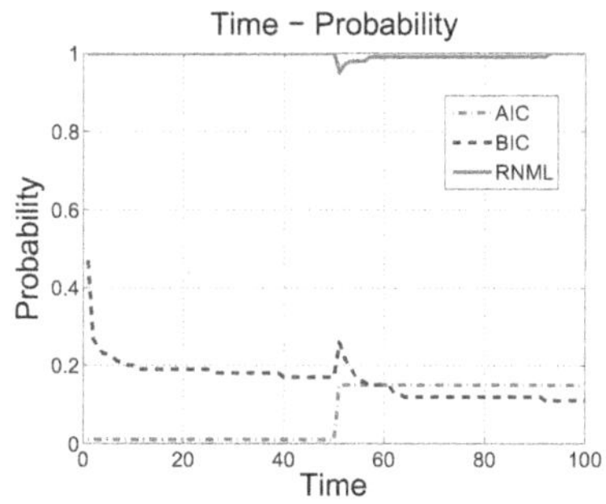

Figure 3.2: Data Set 1: Accuracy Rate Over Time

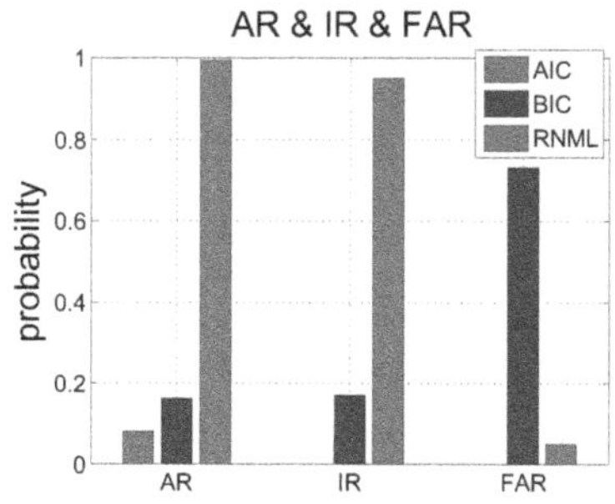

Figure 3.3: Data Set 1: AR, IR, FAR

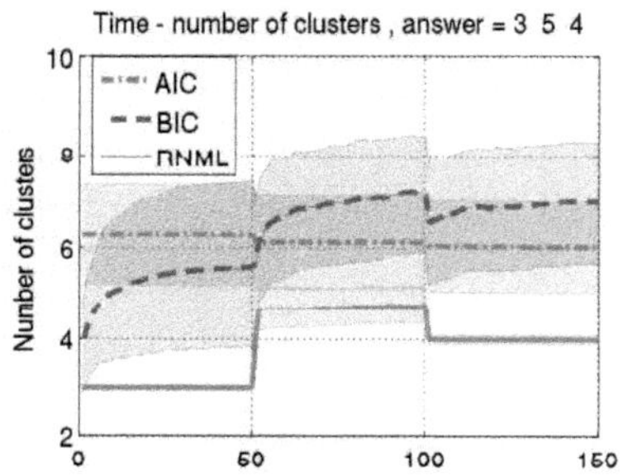

Figure 3.4: Data Set 2: Average Number of Clusters Over Time

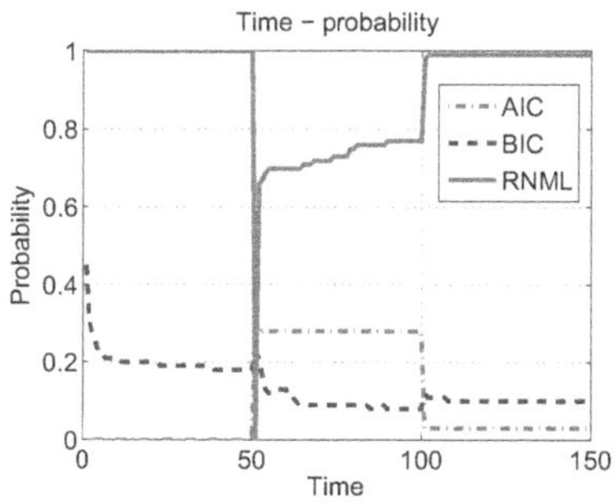

Figure 3.5: Data Set 2: Accuracy Rate Over Time

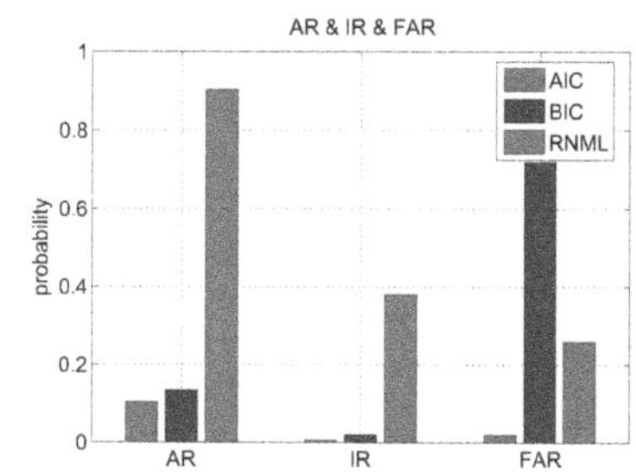

Figure 3.6: Data Set 2: AR, IR, FAR

Algorithm 2 Data Generation Algorithm

STEP 1. At time $t = 1$, generate X_1, Z_1.

STEP 2. At time $t = 2, \ldots, t_1 - 1$, $X_t \leftarrow X_1 + \epsilon, Z_t \leftarrow Z_1$. Here $\epsilon \sim \mathcal{N}(0, \sigma^2 I)$ and I is an identity matrix.

STEP 3. At change-points $t_1, \ldots, t_c$, generate data as follows:

```
for j = 2 to c do
  if K_j = K_{j-1} + 1 then
    at time t_j, choose N_+ data randomly, and assign them
    to a new cluster K_j.
    for t = t_j + 1 to t_{j+1} - 1 do
      X_t <- X_{t_j} + ε
      Z_t <- Z_{t_j}
    end for
  else if K_j = K_{j-1} - 1 then
    at time t_j, choose data belonging to the cluster K_j,
    and assign them to other clusters randomly.
    for t = t_j + 1 to t_{j+1} - 1 do
      X_t <- X_{t_j} + ε
      Z_t <- Z_{t_j}
    end for
  end if
end for
```

3.2.2 Data Set 2

We generated Data Set 2 so that the number of clusters changed as follows:

$$K_t = \begin{cases} 3 & \text{if } 1 \le t \le 50, \\ 5 & \text{if } 51 \le t \le 100, \\ 4 & \text{if } 101 \le t \le 150, \end{cases}$$

This data set was also generated by Algorithm 2. It created 2 new clusters at time 51 (the number of clusters increased from 3 to 5 at time $t = 51$ and an existing cluster disappeared at time 101).

Figures 3.4, 3.5, and 3.6 show the changes of the detected number of clusters and standard deviation, **AR**s per time, and **AR**s, **IR**s, and **FAR**s for RNML, AIC, and BIC.

We observe that RNML was able to identify the true numbers of clusters with higher probability and was able to detect change-points with significantly higher accuracy than AIC and BIC. Meanwhile, as the number of changes increased, the accuracy rates for BIC gradually decreased.

Note that RNML is designed assuming that the number of clusters changes by $\{-1, 0, +1\}$ from time t to $t+1$. We see from Figure 3.4 and 3.5 that even when the number of clusters changes by more than 1, say, 2 from time t to $t+1$, RNML was able to detect the changes step by step within an interval of $[t, t+c]$ for some small c ($c = 2$ in this experiment) for more than 66% data sets.

3.2.3 Comparison with respect to KL-divergence

We evaluated change detection accuracies for RNML, AIC and BIC by varying the Kullback-Leibler divergence (KLD) between the distributions before and after a change point. In general, the larger the KLD is, the more accurately change-points can be detected. We investigated how the detection accuracies varied as the KL-divergence varied. We generated Data Set 3 so that the number of clusters changed as follows:

$$K_t = \begin{cases} 3 & \text{if } 1 \le t \le 50, \\ 4 & \text{if } 51 \le t \le 100. \end{cases}$$

This data set was also generated by Algorithm 2. It created a new cluster at time 51, for which we took various mean values μ_{new}. The KLD between the GMMs before and after a change point was not strictly calculated. Hence we approximated it by the following formula:

$$KLD(f||g) = \sum_a \pi_a \log \frac{\sum_{a'} \pi_{a'} \exp(-D(f_a||f_{a'}))}{\sum_b \omega_b \exp(-D(f_a||g_b))}.$$

It is known from [4] that it gives a tight lower bound on the KLD between GMMs. Here f and g denote GMMs, f_a and g_b denote Gaussian components with indices a and b in f and g, and $D(f_a||g_b)$ denotes the KLD between f_a and g_b.

Figures 3.7–3.9 show **AR**s, **IR**s, and **FAR**s against the KLD, respectively. One plot corresponds to **AR** or **IR** or **FAR** for one mean value μ_{new} of a new cluster.

We observe that RNML was able to detect change-points with significantly higher accuracy than AIC/BIC in almost all plots. We further see that the larger the KLD between GMMs before and after the change-point was, the more accurately it was detected in terms of **AR**, **IR**, and **FAR**. This tendency turned out most clearly in RNML.

3.3 Comparison with Song and Wang's Alg.

We employ Song and Wang's algorithm [14], which we abbreviate as SW, for the comparison with our proposed method. SW is a hypothesis testing based algorithm, which is a different approach to clustering change detection from ours. Below we give its brief sketch. It first employs a GMM to conduct clustering of a newly input data, then makes statistical tests to determine whether the new cluster is identical to an old one or not. If it is, the new cluster is merged into the older one, otherwise it is recognized as a cluster which has newly emerged. SW is shown in Algorithm 3.

Algorithm 3 Algorithm: SW [14]

INPUT $g^N(x)$: a GMM at the latest time, $\mathbf{x}_{N+1}, \ldots, \mathbf{x}_{N+M}$: a newly input data sequence. Here N: data size at the latest time, M: data size of newly input data.
OUTPUT $g^{N+M}(x)$: a GMM.
Generate a GMM $a(x)$ from $\mathbf{x}_{N+1}, \ldots, \mathbf{x}_{N+M}$ where the mixture size K_a is determined by BIC.
for component k in $a(x)$ **do**
  for component j in $g^N(x)$ **do**
    Make a statistical test to determine whether Σ_k is identical to Σ_j.
    If $\Sigma_k = \Sigma_j$, make a statistical test to determine whether μ_k is identical to μ_j or not.
  end for
end for
Compare $g^N(x)$ with $a(x)$ to check if both of the mean and the variance-covariance matrix of one component in $g^N(x)$ are identical to those of another component in $a(x)$.
If they are identical, then merge a new cluster into the older one, and let the merged component be a component of $g^{N+M}(x)$.
Any component that is not merged into any old component be added into $g^{N+M}(x)$ as a new component.
Output a new GMM $g^{N+M}(x)$.

See [14] for the details of statistical tests for fitness of the means and the variance-covariance matrices.

It is assumed in SW that a set of data is newly input every time. In order to meet this setting, we conducted experiments by setting M to be $128, 256, 512, 1024$ in order. In SW the number of clusters is determined on the basis of BIC [12]. Hence we also consider a variant of SW such that BIC is replaced with the RNML criterion for the number of clusters selection criterion.

In summary, we compare the following three algorithms:

1. *Proposed* : Our proposed algorithm.
2. *SW-RNML* : A statistical-test based algorithm using on-line estimation of GMM with the RNML criterion (a variant of SW).
3. *SW-BIC* : A statistical-test based algorithm using on-line estimation of GMM with BIC (original SW).

For comparison, we used the performance indices: **AR**, **IR**, and **FAR**. Tables 3.1–3.3 show results for the three algorithms. Red numerical values indicate the winners.

We observe that our proposed algorithm was the winner in terms of all the indices: **AR**, **IR**, and **FAR** and that it significantly outperformed SW-BIC and SW-RNML. Comparing SW-BIC with SW-RNML, we see that the latter performed significantly better than the former in terms of **AR** and **IR**, while they were comparable in terms of **FAR** when the data size was small. In general, all of the indices for SW-BIC and SW-RNML got better as the data size increased. Meanwhile, our proposed algorithm performed well without depending on the data size so much.

4. MARKET ANALYSIS APPLICATION

4.1 Transaction Data Set

We present an application of clustering change detection to market analysis. The experiment was conducted in corporation with HAKUHODO, Inc. We employed a real data set provided by MACROMILL, Inc. It is specified as follows:

1. *Period* : November 1st 2010 to January 1st 2011.
2. *Number of customers* : 3185 customers.
3. *Data specification* : The data set consists of a number of customers' beer purchase transactions. Each customer's record is specified by a 14-dimensional feature vector, each component of which shows consumption for a certain beer. Brands of beer includes: {Beer-A, Beer-B, Premium-A, Premium-B, Beer-C, Beer-D, Third-A, Third-B, Third-C, Third-D, LM-Beer-A, Off-A, Off-B, Off-C}. Premium-A, B are brands of relatively expensive beer. Third-A,B,C,D are brands of what we call the "third kind" of beer, i.e., beer-taste alcoholic drink. Off-A,B,C are brands of what we call "calorie off" type of beer. LM-Beer-A are beer-type alcoholic drink with relatively low rate of barley.

We constructed a sequence of customers' feature vectors as follows: A time unit is a day. At each time (day) t ($= \tau, \ldots, T$), we denote the feature vector of the i-th customer as $\mathbf{x}_{it} = (x_{it,1}, \ldots, x_{it,d}) \in \mathbb{R}^d$ where $d = 14$. Each $\mathbf{x}_{it,j}$ is the i-th customer's consumption of the j-th brand beer from time $t - \tau + 1$ to t. We denote the set of data at time t as $X_t = (\mathbf{x}_{1t}, \ldots, \mathbf{x}_{n_t t})$, where n_t is the number of customers who purchased the products from time $t - \tau + 1$ to t.

4.2 Market Analysis

We evaluated the clustering change detection algorithms for this data set. Figures 4.1–4.3, and Tables 4.1–4.3 show the results at $\tau = 14$. Numerical values in Tables 4.1 and 4.2 show the average values of consumption where the average is

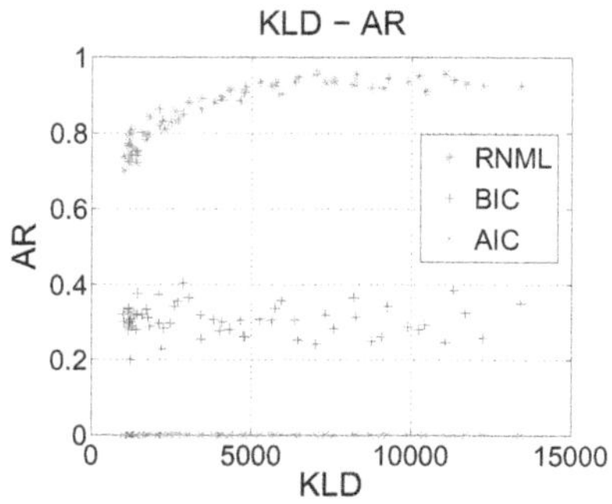

Figure 3.7: AR w.r.t. KLD

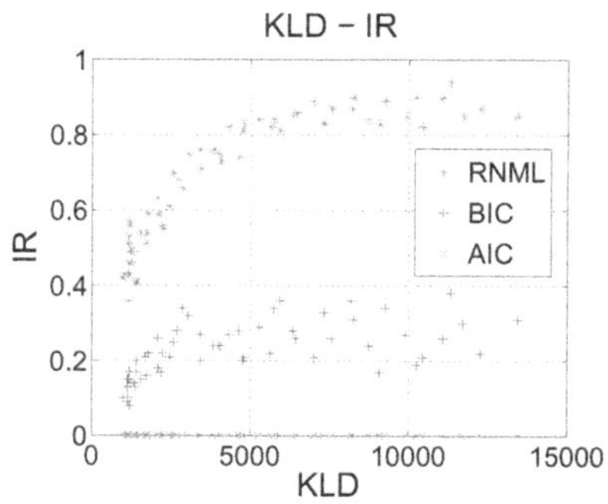

Figure 3.8: IR w.r.t. KLD

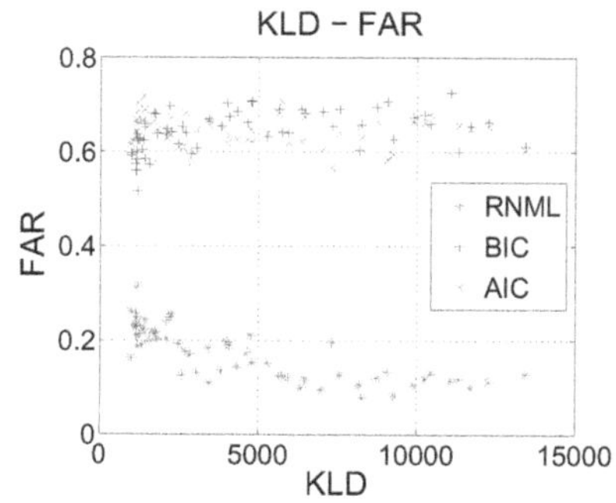

Figure 3.9: FAR w.r.t. KLD

Table 3.1: AR with Various Sample Size in Each Time

Algo. \ M	128	256	512	1024
Proposed	0.972	0.997	0.988	0.975
SW-RNML	0.027	0.238	0.369	0.750
SW-BIC	0.005	0.009	0.019	0.125

Table 3.2: IR with Various Sample Size in Each Time

Algo. \ M	128	256	512	1024
Proposed	1.000	1.000	0.950	0.950
SW-RNML	0.000	0.100	0.300	0.700
SW-BIC	0.000	0.000	0.000	0.050

Table 3.3: FAR with Various Sample Size in Each Time

Algo. \ M	128	256	512	1024
Proposed	0.158	0.025	0.050	0.000
SW-RNML	0.944	0.644	0.503	0.208
SW-BIC	0.964	0.930	0.841	0.550

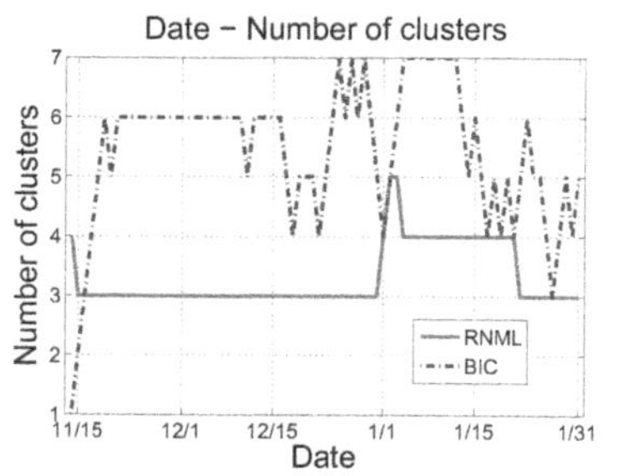

Figure 4.1: Changes of # of Clusters for RNML vs BIC

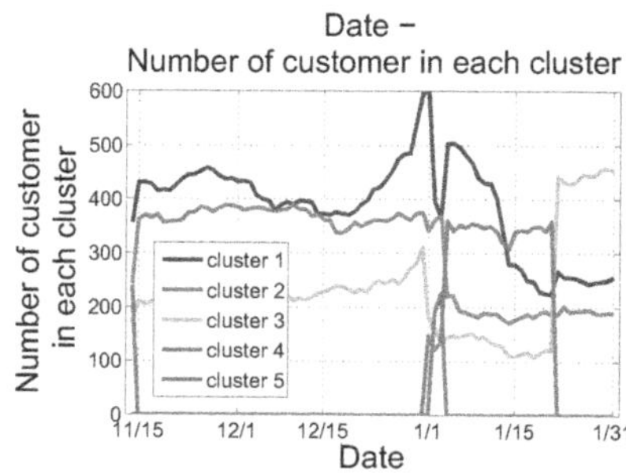

Figure 4.2: Changes of # of Customers within Individual Clusters

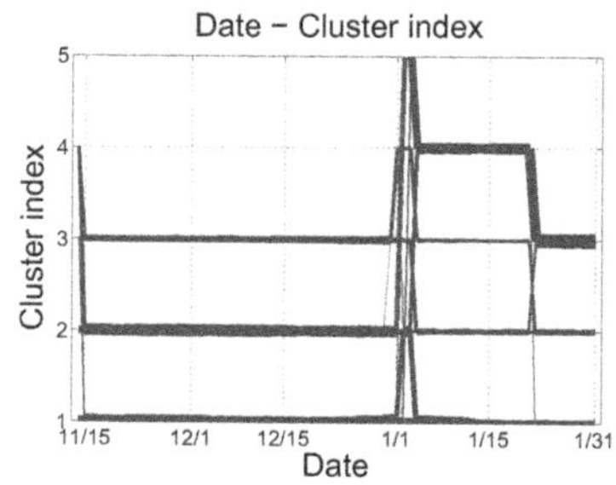

Figure 4.3: Changes of # of Customers among Clusters

taken over all customers within an individual cluster. Figure 4.1 shows the changes of the number of clusters per a day starting from Nov.14th, 2010.

We first compared our proposed algorithm, the sequential DMS with the RNML criterion, with that using BIC. Figure 4.1 shows the results of change detection from Nov. 14th on 2010 to Jan. 31st 2011. We see from Figure 4.1 that the sequential DMS with RNML was able to detect clustering changes that corresponded to the emergence and disappearance of the year's ending demand. Meanwhile, the sequential DMS with BIC detected much more change-points. They included those which were not necessarily related to the year's ending demand. It was so sensitive to irregularities of data that it produced too many change-points. Here is a list of other figures showing the results.

- Figure 4.2: It shows how the number of customers changed over time for individual clusters.
- Figure 4.3: It shows how many customers moved from clusters to clusters. The bolder the line is, the more customers moved. We skipped drawing for the movement of customers when they were not more than 20.

The DMS with RNML detected four change points: Nov. 15th 2010, Jan. 1st 2011, Jan. 2nd 2011, Jan. 4th, and Jan. 22nd 2011. For example, as for the clustering change from Dec. 31st 2010 to Jan. 2nd 2011, Table 4.1 shows the average values of consumption for each beer within individual clusters before the change, while Table 4.2 shows those after the change. In Tables 4.1 and 4.2, $c_1, c_2, \ldots$ denote cluster 1, cluster 2, ..., respectively.

Table 4.3 shows how customers moved from clusters to clusters from Dec. 31st 2010 to Jan. 2nd 2011. In Table 4.3, each row shows a cluster on Dec. 31st 2010 while each column shows a cluster on Jan. 2nd 2011. For example, it is shown that 139 customers moved from the old cluster 1 on Dec. 31st 2010 to the new cluster 5 on Jan. 1st 2011.

We see from Tables 4.1–4.3 that most of customers belonging to the old cluster 3, which had the largest consumption on Dec. 31st, moved into the new clusters 3 and 4.

The cluster 5 newly emerged on Jan. 1st. This cluster had large consumption for Beer A and Third Beer. Most of customers belonging to this cluster came from the old clusters 1 and 2, where the customers belonging to the old cluster 1 had relatively large consumption of Beer(A,B) and Premium-beer(A,B) while the customers belonging to the old cluster 2 had relatively large consumption of other types of beer (Third Beer, LM-Beer, Off-Beer). We see that many of customers belonging to the old clusters 1 and 2 changed their patterns to purchase Beer A and Third Beer at the years' end. Through this analysis, it has turned out that the clustering change detection leads to the understanding of how customer groups changed and how customers moved from clusters to clusters. It was validated by domain experts.

Table 4.1: Clustering Structure on Dec. 31st

Cluster	c 1	c 2	c 3
Beer-A	184	0	117
Beer-B	91	0	95
Premium-A	108	0	80
Premium-B	113	0	43
Beer-C	0	0	126
Beer-D	0	0	140
Third-A	93	41	43
Third-B	0	198	121
Third-C	0	303	103
Third-D	0	120	182
LM Beer-A	0	75	48
Off-A	0	0	157
Off-B	0	114	34
Off-C	0	0	83
Total Volume	589	852	1373
# Customers	598	376	311

Table 4.2: Clustering Structure on Jan. 1st

Cluster	c 1	c 2	c 3	c 4	c 5
Beer-A	84	0	50	131	229
Beer-B	123	0	0	248	0
Premium-A	153	0	73	174	0
Premium-B	176	0	0	105	0
Beer-C	0	0	122	146	0
Beer-D	0	0	192	72	0
Third-A	101	131	0	130	0
Third-B	0	34	0	406	131
Third-C	0	107	46	112	236
Third-D	0	202	0	431	0
LM-Beer A	0	107	0	87	0
Off-A	0	0	138	169	0
Off-B	0	215	0	74	0
Off-C	0	0	83	61	0
Total Volume	637	796	705	2348	596
# Customers	397	190	162	123	363

5. CONCLUDING REMARKS

We have considered the clustering change detection issue. In it we have proposed the sequential DMS algorithm that sequentially tracks changes of clustering structures. The key ideas of the algorithm are; 1) extending DMS (dynamic model selection) into a sequential clustering scenario, and 2) the use of the RNML (renormalized maximum likelihood) code-length in the DMS criterion. The proposed algorithm enables us to deal with merging, splitting, emergence, disappearance, etc. of clusters from a unifying view of the MDL principle. We have empirically demonstrated using artificial data sets that our algorithm is able to detect cluster changes much more accurately than AIC/BIC-based methods and the existing statistical-test based method. We have used real customers' transaction data sets to demonstrate the validity of our algorithm in market analysis.

Acknowledgements

This work was partially supported by MEXT KAKENHI 23240019, Aihara Project, the FIRST program from JSPS, initiated by CSTP, HAKUHODO Inc., MACROMILL, Inc., NTT Corporation, and Microsoft Corporation(CORE6 Project).

Table 4.3: Movement of Customers from Dec. 31st to Jan.1st

cluster	no	c 1	c 2	c 3	c 4	c 5
no purchase	0	22	8	13	3	29
c 1	61	355	26	9	8	139
c 2	45	4	152	1	8	166
c 3	19	16	4	139	104	29

6. REFERENCES

[1] H. Akaike. A new look at the statistical model identification. *IEEE Trans. on Automatic Control*, 19(6):716–723, Dec. 1974.

[2] D.Chakrabrti, R.Kumar. Evolutionary clustering. *Proc.KDD06*, pp:554-560. 2006.

[3] A. P. Dempster, N. M. Laird, and D. B. Rubin. Maximum likelihood from incomplete data via the em. *J. Royal Staitst. Soc. B*, 39:1–38, 1977.

[4] J. Hershey and P. Olsem. Approximating the kullback Leibler divergence between Gaussian mixture models. *Proc. of ICASSP*, 4:317–320, 2007.

[5] S. Hirai and K. Yamanishi. Efficient computation of normalized maximum likelihood coding for Gaussian mixtures with its applications to optimal clustering. *Proc. of IEEE ISIT*, pp.1031–1035, 2011.

[6] S. Hirai and K. Yamanishi. Normalized maximum likelihood coding for exponential family with its applications to optimal clustering. *arXiv:1205.3549*, 2012.

[7] P. Kontkanen and P. Myllymäki. A linear time algorithm for computing the multinomial stochastic complexity. *Inf. Proc. Letters*, 103:227–233, 2007.

[8] Z. G. Krempl and M.Spiliopoulou. Online clustering of high-dimensional trajectories under concept drift. *Proc. ECML-PKDD2011, Part II*, pp. 261–276, 2011.

[9] R. E. Krichevsky and V. K. Trofimov. The performance of universal encoding. *IEEE Trans. Inf. Theory*, 27:199–207, 1981.

[10] J. Rissanen. *Stochastic Complexity in Statistical Inquiries*. World Scientific, 1989.

[11] M. Sato. Online model selection based on the variational bayes. *NC*, 13:1649–1681, 2001.

[12] G. Schwarz. Estimating the dimension of a model. *Annals of Statistics 6 (2)*, pp. 461–464, 1978.

[13] Y. M. Shtarkov. Universal sequential coding of single messages. *Problems of Information Transmission*, 23(3):3–17, 1987.

[14] M. Song and H. Wang. Highly efficient incremental estimation of Gaussian mixture models for online data stream clustering. *Intelligent Computing: Theory and Application*, 2005.

[15] J. Sun, S. Papadimitriou, P. S. Yu, and C. Faloutsos. Graphscope: Parameter-free mining of large time evolving graphs. *Proc. KDD07*, pp: 687–696, 2007.

[16] K. Yamanishi and Y. Maruyama. Dynamic syslog mining for network failure monitoring. *Proc. of KDD2005*, 499–508, 2005.

[17] K. Yamanishi and Y. Maruyama. Dynamic model selection with its applications to novelty detection. *IEEE Trans. on Inf. Theory*, 53(6):2180–2189, 2007.

Subspace Correlation Clustering: Finding Locally Correlated Dimensions in Subspace Projections of the Data

Stephan Günnemann, Ines Färber, Kittipat Virochsiri, and Thomas Seidl
RWTH Aachen University, Germany
{guennemann, faerber, virochsiri, seidl}@cs.rwth-aachen.de

ABSTRACT

The necessity to analyze subspace projections of complex data is a well-known fact in the clustering community. While the full space may be obfuscated by overlapping patterns and irrelevant dimensions, only certain subspaces are able to reveal the clustering structure. Subspace clustering discards irrelevant dimensions and allows objects to belong to multiple, overlapping clusters due to individual subspace projections for each set of objects. As we will demonstrate, the observations, which originate the need to consider subspace projections for traditional clustering, also apply for the task of correlation analysis.

In this work, we introduce the novel paradigm of subspace correlation clustering: we analyze *subspace projections* to find *subsets of objects* showing *linear correlations* among this subset of dimensions. In contrast to existing techniques, which determine correlations based on the full-space, our method is able to exclude locally irrelevant dimensions, enabling more precise detection of the correlated features. Since we analyze subspace projections, each object can contribute to several correlations. Our model allows multiple overlapping clusters in general but simultaneously avoids redundant clusters deducible from already known correlations. We introduce the algorithm SSCC that exploits different pruning techniques to efficiently generate a subspace correlation clustering. In thorough experiments we demonstrate the strength of our novel paradigm in comparison to existing methods.

Categories and Subject Descriptors: H.2.8 Database management: Database applications [Data mining]

Keywords: linear correlations, overlapping clusters

1. INTRODUCTION

The goal of correlation clustering[1] is to identify groups of objects that exhibit dependencies between the features of the dataset. Considering correlations, the attribute values in one dimension depend on the attribute values of other dimensions. In contrast to clustering, the objects do not have to be closely located together but should describe the same regression, e.g., they are located near the same line or plane.

[1]Not to be confused with the term as used in the machine learning community, which refers to a different task [9].

KDD'12, August 12–16, 2012, Beijing, China.

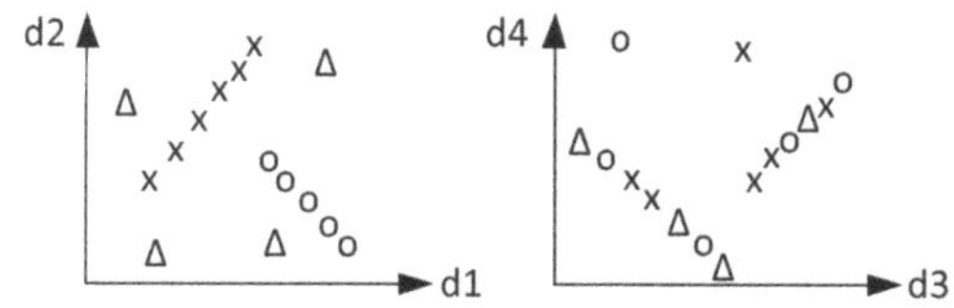

Fig. 1: 4-d database with 15 objects and 4 subspace correlation clusters

Knowing about the dependencies of attributes provides a motive to reason about causalities and is advantageous for, e.g., trend analysis, decision strategies, and prediction.

Mistakenly, in the literature correlation clustering is characterized as generalized subspace clustering [16]. Contrarily, we show in the following how traditional correlation clustering falls short of the fundamental observations and assumptions which originated the research field of subspace clustering and that the actual transfer of the correlation principles towards subspace clustering still needs to be done.

It have been two crucial observations that led the subspace clustering community to the conclusion that solely considering the full-space might deny access to a meaningful clustering structure of the data. First, for high-dimensional data, objects do not necessarily show cohesion regarding all attributes but only w.r.t. a subset of attributes. As each cluster can have its individual set of relevant attributes, global dimensionality reduction does not do the trick. Second, if objects are clustered based on differing characteristics, they can easily belong to multiple clusters when considering different views, i.e., attribute subsets of the data. Given a multitude of overlapping clusters in different subspaces, an immediate consequence is that the clustering structure might be totally obscured in the full-space [10]. This is the key challenge to be solved by subspace clustering and multi-view clustering [18, 16], where clusters highly overlap and multiple partitionings in different views can be determined. Both aspects, the obfuscation of clusters in the full-space and highly overlapping clusters, are not considered by existing correlation clustering methods. Nonetheless, these observations do also hold for correlation clustering as Fig. 1 illustrates. By considering the 2-dim. subspace $\{d1, d2\}$ in Fig. 1, two different (local) correlations can be detected: The objects denoted by a cross are positively correlated on a line, while the objects denoted by a circle are negatively correlated on a different line[2]. Considering the subspace $\{d3, d4\}$, different correlations supported by different sets of objects can be detected. Thus, observable correlations might be fulfilled only for a subset of objects and

[2]Of course our paradigm is not restricted to lines but also detects linear correlations with higher degrees of freedom.

a subset of attributes and also objects might contribute to several correlations of different attributes.

Why do we highlight this problem? One might argue that *given* an appropriate set of objects, correlation clustering can easily determine the subset of correlated dimensions and excludes the irrelevant dimensions by a post-processing. The crux, however, is to *find* the 'appropriate' set of objects in the first place. If patterns are hidden in subspace projections of the data this is an almost impossible task for approaches operating in the full-space. Since correlation clustering analyses the full-space, noisy dimensions and overlapping clusters will obfuscate the local correlations of objects leading to nearly arbitrary groupings in the full-space (similar to traditional full-space clustering). In Fig. 1 it is very unlikely to find a group of objects in the full-space that corresponds to a strong correlation in a subspace. If, however, already wrong sets of objects have been clustered, determining the true subset of correlated dimensions in a post-processing is almost impossible. Thus, correlation clustering will not just miss some clusters, but the resulting clusters are highly questionable as for the traditional full-space clustering approaches.

A novel mining paradigm. In this paper, we show that the observations made for (subspace) clustering also have to be transferred to the task of correlation analysis and we introduce the *novel paradigm of subspace correlation clustering*: First, correlations between dimensions can be restricted to subspace projections, i.e., not the whole set of dimensions is correlated. Second, correlations can be hidden in local and possibly overlapping patterns, i.e., only subsets of the objects may be correlated and objects may contribute to several correlations. With our paradigm we detect locally correlated dimensions in subspace projections. This enables to find more precise local patterns and unfolds the potential of correlation clustering also for higher dimensional datasets.

Challenges for subspace correlation clustering. By analyzing subspace projections, we inherit two crucial challenges of traditional subspace clustering. The first one arises from the exponential number of subspaces to be analyzed. Obviously, a naive exploration of all possible projections is not recommendable. Therefore, we present an efficient algorithm that uses already acquired information to apply pruning strategies. The second challenge is originated by allowing each object to contribute to several correlations. While overlapping clusters are beneficial for detecting multiple patterns in the data, analyzing each subspace projection and simply reporting any pattern, results in highly redundant information. For example a line detected in subspace S is also a line in any of its projections $S' \subseteq S$ (with $|S'| \geq 2$). Since these projections represent similar correlations, they are not beneficial for the user. Even worse, some correlations just exist due to other patterns and, thus, they represent misleading (and redundant) information. Therefore, we have to develop a redundancy model handling these scenarios to ensure interpretable results. Overall, the contributions of our work for the novel paradigm of subspace correlation clustering are:

- we analyze *subspace projections* to find *correlated dimensions* supported by a *subset of objects*
- we allow multiple overlapping clusters, i.e., each object can contribute to several correlations due to different subspace projections
- we avoid redundancy in the clustering result, i.e., we remove clusters representing similar and misleading correlation information

2. RELATED WORK

In the following, we review paradigms related to the topic of subspace correlation clustering. The general clustering objective is to group objects based on their mutual similarity. For traditional clustering, similarity of vector data is determined based on all attributes of the feature space.

Subspace Clustering [16], in contrast, determines clusters that excel by a high compactness or density in projections of the original feature space. The main challenges are to handle the exponentially many subspaces and to avoid redundancy in the result. To reduce the number of potentially relevant subspaces, several techniques exploit the apriori principle [6, 17]. Redundancy is mostly evaluated based on the clusters' similarity w.r.t. objects and attributes [6, 7, 14].

Projected Clustering is related to subspace clustering. However, projected clustering performs an (almost) partitioning of the objects, i.e., for each partition a set of relevant dimensions is detected. As consequence, it misses many of the hidden clusters or the resulting solution is of low quality since it tears multiple clusters apart to fit one partitioning.

Correlation Clustering aims at identifying object groups describing correlations between different features. Since the clusters' dimensions are not restricted to subsets of the original attributes but correspond to arbitrarily oriented subspaces, correlation clustering is often denoted as generalized *subspace* clustering [16]. This, however, is inaccurate; existing methods are rather generalized *projected* clustering methods and have the same limitations: They are not able to find multiple overlapping clusters, since they are limited to find only disjoint or, in the case of [8], nearly disjoint clusters. Even more serious is the ignorance of the obfuscation provoked by highly overlapping clusters in different subspaces, causing most approaches to fail in detecting the true correlation clusters. For completeness, we review existing correlation clustering methods and discuss further limitations. We will restrict to linear correlation clustering in the following. The basic technique utilized by most approaches is PCA. Agglomerative methods (ORCLUS [5], 4C [11], COPAC [4], ERiC [3]) assume that local neighborhoods are in line with a global trend and perform PCA on those neighborhoods, which, however, are strongly influenced by the similarity in the full-space. Therefore these techniques are not appropriate for noise or multiple views in the data as both negatively influence the choice of the neighborhood. To avoid the problem of defining a proper local neighborhood, divisive methods, e.g., [8], were proposed, which, however, usually require the number of clusters to be specified beforehand. The method of [15] is even restricted to find disjoint lines. Instead of PCA, the work of [1] utilizes the Hough transform to detect correlations within the attributes. The paradigm of pattern-based clustering [20, 16] such as co-clustering or biclustering is related; though, it is limited to positive correlations and to one-dimensional correlations.

Overall, none of the existing correlation clustering methods is able to find multiple overlapping subspace correlation clusters as it is possible with our method.

Subspace correlation analysis, e.g. CARE [21] and REDUS [22], tries to identify subsets of attributes in which the *majority* of data entries exhibit a correlation. This differs from clustering in that it does not analyze *several local subsets* of objects. Therefore these methods are restricted to finding only a single correlation per subspace and the datasets have to contain a small degree of noise concerning objects.

3. SUBSPACE CORRELATION CLUSTERS

Generally speaking, a subspace correlation cluster is a set of objects $O \subseteq DB$ that exhibits a correlation in a set of dimensions $S \subseteq Dim$. We call this set of attributes the subspace of the cluster. In Fig. 2 for example, the whole set of objects is correlated in the 2-dim. subspace $\{x, y\}$; the objects form a line. Considering the 3-dim. space, however, we do not have a valid subspace correlation cluster since the attribute z is not correlated to the other ones. Correlation is a measure of the effect of independent variables on a dependent variable [12]. As shown in Fig. 2, however, we cannot draw any conclusion about the attribute values in dimension z given the attribute values in the remaining dimensions. Thus, the plane does not represent a valid subspace correlation cluster. Unlike existing correlation clustering approaches we will not report such invalid correlation clusters as they encourage highly misleading interpretations. Instead we will use this principle of induced clusters for redundancy modeling and efficiency improvements in Section 4.

In Fig. 3, the illustrated plane consisting of all objects in the 3-dim. space, however, is a valid correlation. Given the attribute values of an object in dimension x and y, the attribute value in dimension z is dependent. An object in this correlation is described by *two independent variables.* If we just consider a subset of the objects, we are even able to find a line in the 3-dim. subspace, i.e., given the attribute value in dimension x for example, the attribute values of dimension y and z are completely dependent. For a line we have *one independent variable*, i.e., one degree of freedom.

As shown in the examples, for subspace correlation clusters we have two different types of dimensionalities: First, the *subspace dimensionality*: e.g., the 3-dim. subspace of $\{x, y, z\}$. Second, the *cluster dimensionality*: Within each subspace each cluster/correlation has its own intrinsic dimensionality. E.g., a plane corresponds to a 2-dim. cluster (two degrees of freedom) while a line is a 1-dim. cluster. Thus, in general a subspace correlation cluster is defined by a three-tuple (O, S, λ) with a set of objects $O \subseteq DB$, a set of correlated dimensions $S \subseteq Dim$, and the clusters dimensionality λ, representing the degrees of freedom. We now formalize the definition of such subspace correlation clusters.

3.1 Cluster definition

The basic idea to describe correlations in the data is by considering the data's principal components. We adapt the notions of [2] to define our clusters. Since we design our model to detect linear correlations we will use the term 'correlation' in place of 'linear correlation'.

DEFINITION 1. *Basic notions*
We assume a database $DB \subseteq \mathbb{R}^d$ of d-dimensional objects is given. $Dim = \{1, \ldots, d\}$ is the set of dimensions. With $o_{|S}$ we denote the projection of an object $o \in DB$ to the subspace $S \subseteq Dim$. Accordingly, $O_{|S}$ refers to the projection of a set of objects $O \subseteq DB$. The (sample) covariance matrix for $O_{|S}$, i.e., for a set of objects $O \subseteq DB$ in a subset of dimensions $S \subseteq Dim$, is denoted by $\Sigma_{O,S} \in \mathbb{R}^{|S|} \times \mathbb{R}^{|S|}$. The eigendecomposition of $\Sigma_{O,S}$ is $\Sigma_{O,S} = V_{O,S} \cdot E_{O,S} \cdot V_{O,S}^T$. The eigenvalue matrix $E_{O,S}$ is a diagonal matrix storing the $|S|$ eigenvalues in decreasing order, i.e., $E_{O,S} = diag(e_1, \ldots, e_{|S|})$ with $e_1 \geq e_2 \geq \ldots \geq e_{|S|}$. The eigenvector matrix $V_{O,S}$ is an orthonormal matrix storing the unit eigenvectors v_i corresponding to e_i. Therefore, the i-th principal component is given by $e_i \cdot v_i$.

Given a set of objects O projected to the subspace S, i.e., $O_{|S}$, the minimum number of principal components needed to retain a significant level α of the data's variance corresponds to the cluster's intrinsic dimensionality. Considering the line (defined by a subset of the objects) in the 3-dim. subspace in Fig. 3, we just need one principal component to describe most of the variance. This is indicated by one large eigenvalue and two small ones. In contrast, for the plane we need two principal components. Thus, by using the eigenvalues of the covariance matrix, we are able to determine the cluster dimensionality.

DEFINITION 2. *Cluster dimensionality*
The cluster dimensionality of the (projected) set of objects $O_{|S}$ w.r.t. a significance level α is

$$\lambda(O, S) = \min\{k \in \mathbb{N}^+ \mid \frac{\sum_{i=1}^{k} e_i}{\sum_{i=1}^{|S|} e_i} \geq \alpha\}$$

using the entries e_i of the eigenvalue matrix $E_{O,S}$.

In real world scenarios we cannot expect to observe a set of objects that perfectly fits a line or another linear regression model. Due to errors and noise in the data, the objects slightly deviate from the perfect model. We can measure the strength of a correlation by the degree of variation *not* explained by the regression model. Since the regression model corresponds to the hyperplane spanned by the first $\lambda(O, S)$ principal components with the largest eigenvalues (strong principal components), the distance along the last $|S| - \lambda(O, S)$ principal components with the smallest eigenvalues (weak principal components) determines the strength of a correlation. Intuitively, this corresponds to the distance between an object and, e.g., the perfect line. The smaller these distances, the stronger the correlation. Formally, the correlation distance can be computed by determining the Euclidean distance after projecting the objects and the cluster mean onto the weak principal components (please note: the objects are first projected to the subspace S, i.e., the weak components are linear combinations of the dimensions in S):

DEFINITION 3. *Subspace correlation distance*
The subspace correlation distance of an object $p \in DB$ to a correlation defined by a set of objects O in subspace S is:

$$scdist(p, O, S) = \sqrt{(p_{|S} - \mu_{|S})^T \cdot V_{O,S} \cdot \hat{E} \cdot V_{O,S}^T \cdot (p_{|S} - \mu_{|S})}$$

with mean vector μ of the objects in O, $V_{O,S}$ is the eigenvector matrix, and $\hat{E}$ is a diagonal matrix where the first $\lambda(O, S)$ entries are 0 and the remaining $|S| - \lambda(O, S)$ entries are 1.

Thus, we obtain a strong correlation if each object of the cluster has a small subspace correlation distance. Using these basic ideas, we first introduce our novel cluster definition and afterwards we highlight the important characteristics.

DEFINITION 4. *Subspace correlation cluster*
A subspace correlation cluster $C = (O, S, \lambda)$ is a set of objects $O \subseteq DB$, a set of dimensions $S \subseteq Dim$, and its cluster dimensionality $\lambda = \lambda(O, S)$, such that

1. *the cluster is sufficiently large, i.e., $|O| \geq minSize$*
2. *the subspace correlation distance is small for each object in the cluster, i.e., $\forall o \in O : scdist(o, O, S) \leq \epsilon$*
3. *the set of objects is maximal: any object not in the cluster has a larger subspace correlation distance, i.e., $\forall p \in DB \backslash O : scdist(p, O, S) > \epsilon$*
4. *the cluster dimensionality is smaller than the subspace dimensionality, i.e., $\lambda < |S|$*
5. *uncorrelated dimensions are not included, i.e., $\forall d \in S : \lambda(O, S \backslash \{d\}) = \lambda(O, S)$.*

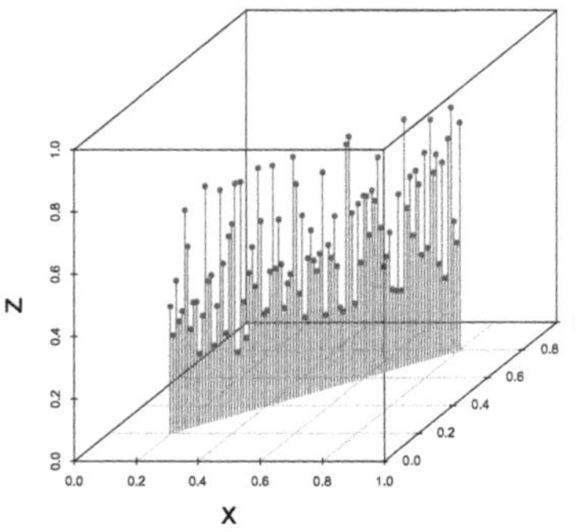

Fig. 2: Valid correlation in subspace $\{x, y\}$, invalid in $\{x, y, z\}$

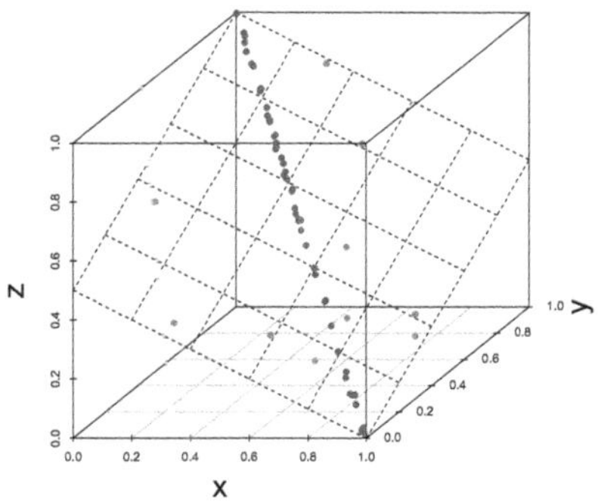

Fig. 3: Redundant plane (induced by the non-redundant line)

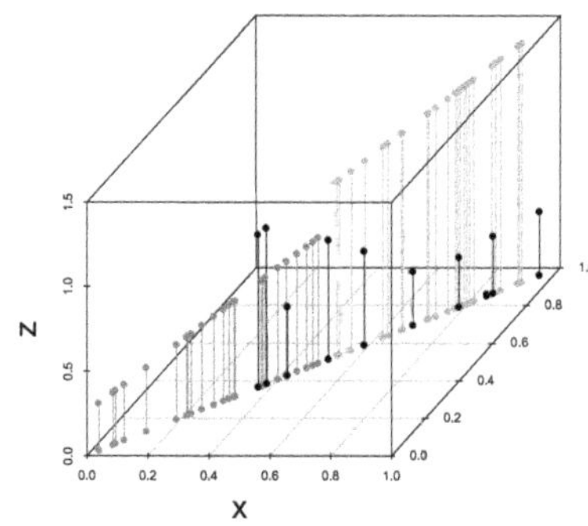

Fig. 4: Redundancy (line in subspace $\{x, y\}$) due to collinearity

The first property ensures that each cluster has sufficiently large support since, e.g., a line composed by only two points is not interesting. By the second property, we ensure that each cluster exhibits a strong correlation; we do not include objects with large subspace correlation distances. Accordingly, we include any object with a small distance, i.e., the cluster should be as large as possible (third property).

The last two properties are the most important ones: With Prop. 4 the case $\lambda = |S|$ is prohibited ($\lambda > |S|$ is not possible by definition). For $\lambda = |S|$, the cluster dimensionality and the subspace dimensionality would be identical. This is not meaningful since each dimension in the current subspace would be an independent variable. Thus, none of the attribute values depends on the others, which does not represent a correlation.

Property 5 is even more important to avoid "meaningless" correlations (and is one large advantage in contrast to traditional correlation clustering). As shown in Fig. 2, the plane is not a valid correlation; dimension z is not correlated to the other ones. This, however, cannot be detected by considering just the eigenvalues. The cluster dimensionality is 2 as for any other plane. Thus, the first 4 properties of the previous definition hold. However, we can detect this invalid correlation by the following principle: Lets assume we have detected a set of objects with dimensionality λ' in subspace $S\backslash\{d\}$. By adding a further dimension, i.e., to get the subspace S, the novel cluster dimensionality obviously has to be either $\lambda' + 1$ or λ'. The first case occurs if we add an uncorrelated/noisy dimension to $S\backslash\{d\}$, e.g., a line in a 2-dim. subspace becomes a plane in a 3-dim. subspace (cf. Fig. 2). The latter case occurs if we add a correlated dimension, e.g., a line still is a line (Fig. 3). Thus, Property 5 checks for each lower-dimensional subspace $S\backslash\{d\}$ whether the cluster dimensionality remains stable. Otherwise ($\lambda(O, S\backslash\{d\}) < \lambda(O, S)$), at least one dimension d would be uncorrelated and the cluster is not valid.

Overall, our cluster definition enables us to detect groups of objects O that are correlated in the set of dimension S with a specific degree of freedom λ by simultaneously excluding uncorrelated dimensions. Note that the *smaller* λ the more interesting is a cluster; a line is better than a plane. Contrarily, the *larger* S the more interesting is a cluster; a 3-dim. subspace is better than a 2-dim. subspace.

3.2 Clustering definition

Based on Def. 4 we are able to determine all valid clusters, which are allowed to group diverse object sets in diverse subspaces. Thus, we allow overlapping clusters in general and we are able to detect multiple different correlations per object, e.g., due to different attribute subsets. We are not limited to disjoint clusters as previous methods. However, simply using the set *All* of all valid subspace correlation clusters according to Def. 4 would lead to an overwhelming result size, containing highly redundant information. This redundancy occurs due to two reasons:

Collinearity: When one dimension $d \in S$ is highly correlated with some other dimension x, the remaining dimensions $S\backslash\{d\}$ will be correlated to x too. This phenomenon is called (multi)collinearity [13]. When this happens, we can derive many clusters describing the same information, e.g., if $\{d1, d2\}$, $\{d2, d3\}$ and $\{d3, d4\}$ are correlated, we directly can infer that $\{d1, d3\}$, $\{d1, d4\}$, ... are correlated as well. Instead of reporting several collinear correlations, we represent them by just one cluster (in a subspace of higher cardinality) and thus avoid redundancy. To handle collinearity, we have to ensure that a correlation cluster in subspace S is not simply a projection of another cluster in a supersubspace $S' \supset S$. As illustrated in Fig. 4, the correlation cluster in subspace $\{x, y\}$ is a projection of two clusters in subspace $\{x, y, z\}$ (the green and red clusters) and a few noise objects (black dots). Such a cluster does not provide much additional insight and therefore should be excluded from the final result.

Induced clusters: With a few extra points, a correlation cluster can induce a cluster of higher dimensionality (e.g., a line induces a plane). In Fig. 3, the 1-dim. correlation cluster (blue line) induces the 2-dim. correlation cluster (plane) which has only a few extra objects. Induced clusters can be misleading as they mainly take credit for another cluster's objects. In this example, the plane is mainly supported by the objects of the line. If we took the line's objects out of consideration, the plane would have too little support to be a valid correlation cluster. The plane is just valid because of the line but not by itself. Thus, we should exclude induced clusters from the final result.

The 'potentially redundant' rule. The main question is, which clusters could lead to a redundancy of other clusters either due to collinearity or due to induction. The following definition clearly states this:

DEFINITION 5. *'Potentially redundant' rule*
A subspace correlation cluster $C = (O, S, \lambda)$ is potentially redundant to $C' = (O', S', \lambda')$, for short $C \prec^{pot}_{red} C'$, iff

$$\lambda - \lambda' \geq |S\backslash S'| \vee \exists S^* \subset S : |S^*| = \lambda + 1 \wedge \lambda - \lambda' > |S^*\backslash S'|$$

We continue by discussing why the above rule covers all clusters C' to which C is potentially redundant to. We distinguish three cases: *(1)* $\lambda < \lambda'$ (the cluster dimensionality of C is lower (better) than the one of C'): In this case, the rule is always evaluated to $false$ as the left sides of both inequalities are negative while their right sides are at least 0. This means a lower dimensional cluster (e.g., a line) is never redundant w.r.t. a higher dimensional cluster (e.g., a plane). This is desirable because high-dim. clusters cannot induce low-dim. ones.

(2) $\lambda = \lambda'$ (both clusters have the same dimensionality): In this case, the rule will be true if and only if $S' \supseteq S$. Otherwise the right side of the first inequality will be greater than 0, and the second part of the rule is violated in any case since a strict $>$ is required. This means a cluster in a higher-dimensional subspace is more important than its projections. As we can derive clusters in lower-dimensional subspaces by simply projecting the cluster of a higher-dimensional subspace, clusters in lower-dimensional subspaces need not to be presented explicitly (cf. collinearity).

(3) $\lambda > \lambda'$ (the cluster dimensionality of C is higher (worse) than the ones of C'): This case is the most complex one and corresponds to induced correlation clusters, e.g., C is a plane while C' is a line. As before, the rule is true for the case $S' \supseteq S$. Though, it can even hold for $S' \not\supseteq S$.

Let us consider an example: C is a 4-dim. cluster in subspace $S = \{1, 2, 3, 4, 5\}$ and C' is a 1d-cluster (line) in subspace $S' = \{1, 2, 3, 8, 9\}$. How does C' look like in S? If we project C' to $\{1, 2, 3\} = S \cap S'$, it has to be still a line. By now adding two further dimensions, e.g., $\{4, 5\}$ to reach S, the dimensionality of the 1d-cluster increases at most by two (if both dimensions are uncorrelated). Thus, in the worst case the dimensionality of C' in S is 1+2=3, which is better than the 4d-cluster C. Hence C' could potentially induce C. In general, this holds if $\lambda' + |S| - |S' \cap S| < \lambda \Leftrightarrow |S \setminus S'| < \lambda - \lambda'$.

But there is more: Assume C to be a 4-dim. cluster in subspace $S = \{1, 2, \ldots, 7\}$. Obviously, the line C' does look like a 5-dim. cluster in S. It cannot induce the cluster C. However, in our model the cluster C represents all of its collinear projections, e.g., also the 4-dim. cluster in subspace $\{1, \ldots, 5\} = S^* \subset S$. As discussed, the cluster in this subspace may be induced by C' and hence could be redundant. Consequently, if the projection S^* is redundant then this information should not be contained in the 'parent' cluster. We also have to denote C as potentially redundant to C'. In general, the equation $\lambda - \lambda' > |S^* \setminus S'|$ has to be checked for any subset $S^* \subset S$ with $|S^*| = \lambda + 1$ since these are the lowest dimensional subspaces represented by collinear information of C.

Overall model. Based on the 'potentially redundant' rule, we define the overall redundancy of a cluster. As discussed and illustrated in Fig. 3, the plane should be discarded as redundant because its support is too small after removing the line. Similarly, in Fig. 4, the line in subspace $\{x, y\}$ should be discarded, since the support is mainly due to the two lines in subspace $\{x, y, z\}$. Thus, we define a cluster C as redundant w.r.t. a set of other clusters *Result* if C's support is too small after removing all objects that are already grouped in clusters $C' \in Result$ to which C is potentially redundant.

DEFINITION 6. *Redundancy of clusters*
A subspace correlation cluster $C = (O, S, \lambda)$ is redundant to a set of clusters Result, for short $C \prec_{red}$ Result, iff

$$|O \setminus \bigcup_{C'=(O', S', \lambda') \in Red} O'| < minSize$$

with $Red = \{C' \in Result \setminus \{C\} \mid C \prec_{red}^{pot} C'\}$

Finally, we define the overall subspace correlation clustering. The final clustering should be redundancy free, i.e., it should not contain induced clusters or clusters present due to collinearity. Moreover, it should be maximal, i.e., should contain as many clusters as possible without introducing redundancy. Based on these two principles, we define the overall clustering model as follows:

DEFINITION 7. *Subspace correlation clustering*
Given the set All of all valid subspace correlation clusters, a subspace correlation clustering Result $\subseteq$ All fulfills the following conditions:

- *redundancy-free:* $\forall C \in Result : C \not\prec_{red} Result$
- *maximality:* $\forall D \in All \setminus Result : Result \cup \{D\}$ *is not redundancy-free*

Our novel clustering model enables the detection of correlations in subspace projections of the data, it allows objects to contribute to multiple, overlapping correlations, and simultaneously prevents redundant information in the result.

4. THE SSCC ALGORITHM

In the following section we briefly introduce our algorithm SSCC, which determines a clustering result according to Definition 7. We refer to an efficient approximation since, as known from traditional subspace clustering, the number of cluster candidates is exponential in the number of objects and the number of dimensions. Furthermore, generating all cluster candidates in a first step and selecting the final clustering afterwards is highly inefficient since most of the clusters will be rejected as redundant anyway. Thus, our SSCC avoids the bottleneck of generating all possible clusters by trying to directly generate only non-redundant clusters.

The general processing of SSCC is shown in Algo. 1. We first describe the general idea of our approach. Three major principles are used to avoid generating redundant clusters: *(1)* Based on the redundancy definition, a λ-dim. cluster can only be redundant to clusters with dimensionality $\lambda' \leq \lambda$. Thus, we can first mine all (non-redundant) low-dimensional clusters (e.g., lines) before mining higher-dimensional ones (e.g., planes). This is shown in line 2 of the algorithm. *(2)* The support of a non-redundant λ-dim. cluster in subspace S has to be high enough *after* removing the objects contained in clusters that make him potentially redundant (cf. Def. 6). We use this idea for pruning objects: Since we already know the non-redundant λ'-dim. clusters with $\lambda' \leq \lambda$ in similar subspaces, we remove all objects of the database (in this subspace) that are already clustered (line 5). Thus, the set of objects to be considered is dramatically reduced (or even too small; line 6) and finding clusters is more efficient. *(3)* We exploit the fact of collinearity to avoid analyzing the exponential number of possible subspaces. Each λ-dim. cluster in subspace S is also a λ-dim. cluster in any subspace $S' \subseteq S$ with $|S'| = \lambda + 1$. Thus, we only mine λ-dim. clusters in subspaces with cardinality $\lambda + 1$ (cf. lines 4, 7) and we *merge* these clusters to obtain clusters with higher subspace cardinality (line 8). For example, if we have already found similar clusters in subspace $\{d1, d2\}$ and $\{d1, d3\}$, we merge them to $\{d1, d2, d3\}$. If the cluster is still valid here, we do not have to analyze $\{d2, d3\}$ since in our model the collinearly correlated dimensions are represented by a single cluster.

Based on these strategies, the lines 3-10 of Algo. 1 efficiently generate a set of λ-dim. clusters (located in subspaces of arbitrarily high cardinality) that is non-redundant with high probability. To finally guarantee a non-redundant result, this set is refined (lines 11-14): To remove redundant

```
1  Result = ∅ // current result containing non-red. clusters
2  for λ from 1 to d − 1 do // low-dim. clusters first
3      λClusters = ∅
4      for S ⊆ Dim with |S| = λ + 1 do
5          NonPruned_S=PruneObjects(DB,S,Result,λClusters)
6          if |NonPruned_S| < minSize then continue;
7          Tmp=FindλClusters(NonPruned_S, S, λ)
8          λClusters=MergeClusters(Tmp, λClusters) // Alg. 2
9          // λClusters may now contain clusters with
10         // subspace cardinality |S_C| > λ+1
11     for x from d to λ + 1 do // high-d subspaces first
12         for C ∈ λClusters with |S_C| = x do
13             if C is non-redundant to Result then // Def. 6
14                 Result = Result ∪ {C}
```

Algorithm 1: The SSCC algorithm

```
1  input: new clusters Tmp, already known λClusters
2  while Tmp ≠ ∅ do
3      select C = (O, S, λ) ∈ Tmp, CIsRedundant = false
4      PotColl = {C_i ∈ λClusters | |S ∩ S_i| ≥ λ ∧ S_i ⊈ S}
5      for C_i ∈ PotColl do
6          generate C_merge = (O ∩ O_i, S ∪ S_i, λ)
7          if C_merge is valid cluster then
8              Tmp = Tmp ∪ {C_merge}
9              if C_i is redundant to C_merge then
10                 λClusters = λClusters\{C_i}
11             if C is redundant to C_merge then
12                 CIsRedundant = true
13     Tmp = Tmp\{C}
14     if CIsRedundant == false then λClusters.add(C)
```

Algorithm 2: Generate high-dim. subspaces by merging

clusters, we can use an efficient incremental approach since based on Def. 5 we can process the clusters of highest *subspace* cardinality first (line 11,12) and we just have to compare these against the current result set (line 13).

Finding λ-dim. clusters in a $(\lambda+1)$-dim. subspace. As described above, we just have to mine the λ-dim. clusters in $(\lambda+1)$-dim. subspaces. To achieve this, we apply the method of COPAC [4] on the current subspace projection; however, with two important differences: First, COPAC partitions the objects according to their local correlation dimensionality and finds clusters in any of these partitions. Since we are just interested in λ-dim. clusters, we just have to analyze a single partition; the one corresponding to λ. This is far more efficient. Note that we still find clusters of higher dimensionality due to our overall processing. Second, our approach avoids uncorrelated dimensions, i.e., clusters containing principal components that are nearly parallel to any axis of the current subspace are rejected. Overall, we efficiently generate the desired set of λ-dim. clusters.

Merging clusters to higher-dimensional subspaces. By our merging principle we avoid to analyze any possible subspace projection. Given the set Tmp of newly detected λ-dim. clusters (cf. line 7), we try to merge these with the already known $\lambda Clusters$ to reach subspaces of higher cardinality. A pseudo-code for this subroutine is given in Algo. 2. For each cluster $C = (O, S, \lambda) \in Tmp$ we first determine those $C_i = (O_i, S_i, \lambda) \in \lambda Clusters$ that fulfill $|S \cap S_i| \geq \lambda$ and $S_i \not\subseteq S$. Only these clusters are potentially collinear to C. If no such C_i exists, we can simply add C to the current set of $\lambda Clusters$. Otherwise, for each potentially collinear cluster C_i we do the following steps:

We generate the candidate $C_{merge} = (O \cap O_i, S \cup S_i, \lambda)$ and check if it is a valid cluster. If so, we first add C_{merge} to Tmp since it potentially can be merged with further clusters later on (Note: Tmp acts as a queue, where we successively remove and add elements; the method stops if Tmp is empty). Second, we check whether C_i is redundant to C_{merge}. Since the 'potentially redundant' rule is automatically fulfilled, we simply have to test $|O_i| - |O \cap O_i| < minSize$. If C_i is redundant, we remove it from $\lambda Clusters$, ensuring a manageable number of clusters at any time. Similarly, we check the redundancy of C w.r.t. C_{merge}. If it is redundant, we mark C.

If each C_i is processed, i.e., its merging with C has been analyzed, we remove C from Tmp. If C is *not* marked as redundant, we finally add C to the set $\lambda Clusters$.

Note that the termination of the merging principle is guaranteed due to the condition $S_i \not\subseteq S$. Since the subspace cardinality of the merged clusters increases, at some point in time no further merging partners can be found and the set Tmp will become empty. Also note that the merging is invoked *within* the for-loop (Alg. 1, line 4). Thus, the set Tmp is usually small and the clusters in $\lambda Clusters$ may already be of much higher subspace cardinality than $\lambda + 1$. Overall, our merging principle efficiently generates λ-dimensional clusters of subspace cardinality larger than $\lambda + 1$.

Object pruning exploiting the redundancy model. Our pruning lowers the number of objects of the current subspace S that have to be analyzed for clustering structure. According to Def. 6, a non-redundant cluster C_S of dim. λ must have sufficiently high support even if the object sets of some other clusters (based on Def. 5) are removed. Since we already know the non-redundant clusters with dimensionality $\lambda' < \lambda$, we can select those clusters $C' \in Result$ that fulfill the 'potentially redundant' rule w.r.t. the current subspace S, i.e., those clusters C' for which $C_S \prec_{red}^{pot} C'$ holds[3]. Clusters fulfilling the rule might be the reason for *induced* correlation clusters in S and hence their object sets can safely be removed. If C_S is a valid non-redundant cluster in S, it will still be so even after removing the objects determined above.

But we can remove even more objects: The merging step generates clusters with subspaces of cardinality larger than $\lambda+1$. For example, based on clusters in $\{d1, d2\}$ and $\{d1, d3\}$ we may get a cluster C_m in $\{d1, d2, d3\}$; it has the same cluster dimensionality λ but higher subspace cardinality. Thus, before analyzing the subspace $\{d2, d3\}$ we can also remove the objects of C_m since the 'potentially redundant' rule holds for this cluster. In general, we can prune objects contained in clusters $C' \in \lambda Clusters$ with $C_S \prec_{red}^{pot} C'$. This prevents the detection of redundant *collinear* clusters with lower subspace cardinality. Hence, our merging principle introduced above also leads to an efficiency gain within this subroutine. Formally, the set of non-pruned objects is given as

$$NonPruned_S = \{o \in DB \mid \neg\exists C' \in Result \cup \lambda Clusters : C' = (O', ., .) \land o \in O' \land (DB, S, |S|-1) \prec_{red}^{pot} C'\}$$

Please note that dependent on the current subspace S different sets of objects are pruned since the 'potentially redundant' rule may be evaluated differently. Thus, objects can still contribute to several correlations due to different subspace projections as desired by our model.

Overall, for each subspace S a large amount of objects might be already removed based on the clusters in *Result* (to

[3] At this point we do not know which objects O are clustered in C_S. However, since Def. 5 just uses λ and S, and we have $\lambda = |S| - 1$, all necessary information is given. We can, e.g., simply set $C_S = (DB, S, |S| - 1)$.

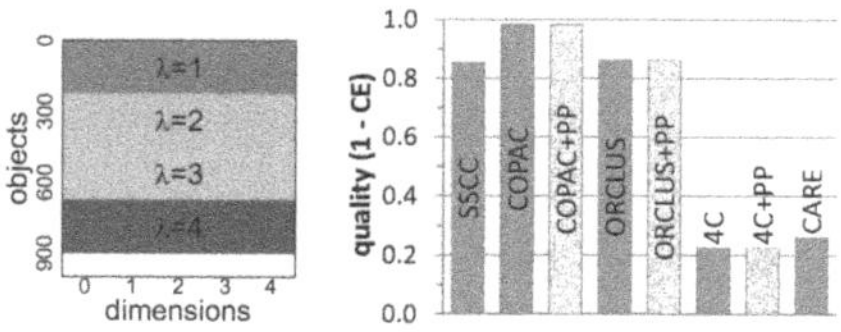

Fig. 5: Scenario A

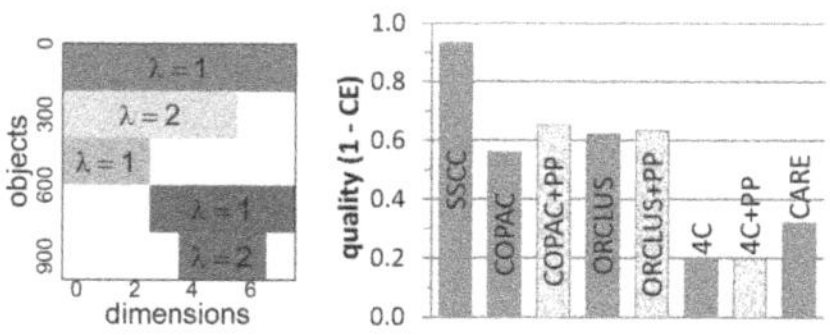

Fig. 6: Scenario B

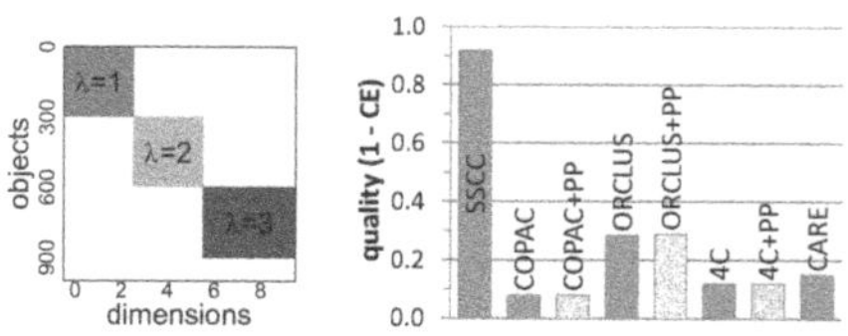

Fig. 7: Scenario C

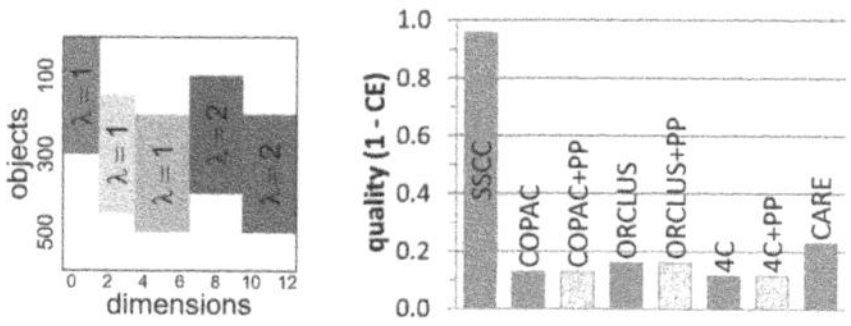

Fig. 8: Scenario D

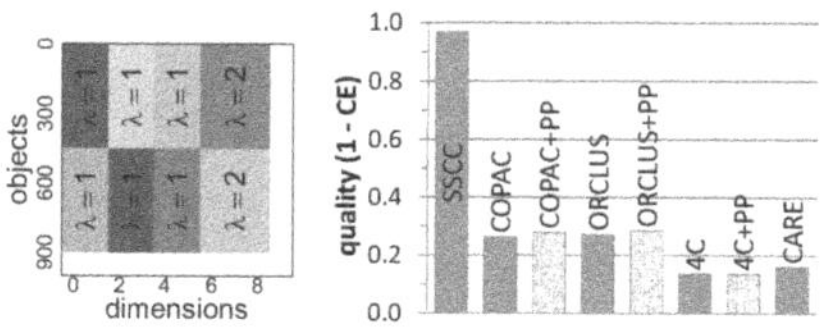

Fig. 9: Scenario E

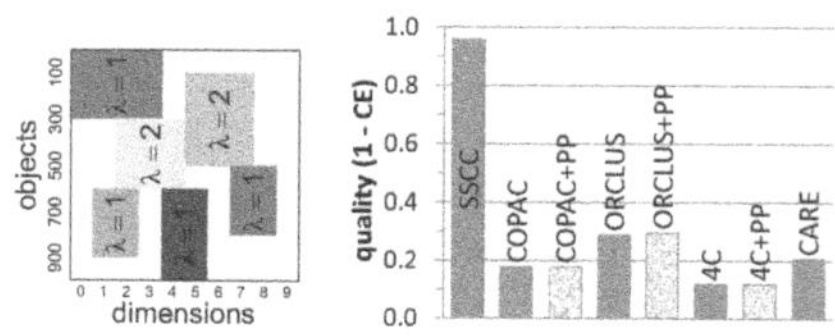

Fig. 10: Scenario F

prevent induced clusters) and $\lambda Clusters$ (to prevent collinear clusters). Only in the remaining set of objects novel clusters have to be detected.

Summary. SSCC generates clusters bottom-up w.r.t. their dimensionality and simultaneously removes redundant clusters top-down w.r.t. their subspace cardinality. Due to the redundancy model and based on the increasing set of known clusters, we are able to prune a large amount of objects that needs not to be considered at all. By utilizing the collinearity phenomenon and merging several clusters, we avoid analyzing many subspace projections. Overall, SSCC efficiently determines a non-redundant subspace correlation clustering.

5. EXPERIMENTAL ANALYSIS

Setup. We compare SSCC against all (non-hierarchical) algorithms implemented in the framework ELKI[4], namely ORCLUS [5], COPAC [4], and 4C [11]. For subspace correlation analysis we choose CARE [21] since, unlike REDUS [22], it is exclusively designed for linear correlations. To revisit our statement of the introduction that simple post-processing is not sufficient in most subspace scenarios to reveal the clustering structure, we implement a post-processing method that discards all dimensions being approximately parallel to the principal components of a cluster and recalculates the cluster's dimensionality. We name this step PP and apply it to all results of full-space correlation clustering methods. We measure clustering quality by the CE measure (clustering error) [19], which also considers the subspaces in its evaluation. For easier interpretation we depict the results of 1-CE, where 1 indicates perfect quality and 0 lowest possible quality. For each algorithm we determine optimal parameter settings w.r.t. the CE value. Efficiency is measured by the approaches' runtime. For comparability all experiments were conducted on Opteron 2.3GHz CPUs using Java6 64bit.

We start by evaluating the approaches based on synthetic data to analyze their performance for the different subspace scenarios. We continue with different scalability experiments and will confirm important observations for the real world datasets 'Wages'[5] and 'Image Segmentation'[6].

Test scenarios for subspace clustering. For Figures 5-10 we examine the algorithms' results for different correlation scenarios, especially for subspace settings. Due to space limitations we provide only visual descriptions of the used datasets attached to the left of the evaluation results of each particular test scenario. Each colored region corresponds to one cluster covering a specific set of objects in a specific subset of dimensions. λ indicates the cluster's dimensionality. Attribute values in white regions are noise.

For the first simple test *scenario A* (Fig. 5), with only full-space clusters, the full-space approaches COPAC and ORCLUS perform better than SSCC. Since clusters are well separated in the full-space but are likely to be merged in subspace projections, the merging strategy of SSCC tends to assign few objects to wrong clusters. Surprisingly, 4C does not yield good results, which probably is originated by its sensitivity to the setting of the neighborhood range, which however might be different for clusters of different dimensionality λ, and its requirement of spatially connectedness of the clusters. Since the CARE approach requires a cluster to comprise the majority of a dataset's objects, it does not perform well for datasets with more than one cluster per subspace, which will be confirmed by the other test cases.

In this scenario, we also examine the importance of *redundancy handling* when considering subspace projections: to this aim, we applied COPAC on each subspace projection. It generated 52 clusters, instead of the four hidden clusters. This matches the observation that each cluster $C = (O, S, \lambda)$ appears as projection in each subspace $S' \subseteq S$ with $|S'| \geq max\{2, \lambda\}$, yielding for this data to the theoretical result of 49 redundant clusters. Clearly, results obfuscated with redundancy would be unmanageable for higher dimensional data; naively using existing correlation clustering in subspace projections is not a choice to detect subspace correlation clusters. In contrast, SSCC detects only the four non-redundant clusters.

Test case B (Fig. 6) shows a simple subspace scenario, where clusters are disjoint and only few dimensions per cluster are noisy. SSCC manages to achieve even better clustering results for this setting. The results of COPAC and ORCLUS are significantly lower compared to scenario A. Noise dimensions obfuscate the clustering structure in the full-space and even *post-processing* only marginally improves the quality. In contrast, CARE is able to achieve better results than for test case A, as clusters overlap less per dimension.

Although *scenario C* (Fig. 7) seems to be the easiest subspace setting, as neither dimensions nor objects of clusters do overlap, it poses severe challenges for full-space algorithms. Since the degree of noise dimensions exceeds the one of relevant dimensions for all clusters, COPAC, ORCLUS, and 4C do not manage to reveal the true clustering structure. Even

[4]Achtert, Kriegel, Zimek. ELKI: A Software System for Evaluation of Subspace Clustering Algorithms, SSDBM, 2008

[5]http://lib.stat.cmu.edu/datasets/CPS_85_Wages

[6]UCI Machine Learning Repos., http://archive.ics.uci.edu/ml

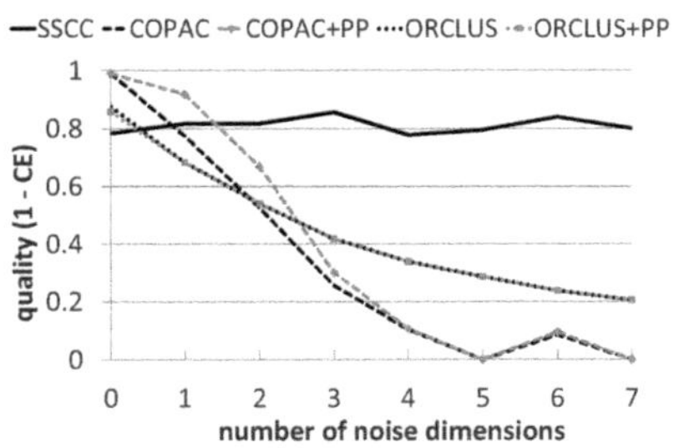

Fig. 11: Effect of noise dimensions

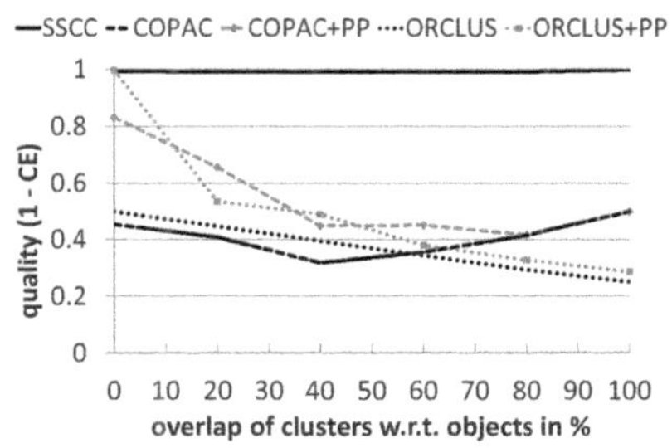

Fig. 12: Effect of cluster overlaps

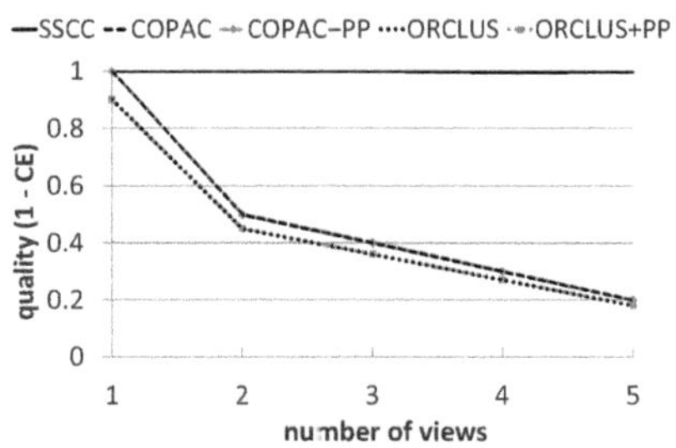

Fig. 13: Effect of multiple views

post-processing achieves no further improvement. SSCC is the only approach being able to uncover the correlations. For the clusters of *scenario D* (Fig. 8) not objects but subspaces are disjoint. As all approaches besides SSCC partition the data, they will not recover the clustering structure by design. However, since the clusters' overlap is arbitrary, the correlations interfere with each other and no clear statement about correlations is possible in the full space. Still, SSCC nearly perfectly recovers the hidden correlations. Although, the degree of overlap of clusters w.r.t objects is increased in *scenario E* (Fig. 9) compared to scenario D, clustering results of COPAC and ORCLUS are better. Clusters either agree perfectly or not at all regarding their objects or dimensions. Therefore the projection into full-space still enables the detection of a certain clustering structure. Thus not only the partitioning of the data hinders the cluster detection for full-space algorithms but also the arbitrary interference shown in scenario D. The last *test case F* (Fig. 10) shows a scenario typically described for subspace clustering. For these combined characteristics of the previous cases, we once more observe that none of the examined approaches but SSCC is able to reveal the underlying correlation clustering structure.

For further experiments we will restrict our comparison of SSCC to COPAC and ORCLUS, as the remaining methods have shown to be not effective to typical subspace scenarios.

Number of noise dimensions. To confirm our observations of scenario B, in Fig. 11 we gradually add noise dimensions to the dataset of Fig. 5. While SSCC is mostly unaffected by noise dimensions, COPAC and ORCLUS increasingly fail to discover the hidden correlations. For few noise dimensions, post-processing slightly increases the quality of COPAC. In general, however, post-processing cannot eliminate the problems of full-space clustering.

Overlap of clusters. In Fig. 12 we increase the percentage of overlapping objects between clusters. For a 4-dim. dataset with 1000 objects, 2 clusters each with 500 objects in disjoint 2-dim. subspaces, we increase the clusters' overlap without varying the clusters' sizes. SSCC shows perfect result in any case. ORCLUS and COPAC with post-proc. are able to reveal the true correlations for small overlap. However, with increasing overlap, both algorithms are destructed by the interference of the two clusters in the full-space, shown by worse post-proc. quality. Even worse, COPAC groups the overlapping objects into a separate cluster, which is more beneficial according to CE than to regard them as noise.

Number of views. In Fig. 13 we increase the number of views for a dataset of 1000 objects and 10 dimensions. Comparably to scenario E (Fig. 9), all views have disjoint, nearly equally sized subspaces and contain two 1-dim. correlation clusters. We observe a fast decrease of clustering quality for COPAC and ORCLUS with increasing number of views. SSCC constantly gets high quality results.

Scalability w.r.t. database size. Fig. 14 (left) shows the results for a varying number of objects in a dataset with 5 dimensions and 4 equally sized full space clusters without noise. All three algorithms scale linearly with the database size. Note the logarithmic scale of *both* axes. Although SSCC has to cope with an exponential number of subspaces, its runtime is still in range of COPAC's runtime.

Scalability w.r.t. dimensionality. For a dataset similar to scenario E (Fig. 9), except that all clusters comprise 500 objects, we consecutively concatenate the dataset to generate datasets of higher dimensionality in Fig. 14 (right). Although the number of subspaces grows exponentially with the number of dimensions, SSCC scales linearly. COPAC shows super linear behavior and thus exceeds SSCC's runtime. We again applied COPAC to any subspace projection to evaluate the *redundancy* and efficiency challenge. Already for the 10-dim. dataset COPAC needed over 4 hours and reported 1013 (redundant) clusters. Thus, removing redundancy, as done by SSCC, is also important for the efficiency.

Real world data. Due to space limitations, we only refer to the results of SSCC and COPAC in the following. For *Wages* (534 objects, 4 numerical attributes, 7 categories) we only use the four numerical attributes. Both algorithms only detected a single 2-dim. cluster, which is visualized in Fig. 15. All clustered objects are colored red, noise is colored blue. For the 2-dim. correlation in the Wages data, SSCC ($\epsilon = 0.002$, $\alpha = 0.85$, $minSize = 80$) captures the objects much better than COPAC. COPAC misses many objects since in the full-space they do not belong to this correlation.

For the *Image Segmentation* data we have 19 numerical attributes describing pixel regions and one class attribute. We removed the class attribute and the constant region-pixel-count attribute. Although, trying a wide range of parameter settings for COPAC, it was not able to detect any cluster for this dataset. For SSCC ($\epsilon = 0.002$, $\alpha = 0.85$, $minSize = 50$) two exemplary clusters out of the eight found ones are plotted in Fig. 16. Clearly, the clusters detected by SSCC correspond to strong correlations, which can be visually verified and are explainable from the dataset's description: the first two dimensions are the measures of excess green and excess blue that are defined as $exgreen.mean = (2G + (R + B))$ and $exblue.mean = (2B + (R + G))$. Here R denotes the average

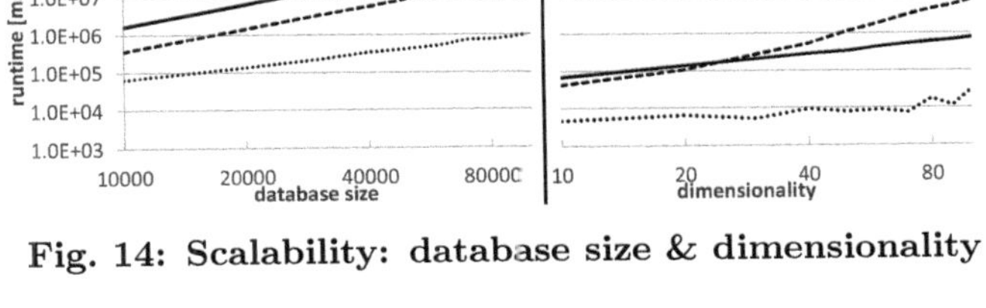

Fig. 14: Scalability: database size & dimensionality

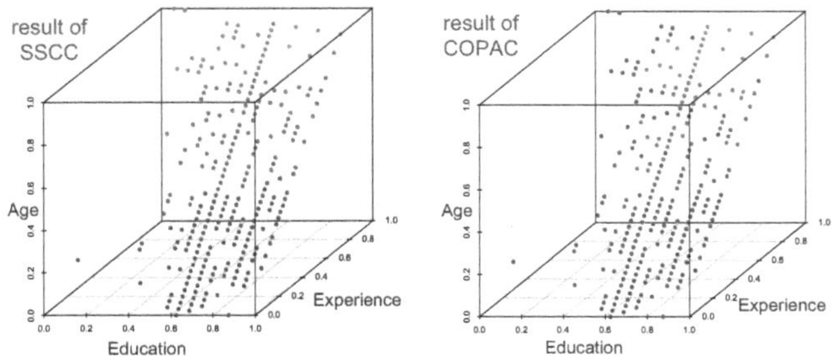

Fig. 15: Results of SSCC and COPAC for Wages

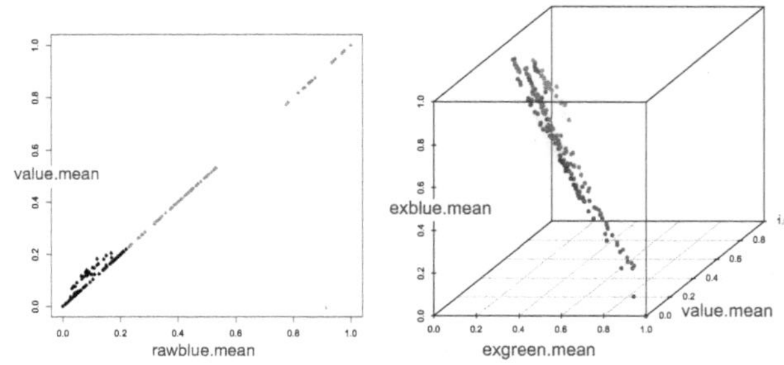

Fig. 16: SSCC results for Image Segmentation

over the raw values of red, B for blue, and G for green. The dimension *value.mean* is a 3-dim. non-linear transformation of the values R, G, and B. Obviously, from the definition of these dimensions we can expect some correlation in this subspace. This correlation is successfully identified by SSCC. Note that these correlations appear only for subsets of the attributes. Thus, full-space approaches are not able to detect these results, confirming the need for our novel subspace correlation clustering paradigm.

6. CONCLUSION

In this work, we have demonstrated that the observations of traditional subspace clustering analogously apply for the paradigm of correlation clustering. A simple post-processing to refine the clustering result determined in the full-space is not sufficient for typical subspace scenarios. Instead we have to analyze *subspace projections* of the data to find meaningful *strong correlations* supported by *subsets of objects*. Our introduced approach reveals linear correlations in subspace projections, allows objects to contribute to multiple correlations, and simultaneously ensures a result of manageable size containing only non-redundant subspace correlation clusters. For this, we carefully differentiate between non-redundant correlation clusters and ones originated due to collinearity or induction. We designed the efficient algorithm SSCC exploiting various pruning techniques. The experiments demonstrate that transferring ideas from the subspace clustering paradigm leads to more precise correlation clustering results compared to state of the art techniques in this domain.

As future work, we will extend our method to also handle non-linear correlations.

Acknowledgment. This work has been partly funded by the DFG grant SE1039/6-1 and by the UMIC Research Centre, RWTH Aachen University, Germany.

7. REFERENCES

[1] E. Achtert, C. Böhm, J. David, P. Kröger, and A. Zimek. Global correlation clustering based on the hough transform. *SADM*, 1(3):111–127, 2008.

[2] E. Achtert, C. Böhm, H.-P. Kriegel, P. Kröger, and A. Zimek. Deriving quantitative models for correlation clusters. In *KDD*, pages 4–13, 2006.

[3] E. Achtert, C. Böhm, H.-P. Kriegel, P. Kröger, and A. Zimek. On exploring complex relationships of correlation clusters. In *SSDBM*, page 7, 2007.

[4] E. Achtert, C. Böhm, H.-P. Kriegel, P. Kröger, and A. Zimek. Robust, complete, and efficient correlation clustering. In *SDM*, 2007.

[5] C. C. Aggarwal and P. S. Yu. Finding generalized projected clusters in high dimensional spaces. In *SIGMOD*, pages 70–81, 2000.

[6] R. Agrawal, J. Gehrke, D. Gunopulos, and P. Raghavan. Automatic subspace clustering of high dimensional data for data mining applications. In *SIGMOD*, pages 94–105, 1998.

[7] I. Assent, R. Krieger, E. Müller, and T. Seidl. Inscy: Indexing subspace clusters with in-process-removal of redundancy. In *ICDM*, pages 719–724, 2008.

[8] M. S. Aziz and C. K. Reddy. A robust seedless algorithm for correlation clustering. In *PAKDD (1)*, pages 28–37, 2010.

[9] N. Bansal, A. Blum, and S. Chawla. Correlation clustering. *Machine Learning*, 56(1-3):89–113, 2004.

[10] K. S. Beyer, J. Goldstein, R. Ramakrishnan, and U. Shaft. When is nearest neighbor meaningful? In *ICDT*, pages 217–235, 1999.

[11] C. Böhm, K. Kailing, P. Kröger, and A. Zimek. Computing clusters of correlation connected objects. In *SIGMOD*, pages 455–466, 2004.

[12] J. Cohen, P. Cohen, S. G. West, and L. S. Aiken. *Applied multiple regression/correlation analysis for the behavioral sciences.* Routledge, 3rd edition, 2002.

[13] R. Freund, W. Wilson, and P. Sa. *Regression analysis: statistical modeling of a response variable.* Academic Press, 2006.

[14] S. Günnemann, E. Müller, I. Färber, and T. Seidl. Detection of orthogonal concepts in subspaces of high dimensional data. In *CIKM*, pages 1317–1326, 2009.

[15] R. Harpaz and R. M. Haralick. Mining subspace correlations. In *CIDM*, pages 335–342, 2007.

[16] H.-P. Kriegel, P. Kröger, and A. Zimek. Clustering high-dimensional data: A survey on subspace clustering, pattern-based clustering, and correlation clustering. *TKDD*, 3(1), 2009.

[17] P. Kröger, H.-P. Kriegel, and K. Kailing. Density-connected subspace clustering for high-dimensional data. In *SDM*, pages 246–257, 2004.

[18] D. Niu, J. G. Dy, and M. I. Jordan. Multiple non-redundant spectral clustering views. In *ICML*, pages 831–838, 2010.

[19] A. Patrikainen and M. Meila. Comparing subspace clusterings. *TKDE*, 18(7):902–916, 2006.

[20] J. Yang, W. Wang, H. Wang, and P. S. Yu. delta-clusters: Capturing subspace correlation in a large data set. In *ICDE*, pages 517–528, 2002.

[21] X. Zhang, F. Pan, and W. Wang. Care: Finding local linear correlations in high dimensional data. In *ICDE*, pages 130–139, 2008.

[22] X. Zhang, F. Pan, and W. Wang. Redus: finding reducible subspaces in high dimensional data. In *CIKM*, pages 961–970, 2008.

Dependency Clustering Across Measurement Scales

Claudia Plant
Florida State University
cplant@fsu.edu

ABSTRACT

How to automatically spot the major trends in large amounts of heterogeneous data? Clustering can help. However, most existing techniques suffer from one or more of the following drawbacks: 1) Many techniques support only one particular data type, most commonly numerical attributes. 2) Other techniques do not support attribute dependencies which are prevalent in real data. 3) Some approaches require input parameters which are difficult to estimate. 4) Most clustering approaches lack in interpretability. To address these challenges, we present the algorithm Scenic for dependency clustering across measurement scales. Our approach seamlessly integrates heterogenous data types measured at different scales, most importantly continuous numerical and discrete categorical data. Scenic clusters by arranging objects and attributes in a cluster-specific low-dimensional space. The embedding serves as a compact cluster model allowing to reconstruct the original heterogenous attributes with high accuracy. Thereby embedding reveals the major cluster-specific mixed-type attribute dependencies. Following the Minimum Description Length (MDL) principle, the cluster-specific embedding serves as a codebook for effective data compression. This compression-based view automatically balances goodness-of-fit and model complexity, making input parameters redundant. Finally, the embedding serves as a visualization enhancing the interpretability of the clustering result. Extensive experiments demonstrate the benefits of Scenic.

Categories and Subject Descriptors

H.2.8 [**Database Applications**]: Data Mining

Keywords

clustering, heterogeneous data, Minimum Description Length

1. INTRODUCTION

In many applications, data are measured on different scales of measurement. For example in biomedicine, we often have binary attributes like sex and categorical attributes, like different genotypes. Moreover, we often have continuous valued attributes like laboratory parameters. To exploit the potential of the available information for knowledge discovery, we need data mining methods which support the integration of different data sources regardless of their measurement scale. As an example, each instance of the data set in Figure 1 is characterized by five attributes: The numerical attributes x and y and three categorical attributes: the attribute *color* with values *red, green* and *blue*; *symbol* with values *box* and *triangle*, and *filling* with values *open* and *filled*, respectively.

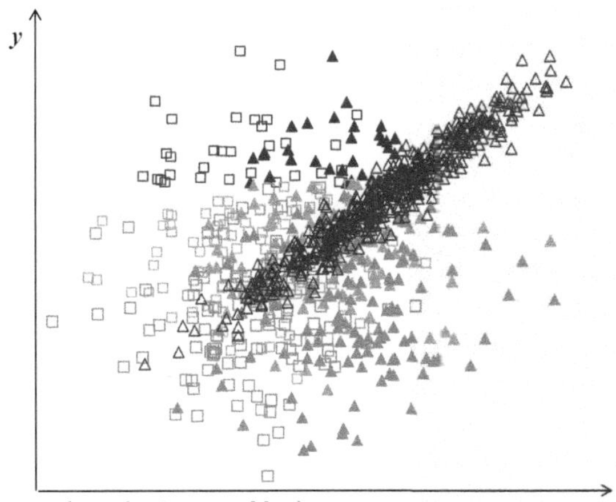

Figure 1: Running Example.

In many cases, the true intrinsic dimensionality of a mixed-type data set is much lower because of attribute dependencies. In complex data sets, attribute dependencies are often not global but exist at the level of single clusters. Our example consists of two clusters, see also Figure 2(a). In Cluster 1, we observe a strong dependency among the numerical x- and y-coordinates. In Cluster 2, there is no dependency among the numerical coordinates but two interesting mixed-type dependencies among numerical and categorical attributes: The attributes *symbol* and *filling* depend on the x value of the objects. For small x values, we mostly observe *open boxes*. The larger x the more likely we have *filled triangles*. Likewise, the attribute *color* depends on the y value: With increasing y we see the transition of colors from *red* over *green* to *blue*. In Cluster 2, the continuous attribute y basically measures the same information as the discrete attribute *color*, however on a different measurement scale. In many real applications, it is up to the expert to select a measurement scale, e.g. for a laboratory parameter either a continuous scale or just record the information whether or not the parameter is within some tolerance range. When integrating data from different sources, we can therefore expect to see a

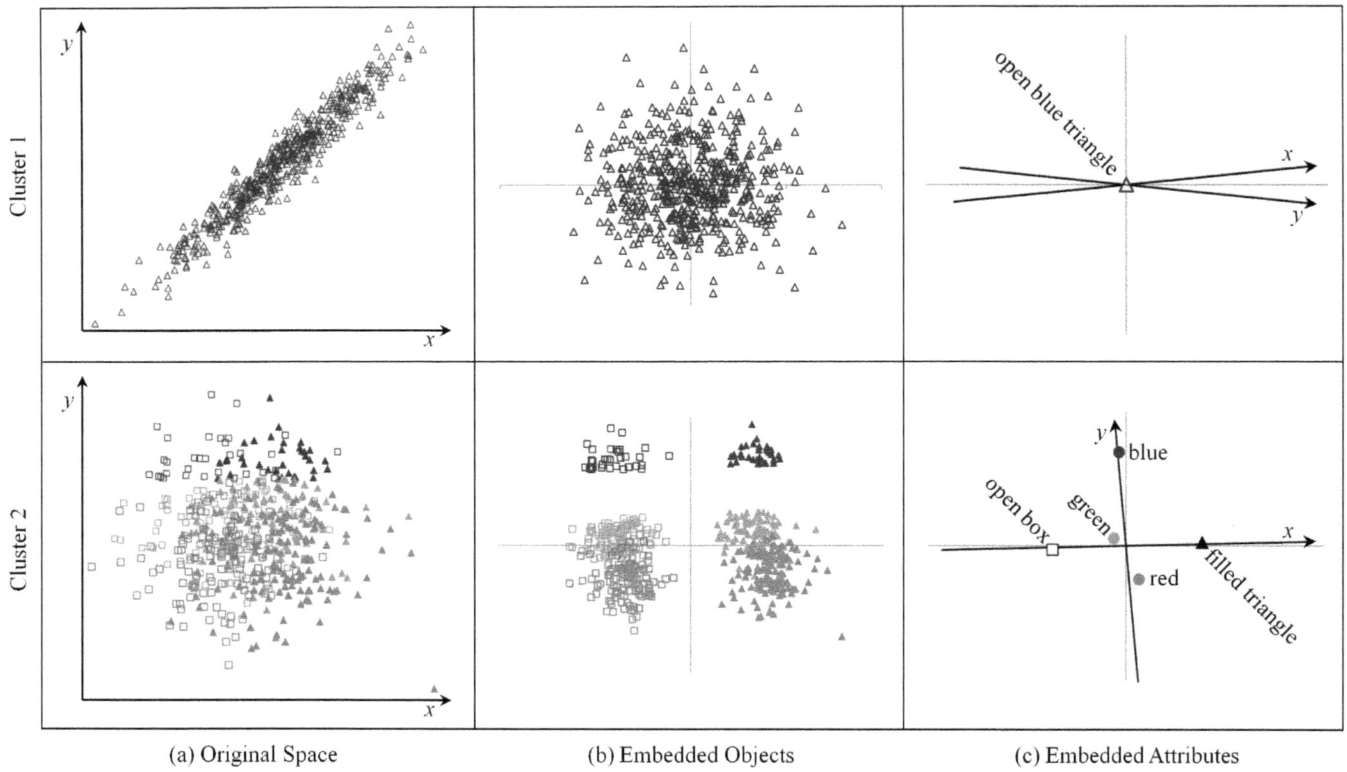

Figure 2: Single Clusters of Running Example: (a) Original space; (b,c) objects and attributes in Attribute-object (AO) space.

wide range of mixed-type attribute dependencies which are very interesting for interpretation. Considering attribute dependencies regardless of the measurement scale opens up novel opportunities in clustering heterogeneous data. In clustering numerical data, *correlation clustering* has attracted much attention. A large volume of research papers, such as the approaches ORCLUS [1], 4C [4] and CURLER [14] have demonstrated the potential of integrating Principal Component Analysis (PCA) into clustering. These techniques detect clusters in arbitrarily oriented subspaces corresponding to unique correlation patterns revealed by PCA. The cluster-specific subspaces are very useful for interpretation since they explain why objects are clustered together. However, all these approaches are suitable for vector data only, i.e. for data of continuous scale level. We therefore introduce a novel cluster notion for mixed-type data.

1.1 Basic Idea

A cluster is a set of objects characterized by a unique attribute dependency pattern. We detect and resolve mixed-type attribute dependency patterns by embedding the data objects and the attributes into a joint low-dimensional vector space, which we call the Attribute-object (AO) space. Attributes and objects are arranged such that the low-dimensional distances between the objects and their corresponding attribute values are minimized. This type of embedding has been proposed in [11], but has so far not been combined with or integrated into clustering. To respect the order and spacing constraints in numerical data, continuous attributes are represented as lines in low-dimensional space and for nominal attributes, every category is embedded. Figures 2(b) and 2(c) display the embedded objects and attributes of the two clusters of our running example. For comparison, Figure 2(a) displays the single clusters in original space. For clarity of presentation, we display the embedding of the objects and of the attributes in separate sub-figures but note that actually all objects and attributes lie in a common vector space. For each cluster a separate embedding is generated to respect the cluster-specific attribute dependencies. The embedding of the attributes in Figure 2(c) reveals at first glance the major characteristics and dependencies of a cluster. Cluster 1 is composed of *open blue triangles*. Therefore these three categories are placed at the center of the display. We can see that both attributes x and y measure similar information, since there is a small angle between the corresponding lines in AO space. The embedding de-correlates the data similar as PCA, c.f. Figure 2(b). Cluster 2 is composed of *open boxes* and *filled triangles* of all colors. The complex mixed-type dependency pattern in Cluster 2 becomes obvious and accessible for interpretation from Figure 2(c). We can clearly see the strong dependency between attribute x and the attributes *filling* and *symbol*. Likewise, we see that the *color* value depends on the y-coordinate. We can even see that the *blue* objects are clearly separated from the remaining colors by the y value, whereas *red* and *green* objects overlap.

Our novel objective function directly relates clustering 1) to unsupervised classification and 2) to data compression. Since each cluster represents a unique attribute dependency pattern, a unique vector space representation of the original attributes is an essential part of the cluster model. We exploit this cluster-specific low-dimensional embedding to reconstruct the original attribute values with high accuracy. Therefore, we search for clusters which predict or explain the original mixed-type attribute values in the data with high accuracy. However, the prediction accuracy alone is not sufficient to comprehensively assess the quality of a clustering result: The more clusters and the more complex the cluster models, i.e. the higher dimensional the vector space representation of each cluster model, the better is the prediction accuracy. To trade off goodness-of-fit and model complexity, we therefore combine the idea of unsupervised classification with the idea of data compression.

1.2 Contributions

The benefits of our approach can be summarized as follows:

- We introduce a novel **cluster notion to support generalized dependency clustering of data measured at different measurement scales.**
- The novel **algorithm Scenic** (Scale-free Dependency Clustering) clusters by embedding objects and attributes in a joint low-dimensional vector space which is very useful for **interpretation** of the result.
- Linking clustering to unsupervised classification and data compression, Scenic produces **valid results without overfitting.**

Notation. In the following we consider a data set DS with n objects. Each object x is represented by d attributes. Attributes are denoted by capital letters and can be either numerical features or categorical variables with two or more values. We denote the number of categorical attributes by d_c and the number of numerical attributes by d_n. For a an attribute A, we denote a value (category or numerical value) by a. We further denote by a_x the value of object x and attribute A. The representation of an object x in AO space is denoted by $\pi(x)$, and the representation of a value a of attribute A by $\pi(a)$. The number of categories of A is denoted by $|A|$. The result of our algorithm is a disjoint partitioning of DS into k clusters $\mathcal{C}_1, ..., \mathcal{C}_k$. The remainder of this paper is organized as follows: In the next section, we elaborate our novel cluster notion and the clustering objective. In Section 3, we introduce the algorithm Scenic. Section 4 is dedicated to an extensive experimental evaluation. Section 5 surveys related work and Section 6 concludes the paper.

2. CLUSTER NOTION AND CLUSTERING OBJECTIVE

In this section, we introduce our cluster model based the Attribute-object space, a low-dimensional vector space representation for mixed-type data suitable for unsupervised classification and data compression. We start by formally introducing the AO space and illustrating its basic properties.

2.1 Basic Properties of the AO Space

DEFINITION 1 (ATTRIBUTE-OBJECT SPACE.). *The AO space of dimensionality d_v of a cluster consists of the following:*

- *The $n \times d_v$ matrix $\Pi(x)$ containing the low-dimensional* object coordinates *$\pi(x)$ of each object x as row-vectors;*
- *the $c \times d_v$ matrix $\Pi(a)$ containing the low-dimensional* attribute coordinates *$\pi(a)$ for each attribute A and each value a, where c denotes the total number of distinguishable attribute values of all numerical and categorical attributes in the data.*

Each numerical attribute A imposes order and spacing constraints on $\pi(a)$:

- Order constraint: *For every pair of values a_1 and a_2, every numerical attribute A and every dimension d of the AO space holds: $a_1 < a_2 \Rightarrow \pi(a_1)_d < \pi(a_2)_d$.*
- Spacing constraint: *For every three values a_1, a_2, a_3 holds: $a_1 = a_2 \cdot a_3 \Rightarrow \pi(a_1)_d = \pi(a_2)_d \cdot \pi(a_3)_d$.*

The goal of the AO space is to represent the major aspects of the complex high-dimensional similarity among mixed-type data objects and attributes in a compact form. Similar as Principle Component Analysis, the transformation to AO space distills the major characteristics from the data by 1) resolving attribute dependencies and 2) removing noise. To learn a suitable AO space, it is essential to respect the fundamental difference in nature between nominal and continuous attributes. The order and spacing constraints guarantee that continuous attributes appear as lines in AO space. Actually, each single value is embedded, but all values lie on a line which we therefore display continuous instead of dotted in Figure 2(c). Only by this restriction, we obtain simple and thus interpretable mixed-type dependencies such that with increasing x we observe more likely *filled triangles* than *open boxes*. Nominal attributes have no order or spacing on their categories and therefore their location in AO space is not restricted. It would be even very counterproductive to restrict their location since by embedding we want to learn their hidden order and spacing from the overall data. It is also not necessary to restrict the location of the objects in any way. Considering Figure 2(b), the objects are clearly not arbitrarily embedded. However, it is important to note that any arbitrary embedding of the objects and the nominal categories would be a valid AO space as long as the order and spacing constraints on the numerical attributes are respected.

2.2 Unsupervised Classification and Data Compression

Definition 1 specifies what a valid AO space is. But what is a good AO space? It is essential to answer this question for the following reasons: Our example demonstrates that especially the embedding of the attributes is very helpful to interpret the cluster content (cf. Figure 2(c)), however we must clarify how much we can trust what we see. We also need a quality measure to compare different AO spaces which are produced as intermediate results of our algorithm, e.g. two sets of AO spaces resulting from different partitioning of the objects into clusters.

A key idea of this paper is to regard clustering as an unsupervised classification problem in a novel way: Given the low-dimensional AO representation of objects and attributes, we want to predict the original attribute values (i.e. the mixed-type input data) with high accuracy. A cluster corresponds to an unknown class of the data. The AO space of a cluster is a specific classification system accustomed to the data distribution in the cluster. The goal of clustering is to find a grouping of objects which maximizes the prediction accuracy.

However, the idea of unsupervised classification alone is not a suitable optimization goal. To see this, consider a clustering where each object is placed in its own singleton cluster. For each singleton cluster, the embedding AO space always provides optimal prediction accuracy. Considering the nominal attributes, each AO space would only contain those categories which the corresponding object has. For the numerical attributes all lines would shrink to points. Thus, each object would be embedded together with its individual attribute values only. No matter what classification scheme we would apply, we could perfectly predict the original values since there are no incorrect answers in the solution space. However, such clustering result would be very bad for interpretation since we learn nothing about the data. Therefore we must take action against overfitting.

To avoid overfitting we combine the idea of unsupervised classification with the idea of data compression, also known as the Minimum Description Length (MDL) Principle. Suppose, we want to transfer the data via a communication channel from a sender to a receiver. A good AO space is a compact model of the data which can drastically reduce the communication costs. The description length DL of a cluster $\mathcal{C}_i$ corresponds to:

$$DL(\mathcal{C}_i) = RE_{\mathcal{C}_i} + MC_{\mathcal{C}_i}.$$

The reconstruction error $RE_{\mathcal{C}_i}$ denotes the number of bits required to reconstruct the original feature information, i.e. the numerical and categorical attribute values of all objects using the AO space as a model. The model complexity $MC_{\mathcal{C}_i}$ corresponds to the number of bits required to encode the AO model itself and includes the bits required to encode the low-dimensional object coordinates as well as the model parameters.

2.2.1 Reconstruction Error

Categorical Attributes. Considering a single object x and categorical attribute A, we determine the reconstruction error $RE_{x,A}$ using Bayes's theorem and Huffman Coding: For each category a of A, the probability to observe a given the representation $\pi(x)$ of x in AOL space is provided by:

$$p(a|\pi(x)) = \frac{p(a) \cdot p(\pi(x)|a)}{p(\pi(x))}.$$

With a suitable model for the probability distribution of category a in AO space, we can specify the probability to observe $\pi(x)$ given that category a. From Section 3.1 it will be evident that applying a Gaussian PDF $\mathcal{N}_a(\mu_a, \Sigma_a)$ with diagonal covariance is an appropriate choice. Thus,

$$p(\pi(x)|a) = (2\pi)^{-\frac{d_v}{2}} \cdot |\Sigma_a|^{-\frac{1}{2}} \exp^{(\pi(x)-\mu_a)^t \cdot \Sigma_a^{-1} \cdot (\pi(x)-\mu_a)}.$$

Applying additionally $p(a) = \frac{|a|}{n}$ and $p(\pi(x)) = \sum_{a \in A} p(\pi(x)|a)$ we can deduce the probability of category a given the AO representation $\pi(x)$. Informally, a good AO space predicts the true category of an object x with high accuracy. This implies, in a good AO space we obtain a very high probability, ideally almost 1, for $p(a_x|\pi(x))$, denoting by a_x the true category of object x, and a very low probability to all remaining categories of attribute A. The reconstruction error of the AO space corresponds to the amount of uncertainty on the categorical attribute values which remains after embedding. To quantify the reconstruction error in bits, we use the principle of Huffman coding summing up over all objects in a cluster $\mathcal{C}_i$ and all categorical attributes:

$$RE_{cat} = \sum_{x \in \mathcal{C}_i} \sum_{A_{cat}} -\log_2(p(a_x|\pi(x))).$$

Numerical Attributes. To quantify the reconstruction error RE_B of a numerical attribute B for the objects of a cluster $\mathcal{C}_i$, we apply multivariate regression where the AO coordinates of the objects $\pi(\mathcal{C}_i)$ are the regressors and the original attribute values $\mathcal{C}_{i,B}$ correspond to the dependent variable:

$$\mathcal{C}_{i,B} = \pi(\mathcal{C}_i) \cdot \beta_B + \epsilon_B.$$

This is a standard linear regression with a Gaussian error distribution. The coding costs therefore correspond to the negative log-likelihood of the error distribution summed up over all objects and attributes:

$$RE_{num} = \sum_{x \in \mathcal{C}_i} \sum_{A_{num}} -\log_2\left(\frac{1}{\sigma_{\epsilon_A}\sqrt{2\pi}} \exp^{-\frac{(x-\mu_{\epsilon_A})^2}{2\sigma_{\epsilon_A}^2}}\right).$$

The overall reconstruction error RE is provided by summing up the numerical and categorical reconstruction errors:
$RE_{\mathcal{C}_i} = RE_{num} + RE_{cat}$.

2.2.2 Model complexity

Following [13], we estimate the costs to encode the model parameters by:

$$P_{cost} = \frac{|m|}{2} \cdot \log_2 |\mathcal{C}_i|,$$

where $|m|$ stands for the number of model parameters. The number of model parameters $|m| = d_v \cdot n + 2 \cdot d_v \cdot |cat| + d_v \cdot d_n$, where the first term corresponds to the costs required to encode the object representations, the second term to the category means and variances and the third term is required for the linear models of the numerical attributes, i.e. the model coefficients β. Besides the model complexity of the cluster-specific embeddings, we need to specify the cluster identifier for each object. Using Huffman coding, these id-costs account for $ID_{cost} = |\mathcal{C}_i| \cdot \log_2(\frac{n}{|\mathcal{C}_i|})$. The overall model complexity is the sum of the parameter costs and the id-costs:

$$MC_{\mathcal{C}_i} = P_{cost} + ID_{cost}.$$

2.2.3 Clustering Objective

The clustering objective is to find a partitioning of the objects into clusters such that the overall description length is minimized:

$$\min \sum_{\mathcal{C}_i \in \mathcal{C}} DL(\mathcal{C}_i).$$

It is important to note that the number of clusters is not an input parameter but is determined by our algorithm at runtime guided by the description length. Likewise, the description length allows us to select a suitable dimensionality of the individual cluster-specific embeddings.

3. ALGORITHM SCENIC

Having specified the cluster notion and clustering objective we now introduce an efficient and effective algorithm to find a good clustering. In particular, our algorithm needs to give answers to the following two questions: How to find a good AO space for a cluster? And: How to find the clusters? This section discusses the answers of our approach Scenic.

3.1 Detecting a Suitable AO Space

Intuitively, it is clear that in an AO space suitable for unsupervised classification and data compression, objects must be embedded as close as possible to the embeddings of their own correct attribute values. At the same time, objects should be as far away as possible from the embeddings of the attribute values they do not have. For example, an object having the value *blue* at the categorical attribute *color* should be embedded as close as possible to the embedding of the category *blue* and at the same time as far away as possible from the values *red* and *green* in order to guarantee correct prediction and effective compression, cf. Section 2.2.1.

Interestingly, the claim that the object should be placed as close as possible to its correct values and as far as possible to the values of other objects resembles a lot to clustering. In clustering, like K-means we claim that objects in a common cluster should be as similar as possible and objects in different clusters should differ as much as possible. As building block to detect a suitable AO space we use the algorithm Princals [11], which is, similar as K-means, an alternating least squares algorithm. Princals first initializes the object coordinates randomly. To avoid the trivial solution that all objects are embedded to the same location, the random coordinates are column-centered and orthogonalized. Princals then iterates two steps until convergence: In step 1), coordinates for the attribute values are determined as the mean of all assigned objects, i.e. all objects having this value. To preserve the order and spacing constraints, the location of the numerical attribute values is corrected by a linear regression using the original attribute values as regressors. In step 2), coordinates for the objects are determined by the mean of all category locations to which the object belongs. After the second step, the object coordinates are orthogonalized, e.g. by using the Gram-Schmidt procedure. When the data is solely numerical, Princals yields the same result as PCA of the centered and normalized data.

```
algorithm Scenic (): set of clusters
  Cluster C_S := k-Scenic (1);
  return REC-SPLIT (C_R) ;
  determine best AO of clusters with MDL ;

algorithm k-Scenic (k): set of k clusters
  {C_1, ..., C_k} := INITIALIZATION (k);
  repeat
    assign every object to C_i with minimum coding cost;
    update AO space as in Section 3.1;
  until convergence;
  return {C_1, ..., C_k};

procedure INITIALIZATION (k): set of k clusters
  k-d Princals;
  obtain l object clusters for each category combination;
  while l > k do
    merge most similar category combination;
  return {C_1, ..., C_k};

procedure REC-SPLIT (Cluster C): set of clusters
  {C_L, C_R} := k-Scenic (2);
  if MDL(C_L) + MDL(C_R) >= MDL(C) then
    return {C};
  else
    return REC-SPLIT (C_L)∪ REC-SPLIT (C_R);
```

Figure 3: The Algorithm Scenic.

Applying a Gaussian PDF in Section 2 is justified by the fact, that Princals embeds each category a at the center of all objects having the value a. Therefore, all category centroids also share a common variance. Moreover, it is appropriate to apply a spherical Gaussian without covariance matrix and to consider each dimension separately because of the orthogonality of the AO dimensions.

3.2 Finding the Clusters

We start by introducing the algorithm k-Scenic for dependency clustering with a fixed number of clusters k and finally introduce Scenic which combines k-Scenic with an effective top-down splitting strategy for parameter-free clustering. Figure 3 summarizes the algorithm in pseudocode.

Since k-Scenic is a k-means-style algorithm which is initialization dependent, we propose the following initialization strategy. Inspired by spectral clustering [10], k clusters can be well separated in a k-dimensional AO space. Similar to PCA, the k first dimensions of the AO space can be regarded as the major dimensions explaining most of the variance. Due to the special properties of the AO space and the algorithmic scheme of Princals, the objects of each category combination form a Gaussian in AO space. If we have more than k category combinations, we greedily merge in each step the most similar category combinations until we end up with k clusters. We merge two category combinations by replacing their multivariate Gaussians with the representative having minimal Kulback-Leibler divergence to both of them. The parameters of this representative can be determined efficiently in closed form, cf. [5].

After initialization, k-Scenic iterates two phases until convergence: 1) Assignment of each object to that cluster where it has the minimal coding costs, and 2) update of the cluster model which involves updating the AO space. Starting with all objects in one cluster, the algorithm Scenic recursively applies 2-Scenic as long we observe an improvement in coding costs. During the splitting phase, clustering is performed in 2-dimensional AO space. In the end, the best AO dimensionality of each individual cluster is determined with MDL.

The runtime complexity of Scenic depends on the number of iterations within the k-Scenic invocations and the number of iterations within Princals. The runtime for k-Scenic is $n \cdot |iter_{kSc}| \cdot (|iter_P| \cdot nd_v^2)$, where the last term represents the time needed for Gram-Schmidt orthogonalization. Since the number of iterations in k-Scenic $|iter_{kSc}|$ and the number of iterations in Princals $|iter_P|$ usually is small (about 10 - 50), the algorithm is efficient.

4. EXPERIMENTS

In this section we perform experiments comparing Scenic to INCONCO [12] and K-Means Mixed [2], two state-of-the-art techniques for clustering mixed-type numerical and categorical data. As a baseline, we also compare to K-means and K-modes. As clustering quality measure we report the Normalized Mutual Information (NMI) [15]. This score scales between 0 and 1. The higher the NMI the better is the clustering.

4.1 Synthetic Data

Figure 4 displays the clusters found by Scenic (a) and the comparison methods (b-d) on our running example. The data set consists of 1,000 objects represented by three nominal and two numerical attributes. Each of the two clusters is composed of 500 objects exhibiting a cluster-specific attribute dependency pattern, see also Figure 1 for the complete data set. In both clusters, the numerical coordinates exhibit a Gaussian distribution, spherical in Cluster 2 and with strong covariance in Cluster 1 (explaining 80% of the variance). Cluster 1 consists of *open blue triangles*. The categorical values of Cluster 2 have been assigned as follows: With probability $p := CDF(x_i)$ of the Gaussian cumulative density function at the x-coordinate of object i we observe *bold triangles*, with (1-p) probability *open boxes*. Analogously for the colors *red* and *green* and the y-coordinate; additionally the color *blue* is assigned for objects with $CDF(y_i) \geq 0.9$.

Scenic is the only method perfectly clustering this data set labeling the objects exactly to the ground truth as generated. Scenic successfully detects the numerical correlation in Cluster 1 and the mixed-type dependency in Cluster 2 and therefore achieves a perfect NMI of 1.0. The embedding of the attributes and the objects is a valuable source of information for interpreting the result. Especially the embedding of the attributes displayed in Figure 2(c) clearly visualizes the core characteristics of the clusters and the attribute dependencies: Categories placed at the center of the display like *open, blue, triangle* in Cluster 1 represent the typical attribute values of a cluster. Analogously, we can see that for Cluster 2, *green* and *red* objects are more frequent than *blue* ones, and the cluster contains *open boxes* as well as *filled triangles*. The complex mixed-type dependency pattern also becomes obvious at first glance: We have a correspondence between numerical x and the probability of observing *open boxes* or *filled triangles* which is displayed in the figure by the placement of those categories at the x-axis; analogously for the colors and the y-axis. Scenic selects to embed Cluster 1 in one-dimensional space and Cluster 2 in two-dimensional space.

The second best result with an NMI of 0.71 is obtained by K-means Mixed [2], cf. Figure 4(b). This clustering is guided by the attribute *color*: All *blue* objects are assigned to Cluster 1. Cluster 2 consists of the remaining *red* and *green* objects. K-means Mixed employs an optimization scheme to decide upon the relative importance of the single attributes for clustering. Among them, *color* best distinguishes between the clusters, since there are only relatively few *blue* objects in Cluster 2. However, only a technique considering dependencies between attributes of arbitrary scale can successfully cluster this data: The *blue* objects wrongly assigned to Cluster 1 by K-means-Mixed do not fit at all into this cluster since they have no correlation among the numerical x- and y-coordinates. How-

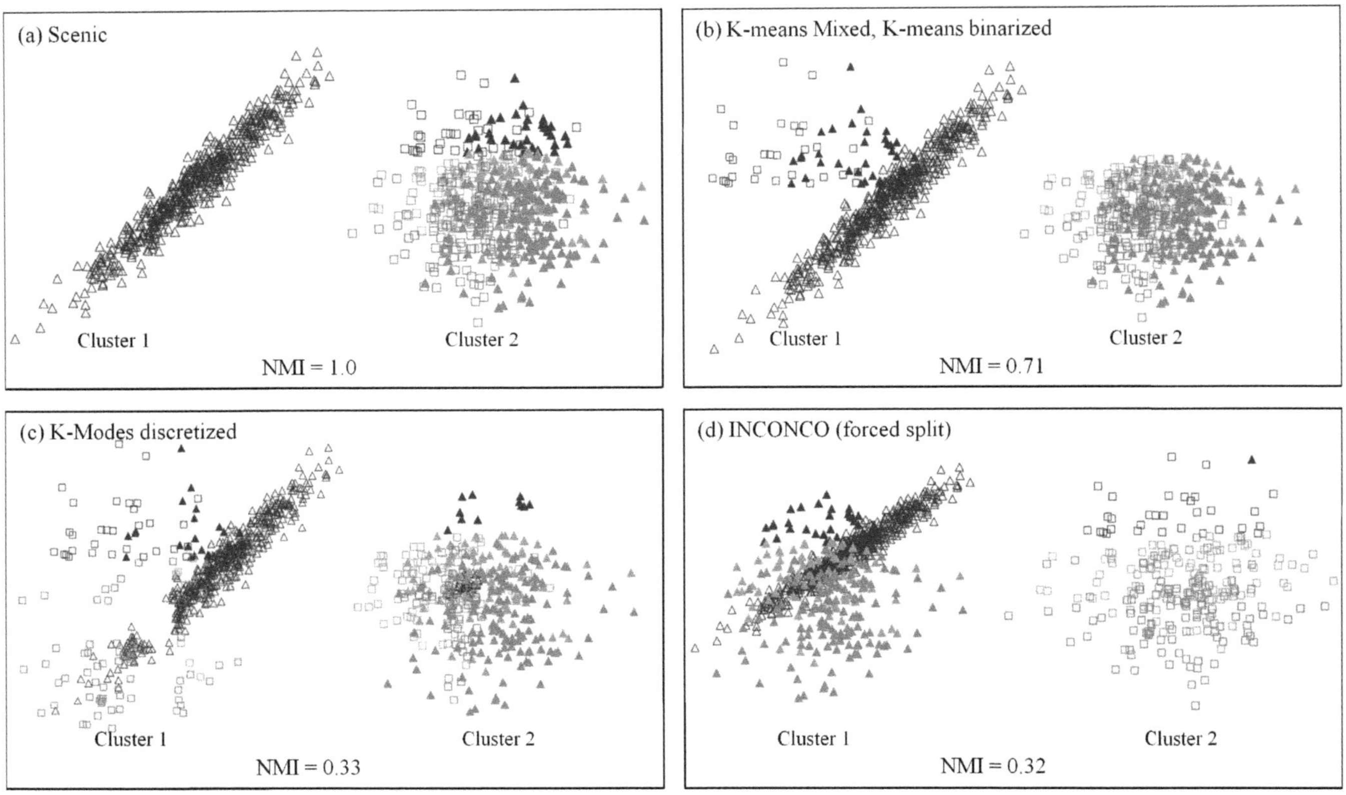

Figure 4: Results on Running Example: single clusters found by Scenic (a) and the comparison methods (b-d). Please also refer to Figure 1 for the complete data set and to Figure 2 for the embedding of objects and attributes performed by Scenic.

ever, these objects fit very well to Cluster 2 because of the transition from *open boxes* to *filled triangles* for increasing x-coordinate. The same result as with K-means Mixed can be obtained with standard K-means when we binarize the categorical attributes. Using solely the two numerical attributes in standard K-means yields a poor result with NMI of 0.18. It is evident that the categorical attributes contain important information for cluster separation, thus integrating both types of attributes improves the clustering result.

Another possibility is using the algorithm K-modes for categorical data and integrating the numerical information by discretizing the numerical attributes. This option yields an NMI of 0.33 using 10 equidistant bins, cf. Figure 4(c). This clustering is mainly guided by the attribute *filling*: Cluster 1 contains in majority *open* objects and Cluster 2 *filled* ones. Since the number of bins is difficult to select we report the result with the best NMI among several trials. Integrating the other source of information by type conversion is not an ideal solution but also helps in this case. Running K-modes solely on the nominal data yields an NMI of only 0.27.

Figure 4(d) shows the result of INCONCO [12]. This algorithm is in principle capable to consider mixed-type attribute dependency patterns, however has a special and limited dependency model: In a mixed-type attribute dependency, all categories of the involved nominal variables must have a unique numerical data distribution which is modeled by a separate Gaussian for each single category. In the cluster model of INCONCO it is not possible that only some of the categories are involved in a dependency. For example in Cluster 2, we observe a transition from *open boxes* to *filled triangles* for increasing x value. This dependency involves the attributes *symbol* and *filling*, but only one of the two categories of each attribute. INCONCO would model this dependency by having an own Gaussian not only for *open boxes* and *filled triangles* but also for *filled boxes* and *open triangles*, attribute combinations which are not existing in this cluster. In addition, the assumption of having a unique Gaussian for each category combination does not fit to the data distribution. As Scenic relying on the MDL, INCONCO selects the number of clusters automatically. Since the data does not fit to the model assumptions of the algorithm, INCONCO prefers to keep all objects in one cluster, a solution having an NMI of 0. To enable comparison, we forced a split into two clusters. The resulting clustering with an NMI of 0.32 is mostly distinguishing *open boxes* (Cluster 2) from the remaining objects (Cluster 1).

Runtime. Scenic is faster than K-means Mixed. However, INCONCO and of course also K-means and K-modes are faster than Scenic. For example to process a data set with 5,000 points and data distribution as the running example, Scenic needs 28 seconds, K-means Mixed 134 seconds, INCONCO, K-modes and K-means less than a second.

4.2 Real Data

We compare to K-means Mixed [2] and INCONCO [12] on two real data sets available at the UCI Machine Learning repository [6]. K-means and K-modes have been left out due to worse results.

4.2.1 Abalone

The abalone data set consists of 4,177 instances which are described by nine attributes: The categorical attribute *sex* with three values *male, female* and *infant*. Further eight numerical attributes represent several measurements of the abalone shell, cf. Figure 5; finally the integer-valued attribute *rings* providing the number of rings of the shell which allows inferring the age of the animal. The data has been originally collected to study the population biology of abalone in Tasmania in an unsupervised way. Since added to the UCI Machine Learning repository [6], the attribute *rings* has been mostly used for evaluation purpose. Therefore, we also excluded

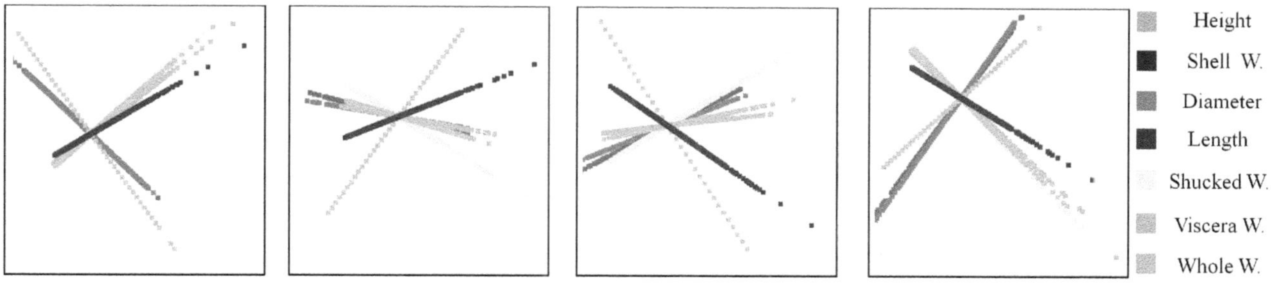

(a) Cl. 1, Infant (b) Cl. 2, Female (c) Cl. 3, Mature Male (d) Cl. 4, Young Male

Figure 5: Cluster-specific Embedding of Attributes on Abalone Data.

this attribute from clustering and used it for evaluation. Scenic detects four clusters on this data set which correspond well to the attribute *sex*. Cluster 1 is purely composed of the 1,342 *infants* and Cluster 2 consists all 1,307 *females*. The *males* are split up into two clusters because Scenic identifies two groups of *male* instances having different attribute dependency patterns. Figure 5 displays the embedding of the attributes for all four clusters. For clarity of presentation, we omitted the attribute *sex*. Since all clusters are *sex*-pure, the corresponding value is embedded at the center of all displays. Note that different rotation in the embedding has no semantic meaning. From Figure 5 it is obvious that we have two general types of dependencies in the data: The young *males* and the *infants* are very similar (Cluster 1, displayed in Figure 5(a) and Cluster 4, cf. Figure 5 (d)). In both clusters, the attributes *length* and *diameter* are strongly correlated. The attributes *shucked weight, viscera weight and whole weight* are also correlated but represent different information. *Height* is rather correlated with *length* and *diameter*; *shell weight* with the other weight attributes. In mature *males* and *females*, cf. Figure 5(b) and 5(c), all attributes with exception of *height* and *shell weight* are rather correlated.

It is probably not surprising that the grouping into *sex*-pure clusters performed by Scenic is informative regarding the evaluation attribute *rings*: Especially the *infant* cluster 1 has with 7.89 a much smaller average number of *rings* than the other clusters (Cluster 2 (*females*): 11.13, Cluster 3 (*males*): 10.95, Cluster 4 (*males*): 10.37). Running a two-sample t-test on the *ring* distribution of each pair of clusters assuming unequal variance provides further evidence that it is reasonable 1) to cluster this data set according to the *sex*, and 2) to split up the *males* into two subgroups. Corrected with Bonferroni for multiple comparisons, almost all pairs of clusters exhibit significant differences in the number of *rings* (at level $\alpha = 0.05$). In particular, Cluster 3 and 4 differ significantly with p-value of 0.001 (corrected). Thus, as already observed above, Cluster 3 represents the mature *males* and Cluster 4 represents the younger *males* having attribute dependencies similar to the *infants*. The only pair of clusters not exhibiting a significant difference in age are Cluster 3 representing the mature *males* and Cluster 4 representing the *females*.

For comparison, we parameterized K-means Mixed to also detect four clusters. The result mainly separates the *infants* from the rest of the data. Cluster 1 consists of 1,337 *infants*. The other three clusters contain *males, females* and the few remaining *infants* to almost equal proportions. Regarding the number of *rings*, the result of K-means mixed is also reasonable since all pairs of clusters differ significantly in a two-sample t-test on this attribute. However, since K-means Mixed does not support attribute dependencies and the only output is the grouping of objects into clusters, the result is difficult to interpret: We do not know why objects are grouped together and which attributes are important for clustering.

INCONCO detects 25 clusters on this data set. The four largest clusters are consist of more than 300 objects. None of these clusters represent a particular *sex*, e.g. the largest cluster with 1,056 instances consists of 554 *males*, 442 *females* and 60 *infants*. Also regarding the number of *rings*, the result is not specific. None of the clusters stands out significantly. Since INCONCO lacks a visual representation of the attribute dependency patterns and detects many small clusters, the detected dependencies are hard to interpret and to compare across clusters. In summary, Scenic achieves all we want: 1) Scenic automatically selects a meaningful number of clusters. 2) The embedding of the attributes clearly visualizes the most important attributes and dependency patterns for clustering. 3) The clusters differ significantly in the evaluation attribute.

4.2.2 Acute Inflammations Data

This data set consists of several measurements relevant for the diagnosis of acute inflammation of the urinary bladder and acute nephritis. Each of the 120 instances represents a patient and is characterized by six attributes. In contrast to the abalone data, besides the *temperature* of the patient which is measured on a continuous scale, all other attributes are binary taking the values *yes* or *no*: occurrence of *nausea, lumbar pain, urine pushing, micturition pain, burning or swelling*. The data contains two binary attributes which can be used as evaluation attributes, the diagnosis *acute inflammation of the urinary bladder* (in the following called Evaluation Attribute 1) and the diagnosis *acute nephritis* (Evaluation Attribute 2). Both diseases can but must not co-occur.

Scenic detects five clusters on this data set. This clustering has an NMI of 0.24 with respect to Evaluation Attribute 1 and an NMI of 0.43 with respect to Evaluation Attribute 2. In particular, Cluster 1 consists of 29 patients suffering from *acute nephritis*, 19 of which also suffer from *acute inflammation of the urinary bladder*. Characteristic for this cluster is the high average *temperature* of 40.6 degrees Celsius and the presence of *nausea*. Cluster 2 consists of 21 patients with *acute nephritis* who do not have *inflammation of the urinary bladder*. The patients in this cluster also have a high average *temperature* of 39.9 degrees but in contrast to those in Cluster 1 do not suffer from *nausea* and also not from *micturition pain*, which makes sense since they do not have *inflammation of the bladder*. Cluster 3 consists of 20 patients suffering from *inflammation of the urinary bladder* but without *nephritis*. These patients are characterized by a normal average *temperature* of 36.9 degrees, and by the fact that they are all having the characteristic symptoms of *pushing*, *micturition pain* and *burning or swelling*. Cluster 4 consists of 20 subjects who have neither *nephritis* nor *inflammation of the bladder*. Cluster 5 consists of 30 subjects which are mostly suffering from *inflammation of the bladder* (20 of 30). None of the subjects in Cluster 5 has *nephritis*. In contrast to Cluster 2, the average *temperature* in Cluster 5 is with 38,5 degrees slightly elevated. Furthermore, in contrast to the subjects in Cluster 3, this

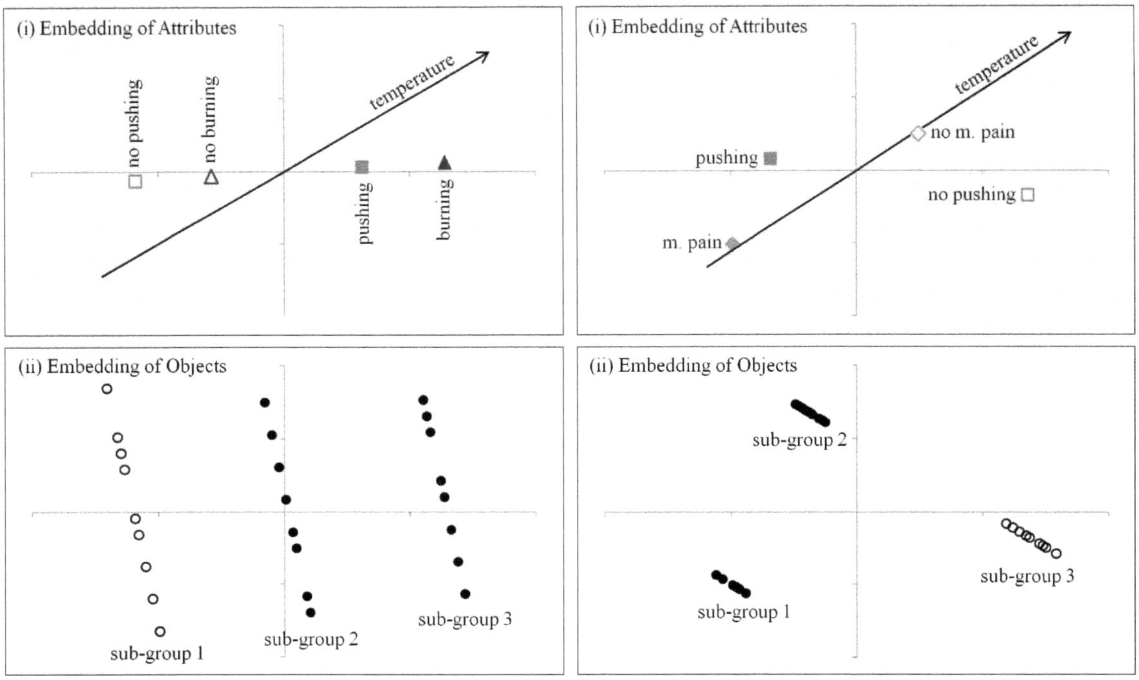

(a) Cluster 1, Nephritis

(b) Cluster 5, no Nephritis

Figure 6: Embedding of Selected Clusters of Acute Inflammations Data. In sub-figures (ii) filled dots represent patients suffering from *inflammation of the bladder*, open dots represent subjects not suffering from this condition.

group is not suffering from *burning or swelling*. Figure 6 displays the embedding of the attributes (i) and of the objects (ii) for Cluster 1 (a) and Cluster 5 (b). As previously, for clarity of presentation, we only show those categories which show a variation inside the corresponding cluster, since all remaining categories are aligned at the origin of the display. Clusters 1 and 5 are the only clusters which are not class-pure with respect to Evaluation Attribute 1, which means that these clusters contain subjects suffering from *inflammation of the bladder* as well as subjects who are not suffering from this condition. In Cluster 1, we observe a strong dependency among the categories *pushing* and *burning* and *no pushing* and *no burning*, respectively. These pairs of categories are grouped together and aligned at the x-axis of the display of Figure 6(a,i). From Figure 6(a,ii) it becomes evident that this axis separates subjects affected from *inflammation of the bladder* from subjects who are not. In the embedding of the objects we can distinguish among three sub-groups. Sub-group 1 has no symptoms and relatively low *temperature* and does not suffer from *inflammation of the bladder*. Sub-groups 2 and 3 suffer from this condition, where sub-group 2 has *no burning* but *pushing* and sub-group 3 has both of those characteristic symptoms. The second axis of the display is spanned mainly by the numerical attribute *temperature*, which has slight dependency to the categorical attributes. Especially patients with the symptoms *pushing* and *burning*, i.e. those who have *nephritis* and *inflammation of the bladder* tend to have a higher *temperature* than patients only having *nephritis*. In Cluster 5, we observe different dependencies. Similar as in Cluster 1, the categories *pushing* and *no pushing* follow approximately the x-axis of the display. However, in contrast to Cluster 1, the binary attribute *micturition pain* strongly depends on the *temperature* and vice versa. Subjects without *micturition pain* have higher *temperature* than the other subjects. As in Cluster 1, the x-axis of the display clearly distinguishes subjects with *inflammation of the bladder* from those without. In Figure 6(b,ii) the subjects form three sub-groups which are class-pure with respect to Evaluation Attribute 1. Sub-groups 1 and 2 consists of patients with *inflammation of the bladder*, where the subjects in sub-group 1 have the symptoms *micturition pain* and *pushing*, and the subjects in sub-group 2 only *pushing* but a higher *temperature*. Sub-group 3 is composed of patients who have an elevated *temperature* but no other symptoms. This group has not been diagnosed with *inflammation of the bladder*.

INCONCO detects 4 clusters with an NMI of 0.11 with respect to Evaluation Attribute 1 and 0.52 with respect to Evaluation Attribute 2. As for Scenic, all clusters detected by INCONCO are class-pure with respect to Evaluation Attribute 2. The only difference explaining the lower NMI of Scenic is the fact that Scenic detects one more cluster than INCONCO. Since the evaluation attributes are binary detecting more clusters has negative effects on NMI. Therefore, we parameterized K-means Mixed to detect 2 clusters. However, the result does not match well any of the two evaluation attributes: K-means Mixed has an NMI of 0.007 with respect to Evaluation Attribute 1 and 0.20 with respect to Evaluation Attribute 2.

In summary, Scenic is the only technique yielding a result which matches well both evaluation attributes. The categorical cluster attribute produced by Scenic well corresponds to the diagnosis *nephritis*. Furthermore, in the leading dimensions of the cluster-specific object embedding, the objects are perfectly separated according to the diagnosis *inflammation of the bladder*.

5. RELATED WORK AND DISCUSSION

In clustering numerical data, considering attribute dependencies has a long history with a lot of well-known approaches like ORCLUS [1] or CURLER [14]. The research area and is often referred to as correlation clustering or generalized subspace clustering. Compared to the large volume of research papers on clustering numerical data, only relatively few approaches focus on categorical data. Recently, some approaches for finding clusters in subspaces of categorical data sets have been proposed like Clicks [17].

However, to the best of our knowledge, the topic of generalized subspace clustering on categorical data is largely unexplored.

Despite the practical relevance integrative mining of data with different measurement scales, only disproportionably few approaches focus on clustering data represented by numerical and categorical attributes. Recently, some approaches to clustering such mixed-type data sets have been proposed, in particular K-prototypes [9], CFIKP [16], CAVE [8], CEBMDC [7], INTEGRATE [3], K-means Mixed [2] and INCONCO [12]. In early approaches like K-prototypes, not only the number of clusters k but also the relative importance of the numerical and categorical attributes in clustering needs to be specified by input parameters. Many later papers set the primary focus on the key question how to balance the relative importance of numerical and categorical information in clustering and developed creative solutions: Ensemble methods in CEBMDC, complex optimization methods in K-means Mixed and elements of information theory in INTEGRATE, CAVE and INCONCO.

In the experimental evaluation, we decided to compare Scenic to K-means Mixed [2] and INCONCO [12], since both algorithms follow different philosophies on how to integrate numerical and categorical information in clustering. K-means Mixed dynamically learns the significance of each single attribute during the clustering process. The objective function of the algorithm formalizes the idea that attributes well separating the data objects are more interesting for clustering. By this attribute weighting scheme, K-means Mixed performs some kind of primitive subspace clustering. To the best of our knowledge, INCONCO is the first step towards making the benefits of generalized subspace clustering available for mixed-type data. As Scenic, INCONCO is based on the MDL Principle however with a different intention. INCONCO does not regard clustering as an unsupervised classification problem but directly compresses the input data. Mixed-type attribute dependencies are revealed by an extended Cholesky Decomposition. However, as mentioned in the experimental section, the cluster model of INCONCO is limited to support certain types of attribute dependencies only. In particular, all categories of all nominal variables involved in a dependency with some numerical variables need to have different Gaussian distributions of the numerical variables. Our experiments on synthetic and real data demonstrate that this condition does often not hold. As additional major benefit over INCONCO, the result of Scenic comprises a clear visualization of the attribute dependencies which is very helpful for interpretation.

6. CONCLUSION

In this paper, we have proposed Scenic, a technique for generalized dependency clustering across measurement scales. The key idea of Scenic is to consider clustering as an unsupervised classification problem. Scenic clusters by constructing low-dimensional joint embeddings of the objects and mixed-type attributes which allow to predict the original attribute values with high accuracy. To avoid overfitting, we combine this idea with data compression. Guided by the Minimum Description Length Principle, Scenic automatically selects the number of clusters as well as the dimensionality of the embeddings. As an additional value-add, the embeddings of objects and attributes are a valuable source of information for interpretation. Especially the embedding of the attributes allows understanding even complex dependencies involving several categorical and numerical attributes at first glance.

Many open challenges remain in mining heterogeneous data: Scenic assigns each object to one distinct cluster. However, objects may belong to several clusters. We therefore focus on fuzzy and subspace clustering with special attention on detecting interesting non-redundant clusterings. Besides clustering, we currently focus on outlier detection methods respecting the dependencies among numerical and categorical attributes. As a long term goal, we want to include further types of attributes, e.g. hierarchical and relational information.

7. ACKNOWLEDGMENTS

C.P. is supported by the Alexander von Humboldt Foundation.

8. REFERENCES

[1] C. C. Aggarwal and P. S. Yu. Finding generalized projected clusters in high dimensional spaces. In *SIGMOD*, pages 70–81, 2000.

[2] A. Ahmad and L. Dey. A k-mean clustering algorithm for mixed numeric and categorical data. *Data Knowl. Eng.*, 63(2):503–527, 2007.

[3] C. Böhm, S. Goebl, A. Oswald, C. Plant, M. Plavinski, and B. Wackersreuther. Integrative parameter-free clustering of data with mixed type attributes. In *PAKDD*, pages 38–47, 2010.

[4] C. Böhm, K. Kailing, P. Kröger, and A. Zimek. Computing clusters of correlation connected objects. In *SIGMOD*, pages 455–466, 2004.

[5] J. V. Davis and I. Dhillon. Differential entropic clustering of multivariate gaussians. In *NIPS*, 2006.

[6] A. Frank and A. Asuncion. UCI machine learning repository, 2010.

[7] Z. He, X. Xu, and S. Deng. Clustering mixed numeric and categorical data: A cluster ensemble approach. *CoRR*, abs/cs/0509011, 2005.

[8] C.-C. Hsu and Y.-C. Chen. Mining of mixed data with application to catalog marketing. *Expert Syst. Appl.*, 32(1):12–23, 2007.

[9] Z. Huang. Extensions to the k-means algorithm for clustering large data sets with categorical values. *Data Min. Knowl. Discov.*, 2(3):283–304, 1998.

[10] U. V. Luxburg, M. Belkin, O. Bousquet, and Pertinence. A tutorial on spectral clustering. *Stat. Comput*, 2007.

[11] G. Michailidis and J. de Leeuw. The gifi system of descriptive multivariate analysis. *STATISTICAL SCIENCE*, 13:307–336, 1998.

[12] C. Plant and C. Böhm. Inconco: interpretable clustering of numerical and categorical objects. In *KDD*, pages 1127–1135, 2011.

[13] J. Rissanen. *Information and Complexity in Statistical Modeling*. Springer, 2007.

[14] A. K. Tung, X. Xu, and B. C. Ooi. CURLER: Finding and visualizing nonlinear correlation clusters. In *SIGMOD*, pages 467–478, 2005.

[15] N. X. Vinh, J. Epps, and J. Bailey. Information theoretic measures for clusterings comparison: is a correction for chance necessary? In *ICML*, pages 1073–1080, 2009.

[16] J. Yin and Z. Tan. Clustering mixed type attributes in large dataset. In *ISPA*, pages 655–661, 2005.

[17] M. J. Zaki, M. Peters, I. Assent, and T. Seidl. Clicks: An effective algorithm for mining subspace clusters in categorical datasets. *Data Knowl. Eng.*, 60(1):51–70, 2007.

A Framework for Summarizing and Analyzing Twitter Feeds

Xintian Yang
The Ohio State University
Columbus, OH
yangxin@cse.ohio-state.edu

Amol Ghoting
IBM T. J. Watson Research Center
Yorktown Heights, NY
aghoting@us.ibm.com

Yiye Ruan
The Ohio State University
Columbus, OH
ruan@cse.ohio-state.edu

Srinivasan Parthasarathy
The Ohio State University
Columbus, OH
srini@cse.ohio-state.edu

ABSTRACT

The firehose of data generated by users on social networking and microblogging sites such as Facebook and Twitter is enormous. Real-time analytics on such data is challenging with most current efforts largely focusing on the efficient querying and retrieval of data produced recently. In this paper, we present a dynamic pattern driven approach to summarize data produced by Twitter feeds. We develop a novel approach to maintain an in-memory summary while retaining sufficient information to facilitate a range of user-specific and topic-specific temporal analytics. We empirically compare our approach with several state-of-the-art pattern summarization approaches along the axes of storage cost, query accuracy, query flexibility, and efficiency using real data from Twitter. We find that the proposed approach is not only scalable but also outperforms existing approaches by a large margin.

Categories and Subject Descriptors

H.2.8 [**Database Applications**]: Data Mining

Keywords

Data Summarization, Analytics, Twitter

1. INTRODUCTION

Microblogging, a lightweight and easy form of communication within social networks such as Facebook, Google+ and Twitter, has become ubiquitous in its use with over 4 billion mobile devices worldwide of which over 1 billion support smart services. An increasing number of organizations and agencies are turning to extract and analyze useful nuggets of information from such services to aid in functions as diverse as emergency response, viral marketing, disease outbreaks, and predicting movie box office success. A fundamental challenge for effective human-computer interaction (querying and analytics) is the scale of the data involved. Twitter for instance has over 200 million users (and growing) and several hundred million tweets per day. Supporting interactive querying and analytics requires novel approaches for filtering and summarizing such data.

Given the diverse nature of applications, a number of queries may be of interest. Queries such as: *What are the currently trending topics?; What did a specific user tweet about today or yesterday?* are straightforward to support since one only needs to maintain recent data to answer such queries. However, often times users and organizations, are interested in capturing high level trends about both current and past activity – particularly highly trending past activity to understand the evolution of user interests and topic trending. For example complex queries of the following form would be of interest: *What topics were people talking about in a specific time interval (2 weeks in the past)?; How has a particular topic evolved across multiple time intervals?; How have a user's or a group's tweets, or topics they tweet on changed over time?* Answers to such questions may enable organizations to understand questions related to the lineage of topic evolution as well as to better understand user interests, their influence, and possibly build a model of trust for specific users and groups.

Answering such queries in real-time is challenging simply because of the scale of the data that is produced – the memory footprint will grow linearly with time and it can easily overwhelm the capacity of even the most powerful computer systems. In this study, we aim to build a summary of microblogging data, focusing on Twitter feeds, that can fit in a limited memory budget and can help to answer complex queries. In our view the desiderata for such a framework include: 1) efficient, incremental summary construction (ideally using a single pass and at pace with data influx rate); 2) budgeted memory which grows at most logarithmically with data influx; and 3) support for complex querying and analytics with low reconstruction error (particularly on more recent data, or on highly trending data). Ideally, we would like to be able to answer queries about the topics in a time interval in the past, and evolutionary events related to specific topics across multiple time intervals.

A novel framework (Figure 1) is proposed to address this desiderata. The elements of our framework include: a) SPUR, a batch summarization and compression algorithm that relies on a novel notion of pattern utility and ranking

KDD'12, August 12–16, 2012, Beijing, China.

which can be incrementally updated; b) D-SPUR, a dynamic variant of SPUR that accordingly merges summaries and maintains pyramidal time frames that grows logarithmically while enabling querying at multiple temporal contexts; and c) TED-SPUR, a topic and event based analytics tool to support complex querying on dynamic data.

We compare the effectiveness of various SPUR variants against state-of-the-art pattern summarization algorithms on a large corpus of Twitter data along the axes of compressability, reconstruction error, efficiency and flexibility in querying. We find that the SPUR variants are up to two orders of magnitude faster and can produce summaries with much lower reconstruction errors than extant approaches. Furthermore, maintaining temporal information in D-SPUR enables the approximate reconstruction of original data over arbitrary time intervals facilitating novel complex queries. We further demonstrate the efficacy of TED-SPUR, in analyzing temporal topic evolution and capturing real-world behavioral events.

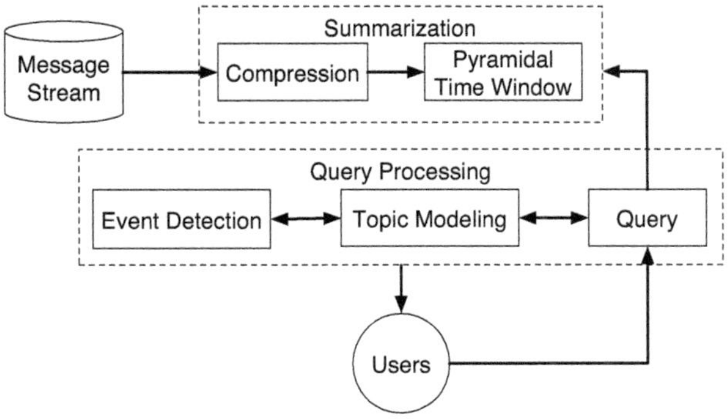

Figure 1: Overview of Summarization via Pattern Utility and Ranking (SPUR) Framework

2. STREAM SUMMARIZATION

In this section, we introduce the summarization component of our proposed stream processing framework.

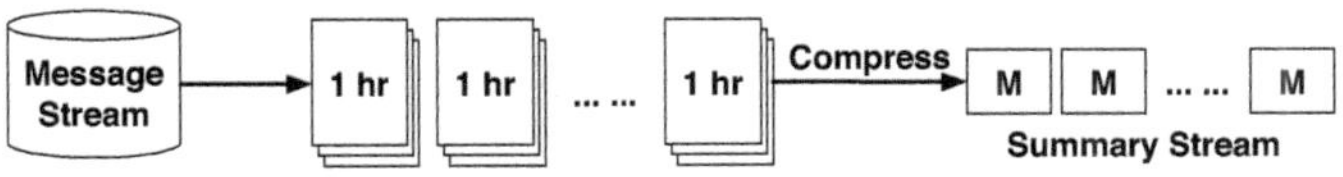

Figure 2: Division and compression of message stream

Given the input message stream with proper word stemming and stop-word removal performed, we divide it into approximately equal-sized batches, e.g. one hour per batch (the first arrow in Figure 2). To compress each batch of messages into a summary object which can fit in a constant memory budget M (the second arrow in Figure 2), we describe our SPUR algorithm in Section 2.1. Then in Section 2.2 we discuss the D-SPUR algorithm which ensures the summary size grows logarithmically with time.

2.1 SPUR

We develop a novel algorithm called SPUR (Summarization via Pattern Utility and Ranking) to summarize a batch of transactions with low compression ratio and high quality in a highly scalable fashion. Our basic idea of compressing a batch of tweets is to replace individual words with frequently used phrases that can cover the original content of the tweets. Consider the example in Figure 3 (left), each column represents a word and each row represents a tweet. The original tweets need 24 words to be stored in memory. However, if we use the frequent phrases as patterns to represent the tweets, we can save 10 of 24 words (Figure 3 right). Our approach represents each tweet as a transaction of words and a batch as a set of transactions. We cast the challenge of finding frequent phrases as a frequent itemset mining problem. To compress a batch of tweets into a summary with memory budget M, we aim to reduce the storage size by covering the transactions with frequent patterns. There are three main challenges one need to address: compressability, scalability and quality (of compressed summary).

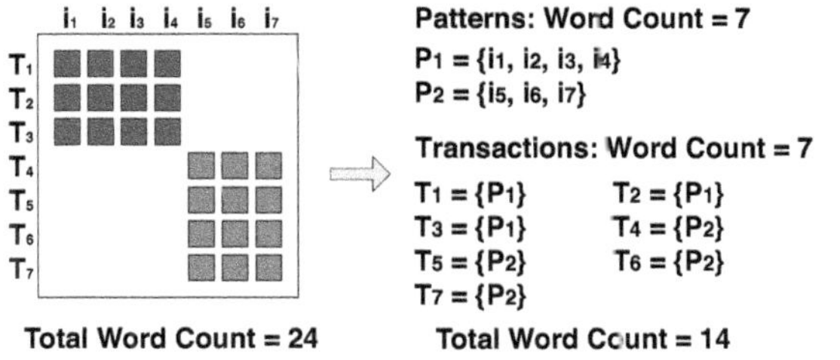

Figure 3: A batch of tweets compressed to a summary

Algorithm 1 provides the pseudo code of SPUR. The algorithm receives a batch of transactions B, a memory budget M, a support threshold σ and a false positive rate f as input. It outputs a summary which can fit in the memory budget M with false positive rate lower than f. First, our algorithm mines frequent itemsets above the support threshold σ as candidate patterns (line 1). We use LCM [13] for our purposes. Second, we define a function to capture the utility of each pattern in terms of compressing the transactions (line 3). Third, we rank all the candidates by their utility values and insert them into a priority queue (lines 2 – 4). Finally, we iteratively select the top ranked pattern to cover the items in transactions until we reach the memory budget M or the top pattern is not cost effective for compression any more (lines 5 – 13).

Algorithm 1 SPUR(B, M, σ, f)

```
1: P ← MineFrequentPatterns(B, σ); Q ← φ; size ← 0;
2: for all p ∈ P do
3:    p.utility = Utility(p, f); Q.insert(p);
4: end for
5: while size < M do
6:    p ← Q.top;
7:    if p.utility ≥ 0 then
8:       Replace(B, p); {Replace items using p}
9:       UpdateRank(Q, p); size = size + p.cost;
10:   else
11:      break;
12:   end if
13: end while
```

A coverage of transaction $T_i \in B$ using pattern p will replace the items in $T_i \cap p$ with a pointer to p. Two types of errors will be introduced: false negative errors are the items in the original data but are not covered by any pattern; false positive errors are items not belonging to a transaction but are introduced by a pattern coverage, i.e. the items in $p \setminus T_i$. False negative/positive rate is the ratio of false negative/positive errors over the total number of items in the transactions. In Algorithm 1, f is a threshold to control false positive rate; and the false negative rate is controlled by σ and M together where σ decides the infrequent items dropped by frequent pattern mining and M controls the selection of frequent items in the summary, thus indirectly determines the frequent items that will be dropped. Next, we will first introduce the definition of pattern utility.

Pattern Utility and Ranking: We define the utility of a pattern p covering a transaction T_i as:

$$u(p, T_i) = |T_i \cap p| - 1 - |p \setminus T_i| \quad (1)$$

where $|T_i \cap p|$ captures the storage saved by p, 1 is the storage cost of a pointer to p in the compressed representation of T_i and $|p \setminus T_i|$ is the amount of false positive errors. Here $|T_i \cap p| - 1$ records the total savings in storage space whereas $|p \setminus T_i|$ penalizes false positive errors [1].

There is also a cost of space for storing pattern p, because we need to record the actual items in p. But this is not a cost for a coverage with an individual transaction, but the cost for a set of transactions. Given a set of transactions $C \subseteq B$, the total utility of covering all transactions in C with p is defined as the sum of the utilities on all transactions in C less the cost of storing pattern p:

$$U(p, C) = \sum_{T_i \in C} u(p, T_i) - |p| \quad (2)$$

The compression utility $Utility(p)$ of pattern p is the maximum value of $U(p, C)$ among all $C \subseteq B$. The *coverage set* $C(p)$ of p is defined as the set of transactions that yields this maximum value. So,

$$Utility(p) = \max_{C \subseteq B} U(p, C) \qquad C(p) = \arg\max_{C \subseteq B} U(p, C) \quad (3)$$

For example, in Figure 3, the best compression using pattern p_1 is to cover transactions T_1, T_2 and T_3. So $C(p_1) = \{T_1, T_2, T_3\}$, $u(p_1, T_i) = |T_i \cap p_1| - 1 - |p_1 \setminus T_i| = 3$ for $i = 1$ to 3 and $Utility(p_1) = \sum_{i=1}^{3} u(p_1, T_i) - |p_1| = 5$. Our compression algorithm needs to find the value of $Utility(p)$ for each pattern p and the transactions in $C(p)$ with the constraint that the false positive rate should be below a threshold f.

Let's first consider a simple case where no false positive errors are allowed in a coverage. In this case p can only cover transactions that contain p. Suppose pattern p with support $\sigma(p)$ and length $l(p)$, if we use $sup(p) = \{T | p \subseteq T\}$ to represent the set of all transactions that contain p, then $C(p) = sup(p)$. Therefore,

$$\begin{aligned} Utility_{no\_fp}(p) &= \sum_{T_i \in sup(p)} (|T_i \cap p| - 1 - |p \setminus T_i|) - |p| \\ &= \sum_{T_i \in sup(p)} (l(p) - 1) - l(p) \\ &= l(p) \cdot \sigma(p) - \sigma(p) - l(p) \end{aligned}$$

Next, let's increase the complexity of the pattern coverage problem by allowing false positive errors but no limitation of the false positive rate. Each transaction T_i will add $u(p, T_i)$ to $Utility(p)$. So the value of $Utility(p)$ is at maximum when all T_i's with $u(p, T_i) \geq 0$ are in p's coverage set $C(p)$. We can rewrite the definition of $u(p, T_i)$ as:

$$\begin{aligned} u(p, T_i) &= |T_i \cap p| - 1 - (|p| - |T_i \cap p|) \\ &= 2 \cdot |T_i \cap p| - 1 - l(p) \end{aligned}$$

[1] A pattern coverage will not introduce false negative errors, because the support threshold in frequent pattern mining decides the infrequent items we dropped.

So the set of transactions that can maximize p's utility is $C(p) = \{T \ s.t. \ |T \cap p| \geq (l(p) + 1)/2\}$. It is inefficient if we intersect all possible pattern and transaction pairs. The following theorem provides a faster way to find $C(p)$ by only considering p and its sub-patterns' supporting transactions.

THEOREM 1. *Suppose* $C'(p) = \{\bigcup sup(p_i) \,|\, p_i \subseteq p$ *and* $l(p_i) \geq (l(p) + 1)/2\}$, *where* $sup(p_i)$ *represents all transactions containing* p_i, *then* $C(p) = C'(p)$.

PROOF. First show $C(p) \subseteq C'(p)$.
$\forall T_i \in C(p)$, $|T_i \cap p| \geq (l(p) + 1)/2$. Let $p' = T_i \cap p$, then $p' \subseteq p$ and $l(p') \geq (l(p) + 1)/2$. $p' \subseteq T_i \Rightarrow T_i \in sup(p') \subseteq C'(p)$. So $C(p) \subseteq C'(p)$.
Then show $C'(p) \subseteq C(p)$.
$\forall T_i \in C'(p)$, $\exists p_i$ s.t. $T_i \in sup(p_i)$, $p_i \subseteq p$ and $|p_i| \geq (l(p)+1)/2$. Then $p_i \subseteq T_i \cap p$ and $|T_i \cap p| \geq |p_i| \geq (l(p)+1)/2 \Rightarrow T_i \in C(p)$. So $C'(p) \subseteq C(p)$. □

Theorem 1 shows that the utility value of a pattern p can be maximized by covering all transactions that contain sub-patterns of p with more than half of the length of p. We essentially replace p's sub-patterns with p in those transactions. This process will reduce the storage size by introducing false positive items. However, we cannot control the upper bound of the false positive rate in this strategy. Next, we will discuss how we can guarantee that the false positive rate in the summary is below a threshold f.

Algorithm 2 Utility(p, f)

```
1: p.utility ← l(p)·σ(p) − σ(p) − l(p); p.coverage_set ← sup(p);
2: p.replaced_patterns ← {p}; area ← l(p)·σ(p); fp_error ← 0; {Safe
   to add transactions without false positive}
3: sub(p) ← all sub-patterns of p;
4: sort sub(p) by pattern length from long to short;
5: for all p_i ∈ sub(p) do
6:    if |p_i| ≥ (|p| + 1)/2 then
7:       transactions ← sup(p_i) \ p.coverage_set; {First find the new
         transactions that can potentially be covered.}
8:       new_area ← area + l(p) · |transactions|;
9:       new_error ← fp_error + (l(p) − l(p_i)) · |transactions|;
10:      if new_error / new_area ≤ f then
11:         p.utility ← p.utility + |transactions| · (2 · l(p_i) − l(p) − 1);
            {Update p's utility}
12:         p.coverage_set ← p.coverage_set ∪ transactions;
13:         p.replaced_patterns ← p.replaced_patterns ∪{p_i};
14:         area ← new_area; fp_error ← new_error;
15:      else
16:         break;
17:      end if
18:   else
19:      break;
20:   end if
21: end for
```

Suppose p_i is a sub-pattern of p, if we replace p_i with p in the transactions that contain p_i but not p, the false positive rate is $1 - l(p_i)/l(p)$. Therefore, longer sub-patterns will introduce lower false positive rate. To control the false positive rate below a threshold f, Algorithm 2 first sorts the sub-patterns of p from long to short (line 3 – 4) and keeps replacing the sub-patterns in this order until the false positive rate is higher than f (line 5 – 21). With this greedy strategy, Algorithm 2 can find the maximum utility of a pattern below a false positive rate threshold. Algorithm 2 also generates the transactions in the coverage (p.coverage_set) as well as the sub-patterns that are replaced by p (p.replaced_patterns). Note: we define the utility of singleton patterns as 0. Instead of making a new pattern with only a single item and storing pointers to it, we can directly store the item id in each transaction and it will cost the same amount of memory as the original data.

The SPUR algorithm calls Algorithm 2 to initialize the ranking of pattern utilities. However, the ranking can change dynamically during the compression iterations. Existing approaches either use a static approximation (e.g. Krimp [11]) or if dynamic, need multiple passes of the data. Hence, they do not fit in the setting of summarizing data streams. Next, we will show how our utility function can be dynamically and efficiently updated without accessing the original data.

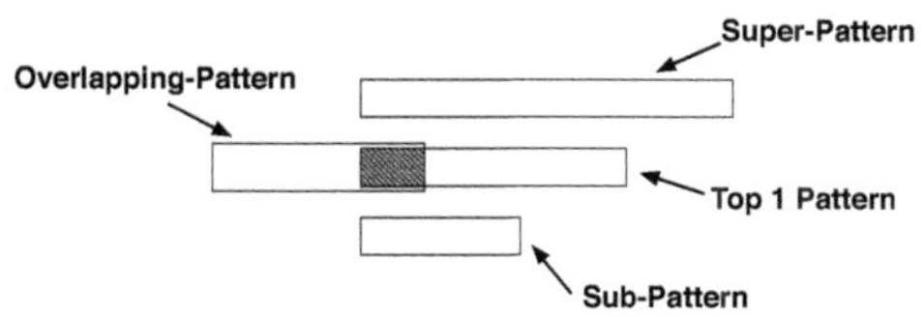

Figure 4: Dynamic adjustment of pattern utility

Compression with Dynamic Ranking Adjustment There are three categories of patterns whose utility values will be affected by a top 1 pattern p: p's super-patterns, sub-patterns and overlapping patterns (Figure 4). Algorithm 3 elaborates how we penalize the utilities of these three types of patterns when p is selected. For an affected pattern p_a, we first find the transactions in the intersection of p_a's and p's coverage sets (line 2). The effective coverage area of p_a will be changed by including p in these transactions, because the common items of p and p_a are already covered by p. Based on the type of p_a, we can penalize its utility value by the total area covered by p already. For a super-pattern p_{super}, the area covered by p is $l(p)$ per transaction (line 4) and $l(p_{overlap} \cap p)$ for a overlapping pattern $p_{overlap}$ (line 12). For a sub-pattern p_{sub}, the area covered by p is $l(p_{sub})$ per transaction. But since the transactions covered by p are not in p_{sub}'s coverage set any more, the space of the pointers to p_{sub} in those transactions are saved. So each transaction is penalized by $l(p_{sub}) - 1$ (line 6). We can see our algorithm only needs to deduct a value of area from a pattern's utility without scanning the items in the transactions.

Algorithm 3 UpdateRank(Q, p)

```
1: for all p_a ∈ p's sub-/super-/overlapping set do
2:     covered_set ← p_a.coverage_set ∩ p.coverage_set;
3:     if p_a is p's super-pattern then
4:         p_a.utility ← p_a.utility - l(p) · |covered_set|;
5:     else if p_a is p's sub-pattern then
6:         p_a.utility ← p_a.utility - (l(p_a) − 1) · |covered_set|;
7:         p_a.coverage_set ← p_a.coverage_set \ covered_set;
8:         if p_a.coverage_set is empty then
9:             Q.remove(p_a); {p_a has been replaced by p.}
10:        end if
11:    else
12:        p_a.utility ← p_a.utility - l(p_a ∩ p) · |covered_set|;
13:    end if
14: end for
```

There are several implementation and performance related issues worth mentioned: First, our algorithm needs to find the sub-/super-/overlapping-pattern relationships among all patterns. However, once these relationships are established, they are reused by the many iterations of the SPUR algorithm. Second, the overlapping-patterns with p are found by taking the union of all super-patterns of p's sub-patterns. Third, we use a max heap to maintain the candidate pattern queue dynamically.

2.2 D-SPUR

We now present D-SPUR, the dynamic version of SPUR. In D-SPUR, we enhance and modify the pyramidal time window suggested by Aggarwal *at al.* [1] for clustering in data streams. Our enhancements center on the fact that we need to find an effective way to manage the stream of summary objects produced by SPUR while limiting the growth of memory footprint and reconstruction error (especially on recent and trending data). D-SPUR summarizes dynamic message streams by maintaining the pyramidal time window in Figure 5.

The input to the pyramidal time window is a stream of summary objects, each with memory size M. (right half of Figure 2). A level of the time window can hold two summary objects. Figure 5 demonstrates how the summary objects are inserted into the time window. Initially, the time window is empty, so Summary 1 and 2 can be directly inserted into Level 1 of the time window (Figure 5(a), (b) and (c)). When Summary 3 is ready, Level 1 of the time window is full (Figure 5(c)). We will *merge* the summary objects on the filled level, expand the time window with one more level, and insert the merged summary objects into the expanded level. In Figure 5(d), Summary 1 and 2 are merged and moved to Level 2, and Sumary 3 is inserted into Level 1. Similarly, Summary 4 is inserted into Level 1 (Figure 5(e)). When Summary 5 is ready, we first merge Summary 3 and 4 into a new summary object Summary 3-4 and insert it into Level 2 of the time window and place Summary 5 on Level 1 (Figure 5(f)). Note that the product of the merging operation (e.g. Summary 1-2 and Summary 3-4) must also fit in the constant memory budget M.

Using the pyramidal time window, the total memory footprint will grow logarithmically. More importantly, historical data is more compressed than recent data, so the summary is more accurate in recent time intervals. Next, we discuss the key operations of maintaining the time window: merging two summaries and maintaining time information.

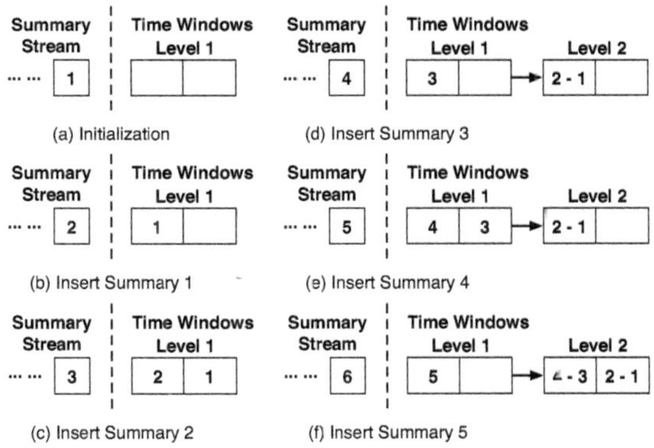

Figure 5: Maintaining pyramidal time window

Merging Two Summary Objects Given two summary objects S_1 and S_2, the corresponding patterns and the transactions represented by the patterns are $S_1 = (P_1, T_1)$ and $S_2 = (P_2, T_2)$. Both S_1 and S_2 are produced by the SPUR algorithm and can fit in a constant memory budget M. When merging S_1 and S_2 in the time window (Figure 5), we want to merge them into a new summary $S = (P, T)$ that can also fit in M. We first combine the pattern sets P_1 and P_2 to a new pattern set P' by removing the duplicate patterns, representing all the transactions in T_1 and T_2 with a unified alphabet P'. Then we merge the transaction sets T_1 and T_2 into a new transaction set T' to get a new summary (P', T').

However, we cannot guarantee that (P', T') can fit in the memory budget M. More compression is needed to meet the budget. We rely on the output of SPUR to perform the compression. Remember the SPUR algorithm outputs a utility value for each pattern. This value measures the compression performance of a pattern. We use a greedy strategy to reduce the memory space of (P', T'). We sort the pattern utility values from low to high. We start with dropping the low utility patterns and removing them from the transactions they cover. This process will stop when the total size of the patterns and transactions left is below M. We output the final merged summary $S = (P, T)$ as our result. D-SPUR uses this merging algorithm to maintain the pyramidal time window in Figure 5. After merging two summaries, however, the time information of the messages is lost since we cannot distinguish the messages between two batches. We will address this problem next.

Maintaining Time It is necessary to maintain time information for the transactions in a summary, otherwise the summary cannot effectively answer a query about an arbitrary time interval. For example, if the state for the summary is as shown in Figure 6, and we want to retrieve messages in batches 3 to 6, the query cannot be answered if no time information is stored with each transaction as the messages in batches 1 to 4 and 5 to 8 are all merged together.

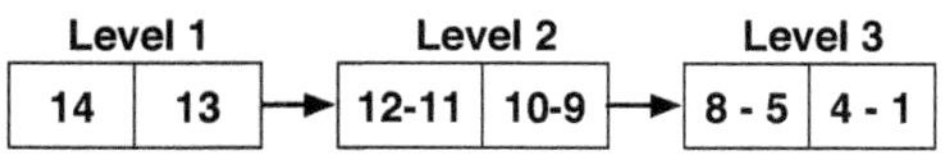

Figure 6: An example of the pyramidal time window

When we compress individual batches to summaries with SPUR, the transactions in the summary are represented by the patterns selected by SPUR. It is likely that two similar but non-identical transactions will be represented by the same set of patterns and they will essentially be identical in the summary. Instead of storing them separately, we store distinct transactions in the summary and associate a count with each transaction to indicate how many times a transaction appeared in a batch.

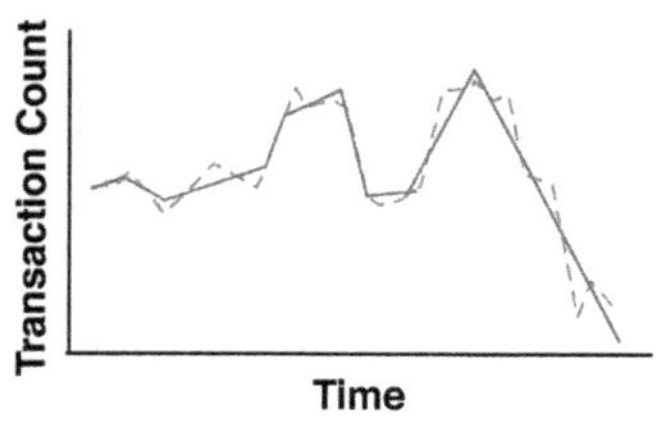

Figure 7: An example of the time series of a transaction

When D-SPUR merges summaries of two adjacent batches, the merging operation combines their transaction sets. If two transactions contain the same set of patterns, they must be from two different batches, because within a batch, we only keep distinct transactions. Instead of summing the count of these two transactions, we could concatenate their counts in time order and form a time series with two points. As D-SPUR combines more summaries, we concatenate more points to each transaction. A time series that spans batches (i.e. the red dashed line in Figure 7) is therefore formed for each transaction, enabling reconstruction of the exact count in any time interval.

However, this time series will grow linearly with time, which will violate the memory budget constraint. We therefore approximate (compress) the time series using a constant number of linear regression lines (blue line in Figure 7). Whenever the number of regression lines exceed a constant k after merging summary objects, D-SPUR will compress the two series for all transactions. We employ methods proposed by Palpanas *et al.* [9] for the purpose of compressing the time series. Their methods can find the optimal approximation when concatenating two adjacent time series.

3. LIVE ANALYTICS WITH TED-SPUR

Next, we present the query processing component of our framework, an analytical tool *TED-SPUR* (Topic and Event detection with D-SPUR), to support complex queries on dynamic data. One typical example of analytical query on text data is to discover topics [3, 10, 12]. Under the dynamic setting of message streams, it is also important to model the evolutionary behaviors [2] of topics. With the in-memory summary produced by D-SPUR, we can approximately reconstruct the original messages to perform those two tasks on arbitrary time interval(s).

We employ an implementation of non-negative matrix factorization (NMF) algorithm [12] to find the topics from the tweets within a query time interval, as NMF has been shown to handle sparse input well. The main idea is to factor a $d \times w$ *document-word* matrix into two non-negative matrices, the first of which a $d \times k$ *document-topic* matrix and the second a $k \times w$ *topic-word* matrix.

Another interesting task of analyzing tweets stream is to discover the evolution of the topics. For this task, we define a series of events to capture the *appearance/disappearance* of a topic, the *growth/ shrinkage/ continuation* of topic popularity and the *merging/ split/ transformation* of topic content. Given two time intervals I_1 and I_2, assume I_2 is after but not necessarily succeeding I_1. Let the mined topic sets from both intervals be T_1 and T_2 respectively. Each topic is further represented as a word distribution z and a support value *sup* indicating how many times it appears in the time interval. We use asymmetric KL-divergence [5] to capture the difference between two topics with regard to their content. The formalization of topic events is as follows:

Appearance: A topic z *appears* in T_2 iff there is no topic z' in T_1 such that $D_{KL}(z, z') < \gamma$, where parameter γ measures the closeness of two topics. The intuition here is that if we cannot find a topic z' in T_1 which is close enough to topic z, we will consider topic z as a novel topic in T_2.

Disappearance: A topic z *disappears* in T_1 iff there is no topic z' in T_2 such that $D_{KL}(z, z') < \gamma$.

Growth: For two topics (z, sup) in T_2 and (z', sup') in T_1, if $D_{KL}(z, z') \leq \delta$, and $sup/sup' \geq 1 + \epsilon$ where $0 < \delta < \gamma$ and $\epsilon > 0$, then topic z *grows* from topic z'. To explain, we find a topic z in T_2 whose content is similar enough to topic z' in T_1 while it is also more frequent than z'. Here the similarity threshold δ should be much lower than γ.

Shrinkage: For two topics (z, sup) in T_2 and (z', sup') in T_1, if $D_{KL}(z, z') \leq \delta$, and $sup/sup' \leq 1 - \epsilon$ where $0 < \delta < \gamma$ and $\epsilon > 0$, then topic z' *shrinks* to topic z.

Continuation: For two topics (z, sup) in T_2 and (z', sup') in T_1, if $D_{KL}(z, z') \leq \delta$, and $1 - \epsilon < sup/sup' < 1 + \epsilon$ where

$0 < \delta < \gamma$ and $\epsilon > 0$, then there is a *continuation* from z' to z. To put it informally, if we can find two topics in T_1 and T_2 with similar enough contents and their strengths are also similar, then we regard the topic in T_2 as the continuation of the topic in T_1.

Merging: Given a topic z in T_2, and a subset of topics $\{z'\}$ from T_1 such that each z' satisfies $\delta < D_{KL}(z, z') < \gamma$. For any pair of topics z'_1 and z'_2 in $\{z'\}$, let the weighted sum of distribution be $Z = \frac{z'_1 \times sup'_1 + z'_2 \times sup'_2}{sup'_1 + sup'_2}$. If $D_{KL}(z, Z) \leq \delta$, then we say z is *merged* from z'_1 and z'_2. The *merging* event deals with topics which can neither be classified as *growth/ shrinkage/ continuation* from a previous topic, nor a newly appeared topic. The explanation is that if the content of a topic is similar enough to that of the weighted combination of two topics from previous time interval, then we consider the new topic to be *merged* from the previous two topics. Note that usually the resultant z's from NMF are divergent from each other, making it unlikely that multiple pairs in $\{z'\}$ merge into the same z.

Split: Given a topic z in T_1, and a set of topics $\{z'\}$ from T_2, such that z' satisfies $\delta < D_{KL}(z', z) < \gamma$. For any pair of topics z'_1 and z'_2 in $\{z'\}$ with the same definition of Z as above, if $D_{KL}(Z, z) \leq \delta$, then z is *split* into z'_1 and z'_2.

Transformation: If a topic z in T_2 is not involved in any of the seven aforementioned events, z is said to be *transformed* from topics $\{z'\}$ in T_1, such that each z' satisfies $\delta < D_{KL}(z, z') < \gamma$. The underlying intuition is that if a topic can find topics in the previous time interval which are partly similar to it and are not involved in any other event, then there is a content transformation to this topic.

By issuing multiple topic modeling queries over subsequent time windows and applying the above event detection algorithms, one can find evolutionary events over time.

4. EXPERIMENTAL RESULTS

Next, we present results for an extensive set of experiments we conducted to evaluate our stream summarization methods and advanced query processing capabilities. We considered several other algorithms as candidates for our baseline. Methods that use a probabilistic models to summarize patterns [15] are not efficient enough to handle the data influx rate we would like to handle. We therefore omit comparisons with these methods. We compare *SPUR* with the following algorithms: a) CDB [16] that uses rectangles to cover a transactional database b) RPMine [17] that tries to cluster the patterns and use the cluster centers to cover the remaining patterns. c) Krimp [11] that generates a static ranking of all patterns first and then summarizes the data using the top ranked patterns. Neither CDB nor RPMine can compress streaming data. Therefore, the *D-SPUR* algorithm is compared only with StreamKrimp [14], the streaming version of Krimp.

4.1 Dataset and Setup

We gathered 2100 hours of Twitter message streams from June to September in 2010[2]. The total data size is 5.9GB. For our evaluation, we partition the message stream into 1-hour batches. There are 100,000 messages per batch and 8 words per message on average after stop word removal and word stemming.

[2]As provided by Twitter, it is a 15% random sample of all messages.

All experiments were performed on a desktop machine with dual boot Red Hat Linux 6 and Windows 7 operating systems. The machine is equipped with an Intel i7 3.4GHz CPU and 16GB of main memory. Except for Krimp and StreamKrimp for which only Windows binaries are available, all algorithms were executed under Linux. All algorithms were implemented in C++.

4.2 Batch Compression With SPUR

In this section we present performance results for compressing a batch of messages to a summary object. Note that we only present results for batch summarization and not for the summary merging procedure. The SPUR algorithm is compared with the three baseline algorithms (**CDB, RPMine and Krimp**). The windows executable for Krimp and the source code for CDB and RPMine were obtained from the authors' websites. As the baseline algorithms cannot compress to a target memory budget, we relax the memory budget constraint in our algorithm by summarizing a batch until the utility of the top pattern is negative. We present results for processing the first 100 batches since they are sufficiently representative of the entire data. Our comparative study focuses on three aspects: execution time, false positive rate (i.e. compression quality) and compression ratio.

4.2.1 Comparison with CDB and RPMine

We first compare SPUR with CDB and RPMine as they all support the trade off between false positive rate and compression ratio. Support level is set to 0.01% for all three methods. We set a low support level because we want the summary to cover as many topical words as possible. We set the maximum false positive rate for SPUR and CDB to 0.1. For RPMine, the pattern cluster tightness parameter is also set to 0.1.

Figure 8a presents the running times for the three methods in log scale. It is easy to see that our method is significantly more efficient – it is at least one order of magnitude faster than RPMine, and two orders of magnitude faster than CDB. SPUR is able to process an hours worth of data in less than one minute, lending itself to our requirement of being able to process the stream in real-time.

We next evaluate the algorithms' false positive rate. Ideally, we want to introduce as few false positives as possible when reducing the data size. We therefore measure the *actual* false positive rate each method exhibits when given the same parameters for support threshold and maximum false positive rate. Figure 8b presents the false positive rate for each batch of the stream. Again, the performance of SPUR is solid – its false positive rate never exceeds 0.005. In contrast, CDB constantly suffers from a higher false positive rate, which is close to the maximum specified value. We also find that RPMine is susceptible to changes in data size, as suggested by the two spikes at batches 41 and 83. With relatively small data size for both batches, false positive rates reach 0.365 and 0.399 respectively.

As for the compression ratio (the lower the better), our method performs midway between CDB and RPMine with a range of 50% to 60% (see Figure 8c). Again note the relatively high compression ratio for RPMine for batches 41 and 83. We conjecture that RPMine tends to cluster singleton patterns with longer patterns for these cases, leading to less reduction in size and a higher false positive rate. Note

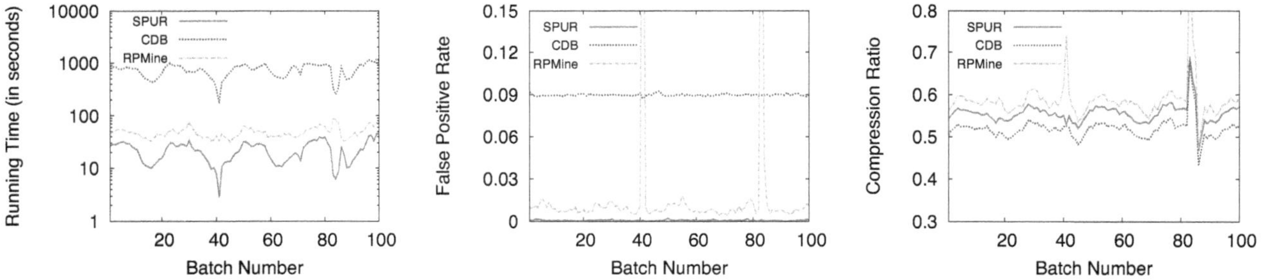

(a) Running time: SPUR vs. CDB vs. RPMine (b) False positive: SPUR vs. CDB vs. RPMine (c) Comp. ratio: SPUR vs. CDB vs. RPMine

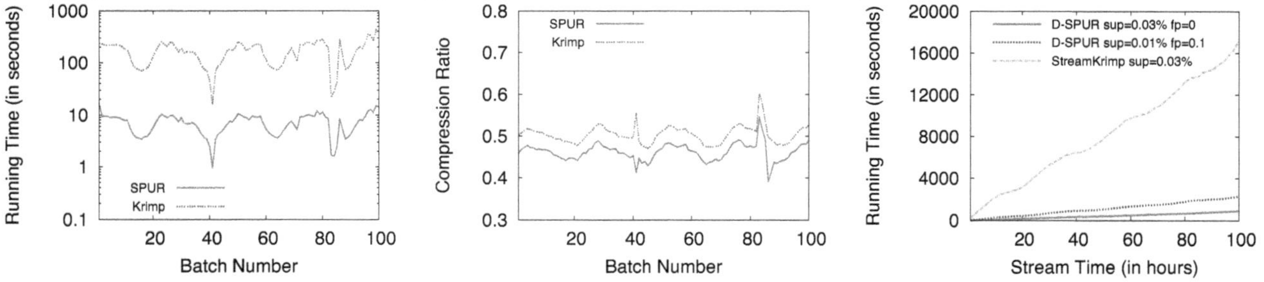

(d) Running time: SPUR vs. Krimp (e) Comp. ratio: SPUR vs. Krimp (f) Running time: stream summarization

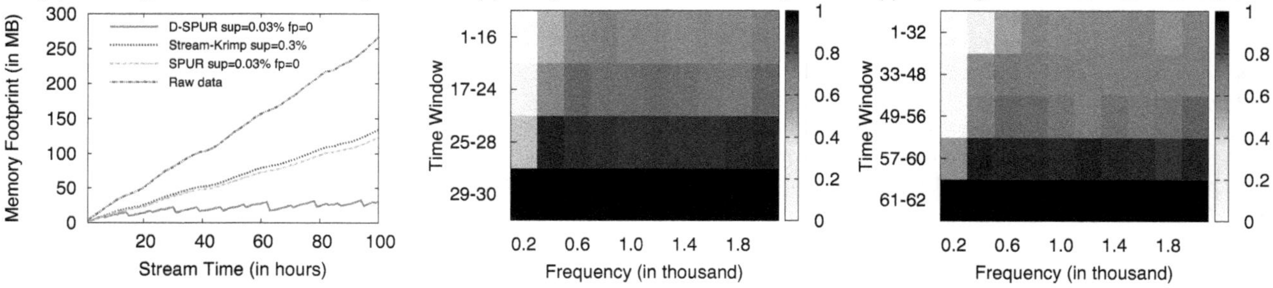

(g) Memory footprint: stream summarization (h) Query accuracy (T=30) (i) Query accuracy (T=62)

Figure 8: Experiment results for batch compression and stream summarization

that the compression quality for our method is more robust against changes in data size, which is a favorable property.

All algorithms achieve exactly the same false negative rate as this only depends on the support level that is set to be same for all algorithms.

4.2.2 *Comparison with Krimp*

For this set of experiments, we compare Krimp with SPUR. We compare KRIMP separately from CDB and RPMine for two reasons. First, it does not allow for false positives during compression. Second, its running time is very large when support level is as low as 0.01%. Therefore, we set the support level to 0.03% in the following set of experiments. For our method, we set the maximum false positive rate to 0.0.

The running times and compression ratios for the two algorithms are shown in 8d and 8e. Our method is always at least 10 times faster than Krimp, and it also bests Krimp in terms of compression ratio.

4.3 Stream Summarization with D-SPUR

In this section, we present the performance of the D-SPUR algorithm on summarizing the Twitter message stream. There is no streaming version for CDB and RPMine, thus we only compared D-SPUR with StreamKrimp at support level = 0.03% and false positive rate = 0. For D-SPUR, the memory budget M is set to 1.2 MB as we find it yields low false negative error rate in the SPUR summarization step. We use 5 linear segments to approximate the time series of the transactions. This configuration leads to a compression ratio of approximately 50% for each batch. We evaluate the algorithms in three aspects: execution time, memory footprint, and quality of the summary.

Execution time: Figure 8f shows the running times for D-SPUR and StreamKrimp. The x-axis represents the batch number and the y-axis shows the time different stream summarization algorithms take to summarize the input stream. We can see D-SPUR is much faster than StreamKrimp at the support level of 0.03%. Even at a lower support level of 0.01%, D-SPUR only takes approximately 40 minutes to summarize 100 hours worth of Twitter messages. Our method can thus process the data faster than it arrives, which is desirable for real-time stream processing.

Memory footprint: As for memory consumption, we plot the storage size of the raw stream together with the memory footprint for different summarization algorithms in Figure 8g. We can see that the memory footprint for D-SPUR grows very slowly – asymptotically it grows logarithmically in the size of the input. Furthermore, the size of D-SPUR's summary is 8 times smaller than the raw data and 3 times smaller than the summary produced by StreamKrimp. This is because the merging of two summaries in D-SPUR is based on the pyramidal time window. If one does not use the pyramidal summarization scheme, the memory footprint grows linearly (see the green line in Figure 8g). Also note that StreamKrimp has an even higher memory footprint than our SPUR algorithm. When a new batch of transactions streams in, the StreamKrimp algorithm first tries to compress the transactions with the codetable used for the previous batches. The old codetable is not always suitable for compressing the new batch and often it is forced to rebuild a new codetable for the new batch. In effect, it ends up maintaining separate summaries for individual batches.

Quality: We evaluate the summary quality by querying the summary with a randomly generated query workload. The query is in the format of a keyword w and a timestamp t. w and t are sampled uniformly at random from all words above the support threshold and all time stamps. We do not consider infrequent words because they are dropped by the frequent pattern mining algorithm and can never be retrieved by any frequent pattern based summarization algorithms. All messages containing keyword w at time t are reconstructed and returned as the query result. We represent the result as a multiset of words, and compute the Jaccard similarity between the query result and the original messages that contain w at time t to measure query accuracy. We expect the query accuracy to be high for both *recent* data and *frequent* keywords.

We present the distribution of query accuracy over time and word frequencies. Figure 8i presents the distribution of query accuracy over time and word frequencies where system time T is 62. The y-axis represents the query time stamps aligned with the pyramidal time window at T and x-axis represents the frequency of the query keywords. The color represents the accuracy at a specific time and word frequency, the darker the better. We can see on recent data, e.g. T = 61 – 62, the accuracy is high on all words; on historical data, e.g. T = 1 – 32, the accuracy is higher on frequent words than infrequent words; the overall accuracy on the recent data is higher than the historical data; and the accuracy on frequent words is generally higher than infrequent words.

Figure 8h shows the distribution of query accuracy when we rewind the system time T to 30. We observe the same trend as the accuracy on recent data for frequent words is higher than that on historical data for infrequent words. Compared with the summary at system time 62 (Figure 8i), we can see the overall query accuracy for batch 1 to 30 is higher, except for the infrequent words for batch 1 to 16. At system time 62, our pyramidal time window compresses the historical data (batch 1 to 30) more, so query accuracy on those batches is low. But at system time 30, the summary can keep more information and is more accurate.

4.4 Analytical Query with TED-SPUR

In this section, we present qualitative evaluations of our algorithm by presenting experimental results for answering topic modeling and event detection queries with our summary on the Twitter data. For these experiments, we apply D-SPUR on subsets of the 2100-hour dataset to answer topic modeling and event detection queries. The data is divided into 6-hour batches with approximately 700K messages per batch. Support threshold is set to 0.01%, false positive rate to 0.1 and M to 20 MB. For the topic modeling algorithm, we use $k = 50$ as the number of topics.

Event Type	Topic ID
Appear	21, 23, 24, 25, 28, 29, 30
Disappear	13, 14, 15, 18, 19, 20
Continue	12 → 22
Merge	(11, 16) → 26
Transform	17 → 27

Table 1: Event detection from the topics in Table 2b and 2c

Topic modeling: We build a summary of data from June 11th to June 26th. All messages generated between 5pm, June 12th and 5pm, June 13th and match the query "world cup" are retrieved from the summary. This time interval is the second day after the World Cup in South Africa began. The top 10 topics returned by NMF are listed in Table 2a, with each topic represented by the top 5 words of the topic's word distribution. There are several topics detected from our summary that are very related to the keywords "world cup". For example, "south africa" indicates the country where the World Cup was held; "vuvuzela" is a handy horn used by South African fans in the World Cup stadiums, and there was a popular debate about whether "vuvuzela" should be banned, because it made an annoying noise. Note that the query time interval is also one day before the game between England and USA. The topic modeling algorithm detected a topic mentioning this game with the keywords "ENG" and "USA". The detected topics show that our summary can approximately reconstruct the messages to support topic modeling queries.

Event Detection: Next, we give an example of an event detection query. A summary is built for data from June 26th to July 11th, and the "world cup" query is run on two time intervals: 5pm, July 3rd to 5pm, July 4th; 5pm, July 4th to 5pm July 5th. We first perform topic modeling on the retrieved messages. The resultant topics are listed in Table 2b and 2c. Note that the first time interval is the day after the quarter-final game between Netherlands and Brazil, and the day before the quarter-final game of Argentina against Germany. From Table 2b, we can see some related keywords of these two games, for example, *NED*, *BRA*, *ARG* and *GER* are abbreviations for the teams, and *Maradona* is the coach of Argentina, *Messi* and *Klose* are the players of Argentina and Germany respectively. In this time interval, we detected topics which discuss the NED vs. BRA game on the day before and predict the ARG vs. GER game. Similarly, the second time interval is the day after Germany beat ARG in the quarter-final and before the semifinal began. Table 2c lists the topics in the second time interval. We also detect topics which discuss previous day's ARG vs. GER game, such as the keywords ARG, GER, Messi and Klose. There are also messages which predict that Germany can enter the final because they defeated Argentina, and messages that predict Spain (ESP) can enter the semi-final.

Next, we apply the event detection algorithms introduced in Section 3 on the topics of the two time intervals. We set the parameters in the algorithm to $\delta = 0.5$, $\gamma = 0.5$ and $\epsilon = 0.3$. The detected events are presented in Table 1. The numbers in the table are topic ids in Table 2b and 2c. Among the events, the newly emerged topics about predicting the semifinal and final games are detected as appear; the topic about the NED vs. BRA game in the day before is categorized as disappear; two same topics about live TV coverage from the two time intervals are detected as continue event; the two topics about the ARG vs. GER game in the first

ID	Words
1	***south***, ***africa***, group, play, now
2	nowplay, yeah, people, twitter, follow
3	watch, big, play, fan, go
4	match, play, win, team, group
5	group, now, ***ENG***, go, ***USA***
6	live, home, real, watch, game
7	***vuvuzela***, watch, annoy, people, game
8	twitter, people, please, org, bit
9	***vuvuzela***, stadium, health, people, ***fifa***
10	bit, photo, show, people, match

(a) 5pm Jun 12th to 5pm Jun 13th.

ID	Words
11	***Messi***, ***German***, today, ***Klose***, goal
12	watch, game, show, tv, live
13	***Maradona***, start, say, people, match
14	fox, soccer, kickoff, down, ***ARG***
15	fan, tv, espn, score, twitter
16	***ARG***, ***GER***, match, goal, ***Klose***
17	***ARG***, out, match, wow, go
18	thank, god, please, today, give
19	tweetphoto, party, nice, look, wow
20	***NED***, ***BRA***, match, play, fly

(b) 5pm Jul 3rd to 5pm Jul 4th.

ID	Words
21	***semifinal***, tv, match, ***ESP***, go
22	watch, game, show, tv, live
23	***german***, ***final***, ***Klose***, play, wow
24	www, home, look, win, play
25	tinyurl, home, play, game, fan
26	***ARG***, ***GER***, ***Messi***, goal, ***Klose***
27	***ARG***, die, game, team, play
28	auction, dasar, demi, goal, otw
29	www, live, show, please, home
30	haha, yeah, watch, gua, cool

(c) 5pm Jul 4th to 5pm Jul 5th.

Table 2: Topics related to "world cup"

time interval are merged to a single topic in the second time interval after Germany defeated Argentina; finally, a thread of topic about Argentina is transformed to a similar topic in the second time interval. We can see that our event detection algorithm can detect evolutionary events which are aligned with events in the real world. These events can help users understand the dynamics of the topics in Twitter messages.

5. RELATED WORK

Since the content generated by social media is available as a stream of timestamped messages, dynamic studies have been conducted to track topics on the stream [7, 6], and find temporal patterns [18]. However, all of these studies assume unlimited amount of memory to store the data. We are interested in summarizing the data stream with a limited memory budget and serving new analytical tasks with the summary. Existing work can also benefit from the summary from approximately reconstructing the original data by querying the summary.

We treat each social media post as a transaction of words and use frequent patterns to summarize. The CDB [16] algorithm uses rectangles to cover a transactional database; RPMine [17] first tries to cluster the patterns and use the cluster centers to cover the remaining patterns. Methods that use a probabilistic model of the patterns [15] are slow and not capable of processing streams that arrive at a fast pace. All the above algorithms do not support mining on data streams. Krimp [11] follows the MDL principle to summarize the data with codetables, which is essentially a static ranking of patterns. StreamKrimp [14], the streaming version of Krimp, can dynamically adjust the codetable for streaming data. Traditional methods of mining frequent patterns on streams [4, 8] focus on either counting item or pattern frequencies rather than summarizing the data.

6. CONCLUSIONS

We proposed an efficient stream summarization framework, which can incrementally build summaries of Twitter message streams with one-pass over the data. We developed a novel algorithm to compress twitter messages with low compression ratio, high quality and fast running time. The memory footprint of our stream summarization algorithm grows approximately logarithmically with time. Our summary allows one to issue queries to retrieve messages over arbitrary time intervals. The original messages can be approximately reconstructed to support topic modeling algorithms. We also defined a suite of events on topics from two time intervals. An event detection algorithm is proposed to find evolutionary events between two time intervals.

Acknowledgments: This material is based upon work supported by the National Science Foundation under Grant No. SoCS-1111118 and IIS-0917070. Any opinions, findings, and conclusions or recommendations expressed in this material are those of the author(s) and do not necessarily reflect the views of the National Science Foundation.

7. REFERENCES

[1] C. Aggarwal, J. Han, J. Wang, and P. Yu. A framework for clustering evolving data streams. In *VLDB '03.*

[2] S. Asur, S. Parthasarathy, and D. Ucar. An event-based framework for characterizing the evolutionary behavior of interaction graphs. In *KDD '07.*

[3] D. M. Blei, A. Y. Ng, and M. I. Jordan. Latent dirichlet allocation. *J. Mach. Learn. Res.*, 3:993–1022, 2003.

[4] T. Calders, N. Dexters, and B. Goethals. Mining frequent items in a stream using flexible windows. *Intell. Data Anal.*, 12(3):293–304, 2008.

[5] Kullback, S. and Leibler, R. A. On Information and Sufficiency. *The Annals of Mathematical Statistics*, 22(1):79–86, 1951.

[6] J. Leskovec, L. Backstrom, and J. Kleinberg. Meme-tracking and the dynamics of the news cycle. In *KDD '09.*

[7] J. Lin, R. Snow, and W. Morgan. Smoothing techniques for adaptive online language models: topic tracking in tweet streams. In *KDD '11.*

[8] G. S. Manku and R. Motwani. Approximate frequency counts over data streams. In *VLDB '02.*

[9] T. Palpanas, M. Vlachos, E. Keogh, D. Gunopulos, and W. Truppel. Online amnesic approximation of streaming time series. In *ICDE '04.*

[10] D. Ramage, S. Dumais, and D. Liebling. Characterizing microblogs with topic models. In *ICWSM*, 2010.

[11] A. Siebes, J. Vreeken, and M. van Leeuwen. Item sets that compress. In *SDM '06.*

[12] V. Sindhwani, A. Ghoting, E. Ting, and R. Lawrence. Extracting insights from social media with large-scale matrix approximations. *IBM J. Res. Dev.*, 55:527–539, Sept. 2011.

[13] T. Uno, M. Kiyomi, and H. Arimura. Lcm ver. 2: Efficient mining algorithms for frequent/closed/maximal itemsets. In *ICDM '04 FIMI Workshop*, 2004.

[14] M. van Leeuwen and A. Siebes. Streamkrimp: Detecting change in data streams. In *ECML/PKDD '08.*

[15] C. Wang and S. Parthasarathy. Summarizing itemset patterns using probabilistic models. In *KDD '06.*

[16] Y. Xiang, R. Jin, D. Fuhry, and F. F. Dragan. Succinct summarization of transactional databases: an overlapped hyperrectangle scheme. In *KDD '08.*

[17] D. Xin, J. Han, X. Yan, and H. Cheng. Mining compressed frequent-pattern sets. In *VLDB '05.*

[18] J. Yang and J. Leskovec. Patterns of temporal variation in online media. In *WSDM '11.*

Entity-Centric Topic-Oriented Opinion Summarization in Twitter

Xinfan Meng[‡*] Furu Wei[†] Xiaohua Liu[†] Ming Zhou[†] Sujian Li[‡] Houfeng Wang[‡]
[‡]MOE Key Lab of Computational Linguistics, Peking University
[†]Microsoft Research Asia
[‡]{mxf, lisujian, wanghf}@pku.edu.cn
[†]{fuwei,xiaoliu,mingzhou}@microsoft.com

ABSTRACT

Microblogging services, such as Twitter, have become popular channels for people to express their opinions towards a broad range of topics. Twitter generates a huge volume of instant messages (i.e. tweets) carrying users' sentiments and attitudes every minute, which both necessitates automatic opinion summarization and poses great challenges to the summarization system. In this paper, we study the problem of opinion summarization for entities, such as celebrities and brands, in Twitter. We propose an entity-centric topic-based opinion summarization framework, which aims to produce opinion summaries in accordance with topics and remarkably emphasizing the insight behind the opinions. To this end, we first mine topics from #hashtags, the human-annotated semantic tags in tweets. We integrate the #hashtags as weakly supervised information into topic modeling algorithms to obtain better interpretation and representation for calculating the similarity among them, and adopt Affinity Propagation algorithm to group #hashtags into coherent topics. Subsequently, we use templates generalized from paraphrasing to identify tweets with deep insights, which reveal reasons, express demands or reflect viewpoints. Afterwards, we develop a target (i.e. entity) dependent sentiment classification approach to identifying the opinion towards a given target (i.e. entity) of tweets. Finally, the opinion summary is generated through integrating information from dimensions of topic, opinion and insight, as well as other factors (e.g. topic relevancy, redundancy and language styles) in an unified optimization framework. We conduct extensive experiments on a real-life data set to evaluate the performance of individual opinion summarization modules as well as the quality of the produced summary. The promising experiment results show the effectiveness of the proposed framework and algorithms.

*Contribution during internship at Microsoft Research Asia.

KDD'12, August 12–16, 2012, Beijing, China.

Categories and Subject Descriptors

I.2.7 [**ARTIFICIAL INTELLIGENCE**]: Natural Language Processing—*Text analysis*

General Terms

Algorithms, Experimentation

Keywords

Opinion summarization, sentiment analysis, topic analysis, #hashtag, Twitter

1. INTRODUCTION

Twitter[1] is a microblogging service that allows people to publish short messages (i.e. tweets) up to 140 characters to share with others what is happening, what is interesting, as well as their feelings and opinions. In the recent several years, Twitter has become an extremely popular site. It has been reported that about 200 million[2] tweets are posted on June 30, 2011. In these tweets, people not only share their daily update information or personal conversation, but also exchange their opinions towards a broad range of topics. For example, they may talk about the newly released electronic products, express their feelings to celebrities, and deliver their comments on politicians or global events, etc. Consequently, we can use Twitter to survey public opinions. In this paper, we are particularly interested in the sentiment towards certain entities , such as celebrities, brands and products. These opinions are extremely useful in many real-life applications. For instance, politicians can study opinions in Twitter in order to know their public image, and company can study opinions in Twitter to obtain customer feedbacks.

The huge volume of tweets carrying sentiments necessitates automatic summarization techniques, which assists users in consuming these opinions. Ideally, we expect the opinion summary to convey the overview of the opinions for a specific entity from the public perspective. However, people may express opinions towards different aspects, or topics, of an entity. Take the US president Obama as an example, people may criticize (in a negative manner) his economic revitalization plans, but firmly support (in a positive attitude) Obama's counter-terrorism polices. This suggests a fine-grained summary, in terms of the different topics, instead of the general summary that mixes up the opinions

[1]http://twitter.com
[2]http://blog.twitter.com/2011/06/200-million-tweets-per-day.html

from all aspects regarding Obama. Furthermore, in Twitter, many tweets simply reveal the sentiment information. For example, "*I love Obama! #libya*". These tweets certainly account for accumulating the overall sentiment for the target, but do not deliver much information for the underlying insight behind the opinions, which are even more important for users. On the other hand, there are tweets in Twitter that explicitly state the factors leading to the positive or negative opinions. We show a typical example: "*I think it is time to say that Barack Obama deserves credit for backing up his words with action on #Libya despite domestic opposition.*" We can clearly understand the reasons underlying the sentiment from the tweet. To summarize, the opinion summary should include three key elements, which are **topic**, **sentiment** and **insight**.

In this paper, we study the problem of opinion summarization for entities in Twitter. In particular, we propose an entity-centric topic-based opinion summarization framework, which aims to produce opinion summaries in accordance with topics and remarkably emphasizing the insight behind the opinions. It has been well-recognized that tweets are short, noisy and ungrammatical, which issues tough challenges for topic analysis, sentiment analysis as well as identifying tweets with insights in Twitter. As for topics analysis, we leverage the human-annotated semantic tags, i.e. #hashtags to assist identifying topics from tweets. #hashtags are created organically by Twitter users as a way to categorize messages and to highlight topics, which is done by simply prefixing a word or a phrase with a symbol # to mark keywords or topics in tweets, such as "#hashtag". For example, in the tweet "*Neelie Kroes, Vice President of European Commission, Digital Agenda Commissioner, will be Keynote speaker at #www2012 : http://www2012.org/*", the author marked up the topic keyword "#www2012" as a #hashtag. Besides, in Twitter, people often group several words together to form a #hashtag, for example, #IraqWar and #HealthCare. Those #hashtags have clear boundaries and often can be viewed as semantic concepts, hence are more suitable as topics than n-gram phrases. The extensive use of #hashtags makes Twitter more expressive and welcomed by people. We measure on a data set with around 0.2 million tweets and find that around 23% of them have at least one #hashtag in each. Among all unique #hashtags, we sample 100 #hashtags and find 75% are useful for topic extraction. The statistics show a great potential for mining topics from #hashtags in Twitter.

Consequently, we integrate #hashtags as weakly supervised information into topic modeling algorithms to obtain better interpretation and representation for calculating the similarity among them, and then adopt Affinity Propagation algorithm to group #hashtags into coherent topics. We develop a target (i.e. entity) dependent sentiment classification approach to identifying the opinion towards a given target (i.e. entity) of tweets. We incorporate the dependency relationship between the sentiment lexicons and the target (i.e. entity) into the lexicon based sentiment classification framework. Subsequently, we use template methods to identify insightful tweets that revealing reasons, expressing demands or reflecting viewpoints to embed deep insights into the opinion summary. However, template methods may suffer from the problem of low recall, we thus employ paraphrasing approach to conduct template expansion. Finally, the opinion summary is generated through integrating information from the above-mentioned dimensions as well as other factors (e.g. redundancy and language styles) in an unified optimization framework.

We conduct extensive experiments on a real-life data set to evaluate the performance of individual opinion summarization modules as well as the quality of the produced summary. The promising experiment results show the effectiveness of the proposed framework and algorithms. To the best of our knowledge, the work in this paper is the first attempt on opinion summarization in Twitter.

2. RELATED WORK

Opinion summarization is a broad and diversified research topic. Most existing work focuses on summarizing opinions from user generated content such as product reviews [11, 12], movie reviews [28] or hotel reviews [26]. They follow the aspect-based opinion summarization paradigm which analyzes sentiment on fine-grained features or aspects of a product. The features can be the functionality of the product, like camera functionality of a mobile phone, or a part of the product, like the screen of a mobile phone. In these work, aspects are extracted from reviews by association rule mining [11, 12] or aspect-sentiment topic models [18, 25, 19], extensions of topic models. Then, the opinion towards each aspect is extracted and summarized. In the simplest case, the summary is a positive or negative label aggregated over the user generated content. Different methods are proposed to assign the sentiment labels for aspects. Some of them leverage existing sentiment classifier, while others directly model aspect-sentiment relation using the aspect-sentiment models [19]. The interested readers are referred to [22] and [16] for a general introduction to opinion summarization, and [14] for a more recent survey on opinion summarization. The above-mentioned work can be viewed as opinion summarization on restricted domain (product reviews, movie reviews, etc.), unlike our approach, which is applied in Twitter, a general domain opinion source.

Sentiment analysis on microblogging services like Twitter is also receiving popularity. Barbosa and Feng conduct sentiment classification on tweets via two-stage SVM classifier [1]. They focus on selecting features and combining different label sources in order to remove noises in Twitter. Davidov et al. incorporate #hashtags and smileys from tweets as sentiment labels [8]. O'Connor et al. determine the sentiments by subjective Lexicon [21] . Jiang et al. study target-dependent Twitter sentiment classification [13]. Wang et al. [27] propose to conduct sentiment classification on #hashtags, which are coarsely regarded as topics in their work. These work mainly focuses on sentiment classification, which apparently differs from the work described in this paper.

3. ENTITY-CENTRIC TOPIC-ORIENTED OPINION SUMMARIZATION

We start this section by a formal definition of the task of entity-centric topic-oriented opinion summarization in Twitter and then present an overview of the proposed approach.

Given a set of tweets $\mathcal{T}$ mentioning an entity e, we aim to produce a opinion summary $O = \{O_1, O_2, \ldots, O_N\}$, where,

- N is the number of topics;
- $O_i, i \in [1, N]$, is a $< label, \{t\} >$ pair, where *label* is

the label of the topic, and $\{t\} \subseteq \mathcal{T}$ is a set of insightful opinionated tweets.

We refer a tweet $t_i \in \{t\}$ as an *insightful opinionated tweet* to indicate a tweet not only conveys opinions but also provides insight. We show an example of insightful opinionated tweet as follows.

> I think it is time to say that Barack Obama deserves credit for backing up his words with action on #Libya despite domestic opposition.

The author not only expresses his/her positive attitude towards President Obama, but also explicitly states that this attitude is the result of Obama's actions on Libya. This type of insightful opinionated tweets conveys the insight behind the opinions, which is especially important for opinion summarization.

Accordingly, we divide the system into two main parts, namely topic extraction and opinion summarization. Firstly, we extract topics for an entity from tweets containing the entity. Secondly, we identify the opinionated tweets with insight information to compose the opinion summary and organize the summary in accordance with topic extraction results.

4. TOPIC EXTRACTION

In this paper, we propose to mine topics from #hashtags. #hashtags are human annotated tags for providing additional context and metadata to tweets, which are used to categorize messages and to highlight topics. We use #hashtags as candidate topics. We conduct a comprehensive study on #hashtags and categorize #hashtags according to their usage in Table 1. In this paper, we focus on **category keywords**, **entities** as well as **events and issues**. We develop a rule-based classifier to identify the #hashtags of these types. Specifically, for category keywords #hashtags, we collect a category dictionary from the Open Directory Project (http://www.dmoz.org/). For person/location #hashtags, we collect a dictionary from Freebase (http://www.freebase.com/). For events/issues #hashtags, we first use a bi-gram language model segmenter[3] to split #hashtags into multiple words. And then we check if some of these words are in our person/location dictionary. If one or more words are in our dictionary, this #hashtag tends to be an event or issue, #LondonRiot and #OccupyChicago for instance. For the remaining #hashtags, we use *tagness*[4] to determine if they are candidate topics. Tagness for a #hashtag is defined as the occurrences of this #hashtag divided by the total occurrences of its content, i.e. without # symbol. For #hashtag may contain multiple words, when computing tagness, we also segment the words and count the occurrences of the segmented word sequences. When the tagness of a #hashtag is smaller than a threshold we set empirically(0.85 in this paper), it will be one of our candidates topic #hashtags. With tagness measurement, we can remove many #hashtags in the other 4 categories, such as #fb and #tcot, since they are always used as #hashtags.

4.1 Graph-based Topic Extraction

In this paper, we model the task of extracting topics as clustering #hashtags into coherent groups. Particularly, we create a weighted undirected graph $G =< \mathcal{H}, \mathcal{E}, f >$. $\mathcal{H}$ is the node set, and each node in the graph is a #hashtag; $\mathcal{E}$ is the edge set, and $f(e = (h_i, h_j) \in \mathcal{E}) \rightarrow \mathcal{R}$, $1 \leq i, j \leq |H|$, is the weight function to measure the relatedness between the two nodes (i.e. #hashtags), h_i and h_j. Then, we run Affinity Propagation [9], a state-of-the-art clustering algorithm on G. The input of the Affinity Propagation clustering algorithm is the #hashtags pairwise relatedness matrix, and the output are the #hashtags clusters and the centroids of clusters.

As for the #hashtags relatedness, we consider three kinds of metrics,namely co-occurrences, context similarity and distributional similarity via weakly supervised topic models.

Co-occurrences Relation.

$$f((h_i, h_j) \in e) = \begin{cases} 1 & \text{if } h_i \text{ and } h_j \text{ co-occur in a tweet} \\ 0 & \text{otherwise.} \end{cases} \quad (1)$$

Context Similarity.

$$f((h_i, h_j) \in e) = \frac{\vec{v}(h_i) \bullet \vec{v}(h_j)}{|\vec{v}(h_i)| \times |\vec{v}(h_j)|} \quad (2)$$

$\vec{v}(h)$ is the centroid context vectors of #hashtags h, which can be obtained from the output of the Affinity Propagation algorithm.

Topic-Aware Distributional Similarity.

Co-occurrences metric discards words that are not #hashtags; context similarity metric assigns equal importance to every word and every #hashtag occurred in a tweet. In order to obtain better representation and interpretation of #hashtags, we use Labeled LDA [23] to learn #hashtags-words correspondence, which associates individual word in a tweet to appropriate #hashtags. We model the #hashtag(s) in a tweet as the label(s) of the tweet and other words as the document for Labeled LDA. We can thus obtain the #hashtag-word distribution, which is similar to topic-word distribution in LDA. Then, we use negative symmetric KL divergence of distribution over words as the similarity between #hashtags. We use Labeled LDA instead of supervised topic model [3], since Labeled LDA can handle multiple-label cases.

$$f((h_i, h_j) \in e) = -\frac{1}{2}\Big[KL(p(W_{h_i})||p(W_{h_j})) + KL(p(W_{h_i})||p(W_{h_j}))\Big] \quad (3)$$

where $p(W_{h_i})$ and $p(W_{h_j})$ are the word distributions of h_i and h_j, respectively.

4.2 Topic Labeling and Assignment

Once we obtain the topics from the previous step, we label each topic with a representative #hashtag. We use the topic centroids output by Affinity Propagation as the topic labels. We assign one or more suitable topics extracted to each tweet. Firstly, for a tweet with #hashtag(s), we assign it the topic(s) corresponding to every #hashtag in the tweet. Hence we may assign multiple topics to a tweet. Secondly, for a tweet without #hashtags, we predict its topic using a SVM classifier trained on tweets that have been assigned topics in the first step. We use bag-of-words features for the classifier.

[3]http://norvig.com/ngrams/

[4]http://energy.twex.poeschko.com/metrics/

Category	Examples	Description
Category keywords	#sports, #economy	General category keywords
Person and location	#Bush, #Libya	People or locations involved
Events and Issues	#LibyaWar, #OccupyWallStreet	Describing events and issues, usually with multiple words
Content clues	#NowPlaying, #WhenIWasAKid	Clues or hints to the tweets content
Sentiment	#fun, #fail	Describing the sentiment expressed in the tweet
Source and media	#fb, #NYT	The sources of the tweets.
Discussion channel	#tcot #tlot	Forwarding the tweets to the related discussion groups

Table 1: #Hashtag categorization

5. OPINION SUMMARIZATION

We use the insightful opinionated tweets to compose the opinion summary. In the following sections, we first describe insightful and opinionated tweets classification and then present an optimization framework to integrate **topic**, **sentiment** and **insight** to generate the opinion summary.

5.1 Insightful Tweet Classification

It is difficult to come to an universal and formal definition of insightful tweets. For our application, we define 7 types of insightful tweets and list them in Table 2, based on the reason that all these types of tweets provide deeper insights and are more useful to the readers.

As a baseline, we use a binary classification approach to select the insightful tweets. In particular, we use LibSVM [5] with bag-of-words features and linear kernel. However, based on our observation of the tweets dataset, only about 10% of the tweets can be regarded as insightful opinionated tweets, which indicates this is an imbalance dataset. In order to alleviate the data imbalance problem, we increase the weight of positive instance [2], but the classifier's performance does not become better.

Alternatively, we can use the patterns defined in Table 2 to identify insightful tweet. A naive pattern matching method is to manually create a pattern list and match the pattern strings against the candidate tweets, and then we predict the matched tweets as insightful. However, this straightforward pattern matching method causes two problems. First, given a tweet containing multiple entities, it makes the same prediction for different entities, irrespective of the syntactic relations between the pattern and the entities. Second, the coverage of manually created pattern list is low.

Therefore, instead of straightforward pattern matching, we use a syntactic-constrained pattern matching approach. We first use Stanford Parser[5] to parse pattern phrases to obtain pattern syntax trees. And then we parse tweets to obtain tweets syntax trees. Finally we match the pattern syntax trees against the pattern syntax trees. To efficiently create a high coverage pattern set without hurting precision too much, we adopt an automatic pattern generalization paradigm. We first define an initial set of patterns and then generate new patterns for each pattern in the initial pattern set. For example, given a pattern "that is why", we generate two new patterns "which is why" and "this is why" and they share the same meaning. To avoid generating grammatically incompatible patterns, we also enforce the syntax constraint, i.e. the pattern generated should have the same syntax tree as the original, in order to ensure the pattern and the new pattern(s) mutually substitutable in the syntax tree. Therefore we use a paraphrase generation algorithm [4], which output patterns having the same syntactic structures to the input patterns by applying syntactic constraints to the underlying phrase extractions and paraphrasing substitution approaches, to generate new patterns.

[5]http://nlp.stanford.edu/software/lex-parser.shtml

5.2 Opinionated Tweet Classification

The opinion summary consists of opinionated tweets, i.e. tweets containing positive or negative sentiment regarding the entity. We thus need an entity (also called target) dependent sentiment classifier to identify the sentiment orientation (positive (P), negative (N) or neutral (O)) of a tweet. In this paper we build the tweet-level sentiment classifier based on sentiment lexicon.

Our lexicon-based sentiment classifier relies on sentiment dictionary matching, or in other words, sentiment lexicon words counting. Specifically, given a sentiment lexicon $\mathcal{D}$, each word in $\mathcal{D}$ is annotated with a prior sentiment orientation, either positive or negative. The lexicon based approach counts the occurrences of the positive (c_p) and negative (c_n) words and determines the sentiment orientation of a sentence (s) simply by aggregating c_p and c_n. However, many named entities contain sentiment words. As a result, we conduct named entity recognition (NER) on sentence, and sentiment words contained in any entity will not be counted.

$$SO(s) = \begin{cases} P & \text{if} c_p > c_n \\ N & \text{if} c_p < c_n \\ O & \text{otherwise.} \end{cases} \quad (4)$$

Here, $SO(s)$ denotes the sentiment orientations of the tweet s. We should pay additional attention to the negation phenomenon in lexicon-based sentiment analysis. Negation expressions in sentences might cause sentiment negation, i.e. reverse the sentiment orientation to its opposite side. Basically, we adopt the categorization for negation as introduced in [7], which categorizes the negation words into two classes: content negation words (such as "not", "never") and function negation words (such as "eliminate", "reduce"). According to both [20] and [7], to incorporate the two types of negators will benefit the accuracy of sentiment classification greatly. We take a simple and heuristic approach to tackling the negation problem in our lexicon-based sentiment analysis. We invert the local sentiment orientation of a sentiment word $w \in \mathcal{D}$ to its opposite orientation whenever a negation expression neg is found preceding w and the distance in words between neg and w is smaller than a predefined threshold (5 in our experiments).

It should be emphasized that we are working on target-dependent sentiment classification. For this purpose, before we count the positive and negative sentiment words, we conduct a classification to determine whether the sentiment word (w) is used to depict the target (e). This is achieved

Category	Example	Example Patterns
Reasoning tweets	"And that is why I voted for President Obama. No more war!"	that is why, because, because of, owing to etc.
Appeal tweets	"Please re-elect President Obama. Dont let these rep. And other blind you with the truth."	I hope, stop, please, etc.
Causal tweets	"Obamacare was, is, and always will be a fatally flawed idea that will only lead to bankruptcy."	lead to, contribute to, result in , etc.
Comparative tweets	"Pinocchio is looking like an honest guy compared to the GOP candidates."	comparing to, compared with, etc.
Opposite opinionated tweets	"@BarackObama I think you are a remarkable man but I come from a family of republicans So I'll be supporting the Republican candidacy"	anyway, however, etc.
Viewpoint tweets	"I wonder how many followers Obama will have after he leaves office and we have another president ? "	I believe, I think, I wonder, I bet, we need to, etc.
Subjunctive mood tweets	"Martin Luther King Jr. would have supported Occupy Wall Street"	would be, would have, etc.

Table 2: Examples of insightful tweets

by a binary SVM classifier which predicts whether the sentiment of e should be dependent on w or not. We design a set of features to facilitate the classification as follows.

- The distance in word between w and e;
- Whether there are other entities between w and e;
- Whether there are punctuation(s) between w and e;
- Whether there are other sentiment word(s) between w and e;
- The relative position of w and e: w is before or after e;
- Whether these is a dependency relation between w and e. We conduct a dependency parsing on the tweet s using the MST Parser[6], and check whether there is dependency link between e and w. We do not consider the dependency relation labels between e and w.

For a given entity e, we only consider the sentiment words w which are classified as dependent to e in the lexicon based sentiment analysis approach as described in Equation 4.

5.3 Optimization-based Summary Generation

By using the techniques described in previous sections, we can already obtain insightful opinionated tweets for each topic towards the given entity. However, these tweets can not be directly output as the opinion summary. First, Many of them are difficult to understand. Unlike news report and other formal text, people use slangs, abbreviations and emoticons extensively in Twitter. Tweets containing too many informal symbols and words are unreadable and should not be included in the opinion summary. Second, they contain highly redundant information, since retweeting is popular in Twitter, which make many tweets extremely similar or even identical.

Consequently, we use an optimization framework to select the most relevant, representative and readable tweets as the final opinion summary. The framework considers three factors simultaneously, namely, relevancy, redundancy and readability of tweets. Intuitively, we model this problem as selecting a subset of tweets from all tweets, so as to minimize the information loss in discarding other tweets. Formally, we define the tweets selection problem as selecting a subset of tweets P from tweet set T_k for topic k to

$$\min_{P \subset T_k} \sum_{t \in T_k - P, p \in P} \left(\operatorname*{argmin}_{p \in P} D(t,p) \right)$$

where $D(t,p)$ is the cost function of representing tweet t with tweet p. This is an NP-hard problem in general, but POPSTAR [6, 24] algorithm can be used to solve this problem approximately. We define the cost function for opinion summarization as

$$D_k(t_i,t_j) = L(t_i) * T_k(t_i) * Re(t_i,t_j)$$

where t_i and t_j are two tweets and k is the topic index. $L(t_i)$ is the language style score of t_i. We favor the more readable tweet.

$$L(t_i) = 1 + \frac{\text{\# of words out of vocabulary}}{\text{tweet length}}$$

$T(t_i)$ is the topic relevance score of t_i, defined as KL divergence between term distribution of t_i and topic label l_k.

$$T(t_i) = KL(t_i, l_k)$$

$Re(t_i,t_j)$ is the redundancy score between tweet t_i and t_j, defined as KL divergence between word distribution of t_i and t_j.

$$Re(t_i,t_j) = KL(t_i,t_j)$$

The final output from our optimization framework are several representative opinionated insightful tweets per topic. Note that we use a asymmetrical cost function here, $D_k(t_i,t_j) \neq D_k(t_j,t_i)$. As a result, the optimization procedure will automatically select the direction with less cost, hence it tends to keep the more readable and relevant tweets.

6. EXPERIMENTAL STUDY

In this section, we present the evaluation results on a real-life data set. We first provide thorough experiments on each component, i.e. topic extraction, insightful tweet classification as well as opinionated tweet classification, and then we present the evaluation results on the final opinion summaries.

[6]http://www.ryanmcd.com/MSTParser/MSTParser.html

6.1 Data

We collect the evaluation data set from 15th September 2011 to 20th October 2011 using the Twitter API[7]. We mainly focus on two types of entities, people (e.g. politicians and celebrities) and brands (e.g. electronic devices company and software company). We select 6 entities, 3 for people and 3 for brands. The entities include, "Obama", "Lady Gaga", "David Cameron", "Microsoft", "Apple", and "Nokia". We use these entities as queries and continuingly crawled tweet mentioning them to build the evaluation corpus. We do not use entity normalization techniques here because the amount of tweets is enormous and we can collect enough data simply through string matching. We collected 201, 234 tweets in total. Table 3 shows the statistics of our data set.

Person	#tweets	Brand	#tweets
Obama	34,980	Apple	39,208
Lady Gaga	43,992	Microsoft	30,993
David Cameron	21,782	Nokia	30,279
Total	100,754	Total	100,480

Table 3: Descriptions of the evaluation corpus

As a preliminary study, we investigate the effectiveness of using #hashtags as topics. We count the number and the percentage of tweets containing zero, one or more #hashtags, and we find out that about 23% of tweets contain #hashtags, and 8% of tweets contain more than 1 #hashtags. These #hashtags can cover a large proportion of the topics in Twitter.

Furthermore, we examine the feasibility of using #hashtags to extract topics. We obtain 15,865 unique #hashtags and 83, 713 #hashtags from the evaluation corpus. Then, we sample 100 #hashtags from the set of the 15,865 #hashtags and manually examine the tags. We discover that 75 #hashtags can be used to represent topics, which supports our proposal of extracting topics from #hashtags.

6.2 Evaluation of Topic Extraction

The aim of the experiments in this section is to evaluate the effectiveness of topic extraction from tweets using the graph-based methods. In particular, we evaluate the performance of topic clustering and topic assignment.

The evaluation of topic extraction is challenging because it is difficult to collect the "gold standard" data set. Though it is possible to identify and label topics from tweets manually, the time cost is prohibitive. Therefore we conduct our evaluation by comparing the topics generated by our methods and baselines.

6.2.1 Evaluation of Topic Clustering

Here we evaluate the effectiveness of topic clustering. The aim is to assess the coherency of the produced #hashtags topics. We conduct the tokenization on the evaluation corpus with ark-tweet-nlp [10], and then remove stopwords, numbers (1.2, 100, $5 etc.), URL and words starting with "@" (accounts in Twitter). Finally we use Porter stemmer[8] to stem the words and #hashtags.

We run the Labeled LDA implementation in the Stanford Topic Modeling Toolbox[9] with the default settings to obtain the #hashtag-word distribution from the preprocessed evaluation corpus. Then we feed the distribution into the Affinity Propagation algorithm[10] and produce the #hashtags clusters.

We evaluate the clustering result by purity [17]. Table 4 shows the result. From the table, we can clearly find that Co-occurrence and Cosine method produce more clusters and smaller clusters than the Labeled LDA method. This indicates that Co-occurrence method and Cosine method can not effectively model the relation between #hashtags and consequently are not capable of finding strong relation information to group similar #hashtags. Moreover, the distributional similarity approach (Labeled LDA) can greatly improve the performance.

6.2.2 Evaluation of Topic Assignment

We evaluate the effectiveness of our topic assignment approach in this section. We sample 100 tweets for 3 topics per entity as the evaluation data set, and collect a corpus of 1,800 tweets in total.

We report the topic assignment accuracy, the number of tweets correctly assigned divided by the total number of tweets, in Table 5. The topics are generated from the Label LDA approach, which gives the best topic extraction results as we have stated in Section 6.2.1. We notice that the accuracy for the singer Lady Gaga is substantially lower than that of politicians. Examining the dataset, we find that the tweets about Lady Gaga contain more noises.

6.3 Evaluation of Opinion Summarization

In this section, we present the evaluation results of opinion summarization. First, we evaluate the performance of identifying insightful tweets and opinionated tweet classification. Then, we assess the quality of opinion summary.

6.3.1 Evaluation of Insightful Tweets Classification

To evaluate the effectiveness of insightful tweets classification, we annotate 300 tweets per entity and obtain a test set of 1,800 tweets.

We conduct experiment on both the SVM baseline and the pattern matching approach. We train the SVM baseline with 100 tweets as training data (14 are insightful tweets). We experiment two setting of our pattern approach. In the first setting, we pick several pattern phrases for each type of insightful tweets and in the end we collect a pattern set of 20 patterns phrases. In the second setting, we use the same pattern phrase set but use the syntactic-constrained paraphrase method to conduct pattern expansion. After pattern expansion, our pattern set expands from 20 to 187. We evaluate the performance of pattern approach without generalization (Pattern_{man}) and pattern approach with generalization (Pattern_{gen}) respectively. We report the performance of these three methods in Table 6. The precision of baseline classification is very low, owing to the data imbalance problem. Meanwhile, patterns selected by human tend to have high precision but very low recall. After pattern expansion, recall increases by 13% while precision only decreases by 4%. This indicates that our pattern expansion method is effective.

[7]https://dev.twitter.com/
[8]http://tartarus.org/martin/PorterStemmer/
[9]http://nlp.stanford.edu/software/tmt/tmt-0.3/
[10]http://scikit-learn.sourceforge.net

	Methods	Obama	Lady Gaga	David Cameron	Microsoft	Apple	Nokia	Average
# of clusters	Labeled LDA	12	16	13	15	19	17	15
	Cosine	35	33	27	17	24	25	27
	Co-occurrence	36	34	19	26	23	34	29
Accuracy	Labeled LDA	0.63	0.54	0.55	0.73	0.65	0.68	0.63
	Cosine	0.35	0.43	0.37	0.47	0.52	0.47	0.435
	Co-occurrence	0.33	0.44	0.48	0.46	0.45	0.41	0.428

Table 4: Performance of #hashtags clustering

Methods	Obama	Lady Gaga	David Cameron	Microsoft	Apple	Nokia	Average
Labeled LDA	76.7%	66.7%	73.3%	83.7%	75.0%	73.7%	75.7%

Table 5: Topic assignment accuracy

Method	Precision	Recall	F1
SVM Baseline	28.0%	46.5%	35.0%
Pattern_{man}	76.0%	37.0%	49.8%
Pattern_{gen}	72.0%	49.8%	58.9%

Table 6: Performance of insightful tweets classification

Precision	Recall	F1-Score
86.5%	80.6%	83.4%

Table 7: Performance of the target-lexicon dependency classification

Classifier	Precision	Recall	F1
Baseline	62.6%	65%	61.7%
System	85.3%	61%	71.1%

Table 8: Performance of the opinionated tweet classification

6.3.2 *Evaluation of Opinionated Tweet Classification*

In this section, we evaluate the performance of opinionated tweet classification as described in Section 5.2. We also present the evaluation result for the dependency classification between target and sentiment word.

In our experiments, we employ the sentiment lexicon from the General Inquirer[11]. We manually annotate 500 tweets which are sampled from the tweets containing the 6 entities as mentioned in Section 6.1. We ask two annotators to conduct the annotation. Each annotator is asked to annotate each tweet as positive, negative or neutral, given the specific target (entity). We also ask the annotators to annotate the dependency between the sentiment word and the target in the tweet. Finally, we obtain 420 tweets, each of which is annotated with the same sentiment label by the two annotators. This indicates the inter-agreement of the annotators is 84%. We use the 420 tweets as our evaluation set for opinionated tweets classification. The evaluation set contains 203 positive tweets, 126 negative tweets and 91 neutral tweets.

Table 7 shows the precision, recall, and F1-Score on 5-fold cross valuation of the target-lexicon dependency classification. As we can see, it yields very encouraging results. Table 8 shows the results for target-dependent tweet-level sentiment analysis results. Since the evaluation data set is also used in the target-lexicon dependency classification, we report the results using the same 5-fold cross validation strategy here. The system and baseline method in Table 8 indicates whether we incorporate the target-lexicon dependency classification into the lexicon based sentiment classification approach or not. As can be seen from the table, the target dependent sentiment classification can greatly improve the performance. Especially, the precision has been significantly improved, which is very important in the context of our work because there will always be huge amount of tweets available and thus we favor precision over recall.

[11]http://www.wjh.harvard.edu/~ inquirer/

6.3.3 *Evaluation of Summary Generation*

Here we evaluate the effectiveness of our method to generate opinion summary in Twitter. To build the evaluation data set, we assume that the topics given by the topic extraction procedure are accurate and select 3 topics for each entity, and then for each topic we select 100 tweets as the corpus for opinion summarization. Then we manually select 5 insightful opinionated tweets from those 100 tweets for each topic as the "ground truth" opinion summary of that topic. Totally we have an evaluation set of 18 opinion summaries on 1800 tweets.

We adopt ROUGE-SU4 measure to evaluate the final summary produced [15]. For comparison, we also experiment a setting of our approach which ignores the language style, i.e. $L(t_i)$ always equals to 1. We compute the average precision, recall and F1-Score of 3 summaries of each entity and report results for both settings in Table 9. The results indicate that employing linguistic knowledge improves the opinion summary quality. We conclude that language style is vital for opinion summarization in Twitter.

7. CASE STUDY

To provide deeper insight into the advantages of topic-oriented insight-based opinion summary, we use the opinion summary towards "Obama" as a case study. Table 10 shows the topic clusters extracted from the tweets, along with their topic labels. We select the #hashtags by its frequency in the clusters. From this table, we observe that the topic labels directly suggest the topics, and other #hashtags in the cluster are also tightly related to the topic. For example, the label of the first topic is "#occupywallst", which immediately suggests that it is a topic about the OccupyWallStreet movement. And other words in this cluster provide fur-

Methods	ROUGE-SU4	Obama	Lady Gaga	David Cameron	Microsoft	Apple	Nokia	Average
Our approach	Precision	0.2392	0.2443	0.2876	0.2764	0.2812	0.2573	0.2643
	Recall	0.2488	0.2132	0.2245	0.2712	0.2324	0.2319	0.2370
	F1	0.2439	0.2277	0.2522	0.2738	0.2545	0.2439	0.2500
-Language	Precision	0.1537	0.1824	0.2128	0.2412	0.1932	0.1754	0.1931
	Recall	0.1871	0.2026	0.2201	0.2207	0.1538	0.1928	0.1961
	F1	0.1688	0.1920	0.2164	0.2305	0.1713	0.1837	0.1946

Table 9: Performance of summary generation

Topic label	Topic
#occupywallst	#wallstreet #occupydenv #fireobama
#iran	#middleeast #israel #nuclear #islam
#obama2012	#hermancain #rickperri #energi #vote

Table 10: Topic cluster for "Obama" with our method

Topic	Top ranking words ranked by $p(words\|topic)$
1	wall street occupi protest support parti ows
2	iran order execut withdraw sign trade plot
3	support elect becaus last fast reelect work

Table 11: Topic cluster for "Obama" with LDA

ther information such as the event location (#wallstreet), the slogan (#fireobama). The topics extracted are easy to interpret and understand.

For a comparison with popular topic extraction methods, we also run LDA on the same dataset and generate Table 11 with K = 12, the same as the number of topics found by our method. We use the LDA implementation in Stanford Topic Modeling Toolbox with the default setting. From the clusters we select 3 example clusters that describe approximately the same topic produced by our method. Topic 1 conveys the same amount of information with more words. In particular, they describe the location with two words, "wall" and "street". Topic 2 in LDA contains many verbs, while the corresponding topic 2 in our approach just contain nouns and/or noun phrases and are easier to interpret. Comparison of Topic 3 demonstrates superior performance of our approach. Topic 3 in LDA contains some common words such as "becaus", "last" and "fast", while our approach select readable topic #hashtags. Moreover, our approach directly provides a topic label to represent the main idea of the topic, which is not available when using LDA.

In Table 12, we present the opinion summaries, consisting of insightful opinionated tweets for each topic. This summary is a tight integration of topic, sentiment and insight. The patterns and clue words for identifying the insightful tweets are highlighted using the bold font. We select 4 representative topics for Obama, namely Libya issue, OccupyWallStreet, HealthCare and jobs plan, covering both domestic and foreign affairs. We can gain many insights from this table. First, the 4 topic labels correctly and concisely summarize the 4 hot debated topics regarding president Obama. Second, on the topic of Libya issue, Obama is praised for saving American soldiers' lives for his intervention policy, though at the same time he is disputed on how he deals with the violence issue in Libya and United States. Third, for the other three topics, Obama is facing criticisms for his ineffective policy. Finally, it can be concluded that Obama receives more supports on foreign affairs than on domestic affairs. We also discover that people tend to provide more insights behind the opinions in their negative tweets.

From this case study, we see that the integration of topic, sentiment and insight provide a powerful way for summarizing opinions regarding entities.

8. CONCLUSION

In this paper, we present an entity-centric topic-oriented opinion summarization framework, which is capable of producing opinion summaries in accordance with topics and remarkably emphasizing the insight behind the opinions in Twitter. We decompose the opinion summarization into three dimensions, namely topic, opinion and insight; the opinion summary is generated by integrating these three dimensions as well as other factors (e.g. redundancy and language styles) in an unified optimization framework. We develop a template based method to effectively identify the insightful tweets with high precision; we use target dependent sentiment classification to identify opinionated tweets regarding the entities. Extensive experiments are conducted to evaluate the performance of both the individual summarization components and the overall summarization results. We also present a case study of the produced opinion summary, which further demonstrates the effectiveness of the proposed opinion summarization framework and algorithms.

In the future, we will further study the semantics underlying #hashtags, which we can make use of to extract more comprehensive and interesting topics. We believe topic based opinions summarization will benefit from the deeper understanding of #hashtags.

9. ACKNOWLEDGMENT

This research was partly supported by National High Technology Research and Development Program of China (863 Program) (No. 2012AA011101) and National Natural Science Foundation of China (No.91024009, No.60973053)

10. REFERENCES

[1] L. Barbosa and J. Feng. Robust sentiment detection on twitter from biased and noisy data. In *Proc. COLING*, pages 36–44, 2010.

[2] A. Ben-Hur and J. Weston. A user's guide to support vector machines. *Methods in Molecular Biology*, 609:223–239, 2010.

[3] D. M. Blei and J. McAuliffe. Supervised topic models. *Advances in Neural Information Processing Systems*, 20:121–128, 2008.

[4] C. Callison-Burch. Syntactic constraints on paraphrases extracted from parallel corpora. In *Proc. EMNLP*, October 2008.

Topic label	Opinion Summaries	Sentiment
#libya	**I think** it is time to say that Barack Obama deserves credit for backing up his words with action on #Libya despite domestic opposition.	Positive
	Thanks to Obama's approach to Libya, not 1 American soldier was lost.	Positive
	Film **comparing** Obama's praise of public protests in Libya/Syria **with** the violence of arrests on Occupy Wall St	Negative
#occupywallst	@BarackObama I'm running out of hope. **Please** replace Geithner w/ Reich or Krugman #wallstreetoutofwhitehouse #OWS.	Negative
	@BarackObama : **Please** recognize the men and women who are occupying wall street.	Negative
	Obama suggests MLK Jr. **would have** backed #occupywallstreet.	Positive
#obamacar	**We need to** completely repeal #Obamacare and start by replacing it with HR 3400! #cnndebate	Negative
	If ObamaCare is not repealed **then** we can **expect** stagnant growth, long term unemployment and record high premiums.	Negative
	Op-ed: **Despite** conservatives' claims, #Obamacare is having little impact on hiring, writes Dean Baker http://t.co/I4pCBEOA #p2	Negative
#jobsnow	**Thanks to** @BarackObama's efforts, 270 businesses have committed over 25,000 jobs to American veterans.	Positive
	Cain creates 11 more jobs in 1 day **than** Obama in a lifetime.	Negative
	Let's be clear, the US economy is horrible **because of** Obama's policies.	Negative

Table 12: A case study of the opinion summary for "Obama"

[5] C. Chang and C. Lin. Libsvm: a library for support vector machines. *ACM Transactions on Intelligent Systems and Technology (TIST)*, 2(3):27, 2011.

[6] J. Cheung, G. Carenini, and R. Ng. Optimization-based content selection for opinion summarization. In *Proceedings of the 2009 Workshop on Language Generation and Summarisation*, pages 7–14, 2009.

[7] Y. Choi and C. Cardie. Learning with compositional semantics as structural inference for subsentential sentiment analysis. In *Proc. EMNLP*, pages 793–801, 2008.

[8] D. Davidov, O. Tsur, and A. Rappoport. Enhanced sentiment learning using twitter hashtags and smileys. In *Proc. COLING*, pages 241–249, 2010.

[9] B. Frey and D. Dueck. Clustering by passing messages between data points. *Science*, 315(5814):972, 2007.

[10] K. Gimpel, N. Schneider, B. O'Connor, D. Das, D. Mills, J. Eisenstein, M. Heilman, D. Yogatama, J. Flanigan, and N. A. Smith. Part-of-speech tagging for twitter: annotation, features, and experiments. In *Proc. ACL-HLT*, pages 42–47, 2011.

[11] M. Hu and B. Liu. Mining and summarizing customer reviews. In *Proc. KDD*, pages 168–177, 2004.

[12] M. Hu and B. Liu. Mining opinion features in customer reviews. In *Proc. AAAI*, 2004.

[13] L. Jiang, M. Yu, M. Zhou, X. Liu, and T. Zhao. Target-dependent twitter sentiment classification. In *Proc. ACL-HLT*, pages 151–160, 2011.

[14] H. Kim, k. Ganesan, P. Sondhi, and C. Zhai. Comprehensive review of opinion summarization.

[15] C. Lin. ROUGE: A package for automatic evaluation of summaries. In *Proceedings of the workshop on text summarization branches out (WAS 2004)*, pages 25–26, 2004.

[16] B. Liu. Opinion mining. In *Encyclopedia of Database Systems*, pages 1986–1990. 2009.

[17] C. Manning, P. Raghavan, and H. Schütze. Introduction to information retrieval. 2008.

[18] R. McDonald, K. Hannan, T. Neylon, M. Wells, and J. Reynar. Structured models for fine-to-coarse sentiment analysis. In *Proc. ACL*, pages 432–439, 2007.

[19] Q. Mei, X. Ling, M. Wondra, H. Su, and C. Zhai. Topic sentiment mixture: modeling facets and opinions in weblogs. In *Proc. WWW*, pages 171–180, 2007.

[20] T. Nakagawa, K. Inui, and S. Kurohashi. Dependency tree-based sentiment classification using crfs with hidden variables. In *Proc. NAACL-HLT*, pages 786–794, 2010.

[21] B. O'Connor, R. Balasubramanyan, B. Routledge, and N. Smith. From tweets to polls: Linking text sentiment to public opinion time series. In *Proc. ICWSM*, pages 122–129, 2010.

[22] B. Pang and L. Lee. Opinion mining and sentiment analysis. *Found. Trends Inf. Retr.*, 2:1–135, January 2008.

[23] D. Ramage, D. Hall, R. Nallapati, and C. Manning. Labeled lda: A supervised topic model for credit attribution in multi-labeled corpora. In *Proc. EMNLP*, pages 248–256, 2009.

[24] M. Resende and R. Werneck. A hybrid heuristic for the p-median problem. *Journal of Heuristics*, 10(1):59–88, 2004.

[25] I. Titov and R. McDonald. A joint model of text and aspect ratings for sentiment summarization. In *Proc. ACL-HLT*, pages 308–316, June 2008.

[26] I. Titov and R. McDonald. Modeling online reviews with multi-grain topic models. In *Proc. WWW*, pages 111–120, 2008.

[27] X. Wang, F. Wei, X. Liu, M. Zhou, and M. Zhang. Topic sentiment analysis in twitter: A graph-based hashtag sentiment classification approach. In *Proc. CIKM*, 2011.

[28] L. Zhuang, F. Jing, and X. Zhu. Movie review mining and summarization. In *Proc. CIKM*, pages 43–50, 2006.

Community Discovery and Profiling with Social Messages

Wenjun Zhou*
University of Tennessee
247 Stokely Mgmt. Center
Knoxville, TN 37996
wzhou4@utk.edu

Hongxia Jin
IBM Research at Almaden
650 Harry Road
San Jose, CA 95120
hongxia@acm.org

Yan Liu
Univ. of Southern California
941 Bloom Walk
Los Angeles, CA 90089
yanliu.cs@usc.edu

ABSTRACT

Discovering communities from social media and collaboration systems has been of great interest in recent years. Existing work show prospects of modeling contents and social links, aiming at discovering social communities, whose definition varies by application. We believe that a community depends not only on the group of people who actively participate, but also the topics they communicate about or collaborate on. This is especially true for workplace email communications. Within an organization, it is not uncommon that employees multifunction, and groups of employees collaborate on multiple projects at the same time. In this paper, we aim to automatically discovering and profiling users' communities by taking into account both the contacts and the topics. More specifically, we propose a community profiling model called COCOMP, where the communities labels are latent, and each social document corresponds to an information sharing activity among the most probable community members regarding the most relevant community issues. Experiment results on several social communication datasets, including emails and Twitter messages, demonstrate that the model can discover users' communities effectively, and provide concrete semantics.

Categories and Subject Descriptors

H.2.8 [**Database Management**]: Database Applications—*Data Mining*

Keywords

Community Discovery, Email, Social Media, Collaboration, Generative Models

1. INTRODUCTION

Given a large collection of social messages, we are interested in profiling a user's communities, which correspond to the user's current focus areas. A focus area is an ad-hoc community, in which several users interact on certain topics. Building such a profile automatically will be helpful for a number of subsequent analytical tasks, such as helping users visualize and organize social communications, classifying new messages into corresponding focus areas, and prioritizing new messages by the user's activeness or relevance in that area.

Current developments in data mining and machine learning provide useful techniques to discover communities from text and social links. For example, topic models can extract topics discussed in documents [9, 5] and represent each topic with a number of ranked key words. On the other hand, social network analysis can identify social relationships according to the communication patterns [10]. Yet many challenges remain to be addressed. First of all, the definition of community has to be well-aligned to application. A community might be a group of people who are closely linked in a social network, or those who share common interests (but not necessarily interact directly with each other). We believe that a semantically meaningful community has to consider both aspects, especially in a collaboration network. Further, most existing work takes a flattened view on social linkage. More specifically, the link between a pair of users is represented by a collapsed evaluation of their relationship, such as closeness or similarity [12], or shared topics [14]. However, communities are usually more than pair-wise connections. The linkage between a pair of users may be sliced into more than one communities being shared. After all, nowadays it is not uncommon that employees of an organization multifunction, and some employees may collaborate on multiple projects at the same time.

In this paper, we propose a community discovery and profiling method based on an extension of the generative model [5]. A key element in this method is a latent community assignment, given which the distributions of topics and social links can be determined. The intuition is that each social message document, when created and shared, corresponds to a sharing activity within the community (both topic-wise and person-wise). More specifically, we extend the topic models and assume the generative process of a latently assigned community for each document. Then, based on the assigned community, words and participants are randomly sampled from the vocabulary and pool of people. Such a Bayesian topic model is trained by Gibbs sampling, so that based on the observed words and people who take active roles in the social media, it can discover most promi-

*The work was done when the author was an intern at IBM Almaden Research Center.

KDD'12, August 12–16, 2012, Beijing, China.

nent topics and participants, as well as obtain best bets on the communities to be assigned.

Our solution has a number of advantages. First of all, it fills the gap of discovering multi-layered social communities, and provide a semantic description (i.e. mixture of topics) of each layer. This can potentially help us find more meaningful communities, which could be missed by existing methods. In addition, because the latent community can serve as an anchor point for mounting information shared across multiple sources and platforms, our model may be applied to other kinds of knowledge sharing systems, such as instant messaging, online discussion forums and group wiki. With this tool, it is possible for users to summarize his or her focus areas in an automatic fashion, so that it is easy to manage the documents, build profiles, find experts [4] and target relevant users in a social network.

The rest of the paper is organized as follows. In Section 2, we discuss the motivation of the study, characteristics of the data, and the state of the art in related studies. Then we describe our model in Section 3, where we provide the technical details. We evaluate our model on real-world datasets, and compare the performances with existing models in Section 4. Finally, we conclude in Section 5.

2. SOCIAL MESSAGES

In this paper, we use the term "social messages," referring to text documents that are associated with a group of people. In the following, we overview the basic characteristics for various types of social messages, with an emphasis on their commonalities.

Social Media A tweet (or Facebook update) is created by a user and broadcasted to his or her followers (or friends), who are allowed to look at and respond to such media. Usually a tweet is visible to many followers, and only a few (compared to all followers) make an active response, such as re-tweet, forward, or comment. Those active responses indicate the interest and relevance of those followers.

Emails We also consider the email as one type of social message, since it also involves multiple people, and helps spread of information. Each email has designated recipients, who are related to the message, at the discretion of the sender. Compared to social media, emails tend to be more targeted by the sender, and all recipients are considered as relevant to some extent.

Collaborative Content This category include publications (with co-authors), patents (with co-inventors), and Wiki pages (with collaborators). They all include text and people, so they can also be modeled with the same structure. The people, whose names are declared, share the same published content, which presumably represent their interest and expertise.

Among the above typical types of social messages, one feature in common is that each document is created and shared among a group of people. If we consider the people as nodes in a graph, then the social links that are being considered are clique-type hyper-edges in that graph. Such social linkage is different from document linkage, such as hyperlinks on blogs that link to other blogs, and references at the end of a paper that link to other papers.

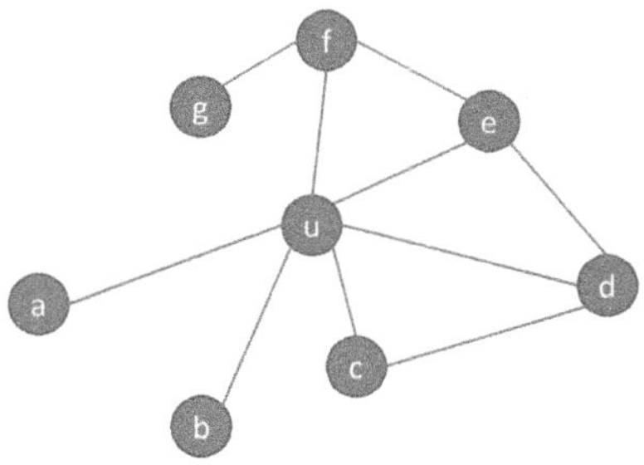

(a) Single-Layer

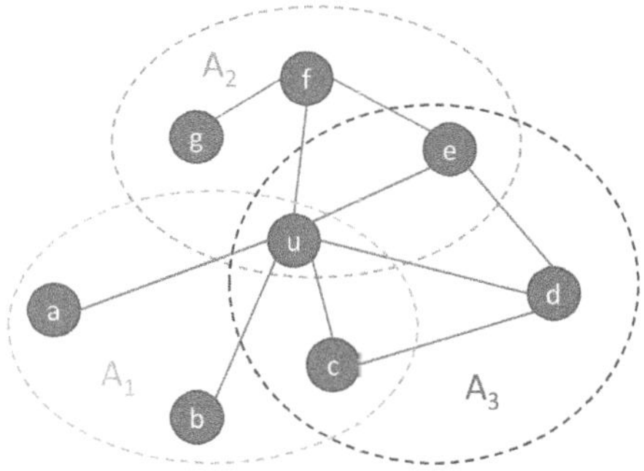

(b) Multi-Layer

Figure 1: A user's social communities.

In the rest of the paper, when referring to social messages, we have taken into account many different types of documents that might be modeled the same way. By unifying different types of social messages, there is the advantage of integrating different sources of information and providing more comprehensive profiles of the users.

2.1 A Motivating Example

Consider a single-user's perspective. Figure 1 illustrates the collaboration network of user u, who resides at the center. All other nodes are his or her visible contacts. There is a link between two nodes if there has been any direct message exchange between them.

Figure 1 (a) shows the traditional single-layer view on pair-wise linkage, where each link is evaluated individually based on this pair only. For example, frequency of messages, number of shared contacts, or important topics.

Figure 1 (b) shows a multi-layered view on u's communities and provides a few examples why it makes more sense than the single-layered view. Imagine that the user u is associated with three communities, A_1, A_2 and A_3, simultaneously. u and e collaborate on communities A_2 and A_3 simultaneously, so their connection should have two different layers that apply to different activity areas, depending on either f is involved or d is involved. Sometimes, a message in community A_3 does not involve all people in that community. For example, u and e, since they work so closely, may exchange emails relevant to community A_3. Without c or d being involved, such messages should still be routed to community A_3 due to the relevance by content. Furthermore, u could see the linkage between f and g since f put g as an additional recipients in some of the emails he or she writes to u. In this case, even if u and g do not exchange emails directly, A_2 should include person g. These results will be missed by purely analyzing linkages.

2.2 Related Work

Discovering communities has been of interest by many previous studies. Being interested in studying collaboration network, we find that social network analysis and topic modeling are both relevant. Specifically, social network analysis typically focuses on closeness of social linkage [7], or evolution of social connections [18]. Due to the complexity of the network, social links are typically simplified into a single-layer of measurement, without consideration of the general context. On the other hand, models for topic discovery from textual documents are also extensively studied, including probabilistic Latent Semantic Analysis (pLSA) [9], Latent Dirichlet Allocation (LDA) [5], variations [8] and applications [11, 3]. Based on the words in a large corpus of documents, these models can extract human comprehensible topics represented by a list of keywords.

Since documents are commonly related to people, recent developments have taken into account people who are related to the topics. For example, the Author-Topic (AT) model [17] considers the interests of each author across multiple documents, and aim to derive the representative topics for individual authors. The Author-Recipient-Topic (ART) model [13, 14] considers topics that are specific to each author-recipient pair. These models focus on profiling individuals or pairwise relation. However, they do not model communities directly. Other works try to augment social network analysis with topic modeling [6, 16, 19, 12], and such models can discover users' mixed membership in various topical communities. However these models are single-layered, without considering the general context of "who are collaborating on what concurrently".

3. THE COMMUNITY MODEL

To discover the latent communities, we develop a generative model, called COCOMP, which stands for COllaborator COMmunity Profiling. It attempts to discover communities in social media documents by considering context in both topics and collaboration groups. The basic rational is to assume that each social media document corresponds to a conversation session within one community, which is defined both by topics and participants. In other words, the topics of a social media document is derived from the community's topic mixture, and the people involved in the thread tend to be those who actively participate in the work area.

3.1 Generative Process

Figure 2 shows the generative process of the latent community model. Like traditional topic models, it is assumed that there are K word distributions $\phi_{1:K}$ which correspond to K latent topics, and are assumed to be Dirichlet distributions with prior β:

$$\phi_k|\beta \sim Dirich(\beta), k = 1, 2, \ldots, K \quad (1)$$

Also, we assume that there are M communities, each of

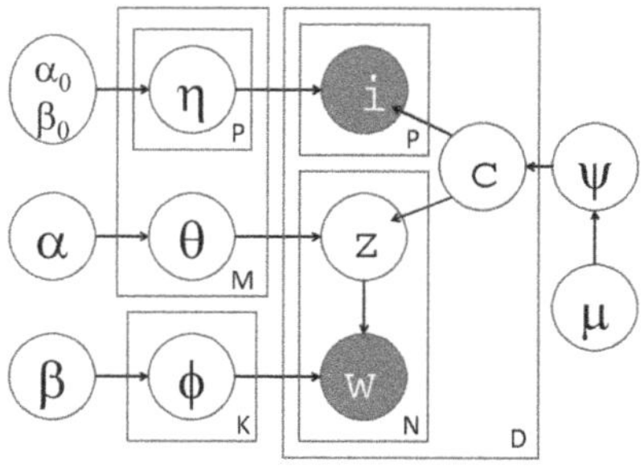

Figure 2: Graphical representation of COCOMP.

which has two components: topic mixture θ and participant mixture η. More specifically, in community m ($m = 1, 2, \ldots, M$):

- The topic mixture θ_m represents the weight of different topics in this community, which has a Dirichlet distribution with hyperparameter α:

$$\theta_m|\alpha \sim Dirich(\alpha). \quad (2)$$

- The participant mixture η_m = represents each person's activeness in this community. In other words, $\eta_{m,p}$, represents person p's activeness in community m ($p = 1, 2, \ldots, P$). We assume that $\eta_{m,p}$ has a Beta distribution with hyperparameters α_0 and β_0:

$$\eta_{m,p}|\alpha_0, \beta_0 \sim Beta(\alpha_0, \beta_0). \quad (3)$$

Finally, there is a community activeness vector ψ, which is assumed a Dirichlet distribution with hyperparameter μ:

$$\psi|\mu \sim Dirich(\mu). \quad (4)$$

Further, we assume the following generative process of this collection of D email documents. For $d = 1, 2, \ldots, D$:

1. A latent community c_d is assigned by tha maximum likelihood of community membership, according to words, topics and people.

$$c_d = \arg\max_c LLH(d, c), \quad (5)$$

   where $LLH(d, c)$ means the log likelihood of document d being assigned to community c.

2. For each person p, run a Bernoulli trial according to his/her personal activeness in community c_d, to see if he or she is involved. Specifically,

$$i_{d,p}|\eta, c_d \sim Bernoulli(\eta_{c_d,p}). \quad (6)$$

   $\forall p = 1, 2, \ldots, P$.

3. Suppose that this document has N_d tokens. For each token in the document, a word is generated in a similar fashion to LDA. Specifically, for $n = 1, 2, \ldots, N_d$:

   (a) Draw a topic assignment $z_{d,n}$ from the c_d-th community's topic mixture:

$$z_{d,n}|\theta, c_d \sim Multi(\theta_{c_d}). \quad (7)$$

   (b) Draw a word $w_{d,n}$ from the $z_{d,n}$-th topic-word distribution:

$$w_{d,n}|z_{d,n}, \phi \sim Multi(\phi_{z_{d,n}}). \quad (8)$$

3.2 Model Training

We used Gibbs sampling for training the model. In this subsection, we derive the conditional posterior distributions for sampling these parameters sequentially.

For document d, the posterior probability for its community assignment will be

$$P(c_d = j|\mathbf{c}_{-d}) = \frac{\mu_j + D_j^{(-d)}}{\sum_{c=1}^{C} \mu_c + D - 1}, \quad (9)$$

where $D_j^{(-d)}$ is number of documents (except the d-th document) that are assigned to community j. After updating the community densities, the document is assigned to the community in which it has the highest likelihood.

For the i-th token in the d-th document, which is assigned to community c_d, the conditional posterior for its latent topic will be

$$P(z_{d,i} = j|\cdot) \propto$$
$$\frac{\beta_{w_{d,i}} + n_{j,w_{d,i}}^{(-d,i)}}{\sum_v \beta_v + \sum_v n_{j,v}^{-(d,i)}} \cdot \frac{\alpha_j + n_{c_d,j}^{(-d,i)}}{\sum_k \alpha_k + \sum_k n_{c_d,k}^{-(d,i)}}, \quad (10)$$

where $n_{j,v}$ is the number of times a unique word type v is assigned to topic k, $n_{c,j}$ is the number of times a token in community c is assigned to topic j, and the superscript $-(d,i)$ means to exclude the i-th token in the d-th document.

After the training process, each parameter is estimated from the ending state:

$$P(c) = \mu'_c = \frac{\mu_c + D_c}{\sum_c \mu_c + D}, \quad (11)$$

$$P(p|c) = \eta' = \frac{\alpha_0 + D_{c,p}}{\alpha_0 + \beta_0 + D_c}, \quad (12)$$

$$P(k|c) = \alpha' = \frac{\alpha_k + n_{c,k}}{\sum_k \alpha_k + n_c}, \quad (13)$$

$$P(v|k) = \beta' = \frac{\beta_v + n_{k,v}}{\sum_v \beta_v + n_k} \quad (14)$$

where $D_{c,p}$ is the number of times a person p is involved in community c.

4. EXPERIMENTS

In this section, we present experiments with the COCOMP model. First, we describe the overall setup of the experiments, and then show discovery results from each dataset.

4.1 Experimental Setup

First, we introduce the setup of the experiments, including data summaries, data preprocessing, implementation and platform, as well as the evaluation metric.

Table 1: Basic Statistics of Example Users

User	# Docs	# Contacts	Source
arnold-j	2,120	2,280	Enron
whalley-g	718	1,560	Enron
zhouw	623	690	IBM
hongxia	607	817	IBM
obama	6,134	6,890	Twitter
justin	5,077	3,228	Twitter

Datasets Our model has been tested with various types of social messages. Given that we are mainly interested in a single user's perspective, we collected individual user's email exchanges and celebrity's Twitter interactions. Table 1 lists some basic statistics of each user's social media dataset.

For each user, we include bi-direction communications. In other words, for email datasets, we include both inbox and outbox; and for twitter datasets, we include tweets written by this user as well as those that mention this user (such as re-tweets).

Preprocessing Basic data preprocessing has been conducted on the raw social media documents, such as parsing and unwrapping HTML tags, removing stopwords, and transforming the text into bag of words. We also excluded a small number of incomplete documents. A document is considered incomplete at the preprocessing stage, if it does not involve at least two different users, or if its remaining bag of words after stopword removal is empty.

Implementation Our model has been implemented in Java, based on modifications of the MALLET [15] package. All experiments are run within Eclipse on a Dell Latitude, running 64-bit Windows 7 Professional with 8.00GB RAM.

Evaluation Metric Perplexity has been a common metric for evaluating language models. For community c, with word sequence $\mathbf{w}_c$, whose length (number of tokens) is N_c, the perplexity can be computed as

$$perplexity(\mathbf{w}_c) = \exp\left\{-\frac{\ln p(\mathbf{w}_c)}{N_c}\right\}. \quad (15)$$

Assuming independence among words, we have

$$\ln p(\mathbf{w}_d) = \sum_{v=1}^{V} n_{c,v}[\ln P(v|k) + \ln P(k|c)], \quad (16)$$

where $P(v|k)$ and $P(v|k)$ are computed as the posterior probability computed at the end of the training.

4.2 Enron Email Dataset

Since the Enron dataset is publicly available, effectiveness of our model can be verified using it as a benchmark. In Table 2 we list the top topics and top people for prominent communities discovered for the user Greg Whalley, assuming that there are 30 topics and 10 communities. For each community, we assign a label corresponding to the topics and the people, which are listed in the last column.

As we can see, most communities include greg.whalley on the top of the contributor list. This means that the user is active in such communities, so his rank is higher. When building his profile, we want to know how relevant a activity area (i.e. community) is to him, so it is desired that this user appears on the top of the contributor list for many communities, which means the communities are his major activity areas. Also, we can see that some topics may rank high in several communities, but the composition of topics and people are different.

From another data source [2], we know that Greg Whalley was the president of Enron, John Lavorato was a CEO, and Louise Kitchen was the president for Enron Online. We don't have information for mark.frevert or liz.taylor, who might be the assistants for Greg Whalley and his contacts. Their roles are consistent to the topics and communities we have discovered.

4.3 Zhouw Email Dataset

Although the Enron dataset is public, the actual social network and communities is not well-known and there is

Table 2: Greg Whalley Communities ($K = 30$, $C = 10$)

Community	Topics			People		Label
2	1	bill, assembl, senat, day, california	.1335	greg.whalley	.5806	legislations
	15	pleas, util, transact, review, date	.0612	john.lavorato	.2500	
	23	today, number, follow, transact, ani	.0511	louise.kitchen	.2016	
5	4	pleas, meet, eb, system, expens	.0942	greg.whalley	.6738	operations
	23	today, number, follow, transact, ani	.0371	mark.frevert	.2032	
	25	inform, servic, avail, email, custom	.0226	liz.taylor	.1497	
6	18	secur, servic, bush, salomon, presid, contract	.0744	greg.whalley	.4300	IT
	25	inform, servic, avail, email, custom, click	.0370	louise.kitchen	.1500	
	16	may, includ, oper, account, result, rais	.0240	mark.frevert	.1200	
7	12	publish, name, memo, target, task	.1913	greg.whalley	.4746	publishing online
	8	itext, img, onlin, valu, pleas	.0863	liz.taylor	.1864	
	22	corpor, com, best, onli, monday	.0089	louise.kitchen	.1441	

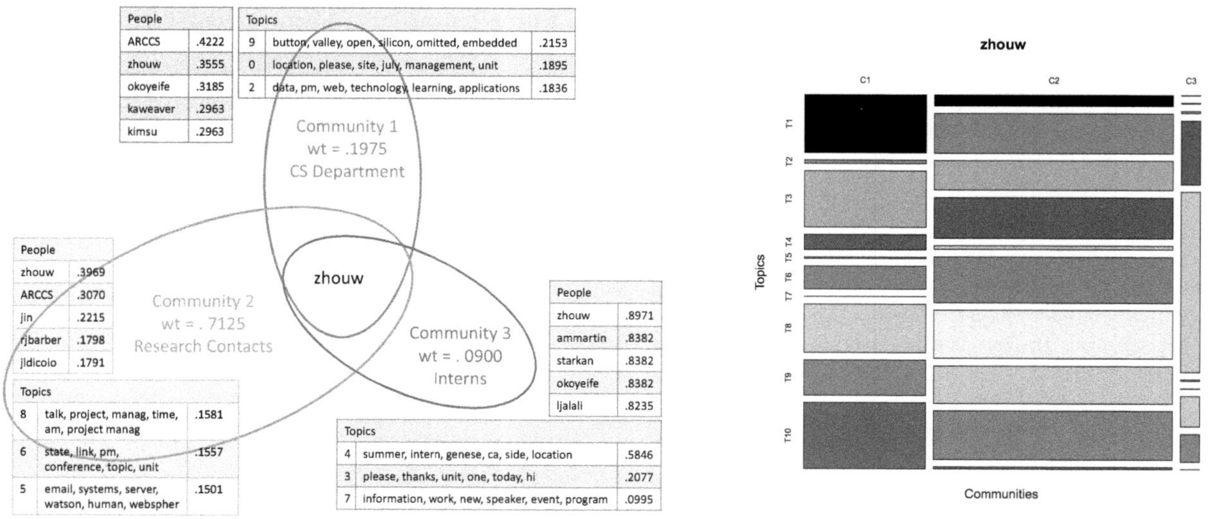

(a) Community Labels

(b) Communities' Topic Distributions

Figure 3: Zhouw communities ($K = 10$, $C = 3$).

no golden standard to check the exact correctness of the important communities found by COCOMP. As a result, we run COCOMP on collections of our own email datasets, which will be presented below.

First, we look at results on the zhouw dataset. This dataset contains one of the authors' emails sent and received during her internship at IBM. Assuming 10 topics and 3 communities, we find communities as shown in Figure 3.

As we can see in Figure 3(a), the three communities discovered are quite clear. It looks like that the first community is the CS department in general, the second community is the smaller research unit, and the third community has to do with the intern group. Both people and keywords make sense. For example, in the intern community, the top contacts are other interns who share similar weights in this community. The top ranked topic, Topic 4, clearly shows that "summer" and "intern" are the top keywords, and "genese" is the summer intern coordinator.

Figure 3(a) is a mosaic plot of the topic distribution in each community. Each other represents a topic, and each column represents a community. We can see clearly that the composition of topics, as indicated by the heights of the rectangles, is very different from one community to another.

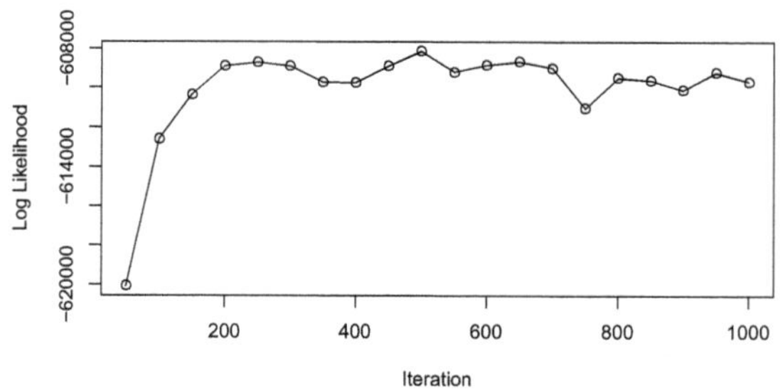

Figure 4: Convergence process.

The widths of the rectangles represent the size of each community. In other words, they are proportional to the number of documents in each community. Clearly, a lot of the emails are related to research.

Despite the fact of being a bit more complex than the plain LDA model, since we consider people in addition, our model converges reasonably fast. Figure 4 shows the convergence process for model training. Although we run 1,000 iterations, the log likelihood begins to stabilize around the 200-th iteration. Other datasets show similar results.

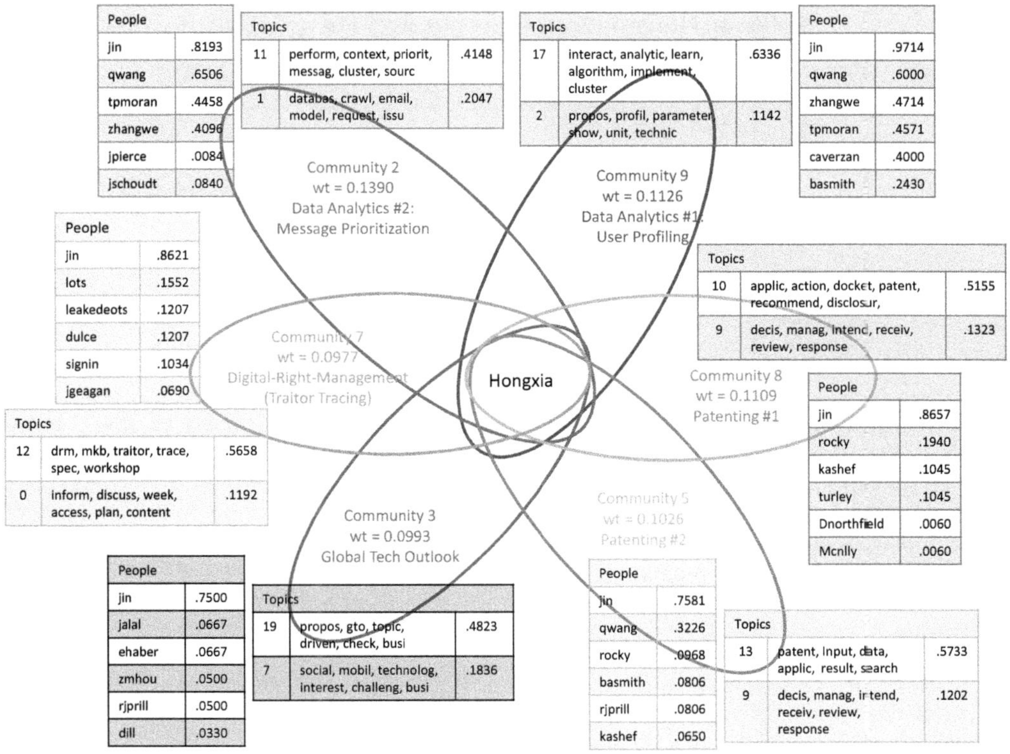

Figure 5: Hongxia communities ($K = 20$, $C = 10$).

In return of handling more complexity by considering the people information, the communities discovered by COCOMP make better sense than those derived directly from by LDA. In order to find three communities, we run the LDA model with the parameter $k = 3$. The basic idea is to identify the topic mixture of each document, and assign the documents to the most important topic. Then based on such document communities, we find the most frequently involved people. The results are listed in Table 3.

Table 3: Zhouw Communities by LDA ($K = 3$)

Community 1	Community 2	Community 3
talk	button	conference
project	valley	systems
manag	open	web
pm	please	data
time	silicon	user
am	embedded	thanks
Software	zhouw	zhouw
rjbarber	Software	jin
Research	okoyeife	okoyeife
vitaly	imber	kimsu
jldicoio	basmith	kaweaver
Storage	Storage	mmejias

The communities, as indicated by the key words, make some sense. For example, Community 1 seems to be the announcement of talks and activities. The top participants include major email lists, to which general announcements are typically sent to. However, a major problem is that the interns group is not found. Despite of the saliently different topics, because there are a small number of emails in the interns community, the LDA fails to capture that community. By considering people (social contacts) in addition, there is clearly the benefit of finding communities that are interesting to the user.

As for the quality of the topics, Figure 6 shows a simple comparison of perplexity for different parameter sets. The three bars on the left correspond to perplexities derived from LDA [5], using $k = 3$, $k = 5$, and $k = 10$, respectively. The two bars on the right represent perplexities derived from COCOMP on the same training data, using 10-topic-3-community ($K = 10$, $C = 3$), and 10-topic-5-community($K = 10$, $C = 5$), respectively. The COCOMP model performs consistently better than LDA for having lower perplexity.

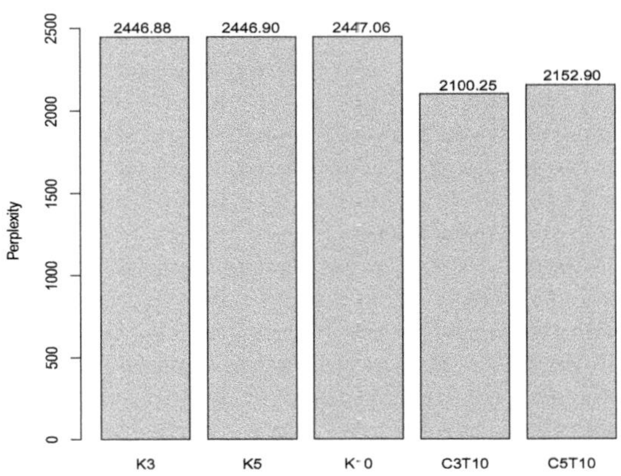

Figure 6: A comparison of perplexity.

Table 4: Hongxia Communities by LDA ($K = 10$)

Topic 5	Topic 3	Topic 1	Topic 7	Topic 4	Topic 2
interact	databas	patent	test	step	context
talk	perform	docket	disclosur	integr	messag
social	crawl	lectur	requir	week	sourc
analysis	women	applic	dlp	cluster	oper
correl	webinar	application	server	servic	result
check	text	seri	miss	june	priorit
jin	jin	jin	jin	jin	jin
tpmoran	tpmoran	rocky	qwang	qwang	qwang
zhangwe	zhangwe	qwang	tpmoran	tpmoran	jschoudt
qwang	qwang	zhangwe	zhangwe	zhangwe	jspierce
caverzan	caverzan	tpmoran	caverzan	caverzan	hbadenes
basmith	basmith	basmith	basmith	basmith	tpmoran

4.4 Hongxia Collaboration Dataset

In this subsection, we apply the COCOMP model on social collaboration data from another author of the paper during a 3-month period. The hongxia dataset contains mostly emails, but also small amounts of data crawled from other social software in IBM, such as wiki and communities. The top 6 communities are shown in Figure 5, assuming 20 latent topics and 10 communities.

As shown in Figure 5, the top 2 communities are both about her big data analytics research activities. Data analytics is her main research direction. Community 2 is focused on the user and community profiling work while community 1 is focused on using user profile to perform context aware prioritization on incoming messages/updates for the user. As one can understand, these research endeavors overlap in the research nature. While she heavily works with 3 other colleagues in both these two areas, some others involved in these two areas are different. Our model clearly detects two overlapping communities that focus on two somewhat overlapping research activities. Moreover, these two activity areas are indeed her most focused activities.

The second major activity for Hongxia is related to patenting. Our model detected two different communities that Hongxia is involved with regarding patenting, namely community 8 and community 5, ranked #3 and #4 respectively in top 6. Again both the topics and the people involved in these two communities overlap. Indeed both Topic 9 is shown in these two communities. Our model managed to clearly detect these two overlapping communities. This indicates the multi-layers of Hongxia's social links with those overlapping members in these two communities, an example of what we illustrated in Figure 1 in Section 2.

Ranked #5 in the detected top 6 communities by our model is Community 3. It is mainly about GTO (Global Technological Outlook) planning activities that she involved. It involves proposal writing, submitting and reviewing. This community consists of a different group of colleagues that she lightly collaborates with.

Lastly, Community 7 is about another light activity area in this 3-month period. It is about Digital Rights Management which was an old research area that Hongxia heavily involved in the past. "Traitor tracing" was the main research topic in this activity area as indicated by Topic #12.

For comparison purpose, we also experiment with LDA using the same dataset. We have LDA detect the top 10 topics and cluster the documents into its dominant topics. We then derive the 10 communities for Hongxia by extracting the top people involved in the corresponding documents clustered into each of those 10 topics. For the sake of comparison, we also illustrate the top 6 communities/topics in Table 4. Again, the weight is calculated based on the number of documents clustered into each community/topic.

As we can see from the table, LDA also detected the two topics/commnities about data analytics, namely Topic 5 and Topic 2. However, the top people involved in both communities are not as precise as the results from our proposed model. More significantly the data analytics activities are not detected very completely. Indeed, many are mixed up with other topics as clearly demonstrated by Topic 3, 4 and 7 in the table. The fact that topics are mixed in the detected communities also means that the documents clustered into each topic are mixed, resulting in the inaccurate weighting of the community. As one can see, LDA result ranks the Topic/Community 2 as the last of the top 6 communities. This rank is incorrect. Similarly, both Topics 3 and 7 are partly about data analytics work but each mixed up with several different actual activities for Hongxia. For example, Topic 7 mixed data analytics with patenting. But these two activities have no overlapping in terms of topics. As a result, the top people shown for these two communities are still those same people involved in the data analytics activity area. Topic/Community 1 is also a mix of topics (mixing with data analytics activities), but to a less extent. It is mainly about patenting. However it mixes the two different groups of people that user Hongxia involved in working with on patenting. In fact some of those people are not shown on top. Instead some of the people involved in data analytics still appear in top 6 participants in this community due to topic mixture. Topic 4 is partly about "traitor tracing" but heavily mixed with other topics (mainly with the data analytics activities). As a result, the correct group of people involved are not even shown on top.

4.5 Twitter Datasets

In order to study the effectiveness of our model on Twitter datasets, we choose two celebrity Twitter users and study their tweet exchange with others Twitter users. One account is the United States President Barack Obama (Figure 7), and the other is a famous singer Justin Beiber (Figure 8). We have crawled all the tweets posted by these two users as well as the replied-to tweets by other users, started from November 1, 2009. As a result, we have collected 6,134 tweets for Barack Obama and 5,077 tweets for Justin Beiber. Twitter users use some structure conventions such as a user-to-message relation (i.e. initial tweet author, via, cc, by), type of message (i.e. Broadcast, conversation,

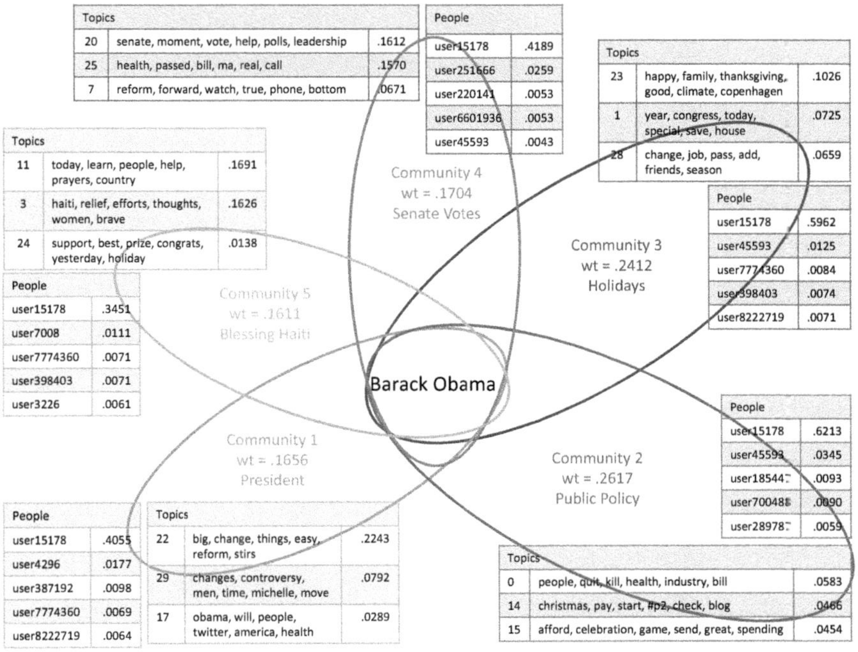

Figure 7: Obama communities ($K = 30$, $C = 5$).

or retweet messages), type of resources (i.e. URLs, hashtags, keywords) to overcome 140 character limit. Since the data are quite noisy with many URLs and acronyms, we preprocessed the data by removing HTML tags and extremely infrequent words.

As shown in Figure 7, if we model Obama's tweets with 30 topics and 5 communities, we can see that his communities from November 2009 to February 2010 can be roughly represented as: President, which is about comments on his advocacy of Presidency; Public Policy, which related to domestic and international politics and policy; Holidays, which is mainly about wishing the best for American families and friends; Senate Votes that has to do with health bills; and Blessing Haiti after the tremendous earthquake. It is interesting to observe that $user45593$ is the Twitter account whitehouse, which is expected to relate to the President regarding domestic and international policies. $user7008$ is Nicki Minaj, a singer who originated from Haiti. Not surprisingly she is most concerned about the tragedy that has happened in her home country. $user251666$ is Martha Coakley, Massachusetts Attorney General, who is on top list of participants in Community 4, which is about law making.

We also show Justin Beiber's Twitter communities in Figure 8. For a pop star like Justin, it is expected that the majority of his "collaborators" are his fans. However, we are able to group those fans into several groups, such as those who like to express emotions (Community #3) and those who does very casual conversations (Commmunity 4). Community 5 is mainly about Justin's broadcasts of media, such as showing his fans some videos. In Communities 1 and 2, different groups of fans were talking about his new album "My World", and his Golden Ticket Concert, respectively.

Finally, we found that Justin Beiber appeared in Barack Obama's Community 1. In that community he was ranked second in the participant list, right after Obama himself. What does Justin have to do with Obama? On Justin's Wikipedia page [1], we found that "Bieber performed Stevie Wonder's *Someday at Christmas* for U.S. President Barack Obama and first lady Michelle Obama at the White House for Christmas in Washington, which was broadcast on December 20, 2009, on U.S. television broadcaster TNT." So probably they are connected because of this event, and also Michelle, who is also in Community 1. For that big event, as a most popular pop star who has countless fans all over the country, Justin is promoted to an activity area of the President. For two very influential twitter users, it is interesting to see how they are connected with each other on Twitter.

5. CONCLUDING REMARKS

In this paper, we design a latent community model, called COCOMP, to uncover the communities of each user as well as their associated topics and communities. In particular, it models each community as a mixture of topics with a corresponding group of users who collaborate together on these topics. With a latent assignment of community membership, we assume that each social media document corresponds to a sharing activity within a community (both topic-wise and person-wise). Experiment results on email and social media datasets demonstrate the effectiveness of our model.

For future work, our model can be extended in various ways. For example, instead of treating all people involved as the same, there is the need of separating active members from passive members (i.e. those who only receive the messages). Also, since the social media contents change over the time, it is meaningful to develop dynamic models to capture the evolving process and online algorithms to monitor the changes over time.

6. ACKNOWLEDGEMENTS

This research is continuing through participation in the Social Media in Strategic Communication (SMISC) program

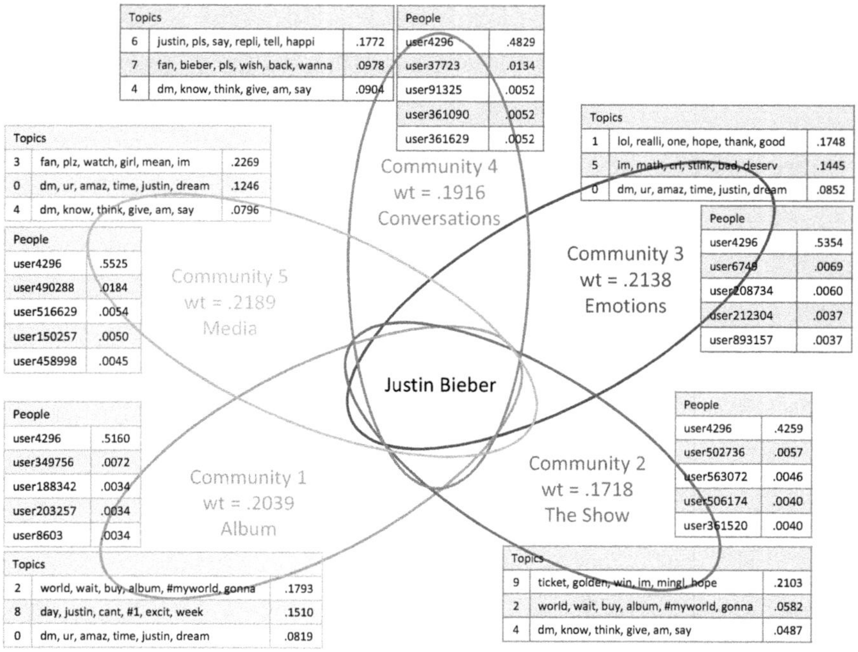

Figure 8: Justin communities ($K = 10$, $C = 5$).

sponsored by the U.S. Defense Advanced Research Projects Agency (DARPA) under Agreement Number W911NF-12-1-0034. The views and conclusions contained herein are those of the authors and should not be interpreted as representing the official policies or endorsements, either expressed or implied, of any of the above organizations or any person connected with them.

7. REFERENCES

[1] http://en.wikipedia.org/wiki/Justin_Bieber, retrieved on October 16th, 2011 at around 5pm.

[2] Enron employee status. Retrieved from http://www.isi.edu/ adibi/Enron/Enron_Employee_Status.xls on May 30th, 2012 at around 9am.

[3] A. Ahmed, E. P. Xing, W. W. Cohen, and R. F. Murphy. Structured correspondence topic models for mining captioned figures in biological literature. In *KDD*, pages 39–48, 2009.

[4] K. Balog and M. de Rijke. Finding experts and their details in e-mail corpora. In *WWW*, pages 1035–1036, 2006.

[5] D. M. Blei, A. Y. Ng, and M. I. Jordan. Latent dirichlet allocation. *J. Machine Learning Res.*, 3:993–1022, 2003.

[6] J. Chang, J. L. Boyd-Graber, and D. M. Blei. Connections between the lines: augmenting social networks with text. In *KDD*, pages 169–178, 2009.

[7] W. de Nooy, A. Mrvar, and V. Batagelj. *Exploratory Social Network Analysis With Pajek*. Cambridge University Press, 2005.

[8] E. Erosheva, S. Fienberg, and J. Lafferty. Mixed-membership models of scientific publications. *Proc. of the National Academy of Sciences*, 101:5220–5227, 2004.

[9] T. Hofmann. Probabilistic latent semantic analysis. In *Proc. of the Fifteenth Conf. on Uncertainty in Artificial Intelligence (UAI'99)*, pages 289–296. Morgan Kaufmann, 1999.

[10] T. Lappas, K. Liu, and E. Terzi. Finding a team of experts in social networks. In *KDD*, pages 467–476, 2009.

[11] Q. Liu, Y. Ge, Z. Li, E. Chen, and H. Xiong. Personalized travel package recommendation. In *ICDM*, pages 407–416, 2011.

[12] Y. Liu, A. Niculescu-Mizil, and W. Gryc. Topic-link lda: joint models of topic and author community. In A. P. Danyluk, L. Bottou, and M. L. Littman, editors, *ICML'09*, volume 382, pages 665–672. ACM, 2009.

[13] A. McCallum, A. Corrada-Emmanuel, and X. Wang. Topic and role discovery in social networks. In *IJCAI*, pages 786–791, 2005.

[14] A. McCallum, X. Wang, and A. Corrada-Emmanuel. Topic and role discovery in social networks with experiments on enron and academic email. *J. Artif. Intell. Res.*, 30:249–272, 2007.

[15] A. K. McCallum. Mallet: A machine learning for language toolkit, 2002. http://mallet.cs.umass.edu.

[16] A. Qamra, B. L. Tseng, and E. Y. Chang. Mining blog stories using community-based and temporal clustering. In *CIKM*, pages 58–67, 2006.

[17] M. Rosen-Zvi, T. L. Griffiths, M. Steyvers, and P. Smyth. The author-topic model for authors and documents. In *Proc. of the 20th Conf. in Uncertainty in Artificial Intelligence*, pages 487–494, 2004.

[18] E. Zheleva, C. Park, and L. Getoor. Co-evolution of social and affiliation networks. In *KDD*, pages 1007–1015, 2009.

[19] D. Zhou, E. Manavoglu, J. Li, C. L. Giles, and H. Zha. Probabilistic models for discovering e-communities. In *WWW*, pages 173–182, 2006.

Finding Trending Local Topics in Search Queries for Personalization of a Recommendation System

Ziad Al Bawab
Yahoo! Labs
Sunnyvale, CA 94089
zalbawab@yahoo-inc.com

George H. Mills
Yahoo! Labs
Sunnyvale, CA 94089
gmills@yahoo-inc.com

Jean-Francois Crespo
Yahoo! Labs
Sunnyvale, CA 94089
jfcrespo@yahoo-inc.com

ABSTRACT

In this paper, we present our approach for geographic personalization of a content recommendation system. More specifically, our work focuses on recommending query topics to users. We do this by mining the search query logs to detect trending local topics. For a set of queries we compute their counts and what we call *buzz* scores, which is a metric for detecting trending behavior. We also compute the entropy of the geographic distribution of the queries as means of detecting their location affinity. We cluster the queries into trending topics and assign the topics to their corresponding location. Human editors then select a subset of these local topics and enter them into a recommendation system. In turn the recommendation system optimizes a pool of trending local and global topics by exploiting user feedback. We present some editorial evaluation of the technique and results of a live experiment. Inclusion of local topics in selected locations into the global pool of topics resulted in more than 6% relative increase in user engagement with the recommendation system compared to using the global topics exclusively.

Categories and Subject Descriptors

H.3 [**Information Storage and Retrieval**]: H.3.1 Content Analysis and Indexing; H.3.3 Information Search and Retrieval; H.4 [**Information Systems Applications**]: H.4.2 Types of Systems;

General Terms

Algorithms, evaluation, live experimentation

Keywords

Trending search queries, clustering, location affinity, personalization, content recommendation

1. INTRODUCTION

Personalization of online content recommendation systems is the task of targeting users with topics tailored to their interests, personal preferences, location, or demography. Internet users engage more with topics that are personally relevant to them, and location is one of the most engaging features that is being exploited heavily by current desktop and mobile applications. For example, users like to know the latest news about their local sports teams and athletes, or like to know about local crimes, elections results, weather events in their area, community festivals or concerts, and local commute disruptions.

Internet portals that recommend content to their users like Yahoo![1], MSN[2], or AOL[3], supply their users with topics and corresponding relevant material to browse for entertainment or to stay up-to-date on current events. Many of these topics are either time-sensitive, hyper-local, or both. In order for personalization to scale for many different locations and to recommend fresh topics in almost real-time, automatic event discovery techniques are highly desirable to power personalized experiences to users.

The search query stream is a valuable and rich source of information about user activity on the internet. It conveys the users' demand for information at a particular time and geographic location. Some of these information needs are time-sensitive, pertaining to current events, or hyper-local, pertaining to local events, or both. Mining the search query stream is one of the most effective ways of finding interesting user *demand*, which recommendation systems can exploit to provide the appropriate *supply* using the content available.

The Trending Now Module on Yahoo!'s front-page, shown in Figure 1, is one of few online trending topic recommendation systems deployed on the internet. The trending topics displayed pertain to different events, mainly globally trending and of interest to a wide user base. Every click on the trending topics takes the user to a search results page where the topic is entered automatically as a query. These topics belong to a larger editorially created pool of topics that are further optimized by the online content recommendation system.

The goal of this paper is to describe the framework we developed to supply trending local topics into the pool of topics used by the Trending Now content recommendation system. This framework will expand the pool of topics and

[1]http://www.yahoo.com
[2]http://www.msn.com
[3]http://www.aol.com

show users from different locations trending topics local to them, in addition to the globally trending topics.

In order to automatically supply local topics to the trending now pool of queries four steps are required. First, we need to detect buzzing queries which are spiking in near real-time. These queries need be distinguished from navigational queries (such as "facebook" or "yahoo"). Queries with fresh news related stories should be given preference. Second, queries need to be clustered around topics ranked according to buzz scores and user views. That is, we need to extract from the buzzing queries the buzzing topics associated with clusters of queries. The third step required for geographic personalization is a mechanism to detect local queries and their affinity to the geographic locations using the geographic information available in the query logs. This is needed so that buzzing topics will be assigned to the locations where their queries are mostly issued from. Finally, the fourth step is to have human editors oversee the selection process. The trending local topics will continuously be refreshed and human editors will select the most interesting topics shown to them on an internal dashboard we created for this task.

To evaluate our framework, we ran two separate tests. The first test was an editorial evaluation of the local topics for selected locations over a period of time. The second was a live test where we included the local topics selected by the editors to be part of the pool of topics for Trending Now. The local topics were added to the global topics, ranked, and presented to users in the respective locations, using the online learning and ranking algorithms described in [10]. A significant increase in user engagement was achieved with the local topics versus the global ones.

In Section 2 we describe related work and motivate the approach that we have taken. In Section 3 we describe the query buzz detection system and in Section 4 we describe the query location affinity detection technique. In Section 5 we describe our approach for query clustering into topics. In Section 6 we describe the editorial evaluation results and in Section 7 we describe the live test experiments and results. We conclude and briefly discuss future work in Section 8.

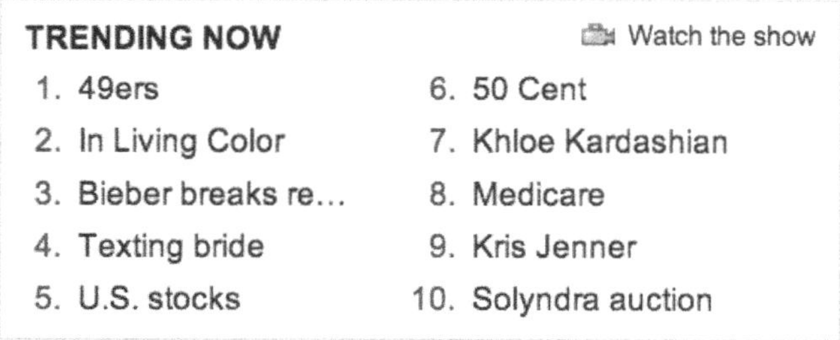

Figure 1: *Trending Now Module on Yahoo! front-page on 11/1/2011 at 3 PM PDT, user logged-in from Sunnyvale CA. Topics T1 and T10 are local topics and the rest are global.*

2. BACKGROUND AND MOTIVATION

The Content Optimization and Relevance Engine (CORE) [1, 2, 3] is the internal engine that drives content recommendation on many Yahoo! properties. It is applied on different content like news stories, today's videos, and trending now topics. There are usually many items in the pool of items for each of these properties and CORE is what decides which of these items to display. CORE implements a partitioning approach to segment the users in real-time into two groups: an exploration and an exploitation group. The exploration group is made of a smaller number of users who provide click-through-rate (CTR) feedback on the content recommended to them according to a random policy. This constitutes the online learning process. The items are then continuously re-ranked according to most engaging and shown to the rest and majority of the users (exploitation). This happens in real-time with models continuously updating. Dong *et al.* [10] discuss applying the CORE technology on the Trending Now Module on Yahoo! front-page.

The CORE powered Trending Now module starts with a pool of topics (or stories) that human editors choose after consulting multiple web resources showing current trends, such as Yahoo! Buzz Index [4] and our internal engine for detection buzzing queries [11]. Using this bounded and fixed pool of topics, CORE optimizes the list by re-ranking it in real-time based on user's engagement. Online personalization is applied where users are segmented into groups based on similarity features like age or gender and the optimal ranking for the topics happens within these segments [10]. Currently there is no consideration of any prior knowledge on the affinity between the topics and the segments. The same list of topics is optimized within the different segments.

The goal of our recommendation framework is to provide the optimal list of trending topics for each user segment, in addition to expanding the pool of topics. Human editors help oversee the selection process in a semi-supervised fashion. The framework we provide allows them to select trending local topics in particular locations and to add them into the corresponding pool of topics. For example, the query "Chicago Cubs", a trending local topic for Chicago, can be added to the pool of topics and be restricted for users from Chicago only. In our experiments, user segmentation is based on geography.

The geographic features derived from the offline search stream can be used as a prior for online optimization. This will help the current optimization approach which suffers from the cold start problem [10], especially for personalization. It starts with a flat prior or equal chance for each topic for each of the user segments. In our work, we tag the topics with the target location. In the example above, Chicago tagged topics will be restricted to users from Chicago according to our framework and hence the re-ranking happens in a fair way. Topics are not demoted due to no-click events from users in other locations who might not be interested in such topics. Similarly, more offline features are to be added like age, gender, and topic category (e.g. sports, finance, shopping, etc.). Figure 2 shows our trending topics detection framework feeding the CORE pool of topics for Trending Now Module.

Trend detection in the search query stream is a technique used to visualize what users are searching for. For example, Google Trends [5] displays a small list of globally trending topics, up to 20 per day. Google Insights[6] provide more flexible analytics and capabilities like trends in different categories,

[4] http://buzzlog.yahoo.com/overall
[5] http://www.google.com/trends
[6] http://www.google.com/insights/search

locations, or variable time intervals. Yet, the smallest interval over which to compute trends provided is seven days. This does not allow for breaking-news detection and might include some stale stories due to the coarse granularity of the selection window. Choi and Varian [7] describe the auto-regressive model used for detecting trends in Google Trends.

Trend detection has also been applied on the Twitter stream of tweets [7]. Like queries, tweets are user generated, and are an effective way to propagate late breaking information. Trendsmap[8] is a tweet based trend visualization service that geographically shows the trending tokens in Twitter. The technique used seems to be token-based which may be noisy and generates tokens that are not news-related. Our buzz detection framework on the other hand makes use of a language modeling [16] approach for detecting buzzing queries [11] as described below. News-related queries buzz scores are boosted. In addition, the trending topics generated by our framework are generalized n-grams, usually more than one token long. This would generate more informative topics for the users to engage with.

Both Google Insights and Trendsmap seem to provide trends for a particular location that could also be globally trending. The work by Welch and Cho [15] uses the lexical information contained in the query itself to identify location. In our work, we use the entropy [8] of the geographic distribution of the topics over all locations and filter out globally trending topics. The local topics our framework provides are those exhibiting the greatest affinity to a particular location. We make use of user logs information that provides the physical location of the users to compute the affinity. This helps enforce location personalization and drive more user engagement. The work in [6, 14] applies query location information to improve web search results ranking. Bennett *et al.* [6] build a location distribution model based on gaussian mixtures for URLs using the users click information and for queries using query logs. They also use entropy as a feature to measure the location affinity of queries. They match the URL and query location distribution to improve the ranking of URLs given a query.

[7]http://twitter.com
[8]http://trendsmap.com

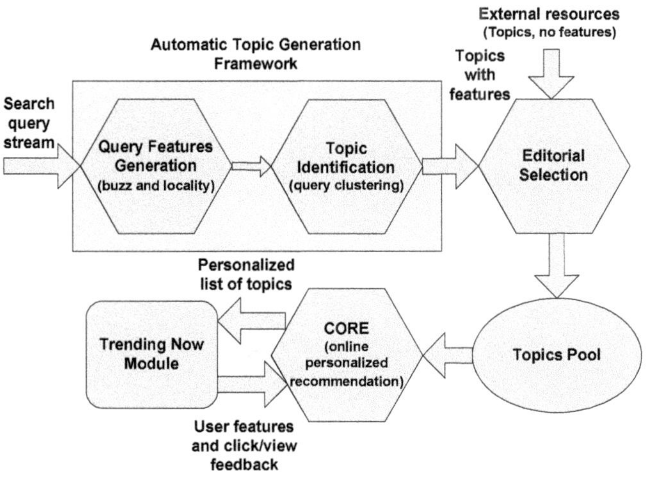

Figure 2: *Our proposed trend detection framework feeding the CORE pool of topics for Trending Now Module.*

3. QUERY BUZZ SCORE

The first component in our framework shown in Figure 2 is responsible for finding buzzing or spiking search queries. It operates in two phases. In the first phase, candidate queries are generated by mining the search logs and selecting queries that integrated a news display in the web search results [9], the top most frequent queries, and all the queries in the last hour with a minimum count and buzz threshold. The buzz score for each query is then computed in the second phase by comparing the query language model scores at the current time window, same time window in the previous day, same time window of the same day one week ago, and the same time window of the same day one month ago. The window size varies between two to six hours depending on the time of the day. The exact window length and the number of top most frequent queries to include were tuned internally. The language models are trained from search queries, queries triggering news displays, and from news feeds. This process is repeated many times per day, and each time produces a "dictionary" which contains the above listed set of queries, their buzz scores, and their counts in the last time window. For more information about buzz score computation refer to [11].

4. QUERY LOCALITY AND DMA PROBABILITY

Our goal is to find queries that have high affinity to specific geographic locations. In our work, we restrict ourselves with the top 50 US Designated Market Areas (DMAs). DMAs are geographic areas defined by Nielsen Media Research company as a group of counties that make up a particular television market. There are 210 Nielsen DMAs in the United States. Examples of DMAs are metropolitan areas (e.g. DMA "Dallas Fort-Worth") or groups of cities (e.g. DMA "San Francisco-Oakland-San Jose") or individual cities (e.g. DMA "Los Angeles", DMA "San Diego", etc.). DMAs are proven (by the television industry) to be effective in targeting geographic audience with customized services.

4.1 Query Location Entropy

We rely on the query location entropy [8, 12] to find local queries as described in Equation 1.

$$entropy(dma \mid q) = -\sum_{i=1}^{N} p(dma_i \mid q) log_2(p(dma_i \mid q)) \quad (1)$$

4.1.1 DMA Posterior Probability

There are two ways to compute the probability of a DMA $p(dma_i \mid q)$ given a query q. The first approach is simply the posterior probability of the DMA given the query as can be computed from the query logs. The internal Yahoo! search query logs provide the physical location (on the DMA level) of the user issuing a query with high accuracy. We aggregate the query DMA volume $v(dma_i, q)$ over 24 hour intervals. For a list of N DMAs, where N is 50 in this case, we compute these probabilities for all the queries in the buzz dictionary (described in Section 3) at the current hour. Queries not making it into the buzz dictionary are excluded.

$$p(dma_i \mid q) = \frac{v(dma_i, q)}{\sum_{j=1}^{N} v(dma_j, q)} \quad (2)$$

4.1.2 DMA Normalized Likelihood

The previous approach does not normalize within a DMA volume. Hence, larger DMAs will be favored. If we assume the DMAs to be equally probable, we arrive at the following normalized likelihood solution, which we adopt for the rest of this paper. This approach favors affinities to smaller DMAs where local topics are more evident relative to the size of the DMA.

$$\begin{aligned} p(dma_i \mid q) &= \frac{p(q \mid dma_i)p(dma_i)}{p(q)} \\ &= \frac{p(q \mid dma_i)p(dma_i)}{\sum_{j=1}^{N} p(q \mid dma_j)p(dma_j)} \\ \widehat{p}(dma_i \mid q) &\approx \frac{p(q \mid dma_i)}{\sum_{j=1}^{N} p(q \mid dma_j)} \end{aligned} \tag{3}$$

where

$$p(q \mid dma_i) = \frac{v(dma_i, q)}{v(dma_i)} \tag{4}$$

4.2 Examples of Local Queries and their Scores

The entropy measure conveys location affinity. Queries with high entropy are global queries and those with low entropy are local. Using the DMAs' normalized likelihoods, we can determine which DMAs the queries are mostly related to. For example running the algorithm on data from December 10, 2010, we get the statistics in Table 1 for a selected list of queries. Since we use only 50 DMAs, the maximum entropy value, which assumes a uniform distribution over DMAs, is $log_2(50) = 5.64$. Buzz scores range between $[0 - 1]$ where the buzzing queries have scores closer to 1.

The first example in Table 1 "ringwood nj murder" has a high buzz score, low entropy, and affinity to DMA "New York", making it a buzzing local query. Similarly the second and third queries are names of a politician and a judge in the states of California and Florida respectively, buzzing around the states' election times. The normalized likelihoods are computed for the 50 DMAs and sum to one. Figure 3 is a scatter plot of the distribution of the buzz and entropy scores of queries. In this figure, queries with count less than 50 for that day are excluded. The majority of the remaining queries are high entropy and low buzz queries (e.g. "amazon", "best buy"). An example of low buzz and low entropy queries is "craigs list san diego". The buzz scores computed do not take location into consideration and are computed over the whole search traffic. Due to data sparsity, some locally trending topics might be missed.

5. TOPIC IDENTIFICATION AND DMA ASSIGNMENT

The previous section described the geographic feature implementation that is added to the current queries dictionary. In addition to the buzz score, the new dictionary includes the query counts in the last 24 hours, the entropy of the query distribution over the 50 DMAs, and the normalized likelihood of the query in each of the DMAs. We use the counts in the last 24 hours to get a more accurate affinity of the queries to the DMAs, whenever these counts are available. To get the topics, the queries need to be clustered and the most prominent DMA for each of the clusters, or topic, need to be identified.

5.1 Topic Clustering

Having identified queries that are buzzing at a particular time, we need a way to cluster those queries around "topics" that users are interested in. For example among the query set ("California Budget", "California Budget Crisis", "California Budget News", and "California State Budget") we wish to single out "California Budget" as "the topic" around which these queries cluster. To determine such topics algorithmically we define a topic score for each query and we choose as our topics those queries with the highest topic scores. The topic score for a query q is defined in terms not just of how many times users searched for exactly q (the volume of q over all DMAs, $v(q)$) but how many times they searched for anything that included q (generalized volume of q over all DMAs, $v^\star(q)$). Thus a search for "California State Budget" would contribute to the generalized volume of "California Budget".

We define two flavors of topic scores for queries, one based on buzz and the other on locality as shown in Equation 5. The locality score $locality(dma \mid q)$ is derived from entropy according to Equation 6. The queries from the new dictionary are sorted according to each of these topic scores separately and the top-n queries (n is tuned internally) from each list form the candidate list of topics. The buzz score will result in a buzzing list of topics and the locality score will result in a local list of topics. Each topic is then associated with the set (or "variants") of queries Q that contain all the words of the topic. Other advanced query clustering techniques have been proposed in the literature [4, 13, 5] which take the search results into consideration and are used for various applications like search assist. The simpler lexically-based solution we use has the advantage of being fast and robust, and proved to be sufficient for our task.

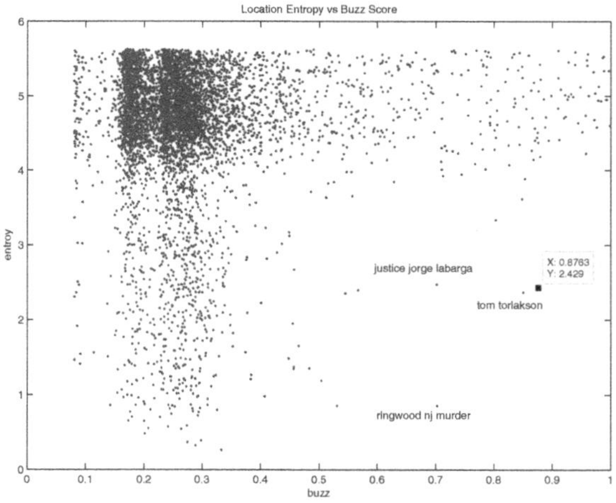

Figure 3: *Buzz versus entropy distribution for December 10, 2010 search queries with count more than 50.*

Table 1: *Query examples and their statistics from December 10, 2010*

Query	Count	Buzz	Entropy	Top DMAs Normalized Likelihood
ringwood nj murder	67	0.70	0.85	New York = 0.84, Philadelphia = 0.06
tom torlakson	73	0.85	2.37	Los Angeles = 0.15, San Francisco = 0.16, Sacramento = 0.36, San Diego = 0.21
justice jorge labarga	66	0.70	2.47	Miami = 0.19, Tampa = 0.17, Orlando = 0.26, Jacksonville = 0.29
craigs list san diego	56	0.27	0.37	San Diego = 0.95

$$\begin{aligned} topic\_buzzscore(q) &= buzz(q) log\{1 + v(q) + v^{\star}(q)\} \\ topic\_localityscore(q) &= locality(dma \mid q) log\{1 + \\ &\quad + v(q) + v^{\star}(q)\} \end{aligned} \quad (5)$$

where

$$locality(dma \mid q) = 1 - \frac{entropy(dma \mid q)}{log_2(N)} \quad (6)$$

5.2 Assigning Topics to DMAs

Once two candidate list of topics are identified according to the two topic scores described in Equation 5, the DMA pertaining to each topic and its query variants set Q is determined. The effective DMA count for each set is computed from the count of each query in the set. The global query count $v(q)$ is used and weighted by the normalized likelihood of the query in that DMA as shown in Equation 7. The effective count $\widehat{count}(Q, dma_i)$ is computed for all 50 DMAs. The DMA with the largest count is chosen as the DMA for this cluster.

$$\widehat{count}(Q, dma_i) = \sum_{q \in Q} \widehat{p}(dma_i \mid q) v(q) \quad (7)$$

Finally the two lists are merged and ranked as shown in Figure 4 which describes the process. We apply certain thresholds on the topics to make sure we retain relevant ones. Topics pass the filtering if their base query count, buzz score, and locality score exceed the thresholds that are tuned separately. The resulting topics and its variant sets are presented in the editorial dashboard we designed so that editors have a good picture about the reason each topic is trending, which is often evident from the query variants that contain it.

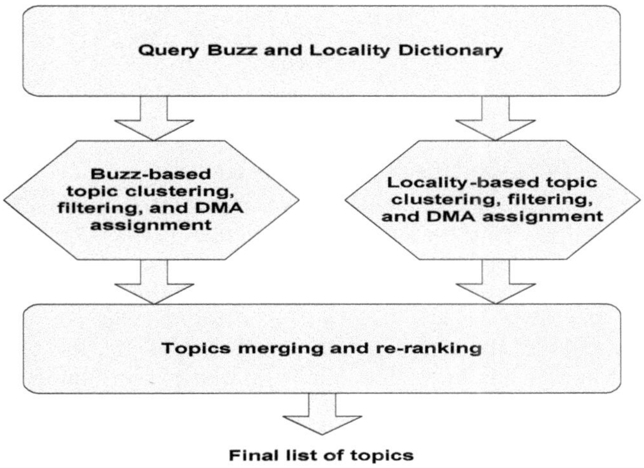

Figure 4: *Topic clustering and merging.*

6. EDITORIAL EVALUATION

Before deploying the framework for a live test, we ran an exhaustive editorial test for the topics chosen for six test DMAs. These DMAs are listed in Table 3. Three editors were chosen for this task. They were asked to judge each topic taking into consideration the DMA assigned to it by the framework. Editors provided grades {"Excellent","Good", "Fair", and "Bad"} to the topics according to preset editorial guidelines. The judgments were influenced by two aspects: recency or buzziness, and local affinity to the corresponding DMA. We prepared an editorial tool which presented the topic sets to each editor and recorded their judgments. The tool allowed editors to view the topic, the queries (or variants) clustered around it, and also allowed them to click on the topics and inspect the web search results page or the news results page. The editors completed a live test from June 1 through June 3, 2011. Table 2 shows the grade distribution for the three editors for one day during the second test period. Each editor was presented with 45 topics from the six DMAs during that day. There were 20% overlap in the topics assigned to each pair of editors so that we keep track on intra-editor differences. "Total with overlap" is sum of the results for the three editors without taking repeating topics into account. The "Aggregate" results take into account the editorial differences. As shown in the results, 25.2% of the topics shown to the editors have a grade of "Excellent" and are suitable to be included into the pool of topics for the Trending Now Module. Around 69.2% of the topics have a grade of "Good" or better (GOB), from which some topics may also be suitable for Trending Now. In addition, the results show a good degree of consistency in the judgments distribution between editors especially for the "Excellent" topics. "Good' topics are usually local and buzzing topics but tailored to a narrow audience or leading to search results with obscene content. "Fair" topics could be local and buzzing but also navigational or unrecognized by most users in that location. "Bad" topics include those that are not local, not buzzing, misspelled, or completely generic.

6.1 DMA Based Breakdown

We ran the editorial test for three days with a fresh list of topics presented to the editors every day containing trending topics that are local to the six DMAs shown in Table 3. The table lists the number of "Excellent" judgments the topics received for the three days in each of the six DMAs. It also shows the average number of "Excellent" topics per day per DMA. It also shows that a similar percentage of the "Excellent" topics is found every day of the test for all of the DMAs. Smaller DMAs like "Cleveland-Akron" and "Detroit" have lower number of "Excellent" topics than larger DMAs like "New York". They make 3% and 4% of the total number of "Excellent" topics found for the three days respectively, versus 39% for DMA "New York".

Table 4 shows the aggregated judgments results for the

Table 2: *Breakdown of editorial test results based on editors for the test on June 2, 2011 starting at 15:00 GMT.*

Editor	Topics	Excellent	Good	Fair	Bad	Good or Better	Excellent %	GOB %
Editor1	45	10	27	6	2	37	22.2%	82.2%
Editor2	45	12	12	18	3	24	26.7%	53.3%
Editor3	45	11	19	9	6	30	24.4%	66.7%
Total with overlap	135	33	58	33	11	91	24.4%	67.4%
Aggregate	107	27	47	24	9	74	25.2%	69.2%

Table 3: *Distribution of "Excellent" topics over DMA for June 1,2 and 3, 2011 starting at 15:00 GMT on each day.*

DMA	06-01-2011	06-02-2011	06-03-2011	Total per DMA	Ave per Day	Topics%
Chicago	6	5	3	14	4.7	20%
Cleveland-Akron	0	1	1	2	0.7	3%
Dallas-Ft. Worth	5	2	6	13	4.3	19%
Detroit	0	1	2	3	1.0	4%
Los Angeles	4	4	2	10	3.3	15%
New York	5	14	8	27	9.0	39%
Total Excellent	20	27	22	69	23.0	100 %
Total Judged	90	107	89	286	95.3	
Excellent %	22.2%	25.2%	24.7%	24.1%	24.1%	

three days. A similar number of "Excellent" topics is found as discussed above. The total judgments for the three days period was 286, out of which 257 are unique. It is expected that some topics repeat from one day to the other. The same judgment aggregation criteria were followed as the one described above. 69 "Excellent" topics were found, out of which 53 are unique, contributing to 20.6% to the total number of unique topics judged during the three days period.

7. LIVE TEST EVALUATION

To evaluate the effectiveness of the local topics our framework provided, we ran a live test on the Trending Now Module on Yahoo!'s front-page shown in Figure 1. The live test covered the six DMAs presented in Table 3. During the test, real-time programming of local topics took place and impacted users in these six DMAs. The traffic for each DMA was split into 45% for the "Test" bucket, 45% for the "Control" bucket, and the remaining 10% for the "Random" exploration (learning) bucket as described in Table 5. The local topics were added in a semi-supervised fashion into the global pool of topics that are programmed daily. The size of the global pool varies daily and at any given time it would be competing with the local topics in the 'Test" buckets for each DMA. The editorial selection of the global topics continued to happen independently of this task. Using the dashboard tool we prepared, human editors selected a subset of the local topics for each of the six DMAs that they deemed suitable according to internal editorial guidelines. The editorial tool refreshes the set of local topics for each of the DMAs in near real-time. Due to time zones differences for the DMAs, one editor took charge of programming topics for DMAs "Cleveland-Akron" and "New York". A second editor programmed topics for DMAs "Chicago" and "Detroit", and a third editor programmed topics for DMAs "Dallas-Ft. Worth" and "Los Angeles". Table 5 describes the 13 buckets we ran. The "Random" bucket contains a randomly shuffled list of global and local topics, out of which 10 topics are displayed to 10% of the users who fall into this bucket from the six DMAs. The global topics are common to all users from the six DMAs, but location-based filtering is applied such that the local topics are shown only to the corresponding DMA users. The users' engagement with the topics is used to re-rank the list of topics continuously. The higher the click through rate (CTR) on the topic the higher is its rank, regardless whether it is a local or a global topic. To assess the impact on the overall module, the top 10 ranked list of local and global topics is displayed to 45% of users who fall into the "Test" bucket in each DMA. The overall module CTR for each of the six "Test" buckets is then computed. In parallel, the local topics are filtered-out and the ranked list of top 10 global topics is displayed to 45% of users who fall into the "Control" bucket. The overall module CTR for each of the six "Control" buckets is then computed. The difference in the CTR between the "Test" and "Control" buckets in each DMA measures the impact of adding the local topics into the pool of global topics. The six DMAs included in the test make about 25% of the total US traffic contributing millions of views daily.

Table 5: *Buckets description*

Bucket Type	Number	Size	Content
Test	6	45%	ranked list of global and local topics
Control	6	45%	ranked list of global topics
Random	1	10%	random list of global and local topics

$$CTR = \frac{Clicks}{Views} \tag{8}$$

7.1 Per-Module Evaluation Results

Table 6 shows the relative increase in CTR on the modules in the "Test" buckets over the modules in the "Control" buckets for each of the DMAs for a period of five days from August 8 through August 12, 2011. The CTR computation for the "Test" buckets included the views and clicks on local and global topics together. The "Control" buckets did not include any local topic. Online learning and re-ranking is applied as described in this paper [10] and included age and gender personalization in the "Control" and "Test" buckets too. Improvements in CTR are observed in the "Test" buckets over the "Control" buckets for all DMAs. This improvement is due to the added local topics in the DMAs "Test" buckets. Overall, there is a 5.91% improvement in

Table 4: *Aggregation of results for June 1,2 and 3, 2011 starting at 15:00 GMT on each day.*

Date	Topics	Excellent	Good	Fair	Bad	Good or Better	Excellent %	GOB %
06-01-2011	90	20	44	21	5	64	22.2%	71.1%
06-02-2011	107	27	47	24	9	74	25.2%	69.2%
06-03-2011	89	22	39	24	4	61	24.7%	68.5%
Total with overlap	286	69	130	69	18	199	24.1%	69.6%
Aggregate	257	53	124	64	16	177	20.6%	68.9%

CTR for all DMAs running this test. The table also shows the DMA volume, which is the ratio of views in the "Control" and "Test" buckets in each of the DMAs to the views in the "Control" and "Test" buckets for all DMAs. In essence, this measures the volume of the DMA relative to the volume of the six DMAs. DMA "Los Angeles" is the largest DMA with 32% DMA volume. A CTR improvement of 5.13% was achieved in DMA "Los Angeles".

Table 6 also shows the total number of local topics programmed during the five days period. There were 78 local topics and 201 global ones programmed during this time. There are some differences in the number of local topics programmed and the rate per day between this period and the period when the editorial test was performed for a few reasons. First, this was a live test in which there were more constraints on the search landing page experience. Second, this is a different time period and the traffic might be different. Third, the editors supervising the selection process were getting more experienced with time. The "Topics%" column in the table presents the ratio between the number of topics programmed for the DMA over the total number of topics programmed for the six DMAs. In essence, this represents the volume of topics programmed for each DMA versus the total topics. The column before the last presents the ratio of this topic volume to the DMA volume. On average, this should be closer to 1.0 for DMAs like "Chicago". This value is 2.51 for DMA "Detroit" which means that more topics were programmed (relative to the other DMAs) in proportion to the volume of this DMA (relative to the volume of the total DMAs). Around 12.86% improvement in CTR occurred for DMA "Detroit" which is correlated with this observation. The trend is reversed for DMA "New York" where this ratio is 0.71 and 3.41% improvement in CTR. In general, the more local queries are programmed in a DMA, relative to the DMA volume, the more improvement in CTR is observed as the results seem to corroborate. The last column shows the ratio of the number of local topics versus the total number of topics, including the global ones, in the pool for each DMA. The local topics compete with the global pool of topics in each DMA independently of other DMAs and form a small portion of the pool (less than 10%) as shown in the table. More analysis on the performance of local versus global queries is below.

Figure 5 shows the relative increase in CTR for the overall Trending Now Module in the "Test" versus "Control" buckets in each of the six test DMAs. We ran the live experiment for a period of more than five weeks. We achieved significant improvements across all DMAs. In DMA "Detroit", one of the smaller DMAs tested, an increase of 12.71% has been achieved overall. The largest CTR increase of 14.85% occurred in the second week of the test (July 25 through 29). This proves the effectiveness of geographic personalization in such locations where users engage well with local events. In addition, an overall increase of 8.58% occurred in DMA "Los Angeles" which is the largest DMA tested. This is also very significant in that it increases the engagement of the largest user segments in the test. On the other hand, the engagement in DMA "New York" was not as strong due to a configuration issue that restricted local topics from appearing at position one in the module. This restriction was later removed but the engagement increase with local events in this DMA continued be be lower than other DMAs. This may indicate that users in DMA "New York" are less interested in local events than users in other DMAs. Yet, the engagement with local topics was still higher than that with the global topics. For all the DMAs, and throughout the five weeks period, an increase of 6.38% was achieved from July 15 through August 20, 2011 [9].

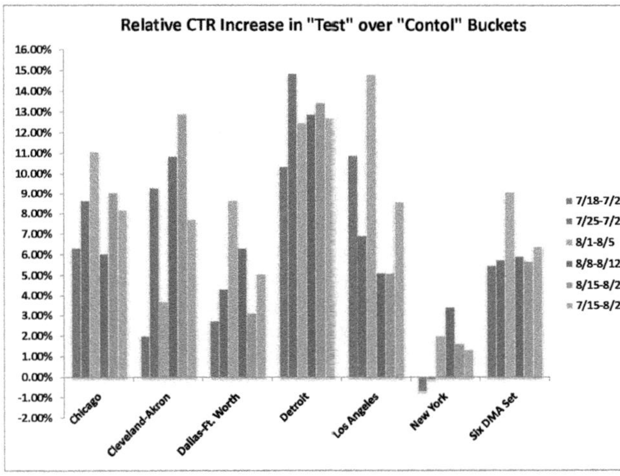

Figure 5: *Relative increase in CTR between the modules in the "Test" and "Control" buckets for the six DMAs and five weeks live test period.*

Figure 6 shows the number of local and global topics programmed in the five DMAs over the five weeks period on a log_2 scale. The largest DMA to receive local topics was DMA "Los Angeles" followed by "Chicago" and "Detroit". The number of local topics programmed was consistent over the five weeks period. The number of global topics programmed was on the order of ten times more in each DMA.

7.2 Local versus Global Topic Analysis

In the previous section, we presented results showing improvements in the overall module CTR when allowing local topics to appear in the "Test" buckets and not in the "Control" buckets. The overall module CTR included clicks on local and global topics together in the "Test" buckets. However, this does not prove that the improvement is solely due

[9]* in Figure 5 denotes excluding weekends.

Table 6: *Bucket test results for the five days programming period from August 8 through August 12, 2011.*

DMA	Module CTR Increase	DMA Volume	Topics Programmed	Topics per Day	Topics%	$\frac{Topics\%}{DMAVolume}$	Local Topics in Pool %
Chicago	6.02%	17%	13	2.6	16.7%	0.99	6.1%
Cleveland-Akron	10.84%	6%	17	3.4	21.8%	3.75	7.8%
Dallas-Ft. Worth	6.28%	11%	6	1.2	7.7%	0.67	2.9%
Detroit	12.86%	7%	14	2.8	17.9%	2.51	6.5%
Los Angeles	5.13%	32%	13	2.6	16.7%	0.53	6.1%
New York	3.41%	27%	15	3.0	19.2%	0.71	6.9%
Six DMAs Set	5.91%	100%	78	15.6	100.0%	1.00	28.0%

to clicks on local topics. There is a very unlikely scenario where users click more on global topics when shown with less attractive local topics in the "Test" buckets. To verify that this is not the case and to assess the performance of the local topics versus global ones we measure the improvement in CTR on the local topics versus the global ones separately. We measure the CTR when a local topic occupies each position on the module shown in Figure 1. We also measure the CTR of the global topics in each position. This provides a direct comparison between the local topics and the global topics. Table 7 reports the relative increase in CTR when local topics occupy each position on the Trending Now Module versus when global topics occupy that position.

For "All-Buckets" we measure the CTR increase between the local topics in "Test" and "Random" buckets versus the CTR of the global topics in all the buckets including the "Control" ones. This shows a relative increase of 61% at all positions, 16% increase at position one and so forth. For the "Test vs Control" we measure the CTR increase between the local topics in "Test" and the global topics in "Control" buckets for all six DMAs. This measures the difference between the ranked list of local topics in "Test" when shown with global topics, versus the ranked list of global topics in "Control" when shown alone with no bias from local topics. A relative improvement of 70% in achieved at all positions. For "Chicago", we measure the CTR difference between the local topics in the "Test" for "Chicago" and the global topics

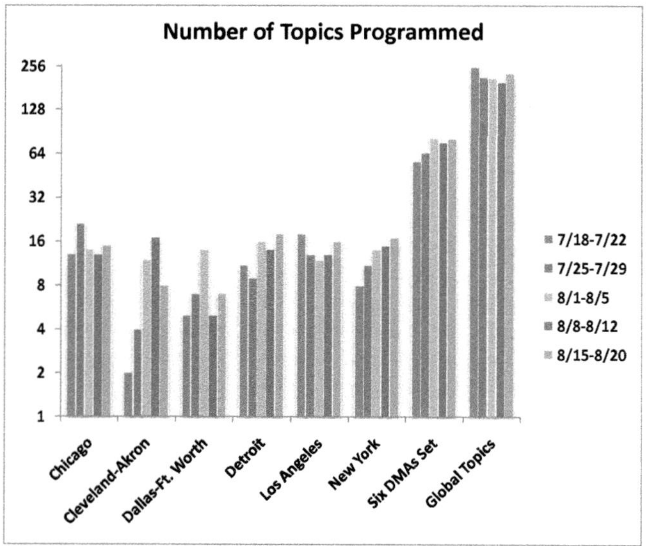

Figure 6: *Number of local and global topics programmed per DMA and week.*

in the "Control" bucket for "Chicago". A relative improvement of 74% is achieved at all positions. There is roughly no difference in engagement at position one when a local or global topic occupies this position. Similarly for DMA "Los Angeles", yet more engagement is achieved at other positions. Notice that the increase is more dramatic at lower positions (on the module counting 1 down to 5 then 6 down to 10) due to the position bias phenomenon [10]: users are more likely to click on position one than on lower positions on the module especially when the ranking of topics is applied. Hence the improvement is more apparent at lower positions. The improvement is more consistent across positions in the "Random" bucket which proves that the local topics are more engaging irrespective of ranking bias. An increase of 39% is achieved in the "Random" bucket across all positions.

Figure 7 shows the distribution of the views and clicks of the local and global topics over the module positions in the "Test" buckets. Recall that "Test" buckets apply topic ranking learned from the "Random" bucket. Local topics are viewed more at top positions than on the lower ones due to the positive feedback they receive in the "Random" bucket and hence are ranked high. Around 18.19% of the views of local topics happened at position one. The views of global topics is flat across positions with almost equal likelihood of 10%. It is interesting to see that the views of global topics at position one is less than 10%, around 9.27% due to the competition with local topics to be displayed at this position. Around 42.15% of clicks on local topics happened on position one, 31.07% of clicks on global topics at this position. This shows the position bias phenomenon and the increased attractiveness of local topics on this position compared to the global topics. The click distribution tapers off at lower positions for both local and global topics.

Figure 8 shows the distribution of the views and clicks of local and global topics in the "Random" bucket. These topics are randomly shuffled and only 10 of them are shown to each user at a time. The figure shows the flat distribution of the views and the position-biased distribution of clicks. Similar distribution is achieved for local and global topics views and clicks since no ranking is applied here.

8. CONCLUSION AND FUTURE WORK

In this paper, we presented a framework that identifies trending local topics for the purpose of personalized Trending Now programming. We described how we computed geographic features for the search queries and how to use these features to detect local queries. We also presented our clustering approach that finds topics from the queries and assigns it to geographic locations. An exhaustive editorial test was performed to assess the quality and quantity of the

Table 7: *Relative increase in CTR of local versus global topics in different buckets and module positions, from August 8 through August 12, 2011.*

Bucket	All-Positions	T1	T2	T3	T4	T5	T6	T7	T8	T9	T10
Test vs Control	70%	17%	23%	35%	17%	92%	28%	36%	143%	56%	57%
Chicago	74%	1%	18%	31%	17%	92%	11%	29%	157%	56%	57%
Cleveland-Akron	112%	39%	35%	31%	15%	92%	19%	38%	171%	89%	75%
Dallas-Ft. Worth	125%	16%	24%	41%	8%	125%	21%	40%	157%	100%	100%
Detroit	136%	22%	40%	54%	31%	142%	45%	60%	214%	133%	88%
Los Angeles	27%	1%	5%	20%	18%	82%	29%	38%	143%	56%	71%
New York	46%	24%	30%	33%	21%	92%	32%	27%	129%	44%	43%
Random	39%	42%	42%	40%	41%	36%	33%	31%	36%	40%	33%
All-Buckets	61%	16%	21%	31%	22%	83%	28%	36%	100%	56%	57%

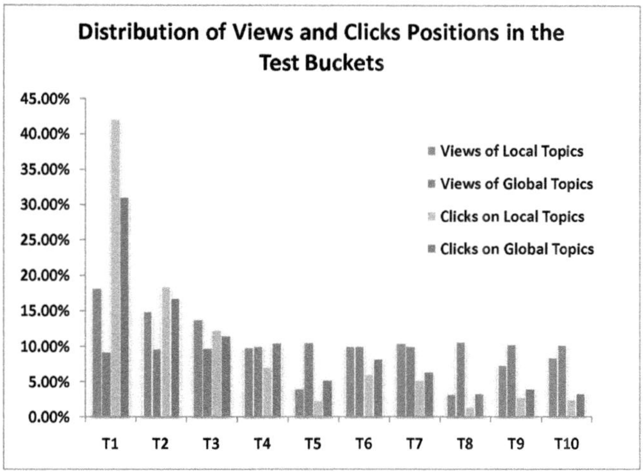

Figure 7: *Distribution of views and clicks of local and global topics over module positions in the "Test" buckets from August 8 through August 12, 2011.*

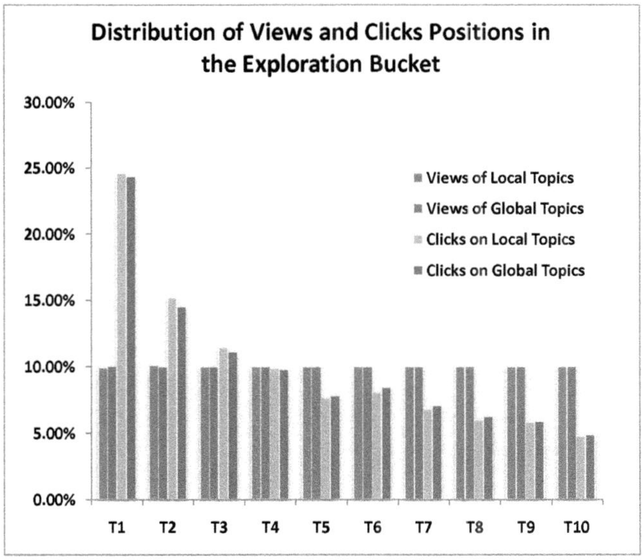

Figure 8: *Distribution of views and clicks of local and global topics over module positions in the "Random" buckets from August 8 through August 12, 2011.*

local topics provided by the framework. The live test showed improvements in CTR in the "Test" buckets compared to the "Control" ones. Significant increase in user engagement was achieved with the local topics versus the global ones. Future work will focus on joint optimization of buzz and locality detection and on combating data sparsity using collaborative filtering techniques. This work has been deployed and powers the Trending Now module on Yahoo! front page as evident in Figure 1 and impacts millions of users in selected locations.

9. REFERENCES

[1] D. Agarwal, B.-C. Chen, and P. Elango. Spatio-temporal models for estimating click-through rate. In *WWW*, pages 21–30, 2009.

[2] D. Agarwal, B.-C. Chen, and P. Elango. Fast online learning through offline initialization for time-sensitive recommendation. In *KDD*, pages 703–712, 2010.

[3] D. Agarwal, B.-C. Chen, P. Elango, N. Motgi, S. taek Park, R. Ramakrishnan, S. Roy, and J. Zachariah. Online models for content optimization. In *Neural Information Processing Systems*, pages 17–24, 2008.

[4] R. A. Baeza-Yates, C. A. Hurtado, and M. Mendoza. Query recommendation using query logs in search engines. In *International Conference on Extending Database Technology*, pages 588–596, 2004.

[5] D. Beeferman and A. L. Berger. Agglomerative clustering of a search engine query log. In *KDD*, pages 407–416, 2000.

[6] P. N. Bennett, F. Radlinski, R. W. White, and E. Yilmaz. Inferring and using location metadata to personalize web search. SIGIR, pages 135–144, 2011.

[7] H. Choi and H. Varian. Predicting the present with google trends. In *Google Inc Technical Report*, 2009.

[8] T. M. Cover and J. A. Thomas. Elements of information theory. 1991.

[9] F. Diaz. Integration of news content into web results. In *WSDM*, pages 182–191, 2009.

[10] A. Dong, J. Bian, X. He, S. Reddy, and Y. Chang. User action interpretation for personalized content optimization in recommender systems. In *CIKM2011*, Stratford-upon-Avon, UK, 2011.

[11] A. Dong, Y. Chang, Z. Zheng, G. Mishne, J. Bai, R. Zhang, K. Buchner, C. Liao, and F. Diaz. Towards recency ranking in web search. In *WSDM*, pages 11–20, 2010.

[12] Q. Mei and K. Church. Entropy of search logs: how hard is search? with personalization? with backoff? WSDM, pages 45–54, 2008.

[13] J. rong Wen, J. yun Nie, and H.-J. Zhang. Query clustering using user logs. *ACM Transactions on Information Systems*, 20:59–81, 2002.

[14] L. Wang, C. Wang, X. Xie, J. Forman, Y. Lu, W.-Y. Ma, and Y. Li. Detecting dominant locations from search queries. SIGIR, pages 424–431, 2005.

[15] M. J. Welch and J. Cho. Automatically identifying localizable queries. In *Research and Development in Information Retrieval*, pages 507–514, 2008.

[16] C. Zhai. Statistical language models for information retrieval: A critical review. *Foundations and Trends in Information Retrieval*, 2:137–213, 2008.

Industry Practice Expo Invited Talk

China's National Personal Credit Scoring System: A Real-Life Intelligent Knowledge Application

Yong Shi
Chinese Academy of Sciences / China Data Technology
China
yshi@gucas.ac.cn

Abstract

Credit Reference Centre (CRC) of People's Bank of China (PBC) has built a big data: the largest personal credit database in the world with 800 million people's accounts collected from all commercial banks in China since 2003. From June 2006 to Sept 2009, Research Centre on Fictitious Economy and Data Science, Chinese Academy of Sciences (CASFEDS) and CRC jointly developed China's National Personal Credit Scoring System, known as "China Score", which is a unique and advanced KDD application under intelligent knowledge management on this big data. The system will be eventually serving all 1.3 billion population of China for their daily financial activities, such as bank accounts, credit card application, mortgage, personal loans, etc. It can become one of the most influential events of KDD techniques to human kind. This talk will introduce the key components of China Score project that includes objectives, modeling process, KDD techniques used in the projects, intelligent knowledge management and experience of the project development. In addition, the talk will also outline a number of policy recommendations based on China Score project which has been potentially impacting Chinese Government on its strategic decision making for China's economic developments.

Categories & Subject Descriptors: H.2.8 [Database Management]: Data Mining.

Author Keywords: Credit Scoring, Risk Models, Knowledge Management.

Bio

Dr Yong Shi a Senior Member of IEEE, Executive Deputy Director, Chinese Academy of Sciences Research Center on Fictitious Economy & Data Science, China. He was the Charles W. and Margre H. Durham Distinguished Professor of Information Technology, College of Information Science and Technology, Peter Kiewit Institute, University of Nebraska, USA from 1999 to 2004. Dr. Shi's research interests include business intelligence, data mining, and multiple criteria decision making. He has published more than 17 books, over 200 papers in various journals and numerous conferences/proceedings papers. He is the Editor-in-Chief of International Journal of Information Technology and Decision Making (SCI), and a member of Editorial Board for a number of academic journals. Dr. Shi has received many awards including the Georg Cantor Award of the International Society on Multiple Criteria Decision Making (MCDM), 2009; Fudan Prize of Distinguished Contribution in Management, 2009; and Outstanding Young Scientist Award, National Natural Science Foundation of China, 2001. He has consulted or worked on business projects for a number of international companies in KDD and intelligent knowledge management.

KDD'12, August 12–16, 2012, Beijing, China.
ACM 978-1-4503-1462-6/12/08.

Industry Practice Expo Invited Talk

Maximizing Return and Minimizing Cost with the Right Decision Management Systems

Rich Holada
IBM
USA
rholada@us.ibm.com

Abstract

The ability to achieve operational efficiency, product leadership, and customer intimacy still eludes many organizations due, in large part, to the chaos of business. Inconsistent prioritization and decision making; poor visibility between systems; processes that are not well controlled; and individual front-line decisions that seem small but, in totality, have a huge impact make it difficult for organizations to link strategy to execution and back. During this presentation, we will demonstrate how automating and optimizing decisions (operational efficiency) with business rules and predictive models enables better data driven results across the enterprise, and how this is implemented at the point of impact (customer intimacy) to transform an organization and support market leadership.

Categories & Subject Descriptors: H.2.8 [Database Management]: Data Mining.

Author Keywords: Automated Decision Management, Predictive Analytics, CRM, ROI.

Bio

Rich Holada heads IBM's predictive analytics group, which includes the SPSS line of software and solutions. Holada is responsible for setting the strategic and technological direction of the group, as well as overseeing its day-to-day operations, from global product development to sales and marketing. With Business Analytics as a key growth area for IBM, Holada is focused on helping customers solve real-world business problems through predictive analytics to create a Smarter Planet.

Previously, Holada was CTO of predictive analytics that included global responsibility for product marketing, product strategy, research and development, and technical support for the IBM SPSS predictive analytics brand. He joined SPSS, prior to its acquisition by IBM, in November 2006 as Senior Vice President of Research & Development, bringing with him nearly 20 years of deep software research and development background and diverse experience in the technology industry.

Previously, Holada has held senior level posts with Oracle Corporation and PeopleSoft, Inc., both leading CRM technology organizations. At PeopleSoft, Inc. he was the senior technical executive responsible for creating the industry-leading PeopleSoft CRM product offering.

KDD'12, August 12–16, 2012, Beijing, China.
ACM 978-1-4503-1462-6/12/08.

Efficient and Domain-Invariant Competitor Mining

Theodoros Lappas
Boston University
tlappas@cs.bu.edu

George Valkanas
University of Athens
gvalk@di.uoa.gr

Dimitrios Gunopulos
University of Athens
dg@di.uoa.gr

ABSTRACT

In any competitive business, success is based on the ability to make an item more appealing to customers than the competition. A number of questions arise in the context of this task: *how do we formalize and quantify the competitiveness relationship between two items? Who are the true competitors of a given item? What are the features of an item that most affect its competitiveness?* Despite the impact and relevance of this problem to many domains, only a limited amount of work has been devoted toward an effective solution. In this paper, we present a formal definition of the competitiveness between two items. We present efficient methods for evaluating competitiveness in large datasets and address the natural problem of finding the top-k competitors of a given item. Our methodology is evaluated against strong baselines via a user study and experiments on multiple datasets from different domains.

Categories and Subject Descriptors

H.2.8 [**Database Management**]: Database applications—*Data Mining*; H.4.m [**Information Systems Applications**]: Miscellaneous

Keywords

competitor mining, competitors, domain-invariant

1. INTRODUCTION

Competitiveness is a challenge that every product or service provider has to face, regardless of the application domain. A significant amount of relevant work has demonstrated the strategic importance of identifying and monitoring an entity's competitors [19]. In fact, a long line of research from the marketing and management community has been devoted to empirical managerial methods for competitor identification [8, 7, 10, 3, 18], as well as to methods for analyzing competitors [5], defending against competitive incursions, and devising appropriate response strategies [11, 6]. Our own work focuses on competitor identification, a key step for any competitiveness-driven study or application. Contrary to the significant amount of available work by the marketing community, the problem has been largely overlooked by computer scientists. For the latter, the challenge is to propose formalizations and competitor-identification algorithms that can utilize the vast amounts of rich data that is nowadays available on the web and other digital sources. Some progress toward this direction has been made by the information systems community [14, 15, 13, 1, 16, 27]. While the proposed approaches help motivate the problem, they present significant shortcomings. These include the lack of a formal definition of competitiveness, as well as the existence of assumptions that limit the applicability of these approaches. Specifically, these techniques are based on mining comparative expressions (e.g. "Item A is better than Item B") from the web or other textual sources. Even though such expressions can be indicators of competitiveness, they are absent in many domains. For example, consider the domain of vacation packages (e.g flight-hotel-car combinations). In this case, the items have no assigned name by which they can be queried or compared with each other. Further, the frequency of textual comparative evidence can vary greatly across domains. For example, when comparing brand names from the domain of technology (e.g. "Google Vs Yahoo" or "Sony Vs Panasonic"), it is indeed likely that comparative patterns can be found by simply querying the web. However, it is trivial to consider other mainstream domains where such findings are extremely scarce, if not non-existent(e.g. shoes, jewelery, hotels, restaurants, furniture). Finally, even in domains where such approaches are applicable, they cannot actually evaluate the competitiveness relationship between *any* two items. Instead, they can only identify a *subset* of the competitors, based on the available evidence. Our own work overcomes these drawbacks, by providing a formal definition of competitiveness that is applicable across domains. On a high-level, the fundamental problem we address in our work is the following:

PROBLEM 1. *We are given a set of items $\mathcal{I}$, defined within the feature space $\mathcal{F}$ of a particular domain. Then, given any pair of items I, I' from $\mathcal{I}$ we want to define a function $C_{\mathcal{F}}(I, I')$ that computes the competitiveness between the two in the context of the domain.*

As mentioned in the statement of the problem, our notion of competitiveness is based on the feature-space $\mathcal{F}$ of the corresponding domain. Our competitiveness paradigm is based on the following observation: *the competitiveness between two items is based on whether they compete for the attention and business of the same group of users (i.e. the same market share), and to what extent.* For example, two restaurants that exist in different countries are obviously not competitive to each other, since there is no overlap between their target groups. In the ideal scenario, we would have access to the complete set of users that could be interested in a given item. Then, given any two items, we could trivially compute their competitiveness based on the overlap of their respective sets. In practice, however, this is clearly not an option. Taking this into consideration, we formalize the competitiveness between two items based on their respective *features*. For example, if the considered items are MP3 Players, $\mathcal{F}$ could consist of the features *price, sound quality, battery life, connectivity, capacity* and *design*. Our motivation is that, regardless of the domain, users compare and evaluate items based on their features. Therefore, by attaching our formalization to the feature space, we ensure the availability of a consistent and informative resource for competitiveness evaluation. We provide a (simplified) overview of our approach in Figure 1.

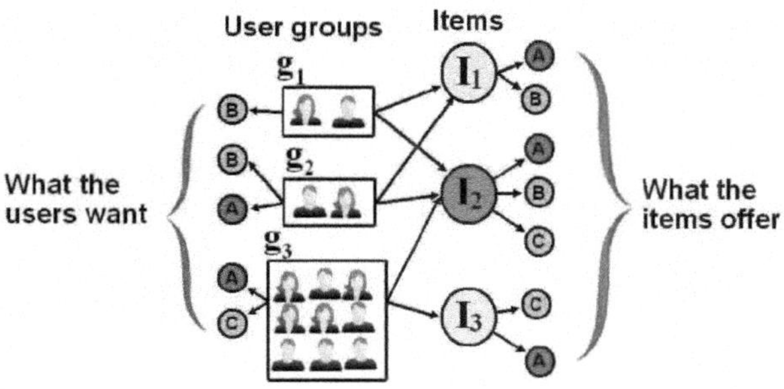

Figure 1: A (simplified) example of our competitiveness paradigm

The figure illustrates the competitiveness between three different items I_1, I_2 and I_3. Each item is mapped to the set of features that it can offer to the users. Three distinct features are considered in this example: A, B and C. Note that, for this simple example, we only consider binary features (i.e. available/not available). Our actual formalization accounts for a much richer space of binary, categorical and numerical features. The left side of the figure shows three groups of users (g_1, g_2, g_3). The example assumes that these are the only groups in existence. Users are grouped based on their preferences with respect to the features. For example, the users in group g_2 are only interested in features A and B. As can be seen by the figure, items I_1 and I_3 are not competitive to each other, since they simply do not appeal to the same groups of users. On the other hand, I_2 is in competition with both I_1 (for groups g_1 and g_2) and I_3 (for g_3). Finally, another interesting observation is that I_2 competes with I_1 for a total of 4 users, and with I_3 for a total of 9 users. In other words, I_3 is a stronger competitor for I_2, since it claims a much larger portion of I_2's market-share than I_1. In our work, we propose ways to deduce these user-groups from sources such as query logs and customer reviews, and describe methods to estimate the size of the market share that they represent. Our work is the first to utilize the opinions expressed in customer reviews as a resource for mining competitiveness.

The formal definition of the competitiveness $C_{\mathcal{F}}(I_i, I_j)$ between two items I_i and I_j, in the context of their domain's feature-space $\mathcal{F}$, is the first contribution of our work. As we demonstrate in our experiments, the evaluation of competitiveness can be a major computational challenge when dealing with real datasets of hundreds or even thousands of items. Motivated by this, we propose an algorithm for the natural problem of finding the top-k competitors of a given item. The proposed framework is geared toward scalability and efficiency, which makes it applicable to domains with large populations of items.

Roadmap

In Section 2 we introduce our competitiveness paradigm. In Sections 3 and 4 we present an efficient framework for finding the top-k competitors of a given item. The experimental evaluation of our work is presented in Section 5. In Section 6 we discuss previous related work. Finally, we conclude the paper in Section 7.

2. FORMALIZING COMPETITIVENESS

In this section, we describe how we can formalize and measure the competitiveness between any two items within a given domain. This formalization serves as the building block of our framework. Note that our definition can be easily extended to handle more than two items at a time.

2.1 Competitiveness via Coverage

In order to synthesize a competitor-mining method that works across domains, we need a formalization of competitiveness that is both accurate and flexible. Motivated by this, we build upon a crucial factor that remains consistent across domains: *user preferences*. In every market, the ultimate goal is to convert users into customers by meeting their individual requirements. Consider a single user u, interested in a specific domain (e.g. restaurants). While the domain may contain numerous items, the user will ultimately choose only one to spend his money on. In a typical scenario, the user follows the following steps:

1. Encode requirements and preferences in a query.
2. Submit the query to a search engine and retrieve the matching items.
3. Process matching items and make the final choice.

We observe that the items that do not match the user's criteria are never considered. In other words, they never get the chance to *compete* for his attention. As far this single user is concerned, the set of competitors consists of the matching items retrieved by the search engine. Consider the following motivating example:

Example: *A user is trying to pick a restaurant for dinner. He has a very limited budget and is only interested in Italian restaurants in the Boston Area. Only the restaurants that satisfy these criteria will compete for the user's attention. On the other hand, Chinese restaurants, restaurants from New York, and expensive establishments are not truly competitors with respect to this particular user, since they are outside the boundaries of his personal requirements and thus never had a chance to be chosen.*

In this example, the user is interested in the features {*price range, location, food type*}. The respective values that encode the user's requirements are {*Cheap, Boston, Italian*}.

Clearly, any other assignment of values could be specified for the same query (e.g. {*Cheap, Chicago, Chinese*}). In fact, each possible value-assignment represents the preferences of a different user. Formally, given a subset of features $\mathcal{F}'$, let $\mathcal{V}_{\mathcal{F}'}$ be the complete space of all possible value assignments over the features in $\mathcal{F}'$. We observe that every item covers a portion of the entire space $\mathcal{V}_{\mathcal{F}'}$, and, hence, covers the corresponding population of users. For example, a cheap restaurant in Boston that serves both Italian and American food *covers* a user who is interesting in cheap Italian food in Boston, as well as a user who is interested in cheap American food in the same city.

In order to evaluate the competitiveness of two given items I_i, I_j in the context of a subset of features $\mathcal{F}'$, we need to compute the number of possible value assignments over $\mathcal{F}'$ that are satisfied by *both* items. Formally, we define pairwise coverage as follows:

DEFINITION 1. **[Pairwise Coverage]** *Given the complete set of features $\mathcal{F}$ in a given domain of interest, let $\mathcal{V}_{\mathcal{F}'}$ be the complete space of all possible value-assignments over the features in a subset $\mathcal{F}' \subseteq \mathcal{F}$. Then, the* coverage *$cov(\mathcal{V}_{\mathcal{F}'}, I_i, I_k)$ of a pair of items I_i and I_j with respect to $\mathcal{V}_{\mathcal{F}'}$ is defined as the portion of $\mathcal{V}_{\mathcal{F}'}$ that is covered by both items.*

Considering the above definition, we observe that the coverage of each dimension (i.e. each feature $F \in \mathcal{F}'$) is independent of the others. Therefore, we first compute the percentage of each dimension that is covered by the pair. We can then optimally compute the coverage of the entire space $\mathcal{V}_{\mathcal{F}'}$ as the product of the respective coverage values $\mathcal{V}_{\{F\}}$ for every $F \in \mathcal{F}'$. Formally:

$$cov(\mathcal{V}_{\mathcal{F}'}, I_i, I_j) = \prod_{F \in \mathcal{F}'} cov(\mathcal{V}_{\{F\}}, I_i, I_j) \quad (1)$$

This computation has a clear geometric interpretation: The portion of the space $\mathcal{V}_{\mathcal{F}'}$ that is covered by a pair of items can be represented as a hyper-rectangle in $|\mathcal{F}'|$-dimensional space. For each dimension F, $cov(\mathcal{V}_{\{F\}}, I_i, I_j)$ gives us the portion of the dimension that is covered by the two items. Finally, by multiplying the individual coverage values, we are essentially computing the volume of the hyper-rectangle that represents the entire space $\mathcal{V}_{\mathcal{F}'}$.

Definition 1 allows us to evaluate the coverage provided by a pair of items to (the value space of) any subset of features $\mathcal{F}'$. Conceptually, $\mathcal{F}'$ captures the fraction of the population that is interested in the features included in $\mathcal{F}'$. In practice, the size of the corresponding population varies across subsets. For example, in the domain of restaurants, the subset {*food quality, price range*} is arguably of interest to more users than the subset {*Wi-Fi availability, delivery options*}. To account for this in our definition of competitiveness, we attach a popularity weight $w(\mathcal{F}')$ to each feature subset. We revisit the computation of these weights in Section 4, where we discuss practical methods for learning the weights from sources such as *query logs* and *customer reviews*. For the remaining of our analysis, we assume that the weights are provided as part of the input. Further, we define $\mathcal{Q}$ to be the collection of subsets with a non-zero weight. Formally: $\mathcal{Q} = \{\mathcal{F}' \in 2^{\mathcal{F}} : w(\mathcal{F}') > 0\}$. Taking the above into consideration, we formally define the competitiveness of two items I_i, I_i as follows:

DEFINITION 2. **[Competitiveness]** *Given the complete set of features $\mathcal{F}$ of a domain of interest, let $\mathcal{Q}$ be the set of all subsets of $\mathcal{F}$ that have a non-zero popularity weight. Then, the competitiveness of two given items I_i and I_i is defined as:*

$$C_{\mathcal{F}}(I_i, I_j) = \sum_{\mathcal{F}' \in \mathcal{Q}} w(\mathcal{F}') \times cov(\mathcal{V}_{\mathcal{F}'}, I_i, I_j) \quad (2)$$

where $cov(\mathcal{V}_{\mathcal{F}'}, I_i, I_j)$ is the portion of $\mathcal{V}_{\mathcal{F}'}$ that is covered by both I_i and I_j.

2.2 Computing Coverage

Our definition of competitiveness between two given items is based on the pairwise coverage that they provide to the value space of the different subsets of features. We observe that the value space is complex, since it can contain different types of features. By supporting virtually every reasonable feature-type (numeric, ordinal, boolean, categorical), our framework guarantees the flexibility required to encode the requirements of virtually *any* potential customer. Next, we discuss the different types of features that we consider in our work, and show how coverage is defined for each of them.

Categorical Features: In our work, we identify two subtypes of categorical features: single-value and multi-value. For a single-value feature F, each item assumes exactly one value from the respective value-space $\mathcal{V}_{\{F\}}$, e.g. the brand of a digital camera. Clearly, boolean features are simply a special case of this group, assuming values from {*YES, NO*}. The pairwise coverage of two items I_i, I_j, given a single-value feature F, is defined as follows:

$$cov(\mathcal{V}_{\{F\}}, I_i, I_j) = \begin{cases} 1 & \text{if } I_i[F] = I_j[F] \\ 0 & \text{otherwise} \end{cases} \quad (3)$$

For a multi-value feature F, each item can be mapped to any *subset* of values from the respective value-space $\mathcal{V}_{\{F\}}$. Assume, for example, the feature *parking* from Table 1, referring to the parking facilities of a restaurant. Since a restaurant can in fact provide any number of these options (even all of them), *parking* is a multi-value categorical feature. We define the pairwise coverage of two items I_i, I_j for a multi-value feature F, as follows:

$$cov(\mathcal{V}_{\{F\}}, I_i, I_j) = \frac{|I_i[F] \cap I_j[F]|}{|\mathcal{V}_{\{F\}}|} \quad (4)$$

Conceptually, the covered portion is defined as the overlap between the sets of values that are mapped to each item, divided by the total number of possible values for F. Clearly, the dividend is always a value in $[0, 1]$.

[Ordinal Features]: The value space $\mathcal{V}_{\{F\}}$ of an ordinal feature F assumes values from a finite *ordered* list: $\mathcal{V}_{\{F\}} = \{v_1, v_2, v_3, ...\}$. Depending on the nature of the feature, higher or lower states may be preferable. For example, for the feature *price range*, lower values are preferable. On the other hand, for the feature *stars rating*, higher values are better.

First, let us introduce two functions that will aid us in our definition of coverage in the context of ordinal features. Given an ordinal feature F and two values $v_1, v_2 \in \mathcal{V}_{\{F\}}$, let $loser(F, v_1, v_2)$ return the least preferable between the two values. In addition, let $weq(F, v_1)$ return the set of values that are worse or equal to v_1. For example, for the *price range* feature discussed above, $weq(F, \$\$\$) = \{\$\$\$, \$\$\$\$\}$. Then, the pairwise coverage of two given items to the value space is defined as follows:

$$cov(\mathcal{V}_{\{F\}}, I_i, I_j) = \frac{|weq(loser(F, I_i[F], I_j[F]))|}{|\mathcal{V}_{\{F\}}|} \quad (5)$$

As in the case of categorical features, $cov(\mathcal{V}_{\{F\}}, I_i, I_j)$ takes values in $[0, 1]$.

[Numeric Features]: A numeric feature F takes values from a continuous pre-defined range. Without loss of generality, we assume that all numeric features are normalized to take values in $[0, 1]$. Higher or lower values may be preferable, depending on the nature of the feature. As in the case of ordinal features, we define $loser(F, v_1, v_2)$ to return the least preferable of two given values for a feature F. Then, given two items I_i, I_j, the pairwise coverage of the value space $\mathcal{V}_{\{F\}}$ is defined as:

$$cov(\mathcal{V}_{\{F\}}, I_i, I_j) = loser(F, I_i, I_j) \quad (6)$$

Conceptually, the value space that is commonly covered by the two items is bounded by the one with the least preferable value. Consider the following example.

Example: Consider the subset of features $\mathcal{F}'$ shown in Table 1. The respective representations for two items I_i, I_j are {\$\$\$, *Boston*, {*Street, Valet*}, 0.8} and {\$\$, *Boston*, {*Street, Priv. Lot*}, 0.6}. Then, following Eq. 1, the pairwise coverage of the two items of is computed as follows:

$$cov(\mathcal{V}_{\mathcal{F}'}, I_i, I_j) = \frac{2}{4} \times 1 \times \frac{1}{3} \times 0.6 = 0.1$$

Table 1: Feature-subsets and their respective value-spaces.

Feature	Type	Value-Set $\mathcal{V}_{\{\mathcal{F}\}}$
price range	ordinal	{\$, \$\$, \$\$\$, \$\$\$\$}
location	categorical (single)	{*Boston, New York*}
parking	categorical (multi)	{*Street, Priv. Lot, Valet*}
food quality	numeric	[0, 1]

3. FINDING THE TOP-K COMPETITORS

In the previous section we presented a formal definition of the competitiveness between any two items. Given this definition, we study the natural problem of finding the top-k competitors of a given item. Formally, the problem is defined as follows:

PROBLEM 2. *We are given a set of items $\mathcal{I}$, defined within the feature space $\mathcal{F}$ of a domain. Then, given a single item $I \in \mathcal{I}$, we want to identify the k items from $\mathcal{I} \setminus \{I\}$, that maximize the pairwise competitiveness with I:*

$$I^* = \underset{I' \in \mathcal{I} \setminus \{I\}}{\text{argmax}}\, C_{\mathcal{F}}(I, I') \quad (7)$$

A naive algorithm for this problem would iterate over all items in $I' \in \mathcal{I} \setminus \{I\}$. For each such item I', it would compute $w(\mathcal{F}') \times cov(\mathcal{V}_{\mathcal{F}'}, I, I')$ for every subset $\mathcal{F}' \in \mathcal{Q}$, where $\mathcal{Q}$ is the collection subsets with a non-zero weight. It would then be trivial to obtain the top-k competitors for the given item. However, considering that $\mathcal{I}$ can contain thousands of items, the computational cost can be overwhelming. We demonstrate this in our experiments, where we compare our own CMiner technique with the naive approach.

3.1 The CMiner Algorithm

Motivated by the inefficiency of the naive approach, we present CMiner, a new algorithm for Problem 2. Our approach combines scalability with the ability to handle the online arrival of new items. The latter is crucial in many mainstream domains. As an example, consider the case when items are vacation packages. In such a domain, an arbitrary number of new packages can be introduced at any point in time. Hence, we would like to preprocess the data in a way that allows us to compute the competitors of a new package without having to repeat the entire computation effort.

First, we define the concept of *item dominance*, which will aid us in our further analysis:

DEFINITION 3. **[Item Dominance]:** *Given two items I_i, I_j from a set $\mathcal{I}$ defined within a feature-space $\mathcal{F}$, we say that an item I_i dominates an item I_j if both of the following conditions are true:*

1. *$I_j[F] \subseteq I_i[F]$, for every multi-value categorical feature $F \in \mathcal{F}$*
2. *$I_i[F] \geq I_j[F]$, for every ordinal, numerical, or single-categorical feature $F \in \mathcal{F}$.*

Conceptually, an item dominates another if it has better values for all features of the considered space $\mathcal{F}$. Clearly, if I_i dominates I_j, then it is also more competitive with respect to any other item from $\mathcal{I}$ (since it covers at least as much coverage to any possible sub-space as I_j). This observation motivates us to utilize the *skyline* of the entire set of items $\mathcal{I}$. The skyline is a well-studied concept that represents the subset of points in a set that are not dominated by any other point in the set [4]. We refer to the skyline of a set of items $\mathcal{I}$ as $Sky(\mathcal{I})$. The concept of the skyline leads to the following lemma:

LEMMA 1. *Given the skyline $Sky(\mathcal{I})$ of a set of items $\mathcal{I}$ and an item $I_i \in \mathcal{I}$, let $\mathcal{Y}$ contain the k items with the highest $C_{\mathcal{F}}(\cdot, I_i)$ values from $Sky(\mathcal{I})$. Then, an item $I_j \in \mathcal{I}$ can only be in the top-k competitors of I_i, if $I_j \in \mathcal{Y}$ or I_j is dominated by one of the items in $\mathcal{Y}$.*

The proof is by contradiction, given the definition of item dominance and the skyline concept. We omit it for lack of space.

By applying Lemma 1, we do not need to consider the entire set of items in order to find the top-k competitors of a given item I^*. Instead, it is sufficient to recursively check for the items that are dominated by the current top-k items from the upper levels. In order to fully utilize this observation, we construct a structure that greatly reduces the number of items that need to be considered for the computation of the top-k competitors set. We refer to this structure as the *skyline pyramid*. This structure is similar to the *dominant graph*, presented by Zou and Chen [29], except that it does not allow multiple parents for each item. The pyramid can be constructed by recursively computing the skyline and removing the skyline points from the current set, until the entire collection of items has been exhausted. Standard techniques can be used for computing the skyline on each iteration [17], as well as for updating the pyramid in case new items are introduced [12]. Each item from the i_{th} layer of the skyline is assigned an inlink from the item from i_{th} level that dominates it. If multiple such dominators exist, we simply choose one randomly. This is simply done to avoid re-checking the dominated item during the competitor-finding process, and does not affect the optimality of the result. A formal proof is trivial and omitted for lack of space.An example of the skyline pyramid is shown in Figure 2.

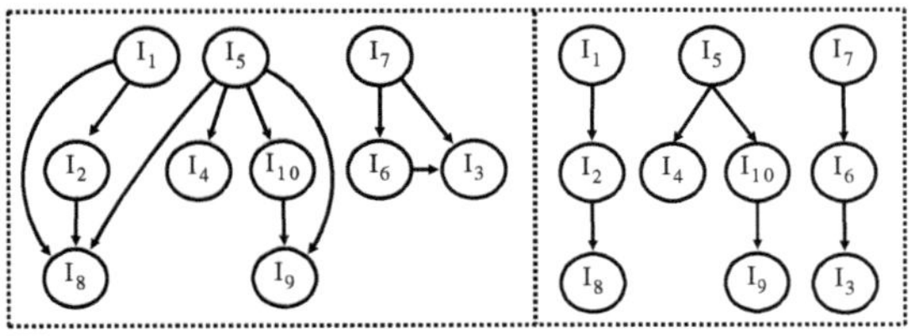

Figure 2: The left side of the figure shows the complete dominance graph for a given set of items. An edge $I_i \rightarrow I_j$ means that I_i dominates I_j. The right side of the figure shows the skyline domination pyramid.

The CMiner Algorithm: Next, we present CMiner, an optimal algorithm for finding the top-k competitors of any given item. Our algorithm makes use of the skyline pyramid described earlier in this section, in order to reduce the number of items that need to be considered and minimize the number of required coverage computation. The intuition is that, since we only care about the top-k competitors, we can incrementally compute the score of each candidate and stop when it is guaranteed that the top-k have emerged. The pseudocode is given in Algorithm 1.

Algorithm 1 CMiner

Input: Set of items $\mathcal{I}$, Item of interest $I^* \in \mathcal{I}$, feature space $\mathcal{F}$, Collection $\mathcal{Q}$ of feature-subsets with non-zero weights, skyline pyramid $\mathcal{D}_\mathcal{I}$, *int k*
Output: Set of top-k competitors for I^* from $\mathcal{I} \setminus \{I^*\}$

1: $TopK \leftarrow masters(I^*)$
2: **if** ($k \leq |TopK|$) **then**
3:     **return** $TopK$
4: $k \leftarrow k - |TopK|$
5: $LB \leftarrow -1$
6: $low(I) \leftarrow 0, \forall I \in \mathcal{X}$.
7: $up(I) \leftarrow \sum_{\mathcal{F}' \in \mathcal{Q}} w(\mathcal{F}') \times (cov(\mathcal{V}'_{\mathcal{F}'}, I^*, I^*)), \forall I \in \mathcal{X}$.
8: $\mathcal{X} \leftarrow$ `getSlaves`$(TopK, \mathcal{D}_\mathcal{I}) \cup \mathcal{D}_\mathcal{I}[0]$
9: **while** ($|\mathcal{X}|$!= 0) **do**
10:     $\mathcal{X} \leftarrow$ `updateTopK`$(k, LB, \mathcal{X})$
11:     **if** ($|\mathcal{X}|$!= 0) **then**
12:         $TopK \leftarrow merge(TopK, \mathcal{X})$
13:         **if** ($|TopK| = k$) **then**
14:             $LB \leftarrow TopK[k]$
15:         $\mathcal{X} \leftarrow$ `getSlaves`$(\mathcal{X}, \mathcal{D}_\mathcal{I})$
16: **return** $TopK$

17: **Procedure** `updateTopK`*(k, LB, $\mathcal{X}$)*
18: $localTopK \leftarrow \emptyset$
19: **for** every $\mathcal{F}' \in \mathcal{Q}$, in sorted order **do**
20:     $sc \leftarrow w(\mathcal{F}') \times cov(\mathcal{V}'_{\mathcal{F}'}, I^*, I^*)$
21:     $localTopK \leftarrow \emptyset$
22:     **for** every item $I \in \mathcal{X}$ **do**
23:         $up(I) \leftarrow up(I) - sc + w(\mathcal{F}') \times cov(\mathcal{V}'_{\mathcal{F}'}, I^*, I)$
24:         **if** ($up(I) < LB$) **then**
25:             $\mathcal{X} \leftarrow \mathcal{X} \setminus \{I\}$
26:         **else**
27:             $low(I) \leftarrow low(I) + w(\mathcal{F}') \times (cov(\mathcal{V}'_{\mathcal{F}'}, I^*, I))$
28:             $localTopK.add(I, low(I))$
29:             **if** ($|localTopK| = k$) **then**
30:                 $LB \leftarrow localTopK[k]$
31:     **if** ($|\mathcal{X}| \leq k$) **then**
32:         **break**
33: **for** every item $I \in \mathcal{X}$ **do**
34:     **for** every remaining $\mathcal{F}' \in \mathcal{Q}$ **do**
35:         $low(I) \leftarrow low(I) + w(\mathcal{F}') \times cov(\mathcal{V}'_{\mathcal{F}'}, I^*, I)$
36:     $localTopK.add(I, low(I))$
37: **return** $localTopK$

Discussion of CMiner: The input to the algorithm includes the set of items $\mathcal{I}$, the set of features $\mathcal{F}$, the item of interest I^*, the number k of top competitors to retrieve, the collection $\mathcal{Q}$ of feature-subsets with non-zero weights, and the skyline pyramid $\mathcal{D}_\mathcal{I}$.

In lines 1-4, the algorithm uses *masters*(I^*) to retrieve the set of items that *dominate* I^*. Note that this set can be easily pre-computed for all the items during the pyramid-construction phase. These items are guaranteed to have the maximum possible competitiveness with I^*. If at least k such items exist, we can just report them and conclude. Otherwise, we append them to the final result and decrement our budget of k accordingly. The LB variable maintains the lowest lower bound from the current top-k set. This is used as pruning threshold for the candidates. In lines 6-7 we initialize the upper and lower bounds for each candidate. In line 8 we initialize the set of candidates $\mathcal{X}$ as the union of the items in the first layer of the pyramid and the items dominated by those in the $TopK$. The latter is returned via calling `getSlaves`$(TopK, \mathcal{D}_\mathcal{I})$.

In every iteration of lines 9-15, the algorithm does the following: (i) it feeds the set of candidates $\mathcal{X}$ routine, which prunes items based on the LB threshold, (ii) updates the $TopK$ set via the *merge*($\cdot$) function, (iii) updates the pruning threshold LB, (iv) expands the set of items by including the items that they dominate.

Discussion of `UpdateTopK()`: This routine processes the items in $\mathcal{X}$ and finds at most k with the highest competitiveness scores among $\mathcal{X}$, subject to the condition that this score is higher than the global pruning threshold LB. The approach uses two bounds *low* and *up*, for every $I \in \mathcal{X}$. $low(I)$ maintains the competitiveness score of item I, as new feature subsets are considered. $up(I)$ is an optimistic upper bound on I's competitiveness score. Therefore, *up* begins with the maximum possible competitiveness score, $\mathcal{C}_\mathcal{F}(I^*, I^*)$.

For every feature subset, we examine all items in $\mathcal{X}$ and update their *up* value. If at any point $up(I) < LB$ (line 24), item I can be safely removed from the $\mathcal{X}$. If, at any point, $|\mathcal{X}|$ becomes less or equal to k, the loop over the subsets comes to a halt. In lines 33-36 we update the lower bounds of the remaining items in $\mathcal{X}$. We do this outside the loop, in order to avoid unnecessary bound checking and improve performance. Observe that the routine processes subsets in *sorted order*. In Section 4, we elaborate on the impact of the ordering on the performance of CMiner.

Complexity: The complexity of CMiner depends on the number of points in each layer of $\mathcal{D}_\mathcal{I}$. According to Bentley et al. [2], for n uniformly-distributed d-dimensional data points (items), the expected size of the skyline is $\Theta(\frac{ln^{d-1}n}{(d-1)!})$. Since we need to examine at most k skyline layers to find the top-k result, this value is upper-bounded by $\Theta(k * \frac{ln^{d-1}n}{(d-1)!})$. This bound naively assumes that each layer should be considered entirely. In practice, however, we only need to check a small fraction of items that are dominated by the items considered in the previous layer. For instance, for a uniform distribution with consecutive skyline layers of similar sizes, the number of points to be considered will be in the order of k, since links will be evenly distributed among the skyline points. As we only expand the top-k items in each step, at most k new items will be introduced. Therefore, for small values of k, the complexity of CMiner is O ($|\mathcal{I}| * |\mathcal{Q}| * k^2$), where $\mathcal{Q}$ is the set of feature subsets with non-zero weights.

4. WEIGHT ESTIMATION

Our analysis has assumed that the weight $w(\mathcal{F}')$ of each subset of features $\mathcal{F}'$ is provided as input. In this section, we discuss methods for computing these weights.

The motivation of assigning a different weight to each subset stems from the observation that not all features are equally important to users. Based on this, a straightforward approach is to consider the weight of each individual feature separately, and then aggregate to the subset level. This aggregation could be achieved by selecting the sum, average, median, maximum or minimum over all the individual features in a set. This approach assumes independence among the features of an item. This assumption, however, is not always valid. For example, it may be the case that people who are interested in the screen resolution of a laptop computer are also more likely to be interested in the included graphics card. This motivates an approach that considers the popularity of *feature-subsets* instead of individual features. We identify two sources from which we can learn the popularity of a subset: *query logs* and *customer reviews.*

Query logs: The first source is the query logs of the search engine on the website where the items are hosted. Regardless of the interface through which the user encodes his preferences in a query, the set of selected feature is always recorded in a dedicated log. Assuming the existence of a large enough user-base, we can simply estimate the popularity of a feature-subset based on the number of times that it was queried upon by the users.

Customer reviews: In cases when query logs are unavailable or inadequate, the weights of the subsets can be estimated by considering the *reviews* that are available for the items in the domain. As an example of such a dataset, consider the union of the review sets that are available for all the digital cameras offered on amazon.com. Each of these reviews comments on a particular subset of attributes from the digital-camera domain. Hence, the review corpus serves as an intuitive way to access user preferences. For example, a user who is greatly interested in the wheelchair-accessibility of a restaurant is more likely to discuss this feature in his review. We implement and employ review mining as a means for estimating the weights of feature-subsets in our experiments. In practice, one can choose to ignore subsets that appear less frequently than a set threshold. In our own experiments, we consider all subsets that appear at least once.

4.1 Subset Ordering

Given an item of interest I^*, CMiner iterates over the given set of subsets and computes the coverage provided by I^* and each candidate item to the value-space that corresponds to each subset. Given our definition of competitiveness, we next consider **IC**, an ordering scheme that processes subsets in descending order by $w(\mathcal{F}') \times cov(\mathcal{V}'_{\mathcal{F}'}, I^*, I^*)$, where I^* is the item of interest. As stated in the following lemma, **IC** achieves the optimal *convergence rate* (i.e. there exists no ordering that leads to a faster convergence).

LEMMA 2. [IC Convergence Rate]: Given two items I_i, I_j, the ordering imposed by the **IC** scheme results in the fastest possible convergence to the target-value $C_{\mathcal{F}}(I_i, I_j)$ (i.e. the true competitiveness between the two items)

PROOF. Assume that we want to compute the competitiveness between the target item I^* and a candidate I'. Let l_i and u_i be the lower and upper competitiveness bounds, after checking $\mathcal{F}'_i$, the i-th feature subset imposed by the **IC** scheme. For ease of notation, we use $C_{\mathcal{F}'_i}(I_1, I_2) = w(\mathcal{F}'_i) \times cov(\mathcal{V}_{\mathcal{F}'_i}, I_1, I_2)$, for any two items. Every time a new subset is considered, l_i and u_i are updated, until finally all the subsets have been evaluated and both variables converge to the actual competitiveness score $C_{\mathcal{F}}(I^*, I')$. We now define $T_i = u_i - l_i$. Since both l_i and u_i ultimately converge to $C_{\mathcal{F}}(I^*, I')$, T_i converges to 0. Also, $T_i \geq 0, \forall i$. The convergence rate of T_i is:

$$\frac{T_i}{T_{i-1}} = 1 - \frac{C_{\mathcal{F}'_i}(I^*, I^*)}{u_{i-1} - l_{i-1}} \tag{8}$$

Also, we know that: $u_i = C_{\mathcal{F}}(I^*, I^*) - \sum_{j=1}^{i} C_{\mathcal{F}'_j}(I^*, I^*) + \sum_{j=1}^{i} C_{\mathcal{F}'_j}(I^*, I^*)$ and $l_i = \sum_{j=1}^{i} C_{\mathcal{F}'_j}(I^*, I')$

By immediate replacement in Eq. 8, the convergence rate becomes:

$$\frac{T_i}{T_{i-1}} = 1 - \frac{C_{\mathcal{F}'_i}(I^*, I^*)}{C_{\mathcal{F}}(I^*, I^*) - \sum_{j=1}^{i-1} C_{\mathcal{F}'_j}(I^*, I^*)} \tag{9}$$

As it can be seen by Eq. 9, the convergence rate depends only on the score of the target item I^*. The **IC** ordering scheme processes subsets in decreasing order of $C_{\mathcal{F}'_j}(I^*, I^*)$, which is the maximum possible coverage that any item can jointly achieve with I^*. Thus, the numerator is equal to the i_{th} maximum possible value among all feature-subsets. Similarly, the difference in the denominator is minimized, since the subtracted sum maintains the highest possible value (and $C_{\mathcal{F}}(I^*, I^*)$ is constant). □

5. EXPERIMENTAL EVALUATION

For our evaluation, we compiled the following datasets:

`Digital Cameras` from `Amazon.com`: The features of this domain include the objective attributes of each camera (e.g. *price, number of megapixels*), as well as numeric attributes representing the opinions of the users on the item's different characteristics (e.g. *photo quality, video quality*). These were extracted via the method by Ding et al. [9], which assigns a numeric opinion-value to each feature of an item, given the corpus of reviews. All scores were normalized to be in $[0, 1]$, with higher scores being preferable. The same method was also used for the datasets from `Booking.com` and `TripAdvisor.com`.

`Hotels` from `Booking.com`: The feature-set for this domain consists of objective features (e.g. *price, location*) and the opinion values extracted from the relevant reviews on different attributes (e.g. *cleanliness, service quality*).

`Restaurants` in New York from `TripAdvisor.com`: The

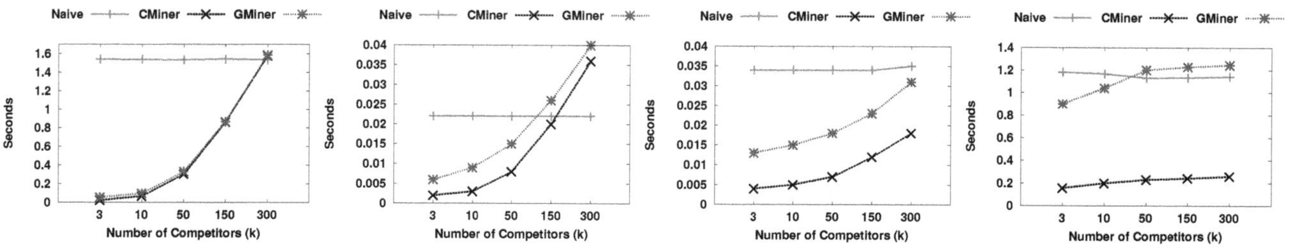

(a) Cameras (b) Hotels (c) Restaurants (d) Recipes

Figure 3: Average time (per item) to compute top-k competitors for the various datasets

feature-set for this domain consists of objective features (e.g. *type of food served*) and the opinion values extracted from the relevant reviews on different attributes (e.g. *food quality,service quality*).

Recipes from Sparkrecipes.com: The feature-set for each recipe consists of the different nutritional values (e.g. *grams of protein and carbohydrates*), as listed on the website.

The datasets were selected from different domains to portray the cross-domain applicability of our approach. Table 5 summarizes some basic statistics for each dataset.

Table 2: Dataset Statistics

Dataset	#Items	#Feats.	#Subsets	Skyline Layers
Cameras	579	21	14779	5
Hotels	1283	8	127	5
Restaurants	4622	8	64	12
Recipes	100000	22	133	22

The second, third, fourth and fifth columns include the number of items, the number of features, the number of distinct feature-subsets, and the number of layers in the respective (complete) skyline pyramid, respectively. The feature subsets were extracted from the set of reviews that is available for each dataset; the frequency of each subset of features is equal to the number of times they were included together in a review. For all four datasets, nearly 99% of the items can be found within the first 4 layers of the pyramid, with the majority of those falling within the first 2 layers. This is due to the large dimensionality of the datasets, which makes domination unlikely. As we show in our evaluation, the skyline pyramid helps CMiner clearly outperform the baselines with respect to the computational cost. This is despite the high concentration of items within the first layers, since CMiner can effectively traverse the pyramid and consider only a small fraction of the included items.

Baselines: We compare our CMiner algorithm with two baselines. The first is the Naive approach described in Section 3. The second is a clustering-based approach that works as follows. First, it iterates over the considered feature-subsets. For each subset $\mathcal{F}'$, it identifies the set of items that have the same value assignment for the features in $\mathcal{F}'$, and places them in the same group. Thus, $\mathcal{F}'$ is mapped to different groups of items with the save value-assignments over its features. The algorithm then iterates over the reported groups. For each group, it updates the pairwise coverage provided to $\mathcal{V}'_{\mathcal{F}}$ by the target item I^* and an arbitrary item from the group (it can be any item, since they all have the same values with respect to $\mathcal{F}'$). The computed coverage is then used to update the competitiveness of all the items in the group. The process continues until the optimal competitiveness scores for all items have been computed. Assuming there are at most M groups per feature-subset, the algorithm's complexity is O($|\mathcal{I}|$ * M * $|\mathcal{Q}|$). Obviously, when each group is a singleton, the algorithm degrades to the Naive case. We refer to this technique as *GMiner*.

Unless otherwise stated, we use the **IC** ordering scheme in our experiments, as described in Section 4.1. All experiments were run on a desktop with a Quad-Core 3.5GHz Processor and 2GB RAM.

5.1 Computational Time

In this experiment we compare CMiner with the two baselines (Naive and GMiner), in terms of computational time. First, we use each of the three algorithms to compute the set of top-k competitors for each item in the four datasets. The process is repeated for $k \in \{3, 10, 50, 150, 300\}$. The results for the four datasets are shown in Figures. 3(a-d). The x-axis holds the different values of k. The y-axis holds the respective computational times (in seconds). We report the average time for each item.

The figures motivate some interesting observations. First, the Naive algorithm consistently reports the same computational time regardless of k, since it naively computes the competitiveness of every single item in the corpus with respect to the target item. Thus, any trivial variations in the required time are due to the process of maintaining the top-k set. In general, Naive is outperformed by the two other algorithms, and is only competitive for very large values of k for the **Hotels Dataset**.

For the **Cameras** dataset, CMiner and GMiner exhibit almost identical running times. This is due to the very large number of distinct feature-subsets for this dataset, which favors GMiner. In particular, this dataset has 14779 different subsets and GMiner identifies, on average, 443.63 groups per subset. This means that the algorithm saves roughly a total of $(579 - 443) \times 14779 = 2009944$ coverage computations per item, allowing it to be competitive to the otherwise superior CMiner. In fact, for the other datasets, CMiner displays a clear advantage. This advantage is maximized for the **Recipes** dataset, which is the most populous of the four, in terms of included items. The experiment on this dataset also illustrates the scalability of the approach with respect to k. For the **Hotels** and **Restaurants** datasets, even though the computational time of CMiner appears to rise as k increases for the other three datasets, it never goes above 0.035 seconds.

5.2 Feature Subsets

In Section 4.1, we described the **IC** ordering scheme, which determines the order in which subsets are processed by CMiner. Two alternatives to this scheme are processing the subsets in descending (**W-DSC**) and ascending (**W-ASC**) order by weight. Next, we evaluate the impact of the three schemes on the efficiency of CMiner. We only show the results for the `Recipes` dataset, which was by far the largest in terms of both size and dimensionality. The findings for the other corpora were identical and are omitted for lack of space. Figure 4 shows the total number of subset-processings

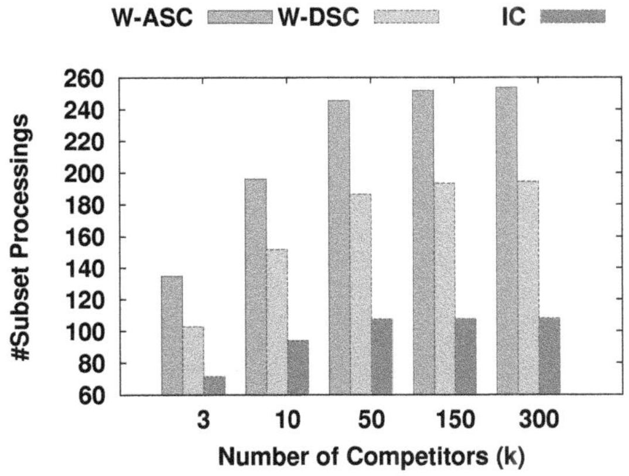

Figure 4: Number of subset processings that required under different ordering schemes.

(i.e. the total number of times the for-loop in line 19 of Algorithm 1 is executed) required by each ordering scheme until CMiner converges to the top-k competitors, for different values of k. We report the average over all items in the corpus. The results demonstrate that **IC** clearly outperforms the two baselines, consistently requiring far less subsets for all values of k. We also obeserve that no more than 110 subsets had to be processed, for all considered values of k. This allows CMiner to quickly converge to the optimal top-k set.

5.3 A User Study

In order to validate our competitiveness paradigm, we conduct a user study as follows. First, we select 10 random items from the `Cameras` corpus. We refer to these 10 items as the *seed.* For each item I^* in the seed, we compute its competitiveness with every other item in the corpus, according to our definition. In addition to our own CMiner approach, we also rank all the items in the corpus based on their distance to I^* in the feature-space. The L_1 distance was used for numeric and ordinal features, and the Jaccard distance was used for categorical attributes. We refer to this as the `NN` approach (i.e. Nearest Neighbor). We then chose the two items with the highest score, the two items with the lowest score, and two items from the middle of the ranked list. This was repeated for both approaches, for a total of 12 candidates per item in the seed (6 per approach). We then created a user study on the online survey-site `kwiksurveys.com`. The survey was taken by 20 different human annotators. Each of the 10 seed-items was paired with each of its 12 corresponding candidates, for a total of 120 different pairs. The pairs were shown in a randomized order to the annotators, who were also given access to a table including the values

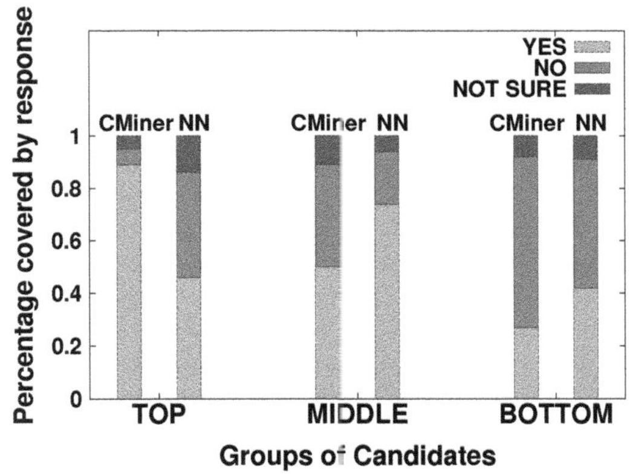

Figure 5: Results of the user study comparing our competitiveness paradigm with the Nearest-Neighbor approach.

of each item for every feature. For each pair, the annotator was asked whether he would consider buying the candidate instead of the seed item. The possible answers were "YES", "NO" and "NOT SURE". The results are shown in Figure 5.

The y-axis holds the percentage covered by each approach. The figure shows 3 pairs of bars. The left bar of each pair corresponds to our CMiner approach, while the right bar to the `NN` approach. The first two bars from the left represent the responses of the users to the top-ranked candidates for each approach. The two bars in the middle represent the responses to the candidates ranked in the middle, and, finally, the two bars on the right represent the responses to the bottom-ranked candidates. Each bar captures the fraction of each of the three possible responses. The lower, middle, and upper part of the bar represent the "YES", "NO" and "NOT SURE" responses, respectively. For example, the first bar on the left, reveals that about 90% of the annotators would consider our top-ranked candidates as a replacement for the seed item. The remaining 10% was evenly divided between the "NO" and "NOT SURE" responses.

The figure motivates some interesting observations. First, we observe that the vast majority of the top-ranked items by our method were identified by the annotators as possible replacements for the seed item. These are thus verified as strong competitors that could deprive the seed item from potential customers. On the other hand, the top-ranked candidates of the NN approach were often rejected by the users, who did not consider these items to be competitive.

The middle-ranked candidates of our approach attracted mixed responses from the annotators, indicating that it was not straightforward to determine whether the item is indeed competitive or not. An interesting observation is that the middle-ranked candidates of the NN approach were more popular than its top-ranked ones. The interpretation is that this approach fails to emulate the way the users perceive the competitiveness between two items.

Finally, the bottom-ranked candidates of our approach were consistently rejected by the annotators, verifying their lack of competitiveness. The bottom-ranked items by the `NN` approach were also frequently rejected, indicating that it is easier to identify items that are *not* competitive to the target. In conclusion, the survey demonstrated the ability of our paradigm to capture the competitiveness between two items. Further, our approach consistently outperformed an intuitive baseline, indicating that the task is non-trivial.

6. RELATED WORK

While our work is the first to consider domain-invariant competitor mining, it has ties to existing relevant literature.

Competitor Mining: Previous work [14, 13, 1, 26] focuses on mining competitors based on comparative expressions found in web results and other textual corpora. The intuition is that the occurrence of expressions like "Item A is better than Item B" "or item A Vs. Item B" is indicative of the competitiveness relationship between the two items. However, as we have already discussed in the introduction, such comparative evidence are typically scarce, or even non-existent in many mainstream domains. As a result, the applicability of such approaches is greatly limited.

Finding Competitive Products: Recent work [22, 23, 28] explored competitiveness in the context of *product design*. The first step in these approaches is the definition of a dominance function that represents the value of a product. This can measure domination of other items or potential customers. The goal is then to use this function to create non-dominated items, or items with the maximum possible dominance value. A similar line of work [25, 24] represents items as points in a multidimensional space and looks for subspaces where the appeal of the item is maximized. While relevant, the above projects have a completely different focus from our own, and hence the proposed approaches are not applicable in our setting (and vice versa).

Skyline computation: Our work leverages concepts and techniques from the extensive literature on skyline computation [4, 12, 17]. These include the dominance concept among items, as well as the construction of the skyline pyramid used by our CMiner algorithm. Our work also has ties to the recent publications in *reverse skyline* queries [20, 21]. Even though the focus of our work is different, we intend to study the advances in this field and evaluate their potential to improve the efficiency of our framework in future work.

7. CONCLUSION

In this work, we presented a formal definition of the competitiveness between two items. Our formalization is applicable across domains, overcoming the shortcomings of previous approaches. We consider a number of factors that have been overlooked by previous approaches, such as the position of the items in the multi-dimensional feature space, and the preferences and opinions of the users. A user study was conducted to verify the validity of our notion of competitiveness. Based on our competitiveness paradigm, we addressed the problem of finding the top-k competitors of a given item. Our framework is designed to be efficient and scalable, in order to be applicable to large populations of items. Our methodology was evaluated via an experimental evaluation on real datasets from different domains.

Acknowledgments

This work was supported by the MODAP and DISFER projects.

8. REFERENCES

[1] S. Bao, R. Li, Y. Yu, and Y. Cao. Competitor mining with the web. *IEEE Trans. Knowl. Data Eng.*, 2008.

[2] J. L. Bentley, H. T. Kung, M. Schkolnick, and C. D. Thompson. On the average number of maxima in a set of vectors and applications. *J. ACM*, 1978.

[3] M. Bergen and M. A. Peteraf. Competitor identification and competitor analysis: a broad-based managerial approach. *Managerial and Decision Economics*, 2002.

[4] S. Börzsönyi, D. Kossmann, and K. Stocker. The skyline operator. In *ICDE*, 2001.

[5] M.-J. Chen. Competitor analysis and interfirm rivalry: Toward a theoretical integration. *Academy of Management Review*, 1996.

[6] M.-J. Chen and I. C. MacMillan. Nonresponse and delayed response to competitive moves: The roles of competitor dependence and action irreversibility. 1992.

[7] B. H. Clark and D. B. Montgomery. Managerial Identification of Competitors. *Journal of Marketing*, 1999.

[8] R. Deshpandé and H. Gatingon. Competitive analysis. *Marketing Letters*, 1994.

[9] X. Ding, B. Liu, and P. S. Yu. A holistic lexicon-based approach to opinion mining. WSDM '08.

[10] W. T. Few. Managerial competitor identification: Integrating the categorization, economic and organizational identity perspectives. *Doctoral Dissertaion*, 2007.

[11] H. Gatignon, E. Anderson, and K. Helsen. Competitive reactions to market entry: Explaining interfirm differences. *Journal of Marketing Research*, 1989.

[12] D. Kossmann, F. Ramsak, and S. Rost. Shooting stars in the sky: an online algorithm for skyline queries. VLDB '02, 2002.

[13] R. Li, S. Bao, J. Wang, Y. Liu, and Y. Yu. Web scale competitor discovery using mutual information. In *ADMA*, 2006.

[14] R. Li, S. Bao, J. Wang, Y. Yu, and Y. Cao. Cominer: An effective algorithm for mining competitors from the web. In *ICDM*, 2006.

[15] Z. Ma, G. Pant, and O. R. L. Sheng. Mining competitor relationships from online news: A network-based approach. *Electronic Commerce Research and Applications*, 2011.

[16] G. Pant and O. R. L. Sheng. Avoiding the blind spots: Competitor identification using web text and linkage structure. In *ICIS*, 2009.

[17] D. Papadias, Y. Tao, G. Fu, and B. Seeger. An optimal and progressive algorithm for skyline queries. SIGMOD '03.

[18] J. F. Porac and H. Thomas. Taxonomic mental models in competitor definition. *The Academy of Management Review*, 2008.

[19] M. E. Porter. *Competitive Strategy: Techniques for Analyzing Industries and Competitors.* Free Press, 1980.

[20] A. Vlachou, C. Doulkeridis, Y. Kotidis, and K. Nørvåg. Reverse top-k queries. In *ICDE*, 2010.

[21] A. Vlachou, C. Doulkeridis, K. Nørvåg, and Y. Kotidis. Identifying the most influential data objects with reverse top-k queries. *PVLDB*, 2010.

[22] Q. Wan, R. C.-W. Wong, I. F. Ilyas, M. T. Özsu, and Y. Peng. Creating competitive products.

[23] Q. Wan, R. C.-W. Wong, and Y. Peng. Finding top-k profitable products. In *ICDE*, 2011.

[24] T. Wu, Y. Sun, C. Li, and J. Han. Region-based online promotion analysis. In *EDBT*, 2010.

[25] T. Wu, D. Xin, Q. Mei, and J. Han. Promotion analysis in multi-dimensional space. *PVLDB*, 2009.

[26] K. Xu, S. S. Liao, J. Li, and Y. Song. Mining comparative opinions from customer reviews for competitive intelligence. *Decis. Support Syst.*, 2011.

[27] D. Zelenko and O. Semin. Automatic competitor identification from public information sources. *International Journal of Computational Intelligence and Applications*, 2002.

[28] Z. Zhang, L. V. S. Lakshmanan, and A. K. H. Tung. On domination game analysis for microeconomic data mining. *ACM Trans. Knowl. Discov. Data*, 2009.

[29] L. Zou and L. Chen. Pareto-based dominant graph: An efficient indexing structure to answer top-k queries. *IEEE Trans. Knowl. Data Eng.*, 23(5):727–741, 2011.

Discriminative Clustering for Market Segmentation

Peter Haider*
Dep. of Computer Science
Univ. of Potsdam, Germany
haider@cs.uni-potsdam.de

Luca Chiarandini†
Web Research Group
Universitat Pompeu Fabra
Barcelona, Spain
chiarluc@yahoo-inc.com

Ulf Brefeld
University of Bonn
Bonn, Germany
brefeld@uni-bonn.de

ABSTRACT

We study discriminative clustering for market segmentation tasks. The underlying problem setting resembles discriminative clustering, however, existing approaches focus on the prediction of univariate cluster labels. By contrast, market segments encode complex (future) behavior of the individuals which cannot be represented by a single variable. In this paper, we generalize discriminative clustering to structured and complex output variables that can be represented as graphical models. We devise two novel methods to jointly learn the classifier and the clustering using alternating optimization and collapsed inference, respectively. The two approaches jointly learn a discriminative segmentation of the input space and a generative output prediction model for each segment. We evaluate our methods on segmenting user navigation sequences from Yahoo! News. The proposed collapsed algorithm is observed to outperform baseline approaches such as mixture of experts. We showcase exemplary projections of the resulting segments to display the interpretability of the solutions.

Categories and Subject Descriptors

I.5.3 [**Clustering**]: Algorithms

General Terms

Algorithms, Experimentation

Keywords

Discriminative Clustering, Market Segmentation

1. INTRODUCTION

Market segmentation reveals divisions in a given market, where a market refers to a population of interest such as people, customers, or organizations. A market segment is a subset of a market that is characterized by similar demands and/or needs based on qualities of a given product such as price or function.

Every segment is required to meet the following criteria. (i) It is homogeneous within the segment, so that individuals within the same segment exhibit common needs and can be targeted jointly with the same marketing strategy. (ii) It is easily distinguishable from other segments to guarantee that different segments have different demands and (iii) serves as a blueprint for distinct targeting strategies. The requirements are often summarized as *homogeneity*, *identifiability*, and *interpretability* (19).

Besides frequently deployed self-organizing maps (SOMs) (13; 7), market segmentation matches the problem setting of model-based clustering approaches. Clustering techniques either minimize the within-cluster similarity (1; 14), maximize the between-cluster similarity (7), or optimize a combination of both (18), and thus aim to produce homogeneous and identifiable solutions. Once segments have been computed, new customers need to be assigned to one of the subgroups to advertise the product accordingly.

Unfortunately, mapping new instances to an existing clustering is often difficult in practice. Intuitively, the new customer should be grouped to the closest segment with respect to some similarity measure. Closeness can for instance be computed as the distance in feature space to the median or the nearest member of a segment (11; 4). However, often at the time of classifying a new instance, not all features are known. Even using the similarity measure that is used by the clustering method itself on all features is frequently observed to perform surprisingly inaccurate, see e.g., (20) and Section 4. Other difficulties are for instance distribution-based clusterings, such as Expectation Maximization (6), which assign probabilities for cluster-memberships. By doing so, customers are probabilistically related to *every* segment. Converting this soft assignment into a hard assignment by taking a *maximum a posteriori* or *winner-takes-all* decision is often suboptimal if the memberships deviate from a point distribution, in which case more than one segments are likely candidates (14).

Optimally, the segmentation is therefore learned together with a classifier that discriminatively maps new instances to clusters; a problem setting which is also known as discriminative clustering (5; 20; 24; 8). The idea is to have the clustering provide the labels for the classifier which is trained in a supervised manner. The joint optimization alters the clustering so that the segments can be easily dis-

*This work was performed during an internship at Yahoo! Research, Barcelona, Spain.

†Also Yahoo! Research, Barcelona, Spain.

KDD'12, August 12–16, 2012, Beijing, China.

criminated from each other by the classifier. Combining the two criteria thus guarantees concise clusterings and accurate classifiers. Existing approaches focus on clustering a population and predicting a cluster label for a new instance. By contrast, market segmentation is more complex. In market segmentation tasks, we need to differentiate between the data that characterizes individuals and the data that characterizes their future behavior. The clustering clearly needs to take all available information into account to generate meaningful segments. However, the classifier does not have access to future events and needs to take a decision on the available information such as gender, income, etc. This observation renders existing approaches to discriminative clustering too restrictive for market segmentation tasks.

In this paper we generalize discriminative clustering for market segmentation tasks using the structured prediction framework. We differentiate between *attributes* of a customer and her *interests/behavior*. *Attributes* are *a priori* available features of individuals of the population such as gender or income. Her *behavior* is a collection of interacting variables describing a segment. As segments need to be interpretable, we model the output data as a complex and structured variable which can be represented as a graphical model. The distinction allows for learning a classifier only on the attributes, computing the clustering on both attributes and behavior, and finally summarizing the segments only in terms of the behavior.

We devise two solutions which are based on the regularized empirical risk minimization framework. The first is a straightforward adaptation of mixtures of experts. Classifier and clustering are optimized using an alternating strategy where we fix one component while optimizing the other. The second solution uses approximations and integrates out parameters of the classifier using collapsed inference for efficiency. Both approaches use generative models for the output structure and, in contrast to conventional discriminative clustering approaches, do not involve trade-off parameters for classification accuracy and cluster consistency (class balance) because the optimization problems are not prone to trivial and degenerate solutions.

Use cases of our methods contain traditional market segmentation tasks. Consider for instance a company that aims at promoting a new product or a hotel chain that intends to lure visitors with special offers. Our methods not only compute a meaningful segmentation of the customers but also allow for devising appropriate targeting strategies from the graphical models. Moreover, our method serves as discriminative clustering for structured variables, where the task is not to output a single class/cluster label but the average structure for every segment. The differentiation between attributes and behavior increases the range of applications that can be addressed. A special – but still novel – case is obtained when attributes and behavior partially overlap.

Empirically, we study our methods on another interesting use case: Segmenting user navigation sessions on the Web for displaying segment-specific website layouts. We experiment on a large click log from Yahoo! News. The attribute data is assembled from meta-information about the session such as the timestamp, the referrer domain, and the first page request. The behavior consists of subsequent navigation actions given by click sequences. The generative representation of the behavior data is interpretable and can be easily transformed into segment-specific layouts.

The remainder of the paper is structured as follows. Section 2 discusses the relationship of our problem setting with previously studied settings and methods. In Section 3 we derive two algorithms to optimize the empirical counterpart of the expected segmented log-likelihood. Section 4 reports on empirical results using a large click log from a commercial news provider and Section 5 concludes.

2. RELATED WORK

Market segmentation tasks are often solved using neural networks such as self-organizing maps (13; 7). Kiang et al. (13) for instance extend self-organizing maps to group customers according to their attitude towards different communications modes. D'Urso and de Giovanni (7) use the natural clustering property of self-organizing maps together with dissimilarity measures which capture temporal structure of the data. In general, clustering data with self-organizing maps and variants thereof inherently implements the homogeneity assumption of market segmentation. However, classifying new instances into the clustering is often difficult and it is not possible to output generative models to summarize the resulting clusters. Additionally, the optimization criterion of self-organizing maps is highly sensitive to the actual initialization and usually converges to different local optima.

Related to market segmentation is the task of estimating a mixture model for observations (6). Introducing selector variables encoding probabilistic cluster-memberships, maximizing the log-likelihood by marginalizing over the selector is usually straightforward. The selector can be modeled in a data-dependent or data-independent fashion but the probabilistic nature of the cluster-memberships render a direct application for market segmentation tasks impossible.

Discriminative clustering simultaneously computes a segmentation of the data at hand *and* a classifier that discriminates the resulting clusters well. Existing approaches include projections into lower-dimensional subspaces (5), joint optimization of max-margin classifiers and clusterings (20; 24), the optimization of scatter metrics (21), and the maximization of an information theoretic criterion to balance class separation and classifier complexity (8). Sinkkonen et al. (17) aim to find clusters that are homogeneous in auxiliary data given by additional discrete variables. The above mentioned approaches do not predict any output variable but focus on the discrete cluster variable. Moreover, in our generalized problem setting, instances are represented as input-output pairs. The classifier discriminates the clusters given only the input, whereas the cluster parameters need to accurately estimate the outputs of the contained instances. Previous work on discriminative clustering does not split instances into two parts. They represent instances as a single input which consequently allows the classifiers to access the whole example at decision time. The same assumption is commonly being made in market segmentation studies that involve model-based clustering approaches, (9; 16; 22) but prohibits a natural solution for market segmentation tasks.

This problem setting can be seen as an alteration of the setting which the Mixture of Experts approach (10; 12) aims to solve, where the behavior y is predicted given the attributes x as a mixture model where the mixture component weights depend again on x. In our case, mixture component weights have to be always point distributions as demanded by the application. Framing the distribution of y given the mixture component as a pure generative model allows us to derive a more efficient algorithm than that of the Mixture of Experts approach.

Zhao et al. (23) proposed a maximum-margin clustering for multivariate loss functions. Minimizing the complex losses allows for capturing structural differences that cannot be expressed in terms of standard misclassification rates. In principle, by defining a loss function that captures the differences of two clusterings, one could possibly solve market segmentation tasks as their approach implicitly favors clusterings that are easily discriminable. However, the loss function cannot be expressed in terms of the contingency table of the two clusterings, and the decoding problem in the inner loop of the algorithm, that is finding the most violated constraint, becomes intractable in practice.

Also related to our problem setting are multi-view clustering approaches, where the data is split into two disjoint feature sets, which are sometimes also called views. Bickel and Scheffer (2) present an intertwined Expectation Maximization algorithm to compute the maximum likelihood solution for one view using the expectations provided by its peer view. The two data views are modeled generatively and the algorithm maximizes the joint marginal likelihood. By contrast, we aim to find a discriminative classifier on the input view and instead of maximizing the marginal likelihood of the output view we seek to maximize the likelihood conditioned on a hard cluster assignment.

3. DISCRIMINATIVE SEGMENTATION

We now present our main contribution, the generalization of discriminative clustering for structured output variables to solve market segmentation problems. We introduce the problem setting in the next section and present a straightforward solution in terms of mixtures of experts in Section 3.2. An efficient approximation is devised in Section 3.3 and Section 3.3.3 discusses scalability issues.

3.1 Preliminaries

We are given a sample $\mathcal{M}$ from a market where individuals are represented by tuples $(x, y) \in \mathcal{X} \times \mathcal{Y}$ encoding attributes x and behavior y. Attributes x may encompass individual features like gender, income, etc while the expressed historic behavior is captured by $y \in \mathcal{Y}$ and represented as a graphical model. The behaviors y are governed by a family of distributions denoted by $P(y|\theta)$ with natural parameter θ.

In our running example on segmenting user navigation on the Web, attributes x encode meta-information about the session such as the timestamp, the referrer domain, and the first page request and is represented as a feature vector. The behavior y encodes sequences of the subsequent Web navigation and can for instance be represented as a Markov-chain where nodes correspond to pageviews and connecting edges visualize clicks.

We aim to find an appropriate segmentation of the market $\mathcal{M}$. Formally, the goal is to find a classifier $h : \mathcal{X} \to \{1, \ldots, k\}$ that maps attributes x to one of k clusters, parameterized by $\boldsymbol{\theta} = (\theta_1, \ldots, \theta_k)$, where the θ_j are chosen to maximize the likelihood of the observed behaviors y of the respective segment. The number of clusters k is assumed to be given by the application at hand, because it constitutes a trade-off between predictive power and effort spent for developing multiple market strategies. As h and $\boldsymbol{\theta}$ are not independent they need to be optimized jointly. Hence, over all classifiers h and parameter collections $\boldsymbol{\theta}$, we aim at maximizing the expected risk functional R that is defined in terms of the segmented log-likelihood

$$R(h, \boldsymbol{\theta}) = \int \log P(y|\theta_{h(x)}) dP(x, y). \quad (1)$$

Since the true joint distribution $P(x, y)$ is unknown, we replace Equation (1) by its empirical counterpart on the finite market sample of size n given by $\mathcal{M} = \{(x_i, y_i)\}_{i=1}^n$

$$\hat{R}(\boldsymbol{\theta}, h) = \sum_{i=1}^{n} \log P(y_i|\theta_{h(x_i)}). \quad (2)$$

Directly maximizing Equation (2) in terms of the component parameters $\boldsymbol{\theta}$ and the classifier h is infeasible, since the objective function is not only highly non-convex and non-continuous but an NP-hard problem because of combinatorial assignments. However, if the classifier h was fixed, the θ_j could be optimized directly, as h provides the segmentation and for each segment j optimal parameters $\hat{\theta}_j$ are trivially computed by

$$\hat{\theta}_j = \underset{\theta}{\operatorname{argmax}} \sum_{i:h(x_i)=j} \log P(y_i|\theta). \quad (3)$$

For many common distribution families, the maximum likelihood estimates $P(y|\theta)$ can be computed easily by counting or averaging over the observations in the segment, respectively. Vice versa, keeping the segment parameters $\theta_1, \ldots, \theta_k$ fixed, learning the classifier h results in a standard multi-class classification scenario. Using linear models, h can be written as

$$h(x) = \underset{j \in \{1 \ldots, k\}}{\operatorname{argmax}} \ w_j^\top x, \quad (4)$$

where each segment has its own weight vector w_j. In the remainder, we will use h and $\boldsymbol{w} = (w_1, \ldots, w_k)^\top$ interchangeably. The next section exploits this observation and presents a joint alternating optimization scheme.

3.2 An Alternating Optimization Scheme

A straightforward approach to solve market segmentation problems is to alternate the optimization of the classifier and the clustering while fixing the other, respectively. As shown in Equation (3), keeping the classifier fixed allows to apply standard maximum likelihood techniques to compute the natural parameters of the segments. We thus focus on deriving the classifier h for a fixed clustering. We make use of the maximum-margin framework and deploy a rescaled variant of the hinge loss to deal with uncertain cluster-memberships (or class labels).

The idea is as follows. Intuitively, an individual (x, y) should be assigned to the segment that realizes the highest log-likelihood with respect to y. However, two or more segments might be competing for the instance and realize

Algorithm 1 Alternating Optimization

1: Input: $(x_1, y_1), \ldots, (x_n, y_n), \lambda > 0, k > 1$
2: Initialize $\boldsymbol{\theta}$ randomly
3: **repeat**
4: E-step: $\boldsymbol{w} \leftarrow \operatorname{argmin}_{\boldsymbol{w}', \boldsymbol{\xi} \geq \mathbf{0}} \ \frac{\lambda}{2}\|\boldsymbol{w}'\|^2 + \frac{1}{n}\sum_{i=1}^{n} \xi_i$
5: s.t. $(w'_{j_i^*} - w'_j)^\top x \geq 1 - \frac{\xi_i}{s(y)}$
6: M-step: $\boldsymbol{\theta} \leftarrow \operatorname{argmax}_{\boldsymbol{\theta}'} \sum_j \sum_{i:h(x_i)=j} \log P(y_i|\theta')$
7: **until** convergence

similar log-likelihoods, in which case a winner-takes-all decision is prohibitive. We thus treat the difference of the log-likelihoods between the most likely segment j^* and cluster $j' \neq j^*$ as a *misclassification score*, given by

$$s(y) = \log P(y|\theta_{j^*}) - \log P(y|\theta_{j'}). \tag{5}$$

These scores can be incorporated in a support vector machine by re-scaling the hinge loss and act like example-dependent costs (3). The re-scaled hinge loss becomes a convex upper bound of the difference of the log-likelihoods,

$$\ell(x) = s(y) \max\left(0, 1 - (w_{j^*} - w_{j'})^\top x\right). \tag{6}$$

Stacking up $\boldsymbol{w} = (w_1, \dots, w_k)^\top$ and $\boldsymbol{\xi} = (\xi_1, \dots, \xi_n)^\top$, we arrive at the following maximum-margin optimization problem

$$\min_{\boldsymbol{w}, \boldsymbol{\xi} \geq \mathbf{0}} \quad \frac{\lambda}{2} \|\boldsymbol{w}\|^2 + \frac{1}{n} \sum_{i=1}^{n} \xi_i$$

$$\text{s.t.} \quad (w_{j_i^*} - w_j)^\top x \geq 1 - \frac{\xi_i}{s(y)},$$

for $1 \leq i \leq n$, $j \in \{1, \dots, k\}$, $j \neq j^*$, $j_i^* = \arg\max_j P(y_i|\theta_j)$, and regularizaion parameter $\lambda > 0$.

Hence, Equation (2) can be optimized by randomly initializing $\boldsymbol{\theta}$ and subsequently alternating between optimizing $\boldsymbol{w}$ and θ_j while fixing the respective peer. Algorithm 1 instantiates the pseudo-code as a member of the Expectation Maximization framework. The alternating optimization scheme can also be interpreted as an adaptation of the EM algorithm for a mixture of experts (12). The classifier h, given as the weight vectors w_j, corresponds to the gating networks. In contrast to the conventional mixture of experts model, it is trained using an SVM to output deterministic decisions, instead of soft decisions. The generative distribution over behaviors differs from the expert networks only in the fact that in our problem setting the prediction of the behavior y is not allowed to depend directly on the attributes x, only via the cluster assignment.

A major drawback of the alternating approach is however the discrete assignment of individuals to only a single segment, even during the intermediate optimization steps. As a consequence, the algorithm is prone to degenerate solutions and poor local optima. Additionally, the optimization is expensive in terms of computational time as it requires the computation of a multi-class SVM until convergence in every step.

3.3 Collapsed Optimization

We now present an efficient approximation of the discriminative segmentation problem by using a continuous relaxation to the original problem formulation. We first show that the parameters of the classifier can be computed in closed-form so that the joint optimization problem depends only on the segment parameters. Second, we devise an EM-like algorithm (6) to optimize the remaining objective.

3.3.1 Eliminating the Classifier Parameters

As the discrete cluster assignments cause many difficulties, we now replacing them by soft assignments using an adjustable soft-max function. The parameter ρ controls the degree of reproducing the maximum, that is for $\rho \to \infty$ we precisely obtain the maximum operator. Incorporating the soft-max in Equation (2) yields the optimization problem

$$\max_{\boldsymbol{\theta}, \boldsymbol{w}} \sum_{i=1}^{n} \log \sum_{j=1}^{k} P(y_i|\theta_j) \frac{\exp(\rho w_j^\top x_i)}{\sum_{j'} \exp(\rho w_{j'}^\top x_i)}, \tag{7}$$

which still contains the mutually dependent variables $\boldsymbol{\theta}$ and $\boldsymbol{w}$. To obtain an efficiently solvable optimization problem, we express the objective as a continuous function of $\boldsymbol{w}$ so that $\boldsymbol{w}$ can be eliminated using collapsed inference. Instead of the hinge loss in Equation (6), we employ another tight convex upper bound in terms of the squared loss,

$$\ell(x) = (\log P(y|\theta_j) - w_j^\top x)^2.$$

Implicitly, introducing the squared loss converts the classifier into a regressor that aims at predicting the log-likelihood for an individual (x, y) and the j-th segment as accurate as possible. Assuming the log-likelihoods were predicted perfectly, the parameters $\boldsymbol{w}$ would not only be optimal for the regression but also for Equation (2) as the classifier h in Equation (4) would still return the most likely segment. Changing the loss function also has the advantage that now the optimal solution for $\boldsymbol{w}$ can be computed analytically. The corresponding regularized optimization problem is also known as regularized least squares regression (RLSR) or ridge regression and is given by

$$\min_{\boldsymbol{w}} \frac{\lambda}{2} \|\boldsymbol{w}\|^2 + \sum_{i=1}^{n} \sum_{j=1}^{k} \left(\log P(y_i|\theta_j) - w_j^\top x_i\right)^2, \tag{8}$$

for $\lambda > 0$. Setting the derivative with respect to $\boldsymbol{w}$ to zero and solving for w_j, we obtain the optimal solution that can be computed in closed-form

$$w_j = X^\top (XX^\top + \lambda I)^{-1} \pi(\theta_j), \tag{9}$$

where $X \in \mathbb{R}^{n \times d}$ contains the stacked attribute vectors and $\pi(\theta_j) = (\log P(y_1|\theta_j), \dots, \log P(y_n|\theta_j))^\top$ is the vector of log-likelihoods for the j-th segment. The computation of the inner product

$$w_j^\top x = \pi(\theta_j)^\top (XX^\top + \lambda I)^{-1} X x$$

can effectively be sped-up by precomputing the linear transformation of the attributes. Introducing auxiliary variables $\bar{x}$ given by

$$\bar{x} = (XX^\top + \lambda I)^{-1} X x,$$

allows to efficiently rewrite the inner product as $w_j^\top x = \pi(\theta_j)^\top \bar{x}$. Further note that $\bar{x}$ depends only on inner products of individual attributes. Hence, the kernel trick can be applied to incorporate non-linearity. Introducing a Mercer kernel κ, the auxiliary matrix $\bar{X}$ can be written in terms of the corresponding kernel matrix K with elements $K_{ij} = \{\kappa(x_i, x_j)\}_{ij}$ as $(K + \lambda I)^{-1} K$. The classifier can then be expressed in terms of a set of dual multipliers α and the kernel function as $h(x) = \arg\max_j \sum_i \alpha_{ji} \kappa(x_i, x_j)$. The dual multipliers can be obtained explicitly as a function of the component parameters as

$$\alpha_j(\theta_j) = \pi(\theta_j)^\top (K + \lambda I)^{-1}. \tag{10}$$

Substituting the obtained observations in Equation (7) results in a simplified optimization problem that does no longer depend on $\boldsymbol{w}$ and that has only the θ_j as free parameters,

$$\max_{\boldsymbol{\theta}} \sum_{i=1}^{n} \log \sum_{j=1}^{k} P(y_i|\theta_j) \frac{\exp(\rho\,\pi(\theta_j)^\top \bar{x}_i)}{\sum_{j'} \exp(\rho\,\pi(\theta_j)^\top \bar{x}_i)}. \quad (11)$$

3.3.2 Optimizing the segment parameters

The optimization problem in Equation (11) can be solved with an EM-like algorithm (6) using auxiliary variables $z_{i,j} \geq 0$, with $\sum_j z_{i,j} = 1$, encoding the belief that the i-th example belongs to the j-th cluster. EM-like algorithms consist of two phases which assign instances to generating segments (E-step) and maximize the segment parameters with respect to the associated instances (M-step), respectively. In the E-step, it therefore suffices to identify the auxiliary variables with the true posterior probabilities given the current $\boldsymbol{\theta}$,

$$z_{i,j} \propto P(y_i|\theta_j) \frac{\exp(\rho\,\pi(\theta_j)^\top \bar{x}_i)}{\sum_{j'} \exp(\rho\,\pi(\theta_j)^\top \bar{x}_i)}.$$

Following the general EM framework, we express the empirical risk functional in Equation (11) in terms of the expectations $z_{i,j}$. This allows us to effectively pull the logarithm into the sum over segments for the M-step; we arrive at the optimization problem

$$\max_{\boldsymbol{\theta}} \sum_i \sum_j z_{i,j} \log \left[P(y_i|\theta_j) \frac{\exp(\rho\,\pi(\theta_j)^\top \bar{x}_i)}{\sum_{j'} \exp(\rho\,\pi(\theta_j)^\top \bar{x}_i)} \right],$$

which can be rewritten as

$$\max_{\boldsymbol{\theta}} \sum_{i,j} z_{i,j}$$
$$\left[\rho\pi(\theta_j)^\top \bar{x}_i - \log \sum_{j'} \exp(\rho\pi(\theta_{j'})^\top \bar{x}_i) + \log P(y_i|\theta_j) \right].$$

The above Equation is to be maximized with respect to $\boldsymbol{\theta}$. Compared to conventional M-steps for mixture model estimation problems, $\boldsymbol{\theta}$ appears not only in $P(y_i|\theta_j)$, but also in what are usually the segment weights for each example. This renders the objective function non-concave and, consequentially, there is no exact analytical solution.

As a remedy, we derive an approximation that is linear and non-decreasing in the $\pi(\theta_j)$, rendering the objective concave in θ_j and thus analytically solvable for common choices of $P(y|\theta_j)$. We begin with approximating the normalization term $Z(\boldsymbol{\theta}) = \log \sum_{j'} \exp(\rho\pi(\theta_{j'})^\top \bar{x}_i)$ by its first-order Taylor expansion around the current $\boldsymbol{\theta}^{old}$ which is given by

$$Z(\boldsymbol{\theta}) \approx \sum_{j'} t_{ij'} \rho\pi(\theta_{j'})^\top \bar{x}_i + C, \quad (12)$$

where the $t_{ij'} = \frac{\exp(\rho\pi(\theta_{j'}^{old})^\top \bar{x}_i)}{\sum_j \exp(\rho\pi(\theta_j^{old})^\top \bar{x}_i)}$ are the Taylor coefficients and C is a constant. Substituting Equation (12) into the objective function of the M-step and collecting the coefficients gives us

$$\underset{\boldsymbol{\theta}}{\operatorname{argmax}} \sum_i \sum_j \log P(y_i|\theta_j) \left[z_{i,j} + \rho \sum_{i'} \bar{x}_{i'i} \Big(z_{i',j} - \sum_{j'} z_{i',j'} t_{i'j'} \Big) \right], \quad (13)$$

which is a linear function of $\log P(y_i|\theta_j)$. For increasing ρ, the Taylor coefficients for each instance approach a point distribution exponentially fast, i.e. $t_{i\cdot} \rightarrow (0, \ldots, 0, 1, 0, \ldots, 0)^\top$. The same holds for the auxiliary variables $z_{i,j}$, which approach t_{ij}. Thus, the second summands of the coefficients in Equation (13) approach zero, and hence for large ρ all the $\log P(y_i|\theta_j)$ have either positive or very small negative coefficients. We clip coefficients below zero to guarantee that the objective function is non-decreasing in the $\log P(y_i|\theta_j)$ and obtain an approximation that approaches the exact solution with increasing ρ.

The softmax factor ρ therefore constitutes a trade-off between accurately approximating the original optimization problem of maximizing $\hat{R}(\boldsymbol{\theta}, h)$ and smoothing the objective function to facilitate finding good local optima.

We deal with this tradeoff by starting the EM-algorithm with $\rho = 1$, and multiplying it by a constant factor each iteration. Preliminary experiments have shown the factor 1.1 to work well. Due to the approximation of the hard decisions with a soft-max, the algorithm is not guaranteed to monotonically increase the true objective value. We thus select the intermediate result with the highest objective value as the final solution for the cluster parameters.

Algorithm 2 Collapsed Optimization Algorithm

1: Input: $(x_1, y_1), \ldots, (x_n, y_n), \lambda$
2: $\rho \leftarrow 1$, $t \leftarrow 1$, initialize $\boldsymbol{\theta}^{(0)}$ randomly
3: **repeat**
4: E-step: $Q(z_i = j) \leftarrow P(z_i = j|x_i, y_i, \rho, \lambda, \boldsymbol{\theta}^{(t-1)})$
5: M-step: $\boldsymbol{\theta}^{(t)} \leftarrow \arg\max_{\boldsymbol{\theta}} \sum_i \sum_j Q(z_i = j) \times$
6: $\log P(y_i, z_i = j|x_i, \rho, \lambda, \boldsymbol{\theta})$
7: $\rho \leftarrow \rho \times 1.1$, $t \leftarrow t + 1$
8: **until** convergence
9: $\hat{\boldsymbol{\theta}} = \operatorname{argmax}_{\boldsymbol{\theta}} \hat{R}(\boldsymbol{\theta}, \alpha(\boldsymbol{\theta}))$
10: $\alpha \leftarrow \alpha(\hat{\boldsymbol{\theta}})$

Algorithm 2 shows the collapsed optimization algorithm in pseudo code. In line 2, the cluster parameters $\boldsymbol{\theta}$ are initialized randomly. Line 4 performs the expectation step of the EM-algorithm, computing the current posterior estimates, given the soft-max factor ρ, the cluster parameters, and implicitly also the classifier h. The maximization step in line 5 boils down to an optimization problem of the form $\sum_i \sum_j c_{ij} \log P(y_i|\theta_j)$, which for non-negative coefficients c_{ij} can be solved analytically for many choices of distribution families. For example if $P(y|\theta)$ is a multinomial distribution over $y \in \{1, \ldots, m\}$ with $P(y = q|\theta_j) = \theta_{j,q}$, the maximum is attained for $\theta_{j,q} = \sum_i c_{ij} [\![y_i = q]\!] / \sum_i c_{ij}$ for all j, q, where $[\![\cdot]\!]$ is the indicator function. Finally, lines 9 and 10 select the best intermediate solution in terms of the true objective, and re-obtain the explicit classifier using Equation (10).

3.3.3 Scalability

The computational bottlenecks of the collapsed optimization algorithm are the computation of the $\bar{x}_i$, involving matrix inversions and multiplications, and the computation of the coefficients in Equation (13), where we have to sum over all pairs of examples, leading to an overall complexity of the algorithm of $O(n^{2.376} + n^2 kT)$.

For applications with a large number of examples the super-quadratic dependence on the sample size n makes the algorithm effectively intractable. We can alleviate this by randomly partitioning the examples in the least-squares estimation in Equation (8) into s disjoint subsets $S^{(1)}, \ldots, S^{(s)}$ of size m. For each subset the weight vectors $\boldsymbol{w}^{(l)}$ are estimated separately, and thus within each subset the vectors $\pi(\theta_j)$ and the transformed examples $\bar{x}$ have only m components. Consequently, in Equation (13) the inner summation over the examples only runs over the m examples in the subset to which example (x_i, y_i) belongs. Finally, we obtain the parameters of the classifier h by averaging the weight vectors over all subsets, $w_j = \frac{1}{s}\sum_l w_j^{(l)}$.

Mixing the separately learned weight vectors is identical to the mixture weight method by Mann et al. (15) that has been shown, theoretically and empirically, to yield results close to learning a weight vector using all examples at once. Note however that $\boldsymbol{\theta}$ is still learned from the whole, unpartitioned training sample. Using the partitioned estimation for the weight vectors, the overall complexity of the algorithm becomes $O(nm^{1.376} + nmkT)$. For $m \ll n$, the computation becomes tractable even for very large sample sizes n.

4. EMPIRICAL EVALUATION

In this section, we evaluate the proposed algorithm using a large data sample from Yahoo! News United Kingdom[1]. The click log contains browsing session logs, where events from the same user are identified by their browser cookies and sessions are split after 25 minutes of inactivity. We use all sessions from June 2011 for training and the first week of July 2011 for testing. Figure 1 shows the categories, such as *politics/world*, *politics/uk*, *science/space*, in the training set, averaged over the four weeks where different colors correspond to different categories[2].

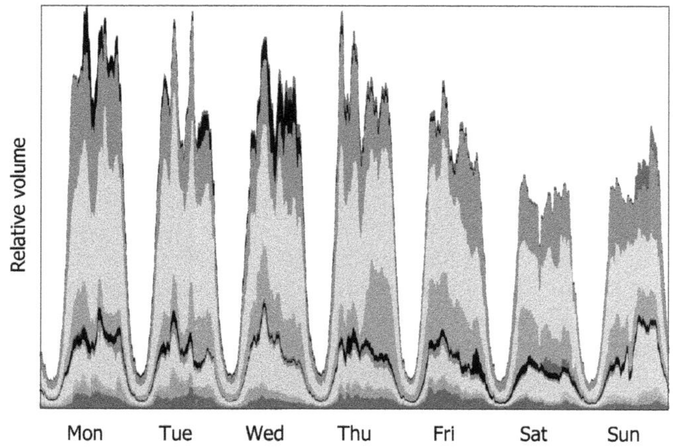

Figure 1: Click volume of categories over time.

The goal of our study is threefold: Firstly, we aim to segment the user sessions of Yahoo! News according to their interests expressed by clicks. Secondly, new sessions need to be classified to one of the segments so that every segment accurately predicts subsequent clicks of the respective user. Finally, the segments need to be interpretable to allow for devising target strategies from the segment description.

[1]All processing is anonymous and aggregated

[2]Colors occur more than once due to the large number of categories.

A typical targeting strategy in our Yahoo! News example could for instance be a dynamic layout of the Web site to advertise news articles of categories that the respective user is probably interested in.

From a data perspective, modeling sequences of clicked categories by Markov processes is straightforward. However, Markov processes, e.g., visualized by transition matrices, are difficult to interpret as the entries encode interests with respect to the previous category. Taking the inferred Markov model properly into account would imply changing the website layout within a session depending on the previous category. A simpler way to obtain interpretable clusters is to use multinomial distributions for the output variables of interest. We use the sequences of user clicks enriched with the respective locations of the clicks. That is, the behavior y consists of the multi-set of subsequently clicked categories c and link sections s. The distribution $P(y|\theta_j)$ is defined as the product of multinomial distributions

$$P(y|\theta) = \prod_l P(c_i|\mu) \prod_j P(s_j|\nu),$$

where μ and ν are the parameter vectors governing the distributions over categories and link sections, respectively.

The attributes x of a session is represented as a binary feature vector encoding the most common referrer domains, the respective category of the first pageview, as well as features encoding the timestamp; we use binary indicators for every day of the week, for each hour of the day, and for each hour of the week. For the collapsed algorithm, we use a linear kernel and randomly partition the training data into disjoint subsets of size 1,000 for computing the predicted log-likelihoods.

4.1 Baselines

We compare the collapsed algorithm with three baselines, the alternating optimization scheme in Section 3.2, a mixture of experts model and a k-means based solution. The *mixture of experts model* (12) minimizes the squared error in terms of the within-cluster log-likelihoods and optimizes the marginal likelihood

$$\sum_i \log \sum_j P(y_i|\theta_j) P(z_i = j|x).$$

Instead of the prior $P(z = j)$ we have a conditional distribution $P(z = j|x)$ which is defined in analogy to the collapsed algorithm as

$$P(z = j|x) \propto \exp(\sum_i \alpha_{j,i} k(x_i, x)).$$

The mixture of experts model is optimized with a standard EM-algorithm and therefore provides only probabilistic cluster assignments and does not take into account that sessions need to be assigned to only a single cluster.

The third baseline is derived from the straightforward, yet somewhat naïve, approach to segment the input space first and only then optimize the generative model in each cluster. The drawback of this non-iterative approach is that it does generally not lead to homogeneous behavior within clusters because the segments are fixed when estimating the generative models. We use k-means for finding the clustering, and estimate segment paramters $\boldsymbol{\theta}$ by maximum likelihood based on the hard cluster assignments. The classifier h classifies a new instance into the cluster with the nearest centroid.

In each setting, every algorithm is deployed 10 times with random parameter initializations and in the remainder we only report the results of the run with highest training likelihood.

4.2 Convergence

In this section, we evaluate the convergence behavior of the collapsed algorithm. Recall that the collapsed algorithm optimizes an approximate objective, where the hard cluster assignments are replaced by a soft-max controlled by an increasing factor ρ. To cancel out effects caused by the approximation, we substitute the resulting $\boldsymbol{\theta}$ into the exact optimization criterion in Equation (2) and measure the respective objective value. Note that the results do not necessarily increase monotonically.

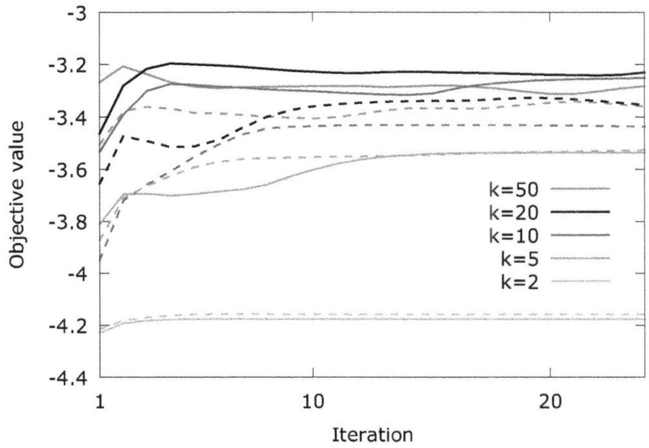

Figure 2: Objective values for the collapsed algorithm (solid) and the mixture of experts baseline (dashed), for different numbers of clusters k.

Figure 2 shows the results for different numbers of clusters for the collapsed algorithm (solid curves). For comparison, we also added the mixture of experts baseline (dashed curves). As expected, the true objective value is not monotonic, since both algorithms optimize an approximation to the exact optimization criterion. The figure also shows that the best values are obtained after at most 20 iterations.

4.3 Predictive Performance

To evaluate the performance of the collapsed algorithm, we measure its predictive accuracy in terms of how well future behavior can be predicted. The classifier and the segmentation are learned jointly as described in Section 3 using the training set and then deployed to the test set. The sessions in the test set are first classified by the classifier in one of the segments which is then used to predict the future clicks of the user. Since the final prediction is a complex variable, we refrain from expressing the performance in terms of error rates and measure the predictive log-likelihood $\log P(y|\theta_{h(x)})$ instead. We compare the collapsed algorithm to the alternating optimization scheme, the mixture of experts model, and the k-means based solution. We report on averages and standard errors over 10 repetitions with different random initializations.

Figure 3 shows the predictive performance for varying numbers of clusters. Not surprisingly, all methods perform

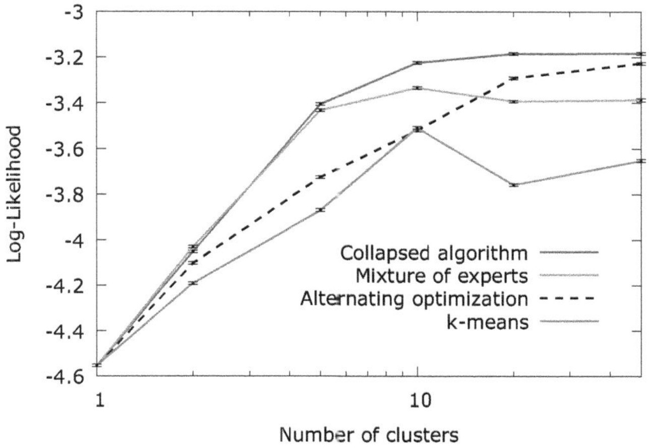

Figure 3: Averaged predictive performance and standard error.

equally worse for only a single cluster. For only a few clusters, the mixture of experts baseline performs about as well as the collapsed algorithm. We credit this finding to the existence of easy-to-reach solutions that do not necessarily require hard cluster assignments in the $\boldsymbol{\theta}$-steps. However, when the number of clusters grows, the performance of the mixture of experts approach decreases slightly while that of the collapsed model increases. Here it becomes more and more important to select the parameters in a way that allows to discriminate well between the clusters, and thus the collapsed algorithm outperforms the baselines significantly. The alternating algorithm and the k-means baseline perform significantly worse than the collapsed algorithm. Only for 20 and more clusters the alternating algorithm produces better results than the mixture of experts model. Note that the k-means performs worst as it does not use an alternating update schema but first learns the clustering and then estimates the generative models using the fixed segments.

It is apparent that the predictive performance levels off after increasing the number of clusters beyond 10. Intuitively, this observation can be explained by a trade-off between classification and segmentation: even if a more fine-grained clustering would be able to predict the future behavior more accurately, the classifier cannot discriminate well between a larger number of similar clusters to identify the best-matching segment. We observe a natural trade-off between predictive power and the effort that has to be spent for developing and maintaining target strategies for a large number of market segments.

The execution time of the collapsed algorithm for a solution with 10 clusters is within the range of 3 hours, compared to about an hour each for the mixture of experts and the k-means baselines. The alternating optimization however takes about 11 hours which renders its application infeasible in practice.

4.4 Discussion

Market segmentation aims at grouping similar individuals of a population together that share the same needs or that have similar demands. The goal is to target individuals within the same segment jointly e.g., to advertise a new product. To this end, the segments need to be interpretable

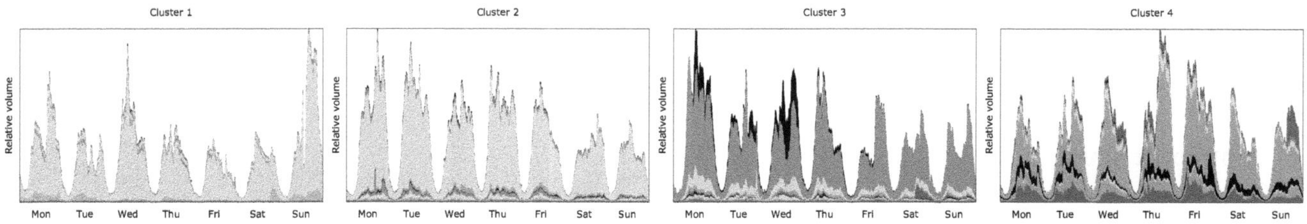

Figure 5: Click volumes of categories over time for the four clusters.

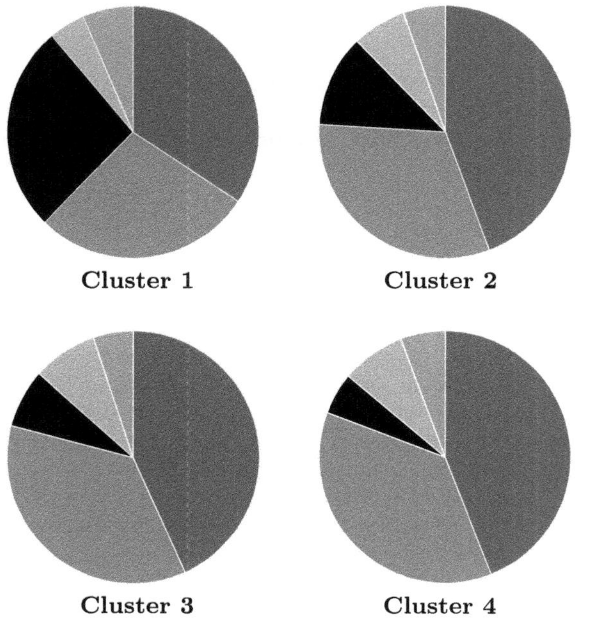

Figure 4: Visualization of click frequencies for the five most frequent link locations using four clusters.

to derive a concise description of the segments that can be converted into a segment-specific targeting strategy.

In our collapsed algorithm, generative models in each segment encode the contained behavior and interest. The flexibility of the probabilistic inference machinery allows us to project the behavior onto discriminative variables to visualize different characteristics of the clusters. In this section we give two examples for such projections to visualize differently distributed user behavior across the clustering. For simplicity, we use a solution with four clusters.

The first example shows a visualization of segment-specific user clicks in terms of their location on the Web page. Including the location of clicks is necessary for altering the layout dynamically as changes in frequently clicked areas will have impact the behavior more than substituting a redundant and less clicked widget. We focus on the five modules of the Web site that receive the highest number of clicks in the data.

Figure 4 shows the results. Segments 2, 3, and 4 exhibit very similar click behavior in terms of the clicked modules. By contrast, cluster 1 differs significantly in the usage of the Web components. On average, users in cluster 1 prefer the location visualized in black over the alternatives compared to users in the other segments. This observation could be exploited to directly devise target strategies. While members of cluster 2–4 should be addressed by changing the content of the modules visualized in gray or dark blue, users in the first segment could also be triggered by the module encoded in black.

Analogously, the behavior could be projected on the categories to visualize the respective distribution of categories for each segment. However, we choose to show a more interesting projection for lack of space. The incorporation of the timestamps of the sessions allows us to visualize the clusters in time. As the feature representation of timestamps encompasses one week, Figure 5 shows the average category distribution across the days of the week where different colors correspond to different categories.[3]

Apparently, the clusters do not only differ in terms of the categories but also specialize on certain periods in time because the segments are optimized using *all* available data, that is, attribute *and* behavior encoding variables. The first cluster clearly specializes on Sundays and is characterized by a clean topic distribution. The three other cluster also possess dominant categories but focuses more on working days than on weekends. Cluster 4 contains the most diverse set of categories and acts like a basin for categories that are not as easy to discriminate. Here it becomes obvious that a solution with only four clusters may not be optimal for the task at hand. When we increase the maximal number clusters, the category distribution of clusters becomes cleaner that is less categories are likely. Additionally, clusters adapt better to specialized periods such as working days or weekends for larger k.

Taking various such projections into account describes segments from different angles and helps to find a concise targeting strategy. For instance, knowing the articles that are likely to be read in an ongoing session helps to address the respective user in various ways including displaying ads. Incorporating context informations such as the click behavior of the segments, finally allows for tailoring web pages to each segment and to increase the overall user experience.

5. CONCLUSION

We studied discriminative clustering for structured and complex response variables that can be represented as generative models. The problem setting matches market segmentation tasks where populations are to be segmented into disjoint groups. Solving market segmentation-like problems appropriately not only involves a clustering of the individuals but also learning a classifier that discriminates well be-

[3]Colors are again reused due to the large number of categories.

tween the segments, for instance to allow for classifying new customers to one of the groups. The two components need to be learned jointly and have access to different pieces of information about the individuals: the classifier needs to group individuals on the basis of *a priori* available informations while the clustering aims at grouping people with similar (future) needs or behavior.

We devised two algorithms based on alternating optimization and collapsed inference, respectively. Empirical results showed that the collapsed variant is not only more efficient but also predicts accurately the click behavior of users for Yahoo! News. The generative nature of the clustering led to interpretable clusters. We showed how projections of the clustering on only a few variables allowed for targeting the detected segments individually and contributed to user understanding.

Our approach is not restricted to Yahoo! News and can generally be applied to arbitrary market segmentation tasks and other Web sites to improve the overall user experience. As our approach is orthogonal to personalized approaches, future work will study the integration of both frameworks.

Acknowledgements

Part of this work was supported by the German Science Foundation under the reference number GA 1615/1-1.

References

[1] N. Bansal, A. Blum, and S. Chawla. Correlation clustering. *Machine Learning*, 56(1-3):89–113, 2004.

[2] S. Bickel and T. Scheffer. Multi-view clustering. In *Proceedings of the IEEE international conference on data mining*. Citeseer, 2004.

[3] U. Brefeld, P. Geibel, and F. Wysotzki. Support vector machines with example dependent costs. In *Proceedings of the European Conference on Machine Learning*, 2003.

[4] R. D'Andrade. U-statistic hierarchical clustering. *Psychometrika*, 4:58–67, 1978.

[5] F. De la Torre and T. Kanade. Discriminative cluster analysis. In *Proceedings of the 23rd international conference on Machine learning*, pages 241–248. ACM, 2006.

[6] A. Dempster, N. Laird, and D. Rubin. Maximum likelihood from incomplete data via the em algorithm. *Journal of the Royal Statistical Society. Series B (Methodological)*, pages 1–38, 1977.

[7] P. D'Urso and L. D. Giovanni. Temporal self-organizing maps for telecommunications market segmentation. *Neurocomput.*, 71:2880–2892, 2008.

[8] R. Gomes, A. Krause, and P. Perona. Discriminative clustering by regularized information maximization. In *Advances in Neural Information Processing Systems*, 2010.

[9] J. Huang, G. Tzeng, and C. Ong. Marketing segmentation using support vector clustering. *Expert systems with applications*, 32(2):313–317, 2007.

[10] R. Jacobs, M. Jordan, S. Nowlan, and G. Hinton. Adaptive mixtures of local experts. *Neural computation*, 3(1):79–87, 1991.

[11] S. C. Johnson. Hierarchical clustering schemes. *Psychometrika*, 2:241–254, 1967.

[12] M. Jordan and R. Jacobs. Hierarchical mixtures of experts and the em algorithm. *Neural computation*, 6(2):181–214, 1994.

[13] M. Y. Kiang, M. Y. Hu, and D. M. Fisher. An extended self-organizing map network for market segmentation – a telecommunication example. *Decision Support Systems*, 42:36–47, 2006.

[14] S. P. Lloyd. Least square quantization in pcm. *IEEE Transactions on Information Theory*, 28(2):129–137, 1982.

[15] G. Mann, R. McDonald, M. Mohri, N. Silberman, and D. Walker. Efficient large-scale distributed training of conditional maximum entropy models. *Advances in Neural Information Processing Systems*, 22:1231–1239, 2009.

[16] M. Namvar, M. Gholamian, and S. KhakAbi. A two phase clustering method for intelligent customer segmentation. In *2010 International Conference on Intelligent Systems, Modelling and Simulation*, pages 215–219. IEEE, 2010.

[17] J. Sinkkonen, S. Kaski, and J. Nikkilä. Discriminative clustering: Optimal contingency tables by learning metrics. *Machine Learning: ECML 2002*, pages 109–137, 2002.

[18] K. Wagstaff, C. Cardie, S. Rogers, and S. Schrödl. Constrained k-means clustering with background knowledge. In *Proceedings of the International Conference on Machine Learning*, 2001.

[19] M. Wedel and W. Kamakura. *Market segmentation: conceptual and methodological foundations*, volume 8. Springer, 2000.

[20] L. Xu, J. Neufeld, B. Larson, and D. Schuurmans. Maximum margin clustering. *Advances in neural information processing systems*, 17:1537–1544, 2005.

[21] J. Ye, Z. Zhao, and M. Wu. Discriminative k-means for clustering. In *Advances in Neural Information Processing Systems*, 2007.

[22] W. Yu and G. Qiang. Customer segmentation of port based on the multi-instance kernel k-aggregate clustering algorithm. In *Management Science and Engineering, 2007. ICMSE 2007. International Conference on*, pages 210–215, 2007.

[23] B. Zhao, J. Kwok, and C. Zhang. Maximum margin clustering with multivariate loss function. In *Data Mining, 2009. ICDM'09. Ninth IEEE International Conference on*, pages 637–646. IEEE, 2009.

[24] B. Zhao, F. Wang, and C. Zhang. Efficient multiclass maximum margin clustering. In *Proceedings of the 25th international conference on Machine learning*, pages 1248–1255. ACM, 2008.

Interacting Viruses in Networks: Can Both Survive?

Alex Beutel, B. Aditya Prakash, Roni Rosenfeld, and Christos Faloutsos
Computer Science Department, Carnegie Mellon University
Pittsburgh, PA, USA
{abeutel, badityap, roni, christos}@cs.cmu.edu

ABSTRACT

Suppose we have two competing ideas/products/viruses, that propagate over a social or other network. Suppose that they are strong/virulent enough, so that each, if left alone, could lead to an epidemic. What will happen when both operate on the network? Earlier models assume that there is perfect competition: if a user buys product 'A' (or gets infected with virus 'X'), she will never buy product 'B' (or virus 'Y'). This is not always true: for example, a user could install and use both Firefox and Google Chrome as browsers. Similarly, one type of flu may give partial immunity against some other similar disease.

In the case of full competition, it is known that 'winner takes all,' that is the weaker virus/product will become extinct. In the case of no competition, both viruses survive, ignoring each other. What happens in-between these two extremes?

We show that there is a phase transition: if the competition is harsher than a critical level, then 'winner takes all;' otherwise, the weaker virus survives. These are the contributions of this paper (a) the problem definition, which is novel even in epidemiology literature [3, 17, 35] (b) the phase-transition result and (c) experiments on real data, illustrating the suitability of our results.

Categories and Subject Descriptors

H.2.8 [**Database management**]: Database applications—*Data mining*

Keywords

Epidemics, Cascades, Competition, Co-existence

1. INTRODUCTION

Given two partially competing products (like Firefox and Google Chrome; or Android and iPhone), is it possible that they both survive?

The well-known Competitive Exclusion Principle in ecology states that when two species are in complete competition under constant conditions, the more fit one will eventually drive the less fit one into extinction. A more common but less well understood scenario is one where the competing species induce partial immunity against one another. There has been significant work trying to elucidate the conditions under which such partial immunity leads to coexistence [25, 11, 26] but a complete theory has not yet emerged.

Here, we study the general case of two virus strains with partial (and symmetric) cross-immunity spreading over a fixed network topology. In addition to the implications for the evolutionary problem discussed above, our results have direct relevance to the spread of rumors and opinions in social networks and market penetration of products.

The contributions of this work are the following:

- the discovery that there is a phase transition, that is, the weaker virus/product may survive, if the cross-immunity satisfies a threshold condition. This seemed to be an open problem even within the epidemiology community [25]
- experiments on real data, showing that our model fits well

Figure 1 shows the time-plots for partially competing products Hulu vs. Blockbuster (a), and Google Chrome vs. Firefox (b). They plot (normalized) count of Google queries, versus time. We fit our model to the data[1] and plot it as well. Notice that it captures the trends well.

The rest of the paper is organized in the usual way: we review related work in § 2 and formulate the problem giving details of our model in § 3. We give the analysis and proof of our phase-transition and coexistence result in § 4 and demonstrate the validity of the results using simulations and real-world case-studies in § 5. Finally, we discuss other subtle aspects of the model in § 6 and conclude in § 7.

2. RELATED WORK

Here we provide a brief overview of the vast literature on epidemiology, influence propagation and population ecology.

Epidemiology and Epidemic Thresholds There are numerous, well-studied epidemiological models, including the so-called *homogeneous models* [4, 27, 3]. They effectively assume that the network is a full clique, that is, every person has the same probability to contact every other person. A large portion of the literature focuses on a single virus, and

[1] Fitted with `www.alexbeutel.com/jsplot/kdd2012.html`

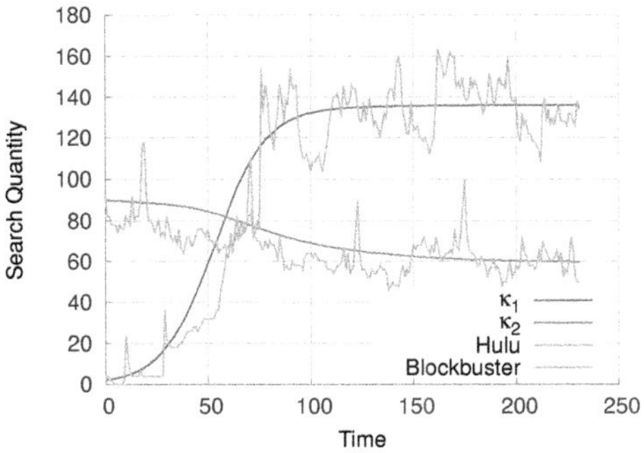

(a) Hulu and Blockbuster

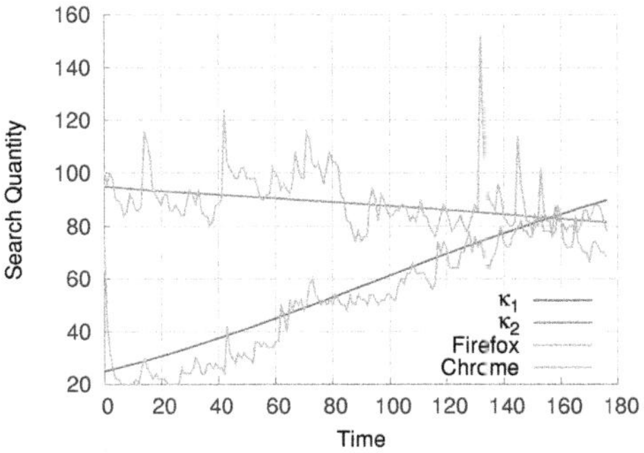

(b) Firefox and Chrome

Figure 1: Plots of real web-search interest vs. time for pairs of competitors with our model fitted to the data.

even then, there are numerous interesting sub-cases. Typical propagation models include SIS (flu-like, with no immunity - Susceptible / Infected / Susceptible), SIR (mumps-like, with lifetime immunity - 'R'= 'recovered'), SIRS (with temporary immunity), and many-many more - see [17] for a detailed survey, or the 700-page book of Anderson and May [3].

A lot of attention focuses on the so-called epidemic threshold: under what conditions will a virus (say, flu-like) become extinct? Earlier works [19, 28] studied specific topologies (e.g., random graphs, power-law graphs, etc). Chakrabarti et al. [10] and Ganesh et al. [13] found that, for arbitrary topologies, and for the flu-like SIS model, the epidemic threshold for any arbitrary graph is determined by the leading eigenvalue of the adjacency matrix of the graph. Prakash et. al. [31] generalized this result to any topology, as well as almost any virus propagation model (SIR, SIRS, etc). However, all of these works focus on single virus models.

Recent work [30] looked at a two-virus SIS model on arbitrary graphs, but focused on the case where there was full mutual immunity between viruses. Their theorem says that, in such a setting, the stronger virus will push the weaker one to extinction ('winner takes all'), even if the weaker one would be able to survive on the network when left alone.

Influence propagation - information diffusion Biological viruses are not the only objects of interest that propagate over the edges of a network. Rumors, ideas, memes, and computer worms behave similarly and have attracted a lot of interest, especially recently thanks to the internet and the web. Research focuses on topics that include (a) information cascades [6, 14], (b) blog propagation [24, 16, 21, 33], and (c) viral marketing and product penetration [23]. Typical cascade models include (a) the independent cascade [18] (essentially an 'SIR' - mumps-like model) and (b) linear threshold [15]. Research work in multiple cascades has examined extensions of the independent cascade model for the case that nodes can not switch from one competitor to the other [5, 20], as well as when they can [29].

There are several fascinating, but remotely-related problems: (a) which nodes to immunize, given a finite count of vaccines [32, 36] (b) which are the best nodes to advertize a new product, to maximize product penetration [12] (c) which nodes are the most likely to be the culprits, when we are given a snapshot of infected nodes in a graph. [22, 34]

Ecology In ecology, the principle of '*competitive exclusion*' espouses that two species can not occupy the same ecological niche in the long term. That is, 'winner takes all', using our earlier terminology. Research has gone into studying this using various propagation models like SIS, SIR, Lotka-Volterra etc. (for example, see [8, 9, 1, 2]). Partial immunity models have received much attention in epidemiology. For example, [25] suggests a differential equation based model and analyzes it via simulation. However, for this and most other models of interest, a complete analytical solution has been beyond reach.

Distinguishing features of current work: In short, none of the previous work fulfills all the conditions of this current work: (a) analytical proof of $\epsilon_{critical}$, the critical value of the competition threshold (b) closed-form steady-state behavior (c) under an SIS (flu-like) model.

3. PROBLEM FORMULATION

In this section, we formulate our problem, giving details about the model used and the assumptions. Table 1 explains the terminology we have used in the paper. Bold letters typically denote matrices (**A**, **M** etc.).

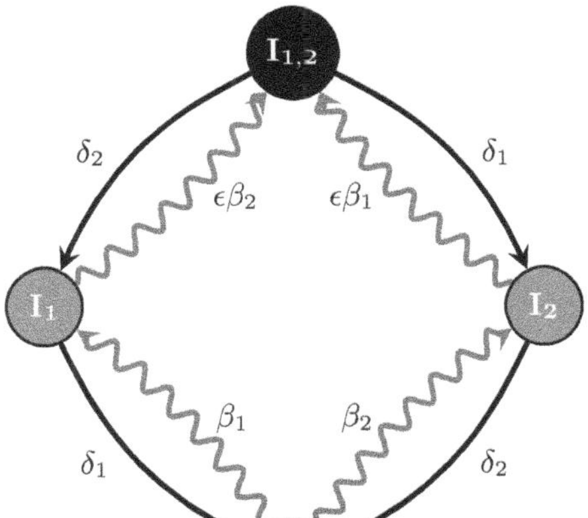

Figure 2: State Diagram for a node in the graph under our partial-competition model.

3.1 The propagation model

We assume that the competing viruses are spreading on the network according to a propagation model, which we describe next. We call our propagation model $SI_{1|2}S$, based on

Table 1: Symbols and Definitions

Symbol	Definition and Description
$SI_{1\|2}S$	our competing viruses model
β_1(or β_2)	attack rate of virus 1 (or virus 2)
δ_1(or δ_2)	cure rate of virus 1 (or virus 2)
ϵ	Interaction factor between virus 1 and 2
$\mathbf{A}$	adjacency matrix of the underlying graph
$\lambda_1(\mathbf{M})$	largest eigenvalue of matrix $\mathbf{M}$
λ	$\lambda_1(\mathbf{A})$
σ_1	$\lambda\beta_1/\delta_1$ (strength of virus 1)
σ_2	$\lambda\beta_2/\delta_2$ (strength of virus 2)
I_1 (or I_2)	The number of nodes infected with only virus 1 (or only virus 2)
$I_{1,2}$	The number of nodes infected with both virus 1 and virus 2
κ_1	Fraction of nodes infected with virus 1 $((I_1 + I_{1,2})/N)$
κ_2	Fraction of nodes infected with virus 2 $((I_2 + I_{1,2})/N)$
i_{12}	Fraction of nodes infected with both viruses $(I_{1,2}/N)$
i_1 (or i_2)	Fraction of nodes infected with virus 1: I_1/N (or virus 2: I_2/N)
$\kappa_1^*, \kappa_2^*, i_{12}^*$	The solution at the coexistence equilibrium (if exists)

the popular "flu-like" SIS (Susceptible-Infected-Susceptible) model [17]. $SI_{1|2}S$ denotes Susceptible - Infected$_{1 \text{ or } 2}$ - Susceptible. Each node in the graph can be in one of four states: Susceptible (healthy), I_1 (infected by virus 1), I_2 (infected by virus 2), or $I_{1,2}$ (infected by both virus 1 and virus 2). The state transition diagram as seen from a node in the network is shown in Figure 2. We could have extended other single virus models as well, but we believe that our model is a reasonable starting point, and we leave the analysis of other models as future work.

Healing (virus death) rate: δ. If a node is in an infected state (I_1, I_2, or $I_{1,2}$), it recovers on its own with some rate, δ_1 for virus 1 or δ_2 for virus 2. The healing rate is inversely related with the virus's strength: a high δ means that nodes that are infected heal quickly. For example, a product that lasts a long time such that people using it rarely consider alternatives would be modeled with a low δ value.

Attack (virus transmission) rate: β. An infected node can spread the virus to its neighboring nodes, and the node susceptibility is captured by β_1 and β_2. Specifically, an infected node transmits its infection to each of its healthy neighbors *independently* at rate β_1 (or β_2). The more often an idea or product is shared with friends, frequently referred to as being "viral," the higher the value for β.

Virus interaction factor: ϵ. A node infected with one virus may be more or less susceptible to being infected by the other virus, as determined by the factor ϵ. The transmission rate for a virus becomes $\epsilon\beta_1$ (or $\epsilon\beta_2$) when a node is already infected with one virus. Specifically, if a node is infected with virus 1, each of its neighbors infected with virus 2 have a transmission rate to it of $\epsilon\beta_2$; a node infected with virus 2 can only be infected with virus 1 at a rate of $\epsilon\beta_1$.

This is a novel generalization of the single-virus SIS model to a multiple-virus scenario. The value of ϵ can describe many different virus interactions. If $\epsilon = 0$ then the viruses are fully mutually immune, and $0 < \epsilon \leq 1$ suggests an amount of competition between viruses.

Fair-play: We assume that the competitors are playing a 'fair game': All nodes in the network have the same model parameters (β's, δ's, ϵ) for each of the viruses and behave according to the state-diagram in Figure 2.

3.2 Problem Statement

We are now in a position to state the problem formally. We assume the underlying network is connected - otherwise we just have separate disconnected problems.

Interacting viruses problem

Given: An undirected connected graph G, and the propagation model ($SI_{1|2}S$) parameters (β_1, δ_1 for virus 1, β_2, δ_2 for virus 2, and ϵ)

Find: What are the possible fixed points for the system? In particular, for what values of ϵ is there a fixed point for which both virus 1 and virus 2 survive?

3.3 Model Formulation for a Clique

For a clique, the following differential equations fully describe the transitions of the system, seen in Figure 2. Here I_1, I_2, and $I_{1,2}$ are the number of nodes infected with only virus 1, only virus 2, and both virus 1 and 2 respectively. N is the total number of nodes, and S is the number of susceptible nodes ($S = N - I_1 - I_2 - I_{12}$).

$$\frac{dI_1}{dt} = \beta_1 S(I_1 + I_{12}) + \delta_2 I_{12} - \delta_1 I_1 - \epsilon\beta_2 I_1(I_2 + I_{12}) \quad (1)$$

$$\frac{dI_2}{dt} = \beta_2 S(I_2 + I_{12}) + \delta_1 I_{12} - \delta_2 I_2 - \epsilon\beta_1 I_2(I_1 + I_{12}) \quad (2)$$

$$\frac{dI_{12}}{dt} = \epsilon\beta_1 I_2(I_1 + I_{12}) + \epsilon\beta_2 I_1(I_2 + I_{12}) - (\delta_1 + \delta_2)I_{12} \quad (3)$$

4. RESULTS AND PROOFS

The goal of our analysis is to find for what values of ϵ is there an equilibrium point for which both virus 1 and virus 2 survive. We find that there is an $\epsilon_{\text{critical}}$ such that if $\epsilon > \epsilon_{\text{critical}}$ then an equilibrium point for which the viruses coexist.

4.1 Formulating the problem

At an equilibrium point, all derivatives are zero. Thus, we can find a simple equation for I_{12}

$$\epsilon(\beta_1 + \beta_2)I_1 I_2 \;=\; (\delta_1 + \delta_2 - \epsilon(\beta_1 I_2 + \beta_2 I_1))I_{12}$$

LEMMA 1. *The number of people infected by both virus 1 and virus 2 will obey the following equation:*

$$I_{12} \;=\; I_1 I_2 \epsilon(\beta_1 + \beta_2)/(\delta_1 + \delta_2 - \epsilon(\beta_1 I_2 + \beta_2 I_1))$$

PROOF. Trivial, given the above. □

Thus we have the expected three equilibrium points

- $I_1 = I_2 = I_{12} = 0$
- $I_1 = I_{12} = 0$, $I_2 = N - \frac{\delta_2}{\beta_2}$
- $I_2 = I_{12} = 0$, $I_1 = N - \frac{\delta_1}{\beta_1}$

and possibly one for which $I_1, I_2 > 0$ and obeys the differential equations outlined:

$$0 = \beta_1 S(I_1 + I_{12}) + \delta_2 I_{12} - \delta_1 I_1 - \epsilon\beta_2 I_1(I_2 + I_{12}) \quad (4)$$
$$0 = \beta_2 S(I_2 + I_{12}) + \delta_1 I_{12} - \delta_2 I_2 - \epsilon\beta_1 I_2(I_1 + I_{12}) \quad (5)$$
$$0 = \epsilon\beta_1 I_2(I_1 + I_{12}) + \epsilon\beta_2 I_1(I_2 + I_{12}) - (\delta_1 + \delta_2)I_{12} \quad (6)$$

We rework these equations to be primarily in terms of κ_1, κ_2, i_{12}, where $\kappa_1 = (I_1 + I_{12})/N$, $\kappa_2 = (I_2 + I_{12})/N$, $i_{12} = I_{12}/N$. As such, each of these terms represent a fraction of the population that is infected. We first convert the constraints to

$$N\kappa_1\beta_1[1 - \kappa_1 - (1-\epsilon)i_2] = \delta_1\kappa_1 \quad (7)$$
$$N\kappa_2\beta_2[1 - \kappa_2 - (1-\epsilon)i_1] = \delta_2\kappa_2 \quad (8)$$
$$\epsilon N(\beta_1\kappa_1 i_2 + \beta_2\kappa_2 i_1) = (\delta_1 + \delta_2)i_{12} \quad (9)$$

where $i_1 = I_1/N$ and $i_2 = I_2/N$.

Manipulating (9) to remove i_1 and i_2, we find

$$\epsilon\kappa_1\kappa_2[\sigma_1\delta_1 + \sigma_2\delta_2] = i_{12}[\delta_1 + \delta_2 + \epsilon\sigma_1\delta_1\kappa_1 + \epsilon\sigma_2\delta_2\kappa_2] \quad (10)$$

Remember, because we are working with a clique the virus strengths are $\sigma_1 = N\beta_1/\delta_1$ and $\sigma_2 = N\beta_2/\delta_2$.

4.2 Results

From these constraints, we look to find a lower bound on ϵ, such that for any less competition there can be coexistence.

THEOREM 1 (EPSILON THRESHOLD THEOREM). *Given a fully connected graph with the $SI_{1|2}S$ model parameters $\sigma_1 \geq \sigma_2$, an equilibrium point for which $\kappa_1, \kappa_2 > 0$ exists if $\epsilon > \epsilon_{\text{critical}}$, where*

$$\epsilon_{\text{critical}} = \begin{cases} \frac{\sigma_1 - \sigma_2}{\sigma_2(\sigma_1 - 1)} & \text{if } \sigma_1 + \sigma_2 \geq 2 \\ \frac{2(1+\sqrt{1-\sigma_1\sigma_2})}{\sigma_1\sigma_2} & \text{if } \sigma_1 + \sigma_2 < 2 \end{cases} \quad (11)$$

PROOF. In Lemma 3 we give the possible fixed point for coexistence. In Lemma 4 we show the constraints for the fixed points to be real, which contribute to the bounds in (11). In Lemmas 5 through 9 we give the proofs for the constraints on the fixed points being positive, and in Lemma 10 we give the proof that the fixed points are less than one. □

Next we describe all of the Lemmas, which contribute to the proof.

LEMMA 2. *If a fourth equilibrium point exists, then it should satisfy the follow equation:*

$$\epsilon(\kappa_2 - \kappa_1) = 1/\sigma_1 - 1/\sigma_2 \quad (12)$$

PROOF. Since we are only looking for non-zero solutions for κ_1 and κ_2, we can eliminate them in (7) and (8).

$$1 - \kappa_1 - (1-\epsilon)i_2 = 1/\sigma_1 \quad (13)$$
$$1 - \kappa_2 - (1-\epsilon)i_1 = 1/\sigma_2 \quad (14)$$

Subtracting, we get the lemma. □

LEMMA 3 (COEXISTENCE LEMMA). *If an equilibrium point exists for which both viruses coexist in the network, $\kappa_1, \kappa_2 > 0$, it will be at:*

$$i_{12} = \epsilon\kappa_1\kappa_2\left[\frac{\sigma_1\delta_1 + \sigma_2\delta_2}{\delta_1 + \delta_2 + \epsilon\sigma_1\delta_1\kappa_1 + \epsilon\sigma_2\delta_2\kappa_2}\right] \quad (15)$$

$$\kappa_1 = \kappa_2 + \frac{1}{\epsilon}\left(\frac{1}{\sigma_2} - \frac{1}{\sigma_1}\right) \quad (16)$$

$$\kappa_2 = \frac{-2\epsilon\sigma_1\sigma_2 + \epsilon^2\sigma_1\sigma_2^2 \pm \epsilon\sqrt{\sigma_1}\sigma_2^{3/2}\sqrt{4-4\epsilon+\epsilon^2\sigma_1\sigma_2}}{2\epsilon^2\sigma_1\sigma_2^2} \quad (17)$$

We will denote the solution to these three equations for fixed-points as i_{12}^*, κ_1^*, and κ_2^* respectively.

PROOF. Equation (15) is a simple rearrangement of equation (10), and equation (16) is a rearrangement of equation (12). Plugging (15) and (16) into (13) allows us to solve for κ_2 resulting in (17).

For κ_2^* (and by extension κ_1^* and i_{12}^*) to be a valid fixed-point, κ_2^* must be: (a) real, (b) $\kappa_2^* \geq 0$, (c) $\kappa_2^* \leq 1$.

LEMMA 4. *In order for fixed-point solution κ_2^*, and by extension κ_1^* and i_{12}^*, to be real valued, either $\sigma_1\sigma_2 > 1$ or*

$$\epsilon < \frac{2(1-\sqrt{1-\sigma_1\sigma_2})}{\sigma_1\sigma_2} \quad \text{or} \quad \epsilon > \frac{2(1+\sqrt{1-\sigma_1\sigma_2})}{\sigma_1\sigma_2}.$$

PROOF. This constraint comes from the square root in equation (17) for κ_2^*. We analyze the quadratic equation $4 - 4\epsilon + \epsilon^2\sigma_1\sigma_2$ (in terms of ϵ) from inside the square root. It is a simple, upward-facing parabola. Solving for the roots of the quadratic equation in terms of ϵ we find

$$\epsilon = \frac{2(1 \pm \sqrt{1-\sigma_1\sigma_2})}{\sigma_1\sigma_2}.$$

For $\sigma_1\sigma_2 > 1$ there is no solution because the equation is positive for all values of ϵ. Thus, if $\sigma_1\sigma_2 > 1$ then κ_2^* must be real valued. For $\sigma_1\sigma_2 < 1$ a portion of the parabola is negative. Therefore, we require that ϵ be in the positive region of the quadratic equation, where ϵ is less than the lower root or greater than the upper root. □

To find when $\kappa_2^* \geq 0$, we consider the cases above for which it is real. As we explained before, we will focus on the lower bound for ϵ.

LEMMA 5. *For strengths $\sigma_1\sigma_2 > 1$, fixed-point κ_2^* is monotonically increasing as a function of ϵ.*

PROOF. Taking the derivative of (17) we get

$$\frac{\pm(-2+\epsilon)\sqrt{\sigma_2} + \sqrt{\sigma_1}\sqrt{4-4\epsilon+\epsilon^2\sigma_1\sigma_2}}{\epsilon^2\sqrt{\sigma_1\sigma_2}\sqrt{4-4\epsilon+\epsilon^2\sigma_1\sigma_2}}.$$

Because $\sigma_1\sigma_2 > 1$, all of the square roots are real valued. The denominator is clearly positive, so to prove that κ_2^* is monotonically increasing, we must show that the numerator is positive. To show that the numerator is always positive we would like to show that

$$\pm(-2+\epsilon)\sqrt{\sigma_2} < \sqrt{\sigma_1}\sqrt{4-4\epsilon+\epsilon^2\sigma_1\sigma_2}$$

or alternatively

$$1 < \frac{\sigma_1}{\sigma_2}\frac{4-4\epsilon+\epsilon^2\sigma_1\sigma_2}{4-4\epsilon+\epsilon^2}.$$

Because $\sigma_1 \geq \sigma_2$ the first term is clearly > 1. For $\sigma_1\sigma_2 > 1$ (and of course $\epsilon > 0$) this is trivially true. □

LEMMA 6. *Fixed-point solution κ_2^-, defined by*

$$\kappa_2^- = \frac{-2\epsilon\sigma_1\sigma_2 + \epsilon^2\sigma_1\sigma_2^2 - \epsilon\sqrt{\sigma_1}\sigma_2^{3/2}\sqrt{4-4\epsilon+\epsilon^2\sigma_1\sigma_2}}{2\epsilon^2\sigma_1\sigma_2^2}, \quad (18)$$

can only be positive when κ_2^+, defined by

$$\kappa_2^+ = \frac{-2\epsilon\sigma_1\sigma_2 + \epsilon^2\sigma_1\sigma_2^2 + \epsilon\sqrt{\sigma_1}\sigma_2^{3/2}\sqrt{4-4\epsilon+\epsilon^2\sigma_1\sigma_2}}{2\epsilon^2\sigma_1\sigma_2^2}, \quad (19)$$

is positive.

PROOF. As a simple case, for $\sigma_1\sigma_2 > 1$, $\kappa_2^- < 0$ and thus invalid for all $\epsilon > 0$. As ϵ approaches 0, it is clear that $\kappa_2^- \to -\infty$, and as $\epsilon \to \infty$, we see that κ_2^- approaches 0. Since from the previous lemma we know that it is monotonically increasing, $\kappa_2^- < 0$ for $\sigma_1\sigma_2 > 1$.

If we do not restrict σ_1 and σ_2, it is still clear that $\kappa_2^- < \kappa_2^+$ for all $\epsilon \geq 0$, since the last term is always positive. We will see later that $\kappa_2^+ < 1$ for all $\epsilon > 0$. Therefore, the range for which κ_2^- is valid is a strict subset of that for which κ_2^+ is valid. □

Because κ_2^- is only valid when κ_2^+ is valid, it has no impact on the phase transition claimed in Theorem 1. As a result, we will focus on κ_2^+ for the remainder of the proof and, with a slight abuse of notation, use κ_2^* to denote κ_2^+.

LEMMA 7. *When strengths $\sigma_1\sigma_2 \geq 1$, the fixed-point for the population infected by virus 2 is positive, $\kappa_2^* > 0$, if and only if*

$$\epsilon \quad > \quad \frac{\sigma_1 - \sigma_2}{\sigma_2(\sigma_1 - 1)}.$$

PROOF. Solving equation (19) for $\kappa_2^* = 0$ produces $\epsilon = \frac{\sigma_1-\sigma_2}{\sigma_2(\sigma_1-1)}$. Because κ_2^* is monotonically increasing in this region ($\sigma_1\sigma_2 > 1$), for all ϵ greater than this solution, $\kappa_2^* > 0$, and for all ϵ less than this solution $\kappa_2^* \leq 0$. □

LEMMA 8. *If virus strengths $\sigma_1 + \sigma_2 < 2$, then the fixed-point for the population infected by virus 2 is positive, $\kappa_2^* > 0$, for*

$$\epsilon > \frac{2(1+\sqrt{1-\sigma_1\sigma_2})}{\sigma_1\sigma_2}.$$

PROOF. For κ_2^* to be positive, the numerator of (19) must be positive. We can reduce this as follows:

$$\begin{aligned}
&-2\epsilon\sigma_1\sigma_2 + \epsilon\sigma_1\sigma_2^2 + \epsilon\sqrt{\sigma_1}\sigma_2^{3/2}\sqrt{4-4\epsilon+\epsilon^2\sigma_1\sigma_2}\\
&= \epsilon\sigma_2(\sqrt{\sigma_1\sigma_2}\sqrt{4-4\epsilon+\epsilon^2\sigma_1\sigma_2} - 2\sigma_1 + \epsilon\sigma_1\sigma_2)\\
&\geq \epsilon\sigma_2(0 - 2\sigma_1 + 2(1+\sqrt{1-\sigma_1\sigma_2}))\\
&= 2\epsilon\sigma_2(-\sigma_1 + 1 + \sqrt{1-\sigma_1\sigma_2})
\end{aligned}$$

For this to be positive we must have $\sqrt{1-\sigma_1\sigma_2} > \sigma_1 - 1$, which is true for $\sigma_1 + \sigma_2 < 2$. □

LEMMA 9. *If virus strengths $\sigma_1 + \sigma_2 \geq 2$ then the fixed-point for the population infected by virus 2 is positive, $\kappa_2^* > 0$, for*

$$\epsilon > \frac{\sigma_1 - \sigma_2}{\sigma_2(\sigma_1 - 1)}.$$

PROOF. Again, for κ_2^* to be positive, the numerator of (19) must be positive. We can reduce this as follows:

$$\begin{aligned}
&-2\epsilon\sigma_1\sigma_2 + \epsilon\sigma_1\sigma_2^2 + \epsilon\sqrt{\sigma_1}\sigma_2^{3/2}\sqrt{4-4\epsilon+\epsilon^2\sigma_1\sigma_2}\\
&= \epsilon\sigma_2(\sqrt{\sigma_1\sigma_2}\sqrt{4-4\epsilon+\epsilon^2\sigma_1\sigma_2} - 2\sigma_1 + \epsilon\sigma_1\sigma_2)\\
&\geq \epsilon\sigma_2\left(\sqrt{\sigma_1\sigma_2}\sqrt{\frac{\sigma_1(-2+\sigma_1+\sigma_2)^2}{\sigma_2(-1+\sigma_1)^2}} - 2\sigma_1 + \sigma_1\sigma_2\left(\frac{\sigma_1-\sigma_2}{\sigma_2(1-\sigma_1)}\right)\right)\\
&= \epsilon\sigma_1\sigma_2\left(\frac{2-\sigma_1-\sigma_2}{1-\sigma_1} - 2 + \frac{\sigma_1-\sigma_2}{1-\sigma_1}\right) = 0
\end{aligned}$$

□

LEMMA 10. *The fixed-point for the population infected by virus 2 is valid, $\kappa_2^* \leq 1$, for $\sigma_1 \geq \sigma_2$ and $\epsilon \geq 0$.*

PROOF. The constraint $\kappa_2^* \leq 1$ is equivalent to

$$-2\epsilon\sigma_1\sigma_2 - \epsilon^2\sigma_1\sigma_2^2 + \epsilon\sqrt{\sigma_1}\sigma_2^{3/2}\sqrt{4-4\epsilon+\epsilon^2\sigma_1\sigma_2} < 0.$$

This can be simplified as follows:

$$\sqrt{\sigma_1\sigma_2}\sqrt{4-4\epsilon+\epsilon^2\sigma_1\sigma_2} < 2\sigma_1 + \epsilon\sigma_1\sigma_2 \quad (20)$$

$$\sigma_1\sigma_2(4-4\epsilon+\epsilon^2\sigma_1\sigma_2) < 4\sigma_1^2 + \epsilon^2\sigma_1^2\sigma_2^2 + 4\epsilon\sigma_1^2\sigma_2 \quad (21)$$

$$\sigma_1\sigma_2 - \epsilon\sigma_1\sigma_2 < \sigma_1^2 + \sigma_1^2\sigma_2 \quad (22)$$

$$\frac{\sigma_2}{\sigma_1}\frac{1-\epsilon}{1+\epsilon\sigma_2} < 1 \quad (23)$$

The simplification to (23) makes it clear that the lemma is true for $\sigma_1 \geq \sigma_2 > 0$. □

As such, for any interaction factor $\epsilon > \epsilon_{\text{critical}}$, we have proved that κ_1^* and κ_2^* are valid equilibrium points for which the population infected by each virus $\kappa_1, \kappa_2 > 0$. **QED**

5. EXPERIMENTS

We demonstrate our result using (a) simulation experiments and (b) case studies using real data in this section.

5.1 Setup

Without loss of generality, in our experiments we assumed that the first virus is the stronger virus. We primarily focus on the case where $\sigma_1 > \sigma_2 > 1$. For our simulations we use $\sigma_1 = 6$ and $\sigma_2 = 4$.

We run a simulation on a fully-connected clique of 1000 nodes. We vary ϵ around our expected threshold and for each value of ϵ perform 10 runs over 4000 time steps. On each run we begin by infecting 30 nodes at random with each virus.

We analyze the results in two ways. First, we create a *steady-state plot* of mean values and standard deviations for κ_1, κ_2, and i_{12} at steady-state over a range of values for ϵ. Over the results of the simulation we draw the behavior predicted by our results. Second, for one $\epsilon > \epsilon_{\text{critical}}$ we track each virus's development over time with a *time-plot.* The time-plot takes the average number of nodes infected (κ_1, κ_2, and i_{12}) at each time step and plots this against time. Although the simulations were run for 4000 time steps, the plots are truncated to give more detail to the initial fluctuations of the virus counts.

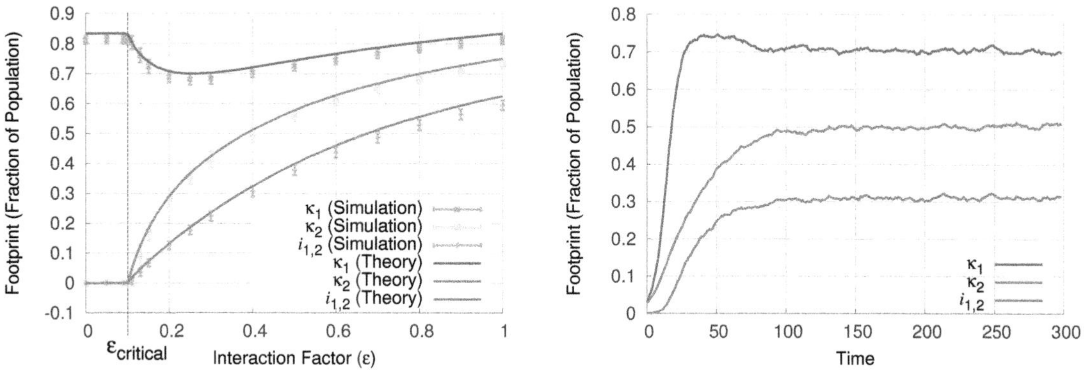

(a) $\sigma_1 = 6$, $\sigma_2 = 4$ (b) $\epsilon = 0.4 > \epsilon_{\text{critical}} = 1$, $\sigma_1 = 6$, $\sigma_2 = 4$

Figure 3: Coexistence is possible: Results from simulations on clique of size 1000 with theoretical fixed points overlayed. (a) shows the steady-state population values, κ_1, κ_2, and i_{12}, for each value of ϵ, with the theoretical $\epsilon_{\text{critical}}$ marked. (b) shows the development of the two viruses over time for $\epsilon > \epsilon_{\text{critical}}$. Notice that both viruses survive as expected.

5.2 Simulation Results

Figure 3 displays our results. In short, the plots agree exactly with our result, as expected. Figure 3(a) shows the steady-state plot for the two viruses, and the theoretical predictions closely match the simulation results. Similarly, the viruses' growth as shown in the time-plot in Figure 3(b) matches what is expected.

For the steady-state plot, we expect the steady-state value to be one of the other fixed points where at least one virus dies out for $\epsilon \leq \epsilon_{\text{critical}}$ and then a co-existence for $\epsilon > \epsilon_{\text{critical}}$. In Figure 3(a) we see for $\sigma_1 > \sigma_2 > 1$ and $\epsilon = 0$, winner takes all, as was proven in [30]. However, for $\epsilon > \epsilon_{\text{critical}}$ we see a coexistence between the viruses as expected; this is true even when the viruses are competing ($\epsilon < 1$). For $\epsilon = 0.4 > \epsilon_{\text{critical}}$ we have the time-plot, Figure 3(b), showing the growth of both viruses to steady-state from a small infection in the system.

5.3 Case-Studies using Real Data

We collected historical data for 'web-search interest' for various competing products from the Google-Insights website[2], which aims to "provide insights into broad search patterns." This allows us to use the data as a proxy for sales/interest for each product. We used the following pairs of rival products:

1. Hulu[3] and Blockbuster[4]: Although not direct competitors, both offer video entertainment services, though under very different models.
2. Firefox[5] and Google Chrome[6]: Two rival web browsers.

We consider both pairs of products to be examples of cases where there is partial mutual immunity; people can use both products, but the use of one we expect would detract from the use of the other. While our model does not describe the situations perfectly, we believe it is a good approximation.

[2] `www.google.com/insights/search/`
[3] `www.hulu.com`
[4] `www.blockbuster.com`
[5] `www.mozilla.org/en-US/firefox/new/`
[6] `www.google.com/chrome`

In Figure 4 we show plots of the web-interest vs. time for both pairs of products, along with our model fitted to the data[7]. In Figure 4(a), we used a virus interaction factor of $\epsilon = 0.7$ (along with virus parameters $\delta_{\text{Hulu}} = 0.04$, $\beta_{\text{Hulu}} = 0.0007$, $\delta_{\text{Blockbuster}} = 0.05$, $\beta_{\text{Blockbuster}} = 0.00045$). In Figure 4(b), we used a virus interaction factor of $\epsilon = 0.6$ (along with virus parameters $\delta_{\text{Firefox}} = 0.01$, $\beta_{\text{Firefox}} = 0.000095$, $\delta_{\text{Chrome}} = 0.01$, $\beta_{\text{Chrome}} = 0.00015$). In Figure 4(c) we use the same model as (b) but let the model continue to see the projected steady state behavior. We note that the plots begin when Hulu and Chrome are first introduced and with Blockbuster and Firefox at a previous steady-state behavior. In each of these fittings we see that our model fits the data well. The fact that the model fits the data well demonstrates the suitability of our $SI_{1|2}S$ model.

6. DISCUSSION

6.1 A general upper bound

CONJECTURE 1 (EPSILON THRESHOLD UPPER BOUND). *Given an arbitrary graph with the $SI_{1|2}S$ model parameters $\sigma_1 \geq \sigma_2 \geq 1$, an equilibrium point for which both virus 1 and virus 2 survive exists if $\epsilon > \epsilon_{\text{critical}}$, where*

$$\epsilon_{\text{critical}} \leq \frac{1}{\sigma_2} \tag{24}$$

Justification: Since $\sigma_1 \geq \sigma_2 \geq 1$ and $0 < \epsilon < 1$, we know that both virus 1 and virus 2 would be strong enough to survive independently but there is some competition between them. Because of the competition, as virus 1 spreads to more nodes, virus 2's attack rate on average decreases and thus its strength decreases. Therefore, if we overestimate the strength or number of people with virus 1, this only makes it more difficult for virus 2 survive and thus decreases the maximum amount of competition virus 2 can handle, increasing $\epsilon_{\text{critical}}$. To simplify the problem, we assume that *every person* is infected with virus 1 (as if virus 1 was infinitely strong). In this case, a node can only be in state I_1

[7] Fitted with `www.alexbeutel.com/jsplot/kdd2012.html`

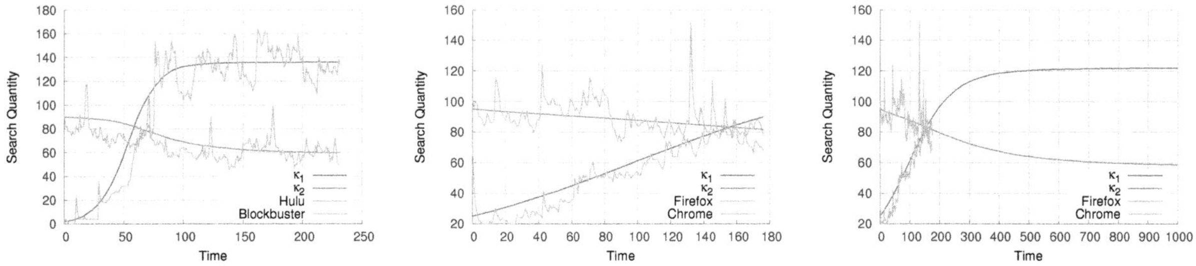

(a) Hulu and Blockbuster (b) Firefox and Chrome (c) Firefox and Chrome (Prediction)

Figure 4: Real web-search interest vs. time plots for pairs of competitors with our model fitted to it. (c) Predicts steady state values based on our model. Data acquired from Google Trends.

or $I_{1,2}$, and the probability of a node with virus 2 infecting a neighbor is always $\epsilon\beta_2$. This is now equivalent to a one virus model where the strength of virus 2 is $\sigma_2' = \epsilon\sigma_2$. Therefore, as shown in previous research [10, 13, 31], if $\sigma_2' > 1$ then virus 2 will survive. In this case, $\epsilon_{\text{critical}} = \frac{1}{\sigma_2}$. However, because this is a relaxation of the original problem, we know that this is an upper bound and in fact $\epsilon_{\text{critical}} \leq \frac{1}{\sigma_2}$.

6.2 Case-Study: Qualitative Analysis

We also consider the example of educational ideas, and specifically sex education, as a virus. Sociology literature analyzing the success of sex education programs notes the impact of network effects and social structure on sex education success [7]. We match education policy to our $SI_{1|2}S$ model and analyze the implications.

Policy 1: Abstinence-Only Education Abstinence-only education teaches abstinence until marriage as the only way to live a healthy life, with students often taking an abstinence pledge. Under our model, virus 1 is believing in abstinence (through education or pledge) and virus 2 is sexual activity. Therefore, those who are in I_1 have taken a pledge of abstinence, those who are in I_2 are sexually active, and those people who are in S do not believe in abstinence but are not sexually active either. It is obviously impossible to both be following an abstinence pledge and to be sexually active so nobody can be in state $I_{1,2}$. Equivalently in this case there is full mutual immunity or $\epsilon = 0$.

Model 1 Predictions and Results Based on this fit, because $\epsilon = 0$, our model predicts 'winner takes all:' the weaker virus dies out and the stronger virus survives. Sociology research [7], studying over 11,000 people over 7 years, notes that of the 2399 people claiming to have taken an abstinence pledge, 1622 (67%) over time forgot. This suggests that $\sigma_{\text{Abstinence}} < \sigma_{\text{Sexual Activity}}$, and as a result, in the long run sexual activity will win over abstinence.

Policy 2: Comprehensive Sex Education Comprehensive sex education teaches numerous methods to have a safe, healthy sex life, discussing both contraception and abstinence. Matching this to our model, virus 1 is being educated in safe-sex practices and valuing their importance and virus 2 is sexual activity. Therefore, those who are in I_1 have been educated about safe-sex practices and believe they are important but are not sexually active, those in I_2 are sexually active but do not practice safe sex, those in $I_{1,2}$ practice safe-sex, and those in S are neither educated on safe-sex practices nor sexually active. Here we expect little to no competition between the two viruses and thus have an ϵ value close to, if not equal to, 1.

Model 2 Predictions and Results Because ϵ is close to 1, we expect that $\epsilon > \epsilon_{\text{critical}}$. As a result, it is possible for there to be coexistence of the two viruses, such that there can be a steady-state in which people are sexually active and practice safe-sex. This appears to match sociology literature claiming that those who initially use condoms will keep using condoms [7].

In summary, our model qualitatively agrees with sociology research and offers a plausible explanation for the results of the study. Additionally, these two cases demonstrate the value of a phase transition. In the first case, the model suggests winner takes all and the ineffectiveness of abstinence-only education. On the contrary, for policy 2, the model predicts coexistence, which agrees with the findings, and is better for society.

6.3 Subtle Points

There are several subtle points, that we deferred until now, for clarity of exposition. Specifically, here we discuss the following issues:

6.3.1 What does it mean for $\epsilon > 1$?

As before, the virus 2 transmission rate for a virus infected with virus 1 becomes $\epsilon\beta_2$ and the virus 1 transmission rate for a virus infected with virus 2 becomes $\epsilon\beta_1$. However, because $\epsilon > 1$ the transmission rate for each virus increases for neighbors that are already infected. We consider this to be a form of cooperation between the viruses (products, ideas, etc.).

This pattern of cooperation between products is common in product ecosystems. An example of this is that people who have an iPod are more likely to buy music and videos through Apple's iTunes. Making use of such cooperation can be seen in 'freebie marketing' or the 'razor and blades business model,' in which the company producing razor blades sells the razors at an artificially low price creating a market for the blades. This method of tightly integrating products is common in a variety of industries.

6.3.2 What happens if σ_2 or $\sigma_1 \leq 1$?

Because $\sigma_1 \geq \sigma_2$ there are two cases we can analyze. The first is when $\sigma_1 \geq 1 > \sigma_2$, in which the second virus is too weak to survive on its own. We will refer to this as the "piggyback setting," because virus 2 can only survive with the help of the first. The second condition is when $1 > \sigma_1 \geq \sigma_2$, where both viruses are independently too weak to survive. We will refer to this as the "teamwork setting," because only through cooperation can both viruses survive.

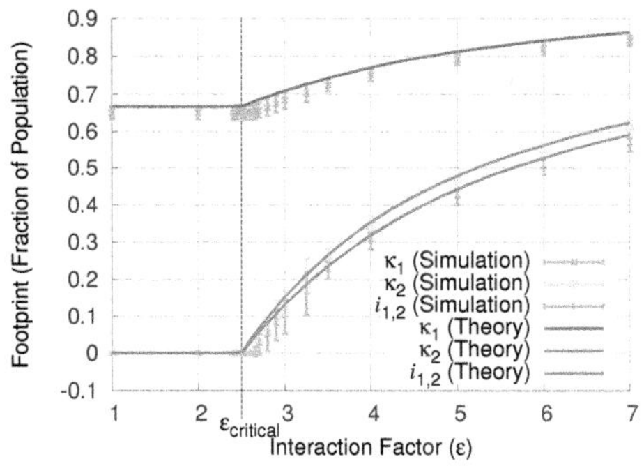

(a) $\sigma_1 = 3$, $\sigma_2 = 0.5$

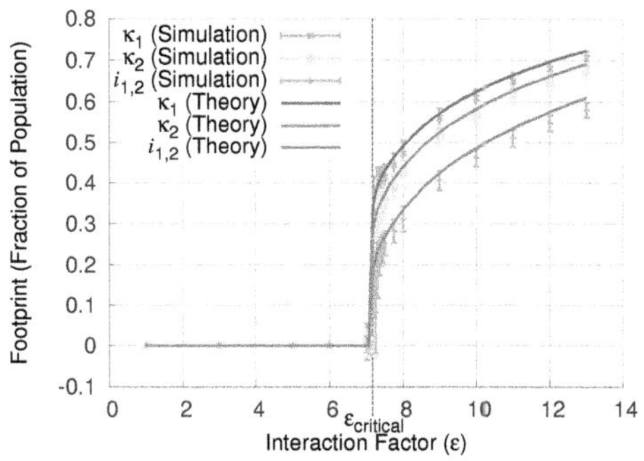

(b) $\sigma_1 = 0.8$, $\sigma_2 = 0.6$

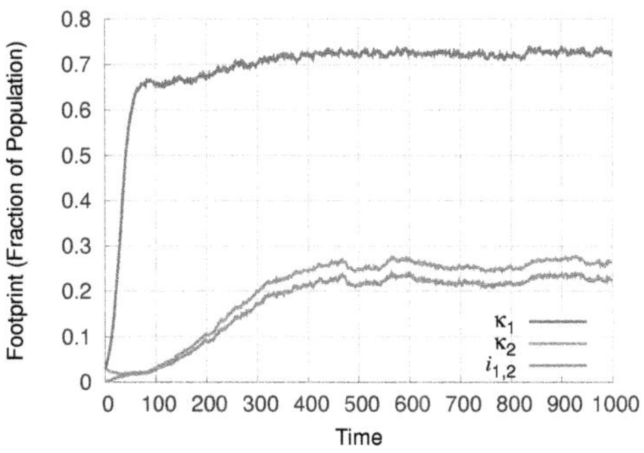

(c) $\epsilon = 3.5$, $\sigma_1 = 3$, $\sigma_2 = 0.5$

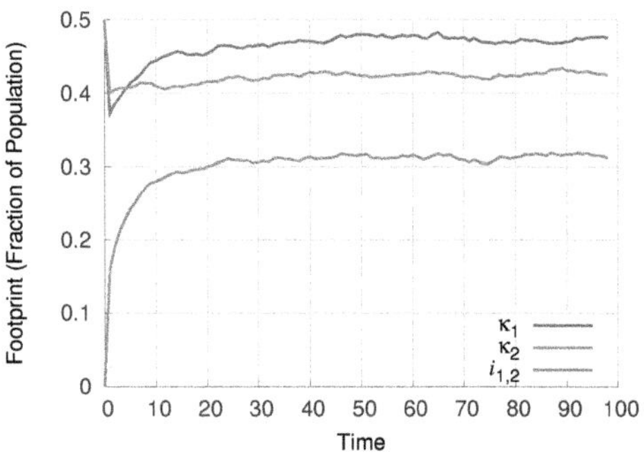

(d) $\epsilon = 8$, $\sigma_1 = 0.8$, $\sigma_2 = 0.6$

Figure 5: With enough collaboration, even weak viruses can survive. Results from simulations on population of $N = 1000$ with theoretical values overlayed, and $1 > \sigma_2$. The first column, (a) and (c), is the "piggyback" case where just virus 2 is too weak to survive. The second column, (b) and (d), is the "teamwork" case where neither virus is on its own strong enough to survive. The top row gives the steady-state plots, showing the steady-state footprint vs. the interaction factor ϵ. The second row gives the time-plots, showing the infection footprint developing over time.

In each of these cases, Theorem 1 still holds - plugging in σ_1 and σ_2 we find an $\epsilon_{\text{critical}}$ for which a fixed point in which $\kappa_1, \kappa_2 > 0$ exists. This suggests that even if both viruses are independently too weak to survive on their own, with enough cooperation they can.

To test our theorem, we ran similar simulations where either one or both viruses were too weak to independently survive. In Figure 5(a) we show the steady-state plot for the piggyback case of $\sigma_1 > 1 > \sigma_2$. As expected, for $\epsilon = 1$ when the viruses are independent, virus 1 survives but virus 2 is not strong enough and dies out. For a sufficient amount of cooperation, $\epsilon > \epsilon_{\text{critical}}$, we find that virus 2 can survive as well. We see in Figure 5(c), the corresponding time-plot where $\epsilon = 3.5 > \epsilon_{\text{critical}}$, that once virus 1 grows, virus 2 is able to survive as well.

We also simulated the teamwork case, where neither virus is independently strong enough to survive, $1 > \sigma_1 \geq \sigma_2$. In Figure 5(b) we show the steady-state plot for this case. Again, the theoretical result and predicted phase-transition match the simulation results. For $\epsilon = 1$, the two viruses are independent and, since they cannot survive on their own, die out. In this case, the phase transition is based on the second part of Theorem 1 where $\sigma_1 + \sigma_2 < 2$, and as such the bound is a result on the restriction of κ_2 being real. As such, at $\epsilon_{\text{critical}}$ both $\kappa_1, \kappa_2 > 0$ rather than equal to 0. We see here at the threshold a large amount of uncertainty in the simulation but as we move away from the threshold the simulation follows this new fixed point. Interestingly, we must initially infect a large portion of the graph for the system to go to this fixed point, and not die out. For $\epsilon = 7.75 > \epsilon_{\text{critical}}$, Figure 5(d) shows the time-plot, demonstrating that both viruses quickly reach steady-state with a high amount of overlap.

7. CONCLUSIONS

We defined and studied the problem of partial competition, where two viruses/products provide partial immunity against each other.

The main contributions of our work are as follows:

1. *Problem Definition*: The problem is novel, in the data mining and web mining communities, and even in the epidemiology literature [3, 17].
2. *Threshold Result and Proof*: We showed that there is a phase transition: 'winner takes all,' until the competition level drops below a critical value. Above this critical value we find a closed-form steady-state solution with coexistence.
3. *Experiments and Case-studies*: We showed results from real settings (like browsers - Firefox vs Google Chrome), which agree with our model.

Acknowledgments: This material is based upon work supported by the Army Research Laboratory under Cooperative Agreement No. W911NF-09-2-0053, the National Science Foundation under Grant No. IIS-1017415, the National Institute of General

Medical Sciences under MIDAS grant 1U54GM088491-0109, and a National Science Foundation Graduate Research Fellowship.

8. REFERENCES

[1] A. Ackleh and L. Allen. Competitive exclusion in sis and sir epidemic models with total cross immunity and density-dependent host mortality. *Discrete and Continuous Dynamical Systems-Series B*, 5, 2005.

[2] R. M. Anderson and R. M. May. Coevolution of hosts and parasites. *Parasitology*, 85, 1982.

[3] R. M. Anderson and R. M. May. *Infectious Diseases of Humans.* Oxford University Press, 1991.

[4] N. Bailey. *The Mathematical Theory of Infectious Diseases and its Applications.* Griffin, London, 1975.

[5] S. Bharathi, D. Kempe, and M. Salek. Competitive influence maximization in social networks. *WINE*, 2007.

[6] S. Bikhchandani, D. Hirshleifer, and I. Welch. A theory of fads, fashion, custom, and cultural change in informational cascades. *Journal of Political Economy*, 100(5):992–1026, October 1992.

[7] H. Brückner and P. Bearman. After the promise: the std consequences of adolescent virginity pledges. *Journal of Adolescent Health*, 2005.

[8] C. Castillo-Chavez, W. Huang, and J. Li. Competitive exclusion in gonorrhea models and other sexually transmitted diseases. *SIAM J. Appl. Math*, 56, 1996.

[9] C. Castillo-Chavez, W. Huang, and J. Li. Competitive exclusion and coexistence of multiple strains in an sis std model. *SIAM J. Appl. Math*, 59, 1999.

[10] D. Chakrabarti, Y. Wang, C. Wang, J. Leskovec, and C. Faloutsos. Epidemic thresholds in real networks. *ACM TISSEC*, 10(4), 2008.

[11] C. Colijn, T. Cohen, C. Fraser, W. Hanage, E. Goldstein, N. Givon-Lavi, R. Dagan, and M. Lipsitch. What is the mechanism for persistent coexistence of drug-susceptible and drug-resistant strains of streptococcus pneumoniae? *Journal of The Royal Society Interface*, 7(47):905–919, 2010.

[12] P. Domingos and M. Richardson. Mining the network value of customers. In *KDD '01: Proceedings of the seventh ACM SIGKDD international conference on Knowledge discovery and data mining*, pages 57–66, New York, NY, USA, 2001. ACM Press.

[13] A. Ganesh, L. Massoulie, and D. Towsley. The effect of network topology in spread of epidemics. *IEEE INFOCOM*, 2005.

[14] J. Goldenberg, B. Libai, and E. Muller. Talk of the network: A complex systems look at the underlying process of word-of-mouth. *Marketing Letters*, 2001.

[15] M. Granovetter. Threshold models of collective behavior. *Am. Journal of Sociology*, 83(6):1420–1443, 1978.

[16] D. Gruhl, R. Guha, D. Liben-Nowell, and A. Tomkins. Information diffusion through blogspace. In *WWW '04*, 2004.

[17] H. W. Hethcote. The mathematics of infectious diseases. *SIAM Review*, 42:599–653, 2000.

[18] D. Kempe, J. Kleinberg, and E. Tardos. Maximizing the spread of influence through a social network. In *KDD '03*, 2003.

[19] J. O. Kephart and S. R. White. Measuring and modeling computer virus prevalence. *IEEE Computer Society Symposium on Research in Security and Privacy*, 1993.

[20] J. Kosta, Y. A. Oswald, and R. Wattenhofer. Word of mouth: Rumor dissemination in social networks. *15 Intl. Coll. on Struct. Inform. and Comm. Complexity SIROCO*, 2008.

[21] R. Kumar, J. Novak, P. Raghavan, and A. Tomkins. On the bursty evolution of blogspace. In *WWW '03: Proceedings of the 12th international conference on World Wide Web*, pages 568–576, New York, NY, USA, 2003. ACM Press.

[22] T. Lappas, E. Terzi, D. Gunopulos, and H. Mannila. Finding effectors in social networks. In *KDD*, pages 1059–1068, 2010.

[23] J. Leskovec, L. A. Adamic, and B. A. Huberman. The dynamics of viral marketing. In *EC*, 2006.

[24] J. Leskovec, M. McGlohon, C. Faloutsos, N. Glance, and M. Hurst. Cascading behavior in large blog graphs: Patterns and a model. In *Society of Applied and Industrial Mathematics: Data Mining*, 2007.

[25] M. Lipsitch, C. Colijn, T. Cohen, W. P. Hanage, and C. Fraser. No coexistence for free: Neutral null models for multistrain pathogens. *Epidemics*, 1(1):2 – 13, 2009.

[26] M. Lipsitch, S. Siller, and M. A. Nowak. The evolution of virulence in pathogens with vertical and horizontal transmission. *Evolution*, 50, 1996.

[27] A. G. McKendrick. Applications of mathematics to medical problems. In *Proceedings of Edin. Math. Society*, volume 14, pages 98–130, 1926.

[28] R. Pastor-Santorras and A. Vespignani. Epidemic spreading in scale-free networks. *Physical Review Letters 86*, 14, 2001.

[29] N. Pathak, A. Banerjee, and J. Srivastava. A generalized linear threshold model for multiple cascades. *ICDM*, 2010.

[30] B. A. Prakash, A. Beutel, R. Rosenfeld, and C. Faloutsos. Winner takes all: Competiting viruses or ideas on fair-play networks. *WWW*, 2012.

[31] B. A. Prakash, D. Chakrabarti, M. Faloutsos, N. Valler, and C. Faloutsos. Threshold conditions for arbitrary cascade models on arbitrary networks. In *ICDM*, 2011.

[32] B. A. Prakash, H. Tong, N. Valler, M. Faloutsos, and C. Faloutsos. Virus propagation on time-varying networks: Theory and immunization algorithms. *ECML-PKDD*, 2010.

[33] M. Richardson and P. Domingos. Mining knowledge-sharing sites for viral marketing, 2002.

[34] D. Shah and T. Zaman. Rumors in a network: Who's the culprit? *IEEE Transactions on Information Theory*, 57(8):5163–5181, 2011.

[35] M. H. H. Stevens. *A Primer of Ecology with R.* Springer Press, 2009.

[36] H. Tong, B. A. Prakash, C. E. Tsourakakis, T. Eliassi-Rad, C. Faloutsos, and D. H. Chau. On the vulnerability of large graphs. In *ICDM*, 2010.

Aggregating Web Offers to Determine Product Prices

Rakesh Agrawal
Microsoft Research, Search Labs
rakesh.agrawal@microsoft.com

Samuel Ieong
Microsoft Research, Search Labs
samuel.ieong@microsoft.com

ABSTRACT

Historical prices are important information that can help consumers decide whether the time is right to buy a product. They provide both a context to the users, and facilitate the use of prediction algorithms for forecasting future prices. To produce a representative price history, one needs to consider all offers for the product. However, matching offers to a product is a challenging problem, and mismatches could lead to glaring errors in price history. We propose a principled approach to filter out erroneous matches based on a probabilistic model of prices. We give an efficient algorithm for performing inference that takes advantage of the structure of the problem. We evaluate our results empirically using merchant offers collected from a search engine, and measure the proximity of the price history generated by our approach to the true price history. Our method outperforms alternatives based on robust statistics both in tracking the true price levels and the true price trends.

Categories and Subject Descriptors

H.2.8 [**Database Management**]: Database Applications—*Data Mining*; J.4 [**Social and Behavioral Sciences**]: Economics

General Terms

Algorithms, Experimentation

Keywords

Data Aggregation, Time Series Analysis

1. INTRODUCTION

The Internet has become one of the most important sources of information for consumers researching for their next purchase. While there are many e-commerce websites dedicated to helping consumers decide what product to buy and where to buy it, few sites exist to help with the question of *when* to buy the product. In [1, 2], the authors proposed a system that addresses this need by providing users with product price history and making recommendations of buy or wait depending on price forecasts and consumer preferences. In their experiments, product prices are obtained through a data vendor. In this paper we investigate the question of how to aggregate web offers to determine representative product prices, thus circumventing the explicit dependence on data vendors.

If the set of all offers correctly matched to the product were given as input, determining the product prices would have been straight-forward: one can simply take the average of the prices (or the minimum, depending on the application). Unfortunately, matching offers to products is known to be a difficult problem, and despite much work in the area (reviewed further in Section 2), it is inevitable that a matching algorithm will make mistakes. We are thus interested in the following question:

> Given a set of offers matched to a product, how do we determine a representative price history for the product, *allowing for some of the matches to be possibly incorrect.*

Note that to produce a good and representative price history, it is not necessary (although it would be sufficient) for an algorithm to identify all of the incorrect matches. For example, if we are interested in the average product price, an incorrectly matched offer with a price close to the average will be mostly harmless. Errors are introduced when we fail to identify incorrect matches with prices significantly different than the average (or in the case of minimum, significantly lower than the true minimum).

As the main challenge in aggregating web offers is due to incorrect offers with prices that are outliers, could the problem be solved using robust statistics [12]? Focusing on determining the average price, for example, could we replace the simple average of product prices by the trimmed mean, where the top and bottom $x\%$ of the data points are discarded before the average is computed, or by the median, often considered to be robust to outliers? It turns out that these solutions are inadequate for two reasons.

First, errors made by matching algorithms are typically not random. A common form of error is confusing one product with another. For example, confusing two models of TVs made by the same manufacturer, or confusing the accessories of a product with the product itself. This form of errors leads to entire sets of offers being (mis)matched to the same product. Another common form of error is due to

KDD'12, August 12–16, 2012, Beijing, China.

products that are configurable. For example, a digital SLR camera may be packaged together with different lenses. The different configurations may be sold at very different prices. Under both form of errors, trimmed mean will remove some offers from both the most and the least expensive sets, but the resulting price will likely remain a mixture of multiple set of offers, and the final price is not representative of a single product. The median will select an offer from one particular set of offers, but as the composition of offers changes over time, it may select an offer from a different set at in the future, leading to inconsistencies and creating discontinuity in the price history when none is present.

Second, a direct application of robust statistics fails to take advantage of the sequential nature of the data. Using all the matched offers across time can help in two ways. First, determining whether an offer is correctly matched or not at an isolated time point is difficult; a valid price can easily be confused with an outlier. By taking into account the entire price history of an offer, we improve our ability to decide whether the offer itself is an outlier. Also, in trying to disambiguate between multiple clusters of prices (with similar number of offers), we can use the historical prices in deciding which cluster is most likely to be correct.

To address these shortcomings, we propose to model offer prices by a generative process motivated by linear Gaussian processes [21]. We model the true product prices as unobserved latent variables that follow some linear dynamics. We associate each offer with a Bernoulli variable that determines whether the offer is correct for this product. If it is correct, the offer prices will be drawn according to a Gaussian distribution with a mean equal to the underlying product prices (and variance to be learned, as different offers exhibit different price volatilities); otherwise the offer prices will be sampled from a background distribution. This model allows us to take advantage of the sequential nature of the data, and by explicitly modeling whether an offer is correctly matched, the solution is sensitive to the type of errors typically made by matching algorithms described above. To ensure efficiency of our learning algorithm, we design an inference algorithm that takes advantage of an independence assumption and allows us to achieve a quadratic speed-up over standard Kalman filter. The technique may be of independent interest.

The rest of the paper is organized as follows. We review related work in offer matching, Kalman filters, and deciding when to buy in Section 2. We then present a probabilistic model of offer prices in Section 3. We consider how to learn the model parameters in Section 4. To speed-up the learning algorithm, we introduce a technique that makes use of the independence assumptions in the model in Section 5. We evaluate the performance of algorithm using merchant offers collected from a search engine over six months in Section 6. We conclude with our main findings and directions for future research in Section 7.

2. RELATED WORK

Matching offers to products is a central problem in ecommerce [16]. Offers for products are often partly structured (including URLs, prices, and sometimes Universal Product Codes (UPCs)) and partly unstructured (offer titles and textual descriptions). There has been much work in the database and data mining communities on matching structured records to other structured records, including record linkage [8, 19, 20, 25], entity resolution [3, 23], and duplicate detection [7, 22]. There has also been some work on matching unstructured text to structured records that uses techniques based on natural language processing [18], segmentation [16, 17], and clustering [4]. Our work builds on these past works and assumes that an initial matching of offers to products has been performed, and takes the output and creates representative product prices for the products. As part of the process, we need to identify incorrect matches where the prices are significantly different than others. While prices can be used as part of the matching process, to our knowledge, there has been no work that uses the sequentiality of the prices in determining the correctness of a match. Our work complements the existing work and can be used to handle matching scenarios where some attribute values of a record are slowly changing over time.

The main modeling technique in this paper is by modeling the offer prices as observations generated from a linear dynamical system (also known as linear Gaussian processes). A good summary of this research area from the machine learning perspective is given in [21]. The study of linear dynamical dates back to early work in signal processing, with the Kalman filter being one of the seminal work in the area [14]. Learning the parameters to a linear dynamical system, also known as system identification, has also been well studied and a review is given in [9]. Many extensions to Kalman filters have been proposed, for example, the extended Kalman Filter [26] and particle filters [11, 13, 15]. While these work relax various assumptions on the linearity of the process and provide efficient algorithms for learning, their models do not consider the possibility of erroneous observations.

In our work, we augment the classical linear dynamical model by allowing for observations to be possibly incorrect. This is related to the robust Kalman filter [27] and Kalman filter with intermittent observations [24]. For the latter work, using a cutoff criteria, one can treat a single outlier as a missing observation. However, in both lines of works, the basic modeling units are individual data points, hence the learned model will not take into account the entire offer (consisting of all offer prices) in deciding whether an observation is an outlier. Closer in spirit to our work is the switching state-space model proposed in [10]. One can view the background prices in our model as a separate state-space model, and that the switching variable of [10] controls whether a set of observations is generated by the background prices or the product prices. However, the learned model will instead group the correct and incorrect observations by time; we are interested in grouping them by offer. As a final note, the technique proposed in Section 5 to speed up the computation of the Kalman Filter under independent observation assumptions is novel to our knowledge, and could be of independent interest.

There has been recent work that investigates the question of helping users to decide when to buy a product [1, 2]. The present study extends this line of work and considers how to obtain representative product prices automatically by aggregating web offers. The history can then be presented to users in response to product queries, be fed as input to forecasting algorithms.

3. MODEL

We now present a generative model of offer prices motivated by linear Gaussian processes. Informally, the model

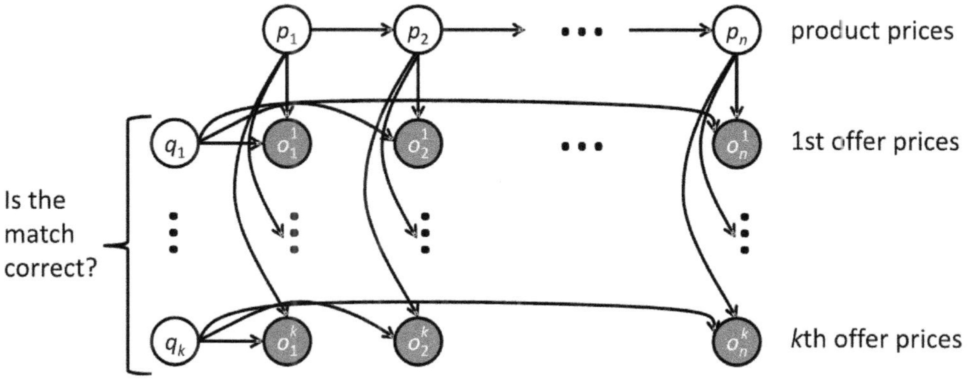

Figure 1: Graphical representation of the generative model of offer prices. The shaded nodes are the observations, which include all of the offer prices $\mathbf{o}^1, \mathbf{o}^2, \ldots, \mathbf{o}^k$. The unshaded nodes are latent variables in the model, which include the product prices p and offer status q. The parameters of the model, not shown here to reduce clutter, are learned to maximize likelihood of the observations.

postulates that there is a set of true but unobserved prices for the product, one for each time step, and that the prices evolve according to some yet-to-be-learned linear dynamics. A set of offers are purportedly matched to the product. An offer is either correctly matched, in which case its prices are drawn according to a distribution parameterized by the product prices, or incorrectly matched, in which case its prices are drawn according to some background price distribution. Our goal is to learn the the underlying prices and the correctness of the matching treating the offer prices as observations.

Formally, we consider a discrete-time generative model as illustrated in Figure 1. Let the true but *unobserved* product prices be denoted $\mathbf{p} = \{p_1, p_2, \ldots, p_n\}$. The prices are generated by a linear Gaussian process, determined by four parameters: μ_0, σ_0^2, α, and σ_α^2, where

$$p_1 \sim N(\mu_0, \sigma_0^2)$$
$$p_t \sim N(\alpha p_{t-1}, \sigma_\alpha^2) \qquad \text{for } 1 < t \leq n$$

and $N(\mu, \sigma^2)$ denotes a Gaussian distribution with mean μ and variance σ^2.

Let the number of offers matched to the product be k, which may vary from product to product. For the i-th offer, its prices $\mathbf{o}^i = \{o_1^i, o_2^i, \ldots, o_n^i\}$ are generated as follows. First, an *unobserved* Bernoulli variable q_i, which we call the *offer status*, is drawn according to parameter π_i. If q_i equals 1, the offer is correctly matched, and the *observed* offer price o_t^i at time t is drawn according to a Gaussian distribution with mean p_t and variance σ_i^2, which we call the *observation variance* of offer i. On the other hand, if q_i equals 0, the offer is incorrectly matched, and the *observed* offer price o_t^i at time t is drawn according to a Gaussian distribution with mean μ_b and variance σ_b^2 that corresponds to some background distribution of prices. We treat this background distribution as exogenously given, and do not learn them in the model as this distribution is estimated using all offers matched to the products of a given category.

Summing up, for each offer i,

$$q_i \sim \text{Bernoulli}(\pi_i)$$
$$o_t^i \sim \begin{cases} N(p_t, \sigma_i^2) & \text{if } q_i = 1 \\ N(\mu_b, \sigma_b^2) & \text{otherwise} \end{cases} \qquad \text{for } 1 \leq t \leq n \quad .$$

Under this model, the probability of a set of observed prices $\mathbf{O} = \{\mathbf{o}^1, \mathbf{o}^2, \ldots, \mathbf{o}^k\}$ can be expressed as a function of the parameters $\Theta = (\mu_0, \sigma_0^2, \alpha, \sigma_\alpha^2, \{\pi_i\}_{i=1}^k \{\sigma_i^2\}_{i=1}^k)$ and background mean and variance μ_b and σ_b^2 by summing out the latent variables, namely,

$$P(\mathbf{O}; \Theta) = \int \sum_{\mathbf{q} \in \{0,1\}^k} P(\mathbf{O}, \mathbf{p}, \mathbf{q}; \Theta) d\mathbf{p}$$

where

$$P(\mathbf{O}, \mathbf{p}, \mathbf{q}; \Theta) = P(p_1; \mu_0, \sigma_0^2) \prod_{t=2}^{n} P(p_t | p_{t-1}; \alpha, \sigma_\alpha^2)$$
$$\prod_{i=1}^{k} \Bigg(\Big(\pi_i \prod_{t=1}^{n} P(o_t^i | p_t; \sigma_i^2)\Big)^{q_i}$$
$$\Big((1 - \pi_i) \prod_{t=1}^{n} P(o_t^i; \mu_b, \sigma_b^2)\Big)^{(1-q_i)} \Bigg) \quad (1)$$

The parameters of the model can be learned, once for each product, by treating the offer prices as observations; this will be discussed further in Section 4. The learned parameters together with the observations can then be used to jointly infer the most likely product prices. In addition, the parameters π_i's, corresponding to the likelihood of an offer being correctly matched, can be used to determine the set of correct matches by comparing its value to a cutoff threshold. The offers deemed correctly matched by the model can then be used to compute the average or the minimum product prices as desired.

Note that in a real running system, offer prices may be missing at times for various reasons, hence we need to make provisions in the generative model to allow for missing observations. We assume that with some fixed probability r an observation may be missing, independent of whether the offer is correctly matched or not. This assumption allows us to simplify the derivation of the inference procedure, as the probability of a missing observation can be factored out from the likelihood function in Equation (1).

4. INFERENCE AND LEARNING

At runtime, given the offer prices, we can learn the values of the parameters of the model by maximizing the likelihood function. As the model consists of both latent and observed variables, we can generalize the Expectation-Maximization (EM) framework [6] to learn the parameters. Following standard EM derivation (see, e.g., Chapter 9 of [5]),

- In the E-Step, we infer the distribution of the latent variables given the parameters, i.e., we compute
$$Q(\mathbf{p}, \mathbf{q}) = P(\mathbf{p}, \mathbf{q} | \mathbf{O}; \Theta)$$
- In the M-Step, we find the values of the parameters that maximizes the likelihood, treating the probability estimates Q as given, i.e., we compute
$$\Theta^{new} = \arg\max_{\Theta} \int \sum_{\mathbf{q} \in \{0,1\}^k} Q(\mathbf{p}, \mathbf{q}) \log P(\mathbf{O}, \mathbf{p}, \mathbf{q}; \Theta) d\mathbf{p}$$

Due to the interactions between the latent variables $\mathbf{q}$ and $\mathbf{p}$, an exact inference is intractable in the E-step. Instead, we consider an approximate inference procedure by variational methods, discussed further in Section 4.1. The optimization of parameters in the M-step are fairly straightforward, and for completeness we present them in Section 4.2. The overall approach is motivated by the learning algorithm for switching state-space models [10], with adaptations to account for the differences in the model.

4.1 The Variational E Step: Inference

Given the observations $\mathbf{O}$, the distribution of the latent product price variables $\mathbf{p}$ and latent offer status variables $\mathbf{q}$ are *not* independent; this can be verified from the graphical structure of the model (Figure 1) that these variables are not *d*-separated given the observations. In order to perform efficient inference, we apply variational approximation in the E-step.

Specifically, we focus on the following structural approximation to $Q^{(j)}(\mathbf{p}, \mathbf{q})$ that decouples the variables $\mathbf{p}$ and $\mathbf{q}$, *viz.*

$$P(\mathbf{p}, \mathbf{q} | \mathbf{O}; \Theta) = Q(\mathbf{p}, \mathbf{q}) = Q(\mathbf{p}) Q(\mathbf{q}) \ .$$

We then find the factors $Q(\mathbf{p})$, $Q(\mathbf{q})$ that minimizes the KL-divergence to the correct non-independent distribution $P(\mathbf{p}, \mathbf{q} | \mathbf{O}; \Theta^{old})$. Using the general result from Chapter 10 of [5], this can be found by iteratively solving the following system until convergence:

$$\log Q(\mathbf{q}) = \mathbb{E}_{\mathbf{p}}[\log P(\mathbf{O}, \mathbf{p}, \mathbf{q}; \Theta)] + \text{constant} \quad (2)$$
$$\log Q(\mathbf{p}) = \mathbb{E}_{\mathbf{q}}[\log P(\mathbf{O}, \mathbf{p}, \mathbf{q}; \Theta)] + \text{constant} \quad (3)$$

where the constants ensure that the factors $Q(\mathbf{p})$ and $Q(\mathbf{q})$ integrates to one.

From Equations (2) and (1), we can verify that $\log Q(\mathbf{q})$ can be expressed as an exact factorization over the individual offer statuses, i.e.,

$$\log Q(\mathbf{q}) = \sum_{i=1}^{k} \log Q(q_i)$$

where

$$\log Q(q_i) = \mathbb{E}_{\mathbf{p}}[\log P(q_i | \mathbf{O}, \mathbf{p}; \Theta)] + \text{constant} \ .$$

Solving for $Q(q_i)$ for each offer i, we find that

$$\begin{aligned} \log Q(q_i = 1) &\propto n \log \frac{1}{\sqrt{2\pi\sigma_i^2}} - \sum_{t=1}^{n} \mathbb{E}_{\mathbf{p}} \left[\frac{(o_t^i - p_t)^2}{2\sigma_i^2} \right] \\ \log Q(q_i = 0) &\propto n \log \frac{1}{\sqrt{2\pi\sigma_b^2}} - \sum_{t=1}^{n} \frac{(o_t^i - \mu_b)^2}{2\sigma_b^2} \end{aligned} \quad (4)$$

which has the natural interpretation that the log odds between $Q(q_i = 1)$ and $Q(q_i = 0)$ is precisely the ratio of the log likelihoods of offer i being generated by the product prices or through the background distribution.

From Equations (3) and (1), we can verify that $\log Q(\mathbf{p})$ can be expressed as an exact factorization according to the linear dynamics that underlie the product prices, i.e.,

$$\log Q(\mathbf{p}) = \log Q(p_1) + \sum_{t=2}^{n} \log Q(p_{t-1}, p_t)$$

where

$$\log Q(p_1) = \mathbb{E}_{\mathbf{q}}[\log P(p_i | \mathbf{O}, \mathbf{q}; \Theta)] + \text{constant}$$

and for $1 < t \leq n$,

$$\log Q(p_{t-1}, p_t) = \mathbb{E}_{\mathbf{q}}[\log P(p_t | p_{t-1}, \mathbf{O}, \mathbf{q}; \Theta)] + \text{constant}$$

As that the factorization preserves the structure of the dynamics, we can apply the forward-backward algorithm (also known as Kalman filter and smoother) for inferring the latent variables given the parameters. To take into account the offer statuses $\mathbf{q}$ (over which we are taking expectations), it is necessary and sufficient to divide the observation variance σ_i^2 of offer i by $Q(q_i = 1)$ in the algorithm (the same has been observed in [10]). This has the effect of decreasing the influence of offer i to the product prices if the likelihood of offer i being correctly matched is low.

Note that just as in the standard derivation of inference for linear dynamical systems, instead of determining the distribution $Q(\mathbf{p})$ exactly, we only determine the required expectations under the distribution. We follow the notations and derivations from [5] with suitable modifications. Formally, let $\mathbf{1}_k$ denote a column vector of ones of length k, and $\mathbf{1}_{k \times k}$ denote a square matrix of all ones of size $k \times k$ (*not* to be confused with the identity matrix of size $k \times k$). Let Σ be a $k \times k$ matrix that corresponds to the modified observation variances, with the i-th diagonal entry equal to $\frac{\sigma_i^2}{Q(q_i=1)}$, and zero elsewhere. Let $\mathbf{o}_t$ denotes all observed offer prices at time t. The forward stage, corresponding to the Kalman filter, can be computed iteratively from $t = 1$ to n, where for $t = 1$,

$$\begin{aligned} K_1 &= \sigma_0^2 \mathbf{1}_k^T (\sigma_0^2 \mathbf{1}_{k \times k} + \Sigma)^{-1} \\ \mu_1 &= \mu_0 + K_1(\mathbf{o}_1 - \mathbf{1}_k \mu_0) \\ v_1 &= (1 - K_1 \mathbf{1}_k) \sigma_0^2 \\ c_1 &= N(\mathbf{o}_1 | \mathbf{1}^k \mu_0, \sigma_0^2 \mathbf{1}_{k \times k} + \Sigma) \end{aligned}$$

and for $1 < t \le n$,

$$p_{t-1} = \alpha^2 v_{t-1} + \sigma_\alpha^2$$
$$K_t = p_{t-1}\mathbf{1}_k^T(p_{t-1}\mathbf{1}_{k\times k} + \Sigma)^{-1}$$
$$\mu_t = \alpha\mu_{t-1} + K_t(\mathbf{o}_t - \mathbf{1}_k\alpha\mu_{t-1})$$
$$v_t = (1 - K_t\mathbf{1}_k)p_{t-1}$$
$$c_t = N(\mathbf{o}_t|\mathbf{1}_k\alpha\mu_{t-1}, p_{t-1}\mathbf{1}_{k\times k} + \Sigma)$$

The backward stage, corresponding to the Kalman smoother, can be computed iteratively from $t = n-1$ down to 1, where

$$j_t = v_t\alpha/p_t$$
$$\hat{\mu}_t = \mu_t + j_t(\hat{\mu}_{t+1} - \alpha\mu_t)$$
$$\hat{v}_t = v_t + j_t^2(\hat{v}_{t+1} - p_t)$$

For both the variational E-step and the subsequent M-step, the required expectations are given by

$$\mathbb{E}_{\mathbf{p}}[p_t] = \hat{\mu}_t$$
$$\mathbb{E}_{\mathbf{p}}[p_t^2] = \hat{\mu}_t^2 + \hat{v}_t$$
$$\mathbb{E}_{\mathbf{p}}[p_t p_{t-1}] = j_{t-1}\hat{v}_t + \hat{\mu}_t\hat{\mu}_{t-1}$$

To sum up, in the variational E-step, we alternate between computing $Q(\mathbf{p})$ and $Q(\mathbf{q})$ until convergence based on the system of equations described in Equations (2) and (3). The factor $Q(\mathbf{p})$ is not determined explicitly, but rather we use the forward-backward algorithm to determine the required expectations. The factor $Q(\mathbf{q})$ is determined explicitly using the log odds described in Equation (4).

Note that the most expensive computation step in the E-step is inverting the $k \times k$ matrices $(\sigma_0^2\mathbf{1}_{k\times k} + \Sigma)$ and $(p_{t-1}\mathbf{1}_{k\times k}+\Sigma)$ in computing the Kalman gain matrices K_t at the forward stage. Note that these are *not* diagonal matrices and hence a direct computation of the inverses will take time $O(k^3)$. However, one can take advantage of the structure of these matrices to avoid the need to take inverses explicitly. This is discussed further in Section 5.

4.2 The M Step: Parameter Learning

In the M-step, we learn the parameters $\Theta = (\mu_0, \sigma_0^2, \mu_a, \sigma_a^2, \{\pi_i\}_{i=1}^k\{\sigma_i^2\}_{i=1}^k)$ by maximizing the likelihood of the observed data. The optimization can be solved analytically by taking the derivative of each of the parameters and setting it to zero. For completeness, the updates to the parameters are

$$\mu_0 = \mathbb{E}_{\mathbf{p}}[p_1] = \hat{\mu}_1$$
$$\sigma_0^2 = \mathbb{E}_{\mathbf{p}}[p_1^2] - \mathbb{E}_{\mathbf{p}}[p_1]\mathbb{E}_{\mathbf{p}}[p_1] = \hat{v}_1$$
$$\alpha = \frac{\sum_{t=2}^n \mathbb{E}_{\mathbf{p}}[p_t p_{t-1}]}{\sum_{t=2}^n \mathbb{E}_{\mathbf{p}}[p_{t-1}^2]}$$
$$\sigma_\alpha^2 = \frac{1}{n-1}\sum_{t=2}^n\Big(\mathbb{E}_{\mathbf{p}}[p_t^2] - 2\alpha\mathbb{E}_{\mathbf{p}}[p_t p_{t-1}] + \alpha^2\mathbb{E}_{\mathbf{p}}[p_{t-1}^2]\Big)$$

and for $1 \le i \le k$,

$$\pi_i = Q(q_i = 1)$$
$$\sigma_i^2 = \frac{1}{n}\sum_{t=1}^n\Big((o_t^i)^2 - 2o_t^i\mathbb{E}_{\mathbf{p}}[p_t] + \mathbb{E}_{\mathbf{p}}[p_t^2]\Big)$$

Putting it altogether, the learning algorithm is given in Algorithm 1.

Algorithm 1: EM Algorithm for learning parameters to generative model of offer prices

input : Offer prices matched to a product $\mathbf{O}$
output: Parameters to the model Θ

Initialize the values of Θ (random or by heuristics);
repeat
  Variational E-step:
  repeat
    Compute required expectations according to $Q(p)$ using forward-backward algorithm;
    Compute $Q(q)$ according to Equation (4);
  until *convergence*;
  M-step: Update Θ according to Section 4.2;
until *convergence*;
return Θ;

5. KALMAN FILTER SPEEDUP

As mentioned in Section 4.1, the dominant computation in the learning algorithm is inverting the matrices needed in the forward stage of the inference algorithm. We now consider how this step can be sped up by avoiding the explicit need to compute the inverse.

As this technique may be of independent interest, we derive it in a case more general than the one considered in Section 4.1. Let s_0 be some scalar quantity, $\mathbf{c} = [c_1, c_2, \ldots, c_k]$ be a column vector of length k, and D be a diagonal matrix of size $k \times k$ with the diagonal elements being $s_1, s_2, \ldots, s_k$. Consider the matrix M formed by

$$M = \mathbf{c}s_0\mathbf{c}^\mathbf{T} + D\ .$$

For convenience of notation, let $c_0 = 1$. We can show by induction the following lemmas related to the matrix M.

Lemma 1. *The determinant of M equals*

$$|M| = \sum_{0\le m\le k}\Big(\prod_{0\le\ell\le k,\ell\ne m} s_\ell\Big)c_m^2\ .$$

Lemma 2. *The inverse of M equals*

$$(M^{-1})_{ij} = \frac{1}{|M|}\begin{cases}\sum_{0\le m\le k,m\ne i}\Big(\prod_{0\le\ell\le k,\ell\ne i,m} s_\ell\Big)c_m^2 & \text{for } i=j\\ \Big(\prod_{0\le\ell\le k,\ell\ne i,j} s_\ell\Big)c_ic_j & \text{for } i\ne j\end{cases}\ .$$

Lemma 3. *The product of vector $a^T = [s_0c_1, s_0c_2, \ldots, s_0c_k]$ and M equals*

$$(a^TM^{-1})_i = \frac{1}{|M|}\Big(\prod_{0\le\ell\le k,\ell\ne i} s_\ell\Big)c_i\ .$$

where $(a^TM^{-1})_i$ is the i-th entry of the vector (a^TM^{-1}).

By setting $\mathbf{c} = \mathbf{1}_k$, $D = \Sigma$, and $s_0 = \sigma_0^2$ or p_{t-1} as appropriate, together with Lemma 3, we can avoid taking the matrix inverse explicitly, and instead compute the Kalman gain filter directly in $O(k)$ time. Note that the evaluation of the determinant of M using Lemma 1 will only take $O(k)$ time, as one can first pre-compute the product $\Big(\prod_{0\le\ell\le k} s_\ell\Big)$ in $O(k)$ time and obtain the required product in the summand by division, thus avoiding taking $O(k)$ time to evaluate each of the k summands. Likewise this applies to the evaluation in Lemma 3.

6. EVALUATION

We now present an empirical evaluation of our technique using real product and offer data obtained from a commerce search engine.

6.1 Experimental Setup

We obtain a set of products related to televisions from a commerce search engine for which we want to create price histories. The products include both televisions and accessories such as remote controls and mounts. For some of these products, we manage to obtain its Universal Product Code (UPC), a unique identifier.

For the products with UPCs, we obtain a set of offers that are matched to each of them according to the search engine. We have also obtained the offer prices over a five-month period from mid July 2011 to mid December 2011. We filter out any product that include offers with prices that exhibit a regime change (prices going up or down by more than 50% from day to day), as these are often due to two offers being confused as one, and are not proper candidate for evaluation.

For some of these offers, we manage to obtain their UPCs, and we treat an offer with a UPC that is equal to that of the product as ground truth. There are certainly limitation to this ground truth set—it is possible that an offer with a missing UPC could be a correct match; it is also possible that the UPC is incorrect. However, obtaining human judgments for whether an offer is correctly matched to the product is a difficult and costly process, and an attempt to obtain judgment via Mechanical Turk has resulted in very noisy labels, hence we settle on employing UPCs as ground truth. To eliminate some of the mistakes due to incorrect UPCs, we filter out cases where the ground truth includes offers for which their prices differ by over 100%, as these are signs that some of the UPCs are incorrect. We also require that a product has to have there are at least three offers in the ground truth set.

To identify aberrations in the ground truth set, we compare the daily average prices according to the ground truth, and the daily average prices according to all offers with prices between the lowest and the highest prices among the offers in the ground truth. *A priori*, there is no reason based on a price argument that an offer within this range is not a correct match. Therefore, if many of the offers are missing, it is an indication that the set of offers in the ground truth for this product is too small. As the usefulness of our metrics depend on a sampling argument (see next subsection), the results measured on products for which this happens are less reliable. We remove from consideration products where the daily averages according to the two computation differs by more than 5% at the peak. After these processing steps, our evaluation is conducted over a total of 700 products.

6.2 Metrics

For each product, we compute the average product price history and the minimum product price history according to the ground truth set. We measure the difference between these price histories (both average and minimum) and the ones generated algorithmically via two metrics.

Our first metric is the mean scaled absolute difference ($MASE$), designed to measure how closely the generated price history tracks the price level of the true price history. Given the price history $\mathbf{p}^*$ computed from ground truth and the algorithmic price history $\mathbf{p}$, the MASE is defined as:

$$MASE(\mathbf{p}^*, \mathbf{p}) = \frac{1}{n}\sum_{t=1}^{n} \frac{|p_t^* - p_t|}{p_t^*} .$$

The lower the MASE, the better the performance of the algorithm. We denote the MASE for the average price history as Avg-MASE and that for the minimum price history as Min-MASE. We report the numbers averaged across all products.

Our second metric is the mean absolute change difference ($MACD$), designed to measure how closely the generated price history tracks the price trends in the true price history. Given the price history $\mathbf{p}^*$ computed from ground truth and the algorithmic price history $\mathbf{p}$, the MACD is defined as:

$$MACD(\mathbf{p}^*, \mathbf{p}) = \frac{1}{n-1}\sum_{t=2}^{n} \left| \frac{p_t^* - p_{t-1}^*}{p_{t-1}^*} - \frac{p_t - p_{t-1}}{p_{t-1}} \right| .$$

This metric captures the average difference between the change in prices according to each history in relative terms. The lower the MACD, the better the performance of the algorithm. We denote the MACD for the average price history as Avg-MACD and that for the minimum price history as Min-MACD. We report the numbers averaged across all products.

As a final note, we discuss how the choice of the ground truth set affects the usefulness of these metrics. If the ground truth set contains all and only correctly matched offers, the metrics will measure the desired difference between the true price histories and the algorithmically genearted ones. Assuming that the correct matches in the ground truth set is only sampled (uniformly) from among all of the correct matches, and that the prices of the correctly matched offers are distributed according to a Gaussian distribution, the average price history based on the ground truth is an unbiased estimator of the true average price history, and hence we expect Avg-MASE and Avg-MACD to be good metrics, provided the samples are sufficiently dense. On the other hand, the minimum price history based on the ground truth will systematically overestimate the true minimum price history. Hence, the Min-MASE and Min-MACD should be interpreted with caution. However, given the importance of minimum price histories for consumers in deciding when to buy a product, we decide to keep these metrics in the evaluation.

6.3 Choices for Our Algorithms

There are two approaches to computing the average price history using the probabilistic model proposed in this paper. First, we can use the inferred latent prices $\mathbf{p}$ computed in the final iteration of the variational E-step in Algorithm 1. In the experiment, we label this method as Latent. Alternatively, we can use the parameters $\{\pi_i\}_{i=1}^k$ that correspond to the likelihoods of the offers being correct matches. Together with a cutoff threshold τ, we can select all offers with $\pi_i > \tau$, and take the average over these offers. In the experiment, we label this method as Match.

To compute the minimum price history, the inferred latent prices are not directly applicable. Therefore, we follow the paradigm of Match as described in the preceding paragraph, and instead of taking the average we take the minimum after offers are selected.

In all of our experiments, we have selected τ to be 0.6.

After inspecting the values of the parameters $\{\pi_i\}_{i=1}^{k}$ for a number of products, we notice that the values are typically very close to 0 or 1. Hence, the choice of τ has minimal effect on the performance of Match.

6.4 Algorithms for Comparison

We compare our approach to three alternatives in our experiments for the evaluation on average price histories. These algorithms are (labels in parentheses):

- Trimmed mean (Trim): for each day, the top and bottom 10% of the offer prices are removed before the average is taken.
- Median (Median): for each day, the median among all offer prices is chosen.
- Postprocessing with Kalman filter and smoother (Post KF): form a price history by taking the daily average of all offer prices, then apply the Kalman filter and smoother to the resulting price history treating it as observations.

We choose the trimmed mean and the median as they are common and popular alternatives to the simple average, and they are considered more robust to outliers. We also choose the Kalman filter and smoother applied as a post-processing step after the average is taken, as it can help to smooth away anomalous averages that are caused by the occasional outliers.

For the evaluation on minimum price histories, the median no longer makes sense. Instead, we select the price of the offer closest to the 10-th percentile as the product price. We call this method as the Trimmed Min (Trim) as it is analogous to removing the top and bottom 10% of the offer prices before taking the minimum. We continue to evaluate the Kalman filter and smoother as a post-processing step applied to the minimum taken over all offer prices.

Finally, as baseline, we consider using the entire set of matched offers to generate the price history. In the experiment, we label that as All.

6.5 Results

The performances of our algorithms, the baseline, and the alternatives are presented in Table 1. Note that while these percentages may appear small, they do matter to prospective consumers. For example, for a \$2,000 TV (a typical price for a brand-named LCD TV), a MASE of 5% corresponds to a difference of \$100 on average between the true price and the reported price each day. Such errors can significantly decrease credibility of the system. Likewise, a MACD of 1% corresponds to a difference of \$20 on average between the true price change and the reported price change. The errors quickly add up and may lead to poor recommendations for consumers who are deciding between buying now or wait.

For each metric, we present its value, followed by % difference from the baseline in the next row. Recall that under all four metrics, the lower the value, the better the performance; improvements over baseline will give a *negative* % difference. Our main findings are:

Metric	All	Trim	Median	Post KF	Latent	Match
Avg-MASE	3.48%	3.77%	4.49%	3.58%	4.84%	**3.34%**
	-	*+8%*	*+29%*	*+3%*	*+39%*	*-4%*
Avg-MACD	0.63%	0.63%	1.00%	0.69%	0.67%	**0.58%**
	-	*0%*	*+59%*	*+9%*	*+6%*	*-9%*
Min-MASE	4.59%	5.14%	N/A	4.85%	N/A	**4.27%**
	-	*+12%*	-	*+6%*	-	*-7%*
Min-MACD	0.80%	0.94%	N/A	0.80%	N/A	**0.59%**
	-	*+18%*	-	*0%*	-	*-26%*

Table 1: Overall Results of All Algorithms Under Four Metrics. The best performing approaches are highlighted in bold.

- Match is the best algorithm overall. The differences in performance under all four metrics between Match and the baseline All are statistically significant under paired t-tests, with $p < 0.1$ for both MASE measures and $p < 0.005$ for both MACD measures. The magnitude of improvements are higher for the minimum price history, and under MACD that measures price trends.
- The baseline All is a difficult baseline to beat. This should perhaps be not too surprising as UPCs constitute an important signal commonly used in matching algorithms. Indeed, none of the alternatives, Trim, Median, or Post KF, has outperformed All on any of the metrics. This shows that the type of errors made by All cannot be addressed by simply applying more robust statistics, or by smoothing away an occasional outliers.
- Although Match and Latent employ the same probabilistic model, Latent performed far worse than Match. This was initially quite puzzling to us. Through an error analysis, we determine the causes were due to the product price dynamics; this is discussed further in Section 6.7.

6.6 Factor Analysis

To better understand when we could expect Match to do well, and under what conditions Match will outperform All and vise versa, we analyze different groupings of the products to identify factors that are highly correlated with performance. We identify two factors—fraction of offers matched in the ground truth, and the difference in prices among matched offers—as the two most influential factors. Their effects on Avg-MASE and Avg-MACD are presented in Figure 2. Their effects on Min-MASE and Min-MACD exhibit the same trends and are omitted due to space limitations. The key observations are:

- The fraction of offers that are matched to a product in the ground truth set is negatively correlated with MASE and MACD for both Match and All, i.e., higher fraction of offers matched lead to better performance. This is unsurprising and can be explained by the experimental setup, as an increasing fraction of offers in the ground truth set increases the likelihood that an offer matched to the product is correct and will contribute to the average product price.

  From the system design viewpoint, an insight from this analysis is that there exists a cross-over point at around 70% when All starts to outperform Match. As most matching algorithm in ecommerce utilizes UPC as one of the features for matching, one can readily

Figure 2: Primary factors that influence the relative performance between Match and All.

use the fraction of offers with matched UPC as a feature, and only apply Match when the fraction falls below some threshold, and derive a hybrid approach that should outperform both.

- The difference between the correctly matched offers with the highest and lowest prices is positively correlated with MASE and MACD for both Match and All, i.e., larger differences lead to worse performance. This points to the increased difficulty of creating representative price histories as the differences in offer prices increase. There is no clear cross-over point like the preceding factor, hence a hybrid approach is unlikely to help with this scenario.

On examining further the set of products with large differences, we discover that there are often fundamental issues with the matching associated with such products. This is discussed further in the next subsection.

6.7 Error Analysis

Examining the cases for which our method performs poorly, we note that a common cause is due to the existence of multiple sets of offers, each with distinct price ranges, being mapped to the same product, and in the ground truth set, offers from two or more sets are deemed correct. This problem often also leads to large differences in the prices of the matched offers, a problem noted before. This leads to poor performance for Match, as the probabilistic model often learns parameters that corresponds to one set of offers, and Match produces an average price history that corresponds only to the set selected.

We find it intuitively unlikely that a set of correctly matched offers should have exhibited such big variations in prices. While it is possible that this is simply a reflection of different pricing strategies by the merchants, we think a more likely explanation is that the offers are fundamentally different in some ways, for example, TVs sold with accessories versus just the TVs, or the price is inclusive of shipping or extended warranty. We believe a representative price history should avoid mixing these different offers, as the underlying product sold is different. Instead, a better solution is to group the like offers together and present separate price histories for each of the groups.

Despite both being based on the same probabilistic model, Latent performs significantly worse than Match. Examining some of the products for which the difference is large, we notice that poor performance often happens when either (1) the composition of the set of offers changes, causing a large discrete jump occurs in the true price history, or (2) there is an offer considered likely to be correct by the model exhibits a temporary change in prices. As the latent price variables attempt to balance the price dynamics of the model (as governed by α and σ_α^2) and the set of new observations, Latent enters into a transition period and adjusts to these changes gradually . The errors during this transition period are high. On the other hand, Match reacts immediately under both situations, and therefore does not suffer from a transition period. As both types of situations are common in our dataset, Latent performs worse than Match.

7. CONCLUSION

We study the problem of how to aggregate web offers to create representative price histories, taking into account that offers that are matched to a product are not always correct. To solve this problem, we propose a probabilistic model for how offer prices are generated, extending the classical linear dynamical system to allow for possibly incorrect observations. We give an EM algorithm for finding the parameters that maximize likelihood, and work around the computationally intractable exact inference needed in the E-step by variational approximation. To further speed up the learning algorithm, we take advantage of the structure of our problem that assumes independence among offers, and establish certain matrix equalities that allow us to circumvent the need to take matrix inverses in computing the Kalman gain filter, leading to quadratic speedup of the algorithm. This technique may be of independent interest.

We conduct an extensive evaluation of our approach using data obtained from a commerce search engine. We consider two metrics in evaluation—MASE for evaluating how well a method tracks the true price level, and MACD for evaluating how well a method tracks the true price trend. Our method significantly outperforms alternatives including the median, the trimmed mean, and post-processing using Kalman filter and smoother. The improvements over the baseline are statistically significant. How the output of the probabilistic model is used has large influence over the performance. We find that it is significantly better to use the learned likelihood of whether offers are correctly matched than to use the latent price variables. This work addresses a limitation of the experiments in [1] which depends on data vendor for product prices, and constitutes a step towards building a system that helps consumers decide when to buy a product.

We conclude with several interesting future research directions. First, can the probabilistic model proposed in the paper be integrated into some matching algorithm to improve the matching process itself? While some proposed matching algorithms in the literature can use price as one of the matching features, we are not aware of any solution that takes advantage of the sequentiality of the offers. Combining a dynamic model of prices like the one presented here with matching will likely be both fruitful and challenging. Second, we have considered only a state-space model with only a single state in our probabilistic model. Better performances may be possible by adopting a higher-dimensional state-space model. One may also want to revisit the generative process for the correctly matched offers, as it is common for merchants to keep offer prices constant for periods of time before adjustments. Finally, looking at the entire set of offers open up new possibility in predicting future product prices. An important direction is to revisit the algorithms proposed in [1], and see if by using all offers one can improve forecasting accuracies, and help make better buy-or-wait recommendations to consumers.

8. REFERENCES

[1] R. Agrawal, S. Ieong, and R. Velu. Ameliorating buyers' remorse. In *Proc. KDD*, 2011.

[2] R. Agrawal, S. Ieong, and R. Velu. Timing when to buy. In *Proc. CIKM*, 2011.

[3] O. Benjelloun, H. Garcia-Molina, D. Menestrina, Q. Su, S. E. Whang, and J. Widom. Swoosh: a generic approach to entity resolution. *The VLDB Journal*, 18(1):255–276, 2009.

[4] M. Bilenko, R. Mooney, W. Cohen, P. Ravikumar, and S. Fienberg. Adaptive name matching in information integration. *IEEE Intel. Sys.*, 18(5):16–23, 2003.

[5] C. M. Bishop. *Pattern Recognition and Machine Learning.* Springer-Verlag New York, 2006.

[6] A. P. Dempster, N. M. Laird, and D. B. Rubin. Maximum likelihood from incomplete data via the em algorithm. *Journal Of The Royal Statistical Society, Series B*, 39(1):1–38, 1977.

[7] A. K. Elmagarmid, P. G. Ipeirotis, and V. S. Verykios. Duplicate record detection: A survey. *IEEE Trans. on Knowl. and Data Eng.*, 19(1):1–16, 2007.

[8] I. P. Fellegi and A. B. Sunter. A theory for record linkage. *Journal of the American Statistical Association*, 64(328):1183–1210, 1969.

[9] Z. Gharamani and G. E. Hinton. Parameter estimation for linear dynamical systems. Technical report, University of Toronto, 1996.

[10] Z. Gharamani and G. E. Hinton. Variational learning for switching state-space models. *Neural Computation*, 12(4):963–996, 2000.

[11] N. J. Gordon, D. J. Salmond, and A. F. M. Smith. Novel approach to nonlinear/non-gaussian bayesian state estimation. *Radar and Signal Processing, IEE Proceedings F*, 140(2):107–113, 1993.

[12] P. J. Huber. *Robust Statistics.* Wiley, 1981.

[13] M. Isard and A. Blake. CONDENSATION — conditional density propagation for visual tracking. *Int. Journal of Computer Vision*, 29(1):5–18, 1998.

[14] R. E. Kalman. A new approach to linear filtering and prediction problems. *Transactions of the ASME–Journal of Basic Engineering*, 82(Series D):35–45, 1960.

[15] K. Kanazawa, D. Koller, and S. Russel. Stochastic simulation algorithms for dynamic probabilistic networks. In *Proc. UAI*, 1995.

[16] A. Kannan, I. E. Givoni, R. Agrawal, and A. Fuxman. Matching unstructured product offers to structured product specifications. In *Proc. KDD*, 2011.

[17] M. Michelson and C. Knoblock. Creating relational data from unstructured and ungrammatical data sources. *Journal of Artificial Intelligence Research*, 31:543–590, 2008.

[18] R. Mitkov. *Anaphora Resolution.* Longman, 2002.

[19] H. B. Newcombe, M. J. Kennedy, S. J. Axford, and A. P. James. Automatic linkage of vital records. *Science*, 130:954–959, October 1959.

[20] P. Ravikumar and W. W. Cohen. A hierarchical graphical model for record linkage. In *UAI*, 2004.

[21] S. Roweis and Z. Ghahramani. A unifying review of linear gaussian models. *Neural Computation*, 1997.

[22] S. Sarawagi and A. Bhamidipaty. Interactive deduplication using active learning. In *KDD*, pages 269–278, 2002.

[23] S. Singh, K. Schultz, and A. McCallum. Bi-directional joint inference for entity resolution and segmentation using imperatively-defined factor graphs. In *ECML-PKDD*, pages 414–429, 2009.

[24] B. Sinopoli, L. Schenato, M. Franceschetti, K. Poolla, M. I. Jordan, and S. Sastry. Kalman filtering with intermittent observations. *IEEE Trans. on Automatic Control*, 49:1453–1464, 2004.

[25] W. E. Winkler. Overview of record linkage and current research directions. Technical report, Bureau of the Census, 2006.

[26] P. Zarchan and H. Musoff. *Fundamentals of Kalman Filtering: A Practical Approach.* AIAA, 2nd ed., 2005.

[27] J. Zhong and S. Sclaroff. Segmenting foreground objects from a dynamic textured background via a robust kalman filter. In *Proc. ICCV*, 2003.

Mining Event Periodicity from Incomplete Observations

Zhenhui Li, Jingjing Wang and Jiawei Han
Department of Computer Science
University of Illinois at Urbana-Champaign
Urbana, Illinois, USA
zli28@uiuc.edu, jwang112@uiuc.edu, hanj@uiuc.edu

ABSTRACT

Advanced technology in GPS and sensors enables us to track physical events, such as human movements and facility usage. Periodicity analysis from the recorded data is an important data mining task which provides useful insights into the physical events and enables us to report outliers and predict future behaviors. To mine periodicity in an event, we have to face real-world challenges of inherently complicated periodic behaviors and imperfect data collection problem. Specifically, the hidden temporal periodic behaviors could be oscillating and noisy, and the observations of the event could be incomplete.

In this paper, we propose a novel probabilistic measure for periodicity and design a practical method to detect periods. Our method has thoroughly considered the uncertainties and noises in periodic behaviors and is provably robust to incomplete observations. Comprehensive experiments on both synthetic and real datasets demonstrate the effectiveness of our method.

Categories and Subject Descriptors

H.2.8 [**Data Management**]: Database Applications - Data Mining; H.4.0 [**Information Systems**]: General

General Terms

Algorithms

Keywords

Periodicity, incomplete observations

1. INTRODUCTION

Periodicity is one of the most common phenomena in the physical world. Animals often have yearly migration patterns; students usually have weekly schedules for classes; and the usage of bedroom, toilet, and kitchen could have daily periodicity, just to name a few. Nowadays, with the rapid development of GPS and mobile technologies, it becomes much easier to monitor such events. For example, cellphones enable us to track human activities [4], GPS devices attached to animals help the scientists to study the animal movement patterns [7], and sensors allow us to monitor the usage of rooms and facilities [14].

Data collected from such tracking and sensor devices provides a valuable resource for ecological study, environmental protection, urban planning and emergency response. An observation of an event defined in this paper is a boolean value, that is, whether an event happens or not. An important aspect of analyzing such data is to *detect true periods* hidden in the observations.

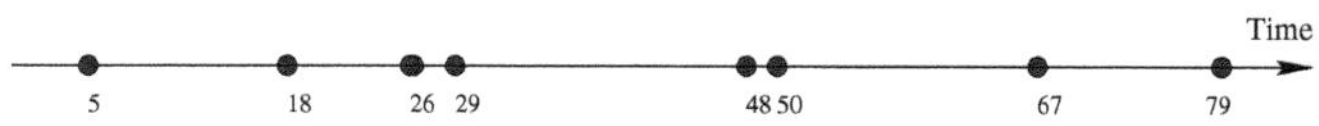

Figure 1: Incomplete observations.

Unfortunately, period detection for an event is a challenging problem, due to the *limitations of data collection methods* and *inherent complexity of periodic behaviors*.

To illustrate the difficulties, let us first take a look at Figure 1. Suppose we have observed the occurrences of an event at timestamps 5, 18, 26, 29, 48, 50, 67, and 79. The observations of the event at other timestamps are not available. It is certainly not an easy task to infer the period directly from these *incomplete* observations. In fact, the issue with incomplete observations is a common problem on data collected from GPS and sensors. For example, a bird can only carry small sensors with one or two reported locations in three to five days. And the locations of a person may only be recorded when he uses his cellphone. Moreover, if a sensor is not functioning or a tracking facility is turned off, it could result in a large portion of missing data. Therefore, we usually have *incomplete observations*, which *are unevenly sampled* and *have large portion of missing data*. Traditional periodicity analysis methods, such as Fourier transform and auto-correlation [11, 15, 1, 7], usually require the data to be *evenly sampled*, that is, there is an observation at every timestamp. Even though some extensions of Fourier transform have been proposed to handle uneven data samples [9, 12], they are still not applicable to the case with very low sampling rate.

Second, the periodic behaviors could be inherently *complicated and noisy*. A periodic event does not necessarily happen at *exactly* the same timestamp in each periodic cycle. For example, the time that a person goes to work in the morning might *oscillate* between 8:00 to 10:00. *Noises*

KDD'12, August 12–16, 2012, Beijing, China.

could also occur when the "in office" event is expected to be observed on a weekday but fails to happen.

In this paper, we take a completely different approach to the period detection problem and handle all the aforementioned difficulties occurring in data collection process and periodic behavior complexity in a unified framework. The basic idea of our method is illustrated in Example 1.

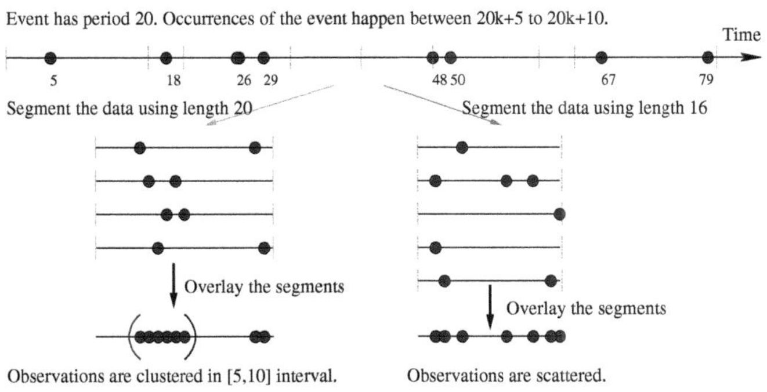

Figure 2: Illustration example of our method.

EXAMPLE 1. *Suppose an event has a period $T = 20$ and we have eight observations of the event. If we overlay the observations with the correct period $T = 20$, we can see that most of the observations concentrate in time interval [5,10]. On the contrary, if we overlay the points with a wrong period, say $T = 16$, we cannot observe such clusters.*

As suggested by Example 1, we could segment the timeline using a potential period T and summarize the observations over all the segments. If most of the observations fall into some time intervals, such as interval $[5, 10]$ in Example 1, T is *likely* to be the true period. In this paper, we formally characterize such likelihood by introducing a probabilistic model for periodic behaviors. The model naturally handles the oscillation and noise issues because the occurrence of an event at any timestamp is now modeled with a probability. Next, we propose a new measure for periodicity based on this model. The measure essentially examines whether the distribution of observations is highly skewed w.r.t a potential period T. As we will see later, even when the observations are incomplete, the overall distribution of observations, after overlaid with the correct T, remains skewed and is similar to the true periodic behavior model.

In summary, our major contributions are as follows. (1) We introduce a probabilistic model for periodic behaviors and a random observation model for incomplete observations. This enables us to model all the variations we encounter in practice in a unified framework. (2) We propose a novel probabilistic measure for periodicity and design a practical algorithm to detect periods directly from the raw data. We further give rigorous proof of its validity under both the probabilistic periodic behavior model and the random observation model. (3) Comprehensive experiments are conducted on both real data and synthetic data. The results demonstrate the effectiveness of our method.

The rest of the paper is organized as follows. We formally define our period detection problem in Section 2 and introduce our probabilistic measure for periodicity in Section 3. Section 4 discusses the implementaion issues and outlines the algorithm. We report our experimental results in Section 5, discuss related work in Section 6 and conclude our study in Section 7.

2. PROBLEM FORMULATION

In this section, we formally define the problem of period detection for events. We first assume that there is an observation at every timestamp. The case with incomplete observations will be discussed in Section 3.2. We use a binary sequence $\mathcal{X} = \{x(t)\}_{t=0}^{n-1}$ to denote observations. For example, if the event is "in the office", $x(t) = 1$ means this person is in the office at time t and $x(t) = 0$ means this person is *not* in the office at time t. Later we will refer $x(t) = 1$ as a *positive observation* and $x(t) = 0$ as a *negative observation*.

DEFINITION 1 (PERIODIC SEQUENCE). *A sequence $\mathcal{X} = \{x(t)\}_{t=0}^{n-1}$ is said to be periodic if there exists some $T \in \mathbb{Z}$ such that $x(t + T) = x(t)$ for all values of t. We call T a period of $\mathcal{X}$.*

A fundamental ambiguity with the above definition is that if T is a period of $\mathcal{X}$, then mT is also a period of $\mathcal{X}$ for any $m \in \mathbb{Z}$. A natural way to resolve this problem is to use the so called *prime period.*

DEFINITION 2 (PRIME PERIOD). *The prime period of a periodic sequence is the smallest $T \in \mathbb{Z}$ such that $x(t + T) = x(t)$ for all values of t.*

For the rest of the paper, unless otherwise stated, we always refer the word "period" to "prime period".

As we mentioned before, in real applications the observed sequences always deviate from the perfect periodicity due to the oscillating behavior and noises. To model such deviations, we introduce a new probabilistic framework, which is based on the *periodic distribution vectors* as defined below.

DEFINITION 3 (PERIODIC DISTRIBUTION VECTOR). *We call any vector $\mathbf{p}^T = [p_0^T, \dots, p_{T-1}^T] \in [0, 1]^T$ other than $\mathbf{0}^T$ and $\mathbf{1}^T$ a periodic distribution vector of length T. A binary sequence $\mathcal{X}$ is said to be generated according to $\mathbf{p}^T$ if $x(t)$ is independently distributed according to Bernoulli($p^T_{\bmod (t,T)}$).*

Here we need to exclude the trivial cases where $\mathbf{p}^T = \mathbf{0}^T$ or $\mathbf{1}^T$. Also note that if we restrict the value of each p_i^T to $\{0, 1\}$ only, then the resulting $\mathcal{X}$ is *strictly* periodic according to Definition 1. We are now able to formulate our period detection problem as follows.

PROBLEM 1 (EVENT PERIOD DETECTION). *Given a binary sequence $\mathcal{X}$ generated according to any periodic distribution vector $\mathbf{p}^{T_0}$, find T_0.*

EXAMPLE 2 (RUNNING EXAMPLE). *We will use a running example throughout the paper to illustrate our method. Assume that a person has a daily periodicity visiting his office during 10am-11am and 2pm-4pm. His observation sequence is generated from the periodic distribution vector with high probabilities at time interval [10:11] and [14:16] and low but nonzero probabilities at other timestamps, as shown in Figure 3.*

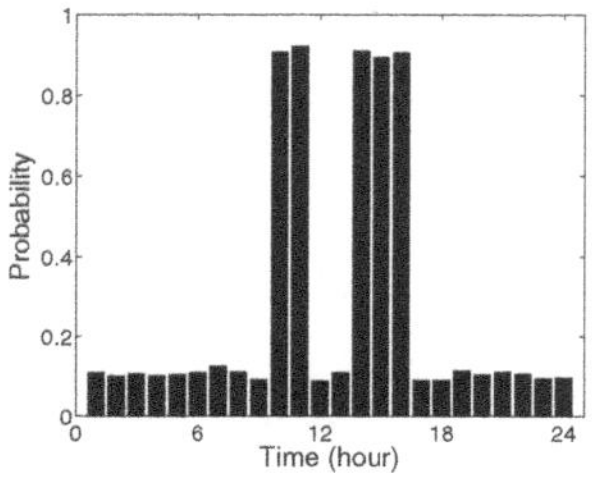

Figure 3: (Running Example) Periodic distribution vector of a event with daily periodicity $T_0 = 24$.

3. A PROBABILISTIC MODEL FOR PERIOD DETECTION

As we see in Example 1, when we overlay the binary sequence with its true period T_0, the resulting sequence correctly reveals its underlying periodic behavior. In this section, we make this observation formal using the concept of periodic distribution vector. Then, we propose a novel probabilistic measure of periodicity based on this observation and prove its validity even when observations are incomplete.

3.1 A Probabilistic Measure of Periodicity

Given a binary sequence $\mathcal{X}$, we define $S^+ = \{t : x(t) = 1\}$ and $S^- = \{t : x(t) = 0\}$ as the collections of timestamps with 1's and 0's, respectively. For a candidate period T, let $\mathcal{I}_T$ denote the power set of $[0 : T-1]$. Then, for any set of timestamps (*possibly non-consecutive*) $I \in \mathcal{I}_T$, we can define the collections of original timestamps that fall into this set after overlay as follows:

$$S_I^+ = \{t \in S^+ : \mathcal{F}_T(t) \in I\}, \quad S_I^- = \{t \in S^- : \mathcal{F}_T(t) \in I\},$$

where $\mathcal{F}_T(t) = \mod(t, T)$, and further compute the ratios of 1's and 0's whose corresponding timestamps fall into I after overlay:

$$\mu_{\mathcal{X}}^+(I,T) = \frac{|S_I^+|}{|S^+|}, \quad \mu_{\mathcal{X}}^-(I,T) = \frac{|S_I^-|}{|S^-|}. \tag{1}$$

The following lemma says that these ratios indeed reveal the true underlying probabilistic model parameters, given that the observation sequence is sufficiently long.

LEMMA 1. *Suppose a binary sequence $\mathcal{X} = \{x(t)\}_{t=0}^{n-1}$ is generated according to some periodic distribution vector $\mathbf{p}^T$ of length T, write $q_i^T = 1 - p_i^T$. Then $\forall I \in \mathcal{I}_T$,*

$$\lim_{n\to\infty} \mu_{\mathcal{X}}^+(I,T) = \frac{\sum_{i\in I} p_i^T}{\sum_{i=0}^{T-1} p_i^T}, \quad \lim_{n\to\infty} \mu_{\mathcal{X}}^-(I,T) = \frac{\sum_{i\in I} q_i^T}{\sum_{i=0}^{T-1} q_i^T}.$$

PROOF. The proof is a straightforward application of the Law of Large Numbers (LLN), and we only prove the first equation. With a slight abuse of notation we write $S_i = \{t : \mathcal{F}_T(t) = i\}$ and $S_i^+ = \{t \in S^+ : \mathcal{F}_T(t) = i\}$. Since $\{x(t) : t \in S_i\}$ are i.i.d. Bernoulli(p_i^T) random variables, by LLN we have

$$\lim_{n\to\infty} \frac{|S_i^+|}{n} = \lim_{n\to\infty} \frac{\sum_{t\in S_i} x(t)}{n} = \frac{p_i^T}{T},$$

where we use $\lim_{n\to\infty} \frac{|S_i|}{n} = \frac{1}{T}$ for the last equality. So,

$$\begin{aligned} \lim_{n\to\infty} \mu_{\mathcal{X}}^+(I,T) &= \lim_{n\to\infty} \frac{|S_I^+|/n}{|S^+|/n} = \lim_{n\to\infty} \frac{\sum_{i\in I} |S_i^+|/n}{\sum_{i=0}^{T-1} |S_i^+|/n} \\ &= \frac{\sum_{i\in I} p_i^T/T}{\sum_{i=0}^{T-1} p_i^T/T} = \frac{\sum_{i\in I} p_i^T}{\sum_{i=0}^{T-1} p_i^T}. \end{aligned}$$

□

Now we introduce our measure of periodicity based on Lemma 1. For any $I \in \mathcal{I}_T$, its discrepancy score is defined as:

$$\Delta_{\mathcal{X}}(I,T) = \mu_{\mathcal{X}}^+(I,T) - \mu_{\mathcal{X}}^-(I,T). \tag{2}$$

Then, the periodicity measure of $\mathcal{X}$ w.r.t. period T is:

$$\gamma_{\mathcal{X}}(T) = \max_{I\in\mathcal{I}_T} \Delta(I,T). \tag{3}$$

It is obvious that $\gamma_{\mathcal{X}}(T)$ is bounded: $0 \le \gamma_{\mathcal{X}}(T) \le 1$. Moreover, $\gamma_{\mathcal{X}}(T) = 1$ if and only if $\mathcal{X}$ is strictly periodic with period T. But more importantly, we have the following lemma, which states that under our probabilistic periodic behavior model, $\gamma_{\mathcal{X}}(T)$ is indeed a desired measure of periodicity.

LEMMA 2. *If a binary sequence $\mathcal{X}$ is generated according to any periodic distribution vector $\mathbf{p}^{T_0}$ for some T_0, then*

$$\lim_{n\to\infty} \gamma_{\mathcal{X}}(T) \le \lim_{n\to\infty} \gamma_{\mathcal{X}}(T_0), \quad \forall T \in \mathbb{Z}.$$

PROOF. Define

$$c_i = \frac{p_i^{T_0}}{\sum_{k=0}^{T_0-1} p_k^{T_0}} - \frac{q_i^{T_0}}{\sum_{k=0}^{T_0-1} q_k^{T_0}},$$

it is easy to see that the value $\lim_{n\to\infty} \gamma_{\mathcal{X}}(T_0)$ is achieved by $I^* = \{i \in [0, T_0 - 1] : c_i > 0\}$. So it suffices to show that for any $T \in \mathbb{Z}$ and $I \in \mathcal{I}_T$,

$$\lim_{n\to\infty} \Delta_{\mathcal{X}}(I,T) \le \lim_{n\to\infty} \Delta_{\mathcal{X}}(I^*, T_0) = \sum_{i\in I^*} c_i.$$

Observe now that for any (I,T),

$$\begin{aligned} \lim_{n\to\infty} \mu_{\mathcal{X}}^+(I,T) &= \sum_{i\in I} \left(\frac{1}{T} \sum_{j=0}^{T_0-1} \frac{p_{\mathcal{F}_{T_0}(i+j\times T)}^{T_0}}{\sum_{k=0}^{T_0-1} p_k^{T_0}} \right), \\ \lim_{n\to\infty} \mu_{\mathcal{X}}^-(I,T) &= \sum_{i\in I} \left(\frac{1}{T} \sum_{j=0}^{T_0-1} \frac{q_{\mathcal{F}_{T_0}(i+j\times T)}^{T_0}}{\sum_{k=0}^{T_0-1} q_k^{T_0}} \right). \end{aligned}$$

Therefore we have

$$\begin{aligned} \lim_{n\to\infty} \Delta_{\mathcal{X}}(I,T) &= \frac{1}{T} \sum_{i\in I} \sum_{j=0}^{T_0-1} \left(\frac{p_{\mathcal{F}_{T_0}(i+j\times T)}^{T_0}}{\sum_{k=0}^{T_0-1} p_k^{T_0}} - \frac{q_{\mathcal{F}_{T_0}(i+j\times T)}^{T_0}}{\sum_{k=0}^{T_0-1} q_k^{T_0}} \right) \\ &= \frac{1}{T} \sum_{i\in I} \sum_{j=0}^{T_0-1} c_{\mathcal{F}_{T_0}(i+j\times T)} \\ &\le \frac{1}{T} \sum_{i\in I} \sum_{j=0}^{T_0-1} \max(c_{\mathcal{F}_{T_0}(i+j\times T)}, 0) \\ &\le \frac{1}{T} \sum_{j=0}^{T_0T-1} \max(c_{\mathcal{F}_{T_0}(i+j\times T)}, 0) \\ &= \frac{1}{T} \times T \sum_{i\in I^*} c_i = \sum_{i\in I^*} c_i, \end{aligned}$$

where the third equality uses the definition of I^*. □

Note that, similar to the deterministic case, the ambiguity of multiple periods still exists as we can easily see that $\lim_{n\to\infty}\gamma_{\mathcal{X}}(mT_0) = \lim_{n\to\infty}\gamma_{\mathcal{X}}(T_0)$ for all m$\in\mathbb{Z}$. But in this paper we are only interested in finding the smallest one.

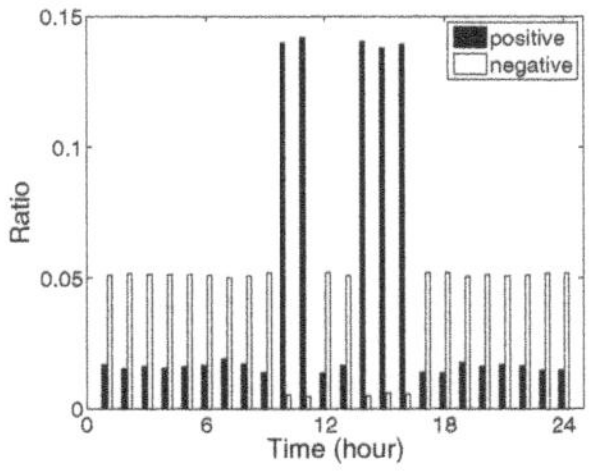

(a) Ratios ($T = 24$)

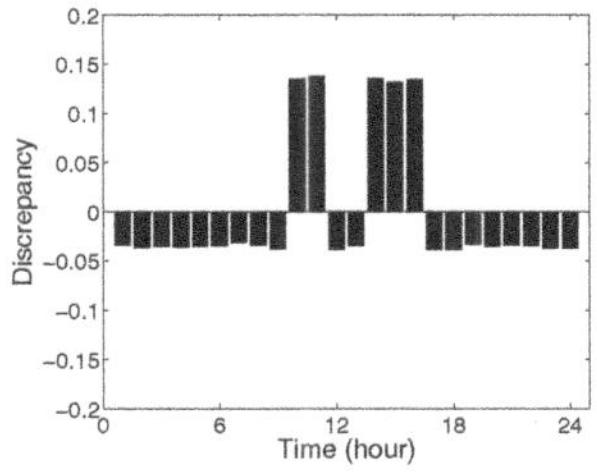

(b) Discrepancy ($T = 24$)

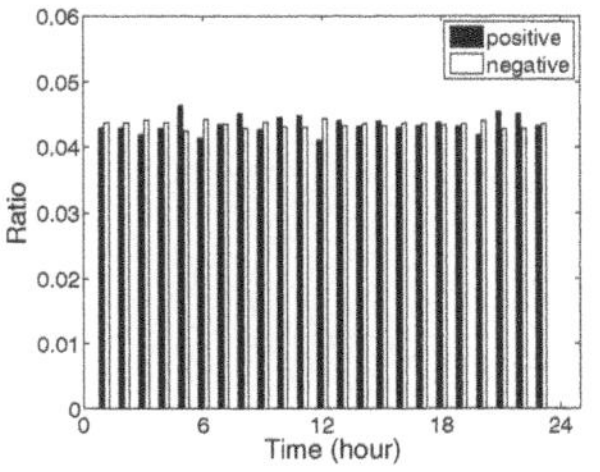

(c) Ratios ($T = 23$)

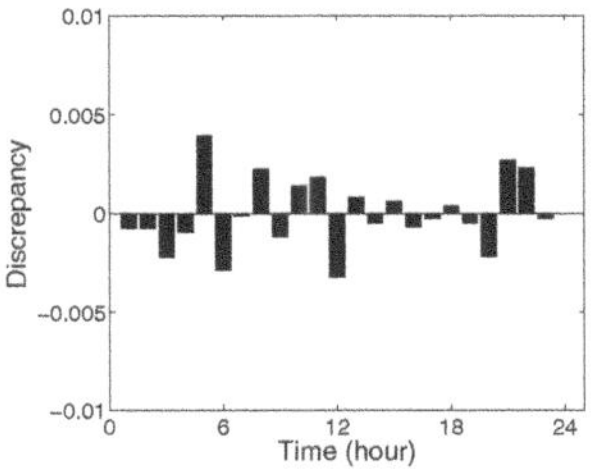

(d) Discrepancy ($T = 23$)

Figure 4: (a) and (c): Ratios of 1's and 0's at a single timestamp (*i.e.*, $\mu^+_{\mathcal{X}}(\cdot,T)$ and $\mu^-_{\mathcal{X}}(\cdot,T)$) when $T = 24$ and $T = 23$, respectively. (b) and (d): Discrepancy scores at a single timestamp (*i.e.* $\Delta_{\mathcal{X}}(\cdot,T)$) when $T = 24$ and $T = 23$.

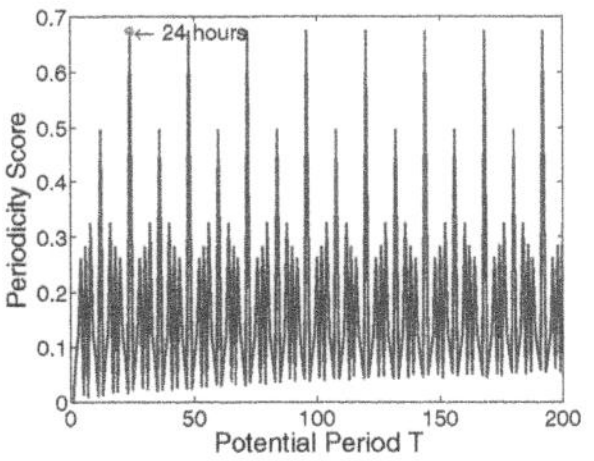

Figure 5: Periodicity scores of potential periods.

EXAMPLE 3 (RUNNING EXAMPLE (CONT.)). *When we overlay the sequence using potential period $T = 24$, Figure 4(a) shows that positive observations have high probability to fall into the set of timestamps: $\{10, 11, 14, 15, 16\}$. However, when using the wrong period $T = 23$, the distribution is almost uniform over time, as shown in Figure 4(c). Similarly, we see large discrepancy scores for T=24 (Figure 4(b)) whereas the discrepancy scores are very small for T=23 (Figure 4(d)). Therefore, we will have $\gamma_{\mathcal{X}}(24) > \gamma_{\mathcal{X}}(23)$. Figure 5 shows the periodicity scores for all potential periods in $[1:200]$. We can see that the score is maximized at $T = 24$, which is the true period of the sequence.*

3.2 Random Observation Model

Next, we extend our analysis on the proposed periodicity measure to the case of incomplete observations with a random observation model. To this end, we introduce a new label "-1" to the binary sequence $\mathcal{X}$ which indicates that the observation is unavailable at a specific timestamp. In the random observation model, each observation $x(t)$ is associated with a probability $d_t \in [0,1]$ and we write $\mathbf{d} = \{d_t\}_{t=0}^{n-1}$.

DEFINITION 4. *A sequence $\mathcal{X}$ is said to be generated according to $(\mathbf{p}^T, \mathbf{d})$ if*

$$x(t) = \begin{cases} \text{Bernoulli}(p^T_{\mathcal{F}_T(t)}) & \text{w.p. } d_t \\ -1 & \text{w.p. } 1-d_t \end{cases} \quad (4)$$

In general, we may assume that each d_t is independently drawn from some fixed but unknown distribution f over the interval $[0,1]$. To avoid the trivial case where $d_t \equiv 0$ for all t, we further assume that it has nonzero mean: $\rho_f > 0$. Although this model seems to be very flexible, in the section we prove that our periodicity measure is still valid. In order to do so, we need the following lemma, which states that $\mu^+_{\mathcal{X}}(I,T)$ and $\mu^-_{\mathcal{X}}(I,T)$ remain the same as before, assuming infinite length observation sequence.

LEMMA 3. *Suppose $\mathbf{d} = \{d_t\}_{t=0}^{n-1}$ are i.i.d. random variables in $[0,1]$ with nonzero mean, and a sequence $\mathcal{X}$ is generated according to $(\mathbf{p}^T, \mathbf{d})$, write $q^T_i = 1 - p^T_i$. Then $\forall I \in \mathcal{I}_T$,*

$$\lim_{n\to\infty}\mu^+_{\mathcal{X}}(I,T) = \frac{\sum_{i\in I} p^T_i}{\sum_{i=0}^{T-1} p^T_i}, \quad \lim_{n\to\infty}\mu^-_{\mathcal{X}}(I,T) = \frac{\sum_{i\in I} q^T_i}{\sum_{i=0}^{T-1} q^T_i}.$$

PROOF. We only prove the first equation. Let $y(t)$ be a random variable distributed according to Bernoulli(d_t) and $z(t) = x(t)y(t)$. Then $\{z(t)\}_{t=0}^{n-1}$ are independent random variables which take value in $\{0,1\}$, with mean $\mathbb{E}[z(t)]$ computed as follows:

$$\begin{aligned}\mathbb{E}[z(t)] &= \mathbf{P}(z(t)=1) = \mathbf{P}(x(t)=1, y(t)=1) \\ &= \mathbf{P}(x(t)=1|y(t)=1)\mathbf{P}(y(t)=1) \\ &= p^T_{\mathcal{F}_T(t)}\mathbf{P}(y(t)=1) = p^T_{\mathcal{F}_T(t)}\mathbb{E}[d_t] = p^T_{\mathcal{F}_T(t)}\rho_f.\end{aligned}$$

Define $S_i = \{t : \mathcal{F}_T(t) = i\}$ and $S^+_i = \{t \in S^+ : \mathcal{F}_T(t) = i\}$, it is easy to see that $|S^+_i| = \sum_{t\in S_i} z(t)$. Using LLN we get

$$\lim_{n\to\infty}\frac{|S^+_i|}{n} = \lim_{n\to\infty}\frac{\sum_{t\in S_i} z(t)}{n} = \frac{p^T_i\rho_f}{T},$$

where we use $\lim_{n\to\infty}\frac{|S_i|}{n} = 1/T$ for the last equality. Therefore,

$$\begin{aligned}\lim_{n\to\infty}\mu^+_{\mathcal{X}}(I,T) &= \lim_{n\to\infty}\frac{|S^+_I|/n}{|S^+|/n} = \lim_{n\to\infty}\frac{\sum_{i\in I}|S^+_i|/n}{\sum_{i=0}^{T-1}|S^+_i|/n} \\ &= \frac{\sum_{i\in I}\frac{p^T_i\rho_f}{T}}{\sum_{i=0}^{T-1}\frac{p^T_i\rho_f}{T}} = \frac{\sum_{i\in I}p^T_i}{\sum_{i=0}^{T-1}p^T_i}.\end{aligned}$$

□

Since our periodicity measure only depends on $\mu^+_{\mathcal{X}}(I,T)$ and $\mu^-_{\mathcal{X}}(I,T)$, it is now straightforward to prove its validity under the random observation model. We summarize our main result as the following theorem.

THEOREM 1. *Suppose $\mathbf{d} = \{d_t\}_{t=0}^{n-1}$ are i.i.d. random variables in $[0,1]$ with nonzero mean, and a sequence $\mathcal{X}$ is generated according to any $(\mathbf{p}^{T_0}, \mathbf{d})$ for some T_0, then*

$$\lim_{n\to\infty}\gamma_{\mathcal{X}}(T) \le \lim_{n\to\infty}\gamma_{\mathcal{X}}(T_0), \quad \forall T \in \mathbb{Z}.$$

The proof is exactly the same as that of Lemma 2 given the result of Lemma 3, hence is omitted here.

Here we make two useful comments on this result. First, the assumption that d_t's are independent of each other plays

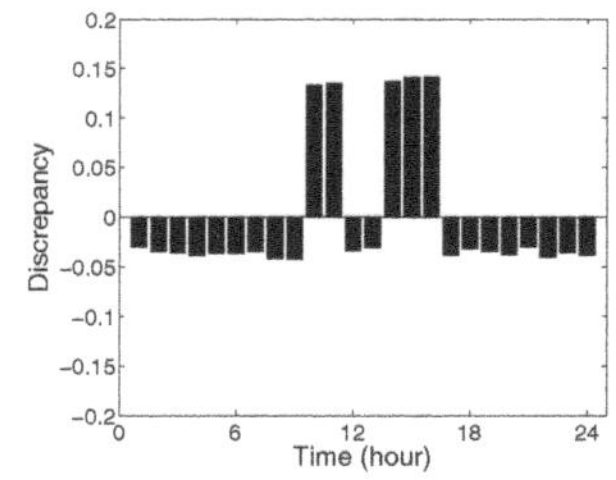

(a) Discrepancy ($T = 24$)

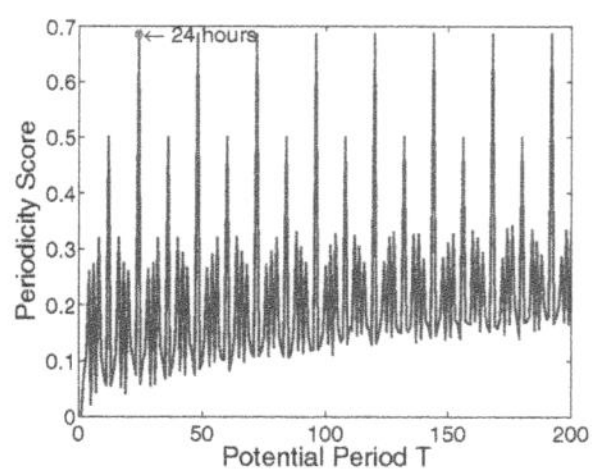

(b) Periodicity scores

Figure 6: Period detection with unknown observations.

an important role in the proof. In fact, if this does not hold, the observation sequence could exhibit very different periodic behavior from its underlying periodic distribution vector. But a thorough discussion on this issue is beyond the scope of this paper. Second, this result only holds exactly with infinite length sequences. However, it provides a good estimate on the situation with finite length sequences, assuming that the sequences are long enough. Note that this length requirement is particularly important when a majority of samples are missing (*i.e.*, ρ_f is close to 0). We will discuss this issue in more detail in Section 4.

EXAMPLE 4 (RUNNING EXAMPLE (CONT.)). *To introduce random observations, we sample the original sequence with sampling rate 0.2. The generated sequence will have 80% of its entries marked as unknown. Comparing Figure 6(a) with Figure 4(b), we can see very similar discrepancy scores over time. Random sampling has little effect on our period detection method. As shown in Figure 6(b), we can still detect the correct period at 24.*

3.3 Handling Sequences Without Negative Samples

In many real world applications, negative samples may be completely unavailable to us. For example, if we have collected data from a local cellphone tower, we will know that a person is in town when he makes phone call through the local tower. However, we are not sure whether this person is in town or not for the rest of time because he could either be out of town or simply not making any call. In this case, the observation sequence $\mathcal{X}$ takes value in $\{1, -1\}$ only, with -1 indicating the missing entries. In this section, we modify our measure of periodicity to handle this case.

Note that due to the lack of negative samples, $\mu_{\mathcal{X}}^-(I,T)$ can no longer be computed from $\mathcal{X}$. Thus, we need find another quantity to compare $\mu_{\mathcal{X}}^+(I,T)$ with. To this end, consider a binary sequence $\mathcal{U} = \{u(t)\}_{t=0}^{n-1}$ where each $u(t)$ is an i.i.d. Bermoulli(p) random variable for some fixed $p > 0$. It is easy to see that for any T and $I \in \mathcal{I}_T$, we have

$$\lim_{n\to\infty} \mu_{\mathcal{U}}^+(I,T) = \frac{|I|}{T}. \tag{5}$$

This corresponds to the case where the positive samples are evenly distributed over all entries after overlay. So we propose the new discrepancy score of I as follows:

$$\Delta_{\mathcal{X}}^+(I,T) = \mu_{\mathcal{X}}^+(I,T) - \frac{|I|}{T}, \tag{6}$$

and define the periodicity measure as:

$$\gamma_{\mathcal{X}}^+(T) = \max_{I\in\mathcal{I}_T} \Delta_{\mathcal{X}}^+(I,T). \tag{7}$$

In fact, with some slight modification to the proof of Lemma 2, we can show that it is a desired measure under our probabilistic model, resulting in the following theorem.

THEOREM 2. *Suppose $\mathbf{d} = \{d_t\}_{t=0}^{n-1}$ are i.i.d. random variables in $[0,1]$ with nonzero mean, and a sequence $\mathcal{X}$ is generated according to any $(\mathbf{p}^{T_0}, \mathbf{d})$ for some T_0, then*

$$\lim_{n\to\infty} \gamma_{\mathcal{X}}^+(T) \le \lim_{n\to\infty} \gamma_{\mathcal{X}}^+(T_0), \quad \forall T \in \mathbb{Z}.$$

PROOF. Define $c_i^+ = \frac{p_i^{T_0}}{\sum_{k=0}^{T_0-1} p_k^{T_0}} - \frac{1}{T_0}$, it is easy to see that the value $\lim_{n\to\infty} \gamma_{\mathcal{X}}^+(T_0)$ is achieved by $I^* = \{i \in [0, T_0-1] : c_i^+ > 0\}$. So it suffices to show that for any $T \in \mathbb{Z}$ and $I \in \mathcal{I}_T$,

$$\lim_{n\to\infty} \Delta_{\mathcal{X}}^+(I,T) \le \lim_{n\to\infty} \Delta_{\mathcal{X}}^+(I^*,T_0) = \sum_{i\in I^*} c_i^+.$$

Observe now that for any (I,T),

$$\lim_{n\to\infty} \mu_{\mathcal{X}}^+(I,T) = \sum_{i\in I} \left(\frac{1}{T} \sum_{j=0}^{T_0-1} \frac{p_{\mathcal{F}_{T_0}(i+j\times T)}^{T_0}}{\sum_{k=0}^{T_0-1} p_k^{T_0}} \right).$$

Therefore we have

$$\begin{aligned}
\lim_{n\to\infty} \Delta_{\mathcal{X}}^+(I,T) &= \frac{1}{T}\sum_{i\in I}\left\{ \sum_{j=0}^{T_0-1} \left(\frac{p_{\mathcal{F}_{T_0}(i+j\times T)}^{T_0}}{\sum_{k=0}^{T_0-1} p_k^{T_0}} \right) - 1 \right\} \\
&= \frac{1}{T}\sum_{i\in I}\sum_{j=0}^{T_0-1} \left(\frac{p_{\mathcal{F}_{T_0}(i+j\times T)}^{T_0}}{\sum_{k=0}^{T_0-1} p_k^{T_0}} - \frac{1}{T_0} \right) \\
&= \frac{1}{T}\sum_{i\in I}\sum_{j=0}^{T_0-1} c_{\mathcal{F}_{T_0}(i+j\times T)}^+ \\
&\le \frac{1}{T}\sum_{i\in I}\sum_{j=0}^{T_0-1} \max(c_{\mathcal{F}_{T_0}(i+j\times T)}^+, 0) \\
&\le \frac{1}{T}\sum_{j=0}^{T_0T-1} \max(c_{\mathcal{F}_{T_0}(i+j\times T)}^+, 0) \\
&= \frac{1}{T} \times T \sum_{i\in I^*} c_i^+ = \sum_{i\in I^*} c_i^+,
\end{aligned}$$

where the fourth equality uses the definition of I^*. □

Note that this new measure $\gamma_{\mathcal{X}}^+(T)$ can also be applied to the cases where negative samples are available. Given the same validity result, readers may wonder if it can replace $\gamma_{\mathcal{X}}(T)$. This is certainly not the case in practice, as our results only hold exactly when the sequence has infinite length. As we will see in experiment results, negative samples indeed provide additional information for period detection in finite length observation sequences.

EXAMPLE 5 (RUNNING EXAMPLE (CONT.)). *In this example we further marked all the negative samples in the sequence we used in Example 4 as unknown. When there is no negative samples, the portion of positive samples at a single timestamp i is expected to be $\frac{1}{T}$, as shown in Figure 7(a). The discrepancy scores when $T = 24$ still have large values at $\{10, 11, 14, 15, 16\}$. Thus the correct period can be successfully detected as shown in Figure 7(b).*

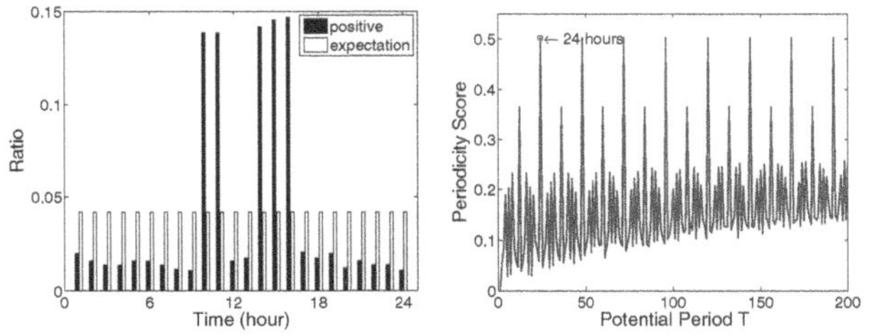

(a) Distribution ($T = 24$) (b) Periodicity scores

Figure 7: (Running Example) Period detection on sequences without negative samples.

4. ALGORITHM

In Section 3, we have introduced our periodicity measure for any potential period $T \in \mathbb{Z}$. Our period detection method simply computes the periodicity scores for every T and report the one with the highest score.

In this section, we first describe how to compute the periodicity score for a potential period and then discuss a practical issue when applying our method to finite length sequence. We will focus on the case with both positive and negative observations. The case without negative observations can be solved in the same way.

As we have seen in Section 3.1, the set of timestamps I^* that maximizes $\gamma_{\mathcal{X}}(T)$ can be expressed as

$$I^* = \{i \in [0, T_0 - 1] : c_i > 0\}, \tag{8}$$

where $c_i = \frac{p_i^{T_0}}{\sum_{k=0}^{T_0-1} p_k^{T_0}} - \frac{q_i^{T_0}}{\sum_{k=0}^{T_0-1} q_k^{T_0}}$. Therefore, to find I^*, it suffices to compute c_i for each $i \in [0, T_0 - 1]$ and select those ones with $c_i > 0$.

Time Complexity Analysis. For every potential period T, it takes $O(n)$ time to compute discrepancy score for a single timestamp (*i.e.*, c_i) and then $O(T)$ time to compute periodicity $\gamma_{\mathcal{X}}(T)$. Since potential period should be in range $[1, n]$, the time complexity of our method is $O(n^2)$. In practice, it is usually unnecessary to try all the potential periods. For example, we may have common sense that the periods will be no larger than certain values. So we only need to try potential periods up to n_0, where $n_0 \ll n$. This will make our method efficient in practice with time complexity as $O(n \times n_0)$.

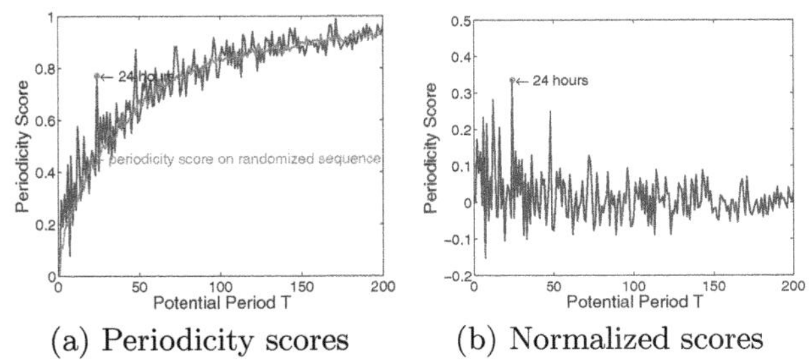

(a) Periodicity scores (b) Normalized scores

Figure 8: Normalization of periodicity scores.

Now we want to point out a practical issue when applying our method on finite length sequence. As one may already notice in our running example, we usually see a general increasing trend of periodicity scores $\gamma_{\mathcal{X}}(T)$ and $\gamma^+_{\mathcal{X}}(T)$ for a larger potential period T. This trend becomes more dominating as the number of observations decreases. For example, the original running example has observations for 1000 days. If the observations are only for 20 days, our method may result in incorrect period detection result, as the case shown in Figure 8(a). In fact, this phenomenon is expected and can be understood in the following way. Let us take $\gamma^+_{\mathcal{X}}(T)$ as an example. Given a sequence $\mathcal{X}$ with *finite number* of positive observations, it is easy to see that the size of I that maximizes $\gamma^+_{\mathcal{X}}(T)$ for any T is bounded above by the number of positive observations. Therefore the value $\frac{|I^*|}{T}$ always decreases as T increases, no matter whether or not T is a true period of $\mathcal{X}$.

To remedy this issue for finite length sequence, we use periodicity scores on *randomized* sequence to normalize the original periodicity scores. Specifically, we randomly permute the positions of observations along the timeline and compute the periodicity score for each potential period T. This procedure is repeated N times and the average periodicity scores over N trials are output as the base scores. The redline in Figure 8(a) shows the base scores generated from randomized sequences by setting $N = 10$, which agree well with the trend.

For every potential period T, we subtract the base score from the original periodicity score, resulting in the normalized periodicity score. Note that the normalized score also slightly favors shorter period, which helps us to avoid detecting duplicated periods (*i.e.*, multiples of the prime period).

5. EXPERIMENT

In this section, we systematically evaluate the techniques presented in this paper on both synthetic and real datasets.

5.1 Synthetic Dataset Generation

In order to test the effectiveness of our method under various scenarios, we first use synthetic datasets generated according to a set of parameter. We take the following steps to generate a synthetic test sequence SEQ.

Step 1. We first fix a period T, for example, $T = 24$. The periodic segment SEG is a boolean sequence of length T, with values -1 and 1 indicating negative and positive observations, respectively. For simplicity of presentation, we write $SEG = [s_1 : t_1, s_2 : t_2, \ldots]$ where $[s_i, t_i]$ denote the i-th interval of SEG whose entries are all set to 1.

Step 2. Periodic segment SEG are repeated for TN times to generate the complete observation sequence, denoted as standard sequence SEQ_{std}. SEQ_{std} has length $T \times TN$.

Step 3 (Random sampling η). We sample the standard sequence with sampling rate η. For any element in SEQ_{std}, we set its value to 0 (*i.e.*, unknown) with probability $(1 - \eta)$.

Step 4 (Missing segments α). For any segment in standard segment SEQ_{std}, we set all the elements in that segment as 0 (*i.e.*, unknown) with probability $(1 - \alpha)$.

Step 5 (Random noise β). For any remaining observation in SEQ_{std}, we reverse its original values (making -1 as 1 and 1 as -1) with probability β.

The input sequence SEQ has values -1, 0, and 1 indicating negative, unknown, and positive observations. In the case when negative samples are unavailable, all the -1 values will be set to 0. Note that here we set negative observations as -1 and unknown ones as 0, which is different from the description in Section 2. The reason is that the unknown entries are set as -1, in the presence of many missing entries, traditional methods such as Fourier transform will be dominated by missing entries instead of actual observations.

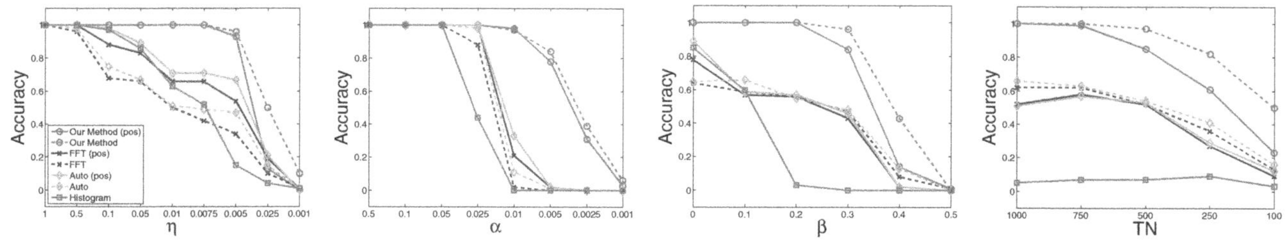

(a) Sampling rate η (b) Observed segements α (c) Noise ratio β (d) Repetitions TN

Figure 9: Comparison results on synthetic data with various parameter settings.

The purpose of such adjustment is to facilitate traditional methods and it has no effect on our method.

5.2 Methods for comparison

We will compare our method with the following methods, which are frequently used to detect periods in boolean sequence [6].

1. Fourier Transform (FFT): The frequency with the highest spectral power from Fourier transform via FFT is converted into time domain and output as the result.

2. Auto-correlation and Fourier Transform (Auto): We first compute the auto-correlation of the input sequence. Since the output of auto-correlation will have peaks at all the multiples of the true period, we further apply Fourier transform to it and report the period with the highest power.

3. Histogram and Fourier Transform (Histogram): We calculate the distances between any two positive observations and build a histogram of the distances over all the pairs. Then we apply Fourier transform to the histogram and report the period with the highest power.

We will use FFT(pos) and Auto(pos) to denote the methods FFT and Auto-correlation for cases without any negative observations. For Histogram, since it only considers the distances between positive observations, the results for cases with or without negative observations are exactly the same.

5.3 Performance Studies

In this section, we test all the methods on synthetic data under various settings. The default parameter setting is the following: $T = 24$, $SEG = [9:10, 14:16]$. $TN = 1000$, $\eta = 0.1$, $\alpha = 0.5$, and $\beta = 0.2$. For each experiment, we report the performance of all the methods with one of these parameters varying while the others are fixed. For each parameter setting, we repeat the experiment for 100 times and report the accuracy, which is the number of correct period detections over 100 trials. Results are shown in Figure 9.

Performance w.r.t sampling rate η. To better study the effect of sampling rate, we set $\alpha = 1$ in this experiment. Figure 9(a) shows that our method is significantly better than other methods in terms of handling data with low sampling rate. The accuracy of our method remains 100% even when the sampling rate is as low as 0.0075. The accuracies of other methods start to decrease when sampling rate is lower than 0.5. Also note that Auto is slightly better than FFT because auto-correlation essentially generates a smoothed version of the categorical data for Fourier transform. In addition, it is interesting to see that FFT and Auto performs better in the case without negative observations.

Performance w.r.t ratio of observed segments α. In this set of experiments, sampling rate η is set as 1 to better study the effect of α. Figure 9(b) depicts the performance of the methods. Our method again performs much better than other methods. Our method is almost perfect even when $\alpha = 0.025$. And when all other methods fail at $\alpha = 0.005$, our method still achieves 80% accuracy.

Performance w.r.t noise ratio β. In Figure 9(c), we show the performance of the methods w.r.t different noise ratios. Histogram is very sensitive to random noises since it considers the distances between any two positive observations. Our method is still the most robust one among all. For example, with $\beta = 0.3$, our method achieves accuracy as high as 80%.

Performance w.r.t number of repetitions TN. Figure 9(d) shows the accuracies as a function of TN. As expected, the accuracies decrease as TN becomes smaller for all the methods, but our method again significantly outperforms the other ones.

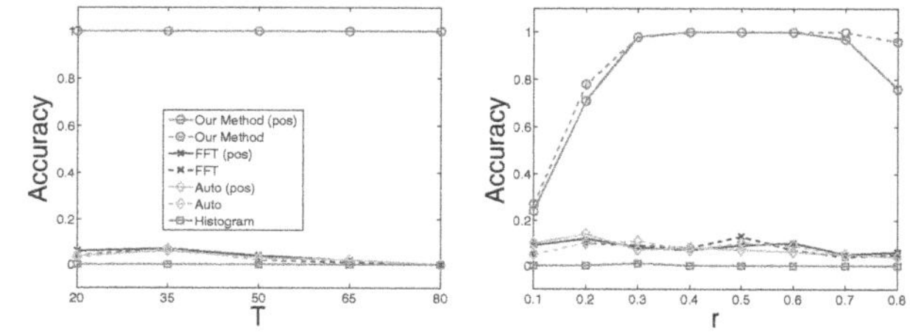

(a) True period T (b) Periodic segment SEG

Figure 10: Comparison results on randomly generated periodic behaviors.

Performance w.r.t periodic behavior. We also study the performance of all the methods on randomly generated periodic behaviors. Given a period T and fix the ratio of 1's in a SEG as r, we generate SEG by setting each element to 1 with probability r. Sequences generated in this way will have positive observations scattered within a period, which will cause big problems for all the methods using Fourier transform, as evidenced in Figure 10. *This is because Fourier transform is very likely to have high spectral power at short periods if the input values alternate between 1 and 0 frequently.* In Figure 10(a) we set $r = 0.4$ and show the results w.r.t period length T. In Figure 10(b), we fix $T = 24$ and show the results with varying r. As we can see, all the other methods fail miserably when the periodic behavior is randomly generated. In addition, when the ratio of positive observations is low, *i.e.* fewer observations, it is more difficult to detect the correct period in general.

Comparison with Lomb-Scargle method. Lomb-Scargle periodogram (Lomb) [9, 12] was introduced as a variation of Fourier transform to detect periods in *unevenly* sampled data. The method takes the timestamps with observations

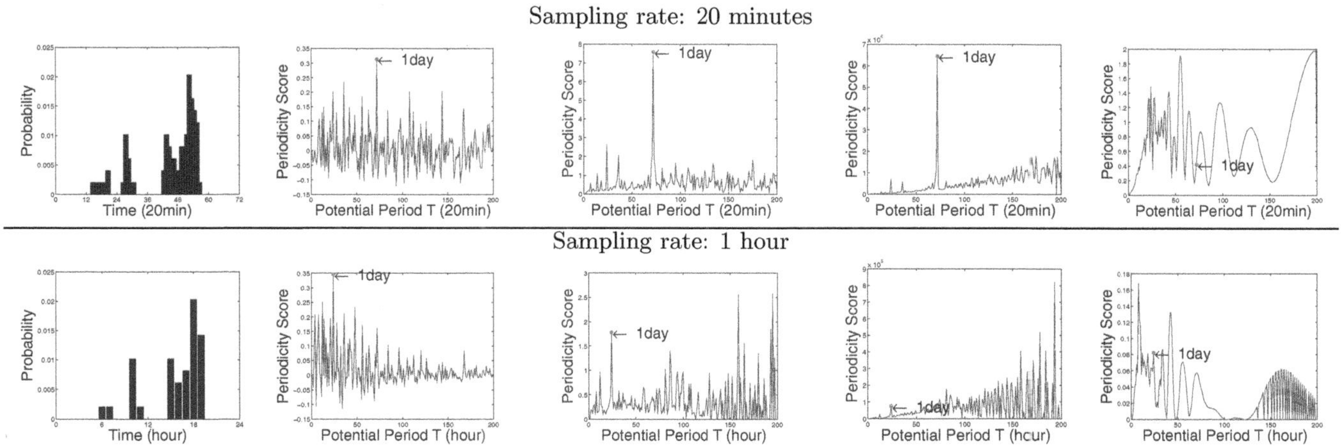

(a) Event (b) Our Method (c) FFT (d) Auto (e) Histogram

Table 1: Comparison of period detection methods on a person's movement data.

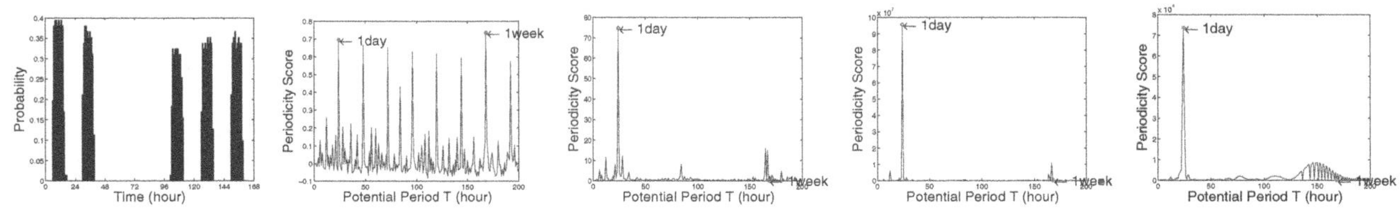

(a) Event (b) Our Method (c) FFT (d) Auto (e) Histogram

Figure 11: Comparion of methods on detecting long period, *i.e.* one week (168 hours).

and their corresponding values as input. It does not work for the positive-sample-only case, because all the input values will be the same hence no period can be detected. The reason we do not compare with this method systematically is that the method performs poorly on the binary data and it is very slow. Here, we run it on a smaller dataset by setting $TN = 100$. We can see from Table 2 that, when $\eta = 0.5$ or $\alpha = 0.5$, our method and FFT perform well whereas the accuracy of Lomb is already approaching 0. As pointed out in [13], Lomb does not work well in bi-modal periodic signals and sinusoidal signals with non-Gaussian noises, hence not suitable for our purpose.

5.4 A Case Study on Real Human Movements

In this section, we use the real GPS locations of a person who has tracking record for 492 days. We first pick one of his frequently visited locations and generate a boolean observation sequence by treating all the visits to this location as positive observations and visits to other locations as negative observations. We study the performance of the methods on this symbolized movement data at different sampling rates. In Table 1, we compare the methods at two sampling rates, 1 hour and 20 minutes. As one can see in Table 1(a), when overlaying this person's activity onto an period of one day, most of the visits occur in time interval [40, 60] for sampling rate of 20 minutes, or equivalently, in interval [15, 20] when the time unit is 1 hour. On one hand, when sampling rate is 20 minutes, all the methods except FFT(pos) and Histogram successfully detect the period of 24 hours, as they all have the strongest peaks at 24 hours (so we take 24 hours as the true period). On the other hand, when the data is sampled at each hour only, all the other methods fail to report 24 hours as the strongest peak whereas our method still succeeds. In fact, the success of our method can be easily inferred from Table 1(a), as one can see that lowering the sampling rate has little effect on the distribution graph of the overlaid sequence. We further show the periods reported by all the methods at various sampling rates in Table 3. Our method obviously outperforms the others in terms of tolerating low sampling rates.

Parameter	Accuracy		
	Our Method	FFT	Lomb
$\eta = 0.5$	1	0.7	0.09
$\eta = 0.1$	1	0.52	0.10
$\alpha = 0.5$	1	1	0.01
$\alpha = 0.1$	0.99	0.35	0

Table 2: Comparison with Lomb-Scargle method.

Method	Sampling rate			
	20min	1hour	2hour	4hour
Our Method (pos)	24	24	24	8
Our Method	24	24	24	8
FFT(pos)	9.3	9	8	8
FFT	24	195	372	372
Auto(pos)	24	9	42	8
Auto	24	193	372	780
Histogram	66.33	8	42	48

Table 3: Periods reported by different methods at various sampling rates.

Next, in Figure 11, we use the symbolized sequence of the same person at a different location and demonstrate the ability of our method in detecting multiple potential periods, especially those long ones. As we can see in Figure 11(a), this person clearly has weekly periodicity w.r.t this location. It is very likely that this location is his office which he only visits during weekdays. Our method correctly detects 7-

day with the highest periodicity score and 1-day has second highest score. But all other methods are dominated by the short period of 1-day. Please note that, in the figures of other methods, 1-week point is not even on the peak. This shows the strength of our method at detecting both long and short periods.

6. RELATED WORK

Fourier transform and auto-correlation are the two most popular methods to detect periods [11]. However, Fourier transform has known problem in detecting the periods from sparse data [6]. It also performs poorly on data with multiple non-consecutive occurrence in a period, as it tends to prefer short periods [15]. Auto-correlation offers accurate estimation for both short and long periods, but is more difficult to find the unique period due to the fact that the multiples of the true period will have the same score as the true period itself. In addition, both Fourier transform and auto-ccorelation require evenly sampled input data. Lomb-Scargle periodogram [9, 12] is proposed as a variation of Fourier transform to handle unevenly spaced data using least-squares fitting of sinusoidal curves. But it suffers the same problems as Fourier transform. In bioinformatics, several methods have been proposed to address the issue of unevenly spaced gene data [3, 8]. However, this issue is only one aspect of our problem whereas the low sampling rate and missing data problem have not been studied in these papers. An interesting previous work [6] has studied the problem of periodic pattern detection in sparse boolean sequences for gene data, where the ratio of the number of 1's to 0's is small. However, sparsity in our problem is a result of low sampling rate and missing data, and we do not make any assumption on the sparsity of original periodic patterns.

Studies on period detection in data mining and database area usually assume the input to be a sequence of symbols instead of real value time series, and most of them have been focused on the *efficiency* of period detection algorithms [5, 1]. The presence of noises in the data has been considered in [10, 16, 2]. Our recent work [7] has studied probabilistic periodic behavior mining for moving objects. But it has been focused on dealing with spatiotemporal data, while period detection is still based on Fourier transform and auto-correlation. In summary, none of previous studies can handle all the practical issues we mentioned in this paper, *i.e.*, the observations are incomplete, and the periodic behavior is complicated and noisy.

7. CONCLUSION

In this paper, we address the important and challenging problem of period detection from incomplete observations. We first propose a probabilistic model for periodic behaviors. Then, we design a novel measure for periodicity and a practical algorithm to detect periods in real scenarios. We give a rigorous proof of its validity for our probabilistic framework. Empirical studies show that our method is robust to imperfectly collected data and complicated periodic behaviors. A case study on real human movement data further demonstrates the effectiveness of our method.

While our approach is designed for binary sequences, one important extension is to handle observation sequences with real values. For example, sensors may not only detect the usage of a room but also report the temperature and humidity, and such data could also be sparse, incomplete and unevenly sampled due to the limitations of sensors. We consider this as interesting future work.

8. ACKNOWLEDGMENTS

The work was supported in part by Boeing company, NASA NRA-NNH10ZDA001N, NSF IIS-0905215 and IIS-1017362, the U.S. Army Research Laboratory under Cooperative Agreement No. W911NF-09-2-0053 (NS-CTA). The views and conclusions contained in this paper are those of the authors and should not be interpreted as representing any funding agencies.

9. REFERENCES

[1] M. G. Elfeky, W. G. Aref, and A. K. Elmagarmid. Periodicity detection in time series databases. *IEEE Trans. Knowl. Data Eng.*, 2005.

[2] M. G. Elfeky, W. G. Aref, and A. K. Elmagarmid. Warp: Time warping for periodicity detection. In *ICDM*, 2005.

[3] E. F. Glynn, J. Chen, and A. R. Mushegian. Detecting periodic patterns in unevenly spaced gene expression time series using lomb-scargle periodograms. In *Bioinformatics*, 2005.

[4] M. C. González, C. A. Hidalgo, and A.-L. Barabás. Understanding individual human mobility patterns. In *Nature*, 2008.

[5] P. Indyk, N. Koudas, and S. Muthukrishnan. Identifying representative trends in massive time series data sets using sketches. In *VLDB*, 2000.

[6] I. Junier, J. Herisson, and F. Kepes. Periodic pattern detection in sparse boolean sequences. In *Algorithms for Molecular Biology*, 2010.

[7] Z. Li, B. Ding, J. Han, R. Kays, and P. Nye. Mining periodic behaviors for moving objects. In *KDD*, 2010.

[8] K.-C. Liang, X. Wang, and T.-H. Li. Robust regression for periodicity detection in non-uniformly sampled time-course gene expression data. In *BMC Bioinformatics*, 2009.

[9] N. R. Lomb. Least-squares frequency analysis of unequally spaced data. In *Astrophysics and Space Science*, 1976.

[10] S. Ma and J. L. Hellerstein. Mining partially periodic event patterns with unknown periods. In *ICDE*, 2001.

[11] M. B. Priestley. *Spectral Analysis and Time Series*. London: Academic Press, 1981.

[12] J. D. Scargle. Studies in astronomical time series analysis. ii - statistical aspects of spectral analysis of unevenly spaced data. In *Astrophysical Journal*, 1982.

[13] M. Schimmel. Emphasizing difficulties in the detection of rhythms with lomb-scargle periodograms. In *Biological Rhythm Research*, 2001.

[14] T. van Kasteren, A. K. Noulas, G. Englebienne, and B. J. A. Kröse. Accurate activity recognition in a home setting. In *UbiComp*, 2008.

[15] M. Vlachos, P. S. Yu, and V. Castelli. On periodicity detection and structural periodic similarity. In *SDM*, 2005.

[16] J. Yang, W. Wang, and P. S. Yu. Mining asynchronous periodic patterns in time series data. In *KDD*, 2000.

Towards Heterogeneous Temporal Clinical Event Pattern Discovery:A Convolutional Approach

Fei Wang[1], Noah Lee,[1,2], Jianying Hu[1], Jimeng Sun[1], Shahram Ebadollahi[1]
[1]Healthcare Analytics Research Group, IBM T.J. Watson Research Center
[2]Department of Biomedical Engineering, Columbia University
fwang,jyhu,jimeng,ebad@us.ibm.com,nl2168@columbia.edu

ABSTRACT

Large collections of electronic clinical records today provide us with a vast source of information on medical practice. However, the utilization of those data for exploratory analysis to support clinical decisions is still limited. Extracting useful patterns from such data is particularly challenging because it is *longitudinal*, *sparse* and *heterogeneous*. In this paper, we propose a *Nonnegative Matrix Factorization* (NMF) based framework using a convolutional approach for open-ended temporal pattern discovery over large collections of clinical records. We call the method *One-Sided Convolutional NMF* (OSC-NMF). Our framework can mine common as well as individual *shift-invariant* temporal patterns from heterogeneous events over different patient groups, and handle sparsity as well as scalability problems well. Furthermore, we use an event matrix based representation that can encode quantitatively all key temporal concepts including order, concurrency and synchronicity. We derive efficient *multiplicative update* rules for OSC-NMF, and also prove theoretically its convergence. Finally, the experimental results on both synthetic and real world electronic patient data are presented to demonstrate the effectiveness of the proposed method.

Categories and Subject Descriptors

J.3 [**Life and Medical Sciences**]: Health; I.5 [**Pattern Recognition**]: Design Technology—*Pattern analysis*

General Terms

Agorithms

Keywords

Pattern Discovery, NMF, Convolution

1. INTRODUCTION

Electronic Health Records (EHR) are systematic collections of longitudinal patient health information generated by one or more encounters in any care delivery setting. Included in this information are patient demographics, encounter records such as claims, progress notes, problems, medications, vital signs, immunizations, laboratory data and radiology reports, etc. Fig.1 illustrates an example of a temporal event record of a diabetic patient over one year, where 30 key event factors are recorded, including procedures (CPTs), lab results (LABs), visits to primary care physician (PCP) and various specialists (SPEC).

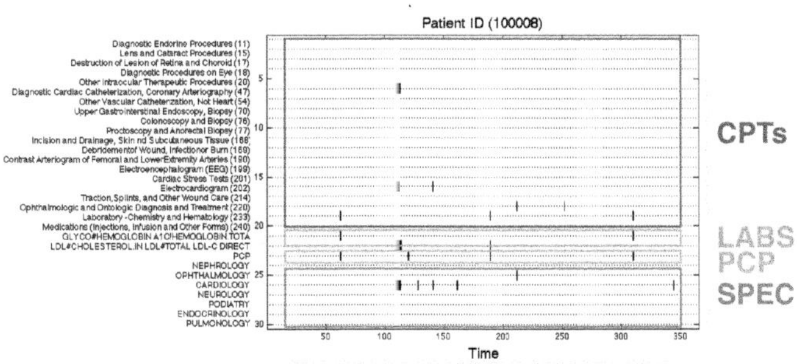

Figure 1: An example of a diabetic patient's electronic record over one year. The x-axis corresponds to the day index, the y-axis represents different types of recorded events, which can be categorized into 4 groups including procedures (CPTs), lab results (LABs), visits to primary care physician (PCP) and visits to specialists (SPEC). The dots in the figure indicate the corresponding events happening at corresponding dates.

In this paper, we study *Temporal Pattern Discovery* (TPD) for EHR data, which aims at finding temporal patterns of one or more groups of patients. TPD is an open-ended problem in the sense that the mined patterns can be utilized in various scenarios such as predictive modeling [1], information visualization [29] and comparative effectiveness research [25]. TPD is also an active research direction that has attracted a lot of interests from data mining related applications including financial marketing [6], video content analysis [4] and social network analysis [19]. Many challenges in TPD are shared by these applications, however some are particularly pronounced in the medical domain when performing TPD from medical data. These include

(1) ***Shift-Invariance.*** EHR for all patients are not temporally aligned. Moreover, due to various complexities such as comorbidities, the trajectories for different patients are very different over a long time period. However, it is possible to extract time-invariant patterns within a shorter timeframe across patients. Thus an appropriate TPD approach should not be affected by the absolute time stamps.

(2) *Heterogeneity*. The EHR data contain multiple types of events (e.g., diagnosis, medication, lab). The method needs to be able to mine patterns from the combination of all types of events and capture the relationship among them.

(2) *Sparsity and Irregularity*. The EHR data are usually very sparse with irregular intervals, as most of the patients do not have frequent events (e.g., the patient shown in Fig.1 only has around 20 events in a year) or with high regularity.

(4) *Quantitative Nature*. In clinical settings qualitative relations such are event A is followed by event B is important but typically insufficient. Quantitative measures of the duration of a given event and the interval between multiple events are often of key importance.

(5) *Scalability*. We may face a large patient population, and each patient may has a long longitudinal record (e.g., chronic disease) and many different event factors. The algorithm needs to be able to efficiently learn patterns from such a large volume of data.

We propose a novel *geometric* framework for EHR representation and perform the TPD task based on that. Specifically, we model the EHR record as an image matrix like Fig.1, where the x-axis corresponds to the time stamps and y-axis corresponds to the event values. Note that different events can have different value ranges and types (e.g., blood pressure has continuous values, while PCP visits has non-negative integer values)[1]. Furthermore, each event could be either instantaneous (represented by a single pixel), or with a certain duration (represented by a line segment in the image). This provides a succinct representation that can effectively encode a large range of temporal information including event value, time and duration, relationships among different events, and intervals between pairwise events using an image. We call such a representation an *event matrix*.

Based on the event matrix representation, we propose a novel approach, *One-Sided Convolutional Nonnegative Matrix Factorization* (*OSC-NMF*), to detect temporal patterns from EHR. NMF is a powerful tool for identifying underline structures in a matrix through regularized decomposition and has been successfully applied to many applications including clustering, metric learning, and classification [13][14]. In order to apply this tool to our problem setting, where each patient is represented by an event matrix with fix number of rows (determined by the events of interested) but varying number of columns (determined by the length of the longitudinal record of the patient), we adapt a convolutional approach. Our approach assumes that each patient matrix is generated by the superposition and concatenation of a set of temporal pattern matrices over the time axis. The method is called *one-sided* because the convolution only occurs along the time axis but not on event side. Each pattern matrix essentially encodes a composite temporal pattern with the inherent order, concurrency and synchronicity relations among different events.

To carry out this convolutional decomposition approach we introduce a methodology to minimize the β-divergence [9] between the convoluted matrix and the original patient matrix to obtain the optimal pattern matrices under nonnegativity constraints. β-divergence is a general divergence measure that includes many common measures such as KL-divergence and Euclidean distance as special cases. We provide efficient multiplicative update rules for solving the optimal patterns based on this general measure, and rigorous proofs for the algorithm convergence. Experimental results on applying OSC-NMF to both synthetic and real world data are presented to demonstrate its effectiveness.

It is worthwhile to highlight the strength of OSC-NMF.

(1) *The mined patterns are shift invariant*. Because of the convolutional nature of OSC-NMF, the mined temporal patterns are independent of the absolute time stamps.

(2) *The mined patterns are comprehensive*. The mined pattern matrices represent relationships among all different types of events recorded in the patient matrices.

(3) *OSC-NMF can incorporate sparsity constraints*. OSC-NMF can easily handle the high sparsity in the data by adding sparsity regularization terms in the objective.

(4) *The mined patterns are quantitative*. The pattern matrices can naturally encode quantitative relationships among all different events, including duration of events as well as interval and overlap between events.

(5) *OSC-NMF can handle large scale data set*. We provide an efficient *stochastic* learning framework for OSC-NMF, which processes one or a small portion of the data matrices each time, thus results in a constant memory cost.

The rest of this paper is organized as follows. Section 2 introduces related work. Algorithm details and extensions are described in section 3. Section 4 presents the experimental results, is followed by the conclusion in section 5.

2. RELATED WORK

In this section we briefly review some previous work that are closely related to our work in this paper.

A lot of work has been done for temporal sequence representation and mining. For example, Keogh *et al.* proposed *symbolic aggregate approximation* (SAX) [15] to represent time series using symbolic sequences. However, SAX cannot take into account the relationships among heterogeneous time sequences. [17] proposed a temporal knowledge representation method with symbolic languages and grammars. [5] proposed a TPD approach based on first-order temporal logic under regular expression constraints. These methods is that they specify some explicit symbolic languages and temporal grammars according to prior knowledge. Frequent item set [22][11] or sub-sequence [30] mining are also closely related to the work in this paper. However, in these approaches, the time intervals between pairwise events are not considered. In our case, this pairwise event intervals are of key importance (e.g., two events happen in a week and a year are completely different disease condition signals).

In medical domain, [20] proposed a statistical approach for summarizing and visualizing the temporal associations between the prescription of a drug and the occurrence of a medical event. [24] proposed a *temporal abstraction* approach for medical TPD. Similar to [17], this method also requires predefined temporal grammar and logic with prior knowledge. [8] proposed a visual interface for finding temporal patterns in multivariate temporal clinical data. The interface was further used in [23] for searching temporal patterns in patient histories, but the user needs to specify the structure of the pattern on the interface.

On the methodology side, *Nonnegative Matrix Factorization* (NMF) [13][14], which aims at factorizing a nonnegative

[1]In this paper, we only consider binary event values, i.e., the (i, j)-th element of the patient matrix is 1 if the i-th event happens at time j, otherwise its value would be 0.

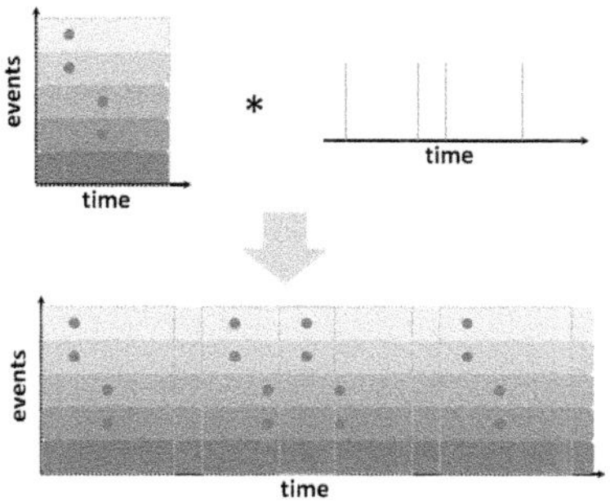

Figure 2: A graphical illustration of one-side convolution. The top left figure shows temporal pattern, and the top right figure is the time axis where we use green bars to represent the position where the pattern appears. The bottom figure is the one-side convolution result, where each dotted line rectangle corresponds to a pattern.

matrix into the product of two low-rank nonnegative matrices, has attracted considerable interests from data mining in recent years. There are also a lot of NMF variants that are related to our work. For instance, [12][7] proposed to enforce sparsity regularizations on the decomposed matrices to obtain sparse solutions. [10], [21], [26] and [18] proposed *convolutional* sparse NMF to discover the shift-invariant temporal patterns from acoustic signals and images. However their approach is designed for time series data and is not applicable to heterogeneous event sequences. Furthermore, all prior methods measure the factorization quality using matrix Frobenius norm, and obtain a common set of patterns by batch learning methods. On the contrary, our method proposed in this paper (1) is based on a general β-divergence loss; (2) can detect common and individual patterns from different data groups, and (3) can be trained with efficient stochastic learning scheme.

3. ONE-SIDED CONVOLUTIONAL NMF

We now describe the *One-Sided Convolutional NMF* (OSC-NMF) algorithm in detail.

3.1 Preliminaries

Suppose we have a patient matrix $\mathbf{X} \in \mathbb{R}^{n\times t}$, where n is the number of event factors, t is the length of the patient clinical history. As mentioned in section 1, we assume $\mathbf{X}$ is the superposition of the one-side convolution of a set of hidden patterns $\mathcal{F} = \{\mathbf{F}^{(r)}\}_{r=1}^{R}$ across the time axis. We define the one-side convolutional operator $*$ as follows.

Definition 1. (One-Sided Convolution). *The one-sided convolution of* $\mathbf{F} \in \mathbb{R}^{n\times m}$ *and* $\mathbf{g} \in \mathbb{R}^{t\times 1}$ *is an* $n \times t$ *matrix with*

$$(\mathbf{F} * \mathbf{g})_{ij} = \sum\nolimits_{k=1}^{t} g_{j-k+1} F_{ik} \quad (1)$$

Note that $g_j = 0$ *if* $j \leqslant 0$ *or* $j > t$, *and* $F_{ik} = 0$ *if* $k > m$.

Thus we can see that one-side convolution is the operation between a matrix and a vector. This operator is specially designed for our scenario on TPD from electronic clinical records. As in our case, we are interested in patterns composed of all events, thus there is no convolution on the vertical axis. Fig.2 gives us an intuitive graphical illustration of the procedure of one-side convolution, where the bottom image is obtained through the one-side convolution of the pattern top-left and the time vector top-right.

Another important definition is the matrix β-divergence.

Definition 2. (β-divergence [9]) *The* β*-divergence between two matrices* $\mathbf{A}$ *and* $\mathbf{B}$ *with the same size is*

$$d_\beta(\mathbf{A},\mathbf{B}) = \frac{1}{\beta(\beta-1)} \sum\nolimits_{ij} \left(A_{ij}^{\beta} + (\beta-1)B_{ij}^{\beta} - \beta A_{ij} B_{ij}^{\beta-1}\right) \quad (2)$$

where $\beta \geqslant 0$ *is a constant.*

For completeness, by making use of the limit theory, we define $d_\beta(\mathbf{A},\mathbf{B})$ for $\beta = 0$ and $\beta = 1$ as follows.

$$\begin{aligned} d_0(\mathbf{A},\mathbf{B}) &= \lim_{\beta\to 0} \sum\nolimits_{ij} \left(A_{ij}\frac{B_{ij}^{\beta-1}}{1-\beta} - \frac{A_{ij}^{\beta} - B_{ij}^{\beta}}{\beta}\right) + \frac{A_{ij}^{\beta}}{\beta-1} \\ &= \sum\nolimits_{ij} A_{ij}(\log A_{ij} - \log B_{ij}) + (B_{ij} - A_{ij}) \quad (3) \\ d_1(\mathbf{A},\mathbf{B}) &= \lim_{\beta\to 1} \sum\nolimits_{ij} \left(A_{ij}\frac{A_{ij}^{\beta-1} - B_{ij}^{\beta-1}}{\beta-1} + \frac{B_{ij}^{\beta} - A_{ij}^{\beta}}{\beta}\right) \\ &= \sum\nolimits_{ij} A_{ij}(\log A_{ij} - \log B_{ij}) + (B_{ij} - A_{ij}) \quad (4) \end{aligned}$$

β-divergence is a very general divergence: $d_0(\mathbf{A},\mathbf{B})$, $d_1(\mathbf{A},\mathbf{B})$, $d_2(\mathbf{A},\mathbf{B})$ correspond to the *Itakura-Saito distance*, *generalized Kullback-Leighbler divergence* and *Euclidean distance*.

3.2 The Algorithm

Now coming back to our problem, we first introduce how to make use of OSC-NMF to detect temporal patterns from a single patient's EHR. Second, we extend OSC-NMF to detect patterns from the EHR of multiple groups of patients.

Recall we suppose the patient EHR matrix $\mathbf{X}$ is constructed by the superposition of the one-side convolution of a set of patterns $\mathcal{F} = \{\mathbf{F}^{(r)}\}_{r=1}^{R}$ across the time axis. Then we propose to detect them by minimizing

$$\mathcal{J} = d_\beta\left(\mathbf{X}, \sum\nolimits_{r=1}^{R} \mathbf{F}^{(r)} * \mathbf{g}^{(r)}\right) \quad (5)$$

where $\mathbf{g}^{(r)} \in \mathbb{R}^t$ is the coding matrix for pattern $\mathbf{F}^{(r)}$. The problem our algorithm aims to solve is

$$\min_{\mathbf{F}^{(r)}\geqslant 0,\ \mathbf{g}^{(r)}\geqslant 0} \mathcal{J} \ (\forall r = 1,2,\cdots,R) \quad (6)$$

Since the patient matrix $\mathbf{X}$ is nonnegative, we also require $\{\mathbf{F}^{(r)}, \mathbf{g}^{(r)}\}_{r=1}^{R}$ to be nonnegative. With the definition of β divergence (Eq.(2)), we have

$$\frac{\partial \mathcal{J}}{\partial F_{ik}^{(r)}} = \sum\nolimits_{j=1}^{t} \left(Y_{ij}^{\beta-1} - X_{ij}Y_{ij}^{\beta-2}\right) \frac{\partial Y_{ij}}{\partial F_{ik}^{(r)}} \quad (7)$$

where we define

$$\mathbf{Y} = \sum\nolimits_{r=1}^{R} \mathbf{F}^{(r)} * \mathbf{g}^{(r)} \quad (8)$$

Combining Eq.(1) and Eq.(8), we have $\partial Y_{ij}/\partial F_{ik}^{(r)} = g_{j-k+1}^{(r)}$. Thus we can update $F_{ik}^{(r)}$ by

$$F_{ik}^{(r)} \leftarrow F_{ik}^{(r)} \left(\frac{\sum_{j=1}^{t} X_{ij} Y_{ij}^{\beta-2} g_{j-k+1}^{(r)}}{\sum_{j=1}^{t} Y_{ij}^{\beta-1} g_{j-k+1}^{(r)}}\right)^{\eta(\beta)} \quad (9)$$

where $\eta(\beta)$ is the learning rate defined as

$$\eta(\beta) = \begin{cases} \frac{1}{2-\beta} & \beta < 1 \\ 1, & 1 \leqslant \beta \leqslant 2 \\ \frac{1}{\beta-1} & \beta > 2 \end{cases} \quad (10)$$

On the other hand, we have $\frac{\partial \mathcal{J}}{\partial g_k^{(r)}} = \sum_{i=1}^{n}\sum_{j=1}^{t}\left(Y_{ij}^{\beta-1} - X_{ij}Y_{ij}^{\beta-2}\right)F_{i,j-k+1}^{(r)}$, therefore

$$g_k^{(r)} \leftarrow g_k^{(r)}\left(\frac{\sum_{i=1}^{n}\sum_{j=1}^{t}X_{ij}Y_{ij}^{\beta-2}F_{i,j-k+1}^{(r)}}{\sum_{i=1}^{n}\sum_{j=1}^{t}Y_{ij}^{\beta-1}F_{i,j-k+1}^{(r)}}\right)^{\eta(\beta)} \tag{11}$$

We have the following theorem (which is proved in the Appendix) to guarantee the convergence of the updates.

Theorem 1. *Starting from some initial guess on $\{\mathbf{F}^{(r)}, \mathbf{g}^{(r)}\}_{r=1}^{R}$ and iteratively update them with Eq.(9) and Eq.(11) will finally converge to a stationary point.*

Complexity Analysis

For the storage complexity, during the iterations, it is good to hold $\mathbf{X}$ and $\mathbf{Y}$ in the memory, which costs $O(s_X + s_Y)$ space, where s_X and s_Y are the number of nonzero elements in $\mathbf{X}$ and $\mathbf{Y}$. We also need to hold $\mathbf{F}^{(r)}$ and $\mathbf{g}^{(r)}$ when updating themselves, which brings an additional $O(\bar{s}_F + \bar{s}_g)$ space. Here $\bar{s}_F$ and $\bar{s}_g$ are the averaged number of nonzero elements over $\{\mathbf{F}^{(r)}\}_{r=1}^{R}$ and $\{\mathbf{g}^{(r)}\}_{r=1}^{R}$. So the total storage complexity is $O(s_X+s_Y+\bar{s}_F+\bar{s}_g)$.

For computational complexity, we need $O(\bar{s}_F\bar{s}_g)$ time to compute $\mathbf{Y}$, $O(2\bar{s}_F\bar{s}_g)$ time to update each $\mathbf{F}^{(r)}$ at every iteration, thus update all $\mathcal{F} = \{\mathbf{F}^{(r)}\}_{r=1}^{R}$ over one step costs $O((2R+1)\bar{s}_F\bar{s}_g)$ time, and the complexity for updating all $\mathcal{G} = \{\mathbf{g}^{(r)}\}_{r=1}^{R}$ over one iteration is the same. Thus the total computational complexity for OSC-NMF over T iterations is $O((4R+2)T\bar{s}_F\bar{s}_g)$.

Imposing the Sparsity Constraints

As shown in Fig.1, the patient EHR matrices are very sparse. Therefore it is natural to assume that the learned temporal pattern matrices and the convolutional coefficients are also sparse. Similar to [12] and [7], we can enforce the sparsity constraints by adding ℓ_1 regularization terms to the objective in Eq.(5). As a consequence, we can solve for the optimal patterns and codes by minimizing

$$\mathcal{J}_1 = d_\beta\left(\mathbf{X}, \sum_{r=1}^{R}\mathbf{F}^{(r)} * \mathbf{g}^{(r)}\right) + \lambda_1\sum_{r=1}^{R}\|\mathbf{F}^{(r)}\|_1 + \lambda_2\sum_{r=1}^{R}\|\mathbf{g}^{(r)}\|_1 \tag{12}$$

where $\lambda_1 > 0$ and $\lambda_2 > 0$ are the regularization parameters. Then the problem we want to solve becomes

$$\min_{\mathbf{F}^{(r)}\geqslant 0,\ \mathbf{g}^{(r)}\geqslant 0} \mathcal{J}_1\ (\forall r = 1, 2, \cdots, R) \tag{13}$$

Similar to the previous subsection, we can get the update rules for $\mathbf{F}$ and $\mathbf{g}$ as follows.

$$F_{ik}^{(r)} \leftarrow F_{ik}^{(r)}\left(\frac{\sum_{j=1}^{t}X_{ij}Y_{ij}^{\beta-2}g_{j-k+1}^{(r)}}{\sum_{j=1}^{t}Y_{ij}^{\beta-1}g_{j-k+1}^{(r)} + \lambda_1}\right)^{\eta(\beta)} \tag{14}$$

$$g_k^{(r)} \leftarrow g_k^{(r)}\left(\frac{\sum_{i=1}^{n}\sum_{j=1}^{t}X_{ij}Y_{ij}^{\beta-2}F_{i,j-k+1}^{(r)}}{\sum_{i=1}^{n}\sum_{j=1}^{t}Y_{ij}^{\beta-1}F_{i,j-k+1}^{(r)} + \lambda_2}\right)^{\eta(\beta)} \tag{15}$$

We can also observe that the storage and computational complexities of OSC-NMF after imposing those sparsity constraints remains the same as simple OSC-NMF.

However, as pointed out by [7], purely solving problem (13) may cause a scaling problem, as we can always scale $\mathbf{F}$ and $\mathbf{G}$ to get the same cost function value. To avoid this, we propose an normalization invariant formulation of problem (13) in the following.

Normalization Invariant Formulation

For the normalization invariant sparse OSC-NMF, we need to minimize the following objective with nonnegativity constraints.

$$\mathcal{J}_1^n = d_\beta\left(\mathbf{X}, \sum_{r=1}^{R}\widehat{\mathbf{F}}^{(r)} * \mathbf{g}^{(r)}\right) + \lambda_1\sum_{r=1}^{R}\|\widehat{\mathbf{F}}^{(r)}\|_1 + \lambda_2\sum_{r=1}^{R}\|\mathbf{g}^{(r)}\|_1 \tag{16}$$

where $\widehat{\mathbf{F}}^{(r)}$ is the r-th normalized pattern matrix. In this paper, we will consider two types of normalization.

- *Individual Normalization.* Each pattern matrix is normalized to unit Frobenius norm, i.e., $\widehat{F}_{ij}^{(r)} = F_{ij}^{(r)}/\sqrt{\sum_{ij}F_{ij}^{(r)2}}$
- *Total Normalization.* Each pattern matrix is normalized by the total Frobenius norm of all the pattern matrices, i.e., $\widehat{F}_{ij}^{(r)} = F_{ij}^{(r)}/\sqrt{\sum_r\sum_{ij}F_{ij}^{(r)2}}$

Using the same trick as in [7], we can update $\mathcal{F}$ and $\mathcal{G}$ by

$$F_{ik}^{(r)} \leftarrow F_{ik}^{(r)}\left(\frac{\sum_{j=1}^{t}\left(X_{ij}+\widehat{Y}_{ij}\widehat{F}_{ik}^{(r)2}\right)\widehat{Y}_{ij}^{\beta-2}g_{j-k+1}^{(r)} + \lambda_1\widehat{F}_{ik}^{(r)2}}{\sum_{j=1}^{t}\left(\widehat{Y}_{ij}+X_{ij}\widehat{F}_{ik}^{(r)2}\right)\widehat{Y}_{ij}^{\beta-2}g_{j-k+1}^{(r)} + \lambda_1}\right)^{\eta(\beta)}$$

$$g_k^{(r)} \leftarrow g_k^{(r)}\left(\frac{\sum_{i=1}^{n}\sum_{j=1}^{t}X_{ij}\widehat{Y}_{ij}^{\beta-2}\widehat{F}_{i,j-k+1}^{(r)}}{\sum_{i=1}^{n}\sum_{j=1}^{t}\widehat{Y}_{ij}^{\beta-1}\widehat{F}_{i,j-k+1}^{(r)} + \lambda_2}\right)^{\eta(\beta)}$$

where $\widehat{Y}_{ij} = \sum_{r=1}^{R}\sum_{k=1}^{t}g_{j-k+1}\widehat{F}_{ik}^{(r)} = \left[\sum_{r=1}^{R}\widehat{\mathbf{F}}^{(r)} * \mathbf{g}^{(r)}\right]_{ij}$.

We can see that this normalization invariant formulation does not bring any extra storage burden, but brings an extra $O(2R\bar{s}_F)$ computational overhead at each iteration.

3.3 OSC-NMF on Data Groups

In the medical domain, patients are often characterized by multiple groups based on characteristics such as diagnosis or treatments. More formally we consider the case where the patient matrices are composed of C groups. We use $\mathcal{X}_c = [\mathbf{X}_{c_1}, \mathbf{X}_{c_2}, \cdots, \mathbf{X}_{c_{n_c}}]$ to represent the c-th patient group, with $\mathbf{X}_{c_l}$ representing the l-th data point in this group. n_c is the number of patient in the c-th group. In many real world applications we are also interested in finding patterns hidden in those groups. In this section we will extend our one-side convolutional NMF to these scenarios.

(1). TPD From One Group

We first consider the case of detecting common patterns from one group, i.e., $C = 1$, which is the same setting as in group sparse coding [2]. If we still denote the hidden pattern set as $\mathcal{F} = \{\mathbf{F}^{(r)}\}_{r=1}^{R}$, then the problem we want to solve becomes (here we directly give the sparsity constrained objective as the non-sparse case just correspond to $\lambda_1 = \lambda_2 = 0$)

$$\begin{aligned}\min\nolimits_{\mathcal{F},\{\mathcal{G}_c\}_{c=1}^{C}}\ & \mathcal{J}_3 \\ s.t.\ & \forall r = 1,\cdots,R; l = 1,\cdots,n_1, \\ & \mathbf{F}^{(r)} \geqslant 0, \mathbf{g}_l^{(r)} \geqslant 0\end{aligned} \tag{17}$$

where $\mathcal{G} = \{\mathbf{g}_l^{(r)}\}_{i=1}^{n_1}$ is the convolution coefficients for the data, n_1 is the size of the group. Then the objective we want to minimize is

$$\mathcal{J}_3 = \sum_{l=1}^{n_1}d_\beta\left(\mathbf{X}_l, \sum_{r=1}^{R}\mathbf{F}^{(r)} * \mathbf{g}_l^{(r)}\right) + \lambda_1\sum_{r=1}^{R}\|\mathbf{F}^{(r)}\|_1 + \lambda_2\sum_{l=1}^{n_1}\sum_{r=1}^{R}\|\mathbf{g}_l^{(r)}\|_1 \tag{18}$$

By defining $\mathbf{Y}_l = \sum_{r=1}^{R} \mathbf{F}^{(r)} * \mathbf{g}_l^{(r)}$, we can obtain the update rules for $\mathcal{F}$ and $\mathcal{G}$ as follows.

$$F_{ik}^{(r)} \leftarrow F_{ik}^{(r)} \left(\frac{\sum_{l=1}^{n_1} \sum_{j=1}^{t} X_{l_{ij}} Y_{l_{ij}}^{\beta-2} g_{l_{j-k+1}}^{(r)}}{\sum_{l=1}^{n_1} \sum_{j=1}^{t} Y_{l_{ij}}^{\beta-1} g_{l_{j-k+1}}^{(r)} + \lambda_1} \right)^{\eta(\beta)} \quad (19)$$

$$g_{l_k}^{(r)} \leftarrow g_{l_k}^{(r)} \left(\frac{\sum_{i=1}^{n} \sum_{j=1}^{t} X_{c_{l_{ij}}} Y_{c_{l_{ij}}}^{\beta-2} F_{i,j-k+1}^{(r)}}{\sum_{i=1}^{n} \sum_{j=1}^{t} Y_{c_{l_{ij}}}^{\beta-1} F_{i,j-k+1}^{(r)} + \lambda_2} \right)^{\eta(\beta)} \quad (20)$$

If we want to find normalized patterns, we can use the same trick as in [7] and derive the following update rules

$$F_{ik}^{(r)} \leftarrow F_{ik}^{(r)} \left(\frac{\sum_{l,j} \left(X_{l_{ij}} + \widehat{Y}_{l_{ij}} \widehat{F}_{ik}^{(r)^2} \right) \widehat{Y}_{l_{ij}}^{\beta-2} g_{l_{j-k+1}}^{(r)} + \lambda_1 \widehat{F}_{ik}^{(r)^2}}{\sum_{l,j} \left(\widehat{Y}_{l_{ij}} + X_{l_{ij}} \widehat{F}_{ik}^{(r)^2} \right) \widehat{Y}_{l_{ij}}^{\beta-2} g_{l_{j-k+1}}^{(r)} + \lambda_1} \right)^{\eta(\beta)}$$

$$g_{l_k}^{(r)} \leftarrow g_{l_k}^{(r)} \left(\frac{\sum_{i=1}^{n} \sum_{j=1}^{t} X_{l_{ij}} \widehat{Y}_{l_{ij}}^{\beta-2} \widehat{F}_{i,j-k+1}^{(r)}}{\sum_{i=1}^{n} \sum_{j=1}^{t} \widehat{Y}_{l_{ij}}^{\beta-1} \widehat{F}_{i,j-k+1}^{(r)} + \lambda_2} \right)^{\eta(\beta)}$$

where $\widehat{\mathbf{Y}}_l = \sum_{r=1}^{R} \widehat{\mathbf{F}}^{(r)} * \mathbf{g}_l^{(r)}$.

Complexity Analysis

Similar to the simple OSC-NMF case, we can analyze that the storage complexity of group OSC-NMF is $O(n_1(\bar{s}_X + \bar{s}_Y + \bar{\bar{s}}_g) + \bar{s}_F)$, where n_1 is the size of the group, $\bar{s}_X, \bar{s}_Y$ are the averaged number of nonzero elements in $\{\mathbf{X}_l\}_{l=1}^{n_1}$ and $\{\mathbf{Y}_l\}_{l=1}^{n_1}$, and $\bar{\bar{s}}_g$ is the averaged number of nonzero elements of all $\{\mathbf{g}_l^{(r)}\}_{r=1,l=1}^{R,n_1}$. The total computatioinal complexity is $O((4R+2)Tn_1\bar{s}_F\bar{\bar{s}}_g)$. For normalized cases, we just need an extra $O(2R\bar{s}_F)$ time for pattern normalization.

A Stochastic Learning Scheme

We can see that group OSC-NMF is storage and time consuming if the group size n_1 is very large. In this case, we can adopt the stochastic (online) learning scheme in [16][3][28], i.e., at each time t, the algorithm only (randomly) receives one or a small number of matrices $\mathcal{X}_t$ from the data pool, then proceeds the following steps:

(1) Estimate the convolution coefficients $\mathcal{G}_t$ for $\mathcal{X}_t$ based on the current $\mathcal{F}_t$. This can be done by starting from some random of $\mathcal{G}_t$, then iterating with Eq.(20) (or its normalized version) several times.

(2) Integrating $\mathcal{X}_t$ and $\mathcal{G}_t$ with the previously received data and their estimated convolution coeffients to update $\mathcal{F}$ with Eq.(19) (or its normalized version) only *once*.

With this scheme, when estimating $\mathcal{G}_t$ at step t, we need $O(n_t(\bar{s}_X + \bar{s}_Y) + \bar{s}_F)$ space, with n_t being the size of $\mathcal{X}_t$ and usually $n_t \ll n_1$. We also need $O(n_t(2R+1)\bar{s}_F\bar{\bar{s}}_g)$ computational time. For updating $\mathcal{F}$ from Eq.(19) (or Eq.(21)), we need to sum over all received data matrices for both numerator and denominator, thus we can save the summation results on the nominator and denominator in the previous step. Therefor, we just need to compute the corresponding summation terms on $\mathcal{X}_t$. For each round of updating $\mathbf{F}$, we need $O(n_t(\bar{s}_X + \bar{s}_Y + \bar{\bar{s}}_g) + 2\bar{s}_F)$ space and $O(n_t(2R+1)\bar{s}_F\bar{\bar{s}}_g)$ time. To conclude, the total storage complexity for this online scheme is $O(n_t(\bar{s}_X + \bar{s}_Y + \bar{\bar{s}}_g) + 3\bar{s}_F)$, and the total computational complexity is $O((4R+2)Tn_t\bar{s}_F\bar{\bar{s}}_g)$. For normalized cases, we just need to add additional $O(2R\bar{s}_F)$ computational time for pattern normalization.

(2). TPD From Multiple Data Groups

Now assume there are C $(C > 1)$ data groups, and we want to find a common pattern dictionary $\mathcal{F}^S$ across all data groups, as well as an individual pattern dictionary $\{\mathcal{F}_c^I\}_{c=1}^{C}$ for each data group, then we need to solve

$$\min_{\mathbf{F}_S^{(r)} \geqslant 0, \mathbf{g}_{S_{cl}}^{(r)} \geqslant 0, \mathbf{F}_{I_c}^{(v)} \geqslant, \mathbf{g}_{I_{cl}}^{(v)} \geqslant 0} \quad \mathcal{J}_4 \quad (21)$$
$$s.t. \quad \forall r = 1, \cdots, R; c = 1, \cdots, C; l = 1, \cdots, n_c; v = 1, \cdots, V$$

where we use r to index the common patterns (whose total number is R), v to index the individual patterns in the c-th group (whose total number is V_c), and l to index the data within each group. The objective we want to minimize is

$$\mathcal{J}_4 = \sum_{c=1}^{C} \left[\sum_{l=1}^{n_c} d_\beta \left(\mathbf{X}_{c_l}, \sum_{r=1}^{R} \mathbf{F}_S^{(r)} * \mathbf{g}_{S_{c_l}}^{(r)} - \sum_{v=1}^{V} \mathbf{F}_{I_c}^{(v)} * \mathbf{g}_{I_{c_l}}^{(v)} \right) \right] + \lambda_S \sum_{r=1}^{R} \left\| \mathbf{F}_S^{(r)} \right\|_1$$
$$+ \sum_{c=1}^{C} \sum_{l=1}^{n_c} \left(\gamma_S \sum_{r=1}^{R} \left\| \mathbf{g}_{S_{c_l}}^{(r)} \right\|_1 + \gamma_I \sum_{v=1}^{V} \left\| \mathbf{g}_{I_{c_l}}^{(v)} \right\|_1 \right) + \lambda_I \sum_{c=1}^{C} \sum_{v=1}^{V} \left\| \mathbf{F}_{I_c}^{(v)} \right\|_1$$

Let $\widetilde{\mathbf{Y}} = \sum_{r=1}^{R} \mathbf{F}_S^{(r)} * \mathbf{g}_{S_{c_l}}^{(r)} + \sum_{v=1}^{V} \mathbf{F}_{I_c}^{(v)} * \mathbf{g}_{I_{c_l}}^{(v)}$, then we can get the update rules for unnormalized case

$$F_{S_{ik}}^{(r)} \leftarrow F_{S_{ik}}^{(r)} \left(\frac{\sum_{c,l,j} X_{c_{l_{ij}}} \widetilde{Y}_{c_{l_{ij}}}^{\beta-2} g_{S_{cl_{j-k+1}}}^{(r)}}{\sum_{c,l,j} \widetilde{Y}_{c_{l_{ij}}}^{\beta-1} g_{S_{cl_{j-k+1}}}^{(r)} + \lambda_S} \right)^{\eta(\beta)} \quad (22)$$

$$F_{I_{cik}}^{(v)} \leftarrow F_{I_{cik}}^{(v)} \left(\frac{\sum_{l,j} X_{c_{l_{ij}}} \widetilde{Y}_{c_{l_{ij}}}^{\beta-2} g_{I_{cl_{j-k+1}}}^{(v)}}{\sum_{l,j} \widetilde{Y}_{c_{l_{ij}}}^{\beta-1} g_{I_{cl_{j-k+1}}}^{(v)} + \lambda_I} \right)^{\eta(\beta)} \quad (23)$$

$$g_{S_{clk}}^{(r)} \leftarrow g_{S_{clk}}^{(r)} \left(\frac{\sum_{i,j} X_{c_{l_{ij}}} \widetilde{Y}_{c_{l_{ij}}}^{\beta-2} F_{S_{i,j-k+1}}^{(r)}}{\sum_{i,l,j} \widetilde{Y}_{c_{l_{ij}}}^{\beta-1} F_{S_{i,j-k+1}}^{(r^S)} + \gamma_S} \right)^{\eta(\beta)} \quad (24)$$

$$g_{I_{clk}}^{(v)} \leftarrow g_{I_{clk}}^{(v)} \left(\frac{\sum_{i,j} X_{c_{l_{ij}}} \widetilde{Y}_{c_{l_{ij}}}^{\beta-2} F_{I_{ci,j-k+1}}^{(r_c^I)}}{\sum_{i,l,j} \widetilde{Y}_{c_{l_{ij}}}^{\beta-1} F_{I_{ci,j-k+1}}^{(v)} + \gamma_I} \right)^{\eta(\beta)} \quad (25)$$

Let $\widehat{\widetilde{\mathbf{Y}}} = \sum_{r=1}^{R} \widehat{\mathbf{F}}_S^{(r)} * \mathbf{g}_{S_{c_l}}^{(r)} + \sum_{v=1}^{V} \widehat{\mathbf{F}}_{I_c}^{(v)} * \mathbf{g}_{I_{c_l}}^{(v)}$, where $\widehat{\mathbf{F}}_S$ and $\{\widehat{\mathbf{F}}_{I_c}\}$ are normalized basis, then we have the following updating rules for normalized cases

$$F_{S_{ik}}^{(r)} \leftarrow F_{S_{ik}}^{(r)} \left(\frac{\sum_{c,l,j} \left(X_{c_{l_{ij}}} + \widehat{\widetilde{Y}}_{c_{l_{ij}}} \widehat{F}_{S_{ik}}^{(r)^2} \right) \widehat{\widetilde{Y}}_{c_{l_{ij}}}^{\beta-2} g_{S_{cl_{j-k+1}}}^{(r)} + \lambda_S \widehat{F}_{S_{ik}}^{(r)^2}}{\sum_{c,l,j} \left(\widehat{\widetilde{Y}}_{c_{l_{ij}}} + X_{c_{l_{ij}}} \widehat{F}_{S_{ik}}^{(r)^2} \right) \widehat{\widetilde{Y}}_{c_{l_{ij}}}^{\beta-2} g_{S_{cl_{j-k+1}}}^{(r)} + \lambda_S} \right)^{\eta(\beta)}$$

$$F_{I_{cik}}^{(v)} \leftarrow F_{I_{cik}}^{(v)} \left(\frac{\sum_{l,j} \left(X_{c_{l_{ij}}} + \widehat{\widetilde{Y}}_{c_{l_{ij}}} \widehat{F}_{I_{cik}}^{(r)^2} \right) \widehat{\widetilde{Y}}_{c_{l_{ij}}}^{\beta-2} g_{I_{cl_{j-k+1}}}^{(v)} + \lambda_I \widehat{F}_{I_{cik}}^{(r)^2}}{\sum_{l,j} \left(\widehat{\widetilde{Y}}_{c_{l_{ij}}} + X_{c_{l_{ij}}} \widehat{F}_{I_{cik}}^{(r)^2} \right) \widehat{\widetilde{Y}}_{c_{l_{ij}}}^{\beta-2} g_{I_{cl_{j-k+1}}}^{(v)} + \lambda_I} \right)^{\eta(\beta)}$$

$$g_{S_{clk}}^{(r)} \leftarrow g_{S_{clk}}^{(r)} \left(\frac{\sum_{i,j} X_{c_{l_{ij}}} \widehat{\widetilde{Y}}_{c_{l_{ij}}}^{\beta-2} \widehat{F}_{S_{i,j-k+1}}^{(r)}}{\sum_{i,l,j} \widehat{\widetilde{Y}}_{c_{l_{ij}}}^{\beta-1} \widehat{F}_{S_{i,j-k+1}}^{(r)} + \gamma_S} \right)^{\eta(\beta)}$$

$$g_{I_{clk}}^{(v)} \leftarrow g_{I_{clk}}^{(v)} \left(\frac{\sum_{i,j} X_{c_{l_{ij}}} \widehat{\widetilde{Y}}_{c_{l_{ij}}}^{\beta-2} \widehat{F}_{I_{ci,j-k+1}}^{(v)}}{\sum_{i,l,j} \widehat{\widetilde{Y}}_{c_{l_{ij}}}^{\beta-1} \widehat{F}_{I_{ci,j-k+1}}^{(r_c^I)} + \gamma_I} \right)^{\eta(\beta)}$$

The complexity of this multi-group OSC-NMF can be analyzed similarly as our analysis in previous sections, thus we omit the details here. Note that when facing with large data groups, we can also adopt the stochastic learning scheme.

4. EXPERIMENTS

In this section we present the experimental evaluation results for OSC-NMF and its variants.

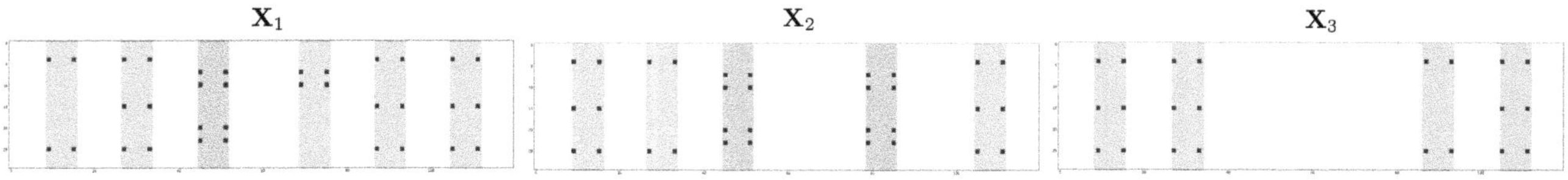

(a) Sample 1 (b) Sample 2 (c) Sample 3

Figure 3: Synthetic data set I. There are three samples $\{\mathbf{X}_i\}_{i=1}^3$ of size 30×120 with binary values. We use black dots to denote value 1, and the 4 types of temporal patterns are shaded with different colors.

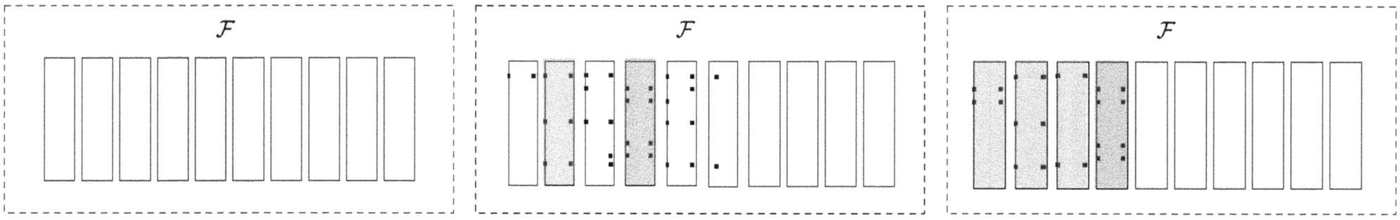

(a) GOSC-NMF (b) GOSC-NMF-IN (c) GOSC-NMF-TN

Figure 4: Detected patterns. GOSC-NMF-TN algorithm can identify all four types successfully.

4.1 Synthetic Data

We generated two synthetic data sets to validate the effectiveness of the proposed methods. The first one is designed to test whether Group OSC-NMF series methods can detect common temporal patterns contained in the data samples. The data set is illustrated in Fig.3, which is composed of one group of three data samples with size 30×120. There are four types of common patterns present in the data samples indicated by windows of different color in Fig.3. These samples are binary, with black dots representing 1.

The following algorithms were applied to this first synthetic data set to evaluate their effectiveness.

(1) **Group OSC-NMF (GOSC-NMF)**. The algorithm is introduced in section 3.3 with $\beta = 0.5$, $R = 11$, $\lambda_1 = \lambda_2 = 0$. All $\{\mathbf{F}^{(r)}, \mathbf{g}^{(r)}\}_{r=1}^R$ are randomly initialized.

(2) **Group OSC-NMF with Individual Normalization (GOSC-NMF-IN)**. The algorithm is the same as in GOSC-NMF except that we use normalization invariant updates with individual normalization introduced in section 3.3, and $\lambda_S = \lambda_I = 0.5$.

(3) **Group OSC-NMF with Total Normalization (GOSC-NMF-TN)**. The algorithm is the same as in GOSC-NMF-IN except we use normalization invariant updates with total normalization introduced in section 3.3, and $\lambda_S = \lambda_I = 0.5$.

For all three algorithms, we set the window length to $m = 7$ and the number of iterations to $T = 100$.

Fig.4 shows the learned patterns by those algorithms. Fig.4(a) shows the patterns learned by simple GOSC-NMF, from which we can see that all of them are null patterns. This is because the three original data samples are all very sparse. By convolving those null patterns over the time axis we get a zero matrix, and the total β-divergence ($\beta = 0.5$) between the data samples to this zero matrix is very small. This makes GOSC-NMF trapped in this local optimum.

Fig.4(b) demonstrates that sparse GOSC-NMG with individual normalization correctly learns two repeating patterns appearing in the original data samples, while Fig.4(c) shows that sparse GOSC-NMG with total normalization correctly learns all temporal patterns. It can be observed that by adding the sparsity regularizations, the learned patterns are much better. More interestingly, we can see that GOSC-NMF-TN identify all 4 patterns.

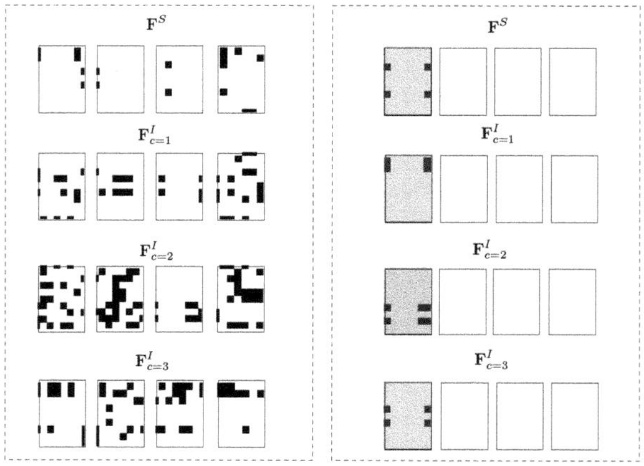

(a) MGOSC-NMF-IN (b) MGOSC-NMF-TN

Figure 6: Group Patterns Discovery: MGOSC-NMF-TN can successfully identify all patterns including shared pattern (red, first row) and all individual patterns from each group (row 2-4).

The second data set is designed to test whether our multi-group OSC-NMF series algorithms introduced in section 3.3 can detect both common and individual temporal patterns contained in different data groups. The data is shown in Fig.5. We tested three algorithms: (1) **MGOSC-NMF**. Simple multi-group OSC-NMF with $\lambda_S = \lambda_I = 0$; (2) **MGOSC-NMF-IN**. MGOSC-NMF with individual normalization, and $\lambda_S = \lambda_I = 0.5$; (3) **MGOSC-NMF-TN**. MGOSC-NMF with total normalization, and $\lambda_S = \lambda_I = 0.5$. For all three methods, we set $\beta = 0.5$, $T = 100$, $R = V = 4$. All pattern images and convolution coefficients are randomly initialized. The results are shown in Fig.6, from which we can make similar observations as in Fig.4. We do not show the learned patterns from simple MGOSC-NMF because all of them are zero. MGOSC-NMF-IN can learn a rich set of pattern images, but not all of them are correct. Finally MGOSC-NMF-TN correctly learns all individual and common patterns.

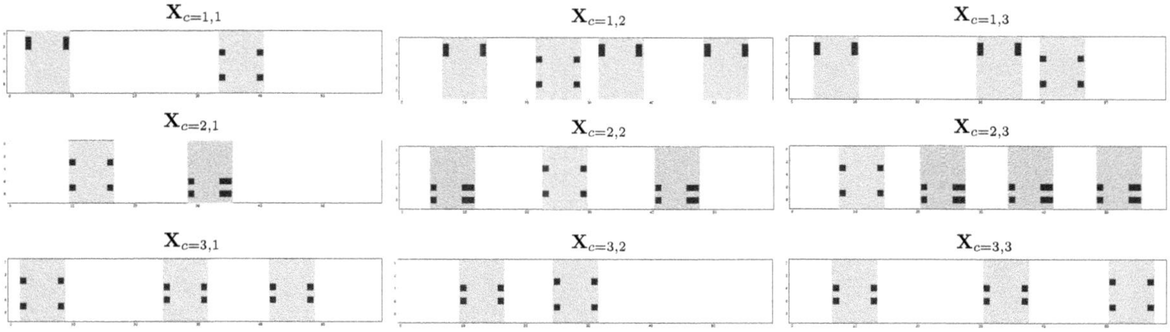

Figure 5: Synthetic data set II. Each row is a data group containing three data samples. All three data groups share a common temporal pattern shaded in red color, while the data within each group has one individual pattern shaded in different colors.

4.2 Real World Data

The real-world dataset consists of records from 21K diabetes patients collected over a period of up to one year. The patients are stratified into three groups A, B, and C based on their specific type of diabetes diagnosis using ICD9 code. Group A (with size 16K) consists of patients with no complications, group B (with size 4,925) consists of patients with chronic disease complications, and group C has patients (with size 254) with acute complications. To evaluate the clinical relevance of the temporal patterns mined by our algorithm, we treat the diagnoses as labels. We then use the mined temporal patterns as additional features for predicting the diagnoses, and compare the performance against a baseline classifier using the aggregate clinical features without consideration of any temporal relations. The hypothesis is that if the temporal patterns mined by our algorithm indeed contain useful clinical information, then their inclusion should improve the classification performance.

For all three groups, 30 different event conditions were selected as being relevant to the progress of diabetes based on consultations with physicians. The events fall into four different groups: medical procedures (CPTs), lab results (LABS), primary care physician visits (PCP), and visits to various specialists (SPEC). One typical patient EHR example is shown in Fig.1. We show some examples of repeating patterns (with one week window length) for each group in Fig.7, which have been identified manually by domain experts. Note that in this case, each patient is represented by a $30 \times T$ matrix, where $T = 365$, and the total patient population is represented by 21k such matrices, and we adopt the stochastic learning strategy for learning the patterns.

To quantitatively evaluate the performance, we randomly selected 70% of the data samples from each group to form the training set, and used the rest data for testing. In this experiment, we set $\beta = 0.5$ and $T = 10000$. The mini-batch size when performing stochastic learning was set to 20. We applied OSC-NMF series methods to construct different feature representations for the data and then used *Nearest Neighbor* (NN) classifier (with Euclidean distance) to classify the test samples. We repeated the experiments 50 times using random partitioning, and report the average classification accuracy compared against the baseline (which is the performance using aggregate clinical features alone, with no considerations of any temporal relations).

Both single group (GOSC-NFM-IN and GOSC-NMF-TN) and multi-group (MGOSC-NMF-IN and MGOSC-NMF-TN) series were tested. For GOSC-NMF-IN and GOSC-NMF-TN, the algorithms were applied to all training data each time and $R = 30$ patterns were learned (null patterns were discarded). Each sample was then represented by a 30 (or less if there are zero patterns) dimensional vector with the value on each dimension equal to the sum of the convolution coefficients $\mathbf{g}$ of the corresponding pattern on this sample. This is very similar to the *bag-of-words* representation for text data. For MGOSC-NMF-IN and NGOSC-NMF-TN, we learned both common and individual patterns for all groups, and discarded the common patterns (since they are not important for classification across groups), using only the individual patterns to construct the dictionary. We set the number of patterns $R = V = 30$ and discarded the null patterns. Thus each sample was represented by a 90 (or less) dimensional vector. For comparison purpose, we also implemented Group and Multi-Group PrefixScan [22] (G-PrefixScan and MG-PrefixScan), i.e., we use a sliding window (with the same length as we used for OSC-NMF methods) to segment the patient record sequence into a set of overlapping transactions, and then apply PrefixScan to mine frequent item sets from all these transactions. For G-PrefixScan, we mine 30 most frequent patterns from all training data, while for MG-PrefixScan, we mine 30 most frequent patterns for the training data in each class. Then we also construct the bag-of-pattern matrix for each patient

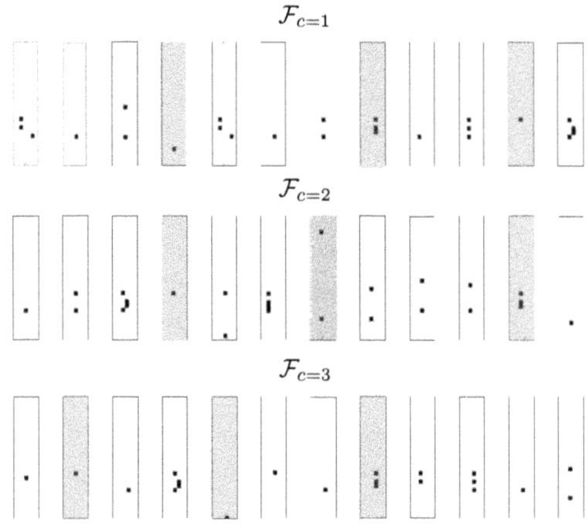

Figure 7: Patient samples from three groups. Shaded windows are manually identified clinical patterns. Red are common patterns across three groups. The other colors are group specific patterns.

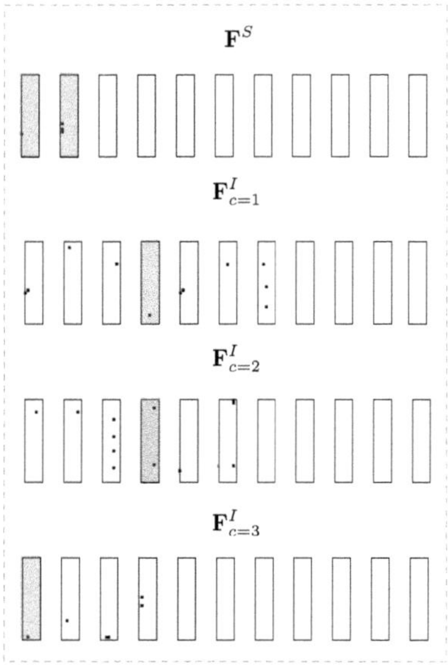

Figure 8: Common and individual patterns are correctly identified by MGOSC-NMF-TN with one week window length. Row 1 are two common patterns, and row 2-4 are group specific patterns. Besides the 5 known patterns, MGOSC-NMF-TN also reveals some unknown patterns, which can potentially lead to new clinical discovery.

(each patient is a 30 dimensional vector with the value on each dimension representing the number of times the corresponding pattern appears within the patient records) for classification.

Table 1 shows the averaged classification performance measured by *Areas Under the Curve* (AUC) with pattern window length set to one week, two weeks and one month. The results show that (1) the classification performances with the inclusion of temporal pattern based features are indeed much better compared to the baseline representation; (2) longer window patterns are more effective, which is likely due to the fact that the progression of diabetes is slow, making the patterns more salient when we increase the window length; (3) multi-group methods tend to perform better, as they extract more discriminative patterns for each group; (4) our matrix approximation based approaches perform better than traditional PrefixScan type methods.

5. CONCLUSION

In this paper we propose an One-Sided Convolutional Nonnegative Matrix Factorization (OSC-NMF) approach for temporal pattern discovery in longitudinal clinical records. We present how to adapt OSC-NMF to extract patterns from one data sample, a group of data samples and multiple groups of data samples. The experimental results on both synthetic and real world data sets are presented to demonstrate the effectiveness of the proposed approaches.

Appendix: Convergence Proof

With $\mathbf{Y}$ defined in Eq.(8), we can expand $d_\beta(\mathbf{X}, \mathbf{Y})$ using Eq.(2). For a power function $f(x) = x^\beta$ with $\beta \geqslant 1$, $f(x)$ is convex; otherwise $f(x)$ is concave. Therefore, when $\beta \geqslant 1$, we have the following conclusion according to *Jensen's inequality*

$$Y_{ij}^\beta = \left(\sum_r \sum_k g_{j-k+1}^{(r)} F_{ik}^{(r)}\right)^\beta \leqslant \sum_r \sum_k \alpha_{ijk}^{(r)} \left(\frac{g_{j-k+1}^{(r)} F_{ik}^{(r)}}{\alpha_{ijk}^{(r)}}\right)^\beta$$

when $1 \leqslant \beta \leqslant 2$, where $\alpha_k \geqslant 0$ and $\sum_k \alpha_k = 1$. The equality holds when

$$\alpha_{ijk}^{(r)} = g_{j-k+1}^{(r)} F_{ik}^{(r)} / \sum_r \sum_k g_{j-k+1}^{(r)} F_{ik}^{(r)}$$

On the other hand, when $\beta < 1$, $f(x) = x^\beta$ is concave, and we have that [27] for any z, $f(x) \leqslant f'(z)(x - z) + f(z)$. Therefore in this case

$$Y_{ij}^\beta \leqslant \beta Z_{ij}^{\beta-1} \left(\sum_r \sum_k g_{j-k+1}^{(r)} F_{ik}^{(r)} - Z_{ij}\right) + Z_{ij}^\beta \tag{26}$$

The equality holds when$Z_{ij} = Y_{ij} = \sum_r \sum_k g_{j-k+1}^{(r)} F_{ik}^{(r)}$. Similarly, $f(x) = -x^\beta$ is convex, if $\beta < 1$; and it is concave, if $\beta \geqslant 1$. Hence

$$-Y_{ij}^\beta \leqslant \begin{cases} -\beta Z_{ij}^{\beta-1}\left(\sum_r \sum_k g_{j-k+1}^{(r)} F_{ik}^{(r)} - Z_{ij}\right) - Z_{ij}^\beta, & \text{if } \beta < 1 \\ -\sum_r \sum_k \alpha_{ijk}^{(r)} \left(\frac{g_{j-k+1}^{(r)} F_{ik}^{(r)}}{\alpha_{ijk}^{(r)}}\right)^\beta, & \text{if } \beta \geqslant 1 \end{cases}$$

Now let's define the following terms for notational convenience.

$$\mathcal{P}_{ij}^\beta(\mathbf{F}, \alpha) = \sum_r \sum_k \alpha_{ijk}^{(r)} \left(g_{j-k+1}^{(r)} F_{ik}^{(r)} / \alpha_{ijk}^{(r)}\right)^\beta$$
$$\mathcal{Q}_{ij}^\beta(\mathbf{F}, Z) = \beta Z_{ij}^{\beta-1} \left(\sum_r \sum_k g_{j-k+1}^{(r)} F_{ik}^{(r)} - Z_{ij}\right) + Z_{ij}^\beta$$

We designed the following function

$$\mathcal{W}^\beta(\mathbf{F}, \alpha, Z) = \sum_{ij} \left(X_{ij}^\beta + \mathcal{I}_{ij}^\beta(\mathbf{F}, \alpha, Z)\right) / \beta(\beta - 1) \tag{27}$$

where
$$\mathcal{I}_{ij}^\beta(\mathbf{F}, \alpha, Z) = \begin{cases} (\beta - 1)\mathcal{Q}_{ij}^\beta(\mathbf{F}, Z) - \beta X_{ij} \mathcal{P}_{ij}^{\beta-1}(\mathbf{F}, \alpha), & \beta < 1 \\ (\beta - 1)\mathcal{P}_{ij}^\beta(\mathbf{F}, \alpha) - \beta X_{ij} \mathcal{P}_{ij}^{\beta-1}(\mathbf{F}, \alpha), & 1 \leqslant \beta \leqslant 2 \\ (\beta - 1)\mathcal{P}_{ij}^\beta(\mathbf{F}, \alpha) - \beta X_{ij} \mathcal{Q}_{ij}^{\beta-1}(\mathbf{F}, Z), & \beta > 2 \end{cases}$$

Consequently, if we treat $\mathcal{W}(\mathbf{F}, \alpha, Z)$ as a function of $\mathbf{F}$, we have

$$\frac{\partial \mathcal{W}(\mathbf{F}, \alpha, Z)}{\partial F_{ik}^{(r)}} = \begin{cases} \sum_j \left(Z_{ij}^{\beta-1} \bar{g}_{j-k+1} - \bar{F}_{ik}^{\beta-2} \bar{g}_{j-k+1}^{\beta-1} \bar{\alpha}_{ijk}^{2-\beta} X_{ij}\right), & \beta < 1 \\ \sum_j \left(\bar{F}_{ik}^{\beta-1} \bar{g}_{j-k+1}^{\beta} \bar{\alpha}_{ijk}^{1-\beta} - Z_{ij}^{\beta-2} \bar{g}_{j-k+1} X_{ij}\right), & \beta > 2 \\ \bar{F}_{ik}^{\beta-2} \sum_j \bar{g}_{j-k+1}^{\beta-1} \bar{\alpha}_{ijk}^{1-\beta} \left(\bar{F}_{ik} \bar{g}_{j-k+1} - \bar{\alpha}_{ijk} X_{ij}\right), & \text{else} \end{cases}$$

where to avoid the notational clutter, we use an overhead bar to replace the superscript (r), i.e., $\bar{F}_{ik} = F_{ik}^{(r)}, \bar{g}_k = g_k^{(r)}, \bar{\alpha}_{ijk} = \alpha_{ijk}^{(r)}$. In the following we will use these two symbols interchangablly. Then the *Hessian* matrix

$$\frac{\partial \mathcal{W}(\mathbf{F}, \alpha, Z)}{\partial F_{ik}^{(r)} \partial F_{i'k'}^{(r)}} = \begin{cases} -\delta_{i,i'}^{k,k'} (\beta - 2) \bar{F}_{ik}^{\beta-3} \sum_k \bar{g}_{j-k+1}^{\beta-1} \bar{\alpha}_{ijk}^{2-\beta} X_{ij}, & \beta < 1 \\ \delta_{i,i'}^{k,k'} \bar{F}_{ik}^{\beta-3} \sum_j \bar{g}_{j-k+1}^{\beta-1} \bar{\alpha}_{ijk}^{1-\beta} \bar{f}_{ijk}^{\beta}, & 1 \leqslant \beta \leqslant 2 \\ \delta_{i,i'}^{k,k'} (\beta - 1) \sum_j \bar{F}_{ik}^{\beta-2} \bar{g}_{j-k+1}^{\beta} \bar{\alpha}_{ijk}^{1-\beta}, & \beta > 2 \end{cases}$$

where
$$\delta_{i,i'}^{k,k'} = \begin{cases} 1, & \text{if } i = i', k = k' \\ 0, & \text{otherwise} \end{cases} \tag{28}$$

and
$$f_{ijk}^\beta = (\beta - 1) \bar{F}_{ik} \bar{g}_{j-k+1} - (\beta - 2) \bar{\alpha}_{ijk} X_{ij} \tag{29}$$

Thus $\mathcal{W}(\mathbf{F}, \alpha, Z)$ is convex with respect to $\mathbf{F}$, whose minumum value can be achieved at the point when $\partial \mathcal{W}(\alpha, Z, \mathbf{F}) / \partial \mathbf{F} = \mathbf{O}$, from which we can get

$$F_{ik}^{(r)*} = \begin{cases} \left(\frac{\sum_j X_{ij} \bar{g}_{j-k+1}^{\beta-1} \bar{\alpha}_{ijk}^{2-\beta}}{\sum_j Z_{ij}^{\beta-1} \bar{g}_{j-k+1}}\right)^{\frac{1}{2-\beta}}, & \beta < 1 \\ \frac{\sum_j X_{ij} \bar{g}_{j-k+1}^{\beta-1} \bar{\alpha}_{ijk}^{2-\beta}}{\sum_j \bar{g}_{j-k+1}^{\beta} \bar{\alpha}_{ijk}^{1-\beta}}, & 1 \leqslant \beta \leqslant 2 \\ \left(\frac{\sum_j X_{ij} \bar{g}_{j-k+1} Z_{ij}^{\beta-2}}{\sum_j \bar{g}_{j-k+1}^{\beta} \bar{\alpha}_{ijk}^{1-\beta}}\right)^{\frac{1}{\beta-1}}, & \beta > 2 \end{cases} \tag{30}$$

Therefore for any specific α, Z, we have $\mathcal{W}(\mathbf{F}^*, \alpha, Z) \leqslant \mathcal{W}(\mathbf{F}, \alpha, Z)$. Now let's treat $\mathcal{W}(\mathbf{F}^*, \alpha, Z)$ as a function of α, Z, we know that its minimum can be achieved with

$$\alpha_{ijk}^{(r)*} = \frac{g_{j-k+1}^{(r)} F_{ik}^{(r)*}}{\sum_r \sum_k g_{j-k+1}^{(r)} F_{ik}^{(r)*}}, \quad Z_{ij}^* = \sum_r \sum_k g_{j-k+1}^{(r)} F_{ik}^{(r)*} \tag{31}$$

Table 1: Averaged AUC Values

	1 Week	2 Weeks	1 Month	2 Months
Baseline	0.5703 ± 0.1236	0.5703 ± 0.1236	0.5703 ± 0.1236	0.5703 ± 0.1236
G-PrefixScan	0.5971 ± 0.0536	0.6018 ± 0.0479	0.6208 ± 0.0405	0.6227 ± 0.0317
MG-PrefixScan	0.6002 ± 0.0484	0.6021 ± 0.0369	0.6230 ± 0.0410	0.6231 ± 0.0420
GOSC-NMF-IN	0.5996 ± 0.0408	0.6045 ± 0.0458	0.6219 ± 0.0347	0.6223 ± 0.0258
GOSC-NMF-TN	0.6004 ± 0.0506	0.6152 ± 0.0352	0.6218 ± 0.0376	0.6315 ± 0.0308
MGOSC-NMF-IN	0.6147 ± 0.0374	$\mathbf{0.6436 \pm 0.0405}$	0.6386 ± 0.0350	0.6432 ± 0.0324
MGOSC-NMF-TN	$\mathbf{0.6208 \pm 0.0406}$	0.6377 ± 0.0370	$\mathbf{0.6417 \pm 0.0290}$	$\mathbf{0.6440 \pm 0.0312}$

Therefore $\mathcal{J}(\mathbf{F}^*, \mathbf{g}) = \mathcal{W}(\mathbf{F}^*, \alpha^*, Z^*) \leqslant \mathcal{W}(\mathbf{F}^*, \alpha, Z)$. Actually if we combine Eq.(30) and Eq.(31) together, we obtain

$$F_{ik}^{(r)} \leftarrow F_{ik}^{(r)} \left(\frac{\sum_{j=1}^{t} X_{ij} Y_{ij}^{\beta-2} g_{j-k+1}^{(r)}}{\sum_{j=1}^{t} Y_{ij}^{\beta-1} g_{j-k+1}^{(r)}} \right)^{\eta(\beta)} \tag{32}$$

where $\eta(\beta)$ is defined as in Eq.(10). In this way, assume the current iteration step is from t to $t+1$, then we have

$$\begin{aligned} &\mathcal{J}(\mathbf{F}(t+1), \mathbf{g}) = \mathcal{W}(\mathbf{F}(t+1), \alpha(t+1), Z(t+1)) \\ &\leqslant \mathcal{W}(\mathbf{F}(t+1), \alpha(t), Z(t)) \leqslant \mathcal{W}(\mathbf{F}(t), \alpha(t), Z(t)) = \mathcal{J}(\mathbf{F}(t), \mathbf{g}) \end{aligned}$$

Thus with the updating rules, the objective is monotonically decreasing, and clearly it is lower bounded by 0, thus the iterations will converge to a stationary point.

6. REFERENCES

[1] I. Batal, L. Sacchi, R. Bellazzi, and M. Hauskrecht. A temporal abstraction framework for classifying clinical temporal data. In *AMIA*, pages 29–33, 2009.

[2] S. Bengio, F. Pereira, Y. Singer, and D. Strelow. Group sparse coding. In *NIPS*, 2009.

[3] B. Cao, D. Shen, J.-T. Sun, X. Wang, Q. Yang, and Z. Chen. Detect and Track Latent Factors with Online Nonnegative Matrix Factorization. In *Proceedings of the 20th IJCAI*, pages 2689–2694, 2007.

[4] M. Cooper, T. Liu, and E. Rieffel. Video Segmentation via Temporal Pattern Classification. *IEEE TMM*, 9(3):610–618, 2007.

[5] S. de Amo and D. A. Furtado. First-order temporal pattern mining with regular expression constraints. *Data & Knowledge Engineering*, 62(3):401–420, 2007.

[6] X. Du, R. Jin, L. Ding, V. E. Lee, and J. H. T. Jr. Migration motif: a spatial - temporal pattern mining approach for financial markets. In *KDD*, pages 1135–1144, 2009.

[7] J. Eggert and E. Körner. Sparse coding and nmf. In *IJCNN*, pages 2529–2533, 2004.

[8] J. Fails, A. Karlson, L. Shahamat, and B. Shneiderman. A Visual Interface for Multivariate Temporal Data: Finding Patterns of Events across Multiple Histories. In *Visual Analytics Science And Technology, 2006 IEEE Symposium On*, pages 167–174, 2006.

[9] C. Févotte and J. Idier. Algorithms for nonnegative matrix factorization with the beta-divergence. *arXiv:1010.1763*, 2010.

[10] R. Grosse, R. Raina, H. Kwong, and A. Y. Ng. Shift-invariant Sparse Coding for Audio Classification. In *UAI*, 2007.

[11] J. Han, J. Pei, Y. Yin, and R. Mao. Mining Frequent Patterns without Candidate Generation: A Frequent-Pattern Tree Approach. *DMKD*, 8(1):53–87, 2004.

[12] P. O. Hoyer. Non-negative matrix factorization with sparseness constraints. *JMLR*, 5:1457–1469, 2004.

[13] D. D. Lee and H. S. Seung. Learning the parts of objects by non-negative matrix factorization. *Nature*, 401(6755):788–791, 1999.

[14] D. D. Lee and H. S. Seung. Algorithms for Non-negative Matrix Factorization. In *NIPS 13*, pages 556–562, 2001.

[15] J. Lin, E. Keogh, S. Lonardi, and B. Chiu. A symbolic representation of time series, with implications for streaming algorithms. In *Proceedings of the 8th ACM SIGMOD workshop on Research issues in data mining and knowledge discovery*, pages 2–11, 2003.

[16] J. Mairal, F. Bach, J. Ponce, and G. Sapiro. Online Learning for Matrix Factorization and Sparse Coding. *Journal of Machine Learning Research*, 11:10–60, 2010.

[17] F. Mörchen and A. Ultsch. Efficient mining of understandable patterns from multivariate interval time series. *DMKD*, 15(2):181–215, 2007.

[18] M. Mørup, M. N. Schmidt, and L. K. Hansen. Shift invariant sparse coding of image and music data. Technical report, 2008.

[19] P. N. E. Nohuddin, F. Coenen, R. Christley, and C. Setzkorn. Detecting temporal pattern and cluster changes in social networks: A study focusing uk cattle movement database. In *IFIP Advances in Information and Communication Technology*, pages 163–172, 2010.

[20] G. Norén, J. Hopstadius, A. Bate, K. Star, and I. Edwards. Temporal pattern discovery in longitudinal electronic patient records. *DMKD*, 20(3):361–387, 2010.

[21] P. D. O'Grady and B. A. Pearlmutter. Discovering convolutive speech phones using sparseness and non-negativity. In *ICA*, 2007.

[22] J. Pei, J. Han, B. Mortazavi-Asl, J. Wang, H. Pinto, Q. Chen, U. Dayal, and M. Hsu. Mining sequential patterns by pattern-growth: The prefixspan approach. *IEEE TKDE*, 16(11):1424–1440, 2004.

[23] C. Plaisant, S. Lam, B. Shneiderman, M. S. Smith, D. Roseman, G. Marchand, M. Gillam, C. Feied, J. Handler, and H. Rappaport. Searching electronic health records for temporal patterns in patient histories: a case study with microsoft amalga. In *AMIA*, pages 601–605, 2008.

[24] M. Robert Moskovitch and Y. Shahar. Medical temporal-knowledge discovery via temporal abstraction. In *AMIA*, pages 452–456, 2009.

[25] B. R. Shah, J. Drozda, and E. D. Peterson. Leveraging observational registries to inform comparative effectiveness research. *American Heart Journal*, 160(1):8–15, 2010.

[26] P. Smaragdis. Non-negative matrix factor deconvolution; extraction of multiple sound sources from monophonic inputs. In *ICA*, pages 494–499. 2004.

[27] H. A. Varian. *Microeconomic Analysis Third Edition.* W.W. Norton and Company, 1992.

[28] F. Wang, C. Tan, P. Li, and C. König. Efficient document clustering via online nonnegative matrix factorization. In *Proceedings of the 11th SDM*, 2011.

[29] T. Wang, C. Plaisant, A. Quinn, R. Stanchak, B. Shneiderman, and S. Murphy. Aligning temporal data by sentinel events: Discovering patterns in electronic health records. In *Proc. of ACM Conference on Human Factors in Computing Systems*, pages 457–466, 2008.

[30] M. J. Zaki. Spade: An efficient algorithm for mining frequent sequences. *Machine Learning*, 42:31–60, 2001.

The Long and the Short of It: Summarising Event Sequences with Serial Episodes

Nikolaj Tatti Jilles Vreeken

Department of Mathematics and Computer Science
Universiteit Antwerpen
{firstname.lastname}@ua.ac.be

ABSTRACT

An ideal outcome of pattern mining is a small set of informative patterns, containing no redundancy or noise, that identifies the key structure of the data at hand. Standard frequent pattern miners do not achieve this goal, as due to the pattern explosion typically very large numbers of highly redundant patterns are returned.

We pursue the ideal for sequential data, by employing a *pattern set* mining approach—an approach where, instead of ranking patterns individually, we consider results as a whole. Pattern set mining has been successfully applied to transactional data, but has been surprisingly understudied for sequential data.

In this paper, we employ the MDL principle to identify the set of sequential patterns that summarises the data best. In particular, we formalise how to encode sequential data using sets of serial episodes, and use the encoded length as a quality score. As search strategy, we propose two approaches: the first algorithm selects a good pattern set from a large candidate set, while the second is a parameter-free any-time algorithm that mines pattern sets directly from the data. Experimentation on synthetic and real data demonstrates we efficiently discover small sets of informative patterns.

Categories and Subject Descriptors

H.2.8 [**Database management**]: Database applications–*Data mining*

General Terms

Theory, Algorithms, Experimentation

Keywords

serial episodes, event sequence, pattern mining, pattern set mining

1. INTRODUCTION

Suppose we are analysing an event sequence database, and are interested in its most important patterns. Traditionally, we would apply a frequent pattern miner, and mine all patterns that occur at least so-many times. However, due to the well-known pattern explosion we would then quickly be buried in huge amounts of highly redundant patterns, such that analysing the patterns becomes the problem, as opposed to the solution.

In this paper we therefore adopt a different approach. Instead of considering patterns individually, which is where the explosion stems from, we are after the *set of patterns* that summarises the data best. Desired properties of such a summary include that it should be small, generalise the data well, and be non-redundant. To this end, we employ the Minimum Description Length principle [5], which identifies the best set of patterns as that set by which we can describe the data most succinctly.

This approach has been shown to be highly successful for summarising transaction data [23], where the discovered patterns provide insight, as well as high performance in a wide range of data mining tasks, including clustering, missing value estimation, and anomaly detection [17, 22, 23]. Sequence data, however, poses additional challenges compared to itemsets. For starters, the order of events is important, and we have to take gaps in patterns into account. As such, encoding the data given a cover, finding a good cover given a set of patterns, as well as finding good sets of patterns, is much more complicated for sequences than for itemsets.

We are not the first to consider summarising sequential data. Existing methods, however, are different in that they require a single pattern to generate a full sequence [12], do not consider gaps [2, 12], or do not punish gaps in patterns [9]. In short, none of these methods take the full expressiveness of episodes into account.

As we identify the best model by best lossless compression, and we consider strings as data, standard compression algorithms such as Lempel-Ziv and Huffman coding are related [16]. While general purpose compressors can provide top-notch compression, they do not result interpretable models. In our case, compression is not the goal, but a means: in order to summarise the data well, we are after those serial episodes that describe it most succinctly. We discuss related work in closer detail in Section 5.

In this paper, we introduce a statistically well-founded approach for succinctly summarising event sequences, or SQS for short—pronounced as '*squeeze*'. We formalise how to encode a sequence dataset given a set of episodes, and using MDL identify the best set as the set that describes the data most succinctly. To optimise this score, we give an efficient heuristic to determine which pattern best describes what part of your data. To find good sets of patterns, we introduce two heuristics: SQS-CANDIDATES filters a given candidate collection, and SQS-SEARCH is a parameter-free any-time algorithm that efficiently mines models directly from data.

Experiments on real and synthetic data show SQS efficiently discovers high-quality models that summarise the data well, correctly identify key patterns. The number of returned patterns stays small, up to a few hundred— most importantly, though, the returned mod-

KDD'12, August 12–16, 2012, Beijing, China.

els do not show redundancy, and none of the patterns are polluted by frequent, yet unrelated, events.

Altogether, the long and the short of it is that SQS mines small sets of the most important, non-redundant, serial episodes that together succinctly describe the data at hand.

2. MDL FOR EVENT SEQUENCES

In this section we formally introduce the problem we consider.

2.1 Preliminaries and Notation

As data type we consider *event sequences.* A sequence database D over an event alphabet Ω consists of $|D|$ sequences $S \in D$. Every $S \in D$ is a sequence of $|S|$ events $e \in \Omega$, i.e. $S \in \Omega^{|S|}$. We write $S[i]$ to mean the ith event in S and $S[i,j]$ to mean a subsequence $S[i] \cdots S[j]$. We denote by $||D||$ the sum of the lengths of all $S_i \in D$, i.e. $||D|| = \sum_{S_i \in D} |S_i|$. In this work, we do not explicitly consider time stamps, however we can extend our framework to time stamped events.

The support of an event e in a sequence S is simply the number of occurrences of e in S, i.e. $supp(e \mid S) = |\{i \in S | i = e\}|$. The support of e in a database D is defined as $supp(e \mid D) = \sum_{S \in D} supp(e \mid S)$.

As patterns we consider serial episodes. A serial episode X is a sequence of events and we say that a sequence S contains X if there is a subsequence in S equal to X. Note that we are allowing gap events between the events of X. A singleton pattern is a single event $e \in \Omega$.

All logarithms in this paper are to base 2, and we employ the usual convention of $0 \log 0 = 0$.

2.2 MDL, a brief introduction

The Minimum Description Length principle (MDL) [5] is a practical version of Kolmogorov Complexity [11]. Both embrace the slogan *Induction by Compression.* For MDL, this can be roughly described as follows.

Given a set of models $\mathcal{M}$, the best model $M \in \mathcal{M}$ is the one that minimises $L(M) + L(D \mid M)$, in which $L(M)$ is the length in bits of the description of M, and $L(D \mid M)$ is the length of the data when encoded with model M.

This is called two-part MDL, or *crude* MDL—as opposed to *refined* MDL, where model and data are encoded together [5]. We use two-part MDL because we are specifically interested in the model: the patterns that give the best description. Further, although refined MDL has stronger theoretical foundations, it cannot be computed except for some special cases. Note that MDL requires the compression to be *lossless* in order to allow for fair comparison between different $M \in \mathcal{M}$, and that we are only concerned with code lengths, not actual code words.

To use MDL, we have to define what our models $\mathcal{M}$ are, how a $M \in \mathcal{M}$ describes a database, and how we encode these in bits.

2.3 MDL for Event Sequences

As models we consider *code tables.* A code table is essentially a look-up table, or dictionary, between patterns and associated codes. A code table has four columns, of which the first column contains patterns, the second column consists of codes for identifying these patterns, and the two right-most columns contain pattern-dependent codes for identifying gaps or the absence thereof within an embedding of a pattern. To ensure any sequence over Ω can be encoded by a code table, we require that all the singleton events in the alphabet, $X \in \Omega$, are included in a code table CT.

To refer to the different codes in CT, we write $code_p(X \mid CT)$ when we refer to the code corresponding to a pattern X, as stored in the second column of a code table CT. Similarly, we write $code_g(X \mid CT)$ and $code_n(X \mid CT)$ to resp. refer to the codes stored in the third and fourth column, which indicate whether or not the next symbol is part of a gap in the usage of pattern X. For readability, we do not write CT wherever clear from context.

Our next step is to explain our encoding scheme. As we will see later, there are typically very many ways of encoding a database, apart from using only singletons. Hence, for clarity, we will first explain our encoding scheme by considering how to *decode* an already encoded database, and postpone finding a good encoding, or *cover*, as well as how to find a good code table to Sections 3 and 4.

Decoding a Database

An encoded database consists of two code streams, C_p and C_g, that follow from the cover C chosen to encode the database. The first code stream, the *pattern-stream*, denoted by C_p, is a list of $|C_p|$ codes, $code_p(\cdot)$, for patterns $X \in CT$ corresponding to those patterns chosen by 'cover' algorithm. For example, $code_p(a)\, code_p(b)$ $code_p(c)$ encodes the sequence '*abc*'.

Serial episodes are not simple subsequences, however, as they allow for gaps. That is, a pattern *de* specifies that event *d*, after possibly some other events, is followed by event *e*. As such, this pattern occurs both in sequence '*de*' as well as in sequence '*dfe*'. In the former there is no gap between the two events, and in the latter there is a gap of length one, in which event *f* occurs.

As such, only when we read the code for a singleton pattern X we can directly unambiguously append X to the sequence S_k we are decoding—there can be no gap in a singleton pattern. When X is a non-singleton pattern, on the other hand, we may only append the first symbol x_1 of X to S_k; before appending event x_2 to S_k, we first need to know whether there is a gap between the two events in this usage of X, and if so, what event(s) occur in the gap. This is what the second code stream is for. This stream, the *gap-stream*, denoted by C_g, is a list of codes from the third and fourth column of CT, indicating whether gaps occur when decoding patterns.

Given the gap-stream, we can determine whether the next event of S_k may be read from the current pattern X, or we have to read a singleton pattern to fill the gap. Starting with an empty sequence for S_k, and assuming that we know its final length, we read the code for the first pattern X, $code_p(X)$, from C_p, and append the first event x_1 of X to the sequence we are decoding. If X is a non-singleton pattern, we read from C_g whether the next event is a gap-event, or not. If we read the gap-code $code_g(X)$ from C_g there is indeed a gap, after which we read from C_p the $code(Y)$ for the (singleton) event $Y \in CT$ associated with this gap—and append it to S_k. We then read again from C_g whether there is another gap, etc, until we encounter the no-gap code $code_n(X)$ in C_g indicating we should append the next symbol x_j of X to S_k. Whenever we are finished decoding pattern X, we read the code for the next pattern X from C_p, until we have read as many events as S_k should be long, after which we continue decoding $S_{k+1} \in D$ until C_p is depleted and all $S \in D$ are reconstructed.

Consider the toy example given as Fig. 1. One possible encoding would be to use only singletons, meaning that gap stream is empty. Another encoding is to use patterns. For example, to encode '*abdc*', we first give the code for *abc* in the pattern stream, then a no-gap code (white) in C_g to indicate *b*, then a gap code (black) in C_g, next the code for *d* in C_p, and we finish with a no-gap code in C_g.

Calculating Encoded Lengths

Given the above decoding scheme we know what codes we can expect to read where and when, and hence can now formalise how to

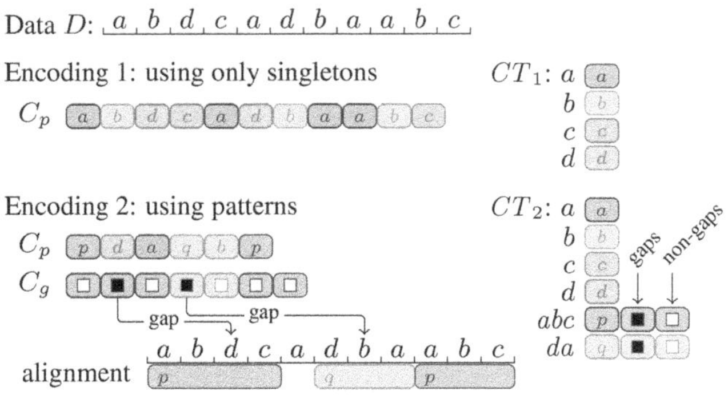

Figure 1: Toy example of two possible encodings. The first encoding uses only singletons. The second encoding uses singletons and two patterns, namely, abc and da

calculate the lengths of these codes, as well as the encoded lengths of the code table and database.

We start with $L(code_p(X))$, the lengths of pattern codes in C_p, which we can look up in the second column of CT. By Shannon Entropy [3] we know that the length, in bits, of the optimal prefix-free code for an event X is $-\log \Pr(X)$, where $\Pr(X)$ is the probability of X. Let us write $usage(X)$ for how often $code_p(X)$ occurs in C_p. That is, $usage(X) = |\{Y \in C_p \mid Y = code_p(X)\}|$. Then, the probability of $code_p(X)$ in C_p is its relative occurrence in C_p. So, we have

$$L(code_p(X) \mid CT) = -\log\left(\frac{usage(X)}{\sum_{Y \in CT} usage(Y)}\right) \quad .$$

Similarly, the lengths of the codes for indicating the presence or absence of a gap in the usage of a pattern X, resp. $L(code_g(X))$ and $L(code_n(X))$, should be dependent on their relative frequency. Let us write $gaps(X)$ to refer to the number of gap events within the usages of a pattern X in the cover of D. We then resp. have

$$fills(X) = usage(X)(|X| - 1) \quad ,$$

for the number of non-gap codes in the usage of a pattern X, and

$$L(code_g(X) \mid CT) = -\log\left(\frac{gaps(X)}{gaps(X) + fills(X)}\right) \quad ,$$

$$L(code_n(X) \mid CT) = -\log\left(\frac{fills(X)}{gaps(X) + fills(X)}\right) \quad ,$$

resp. for the length of a gap and a non-gap code of a pattern X.

We say a code table CT is code-optimal for a cover C of a database D if all the codes in CT are of the length according to their respective usage frequencies in C_p and C_g as defined above.

From the lengths of the individual codes, the encoded length of the code streams now follows straightforwardly, with resp.

$$L(C_p \mid CT) = \sum_{X \in CT} usage(X) L(code_p(X))$$

for the encoded size of the pattern-stream, and

$$L(C_g \mid CT) = \sum_{\substack{X \in CT \\ |X|>1}} \Big(gaps(X)L(code_g(X)) + fills(X)L(code_n(X))\Big)$$

for the encoded size of the gap-stream.

Combining the above, we define $L(D \mid CT)$, the encoded size of a database D given a code table CT and a cover C, as

$$L(D \mid CT) = L_{\mathbb{N}}(|D|) + \sum_{S \in D} L_{\mathbb{N}}(|S|) + L(C_p \mid CT) + L(C_g \mid CT) \quad ,$$

where $|D|$ is the number of sequences in D, and $|S|$ is the length of a sequence $S \in D$. To encode these values, for which we have no prior knowledge, we employ the MDL optimal Universal code for integers [5, 15]. For this encoding, $L_{\mathbb{N}}$, the number of bits required to encode an integer $n \geq 1$, is defined as

$$L_{\mathbb{N}}(n) = \log^*(n) + \log(c_0) \quad ,$$

where $\log^*$ is defined as $\log^*(n) = \log(n) + \log\log(n) + \cdots$, where only the positive terms are included in the sum. To make $L_{\mathbb{N}}$ a valid encoding, c_0 is chosen as $c_0 = \sum_{J \geq 1} 2^{-L_{\mathbb{N}}(j)} \approx 2.865064$ such that the Kraft inequality is satisfied.

Next we discuss how to calculate $L(CT)$, the encoded size of a code table CT. To ensure lossless compression, we need to encode the number of entries, for which we employ $L_{\mathbb{N}}$ as defined above. For later use, and to avoid bias by large or small alphabets, we encode the number of singletons, $|\Omega|$, and the number of non-singleton entries, $|CT \setminus \Omega|$, separately. We disregard any non-singleton pattern with $usage(X) = 0$, as it is not used in describing the data, and has no valid (or infinite length) pattern code.

For the size of the left-hand side column, note that the simplest valid code table consists only of the single events. This code table we refer to as the *standard code table*, or ST. We encode the patterns in the left-hand side column using the pattern codes of ST. This allows us to decode up to the names of events.

As singletons cannot have gaps, the usage of a singleton Y given ST is simply the support of Y in D. Hence, the code length of Y in ST is defined as $L(code_p(Y) \mid ST) = -\log \frac{supp(Y|D)}{||D||}$. Before we can use these codes, we must transmit these supports. We transmit these using a data-to-model code [21], an index over a canonically ordered enumeration of all possibilities; here, the number of ways $||D||$ events can be distributed over $|\Omega|$ labels, where none of the bins may be empty, as $supp(Y \mid D) > 0$. The number of such possibilities is given by $\binom{||D||-1}{|\Omega|-1}$, and by taking a log we have the number of bits required to identify the right set of values. Note that $||D||$ is known from $L(D \mid CT)$. In general, for the number of bits for an index of a number composition, the number of combinations of summing to m with n non-zero terms, we have $L_U(m,n) = \log\binom{m-1}{n-1}$, where for $m = 0$, and $n = 0$, we define $L_U(m,n) = 0$.

Combined, this gives us the information required to reconstruct the left-hand side of CT for the singletons, as well as the information needed to decode the non-singleton patterns of CT. For a pattern X, the number of bits in the left-hand column is the length of X, $|X|$, as encoded by $L_{\mathbb{N}}$, and the sum of the singleton codes

$$L_{\mathbb{N}}(|X|) + \sum_{x_i \in X} L(code(x_i) \mid ST) \quad .$$

Next, we encode the second column. To *avoid* bias, we treat the singletons and non-singleton entries of CT differently. Let us write $\mathcal{P}$ to refer to the non-singleton patterns in CT, i.e. $\mathcal{P} = CT \setminus \Omega$. For the elements of $\mathcal{P}$, we first encode the sum of their usages, denoted by $usage(\mathcal{P})$, and use a data-to-model code like above to identify the correct set of individual usages. With these values, and the singleton supports we know from ST, we can reconstruct the usages of the singletons in CT, and hence reconstruct the pattern codes associated with each pattern in CT.

This leaves us the gap-codes for the non-singleton entries of CT. For reconstructing these, we need to know $gaps(X)$, which we encode using $L_{\mathbb{N}}$. The number of non-gaps then follows from the length of a pattern X and its usage. As such, we can determine $code_g(X)$ and $code_n(X)$ exactly.

Putting this all together, we have $L(CT \mid C, D)$, the encoded size in bits of a code table CT for a cover C of a database D, as

$$\begin{aligned} L(CT \mid C) =& L_{\mathbb{N}}(|\Omega|) + L_U(||D||, |\Omega|) + \\ & L_{\mathbb{N}}(|\mathcal{P}| + 1) + L_{\mathbb{N}}(usage(\mathcal{P}) + 1) + \\ & L_U(usage(\mathcal{P}), |\mathcal{P}|) + \sum_{X \in \mathcal{P}} L(X, CT) \quad , \end{aligned}$$

where $L(X, CT)$, the number of bits for encoding the events, length, and the number of gaps of patterns X in CT, is

$$\begin{aligned} & L(X, CT) \\ & = L_{\mathbb{N}}(|X|) + L_{\mathbb{N}}(gaps(X) + 1) + \sum_{x \in X} L(code_p(x \mid ST)) \quad . \end{aligned}$$

By MDL, we can then define the optimal set of serial episodes for a given sequence database as the set for which the optimal cover and associated optimal code table minimises the total encoded size

$$L(CT, D) = L(CT \mid C) + L(D \mid CT) \ .$$

More formally, we define the problem as follows.

Minimal Code Table Problem *Let Ω be a set of events and let D be a sequence database over Ω, find the minimal set of serial episodes $\mathcal{P}$ such that for the optimal cover C of D using $\mathcal{P}$ and Ω, the total encoded cost $L(CT, D)$ is minimal, where CT is the code-optimal code table for C.*

Clearly, this problem entails a rather large search space. First of all, given a set of patterns, there are many different ways to cover a database. Second, there are very many sets of serial episodes $\mathcal{P}$ we can consider, namely all possible subsets of the collection of serial episodes that occur in D. However, neither the full problem, or these sub-problems, exhibit trivial structure that we can exploit for fast search, e.g. (weak) monotonicity.

We hence break the **Minimal Code Table Problem** into two sub-problems. First, in the next section we discuss how to optimise the cover of a sequence *given* a set of episodes. Then, in Section 4, we will discuss how to mine high quality code tables.

3. COVERING A STRING

Encoding, or covering, a sequence is more difficult than decoding one. The reason is simple: when decoding there is no ambiguity, while when encoding there are many choices, i.e. what pattern to encode a symbol with. In other words, given a set of episodes, there are many valid ways to cover a sequence, where by our problem definition we are after the cover C that minimises $L(CT, D)$.

Due to lack of space, we provide the proofs in the Appendix[1].

3.1 Minimal windows

Assume we are decoding a sequence $S_k \in D$. Assume we decode the beginning of a pattern X at $S_k[i]$ and that the last symbol belonging to this instance of X is, say, $S_k[j]$. We say that $S_k[i, j]$ is an *active* window for X. Let $\mathcal{P}$ be the set of non-singleton patterns used by the encoding. We define an *alignment* A to be the set of all active windows for all non-singleton patterns $X \in \mathcal{P}$ as

$$A = \{(i, j, X, k) \mid S_k[i, j] \text{ is an active window for } X, S_k \in D\} \ .$$

[1]`http://adrem.ua.ac.be/sqs/`

An alignment corresponding to the second encoding given in Figure 1 is $\{(1, 4, abc, 1), (6, 8, da, 1), (9, 11, abc, 1)\}$.

Note that an alignment A does not uniquely define the cover of the sequence, as it does not take into account how the intermediate symbols (if any) within the active windows of a pattern X are encoded. However, an alignment A for a sequence database D does define an equivalence class over covers of the same encoded length. In fact, given a sequence database D and an alignment A, we can determine the number of bits our encoding scheme would require for such a cover. To see this, let X be a pattern and let $W = \{(i, j, X, k) \in A\}$, then

$$usage(X) = |W| \text{ and } gaps(X) = gaps(W) \quad , \qquad (1)$$

where

$$gaps(W) = \sum_{(i,j,X,k) \in W} j - i - |X| - 1 \quad . \qquad (2)$$

The remaining symbols are encoded as singleton patterns. Hence, the usage of a singleton is equal to

$$usage(s) = supp(s \mid D) - \sum_{s \in X} usage(X) \quad . \qquad (3)$$

Given an alignment A for D, we can trivially construct a valid cover C for D, simply by following A and greedily covering S_k with pattern symbols if possible, and singletons otherwise. That is, if for a symbol $S_k[i]$ we have, by A, the choice for covering it as a gap or non-gap of a pattern X, we choose non-gap.

Then, from either C, or directly from A, we can derive the associated code-optimal code table CT. Given an alignment A, let us write $CT(A)$ for this code table. Wherever clear from context, we will write $L(D \mid A)$ to mean $L(D \mid CT(A))$, and similarly $L(D, A)$ as shorthand for $L(D, CT(A))$.

Our next step is to show what kind of windows can occur in the optimal alignment. We say that $W = S[i, j]$ is a minimal window of a pattern X if W contains X but no other proper sub-windows of W contain X. For example, in Figure 1 $S[6, 8]$ is a minimal window for da but $S[6, 9]$ is not.

PROPOSITION 1. *Let A be an alignment producing an optimal encoded length. Then all active windows in A are minimal windows.*

Proposition 1 says that we need to only study minimal windows. Let $\mathcal{F}$ be a set of episodes and let $X \in \mathcal{F}$. Since an event $S_k[i]$ can be a starting point to only one minimal window of X, there are only $\|D\|$ minimal windows of X in D, at most. Consequently, the number of minimal windows we need to investigate is bounded by $\|D\| \, |\mathcal{F}|$. Moreover, we can use FINDWINDOWS in [20] to discover all the minimal windows for a pattern X in $O(|X| \, \|D\|)$ time.

3.2 Finding optimal alignment

Discovering an optimal alignment is non-trivial due to the complex relation between code lengths and the alignment. However, if we fix the alignment, Eqs. 1–3 give us the codes optimising $L(D \mid A)$. In this section we will show the converse, that if we fix the codes, we can easily find the alignment optimising $L(D \mid A)$. In order to do that let $w = (i, j, X, k)$ be a minimal window for a pattern X. We define the gain to be

$$\begin{aligned} gain(w) = & - L(code_p(X)) - (j - i - |X|)L(code_g(X)) \\ & - (|X| - 1)L(code_n(X)) + \sum_{x \in X} L(code_p(x)) \quad . \end{aligned}$$

PROPOSITION 2. *Let D be a dataset and A be an alignment. Then the length of encoding D is equal to*

$$L(D \mid A) = const - \sum_{w \in A} gain(w) \quad ,$$

where const does not depend on A.

This proposition suggests that if we fix the code lengths we need to maximise the total gain. In order for an alignment to be valid, the windows must be disjoint. Hence, given a set of W, consisting of all minimal windows of the given patterns, we need to find a subset $O \subseteq W$ of disjoint windows maximising the gain.

Assume that W is ordered by the first index of each window. For a window w, define $next(w)$ to be the next disjoint window in W. Let $o(w)$ be the optimal total gain of w and its subsequent windows. Let v be the next window of w, then the optimal total gain is $o(w) = \min(o(v), gain(w) + o(next(w)))$. This gives us a simple dynamic program, ALIGN, given as Algorithm 1.

Algorithm 1: ALIGN(W)

input : minimal windows W sorted by the first event
output : mutually disjoint subset of W having the optimal gain

$o(N+1) \leftarrow 0$; $opt(N+1) \leftarrow$ **none**;
foreach $i = N, \ldots, 1$ **do**
  $c \leftarrow 0$;
  if $next(i)$ **then** $c \leftarrow o(next(i))$;
  if $gain(w_i) + c > o(i+1)$ **then**
    $o(i) \leftarrow gain(w_i) + c$; $opt(i) \leftarrow i$;
  else
    $o(i) \leftarrow o(i+1)$; $opt(i) \leftarrow opt(i+1)$;
$O \leftarrow$ optimal alignment (obtained by iterating opt and $next$);
return O;

We can now use ALIGN iteratively. Given the codes we find the optimal alignment and derive the optimal codes given the new alignment. We repeat this until convergence, which gives us a heuristic approximation to the optimal alignment A^* for D using patterns $\mathcal{P}$. As initial values, we use the number of minimal windows as usage and set gap code length to be 1 bit. The pseudo code of SQS, which stands for Summarising event seQuenceS, is given as Algorithm 2.

Algorithm 2: SQS($D, \mathcal{P}$). Summarising event seQuenceS

input : Database of sequences D, set of patterns $\mathcal{P}$
output : Alignment A

foreach $s \in \Omega$ **do** $usage(s) \leftarrow supp(s \mid D)$;
foreach $X \in \mathcal{P}, |X| > 1$ **do**
  $W_X \leftarrow$ FINDWINDOWS(X, D);
  $usage(X) \leftarrow |W_X|$; $gaps(X) \leftarrow |X| - 1$;
$W \leftarrow$ merge sort $\{W_X\}_{X \in \mathcal{F}}$ based on first event;
while changes **do**
  compute gain for each $w \in W$;
  $A \leftarrow$ ALIGN(W);
  recompute usage and gaps from A (Eqs. 1–3);
return A;

The computational complexity of single iteration comes down to the computational complexity of ALIGN(W), which is $O(|W|) \subseteq O(|\mathcal{P}|\, \|D\|)$. Also note that $next$ is precomputed before calling ALIGN and this can be also computed with a single scan, taking $O(|W|)$ steps. Note that the encoded length improves at every iteration, and as there are only finite number of alignments, SQS will converge to a local optimum in finite time. In practice, the number of iterations is small—in the experiments typically less than 10.

4. MINING CODE TABLES

With the above, we both know how to score the quality of a pattern set, as well as how to heuristically optimise the alignment of a pattern set. This leaves us with the problem of finding good sets of patterns. In this section we give two algorithms to do so.

4.1 Filtering Candidates

Our first algorithm, SQS-CANDIDATES, assumes that we have a (large) set of candidate patterns $\mathcal{F}$. In practice, we assume the user obtains this set of patterns using a frequent pattern miner, although any set of patterns over Ω will do. From this set $\mathcal{F}$ we then select that set of patterns $\mathcal{P} \subseteq \mathcal{F}$ such that the optimal alignment A and associated code table CT minimises $L(D, CT)$.

For notational brevity, we simply write $L(D, \mathcal{P})$ as shorthand for the total encoded size $L(D, CT)$ obtained by the code table CT containing a set of patterns $\mathcal{P}$ and singletons Ω, and being code-optimal to the alignment A as found by SQS.

We begin by sorting the candidates $X \in \mathcal{F}$ by $L(D, \{X\})$ from lowest to highest. After sorting, we iteratively greedily test each pattern $X \in \mathcal{F}$. If adding X to $\mathcal{P}$ improves the score, i.e. fewer bits are needed, we keep X in $\mathcal{P}$, otherwise it is permanently removed. The pseudo-code for SQS-CANDIDATES is given as Algorithm 3.

Algorithm 3: SQS-CANDIDATES($\mathcal{F}, D$)

input : candidate patterns $\mathcal{F}$
output : set of non-singleton patterns $\mathcal{P}$ that heuristically minimise the **Minimal Code Table Problem**

order patterns $X \in \mathcal{F}$ based on $L(D, \{X\})$;
$\mathcal{P} \leftarrow \emptyset$;
foreach $X \in \mathcal{F}$ in order **do**
  if $L(D, \mathcal{P} \cup X) < L(D, \mathcal{P})$ **then**
    $\mathcal{P} \leftarrow$ PRUNE($\mathcal{P} \cup X, D,$ **false**);
$\mathcal{P} \leftarrow$ PRUNE($\mathcal{P}, D,$ **true**);
order patterns $X \in G$ by $L(D, \mathcal{P}) - L(D, \mathcal{P} \setminus X)$;
return $\mathcal{P}$;

During the search we iteratively update the code table Hence, it may be that over time, previously included patterns start to harm compression once their role in covering the sequence is taken over by new, more specific, patterns. As such, they become redundant, and should be removed from $\mathcal{P}$.

To this end, we prune redundant patterns (see Algorithm 4) after each successful addition. During pruning, we iteratively consider each pattern $Y \in \mathcal{P}$ in order of insertion. If $\mathcal{P} \setminus X$ improves the total encoded size, we remove X from $\mathcal{P}$. As testing every pattern in $\mathcal{P}$ at every successful addition may become rather time-consuming, we use a simple heuristic: if the total gain of the windows of X is higher than the cost of X in the code table we do not test X.

After SQS-CANDIDATES considered every pattern of $\mathcal{F}$, we run one final round of pruning without this heuristic. Finally, we order the patterns in $\mathcal{P}$ by $L(D, \mathcal{P}) - L(D, \mathcal{P} \setminus X)$. That is, by the impact on the total encoded length when removing X from $\mathcal{P}$. This order tells us which patterns in $\mathcal{P}$ are most important.

Let us consider the execution time needed by SQS-CANDIDATES. Ordering patterns can be done in $O(|\mathcal{F}|\, \|D\|)$ time. Computing $L(D, \mathcal{P} \cup X)$ can be done in $O(|\mathcal{P}|\, \|D\|) \subseteq O(|\mathcal{F}|\, \|D\|)$ time.

Algorithm 4: PRUNE($\mathcal{P}, D, full$)

input : pattern set $\mathcal{P}$, database D, boolean variable *full*, **false** for heuristic scan, **true** for complete scan
output : pruned pattern set $\mathcal{P}$;

foreach $X \in \mathcal{P}$ **do**
  $CT \leftarrow$ code table corresponding to SQS$(D, \mathcal{F})$;
  $CT' \leftarrow$ code table obtained from CT by deleting X;
  $g \leftarrow \sum_{w=(i,j,X,k)\in A} gain(w)$;
  if *full* **or** $g < L(CT) - L(CT')$ **then**
    if $L(D, \mathcal{P} \setminus X) < L(D, \mathcal{P})$ **then** $\mathcal{P} \leftarrow \mathcal{P} \setminus X$;
return $\mathcal{P}$;

Pruning can be done in $O(|\mathcal{P}|^2 \|D\|) \subseteq O(|\mathcal{F}|^2 \|D\|)$. Combined, this gives us a total time complexity of $O(|\mathcal{F}|^3 \|D\|)$. In practice, the algorithm is much faster, however, as first, due to MDL the code tables remain small, and hence $|\mathcal{P}| \ll |\mathcal{F}|$, second, the execution time of SQS is typically faster than $O(|\mathcal{P}| \|D\|)$, and third, the pruning heuristic further reduces the computational burden.

4.2 Directly Mining Good Code Tables

The SQS-CANDIDATES algorithm requires a collection of candidate patterns to be materialised, which in practice can be troublesome; the well-known pattern explosion may prevent patterns to be mined at as low thresholds as desired. In this section we propose an alternative strategy for discovering good code tables directly from data. Instead of filtering a pre-mined candidate set, we now discover candidates on the fly, considering only patterns that we expect to optimise the score given the current alignment.

To illustrate the general idea, consider that we have a current set of patterns $\mathcal{P}$. We iteratively find patterns of form XY, where $X, Y \in \mathcal{P} \cup \Omega$ producing the lowest $L(D, \mathcal{P} \cup \{XY\})$. We add XY to $\mathcal{P}$ and continue until no gain is possible. Unfortunately, as testing each combination takes $O((|\mathcal{P}|+|\Omega|)^2(|\mathcal{P}|+1) \|D\|)$ time, we cannot do this exhaustively and exactly within reasonable time.

Hence, we resort to heuristics.

To guarantee the fast discovery of good candidates, we design a heuristic algorithm that, given a pattern P, will find a pattern PQ of high expected gain in only $O(|\mathcal{P}| + |\Omega| + \|D\|)$ time.

Our first step is to demonstrate that if we take N active windows of P, and N active windows of Q, and convert them into N active windows of PQ, the difference in total encoded length can be computed in constant time.

PROPOSITION 3. *Fix a database D and an alignment A. Let P and Q be two patterns. Let $V = \{v_1, \ldots, v_N\}$ and $W = \{w_1, \ldots, w_N\}$ be two set of candidate windows for P and Q, respectively. Assume that either P (Q) is a singleton or each v_i (w_i) occurs in A. Assume that v_i and w_i occur in the same sequence and write $v_i = (a_i, b_i, P, k_i)$ and $w_i = (c_i, d_i, Q, k_i)$. Assume that $b_i < c_i$. Write $R = PQ$ and let*

$$U = \{(a_1, d_1, R, k_1), \ldots, (a_N, d_N, R, k_N)\} \quad .$$

Assume that U has no overlapping windows and has no overlapping windows with $A \setminus (V \cup W)$. Then the difference

$$L(D, A \cup U \setminus (V \cup W)) - L(D, A)$$

depends only N, $gaps(V)$, $gaps(W)$, and $gaps(U)$ and can be computed in constant time from these values.

The conditions given in Proposition 3 are needed so that $A \setminus (V \cup W)$ is a proper alignment. We denote the aforementioned difference by $diff(V, W, U; A, D)$. Note that this difference partly depends on A and D. However, since we keep these fixed in the proposition they only contribute constant terms. Further note that U should not overlap with $A \setminus (V \cup W)$. We will address this limitation later. We should point out that in practice we do not keep lists of U, V, and W, but instead exploit the gap counts and number of windows, as this is sufficient for computing the difference.

Now that we have a way of computing the gain of using windows for PQ, we need to know which windows to use in the alignment. The following proposition suggest that we should pick the windows with the shortest length.

PROPOSITION 4. *Let D be a database and A be an alignment. Let $v = (i, j, X, k) \in A$. Assume that there exists a window $S_l[a, b]$ containing X such that $w = (a, b\ X, l)$ does not overlap with any window in A and $b - a < j - i$. Then A is not an optimal alignment.*

This proposition gives us an outline of the heuristic. We start enumerating minimal windows of PQ from shortest to largest. At each step we compute the score using Proposition 3, and among these scores we the pick optimal one.

We cannot guarantee linear time if we consider each Q individually. Instead, we scan for all candidates simultaneously. In addition, to guarantee linear time we consider only active windows of P and Q, and do not consider singletons occurring in the gaps. The scan starts by finding all the active windows (ignoring singletons in gaps) of P. We then continue by scanning the patterns occurring after each P. We interleave the scans in such a way that the new minimal windows are ordered, from shortest to longest. We stop the scan after we find next occurrence of P or the end of the sequence.

There are two constraints that we need to take into account. When enumerating minimal windows of PQ we need to make sure that we can add them to the alignment. That is, a new minimal window cannot intersect with other new minimal windows, and the only windows it may intersect in the alignment are the two windows from which it was constructed. The first constraint can only happen when $Q = P$, in which case we simply check if the adjacent scans have already used these two instances of P for creating a minimal window for pattern PP. To guarantee the second constraint, we need to delete the intersecting windows from the alignment. We estimate the effect of deleting w by adding $gain(w)$ (computed from the current alignment) to the score. The pseudo-code for calculating this estimate is given as Algorithm 5.

PROPOSITION 5. ESTIMATE$(P, \emptyset, D)$ *returns a pattern with optimal score.*

Next, let us consider the computational complexity of this approach. The initialisation in ESTIMATE can be done in $O(|\Omega| + |\mathcal{P}| + \|D\|)$, where $\mathcal{P}$ are the current non-singleton patterns. After selecting the next window, each step in the main loop can be done in constant time. The only non-trivial step is picking the next smallest window. However, since the window lengths are integers smaller or equal than $\|D\|$, we can store the candidates into an array of lists, say N_d, where N_d contains the windows of length d. Finding the next window may take more than a constant time since we need to find the next non-empty list N_d but such search may only contribute $\|D\|$ checks in total. Since we stop after encountering P, every event is visited only twice at maximum, hence the running time for ESTIMATE is $O(|\Omega| + |\mathcal{P}| + \|D\|)$.

The actual search algorithm, SQS-SEARCH, calls ESTIMATE for each pattern P. The algorithm, given as Algorithm 6, continues by sorting the obtained patterns based on their estimated scores and attempts to add them into encoding in the same fashion as in

Algorithm 5: ESTIMATE(P, A, D). Heuristic for finding a pattern X used by the current encoding with a low $L(D, A \cup PX)$

input : database D, current alignment A, pattern $P \in CT$
output: pattern PX with $X \in CT$ and a low $L(D, A \cup PX)$

foreach $X \in CT$ **do** $V_X \leftarrow \emptyset$; $W_X \leftarrow \emptyset$; $U_X \leftarrow \emptyset$; $d_X \leftarrow 0$;
$T \leftarrow \emptyset$;
foreach occurrence v of P in the encoding (ignoring gaps) **do**
  $(a, b, P, k) \leftarrow v$;
  $d \leftarrow$ the end index of the active window following v;
  $t \leftarrow (v, d, 0)$; $l(t) \leftarrow d - a$;
  add t into T;
while T is not empty **do**
  $t \leftarrow \arg\min_{u \in T} l(u)$;
  $(v, d, s) \leftarrow t$; $a \leftarrow$ first index of v;
  $w = (c, d, X, k) \leftarrow$ active window of a pattern ending at d;
  if $X = P$ **and** (event at a or d is marked) **then**
    delete t from T;
    continue;
  if $S_k[a, d]$ is a minimal window of PX **then**
    add v into V_X;
    add w into W_X;
    add (a, d, PX, k) into U_X;
    $d_X \leftarrow \min(\mathit{diff}(V, W, U; A) + s, d_X)$;
    if $|X| > 1$ **then** $s \leftarrow s + \mathit{gain}(w)$;
    if $X = P$ **then**
      mark the events at a and d;
      delete t from T;
      continue;
  if w is the last window in the sequence **then**
    delete t from T;
  else
    $d \leftarrow$ the end index of the active window following w;
    update t to (v, d, s) and $l(t)$ to $d - a$;
return PX with the lowest d_X;

Algorithm 6: SQS-SEARCH(D)

input : database D
output: significant patterns $\mathcal{P}$

$\mathcal{P} \leftarrow \emptyset$; $A \leftarrow$ SQS$(D, \emptyset)$;
while changes **do**
  $\mathcal{F} \leftarrow \emptyset$;
  foreach $P \in CT$ **do** add ESTIMATE(P, A, D) to $\mathcal{F}$;
  foreach $X \in \mathcal{F}$ ordered by the estimate **do**
    if $L(D, \mathcal{P} \cup X) < L(D, \mathcal{P})$ **then**
      $\mathcal{P} \leftarrow$ PRUNE$(\mathcal{P} \cup X, D, \textbf{false})$;
    if X is added **then** test recursively X augmented with events occurring in the gaps;
$\mathcal{P} \leftarrow$ PRUNE$(\mathcal{P}, D, \textbf{true})$;
order patterns $X \in G$ by $L(D, \mathcal{P}) - L(D, \mathcal{P} \setminus X)$;
return $\mathcal{P}$;

SQS-CANDIDATES. After each successful addition of pattern X, we scan for the gap events occurring in the active windows of X, and test patterns obtained from X by adding a gap event as intermediate event. The scan can be done in $O(\|D\|)$ time, and in theory we may end up testing $|\Omega| (|X| - 1)$ patterns. In practice, the number is much smaller since accepted patterns typically have small gaps. If any of these patterns in successfully added we repeat this procedure in a recursive fashion. In practice, testing X is relatively fast, and the total computational complexity is dominated by ESTIMATE.

5. RELATED WORK

Discovering frequent sequential patterns is an active research topic. Unlike for itemsets, there are several definitions for frequent sequential patterns. The first approach counts the number of sequences containing a pattern [24]. In such setup, having one long sequence do not make sense. In the second approach we count multiple occurrences within a sequence. This can be done by sliding a window [13] or counting disjoint minimal windows [10].

Mining general episodes, patterns where the order of events are specified by a DAG is surprisingly hard. For example, testing whether a sequence contains a pattern is **NP**-complete [19]. Consequently, research has focused on mining subclasses of episodes, such as, episodes with unique labels [1, 14], and strict episodes [20].

Discovering statistically significant sequential patterns is a surprisingly understudied topic. One reason is that unlike for itemsets, computing an expected frequency under a null-hypothesis is very complex. Using independence assumption as a null-hypothesis has been suggested in [7, 18] and a Markov-chain model has been suggested in [6]. In [1] the authors use information theory-based measure to determine which edges to include in a general episode.

Summarising sequences using segmentation is a well-studied topic. The goal in segmentation is to divide the sequence in large segments of homogenous regions whereas our goal is to find a set of compact patterns that occur significantly often. For an overview in segmentation, see [4], and for a segmentation tool see [8].

Mannila and Meek [12] regard general episodes, as generative models for sequences. Their model generates short sequences by selecting a subset of events from an episode and select a random order compatible with the episode. They do not allow gaps and only one pattern is responsible for generating a single sequence. This is not feasible for our setup, where we may have long sequences and many patterns occurring in one sequence.

SQS draws inspiration from the KRIMP [23] and SLIM [17] algorithms. KRIMP pioneered the use of MDL for identifying good pattern sets; specifically, mining sets of itemsets that describe a transaction database well. As serial episodes are much more expressive than itemsets, we here need a much more elaborate encoding scheme, and in particular, a non-trivial approach for covering the data. For mining the patterns, SQS-CANDIDATES shares the greedy selection over an ordered set of candidates.

Smets and Vreeken recently gave the SLIM algorithm [17] for directly mining KRIMP code tables from data. With SQS-SEARCH we adopt a strategy that resembles SLIM, by considering joins XY of $X, Y \in CT$, and estimating the gain of adding XY to CT. Whereas SLIM iteratively searches for the best addition, for efficiency, SQS-SEARCH adopts a batch-wise strategy.

Lam et al. introduced GOKRIMP [9] for mining sets of serial episodes. As opposed to the MDL principle, they use fixed length codes, and do not punish gaps within patterns—by which their goal is essentially to cover the sequence with as few patterns as possible, which is different from our goal of finding patterns that succinctly summarise the data. Bathoorn et al. [2] also cover greedily, and do not consider gaps at all.

6. EXPERIMENTS

We implemented our algorithms in C++, and provide the source code for research purposes, together with the considered datasets, as well as the generator for the synthetic data.[2] As candidates for SQS-CANDIDATES, we mined frequent serial episodes [10, 20] using disjoint minimal windows of maximal length 15, with minimal support thresholds as low as feasible—i.e. at the point where the number of patterns starts to explode. All experiments were executed single-threaded on a six-core Intel Xeon machine with 12GB of memory, running Linux.

In our experiments we consider both synthetic and real data. Table 1 shows the base statistics per dataset, i.e. number of distinct events, number of sequences, total number of events per database, and the total encoded length by the most simple code table ST.

Synthetic Data. First, we consider the synthetic *Indep*, *Plants-10*, and *Plants-50* datasets. Each consists of a single sequence of 10 000 events over an alphabet of 1 000. In the former, all events are independent, whereas in the latter two we planted resp. 10 and 50 patterns of 5 events 10 times each, with 10% probability of having a gap between consecutive events, but are independent otherwise.

Table 1 shows the results given by SQS-CANDIDATES and SQS-SEARCH. For the *Indep* dataset, while over 9 000 episodes occur at least 2 times, both methods correctly identify the data does not contain significant structure. Similar for *Plants-10* both methods correctly return the 10 planted patterns. *Plants-50* has a very high density of pattern symbols (25%), and hence poses a harder challenge. SQS-CANDIDATES and SQS-SEARCH identify resp. 47 and 46 patterns exactly, the remainder consisting of fragments of correct patterns. The imperfections are due to patterns being partly overwritten during the generation of the data.

Real Data. For the experiments on real data, in order to interpret the patterns, we consider text data. The events are the stemmed words from the text, with stop words removed. *Addresses* contains speeches of American presidents, *JMLR* consists of abstracts of papers from the Journal of Machine Learning Research website,[3] whereas *Moby* contains the novel 'Moby Dick' by Herman Melville.

Let us first consider the number of returned patterns, as shown in Table 1. We see that for all datasets small numbers of patterns are returned, in the order of 100s, two orders of magnitude less than the number of frequent patterns SQS-CANDIDATES considers.

When we consider the gains in compressed size, i.e. $\Delta L = L(D, ST) - L(D, CT)$, we see these few patterns in fact describe a lot of structure of the data; recall that 1 bit of gain corresponds to an increase of factor 2 in likelihood. We note SQS-SEARCH slightly outperforms SQS-CANDIDATES, which is due to the former being able to consider candidates of lower support without suffering from the pattern explosion.

The largest ΔL is recorded for *JMLR*, with almost 30k bits. This is not surprising, as the type of text, abstracts of machine learning papers, has a relatively small vocabulary—the use of which is quite structured, with many key phrases and combinations of words.

Table 2 depicts the top-10 most compressing patterns for *JMLR*, as found by SQS-SEARCH. Here, as ΔL we give the increase in bits the pattern would be removed from CT. Clearly, key machine learning concepts are identified, and importantly, the patterns are neither redundant, nor polluted with common words. In fact, in none of the CTs patterns incorrectly combine frequent events.

Further examples of patterns reported for *JMLR* include '*non neg matrix factor*', '*isotrop log concav distribut*', and '*reproduc[ing] kernel Hilbert space*'. For the presidential *Addresses*, we unsurprisingly see '*unit[ed] stat[es]*' and '*fellow citizen[s]*' as the top-2 patterns. An example of a pattern with many gaps (5.2 gap events, on average), we find the rather current '*economi[c] public expenditur[e]*'. From the *Moby Dick* novel we find the main antagonist's species, '*sperm whale*', and name, '*moby dick*', as well as the phrase '*seven hundr[ed] seventy seventh*' which occurs 6 times.

Table 2: JMLR data. Top-10 patterns by SQS-SEARCH

patterns	ΔL	patterns	ΔL
1. supp. vector machine	850	6. large scale	329
2. machine learning	646	7. nearest neighbor	322
3. state [of the] art	480	8. decision tree	293
4. data set	446	9. neural network	289
5. Bayesian network	374	10. cross validation	279

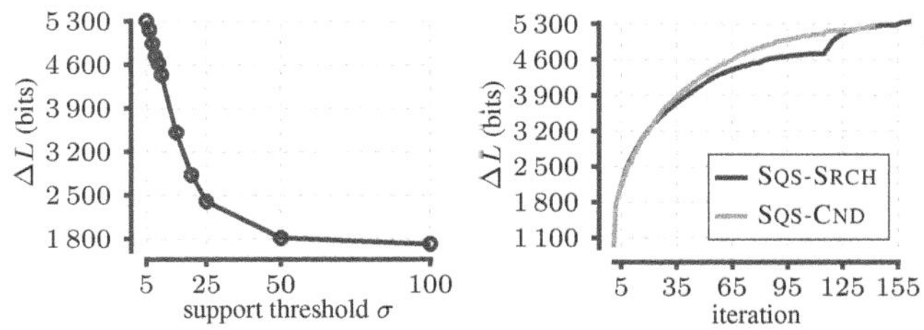

Figure 2: *Addresses* dataset, gain in compression. (left) varying support thresholds for SQS-CANDIDATES. (right) SQS-CANDIDATES and SQS-SEARCH per accepted candidate.

Next, we investigate our search strategies. First, in the left-hand plot of Fig. 2, for SQS-CANDIDATES on the *Moby* data, we show the gain in compression for different support thresholds. It shows that lower thresholds, i.e richer candidate sets, allow for (much) better models—though by the pattern explosion, mining candidates at low σ can be infeasible.

Second, in the right-hand plot, we compare SQS-CANDIDATES and SQS-SEARCH, showing the gain in bits over ST per candidate accepted into CT. It shows both search processes are efficient, considering patterns that strongly aid compression first. The slight dip of SQS-SEARCH around iteration 100 is due to its batch-wise search. At the expense of extra computation, an iterative search for the best estimated addition, like SLIM [17] may find better models.

In these experiments, using these support thresholds, mining the candidates took up to 4 minutes, after which SQS-CANDIDATES took up to 15 minutes to order and filter the candidates. SQS-SEARCH resp. took 10, 18, and 91 minutes. As *Moby* has a large alphabet and is one long sequence, SQS-SEARCH has to consider many possible pattern co-occurrences.

7. DISCUSSION

The experiments show both SQS-CANDIDATES and SQS-SEARCH return high-quality models. By using synthetic data we showed that SQS reveals the true patterns without redundancy, while further not picking up on spurious structure. Analysis of the results on the text data experiments show that key phrases are identified—combinations of words that may be interspersed with 'random' words in the data. Importantly, for all of the datasets, no noisy or redundant patterns are returned. As expected, the more structure a dataset exhibits, the better the attained compression.

With SQS-CANDIDATES we allow the user the freedom to provide a set of candidate serial episodes. In general, lower thresholds correspond to more candidates, more candidates correspond to a larger search space, and hence better models. SQS-SEARCH on the other hand, besides an any-time algorithm, is parameter-free, as it generates and tests patterns that are estimated to improve the score.

[2] http://adrem.ua.ac.be/sqs/
[3] http://jmlr.csail.mit.edu/

Table 1: Basic statistics and results per dataset

					SQS-CANDIDATES				SQS-SEARCH	
Dataset	$\|\Omega\|$	$\|D\|$	$\|\|D\|\|$	$L(D, ST)$	σ	$\|\mathcal{F}\|$	$\|\mathcal{G}\|$	$L(D, CT)$	$\|\mathcal{G}\|$	$L(D, CT)$
Indep	1 000	1	10 000	103 630	2	9 094	0	103 630	0	103 630
Plants-10	1 000	1	10 000	103 340	2	11 957	10	100 629	10	100 629
Plants-50	1 000	1	10 000	102 630	2	25 484	50	91 706	52	91 707
Addresses	5 295	56	62 066	685 593	5	15 506	155	680 287	152	680 236
JMLR	3 846	788	75 646	772 112	5	40 879	580	742 966	565	742 953
Moby	10 277	1	105 719	1 250 149	5	22 559	215	1 240 667	231	1 240 566

Both algorithms are fast, our prototype implementations taking only few minutes on the data here considered. The algorithms have many opportunities for parallelisation: candidates can be estimated or evaluated individually, as can the scanning for minimal windows.

MDL does not provide a free lunch. First of all, although highly desirable, it is not trivial to bound the score. While for Kolmogorov complexity we know this is incomputable, for our models we have no proof one way or another. Furthermore, although MDL gives a principled way to construct an encoding, this involves many choices that determine what structure is rewarded. As such, we do not claim our encoding is suited for all goals, nor that it cannot be improved.

Future work includes the extension of SQS for parallel and general episodes—which surpass serial episodes in expressiveness. Although seemingly opposed to MDL (why describe the same thing twice?) allowing patterns to overlap may provide more succinct summarisations. Last, but not least, we are interested in applying the SQS code tables for clustering and anomaly detection.

8. CONCLUSION

In this paper we employed the MDL principle to mine sets of sequential patterns that summarise the data well. In particular, we formalised how to encode sequential data using set of patterns, and use the encoded length as a quality measure. As search strategy for good models, we adopt two approaches. The first algorithm, SQS-CANDIDATES, selects a good pattern set from a large candidate set, while SQS-SEARCH is a parameter-free any-time algorithm that discovers good pattern sets directly from the data. Experimentation on synthetic and real data showed both methods to efficiently discover small, non-redundant sets of informative patterns.

And that's the long and the short of it.

Acknowledgements

Nikolaj Tatti and Jilles Vreeken are supported by Post-Doctoral Fellowships of the Research Foundation – Flanders (FWO).

9. REFERENCES

[1] A. Achar, S. Laxman, R. Viswanathan, and P. S. Sastry. Discovering injective episodes with general partial orders. *Data Min. Knowl. Disc.*, 2011.

[2] R. Bathoorn, A. Koopman, and A. Siebes. Reducing the frequent pattern set. In *ICDM-Workshop*, pages 1-5, 2006.

[3] T. M. Cover and J. A. Thomas. *Elements of Information Theory*. Wiley-Interscience New York, 2006.

[4] S. Dzeroski, B. Goethals, and P. Panov, editors. *Inductive Databases and Constraint-Based Data Mining*. Springer, 2010.

[5] P. Grünwald. *The Minimum Description Length Principle*. MIT Press, 2007.

[6] R. Gwadera, M. J. Atallah, and W. Szpankowski. Markov models for identification of significant episodes. In *SDM*, pages 404–414, 2005.

[7] R. Gwadera, M. J. Atallah, and W. Szpankowski. Reliable detection of episodes in event sequences. *Knowl. Inf. Sys.*, 7(4):415–437, 2005.

[8] J. Kiernan and E. Terzi. EventSummarizer: a tool for summarizing large event sequences. In *EDBT*, pages 1136–1139, 2009.

[9] H. T. Lam, F. Mörchen, D. Fradkin, and T. Calders. Mining compressing sequential patterns. In *SDM*, 2012.

[10] S. Laxman, P. S. Sastry, and K. P. Unnikrishnan. A fast algorithm for finding frequent episodes in event streams. In *KDD*, pages 410–419, 2007.

[11] M. Li and P. Vitányi. *An Introduction to Kolmogorov Complexity and its Applications*. Springer, 1993.

[12] H. Mannila and C. Meek. Global partial orders from sequential data. In *KDD*, pages 161–168, 2000.

[13] H. Mannila, H. Toivonen, and A. I. Verkamo. Discovery of frequent episodes in event sequences. *Data Min. Knowl. Disc.*, 1(3):259–289, 1997.

[14] J. Pei, H. Wang, J. Liu, K. Wang, J. Wang, and P. S. Yu. Discovering frequent closed partial orders from strings. *IEEE TKDE*, 18(11):1467–1481, 2006.

[15] J. Rissanen. Modeling by shortest data description. *Annals Stat.*, 11(2):416–431, 1983.

[16] D. Salomon and G. Motta. *Handbook of Data Compression*. Springer, 2009.

[17] K. Smets and J. Vreeken. SLIM: Directly mining descriptive patterns. In *SDM*, pages 1–12. SIAM, 2012.

[18] N. Tatti. Significance of episodes based on minimal windows. In *ICDM*, pages 513–522, 2009.

[19] N. Tatti and B. Cule. Mining closed episodes with simultaneous events. In *KDD*, pages 1172–1180, 2011.

[20] N. Tatti and B. Cule. Mining closed strict episodes. *Data Min. Knowl. Disc.*, 2011.

[21] N. Vereshchagin and P. Vitanyi. Kolmogorov's structure functions and model selection. *IEEE TIT*, 50(12):3265– 3290, 2004.

[22] J. Vreeken and A. Siebes. Filling in the blanks: Krimp minimisation for missing data. In *ICDM*, pages 1067–1072, 2008.

[23] J. Vreeken, M. van Leeuwen, and A. Siebes. KRIMP: Mining itemsets that compress. *Data Min. Knowl. Disc.*, 23(1):169–214, 2011.

[24] J. Wang and J. Han. Bide: Efficient mining of frequent closed sequences. *ICDE*, 0:79, 2004.

Efficient Event Pattern Matching with Match Windows

Bruno Cadonna
Free University of Bozen-Bolzano, Italy
cadonna@inf.unibz.it

Johann Gamper
Free University of Bozen-Bolzano, Italy
gamper@inf.unibz.it

Michael H. Böhlen
University of Zurich, Switzerland
boehlen@ifi.uzh.ch

ABSTRACT

In event pattern matching a sequence of input events is matched against a complex query pattern that specifies constraints on extent, order, values, and quantification of matching events.

In this paper we propose a general pattern matching strategy that consists of a pre-processing step and a pattern matching step. Instead of eagerly matching incoming events, the pre-processing step buffers events in a match window to apply different pruning techniques (filtering, partitioning, and testing for necessary match conditions). In the second step, an event pattern matching algorithm, $\mathcal{A}$, is called only for match windows that satisfy the necessary match conditions. This two-phase strategy with a lazy call of the matching algorithm significantly reduces the number of events that need to be processed by $\mathcal{A}$ as well as the number of calls to $\mathcal{A}$. This is important since pattern matching algorithms tend to be expensive in terms of runtime and memory complexity, whereas the pre-processing can be done very efficiently. We conduct extensive experiments using real-world data with pattern matching algorithms for, respectively, automata and join trees. The experimental results confirm the effectiveness of our strategy for both types of pattern matching algorithms.

Categories and Subject Descriptors

H.2.4 [**Database Management Systems**]: Systems—*Query Processing*

Keywords

Event pattern matching, Window, Optimization

1. INTRODUCTION

In event pattern matching a sequence of input events is matched against a complex query pattern that specifies constraints on extent, order, values, and quantification of matching events. Due to its wide applicability in different application domains, such as financial services [3, 8, 12, 15], click stream analysis [12, 15], RFID-based tracking and monitoring [3, 9], RSS feed monitoring [8], health services [5, 11], and workflow monitoring [10], an increasing amount of research is being conducted in this field.

KDD'12, August 12–16, 2012, Beijing, China.
Copyright 2012 ACM 978-1-4503-1462-6/12/08... $15.00.

Chemo

	PID	*L*	*V*	*U*	*T*
e_1	1	C	1672.5	mg	3 Jul
e_2	1	B	7100	$1/\mu l$	4 Jul
e_3	1	P	111.5	mg	5 Jul
e_4	2	B	10100	$1/\mu l$	6 Jul
e_5	2	P	38	mg	8 Jul
e_6	2	D	34	mgl	9 Jul
e_7	2	C	1320	mg	10 Jul
e_8	2	P	98	mg	11 Jul
e_9	1	P	116.5	mg	12 Jul
e_{10}	2	P	38	mg	15 Jul
e_{11}	1	B	3400	$1/\mu l$	17 Jul
e_{12}	2	B	4000	$1/\mu l$	18 Jul
e_{13}	2	B	4900	$1/\mu l$	19 Jul
e_{14}	1	B	3000	$1/\mu l$	22 Jul

Figure 1: Events of Chemotherapy Treatments.

In this paper we propose a two-phase strategy that leverages existing pattern matching algorithms. To illustrate our framework, we use sequenced event set (SES) pattern matching [5], where a query specifies a sequence of event sets and a maximal time interval during which the events must occur. The order of input events that match a single event set is irrelevant, whereas the order of input events that match different event sets must correspond to the order of the sets in the pattern.

Example 1. As a running example, we consider the analysis of chemotherapy data. A chemotherapy is a treatment for cancer patients and consists of a sequence of events, such as the administration of medications and laboratory examinations. Figure 1 shows a sample event relation, Chemo. The attributes represent patient ID (*PID*), event type (*L*), value (*V*) with measurement unit (*U*), and occurrence time (*T*) of an event, respectively. For instance, event e_1 represents the administration of 1672.5 mg of Ciclofosfamide to patient 1 on July 3. To investigate the effect of the medications on the blood count the following query is issued:

> Q1: *For each patient, retrieve the events that match (in any order) one administration of Ciclofosfamide (C) and one or more administrations of Prednisone (P) with monotonically increasing values, followed by a single blood count measurement (B); all events must occur within fifteen days.*

We propose a novel pattern matching strategy that consists of a pre-processing phase and a pattern matching phase. In the pre-processing phase, incoming events are buffered in the match window to apply different pruning techniques, such as filtering, partitioning, and testing for necessary match conditions. The aim of the comparably cheap pre-processing is to reduce the number of input events that need to be processed in the much more expensive pattern matching phase.

First, to eliminate irrelevant events that will never participate in a match we propose a *filtering mechanism*, which can be done very efficiently. Filtering out irrelevant events is particularly effective for the skip-till-next-match and skip-till-any-match event selection strategies that both skip all irrelevant events [3].

Second, a critical aspect of current solutions is that each input event is immediately processed by the pattern matching algorithm. For example, in automaton-based algorithms, each event creates a new automaton instance since each event can potentially start a match. This leads to a large number of automaton instances with a significant amount of state information to be maintained. A first step to improve this is to start an automaton only when it leaves the start state [3]. We achieve a substantial reduction of the number of automata by buffering input events in the *match window*, W, and lazily instantiating an automaton (or equivalently call a pattern matching algorithm $\mathcal{A}$) only when the buffered events satisfy a set of *necessary match conditions* and the window contains all events that need to be considered for matches starting at the first event in the window. We adopt a *summary statistics* based on event counting to efficiently check the necessary match conditions.

Third, although filtering removes irrelevant events, the match window might still contain events that cannot be part of any match starting at the first event in W. For instance, in our example all events in a match must be of the same patient. Thus, all events in W with a patient ID different from the one of the first event do not need to be forwarded to $\mathcal{A}$. We achieve this by *partitioning* incoming events into different windows, based on equality constraints that are derived from the query specification.

In the second phase, an *event pattern matching algorithm*, $\mathcal{A}$, is called for each match window that satisfies the necessary match conditions. This two-phase strategy with a lazy call of the matching algorithm significantly reduces the number of events that need to be processed by $\mathcal{A}$ and the number of calls to $\mathcal{A}$. While pattern matching algorithms tend to be expensive in terms of runtime and memory complexity, pre-processing can be done very efficiently.

We conduct extensive experiments on two real-world datasets, using the automaton-based SES pattern matching algorithm and ZStream which is based on join trees. The experiments show the effectiveness of our strategy for both types of pattern matching algorithms.

The technical contributions can be summarized as follows:

- We propose a general, two-phase pattern matching strategy that can be combined with different pattern matching algorithms.
- We propose an efficient and effective pre-processing step that buffers input events in the match window and applies various pruning techniques (filtering, partitioning, and necessary match conditions). Pre-processing is comparably cheap and significantly reduces the number of events that need to be processed by a more expensive pattern matching algorithm $\mathcal{A}$ as well as the number of calls of $\mathcal{A}$.
- We report the results of an empirical evaluation with an automaton- and join tree-based pattern matching algorithm. For both algorithms, our strategy shows clear performance improvements.

The rest of the paper is organized as follows. Section 2 discusses related work. In Sec. 3 we introduce SES pattern matching. In Sec. 4 we present our two-phase pattern matching strategy together with the pruning techniques. An algorithm that implements this strategy is described in Sec. 5. In Section 6 we report experimental results. Section 7 concludes the paper and points to future work.

2. RELATED WORK

In the past, various approaches have been proposed for processing pattern matching queries, most prominently automaton-based solutions [3, 5, 8, 10] and solutions that use join trees [12]. A common characteristic of these approaches is that incoming events are immediately processed by the pattern matching algorithm. In this paper we advocate a strategy that applies a pre-processing phase followed by a pattern matching phase. Pre-processing significantly reduces the number of events that need to be processed in the pattern matching phase. Our strategy leverages existing pattern matching algorithms and achieves significant performance improvements since pre-processing is cheap when compared to the more expensive pattern matching algorithms.

Sequenced event set (SES) pattern matching [5] allows to specify in the query a sequence of event sets rather than a sequence of single events. For query processing, an approach that uses nondeterministic automata has been proposed. An automaton is created for each input event that matches the beginning of the pattern, which might lead to orders of magnitude more automaton instances than matches, and each input event is passed to all active automaton instances. In this paper we propose an effective pre-processing phase that significantly reduces the number of events that need to be processed by the automaton instances as well as the number of automaton instances.

SASE+ [3] translates a query to a nondeterministic finite state automaton. Specific optimization techniques include partitioning and merging of automaton instances during query execution. Similar to SES automata, SASE+ suffers from the many automaton instances that are created for each incoming event that matches the beginning of the pattern.

The publish/subscribe system Cayuga [8] uses a regular expression like algebra and translates a query into a nondeterministic finite state automaton. Optimization techniques focus on the simultaneous evaluation of multiple queries using indices. By indexing automaton instances, an input event is only processed by those automaton instances that may change state. This is similar to our filter mechanism, but many active automaton instances need to be maintained in memory. To reduce the number of transitions that are evaluated for each incoming event, transitions are indexed on their condition. Cayuga instantiates an automaton for each input event that matches the beginning of the query pattern, and therefore exhibits the same drawbacks as SASE+.

The C-CEP system [10] adopts an automaton-based solution that checks for pattern query unsatisfiability according to pre-existing constraints that are evaluated on the input stream. These constraints originate from the business logic and allow to detect at runtime optimal points to terminate automaton instances that will never produce a match. Different from this work, our pruning techniques need no extra constraints, but exploit the query pattern to filter out irrelevant events and to delay the instantiation of automata until some necessary conditions are satisfied.

The DejaVu system [9] implements a subset of the SQL extension [16] for pattern matching in MySQL. The query processor is extended to use finite state automata for the evaluation of pattern matching queries such that an automaton runs as integral part of the query plan. Specific optimizations for pattern queries (apart from the optimizations of MySQL) are not presented.

ZStream [12] is a cost-based query processor using join trees for matching sequential patterns that are enriched with sequence, conjunction, disjunction, negation, and Kleene closure operators. Operators are arranged in a query tree that processes events from the leaves to the root. Hashing is used to evaluate equality predicates, and a cost-based reordering algorithm is used to find an efficient order of the operators. The algorithm finds an optimal order for patterns that consist of a sequence of single events; this is not guaranteed for queries that consist of sets of more than two events since the reordering does not consider different orders of binary conjunction operators.

Other research work on event pattern matching includes SQL-TS [15], an extension of SQL to process complex sequential patterns in database systems. For efficient query processing, a solution based on the Knuth-Morris-Pratt string matching algorithm has been adopted and optimized. The Event Analyzer [11] is a data warehouse component that allows to analyze event sequences.

Systems for stream processing include Aurora [2, 6], Borealis [1], STREAM [4, 13], and TelegraphCQ [7]. Querying in these systems is limited to a combination of selection, join, and aggregation; pattern queries are not supported. Based on these operations, optimization techniques focus on efficient resource management and load balancing.

3. EVENT PATTERN MATCHING

This section gives an overview of sequenced event set pattern matching (or simply pattern matching), which we use to illustrate our framework. The notation is summarized in Table 1.

Symbol	Description	Example
E	event relation	Chemo in Fig. 1
e	event	$\mathtt{e}_1 = (1, \text{'C'}, 1672.5, \text{mg}, 3\ \text{Jul})$
A	attribute of e	PID with $\mathtt{e}_1.PID = 1$
T	occurrence time of e	$\mathtt{e}_1.T = 3$ Jul
$\vec{e}$	chron. ordered event sequence	$\langle \mathtt{e}_1, \mathtt{e}_2, \mathtt{e}_3 \rangle$
P	pattern	$(\langle \{c, p^+\}, \{b\} \rangle, \Theta, 15\ \text{d})$
B_i	set of variables	$\{c, p^+\}$
v	variable in P	c
Θ	set of constraints	$\{c.L = \text{'C'}, c.PID = p.PID\}$
θ	constraint	$c.L = \text{'C'}$
τ	maximal time span	15 d
γ	substitution	$\{c/\langle \mathtt{e}_1 \rangle, p/\langle \mathtt{e}_3 \rangle, b/\langle \mathtt{e}_{11} \rangle\}$

Table 1: Notation.

An *event* is represented as a tuple with schema $\mathbf{E} = (A_1, \dots, A_l, T)$, where T is a temporal attribute that stores the occurrence time of an event. For T we assume a totally ordered time domain. An *event relation*, E, is a set of events with a total order given by attribute T (see relation Chemo in Fig. 1). A *chronologically ordered sequence of events* is represented as $\vec{e} = \langle e_1, \dots, e_n \rangle$ with e_1 and e_n referring to the first and last event in $\vec{e}$, respectively.

Definition 1. (Pattern) A *pattern*, P, is a triple

$$P = (B, \Theta, \tau),$$

where $B = \langle B_1, \dots, B_k \rangle$, $k \geq 1$, is a sequence of pairwise disjoint sets of variables of the form v or v^+, $\Theta = \{\theta_1, \dots, \theta_l\}$ is a set of constraints over variables in $B_1, \dots, B_k$, and τ is a duration.

A variable, $v \in B_i$, binds a sequence of a single event, $\langle e_1 \rangle$. A quantified variable, $v^+ \in B_i$, binds a sequence of one or more events, $\langle e_1, \dots, e_n \rangle, n \geq 1$. Θ is a set of constraints over variables that must be satisfied by matching events. We distinguish between properties and relationships, i.e., $\Theta = \Theta^{\text{p}} \cup \Theta^{\text{r}}$. *Properties*, $\theta \in \Theta^{\text{p}}$, have the form $(v.A \ \phi \ C)$, where $v.A$ refers to an attribute of a matching event, C is a constant, and $\phi \in \{=, \neq, <, \leq, >, \geq, \}$ is a comparison operator. Properties can be further partitioned by variable, $\Theta^{\text{p}} = \Theta^{\text{p}}_{v_1} \cup \dots \cup \Theta^{\text{p}}_{v_m}$. Each set $\Theta^{\text{p}}_{v_i}$ (also referred to as properties of variable v_i) contains all constraints of the form $(v_i.A \ \phi \ C)$. *Relationships*, $\theta \in \Theta^{\text{r}}$, have the form $(v_i.A_k \ \phi \ v_j.A_l)$ or $(\text{prev}(v.A) \ \phi \ v.A)$. Finally, τ is the maximal time span within which all matching events must occur.

Example 2. Query Q1 is formulated as pattern $P_1 = (\langle \{c, p^+\}, \{b\} \rangle, \Theta, 15\ \text{d})$. The first set, $B_1 = \{c, p^+\}$, contains two variables with the quantifier $^+$ applied to p. The second set, $B_2 = \{b\}$, contains one variable. The maximal time span is fifteen days. The constraints, separated in properties and relationships, are $\Theta = \Theta^{\text{p}}_c \cup \Theta^{\text{p}}_p \cup \Theta^{\text{p}}_b \cup \Theta^{\text{r}}$ with properties $\Theta^{\text{p}}_c = \{c.L = \text{'C'}\}$, $\Theta^{\text{p}}_p = \{p.L = \text{'P'}\}$, and $\Theta^{\text{p}}_b = \{b.L = \text{'B'}\}$ and relationships $\Theta^{\text{r}} = \{c.PID = p.PID, p.PID = b.PID, \text{prev}(p.V) < p.V\}$. Variable c binds a single administration of Ciclofosfamide ($c.L = \text{'C'}$), p^+ binds one or more administrations of Prednisone ($p.L = \text{'P'}$), and b binds a single blood count measurement ($b.L = \text{'B'}$). The first two relationships force the matched events to refer to the same patient. The third relationship requires the amount of Prednisone to be increasing.

To define the matching of a pattern P and an event relation E, we use a *substitution* $\gamma = \{v_1/\vec{e}_1, \dots, v_m/\vec{e}_m\}$. Each pair $v/\vec{e}$ represents a *binding* of variable v to a sequence, $\vec{e} = \langle e_1, \dots, e_n \rangle, n > 0$, of events in E. A substitution contains exactly one binding for each variable in P, and an event can appear in at most one of the bindings. For a constraint $\theta \in \Theta$, $\theta\gamma$ denotes the *instantiation* of θ by γ and is obtained from θ by simultaneously replacing all variables v_i by the corresponding event sequence $\vec{e}_i$. The instantiation of a set of constraints Θ is $\Theta\gamma = \{\theta_1\gamma, \dots, \theta_l\gamma\}$. The truth value of an instantiation is defined through an *interpretation*, $I(\Theta\gamma)$:

- $I(\Theta\gamma) \equiv I(\{\theta_1\gamma, \dots, \theta_l\gamma\}) \equiv I(\theta_1\gamma) \wedge \dots \wedge I(\theta_l\gamma)$,
- $I(\vec{e}.A \ \phi \ C) \equiv \forall x \in \vec{e} \ (x.A \ \phi \ C)$,
- $I(\vec{e}_i.A_i \ \phi \ \vec{e}_j.A_j) \equiv \forall x \in \vec{e}_i, y \in \vec{e}_j \ (x.A_i \ \phi \ y.A_j)$,
- $I(\text{prev}(\vec{e}.A) \ \phi \ \vec{e}.A) \equiv \forall x_{i-1}, x_i \in \vec{e}(x_{i-1}.A \ \phi \ x_i.A)$.

The interpretation of $\Theta\gamma$ is the conjunction of the interpretation of the individual constraints $\theta_i\gamma$. If θ is a property, i.e., $(v.A \ \phi \ C)$, the attribute A of all events bound to v are compared to constant C. If θ is a relationship of the form $(v_i.A_i \phi v_j.A_j)$, all combinations of attributes A_i and A_j of all events bound to v_i and v_j, respectively, are compared. If θ is a relationship of the form $(\text{prev}(v.A) \ \phi \ v.A)$, the attribute A of each pair of consecutive events that are bound to v are compared.

Example 3. Let Θ be the set of constraints of pattern $P_1 = (\langle \{c, p^+\}, \{b\} \rangle, \Theta, 15\ \text{d})$ and $\gamma = \{c/\langle \mathtt{e}_7 \rangle, p/\langle \mathtt{e}_5, \mathtt{e}_8 \rangle, b/\langle \mathtt{e}_{12} \rangle\}$ be a substitution. The instantiation of Θ (cf. Example 2) with γ is

$$\Theta\gamma = \{\langle \mathtt{e}_7 \rangle.L = \text{'C'}, \langle \mathtt{e}_5, \mathtt{e}_8 \rangle.L = \text{'P'}, \langle \mathtt{e}_{12} \rangle.L = \text{'B'}, \\ \langle \mathtt{e}_7 \rangle.PID = \langle \mathtt{e}_5, \mathtt{e}_8 \rangle.PID, \langle \mathtt{e}_5, \mathtt{e}_8 \rangle.PID = \langle \mathtt{e}_{12} \rangle.PID, \\ \text{prev}(\langle \mathtt{e}_5, \mathtt{e}_8 \rangle.V) < \langle \mathtt{e}_5, \mathtt{e}_8 \rangle.V\}.$$

The interpretation of $\Theta\gamma$ is

$$\begin{aligned} I(\Theta\gamma) &\equiv I(\langle e_7\rangle.L = \text{'C'}) \wedge I(\langle e_5, e_8\rangle.L = \text{'P'}) \wedge \cdots \wedge \\ &\quad I(\langle e_5, e_8\rangle.PID = \langle e_{12}\rangle.PID) \wedge \\ &\quad I(\text{prev}(\langle e_5, e_8\rangle.V) < \langle e_5, e_8\rangle.V) \\ &\equiv e_7.L = \text{'C'} \wedge e_5.L = \text{'P'} \wedge e_8.L = \text{'P'} \wedge \cdots \wedge \\ &\quad e_5.PID = e_{12}.PID \wedge e_8.PID = e_{12}.PID \wedge \\ &\quad e_5.V < e_8.V \\ &\equiv \text{'C'} = \text{'C'} \wedge \text{'P'} = \text{'P'} \wedge \text{'P'} = \text{'P'} \wedge \cdots \wedge \\ &\quad 2 = 2 \wedge 2 = 2 \wedge 88 < 98 \\ &\equiv true \end{aligned}$$

Definition 2. (*Match*) Let $P = (B, \Theta, \tau)$ be a pattern with $B = \langle B_1, \ldots, B_k\rangle$ and E be an event relation. A substitution $\gamma = \{v_1/\vec{e}_1, \ldots, v_m/\vec{e}_m\}$ is a *match* of P in E iff the following holds:

$$I(\Theta\gamma) \text{ is true,} \quad (1)$$

$$\forall v_i/\vec{e}_i, v_j/\vec{e}_j \in \gamma(v_i \in B_i \wedge v_j \in B_{i+1} \rightarrow e_{i_n}.T < e_{j_1}.T), \quad (2)$$

$$\forall v_i/\vec{e}_i, v_j/\vec{e}_j \in \gamma\ (|e_{i_1}.T - e_{j_n}.T| \leq \tau). \quad (3)$$

Condition 1 requires that a match satisfies all constraints in Θ. Condition 2 ensures that all events in a match that are bound to a variable in B_i must occur before all events that are bound to any variable in B_{i+1}. No order is imposed on events that are bound to variables in the same B_i, hence any permutation is matched. Condition 3 constrains all events in a match to occur within a time span of τ.

Example 4. Figure 2 illustrates a match of P_1 in relation Chemo. Variables c and b bind a single event each, p binds a sequence of two events. The instantiation $\Theta\gamma$ is satisfied (Cond. 1): e_7 is a 'C' event, e_5 and e_8 are 'P' events, and e_{12} is a 'B' event; all events refer to the same patient; and the value of e_5 is greater than the value of e_8. Events e_5, e_7, and e_8 that match the first event set occur before e_{12} that matches the second event set (Cond. 2). The time span between the first (e_5) and last event (e_{12}) is less than fifteen days (Cond. 3). The complete list of matches is:

$$\begin{aligned} &\{c/\langle e_1\rangle, p/\langle e_3\rangle, b/\langle e_{11}\rangle\}, && \{c/\langle e_1\rangle, p/\langle e_3, e_9\rangle, b/\langle e_{11}\rangle\}, \\ &\{c/\langle e_7\rangle, p/\langle e_5\rangle, b/\langle e_{12}\rangle\}, && \{c/\langle e_7\rangle, p/\langle e_5\rangle, b/\langle e_{13}\rangle\}, \\ &\{c/\langle e_7\rangle, p/\langle e_8\rangle, b/\langle e_{12}\rangle\}, && \{c/\langle e_7\rangle, p/\langle e_8\rangle, b/\langle e_{13}\rangle\}, \\ &\{c/\langle e_7\rangle, p/\langle e_5, e_8\rangle, b/\langle e_{12}\rangle\}, && \{c/\langle e_7\rangle, p/\langle e_5, e_8\rangle, b/\langle e_{13}\rangle\}. \end{aligned}$$

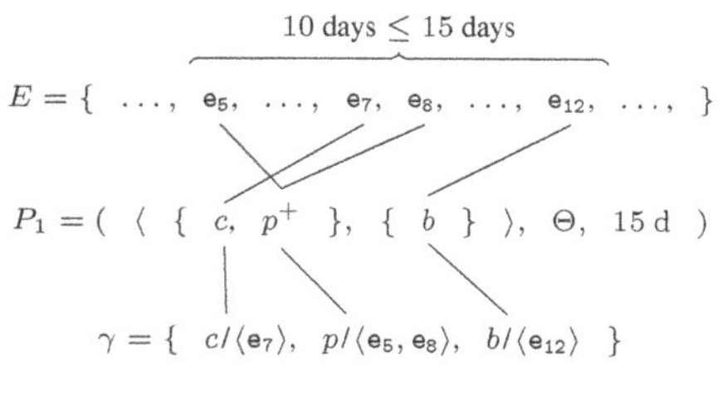

Figure 2: Match for Query Q1.

Definition 2 specifies the set of all possible matches of P in E, but applications might be interested in a subset only. This can be controlled by different *event selection strategies* that have been proposed in the literature [3]. In the running example of this paper we use earliest and maximal matches. A match, $\gamma = \{v_1/\vec{e}_1, \ldots, v_m/\vec{e}_m\}$, is *earliest* iff each $\vec{e}_i$ starts with the earliest possible event after the first event in γ. A match γ is *maximal* iff no $\vec{e}_i$ can be extended with an event that occurs after the start of γ, and γ remains still a match.

Example 5. Match γ in Fig. 2 is earliest and maximal. All bound event sequences start with the earliest possible events and they cannot be extended and still satisfy the conditions of a match. In contrast, match $\{c/\langle e_7\rangle, p/\langle e_5, e_8\rangle, b/\langle e_{13}\rangle\}$ is not earliest, since b binds e_{13} instead of the earlier event e_{12}. Match $\{c/\langle e_7\rangle, p/\langle e_5\rangle, b/\langle e_{12}\rangle\}$ is not maximal, since the event sequence bound to p can be extended with e_8 and still remains a match. The complete list of earliest and maximal matches is:

$$\{c/\langle e_1\rangle, p/\langle e_3, e_9\rangle, b/\langle e_{11}\rangle\}, \quad \{c/\langle e_7\rangle, p/\langle e_8\rangle, b/\langle e_{12}\rangle\}, \quad \{c/\langle e_7\rangle, p/\langle e_5, e_8\rangle, b/\langle e_{12}\rangle\}.$$

4. LAZY EVALUATION USING MATCH WINDOWS

In this section we propose a lazy evaluation strategy for event pattern matching. Instead of eagerly matching incoming events, we advocate a two-phase strategy composed of a pre-processing step and a pattern matching step (see Fig. 3). First, incoming events are buffered in the match window, which allows to apply pruning techniques on the window, such as filtering, partitioning, and testing for necessary match conditions. Second, an event pattern matching algorithm, $\mathcal{A}$, is called that needs to consider only the events in the match window. The pre-processing phase aims at reducing the number of events that need to be processed by $\mathcal{A}$.

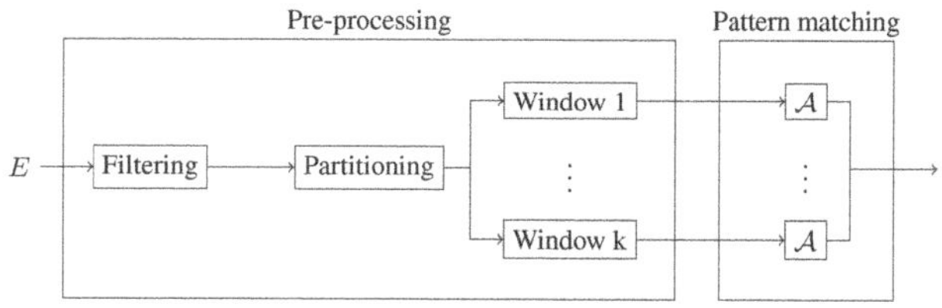

Figure 3: Two-phase Evaluation Strategy.

4.1 Match Window

First, we introduce the match window, which buffers incoming events and aids a lazy call of $\mathcal{A}$.

Definition 3. (*Match Window*) Let E be an event relation and P be a pattern with duration τ. The *match window* starting at event $e_i \in E$ is defined as $W_i = \langle e \in E \mid 0 \leq e.T - e_i.T \leq \tau\rangle$.

A match window W is a maximal subsequence of E that starts at an event e_i and includes all events that are within duration τ.

Example 6. Figure 4 illustrates two match windows, W_1 and W_2, for pattern $P_1 = (\langle\{c, p^+\}, \{b\}\rangle, \Theta, 15\text{ d})$. The match windows start at event e_1 and e_2, respectively. Both match windows contain 12 events, each with a maximal time span of fifteen days between the first and the last event.

Conceptually, a match window slides over the input stream event-by-event and covers at each step all events that are within duration τ from the earliest event in the window. Depending on the

$$E = \mathsf{e}_1, \overbrace{\mathsf{e}_2, \underbrace{\mathsf{e}_3, \mathsf{e}_4, \mathsf{e}_5, \mathsf{e}_6, \mathsf{e}_7, \mathsf{e}_8, \mathsf{e}_9, \mathsf{e}_{10}, \mathsf{e}_{11}, \mathsf{e}_{12}}_{W_1}, \mathsf{e}_{13}}^{W_2}, \mathsf{e}_{14}, \ldots$$

Figure 4: Match Window for Pattern P_1.

density of the input events along the time axis, the number of tuples in the match window might vary.

A match window $W = \langle e_1, \ldots, e_n \rangle$ is a buffer that collects all incoming events that need to be considered for a match that starts at e_1. This includes all events until the time span between the first event e_1 and the current input event exceeds τ. At this point an event pattern matching algorithm is called to compute all matches that start at e_1. Afterwards, e_1 is removed from W.

Definition 4. (*Event Pattern Matching Algorithm*) Let $W = \langle e_1, \ldots, e_n \rangle$ be a match window for a pattern P. An *event pattern matching algorithm*, $\mathcal{A}(P, W)$, takes P and W as input and returns the set of all matches that start at e_1.

$\mathcal{A}$ can be any event pattern matching algorithm that returns matches that start at event e_1. To make the discussion more concrete, we assume an automaton-based algorithm, such as the SES pattern matching algorithm [5]. In the evaluation we also apply our framework to ZStream, which uses join trees.

Example 7. Consider pattern P_1 and the match windows W_1 and W_2 in Fig. 4. $\mathcal{A}(P_1, W_1)$ returns a single match $\{c/\langle \mathsf{e}_1 \rangle, p/\langle \mathsf{e}_3, \mathsf{e}_9 \rangle, b/\langle \mathsf{e}_{11} \rangle\}$ that starts at e_1. In contrast, $\mathcal{A}(P_1, W_2)$ for the second match window returns the empty set since no match starts at e_2.

An eager instantiation of automata for each incoming event might lead to a large number of concurrent instances in memory, whereas a lazy instantiation strategy reduces this number.

4.2 Filtered Match Windows

While the lazy initialization of automata reduces the number of concurrently active automaton instances, filtering aims at reducing the number of events that need to be processed by $\mathcal{A}$. For this we analyse each incoming event for the properties specified in the pattern.

Not all events in the match window are candidates for matching a variable in the query pattern. Events that cannot contribute to any match can be filtered out before they are passed to $\mathcal{A}$. The following theorem specifies a condition that must be satisfied by each event in a match.

THEOREM 1. *Let $P = (B, \Theta, \tau)$ be a pattern with variables $v_1, \ldots, v_m$ and γ be a match of P in E. Each event e in γ satisfies $\Theta^{\mathrm{P}}_{v_1}(e) \vee \cdots \vee \Theta^{\mathrm{P}}_{v_m}(e)$.*

PROOF: see Appendix A.

From Theorem 1 we can conclude that an event $e \in E$ can only be part of a match if $\Theta^{\mathrm{P}}_{v_1}(e) \vee \cdots \vee \Theta^{\mathrm{P}}_{v_m}(e)$ is satisfied for some v_i. Therefore, we can filter out events that do not satisfy this condition, which leads to a reduction of the events that must be processed by algorithm $\mathcal{A}$. Notice that only a subset of Θ need to be checked.

Example 8. Consider pattern $P_1 = (\langle \{c, p^+\}, \{b\} \rangle, \Theta, 15\text{ d})$ and match window W_1 in Fig. 4. All events e_i that contribute to a match must satisfy $\Theta^{\mathrm{P}}_c(e_i) \vee \Theta^{\mathrm{P}}_p(e_i) \vee \Theta^{\mathrm{P}}_b(e_i)$, which is equivalent to $e_i.L =$ 'C' $\vee\ e_i.L =$ 'P' $\vee\ e_i.L =$ 'B'. Referring to relation `Chemo`, we can easily verify that all events except e_6 satisfy this condition. Thus, e_6 can safely be filtered out and need not to be buffered. W_1 and W_2 from Fig. 4 become $W_1' = \langle \mathsf{e}_1, \ldots, \mathsf{e}_5, \mathsf{e}_7, \ldots, \mathsf{e}_{12} \rangle$ and $W_2' = \langle \mathsf{e}_2, \ldots, \mathsf{e}_5, \mathsf{e}_7, \ldots, \mathsf{e}_{13} \rangle$, respectively.

4.3 Candidate Match Windows

While filtering checks for each individual event whether it satisfies the properties of at least one variable, here we consider all events in a match window together and formulate conditions that must be satisfied for a match that starts with the first event in the match window. Match windows that do not satisfy these conditions need not to be passed to $\mathcal{A}$.

4.3.1 Necessary Match Conditions

The following theorem specifies necessary conditions for a match window to contain a match that starts at the first event.

THEOREM 2. (Necessary Match Conditions) *Let $P = (B, \Theta, \tau)$ be a pattern with $B = \langle B_1, \ldots, B_k \rangle$ and variables $v_1, \ldots, v_m$. A match window, $W = \langle e_1, \ldots, e_n \rangle$, that contains a match starting at e_1 satisfies the following conditions:*

$$|W| \geq m, \tag{4}$$

$$\exists v \in B_1\ (\Theta^{\mathrm{P}}_v(e_1)), \tag{5}$$

$$\forall v \in \{v_1, \ldots, v_m\} \exists e_i \in W\ (\Theta^{\mathrm{P}}_v(e_i)), \tag{6}$$

$$\begin{aligned}&\forall v_i \in B_i, v_j \in B_{i+1}\ (\\ &\quad \exists e_i, e_j \in W\ (\Theta^{\mathrm{P}}_{v_i}(e_i) \wedge \Theta^{\mathrm{P}}_{v_j}(e_j) \wedge e_i.T < e_j.T)).\end{aligned} \tag{7}$$

PROOF: see Appendix A.

Theorem 2 allows to selectively pass match windows to algorithm $\mathcal{A}$, thereby reducing the number of calls to $\mathcal{A}$. A match window that does not satisfy the necessary match conditions cannot contain a match that starts with the first event in the window.

Example 9. Consider $P_1 = (\langle \{c, p^+\}, \{b\} \rangle, \Theta, 15\text{d})$ and match window $W_1' = \langle \mathsf{e}_1, \ldots, \mathsf{e}_5, \mathsf{e}_7, \ldots, \mathsf{e}_{12} \rangle$ after filtering out e_6. W_1' is a candidate match window since the necessary match conditions are satisfied: the cardinality of the match window, $|W_1'| = 11$, is greater than the number of variables, which is 3 (Cond. 4); event e_1 satisfies all properties of c in B_1 (Cond. 5); e_1, e_3, and e_{11} satisfy all properties of c, p, and b, respectively (Cond. 6), and their order corresponds to the order of B_1 and B_2 (Cond. 7). Next, consider $W_2' = \langle \mathsf{e}_2, \ldots, \mathsf{e}_5, \mathsf{e}_7, \ldots, \mathsf{e}_{13} \}$, which is not a candidate match window, since e_2 does not satisfy all properties of c or p (Cond. 5). Hence, W_2' cannot contain a match that starts at e_2.

4.3.2 Summary Statistics for Match Windows

Verifying Cond. 4 and 5 of the necessary match conditions is efficient and can be done incrementally as the individual events arrive. This is not the case for Cond. 6 and 7, for which all events in the match window must be considered. We maintain a summary statistics over the match window that can be updated incrementally and allows to efficiently verify the conditions.

Definition 5. (*Summary Statistics*) Let W be a match window and $P = (B, \Theta, \tau)$ be a pattern with $B = \langle B_1, \ldots, B_k \rangle$ and variables $v_1, \ldots, v_m$. A *summary statistics*, $S = \langle (v_1, cnt_1), \ldots, (v_m, cnt_m) \rangle$, is a set of variable-counter pairs such that for each $v_i \in B_i$

$$\begin{aligned}cnt_i = |\{e_i \in W \mid \Theta^{\mathrm{P}}_{v_i}(e_i) \wedge \forall v_j \in B_{i-1} \exists e_j \in W(\\ \Theta^{\mathrm{P}}_{v_j}(e_j) \wedge e_j.T < e_i.T)\}|.\end{aligned} \tag{8}$$

The summary statistics maintains a counter for each variable. The counter for a variable $v_i \in B_i$ records the number of events in W that (1) satisfy all properties of v_i and (2) chronologically follow events in W that satisfy the properties of the variables in the previous set B_{i-1}.

Example 10. Consider $P_1 = (\langle\{c, p^+\}, \{b\}\rangle, \Theta, 15\text{ d})$ and match window $W = \langle e_1, e_2, e_3\rangle$. The summary statistics for W is $S = \langle(c, 1), (p, 1), (b, 0)\rangle$. Events e_1 and e_3 satisfy all properties of c and p, respectively, and there is no previous set B_{i-1} in P_1. Although e_2 satisfies all properties of variable b, its counter is zero since there is no event in W that occurs before e_2 and satisfies the properties of p.

THEOREM 3. *Let P be a pattern with variables $v_1, \ldots, v_m$, W be a match window, and $S = \langle(v_1, cnt_1), \ldots, (v_m, cnt_m)\rangle$ be a summary statistics. The necessary match conditions 6 and 7 are satisfied if $cnt_1 > 0 \wedge \cdots \wedge cnt_m > 0$.*

PROOF: see Appendix A.

The summary statistics is incrementally updated when input events enter or exit W. When a new event e is added, the properties are evaluated. If e satisfies all properties of a variable $v \in B_i$ and the counters of all variables from the previous set B_{i-1} are greater than zero (i.e., W contains a matching event for these variables), cnt_i is incremented by one. When the first event, e, is dequeued from the match window, the counter for each variable whose properties are satisfied by e is decremented. If the counter for a variable $v \in B_i$ becomes zero, the counters of all variables in the sets B_j, $j > i$, are reset to zero.

Example 11. Figure 5 shows the summary statistics for a match window W that buffers events of patient 1. The last four columns show the fulfillment of the necessary match conditions. Event e_1 increments the counter for c. Event e_2 matches b, but has no effect on the statistics, since the counter for p is zero. After reading e_5, all counters are greater than zero, and the necessary match conditions are satisfied. Since the next event exceeds the duration of 15 days, the pattern match algorithm is called with W. Next, e_1 is removed from W and the summary statistics is updated. Since the counter for c becomes zero, the counter for b is reset to zero.

		Match conditions			
W	S	(4)	(5)	(6)	(7)
$\langle e_1\rangle$	$\langle(c,1),(p,0),(b,0)\rangle$	F	T	F	F
$\langle e_1, e_2\rangle$	$\langle(c,1),(p,0),(b,0)\rangle$	F	T	F	F
$\langle e_1, e_2, e_3\rangle$	$\langle(c,1),(p,1),(b,0)\rangle$	T	T	F	F
$\langle e_1, e_2, e_3, e_9\rangle$	$\langle(c,1),(p,2),(b,0)\rangle$	T	T	F	F
$\langle e_1, e_2, e_3, e_9, e_{11}\rangle$	$\langle(c,1),(p,2),(b,1)\rangle$	T	T	T	T
$\langle e_2, e_3, e_9, e_{11}\rangle$	$\langle(c,0),(p,2),(b,0)\rangle$	T	F	F	F

Figure 5: Statistics for $P_1 = (\langle\{c, p^+\}, \{b\}\rangle, \Theta, 15\text{ d})$.

The summary statistics provides an approximate solution and might produce false positives (e.g. due to relationships between variables that are not encoded in the statistics). We show experimentally that the number of match candidates can be significantly reduced.

4.4 Partitioned Match Windows

The last optimization aims to further reduce the number of events in a match window that are processed by algorithm $\mathcal{A}$. The core idea is to remove events that, while fulfilling the properties of a variable, can be excluded from a match since they violate some relationships. If all events in a match must have identical values in one or more attributes, the corresponding equality relationships in Θ can be used to partition a match window W into a set of match windows $W_1, \ldots, W_n$.

To formalize the partitioning of match windows based on equality relationships, we first define the transitive closure of these relationships. Let $P = (B, \Theta, \tau)$ be a pattern with variables $v_1, \ldots, v_m$ and $\Theta_{eq} = \{\theta \mid \theta \in \Theta \wedge \theta \equiv v_i.A_i = v_j.A_i\}$ be the set of all relationships with equality constraints over a single attribute. The *transitive closure* of Θ_{eq} is defined as

$$\Theta_{eq}^{+} = \bigcup_{l \in \mathbb{N}} \Theta_{eq}^{l},$$

where $\Theta_{eq}^0 = \Theta_{eq}$ and $\Theta_{eq}^l = \{v_i.A_i = v_j.A_i \mid \exists v_k((v_i.A_i = v_k.A_i) \in \Theta_{eq}^{l-1} \wedge (v_k.A_i = v_j.A_i) \in \Theta_{eq}^{l-1})\}$.

Definition 6. (*Partitioned Match Windows*) Let W be a match window for a pattern $P = (B, \Theta, \tau)$ with variables $v_1, \ldots, v_m$. Furthermore, let $X = \{A \mid \forall i, j \in [1, m]((v_i.A = v_j.A) \in \Theta_{eq}^{+})\}$. The set of attributes X partitions W into $W_1, \ldots, W_n$ such that for each W_i the following holds:

$$\forall e_i, e_j \in W_i \forall A \in X(e_i.A = e_j.A).$$

X is a maximal set of *partitioning attributes* that have to assume identical values for all events in a match. Accordingly, all events in a partition have identical values in the attributes X.

Example 12. Consider $P_1 = (\langle\{c, p^+\}, \{b\}\rangle, \Theta, 15\text{ d})$. The transitive closure of the equality relationships is $\Theta_{eq} = \{c.PID = p.PID,\ c.PID = b.PID,\ p.PID = b.PID,\ c.PID = c.PID,\ p.PID = p.PID,\ b.PID = b.PID\}$. The set of partitioning attributes is $X = \{PID\}$. That is, all events in a match must have the same patient ID. Partitioning $W_1' = \langle e_1, \ldots, e_5, e_7, \ldots, e_{12}\rangle$ by PID results in two partitions, $\langle e_1, e_2, e_3, e_9, e_{11}\rangle$ containing all events of patient 1 and $\langle e_5, e_7, e_8, e_{10}, e_{12}\rangle$ with all events of patient 2.

Partitioning input events allows two types of optimizations. First, since each partition W_i can be processed independently by algorithm $\mathcal{A}$, parallel event processing is possible. Second, after partitioning, the relationships $v_i.A_i = v_j.A_i$ for all $A_i \in X$ need not to be considered anymore by $\mathcal{A}$. They can be removed from Θ before calling $\mathcal{A}$ to reduce conditions that need to be verified in $\mathcal{A}$.

5. ALGORITHM

Algorithm 1 implements the two-phase pattern matching strategy from the previous section. The input parameters are a pattern P, an event relation E, and an event pattern matching algorithm $\mathcal{A}$. The algorithm returns the set of all matches.

In the initialization phase, an empty hash table H and result set R are created, and the set X of partitioning attributes is determined, which serves as a key for the hash table. H stores triples of the form (K, W, S), where $K = X$ are the grouping attributes, W is a match window, and S is the summary statistics over W.

The main loop iterates over all input events in chronological order. Events that do not satisfy the properties of any variable are immediately filtered out. For events that pass the filter, the corresponding entry in H is retrieved; if no such entry exists, a new entry is added with key set to the values of the partitioning attributes of the current event, an empty match window, and a summary statistics with all counters set to zero. Before inserting the current event e in W, the algorithm ensures that W does not exceed τ when the

Algorithm 1: $\texttt{Match}(P, E, \mathcal{A})$

Input: pattern $P = (\langle B_1, \ldots, B_k \rangle, \Theta, \tau)$ with m variables, event relation E, event pattern matching algorithm $\mathcal{A}$
Output: set of matches

$H \leftarrow \emptyset$; $R \leftarrow \emptyset$;
Compute set $X = (X_1, \ldots, X_k)$ of partitioning attributes;
foreach $e \in E$ *ordered by* T **do**
  if $\Theta^{\mathrm{P}}_{v1}(e)$ *or* ... *or* $\Theta^{\mathrm{P}}_{vm}(e)$ **then**
    $K' \leftarrow (e.X_1, \ldots, e.X_k)$;
    if $\nexists (K, W, S) \in H$ *with* $K = K'$ **then**
      Add $(K', \emptyset, \langle (v_1, 0), \ldots, (v_m, 0) \rangle)$ to H;
    Let (K, W, S) be the entry in H with $K = K'$;
    while $|W| > 0$ *and* $e.T - W[1].T > \tau$ **do**
      // match window exceeds τ with event e
      if $|W| \geq m$ *and* $\exists v \in B_1(\Theta^{\mathrm{P}}_v(W[1]))$
        and $\forall (v, cnt) \in S(cnt > 0)$ **then**
        $R \leftarrow R \cup \mathcal{A}(W, P)$;
      dequeue(W); Update S;
    enqueue(W, e); Update S;
foreach $(K, W, S) \in H$ **do**
  while $|W| \geq m$ *and* $\exists v \in B_1(\Theta^{\mathrm{P}}_v(W[1]))$
    and $\forall (v, cnt) \in S(cnt > 0)$ **do**
    $R \leftarrow R \cup \mathcal{A}(W, P)$;
    dequeue(W);
    Update S;
return R;

event is added. If e's distance from the first event in W exceeds τ, the necessary match conditions are verified; if they are satisfied, algorithm $\mathcal{A}$ is called. Afterwards, the first event is removed from W and the summary statistics is updated. This step is repeated until e fits into W and can be added; the summary statistics is updated.

After reading all input events, the remaining events in the match windows need to be processed. As long as the necessary match conditions are satisfied, $\mathcal{A}$ is called and the first event is removed.

The summary statistics can efficiently be implemented using bit vectors. Let $P = (B, \Theta, \tau)$ be a pattern with $B = \langle B_1, \ldots, B_k \rangle$ and variables $v_1, \ldots, v_m$. We use a bit vector, $\bar{\mathtt{e}}_i$, of length m to mask each incoming event e_i. Each position in the bit vector corresponds to a variable in P. If a bit is 1, the event satisfies all properties of the corresponding variable; otherwise it is set to 0. Similarly, we use a bit vector, $\bar{\mathtt{s}}$, where each position corresponds to a counter in the summary statistics. A 0 bit means that the corresponding counter is greater than zero; otherwise the counter is zero. Finally, we specify a bit mask, $\bar{\mathtt{b}}_i$, for each B_i. It has all bits set to 0 except for the bits that represent the positions of the variables in the previous event set, B_{i-1}. Using these bit vectors in combination allows an efficient update and querying of the summary statistics.

Example 13. Consider $P_1 = (\langle \{c, p^+\}, \{b\} \rangle, \Theta, 15\,\mathrm{d})$ and the events $\mathtt{e}_1$, $\mathtt{e}_2$, and $\mathtt{e}_3$. Event $\mathtt{e}_1$ satisfies all properties of variable c, but not for p and b. The corresponding bit vector is $\bar{\mathtt{e}}_1 = 100$. For the events $\mathtt{e}_2$ and $\mathtt{e}_3$ the bit vectors are, respectively, $\bar{\mathtt{e}}_1 = 001$ and $\bar{\mathtt{e}}_3 = 010$. The bit vector for the summary statistics is $\bar{\mathtt{s}} = 111$ at the beginning and 001 after processing $\mathtt{e}_1$, $\mathtt{e}_2$, and $\mathtt{e}_3$ (cf. Fig. 5). The bit mask for event set B_1 is $\bar{\mathtt{b}}_1 = 000$; for B_2 it is $\bar{\mathtt{b}}_2 = 110$.

6. EXPERIMENTS

In this section, we report the results of an empirical evaluation using real-world data. The experiments have three purposes: (1) to show the effect of the match window on the automaton-based SES pattern matching algorithm [5] that finds earliest and maximal matches and on the join-based ZStream pattern matching algorithm [12] that finds all matches; (2) to show the scalability of the match window in the pattern, and (3) to show the scalability of the match window in the data.

6.1 Setup and Data

We implemented our two-phase matching strategy with the SES algorithm and ZStream algorithm in C. The event relation is stored in an Oracle database, Enterprise Edition 11.1, which is accessed over the OCI API. The experiments were performed on a PC with four AMD Opteron 285 processors with 1.8 and 2.6 GHz and 16 GB memory, on which a 64-bit Linux 2.6.32 is installed.

We use two different real-world data sets. The Onco data set contains 341055 chemotherapy events from the Department of Haematology at the Hospital Meran-Merano. The NYSE data set contains 1M share trades in stock markets over 34 hours [14].

In the experiments, we analyze the scalability by varying the number of variables, the length of τ, and the size of the event relation. For the experiments with a varying number of variables, we use the following two query patterns:

- $P_{\mathrm{seq}} = (\langle \{v_1\}, \{v_2\}, \ldots, \{v_k\} \rangle, \Theta, \tau)$
- $P_{\mathrm{set}} = (\langle \{v_1, v_2, \ldots, v_k\} \rangle, \Theta, \tau)$

The number of variables varies from $k = 1, \ldots, 10$. For each step, we randomly choose ten distinct patterns out of all possible patterns with k variables, and we take the average of the measured throughput. The duration τ is 10 days for the Onco data set and 20 ms for the NYSE data set. P_{seq} is a sequential pattern where the matching events must occur in the same order as the variables in the pattern. In P_{set} the matching events may occur in any order.

For the experiments with a varying length of τ, we use the following patterns.

- $P_{\mathrm{onco}} = (\langle \{c, d\}, \{p^+, r^+\}, \{b, h\} \rangle, \Theta_{\mathrm{onco}}, \tau)$
- $P_{\mathrm{nyse}} = (\langle \{a^+, g^+\}, \{i^+\} \rangle, \Theta_{\mathrm{nyse}}, \tau)$

P_{onco} roughly resembles a cycle of a chemotherapy treatment. b matches white blood cell counts, h red blood cell counts, and the rest different medication administrations. Partitioning is applied on the patient ID. P_{nyse} specifies that a, g, and i match share trades of Apple, Google, and IBM, respectively. The price of the Apple and Google shares must be increasing between trades (i.e., $\mathrm{prev}(a.\mathrm{price}) < a.\mathrm{price}$), followed by a decrease of IBM shares (i.e., $\mathrm{prev}(i.\mathrm{price}) > i.\mathrm{price}$). Apple and Google share trades can occur interleaved. We vary τ from 5 days to 50 days for the Onco data set and from 10 to 100 ms for the NYSE data set.

For the experiments with a varying size of E, we use the pattern P_{nyse} and vary the size of E from 100 to 1000000 events in steps of a factor 10.

6.2 Scalability in the Pattern

In this experiment, we study the scalability of our framework by varying the number of variables and the length of τ in the pattern, respectively. Our hypothesis is that match windows significantly increase the throughput.

We first run the SES and ZStream algorithms with a plain match window without any pruning techniques (baseline), and apply then filtering (f), partitioning (p), and testing for necessary match conditions (c). The performance of the optimizations is measured in terms of throughput increase with respect to the baseline algorithm.

Figures 6 and 7 show the factor of the throughput increase of the various pruning techniques relative to the baseline algorithm.

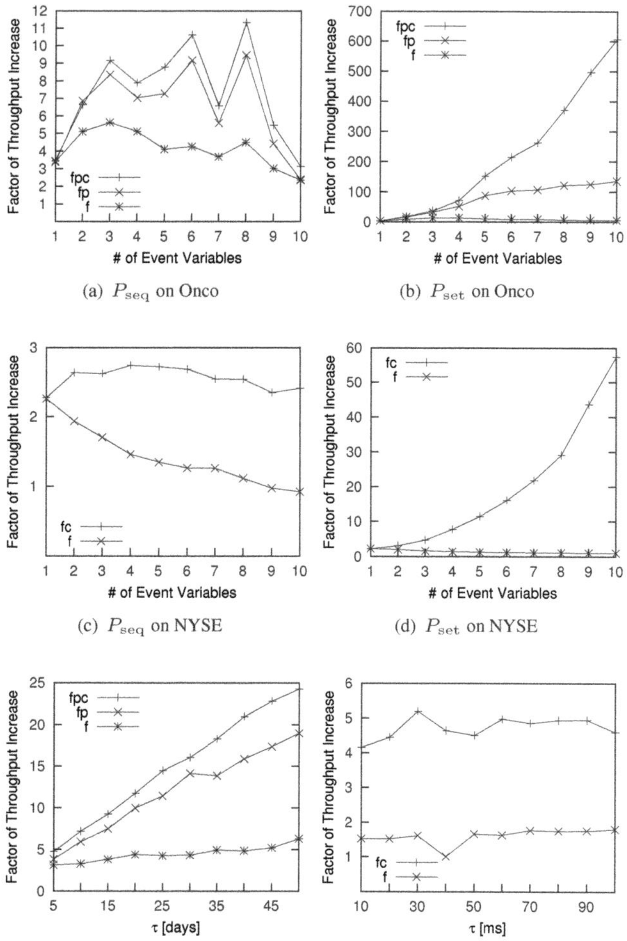

(a) P_{seq} on Onco (b) P_{set} on Onco

(c) P_{seq} on NYSE (d) P_{set} on NYSE

(e) P_{onco} (f) P_{nyse}

Figure 6: Varying the Pattern with SES.

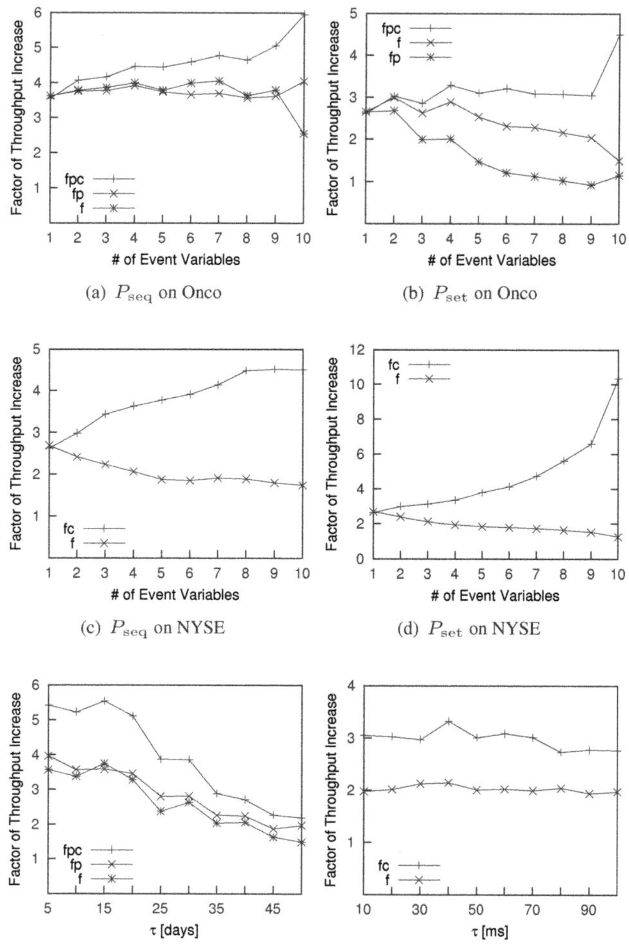

(a) P_{seq} on Onco (b) P_{set} on Onco

(c) P_{seq} on NYSE (d) P_{set} on NYSE

(e) P_{onco} (f) P_{nyse}

Figure 7: Varying the Pattern with ZStream.

The first observation is that the match windows achieve a significant improvement over the baseline solution, up to several orders of magnitudes for P_{set}.

Second, the optimizations are more effective for SES than for ZStream. The reasons are that ZStream implicitly filters new events when they are added to the join tree, and it uses hash tables for the joins on equality predicates. However, filtering, partitioning and testing for necessary conditions together still increase the throughput three to four times.

The third observation is that for SES the optimizations are much more effective for P_{set} (more than two orders of magnitude) than for P_{seq}. With P_{set} and without any pruning techniques, every event that matches any variable starts an automaton instance, yielding a large number of automaton instances, many of which do not lead to a match. With P_{seq}, only events that match the first variable in the pattern start an automaton instance. The match windows have a larger potential to increase the throughput of P_{set} than of P_{seq}.

The fourth observation is that the throughput for P_{onco} increases with increasing duration τ for SES. Events in the Onco data set follow roughly a chemotherapy protocol. Individual chemotherapy treatments are shifted in time, hence the patients are not distributed uniformly over the data. With increasing τ, events of more patients are encountered, hence more partitions of match windows can be created. SES can fully exploit the increasing number of partitions.

6.3 Scalability in the Data

In this experiment, we study the scalability of our framework by varying the number of events in the event relation. Our hypothesis is that the throughput increase remains constant with increasing size of the event relation. Again, we run first the baseline SES and ZStream algorithms on NYSE, and apply then filtering (f) and testing for necessary match conditions (c).

Figure 8 shows the factor of the throughput increase relative to the baseline algorithm. As expected, the throughput increase for our two-phase matching strategy when the pruning techniques are applied remains roughly constant. The reason is that neither the filtering nor the testing for necessary match conditions depends on the length of the event relation. Notice the logarithmic scale on the horizontal axis.

7. CONCLUSION

In this paper we presented a novel pattern matching strategy that consists of a pre-processing phase and a pattern matching phase. In the pre-processing phase, incoming events are buffered in a match window, which allows to apply different pruning techniques, such as filtering, partitioning, and testing for necessary match conditions, and aids a lazy evaluation of a pattern matching algorithm. We conducted extensive experiments using two real-world data sets and two existing event pattern matching algorithms. The results

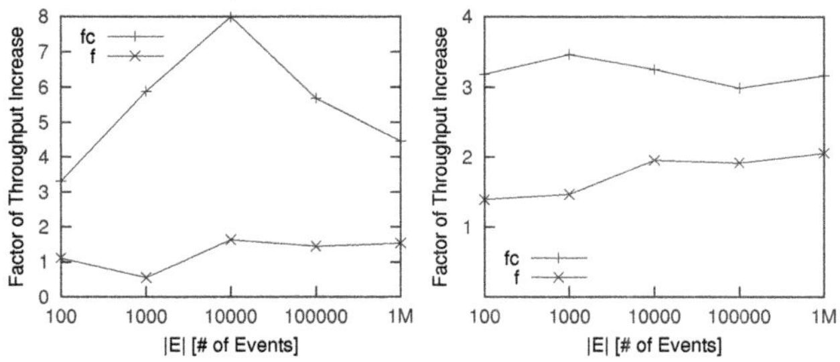

(a) P_{nyse} with SES

(b) P_{nyse} with ZStream

Figure 8: Varying the Data Size.

show that our framework significantly increases the throughput for both algorithms.

Future work is possible in various directions, including the investigation of additional runtime optimizations to efficiently support other event selection strategies (e.g. contiguous matches) as well as to explore space optimizations.

8. ACKNOWLEDGEMENTS

This work has been done within the framework of the MEDAN project, which is funded by the Hospital of Meran-Merano.

9. REFERENCES

[1] D. J. Abadi, Y. Ahmad, M. Balazinska, M. Cherniack, J. hyon Hwang, W. Lindner, A. S. Maskey, E. Rasin, E. Ryvkina, N. Tatbul, Y. Xing, and S. Zdonik. The design of the Borealis stream processing engine. In *CIDR*, pages 277–289, 2005.

[2] D. J. Abadi, D. Carney, U. Çetintemel, M. Cherniack, C. Convey, S. Lee, M. Stonebraker, N. Tatbul, and S. Zdonik. Aurora: a new model and architecture for data stream management. *The VLDB Journal*, 12(2):120–139, 2003.

[3] J. Agrawal, Y. Diao, D. Gyllstrom, and N. Immerman. Efficient pattern matching over event streams. In *SIGMOD*, pages 147–160, 2008.

[4] A. Arasu, S. Babu, and J. Widom. CQL: A language for continuous queries over streams and relations. In *DBPL*, pages 1–19, 2003.

[5] B. Cadonna, J. Gamper, and M. H. Böhlen. Sequenced event set pattern matching. In *EDBT*, pages 33–44, 2011.

[6] D. Carney, U. Çetintemel, M. Cherniack, C. Convey, S. Lee, G. Seidman, M. Stonebraker, N. Tatbul, and S. Zdonik. Monitoring streams: a new class of data management applications. In *VLDB*, pages 215–226, 2002.

[7] S. Chandrasekaran, O. Cooper, A. Deshpande, M. J. Franklin, J. M. Hellerstein, W. Hong, S. Krishnamurthy, S. Madden, V. Raman, F. Reiss, and M. A. Shah. Telegraphcq: Continuous dataflow processing for an uncertain world. In *CIDR*, 2003.

[8] A. J. Demers, J. Gehrke, M. Hong, M. Riedewald, and W. M. White. Towards expressive publish/subscribe systems. In *EDBT*, pages 627–644, 2006.

[9] N. Dindar, B. Güç, P. Lau, A. Ozal, M. Soner, and N. Tatbul. Dejavu: declarative pattern matching over live and archived streams of events. In *SIGMOD*, pages 1023–1026, 2009.

[10] L. Ding, S. Chen, E. A. Rundensteiner, J. Tatemura, W.-P. Hsiung, and K. S. Candan. Runtime semantic query optimization for event stream processing. In *ICDE*, pages 676–685, 2008.

[11] L. Harada and Y. Hotta. Order checking in a CPOE using event analyzer. In *CIKM*, pages 549–555, 2005.

[12] Y. Mei and S. Madden. Zstream: A cost-based query processor for adaptively detecting composite events. In *SIGMOD*, pages 193–206, 2009.

[13] R. Motwani, J. Widom, A. Arasu, B. Babcock, S. Babu, M. Datar, G. S. Manku, C. Olston, J. Rosenstein, and R. Varma. Query processing, approximation, and resource management in a data stream management system. In *CIDR*, 2003.

[14] NYSE. http://www.nyxdata.com/.

[15] R. Sadri, C. Zaniolo, A. Zarkesh, and J. Adibi. Expressing and optimizing sequence queries in database systems. *ACM Trans. Database Syst.*, 29(2):282–318, 2004.

[16] F. Zemke, A. Witkowski, M. Cherniak, and L. Colby. Pattern matching in sequences of rows. Technical report, 2007.

APPENDIX

A. PROOFS

PROOF. *(Theorem 1)* The constraints Θ consist of relationships and properties, i.e., $\Theta = \Theta^{\mathrm{r}} \cup \Theta^{\mathrm{p}}$. The properties can further be partitioned by variable, i.e., $\Theta^{\mathrm{p}} = \Theta^{\mathrm{p}}_{v_1} \cup \cdots \cup \Theta^{\mathrm{p}}_{v_m}$. By Def. 2, a match γ satisfies $I(\Theta\gamma)$. This can be transformed into $I(\Theta^{\mathrm{p}}_{v_1}\gamma) \wedge \cdots \wedge I(\Theta^{\mathrm{p}}_{v_m}\gamma) \wedge I(\Theta^{\mathrm{r}}\gamma)$. Since $I(\Theta^{\mathrm{p}}_{v_i}\gamma) \equiv I(\Theta^{\mathrm{p}}_{v_i}\{v_i/\langle e_1, \ldots, e_n\rangle\}) \equiv I(\Theta^{\mathrm{p}}_{v_i}\{v_i/\langle e_1\rangle\}) \wedge \cdots \wedge I(\Theta^{\mathrm{p}}_{v_i}\{v_i/\langle e_n\rangle\})$, each event in a match satisfies all properties of the variable it is bound to. ☐

PROOF. *(Theorem 2)* Condition 4: Since a given event can only appear once in a match, W needs to contain at least as many input events as variables in the query pattern. Condition 5: By Def. 2, the earliest event in a match is bound to a variable in B_1. Thus, the first event in W must satisfy the properties Θ^{p}_v of a variable $v \in B_1$. Condition 6: By Def. 2, each variable $v_1, \ldots, v_m$ is bound to at least one input event that satisfies the properties $\Theta^{\mathrm{p}}_{v_i}$. Hence, W must contain such an event for each variable. Condition 7: By Def. 2, input events that are bound to variables v_i, v_j in consecutive B_is need to occur in the same chronological order as the B_is in P. ☐

PROOF. *(Theorem 3)* cnt_i is greater than zero iff there exists at least one event in the set specified by Cond. 8. Therefore, $cnt_1 > 0 \wedge \cdots \wedge cnt_m > 0$ is equivalent to

$$\forall v \in B_1 \exists e \in W(\Theta^{\mathrm{p}}_v(e)) \wedge$$
$$\forall v \in B_2, v' \in B_1 \exists e, e' \in W(\Theta^{\mathrm{p}}_v(e) \wedge \Theta^{\mathrm{p}}_{v'}(e') \wedge e'.T < e.T)$$
$$\wedge \cdots \wedge$$
$$\forall v \in B_k, v' \in B_{n-1} \exists e, e' \in W(\Theta^{\mathrm{p}}_v(e) \wedge \Theta^{\mathrm{p}}_{v'}(e') \wedge e'.T < e.T).$$

By applying the rule $\forall x(A \wedge B) \equiv \forall x(A) \wedge \forall x(A \wedge B)$ to all quantified conjuncts we get

$$\forall v \in B_1 \exists e \in W(\Theta^{\mathrm{p}}_v(e)) \wedge \cdots \wedge \forall v \in B_k \exists e \in W(\Theta^{\mathrm{p}}_v(e)) \wedge$$
$$\forall 1 < i \leq n(\forall v \in B_i, v' \in B_{i-1} \exists e, e' \in W($$
$$\Theta^{\mathrm{p}}_v(e) \wedge \Theta^{\mathrm{p}}_{v'}(e') \wedge e'.T < e.T)),$$

which corresponds to Conds. 6 and 7. ☐

Optimal Exact Least Squares Rank Minimization

Shuo Xiang[1,2], Yunzhang Zhu[3], Xiaotong Shen[3], Jieping Ye[1,2]
[1]Center for Evolutionary Medicine and Informatics, The Biodesign Institute, ASU, Tempe, AZ 85281
[2]Department of Computer Science and Engineering, ASU, Tempe, AZ 85281
[3]School of Statistics, University of Minnesota, Minneapolis, MN 55455

ABSTRACT

In multivariate analysis, rank minimization emerges when a low-rank structure of matrices is desired as well as a small estimation error. Rank minimization is nonconvex and generally NP-hard, imposing one major challenge. In this paper, we derive a general closed-form for a global minimizer of a nonconvex least squares problem, in lieu of the common practice that seeks a local solution or a surrogate solution based on nuclear-norm regularization. Computationally, we develop efficient algorithms to compute a global solution as well as an entire regularization solution path. Theoretically, we show that our method reconstructs the oracle estimator exactly from noisy data. As a result, it recovers the true rank optimally against any method and leads to sharper parameter estimation over its counterpart. Finally, the utility of the proposed method is demonstrated by simulations and image reconstruction from noisy background.

Categories and Subject Descriptors

H.2.8 [**Database Management**]: Database Applications-Data Mining

General Terms

Algorithms

Keywords

Nonconvex, global optimality, rank minimization

1. INTRODUCTION

In multivariate analysis, estimation of lower-dimensional structures has received attention in statistics, signal processing and machine learning. One type of such structures is the low-rank of matrices [5, 22], where the rank measures the dimension of a multivariate response. Rank minimization approximates multivariate data with the smallest possible rank of matrices. It has many applications in, for instance, multi-task learning [6, 11], multi-class classification [2], matrix completion [8, 17], collaborative filtering [33, 1], clustering [20, 29], computer vision [35, 21, 18], among others. The central topic this article addresses is least squares rank minimization.

Consider multi-response linear regression in which a k-dimensional response vector $\boldsymbol{z}_i$ follows

$$\begin{aligned} \boldsymbol{z}_i &= \boldsymbol{\Theta}^T \boldsymbol{a}_i + \boldsymbol{\varepsilon}_i; \\ E\boldsymbol{\varepsilon}_i &= \boldsymbol{0}, \quad Cov(\boldsymbol{\varepsilon}_i) = \sigma^2 \boldsymbol{I}_{k\times k}; \quad i = 1, \cdots, n, \end{aligned} \tag{1}$$

where $\boldsymbol{a}_i$ is a p-dimensional design vector, $\boldsymbol{\Theta}$ is a $p \times k$ regression parameter matrix, and components of $\boldsymbol{\varepsilon}_i$ are independent. Model (1) reduces to the widely-used linear model in compressed sensing when $k = 1$ and becomes a multivariate autoregressive model with $\boldsymbol{a}_i = \boldsymbol{z}_{i-1}$. Denote the rank of $\boldsymbol{\Theta}$ as $r(\boldsymbol{\Theta})$ and rewrite (1) in the matrix form as follows:

$$\boldsymbol{Z} = \boldsymbol{A}\boldsymbol{\Theta} + \boldsymbol{e}, \tag{2}$$

where $\boldsymbol{Z} = (\boldsymbol{z}_1, \cdots, \boldsymbol{z}_n)^T \in \mathbb{R}^{n\times k}$, $\boldsymbol{A} = (\boldsymbol{a}_1, \cdots, \boldsymbol{a}_n)^T \in \mathbb{R}^{n\times p}$ and $\boldsymbol{e} = (\boldsymbol{\varepsilon}_1, \cdots, \boldsymbol{\varepsilon}_n)^T \in \mathbb{R}^{n\times k}$ are the data, design and error matrices. In (1), we estimate $\boldsymbol{\Theta}$ based on n pairs of observation vectors $(\boldsymbol{a}_i, \boldsymbol{z}_i)_{i=1}^n$, with *a priori* knowledge that $r(\boldsymbol{\Theta})$ is relatively small in comparison to $\min(n, k, p)$, where the number of unknown parameters k, p can greatly exceed the sample size n.

Least squares rank minimization, as described, solves

$$\begin{aligned} \min_{\boldsymbol{\Theta}} \quad & \|\boldsymbol{A}\boldsymbol{\Theta} - \boldsymbol{Z}\|_F^2 \\ \text{s.t.} \quad & r(\boldsymbol{\Theta}) \le s, \end{aligned} \tag{3}$$

where $\|\cdot\|_F$ is the Frobenius-norm and s is an integer-valued tuning parameter taking values from $[1, \min(n, k, p)]$. The general rank minimization is nonconvex and NP-hard [23], which is like the L_0-minimization in univariate analysis. Therefore an exact global solution to (3) is not known as well as its statistical properties, due primarily to discreteness and non-convexity of the rank function.

Estimation under the restriction that $r(\boldsymbol{\Theta}) = r$ has been studied when $n \to \infty$ with k and p held fixed, see [3, 4, 15, 28, 26]. Two major computational approaches have been proposed for approximating the optimal solution of (3). The first one involves regularization using surrogate function, such as the nuclear-norm, which is a convex envelope of the rank function [13] and can be solved by efficient algorithms [8, 19, 34, 25, 16]. In some cases, the solution of this convex problem coincides with a global minimizer of (3) under certain isometry assumptions [27]. However, these assumptions can be strong and difficult to check. Recently, [7] obtained a global minimizer of a regularized version of (3).

The second approach attacks (3) by approximating the rank function iteratively through calculating the largest singular vector using greedy search [30], or by singular value projection (SVP) through a local gradient method [17]. Under weaker isometry assumptions [27, 10, 9] than that of the nuclear-norm approach, these methods guarantee an exact solution of (3) but suffer from the same difficulties as the regularization method [30], although they have achieved promising results on both simulated and real-world data.

Theoretically, some loss error bounds of the first regularization approach are obtained in [24] under Frobenius-norm, and rank selection consistency is established in [7]. Unfortunately, to our best knowledge, whether similar conclusions hold for our formulation (3) remains largely unknown.

In this paper, we have advanced on two fronts. Computationally, we derive a general closed-form for a global minimizer of (3) in Theorem 1, and give a condition under which (3) and its nonconvex regularized counterpart are equivalent with regard to global minimizers, although these two methods are not generally equivalent. Moreover, we develop an efficient algorithm for computing the entire regularization solution path at the cost of computing only one solution for a single regularization parameter. Theoretically, we establish optimality for a global minimizer of (3). More specifically, the proposed method is optimal against any other ones in that it reconstructs the oracle estimator exactly, thus the true rank, under (1). It is important to note that this exact recovery result is a much stronger property than consistency, which is attributed to the discrete nature of the rank function as well as tuning parameter s. Such a result may not be shared by its regularized counterpart with a continuum tuning parameter. In addition, the method enjoys a higher degree of accuracy for parameter estimation than nuclear-norm rank estimation.

After the first draft of this paper was completed, we were aware that [14] and [32] gave an expression of Theorem 1. However, neither paper considered computational and statistical aspects of the solution. Inevitably, some partial overlaps exist between our Theorem 1 and theirs.

The rest of the paper is organized as follows. Section 2 presents a closed-form solution to (3). Section 3 gives an efficient path algorithm for a regularized version of (3). Section 4 is devoted to theoretical investigation, followed by Section 5 discussing methods for tuning. Section 6 presents proofs for all the theorems we develop and Section 7 presents results of empirical evaluations, where several rank minimization methods are compared. Section 8 concludes the paper.

Notation: Table 1 summarizes the notations used in the rest of the paper.

2. PROPOSED METHOD: CLOSED-FORM SOLUTION

This section derives a closed-form solution to (3). The strategy is to simplify (3) through the singular value decomposition (SVD) of matrix $\boldsymbol{A}$ and utilizing the properties of the rank function. Before proceeding, we present a motivating lemma, known as the Eckart-Young theorem [12].

E A 1. *The best s-rank approximation, in terms of the Frobenius-norm, for a t-rank matrix $\boldsymbol{Z}$ with $t \geq s$, i.e., a global minimizer $\boldsymbol{\Theta}^*$ of*

$$\begin{aligned} \min_{\boldsymbol{\Theta}} \quad & \|\boldsymbol{\Theta} - \boldsymbol{Z}\|_F^2 \\ s.t. \quad & r(\boldsymbol{\Theta}) \leq s \end{aligned} \tag{4}$$

is given by $\boldsymbol{\Theta}^* = \mathcal{P}_s(\boldsymbol{Z}) = \boldsymbol{U}_z \boldsymbol{D}_s \boldsymbol{V}_z^T$, where $\boldsymbol{D}_s$ consists of the largest s singular values of $\boldsymbol{Z}$ given the SVD of $\boldsymbol{Z} = \boldsymbol{U}_z \boldsymbol{D} \boldsymbol{V}_z^T$.

Table 1: Notation used throughout the paper

Notation	Description
$\boldsymbol{A}$	The design matrix
$\boldsymbol{e}$	Error matrix
Θ^0	The ground truth model
$\hat{\Theta}^s$	Estimator obtained by optimizing (3)
$\hat{\Theta}^*_\lambda$	Estimator obtained by optimizing (7)
$r(\boldsymbol{A})$	the rank of matrix $\boldsymbol{A}$
$\mathcal{P}_s(\boldsymbol{Z})$	The best s-rank approximation of matrix Z in terms of the Frobenius-norm

Intuitively $\mathcal{P}_s(\boldsymbol{Z})$ may be viewed as a projection of $\boldsymbol{Z}$ onto a set of matrices whose ranks are no more than s. Note that (4) is a special case of (3) with matrix $\boldsymbol{A}$ being the identity matrix. This motivates us to solve (3) through the simpler problem (4).

When $\boldsymbol{A}$ is nonsingular, clearly (3) has a global minimizer $\boldsymbol{A}^{-1}\mathcal{P}_s(\boldsymbol{Z})$ by rank preserveness of any nonsingular matrix in matrix multiplication. When $\boldsymbol{A}$ is singular, we first assume that $r(\boldsymbol{A}) \geq s$. However, this assumption is by no means mandatory, which will be discussed later. Given the SVD of $\boldsymbol{A} = \boldsymbol{U}\boldsymbol{D}\boldsymbol{V}^T$, with orthogonal matrices $\boldsymbol{U} \in \mathbb{R}^{n\times n}$ and $\boldsymbol{V} \in \mathbb{R}^{p\times p}$ and diagonal matrix $\boldsymbol{D} \in \mathbb{R}^{n\times p}$, we have

$$\|\boldsymbol{A}\boldsymbol{\Theta} - \boldsymbol{Z}\|_F = \|\boldsymbol{U}^T(\boldsymbol{A}\boldsymbol{\Theta} - \boldsymbol{Z})\|_F = \|\boldsymbol{D}\boldsymbol{V}^T\boldsymbol{\Theta} - \boldsymbol{U}^T\boldsymbol{Z}\|_F.$$

This follows from the fact that the Frobenius-norm is invariant under any orthogonal transformation. Let $\boldsymbol{Y} = \boldsymbol{V}^T\boldsymbol{\Theta}$ and $\boldsymbol{W} = \boldsymbol{U}^T\boldsymbol{Z}$, clearly we have $r(\boldsymbol{Y}) = r(\boldsymbol{\Theta})$. Now solving (3) amounts to solving an equivalent form:

$$\begin{aligned} \min_{\boldsymbol{Y}} \quad & \|\boldsymbol{D}\boldsymbol{Y} - \boldsymbol{W}\|_F^2 \\ \text{s.t.} \quad & r(\boldsymbol{Y}) \leq s. \end{aligned} \tag{5}$$

Consequently, a global minimizer of (3) becomes $V\boldsymbol{Y}^*$, where $\boldsymbol{Y}^*$ is a global minimizer of (5) and is given by the following theorem.

HEORE 1. *Let $\boldsymbol{D}$, $\boldsymbol{Y}$, $\boldsymbol{Z}$ and s be as defined above. If $s \leq r(\boldsymbol{A})$, then a global minimizer of (5) is given by*

$$\boldsymbol{Y}^* = \begin{bmatrix} \boldsymbol{D}^{-1}_{r(\boldsymbol{A})}\mathcal{P}_s(\boldsymbol{W}_{r(\boldsymbol{A})}) \\ \mathbf{a} \end{bmatrix}, \tag{6}$$

where $\boldsymbol{D}_{r(\boldsymbol{A})}$ is a diagonal matrix consisting of all the nonzero singular value of $\boldsymbol{A}$, $\boldsymbol{a}$ can be set as the zero matrix, and $\boldsymbol{W}_{r(\boldsymbol{A})}$ consists of the first $r(\boldsymbol{A})$ rows of $\boldsymbol{W}$.

Here are some remarks regarding the above theorem:

Remark 1. The solution to problem (5) is generally not unique. Specifically, the matrix $\boldsymbol{a}$ in (6) need not be fixed at zero, as long as it does not change the rank of Y^*. However, if $\boldsymbol{A}$ is of full column rank, i.e., when $r(\boldsymbol{A}) = p$, then $\boldsymbol{a}$ vanishes and Y^* can be uniquely determined. In this case, the optimal solution of (3) is also unique.

Remark 2. The optimal Y^* can also be computed for the general matrix A with an arbitrary rank, i.e., when $r(\boldsymbol{A}) < s$. See the proof of Theorem 1 in the Section 6.

It is important to note that the value of $\boldsymbol{a}$ is irrelevant for prediction, but matters for parameter estimation. In other words, when $r(\boldsymbol{A}) < p$, a global minimizer is not unique, hence that parameter estimation is not identifiable: see Section 4 for a discussion. For simplicity, we set $\boldsymbol{a} = \boldsymbol{0}$ for $\boldsymbol{Y}^*$ subsequently.

In what follows, our estimator is defined as $\hat{\boldsymbol{\Theta}}^s$, as well as an estimated rank $\hat{r}$. Algorithm 1 below summarizes the main steps for computing $\hat{\boldsymbol{\Theta}}^s$ with regard to $s \leq \min(n, k, p)$, where the LSRM stands for Least Squares Rank Minimization.

Algorithm 1 Exact solution of (3)

Input: $\boldsymbol{A}$, $\boldsymbol{Z}$, $s \leq r(\boldsymbol{A})$
Output: `A global minimizer` $\boldsymbol{\Theta}$ of (3)
Function: `LSRM`($\boldsymbol{A}$, $\boldsymbol{Z}$, s)

if $\boldsymbol{A}$ **is nonsingular then**
  $\boldsymbol{\Theta} = \boldsymbol{A}^{-1}\mathcal{P}_s(\boldsymbol{Z})$
else
  `Perform SVD on` $\boldsymbol{A}$: $\boldsymbol{A} = \boldsymbol{UDV}^T$
  `Extract the first` r `rows of` $\boldsymbol{U}^T\boldsymbol{Z}$ `and denote it as` $\boldsymbol{W}_{r(\boldsymbol{A})}$
  $\boldsymbol{\Theta} = \boldsymbol{V}\begin{bmatrix} \boldsymbol{D}_{r(\boldsymbol{A})}^{-1}\mathcal{P}_s(\boldsymbol{W}_{r(\boldsymbol{A})}) \\ \boldsymbol{0} \end{bmatrix}$
end if
return $\boldsymbol{\Theta}$

The complexity of Algorithm 1 is determined mainly by the most expensive operations–matrix inversion and SVD, specifically, at most one matrix inversion and two SVDs. Such operations roughly require a cubic time complexity [1].

3. REGULARIZATION AND SOLUTION PATH

This section studies a regularized counterpart of (3):

$$\min_{\boldsymbol{\Theta}} \quad \|\boldsymbol{A\Theta} - \boldsymbol{Z}\|_F^2 + \lambda\ r(\boldsymbol{\Theta}), \tag{7}$$

where $\lambda > 0$ is a continuous regularization parameter corresponding to s in (3), and $\boldsymbol{\Theta}_\lambda^*$ is a global minimizer of (7). The next theorem establishes an equivalence between (7) and (3) when $\boldsymbol{\Theta}_\lambda^*$ is unique, occurring when $r(\boldsymbol{A}) = p$. Such a result is not generally anticipated for a nonconvex problem.

HEORE EQUI ALENCE *When $p = r(\boldsymbol{A})$, (7) has a unique global minimizer. Moreover, (7) and (3) are equivalent with respect to their solutions. For any $\boldsymbol{\Theta}_\lambda^*$ with $\lambda \geq 0$, there exists $1 \leq s^* = r(\boldsymbol{\Theta}_\lambda^*)$ such that $\boldsymbol{\Theta}_\lambda^* = \hat{\boldsymbol{\Theta}}^s$, and vice verse.*

Next we develop an algorithm for computing an entire solution path for all values of λ with complexity comparable to that of solving (7) at a single λ-value. For motivation, first consider a special case of the identity $\boldsymbol{A}$ in (7):

$$g(\lambda) = \min_{\boldsymbol{\Theta}} \quad \|\boldsymbol{\Theta} - \boldsymbol{Z}\|_F^2 + \lambda\ r(\boldsymbol{\Theta}). \tag{8}$$

3.1 Monotone property

In (8), $r(\boldsymbol{\Theta})$ decreases as λ increases from 0, where $r(\boldsymbol{\Theta})$ goes through all integer values from $r(\boldsymbol{Z})$ down to 0 when λ becomes sufficiently large. In addition, the value of $g(\lambda)$ is nondecreasing as λ increases. The next theorem summarizes these results.

HEORE MONOTONE RO ERTY *Let $r(\boldsymbol{Z})$ be r. Then the following properties hold:*

(1) There exists a solution path vector $\mathcal{S}$ of length $r+2$ satisfying the following:

$$\mathcal{S}_0 = 0, \quad \mathcal{S}_{r+1} = +\infty, \quad \mathcal{S}_{k+1} > \mathcal{S}_k, \quad k = 0, 1, \cdots, r$$
$$\boldsymbol{\Theta}_\lambda^* = \mathcal{P}_{r-k}(\boldsymbol{Z}), \quad \text{if } \mathcal{S}_k \leq \lambda < \mathcal{S}_{k+1},$$

(2) Function $g(\lambda)$ is nondecreasing and piecewise linear.

The monotone property leads to an efficient algorithm for calculating the pathwise solution of (8). Figure 1 displays the solution path by illustrating the function value $g(\lambda)$ and $r(\boldsymbol{\Theta}_\lambda^*)$ as a function of λ.

3.2 Pathwise algorithm

Through the monotone property, we compute the optimal solution of (8) at a particular λ by locating λ in the correct interval in the solution path vector $\mathcal{S}$, which can be achieved efficiently via a simple binary search. Algorithm 2 describes the main steps.

Algorithm 2 Pathwise solution of (8)

Input: $\boldsymbol{\Theta}$, $\boldsymbol{Z}$
Output: `Solution path vector` $\mathcal{S}$, `pathwise solution` $\boldsymbol{\Theta}$
Function: `pathwise`($\boldsymbol{\Theta}$,$\boldsymbol{Z}$)

`Initialize:` $\mathcal{S}_0 = 0$, $\boldsymbol{\Theta}_0 = \boldsymbol{Z}$, $r = r(\boldsymbol{Z})$
`Perform SVD on` $\boldsymbol{Z}$: $\boldsymbol{Z} = \boldsymbol{UDV}^T$
for $i = r$ **down to** 1 **do**
  $\mathcal{S}_{r-i+1} = \sigma_i^2$
  $\boldsymbol{\Theta}_{r-i+1} = \boldsymbol{\Theta}_{r-i} - \sigma_i u_i v_i^T$
end for
return $\mathcal{S}$, $\boldsymbol{\Theta}$

Algorithm 2 requires only one SVD operation, therefore its complexity is of the same order as that of Algorithm 1 at a single s-value. When $\boldsymbol{Z}$ is a low-rank matrix, existing software for SVD computation such as PROPACK is applicable to further improve computational efficiency.

3.3 Extension to general $\boldsymbol{A}$

For a general design matrix $\boldsymbol{A}$, note that

$$\|A\boldsymbol{\Theta} - \boldsymbol{Z}\|_F^2 = \|\boldsymbol{DY} - \boldsymbol{W}\|_F^2 = \|\boldsymbol{W}'\|_F^2 + \|\boldsymbol{D}_r\boldsymbol{Y}_r - \boldsymbol{W}_r\|_F^2,$$

where $\boldsymbol{W} = \begin{bmatrix} \boldsymbol{W}_r \\ \boldsymbol{W}' \end{bmatrix}$. After ignoring the constant term $\|\boldsymbol{W}'\|_F^2$, we solve

$$\min_{\boldsymbol{Y}_r} \quad \|\boldsymbol{D}_r\boldsymbol{Y}_r - \boldsymbol{W}_r\|_F^2 + \lambda\ r(\boldsymbol{Y}_r).$$

[1]More specifically, for a matrix of dimension $n \times p$, the SVD has a complexity of $O(\min\{n^2p, p^2n\})$, whereas the matrix inversion has a complexity of $O(r(\boldsymbol{A})^3)$, which can be improved to $O(r(\boldsymbol{A})^{2.807})$ when the Strassen Algorithm is utilized.

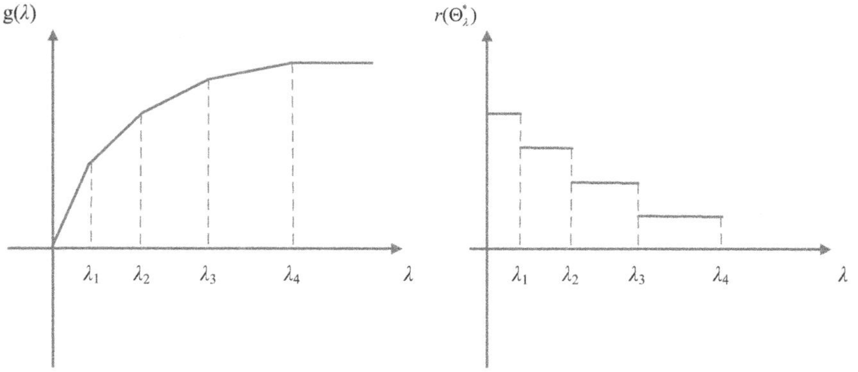

Figure 1: Piecewise linearity of $g(\cdot)$ and the rank of the optimal solution with respect to λ.

Note that $\boldsymbol{D}_r$ is nonsingular, then the problem reduces to the simple case

$$\min_{\hat{\boldsymbol{Y}}} \quad \|\hat{\boldsymbol{Y}} - \boldsymbol{W}_r\|_F^2 + \lambda\ r(\hat{\boldsymbol{Y}}),$$

where $\hat{\boldsymbol{Y}} = \boldsymbol{D}_r \boldsymbol{Y}_r$. The solution path can be obtained directly from Algorithm 2.

4. STATISTICAL PROPERTIES

This section is devoted to the theoretical investigation of least squares rank minimization, which remains largely unexplored, although nuclear-norm regularization has been studied. In particular, we will reveal what is the best performance for prediction as well as the optimal risk for parameter estimation. Moreover, we will establish the optimality of the proposed method. In fact, the proposed method reconstructs the oracle estimator, the optimal one as if the true rank were known in advance. Here the oracle estimator $\hat{\boldsymbol{\Theta}}^0$ is defined as a global minimizer of $\|\boldsymbol{A\Theta} - \boldsymbol{Z}\|_F^2$ subject to $r(\boldsymbol{\Theta}) = r_0$, where $\boldsymbol{\Theta}^0$ and $r_0 = r(\boldsymbol{\Theta}^0) \geq 1$ denote the true parameter matrix and the true rank respectively. This leads to the exact rank recovery, in addition to the reconstruction of the optimal performance of the oracle estimator. In other words, the proposed method is optimal against any other methods such as the nuclear-norm rank regularization.

Given the design matrix $\boldsymbol{A}$, we study the accuracy of rank recovery as well as prediction and parameter estimation. Let $\mathbb{P}$ and $\mathbb{E}$ be the true probability and expectation under $\boldsymbol{\Theta}^0$ given $\boldsymbol{A}$. For rank recovery, we use the metric $\mathbb{P}(\hat{r} \neq r_0)$. For prediction and parameter estimation, we employ the risk $\mathbb{E}K(\hat{\boldsymbol{\Theta}}^s, \boldsymbol{\Theta}^0)$ and $\mathbb{E}\|\hat{\boldsymbol{\Theta}}^s - \boldsymbol{\Theta}^0\|_F^2$ respectively, where

$$K(\hat{\boldsymbol{\Theta}}^s, \boldsymbol{\Theta}^0) = (2\sigma^2 n)^{-1} \sum_{i=1}^{n} \|\boldsymbol{a}_i^T(\hat{\boldsymbol{\Theta}}^s - \boldsymbol{\Theta}^0)\|_2^2$$
$$= (2\sigma^2 n)^{-1} \|\boldsymbol{A}(\hat{\boldsymbol{\Theta}}^s - \boldsymbol{\Theta}^0)\|_F^2$$

is the Kullback-Leibler loss and $\|\cdot\|_2$ is the L_2-norm for a vector. Note that the predictive risk equals to $2\sigma^2 \mathbb{E}K(\hat{\boldsymbol{\Theta}}^s, \boldsymbol{\Theta}^0)$ and parameter estimation is considered when it is identifiable, i.e., $r(\boldsymbol{A}) = p$.

Now we present the risk bounds under (1) without a Gaussian error assumption.

HEORE 4. *Under (1), the oracle estimator is exactly reconstructed by our method in that $\hat{\boldsymbol{\Theta}}^{r_0} = \boldsymbol{\Theta}^0$ under $\mathbb{P}$, when $r_0 \leq min(r(\boldsymbol{A}), p)$. As a result, exact reconstruction of the optimal performance is achieved by our estimator $\hat{\boldsymbol{\Theta}}^{r_0}$. In particular,*

$$\mathbb{E}K(\hat{\boldsymbol{\Theta}}^{r_0}, \boldsymbol{\Theta}^0) \begin{cases} = & \frac{r_0 k}{2n} & \text{if } r_0 = r(\boldsymbol{A}) \\ \leq & \frac{2\mathbb{E}(\sum_{j=1}^{r_0} \sigma_j^2)}{n} & \text{if } r_0 < r(\boldsymbol{A}) \end{cases}$$

and

$$\mathbb{E}\|\hat{\boldsymbol{\Theta}}^{r_0} - \boldsymbol{\Theta}^0\|_F^2 \begin{cases} = & \frac{r_0 k}{\sigma_{\min}^2(\boldsymbol{A}) n} & \text{if } r_0 = r(\boldsymbol{A}) = p \\ \leq & \frac{\mathbb{E}(\sum_{j=1}^{r_0} \sigma_j^2)}{\sigma_{\min}^2 n} & \text{if } r_0 < r(\boldsymbol{A}) = p \end{cases},$$

where σ_j and $\sigma_{\min} > 0$ are the jth largest and the smallest nonzero singular value of $\boldsymbol{e}^\star = \boldsymbol{U}_{r(A)}^T \boldsymbol{e}$ and $n^{-1/2}\boldsymbol{A}$, respectively, and $\boldsymbol{U}_{r(A)}$ denotes the first $r(A)$ rows of $\boldsymbol{U}$.

Remark: In general, $\mathbb{E}\sum_{j=1}^{r_0} \sigma_j^2 \leq r_0 \mathbb{E}\sigma_1^2$.

Theorem 4 says that the optimal oracle estimator is exactly reconstructed by our method. Interestingly, the true rank is exactly recovered from noisy data, which is attributed to discreteness of the rank and is analogous to the maximum likelihood estimation over a discrete parameter space. Concerning prediction and parameter estimation, the optimal Kullback-Leibler risk is $\frac{r_0 k}{n}$ but the risk under the Frobenius-norm is $\frac{r_0 k}{\sigma_{\min}^2 n}$. For prediction, only the effective degrees of freedom $\sum_{j=1}^{r_0} \sigma_j^2$ matters as opposed to p, which is in contrast to a rate $\frac{r_0 kp}{n}$ without a rank restriction. This permits p to be much larger than n, or $k, p \gg n$. For estimation, however, p enters the risk through $\sigma_{\min}^2$, where p can not be larger than n, or $\max(k, p) \leq n$.

5. TUNING

As shown in Section 4, theoretically, exact rank reconstruction can be accomplished through tuning. Practically, we employ a predictive measure for rank selection.

The predictive performance of $\hat{\boldsymbol{\Theta}}^s$ is measured by

$$\text{MSE}(\hat{\boldsymbol{\Theta}}^s) = \frac{1}{n}\mathbb{E}\|\boldsymbol{A}\hat{\boldsymbol{\Theta}}^s - \boldsymbol{Z}\|_F^2,$$

which is proportional to the risk $R(\hat{\boldsymbol{\Theta}}^s)$, where the expectation is taken with respect to $(\boldsymbol{Z}, \boldsymbol{A})$.

To estimate s over integer values in $[0, \cdots, \min(n, p, k)]$, one may cross-validate through a tuning data set, which estimates the MSE. Alternatively, one may use the generalized degrees of freedom [31] through data perturbation without a tuning set.

$$\widehat{\text{GDF}}(\hat{\boldsymbol{\Theta}}^s) = n^{-1}\|\boldsymbol{Z}-\boldsymbol{A}\hat{\boldsymbol{\Theta}}^s\|^2+2n^{-1}\sum_{i=1}^{n}\sum_{l=1}^{k}\widehat{\text{Cov}}(\boldsymbol{z}_{il}, (\boldsymbol{a}_i^T\hat{\boldsymbol{\Theta}}^s)_l), \tag{9}$$

where $\widehat{\text{Cov}}(\boldsymbol{z}_{il}, (\boldsymbol{a}_i^T\hat{\boldsymbol{\Theta}}^s)_l)$ is the estimated covariance between the lth component of $\boldsymbol{z}_i$ and the lth component of $\boldsymbol{a}_i^T\hat{\boldsymbol{\Theta}}^s$. In the case that $\boldsymbol{e}_i$ in (1) follows $N(\boldsymbol{0}, \sigma^2 I_{k\times k})$, the method of data perturbation of [31] is applicable. Specifically, sample $\boldsymbol{e}_i^*$ from $N(\boldsymbol{0}, \sigma^2 I_{k\times k})$ and let

$$\boldsymbol{Z}^* = (1-\tau)\boldsymbol{Z} + \tau\tilde{\boldsymbol{Z}}$$
$$\widehat{\text{Cov}}(\boldsymbol{z}_{il}, (\boldsymbol{a}_i^T\hat{\boldsymbol{\Theta}}^s)_l) = \tau^{-1}\text{Cov}^*(\boldsymbol{z}_{il}^*, (\boldsymbol{a}_i^T\hat{\boldsymbol{\Theta}}^{*s})_l)$$

where $\text{Cov}^*(\boldsymbol{z}_{il}^*, (\boldsymbol{a}_i\hat{\boldsymbol{\Theta}}^{*s})_l)$ is the sample covariance with the Monte Carlo size T. For the types of problems we consider, we fixed T to be n.

6. PROOF OF THEOREMS

In this section we present detailed proofs to the theorems developed in the previous sections. We first present a technical lemma to be used in the proof of Theorem 4.

E A 2. *Suppose* $\boldsymbol{A}$ *and* $\boldsymbol{B}$ *are two* $n_1 \times n_2$ *matrices. Then,*

$$\langle \boldsymbol{A}, \boldsymbol{B}\rangle \le \|\boldsymbol{A}\|_F\|\mathcal{P}_{r(\boldsymbol{A})}(\boldsymbol{B})\|_F, \tag{10}$$

where $\langle A, B\rangle = Tr(A^TB) = Tr(B^TA)$, Tr *denotes the trace, and* $r(\boldsymbol{A})$ *is the rank of* $\boldsymbol{A}$.

PROOF Let the singular value decomposition of $\boldsymbol{A}$ and $\boldsymbol{B}$ be $\boldsymbol{A} = \boldsymbol{U}_1\ _1\boldsymbol{V}_1^T$ and $\boldsymbol{B} = \boldsymbol{U}_2\ _2\boldsymbol{V}_2^T$ where $\boldsymbol{U}_i$ and $\boldsymbol{V}_i, i = 1, 2$, are orthogonal matrices, and Σ_1 and Σ_2 are diagonal matrices with their diagonal elements being the singular values of $\boldsymbol{A}$ and $\boldsymbol{B}$, respectively. Then

$$\begin{aligned}\langle \boldsymbol{A}, \boldsymbol{B}\rangle &= Tr(\boldsymbol{V}_1\ \ _1^T\boldsymbol{U}_1^T\boldsymbol{U}_2\ \ _2\boldsymbol{V}_2^T)\\ &= Tr(\ _1^T\boldsymbol{U}_1^T\boldsymbol{U}_2\ \ _2\boldsymbol{V}_2^T\boldsymbol{V}_1)\\ &\equiv Tr(\ _1^T\boldsymbol{U}\ \ _2\boldsymbol{V}^T),\end{aligned}$$

where $\boldsymbol{U} = \boldsymbol{U}_1^T\boldsymbol{U}_2$ and $\boldsymbol{V} = \boldsymbol{V}_1^T\boldsymbol{V}_2$ continue to be orthogonal. Let the ordered singular values of $\boldsymbol{A}$ be $\sigma_1 \ge \cdots \ge \sigma_{r(\boldsymbol{A})}$ and $\tilde{\boldsymbol{B}} = (\tilde{b}_{ij}) = \boldsymbol{U}\ \ _2\boldsymbol{V}^T$. By Cauchy-Schwarz's inequality,

$$\begin{aligned}Tr(\ _1^T\boldsymbol{U}\ \ _2\boldsymbol{V}^T) &= Tr(\ _1^T\tilde{\boldsymbol{B}})\\ &= \sum_{i=1}^{r(\boldsymbol{A})}\sigma_i\tilde{b}_{ii}\\ &\le \sqrt{\sum_{i=1}^{r(\boldsymbol{A})}\sigma_i^2}\sqrt{\sum_{i=1}^{r(\boldsymbol{A})}\tilde{b}_{ii}^2} \qquad (11)\\ &= \|\boldsymbol{A}\|_F\sqrt{\sum_{i=1}^{r(\boldsymbol{A})}\tilde{b}_{ii}^2}.\end{aligned}$$

Similarly, let the ordered singular values of $\boldsymbol{B}$ be $\eta_1 \ge \cdots \ge \eta_{r(\boldsymbol{B})}$. Then it suffices to show that $\sum_{i=1}^{r(\boldsymbol{A})}\tilde{b}_{ii}^2 \le \sum_{i=1}^{r(\boldsymbol{A})}\eta_i^2$.

Assume, without loss of generality, that $\eta_i = 0$ if $i > r(\boldsymbol{B})$. Let $n = \min(n_1, n_2)$. By Cauchy-Schwarz's inequality,

$$\begin{aligned}\sum_{i=1}^{r(\boldsymbol{A})}\tilde{b}_{ii}^2 &= \sum_{i=1}^{r(\boldsymbol{A})}\Big(\sum_{k=1}^{n}u_{ik}\eta_k v_{ik}\Big)^2\\ &\le \sum_{i=1}^{r(\boldsymbol{A})}\Big(\sum_{k=1}^{n}u_{ik}^2\eta_k^2\Big)\Big(\sum_{k=1}^{n}v_{ik}^2\Big)\\ &\le \sum_{i=1}^{r(\boldsymbol{A})}\Big(\sum_{k=1}^{n}u_{ik}^2\eta_k^2\Big)\\ &= \sum_{k=1}^{n}\eta_k^2\Big(\sum_{i=1}^{r(\boldsymbol{A})}u_{ik}^2\Big)\\ &\le \sum_{k=1}^{r(\boldsymbol{A})}\eta_k^2,\end{aligned}$$

where the last step uses the fact that $\sum_{i=1}^{r(\boldsymbol{A})}u_{ik}^2 \le 1$ and $\sum_{k=1}^{n}\sum_{i=1}^{r(\boldsymbol{A})}u_{ik}^2 = \sum_{i=1}^{r(\boldsymbol{A})}\sum_{k=1}^{n}u_{ik}^2 \le r(\boldsymbol{A})$. A combination of the above bounds lead to the desired results. This completes the proof. □

6.1 Proof of Theorem 1

First partition $\boldsymbol{D}$ and $\boldsymbol{W}$ as follows:

$$\boldsymbol{D} = \begin{bmatrix}\boldsymbol{D}_{r(\boldsymbol{A})} & 0\\ 0 & 0\end{bmatrix}, \quad \boldsymbol{W} = \begin{bmatrix}\boldsymbol{W}_{r(\boldsymbol{A})}\\ \boldsymbol{W}'\end{bmatrix},$$

then

$$\begin{aligned}\boldsymbol{D}\boldsymbol{Y} - \boldsymbol{W} &= \begin{bmatrix}\boldsymbol{D}_{r(\boldsymbol{A})}\boldsymbol{Y}_{r(\boldsymbol{A})}\\ 0\end{bmatrix} - \begin{bmatrix}\boldsymbol{W}_{r(\boldsymbol{A})}\\ \boldsymbol{W}'\end{bmatrix}\\ &= \begin{bmatrix}\boldsymbol{D}_{r(\boldsymbol{A})}\boldsymbol{Y}_{r(\boldsymbol{A})} - \boldsymbol{W}_{r(\boldsymbol{A})}\\ -\boldsymbol{W}'\end{bmatrix}.\end{aligned}$$

Evidently, only the first $r(\boldsymbol{A})$ rows of $\boldsymbol{Y}$ are involved in minimizing $\|\boldsymbol{D}\boldsymbol{Y} - \boldsymbol{W}\|_2^2$, which amounts to computing the global minimizer $\boldsymbol{Y}_{r(\boldsymbol{A})}^*$ of

$$\arg\min_{\boldsymbol{Y}_{r(\boldsymbol{A})}}\|\boldsymbol{D}_{r(\boldsymbol{A})}\boldsymbol{Y}_{r(\boldsymbol{A})} - \boldsymbol{W}_{r(\boldsymbol{A})}\|_F^2.$$

Then $\boldsymbol{Y}_{r(\boldsymbol{A})}^* = \boldsymbol{D}_{r(\boldsymbol{A})}^{-1}\mathcal{P}_s(\boldsymbol{W}_{r(\boldsymbol{A})})$ by non-singularity of $\boldsymbol{D}_{r(\boldsymbol{A})}$ and Lemma 1 with $s \le r(\boldsymbol{A})$. For $s > r(\boldsymbol{A})$, recall that, only the upper part of $\boldsymbol{Y}^*$ is relevant in minimizing (5). The result then follows. This completes the proof.

6.2 Proof of Theorem 2

For any $\boldsymbol{\Theta}_\lambda^*$ with $\lambda > 0$, let $s^* = r(\boldsymbol{\Theta}_\lambda^*)$. Next we prove by contradiction that $\boldsymbol{\Theta}_\lambda^* = \hat{\boldsymbol{\Theta}}^{s^*}$. Suppose $\boldsymbol{\Theta}_\lambda^* \neq \hat{\boldsymbol{\Theta}}^{s^*}$. By uniqueness of $\hat{\boldsymbol{\Theta}}^{s^*}$ given in Theorem 1 and the definition of minimization, $\|\boldsymbol{A}\hat{\boldsymbol{\Theta}}^{s^*}-\boldsymbol{Z}\|_F^2 < \|\boldsymbol{A}\boldsymbol{\Theta}_\lambda^*-\boldsymbol{Z}\|_F^2$. This, together with $r(\hat{\boldsymbol{\Theta}}^{s^*}) = r(\boldsymbol{\Theta}_\lambda^*)$, implies that

$$\|\boldsymbol{A}\hat{\boldsymbol{\Theta}}^{s^*} - \boldsymbol{Z}\|_F^2 + \lambda r(\hat{\boldsymbol{\Theta}}^{s^*}) < \|\boldsymbol{A}\boldsymbol{\Theta}_\lambda^* - \boldsymbol{Z}\|_F^2 + \lambda r(\boldsymbol{\Theta}_\lambda^*).$$

This contradicts to the fact that $\boldsymbol{\Theta}_\lambda^*$ is a minimizer of (7). The converse is revealed in the proof of Theorem 3.

6.3 Proof of Theorem 3

We prove the first conclusion by constructing such a solution path vector $\mathcal{S}$. Let $\mathcal{S}_0 = 0$, $\mathcal{S}_{r+1} = +\infty$. Define $\mathcal{S}_k$ for $1 \le k \le r$ as the solution of equation:

$$\|\mathcal{P}_{r-k+1}(\boldsymbol{Z})-\boldsymbol{Z}\|_F^2+\mathcal{S}_k(r-k+1) = \|\mathcal{P}_{r-k}(\boldsymbol{Z})-\boldsymbol{Z}\|_F^2+\mathcal{S}_k(r-k).$$

It follows that

$$\begin{aligned}\mathcal{S}_k &= \|\mathcal{P}_{r-k}(\boldsymbol{Z}) - \boldsymbol{Z}\|_F^2 - \|\mathcal{P}_{r-k+1}(\boldsymbol{Z}) - \boldsymbol{Z}\|_F^2 \\ &= \sum_{j=r-k+1}^{r} \sigma_j^2 - \sum_{j=r-k+2}^{r} \sigma_j^2 \\ &= \sigma_{r-k+1}^2,\end{aligned} \tag{12}$$

where σ_j is the jth largest non-zero singular value of $\boldsymbol{Z}$. By (12), $\mathcal{S}_k$ is increasing. In addition, by definition of S_k and S_{k+1}, whenever λ falls into the interval $[\mathcal{S}_k, \mathcal{S}_{k+1})$, the rank of a global minimizer $\boldsymbol{\Theta}^*$ of (8) would be no more than $r-k$ and larger than $r-k-1$. In other words, $\boldsymbol{\Theta}_\lambda^*$ is always of rank $r-k$ and is given by $\mathcal{P}_{r-k}(\boldsymbol{Z})$. Therefore, the constructed solution path vector $\mathcal{S}$ satisfies all the requirements in the theorem.

Moreover, when $\mathcal{S}_k \le \lambda < \mathcal{S}_{k+1}$,

$$\begin{aligned}g(\lambda) &= \|\mathcal{P}_{r-k}(\boldsymbol{Z}) - \boldsymbol{Z}\|_F^2 + \lambda\ r(\mathcal{P}_{r-k}(\boldsymbol{Z})) \\ &= \|\mathcal{P}_{r-k}(\boldsymbol{Z}) - \boldsymbol{Z}\|_F^2 + (r-k)\lambda.\end{aligned} \tag{13}$$

Since $\mathcal{P}_{r-k}(\boldsymbol{Z})$ is independent of λ, $g(\lambda)$ is a nondecreasing linear function of λ in each interval $[\mathcal{S}_k, \mathcal{S}_{k+1})$. Combined with the definition of the solution path vector $\mathcal{S}$, we conclude that $g(\lambda)$ is nondecreasing and piecewise linear with each element of $\mathcal{S}$ as a kink point, as shown in Figure 1. The proof is completed.

6.4 Proof of Theorem 4

The proof uses direct calculations. First we bound the Kullback-Leibler loss. By Theorem 1,

$$\boldsymbol{A}\hat{\boldsymbol{\Theta}}^{r_0} = \boldsymbol{U}_{r(\boldsymbol{A})}\mathcal{P}_{r_0}(\boldsymbol{W}_{r(\boldsymbol{A})}),$$

where

$$\boldsymbol{W}_{r(\boldsymbol{A})} = \boldsymbol{D}_{r(\boldsymbol{A})}\left(\boldsymbol{V}^T\boldsymbol{\Theta}^0\right)_{r(\boldsymbol{A})} + \left(\boldsymbol{U}^T\boldsymbol{e}\right)_{r(\boldsymbol{A})}.$$

Denote $\boldsymbol{B} = \boldsymbol{D}_{r(\boldsymbol{A})}\left(\boldsymbol{V}^T\boldsymbol{\Theta}^0\right)_{r(\boldsymbol{A})}$ with rank $r(\boldsymbol{B}) \le r_0$. Since the Frobenius-norm is invariant under orthogonal transformation, it follows that

$$\begin{aligned}&\|\boldsymbol{A}\hat{\boldsymbol{\Theta}}^{r_0} - \boldsymbol{A}\boldsymbol{\Theta}^0\|_F^2 \\ =&\|\boldsymbol{U}_{r(\boldsymbol{A})}\mathcal{P}_{r_0}(\boldsymbol{W}_{r(\boldsymbol{A})}) - \boldsymbol{U}\boldsymbol{D}\boldsymbol{V}^T\boldsymbol{\Theta}^0\|_F^2 \\ =&\|\boldsymbol{U}_{r(\boldsymbol{A})}\mathcal{P}_{r_0}(\boldsymbol{W}_{r(\boldsymbol{A})}) - \boldsymbol{U}_{r(\boldsymbol{A})}\boldsymbol{D}_{r(\boldsymbol{A})}\left(\boldsymbol{V}^T\boldsymbol{\Theta}^0\right)_{r(\boldsymbol{A})}\|_F^2 \\ =&\|\mathcal{P}_{r_0}(\boldsymbol{W}_{r(\boldsymbol{A})}) - \boldsymbol{D}_{r(\boldsymbol{A})}\left(\boldsymbol{V}^T\boldsymbol{\Theta}^0\right)_{r(\boldsymbol{A})}\|_F^2 \\ =&\|\mathcal{P}_{r_0}\left(\boldsymbol{B} + \left(\boldsymbol{U}^T\boldsymbol{e}\right)_{r(\boldsymbol{A})}\right) - \boldsymbol{B}\|_F^2, \\ =&\|\mathcal{P}_{r_0}(\boldsymbol{B} + \boldsymbol{e}^\star) - \boldsymbol{B}\|_F^2,\end{aligned}$$

where $\boldsymbol{e}^\star = \left(\boldsymbol{U}^T\boldsymbol{e}\right)_{r(\boldsymbol{A})}$. From the definition of $\mathcal{P}_{r_0}(\boldsymbol{B} + \boldsymbol{e}^\star)$ we can conclude that:

$$\|\mathcal{P}_{r_0}(\boldsymbol{B} + \boldsymbol{e}^\star) - \boldsymbol{B} - \boldsymbol{e}^\star\|_F^2 \le \|\boldsymbol{B} - \boldsymbol{B} - \boldsymbol{e}^\star\|_F^2 = \|\boldsymbol{e}^\star\|_F^2,$$

which implies that,

$$\begin{aligned}\|\mathcal{P}_{r_0}(\boldsymbol{B} + \boldsymbol{e}^\star) - \boldsymbol{B}\|_F^2 &\le 2\langle\mathcal{P}_{r_0}(\boldsymbol{B} + \boldsymbol{e}^\star) - \boldsymbol{B}, \boldsymbol{e}^\star\rangle \\ &\le 2\|\mathcal{P}_{r_0}(\boldsymbol{B} + \boldsymbol{e}^\star) - \boldsymbol{B}\|_F\|\mathcal{P}_{r_0}(\boldsymbol{e}^\star)\|_F,\end{aligned}$$

where the last inequality follows from Lemma 2. Thus,

$$\|\mathcal{P}_{r_0}(\boldsymbol{B} + \boldsymbol{e}^\star) - \boldsymbol{B}\|_F^2 \le 4\|\mathcal{P}_{r_0}(\boldsymbol{e}^\star)\|_F^2 = 4\sum_{j=1}^{r_0} \sigma_j^2. \tag{14}$$

The risk bounds then follow.

Second we bound $\|\hat{\boldsymbol{\Theta}}^{r_0} - \boldsymbol{\Theta}^0\|_F^2$, which is equal to

$$\begin{aligned}&\|\boldsymbol{V}\begin{bmatrix}\boldsymbol{D}_{r(\boldsymbol{A})}^{-1}\mathcal{P}_{r_0}(\boldsymbol{W}_{r(\boldsymbol{A})}) \\ \boldsymbol{0}\end{bmatrix} - \boldsymbol{\Theta}^0\|_F^2 \\ =&\|\begin{bmatrix}\boldsymbol{D}_{r(\boldsymbol{A})}^{-1}\mathcal{P}_{r_0}(\boldsymbol{W}_{r(\boldsymbol{A})}) \\ \boldsymbol{0}\end{bmatrix} - \boldsymbol{V}^T\boldsymbol{\Theta}^0\|_F^2 \\ =&\|\boldsymbol{D}_{r(\boldsymbol{A})}^{-1}\mathcal{P}_{r_0}(\boldsymbol{W}_{r(\boldsymbol{A})}) - (\boldsymbol{V}^T\boldsymbol{\Theta}^0)_{r(\boldsymbol{A})}\|_F^2 + \|(\boldsymbol{V}^T\boldsymbol{\Theta}^0)_{r(\boldsymbol{A})^c}\|_F^2 \\ \le&\frac{1}{\sigma_{\min}^2 n}\|\mathcal{P}_{r_0}(\boldsymbol{W}_{r(\boldsymbol{A})}) - \boldsymbol{D}_{r(\boldsymbol{A})}(\boldsymbol{V}^T\boldsymbol{\Theta}^0)_{r(\boldsymbol{A})}\|_F^2 \\ &+ \|(\boldsymbol{V}^T\boldsymbol{\Theta}^0)_{r(\boldsymbol{A})^c}\|_F^2,\end{aligned}$$

where $\sigma_{r(\boldsymbol{A})}(n^{-1/2}\boldsymbol{A}) = n^{1/2}\sigma_{\min}$. If $p = r(\boldsymbol{A})$, then the last term vanishes. Thus

$$\begin{aligned}\|\hat{\boldsymbol{\Theta}}^{r_0} - \boldsymbol{\Theta}^0\|_F^2 &\le \frac{1}{\sigma_{r(\boldsymbol{A})}^2 n}\|\mathcal{P}_{r_0}(\boldsymbol{W}_{r(\boldsymbol{A})}) - \boldsymbol{D}_{r(\boldsymbol{A})}(\boldsymbol{V}^T\boldsymbol{\Theta}^0)_{r(\boldsymbol{A})}\|_F^2 \\ &\le \frac{4\sum_{j=1}^{r_0}\sigma_j^2}{\sigma_{\min}^2 n}.\end{aligned}$$

Finally, if $r(\boldsymbol{A}) \ge r_0$, $\mathbb{E}\|\hat{\boldsymbol{\Theta}}^{r_0} - \boldsymbol{\Theta}^0\|_F^2 \le \frac{4}{\sigma_{r(\boldsymbol{A})}^2}\mathbb{E}\left(\sum_{j=1}^{r_0}\sigma_j^2\right)$ and $\mathbb{E}\|\boldsymbol{A}\hat{\boldsymbol{\Theta}}^{r_0} - \boldsymbol{A}\boldsymbol{\Theta}^0\|_F^2 \le 4\mathbb{E}\left(\sum_{j=1}^{r_0}\sigma_j^2\right)$. In particular, if $r(\boldsymbol{A}) = r_0$, then

$$\begin{aligned}\mathbb{E}\|\hat{\boldsymbol{\Theta}}^{r_0} - \boldsymbol{\Theta}^0\|_F^2 &= \frac{1}{\sigma_{\min}^2}\frac{r_0 k}{n} \\ \mathbb{E}\|\boldsymbol{A}\hat{\boldsymbol{\Theta}}^{r_0} - \boldsymbol{A}\boldsymbol{\Theta}^0\|_F^2 &= \frac{r_0 k}{n}.\end{aligned}$$

7. EMPIRICAL EVALUATIONS

This section examines effectiveness of the proposed method and compares it with the nuclear-norm regularization as well as the SVP method [17]. One benefit of our method is that it can evaluate the approximation quality of the inexact ones. For the SVP, we choose a default initial value **0** for this local method since no other choices are guaranteed to deliver better performance. Our numerical experiment, which is not reported in here, suggests that the SVP method is indeed sensitive to the choice of the initial value. For nuclear-norm regularization, we select a suitable regularization parameter value giving the solution satisfying the rank constraint in (3).

7.1 Synthetic Data

Simulations are performed under (2). First, the $n \times p$ design matrix $\boldsymbol{A}$ is sampled, with each entry being iid $N(10, 1)$. Second, the $p \times k$ truth $\boldsymbol{\Theta}^0$ is generated by multiplying a $p \times r$ matrix and an $r \times k$ matrix, each entry of which has a normal distribution over $N(10, 1)$. The data matrix $\boldsymbol{Z}$ is then sampled according to (2) with $\boldsymbol{e}$ following iid $N(0, \sigma^2)$ with $\sigma = 0.5$.

For predictive performance and rank recovery, we compute the MSE $\|\boldsymbol{A}(\boldsymbol{\Theta}^0 - \hat{\boldsymbol{\Theta}}^{\hat{r}})\|_F^2$, the absolute difference $|\hat{r} - r_0|$ and record the training time for each method, averaged over 100 simulation replications on a test set of size $10n$, where $\hat{r}$ is tuned over integers in $[0, \min(n, p)]$ by an independent tuning set of size $2n$. We consider three possible situations, i.e., when $k = r_0 < p$, $k > p > r_0$ and $p > k > r_0$. To illustrate our theoretical conclusion in Theorem 4 that the prediction error bound does not depend on the value of p, we add one more case of $p > k > r_0$ with a larger value of p. The simulation results are summarized in Tables 2-4.

Table 2: Prediction results for the synthetic data: averaged MSEs as well as their standard deviations in parentheses, for three competing methods based on the selected tuning parameters over 100 simulation replications. Our, SVP, and Nuclear-Norm refer to our method, the SVP method and nuclear-norm regularization method.

Set-up	Our	SVP	Nuclear-Norm
$k = r_0 < p, 5 = 5 < 99$	0.0110 (0.0065)	0.4591 (0.0386)	0.4130 (0.0360)
$k > p > r_0, 50 > 40 > 5$	12.0010 (0.6125)	10166.5052 (1236.3237)	7709.0779 (960.6982)
$p > k > r_0, 50 > 40 > 5$	13.1945 (0.5682)	10185.7699 (1132.3515)	8116.2653 (943.6058)
$p > k > r_0, 99 > 40 > 5$	121.4019 (70.3054)	14597.0728 (1185.7200)	13153.3217 (1056.5155)

Table 3: Rank recovery for the synthetic data: averaged values of $|\hat{r} - r_0|$ as well as their standard deviations in parentheses, for three competing methods based on the selected tuning parameters over 100 simulation replications. Our, SVP, and Nuclear-Norm refer to our method, the SVP method and nuclear-norm regularization method.

Set-up	Our	SVP	Nuclear-Norm
$k = r_0 < p, 5 = 5 < 99$	0.8400 (0.8005)	0.0000 (0.0000)	0.0000 (0.0000)
$k > p > r_0, 50 > 40 > 5$	0.0000 (0.0000)	3.5300 (1.6358)	1.6400 (0.6439)
$p > k > r_0, 50 > 40 > 5$	0.0000 (0.0000)	4.0800 (1.3830)	1.6500 (0.5925)
$p > k > r_0, 99 > 40 > 5$	0.0000 (0.0000)	2.9800 (1.9121)	0.2200 (0.4399)

As suggested in Tables 2 and 3, our exact method is much more precise in prediction in all cases and rank recovery except one case of $k = r_0 = 5 < p = 99$, than the other two methods. This is in agreement with the theoretical results in Theorem 4 that exact reconstruction of the oracle estimator is achieved through tuning. Note that the best MSE value does not necessarily yield best rank recovery, as in the case of $k = r_0 = 5 < p = 99$, which is due to the bias/variance trade-off phenomenon. As indicated in Table 4, our method is, on average, 10-20 times faster than the other two.

7.2 MIT logo Recovery

Next we examine the three competing methods for reconstructing the MIT logo image, which was studied in [27, 17]. The original logo is displayed in Figure 2, where we use the gray image of size 44×85 and the image matrix has rank 7.

Figure 2: Original MIT logo image.

Our objective is to reconstruct this image from its noisy version and examine the quality of reconstruction. Towards this end, we sample the design matrix $\boldsymbol{A}$ with each entry being iid $N(0, 1)$, where the sample size n ranges from 20 to 80. To generate a noisy version, we add random error sampled from $N(0, 0.5^2)$ to each element of the sample data. The reconstruction results are displayed in Figure 3 for the three methods with the default initial value $\mathbf{0}$ for the SVP.

Visually, our method delivers highly competitive performance as compared to the other two methods, as displayed in Figure 3, and yields nearly perfect reconstruction when the size of the design matrix $\boldsymbol{A}$ becomes larger, say $n = 60$ and $n = 80$. For all the methods, better reconstruction can be reached as n increases, and comparable results are achieved when n is small, say $n = 20$ and $n = 40$. This conclusion is consistent with our theoretical analysis.

In practice, the exact rank of the matrix to be estimated is unknown but may reasonably be assumed to be small. In this sense, s needs to be tuned or estimated. Next we investigate the effect of estimation of s with regard to the reconstruction quality, measured by the MSE and the recovery rate. The latter is defined as the ratio $\|\hat{\boldsymbol{\Theta}}^s - \boldsymbol{\Theta}^0\|_F / \|\boldsymbol{\Theta}^0\|_F$, commonly used to measure the quality of parameter estimation. In particular, we display both of them as a function of s in Figures 4 and 5, where s is defined in (3).

For the relative recovery error, a clear transition of our solution occurs around $s = 44$, after which a perfect recovery is achieved, whereas no improvement occurs for the other two methods when s increases. In the case of an underdetermined $\boldsymbol{A}$, i.e., $\boldsymbol{A}$ is not of full column rank, all three methods produce similar recovery results. For the MSEs, our method yields the perfect result zero when $s \geq 7$ and a reasonably small value when $s = 3, 5$, whereas the other two methods lead to elevated MSEs as s increases. This is in accordance with our theory which suggests that our method constructs the oracle estimator giving perfect image reconstruction when $s \leq 7$.

8. CONCLUSION

This paper derives an exact closed-form global minimization for nonconvex least squares rank minimization. In addition, an efficient pathwise algorithm is also developed for its regularized counterpart. Moreover, we establish the optimality of the global solution, against any other ones. Experimental results on synthetic and real data demonstrate the efficiency and effectiveness of the proposed algorithm.

An exact global solution seems rare for nonconvex minimization. In future work, we plan to expand the present work to a general loss function, by solving a sequence of weighted least squares rank minimization problems iteratively. We will pursue along this direction for a general rank minimization problem.

Table 4: Run time for the synthetic data: average training time in seconds for three competing methods based on the selected tuning parameters over 100 simulation replications. Our, SVP, and Nuclear-Norm refer to our method, the SVP method and nuclear-norm regularization method.

Set-up	Our	SVP	Nuclear-Norm
$k = r_0 < p, 5 = 5 < 99$	0.0224 (0.0045)	14.1523 (0.3933)	0.9766 (0.0074)
$k > p > r_0, 50 > 40 > 5$	0.0349 (0.0031)	41.2122 (1.8511)	5.8937 (0.2945)
$p > k > r_0, 50 > 40 > 5$	0.0368 (0.0025)	29.5856 (1.1786)	5.7447 (0.1173)
$p > k > r_0, 99 > 40 > 5$	0.0542 (0.0039)	79.9850 (3.6724)	7.6046 (0.1011)

(a) n = 20 (b) n = 40 (c) n = 60 (d) n = 80

Figure 3: Reconstruction of a noisy version of the MIT logo with varying sampling size n. From left to right (for each case of n): SVP; nuclear-norm regularization; our method.

9. ACKNOWLEDGEMENT

This work was supported by NSF grants IIS-0953662 and DMS-0906616, NIH grants R01LM010730, 2R01GM081535-01, and R01HL105397.

10. REFERENCES

[1] J. Abernethy, F. Bach, T. Evgeniou, and J. Vert. Low-rank matrix factorization with attributes. *Arxiv preprint cs/0611124*, 2006.

[2] Y. Amit, M. Fink, N. Srebro, and S. Ullman. Uncovering shared structures in multiclass classification. In *Proceedings of the 24th Annual International Conference on Machine Learning*, pages 17–24. ACM, 2007.

[3] T. Anderson. Estimating linear restrictions on regression coefficients for multivariate normal distributions. *The Annals of Mathematical Statistics*, 22(3):327–351, 1951.

[4] T. Anderson. Asymptotic distribution of the reduced rank regression estimator under general conditions. *The Annals of Statistics*, 27(4):1141–1154, 1999.

[5] T. André, R. Nowak, and B. Van Veen. Low-rank estimation of higher order statistics. *Signal Processing, IEEE Transactions on*, 45(3):673–685, 1997.

[6] A. Argyriou, T. Evgeniou, and M. Pontil. Multi-task feature learning. *Advances in Neural Information Processing Systems*, 19:41, 2007.

[7] F. Bunea, Y. She, and M. Wegkamp. Optimal selection of reduced rank estimators of high-dimensional matrices. *The Annals of Statistics*, 39(2):1282–1309, 2011.

[8] J. Cai, E. Candès, and Z. Shen. A singular value thresholding algorithm for matrix completion. *SIAM Journal of Optimization*, 20(4):1956–1982, 2010.

[9] E. Candes and Y. Plan. Matrix completion with noise. *Arxiv preprint arXiv:0903.3131*, 2009.

[10] E. Candès and B. Recht. Exact matrix completion via convex optimization. *Foundations of Computational Mathematics*, 9(6):717–772, 2009.

[11] J. Chen, J. Liu, and J. Ye. Learning incoherent sparse and low-rank patterns from multiple tasks. In *Proceedings of the 16th ACM SIGKDD international conference on Knowledge discovery and data mining*, pages 1179–1188. ACM, 2010.

[12] C. Eckart and G. Young. The approximation of one matrix by another of lower rank. *Psychometrika*, 1(3):211–218, 1936.

[13] M. Fazel, H. Hindi, and S. Boyd. A rank minimization heuristic with application to minimum order system approximation. In *American Control Conference, 2001. Proceedings of the 2001*, volume 6, pages 4734–4739. IEEE, 2001.

[14] S. Friedland and A. Torokhti. Generalized rank-constrained matrix approximations. *SIAM Journal on Matrix Analysis and Applications*, 29(2):656–659, 2007.

[15] A. Izenman. Reduced-rank regression for the multivariate linear model. *Journal of multivariate analysis*, 5(2):248–264, 1975.

[16] M. Jaggi and M. Sulovský. A Simple Algorithm for Nuclear Norm Regularized Problems. In *Proceedings of the 27th Annual International Conference on Machine Learning*, 2010.

[17] P. Jain, R. Meka, and I. Dhillon. Guaranteed rank minimization via singular value projection. *Advances in Neural Information Processing Systems*, 23:937–945, 2010.

[18] H. Ji, C. Liu, Z. Shen, and Y. Xu. Robust video

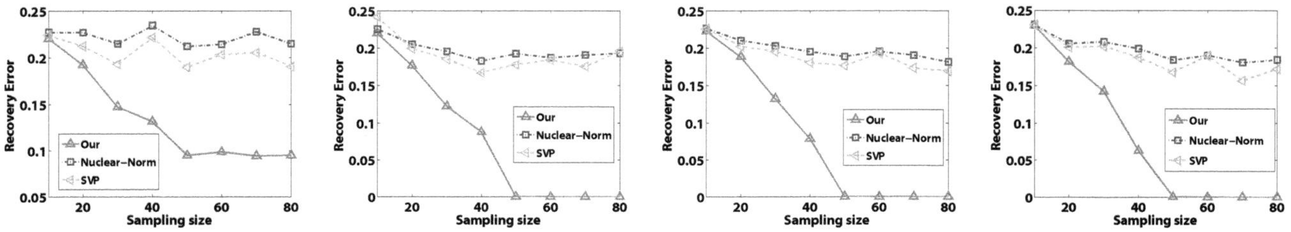

(a) s = 3 (b) s = 5 (c) s = 7 (d) s = 10

Figure 4: Relative recovery error as a function of the sampling size for the MIT logo image under different rank constraints.

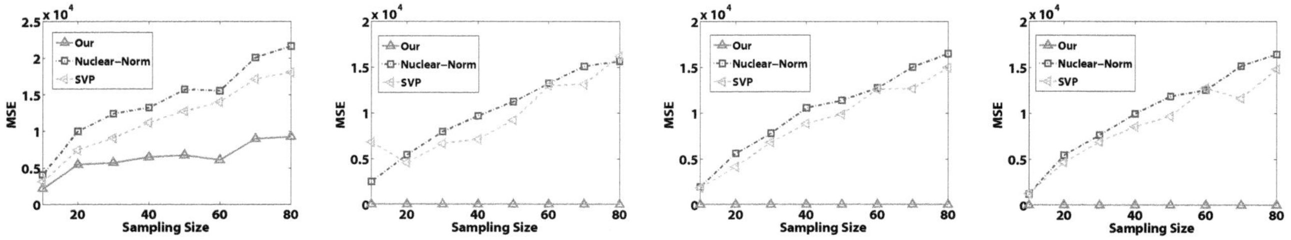

(a) s = 3 (b) s = 5 (c) s = 7 (d) s = 10

Figure 5: MSE as a function of the sampling size for the MIT logo image under different rank constraints. Note that the MSE of our method in (b) is not zero but indistinguishable from zero, which is unlike (c) and (d) in which the MSEs are identical to zero.

denoising using low rank matrix completion. In *Computer Vision and Pattern Recognition (CVPR), 2010 IEEE Conference on*, pages 1791–1798. IEEE, 2010.

[19] S. Ji and J. Ye. An accelerated gradient method for trace norm minimization. In *Proceedings of the 26th Annual International Conference on Machine Learning*, pages 457–464, 2009.

[20] B. Kulis, A. Surendran, and J. Platt. Fast low-rank semidefinite programming for embedding and clustering. In *Eleventh International Conference on Artifical Intelligence and Statistics, AISTATS 2007*, 2007.

[21] G. Liu, Z. Lin, S. Yan, J. Sun, Y. Yu, and Y. Ma. Robust recovery of subspace structures by low-rank representation. *Arxiv preprint arXiv:1010.2955*, 2010.

[22] X. Luo. High dimensional low rank and sparse covariance matrix estimation via convex minimization. *Arxiv preprint arXiv:1111.1133*, 2011.

[23] B. K. Natarajan. Sparse approximation solutions to linear systems. *SIAM J. Comput.*, 24(2):227–234, 1995.

[24] S. Negahban and M. J. Wainwright. Estimation of (near) low-rank matrices with noise and high-dimensional scaling. *Annals of Statistics*, 39(2):1069–1097, 2011.

[25] T. Pong, P. Tseng, S. Ji, and J. Ye. Trace norm regularization: Reformulations, algorithms, and multi-task learning. *SIAM Journal on Optimization*, 20:3465–3489, 2010.

[26] C. Rao. Matrix approximations and reduction of dimensionality in multivariate statistical analysis. *Multivariate analysis*, 5:3–22, 1980.

[27] B. Recht, M. Fazel, and P. Parrilo. Guaranteed Minimum-Rank Solutions of Linear Matrix Equations via Nuclear Norm Minimization. *SIAM Review*, 52(471), 2010.

[28] G. Reinsel and R. Velu. *Multivariate reduced-rank regression: theory and applications*. Springer New York, 1998.

[29] B. Savas and I. Dhillon. Clustered low rank approximation of graphs in information science applications. In *Proceedings of the SIAM Data Mining Conference.*, 2011.

[30] S. Shalev-Shwartz, A. Gonen, and O. Shamir. Large-Scale Convex Minimization with a Low-Rank Constraint. In *Proceedings of the 28th Annual International Conference on Machine Learning*, 2011.

[31] X. Shen and H. Huang. Optimal model assessment, selection, and combination. *Journal of the American Statistical Association*, 101(474):554–568, 2006.

[32] D. Sondermann. Best approximate solutions to matrix equations under rank restrictions. *Statistical Papers*, 27(1):57–66, 1986.

[33] N. Srebro, J. Rennie, and T. Jaakkola. Maximum-margin matrix factorization. *Advances in Neural Information Processing Systems*, 17:1329–1336, 2005.

[34] K. Toh and S. Yun. An accelerated proximal gradient algorithm for nuclear norm regularized linear least squares problems. *Pacific J. Optim*, 6:615–640, 2010.

[35] J. Wright, A. Ganesh, S. Rao, and Y. Ma. Robust principal component analysis: Exact recovery of corrupted low-rank matrices via convex optimization. *Advances in Neural Information Processing Systems*, 2009.

Large-Scale Distributed Non-negative Sparse Coding and Sparse Dictionary Learning

Vikas Sindhwani and Amol Ghoting
IBM T.J. Watson Research Center
Yorktown Heights, NY 10598
{vsindhw,aghoting}@us.ibm.com

ABSTRACT

We consider the problem of building compact, unsupervised representations of large, high-dimensional, non-negative data using sparse coding and dictionary learning schemes, with an emphasis on executing the algorithm in a Map-Reduce environment. The proposed algorithms may be seen as parallel optimization procedures for constructing sparse non-negative factorizations of large, sparse matrices. Our approach alternates between a parallel sparse coding phase implemented using greedy or convex (l_1) regularized risk minimization procedures, and a sequential dictionary learning phase where we solve a set of l_0 optimization problems exactly. These two-fold sparsity constraints lead to better statistical performance on text analysis tasks and at the same time make it possible to implement each iteration in a single Map-Reduce job. We detail our implementations and optimizations that lead to the ability to factor matrices with more than 100 million rows and billions of non-zero entries in just a few hours on a small commodity cluster.

Categories and Subject Descriptors

I.2.6 [**Artificial Intelligence**]: Learning

General Terms

Algorithms, Performance, Experimentation

1. INTRODUCTION

Let us assume that we are given a collection of N data points or signals in a high-dimensional space $\mathbb{R}^D$: $\mathbf{x}_i \in \mathbb{R}^D, 1 \leq i \leq N$. Let $\mathbf{h}_j \in \mathbb{R}^D, 1 \leq j \leq K$ denote a dictionary of K "atoms" which we collect as rows of the matrix $\mathbf{H} = (\mathbf{h}_1 \ldots \mathbf{h}_K)^T \in \mathbb{R}^{K \times D}$. Given a suitable dictionary $\mathbf{H}$, the goal of *sparse coding* is to represent datapoints approximately as *sparse* linear combinations of atoms in the dictionary, i.e., $\mathbf{x}_i \approx \sum_{j=1}^{K} w_{ij}\mathbf{h}_j = \mathbf{H}^T\mathbf{w}_i$, where the coefficient vector $\mathbf{w}_i \in \mathbb{R}^K$ typically only has a few non-zero elements. Of course, the effectiveness of sparse coding in lending a high-quality compact representation to the entire dataset depends on whether the data distribution concentrates around lower-dimensional subspaces, and crucially, on whether the choice of the dictionary appropriately captures this structure.

Spread over several decades, the quest for an appropriate dictionary that is well-suited to a class of signals (e.g. natural images) has generated a vast body of work in Signal Processing and Computational Harmonic Analysis, encapsulating the development of Fourier, DCT, Wavelets and other bases, and matured into the establishment of impactful coding standards. Broadly speaking, in these efforts, dictionary design centers around pre-specified mathematical functions that are justified by optimality proofs and error bounds for the class of signals they attempt to model.

An alternative to the aforementioned approach to modeling is *learning a dictionary* [9] from the data itself. Led by the emergence of the web, we are increasingly encountering new sources of data that more often than not are completely unstructured, very high-dimensional, and expectedly voluminous. Dictionary learning now becomes appealing, as large web-based repositories essentially provide unrestricted samples of natural signals, thereby allowing one to bypass the limitations of analytical formulations that are applicable to restricted signal classes. However, to make dictionary learning feasible, we are confronted with the formidable challenge of scaling associated algorithms to web-scale datasets.

Fortunately, the growing ubiquity of multi-core and cluster systems potentially offers a solution. To make parallel systems more accessible to machine learning researchers and practitioners, recent years have seen the development and adoption of the Map-Reduce (MR) programming model [7]. Map-Reduce programs, when deployed using engines like Hadoop, can be executed on large clusters in a fault tolerant fashion. Higher-level declarative [11] and imperative [10] programming frameworks to ease the implementation of learning algorithms on top of Map-Reduce have also been developed. This paper delves into the problem of carefully designing and implementing large-scale sparse coding and dictionary learning methods that afford efficient parallelizations on distributed computing environments like Hadoop.

We focus on text-like domains that generate very high-dimensional, non-negative, and sparse data matrices. Our framework may also be viewed as providing sparse Non-negative Matrix Factorizations (NMF) [14, 12, 16]. Sparse NMFs and dictionary learning on document collections has recently emerged [13] as an appealing alternative to popular Bayesian topic models such as the Latent Dirichlet Alloca-

KDD'12, August 12–16, 2012, Beijing, China.

tion [4]. In very recent work, [1] present the first theoretical results, under certain assumptions, on provably correct NMF algorithms. For various extensions and applications of NMFs, see [6].

Our contributions may be highlighted as follows: (1) We describe highly efficient parallel algorithms for sparse coding and dictionary learning. These algorithms are implemented using multithreading on a multi-core system and the Map-Reduce programming model on a cluster-system. A hallmark of the method is that it is possible to implement each iteration of the optimization algorithm using a single Map-Reduce job. We note several recent efforts [18, 15, 17] on scaling up related algorithms. (2) Our algorithms alternate between a distributed sparse coding phase and a sequential in-memory dictionary learning phase. For sparse coding, we organize non-negative variants of both Orthogonal Matching Pursuit (OMP) and Lasso [9, 5] around very efficient and light-weight updates. Our work lends a better understanding of the strengths and weaknesses of greedy versus convex methods in the context of parallel sparse non-negative matrix factorizations, a natural comparison that we have not seen reported elsewhere in the literature. (3) In contrast to existing Sparse NMF methods, we also impose hard sparsity constraints on the dictionary atoms. We observe that the related subproblem in coordinate descent can be solved exactly. For textual problems, dictionary sparsity imposes the natural *statistical* prior that meaningful topics have support on only a small, distinctive set of words. As a complimentary *computational* benefit, these dictionary sparsity constraints also enable fast in-memory updates of dictionary atoms. (4) We present empirical results on both small and large problems on multi-core and cluster systems. We show that datasets with more than 6 billion non-zero entries - amongst the largest demonstrations of such techniques - can be factored in a matter of hours on a moderately sized cluster, exhibiting near linear scaling with respect to data size, number of cores, and dictionary size.

2. FORMULATION

We are given N datapoints, $\{\mathbf{x}_i\}_{i=1}^N, \mathbf{x}_i \in \mathbb{R}^D$, and $\mathbf{H} = (\mathbf{h}_1 \dots \mathbf{h}_K)^T \in \mathbb{R}^{K \times D}$ denotes the dictionary matrix comprising of K atoms which are optimization variables in the dictionary learning problem. We denote the associated sparse coding variables by $\{\mathbf{w}_i\}_{i=1}^N, \mathbf{w}_i \in \mathbb{R}^K$ and collect them as rows of the matrix $\mathbf{W} = (\mathbf{w}_1 \dots \mathbf{w}_N)^T$. We will use w_{ij} to denote the jth element of $\mathbf{w}_i$. We pose the following class of joint optimization problems over $\mathbf{W}$ and $\mathbf{H}$,

$$\arg\min_{\mathbf{W},\mathbf{H}} \frac{1}{N} \sum_{i=1}^{N} \|\mathbf{x}_i - \mathbf{H}^T \mathbf{w}_i\|_2^2 + \lambda \|\mathbf{H} - \mathbf{H}^0\|_{fro}^2 \quad (1)$$

subject to the following constraints:

$$\mathbf{w}_i \geq 0 \quad \text{non-negative coding} \quad (2)$$

$$\|\mathbf{w}_i\|_p \leq \gamma \quad \text{sparse coding} \quad (3)$$

$$\mathbf{h}_j \geq 0 \quad \text{non-negative dictionary} \quad (4)$$

$$\|\mathbf{h}_j\|_q \leq \nu \quad \text{sparse dictionary} \quad (5)$$

$$\|\mathbf{h}_j\|_2^2 = 1 \quad \text{uniqueness} \quad (6)$$

where i runs from 1 to N, j runs from 1 to K, $p = \{0, 1\}$, $q = 0$, and λ, γ, ν are real-valued parameters.

The first term in the objective function above, Eqn 1, measures the squared reconstruction error. It is known to be non-convex in $\mathbf{W}$ and $\mathbf{H}$. The second term is a regularizer that enforces the learnt dictionary to be close, in Frobenius norm, to a prior $\mathbf{H}_0$, which may be available e.g., if models are being learnt periodically over time (if $\mathbf{H}^0$ is not available, λ may be set to 0). Equations 2,4 impose non-negativity constraints. The constraint on $\|\mathbf{w}\|_p$ in Eqn 3 implements sparse coding by imposing a bound γ on a sparsity inducing norm ball: $p = 0$ casts this constraint in terms of the l_0 pseudo-norm, i.e., the number of non-zeros in $\mathbf{w}_i$ should not exceed γ, while $p = 1$ uses the l_1 ball of radius γ which is a convex set. Equation 5 imposes similar sparsity constraints on the dictionary elements. We mainly restrict our implementation to hard sparsity constraints, i.e., $q = 0$, and bound the number of non-zeros per atom exactly by ν. As we outline in section 4, the associated rank-one subproblem can actually be solved exactly despite the intractability of working with l_0 norm in general. This allows us to apriori control the memory requirements for maintaining $\mathbf{H}$ as a sparse matrix and turn its updates across iterations into very cheap sequential operations. Our approach therefore enforces *double sparsity* in both the factors. Finally, for vanishing λ and sufficiently large values of γ, ν, it is easy to see that the reconstruction error is invariant under the transformation $\mathbf{H}^T\mathbf{w}_i = \mathbf{H}^T\mathbf{Q}\mathbf{Q}^{-1}\mathbf{w}_i$ for any invertible $K \times K$ scaling matrix $\mathbf{Q}$, making the minimization ill-posed. In particular, for clustering applications, it is common to assign $\mathbf{x}_i$ to the cluster $\arg\max_j w_{ij}$, which can be arbitrarily changed by rescaling. We therefore require dictionary elements to have unit l_2 norm; other constraint sets which are convex can also be instead used [16].

Our optimization strategy is cyclic Block Coordinate Descent (BCD) [3]. Each iteration of the algorithm cycles over the variables $\mathbf{W}$ and $\mathbf{h}_1 \dots \mathbf{h}_K$, optimizing a single variable at a time while holding others fixed. It is easy to see that since the objective function in Eqn. 1 is separable in $\{\mathbf{w}_i\}_{i=1}^N$, i.e. rows of $\mathbf{W}$, they can be optimized in parallel. We call this the PARALLEL SPARSE CODING phase of the algorithm:

PARALLEL FOR $i = 1 \dots N$:

$$\mathbf{w}_i = \arg\min_{\mathbf{w} \geq 0, \|\mathbf{w}\|_p \leq \gamma} \|\mathbf{x}_i - \mathbf{H}^T\mathbf{w}\|_2^2 \quad (7)$$

In the next section, we outline non-negative variations of Orthogonal Matching Pursuit and Lasso to solve these subproblems for $p = 0$ and $p = 1$ respectively.

In the DICTIONARY LEARNING phase of BCD, we cycle sequentially over $\mathbf{h}_1 \dots \mathbf{h}_K$, i.e., rows of $\mathbf{H}$, keeping $\mathbf{W}$ fixed and solve the resulting subproblems. Due to hard sparsity constraints, as well as appropriate aggregations from the sparse coding phase, we can guarantee that dictionary variables can be conveniently held in memory as a sparse matrix $\mathbf{H}$, and manipulated very fast with efficient and exact sequential updates as outlined in section 4. We declare convergence if the overall mean reconstruction error fails to improve significantly relative to its previous value.

In the most general non-convex optimization setting, limit points of a BCD process may not be stationary points of the objective function. Even for a stationary point, apriori theoretical guarantees concerning model quality typically cannot be established. In practice though, such models nonetheless often yield good solutions that turn out to provide valuable empirical insight. We next describe the details of our approach.

3. NON-NEGATIVE SPARSE CODING

Without non-negativity constraints, for a fixed $\mathbf{H}$, Eqn 7 is the classic least-squares sparse regression model, for which greedy orthogonal matching pursuit (OMP) and Lasso are two very well-studied and widely successful algorithmic frameworks [9, 5], with intriguingly similar theoretical guarantees concerning correctness.

Since the dictionary $\mathbf{H}$ is also varying in our setting, the contrast between greedy and convex methods becomes particularly interesting for the following reasons. In each iteration, OMP greedily selects the atom that best helps in reducing the current reconstruction residual. All the atoms are then reoptimized. Lasso, on the other hand, requires numerical optimization procedures, e.g. FISTA [2], that can handle composite objectives with a smooth and a non-differentiable component. Due to its simplicity, OMP tends to be faster than Lasso. The per iteration complexity of OMP involves greedy selection of an atom from upto K candidates, and solving a least squares system for refitting. For Lasso, it involves taking the gradient of the objective and adapting the line search stepsize. OMP, by design, converges in no more than γ iterations while Lasso (using FISTA) converges to an ϵ-optimal solution in $O(\frac{1}{\sqrt{\epsilon}})$ iterations. One advantage of OMP is that it imposes a predictable sparsity structure on $\mathbf{W}$ and hence we know exact memory requirements upfront. However, in the context of the full BCD algorithm, OMP-based sparse coding is not guaranteed to converge (using currently available theoretical results) without making assumptions on the dictionary at every iteration. For sparse coding with Lasso (assuming $q = 1$ or $\nu = D$, convex uniqueness constraints and exact minimization), well-known convergence results [3] imply that the full BCD algorithm will show monotonic decrease and converge to a stationary point. In practice though, OMP may still offer consistent descent to a good solution. We also point out that across BCD iterations, Lasso can utilize warm starts from previously found solutions, while OMP essentially needs to start from scratch. In a distributed setting, it is furthermore worthwhile to investigate if OMP and Lasso offer different load balancing characteristics.

These differences motivate us to study both OMP and Lasso for sparse coding and dictionary learning, and benchmark them in a parallel environment. We next derive very efficient implementations of non-negative versions of these algorithms. For simplicity in the exposition below, we assume that the data points are normalized to unit l_2 norm, i.e., $\|\mathbf{x}_i\|_2 = 1$.

3.1 Non-negative OMP (NOMP)

We are interested in solving $\arg\min_{\mathbf{w}\geq 0, \|\mathbf{w}\|_0 \leq \gamma} R(\mathbf{w})$ where $R(\mathbf{w}) = \|\mathbf{x} - \mathbf{H}^T\mathbf{w}\|_2^2$ denotes the reconstruction error. We will express both Non-negative OMP (NOMP), and also Non-negative Lasso(NLASSO) below, compactly in terms of the following,

$$\mathbf{s} = \mathbf{H}\mathbf{x} \;\text{ and }\; \mathbf{S} = \mathbf{H}\mathbf{H}^T \tag{8}$$

where $\mathbf{s}$ may be interpreted as the vector of cosine similarities between signals and dictionary atoms (since both dictionary elements and data points are unit normalized) and $\mathbf{S}$ is the (small) $K \times K$ matrix of inter-atom similarities. For example note that the objective function can be written as,

$$\begin{aligned} R(\mathbf{w}) &= \|\mathbf{x} - \mathbf{H}^T\mathbf{w}\|^2 = \|\mathbf{x}\|^2 - 2\mathbf{w}^T\mathbf{s} + \mathbf{w}^T\mathbf{S}\mathbf{w} \\ &= 1 - \mathbf{w}^T(\mathbf{s} + \mathbf{u}) \quad \text{where } \mathbf{u} = \mathbf{s} - \mathbf{S}\mathbf{w} \end{aligned} \tag{9}$$

Let $\mathcal{A} \subseteq \{1 \ldots K\}$ denote the support of a candidate solution $\mathbf{w}$, i.e., $\mathcal{A} = \{i : w_i > 0\}$. NOMP starts with $\mathbf{w} = 0$, $\mathcal{A} = \{\}$ and builds the solution by greedily adding variables that help reduce the current residual, $\mathbf{r} = \mathbf{x} - \mathbf{H}^T\mathbf{w} = \mathbf{x} - \sum_{i\in\mathcal{A}} \mathbf{h}_i w_i$. We use $\mathcal{A}^c$ to denote the complement of $\mathcal{A}$. Let $j \in \mathcal{A}^c$ be a candidate variable for inclusion. Its quality is measured how much, acting alone, it can help reduce the current residual. Since $\|\mathbf{h}_j\|_2 = 1$ we can easily see the following: $\arg\min_{w_j\geq 0} \|\mathbf{r} - \mathbf{h}_j w_j\|^2 = \arg\min_{w_j \geq 0}(w_j - (\mathbf{r}^T\mathbf{h}_j))^2$, and hence the minimizing value of w_j is $w_j = \max(\mathbf{r}^T\mathbf{h}_j, 0)$. Furthermore, note that $\mathbf{r}^T\mathbf{h}_j = \mathbf{x}^T\mathbf{h}_j - (\mathbf{H}\mathbf{h}_j)^T\mathbf{w} = u_j$, where $\mathbf{u}$ was defined in Eqn 9. Therefore the OMP selection criteria, quite simply, evaluates to $(u_j - u_{j+})^2$ for a candidate variable j, where we use the notation $u_{j+} = \max(u_j, 0)$. Equivalently, the reduction in residual norm offered is $u_{j+}^2 - 2u_j u_{j+}$ which we can maximize over. As in unconstrained OMP, we now digest the chosen variable into $\mathbf{A}$ and then reoptimize over it with cylic coordinate descent. Given inputs $\mathbf{s}, \mathbf{S}, \gamma$ and convergence parameters ϵ, τ, the entire algorithm, can be organized around very simple and efficient update rules as follows,

Initialize $\mathcal{A} = \{\}, \mathbf{w} = \mathbf{0}_k, \mathbf{u} = \mathbf{s}$, reconstruction error $R = 1$.
while $|\mathcal{A}| < \gamma$

- ◇ Variable selection: $j^\star = \arg\max_{j\in\mathcal{A}^c} \left(u_{j+}^2 - 2u_j u_{+j}\right)$
- ◇ If $\left(u_{j^\star+}^2 - 2u_{j^\star} u_{+j^\star}\right) \leq \epsilon$ return, else continue below.
- ◇ $\mathcal{A} = \mathcal{A} \cup \{j^\star\}$. Refit over $\mathcal{A}$ by cyclic coordinate descent:
  - Cycle over $j \in \mathcal{A}$, reoptimizing w_j as follows:
    - $\delta_j = w_j$, $w_j = \max(u_j + w_j, 0)$, $\delta_j = w_j - \delta_j$
    - $\mathbf{u} = \mathbf{u} - \mathbf{S}_j \delta_j$
  - $R^{old} = R$, $R = 1 - \sum_{j\in\mathcal{A}} w_j\,(s_j + u_j)$
  - Converge if $(R - R^{old}) < \tau R^{old}$ else run another cycle of coordinate descent over $j \in \mathcal{A}$.

The coordinate descent procedure for refitting is guaranteed to converge using standard BCD convergence results [3]. Given inputs $\mathbf{x}$ and $\mathbf{H}$, NOMP offers monotonic decrease in the reconstruction error of $\mathbf{x}$. In the dictionary learning setting, however, what we cannot guarantee is global decrease with respect to the previously found dictionary. Nonetheless, as we report in section 6, in hundreds of experiments on real world data, we always saw stable descent behavior.

3.2 Non-negative Lasso (NLASSO)

We rewrite the NLASSO problem, Eqn 7 with $p = 1$, equivalently as:

$$\arg\min_{\mathbf{w}\in\mathbb{R}^K} R(\mathbf{w}) + \delta(\mathbf{w}) \tag{10}$$

which is a composite objective comprising of a smooth term $R(\mathbf{w})$ and a non-smooth indicator function for the simplex defined as $\delta(\mathbf{w}) = 0$ if $\mathbf{w} \geq 0, \|\mathbf{w}\|_1 \leq \gamma$ and ∞ otherwise. We use an accelerated proximal method, FISTA [2], to handle such an objective function. In proximal methods, the idea is to linearize the smooth component, R, around the current iterate (say $\mathbf{w}^t$), and minimize

$$\min_{\mathbf{w}\in\mathbb{R}^K} R(\mathbf{w}^t) + \nabla R(\mathbf{w}^t)(\mathbf{w} - \mathbf{w}^t) + \frac{L}{2}\|\mathbf{w} - \mathbf{w}^t\|_2^2 + \delta(\mathbf{w})$$

where $\nabla R(\mathbf{w}) = \mathbf{s} - \mathbf{S}\mathbf{w}$ (recall the notation from Eqn. 8). The third term above, called proximal term, keeps the update in a neighborhood of the current iterate $\mathbf{w}^t$ where R is close to its linear approximation. $L > 0$ is a parameter, which should essentially be an upper bound on the Lipschitz constant of ∇R and is typically set with a linesearch. We can rewrite this problem as, $\mathbf{w}^\star = \min_{\mathbf{w} \in \mathbb{R}^K} \frac{1}{2}\|\mathbf{w} - \mathbf{u}\|_2^2 + \delta(\mathbf{w})$ where $\mathbf{u} = \mathbf{w}^t - \frac{1}{L}\nabla R(\mathbf{w}^t)$. The above minimization functional (mapping $\mathbf{u}$ to $\mathbf{w}^\star$) is also called the *proximal operator*. For our purposes, it reduces to the projection operator to the convex set $\mathbf{w} \geq 0, \|\mathbf{w}\|_1 \leq \gamma$. An efficient linear time algorithm for such a projection onto the simplex is given in [8]. The rest of the FISTA details remain unchanged; we point the reader to [2] for more details. It is easy to see that we can also equivalently solve the more familiar penalized form of Lasso: $\arg\min_{\mathbf{w}} \left(R(\mathbf{w}) + \gamma' \sum_j w_j\right) + \delta'(\mathbf{w})$ for some one-to-one correspondence between γ' and γ and with δ' simply being an indicator function for the non-negative orthant $\mathbf{w} \geq 0$. In this case, the associated prox operator simply returns $(\mathbf{w}^t - \frac{1}{L}\nabla R(\mathbf{w}^t) - \frac{\gamma'}{L})_+$. Furthermore, due to our dictionary and data normalization, Lasso screening tests proposed very recently [19] can be immediately adapted to the non-negative case and applied to discard elements of $\mathbf{w}$ upfront that are guaranteed to be zero-valued.

4. SPARSE DICTIONARY LEARNING

We now discuss the dictionary learning phase where we update $\mathbf{H}$. Our strategy for this phase is reminiscent of the Hierarchical Alternating Least Squares (HALS) algorithm [6] which solves rank-one minimization problems to sequentially update both the rows of $\mathbf{H}$ as well as the columns of $\mathbf{W}$ (while we perform parallel row updates for $\mathbf{W}$ by invoking the sparse solvers developed in Section 3).

Let us denote the data matrix as $\mathbf{X} = (\mathbf{x}_1 \dots \mathbf{x}_N)^T \in \mathbb{R}^{N \times D}$ and let $\mathbf{v}_k$ be the kth column of $\mathbf{W}$, i.e., $\mathbf{W} = (\mathbf{v}_1 \dots \mathbf{v}_K)$. Let $\mathbf{R}_k = \left(\mathbf{X} - \sum_{i:i \neq k} \mathbf{v}_i \mathbf{h}_i^T\right)$ be the residual matrix excluding the kth atom. We denote the constraint set for learning dictionaries as

$$\mathcal{C} = \{\mathbf{h} \in \mathbb{R}^D \text{ such that } \mathbf{h} \geq 0, \|\mathbf{h}\|_0 \leq \nu, \|\mathbf{h}\|_2 = 1\}$$

The BCD subproblem of optimizing $\mathbf{h}_k$ keeping other atoms fixed becomes a rank-one matrix approximation problem,

$$\mathbf{h}_k = \arg\min_{\mathbf{h} \in \mathcal{C}} \frac{1}{N} \left\|\mathbf{R}_k - \mathbf{v}_k \mathbf{h}^T\right\|_{fro}^2 + \lambda \|\mathbf{h} - \mathbf{h}_k^0\|_2^2 \quad (11)$$

where $\|\mathbf{A}\|_{fro}$ denotes the Frobenius norm of matrix $\mathbf{A}$. It is easy to see that this reduces to a projection problem, $\mathbf{h}_k = \arg\min_{\mathbf{h} \in \mathcal{C}} \|\mathbf{h} - \mathbf{q}_k\|_2^2$, where the vector $\mathbf{q}_k$ is given by,

$$\mathbf{q}_k = \frac{\frac{1}{N}\mathbf{R}_k^T \mathbf{v}_k + \lambda \mathbf{h}_0}{\frac{1}{N}\|\mathbf{v}_k\|_2^2 + \lambda} \quad (12)$$

Note from the numerator that the residual term and the prior compete for contributing to $\mathbf{q}_k$.

Efficient computation of Residual matrix times a vector: Since $\mathbf{R}_k$ is dense, we want to avoid computing it explicitly and instead use the following,

$$\mathbf{R}_k^T \mathbf{v}_k = \mathbf{X}^T \mathbf{v}_k - \sum_{i \neq k} \mathbf{h}_i (\mathbf{v}_i^T \mathbf{v}_k) \quad (13)$$

The second term, $\sum_{i \neq k} \mathbf{h}_i (\mathbf{v}_i^T \mathbf{v}_k)$, can be expressed compactly and efficiently as follows: Let $\mathbf{G} = \mathbf{W}^T\mathbf{W}$, which is a small $K \times K$ matrix, and let $\mathbf{g} = \mathbf{G}_k$, its kth column. Set $\mathbf{g}_k = 0$. Then its easy to see that $\mathbf{H}^T\mathbf{g} = \sum_{i \neq k} \mathbf{h}_i (\mathbf{v}_i^T \mathbf{v}_k)$. Therefore, we have,

$$\mathbf{q}_k = \frac{\frac{1}{N}\mathbf{R}^T \mathbf{v}_k + \lambda \mathbf{h}_0}{\frac{1}{N}\|\mathbf{v}_k\|_2^2 + \lambda} = \frac{\frac{1}{N}\left(\mathbf{X}^T\mathbf{v}_k - \mathbf{H}^T\mathbf{g}\right) + \lambda \mathbf{h}_0}{\frac{1}{N}\mathbf{G}_{kk} + \lambda} \quad (14)$$

Projection to the set $\mathcal{C}$ of Unit Norm Non-negative Sparse Vectors: We now consider the following projection problem: $\mathbf{h}^\star = \arg\min_{\mathbf{h} \in \mathcal{C}} \|\mathbf{h} - \mathbf{q}\|_2^2$. First, let $\mathbf{h}$ be any ν-sparse vector in $\mathbb{R}^D$ and let $\mathcal{I}(\mathbf{h})$ be its support. Let $i_1 \dots i_D$ be a permutation of the integer set $1 \leq i \leq D$ such that $q_{i_1}, \dots q_{i_D}$ is in sorted order and define $\mathcal{I}^\star = \{i_1, \dots, i_s\}$ where s is the largest integer such that $s \leq \nu$ and $q_{i_1} > \dots > q_{i_s} > 0$. Now its easy to see that,

$$\arg\min_{\mathbf{h} \in \mathcal{C}} \|\mathbf{h} - \mathbf{q}\|_2^2 = \arg\max_{\mathbf{h} \in \mathcal{C}} \sum_{i \in \mathcal{I}(\mathbf{h})} h_i q_i \leq \arg\max_{\mathbf{h} \geq 0, \|\mathbf{h}\|_2 = 1} \sum_{i \in \mathcal{I}^\star} h_i q_i$$

Therefore, the exact solution to this problem given by,

$$\mathbf{h}_{\mathcal{I}^\star}^\star = \arg\min_{\mathbf{h} \in \mathbb{R}^{|\mathcal{I}^\star|}, \|\mathbf{h}\|_2 = 1} \|\mathbf{h} - \mathbf{q}_{\mathcal{I}^\star}\|^2 = \frac{\mathbf{q}_{\mathcal{I}^\star}}{\|\mathbf{q}_{\mathcal{I}^\star}\|}, \; \mathbf{h}_{\mathcal{I}^{\star c}}^\star = 0 \quad (15)$$

where $\mathcal{I}^{\star c}$ denotes the complement of $\mathcal{I}^\star$. Note that if $\mathcal{I}^\star$ turns out to be empty while running dictionary learning phase in BCD, $\mathbf{h}_{\mathcal{I}^\star}^\star$ is undefined, and in this case, we do not update the previous value of that variable. However, we never observed this to happen in practice.

Hence, all we need to solve the projection problem *exactly* is to find upto the top-ν non-negative values of $\mathbf{q}_k$ and normalize them to unit norm. We also note that in the dictionary learning phase we require the summary statistics: $\mathbf{G} = \mathbf{W}^T\mathbf{W} \in \mathbb{R}^{K \times K}$ and columns of the matrix $\mathbf{X}^T\mathbf{W} \in \mathbb{R}^{D \times K}$.

5. IMPLEMENTATION DETAILS

We briefly recap the developments so far and provide an outline for this section. Our parallelization strategy hinges on two observations: (a) the objective function is separable in the sparse coding variables (rows of $\mathbf{W}$) which therefore can be optimized in an embarrassingly parallel fashion, and (b) by enforcing hard sparsity on the dictionary elements, we turn $\mathbf{H}$ into an object that can be manipulated very efficiently in memory. Our implementation is carefully organized around efficient matrix computations and one-pass aggregation of summary statistics. We begin by describing our data structures (summarized in Table 1) and then outline our multicore implementation which requires that the data matrix should fit in memory. We relax this assumption in our cluster implementation sketched in Figure 1 which runs each iteration of the algorithm by making a single pass over the data (i.e., one MapReduce job). Note that our approach generalizes to other large-scale matrix factorization problems where separability, sparsity and in-memory computation can be similarly exploited.

Efficient Matrix Computations: Table 1 records various matrices, their storage schemes, computation strategy and whether they are materialized in memory in our single-node multicore and Hadoop-based cluster implementation. We use compressed row storage for holding the read-only static sparse matrix $\mathbf{X}$. For $\mathbf{H}$, and $\mathbf{W}$ if it is materialized, we use a dynamic sparse matrix data structure which essentially is an array of pointers to the non-zero indices and values for each row, allowing sparsity structure of rows to change across the iterations. Note that sparsity "compresses" the bigger dimension (D) for $\mathbf{H}$ as opposed to the smaller dimension (K) for $\mathbf{W}$, making it reasonable to manipulate $\mathbf{H}$ in-memory. Also note that the maximum memory requirement for $\mathbf{W}$ can be bounded by $O(N\gamma)$ for NOMP, while NLASSO does not offer similar predictability beforehand.

Table 1: Matrices: Storage and Materialization

Matrix	Dims	#Bytes	Storage	Multi-Core	Cluster
$\mathbf{X}$	$N \times D$	$16n_X$	CRS	Y	N
$\mathbf{W}$	$N \times K$	$16N\gamma$	Dyn. Sparse	Y/N	N
$\mathbf{H}$	$K \times D$	$16K\nu$	Dyn. Sparse	Y	Y
$\mathbf{W}^T\mathbf{W}$	$K \times K$	$4K(K+1)$	Dense Symm.	Y	Y
$\mathbf{H}\mathbf{H}^T$	$K \times K$	$4K(K+1)$	Dense Symm.	Y	Y
$\mathbf{X}^T\mathbf{W}$	$D \times K$	$8DK$	Dense	N/Y	N
$\mathbf{H}\mathbf{X}^T$	$K \times N$	$8NK$	Dense	N	N

Recall that in the parallel sparse coding phase, for NOMP and NLASSO, we can carry out computations using $\mathbf{s} = \mathbf{H}\mathbf{x}$ and $\mathbf{S} = \mathbf{H}\mathbf{H}^T$ (see Eqn. 8). The matrix $\mathbf{H}\mathbf{X}^T$ need not be materialized as its columns – which are the $\mathbf{s}$ vectors – can be computed on the fly, used, and then immediately discarded. The matrix $\mathbf{S}$ is a dense symmetric matrix whose lower half is stored in the standard lower-packed storage format, and computed by K sparse matrix-vector products: $\mathbf{H}\mathbf{h}_1 \ldots \mathbf{H}\mathbf{h}_K$. Alternatively, matrix-vector products against $\mathbf{S}$ may be computed in time $O(K\nu)$ implicitly as $\mathbf{S}\mathbf{v} = \mathbf{H}(\mathbf{H}^T\mathbf{v})$. Likewise, note that dictionary learning phase requires $\mathbf{G} = \mathbf{W}^T\mathbf{W}$ and $\mathbf{X}^T\mathbf{W}$. It is profitable to express these matrices as the aggregation of rank-one matrices: $\mathbf{W}^T\mathbf{W} = \sum_{i=1}^N \mathbf{w}_i\mathbf{w}_i^T$ and $\mathbf{X}^T\mathbf{W} = \sum_{i=1}^N \mathbf{x}_i\mathbf{w}_i^T$. These matrices are the summary statistics we need for dictionary learning. Hence, a single pass over the data during the parallel sparse coding phase enables us to perform these aggregations, and prepare these matrices for the dictionary learning phase. Furthermore, in the aggregation above, we exploit the sparsity of $\mathbf{x}_i$ and $\mathbf{w}_i$ by updating only the non-zero cells. Finally, in the projection step of the dictionary learning phase, Eqn 15, we use priority queues for finding top ν non-negative elements in time $O(D\log(\nu))$.

Single-Node In-memory Multicore Implementation: We implemented parallel sparse coding using multithreading to utilize parallelism on a single multicore machine. The data matrix $\mathbf{X}$ is held in memory in its entirety. It is divided into as many blocks as the number of threads, and for each block, a single thread runs NOMP or NLASSO sequentially on the datapoints in that block. Also held in memory are the $K \times K$ dense symmetric matrices, $\mathbf{S} = \mathbf{H}\mathbf{H}^T$ and $\mathbf{G} = \mathbf{W}^T\mathbf{W}$ which we assume are small. Assuming $\nu = O(K)$, $\mathbf{H}$ also similarly requires $O(K^2)$ storage and is held in memory. To maximize the data sizes that our implementation can accommodate, we considered two different execution plans: (a) **Plan 1**: The first plan does not materialize the matrix $\mathbf{W}$, but explicitly maintains the dense $D \times K$ matrix $\mathbf{X}^T\mathbf{W}$. As each invocation of NOMP or NLASSO completes, the associated sparse coding vector $\mathbf{w}_i$ is used to update the summary statistics matrices, $\mathbf{W}^T\mathbf{W}$ and $\mathbf{X}^T\mathbf{W}$, and then discarded since everything needed for dictionary learning is contained in these summary statistics. When $DK \ll N\gamma$, this leaves more room to accommodate larger datasizes in memory. However, not materializing $\mathbf{W}$ means that NLASSO cannot exploit warm-starts from the sparse coding solutions found with respect to the previous dictionary. (b) **Plan 2**: In an alternate plan, we materialize $\mathbf{W}$ instead which consumes lesser memory if $N\gamma \ll DK$. We then serve the columns of $\mathbf{X}^T\mathbf{W}$, i.e., the vectors $\mathbf{X}^T\mathbf{v}_k$ in Eqn 14, by performing a sparse matrix-vector product on the fly. However, this requires extracting a column from $\mathbf{W}$ which is stored in a row-major dynamic sparse format. To make column extraction efficient, we utilize the fact that the indices of non-zero entries for each row are held in sorted order, and the associated value arrays conform to this order. Hence, we can keep a record of where the ith column was found for each row, and simply advance this pointer when the $(i+1)^{th}$ column is required. Thus, all columns can be served efficiently with one pass over $\mathbf{W}$. Two benefits of this plan are: (i) the matrix-vector product of $\mathbf{X}^T$ against the columns of $\mathbf{W}$ can be parallelized and (ii) NLASSO can use warm-starts. Thus, in this plan, both sparse coding and dictionary learning phases benefit from parallelism. To concretize the preceding discussion with some numbers: on a multicore machine with 16-GB RAM, accounting for the matrix storage given in Table 1, both plans can handle around 10 million documents assuming sparsity of 100 words, $\gamma = 5, \nu = 1000$, and 1000 topics need to be learnt. If 15000 topics need to learnt, the first plan can only handle about 2 million documents while the second plan can still manage 9 million by not materializing the dense $D \times K$ matrix $\mathbf{X}^T\mathbf{W}$.

Together, these considerations outlined above, lead to a highly efficient single-node implementation that forms the basis for the cluster version described next.

Cluster Implementation: Unlike the multi-core setting, our cluster implementation does not make the assumption that the data matrix $\mathbf{X}$ fits in main memory. Rather, $\mathbf{X}$ is stored in a distributed file system and our implementation makes one or more passes over it in parallel. Likewise, only small blocks of the large dense matrix $\mathbf{X}^T\mathbf{W}$ are ever materialized at a time and written to disk in parallel in every iteration. We continue making the assumption that the small matrices $\mathbf{W}^T\mathbf{W}$, $\mathbf{H}\mathbf{H}^T$ and the highly sparse matrix $\mathbf{H}$, can be held in-memory on both the control and worker nodes. While there are many choices for the framework one could use to parallelize algorithms, we work with the Map-Reduce paradigm, which fits well with the embarrassingly parallel nature of the sparse coding phase.

The Map-Reduce (MR) programming model was designed to simplify the processing of large files on a parallel system through user-defined Map and Reduce primitives. A MR job consists of two phases: a *Map* phase and a *Reduce* phase. During the Map phase, the user-defined Map primitive transforms the input data into (key, value) pairs in parallel. These pairs are stored and then sorted by the system so as to accumulate all values for each key. During the Reduce phase, the user-defined Reduce primitive is invoked on each unique key with a list of all the values for that key; usually, this phase is used to perform aggregations. Finally, the results are output in the form of (key, value) pairs. Each key can be processed in parallel during the Reduce phase.

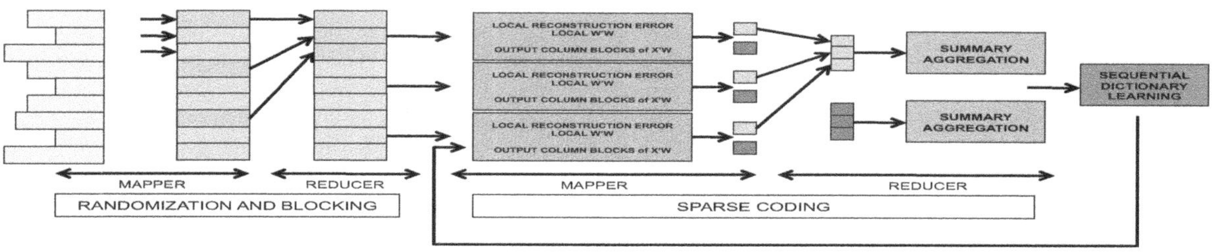

Figure 1: MapReduce implementation

Hadoop (`http://hadoop.apache.org/`), an open-source implementation of the MR programming model, has emerged as a vastly popular platform for parallelization in industry and academia. A user can perform parallel computations by submitting one or more MR jobs to Hadoop. One of the key advantages of Hadoop is that it is capable of running on large commodity clusters and recovering from both data as well as compute node failures.

Hadoop's implementation of the MR programming model targets executions where the input, intermediate (shuffle), and output datasets do not fit in aggregate main memory. Each MR job has to scan the input and intermediate datasets, which is time consuming. Furthermore, each job adds significantly to execution time in the form of startup costs. For these reasons, implementations that require the fewest number of MR jobs are ideal. Our cluster implementation below is driven by this goal.

Figure 1 presents the overall flow for the MR implementation of our algorithms. The execution proceeds in two phases, the preprocessing phase and the learning phase. The preprocessing phase is a one-time step whose objective is to re-organize the data for better parallel execution of the BCD algorithm. The learning phase is iterative and is coordinated by a control node that first spawns NOMP or NLASSO MR jobs on the worker nodes, then runs sequential dictionary learning and finally monitors the global mean reconstruction error to decide on convergence.

The preprocessing step consists of randomization and blocking. The goal of this step is to transform the data set into a set of "blocks" such that each block is a row-wise partition of the input matrix and all the blocks are roughly of the same size and sparsity, implying roughly equal units of work. We block the data set for the following reasons. First, during the learning phase, if one were to provide the input matrix to the Mappers one row at a time, majority of the time spent would go into performing I/O and not actual computation. To amortize the cost of performing I/O, we want to process a block of rows at a time. Second, ensuring these blocks are roughly of the same size and sparsity allows for a load balanced execution. Finally, blocking the input matrix amortizes the cost of writing out blocks of the $\mathbf{X}^T\mathbf{W}$ matrix during the learning phase by allowing one to partially aggregate this matrix for each input block, directly in memory. During the pre-processing step, the Mapper assigns each row to a random block and emits the block id as a key and row as a value. The Reducer then assimilates each block and writes it out to the file system. At the end of the pre-processing phase, we expect to have row-wise blocks of the input matrix that are roughly of same size and sparsity.

The subsequent learning phase proceeds iteratively with each iteration consisting of a parallel sparse coding phase and a sequential dictionary learning phase. The parallel sparse coding phase is implemented using *a single MapReduce job*. To explain its steps, we need the following notation: let $\mathbf{X}^r$ denote the rth block of the $\mathbf{X}$ and R be the number of rows that were assigned to a block by the preprocessing phase. We refer to R as the *row blocking parameter*. A Mapper for the parallel sparse coding phase accepts $\mathbf{X}^r$ and runs NOMP/NLASSO to obtain the associated sparse coding matrix $\mathbf{W}^r$ which can be materialized in memory since the blocks are small. We use the notation $\mathbf{W}^{r,i}$ to denote its ith column. For large D, K, the local summary statistics matrix $\mathbf{X}^{rT}\mathbf{W}^r$ cannot be materialized and written out in one go. Rather, the Mapper computes a set of $D \times C$ matrices, where $C \leq K$: $\mathbf{Q}^{r,j} = X_r^T\left(\mathbf{W}^{r,(j-1)*C+1}, \ldots \mathbf{W}^{r,j*C}\right)$ matrix for $j = 1 \ldots \lceil \frac{K}{C} \rceil$. C is the *column blocking parameter* of our implementation. The Mapper emits the block id j as a key and column block $\mathbf{Q}^{r,j}$ as value. The Reducer then sums up these blocks over the row-blocks: $\mathbf{Q}^j = \sum_r \mathbf{Q}^{r,j}$ which gives the jth block of C columns of the global summary statistics matrix $\mathbf{X}^T\mathbf{W}$. This mechanism to write out column blocks of the local summary statistics matrices (and not all columns) has the following benefits: First, we can constrain the size of the aggregations that need to take place on the Reducers. Second, we get parallelism by having each Reducer perform a complete aggregation for a portion of the columns. In addition to producing the summary statistics matrix, the MR job also writes out the aggregated reconstruction error and $\mathbf{W}^T\mathbf{W}$ matrix. The output of the MR job is delivered to the sequential dictionary learning phase, at the end of which we check for convergence and proceed to the next iteration if necessary. Note that each mapper can writeout its associated $\mathbf{W}^r$ as well to help jumpstart NLASSO in the next iteration.

6. EMPIRICAL STUDIES

We begin with small scale experiments on two classic document collections, the 20 newsgroups collection ($N = 19228$, $D = 18607$ and $K = 20$) and TDT news corpus ($N = 9394$, $D = 19528$ and $K = 30$), that come with manually generated labels with respect to which quality measurements may be made. We then report scalability experiments for our multicore and Hadoop implementations on much larger datasets (New York times and an extended Pubmed Corpora) where extrinsic evaluation cannot be done due to the high cost of labeling.

Statistical Performance on Small Datasets: We explore the effect of double sparsity on the statistical performance of the non-negative sparse coding. We varied dictionary sparsity, covering 5% to 100% of the full data dimensionality. The coding sparsity was varied from 0.05 to 1.0 interpreted as the fraction of the full dictionary size K that NOMP is allowed to use for coding. For NLASSO, the same fractions were used literally as the γ values. Empirically, in this range, NLASSO gave similar degrees of sparsity as NOMP. For each choice of γ, ν, we ran the learning algorithms 10 times with different initialization and averaged the following: (a) the clustering quality in terms of normalized mutual information (NMI) obtained by assigning cluster $\arg\max_j w_{ij}$ to document i, (b) the classification accuracy returned by running linear logistic regression on 5% labeled samples after unsupervised sparse coding, to emulate a semi-supervised learning scenario, and (c) the final objective values attained at convergence. Each choice of γ was associated with the mean sparsity of the final $\mathbf{W}$ across different random initializations.

Figure 2: Results on 20NG (top), TDT2 (bottom)

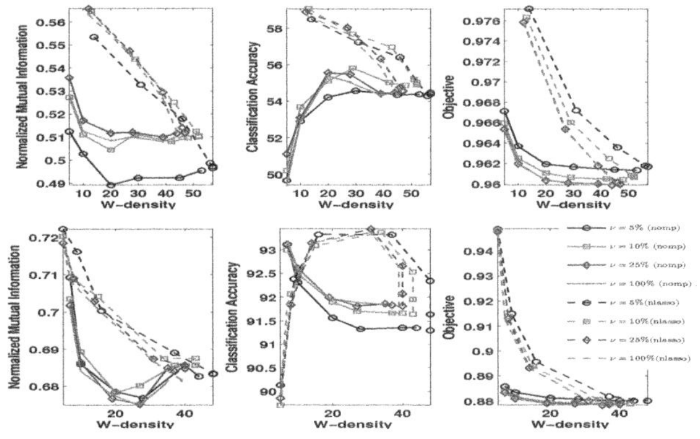

In Figure 2, we plot NMI, Classification accuracy of Logistic Regression and Objective values as a function of percentage of non-zeros in $\mathbf{W}$ for different degrees of percentage of non-zeros in $\mathbf{H}$, for both NOMP and NLASSO. We make the following observations: (1) Our Sparse NMF (both NOMP and NLASSO) demonstrates substantially better clustering and classification performance than NMF which corresponds to the rightmost point on the curves for $\nu = 100\%$. Furthermore, we never observed an increase in objective function with NOMP in these experiments; all runs smoothly converged. (2) Interestingly, we find that on both datasets, NOMP gives substantially better reconstruction error at similar sparsity levels than NLASSO. However, the induced sparse representation does not translate into better clustering performance or classification accuracy. This might seem counter-intuitive at first, but can be reasoned as follows. The NOMP hypothesis space is larger since it does not restrict the magnitude of the weights as NLASSO does. This leads to better mean reconstruction error rates at similar sparsity levels. Indeed, reconstruction error alone does not reflect model utility for these tasks since we know that SVD can do even better without non-negativity and sparsity constraints. The presence of additional weight shrinkage in NLASSO appears to act as an effective regularizer that leads to better statistical performance. (3) We see that the $\nu = 10\%$ curve performs as well or better than the $\nu = 100\%$ curve. This implies a 10-fold storage reduction for $\mathbf{H}$ strongly supporting our choice to maintain it in memory as a light-weight sparse matrix. (4) In Table 2, as a sanity check, we compare clustering performance against popular alternatives. The parameters are $\gamma = 0.05$ (to be interpreted as fraction of K for NOMP) and $\nu = 0.1D$. We see that Sparse NMF with NLASSO performs quite competitively.

Figure 3: Multicore Performance: NYTimes data

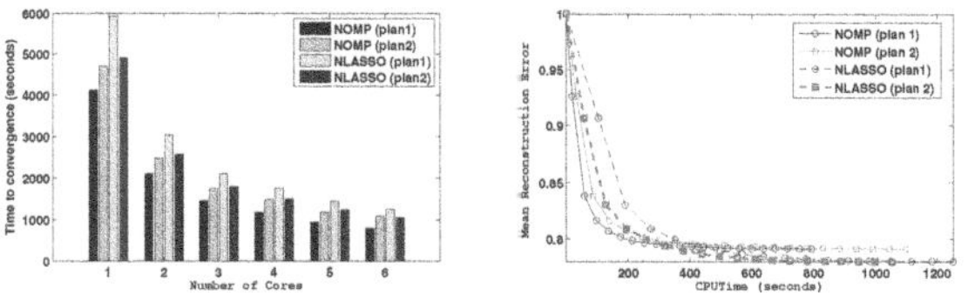

Table 2: Clustering Quality

Algorithm	20NG	TDT2
pLSA	51.5 (2.8)	60.3 (1.6)
LDA	49.4 (1.3)	66.7 (1.5)
K-means	41.4 (14.4)	70.6 (2.3)
NMF	51.0 (1.1)	68.1 (2.1)
SparseNMF (NLASSO)	55.4 (2.4)	72.2(2.5)
SparseNMF (NOMP)	51.3 (2.0)	70.9 (2.2)

Multicore Performance: We next consider computational performance on a commodity hexacore machine with 4GB RAM. For these experiments, we work with the popular NY times corpus (available from UCI Machine Learning Repository) comprising of $N = 299752$ documents indexed over a vocabulary of $D = 102660$ words, with about 70-million nonzero entries in the document-term matrix. We set $\nu = 1000$, $\gamma = 5$ for NOMP and 5 for NLASSO and ran our algorithms for $K = 100$ while increasing the number of cores from 1 to 6. The total time to convergence for both the execution plans is shown in Figure 3 (left). We make the following observations. The use of 6-cores offers the following speedups over a single core: 5.2x for NOMP (plan 1), 4.3x for NOMP (plan 2), 4.7x for both NLASSO (plan 1) and NLASSO (plan 2). Thus, we see near-linear speedups with increasing number of cores. NOMP prefers plan 1 because it cannot utilize warm starts and because dictionary learning is extremely fast (about 0.5 seconds for updating 100 topics per iteration) since it only needs to perform a top-ν operation followed by simple normalization step. NLASSO, on the other hand, prefers plan 2 since warm starts allow it to converge faster. As shown in Figure 3 (right), its iterations start to take lesser and lesser time. The dictionary learning phase for plan 2 takes about 35 seconds in each iteration for 1 core, which reduces to about 13 seconds with 6 cores, due to parallel matrix-vector products as described in section 5.

Hadoop Scaleout: These experiments were performed on IBM's Nadal cluster, which has 48 cores distributed across 12 nodes with 4 GB of RAM per core. All the nodes were running RHEL 5 (kernel 2.6.18-164.el5) with IBM Java v1.6.0 and Hadoop 0.20.2. We measured execution time of the Hadoop implementation on an extended PubMed dataset (also available at UCI repository) containing 106 million documents, 141K words, with more than 6 Billion non-zeros in the document term matrix, as we varied various algorithm and hardware parameters. For these experiments, the row blocking parameter R = 100K rows, the column blocking parameter C = 10 columns, $\gamma = 5$ and $\nu = 1000$, unless otherwise noted.

(a) Varying number of cores: Figures 4 and 5 present execution time for an iteration of NOMP, an iteration of NLASSO, and the blocking phase that is common to both algorithms, for different dataset sizes, as we vary the number of cores from 16 to 48. Speedup for the blocking phase (that is common to both algorithms) varies from 1.53x for 8.2M rows to 2.81x for 106M rows, the maximum possible speedup here being 3x (as we only vary the number of cores from 16 to 48). For 8.2M rows, the speedup is roughly half that of the maximum possible speedup as the data set is small and the system is under utilized. For 106M rows, all cores take part in I/O and the blocking procedure, improving scalability. The blocking phase is thus very efficient and is expected to continue to scale well to larger datasets.

As for the performance of an iteration of NOMP, the speedup is roughly 1.85x for 8.2M rows and 2.7x for 106M rows when K = 100 and 2.1x for 8.2M rows and 3.54x for 106M rows when K = 200. As for the performance of an iteration of NLASSO, the speedup is roughly 1.81x for 8.2M rows and 2.75x for 106M rows when K = 100 and 1.86x for 8.2M rows and 3.02x for 106M rows when K = 200. Keeping K fixed, speedup improves with increasing number of rows as the execution changes from being I/O bound and under utilizing the system to being compute bound. Furthermore, keeping the number of rows fixed, speedup improves as we increase K as there is more computation on offer to better utilize the available parallelism. We observe super linear speedup in some cases likely due to improvements in caching behavior as we increase the number of cores. Given that the execution is compute-bound on large datasets, we expect the implementation to continue to scale on larger number of cores provided the dataset is sufficiently large to make the execution compute-bound.

Figure 4: Varying Number of Cores - 100 Topics

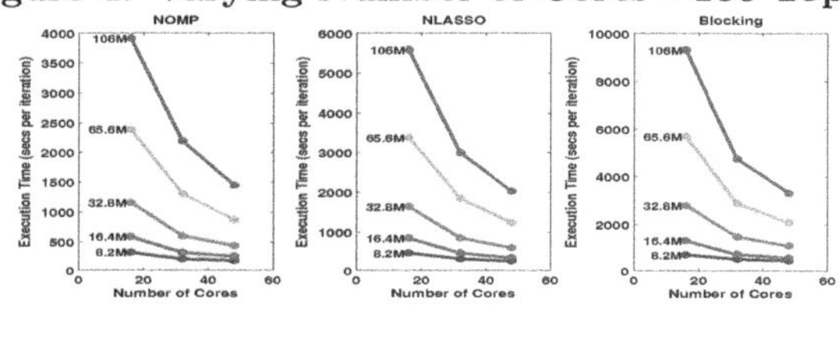

Figure 5: Varying Number of Cores - 200 Topics

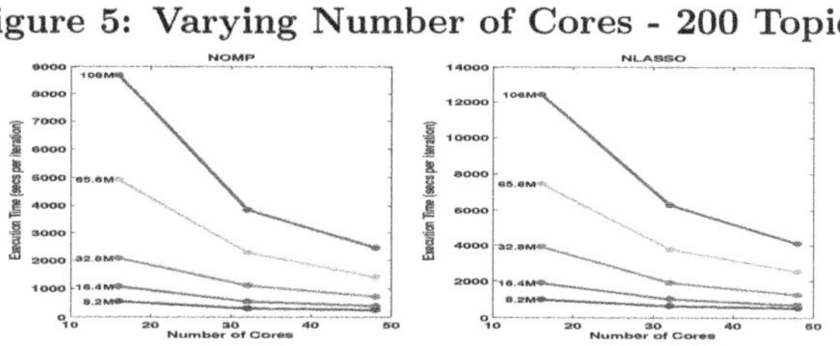

(b) Varying row block size: Figure 6 presents execution times for an iteration of NOMP, an iteration of NLASSO, and the blocking phase that is common to both algorithms, for different values of the row blocking parameter R, as we vary the number of rows in the dataset, keeping number of cores fixed at 48. The performance of the blocking phase improves marginally (from 496 to 373 for 8.2M rows and from 3392 to 3382 for 106M rows) as we increase the size of each block due to the fact that the system needs to sort a fewer keys with fewer blocks. As the performance of the blocking phase is not adversely affected by increasing data sizes, we expect the blocking phase to scale well to larger datasets. However, the performance of an iteration of NOMP and NLASSO varies significantly with varying R. For NOMP, seconds per iteration varies from 200 to 122 for 8.2M rows and from 2099 to 1032 for 106M rows. For NLASSO, seconds per iterations varies from 266 to 180 for 8.2M rows and from 2650 to 1624 for 106M rows. R = 200K can improve performance by nearly 2x when compared to R = 50K. Given that performance of the blocking phase is relatively unaffected by the parameter R, and that the performance of the learning phase is heavily dependent on the value of R, picking the largest possible value for R that allows for an in-memory execution will likely provide the best performance.

Figure 6: Varying Row Block Size

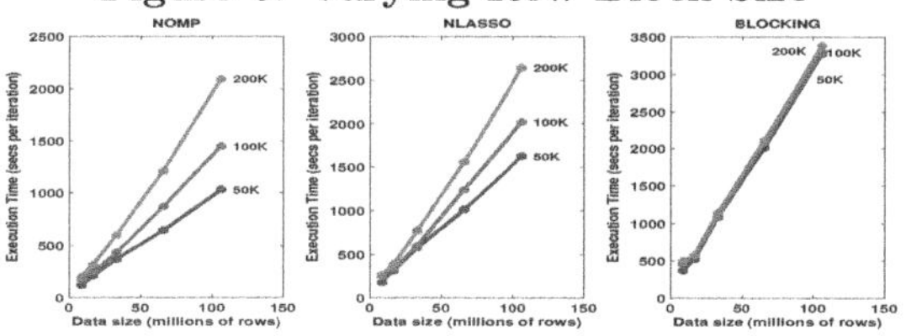

(c) Varying number of topics: Figure 7 presents execution times for an iteration of NOMP, an iteration of NLASSO, for different number of topics K, as we vary the data size, keeping number of cores fixed at 48. For NOMP, at 8.2M rows, execution time increases by 2.76x, and at 106M rows, execution time increases by 4.69x, when going from K = 100 to 400. The execution under utilizes the system at 8.2M rows and hence execution time grows sub-linearly with K. However, at 106M rows, execution time grows near-linearly as the execution is compute bound. Overall, execution time for NOMP grows near-linearly with K. For NLASSO, at 8.2M rows, execution time increases by 5.81x, and at 106M rows, execution time increases by 6.22x, when going from K = 100 to 400. Thus, execution time for NLASSO grows super-linearly with K. We can explain these observations as follows. The per iteration cost of NOMP is linear in K, involving search over K atoms, and the total number of iterations is atmost γ. For NLASSO, the gradient computation involves the dense matrix-vector product $\mathbf{Sw}$ whose complexity depends on the sparsity of $\mathbf{w}$, but for dense iterates is $O(K^2)$. For large K, linear scaling behavior can be recovered for NLASSO by not materializing $\mathbf{S}$, but rather computing $\mathbf{Sw}$ using two *sparse* matrix-vector products $\mathbf{H}(\mathbf{H}^T\mathbf{w})$ which has $O(K\nu)$ cost. Convergence results from [2] show that NLASSO, implemented using FISTA, will take about $O(\sqrt{\frac{1}{\epsilon}})$ iterations to return an ϵ optimal solution, independent of K.

Figure 7: Varying Number of Topics

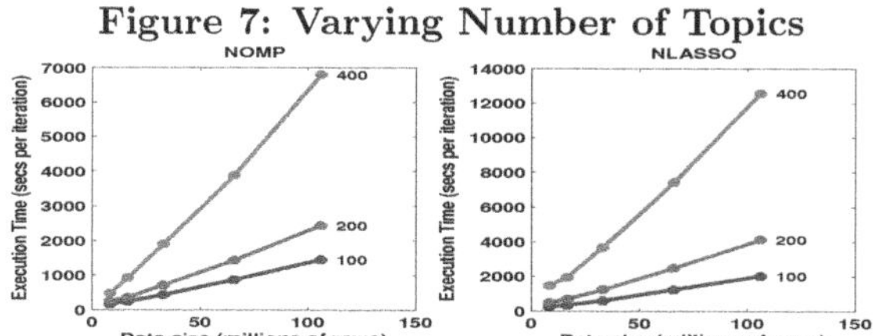

(d) Varying column block size: Figure 8 presents execution times for an iteration of NOMP, an iteration of NLASSO, for different number of topics K (100,400) and column blocking parameter C (5,10,20), as we vary the data size, keeping number of cores fixed at 48. For both NOMP and NLASSO, we observe an interesting trend. When K = 100, C = 5 results in the least execution time as it allows one to leverage a larger number of cores in the Reduce phase of the MR job. However, K = 400, C = 5 results in the largest execution time as it results in an excessively larger number of Reduce tasks, while C = 20 results in the least execution time. These indicate that one must carefully select the parameter C based on the cluster configuration and desired number of topics.

Figure 8: Column Block Size and Topics

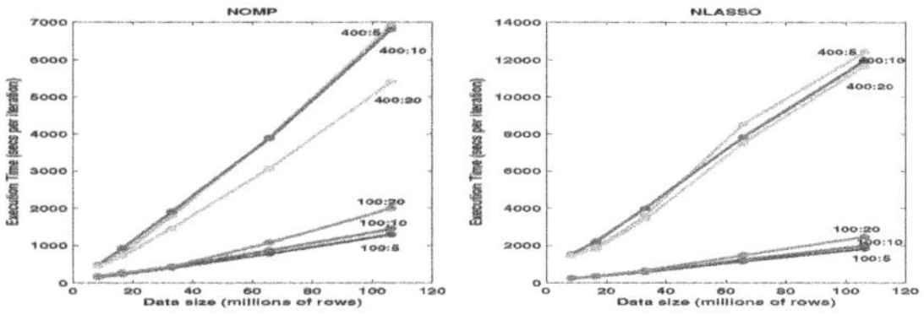

(e) Varying coding sparsity: Figure 9 presents execution times for an iteration of NOMP, an iteration of NLASSO, for $K = 400$, as we vary the data size, keeping number of cores fixed at 48. For NOMP, varying γ from 5 to 20 increases execution time by roughly 1.82x for 106M rows. For NLASSO, varying γ from 0.1 to 1 increases execution time by roughly 1.67x for 106M rows. Thus, for both algorithms, execution time grows sub-linearly with coding sparsity. The per iteration cost of NLASSO is independent of γ and as outlined in (c), it has linear dependence on γ. While the refitting step of NOMP has superlinear dependence on γ, its values are such a small fraction of K that this dependence is "washed out".

Figure 9: Varying Coding Sparsity

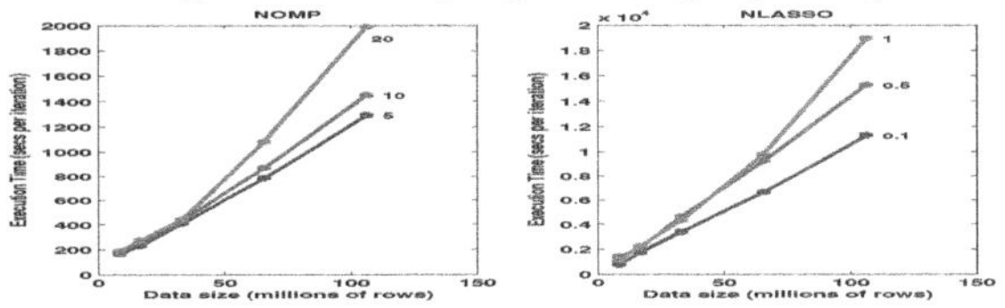

Comparison to related work: On the extended Pubmed corpus with over 106-million rows and more than 6 billion non-zero entries, with $K = 100$ and parameters reported in this section, our fastest algorithms running on 12 nodes (with 48 cores) are expected to converge and complete execution in less than 10 hours. To the best of our knowledge, this is the largest demonstration of sparse coding/dictionary learning algorithms reported to date. Comparing this performance with other related published work has several caveats due to major differences in convergence properties of algorithms benchmarked, actual cluster configuration, characteristics of datasets used, as well as innumerable other lower-level implementation details. In particular, we are not aware of any publically available Hadoop implementation of Sparse NMF and related dictionary learning algorithms to compare against. Nonetheless, to put our performance into perspective, we collect some published results in this section. [15] report running the standard NMF [14] algorithms on a proprietary dataset with around 4.38-billion non-zeros with $K = 10$, on a Hadoop cluster with unspecified configuration. They report 7-hours per iteration each requiring multiple Map-Reduce jobs, which appears to be significantly less efficient than our implementation. [18] parallelize LDA and report about 4.1 hours on 8.2 million Pubmed documents, with $K = 2000$, on a non-dedicated Hadoop cluster with 50 nodes. [17] provide a different MPI-based parallel LDA implementation and report 10-hours for the same dataset on 1024 processors.

Acknowledgments: We thank Prabhanjan Kambadur for several insightful conversations. This research is continuing through participation in the Social Media in Strategic Communication (SMISC) program sponsored by the U.S. Defense Advanced Research Projects Agency (DARPA) under Agreement Number W911NF-12-C-0028.

7. REFERENCES

[1] S. Arora, R. Ge, R. Kannan, and A. Moitra. Computing a nonnegative matrix factorization – provably. In *STOC*, 2012.

[2] A. Beck and M. Teboulle. Gradient-based algorithms with applications to signal recovery problems. *Convex Opt. in Sig. Proc. Comm.. Camb. Univ. Press*, 2010.

[3] D. Bertsekas. *Non-linear Programming.* Athena Scientific, 1999.

[4] David M. Blei, Andrew Y. Ng, and Michael I. Jordan. Latent dirichlet allocation. *JMLR*, 3:993–1022, 2003.

[5] Peter Buhlmann and Sara Van De Geer. *Statistics for High-Dimensional Data.* Springer, 2011.

[6] A. Cichocki, R. Zdunek, A. H. Phan, and S. Amari. *Nonneg. Matrix and Tensor Fact.* Wiley, 2009.

[7] J. Dean and S. Ghemawat. Mapreduce: Simplified data processing on large clusters. In *OSDI*, 2004.

[8] J. Duchi, S. S. Schwartz, Y. Singer, and T. Chandra. Efficient projections onto the l1-ball for learning in high dimensions. In *ICML*, 2008.

[9] M. Elad. *Sparse and Redundant Representations.* Springer, 2010.

[10] A. Ghoting, P. Kambadur, E. Pednault, and R. Kannan. Nimble: a toolkit for the implementation of parallel data mining and machine learning algorithms on mapreduce. In *KDD*, 2011.

[11] A. Ghoting, R. Krishnamurthy, E. Pednault, B. Reinwald, V. Sindhwani, S. Tatikonda, Y. Tian, and S. Vaithyanathan. Declarative machine learning on mapreduce. In *ICDE*, 2011.

[12] P. Hoyer. Non-negative matrix factorization with sparseness constraints. *JMLR*, 5:1457–1469, 2004.

[13] R. Jenatton, J. Mairal, G. Obozinski, and F. Bach. Proximal methods for sparse hierarchical dictionary learning. In *ICML*, 2010.

[14] D. D. Lee and H. S. Seung. Learning the parts of objects by non-negative matrix factorization. *Nature*, 1999.

[15] C. Liu, H. Yang, J. Fan, L. He, and Y. Wang. Distributed nonnegative matrix factorization for web-scale dyadic data analysis on mapreduce. In *WWW*, 2010.

[16] J. Mairal, F. Bach, J. Ponce, and G. Sapiro. Online learning for matrix factorization and sparse coding. *JMLR*, 11:19–60, 2010.

[17] D. Newman, A. Ascuncion, P. Smyth, and M. Welling. Distributed algorithms for topic models. In *JMLR*, 2010.

[18] A. Smola and S. Narayanamurthy. An architecture for parallel topic models. In *VLDB*, 2010.

[19] Z. J. Xiang, H. Xu, and P. J. Ramadge. Learning sparse representations of high-dimensional data on large-scale dictionaries. In *NIPS*, 2011.

Learning Binary Codes for Collaborative Filtering

Ke Zhou
College of Computing
Georgia Institute of Technology
Atlanta, GA 30032
kzhou@gatech.edu

Hongyuan Zha
College of Computing
Georgia Institute of Technology
Atlanta, GA 30032
zha@cc.gatech.edu

ABSTRACT

This paper tackles the efficiency problem of making recommendations in the context of large user and item spaces. In particular, we address the problem of learning binary codes for collaborative filtering, which enables us to efficiently make recommendations with time complexity that is independent of the total number of items. We propose to construct binary codes for users and items such that the preference of users over items can be accurately preserved by the Hamming distance between their respective binary codes. By using two loss functions measuring the degree of divergence between the training and predicted ratings, we formulate the problem of learning binary codes as a discrete optimization problem. Although this optimization problem is intractable in general, we develop effective relaxations that can be efficiently solved by existing methods. Moreover, we investigate two methods to obtain the binary codes from the relaxed solutions. Evaluations are conducted on three public-domain data sets and the results suggest that our proposed method outperforms several baseline alternatives.

Categories and Subject Descriptors

H.3.3 [**Information Search and Retrieval**]: Information filtering; I.2.6 [**Artificial Intelligence**]: Learning

General Terms

Algorithms, Performance, Experimentation

Keywords

Recommender systems, Collaborative filtering, Learning binary codes, Discrete optimization, Relaxed solutions

1. INTRODUCTION

With the rapid growth of E-commerce, hundreds of thousands of products, ranging from books, mp3s to automobiles, are sold through online marketplaces nowadays. In addition, millions of customers with diverse backgrounds and preferences make purchases online, generating great opportunities as well as challenges for E-commerce companies — How to match products to their potential buyers not only accurately but also efficiently. Since collaborative filtering is an essential component for many existing recommendation systems, it has been actively investigated by a wide range of previous studies to improve its accuracy [1, 19]. On the other hand, due to the nature of their applications, collaborative filtering systems are usually required to learn and predict the preferences between a large number of users and items. Therefore, for a given user, it is important to retrieve products that satisfy her preferences efficiently, leading to fast response time and better user experience. Naturally, the problem can be viewed as a similarity search problem where we seek "similar" items for a given user. Recent studies show that binary coding is a promising approach for fast similarity search [9, 13, 14, 17, 21]. The basic idea is to represent data points by binary codes that preserve the original similarities between them. One significant advantage of this approach is that the retrieval of similar data points can be conducted by searching for data points within a small Hamming distance, which can be performed in time that is independent of the total number of data [17]. However, no prior studies have been focused on constructing binary codes for both users and items in the context of collaborative filtering — to the best of our knowledge — a gap we propose to fill in this paper.

One key obstacle that hinders direct exploitation of the existing approaches to learning binary codes to the collaborative filtering context is that most of them assume the similarities between any pairs of data points are given explicitly, e.g., in the form of kernel functions or similarity graphs [13, 21, 24]. However, in collaborative filtering, the similarities between users and items are not known explicitly. In fact, the main goal of collaborative filtering algorithms is to estimate and predict unobserved similarities between users and items from the training data in order to make recommendations. In this paper, we address the problem of learning binary codes for collaborative filtering. Specifically, we propose to learn compact yet effective binary codes for both users and items from the training rating data. Unlike previous works on learning binary codes, we do not assume the similarity between users and items are known explicitly. Therefore, the binary codes we construct not only accurately preserve the observed preferences of users, but they also can be used to *predict* the unobserved preferences, making the proposed method conceptually unique compared with the existing methods.

Our approach is based on the idea that the binary codes

KDD'12, August 12–16, 2012, Beijing, China.

assigned to users and items should preserve the preferences of users over items. Two loss functions are applied to measure the divergence between the training data and the estimates based on the binary codes. Unfortunately, thus formulated, the resulting discrete optimization problem is difficult to solve in general. Through relaxing the binary constraints, it turns out the relaxed optimization problem can be solved effectively by existing solvers. Moreover, we propose two effective methods for rounding the relaxed solutions to obtain binary codes. One key property of the binary codes obtained by the proposed method is that the degree of preferences of a user to items can be measured by the number of common bits between their corresponding binary codes. Hence, the major advantage of representing users and items by binary codes is to enable fast search: In order to provide recommendations for a user, we need only to search items with binary codes within a small Hamming distance to the binary codes of the given user. We evaluated the proposed method over three data sets and compare it with several baseline alternatives. The results show that the binary codes obtained by the proposed method can preserve and predict the preferences of users more accurately than the baselines.

The contributions of this paper are essentially threefold: 1) We propose to learn binary codes for collaborative filtering that accurately preserve the preference of users, which generalizes the existing works of learning binary codes to the context of collaborative filtering. 2) We propose a framework to learning binary codes based on training rating data, which leads to relaxed optimization problems that can be solved effectively by the state-of-the-art optimization techniques. 3) Our experimental evaluations show that the binary codes obtained by the proposed method can preserve the preference of users better than several baseline alternatives.

The rest of the paper is organized as follows: In Section 2, we briefly review existing studies for collaborative filtering and learning binary codes. In Section 3, we first formulate the problem of learning binary codes for collaborative filtering as a discrete optimization problem and introduce the two loss functions used in this work. Then, the learning algorithm proposed with detailed derivations based on transforming and relaxing the discrete optimization problem so that it can be optimized efficiently. Moreover, we discuss two different methods for rounding real-valued solutions to obtain binary codes. The evaluations are described and analyzed in Section 4. We conclude our work and present several future research directions in Section 5.

2. RELATED WORK

2.1 Collaborative Filtering

Many studies on recommender systems have been focused on collaborative filtering approaches. These methods can be categorized into memory-based and model-based. The reader is referred to the survey papers [1, 19] for a comprehensive summary of collaborative filtering algorithms.

Recently, matrix factorization has become a popular direction for collaborative filtering [2, 11, 15, 16]. These methods are shown to be effective in many applications. Specifically, matrix factorization methods seek to associate both users and items with latent profiles represented by vectors in a low dimensional Euclidean space that can capture their characteristics. Specifically, the preference of a user on an item is usually measured by some similarity, such as the dot-product, between their low dimensional profiles. These studies are related to our work in the sense that both of them aim to find certain representations that preserve the preference between users and items. However, one key difference is that our work aims to find binary codes in Hamming space for representing users and items, which has the nice property that the retrieval of interesting items for a user can be performed in time that is independent of the total number of items [17].

Another direction of collaborative filtering investigate the problem of using binary codes to create fingerprints for users [3–5]. The idea is create binary fingerprints for each user using randomized algorithms so that the similarity between users can be approximated according to the fingerprints. However, these studies do not address the problem of simultaneously representing users and items by binary fingerprints. Thus, the preference of users on items can not be estimated directly from these fingerprints. On the other hand, the binary codes learnt by our proposed method can be directly used to measure the preference of users over items.

2.2 Learning Binary Codes

The problem of learning binary codes for fast similarity search has been investigated in several studies [12, 13, 17, 21] Locality sensitive hashing tries to construct binary codes that preserve certain distance (e.g., L_p distance) between different points with high probability, which is usually archived by random projection [6,8]. In [18], the problem of learning effective binary codes is solved by utilizing the idea of boosting. The work of [17] proposes to learn binary codes making use of Restricted Boltzmann Machine (RBM) for fast similarity search of documents. Recent work focuses on constructing binary codes based on a given similarity function [14, 20, 21]. The basic idea is to apply spectral analysis techniques to the data and embedding data points into a low dimension space. For example, the work [21] investigate the requirements for compact and effective binary codes. Their solution relies on spectral graph partition, which can be solved by eigenvalue decomposition of the Laplacian matrix for the graph. It has been shown that these methods archive significant performance improvements in terms of preserving the similarity between data points. Although several extension of this method has been studied [7, 24], these methods only consider the problem of obtaining binary codes for one type of entities. However, in collaborative filtering, two types of entities, users and items, are naturally involved and thus should be consider simultaneously, which makes it difficult to applies these method directly.

The work [23] proposes to learn binary codes for both documents and terms by viewing the term-document matrix as a bipartite graph and apply the method proposed in [21] to obtain the binary codes. However, this method can not deal with the problem of unobserved/missing ratings in collaborative filtering. As shown in our experiments, the binary codes obtained by this method quickly overfit the training data and lead to poor prediction accuracy.

3. LEARNING BINARY CODES

In this section, we describe the proposed method for learning binary codes for collaborative filtering. We first describe the general formulation for this problem through optimization using squared and pairwise loss functions, respectively. Then, the learning method based on solving the relaxed problem is derived in detail. Finally, we discuss two methods to obtain binary codes from the real-valued solutions of the relaxed problems.

3.1 Problem Formulation

The goal of collaborative filtering is to recommend interesting items to users according to their past ratings on the items. Formally, we assume that r_{ui} represents the rating of user $u \in \mathcal{U}$ for item $i \in \mathcal{I}$, where $\mathcal{U}$ and $\mathcal{I}$ are the user and item space, respectively. Without loss of generality, we further assume that r_{ui} is a real number in the interval $[0, 1]$. Moreover, we assign binary codes $f_u \in \{-1, 1\}^B$ for each user u and $h_i \in \{-1, 1\}^B$ for each item i, where B is the length of the binary codes. Our goal is to construct binary codes for users and items that preserve the preferences between them — the degree of preference of user u over item i can be estimated by the similarity between their binary codes f_u and h_i. A natural way to define the similarity between user u and item i is the fraction of common bits in their binary codes f_u and h_i, leading to the similarity function,

$$\text{sim}(f_u, h_i) = \frac{1}{B}\sum_{k=1}^{B} \mathbb{I}(f_u^{(k)} = h_i^{(k)}),$$

where $f_u^{(k)}$ and $h_i^{(k)}$ represent the k-th bit of the binary codes f_u and h_i, respectively. $\mathbb{I}(\cdot)$ denotes the indicator function that returns 1 if the statement in its parameter is true and zero otherwise.

It is easy to check that the following holds for the similarity function $\text{sim}(\cdot, \cdot)$ defined above:

$$\text{sim}(f_u, h_i) = 1 - \frac{1}{B}\text{dist}_{\text{H}}(f_u, h_i),$$

where $\text{dist}_{\text{H}}(f_u, h_i)$ is the Hamming distance between two binary codes f_u and h_i. The above fact suggests that the smaller the Hamming distance is, the more similar their binary codes become. Therefore, in order to find items with similar binary codes to a user represented by f_u, it is sufficient to search items i within a small Hamming distance $\text{dist}_{\text{H}}(f_u, h_i)$. This allows us to find similar items in time that is independent to the total number of items [17].

In order to make accurate recommendations to users, we need to find binary codes f_u and h_i for users and items such that the preferences between them are preserved by the similarities between their respective binary codes. In addition, in collaborative filtering, we only observe a subset of all the possible ratings $\{r_{ui} | (u, i) \in \mathcal{O}\}$ where $\mathcal{O} \subset \mathcal{U} \times \mathcal{I}$ and we need to recommend items to users according to their preferences over items whose ratings are unobserved. Therefore, the key for accurate recommendations is to construct binary codes that can not only preserve the observed ratings but also accurately predict the preferences of users on unobserved items.

Our approach to learn binary codes is to estimate them from observed ratings. Specifically, we propose to construct binary codes that minimize the degree of divergence between the observed ratings and the ratings estimated from the binary codes. To this end, we apply two objective functions to measure the degree of divergence between the observed ratings and the model estimates:

- **Squared Loss.** Using this loss function, we seek to minimize the squared error of the observed ratings and the similarity estimations from the binary codes, which is a commonly used loss function for collaborative filtering:

$$\min_{f_u, h_i \in \{\pm 1\}^B} \mathcal{L}_{sq} = \sum_{(u,i)\in\mathcal{O}} (r_{ui} - \text{sim}(f_u, h_i))^2. \quad (1)$$

- **Pairwise Loss.** Since we are more interested in preserving the relative orders between items rather than their absolute values, it is natural to consider the pairwise loss function described as follows:

$$\min_{f_u, h_i \in \{\pm 1\}^B} \mathcal{L}_{pair} = \sum_{u} \sum_{i,j\in\mathcal{O}_u} \Big((r_{ui} - r_{uj}) - (\text{sim}(f_u, h_i) - \text{sim}(f_u, h_j))\Big)^2, \quad (2)$$

where $\mathcal{O}_u = \{(u, i) \mid (u, i) \in \mathcal{O}\}$. Minimizing the above loss function requires the binary codes to preserve the relative difference between each pair of items rated by the user.

Additionally, we also require the binary codes to be *balanced* — we would like each bit of the binary codes to have equal chance to be 1 or -1. The balance constraint is equivalent to maximizing the entropy of each bit of the binary codes, which indicates that each bit carries as much information as possible. Specifically, we will enforce the following constraints to the binary codes:

$$\sum_u f_u = 0, \quad \text{and} \sum_i h_i = 0.$$

The above constraints motivate the following regularized objective function for learning binary codes. For example, for squared loss, we have the following objective function:

$$\min_{f_u, h_i \in \{\pm 1\}^B} \sum_{(u,i)\in\mathcal{O}} (r_{ui} - \text{sim}(f_u, h_i))^2 + \lambda(\|\sum_u f_u\|^2 + \|\sum_i h_i\|^2), \quad (3)$$

where the first term is the loss over observed ratings and the second term represents that we prefer balanced binary codes. The parameter λ controls the trade-off between minimizing the empirical errors and the enforcement of the constraints. $\|\cdot\|$ indicates Euclidean norm of a vector.

Similarly, we have the following regularized objective function for the pairwise loss function:

$$\min_{f_u, h_i \in \{\pm 1\}^B} \sum_{u} \sum_{i,j\in\mathcal{O}_u} \Big((r_{ui} - r_{uj}) - (\text{sim}(f_u, h_i) - \text{sim}(f_u, h_j))\Big)^2 + \lambda(\|\sum_u f_u\|^2 + \|\sum_i h_i\|^2). \quad (4)$$

3.2 Learning

The objective functions defined in Equation (3) and Equation (4) are defined over the discrete space $\{\pm 1\}^B$, which makes them difficult to optimize in general. Therefore, we propose to solve it approximately by transforming the objective functions and then relaxing the space of solutions to be $[-1, 1]^B$. For the sake of concreteness, we describe our method for solving the squared loss in Equation (3) in detail. The pairwise loss in Equation (4) can be optimized in a similar approach.

First, we notice that for binary codes $f, h \in \{\pm 1\}^B$, the following property holds:

$$\begin{aligned}\mathrm{sim}(f,h) &= \frac{1}{B}\sum_{k=1}^{B}\mathbb{I}(f^{(k)} = h^{(k)}) \\ &= \frac{1}{2B}\left(\sum_{k=1}^{B}\mathbb{I}(f^{(k)} = h^{(k)}) + (B - \sum_{k=1}^{B}\mathbb{I}(f^{(k)} \neq h^{(k)}))\right) \\ &= \frac{1}{2B}\left(B + \sum_{k=1}^{B} f^{(k)}h^{(k)}\right) \\ &= \frac{1}{2} + \frac{1}{2B}f^T h.\end{aligned}$$

Thus, by substituting the above equation into the regularized objective function defined in Equation (3), we can express the objective function for squared loss as follows:

$$\begin{aligned}\min_{f_u, h_i \in \{\pm 1\}^B} \mathcal{L}_{reg} = &\sum_{(u,i)\in\mathcal{O}} (r_{ui} - \frac{1}{2} - \frac{1}{2B}f_u^T h_i))^2 \\ &+ \lambda(\|\sum_u f_u\|^2 + \|\sum_i h_i\|^2). \quad (5)\end{aligned}$$

A widely used approach to obtain approximate solutions to the above discrete optimization problem is to relax the space of solution to be real values and thus enables the application of the continuous optimization techniques to solve the problem. To this end, we first relax the space of solution to be real vectors in $[-1,1]^B$ and then we will round the real-valued solutions into $\{\pm 1\}^B$. The details of rounding are discussed in Section 3.3.

It is also interesting to note that the above formulation also reveals a nice connection between learning binary codes and the matrix factorization approaches that are widely applied in collaborative filtering. In particular, the first term in (5) is the objective function that factorizes the linearly transformed matrix of observed ratings to find low-dimensional representations for users and items. The second term is different from the usual ℓ_2 regularization used in traditional matrix factorization since we would like the binary codes to balanced rather than close to zero in this case.

Given the relaxed problem, the partial derivatives of the objective function $\mathcal{L}_{reg}$ with respect to f_u and h_i can be expressed as follows:

$$\frac{\partial \mathcal{L}_{reg}}{\partial f_u} = -\frac{1}{B}\sum_{i\in\mathcal{O}_u}(r_{ui} - \frac{1}{2} - \frac{1}{2B}f_u^T h_i)h_i + 2\lambda\sum_{u'} f_{u'},$$

$$\frac{\partial \mathcal{L}_{reg}}{\partial h_i} = -\frac{1}{B}\sum_{u\in\mathcal{O}_i}(r_{ui} - \frac{1}{2} - \frac{1}{2B}f_u^T h_i)f_u + 2\lambda\sum_{i'} h_{i'}.$$

The relaxed problem can be solved by methods such as LBFGS [25] and stochastic gradient descent.

3.3 Obtaining Binary Codes

After solving the relaxed optimization problem defined in Equation (5), we obtain real-valued vectors $\tilde{f}_u$ and $\tilde{h}_i \in [-1,1]^B$ for each user u and item i. In this section, we propose two methods to obtain binary codes f_u and $h_i \in \{\pm 1\}^B$ from these real-valued vectors.

3.3.1 Rounding to Closest Binary Codes

A straightforward method is to find binary vectors f_u and $h_i \in \{\pm 1\}^B$ that are closest to $\tilde{f}_u$ and $\tilde{h}_i$. Specifically, we seek to optimize the following objective function to obtain f_u for all $u \in \mathcal{U}$:

$$\min_{f_u \in \{\pm 1\}^B} \sum_u \|f_u - \tilde{f}_u\|^2 \quad (6)$$

subject to $\sum_u f_u = 0$. Similarly, we can obtain h_i for all item $i \in \mathcal{I}$ by:

$$\min_{h_i \in \{\pm 1\}^B} \sum_i \|h_i - \tilde{h}_i\|^2 \quad (7)$$

subject to $\sum_u h_i = 0$.

It turns out that the optimization problems defined in Equation (6) and Equation (7) have the following solution:

$$f_u^{(k)} = \begin{cases} 1, & \tilde{f}_u^{(k)} > \mathrm{median}(\tilde{f}_u^{(k)} : u \in \mathcal{U}), \\ -1, & \text{Otherwise,}\end{cases}$$

and

$$h_i^{(k)} = \begin{cases} 1, & \tilde{h}_i^{(k)} > \mathrm{median}(\tilde{h}_i^{(k)} : i \in \mathcal{I}), \\ -1, & \text{Otherwise,}\end{cases}$$

where $\mathrm{median}(\cdot)$ represents the median of a set of real numbers.

3.3.2 Improved Rounding by Orthogonal Transformations

Another method to obtain the binary codes from the relaxed solution $\tilde{f}_u$ and $\tilde{h}_i$ makes use of the structure of the solutions to the relaxed optimization problem. Similar ideas have been investigated for spectral clustering [22] and we extend the idea to the context of learning binary codes. First, we observe that if $\tilde{f}_u$ and $\tilde{h}_i$ are optimal solutions for (5), then $Q\tilde{f}_u$ and $Q\tilde{h}_i$ are also optimal solutions achieving the same value of the objective function for an arbitrary orthogonal matrix $Q \in \mathbb{R}^{B\times B}$, i.e., $Q^T Q = I$. This observation can be proved as follows:

$$\begin{aligned}&\mathcal{L}_{reg}(Q\tilde{f}_u, Q\tilde{h}_i) \\ &= \sum_{(u,i)\in\mathcal{O}} (r_{ui} - \frac{1}{2} - \frac{1}{2B}(Q\tilde{f}_u)^T(Q\tilde{h}_i))^2 \\ &+ \lambda(\|\sum_u (Q\tilde{f}_u)\|^2 + \|\sum_i (Q\tilde{h}_i)\|^2) \\ &= \sum_{(u,i)\in\mathcal{O}} (r_{ui} - \frac{1}{2} - \frac{1}{2B}\tilde{f}_u^T\tilde{h}_i)^2 + \lambda(\|\sum_u \tilde{f}_u\|^2 + \|\sum_i \tilde{h}_i\|^2) \\ &= \mathcal{L}_{reg}(\tilde{f}_u, \tilde{h}_i),\end{aligned}$$

where the second equation utilizes the fact the Q is an orthogonal matrix. The above observation shows that applying orthogonal transformations to an optimal solution of relaxed optimization problem does not change the value of the objective function, which motives the following method to obtain binary codes from the relaxed solution:

$$\min_{Q, f_u, h_i \in \{\pm 1\}^B} \sum_u \|f_u - Q\tilde{f}_u\|^2 + \sum_i \|h_i - Q\tilde{h}_i\|^2 \quad (8)$$

subject to:

$$\sum_u f_u = 0, \quad \sum_i h_i = 0, \quad Q^T Q = I.$$

Intuitively, instead of directly finding binary codes that are close to the relaxed solutions, we seek binary codes that are close to some orthogonal transformation of the relaxed solutions. Introducing the orthogonal transformation Q not only preserves the optimality of the relaxed solutions but provides us more flexibility to obtain better binary codes.

The optimization problem defined in Equation (8) can be solved by minimizing with respect to f_u, h_i and Q alternatively.

Optimization with respect to f_u and h_i. Specifically, we first fix the orthogonal transformation Q and optimizing with respect to f_u and h_i:

$$\min_{f_u, h_i \in \{\pm 1\}^B} \sum_u \|f_u - Q\tilde{f}_u\|^2 + \sum_i \|h_i - Q\tilde{h}_i\|^2$$

subject to $\sum_u f_u = 0, \sum_i h_i = 0$. The solution can be expressed as follows:

$$f_u^{(k)} = \begin{cases} 1, & (Q\tilde{f}_u)^{(k)} > \text{median}((Q\tilde{f}_u)^{(k)} : u \in \mathcal{U}), \\ -1, & \text{Otherwise,} \end{cases}$$

and

$$h_i^{(k)} = \begin{cases} 1, & (Q\tilde{h}_i)^{(k)} > \text{median}((Q\tilde{h}_i)^{(k)} : i \in \mathcal{I}), \\ -1, & \text{Otherwise} \end{cases}$$

where $(Q\tilde{f}_u)^{(k)}$ represents the k-th element of the transformed vector $Q\tilde{f}_u$.

Optimization with Respect to Q. In this case, we fix f_u and h_i for all $u \in \mathcal{U}$ and $i \in \mathcal{I}$. Then we solve the following optimization problem to update the orthogonal transformation Q:

$$\min_{Q \in \mathbb{R}^{B \times B}} L(Q) = \sum_u \|f_u - Q\tilde{f}_u\|^2 + \sum_i \|h_i - Q\tilde{h}_i\|^2$$
$$= \|F - Q\tilde{F}\|_F^2 + \|H - Q\tilde{H}\|_F^2 \quad (9)$$

subject to the constraint $Q^T Q = I$, where $F = [f_1, \ldots, f_{|\mathcal{U}|}]$, $\tilde{F} = [\tilde{f}_1, \ldots, \tilde{f}_{|\mathcal{U}|}]$, $H = [h_1, \ldots, h_{|\mathcal{I}|}]$ and $\tilde{H} = [\tilde{h}_1, \ldots, \tilde{h}_{|\mathcal{I}|}]$. $\|\cdot\|_F$ indicates the Frobenius norm. The following theorem enables us to solve the optimization problem efficiently by singular value decomposition:

THEOREM 1. *Let UDV^T be the singular value decomposition of the matrix $(F\tilde{F}^T + H\tilde{H}^T)$. Then, $Q = UV^T$ minimizes the objective function defined in Equation (9).*

PROOF. First notice that the objective function $L(Q) = \|F\|^2 + \|\tilde{F}\|^2 - \text{trace}(F\tilde{F}^T Q^T) + \|H\|^2 + \|\tilde{H}\|^2 - \text{trace}(H\tilde{H}^T Q^T)$. Therefore, the optimization problem is equivalent to maximizing the following function subject to the orthogonality constraint $Q^T Q = I$:

$$\text{trace}(F\tilde{F}^T Q^T) + \text{trace}(H\tilde{H}^T Q^T) = \text{trace}((F\tilde{F}^T + H\tilde{H}^T)Q^T).$$

Let us consider the Lagrange

$$L(Q, \Lambda) = \text{trace}((F\tilde{F}^T + H\tilde{H}^T)Q^T) - \frac{1}{2}\text{trace}(\Lambda(Q^T Q - I)),$$

where Λ is a symmetric matrix. By taking the gradient with respect to Q, we have

$$(F\tilde{F}^T + H\tilde{H}^T) - \Lambda Q = 0,$$

Thus, $\Lambda = (F\tilde{F}^T + H\tilde{H}^T)Q^T = UDV^T Q^T$, which implies that $\Lambda^2 = UD^2U^T$. Hence, $\Lambda = UDU^T$. Substituting it into the above equation, we have $Q = UD^{-1}U^T UDV^T = UV^T$. □

In general, we perform the above two steps alternatively until the solution converges and obtain the binary codes f_u and h_i.

4. EXPERIMENTS

In this section, we describe the experiments conducted to evaluate the proposed method for learning binary codes. For the sake of simplicity, we denote the proposed method with squared loss and pairwise loss defined in Equation (3) and Equation (4) by CFCodeReg and CFCodePair, respectively.

4.1 Evaluation Metrics

We apply two evaluation metrics to evaluate the performance of CFCodeReg and CFCodePair. Our goal is to evaluate whether the obtained binary codes can accurately preserve the preferences of users to items. The evaluation metrics are described as follows:

- **Discounted Cumulative Gain (DCG).** DCG [10] is widely used to evaluate the quality of rankings. In order to compute DCG, we sort the items according to the Hamming distance between their binary codes to the binary codes for the user. The DCG value of a ranking list is calculated by the following equation:

$$\text{DCG@n} = \sum_{i=1}^{n} \frac{2^{r_i} - 1}{\log(i+1)},$$

where r_i is the rating assigned by a user to the i-th item in the ranking list. DCG mainly focuses on evaluating whether the obtained binary codes can accurately preserve the relative orders of the of items rated by each user. We use DCG@5 as a evaluation metric in our experiments. When computing DCG, we only consider the observed ratings in the test set.

In order to evaluate the performance of using binary codes for recommending top-K items to users, we apply the following evaluation metrics:

- **Precision:** For each user u, we retrieve the set of items S_u with binary codes within Hamming distance 3 to the binary codes of the user. The precision is defined as the fraction of relevant items in S_u. Formally,

$$\text{Prec} = \frac{|\{i : i \in S_u \text{ and item } i \text{ is relevant to user } u\}|}{|S_u|}.$$

In our experiments, all items with ratings that are greater than or equal to 5 are regarded as relevant items of users.

4.2 Data Sets

We used three data sets to evaluate the performance of CFCodeReg and CFCodePair, MovieLens, EachMovie and Netflix with their statistics summarized in Table 1.

- The MovieLens[1] data set contains 3900 movies, 6040 users and about 1 million ratings. In this data set, about 4% of the user-movie dyads are observed. The ratings are integers ranging from 1 (bad) to 5 (good).
- The EachMovie data set, collected by HP/Compaq Research, contains about 2.8 million ratings for 1628 movies by 72,916 users. The ratings are integers ranging from 1 to 6.

[1]http://www.grouplens.org/node/73

Table 1: Statistics for Data Sets

Dataset	No. Users	No. Items	No. Ratings
MovieLens	6040	3900	1,000,209
EachMovie	72,916	1628	2,811,983
Netflix	480,189	17,770	104,706,033

- The Netflix[2] is one of the largest test bed for collaborative filtering. It contains over 100 million ratings and was split into one training and one test subsets. The training set consists of 100,480,507 ratings for 17,770 movies by 480,189 users. The test set contains about 2.8 million ratings. All the ratings are ranged from 1 to 5.

We split the three data sets into training and test sets as follows: for Movielens and EachMovie, we randomly sample 80% ratings for each user as the training set and the rest 20% is used as the test set. These two data sets are very sparse and thus a lot of ratings are not observed, which may lead to biased evaluation results for precision. Therefore, we also construct a dense data set from the netflix data as follows: We first select 5000 items with the most ratings and then sample 10000 users with at least 100 ratings to construct a relatively dense data set. For this data set, we sample 20% ratings for each users as the training set and the rest ratings are used as the test set. For all three data sets, we generate five independent splits and report the averaged performance in our evaluations. Moreover, we exclude all ratings in the training set and use only the ratings in the test set when computing the evaluation metrics.

4.3 Comparison of Rounding Methods

In Section 3.3, we describe two methods for obtaining binary codes from the approximate real-valued solutions. We now compare the performance of these methods. To this end, we denote the method that rounding to closest binary codes described in Section 3.3.1 as Closest and the method using orthogonal transformation described in Section 3.3.2 by OrthTrans. We apply CFCodeReg and CFCodePair with binary codes of length 10 to all the three data sets and compare the binary codes obtained by Closest and OrthTrans. We report the performance on three data sets measured by precision in Figure 1. From Figure 1, we can see that the binary codes obtained by OrthTrans outperform the corresponding binary codes obtained by Closest, which suggests that the OrthTrans can obtain better approximations for binary codes. Intuitively, OrthTrans is more flexible than Closest through introducing the orthogonal transformation and thus enable us to obtain better approximation. We will use OrthTrans to obtain binary codes in the rest of our evaluations.

4.4 General Performance Results

4.4.1 Baseline Alternative Methods

We compare CFCodeReg and CFCodePair to the following baselines:

- **Spectral Hashing [21] (SH):** This method has been shown to be effective to learning binary codes. Specifically, it formulates the problem of learning binary codes as an eigenvalue problem for the similarity graph. In particular, the training ratings are viewed as the similarities between users and items and a bipartite graph is constructed between nodes representing users and items [23]. Then, spectral hashing is applied to obtain binary codes for users and items based on this graph.

[2]http://www.netflixprize.com/

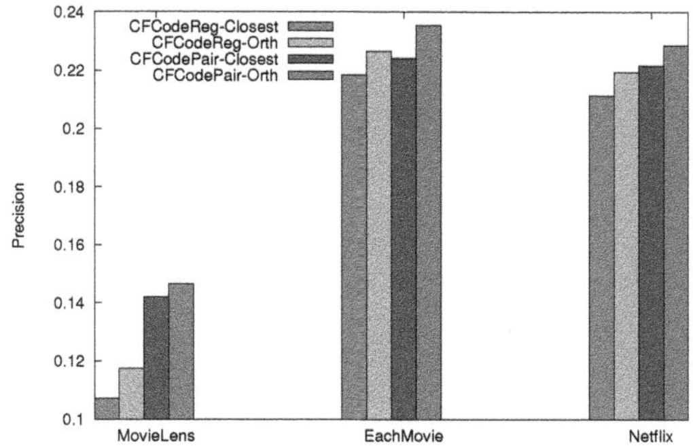

Figure 1: Performance of two rounding methods on MovieLens, EachMovie and Netflix data sets

- **BinMF:** In this baseline, we first apply low-rank matrix factorization to fit the training ratings and obtain low dimensional real-valued latent profiles for users and items. Then, we binarize these vectors to obtain binary codes through the orthogonal transformations described in Section 3.3.2 since it archives better performance as a rounding method.

4.4.2 Performance Analysis

We apply the proposed CFCodeReg and CFCodePair to all three data sets and compare the obtained binary codes to the two baselines described in Section 4.4.1. Specifically, we plot the performance measured by DCG and precision with respect to the length of the binary codes in Figure 2, Figure 3 and Figure 4 for MoveiLens, EachMovie and Netflix data sets, respectively.

We can observe that DCG and precision of both CFCodeReg and CFCodePair increase in most cases with larger length of binary codes. Hence, the performance of CFCodeReg and CFCodePair improves when the number of bits increases. Therefore, we conclude that both methods can utilize the available bits to preserve the preference of users more accurately. We can also observe from the figures that the binary codes obtained by CFCodeReg and CFCodePair outperform other baselines in terms of DCG. Thus, the proposed method can better preserve the relative orders between items according to the preference of users. Moreover, the improvement over baselines in terms of precision indicates that the binary codes obtained by CFCodeReg and CFCodePair can be used to recommend interesting items to users accurately.

Comparing the performance of CFCodeReg and CFCodePair, we can find that CFCodePair outperforms CFCodeReg in most cases, which suggests that the pairwise loss function is more suitable for learning binary codes. This is because the pairwise loss function emphasis more on the orders between different items rather than their absolute ratings, which makes it a more reasonable loss function in the ranking scenario for collaborative filtering.

Another interesting observation is that SH does not work very well in our case. Specifically, it overfits the training data very quickly when the length of binary codes increases.

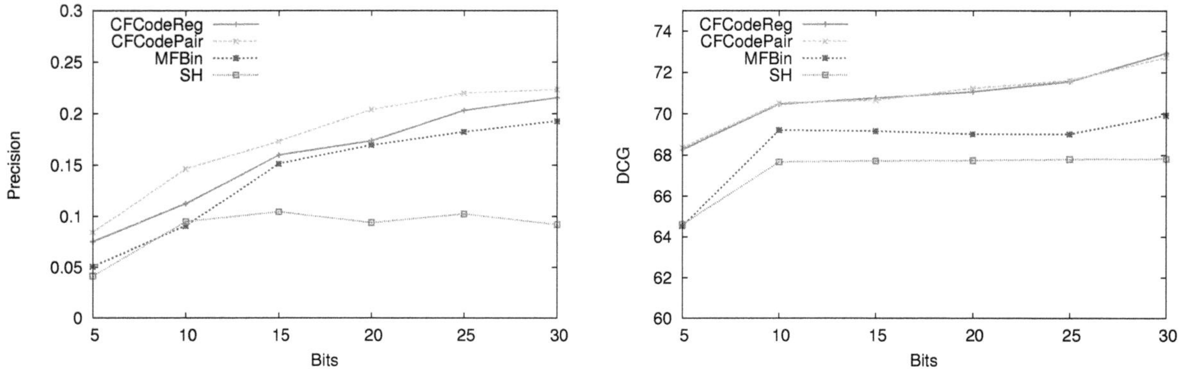

(a) Precision (b) DCG

Figure 2: Performance with respect to the length of binary codes on Movielens data set

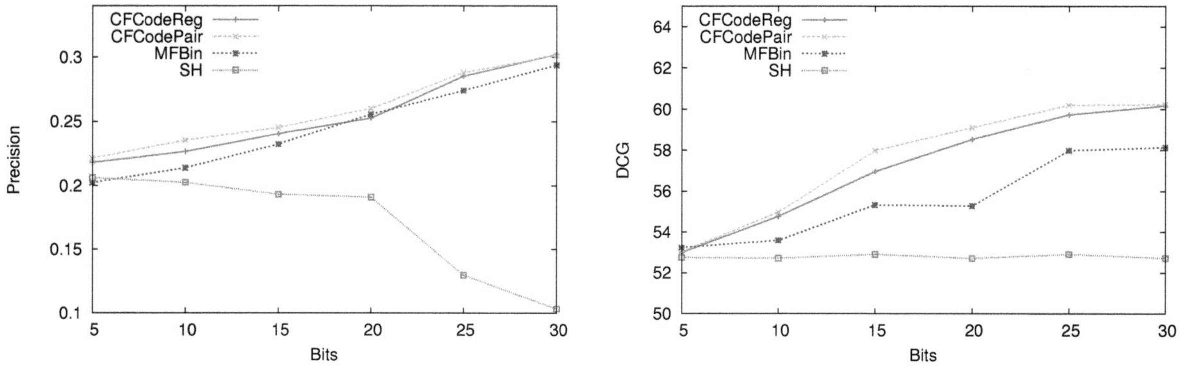

(a) Precision (b) DCG

Figure 3: Performance with respect to the length of binary codes on EachMoive data set

By observing the results, we find that SH usually fits the training data very well. However, it frequently assign similar distances for users and items whose ratings are not in the training set. Therefore, its performance over the test set is reduced. In order to further investigate this point, we vary the length of binary codes and plot the variance of Hamming distances on unobserved ratings for binary codes generated by SH and CFCodeReg in Figure 5. We can observe that the variances produced by SH decrease when the length of binary codes grows. On the other hand, the variance generated by CFCodeReg are generally much higher than those generated by SH, which indicates that CFCodeReg generates more diverse codes when the length of binary codes increases. We think the reason is that SH usually fits the observed similarities while fails to predict the unobserved ones. This observation verifies that CFCodeReg can not only fit the observed preferences very well, but it also can predict the unobserved preference accurately.

4.4.3 *Impact of Parameters*

We investigate the impact of the regularization parameter λ for the propose methods. To this end, we report the performance of CFCodeReg and CFCodePair measured by DCG with respect to different values of λ in Figure 6. We only show the results on the MovieLens data set due to the lack of space. From Figure 6, we can observe that the performance measured by DCG first increases and then decreases in most cases, which indicates that a good value of λ can enhance the learning process and thus improves the accuracy of learnt binary codes. In general, the value of λ can be determined by *cross validation*.

In our experiments, the relaxed optimization problem of Equation (5) is solved by LBFGS, which is an effective iterative solver for optimization problems. In Figure 7, we present the performance measured by DCG with respect to the number of iterations on MovieLens data set. We can observe from Figure 7 that the performance measured by DCG both training and test set increases when the number of iterations grows. The training process usually converges in about one hundred iterations.

4.4.4 *Compare with Low-rank Matrix Factorizations*

It is also interesting to compare CFCodeReg to the low-rank matrix factorization method that is widely exploited for collaborative filtering. Since CFCodeReg is restricted to use binary codes in order to facilitate fast search, it can be viewed as an approximation of the low-rank factorization methods. Thus, it is natural to investigate how close CFCodeReg can approximate the performance of low-rank matrix factorization. To this end, we vary to length of the binary codes from 10 to 110 and report the performance measured by DCG on MovieLens data set in Figure 8. We also report the performance of low-rank matrix factorizations when varying the rank of the factorization. We can see that the performance of CFCodeReg increases in general when the length of the binary codes grows and become very close to the performance of low-rank matrix factorizations. On the other hand, the performance of low-rank matrix factorizations is slightly reduced when the number of latent dimensions increases which is generally explained by the overfitting of the training data.

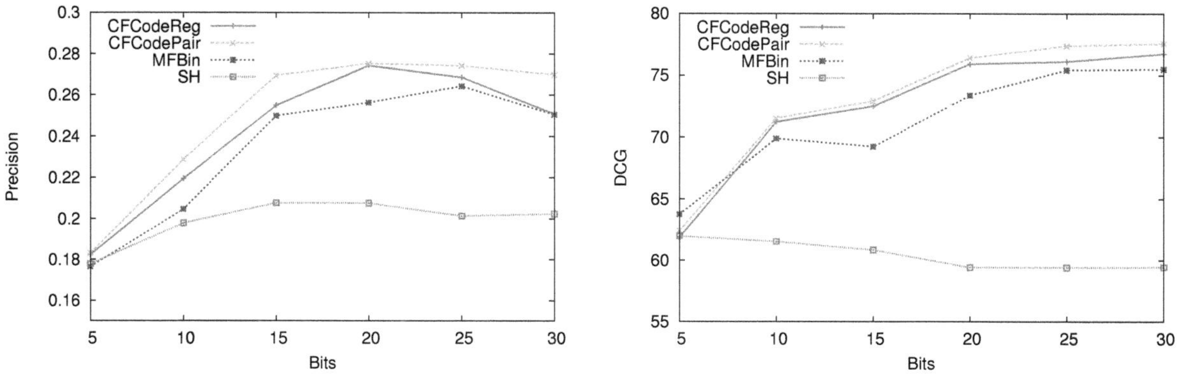

(a) Precision (b) DCG

Figure 4: Performance with respect to the length of binary codes on Netflix data set

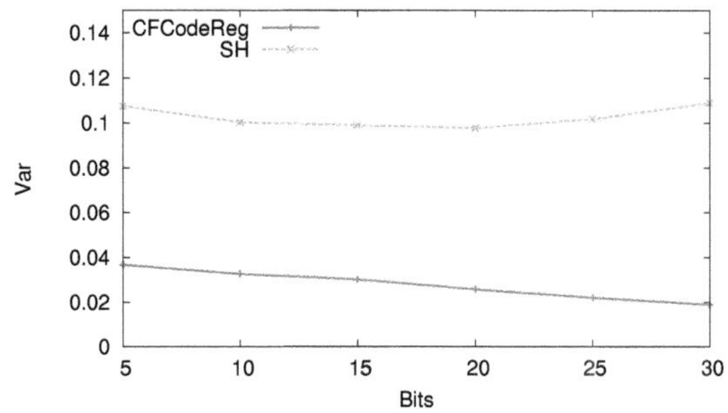

Figure 5: Variance of predicted similarity on unknown ratings with respect to the length of binary codes

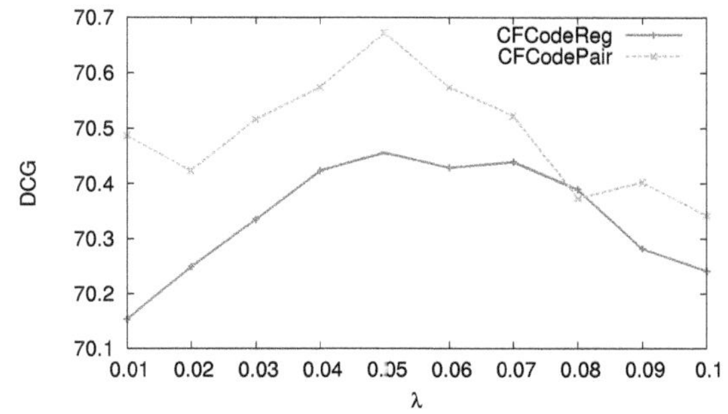

Figure 6: Performance measured by DCG with respect to the regularization parameter λ on MovieLens data set

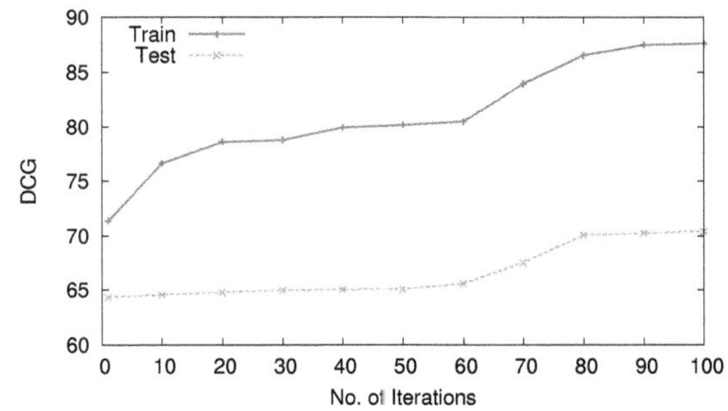

Figure 7: Performance measured by DCG with respect to the number of iterations on MovieLens data set

4.5 Recommendation Efficiency

We also compare the efficiency of obtaining top-K recommendations. In particular, for MF we compute the predicted scores for every item for a given user and then select top-K items with the highest scores. For CFCodeReg, we retrieve items with binary codes within Hamming distance 3 to the binary codes of the user. We measure efficiency by the total time required to generate recommendations for all users. To this end, we run the recommendation program for 10 times and report the average running time. The evaluation is conducted on a server with 16G main memory and use one of its eight 2.5GHz cores. On MovieLens data set, CFCodeReg takes 0.586 seconds to process all users while MF takes 64.9 seconds. The significant efficiency improvement is expected and can be explained by the fact that CFCodeReg only goes through a small fraction of items while MF computes the prediction for all items. This confirms that recommendation efficiency can be significantly improved by utilizing binary codes.

5. CONCLUDING REMARKS

In this paper, we address the problem of learning binary codes that preserves the preferences of users to items. In particular, we propose a framework that constructs binary codes such that the Hamming distances of a user and her preferred items are small. By applying two loss functions, the problem is formulated as a discrete optimization problem defined on the training ratings data set. It turns out that the resulting optimization problem can be solving approximately by transforming the objective function and relaxing the variables to real values. Moreover, we study two methods to obtain the binary codes from the real-valued approximations. Experiments on three data sets show that the proposed methods outperform several baselines and thus and can preserve the preference of users more accurately.

For future research directions, we plan to further investigate other methods for solving the discrete problem more accurately. Specifically, we can investigate how to apply semidefinite programming for relaxing the original problem. Another direction is to study how to learn binary codes incrementally. In particular, we would like to construct the binary codes bit by bit in a sequential and incremental manner. It has the advantage that new bits of binary codes can be introduced to improve the accuracy without re-training all of the bits. Finally, the problem of incorporating features for users and items, such as demographical features for users and descriptions of items, to learn the binary codes can be also very interesting.

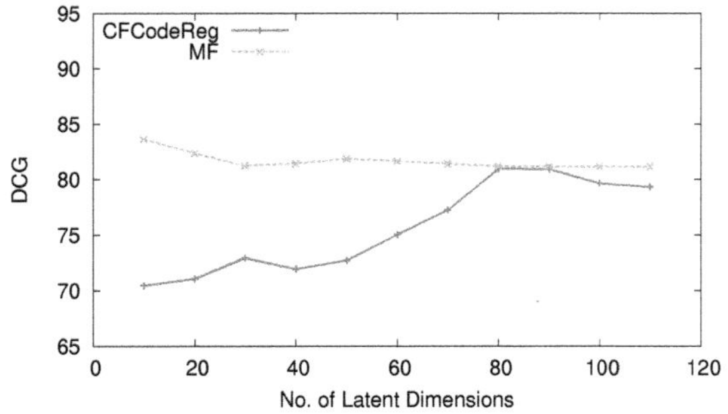

Figure 8: Comparison of low-rank matrix factorization and CFCodeReg on MovieLens data set

6. ACKNOWLEDGEMENT

Part of the work is supported by NSF IIS-1116886, NSF IIS-1049694 and NSFC 61129001/F010403.

7. REFERENCES

[1] G. Adomavicius and a. Tuzhilin. Toward the next generation of recommender systems: a survey of the state-of-the-art and possible extensions. *IEEE Transactions on Knowledge and Data Engineering*, 17(6):734–749, June 2005.

[2] D. Agarwal, B. Chen, and P. Elango. Fast online learning through offline initialization for time-sensitive recommendation. In *Proceedings of the 16th ACM SIGKDD international conference on Knowledge discovery and data mining*, pages 703–712. ACM, 2010.

[3] Y. Bachrach and R. Herbrich. Fingerprinting Ratings For Collaborative Filtering Theoretical and Empirical Analysis. *String Processing and Information Retrieval*, pages 25–36, 2010.

[4] Y. Bachrach, E. Porat, and J. Rosenschein. Sketching techniques for collaborative filtering. In *Proceedings of the 21st international joint conference on Artifical intelligence*, pages 2016–2021. Morgan Kaufmann Publishers Inc., 2009.

[5] A. S. Das, M. Datar, A. Garg, and S. Rajaram. Google news personalization: scalable online collaborative filtering. In *Proceedings of the 16th international conference on World Wide Web - WWW '07*, page 271, New York, New York, USA, 2007. ACM Press.

[6] M. Datar, N. Immorlica, P. Indyk, and V. S. Mirrokni. Locality-sensitive hashing scheme based on p-stable distributions. In *Proceedings of the twentieth annual symposium on Computational geometry - SCG '04*, page 253, New York, New York, USA, 2004. ACM Press.

[7] J. He and W. Liu. Scalable similarity search with optimized kernel hashing. *Proceedings of the 16th ACM SIGKDD*, pages 1129–1138, 2010.

[8] P. Indyk and R. Motwani. Approximate nearest neighbors: towards removing the curse of dimensionality. In *Proceedings of the thirtieth annual ACM symposium on Theory of computing - STOC '98*, pages 604–613, New York, New York, USA, 1998. ACM Press.

[9] H. Jégou, T. Furon, and J.-J. Fuchs. Anti-sparse coding for approximate nearest neighbor search. *Arxiv preprint arXiv:1110.3767*, (October):577–580, Oct. 2011.

[10] J. Kekäläinen. Binary and graded relevance in IR evaluations - Comparison of the effects on ranking of IR systems. *Information Processing and Management*, 41:1019–1033, 2005.

[11] Y. Koren. Factor in the neighbors: Scalable and accurate collaborative filtering. *ACM Transactions on Knowledge Discovery from Data (TKDD)*, 4(1):1–24, 2010.

[12] B. Kulis and T. Darrell. Learning to hash with binary reconstructive embeddings. *Proceedings of Advances in Neural Information Processing Systems*, 2009.

[13] W. Liu, J. Wang, S. Kumar, and S. Chang. Hashing with Graphs. In *Proceedings of the 28th International Conference on Machine Learning*, 2011.

[14] M. Norouzi and D. Fleet. Minimal Loss Hashing for Compact Binary Codes. In *Proceedings of the 28th International Conference on Machine Learning*, volume 1, 2011.

[15] A. Paterek. Improving regularized singular value decomposition for collaborative filtering. In *Proceedings of KDD Cup and Workshop*, volume 2007, pages 5–8. Citeseer, 2007.

[16] S. Rendle, C. Freudenthaler, and L. Schmidt-Thieme. Factorizing personalized Markov chains for next-basket recommendation. *Proceedings of the 19th international conference on World wide web - WWW '10*, page 811, 2010.

[17] R. Salakhutdinov and G. Hinton. Semantic hashing. *International Journal of Approximate Reasoning*, 50(7):969–978, July 2009.

[18] G. Shakhnarovich, P. Viola, and T. Darrell. Fast pose estimation with parameter-sensitive hashing. In *Proceedings Ninth IEEE International Conference on Computer Vision*, pages 750–757 vol.2. IEEE, 2003.

[19] X. Su and T. M. Khoshgoftaar. A Survey of Collaborative Filtering Techniques. *Advances in Artificial Intelligence*, 2009(Section 3):1–20, 2009.

[20] J. Wang and S. Kumar. Sequential projection learning for hashing with compact codes. *International Conference on Machine Learning*, 2010.

[21] Y. Weiss, A. Torralba, and R. Fergus. Spectral hashing. In *Neural Information Processing Systems*, number 1, pages 1–8, 2008.

[22] S. X. Yu and J. Shi. Multiclass spectral clustering. In *Proceedings Ninth IEEE International Conference on Computer Vision*, number 0, pages 313–319 vol.1, Washington, DC, USA, 2003. IEEE.

[23] D. Zhang, J. Wang, D. Cai, and J. Lu. Laplacian co-hashing of terms and documents. *Advances in Information Retrieval*, pages 577–580, 2010.

[24] D. Zhang, J. Wang, D. Cai, and J. Lu. Self-taught hashing for fast similarity search. In *Proceeding of the 33rd international ACM SIGIR conference on Research and development in information retrieval*, pages 18–25. ACM, 2010.

[25] C. Zhu, R. H. Byrd, P. Lu, and J. Nocedal. Algorithm 778: L-BFGS-B: Fortran subroutines for large-scale bound-constrained optimization. *ACM Transactions on Mathematical Software*, 23(4):550–560, Dec. 1997.

Low Rank Modeling of Signed Networks

Cho-Jui Hsieh
Dept. of Computer Science
University of Texas at Austin
Austin, TX 78712-1188, USA
cjhsieh@cs.utexas.edu

Kai-Yang Chiang
Dept. of Computer Science
University of Texas at Austin
Austin, TX 78712-1188, USA
kychiang@cs.utexas.edu

Inderjit S. Dhillon
Dept. of Computer Science
University of Texas at Austin
Austin, TX 78712-1188, USA
inderjit@cs.utexas.edu

ABSTRACT

Trust networks, where people leave trust and distrust feedback, are becoming increasingly common. These networks may be regarded as signed graphs, where a positive edge weight captures the degree of trust while a negative edge weight captures the degree of distrust. Analysis of such signed networks has become an increasingly important research topic. One important analysis task is that of sign inference, i.e., infer unknown (or future) trust or distrust relationships given a partially observed signed network. Most state-of-the-art approaches consider the notion of structural balance in signed networks, building inference algorithms based on information about links, triads, and cycles in the network. In this paper, we first show that the notion of weak structural balance in signed networks naturally leads to a global low-rank model for the network. Under such a model, the sign inference problem can be formulated as a low-rank matrix completion problem. We show that we can perfectly recover missing relationships, under certain conditions, using state-of-the-art matrix completion algorithms. We also propose the use of a low-rank matrix factorization approach with generalized loss functions as a practical method for sign inference — this approach yields high accuracy while being scalable to large signed networks, for instance, we show that this analysis can be performed on a synthetic graph with 1.1 million nodes and 120 million edges in 10 minutes. We further show that the low-rank model can be used for other analysis tasks on signed networks, such as user segmentation through signed graph clustering, with theoretical guarantees. Experiments on synthetic as well as real data show that our low rank model substantially improves accuracy of sign inference as well as clustering. As an example, on the largest real dataset available to us (Epinions data with 130K nodes and 840K edges), our matrix factorization approach yields 94.6% accuracy on the sign inference task as compared to 90.8% accuracy using a state-of-the-art cycle-based method — moreover, our method runs in 40 seconds as compared to 10,000 seconds for the cycle-based method.

Categories and Subject Descriptors

H.2.8 [**Database Management**]: Database Applications—*Data Mining*

Keywords

Signed Networks, Structural Balance, Low Rank Model

1. INTRODUCTION

Social network analysis has received a lot of attention recently. Traditionally, online networks such as Facebook or World Wide Web can be viewed as graphs, with nodes representing entities, and edges representing relationships between entities. Recently, trust networks have also become increasingly common where two opposite kinds of relationships exist between entities. For example, online review websites such as Epinions allow users to either like or dislike others' reviews. Such networks can be modeled as *signed networks*, where edge weights are $+1$ or -1, representing positive or negative relationships respectively.

Perhaps the most basic yet significant belief in signed networks is *structural balance* [11, 4]. Structural balance states that people in signed networks tend to follow patterns such as "an enemy of my friend is my enemy" and "an enemy of my enemy is my friend", and so on [4]. It is important to note that since balance notion applies only to signed networks, therefore, algorithms for signed networks can be somewhat different from algorithms for unsigned networks. Structural balance has been shown to be useful for analysis tasks for signed networks. For instance, the *sign inference problem*, which aims to infer the unknown relationship between two entities, can be achieved by learning from balance information of signed networks [17, 5]. Nevertheless, these state-of-the-art methods for sign inference problem mainly consider structural balance, while a more general notion - weak balance [7] - is not taken into account. Therefore, it is natural to ask what can be further inferred from weak balance.

In this paper, we propose a *low rank model* by observing that complete weakly balanced networks have a low-rank structure. Therefore, many analysis tasks such as sign inference and clustering can be posed as low-rank matrix completion. The advantages of taking a matrix completion approach are as follows. First, many matrix completion algorithms provide theoretical recovery guarantees under certain conditions [19, 12]. Moreover, many algorithms such as Alternating Least Squares (ALS) and Stochastic Gradient Descent (SGD) can efficiently find effective solutions for problems with billions of nonzero entries [14]. We will empirically demonstrate that our proposed low rank model is both accurate and scalable in many applications.

We summarize the contributions of this paper:

- We explore a new model for signed networks - the low rank model - from both theoretical and practical points of view. We show that the low-rank structure arises naturally from weak balance theory. In practice, we show that real-life signed networks tend to have low-rank structure, so it is natural to apply the low rank model to real datasets.
- We show that the sign inference problem can be formulated as a low-rank matrix completion problem. Under certain conditions, we prove that matrix completion can perfectly recover missing links. We also apply matrix factorization algorithms to sign inference problems, and these turn out to be much more accurate and efficient than other inference methods.
- We show that our low rank model can be used for clustering. Our algorithm first infers missing values using matrix completion, and then performs the clustering, thus enabling us to get guarantees for clustering under certain conditions. This theoretical guarantee cannot be achieved by other spectral methods [15].

The paper is organized as follows. In Section 2, we review some recent work related to this paper. In Section 3, we propose our low rank model, and show that the sign inference problem can be modeled as a low-rank matrix completion problem. We present two approaches; matrix completion and matrix factorization. In Section 4, we show how to do clustering using the low rank model. In Section 5, we conduct experiments which convincingly demonstrate that our low rank model improves sign inference accuracy as well as clustering results. Finally, we present our conclusions in Section 6.

2. RELATED WORK

Signed network analysis has a rich history dating back to the 1950s — the notion of structural balance was formulated and analyzed by Harary and Carwright [11, 4], who formally defined balanced triads and proved global structural results for signed balanced networks (stated as Theorem 1 in Section 3). Davis [7] further generalized the notion of balance to weak balance, by allowing triads where all edges are negative. In Section 3, we will elaborate on weak balance and show that it naturally leads to our proposed low-rank model.

An important analysis task on signed networks is the sign inference problem. This problem was first considered by Guha et al.[9]. More recently, Kunegis et al.[15, 16] reconsidered this problem by using varied similarity functions and kernels such as matrix exponential and signed Laplacian, on the signed link structure of the network. Leskovec et al.[17] proposed a machine learning formulation of this problem, arguing that learning from only local triangular structure of edges can achieve high accuracy. Chiang et al.[5] generalized [17] by showing that longer cycles in the signed network reveal balance information in the network — using these additional "features" for learning led to an improvement in inference accuracy. Our modeling approach in this paper is distinct from existing work, as we first show that the global viewpoint of structural balance (as opposed to the local triad structure) naturally leads to a low-rank model for the network, and then show that the sign inference problem may be regarded as a low-rank matrix completion problem. Our approach is much more scalable than previous approaches, and leads to higher inference accuracy as well. Some recent work also considers the link inference problem as network completion [10, 13]. The goal in [10, 13] is to reconstruct the underlying (unsigned) network topology given partially observed links and/or nodes. In contrast, the main goal of our work is to infer the (unobserved) signed relationships between all pairs of entities. Moreover, our low-rank matrix completion approach arises from the notion of weak structural balance, which only applies in signed networks.

Clustering or community detection is another important task in network analysis, and has been well studied for unsigned social networks using many varied approaches [18, 8]. However, extending these algorithms to signed networks is not obvious since it has been shown that clustering on signed networks is highly related to (weak) balance theory [11, 4, 7]. Thus several tailored approaches have been proposed for clustering of signed networks [20]. Recently, Kunegis et al.[16] proposed a spectral approach using the so-called "signed" Laplacian, and showed that partitioning signed networks using the signed Laplacian kernel is analogous to considering ratio cut on unsigned networks. Our approach is somewhat similar to [16] in that we also consider the spectra of signed graphs. However, our clustering algorithm proceeds by first completing the underlying graph using low-rank matrix completion, and then performing the clustering. This important difference makes our clustering results much more reliable, especially on graphs where the observed signed relationships are sparse.

Sign inference using our low rank model is closely related to matrix completion problem. In the last five years, there has been substantial research that has studied exact recovery conditions for this problem [19, 3, 2], and algorithms with theoretical guarantees have also been proposed [1, 12]. Matrix factorization is another approximation technique for matrix completion. Though this approach is notoriously hard to analyze, it is very competitive in practice [14]. While the matrix completion problem is considered mostly in collaborative filtering, our low rank model arises naturally from weak balance of signed networks. We will discuss the details of matrix completion and matrix factorization in Section 3.

3. LOW RANK MODELING

In this section, we investigate the structure of signed networks and show that a low-rank structure intuitively emerges when we consider so-called weakly balanced networks. First, we introduce a few preliminaries before going into details.

We will consider a signed network to be a graph $G = (V, E, A)$, where V is the vertex set of size n, E is the edge set of size m, and $A \in \mathbb{R}^{n \times n}$ is the signed adjacency matrix associated with G. The entries of A are as follows:

$$A_{ij} = \begin{cases} 1, & \text{if } i \ \& \ j \text{ trust each other,} \\ -1, & \text{if } i \ \& \ j \text{ distrust each other,} \\ 0, & \text{if relationship of } (i,j) \text{ is unknown (or missing)} \end{cases}$$

For now we restrict ourselves to symmetric relationships, i.e., A is a symmetric matrix, although asymmetric relationships are possible. Note that for us, $A_{ij} = 0$ does not imply no relationship between i and j; it just means we do not currently observe the relationship. We denote the set of known entries by Ω, i.e. $(i,j) \in \Omega$ iff A_{ij} is observed. A network is complete if all entries in A are observed.

We first review some basics of structural balance. A complete network is called (strongly) *balanced* if all triads in the graph have (i) all positive edges or (ii) only one posi-

$$\begin{pmatrix} 1 & 1 & 1 & -1 & -1 & -1 \\ 1 & 1 & 1 & -1 & -1 & -1 \\ 1 & 1 & 1 & -1 & -1 & -1 \\ -1 & -1 & -1 & 1 & -1 & -1 \\ -1 & -1 & -1 & -1 & 1 & 1 \\ -1 & -1 & -1 & -1 & 1 & 1 \end{pmatrix} = \begin{pmatrix} -1.045 & 0.265 & -0.402 \\ -1.045 & 0.265 & -0.402 \\ -1.045 & 0.265 & -0.402 \\ 0.319 & -1.259 & -0.830 \\ 0.919 & 0.607 & -0.541 \\ 0.919 & 0.607 & -0.541 \end{pmatrix} \begin{pmatrix} -1.045 & -1.045 & -1.045 & 0.319 & 0.919 & 0.919 \\ 0.265 & 0.265 & 0.265 & -1.259 & 0.607 & 0.607 \\ -0.402 & -0.402 & -0.402 & -0.830 & -0.541 & -0.541 \end{pmatrix}$$

Figure 1: An illustrative example of low-rank structure of a 3-weakly balanced network. The network can be represented as a product of two rank-3 matrices, which implies that the adjacency matrix has rank no more than 3.

tive edge. With this local definition, it can be shown that complete balanced networks have a special global structure:

Theorem 1 (Global "Strong Balance" Structure [11]) *A complete network is balanced iff all edges are positive, or the vertices can be divided into two different groups such that all edges within the same group are positive, and all edges between the two groups are negative.*

The assumption that strong structural balance exists in a real signed network might be too extreme, so a more relaxed notion of balance is the so-called "weak" structural balance theory. The formal definition of weak balance is as follows:

Definition 1 (Weak Balance for Complete Graphs [7]) *A complete signed network is weakly balanced iff there is no triad in the network that contains two positive edges and one negative edge.*

Similar to Theorem 1, this local definition implies a simple global structure of weakly balanced networks:

Theorem 2 (Global "Weak Balance" Structure [7]) *A complete signed network is weakly balanced iff all edges are positive, or the vertices can be divided into several groups such that within-group edges are positive and between-group edges are negative.*

Thus we can say that a network is k-weakly balanced iff it can be perfectly divided into k groups, $k \in \mathbb{N}$. Note that Theorem 1 can be regarded as a special case of Theorem 2 with $k \leq 2$. We now show that the adjacency matrix A of a complete k-weakly balanced network is low rank. With a suitable reordering of nodes, A can be represented as a block-diagonal matrix where all entries within the diagonal blocks are $+1$'s, and all entries within off-diagonal blocks are all -1's. The following theorem proves that the adjacency matrix of a complete k-weakly balanced network has rank up to k.

Theorem 3 (Low Rank Structure of Signed Networks) *The adjacency matrix A of a complete k-weakly balanced network has rank 1 if $k \leq 2$, and has rank k for all $k > 2$.*

PROOF. Since A is k-weakly balanced, the nodes can be divided into k groups, say $S^{(1)}, S^{(2)}, \ldots, S^{(k)}$. Suppose group $S^{(i)}$ contains nodes $s_1^{(i)}, s_2^{(i)}, \ldots, s_{n_i}^{(i)}$, then the column vectors $A_{:,s_1^{(i)}}, \ldots, A_{:,s_{n_i}^{(i)}}$ are all identical to the following form (after suitable reordering of nodes):

$$\mathbf{b}_i = [-1 \ \cdots \ -1 \underbrace{1 \ \cdots \ 1}_{\text{the } i^{th} \text{ group}} -1 \ \cdots \ -1]^T,$$

and so the column space of A is spanned by $\{\mathbf{b}_1, \ldots, \mathbf{b}_k\}$.

First let us consider $k \leq 2$, i.e., the network is strongly balanced. If $k = 1$, it is easy to see that $\text{rank}(A) = 1$. If $k = 2$, then $\mathbf{b}_1 = -\mathbf{b}_2$. Therefore, $\text{rank}(A)$ is again 1. Now consider $k > 2$. In this case, we argue that $\text{rank}(A) = k$ by showing that $\mathbf{b}_1, \ldots, \mathbf{b}_k$ are linearly independent. We consider the following $k \times k$ square matrix:

$$M = \begin{bmatrix} 1 & -1 & \cdots & -1 & -1 \\ -1 & 1 & \cdots & -1 & -1 \\ \vdots & \vdots & \ddots & \vdots & \vdots \\ -1 & -1 & \cdots & 1 & -1 \\ -1 & -1 & \cdots & -1 & 1 \end{bmatrix}$$

It is obvious that $\mathbf{1} = [1\,1 \cdots 1]^T$ is an eigenvector of M with eigenvalue $-(k-2)$. We can further construct $k-1$ linearly independent eigenvectors all with eigenvalue 2:

$$\mathbf{e}_1 - \mathbf{e}_2, \ \mathbf{e}_1 - \mathbf{e}_3, \ \ldots, \ \mathbf{e}_1 - \mathbf{e}_k,$$

where $\mathbf{e}_i \in \mathbb{R}^k$ is the ith column of the $k \times k$ identity matrix. These $k-1$ eigenvectors are clearly linearly independent. Therefore, $\text{rank}(M) = k$.

From the above we can show that $\text{rank}(A) = k$. Suppose that $\mathbf{b}_1, \ldots, \mathbf{b}_k$ are not linearly independent, then there exists $\alpha_1, \ldots, \alpha_k$, with some $\alpha_i \neq 0$, such that $\sum_{i=1}^k \alpha_i \mathbf{b}_i = 0$. Using this set of α's, it is easy to see that $\sum_{i=1}^k \alpha_i M_{:,i} = 0$, but this contradicts the fact that $\text{rank}(M) = k$. Therefore, $\text{rank}(A) = k$. ☐

Figure 1 is an example of a complete 3-weakly balanced network. As shown, its adjacency matrix can be expressed as a product of two rank-3 matrices, indicating its rank is no more than three. By Theorem 3, we can conclude that $\text{rank}(A) = 3$.

The above reasoning shows that complete weakly balanced graphs are low rank, however, most real networks are not complete graphs. One way to define balance on graphs that are not complete is to try to fill in the unobserved or missing edges(relationships) so that balance is obtained:

Definition 2 (Weak Balance for General Graphs) *A signed network is weakly balanced iff it is possible to add missing edges to the network, with appropriate sign, so that the resulting complete graph is weakly balanced.*

Hence, sign inference in trust networks can be thought of as a low-rank matrix completion problem. Specifically, given a signed network with observed edges A_{ij}, $(i,j) \in \Omega$, we want to find a complete matrix by assigning ± 1 to every unknown entry, such that the resulting complete graph is (nearly) weakly balanced and hence, the completed matrix is low rank. Thus, our missing value estimation problem can be formulated as:

$$\begin{aligned} \text{minimize} \quad & \text{rank}(X) \\ \text{s.t.} \quad & X_{ij} = A_{ij}, \ \forall\, (i,j) \in \Omega, \\ & X_{ij} \in \{\pm 1\}, \ \forall\, (i,j) \notin \Omega. \end{aligned} \tag{1}$$

Once we obtain the minimizer of (1), which we will denote by X^*, we can infer the missing relationship between i and j by simply looking up the sign of the entry X^*_{ij}. However, it is known that solving (1) is NP-hard in general. Recent research on low-rank matrix completion has shown the surprising result that in many cases, problem (1) can be solved to yield the *global* optimal in polynomial time [3]. In the following subsections, we identify such conditions as well as approaches to approximately solve (1) for real-world signed networks.

3.1 Inference via Matrix Completion

One possible approximate solution for (1) can be obtained by dropping the discrete constraints and replacing rank(X) by $\|X\|_*$, where $\|X\|_*$ denotes the trace norm of X, which is the tightest convex relaxation of rank. Thus, a convex relaxation of (1) is:

$$\text{minimize } \|X\|_* \text{ s.t. } X_{ij} = A_{ij},\ \forall\ (i,j) \in \Omega. \quad (2)$$

It turns out that, under certain condition, by solving (2) we can recover the *exact* missing relationships from the underlying complete signed network. This surprising result is the consequence of recent research [3, 2] which has shown that perfect recovery from the observations is possible if the observed entries are uniformly sampled and X^* has high incoherence, which may be defined as follows:

Definition 3 (Incoherence)
An $m \times n$ matrix X^* with singular value decomposition $X^* = USV^T$ is μ-incoherent if

$$\max_{i,j} |U_{ij}| \le \sqrt{\mu}/\sqrt{m} \text{ and } \max_{i,j} |V_{ij}| \le \sqrt{\mu}/\sqrt{n}. \quad (3)$$

Intuitively, higher incoherence (smaller μ) means that large entries of X^* are not concentrated in a small part of the matrix, and so uniform sampling is sufficient to recover X^*. The following theorem summarizes the exact recovery condition that we will use in this paper:

Theorem 4 (Recovery Condition [2])
Let X^* be a matrix of bounded rank ($k = O(1)$) with singular value decomposition $X^* = USV^T$. Assume X^* is μ-incoherent and more than $C\mu^4 n \log^2 n$ entries are uniformly sampled, then with probability at least $1 - n^{-3}$, X^* is the unique optimizer of (2).

Based on Theorem 4, we now show that the notion of incoherence can be connected to the relative sizes of the clusters in signed networks. As a result, by solving (2), we can recover the underlying signed network with high probability if there are no extremely small groups. More precisely, we define the *group imbalance* of a signed network as follows:

Definition 4 (Group Imbalance)
Let X^* be the adjacency matrix of a complete k-weakly balanced network with n nodes, and let $n_1, \ldots, n_k$ be the sizes of the groups. Group imbalance τ of X^* is defined as

$$\tau \equiv \max_{i=1,\ldots,k} n/n_i. \quad (4)$$

By definition, $k \le \tau \le n$. Intuitively, larger group imbalance τ indicates the presence of a very small group, which would make recovery of the underlying network harder (under uniform sampling). For example, consider an extreme scenario that a k-weakly balanced network contains n nodes, with two groups containing only one node. Then the adjacency matrix of this network has group imbalance $\tau = n$ with the following form:

$$X^* = \begin{bmatrix} 1 & \cdots & \cdots & -1 & -1 \\ \vdots & \ddots & & \vdots & \vdots \\ \vdots & & \ddots & -1 & -1 \\ -1 & \cdots & -1 & 1 & -1 \\ -1 & \cdots & -1 & -1 & 1 \end{bmatrix}$$

However, without observing $X^*_{n,n-1}$ or $X^*_{n-1,n}$, it is impossible to determine whether the last two nodes are in the same cluster, or each of them belongs to an individual cluster. When n is very large, the probability of observing one of these two entries will be extremely small. Therefore, no matrix completion algorithm can exactly recover this network under uniform sampling.

Motivated by this example, we now analytically show that group imbalance τ determines the possibility of recovery. We first show the connection between τ and incoherence μ.

Theorem 5 (Incoherence of Signed Networks)
Any complete k-weakly balanced network is τ-incoherent where τ is the group imbalance measurement.

PROOF. Let X^* be the adjacency matrix of a k-weakly balanced complete network. Recall from Definition 3 that μ is defined as the maximum absolute value in the (normalized) singular vectors of X^*, which are the same as eigenvectors of X^* since the adjacency matrix is symmetric.

Let $\mathbf{u}$ be any eigenvector of $X^*(\|\mathbf{u}\|_2 = 1)$ with eigenvalue λ. Suppose i and j are in the same group, namely $X^*_{i,:} = X^*_{j,:}$, we have $u_i = X^*_{i,:}\mathbf{u}/\lambda = X^*_{j,:}\mathbf{u}/\lambda = u_j$. Thus, $\mathbf{u}$ has the following form:

$$\mathbf{u} = [\underbrace{v_1, v_1, \ldots, v_1}_{n_1}, \underbrace{v_2, \ldots, v_2}_{n_2}, \ldots, \underbrace{v_k, \ldots, v_k}_{n_k}]^T. \quad (5)$$

Since $\|\mathbf{u}\|_2 = 1$, $\sum_{i=1}^k n_i v_i^2 = 1$, and so $n_i v_i^2 \le 1$, $\forall i$, which implies $|v_i| \le 1/\sqrt{n_i}$, $\forall i$. Thus,

$$\max_i |u_i| = \max_j |v_j| \le \max_j \frac{1}{\sqrt{n_j}} = \max_j \frac{\sqrt{n/n_j}}{\sqrt{n}} \le \frac{\sqrt{\tau}}{\sqrt{n}}.$$

Therefore, X^* is τ-incoherent. □

Putting together Theorems 4 and 5, we now have the main theorem of this subsection:

Theorem 6 (Recovery Condition for Signed Networks)
Suppose we observe edges A_{ij}, $(i,j) \in \Omega$, from an underlying k-weakly balanced signed network X^*, and suppose that the following assumptions hold:
A. k is bounded ($k = O(1)$),
B. the set of observed entries Ω is uniformly sampled, and
C. number of samples is sufficiently large, i.e. $|\Omega| \ge C\tau^4 n \log^2 n$, where τ is the group imbalance of the underlying complete network X^*.
Then X^* can be perfectly recovered by solving (2), with probability at least $1 - n^{-3}$.

In particular, if n_i/n is lower bounded so that τ is a constant, then we only need $O(n \log^2 n)$ observed entries to *exactly* recover the complete k-weakly balanced network.

It is known that the convex problem (2) can be exactly solved by an SDP. However, the computational cost of SDP might be too prohibitive in practice. Recent research provides more efficient algorithms to approximately solve (1) [1, 12]. In our experiment, we use the SVP algorithm proposed by Jain et al.[12] which attempts to solve matrix completion problem in an efficient manner. Experimental evidence in [12] shows that all iterates of the SVP algorithm are μ-incoherent, in which case the matrix completion problem (1) can be exactly solved by SVP. In Section 5, we will see that SVP performs well in recovering weakly balanced networks.

3.2 Inference via Matrix Factorization

Though matrix completion algorithms can guarantee recovery for weakly balanced networks under certain conditions, convex relaxation (2) does not work very well in real-life applications, where observed values are not uniformly distributed, which violates one of the assumptions in Theorem 6. In addition, the methods for solving (2) cannot scale to very large datasets. Thus, we use a gradient based matrix factorization approach as an approximation to the signed network completion problem. In Section 5, we will see that a matrix factorization approach can not only boost the accuracy of estimation but also scale to large real networks.

In the matrix factorization approach, we consider the following problem:

$$\min_{W,H \in \mathbb{R}^{k \times n}} \sum_{(i,j)\in\Omega} (A_{ij} - (W^T H)_{ij})^2 + \lambda \|W\|_F^2 + \lambda \|H\|_F^2. \quad (6)$$

Although problem (6) is non-convex, it is widely used in practical collaborative filtering applications as the performance is competitive or better as compared to trace-norm minimization, while scalability is much better. For example, to solve the Netflix problem, (6) has been applied with a fair amount of success to factorize the dataset with 100 million ratings [14].

Nevertheless, there is an issue when modeling signed networks using (6): the square loss in the first term of (6) tends to force entries of $W^T H$ to be either $+1$ or -1. However, what we care about in this completion task is the consistency between $\text{sign}((W^T H)_{ij})$ and $\text{sign}(A_{ij})$ rather than their difference. For example, $(W^T H)_{ij} = 10$ should have zero loss when $A_{ij} = +1$ if only the signs are important.

To resolve this issue, instead of using the squared loss, we use a loss function that only penalizes the inconsistency in *sign*. More precisely, objective (6) can be generalized as:

$$\min_{W,H \in \mathbb{R}^{k \times n}} \sum_{(i,j)\in\Omega} \ell(A_{ij}, (W^T H)_{ij}) + \lambda \|W\|_F^2 + \lambda \|H\|_F^2. \quad (7)$$

In order to penalize inconsistency of sign, we can change the loss function to be the sigmoid or squared-hinge loss:

$$\ell_{\text{sigmoid}}(x, y) = 1/(1 + \exp(xy)),$$
$$\ell_{\text{square-hinge}}(x, y) = (\max(0, 1 - xy))^2. \quad (8)$$

In Section 5, we will see that applying sigmoid or square-hinge loss functions slightly improves prediction accuracy.

Time complexity. There are two main optimization techniques for solving (7) for large-scale data: Alternating Least Squares (ALS) and Stochastic Gradient Descent (SGD) [14]. ALS solves the squared loss problem (6) by alternately minimizing W and H. When one of W or H is fixed, the optimization problem becomes a least squares problem with respect to the other variable, so that we can use well developed least squares solvers to solve each subproblem. Given an $n \times n$ observed matrix with m observations, the time complexity for each subproblem requires $O(mk^2)$ operations to form the Hessian matrices, and $O(nk^3)$ to solve the least squares problem. Therefore, the time complexity of ALS is $O(t_1(mk^2 + nk^3))$ where t_1 is the number of iterations.

However, ALS can only be used when the loss function is square loss. To solve the general form (7) with various loss functions, we use stochastic gradient descent (SGD).In SGD, for each iteration, we pick an observed entry (i, j) at random, and only update the ith column of W and the jth column of H, denoted by $\mathbf{w}_i$ and $\mathbf{h}_j$, respectively. The update rule for $\mathbf{w}_i$ is given by:

$$\mathbf{w}_i \leftarrow \mathbf{w}_i - \eta \left(\frac{\partial \ell(A_{ij}, (W^T H)_{ij})}{\partial \mathbf{w}_i} + \lambda \mathbf{w}_i \right), \quad (9)$$

where η is a small step size. The update rule for $\mathbf{h}_j$ is similar to (9). Since each SGD update (9) costs $O(k)$ time, after a sweep through all known entries it will take $O(mk)$ time. Therefore, the time complexity for SGD is $O(t_2 mk)$, where t_2 is the number of iterations taken by SGD to converge. Notice that although the complexity of SGD is linear in k, it usually takes many more iterations to converge compared with ALS, i.e., $t_2 > t_1$.

On the other hand, all previous link or cycle-based sign inference algorithms [17, 5] require time at least $O(nm)$ because all of them contain some $n \times n$ sparse matrix multiplication steps in model construction. Moreover, for all length-l paths, the number of features is exponential in l. Therefore, assuming the number of features in consideration is d, the time complexity for various methods will be $O(dnm)$. The time complexity is summarized in the following table:

HOC	ALS	SGD
$O(dnm)$	$O(t_1(nk^3 + mk^2))$	$O(t_2 km)$

Since in real large-scale social networks, $m > n \gg t_1, t_2, k$, this shows our alternative minimization approach is much more efficient for sign inference.

3.3 Low Rank Structure in Real Datasets

We now show that real networks tend to exhibit low-rank structure to a much greater extent than random networks. We consider three large-scale online social networks – Wikipedia, Epinions[17], and Slashdot[15][1]. Table 1 shows the statistics of these datasets. We compare these real networks with random networks as the baseline. The random network is created using the Erdös-Rényi model with sparsity equal to the Wikipedia network.

Table 1: Network Statistics

	# nodes	# edges	+ edges	- edges
Wikipedia	7,065	103,561	78.7%	21.2%
Slashdot	82,144	549,202	77.4%	22.6%
Epinions	131,828	840,799	85.0%	15.0%

To measure the closeness of observed entries between the original network and the completed matrix, we first derive the low-rank complete matrix A^* by conducting matrix completion using the observed entries A_{ij}. Then, we look at the relative error on the observed set Ω: $\text{err}_\Omega = \|W \circ (A^* - A)\|_F / \|A\|_F$, where $W_{ij} = 1$ if $(i, j) \in \Omega$ and $W_{ij} = 0$ otherwise, and $\circ$ denotes element-wise multiplica-

[1]All the three data sets can be downloaded from SNAP (`http://snap.stanford.edu`)

tion. Clearly, smaller err_Ω indicates better approximation for the observed entries.

In our experiment, we choose matrix factorization approach for matrix completion, with ranks $k = 1, 2, 4, 8, 16$ and 32. For each network (three real datasets and the random network), we complete the network with different k and compute err_Ω. The result is shown in Figure 2. Compared with the purely random network, the three real-life networks achieve much smaller err_Ω for each small k. This suggests that low-rank matrices provide a better approximation of the observed entries for each real-life network, as compared to random Erdös-Rényi graphs.

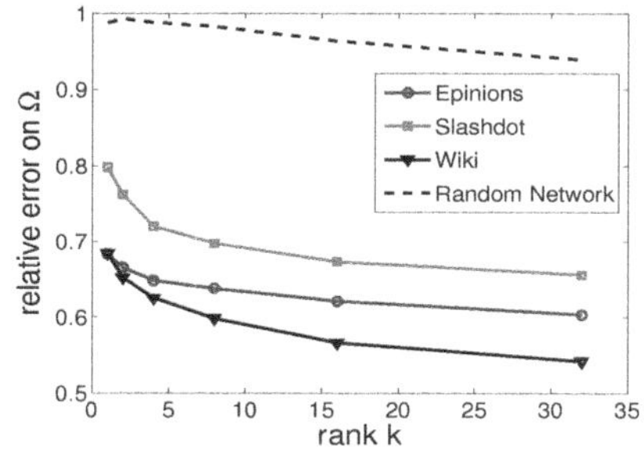

Figure 2: Relative error between adjacency matrix and completed matrix with respect to observed entries, for real-life networks versus a random network. Real-life networks achieve much smaller relative error for every k as compared with the random network.

4. CLUSTERING

In this section, we see how to take advantage of the low-rank structure of signed networks to find clusters. Based on weak balance theory, the general goal of clustering for signed graphs is to find a k-way partition such that most within-group edges are positive and most between-group edges are negative. One of the state-of-the-art clustering algorithms [16] extends the notion of Laplacian to signed networks, and proposes a spectral clustering algorithm based on a signed Laplacian matrix. Given a partially observed signed network A, the signed Laplacian is defined as $\bar{D} - A$, where $\bar{D}$ is a diagonal matrix in which $\bar{D}_{ii} = \sum_{j \neq i} |A_{ij}|$. By this definition, the ratio cut of signed networks can be derived by computing the top k eigenvectors of $\bar{L}$, say $U \in \mathbb{R}^{n \times k}$, and subsequently running the k-means algorithm on U to get the clusters. This procedure is analogous to the standard spectral clustering algorithm on unsigned graphs; the only difference being that the usual graph Laplacian is replaced by the signed Laplacian.

However, there is no theoretical guarantee that the use of the signed Laplacian can recover the true groups in a weakly-balanced signed network. To overcome this theoretical defect, we now give an algorithm which, under certain conditions, is able to recover the real structure even with partial observations. The key idea is that since in Theorem 3 we proved that the k-weakly balanced graphs have rank up to k, we can obtain good clustering by first running a matrix completion algorithm, say trace-norm minimization, on A. The following theorem shows that the eigenvectors of the completed matrix possess a desirable property:

Theorem 7
Let A_{ij}, $(i,j) \in \Omega$, be entries observed from a complete k-weakly balanced network X^*, and assume that the solution of (2) is X with eigenvectors $U = [\mathbf{u}_1, \mathbf{u}_2, \cdots, \mathbf{u}_k]$. If the assumptions in Theorem 6 are all satisfied, then with high probability $U_{i,:} = U_{j,:}$ iff i and j are in the same cluster in X^*.

Algorithm 1: Clustering with Matrix Completion

Input: Adjacency matrix A, number of clusters k
Output: Cluster indicators
1. $X \leftarrow$ Completion(A) with any matrix completion algorithm.
2. $U \leftarrow$ Top k eigenvectors of X.
3. Run any feature-based clustering algorithm on U.

PROOF. From Theorem 6, we know the recovered matrix X will be X^* with high probability. Suppose $\mathbf{u}_1, \ldots, \mathbf{u}_k$ are the k eigenvectors of X^*. From the proof of Theorem 5, the eigenvectors will have the form in (5), which means $U_{i,:} = U_{j,:}$ if i and j are in the same cluster. Furthermore, when i and j are in different clusters, $X^*_{i,:} \neq X^*_{j,:}$, so $U_{i,:}$ cannot equal to $U_{j,:}$. This proves the theorem. □

Following this theorem, the true clusters can be identified from the eigenvectors of X when the assumptions in Theorem 6 hold. Therefore, perfect clustering is guaranteed in this scenario.

More generally, we can use any matrix completion method discussed in Section 3 to complete A. For example, if we take SVP as the matrix completion approach, we can derive perfect clustering result if all iterates of the algorithm are μ-incoherent. This is because under this condition, SVP can recover X^* exactly, so the property of eigenvectors in Theorem 7 can again be used. Our clustering algorithm that uses matrix completion is summarized in Algorithm 1.

It should not be surprising that our clustering algorithm is superior to (signed) spectral clustering. In some sense, our approach can be viewed as a spectral method, except that it first generates missing links from the training data by doing matrix completion. This step is simple yet crucial in signed networks as it overcomes the sparsity of the network. We will see that our clustering algorithm outperforms the (signed) spectral clustering method in Section 5.

5. EXPERIMENTAL RESULTS

In this section, we perform experiments on synthetic and real networks, and show that our proposed low-rank model for signed networks outperforms other methods on the tasks of sign inference and clustering. To ensure that our results are reliable, we conduct all experiments 10 times, and average the result from all of the trials.

5.1 Sign Inference

Recall that given a partially observed signed graph A, the sign inference task is to predict the signs of the missing links. Although in Section 3 we focused on undirected graphs when introducing our low rank model, we can easily extend our sign inference algorithms to directed graphs since matrix completion and matrix factorization algorithms are easily adapted to the directed case. Therefore, our sign inference experiments are all on networks that are directed.

5.1.1 Algorithms and Parameter Setting

We consider two low-rank modeling approaches proposed in Section 3: Matrix Completion (MC) and Matrix Factorization (MF). For MC methods, we use Singular Value Projection (MC-SVP) since it is efficient and effective in practice [12]. For MF methods, we mainly consider Alternating Least Square (MF-ALS) which uses the squared loss in (7). In real datasets, we also use Stochastic Gradient Descent (SGD) to solve (7) with sigmoid and square-hinge losses, denoted as MF-SGDSIG and MF-SGDSH respectively.

We compare the performance of our low rank model to state-of-the-art approaches, such as cycle-based methods, for the sign inference problem [17, 5]. The first cycle-based methods are the so-called measure of social imbalance (MOI), which predict the sign of an edge so that more cycles become balanced [5]. If we consider cycles of arbitrary length, and exponentially damp their importance based on length, we get a measure we call (MOI-∞), which infers the sign of (i, j) as $\text{sign}\big(((I-\beta A)^{-1}-I-\beta A)_{ij}\big)$. The second cycle-based approach we consider is a supervised learning approach based on high order cycles (HOC), with features derived from cycles of length 3 (i.e. triangles) [17], length 4 and length 5 (see [5] for more details). As in [5], we use HOC-3, HOC-4 and HOC-5 to denote these methods.

Some of these models require parameter setting beforehand, such as the regularization parameter λ in MF (see (7)) and β in MOI-∞. To select these parameters, we conduct a 3-fold cross validation on the training set. With the selected parameters, we then construct the model based on the whole training set and conduct sign inference on the testing data.

5.1.2 Synthetic Datasets

We first compare all categories of approaches on synthetic datasets. We choose MC-SVP, MC-ALS, MOI-∞ and HOC-3 as representatives of MC, MF, MOI-based and HOC-based methods respectively. We fix the underlying signed network X^* to be a complete 5-weakly balanced network, where the five clusters have sizes 100, 200, 300, 400 and 500. Instead of observing all of X^*, we assume that we only observe a partial network by sampling some entries from X^* using three sampling procedures: uniform sampling, uniform sampling with noise, and sampling with power-law distribution. For each inference algorithm, we input the observed entries as training data and calculate the sign inference accuracy on the rest of elements.

Uniform sampling: In this scenario, we randomly sample n^2p entries from X^*, where $p \in (0, 1)$ is the fraction of observed entries. We vary p from 0.001 to 0.1 and plot the inference accuracy in Figure 3(a). Clearly, MC-SVP and MF-ALS outperform the cycle-based methods. MOI-∞ performs the worst with accuracy only 50%-70%. This is because MOI uses cycle-based measurements to make more cycles become *balanced*. This inference policy can work only when $k = 2$ (that is, the underlying network has strong balance), but performs poorly when the underlying network is weakly balanced. HOC-3 works much better than MOI-∞ since it learns a classifier from cycle-based features rather than simply making cycles balanced, but its accuracy drops dramatically when p is less than 0.05. On the other hand, both MC-SVP and MF-ALS show high accuracy for all $p \geq 0.01$. In particular, MC-SVP can achieve 100% accuracy when $p > 0.07$, which reconfirms the theoretical recovery guarantee stated in Theorem 6. Moreover, although MF-ALS has no theoretical guarantee, it can still recover the ground truth, an observation that is consistent with previous results.

Uniform sampling with noise: To make the synthetic data more similar to real data, we further add noise into observations. Specifically, in this scenario, each observed entry A_{ij} has sign that is opposite to the true value X^*_{ij} with probability r. For clarity, we fix the fraction of observed entries $p = 0.1$, and increase r from 0.01 to 0.25. The result is shown in Figure 3(b). We can see that our low-rank modeling approaches are still clearly better than cycle-based methods when noise level becomes higher. Moreover, MC-SVP can still perfectly recover X^* when the noise level $r < 0.05$, and MF-ALS can also achieve perfect recovery with a smaller r.

Sampling with power-law distribution: As Section 3 mentioned, the good performance of matrix completion crucially relies on the assumption that observed entries are uniformly sampled. However, in most real networks (for example, Slashdot in [15]), the degree distribution follows power law. Therefore, we examine how all approaches perform on power-law distributed networks. We generate power-law distributed networks using the Chung-Lu-Vu (CLV) model proposed in [6], which allows one to generate random graphs with arbitrary expected degree sequence. Similar to the uniform sampling case, we vary the fraction of observed entries and plot the inference accuracy in Figure 3(c). We can see MOI-∞ still has poor performance for weakly balanced graphs. However, distinct from uniform sampling case, MC-SVP has lower accuracy rate compared to HOC-3 when $p < 0.1$. This shows that MC-SVP cannot work well given non-uniform distributed observations. On the other hand, MF-ALS still performs better than all other methods in power-law distributed graphs.

From all experiments on synthetic data shown in Figure 3, we can conclude that low rank modeling approaches generally do better than cycle-based methods, and the matrix factorization approach (MF-ALS) performs the best in most cases, even in non-uniform distributed networks. This indicates MF approach should be superior than others in real networks. This will be confirmed in the following subsection.

5.1.3 Real-life Datasets

Next we demonstrate that our low rank model is more effective than existing methods in real datasets also. Already in Figure 3(c) we have seen that MC-SVP fails to perform well under power-law distributed networks, so we consider the more robust MF approaches, including MF-ALS, MF-SGDSIG and MF-SGDSH, for experiments on real datasets. We compare these proposed methods with the best cycle-based methods, HOC-3, HOC-4 and HOC-5. Again we use Wikipedia, Slashdot and Epinions to examine sign inference algorithms on real networks. These three datasets have previously been used as benchmarks on sign inference [17, 5].

To make the comparison fair, we conduct a 10-fold cross validation and report the average inference accuracy for each dataset in Table 2. We observe that MF-based algorithms clearly outperform cycle-based methods. In particular, we observe that HOC-5 only improves HOC-3 by less than 1.5%, while MF-based algorithms consistently improve the accuracy of HOC-5 by more than 2% over all datasets. In addition, MF-SGDSIG and MF-SGDSH further improve the accuracy of MF-ALS slightly. This shows that the sigmoid loss and square-hinge are more suitable for sign inference, which supports the discussion in Section 3.2.

In Figure 4, we further examine the performance of these algorithms with different levels of edge embeddedness. Embeddedness of edge (i, j) is defined as the number of common neighbors of the nodes i and j, and can be thought as a mea-

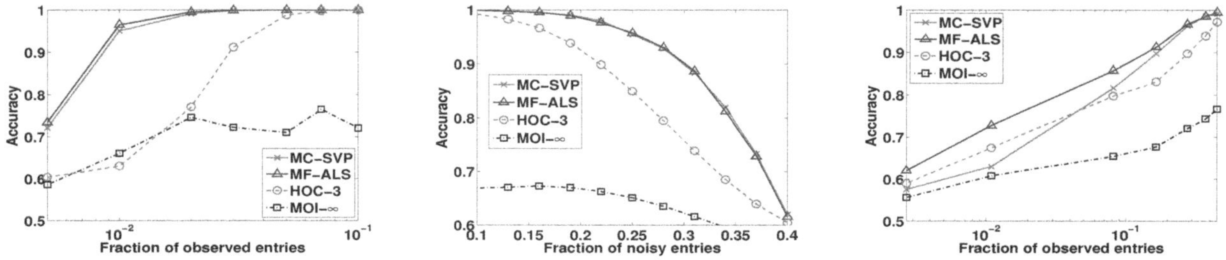

(a) Uniformly sample without noise (b) Uniformly sample with noise (c) Power-law distributed Networks

Figure 3: Accuracy of sign inference algorithms on synthetic datasets. In general, we can see that MC-SVP and MF-ALS outperform cycle-based methods such as MOI-∞ and HOC-3. In addition, MF-ALS is more robust than MC-SVP when the observations are sampled from a power-law distribution.

Table 2: The sign inference accuracy for MF-based algorithms and cycle-based algorithms. We can see that the MF-based algorithms are better than cycle-based algorithms.

	Epinions	Slashdot	Wikipedia
HOC-3	0.9014	0.8303	0.8424
HOC-5	0.9080	0.8469	0.8605
MF-ALS	0.9374	0.8774	0.8814
MF-SGDSIG	**0.9465**	0.8789	**0.8830**
MF-SGDSH	0.9437	**0.8835**	0.8810

sure of the proximity between i and j. One might expect that cycle-based approaches should perform better on edges with higher embeddedness because more cycle information is available. However, surprisingly MF-ALS achieves higher inference accuracy regardless of the embeddedness. The performance of MF-SGDSIG and MF-SGDSH is similar to MF-ALS so they are not shown in Figure 4 for clarity.

5.1.4 Computation Time

In addition to inference accuracy, we now compare the running time required by the different methods. As discussed in Section 3.2, matrix factorization methods are more efficient than cycle-based algorithms in terms of time complexity. Here, we further show that MF-based methods are empirically much faster than cycle-based algorithms. The running times are summarized in Table 3. To conduct timing tests on a large signed network, in addition to the three real datasets as described in Table 1, we further construct a large-scale synthetic dataset called Cluster10 where number of edges is 100 times more than Epinions. Cluster10 is generated from a 10-weakly balanced network, in which clusters have sizes 20000, 40000,..., 200000 respectively. There are totally 1.1 million nodes and 120 million edges uniformly observed from the complete graph. We construct this synthetic data to show that our matrix factorization approach can easily scale up to massive graphs compared to HOC-3 and HOC-5. For matrix factorization approach, we report the time needed to solve the model by SGD (with sigmoid and square-hinge) and ALS (with square loss). For HOC methods which build classifiers from cycle-based features, since the time for training phase depends on the classifier, we only report the time for computation of features. Thus the reported time for HOC is an underestimation for constructing the HOC model; even then we can see that the time required by MF-based algorithms is much lower than HOC methods.

In conclusion, for the sign inference problem, we can see

Table 3: Running time (in seconds) for our MF approach and HOC on real datasets and a 1.1 million node synthetic data Cluster10. For HOC methods, we only consider the time for feature computation before the model training, while for MF-based methods we report the total time for constructing the model. We can see that MF-based methods are clearly more efficient than cycle-based algorithms.

	HOC-3	HOC-4	HOC-5	ALS	SGD
Wiki	18.08	74.52	462.92	**2.26**	2.41
Slashdot	133.4	1936.0	>10,000	**17.4**	24.7
Epinions	560.64	6156.8	>10,000	**28.67**	37.2
Cluster10	>10,000	>10,000	>10,000	**455.1**	1152

that our low rank model outperforms other traditional inference methods. In particular, the matrix factorization approach is clearly the most competitive method in terms of accuracy and scalability.

5.2 Clustering

In this subsection, we show that our proposed clustering approach, which completes the low-rank structure of signed networks before performing clustering, outperforms spectral clustering based on the signed Laplacian [16]. Similar to Section 5.1.2, we conduct experiments on synthetic data generated from weakly balanced networks (note that we do not have ground truth for clustering in the real-life datasets). We consider a 10-weakly balanced network X^* where size of each group is 100. We then observe entries from X^* with two sampling procedures: uniform sampling and uniform sampling with noise.

To measure the performance of clustering, we calculate the number of edges that satisfy the ground-truth clustering, which is defined by

$$\sum_{i,j:s_i=s_j} I(\bar{s}_i = \bar{s}_j) + \sum_{i,j:s_i\neq s_j} I(\bar{s}_i \neq \bar{s}_j).$$

where $s_1, \ldots, s_n$ denote the ground-truth clustering assignment for each node, and $\bar{s}_1, \ldots, \bar{s}_n$ are the clustering results given by the clustering algorithm.

Following the procedure outlined in the previous subsection, in the uniform sampling case, we draw pn^2 i.i.d. samples from all the n^2 edges. Similarly, in sampling with noise, we flip the sign of each observed edge with probability r. The results of these two scenarios are shown in Figure 5. In both scenarios, our proposed clustering approach is significantly better than clustering based on the signed Laplacian. This shows that recovering the low-rank structure of signed networks leads to improved clustering results.

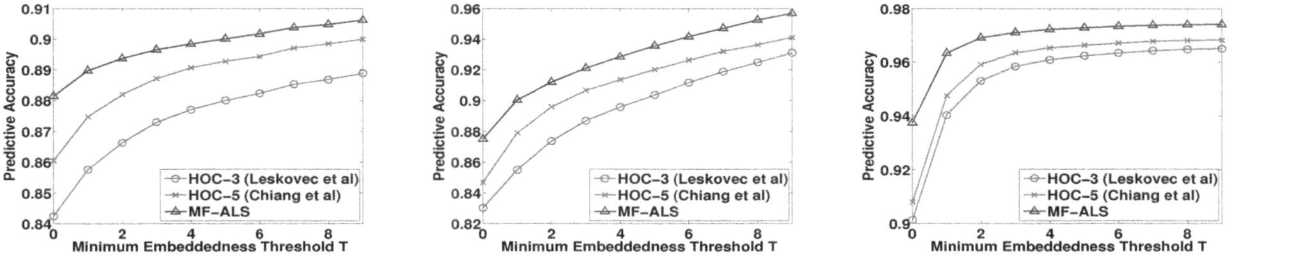

(a) Wiki (b) Slashdot (c) Epinions

Figure 4: Accuracy of sign inference algorithms with different levels of embeddedness. These plots show the accuracy for edges whose embeddedness is at least T. We can see that MF-ALS consistently gives us higher accuracy for all thresholds T.

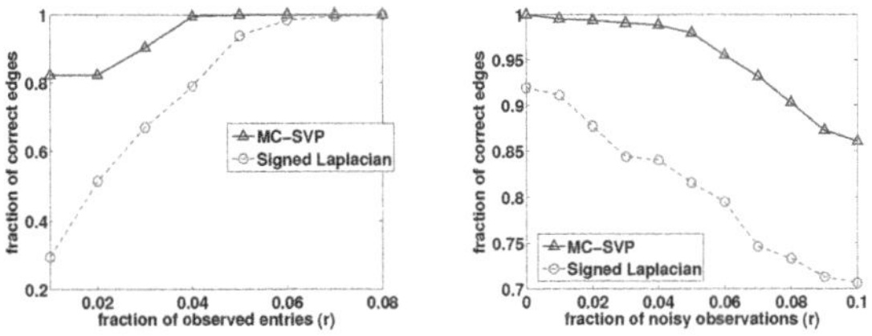

(a) Data without noise (b) Data with noise

Figure 5: Clustering partially observed synthetic data. Figure 5(a) is the result without noise and Figure 5(b) is the result with noise. In both cases, clustering with MC-SVP performs significantly better than using signed Laplacian.

6. CONCLUSIONS

In this paper, we have proposed a low rank modeling approach for signed network analysis. We have shown that the low-rank structure of signed networks naturally emerges from weak balance theory. The sign inference problem in such networks can thus be modeled as a low-rank matrix completion problem. We first showed that missing links in a signed network can be exactly recovered by matrix completion algorithms under certain conditions, and then introduced a more efficient matrix factorization approach for sign inference. Furthermore, we showed that the low rank model can also be used for clustering. Experiments conducted on both synthetic data and real networks show that our low rank model improves sign inference significantly, in terms of both accuracy and speed. Clustering results also become more favorable by making use of the low rank model.

7. ACKNOWLEDGEMENT

This research was supported by NSF grants CCF-0916309, CCF-1117055 and DOD Army grant W911NF-10-1-0529.

8. REFERENCES

[1] J.-F. Cai, E. J. candés, and Z. Shen. A singular value thresholding algorithm for matrix completion. *Society for Industrial and Applied Mathematics (SIAM)*, 20(4):1956–1982, 2010.

[2] E. J. Candés and T. Tao. The power of convex relaxation: Near-optimal matrix completion. *IEEE Trans. Inform. Theory*, 56(5):2053–2080, 2009.

[3] E. J. Canés and B. Recht. Exact matrix completion via convex optimization. *Found. of Comput. Math.*, 9:712–772, 2008.

[4] D. Cartwright and F. Harary. Structure balance: A generalization of Heider's theory. *Psychological Review*, 63(5):277–293, 1956.

[5] K.-Y. Chiang, N. Natarajan, A. Tewari, and I. S. Dhillon. Exploiting longer cycles for link prediction in signed networks. In *CIKM*, 2011.

[6] F. Chung, L. Lu, and V. Vu. Spectra of random graphs with given expected degrees. *Internet Mathematics*, 1, 2004.

[7] J. A. Davis. Clustering and structural balance in graphs. *Human Relations*, 20(2):181–187, 1967.

[8] I. S. Dhillon, Y. Guan, and B. Kulis. Weighted graph cuts without eigenvectors: A multilevel approach. *IEEE Trans. on pattern analysis and machine intelligence*, 29(11):1944–1957, 2007.

[9] R. V. Guha, R. Kumar, P. Raghavan, and A. Tomkins. Propagation of trust and distrust. In *WWW*, 2004.

[10] S. Hanneke and E. P. Xing. Network completion and survey sampling. In *AISTATS*, 2009.

[11] F. Harary. On the notion of balance of a signed graph. *Michigan Mathematical Journal*, 2(2):143–146, 1953.

[12] P. Jain, R. Meka, and I. Dhillon. Guaranteed rank minimization via singular value projection. In *NIPS*, pages 934–945, 2010.

[13] M. Kim and J. Leskovec. The network completion problem: infering missing nodes and edges in networks. In *SDM*, 2011.

[14] Y. Koren, R. M. Bell, and C. Volinsky. Matrix factorization techniques for recommender systems. *IEEE Computer*, 42:30–37, 2009.

[15] J. Kunegis, A. Lommatzsch, and C. Bauckhage. The slashdot zoo: Mining a social network with negative edges. In *WWW*, pages 741–750, 2009.

[16] J. Kunegis, S. Schmidt, A. Lommatzsch, J. Lerner, E. W. DeLuca, and S. Albayrak. Spectral analysis of signed graphs for clustering, prediction and visualization. In *SDM*, pages 559–570, 2010.

[17] J. Leskovec, D. Huttenlocher, and J. Kleinberg. Predicting positive and negative links in online social networks. In *WWW*, 2010.

[18] A. Y. Ng, M. Jordan, and Y. Weiss. On spectral clustering: Analysis and an algorithm. In *NIPS*, 2001.

[19] B. Recht, M. Fazel, and P. A. Parrilo. Guaranteed minimum-rank solutions of linear matrix equations via nuclear norm minimization. *SIAM Review*, 52(3):471–501, 2010.

[20] B. Yang, W. Cheung, and J. Liu. Community mining from signed social networks. *IEEE Trans. on knowledge and data engineering*, 19(10):1333–1348, 2007.

A Structural Cluster Kernel for Learning on Graphs

Madeleine Seeland
Technische Universität München
Institut für Informatik I12
Boltzmannstr. 3
85748 Garching b. München, Germany
madeleine.seeland@in.tum.de

Andreas Karwath
Johannes Gutenberg-Universität Mainz
Institut für Informatik
Staudingerweg 9
55128 Mainz, Germany
karwath@informatik.uni-mainz.de

Stefan Kramer
Johannes Gutenberg-Universität Mainz
Institut für Informatik
Staudingerweg 9
55128 Mainz, Germany
kramer@informatik.uni-mainz.de

ABSTRACT

In recent years, graph kernels have received considerable interest within the machine learning and data mining community. Here, we introduce a novel approach enabling kernel methods to utilize additional information hidden in the structural neighborhood of the graphs under consideration. Our novel structural cluster kernel (SCK) incorporates similarities induced by a structural clustering algorithm to improve state-of-the-art graph kernels. The approach taken is based on the idea that graph similarity can not only be described by the similarity between the graphs themselves, but also by the similarity they possess with respect to their structural neighborhood. We applied our novel kernel in a supervised and a semi-supervised setting to regression and classification problems on a number of real-world datasets of molecular graphs. Our results show that the structural cluster similarity information can indeed leverage the prediction performance of the base kernel, particularly when the dataset is structurally sparse and consequently structurally diverse. By additionally taking into account a large number of unlabeled instances the performance of the structural cluster kernel can further be improved.

Categories and Subject Descriptors

H.2.8 [**Database Applications**]: Data Mining

General Terms

Algorithms, Experimentation, Performance

Keywords

Cluster Kernels, Graph Kernels, Structural Graph Clustering, Cheminformatics, QSAR

1. INTRODUCTION

The topic of graph similarity and in particular kernel approaches have attracted considerable interest in recent years [13, 18, 20, 25]. To determine the similarity of two graphs, most approaches decompose the graphs in different ways: either into a potentially very large set of smaller subgraphs or related graph features, or into one or more larger common subgraphs (connected or disconnected). In this paper, we investigate the question whether the structural neighborhood of two graphs can also contribute to similarity searches and consequently to improve prediction performance. In our setting, the structural neighborhood of a graph is determined by a recently proposed structural graph clustering approach called PSCG [21, 22].

In the work presented here, we propose a novel kernel called *structural cluster kernel* (SCK) which, in addition to existing kernel approaches, measures the similarity between two graphs, by their assignment to structural clusters found with PSCG. Our approach first employs the structural clustering algorithm to determine small, structurally homogeneous regions in the input space, and then uses the pairwise similarities between these regions to define a similarity measure for graphs. The approach taken here is to extend two state-of-the-art graph kernels using this structural distance measure: the weighted decomposition kernel (WDK) [18] and the neighborhood subgraph pairwise distance kernel (NSPDK) [10].

To study the effectiveness of the SCK, we measured the prediction performance in the regression and classification setting, by employing several real-world datasets of molecular graphs within our experiments. To show the advantage of combining graph similarity and structural cluster similarity, we compare our approach with the base kernels using graph similarity alone. Furthermore, we compare the SCK to a different approach also employing structural clustering during model construction. We also investigate the performance of the SCK approach in the semi-supervised setting, where the base kernel is deformed by a cluster kernel encoding similarities between both labeled and unlabeled examples.

This paper is organized as follows: After discussing related work in Section 2, we introduce our proposed structural cluster kernel in Section 3. Section 4 presents and discusses our experimental results, before we conclude in Section 5.

2. RELATED WORK

The idea of combining kernels to improve prediction performance has attracted attention recently. Several types of cluster kernels, relying on different clustering algorithms, have been proposed by Chapelle *et al.* [6]. The authors present a general framework for constructing cluster kernels which implements the cluster assumption, i.e., the induced distance depends on whether the points are in the same cluster or not. Weston *et al.* [26] investigated the use of cluster kernels for protein classification by developing two simple and scalable methods for modifying a base kernel. The neighborhood kernel uses averaging over a neighborhood of sequences defined by a local sequence similarity measure, and the bagged kernel uses bagged clustering of the full sequence dataset to modify the base kernel. In both the semi-supervised and transductive settings, these techniques greatly improve the classification performance when used with mismatch string kernels. In work by Bodo and Csato [3] a kernel construction algorithm for supervised and semi-supervised learning was proposed, which constitutes a general framework for semi-supervised kernel construction. The technique clusters the labeled and unlabeled data by an agglomerative clustering technique, and uses the linkage distances induced by the clustering hierarchy to construct the kernel. Bodo and Csato [4] proposed two cluster kernel methods for semi-supervised learning which can be used for different types of datasets: one using hierarchical clustering, and another kernel for reweighting an arbitrary base kernel taking into account the cluster structure of the data.

Similar to Weston *et al.* [26] and Bodo and Csato [4], the cluster kernel proposed in this paper leverages information of a clustering algorithm to modify a base kernel. However, our approach differs from existing work in several respects. First, our structural cluster kernel can be applied in the domain of graphs. Second, it builds on two state-of-the-art graph kernels and a recently proposed structural graph clustering algorithm to determine small, structurally homogeneous neighborhoods of the input space. The pairwise similarities between these neighborhoods are used to define a similarity measure for graphs which in turn is used to improve a base kernel. Third, the proposed cluster kernel can be used for both graph classification and regression, whereas the above mentioned cluster kernels were only tested on classification tasks.

3. METHOD

3.1 Structural Graph Clustering

Parallel Structural Clustering of Graphs (PSCG) [21, 22] investigates the problem of finding groups of graphs sharing some structural similarity. Graphs with similar structures are expected to be in the same cluster provided that their common substructures match to a satisfactory extent. The common substructure of a cluster can be considered as a scaffold present in all cluster members. Only connected substructures are considered as common substructures. The sizes of these common substructures are used as a measure of similarity between the graphs. A graph is assigned to a cluster provided that there exists at least one common substructure whose size is equal or greater than a user-defined threshold. In this way, a graph can simultaneously belong to multiple clusters (overlapping clustering) if the size of at least one common substructure with these clusters is equal or greater than the defined threshold. If a graph does not meet the threshold to share a common substructure with any cluster, the graph is not included in any cluster (non-exhaustive clustering). For one graph after the other, it is decided whether it belongs to an existing cluster or whether a new cluster should be created. Formally, the problem of structural clustering is defined as follows: given a set of graphs, $X = \{x_1, \ldots, x_n\}$, we assign each graph x_i to a cluster C_j, such that the similarity between graphs is based on their structural similarity, including multiple, or overlapping cluster assignments. In graph clustering, one objective considered is to maximize the average number of graphs contained in a cluster, such that for each cluster C_j there exists at least one common substructure that makes up a specific proportion, θ, of the size of each cluster member. Considering the state of a cluster $C = \{x_1, \ldots, x_m\}$[1] at any point in time, the criterion can formally be defined as:

$$\exists s \in cs(\{x_1, \ldots, x_m\}) \forall x_i \in C : |s| \geq \theta |x_i| \quad (1)$$

where cs determines all common subgraphs of a set of graphs, and $\theta \in [0, 1]$ is a user-defined similarity coefficient. If a new graph x_{m+1} is to be tested for inclusion in cluster C, we can thus infer a minimum size threshold for the substructures shared by this graph and the graphs in the cluster:

$$minSize = \theta \ max(|x_{max}|, |x_{m+1}|), \quad (2)$$

where $\theta \in [0, 1]$ and x_{max} is the largest graph in the cluster. To obtain meaningful and interpretable results, the minimum size of a graph considered for cluster membership is further constrained by a minimum graph size threshold. It excludes graphs that are too small from clustering. Thus, the identification of the cluster scaffold will not be impeded by the presence of a few graph structures whose shared common substructure is much smaller than the one the majority of the cluster members share. For computing common substructures in graphs, we modified the graph mining algorithm gSpan [16, 27] that mines frequent substructures in a database of graphs satisfying a given minimum frequency constraint. For details of these modifications, the structural clustering algorithm and its performance, we refer the interested reader to the original publications [21, 22].

3.2 Weighted Decomposition Kernel

The basic idea of the Weighted Decomposition Kernel (WDK) [18] is to focus on relatively small parts of a structure, called *selectors*, that are matched according to an equality predicate. The importance of the match is then weighted by a factor that depends on the similarity of the *context* in which the matched selectors occur.

More formally, a weighted decomposition kernel is characterized by a decomposition $R(s, z, x)$ where s is a subgraph of x called the selector and z is a subgraph of x called the context of occurrence of s in x. This setting results in the following general form of the kernel:

$$K(x, x') = \sum_{(s,x) \in R^{-1}(x)} \ \sum_{(s',x') \in R^{-1}(x')} \delta(s, s') \kappa(z, z'), \quad (3)$$

where κ is a kernel on contexts and δ is the exact matching kernel applied to selectors.

In this paper, selectors are single atoms and the matching kernel $\delta(s, s')$ is defined by the coincidence between the type of s and s'. The context kernel k is based on a soft match between substructures, defined by the distributions of label

[1]In slight abuse of notation, we use the same indices as above.

contents after discarding topology. In this paper, we use the following attributes labeling vertices and edges: atom type, atom charge and bond type. Contexts are formed as follows: Given a vertex $v \in V$ and an integer $r \geq 0$, called the context radius. We denote by $x(v, r)$ the substructure of x composed of the vertices within distance r from vertex v, and the set of all edges that have at least one end in the vertex set of $x(v, r)$. More formally, we define the decomposition relation depending on r as $R_r = \{(s, z, x) : x \in X, s = \{v\}, z = x(v, r), v \in V\}$, where s is the selector and z is the context for vertex v. In our case, the matching kernel $\delta(v, v')$ returns 1 if the two vertices v and v' have the same label.

3.3 Neighborhood Subgraph Pairwise Distance Kernel

The Neighborhood Subgraph Pairwise Distance Kernel (NSPDK) [10] is based on exact matching between pairs of small subgraphs. Formally, let $R_{r,d}(A^v, B^u; G)$ denote the relation between two rooted graphs A^v,B^u and a graph G to be true iff both A^v and B^u are in $\{N_r^v : v \in V(G)\}$, where A^v (B^u) is isomorphic to some N_r and $D(u, v) = d$. In words: the relation $R_{r,d}$ selects all pairs of neighborhood graphs of radius r whose roots are at distance d in a given graph G.

We define $\kappa_{r,d}$ over $G \times G$ as the decomposition kernel on the relation $R_{r,d}$, i.e.,

$$\kappa_{r,d}(G, G') = \sum_{\substack{A^v, B^u \in R_{r,d}^{-1}(G) \\ A'^{v'}, B'^{u'} \in R_{r,d}^{-1}(G')}} \delta(A^v, A'^{v'})\delta(B^u, B'^{u'}) \quad (4)$$

where δ is the exact matching kernel. In words: $\kappa_{r,d}$ counts the number of identical pairs of neighboring graphs of radius r at distance d between two graphs.

The NSPDK is finally defined as:

$$K(G, G') = \sum_r \sum_d \kappa_{r,d}(G, G'). \quad (5)$$

In this work we impose an upper bound on the radius and the distance: $K_{r^*,d^*}(G, G') = \sum_{r=0}^{r^*} \sum_{d=0}^{d^*} \kappa_{r,d}(G, G')$ that is, NSPDK is limited to the sum of the $\kappa_{r,d}$ kernels for all increasing values of the radius (distance) parameter up to a maximum given value r^* (d^*).

3.4 Structural Cluster Kernel

In this section, we introduce a novel kernel, called structural cluster kernel, that leverages information of a clustering algorithm to improve a base kernel representation. The main idea is to change the similarity metric of a base kernel so that the relative similarity between two points is higher if the points are in the same cluster. Our kernel uses a combination of two similarity measures: (1) a base kernel that computes structural similarity between pairs of graphs and (2) a cluster based similarity measure that describes how close examples are to each other in terms of the similarities between the clusters they belong to. The similarity between two clusters is computed by taking the average of the similarities between the cluster instances. In our application to molecule regression and classification, we use the WDK and NSPDK (see Section 3.2 and 3.3) as the base kernel. For the cluster based kernel, we use the structural clustering algorithm introduced in section 3.1 that clusters a dataset of graphs based on structural similarity. The cluster similarity information is used to improve pointwise similarities, based on which we construct the final kernel.

In the following, we describe the steps which are necessary to build the structural cluster kernel. Let $D_{Trg} = \{(x_1, y_1), \dots, (x_t, y_t)\}$ denote the training data, where $x_i \in X$ represent the data points and y_i their labels, respectively. Further, let $D_{Tst} = \{x_{t+1}, \dots, x_n\}$ denote the set of test points. We first cluster the training set with the structural clustering procedure PSCG presented in Section 3.1. The resulting clusters are used to build a kernel representing the pairwise similarities between all clusters. In this kernel representation, each of the pairwise sets of the structural clusters is seen as a single data point, and a higher level kernel is designed so as to compare the two clusters. The similarity between two clusters is computed by taking the average of the sum of the pairwise similarities between all graph instances in both clusters. The kernel $K(C_i, C_j)$ is defined as

$$K(C_i, C_j) = \begin{cases} \frac{1}{|C_i||C_j|} \sum\limits_{x_k \in C_i} \sum\limits_{x_l \in C_j} K_b(x_k, x_l) & \text{if } i \neq j \\ 1 & \text{if } i = j, \end{cases} \quad (6)$$

where $K_b(x_k, x_l)$ represents the base kernel and $C_i, C_j \in \{C_1, \dots, C_p\}$. As mentioned earlier, we use the WDK and NSPDK as base kernel to compute the pairwise similarities between graphs. In the next step, we build a kernel representation $K_{Cl}(x_i, x_j)$ based on the averaged pairwise similarities between the clusters x_i and x_j belong to. $K_{Cl}(x_i, x_j)$ is defined as

$$K_{Cl}(x_i, x_j) = \begin{cases} \frac{1}{|n_{x_i}||n_{x_j}|} \sum\limits_{C_k : x_i \in C_k} \sum\limits_{C_l : x_j \in C_l} K(C_k, C_l) & \text{if } i \neq j \\ 1 & \text{if } i = j \end{cases} \quad (7)$$

where n_{x_i} denotes the number of clusters containing x_i, n_{x_j} denotes the number of clusters containing x_j and $C_k, C_l \in \{C_1, \dots, C_p\}$. Thus, we map the points to a feature space where the pointwise similarities are equal to the cluster similarities in the input space. The points belonging to the same cluster will result in matrix entries close to one, whereas for the points from different clusters, the entries will be close to zero. Figure 1 illustrates the cluster kernel concept.

The cluster similarity weights $K_{Cl}(x_i, x_j)$ are combined with the values of the base kernel $K_b(x_i, x_j)$, thus forming the final kernel matrix. To sum up, the new structural cluster kernel is

$$K_{SC}(x_i, x_j) = K_b(x_i, x_j) \times K_{Cl}(x_i, x_j) \quad (8)$$

We are faced with two problems in the construction of the above structural cluster kernel: (i) the base kernel matrix has to be positive semi-definite and (ii) the structural cluster kernel must be positive semi-definite. The first requirement is obvious, since we use the WDK and NSPDK as base kernels, which are known to be valid kernels. In the following, we provide a proof sketch to show that the structural cluster kernel is a valid kernel.

Proof Sketch:.

K_{Cl} is a valid kernel, since each kernel value $K_{Cl}(x_i, x_j)$ contains the average sum of pairwise similarities between all

Algorithm 1 Structural Cluster Kernel

Given: training points $D_{Trg} = \{(x_1, y_1), \ldots, (x_t, y_t)\}$ and test points $D_{Tst} = \{x_{t+1}, \ldots, x_n\}$, $x_i \in \mathbb{R}^n$, $i = 1, \ldots, n$

a) Cluster training points using PSCG [22, 21]

c) Build cluster matrix on the training set
$K_{Cl}(x_i, x_j) = \frac{1}{|n_{x_i}||n_{x_j}|} \sum_{C_k: x_i \in C_k} \sum_{C_l: x_j \in C_l} K(C_k, C_l)$, $i, j \in \{1, \ldots, t\}$

d) Build the SCK on the training dataset by taking the product between the base kernel K_b and the cluster kernel K_{Cl}
$K_{SC}(x_i, x_j) = K_{Cl}(x_i, x_j) \times K_b(x_i, x_j)$, $i, j \in \{1, \ldots, t\}$

e) Compute cluster assignments for all test points

f) Compute $K_{SC}(x_j, x_i)$ between each test point x_j and all training points x_i, $i = 1, \ldots, t$.

clusters, which in turn encompass the average sum of all training instances $x_i \in \{x_1, \ldots, x_t\}$.

For each pair of clusters, we define one kernel that returns the average similarity between the two clusters for the first instance in cluster one and the second in cluster two. For all other instances, it returns zero. As the sum of two valid kernels is again a valid kernel, the resulting function is a valid kernel as well. Applying the kernel to two instances, we only consider the clusters to which the two instances are assigned, consequently most of the summands are equal to zero:

$$\begin{aligned} K_{Cl}(x_i, x_j) =& \frac{1}{|n_{x_i}||n_{x_j}|} \sum_{C_k: x_i \in C_k} \sum_{C_l: x_j \in C_l} K(C_k, C_l) \\ =& \frac{1}{|n_{x_i}||n_{x_j}|} \sum_{C_k: x_i \in C_k} \sum_{C_l: x_j \in C_l} K(C_k, C_l) \\ &+ \frac{1}{|m_{x_i}||m_{x_j}|} \underbrace{\sum_{C_k: x_i \notin C_k} \sum_{C_l: x_j \notin C_l} K(C_k, C_l)}_{0} \\ &+ \frac{1}{|n_{x_i}||m_{x_j}|} \underbrace{\sum_{C_k: x_i \in C_k} \sum_{C_l: x_j \notin C_l} K(C_k, C_l)}_{0} \\ &+ \frac{1}{|m_{x_i}||n_{x_j}|} \underbrace{\sum_{C_k: x_i \notin C_k} \sum_{C_l: x_j \in C_l} K(C_k, C_l),}_{0} \end{aligned} \tag{9}$$

where n_{x_i} denotes the number of clusters containing x_i and m_{x_i} denotes the number of clusters not containing x_i.

In kernel methods, for predicting the label of a new test point we need to perform kernel function calculations only between the test points and the training points. For computing the kernel entries, we first need to assign each test point to one or more clusters using the structural clustering procedure to compute $K_{Cl}(x_i, x_t)$. Based on this cluster assignment the similarity $K_{Cl}(x_i, x_t)$ between the test point x_t and all training points x_i is computed by averaging the pairwise similarities between all clusters x_t and x_i are assigned to (Equation 7). The kernel matrix K_{SC} is extended by taking the inner product between $K_{Cl}(x_i, x_t)$ and $K_b(x_i, x_t)$ between each test point x_t and all training points x_i, $i = 1, \ldots, t$.

The steps needed for the calculation of the structural cluster kernel are shown in Algorithm 1.

3.5 Semi-Supervised Setting

In semi-supervised learning, one tries to improve a classifier trained on labeled data by exploiting a relatively large set of unlabeled data. If unlabeled data is added to the relatively small labeled dataset, we expect that the new similarity, obtained via structural clustering and the use of unlabeled data, induces a better representational space for classification and regression than using only the labeled data. Therefore, we extend on the kernel construction in Section 3.4 by involving a large number of unlabeled data. The structural cluster kernel is constructed as follows: We first cluster both the labeled and unlabeled training data with the structural clustering procedure to determine small, structurally homogeneous neighborhoods of the input space. The resulting clusters are then used to build a kernel representing the pairwise similarities between all clusters. As in the supervised setting, the cluster similarity information is used to improve pointwise similarities between the labeled data samples, based on which the final structural cluster kernel is constructed.

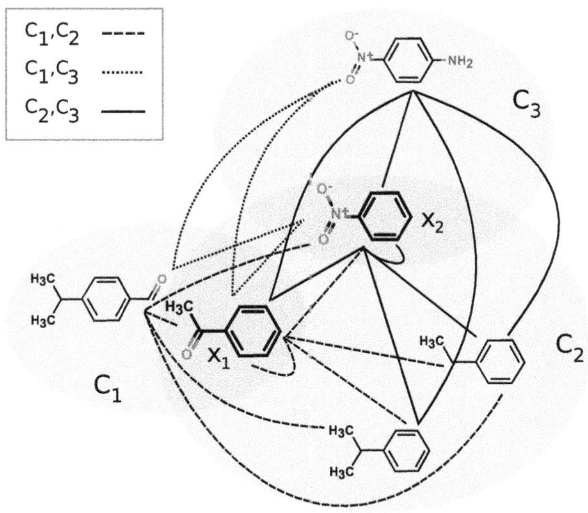

Figure 1: Illustration of the cluster kernel concept. The cluster based similarity $K_{Cl}(x_1, x_2)$ between the highlighted structures x_1 and x_2 is computed based on the averaged pairwise similarities between the clusters they belong to. x_1 belongs to C_1 and C_2, x_2 to C_2 and C_3. Thus, we need to compute the pairwise similarities between the cluster instances of cluster C_1C_2, C_1C_3, C_2C_2 (which equals 1) and C_2C_3.

4. EXPERIMENTAL RESULTS

In this section, we first study the performance of our proposed structural cluster kernel in a supervised setting. Next, we investigate the cluster kernel approach in a semi-supervised setting to test if the prediction performance can be improved by including a large amount of unlabeled data. For all experiments, we employed the chemical domain as our application area by using real datasets of molecular graphs. In Table 1 an overview of the datasets is provided.

Table 1: Overview of the datasets used for assessing our structural cluster kernel. n denotes the number of molecular graphs in the respective dataset.

Dataset	n	class.(SAR)/ regr.(QSAR)	Reference
4QSAR COX2	282	regression	4QSAR database [24]
4QSAR DHFR	362	regression	4QSAR database [24]
CPD MOUSE	442	regression	ACD DSSTox databases [14]
CPD RAT	580	regression	ACD DSSTox databases [14]
ISS MOUSE	316	regression	Benigni/Vari Carcinogenicity [2]
ISS RAT	375	regression	Benigni/Vari Carcinogenicity [2]
Suth COX2	414	regression	Sutherland dataset [23]
Suth DHFR	672	regression	Sutherland dataset [23]
Suth ER TOX	410	regression	Sutherland dataset [23]
FDAMDD	1216	regression	ACD DSSTox databases [17]
Biodeg	328	regression	Biodegradability dataset [11]
Tox09	1213	regression	Environmental Toxicity Prediction Challenge 2009 [1]
ER_LIT	381	regression	Sutherland dataset [23]
CYP INH 2C9	700	classification	Yap and Chen [28]
CYP SUB 2C9	700	classification	Yap and Chen [28]
Fontaine	435	classification	Fontaine *et al.* [12]
NCI AIDS	1000	classification	DTP AIDS Antiviral Screen [9]
CPDB MUT	684	classification	Mutagenicity dataset [15]

4.1 Supervised Setting

In this section, we empirically compare the performance of our structural cluster kernel approach against five methods.

1. **WDK**: The Weighted Decomposition Kernel is used to build a classification or regression model. Section 3.2 provides a detailed description of the WDK.

2. **NSPDK**: The Neighborhood Subgraph Pairwise Distance Kernel (see Section 3.3) is used to build a classification or regression model.

3. **LoMoGraph**: LoMoGraph [5] combines clustering and classification or regression for making predictions on graph structured data. The approach consists of two steps: First, the structural clustering procedure PSCG [22] is applied to find groups of graphs in a structural space that share a common structural scaffold with a minimum size. The sizes of these common subgraphs are used as a measure of similarity between the graphs. A graph is assigned to a cluster provided that there exists at least one common subgraph, whose size is equal or greater than a user-defined threshold θ. Second, one local model is learned per structural cluster using a feature-vector representation of the graphs where the features encode standard chemical descriptors in our setting of molecular graphs. In the prediction step, the query graph is assigned to one or more clusters using PSCG. Based on this assignment, the prediction is made. Since the structural clustering procedure is overlapping and non-exhaustive, a graph can fall into no cluster, one cluster or multiple clusters. If it falls into no cluster, a global model is applied for prediction. If the query graph falls into a single cluster, the local model based on this cluster is used for prediction, and if it is assigned to multiple clusters, weighted local models are used dependent on cluster membership. The weight for a cluster is linearly dependent on its size. Thus, larger weights are assigned to larger clusters, assuming that the more graphs a cluster has, the more reliable the corresponding model is.

4. **LoMoGraph WDK**: The method combines LoMoGraph with WDK. More precisely, one local model is learned per structural cluster based on the WDK.

5. **LoMoGraph NSPDK**: The method combines LoMoGraph with NSPDK, i.e., one local model is learned per structural cluster based on the NSPDK.

We investigated our structural cluster kernel approach using both NSPDK and WDK as base kernel. For SCK with NSPDK and SCK with WDK, we investigated not only the approach with the diagonal elements in the kernel matrices $K(C_i, C_j)$ (Equation 6) and $K_{Cl}(x_i, x_j)$ (Equation 7) set to one, but also a second approach, where the diagonal elements are computed in the same way as the non-diagonal elements. We refer to these four approaches as SCK NSPDK (d=1), SCK NSPDK (d≠1), SCK WDK (d=1) and SCK WDK (d≠1).

In the experiments, regression and classification were performed using the Support Vector Machine (SVM) algorithm. Several user parameters were optimized by internal cross-validation. For SCK WDK, SCK NSPDK, WDK, NSPDK, LoMoGraph WDK, and LoMoGraph NSPDK, the trade-off between training error and margin, C, was selected from $\{10^{-3}, 10^{-2}, 10^{-1}, 10^{0}, 10^{1}, 10^{2}\}$. Further, we optimized the radius r for WDK in $\{1, 2, 3, 4\}$. The parameter combination resulting in the lowest mean absolute error (the highest accuracy) was then used for building the final model. All other SVM parameters were left at their default values. For NSPDK, the maximum radius r^* was set to 2, and the maximum distance d^* to 5. For the SCK approaches, we set the similarity coefficient θ of PSCG to 0.5. For FDAMDD and NCI AIDS we made an exception and set θ to 0.3 to take into account the size and structural heterogeneity of the datasets. As for LoMoGraph, the parameters that were used for clustering were defined based on a set of criteria: the similarity coefficient of PSCG was chosen such that the local models consist of minimally 5% and maximally 20% of the training data. The rationale behind this choice is that a too small value of θ results in large, heterogeneous clusters whereas a too big value of θ produces very few, small clusters or no clusters at all. In both cases the predictivity of LoMoGraph would be negatively affected. For the experiments on SCK, we used the same values for θ for all datasets. Another parameter called minimum cluster size controls how many graphs a cluster must have at least so that a local model can be learned. This parameter was chosen greater than or equal to 20 as a lower bound for the number of graphs that are needed to train meaningful models.

Performance estimates are obtained using 100 times hold-out validation with a training set fraction of 66%. This means that 2/3 of the data are used for training a model while the remaining 1/3 is reserved for testing. To quantify predictive accuracy, we choose the relative mean error (regression) and classification accuracy (classification), which are standard measures in regression and classification settings. The Wilcoxon signed-rank test and the corrected re-

Table 2: Mean absolute errors with standard deviations of SCK NSPDK, NSPDK, LoMoGraph NSPDK and LoMoGraph on the regression datasets. Statistically significant results are reported using both the Wilcoxon signed-rank test and the corrected resampled t-test (separated by a '|').

Dataset	*SCK NSPDK (d≠1)*	SCK NSPDK (d=1)	NSPDK	LoMoGraph NSPDK	LoMoGraph
4QSAR COX2	*0.607 ± 0.055*	0.625 ± 0.055 •|	0.601 ± 0.054 ◦|	0.628 ± 0.055 •|	0.868 ± 0.135 •|•
4QSAR DHFR	*0.551 ± 0.035*	0.572 ± 0.037 •|•	0.541 ± 0.033 ◦|	0.562 ± 0.035 •|	0.955 ± 0.102 •|•
CPD MOUSE	*0.751 ± 0.041*	0.760 ± 0.041 •|	0.764 ± 0.040 •|	0.775 ± 0.039 •|•	1.276 ± 0.154 •|•
CPD RAT	*0.868 ± 0.045*	0.870 ± 0.044 •|	0.887 ± 0.043 •|•	0.877 ± 0.042 |	1.529 ± 0.116 •|•
ISS MOUSE	*0.738 ± 0.046*	0.740 ± 0.046 |	0.753 ± 0.045 •|•	0.761 ± 0.048 •|•	1.197 ± 0.111 •|•
ISS RAT	*0.860 ± 0.050*	0.863 ± 0.047 |	0.900 ± 0.046 •|•	0.873 ± 0.051 •|	1.371 ± 0.109 •|•
Suth COX2	*0.559 ± 0.039*	0.586 ± 0.041 •|•	0.552 ± 0.038 ◦|◦	0.573 ± 0.040 •|	0.905 ± 0.137 •|•
Suth DHFR	*0.504 ± 0.026*	0.519 ± 0.030 •|•	0.493 ± 0.026 ◦|◦	0.498 ± 0.027 ◦|	0.941 ± 0.066 •|•
Suth ER TOX	*0.828 ± 0.046*	0.842 ± 0.045 •|	0.820 ± 0.042 |	0.847 ± 0.052 •|	1.216 ± 0.141 •|•
FDAMDD	*0.629 ± 0.029*	0.647 ± 0.023 •|•	0.612 ± 0.024 ◦|◦	0.621 ± 0.026 ◦|	0.951 ± 0.051 •|•
Biodeg	*0.844 ± 0.051*	0.875 ± 0.055 •|•	0.867 ± 0.050 •|•	0.874 ± 0.053 •|•	-
Tox09	*0.345 ± 0.015*	0.386 ± 0.016 •|•	0.342 ± 0.015 |	0.367 ± 0.016 •|•	-
ER_LIT	*0.492 ± 0.039*	0.499 ± 0.035 •|	0.495 ± 0.039 |	0.495 ± 0.041 |	-

•,◦ statistically significant improvement, or degradation of SCK NSPDK (d≠1) with respect to the other methods

Table 3: Mean absolute errors with standard deviations of SCK WDK, WDK, LoMoGraph WDK and LoMoGraph on the regression datasets. Statistically significant results are reported using both the Wilcoxon signed-rank test and the corrected resampled t-test (separated by a '|').

Dataset	*SCK WDK (d=1)*	SCK WDK (d≠1)	WDK	LoMoGraph WDK	LoMoGraph
4QSAR COX2	*0.673 ± 0.088*	0.691 ± 0.056 •|•	0.683 ± 0.055 |	0.676 ± 0.053 |	0.868 ± 0.135 •|•
4QSAR DHFR	*0.669 ± 0.054*	0.805 ± 0.132 •|•	0.733 ± 0.051 •|•	0.702 ± 0.047 •|	0.955 ± 0.102 •|•
CPD MOUSE	*0.827 ± 0.052*	0.874 ± 0.085 •|	0.888 ± 0.063 •|•	0.880 ± 0.052 •|•	1.276 ± 0.154 •|•
CPD RAT	*1.002 ± 0.048*	1.070 ± 0.103 •|	1.129 ± 0.154 •|•	1.043 ± 0.048 •|•	1.529 ± 0.116 •|•
ISS MOUSE	*0.798 ± 0.049*	0.826 ± 0.053 •|•	0.850 ± 0.056 •|•	0.859 ± 0.062 •|•	1.197 ± 0.111 •|•
ISS RAT	*0.977 ± 0.064*	1.018 ± 0.074 •|•	1.031 ± 0.061 •|•	1.022 ± 0.062 •|•	1.371 ± 0.109 •|•
Suth COX2	*0.612 ± 0.042*	0.620 ± 0.047 •|	0.603 ± 0.041 ◦|	0.610 ± 0.044 |	0.905 ± 0.137 •|•
Suth DHFR	*0.625 ± 0.036*	0.639 ± 0.086 •|	0.633 ± 0.032 •|	0.610 ± 0.031 ◦|	0.941 ± 0.066 •|•
Suth ER TOX	*0.993 ± 0.064*	1.301 ± 0.439 •|•	1.175 ± 0.071 •|•	1.130 ± 0.076 •|•	1.216 ± 0.141 •|•
FDAMDD	*0.727 ± 0.029*	0.809 ± 0.077 •|•	0.833 ± 0.329 •|•	0.727 ± 0.029 |	0.951 ± 0.051 •|•
Biodeg	*1.011 ± 0.072*	1.051 ± 0.119 •|	1.110 ± 0.071 •|•	1.086 ± 0.080 •|•	-
Tox09	*0.440 ± 0.021*	0.643 ± 0.168 •|•	0.464 ± 0.017 •|•	0.425 ± 0.017 ◦|	-
ER_LIT	*0.594 ± 0.040*	0.590 ± 0.058 ◦|	0.609 ± 0.040 •|	0.591 ± 0.043 •|	-

•,◦ statistically significant improvement, or degradation of SCK WDK (d=1) with respect to the other methods

Table 4: Classification accuracies with standard deviations of SCK NSPDK, NSPDK, LoMoGraph NSPDK and LoMoGraph on the classification datasets. Statistically significant results are reported using both the Wilcoxon signed-rank test and the corrected resampled t-test (separated by a '|').

Dataset	*SCK NSPDK (d≠1)*	SCK NSPDK (d=1)	NSPDK	LoMoGraph NSPDK	LoMoGraph
CYP INH	*76.33 ± 2.35*	75.62 ± 2.52 •|	75.55 ± 2.50 •|	75.88 ± 2.56 •|	74.08 ± 2.55 •|•
CYP SUB	*76.84 ± 2.28*	75.11 ± 2.84 •|•	75.95 ± 2.17 •|	76.21 ± 1.99 •|	71.37 ± 2.46 •|•
Fontaine	*95.56 ± 1.57*	95.37 ± 1.57 •|	95.71 ± 1.66 |	95.62 ± 1.60 |	92.08 ± 2.01 •|•
NCI AIDS	*90.13 ± 1.58*	89.86 ± 1.69 •|	90.58 ± 1.35 •|	89.02 ± 1.62 •|•	84.93 ± 1.61 •|•
CPDB MUT	*76.71 ± 2.10*	75.15 ± 2.20 •|•	77.25 ± 2.12 ◦|	73.85 ± 2.50 •|•	-

•,◦ statistically significant improvement, or degradation of SCK NSPDK (d≠1) with respect to the other methods

Table 5: Classification accuracies with standard deviations of SCK WDK, WDK, LoMoGraph WDK and LoMoGraph on the classification datasets. Statistically significant results are reported using both the Wilcoxon signed-rank test and the corrected resampled t-test (separated by a '|').

<table>
<tr><th>Dataset</th><th>SCK WDK (d=1)</th><th>SCK WDK (d≠1)</th><th>WDK</th><th>LoMoGraph WDK</th><th>LoMoGraph</th></tr>
<tr><td>CYP INH</td><td>74.05 ± 3.02</td><td>70.78 ± 3.85 •|•</td><td>75.05 ± 2.51 ∘|</td><td>75.42 ± 2.42 ∘|</td><td>74.08 ± 2.55 |</td></tr>
<tr><td>CYP SUB</td><td>72.07 ± 3.84</td><td>70.63 ± 4.63 •|</td><td>75.77 ± 2.38 ∘|∘</td><td>75.74 ± 2.46 ∘|∘</td><td>71.37 ± 2.46 •|</td></tr>
<tr><td>Fontaine</td><td>94.01 ± 1.86</td><td>94.48 ± 1.83 ∘|</td><td>94.41 ± 1.54 ∘|</td><td>93.03 ± 5.14 •|</td><td>92.08 ± 2.01 •|•</td></tr>
<tr><td>NCI AIDS</td><td>84.28 ± 2.04</td><td>83.67 ± 2.20 •|</td><td>79.97 ± 8.32 •|•</td><td>82.27 ± 1.82 •|•</td><td>84.93 ± 1.61 •|</td></tr>
<tr><td>CPDB MUT</td><td>72.80 ± 2.48</td><td>71.51 ± 2.88 •|</td><td>73.29 ± 2.57 |</td><td>70.85 ± 2.64 •|</td><td>-</td></tr>
</table>

•,∘ statistically significant improvement, or degradation of SCK WDK (d=1) with respect to the other methods

sampled t-test [19] are applied to test for significant differences at a significance level of 5%.

Tables 2, 3, 4 and 5 show the detailed experimental results in terms of relative mean absolute error (regression) and accuracy (classification) for the various methods on all datasets. The results for LoMoGraph are taken from the original publication [5]. Since not all datasets were used in this paper, the table contains missing values. In the same tables the second column shows the performance of the respective SCK method as baseline to compare against. For better illustration we highlight the reference method in italic. We indicate whether the respective SCK method is significantly better or worse than the comparison methods at $p < 0.05$ using both the Wilcoxon signed-ranked test and the corrected resampled t-test. In the following, we discuss the results based on the more conservative corrected resampled t-test. Overall, our experimental results show that the structural cluster kernel with NSPDK as base kernel performs always better than all comparison methods using WDK as base kernel. This demonstrates that NSPDK is a much more powerful base kernel compared to WDK. Moreover, we observe that the choice of setting the diagonal entries in the kernel matrix has a different effect on both SCK methods. Whereas setting the diagonal entries of the kernel matrix unequal to one leads to better predictive performance for SCK NSPDK, setting the diagonal entries equal to one results in better predictive performance for SCK WDK. In the following, we analyze the performance of the SCK approaches on the different datasets. On the COX2 datasets, we observe no performance improvement of SCK NSPDK and SCK WDK over the respective base kernel. The datasets contain extremely similar molecules, often differing in only one atom. Hence, the base kernel cannot be improved by the similarities induced by the structural clustering procedure. For the CPD, ISS and Biodeg datasets, a comparison between the mean absolute errors shows a clear performance advantage of SCK using both WDK and NSPDK as base kernel. Primarily, we explain this positive effect as a result of the structurally heterogeneity of the datasets consisting of many small molecules ($\sim$ up to 10 atoms). Hence, the NSPDK alone is not suited to determine similarity between graphs. As a consequence, for these datasets the pairwise similarities between the small, structurally homogeneous neighborhoods can contribute to similarity and consequently to predictive performance. On FDAMDD, the proposed structural cluster kernel with NSPDK as base kernel yields performance degradation compared to NSPDK. This shows that taking into account the similarities induced by PSCG has an adverse effect on the predictive performance. Although for this dataset a significant performance gain of SCK over the base kernel can be achieved by using WDK as base kernel, SCK WDK still has a higher mean absolute error compared to NSPDK. This demonstrates that NSPDK is much more powerful compared to WDK. For NCI AIDS and both CYP datasets the results on classification are clearly in favor of SCK NSPDK. On these datasets the structural cluster kernel with NSPDK improves over all other compared methods. However, for the corrected resampled t-test only four of the nine wins are statistically significant. Using WDK as base kernel, SCK can only achieve strong performance improvements on NCI AIDS. On the remaining classification datasets taking into account similarities induced by PSCG has either no significant effect or an adverse effect on predictive accuracy compared to the baseline methods (except for LoMoGraph on the Fontaine dataset). In summary, our structural cluster kernel approach is comparative to other methods, yet shows a strong performance increase on structurally more sparse datasets, i.e., chemically and structurally more diverse datasets. On these datasets the base kernel alone is not suited to determine similarities between graphs due to the high structural heterogeneity within the dataset. Hence, the structural neighborhood of two graphs can substantially contribute to graph similarity and therefore to predictive performance of the constructed models.

4.2 Semi-Supervised Setting

In this section, we investigate whether incorporating unlabeled data in the clustering process can positively contribute to predictive performance. Since semi-supervised methods potentially give the greatest benefit when a large amount of unlabeled data is used, we tested our structural cluster kernel approach in large-scale experiments, enriching the training data by a large number of molecules from the vast chemical space. For this, we employed the ChemDB database, which contains nearly 5 M commercially available small molecules [7, 8], as a source of unlabeled data, randomly sampling 100,000 structures from it. Since in the supervised setting, SCK NSPDK (d≠1) performs always better than or equal to all methods using WDK as base kernel as well as to SCK NSPDK (d=1), LoMoGraph NSPDK and LoMoGraph, we only compared SCK in the semi-supervised setting against SCK NSPDK (d≠1) and NSPDK. As in the supervised setting, the SVM complexity constant, C, was selected from $\{10^{-3}, 10^{-2}, 10^{-1}, 10^{0}, 10^{1}, 10^{2}\}$. Further, we used the same parameter setting for the NSPDK and the similarity coefficient θ.

The experimental results are shown in Tables 6 and 7 and in the bar charts in Figure 2. For completeness, the bar charts also depict the results for LoMoGraph NSPDK and LoMoGraph. The following discussion is based on the corrected resampled t-test. The results show that in the semi-supervised setting, SCK NSPDK achieves a strong performance gain on all datasets over the supervised approach: 10 of the 18 wins are statistically significant. For regression, the best results can be achieved on the toxicity datasets consisting of structurally more heterogeneous graphs. The results indicate that incorporating a large set of unlabeled data into the structural clustering process has a definite positive effect on the predictive performance. As opposed to the supervised setting, SCK NSPDK can improve over the base kernel on the FDAMDD dataset. This dataset is the largest one, comprising structurally heterogeneous molecules. Hence, exploiting a large set of unlabeled data in the clustering step can contribute to graph similarity. The strongest performance gains with respect to NSPDK can be achieved on the classification datasets. Whereas in the supervised setting SCK NSPDK was not able to gain significantly with respect to the base kernel on the classification datasets, the semi-supervised approach shows significant improvements over NSPDK in three out of five cases.

Table 6: Mean absolute errors with standard deviations of SCK NSPDK in both the semi-supervised and supervised setting and NSPDK on the classification datasets. Statistically significant results are reported using the Wilcoxon signed-rank test and the corrected resampled t-test (separated by a '|').

Dataset	*SCK NSPDK Semi-Sup*	SCK NSPDK ($d \neq 1$)	NSPDK
4QSAR COX2	*0.606 ± 0.055*	0.607 ± 0.055 |	0.601 ± 0.054 ∘|
4QSAR DHFR	*0.548 ± 0.033*	0.551 ± 0.035 |	0.541 ± 0.033 ∘|
CPD MOUSE	*0.746 ± 0.043*	0.751 ± 0.041 •|	0.764 ± 0.040 •|•
CPD RAT	*0.861 ± 0.046*	0.868 ± 0.045 •|•	0.887 ± 0.043 •|•
ISS MOUSE	*0.731 ± 0.049*	0.738 ± 0.046 •|•	0.753 ± 0.045 •|•
ISS RAT	*0.850 ± 0.050*	0.860 ± 0.050 •|•	0.900 ± 0.046 •|•
Suth COX2	*0.556 ± 0.040*	0.559 ± 0.039 •|	0.552 ± 0.038 |
Suth DHFR	*0.501 ± 0.025*	0.504 ± 0.026 |	0.493 ± 0.026 ∘|∘
Suth ER TOX	*0.808 ± 0.041*	0.828 ± 0.046 •|•	0.820 ± 0.042 •|•
FDAMDD	*0.608 ± 0.020*	0.629 ± 0.029 •|•	0.612 ± 0.024 •|
Biodeg	*0.840 ± 0.051*	0.844 ± 0.051 •|•	0.867 ± 0.050 •|•
Tox09	*0.339 ± 0.014*	0.345 ± 0.015 •|•	0.342 ± 0.015 •|
ER_LIT	*0.492 ± 0.039*	0.492 ± 0.039 |	0.495 ± 0.039 •|

•,∘ statistically significant improvement, or degradation of SCK NSPDK Semi-Sup with respect to the other methods

Table 7: Classification accuracies with standard deviations of SCK NSPDK in both the semi-supervised and supervised setting and NSPDK on the classification datasets. Statistically significant results are reported using the Wilcoxon signed-rank test and the corrected resampled t-test (separated by a '|').

Dataset	*SCK NSPDK Semi-Sup*	SCK NSPDK ($d \neq 1$)	NSPDK
CYP INH	*77.37 ± 2.26*	76.33 ± 2.35 •|•	75.55 ± 2.50 •|•
CYP SUB	*78.78 ± 2.16*	76.34 ± 2.28 •|•	75.95 ± 2.17 •|•
Fontaine	*95.80 ± 1.42*	95.56 ± 1.57 |	95.71 ± 1.66 |
NCI AIDS	*90.92 ± 1.00*	90.13 ± 1.58 •|	90.58 ± 1.35 •|
CPDB MUT	*78.47 ± 2.40*	76.71 ± 2.10 •|•	77.25 ± 2.12 •|•

•,∘ statistically significant improvement, or degradation of SCK NSPDK Semi-Sup with respect to the other methods

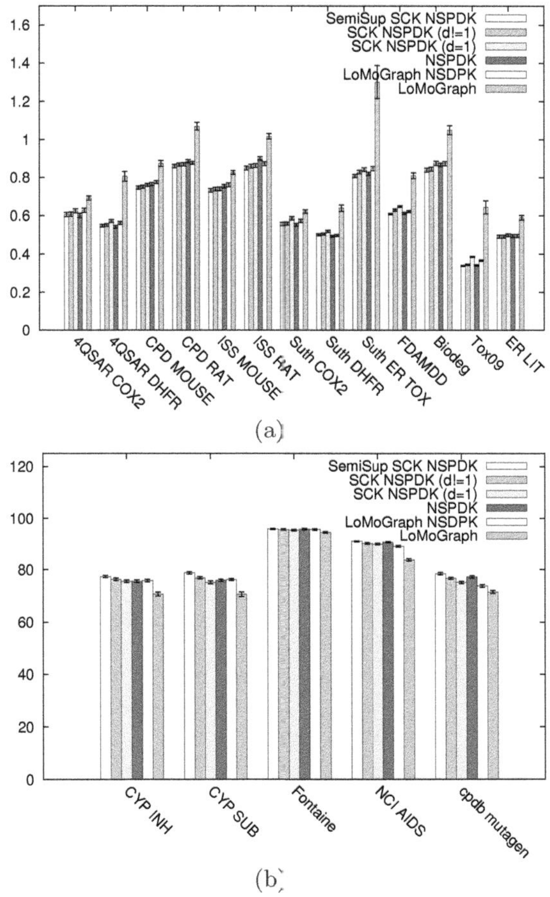

Figure 2: a) Mean absolute errors with 95% confidence intervals and b) classification accuracies with 95% confidence intervals on the different comparison methods for the data sets in Table 1.

5. CONCLUSION

In the work presented here, we proposed a novel graph kernel approach that incorporates similarity information based on structural graph clustering [21, 22] to improve state-of-the-art graph kernels. The proposed kernel is based on the idea that graph similarity can not only be determined by the similarity of the graphs alone, i.e., their structure, but also by the similarity of the graphs' structural neighborhood. We investigated the performance of the structural cluster kernels for regression and classification by using several real-world datasets of molecular graphs. In our experiments we performed a comparison with the weighted decomposition kernel, the neighborhood subgraph pairwise distance kernel, and a learning method combining clustering with classification or regression for the prediction task. The results demonstrate that the proposed kernel approach yields an increase in performance on a number of datasets, in particular on structurally more diverse datasets. We also investigated the performance of our approach in the semi-supervised setting, by enriching relatively small labeled datasets by a large set of unlabeled data instances from the vast chemical space. The results show that within the semi-supervised setting our approach achieves gains in performance when compared to the supervised version as well as to the pure base kernel, in particular for classification. We believe that the approach presented is general as such, and can also be employed in conjunction with a variety of different kernels and clustering approaches and is therefore not restricted to graph mining alone.

6. REFERENCES

[1] Environmental Toxicity Prediction Challenge, `http://www.cadaster.eu/node/65`.

[2] R. Benigni, C. Bossa, and M. Vari. Chemical Carcinogens: Structures and Experimental Data, `http://www.iss.it/binary/ampp/cont/ISSCANv2aEn.1134647480.pdf`.

[3] Z. Bodo. Hierarchical cluster kernels for supervised and semi-supervised learning. In *4th International Conference on Intelligent Computer Communication and Processing*, ICCP 2008, pages 9–16, 2008.

[4] Z. Bodo and L. Csato. Hierarchical and reweighting cluster kernels for semi-supervised learning. *Int. J. Comput. Comm. Contr.*, 5(4):469–476, 2010.

[5] F. Buchwald, T. Girschick, M. Seeland, and S. Kramer. Using local models to improve (Q)SAR predictivity. *Mol. Inf.*, 30(2-3):205–218, 2011.

[6] O. Chapelle, J. Weston, and B. Schölkopf. Cluster kernels for semi-supervised learning. In *Advances in Neural Information Processing Systems*, volume 15 of *NIPS 2002*, pages 585–592. MIT Press, 2003.

[7] J. Chen, S. J. Swamidass, Y. Dou, and P. Baldi. ChemDB: a public database of small molecules and related chemoinformatics resources. *Bioinf.*, 21:4133–4139, 2005.

[8] J. H. Chen, E. Linstead, S. J. Swamidass, D. Wang, and P. Baldi. ChemDB update – full text search and virtual chemical space. *Bioinf.*, 23:2348–2351, 2007.

[9] J. M. Collins. The DTP AIDS Antiviral Screen Program 1999, `http://dtp.nci.nih.gov/docs/aids/aidsdata.html`.

[10] F. Costa and K. De Grave. Fast neighborhood subgraph pairwise distance kernel. In *Proc. 26th International Conference on Machine Learning*, ICML'10, pages 255–262, 2010.

[11] S. Dzeroski, H. Blockeel, B. Kompare, S. Kramer, B. Pfahringer, and W. Van Laer. Experiments in predicting biodegradability. In *Applied Artificial Intelligence*, pages 80–91. Springer, 1999.

[12] F. Fontaine, M. Pastor, I. Zamora, and F. Sanz. Anchor-GRIND: Filling the gap between standard 3D QSAR and the GRid-INdependent descriptors. *J. Med. Chem.*, 48(7):2687–2694, 2005.

[13] T. Gärtner. *Kernels for Structured Data*. PhD thesis, Universität Bonn, 2005.

[14] L. Gold, T. Slone, B. Ames, N. Manley, G. Garfinkel, and L. Rohrbach. *Handbook of Carcinogenic Potency and Genotoxicity Databases*, chapter Carcinogenic Potency Database, pages 1–605. 1997.

[15] C. Helma, T. Cramer, S. Kramer, and L. De Raedt. Data mining and machine learning techniques for the identification of mutagenicity inducing substructures and structure activity relationships of noncongeneric compounds. *J. Chem. Inf. Comput. Sci.*, 44(4):1402–1411, 2004.

[16] K. Jahn and S. Kramer. Optimizing gSpan for molecular datasets. In *Proc. 3rd International Workshop on Mining Graphs, Trees and Sequences*, 2005.

[17] E. Matthews, N. Kruhlak, R. Benz, and J. Contrera. Assessment of the health effects of chemicals in humans: I. QSAR estimation of the maximum recommended therapeutic dose (MRTD) and no effect level (NOEL) of organic chemicals based on clinical trial data. *Curr. Drug. Disc. Tech.*, 1(1):61–76, 2004.

[18] S. Menchetti, F. Costa, and P. Frasconi. Weighted decomposition kernels. In *Proc. 22nd International Conference on Machine Learning*, ICML 2005, pages 585–592. ACM Press, 2005.

[19] C. Nadeau and Y. Bengio. Inference for the generalization error. *Mach. Learn.*, 52:239–281, 2003.

[20] U. Rückert, T. Girschick, F. Buchwald, and S. Kramer. Adapted transfer of distance measures for quantitative structure-activity relationships. In *Proc. 13th International Conference on Discovery Science*, DS 2010, pages 341–355. Springer-Verlag, 2010.

[21] M. Seeland, S. A. Berger, A. Stamatakis, and S. Kramer. Parallel structural graph clustering. In *Proc. 2011 European Conference on Machine Learning and Knowledge Discovery in Databases*, ECML/PKDD 2011, pages 256–272, 2011.

[22] M. Seeland, T. Girschick, F. Buchwald, and S. Kramer. Online structural graph clustering using frequent subgraph mining. In *Proc. 2010 European Conference on Machine Learning and Knowledge Discovery in Databases*, ECML/PKDD 2010, pages 213–228, 2010.

[23] J. J. Sutherland, L. A. O'Brien, and D. F. Weaver. Spline-fitting with a genetic algorithm: A method for developing classification structure-activity relationships. *J. Chem. Inf. Comput. Sci.*, 43(6):1906–1915, 2003.

[24] J. J. Sutherland, L. A. O'Brien, and D. F. Weaver. A comparison of methods for modeling quantitative structure-activity relationships. *J. Med. Chem.*, 47(22):5541–5554, 2004.

[25] S. V. N. Vishwanathan, N. N. Schraudolph, R. Kondor, and K. M. Borgwardt. Graph kernels. *J. Mach. Learn. Res.*, 11:1201–1242, 2010.

[26] J. Weston, C. Leslie, E. Ie, D. Zhou, A. Elisseeff, and W. S. Noble. Semi-supervised protein classification using cluster kernels. *Bioinf.*, 21(15):3241–3247, 2005.

[27] X. Yan and J. Han. gSpan: Graph-based substructure pattern mining. In *Proc. 2002 IEEE International Conference on Data Mining*, pages 721–724, 2002.

[28] C. W. Yap and Y. Z. Chen. Prediction of cytochrome P450 3A4, 2D6, and 2C9 inhibitors and substrates by using support vector machines. *J. Chem. Inf. Model.*, 45(4):982–992, 2005.

Multi-Label Hypothesis Reuse*

Sheng-Jun Huang, Yang Yu, and Zhi-Hua Zhou
National Key Laboratory for Novel Software Technology
Nanjing University, Nanjing 210046, China
{huangsj, yuy, zhouzh}@lamda.nju.edu.cn

ABSTRACT

Multi-label learning arises in many real-world tasks where an object is naturally associated with multiple concepts. It is well-accepted that, in order to achieve a good performance, the relationship among labels should be exploited. Most existing approaches require the label relationship as prior knowledge, or exploit by counting the label co-occurrence. In this paper, we propose the MAHR approach, which is able to automatically discover and exploit label relationship. Our basic idea is that, if two labels are related, the hypothesis generated for one label can be helpful for the other label. MAHR implements the idea as a boosting approach with a *hypothesis reuse* mechanism. In each boosting round, the base learner for a label is generated by not only learning on its own task but also reusing the hypotheses from other labels, and the amount of reuse across labels provides an estimate of the label relationship. Extensive experimental results validate that MAHR is able to achieve superior performance and discover reasonable label relationship. Moreover, we disclose that the label relationship is usually asymmetric.

Categories and Subject Descriptors

I.2.6 [**Artificial Intelligence**]: Learning; H.2.8 [**Database Management**]: Database Applications—*Data mining*; I.5.2 [**Pattern Recognition**]: Design Methodology—*classifier design and evaluation*

General Terms

Algorithm, Experimentation

Keywords

Multi-label learning, label relationship, hypothesis reuse

*This research was supported by the 973 Program (2010CB327903), NSFC (61073097, 60975043), JiangsuSF (BK2011566) and Baidu fund.

KDD'12, August 12–16, 2012, Beijing, China.

1. INTRODUCTION

In traditional supervised classification, one instance is associated with one target concept, whereas in many real-world applications, one instance is naturally associated with multiple concepts. For example, in scene classifications (e.g., [1]) a natural scene picture can be annotated as *sky*, *trees*, *mountains*, *lakes* and *water* simultaneously; in text categorizations (e.g., [25]) a piece of news on global warming issue can be categorized as *global warming*, *environment*, *economics* and *politics*.

Multi-label learning tries to address such kind of tasks. The most straightforward solution to multi-label learning is to decompose the task into a series of binary classification problems, each for one label [1]; however, such a solution neglects the relationship among labels, whereas previous studies [8, 16] have revealed that the label relationship is quite helpful and should be considered. Later on, most multi-label learning approaches try to exploit label relationship explicitly. Some approaches [4, 12, 19, 5] rely on external knowledge resources, such as knowledge on label hierarchies from which the label relationship is derived; label relationship obtained in this way is generally helpful, however, label hierarchies are often unavailable in real applications. Some other approaches [10, 24] try to exploit label relationship by counting the co-occurrence of labels in training data; although such approaches can be effective in some cases, there are high risks of overfitting the training data.

In this paper, we propose a novel multi-label learning approach named MAHR (MultI-lAbel Hypothesis Reuse), which is able to discover and exploit label relationship automatically in the learning process. Our basic idea is that, if two labels are related, the hypothesis generated for one label can be helpful for the other. MAHR implements the idea as a boosting approach with a *hypothesis reuse* mechanism. It trains multiple boosted learners simultaneously, each for one label. In each boosting round, in addition to generating a base learner for each label from its own hypothesis space, MAHR tries to *reuse* the hypotheses generated for other labels. The reuse process takes into account all trained hypotheses from all other labels via weighted combination, and helpful hypotheses are identified and reused with large weights through minimizing the loss on the concerned label. The *reuse score*, which is calculated from the weights of cross-label hypothesis reuse throughout the boosting process, provides an estimate of label relationship.

Extensive experiments show that the MAHR approach is superior or highly competitive to state-of-the-art multi-label learning approaches. In addition to the superior predictive performance, as a prominent advantage, MAHR is able to discover reasonable label relationship. Moreover, it is worth mentioning that our study disclose that the label relationship is usually asymmetric, quite different from symmetric label relationship assumed in many previous studies.

The rest of the paper is organized as follows. Section 2 introduces related work, Section 3 presents MAHR, Section 4 reports on experiments, and Section 5 concludes.

2. RELATED WORK

During the past few years, many multi-label approaches have been developed [17], such as the decomposition-based approaches [1], ranking-based approaches [3], common subspace approaches [14], generative approaches [16, 25], etc.

Some approaches assume that the label relationship can be provided by external knowledge resources as prior knowledge. For example, label hierarchies are required by [4, 19, 5], and a label similarity matrix is required as an input in [12]. In most real-world tasks, however, prior knowledge of label relationship is often unavailable.

Some approaches try to model the label relationship directly. For example, Ghamrawi and McCallum [10] tried to model the impact of an individual feature on the co-occurrence probability of label pairs. Sun et al. [23] used a hypergraph to model the correlation information of labels. Zhang and Zhang [28] used Bayesian network structure to encode the conditional dependencies of both the labels and feature sets. Usually, the label relationship is estimated by considering the co-occurrence or some kinds of equivalence of the labels, and is easy to overfitting the training data.

Tsoumakas et al. [24] proposed the 2BR approach and utilized label relationship to prune stacked single-label classifiers. The label relationship can be measured based on co-occurrence, or their proposed ϕ-coefficient. The ϕ-coefficient for two labels L_i and L_j is defined as $\phi(i,j) = (AD - BC)/\sqrt{(A+B)(C+D)(A+C)(B+D)}$, where A, B, C and D are the frequency counts of $L_i \wedge L_j$, $L_i \wedge \neg L_j$, $\neg L_i \wedge L_j$ and $\neg L_i \wedge \neg L_j$, respectively. We will employ the 2BR approach as a test bed to compare the effectiveness of the *reuse score* generated by our MAHR approach with that of the label co-occurrence and the ϕ-coefficient.

Boosting is a family of learning algorithms with sound theoretical foundation and wide applications. In [20], two boosting approaches for multi-label learning, AdaBoost.MH and AdaBoost.MR, were proposed. They both train additive models to directly optimize multi-label losses, i.e., *hamming loss* for AdaBoost.MH and *ranking loss* for AdaBoost.MR. AdtBoost.MH [6], an extension of AdaBoost.MH, is able to produce a set of comprehensible rules through employing alternating decision trees. MSSBoost [27] maintains a shared pool of base classifiers to reduce the redundancy among labels, where each base classifier is trained in a random subspace and with a random sample; in each round, it selects the best classifier from the pool and takes it as the base classifier for all the labels.

A common idea of these boosting approaches lies in the fact that, in each learning round, one base classifier is generated for all the labels (while only the output threshold may be adjusted for each label). Such a process may suffer from some deficiencies. First, in many cases, especially when there are lots of labels, it is quite difficult to generate a base classifier that can deal well with all the labels simultaneously. Second, it is rare that all labels are strongly related [13], and thus it is not very reasonable to try to generate one base classifier for all labels. In contrast, our MAHR approach generates one base classifier for each label in each round, and does not assume that all labels are strongly related. Moreover, MAHR does not require label relationship as input, and instead, it will produce estimate of the label relationship as output.

3. MAHR

We denote by $\mathcal{D} = \{(\boldsymbol{x}_1, Y_1), (\boldsymbol{x}_2, Y_2), \cdots, (\boldsymbol{x}_m, Y_m)\}$ a multi-label data set of m instances and L possible labels, where $\boldsymbol{x}_i$ is the i-th instance and the corresponding Y_i is a label vector of dimension L, $Y_i(l) = 1$ if the l-th label is a proper label of $\boldsymbol{x}_i$, and -1 otherwise.

3.1 The Algorithm

MAHR, as shown in Algorithm 1, maintains the general outline of boosting. MAHR generates base hypotheses in an iterative manner (the loop from line 3 to line 12). In the round t, it generates a base hypothesis for each label (the loop from line 4 to line 11). For the l-th label, it firstly trains a hypothesis $\hat{h}_{t,l}$ from its own hypothesis space (line 5), and then invokes a *reuse function* R (line 6) to generate another hypothesis $h_{t,l}$ from both $\hat{h}_{t,l}$ and the reuse of the hypotheses in the candidate set $Q_{t,l}$. After that, $h_{t,l}$ is treated as the base hypothesis for label l in round t, and the *edge* of its training error (i.e., 0.5 minus the training error) and the combination weight are calculated (line 7). The training set is then updated for the next round (line 8). Note that the candidate set for reuse in round $t+1$ on label l is defined as $Q_{t+1,l} = \{H_{t,k} | k \neq l\} \cup \{-H_{t,k} | k \neq l\}$ (line 10), where $H_{t,k}$ is the combined hypothesis for label k up to round t (line 9). Here, $-H_{t,k}$ is included in $Q_{t+1,l}$ for simplicity of optimization.

The *reuse function* R is utilized to combine multiple hypotheses, and it can be implemented in different ways. In this paper, we implement R via weighted linear combination. Such a simple implementation leads to decent performance in experiments, and a better implementation of R may even improve the performance. Formally, given a hypothesis pool $Q_{t,l}$ and a newly generated hypothesis $\hat{h}_{t,l}$ at the t-th round on the l-th label, we define a parameterized reuse function $R_{\boldsymbol{\beta}_{t,l}}$ as

$$R_{\boldsymbol{\beta}_{t,l}}(\hat{h}_{t,l}, Q_{t,l}) = \boldsymbol{\beta}_{t,l}(\hat{h}_{t,l}) \cdot \hat{h}_{t,l} + \sum_{H \in Q_{t,l}} \boldsymbol{\beta}_{t,l}(H) \cdot H, \quad (1)$$

where $\boldsymbol{\beta}_{t,l}$ is a vector of reuse weights to be determined and $\boldsymbol{\beta}_{t,l}(H)$ denotes the element of $\beta_{t,l}$ corresponding to H. Different strategies can be employed to solve the parameter $\boldsymbol{\beta}$, aiming to minimize different multi-label losses (e.g., hamming loss and ranking loss).

For hamming loss, which concerns about how each predicted label is consistent with the ground-truth label additively, $\boldsymbol{\beta}_{t,l}$ can be obtained by:

$$\begin{aligned} \min_{\boldsymbol{\beta}_{t,l},\ \xi_i} \ & \sum\nolimits_{i=1}^{m} D_{t,l}(i) \cdot \xi_i \quad (2) \\ s.t.\ \ & Y_i(l) R_{\boldsymbol{\beta}_{t,l}}(\boldsymbol{x}_i) \geq 1 - \xi_i \ (\forall i) \\ & \boldsymbol{\beta}_{t,l}(\hat{h}_{t,l}) + \sum\nolimits_{H \in Q} \boldsymbol{\beta}_{t,l}(H) = 1 \\ & \boldsymbol{\beta}_{t,l}(\hat{h}_{t,l}),\ \boldsymbol{\beta}_{t,l}(H),\ \xi_i \geq 0 \ (\forall H, i) \end{aligned}$$

Algorithm 1 The MAHR algorithm

1: **Input:** Training set $\mathcal{D} = \{(\boldsymbol{x}_i, Y_i)\}_{i=1}^{m}$, base learning algorithm $\mathcal{L}$, reuse function R, number of rounds T
2: $D_{1,l}(i) = \frac{1}{m}$, $Q_{1,l} = \emptyset$ $(i = 1, \cdots, m,\ l = 1, \cdots, L)$
3: **for** $t = 1$ **to** T **do**
4:   **for** $l = 1$ **to** L **do**
5:     $\hat{h}_{t,l} \leftarrow \mathcal{L}(\mathcal{D}, D_{t,l})$
6:     $h_{t,l} \leftarrow R(\hat{h}_{t,l}, Q_{t,l})$ such that $h_{t,l}(\cdot) \in [-1, 1]$
7:     $\gamma_{t,l} = \frac{1}{2} \sum_i D_{t,l}(i) h_{t,l}(\boldsymbol{x}_i) Y_i(l)$; $\alpha_{t,l} = \frac{1}{2} \ln(\frac{0.5+\gamma_{t,l}}{0.5-\gamma_{t,l}})$
8:     $D_{t+1,l}(i) = \left(1 + \exp\left(Y_i(l) \sum_{j=1}^{t} \alpha_{j,l} h_{j,l}(x_i)\right)\right)^{-1}$
9:     $H_{t,l} = \sum_{j=1}^{t} \alpha_{j,l} h_{j,l}$
10:     $Q_{t+1,l} = \{H_{t,k} | k \neq l\} \cup \{-H_{t,k} | k \neq l\}$
11:   **end for**
12: **end for**
13: **Output:** $H_l(\boldsymbol{x}) = \sum_{t=1}^{T} \alpha_{t,l} h_{t,l}(\boldsymbol{x})$ $(l = 1, \cdots, L)$

For ranking loss, which concerns about whether the relevant labels are ordered before irrelevant ones, we can obtain $\boldsymbol{\beta}_{t,l}$ with the following optimization problem, which enforces the combined hypothesis to order the label pairs correctly:

$$\min_{\boldsymbol{\beta}_{t,l},\ \xi_{i,j}} \sum_{i=1}^{m} \sum_{j=1}^{L} D_{t,l}(i) \cdot \xi_{i,j} \quad (3)$$

$$s.t.\ (Y_i(l) - Y_i(j))(R_{\boldsymbol{\beta}_{t,l}}(\boldsymbol{x}_i) - H_{t-1,j}(\boldsymbol{x}_i)) \geq 1 - \xi_{i,j} (\forall i, j)$$

$$\boldsymbol{\beta}_{t,l}(\hat{h}_{t,l}) + \sum_{H \in Q} \boldsymbol{\beta}_{t,l}(H) = 1$$

$$\boldsymbol{\beta}_{t,l}(\hat{h}_{t,l}),\ \boldsymbol{\beta}_{t,l}(H),\ \xi_{i,j} \geq 0\ (\forall H, i, j)$$

In this paper, we focus on hamming loss, and implement MAHR according to Eq. 2.

We then look into the combination weight and the distribution update rule shown in line 7 and line 8, respectively. To optimize the hamming loss, we can equivalently optimize the zero-one loss on each label. The zero-one loss, however, is hard to optimize directly, and thus we try to optimize the logistic loss for each label instead:

$$\ell_{\ln}(H_l, \boldsymbol{x}_i, Y_i, l) = \ln(1 + \exp(-Y_i(l) \cdot H_l(\boldsymbol{x}_i)))$$

which is a surrogate loss function for zero-one loss. By differentiating the logistic loss function, the combination weight and the update rule can be derived, as similarly done in FilterBoost [2]. One can use other surrogate loss functions such as the exponential loss. Also, as similar as FilterBoost, the distribution of MAHR in line 8 is a probability distribution, and thus normalization is not needed.

Note that the MAHR approach trains L models each for one label, these models may or may not have common base hypotheses, depending on the learning task. In contrast, other multi-label boosting approaches, such as MSSBoost, AdaBoost.MH and AdaBoost.MR, use the same base hypothesis for all the labels. This is a significant difference between MAHR and other approaches. The constraint that all labels share the same base hypothesis might be overly restrictive, and it may even injure the learning performance when some of the labels are not closely related.

For a test instance, we follow the training order and calculate the predictions of base hypotheses round-by-round until the final prediction is obtained. In such a way, the output of any hypothesis needs to be calculated only once, and there is no extra computational cost in the test phase comparing with multiple single-label boosting.

3.2 Estimating Label Relationship

Since MAHR reuses hypotheses across labels, the amount of reuse can be considered as a measure of label relationship. If two labels are independent, the hypothesis for one label may have a large error on the other label, and thus the reuse function for the other label will assign a very small weight to that hypothesis; if two labels are strongly related, the hypothesis for one label may have a small error on the other label, and thus the reuse function will assign a large weight to incorporate the hypothesis. Therefore, we assess the label relationship by the reuse weight, i.e., the $\boldsymbol{\beta}$ in Eq. 1. We define the *reuse score* from label j to i as

$$S(i,j) = \sum_{t=2}^{T} \alpha_{t,i} \left(\boldsymbol{\beta}_{t,i}(H_{t-1,j}) - \boldsymbol{\beta}_{t,i}(-H_{t-1,j})\right), \quad (4)$$

where $\boldsymbol{\beta}_{t,i}(\cdot)$ is weighted by $\alpha_{t,i}$ (the weight of $h_{t,i}$). Here, t starts from 2 because there is no hypothesis for reuse in the first round. Note that $\boldsymbol{\beta}_{t,i}(\cdot)$ is constrained to be positive in the optimization, and $\boldsymbol{\beta}_{t,i}(-H_{\cdot,j})$, the weight of the negation of $H_{\cdot,j}$, actually reflects the degree of label j being negatively reused by label i, and therefore, we do subtraction in Eq. 4.

The reuse score $S(i,j)$ assesses how much label j can help the learning of label i. It is worth noting that, unlike the commonly used relationship, such as co-occurrence and ϕ-coefficient, the reuse score is not constrained to be symmetric, i.e., $S(i,j)$ does not necessarily equal $S(j,i)$.

3.3 Convergence Analysis

Suppose the multi-label learning task has L underlying hypotheses $(f_1, \cdots, f_L)$, each corresponds to one label. Given the training set and a hypothesis space $\mathcal{H}$, an algorithm tries to find a set of hypotheses, each approximating one of the underlying hypothesis. We concern about the training hamming loss $\widehat{err}_{hl} = \frac{1}{mL} \sum_{i=1}^{m} \sum_{l=1}^{L} I(sign(H_l(\boldsymbol{x}_i)) \neq Y_i(l))$ and the generalization hamming loss $err_{hl} = \mathbb{E}_{(\boldsymbol{x},Y)}[\frac{1}{L} \sum_{l=1}^{L} I(sign(H_l(\boldsymbol{x})) \neq Y(l))]$, where $I(\cdot)$ denotes the indicator function.

Lemma 1. [2] *Let $\gamma = \min_t |\gamma_t|$, where γ_t is the edge of h_t, and let ϵ be the target error. If the number of boosting rounds $T > 2ln(2)/\epsilon/(1 - 2\sqrt{1/4 - \gamma^2})$, then $err_t < \epsilon$ for some $t, 1 \leq t \leq T$. Particularly it is true for $T > \frac{ln(2)}{2\epsilon\gamma^2}$.*

With Lemma 1, we get Theorem 1 which guarantees the convergence rate of MAHR on the training set.

Theorem 1. *Let $\gamma = \min_{t,l} |\gamma_{t,l}|$, for any $\epsilon > 0$, MAHR achieves the hamming loss $\widehat{err}_{hl} < \epsilon$ on the training set within the number of rounds $T > 0.5 \ln 2 \cdot \epsilon^{-1} \cdot \gamma^{-2}$.*

Proof. When MAHR achieves the zero-one loss ϵ on every label, it also achieves hamming loss ϵ because the hamming loss is the average of the zero-one loss over all labels. Therefore, we focus on the number of rounds for MAHR to achieve ϵ zero-one loss on a label; it is at most $0.5 \ln 2 \cdot \epsilon^{-1} \cdot \gamma^{-2}$ according to Lemma 1. □

Theorem 1 shows that MAHR efficiently achieves a training hamming loss. Then, based on Lemma 2, we get Theorem 2 for the generalization ability of MAHR.

LEMMA 2. [9] *Let H be a class of binary functions of VC-dimension $d \geq 2$. Then the VC-dimension of $\Theta_T(H)$ is at most $2(d+1)(T+1)\log_2(e(T+1))$ (where e is the base of the natural logarithm). Therefore, if the hypotheses generated by weak learner are chosen from a class of VC-dimension $d \geq 2$, then the final hypotheses after T iterations belong to a class of VC-dimension at most $2(d+1)(T+1)\log_2[e(T+1)]$.*

THEOREM 2. *Let $\gamma = \min_{t,l}|\gamma_{t,l}|$ and d be the VC-dimension of the hypothesis space $\mathcal{H}$. For any $\epsilon > 0$, with probability δ the generalization hamming loss of MAHR is bounded by*

$$err_{hl} \leq \epsilon + 2\sqrt{\frac{1}{m}(\ln\frac{9}{\delta} + D(\ln\frac{2m}{D} + 1))}$$

where $D = 2(d+1)(\frac{0.5\ln 2}{\epsilon \cdot \gamma^2} + 1)\log_2(e(\frac{0.5\ln 2}{\epsilon \cdot \gamma^2} + 1)) + L$.

PROOF. The generalization inequality is directly adapted from the Theorem 6.7 in [26]. The capacity D of the learning system depends on the complexity of the base hypothesis space and the number of hypotheses combined. The VC-dimension d of $\mathcal{H}$ and the total number of hypotheses $T \cdot L$ results in the capacity $2(d+1)(\frac{0.5\ln 2}{\epsilon \cdot \gamma^2}+1)\log_2(e(\frac{0.5\ln 2}{\epsilon \cdot \gamma^2}+1))$ according to Lemma 2. Moreover, the reuse of the other $L-1$ labels through linear combination results in the capacity L. Therefore, quantity of D in Theorem 2 is derived. □

Note that Theorems 1 and 2 are derived for a general case. We then analyze how the hypothesis reuse can be helpful. We characterize the ground-truth label relationship between two labels l_1 and l_2 by their output correlation

$$\kappa(l_1, l_2) = \frac{1}{m}\sum\nolimits_{i=1}^{m} f_{l_1}(\boldsymbol{x}) f_{l_2}(\boldsymbol{x}). \tag{5}$$

Then we have the generalization bound in Theorem 3, which shows that the hypothesis reuse in MAHR can utilize the label relationship to reduce the capacity of the learning system and thus leads to a better generalization ability.

THEOREM 3. *Let $\gamma = \min_{t,l}|\gamma_{t,l}|$, d be the VC-dimension of the hypothesis space $\mathcal{H}$, $\tilde{\kappa} = \min_{l_1,l_2}\kappa(l_1,l_2)$, and $\tilde{w}$, $\tilde{\epsilon}$ be the minimum weight and the maximum training error among all the cross-label hypotheses, respectively. For any $\epsilon > 0$, with probability δ the generalization hamming loss of MAHR is bounded by*

$$err_{hl} \leq \epsilon + 2\sqrt{\frac{1}{m}\left(\ln\frac{9}{\delta} + D\left(\ln\frac{2m}{D} + 1\right)\right)}$$

where $D = 2(d+1)\left(\frac{0.5\ln 2}{\epsilon' \cdot \gamma^2}+1\right)\log_2\left(e\left(\frac{0.5\ln 2}{\epsilon' \cdot \gamma^2}+1\right)\right) + L$ *and* $\epsilon' = 0.5 - \frac{1-2\epsilon}{2\tilde{w}} + \frac{(L-1)\tilde{w}(\tilde{\kappa}-2\tilde{\epsilon})}{2\tilde{w}}$.

PROOF. Suppose we have obtained the hypothesis h_l for the l-th label ($l = 2, \cdots, L$) such that

$$\widehat{err}(h_l \mid f_l) = \frac{1}{m}\sum\nolimits_{i=1}^{m} I[h_l(\boldsymbol{x}_i) \neq f_l(\boldsymbol{x}_i)] \leq \epsilon_l,$$

where $h_l(\boldsymbol{x}_i) \in \{+1, -1\}$. Thus, we have

$$\frac{1}{m}\sum\nolimits_{i=1}^{m} h_l(\boldsymbol{x}_i) f_l(\boldsymbol{x}_i) \geq 1 - 2\epsilon_l. \tag{6}$$

Then, we want to learn the first label up to the error ϵ_1. According to the reuse function, the hypothesis for the first label is $h_1 = sign[w_1\hat{h}_1 + \sum_{l=2}^{L} w_l h_l]$, and the following condition should be satisfied:

$$\frac{1}{m}\sum\nolimits_{i=1}^{m} f_1(\boldsymbol{x}_i) sign[w_1\hat{h}_1(\boldsymbol{x}_i) + \sum\nolimits_{l=2}^{L} w_l h_l(\boldsymbol{x}_i)] \geq 1 - 2\epsilon_1.$$

By the constraint of Eq. 2, it holds that $w_1\hat{h}_1 + \sum_{l=2}^{L} w_l h_l \in [-1, 1]$, and thus we can get a stronger requirement to guarantee the error:

$$\frac{1}{m}\sum\nolimits_{i=1}^{m} f_1(\boldsymbol{x}_i)(w_1\hat{h}_1(\boldsymbol{x}_i) + \sum\nolimits_{l=2}^{L} w_l h_l(\boldsymbol{x}_i)) \geq 1 - 2\epsilon_1$$

$$\Leftarrow \sum_{i=1}^{m}\frac{w_1}{m} f_1(\boldsymbol{x}_i)\hat{h}_1(\boldsymbol{x}_i) \geq 1 - 2\epsilon_1 - \sum_{l=2}^{L}\sum_{i=1}^{m}\frac{w_l}{m} f_1(\boldsymbol{x}_i) h_l(\boldsymbol{x}_i)$$

$$\Leftarrow \frac{1}{m}\sum_{i=1}^{m} f_1(\boldsymbol{x}_i)\hat{h}_1(\boldsymbol{x}_i) \geq \frac{1-2\epsilon_1}{w_1} - \sum_{l=2}^{L}\frac{w_l}{w_1}(\kappa(1,l) - 2\epsilon_l),$$

where the last derivation is obtained by applying Eqs. 5 and 6 together. Here, $A \Leftarrow B$ means that A can be guaranteed if B holds. The last inequality implies that we only need to learn the hypothesis $\hat{h}_1$ to approximate f_1 up to the error $\epsilon' = 0.5 - \frac{1-2\epsilon_1}{2w_1} + \sum_{l=2}^{L}\frac{w_l}{2w_1}(\kappa(1,l) - 2\epsilon_l)$, which can be larger than ϵ_1 when $\kappa(1,l)$ is large and ϵ_l is small. Incorporating the error into Theorem 2, we get Theorem 3. □

Theorem 3 suggests that the hypothesis reuse mechanism works when the labels are not independent and the number of rounds in MAHR is large, such that we have fit some labels well enough for reuse. Correspondingly, the number of rounds for achieving the error ϵ on one label is $0.5\ln 2\left(0.5 - \frac{1-2\epsilon_1}{2w_1} + \sum_{l=2}^{L}\frac{w_l}{2w_1}(\kappa(1,l) - 2\epsilon_l)\right)^{-1}\gamma^{-2}$. Also, from the proof of Theorem 3 we can find that with the related and well-learned hypotheses on other labels, the learning of the base hypothesis becomes easier. Note that if labels are independent, Theorem 3 is as same as Theorem 2.

3.4 Discussion on Improving Efficiency

MAHR requires more computational cost than other boosting approaches such as AdaBoost.MH, because in each round of boosting, the optimization of Eq. 2 needs to be addressed for each label. Fortunately, the optimization is a linear programming problem, and thus it can be solved efficiently. MAHR may train more base classifiers than other boosting approaches, however, this can be compensated in a parallel computing system. Unlike other boosting approaches that are relatively hard to be parallelized, in each round of MAHR, the line 5 to line 10 of Algorithm 1 can be executed for each label in parallel, because there is no interaction among labels in one round. Thus, the total execution time of the default implementation of MAHR can be close to that of AdaBoost.MH.

Moreover, since MAHR employs logistic loss, it can utilize the filtering mechanism of FilterBoost [2] to deal with large-scale data efficiently. We can have a filtering version of the MAHR algorithm: given the data set for training and evaluating the base hypothesis, it uses a *Filter* function to collect a set of training instances according to the number of training instances m, the target training error $\epsilon \in (0, 1)$, the confidence $\delta \in (0, 1)$ upper-bounding the probability of failure, and the error in edge estimation $\tau \in (0, 1)$.

4. EXPERIMENTS

We introduce the experimental settings in Section *4.1*, and then compare MAHR with state-of-the-art multi-label learning approaches in Section *4.2*. In Section *4.3*, we study the label relationship discovered by MAHR. We also study the influence of the number of boosting rounds in Section *4.4*, and the computational cost in Section *4.5*.

Table 1: Comparison of MAHR with state-of-the-art multi-label learning approaches on five evaluation criteria. •(◦) indicates that MAHR is significantly better (worse) than the corresponding method (pairwise t-tests at 95% significance level). Note that AdtBoost.MH could not output ranking loss values.

Data	Boosting-style methods						ML-kNN	RankSVM	ECC
	MAHR	MAHR-id	AdaBoost.MH	AdaBoost.MR	AdtBoost.MH	MSSBoost			
Hamming loss (the smaller, the better)									
Image	.169±.011	.190±.015•	.176±.007•	.754±.004•	.190±.007•	.210±.009•	.175±.007•	.339±.021•	.180±.010•
Image2	.191±.008	.229±.014•	.200±.008•	.752±.003•	.210±.006•	.230±.007•	.191±.006	.219±.021•	.205±.009•
Scene	.084±.004	.108±.019•	.091±.003•	.821±.001•	.111±.003•	.134±.004•	.090±.003•	.251±.017•	.095±.004•
Reuters	.030±.003	.046±.006•	.031±.003	.835±.002•	.055±.005•	.096±.008•	.049±.003•	.157±.031•	.062±.007•
Yahoo	.039±.012	.043±.014•	.046±.016•	.901±.052•	.044±.013•	.044±.014•	.043±.014•	.042±.014•	.049±.017•
Yeast	.204±.004	.222±.007•	.228±.004•	.697±.002•	.210±.003•	.227±.005•	.196±.003◦	.196±.003◦	.208±.005•
Enron	.047±.002	.053±.002•	.050±.002•	.932±.009•	.054±.002•	.051±.002•	.051±.002•	.311±.367•	.055±.002•
One error (the smaller, the better)									
Image	.301±.024	.355±.046•	.313±.021•	.307±.020•	.363±.021•	.375±.023•	.325±.024•	.708±.052•	.300±.022
Image2	.368±.019	.493±.063•	.378±.022	.378±.018•	.436±.019•	.427±.018•	.370±.017	.400±.063•	.350±.019◦
Scene	.217±.011	.265±.060•	.226±.010•	.215±.012	.293±.012•	.291±.009•	.238±.012•	.457±.065•	.232±.011•
Reuters	.063±.010	.087±.015•	.055±.008◦	.059±.008◦	.120±.017•	.280±.035•	.126±.012•	.228±.192•	.156±.020•
Yahoo	.398±.122	.506±.188•	.452±.141•	.487±.118•	.483±.148•	.481±.149•	.471±.157•	.412±.130	.391±.133
Yeast	.243±.011	.253±.010•	.291±.012•	.319±.015•	.247±.010	.272±.010•	.235±.012◦	.224±.009◦	.180±.012◦
Enron	.234±.030	.309±.035•	.293±.039•	.362±.035•	.317±.036•	.273±.033•	.299±.031•	.855±.020•	.228±.036
Coverage (the smaller, the better)									
Image	.921±.060	1.06±.122•	.922±.058	.930±.062	1.04±.062•	1.06±.046•	.972±.062•	2.10±.065•	.998±.056•
Image2	1.05±.055	1.49±.180•	1.06±.051	1.09±.048•	1.22±.050•	1.20±.046•	1.08±.048•	1.17±.163•	1.13±.055•
Scene	.471±.032	.555±.132•	.463±.022	.450±.020◦	.633±.040•	.582±.028•	.505±.029•	1.15±.195•	.570±.026•
Reuters	.276±.027	.316±.040•	.268±.026	.270±.025	.409±.047•	.891±.105•	.440±.035•	.801±.780•	.664±.083•
Yahoo	4.56±1.60	7.74±2.96•	4.22±1.29◦	4.54±1.27	4.27±1.36	4.14±1.32◦	4.09±1.23◦	4.60±1.47	8.52±1.79•
Yeast	6.70±.092	7.30±.309•	6.66±.087◦	7.11±.083•	6.50±.074◦	6.71±.097	6.28±.086◦	6.62±.134◦	7.16±.127•
Enron	14.2±1.07	20.2±1.22•	11.5±.772◦	13.5±.865◦	14.0±.813	12.5±.898◦	13.0±.850◦	26.5±1.32•	20.7±1.09•
Ranking loss (the smaller, the better)									
Image	.166±.012	.198±.029•	.164±.011	.171±.012•	N/A	.199±.010•	.177±.013•	.463±.018•	.247±.016•
Image2	.198±.012	.303±.047•	.200±.011	.213±.011•	N/A	.233±.011•	.203±.010•	.225±.041•	.282±.021•
Scene	.077±.006	.093±.026•	.075±.004	.075±.004◦	N/A	.099±.005•	.083±.006•	.214±.039•	.139±.008•
Reuters	.019±.003	.025±.005•	.017±.003◦	.018±.003	N/A	.119±.018•	.045±.004•	.104±.128•	.105±.014•
Yahoo	.109±.046	.206±.100•	.103±.040	.116±.040	N/A	.103±.042	.102±.045	.112±.047	.332±.084•
Yeast	.184±.005	.209±.014•	.194±.005•	.232±.005•	N/A	.195±.006•	.168±.006◦	.172±.006◦	.279±.011•
Enron	.098±.010	.145±.011•	.076±.008◦	.100±.008	N/A	.085±.009◦	.091±.008◦	.267±.019•	.246±.018•
Average Precision (the larger, the better)									
Image	.804±.014	.766±.029•	.798±.013•	.796±.013•	.766±.013•	.758±.013•	.788±.014•	.516±.011•	.789±.014•
Image2	.764±.012	.669±.043•	.759±.012	.751±.011•	.718±.012•	.723±.011•	.759±.011•	.739±.041•	.753±.013•
Scene	.869±.008	.841±.038•	.866±.006•	.869±.007	.822±.008•	.828±.006•	.857±.007•	.698±.047•	.846±.007•
Reuters	.962±.005	.948±.009•	.966±.005◦	.964±.004◦	.925±.011•	.815±.022•	.920±.007•	.846±.145•	.884±.013•
Yahoo	.660±.098	.543±.159•	.634±.109•	.595±.091•	.617±.113•	.618±.112•	.625±.117•	.658±.103	.616±.092•
Yeast	.749±.007	.717±.015•	.727±.008•	.693±.007•	.740±.006•	.729±.007•	.762±.007◦	.767±.007◦	.731±.007•
Enron	.678±.020	.601±.019•	.681±.021	.596±.021•	.596±.027•	.661±.018•	.636±.015•	.262±.017•	.637±.021•

4.1 Settings

To examine the effectiveness of hypothesis reuse, we compare MAHR with a degenerated version MAHR-id, which is as same as MAHR except that it does not reuse hypothesis (i.e., it does not invoke the reuse function) and learns every label independently. We also compare MAHR with state-of-the-art multi-label learning approaches that are divided into two groups: the boosting group including AdaBoost.MH [20], AdaBoost.MR [20], AdtBoost.MH [6] and MSSBoost [27], and the non-boosting group including ML-kNN [29] which considers the first-order correlation, RankSVM [8] which considers the second-order correlation, and ECC [18] which considers higher-order correlation. For the compared approaches, the best parameters reported in their corresponding literatures [20, 6, 27, 29, 8, 18] are used. For MAHR, the base learning algorithm is *decision stump* implemented in Weka [11], the number of rounds, i.e., the parameter T in Algorithm 1 is set as default to $2\times\#feature$ for all the data sets. Note that the influence of the number of learning rounds will be studied in Section 4.4.

There are different criteria for evaluating the performances of multi-label learning. In our experiments, we employ five commonly used criteria, i.e., *hamming loss*, *one error*, *coverage*, *ranking loss* and *average precision*. The definition of these criteria can be found in [21, 7, 30].

Seventeen data sets are used in our experiments. These data sets spanned a broad range of applications: *Image* [29], *Image2* [30] and *Scene* [1] for image classification, *Reuters* [22] for text categorization, *Yeast* [8] for gene function prediction, *Enron* [15] for email analysis, and *Yahoo* [25] for web page categorization. Note that *Yahoo* consists of 11 independent data sets, i.e., *Arts*, *Business*, *Computers*, *Education*, *Entertainment*, *Health*, *Recreation*, *Reference*, *Science*, *Social* and *Society*. For *Yahoo*, the data sets are pre-separated into training and test sets [25]; for the other data sets, we randomly select 1,500 instances for training and use the remaining data for testing. The data partition is repeated randomly for thirty times, and the average results as well as standard deviations over the thirty repetitions are recorded.

4.2 Comparison Results

The comparison results are shown in Table 1. Due to page limit, for *Yahoo* we only report the average results over the eleven data sets. Note that we are mostly interested in *hamming loss* because the current implementation of MAHR is designed for this loss.

Comparing with MAHR-id, MAHR achieves significantly better performance over all the five criteria on all the data sets. This validates the usefulness of the hypothesis reuse mechanism on exploiting label relationship.

Comparing with other approaches, MAHR achieves the best performance on hamming loss in most cases; particularly, it outperforms AdaBoost.MH and AdtBoost.MH that were also designed for optimizing hamming loss. For the other four criteria, MAHR also achieves excellent performances although it was not implemented to optimize these criteria. It is superior to the compared approaches on both one error and average precision in most cases. On coverage, it performs better than ECC, comparable with other approaches, worse than only AdaBoost.MH. On ranking loss, it outperforms ECC and achieves comparable performances with other approaches.

Overall, by exploiting label relationship with the hypothesis reuse mechanism, MAHR drastically improves the performance of its non-reuse counterpart MAHR-id over all criteria. Comparing with other approaches, MAHR is the best approach for optimizing hamming loss, and is highly competitive over the other criteria. These observations suggest that label relationship does help multi-label learning, and the hypothesis reuse mechanism is useful. Note that, currently we just implement R in a simple form of linear combination, and it is expected that better performance can be obtained with better designs of reuse functions. Also, one can incorporate different multi-label learning mechanisms or optimize different objectives in Eq. 2 when other evaluation criteria rather than hamming loss are concerned.

4.3 Label Relationship Discovered

To examine whether the reuse score reflects reasonable label relationship, since we were not given with ground-truth label relationship for real-world data, we first study three synthetic data sets, for which we know the ground-truth label relationship. All the three data sets have five labels, L_1 to L_5, and the 5-th label is assigned to an instance if it has none of L_1 to L_4. In *data-inde*, the first four labels are independent to each other, each label is associated with five different features, and a label is assigned to an instance if the summed value of the corresponding five features is larger than a specified threshold. In *data-equal*, $L_1 = L_2$ and $L_3 = L_4$. In *data-union*, the labels L_2 to L_4 are independent to each other, and L_1 is assigned to an instance if it has at least one of L_2 to L_4, i.e., $L_1 = L_2 \vee L_3 \vee L_4$. We generate 10,000 instances, and randomly divide them into two parts of equal size, using one part for training and the other for testing. The experiments are repeated for 10 times, each with a random partition of the data set, and the average reuse scores are recorded in Tables 2 to 4 for the three data sets, respectively. Note that the values are normalized such that each label has a reuse score 1 for itself.

It is obvious that all the diagonal entries of the tables are larger than the other entries, implying that each boosted learner mainly relies on its own task. It can be found that in the last row of all three tables, when learning L_5, it takes the other labels as negative references. This is in our expectation because L_5 is assigned to an instance when no other label is assigned. Excluding the diagonal entries, in Table 2, the entries in the first four rows of the first four columns are close to zero, indicating that L_1 to L_4 are not helpful to each other; this is consistent with the ground-truth that these labels are independent. In Table 3 the entries $S(L_1, L_2), S(L_2, L_1), S(L_3, L_4)$ and $S(L_4, L_3)$ show relatively large positive values, and in Table 4 the entries $S(L_1, L_2), S(L_1, L_3)$ and $S(L_1, L_4)$ show large positive values; these results are consistent with the ground-truth label relationship. Particularly, in Table 4 the sum of $S(L_1, L_2)$, $S(L_1, L_3)$ and $S(L_1, L_4)$ exceeds the entry $S(L_1, L_1)$, implying the great impact of labels L_2 to L_4 on L_1.

As shown in Tables 2 to 4, unlike co-occurrence or ϕ-coefficient, the reuse score is asymmetric. In *data-union*, since we set L_1 to appear if any of L_2, L_3 and L_4 appears, L_2 to L_4 are helpful for determining L_1; however, the inverse is not true. Table 4 shows that the reuse scores clearly reflect this asymmetric relationship. In real-world tasks, label relationship is usually asymmetric, for example, the label "lake" implies the label "water", but the inverse may not be true. Therefore, asymmetric relationship is more consistent with realistic situations.

We also examine the reuse scores on two real data sets, i.e., *Image* and *Enron*. *Image* contains five labels: *desert*, *mountains*, *sea*, *sunset* and *trees*. Figure 1 shows some example images, each column for one label. The reuse scores are shown in Table 5. Again, all the entries at the diagonal are large positive values. An interesting observation is that most elements are negative, suggesting that the mutually

Table 2: Reuse score on *data-inde* (L_1 to L_4 are independent)

Target label	Reuse label				
	L_1	L_2	L_3	L_4	L_5
L_1	1.00	-0.00	-0.00	0.00	-0.13
L_2	-0.00	1.00	0.00	-0.01	0.02
L_3	0.00	0.00	1.00	-0.01	0.02
L_4	0.01	-0.00	-0.00	1.00	-0.14
L_5	-0.63	-0.33	-0.32	-0.88	1.00

Table 3: Reuse score on *data-equal* ($L_1 = L_2$, $L_3 = L_4$)

Target label	Reuse label				
	L_1	L_2	L_3	L_4	L_5
L_1	1.00	0.25	0.00	-0.00	0.04
L_2	0.28	1.00	-0.00	-0.00	0.05
L_3	0.00	-0.01	1.00	0.20	0.00
L_4	0.00	-0.00	0.19	1.00	0.00
L_5	-0.25	-0.28	-0.24	-0.25	1.00

Table 4: Reuse score on *data-union* ($L_1 = L_2 \vee L_3 \vee L_4$)

Target label	Reuse label				
	L_1	L_2	L_3	L_4	L_5
L_1	1.00	0.45	0.43	0.51	-0.03
L_2	-0.00	1.00	0.00	-0.01	-0.01
L_3	0.00	0.00	1.00	-0.02	-0.01
L_4	0.10	-0.01	-0.01	1.00	-0.09
L_5	-0.03	-0.44	-0.47	-0.58	1.00

Figure 1: Example images of *Image* data set

Table 5: Reuse score on *Image* data set

Target label	Reuse label				
	desert	*mount.*	*sea*	*sunset*	*trees*
desert	1.00	-0.08	-0.05	-0.11	-0.03
mountains	-0.06	1.00	-0.10	-0.07	-0.06
sea	-0.16	-0.10	1.00	0.01	-0.14
sunset	-0.04	-0.07	-0.00	1.00	-0.06
trees	-0.02	0.06	-0.09	-0.11	1.00

exclusive relationship among labels is important when dealing with multi-label image classification tasks, and is worth paying more attention. Besides the diagonal entries, there are two positive entries. The entry $S(trees, mountains)$ is relatively large, which can be understand by the fact that when there are *mountains* in an image, *trees* are likely to appear, as can be recognized from Figure 1. On the contrary, the entry $S(mountains, trees)$ is negative, because *trees* do not imply *mountains*, which again shows asymmetric property of label relationship. Similarly, the entry $S(sea, sunset)$ is positive, which may be understand by the fact that the *sunset* photos are often taken at *sea*; meanwhile, *sea* does not imply *sunset*, as can be recognized from Figure 1. It is noticed that strong negative entries imply relationship as well. For example, when *desert* occurs in an image, it is unlikely to find *sea* in the image; this explains the strong negative entry $S(sea, desert)$.

Enron is a collection of email messages written by the employees of Enron. Different from the results on *Image* data, there are more positive reuse scores than negative ones in *Enron*, and the absolute values of the negative scores are relatively small. So, we focus on the positive relationship. Since there are too many labels, we only show the results on a part of example labels. Table 6 presents the three most positively related labels for each example label. It can be seen that the discovered relationship is reasonable. For example, an email about *company business*, *newsletters* and *secrecy* is usually sent to *alliance* members or *partners*; the emotion *pride* is likely to come through an email about *jubilation*, *contributions* and *admiration*; etc. It is also worth noting that MAHR discovers high-order relationship among labels; for example, with different accompanying labels, the label *talking points* can be positively related with *admiration* as well as *sadness, despair*.

While the results on the two real data sets provide an intuitive evaluation of the reuse score, we can further have a quantitative evaluation. The 2BR approach [24] trains multiple classifiers, each for one label, and then prunes some classifiers and uses the remaining ones for a second-level stacking classifier. The pruning is based on the label relationship. Therefore, we can incorporate different label relationships into 2BR, and then evaluating the performances. Here, three kinds of relationships are compared, i.e., the reuse score returned by MAHR, the co-occurrence relationship, and the ϕ-coefficient relationship which is used in [24]. As in [24], we report the results on *Yeast* and *Enron* which have many labels for pruning. Decision tree implemented in Weka is used for the base-level and the stacking classifiers. Figure 2 shows the hamming loss with varied number of stacked classifiers. According to [24], the number of stacked classifiers increases from 3 to 12 for *Yeast* and from 3 to 19 for *Enron*.

First, we observe that pruning based on any of the three relationships improves the performance of stacking all the classifiers (corresponding to the dashed line in Figure 2). Comparing with the baselines, MAHR lead to the best per-

Table 6: Top 3 positively related labels for some example labels in *Enron* data set

Label	Most related labels
alliances, partnerships	1. *company business, strategy* 2. *newsletters* 3. *secrecy, confidentiality*
gratitude	1. *friendship, affection* 2. *alliances, partnerships* 3. *forwarded email(s) including replies*
legal advice	1. *alliances, partnerships* 2. *government action(s)* 3. *secrecy, confidentiality*
admiration	1. *jubilation* 2. *talking points* 3. *pride*
jokes, humor (related to business)	1. *humor* 2. *sarcasm* 3. *talking points*
pride	1. *jubilation* 2. *political influence, contribution* 3. *admiration*
company image changing, influence	1. *company business, strategy* 2. *talking points* 3. *worry, anxiety*
meeting minutes	1. *regulations and regulators* 2. *company business, strategy* 3. *talking points*
secrecy, confidentiality	1. *worry, anxiety* 2. *talking points* 3. *dislike, scorn*
sadness, despair	1. *secrecy, confidentiality* 2. *political influence, contribution* 3. *talking points*

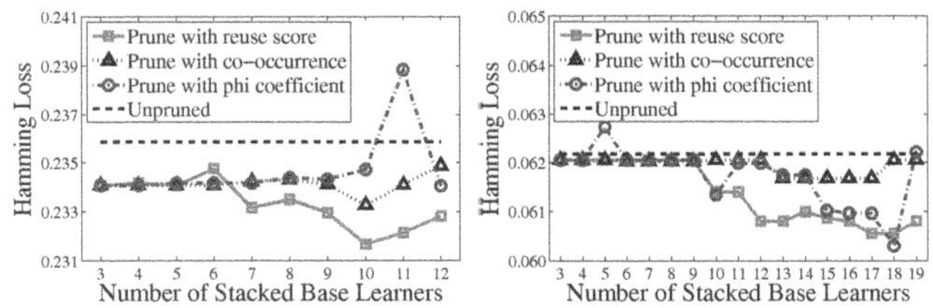

Figure 2: Comparison of three kinds of label relationships with the 2BR approach

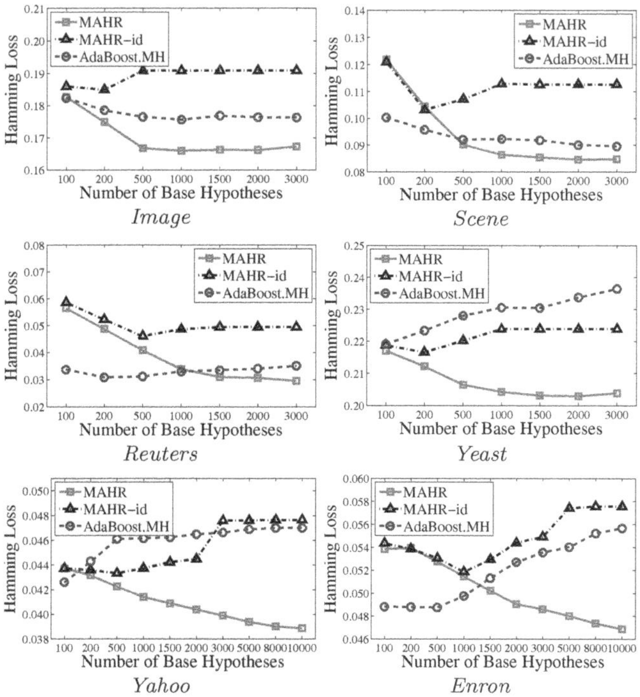

Figure 3: Hamming loss of MAHR, MAHR-id and AdaBoost.MH under varying number of base hypotheses

formance, particularly when the number of stacked classifiers is not too small. This observation further validates the advantage of MAHR on exploiting label relationship.

4.4 Influence of Learning Rounds

An important parameter of boosting algorithms is the number of learning rounds, or in other words, the number of base hypotheses. According to the analysis in [9], to achieve a good performance, the classifier should have low training error and a small number of base hypotheses, whereas a large number of base hypotheses will make the classifier overly complex and may lead to overfitting.

Considering that MAHR and MAHR-id train L (label size) times more hypotheses than the other boosting approaches in each round, to be fair, we compare their performances with the same number of hypotheses. We evaluated three boosting approaches, i.e., MAHR, MAHR-id and AdaBoost.MH, all optimizing hamming loss, up to involving 3,000 base hypotheses for *Image*, *Scene*, *Reuters* and *Yeast*, and 10,000 base hypotheses for *Yahoo* and *Enron*. The hamming loss curves are plotted in Figure 3. (figure for *Image2* is similar with that of *Image*, and thus is not presented due to page limit).

As shown in Figure 3, MAHR significantly improves the performance of MAHR-id with various number of boosting rounds. Contrasting with AdaBoost.MH, MAHR can achieve a better performance after sufficient boosting rounds. Moreover, while MAHR-id and AdaBoost.MH seem suffering from overfitting after a number of rounds, MAHR keeps on improving performance in most cases. We attribute this phenomenon to the fact that MAHR considers high-order relationship among labels, as illustrated in the previous subsection, and thus it can tolerant more complex models.

Table 7: Average CPU time (in seconds) of boosting-style approaches

Methods	*image*	*scene*	*reuters*	*yahoo*	*yeast*	*enron*
MAHR	500	360	255	441	106	488
MAHR-id	50	44	32	23	15	11
AdaBoost.MH	99	127	21	308	92	446
AdaBoost.MR	15	18	10	118	14	188
AdtBoost.MH	1,153	1,578	441	3,036	1,039	2,923
MSSBoost	110	165	226	8,304	952	12,486

4.5 Time Cost

We study the time cost of multi-label boosting approaches. All the experiments are performed with MATLAB 7.6 on a machine with 8×2.60 GHz CPUs and 16GB main memory. The average time cost of each round on one label for MAHR-id and MAHR are 0.73 and 0.91 seconds, respectively, confirming that the hypothesis reuse procedure is efficient. The average CPU time (in seconds) of each boosting approach on each data set is shown in Table 7. It can be seen that AdtBoost.MH is relatively time consuming, and MSSBoost costs more time on some data sets because it employs SVM as base classifier. Benefitting from parallel computing, although MAHR performs more boosting rounds, its computational cost is comparable with other boosting approaches.

5. CONCLUSION

In this paper, we propose a novel multi-label learning approach, MAHR, which does not require the input of label relationship but it is able to discover reasonable label relationship automatically, in addition to achieving a high predictive performance. The key of MAHR is a hypothesis reuse mechanism which offers an effective way to discover and exploit label relationship. This mechanism is implemented as a boosting style approach, where multiple boosted learners are trained, each for one label; each learner not only looks into its own single-label task, but also reuses the trained hypotheses from other labels.

Experiments validate that MAHR is superior or highly competitive to state-of-the-art multi-label approaches, and it drastically improves the performance of MAHR-id, which learns single-label tasks independently. Moreover, experiments show that MAHR discovers reasonable and useful label relationship, and suffers little from overfitting even with a large number of base hypotheses. It is worth noting that our study disclose that the label relationship is usually asymmetric, quite different from symmetric label relationship assumed by previous studies.

It is not difficult to develop variant algorithms of MAHR to optimize other multi-label losses, such as the ranking loss, and it is also possible to reuse hypotheses in forms other than weighted combination in the future.

6. REFERENCES

[1] M. R. Boutell, J. Luo, X. Shen, and C. M. Brown. Learning multi-label scene classification. *Pattern Recognition*, 37(9):1757–1771, 2004.

[2] J. K. Bradley and R. E. Schapire. Filterboost: regression and classification on large datasets. In *Advances in Neural Information Processing Systems 20*, pages 185–192. MIT Press, Cambridge, MA, 2008.

[3] K. Brinker and E. Hüllermeier. Case-based multilabel ranking. In *Proceedings of the 20th International Joint Conference on Artificial Intelligence*, pages 702–707, Hyderabad, India, 2007.

[4] L. Cai and T. Hofmann. Hierarchical document categorization with support vector machines. In *Proceedings of the 13th ACM International Conference on Information and Knowledge Management*, pages 78–87, Washington, DC, 2004.

[5] N. Cesa-Bianchi, C. Gentile, and L. Zaniboni. Hierarchical classification: Combining Bayes with SVM. In *Proceedings of the 23rd International Conference on Machine Learning*, pages 177–184, Pittsburgh, PA, 2006.

[6] F. D. Comité, R. Gilleron, and M. Tommasi. Learning multi-label altenating decision tree from texts and data. In *Proceedings of the 3rd International Conference on Machine Learning and Data Mining in Pattern Recognition*, pages 35–49, Leipzig, Germany, 2003.

[7] A. de Carvalho and A. Freitas. A tutorial on multi-label classification techniques. In A. Abraham, A.-E. Hassanien, and V. Snael, editors, *Foundations of Computational Intelligence, Vol.5*, pages 177–195. Springer, 2009.

[8] A. Elisseeff and J. Weston. A kernel method for multi-labelled classification. In *Advances in Neural Information Processing Systems 14*, pages 681–687. MIT Press, Cambridge, MA, 2002.

[9] Y. Freund and R. Schapire. A decision-theoretic generalization of on-line learning and an application to boosting. *Journal of Computer and System Sciences*, 55(1):119–139, 1997.

[10] N. Ghamrawi and A. Mccallum. Collective multilabel classification. In *Proceedings of the 14th ACM International Conference on Information and Knowledge Management*, pages 195–200, Bremen, Germany, 2005.

[11] M. Hall, E. Frank, G. Holmes, B. Pfahringer, P. Reutemann, and I. Witten. The WEKA data mining software: An update. *ACM SIGKDD Explorations*, 11(1):10–18, 2009.

[12] B. Hariharan, L. Zelnik-Manor, S. V. N. Vishwanathan, and M. Varma. Large scale max-margin multi-label classification with priors. In *Proceedings of the 27th International Conference on Machine Learning*, pages 423–430, Haifa, Israel, 2010.

[13] S.-J. Huang and Z.-H. Zhou. Multi-label learning by exploiting label correlations locally. In *Proceedings of the 26th AAAI Conference on Artificial Intelligence*, Toronto, Canada, 2012.

[14] S. Ji, L. Tang, S. Yu, and J. Ye. Extracting shared subspace for multi-label classification. In *Proceedings of the 14th ACM SIGKDD International Conference on Knowledge Discovery and Data Mining*, pages 381–389, Las Vegas, NV, 2008.

[15] B. Klimt and Y. Yang. Introducing the enron corpus. In *Proceedinds of the 1st Conference on Email and Anti-Spam*, Mountain View, CA, 2004.

[16] A. McCallum. Multi-label text classification with a mixture model trained by EM. In *Working Notes of the AAAI'99 Workshop on Text Learning*, Orlando, FL, 1999.

[17] J. Petterson and T. Caetano. Submodular multi-label learning. In *Advances in Neural Information Processing Systems 24*. MIT Press, Cambridge, MA, 2011.

[18] J. Read, B. Pfahringer, G. Holmes, and E. Frank. Classifier chains for multi-label classification. *Machine Learning*, 85(3):333–359, 2011.

[19] J. Rousu, C. Saunders, S. Szedmak, and J. Shawe-Taylor. Learning hierarchical multi-category text classifcation models. In *Proceedings of the 22nd International Conference on Machine Learning*, pages 774–751, Bonn, Germany, 2005.

[20] R. E. Schapire and Y. Singer. Improved boosting algorithms using confidence-rated prediction. *Machine Learning*, 37(3):297–336, 1999.

[21] R. E. Schapire and Y. Singer. BoosTexter: A boosting-based system for text categorization. *Machine Learning*, 39(2-3):135–168, 2000.

[22] F. Sebastiani. Machine learning in automated text categorization. *ACM Computing Surveys*, 34(1):1–47, 2002.

[23] L. Sun, S. Ji, and J. Ye. Hypergraph spectral learning for multi-label classification. In *Proceedings of the 14th ACM SIGKDD International Conference on Knowledge Discovery and Data Mining*, pages 668–676, Las Vegas, NV, 2008.

[24] G. Tsoumakas, A. Dimou, E. Spyromitros, and V. Mezaris. Correlation-based pruning of stacked binary relevance models for multi-label learning. In *Proceedings of the 1st International Workshop on Learning from Multi-Label Data*, pages 101–116, Bled, Slovenia, 2009.

[25] N. Ueda and K. Saito. Parametric mixture models for multi-labeled text. In *Advances in Neural Information Processing Systems 15*, pages 721–728. MIT Press, Cambridge, MA, 2003.

[26] V. N. Vapnik. *Estimation of Dependences Based on Empirical Data*. Springer-Verlag, New Yorks, NY, 1982.

[27] R. Yan, J. Tešić, and J. R. Smith. Model-shared subspace boosting for multi-label classification. In *Proceedings of the 13th ACM SIGKDD Conference on Knowledge Discovery and Data Mining*, pages 834–843, San Jose, CA, 2007.

[28] M.-L. Zhang and K. Zhang. Multi-label learning by exploiting label dependency. In *Proceedings of the 16th ACM SIGKDD Conference on Knowledge Discovery and Data Mining*, pages 999–1007, Washington, DC, 2010.

[29] M.-L. Zhang and Z.-H. Zhou. ML-kNN: A lazy learning approach to multi-label learning. *Pattern Recognition*, 40(7):2038–2048, 2007.

[30] Z.-H. Zhou, M.-L. Zhang, S.-J. Huang, and Y.-F. Li. Multi-instance multi-label learning. *Artificial Intelligence*, 176(1):2291–2320, 2012.

Rank-Loss Support Instance Machines for MIML Instance Annotation

Forrest Briggs
Oregon State University
School of EECS
Corvallis, Oregon
briggsf@eecs.oregonstate.edu

Xiaoli Z. Fern
Oregon State University
School of EECS
Corvallis, Oregon
xfern@eecs.oregonstate.edu

Raviv Raich
Oregon State University
School of EECS
Corvallis, Oregon
raich@eecs.oregonstate.edu

ABSTRACT

Multi-instance multi-label learning (MIML) is a framework for supervised classification where the objects to be classified are bags of instances associated with multiple labels. For example, an image can be represented as a bag of segments and associated with a list of objects it contains. Prior work on MIML has focused on predicting label sets for previously unseen bags. We instead consider the problem of predicting instance labels while learning from data labeled only at the bag level. We propose Rank-Loss Support Instance Machines, which optimize a regularized rank-loss objective and can be instantiated with different aggregation models connecting instance-level predictions with bag-level predictions. The aggregation models that we consider are equivalent to defining a "support instance" for each bag, which allows efficient optimization of the rank-loss objective using primal sub-gradient descent. Experiments on artificial and real-world datasets show that the proposed methods achieve higher accuracy than other loss functions used in prior work, e.g., Hamming loss, and recent work in ambiguous label classification.

Categories and Subject Descriptors

H.3.3 [**Information Systems**]: Information Search and Retrieval; I.5.2 [**Design Methodology**]: Classifier Design and Evaluation

General Terms

Algorithms, Performance, Experimentation

Keywords

instance annotation, image annotation, multi-instance, multi-label, support vector machine, sub-gradient, bioacoustics

1. INTRODUCTION

Many problems in supervised classification have a certain structure, where the objects of interest (e.g., images or text documents) can naturally be decomposed into a collection of parts or formally, a bag-of-instances representation. For example, in image classification, an image is typically a bag, and the pixels or segments in it are instances. This structure motivates multiple-instance learning (MIL) [7]. The original formulation of MIL concerns problems where bags are associated with a single binary label. Zhou and Zhang [30] proposed multi-instance multi-label learning (MIML), where bags are instead associated with a set of labels. For example, an image might be associated with a list of the objects it contains.

MIML arises in situations where the cost of labeling individual instances becomes prohibitive and consequently multiple instances are grouped and associated with a set of labels. For example, labeling individual pixels in an image takes minutes, but assigning a few words to an image can be accomplished in seconds. In MIML, the training dataset consists of a collection of bags of instances, where each bag is associated with multiple labels. The goal is to learn a classifier that predicts the label set for a previously unseen bag. Numerous algorithms for MIML have been proposed and applied to image and text domains [30, 31, 27, 14, 20].

A related problem which has received little attention [29] is learning to predict instance labels from MIML training data. For example, one might train a classifier on a collection of images paired with lists of object names in each image, then make predictions about the label for each region in an image. This problem is called the *instance annotation* problem for MIML. The key issue in instance annotation is how to learn an instance-level classifier from a MIML dataset (which presents only bag-level labels).

A common strategy in designing MIML algorithms is to learn an instance-level model by minimizing a loss function defined at the bag level. For example, several MIML algorithms minimize bag-level Hamming loss, which captures the disagreement between a ground-truth label set, and a predicted label set. For instance annotation, typically the instance-level classifier outputs a score for each class, and the instance label is predicted as the highest scoring class. Therefore the predicted label depends on the ranking of class scores. Hamming loss is not appropriate in this context, despite its success at bag-level predictions, because it lacks a mechanism to calibrate the scores between different classes. This observation motivates us to introduce a rank-loss objective for instance annotation, which directly optimizes the ranking of classes.

In order to learn an instance-level classifier using a bag-level loss function, it is necessary to define an aggregation model that connects instance-level predictions with bag-level predictions. In this paper, we examine two different aggregation models, which are equivalent to defining a "support instance" for each bag. Therefore, we name our methods Rank-Loss Support Instance Machines (SIM). In this paper, we make the following contributions:

- We propose a general rank-loss objective for instance annotation that can be instantiated with different aggregation models (Sec. 4).
- We propose an optimization procedure for the rank-loss objective which alternates between updating the support instances and solving a convex optimization problem. Using the Pegasos framework [18, 19], we show that a primal sub-gradient descent algorithm finds a solution to the convex problem within ϵ of optimal, with runtime linear in the number of bags, and $\frac{1}{\epsilon}$ (Sec. 4.2.2). The alternating optimization is also linear in the total number of instances.
- Experiments show that Rank-loss SIM achieves higher accuracy than Hamming loss, or ambiguous loss (a comparable state-of-the-art approach [5, 6]), and a novel `softmax` aggregation model outperforms the `max` model which has been used in prior work (Sec. 5).
- We introduce a real-world MIML dataset for instance annotation derived from over 90 minutes of bird song recordings collected in the field, containing multiple simultaneously vocalizing birds of different species. Rank-Loss SIM with the `softmax` model achieves over 80% accuracy in predicting the species of bird responsible for each sound in the recordings (given the list of species present in the recording).

2. PROBLEM STATEMENT

In this section we formalize the instance annotation problem and contrast it with several related problems.

We are given a training set of n bags $(X_1, Y_1), \ldots, (X_n, Y_n)$. Each X_i is a bag of n_i instances, i.e., $X_i = \{\mathbf{x}_{i,1}, \cdots, \mathbf{x}_{i,n_i}\}$, with $\mathbf{x}_{i,q} \in \mathcal{X}$, where $\mathcal{X} = \mathbb{R}^d$ is a d-dimensional feature space. Each bag X_i is associated with a label set $Y_i \subseteq \mathcal{Y}$ where $\mathcal{Y} = \{1, \cdots, c\}$ and c is the total number of classes. The goal of instance annotation in MIML is to learn an instance level classifier $f_{IA} : \mathcal{X} \rightarrow \mathcal{Y}$ that maps an element of the input space $\mathcal{X}$ to its corresponding class label.

The instance annotation problem is different from the traditional MIML learning problem studied by Zhou and Zhang [30] and many others, where the goal is to learn a bag-level classifier $F_{MIML} : 2^{\mathcal{X}} \rightarrow 2^{\mathcal{Y}}$. However, the design principles of many traditional MIML algorithms can be used to learn instance-level classification models, which is the approach we take in this paper.

Instance annotation is closely related to the classic supervised classification problem, where the goal is to learn an instance classifier, but using training data that does not have a bag structure and has each instance labeled individually. In contrast to MIML, this classic setting is often referred to as single-instance single-label (SISL) learning.

Ambiguous label classification (ALC) [13, 6] is another related framework. In ALC, there are no bags; instead instances are paired with a set of possible labels, only one of which is correct. An ALC dataset is $(\mathbf{x}_1, Y_1), \ldots, (\mathbf{x}_m, Y_m)$, where $\mathbf{x}_i \in \mathcal{X}$ and $Y_i \subseteq \mathcal{Y}$. In ALC the goal is to learn a classifier that predicts instance labels, hence an ALC classifier is a function $f_{ALC} : \mathcal{X} \rightarrow \mathcal{Y}$. A MIML instance annotation problem can be transformed into a ALC problem by creating one ALC instance for each instance in a MIML bag, paired with all of the labels from the bag. Hence ALC algorithms can be applied to MIML instance annotation problems. However, this reduction may discard useful bag-level structure in the MIML data.

3. BACKGROUND

Here we discuss some design patterns in traditional MIML algorithms (aimed at bag-level predictions) that contribute to our proposed methods (see Sec. 6 for different approaches to instance annotation, e.g., graphical models).

One common approach in MIML algorithms is to make bag-level predictions based on the outputs of instance-level models. Many algorithms leverage an assumption that the bag label set is equal to the union of the instance labels (i.e. there are no missing or spurious labels). This assumption is used in several MIML algorithms including M^{3}MIML [28], and D-MimlSvm [31]. The following formulation is frequently used to capture this assumption. Let $f_j(\mathbf{x}) : \mathcal{X} \rightarrow \mathbb{R}$ be a function which takes an instance and returns a real-valued score for class j. The output at the bag-level for class j is defined to be $F_j(X) = \max_{\mathbf{x} \in X} f_j(\mathbf{x})$. A bag-level classifier can be obtained by applying a threshold (e.g., 0) to the bag-level scores, i.e. $F(X) = \{y \in \mathcal{Y} : F_y(X) > 0\}$. Note that if an instance $\mathbf{x}^*$ within bag X is predicted to belong to class j, i.e., $f_j(\mathbf{x}^*) > 0$, the predicted label set for bag X will necessarily contain j because $F_j(X) = \max_{\mathbf{x} \in X} f_j(\mathbf{x}) \geq f_j(\mathbf{x}^*) > 0$. Hence, connecting instance and bag-level scores via the max function is equivalent to defining the bag label set as the union of the instance labels.

In contrast with SISL or instance annotation which are evaluated based on instance-level accuracy, MIML algorithms are evaluated based on their label set predictions. Two common performance measures are Hamming loss, and rank loss [31]. Hamming Loss is the number of false positives and false negatives, averaged over all classes and bags,

$$\frac{1}{nc} \sum_{i=1}^{n} \sum_{j=1}^{c} I[j \in F(X_i), j \notin Y_i] + I[j \notin F(X_i), j \in Y_i]$$

Rank loss captures the number of label pairs that are incorrectly ordered by the scores of the MIML classifier. Classes in the true label set should receive higher scores than classes that are not. Let $\bar{Y}$ denote the complement of Y. Rank loss is defined as

$$\frac{1}{n} \sum_{i=1}^{n} \frac{1}{|Y_i||\bar{Y}_i|} \sum_{j \in Y_i, k \in \bar{Y}_i} I[F_j(X_i) \leq F_k(X_i)] \tag{1}$$

These objectives are difficult to optimize directly because they are not continuous. Several algorithms for MIML can be viewed as optimizing a surrogate for Hamming loss. For example, D-MimlSvm [31] and M^{3}MIML [28] optimize variations of the following loss function (with different regularization terms)

$$\frac{1}{nc} \sum_{i=1}^{n} \sum_{j=1}^{c} \max\{0, 1 - Y_i^j F_j(X_i)\} \tag{2}$$

where $Y_i^j = +1$ if $j \in Y_i$ and -1 if $j \notin Y_i$.

The hinged Hamming-loss objective (2) can be decomposed into an independent MIL problem for each class, so it does not calibrate the scores between classes, which could make predicting an instance label based on the highest scoring class unreliable. To overcome this limitation, we consider rank loss instead. We are not aware of any MIML algorithms that learn an instance-level model by minimizing rank loss (i.e. rank loss has only been used as a performance measure, not as an objective). Rank loss has been used as an objective for (single-instance) multi-label SVMs [9].

4. PROPOSED METHODS

We consider classifiers for instance annotation that use one instance-level model for each class $f_j(\mathbf{x}) = \mathbf{w}_j \cdot \mathbf{x}$, and predict a specific label via $f(\mathbf{x}) = \arg\max_j f_j(\mathbf{x})$. The goal is to learn the weights $\mathbf{W} = [\mathbf{w}_1, \ldots, \mathbf{w}_c]$ (note $\mathbf{x} \in \mathbb{R}^d$, $\mathbf{w}_j \in \mathbb{R}^d$, and $\mathbf{W} \in \mathbb{R}^{cd}$). The predicted instance label depends on the ranking of scores for each class, so we propose to directly optimize this ranking.

4.1 Rank-Loss Support Instance Machines

Because we are learning from a MIML dataset, we can only use a loss function that evaluates predictions at the bag level, i.e. the loss function measures the agreement between a bag label set and the bag-level scores $F_j(X_i)$. We propose a regularized surrogate for the rank loss (1):

$$g_{rank}(\mathbf{W}) = \frac{\lambda}{2}||\mathbf{W}||^2 + \frac{1}{n}\sum_{i=1}^{n}\frac{1}{|Y_i||\bar{Y}_i|}\sum_{j\in Y_i, k\in\bar{Y}_i}\max\{0, 1 - (F_j(X_i) - F_k(X_i))\}$$

This objective is designed to encourage a correct ranking of the bag-level scores for each class. For a bag X_i with corresponding label set Y_i, if $j \in Y_i$ and $k \in \bar{Y}_i$, then the loss is zero only if $F_j(X_i) > F_k(X_i) + 1$ (requiring a difference of at least 1 promotes a large-margin solution). The objective is also designed to facilitate primal sub-gradient descent optimization methods, which we discuss in the next section.

This objective can be instantiated with various aggregation models that compute bag-level scores from instance-level scores. For example, the `max` model, which has been used in prior work, with a linear instance classifier is

$$F_j(X_i) = \max_{\mathbf{x}_{i,q}\in X_i} f_j(\mathbf{x}_{i,q}) = \max_{\mathbf{x}_{i,q}\in X_i} \mathbf{w}_j \cdot \mathbf{x}_{i,q}$$

It is equivalent to write $F_j(X_i) = \mathbf{w}_j \cdot \hat{\mathbf{x}}_{i,j}$, where

$$\hat{\mathbf{x}}_{i,j} = \arg\max_{\mathbf{x}_{i,q}\in X_i} \mathbf{w}_j \cdot \mathbf{x}_{i,q} \tag{3}$$

We refer to $\hat{\mathbf{x}}_{i,j}$ as the "support instance" for bag X_i, class j, because the bag-level output for X_i depends only on the support instance for each class (analogous to a support vector). Therefore we name our proposed method Rank-Loss Support Instance Machines (SIM).

The `max` model represents each bag with the most characteristic instance of each class. This approach can ignore other instances that are also useful for learning, and may not be appropriate when the assumption that the bag label set is equal to the union of instance labels does not hold. We propose an alternative `softmax` model, which can also be expressed in terms of support instances, but has the advantage of basing the support on more than one instance per class for each bag. The `softmax` model represents each bag as a weighted average of the instances, with weights specific to each class:

$$F_j(X_i) = \sum_{\mathbf{x}_{i,q}\in X_i} \alpha_{i,q}^j f_j(\mathbf{x}_{i,q}) = \sum_{\mathbf{x}_{i,q}\in X_i} \alpha_{i,q}^j \mathbf{w}_j \cdot \mathbf{x}_{i,q}$$

The weights are defined according to a softmax rule,

$$\alpha_{i,q}^j = \frac{e^{\mathbf{w}_j\cdot\mathbf{x}_{i,q}}}{\sum_{\mathbf{x}'\in X_i} e^{\mathbf{w}_j\cdot\mathbf{x}'}}$$

We can also write the `softmax` model as $F_j(X_i) = \mathbf{w}_j \cdot \hat{\mathbf{x}}_{i,j}$, with the support defined as

$$\hat{\mathbf{x}}_{i,j} = \sum_{\mathbf{x}_{i,q}\in X_i} \alpha_{i,q}^j \mathbf{x}_{i,q} \tag{4}$$

4.2 Optimization

We can rewrite the rank-loss objective in terms of support instances as

$$\hat{g}_{rank}(\mathbf{W}) = \frac{\lambda}{2}||\mathbf{W}||^2 + \frac{1}{n}\sum_{i=1}^{n}\frac{1}{|Y_i||\bar{Y}_i|}\sum_{j\in Y_i,k\in\bar{Y}_i}\max\{0, 1 + \mathbf{w}_k\cdot\hat{\mathbf{x}}_{i,k} - \mathbf{w}_j\cdot\hat{\mathbf{x}}_{i,j}\}$$

If $\hat{\mathbf{x}}_{i,j}$ is constant, this objective is convex. However, using the `max` and `softmax` models, $\hat{\mathbf{x}}_{i,j}$ is a function of $\mathbf{w}_j$, and the objective is non-convex. We can still use convex optimization techniques by alternating between updating the support and keeping the support constant while optimizing the objective. The MI-SVM algorithm for MIL (single-label) also uses the max function to connect instance and bag labels, and alternates between computing the support and optimizing the resulting objective [1].

4.2.1 *Sub-Gradient Descent*

To optimize $\hat{g}_{rank}$, we use a sub-gradient descent method similar to Pegasos, an algorithm for training linear two-class SVMs [19]. The Pegasos algorithm is based on a general framework for optimizing regularized convex objectives [18]. This framework can be applied to convex optimization problems in the form:

$$\min_{\mathbf{W}\in S} g(\mathbf{W}) \text{ where } g(\mathbf{W}) = \frac{\lambda}{2}||\mathbf{W}||^2 + loss(\mathbf{W})$$

For such problems, the following algorithm can be applied:

Projected Sub-Gradient Algorithm:

Initialize $\mathbf{W}^0 \in S$

for $t = 1, 2, \ldots, T$:

  Compute a sub-gradient $\mathbf{V} \in \partial g(\mathbf{W}^{t-1})$

  $\mathbf{W}^t \leftarrow P[\mathbf{W}^{t-1} - \frac{1}{\lambda t}\mathbf{V}]$

The feasible space is S; $P[\mathbf{W}] = \arg\min_{\mathbf{W}'\in S} ||\mathbf{W} - \mathbf{W}'||^2$ is a projection back into the feasible space. Note that when $S = \{\mathbf{W} : ||\mathbf{W}|| \leq r\}$, the projection simplifies to $P[\mathbf{W}] = \min\{1, \frac{r}{||\mathbf{W}||}\}\mathbf{W}$ (this will be the case for our objective).

This algorithm can be considered an example of the projected sub-gradient method [2] with learning rate $\frac{1}{\lambda t}$. Let $\mathbf{W}^*$ be the optimal solution i.e. $\mathbf{W}^* = \arg\min_{\mathbf{W}\in S} g(\mathbf{W})$. Shalev-Shwartz and Singer [18] showed the following convergence rate for this algorithm,

$$\min_t g(\mathbf{W}^t) \leq g(\mathbf{W}^*) + O(\frac{\log T}{T}\frac{L}{\lambda})$$

where L is a constant bounding the magnitude of the sub-gradient i.e. $\forall t, \frac{1}{2}||\mathbf{V}||^2 \leq L$. For practical purposes, the number of iterations of sub-gradient descent T is small enough to treat $\log T$ as constant, hence to obtain a solution that is within ϵ of optimal, it suffices to run $T \approx O(\frac{L}{\lambda\epsilon})$ iterations of the above algorithm [18].

Treating the support instances as constant, we can apply the Pegasos framework for sub-gradient descent to minimize the rank-loss objective $\hat{g}_{rank}$. We denote the component of the sub-gradient corresponding to $\mathbf{w}_q$ as $\mathbf{v}_q^{rank}$, where $q = 1, \ldots, c$. The full sub-gradient is $\mathbf{V}^{rank} = [\mathbf{v}_1^{rank}, \ldots, \mathbf{v}_c^{rank}]$.

$$\mathbf{v}_q^{rank} = \lambda \mathbf{w}_q + \frac{1}{n}\sum_{i=1}^{n}\frac{1}{|Y_i||\bar{Y}_i|}\sum_{j\in Y_i, k\in \bar{Y}_i} \quad (5)$$

$$I[1 + \mathbf{w}_k \cdot \hat{\mathbf{x}}_{i,k} > \mathbf{w}_j \cdot \hat{\mathbf{x}}_{i,j}] \begin{cases} \hat{\mathbf{x}}_{i,q} & \text{if } q = k \\ -\hat{\mathbf{x}}_{i,q} & \text{if } q = j \\ 0 & \text{otherwise} \end{cases}$$

In order to prove sub-gradient descent converges, we must establish L, the bound on the sub-gradient. We begin by showing the following Lemma:

Lemma 1: Consider any objective of the form $g(\mathbf{W}) = \frac{\lambda}{2}||\mathbf{W}||^2 + loss(\mathbf{W})$, such that $loss(\mathbf{W}) \geq 0$ and $loss(\mathbf{0}) = 1$. Let the optimal solution be $\mathbf{W}^* = \arg\min_{\mathbf{W}} g(\mathbf{W})$. Then $||\mathbf{W}^*||^2 \leq \frac{2}{\lambda}$.

Proof: The optimal solution must be at least as good as $\mathbf{W} = \mathbf{0}$, therefore $g(\mathbf{W}^*) \leq 1$. Furthermore, $loss(\mathbf{W}^*) \leq 1$ (assuming the contrary implies $g(\mathbf{W}^*) > 1$, which is a contradiction). Because the loss is non-negative, $0 \leq loss(\mathbf{W}^*) \leq 1$. We will use this property to finish the proof:

$$\begin{aligned} g(\mathbf{W}^*) = \frac{\lambda}{2}||\mathbf{W}^*||^2 + loss(\mathbf{W}^*) &\leq 1 \\ \frac{\lambda}{2}||\mathbf{W}^*||^2 &\leq 1 - loss(\mathbf{W}^*) \leq 1 \\ ||\mathbf{W}^*||^2 &\leq \frac{2}{\lambda} \end{aligned}$$

The $\hat{g}_{rank}$ objective satisfies the criteria of Lemma 1, so we can replace unconstrained minimization of $\hat{g}_{rank}$ with minimization restricted to the set $S = \{\mathbf{W} : ||\mathbf{W}||^2 \leq \frac{2}{\lambda}\}$ without changing the solution. It is also necessary to bound the magnitude of an instance feature vector, $||\mathbf{x}|| \leq R$. Note that $\mathbf{W} \in S$ implies $||\lambda \mathbf{w}_q|| \leq \lambda\sqrt{\frac{2}{\lambda}} = \sqrt{2\lambda}$ (using Lemma 1). Also, $\frac{1}{|Y_i||\bar{Y}_i|} \leq \frac{1}{c-1}$ provided $Y_i \neq \mathcal{Y}$ and $Y_i \neq \{\}$ (if this is not true, the objective is undefined). Using the above, we can derive the bound L:

$$\begin{aligned} ||\mathbf{v}_q^{rank}|| &\leq \sqrt{2\lambda} + R \\ ||\mathbf{v}_q^{rank}||^2 &\leq \left(\sqrt{2\lambda} + R\right)^2 \\ ||\mathbf{V}^{rank}||^2 &= \sum_{j=1}^{c}||\mathbf{v}_j^{rank}||^2 \\ ||\mathbf{V}^{rank}||^2 &\leq c\left(\sqrt{2\lambda} + R\right)^2 \end{aligned}$$

Therefore $L = \frac{c}{2}\left(\sqrt{2\lambda} + R\right)^2$ suffices.

4.2.2 *Runtime of Sub-Gradient Descent*

To compute $\mathbf{V}^{rank}$, one could compute $\mathbf{v}_1^{rank}, \ldots, \mathbf{v}_c^{rank}$ from (5), but this will take $O(nc^3)$ time; where n is the number of bags and c is the number of classes. We give an $O(nc^2)$ algorithm below:

Rank-Loss Sub-Gradient Algorithm:

- for $j = 1, \ldots, c$:
  - $\mathbf{v}_j^{rank} \leftarrow \lambda \mathbf{w}_j$
- for $i = 1, \ldots, n; j \in Y_i, k \in \bar{Y}_i$:
  - if $1 + \mathbf{w}_k \cdot \hat{\mathbf{x}}_{i,k} > \mathbf{w}_j \cdot \hat{\mathbf{x}}_{i,j}$:
    - $\mathbf{v}_j^{rank} \leftarrow \mathbf{v}_j^{rank} - \frac{\hat{\mathbf{x}}_{i,j}}{n|Y_i||\bar{Y}_i|}$
    - $\mathbf{v}_k^{rank} \leftarrow \mathbf{v}_k^{rank} + \frac{\hat{\mathbf{x}}_{i,k}}{n|Y_i||\bar{Y}_i|}$

Running $T = O(\frac{L}{\lambda\epsilon})$ iterations with a runtime of $O(nc^2)$ per iteration of sub-gradient descent gives an upper bound of $O(\frac{nc^3}{\epsilon\sqrt{\lambda}})$ time to find a solution within ϵ of optimal, i.e. linear in the number of bags and $\frac{1}{\epsilon}$. In practice, $T = 100$ iterations is sufficient for many datasets (Fig. 1).

4.2.3 *Updating the Support Instances*

For the `max` and `softmax` models, we run K phases, where each phase consists of updating the support, then running T iterations of projected sub-gradient descent. For the first phase, we start with $\mathbf{W} = \mathbf{0}$ and compute the support as the average of the instances in each bag (to compute the support for the `max` and `softmax` models, we require some prior non-zero $\mathbf{W}$). Going from one phase to the next, we use the final weights from the earlier run of sub-gradient descent as the initial weights for the next run. Note that convergence analysis only applies to the sub-gradient descent part of each phase (it does not describe changes in the support over multiple phases). We summarize the proposed algorithm below.

Rank-Loss Support Instance Machine Algorithm:

- for *phase* $= 1, \ldots, K$:
  - if *phase* $= 1$:
    - $\mathbf{W} \leftarrow \mathbf{0}$
    - initialize $\hat{\mathbf{x}}_{i,j} \leftarrow \frac{1}{n_i}\sum_{\mathbf{x}_{i,q}\in X_i}\mathbf{x}_{i,q}$
  - else:
    - compute $\hat{\mathbf{x}}_{i,j}$ using `max` (3) or `softmax` (4)
  - for $t = 1, \ldots, T$:
    - compute a sub-gradient $\mathbf{V}^{rank} \in \partial\hat{g}_{rank}(\mathbf{W})$
    - $\mathbf{W} \leftarrow \mathbf{W} - \frac{1}{\lambda t}\mathbf{V}^{rank}$
    - $\mathbf{W} \leftarrow \min\{1, \sqrt{\frac{2}{\lambda}}/||\mathbf{W}||\}\mathbf{W}$

Computing the support takes $O(m)$ time where m is the total number of instances, and this must be done K times.

5. EXPERIMENTS

We conduct experiments on artificial and real-world MIML datasets. The goals of our experiments are to (1) compare the proposed rank-loss objective with alternative Hamming loss and ambiguous loss; and (2) compare the `max` and `softmax` aggregation models.

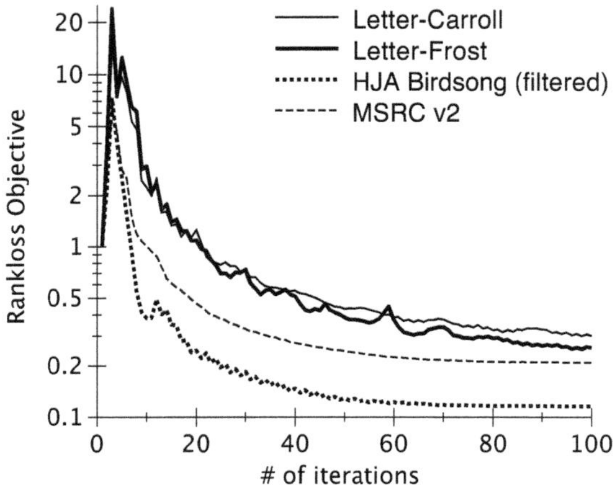

Figure 1: Convergence of sub-gradient descent for rank loss, average model (transductive).

Table 1: MIML datasets used in our experiments.

Dataset	Classes	Dimension	Bags	Instances
HJA Birdsong	13	38	548	10,232
MSRC v2	23	48	591	1,758
Letter-Carroll	26	16	166	717
Letter-Frost	26	16	144	565

5.1 Experimental Setup

We describe the setup of our experiments below.

5.1.1 Transductive vs. Inductive

We consider instance annotation in two different settings: transductive and inductive. In the transductive setting, the goal is to predict the instance labels for bags with known label sets. In this setting, the instance-level classifiers can only predict labels that appear in the bag label set. Formally, the instance classifier in the transductive setting is $f(\mathbf{x}_{i,q}) = \arg\max_{j \in Y_i} f_j(\mathbf{x}_{i,q})$. In the inductive setting, the goal is to predict instance labels in previously unseen bags (with unknown label sets). There is no restriction on which label an instance may be given in this case.

For both modes, we compute classifier accuracy as the fraction of instances correctly classified. For the inductive mode, we run 10-fold cross-validation and report average accuracy $\pm$ standard deviation in accuracy between folds.

5.1.2 Datasets

Table 1 summarizes the properties of each dataset used in our experiments. All of these datasets are available online.[1]

HJA Bird Song. Our collaborators have collected audio recordings of bird song at the H. J. Andrews (HJA) Experimental Forest, using unattended microphones. Our goal is to automatically identify the species of bird responsible for each utterance in these recordings, thereby generating an automatic acoustic survey of bird populations. This problem is a natural fit for the MIML instance annotation framework. We treat a 10-second audio recording as a bag with labels

[1] `http://web.engr.oregonstate.edu/~briggsf/kdd2012datasets`

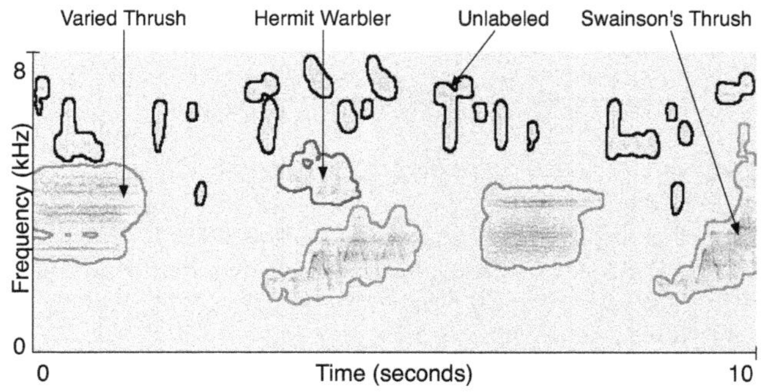

Figure 2: An example spectrogram from the HJA Birdsong dataset. This spectrogram corresponds to one bag. Each outlined region is an instance.

corresponding to the set of species present in the recording. The instances are segments in a spectrogram. A spectrogram is a graph of the spectrum of a signal as a function of time (computed by applying the Fast Fourier Transform to successive overlapping frames of the audio signal). Figure 2 shows an example spectrogram for a 10-second audio recording containing several species of birds.

Starting with a 10-second audio recording, we first convert it to a spectrogram. A series of preprocessing steps are then applied to the spectrogram to reduce noise, and to identify bird song segments in the audio [15]. Each segment is considered an instance and described by a 38-dimensional feature vector characterizing the shape of the segment, its time and frequency profile statistics, and a histogram of gradients.

This dataset contains 548 10-second recordings (bags), and a total of 10,232 segments (instances), of which 4,998 are labeled, and the rest are unlabeled. The available instance labels were provided by a human expert. Some instances were left unlabeled because they correspond to segmentation errors (i.e. noise rather than bird song), because they are too difficult to identify in the presence of other sounds, or because it is extremely time-consuming to produce these labels. The bag-level label sets are formed by taking the union of the instance labels (not including any unlabeled instances).

The presence of the unlabeled instances which are not accounted for by the bag label set presents an additional challenge for instance annotation. To evaluate how well various algorithms handle this problem, we consider two variants of this dataset: "filtered" and "unfiltered". For the filtered variant, all of the unlabeled instances are removed, and in the unfiltered variant they are left in during the training process. In both variants, the accuracy is measured only on the labeled instances.

Image Dataset: MSRC v2. A subset of the Microsoft Research Cambridge (MSRC) image dataset[2] [23] named "v2" contains 591 images and 23 classes. The MSRC v2 dataset is useful for the instance annotation problem, because pixel-level labels are included (Fig. 3). Several authors used MSRC v2 in MIML experiments [27, 24, 22].

We construct a MIML dataset from MSRC v2 as follows: We treat each image as a bag. The bag label set is the list of all classes present in the ground-truth segmentation (i.e. the

[2] `http://research.microsoft.com/en-us/projects/objectclassrecognition/default.htm`

Figure 3: An image from MSRC v2 and the corresponding pixel-level labeling. The classes in this image are 'sky', 'trees, 'grass', 'body', and 'car'. The black regions are 'void'; we discard void regions.

union of the instance labels). The instances correspond to each contiguous region in the ground-truth segmentation (to simplify the experiment, we use the ground-truth segmentation rather than automatic segmentation). Each instance is described by a 16-dimensional histogram of gradients, and a 32-dimensional histogram of colors.

Synthetic MIML Datasets. Limited availability of MIML datasets with instance labels has been a barrier to studying instance annotation (because instance labels are needed to evaluate accuracy). Using the Letter Recognition dataset [11] from the UCI Machine Learning repository, we construct two synthetic MIML datasets. The Letter Recognition dataset consists of 20,000 instances with 16-dimensional features, and 26 classes. Note that randomly forming the bags will not be realistic because real-world MIML problems often have correlations between labels. Instead, we generate datasets derived from the words in two poems, "Jabberwocky" [3], and "The Road Not Taken" [12]. We call these datasets Letter-Carroll and Letter-Frost. For each word in these poems, we create a bag, with instances corresponding to the letters in the word. For each instance, we sample (without replacement), an example from the Letter Recognition dataset with the corresponding letter. The bag-level labels are the union of the instance labels. For example, the word "diverged" is transformed into a bag with 8 instances, and the label set {d, i, v, e, r, g}.

Preprocessing. For all datasets, we apply the following preprocessing to the instance features. First, we transform each feature to the range $[0, 1]$. Next, we apply the same feature rescaling process used in the *Convex Learning from Partial Labels Toolbox* (for ALC [6]), which centers the data and scales each feature by $\frac{1}{\sqrt{\sum_{i=1}^{m}||\mathbf{x}_i||^2}}$.

5.1.3 Base Line Methods

We compare our proposed Rank-Loss SIM methods with a Hamming-Loss SIM, and the Ambiguous Label Classification algorithm proposed by Cour et al. [6]. As a reference, we also consider a SISL classifier, which will have the unfair advantage of learning directly from instance labels.

Hamming-Loss SIM. To compare Hamming loss to rank loss, we use the following Hamming-loss objective, with both `max` and `softmax` aggregation models:

$$g_{ham}(\mathbf{W}) = \frac{\lambda}{2}||\mathbf{W}||^2 + \frac{1}{nc}\sum_{i=1}^{n}\sum_{j=1}^{c}\max\{0, 1 - Y_i^j F_j(X_i)\}$$

or in terms of support instances,

$$\hat{g}_{ham}(\mathbf{W}) = \frac{\lambda}{2}||\mathbf{W}||^2 + \frac{1}{nc}\sum_{i=1}^{n}\sum_{j=1}^{c}\max\{0, 1 - Y_i^j \mathbf{w}_j \cdot \hat{\mathbf{x}}_{i,j}\}$$

We use a similar projected sub-gradient descent algorithm to optimize this objective (and update the support in the same way as for the rank-loss objective over multiple phases). The conditions for Lemma 1 are also met by this objective. We compute the following sub-gradient

$$\mathbf{v}_q^{ham} = \lambda \mathbf{w}_q - \frac{1}{nc}\sum_{i=1}^{n} I[Y_i^q \mathbf{w}_q \cdot \hat{\mathbf{x}}_{i,q} < 1] Y_i^q \hat{\mathbf{x}}_{i,q}$$

In this case, the bound on the magnitude of the sub-gradient is $L = \frac{c}{2}\left(\sqrt{2\lambda} + \frac{R}{c}\right)^2$.

Ambiguous Label Classification (ALC). Cour et al. [5, 6] proposed an SVM formulation for the ALC problem. We compare our proposed method to Cour's ALC algorithm because they both learn one linear model per class $f_j(\mathbf{x}) = \mathbf{w}_j \cdot \mathbf{x}$ and predict the instance label as $\arg\max_j f_j(\mathbf{x})$, and both use an L_2 regularized loss function. The primary difference in Cour's ALC method is that the loss function is designed for use with ALC data (instead of the bag-level loss functions we use for MIML data). The ALC loss function is a convex upper bound to the 0/1 loss with respect to the true (unknown) instance labels, $L(f, \mathbf{x}, Y) =$

$$\max\{0, 1 - \frac{1}{|Y|}\sum_{j \in Y} f_j(\mathbf{x})\}^2 + \sum_{j \notin Y}\max\{0, 1 + f_j(\mathbf{x})\}^2$$

Minimizing regularized ambiguous loss can be converted into an equivalent SISL SVM problem with squared hinge-loss, and solved using an off-the-shelf linear SVM [10].

Comparison to SISL. We also run a SISL SVM for the inductive setting, whose performance can be interpreted as an empirical upper bound for inductive instance annotation because it is trained using unambiguously labeled instances. For this experiment, we use LIBSVM [4] with a linear kernel. Note that LIBSVM uses one linear model for each pair of classes rather than one for each class. For the HJA Birdsong dataset, we only run the SISL SVM on the filtered variant, because we cannot use the unlabeled instances.

5.1.4 Parameter Selection

The Hamming and rank-loss objectives have a regularization parameter λ. Similarly, Cour's ALC method has a regularization parameter C, which achieves roughly the same effect when $C = \frac{1}{\lambda}$. To obtain a fair comparison of different methods regardless of the parameter settings, we repeat all experiments for each value of $\lambda \in \{10^{-1}, 10^{-2}, \ldots, 10^{-9}\}$, and corresponding C values, and report the maximum accuracy achieved by each method.

In practice one could use cross-validation (on the bag-level labels) to select the regularization parameter. However, our results suggest that it maybe sufficient to use a default parameter for many datasets. For example, setting λ to 10^{-7} or 10^{-8} tends to work well for all datasets that we considered (Fig. 4). This approach is consistent with prior work using Cour's ALC method where a fixed value of C is used in all experiments.[3]

For the SISL SVM, the regularization parameter C is optimized by nested 10-fold cross-validation (within each fold

[3]Cour et al. used $C = 10^3$ for all experiments in prior work. Our results support this choice.

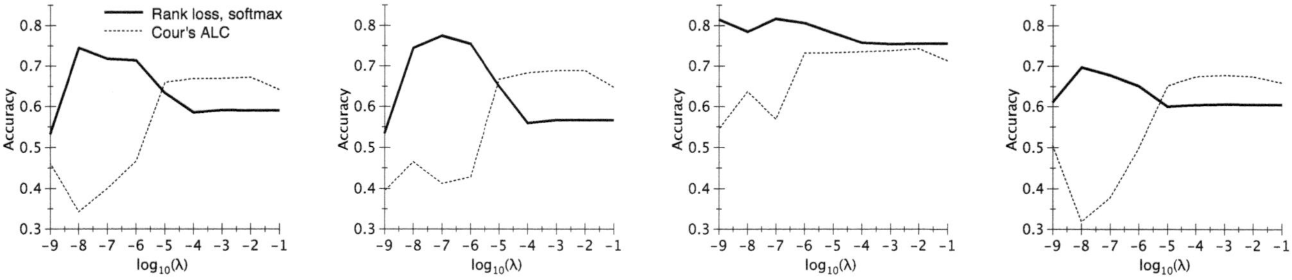

(a) Letter-Carroll (b) Letter-Frost (c) HJA Birdsong (filtered) (d) MSRC v2

Figure 4: Accuracy vs. regularization parameter (transductive).

of 10-fold cross validation, we run 10-fold cross validation in the training set to select the parameter). We search over the range $C \in \{10^1, 10^2, \ldots, 10^7\}$.

For the SIM algorithms, we use $K = 10$ phases, with $T = 100$ iterations of sub-gradient descent in each iteration. Figure 1 shows the rank-loss objective vs. number of iterations of sub-gradient descent with a fixed set of support instances on each dataset. These results show that most of the improvement in the objective occurs within 100 iterations. Note the convergence analysis does not guarantee the objective will decrease monotonically (only that an upper bound decreases monotonically).

5.2 Results and Discussions

Table 2 lists results in the transductive setting, and Table 3 lists results in the inductive setting.

Comparing Different Loss Functions. First, we focus on the transductive setting. Rank-loss methods generally outperform Hamming loss and ambiguous-loss methods. In particular, when used with the same aggregation model, rank loss consistently outperforms Hamming loss on all datasets. The performance differences of these two methods for the `softmax` aggregation model range from 4% for HJA filtered to 15% for Letter-Carroll, and are even more pronounced for the `max` model. These results support our claim that rank loss is more appropriate than Hamming loss for instance annotation. Rank loss with either aggregation model also consistently outperforms ambiguous loss (ALC) in the transductive setting.

In the inductive setting, the performance generally is lower than the transductive setting, which is expected because in the transductive setting predictions are made with extra bag-level label information. However, rank-loss methods still achieve the best overall performance (excluding SISL SVM, which learns from instance labels). The performance of the Hamming-loss based methods is degraded most severely (possibly because Hamming loss does not calibrate scores between classes, so its predictions become less reliable without the restriction on which classes may be selected imposed by the bag label sets).

Comparing Different Aggregation Models. The `softmax` model generally outperforms `max` for both rank loss and Hamming-loss objectives. In fact, rank loss with `softmax` achieves the best performance for all five datasets in both settings (except for the inductive HJA Birdsong filtered dataset, where the difference in accuracy between rank loss with `softmax` and ALC is within the margin of uncertainty). The difference between the two aggregation models is more pronounced for the Hamming-loss objective.

The Effect of Unlabeled Instances. Comparing the filtered and unfiltered variants of the HJA dataset, all methods suffer some accuracy degradation when we include the unlabeled instances. This is not surprising as these unlabeled instances introduce noise both at the instance level (because they may not correspond to any of the defined classes) and at the bag level (because the label set may be incomplete). The rank loss / `softmax` method suffers less than other algorithms in the presence of the unlabeled instances. For example, in the transductive setting the difference in accuracy is 0.4% for rank loss / `softmax` and 6.4% for Cour's ALC. Note that ALC assumes that every instance is associated with one of the labels of the bag. This assumption is violated by the unlabeled instances that are not accounted for by the bag label set, making ALC more sensitive to the presence of such instances. The `softmax` model suffers less than the `max` model, possibly due to the fact that `max` can mistakenly select the unlabeled instances as support instances.

To summarize, we observe that the rank loss / `softmax` method achieves the best overall performance. This result is verified in both transductive and inductive settings. The rank loss / `softmax` method is also the most robust in the presence of instance and label noise introduced by the unlabeled instances in the HJA Birdsong dataset.

6. RELATED WORK

MIML algorithms are developed under multiple frameworks, some of which naturally lend themselves to instance annotation. One such framework is graphical models, which have been previously used to perform bag and instance-level classification. Such models often treat instance labels as latent variables. Inference over such models allows the classification of instances. While a variety of algorithms exists, we highlight some representative examples of recent work. Dirichlet-Bernoulli Alignment [26] and the Exponential Multinomial Mixture model [25] are topic models for MIML datasets and use variational inference to perform instance labeling. Zha et al. [27] proposed the MLMIL algorithm, a conditional random field model for MIML image annotation that uses Gibbs sampling to infer instance labels. Du et al. [8] propose another application of graphical models to simultaneous image annotation and segmentation.

Table 2: Transductive setting accuracy.

Algorithm	Letter-Carroll	Letter-Frost	HJA Birdsong (filtered)	(unfiltered)	MSRC v2
Rank loss, `softmax`	0.745	0.775	0.817	0.813	0.697
Rank loss, `max`	0.728	0.773	0.809	0.779	0.697
Hamming loss, `softmax`	0.591	0.588	0.776	0.755	0.614
Hamming loss, `max`	0.459	0.48	0.709	0.59	0.55
Cour's ALC	0.672	0.688	0.742	0.678	0.678

Table 3: Inductive mode, accuracy ± standard deviation over 10-fold cross-validation.

Algorithm	Letter-Carroll	Letter-Frost	HJA Birdsong (filtered)	(unfiltered)	MSRC v2
Rank loss, `softmax`	0.540 ± 0.066	0.575 ± 0.050	0.619 ± 0.042	0.555 ± 0.053	0.467 ± 0.044
Rank loss, `max`	0.528 ± 0.049	0.561 ± 0.051	0.590 ± 0.044	0.525 ± 0.071	0.439 ± 0.043
Hamming loss, `softmax`	0.347 ± 0.065	0.338 ± 0.041	0.479 ± 0.052	0.438 ± 0.052	0.337 ± 0.034
Hamming loss, `max`	0.142 ± 0.041	0.150 ± 0.044	0.243 ± 0.052	0.119 ± 0.027	0.179 ± 0.064
Cour's ALC	0.474 ± 0.063	0.506 ± 0.063	0.621 ± 0.038	0.542 ± 0.039	0.431 ± 0.036
SISL SVM	0.772 ± 0.049	0.753 ± 0.038	0.772 ± 0.032	–	0.638 ± 0.045

While graphical models offer intuitive probabilistic interpretation, the computational complexity of inference in such models is one of the standing challenges. In this paper, we focus on another class of MIML approaches based on regularized loss minimization. Hamming-Loss SIM can be viewed as alternative approach for optimizing a similar objective to the M^3MIML algorithm [28] (which learns an instance-level model, but was not designed for instance annotation). Also note that Cour's ALC method follows the same framework of regularized loss minimization (but using a loss function designed for ALC).

There are a small number of other works that address MIML instance annotation [21, 22]. Vijayanarasimhan and Grauman [22] developed a MIML SVM that learns a bag-level model with a set kernel (it does not learn a model of the instance feature space). Their algorithm makes predictions at either the bag or instance level by treating an instance as a bag of one instance. Vezhnevets and Buhmann [21] proposed an algorithm for instance annotation in MIML data where images are represented as a bag of pixels. Their algorithm alternates between sampling instance labels from an estimated distribution, and training an ensemble of decision trees on the sampled labels. Similarly, Nguyen [16] proposed a MIML SVM algorithm which alternates between assigning instance labels and maximizing margin given the assigned labels (although they did not conduct experiments on instance annotation).

7. CONCLUSION AND FUTURE WORK

We introduce Rank-Loss Support Instance Machines for instance annotation of MIML datasets. The key to our approach is a loss function that is measured at the bag-level and encourages the correct ranking of classes such that classes present in the label set of a bag score higher than classes that are not present. This general objective can be instantiated with different aggregation models including the previously used `max` model or a newly proposed `softmax` model. Both models can be viewed as representing each bag with a support instance for each class. We alternate between computing this support, and optimizing a convex rank-loss objective using an efficient primal sub-gradient descent method. Experiments demonstrate that Rank-Loss SIM achieves higher accuracy than similar Hamming or ambiguous-loss based methods, and the `softmax` aggregation model achieves higher accuracy than the `max` model.

Our empirical evaluation focuses on methods based on regularized loss minimization. Comparisons to other types of methods including graphical models will be a topic of future work. We only consider linear models in this work, but our proposed methods could be extended to use kernels for non-linear classification. One possibility is to use the standard kernel trick with a dual optimization method. Shalev-Shwartz et al. [19] proposed a way of kernelizing Pegasos that could be applied to our algorithms. A third possibility proposed by Rahimi and Recht [17] is to map the original features into a feature space such that inner products in the new space are approximately equal to a kernel (e.g., a radial basis function kernel). Further work is needed to determine which of these methods works well for instance annotation, and in what circumstances.

8. ACKNOWLEDGMENTS

This work is partially funded by the Ecosystems Informatics IGERT program via NSF grant DGE 0333257, NSF grant 1055113 to X. Z. F., and the College of Engineering, Oregon State University. We would also like to thank Matthew Betts, Sarah Frey, Adam Hadley, and Jay Sexsmith for their help in collecting HJA data, Iris Koski for labeling the data, Katie Wolf for her work on noise reduction, and Lawrence Neal for his work on segmentation.

9. REFERENCES

[1] S. Andrews, I. Tsochantaridis, and T. Hofmann. Support vector machines for multiple-instance learning. *Advances in Neural Information Processing Systems*, 15:561–568, 2002.

[2] S. Boyd and L. Vandenberghe. *Convex optimization.* Cambridge Univ Pr, 2004.

[3] L. Carroll. *Through the looking-glass : and what Alice found there.* 1896.

[4] C.-C. Chang and C.-J. Lin. *LIBSVM: a library for support vector machines*, 2001.

[5] T. Cour, B. Sapp, C. Jordan, and B. Taskar. Learning from ambiguously labeled images. In *Computer Vision and Pattern Recognition, 2009. CVPR 2009. IEEE Conference on*, pages 919–926. IEEE, 2009.

[6] T. Cour, B. Sapp, and B. Taskar. Learning from partial labels. *Journal of Machine Learning Research*, 12:1225–1261, 2011.

[7] T. Dietterich, R. Lathrop, and T. Lozano-Pérez. Solving the multiple instance problem with axis-parallel rectangles. *Artificial Intelligence*, 89(1-2):31–71, 1997.

[8] L. Du, L. Ren, D. Dunson, and L. Carin. A bayesian model for simultaneous image clustering, annotation and object segmentation. *Advances in Neural Information Processing Systems*, 22:486–494, 2009.

[9] A. Elisseeff and J. Weston. A kernel method for multi-labelled classification. *Advances in Neural Information Processing Systems*, 14:681–687, 2001.

[10] R.-E. Fan, K.-W. Chang, C.-J. Hsieh, X.-R. Wang, and C.-J. Lin. LIBLINEAR: A library for large linear classification. *Journal of Machine Learning Research*, 9:1871–1874, 2008.

[11] P. W. Frey and D. J. Slate. Letter recognition using holland-style adaptive classifiers. *Machine Learning*, 6:161, 1991.

[12] R. Frost. *Mountain Interval*. 1916.

[13] E. Hüllermeier and J. Beringer. Learning from ambiguously labeled examples. *Intelligent Data Analysis*, 10(5):419–439, 2006.

[14] Y. Li, S. Ji, S. Kumar, J. Ye, and Z. Zhou. Drosophila gene expression pattern annotation through multi-instance multi-label learning. In *Proceedings of the 21st International Joint Conference on Artificial Intelligence, Pasadena, CA*, 2009.

[15] L. Neal, F. Briggs, R. Raich, and X. Fern. Time-frequency segmentation of bird song in noisy acoustic environments. In *Proc. IEEE Int. Conf. Acoust., Speech, and Signal Processing*, 2011.

[16] N. Nguyen. A new svm approach to multi-instance multi-label learning. In *Tenth IEEE International Conference on Data Mining. ICDM'10*, pages 384–392, 2010.

[17] A. Rahimi and B. Recht. Random features for large-scale kernel machines. *jAdvances in Neural Information Processing Systems*, 20:1177–1184, 2007.

[18] S. Shalev-Shwartz and Y. Singer. Logarithmic regret algorithms for strongly convex repeated games. *The Hebrew University, Technical Report*, 2007.

[19] S. Shalev-Shwartz, Y. Singer, and N. Srebro. Pegasos: Primal estimated sub-gradient solver for svm. In *Proceedings of the 24th international conference on Machine learning*, pages 807–814. ACM, 2007.

[20] C. Shen, J. Jiao, B. Wang, and Y. Yang. Multi-Instance Multi-Label Learning For Automatic Tag Recommendation. In *Proceedings of the 2009 IEEE International Conference on Systems, Man, and Cybernetics (SMC 2009)*, 2009.

[21] A. Vezhnevets, J. Buhmann, and E. Zurich. Towards Weakly Supervised Semantic Segmentation by Means of Multiple Instance and Multitask Learning. In *Conference on Computer Vision and Pattern Recognition*, 2010.

[22] S. Vijayanarasimhan and K. Grauman. What's it going to cost you?: Predicting effort vs. informativeness for multi-label image annotations. 2009.

[23] J. Winn, A. Criminisi, and T. Minka. Object categorization by learned universal visual dictionary. In *Tenth IEEE International Conference on Computer Vision, 2005. ICCV 2005*, pages 1800–1807, 2005.

[24] O. Yakhnenko. *Learning from Text and Images: Generative and Discriminative Models for Partially Labeled Data*. PhD thesis, Iowa State University, 2009.

[25] S. Yang, J. Bian, and H. Zha. Hybrid Generative/Discriminative Learning for Automatic Image Annotation. In *Conference on Uncertainty in Artificial Intelligence*, 2010.

[26] S. Yang, H. Zha, and B. Hu. Dirichlet-Bernoulli Alignment: A Generative Model for Multi-Class Multi-Label Multi-Instance Corpora. 2010.

[27] Z. Zha, X. Hua, T. Mei, J. Wang, G. Qi, and Z. Wang. Joint multi-label multi-instance learning for image classification. In *IEEE Conference on Computer Vision and Pattern Recognition, 2008. CVPR 2008*, pages 1–8, 2008.

[28] M. Zhang and Z. Zhou. M3MIML: A maximum margin method for multi-instance multi-label learning. In *Eighth IEEE International Conference on Data Mining. ICDM'08*, pages 688–697, 2008.

[29] Z. Zhou. Multi-instance learning: A survey. Technical report, National Laboratory for Novel Software Technology, Nanjing University, 2010.

[30] Z. Zhou and M. Zhang. Multi-instance multi-label learning with application to scene classification. *Advances in Neural Information Processing Systems*, 19:1609, 2007.

[31] Z. Zhou, M. Zhang, S. Huang, and Y. Li. Multi-instance multi-label learning. *Artificial Intelligence*, 176(1):2291–2320, 2012.

Inductive Multi-task Learning with Multiple View Data

Jintao Zhang
Center for Bioinformatics
University of Kansas
Lawrence, KS
jtzhang@ku.edu

Jun Huan
Department of Electrical Engineering and Computer Science
University of Kansas
Lawrence, KS
jhuan@ittc.ku.edu

ABSTRACT

In many real-world applications, it is becoming common to have data extracted from multiple diverse sources, known as "multi-view" data. Multi-view learning (MVL) has been widely studied in many applications, but existing MVL methods learn a single task individually. In this paper, we study a new direction of multi-view learning where there are multiple related tasks with multi-view data (i.e. multi-view multi-task learning, or MVMT Learning). In our MVMT learning methods, we learn a linear mapping for each view in each task. In a single task, we use co-regularization to obtain functions that are in-agreement with each other on the unlabeled samples and achieve low classification errors on the labeled samples simultaneously. Cross different tasks, additional regularization functions are utilized to ensure the functions that we learn in each view are similar. We also developed two extensions of the MVMT learning algorithm. One extension handles missing views and the other handles non-uniformly related tasks. Experimental studies on three real-world data sets demonstrate that our MVMT methods significantly outperform the existing state-of-the-art methods.

Categories and Subject Descriptors

H.4 [**Information Systems Applications**]: Miscellaneous; I.2.6 [**Artificial Intelligence**]: Learning—*performance measures*

General Terms

Algorithms,Experimentation

Keywords

Multi-view learning, co-regularization, missing view, inductive multi-task learning, task relationship learning

1. INTRODUCTION

In many real-world applications, it is becoming common to have data extracted from multiple diverse sources, known as "multi-view" data. Each data source is referred as a *view* [13]. Mining and learning with multi-view data (i.e. multi-view learning, or MVL) has been studied extensively [2, 6, 13, 18, 21, 22]. For instance, in multi-lingual text categorization [2], each language represents a view. For scientific document categorization, each paper has two views: the bag-of-words features and their citations [18]. In classifying webpages [6], we may have three views for a given webpage: the content of the webpage, the text of any webpages linking to this webpage, and the link structure of all linked pages. The limitation of these MVL methods is that they essentially learn a single task individually at a time.

In this paper, we study a new direction of multi-view learning where there are multiple related tasks with multi-view data (i.e. multi-view multi-task learning, or MVMT Learning). MVMT Learning has many real-world applications. For instance, sentiment classification for music reviews and news comments is two related tasks, and they both share word features from the comments or reviews. In protein functional classification, each protein has features from multiple views (e.g. protein sequences, 3D structures) and may be associated with multiple functional classes. In image annotation [7], each image has features extracted from multiple sources and can be annotated with multiple objects such as a boat, a bird and etc. The interplay of multiple views and multiple tasks in the same learning problem motivates us to investigate multi-task learning in the multi-view framework.

Despite the wide application areas, multi-task learning (MTL) with multi-view data only caught the attention of the research community recently. Cavallanti *et al.* [8] developed linear algorithms for online multi-task learning. Though there may be multiple views, each task has only one view in their settings. He *et al.* [16] proposed a graph-based iterative algorithm (IteM^2) for multi-view multi-task learning with applications to text classification. The IteM^2 algorithm projects any two tasks to a new Reproducing Kernel Hilbert Space (RKHS) based on the common views shared by the given two tasks. Though impressive preliminary results have been obtained in text categorization applications, the treatment of MVMT learning in IteM^2 is limited. First IteM^2 is a transductive learning method, hence it is unable to generate predictive models on independent, unknown testing samples. A consequence of the transductive learning is that the training data set must have the same fraction of positive samples as in the testing data set. In addition, the method is designed primarily for text categorization where the feature values are all non-negative [1], since otherwise Proposition 4.1 and Theorem 4.2 in [16] will not hold. There are many real-world data sets with a significant portion of features with negative values that the IteM^2 method is unable to handle. In this paper IteM^2 is the most important competing method that our proposed MVMT method will compare with.

[1]Refer to page 3 in He *et al.* [16]

We propose an inductive learning framework to address the general MVMT learning problem. Our starting point is a MVL framework based on co-regularization where we train multiple classifiers, one for each view, with the goal to obtain those classifiers that are in-agreement with one another on the unlabeled samples and achieve minimal classification errors on the labeled samples simultaneously [21, 22]. We add a couple of regularization factors (e.g. ℓ_2 regularization [15]) to ensure the functions that we learn from each task are similar to each other, resulting in a convex objective function, which makes the subsequent optimization easy. In addition, our algorithm is flexible when one view is completely missing for a task. In many application we may have structured view missing, and our algorithm extends to these cases naturally with the regularization function that we use. Moreover, it is quite often that not all tasks in multi-task learning are uniformly related to each other [10, 17]. To handle this, we introduce a positive semi-definite matrix to capture the relationship of tasks that may not be uniformly related to each other.

In summary, the main contributions of this paper are two-fold. First we propose a general inductive learning framework for the challenging multi-view multi-task problems using co-regularization and task relationship learning. Secondly we design efficient algorithms to optimize the objective function with either close-form solutions or iterative optimization solutions. We conducted comprehensive experimental evaluations of our MVMT methods on three real-world MVMT data sets, and compared our MVMT methods with the state-of-the-art methods, including the competing IteM^2 method.

The rest of this paper is organized as follows. In Section 2, we briefly review related work on multi-view learning and multi-task learning. We explain our co-regularized MVMT algorithms and their implementations in details in Section 3. We have experimentally evaluated our methods on three real-world data sets and compared our results with those from the state-of-the-art methods. We present the results in Section 4 and conclude our work in Section 5.

2. RELATED WORK

Multi-view semi-supervised learning has attracted significant research interest in recent years [1, 5, 11, 14, 19, 23, 24]. The underlying assumption of multi-view algorithm is that each view is conditionally independent from other views [6] and is sufficient for constructing a predictive model [2, 14]. We briefly overview MVL methods that are widely used. Based on how information from multiple views is integrated, existing MVL algorithms can be roughly classified into a variety of categories. Co-training [6] iteratively labels unlabeled examples using the models built from existing labeled examples, and expands the pool of labeled examples until convergence of performance [14, 20]. Manifold co-regularization [22] was proposed based on a reproducing kernel Hilbert space with a data-dependent co-regularization norm to explore the structure of unlabeled multi-view data. Recently co-regularization [21] attracted the attention of the community due to its simplicity of optimizing a single regularized objective function.

When each task has only a limited number of samples, multi-task learning has been empirically as well as theoretically shown to provide better predictive models with closely related tasks [3, 4]. Some early MTL approaches assumed that either the function parameters of different tasks are similar [15] or multiple tasks share a subset of features [4]. These MTL methods imposed a regularization term to enforce the difference between multiple task functions to be small. Recent studies on MTL proposed that the relatedness of multiple tasks has a structure such as a graph or a tree [10, 17], or different tasks share a common subspace representation [9]. Another group of MTL methods [25] pose no assumption on the structure of task relatedness, and learn task relationship automatically from the input data, and provide more modeling flexibility.

3. INDUCTIVE MULTI-VIEW MULTI-TASK LEARNING

In this section, we propose a general inductive learning framework for multi-task learning with multiple view data. We apply co-regularized MVL within each task, and the multiple related tasks are learned jointly using task regularization or task relationship learning. We handle the special case that some entire views are missing from some tasks, analyze the complexity of our MVMT methods, and develop efficient optimization algorithms to achieve optimal solutions.

3.1 Notations

In this paper, we use bold capital letters (e.g. $\mathbf{X}$) to represent a matrix and bold lowercase letters (e.g. $\mathbf{x}$) to denote a vector. Lowercase letters (e.g. x) are used for scalars, and Greek letters (e.g λ) for regularization parameters. We use $[m : n]$ $(n > m)$ to denote a set of integers in the range of m to n inclusively. Unless stated otherwise, all vectors are column vectors.

Suppose we are given a set of N labeled and M unlabeled data samples for T tasks. In general we have limited supply of labeled examples but abundant supply of unlabeled examples, i.e. $M \gg N$. We use N_t and M_t denote the number of labeled and unlabeled examples in task $t \in [1 : T]$, thus we have $N = \sum_t N_t$ and $M = \sum_t M_t$. Each example has features from V views and the total number of features from all the V views is denoted as D. Let D_v be the number of features in the view $v \in [1 : V]$, and we have $D = \sum_v D_v$.

For each view v present in task t, the feature matrix of the labeled examples is $\mathbf{X}_t^v \in \mathbb{R}^{N_t \times D_v}$. The feature matrix of the unlabeled examples is $\mathbf{U}_t^v \in \mathbb{R}^{M_t \times D_v}$. Let $\mathbf{y}_t \in \{1, -1\}^{N_t \times 1}$ be the label vector of the labeled examples in the task t. We write $\mathbf{X}_t = (\mathbf{X}_t^1, \mathbf{X}_t^2, \ldots, \mathbf{X}_t^V)$, and $\mathbf{U}_t = (\mathbf{U}_t^1, \mathbf{U}_t^2, \ldots, \mathbf{U}_t^V)$, corresponding to the concatenated feature matrix of the labeled and unlabeled examples for task t, respectively. It is common that in some applications not all tasks have features available from all the V views, so we introduce an indicator matrix $\mathbf{I_d} \in \{1, 0\}^{T \times V}$ to mark which view is missing from which task, i.e. $\mathbf{I}_d(t, v) = 0$ if the view v is missing from task t, and = 1 otherwise. Using this notation, we only handle "structured" missing views in the sense that if a view is present in a task, it is present in all the samples in the task; if a view is missing from a task, it is missing in all the samples in the task. Throughout the paper we use subscripts to denote tasks and superscripts to denote views.

3.2 Problem and Algorithm Overview

We illustrate the problem of learning multiple related tasks with multi-view data in Figure 1. We hypothesize that we can construct better classification models by considering information from multiple views and learning multiple related tasks simultaneously. In our method we learn one linear mapping function $\mathbf{f}_t^v : \mathbb{R}^{D_v} \rightarrow \{1, -1\}$ for each view v present in the task t. We search those mapping functions based on two intuition. First, for a given task t, we expect that the mapping functions $\mathbf{f}_t^v$'s from all its views agree with one another as much as possible on the unlabeled samples. Second, for a given view, we expect that all the mapping functions in different tasks behave similarly. We formalize the two intuitions using regularization functions in a supervised learning framework.

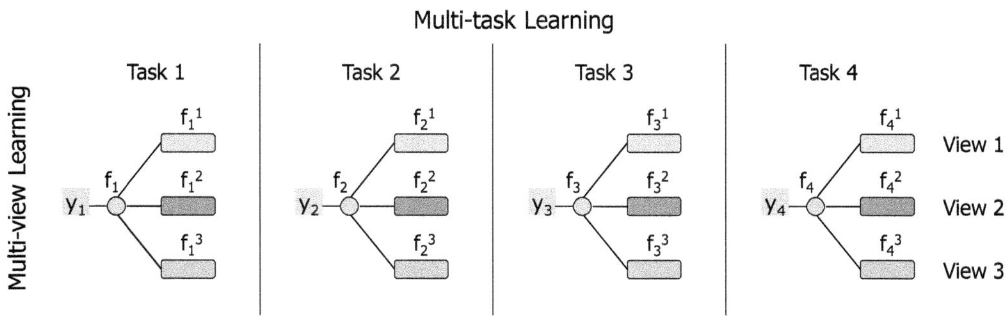

Figure 1: Graphical representation of the multi-view multi-task learning framework.

The details of the regularization, as well as our supervised learning framework, are introduced below.

3.3 Co-regularized Multi-view Learning

The basic assumption underlying multi-view learning for a single task is that the multiple views are conditionally independent and each view generates a predictive model that can be used to make predictions on data examples, while the final models are obtained from these view models. Without prior knowledge on which view contributes more to the final models than other views, we assume that all views contribute equally, following [21,22]. The final models are obtained by averaging the prediction results from all view functions as follows:

$$f(\mathbf{x}) = \frac{1}{V}\sum_{v=1}^{V} f^v(\mathbf{x}^v), \tag{1}$$

where $\mathbf{x}$ has totally V views, $\mathbf{x}^v$ is the set of features for view v, and f^v is the view function generated on view v.

In multi-view learning, we want the models built on each single view to agree with one another as much as possible on unlabeled examples. Co-regularization is a technique to enforce such model agreement on unlabeled examples. The view functions $\mathbf{f}^v$ for all views v's are obtained from the following objective function,

$$\min_{f^v} L(\mathbf{y}, f(\mathbf{X})) + \frac{\lambda}{2}\|f\|^2 + \frac{\mu}{2}\sum_{v'\neq v}\|f^{v'}(\mathbf{U}^{v'}) - f^v(\mathbf{U}^v)\|^2, \tag{2}$$

where $\|.\|$ denotes the ℓ_2 norm. $L(.,.)$ is the loss function that penalizes the misclassification on labeled examples. $f^v(\mathbf{U}^v)$ is the prediction results by applying the function f^v to each sample in the unlabeled data for the view v. λ is the parameter that regulates the strength of the ℓ_2-norm regularization on view functions, and μ is the coupling parameter that regularizes the disagreement of different views. By minimizing the three terms jointly, an optimal set of view functions that minimize the misclassification of labeled examples and maximize the agreement on the prediction results on unlabeled examples can be identified.

3.4 Task Regularization in MVMT Learning

Given multiple related tasks with multi-view data, it is advantageous to learn these tasks in the same framework to achieve the benefits of both multi-task learning and multi-view learning. One approach to extend the co-regularized MVL framework is to learn each of the multiple task individually, as presented below.

$$\min_{f_t^v} \sum_t L(\mathbf{y_t}, f_t(\mathbf{X_t})) + \frac{\lambda}{2}\|f_t\|^2 + \frac{\mu}{2}\sum_{v'\neq v}\|f_t^v(\mathbf{U}_t^v) - f_t^{v'}(\mathbf{U}_t^{v'})\|^2, \tag{3}$$

where f_t^v is a view specific mapping function for the view v in the task t.

Apparently the formula does not take advantage of the presence of multiple related tasks. In order to get benefit from the additional information, we apply an additional regularization function that penalizes the difference of the view specific functions on the same view across different tasks. For each view $v \in [1:V]$ in task $t \in [1:T]$, we learn a linear mapping function indexed by a parameter $\mathbf{w}_t^v \in \mathbb{R}^{D_v\times 1}$. We denote $\mathbf{w}_t \in \mathbb{R}^{D\times 1}$ as the column vector by concatenating all $\mathbf{w}_t^v$ for the task t, and we have:

$$\begin{aligned} f_t(\mathbf{X}_t) &= \frac{1}{V}\sum_{v=1}^{V} f^v(x^v) \\ &= \frac{1}{V}\sum_{v=1}^{V}\mathbf{X}_t^v\mathbf{w}_t^v = \frac{\mathbf{X}_t\mathbf{w}_t}{V}. \end{aligned} \tag{4}$$

Using the least square loss function, we have the objective function for the T tasks with V views for each task as follows:

$$\begin{aligned} \min_{\{\mathbf{w}_t^v\}} & \sum_{t=1}^{T}\frac{1}{2}\|\mathbf{y}_t - \frac{\mathbf{X}_t\mathbf{w}_t}{V}\|^2 + \frac{\mu}{2}\sum_{v'\neq v}^{V}\|\mathbf{U}_t^v\mathbf{w}_t^v - \mathbf{U}_t^{v'}\mathbf{w}_t^{v'}\|^2 \\ & + \frac{\lambda}{2}\sum_{v=1}^{V}\|\mathbf{w}_t^v\|^2 + \frac{\gamma}{2}\sum_{t'\neq t}^{T}\|\mathbf{w}_t^v - \mathbf{w}_{t'}^v\|^2, \end{aligned} \tag{5}$$

where w_t^v, w_t, λ, and μ were explained before. γ is a new regularization parameter to penalize the difference of view mapping function across different tasks for the same view. We call this formalization "the regularized multi-view multi-task learning" (*regMVMT*).

To solve the related optimization problem of *regMVMT*, we denote the objective function as F, and compute its derivative regarding to each $\mathbf{w}_t^v$ as follows:

$$\begin{aligned} \frac{\partial F}{\partial \mathbf{w}_t^v} &= \frac{1}{V}\mathbf{X}_t^{vT}(\frac{\mathbf{X}_t\mathbf{w}_t}{V} - \mathbf{y}_t) + \gamma\sum_{t'\neq t}^{T}(\mathbf{w}_t^v - \mathbf{w}_{t'}^v) \\ & + \lambda\mathbf{w}_t^v + \mu\mathbf{U}_t^{vT}\sum_{v'\neq v}^{V}(\mathbf{U}_t^v\mathbf{w}_t^v - \mathbf{U}_t^{v'}\mathbf{w}_t^{v'}). \end{aligned} \tag{6}$$

Set Eq.(6) to zero, rearrange the terms and we have:

$$E_{tv} = A_{tv}\mathbf{w}_t^v + \sum_{v' \neq v} B_{vv'}^t \mathbf{w}_t^{v'} + \sum_{t' \neq t} C_{t'v}\mathbf{w}_{t'}^v,$$

$$A_{tv} = \lambda + \gamma(T-1) + \mu(V-1)\mathbf{U}_t^{vT}\mathbf{U}_t^v + \frac{\mathbf{X}_t^{vT}\mathbf{X}_t^v}{V^2},$$

$$B_{vv'}^t = \frac{\mathbf{X}_t^{vT}\mathbf{X}_t^{v'}}{V^2} - \mu\,\mathbf{U}_t^{vT}\mathbf{U}_t^{v'},$$

$$C_{t'v} = -\gamma I_{D_v}, \quad E_{tv} = \frac{\mathbf{X}_t^{vT}\mathbf{y}_t}{V}, \tag{7}$$

where I_{D_v} is a $D_v \times D_v$ identity matrix. Note that we can have such an equation for each view v in the task t. To learn $\mathbf{w}_t^v$, we must also learn $\mathbf{w}_t^{v'}$ from other views v' ($v' \neq v$) in the task t and $\mathbf{w}_{t'}^v$ from other tasks $t' \neq t$ on the view v. Eventually we have to learn all $\mathbf{w}_t^v$'s jointly from a large set of equations as in Eq.(7) by taking derivatives regarding to each view in each task, as in the following linear equation system:

$$\mathcal{L}\mathcal{W} = \mathcal{R}, \tag{8}$$

where $\mathcal{L} \in \mathbb{R}^{TD \times TD}$ is a sparse block matrix with $TV \times TV$ blocks. Each block corresponds to a view in a task and its size is the feature dimensionality of the view.

Matrix $\mathcal{L}$ has the following form:

$$\begin{bmatrix} A_{11} & B_{12}^1 & \dots & B_{1V}^1 & \cdot\;\cdot\;\cdot & C_{T1} & 0 & \dots & 0 \\ B_{21}^1 & A_{12} & \dots & B_{2V}^1 & \cdot\;\cdot\;\cdot & 0 & C_{T2} & \dots & 0 \\ \dots & \dots & \dots & \dots & \cdot\;\cdot\;\cdot & \dots & \dots & \dots & \dots \\ B_{V1}^1 & B_{V2}^1 & \dots & A_{1V} & \cdot\;\cdot\;\cdot & 0 & 0 & \dots & C_{TV} \\ \cdot & \cdot & \cdot & \cdot & \cdot & \cdot & \cdot & \cdot & \cdot \\ \cdot & \cdot & \cdot & \cdot & \cdot & \cdot & \cdot & \cdot & \cdot \\ \cdot & \cdot & \cdot & \cdot & \cdot & \cdot & \cdot & \cdot & \cdot \\ C_{T1} & 0 & \dots & 0 & \cdot\;\cdot\;\cdot & A_{T1} & B_{12}^T & \dots & B_{1V}^T \\ 0 & C_{T2} & \dots & 0 & \cdot\;\cdot\;\cdot & B_{21}^T & A_{T2} & \dots & B_{2V}^T \\ \dots & \dots & \dots & \dots & \cdot\;\cdot\;\cdot & \dots & \dots & \dots & \dots \\ 0 & 0 & \dots & C_{TV} & \cdot\;\cdot\;\cdot & B_{V1}^T & B_{V2}^T & \dots & A_{TV} \end{bmatrix}$$

$$\mathcal{W} = \text{Vec}([W_1^1, ..., W_1^V, E_2^1, ..., E_2^V, ..., E_T^1, ..., E_T^V]),$$
$$\mathcal{R} = \text{Vec}([E_{11}, ..., E_{1V}, E_{21}, ..., E_{2V}, ..., E_{T1}, ..., E_{TV}]), \tag{9}$$

where Vec() denotes the function stacking the column vectors in a matrix to a single column vector. Here column vector $\mathcal{W}$ and $\mathcal{R}$ are generated by stacking all column vectors $\mathbf{w}_t^v$ and E_t^v, respectively. Note that $\mathcal{L}$ is a sparse block matrix with $TV \times TV$ blocks, and block matrix A_{tv}, $B_{vv'}^t$, and $C_{t'v}$ are defined in Eq.(7). The analytic solution of $\mathcal{W}$ can be easily obtained from Eq.(8) by taking the inverse of matrix $\mathcal{L}$. When there is a new data example from task t with $\mathbf{x}_t^*$ as the concatenated row feature vector of all the V view, the predictive outputs $\mathbf{y}_t^*$ is given by:

$$y_t^* = \text{sign}(\mathbf{x}_t^*\mathbf{w}_t). \tag{10}$$

Note that by setting $\gamma = 0$ the *regMVMT* algorithm degenerates to the co-regularized multi-view learning algorithm. Similarly set $\mu = 0$ the *regMVMT* algorithm degenerates to the regularized multi-task learning algorithm. These two methods are special cases of our MVMT method when there is only one task or one view for each task, and we will implement them as comparison baseline methods. In Figure 2 we show a comparison between the *regMVMT* method and the competing transductive IteM^2 method on a data set for webpage classification. Here we could see that *regMVMT* improves significantly upon the IteM^2 method. Detailed experimental studies are in Section 4.

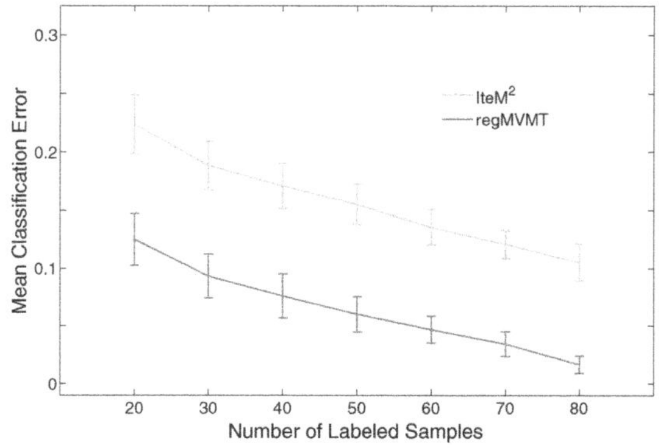

Figure 2: Preliminary results on the WebKB data set.

3.5 Learning Task Relationships in the MVMT Framework

In many MTL applications, tasks may not be uniformly related to each other. A remedy to those situation, as we investigate here, is to introduce a task relationship inference component [25]. The basic idea is to use a positive semi-definite $\mathbf{\Omega} \in \mathbb{R}^{T \times T}$ to model the similarity among T related tasks, and hence $\mathbf{\Omega}$ must be with finite complexity. For single-view MTL problem, we may utilize $\mathbf{\Omega}$ in the following objective function:

$$\min_{\mathbf{W},\mathbf{\Omega}} \sum_t^T \frac{1}{2}\|\mathbf{y}_t - \mathbf{X}_t\mathbf{w}_t\|^2 + \frac{\lambda}{2}\|\mathbf{W}\|_F^2 + \frac{\gamma}{2}\text{tr}(\mathbf{W}\mathbf{\Omega}^{-1}\mathbf{W}^T),$$
$$\text{s.t.} \quad \mathbf{\Omega} \succeq 0, \ \text{tr}(\mathbf{\Omega}) = 1, \tag{11}$$

where $\mathbf{W}$ is a matrix whose t_{th} column is $\mathbf{w}_t$ for task t. $\|.\|_F$ is the matrix Frobenius norm. $tr()$ is the trace of a matrix.

When we have V views for the T task, we learn a task similarity matrix $\mathbf{\Omega}_v$ for each view v of the T tasks, and the MVMT objective function is as follows:

$$\min_{\mathbf{W},\mathbf{\Omega}} \sum_t^T \frac{1}{2}\|\mathbf{y}_t - \mathbf{X}_t\mathbf{w}_t\|^2 + \frac{\mu}{2}\sum_{v'>v}^V \|\mathbf{U}_t^v\mathbf{w}_t^v - \mathbf{U}_t^{v'}\mathbf{w}_t^{v'}\|^2$$
$$+\frac{\lambda}{2}\sum_{v=1}^V \|\mathbf{w}_t^v\|^2 + \frac{\gamma}{2}\sum_{v=1}^V \text{tr}(\mathbf{W}^v\mathbf{\Omega}_v^{-1}\mathbf{W}^{vT}),$$
$$\text{s.t.} \quad \mathbf{\Omega}_v \succeq 0, \ \text{tr}(\mathbf{\Omega}_v) = 1, v \in [1:V], \tag{12}$$

where $\mathbf{w}_t$ is a column vector concatenated from $\mathbf{w}_t^v$'s for all $v \in [1:V]$, and $\mathbf{W}^v$ is a matrix whose t_{th} column is $\mathbf{w}_t^v$ for all $t \in [1:T]$. The inverse of $\mathbf{\Omega}_v$ is a $T \times T$ matrix whose element at (i,j) is the similarity between task i and j.

Though the objective function is convex regarding to both $\{\mathbf{w}_t\}$ and $\{\mathbf{\Omega}_v\}$, simultaneous optimization of them is technically and computationally challenging. Alternate optimization of $\mathbf{w}_t$'s and $\mathbf{\Omega}_v$'s individually can achieve the optimal solutions efficiently. If we fix the $\{\mathbf{w}_t\}$'s and optimize the $\{\mathbf{\Omega}_v\}$, take the partial derivative of the objective function in Eq.(12) with regard to $\{\mathbf{\Omega}_v\}$, and set it to zero. The analytic solution to $\{\mathbf{\Omega}_v\}$ is:

$$\mathbf{\Omega}_v = \frac{(\mathbf{W}^{vT}\mathbf{W}^v)^{\frac{1}{2}}}{\text{tr}((\mathbf{W}^{vT}\mathbf{W}^v)^{\frac{1}{2}})}. \tag{13}$$

Once $\mathbf{\Omega}_v$ is learned, we can use the same algorithm that we have derived in Eq. 7. We find that only the block matrix A_{tv} and $C_{t'v}$ are different from the formulas in Eq.(7), while the formulas of matrix $B_{vv'}^t$ and E_{tv} remain unchanged. The new A_{tv} and C_{tv} are as follows:

$$A_{tv} = \lambda + \mu(V-1)\mathbf{U}_t^{vT}\mathbf{U}_t^v + \frac{\mathbf{X}_t^{vT}\mathbf{X}_t^v}{V^2},$$
$$C_{t'v} = \gamma c_{tt'}^v I_{D_v}, \tag{14}$$

where c_{ij}^v denote the element (i,j) of the inverse of matrix $\mathbf{\Omega}_v$, and it is a scalar constant in each iteration. We denote this approach *regMVMT+* since it is a variant extension of the *regMVMT* method.

3.6 Dealing with Missing-view Data

In the previous subsections, we consider the ideal case that all tasks in a data set have complete data. When we have incomplete data, the MVMT learning problem becomes more challenging. Missing value imputation has been widely discussed, and here we are not concerned about randomly missed feature values. We aim to handel the case of "structured" missing views. In the context of this discussion, we focus on completely missing views for a task in the sense that if a view is present in a task, it is present in all the samples in the task; if a view is missing from a task, it is missing in all the samples in the task. We recognize that there is a more challenging case where we have partially observed views (i.e. some views are missing from some samples in a task). Partially observed views is beyond the scope of this paper. A straightforward strategy to handel structured missing views is to remove any tasks with missing views, which, however, will significantly reduce the number of related tasks available and also discard useful information present in the remaining views of those tasks.

To handel structured missing views, we introduce an indicator matrix $\mathbf{I}_d \in 1,0^{T\times V}$ to mark the missing views for the T tasks with a total of V views for each task, i.e. $\mathbf{I}_d(t,v) = I_{tv} = 0$ if the view $v \in [1:V]$ is missing in the task $t \in [1:T]$, and $I_{tv} = 1$ otherwise. Let $V_t \leq V$ and $T_v \leq T$ denote the real number of views in task t and the number of tasks for view v, and we need to use V_t and T_v to replace V and T in all the above equations, respectively. In addition, the indicator scalars $I_{tv}, I_{t'v}$, and $I_{tv'}$ must be associated with the corresponding matrices from $\mathbf{X}$ and $\mathbf{U}$. In matrix $\mathbf{\Omega}_v$, a task is considered uncorrelated to any other tasks in terms of view v if it does not has the view v, and the dimension of $\mathbf{\Omega}_v$ will be reduced by one row and one column. Though $\mathbf{\Omega}_v$ may have different dimensionality for different v, we learn each $\mathbf{\Omega}_v$ individually and we only need the trace of the resulting product matrix.

If view v is missing from task t, $\mathbf{w}_t^v$ in $\mathcal{W}$, $\mathbf{E}_t^v$ in $\mathcal{R}$, and the $((t-1)V+v)$-th block row and block column in matrix $\mathcal{L}$ are all-zero matrices. After removing these all-zero blocks from $\mathcal{L}$, $\mathcal{W}$, and $\mathcal{R}$, we have their compact versions $\mathcal{L}'$, $\mathcal{W}'$, and $\mathcal{R}'$, respectively. Eq.(8) is converted to:

$$\mathcal{L}'\mathcal{W}' = \mathcal{R}'. \tag{15}$$

Solving this equation is similar to Eq.(8).

3.7 Analysis of the *regMVMT* Algorithm

The objective function in Eq.(5) is convex regarding to $\mathbf{w}_t$'s, hence it has a global minimum. From the derivation of the matrix $\mathcal{L}$, we can tell that it is symmetric. Since matrix $\mathcal{L}$ is obtained from the derivative of a convex function, it must be at least positive semi-definite. If there is no all-zero row or column in matrix $\mathbf{I}_d$, i.e. each task has at least one view and each view present in at least one task, matrix $\mathcal{L}'$ is also positive semi-definite.

The implementation of the *regMVMT* algorithm is straightforward with the analytic solution. We first calculate the block matrices $A_t^v, B_{vv'}^t, C_t^v$, and the column vector E_t^v for each view v present in each task t, construct the large sparse square matrix $\mathcal{L}$ and the long column vector $\mathcal{R}$ according to the equations in Eq.(9). We then easily obtain the solutions $\mathbf{w}_t$'s as in Eq.(8) by computing the inverse of matrix $\mathcal{L}$ for a given set of regularization parameters. The parameters λ, μ, and γ will be optimized using standard cross validation. Note that the first column of each input feature matrix is an extra added unit vector to offset the intercepts (b) of linear functions. Since the intercepts are not included in any regularization terms, an identity matrix with the first diagonal element as 0 is multiplied with the constant terms ($\lambda+\gamma(T-1)$ and $-\gamma$) in Eq.(7) when constructing the matrix A_{tv} and C_{tv}.

Let D_T denote the number of rows or columns in $\mathcal{L}$, and we have $D_T = \sum_{t,v=1}^{T,V} I_{tv}D_v$, where D_v is the number of features in view v. When there is no missing view in any task, we have $D_T = T\times D$. Though the process of constructing square matrix $\mathcal{L}$ is complex, the speed-limiting step of the *regMVMT* algorithm is the inversion of the large sparse matrix $\mathcal{L}$ in Eq.(9). The construction of matrix $\mathcal{L}$ has a time complexity of $\mathbf{O}(T(T-1)D^2 + 2(N+M)D^2)$, and computing its inverse matrix is of complexity $\mathbf{O}(D_T^3)$, so the total number of features instead of the number of data examples dominates the time complexity. Matrix $\mathcal{L}$ is highly sparse, symmetric, and positive semi-definite, and the overall time complexity of the *regMVMT* algorithm is dependent on its sparsity structure.

LEMMA 3.1. *The time complexity of the* regMVMT *algorithm is* $\mathbf{O}((1+2\bar{n}/T)D_T^2 + \frac{1}{3}D_T^3)$*, where* $\bar{n}$ *is the average number of samples in each task,* $D_T = \sum_{t,v=1}^{T,V} I_{tv}D_v$.

PROOF. It is straightforward that constructing matrix $\mathcal{L}$ and vector $\mathcal{R}$ has time complexity of $\mathbf{O}((1+2\bar{n}/T)D_T^2)$, and the inversion of the positive semi-definite matrix $\mathcal{L}$ has time complexity of $\mathbf{O}(\frac{1}{3}D_T^3)$ using Chomsky decomposition. Hence we have the described overall time complexity. □

The constant factor hidden behind the asymptotic complexity depends on the sparsity structure of matrix $\mathcal{L}$. Since D_T is generally much greater than T, V, N, and M, the running time is determined by the total number of features D_T from all views present in all tasks. In addition, when we store matrices in sparse matrix format, the space complexity of our algorithm is dependent on the number of non-zero elements in matrix $\mathcal{L}$ and the space used by other much small matrices is eligible. We can easily obtain the space complexity from the structure of matrix $\mathcal{L}$.

PROPOSITION 3.1. *The space complexity of the* regMVMT *algorithm is approximately* $\mathbf{O}(\sum_t D_t^2 + D_tT(T-1))$.

In real-world data sets, the number of views V is usually small ($2\sim 5$), and the total number of features D from all views is generally much greater than the number of tasks T. Generally D can be in the range of a few hundred to thousands, and feature selection approaches are needed when it is even larger. Due to the limit of the matrix size in most computer systems, our algorithm can only handle up to tens of tasks, and learning problems with hundreds of tasks or more are hence beyond the scope of this paper.

3.8 The *regMVMT+* Implementation

The implementation of the *regMVMT+* algorithm is similar to *regMVMT* algorithm. One difference is the construction of block matrix $\mathbf{A}_{tv}$'s and $\mathbf{C}_{tv}$'s. An additional difference is that *regMVMT+* is an iterative algorithm, and within each iteration the optimization of $\mathbf{w}_t$'s uses a procedure that is very similar to the *regMVMT* algorithm. We repeat the procedure until the predefined convergence thresholds of $\mathbf{w}_t$'s and $\mathbf{\Omega}_v$'s have been met or we have reached a

Algorithm 1 The *regMVMT+* Algorithm

Input: $\{\mathbf{y}_t\}_{t=1}^T, \{\mathbf{X}_t\}_{t=1}^T, \{\mathbf{U}_t\}_{t=1}^T, \lambda, \mu, \gamma, N_{it}, \epsilon$
Output: $\{\mathbf{W}_t\}_{t=1}^T, \{\mathbf{\Omega}_v\}_{v=1}^V$
Initialize $\mathbf{W}_0 := 0$ and $\mathbf{\Omega}_{v0} := \frac{1}{T} I_T$ for $v \in [1:V]$
for $it = 1$ to N_{it} **do**
  for $(t, v) \in [1:T] \times [1:V]$ **do**
    Construct matrix A_{tv} in Eq.(14) and vector E_{tv} in Eq.(7)
    Construct matrix $B_{vv'}^t$ in Eq.(7) and $C_{t'v}$ in Eq.(14) for each $v' \neq v, t' \neq t$
  end for
  Construct square matrix $\mathcal{L}$ and column vector $\mathcal{R}$ in Eq.(9)
  Compute $\mathbf{W} := \mathcal{L}^{-1}\mathcal{R}$
  Update $\mathbf{\Omega}_v$ using Eq.(13) for each $v \in [1:V]$
  if $\|\mathbf{W} - \mathbf{W}_0\|_1 < \epsilon$ & $\|\mathbf{\Omega}_v - \mathbf{\Omega}_{v0}\|_1 < \epsilon$ **then**
    break
  else
    $\mathbf{W}_0 := \mathbf{W}$
    $\mathbf{\Omega}_{v0} := \mathbf{\Omega}_v$ for each $v \in [1:V]$
  end if
end for
Split $\mathbf{W}$ into T vectors, and return $\{\mathbf{W}_t\}_{t=1}^T$ and $\{\mathbf{\Omega}_v\}_{v=1}^V$

maximal number of iterations. It is expected that this method needs significantly more computational time for the numerical solutions.

We design an efficient iterative algorithm to optimize both $\mathbf{w}_t$'s and $\mathbf{\Omega}_v$'s alternately and implement it as in "The *regMVMT+* Algorithm" pseudo code block 3.8. First $\mathbf{\Omega}_v$ is initialized to $\frac{1}{T} I_T$ (I_T is the $T \times T$ identity matrix) for each view v, which corresponds to the assumption that all tasks are initially uncorrelated. We optimize the convex objective function in Eq.(12) over $\mathbf{w}_t$'s, update $\mathbf{\Omega}_v$'s using Eq.(13), and then plug in the new $\mathbf{\Omega}_v$'s to Eq.(12) to optimize $\mathbf{w}_t$'s again. The procedure is repeated until the convergence of both $\mathbf{w}_t$'s and $\mathbf{\Omega}_v$'s under a predefined threshold.

4. EXPERIMENTAL RESULTS

In this section, we present the experimental results of the two proposed MVMT methods and four baseline methods on three real-world multi-view data sets with multiple tasks. The baseline methods that we used are detailed below.

Regularized MTL (regMT): If we consider no co-regularization on different views in a given task, we convert the MVMT learning problem into the single-view MTL problem [15] by concatenating the feature vectors from all views to a single feature vector and merging multiple views into one view. Comparison with this baseline method can help demonstrate the benefits from using multiple views instead of a single view.

Co-regularized MVL (coMV): By ignoring the multi-task relatedness, we apply the co-regularized MVL method [21] on each task. The implementation is obtained by setting the parameter $\gamma = 0$ in the *regMVMT* formulation.

Multi-task Relationship Learning (regMT+): We may learn the task relationships among the multiple related tasks from the input data when we consider no regularization on different views in a given task. The implementation is obtained by setting the parameter $\mu = 0$ in the *regMVMT+* formulation.

Iterative MVMT (IteM[2]): We also compare our methods with the state-of-the-art MVMT method proposed by He *et al.* [16]. The authors didn't release the software, and we implemented it according to the pseudo-code provided in the IteM[2] algorithm in the original paper. This is the most important competing method that our methods will compare with.

4.1 Data Sets

We collected three multi-view data sets with multiple tasks. The first one is the WebKB data set [6] with 1,051 webpages collected from four universities, and the goal is to classify whether each webpage is course related or not. Here each university is a task, and we have four tasks. There are three views for each webpage: the bag-of-word features from the webpage title, from the webpage main text, and from the main text of the webpage with hyperlinks to the given webpage. There is no missing views in this data set.

The second one is the email spam data set in the ECML 2006 Discovery Challenge [2], and the goal is to classify if each email is spam or not. There are three email users with 2,500 emails for each user, and each user is considered a task. Four bag-of-words views are created: one common view shared by all three tasks, and three task specific views with each for a task. The common view consists of the common vocabulary that exists in all the three tasks, while each task specific view consists of the vocabulary unique to each task, as discussed in He *et al.* [16]. Each task has two missing views, which are the two views specific to the other two tasks.

The third data set is extracted from the NUS-WIDE Object web image database [12] where each image is annotated by objects such as "book", "bird", and etc. We removed all images that are associated with zero or only one object, resulting in an object data set consisting of 3,545 samples in 31 tasks. We used a total of 634 features extracted from images [12], which can be considered as five views: 64-dim color histogram, 144-dim color correlogram, 73-dim edge direction histogram, 128-dim wavelet texture, and 225-dim block-wise color moments. We merged the five types of features for each sample into two views with the 225-dim block-wise color moments as one view and the rest as the other view. By removing those tasks with too few positive or negative examples, we obtained a multi-view data set with 11 tasks. Since this data set consists of a significant portion of negative features, when we applied the IteM[2] method to it, we added a positive constant to the values of negative features of all samples so that all negative features become non-negative. There is no missing views in this data set.

The three data sets are summarized in Table 1, where N_p and N_n denote the total number of positive and negative examples available in each data set. As stated in Section 3, T is the number of tasks, V is the number of views, and D is the total number of features from all views.

Table 1: Statistics of Data Sets Used.

Data Set	WebKB	ECML2006	NUS-WIDE Object
V	3	4	$2 \sim 5$
T	4	3	11
View Missing?	No	Yes	No
N_p	230	2,543	$389 \sim 1325$
N_n	821	2,929	$2220 \sim 3156$
D	2,096	5,597	634

4.2 Model Construction and Evaluation

In each MVMT data set we randomly select the same number n of labeled samples and the same number m of unlabeled samples for each task, where n is varying in the range [20,80] with the increment of 10, and m is generally $2 \sim 4$ times of n. For each subset consisting of n labeled samples and m unlabeled samples for each task, we first randomly selected 20% labeled samples as the independent testing set, and the remaining 80% labeled and all unlabeled samples are the training set.

[2]http://www.ecmlpkdd2006.org/challenge.html

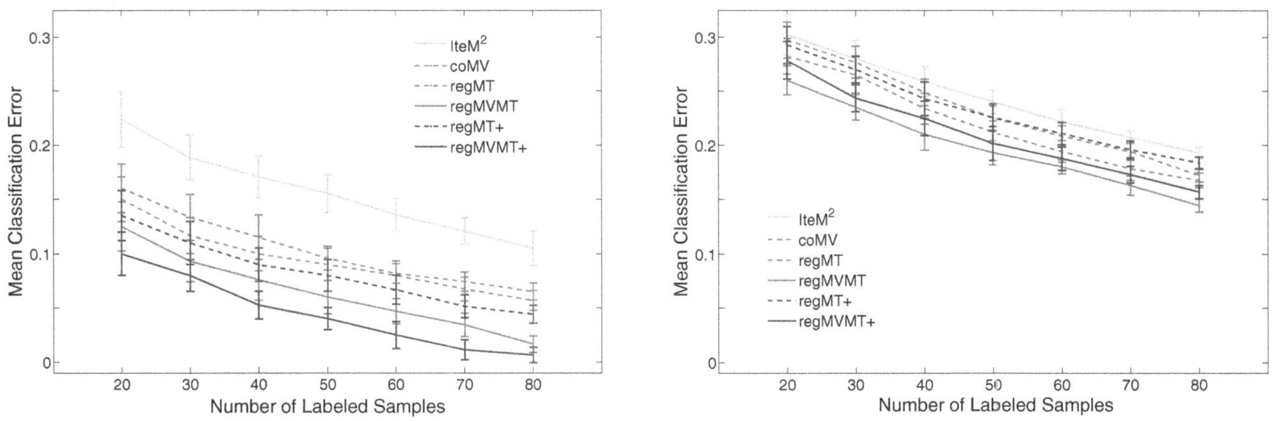

Figure 3: Experimental results on the WebKB data set (left) and on the NUS-WIDE Object data set (right).

The regularization parameters in our methods allow flexible tradeoffs between different regularization terms. We apply five-fold cross validation on the training set to optimize the parameters for each method discussed in this paper: λ, μ and γ for *regMVMT* and *regMVMT+*, λ and γ for *regMT* and *regMT+*, and λ and μ for *coMV*. For the IteM^2 method, we performed five-fold cross validation to optimize the parameter μ and b, but found not much difference. We simply used the optimal values of parameter $\mu = 0.01$ and $b = 1$ that were set in the original paper [16]. We applied grid searching to identify optimal values for each regularization parameter.

After obtaining the optimal parameters for each method, we construct a predictive model using all the training samples and calculate the classification error for each task on the independent testing set using the final task functions in Eq.(9). Each experiment was repeated for 10 times, the mean classification error for each task was calculated separately, and the mean and standard deviation of the classification errors across all tasks in each data set were reported. Here classification error $= 1 - (TP + TN)/N$, where TP, TN, and N stand for the number of true positives, true negatives, and the total number of samples in the testing set, respectively.

4.3 Learning with Complete-view Data

We first consider the ideal case that all tasks have complete-view data, i.e. each of the T tasks has features from all the V views and the indicator matrix I_d is a unit matrix. We perform experiments on the WebKB data set which has four tasks ($T = 4$) and each task shares all the three views ($V = 3$). The left panel in Figure 3 shows for each method how the mean classification error changes with regard to the number of labeled samples. Note that the standard deviations are marked as error bars in each curve.

We observe a common trend that the classification errors and the variances for all methods decrease as the number of labeled samples for training increases. The two MTL baseline methods (*regMT* and *regMT+* perform marginally better than the MVL baseline method (*coMV*), but the performance difference among the three baseline methods is not significant in a two-sample t-test. We test the significance of the results between *regMVMT* and the two baselines *regMT* and *coMV* with two-sample t-test, and find that *regMVMT* significantly outperform *regMT* and *coMV* at the 5% significance level. Similarly t-test shows that *regMVMT+* is significantly better than the baseline *regMT+*. Our proposed inductive MVMT methods (*regMVMT* and *regMVMT+*) significantly outperform the transductive MVMT method (IteM^2) by He *et al.* with the improvement margin of up to $9 \sim 12\%$.

Next we investigate the performance of our MVMT methods on the NUS-WIDE Object data set. We conduct similar experiments and present the results in the right panel in Figure 3. We observe similar trends to the results of the WebKB data set. Our proposed MVMT methods (*regMVMT* and *regMVMT+*) perform better than all the the baselines, especially the IteM^2 method, and the difference is statistically significant with a two-sample t-test.

Different from the previous data set, the *regMVMT* method with ℓ_2 regularization performs slightly better than the variant MVMT method with task relationship learning (*regMVMT+*), but the difference is not significance in the t-test. The performance of the three MTL/MVL baseline methods are close and their curves are entangled. In this data set the improvement margin of our MVMT methods is up to 8% over the transductive counterpart.

4.4 Learning with Missing-view Data

As we discussed earlier, it is common that the multiple tasks in real-world data sets do not share all views. We would like to examine the performance of our MVMT methods compared with the IteM^2 method and other baseline methods in this setting. In the WebKB data set, we randomly select one view in each task and masked it as a missing view. Hence a multi-view data set with missing views is artificially created. Here we enforce a constraint that no more than two tasks miss the same view. We perform the same experiments on this new data set using all the methods, and present the results in the left panel in Figure 4. First we observe that the trend of the performance curves of all methods are very similar to the left panel in Figure 3. Due to the information loss in the missing views, the performance of all methods decreases for about 5%. Our proposed MVMT methods build accurate models using the existing views in each task, and significantly outperform the IteM^2 method with an improvement margin of up to 12%. In addition, the *regMVMT+* method slightly performs better than the *regMVMT* method, maybe due to the more flexible modeling of task relationships.

We then conduct experiments on the ECML2006 Email data set which consists of three task and four views. There is one common vocabulary view that is shared by all the three tasks, while each of the other three views is task specific and owned by only a particular task. Since the four views are not shared by all the three tasks, it is equivalent to the case there are two entire views missing from each of the three tasks. The experimental results of all methods are plotted in the right panel in Figure 4. Our MVMT methods performs better than the three baseline methods and the transductive MVMT method IteM^2 with the margin of up to 7%, and repeated measures

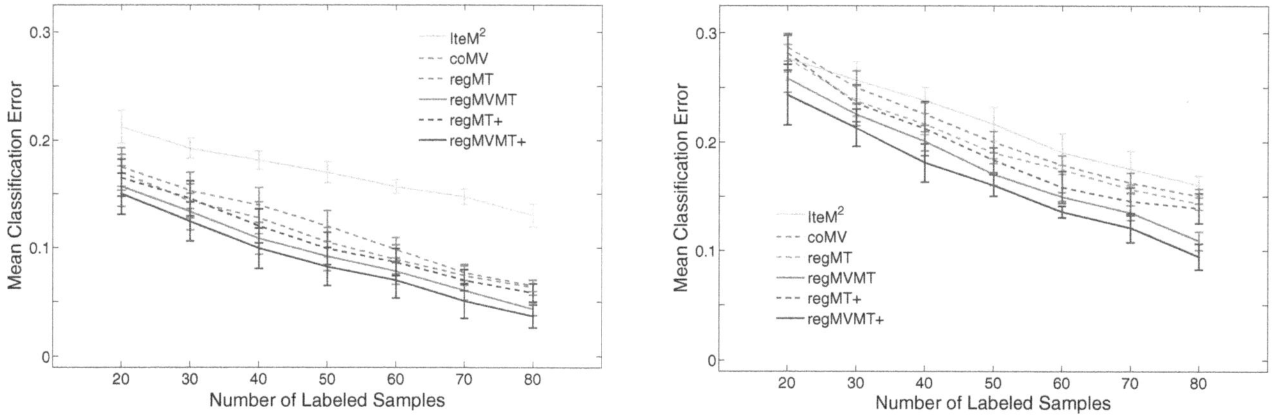

Figure 4: Experimental results on the WebKB data set with one missing view for each task (left) and on the ECML2006 Email data set that has two missing views for each task (right).

t-test (paired two-sample t-test) demonstrates that the difference is statistically significant. All other similar trends are also observed. Since there are more missing views in each task, the overall performance of all methods shrinks more significantly.

4.5 Task Relationship Modeling

We perform a case study to understand how our methods learn task relationships using the NUS-WIDE Object data set with 11 tasks. For any two tasks, we calculate the pairwise correlation using the fraction of samples that are simultaneously active or inactive to the two tasks. For the *regMVMT* method, we calculate the learned relationship between any two tasks using the Gaussian kernel of the ℓ_2 norm of the difference between their decision functions as in Eq.(5). We make a 2D plot with each dot representing a pair of tasks, as presented in Figure 5. The correlation coefficient $R = 0.8978$ reveals the learned task relationships (y-axis) are highly correlated to the pairwise task correlation from the data (x-axis).

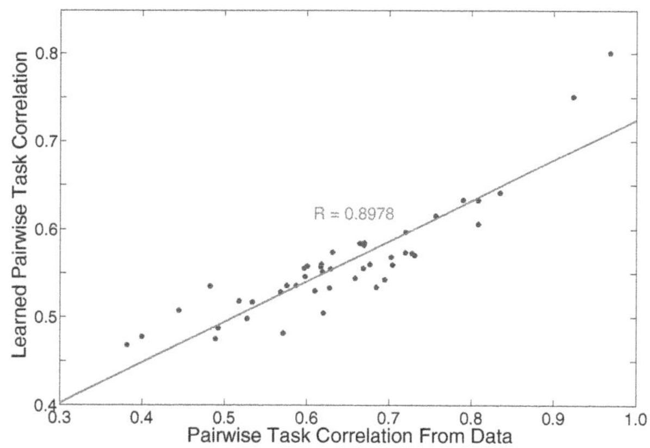

Figure 5: Correlation analysis (*regMVMT*) on the Object data set.

Looking into the 11 tasks, we find that they form three clusters: animals (5 tasks), vehicles (3 tasks), and plants (3 tasks). We then apply the *regMVMT+* algorithm on this data set and obtain the matrices $\mathbf{\Omega}_v$'s that model the task relationships of the 11 tasks. After taking the mean of all task relationship matrices $\mathbf{\Omega}_v, v = 1, 2$, we obtain the learned task relationship matrix whose element (i, j) indicates the relationship index of task i and j. For each task in the animal cluster, we identify the four most significantly correlated tasks, which are found mostly also the tasks in the animal class with only two violations. For the vehicle class and the plant class, we also find two violations that are not in the same class as the seed task, one in each class. The experiments demonstrate that the *regMVMT+* method can well model the task relationships through the learning process.

5. CONCLUSIONS

In this paper, we proposed an inductive multi-view learning algorithm for multiple related tasks. In our algorithm we developed a co-regularized framework. We utilized several regularization functions to control the complexity of the learning algorithms. We also developed two extensions. One handles structured missing views and the other handles non-uniformly related tasks. Experimental results demonstrated that our MVMT methods significantly outperform the state-of-the-art MVMT method IteM^2 and other baseline methods. In the future, we will further extend our work to different types of missing values.

Acknowledgments

This work has been supported by the KU Specialized Chemistry Center (NIH U54 HG005031) and the NSF grant IIS 0845951.

6. REFERENCES

[1] S. Abney. Bootstrapping. In *Proceedings of the 40th Annual Meeting on Association for Computational Linguistics*, pages 360–367, 2002.

[2] M.-R. Amini, N. Usunier, and C. Goutte. Learning from multiple partially observed views - an application to multilingual text categorization. In *NIPS'09*, pages 28–36, 2009.

[3] R. Ando and T. Zhang. A framework for learning predictive structures from multiple tasks and unlabeled data. *J. Mach. Learn. Res.*, 6:1817–1853, 2005.

[4] A. Argyriou, T. Evgeniou, and M. Pontil. Multi-task feature learning. In *NIPS'06*, pages 41–48, 2006.

[5] M.-f. Balcan and A. Blum. A pac-style model for learning from labeled and unlabeled data. In *Proceedings of COLT'05*, pages 111–126, 2005.

[6] A. Blum and T. Mitchell. Combining labeled and unlabeled data with co-training. In *COLT'98*, pages 92–100, 1998.
[7] M. R. Boutell, J. Luo, X. Shen, and C. M. Brown. Learning multi-label scene classification. *Pattern Recognition*, 37(9):1757–71, 2004.
[8] G. Cavallanti, N. Cesa-Bianchi, and C. Gentile. Linear algorithms for online multitask classification. *J. Mach. Learn. Res.*, 11:2901–2934, 2010.
[9] J. Chen, J. Liu, and J. Ye. Learning incoherent sparse and low-rank patterns from multiple tasks. In *KDD'10*, pages 1179–1188, 2010.
[10] X. Chen, S. Kim, Q. Lin, J. Carbonell, and E. Xing. Graph-structured multi-task regression and an efficient optimization method for general fused lasso. *Stat.*, 1050:21, 2010.
[11] C. M. Christoudias, R. Urtasun, and T. Darrell. Multi-view learning in the presence of view disagreement. In *Proceedings of UAI'08*, 2008.
[12] T.-S. Chua, J. Tang, R. Hong, H. Li, Z. Luo, and Y.-T. Zheng. Nus-wide: A real-world web image database from national university of singapore. In *CIVR'09*, 2009.
[13] M. Culp, G. Michailidis1, and K. Johnson. On multi-view learning with additive models. *Ann. Applied Stat.*, 3(1):292–318, 2009.
[14] S. Dasgupta, M. Littman, and D. McAllester. Pac generalization bounds for co-training. In *NIPS'01*, pages 375–382, 2001.
[15] T. Evgeniou and M. Pontil. Regularized multi-task learning. In *KDD'04*, pages 109–117, 2004.
[16] J. He and R. Lawrence. A graph-based framework for multi-task multi-view learning. In *ICML'11*, 2011.
[17] S. Kim and E. P. Xing. Tree-guided group lasso for multi-task regression with structured sparsity. In *ICML'10*, pages 543–550, 2010.
[18] A. McCallum, K. Nigam, J. Rennie, and S. Kim. Automating the construction of internet portals with machine learning. *Information Retrieval*, 3:127–163, 2000.
[19] I. Muslea, S. Minton, and C. A. Knoblock. Adaptive view validation: A first step towards automatic view detection. In *Proceedings of ICML'02*, pages 443–450, 2002.
[20] K. Nigam and R. Ghani. Analyzing the effectiveness and applicability of co-training. In *CIKM'00*, pages 86–93, 2000.
[21] V. Sindhwani and P. Niyogi. A co-regularized approach to semi-supervised learning with multiple views. In *ICML Workshop on Learning with Multiple Views*, 2005.
[22] V. Sindhwani and D. Rosenberg. An rkhs for multi-view learning and manifold co-regularization. In *ICML'08*, pages 976–983, 2008.
[23] W. Wang and Z. H. Zhou. Analyzing co-training style algorithms. In *Proceedings of ECML'07*, pages 454–465, 2007.
[24] W. Wang and Z. H. Zhou. A new analysis of co-training. In *Proceedings of ICML'10*, 2010.
[25] Y. Zhang and D.-Y. Yeung. A convex formulation for learning task relationships in multi-task learning. In *Proceedings of UAI'10*, pages 733–442, Corvallis, Oregon, 2010.

Scalable Misbehavior Detection in Online Video Chat Services

Xinyu Xing [1], Yu-li Liang [2], Sui Huang [3], Hanqiang Cheng [4], Richard Han [2], Qin Lv [2], Xue Liu [4], Shivakant Mishra [2], Yi Zhu [5]
[1]Georgia Institute of Technology, [2]University of Colorado - Boulder, [3]Ohio State University, [4]McGill University, [5]Tsinghua University
xxing8@gatech.edu, {richard.han, qin.lv}@colorado.edu, xueliu@cs.mcgill.ca

ABSTRACT

The need for highly scalable and accurate detection and filtering of misbehaving users and obscene content in online video chat services has grown as the popularity of these services has exploded in popularity. This is a challenging problem because processing large amounts of video is compute intensive, decisions about whether a user is misbehaving or not must be made online and quickly, and moreover these video chats are characterized by low quality video, poorly lit scenes, diversity of users and their behaviors, diversity of the content, and typically short sessions. This paper presents EMeralD, a highly scalable system for accurately detecting and filtering misbehaving users in online video chat applications. EMeralD substantially improves upon the state-of-the-art filtering mechanisms by achieving much lower computational cost and higher accuracy. We demonstrate EMeralD's improvement via experimental evaluations on real-world data sets obtained from Chatroulette.com.

Categories and Subject Descriptors

K.4.1 [**Computers and Society**]: Public Policy Issues–abuse and crime involving computers; K.4.2 [**Computers and Society**]: Public Policy Issues–human safety, abuse and crime involving computers

Keywords

Online video chat, misbehavior detection, video safety

1. INTRODUCTION

The popularity of online video chat services has been increasing over the last few years. Web services such as Chatroulette [1], myYearbook [2], Omegle [3] and TinyChat [4] have all been experiencing aggressive membership growth. For example, Chatroulette had more than 20 million visitors per month by May 2011 [5], which is three times the number of visitors in July 2010 [6]. The common feature of an online video chat website is that it *randomly* pairs online users from around the world for webcam-based conversations. These users can then conduct online chat via video, audio and text with one another. At any point, each user may leave the current chat and seek another random user for chatting. In general, such websites are offered for free and are easy to use, which enhances their popularity.

KDD'12, August 12–16, 2012, Beijing, China.

However, a critical problem encountered by these online video websites is that they attract a large number of misbehaving users who expose themselves, and/or broadcast offensive, obscene or pornographic content. For instance, our observation on a typical weekend (summer 2011) from a representative online video chat website (Omegle) indicates that 35% of the videos broadcast by this website have nudity in them. This is a major problem since a large fraction of the online video chat users are underage minors – about 1/4th by our estimates – and are thus exposed, perhaps illegally, to content unsuitable for their age.

Researchers have recently begun to address this problem of detecting and filtering misbehaving users and inappropriate content in online video chat systems. The SafeVchat system [7] employs a fusion technique that integrates the results from multiple image-based classifiers to develop a stronger inference about whether a particular video chat user is misbehaving or not. This fusion approach overcomes several major challenges in detecting and filtering misbehaving users in online video chat systems, including low quality Webcam video, poorly lit scenes, and diversity of users and their behaviors. Starting in early 2011, this system was successfully deployed on Chatroulette.com, the leading random video chat site on the Web, and has helped reduce the percentage of misbehaving users from about 30% down to about 2-5% today.

However, there are a number of key limitations with prior work. Experiences with deployment in Chatroulette.com have shown that SafeVchat requires over a hundred servers working at near full CPU utilization 24 hours a day to handle the Chatroulette user load. Chatroulette has found this to be an expensive solution that is also not very scalable. Furthermore, Chatroulette has found that SafeVchat's accuracy was only acceptable enough to identify normal users with high accuracy, not misbehaving users. Given that most users are normal users, Chatroulette employs a two-stage solution: SafeVchat is first used to identify and filter out most normal users; in the second stage, a large number of online human users are employed to review any remaining sessions, which could have either misbehaving users or normal ones missed by the first stage. The large bank of human reviewers introduces a second cost factor, and is also not scalable, especially for many of the smaller companies emerging in this application domain. Only well-funded Web companies like Chatroulette can afford such a server-intensive and human-intensive solution. As a result of these costs, another leading video chat site, Omegle chose not to deploy this solution.

In this paper, we present a new approach to misbehavior detection in online video chat systems that significantly improves upon the state of the art in terms of its increased scalability while also achieving higher accuracy. We term our approach EMeralD (Efficient Misbehavior Detection). The key problem that EMeralD solves is how to improve scalability while preserving or even improving accuracy. It is easy to improve scalability of misbehavior detection by simply performing less classification, but this reduces accuracy. The challenge is to improve scalability while simultaneously minimizing the impact on accuracy. We accomplish this by first observing that the reason SafeVchat is not very scalable is that it executes every classifier on every image snapshot before performing its fusion algorithm. Given N classifiers, it fails to note which of the N classifiers causes the overall decision to exceed the probability threshold for making a decision. As a result, some classifiers are executed that do not need to be, and these may be computationally intensive. For example, a face classifier may be sufficient to prove the existence of a normal user, while additional information from the skin classifier may be unnecessary.

EMeralD implements a more efficient approach by measuring at each step whether the execution of a particular classifier (in reality, EMeralD uses rules that aggregate classifiers) has put the overall decision probability over the acceptable threshold for identification, in our case for normal users. In this way, we are able to execute fewer rules/classifiers and thus improve the computational efficiency and scalability while achieving the same probability threshold of success that was acceptable for SafeVchat. A difficult problem that EMeralD solves is what is the optimal ordering of rule execution that minimizes the computational latency? What makes this problem challenging is that each rule has a different coverage, namely the number of normal users with features who could be filtered out by that rule. Thus, the number of users remaining after the previous stage of rule filtering changes as the permutation of rules is changed. EMeralD proposes to use an A*-search algorithm to determine the optimal ordering of the rules to minimize computational latency by exploiting coverage relationships.

However, we noticed that there was a further opportunity to improve accuracy even as we were improving scalability. First, we observed that a key missed opportunity with prior work was that each classifier was viewed as independent from others, and thus failed to exploit semantic correlations between the classification results. EMerald instead exploits these correlations, such as spatial correlations and size correlations between different image features. For example, we know that a mouth should reside within a face. Therefore, if a face classifier finds a face in an image, and a mouth classifier detects a mouth in the same image, then EMerald makes a stronger inference that there is indeed a human face in the image if the mouth's location is within the face's location. Such semantic correlations are exploited by EMeralD to improve the accuracy of classification while using the same OpenCV classifiers as SafeVchat.

EMeralD has been extensively evaluated in terms of its accuracy (precision/recall) and computational cost on real-world datasets obtained from Chatroulette. This evaluation demonstrates that EMeralD outperforms by a large margin the current state-of-the-art detection and filtering techniques such as PicBlock and Bag-of-Visual-Words-based detection. Furthermore, EMeralD is shown to be much more computationally efficient (31%-79% reduction in per-user latency) and scalable than SafeVchat, while also achieving greater accuracy than SafeVchat. For example, to process 11,000,000 image snapshots per hour, Chatroulette requires 182 servers with full CPU usage to detect misbehaving users with SafeVchat, while only 57 servers are needed with EMeralD. By improving both scalability and accuracy, EMeralD makes misbehaving user detection software much more practical and affordable to a wider range of online video chat services. EMeralD is currently being evaluated by three industrial companies at present under an evaluation license, including Chatroulette. In general, EMeralD's accuracy and scalability makes it suitable for most video-based, realtime interactive applications on the Internet.

2. RELATED WORK

Techniques to detect pornographic content can be divided into three categories: manual crowd-sourcing, skin color based detection, and Bag-of-Visual-Words (BoVW) based detection. Manual crowd-sourcing consists of human reviewers inspecting video snapshots. YouTube [8], for example, allows users to flag and report inappropriate content presented on their website [9], which are then reviewed by moderation teams of YouTube. Crowd-sourcing has also been used in online video chat websites such as Chatroulette [1], myYearbook [2] and Tinychat [4]. However, this approach incurs high economic cost and thus is not scalable, is not applied uniformly, i.e., only images that are "reported" are actually inspected, does not report all misbehaving users, and falsely reports some normal users due to pranksters. Online video chat services have stopped using this mechanism for these limitations.

Skin color based detection mechanisms are broadly used and achieve acceptable performance in terms of precision and recall for pornographic content detection [10][11][12][13][14]. This approach identifies skin exposure regions in an image using a statistical color model. Size, texture and shape of the skin exposure regions are sometimes considered to further improve performance.

While skin color based detection mechanism has proved to be effective and efficient in the context of pornographic image detection, its effectiveness is limited in the context of online video chat systems. Due to the diverse quality of snapshot images captured from online video chat systems, the statistical color model is insufficient for identifying misbehaving users. While pornographic images are usually taken by professional cameras under good lighting conditions, the images in online video chat services are taken by chatters' poor-quality webcams, which significantly affects the appearance of the skin. In addition, since different users may be under fairly diverse illumination conditions, skin color in snapshot images have significant variance. Indeed, a recent survey [15] concludes that skin color based detection mechanism may only be used as a preprocessor for pornographic content detection, and other content types such as textual content [12], motion analysis [16] and structural content [11] need to be incorporated to improve accuracy.

There are two recently-proposed systems that harness the Bag of Visual Words model (BoVW framework) to detect pornographic images [17][18]. In a BoVW framework, the Scale-Invariant Feature Transform (SIFT) [19] extracts feature descriptors of an image. Experimental results over data sets containing commercial pornographic content, shown in [17][18], demonstrate a significant performance improvement in terms of precision and recall. However, our experiments (described in Section 6) indicate that a BoVW-based detection mechanism performs poorly in the context of online video chat systems. First, SIFT descriptors are keypoint descriptors that are good at describing salient regions. However, in images that are taken under dark illumination conditions (a relatively common condition in online video chat systems), only a few salient keypoints can be found. Second, the problem we confront here is more difficult than the pornography detection problem due to the smaller inter-class distance between different categories. For example, the "difference", or visual distance, between the fully clothed category and the nude body trunk category is large. However, for our problem, the difference between misbehaving users and normal users is not that clear. Both normal and misbehaving users can be partially clothed (normal male users show partially naked upper body while misbehaving ones their genitals partially clothed). Third, the BoVW based detection mechanism is compute intensive. We implemented "BoVW + HueSIFT" approach proposed in [18] using the implementation of HueSIFT proposed in [20], and found that it takes 1960 milliseconds to classify one image.

To address the drawbacks of these detection mechanisms, we proposed SafeVchat [21]. SafeVchat harnesses Dempster-Shafer Theory to calculate the probability that a user is misbehaving. Though SafeVchat provides acceptable classification performance in terms of precision and recall, it suffers from two key limitations. First, it incurs over 1200 milliseconds of computational latency for each user, which results in large computational resource requirements. Second, it results in 3% leakage of detecting misbehaving users. A detailed analysis is provided in Section 6.

3. SYSTEM OVERVIEW

3.1 Design Requirements

Our obscene content detection system should satisfy two key requirements - scalability and precise classification. Based on our experiences, online video chat systems are capable of providing periodic image snapshots of users (it is once every 30 seconds for Chatroulette). However, image processing is quite computationally intensive, and as mentioned earlier requires a large array of servers all working near full CPU utilization. Therefore, our first design objective is to limit EMeralD's consumption of computational resources. This is achieved by intelligently choosing which filters to activate and in what order.

Second, our goal is to achieve high precision and recall in terms of correctly classifying misbehaving users. The precision should be high because in a system such as Chatroulette, all users classified as misbehaving will be subject to manual review by human monitors. If too many normal users are incorrectly classified as misbehaving, then the burden of these false positives on the human monitors will be high, incurring a high labor cost. Recall should also be high, i.e., most misbehaving users should be detected and only limited few may be falsely classified as normal and appear in the chat system.

Our design leverages our observations of users of the online video chat systems Chatroulette, Omegle, and myYearbook. Misbehaving users on online video chat systems usually hide their faces during the conversation. Some misbehaving users do not completely expose themselves, e.g. expose only their genitals in front of the webcam and stay partially clothed. Chatters who present their faces in front of webcams are mostly normal users because a majority of webcams only provide a narrow field of view (i.e., no wide angle lens are installed onto webcams); thus showing both the body trunk and the face of a user requires the user placing his/her webcam far from the user. However, chatters who do not show their faces may not be flashers. A fair amount of chatters do not show their faces clearly, i.e. only a partial face is presented in front of the webcam. Webcams are usually set up in a fixed position and are not moved often.

3.2 System Architecture

The key contribution of EMeralD is to offer a system that can optimize for latency/scalability while enhancing accuracy. Earlier systems had to execute every individual classifier before a fusion decision - misbehaving or not - could be made [7]. Having to execute every classifier incurred a large computational expense. Instead, EMeralD orders its filtering rules in an optimal sequence that minimizes the overall latency incurred during classification. In our new approach, not all individual classifiers need be executed in order to arrive at an overall classification decision.

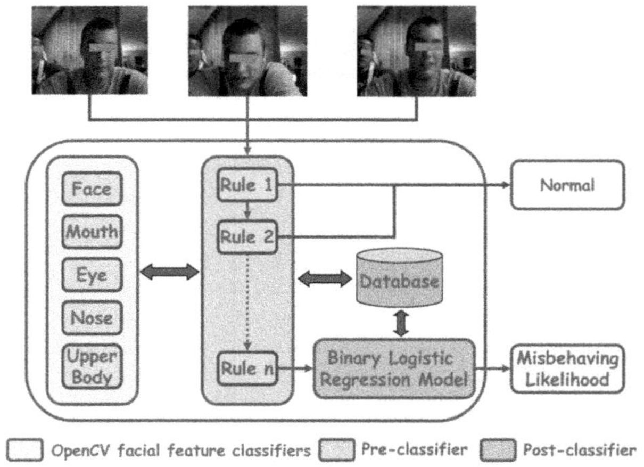

Figure 1: EMeralD: System architecture for detecting misbehaving users in online video chat services.

As shown in Figure 1, we partition the system into a rule-based pre-classifier or front end and a binary logistic regression model or back end. The rule-based pre-classifier leverages data obtained from five OpenCV facial feature classifiers (face, mouth, eye, nose, upper body). Three sequential snapshot images from a user are first delivered to the pre-classifier. In the pre-classifier, a set of association rules are defined in advance and the user's three snapshot images are sequentially examined by pre-defined rules. During the examination of the rules, the facial feature classifiers of OpenCV are called. The pre-classifier stores the classification output from each of the facial feature classifiers into a centralized database.

The rule checking in the pre-classifier is performed following a specific sequence, so that when the user's three snapshot images satisfy a specific rule, the user will be immediately classified as a normal user and the rest of the rule checking operations will not be performed. Therefore, the rule examination in the pre-classifier can filter out a significant number of normal users whose snapshot images do not need to pass all the operations of the facial feature classifiers. Notice that each rule in the pre-classifier needs to use the outputs of partial facial feature classifiers. To circumvent redundant computation from the facial feature classifiers of OpenCV, we cache the outputs of facial feature classifiers in a centralized database, so they can be reused by other classifiers.

In EMeralD, if there are no rules matching with the user's snapshots, then the binary logistic regression of the post-classifier is invoked. After obtaining the user's three snapshot images, the post-classifier will first retrieve the outputs of the facial feature classifiers for these three snapshots from the centralized database. It then calls a motion-based skin color detector [21] to obtain the skin exposure proportions of the user. By combining both the skin exposure proportions of a user and the user's facial features, the post-classifier harnesses a binary logistic regression model to predict the probability of being a misbehaving user for the user. Binary logistic regression is adept at identifying misbehaving users, but is costly to compute, and thus we do not invoke this operation until a large fraction of normal users have already been filtered out.

4. RULE-BASED PRE-CLASSIFIER

In order to improve scalability, we take advantage of early classification results, thereby exiting the decision-making process as soon as an identification threshold is reached, rather than executing

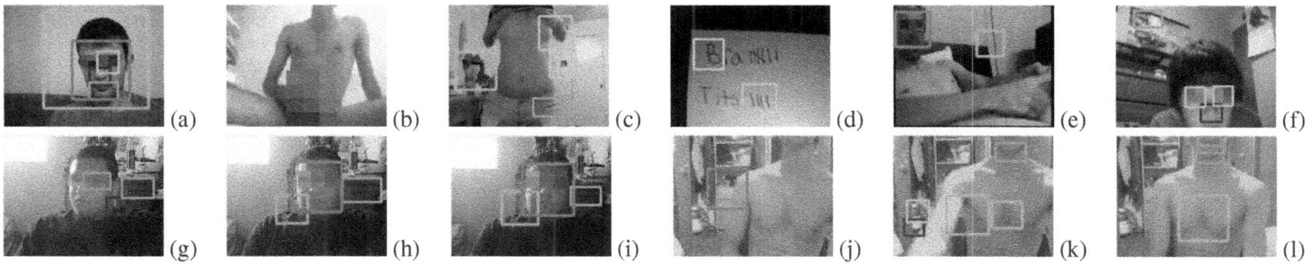

Figure 2: Facial feature classification results of OpenCV for snapshot images from Chatroulette – upper body (green square), face (red square), mouth (pink square), nose (blue square) and eye (purple square).

every single classifier, as in prior systems. We wish to avoid executing any more classifiers than we are required to execute. To do this, we first identify important higher-level discriminative features. We then extract rules for the most frequently occurring joint patterns among these discriminative features, using a set of representative training data. Finally, we consider all rules that achieve greater than the threshold accuracy for correctly identifying normal users, and reorder them so as to minimize overall computational latency. If any such rule identifies a user as normal, then we know that we can trust this result to be at least accurate above the threshold, and can therefore terminate the classification process early, without executing any subsequent rules.

4.1 Identifying Discriminative Characteristics

We need to first develop higher-level discriminative characteristics that exploit the semantic knowledge of facial features in order to improve the accuracy of EMeralD over prior work. Using the raw OpenCV classifiers, or rules based just on these classifiers, without exploiting semantic knowledge, misses the opportunity to improve the accuracy of misbehavior detection. One reason that limits the accuracy of such non-semantic approaches is that the OpenCV classifiers themselves can be inaccurate when taken in isolation, as shown in Figure 2. Thus, rules based on non-semantic approaches will also be limited in accuracy. For example, the eye classifier of OpenCV misclassifies a black character written on white paper as an eye (see Figure 2(d)). Thus, we extract higher-level discriminative characteristics from the basic outputs of facial feature classifiers of OpenCV.

Since filtering misbehaving users in the video chat context is a novel research area, there is a paucity in prior work that could guide us about which features we should consider to classify misbehaving users. Our extensive observations help us identify a long list of initial correlates to the user being a normal one or not. However, we do not make our decision simply by this heuristic examination. We relied on the statistical test results of the relationship. Only the correlates that show statistically significant relationship with the user's identity are included into our association rules. We summarize our new discriminative characteristics as follows.

(1) The presence of a face in a non-facial region is usually an occurrence by chance. As shown in Figure 2(g)-(l), mis-identified faces in non-facial regions usually only appear in one snapshot image of a user, while true faces can be correctly identified in multiple snapshot images of a user. Therefore, we define a discriminative characteristic $Face[n]$, where $n \in \{0, 1, 2, 3\}$ is the number of snapshot images of a user with at least one identified face by OpenCV. For example, the user whose snapshot images are shown in Figure 2(g)-(i) has $Face[2]$.

(2) The face classifier of OpenCV may identify multiple faces in a snapshot, and there is an extremely low random chance that the face classifier mistakenly identifies two or more faces in non-facial regions of one snapshot image. Therefore, we consider whether multiple faces appear in at least one snapshot image of a user, denoted as $MultiFace[n], n \in \{Yes, No\}$.

(3) Although a user has 0.99 likelihood of being normal when a face is present in his or her snapshot images, there are still a small number of misbehaving users who present their faces in front of the webcam. Since webcams have a narrow view angle, to show both their face and genitals, a misbehaving user has to stay far away from the webcam. Our analysis shows that faces of this type of misbehaving users are usually placed on the corner of their snapshots. Therefore, we also consider the positions of the user's faces in the user's three snapshots as a discriminative characteristic. To describe face position efficiently, we first calculate the centroid coordinate of a face. We then calculate the distance from the centroid coordinate to the bottom-left (and bottom-right) corner of the snapshot image, called "left distance" (and "right distance"). The larger of these two distances is selected as the face distance of the snapshot. Since the length of an upper body is at least two times longer than that of a face, it is difficult for a user to show both his genital and face when his face has a large face distance. We divide the face distance by the length of the face in the snapshot and use the quotient as the position of the face in the snapshot. Note that for a snapshot image with zero or multiple faces, the position of the face is defined as ∞ and 0. Face positions can be ranked and we select the maximum face position to represent the face position of the user within user's three snapshot images. The face position of a user is a continuous variable. To use this discriminative characteristic for association rules, we quantize the continuous values into four categories (bins), denoted as $FacePos[n], n \in \{B_1, B_2, B_3, B_4\}$.

(4) Further observations on the output of the upper body classifier of OpenCV indicate that an upper body detected in a snapshot is usually wrong, especially when the detected upper body is fairly small (see Figure 2(c)). In contrast, when the upper body classifier identifies a large region in a snapshot as an upper body, the labeled region is typically correct (see Figure 2(a)). To use the presence of an upper body as a discriminative characteristic, we consider the largest OpenCV-labeled upper body size of a user within the user's three snapshots and denote this characteristic as $UpperBody[n], n \in \{B_0, B_1, B_2, B_3, B_4\}$. Similar to the face position characteristic, we also quantize continuous upper-body size values into 5 bins and make it a categorical variable.

(5) Although the eye's visual characteristic – a center-surround pattern – is common in non-facial regions, the presence of OpenCV-labeled double eyes in a correct relative position generally represent true eyes of a user (see Figure 2(f) versus 2(d)). We consider how many snapshot images of a user contain OpenCV-labeled double eyes in a correct relative position. We denote this discriminative characteristic as $DoubleEye[n], n \in \{0, 1, 2, 3\}$ where n is the number of snapshot images of a user with OpenCV-labeled double eyes in a correct relative position.

(6) Similar to eye's visual characteristic, nose, mouth, face and upper body's visual characteristics are also commonly present in

non-facial regions (see Figure 2(c), 2(j) and 2(k)). One other approach to reduce the mislabeling of the OpenCV facial feature classifiers is to combine the outputs of two facial feature classifiers and examine whether the outputs of two classifiers are in a correct relative position. A correct relative position for two different facial characteristics should satisfy at least one of the position relationships (e.g., Figure 2(a), 2(f)). Specifically, we consider 6 pairs of facial feature relationships as discriminative characteristics: a nose in a face, an eye in a face, a mouth in a face, a face in an upper body, an eye on upper left/right of a nose, and a nose on top of a mouth. Since these combinations may still appear by chance, we count the combination in user's three snapshot images and denote these combined discriminative characteristics as $NoseFace[n]$, $EyeFace[n]$, $MouthFace[n]$, $EyeNose[n]$, $FaceUpperBody[n]$, $NoseMouth[n]$, $n \in \{0, 1, 2, 3\}$.

4.2 Creating Association Rules

Based on the discriminative characteristics, we harness the Apriori algorithm [22] to create association rules which are used in the pre-classifier of EMeralD. We first describe each user as an 11-element vector and each element represents a discriminative characteristic. For example, the user whose snapshot images are shown in Figure 2(g)~2(i) is described as $\{Face[2]$, $MultiFace[No]$, $FacePos[B_1]$, $UpperBody[B_0]$, $DoubleEye[0]$, $NoseFace[0]$, $EyeFace[0]$, $MouthFace[0]$, $FaceUpperBody[0]$, $EyeNose[0]$, $NoseMouth[0]\}$. The Apriori algorithm attempts to find all frequent k-itemsets ($k = 1, \ldots, 12$) and uses the corresponding frequent itemsets to create association rules. Note that there are frequent 12-itemsets because we investigate the relationship between 11 discriminative characteristics and the hypothesis of being a normal user. For a frequent k-itemset, the higher the value of k, the more computation cost an association rule will involve, because the examination of an association rule needs to involve the operations of facial feature classifiers of OpenCV which are usually compute-intensive. Rule $Face[2] \Longrightarrow User[Normal]$, for example, only involves the operation of the face classifier, while rule $Face[2]\&EyeNose[1] \Longrightarrow User[Normal]$ involves the computation of face, nose and eye classifiers. To involve as little computation and filter as many users as possible, our association rule generation and selection, in practice, have to satisfy the following conditions:

• Since we observed not all the normal users present their faces and the facial feature classifier of OpenCV may not be able to identify their facial characteristics even when they present their faces in front of webcams, we empirically set the minimum support value to 100 out of 10,000 (1%).

• An online video chat system like Chatroulette and myYearbook usually skips the costly human review process for users with high likelihood of being normal; therefore, the minimum confidence for generating association rules is 0.99.

• The association rules that are used in the pre-classifier of EMeralD have to follow the form $X_1\&X_2\&...\&X_i \Longrightarrow User[Normal]$ where X denotes a discriminative characteristic and $User[Normal]$ represents the hypothesis that *a user is normal.*

• To reduce computation cost, we limit the operations of some facial feature classifiers of OpenCV for each association rule. For each association rule that is selected to use in the pre-classifier of EMeralD, we designate the number of facial feature classifiers involved by the rule to be no greater than two.

• We also constrain that the association rules used in the pre-classifier cannot be redundant. An association-rule set is non-redundant when the following is true. If there is association rule r' which is generated from frequent itemsets Ω' and has confidence value c', then there is no other association rule r which is generated from frequent itemsets Ω ($\Omega' \subset \Omega$) and has confidence value c ($c' > c$). Here, if rule r is redundant, the dataset that rule r covers is also covered by rule r'.

4.3 Minimizing Computational Latency

After creating the association rules, we need to further determine the operation sequence of all the association rules, i.e., in what order should the rules be examined. Each association rule has its computation cost and support (i.e., the users covered by the association rule), and a user might be covered by several different association rules because of OpenCV-labeled multiple facial features. In addition, each facial feature classifier that is used by multiple rules only need to be computed once, thus saving the computation cost. Therefore, the computation cost is significantly dependent upon the *order of rule execution.* For example, in Figure 3(a), assume that three association rules r_1, r_2 and r_3 can filter 257 users from a 300-Chatroulette-user dataset and label them as normal users. Each of the association rules has its own computation cost. We consider two examination sequences for these three association rules. The first examination sequence follows r_2, r_3 and r_1, which takes 69.60 seconds to filter out 257 users. In another sequence - r_3, r_2, r_1, the entire processing time for filtering out the same number of users is 41.78 seconds, which is 40% less than that of the first sequence.

To determine the order of rule execution that minimizes the computational latency, we model the problem as a path finding and graph traversal problem and apply the A* search algorithm [23] to find the least-cost path. First, we define two sub-datasets, s_1 and s_2. These sub-datasets contain those user datasets that do not affect our computation latency no matter what sequence the association rules are examined in. The sub-dataset s_1 is the sub-dataset which is covered by all the association rules. No matter which association rule is examined first, sub-dataset s_1 will be filtered. Therefore, this sub-dataset does not involve extra examination cost for other association rules irrespective of which association rule in the pre-classifier is examined first. We ignore this sub-dataset in our modeling. In Figure 3(a), there are 105 such users. The second sub-dataset - s_2 - is the sub-dataset which is not covered by any association rule in the pre-classifier. All datasets in this sub-dataset will be examined by all association rules, which involves the maximum computation cost (i.e. all facial feature classifiers of OpenCV will be performed for examining sub-dataset s_2). In Figure 3(a), there are 43 such users. In addition to sub-dataset s_1, our model also ignores the computation cost of the classifier which all the association rules involve. For example, Figure 3(a) indicates all three association rules involve the operations of the face classifier. No matter which association rule is examined first, the face classifier has to be used for labeling the face regions for all the 300-Chatroulette users.

Since any association rule can only cover a part of a dataset, selection of an association rule involves extra computation cost, which is the cost of applying that rule on all users not filtered out by it. For example, association rule r_1 does not cover 93+43 users. So, the extra commutation cost of selecting r_1 is $(93+43) \times 81ms$. Notice that we have not considered the cost of face classifier, as face classifier is included in all association rules. Similarly, extra computation cost of selecting rule r_1 followed by rule r_2 is the extra computation cost of selecting r_1 plus $(44+43) \times 52ms$, where 44+43 is the number of users not covered by r_1 or r_2. Finally, the extra computation cost of selecting the sequence r_1, r_2, r_3 is the extra computation cost of selecting r_1 followed by r_2 plus $43 \times 36ms$, where 43 is the number of users not covered by any of the three rules, i.e. sub-dataset s_2.

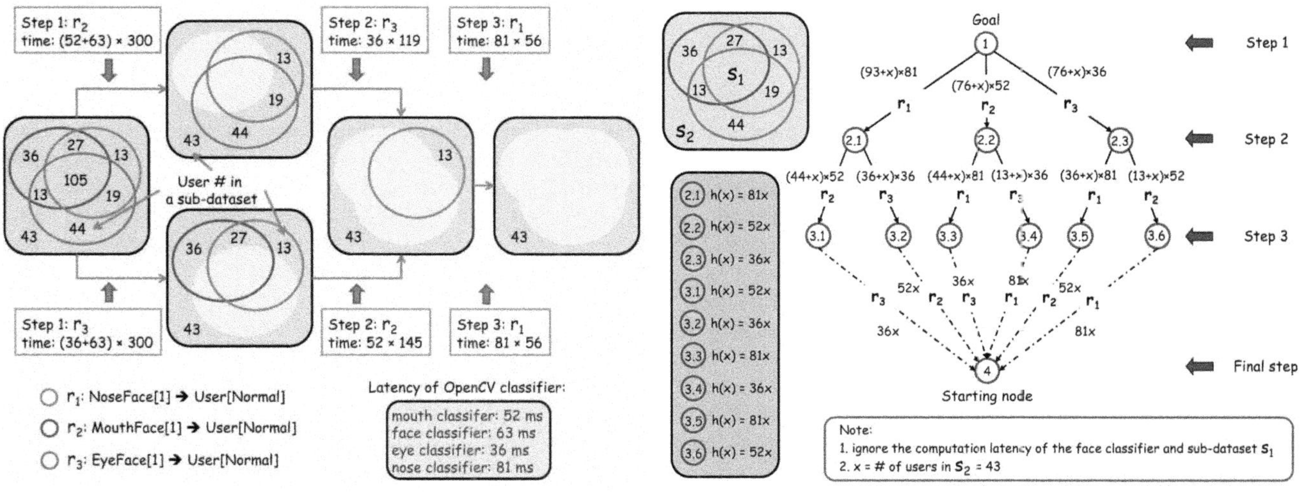

(a) Two examination sequences of three association rules.

(b) Modeling the least computation cost for three association rules.

Figure 3: Understanding and modeling the computation cost of three association rules.

We use the extra computation cost of each association rule and association-rule-selection steps to model a graph. Each edge in this graph represents a selection of an association rule. The weight on an edge is the extra communication cost of selecting this rule in the sequence starting from the root. In general, weight of an edge with rule r is dependent on the number of users (K) that have not yet been filtered out and are not covered by rule r and the cost (δt) of applying r, i.e. the edge weight is ($w = K \cdot \delta t$). Note that the weight of the edge for the same association rule is different because the value of K and δt may vary in each association-rule-selection step. For example, Figure 3(a) demonstrates that association rule r_2 which is examined in two different sequences has different value of K ($K = 119$ and $K = 56$) and same value of δt [1]. The connection of the nodes in the graph follows the steps of selecting the association rules (i.e., in any path of the graph from the first step to the last, each association rule can only appear once; further, a path from the first step to the last has to contain all the association rules that are used in the pre-classifier.). Figure 3(b) shows a graph which represents the example case shown in Figure 3(a).

Since A* search algorithm uses a distance-plus-cost heuristic function that contains an admissible heuristic function $h(x)$, we further define the admissible heuristic function $h(x) = \delta t \cdot x$ where x is the total number of users in sub-dataset s_2. It is obvious that function $h(x)$ is not an admissible heuristic if we take the step-one node as the starting node and the final-step node as the goal. To ensure function $h(x)$ does not overestimate the distance to the goal, we designate the final-step and step-one nodes as the starting node and the goal, respectively.

5. PROBABILISTIC POST-CLASSIFIER

In stage two, all remaining users not filtered out as normal by the pre-classifier are subject to the probabilistic post-classifier, in order to identify misbehaving users.

To identify the appropriate statistical model, we need to understand the distributional characteristics of variables of interest. Since our goal is to establish a model to identify flashers, a user being a flasher or not is our dependent variable. It is a binary response with 2 categories (0, 1) and thus follows a binomial distribution. A simple linear regression model, which assumes normal distribution of dependent variable, is not appropriate for our system. Instead, we consider a binary logistic regression model, which is a special case of the general linear model, yet it does not impose strict assumptions on the distributions of the independent variables. The random component for the (success, failure) outcomes has a binomial distribution [24]. The logit of the probability of success in outcome (i.e., being a flasher in our study) is expressed by a linear function of continuous or categorical predictors. The logit model is $\log \frac{p(x)}{1-p(x)} = \alpha + \beta(x)$.

Our previous work has successfully established the connection between video chat users' skin exposure and being flasher or not. EMeralD defines 3 different variables of Skin Proportion 1, 2, and 3 (SP_1, SP_2, SP_3) to represent users' skin exposure percentages captured by 3 different skin-color spaces. In this paper, we extend the model further by integrating facial features in identifying misbehaving users. We use the 10 discriminative characteristics (facial features) introduced in Section 4.1 as ordinal variables. The value of a variable is dependent upon how the corresponding discriminative characteristic is presented in user's snapshots. For example, the value of variable $NoseMouth[n]$ is 2 if $NoseMouth[2]$ is presented in user's snapshots. To sum up, our theoretical model can be expressed as

$$\log \frac{p(flasher)}{1 - p(flasher)} = \alpha + \beta_1 \cdot facialfeature + \beta_2 \cdot skinportion \quad (1)$$

Inter-variable correlations and multicollinearity diagnostic statistics (Variance Inflation Factor - VIF, Tolerance, Condition Index) [25] have been calculated to evaluate the threat of multicollinearity. While there is no formal cutoff value to use with VIF for determining the presence of multicollinearity, values of VIF exceeding 10 and Condition Index exceeding 15 often indicate multicollinearity, but in weaker models, which is often the case in logistic regression, VIF values above 2.5 may be a cause for concern.

Our multicollinearity diagnostic statistics show that multicollinearity threats do exist among several independent variables, namely $FacePos[n]$, $Face[n]$ and three skin portion measures. Common solutions for multicollinearity include dropping one or more correlated variables and combining variables. In this study, we noticed that $FacePos[n]$ and $Face[n]$ have high information overlap – both loaded high on the same dimension, with condition index ex-

[1]The operation of the face classifier has been ignored.

ceeding 15. Since it is neither practical nor meaningful to combine these two ordinal variables, we choose to keep only one of them in the final model to avoid the multicollinearity issue.

When capturing users' exposed skin portions, we apply three aforementioned measures [21]. These three measures provide slightly different information about the degree of skin exposure and are all included in our theoretical model. However, correlation analysis and multicollinearity diagnostics revealed multicollinearities among these measures. To reduce the threats of multicollinearity yet to consider all three measures at the same time, we conduct principal component analysis – a mathematical procedure that transforms multiple correlated continuous variables into a smaller number of uncorrelated variables – on these three predictors before we proceed in the model building process.

We used the principal component analysis procedure in IBM SPSS 19.0 [26] to transform three measures of skin exposure. Kaiser Criterion (Eigen value > 1) was followed when selecting components and Scree Plot was used to confirm the dimensions identified. We extracted one component (skinexpcomp) to represent the 3 aforementioned measures of skin exposure according to Eigen values and the elbow point identified in scree plot. When subsequently building our binary logistic regression model, we include only the skin exposure composite (skinexpcomp) which is a linear function of normalized measure scores:

$$skinexpcomp = 0.349 \cdot SP_1 + 0.366 \cdot SP_2 + 0.346 \cdot SP_3 \quad (2)$$

A training sample data was analyzed with the stepwise binary logistic regression procedure in statistical package IBM SPSS 19.0. Maximum Likelihood Estimation with EM algorithm was utilized to estimate the model coefficients. Stepwise logistic regression procedure in SPSS was able to provide multiple models with different combination of independent variables. We identified the optimal model by comparing their goodness of fit indices such as deviance score, AIC (Akaike Information Criterion) and BIC (Bayesian Information Criterion).

6. EVALUATION

In this section, we conduct detailed experiments to answer the question of whether our EMeralD system achieves our design goals – both *high accuracy* and *high efficiency* when detecting and filtering misbehaving users in online video chat services. We first compare the accuracy (in terms of precision and recall) of our EMeralD system with state-of-the-art techniques. We then focus on the overall run-time efficiency of EMeralD and its execution cost.

6.1 Classifier Performance

In our evaluations, we use a real-world dataset containing 20,000 Chatroulette users' snapshots and randomly split the 20,000 samples into two groups: a 10,000-user training set used to train our pre-classifier and post-classifier; and a 10,000-user testing set to evaluate these classifiers. The 20,000-Chatroulette-user dataset was obtained from Chatroulette system in September 2010 when there were approximately 35% misbehaving users.

Table 1: Ordering of Association Rules Used in EMeralD

Order	Association Rule	Confidence
1	$MultiFace[Yes] \Longrightarrow User[normal]$	1.00
2	$Face[3]\&FacePos[B_2] \Longrightarrow User[normal]$	1.00
3	$Face[3]\&FacePos[B_3] \Longrightarrow User[normal]$	1.00
4	$Face[3]\&FacePos[B_4] \Longrightarrow User[normal]$	1.00
5	$DoubleEye[3] \Longrightarrow User[normal]$	1.00
6	$DoubleEye[2] \Longrightarrow User[normal]$	1.00
7	$UpperBody[B_4] \Longrightarrow User[normal]$	0.99
8	$FaceMouth[3] \Longrightarrow User[normal]$	1.00
9	$FaceMouth[2] \Longrightarrow User[normal]$	0.99

We compare the precision and recall of EMeralD with that of the state-of-the-art skin color based detection technique (PicBlock [27]) as well as the integration of SIFT and a Bag-of-Visual-words framework (SIFT+BoVW, Dense-SIFT+BoVW), and our earlier system SafeVchat, which is currently deployed on Chatroulette. As shown in Figure 4, EMeralD significantly outperforms PicBlock [27], because the skin colors in snapshot images captured from online video chat systems are very diverse and the statistical skin-color model used in PicBlock cannot provide effective discriminative characteristics for misbehaving user classification.

While SIFT+BoVW performs better than PicBlock, it still cannot satisfy the requirement of online video chat systems. Figure 4(a) shows that the recall for classifying normal users is fairly low when the classification precision remains at a high level (e.g., > 0.95). As a result, a large number of normal users have to be manually reviewed by human moderators. The main reason behind the poor classification results of SIFT+BoVW is that the SIFT descriptor is a sparse feature representation, which may cause a loss of some discriminative characteristics. To address this issue, we replace the SIFT descriptor with the Dense SIFT descriptor [28] and repeat the experiment of SIFT+BoVW. As shown in Figure 4(a), the recall of Dense-SIFT+BoVW for classifying normal users has increased to 0.50 when precision is high. However, compared with SafeVchat and EMeralD, Dense-SIFT+BoVW still has lower precision and recall, since snapshot images have smaller inter-class distance between normal and misbehaving users.

Finally, we compare the performance between SafeVchat and EMeralD. As shown in Figure 4, the classification performance of EMeralD is slightly higher than that of SafeVchat in terms of precision and recall. Still, this performance improvement is quite beneficial. SafeVchat uses a threshold for the likelihood of being a normal user. This threshold is used to automatically filter out normal users, thus saving human review cost. As shown in Figure 4(a), SafeVchat provides 0.97 precision for classifying normal users with 0.70 recall, while EMeralD reaches 0.997 precision. This indicates that EMeralD only misses (misclassifies) 0.3% of misbehaving users, while automatically and correctly filtering out 70% of normal users – one order of magnitude lower than that of SafeVchat (3% versus 0.3%). To illustrate this improvement, we again take the Chatroulette system as an example. Chatroulette reports that there are approximately 20,000 $\sim$ 40,000 online users at any given time. By using both EMeralD and SafeVchat[2], Chatroulette can automatically filter out about 70% of normal users without involving human reviewers. EMeralD mistakenly leaves only 40 $\sim$ 80 misbehaving users while SafeVchat leaves 400 $\sim$ 800 misbehaving users. Furthermore, we observe that the classification performance of EMeralD for misbehaving users has 5% $\sim$ 8% of improvement on average (see Figure 4(b)). The reasons for these improvements are summarized as follows. (1) The discriminative characteristics that we use in EMeralD is more powerful than the features we used in SafeVchat. One example is that we consider face position as a discriminative characteristic while SafeVchat ignores spatial information. (2) The rule-based pre-classifier provides higher classification capacity for normal users, which dominates the improvement of classification performance. Figure 5 shows that rule-based pre-classifier has high classification precision. The more the rules are harnessed, the higher the classification recall is. (3) Though the classification precision drops when the probabilistic post-classifier is executed, we still observe that our probabilistic post-classifier contributes 6% of recall improvement while maintaining 0.997 precision.

[2]Chatroulette ignores their human review process for the users' snapshots whose likelihoods of being normal users are above 0.97.

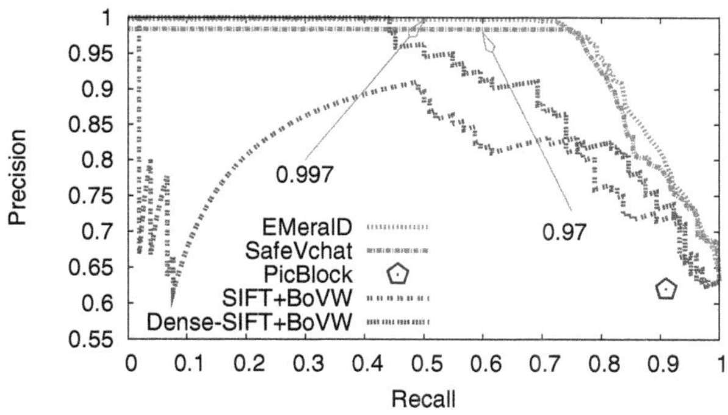

(a) Classification results for normal users.

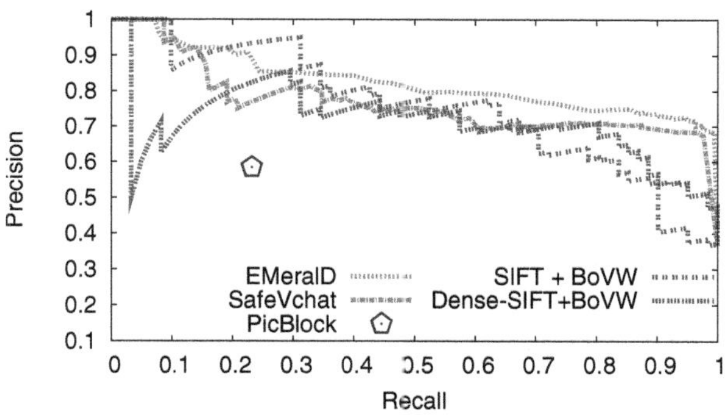

(b) Classification results for misbehaving users.

Figure 4: Classification performance in terms of precision and recall.

6.2 Run Time Performance

Since PicBlock, SIFT+BoVW and Dense-SIFT+BoVW perform extremely poorly (low precision and recall) in detecting misbehaving users, we have only considered SafeVchat for comparison to evaluate EMeralD's runtime performance. We used EMeralD for two Chatroulette datasets: one is the 20,000-Chatroulette-user dataset that we used for precision and recall evaluation, and the other is a recently collected 30,000-Chatroulette-user dataset that contains 2% misbehaving users. As shown in Table 2, compared to the computation latency of SafeVchat (1276 milliseconds per user), EMeralD system can reduce computation latency by 31.15% on the 20,000-Chatroulette-user dataset. Figure 5 explains the reason behind this. Rule-based pre-classifier is first used to examine users' snapshots. As shown in this figure, the first four association rules successfully filter out 53% of normal users by running only the face classifier of OpenCV. This filtering of 53% of normal users saves the subsequent computation overhead of other OpenCV classifiers. Similar saving is also applied to the other rules except for rule 8 and 9. Note that rule 8 and 9, though correctly filter out 68% of the normal users, do not save computation overhead because the dataset that rule 8 and 9 process has already been examined by all the OpenCV classifiers except the mouth classifier of OpenCV. We can also observe from Table 2 that the latency reduction of EMeralD is affected by the fraction of misbehaving users (i.e., 30,000-Chatroulette-user dataset achieves 48.86% of latency reduction while the other dataset has 31.15% of latency reduction). To further investigate the relationship between the fraction of misbehaving users and the average computation latency, we randomly select 1,000 users from the 20,000-user dataset and manually tune the fraction of misbehaving users. We observe that the average computation latency per user has a linear relationship with the fraction of misbehaving users (Figure 6). The higher the fraction of misbehaving users, the more is the computation latency. The reason behind this is quite straightforward – misbehaving users usually have to be examined by the probabilistic model which uses the outputs of all OpenCV facial feature classifiers which are computation intensive. Another surprising observation from Table 2 is that the average computation latency reduction per user can reach 79.45% when the confidence threshold (minimum confidence) that is used for association rule selection in the pre-classifier is decreased from 99% to 97%. Figure 6 indicates that lower confidence threshold typically results in lower computation latency, because more association rules will be selected to use in the pre-classifier of EMeralD, which makes more users filtered out and labeled as normal users. Note however the decrease in the confidence threshold also gives rise to the decrease in classification precision of the pre-classifier.

Table 2: Comparison of Computation Latency

Confidence	Chatroulette dataset	30,000 users	20,000 users
	% of Misbehaving users	2%	35%
0.99	Avg. latency per user	653 ms	878 ms
	Latency reduction	48.86%	31.15%
0.97	Avg. latency per user	262 ms	782 ms
	Latency reduction	79.45%	38.67%

Table 3: Performance Comparison of EMeralD and SafeVchat

	# of instances	Throughput per instance	Total cost per month
EMeralD	57	190,350 snapshots per hour	$5,089
SafeVchat	182	59,424 snapshots per hour	$16,249

To test how EMerald performs on a large scale, we deployed EMeralD on 57 large instances on Amazon's EC2 infrastructure. These server instances were driven by a large collection of PlanetLab clients generating image snapshots to emulate the Chatroulette workload of about 11 million snapshots per hour. Each instance that the EMeralD code executed on had 7.5 GB of memory and 4 EC2 Compute Units, running a 64-bit version of SUSE Linux Enterprise 11. Each instance processes the snapshots of 8 $\sim$ 10 Chatroulette users in parallel with 85.32% $\sim$ 93.01% of CPU utilization. Using this deployment, we on average process 190,350 Chatroulette snapshots per hour for every instance. As shown in Table 3, this throughput is three times that of SafeVchat, which has 59,424 snapshots per hour for every instance, and used 182 EC2 instances as of December 2010. This three-fold improvement in throughput at a large scale mainly results from the reduction of computational complexity.

We also estimate the cost savings of using EMeralD in Table 3. Under current cost assumptions at Amazon for large VM instances, we estimate that EMeralD would only cost Chatroulette $5,089 per month in computation, whereas we estimate SafeVchat currently costs Chatroulette about $16,249 per month for the current user workload, generating 11 million snapshots per month. Note that though tens of millions of snapshots stream into Chatroulette, extra storage instances are not necessary because the size of a user's snapshot is relatively small. Every 15,000 snapshots need approximately 100 MB of storage space and a large instance has 850 GB of local storage. 57 large instances can store users' snapshots for a month without being overwritten. In practice, Chatroulette only keeps users' snapshots for several hours. Therefore, this cost analysis only involves the cost of computation resources for Chatroulette.

7. CONCLUSION

We have presented EMeralD, a novel system for misbehavior detection in online video chat systems that substantially improves scalability while improving accuracy. In EMeralD's two-stage approach, first a rule-based pre-classifier identifies and filters out nor-

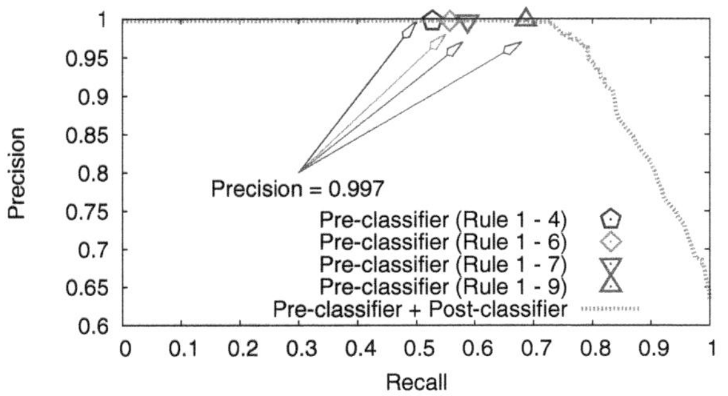

Figure 5: Classification performance for individual classification components.

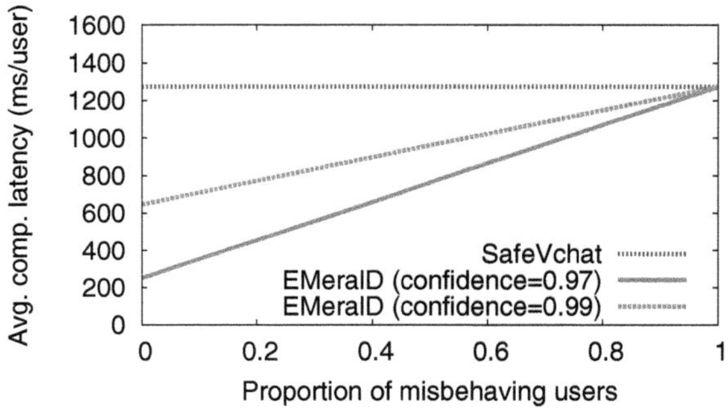

Figure 6: Proportion variance of misbehaving users versus computation latency of EMeralD.

mal users by executing only as many classifiers as are needed to reach a probability threshold for identification, thus saving on needless computation. Moreover, the rules are reordered using an A* search algorithm to minimize latency. In stage two, remaining users are processed by a post-classifier using binary logistic regression to accurately identify misbehaving users. Using the real-world image datasets obtained from Chatroulette, we demonstrate compared to prior work that (1) EMeralD achieves improved precision and recall of identifying misbehaving users, (2) EMeralD lowers the computational latency by at least 31-49%, and (3) EMeralD scalably achieves 3 times higher throughput on a large scale Amazon EC2 server deployment.

Acknowledgment

We thank Andrey Ternovskiy, the founder of Chatroulette.com, for providing us with these otherwise unobtainable internal data traces. We also thank Wenke Lee for providing computation resources in Georgia Institute of Technology. This work is supported in part by the unrestricted gift funds from Chatroulette and the US National Science Foundation (NSF) through grant number CiC 1048298.

8. REFERENCES

[1] "Chatroulette web site," http://www.chatroulette.com/.

[2] "myYearbook live web site," http://live.myyearbook.com/.

[3] "Omegle web site," http://www.omegle.com/.

[4] "Tinychat web site," http://tinychat.com/.

[5] "Chatroulette parts with private parts, looking for a new look," http://techcrunch.com/2011/05/04/chatroulette-parts-with-private-parts-looking-for-a-new-look/.

[6] "Can Chatroulette get it up again?" http://techcrunch.com/2010/08/23/chatroulette-up-again/.

[7] "Flasher detection algorithm aims to clean up video chat," http://www.technologyreview.com/blog/arxiv/26281/.

[8] "YouTube web site," http://www.youtube.com/.

[9] "Flag violations and manual inspection on YouTube," http://www.google.com/support/youtube/bin/answer.py?answer=118747.

[10] M. J. Jones and J. M. Rehg, "Statistical color models with application to skin detection," in *International Journal of Computer Vision*, 1999, pp. 274–280.

[11] M. Hammami, Y. Chahir, and L. Chen, "Webguard: A web filtering engine combining textual, structural, and visual content-based analysis," *IEEE Trans. on Knowl. and Data Eng.*, vol. 18, pp. 272–284, 2006.

[12] W. Hu, O. Wu, Z. Chen, Z. Fu, and S. Maybank, "Recognition of pornographic web pages by classifying texts and images," *IEEE Trans. on Pattern Analysis and Machine Intelligence*, pp. 1019–1034, 2007.

[13] H. Zheng, M. Daoudi, and B. Jedynak, "Blocking adult images based on statistical skin detection," in *Electronic Letters on Comp. Vision & Image Analysis*, 2004, pp. 1–14.

[14] J.-S. Lee, Y.-M. Kuo, P.-C. Chung, and E.-L. Chen, "Naked image detection based on adaptive and extensible skin color model," *Pattern Recog.*, vol. 40, pp. 2261–2270, 2007.

[15] P. Kakumanu, S. Makrogiannis, and N. Bourbakis, "A survey of skin-color modeling and detection methods," *Pattern Recog.*, 2007.

[16] C. Jansohn, A. Ulges, and T. M. Breuel, "Detecting pornographic video content by combining image features with motion information," in *Multimedia*, 2009.

[17] T. Deselaers, L. Pimenidis, and H. Ney, "Bag of visual words models for adult image classification and filtering," in *ICPR*, 2008, pp. 1–4.

[18] A. Lopes, S. Avila, and A. Peixoto, "A bag-of-features approach based on hue-sift descriptor for nude detection," in *Proc. of the 17th European Signal Processing Conf.*, 2009, pp. 1552–1556.

[19] D. Lowe, "Object recognition from local scale-invariant features," in *Proc. of Int'l Conf. on Computer Vision*, vol. 2, 1999, pp. 1150–1157.

[20] K. Van De Sande, T. Gevers, and C. Snoek, "Evaluating color descriptors for object and scene recognition," *IEEE Trans. on Pattern Analysis and Machine Intelligence*, pp. 1582–1596, 2009.

[21] X. Xing, Y. Liang, H. Cheng, J. Dang, S. Huang, R. Han, X. Liu, Q. Lv, and S. Mishra, "SafeVchat: Detecting obscene content and misbehaving users in online video chat services," in *WWW*, 2011.

[22] R. Agrawal and R. Srikant, "Fast algorithms for mining association rules in large databases," in *VLDB*, 1994.

[23] P. E. Hart, N. J. Nilsson, and B. Raphael, "A formal basis for the heuristic determination of minimum cost paths," *IEEE Trans. on Systems, Science, and Cybernetics*, 1968.

[24] A. Agresti, *Analysis of Ordinal Categorical Data*. Wiley, 1984.

[25] "Detection of multicollinearity," http://en.wikipedia.org/wiki/Multicollinearity.

[26] "IBM SPSS," http://www-01.ibm.com/software/analytics/spss/.

[27] "Picblock," http://www.cinchworks.com/.

[28] D. G. Lowe, "Distinctive image features from scale-invariant keypoints," *Int'l J. of Computer Vision*, pp. 91–110, 2004.

Keyword-Propagation-Based Information Enriching and Noise Removal for Web News Videos

[1]Jun Zhang [2]Xiaoming Fan [3]Jianyong Wang [4]Lizhu Zhou
Tsinghua National Laboratory for Information Science and Techno ogy
Department of Computer Science and Technology
Tsinghua University, Beijing 100084, China
{[1]zhangjun03, [2]xmFan1983}@gmail.com
{[3]jianyong, [4]dcszlz}@tsinghua.edu.cn

ABSTRACT

The volume of Web videos have increased sharply through the past several years because of the evolvement of Web video sites. Enhanced algorithms on retrieval, classification and TDT (abbreviation of *Topic Detection and Tracking*) can bring lots of convenience to Web users as well as release tedious work from the administrators. Nevertheless, due to the the insufficiency of annotation keywords and the gap between video features and semantic concepts, it is still far away from satisfactory to implement them based on initial keywords and visual features. In this paper we utilize a keyword propagation algorithm based on manifold structure to enrich the keyword information and remove the noise for videos. Both text similarity and temporal similarity are employed to explore the relationship between any pair of videos and to construct the propagation model. We explore three applications, i.e., TDT, Retrieval and Classification based on a Web news video dataset obtained from a famous online video-distributing website, *YouKu*, and evaluate our approach. Experimental results demonstrate that they achieve satisfactory performance and always outperform the baseline methods.

Categories and Subject Descriptors

H.3.3 [**Information Systems**]: Information Storage and Retrieval—*Information Search and Retrieval*

General Terms

Algorithms, Experimentation, Performance

Keywords

Information Enrichment, Noise Removal, Keyword Propagation

1. INTRODUCTION

Due to the fast advancement of multimedia technology and the great progress of Web 2.0, the volume of Web news videos on online video-distributing websites has been growing explosively through the past several years. Web users upload a large number of videos, share the videos of interests with and recommend them to friends all over the world. *YouTube* [5], one of the most popular online video-distributing websites, according to *YouTube Report 2009* [6] released by *Camscore* (a famous marketing research company in U.S.), has reached 100 million viewers. In January 2009, 14.8 billion online videos were watched by 147 million U.S. Internet users, with an average of 101 videos per person in this month alone. *YouTube* led the growth change, accounting for 91 percent of the incremental gain in the number of videos viewed versus December 2008, as it surpassed 100 million viewers for the first time. In China, there are many YouTube-style video-distributing websites emerged in the past several years, such as *YouKu* [4], *TuDou* [3], etc. *YouKu*, a dominant one of all the counterparts of *YouTube* in China, has increased by 20 times in terms of website traffic last year, and attracted an average of more than 10 million Internet users to visit videos of interests per day in the last three months [1]. Fig.1 shows the two video-distributing websites, i.e., *YouTube* and *YouKu*, and takes some hot news videos as examples, i.e., Beijing Olympic Games and China National Day.

In many cases, rather than surfing websites to read news documents, people prefer to watch Web news videos to know the progress of a hot event or topic. It is not satisfactory to recommend all new-coming unstructured videos to the users, because it is really daunting for the users to view from a video to another to select the hot ones of interests. Furthermore, once a video representing a hot event or a topic is encountered, the users always get curious to know the background, current progress, public opinions and potential trends. Thus tracking hot topics seems much promising to enhance the service of video recommendation. From the perspective of administrators by whom topic structures are manually generated, it is also difficult to do TDT on such a massive video database containing topics of many categories.

Sometimes, Web users submit a query with several keywords to search for the videos of interests. Satisfactory ranking results would come up with the best videos that the user wants most at the top of ranking list. Therefore, an effective and efficient information retrieval system can bring lots of convenience to Web users. Similarly, auto classification for

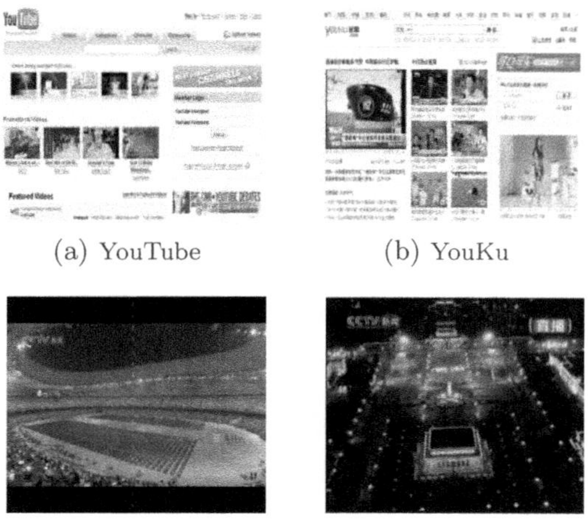

(a) YouTube (b) YouKu (c) Beijing Olympics (d) China National Day

Figure 1: Famous video websites and some hot news videos. *YouKu* is a counterpart of *YouTube* in China

Web news videos definitely cuts down sharply the man-hours for administrators when they organize the video dataset and release human efforts for Web users when they try to watch videos of the same classes.

In a word, automatic TDT, Retrieval and Classification for Web news videos can benefit both administrators and Web users.

Actually, research efforts have been devoted to TDT, Retrieval and Classification on text-rich documents. Take TDT for example. The problem was firstly proposed by NIST in 1990s [2, 28, 29, 7], and encouraging results were reported [9, 12, 10]. TDT is a specialization of cluster analysis to facilitate the task of information analysis [25], thus models employed in information retrieval were borrowed to calculate similarity between two documents. Single-pass clustering [28] and hierarchical clustering [10] algorithms are among the most frequently used methods. For Web videos, however, there is much less text information to represent them, and it becomes useless to turn to traditional approaches in a straightforward way.

To survive this challenge in TDT, Retrieval and Classification, many researchers tried to extract semantic concepts from low-level visual features [21, 30, 14], but as we know, it is not a trival task to extract low-level features (e.g., color, texture, shape, etc.) from videos. Moreover, such low-level features are also far from sufficient to represent videos. Although some video search systems [17, 15] utilized not only text information but also other low-level features such as image content, audio, and have improved their performance, meanwhile they also required large amounts of data for training and consumed a large amount of time. In a word, they only achieved minor improvement because of the well-known gap between visual features and semantic concepts. Last but not least, most Web news videos are amateur-made, thus it would be less efficient to extract semantic features from them.

In this paper, given the title, tags, and creation time with any video, we firstly generate keywords with weights from title and tags to initially represent the videos' features. Nevertheless, the keywords of Web news videos are provided by the users with different backgrounds when they uploaded videos. These keywords are not enough to represent all items of interest in a video story. What is even worse, to attract more attention and pageviews or just to do advertisement, misleading or irrelevant keywords are sometimes intermingled with the normal ones by malicious users. As a result, the keywords are always insufficient, limited and noisy. Thus to overcome the difficulties stated above, we employ a manifold-based structure to propagate keywords between any pair of videos about a topic and re-rank them in order to filter out noisy keywords, and enrich keyword information such as involved people, places, and other items of interest.

The key point of our approach is that every video spreads its keywords and weights to their neighboring videos, then its neighbors spread its keywords further to their neighbors. The keyword propagation continues until a global stable state is achieved. Our main contributions are summarized as follows:

- we utilize a manifold-based keyword propagation model to enrich keyword information and remove noise for Web news videos. Two videos are considered as neighbors if and only if they emerge closely in time and share one common keywords at least, and are connected by an edge with a weight value. The manifold is composed of such video points and edges, within which keyword propagation is performed.
- Three applications (Topic Detection and Tracking, Retrieval, and Classification) for Web news videos are performed on the processed videos, and extensive experiments demonstrate that they all achieve significant improvements and outperform the baseline methods.

The rest of this paper is organized as follows. Some related works are discussed in Section 2, and we give some notations in Section 3. In Section 4 we describe the proposed algorithm and framework in details. Section 5 presents the three typical applications, and we analyze the experimental results in Section 6. Section 7 concludes this paper and points out the future work.

2. RELATED WORK

A manifold is a topological space that is typically endowed with a differentiable structure that allows one to measure distances by Euclidean distances. Data points on a manifold structure hold close connections to each other. Furthermore, if two data points were strongly connected to an intermediary data point respectively, they would be considered to have close relationship even if the Euclidean distance between them is large. In other words, the link structure of data points provides us with effective information to understand the environment of data points. Mathematically speaking, by an one-to-one map operation, any pair of data points in the high-dimensional space should be close to each other in a low-dimensional one.

The semi-supervised learning algorithm which employs relationship among data points in [8, 31, 27] is based on the concept of manifold, and achieves significant improvement. Such a learning algorithm satisfies the assumption of local and global consistency, thus the points on the same manifold structure can spread their messages to the neighboring points and reach a stable state. As a result, the idea of propagation model on a manifold has been widely used in several

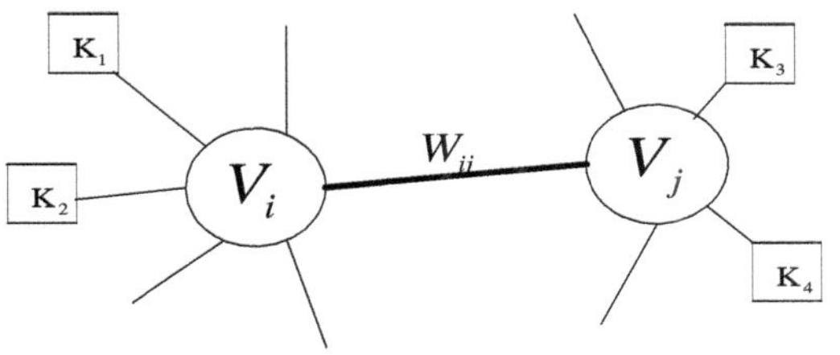

Figure 2: Keyword Propagation Model

research fields, among which are image retrieval, document classification [32, 24, 13, 22], and so on.

Take [31] for example to get more details. As Zhou et al. stated, since it is possible for a data point to spread its labels to those with long distances in space by many intermediary neighbors on the same manifold, the authors designed a classifying function, and generated a toy dataset with a pattern of two intertwining moons in order to evaluate the effectiveness. Classification results on the toy dataset demonstrate that the manifold-based algorithm outperforms the SVM algorithm. Similary in [32], the authors proposed a method to rank on data manifolds, which also achieved higher performance than other baseline methods. This related work encouraged us to develop a manifold-based algorithm for applications of Web news videos. More exhaustive details can be found in the following sections.

3. NOTATIONS

Before we present our keyword propagation model, we first introduce some notations.

Given a news video set $\mathcal{V} = \{v_1, v_2, \dots, v_n\} \subset R^c$ and a keyword set $\mathcal{T} = \{t_1, t_2, \dots, t_c\}$, any video $V_i (1 \leq i \leq n)$ has its own keyword set $K_i \subseteq \mathcal{T}$. Let $\mathcal{F}$ denote the set of matrices of $n \times c$ with nonnegative entries. The keyword distribution matrix is defined as an $n \times c$ matrix $F = [F_1^T, F_2^T, \dots, F_n^T]^T \in \mathcal{F}$, where F_j means the keyword distribution state of the jth video, and each entry of the matrix denotes the corresponding *weight* value. Namely, F can be viewed as a vectorial function $F : \mathcal{V} \to R^c$, which maps a vector F_i to each video v_i. F_{ij} is the weight of the ith video (i.e., v_i) with respect to the jth keyword (i.e., t_j), and it must be a nonnegative number.

Furthermore, $\sum_{k=1}^{c} F_{ik} = 1$, that means the sum of probabilities of the ith video with respect to each keyword should be full. Most of F_{ij}'s are zero because of the sparseness property of F. Each video only has a few keywords of a large keyword set. We define a matrix $Y \in \mathcal{F}$ with $Y_{ij} = w_{ij}$ if v_i has the jth keyword with weight value w_{ij} (defined in Section 4.1) and $Y_{ij} = 0$ otherwise. Generally speaking, Y is consistent with the initial keyword distribution.

As we stated in Section 2, data points on a manifold structure can spread their keywords to the neighboring points. Fig. 2 shows an example of keyword propagation. v_i and v_j are two Web news videos. w_{ij} is the similarity between video i and video j, and it can be regarded as the keyword transition probability from v_i to v_j. In the process of propagation, the model will propagate keywords from v_i to v_j with probability w_{ij}. Excitingly, the keywords of v_i can be propagated to v_k though v_j exactly. The algorithm for keyword propagation will be described in details in the next section.

4. ALGORITHM AND FRAMEWORK

4.1 Pre-Processing

First of all, we tokenize words (word segmentation is performed when dealing with Chinese texts), perform part-of-speech tagging, recognize named entities, remove stop words, and filter out adjective, adverb, etc. Finally a keyword vector is created for each video. To generate a weight for a keyword with respect to each video, we collected 584 days worth of video data from website Youku as a training corpus and compute *video frequency* (a counterpart of *document frequency*) for each keyword, then a weight is computed as Equation 1 which is described in [26].

$$w(t, v) = \frac{tf(t, v)log((|V| + 1)/(vf(t) + 0.5))}{\sqrt{\sum_{v' \in V} (tf(t, v')log((|V| + 1)/(vf(t) + 0.5)))^2}} \quad (1)$$

where $tf(t, v)$ represents how many times term t appears in video v, $vf(t)$ represents video frequency of term t in corpus, and $|V|$ is equal to the number of videos in the dataset, that is $2,654,470$ in our experiments. Note that the vector is normalized so that it is of unit length. More detail can be found in [26].

4.2 Manifold-based Propagation Model

As we stated in Section 1, it is essential to filter out noisy keywords and enrich relevant ones to the video, thus we use a manifold-based keyword propagation method inspired mainly from work [31] and [32]. But before diving into more details of the algorithm, we present two prior assumptions that are critically necessary.

As we know, it is a characteristic of news reporting that stories about the same topic often occur in clumps close in time [7], and gradually fade away. Thus it seems that:

1. videos on the same category (event or topic) are likely to share some common keywords, and

2. neighboring news videos that emerge closely in time are more likely about the same topic.

Based on the two assumptions, besides creation time, only keywords obtained from titles and tags are utilized here. Firstly, we need to form a weighted graph based on Web news videos, and to assign a positive similarity score to the edge connecting each pairwise, which is used to construct affinity matrix in our algorithm. To simplify the algorithm, we connect two points with an edge if they are neighbors. It ensures enough connection for each point while preserving the sparse property of the weighted graph.

Given the notations in Section 3, we present the detailed algorithm for the task of keyword propagation in Algorithm 1. Note the algorithm was first proposed in [31] and [32], and has been used for image retrieval in [13] and [24].

In step 1, we establish a connected graph and the distances in Equation 4 are used to calculate the distances between videos. In the second step, we set the diagonal elements of affinity matrix to zero to avoid *self-reinforcement.* The affinity matrix is symmetrically normalized in step 3 and the algorithm really begins to spread keywords among all videos in step 4. In practice, all videos spread their keywords to their neighbors via the linked network. The spread process

Algorithm 1 Manifold-based Keyword Propagation

1. Sort the pair-wise distances ($d(v_i, v_j) = ||v_i - v_j||$) among videos in ascending order. Repeat connecting two videos with an edge according to the order until a connected graph is obtained.

2. Form the affinity matrix W defined by $W_{ij} = exp[-d^2(v_i, v_j)/(2\sigma^2)]$ if there is an edge linking v_i and v_j. Let $W_{ii} = 0$.

3. Symmetrically normalize W by $S = D^{-1/2}WD^{1/2}$ in which D is the diagonal matrix with (i,i)-element equal to the sum of the ith row of W.

4. Iterate $F(t+1) = \alpha SF(t) + (1-\alpha)Y$ until convergence, where α is a parameter in $[0,1)$ and $Y = F(0)$.

is not stopped until a global state is achieved. By the way, the parameter α and the number of iterations are very important for the algorithm's convergence. Some details will be discussed in Section 6.5.

As we can see from step (2), $W_{ij} \in (0,1]$, which implies that W is a positive and irreducible matrix, so is S. Since $0 < \alpha < 1$ and the eigenvalue of S in $[-1,1]$, according to *Perron-Frobenius Theory* [23] and comprehensive discussions in [18, 31, 32, 13], we come to a conclusion that $\{F(i)\}$ converges to

$$F^* = (1-\alpha)(I-\alpha S)^{-1}Y \tag{2}$$

Although F^* can be expressed in a closed form, we can expand it by Taylor expansion method:

$$\begin{aligned} F^* &= (I + \alpha S + \alpha^2 S^2 + \cdots)Y \\ &= Y + \alpha SY + \alpha S(\alpha SY) + \cdots \end{aligned} \tag{3}$$

From Equation 3, F^* can be regarded as the sum of infinite terms. The first term is the initial (keyword, weight) pairs for each video, the second term is to spread the (keyword, weight) pairs of each video to its neighbors, the third term is to spread the pairs further, and so on. Parameter α specifies the relative amount of the information from its neighbors and its initial information. The spread process is repeated until a global stable state is reached, and all the videos have their own keywords and corresponding weights. It is possible that a video receives dozens of keywords, but in our experiments only the top K dominant words (with high weights) would be reserved to represent the features to speed the propagation of keywords. And the last keywords in sorted keywords list with low weights are removed. Therefore the weight of some important keywords will be increased due to that the neighbors spread these keywords, in contrast, some noisy keywords will be removed due to low weight. Although F^* has a concise expression in Equation 2, for large scale problems, the iteration algorithm expressed in Equation 3 is preferable in considering the computational efficiency. In practice, however, we make some modifications as follows.

First, it is not necessary to calculate all distances between any pair of videos and ensure a totally connected graph. Actually, videos with few keywords in common in different class are far away in space, the graph constructed may contains many strong connected components. Therefore, if two videos are far away in space, keyword propagation seems to bring no effect to change the top K dominant keywords and their relative orders. That is to say, it does no harm to performance if keywords coming last in the keyword ranking list are removed, or even if no propagation is performed for them. Consequently, it may lead to reducible matrices W and S, which results in an iterative process that converges slowly, or even a state of oscillation around a stable dominant value.

Second, instead of the closed form without iterations, we choose the iterative method stated in Equation 3 to work out a final result. Although it is not necessarily equal to the stable F^*, we can get a satisfactory one by giving a constant number of iterations or an acceptable error threshold as the termination condition.

Third, an intuitive distance function incorporating time and keyword information is defined to generate the matrix W. Since it is a characteristic of news reporting that videos about the same event come out in the form of a burst, only those pairs that the creation time gap does not exceed a limit (e.g., N days) are taken into consideration. Meanwhile, σ^2 in step (2) of Algorithm 1 is described as a human-specified parameter, thus we incorporate it into the distance metric to reduce it. Given a weight threshold w_d,

$$d(v_i, v_j) = \sqrt{2}\sigma/(w_C(i,j) - w_d) \tag{4}$$

if the sum of the dot product of common keywords ($C = \{t | t \in v_1 \cap v_2\}$), $w_C(i,j)$, is larger than the given threshold w_d, otherwise $d(v_i, v_j) = \infty$.

5. TYPICAL APPLICATIONS

In this section we will explore three typical applications of the keyword propagation framework proposed in preceding section, i.e., topic detection and tracking, retrieval, and classification. We will evaluate the effectiveness of the proposed model based on the experimental results over a Web news videos dataset obtained from an online video-distributing website, *YouKu*, which contains 2,654,473 news videos. For any video, only the title, tags, and the creation time are utilized. We will describe the experimental results and discuss them in the following sections.

5.1 Topic Detection and Tracking

5.1.1 Story, Event, and Topich

In [11], the authors described the concept of story, event, TDT and so on. TDT mainly process news streams (either in the form of documents or of videos) and group news reports into different events and topics. The basic units are stories (More detail in [11]). Typically, a news document text or a Web news video is treated as a single story, for example, Figures 1(c) (Beijing Olympics) and 1(d) (China National Day) can be treated as stories. An *event* identifies something (non-trivial) happening in a certain place at a certain time [28], and each event should contain one or more stories that describe it. Obviously, all stories in an event always are close in time and emerge in the form of a burst. Finally, one or more directly related events form a broad *topic*, and it is allowed that there are relatively long time gaps between any two topically similar events. And for simplicity, we say a topic is the *super-unit* of multiple

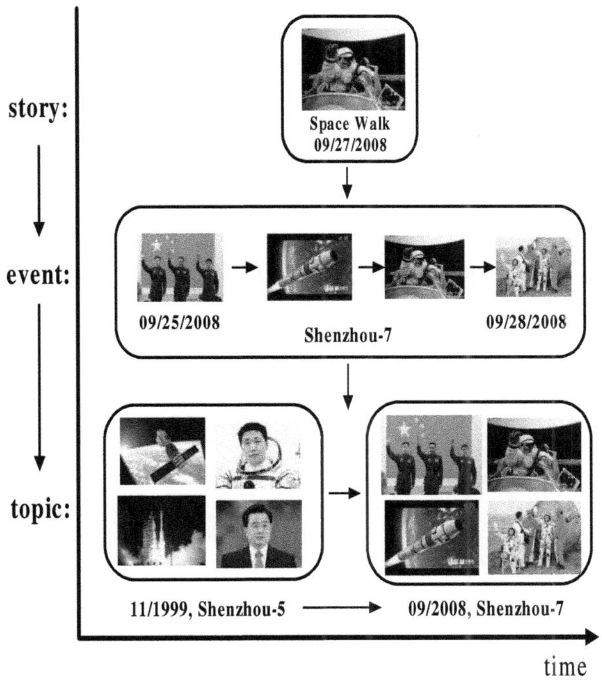

Figure 3: Shenzhou-Series Manned Spacecraft of China

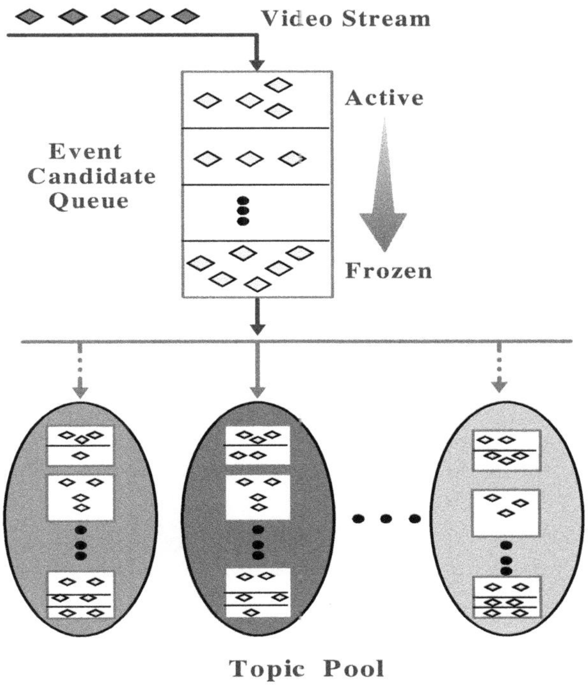

Figure 4: Procedure of Topic Detection and Tracking

events, and an event is the *super-unit* of multiple stories. As a good example, Figure 3 illustrates the three concepts.

News stories discussing the same event tend to be temporally proximate, thus instead of the whole collection, only *local* events are selected to compare with the current story to do *New Event Detection*, which is different from *Topic Tracking* requiring to compare the new event with all historical topics.

5.1.2 *Procedure*

As we mentioned in Section 5.1.1, an event contains one or more stories close in time, and a topic contains several events. Events are represented as keyword vectors defined as the arithmetic average of keyword vectors of all stories within them, and only the top K dominant keywords are reserved for each event, so are the topics. Cosine similarity in [26] is employed here to calculate the similarities between any two *units*. Since the vectors are all normalized, it can be formulated as:

$$similarity(u_1, u_2) = \sum_{t \in u_1 \cap u_2} w(t, u_1) \times w(t, u_2) \quad (5)$$

The procedure of TDT for Web news videos is illustrated in Figure 4. And we explain it more formally step by step in the following:

1. Once a new video arrives (either an original video or an enriched video), calculate the similarities between the video and every event in the *Event Candidate Queue*. If the similarity between the current video and the most similar event is below a given threshold, it indicates that the story is *new* and a new event is detected; otherwise the video will be assigned to the event. With regard to the former case, a new event will be created and pushed into the queue, while in the latter case, we re-calculate the representative keywords for the updated event, and place it at the head of the queue where it is recently activated.

2. Pop out the last event in the *queue*, and judge whether it has been frozen for N days. If yes, it means no story was assigned to the event through the past N days and it is time to remove the event from the *Event Candidate Queue*, and relate it to a historical topic.

3. Once an event needs to be assigned to a topic, we calculate the similarities between the event and every topic in the *Topic Pool*. Note that any event or topic is represented as a keyword vector that has only K dominant keywords, thus it is a trivial task to do the real-time similarity calculation. If and only if the similarity between the event and the most similar topic is larger than the given threshold, it will be assigned to the topic and the topic will be updated, otherwise, a new topic will be generated and inserted into the *Topic Pool*.

5.2 Video Retrieval

Information retrieval aims to find out some objects such as Web pages, images, videos, which are hit by the keywords within a submitted query, and to rank them in order to put the most satisfactory one on the top of the result list. Traditionally, video retrieval task is performed on the initial keywords that come up with the titles, tags. But in this paper, the manifold-based keyword propagation algorithm is used here to enrich the keyword information and remove noisy keywords for Web news videos, and we expect it to work better than traditional baseline methods.

In this experiment, we propose a retrieval problem for Web news videos by selecting several query keywords randomly and evaluating the performance improvements. We implement our system as follows.

1. According to Section 4.2, we spread keywords iteratively until the keyword distribution converges to a stable state. Although it is possible for a video to receive dozens of keywords, only the top K dominant keywords are reserved while the last ones in the sorted keywords list with low weights are considered as noisy ones and removed.
2. Calculate the similarity value between the query vector (keyword vector) and each video vector. And a result ranking list is generated in descending order in terms of both creation time and similarity relevance. In other words, the higher similarity value is, the more relevant with the video is.

Note that we employ cosine similarity to calculate the similarity between a query and a news video as shown in Equation 6. Specifically, given a submitted query q, it is parsed into some text tokens which are considered to form a keyword vector. According to the Eqation 6 we calculate the similarity between the keyword vector of query q and that of a video u.

$$similarity(q, u) = \sum_{k \in q \cap u} w(k, q) \times w(k, u) \qquad (6)$$

Notice that notation k denotes the common words shared by query keywords and video ones.

5.3 Classification

In this section we investigate the task of classification for Web news videos. We select a dataset which contains three categories, i.e., Shenzhou Series (Space Flight), World Cup (Football), Moon Craft (Chang E). After keywords propagation and noise removal, we obtain 2113 video vectors, which are normalized into *TF-IDF* representation as shown in Equation 1.

We explore two popular classification algorithms, KNN and SVM, to handle the classification problem. For KNN and SVM, we firstly do the same as we did in the retrieval task, i.e., keywords propagation. However the following steps in these two methods are not identical. For KNN, we calculate the similarity between the test video and each training video, and then a vote is taken by the most similar K training videos, which assigns a label to the test video. On the contrary, SVM predicts the label of the test videos in a straightforward way.

The similarity between videos v_i and v_j is defined as Equation 5 indicates, and the K in KNN is set to 1. The width of the RBF kernel for SVM is set to 5. The discriminating process repeated several times (with different random samples of training data) and more details are described in Section 6.

6. RESULTS AND DISCUSSIONS

The baseline methods are taken on the original keywords of videos, and are compared with the enriched approaches based on the keywords after propagation. Three applications, i.e., TDT, Retrieval and Classification, are explored on the same algorithms but on different datasets.

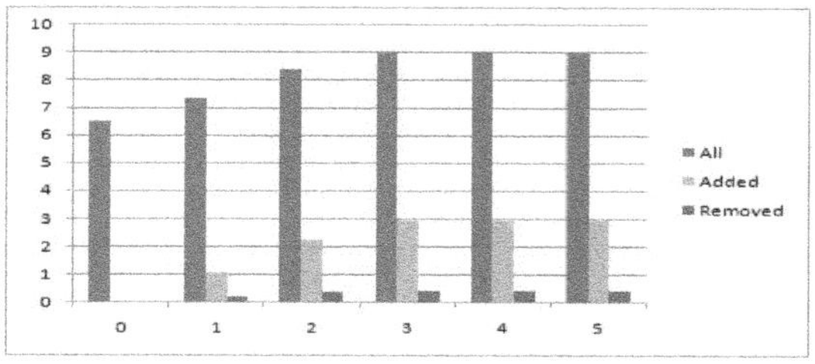

Figure 5: The average number of keywords versus Iteration number of the propagation algorithm.

Firstly, we compare the average number of keywords after propagation with that of the initial ones. As Figure 5 shows, the average keyword number of the initial videos is 6.5 (when iteration number is 0) while the average length of keyword list of videos increases to 9 after propagation. The average number of keywords added and removed are 2.9 and 0.4 respectively. This means that our method enriches information of news videos (by keyword propagation) indeed. In fact, when we check the keyword list of videos after propagation carefully, we find that the algorithm adds some new topic-relevant keywords of videos and also removes some noisy keywords. As the iteration process continues, the average number of keywords increases gradually. Note that the number of keywords would not increase after the iteration number reaches 3, because the relative order of dominant keywords gets stable and arrives at the termination condition at this moment.

6.1 Topic Detection and Tracking

Since whether a video belongs to an event or an event is relevant to a topic is subjective, we invite nine participants to decide which event a story belongs to, and which topic an event belongs to. Every final decision goes to the choice proposed by the majority. Based on the procedure in Figure 4, we performed TDT for the original video stream (Baseline for abbr.), and for the enriched video stream (Enriched for abbr.), respectively. *False Alarm* (*fa* for abbr.), *Miss*, and *Precision* measures [28, 20] are adopted for evaluation.

Firstly we do *New Event Detection* on 93,003 videos that all emerged in year 2007. Since it is not necessary to judge whether any video in year 2007 belongs to a specified event, we collected videos which emerged between the first story and the last story of the current event, and evaluated the effectiveness based on them. In Table 1 we list four bursty events that have been detected. It demonstrates that the proposed method outperforms, or at least be comparable to, the baseline over all four events in terms of *false alarm* and *miss*. Interestingly in Event 3, the baseline does well as the enriched one since both *fa* and *miss* are zero in these two methods, because there are so few videos belonging to this event that it is in vain practically to propagate keywords.

Nevertheless, a topic spans long compared with a bursty event, resulting in the inability to find every topic-relevant video from the massive video stream. Since it is not difficult for us to judge whether a video is relevant to a specified topic, we only adopt *precision* to evaluate the task *Topic Tracking*. Seven prominent topics are listed in Table 2 ("#" denotes the number of videos within the topic). As the figure indicates, the most significant improvement is for *Topic* 7, and the least for *Topic* 6 is about 2.4%. As a result, the

Event	Dominant Keywords (enriched)	Baseline		Enriched	
		miss	*fa*	*miss*	*fa*
1	Womens' World Cup, FIFA, China, Germany, Marta, Brazil	16.7%	8.8%	5.3%	2.6%
2	North Korea, Nuclear Power, Threat, US, Six-Party Talk	25.0%	4.9%	4.9%	3.8%
3	Virus, Nimaya, Safety, Spread, Internet	0.0%	0.0%	0.0%	0.0%
4	Shenzhou-7, Rocket Spacecraft, Test, Astronauts	6.5%	0.0%	2.3%	0.0%

Table 1: Comparison of the Detected Events result between the Baseline and the Enriched

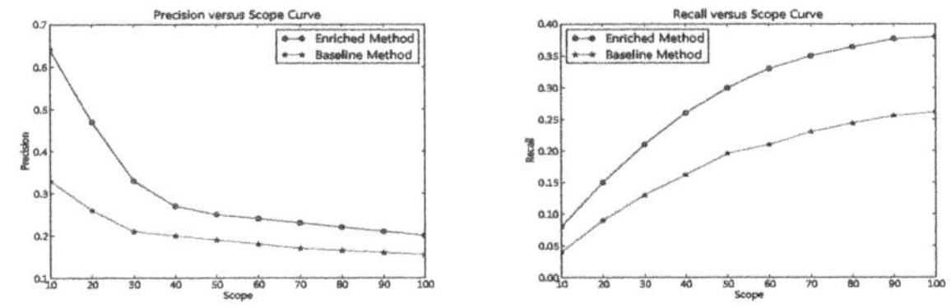

Figure 6: Comparison of the retrieval result between the Enriched method and the baseline method.

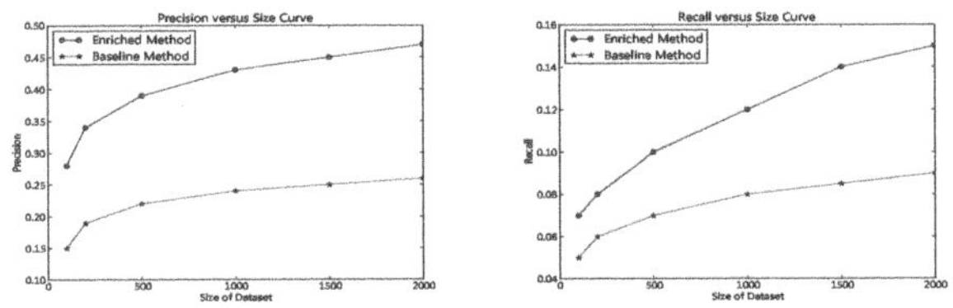

(a) (b)

Figure 7: Comparison of the retrieval result between the Enriched method and the baseline method under different size of data. 7(a) P20 versus the percentage of data. 7(b) R20 versus the percentage of training data.

overall *precision* measure increases sharply from 43.0% to 82.3%. In a word, the keyword propagation method helps improve the effectiveness by a large margin in terms of both the number of retrieved videos and the *precision* measure.

Topic	Dominant Keywords	Baseline		Enriched	
		# v	p (%)	# v	p (%)
1	FIFA World Cup 2006, Goals, Germany, Italy,France, Zidane	301	64.2	356	81.8
2	Yao Ming, Rockets, score, NBA, dunk, McGrady, playoffs	544	87.5	731	90.0
3	Shenzhou Series, Spacecraft, China, Astronaut Yang,rocket	117	72.3	142	87.6
4	Palestine, Israel, conflicts, suicide, bomb, revenge, battle	143	79.6	167	92.2
5	Beijing, Olympics, preparation, ticket, stadium, torch bearer	282	94.0	319	96.9
6	Premier League, ManUtd, Liverpool, Chelsea, Arsenal	317	89.6	346	91.9
7	Iran, US, Bush, Nuclear Plan, sanction, Force, debate	270	43.0	331	72.3

Table 2: Comparison of the Detected Topics result between the Baseline and the Enriched

More interestingly, we find out many videos get associated with some new keywords after propagation, which were not contained initially. For example, before spreading, a video consisted of six keywords, i.e., *NBA, Yao, Rocket, Star, Game, Advertisement*, but they become *NBA, Yao, Rocket, Star, Game, and Basketball.* Obviously the keyword *Basketball* joins the keyword list, and such noisy keywords as *Advertisement* have been filtered out, that does a great favor to detect the relevant event.

6.2 Video Retrieval

In this experiment, we use *precision versus scope* and *recall versus scope* curve to evaluate the performance of the baseline method and the enriched one. Considering the randomness of the selected query keywords, we ran 10 times of ten different queries and recorded each result. Then we computed the average of the results over all the 10 queries.

Firstly the initial retrieval is evaluated. The *precision (recall) versus scope curve* is shown in Figure 6, where the scope stands for the range of the top K retrieval results. In order to perform a systematic evaluation, we varied the size of dataset and compared the *average precision* (P20) and *recall* (R20) of the top 20 retrieved videos of the enriched method with those of the baseline one. The *precision* (*recall*) versus the size of dataset is demonstrated in Figure 7. As the figures indicate, our propagation method outperforms the baseline method by a large margin. What is more important, the improvement was still very significant even when only a small number of videos were employed.

As mentioned in Section 6.1, we expect that the example video without the keyword *basketball* would validate the effectiveness of our method. Actually, it is exciting to find that if we take *basketball* as the query, the example video will be found out while we know the baseline method will not.

6.3 Classification

We explored two classification algorithms, KNN and SVM, to conduct our experiments. For KNN, we firstly calculated the similarity between the test video and the training one, selected the most similar video, and assigned its label to the test one. In other words, the K was set to 1. For SVM, we used keyword vectors with weight as input data, and selected the RBF kernel as the kernel of SVM, which was set to 5. The classifier was expected to predict the label of the test data with three categories. The *precision* is utilized to evaluate the performance and experimental result is shown in Figure 8. We also change the size of training data and compare the *precision* of these two methods. From the experimental results demonstrated in these two figures, it is obvious that our method outperforms the baseline approach significantly.

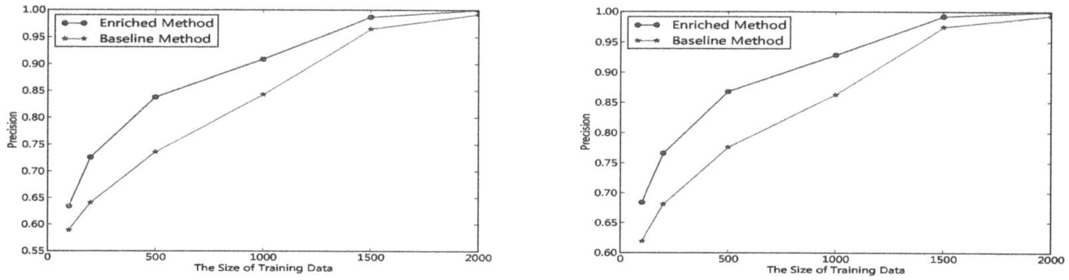

(a) KNN (b) SVM

Figure 8: Comparison of the classification result (precision versus the size of training data) between the Enriched method and the baseline method.

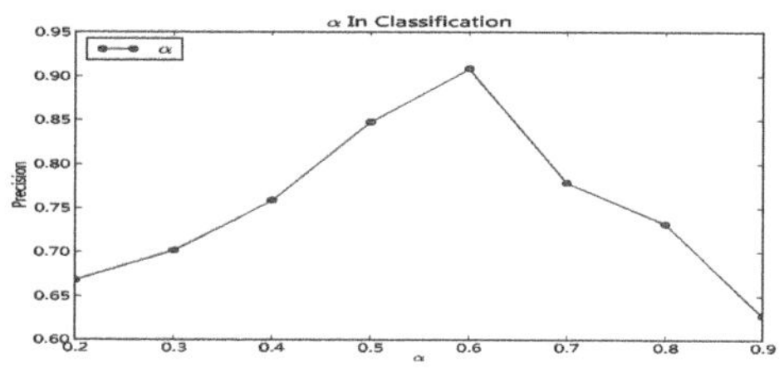

Figure 9: Classification precision versus parameter α in our Enriched method.

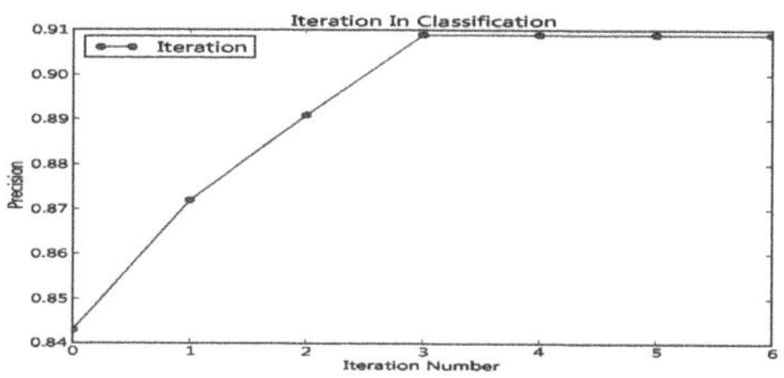

Figure 10: Classification precision versus Iteration number in our Enriched method.

6.4 Time complexity of propagation

A single iteration of propagation (cf. Section 4) consists of a single matrix multiplication $SF(t)$ which is an $O(n^2c)$ operation, where n is the number of videos, c denotes the size of keyword vector, and typically they are about several thousand in the experiments. In our implementation, the keyword distribution converges within a few iterations ranging from 3 to 6, and it takes less than one minute in a regular desktop computer. While for large scale datasets, there are several advanced implementation techniques for matrix multiplication, such as $PowerMethod$ [19].

6.5 Parameter sensibility

6.5.1 α Parameters

The use of α in Equation 3 plays an important role in balancing the initial distribution weight and propagation weight. The value of α also has an impact on the performance and speed of convergence. With α close to 1, the keyword distribution relies almost entirely on the spreading process. Based on our experimental comparisons in Figure 9, the best value for parameter α is 0.6, which is also close to the empirical value in large-scale Web applications [16, 18].

6.5.2 Number of Iterations

The number of iterations is also important for the propagation method, since it has an impact on the performance and the speed of convergence. As the iteration number increases to 3, the keyword distribution gets to a satisfactory and stable state. According to the experimental comparisons in Figure 10, the best value for iteration number is 3, which also means that our method helps the distribution converge to a stable one in a short period of time (less than 1 minute in these experiments).

7. CONCLUSION AND FUTURE WORK

In this paper we have introduced a manifold-based keyword propagation algorithm for Web news videos, in order to enrich the keyword information by adding new topic-relevant keywords and filter out noisy keywords. Both text similarity and temporal similarity are employed to explore the relationship between any pair of videos and to construct the propagation model. Three typical applications, i.e., *Topic Detection and Tracking*, *Retrieval* and *Classification* have been explored in details on a Web news video dataset. Extensive experimental results demonstrate the higher effectiveness of keyword propagation model.

Nevertheless, there are still some issues that are not discussed in this paper. First, we suppose that there is a short time gap between the time when the video's story really took place and the video's creation time, however, it is actually not the case. Thus our future work will focus on how to automatically detect whether they are synchronized, or at least lay in a relatively short period. Second, as the sizes of datasets increase, the dimensions of matrix in propagation model will get much huge and the speed of convergence gets lower. Therefore, to run our model in large-scale video datasets will also be a challenge.

8. ACKNOWLEDGMENTS

This work was supported in part by National Basic Research Program of China (973 Program) under Grant No. 2011CB302206, and National Natural Science Foundation of China under Grant No. 60833003.

9. REFERENCES

[1] http://www.alexa.com/siteinfo/youku.com.

[2] http://www.itl.nist.gov/iad/mig/tests/tdt/.

[3] http://www.tudou.com.

[4] http://www.youku.com.

[5] http://www.youtube.com.

[6] http://youtubereport2009.com/category/youtube-statistics.

[7] J. Allan, R. Papka, and V. Lavrenko. On-line new event detection and tracking. In *SIGIR'98*, pages 37–45, 1998.

[8] M. Belkin and P. Niyogi. Semi-supervised learning on riemannian manifolds. In *Machine Learning*, volume 56, pages 209–239, 2004.

[9] T. Brants, F. Chen, and A. Farahat. A system for new event detection. In *SIGIR '03*, pages 330–337, 2003.

[10] M. Connell, A. Feng, G. Kumaran, H. Raghavan, C. Shah, and J. Allan. Umass at tdt 2004. In *Working Notes of the TDT-2004 Evaluation*, 2004.

[11] A. Feng and J. Allan. Hierarchical topic detection in tdt-2004. IR 389, University of Massachusetts, 2005.

[12] G. P. C. Fung, J. X. Yu, H. Liu, and P. S. Yu. Time-dependent event hierarchy construction. In *KDD '07*, pages 300–309, 2007.

[13] J. He, M. Li, H. Zhang, H. Tong, and C. Zhang. Manifold-ranking based image retrieval. In *ACM Multimedia*, pages 9–16, 2004.

[14] W. H. Hsu and S.-F. Chang. Topic tracking across broadcast news videos with visual duplicates and semantic concepts. In *ICIP*, pages 141–144, 2006.

[15] W. H. Hsu, L. S. Kennedy, and S.-F. Chang. Video search reranking through random walk over document-level context graph. In *ACM Multimedia*, pages 971–980, 2007.

[16] S. D. Kamvar, T. H. Haveliwala, C. D. Manning, and G. H. Golub. Extrapolation methods for accelerating pagerank computations. In *WWW*, pages 261–270, 2003.

[17] L. S. Kennedy and S.-F. Chang. A reranking approach for context-based concept fusion in video indexing and retrieval. In *CIVR*, pages 333–340, 2007.

[18] A. N. Langville and C. D. Meyer. A survey of eigenvector methods for web information retrieval. In *SIAM Review*, volume 47, pages 135–161, 2005.

[19] J. J. Leader. *Numerical Analysis and Scientific Computation.* Addison Wesley, 2004.

[20] L. Liu, L. Sun, Y. Rui, Y. Shi, and S. Yang. Web video topic discovery and tracking via bipartite graph reinforcement model. In *WWW '08*, pages 1009–1018, 2008.

[21] G. Luo, R. Yan, and P. S. Yu. Real-time new event detection for video streams. In *CIKM '08*, pages 379–388, 2008.

[22] S. A. Macskassy and F. Provost. Classification in networked data: A toolkit and a univariate case study. In *Journal of Machine Learning*, volume 8,(May), pages 935–983, 2007.

[23] C. D. Meyer. *Matrix Analysis and Applied Linear Algebra.* SIAM, February 2001.

[24] H. Tong, J. He, M. Li, W. Ma, H. Zhang, and C. Zhang. Manifold-ranking based keyword propagation for image retrieval. volume 21, pages 1–10 Special Issue on Information Mining from Multimedia Database, 2006.

[25] D. Trieschnigg and W. Kraaij. TNO hierarchical topic detection at TDT 2004. Technical report, 2004. TDT 2004 workshop notes.

[26] C. Wang, M. Zhang, S. Ma, and L. Ru. Automatic online news issue construction in web environment. In *WWW*, pages 457–466, 2008.

[27] F. Wang and C. Zhang. Label propagation through linear neighborhoods. In *Proceedings of the 23rd international conference on Machine learning*, pages 985–992, 2006.

[28] Y. Yang, J. Carbonell, R. Brown, T. Pierce, B. T. Archibald, and X. Liu. Learning approaches for detecting and tracking news events. *IEEE Intelligent Systems*, 14(4):32–43, 1999.

[29] Y. Yang, T. Pierce, and J. Carbonell. A study of retrospective and on-line event detection. In *SIGIR'98*, pages 28–36, 1998.

[30] Y. Zhai and M. Shah. Tracking news stories across different sources. In *ACM MM '05*, pages 2–10, 2005.

[31] D. Zhou, O. Bousquet, T. N Lal, J. Weston, B. Schölkopf, and B. S. Olkopf. Learning with local and global consistency. In *NIPS '03*, pages 321–328. MIT Press, 2003.

[32] D. Zhou, J. Weston, A. Gretton, O. Bousquet, and B. Schölkopf. Ranking on data manifolds. In *NIPS '04*. MIT Press, 2004.

Harnessing the Wisdom of the Crowds for Accurate Web Page Clipping*

Lei Zhang[†‡], Linpeng Tang[♭‡], Ping Luo[‡], Enhong Chen[†],
Limei Jiao[‡], Min Wang[‡] and Guiquan Liu[†]
[†]University of Science and Technology of China, [♭]Shanghai Jiao Tong University, [‡]HP Labs China
[†]{stone, cheneh, gqliu }@ustc.edu.cn,
[‡]{linpeng.tang, ping.luo, li-mei.jiao, min.wang6}@hp.com

ABSTRACT

Clipping Web pages, namely extracting the informative clips (areas) from Web pages, has many applications, such as Web printing and e-reading on small handheld devices. Although many existing methods attempt to address this task, most of them can either work only on certain types of Web pages (e.g., news- and blog-like web pages), or perform semi-automatically where extra user efforts are required in adjusting the outputs. The problem of clipping any types of Web pages accurately in a totally automatic way remains pretty much open. To this end in this study we harness the wisdom of the crowds to provide accurate recommendation of informative clips on any given Web pages. Specifically, we leverage the knowledge on how previous users clip similar Web pages, and this knowledge repository can be represented as a *transaction database* where each transaction contains the clips selected by a user on a certain Web page. Then, we formulate a new pattern mining problem, *mining top-1 qualified pattern*, on transaction database for this recommendation. Here, the recommendation considers not only the pattern *support* but also the pattern *occupancy* (proposed in this work). High support requires that patterns appear frequently in the database, while high occupancy requires that patterns occupy a large portion of the transactions they appear in. Thus, it leads to both precise and complete recommendation. Additionally, we explore the properties on occupancy to further prune the search space for high-efficient pattern mining. Finally, we show the effectiveness of the proposed algorithm on a human-labeled ground truth dataset consisting of 2000 web pages from 100 major Web sites, and demonstrate its efficiency on large synthetic datasets.

Categories and Subject Descriptors

H.2.8 [**Database Application**]: Data Mining

General Terms

Algorithms, Design, Experimentation

*The work was done when Lei Zhang and Linpeng Tang were visiting HP Labs China.

KDD'12, August 12–16, 2012, Beijing, China.

Keywords

Occupancy, Frequent and Dominant Pattern, Web Page Clipping, Wisdom of the Crowds

1. INTRODUCTION

Many people use the World Wide Web as the primary information source in their daily lives. However, Web pages encoded by the HTML language are designed for viewing on PC screen and may not be suitable for other purposes, such as Web printing and e-reading on small handheld devices. Thus, extracting informative *clips* (referring to content areas in Web pages) attracts many research works [12, 14, 3, 10, 9]. However, most of these previous works focus on extracting *article* Web pages, such as news stories, encyclopedia entries, and blog posts. In these article pages, the informative contents include the title, text-body, content-related images and image captions and so on. These content items usually appear in the similar layouts and formats in the article Web pages. For example, the article body usually consists of contiguous paragraph blocks, which occupy the main area of the Web page. The article title is usually placed above the text-body in a more standout font. Thus, these commonly-shared visual features can be used to extract these informative items with high accuracy [3].

Besides article pages, there are a large number of *non-article* Web pages (e.g., online shopping pages, job recruiting pages and recipe pages). For these *non-article* pages the informative clips are scattered irregularly, thus it is hard to summarize the visual features, which makes the automatic extraction of these informative clips impossible. For example, in a product Web page users are usually interested in the product name, brief description, product image, and price. However, these informative items are formatted in diverse manners in different Web sites. Thus, an expedient solution to clipping non-article Web pages is a semi-automatic process, where users can manually select the informative areas in an interactive interface. This is exactly what the tool of *Smart Print*[1] provides for Web page printing [9].

Let us see how *Smart Print* works using the example in Figure 1. When a user opens the recipe Web page[2] and clicks *Smart Print* button, it recommends a valuable area, which is highlighted in a white rectangle (Figure 1(a)). The user can also preview the recommended print content (Figure 1(b)) at this time. Then, the user can interactively add or remove any content blocks on this page. For example, as shown in Figure 1(c) the recipe title "sausage-strata" is added and some uninformative clips, i.e. the six black rectangles

[1]An extension of Web browser, download from http:www.hp.com/go/smartprint

[2]http://www.diabeticlifestyle.com/recipes/breakfast/sausage-strata

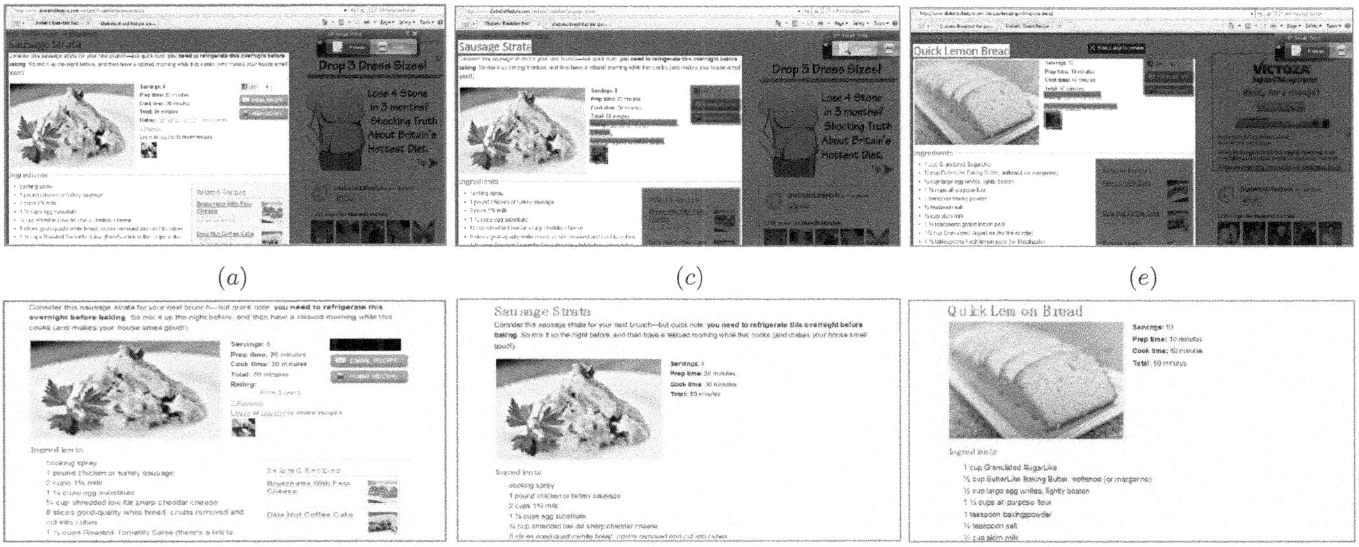

(a) (c) (e)

(b) (d) (f)

Figure 1: The Screenshoots of SmartPrint.

inside the big white rectangle, are removed. Finally, you can see that we get exactly what we want by the current print preview as shown in Figure 1(d)). Through this whole process, we see clearly that, many tedious user efforts are still required in *Smart Print*. And what is more, when we want to print similar Web pages, e.g. print another recipe from the same Web site, we have to do the tedious selection again. It means that in current *Smart Print* users' efforts are utilized only once and then discarded. But in fact these users' selections are very valuable to help us to understand users' interests and printing intentions.

Therefore, a more intelligent solution to clipping Web pages is in urgent need, where the user efforts in selecting the content areas are eliminated or greatly alleviated. Ideally, only one click is required in Clipping any Web page. To this end we leverage the wisdom of the crowds for more accurate recommendation. Here, the wisdom of the crowds comes from the log data on how previous users clip the Web pages. The print logs can be collected by *Smart Print* with users' permission. At a high level, we want to learn from the print log what other users were printing for a particular Web page and then recommend the learned selection to the current user. For example, assume that the selection on the "sausage-strata" Web page (Figure 1(c)) is shared to our knowledge repository. Then, if another user wants to print another recipe page about "quick-lemon-bread"[3], by leveraging the print logs our method can directly recommend the perfect informative clips (as shown in Figure 1(e)(f)) without manual selection. Interested readers can also watch a demo video[4] of this work to taste its effectiveness.

Table 1: The transaction database for Figure 1(c) and 1(e)

Transaction	Items
Figure 1(c)	{A B C D E F G H}
Figure 1(e)	{A B C D E F G}

In fact, these log data can be represented as a *transaction database* where each transaction contains the content clips selected by a user on a Web page. For example, Table 1 shows a transaction database for the content clips selected in Figure 1(c) and 1(e), where items A and B represent the two white rectangles (clips) and items C,D,E,F,G,H represent the six black rectangles. Then, with this transaction database we formulate a novel pattern mining problem, *mining top-1 qualified pattern*, for accurate informative clips recommendation on any given Web pages. It considers both the pattern *support* and the pattern *occupancy*. Previous studies widely consider support as the primary measure of pattern interestingness. In this study we introduce an another measure, *occupancy*, which requires that patterns should occupy a large portion of the transactions they appear in. Thus, intuitively the patterns with both high support and high occupancy may lead to both precise and complete recommendation. We summarize our contributions in this study as follows:

- We harness the wisdom of the crowds for more accurate Web page clipping. We formulate this task as a pattern mining problem on transaction databases. Besides the widely-studied pattern support, we propose a new concept, pattern *occupancy*, which measures the occupancy degree of a pattern inside the transactions it appears in. Thus, pattern support together with occupancy may lead to both precise and complete recommendation.
- We propose an efficient algorithm for this pattern mining problem with the constraints of both support and occupancy. Specifically, we explore the properties on occupancy, which can further prune the search space compared with the search process of frequent pattern mining.
- We demonstrate the effectiveness of the proposed algorithm on a human-labeled ground truth dataset consisting of 2000 Web pages from 100 major print-worthy Web sites. The average precision and recall of the proposed method reach more than 90%. Compared with the baseline method without the support of the wisdom of the crowds the precision increases 23.8% and the recall increases 5.1%. In addition, we also show the efficiency of the proposed algorithm on large synthetic datasets. Our algorithm runs faster than the baseline method by several orders of magnitude.

The rest of the paper is organized as follows. We describe the related work in Section 2. We formulate the task of clipping Web pages as a pattern mining problem in Section 3 and propose the efficient algorithm to solve it in Section 4. We address the issues on how to identify and represent informative clips in Web pages in Section 5 and summarize the whole solution in Section 6. We report an empirical study in Section 7 and finally conclude the paper in Section 8.

[3]http://www.diabeticlifestyle.com/recipes/bread/quick-lemon-bread

[4]http://goo.gl/VixPl

2. RELATED WORKS

Web page clipping has received substantial interests in literature [12, 14, 3, 10, 8, 16, 9]. Most existing methods only attempt to focus on extracting *article* Web pages. For example, Pasternack and Roth [12] proposed a method based on the maximum subsequence segmentation to generate scores for words using features of tri-grams and tags. Wang et al.[14] proposed a SVM-based template-independent wrapper with the content and spatial features to identify two minimum sub-trees containing title and article body. Luo et al. [10] utilized the visual and DOM tree based features to identify paragraphs as basic elements and then find the region for the main content by the maximum subsequence algorithm. Furthermore, some other heuristics are used to filter out the non-informative clips within the main content region. Fan et al. proposed a full-fledged system to extract title, text-body, content-related images and image captions from any article Web page [3] and achieved a high extraction accuracy.

However, such methods make use of the some prior assumptions on the layouts and formats of article Web pages and only work well for text-dominant Web pages such as news and blogs. They may not work well on non-article Web pages such as shopping, recipes or other types of Web pages where the informative clips are scattered irregularly in different formats. For non-article pages Lim et al. [9] proposed a semi-automatic tool *Smart Print* which can automatically select the main content of the web page in the first round and then allows the users to make adjustments. All of these previous works leverage the features of DOM tree, text or visual information on the given Web page. To our best knowledge, this work is the first study to show the log data on how previous users clip the Web pages can greatly improve the accuracy in clipping any Web page.

Pattern mining algorithms are adopted for the recommendation of informative clips. Frequent pattern mining [1] has been well recognized to be fundamental to many important data mining tasks. There is a great amount of work that studies efficient mining of frequent patterns [5, 6, 7, 2, 11]. These algorithms can be classified into mining frequent patterns [5, 6, 7], frequent maximal patterns [2], and frequent closed patterns [11]. To reduce the number of frequent patterns some interestingness measures and constraints are proposed [13, 4]. The concept of occupancy proposed in this paper can be viewed as a new interestingness measure. However, it is not *anti-monotonic*, *monotonic*, *convertible*, and *succinct* [4], thus, no previous methods can be leveraged. In this study we explored the properties on occupancy and show how it can be used to greatly prune the search space. The experimental result shows its superiority in efficiency over the other methods.

3. WEB PAGE CLIPPING BASED ON PATTERN MINING

In this section we will detail how to transform our task of Web page clipping based on the print logs into a pattern mining problem. First, we will briefly describe this task as follows.

3.1 Brief Description

The task of Web page clipping is actually to recommend a set of informative clips for the given Web page. In this application we assume that a log database is given for the Web pages from a Web site, where each piece of log records all informative clips a previous user selected on one of these Web pages. If we consider each clip as an *item*, then any piece of log becomes a *transaction* (set) of items and the log database becomes a *transaction database* [1]. The details on how to identify a clip in a Web page will be addressed later in Section 5.

Although the selections from different users may be different due to their own use habits and interests, generally their selections on similar Web pages may reach certain degree of consensus since the user intensions in clipping certain Web pages may be similar. Then, our task is to mine users' interests and intensions in clipping these Web pages and then provide more accurate recommendation.

The key question to this task is how to measure the *quality* of a clipping pattern (a set of items). On one hand, the more frequently a pattern appears in the database (it means a large number of users select this set of informative clips), the better it is. Thus, the *support* of a pattern is a key factor to its quality. On the other hand, we prefer the pattern which occupies a large portion of the transactions it appears in. Note that besides the items in a given pattern a transaction may include some other ones. If we apply the pattern onto the Web page corresponding to this transaction, all these other items will be missed. Intuitively, the patterns with high occupancy may lead to more complete recommendations. Thus, it is another factor of its quality. Altogether, patterns with bigger values of support and occupancy are preferred. With this motivation we give some definitions and notations as follows, and then formulate the problem.

3.2 Definitions and Notations

A *transaction database*[5] is a set of transactions, where each *transaction* is a set of items. Let $\mathcal{I}$ be the complete set of distinct items and $\mathcal{T}$ be the complete set of transactions. Any non-empty set of items is called an *itemset* and any set of transactions is called a *transaction set*. The transactions that contain all the items in an itemset X are the *supporting transactions* of X, denoted as $\mathcal{T}_X$. The *frequency* of an itemset X (denoted as $freq(X)$) is the number of transactions in $\mathcal{T}_X$.

The following two definitions are adopted from [1].

Definition 1 (Support): The *support* of X is defined as

$$\sigma(X) = freq(X)/|\mathcal{T}| \qquad \blacksquare$$

Definition 2 (Frequent Itemset): For a given minimum support threshold α ($0 < \alpha \leq 1$), X is said to be *frequent* if $\sigma(X) \geq \alpha$. ■

In this application, the itemset we intend to find should also occupy a large portion of the transactions in which it appears. We can calculate the occupancy degree as follows. For an itemset X we identify all its supporting transactions $\mathcal{T}_X$. For each transaction $t \in \mathcal{T}_X$ we calculate the ratio of $\frac{|X|}{|t|}$, where $|X|$ and $|t|$ represents the number of items in X and t, respectively. We then aggregate these ratios to compute a single value of occupancy for X. In this paper we focus on the *harmonic* average of these ratios while other aggregate functions such as *quantile* or *min* may also be considered. The definition of occupancy is given as follows.

Definition 3 (Occupancy): Formally, the *occupancy* of an itemset X is defined as

$$\phi(X) = \frac{freq(X)|X|}{\sum_{t \in \mathcal{T}_X} |t|}$$

where t is any support transaction of X. ■

In other words, the occupancy of an itemset X is the ratio of the occurrences of the items in X to the total number of the items in $\mathcal{T}_X$ (the supporting transactions of X). The high value of the

[5]This term is commonly used by the frequent pattern mining community, such as [1].

occupancy indicates that besides the items in X there are only a small number of items left inside the supporting transactions of X. Thus, the itemset with high occupancy is preferred.

Take the transaction database in Figure 2 as an example. Consider the itemset $\{BC\}$. Its supporting transactions are $\{1, 2, 4, 6\}$, the support $\sigma(\{BC\}) = \frac{4}{6}$, and the occupancy $\phi(\{BC\}) = \frac{4\times 2}{3+2+2+3} = \frac{4}{5}$.

In some sense, occupancy describes the *relative size* of an itemset to its supporting transactions. One may compare it to the *absolute size* of an itemset, i.e., the number of items it contains. For example, in [15], Wang et al. formulated the problem of finding the top-k frequent itemsets that have absolute size larger than min_l, so the absolute size of a itemset was used as measure on its quality. However, in many cases where transactions in the database varies in sizes, occupancy provides a more accurate and normalized score on the quality of the itemset. Later we will also empirically prove the superiority of occupancy over absolute size of an itemset on the application of web-print recommendation.

One may think that the itemset with a larger absolute size leads to a bigger value of occupancy. However, it is not always true. Here, we generate another transaction database based on the one in Figure 2. There are also 6 transactions in it, where the first 5 ones are the same with the ones in Figure 2 and the last one changes to $\{BCDEFGHI\}$. In this new transaction database $\phi(\{BC\})$ changes to $\frac{4\times 2}{3+2+2+8} = \frac{8}{15}$ while $\phi(\{BCD\}) = \frac{3}{8}$. Clearly, $\phi(\{BCD\}) < \phi(\{BC\})$. The reason is that BCD only appears in large transactions where it only occupies a small fraction, while BC appears in many smaller transactions where it occupies a large fraction. Thus, occupancy does not always increase monotonically when we add more items to an itemset. Similarly, we can show that occupancy does not always decrease monotonically when we add more items to an itemset either. This non-monotonic property of occupancy is in contrast to that of support in frequent pattern mining.

Definition 4 (Dominant Itemset): For a given minimum occupancy threshold β ($0 < \beta \leq 1$), X is said to be *dominant* if $\phi(X) \geq \beta$. ■

With the definition of support and occupancy we can measure the *quality* of an itemset by combining these two factors.

Definition 5 (Quality): The *quality* of an itemset X is defined as $q(X) = \sigma(X) + \lambda\phi(X)$, where occupancy weight $0 \leq \lambda < +\infty$ is a user defined parameter to capture the relative importance of support and occupancy. ■

Definition 6 (Qualified Itemset): For a given minimum support threshold α and a minimum occupancy threshold β ($0 < \alpha, \beta \leq 1$), X is said to be *qualified* if $\sigma(X) \geq \alpha$ and $\phi(X) \geq \beta$. ■

Assume that we have the log database which records how previous users clipped the Web pages from a Web site. Given a Web page from the same Web site, we aim to recommend the informative clips for this Web page. More specifically, let $\mathcal{I}$ be the complete set of distinct clips in the database. For a given Web page we can get a set $Q \subseteq \mathcal{I}$ of clips which are included in this Web page. It is meaningless to recommend the informative clips which are not in the given Web page (how to determine Q will be addressed in Section 5). Thus, our task is to select a subset of Q for the clip recommendation.

In this application it is required that interesting patterns should be both frequent and dominant. On one hand, if a pattern F is frequent it means that there are enough cases such a pattern appears in the transaction database. Thus, it may improve the recommendation precision. On the other hand, if X is dominant it indicates that the recommendation of X is complete enough. Therefore, with the definition of support and occupancy, we formulate the problem of mining top-1 qualified patterns as follows.

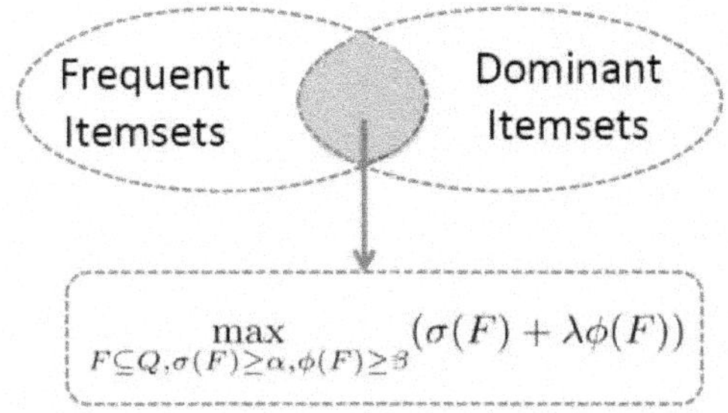

Figure 3: The problem of mining top-1 qualified pattern

3.3 Problem Formulation

Mining Top-1 Qualified Pattern. With the definition of support, occupancy and quality, we describe our recommendation method as follows. The recommended itemset is $F \subseteq Q$ which has the maximal quality value among the qualified itemsets (for a given support threshold α and a occupancy threshold β). Formally, it is

$$\arg\max_{F: F\subseteq Q, \sigma(F)\geq\alpha, \phi(F)\geq\beta} (\sigma(F) + \lambda\phi(F)) \quad (1)$$

This problem formulation is illustrated in Figure 3. Actually, we aim to find the top-1 qualified itemset among the intersection area of frequent and dominant itemsets.

There are three parameters in the definition of the top-1 qualified pattern, namely α, β, λ. If there is no itemset that is both frequent and dominant with respect to α, β, the top-1 qualified pattern does not exist and it will not output any result since no non-empty pattern exists that meets the quality requirements. Parameter λ, the occupancy weight, is a user defined parameter to capture the relative importance of support and occupancy.

One may think that dominant patterns with high occupancy usually contain a large number of items and thus methods based on *Maximal Frequent Itemset* (an itemset X is a maximal frequent itemset if X is frequent and no superset of X is frequent [2]) mining may also work in this application. Specifically, given a support threshold we can get multiple maximal frequent itemsets. Among them we can select the one with the largest number of items for the recommendation. Is this a valid method for our task? The answer is "no" for the following reasons. First, in methods based on mining maximal frequent itemsets, the number of items in a pattern is used as a measure in pattern selection. Compared with the concept of occupancy, this is actually the *absolute* size of an itemset while occupancy is the *relative* size of an itemset to the number of items in its supporting transactions. Among all the frequent itemsets, the maximal frequent itemset selected usually has very low support, thus leading to a low precision in recommendation. Secondly, in mining top qualified pattern a weighted sum of both support and occupancy is used as the interestingness measure, which may lead to better recommendation performance compared to the patterns selected by methods based on maximal frequent itemsets. The experimental results in Section 7 further validate our analysis here.

As mentioned before, Wang et al. [15] formulated a similar pattern mining task, i.e. the top-k frequent itemset with sizes larger than a minimum threshold. Here we can immediately see the differences of our problem to that problem: first, we use occupancy, the relative size, rather the absolute size of an itemset as an interesting-

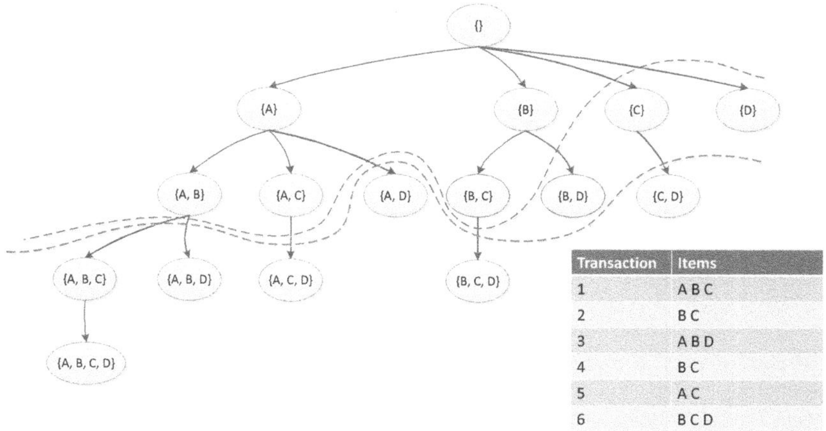

Transaction	Items
1	A B C
2	B C
3	A B D
4	B C
5	A C
6	B C D

Figure 2: The example of the transaction database and lexicographic subset tree ($\alpha = 0.2, \beta = 0, \lambda = 2$)

ness measure; second, we use the the weighted sum of support and occupancy, rather than just the support as the quality of an itemset.

Next we will propose an efficient algorithm to this new pattern mining problem.

4. EFFICIENT PATTERN MINING ALGORITHM

The straightforward solution to the pattern mining problem is to first generate all the frequent itemsets, calculate the occupancy value for each frequent itemset, and then select the qualified itemset with maximum quality value. In this section we will show how the properties on occupancy and quality measures can be injected deeply into the search process and greatly prune the search space.

Pattern mining algorithms usually adopt the *lexicographic subset tree* [2, 11] to guide the search process. See Figure 2 as an example for four items A, B, C, D. The top element in the lattice is the empty set and each lower level l contains all the l-itemsets (itemsets with exactly l items). The l-itemsets are ordered lexicographically on each level. Generating children in this manner enumerates all the distinct itemsets to be considered without redundancy. As there are 4 items, there are in total $2^4 = 16$ itemsets for consideration. Thus, in the lexicographic subset tree there are 16 nodes, each of which corresponds to an itemset. Frequent pattern mining usually leverages the *monotonic decreasing* property of support values when adding more items to a given itemset. That is, if an itemset X is not frequent then all the supersets of X are not frequent either. Thus, the traversal in the tree is to find a cut (the red line in Figure 2) such that all the nodes (itemsets) above the cut are frequent, and all the nodes below the line are infrequent.

Note in our task of clip recommendation we only consider the items in Q, namely the clips identified in the given Web page (here, $\mathcal{I}$ may contain the distinct clips in the logs from the same Web site). Thus, the lexicographic subset tree only includes the items in Q. The search space becomes much smaller compared with the one on the complete set of distinct items.

4.1 Algorithm Overview

With the proposed occupancy and quality measure we can further prune the search space. Specifically, we can give the upper bounds of the occupancy and quality values for all the nodes in a subtree. In other words, the occupancy or quality of any node in a given subtree will be no bigger than its upper bound. If the upper bound on the occupancy is smaller than the occupancy threshold β, the corresponding subtree will be pruned. Also, we can maintain the current biggest quality value in the search process, denoted by $q*$. Then, the subtrees with the upper bounds less than $q*$ will be pruned.

Take the subtree with the root $\{C\}$ in Figure 2 as an example. We can give an upper bound of the quality for all the nodes in the subtree, including $\{C\}, \{CD\}$. Currently, this upper bound is less than the quality of node $\{BC\}$. Thus, this subtree is trimmed. The blue line (which is above the red one) in Figure 2 is the cut line for our problem. Clearly, it further reduces the search space.

Next, we will propose the properties to show how the upper bounds on occupancy and quality are computed.

4.2 The Upper Bounds on Occupancy and Quality

First, we give the notations which will be widely used in the following properties. For any subtree, let X be the itemset for the subtree root, Y be the itemset including all the new items which will be extended in all the descendants of this subtree. For example, for the subtree root $X = \{A\}$ there are three new items B, C, D which will appears in the descendants. Thus, $Y = \{BCD\}$. Then, we have the following properties.

Lemma 1: For any itemset W in the subtree of X let u be the frequency of W. Then, the occupancy of W satisfies that

$$\phi(W) \le \frac{u|X| + \max_{l_1,\cdots,l_u}\sum_{i=1}^{u}|t_{l_i}\cap Y|}{\min_{l_1,\cdots,l_u}\sum_{i=1}^{u}|t_{l_i}\cap(\mathcal{I}-Y)| + \max_{l_1,\cdots,l_u}\sum_{i=1}^{u}|t_{l_i}\cap Y|}, \quad (2)$$

where t_{l_i} is any supporting transaction for X and $\mathcal{I}$ is the complete set of distinct items. ∎

Proof: Remember that Y is the itemset including all the new items which will be extended in the descendants, X is the root of the subtree. Now we consider the occupancy of W.

$$\phi(W) = \frac{u|W|}{\sum_{t\in\mathcal{T}_W}|t|} \quad (3)$$

$$= \frac{u|X| + \sum_{t\in\mathcal{T}_W}|t\cap(W-X)|}{\sum_{t\in\mathcal{T}_W}|t|} \quad (4)$$

$$\le \frac{u|X| + \sum_{t\in\mathcal{T}_W}|t\cap Y|}{\sum_{t\in\mathcal{T}_W}|t\cap(\mathcal{I}-Y)| + \sum_{t\in\mathcal{T}_W}|t\cap Y|} \quad (5)$$

$$\le \frac{u|X| + \max_{l_1,\cdots,l_u}\sum_{i=1}^{u}|t_{l_i}\cap Y|}{\sum_{t\in\mathcal{T}_W}|t_{l_i}\cap(\mathcal{I}-Y)| + \max_{l_1,\cdots,l_u}\sum_{i=1}^{u}|t_{l_i}\cap Y|} \quad (6)$$

$$\le \frac{u|X| + \max_{l_1,\cdots,l_u}\sum_{i=1}^{u}|t_{l_i}\cap Y|}{\min_{l_1,\cdots,l_u}\sum_{i=1}^{u}|t_{l_i}\cap(\mathcal{I}-Y)| + \max_{l_1,\cdots,l_u}\sum_{i=1}^{u}|t_{l_i}\cap Y|} \quad (7)$$

where $t_{l_1},\cdots,t_{l_u}$ be any supporting transactions of X.

Inequality (5) comes from $Z - X \subseteq Y$. Inequality (6) comes from the inequality that if $b > a > 0, \gamma \ge 0$, then $\frac{a}{b} \le \frac{a+\gamma}{b+\gamma}$. ∎

Note that the right hand side of Equation (7) is only dependant on u, X, Y. Thus, it can be denoted as $F(u, X, Y)$. Then, we also have

Lemma 2: $F(u+1, X, Y) \leq F(u, X, Y)$ ■

Proof: Let α_k be the k-th largest value in the vector $\langle |t \cap Y| : t \in \mathcal{T}_W \rangle$, and β_k be the k-th smallest value in the vector $\langle |t \cap (\mathcal{I} - Y)| : t \in \mathcal{T}_W \rangle$. Then, by this definition we have $\alpha_{k+1} \leq \alpha_k$, $\beta_{k+1} \geq \beta_k$. Clearly,

$$F(u+1, X, Y) = \frac{\sum_{i=1}^{u+1}(|X| + \alpha_i)}{\sum_{i=1}^{u+1}(\beta_i + \alpha_i)} \tag{8}$$

For any k $(1 \leq k \leq u)$ we have

$$\frac{|X| + \alpha_k}{\beta_k + \alpha_k} \geq \frac{|X| + \alpha_k}{\beta_{u+1} + \alpha_k} \geq \frac{|X| + \alpha_{u+1}}{\beta_{u+1} + \alpha_{u+1}} \tag{9}$$

Then,

$$F(u, X, Y) = \frac{\sum_{i=1}^{u}(|X| + \alpha_i)}{\sum_{i=1}^{u}(\beta_i + \alpha_i)} \geq \frac{|X| + \alpha_{u+1}}{\beta_{u+1} + \alpha_{u+1}} \tag{10}$$

So

$$F(u, X, Y) \geq \frac{\sum_{i=1}^{u}(|X| + \alpha_i) + |X| + \alpha_{u+1}}{\sum_{i=1}^{u}(\beta_i + \alpha_i) + \beta_{u+1} + \alpha_{u+1}} = F(u+1, X, Y) \tag{11}$$

Inequality (10) comes from the property that if $1 \geq \frac{a_i}{b_i} \geq \frac{c}{d}$ for any i, then $\frac{\sum a_i}{\sum b_i} \geq \frac{c}{d}$.
Inequality (11) comes from the property that if $1 \geq \frac{a}{b} \geq \frac{c}{d}$, then $\frac{a}{b} \geq \frac{a+c}{b+d}$. ■

It is required that itemset W be frequent. Thus, the frequency of W is not smaller than $\alpha \cdot |\mathcal{T}|$. As shown in Lemma 2, $F(u, X, Y)$ will not decrease along the decrease of u. Then, we have

Theorem 1:

$$\phi(W) \leq F(u, X, Y) \leq F(u', X, Y)$$

where u' is the minimal integer which is not smaller than $\alpha \cdot |\mathcal{T}|$. ■

In other words, u' is the minimal frequency value which satisfies the support threshold α. Theorem 1 actually gives an upper bound on the occupancy values of the itemsets in the subtree.

Theorem 2:

$$q(W) \leq \max_{\alpha \cdot |\mathcal{T}| \leq k \leq |\mathcal{T}_X|} \left(\frac{k}{|\mathcal{T}|} + \lambda F(k, X, Y)\right),$$

where k is an integer between $\alpha \cdot |\mathcal{T}|$ and $|\mathcal{T}_X|$. ■

Proof: Let u be the frequency of W. Then,

$$q(W) = \frac{u}{|\mathcal{T}|} + \lambda\phi(W) \leq \frac{u}{|\mathcal{T}|} + \lambda F(u, X, Y) \tag{12}$$

It is required that itemset W be frequent. Thus, $\alpha \cdot |\mathcal{T}| \leq u \leq |\mathcal{T}_X|$. Then,

$$\frac{u}{|\mathcal{T}|} + \lambda F(u, X, Y) \leq \max_{\alpha \cdot |\mathcal{T}| \leq k \leq |\mathcal{T}_X|} \left(\frac{k}{|\mathcal{T}|} + \lambda F(k, X, Y)\right) \tag{13}$$

It follows the conclusion. ■

Theorem 2 actually gives an upper bound on the quality values of the itemsets in the subtree.

5. IDENTIFICATION OF WEB PAGE CLIP-S

So far we assume that the transaction database of print logs is provided in advance. In this section we will detail how to identify the clips in a Web page. We first give some preliminaries on Web page analysis before we address these details.

5.1 Preliminaries on Web Page Analysis

Here, we provide some preliminaries for DOM (Document Object Model) tree, DOM tree path and Web page rendering, which are the key concepts in Web page analysis.

DOM Tree. A DOM tree for any HTML or XML document is defined as a tuple $T = \{V, E, L_V, F_V\}$, where V is the set of vertices, $E \subseteq V \times V$ is the set of edges, L_V is the set of vertex labels, and $F_V : V \rightarrow L_V$ maps the vertices to their labels. Figure 4(a) shows an example of DOM tree.

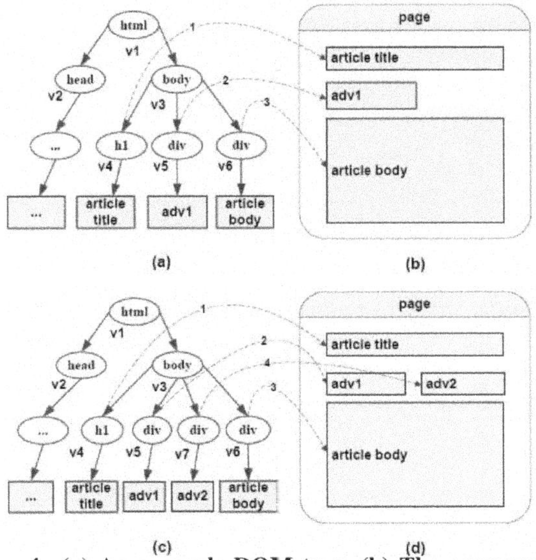

Figure 4: (a) An example DOM tree; (b) The corresponding Web page for Figure 1(a); (c) Another example DOM tree with one more adv; (d) The corresponding Web page for Figure 1(c).

DOM Tree Path. A DOM Tree Path (DTPath for short) for a node v in a DOM tree T is a sequence of label-position pairs, i.e. $P_v = ((l_1, k_1), \cdots, (l_n, k_n))$, where l_i is the combination of HTML tag and attributes of $node_i$ and k_i is the relative position among its sibling nodes. It records the path from the root of T to node v. For example, the DTPath of the node v_5 and v_6 in Figure 4(a) is *((html,1),(body,1),(div,1))* and *((html,1),(body,1),(div,2))* respectively. Note that in this example the attributes on each node are omitted from the DTPath just for description convenience. S-ince the node attributes contain much format and style information especially when CSS (Cascading Style Sheets) is more and more popular in Web page design, practically they help to identify the informative clips more precisely.

Matching. The DTPath P is *matched* in a DOM tree T, denoted by $P \sqsubset T$, if and only if there exists a path from the root node to an internal node in T such that the sequence along this path is exactly P. Consider Figure 4(a) again. We can say the DTPath $((html, 1), (body, 1), (h1, 1))$ can be matched in this tree since along this path we reach node v_4. However, the DTPath $((html, 1), (body, 1), (div, 3))$ can not be matched in this tree.

Web Page Rendering. The whole HTML document appears in a Web browser after *rendering*. The rendering process actually assigns each DOM tree node a *bounding rectangle*, identifying where the content inside the node is displayed in the browser. Thus, a node v also corresponds to a unique bounding rectangle. Figure 4(b) shows the Web page corresponding to the DOM tree in Figure 4(a). As you can see, v_4, v_5, v_6 corresponds to the three rectangles of *article title*, *adv1*, and *article body* respectively.

The tool of Smart Print provides the interactive interface in a Web browser, where users can select the informative clips in a Web page. Actually, each clip is identified by a bounding rectangle, which then corresponds to a node in the DOM tree of the Web page. Thus, any clip can be identified by the DTPath of the selected node in the DOM tree. Then, a piece of clipping log actually contains a set of DTPaths.

5.2 Match a Set of DOM Tree Paths

To recommend informative clips we need to get all the clips which are included in a given Web page. Recommending the informative clips which are not in the given Web page is meaningless. As each clip is represented by its DTPath, this task is to match a set of DTPaths to a given DOM tree. More specifically, let $\mathcal{I}$ be the complete set of distinct DTPaths in the database. We aim to find all the DTPaths in $\mathcal{I}$, which can be matched in the given DOM tree T. Formally, this set Q is $\{P|P \in \mathcal{I} \cap P \sqsubset T\}$. These clips are the recommendation candidates in the given Web pages.

A straightforward method to this task is to consider each DTPath separately. Then, its complexity to n DTPaths is $o(\sum_{i=1}^{n} N_i)$ where N_i is the number of nodes in the i-th DTPath.

5.3 Generalized DOM Tree Paths

So far the DTPath considers the HTML tag and attributes of a node, and also its relative position among its siblings. However, the match of such DTPaths is not robust to the change of DOM tree structures. See the examples in Figure 4. The Web page in Figure 4(b) contains one advertisement, and the DTPath for *article body* is

$$P : ((html, 1), (body, 1), (div\{id = \text{“}article\_body\text{”}\}, \mathbf{2}))$$

The Web page in Figure 4(d) has the same Web page template with the one in Figure 4(b). However, one more advertisement is inserted into the page. Thus, the DTPath for *article body* in Figure 4(d) changes to

$$P' : ((html, 1), (body, 1), (div\{id = \text{“}article\_body\text{”}\}, \mathbf{3}))$$

P and P' are two distinct items in the transaction database even though they refer to the same type of content clips. It indicates that the transaction database generated by such DTPathes will be very sparse. Additionally, the clip for *article body* in Figure 4(d) will be missed if we apply P to match it. Thus, such DTPathes are vulnerable to the change of DOM tree structures.

After some empirical studies we find that this situation happens quite often, and is worth careful consideration. We address this issue by proposing *generalized* DTPaths by which we do not consider the relative positions for some nodes during the matching process. Specifically, we require that two distinct DTPathes should be combined as a generalized one when they are different only at the position indexes for some nodes in the pathes. For example, except the position indexes of the third nodes the other parts of the two paths P and P' are the same. Thus, they should be combined as a generalized DTPath

$$P^* : ((html, 1), (body, 1), (div\{id = \text{“}article\_body\text{”}\}, *))$$

where $*$ can be any integer. It indicates that we will not consider the position index of the third node in this path when matching. Using the generalized DTPath P^* the clips of *article body* in Figures 4(b) and (d) can be identified successfully. Readers may also worry that some more clips will be matched by the generalized DTPaths since a generalized DTPath can match multiple clips. We argue that this situation is acceptable since the identified clips by a generalized DTPath appear in the same format and style (remember that the attributes of the HTML nodes are used here).

After this combination the number of distinct generalized DTPaths is much smaller than that of the original DTPaths. Thus, the item size of the corresponding transaction database becomes much smaller, leading to more efficient pattern mining. Additionally, the database becomes more dense, which definitely helps to find the patterns in clipping the Web pages by users.

6. SOLUTION SUMMARY

We summarize the solution framework in Figure 5.

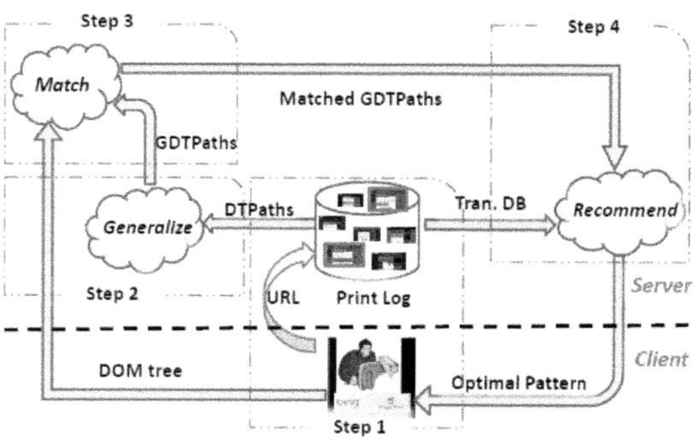

Figure 5: The Solution Framework.

Step 1. After a clipping request is fired, the client first sends the url and DOM tree of the current Web page to the server. Then, the server looks up in the log database to collect the print logs from the same Web site of the give URL. Based on these logs, it construct the corresponding transaction database $\mathcal{T}$ and all the distinct DTPaths $\mathcal{P}$ in these logs are also identified.

Step 2. Given the complete set $\mathcal{P}$ of distinct DTPaths we combine them to a set $\mathcal{P}^*$ of generalized DTPaths. Accordingly, we generate the transaction database based on the generalized DTPaths. See the details in Section 5.3.

Step 3. Identify the generalized DTPaths which is matched in the current DOM tree T. The set of the matched generalized DTPaths is denoted by Q. See the details in Section 5.2.

Step 4. Generate the pattern F in Equation 1 using the efficient algorithm in Section 4. Finally, the clips identified by the generalized DTPaths in F are recommended to the given Web page.

7. EXPERIMENTAL STUDY

In this section we present an empirical evaluation of our proposed method. Specifically, we show the effectiveness of the proposed pattern mining algorithm on a human-labeled ground-truth dataset including 2000 Web pages, discuss the impact from the method parameters and show the efficiency of our method on the synthetic datasets.

7.1 Data and Baseline Methods

A human-labeled ground truth dataset [6] consisting of 2000 Web pages was collected from 100 major print-worthy Web sites. These Web sites were selected from the 10 Web site types, namely *DIY, Recipe, Shopping, News, Jobs, Science, Article, Leaning, Travel and Sports*. They are top Web site types, which attract large numbers of Web page printing. For each Web site type we selected 10 Web sites, and for each Web site we selected 20 Web pages. The

[6]http://home.ustc.edu.cn/ stone/files/Publications/Data.zip

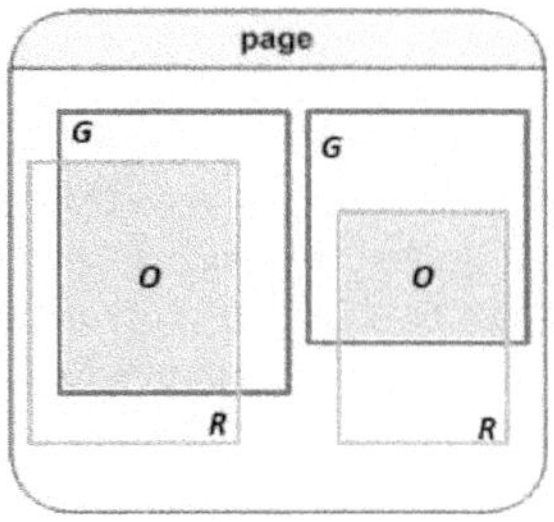

Figure 6: The region overlap

Web pages from the same Web site may have the different Web templates. On each Web page we manually select the informative clips as the ground truth.

We compare the proposed solution Clipping via Crowd Intelligence (**CIC** for short) with two baseline methods. The first one is the method used in the tool of Smart Print [9] (**SP** for short). This tool analyzes the visual features of a given Web page and aims to select one clip for the *main content* as recommendation. This recommendation usually covers a big area, inside which it may contain un-informative junks. Note that this is a method without the support of the wisdom of the crowds. The other baseline method is based on Maximal Frequent Itemset mining (**MFI** for short) over the transaction database for the clipping log data. Specifically, we can first generate all the maximal frequent itemsets and among them select the one with the largest number of items for recommendation.

7.2 Evaluation Method and Measure

We use leave-one-out cross validation to evaluate the accuracy of the methods on the data-sets. For the 20 Web pages from a Web site, we iteratively select one page as query and the log data on the remaining 19 Web pages are used to generate the transaction database for recommendation. The result is then compared against the ground truth of the query page.

A recommendation result actually refers to a set of content clips on the given Web page. Thus, we can evaluate its effectiveness by calculating the overlap area between the recommended clips and the ground truth. Note that each clip corresponds a bounding rectangular (area) with four coordinates (i.e. x, y, height and width) after rendering in the browser and we can easily get those coordinates. See the evaluation example in Figure 6. The two blue rectangles refers to the two clips selected by a user, and the two green ones refers to the two clips recommended by our methods. Thus, the Area O is their overlap area. Then, with the overlap area we can calculate the precision P, recall R and $F1$ score of the recommendation in terms of area size. Specifically,

$$P = \frac{|A_G \cap A_R|}{|A_R|}, R = \frac{|A_G \cap A_R|}{|A_G|}, F1 = 2 \times \frac{P \times R}{P + R}$$

Where A_G is the clipping region of ground truth, A_R is the clipping region of the recommendation result and $|\ldots|$ denotes the region size. If the precision is less than 1, it means that we need to remove some areas from the recommendation. If the recall is less than 1, it indicates that we need to add some contents to get the exact clipping areas.

7.3 Experimental Results

Effectiveness. Table 2 records the average precision, recall and F1 score of the three methods on each Web site type. Specifically, we average the performance values over the 200 Web pages from each Web site type. In the recommendation we set $\alpha = 0.01$, $\beta = 0.1$ and $\lambda = 2$. The average precision and recall over all the 2000 Web pages of CIC reach 92.46% and 94.93% respectively. Compared with the SP method, CIC increases 23.81% in precision and 5.14% in recall. This clearly shows that leveraging the wisdom of the crowds greatly improves the recommendation performance. Compared with the best MFI result ($\alpha = 0.1$) in Table 3, CIC increases 1.34% in recall and 0.42% in precision. It indicates that CIC helps to find better patterns for recommendation. The reason why CIC can find better pattern has been detailed discussed in Section 3.3.

Table 2: The average recommendation performance (%) of CIC and SP on each Web site type ($\alpha = 0.01$, $\beta = 0.1$ and $\lambda = 2$)

WebSite Type	CIC			SP		
	P	*R*	*F1*	*P*	*R*	*F1*
DIY	89.34	93.7	89.85	70.14	93.31	76.43
Recipe	92.82	96.7	94.23	70.94	96.91	78.56
Shopping	80.96	89.69	83.11	34.81	81.61	41.47
News	93.3	94.82	93.36	68.99	78.14	66.23
Jobs	95.51	94.48	94.16	85.17	97.21	89.11
Science	91.56	92.95	90.96	71.02	89.4	72.01
Article	93.51	95.9	94.3	70.06	89.37	72.13
Learning	95.82	95.28	94.16	69.88	96.77	74.62
Travel	97.44	98.79	97.82	69.25	83.08	64.73
Sports	94.38	97.0	94.76	76.19	92.09	79.59
Average	**92.46**	**94.93**	**92.67**	**68.65**	**89.79**	**71.49**

Table 3: The average recommendation performance (%) of MFI and CIC with different α on the 2000 Web pages

α	MFI			CIC ($\beta = 0.1$,$\lambda = 2$)		
	P	*R*	*F1*	*P*	*R*	*F1*
0.01	91.51	93.16	90.73	**92.46**	**94.93**	**92.67**
0.1	**92.04**	**93.69**	**91.85**	91.64	93.58	91.66
0.2	90.77	90.78	89.52	91.36	93.09	90.97
0.3	90.25	90.63	88.89	89.78	91.27	89.15
0.4	87.8	87.56	86.06	87.79	88.61	86.65
0.5	83.26	81.07	79.36	82.84	83.45	81.32

Table 4: Results of CIC (%) with different λ ($\alpha = 0.01$ and $\beta = 0.1$)

λ	*P*	*R*	*F1*
0.1	91.23	78.66	77.08
0.2	91.54	83.01	80.89
0.4	92.66	85.29	83.54
0.8	92.96	89.9	87.86
1.0	92.49	92.86	90.59
2.0	**92.46**	**94.93**	**92.67**
4.0	92.37	94.19	92.25
8.0	92.15	94.12	92.08
$+\infty$	90.77	91.67	89.53

Impact from λ. The parameter λ decides the trade-off between support and occupancy in the quality measure. Here, we also evaluate its impact on the recommendation performance. Table 4 shows the average performance over 2000 Web pages when λ changes from 0.1 to $+\infty$. $\lambda = +\infty$ means that we only consider occupancy in the quality measure. Clearly, we can see when λ increases from 0.1 to 2 both the precision and recall increase. When λ continues to increase from 2, both the precision and the recall drop. Usually, too much emphasis on frequency will typically recommend informative but uncomplete itemset, in other word, the recommend area R in Figure 6 is small and almost overlap with the overlap area O (Note that the ground truth area G is fixed). Thus, the precision is high and the recall is low when λ is small. With the increase

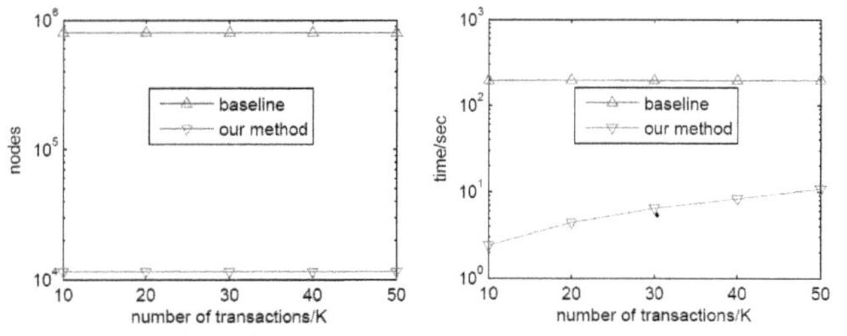

(a) Number of Nodes (b) Running Time

Figure 7: The effects of the number of transactions on MAFIA and our method

of λ from 0.1 to 2, both recommend area R and the overlap area O grow, leading to the large improvement on recall and the slight increase on precision. In contrast, too much emphasis on occupancy will recommend an over-complete itemset with too many items. However, in our application of *Smart Print* there are actually two kinds of items in the database—the positive items (the clips that users select) and the negative items (the clips that users de-select). When λ is increasing from 2 to $+\infty$, the recommendation will include many such negative items, leading to the decrease of overlap area O. Thus, both the precision and the recall drop. For our 2000 Web page data set, $\lambda = 2$ achieves the best result. In practice, λ can be chosen by cross validation to achieve the best performance in similar manners.

Efficiency. To show the efficiency of the proposed pruning methods in Section 4 we compare its running time with the straightforward method to our problem on the synthetic transaction databases with different numbers of transactions. The data sets used in the experiment are generated by the IBM synthetic data generator[7] for itemset patterns. Here, the straightforward method is simply frequent pattern mining with the check on occupancy. The implementation of MAFIA [2], a highly efficient method for finding frequent patterns, is adopted in this comparison. Our method leverages the properties in Section 4 to further prune the search space, thus may achieve better efficiency.

Here, we generate a database of $N = 10000$ transactions and scale it up by vertical concatenation of the database. The results are shown in Figure 7, including the running time and the number of nodes in the subset tree searched by the baseline and our method. Note that in this experiments we only duplicate the database to increase its size. Thus, the number of nodes visited in the subset tree is expected to stay unchanged. As can be seen from Figure 7(a), our method only searches about 1.4% nodes of those searched by the baseline. With respect to running time, our algorithm's running time grows linearly, from 2.45 seconds for 10000 transactions to 10.34 seconds for 50000 transactions. What is interesting is that the baseline's running time remains stable when the number of transactions grows. After careful investigation, we think it is due to the extreme efficiency of bit operators used extensively by MAFIA. However, since it takes the baseline about 195 seconds to run the experiment for each data set, our algorithm is still much faster.

8. CONCLUSIONS

In this work we harness the wisdom of the crowds for accurate Web page clipping. The crowd intelligence comes from the log data on how previous users clip Web pages. We formulate this problem as a new pattern mining task, *mining top-1 qualified pattern*, which considers both the support and occupancy in pattern recommendation. Along this line, we propose the properties on occupancy which helps to greatly prune the search space for high efficiency. In addition, we propose the generalized DOM tree paths to identify content clips in Web pages, and show its robustness to the change of DOM tree structures. Compared with previous works our method significantly improves the accuracy in Web page clipping, which is shown by the experimental study on the 2000 Web pages.

It is worth mentioning that the proposed problem of mining top-K qualified pattern can be useful to other pattern mining applications where each transaction corresponds to a set of actions for a task. Also, we can extend this concept of occupancy in sequential mining.

[7]http://www.cs.rpi.edu/ zaki/www-new/pmwiki.php/Software

9. ACKNOWLEDGEMENTS

The authors Lei Zhang, Enhong Chen and Guiquan Liu are supported by grants from Natural Science Foundation of China (Grant No. 60775037), The National Major Special Science & Technology Projects (Grant No. 2011ZX04016-071), The HeGaoJi National Major Special Science & Technology Projects (Grant No. 2012ZX01029001-002) and Research Fund for the Doctoral Program of Higher Education of China (20093402110017).

10. REFERENCES

[1] R. Agrawal, T. Imielinski, and A. Swami. Mining association rules between sets of items in large databases. In *Proceedings of the ACM SIGMOD*, pages 207–216, 1993.

[2] D. Burdick, M. Calimlim, and J. Gehrke. Mafia: A maximal frequent itemset algorithm for transactional databases. In *Proceedings of the IEEE ICDE*, pages 443–452, 2001.

[3] J. Fan, P. Luo, S. H. Lim, S. Liu, P. Joshi, and J. Liu. Article clipper-a system for web article extraction. In *Proceedings of the ACM SIGKDD*, pages 743–746, 2011.

[4] K. Gade, J. Wang, and G. Karypis. Efficient closed pattern mining in the presence of tough block constraints. In *Proceedings of the ACM SIGKDD*, pages 138–147, 2004.

[5] B. Goethals and M. J.Zaki. Frequent itemset mining implementations. In *Proceedings of the ICDM workshop on Frequent Itemset Mining Implementations*, 2003.

[6] J. Han, J. Pei, and Y. Yin. Mining frequent patterns without candidate generation. In *Proceedings of the ACM SIGMOD*, pages 1–12, 2000.

[7] J. Han, J. Pei, Y. Yin, and R. Mao. Mining frequent patterns without candidate generation: A frequent-pattern tree approach. *Data Mining and Knowledge Discovery*, pages 53–87, 2005.

[8] Y. Hu, G. Xin, R. Song, G. Hu, S. Shi, Y. Cao, and H. Li. Title extraction from bodies of html documents and its application to web page retrieval. In *Proceedings of the ACM SIGIR*, pages 250–257, 2005.

[9] S. H. Lim, L. Zheng, J. Jin, H. Hou, J. Fan, and J. Liu. Automatic selection of print-worthy content for enhanced web page printing experience. In *Proceedings of the ACM DocEng*, pages 165–168, 2010.

[10] P. Luo, J. Fan, S. Liu, F. Lin, Y. Xiong, and J. Liu. Web article extraction for web printing: a dom+visual based approach. In *Proceedings of the ACM DocEng*, pages 66–69, 2009.

[11] N. Pasquier, Y. Bastide, R. Taouil, and L. Lakhal. Discovering frequent closed itemsets for association rules. In *Proceedings of the ACM ICDT*, pages 398–416, 1999.

[12] J. Pasternack and D. Roth. Extracting article text from the web with maximum subsequence segmentation. In *Proceedings of the ACM WWW*, pages 971–980, 2009.

[13] J. Pei, J. Han, and L. Lakshmanan. Mining frequent itemsets with convertible constraints. In *Proceedings of the IEEE ICDE*, pages 433–442, 2001.

[14] J. Wang, C. Chen, C. Wang, J. Pei, J. Bu, Z. Guan, and W. V. Zhang. Can we learn a template-independent wrapper for news article extraction from a single training site? In *Proceedings of the ACM SIGKDD*, pages 1345–1354, 2009.

[15] J. Wang, J. Han, S. Member, Y. Lu, and P. Tzvetkov. Tfp: An efficient algorithm for mining top-k frequent closed itemsets. *IEEE Trans. on Knowledge and Data Engineering*, 17:2005, 2005.

[16] J. Xiao and J. Fan. Printmarmoset: Redesigning the print button for sustainability. In *Proceedings of the ACM CHI*, pages 109–112, 2009.

Bootstrapped Language Identification for Multi-Site Internet Domains

Uwe F. Mayer
eBay Research Labs
2145 Hamilton Ave
San Jose, CA 95125
1-408-558-7400
uwemayer@ebay.com

ABSTRACT
We present an algorithm for language identification, in particular of short documents, for the case of an Internet domain with sites in multiple countries with differing languages. The algorithm is significantly faster than standard language identification methods, while providing state-of-the-art identification. We bootstrap the algorithm based on the language identification based on the site alone, a methodology suitable for any supervised language identification algorithm. We demonstrate the bootstrapping and algorithm on eBay email data and on Twitter status updates data. The algorithm is deployed at eBay as part of the back-office development data repository.

Categories and Subject Descriptors
I.2.7 [**Computing Methodologies**]: Artificial Intelligence – Natural Language Processing.

General Terms
Algorithms, Performance, Design.

Keywords
Language identification, large data, statistical model, boosting.

1. INTRODUCTION
In today's interconnected global Internet community it is quite common that Internet-based businesses (e.g., eBay, Twitter) operate sites in different languages (e.g., ebay.com, ebay.de, ebay.fr, etc., or twitter.com, twitter.com/?lang=de, twitter.com/?lang=fr, etc.). Many such sites have user-contributed content data, private or public, such as web postings, reviews, blogs, or emails. Usually, but not always, either the site which the user employs to generate the content or more often the site on which it is to appear (or which the recipient uses in case of a message) dictates the language used by the creator of the content. Typically one may expect that knowing the site language alone allows language identification of user-provided content with high precision. On the other hand this approach is not expected to be perfect, and one can employ standard language identification algorithms, which even if not specifically trained for the corpus at hand, also achieve usually still high precision. The task is to improve over either approach to determine the language of the user-created documents.

KDD'12, August 12–16, 2012, Beijing, China.

The general idea, of course, is to combine the language identification based on the site language or language from a user profile with some other supervised algorithm. In particular in a web setting one usually has lots of data, however obtaining suitable accurate labels constitutes the bottleneck. Our approach is to use data labeled by the site or the user profile alone for training, and we build a custom model using a supervised algorithm. Then we combine the language identification based on the site or user profile language with the newly trained supervised model to create a final model. The method of combination could be as simple as a linear model.

Most algorithms for language identification, and in particular most modern ones, employ a statistical approach, often not word (dictionary) based, but rather character or n-gram based [1,2,3]. However, these algorithms often perform not optimally if the documents to be classified are short [4].

The archetypical example of shorts text on the web nowadays are Twitter status updates (so-called tweets), which by design are limited to 140 characters. On the other hand, tweets are not the only short prevalent documents on the web. This research grew out of the need to accurately identify the language of user-to-user email communications on eBay. We found that these often also are rather short. This may well be due to the limited setting of what the messages are usually about (e.g., "do you have this also in a different color?" or "would you ship the item to Europe?", or the complete email could also just be the single word "yes"). It turns out that on these user-to-user email messages a dictionary-based approach does indeed perform very well. We then also apply our methodology to Twitter status updates, which besides being short, are also well known to be difficult to classify due to the vast amount of Twitter-specific slang and abbreviations.

Our specific approach is to look only at the first two and the last two words of the documents (emails, tweets), and use the site or user profile determined language to build frequency tables on a training set. In the email setting, the intuition of looking at the opening word of a message was the observation that many users start their text with one of only relatively few and very language-specific terms, such as hello, bonjour or goedendag. Then again, starting an email with the name of the recipient is also very frequent, which leads to a dilution of the signal captured by the first word. This is why we also consider the second word, which then in turn tends to be language-specific. An analogous reasoning applies to the end of the messages, common endings are strongly indicative of the language, such as good-bye, ciao, or Tschüß. However, if the email is ended with the name of the sender, then the second-to-last word carries this signal.

This approach also works quite well for tweets, which start often with common opening words or abbreviations and often finish with common ending words or abbreviations. For example in English common opening words or abbreviations are I, lol, you, my, …, while common ending words or abbreviations are you, now, me, smh, …, and similarly for other languages.

Normalizing these frequency tables across the languages for each word separately leads to estimated language probabilities, and summing up these probabilities with suitable weights creates a dictionary-based language identification model, with weights on the opening and closing words only. Combination with the site or user profile language identification is easy, the indicator variable is just another (binary) probability weighted into the sum.

Because in the end only the first two and the last two words of a document need to be investigated, the algorithm is computationally very lightweight during scoring, and correspondingly very fast. Additionally our method needs no human-labeled training data, rather it bootstraps itself from the (hopefully relatively strong) learner given by language identification based on the site or user profile alone. This is also where the nature of today's high-volume web sites helps our approach: the hosting domain generally captures vast amounts of such trivially machine-labeled data for free. Furthermore, as a consequence of being built on large amounts of data, the resulting models are very stable. On the eBay data where we have access to a longer period of data, the model still performs exceptionally well one year after fitting. The algorithm is deployed at eBay as part of the back-office development data repository.

With the investigation of the Twitter data, which has the relatively weaker language identifier given by the user profile language, we conclude that the (a-priori) precision of the site or user profile language determination is a key ingredient to our approach: the stronger the site or user profile language learner, the better the algorithm and bootstrapping.

Applications of language identification are not subject of this paper, but of course could include the obvious ones, from spam filtering, fraud detection, sentiment analysis, to customer service queue routing, among others.

2. EBAY MEMBER TO MEMBER EMAILS

The specific data leading to the development of the algorithm were the (non-public) emails between sellers and buyers (or interested members, in case of a pre-sale communication). These are all called member-to-member emails (or messages), in short, M2M emails. The eBay sites that are part of this study use one of the following seven languages: English, German, Italian, French, Spanish, Dutch, or Polish. This glosses over subtle differences, for example, British English, Australian English, and American English are simply identified as English, similarly for French being spoken in France, parts of Canada, parts of Switzerland, and parts of Belgium, the same holds for German being used in Germany, Austria, and parts of Switzerland, and finally Dutch for the Netherlands and parts of Belgium.

M2M messages on eBay usually are generated within the MyMessages facility, which wraps each message with a template. What the template precisely contains is not important, with the exception that the template header before the message ends on "Dear recipient-user-name", and the footer template after the message starts with a signature of the form "- sender-user-name". Hence many eBay members do not include the recipient name as part of their message, and neither do they include their own sender name as a signature. This is important for our algorithm, as otherwise if one looks just at the beginning and the ending of a typical email message one would generally have to discard (and identify!) user names in order to derive a generalizable model. On the other hand, as explained in the introduction, we consider the leading two words and the ending two words, just in case a greeting by name or a signature user name is still present in the message.

A key feature of the eBay M2M data is that it contains many short documents; one- and two-word documents are not uncommon.

Obviously, the strongest indicator of the email language is the site. In our setting we extract the site from the email template, thus avoiding a user database lookup to find the registered site of the user. However, in particular because of a small percentage of template-free emails this results in missing values for some of the records. Also, some users write emails in a language different from their site language, which combined with the missing values ultimately gives a site-language accuracy of about 96% in identifying the language of emails. More precisely, in case the sites of the sender and the recipient differ, this is based on the site of the recipient, which has proven to give slightly better language identification performance. This percentage was established on a random un-biased sample of about 15K emails from June 2010 which were human-labeled into the seven languages considered. For the eBay data, our goal is to improve on this 96% accuracy rate.

3. TWITTER STATUS UPDATES

As the obvious source of short web documents in multiple languages, we also consider Twitter status updates. We used the streaming API to capture a 1% sample of public status updates made freely available by Twitter, commonly known as the "Sprinkler" data feed [6].

For this study we excluded several languages that could easily be separately handled from the Twitter data feed because these languages use a different font encoding: Japanese (ISO 639-1 code "ja"), Chinese (both "zh-cn" and "zh-tw"), Korean ("ko") and Russian ("ru"). Similarly to how we grouped all different flavors of English from eBay's data into simply one English language, we mapped the intricately related macro-languages Malay ("msa") and Indonesian ("id") simply into Indonesian ("id"). The Twitter user profile languages (in the following often called "site languages") that are part of this study were determined on the training set and comprise the following eleven languages: English, Spanish, Portuguese, French, Dutch, Turkish, Indonesian, German, Italian, Filipino, and Hindi. In the end there actually was not a single Twitter status update in Hindi in the test sets, however all code used all eleven languages.

An important point is that while there are no missing values in the language field in the Twitter user profiles, the language specified in the user profile is only about 80% accurate if used to identify the language used for status updates. However, the public user profile distributed by Twitter as part of the streaming API also contains a location field. This field is populated for about three quarters of all status updates, but of these about absolute 15% of the values contain not even a single letter (e.g., contain a "smiley face"), leaving about 60% of locations with potentially identifiable values. Not all of these values map to an actual physical location on a map, but some contain other whimsical entries (e.g., "in my kitchen"). In the end, we prepared a simple parsing model on the location field by using both the geographic location and the language used to specify the location to assign a language to the location (e.g. both "Chicago" and "in my kitchen" would be assigned "English"). We managed to map about 50% of status updates to a location language (from an upper limit of 60%). Finally, we assigned this location language (if present) as the site-language, thus overriding the user profile language. As it turns out, the majority of Twitter users in Indonesia and in the Philippines post in English, and hence for these two locations we did not override the user language from the profile with the location language. With this improved site language from using both the language field and the location field from the user profile, the combined prediction accuracy if using it to predict the language used for the status updates is about 87%, comparing favorably to the 80% accuracy if using the user profile language alone.

In the rest of this study we use both of these Twitter site languages (user profile language alone, or user profile language and location language combined), and we list the results in separate tables.

4. THE ALGORITHM

4.1 Data Preparation

The algorithm expects only absolutely minimal data cleaning. Generally, digits and letters including umlauts and accented letters make up the words, anything else is a word break. For the eBay message data, after breaking the document into words, all words containing a digit were removed, which removed many user-selected user ids and names. For the Twitter data, on the other hand, numbers are often used as abbreviations (e.g., "gr8" for "great"), and hence these words were allowed. As a further concession to the abbreviated nature of Twitter status updates, we also allowed apostrophes (e.g., in this study "I'm" is considered one word in the Twitter data, but two words in the eBay data). Similar to the eBay data we removed Twitter user names from the status updates (e.g., "@Example") and we saw a slight improvement in the language identification. Finally all the letters are transformed into a uniform case (lower case, for example). On the other hand, no stemming or aliasing is performed.

4.2 Learning of Frequency Tables

After pre-processing, we collect site or user language counts for each of the first two words and each of the last two words of each document. For the eBay M2M data we found during our experimentations that it helps slightly to combine the frequencies from the last two words into a single table. Hence for the eBay M2M data we created only three frequency tables, one each for the first words, the second words, and one for the combined collection of second-to-last and last words. The likely reason for this improvement is that in the combined frequency table stray entries from signature user names will obtain relatively less dominance as they would in a last-word-only table. The Twitter status update data contains no signatures at the end of tweets, and we observed no such improvement by combining the last two words into a single frequency table. We kept those tables separate.

The frequency tables can be both pre- and post-processed. The most obvious post-processing is to remove entries with insufficient total frequency. For both the eBay M2M data and the Twitter status updates data, we collected the frequency tables on a training set of several million documents, and we set the minimum frequency to 50 for the individual (first, second, second-to-last, last) word tables, and to 100 for the combined last words table in the case of eBay M2M data. Additional pre-processing may include removal of undesirable words (e.g., words which are known to carry no signal) from the document before extraction of the leading and terminating words for the frequency tables. For example, for the eBay M2M data we excluded the words ebay and paypal, while for the Twitter data we excluded the abbreviation RT (short for Re-Tweet).

4.3 Scoring

Assigning a language to a given document is highly efficient. It amounts to extracting the first two and the last two words of the document, and for each of these four words w_k ($k = 1,\ldots,4$) and for each of the predetermined set of languages L looking up the corresponding frequency $f_{kL}(w_k)$ in the count tables k ($k = 1,\ldots,4$), and computing a linear weighted sum. Recall that for the eBay M2M data we created one combined table for the last two words ($k = 3,4$), which is to say in this case $f_{3L}(w) = f_{4L}(w)$ for all languages L and all words w.

Let $f_k(w)$ denote the sum of the frequencies for a word w in table k across all languages. Given weights W_k ($k = 1,\ldots,4$), the language score is computed for each language L as

$$s_L = W_1 f_{1L}(w_1) / f_1(w_1) + W_2 f_{2L}(w_2) / f_2(w_2) +$$

$$W_3 f_{3L}(w_3) / f_3(w_3) - W_4 f_{4L}(w_4) / f_4(w_4).$$

Lacking any prior, we chose all weights $W_k = 1$. The final language assigned is the language with the highest score. In case of a score tie, a predetermined preference order based on the expected distribution of languages could be used.

4.4 Combination with the Site Language

We chose a simple approach and combined the above language identification scores s_L in a linear fashion with the site language. Let $\delta(L)$ be the indicator function for the site language (value = 1 if L is the site language, 0 otherwise), and let W_S be a pre-chosen site weight, then the combined site and algorithm score is

$$s_{LS} = W_S\, \delta(L) + s_L.$$

For both the eBay M2M and the Twitter status data, we chose $W_S = 1.75$, with the idea that the site or user profile language is by itself already very accurate, and this way at least two of the features in the weighted sum s_L have to trigger at values close to 1 to override the site or user profile language.

5. EVALUATION ON EBAY DATA

5.1 Data

As a first evaluation of our approach, we fitted the models and tested the algorithm on proprietary eBay M2M data. Specifically we used the samples listed in the table below.

Table 1. eBay Data Sets

Time Period	Volume	Filter	Labeled By
June 2010	Several million	No	Site language
June 2010	1K per language	Biased	Site language
June 2010	15K	Cleaned	Human
Sept 30, 2010	20K	Cleaned	Human
June 2011	21K	Cleaned	Human

In the table above, "Cleaned" means that records that were using more than one language, or that were ambivalent were removed (e.g., a message consisting of digits only could be any language). "Biased" means that the given distribution of languages was ignored, and rather a specific number of documents was extracted for all languages in order to generate a reference set; these were also filtered so that each sender was allowed only one message in order to capture as much different user behavior as possible. The data set listed in row 1 is a superset of those in rows 2 and 3. No attempt has been made to keep the data sets from rows 2 and 3 disjoint.

5.2 Comparison Algorithms on eBay Data

We compared our algorithm to two industry-standard algorithms, which we also combined with the site language determination for further competitiveness.

5.2.1 Standalone Zipping

We prepared a set of reference documents for each of the seven languages, these are the 1,000 documents each from June 2010 in row 2 of Table 1. We used Gzip as the compression tool, and pruned the 1K reference document files so that for each of the seven languages the resulting gzipped reference set had roughly the same byte count (about 64KB each). We also used a much smaller reference set (about 2KB each) as a second classifier. Classification is as follows: Given a document, for each of the language reference sets add the given document and compress the resulting document set using gzip. Among the seven resulting document sets that one reference set that grew relatively the least must have had similar statistical byte patterns, and its language is selected [4]. One immediate drawback of this algorithm is that even for a one-word message the algorithm needs to compress seven 64KB (or 2KB, respectively) data sets, which is a relatively huge computational effort. Thus the expected run-time performance is expected to be very poor if compared to other methods.

5.2.2 Combination Zipping with Site Language

For the Zipping algorithm, a voting scheme determines whether to use the gzip-determined language or the site language. The voting scheme is as follows. For any language L, let r_L be the ratio of the size of the gzipped reference set with the document attached to the size of the gzipped reference set without the document attached. Let r_{L_2} be the second smallest ratio and r_{L_1} be the smallest ratio (for the given document), and let W_g be a pre-determined weight. The voting scheme is testing $W_g < r_{L_1} / r_{L_2}$, if true it uses the site language, otherwise the gzip language. The ratio of the two smallest ratios is thus taken as a measurement of how sure the gzip determination is of its result. For the 64K (2K) sized reference sets we experimentally fit W_g = 0.999925 (0.997, respectively) using the human-labeled June 2010 data (row 3 of Table 1). Note that this combination is not bootstrapped but uses a human-labeled dataset to obtain the optimal combination weight. It is included here for comparison purposes only, and not to illustrate the methods described in this paper.

5.2.3 Standalone Character n-gram Naïve Bayesian

We used the publicly available implementation from Cybozu Labs [2]. This Java software comes out-of-the box pre-trained for 49 languages, the training being based on Wikipedia documents. We used the tool as it is, but also used it with the 49 languages restricted to just the seven languages under consideration, and finally, we also retrained the underlying classifier using a sample of the eBay M2M data, using the same reference sets as for the Zipping classifier from June 2010. The classifier software drops short documents during training, in order to avoid this, we repeated any short message inside the eBay M2M reference training set until it exceeded that drop cut-off (a simple study showed this repetition did improve the performance because it increased the training data size). Note that this custom language profile generation follows the same bootstrapping philosophy as we used for our algorithm, no human-labeled data was needed.

5.2.4 Combination Bayesian with Site Language

The software described in the previous section outputs a probability score for the assigned language. If this score exceeds the prior precision known of the site language (0.96 for the eBay M2M data), then the language assigned by the Bayesian model was used, otherwise the site language was used.

Table 2. Models for eBay Data

Name	Description
Site	Language based on recipient site
Gzip64	Zipping 64K reference docs
Gzip64Site	Zipping 64K with site
Gzip2	Zipping 2K reference docs
Gzip2Site	Zipping 2K with site
Bayes49W	Naïve Bayes 49 languages, Wikipedia profile
Bayes7W	Naïve Bayes 7 languages, Wikipedia profile
Bayes7M	Naïve Bayes 7 languages, M2M profile
Bayes49WSite	Naïve Bayes 49 languages with site, Wikipedia profile
Bayes7WSite	Naïve Bayes 7 languages with site, Wikipedia profile
Bayes7MSite	Naïve Bayes 7 languages with site, M2M profile
Algo	Our algorithm
AlgoSite	Our algorithm with site

5.3 Results on eBay Data

Based on the discussions and explanations of the previous sections, Table 2 on the previous page lists the models we compared. Below are various result tables. Note that the June 2010 data is the training data, while the other data sets are unseen test data (out of sample, out of time).

Table 3. Runtime on a 32 Bit 2.66 GHz System

Name	1 record	15K records	100K records
Gzip64Site	0m 0.5s	30m 0s	(not performed)
Gzip2Site	0m 0.4s	0m 34s	3m 29s
Bayes7MSite	0m 0.3s	0m 3.5s	0m 19s
AlgoSite	0m 1.2s	0m 1.9s	0m 4.3s

Runtimes of the "without site" models are essentially equivalent.

Table 4. Precision on Human-labeled eBay Data

Name	June 2010	Sept 2010	June 2011
Site	0.960	0.958	0.956
Gzip64	0.971	0.974	0.972
Gzip64Site	0.987	0.986	0.988
Gzip2	0.962	0.960	0.958
Gzip2Site	0.988	0.986	0.987
Bayes49W	0.968	0.971	0.970
Bayes7W	0.979	0.981	0.981
Bayes7M	0.992	0.992	0.991
Bayes49WSite	0.984	0.986	0.986
Bayes7WSite	0.987	0.988	0.987
Bayes7MSite	0.995	0.995	0.994
Algo	0.995	0.994	0.996
AlgoSite	0.997	0.996	0.997

Table 5. Precision by Language on June 2011 eBay Data

Grouped True Language	True Count	Correct by Bayes7MSite	Correct by AlgoSite
English German	19,230	19,118 (0.994)	19,196 (0.998)
Dutch French Italian Polish Spanish	1,588	1,580 (0.995)	1,561 (0.983)
ALL	20,818	20,698 (0.994)	20,757 (0.997)

6. EVALUATION ON TWITTER DATA

6.1 Data

As a second cross-domain application, we determined the language profiles and tested the algorithm on public Twitter status update data. Specifically we used the following samples listed in the Table 6. In this table, "Cleaned" means that records that were using more than one language, or that were ambivalent were removed (e.g., a message consisting only of a smiley face could be any language). Additionally all languages not part of the set of eleven Twitter languages considered were removed.

The data from October 2011 was used to generate the location to language mapping explained at the end of Section 3. It was not otherwise used.

The November 2011 data was used in several ways. First, it was used to generate the word frequency tables. Second, a subset was used to generate custom profiles for the Character n-gram Naïve Bayesian classifier.

The December 2011 data was used as a near-term small test set, in particular as a sanity check, while the January 2012 data was used as a longer-term test set.

Table 6. Twitter Data Sets

Time Period	Volume	Filter	Labeled By
Oct 29-31, 2011	750K	No	Not labeled
Nov 13-19, 2011	14.6 million (100% of "Sprinkler" = 1% of all Twitter status data)	No	(a) User profile language (b) User profile language and location
Dec 11-17, 2011	1.2K (0.001% of "Sprinkler")	Cleaned	Human
Jan 8-10, 2012	6.5K (0.01% of "Sprinkler")	Cleaned	Human

6.2 Comparison Algorithms on Twitter Data

We followed our approach to evaluating our method on the eBay M2M data, and compared our algorithm to the industry-standard Standalone Character n-gram Naïve Bayesian classifier, which as for the eBay data we also combined with the site language (in the user profile sense, see Section 3) for further competitiveness. We did not evaluate the Zipping algorithm on the Twitter data as it had proved to be non-competitive on the eBay data.

6.2.1 Standalone Character n-gram Naïve Bayesian

As before, we used the publicly available implementation from Cybozu Labs [2], and as for the eBay data used it with all 49 languages, the training being based on Wikipedia documents, and also restricted to just the subset of the considered eleven Twitter site-languages. Similar to the eBay data we also retrained the underlying classifier using a sample of the Twitter data. For this we generated two sets of language profiles, once using the user profile language as the label, and once using the language determined from the location and language from the user profile as the label (see Section 3). The language profiles were generated on the November 2011 data, limited to at most 100K records per language (some less-used languages stayed significantly below this). As before for the eBay M2M data we appended to itself any short message inside the Twitter reference training set until it exceeded the software's internal minimum message-length cut-off, and as for the eBay data a simple study showed this repetition did improve the performance. Once again this implements the same bootstrapping philosophy as we used for our algorithm, no human-labeled data was needed.

6.2.2 Combination Bayesian with Site Language

As previously explained, the software described in the section above outputs a probability score for the assigned language, and if this score exceeds the prior precision known of the pre-assigned site language, then the language assigned by the Bayesian model was used, otherwise the site language was used. "Pre-assigned site language" in the previous sentence means either (a) the language from the user profile with an accuracy estimate of 80%, or (b) the language determined from the combination of user location and profile language with an accuracy estimate of 87%.

Table 7. Models for Twitter Data

Name	Description
Site	Language based on user site (a) or (b) as explained above
Bayes49W	Naïve Bayes 49 languages, Wikipedia profile
Bayes11W	Naïve Bayes 11 languages, Wikipedia profile
Bayes11T	Naïve Bayes 11 languages, Twitter profile
Bayes49WSite	Naïve Bayes 49 languages with site, Wikipedia profile
Bayes11WSite	Naïve Bayes 11 languages with site, Wikipedia profile
Bayes11TSite	Naïve Bayes 11 languages with site, Twitter profile
Algo	Our algorithm
AlgoSite	Our algorithm with site

6.3 Results on Twitter Data

Based on the discussions and explanations of the previous sections, Table 7 above lists the models we compared, and below are the result tables. There are two sets of all results (Tables 8a and b), corresponding to the two site-language strategies: (a) the site language is the language from the user profile, or (b) the site language is the language determined from the combination of language and location from the user profile.

Table 8a. Precision on Human-labeled Twitter Data with Site-language = User Profile Language

	Dec 2011	Jan 2012
Algo	0.657	0.664
Bayes11T	0.821	0.810
Bayes49W	0.820	0.816
Site	**0.793**	**0.828**
AlgoSite	0.804	0.830
Bayes11TSite	0.858	0.848
Bayes49WSite	0.864	0.860
Bayes11W	0.873	0.863
Bayes11WSite	0.902	0.897

Table 8b. Precision on Human-labeled Twitter Data with Site-language = Language from Location and Language from User Profile

	Dec 2011	Jan 2012
Algo	0.679	0.689
Bayes49W	0.820	0.816
Bayes11T	0.853	0.834
Bayes11W	0.873	0.863
Site	**0.878**	**0.869**
Bayes11TSite	0.900	0.885
Bayes49WSite	0.893	0.889
AlgoSite	0.904	0.897
Bayes11WSite	0.917	0.914

Table 9. Precision by Language on Jan 2012 Twitter Data

True Language	True Count	Correct by Bayes11WSite	Correct by AlgoSite
English	3596	3390 (0.94)	3566 (0.99)
Portuguese	794	670 (0.84)	639 (0.80)
Spanish	674	595 (0.88)	601 (0.89)
Indonesian	411	355 (0.86)	247 (0.60)
Dutch	184	168 (0.91)	68 (0.37)
Turkish	55	52 (0.95)	49 (0.89)
French	53	48 (0.91)	36 (0.68)
Italian	22	19 (0.86)	11 (0.50)
German	20	18 (0.90)	8 (0.40)
Filipino	16	12 (0.75)	0 (0.00)
ALL	5825	5330 (0.914)	5225 (0.897)

7. DISCUSSION / CONCLUSIONS

As is apparent from comparing Tables 4, 8a and b, there are significant differences between the eBay M2M data, and the Twitter status data. On the positive side, on all data sets all models / approaches are very stable, and show no over-fitting. Scoring eBay M2M data one year out from the training period achieves the same precision, showing that the underlying patterns are well captured by all approaches. The Twitter data was evaluated on a shorter timeframe, but the models also appear stable.

On the eBay M2M data the Bayesian model shows, as expected, that a custom model (Bayes7M) performs better than a generic model (Bayes7W). On the other hand, this is not the case on the Twitter status data, where the generic profile (Bayes11W) outperforms the custom profile (Bayes11T). The email messages in the eBay M2M data are fairly clean text with highly accurate site language identification labels, certainly if compared to Twitter status updates, where abbreviations and creative slang are the norm and where the user profile language (and location) information is less accurate in identifying the language of status updates. In other words, the major differences between the eBay M2M and the Twitter status update data sets seem to be the cleanliness of the data and the vast difference in the labeling accuracy by the site language. It stands to reason that this noisy signal confuses both the Bayesian model's language profiles when built on the Twitter data, and also our dictionary-based model's frequency tables. Indeed, on the Twitter status update data labeled by the user profile language, which has the lowest accuracy of all site-languages considered in this study, both modeling approaches perform poorly when evaluated stand-alone. For the Bayesian model using an off-the-shelf profile avoids this pitfall.

From a pure run-time consideration (Table 3), the Zipping method is not competitive in a real-time high-volume application. While the Bayesian model has a shorter load time as compared to our model, which must load the more extensive count tables, once the model is loaded, scoring with the Bayesian model is more than an order of magnitude slower as compared to scoring with our model.

Our observation of the poor run-time performance of the Zipping method along with its also relatively poor language identification performance validates a previous observation from the literature dated shortly after the original publication of the Zipping algorithm [6].

Maybe surprisingly, our simple custom model performed in the same ballpark as all the other models, in an overall sense, at least if the underlying site language classifier was strong. Its natural role thus is as a boost to an already existing strong language detector. A more detailed breakdown (Tables 5 and 9) shows that it roughly matched or outperformed the best competing model on the popular languages, while having a (slightly) higher error rate on the less popular languages. This imbalance was more pronounced on the more noisy Twitter data. As to specific languages, the main root cause of the poor language identification performance of our algorithm on the Twitter data, even when combined with the site, in particular on the Filipino language (Table 9) is that all users tweeting in Filipino had English as their site language from their user profile. Because of the rarity of the Filipino language there was insufficient evidence in the frequency tables to override this dominant site language. The same explanation applies on the Twitter data to the lower identification rate of the Dutch language where more than half of the users have English as their site language, and also to German, where just under half of the users have English as their site language.

The performance on the Twitter data indicates that our word-frequency based approach has a strong dependency on the accuracy of the classifier based on the site-language. When this accuracy is lower, this lack of accuracy transports itself into the frequency tables, and the algorithm's performance suffers significantly (Table 8a). On the other hand, the boot-strapping procedure using an existing strong classifier based on the site-language works well, for all of the algorithms considered (Tables 4 and 8b). Indeed, even on noisy Twitter data the bootstrapping procedure boosts the precision to roughly the 90% range (Tables 8a and 8b), which is significantly better than the roughly 80% accuracy one obtains from the user profile language alone.

One key point is that both our algorithm and our bootstrapping are completely unsupervised in the classical sense that no human-labeled data is needed, instead the site provides the necessary labeling. The weights in our algorithm including the weight for the combination with the site language have not been optimized but were set based only on insight into the model structure, and could likely be improved. The combination of the Bayesian model with the site-language classifier requires a single a-priori estimate on the precision of the site-language classifier, but nothing else in form of labeled data, and it boosts the performance measurably.

In summary, we presented a simple, stable, and highly runtime-efficient algorithm for language identification, which does not need any human-labeled training data, provided there already exists a strong language identifier based on a site language or user language. While it is at heart a statistical method based on frequency tables on a machine-generated dictionary, the decision of building the dictionary only on the opening and closing words of a message was driven by human insight into the problem structure. The method shines on web-scale data, validating once more that bigger data is better data, and that, when combined with human understanding of the problem domain, bigger data is even better data. Our approach in particular works well for short documents, and its precision is on-par with state-of-the-art language identification.

8. ACKNOWLEDGMENTS

Our thanks go to Cybozu Labs, Inc. for publicly posting their implementation of a character n-gram Bayesian language classifier, thus allowing us to easily compare our method to a state-of-the-art classifier.

9. REFERENCES

[1] Dunning, Ted. 1994. *Statistical Identification of Language.* Technical Report MCCS 94-273. Computing Research Laboratory, New Mexico State University.

[2] Shuyo, Nakatani. 2010. *Language Identification Library.* Technical Presentation and Java Implementation. Cybozu Labs, Inc. http://code.google.com/p/language-detection/.

[3] Benedetto, Dario, Caglioti Emanuele and Loreto, Vittorio. 2002. *Language trees and zipping.* Physical Review Letters, 88:4.

[4] Řehůřek, Radim and Kolkus, Milan. 2009. *Language Identification on the Web: Extending the Dictionary Method.* Computational linguistics and intelligent text processing. Lecture Notes in Computer Science, 2009, Volume 5449/2009, 357-368, DOI: 10.1007/978-3-642-00382-0_29.

[5] Twitter, *Streaming API.* Online documentation at https://dev.twitter.com/docs/streaming-api.

[6] Goodman, Joshua, 2002. *Extended comment on "Language Trees and Zipping".* Microsoft Research, Feb 21 2002.

Semantic Search and a New Moore's Law Effect in Knowledge Engineering

Wei-Ying Ma
Microsoft Research Asia
wyma@microsoft.com

Abstract

In history, the Moore's law effect has been used to describe phenomena of exponential improvement in technology when it has a virtuous cycle that makes technology improvement proportional to technology itself. For example, chip performance had doubled every 18-24 months because better processors support the development of better layout tools that support the development of even better processors. I will describe a new Moore's law effect that is being created in knowledge engineering and is driven by the self-reinforcing nature of three trends and technical advancements: big data, machine learning, and Internet economics. I will explain how we can take advantage of this new effect to develop a new generation of semantic and knowledge-based search engines. Specifically, my presentation will cover the following three areas:

Knowledge acquisition – our goal is to build a comprehensive entity graph and knowledge graph to complement the web and social graphs. I will introduce techniques for entity extraction and knowledgebase construction through automatic and interactive mining and crowdsourcing.

Managing knowledge – our goal is to support advanced analytical queries by combining probabilistic knowledge with a distributed platform. I will focus on technology for both online knowledge serving and offline knowledge inference.

Knowledge-empowered search and applications – the knowledge we have acquired and curated enables applications like query understanding, entity-centric search experiences, and answers to natural language queries.

Categories & Subject Descriptors: H.2.8 [Database Management]: Data Mining.

Author Keywords: Knowledge Acquisition, Semantic Search, Query Understanding.

Bio

Dr. Wei-Ying Ma is an Assistant Managing Director at Microsoft Research Asia where he oversees research groups in Web Search, Data Mining, and Natural Language Computing. He has developed several key technologies for Microsoft's Bing Search Engine. He has published over 250 papers at international conferences and journals. He is a Fellow of the IEEE and a Distinguished Scientist of the ACM. He currently serves on the editorial boards of ACM Transactions on Information System (TOIS) and ACM/Springer Multimedia Systems Journal. In recent years, he served as general chair of ACM SIGIR 2011, program co-chair of WWW 2008, program co-chair of Pacific Rim Conference on Multimedia (PCM) 2007, and general co-chair of Asia Information Retrieval Symposium (AIRS) 2008. Before joining Microsoft in 2001, Wei-Ying was with Hewlett-Packard Labs in Palo Alto, California where he worked on multimedia content analysis and adaptation. He received a bachelor of science in electrical engineering from the National Tsing Hua University in Taiwan in 1990. He earned a Master of Science degree and doctorate in electrical and computer engineering from the University of California at Santa Barbara in 1994 and 1997, respectively.

KDD'12, August 12–16, 2012, Beijing, China.
ACM 978-1-4503-1462-6/12/08.

Industry Practice Expo Invited Talk

Key Lessons Learned Building Recommender Systems for Large-scale Social Networks

Christian Posse
LinkedIn Inc.
cposse@linkedin.com

Abstract

By helping members to connect, discover and share relevant content or find a new career opportunity, recommender systems have become a critical component of user growth and engagement for social networks. The multidimensional nature of engagement and diversity of members on large-scale social networks have generated new infrastructure and modeling challenges and opportunities in the development, deployment and operation of recommender systems. This presentation will address some of these issues, focusing on the modeling side for which new research is much needed while describing a recommendation platform that enables real-time recommendation updates at scale as well as batch computations, and cross-leverage between different product recommendations. Topics covered on the modeling side will include optimizing for multiple competing objectives, solving contradicting business goals, modeling user intent and interest to maximize placement and timeliness of the recommendations, utility metrics beyond CTR that leverage both real-time tracking of explicit and implicit user feedback, gathering training data for new product recommendations, virality preserving online testing and virtual profiling.

Categories & Subject Descriptors: H.2.8 [Database Management]: Data Mining.

Author Keywords: Recommender Systems, Real-time updates, Multi-Objective Optimization, User Intent Modeling, Online Testing.

Bio

Dr. Christian Posse is Principal Scientist at LinkedIn Inc. where he leads the development of recommendation solutions as well as the next generation online experimentation platform. Prior to LinkedIn, Dr. Posse was a founding member and technology lead of Cisco Systems Inc. Network Collaboration Business Unit where he designed the search and advanced social analytics of Pulse, Cisco's network-based search and collaboration platform for the enterprise. Prior to Cisco, Dr. Posse worked in a wide range of environments, from holding faculty positions in US universities, to leading the R&D at software companies and a US National Laboratory in the social networks, biological networks and behavioral analytics fields. His interests are diverse and include predictive analytics, search and recommendation engines, social networks analytics, computational social and behavioral sciences, computational linguistics, and information fusion. He has written over 40 scientific peer-reviewed publications and holds several patents in those fields. Dr. Posse has a PhD in Statistics from the Swiss Federal Institute of Technology, Switzerland.

KDD'12, August 12–16, 2012, Beijing, China.
ACM 978-1-4503-1462-6/12/08.

Magnet Community Identification on Social Networks

Guan Wang † Yuchen Zhao† Xiaoxiao Shi † Philip S. Yu†*
†University of Illinois at Chicago, USA *King Abdulaziz University, Saudi Arabia
{gwang26, yzhao24, xshi9, psyu}@uic.edu

ABSTRACT

Social communities connect people of similar interests together and play essential roles in social network applications. Examples of such communities include people who like the same objects on Facebook, follow common subjects on Twitter, or join similar groups on LinkedIn. Among communities, we notice that some of them are *magnetic* to people. A *magnet community* is such a community that attracts significantly more people's interests and attentions than other communities of similar topics. With the explosive number of self-formed communities in social networks, one important demand is to identify magnet communities for users. This can not only track attractive communities, but also help improve user experiences and increase their engagements, e.g., the login frequencies and user-generated-content qualities. In this paper, we initiate the study of magnet community identification problem. First we observe several properties of magnet communities, such as attention flow, attention qualify, and attention persistence. Second, we formalize these properties with the combination of community feature extraction into a graph ranking formulation based on constraint quadratic programming. In details, we treat communities of a network as super nodes, and their interactions as links among those super nodes. Therefore, a network of communities is defined. We extract community's magnet features from heterogeneous sources, i.e., a community's standalone features and its dependency features with other communities. A graph ranking model is formulated given these features. Furthermore, we define constraints reflecting communities' magnet properties to regularize the model. We demonstrate the effectiveness of our framework on real world social network data.

Categories and Subject Descriptors

H.2.8 [**Database Management**]: Database Applications–Data Mining

Keywords

Magnet community, social networks

KDD'12, August 12–16, 2012, Beijing, China.

1. INTRODUCTION

Community is an important building-block of social networks. It attracts people with common backgrounds, goals or interests, and it is the key element of social media's dominating success. For instance, college-level social community leads to the success of social-media giant Facebook; company-level social community initiates the popularity of professional network LinkedIn; business-level social community boosts the development of peer-to-peer business such as eBay. Moreover, in academic field, countless communities are formed to improve the academic society, such as the special interest group (SIG) for computer scientists, the Society for Industrial and Applied Mathematics (SIAM), etc.

Among all social communities, we notice that some of them attract people's interests more than the others, and we call them *magnet communities*. More specifically, *magnet communities* are such communities that draw significantly more attention than others even if they are all about the same topic. Examples of magnet communities include the magnet colleges with over 20,000 talented applicants each year (e.g., Stanford, MIT, etc), magnet research communities with over 1000 high quality paper submissions (e.g., KDD), and magnet companies professionals would love to work for. Communities draw people's attention from each other and form an interesting network. For example, Figure 1 depicts such a network where the employees migrate among some prestige IT companies/communities [1]. According to this statistics, every time there is one person joining Google from Facebook, there are 15.5 people joining Facebook from Google. Though we are not discussing which company is "*better*" from the figure, we notice that Facebook is one of the *magnet* communities that people prefer to join.

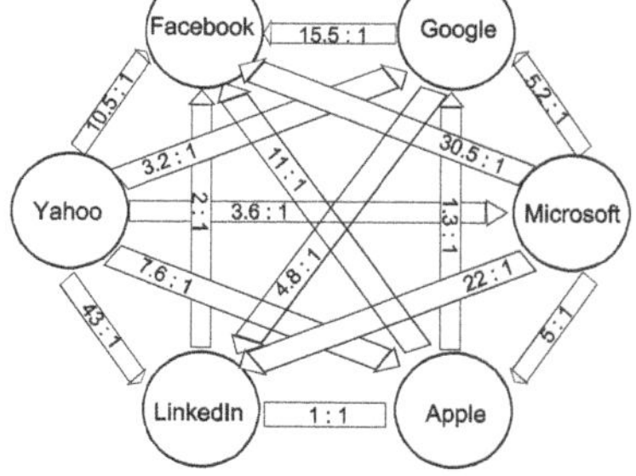

Figure 1: Community Interactions

Identifying magnet communities in a specific domain is an important task. First, the magnet communities help people understand the trends of their domains, e.g., which topics are hot, what

[1]The information is from [4]

kinds of new interests people are developing, and which types of new communities are forming. Second, they help people make decisions when joining communities. For example, irrelevant to communities' sizes or histories, people may want to join magnet ones that represent energetic present and promising future. These two functions of magnet community identification can further serve as building blocks of many other applications, e.g., community recommendation, etc. Despite its importance, magnet community identification problem has not been studied before, to the best of our knowledge. Researchers have focused on community detection in various scenarios. Given a network, their goal is to detect subnetworks of similar nodes as communities. Our goal is one step further to identify magnet communities in a given domain through quantitative analysis. More specifically, given communities in a domain, we want to rank them based on their attractiveness to people among the communities of that domain. In the end, the top ranked communities are the ones people tend to adhere to.

To solve this problem, a quick path to go down is the classic random walk scheme. PageRank or its variations seems to be the simple and right choice. However, we demonstrate their incompetence on this problem using Table 1, where we list 3 ranking results based on different mechanisms. The first column lists the companies with highest PageRank scores among 6853 IT companies in the employee migration network that we have. Interestingly enough, they are also the 5 largest companies in terms of employee numbers in our dataset. Therefore, standard PageRank skews heavily towards the size of a community. What about we simply normalize the migration flow by community size? The second column of Table 1 lists the results after normalization. The top ranked companies become tiny start-ups with about 100 employees. The third column are the companies recognized as "ideal employers" according to a survey result from Universumglobal [2]. It aligns better with people's common sense about IT industry. As we have seen, the classic random walk schemes cannot accurately measure the attractiveness of communities. Although the survey result can create better performance, it takes a lot of efforts and manual works, which becomes infeasible for large-scale identification tasks.

Rank	PageRank	Normalized PR	Survey Result
1	Hewlett Packard	Zuora	Google
2	IBM	Silver Peak Systems	Microsoft
3	Oracle	Kony Solutions	Apple
4	Microsoft	Palo Alto Networks	Facebook
5	Cisco Systems	Quickoffice	IBM

Table 1: Top Ranked IT Companies

Therefore, the magnet community identification task is more challenging than it appears to be. First, there is no single criterion that we could rely on to determine the attractiveness of a community. For example, we cannot blindly say that a larger community is magnetic while a smaller one is not. Therefore, the first challenge is how to extract features from these heterogeneous sources of impacting factors of a community's attractiveness. The second challenge is how to naturally combine all heterogeneous information into a unified ranking model that also depicts attractive properties. For example, some features are only related to each individual community, e.g., size or specific topic, which have little to do with other communities; while others depend on other communities, e.g., people's preferences. The third challenge is the noise handling. People may have different tastes about communities. It is possible that a few people may prefer the less attractive communities. However, we are focusing on the major trend.

[2]www.universumglobal.com/Top50

We attack the problem by first identify some common properties of magnet communities and design appropriate solution accordingly. First, we notice that a community's attractiveness associates with its *attention flow*. A community is attractive when it draws more people's attentions than losing attentions to other communities. In other words, the in-flow of people's attentions could be larger than out-flow for magnet communities. Second, a community's attractiveness associates with *attention quality*. It goes higher if it could draw people's attention from other magnet communities. Therefore, magnet communities could not only attract people, but also attract them from other attractive communities. Third, a community's attractiveness also associates with the *persistence* of people's attention. Being able to have the first two properties for only a short period does not make a real magnet community. When a community can persistently sustain the two properties, it becomes a magnet one. With these observations, we formulate the magnet community identification problem as a constrained graph ranking problem with heterogeneous information from nodes and edges, where constraints represent the relations between these features and magnet properties we just discussed. The whole model becomes an optimization framework of a synthesis measure of attractiveness of communities, which we will go into details later.

We summarize our contributions in three folds:

- We propose a new direction on social network analysis, namely magnet community identification. We believe that the work towards this direction is of huge demands of social network applications, since it can improve user experiences, increase their engagements to social network platforms, and enrich application features on these platforms.
- We propose one definition of magnet communities by identifying their properties. We develop a framework for large community graphs, which models both community features and the attractiveness properties together to identify magnet communities that reflect people's preferences among them.
- We demonstrate the effectiveness of our framework on a particular domain of magnet community identification, namely company's employee magnet community identification. As a tip of the iceberg of general magnet community identification, this domain specific example could serve as an interesting topic by itself, which further proves the wide range of applications magnet community identification may have.

This paper is organized as follows. In the next section, we formally define the magnet community identification problem and propose our framework in details. In section 3, we show our experiment results on real world social network data. In section 4, we explain the relationship between our work and previous related ones. Section 5 is the conclusion.

2. MAGNET COMMUNITY IDENTIFICATION FRAMEWORK

Starting from a bird's-eye view of the magnet community identification framework, we will go deeply through the formulation of our model in this section.

We first represent a social network as a graph $G(V, E, f_V, f_E)$, where V and E are vectors of nodes and edges, and f_V and f_E are features of nodes and edges respectively. To deal with the large scale nature of social networks, we define a summarization function $\mathscr{L}: G \rightarrow \mathcal{G}_C$ that maps an original graph to its condensed graph $\mathcal{G}_C(\mathcal{V}, \mathcal{E}, \mathcal{F}_\mathcal{V}, \mathcal{F}_\mathcal{E})$, where $\mathcal{V} = \{\mathcal{V}_1, \mathcal{V}_2, ..., \mathcal{V}_k\}$ $(\forall i, \mathcal{V}_i \subset V)$ and $\mathcal{E} = \{\mathcal{E}_1, \mathcal{E}_2, ..., \mathcal{E}_n\}$ $(\forall i, \mathcal{E}_i \subset E)$ are subsets of nodes and edges of original graph. Moreover, $\mathcal{F}_\mathcal{V}$ and $\mathcal{F}_\mathcal{E}$ are aggregated nodes' and edges' features in the condensed graph. For the sake of modeling simplicity, we further require $\forall i, j, \mathcal{V}_i \cap \mathcal{V}_j = \emptyset$. Therefore, every element in $\mathcal{V}$ is a community, and every element in $\mathcal{E}$ is a hyper-connection between two communities (a set of edges across the two communities in original graph). Such connections could be defined in various ways, e.g., their domain relation, or people's preference on each other. Figure 2 illustrates such a compression process. Community detection algorithms could be applied in this process. However, it is not the emphasis of this paper. We directly focus on magnet community identification on $\mathcal{G}_\mathcal{C}$.

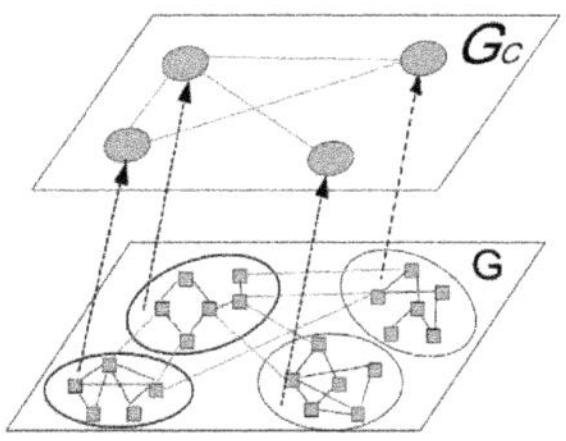

Figure 2: Graph Compression

2.1 Basic definitions

Generally speaking, magnet communities are the ones that people prefer to pay attention to among all social communities. In order to quantitatively identify magnet communities, we first give some more precise definitions related to them, from which we formally depict magnet communities later on in our model.

DEFINITION 2.1. *(Attention to a community) People's attention to a community is a generic representation of their selectively concentration on the community while ignoring others.*

In other words, we assume one person only pays attention to one community at a given time. The person's attention may change from one community to another from time to time, but one at a time. Paying attention has generic meaning, e.g., working for a particular company, or submitting paper to a special interest group. When we mention that a community is observed to attract people's attention, we assume that the people being attracted only pay attention to that community but not others at the time of observation.

DEFINITION 2.2. *(Attention migration flow among communities) Attention migration flow is the overall changes of people's attentions among communities, at the time of observation.*

When a person loses her interest in one community and starts to pay attention to another, there is an attention migration. For one community, its *in-flow* represents the total attentions drawn from other communities, and *out-flow* represents the total attentions lost to other communities.

DEFINITION 2.3. *(Magnet community) A community is a magnet community, i.e., with high attractiveness level, if it has the following properties.*

- *Attention flow: Its in-flow is larger than the out-flow.*
- *Attention quality: The in-flow comes from other communities with high attractiveness levels.*
- *Attention persistency: Its first two properties should be persistent.*

The first property ensures that the size of a magnet community should be growing, because it could attract more and more people. The second property tells the fact that a community's attractiveness should depend on other communities as well. It is more attractive if it could draw people's attention over other attractive ones. The third property, persistence, guarantees that we identify true magnet communities rather than some communities only with a momentarily attention burst. We also notice that the community size does not directly contribute to the attractiveness value. However, magnet communities usually have a certain size that is neither too small nor too large. On the one hand, the persistence property will ensure an accumulative effect of community growth to make itself become larger. On the other hand, when the community has grown into a large one, it is hard to keep in-flow larger than out-flow. That is the reason that very large communities tend to become less attractive due to the loss of people's attention. For example, one particular friendship community of a person may be more attractive when it contains certain number of friends sharing information, but when it grows too large and interesting information get diluted, it becomes less attractive.

2.2 Attractiveness computation framework

We use a vector $\mathcal{M} = (m_1, m_2, ..., m_k)$ to denote the set of estimated attractiveness levels for all communities. As we mentioned, attractiveness level of a community m_i is determined not only by heterogeneous features $\mathcal{F}_\mathcal{V}$ and $\mathcal{F}_\mathcal{E}$ from nodes and edges in the condensed community graph, but also by the attractiveness values of other communities in the same domain. Therefore, we have an abstract representation of $\mathcal{M}$ as

$$\mathcal{M} = f(\mathcal{F}_\mathcal{V}, \mathcal{F}_\mathcal{E}, \mathcal{M}) \tag{1}$$

Let $\mathcal{M}^*$ be the real attractiveness values. Our goal is to make the gap between the real values and the estimated ones as small as possible. Therefore, our objective function at high level is to minimize the Frobenius norm of the two, with the constraint φ to ensure that the final attractiveness levels for communities are consistent with their magnet properties.

$$min||\mathcal{M}^* - \mathcal{M}||_F^2 \tag{2}$$

$$s.t., \varphi(\mathcal{M}, \mathcal{F}_\mathcal{V}, \mathcal{F}_\mathcal{E}) \geq 0 \tag{3}$$

In the following subsections, we will concentrate on more details about feature extractions and concrete formula of our objective function and its constraint.

2.3 Attractiveness features

2.3.1 *Standalone features*

As the name indicates, a community's standalone features are those not depending on other communities. For example, the topic of a community is a standalone feature. For example, if a group on LinkedIn is about text mining, it is very unlikely that it changes that topic due to other groups' activities.

Suppose we have h standalone features $\Gamma = \{\gamma_1, ..., \gamma_h\}$, the score of standalone features of community i is a function of Γ_i. $f_i = g(\Gamma_i)$, where Γ_i is the values of the standalone features of community i. Therefore, $\mathcal{F}_\mathcal{V} = (f_1, f_2, ..., f_k)$ becomes the standalone feature vector for all the nodes in $\mathcal{G}_\mathcal{C}$.

2.3.2 *Attention migrating matrix as dependency features*

We call a community magnet because it can draw people's attention from other communities. Thus, a straightforward way to derive dependency features is to start from people's attention migration flow. People in one community may stay active in that community, or become inactive because some other communities draw their attention away, so that they become active in somewhere else. Therefore, communities draw people's attention among each other. This unique relation is modeled as an attention migrating matrix $D = (d_{ij})_{k*k}$, where d_{ij} is the actual number of people who *depart* from community i and *join* j. Departing from i means the person becomes inactive in community i. Respectively, joining j means the person becomes active in j. Note that what we assume here is that every person could only be active in one community at one time. Let vector $A = (a_i)_{k*1} = D \cdot e$ be the attention vector, where e is a k-by-1 unit vector. Thus, a_i is the total number of people who depart from community i. Let $\mathcal{A}$ be the element-wise inverted vector of A, where $\mathcal{A} = (a_i^{-1})_{k*1}$. We have dependency features of communities as $\mathcal{F_E} = \mathcal{A} \circ D^T$, which is the Hadamard product of $\mathcal{A}$ and D.

The dependency matrix, or edge feature, $\mathcal{F_E}$ is a probabilistic transitional matrix [3]. Each column of $\mathcal{F_E}$ is the distribution of people whose attentions are migrating to other communities.

2.4 Concrete formula of magnet community ranking framework

One way to model the attractiveness of a community, i.e., a node in $\mathcal{G_C}$ is to use random walk with restart. A node's attractiveness value depends on the probability of it being visited from other nodes. In other words, it is the probability that people's attention would arrive from other communities. Upon combining heterogeneous features about node and edge on $\mathcal{G_C}$, we have

$$\mathcal{M} = \alpha\mathcal{F_E}\mathcal{M} + (1-\alpha)\mathcal{F_V}, 0 \le \alpha \le 1 \quad (4)$$

where α is a weighting parameter. With that formula, we can rewrite the objective function as

$$min\ ||\mathcal{M}^* - \mathcal{M}||_F^2 \quad (5)$$

$$= min\ ||\alpha\mathcal{F_E}\mathcal{M} + (1-\alpha)\mathcal{F_V} - \mathcal{M}||_F^2 \quad (6)$$

$$= min\ ||(\alpha\mathcal{F_E} - I)\mathcal{M} + (1-\alpha)\mathcal{F_V}||_F^2 \quad (7)$$

Now let us focus on the constraint for the above objective function. When we say one community is more magnetic than the other, at least one of the following two conditions are very likely to happen. First, this community has better standalone features. Second, it draws people's attention out of other similar communities. On the contrast, it is unlikely for a community to be more magnetic than others if it is inferior on both conditions. Formally, when i is more magnetic than j, i.e., $m_i - m_j > 0$, we want at least one of the following conditions hold.

- $f_i > f_j$
- $\frac{d_{ji}}{S_i} > \frac{d_{ij}}{S_j}$

The first condition is straightforward. It simply states that i's standalone feature should be higher than j's, if i has high attractiveness level than j. The second one needs more explanation. When people depart from community i and join j, we say that i has contribution to j. If community i is more attractive than j, j's contribution to i should be larger than i's contribution to j. The significance of this contribution depends on two factors: the number of migrated people from j and the size of i. Larger communities are harder to be contributed significantly than smaller ones with the same size of in-flow (see Figure 3). Therefore, we call the second condition *contribution imbalance*.

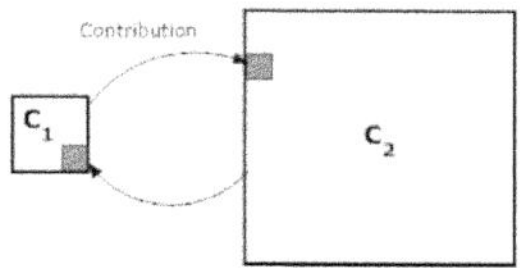

Figure 3: Contribution imbalance

Although it is possible for people to move from i to j if only one of the above conditions is true, it is very unlikely for them to prefer i over j if none of the two condition is true. Thus, we make our constraint as follows, where μ is a weighting parameter and ζ is a lower bound.

$$\sum_{(i,j)} (m_i - m_j) * (\mu(\frac{d_{ji}}{S_i} - \frac{d_{ij}}{S_j}) + (1-\mu)(f_i - f_j)) \ge \zeta \quad (8)$$

Therefore, the three properties of magnet communities are captured into Eq. 7 and Eq. 8 in a subtle way. Eq. 7 states that a community would have better chance to be a magnet one if it attracts attentions from other high magnet communities, which implies the second property. Eq. 8 constraints the magnet computation results must consistent with the first and third properties in Definition 2.3, which are reflected by the term $\frac{d_{ji}}{S_i} - \frac{d_{ij}}{S_j}$.

We rewrite the constraint after combining like terms as

$$\sum_{i=1}^{n} \left(\sum_{u \in n_{in}^i} \varphi_{iu} - \sum_{v \in n_{out}^i} \varphi_{vi} \right) m_i \ge \zeta \quad (9)$$

where n_{in}^i is node i's in-degree neighbors in $\mathcal{G_C}$ and

$$\varphi_{iu} = \mu(\frac{d_{ui}}{S_i} - \frac{d_{iu}}{S_u}) + (1-\mu)(f_i - f_u)$$

n_{out}^i is node i's out-degree neighbors in $\mathcal{G_C}$, and φ_{vi} has similar meaning with φ_{ui}.

We organize Eq. 9 in a more abstract form as

$$\Phi\mathcal{M} \ge \zeta \quad (10)$$

Here, $\mathcal{M}$ is the vector of $\{m_i\}_{1*n}$ and Φ is its coefficient vector.

Now we discuss how to solve the optimization framework.

THEOREM 1. *Our optimization framework is equivalent to the following canonical quadratic programming form:*

$$min \left(\mathcal{M}^T Q \mathcal{M} - 2u^T \mathcal{M} \right) \quad (11)$$

$$s.t., H\mathcal{M} \le \xi \quad (12)$$

PROOF. The objective function of Eq. 7 can be rewritten as

$$||(\alpha\mathcal{F_E} - I)\mathcal{M} + (1-\alpha)\mathcal{F_V}||_F^2$$

$$= tr(\mathcal{M}^T(\alpha\mathcal{F_E}^T - I)(\alpha\mathcal{F_E} - I)\mathcal{M} + (1-\alpha)\mathcal{M}^T(\alpha\mathcal{F_E}^T - I)\mathcal{F_V}$$

$$+ (1-\alpha)\mathcal{F_V}^T(\alpha\mathcal{F_E} - I)\mathcal{M} + (1-\alpha)^2\mathcal{F_V}^T\mathcal{F_V})$$

Notice that the first three terms here are single number variables, and the fourth term is a constant. Therefore, above objective equation is equivalent to the form below:

$$(\mathcal{M}^T(\alpha\mathcal{F_E}^T - I)(\alpha\mathcal{F_E} - I)\mathcal{M} + 2(1-\alpha)\mathcal{F_V}^T(\alpha\mathcal{F_E} - I)\mathcal{M}$$

[3] If two nodes are unreachable, we add a small probability for them to directly reach each other to make $\mathcal{F_E}$ irreducible and aperiodic. (PageRank computation has a similar procedure [18])

Let $Q = (\alpha\mathcal{F_E}^T - I)(\alpha\mathcal{F_E} - I)$, $u = (1-\alpha)(\alpha\mathcal{F_E}^T - I)\mathcal{F_V}$, $H = -\Psi$, and $\xi = -\zeta$. We have our optimization framework reduced to the target form. □

Next, we explore the property of the solution of our optimization, i.e., whether it has feasible solution, or whether the global minimal exist, and the complexity of solving the optimization.

LEMMA 1. *Q in the optimization framework is positive definite, if $\alpha \neq 0$ and $\alpha \neq \frac{1}{\lambda}$, where $\lambda \neq 0$ is the eigenvalue of $\mathcal{F_E}$.*

PROOF. Since $\mathcal{F_E}$ is a stochastic matrix, $|\mathcal{F_E}| \neq 0$. We have $\mathcal{F_E}X = \lambda X$. Therefore, $(\alpha\mathcal{F_E} - I)X = \alpha\mathcal{F_E}X - X = (\alpha\lambda - 1)X$. We have the eigenvalue of $(\alpha\mathcal{F_E} - I)$ is $\alpha\lambda - 1$. Thus, $|\alpha\mathcal{F_E} - I| = \alpha\lambda - 1 \neq 0$. Since $Q = (\alpha\mathcal{F_E} - I)^T(\alpha\mathcal{F_E} - I)$, Q is positive definite. □

THEOREM 2. *Our objective function is strictly convex and it has a unique local minimum which is also a global minimum. Ellipsoid method can find global minimum of the objective function in polynomial time.*

PROOF. The convexity of objective function and the existence of global minimum are guaranteed by the positive definite Q, which also ensures there are polynomial time algorithms can find the minimum solution [7]. □

With the solution techniques, attractiveness computation framework for communities can be formally illustrated below.

Algorithm 1 Attractiveness Computation Framework

Input: The social network with node and edge features $G(V, E, f_V, f_E)$
Output: The magnet vector $\mathcal{M}$
Define the graph transformation function $\mathcal{L}$, generate condensed graph $\mathcal{G_C} = \mathcal{L}(G)$
$\mathcal{F_V} \leftarrow$ Standalone features extraction from $\mathcal{G_C}$
$\mathcal{F_E} \leftarrow$ Dependency features extraction from $\mathcal{G_C}$
Constraint generation from graph $\mathcal{G}(\mathcal{V}, \mathcal{E}, \mathcal{F_V}, \mathcal{F_E})$
Solve the optimization problem using Eq. 7 and Eq. 10, based on $\mathcal{F_V}$ and $\mathcal{F_E}$

3. EVALUATION

In this section, we apply the magnet community identification framework to one real world application, namely magnet company identification, on a social network of professional relations in two industries. Magnet company identification is an interesting research topic by itself. As it serves as a good instance for our framework as well, we select this unique angle to show the effectiveness of our model. All experiments are conducted on machines with Intel Xeon^{TM} Quad-Core CPUs of 2.27 GHz and 24 GB RAM. We use the Matlab optimization toolbox as the solver for our framework.

3.1 Data collection and features extraction

3.1.1 Data collection

We crawl the company community data from the world's largest online professional network platform www.linkedin.com. It provides information about many aspects of companies, one of which is the employee flow (Figure 4). For most companies with certain size or reputation, LinkedIn lists up to top 5 companies of their employee sources and destinations. With this publicly available information, we can construct the raw departure matrix. LinkedIn also displays an estimated size of every company. Therefore, we can piece the information together to have our contribution matrix, which serves as the dependency features. Although LinkedIn only

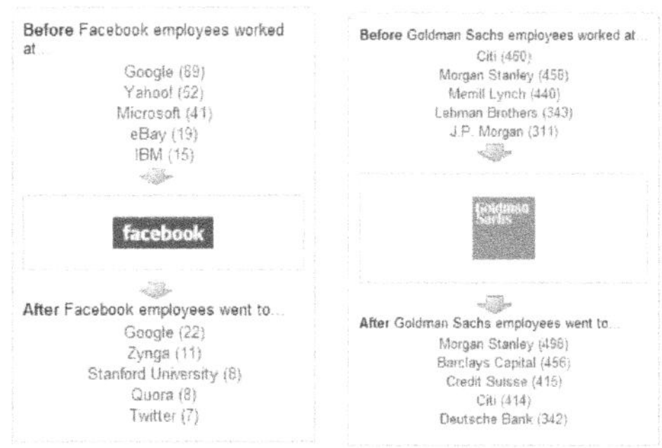

(a) Facebook employee flow (b) Goldman Sachs employee flow

Figure 4: Employee Migration Flows on Linkedin

contains partial information about these companies (not all the employees have LinkedIn accounts), it is a close estimation of real world situation and a good sample of the ground truth data.

For standalone features, we select a company's revenue per employee [4] (a commonly used factor to describe company efficiency [6]), industry, location, and age as its raw features. We believe the four factors contribute much to one's decision about joining a company.

Notice that we can directly consider the information we crawled the features on condensed graph $\mathcal{G_C}$. In fact, in this application domain, the original graph G should be the whole professional network, including users features and their connections. Since that information is not publicly available, we could omit the graph compression process. However, we argue that the performance of our model may not be impacted significantly, because the publicly available information is already an aggregated representation of the hidden condensed graph we need. As a result, the different aspects of information about company communities we crawled can be plugged right in to the optimization framework. In total, we have 39527 companies' information in 142 industries.

3.1.2 Feature extraction

Our raw features for community standalone features in this case are a company's revenue-per-employee, industry, location, and founded year. They are categorical valued except for the first feature. Now we discuss how we translate them into numerical forms.

For each industry, we count how many people flow into it and out of it, using company level departure and arrival data. With that data normalized by industry size, we have the percentage growth of each industry. This percentage indicates the attractiveness of the industries. Table 2 is such an example. It lists growth of all industries related to IT and Finance. We use this growth rate as the industrial feature value.

For locations, we measure their popularities. If a location has more companies nearby, it is more popular. For example, Silicon Valley and New York City are two popular places for IT and finance industries, respectively. A company should be more attractive if it is at a more popular location. We use the number of companies of a location as its feature. We further normalize it to the range (0,1).

Founded year feature is treated similar to location features. For example, people in high-tech industry would like to work for companies that are not only mature enough to be stable, but also not founded too long ago to be active. Thus, we count the number of

[4]Since LinkedIn does not have this information, we crawl that from www.reuters.com/finance.

IT Industry	Growth	Financial Industry	Growth
hardware	3%	banking	1%
software	3%	insurance	0%
network	6%	finance	2%
internet	11%	real estate	0%
semiconductor	2%	investment banking	3%
telecomm.	-2%	investment mngt.	3%
electronics	0%	accounting	1%
information service	1%	venture capital	5%
online game	6%	commercial real estate	6%
information security	4%	capital markets	-1%

Table 2: Industry Growth

companies founded for each year. We use normalized value to represent year feature.

After the categorical-numerical translation, we use a linear combination of the values from the four features as the standalone feature. The dependency features are from the transition data we mentioned in data collection section.

3.2 Ranking performance

3.2.1 Baseline Description

We choose PageRank with one simple but important variation as our baseline. We replace its originally binary adjacent matrix with $\mathcal{F}_{\mathcal{E}}$, and its uniform distributed restart vector with $\mathcal{F}_{\mathcal{V}}$. We still call it PageRank for the ease of presentation. However, this variation captures more information than original PageRank and slightly improves its results, so it serves better as a baseline.

It makes more sense to compare companies in the same industries. Therefore, we pick two representative industries, IT and financial, to conduct our experiments. Although there are divisions within each meta industry (e.g., IT has segments of software, hardware, etc), they are comparable because they share many common properties and attract similar employees. Since our objective is to identify *magnet* companies, the desired result should be companies that have the most potential at current time, which will accelerate the new technology development, produce new ideas, and significantly change people's lives. They are not necessarily giant or well-established ones, but rather innovative and attractive to talents. We searched through media for such rankings as the ground truth. Unfortunately, despite many kinds of company rankings, there is no one directly based on the criteria we mentioned above. Take the arguably most recognized company ranking system *Fortune Magazine* as an example. The famous *Fortune 500* is for largest corporations, because it is based on size and revenue. Other simple rankings proposed by Fortune are based on straightforward criteria. For example, its "best companies to work for" is a series of rankings each of which is based on one of the conditions like *job growth, no layoffs, best for women, big pay*, etc. Out of our best effort, we found no single ranking that takes as many aspects of *attractiveness* level as we did. Nevertheless, we found two rankings that are related to our criteria. One such ranking is the 2011 *ideal employer ranking* proposed by *Universumglobal*while the other is the 2011 most admired company ranking by Fortune [5]. Both of them are based on survey results from professionals and university students. We will use them as our reference sets to compare the effectiveness of our results with PageRankresults. Before that, we would like to first demonstrate some interesting case studies. This provides intuitions and insights of the performance of our magnet community identification model, and why it identifies real magnet companies that attract talents.

[5] money.cnn.com/magazines/fortune/mostadmired/2011/index.html

3.2.2 Case studies

First we want to be clear that, in this study, we are not judging which companies are better. We only neutrally comment on the trend of the companies attractiveness on talents.

IT magnet companies general trend. Table 3 lists the top-10 ranked companies by PageRank and magnet identification model (MIM) results, along with the survey results from Universumglobal and Fortune about ideal employer and most admired companies, respectively. The magnet company list we identified contains both well-established companies, such as Google, Apple, and Microsoft, and energetic start-ups such as Facebook, Salesforce, and LinkedIn. As we know, the technology trend of IT industry is migrating from software to internet in the early 2000s, and from internet to mobile applications and social networks in recent years. The top magnet companies that we identified correctly reflect this trend. For example, software company Microsoft has become less magnetic than internet company Google; Apple is attractive because of the popularity of mobile applications; and social network company Facebook is catching up with other prestigious companies on attractiveness level even if it was just founded a few years ago. In contrast, PageRank prefers big companies because they have far more employee flows than small companies. The PageRank's score depends heavily on a company's size, which is why IBM and Hewlett Packard outrank Microsoft, and Microsoft outranks Google. Compact yet competitive companies like Apple do not earn the chance to get into top 10. These clearly counter people's general understanding of these IT companies and the industry trend. Moreover, in its top 10 list, PageRank does not identify small but promising companies.

We also notice that our result has some important differences with the two survey results, even if our results are already closer to them than with PageRank's result. In the survey results, well-established companies trend to have higher ranks, maybe because people are more familiar with them. For example, companies such as Cisco, Intel, and Texas Instruments will be more recognized due to their legacies. However, well-established companies do not necessarily correspond to magnet companies. Sometimes small or medium start-ups represent the direction of brand new trends which may not even be realized by majority of the population taking the survey. Therefore, these kinds of surveys could not capture this phenomenon. That is why MIM works better than them. For example, we are able to identify promising companies such as Facebook, Salesforce.com and LinkedIn in top 10, and Twitter, Zynga in top 25, where they are hardly recognized by the survey results.

Micro-level case study It is interesting to note that our model, in its top 10 list, is able to identify all the companies in Figure 1 that is generated from a separate source [4]. From that figure, we can see Yahoo! is contributing its talents to all others, and Facebook and LinkedIn are drawing talents from the rest of the companies. That phenomenon has been captured in our list. First, according to our result, Yahoo! is less magnetic than all the companies in the figure (except LinkedIn). Second, Facebook and LinkedIn already make themselves in the top 10 list, despite the fact that they are much younger and smaller than others. They have not outranked others due to other factors, since we are not only using talent traffic as it does in Figure 1.

Financial industry general trend. Table 4 lists the top 10 finance companies identified by PageRank and MIM results. J.P. Morgan

Rank	PageRank	MIM	Ideal Employer	Admired Company
1	IBM	**Google**	Google	Apple
2	Hewlett Packard	**Amazon.com**	Microsoft	Google
3	Oracle	**Apple**	Apple	Amazon.com
4	Microsoft	**Microsoft**	Facebook	IBM
5	Cisco Systems	**Facebook**	IBM	Qualcomm
6	Google	**Salesforce.com**	Electronics Arts	Intel
7	Tata Consult. Services	**Cisco Systems**	Amazon	Texas Instruments
8	Cognizant Tech. Solu.	**Juniper Networks**	Cisco Systems	Cisco Systems
9	Dell	**Yahoo!**	Intel	Adobe Systems
10	EMC	**Linkedin**	Sony	Oracle

Table 3: Top 10 IT Companies

Rank	PageRank	MIM	Ideal Employer	Admired Company
1	J.P. Morgan Chase	**J.P. Morgan Chase**	Goldman Sachs	US Bank
2	Citigroup	**Goldman Sachs**	J.P. Morgan Chase	Goldman Sachs
3	HSBC	**Morgan Stanley**	Boston Consult. Grp.	J.P. Morgan Chase
4	PWC	**Citigroup**	Deloitte	Merrill Lynch
5	Merrill Lynch	**Merrill Lynch**	Merrill Lynch	Northern Trust Corp.
6	Ernst & Young	**CB Richard Ellis**	Ernst & Young	Credit Suisse
7	Deutsche Bank	**Wells Fargo**	Morgan Stanley	CB Richard Eills
8	Credit Suisse	**PWC**	PWC	HSBC
9	Barclays Capital	**Jones Lang LaSalle**	American Express	Barclays
10	Goldman Sachs	**Blackrock**	Bain & Company	Jones Lang LaSalle

Table 4: Top 10 Finance Companies

Chase and Goldman Sachs are relatively unscathed by the recent financial crisis. That means the two companies stay attractive to talents because of their stabilities and capital power. Our model correctly identifies them as the top two. Goldman Sachs is widely recognized as one of the best financial companies, but PageRank fails to give it a proper rank. That's a clear advantage of our method in terms of magnet community identification.

We also have good diversity in the list in terms of segments and sizes. For example, we have leading companies of banks, real estates, financial services, and accounting. CB Richard Ellis and Jones Lang LaSalle are the well-known top 2 leaders in real estate segment. Blackrock is the leader in assess management segment. PWC (PriceWaterhouseCooper) is known as one of the "big four" accounting firms. Unlike IT industry where small start-ups may attract talents by their innovations, financial companies may be attractive due to their capitalization and customer relations, which makes smaller firms harder to stand out as magnet ones. Despite that fact, we also discover some smaller boutique ones in addition to big firms, such as Blackrock. Although it is a much younger and smaller company than others in the list, it has grown to be the world's largest asset manager and one of the leading investment management companies. PageRank's performance is similar to that of IT industry. It heavily prefers big cooperations, e.g., large banks, while ignoring the top companies in segments other than banking. Since big firms tend to be magnet ones in financial industry, PageRank's performance becomes better in financial industry compared to IT industry. We observe that in financial industry, the most admired companies and ideal employers survey results are not as consistent as that of IT industry. The reason for this phenomenon may be that, despite they have some basic functionalities in common, financial companies are more specialized than IT companies, which makes the attraction criteria vary more than that of IT.

3.2.3 Overall Correctness measures

We use discounted cumulative gain (DCG [11]) to evaluate the ranking quality. It emphasizes the correctness of high ranked entities, which is the major goal of many information retrieval tasks. Figure 5(a) and (b) compare the marginal gain on DCG values at different cut-off positions on both ideal employer and admired company data in *IT industry*. As it shows, MIM outperforms PageRank significantly, because it identifies much more top-ranked companies correctly in the beginning. In the rank list generated by PageRank, the top-ranked companies are not the top in both datasets.

On aggregated level, we define a *weighted pairwise distance* measure of retrieved list L_1 and relevant list L_2, which emphasizes more on ranking order and correctness. $wDist(L_1, L_2) = \sum_{a_i \in L_2} (|L_2| - i + 1)(|i - \Lambda(a_i)|)$, where $\Lambda(a_i)$ is the rank of a_i in L_1. Based on this definition, if an algorithm misplaces top-ranked entities, it will receive more penalties than another algorithm which misplaces low-ranked entities. Hence the smaller the value, the better the performance, Figure 5(c) shows MIM result has smaller weighted distance than PageRank result.

Similar to IT industry, we also examine the performance of MIM on financial industry. Figure 6(a) and (b) show its marginal DCG gain results comparing with PageRank. The performance is similar to IT industry, where MIM dominates PageRank performance in high-ranked company set.

Figure 6(c) shows average weighted distance results. We notice that MIM does not outperforms as much as it does in IT industry data. We suspect two reasons for this phenomenon. First, the two benchmark data, i.e., survey results, are based on ad hoc criteria and not as diverse as MIM result. They always biased towards large corporations in banking and accounting. Moreover, some of their results are not consistent with people's usual understanding of the industry, e.g., US Bank ranks higher than any other prestigious financial firms. If the benchmark needs calibration, the comparison results may be affected. Second, in financial industry, well-established ones tend to be magnetic automatically. In that sense, PageRank also does well because it identifies large companies. Even so, MIM still outperforms PageRank by a wide margin in terms of average weighted distance. This comparison between IT industry and financial industry clarifies that, when large communities are not necessarily the magnet targets, MIM is the ideal tool to discover magnet communities.

3.2.4 Parameter sensitivity

According to Eq. 7 and Eq. 8, the MIM algorithm has two parameters α and μ. Now we study how sensitive our model is to

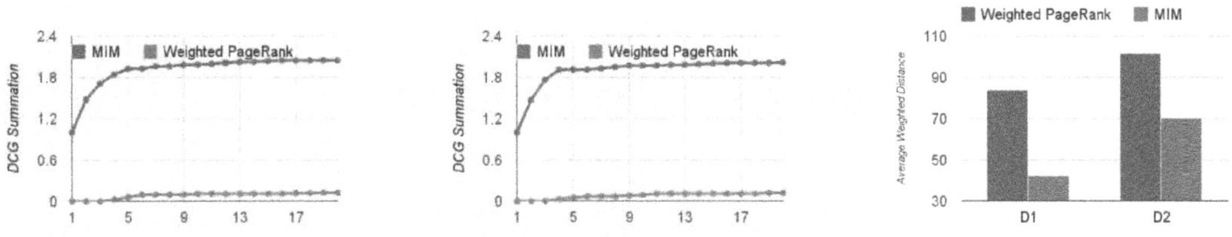

(a) DCG on IT Ideal Employers (b) DCG on IT Admired Companies (c) Average Weighted Distance on IT

Figure 5: Performance on IT Industry

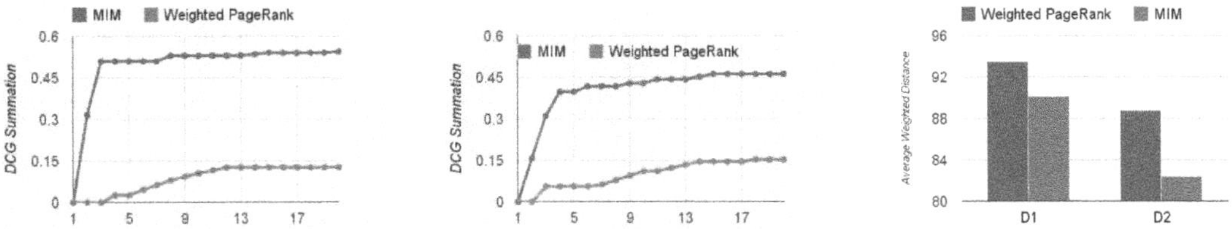

(a) DCG on Finance Ideal Employers (b) DCG on Finance Admired Corp. (c) Avg Weighted Dist. on Finance

Figure 6: Performance on Finance Industry

the two parameters. Due to space limitation, we only show the results on IT industry data and using admired company list as comparison. (Financial industry data give similar results.) Since we care more on high ranked entities, in addition to weighted distance, we also measure the model's performance on average precision $EP = \sum_{k=1}^{n} P(k)\Delta R(k)$, where $P(k)$ is the precision at cut-off k and $\Delta R(k)$ is the change of recall from position $k-1$ to k. We further normalize $wDist$ using $nwDist = \frac{1}{Z} wDist$, where Z is a normalization factor to make it align in the same scale as EP. In Figure 7 we can see that our model performs consistently on different α values. The fluctuations are in a small range. We also observe that the best performances are achieved at $\alpha = 0.6$.

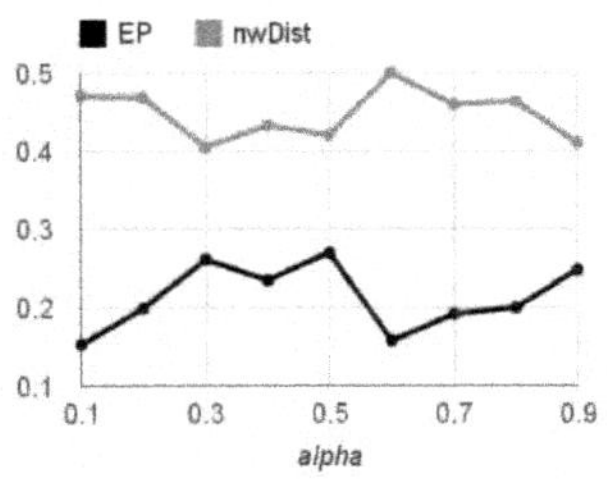

(a) EP and $nwDist$ on α

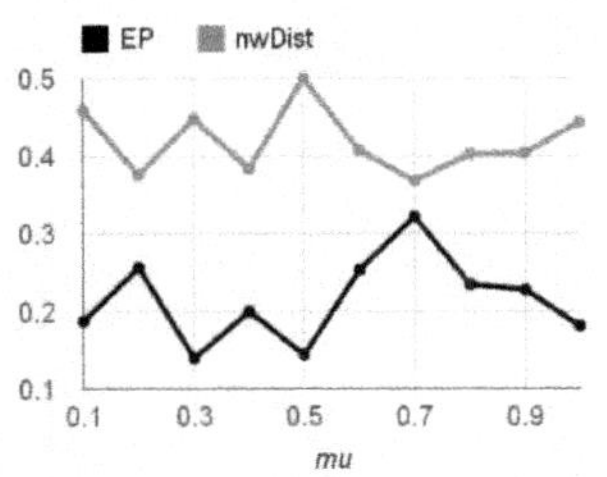

(b) EP and $nwDist$ on μ

Figure 7: Sensitivity Evaluation

Figure 7 also shows that μ has similar effects as α. Though the performance varies on different μ values, they are bounded by a small range. The highest average precision and smallest distance are achieved simultaneously at $\mu = 0.5$. Therefore, we assign 0.6 and 0.5 to α and μ to generate results of IT industry, and 0.2 and 0.7 to them for the same reason for financial industry in case studies.

4. RELATED WORK

Network community analysis has been an active research field for a long time. However, previous works mainly focus on static or dynamic community detection, or most recently community evolution. To our best knowledge, there is no previous work directly related to *magnet community* identification.

Initially, people paid great attention on community detection via the structural properties of communities within a network, e.g., connection densities, etc [15]. While majority of community detection has been done on static networks, new topics and methods addressing dynamic networks are proposed. Rosvall, et.al [19] used random walks to identify the structure of communities. Their work could also rank communities by their structural relations. However, their method also prefers large communities. Aggarwal, et.al. [3] captured the changing phenomena of groups of nodes in a network. They intent to track the gradual changes of one given community. Sun et.al. [20] identified communities that are locally static. The work in [21] identified communities with social interaction and their dynamics based an optimization model that minimizes social cost within communities. The work in [16] also tried to discover dynamic communities, such as growing or birthing communities from hidden member relations. Other studies focused on the discovery of inter-community structure using learning algorithms based on Markov process, which maximize the likelihood of interaction data [17, 23].

The goals of static and dynamic community detections are similar, which is to identify communities. They do not go beyond that to further analyze properties of identified communities, e.g., how magnet community is forming. Therefore, we are addressing a totally different problem where identifying community is only the starting point of our framework.

Another somewhat related direction is to discover the trend or properties related to community members. Falkowski et. al, tried to answer the question of how inactively participating a community would represent a user's interests [9]. It focused on the fluctuation of members on a single community and the insights of the member-community interplay. Although our work also reflects members' interests about communities, it is about their selective attention over multiple communities. Furthermore, we are not emphasizing on the growth or demise of one single community, but the magnet interactions among multiple communities. Another work stood on a single node's (or a small subset of nodes') point of view to analyze how critical events affect *one* dynamic network [5]. In our model, we take account of majority members' attentions rather than a small set of them to help determine the attractiveness levels of *many* communities. The authors in [13] studied the bursts of a short lived "community", or transient crowd, when a hot news emerges on a social network. Their work is mainly about detecting a special type of community of highly dynamic nature. In our case, the communities are not transformed that rapidly. Also, they are not considering anything related to *magnet communities*.

Regarding to our solution technique, constraint optimization formulation in link based graph data ranking has been proposed before with different intentions and design emphasis. The work in [8] constrains HITS algorithm [14] on user opinions about authorities. The work in [22] constrains PageRank algorithm on teleportation parameters to reflect personalization. The work in [1] learns parameters on transition matrix among nodes. The work in [2] tries to rank the whole set of nodes based on the known rankings of a small subset of them. The work in [10] proposes a more complete framework on utilizing meta data such as node and edge features and user preferences, which has never been completely considered in one work before. Our solution differs from the above on several points. First, our work is unsupervised. We don't have labels that indicate which communities are *magnetic*, or which one should absolutely has more attractiveness value than the other. Second, our constraint is derived on meta data, in addition to pairwise preferences. On the comparison with unsupervised approaches, e.g., [12, 18], our method considers more meta data such as node and edge features and magnet properties.

5. CONCLUSION

We introduced the magnet community identification problem. It is not only an important problem for social network research, but also a potential building-block for other analysis. We formulate the problem by graph ranking with heterogeneous information and constraints. Our model takes dependency and standalone features, as well as the magnet properties of communities to generate reasonable communities' attractiveness values. Tailored for this type of ranking, our model outperforms classical link based ranking algorithm, i.e., PageRank and its variation. This paper is only an initial step towards the new direction of research on social network communities. Possible future expansions include applying our framework to other heterogeneous network or analyzing business problems with company attractiveness as a starting point.

6. ACKNOWLEDGE

This work is supported in part by NSF through grants IIS-0905215, IIS-0914934, CNS-1115234, DBI-0960443 and OISE-1129076, US Department of Army through grant W911NF-12-1-0066, and Google Mobile 2014 Program. Thank Xiangnan Kong for providing computation resources.

7. REFERENCES

[1] A. Agarwal, S. Chakrabarti, and S. Agarwal. Learning to rank networked entites. In *KDD'06*.

[2] S. Agarwal. Ranking on graph data. In *ICML'06*.

[3] C. C. Aggarwal and P. S. Yu. Online analysis of community evolution in data streams. In *The 5th SIAM International Conference on Data Mining*, 2005.

[4] Alex, Andrew, and Courtney. http://blog.topprospect.com/2011/06/the-biggest-talent-losers-and-winners.

[5] S. Asur and S. Parthasarathy. A viewpoint-based approach for interaction graph analysis. In *KDD'09*.

[6] A. Barua, P. Konana, A. B. Whinston, and F. Yin. Driving e-business excellence. *MIT Sloan Management Review*, 2001.

[7] S. P. Boyd and L. Vandenberghe. Convex optimization. *Cambridge University Press*, 2004.

[8] H. Chang, D. Cohn, and A. K. McCallum. Learning to create customized authority lists. In *ICML'00*.

[9] T. Falkowski and Myra Spiliopoulou. Users in volatile communities: Studying active participation and community evolution. *Lecture Notes in Computer Science*, 4511.

[10] B. Gao, T. Liu, W. Wei, T. Wang, and H. Li. Semi-supervised ranking on very large graph with rich metadata. In *KDD'11*.

[11] K. Jarvelin and J. Kekalainen. Cumulated gain-based evaluation of ir techniques. 2002.

[12] T. Joachims. Optimizing search engines using clickthrough data. In *KDD'02*.

[13] K. Y. Kamath and J. Caverlee. Transient crowd discovery on the real-time social web. In *WSDM'11*.

[14] JM Kleinberg. Authoritative sources in a hyperlinked environment. In *Journal of the ACM (JACM)*, 1999.

[15] A. Lancichinetti and S. Fortunato. Community detection algorithms: A comparative analysis. 2009.

[16] J. Li, W.K. Cheung, J. Liu, and C.H. Li. On discovering community trends in social networks. In *WI-IAT'09*.

[17] Y. Lin, Y. Chi, S. Zhu, H. Sundaram, and B. L. Tseng. Facetnet: a framework for analyzing communities and their evolution in dynamic networks. In *WWW'08*.

[18] L. Page, S. Brin, R. Motwani, and T. Winograd. The pagerank citation ranking: Bringing order to the web. In *Technical Report, Stanford Digital Library Technologies Project*, 1998.

[19] Martin Rosvall and Carl T. Bergstrom. Maps of random walks on complex networks reveal community structure. *PNAS*, 2008.

[20] J. Sun, S. Papadimitriou, P.S. Yu, and C. Faloutsos. Graphscope: Parameter-free mining of large time-evolving graphs. In *KDD'07*, 2007.

[21] C. Tantipathananandh, T. B. Wolf, and D. Kempe. A framework for community identification in dynamic social networks. In *KDD'07*.

[22] A. C. Tsoi, G. Morini, F. Scarselli, M. Hagenbuchner, and M. Maggini. Adaptive ranking of web pages. In *WWW'03*.

[23] T. Yang, Y. Chi, S. Zhu, Y. Gong, and R. Jin. Detecting communities and their evolutions in dynamic social networks–a bayesian approach. *Mach Learn*.

Vertex Neighborhoods, Low Conductance Cuts, and Good Seeds for Local Community Methods

David F. Gleich*
Purdue University
Computer Science Department
dgleich@purdue.edu

C. Seshadhri†
Sandia National Laboratories‡
Livermore, CA
scomand@sandia.gov

ABSTRACT

The communities of a social network are sets of vertices with more connections inside the set than outside. We theoretically demonstrate that two commonly observed properties of social networks, heavy-tailed degree distributions and large clustering coefficients, imply the existence of vertex neighborhoods (also known as egonets) that are themselves good communities. We evaluate these neighborhood communities on a range of graphs. What we find is that the neighborhood communities can exhibit conductance scores that are as good as the Fiedler cut. Also, the conductance of neighborhood communities shows similar behavior as the network community profile computed with a personalized PageRank community detection method. Neighborhood communities give us a simple and powerful heuristic for speeding up local partitioning methods. Since finding good seeds for the PageRank clustering method is difficult, most approaches involve an expensive sweep over a great many starting vertices. We show how to use neighborhood communities to quickly generate a small set of seeds.

Categories and Subject Descriptors

I.5.3 [**Pattern Recognition**]: Clustering—*Algorithms*

General Terms

Algorithms, Theory

Keywords

clustering coefficients, triangles, egonets, conductance

*Supported by NSF CAREER award 1149756-CCF.

†Supported by the Sandia LDRD program (project 158477) and the applied mathematics program at the Dept. of Energy.

‡Sandia National Laboratories is a multi-program laboratory managed and operated by Sandia Corporation, a wholly owned subsidiary of Lockheed Martin Corporation, for the U.S. Department of Energy's National Nuclear Security Administration under contract DE-AC04-94AL85000.

KDD'12, August 12–16, 2012, Beijing, China.

1. INTRODUCTION

Community detection, loosely speaking, is any process that takes a graph or network and picks out sets of related nodes. An incredibly variety of techniques exist for this single task, which has a variety of names as well: community detection, graph clustering, and graph partitioning. Thus, we use community and cluster interchangeably. For more information about approaches for this problem, see the recent survey by Schaeffer [33]. In many techniques, a community is a set with a good score under a quality measure that reflects the connectivity between the set and the rest of the network. Common measures are based on density of local edges, deviance from a random null model, the behavior of random walks, or graph cuts. Mostly, these measures are NP-hard to optimize.

To keep this manuscript simple, we shall evaluate communities using their *conductance score*. Schaeffer identified this measure as one of the most important cut-based measures and it has been studied extensively in a variety of disciplines [11, 17, 35]. Work by Leskovec et al. has recently demonstrated that, although different quality measures produce differences in terms of specific communities, strong communities persist under a variety of measures [26].

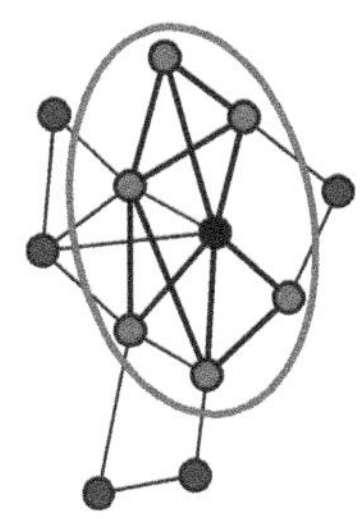

A vertex neighborhood of a vertex v is the set of vertices directly connected to v via an edge and v itself. For example, see the green and black vertices at right. *What we show here is that the presence of two commonly observed properties of modern information networks – a large global clustering coefficient [38] and a heavy tailed degree distribution [5] – implies the existence of vertex neighborhoods with good conductance scores.* We make this statement precise in Theorem 4.6, and the discussion surrounding it in Section 4. These results can be seen as an extension of the simple observation that, in the extreme case when the global clustering coefficient of a network is 1, the network must be a union of cliques. Neighborhoods define ideal communities in this case. We mathematically show that this argument can be extended to the case when the graph has a heavy tailed degree distribution and a large clustering coefficient. The significance of this finding is that robust community detection need not employ complicated algorithms. Instead, a straightforward approach that just involves counting triangles – a function that is easy to implement in MapReduce [12] and easy to approximate [21], suffices to identify communities. It is intriguing that arguably the two most important measurable quantities of social networks imply that communities are very easy to find. This may lead to more mathematical work explaining the success of community detection algorithms, given that the problem is in general NP-hard. We note that unfortunately, our theoretical bounds reflect a worst case behavior and are weaker than required for practical use. Consequently, in the remainder of the paper we explore the utility of neighborhood communities empirically on 15 public real-world networks including collaboration networks, social networks, technological networks, and web networks – see Section 5 for a discussion.

Our empirical investigation of neighborhood clusters begins in Section 6. We first exhibit the conductance scores for the set of neighborhood communities for a few graphs (e.g. Figure 2). We find that neighborhood communities reflect the shape of the network community plot observed by Leskovec et al. [24, 25] at small size scales. We next compare the best neighborhood communities to those discovered by four other procedures: the Fiedler community, the best personalized PageRank community (§2.3), the best network whisker (§2.3), and the best clusters from METIS [18]. In one third of the cases, a neighborhood community is as good as the best of any of the other algorithms.

Motivated by the success of the neighborhood communities at small size scales, we explore using the best vertex neighborhoods as *seeds* for the Andersen-Chung-Lang algorithm in Section 7. Here, we find that these procedures, when seeded with an easy-to-identify set of neighborhood communities, produce larger clusters that decay as expected by the results in Leskovec et al. [24, 25]

The technical discussion of the manuscript begins next by introducing our notation and precisely defines the quantities we examine, such as clustering coefficients, due to variability in the definitions of these measures. We also discuss the Andersen-Chung-Lang personalized PageRank clustering scheme [2] and the network whiskers from Leskovec et al. [24, 25]. We utilize the latter two algorithms as reference points for the success of our community detection.

We make all of our algorithm and experimental code, the majority of the data for the experiments, and many extra figures that did not fit into the paper available:

`www.cs.purdue.edu/homes/dgleich/codes/neighborhoods`

These codes are easy to use. Given the adjacency matrix of a network `A`, the single Matlab command

```
>> ncpneighs(A)
```

will produce a figure like those in this paper.

Summary of contributions.

- We theoretically motivate the study of neighborhood communities by showing they often have a low conductance in graphs with a heavy tailed degree distribution and large clustering coefficients.
- We empirically evaluate these neighborhood communities and find them comparable to those communities found by other algorithms at small size scales.
- We find a small set of neighborhood communities that can be grown into larger communities using a PageRank based community detection algorithm. The results match those communities found with a more expensive sweep over all communities.

Table 1: A summary of the notation.

$n = \|V\|$	the number of vertices
$m = \|E\|$	the number of edges
d_v	the degree of vertex v
f_d	the number of vertices of degree d
W	the set of wedges in a graph
W_v	the set of wedges centered at vertex v
κ	the global clustering coefficient
$\bar{C}$	the mean local clustering coefficient
C_v	the local clustering coefficient for vertex v
$N_r(v)$	the set of vertices within distance r or v
$E(S,T)$	the set of edges between S and T
$\texttt{cut}(S)$	the size of the cut around vertex set S
$\texttt{vol}(S)$	the sum of degrees (volume) of vertices in S
$\texttt{edges}(S)$	twice the number of edges among vertices in S
$\phi(S)$	the conductance of vertex set S

2. FORMAL SETTING AND NOTATION

All of the key notation is summarized in Table 1, and we briefly review it here. Let $G = (V, E)$ be a loop-less, undirected, unweighted graph. We denote the number of vertices by $n = |V|$ and the number of edges by $m = |E|$. In terms of the adjacency matrix, m is half the number of non-zeros entries. For a vertex v, let d_v be the degree of v. For any positive integer d, let f_d be the number of vertices of degree d, that is, the frequency of d in the degree distribution. The maximum degree is denoted by $d_{\max}$. Let $D_r(v)$ to be the distance r-neighborhood of v. This is the set of vertices whose shortest path distance from v is exactly r. Then, we define the ball of distance r around v, denoted by $N_r(v)$, as the set $\bigcup_{i \le r} D_r(v)$.

2.1 Clustering coefficients

A *wedge* is an unordered pair of edges that share an endpoint. The *center* of the wedge is the common vertex between the edges. A wedge $\{(s,t),(s,u)\}$ is *closed* if the edge (t,u) exists, and is open otherwise. We use W to denote the set of wedges in G, and W_v for the set of wedges centered at V. Note that $|W_v| = \binom{d_v}{2}$. We set $p_v = |W_v|/|W|$.

Social networks often have large *clustering coefficients* [38]. Because of the varying definitions of this term that are used, we will denote by κ the *global clustering coefficient*. This quantity is a normalized count of triangles that we interpret as the probability that a uniform random wedge w is closed:

$$\kappa = \Pr_{w \sim W}[w \text{ is closed}] = \frac{\text{number of closed wedges}}{|W|}$$

In terms of triangles, $\kappa = 3 \cdot \text{number of triangles}/|W|$. For any vertex v, C_v is the *local clustering coefficient of* v, or the probability that a uniform random wedge w from W_v is closed. Formally,

$$C_v = \Pr_{w \sim W_v}[w \text{ is closed}] = \frac{\text{number of closed wedges in } W_v}{|W_v|}$$

2.2 Cuts and Conductance

Given a set of vertices S, the set $\bar{S}$ is the complement set, $\bar{S} = V \backslash S$. For disjoint sets of vertices S, T, $E(S,T)$ denotes the edges between S and T. For convenience, we denote *the size of the cut induced by a set* $|E(S,\overline{S})|$ by $\texttt{cut}(S)$.

The conductance of a cluster (a set of vertices) measures the probability that a one-step random walk starting in that cluster leaves that cluster. Let $\texttt{vol}(S)$ denotes the sum of degrees of vertices in S and $\texttt{edges}(S)$ denotes twice the number of edges among vertices in S so that

$$\texttt{edges}(S) = \texttt{vol}(S) - \texttt{cut}(S).$$

Then the conductance of set S, denoted $\phi(S)$, is

$$\phi(S) = \frac{\texttt{cut}(S)}{\min(\texttt{vol}(S), \texttt{vol}(\bar{S}))}.$$

Conductance is measured with respect to the set S or $\bar{S}$ with smaller volume, and is the probability of picking an edge from the smaller set that crosses the cut. Because of this property, conductance is preserved on taking complements: $\phi(S) = \phi(\bar{S})$. For this reason, when we refer to the number of vertices in a set of conductance ϕ, we always use the smaller set $\min(|S|, |\bar{S}|)$. Figure 1 shows a few communities and their associated cuts and conductance scores from our methods and two points of comparison.

2.3 Finding good conductance communities

We briefly review three ways of identifying a community with a good conductance score.

Fiedler set. The well-known Cheeger inequality defines a bound between the second smallest eigenvalue of the normalized Laplacian matrix and the set of smallest conductance in a graph [11]. Formally,

$$(1/2)\lambda_2 \leq \min_{S \subset V} \phi(S) \leq \sqrt{2\lambda_2}$$

where λ_2 is the second smallest eigenvalue of the normalized Laplacian. The proof is constructive. It identifies a set of vertices that obeys the upper-bound using a *sweep* cut. This is the smallest conductance cut among all cuts induced by ordering vertices by increasing values of $\sqrt{d_v}x_v$, where x_v is the component of the eigenvector associated with λ_2. This is the same idea used in normalized cut procedures [35]. We refer to the set identified by this procedure as the *Cheeger* community or *Fiedler* community. The latter term is based on Fiedler's work in using the second smallest eigenvalue of the combinatorial Laplacian matrix [14]. Figure 1b shows the Fiedler community for the Les Misérables network.

Personalized PageRank communities. Another successful scheme for community detection based on conductance uses personalized PageRank vectors. A personalized PageRank vector is the stationary distribution of a random walk that follows an edge of the graph with probability α and "teleports" back to a fixed seed vertex with probability $1 - \alpha$. We use $\alpha = 0.99$ in all experiments. The essence of the induced community is that an inexact personalized PageRank vector, computed via an algorithm that "pushes" rank round the graph, will identify good bottlenecks nearby a seed vertex. These bottlenecks can be formalized in a Cheeger-like bound [2]. The procedure to find a personalized PageRank community is: i) specify a value of α, a seed vertex v, and a desired cluster size σ; ii) solve the personalized PageRank problem using the algorithm from [2] until a degree-weighted tolerance of $\tau = 1/(10\sigma)$; and iii) sweep over all cuts induced by the ordering of the personalized PageRank vector (normalized by degrees) and choose the best. Personalized PageRank communities (PPR communities, for short) were used to identify an interesting empirical property of communities in large networks [24, 25]. To generate these plots, those authors examined a range of values of σ for a large number of vertices of the graph and summarized the best communities found at any size scale in a network community plot. Figure 1c shows the best personalized PageRank community for the network of character interactions in Les Misérables.

Whisker communities. Perhaps the best point of comparison with our approach are the *whisker communities* defined by Leskovec et al. [24,25]. These communities are small dense subgraphs connected by a single edge. They can be found by looking at any subgraph connected to the largest biconnected component by a single edge. Note that the largest biconnected component is not necessarily a 2-core of the graph. (Here, a graph k-core is a subset of vertices where all nodes have degree at least k [34].) Leskovec et al. observed that many of these subgraphs are rather dense. Each subgraph has a cut of exactly one, and consequently, a productive means of finding sets with low conductance is to sort these subgraphs by their volume. The best whisker cut is the single subgraph with largest volume.

3. RELATED WORK

Egonets, homophily, and structural holes. In the context of social networks, vertex neighborhoods are often called egonets because they reflect the the state of the network as perceived by a single vertex. Their analysis is a key component in the study of social networks [37], especially in terms of data collection. Studies of these networks often focus on the theory of structural holes, which is the notion that an individual can derive an advantage from serving as a bridge between disparate groups [9]. These bridge roles are interesting because they contradict homophily in social ties. Homophily, or the principle that similar individuals form ties, is the mechanism that is expected to produce networks with large local clustering coefficients [28]. These social theories have prompted the development of new methods to tease apart some of these effects in real-world networks [22], and to develop network models that capture structural holes [19].

Clustering and communities. Vertex neighborhoods often play a role in other techniques to find community or clustering structure in a network. Overlap in the neighborhood sets of vertices is a common vertex similarity metric used to guide graph clustering algorithms [33]. Other schemes utilize vertex neighborhoods as good *seed sets* for local techniques to grow communities [16, 32]. We explore using a carefully chosen set of neighborhoods for this purpose in our final empirical discussion (§7). Perhaps the most closely related work is a recent idea to utilize the connected components of egonets, after their ego vertex is removed, to produce a good set of overlapping communities [31]. Our theoretical results establish that these ideas are highly likely to succeed in networks with local clustering and heavy tailed degree distributions.

Graph properties. Much of the modern work on networks rests on surprising empirical observations about the structure of real world connections. For instance, information networks were found to have a heavy tailed in the degree distribution [5, 13]. These same networks were also found to have considerable local structure in the form of large clustering coefficients [38], but retained a small global diameter. Our theory shows that a third potential observation – the existence of vertex neighborhood with low conductance – is in fact implied by these other two properties. We formally show that heavy tailed degree distributions and high clustering coefficients imply the existence of large dense cores.

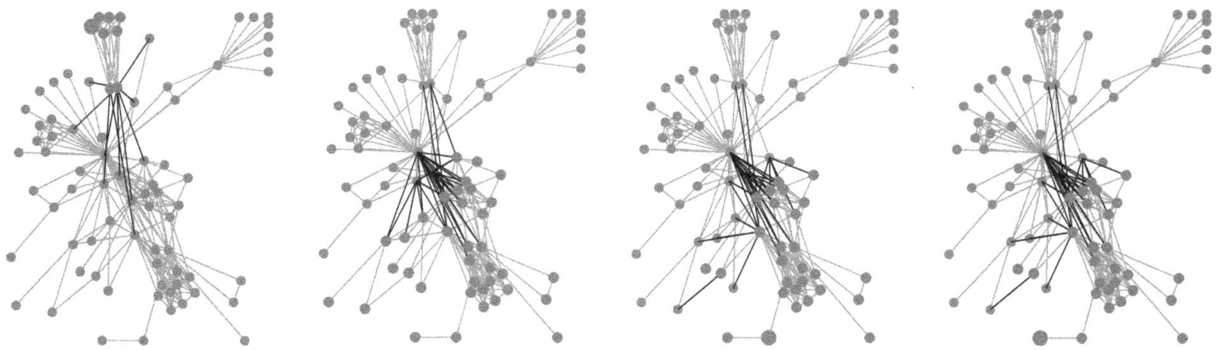

(a) Best neighborhood size=8, cut=10, ϕ=0.15

(b) Fiedler community size=36, cut=29, ϕ=0.13

(c) Best PPR community size=28, cut=31, ϕ=0.12

(d) Best seeded community size=28, cut=31, ϕ=0.12

Figure 1: A series of vertex sets and their associated sizes and conductance score on the graph of characters from *Les Misérables* [20]. The best neighborhood and best seeded community are discussed further in §6 and §7, respectively. See §2.3 for more on the Fiedler and PPR communities. Finding (d) is faster than (c).

Anomaly detection. Predictable behavior in the structure of egonets makes them a useful tool for detecting anomalous patterns in the structure of the network. For instance, Akoglu et al. [1] compute a small collection of measures on each egonet, such as the average degree and largest eigenvalues. Outliers in this space of vertices are often rather anomalous vertices. Our work is, in contrast, a precise statement about the regularity of the egonets, and says that we always expect a large egonet to be a good community.

Summary. Although we are not the first to study neighborhood based communities, the relationship between the local clustering, heavy tailed degree distributions, and large neighborhoods with small conductance does not appear to have been noticed before.

4. THEORETICAL JUSTIFICATION FOR NEIGHBORHOOD COMMUNITIES

The aim of this section is to provide some mathematical justification for the success of neighborhood cuts. Our aim is to show that heavy tailed degree distributions and large clustering coefficients imply the existence of neighborhood cuts with low conductance and large dense cores. *We stress that the exact bounds obtained are weak and only hold when the clustering coefficient is extremely large. Nonetheless, the proofs give significant intuition into* why *neighborhoods are good communities.* The theory is truly tested with the experimental work in the next sections.

We begin with the extreme case when the value of κ is 1, when *every* wedge is closed, for the following simple claim.

CLAIM 4.1. *Suppose the global clustering coefficient of G is 1. Then G is the union of disjoint cliques.*

PROOF. Consider two vertices u and v that are connected. Suppose the shortest path distance between them is $\ell > 1$. Then the shortest path has at least 3 distinct vertices (including u and v). Take the last three vertices on this path, v_1, v_2, v. This forms a wedge at v_2, and must be closed (since the clustering coefficient is 1). Hence, the edge (v_1, v) exists and there exists a path between u and v of length less than ℓ, contradicting the assumption. Hence, any two connected vertices have a shortest path distance of 1, i.e., are connected by an edge and the graph is a disjoint union of cliques. □

Note that the neighborhood of any vertex in the above claim forms a clique disconnected from the rest of G. Therefore, all neighborhoods form perfect communities, in this extremely degenerate case. We prove this for more general settings.

Define $p_v = |W_v|/|W|$, and observe that it forms a distribution over the set of vertices. We show a simple claim about these values. We remind the reader that κ is the global clustering coefficient of G.

CLAIM 4.2. $\sum_v p_v C_v = \kappa$

PROOF.

$$\begin{aligned}\sum_v p_v C_v &= \sum_v \frac{|W_v|}{|W|} \cdot \frac{\text{number of closed wedges in } W_v}{|W_v|} \\ &= \frac{\sum_v (\#\text{ closed wedges in } W_v)}{|W|} = \kappa. \quad \square\end{aligned}$$

We come to an important lemma. This argues that, on average, neighborhood cuts must have low conductance.

LEMMA 4.3.

$$\sum_v \left(p_v \frac{\texttt{cut}(N_1(v))}{|W_v|} \right) = 2(1-\kappa)$$

PROOF. We express the sum of $\texttt{cut}(N_1(v))$ as a double summation, and perform some algebraic manipulations.

$$\begin{aligned}\sum_v \texttt{cut}(N_1(v)) &= \sum_v \sum_{u \in N_1(v)} |N_1(u) \setminus (N_1(v) \cup \{v\})| \\ &= \sum_u \sum_{v \in N_1(u)} |N_1(u) \setminus (N_1(v) \cup \{v\})| \\ &= \sum_u \sum_{v \in N_1(u)} (\#\text{ open wedges centered} \\ &\qquad \text{at } u \text{ involving edge } (u,v)) \\ &= 2\sum_u (\#\text{ open wedges centered at } u) \\ &= 2(1-\kappa)|W|\end{aligned}$$

We complete the proof with the following simple observation:

$$\sum_v \left(p_v \frac{\texttt{cut}(N_1(v))}{|W_v|} \right) = \frac{\sum_v \texttt{cut}(N_1(v))}{|W|}. \quad \square$$

So far, the discussion and proofs hold for any graph with clustering coefficient κ. We now bring in the heavy-tailed degree distribution of G. Since we are performing an asymptotic analysis, we will use $o(1)$ to denote any quantity that becomes negligible as the graph size increases. We will choose β to be a constant less than 1. The asymptotics hold for any β, but from a practical standpoint, we think of β as a constant such that most edges are incident to a vertex of degree at least $d_{\max}^{\beta}$, 2/3 is usually a reasonable value.

Let us formalize the notion that the degree distribution is heavy tailed. This is sometimes expressed as a power law, but that is a fairly contested assertion. Power laws often do not fit real-world degree distributions, but they nonetheless give a rough guide. So we will assume that there is a power law that *approximately bounds* the degree distribution. We formalize this as *Condition* (*).

CONDITION (*) (i) For all d, $f_d \in [\alpha_1 n/d^{\gamma}, \alpha_2 n/d^{\gamma}]$, for some α_1, α_2, and $\gamma < 3$. (ii) The global clustering coefficient of G is κ.

CLAIM 4.4. *Suppose G satisfies Condition (*). Let S be the set of vertices with degrees more than $d_{\max}^{\beta}$. Then, $\sum_{v \in S} p_v = 1 - o(1)$.*

PROOF. We can set $p_v = (2|W_v|)/(2|W|)$. We have $2|W| = \sum_{d>1}^{d_{\max}} d(d-1) f_d$ and $2|W_S| := \sum_{v \in S} 2|W_v| = \sum_{d=d_{\max}^{\beta}}^{d_{\max}} d^2 f_d$. Note that $\sum_{v \in S} p_v = 2|W_S|/2|W|$. It suffices to show that $2|W| - 2|W_S| = o(|W|)$. By the heavy tail condition,

$$2|W| = \sum_{v} 2|W_v| = \sum_{d>1}^{d_{\max}} d(d-1) f_d$$

$$\geq (\alpha_1 n/2) \sum_{d>1}^{d_{\max}} d^{2-\gamma} \geq (\alpha_1 n/2^{4-\gamma}) d_{\max}^{3-\gamma}$$

$$2(|W| - |W_S|) = \sum_{d>1}^{d_{\max}^{\beta}} d(d-1) f_d \leq \alpha_2 n \sum_{d>1}^{d_{\max}^{\beta}} d^{2-\gamma} \leq \alpha_2 n d_{\max}^{\beta(3-\gamma)}$$

Note that $3 - \gamma > 0$ and $\beta < 1$. So the latter is asymptotically smaller than the former, i.e. $2|W| - 2|W_S| = o(|W|)$. □

We next state a cute result that can be derived from our calculations. It is not applied anywhere later, but shows that graphs with heavy tails and large clustering coefficients have large cores. See the online version for the proof.

THEOREM 4.5. *Consider a graph G satisfying Condition (*). There exists a k-core in G for $k \geq \kappa d_{\max}^{\beta}/2$.*

We come to our main theorem that proves the existence of a neighborhood cut with low conductance. When $\kappa = 1$, we get back the statement of Claim 4.1, since we have a set of conductance 0. But this theorem also gives non-trivial bounds for (very) large values of κ. As we mentioned earlier, when κ becomes small, this bound is not useful any longer. Again, it is the intuition of this theorem that is important, not the exact constant that it provides.

THEOREM 4.6. *Consider a graph G satisfying Condition (*). There exists a neighborhood cut with conductance at most $4(1-\kappa)/(3-2\kappa)$.*

PROOF. The proof uses the probabilistic method, given the bounds of Lemma 4.3 and Claim 4.2. Suppose we choose a vertex v according to the probability distribution given by p_v. Let X denote the random variable $\texttt{cut}(N_1(v))/|W_v|$, so $\mathbf{E}[X] = 2(1-\kappa)$ (Lemma 4.3). By Markov's inequality, $\Pr[X > 4(1-\kappa)] \leq 1/2$.

Set $\xi = 2\kappa - 1$, and set $\Pr[C_v < \xi] = p$. Let S_ξ denote the set $\{v | C_v < \xi\}$. (So $\sum_{v \in S_\xi} p_v = p$.) Now, starting with Claim 4.2,

$$\kappa = \sum_{v} p_v C_v = \sum_{v \in S_\xi} p_v C_v + \sum_{v \notin S_\xi} p_v C_v$$

$$< \xi \sum_{v \in S_\xi} p_v + \sum_{v \notin S_\xi} p_v = p\xi + (1-p)$$

$$\Longrightarrow p < (1-\kappa)/(1-\xi) = 1/2$$

By the union bound, the probability that $\texttt{cut}(N_1(v))/|W_v| > 4(1-\kappa)$ *or* $C_v < \xi$ is less than 1. Hence, there exists some vertex v such that $\texttt{cut}(N_1(v)) \leq 4(1-\kappa)|W_v|$ and $C_v \geq \xi$ (we can also show that $d_v \geq n^{\beta}$). Let E be the set of edges in the subgraph induced on $N_1(v)$. Since $C_v \geq \xi$, $|E| \geq \xi |W_v|$. We can bound the conductance of $N_1(v)$,

$$\frac{\texttt{cut}(N_1(v))}{|E| + \texttt{cut}(N_1(v))} \leq \frac{4(1-\kappa)|W_v|}{\xi |W_v| + 4(1-\kappa)|W_v|} = \frac{4-4\kappa}{3-2\kappa}. \quad \square$$

Table 2: Datasets for our experiments. The five types are: collaboration networks, social networks, technological networks, and web graphs.

Graph	Verts	Edges	Avg. Deg.	Max Deg.	κ	$\bar{C}$
ca-AstroPh	17903	196972	22.0	504	0.318	0.633
email-Enron	33696	180811	10.7	1383	0.085	0.509
cond-mat-2005	36458	171735	9.4	278	0.243	0.657
arxiv	86376	517563	12.0	1253	0.560	0.678
dblp	226413	716460	6.3	238	0.383	0.635
hollywood-2009	1069126	56306653	105.3	11467	0.310	0.766
fb-Penn94	41536	1362220	65.6	4410	0.098	0.212
fb-A-oneyear	1138557	4404989	7.7	695	0.038	0.060
fb-A	3097165	23667394	15.3	4915	0.048	0.097
soc-LiveJournal1	4843953	42845684	17.7	20333	0.118	0.274
oregon2-010526	11461	32730	5.7	2432	0.037	0.352
p2p-Gnutella25	22663	54693	4.8	66	0.005	0.005
as-22july06	22963	48436	4.2	2390	0.011	0.230
itdk0304	190914	607610	6.4	1071	0.061	0.158
web-Google	855802	4291352	10.0	6332	0.055	0.519

5. DATA

Data for our empirical investigation comes from a variety of sources. See Table 2 for a summary of the networks and their basic statistics. All networks are undirected and were symmetrized if the original data were directed. Also, any self-loops in the networks were discarded. We only look at the largest connected component of the network. There are four types of networks here. We investigate forest-fire models [23] in the online figures.

Collaboration networks. In these networks, the nodes represent people. The edges represent collaborations, either via a scientific publication (ca-AstroPh [23], cond-mat-2005 [30], arxiv [8], dblp [6, 7]), an email (email-Enron [25]), or a movie (hollywood-2009 [6, 7]). These networks have large global clustering coefficients and large mean clustering coefficients.

Social networks. The nodes are people again, and the edges are either explicit "friend" relationships (fb-Penn94 [36], fb-A [39], soc-LiveJournal [4]) or observed network activity over edges in a one-year span (fb-A-oneyear [39]).

Technological networks. The nodes act in a communication network either as agents (p2p-Gnutella25 [27]) or as routers (oregon2 [23], as-22july06 [29], itdk0304 [10]). The edges are observed communications between the nodes.

Web graphs. The nodes are web-pages, and the edges are symmetrized links between the pages [25].

6. EMPIRICAL NEIGHBORHOOD COMMUNITIES

6.1 Computation

We first show that we can adapt any procedure to compute all local clustering coefficients to compute the conductance scores for each neighborhood in the graph. Most of the work to compute a local clustering coefficient is performed when finding the number of triangles at the vertex. We can express the number of triangles with v as:

$$\texttt{edges}(N_1(v) \setminus \{v\})/2$$

because each edge among v's neighbors produces a triangle (recall that the edges function double-counts). Note also that $\texttt{edges}(N_1(v) \setminus \{v\})/2 = \texttt{edges}(N_1(v))/2 - d_v$. Then $\texttt{cut}(N_1(v)) = \texttt{vol}(N_1(v)) - \texttt{edges}(N_1(v))$. And so, given the number of triangles, we can compute the cut given the volume of the neighborhood as well. This is easy to do with any graph structure that explicitly stores the degrees.

6.2 Quality of neighborhood communities

We use Leskovec et al.'s [24] network community plot to show the information on all neighborhood communities simultaneously. These plots will help us understand if the neighborhood communities are high quality (low conductance), and how they compare to other community detection methods. Given the conductance scores from all the neighborhood communities and their size in terms of number of vertices, we first identify the best community at each size. The network community plot shows the relationship between best community conductance and community size on a log-log scale. In Leskovec et al., they found that these plots had a characteristic shape for modern information networks: an initial sharp decrease until the community size is between 100 and 1000, then a considerable rise in the conductance scores for larger communities. In our case, neighborhood communities cannot be any larger than the maximum degree plus one, and so we mark this point on the figures. We always look at the smaller side of the cut, so no community can be larger than half the vertices of the graph. We also mark this location on the plots. Each subsequent figure in this paper utilizes this size-vs-conductance plot, and we will continually layer information from new methods above results from old methods. The result are information-dense plots that need slightly more study than would be ideal, however, we point out the salient features in each plot in the text. Note also that we deliberately attempt to preserve the axes limits across figures to promote comparisons. However, some figures *have different axis limits* to exhibit the range of data.

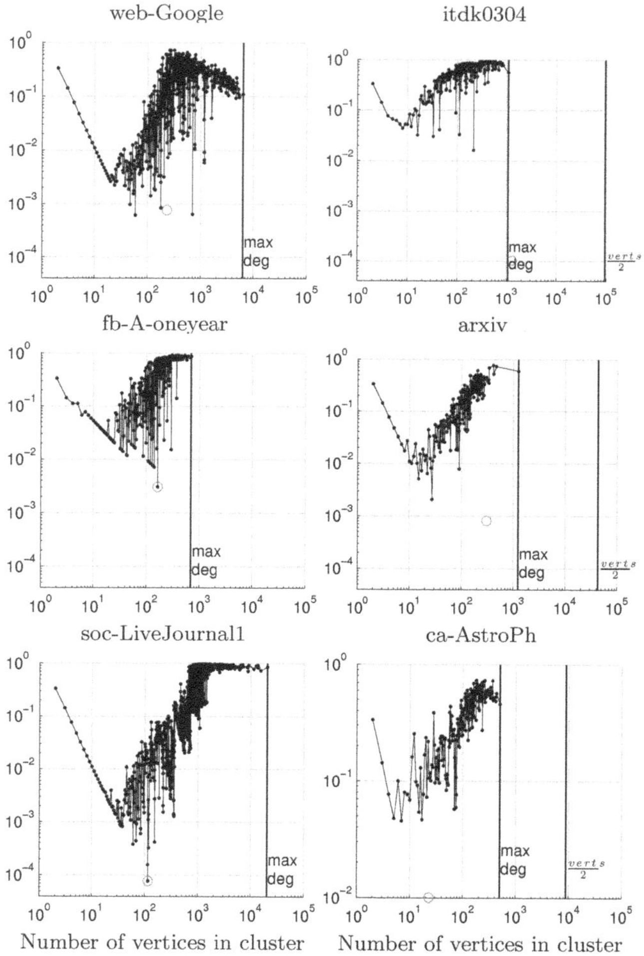

Figure 2: The best neighborhood community conductance at each size (black) and the Fiedler community (red). (Note the axis limits on ca-AstroPh).

First, we show these network community plots for six of the networks in Figure 2. These figures are representative of the best and worst of our results. Plots for other graphs are available on the website given in the introduction.

The three graphs on the left show cases where a neighborhood community *is or is nearby* the best Fiedler community (the red circle). The three graphs on the right highlight instances where the Fiedler community is much better than any neighborhood community. We find it mildly surprising that these neighborhood communities *can be* as good as the Fiedler community. The structure of the plot for both fb-A-oneyear and soc-LiveJournal1 is instructive. Neighborhoods of the *highest degree* vertices are not community-like – suggesting that these nodes are somehow exceptional. In fact, by inspection of these communities, many of them are nearly a star graph. However, a few of the large degree nodes define strikingly good communities (these are sets with a few hundred vertices with conductance scores of around 10^{-2}). This evidence concurs with the intuition from Theorem 4.6.

6.3 Comparison to PPR communities

Note that these plots show the same shape as observed by Leskovec et al. [24]. Consequently, in the next set of figures, and in the remainder of the empirical investigation,

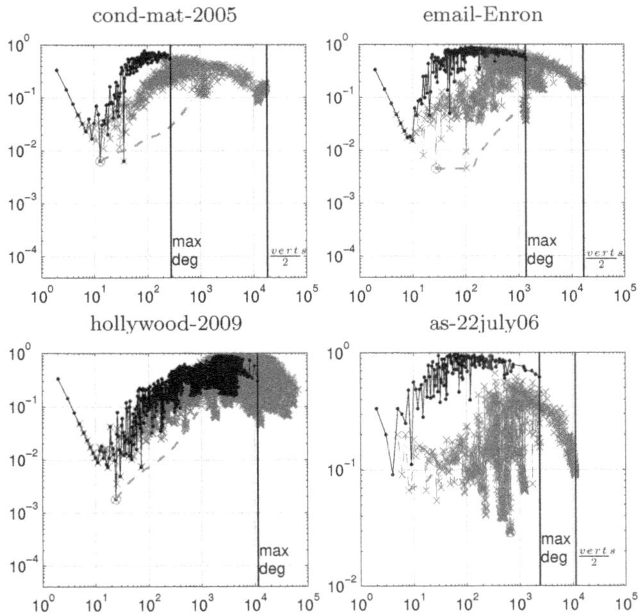

Figure 3: A comparison of neighborhood communities (black) personalized PageRank communities (blue), and whiskers (green).

we compare our neighborhood communities against those computed via the personalized PageRank community scheme employed in that work and described in Section 2.3. Figure 3 compares the neighborhood communities to those computed by running the local personalized PageRank algorithm for all vertices as described by Leskovec et al. [24]. We also show the behavior of the whisker communities in this plot as well. The plot adopts the same style of figure. The PageRank communities are in a deep blue color, and the whisker communities are show in a shade of green. Here, we see that the neighborhood communities show similar behavior at small size scales (less than 20 vertices), but the personalized PageRank algorithm is able to find larger communities of smaller, or similar conductance. In these four cases (which are representative of the others), a personalized PageRank community was also the Fiedler community.

6.4 The best community found

Based on this observation, we wanted to understand how the best community identified by a range of algorithms compares to the neighborhood communities. The results are shown in Table 3. We computed a set of communities with METIS by repeatedly calling the algorithm, asking it to use *more* partitions each time, and saved the best. See our online codes for the precise details of which partitions were used. The seeded community results are described in the next section.

By-and-large, all methods, except neighborhoods, tend to identify similar communities as the best. The Penn94 graph shows a large difference where the Fiedler community is much larger than the best PageRank community *and* it has better conductance. When a neighborhood has conductance that's as good as the rest, then it is always a whisker as well. In the following full section, we explore using these neighborhood communities as *seeds* for the PageRank algorithms. These seeded communities are just as good as the other methods.

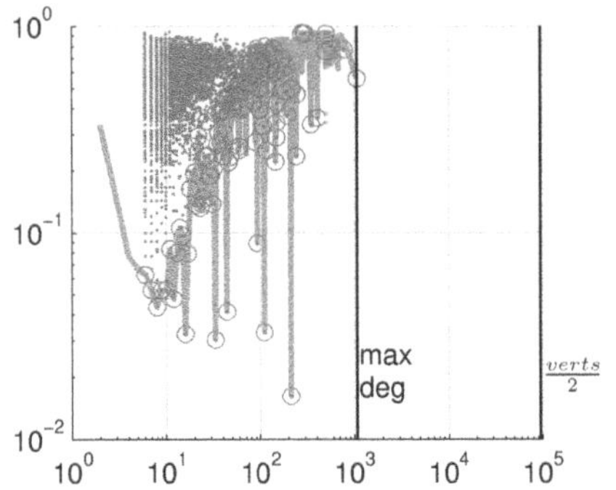

Figure 4: The conductance of locally minimal communities in the itdk0304 graph (red). Note that these capture most of the local minima (downward spikes) in the profile.

7. SEEDED COMMUNITIES

Many of the theorems about extracting local communities from seed sets [2,3] require that the seed set itself be a good community. This is precisely what our theoretical results justify for neighborhood communities. Consequently, in this section, we look at *growing* the neighborhood communities using the local personalized PageRank community algorithm from a set of carefully chosen seeds.

One of the key problems with using the personalized PageRank algorithms is that finding a good set of seeds is not easy. Leskovec et al. [25] used exhaustive enumeration over all seeds, and [15] describes a way to do this using the most popular videos on YouTube. Such a meaningful heuristic is not always available. We begin this section by empirically showing that there is an easy-to-identify set of neighborhood communities that are local extrema in the network community plot of the neighborhood communities.

First, some quick terminology: we say a neighborhood community is a local minima, or locally minimal, if the conductance of the neighborhood of a vertex is smaller than the conductance of any of the adjacency neighborhood communities. Formally,

$$\phi(N_1(v)) \le \phi(N_1(w)) \quad \text{for all } w \text{ adjacent to } v$$

is true for any locally minimal communities. These can be found by looking at each edge in the graph once. We find there are only a small set of locally minimal communities with more than 6 vertices. Shown in Figure 4 are the conductance and sizes of the roughly 7000 communities identified by this measure for the itdk0304 graph. Indeed, among all of the graphs with at least 85,000 vertices, this heuristic picks out about 3% of the vertices as local minima. In the worst case, it picked out 100,000 seeds for soc-LiveJournal1. Increasing the minimum size to 10 vertices reduces this down to 50,000 seeds. We then use these locally minimal neighborhoods as seed sets for the personalized PageRank community detection procedure. Each locally minimal neighborhoods is grown by up to 50-times its volume by solving for communities using values of σ up to 50. In some experiments motivated by Theorem 4.5, we also found interesting results by looking at graph k-cores, and so we also explore growing the k-cores of a graph by up to 5 times their volume.

Figure 5 shows the results. In these figures, we leave the baseline neighborhood communities in for comparison.

Table 3: The best community detected by the six methods explored. The first (§6) and last (§7) are ours.

Graph	Neighborhood		Fiedler		PageRank		Whisker		Metis		Seeded	
	Cond.	Size	Cond.	Size	Cond.	Size	Cond.	Size	Cond.	Size	Cond.	Size
ca-AstroPh	0.0455	7	0.0101	23	0.0101	23	0.0101	23	0.0101	23	0.0101	23
email-Enron	0.0154	10	0.0045	28	0.0045	28	0.0045	28	0.0080	16	0.0045	28
cond-mat-2005	0.0064	13	0.0064	13	0.0064	13	0.0064	13	0.0154	11	0.0064	13
arxiv	0.0021	27	0.0008	303	0.0014	304	0.0021	27	0.0021	27	0.0019	306
dblp	0.0038	24	0.0038	25	0.0034	83	0.0038	25	0.0041	17	0.0034	83
hollywood-2009	0.0018	24	0.0018	24	0.0018	24	0.0018	24	0.0018	24	0.0018	24
Penn94	0.3333	2	0.1898	7191	0.1966	41	0.3333	2	0.1986	6923	0.2009	39
fb-A-oneyear	0.0031	164	0.0031	164	0.0031	164	0.0031	164	0.0090	56	0.0031	164
fb-A	0.0345	8	0.0084	647	0.0084	647	0.0133	38	0.0130	77	0.0084	647
soc-LiveJournal1	0.0001	115	0.0001	115	0.0001	115	0.0001	115	0.0001	115	0.0001	115
oregon2-010526	0.1368	12	0.0467	316	0.0438	318	0.1429	4	0.0553	3820	0.0443	319
p2p-Gnutella25	0.1429	10	0.0417	24	0.0417	24	0.0588	9	0.0417	24	0.0417	24
as-22july06	0.0909	4	0.0289	661	0.0286	654	0.0667	8	0.0296	657	0.0285	656
itdk0304	0.0162	213	0.0001	1306	0.0002	1188	0.0001	1306	0.0046	152	0.0002	1188
web-Google	0.0006	59	0.0008	234	0.0006	59	0.0006	59	0.0006	59	0.0006	59

This leaves the figures rather noisy, but the key insight is that the dark black line (neighborhood seeded communities) closely tracks the the outline of the pure-PageRank based community profile (light blue). That profile was computed by using every vertex in the graph as a seed (although, some vertices were skipped after 10 other clusters had already visited that vertex). This effect is most clearly illustrated by the email-Enron dataset. The dark black line identifies almost all of the local minima from the full PageRank sweep (there are a few it misses). A weakness of these minimal seeds for PageRank is that they may not capture the *largest* communities. However, we found that growing communities from a k-core instead (red line with circles) of a vertex neighborhood do seem to capture this region of the profile (e.g. arxiv), although ca-AstroPh is an exception.

8. CONCLUDING DISCUSSIONS

We recap. Community detection is the problem of finding cohesive collections of nodes in a network. We formalize this as finding vertex sets with small conductance. Modern information networks have many distinctive properties, including a large clustering coefficient and a heavy-tailed degree distribution. We derive a set of theoretical results that show these properties imply that such networks will have vertex neighborhoods that are *themselves* sets of small conductance. Although our theoretical bounds are weak, they suggest measuring the conductance of vertex neighborhoods.

Algorithms to compute *all such conductance scores* are easy to implement by modifying a routine for computing local clustering coefficients. We evaluate these communities on a set of real-world networks. In summary, our results support the idea that there are many neighborhood communities which are *good communities* in a conductance sense. They may be smaller than desired, however.

We next investigate finding a set of locally minimal communities. These communities represent the *best of the neighborhood*. We find that these locally minimal communities, of which there are many fewer than vertices in the graph (usually around 3%), capture the local minimal in the network community profile plot. More importantly, they can be enlarged using a local personalized PageRank community detection procedure. Afterwards, the profile of these "grown" neighborhoods is strikingly close to the profile of the PageRank communities when seeded with all vertices individually. While we do not discuss timing due to the variability in the quality of implementations, this later procedure is much faster in our experiments.

These findings have implications for future studies in community detection. One explanation for the results with the PageRank seeds is that vertex neighborhoods form the base of *any* good community in the network. This idea may guide future research into social network communities.

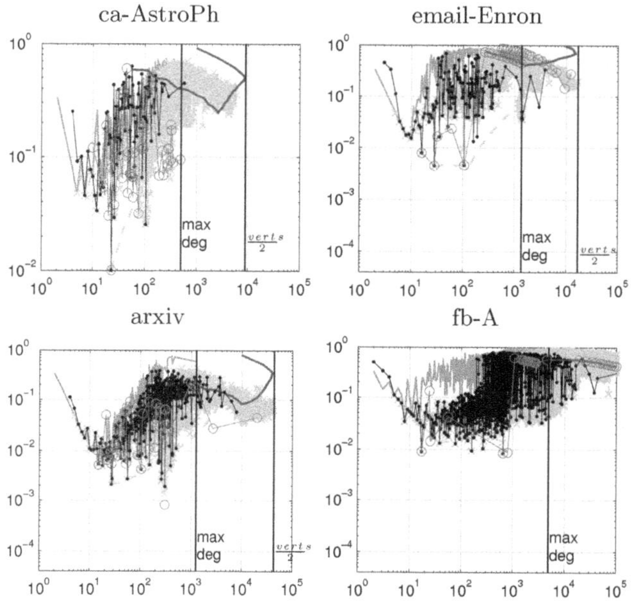

Figure 5: Network community plots with neighborhood communities (gray), PageRank communities (light blue), whiskers (green), k-cores (purple), locally minimal seed PageRank communities (black), and k-core seeded PageRank communities (red).

9. REFERENCES

[1] L. Akoglu, M. McGlohon, and C. Faloutsos. oddball: Spotting anomalies in weighted graphs. In M. Zaki, J. Yu, B. Ravindran, and V. Pudi, editors, *Advances in Knowledge Discovery and Data Mining*, volume 6119 of *Lecture Notes in Computer Science*, pages 410–421. Springer, 2010.

[2] R. Andersen, F. Chung, and K. Lang. Local graph partitioning using PageRank vectors. In *Proceedings of the 47th Annual IEEE Symposium on Foundations of Computer Science*, 2006.

[3] R. Andersen and K. J. Lang. Communities from seed sets. In *Proceedings of the 15th international conference on the World Wide Web*, pages 223–232. ACM Press, 2006.

[4] L. Backstrom, D. Huttenlocher, J. Kleinberg, and X. Lan. Group formation in large social networks: membership, growth, and evolution. In *Proceedings of the 12th ACM SIGKDD international conference on Knowledge discovery and data mining*, KDD '06, pages 44–54. ACM, 2006.

[5] A.-L. Barabási and R. Albert. Emergence of scaling in random networks. *Science*, 286(5439):509–512, 1999.

[6] P. Boldi, M. Rosa, M. Santini, and S. Vigna. Layered label propagation: A multiresolution coordinate-free ordering for compressing social networks. In *Proceedings of the 20th WWW2011*, pages 587–596, March 2011.

[7] P. Boldi and S. Vigna. The Webgraph Framework I: Compression techniques. In *Proceedings of the 13th international conference on the World Wide Web*, pages 595–602. ACM Press, 2004.

[8] F. Bonchi, P. Esfandiar, D. F. Gleich, C. Greif, and L. V. S. Lakshmanan. Fast matrix computations for pair-wise and column-wise commute times and katz scores. *Internet Mathematics*, To appear., 2011.

[9] R. Burt. *Structural Holes: The Social Structure of Competition*. Harvard University Press, 1995.

[10] T. CAIDA. `http://www.caida.org/tools/measurement/skitter/router_topology/`. Accessed in 2005.

[11] F. R. K. Chung. *Spectral Graph Theory*. American Mathematical Society, 1992.

[12] J. Cohen. Graph twiddling in a MapReduce world. *Computing in Science and Engineering*, 11(4):29–41, 2009.

[13] M. Faloutsos, P. Faloutsos, and C. Faloutsos. On power-law relationships of the internet topology. *SIGCOMM Comput. Commun. Rev.*, 29:251–262, August 1999.

[14] M. Fiedler. Algebraic connectivity of graphs. *Czechoslovak Mathematical Journal*, 23(98):298–305, 1973.

[15] U. Gargi, W. Lu, V. Mirrokni, and S. Yoon. Large-scale community detection on YouTube for topic discovery and exploration. In *Proceedings of Fifth International AAAI Conference on Weblogs and Social Media*, 2011.

[16] J. Huang, H. Sun, Y. Liu, Q. Song, and T. Weninger. Towards online multiresolution community detection in large-scale networks. *PLoS ONE*, 6(8):e23829, August 2011.

[17] R. Kannan, S. Vempala, and A. Vetta. On clusterings: Good, bad and spectral. *J. ACM*, 51(3):497–515, May 2004.

[18] G. Karypis and V. Kumar. A fast and high quality multilevel scheme for partitioning irregular graphs. *SIAM J. Sci. Comput.*, 20(1):359–392, 1998.

[19] J. Kleinberg, S. Suri, E. Tardos, and T. Wexler. Strategic network formation with structural holes. In *Proceedings of the 9th ACM conference on Electronic commerce*, EC '08, pages 284–293. ACM, 2008.

[20] D. E. Knuth. *The Stanford GraphBase: A Platform for Combinatorial Computing*. Addison-Wesley, 1993.

[21] M. Kolountzakis, G. Miller, R. Peng, and C. Tsourakakis. Efficient triangle counting in large graphs via degree-based vertex partitioning. In *Algorithms and Models for the Web-Graph*, volume 6516 of *Lecture Notes in Computer Science*, pages 15–24. Springer, 2010.

[22] T. La Fond and J. Neville. Randomization tests for distinguishing social influence and homophily effects. In *Proceedings of the 19th international conference on World wide web*, WWW '10, pages 601–610. ACM, 2010.

[23] J. Leskovec, J. Kleinberg, and C. Faloutsos. Graph evolution: Densification and shrinking diameters. *ACM Trans. Knowl. Discov. Data* 1:1–41, March 2007.

[24] J. Leskovec, K. J. Lang, A. Dasgupta, and M. W. Mahoney. Statistical properties of community structure in large social and information networks. In *WWW '08: Proceeding of the 17th international conference on World Wide Web*, pages 695–704. ACM, 2008.

[25] J. Leskovec, K. J. Lang, A. Dasgupta, and M. W. Mahoney. Community structure in large networks: Natural cluster sizes and the absence of large well-defined clusters. *Internet Mathematics*, 6(1):29–123, September 2009.

[26] J. Leskovec, K. J. Lang, and M. Mahoney. Empirical comparison of algorithms for network community detection. In *Proceedings of the 19th international conference on World wide web*, WWW '10, pages 631–640. ACM, 2010.

[27] R. Matei, A. Iamnitchi, and P. Foster. Mapping the Gnutella network. *Internet Computing, IEEE*, 6(1):50–57, January 2002.

[28] M. McPherson, L. Smith-Lovin, and J. M. Cook. Birds of a feather: Homophily in social networks. *Annual Review of Sociology*, 27:415–444, 2001.

[29] M. Newman. `http://www-personal.umich.edu/~mejn/netdata/`, 2006.

[30] M. E. J. Newman. Scientific collaboration networks. II: Shortest paths, weighted networks, and centrality. *Phys. Rev. E*, 64:016132, Jun 2001.

[31] B. S. Rees and K. B. Gallagher. Overlapping community detection by collective friendship group inference. In *International Conference on Advances in Social Network Analysis andMining*, pages 375–379, Los Alamitos, CA, USA, 2010. IEEE Computer Society.

[32] S. E. Schaeffer. *Algorithms for Nonuniform Networks*. PhD thesis, Helsinki University of Technology, 2006.

[33] S. E. Schaeffer. Graph clustering. *Computer Science Review*, 1(1):27–64, 2007.

[34] S. B. Seidman. Network structure and minimum degree. *Social Networks*, 5(3):269–287, 1983.

[35] J. Shi and J. Malik. Normalized cuts and image segmentation. *Pattern Analysis and Machine Intelligence, IEEE Transactions on*, 22(8):888–905, August 2000.

[36] A. L. Traud, P. J. Mucha, and M. A. Porter. Social structure of facebook networks. *arXiv*, cs.SI:1102.2166, 2011.

[37] S. Wasserman and K. Faust *Social network analysis: methods and applications*. Cambridge University Press, 1994.

[38] D. J. Watts and S. H. Strogatz. Collective dynamics of "small-world" networks. *Nature*, 393(6684):440–442, 1998.

[39] C. Wilson, B. Boe, A. Sala, K. P. Puttaswamy, and B. Y. Zhao. User interactions in social networks and their implications. In *Proceedings of the 4th ACM European conference on Computer systems*, EuroSys '09, pages 205–218. ACM, 2009.

Overlapping Community Detection via Bounded Nonnegative Matrix Tri-Factorization

Yu Zhang and Dit-Yan Yeung
Department of Computer Science and Engineering
Hong Kong University of Science and Technology
Clear Water Bay, Kowloon, Hong Kong
{zhangyu, dyyeung}@cse.ust.hk

ABSTRACT

Complex networks are ubiquitous in our daily life, with the World Wide Web, social networks, and academic citation networks being some of the common examples. It is well understood that modeling and understanding the network structure is of crucial importance to revealing the network functions. One important problem, known as community detection, is to detect and extract the community structure of networks. More recently, the focus in this research topic has been switched to the detection of overlapping communities. In this paper, based on the matrix factorization approach, we propose a method called bounded nonnegative matrix tri-factorization (BNMTF). Using three factors in the factorization, we can explicitly model and learn the community membership of each node as well as the interaction among communities. Based on a unified formulation for both directed and undirected networks, the optimization problem underlying BNMTF can use either the squared loss or the generalized KL-divergence as its loss function. In addition, to address the sparsity problem as a result of missing edges, we also propose another setting in which the loss function is defined only on the observed edges. We report some experiments on real-world datasets to demonstrate the superiority of BNMTF over other related matrix factorization methods.

Categories and Subject Descriptors

I.2.6 [**Artificial Intelligence**]: Learning; H.2.8 [**Database Management**]: Database Applications—*Data mining*

General Terms

Algorithms

Keywords

Network Analysis, Community Detection, NMF, BNMTF

KDD'12, August 12–16, 2012, Beijing, China.

1. INTRODUCTION

Complex networks are ubiquitous in our daily life. For example, the World Wide Web, social networks, and academic citation networks are some of the commonly encountered ones. In these networks, links or edges connecting entities represent relations between them, such as hyperlinks between webpages, friend relations between people, and citations in academic publications. It is well understood that modeling and understanding the network structure is of crucial importance to revealing the network functions. One important problem in understanding the structure of a network is to detect and extract its modular structure consisting of communities, which is often known as community detection [7]. Although the problem is intuitively easy to understand, what constitutes a community in a network does not yet have a well-accepted definition. In this paper, similar to the notion used in [7], we regard communities in a network as densely connected subsets of vertices with a relatively high ratio of the number of intra-community edges to the number of inter-community edges.

Over the past decade, research on community detection has mostly adopted the assumption that each node or vertex in a network belongs to one and only one community. We refer to this as the non-overlapping community detection problem [7, 13], which is similar in many ways to clustering in a lot of data mining applications. Some of the popular community detection methods in this category make use of a quality measure called modularity [4, 2] to evaluate the quality of the community structure found, possibly by directly maximizing an objective function which is based on the modularity measure. This assumption is apparently too restrictive. In many real-world networks such as social networks, it is not uncommon to find entities belonging to multiple groups or communities. In other words, the communities are not disjoint but do overlap. By relaxing the assumption, the community detection problem becomes more general and we refer to it as the overlapping community detection problem. The first method for this problem, called the clique percolation method (CPM), was proposed in [16]. CPM is based on the assumption that each community is a union of adjacent k-cliques. It is an influential method with many extensions proposed subsequently, e.g., [6, 17]. More recently, several methods have been developed based on matrix factorization. For example, nonnegative matrix factorization (NMF) [10] has been applied to develop some methods which deliver promising performance [18, 19].

Even though the NMF-based methods in [18, 19] exhibit good performance on some overlapping community detection applications, they do have drawbacks. For example, the method in [18] uses the conventional NMF model and hence the physical meaning of the parameters is not very clear for the overlapping community detection problem, and the method in [19] has to use different formulations for directed and undirected networks. Moreover, methods in [18, 19] only consider one loss function, i.e., generalized KL-divergence in [18] and squared loss in [19], but in applications we still have no idea which loss function is a more suitable choice for the task at hand. In this paper, our goal is to overcome these drawbacks within the matrix factorization approach. We propose a method called bounded nonnegative matrix tri-factorization (BNMTF). Specifically, from the matrix factorization perspective, we use tri-factorization, i.e., three-factor factorization, in the form $\mathbf{UBU}^T$, where $\mathbf{U}$ represents the membership of each node in each community and $\mathbf{B}$ represents the interaction among all communities. Each entry in $\mathbf{U}$ corresponds to the probability that a node belongs to a community and hence its value is restricted to the range $[0, 1]$, i.e., $\mathbf{U}$ is bounded. Obviously, the physical meaning of $\mathbf{U}$ and $\mathbf{B}$ is very clear. We also note that the same tri-factorization form can be used for both directed and undirected networks. The only difference lies in $\mathbf{B}$, which is required to be symmetric for undirected networks. Unlike the previous methods [18, 19], we consider both the squared loss and generalized KL-divergence as loss functions. Moreover, we note that there is intrinsic ambiguity when an edge is missing between two vertices. While the two vertices involved may indeed be unrelated, it is also possible that the relation between them has not been observed. In the same spirit as many methods for collaborative filtering, we also consider another setting in which the loss function is defined on the edges with nonzero weights only. We will report some experiments on real-world datasets to demonstrate the superiority of BNMTF over existing NMF-based methods.

Notations. Throughout the paper, we use lowercase letters for scalars, bold lowercase letters for vectors, and bold uppercase letters for matrices. We use $\text{tr}(\mathbf{M})$ to denote the trace of a square matrix $\mathbf{M}$. For vector and matrix norms, we use $\|\mathbf{M}\|_1$ to denote the l_1 norm of a matrix $\mathbf{M}$, which is equal to the sum of the absolute values of all the elements of $\mathbf{M}$, $\|\mathbf{M}\|_F$ to denote the Frobenius norm of $\mathbf{M}$, and $\|\mathbf{a}\|_1$ and $\|\mathbf{a}\|_2$ to denote the l_1 and l_2 norms, respectively, of a vector $\mathbf{a}$. To characterize a matrix, we write $\mathbf{M} \geq 0$ to mean that all elements in $\mathbf{M}$ are nonnegative, and $\mathbf{M}_1 \geq (\leq) \mathbf{M}_2$ to denote elementwise inequality between $\mathbf{M}_1$ and $\mathbf{M}_2$. We use $\mathbf{0}$ and $\mathbf{1}$ to denote a vector or matrix consisting of all zeros and ones, respectively, of the appropriate size. The identity matrix of an appropriate size is denoted by $\mathbf{I}$ and the Hadamard or elementwise product is denoted by $\odot$.

2. COMMUNITY DETECTION VIA BNMTF

In this section, we present the BNMTF model and put it in the context of related methods for overlapping community detection. Details on how to solve the optimization problem for parameter learning will be presented in the next section.

2.1 Model Formulation

Let us denote a network by $\mathcal{N} = (\mathcal{V}, \mathcal{E})$, where $\mathcal{V}$ is a set of n vertices and $\mathcal{E}$ is a set of m edges with each of them connecting a pair of vertices in $\mathcal{V}$. The adjacency matrix is a nonnegative matrix $\mathbf{G} \in \mathbb{R}_+^{n\times n}$ whose (i,j)th entry g_{ij} represents the edge weight between the ith and jth vertices.

Depending on whether the network is directed or undirected, $\mathbf{G}$ is asymmetric or symmetric accordingly. Moreover, the network is usually far from being a fully connected network, implying that $\mathbf{G}$ is sparse and hence $m \ll n(n-1)/2$.

We assume that the maximum number of possible communities, denoted by k, is given. In our opinion, a maximum number is much easier to set than the exact number. We use a matrix $\mathbf{U} \in \mathbb{R}_+^{n\times k}$ to denote the community membership of the n vertices in $\mathcal{V}$ and $\mathbf{B} \in \mathbb{R}_+^{k\times k}$ to denote the community interaction matrix. For each entry u_{ij} in $\mathbf{U}$, we interpret it as the probability that the ith vertex belongs to the jth community. The higher the value of u_{ij}, the more active is the ith entity in the jth community. We thus have the following bounded constraint on each element of $\mathbf{U}$:

$$0 \leq u_{ij} \leq 1 \text{ or equivalently } \mathbf{0} \leq \mathbf{U} \leq \mathbf{1}. \tag{1}$$

The matrix $\mathbf{B}$ represents the relations between communities. For example, the communities (or interest groups) 'Economics' and 'Politics' are strongly related and hence we expect a large value for the corresponding entry in $\mathbf{B}$; on the contrary, the communities 'Movies' and 'Politics' are only weakly related and hence the corresponding entry in $\mathbf{B}$ is likely to be small. The product form $\mathbf{UBU}^T$ represents the relation between any two vertices in terms of the community structure. We want to use it to approximate the adjacency matrix $\mathbf{G}$. In other words, we approximate $\mathbf{G}$ by a nonnegative matrix tri-factorization $\mathbf{UBU}^T$ with bounded $\mathbf{U}$:

$$\mathbf{G} \approx \hat{\mathbf{G}} \equiv \mathbf{UBU}^T.$$

Two loss functions, namely, squared loss and generalized KL-divergence, are used to measure the approximation error. Specifically, they are defined as

$$L_{sq}(\mathbf{G}, \mathbf{U}, \mathbf{B}) = \|\mathbf{G} - \hat{\mathbf{G}}\|_F^2 \tag{2}$$

$$L_{kl}(\mathbf{G}, \mathbf{U}, \mathbf{B}) = \sum_{i,j} \left(g_{ij} \ln \frac{g_{ij}}{\hat{g}_{ij}} - g_{ij} + \hat{g}_{ij} \right), \tag{3}$$

where $\hat{g}_{ij}$ is the (i,j)th entry of $\hat{\mathbf{G}}$.

As discussed above, $\mathbf{G}$ is usually sparse. In previous community detection methods, the zero entries in $\mathbf{G}$ are often interpreted as having no edges between the corresponding vertices. However, it is also possible that some otherwise nonzero entries have not been observed during the data collection process. If a loss function is defined on the whole matrix $\mathbf{G}$, then even the second case will be treated as the first case, bringing additional noise to the learning process. Here we propose another loss function which is defined only on the edges with $g_{ij} > 0$:

$$l_{sq}(\mathbf{G}, \mathbf{U}, \mathbf{B}) = \sum_{g_{ij}>0} (g_{ij} - \hat{g}_{ij})^2 \tag{4}$$

$$l_{kl}(\mathbf{G}, \mathbf{U}, \mathbf{B}) = \sum_{g_{ij}>0} \left(g_{ij} \ln \frac{g_{ij}}{\hat{g}_{ij}} - g_{ij} + \hat{g}_{ij} \right). \tag{5}$$

In real networks, usually each vertex does not participate in too many communities and so $\mathbf{U}$ is sparse. To enhance the sparsity of $\mathbf{U}$, we use the l_1 norm to regularize it, i.e., $\|\mathbf{U}\|_1 = \mathbf{1}^T\mathbf{U}\mathbf{1}$ due to the nonnegativity of $\mathbf{U}$. Moreover, by utilizing the l_1 norm of $\mathbf{U}$, we can reduce the effective number of free parameters in $\mathbf{U}$ and hence control the complexity of the model.

Combining the several considerations above, the optimization problem underlying BNMTF can be formulated as

$$\min_{\mathbf{U},\mathbf{B}} L(\mathbf{G}, \mathbf{U}, \mathbf{B}) + \lambda \mathbf{1}^T\mathbf{U}\mathbf{1} \text{ s.t. } \mathbf{0} \leq \mathbf{U} \leq \mathbf{1}, \mathbf{B} \geq \mathbf{0}. \tag{6}$$

In the objective function, the loss function $L(\mathbf{G}, \mathbf{U}, \mathbf{B})$ can be any of the loss functions defined in Eqs. (2) to (5) and the regularization parameter $\lambda > 0$ balances the tradeoff between the approximation error and the complexity of $\mathbf{U}$.

2.2 Related Methods

As discussed above, two NMF-based community detection methods have been developed. In this subsection, we give a more in-depth review of these two methods to put the BNMTF model in perspective.

Psorakis et al. [18] used the conventional NMF model which has two factors. Specifically, using the generalized KL-divergence as in Eq. (3), the model approximates $\mathbf{G}$ using $\mathbf{X}\mathbf{Y}^T$ for directed networks and $\mathbf{X}\mathbf{X}^T$ for undirected networks. One disadvantage of this formulation is that the physical meaning of $\mathbf{X}$ and $\mathbf{Y}$ is not very clear, because $\mathbf{X}$ and $\mathbf{Y}$ cannot be interpreted directly as representing community membership since different entries are of different scales. From the perspective of BNMTF, $\mathbf{X}$ (or $\mathbf{Y}$) may take the form $\mathbf{U}\mathbf{V}$ where $\mathbf{V}$ is related to $\mathbf{B}$. Thus, $\mathbf{X}$ (or $\mathbf{Y}$) captures both $\mathbf{U}$ and $\mathbf{B}$, making its physical meaning unclear. For undirected networks, using a positive semidefinite (PSD) matrix $\mathbf{X}\mathbf{X}^T$ to approximate the symmetric matrix $\mathbf{G}$ is not very suitable in some sense. For example, the diagonal elements of $\mathbf{X}\mathbf{X}^T$ are usually positive but those of $\mathbf{G}$ are almost zero. Moreover, the eigenvalues of $\mathbf{X}\mathbf{X}^T$ are all nonnegative but $\mathbf{G}$ can have negative eigenvalues. For directed networks, the number of parameters ($2nk$) is much larger than that of the undirected case (nk) and also that of BNMTF ($nk+k^2$). As a result, its model complexity is also higher accordingly. Moreover, since $\mathbf{X}\mathbf{Y}^T = (\mathbf{X}\mathbf{D})(\mathbf{Y}\mathbf{D}^{-1})^T$ where $\mathbf{D}$ can be any diagonal matrix with positive diagonal elements, this factorization also faces the nonidentifiability problem and hence slows down the convergence of the algorithm.

In [19], the authors treated directed and undirected networks differently. For undirected networks, like in [18], the factorization form $\mathbf{X}\mathbf{X}^T$ is used but with the squared loss as in Eq. (2). For directed networks, however, a different form $\mathbf{X}\mathbf{A}\mathbf{X}^T$ is used. On the contrary, BNMTF has a unified formulation for both directed and undirected networks, with the only difference being that $\mathbf{B}$ is symmetric or asymmetric according to whether the network is undirected or directed. With a unified formulation, we can gain a better understanding of our model under different settings. Moreover, from the implementation point of view, having a unified formulation is also favorable due to the high degree of code reusability. For undirected networks, because the model in [19] is similar to that in [18], it has the same drawbacks as discussed above. For directed networks, even though their formulation appears to be similar to ours, there exist some crucial differences. For example, their method implicitly assumes that each row of $\mathbf{X}$ represents the probability distribution that the corresponding vertex belongs to each of the communities because a postprocessing step makes the probabilities sum to 1. They do not impose constraints on $\mathbf{X}$ directly because doing so would make the optimization problem even more difficult due to the nonexistence of an analytical solution. However, in order to model overlapping communities, we believe the probabilities of each vertex belonging to different communities should not be constrained as in [19]. For instance, a vertex may belong to the community 'Politics' with probability 0.9 and the community 'Economics' with probability 0.8, due to the strong relation between these two communities. An entity can be very active in multiple communities, but this scenario cannot be modeled well if we impose the constraint that the row sum be equal to 1.

Besides, the network sparsity problem has not been addressed by both methods in [18, 19].

In summary, compared with [18, 19], BNMTF has some appealing advantages:

1) The use of a tri-factorization form in BNMTF gives clear physical meaning to each factor.
2) A unified formulation is used for both directed and undirected networks.
3) BNMTF addresses the network sparsity problem explicitly by using a loss function, as in Eq. (4) or (5), based only on the observed data.

We note that nonnegative matrix tri-factorization has been investigated by some other researchers. For example, Ding et al. [5] proposed an orthogonal nonnegative matrix tri-factorization method for clustering problems by placing an orthogonal constraint on $\mathbf{U}$. However, their method is not suitable for overlapping community detection because it assumes that each vertex can only belong to one community. To the best of our knowledge, there does not exist any nonnegative matrix tri-factorization method with bounded constraints imposed.

3. PARAMETER LEARNING

In this section, we discuss how to solve the optimization problem (6) efficiently.

In general, three types of optimization methods have been used for solving NMF-based methods, namely, auxiliary function methods [11], which are similar to the majorization-minimization approach [9] in statistics, projected gradient methods [12], and the newly emerging coordinate descent methods [3, 8]. Among these three approaches, auxiliary function and coordinate descent methods are very popular due to their efficiency and the existence of analytical solutions. In what follows, we will develop coordinate descent and auxiliary function methods for the BNMTF model.

3.1 Squared Loss

We first discuss how to solve problem (6) when the loss function is the squared loss as in Eq. (2) or (4). For convenience, let us unify Eqs. (2) and (4) to the following form:

$$L(\mathbf{G}, \mathbf{U}, \mathbf{B}) = \sum_{(i,j)\in\mathcal{I}} (g_{ij} - \hat{g}_{ij})^2, \tag{7}$$

where $\mathcal{I}$ is an index set of the available entries in $\mathbf{G}$. More specifically, for the squared loss defined in Eq. (2), $\mathcal{I}$ denotes the set of all indices in $\mathbf{G}$ for directed networks and the set of all indices in the upper-triangular portion of $\mathbf{G}$ for undirected networks. For the squared loss defined in Eq. (4), $\mathcal{I}$ denotes the set of indices of all the nonzero entries of $\mathbf{G}$ for directed networks and the set of indices of all nonzero entries in the upper-triangular portion of $\mathbf{G}$ for undirected networks.

Here we use the coordinate descent method to solve problem (6) with the unified squared loss function as in Eq. (7).[1]

[1]We have also tried to devise an auxiliary function method. However, due to the existence of l_1 regularization and the bounded constraint on $\mathbf{U}$, we have not been able to find a good auxiliary function, as an upper bound of the objective function of problem (6), with an analytical solution.

For the matrix $\mathbf{U}$, the coordinate descent method considers a one-variable update for problem (6) as

$$\begin{aligned} \min_{t} \quad & f_{pq}^{U}(t) = L(\mathbf{G}, \mathbf{U} + t\mathbf{O}_{nk}^{pq}, \mathbf{B}) + \lambda \mathbf{1}^T(\mathbf{U} + t\mathbf{O}_{nk}^{pq})\mathbf{1} \\ \text{s.t.} \quad & 0 \le u_{pq} + t \le 1, \end{aligned} \tag{8}$$

where $\mathbf{O}_{nk}^{pq}$ denotes an $n \times k$ matrix with all entries equal to 0 except the (p,q)th entry which is equal to 1, and u_{pg} denotes the (p,q)th entry of $\mathbf{U}$. By introducing a weight matrix $\mathbf{W}$ whose (i,j)th entry equals 1 when $(i,j) \in \mathcal{I}$ and 0 otherwise, we rewrite the unified squared loss as

$$L(\mathbf{G}, \mathbf{U}, \mathbf{B}) = \|\mathbf{W} \odot (\mathbf{G} - \mathbf{U}\mathbf{B}\mathbf{U}^T)\|_F^2$$

and then simplify $f_{pg}^{U}(t)$ to

$$\begin{aligned} & f_{pq}^{U}(t) \\ =& \left\| \mathbf{W} \odot \left(\mathbf{G} - (\mathbf{U} + t\mathbf{O}_{nk}^{pq})\mathbf{B}(\mathbf{U} + t\mathbf{O}_{nk}^{pq})^T \right) \right\|_F^2 + \lambda t + \lambda \mathbf{1}^T\mathbf{U}\mathbf{1} \\ =& \|\mathbf{W} \odot (\mathbf{Z}_0 + t\mathbf{Z}_1 + t^2\mathbf{Z}_2)\|_F^2 + \lambda t + \lambda \mathbf{1}^T\mathbf{U}\mathbf{1} \\ =& \text{tr}\left((\mathbf{W} \odot (\mathbf{Z}_0 + t\mathbf{Z}_1 + t^2\mathbf{Z}_2)) \, (\mathbf{W} \odot (\mathbf{Z}_0 + t\mathbf{Z}_1 + t^2\mathbf{Z}_2))^T \right) \\ & + \lambda t + \lambda \mathbf{1}^T\mathbf{U}\mathbf{1} \\ =& at^4 + bt^3 + ct^2 + dt + e, \end{aligned} \tag{9}$$

where $\mathbf{Z}_0 = \mathbf{U}\mathbf{B}\mathbf{U}^T - \mathbf{G}$, $\mathbf{Z}_1 = \mathbf{O}_{nk}^{pq}\mathbf{B}\mathbf{U}^T + \mathbf{U}\mathbf{B}(\mathbf{O}_{nk}^{pq})^T$, $\mathbf{Z}_2 = \mathbf{O}_{nk}^{pq}\mathbf{B}(\mathbf{O}_{nk}^{pq})^T$, $a = \text{tr}((\mathbf{W} \odot \mathbf{Z}_2)(\mathbf{W} \odot \mathbf{Z}_2)^T)$, $b = 2\text{tr}((\mathbf{W} \odot \mathbf{Z}_1)(\mathbf{W} \odot \mathbf{Z}_2)^T)$, $c = 2\text{tr}((\mathbf{W} \odot \mathbf{Z}_0)(\mathbf{W} \odot \mathbf{Z}_2)^T) + \text{tr}((\mathbf{W} \odot \mathbf{Z}_1)(\mathbf{W} \odot \mathbf{Z}_1)^T)$, $d = 2\text{tr}((\mathbf{W} \odot \mathbf{Z}_0)(\mathbf{W} \odot \mathbf{Z}_1)^T) + \lambda$, and $e = \text{tr}((\mathbf{W} \odot \mathbf{Z}_0)(\mathbf{W} \odot \mathbf{Z}_0)^T) + \lambda \mathbf{1}^T\mathbf{U}\mathbf{1}$. We can further simplify a, b, c and d by noting the following:

$$\begin{aligned} \text{tr}\left((\mathbf{W} \odot \mathbf{Z}_i)^T(\mathbf{W} \odot \mathbf{Z}_j) \right) &= \text{tr}\left((\mathbf{W} \odot \mathbf{Z}_i \odot \mathbf{W})^T\mathbf{Z}_j \right) \\ &= \text{tr}\left((\mathbf{W} \odot \mathbf{Z}_i)^T\mathbf{Z}_j \right), \end{aligned}$$

where the first equation follows from a property of the Hadamard product that $\text{tr}(\mathbf{A}^T(\mathbf{C} \odot \mathbf{D})) = \text{tr}((\mathbf{A} \odot \mathbf{C})^T\mathbf{D})$, and the second equation follows from another property of the Hadamard product that $\mathbf{A} \odot \mathbf{C} \odot \mathbf{D} = \mathbf{A} \odot \mathbf{D} \odot \mathbf{C}$ and a property of $\mathbf{W}$ that $\mathbf{W} \odot \mathbf{W} = \mathbf{W}$ because $\mathbf{W} \in \{0,1\}^{n \times n}$ is a binary matrix. If there is no constraint in problem (8), we can set the derivative of $f_{pg}^{U}(t)$ with respect to t to 0 and get

$$h(t) = 4at^3 + 3bt^2 + 2ct + d = 0, \tag{10}$$

which amounts to solving a root finding problem. It is easy to show that $a, b \ge 0$. Since different values of a, b, c and d affect the result of the root finding problem, we discuss it separately for the following cases:

1) $a > 0$
2) $a = 0, b > 0$
3) $a = 0, b = 0, c \neq 0$
4) $a = 0, b = 0, c = 0, d \neq 0$.

The solutions for these four cases are depicted in Tables 1 to 4 separately.

For the matrix $\mathbf{B}$, we consider two situations depending on whether the network is directed. When it is directed, $\mathbf{B}$ is a general nonnegative matrix and the objective function for each step of the coordinate descent method is formulated as

$$\begin{aligned} \min_{t} \quad & f_{pq}^{B}(t) = L(\mathbf{G}, \mathbf{U}, \mathbf{B} + t\mathbf{O}_{kk}^{pq}) + \lambda \mathbf{1}^T\mathbf{U}\mathbf{1} \\ \text{s.t.} \quad & b_{pq} + t \ge 0, \end{aligned} \tag{11}$$

Table 1: Algorithm for solving problem (8) when $a > 0$.

calculate $r = \frac{c}{2a} - \frac{3b^2}{16a^2}$;
calculate $s = \frac{b^3}{32a^3} - \frac{bc}{8a^2} + \frac{d}{4a}$;
calculate $\Delta = \frac{r^3}{27} + \frac{s^2}{4}$;
if $\Delta > 0$
  calculate $t_1 = \sqrt[3]{\sqrt{\Delta} - \frac{s}{2}} - \sqrt[3]{\sqrt{\Delta} + \frac{s}{2}} - \frac{b}{4a}$;
  $t = \max(-u_{pq}, \min(1 - u_{pq}, t_1))$;
elseif $\Delta == 0$
  $t_1 = -2\sqrt[3]{\frac{s}{2}} - \frac{b}{4a}$;
  $t_2 = \sqrt[3]{\frac{s}{2}} - \frac{b}{4a}$;
  if $s == 0$
    $t = \max(-u_{pq}, \min(1 - u_{pq}, t_1))$;
  else
    if $t_1 \in [-u_{pq}, 1 - u_{pq}]$ and $t_2 \in [-u_{pq}, 1 - u_{pq}]$
      $t = \begin{cases} t_1 & \text{if } f_{pq}^{U}(t_1) <= f_{pq}^{U}(t_2) \\ t_2 & \text{otherwise} \end{cases}$;
    elseif $t_1 \in [-u_{pq}, 1 - u_{pq}]$
      $t = t_1$;
    elseif $t_2 \in [-u_{pq}, 1 - u_{pq}]$
      $t = t_2$;
    elseif $t_1 < -u_{pq}$
      $t = -u_{pq}$;
    else
      $t = 1 - u_{pq}$;
    end
  end
else
  calculate $\rho = \sqrt{\frac{s^2}{4} - \Delta} = \sqrt{-\frac{r^3}{27}}$;
  calculate ϕ according to $cos(\phi) = -\frac{s}{2\rho}$;
  calculate $t_i = 2\rho^{\frac{1}{3}} \cos\left(\frac{\phi + 2(i-1)\pi}{3}\right) - \frac{b}{4a}$, for $i = 1, 2, 3$,
  assumed $t_1 < t_2 < t_3$;
  if $t_1 \in [-u_{pq}, 1 - u_{pq}]$ and $t_3 \in [-u_{pq}, 1 - u_{pq}]$
    $t = \begin{cases} t_1 & \text{if } f_{pq}^{U}(t_1) <= f_{pq}^{U}(t_3) \\ t_3 & \text{otherwise} \end{cases}$;
  elseif $t_1 \in [-u_{pq}, 1 - u_{pq}]$
    $t = t_1$;
  elseif $t_3 \in [-u_{pq}, 1 - u_{pq}]$
    $t = t_3$;
  elseif $t_2 \in [-u_{pq}, 1 - u_{pq}]$
    $t = \begin{cases} -u_{pq} & \text{if } f_{pq}^{U}(-u_{pq}) <= f_{pq}^{U}(1 - u_{pq}) \\ 1 - u_{pq} & \text{otherwise} \end{cases}$;
  elseif $t_1 > 1 - u_{pq}$
    $t = 1 - u_{pq}$;
  elseif $t_3 < -u_{pq}$
    $t = -u_{pq}$;
  elseif $t_2 > 1 - u_{pq}$
    $t = -u_{pq}$;
  else
    $t = 1 - u_{pq}$;
  end
end

where b_{pq} is the (p,q)th entry of $\mathbf{B}$. We simplify $f_{pq}^{B}(t)$ as

$$\begin{aligned} & f_{pq}^{B}(t) \\ =& \left\| \mathbf{W} \odot \left(\mathbf{G} - \mathbf{U}(\mathbf{B} + t\mathbf{O}_{kk}^{pq})\mathbf{U}^T \right) \right\|_F^2 + \lambda \mathbf{1}^T\mathbf{U}\mathbf{1} \\ =& \|\mathbf{W} \odot (t\mathbf{P}_0 + \mathbf{P}_1)\|_F^2 + \lambda \mathbf{1}^T\mathbf{U}\mathbf{1} \\ =& t^2\text{tr}((\mathbf{W} \odot \mathbf{P}_0)^T\mathbf{P}_0) + 2t\text{tr}((\mathbf{W} \odot \mathbf{P}_1)^T\mathbf{P}_0) + \text{tr}((\mathbf{W} \odot \mathbf{P}_1)^T\mathbf{P}_1) \\ & + \lambda \mathbf{1}^T\mathbf{U}\mathbf{1}, \end{aligned}$$

where $\mathbf{P}_0 = \mathbf{U}\mathbf{O}_{kk}^{pq}\mathbf{U}^T$ and $\mathbf{P}_1 = \mathbf{U}\mathbf{B}\mathbf{U}^T - \mathbf{G}$. We note that $f_{pq}^{B}(t)$ is a quadratic function of t. It is easy to show that the solution to problem (11) can be calculated as

$$\begin{aligned} t &= \max\left(-b_{pq}, -\frac{\text{tr}((\mathbf{W} \odot \mathbf{P}_1)^T\mathbf{P}_0)}{\text{tr}((\mathbf{W} \odot \mathbf{P}_0)^T\mathbf{P}_0)} \right) \\ &= -\min\left(b_{pq}, \frac{\text{tr}((\mathbf{W} \odot \mathbf{P}_1)^T\mathbf{P}_0)}{\text{tr}((\mathbf{W} \odot \mathbf{P}_0)^T\mathbf{P}_0)} \right). \end{aligned}$$

Table 2: Algorithm for solving problem (8) when $a = 0, b > 0$.

```
if c^2 < 3bd
    t = -u_pq;
elseif c^2 > 3bd
    calculate t1 = (-c + sqrt(c^2 - 3bd)) / (3b);
    calculate t2 = (-c - sqrt(c^2 - 3bd)) / (3b);
    if t1 ∈ [-u_pq, 1 - u_pq]
        t = t1;
    elseif t2 ∈ [-u_pq, 1 - u_pq]
        t = { -u_pq      if f^U_pq(-u_pq) <= f^U_pq(1 - u_pq)
            { 1 - u_pq   otherwise                              ;
    elseif t1 < -u_pq or t2 > 1 - u_pq
        t = -u_pq;
    else
        t = 1 - u_pq;
    end
else
    calculate t1 = -c/(3b);
    if t1 ∈ [-u_pq, 1 - u_pq]
        t = t1;
    else
        t = -u_pq;
    end
end
```

Table 3: Algorithm for solving problem (8) when $a = 0, b = 0, c \neq 0$.

```
calculate t1 = -d/(2c);
if c > 0
    t = max(-u_pq, min(1 - u_pq, t1));
else
    t = { -u_pq      if |-u_pq - t1| >= |1 - u_pq - t1|
        { 1 - u_pq   otherwise                          ;
end
```

Table 4: Algorithm for solving problem (8) when $a = 0, b = 0, c = 0, d \neq 0$.

$$t = \begin{cases} -u_{pq} & \text{if } d > 0 \\ 1 - u_{pq} & \text{otherwise} \end{cases};$$

When the network is undirected, $\mathbf{B}$ is symmetric and the objective function for a non-diagonal entry b_{pq} $(p \neq q)$ is given by

$$\begin{aligned} \min_t \quad & f^B_{pq}(t) = L(\mathbf{G}, \mathbf{U}, \mathbf{B} + t\mathbf{O}^{pq}_{kk} + t\mathbf{O}^{qp}_{kk}) + \lambda \mathbf{1}^T \mathbf{U} \mathbf{1} \\ \text{s.t.} \quad & b_{pq} + t \geq 0, \end{aligned} \tag{12}$$

where the objective function can be simplified to

$$\begin{aligned} & f^B_{pq}(t) \\ =& \left\| \mathbf{W} \odot \left(\mathbf{G} - \mathbf{U}(\mathbf{B} + t\mathbf{O}^{pq}_{kk} + t\mathbf{O}^{qp}_{kk})\mathbf{U}^T \right) \right\|_F^2 + \lambda \mathbf{1}^T \mathbf{U} \mathbf{1} \\ =& \|\mathbf{W} \odot (t\mathbf{P}_2 + \mathbf{P}_1)\|_F^2 + \lambda \mathbf{1}^T \mathbf{U} \mathbf{1} \\ =& t^2 \mathrm{tr}((\mathbf{W} \odot \mathbf{P}_2)^T \mathbf{P}_2) + 2t\mathrm{tr}((\mathbf{W} \odot \mathbf{P}_1)^T \mathbf{P}_2) + \mathrm{tr}((\mathbf{W} \odot \mathbf{P}_1)^T \mathbf{P}_1) \\ & + \lambda \mathbf{1}^T \mathbf{U} \mathbf{1}, \end{aligned}$$

with $\mathbf{P}_2$ defined as $\mathbf{P}_2 = \mathbf{U}(\mathbf{O}^{pq}_{kk} + \mathbf{O}^{qp}_{kk})\mathbf{U}^T$. Then the optimal t can be calculated as

$$t = -\min\left(b_{pq}, \frac{\mathrm{tr}((\mathbf{W} \odot \mathbf{P}_1)^T \mathbf{P}_2)}{\mathrm{tr}((\mathbf{W} \odot \mathbf{P}_2)^T \mathbf{P}_2)} \right).$$

For each diagonal entry b_{pp}, the update rule is identical to that for directed networks and we omit the derivation here.

3.1.1 Some Implementation Issues

For the update of $\mathbf{U}$, we need to efficiently compute the coefficients in Eq. (9) or, equivalently, the matrices $\mathbf{Z}_0$, $\mathbf{Z}_1$ and $\mathbf{Z}_2$. According to the definition of $\mathbf{Z}_2$, it is a zero matrix with only one nonzero element indexed by (p, p) as b_{qq}. $\mathbf{Z}_0$ measures the approximation residual and we can keep track of $\mathbf{Z}_0$ and update it whenever each entry in $\mathbf{U}$ and $\mathbf{B}$ changes. Since $\mathbf{Z}_1$ is related to $\mathbf{UB}$ and $\mathbf{BU}^T$, similar to $\mathbf{Z}_0$, we also keep track of $\mathbf{UB}$ and $\mathbf{BU}^T$. By taking advantage of the extreme sparsity of the matrices involved, we can compute the coefficients in Eq. (9) efficiently.

For the update of $\mathbf{B}$, we need to compute $\mathbf{P}_0$, $\mathbf{P}_1$ and $\mathbf{P}_2$. Note that $\mathbf{P}_1$ is equal to $\mathbf{Z}_0$ which is kept as a global variable and needs no additional computation. For $\mathbf{P}_0$, it is easy to show that $\mathbf{P}_0 = \mathbf{u}_p \mathbf{u}_q^T$ according to its definition, where $\mathbf{u}_p$ is the pth column of $\mathbf{U}$, and hence we can compute $\mathbf{P}_0$ more efficiently. Similar to $\mathbf{P}_0$, $\mathbf{P}_2$ can be computed as $\mathbf{P}_2 = \mathbf{u}_p \mathbf{u}_q^T + \mathbf{u}_q \mathbf{u}_p^T$ in an efficient way.

3.2 Generalized KL-Divergence

Similar to the squared loss, we first give a unified form of the generalized KL-divergence as follows

$$L(\mathbf{G}, \mathbf{U}, \mathbf{B}) = \sum_{(i,j) \in \mathcal{I}} \left(g_{ij} \ln \frac{g_{ij}}{\hat{g}_{ij}} - g_{ij} + \hat{g}_{ij} \right). \tag{13}$$

According to [3, 8], the coordinate descent method has no closed-form solution and so we resort to an auxiliary function method. We first give the definition of an auxiliary function.

Definition 1. *$G(\mathbf{h}, \mathbf{h}_0)$ is an auxiliary function for a function $F(\mathbf{h})$ if the conditions*

$$G(\mathbf{h}, \mathbf{h}_0) \geq F(\mathbf{h}); \quad G(\mathbf{h}, \mathbf{h}) = F(\mathbf{h})$$

are satisfied.

For the minimization of $F(\mathbf{h})$, we can minimize $G(\mathbf{h}, \mathbf{h}_0)$ instead based on the following lemma from [9, 11].

Lemma 1. *For an estimate $\mathbf{h}_0$ of $F(\mathbf{h})$, we can update it to $\mathbf{h}_1$ with $F(\mathbf{h}_1) \leq F(\mathbf{h}_0)$ where $\mathbf{h}_1$ satisfies*

$$\mathbf{h}_1 = \arg\min_{\mathbf{h}} G(\mathbf{h}, \mathbf{h}_0).$$

With $\mathbf{B}$ fixed, the objective function for $\mathbf{U}$ is formulated as

$$F(\mathbf{U}) = \sum_{(i,j) \in \mathcal{I}} ([\mathbf{UBU}^T]_{ij} - g_{ij} \ln[\mathbf{UBU}^T]_{ij}) + \lambda \mathbf{1}^T \mathbf{U} \mathbf{1},$$

where $[\mathbf{A}]_{ij}$ denotes the (i, j)th element of $\mathbf{A}$. Then we define the auxiliary function for $F(\mathbf{U})$ in the following theorem.

Theorem 1.

$$\begin{aligned} & G(\mathbf{U}, \hat{\mathbf{U}}) \\ =& \sum_{(i,j) \in \mathcal{I}} \left(\sum_{r=1}^k \sum_{s=1}^k b_{rs} \left(\frac{(\hat{u}_{js} + \epsilon)(u_{ir} + \epsilon)^2}{2(\hat{u}_{ir} + \epsilon)} + \frac{(\hat{u}_{ir} + \epsilon)(u_{js} + \epsilon)^2}{2(\hat{u}_{js} + \epsilon)} \right) \right. \\ & \left. - \sum_{r=1}^k \sum_{s=1}^k (\epsilon b_{rs} u_{js} + \epsilon b_{rs} u_{ir} + \epsilon^2 b_{rs}) - g_{ij} \sum_{r,s} \alpha^{ij}_{rs} \ln \frac{u_{ir} b_{rs} u_{js}}{\alpha^{ij}_{rs}} \right) \\ & + \lambda \mathbf{1}^T \mathbf{U} \mathbf{1}, \end{aligned}$$

where ϵ is a positive constant, $\hat{u}_{ij}$ is the (i,j)th element of $\hat{\mathbf{U}}$, and $\alpha^{ij}_{rs} = \frac{\hat{u}_{ir}b_{rs}\hat{u}_{js}}{\sum_{r,s}\hat{u}_{ir}b_{rs}\hat{u}_{js}}$ is the auxiliary function of $F(\mathbf{U})$.

In Theorem 1, we add ϵ to each $\hat{u}_{rs}$ to increase numerical stability because $\hat{u}_{rs}$ may be equal or very close to 0. Then we need to minimize $G(\mathbf{U},\hat{\mathbf{U}})$ with respect to $\mathbf{U}$ where $\hat{\mathbf{U}}$ is the current estimate of $\mathbf{U}$. For each entry of $\mathbf{U}$, the optimization problem is formulated by rewriting $G(\mathbf{U},\hat{\mathbf{U}})$ as

$$\begin{aligned} \min_{u_{pq}} \quad & f(u_{pq}) = \frac{a}{2}u_{pq}^2 + bu_{pq} - c\ln u_{pq} \\ \text{s.t.} \quad & 0 \le u_{pq} \le 1, \end{aligned} \tag{14}$$

where

$$\mathcal{I}_p^+ = \{j \mid (p,j)\in\mathcal{I}\},\ \ \mathcal{I}_p^- = \{i \mid (i,p)\in\mathcal{I}\}$$

$$a = \sum_{j\in\mathcal{I}_p^+}\sum_{s=1}^{k}\frac{(\hat{u}_{js}+\epsilon)b_{qs}}{\hat{u}_{pq}+\epsilon} + \sum_{i\in\mathcal{I}_p^-}\sum_{r=1}^{k}\frac{b_{rq}(\hat{u}_{ir}+\epsilon)}{\hat{u}_{pq}+\epsilon}$$

$$b = \epsilon(a - \sum_{i\in\mathcal{I}_p^-}\sum_{r=1}^{k}b_{rq} - \sum_{j\in\mathcal{I}_p^+}\sum_{s=1}^{k}b_{qs}) + \lambda$$

$$c = \sum_{j\in\mathcal{I}_p^+}\sum_{s=1}^{k}g_{pj}\alpha^{pj}_{qs} + \sum_{i\in\mathcal{I}_p^-}\sum_{r=1}^{k}g_{ip}\alpha^{ip}_{rq}.$$

If $a = 0$ and $b = 0$, $f(u_{pq})$ degenerates to $f(u_{pq}) = -c\ln u_{pq}$. It is easy to show that the optimal solution is $u_{pq} = 1$ because $c \ge 0$.

If $a = 0$ and $b > 0$, we set the derivative of $f(u_{pq})$ with respect to u_{pq} to 0 and get the solution as $u_{pq,1} = \frac{c}{b}$. If $c \le b$, we can get $u_{pq,1} \in [0,1]$ and since the second-order derivative $f''(u_{pq,1}) = \frac{c}{u_{pq,1}^2} \ge 0$, $u_{pq,1}$ is the optimal solution. If $c > b$, we can get $f'(u_{pq}) = b - \frac{c}{u_{pq}} < 0$ for $u_{pq} \in [0,1]$, implying that $f(u_{pq})$ is nonincreasing and hence 1 is the optimal solution.

If $a = 0$ and $b < 0$, $f'(u_{pq}) = b - \frac{c}{u_{pq}} < 0$ over $[0,1]$, which implies that $f(u_{pq})$ is nonincreasing and hence $u_{pq} = 1$ is the optimal solution.

When $a > 0$,[2] the situation is more complicated. If there is no constraint in problem (14), we can set the derivative of $f(u_{pq})$ with respect to u_{pq} to 0 and obtain the solutions for u_{pq} as

$$u_{pq,1} = \frac{-b+\sqrt{b^2+4ac}}{2a},\ \ u_{pq,2} = \frac{-b-\sqrt{b^2+4ac}}{2a}.$$

It is easy to show that $u_{pq,1} \ge 0$ and $u_{pq,2} \le 0$ since $a > 0$ and $c \ge 0$. When $u_{pq,1} \in [0,1]$, we have $f''(u_{pq}) = a + \frac{c}{u_{pq}} > 0$, implying that $u_{pq,1}$ is the optimal solution of problem (14). When $u_{pq,1} \notin [0,1]$ or equivalently $u_{pq,1} > 1$ since $u_{pq,1} \ge 0$, the derivative of $f(\cdot)$ denoted by $f'(u_{pq})$ is negative over $[0,1]$ since $f'(u_{pq}) = \frac{a}{u_{pq}}(u_{pq}-u_{pq,1})(u_{pq}-u_{pq,2})$ due to $u_{pq,1} > 1$ and $u_{pq,2} \le 0$. This implies that $f(u_{pq})$ is nonincreasing over $[0,1]$ and hence $u_{pq} = 1$ is the optimal solution to problem (14).

When $\mathbf{U}$ is fixed, the objective function for $\mathbf{B}$ is formulated as

$$F(\mathbf{B}) = \sum_{(i,j)\in\mathcal{I}}([\mathbf{UBU}^T]_{ij} - g_{ij}\ln[\mathbf{UBU}^T]_{ij}).$$

For the auxiliary function of $F(\mathbf{B})$, we have the following result.

[2]By definition a cannot be negative.

THEOREM 2.

$$G(\mathbf{B},\hat{\mathbf{B}}) = \sum_{(i,j)\in\mathcal{I}}\left(\sum_{r=1}^{k}\sum_{s=1}^{k}b_{rs}u_{ir}u_{js} - g_{ij}\sum_{r=1}^{k}\sum_{s=1}^{k}\beta^{ij}_{rs}\ln\frac{b_{rs}u_{ir}u_{js}}{\beta^{ij}_{rs}}\right),$$

where $\hat{b}_{rs}$ is the (r,s)th element of $\hat{\mathbf{B}}$ and $\beta^{ij}_{rs} = \frac{\hat{b}_{rs}u_{ir}u_{js}}{\sum_{r,s}\hat{b}_{rs}u_{ir}u_{js}}$ is the auxiliary function of $F(\mathbf{B})$.

Then we need to minimize $G(\mathbf{B},\hat{\mathbf{B}})$, where $\hat{\mathbf{B}}$ is the current estimate of $\mathbf{B}$, with the objective function for each entry b_{pq} of $\mathbf{B}$ formulated as

$$\begin{aligned} \min_{b_{pq}} \quad & f(b_{pq}) = b_{pq}\sum_{(i,j)\in\mathcal{I}}u_{ip}u_{jq} - \left(\sum_{(i,j)\in\mathcal{I}}g_{ij}\beta^{ij}_{pq}\right)\ln b_{pq} \\ \text{s.t.} \quad & b_{pq} \ge 0. \end{aligned}$$

When the network is directed, $\mathbf{B}$ is asymmetric and we set the derivative of $f(b_{pq})$ with respect to b_{pq} to 0 to get the solution as

$$b_{pq} = \frac{\sum_{(i,j)\in\mathcal{I}}g_{ij}\beta^{ij}_{pq}}{\sum_{(i,j)\in\mathcal{I}}u_{ip}u_{jq}},$$

which is nonnegative and hence satisfies the constraint. When the network is undirected, $\mathbf{B}$ is symmetric. We set the derivative of $f(b_{pq})$ with respect to b_{pq} and b_{qp} to 0 and get the solution as

$$b_{pq} = \begin{cases} \frac{\sum_{(i,j)\in\mathcal{I}}g_{ij}\beta^{ij}_{pq}}{\sum_{(i,j)\in\mathcal{I}}u_{ip}u_{jq}} & \text{if } p = q \\ \frac{\sum_{(i,j)\in\mathcal{I}}g_{ij}(\beta^{ij}_{pq}+\beta^{ij}_{qp})}{\sum_{(i,j)\in\mathcal{I}}(u_{ip}u_{jq}+u_{iq}u_{jp})} & \text{otherwise.} \end{cases}$$

3.2.1 Some Implementation Issues

Even though the derivation above appears complicated, it can actually be summarized as an elegant matrix formulation which can be implemented efficiently using some matrix-based software such as MATLAB.

For the update of $\mathbf{U}$, we need to compute the coefficients in the objective function of problem (14). We stack the coefficients for all $\{u_{pq}\}$ in three matrices, namely, $\mathbf{M}_a$, $\mathbf{M}_b$ and $\mathbf{M}_c$, which are all of size $n \times k$. Then we can compute them as

$$\mathbf{M}_a = \frac{\mathbf{W}(\mathbf{U}+\epsilon\mathbf{E}_{nk})\mathbf{B}^T + \mathbf{W}^T(\mathbf{U}+\epsilon\mathbf{E}_{nk})\mathbf{B}}{\mathbf{U}+\epsilon\mathbf{E}_{nk}}$$

$$\mathbf{M}_b = \epsilon(\mathbf{M}_a - \mathbf{W}^T\mathbf{E}_{nk}\mathbf{B} - \mathbf{W}\mathbf{E}_{nk}\mathbf{B}^T) + \lambda\mathbf{E}_{nk}$$

$$\mathbf{M}_c = \mathbf{U}\odot\left(\frac{\mathbf{G}}{\mathbf{UBU}^T}\mathbf{UB}^T + \left(\frac{\mathbf{G}}{\mathbf{UBU}^T}\right)^T\mathbf{UB}\right),$$

where $\mathbf{E}_{nk}$ denotes an $n \times k$ matrix of all ones, and $\frac{\mathbf{M}_1}{\mathbf{M}_2}$ for matrices $\mathbf{M}_1$ and $\mathbf{M}_2$ denotes elementwise division. When we utilize all the elements in $\mathbf{G}$, $\mathbf{W}$ becomes $\mathbf{E}_{nn}$ and we can further simplify the formulation. After getting $\mathbf{M}_a$, $\mathbf{M}_b$ and $\mathbf{M}_c$, we can easily obtain the estimate of $\mathbf{U}$.

For the update of $\mathbf{B}$, we unify the update rule for directed and undirected networks as

$$\tilde{\mathbf{B}} = \frac{\mathbf{B}\odot\left(\mathbf{U}^T\frac{\mathbf{G}}{\mathbf{UBU}^T}\mathbf{U}\right)}{\mathbf{U}^T\mathbf{WU}},$$

where $\tilde{\mathbf{B}}$ is the updated solution for $\mathbf{B}$.

4. EXPERIMENTS

In this section, we report the empirical performance of BNMTF by comparing it with the two related NMF-based methods mentioned before, denoted by NMF_{sq} [19], which uses the squared loss, and by NMF_{kl} [18], which uses the generalized KL-divergence. The two variants of BNMTF are denoted by BNMTF_{sq} and BNMTF_{kl} which use the squared loss and generalized KL-divergence, respectively. The implementation of our method can be downloaded from `http://www.cse.ust.hk/~dyyeung/code/BNMTF.zip`.

The first performance measure is modularity which was proposed by Newman and Girvan in [14]. The modularity measure Q is defined as

$$Q(\mathbf{Y}) = \frac{1}{2m}\sum_{i,j,l}\Big(g_{ij} - \frac{d(i)d(j)}{2m}\Big)y_{il}y_{jl} = \frac{1}{2m}\text{tr}(\mathbf{Y}^T\mathbf{X}\mathbf{Y}),$$

where $d(i)$ denotes the degree of node i, y_{il} is the (i,l)th element of the membership matrix $\mathbf{Y}$, and $\mathbf{X}$ is a matrix with the (i,j)th element $x_{ij} = g_{ij} - \frac{d(i)d(j)}{2m}$. The larger the modularity, the better the performance. Since modularity was originally designed for non-overlapping community detection, only one entry in each row of $\mathbf{Y}$ is 1 while all other entries are 0. So all the methods compared need a postprocessing step to obtain $\mathbf{Y}$ as

$$y_{ik} = \begin{cases} 1 & k = \arg\max_t u_{it} \\ 0 & \text{otherwise} \end{cases}$$

where $\mathbf{U}$ is the membership matrix returned by any method compared and u_{it} is an element of $\mathbf{U}$. The modularity measure may be viewed as a criterion to measure the confidence of the community structure returned by each method. Besides modularity, we also propose another measure which is the area under curve (AUC) score based on modularity. AUC score is to measure the accuracy of the finding of multiple communities by each method. We first scale the entries in each column of the membership matrix $\mathbf{U}$ to $[0,1]$ to make the membership value of the most active node in one community as 1.We then vary a threshold from 0 to 1 and set all those entries in $\mathbf{U}$ that exceed the threshold to 1 and 0 otherwise. Finally we compute the modularity $Q(\mathbf{U})$ and also the AUC score. We use several benchmark datasets[3] (see Table 5) from real-world applications for the experiments.

Table 5: Characteristics of 12 datasets.

Dataset	n	m
Book US politics	105	441
C. elegans metabolic	453	2025
American college football	115	613
Dolphins	62	159
Jazz musicians	198	2742
Les Misérables	77	254
Word adjacencies	112	425
Neural network	297	2345
Email	1133	5451
Coauthorships in network science	1589	2742
Power grid	4941	6594
High-energy theory collaborations	8361	15751

[3] `http://www-personal.umich.edu/~mejn/netdata/`

4.1 Comparison with NMF-based Methods

We first compare BNMTF with NMF_{sq} and NMF_{kl} based on the modularity and AUC score. The results are summarized in Tables 6 and 7. Using the generalized KL-divergence, BNMTF_{kl} is either comparable to or better than NMF_{kl} on every dataset with respect to both performance measures. The result is similar when the squared loss is used. We also compare the two variants of BNMTF. Out of 12 benchmark datasets, BNMTF_{kl} outperforms BNMTF_{sq} on eight in terms of modularity measure while for AUC score, BNMTF_{kl} outperforms BNMTF_{sq} on seven datasets. The result seems to suggest that both loss functions are comparable in performance.

4.2 Comparison of Two Strategies to deal with Sparsity

The methods BNMTF_{kl} and BNMTF_{sq} utilize the whole graph. Here we also consider another setting in which the loss function is defined only on the edges with nonzero weights, i.e., Eqs. (4) and (5). The corresponding methods are denoted by sBNMTF_{sq} and sBNMTF_{kl}. The results are also shown in Tables 6 and 7. We note that sBNMTF_{kl} and sBNMTF_{sq} are generally better than BNMTF_{kl} and BNMTF_{sq} in terms of the AUC score but worse in terms of modularity. This suggests that sBNMTF_{kl} and sBNMTF_{sq} seem to be better for identifying the community structure but worse for finding the most confident communities. Moreover, the performance of sBNMTF_{kl} and sBNMTF_{sq} is unsatisfactory in some cases, e.g., on the 'Word adjacencies' dataset. One possible reason for this is that the network is so sparse that there are only very few edges with nonzero weights.

4.3 Sensitivity Analysis

The free parameters in BNMTF include the rank parameter k, the regularization parameter λ, and ϵ which is added to the denominator in BNMTF_{kl}. Here we conduct some experiments on the 'Dolphins' and 'American college football' datasets to study the sensitivity of these parameters.

We vary the rank parameter k from 3 to 100 and the results are shown in Figures 1(a) and 1(b). When k does not exceed 10, the performance change is small. The performance deteriorates very fast as k increases. This is not surprising because the total number of communities is generally very small.

For the regularization parameter λ, we vary it from 0.01 to 100. Figures 2(a) and 2(b) show the results. We find that the performance is very stable except with some slight degradation as λ approaches 100. Because the performance is not sensitive to λ, setting its value is quite easy.

Figures 3(a) and 3(b) show the results when ϵ varies from 0 to 1. The performance increases significantly as it increases from 0 to 0.2, showing that a nonzero value can help to enhance the numerical stability of BNMTF. Beyond 0.2, the performance is generally insensitive to its value and hence its value is also easy to set.

5. CONCLUSION

By using matrix tri-factorization, BNMTF explicitly models the community membership of each node and the interaction among communities, making it outperform other NMF-based methods in our empirical comparative study.

Table 6: **Comparison in terms of modularity.**

Dataset	NMF_{kl}	$BNMTF_{kl}$	$sBNMTF_{kl}$	NMF_{sq}	$BNMTF_{sq}$	$sBNMTF_{sq}$
Book US politics	0.4051	**0.4802**	0.3893	0.4613	**0.4924**	0.4530
C. elegans metabolic	0.1146	**0.1399**	0.1111	**0.1445**	0.1135	0.0925
American college football	0.5566	**0.5584**	0.4789	0.5584	**0.5733**	0.4315
Dolphins	0.4125	**0.4740**	0.3544	**0.5067**	**0.5067**	0.4125
Jazz musicians	0.2024	**0.2184**	0.2070	0.1133	0.1118	**0.1655**
Les Misérables	0.1565	**0.2146**	0.1772	0.1247	0.1031	**0.1763**
Word adjacencies	-0.0948	**0.1459**	0.0099	0.2539	**0.2677**	-0.0003
Neural network	0.1544	**0.1877**	0.1365	0.0647	**0.1021**	0.0654
Email	0.4992	**0.5108**	0.4210	0.4854	**0.4950**	-0.0020
Coauthorships in network science	0.6936	**0.7827**	0.6835	0.6607	**0.7413**	0.5552
Power grid	0.1530	**0.4646**	0.1217	0.3417	**0.3682**	0.3012
High-energy theory collaborations	0.4803	**0.6053**	0.4444	0.5648	**0.6004**	0.5413

Table 7: **Comparison in terms of AUC score.**

Dataset	NMF_{kl}	$BNMTF_{kl}$	$sBNMTF_{kl}$	NMF_{sq}	$BNMTF_{sq}$	$sBNMTF_{sq}$
Book US politics	0.0981	0.1024	**0.2352**	0.1415	0.1527	**0.2000**
C. elegans metabolic	0.0028	0.0044	**0.0188**	0.0036	0.0026	**0.0268**
American college football	0.2135	0.2103	**0.2178**	0.2125	**0.2158**	0.0180
Dolphins	0.1118	0.1284	**0.1984**	0.1504	0.1501	**0.1911**
Jazz musicians	0.0416	0.0848	**0.1179**	0.0710	0.0620	**0.2219**
Les Misérables	0.0339	0.0809	**0.0877**	0.0679	0.0529	**0.0896**
Word adjacencies	-0.0262	**0.0208**	-0.0025	0.0513	**0.0560**	-0.0009
Neural network	0.0261	0.0285	**0.0344**	0.0061	0.0127	**0.0278**
Email	0.0782	0.0790	**0.1477**	**0.0829**	0.0808	0.0706
Coauthorships in network science	0.0394	0.0430	**0.0431**	0.0175	0.0162	**0.0487**
Power grid	0.0187	**0.0385**	0.0101	0.0159	**0.0168**	0.0149
High-energy theory collaborations	0.0231	**0.0258**	0.0160	0.0053	**0.0181**	0.0172

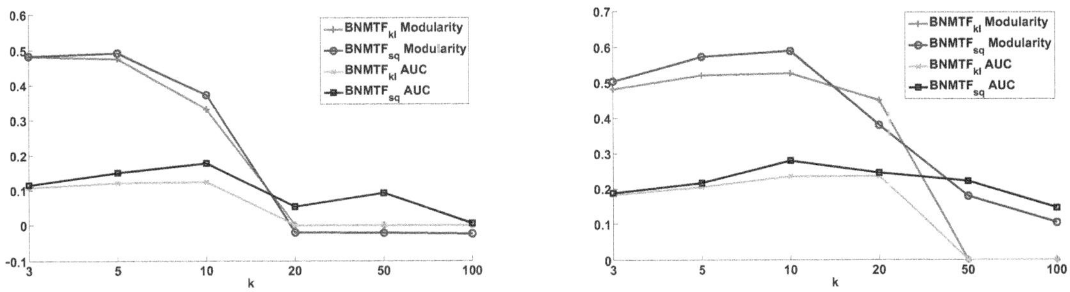

(a) Dolphins (b) American college football

Figure 1: Sensitivity analysis with respect to rank parameter k on 'Dolphins' and 'American college football' datasets.

Currently, BNMTF requires the maximum number of communities to be set in advance. One possible extension in the future is to allow the actual number of communities to be determined automatically. For example, we may pursue a probabilistic reformulation of BNMTF so that methods such as automatic relevance determination [1] can be incorporated to learn the number of communities. Moreover, the current paper focuses on the static community detection problem. Another interesting direction is to extend BNMTF to dynamic community detection [15] by modeling dynamic network evolution over time.

Acknowledgments

This research has been supported by General Research Fund 621310 from the Research Grants Council of Hong Kong.

6. REFERENCES

[1] C. M. Bishop. *Pattern Recognition and Machine Learning*. Springer, New York, 2006.

[2] V. D. Blondel, J.-L. Guillaume, R. Lambiotte, and E. Lefebvre. Fast unfolding of communities in large networks. *Journal of Statistical Mechanics: Theory and Experiment*, 2008(10):P10008, 2008.

[3] A. Cichocki and A.-H. Phan. Fast local algorithms for large scale nonnegative matrix and tensor factorizations. *IEICE Transaction on Fundamentals*, E92-A(3):708–721, 2009.

[4] A. Clauset, M. E. J. Newman, and C. Moore. Finding community structure in very large networks. *Physical Review E*, 70(6):066111, 2004.

[5] C. Ding, T. Li, W. Peng, and H. Park. Orthogonal

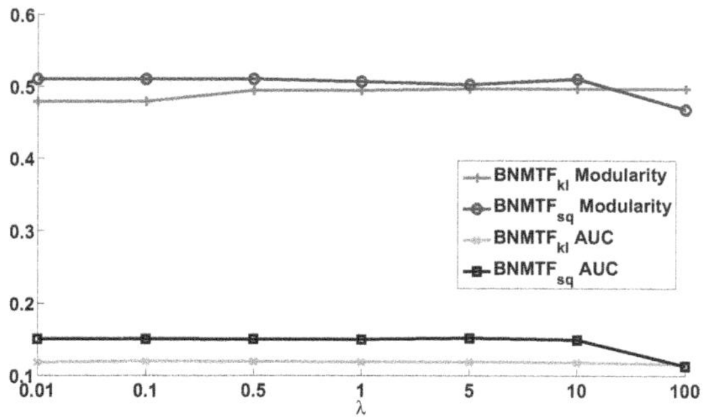

(a) Dolphins

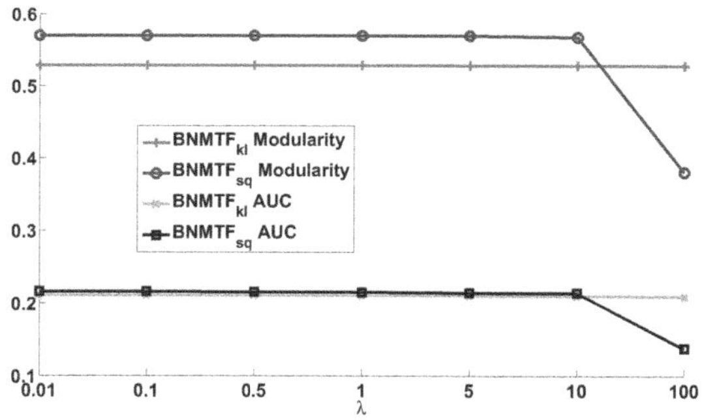

(b) American college football

Figure 2: Sensitivity analysis with respect to regularization parameter λ on 'Dolphins' and 'American college football' datasets.

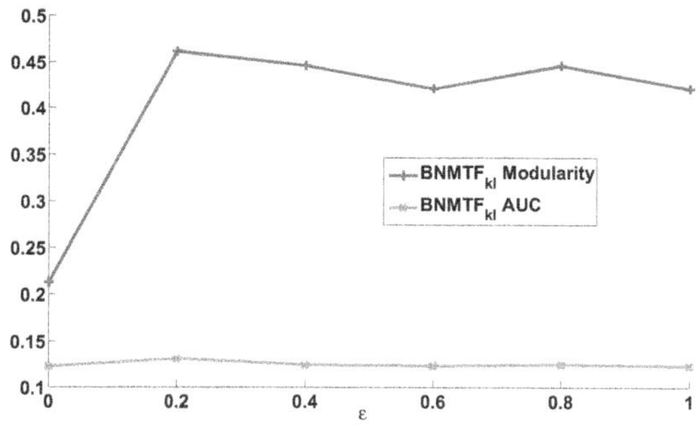

(a) Dolphins

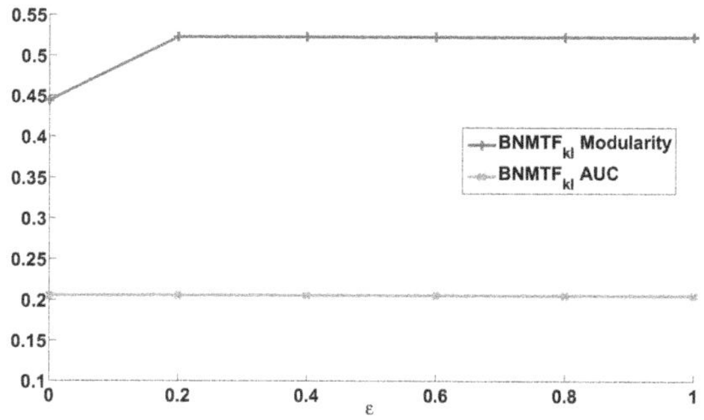

(b) American college football

Figure 3: Sensitivity analysis with respect to ϵ on 'Dolphins' and 'American college football' datasets.

nonnegative matrix tri-factorizations for clustering. In *Proceedings of the Twelfth ACM SIGKDD International Conference on Knowledge Discovery and Data Mining*, pages 126–135, Philadelphia, PA, USA, 2006.

[6] I. J. Farkas, D. Ábel, G. Palla, and T. Vicsek. Weighted network modules. *New Journal of Physics*, 9:180, 2007.

[7] M. Girvan and M. E. J. Newman. Community structure in social and biological networks. *Proceedings of the National Academy of Sciences*, 99(12):7821–7826, 2002.

[8] C.-J. Hsieh and I. S. Dhillon. Fast coordinate descent methods with variable selection for non-negative matrix factorization. In *Proceedings of the 17th ACM SIGKDD International Conference on Knowledge Discovery and Data Mining*, pages 1064–1072, San Diego, CA, USA, 2011.

[9] K. Lange, D. R. Hunter, and I. Yang. Optimization transfer using surrogate objective functions. *Journal of Computational and Graphical Statistics*, 9(1):1–59, 2000.

[10] D. D. Lee and H. S. Seung. Learning the parts of objects by non-negative matrix factorization. *Nature*, 401(6755):788–791, 1999.

[11] D. D. Lee and H. S. Seung. Algorithms for non-negative matrix factorization. In T. K. Leen, T. G. Dietterich, and V. Tresp, editors, *Advances in Neural Information Processing Systems 13*, pages 556–562, Denver, CO, USA, 2000.

[12] C.-J. Lin. Projected gradient methods for nonnegative matrix factorization. *Neural Computation*, 19(10):2756–2779, 2007.

[13] M. E. J. Newman. Fast algorithm for detecting community structure in networks. *Physical Review E*, 69(6):066133, 2004.

[14] M. E. J. Newman and M. Girvan. Finding and evaluating community structure in networks. *Physical Review E*, 69:026113, 2004.

[15] G. Palla, A.-L. Barabási, and T. Vicsek. Quantifying social group evolution. *Nature*, 446:664–667, 2007.

[16] G. Palla, I. Derényi, I. Farkas, and T. Vicsek. Uncovering the overlapping community structure of complex networks in nature and society. *Nature*, 435:814–818, 2005.

[17] G. Palla, I. J. Farkas, P. Pollner, I. Derényi, and T. Vicsek. Directed network modules. *New Journal of Physics*, 9:186, 2007.

[18] I. Psorakis, S. Roberts, M. Ebden, and B. Sheldon. Overlapping community detection using Bayesian non-negative matrix factorization. *Physical Review E*, 83, 2011.

[19] F. Wang, T. Li, X. Wang, S. Zhu, and C. H. Q. Ding. Community discovery using nonnegative matrix factorization. *Data Mining and Knowledge Discovery*, 22(3):493–521, 2011.

DEMON: a Local-First Discovery Method for Overlapping Communities

Michele Coscia
CID - Harvard Kennedy School
79 JFK Street, Cambridge, MA, US
michele_coscia@hks.harvard.edu

Giulio Rossetti
KDDLab University of Pisa
Largo B. Pontecorvo 3, Pisa, Italy
giulio.rossetti@isti.cnr.it

Fosca Giannotti
KDDLab ISTI-CNR
Via G. Moruzzi 1, Pisa, Italy
fosca.giannotti@isti.cnr.it

Dino Pedreschi
KDDLab University of Pisa
Largo B. Pontecorvo 3 Pisa, Italy
pedre@di.unipi.it

ABSTRACT

Community discovery in complex networks is an interesting problem with a number of applications, especially in the knowledge extraction task in social and information networks. However, many large networks often lack a particular community organization at a global level. In these cases, traditional graph partitioning algorithms fail to let the latent knowledge embedded in modular structure emerge, because they impose a top-down global view of a network. We propose here a simple local-first approach to community discovery, able to unveil the modular organization of real complex networks. This is achieved by democratically letting each node vote for the communities it sees surrounding it in its limited view of the global system, i.e. its ego neighborhood, using a label propagation algorithm; finally, the local communities are merged into a global collection. We tested this intuition against the state-of-the-art overlapping and non-overlapping community discovery methods, and found that our new method clearly outperforms the others in the quality of the obtained communities, evaluated by using the extracted communities to predict the metadata about the nodes of several real world networks. We also show how our method is deterministic, fully incremental, and has a limited time complexity, so that it can be used on web-scale real networks.

Categories and Subject Descriptors

I.5.3 [**Clustering**]: Algorithms

Keywords

complex networks, data mining, community discovery

1. INTRODUCTION

Complex network analysis has emerged as one of the most exciting domains of data analysis and mining over the last decade. One of the most prolific sub field is community discovery in complex network, or *CD* in short. The concept of a "community" in a (web, social, or informational) network is intuitively understood as a set of individuals that are very similar, or close, to each other, more than to anybody else outside the community [6]. This has often been translated in network terms into finding sets of nodes densely connected to each other and sparsely connected with the rest of the network. Community discovery can be seen as a network variant of traditional data clustering. To efficiently detect these structures is very useful for a number of applications, ranging from targeted vaccinations and outbreak prevention [23], to viral marketing [16] and to many web data analysis tasks such as finding tribes in online information exchanges [12, 25], data compressing, clustering [4] and sampling [14].

The classical problem definition of community discovery finds a very intuitive counterpart for small networks, where the denser areas are easily identifiable by visual inspection, while the problem becomes much harder for medium and large scale networks. At the global level, very little can be said about the modular structure of the network, because on larger scales the organization of the system becomes simply too complex. The friendship graph of Facebook includes more than 845 millions nodes as of February 2012[1], but the difficulty of the CD task can be appreciated even considering a tiny fragment of the Facebook friendship graph, illustrated in Figure 1(a). We depicted the connections among 15,000 nodes, i.e., less than 0.002% of the total network. Even in this small subset of the network, no evident organization can be identified easily. Big networks are not analyzable with the naked eye. Very often, a visualization of ten thousands nodes results in a *structureless* hairball. In cases like this, also generic community discovery algorithms tend to return not meaningful communities, as they typically try to cluster the whole structure and return some huge communities and a long list of small branches (see [6]). Often, superimposing an order with a top-down approach leads to failure.

On the contrary, human eyes are good in finding denser areas in simple networks, i.e., the structure of cohesive groups of nodes that emerge considering a *local* fragment of an otherwise big network. But what does *local* mean? Commonsense goes that people are good at identifying the reasons why they know the people they know; therefore, each node

KDD'12, August 12–16, 2012, Beijing, China.

[1]http://newsroom.fb.com/content/default.aspx?NewsAreaId=22

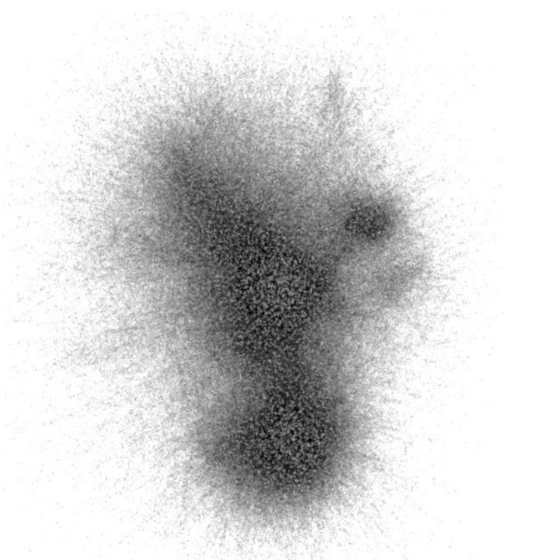

(a) A global view of the Facebook graph from 15k users.

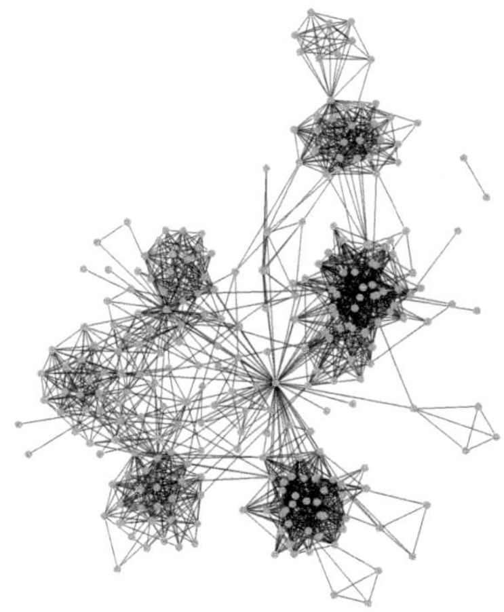

(b) The "ego minus ego" network of one Facebook user among the 15k.

Figure 1: The real world example of the "local vs global" structure intuition.

has presumably an incomplete, yet clear, vision of the social communities it is part of, and that surrounds it. The consequences of exploiting this idea for the CD problem is effectively illustrated by Figure 1(b). Here, we chose one of the 15k nodes from the previous example and extracted what we call its "ego minus ego" network, i.e. its ego network in which the ego node has been removed, together with all its attached edges. Suddenly, everything around the ego makes sense and some groups can be easily spotted. These groups correspond to the high school and university friends, mates from different workplaces and the members of an online community (we know all these details because the chosen ego is one of the authors of this paper). The ego is part of all these communities and knows that particular subsets of its neighborhood are part of these communities too. Probably, different egos have different perspectives over the same neighbors and it is the union of all these perspectives that creates an optimal partition of the network. In other words: if node A and node B are considered in the same communities by all the nodes connected to both A and B, then they should be grouped in the same community. This is achieved by a *democratic* bottom-up mining approach: in turn, each node gives the perspective of the communities surrounding it and then all the different perspectives are merged together in an overlapping structure.

In the vast CD literature, the general approach for the detection of the modular structure of a network is usually to develop a particular (greedy) algorithm, testing a general quality function with a particular heuristic and then return a set of communities extracted from the global structure (we discuss some of these methods in Section 2). This approach generally fails for large networks due to the difference in structural organization at global and local scale. To cope with this difficulty, we propose a change of mentality. Since our community definition works perfectly in the small scale, then it should be applied only at this small scale. We propose a simple local-first approach to community discovery in complex networks by letting the hidden modular organization of a network emerge from local patterns.

Essentially, we adopt a *democratic* approach to the discovery of communities in complex networks. We ask each node to vote for the communities present in its local view of the network. For this reason, we chose to name our algorithm **D**emocratic **E**stimate of the **M**odular **O**rganization of a **N**etwork, or *DEMON* in short. In practice, we extract the ego network of each node and apply a Label Propagation CD algorithm [21] on this structure, ignoring the presence of the ego itself, that will be judged by its peers neighbors. We then combine, with equity, the vote of everyone in the network. The result of this combination is a set of (overlapping) modules, the guess of the real communities in the global system, made not by an external observer, but by the actors of the network itself. Our democratic algorithm is *incremental*, allowing to recompute the communities only for the newly incoming nodes and edges in an evolving network. Nevertheless, *DEMON* has also a low theoretical linear time complexity. The main core of our method has also the interesting property of being easily *parallelizable*, since only the ego network information is needed to perform independent computations, and it can be easily combined in a MapReduce framework [7]; although the post-process Merge procedure is not trivially solvable in a MapReduce framework (and for this reason we leave a discussion about the parallel implementation as future work). The properties of *DEMON* support its use in massive real world scenarios.

We provide an extensive empirical validation of *DEMON*. In our experimental setting, we are particularly interested in investigating what useful knowledge we can discover. We test the results obtained with our method against selected state-of-the-art algorithms, both overlapping and not overlapping, since we believe that the possibility to cluster the same nodes in different communities is one of the crucial properties that a community discoverer should allow: online social networks have proved that individuals are part of many different communities and groups of interest. To evaluate this knowledge, we make use of a multilabel predictor fed with the extracted communities as input, with the aim of correctly classifying the metadata attached to the nodes in real life. Our datasets include the international store Amazon, the database of collaborations in movie industry IMDb, and the register of the activities of the US Congress GovTrack.us.

The rest of the paper is organized as follows: in Section 2 we present related works in community discovery literature. Section 3 is dedicated to the problem representation and definition. Section 4 describe the *DEMON* algorithm structure, with algorithmic details and an account of the formal properties of the method. Our experiments are presented in Section 5, and finally Section 6 concludes the paper.

2. RELATED WORK

The problem of finding communities in complex networks is very popular among network scientists, as witnessed by an impressive number of valid works in this field. A huge survey by Fortunato [9] explores all the most popular techniques to find communities in complex networks. Traditionally, a community is defined as a dense subgraph, in which the number of edges among the members of the community is significantly higher than the outgoing edges. However, this definition does not cover many real world scenarios, and in the years many different solutions started to explore alternative definitions of communities in complex networks [6].

A variety of CD methods are based on the *modularity* concept, a quality function of a partition proposed by Newman [5, 18]. Modularity scores high values for partitions in which the internal cluster density is higher than the external density. Hundreds of papers have been written about modularity, either using it as a quality function to be optimized, or studying its properties and deficiencies. One of the most advanced examples of modularity maximization CD is [17], where the authors use an extension of the modularity formula to cluster multiplex (evolving and/or multirelational) networks. A fast and efficient greedy algorithm, Modularity Unfolding, has been successfully applied to the analysis of huge web graphs of millions of nodes and billions of edges, representing the structure in a subset of the WWW [3].

Many algorithms have been proposed that are unrelated to modularity. Among them, a particular important field is the application of information theory techniques, as for example in Infomap [22] or Cross Associations [19]. In particular, Infomap has been proven to be one among the best performing non overlapping algorithms [15]. For this reason we chose Infomap as alternative to modularity approaches as a baseline method. Further, modularity approaches are affected by known issues, namely the resolution problem and the degeneracy of good solutions [10]. Similarly to Infomap, Walktrap [20] is based on flow methods and random walks.

A very important property for community discovery is the ability to return overlapping partitions, i.e., the possibility of a node to be part of more than one community. This property reflects the common sense intuition that each of us is part of many different communities, including family, work, and probably many hobby-related communities. Specific algorithms developed over this property are Hierarchical Link Clustering [1], HCDF [13] and k-clique percolation [8].

Finally, an important approach is known as Label Propagation [21]: in this work authors detect communities by spreading labels through the edges of the graph and then labeling nodes according to the majority of the labels attached to their neighbors, iterating until a general consensus is reached. With a reasonable good quality on the partition, this algorithm is extremely fast and known to be one of the very few quasi-linear solutions to the community discovery problem, even if its plain application leads to worse results than Infomap and it does not return an overlapping partition. A related work is also [2], whose aim is also to discover local communities. However, authors are only interested in those local communities and they do not return any global structure modular organization.

To to extract useful knowledge from the modular structure of networked data is also a prolific track of research. We recall the GuruMine framework, whose aim is to identify leaders in information spread and to detect groups of users that are usually influenced by the same leaders [12]. Many other works investigate the possibility of applying network analysis for studying, for instance, the dynamics of viral marketing [16].

3. NETWORKS AND COMMUNITIES

We model networks and their properties in terms of simple graphs. For the sake of simplicity, a network is represented as an undirected, unlabeled and unweighted simple graph, denoted by $\mathcal{G} = (V, E)$ where V is a set of nodes and E is a set of edges, i.e., pairs (u, v) representing the fact that there is a link in the network connecting nodes u and v. It should be noted, however, that our method can handle weighted, directed and labeled multi-graphs.

In general terms, our problem definition is to find communities in complex networks. However, this is an ambiguous goal, as the definition itself of "community" in a complex network, similarly to the notion of clustering in statistics and data mining, is not unique [6]. Furthermore, in a complex and semantically rich setting as the modern Web, one may want to cluster many different kinds of objects for many different reasons. Therefore, we need to narrow down our problem definition as follows.

We define two basic graph operations. The first one is the Ego Network extraction EN. Given a graph $\mathcal{G}$ and a node $v \in V$, $EN(v, \mathcal{G})$ is the subgraph $\mathcal{G}'(V', E')$, where V' is the set containing v and all its neighbors in E, and E' is the subset of E containing all the edges (u, v) where $u \in V' \wedge v \in V'$. The second operation is the Graph-Vertex Difference $-g$: $-g(v, \mathcal{G})$ will result in a copy of $\mathcal{G}$ without the vertex v and all edges attached to v. The combination of these two functions yields the $EgoMinusEgo$ function: $EgoMinusEgo(v, \mathcal{G}) = -g(v, EN(v, \mathcal{G}))$. Given a graph $\mathcal{G}$ and a node $v \in V$, the set of *local communities* $\mathcal{C}(v)$ of node v is a set of (possibly overlapping) sets of nodes in $EgoMinusEgo(v, \mathcal{G})$, where each set $C \in \mathcal{C}(v)$ is a community according to node similarity: each node in C is more similar to any other node in C than to any other node in $C' \in \mathcal{C}(v)$, with $C \neq C'$. Finally, we define the set of *global communities*, or simply communities, of a graph $\mathcal{G}$ as:

$$\mathcal{C} = Max(\bigcup_{v \in V} \mathcal{C}(v)) \tag{1}$$

where, given a set of sets $\mathcal{S}$, $Max(\mathcal{S})$ denotes the subset of $\mathcal{S}$ formed by its maximal sets only; namely, every set $S \in \mathcal{S}$ such that there is no other set $S' \in \mathcal{S}$ with $S \subset S'$. In other words, by equation (1) we generalize from local to global communities by selecting the maximal local communities that cover the entire collection of local communities, each found in the $EgoMinusEgo$ network of each individual node.

Algorithm 1 The pseudo-code of *DEMON* algorithm.

Require: $\mathcal{G} : (V, E)$; $\mathcal{C} = \emptyset$; $\epsilon \in [0..1]$
Ensure: set of overlapping communities $\mathcal{C}$

```
1: for all v ∈ V do
2:    e ← EgoMinusEgo(v, G)
3:    C(v) ← LabelPropagation(e)
4:    for all C ∈ C(v) do
5:       C ← C ∪ v
6:       C ← Merge(C, C, ϵ)
7:    end for
8: end for
9: return C
```

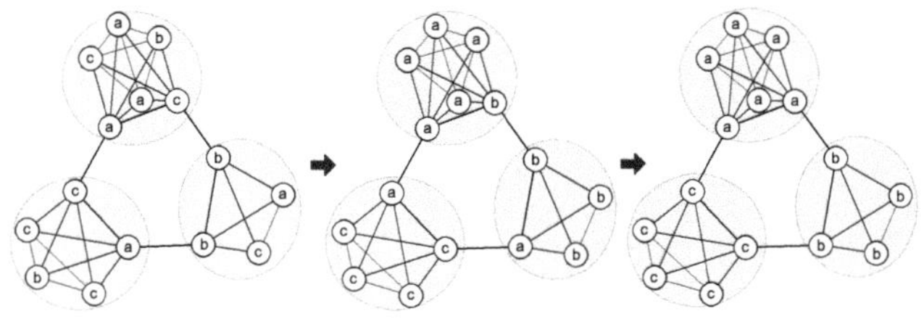

Figure 2: A simple simulation of the Label Propagation process for community discovery.

4. THE ALGORITHM

In this section we present our solution to the community discovery problem. The pseudo code of *DEMON* is specified in Algorithm 1.

4.1 The Core of the Algorithm

The set of discovered communities $\mathcal{C}$ is initially empty. The external (explicit) loop of *DEMON* cycles over each individual node, and it is necessary to generate all the possible points of view of the structure and get a complete coverage of the network itself. For each node v, we apply the $EgoMinusEgo(v, \mathcal{G})$ operation defined in Section 3, obtaining a graph e. We cannot apply simply the ego network extraction $EN(v, \mathcal{G})$ because the ego node v is directly linked to all nodes $\in EN(v, \mathcal{G})$. This would lead to noise in the subsequent steps of *DEMON*, since by our definition of local community the nodes would be put in the same community if they are close to each other. Obviously a single node connecting the entire sub-graph will make all nodes very close, even if they are not in the same community. For this reason, we remove the ego from its own ego network.

Once we have the e graph, the next step is to compute the communities contained in e. We chose to perform this step by using a community discovery algorithm borrowed from the literature. Our choice fell on the Label Propagation (LP) algorithm [21]. This choice has been made for the following reasons:

1. LP shares with this work the definition of what is a community.

2. LP is known as the least complex algorithm in the literature, reaching a quasi-linear time complexity in terms of nodes. However,

3. LP will return results of a quality comparable to more complex algorithms [6].

Reason #2 is particularly important, since Step #3 of our pseudo code needs to be performed once for every node of the network. It is unacceptable to spend a superlinear time for each node at this stage, if we want to scale up to millions of nodes and hundreds of millions edges. Given the linear complexity of Step #3, we refer to this as the internal (implicit) loop for finding the local communities.

We briefly describe in more detail the LP algorithm, given its importance in the *DEMON* algorithm, following the original article [21]. Suppose that a node v has neighbors $v_1, v_2, ..., v_k$ and that each neighbor carries a label denoting the community that it belongs to. Then v determines its community based on the labels of its neighbors. A three-step example of this principle is shown in Figure 2. The authors assume that each node in the network chooses to join the community to which the maximum number of its neighbors belong. As the labels propagate, densely connected groups of nodes quickly reach a consensus on a unique label. At the end of the propagation process nodes with the same labels are grouped together as one community. Clearly, a node with an equal maximum number of neighbors in two or more communities can belong to both communities, thus identifying possible overlapping communities. The original algorithm does not handle this situation. For clarity, we report here the procedure of the LP algorithm, that is the expansion of Step #3 of Algorithm 1 and represents our inner loop:

1. Initialize the labels at all nodes in the network. For any given node v, $C_v(0) = v$.

2. Set $t = 1$.

3. Arrange the nodes in the network in a random order and set it to V.

4. For each $v_i \in V$, in the specific order, let $C_{v_i}(t) = f(C_{v_{i1}}(t-1), \ldots, C_{v_{ik}}(t-1))$. f here returns the label occurring with the highest frequency among neighbors and ties are broken uniformly randomly.

5. If every node has a label that the maximum number of their neighbors have, or t hits a maximum number of iterations t_{max} then stop the algorithm. Else, set $t = t + 1$ and go to (3).

4.2 The Merge Function

The result of Step #3 of Algorithm 1 is a set of local communities, according to the perspective of node v: at the end of the LP algorithm we reintroduce, in each local community, the node v. These communities are likely to be incomplete and should be used to enrich what *DEMON* already discovered so far. Thus, the next step is to merge each local community of $\mathcal{C}$ in order to obtain the result set. The $Merge$ operation is defined as follows.

Two communities C and I are merged if and only if at most the ϵ% of the smaller one is not included in the bigger one; in this case, C and I are removed from $\mathcal{C}$ and their union is added to the result set. The ϵ factor is introduced to vary the percentage of common elements provided from each couple of communities: $\epsilon = 0$ ensure that two communities are merged only if one of them is a proper subset of the other, on the other hand with a value of $\epsilon = 1$ even communities that do not share a single node are merged together.

Algorithm 2 The pseudo-code of Merge function.

Require: $\mathcal{C} = Community\ set; C = Community; \epsilon \in [0..1]$
Ensure: set of overlapping communities $\mathcal{C}$

```
1: for all I ∈ 𝒞 do
2:    if C.size ≤ I.sizeandC ⊆_ε I then
3:       u = C ∪ I;
4:       𝒞 − C; 𝒞 − I;
5:       𝒞 = 𝒞 ∪ u;
6:    end if
7: end for
8: return 𝒞
```

4.3 DEMON Properties

To prove the correctness of the *DEMON* algorithm w.r.t. the problem definition in Section 3, we prove by induction that the following holds:

PROPERTY 1. *At the k-th iteration of the outer loop of DEMON, for all $k \geq 0$:*

$$\mathcal{C} = Max\left(\bigcup_{v=v_1,\ldots,v_k} \mathcal{C}(v) \right) \quad (2)$$

where $v_1, \ldots, v_k$ are the nodes visited after k iterations.

Property (1) trivially holds for $k = 0$, i.e., at initialization stage. For $k > 0$, assume that the property holds up to $k - 1$. Then $\mathcal{C}$ contains the maximal local communities of the subgraph with nodes $v_1, \ldots, v_{k-1}$. By merging every local community C of node v_k into $\mathcal{C}$, we guarantee that C is added to the result only if it is not covered by any preexisting community, and, if added, any preexisting community covered by C is removed from $\mathcal{C}$. As a result, after merging all communities in $\mathcal{C}(v_k)$ into $\mathcal{C}$ in Steps #4-6, the latter is the set of maximal communities covering all local communities discovered in $v_1, \ldots, v_k$. Therefore, we can conclude that *DEMON* is a correct and complete implementation of the CD problem stated by equation (1). More generally, denoting by $DEMON(\mathcal{G}, \mathcal{C})$ the set of communities $\mathcal{C}'$ obtained by running the *DEMON* algorithm on graph $\mathcal{G}$ starting with the (possibly non-empty) set of communities $\mathcal{C}$, the following properties hold.

PROPERTY 2. **Correctness** *and* **Completeness.** *If $DEMON(\mathcal{G}, \mathcal{C}) = \mathcal{C}'$, where $\mathcal{G} = (V, E)$, then*

$$\mathcal{C}' = Max\left(\mathcal{C} \cup \bigcup_{v \in V} \mathcal{C}(v)\right) \quad (3)$$

In other words, given a preexisting set of communities $\mathcal{C}$ and a graph $\mathcal{G}$, *DEMON* returns all and only the communities obtained extending $\mathcal{C}$ with the communities found in $\mathcal{G}$, coherently with the definition of communities given in equation (1).

PROPERTY 3. **Determinacy** *and* **Order insensitivity**. *There exists a* unique $\mathcal{C}' = DEMON(\mathcal{G}, \mathcal{C})$ *for any given $\mathcal{G}$ and $\mathcal{C}$, disregarding the order of visit of the nodes in $\mathcal{G}$.*

This is a direct corollary of property (2) and of the uniqueness of the set $Max(\mathcal{S})$ for any set of sets $\mathcal{S}$, under the assumption that the set of local communities $\mathcal{C}(v)$ is also uniquely assigned, for any node v. Therefore, the order in which the nodes in $\mathcal{G}$ are visited by *DEMON* is irrelevant.

PROPERTY 4. **Compositionality**. *Consider any partition of a graph $\mathcal{G}$ into two subgraphs $\mathcal{G}_1$, $\mathcal{G}_2$ such that, for any node v of $\mathcal{G}$, the entire ego network of v in $\mathcal{G}$ is fully contained either in $\mathcal{G}_1$ or $\mathcal{G}_2$. Then, given an initial set of communities $\mathcal{C}$:*

$$DEMON(\mathcal{G}_1 \cup \mathcal{G}_2, \mathcal{C}) = Max(DEMON(\mathcal{G}_1, \mathcal{C}) \cup DEMON(\mathcal{G}_2, \mathcal{C})) \quad (4)$$

This is a consequence of two facts: *i*) each local community $\mathcal{C}(v)$ is correctly computed under the assumption that the subgraphs do not split any ego network, and *ii*) for any two sets of sets $\mathcal{S}_1, \mathcal{S}_2$, $Max(\mathcal{S}_1 \cup \mathcal{S}_2) = Max(Max(\mathcal{S}_1) \cup Max(\mathcal{S}_2))$.

PROPERTY 5. **Incrementality**. *Given a graph $\mathcal{G}$, an initial set of communities $\mathcal{C}$ and an incremental update $\Delta\mathcal{G}$ consisting of new nodes and new edges added to $\mathcal{G}$, where $\Delta\mathcal{G}$ contains the entire ego networks of all new nodes and of all the preexisting nodes reached by new links, then*

$$DEMON(\mathcal{G} \cup \Delta\mathcal{G}, \mathcal{C}) = DEMON(\Delta\mathcal{G}, DEMON(\mathcal{G}, \mathcal{C})) \quad (5)$$

This is a consequence of the fact that only the local communities of nodes in $\mathcal{G}$ affected by new links need to be reexamined, so we can run *DEMON* on $\Delta\mathcal{G}$ only, avoiding to run it from scratch on $\mathcal{G} \cup \Delta\mathcal{G}$.

Properties (4) and (5) have important computational repercussions. The compositionality property entails that the core of *DEMON* algorithm as described in subsection 4.1 is highly parallelizable, because it can run independently on different fragments of the overall network with a relatively small combination work. Each node of the computer cluster needs to obtain a small fragment of the network, as small as the ego network of one or a few nodes. The Map function is simply the LP algorithm. The incrementality property entails that *DEMON* can efficiently run in a streamed fashion, considering incremental updates of the graph as they arrive in subsequent batches; essentially, incrementality means that it is not necessary to run *DEMON* from scratch as batches of new nodes and new links arrive: the new communities can be found by considering only the ego networks of the nodes affected by the updates (both new nodes and old nodes reached by new links). This does not trivially hold for the Merge function presented in subsection 4.2, therefore the actual parallel implementation of *DEMON* is left as future work. However, different and simpler Merge functions can be define to combine the results provided by the core of the algorithm, thus preserving its possibility to scale up in a parallel framework.

4.4 Complexity

We now evaluate the time complexity of our approach. *DEMON* core (Section 4.1) is based on the Label Propagation algorithm, whose complexity is $\mathcal{O}(n + m)$ [21], where n is the number of nodes and m is the number of edges. LP is performed once for each node. Let us assume that we are working with a scale free network, whose degree distribution is $p_k = k^{-\alpha}$. This means that there are $\frac{n}{k^\alpha}$ nodes with degree k. If K is the maximum degree, the complexity would be $\sum_{k=1}^{K}(\frac{n}{k^\alpha} \times (k + \frac{k(k-1)}{2}))$ because for each node of degree k we have an ego network of k nodes and at worst $\frac{k(k-1)}{2}$ edges. This number is very small for the vast majority of nodes, being the degree distribution right skewed, thus many nodes have degree 1 or 2. We omit the solution of the sum with the integral and we report that the complexity is then dominated by a single term, ending up to be $\mathcal{O}(nK^{3-\alpha})$. This means that the stronger is the α exponent, the faster is *DEMON*: with $\alpha = 3$ we have few super-hubs for which we basically check the entire network few times and the rest of nodes add nothing to the complexity; with $\alpha = 2$ we have many high degree nodes and we end up with higher complexity, but still subquadratic in term of nodes (as, with $\alpha = 2$, $K << n$).

5. EXPERIMENTS

We now present our experimental findings. We make use of three networked datasets, representing very different phenomena. We first concentrate on evaluating the quality of a set of communities discovered in these datasets, comparing the results with those of other competing methods in terms of the predictive power of the discovered communities. Since real world data are enriched with annotated information, we measure the ability of each community to predict the semantic information attached with the metadata of the nodes within the community itself.

Next, we assess the community quality using a global measure of community cohesion, based on the intuition that nodes into the same community should possess similar semantic properties in terms of attached metadata.

The selected competitors for our assessment are: Hierarchical Link Clustering (HLC) [1], that has been proven able to outperform all the overlapping algorithms, including the k-clique Propagation algorithm by Palla et al [8]; two random walks based methods, one focusing on minimizing random walk entropy (Infomap [22]) and the other relying on a general flow method (Walktrap [20]); a leading eigenvector-based community discovery, namely Modularity maximization in the fast greedy implementation introduced in [5]. Finally, we present some examples of knowledge that we are able to extract from the communities found by the *DEMON* algorithm.

Note that we are not able to provide the analytic evaluation for Amazon dataset: for that network HLC algorithm was not able to provide results due to memory consumption problems, while the other community discovery algorithms usually returned some huge communities that was not possible to analyze (see Section 5.2 and particularly Figure 4 for more information).

The experiments were performed on a Dual Core Intel i7 64 bits @ 2.8 GHz, equipped with 8 GB of RAM and with a kernel Linux 3.0.0-12-generic (Ubuntu 11.10). The code was developed in Java and it is available for download with the network datasets used[2]. For performances purposes, we mainly refer to the biggest dataset, i.e. Amazon: the core of the algorithm (Section 4.1) took less than a minute, while the Merge function (Section 4.2) with increasing thresholds can take from one minute to one hour.

5.1 Networks

We tested our algorithms on three real world complex networks extracted from available web services of different domains. A general overview about the statistics of these networks can be found in Table 1, where: $|V|$ is the number of nodes, $|E|$ is the number of edges and $\bar{k}$ is the average degree of the network. Congress and IMDb networks are similar to the ones used in [1], generally updating the source dataset with a more recent set of data, and we refer to that paper for a deeper description of them. The networks were generated as follows:

Network	$\|V\|$	$\|E\|$	$\bar{k}$
Congress	526	14,198	53.98
IMDb	56,542	185,347	6.55
Amazon	410,236	2,439,437	11.89

Table 1: Basic statistics of the studied networks.

Congress. The network of legislative collaborations between US representatives of the House and the Senate during the 111st US congress (2009-2011). We downloaded the data about all the bills discussed during the last Congress from GovTrack[3], a web-based service recording the activities of each member of the US Congress. The bills are usually cosponsored by many politicians. We connect politicians if they have at least 75 co-sponsorships and delete all the connections that are created only by bills with more than 10 co-sponsors. Attached to each bills in the Govtrack data we have also a collection of subjects related to the bill. The set of subjects a politicians frequently worked on is the *qualitative attribute* of this network.

IMDb. We downloaded the entire database of IMDb from their official APIs[4] on August 25th 2011. We focus on actors who star in at least two movies during the years from 2001 to 2010, filtering out television shows, video games, and other performances. We connect actors with at least two movies in which they both appear. This network is weighted according to the number of co-appearances. Our *qualitative attributes* are the user assigned keywords, summarizing the movies each actor has been part of.

Amazon. We downloaded Amazon data from the Stanford Large Network Dataset Collection[5]. In this dataset, frequent co-purchases of products are recorded for the day of May 5th 2003. We transformed the directed network in an undirected version. We also downloaded the metadata information about the products, available in the same repository. Using this metadata, we can define the *qualitative attributes* for each product as its categories.

5.2 Quality Evaluation via Label Prediction

We first assess *DEMON* performances using a classical prediction task. We attach the community memberships of a node as known attributes, then its qualitative attributes (real world labels) as target to be predicted; we then feed these attributes to a state-of-the-art label predictor and record its performance. Of course, a node may have one or more known attributes, as both *DEMON* and HLC are overlapping community discoverers; and it may have also one or more unknown attributes, as it can carry many different labels.

For this reason, we need a multilabel classificator, i.e. a learner able to predict multiple target attributes [24]. We chose to use the Binary Relevance Learner. The BRL learns $|L|$ binary classifiers $H_l : X \to \{l, \neg l\}$, one for each different label $l \in L$. It transforms the original data set into $|L|$ data sets D_l that contain all examples of the original data set,

[2]http://www.di.unipi.it/~coscia/demon/

[3]http://www.govtrack.us/developers/data.xpd

[4]http://www.imdb.com/interfaces

[5]http://snap.stanford.edu/data/index.html

Network	*DEMON*	HLC	Infomap	Modularity	Walktrap
Congress	**0.21275**	0.14740	0.00535	0.00099	0.00725
IMDb	**0.44252**	0.43078	0.38470	0.10692	0.17488

Table 2: The F-Measure scores for Congress and IMDb dataset and each community partition.

labeled as l if the labels of the original example contained l and as $\neg l$ otherwise. It is the same solution used in order to deal with a single-label multi-class problem using a binary classifier. Note that this classifier does not penalize per se non-overlapping partitions, as each target label is classified independently, and this property is requested to fairly confront overlapping algorithms such as *DEMON* and HLC, with the other non-overlapping algorithms. We used the Python implementation provided in the Orange software[6]. For time and memory constraints due to the BRL complexity, for IMDb we used as input only the biggest communities (with more than 15 nodes) and eliminating all nodes that are not part of any of the selected communities.

Multi-label classification requires different metrics than those used in traditional single-label classification. Among the measures that have been proposed in the literature, we use the multi-label version of the standard Precision and Recall measures. Let D_l be our multi-label evaluation data set, consisting of $|D_l|$ multi-label examples $(x_i, Y_i), i = 1..|D_l|, Y_i \subseteq L$. Let H be our BRL multi-label classifier and $Z_i = H(x_i)$ be the set of labels predicted by H for x_i. Then, we can evaluate Precision and Recall of H as:

$$Precision(H, D_l) = \frac{1}{|D_l|} \sum_{i=1}^{|D_l|} \frac{|Y_i \cap Z_i|}{|Z_i|},$$

$$Recall(H, D_l) = \frac{1}{|D_l|} \sum_{i=1}^{|D_l|} \frac{|Y_i \cap Z_i|}{|Y_i|}.$$

We then derive the F-measure from Precision and Recall. For alternatives multi-label evaluations, we refer to [11]. The results are reported in Table 2 and show how *DEMON* outperforms its competitors. We did not test Amazon network as HLC was not able to provide results due to its complexity and further the BRL classifier was not able to scale for the overall number of nodes and labels.

For IMDb dataset, HLC was able to score almost like *DEMON*. However, there is an important distinction to be made about the quantity of the results: if the community discovery returns too many communities, then it is difficult to actually extract useful knowledge from them. We reported in Table 3 the basic statistics about the partitions returned by the algorithms: number of communities ($|\mathcal{C}|$) and average community size ($|\bar{c}|$). For *DEMON*, we report the statistics of the communities extracted with $\epsilon = 0$. As we can see, not only *DEMON* scores better results, but it does with 70-80% less communities than HLC and with an average community size more manageable than Infomap.

We report in Table 3 the results for $\epsilon = 0$. However, we vary the ϵ threshold and see what happens to the number of communities and to the quality of the results. We can see that for both Congress and IMDb the Precision, Recall and F-Measure scores remains constant (and actually F-Measure peaks at $\epsilon = 0.076$ and $\epsilon = 0.301$ for Congress

[6]http://orange.biolab.si/

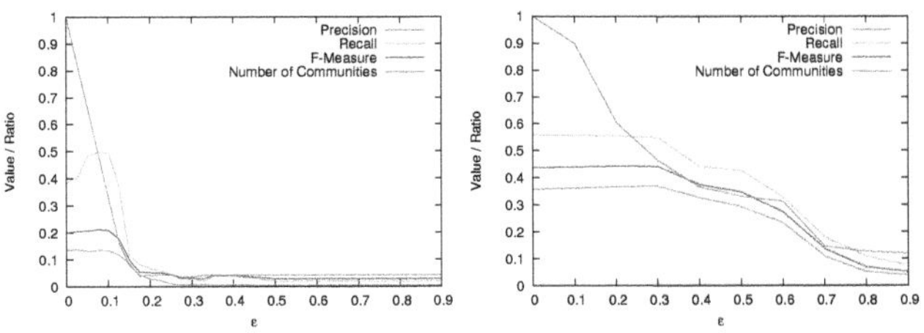

(a) Congress (b) IMDb

Figure 3: Precision, Recall, F-Measure and number of communities for different ϵ values.

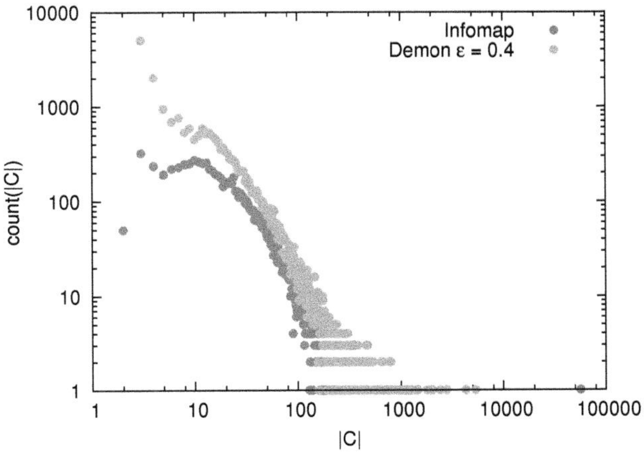

Figure 4: The distribution of the community sizes for DEMON and Infomap in the Amazon network.

and IMDb respectively) before falling for increasing ϵ values, while the relative number of communities dramatically drops. For Congress, we have the maximum F-Measure with only 175 communities; while for IMDb F-Measures peaks with 6,508 communities (in both cases, less than 50% of the communities at $\epsilon = 0$ and than an order of magnitude of HLC).

A final consideration is needed about the size distribution of the communities detected by *DEMON* and the other community discovery algorithms. In Figure 4 we depicted the community size distribution for *DEMON* and Infomap for the Amazon network. As we can see, Infomap returned, among the others, a giant community, one order of magnitude greater than the biggest one returned by *DEMON*. To analyze such a community has been proved impossible, and this is another reason why we are not able to provide an analitycal evaluation of the results extracted from the Amazon network.

We can conclude that *DEMON* with a manageable number of communities is able to outperform more complex methods and the choice of ϵ can make the difference in obtaining a narrower set of communities with the same (or greater) overall quality.

5.3 Quality Evaluation via Community Cohesion

As presented at the beginning of this section, the networks studied here possess *qualitative attributes* that attaches a

Network	Demon		HLC		Infomap		Modularity		Walktrap	
	$\|\mathcal{C}\|$	$\|\bar{c}\|$	$\|\mathcal{C}\|$	$\|\bar{c}\|$	$\|\mathcal{C}\|$	$\|\bar{c}\|$	$\|\mathcal{C}\|$	$\|\bar{c}\|$	$\|\mathcal{C}\|$	$\|\bar{c}\|$
Congress	425	63.3671	1,476	4.5867	6	87.6667	3	175.3333	7	71.8571
IMDb	14,004	12.6824	88,119	8.3426	5,991	27.1574	4,746	11.9157	7,877	7.1781

Table 3: Statistics of the community set returned by the different algorithms.

Network	*DEMON*	HLC	Infomap	Modularity	Walktrap
Congress	**1.1792**	1.1539	1.0229	1.0373	1.0532
IMDb	**5.6158**	5.1589	0.1400	1.4652	0.0211

Table 4: The Community Quality scores for Congress and IMDb dataset and each community partition.

small set of annotations or tags to each node. Assuming that these qualitative attributes form a description of the node, beyond the network itself, we can reasonably state that "similar" nodes share more *qualitative attributes* than dissimilar nodes. This procedure is not standard in community discovery results evaluation. Usually authors prefer to use the established measure of Modularity. However, Modularity is strictly (and exclusively) dependent on the graph structure. What we want evaluate is not how a graph measure is maximized, but how good is our community partition in describing real world knowledge about the clustered entities.

We quantify the matching between a community partition and the metadata by evaluating how much higher are on average the Jaccard coefficient of the set of *qualitative attributes* for pair of nodes inside the communities over the average of the entire network, or:

$$CQ(P) = \frac{\sum_{(n_1,n_2)\in P} \frac{|QA(n_1)\cap QA(n_2)|}{|QA(n_1)\cup QA(n_2)|}}{\sum_{(n_1,n_2)\in E} \frac{|QA(n_1)\cap QA(n_2)|}{|QA(n_1)\cup QA(n_2)|}},$$

where P is the set of node pairs that share at least one community, $QA(n)$ is the set of qualitative attributes of node n and E is the set of all edges. If $CQ(P) = 1$, then there is no difference between P and the average similarity of nodes, i.e. P is practically random. Lower values implies that we are grouping together dissimilar nodes, higher values are expected for an algorithm able to group together similar nodes.

To calculate the Jaccard coefficient for each pair of the network is computationally prohibitive. Therefore, for IMDb we chose a random set of 400k pairs. Moreover, CQ is biased towards algorithms returning more communities. For this reason, we just collected random communities from the community pool, trying to avoid too much overlap as we want also to maximize the number of nodes considered by CQ (i.e. we try not to consider more than one community per node). We apply this procedure for each algorithm and calculated the CQ value. We repeated this process for 100 iterations and we report in Table 4 the average value of the CQ obtained. Also in this case, *DEMON* was able to easily outperform all the other algorithms.

5.4 Interpretation of Discovered Communities

In this Section we present a brief case study using the communities extracted for the previously exposed evaluation of *DEMON*. Aim of the section is to demonstrate that the extracted communities have practical applications in the extraction of knowledge from real world scenarios. In the

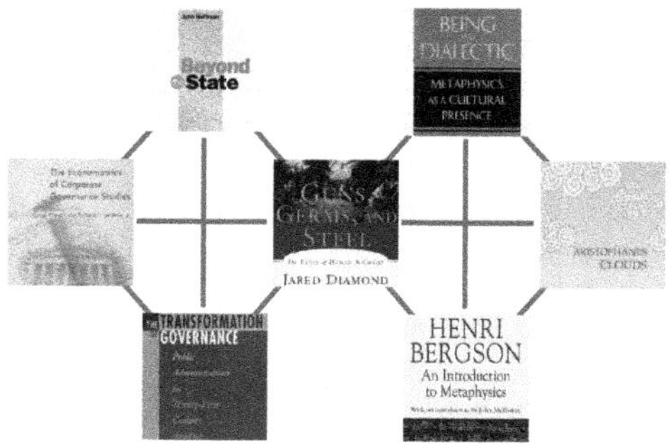

Figure 5: A representation of parts of the two communities surrounding our case study in the amazon network.

Amazon network to have different communities for each item is very useful. A recommendation system is able to better discern if a user may be interested in a product or not given that he bought something else; however being part of one community of products does not mean that that particular community describes all aspects of a particular product.

Let us consider, as an example, the case of Jared Diamond's best selling book "Guns, Germs, and Steel: The Fates of Human Societies". Clearly, it is difficult to say that the people interested in this book are always interested in the same things. Checking the communities to which it belongs, we find two very different big communities (a depiction of the two communities is provided by Figure 5). These communities have some sort of overlap, however they can be characterized by looking at the products that appear exclusively in one or in the other. In the first one we find books such as: "Beyond the State: An Introductory Critique", "The Econometrics of Corporate Governance Studies" and "The Transformation of Governance: Public Administration for Twenty-First Century America". This is clearly a community composed mainly by purchases made by the people more interested in the socioeconomic aspects of Diamond's book. The second community hosts products such as: "An Introduction to Metaphysics", "Aristophanes' Clouds Translated With Notes and Introduction" and "Being and Dialectic: Metaphysics and Culture". This second communities is apparently composed by the purchases of customers more attracted by the underlying philosophical implications of Diamond's study. Products in one communities may have something in common, but they are part of two distinct and very well characterized groups, and the one in one group are not expected to be found in the other.

This is of course one of the many cases. We report as an additional example the two communities around the historical novel "The Name of the Rose" by Umberto Eco: one community is characterized by history related products (such as "Ancestral Passions : The Leakey Family and the Quest for Humankind's Beginnings"), the other by costume fiction (for example the 1932 Dreyer's movie "Vampyr").

6. CONCLUSION AND FUTURE WORKS

In this paper we proposed a new method for solving the problem of detecting latent knowledge from significant communities in complex networks. We propose a democratic approach, where the peer nodes judge where their neighbors should be clustered together. This approach has robust theoretical properties, including correctness and completeness w.r.t. a precise community definition, determinacy, compositionality and incrementality, that make it amenable to challenge the conceptual and computational challenge to analyze networks with millions of nodes. We have shown in the experimental section that this method allows a discovery of communities in different real world networks collected from information rich datasets. The quality of the overlapping partition, a partition that allows nodes to be in different communities at the same time, is improved w.r.t state-of-the-art algorithms, evaluated using the communities to predict the metadata attached to the nodes, and according to a quantitative quality function, also metadata-based.

Many lines of research remain open for future work, such as an efficient parallel implementation that may make *DEMON* the first community discovery algorithm able to scale to billions of nodes; different merging strategies that may further improve the quality of the results; different hosted algorithms can be used instead of the Label Propagation algorithm in the inner loop of *DEMON*, to extract communities according to different definitions.

Acknowledgments. Michele Coscia is a recipient of the Google Europe Fellowship in Social Computing, and this research is supported in part by this Google Fellowship. This work has been partially supported by the European Commission under the FET-Open Project n. FP7-ICT-270833, DATA SIM - DATa science for SIMulating the era of electric vehicles http://www.datasim-fp7.eu/.

7. REFERENCES

[1] Yong-Yeol Ahn, James P. Bagrow, and Sune Lehmann. Link communities reveal multiscale complexity in networks. *Nature*, 466(7307):761–764, June 2010.

[2] James P. Bagrow and Erik M. Bollt. Local method for detecting communities. *Physical Review E*, 72(4):046108+, October 2005.

[3] Vincent D. Blondel, Jean-Loup Guillaume, Renaud Lambiotte, and Etienne Lefebvre. Fast unfolding of communities in large networks. *J.STAT.MECH.*, page P10008, 2008.

[4] Paolo Boldi, Marco Rosa, Massimo Santini, and Sebastiano Vigna. Layered label propagation: a multiresolution coordinate-free ordering for compressing social networks. In *WWW*, pages 587–596, 2011.

[5] Aaron Clauset, M. E. J. Newman, and Cristopher Moore. Finding community structure in very large networks. *Physical Review E*, 70:066111, 2004.

[6] Michele Coscia, Fosca Giannotti, and Dino Pedreschi. A classification for community discovery methods in complex networks. *Statistical Analysis and Data Mining*, 4(5):512–546, 2011.

[7] Jeffrey Dean and Sanjay Ghemawat. MapReduce: Simplified data processing on large clusters. *OSDI*, pages 137–150, 2004.

[8] Imre Derényi, Gergely Palla, and Tamás Vicsek. Clique Percolation in Random Networks. *Physical Review Letters*, 94(16):160202+, April 2005.

[9] S. Fortunato. Community detection in graphs. *Physics Reports*, 486:75–174, February 2010.

[10] Santo Fortunato and Marc Barthélemy. Resolution limit in community detection. *PNAS*, 104(1):36–41, January 2007.

[11] Shantanu Godbole and Sunita Sarawagi. Discriminative methods for multi-labeled classification. In *PAKDD*, pages 22–30, 2004.

[12] Amit Goyal, Byung-Won On, Francesco Bonchi, and Laks V. S. Lakshmanan. Gurumine: A pattern mining system for discovering leaders and tribes. *ICDE*, 0:1471–1474, 2009.

[13] Keith Henderson, Tina Eliassi-Rad, Spiros Papadimitriou, and Christos Faloutsos. Hcdf: A hybrid community discovery framework. In *SDM*, pages 754–765, 2010.

[14] Liran Katzir, Edo Liberty, and Oren Somekh. Estimating sizes of social networks via biased sampling. In *WWW*, pages 597–606, 2011.

[15] A. Lancichinetti and S. Fortunato. Community detection algorithms: A comparative analysis. *Physical Review E*, 80(5):056117–+, November 2009.

[16] Jure Leskovec, Lada A. Adamic, and Bernardo A. Huberman. The dynamics of viral marketing. *ACM Trans. Web*, 1, May 2007.

[17] Peter J. Mucha, Thomas Richardson, Kevin Macon, Mason A. Porter, and J-P Onnela. Community structure in Time-Dependent, multiscale, and multiplex networks. *Science*, 328(5980):876–878, 2010.

[18] M. E. J. Newman. Modularity and community structure in networks. *Proceedings of the National Academy of Sciences*, 103(23):8577–8582, June 2006.

[19] Spiros Papadimitriou, Jimeng Sun, Christos Faloutsos, and Philip S. Yu. Hierarchical, parameter-free community discovery. In *ECML PKDD*, pages 170–187, 2008.

[20] Pascal Pons and Matthieu Latapy. Computing communities in large networks using random walks. *J. Graph Algorithms Appl.*, 10(2):191–218, 2006.

[21] Usha N. Raghavan, Réka Albert, and Soundar Kumara. Near linear time algorithm to detect community structures in large-scale networks. *Physical Review E*, 76(3):036106+, September 2007.

[22] Martin Rosvall and Carl T. Bergstrom. Maps of random walks on complex networks reveal community structure. *PNAS*, 105(4):1118–1123, January 2008.

[23] Jianhua Ruan and Weixiong Zhang. An efficient spectral algorithm for network community discovery and its applications to biological and social networks. *Data Mining, IEEE International Conference on*, 0:643–648, 2007.

[24] G. Tsoumakas and I. Katakis. Multi label classification: An overview. *International Journal of Data Warehousing and Mining*, 3(3):1–13, 2007.

[25] Dashun Wang, Zhen Wen, Hanghang Tong, Ching-Yung Lin, Chaoming Song, and Albert-László Barabási. Information spreading in context. In *WWW*, pages 735–744, 2011.

On the Separability of Structural Classes of Communities

Bruno Abrahao Sucheta Soundarajan John Hopcroft Robert Kleinberg

Department of Computer Science
Cornell University
Ithaca, NY, 14850, USA
{abrahao, sucheta, jeh, rdk}@cs.cornell.edu

ABSTRACT

Three major factors govern the intricacies of community extraction in networks: (1) the application domain includes a wide variety of networks of fundamentally different natures, (2) the literature offers a multitude of disparate community detection algorithms, and (3) there is no consensus characterizing how to discriminate communities from non-communities. In this paper, we present a comprehensive analysis of community properties through a class separability framework. Our approach enables the assessement of the structural dissimilarity among the output of multiple community detection algorithms and between the output of algorithms and communities that arise in practice. To demostrate this concept, we furnish our method with a large set of structural properties and multiple community detection algorithms. Applied to a diverse collection of large scale network datasets, the analysis reveals that (1) the different detection algorithms extract fundamentally different structures; (2) the structure of communities that arise in practice is closest to that of communities that random-walk-based algorithms extract, although still siginificantly different from that of the output of all the algorithms; and (3) a small subset of the properties are nearly as discriminative as the full set, while making explicit the ways in which the algorithms produce biases. Our framework enables an informed choice of the most suitable community detection method for a given purpose and network and allows for a comparison of existing community detection algorithms while guiding the design of new ones.

Categories and Subject Descriptors

I.5.1 [**Computing Methodology**]: Pattern Recognition — *Design Methodology*

Keywords

Networks, Community Structure, Detection Algorithms, Class Separability

1. INTRODUCTION

Community structure captures the tendency of entities in a network to group together in meaningful subsets whose members have a distinctive relationship to one another. The identification of these subsets allows for the analysis of networks at different levels of detail, which is instrumental in illuminating the structure underlying large-scale systems [5, 9, 10, 22, 23].

Despite playing a fundamental role in the structure and function of networks, community structure has proved to be frustratingly difficult to define, quantify, and extract. In addition to challenges related to computational tractability, three major factors account for the intricacies of community extraction. First, the application domain includes a wide variety of networks of fundamentally different natures. Each of these networks possesses meaningful communities that may possess their own distinctive structural profiles. Second, the literature offers a multitude of disparate community detection algorithms. Due to differences in concept and design, the output of these procedures exhibits high structural variability across the collection. Last, there is no established consensus on the question of what properties distinguish subgraphs that are communities from those that are not communities.

In this paper, we tackle these challenges through a comprehensive analysis of community properties. We present a framework that enables researchers and practitioners to assess the structural dissimilarity among the output of multiple community detection algorithms and between the output of algorithms and communities that arise in practice. Our approach analyzes communities by taking account of a broad spectrum of structural properties. The analysis reveals nuances of the structure of real and extracted communities.

We frame our approach as a class separability problem, which simultaneously handles many classes of communities and a diverse set of structural properties. To this end, we specify a learning problem in which we map the distinct communities into a feature space, where the dimensions represent measures that characterize a community's link structure. The separability of classes provides information on the extent to which different communities come from the same (or fundamentally different) distributions of feature values. We extract different classes of communities that can be grouped into two categories: intrinsically-defined and extrinsically-defined communities.

We define the first set of communities by properties intrinsic to their link structure. For our purposes, these are the sets that community detection algorithms may output.

Each class of intrinsically defined communities comprises a set of examples that a specific algorithm extracts. The separability of these classes demonstrates the extent to which different algorithms output structurally distinguishable subgraphs. A feature selection analysis can then be employed to highlight the properties that exhibit the highest degree of inter-class variability, thereby making explicit the structural bias produced by different algorithms.

We also define communities by the context, the dynamics, or the function associated with the networks, but extrinsic to the link structure. We identify these communities through meaningful annotations provided with the datasets, such as explicit declaration of membership, product categories, grouping by protein function, and so on. In this fashion, for each network, we form a class of extrinsically-defined communities, henceforth called *annotated communities*. These communities enable a large-scale rigorous analysis of community detection methods. The separability of the class comprising annotated communities from the classes of intrinsically-defined communities determines the extent to which community detection algorithms succeed in extracting subgraphs that are structurally comparable to the communities formed by nodes sharing extrinsic properties in common.

To demonstrate our approach, we furnish our framework with a large set of structural properties and ten different community detection procedures to produce examples of different structural classes. Our selection is representative of categories of popular algorithms available in the literature. We consider a diverse collection of large scale real networks whose domains span biology, on-line shopping, and social systems. Assessing separability using supervised classifiers both parametric, namely Support Vector Machines [30], and nonparametric, namely k-Nearest Neighbors [1], together with a feature selection analysis using correlation-based methods [11], we reach the following conclusions about the communities in question. First, for all networks, the strong cross validation performance indicates that the different community detection algorithms produce fundamentally different structures that are separable on the feature space defined. Second, we observe that in nearly all cases, the annotated communities are structurally distinguishable from the output of all community detection algorithms. Nevertheless, the communities bearing the closest structural resemblance to annotated communities are those that random-walk-based algorithms extract. Surprisingly, in spite of the diversity of the domains from which our networks are drawn, this observation applies to all of the networks, except to two of them for which we have a small population size. Finally, a small subset of the features is consistently observed as the most discriminative. This observation allows for a dimensionality reduction by a factor as large as 4, preserving an equivalent 10-fold cross validation performance. The most discriminative features identify the ways in which the different algorithms produce biases. As illustrated by our experiments, by producing artificial or real examples of communities that possess the structure we wish to find, we can use our framework to enable an informed choice of the most suitable community detection method for a given network. In addition, it allows for a comparison of existing community detection algorithms and may guide the design of new ones.

This paper is organized as follows. Section 2 discusses background information and related work. Section 3 introduces the datasets we use, the algorithms we consider, and the measures we apply to construct the feature space. Section 4 describes the heart of our framework and presents an experimental analysis thereof. Next, this section closes with a feature selection analysis. Finally, Section 5 offers our concluding remarks.

2. BACKGROUND AND RELATED WORK

The work by Girvan and Newman [10] has recently sparked a wave of interest in the notion of *community structure* as a decomposition of a network that reflects meaningful properties of the underlying system [9]. Nevertheless, this area has its roots in the related problem of graph partitioning whose initial contributions date back to the 1970s [14].

Given the diverse nature of networks, the notion of meaningful communities is necessarily context dependent, involving interpretations and expectations of domain experts. Therefore, many attempts to define communities are grounded on the notion of mathematical optimization. Starting with an a priori expectation about what a community should look like, researchers specify an objective function for a search method, whose solution for a given instance provides the desired communities. This process has given rise to a a large collection of community detection algorithms, which aim at optimizing various objective functions. As mentioned in the previous section, the multitude of community structure definitions represents a source of high variability between the output of different community detection algorithms.

Among the objective functions introduced in previous work, the notion of *modularity* [10] has become an influential one. Modularity assigns high scores to communities whose internal edges outnumber the ones established in expectation by a random-network model that preserves the degree distribution of the original network. A related notion inspired by electrical networks is that of *conductance* [5]. The conductance of a set S with complement S^C is the ratio of the number of edges connecting nodes in S to nodes in S^C by the total number of edges incident to S or to S^C (whichever number is smaller). The common theme underlying the preceding notions is the search for node sets that are internally cohesive and yet sparsely connected to the rest of the network. Therefore, these measures tend to penalize sets having a large number of edges crossing the set relative to the count of internal edges.

Communities in general, however, display features that modularity and conductance may not capture, such as a preponderance of links to the outside over internal links and an arbitrary degree of overlap. This fact is substantiated by an investigation of real networks revealing that they do not split well into low-conductance communities [17] as most networks are expander-like [12]. These considerations lead to the development of alternative definitions, such as (α, β)-*community* [20], and algorithms, such as *Link Communities* [2] and *Clique Percolation* [24].

Communities in real networks often emerge as a result of multiple driving forces that make up the underlying complex system. Therefore, the attempt to capture community structure by maximizing a given objective function may represent an unrealistic expectation. As a consequence, communities identified by methods that reflect mathematical constructs may differ structurally from real communities that arise in practice. Despite the vast literature on community detection, the work by Ahn et al. [2], as well as ours, are among the few that attempt to analyze the structural resemblance between communities extracted by algorithms and annotated communities, which represent examples of meaningful communities in various domains.

Even though network analysts expect the outputs of the different algorithms to display dissimilar structural profiles due their conceptual diversity, the structural variability does not hinge simply on the choice of optimization problem. In most cases of interest, the search for a collection of node sets that maximize a given objective function is computationally intractable [9]. Therefore, in an attempt to handle the massive scale of today's networks, popular methods of community detection rely on efficient heuristics. As a consequence, previous work have quantified a significant output variability among different approximation algorithms that aim at maximizing the exact same function [15, 18].

In the spirit of studying the structural variability exhibited by different algorithms, closest to ours is the work by Leskovec et al. [17], which discusses properties of communities produced by multiple algorithms that aim at maximizing conductance. They consider the values of a handful of features, e.g., set compactness and internal conductance, produced by different algorithms. In contrast, here we present the first study that is simultaneously comprehensive with respect to the diversity of structural properties, of domains, of algorithms, and of scale. We take account of a set of 36 features, measured from the output produced by 10 different community detection processes, which are representative of classes of available algorithms that aim at maximizing various different objective functions in the literature. We derive our results from a diverse collection of datasets from large-scale networks arising from multiple domains.

3. BUILDING STRUCTURAL CLASSES

Before describing our framework and delving into our analysis, in this section we present the datasets we use, as well as our methodology for building structural classes of communities from the network data. We also define the feature space for our learning problem.

3.1 Datasets

We analyze eight large scale datasets, namely DBLP, LiveJournal, two portions of the Facebook network (denoted by Facebook — Rice University Undergraduate and Graduate), Amazon, and three biological networks denoted by HS, SC, and Fly. The collection encompasses different forms of entities and relationships and originate from diverse domains.

The LiveJournal dataset consists of a snapshot of a large network of bloggers, previously explored in [3]. The snapshot includes 4,847,571 bloggers who explicitly declare their friendship links. Due to the massive size of this dataset, we consider two portions of it, which we obtain by starting at a random node and performing a breadth-first search from that node. The datasets, henceforth named LJ1 and LJ2, contain 500,000 nodes each. LJ1 and LJ2 contain 10,736,588 and 10,640,429 edges, respectively.

DBLP data is publicly collectible and our dataset consists of a snapshot taken in May 2009 of the on-line publications database site DBLP. The data include a collection of editions of publication venues (i.e., conferences and journals) in computer science. A pair of the 744,386 authors present in the dataset are linked if they have co-authored at least one paper in any of the venues.

Facebook — Rice University Undergraduate (Ugrad) and Graduate (Grad) are an anonymized portion of the Facebook network which include Rice University students, collected by crawling public friends lists on Facebook on May 17, 2008. They consist of two disjoint sets of 1220 undergraduate students and 503 graduate students, respectively. Mislove et al. [21] present a detailed description of these datasets.

The Amazon dataset [16] is a product co-purchasing network from the on-line retailer Amazon.com. Each node represents a book, and an edge exists between two nodes if one was frequently purchased with the other. The network contains 270,347 nodes and 741,142 edges. For each book, Amazon.com reports up to 5 other items that were frequently purchased with the book.

Biological networks HS, SC, and Fly describe protein-protein interactions for *H. Sapiens* (human), *S. Cerevisiae* (a type of yeast), and *Drosophila* (a fruit fly species) [25], respectively. In these networks, a node represents a protein, and two nodes are connected if scientific evidence of their interaction exists. HS contains 10,298 nodes and 54,655 edges, SC contains 5523 nodes and 82,656 edges, and Fly contains 15,326 nodes and 486,970 edges.

3.1.1 *Annotated communities*

The networks we analyze contain annotations reflecting examples of communities that arise in these domains[1]. Some of these sets are user-defined, i.e., users explicitly declare their participation in the community, while others reflect contextual information of the underlying process or organization, e.g., department, protein function, product category, etc.. Below we describe how we identify and clean the annotated communities for each dataset.

For the social networks, in LiveJournal, users explicitly declare their membership in zero or more communities created and administered by users. In DBLP, conferences where authors publish their research work reflect the community memberships. Finally, for Facebook — Rice University Undergraduate and Graduate, users who possess common academic attributes, such as department, major, or dormitory, form the communities. These attributes were obtained by matching Facebook names with student records from the university's directory [21].

For each item in Amazon.com, the on-line store provides several product categories, such as "Photo Essays" or "Landscape Architecture Textbooks". We identify a set of nodes possessing a common categorical label as a community.

For HS, SC, and Fly, a number of proteins (though not all) have annotations regarding one or more gene ontology IDs describing the known functions that the protein serves (e.g., metabolic regulation). We use these gene ontology values to identify the communities.

Since we define annotated communities extrinsically to the link structure, the sets formed by the preceding definitions may induce disconnected graphs. However, it is reasonable to limit the definition of community to include only connected subgraphs of the network. Therefore, to capture the community information implicit in the annotations, we consider each connected component of the graph induced by a node set possessing a common label as an annotated community by itself. Moreover, since we are interested in the

[1]These communities, however, may not represent an unbiased sample of communities in these networks as other communities that are not annotated might also exist.

structure of reasonably sized communities, we filtered out small communities with less than 10 members.

Overall, we identified 29,955 annotated communities for LJ1, 39,598 for LJ2, 10,595 for DBLP, 24 for RICE-grad, and 41 for RICE-ugrad, 9439 for Amazon, 64 for HS, 76 for SC, and 54 for Fly.

3.2 Structural classes and feature space

In this section we describe how to produce examples that constitute the structural classes and how to build the feature space for our learning framework. The process consists of two steps. First, we produce the examples by applying community detection algorithms, one for each class, to the network data. Second, we extract features by measuring a broad spectrum of properties of the subgraphs induced by communities. This latter step uses a set of examples consisting of the output produced in the previous step along with the set of annotated communities.

3.2.1 Producing the examples

To study classes of intrinsically defined communities, we selected a collection of 10 community detection procedures, which are representative of strategies employed by a broad range of algorithms in the literature. We applied these procedures to each of the nine network datasets to extract examples of subgraphs produced by these methods. We labeled examples with the identity of the community detection procedure that produced them. In total, for each network, we created 11 structural classes of communities: one class of extrinsically-defined communities, which comprises examples of annotated communities, and each of the other 10 classes corresponding to intrinsically-defined communities, which comprise examples extracted by each of the 10 community detection algorithms respectively. Below we briefly describe the community detection procedures we consider.

1. **Breadth First Search (BFS):** To establish a baseline, we use breadth first search to extract sets that serve as examples of random connected communities. To create one BFS community of size k, we begin with a randomly selected node and perform a breadth first search from that node until we visit k elements.
2. **Random Walk 0 (RW0):** The central idea in many community detection algorithms is that random walks tend to concentrate within a community [26, 31]. To create communities of size k, we begin with a random node and perform a uniform–random walk from that node until k different nodes are visited.
3. **Random Walk 0.15 (RW15):** This is similar to the preceding method with the twist that at each step we restart the walk from the starting node with 0.15 probability. RW15 concentrates the random walk distribution around a center, thereby forming more compact sets, whereas RW0 communities tend to spread out.
4. (α, β) **(AB)**: An (α, β)-community, for $\alpha < \beta$, requires every member of the community to be connected to at least β other members while nonmembers have at most α links to the community [20]. This definition allows for overlapping communities whose out-links may outnumber the in-links. To produce an AB community of size k, we produce a BFS community of size k and then apply a limited number of sequential node swaps that aim at making the set an approximate or exact (α, β)-community. In each step we remove the community node with the fewest member neighbors and add the fringe node with the most member neighbors.
5. **Link Communities (LC):** In contrast with the majority of the available algorithms, Link Communities [2] aims at addressing the overlapping and hierarchical nature of community structure by treating communities as groups of links rather than nodes. We extract examples of this structure by applying a standard implementation of this algorithm to our networks.
6. **Infomap (IM):** The Infomap algorithm [27] views the problem of finding communities as akin to the problem of a map-maker deciding on a level of granularity. The communities and the nodes therein have names. A random walk in the network is described by appending the community name followed by the name of nodes visited while in the community to a transcript. The goal is to find the community structure that minimizes the expected length of the description. Intuitively, such a structure would cause random walks to rarely escape communities.
7. **Louvain:** The Louvain method [4] is a popular method for greedy modularity optimization. The algorithm consists of iteratively aggregating nodes into communities whenever this move locally improves modularity. The process outputs communities when no further merge produces a significant gain in modularity.
8. **Newman-Clauset-Moore (Newman):** This method is another example of greedy modularity maximization [6]. Unlike the Louvain method, which considers merges that locally improve modularity, Newman-Clauset-Moore identifies a hierarchical community structure from which communities are extracted by cutting the dendrogram that reflects the hierarchy at the level that maximizes a global value of modularity.
9. **Markov Clustering Algorithm (MCL):** MCL [7] is a random-walk-based method. It consists of two alternating steps. It begins with the random-walk matrix of a graph (the normalized adjacency matrix). The first step, namely "expansion", squares this matrix; this corresponds to computing the flow between clusters. The second step called "inflation", squares each element of the matrix individually, and then renormalizes; this step corresponds to increasing the strength of intra-community ties. This process converges to a stationary matrix with several connected components, which the algorithm output as the communities.
10. **Metis:** Metis [13] is a graph partitioning method which is a variation of the Kernighan-Lin algorithm [14]. Metis partitions a node-weighted network into a specified number of equal weight sets while minimizing the number of edges between the sets. Here we used a version of Metis we adapted for finding high-conductance sets.

In the process of generating examples, we discard communities of size less than 10 or greater than 1000, as well as those communities that contain multiple components. The number of examples extracted varies among the procedures. However, the methods we use for class separability are sensitive to class imbalance. Thus, we under-sample the large

#	Feature	Description
1	n	Number of nodes
2	m	Number of edges
3	Diameter	Greatest distance between two nodes by traversing shortest paths
4	Edge Density	Ratio of m to the maximum possible number of edges
5	Conductance	Ratio of m to the sum of the total degrees of the n nodes, including edges to rest of the network
6	Transitivity	Ratio of the number of 3-node cycles (triangles) to the number of 2-hop paths (open triangles)
7	Triangle Density	Ratio of the number of 3-node cycles (triangles) to the number of possible node triples
8-11	Shortest Path	All pairs shortest paths The features are the three quartiles and the maximum.
12-15	Edge Betweenness	For each edge, fraction of all-pairs shortest paths that include that edge The features are the three quartiles and the maximum.
16-20	Node Betweenness	For each node, fraction of all-pairs shortest paths that include that node The features are the minimum, the three quartiles, and the maximum.
21-25	α	For each nonmember on the fringe of the community, number of members that this node is connected to; The features are the minimum, the three quartiles, and the maximum.
26-30	β	For each member, number of other members this node is connected to The features are the minimum, the three quartiles, and the maximum.
31	Treesum	Total number of spanning trees of the community graph, divided by the total number of spanning trees of a K_n-clique (computed using Kirchoff's matrix tree theorem [19])
32-36	Information Centrality	For each node, its Stephenson and Zelen's information centrality index [28] The features are the minimum, the three quartiles, and the maximum.

Table 1: List of features corresponding to measures of the subgraphs that communities induce.

classes and to a lesser extent over-sample small classes to reduce this source of bias.

Our algorithm selection has the purpose of illustrating the applicability of our framework. The approach, however, is not limited to the list we consider. Our method scales to a large number of classes, and a collection of classes should include enough information to reflect the analysis intended. As discussed in the next section, a pair of classes may be highly correlated to each other (e.g., RW0 and RW15). As a result, they may split the predictions in such a way as to obfuscate the interpretation of the outcome. To avoid this pitfall, an inter-class correlation analysis can be employed to assess the independence of the algorithm selection [29].

3.2.2 Feature Extraction

In the feature extraction phase, we measure the subgraphs induced by the communities produced in the previous step and those induced by annotated communities. We use a large spectrum of measurements that cover many properties of both the internal link structure and the external interaction of the community with the rest of the network. Each measurement corresponds to a dimension of our feature space. Table 1 lists the features and describes their corresponding measures.

Most of the features can be understood from their table description. The feature Information Centrality, however, deserves further explanation. This measure captures a node's degree of centrality as a function of how fast its information can sequentially reach every other node in the network. For a given node, the information centrality computes a harmonic mean of the amount of "signal" that a node receives from other nodes. A signal between two nodes corresponds to a path between them, which varies according to the "noise", instantiated here as the path length [28].

By measuring the structural properties described in Table 1 for each example of a community derived in the previous phase, we obtain 11 classes of labeled examples in feature space, which constitute the input in our framework.

4. FRAMEWORK AND APPLICATION

In this section we present an experimental application using the data we processed through the steps described in the previous section.

4.1 Class Separability Measures

Methods for measuring class separability are popular in machine learning for guiding feature selection analysis. Accordingly, effective feature sets for classification tasks are the ones that simultaneously lead to high inter-class and low intra-class variability [29]. Methods of class separability allow for a rigorous analysis of independence among classes. Unfortunately, many of these methods are computationally demanding or dependent on assumptions which are often mismatched with applications [8].

In this work, we frame the research question of discriminating the structure of different communities as a class separability problem. The separability of structural classes of communities provides information on whether different communities come from the same (or fundamentally different) distributions of feature values. This analysis is informative of the extent to which different algorithms produce structural differences and the extent to which community detection algorithms succeed in producing sets that resemble annotated communities. Aiming at achieving computational scalability and fine-grained separability information,

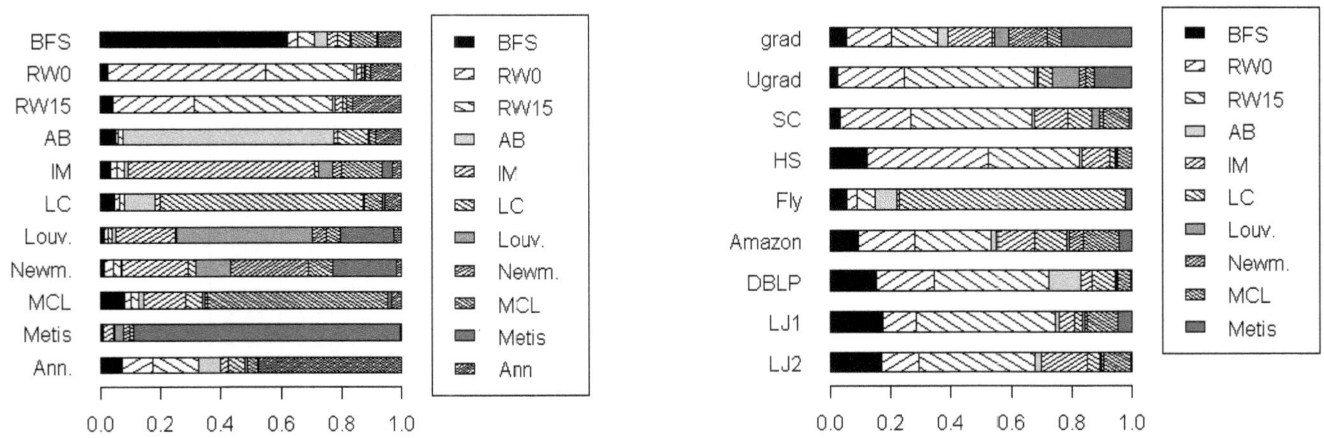

(a) Class separability via cross validation (DBLP).

(b) Classification of annotated communities.

Figure 1: Distribution of probability mass resulting from the SVM (a) cross validation on the 11 classes, and (b) classification of annotated communities examples and trained on the 10 classes of algorithms.

we use the performance of existing supervised classifiers as a measure of class separability. To our definition, classes are separable to the extent that a classifier can correctly distinguish their structure by exhibiting an accurate classification. More specifically, we employ two techniques, one parametric, namely Support Vector Machines (SVM) [30], and one nonparametric, namely k-Nearest-Neighbors (kNN) [1], to confirm each other's outcomes while ruling out variability due to the specifics of each algorithm. We select hyperparameters in both cases via grid search using the performance of 10-fold cross validation as the objective function. Both methods are capable of handling a large number of classes and scale to a large volume of data.

We measure class separability using the performance of a 3-fold cross-validation. For each network, we train a multiclass classifier on a set containing two thirds of the examples, which are selected at random, and then evaluate the performance of the model on the remaining third, which constitute the test set. We perform 3 rounds of this process and average the outcomes. For each element in a test set, the probabilistic SVM model outputs a probability mass vector indicating the probability that each data point belongs to each class.

4.2 Experimental Analysis

Our primary goal is to gain insight into whether the classes are separable in the feature space defined. Second, building on the preceding observations, we are interested in finding the algorithms whose output structurally reflects the annotated communities. Finally, we study the features that are most useful for distinguishing between the structural classes of network communities.

Our first experiment performs the cross-validation on all the 11 classes. We first observe that the experiments suffer little variability between the two classifiers.

To illustrate the method's output, Figure 1(a) presents the analysis of the outcome produced by the SVM-based method applied to the DBLP network. In the picture, we show a bar graph of the distribution of probability mass for each class derived from the network DBLP. This graph visually demonstrates that the bulk of the probability mass from each class was correctly classified. Table 2 contains a summary of results for all networks. Each entry in the table represents the fraction of probability mass from that class that was correctly assigned. When a value appears in parentheses, this indicates that most of the probability mass was assigned to some other class. While the the SVM provides a breakdown of values by classes, the last two rows present global scores of separability computed using *scatter matrices* [29], which is a standard measure of class separability in pattern recognition[2]. The last row presents a reference point of little separability for each network, where we shuffle the labels of points before computing the score.

As this table shows, only 17 out of 99 network-class pairs failed to have a plurality of the probability mass correctly classified. Newman Modularity is frequently misclassified; however, it is a small class in all networks, especially on the smaller ones (e.g., on network SC, Newman Modularity found only 3 communities of size between 10 and 1000). In the case of annotated communities a plurality of their corresponding classes tends to be correctly classified, with the exception of network Fly. Figure 1(a) serves as a visual reference of a network whose classes have global separability score of 22.7. The other networks exhibit comparable scores, with the exception of network Fly, whose classes are not well separated.

The previous experiment shows that annotated communities tend to form their own, separable class that is significantly distinct from all other classes. However, a question

[2]We use a criterion referred to as J_3 by [29].

	Grad	Ugrad	HS	SC	Fly	DBLP	Amaz	LJ1	LJ2
BFS	60%	88%	73%	70%	(40%)	63%	55%	86%	81%
RW0	44%	55%	43%	(39%)	(27%)	52%	43%	61%	63%
RW15	40%	(29%)	44%	42%	34%	46%	39%	57%	57%
AB	83%	91%	90%	71%	60%	70%	74%	90%	89%
IM	27%	(23%)	72%	73%	(2%)	62%	51%	82%	66%
LC	68%	96%	83%	85%	83%	67%	56%	90%	89%
Louv.	24%	(3%)	49%	(1%)	(0%)	45%	58%	38%	49%
Newm.	(14%)	(25%)	(15%)	(0%)	90%	26%	39%	45%	56%
MCL	19%	(22%)	57%	28%	(34%)	59%	46%	80%	74%
Metis	61%	73%	81%	90%	(42%)	88%	66%	92%	86%
Annot.	37%	33%	50%	46%	(8%)	47%	40%	72%	71%
Global	**19.2**	**22.3**	**26.0**	**27.4**	**6.3**	**22.7**	**16.4**	**19.7**	**21.9**
Ref.	14.7	13.1	13.0	13.0	12.9	13.0	12.9	12.9	12.9

Table 2: Percentage of the probability mass of classification of elements in the test set into the correct class, using SVM, for all networks. The last two rows present global separability scores using scatter matrices.

Network		Grad	Ugrad	HS	SC	Fly	DBLP	Amaz	LJ1	LJ2
Number of Features Selected		**6**	**7**	**10**	**5**	**6**	**10**	**8**	**12**	**11**
Rank	**Feature**									
1	**Conductance**	1	1	1	1		1	1	1	1
1	**Diameter**		1	1	1	1	1	1	1	1
3	**Info Centrality***	2	2	3	1	1	2	1	2	2
4	**Node Betweenness***			2	2		2	1	5	5
5	**Shortest Path***			1		3	2	1	1	1
6	β^*	1	1	1			2	1	1	1
7	α^*	1		1		1		2	1	
Other features**		#6	#4, #7							

Table 3: Summary of the feature selection results. Features are ranked in order of their frequency in the selection list over the networks. (∗ reporting how many quartiles of the property were selected. ∗∗ feature number according to Table 1.)

of interest to the design and application of community detection procedures is what algorithms output communities bearing the closest structural resemblance to the annotated communities. To answer this question we perform a variation of the classification task previously described. We train a classifier on the 10 classes corresponding to the community detection algorithms and leave the class of annotated communities out of the training set. The goal of this experiment is to evaluate to which class of intrinsically defined communities the annotated examples of the test set are classified.

Figure 1(b) shows the distribution of probability mass of the annotated communities classified into the different classes corresponding to community detection algorithms. The structure that random-walk-based algorithms produce is clearly the most similar to that of the annotated communities. For 7 of the 9 networks, a plurality of the probability mass from the annotated communities was assigned to the classes RW15 and RW0. Due to their high similarity, the classifier confuses these two random-walk-based algorithms as shown in Figure 1(a). The exceptions to this are networks Grad and Fly. For Grad, their annotated communities' probability is spread across all classes, where Metis received the plurality of the mass. In the Fly network, the greatest share of the mass of annotated communities is assigned to LC. These exceptions are associated with small network datasets, therefore the variability could be due to small population sample size. Given the diverse nature of these networks, it is perhaps surprising that in virtually all domains the random-walk communities bear the closest structural resemblance to the annotated communities.

4.2.1 Feature Selection

As we have seen in the preceding experiment, each community detection algorithm extracts a distinct structure, which our method is able to separate when projected onto the feature space we define. In this section, we are concerned with identifying the ways in which the algorithms produce bias by finding which properties exhibit the highest degree of between-class variability.

To address this question we use the Correlation-based Feature Selection algorithm (CFS) [11] to identify subsets of the most discriminative features for each network. CFS is intended to give a high score to sets of features that are highly predictive of the class and are not redundant with one another. CFS begins with no nodes in the feature set, and it then employs a hill-climbing algorithm to search the space of feature subsets.

Table 3 lists the features selected by CFS for each net-

	Grad	Ugrad	HS	SC	Fly	DBLP	Amaz	LJ1	LJ2
All Features	62.9%	86%	82.2%	80.9%	93.6%	81.3%	65.3%	89.1%	88.5%
With selection	61.5%	84.7%	85.1%	81%	90.6%	79.4%	63%	78.8%	76%

Table 4: k-Nearest-Neighbors classification performance using both the full set of features and the subset of the most discriminative features selected by CFS.

work ranked in order of the frequency with which they appear in the selection over the networks. The table lists the most frequent features, or sets of features for those properties calculated with quartiles. The entries for row "Features" and column "Network" that contain the value 1 indicate the presence of that feature in the feature selection applied to that particular network data, whereas empty cells indicate the absence thereof. Integers larger than 1 can be found in some of the entries and indicate the number of quartiles from that feature that were selected by CFS. In nearly every network, conductance, diameter, information centrality, and node betweeness were the most discriminative features.

Surprisingly, in several cases, multiple quartiles of a feature appear: e.g., Fly has 3 path length quartiles, and LJ1 and LJ2 each contain all 5 node betweenness features. We had expected that different quartiles of the same feature would be highly correlated to each other, and therefore they would be unlikely to co-occur among the features selected by CFS. Instead, these results suggest that varying the choice of community detection algorithm results in fine-grained variation in the distribution of such features.

To assess the effectiveness of the features CFS found, Table 4 presents for all networks the classification performance of the kNN cross validation using both the full set of features and the subset of features found by CFS. We see that in most cases, there is very little loss in accuracy. We observe a similar qualitative outcome for the SVM cross validation. In the table, the largest drops happened for LJ1 and LJ2 and reduced the accuracy by less than 15%. Being nearly as discriminative as the full set, a reduced set containing a handful of features retains the relevant information needed to analyze the bias produced by different algorithms.

We use the sets of the most discriminative features to study which tendencies in feature values are associated with which algorithms. To this end, we conducted a range analysis which distinguishes the different algorithms according to the value of their features. In the interest of space, we summarize the qualitative outcome of this experiment in Table 5. The entries correspond to the bias produced by each of the algorithms, considering all networks. Features take on a varying range of values across different networks. Thus, to label the magnitude of features, we compute the mean value of each class and compute a global median of these averages over all classes. The averages occurring between the 33rd and 67th percentile constitute the *medium* denomination; whereas those below the 33rd and above the 67th constitute *low* and *high*, respectively. Finally, we count how many times each feature produced each of the denominations across all the networks. From this count, we determine the most frequent tendency which make up the entries we present in the table.

Using this analysis, we are able to group algorithms with similar behavior. For example, the random-walk-based algorithms produce the same structural bias. The same holds for Louvain and Newman; and AB and LC. The profile of annotated communities is close to that of random-walk-based algorithms, with a few nuances. Annotated communities exhibit medium conductance whereas RW0 and RW15 extract low conductance sets. In addition, the diameter of annotated communities was measured as high for four of the networks, medium for one of them, and low for the remaining four. This contrasts with RW0 and RW15, which produce set with high diameter. Nevertheless, the similarity due to other features explains the ways in which annotated communities resemble the output of random-walk-based algorithms. Finally, Metis and IM differ only in behavior of the node betweenness feature.

Algorithm	Conduct.	Diam.	Nd.Betw.	Inf.Cent.
Annotated	Medium	High/Low	High	Low
RW0, RW15	Low	High	High	Low
Louvain	High	High	Low	Medium
Newman	High	High	Low	Medium
AB	Medium	Low	Medium	High
LC	Medium	Low	Medium	High
Metis	High	Medium	Medium	Medium
IM	High	Medium	High	Medium

Table 5: Tendency of different algorithms with respect to the most discriminative features.

5. DISCUSSION

In this paper we tackle the complexity involved in the task of extracting communities in networks by illuminating structural properties of different algorithms and communities that arise in networks across a diverse set of domains. Our approach differs fundamentally from previous work in the area due to its supervised nature. The existing community detection algorithms treat the problem as an unsupervised decomposition of a network with little sensitivity to different purposes, structures of interest, and the various domains of application. Accordingly, our supervised approach may be used by a practitioner to make an informed decision about the most suitable algorithm for a given network in the following way. First, we produce a test set comprising examples of the communities we are interested in finding, which could be either real or synthetic. Second, we choose a set of algorithms we want to evaluate. Finally, we apply our approach using the target network and present the classifier with the test set. The classifier assigns the probability mass of the test set to the class of algorithm that bears close resemblance to the examples. The algorithm that receives the bulk of the mass is the algorithm that may succeed in extracting communities that structurally resemble the ones we are interested in. Researchers may also benefit from our methodology when designing new community detection algorithms as a way to compare the behavior of new methods with existing ones.

Structural similarity is a weaker requirement than accuracy. In other words, communities with similar properties to real communities may not correspond exactly to the communities we may expect to find. Nevertheless, mastering structure is a fundamental stepping stone in the development of algorithms to accurately find the communities of interest.

Finally, our approach suggests a change in the way we approach the problem of community detection. Instead of developing multiple general purpose algorithms that find a particular type of community, one could use a supervised approach that allows the user to specify what they intend to find through examples. Then, one could develop an algorithm that learns from these examples and retrieves similar structures. This is part of our agenda for future work.

Acknowledgments

We are grateful to Eduardo Valle for valuable discussions. Support for this research is provided by AFOSR grants FA9550-09-1-0100 and FA9550-09-1-0675.

6. REFERENCES

[1] D. W. Aha, D. Kibler, and M. K. Albert. Instance-based learning algorithms. *Machine Learning*, 6:37–66, January 1991.

[2] Y. Ahn, J. P. Bagrow, and S. Lehmann. Link communities reveal multiscale complexity in networks. *Nature*, 466(7307):761–764, 2010.

[3] L. Backstrom, D. Huttenlocher, J. Kleinberg, and X. Lan. Group formation in large social networks: Membership, growth, and evolution. In *Proceedings of the 12th ACM SIGKDD Conference on Knowledge Discovery and Data Mining*, 2006.

[4] V. D. Blondel, J. Guillaume, R. Lambiotte, and E. Lefebvre. Fast unfolding of communities in large networks. Mar. 2008. Journal of Statistical Mechanics.

[5] F. R. K. Chung. *Spectral Graph Theory.* American Mathematical Society, Dec. 1996.

[6] A. Clauset, M. E. J. Newman, and C. Moore. Finding community structure in very large networks. *Physical Review E*, 70(6):066111+, Dec. 2004.

[7] S. V. Dongen. Graph clustering via a discrete uncoupling process. *SIAM Journal on Matrix Analysis and Applications*, 30(1):121–141, 2008.

[8] N. Fatemi-Ghomi, P. Palmer, and M. Petrou. The two-point correlation function: A measure of interclass separability. *Journal of Mathematical Imaging and Vision*, 10:7–25, 1999. 10.1023/A:1008362414568.

[9] S. Fortunato. Community detection in graphs. *0906.0612*, June 2010. Phys. Reports 486, 75-174.

[10] M. Girvan and M. Newman. Community structure in social and biological networks. *Proc. of the National Academy of Sciences*, 99(12):7821 –7826, June 2002.

[11] M. A. Hall. *Correlation-based Feature Subset Selection for Machine Learning.* PhD thesis, Department of Computer Science, University of Waikato, 1999.

[12] S. Hoory, N. Linial, and A. Wigderson. Expander graphs and their applications. *Bulletin of the American Mathematical Society*, 43(4):439, 2006.

[13] G. Karypis and V. Kumar. A fast and high quality multilevel scheme for partitioning irregular graphs. *SIAM J. Sci. Comput.*, 20:359–392, December 1998.

[14] B. W. Kernighan and S. Lin. An efficient heuristic procedure for partitioning graphs. *The Bell System Technical Journal*, 49(1):291–307, 1970.

[15] A. Lancichinetti and S. Fortunato. Community detection algorithms: A comparative analysis. *Physical Review E*, 80:056117, Nov 2009.

[16] J. Leskovec, L. Adamic, and B. Huberman. The dynamics of viral marketing. In *Proceedings of the 7th ACM Conference on Electronic Commerce*, 2006.

[17] J. Leskovec, K. Lang, A. Dasgupta, and M. Mahoney. Statistical properties of community structure in large social and information networks. In *Proc. of the 17th Intl. Conf. on World Wide Web*, 2008.

[18] J. Leskovec, K. Lang, and M. Mahoney. Empirical comparison of algorithms for network community detection. In *Proceedings of the 19th Intl. Conference on World Wide Web*, 2010.

[19] R. Lyons and Y. Peres. *Probability on Trees and Networks.* Cambridge University Press, 2012.

[20] N. Mishra, R. Schreiber, I. Stanton, and R. Tarjan. Finding strongly knit clusters in social networks. *Internet Mathematics*, 5(1):155–174, Jan. 2008.

[21] A. Mislove, B. Viswanath, K. Gummadi, and P. Druschel. You are who you know: Inferring user profiles in online social networks. In *Proc. 3rd ACM Intl. Conf. on Web Search and Data Mining*, 2010.

[22] M. Newman. Detecting community structure in networks. *The European Phys. Journal B*, 38(2):321–330–330, Mar. 2004.

[23] M. Newman. Modularity and community structure in networks. *Proceedings of the National Academy of Sciences*, 103(23):8577 –8582, June 2006.

[24] G. Palla, I. Derenyi, I. Farkas, and T. Vicsek. Uncovering the overlapping community structure of complex networks in nature and society. *Nature*, 435(7043):814–818, June 2005.

[25] D. Park, R. Singh, M. Baym, C.-S. Liao, and B. Berger. IsoBase: a database of functionally related proteins across PPI networks. *Nucleic Acids Research*, (suppl 1):D295–D300.

[26] P. Pons and M. Latapy. Computing communities in large networks using random walks. *J. of Graph Algorithms and Applications*, 10(2):191–218, 2006.

[27] M. Rosvall and C. Bergstrom. Multilevel compression of random walks on networks reveals hierarchical organization in large integrated systems. *PLoS ONE*, 6(4):e18209, 04 2011.

[28] K. Stephenson and M. Zelen. Rethinking centrality: Methods and examples. *Social Networks*, 11(1):1–37, Mar. 1989.

[29] S. Theodoridis and K. Koutroumbas. *Pattern Recognition.* Academic Press, 4th edition, Nov. 2008.

[30] V. N. Vapnik. *Statistical Learning Theory.* Wiley-Interscience, 1st edition, Sept. 1998.

[31] E. Weinan, T. Li, and E. Vanden-Eijnden. Optimal partition and effective dynamics of complex networks. *Proceedings of the National Academy of Sciences*, 105(23):7907–7912, June 2008.

Discovering Lag Intervals for Temporal Dependencies

Liang Tang Tao Li
School of Computer Science
Florida International University
11200 S.W. 8th Street
Miami, Florida, 33199
U.S.A
{ltang002,taoli}@cs.fiu.edu

Larisa Shwartz
IBM T.J Watson Research Center
19 Skyline Drive
Hawthorne, NY, 10532
U.S.A
lshwart@us.ibm.com

ABSTRACT

Time lag is a key feature of hidden temporal dependencies within sequential data. In many real-world applications, time lag plays an essential role in interpreting the cause of discovered temporal dependencies. Traditional temporal mining methods either use a predefined time window to analyze the item sequence, or employ statistical techniques to simply derive the time dependencies among items. Such paradigms cannot effectively handle varied data with special properties, e.g., the interleaved temporal dependencies.

In this paper, we study the problem of finding lag intervals for temporal dependency analysis. We first investigate the correlations between the temporal dependencies and other temporal patterns, and then propose a generalized framework to resolve the problem. By utilizing the sorted table in representing time lags among items, the proposed algorithm achieves an elegant balance between the time cost and the space cost. Extensive empirical evaluation on both synthetic and real data sets demonstrates the efficiency and effectiveness of our proposed algorithm in finding the temporal dependencies with lag intervals in sequential data.

Categories and Subject Descriptors

H.2.8 [**Database applications**]: Data mining

Keywords

Temporal dependency, Time lag

1. INTRODUCTION

Sequential data is prevalent in business, system management, health-care and many scientific domains. One fundamental problem in temporal data mining is to discover hidden temporal dependencies in the sequential data [23] [11] [13] [8] [29]. In temporal data mining, the input data is typically a sequence of discrete items associated with time stamps [24] [23]. Let A and B be two types of items, a temporal dependency for A and B, written as $A \to B$, denotes that the occurrence of B depends on the occurrence of A. The dependency indicates that an item A is often followed by an item B. Let $[t_1, t_2]$ be the range of the lag for two dependent A and B. This temporal dependency with $[t_1, t_2]$ is written as $A \to_{[t_1,t_2]} B$ [7]. For example, in system management, disk capacity alert and database alert are two item types. When the disk capacity is full, the database engine often raises a database alert in the next 5 to 6 minutes as shown in Figure 1. Hence, the disk capacity has a temporal dependency with the database. $[\mathtt{5min}, \mathtt{6min}]$ is the lag interval between the two dependent system alerts. $disk\_capacity\_alert \to_{[\mathtt{5min},\mathtt{6min}]} database\_alert$ describes the temporal dependency with the associated lag interval. This paper studies the problem of finding appropriate lag intervals for two dependent item types.

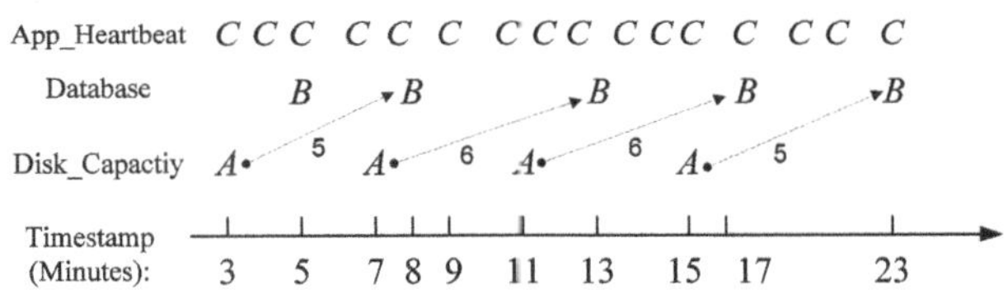

Figure 1: Lag Interval for Temporal Dependency

Temporal dependencies are often used for prediction. In Figure 1, $[\mathtt{5min}, \mathtt{6min}]$ is the predicted time range, indicating when a database alert occurs after a disk capacity alert is received. Furthermore, the associated lag interval characterizes the cause of a temporal dependency. For example, if the database is writing a huge temporal log file which is larger than the disk free space, the database alert is immediately raised in $[\mathtt{0min}, \mathtt{1min}]$. But if the disk free capacity is consumed by other applications, the database engine can only detect this alert when it runs queries. The associate time lags in such a case would be larger than 1 minute.

Previous work for discovering temporal dependencies does not consider interleaved dependencies [17] [4] [21]. For $A \to B$, they assume that an item A can only have a dependency with its first following B. However, it is possible that an item A has a dependency with any following B. For example, in Figure 1, the time lag for two dependent A and B is 5 to 6 minutes, but the time lag for two adjacent A's is only 4 minutes. All A's have a dependency with the second following B, not the first following B. Hence, the dependencies among these dependent A and B are interleaved. For two item types, the numbers of time stamps are both $O(n)$, The number of possible time lags is $O(n^2)$. Thus, the number of lag intervals is $O(n^4)$. The challenge of our work is how to efficiently find appropriate lag intervals over the $O(n^4)$ candidates.

1.1 Contributions

In this paper, we study the problem of finding appropriate lag intervals for temporal dependency analysis. The contribution of this paper is summarized as follows:

- Investigates the relationship among the lag intervals and other existing temporal patterns proposed in previous work. It shows that, many existing temporal patterns can be expressed as special cases of temporal dependencies with lag intervals.
- Develops an algorithm for discovering appropriate lag intervals. The time complexity is $O(n^2 \log n)$ and the space complexity is $O(N)$, where N is the number of items, and n is the number of distinct time stamps. This paper also proves that, there is no algorithm can solve this problem with an $o(n^2)$ time complexity.
- Conducts extensive experiments on synthetic and real data sets. The experimental results confirm the theoretical analysis of this paper and show that the performance of the proposed algorithm outperforms baseline algorithms.

1.2 Road Map

The rest of the paper is organized as follows: Section 2 summarizes the related work for temporal pattern mining and discusses the relationships with other existing temporal patterns. Section 3 defines the lag interval that we try to find. Section 4 presents several algorithms for finding appropriate lag intervals and analyzes the complexity of our problem. In Section 5, we present the experimental studies on synthetic and real data sets. Finally, Section 6 concludes our paper and discusses the future work.

2. RELATED WORK

Previous work of temporal dependency discovery can be categorized by the data set type. The first category is for market basket data, which is a collection of transactions [29] where each transaction is a sequence of items. The purpose of this type of temporal dependency discovery is to find frequent subsequences which are contained by a certain amount of transactions. Typical algorithms are GSP [28], FreeSpan[9], PrefixSpan[26], and SPAM[3]. The second category is for the time series data. A temporal dependency of this category is seen as a correlation on multiple time series variables [32] [5], which determines whether one time series is useful in forecasting another. Our work belongs to the third category, which is for temporal symbolic sequences. The input data is an item sequence and each item is associated with a time stamp. An item may represent an event or a behavior in history [18] [24] [23] [25][16]. The purpose is to find various temporal relationships among these events or behaviors. Many temporal patterns proposed in previous work can be considered as special cases of temporal dependencies with different lag intervals.

2.1 Relation with Other Temporal Patterns

Table 1 lists several types of temporal patterns proposed in the literature and their corresponding temporal dependencies with lag intervals. A mutually dependent pattern (**m-pattern**) $\{A, B\}$, can be described as two temporal dependencies $A \rightarrow_{[0,\delta]} B$ and $B \rightarrow_{[0,\delta]} A$. Items of A and B in an **m-pattern** appear almost together so that $t_1 = 0, t_2 \leq \delta$, where δ is the time tolerance. A partially periodic pattern (**p-pattern**) [20] for a single item A, can be expressed as a temporal dependency $A \rightarrow_{[p-\delta,p+\delta]} A$, where p is the period. Frequent episodes $A \rightarrow B \rightarrow C$ can be separated to $A \rightarrow_{[0,p]} B$ and $B \rightarrow_{[0,p]} C$ where p is the parameter of the time window length [21]. [17] proposes *loose temporal pattern* and *stringent temporal pattern*. As shown in Table 1, the two types of temporal patterns can be explained by two temporal dependencies with particular constraints on the lag intervals. One common problem of these algorithms is how to set the precise parameter about the time window [21] [20] [4]. For example, for discovering partially periodic patterns, if δ is too small, the identification of partially periodic patterns would be too strict and no result can be found; if the δ is too large, many false results would be found. [15] [14] [22] directly find frequent episodes according to the occurrences of episodes in the data sequence. The discovered frequent episode may not have fixed lag intervals for the represented temporal dependency. Our method proposed in this paper does not require users to specify the parameters about the time window and is able to discover interleaved temporal dependencies.

3. QUALIFIED LAG INTERVAL

Given an item sequence $S = x_1 x_2 ... x_N$, x_i denotes the type of the i-th item, and $t(x_i)$ denotes the time stamp of x_i, $i = 1, 2, ..., N$. Intuitively, if there is a temporal dependency $A \rightarrow_{[t_1,t_2]} B$ in S, there must be a lot of A's that are followed by some B with a time lag in $[t_1, t_2]$. Let $n_{[t_1,t_2]}$ denote the observed number of A's in this situation. For instance, in Figure 1, every A is followed by a B with a time lag of 5 or 6 minutes, so $n_{[5,6]} = 4$. Only the second A is followed by a B with a time lag of 0 or 1 minute, so $n_{[0,1]} = 1$. Let $r = [t_1, t_2]$ be a lag interval. One question is that, what is the minimum required n_r that we can utilize to identify the dependency of A and B with r. In this example, the minimum required n_r cannot be greater than 4 since the sequence has at most 4 A's. However, if let $r = [0, +\infty]$, we can easily have $n_r = 4$. [20] proposes a chi-square test approach to determine the minimum required n_r, where the chi-square statistic measures the degree of the independence by comparing the observed n_r with the expected n_r under the independent assumption. The null distribution of the statistic is approximated by the chi-squared distribution with 1 degree of freedom. Let χ^2_r denote the chi-square statistic for n_r. A high χ^2_r indicates the observed n_r in the given sequence cannot be explained by randomness. The chi-square statistic is defined as follows:

$$\chi^2_r = \frac{(n_r - n_A P_r)^2}{n_A P_r (1 - P_r)}, \tag{1}$$

where n_A is the number of A's in the data sequence, P_r is the probability of a B appearing in r from a random sequence. Hence, $n_A P_r$ is the expected number of A's that are followed by some B with a time lag in r. $n_A P_r(1-P_r)$ is the standard deviation. Note that the random sequence should have the same sampling rate for B as the given sequence S. The randomness is only for the positions of B items. It is known that a random sequence usually follows the Poisson process, which assumes the probability of an item appearing in an

Table 1: Relation with Other Temporal Patterns

Temporal Pattern	An Example	Equivalent Temporal Dependency with Lag Interval
Mutually dependent pattern [19]	$\{A, B\}$	$A \to_{[0,\delta]} B$, $B \to_{[0,\delta]} A$
Partially periodic pattern [20]	A with periodic p and a given time tolerance δ	$A \to_{[p-\delta,p+\delta]} A$
Frequent episode pattern [21]	$A \to B \to C$ with a given time window p	$A \to_{[0,p]} B$, $B \to_{[0,p]} C$
Loose temporal pattern [17]	B follows by A before time t	$A \to_{[0,t]} B$
Stringent temporal pattern [17]	B follows by A about time t with a given time tolerance δ	$A \to_{[t-\delta,t+\delta]} B$

interval is proportional to the length of the interval [27]. Therefore,

$$P_r = |r| \cdot \frac{n_B}{T}, \tag{2}$$

where $|r|$ is the length of r, $|r| = t_2 - t_1 + w_B$, w_B is the minimum time lag of two adjacent B's, $w_B > 0$, and n_B is the number of B's in S. For lag interval r, the absolute length is $t_2 - t_1$. w_B is added to $|r|$ because without w_B when $t_1 = t_2$, $|r| = 0$, P_r is always 0 no matter how large the n_B is. As a result, χ_r^2 would be overestimated. In reality, the time stamps of items are discrete samples and w_B is the observed sampling period for B items. Hence, the probability of a B appearing in $t_2 - t_1$ time units is equal to the probability of a B appearing in $t_2 - t_1 + w_B$ time units.

The value of χ_r^2 is defined in terms of a confidence level. For example, 95% confidence level corresponds to $\chi_r^2 = 3.84$. Based on Eq.(1), the observed n_r should be greater than $\sqrt{3.84 n_A P_r (1 - P_r)} + n_A P_r$. Note that we only care positive dependencies, so

$$n_r - n_A P_r > 0. \tag{3}$$

To ensure a discovered temporal dependency fits the entire data sequence, *support* [2] [28] [20] is used in our work. For $A \to_r B$, the support $supp_A(r)$ (or $supp_B(r)$) is the number of A's (or B's) that satisfy $A \to_r B$ divided by the total number of items N. *minsup* is the minimum threshold for both $supp_A(r)$ and $supp_B(r)$ specified by the user [28] [20]. Based on the two minimum thresholds χ_c^2 and *minsup*, Definition 1 defines the qualified lag interval that we try to find.

DEFINITION 1. *Given an item sequence S with two item types A and B, a lag interval $r = [t_1, t_2]$ is qualified if and only if $\chi_r^2 > \chi_c^2$, $supp_A(r) > minsup$ and $supp_B(r) > minsup$, where χ_c^2 and minsup are two minimum thresholds specified by the user.*

4. LAG INTERVAL DISCOVERY

In this section, we first develop a straightforward algorithm for finding all qualified lag intervals, a *brute-force* algorithm. Then, *STScan* and *STScan** algorithms are proposed which are much more efficient. We also present a lower bound of the time complexity for finding qualified lag intervals. Finally, we discuss how to incorporate the domain knowledge to speed up the algorithms.

4.1 Brute-Force Algorithm

To find all qualified lag intervals, a straightforward algorithm is to enumerate all possible lag intervals, compute their χ_r^2 and supports, and then check whether they are qualified or not. This algorithm is called *brute-force*. Clearly, its time cost is very large. Let n be the number of distinct time stamps of S, $r = [t_1, t_2]$. The numbers of possible t_1 and t_2 are $O(n^2)$, and then the number of possible r is $O(n^4)$. For each lag interval, there is at least $O(n)$ cost to scan the entire sequence S to compute the χ_r^2 and the supports. Therefore, the overall time cost of the *brute-force* algorithm is $O(n^5)$, which is not affordable for large data sequences.

4.2 STScan Algorithm

To avoid re-scanning the data sequence, we develop a sorted table based algorithm. A sorted table is a sorted linked list with a collection of sorted integer arrays. Each entry of the linked list is attached to two sorted integer arrays. Figure 2 shows an example of the sorted array. In our algo-

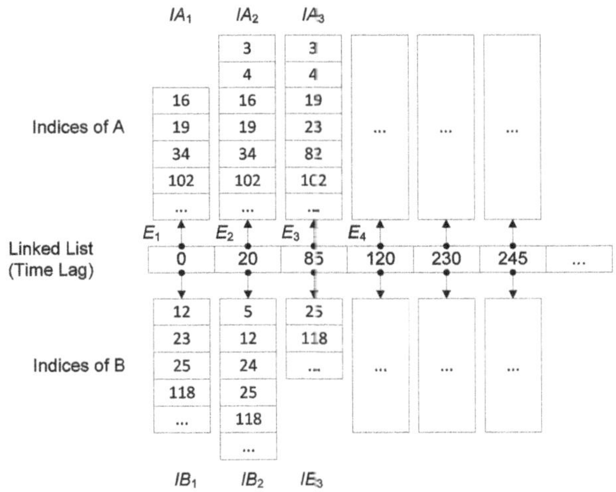

Figure 2: Sorted Table

rithm, we store every time lag $t(x_j) - t(x_i)$ into each entry of linked list, where $x_i = A$, $x_j = B$, i, j are integers from 1 to N. Two arrays attached to the entry $t(x_j) - t(x_i)$ are the collections of i and j. In other words, the two arrays are the indices of A's and B's. Let E_i denote the i-th entry of the linked list and $v(E_i)$ denote the time lag stored at E_i. IA_i and IB_i denote the indices of A's and B's that are attached to E_i. For example in Figure 2, $x_3 = A$, $x_5 = B$, $t(x_5) - t(x_3) = 20$. Since $v(E_2) = 20$, IA_2 contains 3 and IB_2 contains 5. Any feasible lag interval can be represented as a subsegment of the linked list. For example in Figure 2, $E_2E_3E_4$ represents the lag interval $[20, 120]$.

To create the sorted table for a sequence S, each time lag between an A and a B is first inserted into a red-black tree. The key of the red-black tree node is the time lag, the value is the pair of indices of A and B. Once the tree is built, we traverse the tree in ascending order to create the linked list of the sorted table. In the sequence S, the number A and B are both $O(N)$, so the number of $t(x_j)-t(x_i)$ is $O(N^2)$. The time cost of creating the red-black tree is $O(N^2 \log N^2) = O(N^2 \log N)$. Traversing the tree costs $O(N^2)$. Hence, the overall time cost of creating a sorted table is $O(N^2 \log N)$, which is the known lower bound of sorting $X+Y$ where X and Y are two variables [10]. The linked list has $O(N^2)$ entries, and each attached integer array has $O(N)$ elements, so it seems that the space cost of a sorted table is $O(N^2 \cdot N) = O(N^3)$. However, Lemma 1 shows that the actual space cost of a sorted table is $O(N^2)$, which is same as the red-black tree.

E A 1. *Given an item sequence S having N items, the space cost of its sorted table is $O(N^2)$.*

PROOF Since the numbers of A's and B's are both $O(N)$, the number of pairs (x_i, x_j) is $O(N^2)$, where $x_i = A$, $x_j = B$, $x_i, x_j \in S$. Every pair associated with three entries in the sorted table: the time stamp distance, the index of an A and the index of a B. Therefore, each pair (x_i, x_j) introduces 3 space cost. The total space cost of the sorted table is $O(3N^2) = O(N^2)$. □

Once the sorted table is created, finding all qualified lag intervals is scanning the subsegments of the linked list. However, the number of entries in the linked list is $O(N^2)$, so there are $O(N^4)$ distinct subsegments. Scanning all subsegments is still time-consuming. Fortunately, based on the minimum thresholds on the chi-square statistic and the support, the length of a qualified lag interval cannot be large.

E A 2. *Given two minimum thresholds χ^2_c and minsup, the length of any qualified lag interval is less than $\frac{T}{N} \cdot \frac{1}{minsup}$.*

PROOF Let r be a qualified lag interval. Based Eq.(1) and Inequality.(3), χ^2_r increases along with n_r. Since $n_r \leq n_A$,

$$\frac{(n_A - n_A P_r)^2}{n_A P_r (1-P_r)} \geq \chi^2_r > \chi^2_c \implies P_r < \frac{n_A}{\chi^2_c + n_A}.$$

By substituting Eq. 2 to the previous inequality,

$$|r| < \frac{n_A}{\chi^2_c + n_A} \cdot \frac{T}{n_B}.$$

Since $n_B > N \cdot minsup$, $\chi^2_c > 0$, we have

$$|r| < \frac{T}{N} \cdot \frac{1}{minsup} = |r|_{max}.$$

□

$\frac{T}{N}$ is exactly the average period of items, which is determined by the sampling rate of this sequence. For example, in system event sequences, the monitoring system checks the system status for every 30 seconds and records system events into the sequence. The average period of items is 30 seconds. Therefore, we consider $\frac{T}{N}$ as a constant. $minsup$ is also a constant, so $|r|_{max}$ is a constant.

Algorithm *STScan* states the pseudocode for finding all qualified lag intervals. $len(ST)$ denotes the number of entries of the linked list in sorted table ST. This algorithm sequentially scans all subsegments starting with E_1, E_2, ..., $E_{len(ST)}$. Based on Lemma 2, it only scans the subsegment with $|r| < |r|_{max}$. To calculate the χ^2_r and the supports, for each subsegment, it cumulatively stores the aggregate indices of A's and B's and the corresponding lag interval r. For each subsegment, $n_r = |IA_r|$, $supp_A(r) = |IA_r|/N$, $supp_B(r) = |IB_r|/N$.

Algorithm 1 *STScan* $(S, A, B, ST, \chi^2_c, minsup)$

Input: S : input sequence; A, B: two item types; ST : sorted table; χ^2_c: minimum chi-square statistic threshold; *minsup*: minimum support.
Output: a set of qualified lag intervals;

$R \leftarrow \emptyset$
Scan S to find w_B
for $i = 1$ to $len(ST)$ **do**
  $IA_r \leftarrow \emptyset$, $IB_r \leftarrow \emptyset$
  $t_1 \leftarrow v(E_i)$
  $j \leftarrow 0$
  while $i + j \leq len(ST)$ **do**
    $t_2 \leftarrow v(E_{i+j})$
    $r \leftarrow [t_1, t_2]$
    $|r| \leftarrow t_2 - t_1 + w_B$
    if $|r| \geq |r|_{max}$ **then**
      break
    end if
    $IA_r \leftarrow IA_r \cup IA_{i+j}$
    $IB_r \leftarrow IB_r \cup IB_{i+j}$
    $j \leftarrow j + 1$
    if $|IA_r|/N \leq minsup$ **or** $|IB_r|/N \leq minsup$ **then**
      continue
    end if
    Calculate χ^2_r from $|IA_r|$ and $|r|$
    if $\chi^2_r > \chi^2_c$ **then**
      $R \leftarrow R \cup r$
    end if
  end while
end for
return R

E A 3. *The time cost of* STScan *is $O(N^2)$, where N is the number of items in the data sequence.*

PROOF For each entry E_{i+j} in the linked list, the time cost of merging IA_{i+j} and IB_{i+j} to IA_r and IB_r is $|IA_{i+j}| + |IB_{i+j}|$ by using a hash table. Let l_i be the largest length of the scanned subsegments starting at E_i. Let l_{max} be the maximum l_i, $i = 1, ..., len(ST)$. The total time cost is:

$$\begin{aligned} T(N) &= \sum_{i=1}^{len(ST)} \sum_{j=0}^{l_i - 1} (|IA_{i+j}| + |IB_{i+j}|) \\ &\leq \sum_{i=1}^{len(ST)} \sum_{j=0}^{l_{max}-1} (|IA_{i+j}| + |IB_{i+j}|) \\ &\leq l_{max} \cdot \sum_{i=1}^{len(ST)} (|IA_i| + |IB_i|) \end{aligned}$$

$\sum_{i=1}^{len(ST)}(|IA_i| + |IB_i|)$ is exactly the total number of integers in all integer arrays. Based on Lemma 1, $\sum_{i=1}^{len(ST)}(|IA_i| + |IB_i|) = O(N^2)$. Then $T(N) = O(l_{max} \cdot N^2)$. Let $E_k ... E_{k+l}$ be the subsegment for a qualified lag interval, $v(E_{k+i}) \geq 0$, $i = 0, ..., l$. The length of this lag interval is $|r| = v(E_{k+l_{max}}) - v(E_k) < |r|_{max}$, then $l_{max} < |r|_{max}$ and l_{max} is not depending on N. Assume Δ_E is the average $v(E_{k+1}) - v(E_k)$, $k = 1, ..., len(ST) - 1$, we obtain a tighter bound of l_{max}, i.e., $l_{max} \leq |r|_{max}/\Delta_E \leq \frac{T}{N \cdot \Delta_E} \cdot \frac{1}{minsup}$. Therefore, the overall time cost is $T(N) = O(N^2)$. □

4.3 STScan* Algorithm

To reduce the space cost of *STScan* algorithm, we develop an improved algorithm *STScan** which utilizes the increment sorted table and sequence compression.

4.3.1 Incremental Sorted Table

Lemma 1 shows the space cost of a complete sorted table is $O(N^2)$. Algorithm *STScan* sequentially scans the subsegments starting from E_1 to $E_{len(ST)}$, so it does not need to access every entry at every time. Based on this observation, we develop an incremental sorted table based algorithm with an $O(N)$ space cost. This algorithm incrementally creates the entries of the sorted table along with the subsegment scanning process.

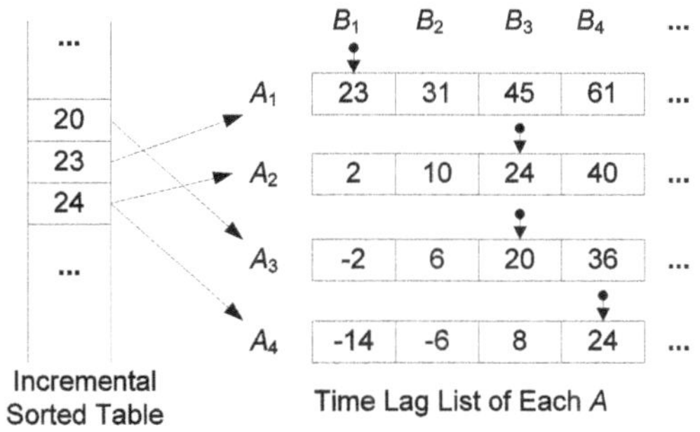

Figure 3: Incremental Sorted Table

The linked list of a sorted table can be created by merging all time lag lists of A's (Figure 3), where A_i and B_j denote the i-th A and the j-th B, $i, j = 1, 2, ...$ The j-th entry in the list of A_i stores $t(B_j)-t(A_i)$. The time lag lists of all A's are not necessary to be created in the memory because we only need to know $t(B_j)$ and $t(A_j)$. This can be done just with an indices arrays of all A's and all B's respectively. By using N-way merging algorithm, each entry of the linked list would be created sequentially. The indices of A's and B's attached to each entry are also recorded during the merging process. Base on Lemma 2, the length of a qualified lag interval is at most $|r|_{max}$, therefore, we only keep track of the recent l_{max} entries. The space cost for storing l_{max} entries is at most $O(l_{max} \cdot N) = O(N)$. A heap used by the merging process costs $O(N)$ space. Then, the overall space cost of the incremental sorted table is $O(N)$. The time cost of merging $O(N)$ lists with total $O(N^2)$ elements is still $O(N^2 \log N)$.

4.3.2 Sequence Compression

In many real-world applications, some items may share the same time stamp since they are sampled within the same sampling cycle. To save the time cost, we compress the original S to another compact sequence S'. At each time stamp t in S, if there are k items of type I, we create a triple (I, t, k) into S', where k is the cardinality of this triple. To handle S', the only needed change of our algorithm is that the $|IA_r|$ and $|IB_r|$ become the total cardinalities of triples in IA_r and IB_r respectively. Clearly, S' is more compact than S. S' has $O(n)$ triples, where n is the number of distinct time stamps of S, $n \leq N$. Creating S' costs an $O(N)$ time complexity. By using S', the time cost of *STScan** becomes $O(N + n^2 \log n)$ and the space cost of the incremental sorted table becomes $O(n)$.

4.4 Time Complexity Lower Bound

For analyzing large sequences, an $O(n)$ or $O(n \log n)$ algorithm is needed. However, we find that the time complexity of any algorithm for our problem is at least $O(n^2)$ (Lemma 4). The proof is to reduce the 3SUM$'$ problem to our problem, and the 3SUM$'$ has no $o(n^2)$ solution [6]. To answer whether $O(n^2)$ is the tightest lower bound or not, a further study is needed.

LEMMA 4. *Finding a qualified lag interval cannot be solved in $o(n^2)$ in the worst case, where n is the number of distinct time stamps of the given sequence.*

PROOF Assume that an algorithm **P** can find a qualified lag interval in $o(n^2)$ in any case, we can construct an algorithm to solve the 3SUM$'$ problem in $o(n^2)$ as follows. Given three sets of integers X, Y, and Z such that $|X| + |Y| + |Z| = n$, we construct a compressed sequence S' of items which only has two item types A and B as follows:

1. For each x_i in X, create an A at time stamp x_i.
2. For each y_i in Y, create a B at time stamp y_i.
3. For each z_i in Z, create $n+1$ A's at time stamp $\beta(i+1)+z_i$ and $n+1$ B's at time stamp $\beta(i+1)$, where β is the diameter of set $X \cup Y$, which is the largest integer minus the smallest integer in $X \cup Y$.

Only the lag intervals created from z_i have $n_r \geq n+1$. If there are three integers $y_j \in Y$, $x_k \in X$, $z_i \in Z$ such that $y_j - x_k = z_i$, the lag interval of z_i must have $n_r \geq n+2$. Then, we substitute $n_r = n+2$ into Eq. 1 to find the appropriate threshold χ^2_c, and call algorithm **P** to find all z_i that have $n_r \geq n+2$. By filtering out the situations of $y_j - y_k = z_i$ and $x_j - x_k = z_i$, we can obtain the desired three integers such that $y_j - x_k = z_i$ if they exist. S' has at most $2n$ distinct time stamps. The time cost of creating S' is $O(2n) = O(n)$. **P** is an $o(n^2)$ algorithm. Filtering the result of **P** is $O(n)$ since $|Z| \leq n$. Therefore, the overall solution for the 3SUM$'$ problem is $O(n) + o(n^2) + O(n) = o(n^2)$. However, it is believed that the 3SUM$'$ problem has no $o(n^2)$ solution [6]. Therefore, the algorithm **P** does not exist. □

4.5 Finding Lag Interval with Constraints

As discussed in Section 2, most existing temporal patterns can be described as temporal dependencies with some constraints on the lag interval. In many real-world applications, the users have the domain knowledge or other requirements for desired lag intervals, which are helpful to speed up the algorithm. For example, in system management, the temporal dependencies of certain events can be used to identify false alarms [31]. However, SLA(Service Level Agreement) requires that any real system alarms must be acknowledged within K hours, and K is specified in the contract with customers. If a discovered lag interval is greater than K hours, the corresponding temporal dependency is trivial and can not be used for false alarm identification.

Generally, the constraints for a qualified lag interval $[t_1, t_2]$ can be expressed as a set of inequalities:

$$f_i(t_1, t_2) \leq d_i, \text{for } i = 1, ..., m,$$

where m is the number of constraints, $f_i(t_1, t_2) \leq d_i$ are constraint functions that need to be satisfied. For example, the constraint for the partially periodic pattern is $|t_1 - t_2| \leq \delta$.

The constraints for the predefined time window based temporal pattern are $t_1 = 0$, $t_2 \le p$, where p is the window length. To incorporate the constraints to our algorithm, a straightforward approach is to filter discovered qualified lag interval by the given constraints. However, this approach does not make use of the constraints to reduce the search space of the problem. On the other hand, since the constraint function $f_i(\cdot,\cdot)$ can be any complex function about t_1 and t_2, there is no generalized and optimal approach for using them. We only consider two typical cases: $|t_1 - t_2| \le \delta$ and $t_2 \le p$. The first case can be utilized in the subsegment scanning. It provides a potential tighter bound than l_{max} if $\delta < l_{max}$, but does not change the order of the overall time cost. The second case can be utilized to reduce the length of the linked list of the sorted table. When $t_2 < p$, each time lag list of A_i has at most $O(p/\Delta_E)$ entries. Then, the overall time cost can be reduced to $O(n \log n \cdot p/\Delta_E) = O(n \log n)$.

5. EVALUATION

This section presents our empirical study of discovering lag intervals on both synthetic data sets and real data sets in terms of the effectiveness and efficiency.

5.1 Experimental Platform and Algorithms

All comparative algorithms are implemented in Java 1.6 platform. Table 2 summarizes our experimental environment. At present, the most dedicated algorithm for finding

Table 2: Experimental Machine

OS	CPU	bits	Memory	JVM Heap Size
Linux 2.6.18	Intel Xeon(R) @ 2.5GHz, 8 core	64	16G	12G

lag intervals is the inter-arrival clustering method [17] [20], denoted by *inter-arrival*. For $A \to B$, an inter-arrival is the time lag of an A to its first following B. A dense cluster created from all inter-arrivals indicates its time lag frequently appears in the sequence. Thus, a qualified lag interval is probably around this time lag. This algorithm is very efficient and only has a linear time cost, however, it does not consider the interleaved dependencies. We also implement the four algorithms, *brute-force*, *brute-force**, *STScan* and *STScan**, to compare with in this experiment. *brute-force** is the improved version of *brute-force* which utilizes the pruning strategy about $|r|_{max}$ mentioned in Lemma 2.

For each test, we enumerate all pairwise temporal dependencies for discovering qualified lag intervals.

5.2 Synthetic Data

The synthetic data consists of 7 data sequences. Each sequence is first generated from a random item sequence with 8 item types, denoted by I_1,...,I_8. The average sample period of items is 100. Three predefined temporal dependencies are randomly embedded into each random sequence and shown in Table 3. For each temporal dependency $I_i \to_{[t_1,t_2]} I_j$, we

Table 3: Embedded Temporal Dependencies

Embedded Temporal Dependencies	Support
$I_1 \to_{[400,500]} I_2$	0.1
$I_2 \to_{[1000,1100]} I_3$	0.12
$I_4 \to_{[5500,5800]} I_5$	0.15

first randomly choose an item x_i and an integer $t \in [t_1, t_2]$, and then let $x_i = I_i$ and the item at $t(x_i) + t$ be I_j. We repeat this process until $\chi^2_{[t_1,t_2]}$ and the support are greater than the specified thresholds. Note that the time lags in these lag intervals are larger than the average sample period of items, so all three temporal dependencies are very likely to be interleaved dependencies.

5.2.1 *Effectiveness*

The effectiveness of the algorithm result is validated by comparing the discovered results with the embedded lag intervals and measured by the recall [29]. We do not care the precision because every algorithm can achieve the 100% precision if this algorithm is correct. We let $\chi^2_c = 10.83$ which represents a 99.9% confidence level, $minsup = 0.1$. There is no surprise that all the algorithms proposed in this paper, *brute-force*, *brute-force**, *STScan* and *STScan**, find all the embedded lag intervals since they scan the entire space of the lag interval. Thus, the recalls of these methods are 1.0. The parameter δ of *inter-arrival* is varied from 1 to 2000. However, *inter-arrival* does not find any qualified lag interval in the synthetic data and its recall is 0. The reason is that, the qualified lag intervals are [400,500], [1000,1100] and [5500,5800], but most inter-arrivals in the sequence are close to the average sample period 100. Thus, *inter-arrival* can only probe the lag intervals around 100.

5.2.2 *Efficiency*

The empirical efficiency is evaluated by the CPU running time (Figure 4). *inter-arrival* is a linear algorithm, so it runs much faster than other algorithms. The running time of the *brute-force* algorithm increases extremely fast so that it can only handle very tiny data sets. By adding the pruning strategy about $|r|_{max}$ to *brute-force*, the *brute-force** algorithm runs a little bit faster than the *brute-force* algorithm, but it still can only handle small data sets. *STScan** compresses the sequence before the lag interval discovering, therefore, *STScan** is a little bit more efficient than *STScan*.

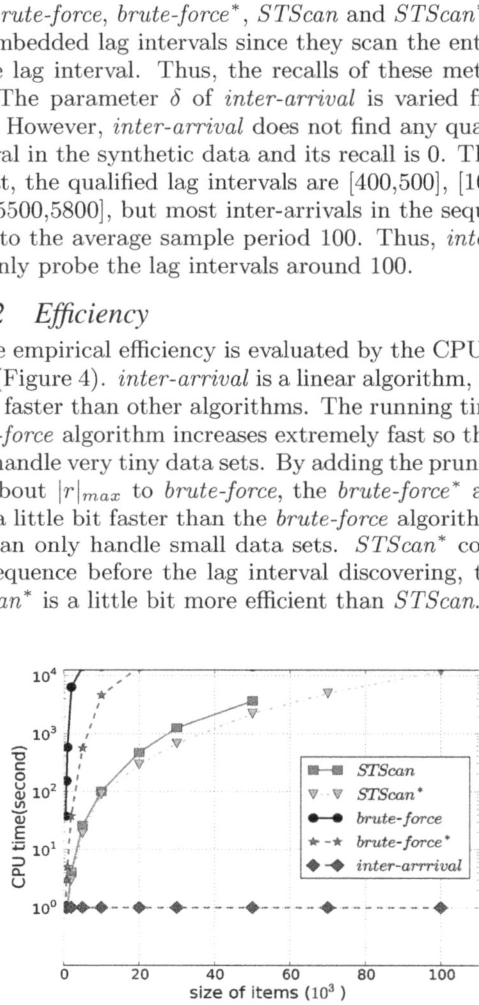

Figure 4: Runtime on Synthetic Data

STScan has not finish the tests for larger data sets because it runs out of memory. Table 5 lists the approximate peak numbers of allocated objects in Java heap memory (not including the data sequence). It confirms Lemma 1 that the sorted table takes an $O(N^2)$ space cost. It also shows that, the space costs of *STScan**, *brute-force* and *brute-force** are all $O(N)$ as mentioned in Section 4. Assuming each Java object only occupies an integer(8 bytes), *STScan* would cost

Table 4: Discovered Temporal Dependencies with Lag Intervals

Data set	Dependency	χ_r^2	*support*
Account1	$MSG\_Plat\_APP \rightarrow_{[3600,3600]} MSG\_Plat\_APP$	> 1000.0	0.07
	$Linux\_Process \rightarrow_{[0,96]} Process$	134.56	0.05
	$SMP\_CPU \rightarrow_{[0,27]} Linux\_Process$	978.87	0.06
	$AS\_MSG \rightarrow_{[102,102]} AS\_MSG$	> 1000.0	0.08
Account2	$TEC\_Error \rightarrow_{[0,1]} Ticket\_Retry$	> 1000.0	0.12
	$Ticket\_Retry \rightarrow_{[0,1]} TEC\_Error$	> 1000.0	0.12
	$AIX\_HW\_ERROR \rightarrow_{[25,25]} AIX\_HW\_ERROR$	282.53	0.15
	$AIX\_HW\_ERROR \rightarrow_{[8,9]} AIX\_HW\_ERROR$	144.62	0.24

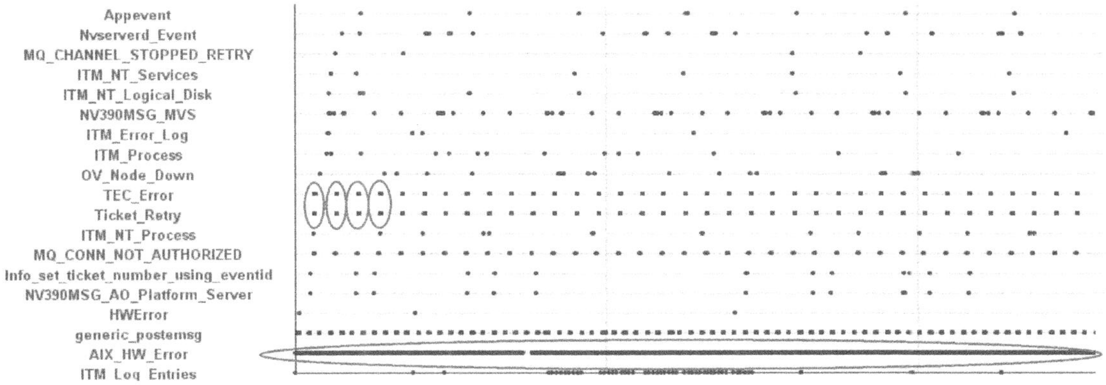

Figure 5: Plotting for Account2 Data

Table 5: Space Cost on Synthetic Data

Data size / Algorithm	10^3	10×10^3	50×10^3	100×10^3
STScan	3×10^4	3×10^6	8×10^7	OutOfMemory
*STScan**	10^3	10^4	5×10^4	10^5
brute-force	9×10^2	10^4	5×10^4	9×10^4
*brute-force**	9×10^2	10^4	5×10^4	9×10^4
inter-arrival	$< 10^2$	$< 10^2$	$< 10^2$	$< 10^2$

over 10G bytes memory for 50×10^3 items. Hence, it runs out of memory when the data size becomes larger. However, by using the incremental sorted table, for the same data set, *STScan** only costs 10M memory. *inter-arrival* only stores the clusters of all inter-arrivals, so its space cost is small.

5.3 Real Data

Table 6: Real System Events

Data set	Time Frame	#Events	#Event Types
Account1	54 days	1,124,834	95
Account2	32 days	2,076,408	104

Two real data sets are collected from IT outsourcing centers by IBM Tivoli monitoring system [1] [30], denoted as Account1 and Account2. Each data set is a collection of system events from hundreds of application servers and data server. These system events are mostly system alerts triggered by some monitoring situations (e.g. the CPU utilization is above a threshold). Table 6 shows the time frames and the sizes of the two real data sets. To discover the temporal dependencies with qualified lag intervals, we let $\chi_c^2 = 6.64$ which corresponds to the confidence level 99%, and $minsup = 0.05$. A constraint that $t_2 \leq$ `1hour` is applied to this testing from the domain experts. δ of *inter-arrival* is varied from 1 to 2000.

Figures 6 and 7 show the running times of all algorithms on the two real data sets. As for *STScan* and *STScan**, the running times grow slower than in Figure 4 because the constraint $t_2 \leq$ `1hour` reduces their time complexities. Table 7 lists the peak numbers of allocated memory objects in JVM on Account2 data. The results on Account1 data is similar to this table.

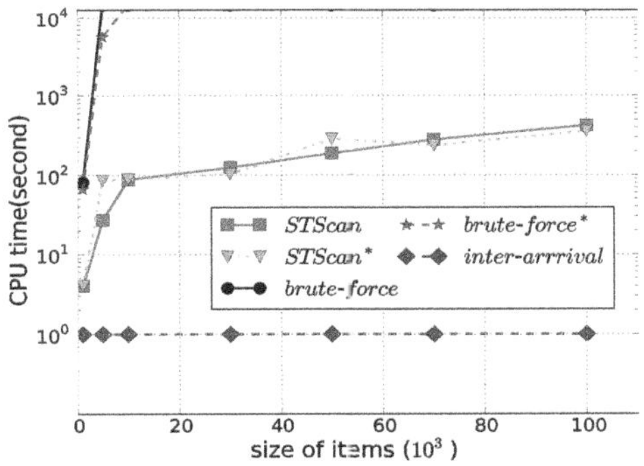

Figure 6: Running Time on Account1 Data

Table 7: Space Cost on Account2 Data

Data size / Algorithm	10^3	10×10^3	50×10^3	100×10^3
STScan	4×10^4	3×10^6	1×10^7	3×10^7
*STScan**	10^3	6×10^3	5×10^4	10^5
brute-force	9×10^2	3×10^3	3×10^3	3×10^3
*brute-force**	9×10^2	3×10^3	3×10^3	3×10^3
inter-arrival	$< 10^2$	$< 10^2$	$< 10^2$	$< 10^2$

Table 4 lists several discovered temporal dependencies with qualified lag intervals. *inter-arrival* only finds the first two temporal dependencies on Account2 data. The reason is

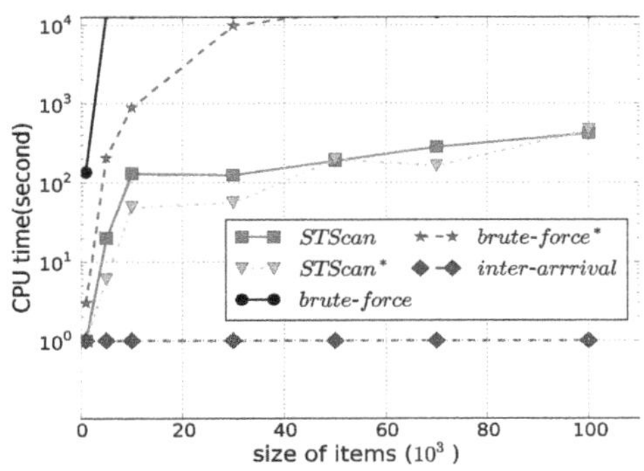

Figure 7: Running Time on Account2 Data

that, only the two temporal dependencies have very small lag intervals which are just the inter-arrivals of the events. However, the lag intervals for other temporal dependencies are larger than most inter-arrivals, so *inter-arrival* fails.

In Table 4, the first discovered temporal dependency for Account1 shows that MSG_Plat_APP is a periodic pattern with a period of 1 hour. This pattern indicates this event MSG_Plat_APP is a heartbeat signal from an application. The second and third discovered temporal dependencies can be viewed as a case study for event correlation [12]. Since most servers are Linux servers, so the alerts from processes must be also from Linux processes. Therefore, for Account1, process events and Linux process events can be automatically correlated. High CPU utilization alerts (*SMP_CPU*) can only be triggered by abnormal processes, so SMP_CPU events can also be correlated with *Linux_Process* events. In Account2, the first two temporal dependencies compose a mutual dependency pattern between *TEC_Error* and *Ticket_Retry*. It can be explained by a programming logic in IBM Tivoli monitoring system. When the monitoring system fails to generate the incident ticket to the ticketing system, it will report a *TEC* error and retry the ticket generation. Therefore, *TEC_Error* and *Ticket_Retry* events are often raised together. The third and fourth discovered temporal dependencies for Account2 are related to a hardware error of an AIX server but with different lag intervals. This is caused by a polling monitoring situation. When an AIX server is down, the monitoring system continuously receive *AIX_HW_Error* events when polling that AIX server. Thus, this *AIX_HW_Error* event exhibits a periodic pattern. To validate the discovered results, we plot the temporal events into a graphical chart. Figure 5 is a screen shot of the plotting for Account2 data. The x-axis is the time stamp, the y-axis is the event type. As shown by this figure, *TEC_Error* and *Ticket_Retry* exhibit a mutually dependency since they are always generated at the almost same time. *AIX_HW_Error* is a polling event.

5.3.1 Parameter Sensitivity

To test the sensitivity of parameters, we vary χ_c^2 and *minsup* and test the numbers of discovered temporal dependencies (Figures 8 and Figure 9) and the running time (Figure 10 and Figure 11). When varying χ_c^2, $minsup = 0.05$; When varying *minsup*, $\chi_c^2 = 6.64$ (with 99% confidence level). χ_c^2 is not sensitive to the algorithm result because the associated confidence level is only from 95% to 99.99% although χ_c^2 is varied from 3.84 to 100. By varying *minsup*, the number of discovered temporal dependencies exponentially decreases as shown in Figure 9. As mentioned in [20], the effective choice of *minsup* is 0.001 to 0.1.

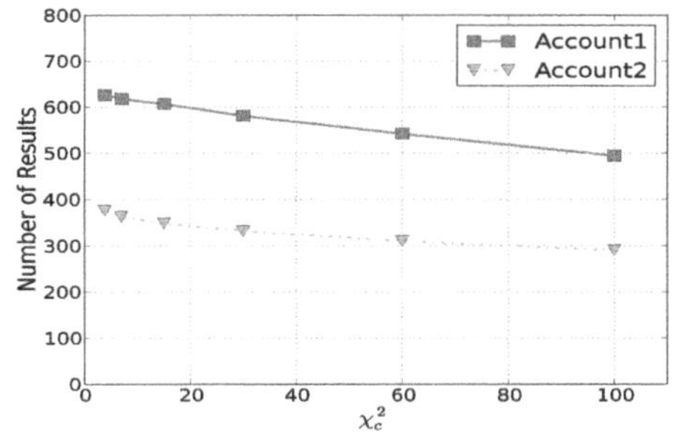

Figure 8: Num. of Results by Varying χ_c^2

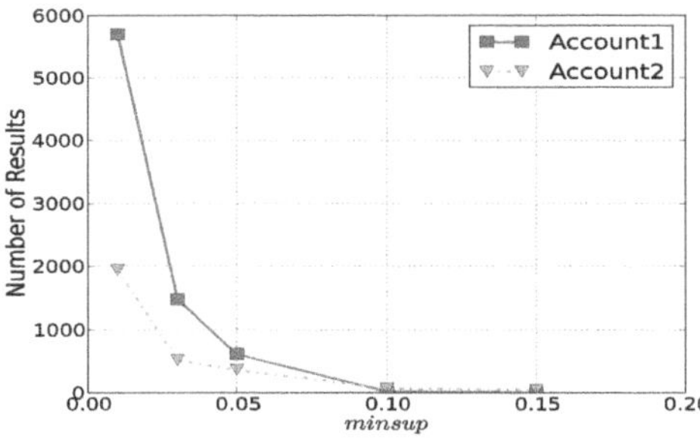

Figure 9: Num. of Results by Varying *minsup*

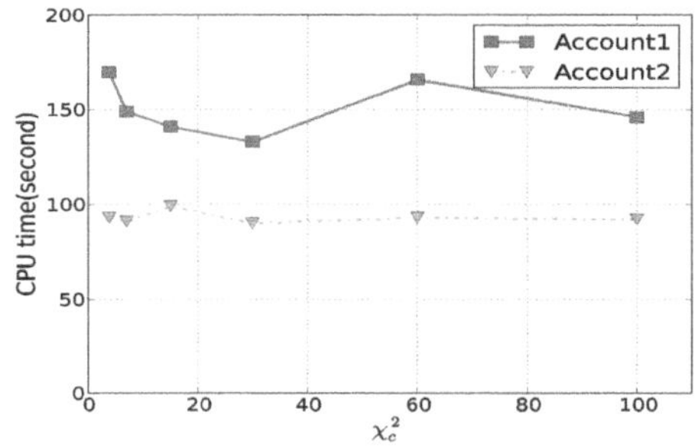

Figure 10: Running time by Varying χ_c^2

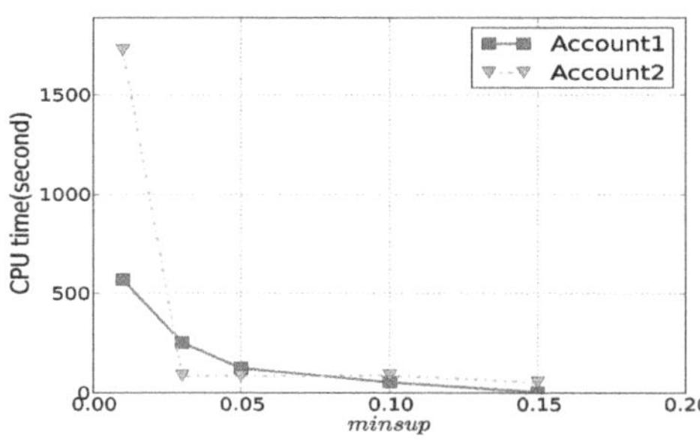

Figure 11: Running time by Varying *minsup*

6. CONCLUSION AND FUTURE WORK

In this paper, we study the problem of finding appropriate

lag intervals for temporal dependencies over item sequences. We investigate the relationship between the temporal dependency with other existing temporal patterns. Two algorithms *STScan* and *STScan** are proposed to efficiently discover the appropriate lag intervals. Extensive empirical evaluation on both synthetic and real data sets demonstrates the efficiency and effectiveness of our proposed algorithm in finding the temporal dependencies with lag intervals in sequential data. As for the future work, we will continue to investigate more efficient algorithms that can handle large data sequences. We hope to find an $O(n^2)$ time complexity algorithm with a linear or constant space cost.

Acknowledgement

The work is supported in part by NSF grants IIS-0546280 and HRD-0833093.

7. REFERENCES

[1] IBM Tivoli Monitoring. `http://www-01.ibm.com/software/tivoli/products/monitor/`.

[2] R. Agrawal and R. Srikant. Fast algorithms for mining association rules in large databases. In *Proccedings of VLDB*, pages 487–499, 1994.

[3] J. Ayres, J. Flannick, J. Gehrke, and T. Yiu. Sequential pattern mining using a bitmap representation. In *Proceedings of KDD*, pages 429–435, 2002.

[4] K. Bouandas and A. Osmani. Mining association rules in temporal sequences. In *Proceedings of CIDM*, pages 610–615, 2007.

[5] A. Dhurandhar. Learning maximum lag for grouped graphical granger models. In *ICDM Workshops*, pages 217–224, 2010.

[6] A. Gajentaan and M. H. Overmars. On a class of $O(n^2)$ problems in computational geometry. *Computational Geometry*, 5:165–185, 1995.

[7] L. Golab, H. J. Karloff, F. Korn, A. Saha, and D. Srivastava. Sequential dependencies. *PVLDB*, 2(1):574–585, 2009.

[8] R. Gwadera, M. J. Atallah, and W. Szpankowski. Reliable detection of episodes in event sequences. In *Proccedings of ICDM*, pages 67–74, 2003.

[9] J. Han, J. Pei, B. Mortazavi-Asl, Q. Chen, U. Dayal, and M. Hsu. Freespan: frequent pattern-projected sequential pattern mining. In *Proccedings of KDD*, pages 355–359, 2000.

[10] A. Hernandez-Barrera. Finding an $o(n^2 \log n)$ algorithm is sometimes hard. In *Proceedings of the 8th Canadian Conference on Computational Geometry*, pages 289–294, August 1996.

[11] E. J. Keogh, S. Lonardi, and B. Y. chi Chiu. Finding surprising patterns in a time series database in linear time and space. In *Proccedings of KDD*, pages 550–556, 2002.

[12] S. Kliger, S. Yemini, Y. Yemini, D. Ohsie, and S. J. Stolfo. A coding approach to event correlation. In *Integrated Network Management*, pages 266–277, 1995.

[13] S. Laxman and P. S. SASTRY. A survey of temporal data mining. *Sadhana*, 31(2):173–198, 2006.

[14] S. Laxman, P. S. Sastry, and K. P. Unnikrishnan. Discovering frequent episodes and learning hidden markov models: A formal connection. *IEEE Trans. Knowl. Data Eng.*, 17(11):1505–1517, 2005.

[15] S. Laxman, P. S. Sastry, and K. P. Unnikrishnan. A fast algorithm for finding frequent episodes in event streams. In *Proceedings of ACM KDD*, pages 410–419, August 2007.

[16] T. Li, F. Liang, S. Ma, and W. Peng. An integrated framework on mining logs files for computing system management. In *Proceedings of ACM KDD*, pages 776–781, August 2005.

[17] T. Li and S. Ma. Mining temporal patterns without predefined time windows. In *Proceedings of ICDM*, pages 451–454, November 2004.

[18] Z. Li, B. Ding, J. Han, R. Kays, and P. Nye. Mining periodic behaviors for moving objects. In *Proccedings of KDD*, pages 1099–1108, 2010.

[19] S. Ma and J. L. Hellerstein. Mining mutually dependent patterns. In *Proceedings of ICDE*, pages 409–416, 2001.

[20] S. Ma and J. L. Hellerstein. Mining partially periodic event patterns with unknown periods. In *Proceedings of ICDE*, pages 205–214, 2001.

[21] H. Mannila, H. Toivonen, and A. I. Verkamo. Discovery of frequent episodes in event sequences. *Data Mining and Knowledge Discovery*, 1(3):259–289, 1997.

[22] N. Méger and C. Rigotti. Constraint-based mining of episode rules and optimal window sizes. In *Proccedings of PKDD*, pages 313–324, 2004.

[23] T. Mitsa. *Temporal Data Mining*. Chapman and Hall/CRC, 2010.

[24] F. Mörchen. Algorithms for time series knowledge mining. In *Proccedings of KDD*, pages 668–673, 2006.

[25] F. Mörchen and D. Fradkin. Robust mining of time intervals with semi-interval partial order patterns. In *Proccedings of SDM*, pages 315–326, 2010.

[26] J. Pei, J. Han, B. Mortazavi-Asl, H. Pinto, Q. Chen, U. Dayal, and M. Hsu. Prefixspan: Mining sequential patterns by prefix-projected growth. In *Proceedings of EDBT*, pages 215–224, 2001.

[27] S. M. Ross. *Stochastic Processes*. Wiley, 1995.

[28] R. Srikant and R. Agrawal. Mining sequential patterns: Generalizations and performance improvements. In *Proceedings of EDBT*, pages 3–17, 1996.

[29] P.-N. Tan, M. Steinbach, and V. Kumar. *Introduction to Data Mining*. Addison Wesley, 2005.

[30] L. Tang, T. Li, F. Pinel, L. Shwartz, and G. Grabarnik. Optimizing system monitoring configurations for non-actionable alerts. In *Proceedings of IEEE/IFIP Network Operations and Management Symposium*, 2012.

[31] W. Xu, L. Huang, A. Fox, D. A. Patterson, and M. I. Jordan. Mining console logs for large-scale system problem detection. In *SysML*, December 2008.

[32] W.-X. Zhou and D. Sornette. Non-parametric determination of real-time lag structure between two time series: The 'optimal thermal causal path' method with applications to economic data. *Journal of Macroeconomics*, 28(1):195 – 224, 2006.

Testing the Significance of Spatio-temporal Teleconnection Patterns

Jaya Kawale*, Snigdhansu Chatterjee‡, Dominick Ormsby*, Karsten Steinhaeuser*
Stefan Liess†, Vipin Kumar*

*Department of Computer Science ‡ School of Statistics † Department of Soil, Water & Climate
University of Minnesota
{kawale,ormsby,ksteinha,kumar}@cs.umn.edu chatterjee@stat.umn.edu liess@umn.edu

ABSTRACT

Dipoles represent long distance connections between the pressure anomalies of two distant regions that are negatively correlated with each other. Such dipoles have proven important for understanding and explaining the variability in climate in many regions of the world, e.g., the El Niño climate phenomenon is known to be responsible for precipitation and temperature anomalies over large parts of the world. Systematic approaches for dipole detection generate a large number of candidate dipoles, but there exists no method to evaluate the significance of the candidate teleconnections. In this paper, we present a novel method for testing the statistical significance of the class of spatio-temporal teleconnection patterns called as dipoles. One of the most important challenges in addressing significance testing in a spatio-temporal context is how to address the spatial and temporal dependencies that show up as high autocorrelation. We present a novel approach that uses the wild bootstrap to capture the spatio-temporal dependencies, in the special use case of teleconnections in climate data. Our approach to find the statistical significance takes into account the autocorrelation, the seasonality and the trend in the time series over a period of time. This framework is applicable to other problems in spatio-temporal data mining to assess the significance of the patterns.

Categories and Subject Descriptors

H.2.8 [**Databse Management**]: Database Applications—*Data mining*

Keywords

Significance testing

1. INTRODUCTION

Pressure dipoles are important long distance climate phenomena (*teleconnection*) characterized by anomalies[1] of opposite polarity appearing at two different locations at the same time. Dipoles are of great importance in understanding climate variability and are known to impact precipitation and temperature anomalies throughout the globe. Fig. 1 shows the pressure anomaly time series at Tahiti and Darwin representing one of the most well-known dipoles - the El Niño Southern Oscillation which is known to drive precipitation and temperature anomalies worldwide. The anomaly time series of the two regions are in the opposite direction representing an oscillation.

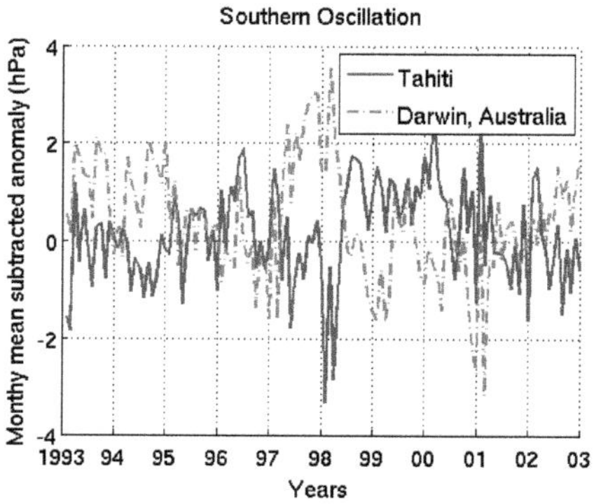

Figure 1: Pressure anomaly time series at the two ends of the Southern Oscillation.

Historically, these dipoles have been discovered by direct observation of some climate phenomenon on land and have been defined using single point locations [1]. Later on, pattern analysis techniques such as the EOF [2] have been used to identify individual dipoles over a limited region, such as Arctic Oscillation (AO). However, there are several limitations associated with EOF and other types of eigenvector analysis; namely, it only finds a few of the strongest signals and the physical interpretation of such signals can be difficult due to the orthogonality of EOFs, whereas signals in climate are not necessarily orthogonal to each other. Systematic approaches for dipole discovery have been proposed in [3, 4, 5]. Kawale et al. [3, 4] present a graph based approach to find dipoles in the climate data and are able to match the existing dipole indices used by climate scien-

[1] Anomalies are computed from raw data by subtracting the long term monthly means and are widely used in climate studies to take care of the seasonality in the data.

KDD'12, August 12–16, 2012, Beijing, China.

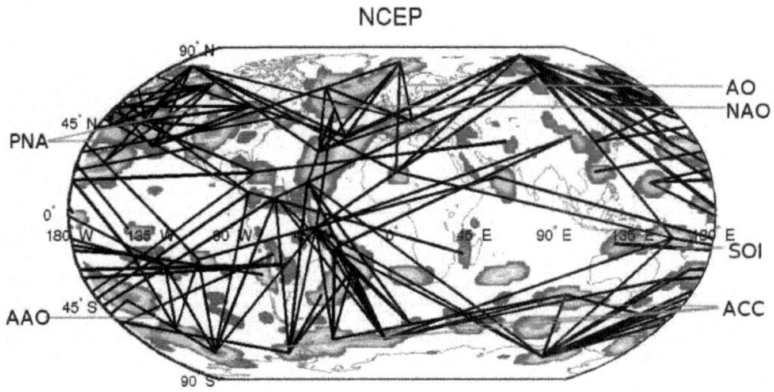

Figure 2: Dipole edges with correlation < -0.2 in the NCEP sea level pressure data taken from [3].

tists with a very high precision and are able to provide region based definitions for dipoles defined earlier using EOF analysis. An important utility of the dynamic dipoles defined using this approach is that they are able to capture the dynamics of the climate phenomenon unlike the existing approaches that are based on pre-specified regions. Hence these dynamic dipoles tend to capture greater amount of climate variability at the global level [3, 4]. Further, they have been shown to be important in understanding the structure of the various General Circulation Models (GCMs) which are used to understand global climate change [3]. It is imperative to have a significance testing to rule out spuriously connected regions, correlated by random chance. This can help in discovering a new dipole phenomenon, previously not known to climate scientists. Given the importance of the teleconnections in influencing extreme weather events like tropical cyclones, droughts, hurricanes, etc., a previously unknown connection provides a critical missing link to the climate scientists.

Systematic approaches for dipole discovery generate a large number of *candidate* dipoles, i.e. two regions that are connected by negative correlation in their anomalies, that might possibly represent a physical phenomenon. Fig. 2 shows the dipoles generated by the algorithm given in [3]. The edges represent a connection between the two opposing ends of the dipoles. The figure captures most of the dipoles known to climate scientists, however, it also shows a large number of edges that do not correspond to any known dipole phenomenon. Some of these might represent mechanisms unknown to climate scientists, but it is likely that most of them are spurious patterns. Indeed, because there are thousands of locations and hence tens of millions of possible pairs; thus the chances of finding strong negative correlations among pairs or even regions is quite high. To differentiate interesting dipoles (some of which may be unknown) from spurious ones, a method to evaluate their statistical significance is required. However, to our knowledge there are no such approaches in the literature that can incorporate all the nuances of climate dipoles.

1.1 Challenges in Significance Testing

Statistical significance testing determines whether a given result is likely to occur by random chance and thus implies whether a result is of statistical importance, and therefore would generalize to other contexts. Historically, significance testing has been widely studied in statistics and there are several classical analytical hypothesis testing methods available. Analytical methods of hypothesis testing such as the *t-test* generally involve computing a test statistic from the observed data and computing a probability value to test if the observed data was derived from a *null hypothesis*. The null hypothesis is rejected in favor of the alternate one if the probability value is below the *significance level*. However, a main drawback of these approaches is that they impose a distribution structure on the data. Technically, t-tests are valid only for i.i.d. normally distributed data and are very sensitive to outliers.

An alternate method of significance testing widely used in data mining is empirical testing using randomization to determine the null model. Randomization tests proceed by following the sequence of steps: (i) rearrange or shuffle the observed value in each sample, (ii) compute the statistics for the randomized data, (iii) repeat it k times (e.g. 1000), and (iv) compare the test statistic generated from the original data and the random distribution to rule out patterns generated by random chance. The intuition behind generating a large sample of the datasets is to create a null model from the data. If the computed test statistics differ widely from the measurements on random datasets then we can reject the null hypothesis and declare the result to be significant.

Randomization tests [6] have been successfully used in many contexts in data mining to find interesting patterns in graphs [7], association rule mining [8], motif mining [9, 10, 11], etc. In ecology, significance testing has been used to study the analysis of species nestedness patterns [12] and to study the diffusion of a spatial phenomenon [13] and spatial gradients [14]. Monte Carlo tests to test the significance of spatial patterns has been discussed in [15]. However, there are many challenges in using randomization tests for spatio-temporal patterns, some of which are listed below:

1.1.1 Data independence

One of the underlying assumptions in randomization testing is i.i.d. data. However, in the spatio-temporal context, generally there is a high spatial and temporal autocorrelation and homogeneity, thus violating the assumption of data independence.

1.1.2 Heteroscedasticity

Heteroscedasticity refers to the problem of different variances in a sub-population and the tests of randomization are sensitive to it. Heteroscedasticity exists in Earth science data in both space and time, i.e., not only the sub-population variances may be different for different locations but they can also vary over time for the same location [16].

1.1.3 Seasonality and trends

In a spatio-temporal context, there are other influencing factors like seasonality, trends, etc. which greatly impact the values in a time series. This can make the tests of randomization either too liberal or too conservative (Type I vs Type II errors). A possible strategy to get rid of trends could be to de-trend the time series. However, de-trending of non-stationary time series data itself has several issues and may result in removing certain dipoles or adding spurious ones, which might require a detailed investigation [17, 18]. Results also depend upon the nature of trends, whether unit roots are present or not, and the nature of possible co-integrating relations, see Engle and Granger [17, 18] for further details. Seasonality is generally handled in climate data by creating an anomaly time series. However, even then there is annual cycle still left in the anomaly time series of some locations on the Earth which could result in the formation of spurious dipoles [19].

1.1.4 Null model

We want the data generating process for drawing random samples to be as close as possible to the true data generating process which generated the observed values. While randomization tests are very often better than simple methods like the t-test, it is very hard to verify the assumption that (and is generally not true that) the multiple datasets created by randomization come from a null model representing the true data generating process.

1.2 Our Contribution

To the best of our knowledge, there are no existing approaches for testing the significance of spatio-temporal patterns that systematically model the spatio-temporal data and handle various aspects like auto-correlation, trends, etc. In this paper, we provide a systematic approach to test the significance of the spatio-temporal teleconnection patterns that overcomes the challenges mentioned above. Our approach uses the general framework provided by the wild bootstrap procedure [20, 21] which is traditionally applied for heteroscedastic problems to present a technique that takes into account the various aspects of climate data like auto-correlation, trends, etc. One novel aspect of our approach is that we translate the space time problem to one where the errors can be modeled as independent but heteroscedastic. We capture the spatial dependence of each region of a dipole via a unified function and capture the temporal dependencies through a first order Markovian distribution. We show the utility of our approach by using it to test the significance of dipoles generated in the NCEP sea level pressure dataset. While we mainly use our algorithm to test the significance of teleconnection patterns, our approach can be instructive to other pattern mining algorithms in the spatio-temporal context to test the significance.

2. PROPOSED APPROACH

As we saw in the previous section, a significance testing based on randomizing time series would not be appropriate for climate data. Instead, it would be more desirable to compute the significance amongst those random series that preserve the same properties as the underlying climate data time series. Our approach for randomization is inspired from the wild bootstrap procedure [20, 21]. The wild bootstrap is a technique where random weights are multiplied to the residuals from the data after fitting a statistical model, then artificial datasets are created using these randomly weighted residuals, and inference is based on repeating the statistical model fitting exercise on these artificial datasets. The wild bootstrap has been mathematically proven to be consistent, and successfully applied to a variety of problems where the data may be heteroscedastic in nature, and the parameter dimension may be large compared to the sample size.

We present a novel approach that uses the wild bootstrap and capture the spatio-temporal dependencies, in the special use case of teleconnections in climate data. First, we develop a small area or state-space type decomposition of the spatio-temporal data to extract the underlying time series that governs teleconnection patterns, against the background of local noise variations. Our approach implicitly takes into account the space dependence of the data as we require each end of the dipole (consisting of many single point locations) to share the same global component. We account for the time dependencies by incorporating an auto-regressive term assuming a first order Markovian dependency in our time series decomposition. Once we extract out the properties (or dominant signals), we test the significance by examining the residual correlation at both the ends of the dipole and thus it helps us in identifying that the negative correlation between the two regions at the two ends is indeed coming from an underlying phenomenon or is just an artifact of the dominant properties. We assign a degree of confidence to our conclusions using a test of randomization. Further details of our approach are mentioned in the following subsections:

2.1 Notation

Let A and B represent the two ends of the dipole and let n_A and n_B represent the number of points at the two ends. Let X_{it} $t = 1, \ldots, T, i = 1, \ldots, n_A$ represent the time series for T time steps at the n_A points of region A. Similarly, let Y_{it} $t = 1, \ldots, T, i = 1, \ldots, n_B$ represent the time series for T time steps at the n_B points of region B.

2.2 Step 1: Time Series Decomposition

The first step in the significance testing of dipoles is a temporal decomposition that captures the spatial as well as the temporal bindings of the two ends of the dipoles. We begin by noting two key properties of the dipole anomaly time series.

1. **Trend**: Many locations on Earth experience a general linear trend in their anomalies over time. For some locations, the trend increases and for some it decreases over time and this pattern can vary with different magnitude at different locations.

2. **Seasonality**: Typically, Earth science data has seasonality in it. Apart from the annual seasonality which is accounted for by constructing the anomaly time series, the data typically has sinusoidal patterns of various periodicities and of varying strengths across regions. If we examine the periodicities of the anomaly time series using the power spectrum, we see that quite of few of them have a period of 12 months [19].

In order to model these two key characteristics of dipole locations, we propose a temporal function $f(t)$, defined as follows:

$$f(t) = \alpha + \beta t + \gamma \sin\left(\frac{2\pi(t+\delta)}{12}\right) \quad (1)$$

The function $f(t)$ captures the trend through the βt component and the seasonality through the $\gamma \sin(\cdot)$ component. The α component ensures that the constant effect due to altitude, latitude and other unknown phenomena is also captured. $f(\cdot)$ only captures the temporal fluctuations at a given location independent of any spatial or temporal bindings.

Recall that a dipole consists of two regions, A and B, with opposite climate phenomenon. All the locations in a given region have a highly positive correlation in their anomalies and they are driven by the same underlying phenomenon. Let that underlying phenomenon for a specific end of dipole (say A) be indicated by U, where size of U is $T \times 1$. This results in the following linear heteroscedastic decomposition:

$$\forall_{i \in A} \; X_i = U + r_i \tag{2}$$

where r_i is the error term representing the local phenomenon at a location $i \in A$. Moreover, depending on how far a location i lies from the dipole center, its anomaly time series would be influenced accordingly. Let $w(i)$ indicate the weight or influence of U on X_i. The goal in this case is to reduce the residue of a given region.

$$SE_r = Tr\left[(X - U\mathbf{1})^T \; W \; (X - U\mathbf{1})\right] \tag{3}$$

where X is a $T \times N$ matrix with column i indicating anomaly time series of location $i \in A$, $\mathbf{1}$ is a matrix of size $1 \times N$ with all elements $= 1$, W is a diagonal matrix with $W_{ii} = w(i)$.

Equation 2 allows us to capture the spatial bindings of a dipole region and provides a unified anomaly time series U. It does not capture the temporal correlations of U. In order to do this, we consider the following auto-regressive formulation:

$$U_t = f(t) + \phi[U_{t-1} - f(t-1)] + \epsilon_t \tag{4}$$

Similar to equation 3, we aim to reduce the residue ϵ, such that the decomposition captures all the spatial and temporal properties of the dipole. We define the squared error of ϵ as

$$SE_\epsilon = \sum_t (V_t - \phi V_{t-1})^2 \tag{5}$$

where $V_t = U_t - f(t)$. The mathematical properties of the dipole detection algorithm is primarily governed by the bivariate time series

$$\mathbf{V}_t = \begin{pmatrix} V_{At} \\ V_{Bt} \end{pmatrix}, t = 1, 2, \dots T.$$

This is a non-stationary time series, since the innovations for this time series are given by the independent bivariate random variables

$$\epsilon_t = \begin{pmatrix} \epsilon_{At} \\ \epsilon_{Bt} \end{pmatrix} \overset{ind}{\sim} \mathcal{N}_2 \left(\begin{pmatrix} 0 \\ 0 \end{pmatrix}, \begin{pmatrix} \sigma_{At}^2 & \rho_{AB}\sigma_{At}\sigma_{Bt} \\ \rho_{AB}\sigma_{At}\sigma_{Bt} & \sigma_{Bt}^2 \end{pmatrix} \right).$$

A variation of the Kolmogorov consistency theorem is used to establish the existence of the second order stochastic process $\{\mathbf{V}_t\}$. The properties of the dipole are dictated by the innovation correlation coefficient ρ_{AB}, which takes a high negative value for true dipoles.

We model $\mathbf{V}_t = \mathbf{\Phi} \mathbf{V}_{t-1} + \epsilon_t$ where we assume $\mathbf{\Phi}$ is a diagonal matrix with diagonal entries ϕ_A and ϕ_B. The deterministic trend functions $\{f_A(\cdot)\}$ and $\{f_B(\cdot)\}$ and the local noise perturbation terms $\{r_{Ai}(\cdot), i = 1, \dots, n_A\}$ and $\{r_{Bi}(\cdot), i = 1, \dots, n_B\}$ do not contribute towards the properties of a dipole, but are important nuisance factors in studying dipoles. Needless to say, we could adopt a more complicated model for the time series properties of $\mathbf{V}_t$, the deterministic trends or the local noise, and include co-integration and other complex features. However, in the context of the present application, such additional complexity seems unnecessary.

Our aim is to reduce the squared error SE_r and SE_ϵ and we do it by minimizing them in turn. The residue term ϵ_t represents error that is independent and heteroscedastic. Thus we are able to effectively translate the space time problem into one where we are able to model the errors as independent but heteroscedastic. We use a simplistic approach to obtain an approximate solution that minimizes Equation 3 and 5. The idea is to minimize SE_r independent of U_t's auto-regressive property and obtain estimates of α, β, γ for a fixed choice of δ. After that, using U_t's auto-regressive properties estimate ϕ and compute ϵ. The attractive property of this approach is that it leads to a closed form solution for the parameters. We get,

$$\sum_t g_k(t) \cdot f(t) = \frac{\sum_{i,t} g_k(t) \cdot w(i) \cdot X_{it}}{Tr(W)}, k = 1, 2, 3 \tag{6}$$

where $g_1(t) = 1$, $g_2(t) = t$, $g_3(t) = \sin(\frac{2\pi(t+\delta)}{12})$. The three equations can be easily solved for a fixed δ using linear regression. Additionally, we get a closed form for ϕ as,

$$\phi = \frac{\sum_{t=2}^T V_t \cdot V_{t-1}}{\sum_{t=2}^T V_{t-1}^2} \tag{7}$$

In order to estimate the optimal δ, we begin with an estimate by varying it from $1, \dots, 12$ and pick the one that minimizes $E[\epsilon_t]$.

2.3 Step 2: Residual correlation

After finding the residue at each end of the dipole, our next goal is to examine the residual correlation at the two ends of the dipole to check if the regions involved form a true dipole. The residue at the two ends represents the time series signal after extracting trend and the seasonality. We compute the pairwise correlation ρ_{ij} between all the nodes in ϵ_{it} and ϵ'_{jt}. We can use the raw correlation values to test the significance of the dipoles. However, we use a more stable transformation provided by Fisher to transform the correlation into Z_{ij} as described in the following subsection.

Fisher transformation

The Fisher transformation [22] is generally used in statistics to test the hypothesis about the correlation coefficient ρ between two variables. The transformation changes the probability density function (pdf) of any waveform so that the transform output has an approximately Gaussian pdf. The transformation is defined as follows:

$$Z_{ij} = \frac{1}{2} log \frac{1 + \rho_{ij}}{1 - \rho_{ij}} \tag{8}$$

The Fisher transformation is a variance stabilizing transformation and converges to a normal distribution much faster.

2.4 Step 3: Assessing dipole statistical significance

In testing the significance of dipoles, the null hypothesis means that the dipole pattern is spurious or uninteresting. Our task is to generate the p-value to specify a confidence measure on whether the dipole is significant. Using our time series decomposition, we devise the following method of randomization inspired from the wild bootstrap algorithm [23] in which re-samples are generated by multiplying random noise to the residuals in order to preserve heteroscedasticity. The details of the steps are mentioned as follows:

1. Step 1: Compute the time series decomposition and the parameters, α, β, γ and δ. Compute the residue

ϵ_A and ϵ_B at the two ends and the Fisher transformed correlation Z_{AB}.

2. Step 2: Generate random perturbations in the residual data such that the variance of the residual data is still σ_ϵ^2. This can be done by multiplying i.i.d. random noise $\mathcal{N}(0,1)$ to the original residue ϵ_A and ϵ_B.

$$\begin{aligned} E[(\psi\epsilon - E[\psi\epsilon])^2] &= E[(\psi\epsilon)^2] - (E[\psi]E[\epsilon])^2 \\ &= E[(\psi\epsilon)^2] = \sigma_\epsilon^2 \end{aligned}$$

here we have used $E[\psi] = 0, E[\psi^2] = 1, E[\epsilon] = 0$.

3. Step 3: Recompute $X_{it}^{'}$ and $Y_{it}^{'}$ using α, β, γ and δ.

4. Step 4: Recompute the decomposition to generate $\alpha^{'}$, $\beta^{'}$, $\gamma^{'}$ and $\delta^{'}$. Compute the residue $\epsilon_A^{'}$ and $\epsilon_B^{'}$ at the two ends and the Fisher transformed correlation $Z_{AB}^{'}$.

5. Step 5: Repeat steps 2 to 5 $N = 10,000$ times and generate the p-value as follows:

$$p_{AB} = \frac{1}{N}\sum_{i=1}^{N} I_{(Z_{AB} \geq Z_{AB}^{'})} \tag{9}$$

Let $Z_{AB} = \frac{1}{2}log\frac{1+\rho_{AB}}{1-\rho_{AB}}$ and similarly define $\hat{Z}_{AB}$, and $T_n = T^{1/2}(\hat{Z}_{AB} - Z_{AB})$ where T is the observed length of the time-series. From the wild-bootstrap based generation, we obtain similar estimates from each resample, and let $\hat{Z}_{AB}^*$ be the equivalent of $\hat{Z}_{AB}$ from the resample. Define $T_n^* = T^{1/2}(\hat{Z}_{AB}^* - \hat{Z}_{AB})$. We have the following result as the theoretical counterpart of our algorithm:

THEOREM 2.1. *In the framework presented above, the following hold:*

1. *The distribution of the statistic T_n converges weakly to the standard Normal distribution $N(0,1)$.*

2. *The distribution of the statistic T_n^*, conditionally on the observed data from regions A and B, converges weakly to the standard Normal distribution $N(0,1)$ almost surely.*

The second part of the above theorem states that for all possible data sets arising from regions A and B, the convergence of the wild bootstrap-based statistic T_n^* to the same distribution as that of the original statistic T_n is guaranteed with probability one. The proof of the above theorem is omitted here due to the lack of space.

2.5 Step 4: Multiple Hypotheses

Multiple comparisons is an important issue in dipole significance testing as there are a set of statistical inferences computed simultaneously. Multiplicity leads to false positives or the type I errors, i.e., the errors committed by incorrectly rejecting the null hypothesis. In order to control the false discovery rate (FDR), we use the standard procedure by Benjamini-Hochberg-Yekutieli [24] which controls the false discovery when the m hypothesis tests are dependent, which is true in our case. The method refines the threshold of p-values to find the largest k such that:

$$P_{(k)} \leq \frac{k}{m \cdot c(m)} * \alpha \tag{10}$$

We compute c(m) by examining the correlation between the 10000 random values generated for each end of the dipole. As they are positively correlated, we set c(m) to 1. We discard all the dipoles having a p-value less that $P_{(k)}$.

3. EXPERIMENTS AND RESULTS

3.1 Dataset

We use the data from the NCEP/NCAR Reanalysis project provided by the NOAA/ESRL [25]. The NCEP reanalysis product uses an assimilation scheme embedded in a physical model to interpolate global observations from 1948 onward into a gridded projection of the state of the atmosphere. The reanalysis datasets are created by assimilating remote and in situ sensor measurements using a numerical climate model to achieve physical consistency and interpolation to global coverage; they are considered the best available proxy for global observations. We use the monthly resolution of data and it has a grid resolution of 2.5° longitude x 2.5° latitude on the globe. We use the sea level pressure (SLP) data to find the dipoles because most of the important climate indices are based upon pressure variability. For the analyses and results presented here, we use the 50 year of data starting from 1951 to 2000.

3.2 Results

We ran the dipole algorithm using the NCEP dataset and the algorithm mentioned in [3] and obtained all the dipoles at a correlation threshold of -0.25. We ran our approach on significance testing for this data to generate the residual correlation and obtained the p-values. Fig. 3 shows the scatter plot of original correlation versus the residual correlation amongst the dipoles found in the dataset. From the figure, we see that a high negative original correlation does not necessarily transform to a high negative residual correlation. Fig. 4(a) shows an example of a dipole having an original correlation of -0.32 but a residual correlation of 0.1359 (p-value = 1). If we examine the time series at the two centres of the dipole (see Fig. 4(b), we see that there is a linear trend in the opposite direction which the model is able to effectively capture. Fig. 5 shows an example dipole that did not have significant trends but was discarded due to the seasonality component γ. The original correlation of the dipole is -0.24, whereas the residual correlation is 0.0219.

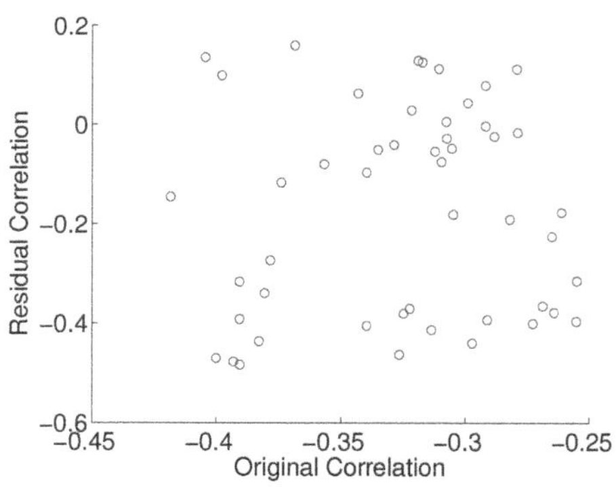

Figure 3: Scatter plot showing original vs residual correlation.

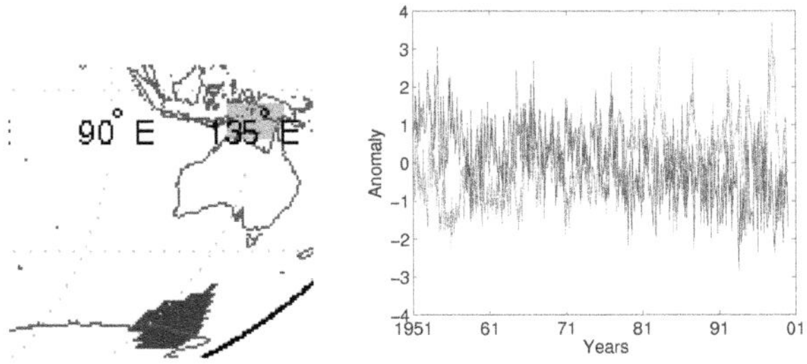

(a) Dipole having a correlation of -0.32 but a residual correlation 0.1359 (b) Time series at the two centres

Figure 4: Dipole rejected due to linear trend.

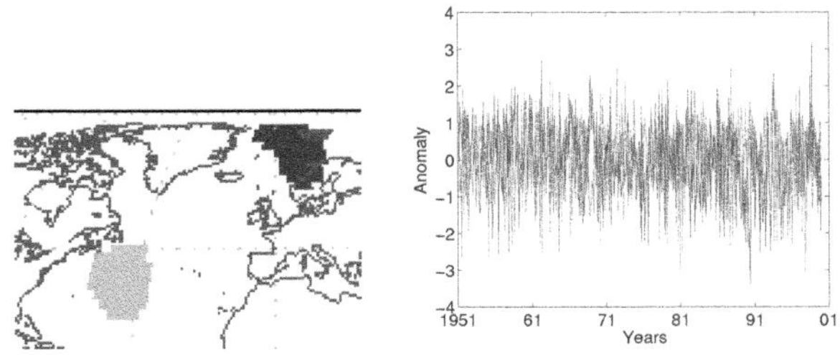

(a) Dipole having an original correlation of -0.24 but a residual correlation of 0.0219 (b) Time series at the two centres

Figure 5: Dipoles discarded due to seasonality filtering.

On the other hand, Fig. 6 shows an example of a dipole that had an original correlation of -0.25 but has a higher negative residual correlation of -0.39 (p-value = 0). This dipole represents one of the known connections AAO and has a correlation of 0.8 with the AAO index defined by the CPC [26]. We see that the approach effectively eliminates about 16 dipoles with a p-value ≥ 0.01. Further, it declares all the known connections as significant. However, we see that there are still a few dipoles (10) left that require post-processing which is described below.

3.3 Post Processing Using Domain Knowledge

Our model for deterministic trend accommodates a linear function and a sinusoidal component at each end-point of a potential dipole. A careful analysis of some of these time series show that non-linear trends may occasionally exist. Fig. 7(a) shows an example of a dipole that had an original correlation of -0.39 but has high non-linear trends. Fig. 7(b) shows the time series at the two centres of the dipole. From the figure, we see that the trends in the two dipole ends are not linear, thus making the post processing necessary. One end of the dipole corresponds to the Sahel region in Africa which underwent an abrupt change a long period of drought around 1969 [27] which is also reflected in the time series as shown in the Fig. 7(b). Based on domain knowledge and prior experience, we know that this dipole does not make physical sense. De-trending the data before applying the dipole detection algorithm might appear to be a solution. However, as we discussed earlier,

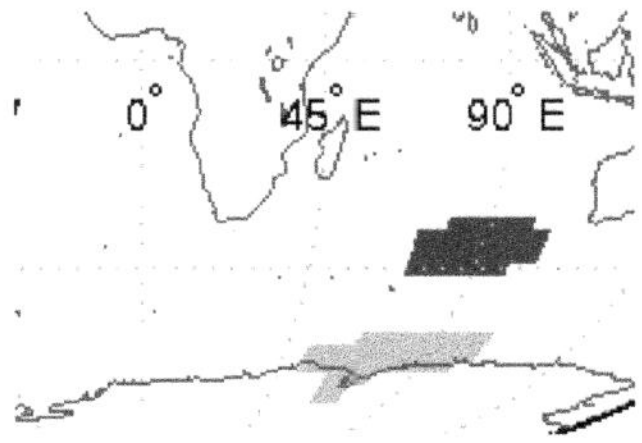

Figure 6: Dipole having an original correlation -0.25 but a residual correlation -0.39 corresponds to the known dipole AAO.

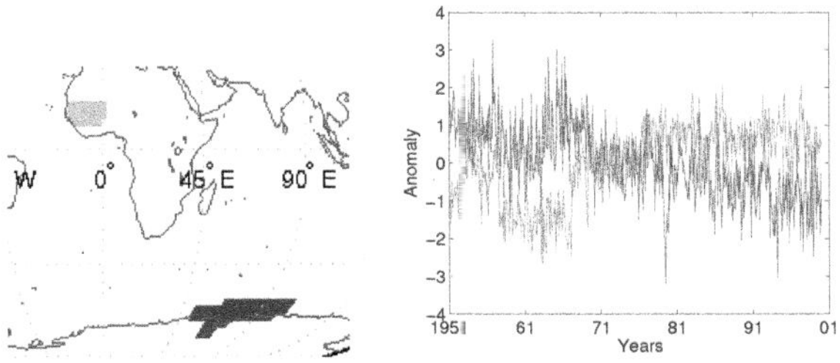

(a) Dipole having a correlation of -0.39 (b) Time series at the two centres of the dipole

Figure 7: Dipole showing non-linear trend corresponding to abrupt change due to the Sahel drought

detrending of climate data has many challenges and can lead to adding spurious connections especially when the trends are non-linear. Using domain knowledge, we want to further eliminate these trend dipoles in order to identify the real dipole structure.

Our parametric form comes to rescue in this case as this allows us to put bound on the value β can take. We use a simple method to examine the β values at the two ends. If the difference in β values at the two ends of the dipole is greater than a threshold, we discard them.

$$Discard\ dipoles\ if\ |\beta_A - \beta_B| \geq \hat{\beta} \tag{11}$$

In order to compute $\hat{\beta}$, we considered the 6 well known dipoles and computed the absolute difference in their beta values and selected our threshold of $\hat{\beta}$ based upon that. With the use of this filtering, a number of trended dipoles mainly starting from the Sahel region in Africa that initially passed the significance threshold were eliminated. This intuitively makes sense because our parametric form removes trend as well as cyclic patterns from the data but not the small local oscillations (which are captured by ϵ). There is a possibility that one end of the spurious dipole is influenced by one end of a true dipole. In this case, those local oscillations as captured by epsilon could be of opposite polarity and hence manage to pass the significance test. The above filtering mechanism using $\hat{\beta}$ seems like a simple way to eliminate such cases.

3.4 Comprehensive Evaluation

Table 1 shows the summary of the number of dipoles declared as significant using a significance level $\alpha = 0.01$ and the post-processing that we described above. From the table, we see that 23 dipoles are declared as significant in the dataset having a correlation < -0.25. Figures 8 shows

	NCEP -0.25		NCEP -0.2	
Total	49		85	
	p < 0.01	p ≥ 0.01	p < 0.01	p ≥ 0.01
No trends	**23**	4	**31**	13
Trends	10	12	23	18

Table 1: Number of dipoles declared as significant using our approach in the NCEP data.

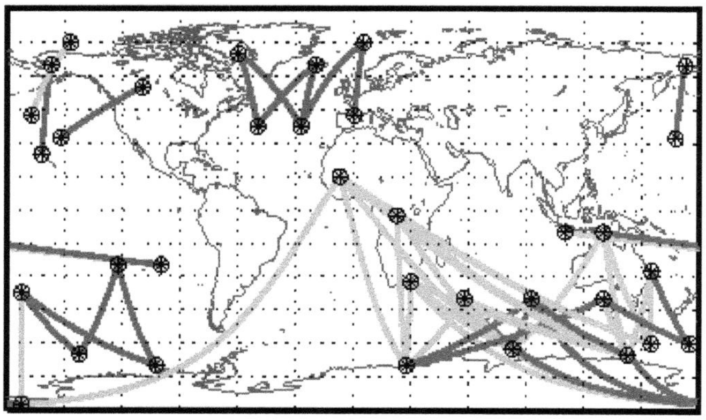

Figure 8: Dipoles declared significant in the NCEP dataset at a threshold of -0.25. Red denotes significant dipoles and green denotes insignificant dipoles.

the dipoles declared significant in the NCEP dataset at a threshold of -0.25. From a quick visual inspection of the figures, we see that the well-known dipoles like North Atlantic Oscillation (NAO), Southern Oscillation (SO), Western Pacific (WP), Pacific North America pattern (PNA) and Antarctic Oscillation (AAO) are all identified as significant. Fig 9 shows the dipoles declared as significant at a lower threshold of -0.2. From the figure, we see that apart from the well known dipoles, other weaker connections start appearing as significant, for example the Scandinavia pattern starting around Russia and ending at the Atlantic.

Our next goal is to check whether our algorithm has a bias to declare dipoles having a higher negative correlation as significant. Fig. 10 shows the histogram of correlation values of dipoles declared as significant and insignificant in the NCEP data. The histogram shows that at times the algorithm even declares dipoles with higher negative correlation as insignificant. However, using our approach, we are still able to remove about $1/2$ of the dipoles from the NCEP data having a correlation < -0.25 as insignificant. Also the histogram of correlations of significant and insignificant correlations shows that the algorithm has no particular bias. Next, we examine closely the two reasons in our algorithm to label the dipoles as insignificant.

Recall, that the β values capture the linear trend present in the data. Spurious dipoles can be formed if the two regions involved in the dipole have significant trends in the opposite direction and the negative correlation between the two regions is accounted for by the negative trends and not a periodic oscillation. Fig. 11 shows a plot of β values for the NCEP dataset. From the figure, we see that there are quite a few dipoles with strikingly opposite trends in the NCEP data and most of them going to the southern hemisphere. This also conforms with the existing knowledge about the

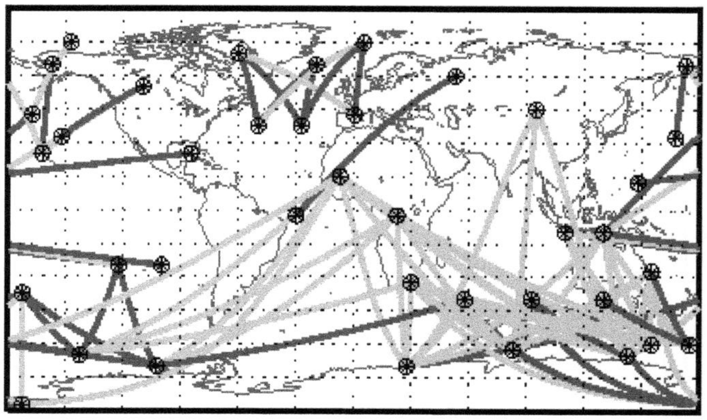

Figure 9: Dipoles declared significant in the NCEP dataset at a threshold of -0.2. Red denotes significant dipoles and green denotes insignificant dipoles.

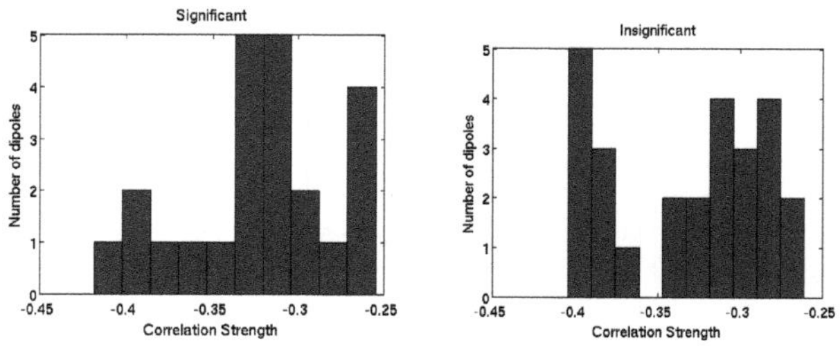

Figure 10: Histogram of correlation strengths for significant and insignificant dipoles.

NCEP data from the climate science [28] about the presence of significant spurious trends in the southern hemisphere.

Table 1 shows that half of the rejected dipoles have significant trends in the opposite direction. Apart from the dipoles with trends, the other dipoles which are discarded using our algorithm are the ones with very little negative residual correlation left in them (see Table 1). Seasonality in the dipoles could be one possible reason. Fig. 12 shows the gamma values of the dipoles. From the figure, we see that quite a few of them have significant value of gamma.

3.4.1 *p-value for the known dipoles*

A good measure of evaluation is to examine the p-values generated for the 6 of the most well known dipoles - SOI, NAO, AO, AAO, WP, PNA. The existence and the impact of these dipoles has been well established in literature from climate science. At first, we pick up a data driven dipole which represents the static index of the closest in correlation. After that, we examine the p-values generated for the data driven dipole closely matching the static index. Table 2 shows the p-values generated for the known dipoles using our approach. From the table, we see that all of the 6 well known dipoles are declared significant using our algorithm and have a p-value of 0 up to the order of machine precision. Further the residual correlation at the two ends of the dipole generated by removing $f(t)$ from the time series at the two ends is also very highly negative for the known dipoles. This provides empirical evidence that our approach to estimate the statistical significance works well in practice.

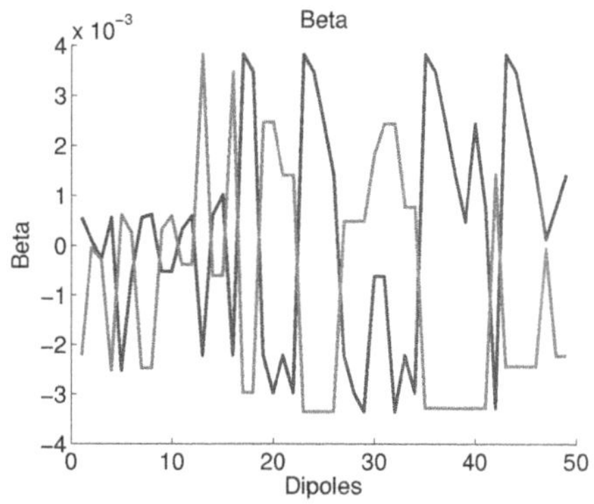

Figure 11: Beta values at the two ends of the dipoles for the NCEP dataset.

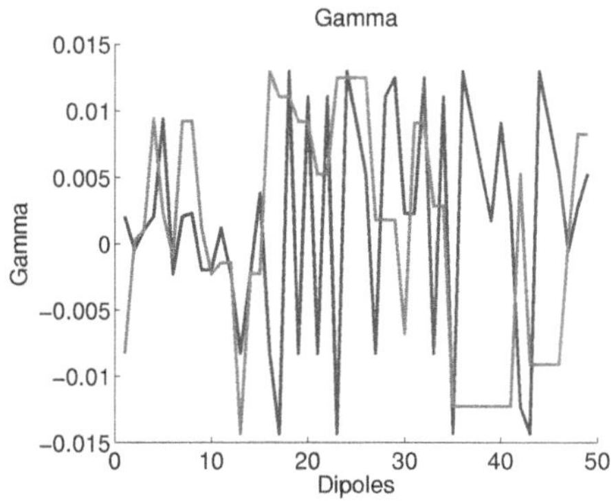

Figure 12: Gamma values at the two ends of the dipoles for the NCEP dataset.

3.4.2 Correlation with Static indices

In order to further assess the quality of the extracted dipoles, we did another experiment to understand the nature of the dipoles. Most of the candidate dipoles should be a representative of some known phenomenon. We considered 6 teleconnection patterns identified by the Climate Prediction Centre website [26]. From the NCEP data, we considered two sets of dipoles significant and insignificant. There were about 25 dipoles in each subset. We computed the correlation of each of these dipoles with the 6 known climate indices. Fig. 13 shows the maximum correlation of the two groups of dipoles with the known indices. From the figure, we see that all the surrogates of the known phenomenon are captured very well in the significant group as compared to the insignificant one. PNA is not captured with a very high correlation in both the groups as the actual phenomenon consists of three epicenters and is not a dipole. AAO has high correlation with significant as well as insignificant group. This might be due to trends in the insignificant group.

3.4.3 A new dipole ?

A larger implication of our work on significance testing lies in identifying potentially new teleconnection patterns not known to climate scientists so far. A careful evaluation of all the dipoles from Fig. 8 shows that most of them have a very high correlation with the known climate indices and thus are some variant of the known phenomenon. However,

	NCEP/NCAR		
	p-value	Residual Corr	Fisher transform
SOI	1.2897e-13	-0.1814	-10.3147
NAO	0	-0.4137	-54.2486
AO	0	-0.3092	-19.913
AAO	0	-0.39	-32.4990
WP	0	-0.1755	-9.2258
PNA	0	-0.0968	-8.4194

Table 2: p-values for the known dipoles using the random approximation along with residual correlation.

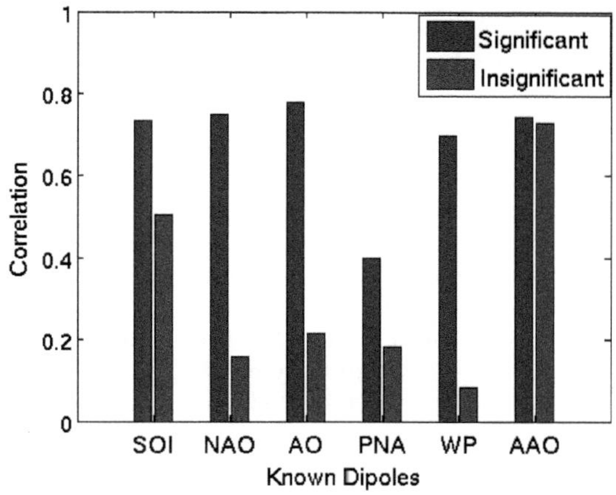

Figure 13: Maximum correlation with known indices in the two sets of dipoles.

there are some teleconnection patterns that are declared as significant and that do not have a high correlation with any known phenomenon. One such striking dipole is a dipole near Australia as shown in the Fig. 14. It appears as significant in the NCEP data and its correlation with the known indices is also very low (see Fig. 15). Further, it is not supported by the existing literature on teleconnections. This might represent a new dipole phenomenon not known to climate scientists so far. Our preliminary investigations show that this dipole also has a different impact on land temperature as compared to other known dipoles. A comprehensive evaluation of the physical significance of the phenomenon is a part of our future work.

4. DISCUSSION AND CONCLUSION

Significance testing in spatio-temporal data presents many

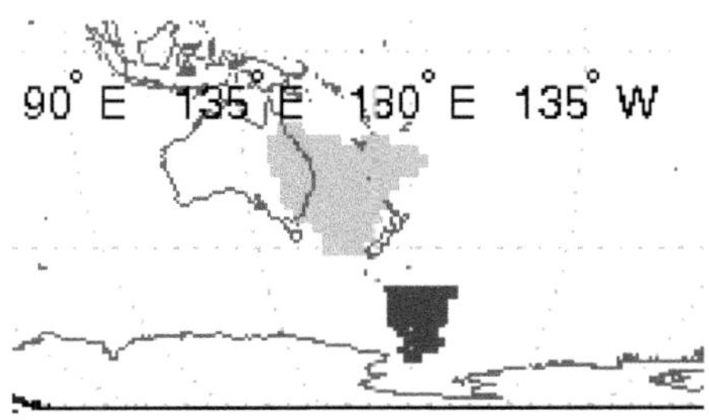

Figure 14: Dipole near Australia shows up as statistically significant.

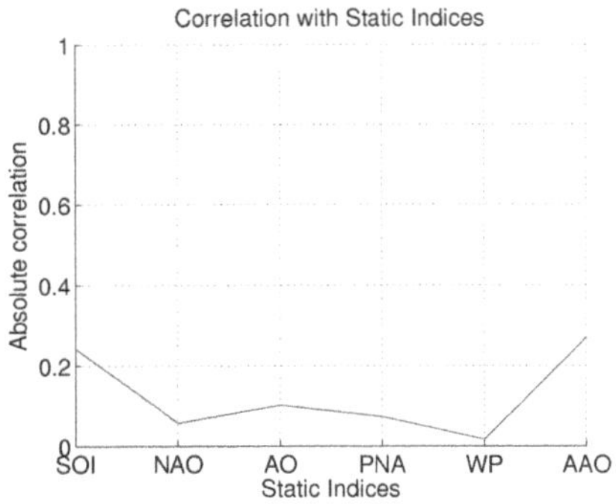

Figure 15: Correlation of the dipole near Australia with known indices

challenges due to the inherent autocorrelation dependencies in time and space. However, significance testing of spatio-temporal patterns has received little attention. In this paper, we present a systematic approach to detect the significance of spatio-temporal teleconnection patterns. We ran our algorithm on the NCEP sea level pressure data. From our results, we see that our algorithm is able to capture the known dipoles. We show the utility of using a simple model to extract out the characteristics of climate data time series. A larger implication of our work is that the algorithm can be instructive to other researchers in the spatio-temporal domain to test the significance of patterns. A part of the future work involves handling non-linear trends. Another limitation of the model is that the marginal analysis of the periodic component distort co-periodicity properties. We propose to address this in our future research work. In particular, we propose to simultaneously model the deterministic trends and periodic components at the two ends of a dipole, along with the stochastic components of the bivariate time series. Two-dimensional wavelets would be used for this purpose, since evidence shows some erratic patterns and discontinuities. Also, as part of our future work, we would like to explore if some potential dipoles are governed by co-integrating relations. We also propose to explore the choice of resampling weights for which the wild bootstrap inference would be second order accurate. Another future direction is to integrate the significance testing into the algorithm for dipole detection and thus not allow spuriously connected regions to be declared as candidate dipoles.

Acknowledgments

This work was partially supported by NSF grants IIS-0905581, IIS-1029711 and SES-0851705. Access to computing facilities was provided by the University of Minnesota Supercomputing Institute.

5. REFERENCES

[1] J.M. Wallace and D.S. Gutzler. Téléconnexions in the geopotential height field during the northern hemisphere winter. *Mon. Wea. Rev*, 109:784–812, 1981.

[2] H. Von Storch and F.W. Zwiers. *Statistical analysis in climate research.* Cambridge Univ Pr, 2002.

[3] J. Kawale, S. Liess, A. Kumar, M. Steinbach, A. Ganguly, N.F. Samatova, F. Semazzi, P. Snyder, and V. Kumar. Data guided discovery of dynamic climate dipoles. In *CIDU*, pages 30–44, 2011.

[4] J. Kawale, M. Steinbach, and V. Kumar. Discovering dynamic dipoles in climate data. In *SIAM Conference on Data Mining, SDM*, pages 107–118, 2011.

[5] M. Steinbach, P.N. Tan, V. Kumar, S. Klooster, and C. Potter. Discovery of climate indices using clustering. In *Proceedings of the ninth ACM SIGKDD international conference on Knowledge discovery and data mining*, pages 446–455. ACM, 2003.

[6] E.S. Edgington. *Randomization tests*, volume 147. CRC Press, 1995.

[7] S. Hanhijarvi, G. Garriga, and K. Puolamaki. Randomization techniques for graphs. 2009.

[8] A. Gionis, H. Mannila, T. Mielik "ainen, and P. Tsaparas. Assessing data mining results via swap randomization. *ACM Transactions on Knowledge Discovery from Data (TKDD)*, 1(3):14–es, 2007.

[9] Nuno Castro and Paulo J. Azevedo. Time series motifs statistical significance. In *SDM*, pages 687–698, 2011.

[10] P. Ferreira, P. Azevedo, C. Silva, and R. Brito. Mining approximate motifs in time series. In *Discovery Science*, pages 89–101. Springer, 2006.

[11] T. Oates. Peruse: An unsupervised algorithm for finding recurrig patterns in time series. 2002.

[12] W. Ulrich and N.J. Gotelli. Null model analysis of species nestedness patterns. *Ecology*, 88(7):1824–1831, 2007.

[13] A. Waldron. Null models of geographic range size evolution reaffirm its heritability. *American Naturalist*, pages 221–231, 2007.

[14] J.A. Veech. A null model for detecting nonrandom patterns of species richness along spatial gradients. *Ecology*, 81(4):1143–1149, 2000.

[15] J. Besag and P.J. Diggle. Simple monte carlo tests for spatial pattern. *Applied Statistics*, pages 327–333, 1977.

[16] D.S. Wilks. *Statistical methods in the atmospheric sciences*, volume 100. Academic press, 2011.

[17] R.F. Engle and C.W.J. Granger. Co-integration and error correction: representation, estimation, and testing. *Econometrica: Journal of the Econometric Society*, pages 251–276, 1987.

[18] C.W.J. Granger. Some properties of time series data and their use in econometric model specification. *Journal of econometrics*, 16(1):121–130, 1981.

[19] E.C. Weatherhead, G.C. Reinsel, G.C. Tiao, X.L. Meng, D. Choi, W.K. Cheang, T. Keller, J. DeLuisi, D.J. Wuebbles, J.B. Kerr, et al. Factors affecting the detection of trends: Statistical considerations and applications to environmental data. *Journal of Geophysical Research*, 103(D14):17–149, 1998.

[20] C.F.J. Wu. Jackknife, bootstrap and other resampling methods in regression analysis. *The Annals of Statistics*, 14(4):1261–1295, 1986.

[21] E. Mammen. Bootstrap and wild bootstrap for high dimensional linear models. *The Annals of Statistics*, 21(1):255–285, 1993.

[22] R.A. Fisher et al. On the" probable error" of a coefficient of correlation deduced from a small sample. *Metron*, 1:3–32, 1921.

[23] W. Hardle and E. Mammen. Comparing nonparametric versus parametric regression fits. *The Annals of Statistics*, 21(4):1926–1947, 1993.

[24] Y. Benjamini and D. Yekutieli. The control of the false discovery rate in multiple testing under dependency. *Annals of statistics*, pages 1165–1188, 2001.

[25] E. Kalnay and et al. The ncep/ncar 40-year reanalysis project. *Bull. Amer. Meteor. Soc.*, 77:437–471, 1996.

[26] Climate prediction centre, http://www.cpc.ncep.noaa.gov/.

[27] J.E. Janowiak. An investigation of interannual rainfall variability in africa. *Journal of Climate*, 1:240–255, 1988.

[28] K.M. Hines, D.H. Bromwich, and G.J. Marshall. Artificial surface pressure trends in the ncep–ncar reanalysis over the southern ocean and antarctica. *J. Climate*, 13(22):3940–3952, 2000.

SeqiBloc: Mining Multi-time Spanning Blockmodels in Dynamic Graphs*

Jeffrey Chan, Wei Liu, Christopher Leckie, James Bailey, Kotagiri Ramamohanarao
Department of Computing and Information Systems, University of Melbourne, Australia
{jeffrey.chan, wei.liu, caleckie, baileyj, kotagiri}@unimelb.edu.au

ABSTRACT

Blockmodelling is an important technique for decomposing graphs into sets of roles. Vertices playing the same role have similar patterns of interactions with vertices in other roles. These roles, along with the role to role interactions, can succinctly summarise the underlying structure of the studied graphs. As the underlying graphs evolve with time, it is important to study how their blockmodels evolve too. This will enable us to detect role changes across time, detect different patterns of interactions, for example, weekday and weekend behaviour, and allow us to study how the structure in the underlying dynamic graph evolves. To date, there has been limited research on studying dynamic blockmodels. They focus on smoothing role changes between adjacent time instances. However, this approach can overfit during stationary periods where the underlying structure does not change but there is random noise in the graph. Therefore, an approach to a) find blockmodels across spans of time and b) to find the stationary periods is needed. In this paper, we propose an information theoretic framework, SeqiBloc, combined with a change point detection approach to achieve a) and b). In addition, we propose new vertex equivalence definitions that include time, and show how they relate back to our information theoretic approach. We demonstrate their usefulness and superior accuracy over existing work on synthetic and real datasets.

Categories and Subject Descriptors

H.2.8 [**Database Applications**]: Data Mining; E.1 [**Data Structures**]: Graphs and Networks

General Terms

Algorithms

*This research was supported under Australian Research Council's Discovery Projects funding scheme (project number DP110102621).

KDD'12, August 12–16, 2012, Beijing, China.
Copyright 2012 ACM 978-1-4503-1462-6 /12/08 ...$10.00.

Keywords

Blockmodel, Dynamic Graphs, Minimum Description Length, Structural Equivalence

1. INTRODUCTION

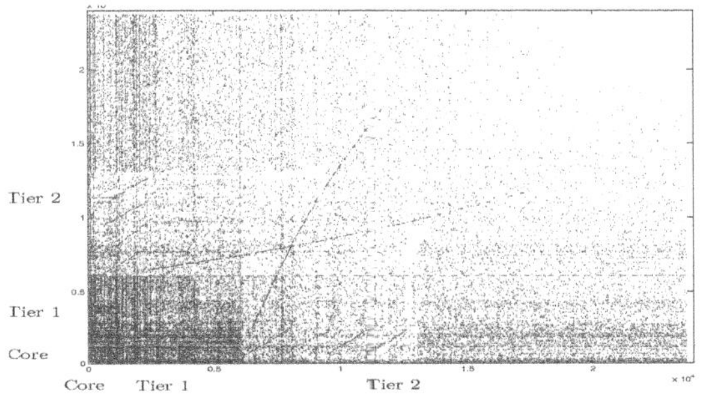

(a) Adjacency matrix and the blockmodel decomposition. Red dotted lines delimit the boundaries of each role. The 3 roles are Core, Tier 1 and Tier 2.

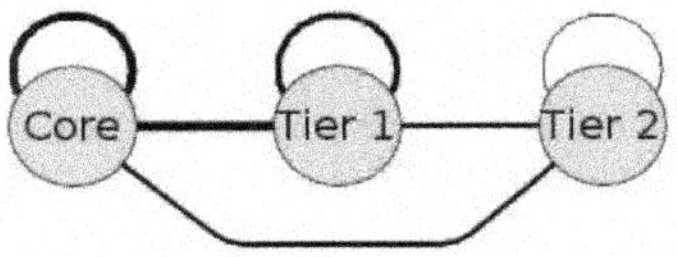

(b) Image diagram of the 3 roles and their role to role relationships.

Figure 1: Blockmodel decomposition of a BGP connectivity graph over November 2011.

Blockmodelling has been studied for many years in the social sciences [16]. Blockmodelling is a powerful approach to decompose social networks and graphs into partitions and common roles. Vertices playing the same role, or are equivalent, if they have similar connections to other vertices. These roles, along with the role to role interactions, summarises the underlying structure of a graph succinctly. For example, consider Figure 1, which shows a blockmodel decomposition of the Internet routing graph in November 2011. Figure 1a shows the adjacency matrix of the graph, along with the partition into roles, delimited by the red dotted lines. We label the roles into 'Core', 'Tier 1' and 'Tier 2'. The decomposition shows the Core vertices are highly connected among themselves and to vertices in other roles. Tier 1 vertices are highly connected among themselves and connected to some Tier 2 vertices. The overall structure is a core-periphery, which can be succinctly summarised by the image diagram in Figure 1b, which shows the roles as vertices, and the inter role interactions as edges (the amount of connectivity between roles is expressed by the thickness of the edges in the image diagram). As can be seen, blockmodels summarise the structure of a graph succinctly, allowing us to understand and characterise the underlying structure (e.g., it is a core-periphery), discover the important roles (e.g., the Core role is highly connected to all other roles and hence routes most of the traffic) and compare with other graphs.

A community decomposition seeks to find roles that are densely connected within themselves and sparsely connected to vertices of other roles. Such a type of decomposition is not able to find the structure in Figure 1b. For example, the connections between the Core vertices to the Tier 1 vertices are more dense than among the Tier 1 vertices, so it is likely that the Core and Tier 1 vertices are incorrectly merged into one role. Blockmodelling, on the other hand, can find community decompositions, and hence, it can be considered as a generalisation of community finding for graphs.

The vertex equivalence used in the previous example is called *structural equivalence*; there are several others, but we concentrate on this type of equivalence in this paper as it is the most common and easiest to interpret. Equivalent vertices have similar in and out neighbours. For example, the vertices labelled 2 and 3 in Figure 2a are structurally equivalent because they have the same out neighbours (1,2,3,4) and the same in neighbours (1,2,3,4).

As the underlying graphs are not static, it is essential to fit and track blockmodels across time. For example, in the dynamic graph representing the email communications in Enron, it is known that during the crisis, communication patterns and intensity among different employee roles experienced large shifts [8]. Hence if we used a single blockmodel to describe the whole sequence we will not detect or see these changes.

There are several open challenges in fitting dynamic blockmodels. Unlike the case of static blockmodelling where there is a strong formalism between the vertex equivalences and what type of blockmodels will satisfy those equivalences [16], there are no equivalence definitions for dynamic blockmodels. These formalisms are important, because they provide the theoretical underpinnings between (intuitive) definitions of vertex equivalences (i.e., what defines a group of vertices playing the same role) and how they relate to structure seen in the adjacency matrix. In this paper, we introduce two formal definitions of evolving structural equivalence and provide lemmas on how this is reflected in the block structure of a blockmodel decomposition.

In addition, dynamic blockmodels have only been recently studied [17]. In these works, each snapshot in the dynamic graph is modelled by a blockmodel, with smoothing applied on the membership of the roles (for the rest of the paper, we will use roles and positions, which is the term from social sciences, interchangeably). However, this might not be the optimal model to represent a dynamic graph. Consider the following scenarios, using the Enron email network as an example. If we used a single blockmodel to represent the whole graph sequence, it will be the simplest blockmodel, but it will be unlikely to model the communication changes inside Enron. On the other hand, if we represented each snapshot

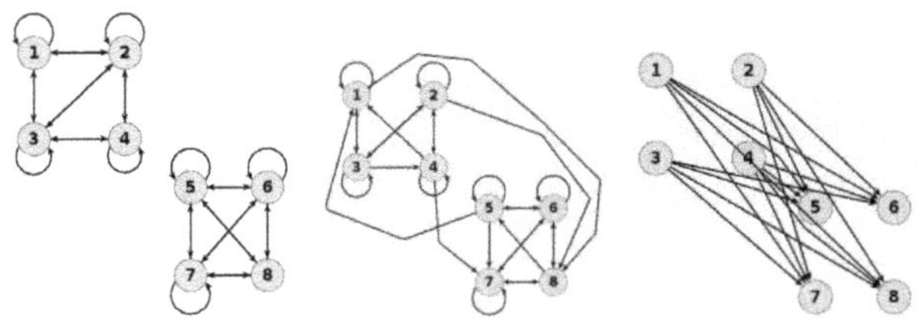

(a) T1 Snapshot. (b) T2 Snapshot. (c) T3 Snapshot.

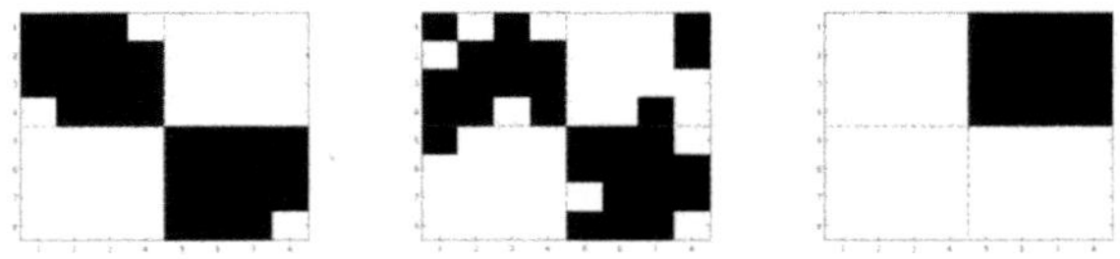

(d) T1 Adj matrix. (e) T2 Adj matrix. (f) T3 Adj matrix.

Figure 2: A dynamic graph example of 3 snapshots. The top and bottom rows illustrate the snapshots and corresponding adjacency matrices respectively.

with its own blockmodel, this will accurately model the underlying dynamic graph, but at the expense of overfitting. Hence, it is desirable to find a balance between accuracy and generality. During periods where the edges within the graph undergo minor noisy fluctuations, it is better to use one blockmodel to represent these periods. On the other hand, when the underlying graph is going through a fundamental shift, then using multiple blockmodels to represent this period might be preferable. This shows the importance of having a) an approach to quantify and find a tradeoff between model complexity and model accuracy; b) a method to fit blockmodels over subsequences of snapshots and c) a way to find where best to segment a graph sequence.

In this paper, we present an information theoretic approach to address these challenges. Using the minimum description length principle [14] to quantify the tradeoff between model complexity and accuracy, we propose four different encoding schemes that are used as objectives for finding blockmodels over subsequences, for our two proposed definitions of evolving structural equivalence. In addition, we propose a new, fast, change point detection based approach and a new blockmodel comparison measure to segment the graph sequence. Using generated and three real datasets, we show that our approach can accurately determine good locations to segment the dynamic graph sequence and find interesting dynamic blockmodels. We call our framework SeqiBloc (**Subsequence Information** Theoretic **Block**modelling).

We present the following contributions in this paper:

- We introduce two formal definitions of evolving structural equivalences, describe when they are applicable, and show their corresponding matrix form.
- We propose four different information theoretic encodings that quantify the tradeoff between model complexity and accuracy and conform to the new equivalence definitions.
- Using our encoding schemes, we propose a blockmodel comparison measure and a fast and accurate change point detection based segmenting approach to determine when new blockmodels need to be learnt.

2. RELATED WORK

In this section, we describe related work in static and dynamic blockmodelling and finding dynamic communities.

Blockmodelling was initially introduced in sociology to model social networks [16]. Later, stochastic blockmodels [2] were proposed to relax the presumption of exact vertex equivalences. Edges, the position of vertices and other variables are modelled as random variables. The assumptions made about the variables modelled, the dependencies between random variables and the parametric distributions of the probabilities lead to different formulations and probabilistic models. For example, Airolid et al. [2] introduced a model that allowed vertices to belong to multiple positions In [17], Xing et al. extended the mixed membership model of [2] to dynamic networks, where there is one blockmodel per snapshot. The positions of vertices are allowed to change with time and be smoothed between adjacent snapshots. This is similar to one of the dynamic equivalence definitions we propose. To improve the fitting complexity, Yang et al. [18] performed the fitting using Bayesian inference.

Statistical approaches can infer insightful models, but their fitting process can be computationally demanding. More importantly, the dynamic blockmodel techniques fit one blockmodel per snapshot, which is likely overfit.

There are a variety of approaches proposed for finding and tracking communities across time. Initially, static methods were applied to each individual snapshot and the amount of overlap between the communities of adjacent snapshots were used to categorise community events such as growth, decay and stability [11]. Subsequent approaches used the idea of smoothing from evolutionary clustering [4] to find communities that are good for the current snapshot but also close to the communities found from the previous snapshot. Work in this area includes [5], which extended static spectral community finding to this framework.

Dinh et al. [9] proposed an incremental algorithm to update existing communities when a new snapshot arrives. Similarly, [1] introduced efficient ways to maintain a set of communities in massive graph streams. The emphasis is on incrementally maintaining the best current set of communities, not on finding communities across a subsequence.

Algorithms for finding dynamic communities generally do not work with dynamic blockmodels, as finding communities is only one type of blockmodel and there are many other interesting types, like the core-periphery structure of the BGP example.

To the best of our knowledge, only [15] represents a graph sequence as a series of models. Graphscope [15] uses a minimum description length coding formulation to find evolving co-clusters in bi-partite graphs. The sequence of graphs is partitioned into segments where a single co-clustering holds. This is similar to our approach, and as a baseline we have adapted Graphscope to finding unipartite blockmodels. However, the original Graphscope can only find one type of dynamic equivalence and its greedy lookahead segmenting approach misses many segmenting points in synthetic and real datasets. In addition, the blockmodels it found for real datasets have an unreasonably high number of positions. In contrast, we propose four different encodings to find our proposed dynamic equivalences, and our change point detection approach can accurately segment the graph sequences and find blockmodels that have a reasonable number of positions.

Symbol	Description
G	A graph with vertex set $V$and edge set E.
$<G^{ts,te}>$	A continuous graph sequence of snapshots.
v_i	A vertex.
$e_{i,j}$	An edge from vertex v_i to v_j.
$\mathbf{A}_t$	Adjacency matrix of G^t.
n	Number of vertices.
$\mathcal{C}^L$	A set of vertex positions with index L.
C_i	A vertex position.
$\mathbf{A}^t(C_i, C_j)$	A block with rows from C_i and columns from C_j, from graph snapshot G^t.
$m_1(\mathbf{A}^t(C_i, C_j))$	The number of 1's in block $\mathbf{A}^t(C_i, C_j)$.
H(X)	Entropy of random variable X.

Table 1: Description of symbols used in this paper.

3. BACKGROUND

In this section, we formally introduce the ideas of blockmodelling and structural equivalence, their dynamic variants, and the notation we use in this paper (see Table 1).

A **graph** G consists of a set of vertices V, and a set of edges E, $E : V \times V$. In this paper, the graphs we study are uniquely labelled and the set of vertices do not change (we leave this to future work). A graph can also be modelled by its adjacency matrix $\mathbf{A}$. A **dynamic graph** is represented as a sequence of snapshots $< G^{1,T} >=< G^1, \ldots, G^t, \ldots, G^T >$, $1 < t < T$ (T can be ∞).

3.1 Blockmodelling

We start by describing the traditional, static definition of blockmodelling. Recall that a blockmodel partitions the vertices of a graph into a set of positions, based on notions of vertex equivalence. The positions in turn divide the adjacency matrix of the graph into a set of blocks. Each block defines the edge interactions between two positions.

Let the set of positions be denoted by $\mathcal{C} = \{C_1, C_2, \ldots, C_k\}$, e.g., C_1 in Figure 2d is $\{1, 2, 3, 4\}$. A block $\mathbf{A}(C_i, C_j)$ is a submatrix of the adjacency matrix $\mathbf{A}$, and represents the edges from the vertices of position C_i to the vertices of position C_j. An example block is $\mathbf{A}(C_1, C_1)$ from Figure 2d, which occupies the top left of the adjacency matrix.

A **blockmodel** is defined as $\mathbf{B}(\mathbf{A}, \mathcal{C})$, where the rows and columns of $\mathbf{A}$ are rearranged into blocks according to the set of positions $\mathcal{C}$, such that the vertices in the same position are (structurally) equivalent.

3.2 Evolving Blockmodels

As explained in Section 1, evolving structural equivalence has not been explored in the literature hence it is not clear what it means to have dynamic structural equivalence. Therefore, in this section, we propose and define two definitions of dynamic structural equivalence.

The most strict definition, **block preserving structural equivalence**, asserts that two vertices are equivalent over a span of time if they have the same neighbours over that span of time.

Definition 1. Two vertices v_i and v_j are **block preserving structurally equivalent** over the continuous time span of $[ts, te]$, where $ts \leq te$, if for t and t', where $ts \leq t \leq te, ts \leq t' \leq te$, and for $v_k, v_l \in V$:

1. $e^t_{i,k} \in E^t$ iff $e^{t'}_{j,k} \in E^{t'}$ and $e^t_{l,i} \in E^t$ iff $e^{t'}_{l,j} \in E^{t'}$;
2. $e^t_{i,k} \notin E^t$ iff $e^{t'}_{j,k} \notin E^{t'}$ and $e^t_{l,i} \notin E^t$ iff $e^{t'}_{l,j} \notin E^{t'}$.

For example, in Figure 2, vertices 2 and 3 are block preserving equivalent over T1 and T2, but not T3, because their neighbourhood in T3 is different from T1 and T2. Next, we relate this definition of equivalence with the density of the blocks of the corresponding blockmodel.

LEMMA 1. *Let a block consisting of all 1s be denoted by* **1**, *and all 0s be denoted by* **0**. *Let V be partitioned into block preserving structurally equivalent positions,* $\mathcal{C}$, *over the span* $[ts, te]$. *Then for all* t, t', $ts \leq t, t' \leq te$, *and* $\forall C_x, C_y \in \mathcal{C}$

1. $\mathbf{A}^t(C_x, C_y) = \mathbf{1}$ *or* $\mathbf{0}$;

2. $\mathbf{A}^t(C_x, C_y) = \mathbf{A}^{t'}(C_x, C_y)$.

The inverse direction holds true also.

PROOF. Consider the vertices v_i and $v_j \in C_x$ and $v_k \in C_y$, $\forall C_x, C_y \in \mathcal{C}$. Since v_i and v_j are equivalent, then they must either both have an edge, or both have no edge to v_k over all t. This means condition 1, and since it is over all t, condition 2 of the lemma are both true. To show the inverse direction, consider a block $\mathbf{A}^t(C_x, C_y)$. If it is equal to **1**, then there is an edge from all vertices $v_i \in C_x$ to all vertices $v_j \in C_y$. As the blocks are equal across all t, then the edge $e_{i,j}$ must exist over all t, satisfying first part of condition 1 of Definition 1. Similar reasoning can be used to show the second part of condition 1 and condition 2 of Definition 1 ($\mathbf{A}^t(C_x, C_y) = 0$ case) holds also. □

The second definition, **position preserving structural equivalence**, asserts that two vertices are equivalent over a span of time if for every time instance in the span, the two vertices are structurally equivalent. Note that the set of neighbours of equivalent vertices can be different at different time instances, but must be the same at the same time instance. For example, vertices 2 and 3 are position preserving equivalent over T1 to T3 in Figure 2. This equivalence is useful for finding dynamic equivalences that might not maintain the same connectivity throughout a span of time.

For example, we could represent the replying between a group of experts and newbies in a Q&A forum as a dynamic graph with one snapshot per hour. During the day, the experts are active, but they go to sleep at night. Using a position preserving structural equivalence definition, the experts are considered equivalent throughout a 24 hour period because they are structurally equivalent for each snapshot. They are still regarded as experts when they go to sleep. However, applying a block preserving definition, their behaviour means they are equivalent in two subsequences - one for the day, when they are highly active, and one for night, when they are inactive and likely to have the same replying behaviour as newbies (and be equivalent to them). This equivalence asserts that the experts are only considered experts when they are actively answering questions.

Definition 2. Two vertices v_i and v_j are **position preserving structurally equivalent** over the continuous time span of $[ts, te]$, where $ts \leq te$, if $\forall t, ts \leq t \leq te$, and for $v_k, v_l \in V$:

1. $e^t_{i,k} \in E^t$ iff $e^t_{j,k} \in E^t$ and $e^t_{l,i} \in E^t$ iff $e^t_{l,j} \in E^t$;

2. $e^t_{i,k} \notin E^t$ iff $e^t_{j,k} \notin E^t$ and $e^t_{l,i} \notin E^t$ iff $e^t_{l,j} \notin E^t$.

LEMMA 2. *Let V be partitioned into position preserving structurally equivalent positions,* $\mathcal{C}$, *over the span* $[ts, te]$. *Then for all* t, $ts \leq t \leq te$ *and* $\forall C_x, C_y \in \mathcal{C}$,

1. $\mathbf{A}^t(C_x, C_y) = \mathbf{1}$ *or* $\mathbf{0}$.

The inverse direction holds true also.

PROOF. The proof is similar to Lemma 1 and due to space limitations, we omit it. □

4. INFORMATION THEORETIC BLOCKMODELLING

In this section, we describe our information-theoretic framework to evaluate how well blockmodels conform to our proposed equivalence definitions.

Given data and a model, the idea is to evaluate a model by the amount of compression it can achieve on the data against how complex the model is. The more compression that is achieved, the lower the cost to encode the model, and the more accurate the model is. This is balanced against the complexity of the model (the more complexity, the higher the encoding costs). Using the minimum description length principle, we can combine the two ideas as C(graph, position) = C(position) + C(graph | position). A blockmodel (described by its set of positions) is the best tradeoff between accuracy and complexity if it minimises this expression.

In this work, we assume an unweighted, directed graph representation. Note that we can extend our representation to weighted graphs; we describe this in Section 7. Next, we describe the different encoding schemes.

4.1 Individual Encodings

As a baseline and for our change point detection approach, we first present two encodings that encode each snapshot of a graph sequence with a blockmodel.

4.1.1 Individual Snapshot Encoding

Let $\mathcal{C}^t$ denotes the set of positions (blockmodel) for snapshot G^t. Then the total encoding cost is:

$$C_{\texttt{Ind}}(< G^{1,T} >, \{\mathcal{C}^1, \ldots \mathcal{C}^T\}) = C(n) + \sum_{t=1}^{T} C(\mathcal{C}^t) + C(G^t|\mathcal{C}^t)$$

where $C(n)$ is the cost to send the number of vertices (needed to decode the sizes of the positions), $C(\mathcal{C}^t)$ is the cost to encode the positions, and $C(G^t|\mathcal{C}^t)$ is the cost to encode the snapshot G^t using $\mathcal{C}^t$.

Next, we describe the position description cost $C(\mathcal{C}^t)$. Let the random variable $\Psi(\mathcal{C})$ represent the distribution of the position memberships of $\mathcal{C}$; i.e., $p(\Psi(\mathcal{C}) = i) = \frac{|C_i|}{n}$, where $C_i \in \mathcal{C}$. Let H(X) denote the entropy of random variable X. From information theory [7], we know we can design lossless codes that uses $H(\Psi(\mathcal{C}^t))$ bits, on average, to encode the position of a vertex, and $n * H(\Psi(\mathcal{C}^t))$ to encode the positions of all vertices. In order to be able to recover the memberships fully, we also need the number of positions, which can be encoded as an integer [7] with cost $C(|\mathcal{C}^t|)$. Then the cost to send the position information is : $C(\mathcal{C}^t) = C(|\mathcal{C}^t|) + n * \mathrm{H}(\Psi(\mathcal{C}^t))$.

Next, we explain how to compute $C(G^t|\mathcal{C}^t)$. Given a blockmodel, the snapshot can be described as a sequence of its blocks[1].

[1]In row or column order - we use row order

$$C(G^t|\mathcal{C}^t) = \sum_{C_i \in \mathcal{C}^t} \sum_{C_j \in \mathcal{C}^t} C(\mathbf{A}^t(C_i, C_j))$$

We can treat each timesliced block as a vector, and encode it using single symbol encoding. Let $m_1(\mathbf{A}^t(C_i, C_j))$ denote the number of 1's in the block $\mathbf{A}^t(C_i, C_j)$. Let the random variable $\Phi(\mathbf{A}^t(C_i, C_j))$ represent the distribution of 0's and 1's in the block $\mathbf{A}^t(C_i, C_j)$; i.e, $p(\Phi(\mathbf{A}^t(C_i, C_j)) = 1) = \frac{m_1(\mathbf{A}^t(C_i,C_j))}{|C_i|*|C_j|}$. Then the cost to send one block is:

$$C(\mathbf{A}^t(C_i, C_j)) = C(m_1(\mathbf{A}^t(C_i, C_j))) + |C_i| * |C_j| * H(\Phi(\mathbf{A}^t(C_i, C_j)))$$

Again, we need the number of edges (1's) in the block, sent with cost $C(m_1(\mathbf{A}^t(C_i, C_j)))$, in order to fully reconstruct the edges in the block.

4.1.2 *Smoothed Individual Encoding*

This model is based on ideas from evolutionary clustering, to smooth out position changes between two consecutive snapshots. Similar to the individual snapshot encoding, we can write the overall encoding cost as:

$$C_{\text{sInd}}(< G^{1,T} >, \{\mathcal{C}^1, \ldots \mathcal{C}^T\}) = C(n) + C(\mathcal{C}^1) + \sum_{t=2}^{T} C(\mathcal{C}^{t-1}|\mathcal{C}^t) + C(G^t|\mathcal{C}^t)$$

The only term that is different from the individual snapshot encoding is $C(\mathcal{C}^{t-1}|\mathcal{C}^t)$, which is the encoding cost of describing the changes in position between $\mathcal{C}^t$ and $\mathcal{C}^{t-1}$. This can be encoded using a membership difference vector of length n, where we can encode each symbol with an average cost of $H(\Psi(\mathcal{C}^t) \mid \Psi(\mathcal{C}^{t-1}))$ bits:

$$C(\mathcal{C}^{t-1}|\mathcal{C}^t) = C(|\mathcal{C}^t|) + n * H(\Psi(\mathcal{C}^t)|\Psi(\mathcal{C}^{t-1}))$$

4.2 Subsequence Encodings

These encodings are used to describe blockmodels that span more than one snapshot and measure how close they are to being block preserving and position preserving equivalent. The graph sequence is represented as a series of continuous subsequences, where a single blockmodel holds for each subsequence.

4.2.1 *Block Preserving Encoding*

This encoding scheme is designed to find block preserving equivalent blockmodels. Let the subsequence be delimited by the timing indices $t_1, t_2, \ldots, t_L$, where $t_1 < t_2, \ldots, < t_L$ (with $t_1 = 1$ and $t_L = T$) and L is the number of subsequences up to time index T. Then the graph sequence $<G^{1,T}>$ is divided into a series of subsequences, $< G^{t_1,t_2} > \cdot < G^{t_2,t_3} > \ldots < G^{t_{L-1},t_L} >$. Let $\mathcal{C}^s$ represent the set of positions for the subsequence $< G^{t_s,t_{s+1}} >$, $1 \le s \le T-1$. The the overall encoding cost is:

$$C(< G^{1,T} >, \{\mathcal{C}^1, \ldots \mathcal{C}^L\}) = C(n) + \sum_{s=1}^{L} C(t_{s+1} - t_s) + C(\mathcal{C}^s) + C(< G^{t_s,t_{s+1}} > |\mathcal{C}^s)$$

Most of the cost terms are the same as the individual encodings, apart from $C(t_{s+1} - t_s)$, which is the cost to encode the length of the subsequence $<G^{t_s,t_{s+1}}>$, and the block encoding cost $C(< G^{t_s,t_{s+1}} > |\mathcal{C}^s)$. Let $\mathbf{A}^{t_s,t_e}(C_i, C_j)$ denote the multi-time slices of the adjacencies of the snapshots G^{t_s} to G^{t_e}, between the positions C_i and C_j. Then the graph description cost is:

$$C(< G^{t_s,t_{s+1}} > |\mathcal{C}^s) = \sum_{C_i \in \mathcal{C}^s} \sum_{C_j \in \mathcal{C}^s} C(\mathbf{A}^{t_s,t_{s+1}}(C_i, C_j))$$

Each multi-time sliced block is encoded as one string. An useful way to think of this is that we unroll each block of each snapshot into a string. The strings are concatenated and then encoded as a single string. The cost is:

$$C(\mathbf{A}^{t_s,t_{s+1}}(C_i, C_j)) = C(m_1(\mathbf{A}^{t_s,t_{s+1}}(C_i, C_j))) + |C_i| * |C_j| * H(\Phi(\mathbf{A}^{t_s,t_{s+1}}(C_i, C_j)))$$

When $C(< G^{t_s,t_{s+1}} > |\mathcal{C}^s)$ is minimal $(H(\Phi(\mathbf{A}^{t_s,t_{s+1}}(C_i, C_j))) = 0, \forall C_i, C_j \in \mathcal{C}^s)$, then the multi-sliced blocks must be all 0s or all 1s. This means the two conditions of Lemma 1 are satisfied, which means the decomposition is block preserving equivalent. Therefore this encoding is a measure of block preserving equivalence.

4.2.2 *Position Preserving Encoding*

This encoding implements the position preserving equivalence. The overall encoding cost formulation is similar to the block preserving encoding, except for how the multi-time block slices are encoded:

$$C(\mathbf{A}^{t_s,t_{s+1}}(C_i, C_j)) = \sum_{t=t_s}^{t_{s+1}} \Big(|C_i| * |C_j| * H(\mathbf{A}^t(C_i, C_j)) + C(m_1(\mathbf{A}^t(C_i, C_j))) \Big)$$

The blocks are encoded per snapshot. Again, $C(\mathbf{A}^{t_s,t_{s+1}}(C_i, C_j))$ is minimal when $H(\mathbf{A}^t(C_i, C_j)) = 0$, which occurs when the position preserving condition of Lemma 2 is true, hence this encoding is a measure of position preserving equivalence.

5. FINDING OPTIMAL BLOCKMODELS

In this section, we describe our common approach to optimising the encodings and finding optimal blockmodels. We use a similar approach to [15] to optimise our encodings over subsequences, but we introduce a change point detection approach to segmenting the graph sequence, which we will show is more accurate and faster than the one lookahead approach of Graphscope.

Given a subsequence segment, the greedy algorithm approach used to optimise the positions will iteratively try to merge positions, split them and move vertices between positions to minimise the encoding cost.

5.1 Determining the Optimal Segments

Graphscope determines a change point by comparing the encoding costs of extending the existing, single model against the costs of two models, the existing model up to the change point and a new model for describing the rest of the sequence (the lookahead subsequence). Graphscope uses a lookahead of 1 snapshot, and as our results show, it can sometimes miss change points. Once a change point is missed, the objective generally favours extending the current subsequence,

Algorithm 1 Main procedure in SeqiBloc.

Input: New snapshot G^t, **Current subsequence** $<G^{ts,te}>$, **prev. blockmodel** $\mathcal{C}^{t-1}$
Output: $\mathcal{C}^{ts}$
// Compute partitioning on single snapshot
$\mathcal{C}^t$ = updatePos(G^t)
deltaCost = $M(\mathcal{C}^t, \mathcal{C}^{t-1})$
if isChangePoint(deltaCost) **then**
    $\mathcal{C}^{ts}$ = updatePos($<G^{ts,t}>$)
end if
updateTimeSeries(deltaCost)

because the lookahead is too short. Hence, a greater lookahead is needed, but there is no principled and inexpensive way to determine the appropriate lookahead, and the optimal lookhead is likely to change across time.

Instead, we propose a simple change point detection approach (see Algorithm 1 for an overview). First, note that a new blockmodel should only be induced when there is a change point and the existing one is no longer accurate for describing the new snapshots. This means that the optimal blockmodel over the new snapshots varies significantly from the existing blockmodel. Conversely, when there is no change point and only (uniformly) random noise, then the likelihood of dense or sparse sub-blocks appearing by chance is low and therefore the blockmodel over the new snapshots is likely to be similar to the existing blockmodel. Therefore, if we found the best blockmodels for each snapshot (using one of the individual encodings), and monitored the differences between consecutive blockmodels (see next section), then the actual change points are likely to occur when there are significant spikes in the difference, which can be detected using traditional change point detection methods.

5.1.1 Blockmodel Difference Measures

In this subsection, we describe the two measures we used to determine the change points in the graph streams.

To detect the change points of position preserving blockmodels, we monitor for differences in the positions of two time-adjacent blockmodels. Existing measures from external clustering validation can be used to measure this position difference. We found that the Variation of Information (VI) measure [13] performed well for this task. We denote this change point approach with the VI measure as *pos-cp*.

To detect change points in block preserving blockmodels, we know from Lemma 1 that we need to monitor for changes in the positions and the block densities. There are no measures that satisfy our requirements; the closest are spatially aware cluster comparison techniques [6], but these assume the entities are points embedded in a Euclidean space, which is generally non-trivial to map from graphs.

Hence, we propose a measure, called BMDD that compares the differences in densities across the blocks of the two blockmodels. We cannot directly compare blocks, because the positions and blocks between two models might not align. Instead, we compute the expected difference in densities across the blocks of the two models. Recall that $\Psi(\mathcal{C})$ is the random variable of the position memberships and event space of $\mathcal{C}$. Let $d()$ denote a distance between densities (we will elaborate shortly) and the probability $p(\Psi(\mathcal{C}^t) = i, \Psi(\mathcal{C}^t) = j, \Psi(\mathcal{C}^{t-1}) = x, \Psi(\mathcal{C}^{t-1}) = y)$ be simplified to $p(i, j, x, y)$. Then BMDD is defined as

$$\begin{aligned} & BMDD(\mathcal{C}^t, \mathcal{C}^{t-1}) \\ = & \sum_{r1,c1,r2,c2} p(r1, c1, r2, c2) d(\mathbf{A}^t(C_{r1}, C_{c1}), \mathbf{A}^{t-1}(C_{r2}, C_{c2})) \\ = & \sum_{r1,c1,r2,c2} p(r1, r2) p(c1, c2) d(\mathbf{A}^t(C_{r1}, C_{c1}), \mathbf{A}^{t-1}(C_{r2}, C_{c2})) \end{aligned}$$

where $p(r1, r2) = \frac{|C_{r1} \cap C_{r2}|}{n}$ and $p(c1, c2) = \frac{|C_{c1} \cap C_{c2}|}{n}$. BMDD effectively weighs the difference between block densities based on the amount of overlap the two blocks have.

For the density distance dd, we used the absolute difference of their densities $d(\mathbf{A}^t(C_{r1}, C_{c1}), \mathbf{A}^{t-1}(C_{r2}, C_{c2})) = |\mathbf{A}^t(C_{r1}, C_{c1}) - \mathbf{A}^{t-1}(C_{r2}, C_{c2})|$, which we found to work well. We denote this change point approach with the BMDD measure as *pos-cp*.

5.1.2 Change Point Detection Approaches

The change point we seek is a large, significant spike. There are many different change point measures we can use (our framework can accommodate any that can detect spikes), but we found the basic control chart measure [3] worked well. The control chat measure tracks the mean and standard deviation of our blockmodel difference measures, and flags a change point when the standard deviation is significantly ($\Delta * \sigma$, where Δ is the alarm threshold) above the mean. Because we do not make any assumptions on the underlying graph stream, we cannot use techniques like generalised likelihood tests to quantify significance. Hence, the alarm threshold is the only parameter in our approach. We found $\Delta = 0.5$ works well for many datasets, and this can be used as the default value.

6. EVALUATION

In this section, we will show that our change point detection based algorithms, *pos-cp* and *pos-cp*, are more accurate and efficient than the corresponding Graphscope algorithms at detecting change points and learning new blockmodels. In addition, we demonstrate the difference between the block and position preserving formulations. We use a combination of synthetic data and three real datasets.

We evaluate against two baseline Graphscope algorithms, *block-gs* and *pos-gs*. *block-gs* and *pos-gs* use the one-lookahead approach of Graphscope to optimise the block preserving and position preserving encodings respectively.

6.1 Synthetic Evaluation

To construct the synthetic graphs, we use a static stochastic blockmodel algorithm [2] to generate initial static blockmodels of 250 vertices, 10 uniformly sized positions, 30% of blocks having 75% density and rest having 5% density. We then introduced change points at 10 uniformly random locations, where we change the underlying blockmodel by moving vertices between positions, flipping the densities of some blocks (e.g., 0.75 to 0.25) or adding or deleting a position. Each subsequence (of 100 snapshots) is then generated from a static blockmodel, with some uniformly distributed noise (flipping of edges) added to the snapshots between the change points. For each parameter setting, we generated three blockmodels, and from each, three subsequences, and ran each of the algorithms three times, for a total of 27 runs per algorithm for each dataset[2] setting.

[2]Available at `http://eng.unimelb.edu.au/jeffreyc/data`

Algor.	Precision	Recall	VI / sshot
pos-cp	1.000(0.000)	0.733(0.267)	4.101(1.931)
pos-cp	0.626(0.000)	1.000(0.000)	3.990(1.992)
block-gs	0.500(0.000)	0.933(0.047)	4.956(0.936)
pos-gs	0.000(0.000)	0.000(0.000)	5.035(0.843)

(a) Results for datasets with 5% noise, and an average of 1 position addition/deletion and 5% position membership changes at the change points.

Algor.	Precision	Recall	VI / sshot
pos-cp	0.222(0.416)	0.033(0.067)	5.550(0.357)
pos-cp	0.717(0.081	0.989(0.031)	5.529(0.442)
block-gs	0.500(0.000)	0.900(0.000)	5.677(0.242)
pos-gs	0.000(0.000)	0.000(0.000)	5.689(0.148)

(b) Results for datasets with 5% noise, and no position additions/deletions and 5% block density flips at the change points.

Algor.	Precision	Recall	VI / sshot
pos-cp	1.000(0.000)	1.000(0.000)	5.663(0.227)
pos-cp	0.627(0.023)	1.000(0.000)	5.739(0.257)
block-gs	0.500(0.000)	0.900(0.082)	5.794(0.184)
pos-gs	0.000(0.000)	0.000(0.000)	5.792(0.190)

(c) Results for datasets with 5% noise, and no position additions/deletions and 5% position membership changes at the change points.

Table 2: Segmenting results for generated datasets. Results are reported as average (std. deviation).

6.1.1 Measures

To evaluate the ability of the algorithms to detect the introduced change points, we use the precision and recall measures. Let I^{true} and I^{act} denote the set of true and detected change points respectively. Then precision $= \frac{|I^{true} \cap I^{act}|}{|I^{act}|}$ and recall $= \frac{|I^{true} \cap I^{act}|}{|I^{true}|}$. We measure how similar the detected and generated blockmodels are by comparing their sets of positions across the snapshots and averaging the results. We use the average variation of information (VI) per snapshot as our comparison measure. Lower VI means more similar sets of positions. Although the mean of the total objective values for the change point algorithms are 20–30% lower than the corresponding Graphscope variants, we do not report these values because we found they vary greatly between the datasets (large variance) and hence are inconclusive for our analysis.

6.1.2 Results

In this subsection, we evaluate the segmenting accuracy of SeqiBloc. We first evaluate its ability to locate the introduced change points, varying the amount of noise and the size of the blockmodel shift at the change points.

We first changed the amount of noise introduced from 1% of edges to 10% of edges. We found that the algorithms were mostly invariant to the amount of noise introduced, hence we only show one of the results (5% of edges changed) in Table 2a. The results indicate that when *pos-cp* detects a change, it is always correct in these tests (100% precision), but it can sometimes miss some change points (73% recall). On the other hand, *pos-cp* is able to detect all the introduced changed points (100% recall), but is sometimes oversensitive and makes a false detection (62.6% precision). *block-gs* has less precision and recall than both our algorithms, indicating it is overly sensitive due to its greedy nature. *pos-gs* cannot detect any change points at all. The variation of information values indicate that both *pos-cp* and *pos-cp* obtained blockmodels that are significantly closer to the true blockmodels than the Graphscope variants.

Next, we show the results of experiments where we only change the block densities (Table 2b) and the position memberships (Table 2c). The first test should favour *pos-cp*, as *pos-cp* and its position-preserving formulation generally cannot detect change points with block densities changes only. The results in Table 2b confirm this. The second test should favour *pos-cp*, as it only involves position change and our measure BMDD monitors for a change in position and density. Again, the results confirm this. Note that for both tests, *pos-gs* could not detect any change points, and when comparing the block-preserving algorithms, *block-gs* is always less accurate than the equivalent *pos-cp*.

The synthetic results show that the change point algorithms are more accurate than their Graphscope counterparts.

Dataset	Vert. #	Seq. Length	Resolution
Reality Mining	97	290	day
Enron	141	209	week
BGP	30k	13	2 days

Table 3: Real datasets statistics.

6.2 Real Data Evaluation

In this subsection, we demonstrate the blockmodels and segmenting produced by the different formulations for the MIT reality mining proximity graphs [10], the Enron email graph [8] and the BGP Internet routing network [12]. Their statistics are described in Table 3.

The Reality Mining graph measures the proximity of users in a laboratory environment over a period of a few months. Each vertex in the graph represents a user, and an undirected edge represents proximity. The Enron email graph tracks the email communications among Enron employees[3]. Each vertex in the Enron graph represents a person, and a directed edge represents sending at least one email from the person represented by the source vertex to the person representing the target vertex. Finally, the BGP Internet routing graph represents the connectivity among organisations in the Internet. A vertex represents an organisation, and an undirected edge represents connectivity between them. The time spanned by each snapshot of the Reality Mining, Enron and BGP graphs are one day, one week and two days respectively. The datasets span a variety of data types, with the MIT and Enron data being unstable and noisy in general and the BGP data being larger and relatively stable.

6.2.1 Reality Mining

To provide an illustration of the blockmodels found, we first show a 10 day graph sequence of the proximity network, with each snapshot spanning a day. We show the results from the *pos-cp*, *pos-cp* and *block-gs* algorithms (Figures 3a to 3c). Each figure shows the adjacency matrix of each snapshot, with the red dotted lines as delimiters of the positions/blocks. Time runs top to bottom, left to right. We used a basic matching algorithm to align the blocks and vertices as best we can, but vertices of different snapshots that

[3]We use the version of dataset that only tracks the internal communications within Enron

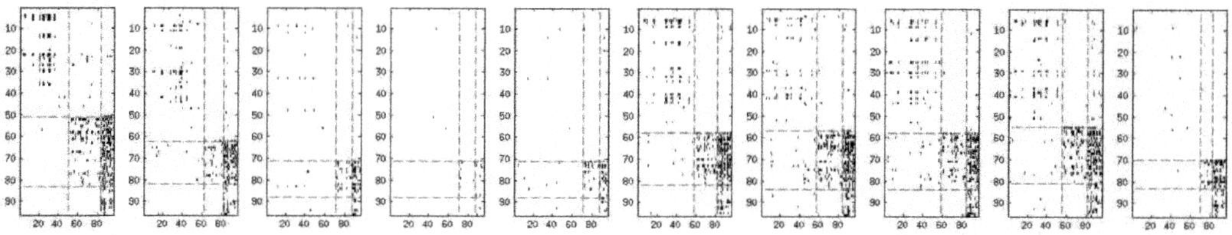

(a) Blockmodels obtained using *pos-cp*.

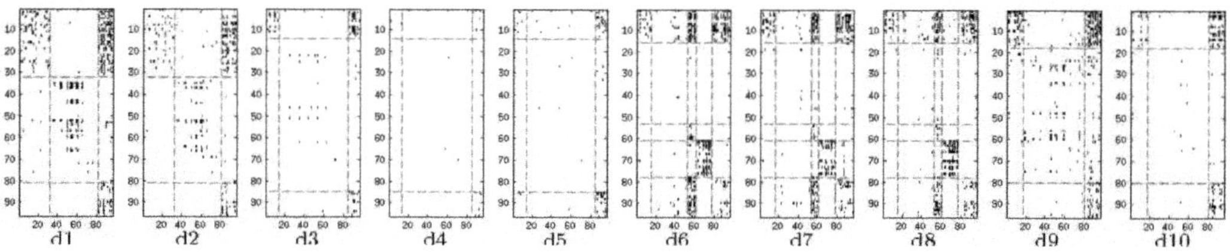

(b) Blockmodels obtained using *pos-cp*.

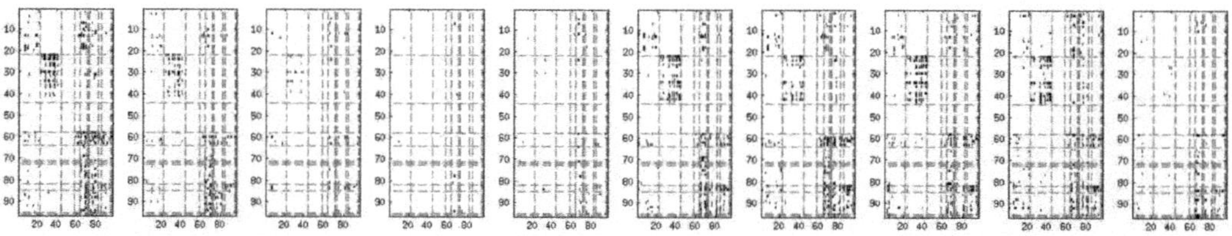

(c) Blockmodels obtained using *block-gs*.

Figure 3: Adjacency matrices of a 10 day graph sequence extracted from the Enron graph. Red dotted lines delimit blockmodel decompositions of each snapshot.

have the same labels in the figures might not correspond to the same actual vertex.

As the Figure 3c shows, *block-gs* fragments very easily. Once the number of positions increases, the greedy algorithm is unable to recover and all subsequent parts of the graph sequence are lumped into one blockmodel.

Now consider the blockmodels obtained from *pos-cp* and *pos-cp* (Figures 3a and 3b respectively). They clearly reflect the weekday (5 days of high levels of proximity) and weekends (almost no proxmity detected). Because the position preserving equivalence is easier to satisfy, *pos-cp* is generally able to find blockmodels of longer lengths (e.g. d6–d9 in Figure 3b vs. individual blockmodels over the same period in Figure 3a). In contrast, the block preserving equivalence is less likely to fragment (compare the subsequence d1–d8). Both equivalences are able to produce blockmodels that appear to be visually reasonable.

To analyse the amount of fragmentation and the length of segments obtained, we analysed the number of segments, their average length and the number of positions found over time. The results are in Table 4a and Figure 4a, which shows the number of positions found across time.

The results in Table 4a and Figure 4a confirm that *block-gs* cannot segment the proximity graph sequence and only managed two fragmented segments. *pos-cp*, being more strict than *pos-cp*, had more segments, but the larger standard deviation of segment lengths show that they vary more in length than ones obtained from *pos-cp*. The reason for this is that *pos-cp* tends to be more sensitive to changes (recall the synthetic results), hence more likely to segment during

Algor.	Seg. #	Seg. len.	Run time	Obj. Val.
pos-cp	125	2.33 (4.51)	5.316s	212572
pos-cp	97	3.0 (3.09)	8.873s	188077
block-gs	2	146 (89)	52.384s	348253

(a) Reality Mining Results.

Algor.	Seg. #	Seg. len.	Run time	Obj. Val.
pos-cp	90	2.32 (4.96)	5.036s	155959
pos-cp	59	3.54 (4.75)	7.732s	137817
block-gs	1	209 (0.0)	704.178s	286972

(b) Enron Results.

Table 4: Segmenting results for Reality Mining and Enron. Segment length results are reported as average (standard deviation).

fluctuating periods than *pos-cp*. In addition, both change point models used much less positions to describe the data than *block-gs*, even after we capped the maximum number of positions to 51. The lower objective value of *pos-cp* over *block-gs* suggest that the evolving blockmodels found by *pos-cp* are a better fit. The running time of *block-gs* is much slower than the other two algorithms, because the optimising algorithm's complexity scales at least quadratically with the number of positions.

6.2.2 *Enron*

We repeat the previous analysis to evaluate the segmenting quality on the Enron data. Consider Table 4b and Figure 4b. They show that *block-gs* is unable to segment the stream at all, producing one segment for the whole stream.

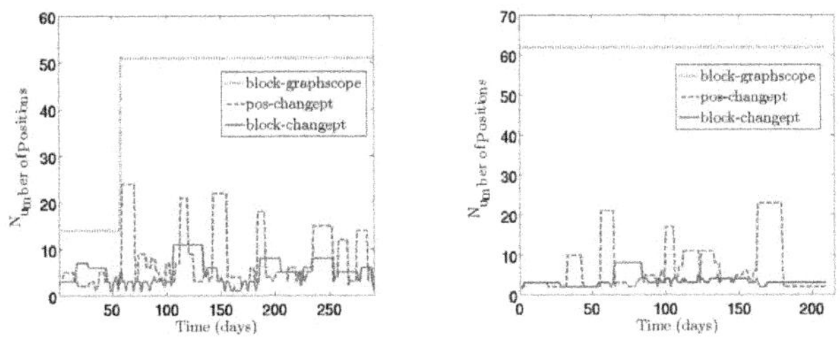

(a) Reality Mining. (b) Enron.

Figure 4: Plots of the number of partitions vs. time for the Reality Mining and Enron datasets.

This caused the single blockmodel to fragment into many positions and causing the run time to grow to 700 seconds. In contrast, both *pos-cp* and *pos-cp* were able to segment the sequence into a number of segments, with *pos-cp* producing more segments again. Again, it shows *block-gs* fragmenting and not being able to produce meaningful blockmodel decompositions, *pos-cp* having more positions in general while *pos-cp* being the most stable of the three, in terms of number of positions.

6.2.3 BGP

The BGP data is largely stable, and for the period we analysed over November 2011, there was no known outages. For both *pos-cp* and *pos-cp* we correctly found one segment, with the set of positions found illustrated in Figure 1. The running time was several hours, which is about 10-100 times more scalable than state of the art blockmodelling algorithms [17].

In summary, both *pos-cp* and *pos-cp* can mine blockmodels that are a balance between accuracy (one blockmodel per snapshot) and simplicity (one blockmodel for the whole sequence). We found weekday/weekend structure in the Reality Mining data, a stable hierarchical structure for the BGP graph, and showed that the change point formulations in SeqiBloc performed well in synthetic datasets and do not fragment like Graphscope does.

7. CONCLUSION

In conclusion, we have presented a novel framework, SeqiBloc, to decompose a dynamic graph into a series of multi-snapshot blockmodels that summarises the evolving structural patterns. In this framework, we have introduced two new definitions of dynamic structural equivalence and showed what this means in terms of adjacency matrix structure and blockmodelling. Based on these definitions, we have formulated four different information theoretic encodings that correspond to the new equivalence definitions and provide an intuitive tradeoff between the number of positions in a blockmodel, the time it spans and how well it fits the subsequence spanned. We then introduced a change point detection approach with a new blockmodel comparison measure, BMDD, to find the appropriate length of these blockmodels. Using synthetic and real datasets like the Reality Mining, Enron and BGP dynamic graphs, we showed our approach can find relevant segments and discover interesting and intuitive blockmodels across time.

For future work, it will be interesting to mine for frequent multi-snapshot blockmodels. For example, in the Reality Mining results, we saw there were clear weekday and weekend structural patterns. If we can group the similar weekend and weekday behaviours (in terms of blockmodels), then we can find normal patterns of interactions and detect outliers.

Another possible future direction is to extend the framework to weighted blockmodels. There are no standard definitions of weighted equivalences and blockmodels, hence there is a need to find intuitive definitions of weighted equivalences.

8. REFERENCES

[1] C. C. Aggarwal, Y. Zhao, and P. S. Yu. On Clustering Graph Streams. In *Proceedings of SDM*, 2010.

[2] E. M. Airoldi, D. M. Blei, S. E. Fienberg, and E. P. Xing. Mixed membership stochastic blockmodels. *J. of Machine Learning Research*, 9, June 2008.

[3] B. Brodsky and B. Darkhovsky. *Nonparametric Methods in Change Point Problems*. Springer, 1993.

[4] D. Chakrabarti, R. Kumar, and A. Tomkins. Evolutionary clustering. In *Proceedings of KDD*, 2006.

[5] Y. Chi, X. Song, D. Zhou, K. Hino, and B. L. Tseng. Evolutionary spectral clustering by incorporating temporal smoothness. In *Proceedings of KDD*, 2007.

[6] M. Coen, H. Ansari, and N. Fillmore. Comparing clusterings in space. In *Proceedings of ICML*, 2010.

[7] T. Cover and J. Thomas. *Elements of Information Theory*. Wiley-Interscience, 2006.

[8] J. Diesner, T. Frantz, and K. Carley. Communication Networks from the Enron Email Corpus It's Always About the People. Enron is no Different. *Comp. & Math. Org. Theory*, 11(3), 2005.

[9] T. N. Dinh, I. Shin, N. K. Thai, M. T. Thai, and T. Znati. *A General Approach for Modules Identification in Evolving Networks*. Springer, 2010.

[10] N. Eagle and A. (Sandy) Pentland. Reality mining: sensing complex social systems. *Personal Ubiquitous Comput.*, 10, March 2006.

[11] D. Greene, D. Doyle, and P. Cunningham. Tracking the Evolution of Communities in Dynamic Social Networks. In *Proceedings of ASONAM*, 2010.

[12] Y. Hyun, B. Huffaker, D. Andersen, E. Aben, M. Luckie, kc claffy, and C. Shannon. The IPv4 Routed /24 AS Links Dataset - November 2011.

[13] M. Meila. Comparing clusterings by the variation of information. In *Proceedings of the 16th Annual Conference on Learning Theory and 7th Kernel Workshop*, page 173. Springer Verlag, 2003.

[14] J. Rissanen. Modeling by shortest data description. *Automatica*, 14, 1978.

[15] J. Sun, C. Faloutsos, S. Papadimitriou, and P. S. Yu. Graphscope: parameter-free mining of large time-evolving graphs. In *Proceedings of KDD*, 2007.

[16] S. Wasserman and K. Faust. *Social Network Analysis: Methods and Applications*. Cambridge Uni. Pr., 1994.

[17] E. P. Xing, W. Fu, and L. Song. A State-Space Mixed Membership Blockmodel for Dynamic Network Tomography. *Annals of Applied Statistics*, 4(2), 2010.

[18] T. Yang, Y. Chi, S. Zhu, Y. Gong, and R. Jin. Detecting communities and their evolutions in dynamic social networks - a Bayesian approach. *Machine Learning*, 82, 2011.

USpan: An Efficient Algorithm for Mining High Utility Sequential Patterns

Junfu Yin
Advanced Analytics Institute
University of Technology,
Sydney, Australia
junfu.yin@student.uts.edu.au

Zhigang Zheng
Advanced Analytics Institute
University of Technology,
Sydney, Australia
zgzheng@it.uts.edu.au

Longbing Cao*
Advanced Analytics Institute
University of Technology,
Sydney, Australia
longbing.cao@uts.edu.au

ABSTRACT

Sequential pattern mining plays an important role in many applications, such as bioinformatics and consumer behavior analysis. However, the classic frequency-based framework often leads to many patterns being identified, most of which are not informative enough for business decision-making. In frequent pattern mining, a recent effort has been to incorporate *utility* into the pattern selection framework, so that high utility (frequent or infrequent) patterns are mined which address typical business concerns such as dollar value associated with each pattern. In this paper, we incorporate utility into sequential pattern mining, and a generic framework for high utility sequence mining is defined. An efficient algorithm, USpan, is presented to mine for high utility sequential patterns. In USpan, we introduce the lexicographic quantitative sequence tree to extract the complete set of high utility sequences and design concatenation mechanisms for calculating the utility of a node and its children with two effective pruning strategies. Substantial experiments on both synthetic and real datasets show that USpan efficiently identifies high utility sequences from large scale data with very low minimum utility.

Categories and Subject Descriptors

H.2.8 [**Database Applications**]: Data mining

General Terms

Algorithms

Keywords

High utility sequential pattern mining, Sequential pattern mining

*Author for correspondence.

KDD'12, August 12–16, 2012, Beijing, China.

1. INTRODUCTION

Sequential pattern mining has emerged as an important topic in data mining. It has proven to be very essential for handling order-based critical business problems, such as behavior analysis, gene analysis in bioinformatics and weblog mining. For example, sequence analysis is widely employed in DNA and protein to discover interesting structures and functions of molecular or DNA sequences. The selection of interesting sequences is generally based on the frequency/support framework: sequences of high frequency are treated as significant. Under this framework, the *downward closure property* (also known as *Apriori property*) [1] plays a fundamental role for varieties of algorithms designed to search for frequent sequential patterns [10, 14, 5].

In practice, many patterns are identified by frequent sequential pattern mining algorithms. Most of them may not be informative to business decision-making, since they do not show the business value and impact. In some cases, such as fraud detection, some truly interesting sequences may be filtered because of their low frequencies. For example, in retail business, selling a car generally leads to much higher profit than selling a bottle of milk, while the frequency of cars sold is much lower than that of milk. In online banking fraud detection, the transfer of a large amount of money to an unauthorized overseas account may appear once in over one million transactions, yet it has a substantial business impact. Such problems cannot be tackled by the frequency/support framework.

This brings about an interesting question: how to mine sequential patterns of business interest? In the related area, *utility* is introduced into frequent pattern mining to mine for patterns of high utility by considering the quality (such as profit) of itemsets. This has led to *high utility pattern mining* [13], which selects interesting patterns based on minimum utility rather than minimum support. Let us use a toy example to illustrate. Table 1 shows the items and their respective weights or profit (quality) appearing in an online retail store. Table 2 collects several shopping sequences with quantities; each transaction in the sequence consists of one to multiple items, and each item is associated with a quantity showing how many of this item were purchased. For instance, the first sequence $(e,5)[(c,2)(f,1)](b,2)$ shows three itemsets $(e,5)$, $[(c,2)\ (f,1)]$ and $(b,2)$, and the quantity purchased of item, e.g. the quantity of e is 5. Following the high utility pattern mining concept, a possible calculation of utility of an itemset is to consider its total profit.

Table 1: Quality Table

item	a	b	c	d	e	f
weight/quality	2	5	4	3	1	1

Table 2: Quantitative Sequence Database

sid	q-sequence
1	$\langle(e,5)[(c,2)(f,1)](b,2)\rangle$
2	$\langle[(a,2)(e,6)][(a,1)(b,1)(c,2)][(a,2)(d,3)(e,3)]\rangle$
3	$\langle(c,1)[(a,6)(d,3)(e,2)]\rangle$
4	$\langle[(b,2)(e,2)][(a,7)(d,3)][(a,4)(b,1)(e,2)]\rangle$
5	$\langle[(b,2)(e,3)][(a,6)(e,3)][(a,2)(b,1)]\rangle$

Accordingly, the utility of a single item can be defined as its purchased quantity times its profit. The utility of an itemset is the sum of the utilities of all its items. Since each item in a sequence may have multiple utility values, the utility of a sequence may have multiple values. For instance, the utility of $\langle ea\rangle$ in sequence 2 is $\{(6\times 1+1\times 2), (6\times 1+2\times 2)\}=\{8,10\}$. The utility of $\langle ea\rangle$ in the database is $\{\{\},\{8,10\},\{\},\{16,10\},\{15,7\}\}$. We select the highest utility in each sequence and add them together to represent the maximum utility of the sequence in a given sequence database. The maximum utility of $\langle ea\rangle$ is $10+16+15=41$. A sequence is of high utility only if its utility is no less than a user-specified *minimum utility*. Following the high utility pattern mining approach, our goal is to mine for highly profitable sequential purchasing; the identified shopping patterns are more informative for retailers in determining their marketing strategy.

High utility sequential pattern mining is substantially different and much more challenging than high utility itemset mining. If the order between itemsets is considered, e.g. $(e,5)$, $[(c,2)(f,1)]$ and $(b,2)$ in record $sid=1$ occurring sequentially, it becomes the problem of mining high utility sequential patterns. This is substantially different and much more challenging than mining frequent sequences and high utility itemsets. First, as with high utility itemset mining, the downward closure property does not hold in utility-based sequence mining. This means that most of the existing algorithms cannot be directly transferred, e.g. from frequent sequential pattern mining to high utility sequential pattern mining. Second, compared to high utility itemset mining, utility-based sequence analysis faces the critical combinational explosion and computational complexity caused by sequencing between sequential elements (itemsets).

So far, only very preliminary work has been proposed to mine for high utility sequential patterns [2, 4, 11]. It is in a very early stage since there is no systematic problem statement available. The proposed algorithms are rather specific and focus on simple situations, and still need substantial effective scanning and pruning strategies to improve performance. Basically, we can see that this is a new and promising area expecting much substantial exploration from problem definition to algorithm development and applications.

In this paper, we formalize the problem of high utility sequential pattern mining, and propose a generic framework and an efficient algorithm, USpan, to identify high utility sequences.

- We build the concept of sequence utility by considering the quality and quantity associated with each item in a sequence, and define the problem of mining high utility sequential patterns;
- A complete lexicographic quantitative sequence tree (LQS-tree) is used to construct utility-based sequences; two concatenation mechanisms I-Concatenation and S-Concatenation generate newly concatenated sequences;
- Two pruning methods, width and depth pruning, substantially reduce the search space in the LQS-tree;
- USpan traverses LQS-tree and outputs all the high utility sequential patterns.

Substantial experiments on both synthetic and real datasets show that the proposed framework and the USpan algorithm can efficiently identify high utility sequences from large scale data with very low minimum utility.

The paper is organized as follows. Section 2 reviews the related work. Section 3 proposes a sequence utility framework and defines the problem of mining high utility sequential patterns. Section 4 details the USpan algorithm. Experimental results and evaluation are presented in Section 5. Section 6 concludes the work.

2. RELATED WORK

2.1 Utility Itemset/Pattern Mining

Utility itemset mining, also generally called utility pattern mining, was first introduced in [13]. Every item in the itemsets is associated with an additional value, called internal utility which is the quantity (i.e. count) of the item. An external utility is attached to an item, showing its quality (e.g. price). With such a utility-based database, high utility itemsets (patterns) are mined, including those satisfying the minimum utility. Mining high utility itemsets is much more challenging than discovering frequent itemsets, because the fundamental downward closure property in frequent itemset mining does not hold in utility itemsets.

Several algorithms are available. UMining was proposed in 2004 for mining high utility patterns, but it cannot extract the complete set of them. A transaction-weighted downward closure property was introduced in [8], in which a two-phase algorithm was proposed with a pruning strategy, which makes it faster and more efficient than UMining. IHUP [3] maintains the high utility patterns in an incremental environment; since it avoids multiple scans of the database, its efficiency is far better than [8]. UP-Growth [12] also uses a tree structure, UP-Tree, to mine high utility patterns. Compared to IHUP, UP-Growth is more efficient, since it further reduces the number of promising patterns which cannot be pruned in IHUP.

The above algorithms can only handle utility itemsets, and do not involve the ordering relationships between items. The addition of ordering information in sequences makes it fundamentally different and much more challenging than mining utility itemsets.

2.2 Utility-based Sequential Pattern Mining

Frequent sequential pattern mining is a very popular topic [1, 9], with quite a few algorithms, such as SPADE [14], Prefixspan [10] and SPAM [5], proposed on the support/frequency framework. Algorithms for mining frequent sequences often result in many patterns being mined; most of them may not make sense to business, and those with frequencies lower than the given minimum support are filtered. This limits the actionability [6] of discovered frequent patterns.

The integration of utility into sequential pattern mining aims to solve the above problem and has only taken place very recently. In total, we found only three papers in the literature. UMSP [11] was designed for mining high utility mobile sequential patterns. Each itemset in a sequence is associated with a location identifier. With this feature, the utility of a mobile sequential pattern is also a single value. UMSP searches for patterns within a structure called MTS-Tree, which is efficient. However, due to the specific constraint on the sequences, this algorithm can only handle specific sequences with simple structures (single item in each sequence element, and a single utility per item).

In [2], an algorithm is specifically designed for utility web log sequences. The utility of a pattern can have multiple values, and the authors choose the utility with maximal values to represent a pattern's utility with two tree structures, i.e. UWAS-tree and IUWAS-tree. However, sequence elements with multiple items such as $[(c,2)(b,1)]$ cannot be supported, and the scenarios considered are rather simple, which limit the algorithm's applicability for complex sequences.

UI and US [4] extends traditional sequential pattern mining. A pattern utility is calculated in two ways. The utilities of sequences having only distinct occurrences are added together, while the highest occurrences are selected from sequences with multiple occurrences and used to calculate the utilities. However, the problem defintion in [4] is rather specific. No generic framework is proposed which has a clear process to transfer from sequential pattern mining to high utility sequence analysis.

It is obvious that mining high utility sequences is a very open and challenging area. Substantial research topics ranging from problem definition to algorithm development and applications are worthwhile to explore.

3. PROBLEM STATEMENT

3.1 Sequence Utility Framework

Let $\mathcal{I} = \{i_1, i_2, ..., i_n\}$ be a set of distinct *items*. Each item $i_k \in \mathcal{I}(1 \leqslant k \leqslant n)$ is associated with a *quality* (or *external utility*), denoted as $p(i_k)$, which may be the unit profit or price of i_k. A *quantitative item*, or *q-item*, is an ordered pair (i, q), where $i \in \mathcal{I}$ represents an item and q is a positive number representing the *quantity* or *internal utility* of i, e.g. the purchased number of i. A *quantitative itemset*, or *q-itemset*, consists of more than one q-item, which is denoted and defined as $l = [(i_{j_1}, q_1)(i_{j_2}, q_2)...(i_{j_{n'}}, q_{n'})]$, where (i_{j_k}, q_k) is a q-item for $1 \leqslant k \leqslant n'$. For brevity, the brackets are omitted if a q-itemset has only one q-item. Since the items in a set can be listed in any order, without loss of generality, we assume that q-items are listed in alphabetical order. A *quantitative sequence*, or *q-sequence*, is an ordered list of q-itemsets, which is denoted and defined as $s = \langle l_1 l_2 \ ... \ l_m\rangle$, where $l_k(1 \leqslant k \leqslant m)$ is a q-itemset. A *q-sequence database* $\mathcal{S}$ consists of sets of tuples $\langle sid, s\rangle$, where sid is a unique identifier of s, which is a q-sequence.

We use the examples in Table 1 and Table 2 to illustrate the concepts, to show items and corresponding qualities and q-sequences respectively. In $sid = 1$ q-sequence, $(e,5)$, $(c,2)$, $(f,1)$ and $(b,2)$ are q-items; $[(c,2)\ (f,1)]$ is a q-itemset with two q-items. For convenience, in this paper, "sequence" refers to ordered itemsets without quantities, i.e. the same meaning in sequence analysis; similarly, "item" and "itemset" do not involve quantity either. We use "q-" to name the object associated with quantity. We denote the $sid = 1$ q-sequence in Table 2 as s_1; other q-sequences are numbered accordingly. We use the following definitions to construct the sequence utility framework.

Definition 1. (Q-itemset Containing) Given two q-itemsets $l_a = [(i_{a_1}, q_{a_1})(i_{a_2}, q_{a_2})...(i_{a_n}, q_{a_n})]$ and $l_b = [(i_{b_1}, q_{b_1})(i_{b_2}, q_{b_2})...(i_{b_m}, q_{b_m})]$, l_b *contains* l_a iff there exist integers $1 \leq j_1 \leq j_2 \leq ... \leq j_n \leq m$ such that $i_{a_k} = i_{b_{j_k}} \wedge q_{a_k} = q_{b_{j_k}}$ for $1 \leq k \leq n$, denoted as $l_a \subseteq l_b$.

For example, q-itemset $[(a,4)(b,1)(e,2)]$ contains q-itemsets $(a,4)$, $[(a,4)(e,2)]$ and $[(a,4)(b,1)(e,2)]$, but does not contain $[(a,2)(e,2)]$ or $[(a,4)(c,1)]$.

Definition 2. (Q-sequence Containing) Given two q-sequences $s = \langle l_1, l_2, ..., l_n\rangle$ and $s' = \langle l'_1, l'_2, ..., l'_{n'}\rangle$, we say s' *contains* s or s is a *q-subsequence* of s' iff there exist integers $1 \leq j_1 \leq j_2 \leq ... \leq j_n \leq n'$ such that $l_k \subseteq l'_{j_k}$ for $1 \leq k \leq n$, denoted as $s \subseteq s'$.

For example, $\langle(b,2)\rangle$, $\langle[(b,2)(e,3)]\rangle$, $\langle[(b,2)][(e,3)](a,2)\rangle$ are the q-subsequences of q-sequence s_5 ($sid = 5$), while $\langle[(b,4)(e,3)]\rangle$ and $\langle(b,2)(b,6)\rangle$ are not.

Definition 3. (Length and Size) A (q-)sequence is called k-(q)sequence i.e. its length is k iff there are k (q-)items in the (q-)sequence; the size of a (q-)sequence is the number of (q-)itemsets in the (q-)sequence.

For example, $\langle(e,5)[(c,2)(f,1)](b,2)\rangle$ is a 4-q-sequence with size 3. $\langle ea\rangle$ is a 2-sequence with size 2.

Definition 4. (Matching) Given a q-sequence $s = \langle(s_1, q_1)(s_2, q_2)...(s_n, q_n)\rangle$ and a sequence $t = \langle t_1 t_2 ... t_m\rangle$. s matches t iff $n = m$ and $s_k = t_k$ for $1 \leq k \leq n$, denoted as $t \sim s$.

Due to the variety of quantities, two q-items can be different even though their items are the same. That is, there could be multiple q-subsequences of a q-sequence matching a given sequence. For example, if we want to find the q-subsequences in q-sequence s_4 ($sid = 4$) in Table 2 which matches the sequence $\langle b\rangle$, we obtain $\langle(b,2)\rangle$ in the first q-itemset and $\langle(b,1)\rangle$ in the third q-itemset. Sometimes, two q-items can be exactly the same and appear in one q-sequence. For example, q-item $(e,2)$ appears in both the first and third q-itemsets in q-sequence s_4.

Definition 5. (Q-item Utility) The *q-item utility* is the utility of a single q-item (i, q), denoted and defined as $u(i, q)$:

$$u(i,q) = f_{u_i}(p(i), q) \tag{1}$$

where f_{u_i} is the function for calculating q-item utility.

Definition 6. (Q-itemset Utility) Q-itemset utility is the utility of an q-itemset $l = [(i_1, q_1)\ (i_2, q_2)\ ...\ (i_n, q_n)]$, denoted and defined as $u(l)$:

$$u(l) = f_{u_{is}}(\bigcup_{j=1}^{n} u(i_j, q_j)) \tag{2}$$

$f_{u_{is}}$ is the function for calculating q-itemset utility.

Definition 7. (Q-sequence Utility) For a q-sequence $s = \langle l_1 l_2 ... l_m \rangle$, the q-sequence utility is $u(s)$:

$$u(s) = f_{u_s}(\bigcup_{j=1}^{m} u(l_j)) \quad (3)$$

where f_{u_s} is the utility function for q-sequences.

Definition 8. (Q-sequence Database Utility) For a utility-oriented sequence database $\mathcal{S} = \{\langle sid_1, s_1 \rangle, \langle sid_2, s_2 \rangle, ..., \langle sid_r, s_r \rangle\}$, the q-sequence database utility is $u(\mathcal{S})$:

$$u(\mathcal{S}) = f_{u_{db}}(\bigcup_{j=1}^{r} u(s_j)) \quad (4)$$

$f_{u_{db}}$ is the function for aggregating utilities in the database.

In the above, utility functions f_{u_i}, $f_{u_{is}}$, f_{u_s} and $f_{u_{db}}$ are all application-dependent, which may be determined through collaboration with domain experts.

Definition 9. (Sequence Utility) Given a utility-oriented database $\mathcal{S}$ and a sequence $t = \langle t_1 t_2 ... t_n \rangle$, t's utility in q-sequence $s = \langle l_1 l_2 ... l_m \rangle$ from $\mathcal{S}$ is denoted and defined as $v(t, s)$, which is a utility set:

$$v(t, s) = \bigcup_{s' \sim t \wedge s' \subseteq s} u(s') \quad (5)$$

The utility of t in $\mathcal{S}$ is denoted and defined as $v(t)$, which is also a utility set:

$$v(t) = \bigcup_{s \in \mathcal{S}} u(t, s) \quad (6)$$

For example, let sequence $t = \langle ea \rangle$, t's utility in the s_4 sequence in Table 2 is $v(t, s_4) = \{u(\langle (e, 2)(a, 7) \rangle), u(\langle (e, 2)(a, 4) \rangle)\} = \{16, 10\}$. t's utility in $\mathcal{S}$ is $v(t) = \{u(t, s_2), u(t, s_4), u(t, s_5)\} = \{\{8, 10\}, \{16, 10\}, \{15, 7\}\}$. This shows that there may be multiple utility values for a sequence within the utility sequence framework. For instance, $t = \langle ea \rangle$ has 2 utility values 16 and 10 for s_4. This is very different from frequent sequential pattern mining, in which there is only one support associated with a sequence.

3.2 High Utility Sequential Pattern Mining

In the utility Definitions 5-8, we did not provide the utility functions f_{u_i}, $f_{u_{is}}$, f_{u_s} and $f_{u_{db}}$. Here, we first specify them, and then state the problem of high utility sequential pattern mining. Although there may be various ways, we here define the above functions as

$$f_{u_i}(p(i), q) = p(i) \times q, \quad (7)$$

$$f_{u_{is}}(\bigcup_{j=1}^{n} u(i_j)) = \sum_{j=1}^{n} u(i_j), \quad (8)$$

$$f_{u_s}(\bigcup_{j=1}^{m} u(t_j)) = \sum_{j=1}^{m} u(l_j), \quad (9)$$

$$f_{u_{db}}(\bigcup_{j=1}^{r} u(s_i)) = \sum_{j=1}^{r} u(s_j) \quad (10)$$

Definition 10. (High Utility Sequential Pattern) Because a sequence may have multiple utility values in the q-sequence context, we choose the *maximum utility* as the sequence's utility. The *maximum utility* of a sequence t is denoted and defined as $u_{max}(t)$:

$$u_{max}(t) = \sum \max\{u(s') | s' \sim t \wedge s' \subseteq s \wedge s \in \mathcal{S}\} \quad (11)$$

Sequence t is a high utility sequential pattern if and only if

$$u_{max}(t) \geq \xi \quad (12)$$

where ξ is a user-specified *minimum utility*. Therefore, given a utility sequence database $\mathcal{S}$ and the minimum utility ξ, the problem of mining high utility sequential patterns is to extract all high utility sequences in $\mathcal{S}$ satisfying ξ.

Here we illustrate the utility definitions in Section 3.1 and the above utility functions through their use in the retail business. In Tables 1 and 2, the utility of a shopped item (q-item) is its profit, equal to the unit profit (weight or quality) of the item times the quantity of the item shopped. The profit (q-itemset utility) of a series of purchased items (q-itemset) is the sum of the profits of all items. Similarly, we can calculate the profit (utility) for a shopping sequence and for a shopping database. For example, for s_1, the utility of q-item $(e, 5)$ is $u(e, 5) = 5 \times 1 = 5$, which is also the utility of the first itemset's utility. Similarly, the utility of s_1 and $\mathcal{S}$ are $u(s_1) = u(e, 5) + u(c, 2) + u(f, 1) + u(b, 2) = 5 \times 1 + 2 \times 4 + 1 \times 1 + 2 \times 5 = 24$ and $u(\mathcal{S}) = u(s_1) + u(s_2) + u(s_3) + u(s_4) + u(s_5) = 24 + 41 + 27 + 50 + 37 = 179$ respectively. The utility of sequence ea is $u_{max}(\langle ea \rangle) = 10 + 16 + 15 = 41$. If the minimum utility is $\xi = 40$, then the shopping sequence $s = \langle ea \rangle$ is a high utility sequential pattern since $u_{max}(s) = 41 \geq \xi$.

The utility Definitions 5-9 and the utility functions defined in Equations (7)-(10) define the problem of utility sequence mining. The high utility sequential pattern mining specification defined in Equations (11) and (12) is a special case of utility sequence mining. Based on different definitions of sequence utility calculation, other metrics can be defined for selecting high utility sequences. In fact, the traditional frequent sequence mining problem can also be viewed as a special case of the above utility-based framework. Suppose we set the quantity of all items as 1, and define the utility functions in Equations (7)-(10) as

$$f_{u_i}(i, q) = p(i) \times q, \quad (13)$$

$$f_{u_{is}}(\bigcup_{j=1}^{n} u(i_j)) = \prod_{j=1}^{n} u(i_j), \quad (14)$$

$$f_{u_s}(\bigcup_{j=1}^{m} u(t_j)) = \prod_{j=1}^{m} u(l_j), \quad (15)$$

$$f_{u_{db}}(\bigcup_{j=1}^{r} u(s_i)) = \sum_{j=1}^{r} u(s_j) \quad (16)$$

then the sequence utility is equal to its support. We can also prove that the specific algorithms proposed in the related work [4, 11, 2] are special cases of our proposed utility sequence mining framework.

4. USPAN ALGORITHM

Here we specify and present an efficient algorithm, USpan, for mining high utility sequential patterns. USpan is composed of a lexicographic q-sequence tree, two concatenation mechanisms, and two pruning strategies.

4.1 Lexicographic Q-sequence Tree

For utility-based sequences, we adapt the concept of the Lexicographic Sequence Tree in [5] to the characteristics of q-sequences, and come up with the Lexicographic Q-sequence Tree (LQS-Tree) to construct and organize utility-based q-sequences.

Suppose we have a k-sequence t, we call the operation of appending a new item to the end of t to form (k+1)-sequence *concatenation*. If the size of t does not change, we call the operation *I-Concatenation*. Otherwise, if the size increases by one, we call it *S-Concatenation*. For example, $\langle ea \rangle$'s I-Concatenate and S-Concatenate with b result in $\langle e(ab) \rangle$ and $\langle eab \rangle$, respectively. Assume two k-sequences t_a and t_b are concatenated from sequence t, then $t_a < t_b$ if

i) t_a is I-Concatenated from t, and t_b is S-Concatenated from t, or

ii) both t_a and t_b are I-Concatenated or S-Concatenated from t, but the concatenated item in t_a is alphabetically smaller than that of t_b.

For example, $\langle (ab) \rangle < \langle (ab)b \rangle$, $\langle (abc) \rangle < \langle (ab)b \rangle$, $\langle (ab)c \rangle < \langle (ab)d \rangle$ and $\langle (ab)(de) \rangle < \langle (ab)(df) \rangle$.

Definition 11. (Lexicographic Q-sequence Tree) An lexicographic q-sequence tree (LQS-Tree) T is a tree structure satisfying the following rules:

- Each node in T is a sequence along with the utility of the sequence, while the root is empty
- Any node's child is either an I-Concatenated or S-Concatenated sequence node of the node itself
- All the children of any node in T are listed in an incremental and alphabetical order

Additionally, if we set $\xi = 0$, then the complete set of the identified high utility sequential patterns forms a *complete-LQS-Tree*, which covers the complete search space.

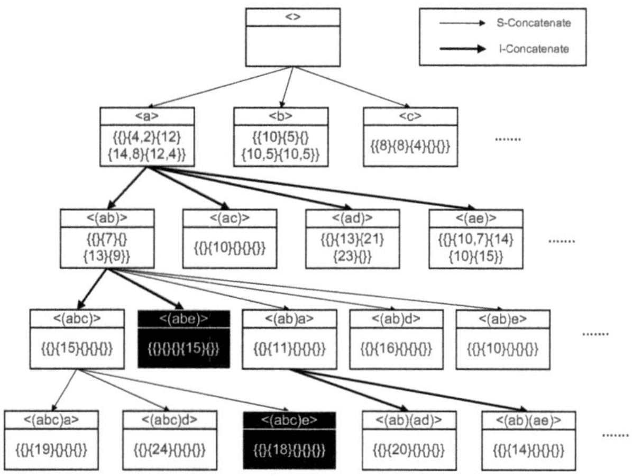

Figure 1: The Complete-LQS-Tree for the Example in Table 2

Figure 1 is an example of LQS-Tree. The root is an empty q-sequence, while the nodes in the black boxes such as $\langle (abe) \rangle$ are leaves in the LQS-Tree. The bold lines and the light lines represent I-Concatenation and S-Concatenation, respectively. Nodes within the same parent are arranged in increasing order. The utilities of the sequences are in the bottom of the respective boxes.

Given a sequence t and a sequence database $\mathcal{S}$, calculating $v(t)$ in $\mathcal{S}$ is easy without any prior knowledge. For example, if we want to calculate $v(\langle ea \rangle)$, we simply find all the q-subsequences in each q-sequence that match $\langle ea \rangle$, and calculate and aggregate the utilities of those q-subsequences. We obtain $v(\langle ea \rangle) = \{\{8, 10\}, \{16, 10\}, \{15, 7\}\}$ and $u_{max}(\langle ea \rangle) = 41$. Once we have $u_{max}(\langle ea \rangle)$, a very natural question is, "Can any $\langle ea \rangle$'s child's maximum utility be calculated by simply adding the highest utility of the q-items after $\langle ea \rangle$ to $u_{max}(\langle ea \rangle)$?". Unfortunately, the answer is no.

In frequent sequential pattern mining, the *downward closure property* serves as the foundation of pattern mining algorithms. However, this property does not hold in the high utility pattern mining problem. In Table 2, $u_{max}(\langle ea \rangle) = 41$, but $u_{max}(\langle e \rangle) = 5 + 6 + 2 + 2 + 3 = 18$, which is lower than its super-pattern. Thus, any frequent sequential pattern mining algorithms built on this property, such as prefixspan [10] and SPADE [14], cannot mine for high utility sequences. What is more, if we check the maximum utilities of a path in the complete-LQS-Tree, we find that the utilities of the sequential patterns $\langle (ae) \rangle$, $\langle (ae)a \rangle$, $\langle (ae)(ab) \rangle$, $\langle (ae)(abc) \rangle$ and $\langle (ae)(abc)a \rangle$ are 49, 33, 41, 25 and 29 respectively. There is no such property as anti-monotonicity in the maximum utilities. Therefore, it is not surprising that given $\xi > 0$, the high utility sequences may not form an complete-LQS-Tree. For example, for $\xi = 60$, the high utility sequential patterns are $\{(be)a(ab)\}$, $\{ba(ab)\}$, $\{(be)aa\}$ and $\{(be)ab\}$. Obviously, these four patterns cannot form an complete-LQS-Tree.

USpan consequently uses a depth-first search strategy to traverse the LQS-Tree to search for high utility patterns. As shown in Figure 1, USpan first generates the children of the root. It then takes $\langle a \rangle$ as the current node, checks whether $\langle a \rangle$ is a high utility pattern, and scans for $\langle a \rangle$'s possible children. If $\langle a \rangle$'s first children, i.e. $\langle (ab) \rangle$, are not taken as the current node, the same operations will apply to $\langle (ab) \rangle$. This procedure will be recursively invoked until there is no other node in the LQS-Tree to visit.

Three important things about USpan need to be addressed. First, knowing the utility of a node, how can we generate the node's children's utilities by concatenating the corresponding items? The answer is provided in Section 4.2. Second, how can we avoid checking unpromising children? We discuss this in Section 4.3. Finally, when should USpan stop the search of deeper nodes? This is discussed in Section 4.4.

4.2 Concatenations

At this point, we discuss how to generate the children's utility based on the utility of its parent, in other words, through I-Concatenation and S-Concatenation. We introduce a *utility matrix* to represent the utility of a q-sequence. Table 3 is the utility matrix of q-sequence s_4 in Table 2. Each element in the matrix is a tuple; the first value shows the utility of the q-item, and the second is the utility of the remaining items in the q-sequence; we call it *remaining utility*, which will be discussed in Section 4.4. The items that do not appear in the q-sequence are given zero utility value. We illustrate the concatenations with q-sequence s_4; other sequences can be conducted in the same way. Let us look at the record for item b in Table 3. Clearly, q-

Table 3: Utility Matrix of Q-sequence s_4 in Table 2

items	q-itemset 1	q-itemset 2	q-itemset 3
a	(0,50)	(14,24)	(8,7)
b	(10,40)	(0,24)	(5,2)
d	(0,40)	(9,15)	(0,2)
e	(2,38)	(0,15)	(2,0)

subsequences $\langle(b,2)\rangle$ and $\langle(b,1)\rangle$ match the sequence $\langle b\rangle$, so $v(\langle b\rangle, s_4) = \{10, 5\}$. Items can either I-Concatenate or S-Concatenate to an existing pattern.

We start from the I-Concatenation. In the example, only items larger than b can be I-Concatenated, i.e. entries in the rectangle from $d1$ (meaning d in itemset 1) to $e3$ are possible items. More precisely, only itemsets 1 and 3 have b, so items corresponding to $e1 = (2, 38)$ to $e3 = (2, 0)$ can be used to form the q-subsequences that match the sequence $\langle(be)\rangle$. The utilities of $\langle(be)\rangle$ are the utilities of $u(\langle b\rangle, s_4)$ plus the newly added q-items' utilities $e1 = (2, 38)$, $e3 = (2, 0)$, i.e. $v(\langle(be)\rangle, s_4) = \{10 + 2, 5 + 2\} = \{12, 7\}$. Similarly, we have $v(\langle a\rangle, s_4) = \{14, 8\}$, and utilities for its I-Concatenated sequences $v(\langle(ab)\rangle, s_4) = \{13\}$, $v(\langle(ad)\rangle, s_4) = \{23\}$, $v(\langle(ae)\rangle, s_4) = \{10\}$, etc.

S-Concatenation is a little more complicated. We continue with $\langle(be)\rangle$. As we can see from the utility matrix, there is no other literal that can be I-Concatenated to $\langle(be)\rangle$. Q-items that can be S-Concatenated to the q-subsequences are located in the rectangle region from $a1$ to $e3$. Thus, sequences such as $\langle(be)a\rangle$, $\langle(be)b\rangle$, $\langle(be)d\rangle$ and $\langle(be)e\rangle$ are the candidates. $\langle[(b,2)(e,2)](a,7)\rangle$ and $\langle[(b,2)(e,2)](a,4)\rangle$ match sequence $\langle(be)a\rangle$, whose utilities are $v(\langle(be)a\rangle, s_4) = \{12 + 14, 12 + 8\} = \{26, 20\}$. We also have $v(\langle(be)b\rangle, s_4) = \{17\}$, $v(\langle(be)d\rangle, s_4) = \{21\}$, $v(\langle(be)e\rangle, s_4) = \{14\}$.

From the above two examples, we conclude that a sequence's children's utilities can be calculated in terms of the utility of a sequence and the positions of the last q-items of q-subsequences that match the sequence. For example, to generate the utility of $\langle(be)a\rangle$ based on $\langle(be)\rangle$ in s_4, we only need to know the following information from $\langle(be)\rangle$: i) $e1$ and $e3$ are the two last q-items of q-subsequences which match the sequence $\langle(be)\rangle$, and ii) the utilities are 12 and 7 respectively. As for which q-items matches b, this is not important. Additionally, we call $e1$ *pivot*, because it is the first place where the q-subsequences that match $\langle(be)\rangle$ end. Items that are similar to $e3$ are called *ending q-items.*

Figure 2 presents the data representation in USpan. Every sequence is stored in the memory in the form of a utility matrix. We omit the entries in the figure for simplicity. The pivot in q-sequence 1 is the black dot; other ending q-items are the black solid boxes on the right side of the dot.

4.3 Width Pruning

The above section discusses how to concatenate items to a sequence, a remaining issue is what kind of items are qualified to be concatenated. This section presents the scanning function of USpan, and proposes a width pruning strategy to further select the promising items.

As shown in Figure 2, those located at the left side of the pivot (inclusive) are called *projected q-items.* Clearly, it is not possible to concatenate these projected q items. The qualified items are at the right side of the pivot. They are I-Concatenation items right under the pivot and the ending q-items, and S-Concatenation q-items are on the right side of the pivot. For each sequence in $\mathcal{S}$, those items should be scanned and inserted into the corresponding I-Concatenation and/or S-Concatenation lists.

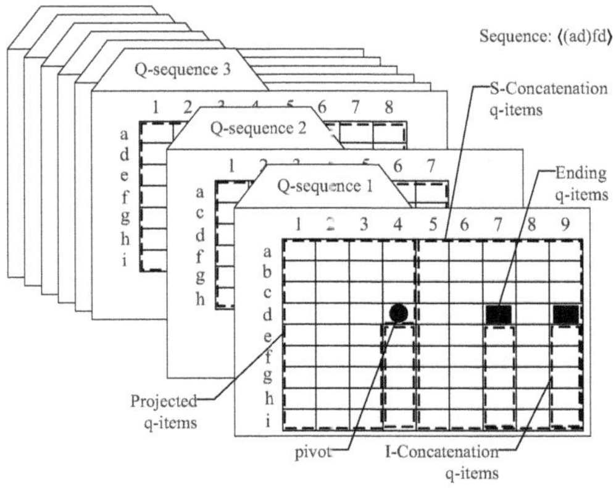

Figure 2: Data Representation in USpan

Not every qualified item is a promising item. For example, f is qualified to concatenate to several sequences, but it appears once only in the whole database, i.e. $(f, 1)$ in q-sequence 1. The maximum utility of any sequence containing f will be no more than the utility of q-sequence 1, so any sequence concatenating with f will, if it can, make itself a low utility pattern.

To avoid selecting the unpromising items, we propose a *width pruning strategy* for the scanning subroutine. This is based on the *sequence-weighted downward closure property* (SDCP), which is similar to the *transaction-weighted downward closure property* (TDCP) in [8]. Before introducing SDCP, we give a definition to the *sequence-weighted utilization* (SWU) of a sequence.

Definition 12. (SWU) SWU of a sequence t in $\mathcal{S}$ is denoted and defined as $SWU(t)$

$$SWU(t) = \sum_{s' \sim t \wedge s' \subseteq s \wedge s \subseteq \mathcal{S}} u(s) \tag{17}$$

For example, $SWU(\langle f\rangle) = u(s_1) = 24$ and $SWU(\langle ea\rangle) = u(s_2) + u(s_4) + u(s_5) = 41 + 50 + 37 = 128$.

THEOREM 1. *(Sequence-weighted Downward Closure Property) Given a utility-based sequence database $\mathcal{S}$, and two sequences t_1 and t_2, where t_2 contains t_1, then*

$$SWU(t_2) \leqslant SWU(t_1) \tag{18}$$

PROOF. Let $s_2 \subseteq s_j \in \mathcal{S}$ be a subsequence matching the sequence t_2. Since t_2 contains t_1, we know that there must be a subsequence $s_1 \subseteq s_2$ matching t_1. Therefore, a sequence containing subsequences such as s_2 is a subset of that containing s_1, i.e

$$\bigcup_{s_2 \sim t_2 \wedge s_2 \subseteq s_j \wedge s_j \subseteq \mathcal{S}} s_j \subseteq \bigcup_{s_1 \sim t_1 \wedge s_1 \subseteq s_i \wedge s_i \subseteq \mathcal{S}} s_i \tag{19}$$

We derive,

$$\sum_{s_2 \sim t_2 \wedge s_2 \subseteq s_j \wedge s_j \subseteq \mathcal{S}} u(s) \leqslant \sum_{s_1 \sim t_1 \wedge s_1 \subseteq s_i \wedge s_i \subseteq \mathcal{S}} u(s_i) \tag{20}$$

and obtain $SWU(t_2) \leqslant SWU(t_1)$. □

Based on Theorem 1, we define whether an item is "promising". Imagine we have a k-sequence t, a new item i concatenates to t and results in a (k+1)-sequence t'. If $SWU(t') \geqslant \xi$, we say item i is a *promising item* to t. Otherwise, i is called an *unpromising item*. In the implementation, to test whether an item is promising, we do not have to generate the new sequence to test whether an item is promising. We simply add the utilities of all the sequences; this is equal to the SWU of the new sequence.

4.4 Depth Pruning

The width pruning strategy avoids constructing unpromising patterns into the LP-Tree; a depth pruning strategy stops USpan from going deeper by identifying the leaf nodes in the tree. Imagine the following scenario: the pivots are approaching the end of q-sequences; meanwhile, the maximum utility of the sequence is much less than ξ. The gap is so large that even if all the utilities of the remaining q-items are counted into the utility of the sequence, the cumulative utility still cannot satisfy ξ. In this situation, we use the depth pruning strategy to backtrack USpan instead of waiting to go deeper and returning with nothing.

We use the notation $u_{rest}(i, s)$ to refer to the remaining utility at q-item i (exclusive) in q-sequence s. In the utility matrix, the *remaining utility* appears in the second element in each entry, as shown in Table 3, e.g. $u_{rest}(b1, s_4) = 40$, $u_{rest}(d2, s_4) = 15$.

THEOREM 2. *Given a sequence t and $\mathcal{S}$, the maximum utilities of t and t's offsprings are no more than*

$$\sum_{i \in s' \wedge s' \sim t \wedge s' \subseteq s \wedge s \in \mathcal{S}} (u_{rest}(i, s) + u(s')), \qquad (21)$$

where i is the pivot in s of t, $i \in s'$ and $s' \subseteq s$.

PROOF. Suppose we have the utility of sequence t in $\mathcal{S}$, we can divide each sequence $s \in \mathcal{S}$ into two parts from the pivots, where the pivots are in the left part. Assume $s' \subseteq s$ and pivot $i \in s'$, in other word, s' is the far left subsequence in s that matches t. t's offsprings can be only concatenated from the right side of the pivot. Correspondingly, it is easy to understand that the maximum utilities of the concatenated items are no more than $u_{rest}(i, s)$. Hence, the utility of any item concatenated from s is no more than $u_{rest}(i, s) + u(s')$. Similarly, the highest utility of other sequences in $\mathcal{S}$ can be calculated in the same way. Thus, the theorem holds. □

Based on Theorem 2, if the utility upper bound, i.e. the sum of remaining utilities and utilities of far left subsequences, is less than ξ, we can simply stop USpan from going deeper and backtrack the search procedure.

4.5 USpan Algorithm

The USpan algorithm is illustrated in Algorithm 1. The input for USpan is a database $\mathcal{S}$ and a minimum utility threshold ξ; the output includes all the high utility patterns.

Lines 1 describes the depth pruning strategy. A node is judged as a leaf or not based on the comparison between the value of Equation (21) and ξ; if it is lower than ξ then it returns to its parent nodes. Lines 2 to 4 are the scanning subroutine with the width pruning in Line 5. Once the concatenation items are collected, the unpromising items are omitted from the respective lists. Lines 7 and 12 construct the I-Concatenation and S-Concatenation children respectively. It invokes the concatenation to generate the utilities of sequences; the positions are also maintained. USpan then outputs the high utility sequences if qualified, and recursively invokes itself to go deeper in the LQS-Tree.

Algorithm 1 USpan($t, v(t)$)

Input: A sequence t, t's utility $v(t)$, a utility-based sequence database $\mathcal{S}$, the minimum utility threshold ξ.
Output: All high utility sequential patterns

1: **if** p is a leaf node **then return**
2: scan the projected database $\mathcal{S}(v(t))$ once to:
3:     a).put I-Concatenation items into *ilist*, or
4:     b).put S-Concatenation items into *slist*
5: remove unpromising items in *ilist* and *slist*
6: **for each** item i in *ilist* **do**
7:     $(t', v(t')) \leftarrow$ I-Concatenate(p,i)
8:     **if** $u_{max}(t') \geqslant \xi$ **then**
9:         output t'
10:     USpan(t', $v(t')$)
11: **for each** item i in *slist* **do**
12:     $(t', v(t')) \leftarrow$ S-Concatenate(p,i)
13:     **if** $u_{max}(t') \geqslant \xi$ **then**
14:         output t'
15:     USpan(t', $v(t')$)
return

5. EXPERIMENTS

The USpan algorithm was implemented in C++ of Visual Studio 2010. All experiments were conducted on a desktop computer with Intel Core 2 CPU of 2.80GHz, 4GB memory and Windows XP Professional SP3. Both real and synthetic datasets are used to evaluate the efficiency of USpan.

5.1 Data Sets

Four source datasets are used for the experiments. They include two synthetic datasets $DS1, DS2$ generated by the IBM data generator [1].

DS1 is C10T2.5S4I2.5DB10kN1k.

DS2 is C8T2.5S6I2.5DB10kN10k.

The parameters in DS1(DS2) mean that the average number of elements in a sequence is 10(8), the average number of items in an element is 2.5(2.5), the average length of a maximal pattern consists of 4(6) elements and each element is composed of 2.5(2.5) items average. The data set contains 10k(10k) sequences, the number of items is 1000(10k).

We also test two real datasets $DS3, DS4$.

DS3 is a real dataset consisting of online shopping transactions. Each customer has a sequence of records containing the information about product ID, the amount of the products and its unit price. There are 811 distinct products, 350,241 transactions and 59,477 customers in the dataset. The average number of elements in a sequence is 5. The max length of a customer's sequence is 82. The most popular product has been ordered 2176 times. We test USpan by selecting online shopping sequences with high sale turnover.

DS4 is a real dataset that includes mobile communication transactions. The dataset is a 100,000 mobile-call history from a specific day. There are 67,420 customers in the dataset. The maximum length of a sequence is 152.

5.2 Performance Evaluation

We conduct intensive experiments to evaluate the performance of USpan in terms of computational cost, memory

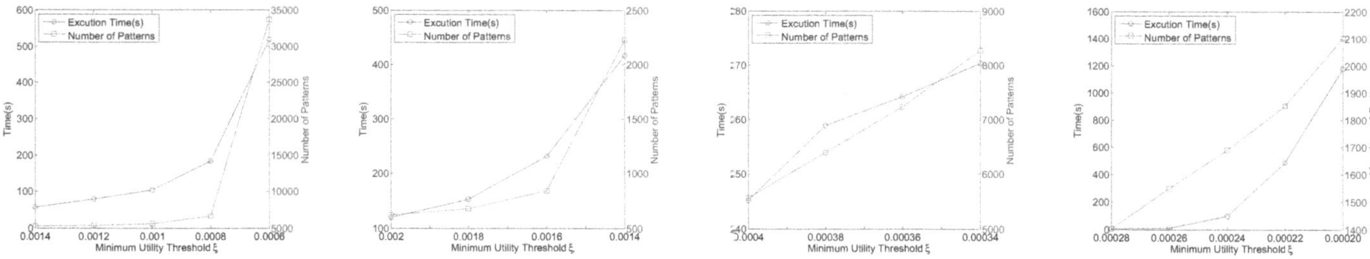

(a) DS1 (b) DS2 (c) DS3 (d) DS4

Figure 3: Evaluation of Execution Time and Number of Patterns on the Four Datasets

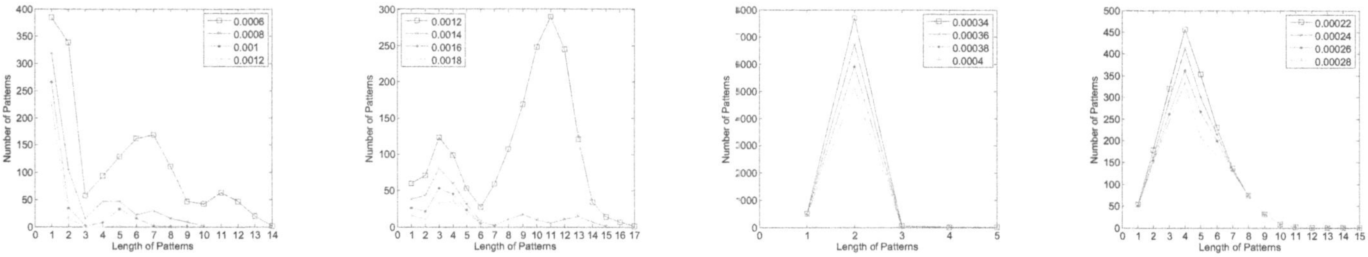

(a) DS1 (b) DS2 (c) DS3 (d) DS4

Figure 4: Distribution of Discovered High Utility Sequential Patterns

usage, number of high utility patterns, and length of patterns on different datasets.

The execution times of mining high utility sequential patterns by USpan on $DS1$ to $DS4$ are shown in Figure 3; the figure also includes the number of patterns. When the minimum utility threshold decreases, more execution time is required since we can obtain many more high utility sequential patterns. The results also show that USpan can extract high utility sequences under very low minimum utility (for instance, 0.0006 for $DS1$ and 0.0002 for $DS2$).

Figure 4 shows the distribution of the high utility sequential patterns discovered in terms of pattern length. It shows that the maximum length of identified high utility sequences increases dramatically with the decrease of minimum utility. It is also clear that high utility sequential pattern mining shows a very different trend of pattern distribution against minimum utility from that of frequent sequential pattern mining against minimum support, e.g. when the pattern length is 11, we find the largest number of identified utility sequences in $DS2$. This shows that the Apriori property does not hold in utility sequence mining.

5.3 Evaluation of Pruning Strategies

We test the computational costs of the two proposed pruning methods on $DS1$ and $DS2$. Three type of pruning strategies are evaluated. The first only uses depth-pruning, the second only uses width-pruning, and the third uses both depth and width pruning. The results of these three strategies are shown in Figure 5.

On both datasets, the depth-pruning method is very sensitive to the minimum utility. When the threshold is high, the pruning is very effective, because it only goes deeper when there is a higher remaining utility value. It can greatly ignore invalid searches by pruning patterns whose pivots appear at the end of sequences. However, when the threshold decreases, the search space in LQS-Tree grows exponentially.

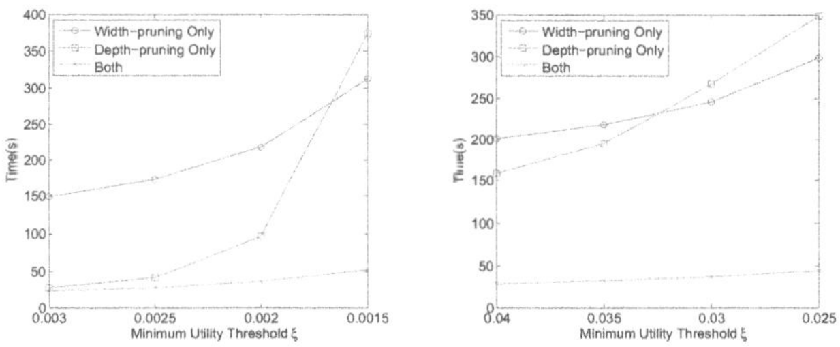

(a) DS1 (b) DS2

Figure 5: Comparison of Pruning Methods

In contrast, width pruning is more stable with the decrease of the threshold. The reason is that width pruning always prevents unpromising items from getting into the concatenation lists. It can control the width of the trees very well, however it cannot control whether the current sequence is promising until it reaches the very end of the LQS-Tree. The combination of both width and depth pruning strategies leads to extremely improved efficiency compared to either of them, and result in up to eight times the difference in execution time, because the two kinds of pruning strategies can compensate for the shortcomings of each other. In addition, since the high utility sequential pattern mining algorithm in [4] is essentially based on width-pruning, the experimental results indirectly show that USpan is much more efficient.

5.4 Scalability Test

The scalability test is conducted to test USpan's performance on large-scale datasets. Figure 6 shows the results on datasets $DS1$ and $DS2$ in terms of different data sizes: 50K to 200K sequences are extracted from $DS1$ and $DS2$, by setting $\xi = 0.006$ on $DS1$ and $\xi = 0.003$ on $DS2$.

On both datasets, the execution time and memory usage

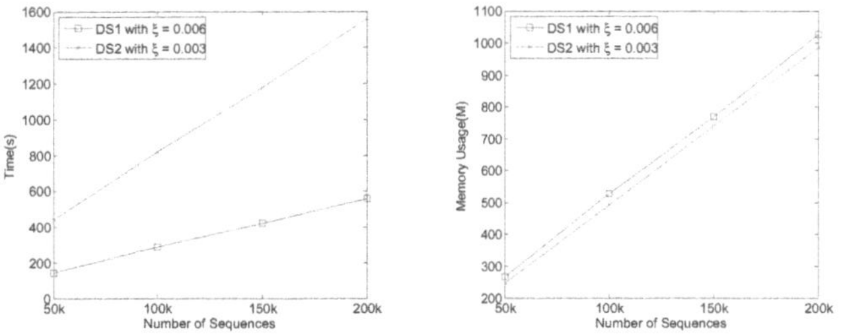

(a) Execution Time (b) Memory Usage

Figure 6: Results of Scalability Test

are exactly linear with the number of transactions, as shown in Figure 6. USpan stores the whole dataset, and the running time is directly related to the size of the LQS-Tree.

5.5 Utility Comparison with Frequent Pattern Mining

This experiment tests the utility difference between the patterns identified by USpan and that the patterns identified purely by frequent sequential pattern mining.

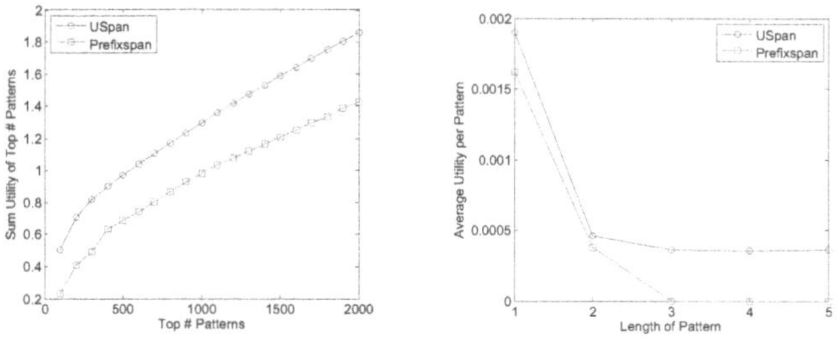

(a) Sum (b) Average

Figure 7: High Utility vs. Frequent Sequential Patterns

Figure 7(a) shows the utilities of two groups of identified patterns, one by prefixspan and the other by USpan. The x axis refers to the top n number of frequent vs. high-utility patterns selected from the two groups, while the y axis shows the sum of the utilities of the top n patterns. Figure 7(b) shows the average utilities of patterns with different lengths from prefixspan and USpan. The x axis refers to the lengths of patterns; while the y axis shows the average utilities per pattern. The results show that USpan can identify higher utility patterns more efficiently, and it can extract top patterns with higher average utility per pattern.

6. DISCUSSION AND CONCLUSIONS

Frequent sequential pattern mining leads to patterns which do not show business value and impact, and thus are not actionable for business decision-making. In this paper, we have provided a systematic statement of a generic framework, and an efficient algorithm, USpan, for mining high utility sequential patterns. Substantial experiments on both synthetic and real datasets have shown that USpan can efficiently identify high utility sequences in large-scale data with low minimum utility. For USpan, the metrics in Equation (11) can be changed to some other proper metrics such as minimum or average utility. The corresponding functions in lines 8 and 13 will be modified as well to fit the new frameworks, and the complexities are in the same level. In fact, USpan stores the positions and utilities of the candidates, a range of different functions can be applied on them with different purposes in such a framework. Our future work is on designing algorithms for even bigger datasets and better pruning strategies.

7. ACKNOWLEDGEMENTS

This work is sponsored in part by Australian Research Council Discovery Grant (DP1096218) and ARC Linkage Grant (LP100200774).

8. REFERENCES

[1] R. Agrawal and R. Srikant, *Mining sequential patterns*, ICDE 1995, pp. 3-14.

[2] C. F. Ahmed, S. K. Tanbeer and B. Jeong, *Mining High Utility Web Access Sequences in Dynamic Web Log Data*, SNPD 2010, pp.76-81.

[3] C. F. Ahmed, S. K. Tanbeer, J. Byeong-Soo and L. Young-Koo, *Efficient tree structures for high utility pattern mining in incremental databases*, TKDE 2009, vol. 21, pp. 1708-1721.

[4] C. F. Ahmed, S. K. Tanbeer and B. Jeong, *A Novel Approach for Mining High-Utility Sequential Patterns in Sequence Databases*, ETRI Journal, 2010, vol.32, no.5, pp.676-686.

[5] J. Ayres, J. Flannick, J. Gehrke and T. Yiu, *Sequential PAttern mining using a bitmap representation*, ICDM 2002, pp. 429-435.

[6] L. Cao, P. Yu, C. Zhang and Y Zhao. *Domain Driven Data Mining*. Springer, 2010.

[7] Y. Li, J. Yeh and C. Chang, *Isolated items discarding strategy for discovering high utility itemsets*, Data and Knowledge Engineering, Vol. 64, Issue 1, pp.198-217, Jan., 2008.

[8] Y. Liu, W. Liao and A. Choudhary, *A two-phase algorithm for fast discovery of high utility itemsets*, PAKDD 2005, vol. 3518, pp. 689-695.

[9] N. R. Mabroukeh and C. I. Ezeife, *A taxonomy of sequential pattern mining algorithms*, ACM Comput. Surv., 2010, vol. 43, pp. 1-41.

[10] J. Pei, J. Han, B. Mortazavi-Asl, J. Wang, H. Pinto, Q. Chen, U. Dayal and M.C. Hsu.,*PrefixSpan: mining sequential patterns efficiently by prefix-projected pattern growth*, ICDE 2001, pp. 215-224.

[11] B. Shie, H. Hsiao, V. S. Tseng and P. S. Yu, *Mining high utility mobile sequential patterns in mobile commerce environments*, DASFAA 2011, pp.224-238.

[12] V. S. Tseng, C.-W. Wu, B.-E. Shie and P. S. Yu, *UP-Growth: an efficient algorithm for high utility itemset mining*, KDD 2010, pp. 253-262.

[13] H. Yao, H. J. Hamilton and C. J. Butz, *A foundational approach to mining itemset utilities from databases*, ICDM 2004, pp. 482-486.

[14] M. J. Zaki, *SPADE: An Efficient Algorithm for Mining Frequent Sequences*, Machine Learning, 2001, vol. 42, pp. 31-60.

Mining Large-Scale, Sparse GPS Traces for Map Inference: Comparison of Approaches

Xuemei Liu*
Shanghai Jiao Tong University
Shanghai, China
xuemeiliu@sjtu.edu.cn

James Biagioni Jakob Eriksson
University of Illinois at Chicago
Chicago, IL, USA
{jbiagi1,jakob}@uic.edu

Yin Wang George Forman
Hewlett-Packard Labs
Palo Alto, CA, USA
{yin.wang,george.forman}@hp.com

Yanmin Zhu
Shanghai Jiao Tong University
Shanghai, China
yzhu@sjtu.edu.cn

ABSTRACT

We address the problem of inferring road maps from large-scale GPS traces that have relatively low resolution and sampling frequency. Unlike past published work that requires high-resolution traces with dense sampling, we focus on situations with coarse granularity data, such as that obtained from thousands of taxis in Shanghai, which transmit their location as seldom as once per minute. Such data sources can be made available inexpensively as byproducts of existing processes, rather than having to drive every road with high-quality GPS instrumentation just for map building—and having to re-drive roads for periodic updates. Although the challenges in using opportunistic probe data are significant, successful mining algorithms could potentially enable the creation of continuously updated maps at very low cost.

In this paper, we compare representative algorithms from two approaches: working with individual reported locations vs. segments between consecutive locations. We assess their trade-offs and effectiveness in both qualitative and quantitative comparisons for regions of Shanghai and Chicago.

Categories and Subject Descriptors

I.5.2 [**Pattern Recognition**]: Design methodology; H.2.8 [**Database Management**]: Applications—*Data mining; Spatial databases and GIS*

General Terms

Algorithms, Experimentation, Performance

Keywords

spatial data mining, GPS, map inference, road maps

*The work was performed while visiting HP Labs, Palo Alto.

KDD'12, August 12–16, 2012, Beijing, China.

1. INTRODUCTION

Accurate road maps are crucial for travel efficiency and safety. Existing maps are mostly drawn from geographical surveys. Such maps are updated infrequently due to the high cost of surveys, and thus lag behind road construction substantially. This problem is most prominent in developing countries, where there is often a combination of inferior survey quality as well as booming growth. Even for developed countries, frequent road reconfigurations and closures often confuse GPS navigation, and have caused fatal accidents even with experienced drivers [4]. As an alternative, OpenStreetMap (OSM) has attracted an online community to manually draw street maps from aerial images and collected GPS traces [2]. Though less expensive, this volunteer-driven process is extremely labor intensive. It also suffers from significant variability in both the skill level and availability of volunteers in different parts of the world.

The past decade has witnessed considerable interest in building road maps automatically from GPS traces. Given sequences of GPS coordinates from instrumented probe vehicles, the problem is to extract the roads covered by these probes. Existing methods can be largely divided into three categories [7]: *k-means*, which finds clusters along roads and links their centers to produce the road centerlines [13, 21, 25, 5]; *kernel density estimation* (KDE), which builds a 3D density map from traces and uses its contour lines to calculate the road centerlines [12, 10, 22]; and *trace merging*, which clusters traces by roads and approximates their centerlines using various fitting methods [9, 20, 26]. Recently, the accuracy of these three categories of methods were compared using GPS traces from shuttle buses in Chicago [7]. The above methods were largely developed for and evaluated against GPS data that is sampled with high frequency, e.g. every second. Where a slightly slower sampling rate was used, e.g. every ten seconds, probe data was only used to update an existing base map [21, 26]. Further, the traces studied typically have good accuracy, with a standard deviation less than five meters [9]. In this paper, we use opportunistically collected GPS traces with coarser recorded precision and sampling.

With the ever increasing use of GPS-enabled smart phones and telematics systems, vehicles equipped with these devices cover road networks around the globe. Often large-scale GPS traces are readily available from these vehicles. For

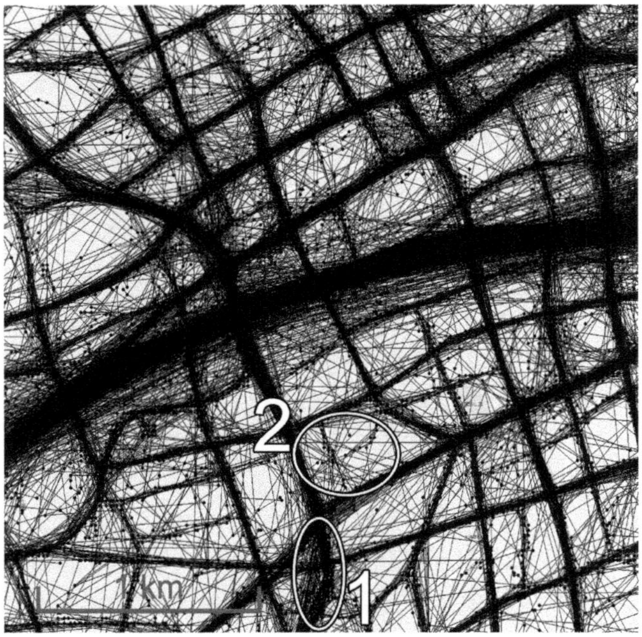

Figure 1: Sample raw input data from a dataset of 2,300 taxis in Shanghai emitting GPS samples every 16 to 61 seconds for six hours. Lines connect consecutive samples, represented by small dots.

example, taxi dispatching that utilizes GPS technology has been around for more than a decade [15], and real-time taxi traces are available in many major cities [16, 8, 6, 24]. These traces enable an unprecedented opportunity to build and dynamically update large-scale maps.

However, the nature of these GPS traces differs significantly from those used in the literature. Most importantly, due to bandwidth and storage cost concerns, sampling rates much lower than 1 Hz are common [18, 24]. In addition, precision and accuracy may sometimes be degraded due to further cost and bandwidth conserving measures. Although the much larger volume of probe data may well compensate for these limitations, none of the above-mentioned algorithms are designed for this type of data. For example, a crucial design tradeoff in map building is whether to use probe coordinates alone [13, 21, 25, 10, 22, 5] or the edges that connect consecutive probe samples [12, 20, 9]. Using individual coordinates alone, sparsely sampled roads may be fragmented or missed entirely. Using segments, one may recover sparsely sampled roads. Here, the drawback is that segments may pass over areas where there is no actual road. For example, two samples taken on either side of a right-angle turn may suggest a non-existent diagonal street.

Fig. 1 illustrates this tradeoff with sparse taxi data from Shanghai [3], overlaid on top of OSM map tiles. We use six hours of data from 8AM to 2PM on Feb. 18, 2007. There are 2,300 taxis reporting their locations. The sampling rate is 16 seconds when vacant, and 61 seconds when occupied [24]. The area shown in the figure is between latitude [31.21, 31.235] and longitude [121.43, 121.46]. We draw each sample as a black dot, and connect consecutive samples by line segments. For better clarity, the figure does not include samples whose straight-line speed exceeds 180 km/h. Most dots and lines are well aligned with roads. The thick horizontal curve in the center corresponds to an elevated freeway. Its greater thickness is due to several factors, including road width, number of samples, and lines connecting these samples that widen the curve inward. The latter issue is most prominent in area 1. Area 2 illustrates the problem with uneven distribution of samples. There are two local roads that intersect orthogonally inside the area, and which are covered by samples with a density much lower than major roads, almost on par with noise density. We cannot visually detect such roads without connecting consecutive samples or obtaining a great deal more data.

In light of these issues, we investigate two new techniques for map inference from sparse data. First, the existing KDE-based algorithm by Davies et al. [12] was previously shown to be robust against high GPS noise [7]. We describe a sparse-data adaptation of this algorithm. Second, we evaluate TC1 [17], a map inference method specifically designed for sparse data. For completeness, we also include the less competitive K-means algorithm [13] in our evaluation.

Below we offer a qualitative and quantitative comparison of these map inference methods on sparse data. As a first step, we use densely sampled trace data from shuttle buses at the University of Illinois at Chicago, together with a hand-verified ground truth map. Using this data we study the performance of the three algorithms for varying sampling intervals, amounts of data, and control parameters, to learn about algorithm characteristics and parameter sensitivity.

However, this dataset is relatively small both in terms of the number of probe vehicles and the number of road segments traversed, as well as being a somewhat controlled environment. For a large-scale evaluation, we use up to one month's worth of opportunistically collected GPS traces from 2,300 taxis in Shanghai. We tune each algorithm on a training region of Shanghai and evaluate its performance on a separate test region to get a picture of the overall map generation performance of these algorithms.

The main contribution of this paper is to provide the first evaluation of existing map building methods on sparse, passively collected data. We also contribute a simple variant of KDE-based map inference for sparse GPS traces.

The remainder of this paper is structured as follows. Section 2 provides background and related work, summarizing the three main categories of map building algorithms. Section 3 describes the key algorithms evaluated here. Section 4 describes the evaluation methodology, with the results and discussion of findings in Section 5. Finally, Section 6 concludes with an eye toward future work.

2. RELATED WORK

In a recent survey of the existing literature [7], three categories of map inference algorithms are identified:

K-means style algorithms begin by performing a traditional k-means style clustering of the GPS samples, where the distance measure may involve both the geometric distance to the cluster center, as well as its GPS bearing. A second phase links appropriate cluster centers to find roads, based on the traces that pass through the clusters. Representative algorithms in this class include work by Edelkamp and Schrödl [13], Schrödl et al. [21], Worrall and Nebot [25], and Agamennoni et al. [5].

Kernel density estimation (KDE) methods begin by transforming the individual samples or traces into a discretized image representing the density of samples or segments at each pixel. Using a binary threshold, they produce

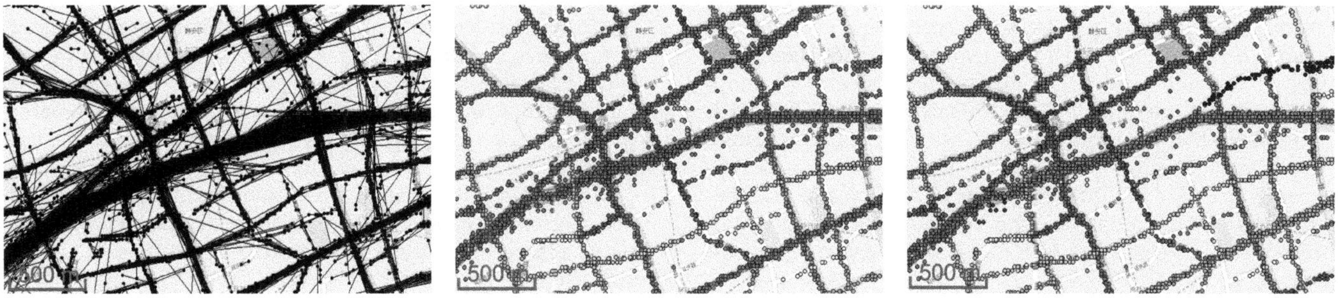

(a) Trace segment selection (b) Clustering (c) Y-split separation

Figure 2: The three steps of the trace clustering algorithm, TC1.

a binary image of the roads in the region, and proceed to find road centerlines by a variety of methods, e.g. via Voronoi partitioning. Algorithms in this class include work by Davies et al. [12], Chen and Cheng [10], Shi et al.[22], and Steiner and Leonhardt [23].

Trace merging algorithms generally accumulate traces into a growing road network, where each addition meets the location and bearing constraints of existing roads so far. A post-processing phase removes relatively unsupported road findings. Representative algorithms in this class include works by Cao and Krumm [9], and Niehofer et al. [20].

In addition to the above references, Zhang et al. [26] use GPS traces to continuously refine existing road maps, with a method similar to trace merging. With assumptions on GPS sample coverage and error bounds, as well as road geometry, Chen et al. [11] formulates road inference as a geometric problem. They propose a map inference algorithm with accuracy guarantees based on finding shared sub-paths from the input traces.

Experiments using controlled GPS traces are common, e.g., a probe vehicle following a certain route. The GPS data produced by these probes is typically of high quality, e.g., with a standard deviation of 4.07 m [19] or 3.3 m [14], and sampled at 1 Hz. By contrast, we address the sparse, low-quality data currently available in large quantities.

3. MAP INFERENCE USING SPARSE DATA

Until now, the map inference literature has focused primarily on dense trace data. In this section, we describe two map inference methods for sparse trace data. One is a modification to an existing KDE algorithm [12]. The other is a new trace merging algorithm [17], designed specifically for sparse data. Finally, we briefly discuss problems encountered when applying dense-data algorithms to sparse data.

3.1 Kernel Density Estimation

We implement two variants of the KDE map inferencing algorithm in [12]: point-based KDE and segment-based KDE. In both cases, the map is represented by a fine grid of cells. A 2-dimensional histogram is produced by counting, in the case of point-based KDE, how many samples are within each cell, or in the case of line-based KDE, how many segments pass through each cell. Here, the line-based KDE is the original method as proposed in [12], and the point-based method is our modified version targeted at sparse data.

The histogram produced above is then convolved with a Gaussian smoothing function to produce a density map. With a small enough cell size, our discretized density map closely approximates the real density. Next we find the contour line based on a given threshold, and the road centerlines are extracted from the Voronoi diagram of sample points evenly distributed along the contour line. A post-processing step removes centerlines outside the contour, as well as any dead ends or "spurs" in the map.

Besides the choice of using either points or line segments, the fundamental control parameter is the global threshold used to find the contour lines. A high threshold may miss roads with few samples, and a low threshold may produce spurious roads due to noise. This problem is prominent with the taxi data, illustrated by Fig. 1. We evaluate these design choices in detail in Section 5. To ensure portability of thresholds between datasets, we express thresholds in terms of density percentiles, rather than absolute values. For example, grid cells with a density above the 80th percentile may be considered roads, independent of the size of the map, or number of sample points.

3.2 Trace Clustering Algorithm (TC1)

For sparse GPS traces, the straight line between successive samples does not necessarily correspond to the actual road driven. Consider a car turning a corner. With one sample well before the turn, and one sample well after the turn, the straight line between samples would be likely to cut straight through a building. There is a natural precision-recall tradeoff between using the sample locations alone vs. also using the line segments of the trace paths: If an algorithm uses the samples alone, it risks having lower recall for roads less traveled. For example, consider area 2 labeled in Fig. 1. Such a road may be better detected by an algorithm that takes into account the line segment between samples. However, due to turns and curvy roads, this is likely to result in lower precision, as illustrated by area 1 of Fig. 1.

To explore the use of line segments for sparse GPS traces, we have previously designed a trace clustering algorithm, TC1 [17]. It operates in four main steps, as described below. Prior to this, all data is pre-processed to discard segments over 1.5 km long or that imply more than 120 km/h in straight-line speed.

Step 1: Segment Selection. As a first step, segments that are likely to fall on an actual road, as opposed to across a building, are selected using a simple heuristic. Intuitively, for a given pair of GPS points (a, b), if a has roughly the same bearing as b and is consistent with the segment's orientation, then the vehicle likely followed the straight line from a to b. Fig. 2a demonstrates the effect of segment selection on the dataset illustrated in Fig. 1.

Step 2: Clustering. After segment selection, the remaining segments are clustered using a method based on single-linkage clustering. Initially, each segment represents its own cluster, and clusters are iteratively merged that are highly similar in both orientation and geographic distance. Two clusters A and B are merged if there exists a pair of segments $a \in A, b \in B$ such that their difference in orientation and geographic distance are below their corresponding thresholds. The segments of Fig. 2a have been replaced by their end-points in Fig. 2b, and clustered (represented by their color). After this step, segments are no longer used, and therefore we display each cluster by samples alone.

Step 3: Y-split separation. Step 2 performs well for orthogonal roads, but for roads that have Y-splits of a sufficiently narrow angle, multiple roads become merged into one cluster. To separate these Y-splits, the major axis of each cluster is traversed, building a polyline incrementally with nodes at least 100m apart, selected so that pairs of adjacent segments do not turn excessively. The process is repeated with any remaining samples of the original cluster. For example, the big cluster that covers the horizontal freeway in Fig. 1, shown in blue (navy) in Fig. 2b, is separated into several sub-clusters representing distinct roads, as shown by different colors in Fig. 2c.

Step 4: Centerline fitting. The centerline of each road is computed using *B-spline fitting* [21]. The end result is that the road centerlines curve naturally to fit the actual GPS probe points, which we display later in Fig. 9c. Similar to the contour threshold used by KDE, a global threshold determines the minimum support needed to fit a cluster, called the *support threshold* hereafter.

3.3 Other Map Inference Algorithms

Map inference algorithms designed for high-density, high-accuracy data typically work poorly on low-density or low-accuracy data. For example, our implementation of a K-means algorithm [13] and a trace merging algorithm [9] produce numerous spurious roads when applied to high-error samples obtained near high-rise buildings [7].

These algorithms perform even worse when both errors and sampling intervals are high. For example, we applied the K-means algorithm described in [13] to our Shanghai taxi data set. The clustering step is able to locate many clusters near road centers after several iterations, but the topology discovery step produces an almost completely connected graph among all cluster centers. This is because a vehicle may travel through multiple clusters between two sparse samples, and the algorithm simply connects the two end points. Finding the correct sequence of clusters it passed through is non-trivial.

4. EVALUATION FRAMEWORK

To evaluate the quality of a result from a road inference algorithm, we perform both qualitative evaluation as well as quantitative measurements of performance. So far, the literature has largely relied on the former ("eyeball" tests) for a variety of reasons: it is simple to draw the inferred roads on top of a ground-truth background image, it does not require having a ground-truth map that accurately captures the road centerlines, and it gives a good, high level perspective that may not be captured by various evaluation methods (or these may not capture salient differences in an intuitive way). But, going forward it will be increasingly important to also perform a quantitative measurement of performance to enable: (a) measurement of progress in the field, (b) comparison of many algorithms in one plot, and (c) use of machine learning techniques to derive parameter choices from training data. As ground-truth data, we use manually verified portions of OpenStreetMap.

We perform our quantitative evaluation by measuring the precision and recall of each inferred road map M with respect to the ground truth map $Truth$. To do this, we determine the *true positive length* $tp = M \bigcap Truth$, as a measure of common road length, which we define shortly. Then we compute

$$recall = \frac{tp}{||Truth||}, \quad precision = \frac{tp}{||M||}$$

where $|| \cdot ||$ measures the total length of the roads in the set. As is ubiquitous in information retrieval evaluation, we combine these two measurements into a single, scalar value by computing their harmonic average:

$$F\text{-}measure = \frac{2 \times precision \times recall}{precision + recall}$$

F-measure has a nice *AND*-like property: it only gives a high score when both precision and recall are high.

It remains only to explain the computation of the intersection $M \bigcap Truth$. We walk each ground-truth line segment $t \in Truth$ taking samples at every meter along t to determine what fraction of those samples are within a perpendicular distance threshold m to a (nearest) segment $t' \in M$, such that the orientation difference between t and t' does not exceed 60°. The angle restriction avoids matching portions of roads that cross at intersections, but allows for substantial misalignment of the inferred road. (This wide angle margin is needed for the zigzag road centerlines that the Voronoi algorithm sometimes produces in the KDE method.) Note that even if the inferred road has a high frequency zigzag pattern next to a straight ground-truth road, the true positive length tp will not exceed the length of the ground-truth road. Consider a situation where two inferred roads lie close to a single ground-truth centerline (within the distance m). The evaluation will find that 100% of the ground-truth road is accounted for, but the precision for this portion will be 50%, as we would expect, since twice as many kilometers will have been inferred than are actually present.

In order to measure the typical road centerline offsets from ground-truth, we separately compute the histogram of perpendicular road distances from each 1m sample from each segment $t' \in M$ to the nearest road segment $t \in Truth$ (with replacement this time). For an inferred map with accurate centerline positions, we would obtain a sharp histogram within a small distance from the centerline.

Note that the evaluation here tests the geometric accuracy of inferred road centerlines, but does not test the algorithm's ability to detect one-way vs. two-way roads, individual freeway lanes, turn restrictions at intersections, or the presence of an intersection node where two road segments cross (cf. [7]). We are not aware of any map inference method that can detect such topological information in sparse data with reasonable accuracy.

Finally, as a matter of protocol when employing quantitative measurements, it is even more important that the debugging, development, and parameter tuning of each algorithm is *not* performed on the same geographical region as the testing region. We have observed this in our experiments using separate datasets with distinctive features.

5. EXPERIMENTAL RESULTS

In this section we compare multiple algorithms on multiple datasets, using both qualitative evaluation and quantitative performance measurement. The algorithms under consideration are the variants of KDE and the trace clustering algorithm TC1, discussed in Section 3.

5.1 Datasets and Ground-Truth Map

We use two different datasets for evaluation: 118 hours of traces from the UIC campus shuttles [1], and one month of traces from 2,300 taxis in Shanghai [3].

The Chicago data is sampled at 1 Hz, using commodity, low-cost SiRF-3 GPS receivers installed in 13 vehicles. Spatial resolution of this data is 0.000001 degrees latitude and longitude (less than 0.1m), offset by GPS noise with a standard deviation of 3.3m. Certain portions of the Chicago data contain significant noise (tens of meters) due to nearby high-rise buildings [7]. This dataset represents the best quality data one might expect to receive from passive data collection using non-survey grade equipment. However, the coverage of this dataset is severely limited, due to the small number of vehicles and their regular driving patterns.

The Shanghai data was collected by 2,300 taxis, providing excellent coverage of the freeways and arterials. However, the quality of the recorded data is decidedly less stellar. The taxis report their location at various intervals, the most common being 16 seconds (when vacant) and 61 seconds (when occupied). These longer sampling intervals are quite common among the taxi dispatching systems we are aware of [16, 18, 8, 6]. In addition to this, the spatial resolution of these traces varies between 0.0001 and 0.0002 degrees latitude and longitude, or about 10-20 meters, and bearing is reported at a resolution of 45 degrees [24]. We speculate that the taxis were using an early generation of GPS devices, resulting in these poor specifications. The test-area for the Shanghai dataset is displayed in Fig. 1.

For ground truth, we select portions of OpenStreetMap (OSM) data that we have manually verified. The OSM map typically represents freeways and arterial roads by multiple parallel polylines corresponding to opposite lanes. We manually remove duplicate lanes from the ground-truth for this evaluation. With the Chicago dataset, roads not covered by shuttle routes were removed as well. Curiously, judging by our raw GPS traces, the OSM map in the Shanghai area suffers from a bias to the northeast, which is visible in Fig. 1 viewed at high magnification. We observe that most roads in Shanghai agree with the aerial images and were likely created by manually tracing the shape of the roads on the satellite imagery. This suggests that the aerial images are misaligned; see [24] for detail. Based on the visual comparison with the locations reported by the taxi fleet, we shift the ground-truth map 15 m to the east and 12 m to the north for more faithful evaluation.

As discussed in Section 3, we need to determine the *contour threshold* for KDE methods and the support threshold for TC1. In addition to these map-inference control parameters, we need to pick a *matching distance threshold* for the evaluation, i.e., the maximum distance between generated and ground-truth roads that we consider as a match. Our Chicago dataset is relatively small in terms of the size and the area covered. Therefore, we do not separate training and testing data for parameter tuning. Instead, we set the matching distance threshold to 20 m, based on typical GPS error ranges and road widths [24], and pick the optimal contour threshold and support threshold for the experiments. We use this dataset mostly to evaluate the accuracy of different algorithms under different temporal resolutions. On the other hand, our Shanghai dataset covers the entire metropolis for one month. We first examine each algorithm threshold separately to understand its effect. Then we use data from a different area in Shanghai for training, and apply the tuned parameters for a fair comparison of all algorithms. The Shanghai GPS data and its road network are much more diverse than the Chicago dataset. For example, the Chicago dataset covers only straight roads aligned to the four cardinal directions, while the Shanghai dataset covers curved roads, Y-splits, five-way intersections, and all road types. Moreover, the GPS samples in Chicago are somewhat evenly distributed along shuttle bus routes, while there is a great degree of uneven distribution in Shanghai. In summary, "stress testing" using the Shanghai dataset exhibits many important issues for map inference using sparse data.

5.2 Results for the Chicago Shuttle Bus Data

The Chicago dataset in its original form has high resolution in both the spatial and temporal dimensions. To better understand how temporal resolution impacts map inference, we vary the temporal resolution of this data via subsampling. Fig. 3a shows the F-measure of each algorithm at sampling intervals of 1, 2, 4, ..., 256 seconds.

As the sampling interval increases, the performance of KDE-based methods gradually decreases, with the line-based method dropping off considerably when sampled at 32 second intervals and beyond. Intuitively, for larger intervals, the line based method is likely to produce many diagonal segments, cutting across buildings instead of following the roads. This intuition is corroborated by Fig. 3b, where the precision of the line-based KDE method drops off quickly at 32 seconds or more, while recall decays more slowly, as seen in Fig. 3c.

The point-based KDE variant shows somewhat increased tolerance for temporal sparsity. Overall its F-measure is better maintained up to the 64 second interval. Beyond 64 seconds, the decreased density fails to fully cover the streets, resulting in a map with poor recall. However, for the roads it does infer, their precision remains high up until 256, where no roads were found at all. Both KDE methods suffer from a relatively low recall: a large section of the ground-truth map is very lightly traveled compared to the rest of the map, which the global contour threshold discards as noise.

The TC1 algorithm offered the best overall performance, with both high recall and precision. Interestingly, TC1 performance does not consistently improve with higher sampling rates. We discovered that dense data at a turn sometimes links the two perpendicular roads into one cluster, and the centerline extracted from the linked cluster matches neither. Exploring alternatives to single-linkage clustering may lead to further improvements in TC1 performance.

The K-means algorithm produced poor results overall. We believe that this class of algorithms is unsuitable for sparse data, due to its strong tendency to produce spurious segments as data sparsity increases. This is evidenced by the very low precision offered by this algorithm. Due to its poor

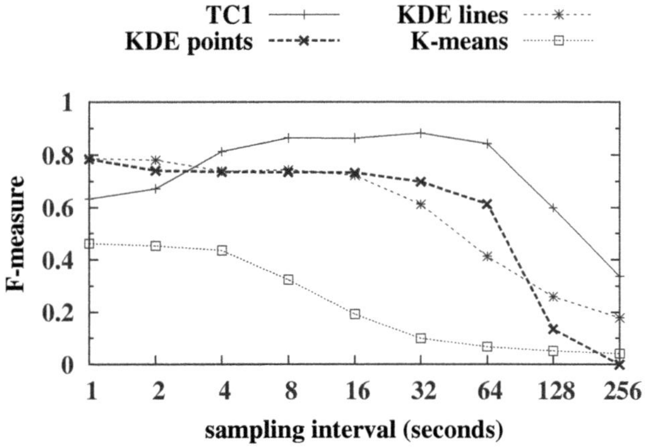

(a) F-measure for varying sampling interval

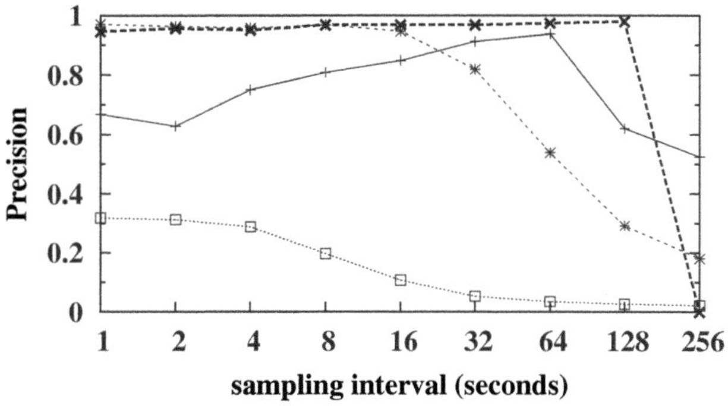

(b) Precision for varying sampling interval

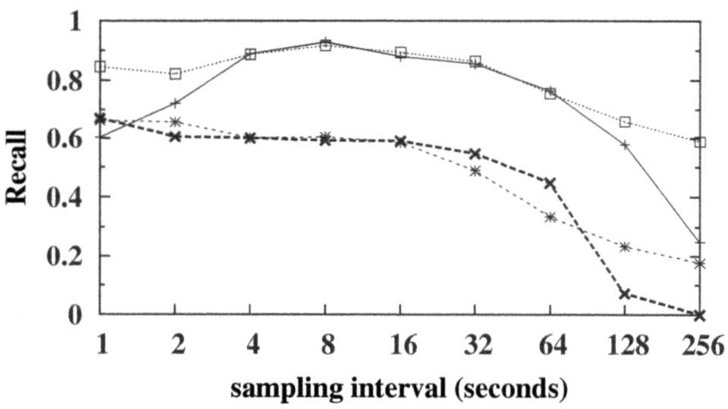

(c) Recall for varying sampling interval

Figure 3: Performance results from various algorithms on Chicago Shuttle Bus dataset.

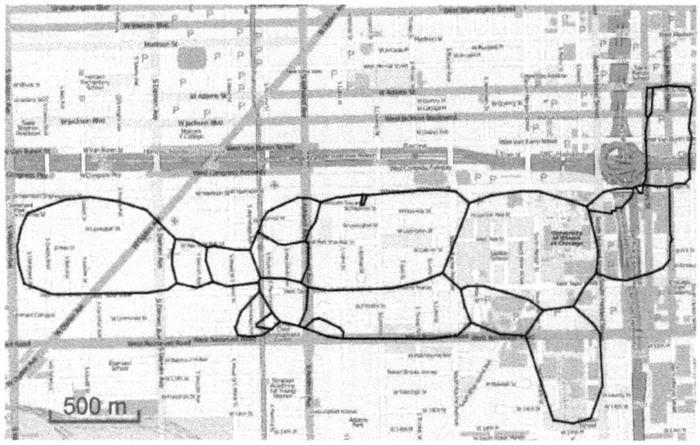

(a) line-based KDE, low threshold

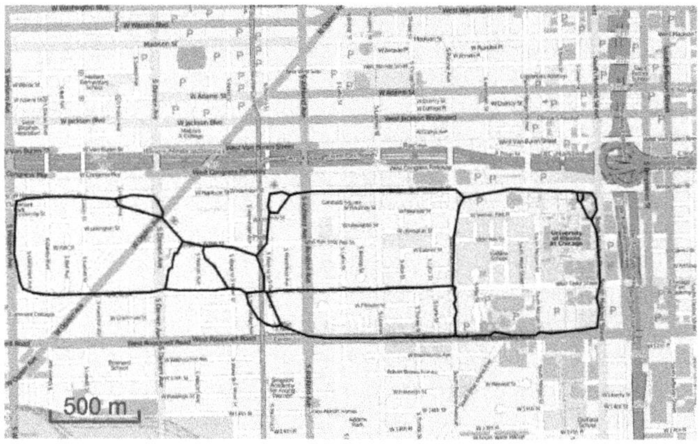

(b) line-based KDE, high threshold

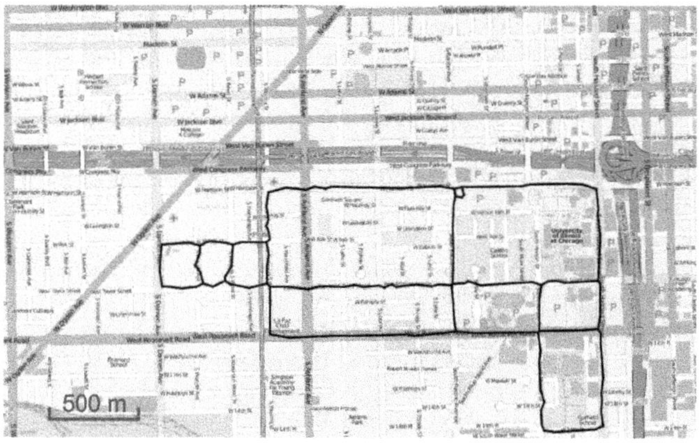

(c) point-based KDE, lowest threshold

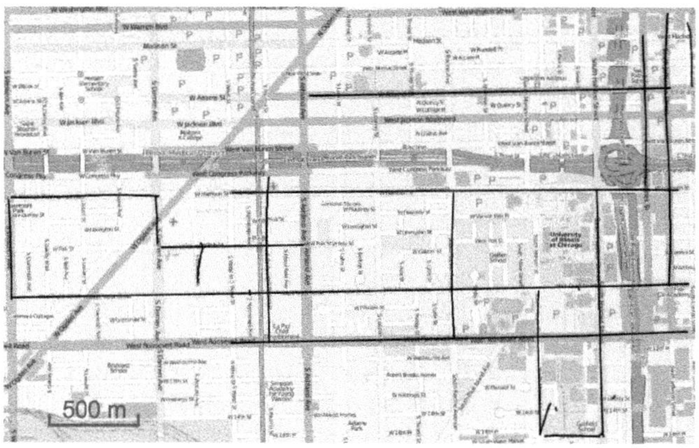

(d) TC1

Figure 4: map inference results in Chicago

performance in this initial evaluation, we omit K-means in our comparison for the rest of the paper.

Fig. 4 shows the generated roads overlaid on OSM, using various algorithms at a 60 second sampling interval. Here, it is clear how the line-based KDE method suffers from large numbers of spurious edges, as corners are pulled inward along shuttle routes. A higher contour threshold mitigates this problem, but reduces coverage instead. The point-based KDE does not suffer from the corner problem and produces a high-precision map, but it cannot discover roads that are not *entirely* covered by samples. Since the point-based KDE is less prone to producing spurious density, it tends to produce better results with a low contour

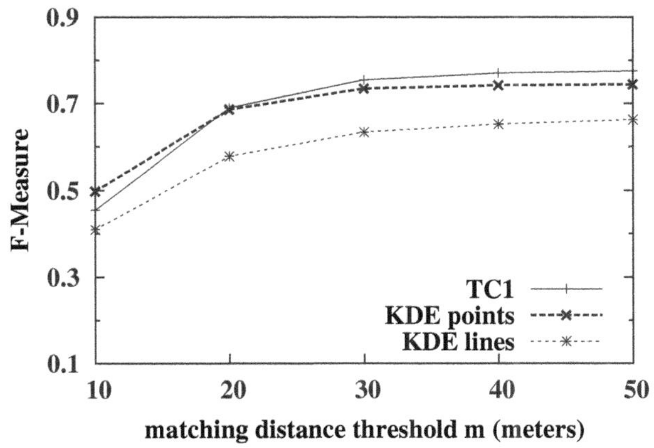

Figure 5: F-measure for each algorithm on a 6-hour dataset, for varying matching distance thresholds. All three algorithms level out around 20 meters.

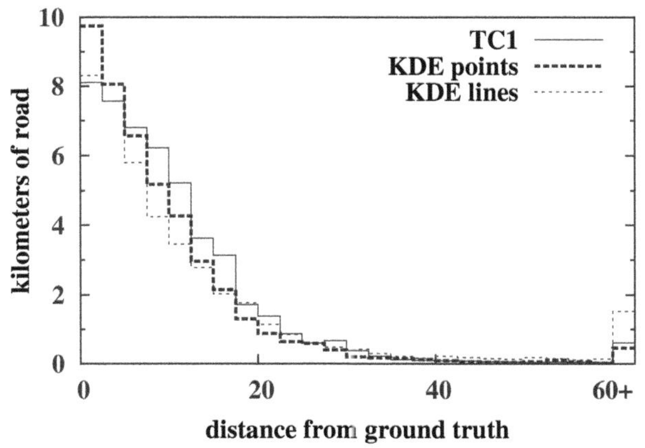

Figure 6: Histogram of distance between generated roads and ground truth.

threshold. Finally, TC1 has good coverage, producing centerlines that match the road shape as the result of B-spline fitting. Qualitatively, we observe a large number of small gaps where line segments meet—an artifact of deliberately discarding turns. This does not impact precision and recall, and simply connecting nearby segments may resolve this issue. Similarly, there are two short vertical road segments on the middle left-hand side that are covered by both KDE methods but not TC1. Here, the bus route turns both immediately before and after the short vertical segment, such that there is typically only one sample on the segment itself. TC1 discards such point pairs, and thus cannot form a cluster.

5.3 Shanghai Taxi Dataset

The Shanghai dataset presents a much larger and more complex problem than the previous Chicago dataset. Here, we first study how the matching distance threshold affects the evaluation results. Recall that the Shanghai dataset represents locations in 0.0001–0.0002 increments of latitude and longitude, resulting in a 10–20 meter granularity.

Fig. 5 shows, for each algorithm, how the F-measure varies with the matching distance threshold. These results are based on a 6-hour dataset from the area shown in Fig. 1. We pick the contour thresholds for KDE methods and the support threshold for TC1 that produce the highest scores. A larger matching distance naturally increases the number of matched roads, allowing both precision and recall to monotonically increase. However, we note that the increase levels off near the 20 meter threshold used elsewhere in this paper.

Based on the same dataset and algorithm parameters, Fig. 6 shows the histogram of distance between generated roads and ground truth for the three algorithms. Again, for all three algorithms, few generated roads fall outside our default 20 meter matching distance threshold. However, there is a relatively heavy tail of distances over 60 meters, suggesting room for further improvement.

Fig. 7 illustrates the trade-off in selecting the contour threshold for KDE and the support threshold for TC1, using the same 6-hour dataset. Here, we see that for the KDE methods, increasing the threshold reduces the number of spurious roads (increasing precision), but also discards roads less frequently traveled (reducing recall). Perhaps counter-

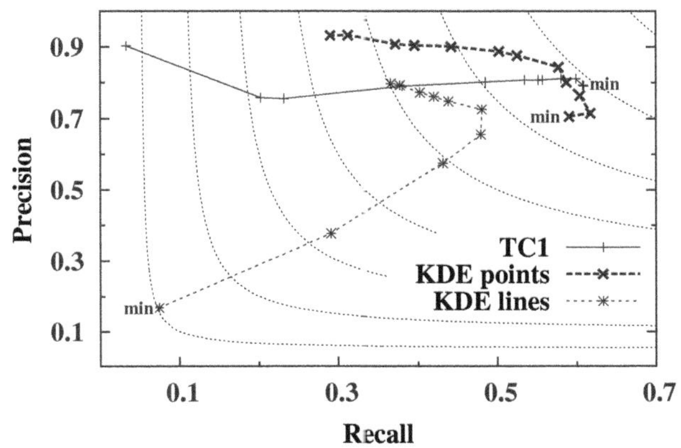

Figure 7: Precision/recall trade-off as we vary the contour threshold for KDE, and the support threshold for TC1. For each algorithm, the threshold monotonically increases from "min" along the line. The background curves show isoclines of equal F-measure, with greatest performance in the top right.

intuitively, KDE-lines is unable to match the recall performance of KDE-points despite drawing the full line between each pair of points. This apparent contradiction is explained by the centerline-finding step in the KDE algorithm: with a low threshold, KDE-lines will produce large areas of solid "road surface," for which the centerline-finding method then produces a single road, significantly limiting recall for this algorithm. A lower support threshold increases the recall of TC1 as well, but it is less correlated with the precision. The pruning step of TC1 removes most of the noise, and the clusters obtained afterwards are usually accurate. As F-measure is the harmonic average of precision and recall, the best F-measure is attained towards the top right corner; the isoclines in the background connect precision-recall points with equal F-measure.

Next we study how each algorithm performs as we vary the amount of input data. We select a different training area of similar size in Shanghai for parameter tuning. We find the contour thresholds for KDE methods and the support threshold for TC1 that produce the best F-measures on the training area. For TC1, the same threshold is then used for

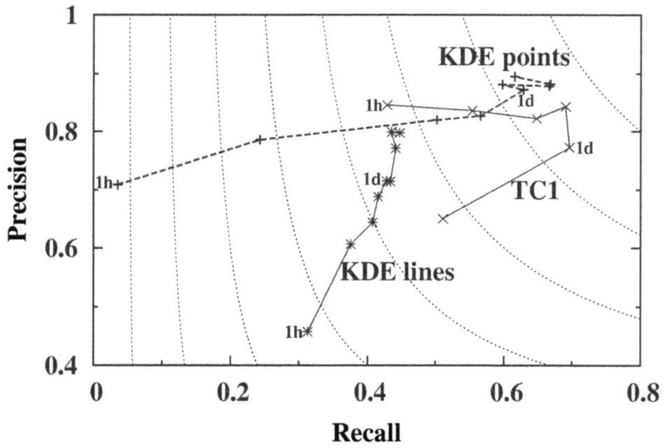

Figure 8: Precision and recall as we vary the number of hours of Shanghai taxi data: 1, 2, 4, 8 hours, 1, 2 days, and (for KDE only) 1, 2, 4 weeks. Isoclines show F-measure.

the test area of Fig. 1. For KDE, the density percentile of the threshold is preserved, rather than the absolute value. Fig. 8 shows the precision, recall, and F-measure results as we vary the input data from one hour to one month.

As one might expect, recall initially increases rapidly as trace coverage improves. Overall, increasing the amount of data has relatively little effect on precision: we train the algorithms separately for each data size, which automatically adjusts the thresholds to compensate for the extra data. However, the performance improvement starts to fizzle around one week of data (for KDE-points), and 24 hours (for TC1). For TC1, this can be explained by the use of single-linkage clustering: additional data increases the diversity of points, which raises the probability of nearby clusters merging incorrectly. We did not run TC1 for datasets larger than two days due to its high runtime complexity.

For KDE-points, over-fitting to training data appears to be one culprit: for the larger datasets, a lower threshold than what training produced results in a considerably better map for the test area. This suggests that there is room for improvement in the way the KDE-points classifier is trained. Overall, we find that KDE-points and TC1 exhibit similar numerical performance, with KDE-lines falling far behind.

Finally, Fig. 9 shows the inferred maps from the three algorithms overlaid on OSM map tiles, using the bounding box from Fig. 1. This yields some valuable qualitative insight into the relative performance of the three algorithms. KDE-lines by necessity chooses a high threshold in order to distinguish between roads. This, in turn, reduces recall leading to a clean, but sparse-looking map. KDE-points produces what from a distance appears to be a very accurate map, with very few spurious road segments. This is somewhat surprising, given the merely 90% precision reported in Fig. 8. However, upon closer inspection, the KDE-points map exhibits severe jaggedness in many places, significantly increasing total road length, thus reducing precision according to the definition in Section 4.

The TC1 map (Fig. 9c) shows very good coverage, but precision is hampered by a number of spurious road segments. This map also exhibits the disconnected road segments discussed in Section 5.2.

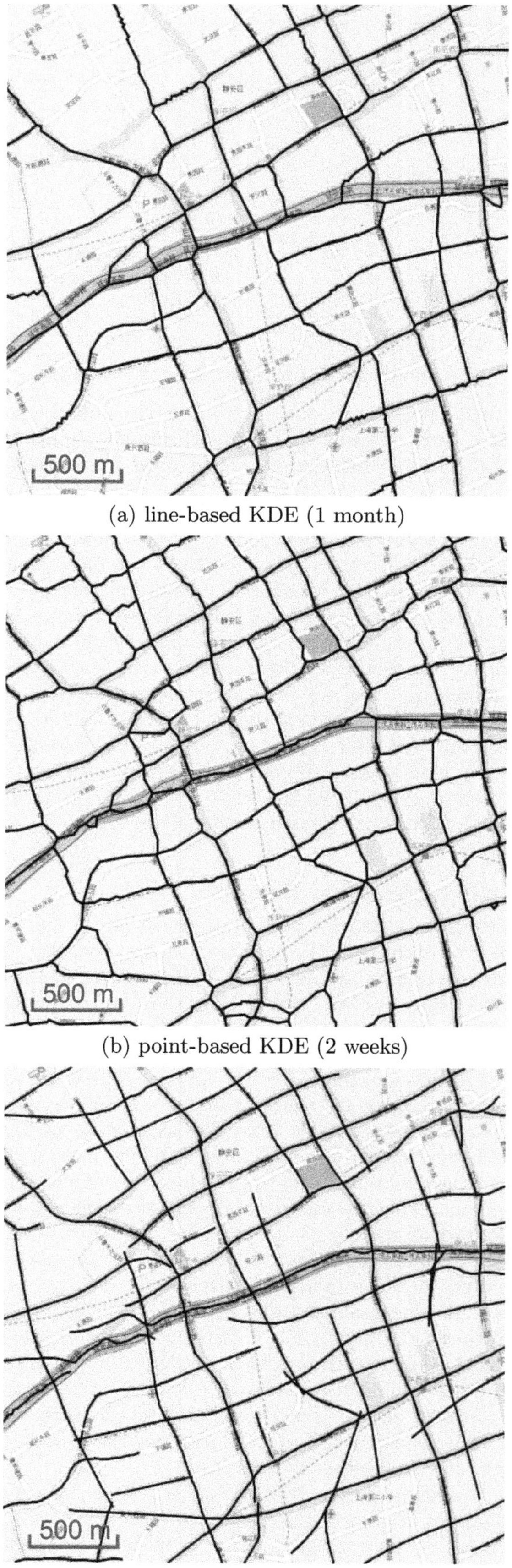

(a) line-based KDE (1 month)

(b) point-based KDE (2 weeks)

(c) TC1 (8 hours)

Figure 9: Inferred maps overlaid on OSM map tiles.

6. CONCLUSIONS AND FUTURE WORK

We have highlighted the problem of inferring road maps from inexpensive, large-scale, *coarse-grained* GPS trace data, which will increasingly become available as a byproduct of other processes. Given the continuing desire to minimize communication costs and the very large install base of sparsely recording GPS tracking systems, we hold that there will be an ongoing need for inference algorithms that can deal with sparse data. Such robust algorithms may succeed partly by the large volume of data available in this form.

While this paper has assessed existing algorithms, the results show there is ample space for ongoing algorithms research. Future work will need to produce high quality, *navigable* maps, including turn restrictions—all from sparse, coarse-grained data. Furthermore, to obtain data volume large enough to have good coverage over all the roads in a city, future system designers will likely wish to include heterogeneous data sources, such as taxis, public transportation vehicles, emergency vehicles, and (by opt-in) cell phones and touch-pad devices. Even with homogeneous data sources, working with large-scale, real-world datasets always involves a substantial effort in data cleaning [24]. Thus, another avenue of future research is to automate the data cleaning processes, especially for heterogeneous data.

The ability to automatically and quantitatively evaluate inferred maps opens the door to machine learning approaches, which require goodness-of-fit measures. It is hoped that by exposing this work to the KDD community, we may encourage future research in this direction.

7. ACKNOWLEDGMENTS

We acknowledge HP Open Innovation Program, Shanghai Pu Jiang Talents Program (10PJ1405800), and NSFC (No. 61170238, 60903190, and 61027009) for the support of Xuemei Liu and Dr. Yanmin Zhu. Also, this material is based upon work supported by the U.S. National Science Foundation under Grants CNS-1017877, CNS-1149989, and DGE-0549489.

8. REFERENCES

[1] BITS lab trace data. `http://www.cs.uic.edu/Bits/Software`.

[2] Open StreetMap. `http://www.openstreetmap.org`.

[3] SUVnet-trace data. `http:/wirelesslab.sjtu.edu.cn`.

[4] More than 50 crashes on Bay Bridge curve. `http://www.usatoday.com/news/nation/2009-11-18-bay-bridge_N.htm`, 2009. USA Today.

[5] G. Agamennoni, J. I. Nieto, and E. M. Nebot. Robust inference of principal road paths for intelligent transportation systems. *IEEE Trans. on Intelligent Transportation Systems*, 12(1):298–308, 2011.

[6] R. K. Balan, K. X. Nguyen, and L. Jiang. Real-time trip information service for a large taxi fleet. In *MobiSys*, 2011.

[7] J. Biagioni and J. Eriksson. Inferring road maps from GPS traces: Survey and comparative evaluation. In *Transportation Research Board, 91st Annual*, 2012.

[8] A. Biem, E. Bouillet, H. Feng, A. Ranganathan, A. Riabov, O. Verscheure, H. N. Koutsopoulos, and C. Moran. IBM infosphere streams for scalable, real-time, intelligent transportation services. In *ACM SIGMOD*, 2010.

[9] L. Cao and J. Krumm. From GPS traces to a routable road map. In *ACM SIGSPATIAL GIS*, 2009.

[10] C. Chen and Y. Cheng. Roads digital map generation with multi-track GPS data. In *Int'l. Workshop on Geoscience and Remote Sensing*, 2008.

[11] D. Chen, L. J. Guibas, J. Hershberger, and J. Sun. Road network reconstruction for organizing paths. In *SODA*, 2010.

[12] J. J. Davies, A. R. Beresford, and A. Hopper. Scalable, distributed, real-time map generation. *IEEE Pervasive Computing*, 5(4):47–54, 2006.

[13] S. Edelkamp and S. Schrödl. Route planning and map inference with global positioning traces. In *Computer Science in Perspective*, pages 128–151, 2003.

[14] J. Eriksson, L. Girod, B. Hull, R. Newton, S. Madden, and H. Balakrishnan. The pothole patrol: using a mobile sensor network for road surface monitoring. In *MobiSys*, 2008.

[15] Z. Liao. Real-time taxi dispatching using global positioning systems. *Comm. ACM*, 46(5):81–83, 2003.

[16] K. Liu, T. Yamamoto, and T. Morikawa. Feasibility of using taxi dispatch system as probes for collecting traffic information. *J. Intel. Trans. Sys.: Technology, Planning, and Operations*, 13(1):16–27, 2009.

[17] X. Liu, Y. Zhu, Y. Wang, G. Forman, L. M. Ni, Y. Fang, and M. Li. Road recognition using coarse-grained vehicular footprints. Technical Report HPL-2012-26, HP Labs, 2012.

[18] Y. Lou, C. Zhang, Y. Zheng, X. Xie, W. Wang, and Y. Huang. Map-matching for low-sampling-rate GPS trajectories. In *ACM SIGSPATIAL GIS*, 2009.

[19] P. Newson and J. Krumm. Hidden markov map matching through noise and sparseness. In *ACM SIGSPATIAL GIS*, 2009.

[20] B. Niehoefer, R. Burda, C. Wietfeld, F. Bauer, and O. Lueert. GPS community map generation for enhanced routing methods based on trace-collection by mobile phones. In *1st Int'l. Conf. on Advances in Satellite and Space Communications*, 2009.

[21] S. Schrödl, K. Wagstaff, S. Rogers, P. Langley, and C. Wilson. Mining GPS traces for map refinement. *Data Min. Knowl. Discov.*, 9(1):59–87, 2004.

[22] W. Shi, S. Shen, and Y. Liu. Automatic generation of road network map from massive GPS, vehicle trajectories. In *Intelligent Transportation Systems, International IEEE Conference on*, 2009.

[23] A. Steiner and A. Leonhardt. A map generation algorithm using low frequency vehicle position data. In *Transportation Research Board, 90th Annual*, 2011.

[24] Y. Wang, Y. Zhu, Z. He, Y. Yue, and Q. Li. Challenges and opportunities in exploiting large-scale GPS probe data. Technical Report HPL-2011-109, HP Labs, 2011.

[25] S. Worrall and E. Nebot. Automated process for generating digitised maps through GPS data compression. In *Australasian Conference on Robotics and Automation*, 2007.

[26] L. Zhang, F. Thiemann, and M. Sester. Integration of GPS traces with road map. In *2nd Int'l. Workshop on Computational Transportation Science*, 2010.

Transparent User Models for Personalization

Khalid El-Arini*
Carnegie Mellon University
Pittsburgh, PA

Ulrich Paquet
Microsoft Research
Cambridge, UK

Ralf Herbrich*
Facebook, Inc.
Menlo Park, CA

Jurgen Van Gael*
Rangespan Ltd.
London, UK

Blaise Agüera y Arcas
Microsoft Corp.
Bellevue, WA

ABSTRACT

Personalization is a ubiquitous phenomenon in our daily online experience. While such technology is critical for helping us combat the overload of information we face, in many cases, we may not even realize that our results are being tailored to our personal tastes and preferences. Worse yet, when such a system makes a mistake, we have little recourse to correct it.

In this work, we propose a framework for addressing this problem by developing a new user-interpretable feature set upon which to base personalized recommendations. These features, which we call *badges*, represent fundamental traits of users (e.g., "vegetarian" or "Apple fanboy") inferred by modeling the interplay between a user's behavior and self-reported identity. Specifically, we consider the microblogging site Twitter, where users provide short descriptions of themselves in their profiles, as well as perform actions such as tweeting and retweeting. Our approach is based on the insight that we can define badges using high precision, low recall rules (e.g., "Twitter profile contains the phrase 'Apple fanboy'"), and with enough data, generalize to other users by observing shared behavior. We develop a fully Bayesian, generative model that describes this interaction, while allowing us to avoid the pitfalls associated with having positive-only data.

Experiments on real Twitter data demonstrate the effectiveness of our model at capturing rich and interpretable user traits that can be used to provide transparency for personalization.

Categories and Subject Descriptors

G.3 [**Mathematics of Computing**]: Probability and Statistics

*Work done while at Microsoft Research, Cambridge, UK.

Keywords

personalization, Twitter, graphical models, transparency

1. INTRODUCTION

Whether we are reading news, searching the Web or connecting with our friends on a social network, personalization plays an important—if often hidden—role in shaping our experience. As the scale of online content grows, the ability to tailor information to the tastes and preferences of individual users is becoming critical for maintaining a positive user experience. For example, different users may prefer news articles from different blogs, diners with different tastes may trust different restaurant reviews, and so on.

However, along with the promise of personalization come many challenges, both technical and social, that hinder its potential:

- Users often do not know that their results are being personalized in the first place, and as such, may not understand why their Web experience is different from (and perhaps worse than) that of their friends.
- Even if they are aware that their results are personalized, users are rarely provided with information about how the particular site or service perceives them, and, as such, have little recourse to make corrections, if necessary. For example, in a famous critique of personalization as applied to television show recommendation in TiVo[1], Zaslow describes the drastic steps users feel they need to take in order to correct misperceptions that the system has of them, reaching the conclusion that "there's just one way to change its 'mind': outfox it," [16].
- Even when a system correctly models a user's interests and tastes, it may not always be desirable to use such information. Whether because of privacy concerns or to avoid groupthink (cf. Pariser's *The Filter Bubble* [10]), users may wish to selectively inhibit certain signals or attributes from being used for personalization.

In this work, we seek to address these challenges by making personalization more *transparent*. In other words, users should know, (1) *when* personalization is happening, and, (2) *how* they are perceived by the system (with the ability to correct this perception as necessary).

We provide this transparency by representing each user as a set of interpretable, explainable attributes (e.g., "veg-

[1]`http://www.tivo.com`

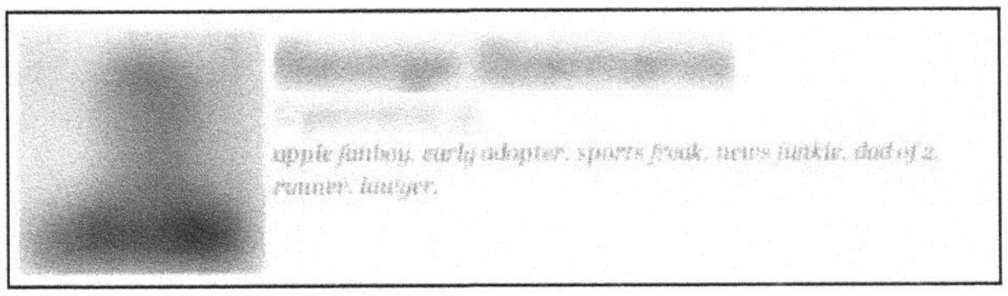

Figure 1: An example Twitter profile, showing an anonymized user's self-reported description. Here, if we are interested in the "Apple fanboy" badge, we can observe this user's actions on Twitter to help us figure out what it means to be an Apple fanboy.

etarian," "hipster," or "Apple fanboy") that we learn from user behavior. It is important that both the *meaning* of these attributes and *why they were assigned* to the user be readily apparent. Following the paradigm made popular by location-aware social networks such as Foursquare[2], we refer to these attributes as *badges*.

In particular, we consider the microblogging site Twitter[3], and we associate each badge with a characteristic *label* (e.g., "Apple fanboy") that a user might use to describe himself in his Twitter profile. For any user, we can observe his or her profile and determine whether or not it contains a particular label. For example, the user profile in Figure 1 contains the label "Apple fanboy," which we might associate with an Apple fanboy badge. It is important to note that there is a *probabilistic* relationship between labels and the badges they correspond to. For example, most users who adore Apple products will not explicitly identify themselves with "Apple fanboy" in their Twitter profiles[4]. Nevertheless, we wish to use the actions of those *self-identified* Apple fanboys to help us learn what it means to be one. We can then hope to predict which other users might also be Apple fanboys, even if they don't identify themselves as such.

Moreover, in this paper, we take the view that the set of possible badges (and their corresponding labels) are defined *a priori* in a supervised manner. Specifically, we assume we are *given* some set of possible badges (e.g., as in Table 1), and wish to *infer*: (1) their presence or absence for each user, and, (2) how they manifest themselves in terms of Twitter behavior.

In the remainder of this paper, we describe how we learn badges from user activity on Twitter, using a Bayesian framework to explicitly model uncertainty. We show experimental results on real Twitter users, and present both quantitative evidence and qualitative anecdotes demonstrating the effectiveness of our method.

2. MODELING BADGES

We describe each user as a set of *latent* badges that, collectively, explain the user's behavior. The fundamental problem we seek to solve is: *how do we infer the badges for each user based on observed actions and labels?*

For each user u, we observe two binary vectors:

1. The label vector $\boldsymbol{\lambda}^{(u)}$, with $\lambda_i^{(u)} = 1$ indicating that the Twitter profile of user u contains the label corresponding to badge i. As an example, if we let badge i correspond to the "runner" label, then $\lambda_i^{(u)} = 1$ if the Twitter profile of user u contains the word "runner," and $\lambda_i^{(u)} = 0$ otherwise.
2. The action vector $\boldsymbol{a}^{(u)}$, where $a_j^{(u)} = 1$ if user u is observed performing action j. In our Twitter domain, we take the set of possible actions to include all hashtags and retweets. For example, action j might correspond to tweeting with the hashtag `#runkeeper`, and $a_j^{(u)} = 1$ for users u that have such a tweet.

We model these observations as probabilistically arising from a latent set of badges $\boldsymbol{b}^{(u)}$, where $b_i^{(u)} \in \{0, 1\}$ indicates whether or not user u has badge i. In particular, we elect to define a generative—rather than discriminative—model; while the high precision labels may provide us with positive training examples, their low recall leads to no meaningful negative examples. Moreover, if a user chooses to decline a badge that we predict for him (e.g., he might not really be an Apple fanboy), this simply corresponds in our model to observing the latent variable $b_i^{(u)} = 0$. Additionally, we note that our model differs from traditional unsupervised latent variable models, such as topic models [2], in that the badge labels provide identifiability that we would not otherwise achieve. Thus, for example, if we define the label for badge i to correspond to those users with "runner" in their Twitter profile, then the actions explained by badge i will always correspond to (our view of) runners, which is a property we do not get with fully unsupervised topic models, such as latent Dirichlet allocation [3].

2.1 Generating labels

Given a particular user's badge assignments, the generative process for labels encodes our intuition that each label $\boldsymbol{\lambda}_i$ is a high precision, low recall indicator of the presence or absence of a badge. Specifically, "high precision" here means that it is very unlikely for someone without badge i (i.e., with $b_i^{(u)} = 0$) to use the corresponding label (i.e., $\lambda_i^{(u)} = 1$) in his profile, while "low recall" indicates that many users u with $b_i^{(u)} = 1$ nevertheless have $\lambda_i^{(u)} = 0$. For example, while most vegetarians on Twitter do not describe themselves as "vegetarian" in their Twitter profiles, it is much more rare (but not impossible) for non-vegetarians to have the word "vegetarian" in their profiles.

As such, we model label $\lambda_i^{(u)}$ as being *a priori* present with a true positive rate γ_i^{T} and false positive rate γ_i^{F} (with $\gamma_i^{\mathrm{F}} \ll \gamma_i^{\mathrm{T}} < 1$ and $\gamma_i^{\mathrm{F}} \approx 0$). Formally, we have:

$$p(\lambda_i^{(u)} = 1 \,|\, b_i^{(u)}, \gamma_i^{\mathrm{T}}, \gamma_i^{\mathrm{F}}) = \mathsf{Bernoulli}(b_i^{(u)}\gamma_i^{\mathrm{T}} + (1 - b_i^{(u)})\gamma_i^{\mathrm{F}}),$$

given the user's badge $b_i^{(u)}$. In other words, the presence of a badge does not necessarily imply its appearance in a user's profile, and it is precisely these badges that we aim to infer.

2.2 Generating actions

We assume that the observed actions $a_j^{(u)} \in \{0, 1\}$ of a user u can be explained by one or more of his latent badges $b_i^{(u)}$. In the Twitter domain, possible actions j might include a user *re-tweeting* some author or using a particular *hashtag*.

For each possible badge i and action j, there is a probability $s_{ij}\phi_{ij}$ of associating them; it is decomposed into a context-specific rate $\phi_{ij} \in (0, 1)$ and a sparsity prior $s_{ij} \in \{0, 1\}$. The $\mathbf{s}_i$ variables for a badge i act as a mask, delineat-

[2]`http://www.foursquare.com`

[3]`http://www.twitter.com`

[4]This stands in contrast to Foursquare, where badges are deterministic (e.g., five check-ins at an airport *guarantee* the "jet-setter" badge).

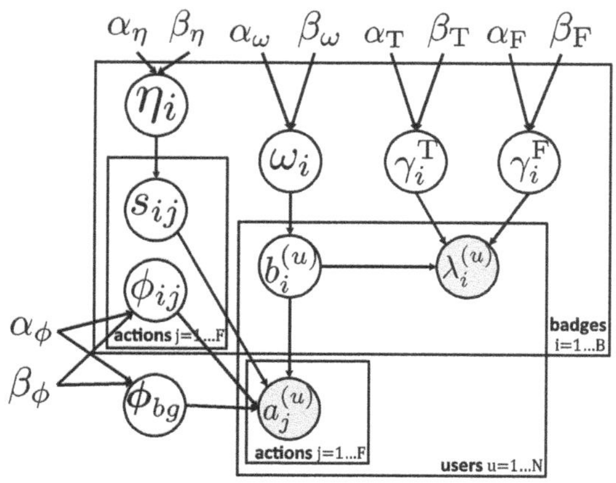

for all badges $i = 1, \ldots, B$ **do**
  $\omega_i \sim \text{Beta}(\alpha_\omega, \beta_\omega)$
  $\gamma_i^{\text{T}} \sim \text{Beta}(\alpha_{\text{T}}, \beta_{\text{T}})$
  $\gamma_i^{\text{F}} \sim \text{Beta}(\alpha_{\text{F}}, \beta_{\text{F}})$
  $\eta_i \sim \text{Beta}(\alpha_\eta, \beta_\eta)$
  for all actions $j = 1, \ldots, F$ **do**
    $s_{ij} | \eta_i \sim \text{Bernoulli}(\eta_i)$
    $\phi_{ij} \sim \text{Beta}(\alpha_\phi, \beta_\phi)$
for all actions $j = 1, \ldots, F$ **do**
  $\phi_{\text{bg},j} \sim \text{Beta}(\alpha_\phi, \beta_\phi)$
for all users $u = 1, \ldots, N$ **do**
  for all badges $i = 1, \ldots, B$ **do**
    $b_i^{(u)} | \omega_i \sim \text{Bernoulli}(\omega_i)$
    $\lambda_i^{(u)} | b_i^{(u)}, \gamma_i^{\text{F}}, \gamma_i^{\text{T}} \sim \text{Bernoulli}\left(b_i^{(u)} \gamma_i^{\text{T}} + (1 - b_i^{(u)}) \gamma_i^{\text{F}}\right)$
  for all actions $j = 1, \ldots, F$ **do**
    $a_j^{(u)} | \boldsymbol{b}^{(u)}, \boldsymbol{\phi}_{\bullet j}, \mathbf{s}_{\bullet j} \sim \text{Bernoulli}\left(1 - (1 - \phi_{\text{bg},j}) \prod_{i:b_i^{(u)}=1} (1 - \phi_{ij} s_{ij})\right)$

Figure 2: Plate diagram and generative model.

ing which actions can be explained by this particular badge, and their sparsity is controlled by a badge-specific prior η_i. Given that $s_{ij} = 1$, the variable ϕ_{ij} represents the probability that a user with badge i undertakes action j, in the absence of any other badges. For example, if a user only has the "runner" badge active, and $s_{\text{runner},\#\text{runkeeper}} = 1$, meaning that the "runner" badge can explain tweeting **#runkeeper**, then our user will tweet **#runkeeper** with probability $\phi_{\text{runner},\#\text{runkeeper}}$.

As a user may have more than one badge active that can explain a particular action, we combine their influence in a noisy-or fashion, indicating that a user performs an action j if at least one of his badges induce him to do so. Moreover, it is plausible that a user's behavior is influenced not just by his particular attributes, but by the environment at large, and thus we assume a background model $\phi_{\text{bg},j}$, acting as a badge that every user shares, that has some probability of explaining every action.

Thus, formally, action $a_j^{(u)}$ is observed if it is explained by either the background or at least one of the badges of user u, which we can write as follows[5]:

$$p(a_j^{(u)} = 1 \mid \boldsymbol{b}^{(u)}, \boldsymbol{\phi}_{\bullet j}, \mathbf{s}_{\bullet j}) = \text{Bernoulli}\left(1 - (1 - \phi_{\text{bg},j}) \prod_{i:b_i^{(u)}=1} (1 - \phi_{ij} s_{ij})\right).$$

2.3 Prior probabilities

Keeping with a proper Bayesian approach, we specify prior distributions on our badge assignments $\boldsymbol{b}$, rates $\boldsymbol{\gamma}^{\text{T}}$ and $\boldsymbol{\gamma}^{\text{F}}$, sparsity masks $\mathbf{s}$ and action probabilities $\boldsymbol{\phi}$ encoding our modeling assumptions.

First, as some badges are more prevalent than others (e.g., there are likely more vegetarians on Twitter than machine learning enthusiasts), we assume that each badge assignment $b_i^{(u)}$ is drawn from a beta-distributed prior rate ω_i, shared across all users for each badge i.

Second, to encode that we expect the false positive rate to be considerably lower than the true positive rate, we place separate beta priors on $\boldsymbol{\gamma}^{\text{T}}$ and $\boldsymbol{\gamma}^{\text{F}}$, setting the hyperparameters accordingly.

Third, as we want each badge i to explain only a sparse set of actions, we place badge-specific beta-distributed prior rates η_i from which we sample s_{ij}, allowing different badges to have different degrees of sparsity.

Finally, we place vague beta priors on the action probabilities $\boldsymbol{\phi}$ seeking to learn these primarily from data.

A depiction of our graphical model and a summary of the full generative process can be found in Figure 2.

2.4 Badge inference

Given our model and the observations from each user, we wish to infer the latent badge assignments $\boldsymbol{b}$, as well as which actions are explained by each badge (and to what degree). As computing the exact posterior probabilities in a graphical model such as this is intractable, we employ Markov Chain Monte Carlo (MCMC) methodology and estimate the posterior probabilities on $\boldsymbol{b}$, $\mathbf{s}$ and $\boldsymbol{\phi}$ by deriving a Gibbs sampler with interleaved Metropolis-Hastings steps. In particular, we derive a *collapsed* Gibbs sampler, marginalizing out $\boldsymbol{\eta}$, $\boldsymbol{\omega}$, $\boldsymbol{\gamma}^{\text{T}}$ and $\boldsymbol{\gamma}^{\text{F}}$, leaving only the variables of interest. This results in the following sampler:

1. *Sample* $\boldsymbol{b}$. We sample each badge assignment $b_i^{(u)}$ for a particular user u from its conditional distribution, which we can write as proportional to the product of an action likelihood, a label likelihood and a prior:

$$p(b_i^{(u)} | \boldsymbol{a}^{(u)}, \boldsymbol{\lambda}_i, \boldsymbol{b}_i^{(-u)}, \boldsymbol{\phi}, \mathbf{s}, \boldsymbol{b}_{-i}^{(u)}) \propto p(\boldsymbol{a}^{(u)} | \boldsymbol{b}^{(u)}, \boldsymbol{\phi}, \mathbf{s}) \cdot p(\boldsymbol{\lambda}_i | \boldsymbol{b}_i) \cdot p(b_i^{(u)} | \boldsymbol{b}_i^{(-u)}). \quad (1)$$

2. *Sample* $\mathbf{s}$. We sample the binary variable s_{ij} from its conditional distribution, which we can write as follows:

$$p(s_{ij} | \boldsymbol{a}_j, \mathbf{s}_{(-ij)}, \boldsymbol{\phi}, \boldsymbol{b}) \propto p(s_{ij} | \mathbf{s}_{i(-j)}) \cdot p(\boldsymbol{a}_j | \boldsymbol{\phi}, \mathbf{s}, \boldsymbol{b}), \quad (2)$$

which is a product of a prior on s_{ij} and an action likelihood term. In practice, for statistical efficiency (and following Fox [5]), rather than sampling from the conditional distribution directly, we employ a Metropolis Hastings step with a deterministic proposal of flipping s_{ij} from some value s to its complement, $\bar{s}$ [6, 8].

[5]We note that, by assuming the influence of the badges to be independent of each other for a particular user, we can write this "at least one" clause as the complement of a product of complements. While this assumption may be violated in practice, we posit that the computational savings we achieve by this simplification will outweigh the induced bias.

Table 1: The 31 badges we defined for our experiments, as specified by their corresponding labels.

1	vegetarian	17	entrepreneur
2	Apple fanboy	18	golfer
3	cyclist	19	wine lover
4	gamer	20	book worm
5	runner	21	coffee
6	hacker	22	Harry Potter
7	feminist	23	Ruby on Rails
8	photographer	24	Manchester United
9	teacher	25	Hello Kitty
10	artist	26	anime
11	foodie	27	Warcraft
12	hipster	28	jetsetter
13	NASCAR	29	Taylor Swift
14	redneck	30	Lady Gaga
15	country music fan	31	jQuery
16	yoga		

3. *Sample* $\boldsymbol{\phi}_i$. To sample ϕ_{ij}, we first write its conditional distribution as a product of a prior and an action likelihood term:

$$p(\phi_{ij}|\boldsymbol{a}_j, \boldsymbol{\phi}_{-(ij)}, \mathbf{s}, \boldsymbol{b}) \propto p(\phi_{ij}) \cdot p(\boldsymbol{a}_j|\boldsymbol{\phi}, \mathbf{s}, \boldsymbol{b}). \quad (3)$$

We use a Metropolis Hastings step here to obtain our sample, with a beta-distributed proposal distribution:

$$q(\phi'_{ij}|\phi_{ij} = \phi) = \mathsf{Beta}(\phi'_{ij}; \phi\nu, (1-\phi)\nu), \quad (4)$$

parameterized with mean ϕ and effective sample size ν, meaning that each proposal is centered around the ϕ of the previous step.

4. *Sample* $\boldsymbol{\phi}_{\text{bg}}$. We sample the background action probability, $\phi_{\text{bg},j}$, in the same manner that we sample the per badge action probability, using a Metropolis Hastings step with the same proposal distribution.

Further details of our sampling algorithm, including complete derivations of all conditional distributions, can be found in the supplemental material [4].

3. EXPERIMENTAL RESULTS

3.1 Data

We evaluate our model on a data set of approximately seven million active Twitter users by monitoring Twitter's "firehose" stream in early August 2011, recording users with non-empty profiles. We scanned through these seven million users–which at the time of collection represented approximately 3.5 percent of all Twitter users–and manually defined a set of 31 badges by specifying a label for each one, based on the occurrence of a particular phrase or word in each user's Twitter profile. For example, we define a "vegetarian" badge by specifying:

$\lambda^{(u)}_{\text{vegetarian}} = 1$ *if user u has the word "vegetarian" in her Twitter profile.*

Table 1 contains a full listing of our 31 badges. We note that while these badges were defined as a proof of concept by the authors, a real personalization system would include a principled method for defining a large quantity of badges, as discussed further in Section 5.

Of the seven million users in our data set, we identified 376,916 that had at least one of the 31 labels in their profiles. We took this subset of users and monitored the firehose for one week, from 5 August 2011 to 12 August 2011, collecting every tweet and retweet by these users. This resulted in a set of approximately two million tweets. From these tweets, we extracted all unique hashtags (e.g., #`runkeeper`) and retweeted users (e.g., `@MacRumors`), defining a vocabulary of actions. We culled this vocabulary to remove any actions belonging to just a single user, leaving us with a final vocabulary of 32,030 actions (broken down into 18,003 hashtags and 14,027 retweets), performed by 75,880 different users. The most common action over this time period was the hashtag #`londonriots`, referring to the riots that took place in the British capital during the week of our data collection. Moreover, Figure 3(a) shows how many users in the data set described themselves using each of the 31 labels, with the most common being "artist."

Finally, we note that our model is not dependent on Twitter, as both the labels and the actions could be defined to take advantage of any other user signals one has access to, including location, shopping patterns, clicks, query logs and so on[6]. Twitter is, however, a convenient open platform for experimentation.

3.2 Evaluation

We ran our sampler on the data set described above, estimating posterior probabilities of badge assignments ($\boldsymbol{b}$) and badge definitions ($\boldsymbol{\phi}$ and $\mathbf{s}$) under our modeling assumptions. For each iteration, our sampler has time complexity $O(B(F+N))$. Our implementation in the F# functional programming language achieves a runtime of approximately 3.5 minutes per sample, which is the time it takes to make a single, complete pass over more than 3.3 million random variables. Our hyperparameter settings and initialization condition are detailed in the supplemental material [4].

In an effort to compare our methodology to a state-of-the-art alternative, we wanted a model that: (1) can represent multiple labels per user; (2) provides a mechanism for interpreting the definitions of each badge; and, (3) can probabilistically infer badge assignments, especially in cases where the corresponding label is not present for the particular user.

We found the most suitable comparison technique to be the labeled latent Dirichlet allocation (labeled LDA) model of Ramage et al. [13]. This model makes a slight, but important, modification to the original LDA model, by assuming that each document is labeled with one or more tags, with each tag associated with one and only one topic. Thus, e.g., a document labeled with tags 1, 2 and 5 is assumed to have been generated from topics 1, 2 and 5, and no others. Like our model, labeled LDA provides a level of identifiability not obtained in traditional unsupervised approaches.

In order to adapt labeled LDA to our setting, we first associate a tag (and thereby a topic) with each badge, as well as an additional tag corresponding to a background topic. In our particular example, this leads to 32 unique tags. We then run labeled LDA twice: once for learning badge defi-

[6]For instance, we can imagine generalizing "labels" to instead represent any high-precision, low-recall *rule* that we intend on associating with a badge, not necessarily based on the content of a user's Twitter profile.

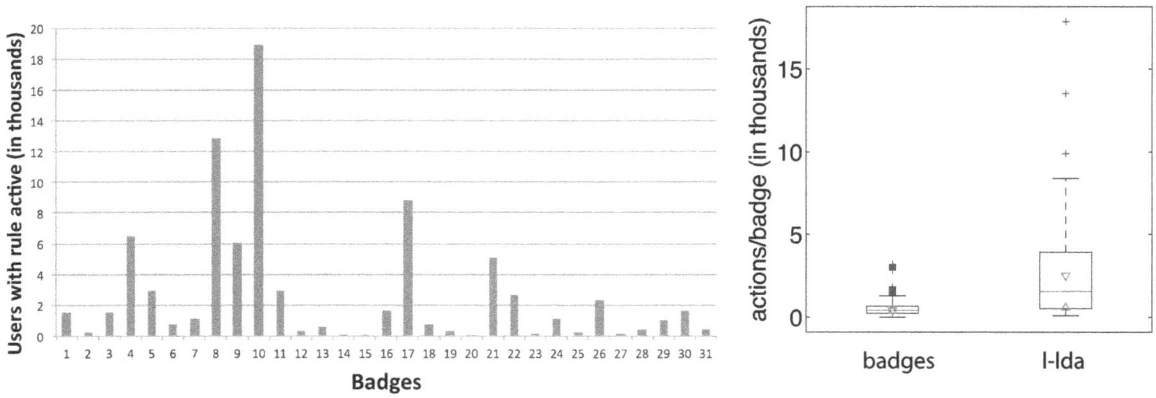

(a) Number of users with each label present in their Twitter profile

(b) Sparsity

Figure 3: (a) A bar chart indicating how many users in our Twitter data set have each of the 31 labels (corresponding to each of our badges.) (b) A box plot showing that the badge definitions we learn are significantly sparser than the topics learned by labeled LDA. The horizontal line in the middle of each box represents the median number of actions per badge, and the triangles delineate confidence intervals, giving us a 5% significance threshold.

nitions, and once for inferring badge probabilities for each user.[7] This two-stage approach contrasts with our model–which performs both functions simultaneously–and is necessary here because the labeled LDA model does not allow us to specify uncertainty in the label assignments.

In the first run of labeled LDA, we assign each user tags corresponding to the labels present in his or her user profile, as well as the background tag. For example, a user with the word "runner" in his Twitter profile would have to be modeled by only two topics: the one corresponding to the "runner" label, and the background topic. This first run learns a topic corresponding to each of the badges, giving the probability that each badge explains each action in our vocabulary. However, as each topic is a multinomial distribution over actions, its probabilities must sum to one, leading to qualitative differences with the badges learned from our model. First, for a given badge i in our model, the probability of each action ϕ_{ij} lies in the set $(0, 1)$, and are conditionally independent of each other given their prior. This allows several actions to have high probability of being explained by the same badge, if that is what can best model the user data. Second, by explicitly modeling sparsity using the $\mathbf{s}$ variables, a badge is not forced to explain actions it is only weakly associated with, simply for the sake of getting its distribution to sum to one. This is a characteristic not only of labeled LDA, but of all such topic models. Figure 3(b) shows the difference in the sparsity of our badge definitions when compared to labeled LDA.

After learning the topics with the first run of labeled LDA, we keep them fixed and infer the badge assignments, this time giving all 32 tags to each user, allowing for badges to be inferred beyond the ones corresponding to observed labels. However, as before, because labeled LDA provides no explicit model of sparsity, and is modeling a multinomial distribution, every user will, in expectation, be assigned to one badge, but this probability mass will be spread over all 32 topics, even if they are all unlikely.

We take the badges learned and inferred by our model and compare it to those from labeled LDA, evaluating both the interpretability of the badge definitions and the correctness of the badge assignments.

3.2.1 Interpretability of Badge Definitions

One important desideratum from our problem description is that, whichever model we use, if we are to bring transparency to the personalization process, we must provide users with meaningful and interpretable answers when they ask, "Why did I get badge X?" A convenient way to visualize badge definitions is via word clouds, with the size of an action proportional to its weight in the badge, concisely summarizing what it means to have a particular badge. Specifically, in our model, the "weight" of action j in badge i refers to the quantity $s_{ij}\phi_{ij}$, while in labeled LDA, the weight is the probability of action j coming from topic i.

Figure 4 shows six examples of badges learned from running our model on the Twitter data set described above.[8] These badges do an excellent job of describing actions that are consistent with their definitions, and are precisely the types of explanations we would hope to expose to the user. For instance, the "runner" badge in Figure 4(d) explains the action `#runkeeper`, which is a hashtag automatically tweeted when using a particular smartphone application[9] that helps manage and track a user's workouts.

However, looking at Figure 4(f), which we learn by generalizing from the actions of self-described "rednecks," we find that while some actions are expected for such a badge (e.g., `#teaparty` and `#tcot`[10]), others are more surprising, (e.g., `#p2`, a popular hashtag among progressives). In fact, looking at other hashtags here such as `#obama`, `#debt` and `#syria`, we see that we actually learn a more general badge, referring to American politics and global affairs, rather than

[7] In both cases, we use the implementation provided by Ramage and Rosen in the Stanford Topic Modeling Toolbox, using the default hyperparameter settings and the CVB0 inference algorithm [14].

[8] A full visualization of all 31 badges learned from our model can be found with the supplemental material [4].

[9] `http://www.runkeeper.com`

[10] "Top Conservatives on Twitter"

(a) Harry Potter (b) Vegetarian (c) Manchester United

(d) Runner (e) Entrepreneur (f) Redneck

Figure 4: Word clouds (generated via `wordle.net`) representing six (of 31) badges learned by our model. Here, the size of a word is proportional to the action probability ϕ_{ij}.

one narrowly focused on rednecks. A plausible explanation for this phenomenon can be found in Figure 3(a), where we see that "redneck," associated with label 14, appears in the Twitter profiles of very few users–perhaps too few to effectively learn what it means to be a "redneck" on Twitter.

Figure 5 shows two other badges corresponding to labels present in very few users. The first example, Figure 5(a), is a more extreme form of overgeneralization than the "redneck" badge, as we see the idea of a wine lover translating to actions representing enjoyable (and often expensive) interests and activities, such as `#swarowski`, `#travel` and `#jewelry`. Figure 5(b), on the other hand, shows the extreme situation where the original label–in this case for "Ruby on Rails"–is present in so few users that the badge can be completely overwhelmed by a more popular topic. Here, we see that this badge has been taken by actions relating to the London riots, which was the most prevalent news item in our data.

When we look at the topics learned by labeled LDA, we find that they also represent interpretable badge descriptions. However, as we described earlier in this section, we do not find the same sparsity that we achieve using our model, because topic modeling approaches assume each topic is a distribution over the entire vocabulary. This contrast is made clear in Figure 6, where we see an extremely sparse badge representation for Apple fanboys, as learned by our model, compared to a much denser distribution over actions, learned by labeled LDA. The badge we learn focuses on a few informative actions, such as following `@MacRumors`, whereas the topic learned using labeled LDA includes, in addition to many Apple-related actions, many actions that are just tangentially related (e.g., `#runkeeper`).

3.2.2 Correctness of Badge Assignments

The fundamental goal of this work is not just to produce interpretable badges, but to accurately assign badges to users based on their actions. After all, badges are only useful for personalization if we infer them correctly. We expect our model to significantly outperform labeled LDA here, as we explicitly model the uncertainty relating badges and their corresponding labels, which labeled LDA does not.

In order to quantitatively measure our performance in this area, and compare it to that of labeled LDA, we retrained both models on the Twitter data set, this time holding out a random tenth of present labels, which we treat as ground truth labels that we seek to recover. Specifically, of all badge-user pairs (i, u) corresponding to present labels $\lambda_i^{(u)} = 1$ (of which there are 83,020), we select 10% uniformly at random, and hold them out. We then take the perturbed data set and run both labeled LDA (two stages, as before) and our model, leading to estimated posterior probabilities of badge assignments, $b_i^{(u)}$.

In order to compare the two models as fairly as possible, we take each user and rank his or her badges from most probable to least probable, and see where the held out points (i, u) appear. When ranking badges for a user u using our model, we rank them by descending posterior probability of $b_i^{(u)} = 1$. When ranking based on the labeled LDA model, we rank the topics for each user by decreasing topic proportion. If label i was held out for user u, then the better of the two models will rank badge i closer to the top.[11] Figure 7(a) demonstrates that our model significantly outperforms labeled LDA on this metric, with the held out badges appearing, on average, approximately four positions higher in the ranking. Moreover, we hypothesize that the more active a user is (i.e., the more actions we observe for her in our data set), the better we will do in predicting the held out badge, as we will have more information to base our inference on. This prediction is confirmed in Figure 7(b), where we see a six position difference in the ranking separating the most active from the least active users.

Moving beyond this quantitative comparison, we observe several qualitative properties of our inferred badges that provide anecdotal support for our model's effectiveness. First, as we model each user's badge assignments as a binary vector, we can use our samples to estimate the posterior marginal probability on *pairs* of badges appearing together in the same user, as predicted by our model. These results, shown in the annotated matrix in Figure 8, indicate that the hot spots of badge co-occurrence correspond to pairs of badges that we would expect to see together. In particular, the top four pairs of badges, ranked by decreasing posterior probability, are:

[11]We note that this is a fairer comparison than directly measuring the posterior badge assignment probability, since the labeled LDA probabilities are constrained to sum to one, giving us an unfair advantage. By ranking the badges, we avoid this problem.

(a) Wine lover: overgeneralization

(b) Ruby on Rails: overwhelmed

Figure 5: Two cases showing current limitations of our model that arise when we have labels present in only a small number of people.

(a) badges

(b) labeled LDA

Figure 6: Two word clouds for the "Apple fanboy" badge, contrasting the sparsity of our learned badge (a) versus the corresponding labeled LDA topic (b).

1. Entrepreneur and jQuery
2. Feminist and "London riots" (originally the "Ruby on Rails" badge)
3. Feminist and "American politics" (the generalized "redneck" badge)
4. Photographer and "London riots."

The matrix shows many other correspondences, for instance, tying together pop icons Taylor Swift and Lady Gaga.

Another view of our inferred badge assignments can be obtained by selecting a population of Twitter users from our data set, and visualizing their collective badge profile in aggregate. Here, the size of a badge label in each word cloud is proportional to its mean posterior probability across the entire population of interest. For example, we can compute the mean probability that someone with the word "conservative" in his Twitter profile is assigned the "entrepreneur" badge. Figure 9(a) shows such a word cloud for precisely this population of conservative Twitter users from our data set. We see a heavy focus on the redneck badge among this population, since it's plausible that those with the word "conservative" in their Twitter profiles are apt to tweet about American politics. Interestingly, this is true even though conservatives are more likely to describe themselves as "teachers" or "entrepreneurs", as shown in Figure 9(b), potentially indicating that an interest in politics plays a larger role in influencing Twitter behavior than, say, being a teacher.

Finally, we can compare the inferred badge profiles of two different populations, and look at the differences between them. Naturally, to contrast with the "conservative" population of Twitter users, we also gather all users in our data set with the word "liberal" in their Twitter profile. We can than take our estimate of the mean posterior probability for each badge in each of the two populations, and visualize the difference between them, which we display in Figures 9(c)

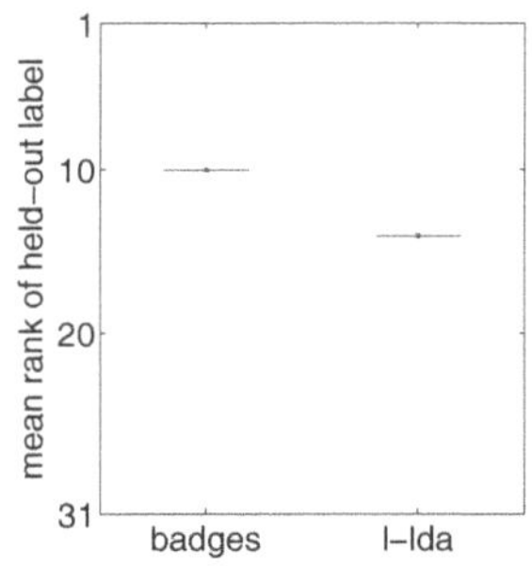

(a)

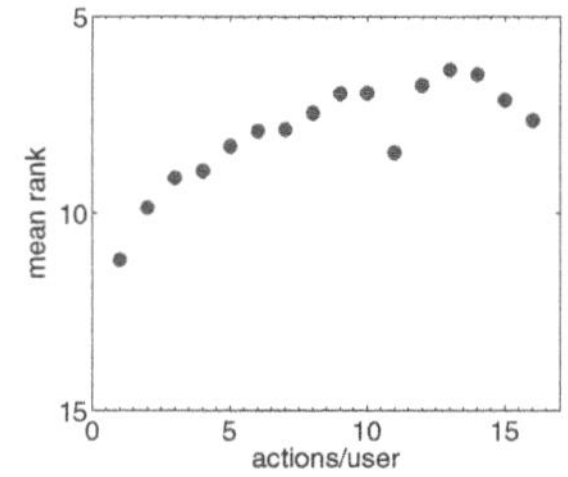

(b)

Figure 7: Results showing that, on a held-out set of labels, (a) our algorithm is better able to recover (approximately) ground truth badges than labeled LDA, and, (b) more active users get better predictions. (Error bars indicating standard error are too small to be visible.)

(conservatives - liberals) and 9(d) (liberals - conservatives). For example, if we look at the word "feminist" in Figure 9(d), its size is proportional to our estimate of the mean posterior difference, $p(b^{(\mathtt{liberals})}_{\mathtt{feminist}}) - p(b^{(\mathtt{conservatives})}_{\mathtt{feminist}})$. As expected, we see, e.g., that the "feminist" badge is the one that is most likely to occur in a liberal and not a conservative.

4. RELATIONSHIP TO PRIOR WORK

Since Zaslow's article on TiVo was published in 2002 [16], many forms of personalization have appeared or intensified on the Web, and they operate with varying degrees of transparency:

- The most transparent and interpretable personalization today is arguably done by Amazon.com. A user gets a selection of "recommended for you" items, with each being associated with a "because you purchased" explanation. If the recommendation is questionable, a user is allowed to correct the system by selecting a "because you purchased" item and indicating "don't use for recommendations." Amazon's feedback is similar to a user revealing the true value of an inferred badge in our model, but more specific. Furthermore, their item-to-item personalization holds the advantage that only user feedback is revealed in any explanations. The reliance on a well-represented catalogue is not feasible in many scenarios, though, and this is most notable where content is user-generated.
- Pandora[12] provides music recommendation based on likes and dislikes of each user, grounded in a "deeply detailed, hand-built musical taxonomy" known as the Music Genome Project[13]. Pandora's personalization service is quite transparent, with each song recommendation accompanied by an explanation for why it was selected, making clear the connection between user feedback and personalization. However, again, a hand-curated feature set like Pandora's is problematic to maintain for more dynamically generated content.
- Google provides users with a Privacy Center[14], from

[12]`http://www.pandora.com`

[13]`http://blog.pandora.com/press/pandora-company-overview.html`

[14]`http://www.google.com/intl/en/privacy/`

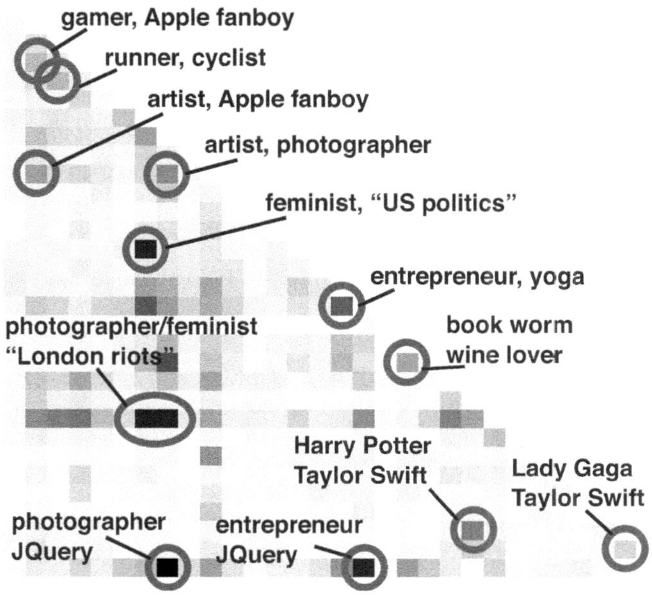

Figure 8: A matrix depicting the posterior marginal probability of badge co-occurrence, as estimated by our model. Darker squares represent higher probabilities. The badges are ordered in the same manner as presented in Table 1.

Figure 9: These four word clouds depict the badges learned for two populations of people: those with the word "conservative" in their Twitter profiles (254 such users in our data set), and those with the word "liberal" in their profiles (327 of them). (a) Shows the mean badge probabilities for self-described conservatives. The size of a badge name is proportional to the mean probability of that badge as estimated by our model. (b) Shows the proportion of "conservatives" that have each of the 31 labels present in their profiles. (c) These badges are more likely for self-described conservatives than self-described liberals, and the size of each badge label is proportional to the absolute difference $(p(b_i^{(\text{conservatives})}) - p(b_i^{(\text{liberals})}))$. (d) Badges more likely for liberals than conservatives. (Recall from Figure 5(b) that the "Ruby on Rails" badge is instantiated as a "London riots" badge.)

which they can opt out of having their Web and search history tracked, which affects personalization of the search results. Additionally, Google has recently allowed its users to see the attributes that it has inferred about them for ad prediction (e.g., "Demographics - Age - 65+"), giving them the option to decline any incorrect or undesired attributes[15]. While in the spirit of what we propose in this paper, this particular dashboard is focused on addressing the quality of personalized advertising, which is not the primary reason users interact with Google. At the time of writing, there does not seem to be any such window for viewing how search results are personalized.

- Bing search[16] is personalized based on search history when signed in with a Microsoft Live account; users see "Search history has changed the ranking of these results. Learn more." on the bottom of their search results. Clicking on "Learn more" provides an opportunity to toggle on or off the personalization, as well as information about how to remove some or all of the search from search history, but it is non-transparent how this affects personalization.
- Social networks such as Facebook and Google+ are (quite openly) repositories of structured personal information, and thus the primary transparency issue with these sites is not what information they infer about their users, but rather how it is used for personalization. For example, at the time of writing, Facebook's News feed is divided into a personalized list of "Top stories" and a timely list of "Recent stories," but there is no way for a user to see why a particular status update appeared in one feed and not the other.

While this is certainly not an exhaustive list, and personalization capabilities are routinely being added and removed from these sites and others, the websites mentioned represent a large portion of user interaction on the Web (e.g., Google and Bing search amounted to 85 percent of all web searches from the United States in September 2011[17], while over 500 million users log on to Facebook per day at the time of writing[18]), demonstrating the importance of studying methods for making personalization more transparent.

From the perspective of methodology, personalization by inferring latent user features has come a long way. While collaborative filtering through factorizing a user-item matrix, and variants thereof, is extremely successful as a backbone of recommender systems [7], the latent features don't have any interpretable meaning. Interpretability often means discretization. In this vein, Porteous et al. extended matrix factorization with discrete class allocations [11], and although we are not aware of its existence, it is entirely feasible to enforce labels to certain class allocations.

When the domain of interest includes user-generated content, like blogs and tweets, latent topic models have frequently provided a successful modeling framework. Unfortunately, as is the case with matrix factorization techniques, the topics learned in such unsupervised models do not lend

[15] `http://googleblog.blogspot.com/2011/10/increasing-transparency-and-choice-with.html`
[16] `http://www.bing.com`
[17] `http://www.comscore.com/Press_Events/Press_Releases/2011/10/comScore_Releases_September_2011_U.S._Search_Engine_Rankings`
[18] `http://newsroom.fb.com`

themselves to interpretability, as they are not identifiable, a problem we avoid by associating each badge with a label. Topic models that incorporate supervision at the topic level, such as labeled LDA, explained in Section 3.2, and the more recent work by Andrzejewski et al. [1], provide a mechanism for such identifiability. For instance, labeled LDA was recently used to model another axis of personalization on Twitter, mapping posts as informative, personal status updates, or inter-user social communication [12].

5. DISCUSSION

In this paper we have presented a Bayesian inference algorithm to learn both a descriptive model and predictor for *badges* based on user activity on a micro-blogging site (Twitter). In our work, a badge is seeded by a label—more generally, a high precision, low recall rule—based on self-reported user information, while our predictive model for badges explicitly relies on the presence or absence of user actions. Both these modeling decisions contribute greatly to the transparency of the prediction and we believe transparency will be a critical building block for personalization systems that users will find acceptable and suitable.

We have shown empirically that our model outperforms state-of-the-art models such as labeled LDA in terms of predictive performance, while producing interpretable descriptions of badges.

There are a number of open questions and challenges that need to be addressed in future work.

- **Scale**: The current inference algorithm is a combination of exact inference (*collapsing* some of the conditional priors; see Section 2.4) and Gibbs sampling with interleaved Metropolis-Hastings steps. The latter is applied for all B badges and F actions. This can become problematic if the number of actions grows unbounded, e.g., if an action is the presence of a word in a status update. In order to scale this approach to real-time streams, a single-pass approximate inference algorithm needs to be developed, with special attention paid to inference algorithms conducted in a distributed setting (cf. [9, 15]).
- **Dynamics**: Currently, our model assumes a fixed but unknown dependency of user actions and badges. In a more realistic setting, this dependency will vary over time. In future work, we will study a time-dependent model, allowing for both "topic drift" as well as the online addition and deletion of badges and actions.
- **Causality**: The proposed model is a purely "correlational" model which bases its inferences about latent badges on observed user activity. This can sometimes lead to *spurious* correlations which we also observed in our experiments, for example, with redneck badges. We have chosen this framework because our analysis is based on logs of activity only. Going forward, we will study causal models of badges by assuming we can influence the choice of actions that a user has (for example, suggest hashtags).
- **Crowd-sourcing**: As badges are defined simply by indicating a label, and in a realistic setting, a large number of them will be needed to model the full spectrum of user behavior, it is natural to consider a crowd-sourced solution for large-scale badge definition. Such an approach would maintain human supervision of badge definition (which we feel is necessary to ensure that badges are meaningful) while scaling our model to be more expressive.

Despite these current limitations and future challenges, our work introduces a promising framework that we believe will be successful in bringing transparency to a myriad of personalized services on the Web.

6. ACKNOWLEDGMENTS

First author was partially supported by ONR grants MURI N000141010934, N000140810752 and PECASE N000141010672.

7. REFERENCES

[1] D. Andrzejewski, X. Zhu, M. Craven, and B. Recht. A framework for incorporating general domain knowledge into latent Dirichlet allocation using first-order logic. In *Proc. IJCAI*, 2011.

[2] D. M. Blei and J. Lafferty. Topic models. In A. Srivastava and M. Sahami, editors, *Text Mining: classification clustering, and applications*. Chapman and Hall, 2009.

[3] D. M. Blei, A. Y. Ng, and M. I. Jordan. Latent Dirichlet allocation. *Journal of Machine Learning Research*, 3:993–1022, 2003.

[4] K. El-Arini, U. Paquet, R. Herbrich, J. Van Gael, and B. Agüera y Arcas. Transparent user models for personalization: Supplemental material. `http://www.cs.cmu.edu/~kbe/badges`.

[5] E. B. Fox. *Bayesian Nonparametric Learning of Complex Dynamical Phenomena*. PhD thesis, Massachusetts Institute of Technology, 2009.

[6] A. Frigessi, P. Di Stefano, C. Hwang, and S. Sheu. Convergence rates of the Gibbs sampler, the Metropolis algorithm and other single-site updating dynamics. *Journal of the Royal Statistical Society, Series B*, pages 205–219, 1993.

[7] Y. Koren, R. M. Bell, and C. Volinsky. Matrix factorization techniques for recommender systems. *IEEE Computer*, 42(8):30–37, 2009.

[8] J. Liu. Peskun's theorem and a modified discrete-state Gibbs sampler. *Biometrika*, 83(3):681–682, 1996.

[9] Y. Low, J. Gonzalez, A. Kyrola, D. Bickson, C. Guestrin, and J. M. Hellerstein. Distributed GraphLab: A framework for machine learning and data mining in the cloud. In *PVLDB*, 2012.

[10] E. Pariser. *The Filter Bubble*. Viking, 2011.

[11] I. Porteous, A. Asuncion, and M. Welling. Bayesian matrix factorization with side information and Dirichlet process mixtures. In *Proc. AAAI*, 2010.

[12] D. Ramage, S. Dumais, and D. Liebling. Characterizing microblogs with topic models. In *Proc. ICWSM*, 2010.

[13] D. Ramage, D. Hall, R. Nallapati, and C. D. Manning. Labeled LDA: A supervised topic model for credit attribution in multi-labeled corpora. In *EMNLP*, 2009.

[14] D. Ramage and E. Rosen. Stanford topic modeling toolbox. `http://nlp.stanford.edu/software/tmt/`.

[15] A. J. Smola and S. Narayanamurthy. An architecture for parallel topic models. *PVLDB*, 3(1):703–710, 2010.

[16] J. Zaslow. If TiVo thinks you are gay, here's how to set it straight. *The Wall Street Journal*, Nov. 26 2002.

Estimating Entity Importance via Counting Set Covers

Aristides Gionis
Yahoo! Research
gionis@yahoo-inc.com

Theodoros Lappas
Boston University
tlappas@cs.bu.edu

Evimaria Terzi
Boston University
evimaria@cs.bu.edu

ABSTRACT

The data-mining literature is rich in problems asking to assess the importance of entities in a given dataset. At a high level, existing work identifies important entities either by *ranking* or by *selection*. Ranking methods assign a score to every entity in the population, and then use the assigned scores to create a ranked list. The major shortcoming of such approaches is that they ignore the redundancy between high-ranked entities, which may in fact be very similar or even identical. Therefore, in scenarios where diversity is desirable, such methods perform poorly. Selection methods overcome this drawback by evaluating the importance of a group of entities *collectively*. To achieve this, they typically adopt a *set-cover* formulation, which identifies the entities in the minimum set cover as the important ones. However, this dichotomy of entities conceals the fact that, even though an entity may not be in the reported cover, it may still participate in many other optimal or near-optimal solutions. In this paper, we propose a framework that overcomes the above drawbacks by integrating the ranking and selection paradigms. Our approach assigns importance scores to entities based on both the *number* and the *quality* of set-cover solutions that they participate in. Our methodology applies to a wide range of applications. In a user study and an experimental evaluation on real data, we demonstrate that our framework is efficient and provides useful and intuitive results.

Categories and Subject Descriptors

H.4 [**Information Systems Applications**]: Miscellaneous; G.2.1 [**Discrete Mathematics**]: Combinatorics—*Combinatorial algorithms, Counting problems*

Keywords

counting, importance sampling, set cover

1. INTRODUCTION

How can we identify a subset of important entities from a given population? This question arises in numerous application domains. For example, how can we select a small subset of reviews to show to a user from over 35,000 reviews hosted on `Amazon.com` for the Kindle Keyboard 3G? Or, as another example, how can we select a set of experts from a large population of skilled individuals registered on sites like `linkedin.com`, `odesk.com` and `guru.com`?

Existing data-mining methods address this type of questions via *entity-ranking* or *entity-selection* methods.

Entity-ranking methods assign a score to each entity and then report to the user the top-k entities with the highest scores. For example, review portals like `Yelp` or `Amazon` rank reviews based on user-submitted helpfulness votes. Such score-assigning schemes ignore the redundancy between the highly-scored entities. For example, the top-k reviews about a laptop may all comment on the battery life and the weight of the laptop, but may provide no information about the quality of its screen or other important features.

Entity-selection methods overcome this drawback by *collectively* evaluating *sets* of entities, and reporting the members of the highest-scoring sets as important. For example, review-selection methods select a small subset of reviews that collectively comment upon all the attributes of a particular product [16, 18, 23]. Similarly, expert-selection methods identify a set of skilled experts that can collectively perform a given task [2, 17]. That is, entity-selection methods identify the entities in the selected subset as important, and naïvely dismiss the rest as unimportant. Such a dichotomy conceals the fact that there may be entities not selected in the discovered solution, but which may participate in equally-good (or almost as good) solutions.

In this paper, we propose a framework that combines the entity-ranking and entity-selection paradigms and overcomes their respective drawbacks. Given a set of entities $\mathcal{C}$, our methods assign an importance score to entities based on the number of *high-quality* solutions that they participate. In particular, we focus on entity-selection problems, which are formalized as *minimum set-cover* problems [1, 14, 16, 17, 21, 23]. The common characteristic of all these formulations is that the input consists of two parts: (i) a universe $U = \{u_1, \ldots, u_n\}$ of items that need to be covered, and (ii) a collection of entities, where each entity is a subset of this universe, i.e., $\mathcal{C} = \{C_1, \ldots, C_m\}$ with $C_i \subseteq U$. Any subset $\mathcal{S}$ of entities whose union contains the entire universe U, i.e., $\cup_{C \in \mathcal{C}'} C = U$, is called a *set cover* or simply a *cover*. The data-mining task is typically mapped to the problem of finding the *minimum set cover*. The assumption in such formulations is that the entities that participate in the minimum cover compose an important subset. Some of the applications this formulation are the following.

Review selection: What are the best reviews to display for a given product? In this application, the universe U consists of all the attributes of the reviewed product. Each review $C \in \mathcal{C}$ comments only on a subset $C \subseteq U$ of the attributes. Given the limited attention-

KDD'12, August 12–16, 2012, Beijing, China.

span of the users, the review-selection problem asks for a small set of reviews that comment on all the attributes of a product [16, 23].

Expert selection: Who are the best experts to select for executing a given task? In this application, the universe U consists of the skills required for a particular task. Each expert $C \in \mathcal{C}$ is represented by the set of his skills $C \subseteq U$. The team-formation problem asks for a small-cardinality team whose members have the required set of skills [2, 17].

The underlying thesis in this paper is that by simply selecting the entities in the minimum set cover and dismissing other set-cover solutions one ignores useful information about the landscape of the solution space. For example, our analysis of the `Guru` dataset[1] revealed that although there are more than 340 000 registered experts, there are only 200 unique combinations of skills. That is, every expert is (on average) identical with approximately 1700 other experts. This means that every set $\mathcal{S}$ of cardinality $|\mathcal{S}|$ is as good as $1700^{|\mathcal{S}|}$ other teams (on average). However, the set-cover formulation naïvely selects to report as important the members of only one of these subsets

In our work, we take into consideration the landscape of solutions by adopting a *counting framework*; instead of focusing on a single optimal solution, we count the number of high-quality set covers that each entity participates. We use the cardinality of a set cover as a measure of its quality; compact covers are preferable, since they lead to lower-cost solutions.

On a high level, we address the following problem.

PROBLEM 1. *We are given a universe of elements U and a set of entities $\mathcal{C}$ where each $C \in \mathcal{C}$ is a subset of U. The goal is to evaluate the importance of each entity by counting the number of compact set covers that it participates.*

In the context of reviews, solving Problem 1 will allow us to to evaluate the utility of each review in the covering of all the attributes of a given product. Intuitively, our methodology will assign high importance to reviews that cover a large number of a product's attributes, or comment on a small number of attributes that are rarely commented by other reviewers. In *expert-management* applications, the scores assigned by our approach will be driven by the number of skills that each individual can contribute, as well as the rarity of these skills. Intuitively, these are the individuals who play a key role in forming effective teams. While we use the domains of reviews and experts to motivate our work, our methodology is applicable to any setting that can be expressed in the terms of the set-covering formulation.

Contribution: Given a set system $X = \langle U, \mathcal{C} \rangle$, where U is a universe of elements and $\mathcal{C}$ is a set of entities defined as subsets of U, our paper proposes a general methodology that assigns importance scores to entities in $\mathcal{C}$. The score of each entity depends both on the number and the quality of the set covers that the entity participates. Enumerating all the set covers that an entity participates is a computationally intractable task. Here, we take advantage of the fact that we are only interested in the *number* of set covers an entity participates. Therefore, we develop practical counting schemes that allow us to accurately estimate this number in polynomial time. More specifically, we propose a counting algorithm that is based on Monte Carlo (MC) sampling. The algorithm builds on existing techniques for counting the number of satisfying assignments of DNF formulas [22]. We significantly extend this technique in the following ways: (i) we modify it so that it can efficiently estimate the number of set covers of *all* entities simultaneously; (ii) we show how we can incorporate weights that capture the size of set cover solutions; (iii) we show how to handle efficiently entities with multiple copies. Finally, our experimental evaluation shows the scalability of our algorithm, and the utility of our methodology in different application domains. Also, our user study demonstrates that our concept of importance is in agreement with human perception regarding important entities.

Roadmap: The rest of the paper is organized as follows. In Section 2 we present an overview of our framework, and in Section 3 we present our algorithms. We present our experimental results in Section 4 and we discuss the related work in Section 5. We conclude the paper with discussion and conclusions in Section 6.

2. THE COUNTING FRAMEWORK

In this paper, we consider problems for which the input consists of two parts: (i) a universe set $U = \{u_1, \ldots, u_n\}$ of items that need to be covered, and (ii) a collection of entities, where each entity is a subset of this universe, i.e., $\mathcal{C} = \{C_1, \ldots, C_m\}$ with $C_i \subseteq U$. We use the notation $X = \langle U, \mathcal{C} \rangle$ to represent such an input. We visualize this type of input using a bipartite graph; the nodes on the one side of the graph correspond to the elements of U, and the nodes of the other side correspond to the entities in $\mathcal{C}$. An edge connects a node $u \in U$ to node $C \in \mathcal{C}$ if $u \in C$. A bipartite-graph representation of input $X = \langle U, \mathcal{C} \rangle$ with $U = \{u_1, u_2, u_3, u_4\}$ and $\mathcal{C} = \{C_1, \ldots, C_5\}$ is shown in Figure 1(a).

DEFINITION 1. *For input $X = \langle U, \mathcal{C} \rangle$ we say that a subset $\mathcal{S}$ of the collection $\mathcal{C}$ ($\mathcal{S} \subseteq \mathcal{C}$) is a* set cover *or simply a* cover *of U if $U \subseteq \bigcup_{C \in \mathcal{S}} C$.*

For the rest of the paper, we will use $\mathbf{L}$ to represent all the subsets of $\mathcal{C}$ and $\mathbf{L}_{sc}$ to represent all possible set covers.

The minimum set cover. A set cover $\mathcal{S}^*$ that has minimum cardinality is called *a minimum set cover.* The problem of finding the minimum set cover, henceforth called SET-COVER, is a well-studied NP-hard problem, which can be approximated within a factor of $O(\log n)$ using a simple greedy algorithm [24].

In many application domains, a solution to SET-COVER is a natural way to select a small subset of $\mathcal{C}$: an entity C of the collection $\mathcal{C}$ is "selected" if and only if C is part of the solution $\mathcal{S}^*$. Then, the entities in $\mathcal{S}^*$ are rendered more "important" than the entities not in the solution. However, such a strict dichotomy can be unfair. For example, an entity C may be part of another minimum or near-minimum set cover. Such a case is shown in the following example.

EXAMPLE 1. *Consider the instance of the* SET-COVER *problem represented by the bipartite graph shown in Figure 1(a) with 4 items in U, 5 entities in $\mathcal{C}$, and $C_1 = \{u_1\}$, $C_2 = \{u_1, u_2\}$, $C_3 = \{u_2, u_3\}$, $C_4 = \{u_3, u_4\}$, and $C_5 = \{u_5\}$. In this case, the minimum set-cover solution is $\mathcal{C} = \{C_2, C_4\}$. The minimum-cardinality solution, in which set C_3 participates, has cardinality 3. Nevertheless, there is no reason to believe that set C_3 is so much less important than C_2 or C_4. After all, C_3 has as many elements as C_2 and C_4.*

Minimal set covers. Instead of focusing on a single minimum-cardinality solution, we could *count the number of solutions* that each entity $C \in \mathcal{C}$ participates. One way of applying this idea is to consider the concept of *minimal set covers.* A set cover $\mathcal{S}$ is *minimal* if $\mathcal{S} \setminus C$ is not a set cover for all $C \in \mathcal{S}$. Minimal set covers have the property that every other cover is a superset of a minimal

[1] `www.guru.com`

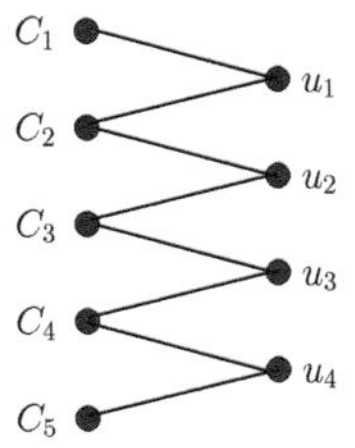

(a) Minimum cardinality set cover

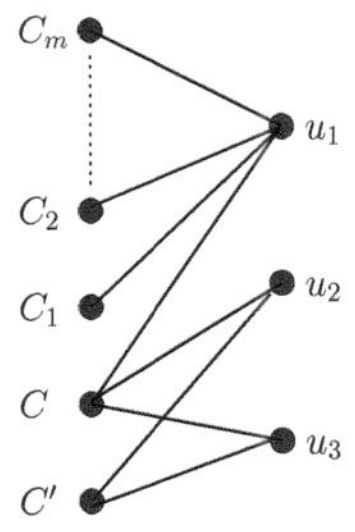

(b) Minimal set covers

Figure 1: Examples used for illustrating the inadequacy of minimum and minimal set covers in value computations.

cover. In order to estimate the importance of a particular entity C, one could count in how many minimal covers it participates. Although this initially looks like a natural approach, the following example indicates that it can lead to unintuitive results.

EXAMPLE 2. *Consider the instance of the* SET-COVER *problem shown in Figure 1(b). In this instance,* $U = \{u_1, u_2, u_3\}$ *and* $\mathcal{C} = \{C', C, C_1, \ldots, C_m\}$, *and* $C_1 = C_2 = \ldots = C_m = \{u_1\}$, $C = \{u_1, u_2, u_3\}$ *and* $C' = \{u_2, u_3\}$. *Observe that* C *can cover all the elements in* U. *Nevertheless, it participates in a single minimal solution* $\{C\}$. *On the other hand,* C' *participates in* m *minimal solutions* $\{C', C_i\}$ *for* $i \in \{1, \ldots, m\}$. *Even though in this case,* C *participates in significantly less minimal solutions than* C', C *is clearly as useful as* C' *(since it is actually a superset of* C'*).*

Counting set covers. We overcome the deficiencies of the above approaches by introducing a score $R(C)$ for every entity $C \in \mathcal{C}$. The *cover score* (or simply *score*) of entity C is defined as follows:

$$R(C) = \sum_{\mathcal{S} \in \mathbf{L}_{sc}} \delta(C, \mathcal{S})\, w(\mathcal{S}). \qquad (1)$$

In the above equation, $\mathbf{L}_{sc}$ represents *all the set covers* of $\langle U, \mathcal{C} \rangle$; the function $\delta(C, \mathcal{S})$ is an indicator variable that takes value 1 if $\mathcal{S}$ is a set cover and takes value 0 otherwise. The term $w(\mathcal{S})$ assigns to every solution $\mathcal{S}$ a weight such that better solutions – smaller cardinality covers – are assigned higher weights. In other words, for two set covers $\mathcal{S}$ and $\mathcal{S}'$ if $|\mathcal{S}| \leq |\mathcal{S}'|$, then $w(\mathcal{S}) \geq w(\mathcal{S}')$. In other words, important entities participate in many good set covers and therefore are assigned higher scores.

In this paper, we consider three weighting schemes:

- *Uniform:* The uniform scheme assigns a weight of 1 to all set covers. Formally: $w(\mathcal{S}) = 1$ for every $\mathcal{S} \in \mathbf{L}_{sc}$. For every other $\mathcal{S}$, $w(\mathcal{S}) = 0$.
- *Step:* The step scheme assigns a weight of 1 to all set covers of size less or equal to a threshold τ. Formally: $w(\mathcal{S}) = 1$ if $\mathcal{S} \in \mathbf{L}_{sc}$ and $|\mathcal{S}| \leq \tau$. Otherwise, $w(\mathcal{S}) = 0$.
- *Cardinality-based:* The cardinality-based scheme assigns a weight that decreases with the cardinality of the set cover. Formally: $w(\mathcal{S}) = w_k > 0$, for every $\mathcal{S} \in \mathbf{L}_{sc}$ and $|\mathcal{S}| = k$; $w(\mathcal{S}) = 0$ for every $\mathcal{S} \notin \mathbf{L}_{sc}$.

From the algorithmic point of view, computing $R(C)$ is computationally intractable; note that there are exponentially many solutions in $\mathbf{L}_{sc}$. More formally, for the uniform weighting scheme, the task of estimating $R(C)$ is identical to the task of counting all set covers for $\langle U, \mathcal{C} \setminus \{C\} \rangle$, which is a #P-complete problem [22].

Discussion: The interpretation of the cover score is the following: if we sample solutions from $\mathbf{L}$ such that every solution $\mathcal{S}$ is sampled with probability proportional to $w(\mathcal{S})$ (i.e., good solutions are sampled with higher probability), then $R(C)$ is proportional to the probability that the sampled solution contains C.

The Equation (1) indicates that the framework we propose bridges Bayesian model-averaging [4] with optimization-based data mining. To draw the analogy, the objective function (expressed via the weight $w(\cdot)$) corresponds to the Bayesian prior. The validity of the solution (expressed via the indicator function $\delta(\cdot, \cdot)$) corresponds to the probability of the data given the model. At a very high level, one can think that $R(C)$ is the average "goodness" of solutions with entity C.

3. ALGORITHMS FOR COUNTING

As already discussed, estimating $R(C)$ is computationally intractable and we cannot hope for computing it exactly in polynomial time. Therefore, we are content with algorithms that approximate the cover score in polynomial time. In this section, we discuss such algorithms for the different weighting schemes.

Apart from $R(C)$ we will also compute the sum of the weights of all the subsets of $\mathcal{C}$. Formally: $R = \sum_{\mathcal{S} \in \mathbf{L}} w(\mathcal{S})$. In some cases, for clarity of presentation, we will use the *uniform weighting scheme*. Under this scheme, R represents the cardinality of set $\mathbf{L}_{sc}$, namely, the number of set covers for $X = \langle U, \mathcal{C} \rangle$.

3.1 Naïve Monte Carlo sampling

We begin by presenting a naïve Monte-Carlo counting algorithm. We discuss why this algorithm fails to compute $R(\cdot)$ under the uniform weighting scheme, but the discussion applies to the other weighting schemes too.

For input $X = \langle U, \mathcal{C} \rangle$ one could compute estimates $R(C)$ using the following procedure: first, set the counters $r = 0$ and $r(C) = 0$ for every $C \in \mathcal{C}$. Then retrieve N samples from $\mathbf{L}$. For each sample $\mathcal{S}$, check if $\mathcal{S}$ is a set cover. If it is, then: (i) increase the value of r by 1 and (ii) increase the value of $r(C)$ by 1 for all $C \in \mathcal{S}$. In the end of the sampling procedure, report the estimate for R to be $2^m r N^{-1}$ and the estimate for $R(C)$ to be $2^m r(C) N^{-1}$, where m is the number of entities in $\mathcal{C}$.

The above algorithm, which we call `NaiveCounter`, is a standard Monte-Carlo sampling method. Using Chernoff bounds, we can state the following fact [22, Theorem 11.1].

FACT 1. *The* `NaiveCounter` *algorithm yields an* ϵ*-approximation to* $R(C)$ *with probability at least* $1 - \delta$, *provided that*

$$N \geq \frac{4}{\epsilon^2 \rho_c} \ln \frac{2}{\delta},$$

where $\rho_c = \frac{R(C)}{2^m}$.

The drawback of `NaiveCounter` is that, as ρ_c becomes smaller, the number of samples N required to obtain a good approximation increases. Since we do not know the value of ρ_c (in fact, this is what we are trying to approximate) we have to rely on a lower bound. In the absence of any evidence, the only reasonable lower bound is $\rho_c \geq \frac{1}{2^m}$. This, however, requires an exponential number of samples, leading to an inefficient and impractical algorithm.

3.2 Importance sampling

We overcome the problem of `NaiveCounter` with a novel and efficient algorithm, based on the principles of *importance sam-*

Algorithm 1 The `CountSimple` algorithm.

Input: $X = \langle U, \mathcal{C} \rangle$ and seed sets $\mathbf{M} = \{\mathcal{M}_1, \ldots, \mathcal{M}_d\}$.
Output: Quantity $R = \sum_{\mathcal{S} \in \mathbf{L}_{sc}} w(\mathcal{S})$.

$r \leftarrow 0$
for iterations N, polynomial in d **do**
  pick $\mathcal{M}_\ell$ from $\mathbf{M}$ with prob $\frac{w(\mathbf{M}_\ell)}{\sum_{j=1}^{d} w(\mathbf{M}_j)}$
  $\mathcal{S} =$ `RandomSample`$(\mathbf{M}_\ell)$
  $\ell^* =$ `CanonicalRepresenative`$(\mathcal{S})$
  if $\ell^* = \ell$ **then** $r \leftarrow r + w(\mathcal{S}_\ell)$
$r \leftarrow r \frac{w(\mathbf{U})}{N}$
return r

pling.[2] We call our algorithm `Compressed-IC`. Our algorithm works for all our weighting schemes and therefore we present it here in its full generality.

The algorithm requires as input a *seed* of d minimal set covers $\mathbf{M} = \{\mathcal{M}_1, \ldots, \mathcal{M}_d\}$. In principle, *all* minimal set covers are required. However, computing all minimal set covers can be a computationally expensive task. Thus, we propose to use as seed a subset of all the minimal covers. As we show in our experiments this is sufficient to accurately estimate the desired counts. Later in the section, we give details on how to obtain such a seed.

In the sections that follow, we give a bottom-up presentation of the `Compressed-IC` algorithm. That is, we describe a sequence of steps that allow us to modify the classic importance sampling algorithm in order to efficiently approximate the cover scores.

3.2.1 *Overview of importance sampling*

We start with an overview of importance sampling for the task of estimating R. For a minimal set cover $\mathcal{M}_\ell$ we define $\mathbf{M}_\ell$ to be the collection of all supersets of $\mathcal{M}_\ell$. Given two (small) positive numbers ϵ and δ, the method provides an ϵ-accurate estimate for R with probability at least $(1 - \delta)$, provided that the following three conditions are satisfied:

1. We can compute $w(\mathbf{M}_\ell) = \sum_{\mathcal{S} \in \mathbf{M}_\ell} w(\mathcal{S})$ for all $\ell = 1, \ldots, d$ in polynomial time.
2. We can obtain a random sample from each $\mathcal{S}_\ell$; where the sampling space is determined by the weighting scheme $w(\mathcal{S})$.
3. We can verify in polynomial time if $\mathcal{S} \in \mathbf{M}_\ell$.

For the weighting schemes we consider in this paper, we have the following lemma.

LEMMA 1. *For the uniform, step, and cardinality-based weighting schemes, all three conditions above are satisfied.*

Due to space constraints, we omit the proof of this lemma.

3.2.2 *The* `CountSimple` *algorithm*

First, we present an algorithm for estimating $R = w(\mathbf{L})$, the sum of the weights of all the subsets in $\mathbf{L}$, i.e., the collections of all possible subsets of $\mathcal{C}$. Recall that all three considered weighting schemes assign a weight of 0 to all subsets that are not set-covers. Therefore, the problem of computing R is reduced to computing the sum of the weights of all the set covers

$$R = w(\mathbf{L}_{sc}) = \sum_{\mathcal{S} \in \mathbf{L}_{sc}} w(\mathcal{S}).$$

The basic idea is to consider the multiset $\mathbf{U} = \mathbf{M}_1 \uplus \ldots \uplus \mathbf{M}_d$, where the elements of $\mathbf{U}$ are pairs of the form $(\mathcal{S}, \ell)$ corresponding to $\mathcal{S} \in \mathbf{M}_\ell$. I.e., for every set cover $\mathcal{S}$, $\mathbf{U}$ contains as many copies of $\mathcal{S}$ as there are $\mathbf{M}_\ell$'s for which $\mathcal{S} \in \mathbf{M}_\ell$. Notice that the total weight of $\mathbf{U}$ can be trivially computed as $w(\mathbf{U}) = \sum_{\ell=1}^{d} w(\mathbf{M}_\ell)$.

The multiset $\mathbf{U}$ is then divided into equivalence classes, where each class contains all pairs $(\mathcal{S}, \ell)$ that correspond to the same set cover $\mathcal{S}$. For each equivalence class, *a single pair* $(\mathcal{S}, \ell)$ is defined to be the *canonical representation* for the class. Now, R can be approximated by generating random elements from $\mathbf{U}$ and estimating the fraction of those that correspond to a canonical representation of an equivalent class. The generation of random samples from $\mathbf{U}$ is done by first picking a minimal set $\mathcal{M}_\ell$ from $\mathbf{M}$ and with probability proportional to the weight of $\mathbf{M}_\ell$. Then, we randomly sample $\mathcal{S}$ from $\mathbf{M}_\ell$. The different weighting schemes imply different sampling methods within $\mathbf{M}_\ell$. However, as Lemma 1 indicates, this sampling can be done in polynomial time.

The pseudocode of this algorithm, named `CountSimple`, is shown in Algorithm 1. The key idea of the algorithm is that instead of sampling from the whole space $\mathbf{L}$, it only draws samples from $\mathbf{U}$. Observe that each cover $\mathcal{S}$ can contribute weight at most $d\, w(\mathcal{S})$ in $w(\mathbf{U})$. Therefore, the ratio $\rho = w(\mathbf{L}_{sc})/w(\mathbf{U})$ is bounded from below by $1/d$. Following a similar argument as in Fact 1, we can estimate the value of $w(\mathbf{L}_{sc})$ using $N \geq \frac{4d}{\epsilon^2} \ln \frac{2}{\delta}$ samples, i.e., the number of samples required is polynomial to the size of $\mathbf{M}$.

Algorithm 2 The `ImportanceCounter` algorithm.

Input: $X = \langle U, \mathcal{C} \rangle$ and seed sets $\mathbf{M} = \{\mathcal{M}_1, \ldots, \mathcal{M}_d\}$.
Output: Quantities R and $R(C)$ for every $C \in \mathcal{C}$.

$R \leftarrow 0$
for $C \in \mathcal{C}$ **do**
  $R(C) \leftarrow 0$
for iterations N, polynomial in d, **do**
  pick $\mathcal{M}_\ell$ from $\mathbf{M}$ with prob $\frac{w(\mathbf{M}_\ell)}{\sum_{j=1}^{d} w(\mathbf{M}_j)}$
  $\mathcal{S} =$ `RandomSample`$(\mathbf{M}_\ell)$
  $\ell^* =$ `CanonicalRepresenative`$(\mathcal{S})$
  if $\ell^* = \ell$ **then**
    $R \leftarrow r + w(\mathbf{M}_\ell)$
    for $C \in \mathcal{S}_\ell$ **do**
      $R(C) \leftarrow R(C) + w(\mathbf{M}_\ell)$
for $C \in \mathcal{C}$ **do**
  $R(C) \leftarrow R(C) \frac{w(\mathbf{U})}{N}$
$R \leftarrow R \frac{w(\mathbf{U})}{N}$
return R, $R(C)$ for every $C \in \mathcal{C}$

3.2.3 *The* `ImportanceCounter` *algorithm*

To estimate the values of $R(C)$, we modify Algorithm 1 as follows: every set $\mathcal{M} \in \mathbf{M}$ needs to be extended so that it contains set C. Using as $\mathbf{M} = \{\mathcal{M}_1 \cup \{C\}, \ldots, \mathcal{M}_d \cup \{C\}\}$, we can then run `CountSimple` for each entity separately and thus compute the number of covers that contain C.

Such an approach, however, is computationally expensive. Each execution of the `CountSimple` algorithm requires N calls to the `CanonicalRepresentative` routine and therefore $O(Nmd)$ time. Since `CountSimple` needs to be executed m times, the total running time is $O(Nm^2d)$. Even if $N = O(d)$ any reasonable seed size is at least $d = O(m)$, implying that the approach needs time $O(m^4)$.

We overcome this computational bottleneck by computing all the score values $R(C)$ for every $C \in \mathcal{C}$ in a single (yet modified) call of the `CountSimple` routine. Algorithm 2 gives the pseudocode of this modified algorithm, which we call `ImportanceCounter`.

[2]See the textbook of Motwani and Raghavan [22] for a detailed discussion on the foundations of this technique.

The main result of this section is that `ImportanceCounter` yields estimates for the m values of $R(C)$ that are as good as executing m times the `CountSimple` algorithm, while it requires almost the same number of samples.

THEOREM 1. *If the weighting scheme satisfies a certain "smoothness" condition, then Algorithm 2 gives an ϵ-approximation of $R(C)$ and R with probability $(1-\delta)$ if*

$$N \geq \frac{(1+\alpha)4d}{\epsilon^2} \ln \frac{2}{\delta},$$

where α is a finite integer greater or equal to 1. Furthermore, for the uniform weighting scheme $\alpha = 1$, for the cardinality-based weighting scheme $\alpha = 2$, while for the the threshold weighting there does not exist a finite α for which the above inequality holds.

Although we do not give the proof of the above theorem, we state the smoothness condition that we require for the weighting scheme $w(\cdot)$, so that the above theorem holds for finite α.

CONDITION 1. *If $\mathcal{S}$ and $\mathcal{T}$ are set covers with $|\mathcal{T}| = |\mathcal{S}| + 1$, then the weighting function satisfies $w(\mathcal{S}) \leq \alpha\, w(\mathcal{T})$ for some $\alpha > 0$. In other words, if $\mathcal{T}$ is larger than $\mathcal{S}$ by one element, the value of the weighting function cannot drop too much.*

Running time: Note that the `ImportanceCounter` algorithm requires only N calls to the `GenerateSuperset` routine, obtaining a factor of $O(m)$ improvement over the naïve approach of executing `CountSimple` m times.

3.2.4 *The* `Compressed-IC` *algorithm*

Even though `ImportanceCounter` is much more efficient than `NaiveCounter`, its running time can still be prohibitive for very large datasets. Here, we present the `Compressed-IC` algorithm, which outputs the same scores as `ImportanceCounter`, but it is much more efficient in practice.

In many of the datasets we considered, we observed that many of the entities in $\mathcal{C}$ are identical. For example, in the case of reviews, there are many identical reviews that comment on the same product attributes. Similarly, in the case of experts, there are many experts who have exactly the same set of skills. `Compressed-IC` takes advantage of this phenomenon while optimizing for running time.

One can observe that, for all our weighting schemes, identical entities are assigned the same cover scores. `Compressed-IC` takes advantage of this observation and compresses all identical entities into into *super-entities*. Then, the algorithm assigns scores to super-entities and in the end it assigns the same score to all the original entities that are part of the same super-entity. The key technical challenge we face here is to design an algorithm that operates on this compressed input and still assigns to all entities the *correct scores*. We say that a score assignment on the compressed input is *correct*, if the scores assigned to entities are identical to the scores that would have been assigned to them by the `ImportanceCounter` algorithm before compression.

A naïve way of dealing with identical entities in $\mathcal{C}$ is to simply ignore their multiplicities. In this case, all identical entities have a single representative and in the end they are all assigned the score of this representative. Although this procedure will reduce the number of entities and the running time of the `ImportanceCounter` algorithm, the output scores will be incorrect. In order to see that these scores are incorrect consider the following example.

EXAMPLE 3. *Assume $X = \langle U, \mathcal{C}\rangle$, where $U = \{u_1, u_2, u_3\}$ and $\mathcal{C} = \{C_0, C_1, \ldots, C_K\}$ with $C_0 = \{u_3\}$ and $C_1 = \ldots = C_K = \{u_1, u_2\}$. If we represent all entities $C_1, \ldots, C_K$ by a single representative $\widehat{C} = \{u_1, u_2\}$ we have a new problem instance $X' = \langle U, \widehat{\mathcal{C}}\rangle$, with $\widehat{\mathcal{C}} = \{C_1, \widehat{C}\}$. If we now compute the cover scores of C_0 and $\widehat{C}$ for input X' and for the uniform weighting scheme, we get that both weights are equal to 1. However, in the original problem instance $X = \langle U, \mathcal{C}\rangle$, the score of C_0 is K times larger than the score of any one of the sets $C_1, \ldots, C_K$.*

Instead of assigning the score of the representative to all the identical entities, we could divide this score by the cardinality of each set of identical entities. This solution also fails to produce the correct cover scores. This is shown in the following example.

EXAMPLE 4. *Consider the problem instance $X = \langle U, \mathcal{C}\rangle$, where $U = \{u_1, u_2, u_3, u_4\}$ and $\mathcal{C} = \{C_1, C_2, C_3, C_4\}$ with $C_1 = C_2 = \{u_1, u_2, u_3\}$, $C_3 = \{u_1, u_2\}$ and $C_4 = \{u_3, u_4\}$. Now assume that we form new set $\widehat{\mathcal{C}} = \{\widehat{C}_{12}, C_3, C_4\}$, where $\widehat{C}_{12} = \{u_1, u_2, u_3\}$. For the problem instance $X = \langle X, \widehat{\mathcal{C}}\rangle$ and uniform weighting scheme, the scores assigned to $\widehat{C}_{12}$, C_3 and C_4 are respectively 3, 3, and 4. Now, if we attempt to find the scores in the original problem by dividing the score of $\widehat{C}_{12}$ equally into C_1 and C_2 we get that the final scores are: $R(C_1) = R(C_2) = 1.5$, $R(C_3 = 3)$ and $R(C_4) = 4$. One can see that these scores are incorrect; they do not correspond to the number of solutions that the different entities participate. Even further, ranking the entities using these scores gives a totally unintuitive ranking: C_1 and C_2 appear to be worse than C_3 although they both cover a superset of the elements that C_3 covers!*

The above two examples illustrate that if we want to form one *super-entity* for each set of identical entities in $\mathcal{C}$, we need to make a very meticulous adaptation of the `ImportanceCounter` algorithm. We describe this adaptation here. First, we transform the input entities $\mathcal{C}$ into $\widehat{\mathcal{C}} = \{\widehat{C}_1, \ldots, \widehat{C}_K\}$ where every $\widehat{C}_j$ is a *super-entity* that represents a set of identical input entities. Each such entity $\widehat{C}_k \in \widehat{\mathcal{C}}$ is characterized by its cardinality T_k. The mechanics of the `Compressed-IC` algorithm are similar to the mechanics of the `ImportanceCounter` algorithm, shown in Algorithm 2. The main differences are explained below.

First, note that every minimal set $\mathcal{M}_\ell$ now consists of super-entities and therefore the probability of $\mathcal{M}_\ell$ being sampled is the weighted sum of the probabilities of all the minimal sets it represents. Once a minimal set $\mathcal{M}_\ell$ is selected, a particular element $\mathcal{S}$ is sampled from $\mathbf{M}_\ell$. The sampling is identical to the corresponding step of the `ImportanceCounter` algorithm. The result of sampling is a set cover $\mathcal{S}$ that consists of j super-entities $\widehat{C}_1, \ldots, \widehat{C}_j$; for each super-entity $\widehat{C}_i$ that participates in $\mathcal{S}$, we know its cardinality T_i as well as the number t_i of actual entities that were sampled from $\widehat{C}_i$. By treating super-entities in the same way as entities, we check whether the canonical representative of the sampled set cover $\mathcal{S}$ is indeed the previously-selected minimal set $\mathcal{M}_\ell$. If this is not the case, no counter is increased. Otherwise, we need to do the following: first, we accept the match with probability $\left(\prod_{\widehat{C}_i \in \mathcal{M}_\ell} t_i\right)^{-1}$. Second, for every entity $C \in \widehat{C}_i$ the score of C is increased by $w(\mathbf{M}_\ell) t_i T_i^{-1}$. The rest of the steps of the `Compressed-IC` algorithm remain identical with those of the `ImportanceCounter` algorithm.

We have the following result.

THEOREM 2. *The cover scores computed by* `Compressed-IC` *are correct. That is, they are identical to the scores computed by the* `ImportanceCounter` *algorithm.*

Although we omit the proof of Theorem 2 we consider this theorem as the second main technical contribution of our work.

The running time of the `Compressed-IC` algorithm depends only on the number of super-entities and not on the actual number of entities. Therefore, for datasets that contain small number of distinct entities the `Compressed-IC` algorithm is extremely efficient, while at the same time it outputs the correct scores for all the individual entities.

From now on, whenever we use the term entities, we will refer to the super-entities that are formed after the compression of the identical input entities.

3.2.5 Selecting the seed of minimal sets

As discussed early in the section, importance sampling requires the complete set $\mathbf{M}$ of all minimal set covers. However, enumerating all the minimal set covers is a computationally expensive task; this problem is known as the *transversal hypergraph* problem. Although we experimented with various available methods for the problem [3, 9, 12], none of them was able to generate all minimal set covers in reasonable time, even for small inputs.

Therefore, we propose to execute `Compressed-IC` with a seed of minimal sets, which is a subset of $\mathbf{M}$. Our intuition is that even a small-cardinality seed is adequate to accurately estimate the counts of the entities in the input. We form such seeds by starting with set $\mathcal{C}$ and randomly removing elements until we reach a minimal solution. We repeat this process until we generate a seed of the desired size. Our experiments indicate that a seed of size moderately larger than m, where m is the total number of entities, is sufficient.

3.2.6 Decomposition into subproblems

Assume that the input can be partitioned into *disjoint connected components*, where a connected component is defined over the bipartite graph representation that we used in Figure 1. In this case, to compute R and $R(C)$ for every $C \in \mathcal{C}$, it is sufficient to compute the $R(C)$'s for all the C's that are in the same connected component separately. Such separate computations are much faster, since they operate on smaller inputs. We can then obtain the final counts by simply computing the product of the values reported for each component. For the datasets we have experimented with, this decomposition alone has yielded significant speedups. For example, in one of our datasets there were 2227 entities, while the largest component included only 705, i.e., about 30%, of them.

3.2.7 Discussion

Oftentimes, counting problems are solved using the Markov chain Monte Carlo method [20], and Metropolis-Hastings [11]. In our setting, such a method would sample elements of $\mathbf{L}_{sc}$ by performing a random walk on the space $\mathbf{L}_{sc}$. Appropriate definitions of the random walk can guarantee unbiased estimates of the required scores. Using the appropriate random walk, we experimented with such a method and found it is very inefficient when compared to `Compressed-IC`. Thus, we do not present this method in detail, neither do we show any experiments for it.

4. EXPERIMENTS

In this section, we describe the experiments we conducted to evaluate the `Compressed-IC` algorithm, in terms of both utility and performance. We also report the results of a user study that demonstrates the validity of our scores and their closeness to the human perception of important entities. All our results are obtained using the step weighting scheme, since it is the obvious choice in applications where the size of the set cover solutions is important.

For all our experiments, we use a machine with 8GB of RAM and 2.66GHz processor speed.

4.1 Datasets

We evaluate our algorithms using three families of datasets, which we describe below.

`GPS` **datasets:** We consider the reviews of the five most-frequently reviewed GPS systems sold on Amazon.com, as of 2010. Thus we compile five different datasets in total. For this dataset family, the universe U is the set of product attributes. Each review C_i comments on a subset of the product attributes. In other words, each review is represented by the set of the attributes discussed in the review. We construct the subsets C_i by parsing the reviews using the method by Hu and Liu [13], which can be shown to extract the review attributes with high accuracy. An attribute is covered if there exists at least one review that discusses this attribute. The cover score $R(C_i)$ expresses the usefulness of the review C_i. In addition to the complete text for each review, the datasets also include the number of the accumulated *helpfulness* votes of each review; we anonymize the five datasets and simply refer to them as `GPS-1`, `GPS-2`, `GPS-3`, `GPS-4` and `GPS-5`. The number of reviews in these datasets are 375, 285, 254, 216 and 222, respectively.

`Guru` **datasets:** We construct the `Guru` datasets by crawling the `www.guru.com` website, which hosts profiles of active freelancers from various professional disciplines, such as software engineering, marketing, etc. We extracted the skills of each each freelancer and we compiled five different datasets as follows: each dataset corresponds to a task that requires c skills, with $c \in \{10, 20, 40, 80, 160\}$. Each dataset consists of all the freelancers who have at least one of the skills required by the respective task. We refer to the five datasets as `Guru-1`, `Guru-2`, `Guru-3`, `Guru-4` and `Guru-5`. The number of freelancers in each one of these datasets is 109 158, 184 520, 239 856, 300 256 and 317 059 respectively.

With the `Guru` datasets, we evaluate the ability of our algorithm to identify the freelancers who are most valuable for a given task. Consequently, the universe U is the set of skills required for the task. Each freelancer C_i is represented by the set of his skills, as they appear in his profile. The cover score $R(C_i)$ given by our algorithm quantifies the usefulness of the freelancer C_i, with respect to the given task and can be used to rank experts.

4.2 Performance of `Compressed-IC`

In this section we provide a comprehensive experimental evaluation of the behavior of the scores $R(C)$ output by `Compressed-IC` as well as the running time of the algorithm.

Inefficiency of the naïve Monte-Carlo sampling: We start the presentation of our experimental results by pointing out that the the naïve Monte-Carlo sampling technique presented in Section 3.1 is impractical. The reason for that is that the naïve sampling rarely succeeds in forming a set from $\mathbf{L}_{sc}$. In practice, for each one of our 10 datasets, we sampled 10 000 sets from $\mathbf{L}$: in 5 out of 10 datasets 0% of the samples were set covers; in 4 out of 10 1% of the samples were set covers and in the remaining one 12% of the samples were set covers. This indicates, that we cannot rely on this technique in order to compute the $R(C)$ scores.

`Compressed-IC` **vs.** `ImportanceCounter`**:** As we discussed in Section 3.2.4, the `Compressed-IC` algorithm gives the same results as `ImportanceCounter`, but it is designed to handle datasets with multiple copies of entities in $\mathcal{C}$. Thus, the only difference between the `Compressed-IC` algorithm and `ImportanceCounter` is that the former keeps a single copy for every set of identical entities, rather than considering each one of them separate-

Table 1: Compressed-IC; GPS and Guru datasets: ratio of the number of super entities considered by Compressed-IC over the number of original set of entities in the dataset.

GPS				
GPS-1	GPS-2	GPS-3	GPS-4	GPS-5
0.808	0.6667	0.7087	0.8009	0.6667
Guru				
Guru-1	Guru-2	Guru-3	Guru-4	Guru-5
0.0001	0.0004	0.0005	0.0036	0.0253

ly. In other words, the Compressed-IC algorithm compresses entities into super-entities. Table 1 shows the corresponding *compression ratio*; that is, the ratio of the number of super-entities (after compression) to the number of total entities (before compression) in all 10 datasets. The smaller the value of this ratio the larger the compression achieved by the super-entities.

The results show that the compression ratio achieved for the GPS datasets ranges from 67% to 81%. For the Guru datasets, this ratio is much smaller, ranging from 0.01% to 2.5%. Such large compressibility can be explained by the nature of this particular data type; recall that, in the Guru datasets, each freelancer is associated with a set of skills. It is much more likely to have multiple freelancers with identical sets of skills; for example, it is expected that all programmers know more or less the same set of programming languages. On the other hand, when it comes to product reviews, it is less likely (although possible) to find reviews that comment on exactly the same set of product attributes.

Effect of the size of the seed of minimal sets: As we discussed in Section 3.2, ImportanceCounter requires as input a set of minimal solutions. While, in principle, the complete set of all such solutions is required, we show here that using a subset is sufficient for the algorithm to converge. First, we run the algorithm with different seed sizes and retrieve the produced cover scores for each individual. Specifically, we try all the seed sizes in $\{m, 10m, 20m, 30m, 40m\}$ (in that order), where m is the total number of entities. We then compare the scores obtained for the different entities after consecutive runs (i.e., m vs. $10m$, $10m$ vs. $20m$, etc.). Since we use these scores to rank entities, we assess the stability of the different runs by comparing the ranked lists induced by the computed scores. For comparing ranked lists, we use the popular Kendall-τ rank correlation coefficient [15]. The measure takes values in [0, 1]; the lower the value the more different the two lists are.

The process is repeated for all 10 datasets. The results are shown in Table 2. Each value is an average of 50 experiments, each using a different seed set. The results show that even though we use very small seed sets, the scores obtained with seeds of different sizes produce very similar ranked lists. In particular, as the size of the seed set grows very moderately most values of τ become very close to 1.00. This behavior is verified across all three families of datasets. Therefore, we conclude that the Compressed-IC algorithm is robust, and the estimated scores produce stable rankings even when considering small-size seed sets.

Effect of the number of samples: Theorem 1 provides a theoretical bound on how many samples are necessary for the ImportanceCounter and Compressed-IC algorithms compute the true values of $R(C)$ under different weighting schemes. In this experiment, we demonstrate that, in practice, even smaller number of sample is sufficient.

Table 2: Kendall-τ rank correlation between rankings induced from cover scores obtained with seeds of different sizes. The results are averages of 50 repetitions, where each repetition uses a different seed.

Dataset	1 vs. 10	10 vs. 20	20 vs. 30	30 vs. 40
GPS-1	0.75	0.77	0.82	0.86
GPS-2	0.77	0.88	0.90	0.90
GPS-3	0.82	0.88	0.9	0.9
GPS-4	0.8	0.9	0.9	0.9
GPS-5	0.79	0.85	0.87	0.89
Guru-1	1.00	1.00	1.00	1.00
Guru-2	0.88	0.93	0.93	0.94
Guru-3	0.84	0.89	0.89	0.90
Guru-4	0.96	0.99	0.99	0.99
Guru-5	0.98	0.98	0.99	0.99

Table 3: Number of samples and time required until the Kendall-τ rank correlation coefficient reaches a value 0.90. The results are averages of 50 repetitions, with 50 different seeds.

Dataset	# entities	# samples	time (sec)
GPS-1	375	3 000	4.222
GPS-2	285	3 000	1.526
GPS-3	254	3 000	1.14
GPS-4	216	3 000	1.130
GPS-5	222	3 000	0.689
Guru-1	109 158	8 640	29.607
Guru-2	184 520	6 600	42.547
Guru-3	239 856	3 920	26.595
Guru-4	300 256	3 100	71.367
Guru-5	317 059	3 060	47.552

Our experimental setting is the following: first we apply the Compressed-IC algorithm to each of the 10 datasets, using a seed of size $20m$. As a convergence criterion, we use the Kendall-τ rank correlation coefficient. We let the algorithm run until the Kendall-τ coefficient reaches a value of 0.90 (while checking the τ coefficient every 1000 samples).

The results of our experiments are summarized in Table 3. Again, the results reported in Table 3 are averages over 50 repetitions, where each repetition considers a different seed set. For each dataset, in the second column of the table, we report the number of entities in the dataset since it has direct impact on the complexity of algorithm.Next, we report the total number of total samples required until reaching Kendall-τ value of 0.90 (third column), as well as the actual computation time in seconds (fourth column).

As shown in Table 3, in most cases a small number of samples is needed: in all cases but one the number of samples required is less than 10 000. This is true even for the Guru datasets, which have three orders of magnitude more sets than the other datasets. Therefore, the number of required samples grows very mildly with the number of sets in the dataset. On the other hand, the number of entities impacts the overall running time of the algorithm. This is expected since the time required for drawing one sample grows linearly with the number of entities in the dataset.

4.3 Evaluating the quality of the results

Here, we compare the scores produced by Compressed-IC with other baselines. Due to space constraints, we only show results for the largest dataset from each family.

For the GPS-1 dataset, we use as baseline score the *helpfulness score* of a review, i.e., the number of users that have declared this review to be helpful. The helpfulness score is a popular criterion for ranking reviews in review-hosting sites (e.g., `amazon.com`). Figure 2(a) shows the scatterplot between the cover and the helpfulness scores; note that the cover scores are normalized, i.e, scores $R(C)$ are divided by R so that the measures are in $[0, 1]$.

We observe that there is no correlation between the cover and helpfulness. For example, helpfulness does not directly consider the contribution of each review in the coverage of an item's attributes. Instead, it relies on the willingness of the users to reward a "good" review by giving a helpfulness vote. In such a scheme, older reviews are more likely to collect higher helpfulness votes, regardless of whether they are more informative [19]. Our scoring scheme, on the other hand, is unaffected by such biases, since it objectively evaluates reviews based on their contribution.

For the `Guru-5` dataset, we select a *frequency-based* baseline score, i.e., the number of skills of each freelancer. The scatter plot between our measure and the baseline is shown in Figure 2(b). This baseline measure can take only one of 5 distinct values {1,2,3,4,5} and considers all freelancers with the same number of skills as equally important. This is an over-simplifying assumption that does not take into consideration factors like the rarity of each skill. For example, one of the freelancers has the following five skills: {*Children's Writing, Writing-Editing & Translation, Reports, Technical Writing, Blogs*}. While this freelancer has the maximum number of skills, all of these skills are very common. This fact is captured by our own measure, since the particular freelancer participates in far less covers than most of his peers. As a result, this freelancer is given one of the lowest observed scores (0.007). On the other hand, a freelancer with only three skill {*Commercial Interior Design, Landscape Design*} is assigned one of the top-30 scores (0.49). This is because his second skill (*Landscape Design*) is a rather rare skill, possessed by only 260 other individuals. Therefore, our scoring scheme can differentiate between individuals with the same number of skills, and it can also identify important experts even when they have small number of skills.

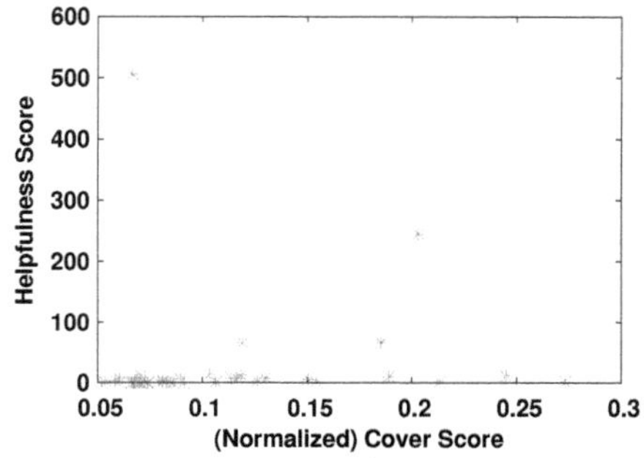

(a) `GPS-1` dataset

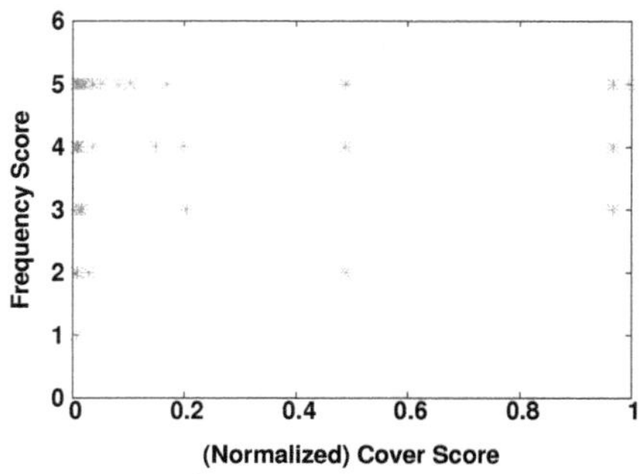

(b) `Guru-5` dataset

Figure 2: Scatterplots of (normalized) scores of entities against their baseline scores.

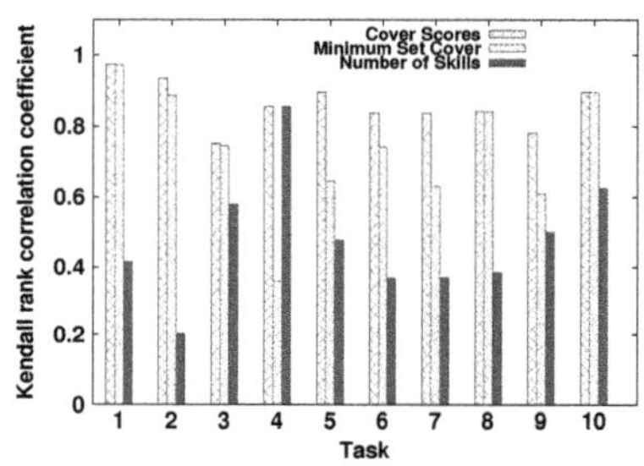

Figure 3: Average Kendall-τ rank-correlation coefficient between human rankings and rankings obtained by cover scores, number of skills and minimum set covers.

4.4 User study

In this section, we present a user study that we conducted in order to validate the assumption that cover scores give rankings that agree with human intuition. Using the original dataset from `Guru`, we sampled 10 small groups of freelancers; the cardinality of each group was randomly selected between 5 and 10. For the i-th group of freelancers we created a task T_i, which was defined as the union of the skills of the freelancers in the i-th group. Using these 10 tasks we set up a survey on `kwiksurveys.com`, in which 30 human subjects participated. The subjects were asked to inspect the skills required for a task and the skills of the freelancers in the corresponding group. The subjects were then asked to rank the freelancers in the group by assigning to every freelancer a numeric "usefulness" score with the following interpretation: 4 if the freelancer is absolutely necessary, 3 if she is very useful, 2 if she is somewhat useful, and 1 if she is not useful. In the instructions it was made clear that the team will have to complete the task repetitively and that the task can only be completed if all the required skills are represented.

Figure 3 shows the average Kendall-τ rank correlation coefficient between the rankings obtained by the humans and the rankings obtained by three automated measures: (i) using the cover scores, (ii) the number of skills per freelancer, and (iii) the minimum set-cover solution; in the latter ranking all freelancers in the minimum set cover were ranked higher than the rest. Recall that the Kendall-τ coefficient takes values in $[0, 1]$, with 1 (resp. 0) denoting the largest (resp. smallest) similarity between the compared rankings. The results indicate that the ranking obtained by cover scores has consistently high Kendall-τ value; this value never drops below 0.8 and it is close to 1 for most of the tasks. On the other hand, with the exception of task T_4, the Kendall-τ coefficients between human rankings and rankings by the number of skills per freelancer are notably low. For task T_4, we observe the highest similarity between these two rankings. This is because the freelancers in the 4-th group are more or less equivalent both in terms of their count scores and in terms of their number of skills (all of them have 1 or 2 common skills). Therefore, the frequency and the cover-score rankings are very similar to each other and also similar to the human rankings. This also explains why for task T_4 the minimum set-cover ranking does not correlate well with the human ranking. Apparently, the single set-cover solution does not reflect the equivalence between the freelancers and the fact that they all participate in many different set-cover solutions. Other than T_4, the minimum set-cover rankings correlate well with the human rankings. This is mostly because for many of the tasks we considered the number of freelancers is small and therefore the majority of the freelancers participate in the minimum cover. Nevertheless, this correlation is not as strong as the one between human and cover-score rankings.

Overall, the user study demonstrates that humans perceive cover scores as a natural ranking mechanism.

5. RELATED WORK

To the best of our knowledge, we are the to formalize framework that allows counting techniques for the evaluation of entity importance. Nonetheless, our work has ties to existing research. We summarize some of this work here.

Counting set covers. There are many theoretical studies on the problem of hitting-set counting, [6, 7, 8, 10] including complexity studies and algorithms for special inputs. Since the hitting set and the set cover problems are isomorphic, these methods can also count set covers. Among these works, the closest to ours is the work of Damaschke and Molokov [8], that proposes a parameterized algorithm for counting all k-hitting sets (i.e, hitting sets of size at most k) in set systems, where the size of the maximum set is at most r. Their algorithm runs in time that is exponential in k and in r, and despite its theoretical elegance, it is impractical for reasonably large datasets.

Review selection. Lappas and Gunopulos [16] considered the problem of finding a small set of reviews that cover *all* product attributes. Tsaparas et. al. [23] studied the problem of selecting a set of reviews that includes both a positive and negative opinion on each attribute. More recently, Lappas and Terzi [18] proposed a scheme for showing to users different covers of the same corpus of reviews. All these works focus on picking a single set of reviews that optimizes a particular function under a set of constraints. On the other hand, our framework evaluates reviews by assigning a score based on the weight of *all* the solutions that each review participates in. Although the notion of coverage is central to our framework, our intuition and methodology are distinct from existing work in the area.

Team formation. The problem of identifying a set of individuals from a pool of experts who are capable of performing a given task has been an active area of research in Operations Research [5, 25, 26]. Our own recent work has introduced the problem in the computer science domain [2, 17]. This work focuses on identifying a single team of experts that collectively meet a certain set of requirements. Our framework is complementary to this: it identifies the marginal value of each expert with respect to a given task. Also, instead of reporting a single solution of the optimization problem at hand, our framework counts *all* solutions. Thus, the technical challenges we face are orthogonal to the those faced when looking for a single good solution.

6. DISCUSSION AND CONCLUSIONS

Our work is motivated by data-mining problems that have been formalized in terms of the set-cover problem. For such formulations, we have developed a novel framework for evaluating the importance of entities. Instead of looking at a single set-cover solution, our framework computes the importance of entities by counting of the number of good set covers an entity participates. Our algorithmic contribution is the design of `Compressed-IC`, which is an efficient algorithm for solving this problem. Our algorithm is proven to provide the correct counts and scales extremely well. Our framework has applications in numerous domains, including those of human-resource management and review-management systems. In a thorough experimental evaluation, we have demonstrated the efficiency and the effectiveness of our methods, using real datasets from such domains.

Acknowledgements. Aristides Gionis was partially supported by the Torres Quevedo Program of the Spanish Ministry of Science and Innovation, co-funded by the European Social Fund, and by the Spanish Centre for the Development of Industrial Technology under the CENIT program, project CEN-20101037, "Social Media" (`http://www.cenitsocialmedia.es/`).

Theodoros Lappas and Evimaria Terzi were supported by the NSF award #1017529, and from gifts from Microsoft, Yahoo! and Google.

7. REFERENCES

[1] F. N. Afrati, A. Gionis, and H. Mannila. Approximating a collection of frequent sets. In *KDD*, 2004.

[2] A. Anagnostopoulos, L. Becchetti, C. Castillo, A. Gionis, and S. Leonardi. Power in unity: forming teams in large-scale community systems. In *CIKM*, 2010.

[3] J. Bailey, T. Manoukian, and K. Ramamohanarao. A fast algorithm for computing hypergraph transversals and its application in mining emerging patterns. In *ICDM*, 2003.

[4] C. Bishop. *Pattern Recognition and Machine Learning*. Springer, 2006.

[5] S.-J. Chen and L. Lin. Modeling team member characteristics for the formation of a multifunctional team in concurrent engineering. *IEEE Transactions on Engineering Management*, 51(2), 2004.

[6] V. Dahllöf, P. Jonsson, and M. Wahlström. Counting models for 2sat and 3sat formulae. *TCS*, 332(1-3), 2005.

[7] P. Damaschke. Parameterized enumeration, transversals, and imperfect phylogeny reconstruction. *TCS*, 351, 2006.

[8] P. Damaschke and L. Molokov. The union of minimal hitting sets: Parameterized combinatorial bounds and counting. *J. Discrete Algorithms*, 7(4), 2009.

[9] T. Eiter and G. Gottlob. Identifying the minimal transversals of a hypergraph and related problems. *SIAM J. Comput.*, 24, 1995.

[10] J. Flum and M. Grohe. The parameterized complexity of counting problems. *SIAM J. of Computing*, 33(4), 2004.

[11] W. K. Hastings. Monte Carlo sampling methods using Markov chains and their applications. *Biometrika*, 57(1), 1970.

[12] C. Hébert, A. Bretto, and B. Crémilleux. A data mining formalization to improve hypergraph minimal transversal computation. *Fundam. Inf.*, 80, 2007.

[13] M. Hu and B. Liu. Mining opinion features in customer reviews. In *AAAI*, 2004.

[14] D. Kempe, J. M. Kleinberg, and É. Tardos. Maximizing the spread of influence through a social network. In *KDD*, 2003.

[15] M. G. Kendall. A New Measure of Rank Correlation. *Biometrika*, 30(1/2), 1938.

[16] T. Lappas and D. Gunopulos. Efficient confident search in large review corpora. In *ECMLPKDD*, 2010.

[17] T. Lappas, K. Liu, and E. Terzi. Finding a team of experts in social networks. In *KDD*, 2009.

[18] T. Lappas and E. Terzi. Toward a fair review-management system. In *ECMLPKDD*, 2011.

[19] J. Liu, Y. Cao, C. Y. Lin, Y. Huang, and M. Zhou. Low-Quality Product Review Detection in Opinion Summarization. In *EMNLP-CoNLL*, 2007.

[20] N. Metropolis, A. W. Rosenbluth, M. N. Rosenbluth, A. H. Teller, and E. Teller. Equation of State Calculations by Fast Computing Machines. *The Journal of Chemical Physics*, 21(6), 1953.

[21] T. Mielikäinen and H. Mannila. The pattern ordering problem. In *PKDD*, 2003.

[22] R. Motwani and P. Raghavan. *Randomized Algorithms*. Cambridge University Press, 1995.

[23] P. Tsaparas, A. Ntoulas, and E. Terzi. Selecting a comprehensive set of reviews. In *KDD*, 2011.

[24] V. Vazirani. *Approximation Algorithms*. Springer, 2003.

[25] H. Wi, S. Oh, J. Mun, and M. Jung. A team formation model based on knowledge and collaboration. *Expert Syst. Appl.*, 36(5), 2009.

[26] A. Zzkarian and A. Kusiak. Forming teams: an analytical approach. *IIE Transactions*, 31, 2004.

ComSoc: Adaptive Transfer of User Behaviors over Composite Social Network*

Erheng Zhong†, Wei Fan‡, Junwei Wang§, Lei Xiao§, and Yong Li§
†Hong Kong University of Science and Technology, Hong Kong
‡IBM T.J.Watson Research Center, New York, USA
§Tencent Inc., Shenzhen, China
ezhong@ust.hk, weifan@us.ibm.com, {jannywang,shawnxiao,nickyyli}@tencent.com

ABSTRACT

Accurate prediction of user behaviors is important for many social media applications, including social marketing, personalization and recommendation, etc. A major challenge lies in that, the available behavior data or interactions between users and items in a given social network are usually very limited and sparse (e.g., $\geq$ 99.9% empty). Many previous works model user behavior from only historical user logs. We observe that many people are members of several social networks in the same time, such as Facebook, Twitter and Tencent's QQ[1]. Importantly, their behaviors and interests in different networks influence one another. This gives us an opportunity to leverage the knowledge of user behaviors in different networks, in order to alleviate the data sparsity problem, and enhance the predictive performance of user modeling. Combining different networks "simply and naively" does not work well. Instead, we formulate the problem to model multiple networks as "composite network knowledge transfer". We first select the most suitable networks inside a composite social network via a hierarchical Bayesian model, parameterized for individual users, and then build topic models for user behavior prediction using both the relationships in the selected networks and related behavior data. To handle big data, we have implemented the algorithm using Map/Reduce. We demonstrate that the proposed composite network-based user behavior model significantly improve the predictive accuracy over a number of existing approaches on several real world applications, such as a very large social-networking dataset from Tencent Inc.

Categories and Subject Descriptors

H.2.8 [**Database Management**]: Database Applications – Data Mining

*Part of the work is done during the first author's internship at Tencent Inc.

[1]`http://www.tencent.com/en-us/ps/imservice.shtml`

KDD'12, August 12–16, 2012, Beijing, China.

Keywords

Social Network Analysis, Transfer Learning

1. INTRODUCTION

An important challenge for user behavior modeling in social media is how to push the right information to the right users at the right time. Accurate user-behavior models enable us to predict users' actions and intents based on data collected from online product purchasing, webpage browsing and ads clicking history, etc. Different approaches of user-behavior modeling, such as collaborative filtering, have been proposed [19]. A major challenge to use these methods lies in the "sparse" nature of historical data, whereby users have interactions with only few other users and items; users may click on only one or two advertisements and listen to a few songs during a time period. For example, the dataset from Tencent has more than 99.9% empty entries in the user-item interaction matrix. The problem with sparse data makes existing methods overfit, and thus fails to model users' behaviors accurately.

With the development of Web 2.0, billions of users are now engaged in multiple online social networks, such as Facebook, Twitter, Tencent's QQ, etc. In many cases, a given user is simultaneously a member of several different networks. These networks form a **composite** social network, where users have various relationships, and can both exhibit different behaviors in each individual network or subnetwork, and share some common latent interests across networks in the same time. Many people use Facebook to communicate with their friends, but post their real-time information on Twitter and browse video uploaded by others on Youtube. Inside a composite social network, links in different sub-networks reflect users' behaviors and relationships from different aspects. For example, friendship relationships on Facebook reflect users' acquaintances in daily life, but contacts on Youtube capture users' common preferences on videos instead. Users tend to build social relations based on interests, and their behaviors are closely related to interests. Thus, one's behaviors can be inferred from that of his/her neighbors. For example, one may want to watch a movie as he/she finds that most friends have watched already. Hence, the knowledge in users' social relationships shed light on solving the sparsity problem.

While interactions in a single social network can be sparse, there is an opportunity to exploit data in multiple networks by considering overlapping users as bridges. Several previous research works have considered combining multiple networks to form a larger network, in which a holistic user

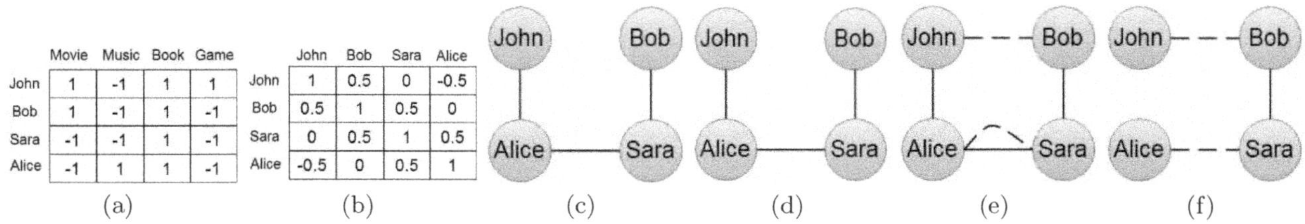

Figure 1: Synthetic example on how to exploit Composite Social Network adaptively. (a) the complete user-item interaction matrix - most items are empty and need to be modeled by recommendation system; (b) the user similarity based on user-item interactions; (c) "Facebook" relationship among them; (d) "Following" relationship on Twitter; (e) the naive combination of (c) and (d); (f) the adaptive combination reflecting the correct user similarity in (b).

model could ideally be built. For example, Pan et al. [16] has proposed to combine multiple user relationships to recommend Apps to users, where the subnetworks are treated uniformly, such that each user-user relationship holds the same importance. However, we observe that in a composite network, the solution by treating each relationship uniformly may likely result in poor prediction performance, due to the following two reasons. First, different networks have their own properties, such as density, degree distributions, clustering coefficient or diameters. If we combine dense and sparse networks together, the information in the sparse network will be overwhelmed inside the dense one. Second, users play different roles and get different levels of influence from their neighbors in individual networks. Some users may prefer Facebook over Twitter for one application, while others may use Twitter more frequently instead. Hence, neighbors in different networks may have different impacts on a given user. To illustrate the idea, a synthetic example is drawn in Figure 1, where there are four users (John, Sara, Bob, Alice) and their preferences on four hobbies: watching movie, listening to music, reading book and playing games. In this figure, "1" represents "like" and "-1" denotes "dislike". Based on the interaction matrix in Figure 1(a), we compute the users' similarities with cosine distance [19], as shown in Figure 1(b). Clearly, John is similar to Bob, Bob is similar to John and Sara, and Sara is similar to both Bob and Alice. Figure 1(c) summarizes their relations under a given relationship, such as the friendship on Facebook while Figure 1(d) shows another one, such as the following relationship on Twitter. Clearly, both of the friendship and following relationships can only partially reflect the similarities in interests. If we simply merge them together, as shown in Figure 1(e), the naively combined network does not reflect the correct similarity among them. For example, John and Alice are dissimilar, but there is still a link between them.

In this paper, we present a hierarchical Bayesian model to cope with the above challenges. It transfers knowledge of behavior models across subnetworks in a composite network, specifically adapted and parameterized for different users. The common users across subnetworks form bridges to enable the transfer. To uncover the common knowledge across different subnetworks, we apply transfer learning techniques [15] to exploit both the topological and topical knowledge in social networks. The basic idea is to integrate relationships adaptively, where different users will be influenced by their neighbors in each subnetwork with personalized weights.

We explain the approach briefly as follows. The model is based on latent Dirichlet allocation (LDA) [1]. Essentially, we model users' interests as latent topics. We maintain two

Table 1: Definition of notations

Group	Notation	Notation Description
Data	$\mathcal{G} = \{G_i\}_{i=1}^{\ell}$	Composite Social Networks
	$\mathbf{U} = \{u_i\}_{i=1}^{T}$	User set of $\mathcal{G}$
	$\mathbf{E} = \cup\{E_i\}_{i=1}^{\ell}$	Link set of $\mathcal{G}$
	$\mathbf{V} = \{v_i\}_{i=1}^{T}$	Item set
	$\mathcal{A} = \{a_i\}_{i=1}^{Q}$	Interaction set
	ℓ	Number of subnetworks of $\mathcal{G}$
	N	Number of users in $\mathbf{U}$
	T	Number of items in $\mathbf{V}$
	Q	Number of interactions in $\mathcal{A}$
	M_i	Number of links in E_i
Model	$\mathbf{Dir}(\cdot)$	Dirichlet distribution
	$\mathbf{Mult}(\cdot)$	Multi-nominal distribution
	$\mathbf{Bern}(\cdot)$	Bernoulli distribution
	θ, ϕ and ψ	Topic proportions
	α, β and ν	Priors
	K	Number of topics

distributions, i.e., users' distributions over topics and topics' distributions over items. These distributions are denoted as $\Pr(t|u)$ and $\Pr(v|t)$, where t, v and u denote topic, item and user respectively. To exploit the relational knowledge among users, we add a constraint on $\Pr(t|u)$ to enforce that one user's distribution over topics should be similar to his/her neighbors'. In addition, we introduce one more measure $\Pr(G_s|u)$ to indicate the importance of a chosen social network G_s for a given user u. This probability is important, since each user is influenced by his/her neighbors in different social networks with different levels of importance. We revisit the synthetic example in Figure 1 to illustrate the idea. By introducing $\Pr(G_s|u)$, each user can adopt relationship from different subnetworks individually according to their similarities to others. For example, Bob adopts the Facebook relationship in Figure 1(c) while Alice adopts the "Following" relationship in Figure 1(d). Hence the adaptively combined network can reflect users' interests correctly, as shown in Figure 1(f). We derive an efficient Gibbs sampling method with a Map/Reduce implementation to compute parameters in the proposed model, and infer the user-topic distribution $\Pr(t|u)$, the item-topic distribution $\Pr(v|t)$ and the user-network distribution $\Pr(G_s|u)$. Extensive experiments were performed to verify the effectiveness and the efficiency of the proposed model, by comparing with state-of-the-art approaches on several large social-networking datasets - such as the actual datasets from Tencent Inc.

2. PROBLEM FORMULATION

First, we formally define the concept of composite social network. The notations are summarized in Table 1. Let $\mathbb{G} = \{G_i = (U_i, E_i)\}_{i=1}^{\ell}$ denote a composite social network, where G_i is the i-th subnetwork, U_i is the user set of G_i, E_i is the user relationship of U_i and ℓ is the number of subnetworks. In addition, we define a complete user set as

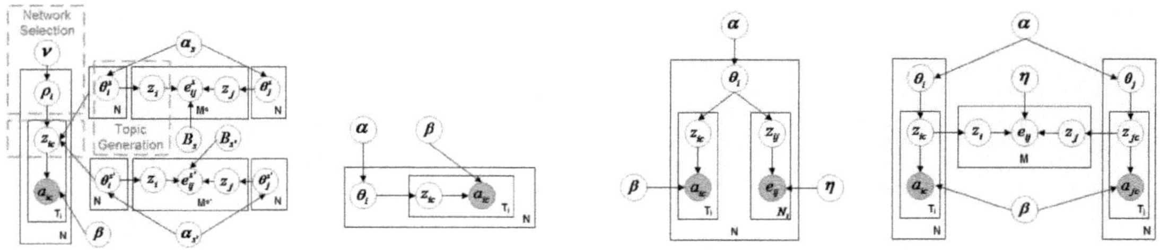

(a) ComSoc (b) LDA (c) LinkLDA (d) RTM

Figure 2: Different Topic Models

$\mathbf{U}$ and a complete link set as $\mathbf{E}$, where $\mathbf{U} = \cup\{U_i\}_{i=1}^{\ell} = \{u_j\}_{j=1}^{N}$ and $\mathbf{E} = \cup\{E_i = \{e_i^j\}_{j=1}^{M_i}\}_{i=1}^{\ell}$. In a composite network, users and links in different subnetworks overlap:

$$U_i \cap U_j \neq \emptyset,\ \forall i \neq j,\ U_i \subseteq \mathbf{U},\ U_j \subseteq \mathbf{U} \tag{1}$$

$$E_i \cap E_j \neq \emptyset,\ \forall i \neq j,\ E_i \subseteq \mathbf{E},\ E_j \subseteq \mathbf{E} \tag{2}$$

These properties are easy to satisfy in practice. For example, users of Facebook and Twitter often overlap, although are not identical. Two users may be friends on Facebook, but may or may not always be followers on Twitter. We notice that in different social networks, a user can have a different set of neighbors, and also have different levels of influence on their neighbors. This depends on how often they interact and the closeness of their relationships. It is a key property to exploit for knowledge transfer in a composite social network, as different subnetworks may capture partial aspects of a given user's behaviors. Consequently, we define the task of user behavior prediction as follows. Let $\mathbf{V} = \{v_j\}_{j=1}^{T}$ be an item set, where v_j is the j-th item, which can be a movie, music, news, advertisement, webpage, etc. Let the matrix $\mathcal{A} = \{a_i = (u_j, v_k)\}_{i=1}^{Q}$ denote the historical user behavior data, where each user-item pair (u_j, v_k) represents the interaction between u_j and v_k, such as clicking, rating, etc., and most the entries in this matrix are empty. Formally, the task of user behavior prediction is to predict the non-existing elements in $\mathcal{A}$ with the help of $\mathbb{G}$.

3. COMPOSITE SOCIAL TOPIC MODEL

We propose a composite social topic model (ComSoc) for selecting subnetworks in a composite social network, in order to adaptively transfer the relationship knowledge. A key point is that, the regularization from different networks is adjusted adaptively depending on the user. This is consistent with the observation that, someone may use Facebook more often than Twitter and hence the neighbors on the Facebook shall have higher level of influence for the given user, while others may be influenced more by their followers on Twitter, as they prefer Twitter over Facebook.

The complete generating process of ComSoc is as follows. Firstly, ComSoc models users' interests as topics and then each user is represented as a distribution over topics, $\Pr(t|u)$. In addition, ComSoc adds one constraint on $\Pr(t|u)$ by enforcing that users' distributions over topics can be used to generate links between users. Intuitively, common interests tend to create relationships among people. For each user in each subnetwork G_d, ComSoc assumes $\Pr(t|u)$, a Multinomial distribution, is generated by a Dirichlet distribution with a prior α_d. Subsequently, a topic indicator is drawn from this distribution for each user. Then every link in each network is generated by a Bernoulli distribution, of which the prior is determined by the topic indicators of the users and a topic compatibility matrix B^d related to G_d, where B^d represents the topic connections. After generating the user-topic distribution $\Pr(t|u)$ for each user in every social networks, to transfer knowledge from social relationships adaptively, we introduce a term of users' distribution over networks, $\Pr(G_d|u)$, in order to represent the probability of how much a user is influenced by a given network. ComSoc models this user-network distribution in a hierarchical manner. At first, for each user u_i, a network proportion ρ_i is drawn from a Dirichlet distribution with a prior ν. Then, for every interaction of a given user, a social network is drawn from a Multinomial distribution according to the network proportion. The user-topic distribution of the selected network, $\Pr(t|u)$, is picked to generate a topic assignment. Finally, ComSoc generates each interaction according to the item-topic distribution, $\Pr(v|t)$, over the chosen topic. We formulate this process as follows.

- For every user u_i in each network G_d:
  - Draw topic proportion $\theta_{id} \sim \mathbf{Dir}(\alpha_d)$
- For every link of (u_i, u_j) in each network G_d:
  - Draw topic indicator $z_i \sim \mathbf{Mult}(\theta_{id})$, $z_j \sim \mathbf{Mult}(\theta_{jd})$
  - Draw binary link indicator $e_{ij}^d \sim \mathbf{Bern}(B_{z_i,z_j}^d)$
- For each user u_i:
  - Draw network proportion $\rho_i \sim \mathbf{Dir}(\nu)$
  - For each interaction $a_{i,k} \in \mathcal{A}$ with item v_k:
    - Draw a network indicator $d \sim \mathbf{Mult}(\rho_i)$
    - Draw assignment $z_{i,k} \sim \mathbf{Mult}(\theta_{id})$
    - Draw interaction $a_{i,k} \sim \mathbf{Mult}(\beta_{z_{i,k}})$

We observe that, each user u_i has her/his own network proportion ρ_i. This means that we choose different subnetworks to transfer knowledge adaptively for each user.

We draw the graphical model of ComSoc, as well as the basic LDA, LinkLDA [7] and RTM [3] in Figure 2. To make the figures clearer, for ComSoc, we draw only two social networks. In contrast to both LinkLDA and RTM, ComSoc follows a novel heuristic to exploit the knowledge in social networks in two levels or hierarchies: (1) it first introduces a network indicator to judge which network is appropriate to transfer behavior data and help the recommendation for each user adaptively - the portion surrounded by the red box in Figure 2(a); (2) for each user, it generates topics from shared user-topic distribution, in order to produce user-item interactions and user-user relations in each subnetwork at the same time - the portions highlighted by the green box. We notice that, this adaptation is not employed in the global merging approach proposed in [16]. To learn the model, we propose an efficient inference algorithm based on Gibbs sampling. In addition, to cope with the massive data issue, we also propose a large-scale implementation based on Map/Reduce [5].

3.1 Inference Algorithm

The basic idea is to update topic assignments from the posterior distribution. To guarantee sampling efficiency, the posterior distribution is represented in collapsed format [18]. We first define a number of statistics. Let $n_{t,v}$ denote the number of the topic t related to an item, and $n^s_{u,t}$ denote the number of the topic t assigned to a user in the s-th network. Formally, for each topic assignment $z_{i,k}$,

$$n_{t,v} = \sum_{i,k}\{z_{i,k} = t; v_k = v\}; n^s_{u,t} = \sum_{k}\{z^s_{i,k} = t\}$$

In addition, we denote $n_t = \sum_v n_{t,v}$, where n_t stores the number of times that items are assigned to the topic t, and n_u, which maintains the number of items interacted with the user u. Lastly, we define another statistic $n_{u,d}$, which is the number of times that a user u utilizes subnetwork G_d in order to regularize her/his distribution over topics.

We express the full joint probability of the interaction data in $\mathcal{A}$ with network indicators as:

$$\begin{aligned}\Pr(\mathcal{A}, z, s|\alpha, \beta, \nu) &= \left[\Pi_{i=1}^{N} \frac{\Pi_{j=1}^{K}\Gamma(\alpha_s + n_{u=i,t=j})}{\alpha_s K + n_{u=i}} \frac{\Gamma(\alpha_s K)}{\Pi_{j=1}^{K}\Gamma(\alpha_s)}\right] \\ &\times \left[\Pi_{i=1}^{K} \frac{\Pi_{j=1}^{T}\Gamma(\beta + n_{t=i,v=j})}{\beta T + n_{t=i}} \frac{\Gamma(\beta T)}{\Pi_{j=1}^{V}\Gamma(\beta)}\right] \\ &\times \left[\Pi_{i=1}^{N} \frac{\Pi_{j=1}^{\ell}\Gamma(\nu + n_{u=i,d=j})}{\nu\ell + n_{u=i}} \frac{\Gamma(\nu\ell)}{\Pi_{j=1}^{\ell}\Gamma(\nu)}\right]\end{aligned}$$

We notice that, different from the inference in LDA [18], the above equation has one additional term to model, which network to be selected, in order to regularize users' distributions over topics. Following the inference in [18], let $\mathbf{z}_{\neg(i,k)}$ denote the topic assignments without the current topic on $a_{i,k}$, and then we rewrite the above equation to obtain the following un-normalized probability, in order to resample the topic $z_{i,k}$ for $a_{i,k}$ between user u_i and item v_k:

$$\begin{aligned}&\Pr(z_{i,k} = t, d = s|\mathcal{A}, \mathbf{z}_{\neg(i,k)}) \qquad (3) \\ \propto\ &(n^s_{i,t,\neg(i,k)} + \alpha_s)(n_{i,s,\neg(i,k)} + \nu)\frac{n_{t,k,\neg(i,k)} + \beta}{n_{t,\neg(i,k)} + T\beta}\end{aligned}$$

The resulting equation is used to update the topic assignments for user-item interactions. In addition, we need to sample users' pairwise topic assignments for user-user relationships in each subnetwork G_s, which regularizes the user-topic distributions for user-item interactions. In each network, we first define the full joint probability as:

$$\begin{aligned}\Pr(\tilde{z}, E_s|B^s, \alpha_s) &= \left[\Pi_{i=1}^{N} \frac{\Pi_{j=1}^{K}\Gamma(\alpha_s + n_{u=i,t=j})}{\alpha_s K + n_{u=i}} \frac{\Gamma(\alpha_s K)}{\Pi_{j=1}^{K}\Gamma(\alpha_s)}\right] \\ &\times \left[\Pi_{i=1}^{N} \frac{\Pi_{j=1}^{K}\Gamma(\alpha_s + n_{u=i,t=j})}{\alpha_s K + n_{u=i}} \frac{\Gamma(\alpha_s K)}{\Pi_{j=1}^{K}\Gamma(\alpha_s)}\right]\end{aligned}$$

Following the same inference process, the un-normalized probability for resampling the pairwise topic for user relationship between u_i and u_j is

$$\begin{aligned}&\Pr(\tilde{z}_{i,j} = t_1, \tilde{z}_{j,i} = t_2|\alpha_s, B^s, E_s, \tilde{\mathbf{z}}_{\neg(i,j)}) \qquad (4) \\ \propto\ &\Pi_{t_1,t_2}\Gamma(n^s_{i,t_1} + \alpha_s)\Gamma(n^s_{j,t_2} + \alpha_s) \\ \propto\ &(n^s_{i,t_1,\neg(i,j)} + \alpha_s)(n^s_{j,t_2,\neg(i,j)} + \alpha_s)\end{aligned}$$

This equation is used to update the pairwise topic assignments for user-user relations. In summary, in each iteration of Gibbs sampling, we update the topic assignments for user-item interactions and user-user relations in each subnetwork alternatively using Eq.(3) and Eq.(4) respectively until convergence. We revisit the synthetic example in Figure 1. After learning the model, to predict the preference of each user, it first selects an appropriate social relationship. For example, Bob adopts the Facebook relationship in Figure 1(c) while Alice adopts the "Following" relationship in Figure 1(d). Then, an adaptively combined network is constructed, as shown in Figure 1(f). The neighbors' knowledge in this network is exploited to help pick a topic. Finally an item is selected to recommend to the given user according to the item proportion of this topic.

Algorithm 1 Inference of ComSoc

Input: Composite network: $\mathcal{G}$, Interactions: $\mathcal{A}$, # of iterations I, # of burn-in, I_b, Priors: α, β and ν
Output: User-topic distribution θ_s for each subnetwork G_s, topic-item distribution ϕ and user-network distribution ψ
Assign topics for user-item pairs randomly
Assign topics for user-user pairs in each subnetwork
Initialize the user-network assignments randomly
Initialize the θ_d, ϕ and ψ with zeros
for $i = 1$ to I **do**
  Update user-item topic assignments using Eq.(3)
  Update user-user topic assignments using Eq.(4)
  IF $I > I_b$ Update θ_s, ϕ, ψ as
    $\theta_{s,i,j} += \frac{1}{I-I_b}\frac{\alpha_s + n_{u=i,t=j}}{\alpha_s K + n_{u=i}}$
    $\phi_{i,j} += \frac{1}{I-I_b}\frac{\beta + n_{t=j,v=i}}{\beta V + n_{v=i}}$
    $\psi_{i,j} += \frac{1}{I-I_b}\frac{\nu + n_{u=i,s=j}}{\nu\ell + n_{u=i}}$
end for
Return θ_s, ϕ and ψ

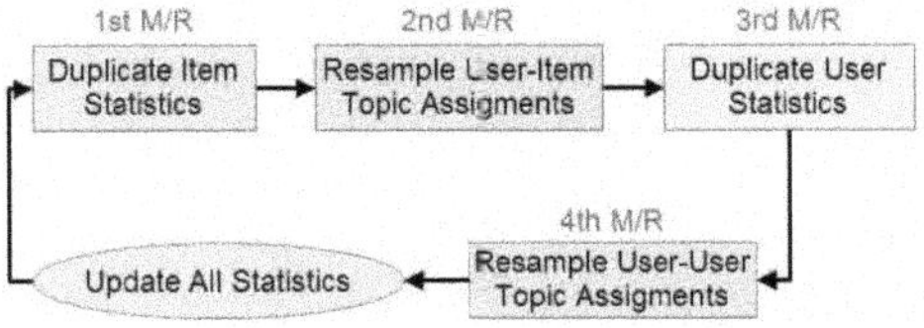

Figure 3: Large Scale Implementation on Map/Reduce

Inference Framework The inference framework of ComSoc can be found in Algorithm 1. At the beginning, it randomly picks topics for user-item interactions and user-user relationships. Afterwards, in each iteration, Eq.(3) and Eq.(4) are utilized to update the topic assignments from user-item interactions and user-user relations in each social network. The iteration is repeated until convergence. In addition, a burn-in process is introduced in the first several iterations to remove unreliable sampling results. The parameters θ_s, ϕ and ψ are used to predict user behaviors.

Time Complexity We analyze the time complexity as follows. Suppose the process needs I iterations to reach convergence. In each iteration, it requires to go through all user-item pairs (Q) in the interaction network and user-user pairs (M_i) in each sub social network. In addition, for each pair, it requires $O(K)$ operations to compute the posterior distribution and sample topics and constant cost to update the statistics. At last, it needs $O(N + T)$ operations to generate topic proportions. Thus, the whole time complexity is $O(I(Q + \sum_{i=1}^{\ell} M_i)K + N + T) = O(I(Q + \sum_{i=1}^{\ell} M_i)K)$.

3.2 Large-scale Implementation

In many real world applications, the number of users (N) can be in the order of several billions, the number of items (T) can be up to millions and the number of user-item inter-

Table 2: Summary of Data Characteristics

Collections	Tencent		Douban		Collections	Tencent		Douban		
Networks	QQ	Microblog	Online	Offline	Behaviors	Music	Profile	Movie	Music	Book
#User	$\sim 1M$		$\sim 50K$		#Item	$\sim 360K$	$\sim 5K$	$\sim 57K$	$\sim 180K$	$\sim 170K$
#Edge	$\sim 80M$	$\sim 32M$	$\sim 5M$	$\sim 4M$	#Interaction	$\sim 55M$	$\sim 13M$	$\sim 5.2M$	$\sim 2.5M$	$\sim 3.2M$

actions (Q) and user-user relations (M_i) can be tens of billions. In a way, these are very big datasets. Thus, the ability to scale up the proposed algorithm is crucial for real-world practice. We implement the inference algorithms of ComSoc based on Map/Reduce [5]. The main idea is to compute the posterior distribution and resample the topic assignments on partial data in each single machine and then aggregate pieces of results. Recall that in Eq.(3) and Eq.(4), several statistics will be updated in the sampling process, including the user-topic count $n^s_{u,\cdot}$ of each user in the s-th network, the user-network count $n_{u,\cdot}$, the topic count n_t, the item-topic count $n_{\cdot,v}$ of each item and the topic assignment $z_{i,k}$ for u_i and v_k. We partition the data by users. For example, if there are D machines, then the whole dataset will be divided into D groups and each group will contain parts of users as well as their relationship and interaction data. As stated in [20], $n^s_{u,\cdot}$, $n_{u,\cdot}$ and $z_{i,k}$ are entirely local to each user and thus do not need to be shared. They can be written to the disk after resampling. In addition, n_t and $n_{\cdot,v}$ change slowly, and hence, a delay in obtaining their up-to-date representations will not affect the sampler significantly. Furthermore, the number of topic statistics, $\{n_t\}_{t=1}^K$, is small, where K is the number of topics. Thus we can keep them in the memory permanently. These observations accomplish the local sampling without losing too much precision. In summary, the distributed implementation of Algorithm 1 is also an iterative approach, but in each iteration, it resamples topic assignments in a distributed manner. Let M/R denote a pair of Map/Reduce operations for simplicity.

Before the start of iterations, the inference algorithm performs distributed initialization. Due to limited space, we omit the details here. The sampling process in each iteration needs four M/R. The main flow can be found in Figure 3. The first M/R is used to duplicate the statistics $n_{\cdot,v}$ of every item for each related user. Similarly, the third M/R is used to duplicate the statistics $n^s_{u,\cdot}$, since each user is linked to multiple users in the s-th social network. For each user u_i, the related statistics $n^s_{u=i,\cdot}$ will be copied $|N^s(u_i)|$ times, where $|N^s(u_i)|$ is the number of its neighbors in the s-th network, and each duplicated statistics is used for the sampling of each neighbor $u_j \in N^s(u_i)$. The second M/R is used to resample the topic assignments for user-item interactions and the last one resamples the topic assignments for user-user relations in each subnetwork. All information related to users and items are represented as $\langle key, value\rangle$ pairs, where *key* can be either user or item identities and *value* can be statistics, topic assignments $z_{i,\cdot}$, item interactions $a_{\cdot,k}$ and user relations information $N^s(u_i)$. Let ξ denote the type of *value* and c indicate whether the value is for a given user or her/his neighbors. Formally, the process is as follows:

- Map-I: Map $\langle v_k, n_{\cdot,v=k}\rangle$ and $\langle v_k, a_{\cdot,k}\rangle$, in the form of $\langle v_k, \{\xi, V\}\rangle$ where V is either $n_{\cdot,v=k}$ or $a_{\cdot,k}$.
- Reduce-I: Take $\langle v_k, \{\xi, V\}\rangle$ and emit $\langle u_i, \{v_k, n_{\cdot,v=k}\}\rangle$ for each user $u_i \in a_{\cdot,k}$.
- Map-II: Map $\langle u_i, \{v_k, n_{\cdot,v=k}\}\rangle$, $\langle u_i, n^s_{u=i,\cdot}\rangle$, the user-network count $\langle u_i, n_{u=i,\cdot}\rangle$ and $\langle u_i, z_{i,\cdot}\rangle$ in the form of $\langle u_i, \{\xi, V\}\rangle$.
- Reduce-II: Take $\langle u_i, \{\xi, V\}\rangle$, compute the topic assignments according to Eq.(3) and emit the updated $\langle u_i, n^s_{u=i,\cdot}\rangle$, $\langle u_i, n_{u=i,\cdot}\rangle$, $\langle u_i, z_{i,\cdot}\rangle$ and the increments of $\langle v_k, n_{\cdot,v=k}\rangle$ and $\langle t, n_t\rangle$.
- Map-III: Map $\langle u_i, n^s_{u=i,\cdot}\rangle$ and $\langle u_i, N^s(u_i)\rangle$, such that statistics with the same user are shuffled to the same machine in the form of $\langle u_i, \{\xi, V\}\rangle$ where V is either $n^s_{u=i,\cdot}$ or $N^s(u_i)$.
- Reduce-III: Take $\langle u_i, \{\xi, V\}\rangle$ and emit $\langle u_j, \{c, n^s_{u=i,\cdot}\}\rangle$ for each user $u_j \in N^s(u_i) \cup u_i$.
- Map-IV: Map $\langle u_i, \{c, n^s_{u=j,\cdot}\}\rangle$ and $\langle u_i, \tilde{z}_{i,\cdot}\rangle$ in the form of $\langle u_i, \{\xi, V\}\rangle$.
- Reduce-IV: Take $\langle u_i, \{\xi, V\}\rangle$, compute the topic assignments according to Eq.(4) and emit the updated $\langle u_i, n^s_{u=i,\cdot}\rangle$ and $\langle u_i, \tilde{z}_{i,\cdot}\rangle$.

Subsequently, the increments for the counts on topics and item-topic pairs will be used to update $n_{\cdot,v=k}$. Finally, n_t in each single machine and the updated statistics will be shuffled to each single machine for the next iteration.

4. EXPERIMENTS

We evaluate the proposed methods on two data collections, one is from Douban[2], and the other is from Tencent; both contain composite social networks and rich user behavior information. We compare the proposed approach with three state-of-the-art methods: latent Dirichlet allocation (LDA) [1], LinkLDA [7] and relational topic models (RTM) [3]. For LinkLDA and RTM, we implement two variations: one is to build models with only one single social network, and the other is to build models with a naive combined social network, of which the edge set is the union of all edges in subnetworks. For the model parameters, we set the priors for topic models as $\alpha = 0.5$, $\beta = 50/K$ and $\nu = 0.5$. In addition, we set the number of topics as $K = 50$. We will study the effectiveness of this parameter later. The results are evaluated based on two criteria: perplexity (perp) and mean average precision (MAP) on the hold-out set $\mathcal{T}$.

$$\text{perplexity} = \exp\Big\{-\frac{\sum_{(u,v)\in\mathcal{T}} \log \Pr(u,v)}{|\mathcal{T}|}\Big\} \quad (5)$$

$$\text{MAP} = \frac{1}{N}\sum_{u\in\mathbf{U}} \frac{\sum_{(u,v)\in\mathcal{T}_u} \frac{1}{T}\sum_{r\in[1,T]} pre_r}{|\mathcal{T}_u|} \quad (6)$$

where pre_r represents the precision on top-r predictions. Behavior records in $\mathcal{T}$ are represented as a list of user-item pairs. For example, for the music listening prediction, one user-item pair represents one user will listen to the given music. Then the task is to predict if such behaviors happen or not, in other words, if the corresponding user-item pairs exist in $\mathcal{T}$ or not. Generally, perplexity measures how precisely the algorithm generates the behaviors in the hold-out set, and MAP measures how well the algorithms rank the behaviors in the hold-out set above non-existing behaviors. In addition, to evaluate the significance in improvement of the proposed model, we randomly split the hold-out set into 10 subsets and then calculate the error bar. We notice that, the observed behaviors are implicit, where we only know which items are interacted by a given user.

[2] `http://www.douban.com`

Table 3: Comparison in MAP and perplexity on Douban Collection (K=50)

Algorithm		LDA	LinkLDA-On	LinkLDA-Off	LinkLDA-C	RTM-On	RTM-Off	RTM-C	ComSoc
Movie	perp	7140.3	7311.1	7342.6	7269.9	7425.1	7433.6	7370.6	**6626.6**
	MAP	0.8407	0.8407	0.8406	0.8415	0.8434	0.8407	0.8517	**0.8581**
Music	perp	43676.8	43506.4	45185.9	43730.3	43511.8	44358.1	43667.4	**34540.5**
	MAP	0.7492	0.7492	0.7489	0.7571	0.7583	0.7493	0.7581	**0.7624**
Book	perp	47541.0	54646.1	58460.9	54627.8	55388.0	57130.3	55386.9	**33624.9**
	MAP	0.7084	0.7088	0.7086	0.7085	0.7091	0.7088	0.7089	**0.7173**

Table 4: Comparison in MAP and perplexity on Tencent Collection (K=50)

Algorithm		LDA	LinkLDA-QQ	LinkLDA-MB	LinkLDA-C	RTM-QQ	RTM-MB	RTM-C	ComSoc
Music	perp	21118.8	21041.2	21032.1	21020.3	21016.8	21042.3	21080.2	**20042.3**
	MAP	0.8497	0.8580	0.8582	0.8677	0.8559	0.8591	0.8681	**0.8795**
Profile	perp	1233.1	1217.9	1189.7	1187.1	1231.2	1198.3	1188.1	**1150.7**
	MAP	0.5745	0.5839	0.5857	0.5861	0.5885	0.5861	0.5866	**0.6064**

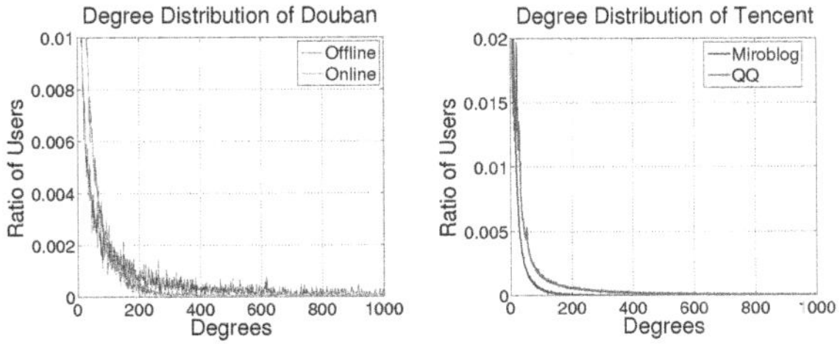

Figure 4: The Long-tail Property

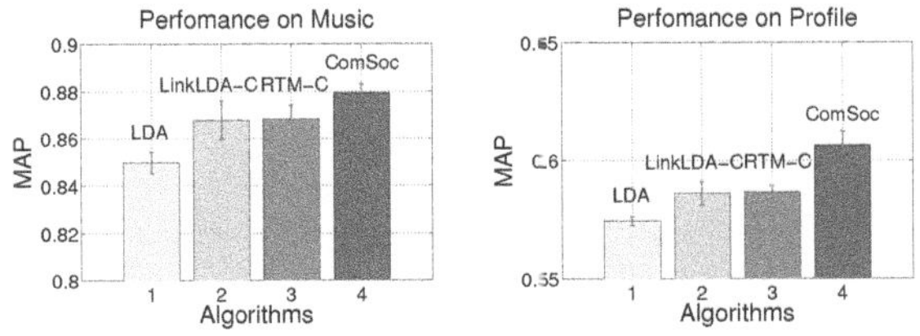

Figure 5: MAP with Error Bars of Tencent Collection (data bars are the means of MAP; the error bars are the upper and lower limits with 95% confidence.)

4.1 Dataset Description

The Douban collection contains two subnetworks. One is the online contact network, representing who pay attention to whom, and the other is the offline physical network, indicating who are familiar with whom in the real world. Since the website does not provide APIs to collect the data of offline relations, we construct the offline network using users' co-occurrence in social gatherings, where people physically meet. If two users take part in the same gatherings more than 20 times, we consider that they know each other. Finally, the task is to predict users' behaviors on movie, music and book domains using their historical behavior logs, as well as the information in the online and offline networks. This dataset can be downloaded[3].

The Tencent collection contains two subnetworks. One is QQ[4], which contains about 1 billion users and 80 billions links, making it the biggest instant messaging network in the world, and the other is Tencent's Microblog network[5], which contains more than 200 millions users, making it one of the biggest Microblog networks in China. We introduce two subtasks: the first one is to predict which songs users will collect in the future, which can be applied to radio applications[6], and the second one is to predict users' profiles, which is crucial to display online advertisements. To generate users' profiles, we recorded the words from three big Web sites: QQ.com, one of the biggest portals in China, qzone[7], the biggest social blogging service in China and wenwen[8], one of the biggest QA systems in China. Subsequently, for a given user, 5,000 words with commercial values, such as insurance, loans, etc., were extracted from webpages that the user has browsed. These words are used to describe users and then each user is represented with a ?/1 vector, where 1 represents a particular user browsing the corresponding word, and the question mark (?) represents unknown. As users' browsing contents can change over time, the task here is to predict which words the user will browse in the future.

Table 2 presents the statistics of the datasets. In summary, the Douban collection contains three types of user behavior: movie watching, music listening, and book reading, while the Tencent collection contains two other types: music collection and user profile modeling. We observe that the user-item interactions and user-user relations in each single network are very sparse. The degree distributions of the social networks in both Douban and Tencent datasets are plotted in Figure 4. We observe that degree distribution of each network follows the power-log distribution, that means each subnetwork is still sparse and most users have limited interactions. Hence we should utilize the knowledge from multiple networks together.

Data Sampling Process For the Douban dataset, we crawled the data through the APIs provided by the website. We randomly retrieved 30 senior users, who registered more than 4 years ago and are still active. Then we performed breadth-first-search based on their online contacts to collect more users iteratively, until the number of users reached a threshold (50,000 in this paper). Subsequently, the contact relations and the social gathering co-occurrence among these users, and their behaviors on music, book and movie domains were recorded. For the Tencent dataset, we firstly picked a user whose number of neighbors is around 100 randomly. Then, this user as well as his/her neighbors on QQ and Microblog networks are retrieved as a seed set. Similar to the Douban data, we performed breadth-first-search on these two networks to extend the user set until the number of users exceeded a threshold. Finally, corresponding social networks of these users, their music collection records and webpages browsing logs within two months were extracted as the experimental data. Behavior data in the final week are hold out as the test set.

4.2 Performance Comparisons

Table 3 and Figure 6 summarize the perplexity and MAP of LDA, LinkLDA, RTM and the proposed ComSoc on the

[3] http://www.cse.ust.hk/TL/dataset/Douban-50000.zip
[4] http://www.tencent.com/en-us/ps/imservice.shtml
[5] http://t.qq.com/?lang=en_US
[6] http://fm.qq.com/
[7] http://qzone.qq.com
[8] http://wenwen.soso.com/

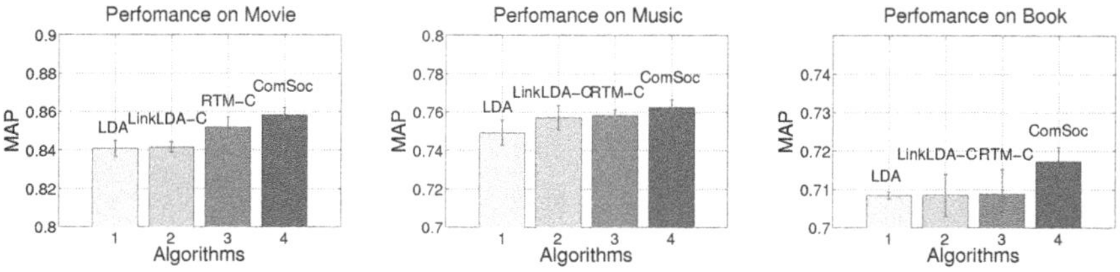

Figure 6: MAP Comparison with Error Bars of Douban Collection

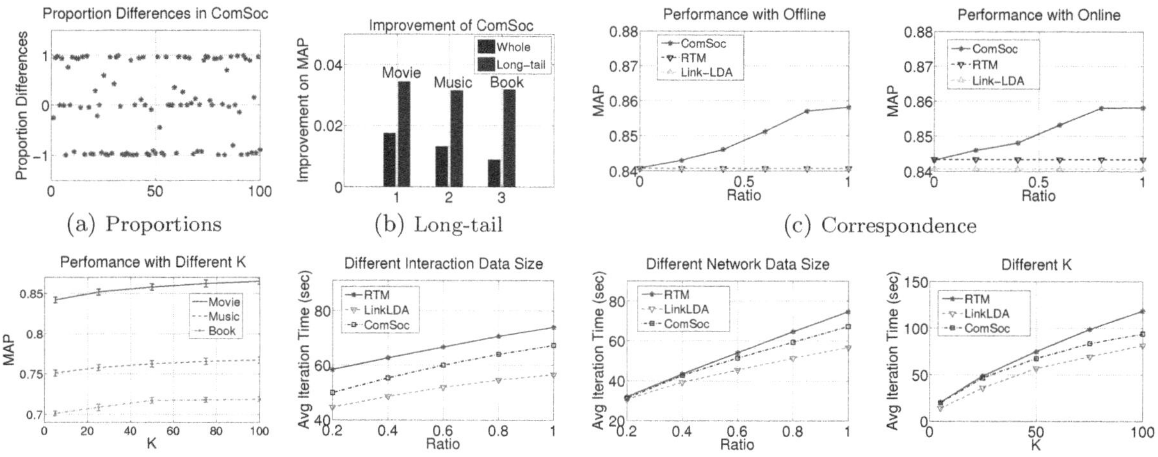

(a) Proportions (b) Long-tail (c) Correspondence

(d) K (e) Efficiency-interactions (f) Efficiency-links (g) Efficiency-K

Figure 7: Performance Analysis

three datasets of the Douban collection. For the Movie dataset, as highlighted in bold, ComSoc consistently outperforms LDA, LinkLDA and RTM on MAP and perplexity. The MAP of ComSoc is at least 0.017 larger than LDA. If we overlook the model differences, compared to its competing methods, ComSoc on average achieves 0.017, 0.016 and 0.007 higher MAP as compared to LDA, LinkLDA and RTM respectively. The better performance of ComSoc over RTM and LinkLDA with one subnetwork, e.g, RTM-Online, etc., can be ascribed to the fact that, ComSoc considers more knowledge from auxiliary networks, and hence, captures more aspects of users' interests. For example, users can share their interests through different subnetworks so some regularization knowledge will be missed if only one network is considered. On the other hand, although RTM-C and LinkLDA-C explore knowledge from multiple networks to improve their accuracies, they assign uniform regularization on users without considering the network differences to each user, i.e., different users actually receive different levels of influence from their neighbors in different social networks. In this sense, RTM-C and LinkLDA-C may introduce unnecessary regularization from unrelated networks. For example, the offline network is less useful to infer users' interests. As shown in Table 3, LinkLDA-Off and RTM-Off do not improve the performance of LDA. However, ComSoc adaptively selects network and hence solve the above problems. Moreover, in all cases, ComSoc outperforms LDA on all three datasets, implying that when the historical interaction knowledge is sparse, social network information can actually improve the prediction performance.

Table 4 and Figure 5 summarize the results on the two datasets from Tencent. Similar to the performance in the Douban collection, ComSoc consistently outperforms RTM, LinkLDA and LDA on both perplexity and MAP for both datasets. For example, on the Profile dataset, ComSoc gets MAP higher than 0.605 while other baselines do not exceed 0.587. In addition, on the Music dataset, the improvement of ComSoc is as high as 0.03 on MAP comparing to LDA. Importantly, the improvement of ComSoc on Tencent collections is more significant. One reason is that, users share more contents through both QQ and Microblog networks, and hence the links in these two networks can reflect more users' interests. These justify the effectiveness of the proposed methods empirically.

4.3 Performance Analysis

We conduct five extensive experiments on the Douban collection to answer the following questions: (1). Does ComSoc transfer knowledge from composite social networks to different users adaptively? (2). Does ComSoc enrich the knowledge in the user-item interaction network and therefore reduce the "sparsity"? (3). How does the correspondence ratio between composite social network and user-item interaction network affect ComSoc's performance? (4) What is the effectiveness of the model parameters?

We answer the first question by examining the network proportions of different users in the Movie dataset captured by ComSoc. We pick 100 users who have the most behavior data, as these users have the highest confidence to derive the weights of different networks. The results are presented in Figure 7(a), where the y-axis represents the proportion difference between online and offline networks of a given user u: $\Pr(\text{network=online}|u) - \Pr(\text{network=offline}|u)$. The differences of most users are not equal to zero, meaning different networks have different impacts to different users and ComSoc utilizes the knowledge in each network adaptively.

We evaluate the results on long-tail users, whose number of behaviors are smaller than 10. These users suffer from the harm of "sparsity" the most, since each of them interacts with only $\leq 0.01\%$ items. The results are presented in Figure 7(b). We observe that, the improvement of ComSoc on long-tail users is at least twice more than the average

Table 5: Different Related Works

	Uniform	Adaptively
Single Network	RTM [3],etc.	-
Multiple Networks	Combined KNN [16]	ComSoc

level. For example, on the Book dataset, the improvement of ComSoc is smaller than 0.01 on MAP on the average level, while larger than 0.03 on long-tail users. One reason is that, for those users who have a large number of interactions, LDA has gained enough knowledge to infer their distributions over topics; but for the long-tail users, ComSoc can significantly exploit knowledge from the composite social network to help enhance the prediction. This provides justification to the argument that ComSoc can enrich the knowledge in the user-item interaction network.

In real world, many people may only use parts of on-line services, i.e., they may exist in one subnetwork but not in all networks. We test the effect of the correspondence ratio between the composite social network and the user-item interaction network, e.g., the number of users who exist in both social and interaction networks. Figure 7(c) presents the results with different ratios between the offline/online networks and the Movie interaction network. ComSoc's performance becomes worse if fewer correspondences are provided across networks. An important observation is that it outperforms LinkLDA consistently if there are corresponding users among networks, implying that ComSoc successfully use the overlapping users as bridges to transfer knowledge.

We analyze the effect to change the number of topics K on the Douban collection. We change K from 5 to 100. The results are illustrated in Figure 7(d). We observe that the performance of ComSoc improves with the increase of K but the increment becomes smaller. The reason is that K represents the model complexity. Thus, when K is too small, the model has limited ability to describe the data. On the other hand, when K exceeds a threshold (e.g, 50, the default value in the experiment), the model is complex enough to handle the data. At this point, it is less helpful to improve the model performance by increasing K. In practice, K can be tuned through cross-validation techniques [25].

4.4 Efficiency Analysis

As analyzed in the end of Section 3.2, the computational time of ComSoc increases linearly with the number interactions between users and items, the number of links in the composite networks, and the number of topics K. We evaluate this empirically as shown in Figure 7(e)$\sim$(g). Three subfigures from left to right illustrate the computational time of LinkLDA-C, RTM-C and ComSoc on the Movie dataset, with different ratio of interactions and links, and different number of topics respectively. We observe that the computational time linearly increases with larger data size and number of topics. For our experiment setting, each iteration takes about 80 seconds in our computer, of which memory is 4G and CPU is 2.0Gz. Although ComSoc has better prediction performance as show in Table 3 and Table 4, it is faster than RTM and has similar time cost with LinkLDA.

5. RELATED WORKS

The proposed methods can be considered as transfer collaborative filtering algorithms based on topic models. We summarize the novelty of the proposed approaches in Table 5. Most previous works either focus on one social network or treat users uniformly, where different users receive the same influence from different social networks, but the proposed model exploits knowledge adaptively in a composite social network, which contains several subnetworks. Although the problem studied in this paper is how to solve the "sparsity" problem, sparse learning [21] is in fact a different formulation that does not solve this problem; it builds models with very few non-zero coefficients to reduce the computation cost, but does not resolve the data sparsity.

Social Networks Analysis [6] has drawn much research interest, ranging from link prediction [12], predicting how likely an unobserved edge exists between an arbitrary pair of nodes; community detection [11, 10], identifying communities of interest and studying their behaviors over time in social networks; to social influence [23], studying how the perceived relationships with other users influence the behavior of a given user. Most previous works of social influence focus on how to measure the social influence [2] or maximize the user influence [4, 8]. However, the proposed methods in this paper instead exploit social influence to help predict users' behaviors. **Collaborative Filtering** (CF) is the process to filter information or patterns using techniques involving collaboration among multiple agents, viewpoints, data sources, etc. The proposed methods in this paper belong to the category of model-based CF which uses the observed user-item interactions to train a compact model that explains the given data. Models in this category include matrix factorization[9] and topic models [22]. Among them, topic models provide an interpretable low-dimensional representation for the interactions between users and items. The simplest topic model is latent Dirichlet allocation (LDA) [1], where a topic is a distribution over items and a user is a distribution over topics. Multiple variants have been proposed to incorporate the relational knowledge [3, 14, 7]. However, these previous works utilize only one single network. **Transfer Learning** solves the lack of class label problem in the target application by "borrowing" knowledge from related domains [15, 24]. It was on collaborative filtering recently. According to the different kinds of auxiliary data, transfer CF can be categorized into three classes. The first one is to exploit the meta data or user/item content [22]. For example, the algorithm in [22] utilizes both articles' content and users' interactions on articles together to perform recommendation. The second one is to borrow knowledge from other CF domains, such as transferring knowledge from a movie to a book domain [17]. The third kind is to exploit users' or items' relationship, such as a single trust network [13]. More recently, the work in [16] utilizes multiple social networks to recommend Apps to users using a nearest neighbor model. However, it needs to enumerate all user-item pairs and hence cannot scale up to handle large datasets. In addition, these previous works either consider one auxiliary source or regularize users modeling uniformly, which ignore the fact that different networks have different influences to different users.

6. CONCLUSION AND FUTURE WORKS

In this paper, we studied a new problem on how to transfer knowledge from composite social network for user behavior prediction, where the behavior data (or user-item matrix) of the target application can be more than 99.9% empty. We defined a composite social network as a set of nested single networks, where users and links in different subnetworks overlap. Each network reflects partial aspects of users' interests and has different properties. For different users, individual networks have a diverse range of influences. Thus, we proposed a hierarchical Bayesian model to transfer knowledge for different users adaptively. The knowledge from the composite social network is utilized to regularize users' distributions over topics. Unlike prior works, the proposed model considers knowledge transfer adaptively. This is formulated into a parametric model that controls the probability of how one user is influenced by a given network. In addition, different from the previous relational topic models, ComSoc exploits user-topic distributions to generate users' social relations. The proposed model is flexible in that, it can be extended to any number of networks. We proposed a large-scale implementation based on Map/Reduce to cope with massive amount of data. We conducted empirical studies on two data collections from Tencent Inc. and Douban, where ComSoc outperforms several state-of-the-art baselines by as high as 0.03 on MAP.

Future Works In this paper, we only build models to predict whether a user will interact with a given item or not. In future work, we plan to extend the proposed model to handle different kinds of behavior, such as rating, multi-class prediction, etc. We will extend the experiments over multiple social networks, such as Facebook + Twitter + MSN. We will consider incorporating heterogeneous auxiliary knowledge together, such as item profiles, user behaviors in auxiliary domains, etc.

Acknowledgement

We thank the support of Hong Kong RGC GRF Projects 621010 and 621211.

7. REFERENCES

[1] D. M. Blei, A. Y. Ng, and M. I. Jordan. Latent dirichlet allocation. *J. Mach. Learn. Res.*, 3:993–1022, 2003.

[2] M. Cha, H. Haddadi, F. Benevenuto, and P. K. Gummadi. Measuring user influence in twitter: The million follower fallacy. In *Proceedings of the 4th International Conference on Weblogs and Social Media*, ICWSM '10, pages 10–17. AAAI, 2010.

[3] J. Chang and D. M. Blei. Relational topic models for document networks. *J. Mach. Learn. Res.*, 5:81–88, 2009.

[4] W. Chen, Y. Wang, and S. Yang. Efficient influence maximization in social networks. In *Proceedings of the 15th ACM SIGKDD International Conference on Knowledge Discovery and Data Mining*, KDD '09, pages 199–208. ACM, 2009.

[5] J. Dean and S. Ghemawat. Mapreduce: simplified data processing on large clusters. *Commun. ACM*, 51:107–113, 2008.

[6] N. Du, H. Wang, and C. Faloutsos. Analysis of large multi-modal social networks: patterns and a generator. In *Proceedings of the 2010 European Conference on Machine learning and knowledge discovery in databases: Part I*, ECML PKDD'10, pages 393–408. Springer-Verlag, 2010.

[7] E. Erosheva, S. Fienberg, and J. Lafferty. Mixed-membership models of scientific publications. *Proceedings of the National Academy of Sciences of the United States of America*, 101(Suppl 1):5220–5227, 2004.

[8] D. Kempe, J. Kleinberg, and E. Tardos. Influential nodes in a diffusion model for social networks. In *Proceedings of the 32nd International Conference on Automata, Languages and Programming*, ICALP'05, pages 1127–1138. Springer-Verlag, 2005.

[9] Y. Koren. Factorization meets the neighborhood: a multifaceted collaborative filtering model. In *Proceedings of the 14th ACM SIGKDD International Conference on Knowledge Discovery and Data Mining*, KDD '08, pages 426–434. ACM, 2008.

[10] J. Leskovec, K. J. Lang, A. Dasgupta, and M. W. Mahoney. Statistical properties of community structure in large social and information networks. In *Proceedings of the 17th International Conference on World Wide Web*, WWW '08, pages 695–704. ACM, 2008.

[11] J. Leskovec, K. J. Lang, and M. Mahoney. Empirical comparison of algorithms for network community detection. In *Proceedings of the 19th International Conference on World Wide Web*, WWW '10, pages 631–640. ACM, 2010.

[12] D. Liben-Nowell and J. Kleinberg. The link prediction problem for social networks. In *Proceedings of the 12th International Conference on Information and Knowledge Management*, CIKM '03, pages 556–559. ACM, 2003.

[13] H. Ma, D. Zhou, C. Liu, M. R. Lyu, and I. King. Recommender systems with social regularization. In *Proceedings of the 4th ACM International Conference on Web Search and Data Mining*, WSDM '11, pages 287–296. ACM, 2011.

[14] R. M. Nallapati, A. Ahmed, E. P. Xing, and W. W. Cohen. Joint latent topic models for text and citations. In *Proceedings of the 14th ACM SIGKDD International Conference on Knowledge Discovery and Data Mining*, KDD '08, pages 542–550. ACM, 2008.

[15] S. J. Pan and Q. Yang. A survey on transfer learning. *IEEE Transactions on Knowledge and Data Engineering*, 22(10):1345–1359, 2010.

[16] W. Pan, N. Aharony, and A. Pentland. Composite social network for predicting mobile apps installation. In *Proceedings of the 25th AAAI Conference on Artificial Intelligence*, AAAI '11, pages 821–827. AAAI, 2011.

[17] W. Pan, E. W. Xiang, N. N. Liu, and Q. Yang. Transfer learning in collaborative filtering for sparsity reduction. In *Proceedings of the 24th AAAI Conference on Artificial Intelligence*, AAAI '10, pages 230–235. AAAI, 2010.

[18] I. Porteous, D. Newman, A. Ihler, A. Asuncion, P. Smyth, and M. Welling. Fast collapsed gibbs sampling for latent dirichlet allocation. In *Proceedings of the 14th ACM SIGKDD International Conference on Knowledge Discovery and Data Mining*, KDD '08, pages 569–577. ACM, 2008.

[19] B. Sarwar, G. Karypis, J. Konstan, and J. Reidl. Item-based collaborative filtering recommendation algorithms. In *Proceedings of the 10th International Conference on World Wide Web*, WWW '01, pages 285–295. ACM, 2001.

[20] A. Smola and S. Narayanamurthy. An architecture for parallel topic models. *Proc. VLDB Endow.*, 3:703–710, 2010.

[21] M. E. Tipping. Sparse bayesian learning and the relevance vector machine. *J. Mach. Learn. Res.*, 1:211–244, 2001.

[22] C. Wang and D. M. Blei. Collaborative topic modeling for recommending scientific articles. In *Proceedings of the 17th ACM SIGKDD International Conference on Knowledge Discovery and Data Mining*, KDD '11, pages 448–456. ACM, 2011.

[23] R. Xiang, J. Neville, and M. Rogati. Modeling relationship strength in online social networks. In *Proceedings of the 19th International Conference on World Wide Web*, WWW '10, pages 981–990. ACM, 2010.

[24] E. Zhong, W. Fan, J. Peng, K. Zhang, J. Ren, D. Turaga, and O. Verscheure. Cross domain distribution adaptation via kernel mapping. In *KDD '09: Proceedings of the 15th ACM SIGKDD International Conference on Knowledge Discovery and Data Mining*, pages 1027–1036. ACM, 2009.

[25] E. Zhong, W. Fan, Q. Yang, O. Verscheure, and J. Ren. Cross validation framework to choose amongst models and datasets for transfer learning. In *Proceedings of the 2010 European Conference on Machine learning and Knowledge Discovery in Databases: Part III*, ECML PKDD'10, pages 547–562. Springer-Verlag, 2010.

Online Learning to Diversify from Implicit Feedback

Karthik Raman
Cornell University
Ithaca, NY
karthik@cs.cornell.edu

Pannaga Shivaswamy
Cornell University
Ithaca, NY
pannaga@cs.cornell.edu

Thorsten Joachims
Cornell University
Ithaca, NY
tj@cs.cornell.edu

ABSTRACT

In order to minimize redundancy and optimize coverage of multiple user interests, search engines and recommender systems aim to diversify their set of results. To date, these diversification mechanisms are largely hand-coded or relied on expensive training data provided by experts. To overcome this problem, we propose an online learning model and algorithms for learning diversified recommendations and retrieval functions from implicit feedback. In our model, the learning algorithm presents a ranking to the user at each step, and uses the set of documents from the presented ranking, which the user reads, as feedback. Even for imperfect and noisy feedback, we show that the algorithms admit theoretical guarantees for maximizing any submodular utility measure under approximately rational user behavior. In addition to the theoretical results, we find that the algorithm learns quickly, accurately, and robustly in empirical evaluations on two datasets.

Categories and Subject Descriptors

H.3.3 [**Information Search and Retrieval**]: Retrieval Models; I.2.6 [**Artificial Intelligence**]: Learning

General Terms

Algorithms, Experimentation, Theory

Keywords

Online Learning, Diversified Retrieval, Submodularity

1. INTRODUCTION

Modeling the dependencies between items in a ranking of results is one of the most promising directions for improving the quality of retrieval and recommendation systems. First, consider the example of a search engine and a query such as "jaguar" or "apple". For such queries, it is important to present a diverse set of results since diversity hedges against uncertainty about the users intent. Such hedging against uncertainty about the user's information need is called *extrinsic diversity* [10]. A second reason for diversity is called *intrinsic diversity* [10] where it is important to avoid redundancy and provide a set of results that cover multiple aspects of an information need. For example, of all the articles in the NY Times on a given day, a user only has time to read a small subset. Therefore, even if the user is interested in the European Debt Crisis, he may not want to read exclusively about this one topic, but rather read one article and also cover other topics. In the following, we focus on problems where such intrinsic diversity is important.

In this paper, we extend the recently proposed coactive learning model [14] to learn diversified results from implicit user feedback. In particular, we develop two algorithms for learning both relevance and the desired amount of diversity from set-valued preference data that can be derived from implicit feedback. The algorithms proposed in this paper are easy to implement and allow theoretical analysis. Furthermore, the ability to learn the desired amount of diversity based on user feedback makes the algorithms attractive for a wide range of applications where the required amount of diversity is not determined apriori. A crucial extension over the methods in [14] is that we now consider models with submodular structure, whose diminishing returns property makes it possible to avoid redundancy and increase novelty.

Coactive learning proceeds in the following online fashion. In each step, a ranking is presented to the user that (approximately) maximizes the current estimate of the submodular utility function. As feedback, the algorithm observes the (possibly diverse) set of documents the user reads in the presented ranking. After receiving this feedback, the algorithm updates its model. Even though we allow user feedback to be imperfect, noisy, and only "weakly informative" (in a specific sense), we are able to prove guarantees on the performance of the algorithm. Unlike the theorems in [14], our guarantees apply even though submodular models only allow for approximate inference. Finally, experiments demonstrate the empirical effectiveness of the proposed approach in learning both relevance and diversity.

2. RELATED WORK

Presenting a diverse set of results is an important goal in both web-search ranking as well as recommender systems research. While much prior work on diversity has focused on non-learning approaches (e.g. [2, 19, 3, 16, 4]), recently developed supervised learning methods for diversity have shown a lot of promise (e.g. [13, 18, 12, 8]). Unfortunately,

KDD'12, August 12–16, 2012, Beijing, China.

supervised learning relies on manually judged training data with multi-topic annotations, which are expensive and difficult to obtain. El-Arini and Guestrin [6] proposed an approach to discover relevant scientific literature based on a set of scientific papers. They retrieve a set of papers based on both diversity and relevance. While their approach also makes use of submodular influence measures, they assume noise-free feedback, which is unrealistic for our problem.

While some online learning methods exist that can exploit click data, those methods either cannot generalize across queries [11] and/or have a hard-coded notion of diversity that cannot be adjusted through learning [15]. Recently, Yue and Guestrin [17] proposed online learning algorithms to maximize submodular utilities and applied them to diversified retrieval. However, their model relies on observing cardinal utilities whereas in our model we only rely on implicit preference feedback. User studies for web search [7] have shown that such preference feedback can be extracted reliably from observable user behavior (e.g. clicks), while attempt to interpret click-data as cardinal utility statements were found to be biased and unreliable.

3. LEARNING PROBLEM AND MODEL

To illustrate our learning model, consider the example of a personalized news reader that users visit on a daily basis. On day t, the news reader suggests a list of articles $\mathbf{y}_t = (d_1, d_2, d_3, d_4, d_5, ...)$ and observes which of these articles are actually read by the user. We assume that the decision to read an article is influenced by two factors. First, the article must be relevant to the user's interest. Second, the decision may have dependencies with other articles in $\mathbf{y}$. For example, the user may be interested in the European debt crisis. But the user may only want to read one article related to this issue, even if $\mathbf{y}$ contains 5 relevant articles.

In this paper, we design an online learning algorithm that can model both relevance as well as interdependencies between documents. The training data we exploit are the sets of documents read by the user each day. Continuing the example from above, the system may observe that the user read articles d_3 and d_5. Obviously, we cannot conclude that $\{d_3, d_5\}$ was the optimal set of articles the user wanted to read on day t, since there may have been other articles far down the list that the user never saw. However, we can conclude that the user would have preferred the ranking $\bar{\mathbf{y}}_t = (d_3, d_5, d_1, d_2, d_4, ...)$ over the ranking $\mathbf{y}_t = (d_1, d_2, d_3, d_4, d_5, ...)$ that was presented. We refer to $\bar{\mathbf{y}}_t$ as the **user feedback ranking**.

We now define the learning problem and the user-interaction model more generally. At each round t, our algorithm presents a ranking $\mathbf{y}_t$ from a corpus $\mathbf{x}_t \in \mathcal{X}$ of candidate documents[1]. We assume that the user acts (approximately) rational according to an unknown utility function $U(\mathbf{x}_t, \mathbf{y}_t)$ that models both relevance of the documents as well as their dependencies (e.g. redundancy). In the context of such a utility function, we can interpret the user feedback as a preference between rankings. This type of preference feedback over multiple rounds t is the input for our learning model. Given the set of candidate documents $\mathbf{x}_t$, the **optimal ranking** is denoted by

$$\mathbf{y}_t^* := \arg\max_{\mathbf{y} \in \mathcal{Y}} U(\mathbf{x}_t, \mathbf{y}). \quad (1)$$

[1]In general, $\mathbf{x}_t$ can also represent a query/context.

Since the user's utility function $U(\mathbf{x}_t, \mathbf{y})$ is unknown, this optimal ranking $\mathbf{y}_t^*$ cannot be computed. The goal of the learning algorithm is to predict rankings with utility close to that of $\mathbf{y}_t^*$. Note, however, that the user feedback does not even give the optimal $\mathbf{y}_t^*$ to the algorithm (as in traditional supervised learning), but only the user feedback ranking $\bar{\mathbf{y}}_t$ is observed. To analyze the learning algorithms in the subsequent sections, we refer to any feedback that satisfies the following inequality as **strictly α-informative feedback**:

$$U(\mathbf{x}_t, \bar{\mathbf{y}}_t) - U(\mathbf{x}_t, \mathbf{y}_t) \geq \alpha \left(U(\mathbf{x}_t, \mathbf{y}_t^*) - U(\mathbf{x}_t, \mathbf{y}_t) \right). \quad (2)$$

The above inequality states that the utility of the user feedback ranking $\bar{\mathbf{y}}_t$ must be slightly better than the utility of the ranking $\mathbf{y}_t$ that was presented as a fraction of the difference between the utility of $\mathbf{y}_t^*$ and the utility of $\mathbf{y}_t$. As demonstrated in the example above, such a slightly improved rankings $\bar{\mathbf{y}}_t$ can be constructed as a reordering of $\mathbf{y}_t$ based on user clicks. The amount of improvement is quantified by $\alpha \in (0, 1]$, which is (an unknown) parameter in the above inequality that controls by what fraction the utility of the feedback ranking $\bar{\mathbf{y}}_t$ is higher than that of the predicted ranking $\mathbf{y}_t$ as compared to the maximum possible utility gain. To allow noisy feedback, we introduce slack variables ξ_t which allow violations of the above condition. This gives the following user feedback, referred to as **α-informative feedback**:

$$U(\mathbf{x}_t, \bar{\mathbf{y}}_t) - U(\mathbf{x}_t, \mathbf{y}_t) = \alpha \left(U(\mathbf{x}_t, \mathbf{y}_t^*) - U(\mathbf{x}_t, \mathbf{y}_t) \right) - \xi_t. \quad (3)$$

The above feedback model can be further relaxed, requiring that it merely holds in expectation over feedback. We refer to this as **expected α-informative feedback**

$$\mathbf{E}[U(\mathbf{x}_t, \bar{\mathbf{y}}_t) - U(\mathbf{x}_t, \mathbf{y}_t)] = \alpha \left(U(\mathbf{x}_t, \mathbf{y}_t^*) - U(\mathbf{x}_t, \mathbf{y}_t) \right) - \bar{\xi}_t, \quad (4)$$

and many of our results can be generalized to his weaker form of feedback as well. Note that the above expectation is over user's choice of $\bar{\mathbf{y}}_t$ given $\mathbf{y}_t$ for corpus $\mathbf{x}_t$ (i.e., distribution $\mathbf{P}_{\mathbf{x}_t}[\bar{\mathbf{y}}_t | \mathbf{y}_t]$). Moreover, $\bar{\xi}_t$ denotes the corresponding slack variable.

To measure the performance of our method we define a notion of **regret** based on the utility of the ranking we present with respect to the utility of the best possible ranking $\mathbf{y}_t^*$ that could have been presented in each step:

$$REG_T := \frac{1}{T} \sum_{t=0}^{T-1} \left(U(\mathbf{x}_t, \mathbf{y}_t^*) - U(\mathbf{x}_t, \mathbf{y}_t) \right). \quad (5)$$

Note that regret is measured with respect to the user's true utility function $U(\mathbf{x}_t, \mathbf{y}_t)$ and the optimal ranking $\mathbf{y}_t^*$, even though neither is ever explicitly revealed to the algorithm. Thus a decreasing regret indicates the utility of the predicted ranking improves over time.

4. MODELING RELEVANCE AND DIVERSITY

A key step in designing a learning algorithm that models both relevance and diversity lies in the design of an appropriate hypothesis space for modeling $U(\mathbf{x}, \mathbf{y})$. In short, the learning algorithm needs to learn an accurate model of how the user values a ranking $\mathbf{y}$ for a given $\mathbf{x}$. Since this relates to metrics for evaluating retrieval systems, we start our design of $U(\mathbf{x}, \mathbf{y})$ based on existing retrieval measures.

While traditional IR metrics are oblivious to diversity (e.g. NDCG, Precision), more recent additions account for diversity in some form (e.g. [16, 11, 18, 1, 5]). We define our hypothesis space based on the family of performance measures proposed in [12], since it subsumes many existing measures. These measures exhibit a *diminishing returns* property (i.e. submodularity), which means that the marginal utility of a document is lower if the intents the document is relevant to are already represented in the ranking.

While [12] focuses on the case of extrinsic diversity, the same model structure also applies to problems with need for intrinsic diversity. In particular, we model $U(\mathbf{x}, \mathbf{y})$ as a function that is linear in its parameters $\mathbf{w} \in \mathbf{R}^m$ with $\mathbf{w} \geq 0$,[2] but submodular (and non-linear) in a feature map $\phi(\mathbf{x}, \mathbf{y}) \in \mathbf{R}^m$ with $\phi(\mathbf{x}, \mathbf{y}) \geq 0$:

$$U(\mathbf{x}, \mathbf{y}) := \mathbf{w}^\top \phi(\mathbf{x}, \mathbf{y}). \tag{6}$$

The parameters $\mathbf{w}$ will be learned by the learning algorithm. The feature vector $\phi(\mathbf{x}, \mathbf{y})$ describes the ranking, but for simplicity of exposition we will consider $\mathbf{y}$ to be the set consisting of the top k results that were viewed by the user, not the full ranking[3]. The function $\phi(\mathbf{x}, \mathbf{y})$ generates a feature vector describing the set $\mathbf{y} = \{d_{i_1}, d_{i_2}, ..., d_{i_k}\}$ under context $\mathbf{x} = \{d_1, d_2, ..., d_{|\mathbf{x}|}\}$ in the following manner: We assume that each document d itself is described by a feature vector $\phi(d)$. These feature vectors are aggregated into the feature vector $\phi(\mathbf{x}, \mathbf{y})$ of $\mathbf{y}$ using an aggregation function F. Let $\phi^j(\mathbf{x}, \mathbf{y})$ be the j-th feature of $\phi(\mathbf{x}, \mathbf{y})$ and $\phi^j(d)$ the j-th feature of $\phi(d)$, then

$$\phi^j(\mathbf{x}, \mathbf{y}) = F(\{\phi^j(d_{i_1}), \phi^j(d_{i_2}), ..., \phi^j(d_{i_k})\}). \tag{7}$$

Examples of the per-feature aggregation function F are:

Name	$F(A)$	Subsumes
LIN	$F(A) = \sum_{a \in A} a$	Precision, DCG
MAX	$F(A) = \max_{a \in A} a$	Coverage

The MAX variant, but not LIN, encourages diversity in the following way. As example, consider a boolean bag-of-words representation of documents $\phi(d)$. The first document to contain a term t will increase the feature value of t in $\phi(\mathbf{x}, \mathbf{y})$ by 1. The second document to contain t, however, will not cause any increase. This models the redundancy of multiple occurrences of t, as it does not give any benefit to all but the first occurrence of t. Note that multiple aggregation functions F can be stacked into $\phi(\mathbf{x}, \mathbf{y})$, which allows the linear model to select a desired diminishing-returns profile. Note also that our model is not restricted to the F listed above, but rather any F can be used that is monotone and submodular [12], including less stringent functions which allows for some redundancy (like square root).

To compute the ranking that maximizes a utility function, i.e. $\mathbf{y} := \arg\max_{\mathbf{y} \in \mathcal{Y}} \mathbf{w}^\top \phi(\mathbf{x}, \mathbf{y})$, one can use the simple and efficient Greedy Algorithm 1. At each step, the algorithm greedily chooses the document with the highest marginal utility to be added to the ranking. Note that $\mathbf{y} \oplus d$ is used to refer to the operator that appends document d to ranking $\mathbf{y}$. Also note that Algorithm 1 computes the exact utility optimizer $\mathbf{y}_t$ for the modular measure LIN, whereas it finds a $1-1/e$ approximate $\mathbf{y}_t$ for any submodular and monotone function F.

[2]Denotes component-wise non-negativity.

[3]A ranking can be viewed as a nested structure of top-k sets, and the greedy algorithm we will later use to compute rankings uniformly optimizes the utility of the sets at any cutoff in the ranking.

Algorithm 1 GreedyRanking($\mathbf{w}, \mathbf{x}$)

```
y ← 0
for i = 1 to k do
  bestU ← −∞
  for all d ∈ x/ y do
    if w⊤(x, y ⊕ d) > bestU then
      bestU ← w⊤φ(x, y ⊕ d)
      best ← d
  y ← y ⊕ best
return y
```

5. ONLINE LEARNING ALGORITHMS

In this section, we present our coactive learning algorithms. In section 5.1, we present a perceptron style algorithm and then a clipped version of it. In section 5.2 we present an exponentiated gradient algorithm. We prove regret bounds for all the proposed algorithms.

5.1 Diversified Perceptron

We now describe our first learning algorithm for minimizing regret (5) for utility functions of the form (6). Algorithm 2, which we call the **Diversifying Perceptron (DP)**, maintains a weight vector $\mathbf{w}_t$ which is initialized to $\mathbf{0}$. At each time step t, DP presents a ranking $\mathbf{y}_t$ from the corpus $\mathbf{x}_t$ using Algorithm 1 with the current estimate $\mathbf{w}_t$. DP then uses the **user feedback ranking** $\bar{\mathbf{y}}_t$ (obtained as outlined in Section 3) to update the weight vector $\mathbf{w}_t$ in the direction of $\phi(\mathbf{x}_t, \bar{\mathbf{y}}_t) - \phi(\mathbf{x}_t, \mathbf{y}_t)$. Note that the α used in modeling user feedback (in Eqns. (2) and (3)) is unknown to the algorithm; it only plays a role in the analysis.

The following theorem describes the generalization performance of the Diversified Perceptron. Note that bound on the worst-case regret is independent of the dimensionality of the feature space, that the regret converges to its asymptote at the rate of $1/\sqrt{T}$ (where T is equal to the number of examples), and that the informativeness α of the feedback enters the bound only linearly. The first term of the bound captures the noise in the feedback.

THEOREM 1. *The average regret of the diversified perceptron algorithm can be upper bounded, for any* $\mathbf{w} \in \mathbf{R}^m$ *with* $\mathbf{w} \geq 0$ *that defines the utility in Eq. (6), as follows:*

$$REG_T \leq \frac{1}{\alpha T}\sum_{t=0}^{T-1} \xi_t + \frac{\beta R\|\mathbf{w}\|}{\alpha} + \frac{\sqrt{2}\sqrt{4-\beta^2}R\|\mathbf{w}\|}{\alpha\sqrt{T}}. \tag{8}$$

Here $\frac{1}{\beta+1}$ *is the approximation factor of the greedy algorithm with* $\beta \leq 2$ *and* $\|\phi(\mathbf{x}, \mathbf{y})\|_{\ell_2} \leq R$.

PROOF. Consider the ℓ_2 norm of $\mathbf{w}_T$:

$$\begin{aligned}\|\mathbf{w}_T\|^2 &= \|\mathbf{w}_{T-1}\|^2 + 2\mathbf{w}_{T-1}^\top(\phi(\mathbf{x}_{T-1}, \bar{\mathbf{y}}_{T-1}) - \phi(\mathbf{x}_{T-1}, \mathbf{y}_{T-1})) \\ &\quad + \|\phi(\mathbf{x}_{T-1}, \bar{\mathbf{y}}_{T-1}) - \phi(\mathbf{x}_{T-1}, \mathbf{y}_{T-1})\|^2 \\ &\leq \|\mathbf{w}_{T-1}\|^2 + 2\beta\, \mathbf{w}_{T-1}^\top \phi(\mathbf{x}_{T-1}, \mathbf{y}_{T-1}) + 4R^2 \\ &\leq \|\mathbf{w}_{T-1}\|^2 + 2\beta\|\mathbf{w}_{T-1}\|R + 4R^2 \end{aligned} \tag{9}$$

The first line comes from the update rule in Algorithm 2. The second line is from the fact: $\mathbf{w}_{T-1}^\top \phi(\mathbf{x}_{T-1}, \bar{\mathbf{y}}_{T-1}) \leq (\beta +$

Algorithm 2 Diversifying Perceptron.

Initialize $\mathbf{w}_0 \leftarrow \mathbf{0}$
for $t = 0$ **to** $T-1$ **do**
  Observe $\mathbf{x}_t$
  Present $\mathbf{y}_t \leftarrow GreedyRanking(\mathbf{w}_t, \mathbf{x}_t)$
  Obtain feedback $\bar{\mathbf{y}}_t$
  Update: $\mathbf{w}_{t+1} \leftarrow \mathbf{w}_t + \phi(\mathbf{x}_t, \bar{\mathbf{y}}_t) - \phi(\mathbf{x}_t, \mathbf{y}_t)$

Algorithm 3 Clipped Diversifying Perceptron.

Initialize $\mathbf{w}_0 \leftarrow \mathbf{0}$
for $t = 0$ **to** $T-1$ **do**
  Observe $\mathbf{x}_t$
  Present $\mathbf{y}_t \leftarrow GreedyRanking(\mathbf{w}_t, \mathbf{x}_t)$
  Obtain feedback $\bar{\mathbf{y}}_t$
  Update: $\bar{\mathbf{w}}_{t+1} \leftarrow \mathbf{w}_t + \phi(\mathbf{x}_t, \bar{\mathbf{y}}_t) - \phi(\mathbf{x}_t, \mathbf{y}_t)$
  Clip: $\mathbf{w}^j_{t+1} \leftarrow \max(\bar{\mathbf{w}}^j_{t+1}, 0) \quad \forall 1 \le j \le m$.

$1)\mathbf{w}_{T-1}^\top \phi(\mathbf{x}_{T-1}, \mathbf{y}_{T-1})$ since the greedy algorithm produces an $\frac{1}{\beta+1}$ approximation and that $\|\phi(\cdot,\cdot)\| \le R$. The third line comes by using the Cauchy-Schwarz inequality.

Let us inductively assume that $\|\mathbf{w}_t\| \le c_1 R(t+c_2)$ for $t = \{0, \dots T-1\}$ where the values $c_1, c_2 \ge 0$ will be determined later. The base case is trivially shown as $\|\mathbf{w}_0\| = 0$. Thus to complete the induction step, we have:

$$\begin{aligned}
\|\mathbf{w}_T\|^2 &\le \|\mathbf{w}_{T-1}\|^2 + 2\beta\|\mathbf{w}_{T-1}\|R + 4R^2 \\
&\le \|\mathbf{w}_{T-2}\|^2 + 2\beta R(\|\mathbf{w}_{T-1}\| + \|\mathbf{w}_{T-2}\|) + 8R^2 \\
&\le \|\mathbf{w}_0\|^2 + 2\beta R \sum_{t=0}^{T-1} \|\mathbf{w}_t\| + 4R^2 T \\
&\le \beta R^2 c_1(T^2 - T) + 2\beta R^2 T c_1 c_2 + 4R^2 T \\
&\le R^2\Big(\beta c_1 T^2 + T(-\beta c_1 + 2\beta c_1 c_2 + 4)\Big)
\end{aligned}$$

We now choose c_1 and c_2 such that the induction step holds. This is done by ensuring that the coefficients of T^2 and T in the above expression are smaller than the corresponding terms in $c_1^2T^2 + 2c_1^2c_2T + c_1^2c_2^2$. First, set $c_1 = \beta + \epsilon$, which will ensure the inequality for T^2. Next, we can ensure $-\beta c_1 + 2\beta c_1 c_2 + 4 \le 2c_1^2 c_2$, by setting $c_2 = \frac{4-\beta(\beta+\epsilon)}{2\epsilon(\epsilon+\beta)}$. We therefore have $\|\mathbf{w}_T\| \le (\epsilon+\beta)TR + \frac{(4-\beta^2)R}{2\epsilon} - \frac{\beta R}{2}$. Minimizing the above bound over ϵ, we get $\epsilon = \sqrt{\frac{4-\beta^2}{2T}}$. Substituting this in the upper bound for $\|\mathbf{w}_T\|$, we get $\|\mathbf{w}_T\| \le (\beta T + \sqrt{4-\beta^2}\sqrt{2T})R$.

Thus using the update rule of Algorithm 2, we have,

$$\begin{aligned}
\mathbf{w}_T^\top \mathbf{w} &= \mathbf{w}_{T-1}^\top \mathbf{w} + U(\mathbf{x}_{T-1}, \bar{\mathbf{y}}_{T-1}) - U(\mathbf{x}_{T-1}, \mathbf{y}_{T-1}) \\
&= \sum_{t=0}^{T-1} U(\mathbf{x}_t, \bar{\mathbf{y}}_t) - U(\mathbf{x}_t, \mathbf{y}_t).
\end{aligned}$$

We now use the fact that $\mathbf{w}_T^\top \mathbf{w} \le \|\mathbf{w}\|\|\mathbf{w}_T\|$ (Cauchy-Schwarz inequality) which implies,

$$\sum_{t=0}^{T-1} U(\mathbf{x}_t, \bar{\mathbf{y}}_t) - U(\mathbf{x}_t, \mathbf{y}_t) \le (\beta T + \sqrt{4-\beta^2}\sqrt{2T})R\|\mathbf{w}\|.$$

The above inequality, along with the condition of *α-informative feedback gives:*

$$\alpha REG_T - \frac{1}{T}\sum_{t=0}^{T-1} \xi_t \le \left(\beta + \sqrt{4-\beta^2}\sqrt{\frac{2}{T}}\right) R\|\mathbf{w}\|$$

from which the claimed result follows. □

For the case of modular utility (LIN), $\beta = 0$ and the above bound resembles the bound in [14]. For submodular utilities, $\beta = 1/(e+1)$ in the worst case, but is typically much smaller in practice. When users provide "clean" feedback according to (2), the first term in the bound (8) vanishes. We can also show a result similar to the one above in the case of expected α-informative feedback (4). We do not provide a proof for this case due to space limitations.

While the above theorem holds whenever there is a $\frac{1}{1+\beta}$-approximation for finding $\mathbf{y}_t$, there is a caveat. In the case of submodular utility, to ensure that the approximation guarantee holds, all the weights in $\mathbf{w}_t$ must be positive. This can be done by an additional clipping step that modifies each weight of $\mathbf{w}_t$ by clipping it at zero if it is negative. The clipped version of the algorithm is shown in Algorithm 3.

For Algorithm 3, assuming that the utility is also defined using a vector $\mathbf{w}$ which has only non-negative components, we can still give a regret bound similar to Theorem 1. Start by observing that, for any t,

$$\|\mathbf{w}_t\|^2 \le \|\bar{\mathbf{w}}_t\|^2 \quad \text{and} \quad \mathbf{w}^\top \mathbf{w}_t \ge \mathbf{w}^\top \bar{\mathbf{w}}_t \tag{10}$$

The first inequality holds because the product of any clipped value with itself is positive. Since all the components of $\mathbf{w}$ are positive and since only negative values in $\bar{\mathbf{w}}_T$ are set to zero in the clipping step, the second inequality holds. With these two steps, the remaining steps in the proof of Theorem 1 follow and we have the following corollary.

COROLLARY 2. *The average regret of the diversified perceptron algorithm can be upper bounded, for any* $\mathbf{w} \in \mathbf{R}^m$ *with* $\mathbf{w} \ge \mathbf{0}$ *that defines the utility, as follows:*

$$REG_T \le \frac{1}{\alpha T}\sum_{t=0}^{T-1} \xi_t + \frac{\beta R\|\mathbf{w}\|}{\alpha} + \frac{\sqrt{2}\sqrt{4-\beta^2}R\|\mathbf{w}\|}{\alpha\sqrt{T}}, \tag{11}$$

where $\frac{1}{\beta+1}$ *is the approximation factor of the greedy algorithm with* $\beta \le 2$ *and* $\|\phi(\mathbf{x}, \mathbf{y})\| \le R$.

We obtained the clipped version of the algorithm to avoid non-negative weights. In the next sub-section, we provide an elegant exponentiated algorithm that naturally maintains non-negative weights.

5.2 Exponentiated Algorithm

Our exponentiated algorithm for learning to diversify from implicit feedback is shown in Algorithm 4. In this algorithm, the weights are initialized uniformly at the start. There is a rate θ associated with each step. The rate depends on the maximum ℓ_∞ norm of the feature vectors (i.e., $\|\phi(\cdot,\cdot)\|_{\ell_\infty} \le S$) and time horizon T.

At each step, a context $\mathbf{x}_t$ is observed and an object $\mathbf{y}_t$ is presented just like in the earlier algorithms. However, once the feedback $\bar{\mathbf{y}}_t$ is obtained, the update rules are multiplicative as shown in Algorithm 4. The weights are normalized to one and the steps of the algorithm repeat. Since the updates are multiplicative and the weights are initially positive, $\mathbf{w}_t$ is guaranteed to remain positive in this algorithm.

We now prove the regret bound for Algorithm 4. While the regret bounds for Algorithms 2 and 3 depended on the ℓ_2 norm of the features, and the ℓ_2 norm of $\mathbf{w}$, the bound

Algorithm 4 Exponentiated Diversifying Algorithm.

Initialize $\mathbf{w}_0^i \leftarrow \frac{1}{m}\ \forall 1 \leq i \leq m$.
$\theta \leftarrow \frac{1}{2S\sqrt{T}}$
for $t = 0$ **to** $T-1$ **do**
  Observe $\mathbf{x}_t$
  Present $\mathbf{y}_t \leftarrow GreedyRanking(\mathbf{w}_t, \mathbf{x}_t)$
  Obtain feedback $\bar{\mathbf{y}}_t$
  Update: $\mathbf{w}_{t+1}^i \leftarrow \mathbf{w}_t^i \exp(\theta(\phi^i(\mathbf{x}_t, \bar{\mathbf{y}}_t) - \phi^i(\mathbf{x}_t, \mathbf{y}_t)))/Z_t$
  where Z_t is such that the weights add to one.

for the exponentiated algorithm depends on the ℓ_∞ norm of the feature vectors and the ℓ_1 norm of $\mathbf{w}$.

THEOREM 3. *For any $\mathbf{w} \in \mathbf{R}^m$ such that $\|\mathbf{w}\|_{\ell_1} = 1$, $\mathbf{w} \geq 0$, the average regret of the exponentiated algorithm can be upper bounded as follows:*

$$REG_T \leq \frac{1}{\alpha T}\sum_{t=0}^{T-1}\xi_t + \frac{S\beta}{\alpha} + \frac{2\log(m)S}{\alpha\sqrt{T}} + \frac{S}{2\alpha\sqrt{T}}, \quad (12)$$

where $\frac{1}{\beta+1}$ is the approximation factor of the greedy algorithm with $\beta \leq 2$ and $\|\phi(\mathbf{x}, \mathbf{y})\|_{\ell_\infty} \leq S$.

PROOF. We look at how the KL divergence between $\mathbf{w}$ and $\mathbf{w}_t$ evolves,

$$KL(\mathbf{w}\|\mathbf{w}_t) - KL(\mathbf{w}\|\mathbf{w}_{t+1}) = \sum_{i=1}^{m}\mathbf{w}^i \log(\mathbf{w}_{t+1}^i/\mathbf{w}_t^i)$$
$$= \sum_{i=1}^{m}\mathbf{w}^i(\theta(\phi^i(\mathbf{x}_t, \bar{\mathbf{y}}_t) - \phi^i(\mathbf{x}_t, \mathbf{y}_t))) - \log(Z_t)$$
$$= \theta\mathbf{w}^\top(\phi(\mathbf{x}_t, \bar{\mathbf{y}}_t) - \phi(\mathbf{x}_t, \mathbf{y}_t)) - \log(Z_t). \quad (13)$$

On the second line, we pulled out $\log(Z_t)$ from the sum since $\sum_{i=1}^m \mathbf{w}^i = 1$. Now, consider the last term in the above equation. Denoting $\phi^i(\mathbf{x}_t, \bar{\mathbf{y}}_t) - \phi^i(\mathbf{x}_t, \mathbf{y}_t)$ by $\Delta^i\phi_t$ for brevity, we have, by definition,

$$\log(Z_t) = \log\left(\sum_{i=1}^{m}\mathbf{w}_t^i \exp(\theta\Delta^i\phi_t)\right)$$
$$\leq \log\left(\sum_{i=1}^{m}\mathbf{w}_t^i(1 + \theta\Delta^i\phi_t + \theta^2\Delta^i\phi_t^{\,2})\right)$$
$$\leq \log\left(1 + \theta\mathbf{w}_t^\top\Delta\phi_t + \theta^2 S^2\right)$$
$$\leq \theta\mathbf{w}_t^\top\Delta\phi_t + \theta^2 S^2. \quad (14)$$

On the second line we used the fact that $\exp(x) \leq 1+x+x^2$ for $x \leq 1$. The rate θ ensures that $\theta(\Delta^i\phi) \leq 1$. On the last line, we used the fact that $\log(1+x) \leq x$. Combing (13) and (14), we get,

$$(\mathbf{w} - \mathbf{w}_t)^\top\Delta\phi_t \leq \frac{KL(\mathbf{w}\|\mathbf{w}_t) - KL(\mathbf{w}\|\mathbf{w}_{t+1})}{\theta} + \theta S^2.$$

Adding the above inequalities, we get:

$$\sum_{t=0}^{T-1}(\mathbf{w} - \mathbf{w}_t)^\top(\phi(\mathbf{x}_t, \bar{\mathbf{y}}_t) - \phi(\mathbf{x}_t, \mathbf{y}_t))$$
$$\leq \sum_{t=0}^{T-1}\frac{KL(\mathbf{w}\|\mathbf{w}_t) - KL(\mathbf{w}\|\mathbf{w}_{t+1})}{\theta} + \sum_{t=0}^{T-1}\theta S^2.$$
$$\leq \frac{KL(\mathbf{w}\|\mathbf{w}_0)}{\theta} + \theta S^2 T. \quad (15)$$

Rearranging the above inequality, and substituting the value of θ from Algorithm 4, we get:

$$\sum_{t=0}^{T-1}(U(\mathbf{x}_t, \bar{\mathbf{y}}_t) - U(\mathbf{x}_t, \mathbf{y}_t))$$
$$\leq \sum_{t=0}^{T-1}\mathbf{w}_t^\top(\phi(\mathbf{x}_t, \bar{\mathbf{y}}_t) - \phi(\mathbf{x}_t, \mathbf{y}_t)) + 2\log(m)S\sqrt{T} + \frac{S\sqrt{T}}{2}$$
$$\leq \sum_{t=0}^{T-1}\beta\mathbf{w}_t^\top\phi(\mathbf{x}_t, \mathbf{y}_t) + 2\log(m)S\sqrt{T} + \frac{S\sqrt{T}}{2}$$
$$\leq \beta ST + 2\log(m)S\sqrt{T} + \frac{S\sqrt{T}}{2}. \quad (16)$$

In the above, we also used the fact that $KL(\mathbf{w}\|\mathbf{w}_0) \leq \log(m)$ since $\mathbf{w}_0$ is initialized uniformly. On line three, we used the fact that the greedy algorithm finds a $\frac{1}{1+\beta}$ approximation. Moreover, from a generalized version of Cauchy-Schwarz inequality, we obtained

$$\mathbf{w}_t^\top\phi(\mathbf{x}_t, \mathbf{y}_t) \leq \|\mathbf{w}_t\|_{\ell_1}\|\phi(\mathbf{x}_t, \mathbf{y}_t)\|_{\ell_\infty} \leq S.$$

The above inequality along with α-informative feedback gives the claimed result. □

Like the result in Theorem 1, Theorem 3 also bounds the regret in terms of the noise in the feedback (first term), the approximation factor of the inference algorithm (second term), and additional terms which converge to zero at the rate $\mathcal{O}(1/\sqrt{T})$. The key difference to Theorem 1 is that the regret bound of the exponentiated algorithm scales logarithmically with the number of features, and with the ℓ_1-norm of $\mathbf{w}$, which can be advantageous if the optimal $\mathbf{w}$ is sparse.

6. EXPERIMENTS

In this section we empirically study different aspects of our proposed algorithms. In particular, we show how using the submodular utility helps achieve diversity. Furthermore, we explore the robustness of our learning method under degraded feedback quality and noise. We also explore learning the *amount* of diversity a user wants and also compare our method against a supervised method. Finally, we compare the three algorithms that we proposed in this paper against each other.

6.1 Experiment Setup

Since there is no large publicly available real-world corpus containing intrinsic diversity judgments[4], we created two artificial datasets from the RCV-1 [9] text corpus and from the 20 newsgroups dataset (abbreviated 20NG).

The RCV-1 corpus contains over 800k documents, each of which is annotated as belonging to one or more of 100+ *topics*. While the original RCV-1 topics are arranged hierarchically, to make the problem non-trivial, we considered only topics from the second level. The 20NG dataset contains about 19k documents (with duplicates removed) with a single class label for each document. We simulate users with multiple different interests, by forming *super-users* with 5 different interests corresponding to 5 different topics/classes. Thus, if a document is relevant to any of these topics it is relevant to that super-user, else it is not. We assume that

[4]Corpora like the TREC WEB corpus are small and contain relevance judgments only for extrinsic diversity.

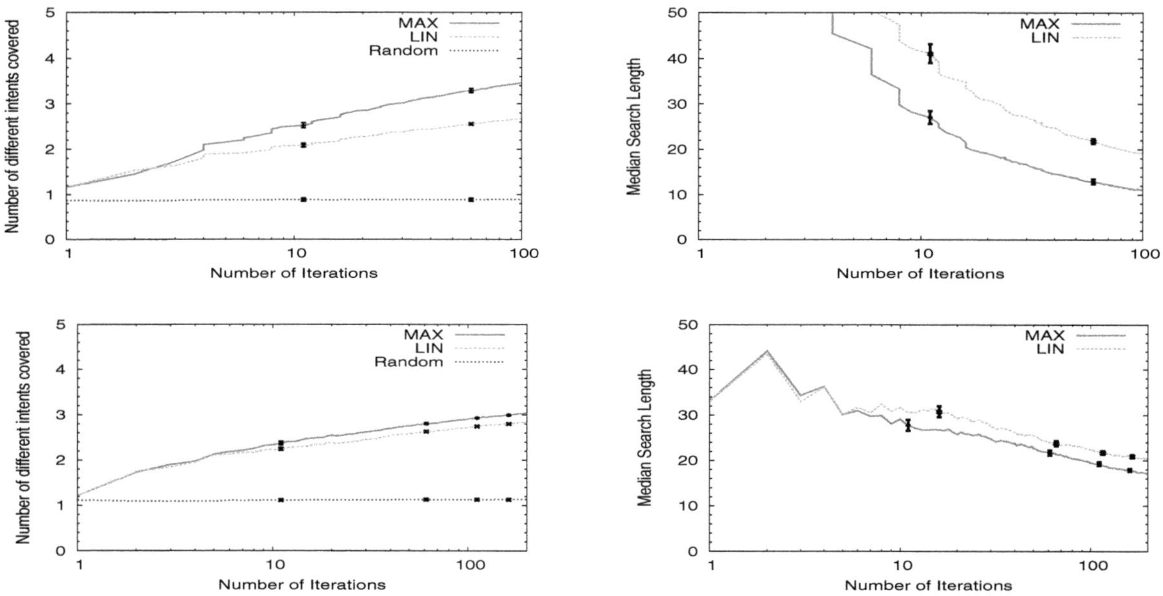

Figure 1: Comparison between the submodular (MAX) and independent (LIN) model for users that are purely seeking diversity; top: RCV-1, bottom: 20NG.

all topics are equally important unless otherwise mentioned. In addition, for a given *super-user* we removed documents relevant to multiple interests. In this manner, producing a diverse set of results would require being able to truly learn each of the interests separately.

We ran the Diversifying Perceptron algorithm with a fresh set of 1000 documents for RCV1 (100 for *20NG*) in each step as the corpus $\mathbf{x}$ and presented a ranking $\mathbf{y}$ from the current corpus. In particular we focus on the top 5 results for all evaluation measures for brevity, though the trends reported in the following hold true for other ranking lengths as well. All results we report are averaged over 50 runs of the algorithm, each for a different *super-user*. Documents are represented as TFIDF vectors. The joint feature map $\phi(\mathbf{x}, \mathbf{y})$ is an aggregation of the document vectors using one (or multiple) of the aggregation functions F described in Section 4.

6.2 Can the algorithm learn to diversify?

We first evaluate if the proposed DP algorithm is really able to learn a function that combines relevance and diversity. In particular, we generated users with 5 different and disjoint interests, and each user wants to read exactly one document relevant to each interest in every iteration. Note that users of this type are seeking maximum diversity in their rankings. To illustrate the performance of the algorithm, we report two quantities. First, we computed how many interests are covered in the top 5 documents of the presented ranking in each iteration. Second, we considered the *median* depth the user needs to search down the ranking to find one document for each of his interests.

We ran the DP algorithm with the **MAX** feature map as defined in Section 4. This is compared against another instance of our algorithm that uses the conventional model **LIN**, which focuses purely on relevance but cannot model diversity directly. For simplicity, we assume $\alpha = 1$ informative feedback. We also compare against a **Random** baseline, which is the performance of a random ranking.

Figure 1 shows the average and standard error of the results for this experiment on the two datasets. The left column shows the number of intents covered in the top 5 positions over time. While the LIN method is far better than the Random method and continues to improve over time, it is outperformed by the MAX method, which is able to learn better.

The right pane further illustrates this result, as it shows how the median search length (required to find at least one document for each intent) starts at high values, but quickly drops to small values after a few iterations. Both learning methods clearly outperform the Random baseline, the value of which is too large to show. In all the plots, the standard errors are small implying statistical significance.

It can be observed that the difference between the MAX and the LIN is much higher in the case of RCV-1 compared to 20NG dataset. This is due to the fact that 20NG has only 20 categories, whereas RCV-1 has more than 100 and is thus much harder to learn for LIN.

6.3 What is the effect of feedback quality?

We next study the effect of the quality of feedback (as described by α) on the performance our method. As real-world users are unlikely to provide perfect feedback, we would like our algorithm to learn even in scenarios where the user-feedback is far from ideal. We varied the quality of the feedback by changing the value of α. A change in α is achieved through the following mechanism: for any intent not covered in the presented ranking, but covered in the optimal ranking, with probability $1 - \alpha$, documents covering that intent are absent in the feedback ranking. This leads to having α-informative feedback in expectation.

Figure 2 shows the results for this experiment. Most notably, the performance is nearly unchanged for larger values of α. In particular, we find that for $\alpha \geq 0.6$ the perfor-

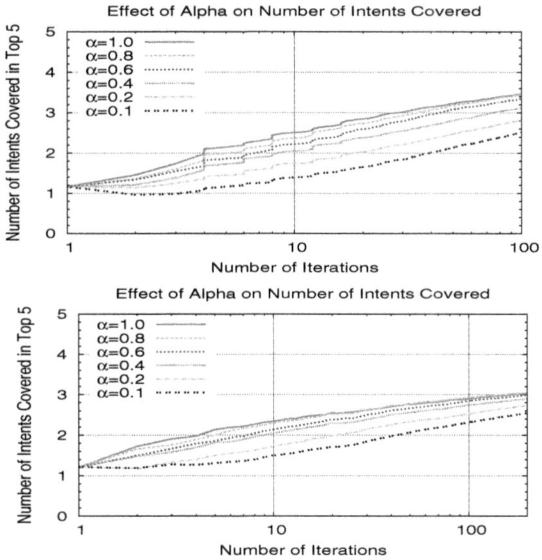

Figure 2: Effect of α on performance of the algorithm for users that are purely seeking diversity; top: RCV-1, bottom: 20NG.

mance is very close to that with perfect feedback ($\alpha = 1.0$). At low values of α such as 0.2 or 0.1, the method still makes reasonable progress over time, albeit at a slower rate. We see that for $\alpha = 0.2$ within 100 iterations the number of intents covered more than doubles. These results indicate that the proposed method is still able to learn even when the informativeness of the user feedback is poor.

6.4 What is the robustness to noise?

While the experiments in the previous section showed robustness to imperfect feedback, we now test the robustness of our algorithm to noisy feedback. One key difference between the two is that with noisy feedback, the user may return a feedback ranking that is worse than the one he was presented. Such a degradation in the quality of the ranking will be captured by the slack variable seen in Eq. (3). We would particularly like the noise introduced to be reflective of that expected in the real-world, where users may sometimes be unsure of the relevance of some documents. Thus we modify the user clicking mechanism that produces the feedback in the following manner:

- Each irrelevant document encountered in the ranking may be considered as relevant with probability η.
- Documents relevant to one of the user's topics may be confused for a different topic with probability $\eta/5$.

Like α, η affects only the quality of the user feedback and not the learning algorithm itself. Figure 3 shows the effect of varying the noise factor η. As seen in the figure, the algorithm is quite robust to noise. For high values of η, such as 0.2, we find that the algorithm is still able to learn quite well. The figures also indicate the expected α of the feedback received after adding noise. However, note that in this scenario, unlike the experiments varying α, the feedback ranking can be significantly worse than the predicted ranking. Thus we see that for $\eta = 0.2$, although $\alpha \sim 0.4$ in expectation, the performance is noticeably worse than for the case of $\alpha = 0.4$.

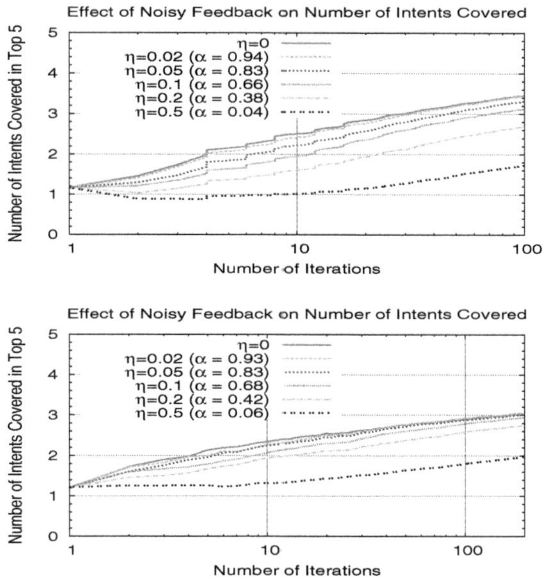

Figure 3: Effect of η on performance of the algorithm for users that are purely seeking diversity (number in bracket indicates the effective α of the feedback); top: RCV-1, bottom: 20NG.

		User-Utility	
		LIN	*MAX*
	RANDOM	.862(±.007)	.756(±.016)
Algo-Util	*LIN*	.137(±.019)	.447(±.005)
	MAX	.169(±.020)	.274(±.011)
	LIN + MAX	.158(±.021)	.310(±.010)

Table 1: Average Regret for different user utilities and algorithm utility functions.

6.5 Learn the desired amount of diversity?

We next explore whether the algorithm can learn how much diversity the user wants Furthermore, it is interesting to know how the algorithm performs in settings where the utility that the user optimizes (to provide feedback) is different from the one the algorithm uses.

To study this question, we experimented with the MAX and LIN utility functions mentioned earlier. We varied the user's inherent utility as well as the algorithm's utility to either of these two values. We also experimented with a *combination* method for the DP algorithm, which simply takes the joint feature vector representations used in the MAX and LIN functions and appends them to form a single vector. We refer to this method as $MAX + LIN$. To ensure difference in feedback between the two user utility functions, we weight the different intents (as done in [18]), which results in the utility being higher if a more *popular* topic is covered instead of a less popular one. We ran the DP algorithm for 100 iterations, where at each iteration the feedback provided by the user is as per the utility they optimize. We report performance in terms of the the average regret over these 100 iterations of the user's utility measure (since that is what the true $\mathbf{w}$ captures), thus *lower the better.*

Table 1 shows the results for RCV1[5]. First, consider the cases where the algorithm *is given the user's true diversity*

[5]We observe similar results for 20NG but omitted it due to space limitations

profile. As expected, the algorithm performs very well, as seen in the case of the LIN-maximizing algorithm performing best for purely-relevance seeking users (and similarly for the MAX-maximizing algorithm and diversity-seeking users). However, an important result of the experiment is that even when the amount of diversity the user requires is unknown, the *combination* algorithm is able to learn the amount of diversity the user wants. It performs nearly as well as the case where the user's diversity needs are known, as can be seen in the last row of the table. This shows that the combination algorithm is able to learn the trade-off between relevance and diversity that the user is looking for. This is very encouraging as it allows for the method to be used in scenarios where there is no a priori information about the desired amount of diversity. While related to recent work on extrinsic diversity [13], our method is an online learning technique and utilizes much weaker feedback than methods in [13] do.

6.6 Exponentiated algorithm

Compared to the other two algorithms, the exponentiated algorithm has a rate θ associated with it. This rate needs to be set appropriately. In practice, we observed that the performance of the exponentiated algorithm is sensitive to the value of the rate. In particular, we multiplied the rate θ by a numerical value and studied how the algorithm behaved. Note that this effectively changes the radius of the data, but seemed to significantly affect the behavior of the exponentiated algorithm. The results of this experiment is shown in Figure 4. The performance of the algorithm first improves and then deteriorates as the rate factor increases.

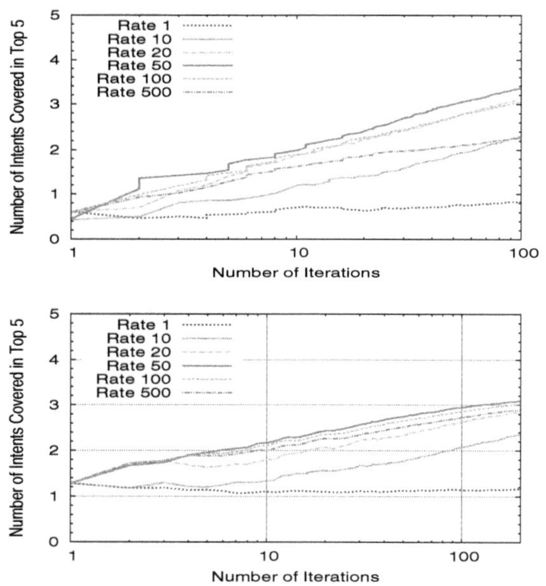

Figure 4: Exponentiated algorithm with different rates; top: RCV-1, bottom: 20NG.

6.7 How do the three algorithms compare?

We proposed three algorithms to learn diversity from implicit feedback. In this section, we study whether there is a difference in performance of these three algorithms. The clipped DP (Algorithm 3) was proposed mainly due to theoretical considerations. To compare the three algorithms, we followed the same setup as in Section 6.2. For the exponentiated algorithm, we considered the best rate parameter from the previous experiment. The results for this experiment are shown in Figure 5. It can be seen that there is not much of a difference between the clipped and the non-clipped algorithms in the case of RCV-1. In the case of 20NG, there is hardly any difference between the three algorithms. Even though restricting weights to positive values is required for theoretical purposes, in practice it does not seem to make much of a difference on these two datasets.

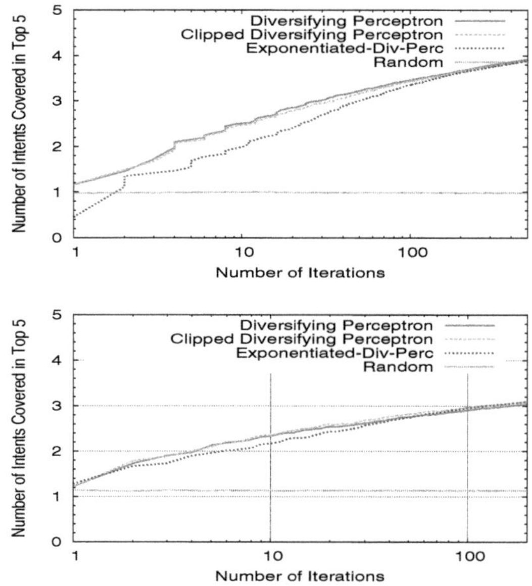

Figure 5: Comparison of the three algorithms; top: RCV-1, bottom: 20NG.

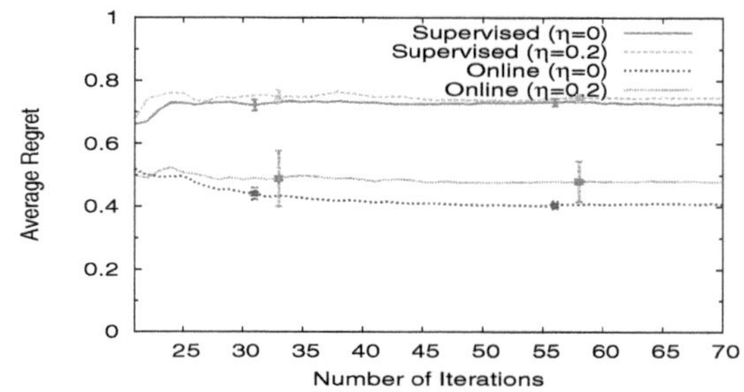

Figure 6: Comparison with supervised learning.

6.8 Comparison to supervised learning

To the best of our knowledge, ours is the first online learning method that can provide a ranking, of required diversity, from a different corpus (i.e. context) in every iteration. Hence there is no suitable online learning baseline to compare against. We thus compare our method against a batch learning method. In particular, we compare against the *one-level* version of the method proposed in [12], which is a generalization of [18].

In this setup, for each maximum diversity-seeking user we obtain the complete document-intent relevance labels for the first 50 (20) iterations for RCV1 (20NG), which is then used in training the SVM-struct based supervised learning method of [12] to obtain the $\mathbf{w}_t$. We train models using the labels from 40 (16) iterations, while utilizing the remaining 10 (4) to select the best value of the C parameter, which is varied from 10^{-2} to 10. The best model is then used to make predictions over the next 100 (50) iterations. We also run the online algorithm over these 150 (70) iterations to compare the two methods. Note that both the online method and the supervised learning method use exactly the same MAX model of user utility and exactly the same document features.

Since the supervised method does not predict rankings for the first 50 (20) iterations, to ensure a fair evaluation, we report the average regret for the next 100 (50) iterations *i.e.*:

$$REG_T := \frac{1}{100}\sum_{t=51}^{150}\left(U(\mathbf{x}_t, \mathbf{y}_t^*) - U(\mathbf{x}_t, \mathbf{y}_t)\right). \qquad (17)$$

We also run both methods with noise introduced using the technique mentioned in subsection 6.4.

As seen in Figure 6, the DP algorithm performs significantly better than the supervised learning method, achieving nearly 25% lower regret when there is no noise for RCV1. This is particularly encouraging given that the amount of feedback the supervised algorithm receives is vastly superior in informativeness to that of the online learning method: While the supervised algorithm receives the relevance labels of each document for each of the user's intent, the DP algorithm only receives a single preference (which has atmost 5 documents) in each iteration. Even for the $\eta = 0.2$ case, the DP algorithm is able to achieve lower regret eventually, indicating that the trend holds even under noisy conditions.

Finally, note that the (per-iteration) training times of the supervised batch method are vastly larger than those of the DP algorithm ($\sim$ 1000s vs. 0.1s). This is because the supervised method solves a more complex optimization problem (the structural SVM objective), while training the Diversifying Perceptron involves just a single update step. Consequently, this makes the DP algorithm especially useful in problem settings where we would like to continuously improve the learned model over time, something that would be prohibitively expensive with the supervised learning method.

7. CONCLUSIONS

We proposed online-learning algorithms for learning diversity in rankings. The proposed algorithms balance diversity and relevance by modeling the utility of the ranking as a submodular function. Using plausible user feedback in the form of preferences between rankings, the algorithms are able to learn rankings that optimize the user's utility. In addition to theoretically characterizing the performance of the algorithms and their robustness to noise, we showed that the algorithms perform well in empirical studies. Future research directions are the deployment of the algorithm in a real system and validation of the feedback model in user studies.

This research was funded in part by NSF Award IIS-0905467.

References

[1] R. Agrawal, S. Gollapudi, A. Halverson, and S. Ieong. Diversifying search results. In *WSDM*, 2009.

[2] J. Carbonell and J. Goldstein. The use of mmr, diversity-based reranking for reordering documents and producing summaries. In *SIGIR*, 1998.

[3] H. Chen and D. R. Karger. Less is more: probabilistic models for retrieving fewer relevant documents. In *SIGIR*, 2006.

[4] C. Clarke, M. Kolla, and O. Vechtomova. An effectiveness measure for ambiguous and underspecified queries. In *Advances in Information Retrieval Theory*, Lecture Notes in Computer Science, 2009.

[5] C. L. Clarke, N. Craswell, and I. Soboroff. Overview of the trec 2009 web track. Technical report, 2010.

[6] K. El-Arini and C. Guestrin. Beyond keyword search: discovering relevant scientific literature. In *KDD*, 2011.

[7] T. Joachims, L. Granka, B. Pan, H. Hembrooke, F. Radlinski, and G. Gay. Evaluating the accuracy of implicit feedback from clicks and query reformulations in web search. *ACM Transactions on Information Systems (TOIS)*, 25(2), April 2007.

[8] A. Kulesza and B. Taskar. Learning determinantal point processes. In *UAI*, pages 419–427, 2011.

[9] D. D. Lewis, Y. Yang, T. G. Rose, and F. Li. RCV1: A new benchmark collection for text categorization research. *JMLR*, 5:361–397, 2004.

[10] F. Radlinski, P. N. Bennett, B. Carterette, and T. Joachims. Redundancy, diversity and interdependent document relevance. *SIGIR Forum*, 43(2):46–52, 2009.

[11] F. Radlinski, R. Kleinberg, and T. Joachims. Learning diverse rankings with multi-armed bandits. In *ICML*, 2008.

[12] K. Raman, T. Joachims, and P. Shivaswamy. Structured learning of two-level dynamic rankings. In *CIKM*, 2011.

[13] R. L. Santos, C. Macdonald, and I. Ounis. Selectively diversifying web search results. In *CIKM*, 2010.

[14] P. Shivaswamy and T. Joachims. Online structured prediction via coactive learning. In *ICML*, 2012.

[15] A. Slivkins, F. Radlinski, and S. Gollapudi. Learning optimally diverse rankings over large document collections. In *ICML*, pages 983–990, 2010.

[16] A. Swaminthan, C. Metthew, and D. Kirovski. Essential pages. In *Technical Report, MSR-TR-2008-15*, Microsoft Research, 2008.

[17] Y. Yue and C. Guestrin. Linear submodular bandits and their application to diversified retrieval. In *Advances in Neural Information Processing Systems (NIPS)*, 2012.

[18] Y. Yue and T. Joachims. Predicting diverse subsets using structural svms. In *ICML*, 2008.

[19] C. X. Zhai, W. W. Cohen, and J. Lafferty. Beyond independent relevance: methods and evaluation metrics for subtopic retrieval. In *SIGIR*, 2003.

Playlist Prediction via Metric Embedding

Shuo Chen
Cornell University
Dept. of Computer Science
Ithaca, NY, USA
shuochen@cs.cornell.edu

Joshua L. Moore
Cornell University
Dept. of Computer Science
Ithaca, NY, USA
jlmo@cs.cornell.edu

Douglas Turnbull
Ithaca College
Dept. of Computer Science
Ithaca, NY, USA
dturnbull@ithaca.edu

Thorsten Joachims
Cornell University
Dept. of Computer Science
Ithaca, NY, USA
tj@cs.cornell.edu

ABSTRACT

Digital storage of personal music collections and cloud-based music services (e.g. Pandora, Spotify) have fundamentally changed how music is consumed. In particular, automatically generated playlists have become an important mode of accessing large music collections. The key goal of automated playlist generation is to provide the user with a *coherent* listening experience. In this paper, we present Latent Markov Embedding (LME), a machine learning algorithm for generating such playlists. In analogy to matrix factorization methods for collaborative filtering, the algorithm does not require songs to be described by features a priori, but it learns a representation from example playlists. We formulate this problem as a regularized maximum-likelihood embedding of Markov chains in Euclidian space, and show how the resulting optimization problem can be solved efficiently. An empirical evaluation shows that the LME is substantially more accurate than adaptations of smoothed n-gram models commonly used in natural language processing.

Categories and Subject Descriptors

I.2.6 [**Artificial Intelligence**]: Learning; I.5.1 [**Pattern Recognition**]: Models

General Terms

Algorithms, Experimentation, Human Factors

Keywords

Music Playlists, Recommendation, User Modeling, Sequences

1. INTRODUCTION

A music consumer can store thousands of songs on his or her computer, portable music player, or smart phone. In addition, when using a cloud-based service like Rhapsody or Spotify, the consumer has instant on-demand access to millions of songs. This has created substantial interest in automatic playlist algorithms that can help consumers explore large collections of music. Companies like Apple and Pandora have developed successful commercial playlist algorithms, but relatively little is known about how these algorithms work and how well they perform in rigorous evaluations.

Despite the large commercial demand, comparably little scholarly work has been done on automated methods for playlist generation (e.g., [13, 4, 9, 11]), and the results to date indicate that it is far from trivial to operationally define what makes a playlist coherent. The most comprehensive study was done by [11]. Working under a model where a coherent playlist is defined by a Markov chain with transition probabilities reflecting similarity of songs, they find that neither audio-signal similarity nor social-tag-based similarity naturally reflect manually constructed playlists.

In this paper, we therefore take an approach to playlist prediction that does not rely on content-based features, and that is analogous to matrix decomposition methods in collaborative filtering [7]. Playlists are treated as Markov chains in some latent space, and our algorithm – called Logistic Markov Embedding (LME) – learns to represent each song as one (or multiple) points in this space. Training data for the algorithm consists of existing playlists, which are widely available on the web. Unlike other collaborative filtering approaches to music recommendation like [13, 4, 19], ours is among the first (also see [1]) to directly model the sequential and directed nature of playlists, and that includes the ability to sample playlists in a well-founded and efficient way.

In empirical evaluations, the LME algorithm substantially outperforms traditional n-gram sequence modeling methods from natural language processing. Unlike such methods, the LME algorithm does not treat sequence elements as atomic units without metric properties, but instead provides a generalizing representation of songs in Euclidean space. Technically, it can be viewed as a multi-dimensional scaling problem [3], where the algorithm infers the metric from a stochastic sequence model. While we focus exclusively on playlist prediction in this paper, the LME algorithm also provides interesting opportunities for other sequence prediction problems (e.g. language modeling).

KDD'12, August 12–16, 2012, Beijing, China.

2. RELATED WORK

Personalized Internet radio has become a popular way of listening to music. A user seeds a new stream of music by specifying a favorite artist, a specific song, or a semantic tag (e.g., genre, emotion, instrument.) A backend playlist algorithm then generates a sequence of songs that is related to the seed concept. While the exact implementation details of various commercial systems are trade secrets, different companies use different forms of music metadata to identify relevant songs. For example, Pandora relies on the content-based music analysis by human experts [17] while Apple iTunes Genius relies on preference ratings and collaborative filtering [2]. What is not known is the mechanism by which the playlist algorithms are used to *order* the set of relevant songs, nor is it known how well these playlist algorithms perform in rigorous evaluations.

In the scholarly literature, two recent papers address the topic of playlist prediction. First, Maillet et al. [9] formulate the playlist ordering problem as a supervised binary classification problem that is trained discriminatively. Positive examples are pairs of songs that appeared in this order in the training playlists, and negative examples are pairs of songs selected at random which do not appear together in order in historical data. Second, McFee and Lanckriet [11] take a generative approach by modeling historical playlists as a Markov chain. That is, the probability of the next song in a playlist is determined only by acoustic and/or social-tag similarly to the current song. We take a similar Markov chain approach, but do not require any acoustic or semantic information about the songs.

While relatively little work has been done on explicitly modeling playlists, considerably more research has focused on embedding songs (or artists) into a similarity-based music space (e.g., [8, 13, 4, 19].) Our work is most closely related to research that involves automatically *learning* the music embedding. For example, Platt et al. use semantic tags to learn a Gaussian process kernel function between pairs of songs [13]. More recently, Weston et al. learn an embedding over a joint semantic space of audio features, tags and artists by optimizing an evaluation metric (Precision at k) for various music retrieval tasks [19]. Our approach, however, is substantially different from these existing methods, since it explicitly models the sequential nature of playlists.

Modeling playlists as a Markov chain connects to a large body of work on sequence modeling in natural language processing and speech recognition. In those applications, a language model of the target language is used to disambiguate uncertainty in the acoustic signal or the translation model. Smoothed n-gram models (see e.g. [6]) are the most commonly used method in language modeling, and we will compare against such models in our experiments. However, in natural language processing and speech recognition n-grams are typically used as part of a Hidden Markov Model (HMM)[14], not in a plain Markov Model as in our paper. In the HMM model, each observation in sequence is governed by an hidden state that evolves in Markovian fashion. The goal for learning to estimate the transition probability between hidden states as well as the probability of the observations conditioned on the hidden states. Using singular value decomposition, recent works on embedding the HMM distribution into a reproducing kernel Hilbert space [16, 5] circumvent the inference of the hidden states and make the model usable as long as kernel can be defined on the domain of observation. While both this work and our work make use of embeddings in the context of Markov chains, the two approaches solve very different problems.

Sequenced prediction also has important applications and related work in other domains. For example, Rendle et al. [15] consider the problem of predicting what a customer would have in his next basket of online purchasing. They model the transition probabilities between items in two consecutive baskets, and the tensor decomposition technique they use can be viewed as embedding in a way. While both are sequence prediction problems, the precise modeling problems are different.

Independent of and concurrent with our work, Aizenberg et al. [1] developed a model related to ours. The major difference lies in two aspects. First, they focus less on the sequential aspect of playlists, but more on using radio playlists as proxies for user preference data. Second, their model is based on inner products, while we embed using Euclidean distance. Euclidian distance seems a more natural choice for rendering an easy-to-understand visualization from the embeddings. Related is also work by Zheleva et al. [21]. Their model, however, is different from ours. They use a Latent Dirichlet Allocation-like graphical model to capture the hidden taste and mood of songs, which is different from our focus.

3. METRIC MODEL OF PLAYLISTS

Our goal is to estimate a generative model of coherent playlists which will enable us to efficiently sample new playlists. More formally, given a collection $\mathcal{S} = \{s_1, ..., s_{|\mathcal{S}|}\}$ of songs s_i, we would like to estimate the distribution $\Pr(p)$ of coherent playlists $p = (p^{[1]}, ..., p^{[k_p]})$. Each element $p^{[i]}$ of a playlist refers to one song from S.

A natural approach is to model playlists as a Markov chain, where the probability of a playlist $p = (p^{[1]}, ..., p^{[k_p]})$ is decomposed into the product of transition probabilities $\Pr(p^{[i]}|p^{[i-1]})$ between adjacent songs $p^{[i-1]}$ and $p^{[i]}$.

$$\Pr(p) = \prod_{i=1}^{k_p} \Pr(p^{[i]}|p^{[i-1]}) \tag{1}$$

For ease of notation, we assume that $p^{[0]}$ is a dedicated start symbol. Such bigram (or n-gram models more generally) have been widely used in language modeling for speech recognition and machine translation with great success [6]. In these applications, the $O(|\mathcal{S}|^n)$ transition probabilities $\Pr(p^{[i]}|p^{[i-1]})$ are estimated from a large corpus of text using sophisticated smoothing methods.

While such n-gram approaches can be applied to playlist prediction in principle, there are fundamental difference between playlists and language. First, playlists are less constrained than language, so that transition probabilities between songs are closer to uniform. This means that we need a substantially larger training corpus to observe all of the (relatively) high-probability transitions even once. Second, and in contrast to this, we have orders of magnitude less playlist data to train from than we have written text.

To overcome these problems, we propose a Markov-chain sequence model that produces a *generalizing representation* of songs and song sequences. Unlike n-gram models that treat words as atomic units without metric relationships between each other, our approach seeks to model coherent

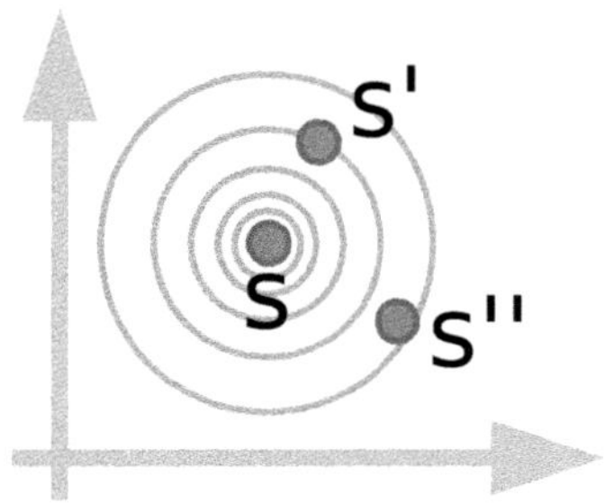

Figure 1: Illustration of the Single-Point Model. The probability of some other song following s depends on its Euclidean distance to s.

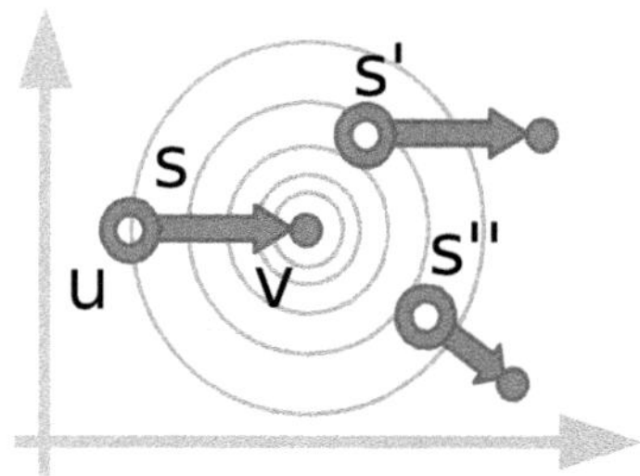

Figure 2: Illustration of the Dual-Point Model. The probability of some other song following s depends on the Euclidean distance from the exit vector $V(s)$ of s to the target song's entry vector $U(\cdot)$.

playlists as paths through a latent space. In particular, songs are embedded as points (or multiple points) in this space so that Euclidean distance between songs reflects the transition probabilities. The key learning problem is to determine the location of each song using existing playlists as training data. Once each song is embedded, our model can assign meaningful transition probabilities even to those transitions that were not seen in the training data.

Note that our approach does not rely on explicit features describing songs. However, explicit song features can easily be added to our transition model as outlined below. We will now introduce two approaches to modeling $\Pr(p)$ that both create an embedding of playlists in Euclidean space.

3.1 Single-Point Model

In the simplest model as illustrated in Figure 1, we represent each song s as a single vector $X(s)$ in d-dimensional Euclidean space $\mathcal{M}$. The key assumption of our model is that the transition probabilities $\Pr(p^{[i]}|p^{[i-1]})$ are related to the Euclidean distance $||X(p^{[i]})-X(p^{[i-1]})||_2$ between $p^{[i-1]}$ and $p^{[i]}$ in $\mathcal{M}$ through the following logistic model:

$$\Pr(p^{[i]}|p^{[i-1]}) = \frac{e^{-||X(p^{[i]})-X(p^{[i-1]})||_2^2}}{\sum_{j=1}^{|S|} e^{-||X(s_j)-X(p^{[i-1]})||_2^2}} \tag{2}$$

We will typically abbreviate the partition function in the denominator as $Z(p^{[i-1]})$ and the distance $||X(s)-X(s')||_2$ as $\Delta(s,s')$ for brevity. Using a Markov model with this transition distribution, we can now define the probability the of an entire playlist of a given length k_p as

$$\Pr(p) = \prod_{i=1}^{k_p} \Pr(p^{[i]}|p^{[i-1]}) = \prod_{i=1}^{k_p} \frac{e^{-\Delta(p^{[i]},p^{[i-1]})^2}}{Z(p^{[i-1]})}. \tag{3}$$

Our method seeks to discover an embedding of the songs into this latent space which causes "good" playlists to have high probability of being generated by this process. This is inspired by collaborative filtering methods such as [7, 18], which similarly embed users and items into a latent space to predict users' ratings of items. However, our approach differs from these methods in that we wish to predict paths through the space, as opposed to independent item ratings.

In order to learn the embedding of songs, we use a sample $D = (p_1, ..., p_n)$ of existing playlists as training data and take a maximum likelihood approach. Denoting with X the matrix of feature vectors describing all songs in the collection $\mathcal{S}$, this leads to the following training problem:

$$X = \underset{X\in\Re^{|S|\times d}}{\operatorname{argmax}} \prod_{p\in D}\prod_{i=1}^{k_p} \frac{e^{-\Delta(p^{[i]},p^{[i-1]})^2}}{Z(p^{[i-1]})} \tag{4}$$

Equivalently, we can maximize the log-likelihood

$$L(D|X) = \sum_{p\in D}\sum_{i=1}^{k_p} -\Delta(p^{[i]},p^{[i-1]})^2 - \log(Z(p^{[i-1]})). \tag{5}$$

In Section 5, we describe how to solve this optimization problem efficiently, and we explore various methods for avoiding overfitting through regularization in Section 3.3. First, however, we extend the basic single-point model to a model that represents each song through a pair of points.

3.2 Dual-Point Model

Representing each song using a single point $X(s)$ as in the previous section has at least two limitations. First, the Euclidean metric $||X(s)-X(s')||_2$ that determines the transition distribution is symmetric, even though the end of a song may be drastically different from its beginning. In this case, the beginning of song s may be incompatible with song s' altogether, and a transition in the opposite direction – from s' to s – should be avoided. Second, some songs may be good transitions between genres, taking a playlist on a trajectory away from the current location in latent space.

To address these limitations, we now propose to model each song s using a pair $(U(s), V(s))$ of points. We call $U(s)$ the "entry vector" of song s, and $V(s)$ the "exit vector". An illustration of this model is shown in Figure 2. Each song s is depicted as an arrow connecting $U(s)$ to $V(s)$. The "entry vector" $U(s)$ models the interface to the previous song in the playlist, while the "exit vector" $V(s)$ models the interface to the next song. The transition from song s to s' is then described by a logistic model relating the exit vector $V(s)$ of song s to the entry vector $U(s')$ of song s'. Adapting our notation for this setting by representing the asymmetric song divergence $||V(s)-U(s')||_2$ as $\Delta_2(s,s')$ and the corresponding dual-point partition function as $Z_2(s)$, we obtain the following probabilistic model of a playlist.

$$\Pr(p) = \prod_{i=1}^{k_p} \Pr(p^{[i]}|p^{[i-1]}) = \prod_{i=1}^{k_p} \frac{e^{-\Delta_2(p^{[i]},p^{[i-1]})^2}}{Z_2(p^{[i-1]})} \tag{6}$$

Similar to Eq. (4), computing the embedding vectors ($U(s)$, $V(s)$) for each song can be phrased as a maximum-likelihood problem for a given training sample of playlists $D = (p_1, ..., p_n)$, where V and U are the matrices containing the respective entry and exit vectors for all songs.

$$(V, U) = \underset{V,U \in \Re^{|S| \times d}}{\text{argmax}} \prod_{p \in D} \prod_{i=1}^{k_p} \frac{e^{-\Delta_2(p^{[i]}, p^{[i-1]})^2}}{Z_2(p^{[i-1]})} \quad (7)$$

As in the single-point case, it is again equivalent to maximize the log-likelihood:

$$L(D|V, U) = \sum_{p \in D} \sum_{i=1}^{k_p} -\Delta_2(p^{[i]}, p^{[i-1]})^2 - \log(Z_2(p^{[i-1]})) \quad (8)$$

3.3 Regularization

While the choice of dimensionality d of the latent space $\mathcal{M}$ provides some control of overfitting, it is desirable to have more fine-grained control. We therefore introduce the following norm-based regularizers that get added to the log-likelihood objective.

The first regularizer penalizes the Frobenius norm of the matrix of feature vectors, leading to

$$X = \underset{X \in \Re^{|S| \times d}}{\text{argmax}} \; L(D|X) - \lambda ||X||_F^2 \quad (9)$$

for the single point model, and

$$(V, U) = \underset{V,U \in \Re^{|S| \times d}}{\text{argmax}} \; L(D|V, U) - \lambda(||V||_F^2 + ||U||_F^2) \quad (10)$$

for the dual point model. λ is the regularization parameter which we will set by cross-validation. For increasing values of λ, this regularizer encourages vectors to stay closer to the origin. This leads to transition distributions $\Pr(p^{[i]}|p^{[i-1]})$ that are closer to uniform.

For the dual-point model, it also makes sense to regularize by the distance between the entry and exit vector of each song. For most songs, these two vectors should be close. This leads to the following formulation,

$$(V, U) = \underset{V,U \in \Re^{|S| \times d}}{\text{argmax}} \; L(D|V, U) - \lambda(||V||_F^2 + ||U||_F^2) \quad (11)$$
$$-\nu \sum_{s \in \mathcal{S}} \Delta_2(s, s)^2$$

where ν is a second regularization parameter.

3.4 Extending the Model

The basic LME model can be extended in a variety of ways. We have already seen how the dual-point model can account for the directionality of playlists. To further demonstrate its modeling flexibility, consider the following extensions to the single-point model. These extension can also be added to the dual-point model in a straightforward way.

Popularity. The basic LME models have only limited means of expressing the popularity of a song. By adding a separate "popularity boost" b_i to each song s_i, the resulting transition model

$$\Pr(p^{[i]}|p^{[i-1]}) = \frac{e^{-\Delta(p^{[i]}, p^{[i-1]})^2 + b_i}}{\sum_j e^{-\Delta(s_j, p^{[i-1]})^2 + b_j}} \quad (12)$$

can separate the effect of a song's popularity from the effect of its similarity in content to other songs. This can normalize the resulting embedding space with respect to popularity, and it is easy to see that training the popularity scores b_i as part of Eq. (12) does not substantially change the optimization problem.

User Model. The popularity score is a simple version of a preference model. In the same way, more complex models of song quality and user preference can be included as well. For example, one can add a matrix factorization model to explain user preferences independent of the sequence context, leading to the following transition model.

$$\Pr(p^{[i]}|p^{[i-1]}, u) = \frac{e^{-\Delta(p^{[i]}, p^{[i-1]})^2 + A(p^{[i]})^T B(u)}}{\sum_j e^{-\Delta(s_j, p^{[i-1]})^2 + A(s_j)^T B(u)}} \quad (13)$$

Analogous to models like in [7], $A(s)$ is a vector describing song s and $B(u)$ is a vector describing the preferences of user u.

Semantic Tags. Many songs have semantic tags that describe genre and other qualitative attributes of the music. However, not all songs are tagged, and tags do not follow a standardized vocabulary. It would therefore be desirable to embed semantic tags in the same Euclidean space as the songs, enabling the computation of (semantic) distances between tags, as well as between tags and (untagged) songs. This can be achieved by modeling the prior distribution of the location of song s based on its tags $T(s)$ in the following way.

$$\Pr(X(s)|T(s)) = \mathcal{N}\left(\frac{1}{|T(s)|} \sum_{t \in T(s)} M(t), \; \frac{1}{2\lambda} I_d\right) \quad (14)$$

Note that this definition of $\Pr(X(s)|T(s))$ nicely generalizes the regularizer in (4), which corresponds to an "uninformed" Normal prior $\Pr(X(s)) = \mathcal{N}(0, \frac{1}{2\lambda} I_d)$ centered at the origin of the embedding space. Again, simultaneously optimizing song embeddings $X(s)$ and tag embeddings $M(t)$ does not substantially change the optimization problem during training. This extended embedding model for songs and tags is described in more detail in [12].

Observable Features. Some features may be universally available for all songs, in particular features derived from the audio signal via automated classification. Denote these observable features of song s as $O(s)$. We can then learn a positive-semidefinite matrix W similar to [10], leading to the following transition model.

$$\Pr(p^{[i]}|p^{[i-1]}) = \frac{e^{-\Delta(p^{[i]}, p^{[i-1]})^2 + O(p^{[i]})^T W O(p^{[i-1]})}}{\sum_j e^{-\Delta(s_j, p^{[i-1]})^2 + O(s_j)^T W O(p^{[i-1]})}} \quad (15)$$

Long-Range Dependencies. A more fundamental problem is the modeling of long-range dependencies in playlists. While it is straightforward to add extensions for modeling closeness to some seed song – either during training, or at the time of playlist generation as discussed in Section 4 – modeling dependencies beyond n-th order Markov models is an open question. However, submodular diversification models from information retrieval (e.g. [20]) may provide interesting starting points.

4. GENERATING PLAYLISTS

From a computational perspective, generating new playlists is very straightforward. Given a seed location in the embedding space, a playlist is generated through repeated sampling from the transition distribution. From a usability perspective, however, there are two problems.

First, how can the user determine a seed location for a playlist? Fortunately, the metric nature of our models gives many opportunities for letting the user specify the seed location. It can be either a single song, the centroid of a set of songs (e.g. by a single artist), or a user may graphically select a location through a map similar to the one in Figure 3. Furthermore, we have shown in other work [12] how songs and social tags can be jointly embedded in the metric space, making it possible to specify seed locations through keyword queries for semantic tags.

Second, the playlist model that is learned represents an average model of what constitutes a good playlists. Each particular user, however, may have preferences that are different from this average model at any particular point in time. It is therefore important to give the user some control over the playlist generation process. Fortunately, our model allows a straightforward parameterization of the transition distribution. For example, through the parameters α, β and γ in the following transition distribution

$$\Pr(p^{[i]}|p^{[i-1]}, p^{[0]}) = \frac{e^{-\alpha\Delta(p^{[i]},p^{[i-1]})^2+\beta b_i-\gamma\Delta(p^{[i]},p^{[0]})^2}}{Z(p^{[i-1]}, p^{[0]}, \alpha, \beta, \gamma)}, \quad (16)$$

the user can influence meaningful and identifiable properties of the playlists that get generated. For example, by setting α to a value that is less than 1, the model will take larger steps. By increasing β to be greater than 1, the model will focus on popular songs. And by setting γ to a positive value, the playlists will tend to stay close to the seed location. It is easy to imagine other terms and parameters in the transition distribution as well.

To give an impression of the generated playlists and the effects of the parameters, we provide an online demo at `http://lme.joachims.org`.

5. SOLVING THE OPTIMIZATION PROBLEMS

In the previous section, the training problems were formulated as the optimization problems in Eq. (5) and (8). While both have a non-convex objective, we find that the stochastic gradient algorithm described in the following robustly finds a good solution. Furthermore, we propose a heuristic for accelerating gradient computations that substantially improves runtime.

5.1 Stochastic Gradient Training

We propose to solve optimization problems (5) and (8) using the following stochastic gradient method. We only describe the algorithm for the dual-point model, since the algorithm for the single-point model is easily derived from it.

We start with random initializations for U and V. We also calculate a matrix T whose elements T_{ab} are the number of transitions from the s_a to s_b in the training set. Note that this matrix is sparse and always requires less storage than the original playlists. Recall that we have defined $\Delta_2(s_a, s_b)$ as the song divergence $||U(s_a) - V(s_b)||_2$ and $Z_2(s_a)$ as the dual-point partition function $\sum_{l=1}^{|S|} e^{-\Delta_2(s_a,s_l)^2}$. We can now equivalently write the objective in Eq. (8) as

$$L(D|U, V) = \sum_{a=1}^{|S|}\sum_{b=1}^{|S|} T_{ab}\, l(s_a, s_b) - \Omega(V, U) \quad (17)$$

where $\Omega(V, U)$ is the regularizer and $l(s_a, s_b)$ is the "local" log-likelihood term that is concerned with the transition from s_a to s_b.

$$l(s_a, s_b) = \quad -\Delta_2(s_a, s_b)^2 - \log(Z_2(s_a)) \quad (18)$$

Denoting with $1^{[x=y]}$ the indicator function that returns 1 if the equality is true and 0 otherwise, we can write the derivatives of the local log-likelihood terms and the regularizer as

$$\frac{\partial l(s_a, s_b)}{\partial U(s_p)} = 1^{[a=p]}2\left[-\vec{\Delta}_2(s_a,s_b) + \frac{\sum_{l=1}^{|S|} e^{-\Delta_2(s_a,s_l)^2}\vec{\Delta}_2(s_a, s_l)}{Z_2(s_a)}\right]$$

$$\frac{\partial l(s_a, s_b)}{\partial V(s_q)} = 1^{[b=q]}2\vec{\Delta}_2(s_a, s_b) - 2\frac{e^{-\Delta_2(s_a,s_q)^2}\vec{\Delta}_2(s_a, s_q)}{Z_2(s_a)}$$

$$\frac{\partial \Omega(V, U)}{\partial U(s_p)} = 2\lambda U(s_p) - 2\nu\vec{\Delta}_2(s_p, s_p)$$

$$\frac{\partial \Omega(V, U)}{\partial V(s_p)} = 2\lambda V(s_p) + 2\nu\vec{\Delta}_2(s_p, s_p)$$

where we used $\vec{\Delta}_2(s, s')$ to denote the vector $V(s) - U(s')$.

We can now describe the actual stochastic gradient algorithm. The algorithm iterates through all songs s_p in turn and updates the exit vectors for each s_p by

$$U(s_p) \leftarrow U(s_p) + \frac{\tau}{N}\left[\sum_{b=1}^{|S|} T_{pb}\frac{\partial l(s_p, s_b)}{\partial U(s_p)} - \frac{\partial \Omega(V, U)}{\partial U(s_p)}\right]. \quad (19)$$

For each s_p, it also updates the entry vector for each possible transition (s_p, s_q) via

$$V(s_q) \leftarrow V(s_q) + \frac{\tau}{N}\left[\sum_{b=1}^{|S|} T_{pb}\frac{\partial l(s_p, s_b)}{\partial V(s_q)} - \frac{\partial \Omega(V, U)}{\partial V(s_q)}\right]. \quad (20)$$

τ is a predefined learning rate and N is the number of transitions in training set. Note that grouping the stochastic gradient updates by exit songs s_p as implemented above is advantageous, since we can save computation by reusing the partition function in the denominator of the local gradients of both $U(s_p)$ and $V(s_q)$. More generally, by storing intermediate results of the gradient computation, a complete iteration of the stochastic gradient algorithm through the full training set can be done in time $O(|\mathcal{S}|^2)$. We typically run the algorithm for $T = 100$ or 200 iterations, which we find is sufficient for convergence.

5.2 Landmark Heuristic for Acceleration

The $O(|\mathcal{S}|^2)$ runtime of the algorithm makes it too slow for practical applications when the size of $\mathcal{S}$ is sufficiently large. The root of the problem lies in the gradient computation, since for every local gradient one needs to consider the transition from the exit song to all the songs in $\mathcal{S}$. This leads to $O(|\mathcal{S}|)$ complexity for each update steps. However, considering all songs is not really necessary, since most songs are not likely targets for a transition anyway. These songs contribute very little mass to the partition function and excluding them will only marginally change the training objective.

We therefore formulate the following modified training problem, where we only consider a subset C_i as possible successors for s_i.

$$L(D|U, V) = \sum_{a=1}^{|S|}\sum_{s_b\in C_a} T_{ab}\, l(s_a, s_b) - \Omega(V, U) \quad (21)$$

This reduces the complexity of a gradient step to $O(|C_i|)$. The key problem lies in identifying a suitable candidate set C_i for each s_i. Clearly, each C_i should include at least most of the likely successors of s_i, which lead us to the following landmark heuristic.

We randomly pick a certain number (typically 50) of songs and call them landmarks, and assign each song to the nearest landmark. We also need to specify a threshold $r \in [0, 1]$. Then for each s_i, its direct successors observed in the training set are first added to the subset C_i^r, because these songs are always needed to compute the local log-likelihood. We keep adding songs from nearby landmarks to the subset, until ratio r of the total songs has been included. This defines the final subset C_i^r. By adopting this heuristic, the gradients of the local log-likelihood become

$$\frac{\partial l(s_a,s_b)}{\partial U(s_p)} = 1^{[a=p]} 2 \left[-\vec{\Delta}_2(s_a,s_b) + \frac{\sum_{s_l \in C_p^r} e^{-\Delta_2(s_a,s_l)^2} \vec{\Delta}_2(s_a,s_l)}{Z^r(s_a)} \right]$$

$$\frac{\partial l(s_a,s_b)}{\partial V(s_q)} = 1^{[b=q]} 2 \vec{\Delta}_2(s_a,s_b) - 2 \frac{e^{-\Delta_2(s_a,s_q)^2} \vec{\Delta}_2(s_a,s_q)}{Z^r(s_a)},$$

where $Z^r(s_a)$ is the partition function restricted to C_a^r, namely $\sum_{s_l \in C_a^r} e^{-\Delta_2(s_a,s_l)^2}$. Empirically, we update the landmarks every 10 iterations[1], and fix them after 100 iterations to ensure convergence.

5.3 Implementation

We implemented our methods in C. The code is available online at `http://lme.joachims.org`.

6. EXPERIMENTS

In the following experiments we will analyze the LME in comparison to n-gram baselines, explore the effect of the popularity term and regularization, and assess the computational efficiency of the method.

To collect a dataset of playlists for our empirical evaluation, we crawled *Yes.com* during the period from Dec. 2010 to May 2011. Yes.com is a website that provides radio playlists of hundreds of stations in the United States. By using the web based API[2], one can retrieve the playlists of the last 7 days for any station specified by its genre. Without taking any preference, we collect as much data as we can by specifying all the possible genres. We then generated two datasets, which we refer to as *yes_small* and *yes_big*. In the small dataset, we removed the songs with less than 20, in the large dataset we only removed songs with less than 5 appearances. The smaller one is composed of 3,168 unique songs. It is then divided into into a training set with 134,431 transitions and a test set with 1,191,279 transitions. The larger one contains 9,775 songs, a training set with 172,510 transitions and a test set with 1,602,079 transitions. The datasets are available for download at `http://lme.joachims.org`.

Unless noted otherwise, experiments use the following setup. Any model (either the LME or the baseline model) is first trained on the training set and then tested on the test set. We evaluate test performance using the average log-likelihood as our metric. It is defined as $\log(\Pr(D_{\text{test}}))/N_{\text{test}}$, where N_{test} is the number of transitions in test set. One should note that the division of training and test set is done so that each song appears at least once in the training set. This was done to exclude the case of encountering a new song when doing testing, which any method would need to treat as a special case and impute some probability estimate.

[1]A iteration means a full pass on the training dataset.
[2]`http://api.yes.com`

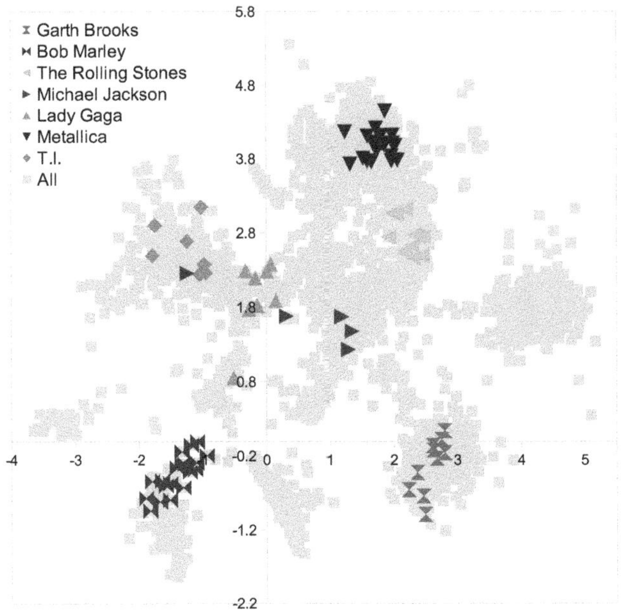

Figure 3: Visual representation of an embedding in two dimensions with songs from selected artists highlighted

6.1 What do embeddings look like?

We start with giving a qualitative impression of the embeddings that our method produces. Figure 3 shows the two-dimensional single-point embedding of the *yes_small* dataset. Songs from a few well-known artists are highlighted to provide reference points in the embedding space.

First, it is interesting to note that songs by the same artist cluster tightly, even though our model has no direct knowledge of which artist performed a song. Second, logical connections among different genres are well-represented in the space. For example, consider the positions of songs from Michael Jackson, T.I., and Lady Gaga. Pop songs from Michael Jackson could easily transition to the more electronic and dance pop style of Lady Gaga. Lady Gaga's songs, in turn, could make good transitions to some of the more dance-oriented songs (mainly collaborations with other artists) of the rap artist T.I., which could easily form a gateway to other hip hop artists.

While the visualization provides interesting qualitative insights, we now provide a quantitative evaluation of model quality based on predictive power.

6.2 How does the LME compare to n-gram models?

We first compare our models against baseline methods from Natural Language Processing. We consider the following models.

Uniform Model. The choices of any song are equally likely, with the same probability of $1/|S|$.

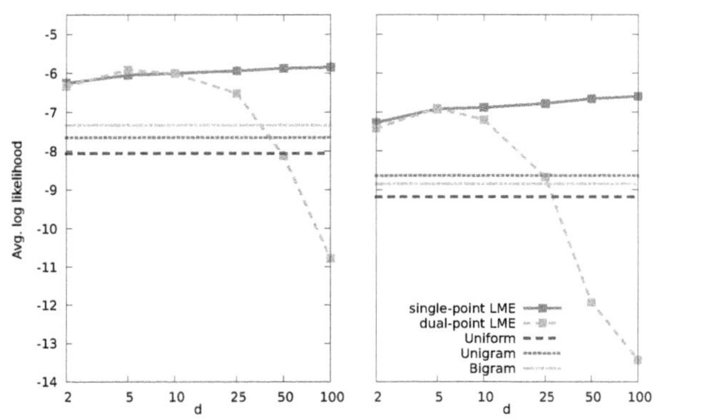

Figure 4: Single/Dual-point LME against baseline on *yes_small*(left) and *yes_big*(right). d is the dimensionality of the embedded space.

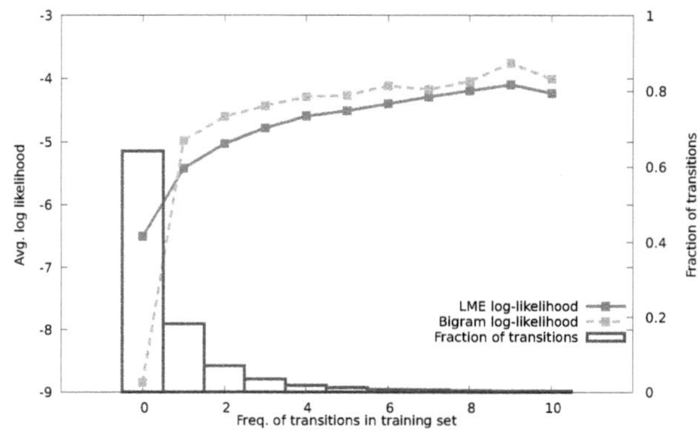

Figure 5: Log likelihood on testing transitions with respect to their frequencies in the training set on *yes_small*

Unigram Model. Each song s_i is sampled with probability $p(s_i) = \frac{n_i}{\sum_j n_j}$, where n_i is the number of appearances of s_i in the training set. $p(s_i)$ can be considered as the popularity of s_i. Since each song appears at least once in the training set, we do not need to worry about the possibility of $p(s_i)$ being zero in the testing phase.

Bigram Model. Similar to our models, the bigram model is also a first-order Markov model. However, transition probabilities $p(s_j|s_i)$ are estimated directly for every pair of songs. Note that not every transition from s_i to s_j in the test set also appears in the training set, and the corresponding $p(s_i|s_j)$ will just give us minus infinity log likelihood contribution when testing. We adopt the Witten-Bell smoothing [6] technique to solve this problem. The main idea is to use the transition we have seen in the training set to estimate the counts of the transitions we have not seen, and then assign them nonzero probabilities.

We train our LME models without heuristic on both *yes_small* and *yes_big*. The resulting log-likelihood on the test set is reported in Figure 4, where d is the dimensionality of the embedding space. Over the full range of d the single-point LME outperforms the baselines by at least one order of magnitude in terms of likelihood. While the likelihoods on the big dataset are lower as expected (i.e. there are more songs to choose from), the relative gain of the single-point LME over the baselines is even larger for *yes_big*.

The dual-point model performs equally well for models with low dimension, but shows signs of overfitting for higher dimensionality. We will see in Section 6.4 that regularization can mitigate this problem.

Among the conventional sequence models, the bigram model performs best on *yes_small*. However, it fails to beat the unigram model on *yes_big* (which contains roughly 3 times the number of songs), since it cannot reliably estimate the huge number of parameters it entails. Note that the number of parameters in the bigram model scales quadratically with the number of songs, while it scales only linearly in the LME models. The following section analyzes in more detail where the conventional bigram model fails, while the single-point LME shows no signs of overfitting.

6.3 Where does the LME win over the n-gram model?

We now explore in more detail why the LME model outperforms the conventional bigram model. In particular, we explore the extent to which the generalization performance of the methods depends on whether (and how often) a test transition was observed in the training set. The ability to produce reasonable probability estimates even for transitions that were never observed is important, since about 64 percent of the test transitions were not at all observed in our training set.

For both the single-point LME and the bigram model on the small dataset, Figure 5 shows the log-likelihood of the test transitions conditioned on how often that transition was observed in the training set. The bar graph illustrates what percentage of test transitions had that given number of occurrences in the training set (i.e. 64% for zero). It can be seen that the LME performs comparably to the bigram model for transitions that were seen in the training set at least once, but it performs substantially better on previously unseen transitions. This is a key advantage of the generalizing representation that the LME provides.

6.4 What are the effects of regularization?

We now explore whether additional regularization as proposed in Section 3.3 can further improve performance.

For the single-point model on *yes_small*, Figure 6 shows a comparison between the norm-based regularizer (R1) and the unregularized models across dimensions 2, 5, 10, 25, 50 and 100. For each dimension, the optimal value of λ was selected out of the set {0.0001, 0.001, 0.01, 0.1, 1, 10, 20, 50, 100, 500, 1000}. It can be seen that the regularized models offer no substantial benefit over the unregularized model. We conjecture that the amount of training data is already sufficient to estimate the (relatively small) number of parameters of the single-point model.

Figure 7 shows the results for dual-point models using three modes of regularization. R1 denotes models with $\nu = 0$, R2 denotes models with $\lambda = 0$, and R3 denotes models trained with $\nu = \lambda$. Here, the regularized models consistently outperform the unregularized ones. Starting from dimensionality 25, the improvement of adding regularization is drastic, which saves the dual-point model from being unusable for high dimensionality. It is interesting to note the effect of R2, which constrains the exit and entry points for each song to be near each other. Effectively, this squeezes

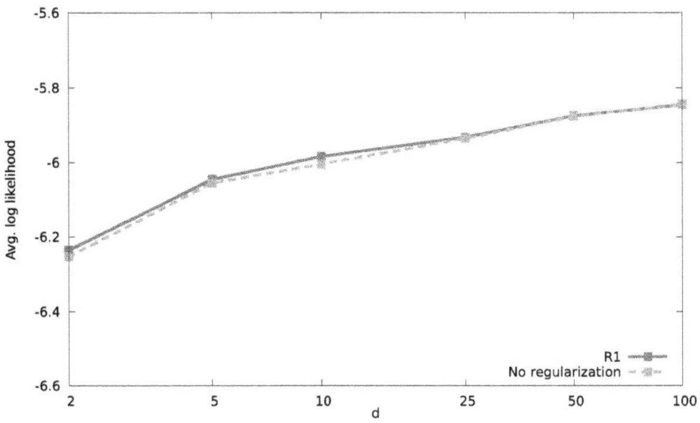

Figure 6: Effect of regularization for single-point model on *yes_small*

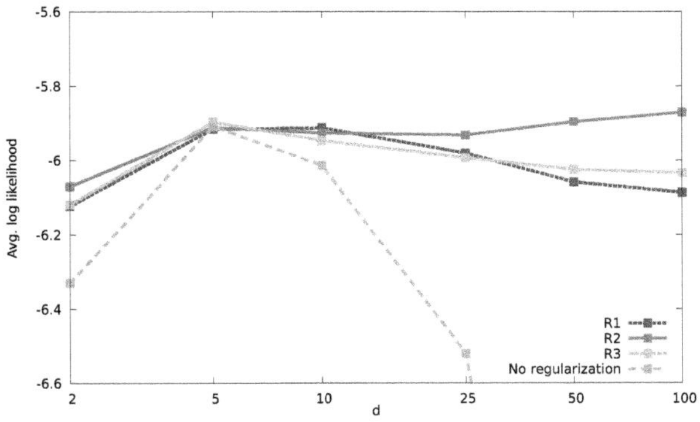

Figure 7: Effect of regularization for dual-point model on *yes_small*

the distance between the two points, bringing the dual-point model closer to the single-point model.

6.5 How directional are radio playlists?

Since the single-point model appears to perform better than the dual-point model, it raises the question of how important directionality is in playlists. We therefore conducted the following experiment. We train the dual-point model as usual for $d = 5$ on *yes_small*, but then reverse all test transitions. The average log-likelihood (over 10 training runs) on the reversed test transition is -5.960 ± 0.003, while the log-likelihood of the test transitions in the normal order is -5.921 ± 0.003. While this difference is significant according to a binomial sign test (i.e. the reversed likelihood was indeed worse on all 10 runs), the difference is very small. This provides evidence that radio playlists appear to not have many directional constraints. However, playlists for other settings (e.g. club, tango) may be more directional.

6.6 What is the effect of modeling popularity?

As discussed in Section 3.4, an added term for each song can be used to separate popularity from the geometry of the resulting embedding. In Figure 8, a comparison of the popularity-augmented model to the standard model (both with single-point) on the two datasets is shown. Adding the popularity terms substantially improves the models for low-dimensional embeddings. Even though the term adds only one parameter for each song, it can be viewed as adding

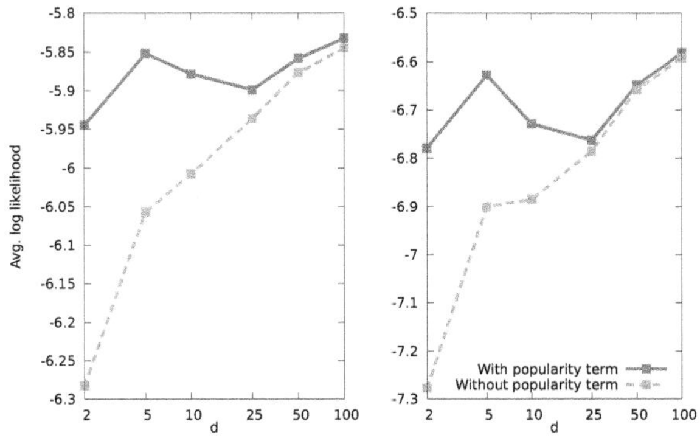

Figure 8: Effect of popularity term on model likelihood in *yes_small* (left) and *yes_big* (right)

as much expressive power as dozens of additional spatial parameters per song.

6.7 How does the landmark heuristic affect model quality?

We take the single-point model with $d = 5$ without regularization as an example in this part. We list the CPU time per iteration and log-likelihood on both datasets in Table 1 and Table 2. The landmark heuristic significantly reduces the training iteration time to what is almost proportional to r. However, for low r we see some overhead introduced by building the landmark data structure. The heuristic yields results comparable in quality to models trained without the heuristic when r reaches 0.3 on both datasets. It even gets slightly better than the no-heuristic method for higher r. This may be because we excluded songs that are very unlikely to be transitioned to, resulting in some additional regularization.

r	CPU time/s	Test log-likelihood
0.1	3.08	-6.421977
0.2	3.81	-6.117642
0.3	4.49	-6.058949
0.4	5.14	-6.043897
0.5	5.79	-6.048493
No heuristic	11.37	-6.054263

Table 1: CPU time and log-likelihood on *yes_small*

r	CPU time/s	Test log-likelihood
0.1	27.67	-7.272813
0.2	34.98	-7.031947
0.3	42.01	-6.925095
0.4	49.33	-6.897925
0.5	56.88	-6.894431
No heuristic	111.36	-6.917984

Table 2: CPU time and log-likelihood on *yes_big*

6.8 Does our method capture the coherency of playlists?

We designed the following experiment to see whether our method captures the coherency of playlists. We train our

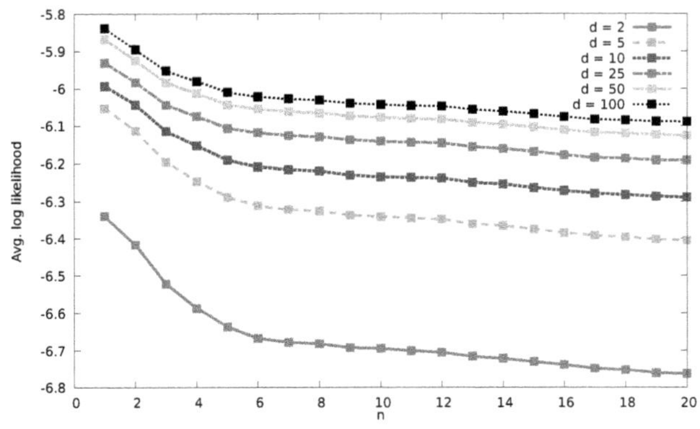

Figure 9: n-hop results on *yes_small*

model on the 1-hop transitions in training dataset, which is the same as what we did before. However, the test is done on the n-hop transitions (consider the current song and the nth song after it as a transition pair) in the test dataset. The experiments was run on *yes_small* for various values of d without regularization. Results are reported in Figure 9.

One can observe that for all values of d, the log-likelihood consistently decreases as n increases. As n goes up to 6 and above, the curves flatten out. This is evidence that our method does capture the coherency of the playlists, since songs that are sequentially close to each other in the playlists are more likely to form a transition pair.

7. CONCLUSIONS

We presented a new family of methods for learning a generative model of music playlists using existing playlists as training data. The methods do not require content features about songs, but automatically embed songs in Euclidean space similar to a collaborative filtering method. Our approach offers substantial modeling flexibility, including the ability to represent song as multiple points, to make use of regularization for improved robustness in high-dimensional embeddings, and to incorporate popularity of songs, giving users more freedom to steer their playlists. Empirically, the LME outperforms smoothed bigram models from natural language processing and leads to embeddings that qualitatively reflect our intuition of music similarity.

8. ACKNOWLEDGMENTS

This work was funded in part by NSF Awards IIS-0812091, IIS-0905467, and IIS-1217686.

9. REFERENCES

[1] N. Aizenberg, Y. Koren, and O. Somekh. Build your own music recommender by modeling internet radio streams. In *Proceedings of the 21st international conference on World Wide Web*, pages 1–10. ACM, 2012.

[2] L. Barrington, R. Oda, and G. Lanckriet. Smarter than genius? human evaluation of music recommender systems. *ISMIR*, 2009.

[3] T. F. Cox and M. A. Cox. *Multidimensional scaling.* Chapman and Hall, 2001.

[4] D. F. Gleich, L. Zhukov, M. Rasmussen, and K. Lang. The World of Music: SDP embedding of high dimensional data. In *Information Visualization 2005*, 2005.

[5] D. Hsu, S. Kakade, and T. Zhang. A spectral algorithm for learning hidden markov models. *Arxiv preprint arXiv:0811.4413*, 2008.

[6] D. Jurafsky and J. Martin. Speech and language processing, 2008.

[7] Y. Koren, R. M. Bell, and C. Volinsky. Matrix factorization techniques for recommender systems. *IEEE Computer*, 42(8):30–37, 2009.

[8] B. Logan. Content-based playlist generation: exploratory ex- periments. *ISMIR*, 2002.

[9] F. Maillet, D. Eck, G. Desjardins, and P. Lamere. Steerable playlist generation by learning song similarity from radio station playlists. In *International Conference on Music Information Retrieval (ISMIR)*, 2009.

[10] B. McFee and G. R. G. Lanckriet. Metric learning to rank. In *ICML*, pages 775–782, 2010.

[11] B. McFee and G. R. G. Lanckriet. The natural language of playlists. In *International Conference on Music Information Retrieval (ISMIR)*, 2011.

[12] J. L. Moore, S. Chen, T. Joachims, and D. Turnbull. Learning to embed songs and tags for playlist prediction. http://www.joachims.org/publications/moore_etal_12a.pdf, April 2012.

[13] J. C. Platt. Fast embedding of sparse music similarity graphs. In *NIPS*. MIT Press, 2003.

[14] L. Rabiner. A tutorial on hidden markov models and selected applications in speech recognition. *Proceedings of the IEEE*, 77(2):257–286, 1989.

[15] S. Rendle, C. Freudenthaler, and L. Schmidt-Thieme. Factorizing personalized markov chains for next-basket recommendation. In *Proceedings of the 19th international conference on World wide web*, pages 811–820. ACM, 2010.

[16] L. Song, B. Boots, S. Siddiqi, G. Gordon, and A. Smola. Hilbert space embeddings of hidden markov models. 2010.

[17] D. Tingle, Y. Kim, and D.Turnbull. Exploring automatic music annotation with "acoustically-objective" tags. In *ACM International Conference on Multimedia Information Retrieval*, 2010.

[18] C. Wang and D. Blei. Collaborative topic modeling for recommending scientific articles. In *SIGKDD*, 2011.

[19] J. Weston, S. Bengio, and P. Hamel. Multi-tasking with joint semantic spaces for large-scale music annotation and retrieval. *Journal of New Music Research*, 2011.

[20] Y. Yue and T. Joachims. Predicting diverse subsets using structural SVMs. In *International Conference on Machine Learning (ICML)*, pages 271–278, 2008.

[21] E. Zheleva, J. Guiver, E. Mendes Rodrigues, and N. Milić-Frayling. Statistical models of music-listening sessions in social media. In *Proceedings of the 19th international conference on World wide web*, pages 1019–1028. ACM, 2010.

Parallel Field Ranking

Ming Ji[†], Binbin Lin[‡], Xiaofei He[‡], Deng Cai[‡], Jiawei Han[†]
[†]Department of Computer Science, University of Illinois at Urbana-Champaign, Urbana, IL, USA
[‡]State Key Lab of CAD&CG, College of Computer Science, Zhejiang University, China
[†]{mingji1, hanj}@illinois.edu, [‡]binbinlin@zju.edu.cn, {xiaofeihe, dengcai}@cad.zju.edu.cn

ABSTRACT

Recently, ranking data with respect to the intrinsic geometric structure (manifold ranking) has received considerable attentions, with encouraging performance in many applications in pattern recognition, information retrieval and recommendation systems. Most of the existing manifold ranking methods focus on learning a ranking function that varies smoothly along the data manifold. However, beyond smoothness, a desirable ranking function should vary monotonically along the geodesics of the data manifold, such that the ranking order along the geodesics is preserved. In this paper, we aim to learn a ranking function that varies linearly and therefore monotonically along the geodesics of the data manifold. Recent theoretical work shows that the gradient field of a linear function on the manifold has to be a parallel vector field. Therefore, we propose a novel ranking algorithm on the data manifolds, called Parallel Field Ranking. Specifically, we try to learn a ranking function and a vector field simultaneously. We require the vector field to be close to the gradient field of the ranking function, and the vector field to be as parallel as possible. Moreover, we require the value of the ranking function at the query point to be the highest, and then decrease linearly along the manifold. Experimental results on both synthetic data and real data demonstrate the effectiveness of our proposed algorithm.

Categories and Subject Descriptors

H.3.3 [**Information Storage and Retrieval**]: Information Search and Retrieval—*Retrieval models*

General Terms

Algorithms, Theory

Keywords

Manifold, Ranking, Vector field

KDD'12, August 12–16, 2012, Beijing, China.

1. INTRODUCTION

Ranking is a fundamental problem in many areas including data mining, machine learning and information retrieval [17, 10, 6]. Given a query, we aim to learn a real-valued function f that ranks the data points according to their relevance to the query. In other words, for any two data points x_i and x_j, $f(x_i) > f(x_j)$ if x_i is more relevant to the query than x_j, and vice-versa.

In many real-world applications, one is often confronted with high dimensional data, such as images, documents and videos [21, 22]. However, there is a strong intuition that the high dimensional data may have a lower dimensional intrinsic representation. Various work in literature have considered the case where the data is sampled from a submanifold embedded in the ambient Euclidean space [2, 19, 23]. In this paper, we are interested in the ranking problem on the data represented by vectors in Euclidean space, under the manifold assumption [28, 1, 29].

Most of the existing ranking algorithms on data manifolds are based on the Laplacian regularization framework [28, 29], with promising performance observed on various data types such as image [9], video [27], and text [25]. These methods usually construct nearest neighbor graphs over the data to model the intrinsic geometric structure, and use the Graph Laplacian [5] to ensure that the ranking function varies smoothly along the manifold. They essentially spread the ranking scores via the graph iteratively until a stationary state is achieved. The Laplacian-based ranking framework has some nice interpretations including close relationships to personalized PageRank [28, 17] and HITS [10]. However, recent theoretical analysis [12, 13] shows that the Laplacian regularizer is way too general for measuring the smoothness of the function. Although it is ensured that data points connected by edges in the graph have similar ranking scores, the actual variation of the ranking function along the geodesics of the data manifold is unknown. Ideally, beyond smoothness, a desirable ranking function should vary monotonically along the geodesics of the manifold. Therefore, the ranking order of the data points along the geodesics of the manifold could be well preserved. Moreover, according to the nature of the ranking problem, no sample in the data set should be more relevant to the query than the query itself. So the ranking function should have the highest value at the query point, and then decrease to other points nearby.

In this paper, we propose a novel ranking algorithm on the data manifolds termed Parallel Field Ranking (PFRank), which learns a ranking function that has the highest value at the query point, and varies linearly and therefore mono-

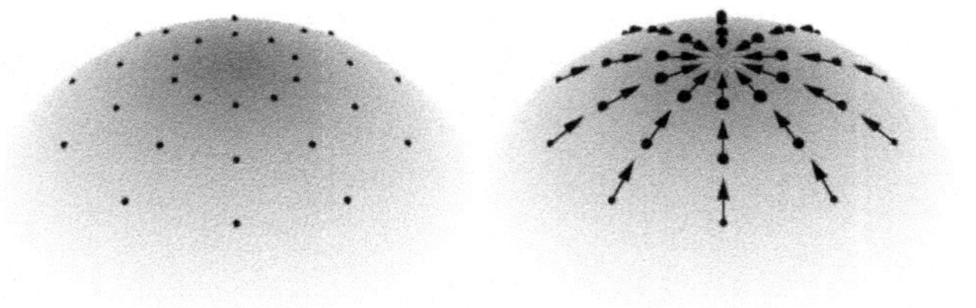

(a) Data samples (b) Ranking results

Figure 1: We aim to design a ranking function that has the highest value at the query point marked by red, and then decreases linearly along the geodesics of the manifold, which is equivalent to its gradient field being parallel along the geodesics. The arrows above denote the gradient field of the ranking function, and the green lines denote the geodesics of the data manifold.

tonically along the geodesics of the data manifold. A function that varies linearly along the geodesics of the manifold is called a linear function on the manifold [18], which could still be nonlinear in the Euclidean space. It was shown that the gradient field of a linear function on the manifold has to be a parallel vector field (or parallel field in short) [18]. Besides, in order to ensure that the query has the highest ranking score, the gradient field of the ranking function should point to the query at the neighborhood around the query, since the value of a function increases towards the direction pointed by its gradient field. Figure 1 shows an example of the ranking function that we aim to learn on a data set sampled from a 2D sphere manifold in the 3D Euclidean space, where the red point denotes the query, the green lines denote the geodesics, and the arrows denote the gradient field of the ranking function. The size of each point denotes the ranking order generated by the ranking function, where large points are ranked higher than small ones. As can be observed, the ranking results generated by a function that has the highest value at the query point and varies linearly along the geodesics are quite reasonable. The gradient field of the function points to the query, and is parallel along the geodesics which pass through the query.

However, it is very difficult to design constraints on the gradient field of a function directly [13]. Instead, motivated by the recent progress in semi-supervised regression [13], we propose to learn a vector field to approximate the gradient field of the ranking function, and then design constraints on the vector field. In this paper, we propose to learn a ranking function and a vector field simultaneously based on three intuitions:

1. The vector field should be close to the gradient field of the ranking function.
2. The vector field should be as parallel as possible.
3. The vector field at the neighborhood around the query should all point to the query.

By encoding the above three intuitions, the gradient field of the learned ranking function should be as parallel as possible, and is forced to point to the query at the neighborhood around the query. Hence the ranking function learned by our method decreases linearly from the query to other points along the geodesics of the data manifold.

The rest of this paper is organized as follows. We briefly review some background knowledge related to ranking under the manifold assumption and vector fields in Section 2. Our Parallel Field Ranking algorithm encoding all the three intuitions proposed above is introduced in Section 3. Section 4 presents an optimization scheme that solves our objective function. Section 5 provides the experimental results on both synthetic data and real data. Finally, we conclude this work in Section 6.

2. BACKGROUNDS

Our algorithm is fundamentally based on vector fields in geometry and vector calculus. Also, for ranking methods under the manifold assumption, the most related work is the Laplacian-based manifold ranking [28]. In this section, we give a brief introduction of [28], and review some background knowledge related to vector fields.

2.1 Laplacian-based Manifold Ranking

Let $\mathcal{M}$ be a d-dimensional submanifold in the Euclidean space $\mathbb{R}^m$. Given n data points $\{x_1, \dots, x_n\} \in \mathbb{R}^m$ on $\mathcal{M}$, where x_q is the query ($1 \le q \le n$), we aim to learn a ranking function $f : \mathcal{M} \to \mathbb{R}$, such that $\forall i, j \in \{1, \dots, n\}$, $f(x_i) > f(x_j)$ if x_i is more relevant to the query x_q than x_j, and vice-versa.

The intuition behind [28] is that if two points x_i and x_j are sufficiently close to each other, then their ranking scores $f(x_i)$ and $f(x_j)$ should be close as well. Let $W \in \mathbb{R}^{n \times n}$ be a symmetric similarity matrix, and $y = [y_1, \dots, y_n]^T$ be an initial ranking score vector which encodes some prior knowledge about the relevance of each data point to the query. Then [28] minimizes the following objective function:

$$J_{MR}(f) = \sum_{i,j=1}^{n} w_{ij} \left(\frac{f(x_i)}{\sqrt{D_{ii}}} - \frac{f(x_j)}{\sqrt{D_{jj}}}\right)^2 + \mu \sum_{i=1}^{n} (f(x_i) - y_i)^2 \quad (1)$$

where w_{ij} denotes the element at the i-th row and j-th column of W, $\mu > 0$ is a regularization parameter and D is a diagonal matrix used for normalization with $D_{ii} = \sum_{j=1}^{n} w_{ij}$. The first term in the above function aims to learn a ranking function that varies smoothly along the data manifold. The second term ensures the final ranking results to be close to the initial ranking score assignment y.

Let $f = [f(x_1), \dots, f(x_n)]^T$. The closed form solution of Eq. (1) is the following:

$$f^* = (\mu I + L)^{-1} y \quad (2)$$

where I is an identity matrix of size $n \times n$. $L = I - D^{-1/2} W D^{-1/2}$ is the normalized Graph Laplacian [5]. We can also obtain the same solution via an iterative scheme:

$$f^{t+1} = \frac{1}{\mu + 1} S f^t + \frac{\mu}{\mu + 1} y \quad (3)$$

where each data point spreads the ranking score to its neighbors iteratively.

The above ranking framework based on Laplacian regularization has enjoyed long-lasting popularity in the community, with successful extensions in content-based image retrieval [9], ranking on both undirected and directed graphs [1], ranking on multi-typed interrelated web objects [8], ranking tags over a tag similarity graph [14], etc. However, for the Laplacian-based ranking framework, we do not exactly know how the ranking function varies, and whether the ranking order of the data points is preserved along the geodesics of the data manifold. [29] points out some drawbacks of [28] and proposes a more robust method by using an iterated graph Laplacian. But [29] still works under the Laplacian-based ranking framework, addressing the smoothness of the function. Besides, the Laplacian-based ranking framework requires the final ranking results to be close to the initial ranking score assignment y. In the situation when there is no prior knowledge about the relevance of each data point, people usually assign $y_i = 1$ if x_i is the query and $y_i = 0$ otherwise. This might not be very reasonable, and the final ranking results are likely to be biased towards the initial ranking score assignment.

2.2 Parallel Fields and Linear Functions

In geometry and vector calculus, a vector field is a mapping from a manifold $\mathcal{M}$ to tangent spaces [18]. We can think of a vector field on $\mathcal{M}$ as an arrow in the same way as we think of the vector field in Euclidean space, with a given magnitude and direction, attached to each point on $\mathcal{M}$, and chosen to be tangent to $\mathcal{M}$.

As discussed before, we aim to learn a ranking function $f : \mathcal{M} \to \mathbb{R}$ that varies linearly along the manifold $\mathcal{M}$. We first review the definitions of parallel fields and linear functions on the manifold [13].

Definition 1. **Parallel Field** [18]. A vector field X on manifold $\mathcal{M}$ is a parallel field if

$$\nabla X \equiv 0,$$

where ∇ is the covariant derivative on $\mathcal{M}$. ■

Definition 2. **Linear Function** [18]. A continuous function $f : \mathcal{M} \to \mathbb{R}$ is said to be linear if

$$(f \circ \gamma)(t) = f(\gamma(0)) + ct \tag{4}$$

for each geodesic γ. ■

In this paper, a function f is linear means that it varies linearly along the geodesics of the manifold. This definition is a natural extension of linear functions on the Euclidean space.

Then the following proposition reveals the relationship between a parallel field and a linear function on the data manifold:

Proposition 1. [18] Let V be a parallel field on the manifold. If it is also a gradient field for function f, $V = \nabla f$, then f is a linear function on the manifold. ■

3. PARALLEL FIELD RANKING

In this section, we propose the objective function which learns a ranking function that decreases linearly from the query to other points along the data manifold.

3.1 Ensuring the Linearity

As discussed before, we aim to design regularization terms that ensure the linearity of the ranking function with respect to the data manifold, which is equivalent to ensuring the parallelism of the gradient field of the function. However, it is very difficult to design constraints on the gradient field of a function directly [13]. Following the above analysis, we propose to learn a vector field to approximate the gradient field of the ranking function, and require the vector field to be as parallel as possible. Let $C^\infty(\mathcal{M})$ denote smooth functions on $\mathcal{M}$. Following [13], we learn a ranking function f and a vector field V on the manifold simultaneously with two constraints, which correspond to the first two intuitions proposed in Section 1:

- The vector field V should be close to the gradient field ∇f of f, which can be formularized as follows:

$$\min_{f \in C^\infty, V} R_1(f, V) = \int_{\mathcal{M}} \|\nabla f - V\|^2 \tag{5}$$

- The vector field V should be as parallel as possible:

$$\min_{V} R_2(V) = \int_{\mathcal{M}} \|\nabla V\|_F^2 \tag{6}$$

where ∇ is the covariant derivative on the manifold, and $\|\cdot\|_F$ denotes the Frobenius norm.

∇V measures the change of the vector field V. If ∇V vanishes, then V is a parallel field. Then the following objective function learns a f that varies linearly along the manifold, from the vector field perspective [13]:

$$\begin{aligned} &\arg\min_{f \in C^\infty(\mathcal{M}), V} \; E(f, V) \\ &= R_0(x_q, y_q, f) + \lambda_1 R_1(f, V) + \lambda_2 R_2(V) \end{aligned} \tag{7}$$

where $\lambda_1 > 0$ and $\lambda_2 > 0$ are two regularization parameters. R_0 is a loss function that ensures the predicted ranking score for the query x_q to be close to a constant positive number y_q. If we remove R_0 from Eq. (7), then if f is an optimal solution to $\arg\min_{f \in C^\infty(\mathcal{M}), V} \lambda_1 R_1(f, V) + \lambda_2 R_2(V)$, it is easy to check that $f + c$ is also an optimal solution, where c could be any constant number. Therefore, by adding the R_0 term, we can get a unique solution of our ranking function f. In principle, y_q could be any positive number. Following [28, 13], we set $y_q = 1$, and use the squared loss $R_0(x_q, y_q, f) = (f(x_q) - y_q)^2$ for simplicity.

3.2 Discretization

Since the manifold $\mathcal{M}$ is unknown, the function f which minimizes Eq. (7) can not be directly solved. Following [13], we introduce how to discretize the continuous objective function (7) in this subsection.

For simplicity, let $f_i = f(x_i)$, $i = 1, \ldots, n$. Then our goal is to learn a ranking score vector $f = [f_1, \ldots, f_n]^T$. We first build a nearest neighbor graph $\mathcal{G}$ among the data. Let W be the corresponding affinity matrix of $\mathcal{G}$. There are many choices of the affinity matrix W. A simple definition is as follows:

$$w_{ij} = \begin{cases} 1 & \text{if } x_i \in N_k(x_j) \text{ or } x_j \in N_k(x_i) \\ 0 & \text{otherwise.} \end{cases} \tag{8}$$

where w_{ij} denotes the element at the i-th row and j-th column of matrix W. $N_k(x_i)$ denotes the set of k nearest neighbors of x_i. Then for each x_i, we can estimate its tangent space $T_{x_i}\mathcal{M}$ by performing PCA on its local neighborhood. We choose the eigenvectors corresponding to the d largest eigenvalues since $T_{x_i}\mathcal{M}$ is d-dimensional. Let $T_i \in \mathbb{R}^{m \times d}$ be the matrix whose columns constitute an orthonormal basis for $T_{x_i}\mathcal{M}$. It is easy to show that $P_i = T_i T_i^T$ is the *unique* orthogonal projection from $\mathbb{R}^m$ onto the tangent space $T_{x_i}\mathcal{M}$ [7]. That is, for any vector $a \in \mathbb{R}^m$, we have $P_i a \in T_{x_i}\mathcal{M}$ and $(a - P_i a) \perp P_i a$.

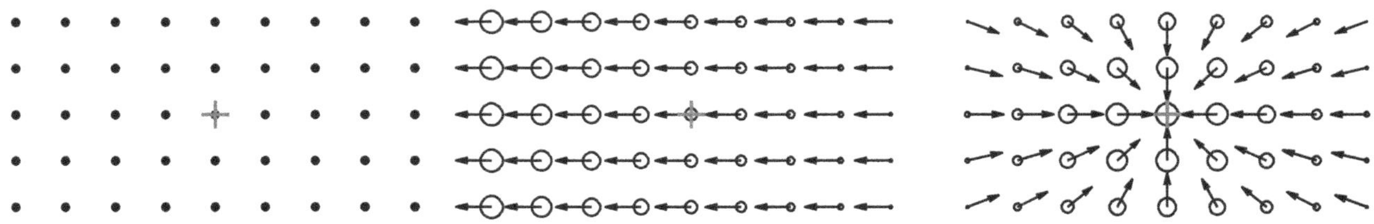

(a) Data samples (b) Ranking results without R_3 (c) Ranking results with R_3

Figure 2: A toy example explaining the reason of adding R_3.

Let V be a vector field on the manifold $\mathcal{M}$. For each point x_i, let V_{x_i} denote the value of the vector field V at x_i, and $\nabla V|_{x_i}$ denote the value of ∇V at x_i. According to the definition of vector field, V_{x_i} should be a vector in tangent space $T_{x_i}\mathcal{M}$. Therefore, it can be represented by the local coordinates of the tangent space, $V_{x_i} = T_i v_i$, where $v_i \in \mathbb{R}^d$. We define $\mathbb{V} = \left[v_1^T, \ldots, v_n^T\right]^T \in \mathbb{R}^{dn}$. In other words, $\mathbb{V}$ is a dn-dimensional column vector concatenating all the v_i's.

Then according to the analysis in [13], R_1 reduces to the following:

$$R_1(f, \mathbb{V}) = \sum_{i,j=1}^{n} w_{ij} \left((x_j - x_i)^T T_i v_i - f_j + f_i \right)^2 \quad (9)$$

And R_2 can be discretized to the following:

$$R_2(\mathbb{V}) = \sum_{i,j=1}^{n} w_{ij} \left\| P_i T_j v_j - T_i v_i \right\|^2 \quad (10)$$

3.3 Objective Function in the Discrete Form

As discussed in Section 1, a function that varies linearly along the manifold is good for ranking. However, merely ensuring the linearity is not enough. Furthermore, we hope that the ranking function has the highest value at the query point, i.e., no sample in our data set is more relevant to the query than the query itself. Therefore, the ranking function should decrease from the query to neighboring data points, which is equivalent to that the gradient field of the ranking function at the neighborhood around the query should all point to the query. Figure 2 presents a simple toy problem to illustrate this idea. Suppose we are given a set of data points sampled from a 2D rectangle as shown in Figure 2(a). The query is marked by '+'. Figure 2(b) shows the ranking results without employing a third regularizer R_3 which addresses our third intuition, where the arrows denote the gradient field of the ranking function, and the size of the circle at each point denotes the ranking order. Points marked by large circles are ranked higher than those marked by small circles. It is easy to see that the ranking function learned in Figure 2(b) varies linearly, and its gradient field is a parallel field. However, some data points are even ranked higher than the query itself, and points far from the query could be ranked higher than those close to the query, which is not reasonable. By addressing the third intuition via R_3, we force the gradient field at the neighborhood around the query to point to the query while still requiring the gradient field to be parallel along the geodesics, generating good ranking results as shown in Figure 2(c).

Since we approximate the gradient field of the ranking function by the vector field V through R_1, we can easily control the gradient field using V. Therefore, we require V at the neighborhood around the query to point to the query. Let $i \sim j$ denote that x_i and x_j are neighbors. We now propose the third regularization term R_3, which addresses the third intuition proposed in Section 1:

$$\begin{aligned} R_3(\mathbb{V}) &= \sum_{j \sim q} \left\| V_{x_j} - P_j(x_q - x_j) \right\|^2 \\ &= \sum_{j \sim q} \left\| T_j v_j - P_j(x_q - x_j) \right\|^2 \end{aligned} \quad (11)$$

Recall that V_{x_j} denotes the value of the vector field V at x_j, which is a vector in tangent space $T_{x_j}\mathcal{M}$. $(x_q - x_j)$ is a vector pointing from a neighboring point x_j to x_q, and $P_j(x_q - x_j)$ is its projection to $T_{x_j}\mathcal{M}$. Therefore, ensuring V_{x_j} and $P_j(x_q - x_j)$ to be similar forces the vector field at x_j to point from x_j to x_q.

Let $\mathbb{I}$ denote a $n \times n$ matrix where the entry at the q-th row and q-th column is 1, and all the other entries are 0. Let $y \in \mathbb{R}^n$ be a column vector where the q-th entry is $y_q (= 1)$, and all the other entries are 0. Then we have:

$$R_0(x_q, y_q, f) = (f - y)^T \mathbb{I} (f - y) \quad (12)$$

Combining R_0 in Eq. (12), R_1 in Eq. (9), R_2 in Eq. (10) and R_3 in Eq. (11), our final objective function can be formulated as follows:

$$\begin{aligned} J(f, \mathbb{V}) &= R_0(x_q, y_q, f) + \lambda_1 R_1(f, \mathbb{V}) + \lambda_2 R_2(\mathbb{V}) + \lambda_3 R_3(\mathbb{V}) \\ &= (f - y)^T \mathbb{I} (f - y) \\ &\quad + \lambda_1 \sum_{i,j=1}^{n} w_{ij} \left((x_j - x_i)^T T_i v_i - f_j + f_i \right)^2 \\ &\quad + \lambda_2 \sum_{i,j=1}^{n} w_{ij} \left\| P_i T_j v_j - T_i v_i \right\|^2 \\ &\quad + \lambda_3 \sum_{j \sim q} \left\| T_j v_j - P_j(x_q - x_j) \right\|^2 \end{aligned} \quad (13)$$

The trade-off among the three regularization terms is controlled by the parameters λ_1, λ_2 and λ_3 in the range of $(0, +\infty)$.

4. OPTIMIZATION

In this section, we discuss how to solve our objective function (13).

Let D be a diagonal matrix where $D_{ii} = \sum_{j=1}^{n} w_{ij}$. Let $L = D - W$ denote the Laplacian matrix [5] of the graph. Then we can rewrite R_1 as follows:

$$\begin{aligned} R_1(f, \mathbb{V}) &= 2 f^T L f + \sum_{i,j=1}^{n} w_{ij} \left((x_j - x_i)^T T_i v_i \right)^2 \\ &\quad - 2 \sum_{i,j=1}^{n} w_{ij} (x_j - x_i)^T T_i v_i s_{ij}^T f \end{aligned} \quad (14)$$

where $s_{ij} \in \mathbb{R}^n$ is a selection vector of all zero elements except for the i-th element being -1 and the j-th element being 1. We further construct a $dn \times dn$ block diagonal matrix G, and a $dn \times n$ block matrix $C = [C_1^T, \dots, C_n^T]^T$. Let G_{ii} denote the i-th $d \times d$ diagonal block of G, and C_i denote the i-th $d \times n$ block of C, we define:

$$G_{ii} = \sum_{j \sim i}^{n} w_{ij} T_i^T (x_j - x_i)(x_j - x_i)^T T_i \quad (15)$$

$$C_i = \sum_{j \sim i}^{n} w_{ij} T_i^T (x_j - x_i) s_{ij}^T \quad (16)$$

With some algebraic transformations, it is easy to check that R_1 in Eq. (14) can be written as follows:

$$R_1(f, \mathbb{V}) = 2f^T L f + \mathbb{V}^T G \mathbb{V} - 2\mathbb{V}^T C f \quad (17)$$

Similarly, in order to rewrite R_2 into a simplified form, we define $Q_{ij} = T_i^T T_j$, $i,j = 1, \dots, n$. Let I denote the identity matrix of size $n \times n$. We further construct a $dn \times dn$ sparse block matrix B. Let B_{ij} denote each $d \times d$ block, $i,j = 1, \dots, n$, then we define

$$B_{ii} = \sum_{j \sim i} w_{ij}(Q_{ij} Q_{ij}^T + I) \quad (18)$$

$$B_{ij} = -2w_{ij} Q_{ij} \quad (19)$$

Then we can rewrite R_2 as follows:

$$R_2(\mathbb{V}) = \mathbb{V}^T B \mathbb{V} \quad (20)$$

For R_3, we construct a $dn \times dn$ block diagonal matrix D, and a $dn \times 1$ block vector $H = [H_1^T, \dots, H_n^T]^T$. Let D_{jj} denote the j-th $d \times d$ diagonal block of D, and H_j denote the j-th $d \times 1$ block of H. We define:

$$D_{jj} = \begin{cases} I_d, & \text{if } j \sim q \\ 0, & \text{otherwise} \end{cases} \quad (21)$$

$$H_j = \begin{cases} T_j^T (x_q - x_j), & \text{if } j \sim q \\ 0, & \text{otherwise} \end{cases} \quad (22)$$

where I_d is an identity matrix of size $d \times d$. Now we can rewrite R_3 as follows:

$$R_3(\mathbb{V}) = \mathbb{V}^T D \mathbb{V} - 2H^T \mathbb{V} + \sum_{j \sim q} \|P_j(x_q - x_j)\|^2 \quad (23)$$

Combining R_1 in Eq. (17), R_2 in Eq. (20) and R_3 in Eq. (23), we get the following simplified form of our objective function:

$$\begin{aligned} & J(f, \mathbb{V}) \\ = \; & (f - y)^T \mathbb{I}(f - y) \\ & + \lambda_1 (2f^T L f + \mathbb{V}^T G \mathbb{V} - 2\mathbb{V}^T C f) \\ & + \lambda_2 \mathbb{V}^T B \mathbb{V} \\ & + \lambda_3 (\mathbb{V}^T D \mathbb{V} - 2H^T \mathbb{V} + \sum_{j \sim q} \|P_j(x_q - x_j)\|^2) \\ = \; & f^T(\mathbb{I} + 2\lambda_1 L) f - 2y^T \mathbb{I} f - 2\lambda_1 \mathbb{V}^T C f \\ & + \mathbb{V}^T (\lambda_1 G + \lambda_2 B + \lambda_3 D) \mathbb{V} - 2\lambda_3 H^T \mathbb{V} \\ & + y^T \mathbb{I} y + \lambda_3 \sum_{j \sim q} \|P_j(x_q - x_j)\|^2 \end{aligned} \quad (24)$$

From Eq. (24), it is easy to compute the partial derivative of $J(f, \mathbb{V})$ with respect to f and $\mathbb{V}$ as follows:

$$\begin{aligned} & \frac{\partial J(f, \mathbb{V})}{\partial f} \\ = \; & 2(\mathbb{I} + 2\lambda_1 L) f - 2y - 2\lambda_1 C^T \mathbb{V} \quad (25) \\ & \frac{\partial J(f, \mathbb{V})}{\partial \mathbb{V}} \\ = \; & -2\lambda_1 C f + 2(\lambda_1 G + \lambda_2 B + \lambda_3 D)\mathbb{V} - 2\lambda_3 H \quad (26) \end{aligned}$$

Requiring that the derivatives vanish, our solution could be obtained by solving the following linear equation system:

$$(\mathbb{I} + 2\lambda_1 L) f - \lambda_1 C^T \mathbb{V} = y \quad (27)$$

$$-\lambda_1 C f + (\lambda_1 G + \lambda_2 B + \lambda_3 D)\mathbb{V} = \lambda_3 H \quad (28)$$

which is further equivalent to solving the following linear system:

$$\begin{pmatrix} \mathbb{I} + 2\lambda_1 L & -\lambda_1 C^T \\ -\lambda_1 C & \lambda_1 G + \lambda_2 B + \lambda_3 D \end{pmatrix} \begin{pmatrix} f \\ \mathbb{V} \end{pmatrix} = \begin{pmatrix} y \\ \lambda_3 H \end{pmatrix} \quad (29)$$

5. EXPERIMENTS

In this section, we empirically evaluate the effectiveness of our proposed Parallel Field Ranking (PFRank) algorithm with comparison to several existing ranking algorithms. Since we focus on learning a ranking function under the manifold assumption, the main comparative method is the Laplacian-based manifold ranking algorithm (MR) [28]. We use the same graph structure according to Eq. (8) and empirically set the number of nearest neighbors to be 15 for both PFRank and MR. The parameter setting of MR is the same as the original paper [28, 9]. We empirically set $\lambda_1 = \lambda_2 = \lambda_3 = 0.01$ in our PFRank algorithm.

We also compare with the SVM method, which has been successfully applied to image retrieval [24]. With the specified relevant/irrelavant information, a maximal margin hyperplane could be built to separate the relevant data points from the irrelevant ones. Then we can return the data points farthest from the SVM boundary as the relevant ones. We use the LIBSVM toolbox [4] in our experiments. However, with a single query, there are no irrelevant data specified by the user. Following [26], we adopt the pseudo relevance feedback strategy [15]. Specifically, the nearest 10 data points to the query measured by the Euclidean distance are considered to be relevant, and the farthest 10 are treated as irrelevant. Then we can run SVM for ranking.

In the following, we begin with a simple synthetic example to give some intuition about how PFRank works.

5.1 Synthetic Example

A simple synthetic example is given in Figure 3. We randomly sample 1500 data points from a Swiss roll with a hole as shown in Figure 3(a). This data set lies on a 2D manifold in the 3D Euclidean space. The query is marked by '+'.

Figure 3(b)~(d) show the ranking order generated by PFRank, MR and SVM, respectively, where the data points marked by warmer color (such as red) are ranked higher than those marked by colder color (such as blue). We can see that SVM does not take the manifold structure of the data into consideration. The ranking functions generated by both PFRank and MR vary smoothly along the data manifold, and PFRank better preserves the ranking order of the data points along the geodesics of the manifold. For example, the

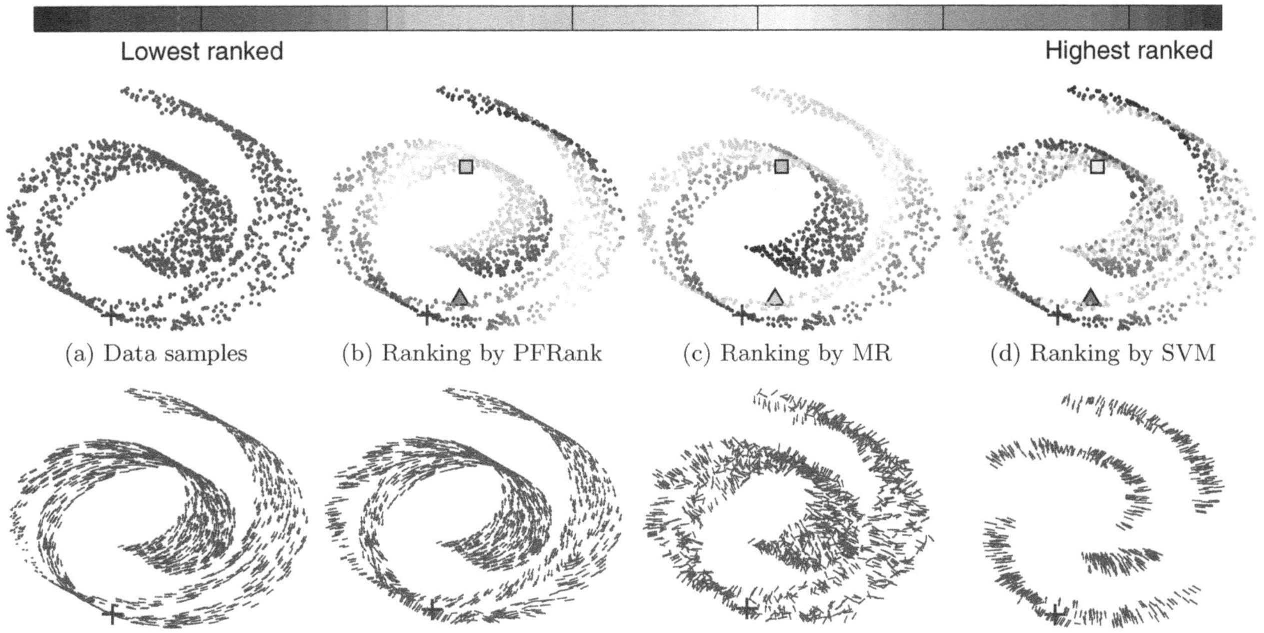

(a) Data samples (b) Ranking by PFRank (c) Ranking by MR (d) Ranking by SVM

(e) Vector field by PFRank (f) Gradient field by PFRank (g) Gradient field by MR (h) Gradient field by SVM

Figure 3: Performance comparison of various ranking algorithms on a toy data set. (a) shows the data set sampled from a Swiss roll with a hole, where the query is denote by '+'. (b) shows the ranking order generated by PFRank. We can see that PFRank successfully preserves the ranking order of the data points along the geodesics of the manifold. For example, the geodesic distance between the query and the point marked by '▲' is smaller than that between the query and the point marked by '■'. So '▲' is ranked higher than '■'. (c) shows the ranking order generated by MR. We can see that '▲' is ranked lower than '■', which is counterintuitive. (d) shows the ranking order generated by SVM, which does not take the manifold structure into consideration. (e) and (f) show the vector field and the gradient field of the ranking function learned by PFRank, respectively, which are quite parallel and point to the query. (g) and (h) show the gradient fields of the ranking functions learned by MR and SVM, respectively, which do not vary smoothly along the manifold.

geodesic distance between the query and the triangle point is smaller than that between the query and the square point. Therefore, the triangle point should rank higher than the square point. However, MR ranks the square point higher than the triangle point, which is counterintuitive.

Note that once the ranking function f is obtained, we can estimate its gradient field reversely. Specifically, the gradient field at each point x_i ($1 \leq i \leq n$), denoted by $\nabla f|_{x_i}$, can be computed by minimizing the following objective function at the local neighborhood of x_i:

$$\nabla f|_{x_i} = \arg\min_{g \in \mathbb{R}^m} \sum_{j \sim i} \left(f(x_j) - f(x_i) - g^T P_i (x_j - x_i) \right)^2 \quad (30)$$

We further plot the vector field learned by PFRank in Figure 3(e), and plot the gradient fields of the ranking functions learned by PFRank, MR and SVM (computed via Eq. (30)) in Figure 3(f)∼(h), respectively. For SVM, many data points have the same ranking scores (i.e., same distance to the SVM boundary), therefore are ranked randomly. And the gradient field of the ranking function has 0 values at many places, therefore are left blank in Figure 3(h). Note that the value of a ranking function increases towards the direction pointed by its gradient field. Therefore, the ranking orders of data points get higher towards the direction pointed by the arrows of the gradient field. It can be observed that both the vector field and the gradient field of the ranking function learned by PFRank point to the query along the geodesics of the manifold, and are quite parallel. On the contrary, the gradient fields of the ranking functions learned by MR and SVM do not vary smoothly along the manifold, and therefore cannot preserve the ranking order.

5.2 Image Retrieval

In this subsection, we apply our proposed ranking algorithm to the image retrieval problem in real world image databases. Given an image as a query, we hope to rank the images in our database according to their relevance to the query. We begin with a description of the data preparation.

5.2.1 Data Preparation

Two real world data sets are used in our experiments. The first one contains 5,000 images of 50 semantic categories, from the COREL database. For each image, we extract a 297-dimensional feature vector which combines the following information:

- Grid Color Moment: Each image is partitioned into 3×3 grids. For each grid, there color moments: mean, variance and skewness are extracted in each color channel (R, G, and B) respectively. Thus, an 81-dimensional grid color moment vector is adopted.
- Edge: The Canny edge detector [3] is used to obtain

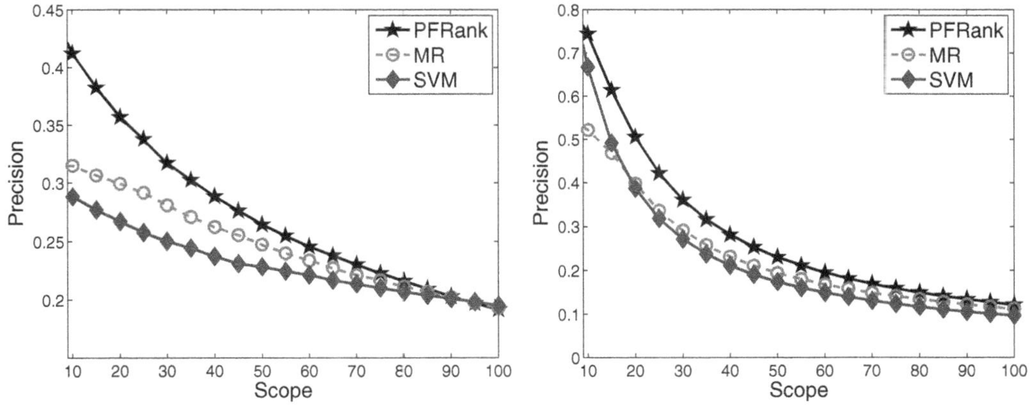

(a) COREL (b) CMU PIE

Figure 4: The average precision-scope curves of different algorithms on the two data sets.

Table 1: Performance comparison using different evaluation metrics on the COREL data set

	NDCG@10	NDCG @20	Recall@10	Recall@20	Recall@50	Recall@100	MAP
SVM	0.297	0.279	0.066	0.121	0.242	**0.404**	0.244
MR	0.312	0.302	0.061	0.116	0.237	0.371	0.237
PFRank	**0.435**	**0.388**	**0.091**	**0.152**	**0.272**	0.394	**0.256**

Table 2: Performance comparison using different evaluation metrics on the CMU PIE data set

	NDCG@10	NDCG @20	Recall@10	Recall@20	Recall@50	Recall@100	MAP
SVM	0.761	0.530	0.503	0.570	0.631	0.695	0.575
MR	0.537	0.446	0.383	0.583	0.698	0.806	0.441
PFRank	**0.786**	**0.605**	**0.572**	**0.750**	**0.847**	**0.889**	**0.729**

the edge map for the edge orientation histogram, which is quantized into 36 bins of 10 degrees each. An additional bin is to count the number of pixels without edge information. Hence, a 37-dimensional vector is used.

- Gabor Wavelets Texture: Each image is first scaled to 64× 64 pixels. The Gabor wavelet transform [11] is then applied on the scaled image with 5 levels and 8 orientations, which results in 40 subimages. For each subimage, 3 moments are calculated: mean, variance and skewness. Thus, a 120-dimensional vector is used.
- Local Binary Pattern: The LBP [16] is a gray-scale texture measure derived from a general texture definition in a local neighborhood. A 59-dimensional LBP histogram vector is adopted.

The second data set is from the CMU PIE face database [20]. This database contains 68 subjects with 41,368 face images as a whole. The face images were captured by 13 synchronized cameras and 21 flashes, under varying pose, illumination and expression. In this experiment, we choose the frontal pose (C27) with varying lighting conditions, which leaves us 21 images per subject. Preprocessing to locate the faces were applied. Original images were normalized (in scale and orientation) such that the two eyes were aligned at the same position. Then the facial areas were cropped into the final image for matching. The size of each cropped image in all the experiments is 32 × 32 pixels, with 256 gray levels per pixel. Therefore, each image can be represented by a 1024-dimensional feature vector in the image space. No further preprocessing is done.

5.2.2 *Experimental Settings*

We describe our experimental setup in this subsection. Both of the two image data sets we use have category labels. In the COREL data set, images from the same category belong to the same semantic concept, such as eagle, bird, elephant, etc. In CMU PIE data set, images from the same category belong to the same person (subject). Therefore, given a query, images that belong to the same category as the query are judged relevant. For each data set, we randomly choose 10 images from each category as queries, and average the retrieval performance over all the queries. It is worth noticing that both PFRank and MR need to construct a nearest neighbor graph among the data and invert a matrix whose size is at least $n \times n$, which is time consuming. In order to make the ranking scheme more efficient, given a query image, we first rank all the images according to the Euclidean distance to the query. Then we choose the top 500 images as candidates and use different ranking algorithms to re-rank them.

We use precision, recall, Mean Average Precision (MAP) [15] and Normalized Discount Cumulative Gain (NDCG) to evaluate the ranking results of different algorithms. Precision is defined as the number of relevant presented images divided by the number of presented images. Recall is defined as the number of relevant presented images divided by the total number of relevant images in our database. Given a query, let r_i be the relevance score of the image ranked at position i, where $r_i = 1$ if the image is relevant to the query and $r_i = 0$ otherwise. Then we can compute the Average

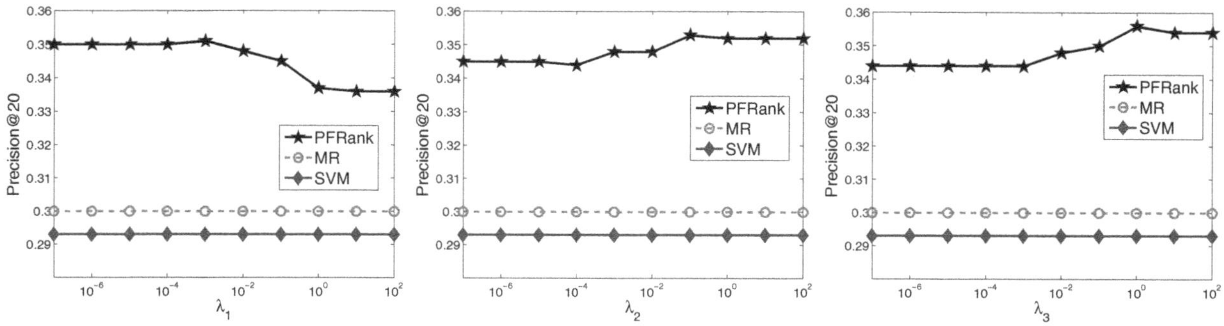

(a) Varying λ_1 (b) Varying λ_2 (c) Varying λ_3

Figure 5: Model selection on the COREL data set.

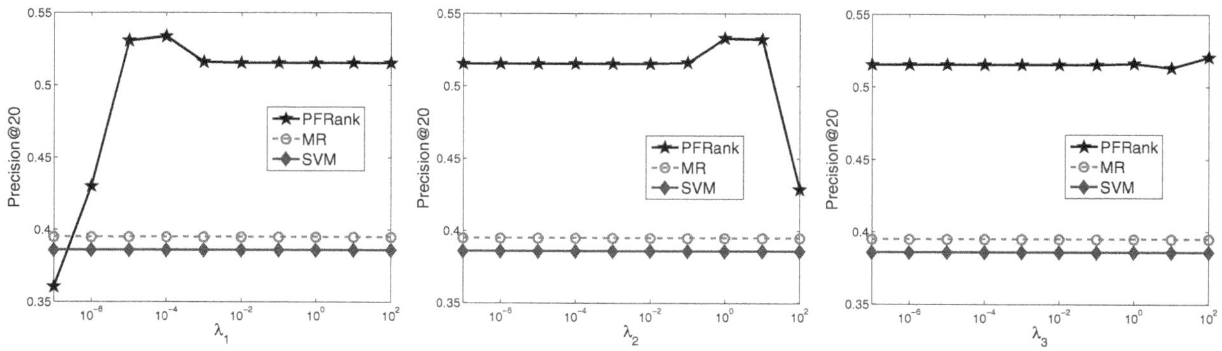

(a) Varying λ_1 (b) Varying λ_2 (c) Varying λ_3

Figure 6: Model selection on the CMU PIE data set.

Precision (AP):

$$\text{AP} = \frac{\sum_i r_i \times \text{Precision@}i}{\#\text{ of relevant images}} \tag{31}$$

MAP is the average of AP over all the queries. And NDCG at position n is defined as:

$$\text{NDCG@}n = Z_n \sum_{i=1}^{n} \frac{2^{r_i} - 1}{\log_2(i+1)} \tag{32}$$

n is also called the scope, which means the number of top-ranked images presented to the user. Z_n is chosen such that the perfect ranking has a NDCG value of 1.

For our PFRank algorithm, the dimensionality of the manifold (d) in the real data is unknown. We perform cross-validation and choose $d = 2$ for the COREL data set, and choose $d = 9$ for the CMU PIE data set, respectively. All the other parameter settings are the same as in the previous experiment.

5.2.3 *Performance Evaluation*

Figure 4 shows the average precision-scope curves of various methods on the two data sets, respectively. The precision-scope curve describes the precision with various scopes, and therefore providing an overall performance evaluation of the algorithms. As can be seen, our proposed PFRank algorithm consistently outperforms the other two algorithms on both data sets. MR generally achieves higher precision than SVM, indicating that considering the manifold structure in the data is useful for image retrieval.

In order to have a comprehensive view of the ranking performance, we present the NDCG, recall and MAP scores of different algorithms on the COREL and CMU PIE data set in Table 1 and Table 2, respectively. Overall, our PFRank method performs the best on both data sets. Although the precision of MR is generally higher than SVM in Figure 4, the NDCG scores of MR are lower than that of SVM on the CMU PIE data set. This is because the precision@n of MR is lower than that of SVM when $n < 20$, and NDCG computes the cumulative relevance scores of the top ranked images. Moreover, the recall and MAP of MR are lower than SVM on the COREL data set. MAP provides a single figure measure of quality across recall levels. Our PFRank achieves the highest MAP on both data sets, indicating reliable performance over the entire ranking list.

5.2.4 *Model Selection*

Model selection is a critical problem in most of the learning problems. In some situations, the learning performance may drastically vary with different choices of the parameters. λ_1, λ_2 and λ_3 are essential parameters in PFRank which control the trade-off among the three regularization terms. We empirically set $\lambda_1 = \lambda_2 = \lambda_3 = 0.01$ in all the previous experiments. In this subsection, we try to study the impact of the parameters on the performance of our PFRank algorithm. Specifically, we fix other parameters the same as before, and let one of $\{\lambda_1, \lambda_2, \lambda_3\}$ vary.

In general, it is appropriate to present 20 images on a screen. Putting more images on a screen might affect the quality of the presented images. Therefore, precision@20 is especially important. Figure 5 and Figure 6 show the precision@20 scores of PFRank with respect to different values of λ_1, λ_2 and λ_3, respectively. As can be seen, our PFRank algorithm is generally not very sensitive to the parameters, and outperforms the other two methods over a wide range of parameters.

6. CONCLUSIONS

In this paper, we propose a novel ranking algorithm on the data manifold from the vector field perspective. Motivated by recent study about the relationship between vector fields and functions on the manifold, we employ vector fields to ensure the linearity of the ranking function with respect to the manifold, as well as requiring the predicted ranking score of the query to be higher than that of its neighboring data points. In this way, the ranking function learned by our method decreases linearly, and therefore monotonically from the query to other points along the geodesics of the data manifold. Hence the ranking order along the geodesics is well preserved. Experimental results on both synthetic data and real data demonstrate the superiority of our method over existing ranking schemes.

There are several interesting directions for extending this work. One important problem is how to efficiently learn a ranking function from the vector field perspective for large-scale retrieval problems. The algorithm proposed in this paper needs to build a nearest neighbor graph among the data, and involves the matrix inversion operation. Given a query that is out of our database, how to update the n-earest neighbor graph and compute the ranking scores efficiently is critical for introducing this technique to real search engines. We may also consider employing distributed computing techniques to further improve the efficiency. Finally, vector fields are very useful to study the geometry and topology of the data manifold. It will be interesting to explore the application of vector fields in many other real-world problems under the manifold assumption, such as face recognition, manifold alignment, recommendation systems and so on.

7. ACKNOWLEDGMENTS

The work was supported in part by the U.S. Army Research Laboratory under Cooperative Agreement No. W911NF-09-2-0053 (NS-CTA), NSF IIS-1017362, U.S. Air Force Office of Scientific Research MURI award FA9550-08-1-0265, and National Basic Research Program of China (973 Program) under Grant 2009CB320801. The views and conclusions contained in this paper are those of the authors and should not be interpreted as representing any funding agencies.

8. REFERENCES

[1] S. Agarwal. Ranking on graph data. In *ICML*, pages 25–32, 2006.
[2] M. Belkin and P. Niyogi. Laplacian eigenmaps and spectral techniques for embedding and clustering. In *NIPS 14*, pages 585–591. 2001.
[3] J. Canny. A computational approach to edge detection. *IEEE Transactions on Pattern Analysis and Machine Intelligence*, 8(6):679–698, 1986.
[4] C.-C. Chang and C.-J. Lin. *LIBSVM: a library for support vector machines*, 2001. Software available at http://www.csie.ntu.edu.tw/~cjlin/libsvm.
[5] F. R. K. Chung. *Spectral Graph Theory*, volume 92 of *Regional Conference Series in Mathematics*. AMS, 1997.
[6] B. Gao, T.-Y. Liu, W. Wei, T. Wang, and H. Li. Semi-supervised ranking on very large graphs with rich metadata. In *KDD*, pages 96–104, 2011.
[7] G. H. Golub and C. F. V. Loan. *Matrix computations*. Johns Hopkins University Press, 3rd edition, 1996.
[8] Z. Guan, J. Bu, Q. Mei, C. Chen, and C. Wang. Personalized tag recommendation using graph-based ranking on multi-type interrelated objects. In *SIGIR*, pages 540–547, 2009.
[9] J. He, M. Li, H.-J. Zhang, H. Tong, and C. Zhang. Manifold-ranking based image retrieval. In *ACM Multimedia*, New York, October 2004.
[10] J. Kleinberg. Authoritative sources in a hyperlinked environment. *Journal of the ACM*, 46(5):604–622, 1999.
[11] M. Lades, J. C. Vorbrüggen, J. M. Buhmann, J. Lange, C. von der Malsburg, R. P. Würtz, and W. Konen. Distortion invariant object recognition in the dynamic link architecture. *IEEE Transactions on Computers*, 42(3):300–311, 1993.
[12] J. Lafferty and L. Wasserman. Statistical analysis of semi-supervised regression. In *NIPS 20*, pages 801–808, 2007.
[13] B. Lin, C. Zhang, and X. He. Semi-supervised regression via parallel field regularization. In *NIPS 24*, pages 433–441. 2011.
[14] D. Liu, X.-S. Hua, L. Yang, M. Wang, and H.-J. Zhang. Tag ranking. In *WWW*, pages 351–360, 2009.
[15] C. D. Manning, P. Raghavan, and H. Schtze. *Introduction to Information Retrieval*. Cambridge University Press, 2008.
[16] T. Ojala, M. Pietikäinen, and D. Harwood. A comparative study of texture measures with classification based on featured distributions. *Pattern Recognition*, 29(1):51–59, 1996.
[17] L. Page, S. Brin, R. Motwani, and T. Winograd. The pagerank citation ranking: Bringing order to the web. Technical report, Stanford University, 1998.
[18] P. Petersen. *Riemannian Geometry*. Springer, 1998.
[19] S. Roweis and L. Saul. Nonlinear dimensionality reduction by locally linear embedding. *Science*, 290(5500):2323–2326, 2000.
[20] T. Sim, S. Baker, and M. Bsat. The cmu pose, illumination, and expression database. *IEEE Transactions on Pattern Analysis and Machine Intelligence*, 25(12):1615–1618, 2003.
[21] D. Tao, X. Li, X. Wu, and S. J. Maybank. Geometric mean for subspace selection. *IEEE Transactions on Pattern Analysis and Machine Intelligence*, 31(2):260–274, 2009.
[22] D. Tao, X. Tang, X. Li, and Y. Rui. Direct kernel biased discriminant analysis: A new content-based image retrieval relevance feedback algorithm. *IEEE Transactions on Multimedia*, 8(4):716–727, 2006.
[23] J. Tenenbaum, V. de Silva, and J. Langford. A global geometric framework for nonlinear dimensionality reduction. *Science*, 290(5500):2319–2323, 2000.
[24] S. Tong and E. Y. Chang. Support vector machine active learning for image retrieval. In *ACM Multimedia*, pages 107–118, 2001.
[25] X. Wan, J. Yang, and J. Xiao. Manifold-ranking based topic-focused multi-document summarization. In *IJCAI*, pages 2903–2908, 2007.
[26] B. Xu, J. Bu, C. Chen, D. Cai, X. He, W. Liu, and J. Luo. Efficient manifold ranking for image retrieval. In *SIGIR*, pages 525–534, 2011.
[27] X. Yuan, X.-S. Hua, M. Wang, and X. Wu. Manifold-ranking based video concept detection on large database and feature pool. In *ACM Multimedia*, pages 623–626, 2006.
[28] D. Zhou, J. Weston, A. Gretton, O. Bousquet, and B. Schölkopf. Ranking on data manifolds. In *NIPS 16*, 2003.
[29] X. Zhou, M. Belkin, and N. Srebro. An iterated graph laplacian approach for ranking on manifolds. In *KDD*, pages 877–885, 2011.

Semi-Supervised Learning with Mixed Knowledge Information

Fanhua Shang, L. C. Jiao
Key Laboratory of Intelligent Perception and Image Understanding of Ministry of Education of China
Xidian University, Xi'an 710071, PR China
shangfanhua@hotmail.com
jlcxidian@163.com

Fei Wang
Healthcare Analytics Research Group,
IBM T. J. Watson Research Center
Hawthorne, NY, USA
feiwang03@gmail.com

ABSTRACT
Integrating new knowledge sources into various learning tasks to improve their performance has recently become an interesting topic. In this paper we propose a novel semi-supervised learning (SSL) approach, called semi-supervised learning with *Mixed Knowledge Information* (SSL-MKI) which can simultaneously handle both sparse labeled data and additional pairwise constraints together with unlabeled data. Specifically, we first construct a unified SSL framework to combine the manifold assumption and the pairwise constraints assumption for classification tasks. Then we present a *Modified Fixed Point Continuation* (MFPC) algorithm with an eigenvalue thresholding (EVT) operator to learn the enhanced kernel matrix. Finally, we develop a two-stage optimization strategy and provide an efficient SSL approach that takes advantage of Laplacian spectral regularization: semi-supervised learning with *Enhanced Spectral Kernel* (ESK). Experimental results on a variety of synthetic and real-world datasets demonstrate the effectiveness of the proposed ESK approach.

Categories and Subject Descriptors
I.2.6 [**Artificial Intelligence**]: Learning; H.2.8 [**Database Management**]: Database Applications—*Data mining*

General Terms
Algorithms, Performance, Experimentation

Keywords
Semi-supervised learning (SSL), Kernel learning, Graph Laplacian, Nuclear norm regularization, Pairwise constraints

1. INTRODUCTION
Semi-Supervised Learning (SSL) has recently received a significant amount of attention in the machine learning and data mining communities [1, 2]. A large amount of SSL approaches have been proposed, including EM with generative mixture models, self-training, co-training, transductive support vector machines (TSVMs), and graph-based methods. Among them, a family of graph-based SSL methods is label propagation techniques [3, 4] or provides graph-based regularization frameworks for learning from labeled and unlabeled data [5, 6]. Although graph-based SSL has been studied extensively, so far there are few comprehensive techniques to integrate weakly labeled data and pairwise constraints together for classification tasks.

KDD'12, August 12 - 16 2012, Beijing, China

In SSL, the class labels of data are the most widely used supervisory information [7]. But labeled instances are often difficult, expensive, or time consuming to obtain, as they require the efforts of the domain experts. Integrating new knowledge sources such as side information into classification tasks with insufficient training data has recently become an interesting topic [8]. In this paper we are particularly interested in how to incorporate additional pairwise constraints to improve classification accuracy. *Pairwise constraints* may be relatively easy to collect, and indicate that some pairs of instances are in the same class and some are not, known as the *Must-Link* (ML) and the *Cannot-Link* (CL), respectively, [1, 9, 10]. Pairwise constraints can also be obtained from data labels where objects with the same label are must-link while objects with different labels are cannot-link. Pairwise constraints have been widely used in various tasks such as clustering [9-12] and distance metric learning [13-15] where it has been shown that the presence of appropriate pairwise constraints can achieve reasonable performance improvement. However, there are relatively fewer works using additional pairwise constraints to support semi-supervised classification tasks [8].

Generally, SSL methods are derived based on two fundamental assumptions: the *cluster assumption* (also called label consistency) and the *manifold assumption*. In the cluster assumption, decision boundaries should not cross high density regions, but instead lie in low density regions. Typical methods include TSVMs [16, 17] and some convex relaxation methods. In the manifold assumption, data are assumed to be sampled from a low-dimensional manifold that is embedded inside of a higher dimensional input space. Many SSL approaches implement such an assumption by using the graph Laplacian of a neighborhood graph which can characterize the underlying manifold structure. Typical methods include Zhu et al.'s Gaussian random fields (GRF) method [3], Zhou et al.'s learning with local and global consistency (LGC) [4], manifold regularization [5, 6], etc. More recently, Li et al. [7] presented a *pairwise constraint assumption* that is very effective for classification tasks together with the cluster assumption. In the pairwise constraint assumption, those unlabeled data points involved in any ML constraint are classified into the same class and those involved in any CL constraint are classified into different classes.

Despite many successes, most graph-based SSL methods mentioned above have a limitation in the difficulty of tuning optimal graph parameters. Specially, with limited labeled data, it may be ineffective to learn kernel parameters by cross-validation from labeled data only [18]. To address this limitation, various kernel learning approaches [7, 18-23] (also called non-parametric kernel learning) are proposed to learn a positive semidefinite (PSD) kernel matrix directly from the data incorporating label or side information. Several existing studies [7, 21] have shown that time complexity of standard interior-point semidefinite programming (SDP) solvers to learn the entire kernel matrix could be as high as $O(n^{6.5})$, where n is the number of data points, which prohibits those approaches for practical applications [18], whereas there are several efficient approaches derived from the spectral decomposition of graph Laplacians, such as the *Order-constrained Spectral Kernel* (OSK) [19, 20], the *Transductive Spectral Kernel* (TSK) [22], and the graph *Laplacian Regularized Kernel* (LRK) [24].

In this paper, we consider a more general problem of semi-supervised classification which can handle sparse labeled data and additional pairwise constraints together with abundant unlabeled data, and propose a novel SSL approach, also called semi-supervised learning with *Mixed Knowledge Information* (SSL-MKI). We first construct a unified SSL-MKI framework to implement both the manifold assumption and the pairwise constraint assumption. Under the SSL-MKI framework, we also present a semi-supervised low-rank kernel learning model with nuclear norm regularization. Then we develop a two-stage optimization strategy and provide an efficient SSL-MKI algorithm that takes advantage of Laplacian spectral regularization: semi-supervised learning with *Enhanced Spectral Kernel* (ESK).

2. NOTATIONS AND BACKGROUND

Given a data set of n instances $X=\{x_1,x_2,\cdots,x_l,x_{l+1},\cdots,x_n\}$, the first small number l points $X_L=\{x_i\}_{i=1}^{l}$ belonging to c classes are labeled, and the remaining points $X_U=\{x_i\}_{i=l+1}^{n}$ are unlabeled, and two sets of pairwise must-link and cannot-link constraints are denoted respectively by $\mathrm{ML}=\{(x_i,x_j)\}$ where x_i and x_j should be in the same class, and $\mathrm{CL}=\{(x_i,x_j)\}$ where x_i and x_j should be in different classes.

Before we go into the details of our method, we will briefly review some of the related works in this section. As mentioned in the previous section, the common denominator of graph-based methods is to model the whole data set as a graph $\mathcal{G}=(\mathcal{V},\mathcal{E})$ with the vertex set $\mathcal{V}=X$, and the weight w_{ij} on the edge $e_{ij}\in\mathcal{E}$ representing the similarity between x_i and x_j. For convenience, we adopt the local scaling parameter trick proposed in [25] to construct $\mathcal{G}$ as a *T*-nearest neighbor (*T*-NN) graph. Let us define a selecting function of the local scale,

$$h(x)=\left\|x-x^{(T)}\right\|, \tag{1}$$

where $x^{(T)}$ is the *T*-th nearest neighbor of x in X. The weight matrix $W\in\mathbb{R}^{n\times n}$ associated with $\mathcal{G}$ is formed subsequently as

$$W_{ij}=\begin{cases}\exp\left(-\dfrac{\left\|x_i-x_j\right\|^2}{h(x_i)h(x_j)}\right), & \text{if } x_j\in N(x_i) \text{ or } x_i\in N(x_j);\\[2mm] 0, & \text{otherwise.}\end{cases} \tag{2}$$

Note that we set $W_{ii}=0$ to avoid self-loops. We further denote the diagonal degree matrix $D\in\mathbb{R}^{n\times n}$ whose entries are given by $D_{ii}=\sum_j W_{ij}$, and the normalized *graph Laplacian* $L=I-D^{-1/2}WD^{-1/2}$.

The regularization framework proposed by Zhou et al. [4] can implement a global classification task as follows:

$$\begin{aligned}\mathcal{Q}(F)&=\mathcal{S}(F)+\mathcal{L}(F)\\ &=\frac{1}{2}\sum_{i,j=1}^{n}W_{ij}\left\|\frac{F_i}{\sqrt{D_{ii}}}-\frac{F_j}{\sqrt{D_{jj}}}\right\|^2+\mu\sum_{i=1}^{n}\left\|F_i-Y_i\right\|^2,\end{aligned} \tag{3}$$

where F is a vectorial function, $F:X\rightarrow\mathbb{R}^c$, to assign a label $f_i=\arg\max_{j\le c}F_{ij}$ to each instance x_i, $\mu>0$ is the regularization parameter, and $Y\in\mathbb{R}^{n\times c}$ is a class indicator matrix, where $Y_{ik}=1$ if x_i is labeled as k, and $Y_{ik}=0$ otherwise. The $\mathcal{S}(\cdot)$ is a regularizer to penalize the smoothness of the classifying function F over the graph, and the $\mathcal{L}(\cdot)$ is a loss function measuring the inconsistency between the predicted and initial label assignment. Then the classification function is

$$F^*=\arg\min_F\mathcal{Q}(F)=(1-\alpha)(I-\alpha S)^{-1}Y, \tag{4}$$

where α ($0<\alpha=1/(1+\mu)<1$) is the regularization parameter and $S=D^{-1/2}WD^{-1/2}$ symmetrically normalizes W. The calculated matrix F^* stacks the final class assignment. But this method is an unreliable approach for model selection if only very few labeled instances are available [26].

In recent years, a large amount of low-rank matrix recovery methods have been proposed for matrix completion [27]-[30] problems. Among of them, there are several representative methods such as SVT [27], FPCA [28], and ALM [29]. And some works also provide theoretical guarantee that the task of the *rank minimization* problem can be accomplished via solving the *nuclear norm* (also known as the trace norm) minimization under some reasonable conditions. Specifically, Candès and Recht [30] proved that a given incomplete low-rank matrix (but unknown) $Z\in\mathbb{R}^{n\times n}$ satisfying certain incoherence conditions can be exactly recovered by the following model (5) with probability at least $1-B_1n^{-3}$ from a subset Ω of uniformly sampled entries $\{Z_{ij}:(i,j)\in\Omega\}$ whose cardinality $|\Omega|$ is of the form $B_2rn^{5/4}\log n$, where r is the rank of the desired matrix, and B_1 and B_2 are two positive constants.

$$\begin{aligned}&\min_K\|K\|_*,\\ &\text{s.t., } M\odot(K-Z)=0,\end{aligned} \tag{5}$$

where $\|\cdot\|_*$ denotes the nuclear norm of a matrix, i.e., the sum of its singular values, the operator $\odot$ denotes element-wise multiplication, and the weight matrix M is defined as

$$M_{ij} = \begin{cases} 1, & \text{if } (i,j) \in \Omega, \\ 0, & \text{otherwise.} \end{cases} \tag{6}$$

3. FRAMEWORK OF SSL-MKI

3.1 A General Framework

As mentioned above, our goal is to use the given labeled data and pairwise constraints together with unlabeled instances for classification tasks. We propose a general SSL-MKI framework as follows:

$$\mathcal{Q}(F,K) = \mathcal{S}(F,K) + \mu_1 \mathcal{L}_1(F) + \mu_2 \mathcal{L}_2(K), \tag{7}$$

where K is a desired "ideal" kernel matrix, $\mathcal{S}(\cdot,\cdot)$ is a regularizer to penalize the smoothness of the classifying function F, $\mathcal{L}_1(F)$ is a loss function penalizing the inconsistency between the predicted and initial label assignment, and $\mathcal{L}_2(K)$ is a loss function to measure the change between the predicted and "ideal" kernels corresponding to the given pairwise constraints, such as the squared loss or hinge loss functions. $\mu_1 > 0$ and $\mu_2 > 0$ are the regularization parameters for $\mathcal{L}_1(F)$ and $\mathcal{L}_2(K)$, respectively. In the unified framework, we can implement both the *manifold assumption* and the *pairwise constraint assumption.*

3.2 Nuclear Norm Regularized Model

Under the squared loss function, the model (7) is formulated as follows:

$$\begin{aligned} \mathcal{Q}(F,K) =& \frac{1}{2}\sum_{i,j=1}^{n} \tilde{K}_{ij} \left\| \frac{F_i}{\sqrt{D_{ii}}} - \frac{F_j}{\sqrt{D_{jj}}} \right\|^2 + \mu_1 \sum_{i=1}^{n} \|F_i - Y_i\|^2 \\ & + \mu_2 \left(\sum_{i=1}^{n} (K_{ii}-1)^2 + \sum_{(x_i,x_j)\in \mathrm{ML}}^{n} (K_{ij}-1)^2 + \sum_{(x_i,x_j)\in \mathrm{CL}}^{n} (K_{ij}-0)^2 \right), \\ =& \frac{1}{2}\sum_{i,j=1}^{n} \tilde{K}_{ij} \left\| \frac{F_i}{\sqrt{D_{ii}}} - \frac{F_j}{\sqrt{D_{jj}}} \right\|^2 + \mu_1 \sum_{i=1}^{n} \|F_i - Y_i\|^2 + \mu_2 \sum_{(x_i,x_j,t_{ij})\in S} (K_{ij} - t_{ij})^2, \end{aligned} \tag{8}$$

where $S = \{(x_i, x_j, t_{ij})\}$ is the set of pairwise constraints, and t_{ij} is a binary variable that takes 1 or 0 to denote x_i and x_j belonging to the same class or not, and

$$\tilde{K}_{ij} = \begin{cases} K_{ij}, & K_{ij} \geq 0; \\ 0, & \text{otherwise.} \end{cases} \tag{9}$$

The time complexity of learning the entire kernel matrix in [7, 21] could be as high as $O(n^{6.5})$. An effective heuristic of speedup is to perform low-rank kernel matrix approximation and matrix factorization [19, 22, 24, 31, 32]. Moreover, the number of the given pairwise constraints is far less than the one which is sufficient to complete the low-rank kernel matrix with high probability. Thus, we incorporate the Laplacian spectral regularization into the above model (8). In other words, we set $K = QUQ^T$, where $Q = (q_1, \ldots, q_n)^T \in \mathbb{R}^{n\times m}$ consists of the m smoothest eigenvectors of the graph Laplacian L, and U is of size $m \times m$. The completion problem of the desired kernel K is then converted into the learning problem of a much smaller matrix U ($m \ll n$), subject to the constraint that $U \geq 0$.

Considering that the desired kernel matrix K is low-rank, and $\|K\|_* = \|QUQ^T\|_* = \|U\|_*$, we present the following nuclear norm regularized problem,

$$\begin{aligned} \mathcal{Q}(F,U) =& \frac{1}{2}\sum_{i,j=1}^{n} \tilde{K}_{ij} \left\| \frac{F_i}{\sqrt{D_{ii}}} - \frac{F_j}{\sqrt{D_{jj}}} \right\|^2 + \mu_1 \sum_{i=1}^{n} \|F_i - Y_i\|^2 + \\ & \mu_2 \left(\mu \|U\|_* + \frac{1}{2} \| M \odot (QUQ^T - Z) \|_F^2 \right), \end{aligned} \tag{10}$$

where μ is a positive regularization parameter, Ω is the set of indices of known entries of Z, which is defined as

$$Z_{ij} = \begin{cases} 1, & i = j; \\ 1, & (i,j) \in \mathrm{ML}; \\ 0, & (i,j) \in \mathrm{CL}. \end{cases}$$

It is generally difficult that the optimization problem (10) is minimized with respect to both variables simultaneously. Thus, we employ an alternating optimization idea to solve the above problem. In the next section, we present a two-stage optimization strategy and provide an efficient *modified fixed point continuous* algorithm to learn the enhanced matrix U.

4. THE ALGORITHM

In this section, we present an effective two-stage optimization strategy for the SSL-MKI model (10). Furthermore, we should first choose to respect the *pairwise constraints assumption* and then the *manifold assumption*, considering that the given pairwise constraints are from reliable knowledge. Then we design an efficient *modified fixed point continuous* algorithm to learn the enhanced matrix U, and present a semi-supervised classification (SSC) algorithm, which aims to solve transduction classification tasks.

The objective function (10) can be approximated by a two-stage optimization strategy as follows:

$$\begin{cases} \min\limits_{U} \mu\|U\|_* + \frac{1}{2}\left\|M \odot (QUQ^T - Z)\right\|_F^2, \\ \min\limits_{F} \frac{1}{2}\sum_{i,j=1}^{n} \tilde{K}_{ij} \left\| \frac{F_i}{\sqrt{D_{ii}}} - \frac{F_j}{\sqrt{D_{jj}}} \right\|^2 + \mu_1 \sum_{i=1}^{n} \|F_i - Y_i\|^2. \end{cases} \tag{11}$$

In other words, the problem (10) can be efficiently solved using the following two stages: the first stage involving only one variable U is to compute the desired enhanced matrix U with the given pairwise constraints; and the second stage is to achieve the classification assignment based on the learned similarity matrix $\tilde{K}$ from the first stage.

4.1 Modified Fixed Point Algorithm

In the first stage, the optimization problem is formulated as follows:

$$\min_U \mu\|U\|_* + \frac{1}{2}\|M \odot (QUQ^T - Z)\|_F^2, \quad \text{s.t.}, \; U \geq 0. \tag{12}$$

While the nuclear norm minimization problem (12) can be converted into a semidefinite programming (SDP) problem, the time complexity of each iteration of standard SDP solvers based on the interior-point method could be at least as $O(m^6)$ [33]. To overcome this issue, many first-order algorithms have been developed to solve those problems, such as FPCA [28], which is a fixed point continuation algorithm. Furthermore, the FPCA method provably converges to the globally optimal solution and has been shown to outperform SDP solvers in terms of matrix recoverability. More recently, Ni et al. [34] proposed an *Augmented Lagrange Multiplier* (ALM) method for solving the low-rank representation problem with a PSD constraint. Our model (12) is also a nuclear norm minimization problem with a PSD constraint. In this part, we propose a *Modified Fixed Point Continuation* (MFPC) algorithm with an eigenvalue thresholding (EVT) operator to learn the enhanced matrix U, also called MFPC. The proposed MFPC algorithm can reduce the number of the auxiliary variables used in the ALM method [29] to accelerate its convergence. In the following subsections, we describe the proposed MFPC algorithm, and discuss the stopping criteria for iterations to acquire the optimal solution.

Inspired by the fixed point continuation algorithm proposed by Ma et al. [28], which has been used to multi-label transductive learning [35], we develop a modified fixed point iterative algorithm with an EVT operator to solve the proposed nuclear norm minimization problem (12).

Let $g(U) := \mu\|U\|_* + \frac{1}{2}\|M \odot (QUQ^T - Z)\|_F^2$, the derivative of the function $g(\cdot)$ with respect to U is given by

$$\partial g = \mu\partial\|U\|_* + H,$$

where $\partial\|U\|_*$ is the set of the subgradients of the nuclear norm, and $H = h(U) := Q^T\left(M \odot (QUQ^T - Z)\right)Q$.

Following [36], an explicit expression of the subdifferential of the nuclear norm at a symmetric matrix is given by the following lemma.

Lemma 1. Let $U \in \mathbb{R}^{m\times m}$ be a real symmetric matrix, then

$$\partial\|U\|_* = \{V^{(1)}[V^{(1)}]^T - V^{(2)}[V^{(2)}]^T + S : [V^{(1)}, V^{(2)}]^T S = 0, \; \|S\|_2 \leq 1\},$$

where $V^{(1)}$ and $V^{(2)}$ are orthogonal eigenvectors associated with the positive and negative eigenvalues of U respectively, and $\|\cdot\|_2$ denotes the spectral norm of a matrix.

In addition, the following optimality condition in [37] can be adopted for the proposed nuclear norm minimization problem (12).

Theorem 1. Let $g(\cdot)$ be a convex function. Then U^* is an optimal solution to the problem (12), if and only if $U^* \geq 0$, and there exists a matrix $E \in \partial g(U^*)$ such that

$$\left\langle E, F - U^*\right\rangle \geq 0, \quad \text{for all } F \geq 0.$$

Based on the above theorem, we can develop a modified fixed point iterative scheme for solving the problem (12) by adopting the operator splitting technique.

The operator $T(\cdot)$ is defined as

$$T(\cdot) := \tau\mu\partial\|\cdot\|_* + \tau h(\cdot),$$

where $\tau > 0$. And $T(\cdot)$ can be split into two parts:

$$T(\cdot) = T_1(\cdot) - T_2(\cdot),$$

where $T_1(\cdot) = \tau\mu\partial\|\cdot\|_* + I(\cdot)$, $T_2(\cdot) = I(\cdot) - \tau h(\cdot)$, and $I(\cdot)$ is an identity operator.

Let $Y = T_2(U)$, then $T(U) = \tau\mu\partial\|U\|_* + U - Y$, and $U \geq 0$. For tackling the proposed model (12), we need to solve the following nuclear norm minimization problem,

$$\min_{U\geq 0} \tau\mu\|U\|_* + \frac{1}{2}\|U - Y\|_F^2. \tag{13}$$

The convex optimization problem (13) has a closed-form optimal solution [34], and the optimal solution is given by the eigenvalue thresholding (EVT) operator which will be defined later:

$$U^* = \mathrm{EVT}_{\tau\mu}(Y).$$

Thus, our modified fixed point scheme for solving the problem (12) can be expressed by the following two-step iteration as follows:

$$\begin{cases} Y^k = U^k - \tau h(U^k), \\ U^{k+1} = \mathrm{EVT}_{\tau\mu}(Y^k). \end{cases} \tag{14}$$

Definition 1 (Eigenvalue thresholding (EVT) operator) Assume $U = U^T \geq 0$, and its eigenvalue decomposition is given by $U = V\mathrm{diag}(\lambda)V^T$, where $V \in \mathbb{R}^{m\times r}$, and $\lambda \in \mathbb{R}_+^r$. Given $v > 0$, $\mathrm{EVT}_v(\cdot)$ is defined as:

$$\mathrm{EVT}_v(U) := V\mathrm{diag}(\max\{\lambda - v, 0\})V^T, \tag{15}$$

where $\max\{\cdot,\cdot\}$ should be understood element-wise.

Theorem 2. Suppose a symmetric matrix $U^* \geq 0$ satisfies:

1. $\|M \odot (QU^*Q^T - Z)\|_F^2 < \mu / m$ for a small positive constant μ.
2. $U^* = \mathrm{EVT}_{\tau\mu}(U^* + \tau h(U^*))$. (16)

Then U^* is the unique optimal solution of the problem (12).

Proof. Please refer to [28, 37]. □

4.2 Implementation

We develop a modified fixed point iterative scheme to learn the enhanced matrix U with a PSD constraint. As suggested in [28, 37], the continuation technique can accelerate the convergence of the fixed point iterative method, and the parameter β determines the rate of reduction of consecutive μ_k,

$$\mu_{k+1} = \max\{\mu_k\beta, \bar{\mu}\}. \tag{17}$$

where $\bar{\mu}$ is a moderately small constant. Thus, the continuation strategy is also adopted by our modified fixed point algorithm, which solves a sequence of the problem (12), easy to difficult, corresponding to a sequence of large to small values of μ_k.

In the implementation of [28], the parameter τ is always set to 1, in contrast, it is set to $\tau \in (0, 2/\|\Psi\|_2)$ for the proposed fixed point continuation algorithm so that our algorithm's convergence is guaranteed, where $\Psi := (Q^T \otimes Q^T) I_\Omega (Q \otimes Q)$, $\otimes$ denotes the Kronecker product of two matrices, and $I_\Omega \in \mathbb{R}^{n^2 \times n^2}$ is a diagonal matrix which entries associated with Ω are set to 1, and 0 otherwise. There are many ways to select the parameter τ to accelerate the convergence of gradient algorithms for compressing sensing tasks. We now specify a strategy, which is based on the *Barzilai-Borwein* (BB) method [38] for choosing the parameter τ_k. The shrinkage iteration (14) first takes a gradient descent step with the step size τ_k along the negative gradient direction h^k of the smooth function $\| M \odot (QUQ^T - Z)\|_F^2 / 2$, and then applies the EVT operator $\mathrm{EVT}_v(\cdot)$ to accommodate the non-smooth term $\|U\|_*$. Therefore, it is natural to choose the parameter τ_k based on the function $\| M \odot (QUQ^T - Z)\|_F^2 / 2$ alone.

Let $H^k = Q^T \left(M \odot (QUQ^T - Z)\right) Q$, $\Delta U = U^k - U^{k-1}$, and $\Delta h = H^k - H^{k-1}$, then the BB step is defined by

$$\tau_k = \frac{\langle \Delta U, \Delta h\rangle}{\langle \Delta h, \Delta h\rangle}, \text{ or } \tau_k = \frac{\langle \Delta U, \Delta U\rangle}{\langle \Delta U, \Delta h\rangle}.$$

To avoid the BB step size τ_k being either too small or too large, we take

$$\tau_k = \max\{\tau_{\min}, \min\{\tau_k, \tau_{\max}\}\}, \tag{18}$$

where $0 < \tau_{\min} < \tau_{\max} < \infty$ are two constants.

Because our ultimate goal is to learn the enhanced matrix U, the accurate solution of the problem (12) is not required. Therefore, we use the following criterion as a stopping rule,

$$\frac{\|U^{k+1} - U^k\|_F}{\max\{1, \|U^k\|_F\}} < tol, \tag{19}$$

where tol is a small positive number. Experiments shows that $tol = 10^{-4}$ is good enough for obtaining the optimal matrix U^*.

Based on the previous analysis, we develop a *Modified Fixed Point Continuation* (MFPC) algorithm to learn the enhanced matrix U, as listed in **Algorithm 1**.

Theorem 3. The sequence $\{U^k\}$ generated by our modified fixed point iterations with $\tau \in (0, 2/\|\Psi\|_2)$ converges to some $\bar{U} \in \Gamma$, where Γ is the set of optimal solutions of the problem (12).

Proof. Please refer to [28, 37]. □

We now claim that our modified fixed-point continuation algorithm converges to an optimal solution of the problem (12).

Algorithm 1: MFPC algorithm

Input: A data set of n instances $X = \{x_1, x_2, \cdots, x_l, x_{l+1}, \cdots, x_n\}$, $X_L = \{x_i\}_{i=1}^l$ are labeled, and $X_U = \{x_i\}_{i=l+1}^n$ are unlabeled. ML$= \{(x_i, x_j)\}$ is the set of must-link constraints, and CL$= \{(x_i, x_j)\}$ is the set of cannot-link constraints. The number of nearest neighbors T and the constant m.

Output: The enhanced matrix U.

Initialize: Given M, U^0, $\bar{\mu}$, β, and tol.

And select $\mu_1 > \mu_2 > \cdots > \mu_L = \bar{\mu} > 0$.

1. Construct the T-NN graph and compute the normalized graph Laplacian $L = I - D^{-1/2} W D^{-1/2}$.
2. Compute the m eigenvectors $\phi_1, \ldots, \phi_m$ of L associated with the first m smallest eigenvalues, and form the spectral representation matrix $Q = [\phi_1, \ldots, \phi_m] \in \mathbb{R}^{n \times m}$.

for $\mu_k = \mu_1, \mu_2, \cdots, \mu_L$, **do**

  while not converged **do**

    1. Choose the BB step size τ_k by Eq. (18).

    2. Update Y^k

$$H^k = Q^T \left(M \odot (QUQ^T - Z)\right) Q, \quad Y^k = U^k - \tau_k H^k.$$

    3. Update U^{k+1}

$$U^{k+1} = \mathrm{EVT}_{\tau_k \mu_k}\left(Y^k\right).$$

  stop condition: $\dfrac{\|U^{k+1} - U^k\|_F}{\max\{1, \|U^k\|_F\}} < tol$.

  end while

end for

4.3 Label Propagation

The enhanced spectral kernel K has been constructed using the above proposed MFPC algorithm, and we would have to take advantage of it to predict the labels of the unlabeled instances. We also present a semi-supervised learning method with *enhanced spectral kernel*, also called ESK, as shown in **Algorithm 2**. Here, our iteration equation can be written as follows:

$$F^{t+1} = \alpha P F^t + (1 - \alpha) Y, \tag{20}$$

where $P = D^{-1/2} \tilde{K} D^{-1/2}$ [1]. We will use the equation (20) to update the labels of each data point until convergence.

We give a toy example to illustrate how our ESK algorithm works, as shown in Figure 1. At first glance, the toy data consists of three separate groups, and is composed of a mixture of Gaussian-like and curve-like groups, as shown in Figure 1(a). Moreover, we also present the comparison between the similarity matrix in the input space and the kernel matrices learned by OSK, TSK, and MFPC, where the data are ordered such that all the instances in two Gaussian-like groups appear first; all the instances in the curve-like group appear second. It can be clearly observed that the enhanced kernel matrix learned by our MFPC algorithm exhibits two clear block structures so that the two classes are well-separated groups. In addition, we can draw a similar

[1] We set the enhanced similarity matrix $\tilde{K}$ by Eq. (9) for the proposed ESK algorithm. However, there is no need to change the enhanced spectral kernel as described above when it is used in traditional kernel machines such as SVMs.

conclusion as [23] that the kernel matrices learned by OSK and TSK have some uninformative eigenvectors even though which are optimally combined according to their own optimization criteria, and they fail to classify data points into the proper class.

Algorithm 2: ESK Algorithm

Input: The enhanced matrix U and the constant α.
Output: The assigned labels of all the data points.

1. Obtain the enhanced matrix U by solving the problem (12) via the proposed MFPC algorithm.
2. Construct the enhanced spectral kernel matrix $K = QUQ^T$, and iterate Eq. (20) until convergence.
3. Let F^* be the limit of the sequence $\{F^t\}$, and assign the labels of each data point x_i by $y(x_i) = \text{argmax}_{k \le c} F^*_{ik}$.

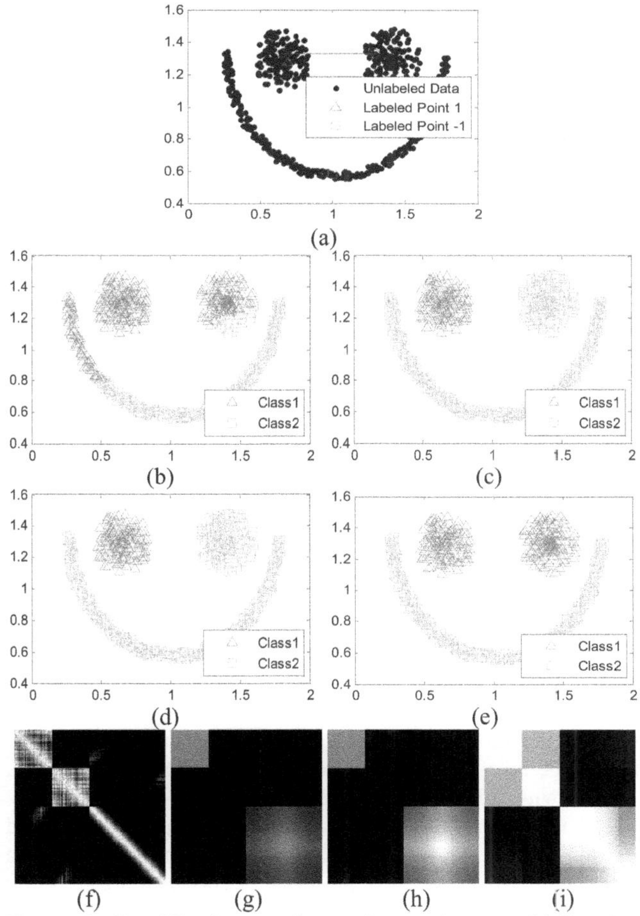

Figure 1: Classification results on the toy data set. (a) Toy data set with two labeled points and one ML constraint. (b)–(e) Classification results using LGC with $\sigma = 0.2$, OSK, TSK, and the proposed ESK algorithm with only one iteration. (f) Similarity matrix for the toy data set in the input space. (g)–(i) Learned kernel matrices by OSK, TSK, and MFPC with the $m = 5$ smoothest eigenvectors of graph Laplacians and a neighborhood size $T = 7$. The brighter a pixel, the greater similarity the pixel represents.

4.4 Valid Kernel

Theorem 4. If a normalized graph Laplacian $L \in \mathbb{R}^{n \times n}$ has the first m eigenvectors $\phi_1, \ldots, \phi_m$ corresponding to the m smallest engenvalues, and the enhanced matrix U obtained by solving the problem (12) for ESK is symmetric positive semidefinite. Then the family of matrices $K = QUQ^T$ is a valid kernel matrix.

Proof: Because $U = U^T \ge 0$, $U = U^{1/2}(U^{1/2})^T$, and $K = QUQ^T = QU^{1/2}(QU^{1/2})^T$, the enhanced spectral kernel matrix K is certainly positive semidefinite and thus a valid kernel matrix. □

Remark: Similar to the existing spectral kernel learning approaches such as OSK and TSK, the kernel matrix K learned by the proposed MFPC algorithm is also nonparametric spectral kernels from the graph Laplacian kernel L, and is referred to as the enhanced spectral kernel. Hence, the enhanced spectral kernel can be used in traditional kernel machines such as SVMs.

4.5 Complexity Analysis

The main running time of the proposed ESK algorithm is consumed by constructing the k-NN graph, computing the enhanced kernel matrix, and iterating the procedure (20). The time complexity of computing the enhanced matrix U by solving the problem (12) is $O(n^2 + t_1 m^2 n - t_1 m^3)$, where t_1 is the number of iterations. The total time complexity of ESK is $O(n^2 + t_1 m^2 n + t_1 m^3 + n^2 m + t_2 n^2 c)$, where t_2 is the number of iterations in the procedure (20). In the ESK algorithm, computing the m smoothest eigenvectors of the sparse matrix L can be efficiently performed using the Lanczos algorithm [39].

5. EXPERIMENTS

In this section, we present a set of experiments on many data sets, including a synthetic data set and many transductive settings.

5.1 Compared Algorithms

We compared the performance of the proposed ESK approach with the existing state-of-the-art SSL algorithms or related SSL methods, and the results averaged over 50 independent runs are reported.

- We use one-versus-rest SVMs[2] (SVM) [40] as the baseline. The width of the RBF kernel for SVM is set using 5-fold cross validation.
- GRF [3] and LGC [4]. The affinity matrix is constructed by a Gaussian function whose width is set by 5-fold cross validation.
- LapSVM[3] [6]: The base kernel is also selected to be Gaussian whose width is set by 5-fold cross validation, and all of the other hyperparameters are set by grid search as in [6].
- TSK [22] and OSK[4] [19]. For TSK, the decay factor γ is set to 2, and other parameters in TSK are set as in our ESK algorithm. For OSK, all parameters in OSK are set as in our algorithm.
- The proposed ESK algorithm. In all of the experiments, we set the constant $\alpha = 0.01$. And the number of nearest neighbors T is set by grid search as in [6].

[2] http://www.csie.ntu.edu.tw/~cjlin/libsvm/.
[3] http://www.dii.unisi.it/~melacci/lapsvmp/.
[4] http://pages.cs.wisc.edu/~jerryzhu/publications.html.

5.2 Real-world Datasets

We use three categories of real-world data sets in our experiments, which are selected to cover a wide range of properties. Specifically, these data sets include:

- *UCI Data*[5]. We perform experiments on five UCI data sets, including Ionosphere, Sonar, Balance, Iris and Glass, and an artificial data set, G50c.
- *Image Data.* We perform experiments on six image data sets: MNIST [41], USPS[6], COIL20 [42], Caltech4[7], ORL[8] and YaleB3 [43].
- *Text Data.* We also perform experiments on two text data sets: 20-newsgroup[9] and WebKB[10].

The basic information of those data sets together with additional randomly chosen pairwise constraints is summarized in Table 1.

Table 1: Descriptions of the data sets.

Category	Data	Class	Feature	Labeled	Size	num_*M*	num_*C*
UCI	G50c	2	50	20	550	10	5
	Ionosphere	2	33	20	351	10	5
	Sonar	2	60	20	208	10	5
	Balance	3	4	20	625	15	15
	Iris	3	4	20	150	15	15
	Glass	6	9	30	214	12	30
Images	MNIST0123	4	784	8	4157	8	12
	USPS0123	4	256	8	3588	8	12
	COIL20	20	1024	40	1440	40	100
	Caltech4	4	4200	20	3479	8	12
	ORL	40	1024	80	400	80	200
	Yale3	3	1200	3	1755	6	6
Text	20-News	4	8014	40	3970	20	30
	Text1	2	7511	20	1946	20	10
	WK-CL	7	4134	70	827	14	72
	WK-TX	7	4029	70	814	14	72
	WK-WT	7	4165	70	1166	14	72
	WK-WC	7	4189	70	1210	14	72

Note that num_*M* and num_*C* denote the numbers of randomly chosen must-link constraints and cannot-link constraints, respectively.

5.3 Transduction Classification Results

The performances of the existing state-of-the-art SSL methods and the proposed ESK algorithm on these real-world data sets and G50c data set are shown in Tables 2, 3, and 4, in which the best performance for each data set is shown in bold. Here, we fairly compare the performance of the proposed ESK algorithm only using the given labeled data (denoted as ESK_L) with four existing state-of-the-art SSL approaches and SVMs. And we also provide the classification results of the proposed ESK algorithm both using the sparse labeled data and additional constraints (denoted as ESK_LC). By applying SVMs as the final classifier, we contrast the enhanced spectral kernel for ESK with two competitive spectral kernels such as OSK and TSK. From these tables, we can observe the following:

- LapSVM usually outperforms SVMs, GRF and LGC, especially on the image data sets, since there are clear nonlinear underlying manifolds behind those data sets, and LapSVM algorithm can make use of both the labeled data and the geometrical structure information contained in data.
- TSK, OSK, and the proposed ESK algorithm are often better than SVMs, GRF, LGC, and LapSVM since the flexible kernel from spectral transforms is more data-driven than the standard kernel, e.g., Gaussian kernel. And TSK has been shown to very effective for text data sets [22].
- The proposed ESK algorithm always performs at least as good as the best of the other algorithms. On the text data sets, ESK usually outperforms all other state-of-the-art SSL algorithms. Additional pairwise constraints have been shown to consistently improve the performance of the proposed ESK algorithm on all data sets since ESK can take advantage of both the given labeled data and pairwise constraints together.
- ESK+SVMs often significantly outperforms the other two learned spectral kernel machines including OSK+SVMs and TSK+SVMs.

In the second part of these experiments, we illustrate classification accuracies using the proposed ESK algorithm on the G50c, USPS0123 and 20-News data sets with the number of randomly labeled points varying from 2 to 20, from 4 to 40, and from 4 to 40, respectively, and against a number of randomly chosen pairwise constraints with only one labeled data point in each class, as shown in Figures 2 and 3. In the figures, the abscissa denotes the number of randomly labeled data or chosen pairwise constraints (we guarantee that there is at least one labeled point in each class), and the ordinate is the classification accuracy value averaged over 50 independent runs. For comparison, the classification results of four state-of-the-art SSL algorithms and SVMs are also plotted in the corresponding figure. It can be clearly observed that the proposed ESK algorithm is very stable, that is, even when we only label a very small fraction of the data, it can still get high classification accuracies and consistently outperforms the other five algorithms with the same amount of labeled data. Moreover, as the number of sparse constraints grows, the classification accuracy of the proposed ESK algorithm can be considerably improved and is better than that of graph Laplacian regularized kernel (LRK) [24]. This confirms that the proposed kernel learning model with nuclear norm regularization can avoid the over-fitting problems of LRK.

6. CONCLUSIONS

In this paper we have proposed a novel semi-supervised learning approach with *Mixed Knowledge Information* (SSL-MKI), which can handle both labeled data and additional pairwise constraints together with unlabeled data. We first constructed a unified SSL-MKI framework that can implement both the manifold assumption and the pairwise constraint assumption. Under the above framework, we also presented a *Modified Fixed Point Continuation* (MFPC) algorithm with an eigenvalue thresholding (EVT) operator to learn the enhanced kernel matrix. Then we developed a two-stage optimization strategy and provided an efficient ESK approach. Unlike the general SSL method, the proposed ESK approach can effectively make use of the given pairwise constraints that can often be obtained with little human effort. Finally, we provided a variety of experiments to show the effectiveness of our ESK approach, from which we found that the proposed ESK algorithm outperforms the state-of-the-art SSL methods.

[5] http://archive.ics.uci.edu/ml/.
[6] http://www.kernel-machines.org/data.html.
[7] http://www.robots.ox.ac.uk/~vgg/data3.html.
[8] http://www.uk.research.att.com/facedatabase.html.
[9] http://people.csail.mit.edu/jrennie/20Newsgroups/.
[10] http://www.cs.cmu.edu/~WebKB/.

Table 2: Classification accuracies (mean and standard deviation, %) on UCI datasets.

Data	G50c	Ionosphere	Sonar	Balance	Iris	Glass
SVM	85.36±2.46	74.54±6.79	66.24±4.83	71.39±6.14	94.35±2.42	57.38±3.64
GRF	57.36±9.36	78.54±6.84	60.82±6.35	67.46±6.93	93.81±2.46	57.81±5.32
LGC	86.78±2.44	83.10±4.39	62.18±6.03	70.03±8.19	93.11±2.40	56.25±3.92
LapSVM	86.65±3.22	82.95±1.84	**68.24±1.28**	63.86±7.43	95.42±1.83	60.11±4.98
TSK	92.69±2.13	76.10±7.19	64.31±5.02	68.41±4.19	93.89±3.88	57.80±4.02
ESK_L	**94.57±0.25**	**84.72±1.52**	66.86±1.43	**71.70±4.06**	**96.10±1.36**	**60.87±3.63**
ESK_LC	94.64±0.27	85.69±1.33	67.54±1.75	72.55±3.87	96.74±1.40	62.21±3.38
OSK+SVM	91.79±3.25	82.43±3.40	64.57±1.66	67.58±8.64	93.83±4.29	58.70±5.94
TSK+SVM	93.09±4.40	86.59±3.15	69.68±2.97	72.82±4.05	94.16±1.35	61.96±8.05
ESK+SVM	95.06±0.21	87.43±2.01	69.22±2.13	73.64±5.61	96.58±1.45	63.49±4.62

Table 3: Classification accuracies (mean and standard deviation, %) on images datasets.

Data	MNIST0123	USPS0123	COIL20	Caltech4	ORL	YALE3
SVM	74.06±4.20	84.35±4.27	74.96±2.11	59.89±7.40	76.82±2.71	91.00±7.22
GRF	68.94±6.03	77.09±7.54	82.36±2.76	65.84±4.40	76.92±2.77	95.18±6.92
LGC	80.13±3.32	90.14±4.14	80.38±2.10	88.00±5.69	76.40±2.39	94.68±5.47
LapSVM	76.36±5.02	87.88±5.75	86.58±1.53	**90.81±4.98**	77.34±2.60	**96.95±0.51**
TSK	93.49±0.73	95.25±1.79	83.19±1.29	87.81±6.98	76.13±3.02	93.35±3.92
ESK_L	**95.56±2.15**	**95.82±0.93**	**87.75±1.26**	90.74±3.87	**78.91±2.31**	96.87±1.13
ESK_LC	95.90±1.86	96.45±0.74	88.66±2.45	91.03±3.62	83.44±2.27	97.35±1.22
OSK+SVM	81.35±6.72	90.57±4.11	86.52±4.51	88.51±8.23	76.34±4.22	95.14±2.69
TSK+SVM	94.08±4.23	95.79±1.26	90.00±3.93	91.96±6.16	82.22±3.63	95.37±7.75
ESK+SVM	96.17±1.65	96.92±3.08	90.39±2.67	91.58±4.70	83.51±4.82	97.60±1.64

Table 4: Classification accuracies (mean and standard deviation, %) on text datasets.

Data	20-News	Text1	WK-CL	WK-TX	WK-WT	WK-WC
SVM	58.88±8.17	76.05±5.18	73.00±0.46	71.92±0.53	79.48±0.25	75.36±0.22
GRF	71.63±1.83	77.55±9.79	73.26±0.36	72.20±0.41	79.57±0.28	75.56±0.29
LGC	73.99±2.48	74.89±9.91	73.15±0.41	71.86±0.31	79.40±0.26	75.40±0.24
LapSVM	74.36±0.18	80.72±1.51	74.62±0.80	72.50±0.52	80.18±0.23	76.25±0.28
TSK	86.07±3.24	87.91±2.93	75.28±2.62	74.98±3.99	80.39±1.92	75.79±1.70
ESK_L	**89.16±0.74**	**89.65±2.63**	**79.53±3.18**	**78.60±4.21**	**82.93±1.57**	**80.49±1.63**
ESK_LC	89.32±0.67	89.77±2.25	79.74±2.85	79.16±3.42	83.46±1.60	81.35±1.49
OSK+SVM	86.19±4.55	82.74±4.82	76.63±2.32	75.50±3.36	81.48±0.76	77.86±1.68
TSK+SVM	89.30±2.90	85.76±3.63	77.25±1.67	76.77±2.82	82.04±2.63	79.93±0.45
ESK+SVM	91.57±0.76	89.93±1.69	81.76±2.96	79.61±3.69	83.78±1.34	82.26±1.55

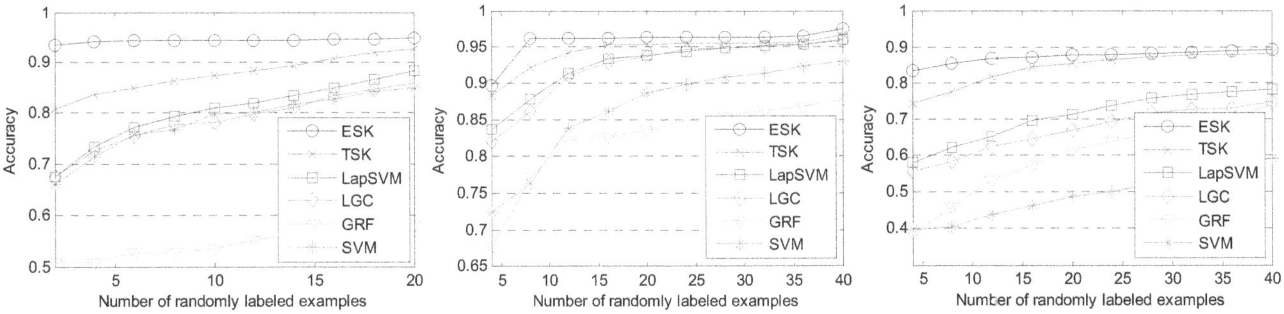

(a) The G50c dataset (b) The USPS0123 dataset (c) The 20-News dataset

Figure 2: Classification results of different algorithms against a number of randomly labeled data points.

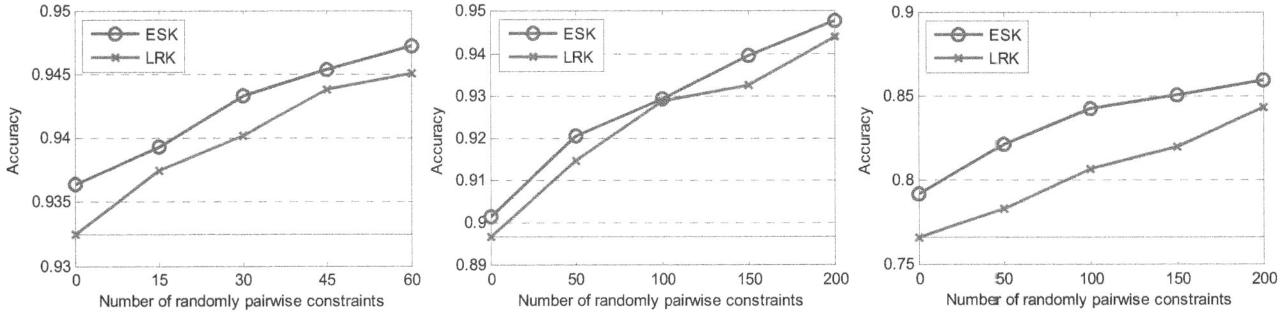

(a) The G50c dataset (b) The USPS0123 dataset (c) The 20-News dataset

Figure 3: Classification results of LRK and ESK algorithms against a number of randomly chosen pairwise constraints.

7. ACKNOWLEDGMENTS

This work is supported by the National Natural Science Foundation of China Nos. 61003198, 60970067; the Fund for Foreign Scholars in University Research and Teaching Programs (the 111 Project) No. B07048; the Program for Cheung Kong Scholars and Innovative Research Team in University No. IRT1170.

8. REFERENCES

[1] O. Chapelle, B. Schölkopf, A. Zien. Semi-Supervised Learning. The MIT Press, Cambridge, MA, 2006.

[2] X. Zhu. Semi-supervised learning literature survey. Tech. rep., Computer Sciences, University of Wisconsin-Madison, 2008.

[3] X. Zhu, Z. Ghahramani, J. Lafferty. Semi-supervised learning using Gaussian fields and harmonic functions. In *ICML*, pages 912–919, 2003.

[4] D. Zhou, O. Bousquet, T. Lal, J. Weston, B. Schölkopf. Learning with local and global consistency. In *NIPS*, pages 321–328, 2004.

[5] M. Belkin, P. Niyogi, V. Sindhwani. Manifold regularization: A geometric framework for learning from labeled and unlabeled examples. *J. Mach. Learn. Res.*, 7:2399–2434, 2006.

[6] S. Melacci, M. Belkin. Laplacian support vector machines trained in the primal. *J. Mach. Learn. Res.*, 12:1149–1184, 2011.

[7] Z. Li, J. Liu, X. Tang. Pairwise constraint propagation by semidefinite programming for semi-supervised classification. In *ICML*, pages 576–583, 2008.

[8] R. Yan, J. Zhang, J. Yang, A. Hauptmann. A discriminative learning framework with pairwise constraints for video object classification. *IEEE Trans. Pattern Anal. Mach. Intell.*, 28(4):578–593, 2006.

[9] K. Wagstaff, C. Cardie. Clustering with instance-level constraints. In *ICML*, pages 1103–1110, 2000.

[10] D. Klein, S. Kamvar, C. Manning. From instance-level constraints to space-level constraints: making the most of prior knowledge in data clustering. In *ICML*, pages 307–314, 2002.

[11] S. Basu, M. Bilenko, R. Mooney. A probabilistic framework for semi-supervised clustering. In *KDD*, pages 59–68, 2004.

[12] B. Kulis, S. Basu, I. Dhillon, R. Mooney. Semi-supervised graph clustering: A kernel approach. In *ICML*, pages 457–464, 2005.

[13] E. Xing, A. Ng, M. Jordan, S. Russell. Distance metric learning, with application to clustering with side-information. In *NIPS*, pages 505–512, 2003.

[14] M. Bilenko, S. Basu, R. Mooney. Integrating constraints and metric learning in semi-supervised clustering. In *ICML*, pages 81–88, 2004.

[15] J. Davis, B. Kulis, P. Jain, S. Sra, I. S. Dhillon. Information theoretic metric learning. In *ICML*, pages 209–216, 2007.

[16] T. Joachims. Transductive inference for text classification using support vector machines. In *ICML*, pages 200–209, 1999.

[17] O. Chapelle, A. Zien. Semi-supervised classification by low density separation. In *AISTATS*, pages 57–64, 2005.

[18] J. Zhuang, I. Tsang, S.C.H. Hoi. A family of simple non-parametric kernel learning algorithms. *J. Mach. Learn. Res.*, 12:1313–1347, 2011.

[19] X. Zhu, J. S. Kandola, Z. Ghahramani, J. D. Lafferty. Nonparametric transforms of graph kernels for semi-supervised learning. In *NIPS*, pages 1641–1648, 2005.

[20] S. Hoi, M. Lyu, E. Chang. Learning the unified kernel machines for classification. In *KDD*, pages 187–196, 2006.

[21] S. Hoi, R. Jin, M. Lyu. Learning nonparametric kernel matrices from pairwise constraints. In *ICML*, pages 361–368, 2007.

[22] W. Liu, B. Qian, J. Cui, J. Liu. Spectral kernel learning for semi-supervised classification. In *IJCAI*, pages 1150–1155, 2009.

[23] E. Hu, S. Chen, D. Zhang, X. Yin. Semisupervised kernel matrix learning by kernel propagation. *IEEE Trans. Neural Netw.*, 21(11):1831–1841, 2010.

[24] X. -M. Wu, A. So, Z. Li, S. Li. Fast graph Laplacian regularized kernel learning via semidefinite-quadratic-linear programming. In *NIPS*, pages 1964–1972, 2009.

[25] L. Zelnik-Manor, P. Perona. Self-tuning spectral clustering. In *NIPS*, pages 1601–1608, 2004.

[26] F. Wang, C. Zhang. Label propagation through linear neighborhoods. *IEEE Trans. Knowl. Data Eng.*, 20(1):55–67, 2008.

[27] J. Cai, E. J. Candès, Z. Shen. A singular value thresholding algorithm for matrix completion. *SIAM J. Optim.*, 20(4):1956–1982, 2010.

[28] S. Ma, D. Goldfarb, L. Chen. Fixed point and Bregman iterative methods for matrix rank minimization. *Math. Program.*, 128(1):321–353, 2011.

[29] Z. Lin, M. Chen, L. Wu. The augmented Lagrange multiplier method for exact recovery of corrupted low-rank matrices. *Math. Program.*, submitted, 2009.

[30] E. J. Candès, B. Recht. Exact matrix completion via convex optimization. *Found. Comput. Math.*, 9(6):717–772, 2009.

[31] K. Q. Weinberger, F. Sha, Q. Zhu, L. K. Saul. Graph Laplacian regularization for large-scale semidefinite programming. In *NIPS*, pages 1489–1496, 2007.

[32] F. Shang, Y. Liu, F. Wang. Learning spectral embedding for semisupervised clustering. In *ICDM*, pages 597–606, 2011.

[33] Z. Liu, L. Vandenberghe. Interior-point method for nuclear norm approximation with application to system identification. *SIAM J. Matrix Anal. Appl.*, 31(3):1235–1256, 2010.

[34] Y. Ni, J. Sun, X. Yuan, S. Yan, L. Cheong. Robust low-rank subspace segmentation with semidefinite guarantees. In *ICDM*, pages 1179–1188, 2010.

[35] A. B. Goldberg, X. Zhu, B. Recht, J. Xu, R. Nowak. Transduction with matrix completion: three birds with one stone. In *NIPS*, 2010.

[36] G. Watson. Characterization of the subdifferential of some matrix norms. *Linear Algebra Appl.*, 170:33–45, 1992.

[37] Y. Ma, L. Zhi. The minimum-rank gram matrix completion via modified fixed point continuation method. In *ISSAC*, pages 241–248, 2011.

[38] J. Barzilai, J. Borwein. Two-point step size gradient methods. *IMA J. Numer. Anal.*, 8:141–148, 1988.

[39] G. H. Golub, C. F. V. Loan. Matrix computations. Third edition, Johns Hopkins University Press, 1996.

[40] C. Chang, C. Lin. LIBSVM: A library for support vector machines, 2001. Available at http://www.csie.ntu.edu.tw/~cjlin/libsvm.

[41] Y. LeCun, C. Cortes. The MNIST database of handwritten digits, 2009. Available: http://yann.lecun.com/exdb/mnist/.

[42] S.A. Nene, S.K. Nayar, J. Murase. Columbia object image library (COIL-20). Tech. rep., CUCS-005-96, Columbia Univ., 1996.

[43] A.S. Georghiades, P.N. Belhumeur, D.J. Kriegman. From few to many: illumination cone models for face recognition under variable lighting and pose. *IEEE Trans. Pattern Anal. Mach. Intell.*, 23(6):643–660, 2001.

Batch Mode Active Sampling based on Marginal Probability Distribution Matching

Rita Chattopadhyay [1], Zheng Wang [1,2], Wei Fan [3],
Ian Davidson [4], Sethuraman Panchanathan [1], Jieping Ye [1,2]
[1]Computer Science and Engineering, Arizona State University, AZ 85287
[2]Center for Evolutionary Medicine and Informatics, The Biodesign Institute, Arizona State University, AZ 85287
[3]IBM T.J. Watson Research Center, Hawthorne, NY 10532
[4]Department of Computer Science, University of California, Davis, CA 95616

ABSTRACT

Active Learning is a machine learning and data mining technique that selects the most informative samples for labeling and uses them as training data; it is especially useful when there are large amount of unlabeled data and labeling them is expensive. Recently, batch-mode active learning, where a set of samples are selected concurrently for labeling, based on their collective merit, has attracted a lot of attention. The objective of batch-mode active learning is to select a set of informative samples so that a classifier learned on these samples has good generalization performance on the unlabeled data. Most of the existing batch-mode active learning methodologies try to achieve this by selecting samples based on varied criteria. In this paper we propose a novel criterion which achieves good generalization performance of a classifier by specifically selecting a set of query samples that minimizes the difference in distribution between the labeled and the unlabeled data, after annotation. We explicitly measure this difference based on all candidate subsets of the unlabeled data and select the best subset. The proposed objective is an NP-hard integer programming optimization problem. We provide two optimization techniques to solve this problem. In the first one, the problem is transformed into a convex quadratic programming problem and in the second method the problem is transformed into a linear programming problem. Our empirical studies using publicly available UCI datasets and a biomedical image dataset demonstrate the effectiveness of the proposed approach in comparison with the state-of-the-art batch-mode active learning methods. We also present two extensions of the proposed approach, which incorporate uncertainty of the predicted labels of the unlabeled data and transfer learning in the proposed formulation. Our empirical studies on UCI datasets show that incorporation of uncertainty information improves performance at later iterations while our studies on 20 Newsgroups dataset show that transfer learning improves the performance of the classifier during initial iterations.

KDD'12, August 12–16, 2012, Beijing, China.

Categories and Subject Descriptors

H.2.8 [**Database Management**]: Database Applications - Data Mining

General Terms

Algorithm

Keywords

Active learning, marginal probability distribution, Maximum Mean Discrepancy

1. INTRODUCTION

Classification has been an active research topic in data mining and machine learning. The availability of a large amount of digital data in recent years, has greatly expanded the opportunities of automated data classification using data mining and machine learning techniques. One of the prerequisites for any data classification framework is the availability of labeled examples. Annotating large quantities of data for developing automated classifiers is a time consuming and expensive process. Hence there is a need to select an optimal set of instances from the pool of unlabeled data for labeling, such that a classifier learned on the selected instances performs well on the unlabeled data and also on unseen data belonging to the same distribution. Randomly selecting a set of unlabeled instances may result in selection of redundant and non-informative instances. *Active learning* methodologies enable selection of a set of most informative unlabeled instances from enormous amount of unlabeled data for manual labeling, with the intention of developing a good classifier with low generalization error. Specifically, the goal of active learning is to label as little data as possible, to achieve a certain classification performance, thus saving considerable annotation cost for training a good learner.

Active learning methodologies iteratively select the most informative data. Informativeness of a data sample or a set of data samples is measured by their potentiality in increasing the performance of a classifier, once their label is known [32]. Many researchers have addressed the active learning problem in various ways [23]. Most have focused on selecting a single most informative unlabeled instance to query each time. The most popular approaches include query-by-committee [24, 7, 9] where a number of distinct classification models are generated and an instance having the most disagreement among the classification models in predicting the label is selected for querying. Another popular approach is querying an instance with maximum uncertainty of labeling measured by the distance from the classification boundary [6, 22, 28] or by the entropy in the predicted label [17, 16].

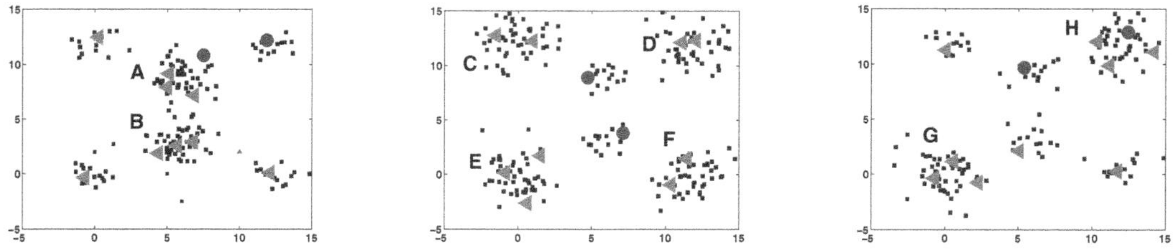

(a) (b) (c)

Figure 1: Three toy data sets with different data distributions (dark green squares) and corresponding selected sets of query data points (red triangles) based on the proposed algorithm, selected in 3 iterations in batches of 3 data points. The two data points represented by blue circles are randomly selected initially available labeled data points (figures best viewed in color).

Most single instance selection methods require to retrain the classifier with each single instance being labeled. The retraining process between queries can make the process very slow. Furthermore, if a parallel labeling system is available, e.g., multiple annotators working parallely, single instance selection would not be able to make the effective use of the resources. A batch-mode active learning strategy, that selects multiple instances each time is more appropriate under these circumstances. However, the challenge in batch-mode active learning is the formulation of the selection criteria for multiple instance selection. Using a single instance selection strategy to select a batch of queries in each iteration by ranking them based on their individual merit may not give good results, as this strategy fails to take into account the information overlap between multiple instances. Hence principles for batch-mode active learning to select a set of instances simultaneously based on their collective merit, need to be developed to address the multi-instance selection *specifically*.

The batch-mode active learning methods are particularly suitable for large scale applications where the data has high redundancy such as text classifications [11], content based image retrieval [14] and image recognition [13] due to high frame rate. The greatest challenge in selecting a set of instances simultaneously is two fold. The first challenge lies in the formulation of a right objective which will be optimized to select the most informative set of samples and the second challenge is concerned with the computational complexity of the NP hard combinatorial integer programming problem for obtaining a good local solution.

Recently, several sophisticated batch-mode active learning methods based on optimizing an information measure have been proposed for classification. Guo [11] selected a batch of query samples based on maximum mutual information with the unlabeled set of data, while Hoi et al. [13] applied Fisher information matrix to select a set of informative instances. Yu et al. [31] selected a set of instances closest to the basis vectors that approximate the set of unlabeled data and Guo and Schuurmans [12] proposed a discriminative approach.

In this paper, we propose a novel batch-mode active learning approach that selects a batch of query instances such that the distribution represented by the selected query set and the available labeled data is closest to the distribution represented by the unlabeled data. The motivation behind this approach is to ensure that a classifier learned by minimizing loss on the selected set of labeled data has good generalization capabilities on the unlabeled data and also on the unseen data coming from the same distribution. In other words, in order to learn a classifier with a budgeted number of labeled data we select a set of samples S from the unlabeled set of data, denoted by U, such that the probability distributions represented by $L \cup S$ and $U \backslash S$, where L is the set of available labeled data, are similar to each other.

We measure the difference in the probability distribution between the two sets of data using the Maximum Mean Discrepancy (MMD) proposed by Borgwardt et al [4, 1, 26]. Maximum Mean Discrepancy is a statistical test based on the fact that two distributions are different if and only if there exists at least one function in a characteristic RKHS [26] having different expectations on the two distributions. MMD has been proven to be very accurate in finding samples that were generated from the same distribution and outperforms its best competitors. MMD has been widely and successfully used in various classification tasks to ensure similarity in distribution between training and test data, specifically in the context of *transfer learning* applications [15, 20]. We use this measure in an optimization formulation to select a subset S out of all candidate subsets, based on minimum distribution difference between $L \cup S$ and $U \backslash S$. To the best of our knowledge, this is the first work that uses MMD in the active learning context.

Figure 1 shows the data points selected by the proposed method (red triangles) under three different distributions of unlabeled data (dark green squares). We created six dense regions of two different densities and kept a budget of nine query points which were selected in batches of three, in three iterations. We started with two randomly selected data samples (blue circles). We observe that the proposed method selects points from every dense region. It is also interesting to note that the number of points that get selected from each dense region is approximately proportional to the density of the region i.e., comparatively more data samples get selected from denser regions, A, B [Figure1 (a)], C, D, E, F [Figure1 (b)], and G, H [Figure1 (c)], thus preserving the distribution of the unlabeled data. We also observe that since available labeled data is considered at every iteration, hence diversity with respect to available data is maintained in query selection, as shown in Figures 1 (b) where no query data gets selected from the small regions in the center as an instance from those regions is already available in the initial labeled set. More details about the properties of query points are provided in Section 2.2. We also observe that the proposed approach decreases MMD monotonically as more data samples are selected from the unlabeled data and the decrease in MMD value corresponded to the increase in classification accuracy on the test set, discussed in detail in Section 4.

The subset selection problem is an NP-hard combinatorial integer programming problem. The proposed formulation is an integer quadratic programming problem. We show that the quadratic formulation can be reformulated as an integer linear programming problem. We then provide two optimization techniques to solve this problem. In the first method, we solve a continuous quadratic programming problem (by relaxing the integer constraint) on a convex function, providing a global solution. This is unlike most of the state-of-the art batch-mode active learning methods which provide a local solution following a gradient descent method [12, 11] or a greedy algorithm [13, 5, 30]. In the second method, we solve a continuous integer programming problem.

We tested our method on publicly available UCI[1] datasets and on a biomedical image dataset, Fly-FISH [18], consisting of images representing different developmental stages in the life cycle of *Drosophila*. The manual annotation of developmental stages of the images of *Drosophila* is an expensive task. Hence active selection of an optimal number of images is crucial for the development of an automatic classifier. The empirical results on UCI and Fly-FISH datasets show that the proposed batch-mode active learning approach achieves superior or comparable performance to the state-of-the-art batch-mode active learning methods. The proposed method is also significantly time efficient compared to the state-of-the-art batch-mode active learning methods.

We further extend the proposed method by incorporating uncertainty of the predicted labels of the unlabeled data and transfer learning in the proposed formulation. Our empirical studies on UCI datasets show that incorporation of uncertainty information improves performance at later iterations while our studies on publicly available 20 Newsgroups dataset[2] show that transfer learning improves the performance of the classifier during initial iterations. The source codes along with synthetic data are available online (www.public.asu.edu/~rchattop/code/MP-AL).

The remainder of the paper is organized as follows. Section 2 introduces the proposed batch-mode active learning framework. Section 3 compares the proposed method with the state-of-the-art active learning methods. Empirical studies are presented in Section 4. We present two extensions of the proposed approach in Section 5, and Section 6 concludes this paper.

2. PROPOSED FRAMEWORK

The key hypothesis in active learning is that if the learning algorithm is allowed to choose the data from which it learns, it will perform better even with less annotation [23]. Given a parametric classification model, the learning algorithms often learn the parameters θ by maximizing the joint probability $P(X,Y|\theta) = P(X|\theta)$ $P(Y|X,\theta)$ where X and Y are represented empirically by the training data $X_{tr} = \{x_1, x_2, \cdots, x_n\}$ and their corresponding labels $Y_{tr} = \{y_1, y_2, \cdots, y_n\}$ and $P(X)$ and $P(Y|X)$ denote the marginal and conditional probability distribution of X and Y respectively. Traditional data mining and machine learning algorithms are based on the assumption that the training data (X_{tr}, Y_{tr}) represents the true underlying distributions of X and Y and hence a model learned on this data works well for the test data (X_{tst}, Y_{tst}) which is also drawn i.i.d. from the same distribution. When the distributions on the training and test set are different the classification model learned on the training data performs poorly on the test data due to model mismatch.

The proposed active learning method addresses this issue by iteratively selecting a set of query instances from the unlabeled data such that the distribution represented by the queried and labeled data (X_{tr}, Y_{tr}), is similar to the probability distribution of the unlabeled data set. In other words, in order to learn a classifier with a budgeted number of labeled data, the proposed method iteratively selects a set of samples S from the unlabeled set of data, denoted by U, such that the joint probability distributions $P(X,Y)$ represented by $X_{tr} = L \cup S$ and $X_{tst} = U \backslash S$, where L is set of available labeled data, are similar to each other. Since the labeling function or the conditional probability $P(Y|X)$ remains the same for both S and $U \backslash S$ as they are drawn from the same underlying distribution, the problem reduces to selecting S such that the marginal probability $P_{S \cup L}(X)$ is similar to $P_{U \backslash S}(X)$. In this paper, we measure the difference in the marginal probability distribution between the two sets empirically using Maximum Mean Discrepancy (MMD) [4, 1, 26]. The difference between the empirical means of two distributions after mapping onto a reproducing kernel Hilbert space, called Maximum Mean Discrepancy, has been shown to be an effective measure of the difference in their marginal probability distributions. We review the basics of MMD below.

2.1 Maximum Mean Discrepancy (MMD)

Let $X = \{x_1, \cdots, x_m\}$ and $Z = \{z_1, \cdots, z_n\}$ be two sets of samples drawn randomly from a target population. Let p and q be the probability distributions defined on the basis of sample sets X and Z respectively. The Maximum Mean Discrepancy (MMD) proposed by Borgwardt et al [4, 1, 26] is a statistical tool that provides a method for testing whether two distributions p and q from which X and Z have been drawn respectively are similar or not.

The principal underlying the Maximum Mean Discrepancy is to find a function that assumes different expectations on two different distributions so that when evaluated empirically on samples drawn from the different distributions it would tell us whether the distributions are similar or not. Let $\mathcal{F}$ be a class of functions $f : \mathcal{X} \to \mathcal{R}$ and let X, Z, p, q be defined as above. Then the Maximum Mean Discrepancy and its empirical estimate are defined as:

$$\text{MMD}[\mathcal{F}, p, q] := \sup_{f \in \mathcal{F}} \left(E_p[f(x)] - E_q[f(z)]\right). \quad (1)$$

$$\text{MMD}[\mathcal{F}, X, Z] := \sup_{f \in \mathcal{F}} \left(\frac{1}{m}\sum_{i=1}^{m} f(x_i) - \frac{1}{n}\sum_{i=1}^{n} f(z_i)\right) \quad (2)$$

Intuitively if $\mathcal{F}$ is 'rich enough', $\text{MMD}[\mathcal{F}, X, Z]$ will vanish if and only if $p = q$. A class of functions for which MMD may easily be computed, while retaining the ability to detect all discrepancies between p and q without making any simplifying assumptions is the complete inner product space $\mathcal{H}$ (i.e., a reproducing kernel Hilbert space (RKHS) [27]) of functions $f : \mathcal{X} \to \mathcal{R}$, where $\mathcal{X}$ is a nonempty compact set and for all $x \in \mathcal{X}$, the linear point evaluation functional mapping $f \to f(x)$ exists and is continuous. In this case, $f(x)$ can be expressed as an *inner product* via

$$f(x) = \langle \phi(x), f \rangle_{\mathcal{H}}. \quad (3)$$

where $\phi : \mathcal{X} \to \mathcal{H}$ is known as the feature space map from $\mathcal{X}$ to $\mathcal{H}$ [4]. When $\mathcal{F}$ is the unit ball in a characteristic RKHS [26], MMD is defined as the difference between the means of two distributions after mapping onto the characteristic RKHS. An empirical estimate of MMD is then obtained as follows:

$$\text{MMD}[\phi, X, Z] := \left\| \frac{1}{m}\sum_{i=1}^{m} \Phi(x_i) - \frac{1}{n}\sum_{i=1}^{n} \Phi(z_i) \right\|_{\mathcal{H}}^2. \quad (4)$$

For more details about Maximum Mean Discrepancy, the related theoretical proofs and comparison with related methods, interested readers may refer to [4, 1, 26].

2.2 Proposed Batch Mode Active Sampling

The proposed batch-mode active sampling method, referred to as *Marginal Probability based Active Learning* (MP-AL) iteratively selects batches of query instances which represent best the distribution of the unlabeled instances so that a classifier learned by minimizing risk on the queried data after labeling, has good generalization performance on the unlabeled data set and on future unseen data that comes from the same distribution. We formulate the problem as an integer quadratic programming problem which can be reformulated as an equivalent integer linear programming problem.

[1] Available at http://www.ics.uci.edu/mlearn/MLRepository.html

[2] Available at http://www.ai.mit.edu/~jrennie/20Newsgroups/

The proposed framework uses MMD to measure the distribution difference between two sets of samples. Let us assume that we have n_u instances of unlabeled data U and n_l instances of labeled data L and we would like to select a batch S of b instances such that the distribution of $L \cup S$ is similar to the distribution of $U \backslash S$. In that case, the MMD between the sets $L \cup S$ and $U \backslash S$ defined by $f(S)$, can be computed using the expression in Equation (4), as follows:

$$f(S) = \left\| \frac{1}{n_l + b} \sum_{j \in L \cup S} \Phi(x_j) - \frac{1}{n_u - b} \sum_{i \in U \backslash S} \Phi(x_i) \right\|_{\mathcal{H}}^2 . \quad (5)$$

Since we want to select a set S that minimizes the mismatch between $L \cup S$ and $U \backslash S$ we propose to select a subset S of U that minimizes $f(S)$. Next we define a binary vector α of size n_u where each entry α_i indicates whether the data $x_i \in U$ is selected or not. If a point is selected, the corresponding entry α_i is 1 else 0. Thus the minimization problem reduces to finding α that minimizes the cost function $f(S)$:

$$\min_{\alpha:\alpha_i \in \{0,1\}, \alpha^T \mathbf{1} = b} \left\| \frac{1}{n_l + b} \left(\sum_{j \in L} \Phi(x_j) + \sum_{i \in U} \alpha_i \Phi(x_i) \right) - \frac{1}{n_u - b} \sum_{i \in U} (1 - \alpha_i) \Phi(x_i) \right\|_{\mathcal{H}}^2 . \quad (6)$$

where $\mathbf{1}$ is a vector of the same dimension as α with all entries 1 and symbol T is used to represent the matrix or vector *transpose* operation. Evidently, the cost function in Equation (6) is an alternative (equivalent) representation of the cost function $f(S)$ in Equation (5). The first term denotes the mean of the mapped features of the labeled and selected points. Note that if a point x_i is not selected in the current set then α_i will be 0 and this term would not get added in the summation. The second term is mean of the mapped features of the unlabeled data set minus the selected query set. The first constraint ensures that each entry in α is either 0 or 1 and the second constraint ensures that exactly b entries of α are 1, meaning exactly b instances are selected from the unlabeled data set, where b is specified a priori by the user. The above formulation can be represented as:

$$\min_{\alpha:\alpha_i \in \{0,1\}, \alpha^T \mathbf{1} = b} \frac{1}{2} \alpha^T K_1 \alpha - k_2^T \alpha + k_3^T \alpha + \text{const.} \quad (7)$$

The various terms in the above expression are given as follows. We denote G as the $(n_u + n_l) * (n_u + n_l)$ kernel Gram matrix over the unlabeled data U and labeled data L, arranged in order, using a kernel function K such that $G(i,j) = K(x_i, x_j)$. Then, $K_1 = G(1 : n_u, 1 : n_u)$, $k_2(i) = \frac{n_l + b}{n_l + n_u} \sum_{j=1}^{n_u} K_1(i,j)$, and $k_3(i) = \frac{n_u - b}{n_l + n_u} \sum_{j=1}^{n_l} G(i, n_u + j)$.

Based on the above expressions, we can draw the following observations regarding the properties of the selected query set:

- The first term ensures that the selected query set has minimum similarity within itself, avoiding *redundancy* in the selected set.
- The second term enforces the selected examples to be similar to the unselected ones, ensuring *representativeness*.
- The third term implies the examples with less similarity with already labeled data are more likely to be selected ensuring *diversity* in the selected set.

Thus the proposed method selects examples which meet all the desirable properties for batch mode active learning. The proposed method can be easily extended to add any other evaluation criteria (M) by adding a corresponding linear term $M^T \alpha$, while still maintaining the quadratic form (see Section 5 for more details). Also the proposed method does not depend on the availability of labeled data to initiate the process of selecting a query set, in which case $n_l = 0$, and the third term $k_3^T \alpha$ in Equation (7) vanishes.

The above optimization formulation is an integer quadratic programming problem. Next, we show that it can be reformulated as an equivalent integer linear programming (ILP) problem.

2.3 Reformulation as an ILP Problem

Due to the binary constraint $\alpha_i \in \{0,1\}, \forall i$, the linear terms in the objective defined in Equation (7) can be absorbed into the quadratic term by subtracting k_2 and adding k_3 terms to the diagonal entries of matrix K_1, forming a D matrix given by: $D(i,j) = K_1(i,j) - k_2(i) + k_3(i)$ for $i = j$ and $D(i,j) = K_1(i,j)$ otherwise. We can thus rewrite the optimization problem in (7) as:

$$\min_{\alpha:\alpha_i \in \{0,1\}, \alpha^T \mathbf{1} = b} \alpha^T D \alpha. \quad (8)$$

We next introduce a binary matrix $Z = (z_{ij})$ with $z_{ij} = \alpha_i \alpha_j$. Thus the optimization in Equation (8) becomes:

$$\begin{aligned} \min_{\alpha, Z} \quad & \sum_{i,j} d_{ij} z_{ij} \\ \text{s.t.} \quad & z_{ij} = \alpha_i \alpha_j, \quad \alpha_i \in \{0,1\} \; \forall i,j, \quad \alpha^T \mathbf{1} = b. \end{aligned} \quad (9)$$

The quadratic equality constraint $z_{ij} = \alpha_i \alpha_j$ makes the problem difficult to solve. We show that this can be represented by a set of linear inequalities. Since d_{ij} can have both negative and positive values, we rewrite the quadratic constraints as follows:

$$\begin{aligned} \min_{\alpha, Z} \quad & \sum_{i,j} d_{ij} z_{ij} \\ \text{s.t.} \quad & -\alpha_i - \alpha_j + 2 z_{ij} \leq 0 \text{ for } d_{ij} < 0 \\ & \alpha_i + \alpha_j - z_{ij} \leq 1 \quad \text{for } d_{ij} \geq 0 \\ & \alpha_i \in \{0,1\} \; \forall i,j, \quad \alpha^T \mathbf{1} = b. \end{aligned} \quad (10)$$

The first constraint ensures that z_{ij} equals zero if the value of α_i or α_j (or both) is zero. If α_i and α_j both equal to one, the value of z_{ij} is free to be either 0 or 1; however, the minimization forces the value of z_{ij} to be 1 since d_{ij} is negative. Similarly, we derive the second constraint when d_{ij} is positive. The second constraint makes the value of z_{ij} equals to 1 if α_i and α_j both equal to one. If any of the α_i and α_j equals zero, then the value of z_{ij} is free to be either 0 or 1; nevertheless, at optimality, z_{ij} must equal 0 since d_{ij} has positive contribution to the objective, which is a minimization of the cost function. Consequently, the relation between z_{ij} and the pair α_i and α_j at optimality is as follows: $z_{i,j} = 1$, if and only if $\alpha_i = 1$ and $\alpha_j = 1$. Thus, the formulation in Equation (10) is equivalent to the original integer quadratic programming problem.

Next, we present two algorithms to solve the integer quadratic and integer linear optimization problems defined in Equation (7) and Equation (10) respectively as quadratic programming (QP) and linear programming (LP) problems by relaxing the binary constraints.

2.4 Quadratic Programming (QP) Problem

The binary constraint on α_i makes the integer quadratic problem defined in Equation (7) NP-hard. A common strategy is to relax the constraints to make it a continuous optimization problem, which can be solved in polynomial time:

$$\min_{\alpha:0 \leq \alpha_i \leq 1, \alpha^T \mathbf{1} = b} \frac{1}{2} \alpha^T K_1 \alpha - k_2^T \alpha + k_3^T \alpha. \quad (11)$$

The minimization problem in (11) is a standard quadratic problem (QP) and can be solved efficiently by applying many existing solvers. We used the 'quadprog' function in MATLAB to solve this QP problem. The overall algorithm for selecting the query set S at any iteration is given in Algorithm 1.

2.5 Linear Programming (LP) Problem

We relax the integral constraint and obtain a linear program (LP) formulation which is a relaxation of the ILP formulation in (10) as follows:

$$\begin{aligned} \min_{\alpha,Z} \quad & \sum_{i,j} d_{ij} z_{ij} \\ \text{s.t.} \quad & -\alpha_i - \alpha_j + 2z_{ij} \leq 0 \text{ for } d_{ij} < 0 \\ & \alpha_i + \alpha_j - z_{ij} \leq 1 \quad \text{for } d_{ij} \geq 0 \\ & \alpha_i, z_{ij} \in [0,1] \ \forall i,j, \quad \alpha^T \mathbf{1} = b. \end{aligned} \tag{12}$$

The LP formulation can be further simplified by incorporating the first constraint into the objective function. Since this is a minimization problem when $d_{ij} < 0$, at optimality, $z_{ij} = \frac{\alpha_i + \alpha_j}{2}$ following the first equality constraint. On the other hand, the second equality constraint for $d_{ij} \geq 0$, may not hold at optimality. Since removing or relaxing a constraint of a minimization program does not reduce the optimal value, the formulation in Equation (12) can be reformulated as follows:

$$\begin{aligned} \min_{\alpha,Z} \quad & \frac{1}{2} \sum_{d_{ij}<0} d_{ij}(\alpha_i + \alpha_j) + \sum_{d_{ij}\geq 0} d_{ij} z_{ij} \\ \text{s.t.} \quad & \alpha_i + \alpha_j - z_{ij} \leq 1 \text{ for } d_{ij} \geq 0 \\ & z_{ij} \in [0,1] \text{ for } d_{ij} \geq 0 \\ & \alpha_i \in [0,1] \ \forall i,j, \quad \alpha^T \mathbf{1} = b. \end{aligned} \tag{13}$$

The problem in Equation (13) is a standard linear programming problem, and can be solved efficiently using any standard LP solver. Since the Hessian matrix K_1 in Equation (7) is a kernel Gram matrix which is positive semi-definite hence both formulations are convex. We used CVX [10] to solve the LP problem. The overall algorithm for selecting the query set S at any iteration using the LP formulation is given in Algorithm 1.

Algorithm 1 MP-AL

1: **Input:** L: set of labeled instances; U: set of unlabeled instances; b: batch size;
2: **Output:** S: query set;
3: Compute K_1, k_2 and k_3 as explained in Section 2.2.
4: **if** QP Problem **then**
5:     Compute α by solving (11).
6: **end if**
7: **if** LP Problem **then**
8:     Form D matrix as explained in Section 2.3.
9:     Compute α by solving (13).
10: **end if**
11: Sort U in descending order of α and select top b instances as S.
12: Update sets L and U: $L \to L \cup S$, $U \to U \backslash S$.

3. COMPARISON WITH RELATED WORK

We compared the performance of the proposed method with state-of-the-art batch-mode active learning methods including *Matrix* [11], *Disc* [12] and *Fisher* [13] which selected a set of instances that are together maximally informative, similar to the proposed approach. We also compared our approach with state-of-the-art batch-mode active learning methods which selected a set of instances in each iteration based on their individual merits such as *svmD* [5] and a multiple criteria based instance selection method [30], referred to in this paper as *MCS* for convenience. Besides, we also compared our method to one transductive experimental design method [31], referred to as *Design*, which is based on regression models. A brief review of each of these methods is presented below.

The *Disc* method selects a set of instances by maximizing the likelihood of labeled and selected instances, while minimizing the uncertainty of unlabeled instances, based on a classifier learned on the labeled and selected instances. The problem formulation is non-convex and a local solution is obtained using the gradient descent method. The *Matrix* method selects a batch of queries S in each iteration by maximizing a mutual information criterion between the selected and labeled instances ($L' = L \cup S$) and unlabeled instances ($U' = U \backslash S$) as follows:

$$S^* = \arg \max_{|S|=b, S\subseteq U} ln|\Sigma_{L'L'}| + ln|\Sigma_{U'U'}|. \tag{14}$$

where $\Sigma_{U'U'}$ and $\Sigma_{L'L'}$ are covariance matrices of U' and L' computed using Gaussian kernel. Similar to the *Disc* method, this formulation is non-convex and a local solution is obtained using the gradient descent method. Similar to proposed approach, this method does not depend on any classifier model. The *Fisher* [13] method selects samples using Fisher information as the criterion. It selects a set of instances such that the difference in Fisher information between the selected set and unlabeled examples is minimum. The formulation is solved using a greedy algorithm.

The *svmD* method [5] selects a set of uncertain and diverse instances for query by ranking each instance in the unlabeled data based on their distance from the margin and maximum angle with the already labeled samples. The angle between two samples is measured using cosine of the angles between the hyperplanes corresponding to the samples. Similar to *svmD*, *MCS* [30] evaluates instances based on their individual merit using multi-criteria, but added a third term to measure the representativeness of each unlabeled data based on average cosine similarity with the unlabeled data. The proposed *MP-AL* method based on distribution matching, addresses both diversity and representativeness, besides addressing redundancy as well. It is also different from these two selection methods as it selects a batch of instances simultaneously which are together maximally informative based on their collective merit.

The *Design* method [31] proposes an experimental design in a *transductive* setting, where the focus is on the predictive performance on known test data. This method selects a set of instances closest to the basis vectors that approximate the set of unlabeled data. This method does not consider already labeled data, when selecting the next set of query, unlike the proposed method.

4. EXPERIMENTS AND RESULTS

Datasets. We evaluated the empirical performance of the proposed *MP-AL* algorithm using eight datasets from the UCI machine learning repository (both binary and multi-class), and a biological image dataset (Fly-FISH). The biological image dataset consists of 1016 images of 7 developmental stages of *Drosophila*, commonly known as fruit-fly. Each stage forms a class. Each image is represented by 3850 textural features that are extracted using Gabor filters [19].

Competing Methods. We compared the performance of the proposed approach with state-of-the-art batch-mode active learning methods which selected a set of instances based on their collective merit including *Matrix* [11], *Fisher* [13] and *Disc* [12]. We also compared our method with state-of-the-art batch-mode active learning methods which selected a set of instances based on their individual merit such as *svmD* [5] and *MCS* [30], besides comparing to one transductive experimental design method, referred to as

Design [31]. We used the sequential design code downloaded from the authors' webpage and denote this method here as *Design*(s), that selects a set of instances sequentially based on their individual merits. A detailed description of each of these methods is provided in Section 3. Comparative performance of a random instance selection algorithm denoted as *Rand*, is also presented for reference.

Experimental Setup. We randomly divided each dataset into two sets. Batch selection based on active learning methodologies was performed on one set referred to as unlabeled set (65%) and the effectiveness of the selection methodologies was measured based on classification accuracy on the other unseen fixed set (35%) referred to as the test set. Table 2 summarizes the sizes of each of the datasets used. We subsampled some of the datasets due to the computational complexity of the several competing methods. We consider a hard case of active learning, where we start with two randomly selected labeled instances per class. All the algorithms start with the same initial labeled set, unlabeled set and test set. For a fixed batch size b, each algorithm repeatedly selected b instances for labeling at each iteration and evaluated the performance of a classifier learned on labeled instances, on the fixed test set. The size of b was fixed at 10 for all datasets except for Vehicles and Iris, where it was fixed at 5 due to their small sizes. The experiments were repeated 10 times and the average results are reported.

We compared the QP and LP formulations by the values of the objective function in Equation (7) and the classification accuracies obtained by the selected query set on the fixed test set. We observed that the values of the objective function obtained by LP were slightly lower than QP, though accuracies obtained were similar. We also noted that the execution time of QP was generally lower than LP. This can be attributed to the larger number of constraints in LP and the specific software package used. As part of the future work, we plan to explore ways to improve the efficiency of the LP formulation. The performance values of the proposed method included in this section are based on the QP formulation. We used a Gaussian kernel with the parameter value selected via cross validation and Support Vector Machines as classification model to evaluate the effectiveness of the queried instances.

Comparative Studies. The comparative performance of the proposed approach on UCI datasets, is shown in Figure 2. We observe that the proposed *MP-AL* performed better than the state-of-the-art batch-mode active learning methods for 6 out of 8 datasets and had comparable performance for the remaining two datasets: Musk and Wine. We also note that for 6 out of 8 datasets the nearest competitors were *Matrix*, *Fisher* and *Disc*, except for Iris and Vehicles where *svmD*, *MCS* and *Design*(s) were nearest competitors.

We conducted another set of experiments on a multi-class, high dimensional biological image dataset (Fly-FISH) for classifying different developmental stages of *Drosophila*. We randomly sampled 511 samples (divided equally among all 7 classes). The batch size b and number of iterations were fixed at 10 and 9 respectively. Figure 4 reports the results of the proposed method *MP-AL* compared to the other active learning methods. We observe that *MP-AL* outperformed all the other active learning methods followed by *Matrix*, *Fisher* and *Disc*. Table 1 presents the results of 2-sided paired t-test of *MP-AL* vs *Matrix*, *Disc* and *Fisher* methods on UCI and Fly-FISH datasets. We compare the accuracies over 10 runs at each evaluation point and present the percentage of evaluation points at which *MP-AL significantly* outperforms or under-performs the compared algorithm, denoted as win % and loss% respectively.

Variation in MMD Vs Number of Selected Samples. We investigated the variation in MMD value between the training set and the unlabeled data at each iteration for all the datasets. Figure 3 presents the results for some of the representative UCI datasets.

Table 1: Win-Loss % of MP-AL in 2-sided paired t-test ($p < 0.05$). The fraction not reported (e.g., 60% for MP-AL vs. Matrix on Heart) corresponds to the cases where the two algorithms are not significantly different at the level of $p < 0.05$.

Dataset	MP-AL vs. Matrix		MP-AL vs. Disc		MP-AL vs. Fisher	
	win%	lose%	win%	lose%	win%	lose%
Heart	40.0	0	60.0	0	60.0	0
Sonar	28.5	0	85.7	0	28.5	0
Waveform	14.3	0	71.4	0	28.5	0
Image Segmentation	20.0	0	60.0	0	40.0	0
Musk	0	20.0	0.0	0	20.0	0
Wine	0.0	0	75.0	0	50.0	0
Vehicles	66.6	0	50.0	0	83.3	0
Iris	80.0	0	80.0	0	100.0	0
Fly-FISH	62.5	0	85.7	0	62.5	0

Similar patterns were observed for the other datasets. We observe that our algorithm decreases MMD value monotonically as more data samples are selected from the unlabeled data and that the decrease in MMD value corresponds to the increase in classification accuracy on the test data as shown in Figure 2. The decrease in MMD value during the initial iterations is more than the decrease towards the later iterations, resulting in the higher increase in accuracy values during the initial iterations than later iterations. We observe for the Vehicles dataset the accuracy value sharply increases between the second and third iteration points. We also observe a sharp decrease in MMD value for the Vehicles dataset at the corresponding iteration points.

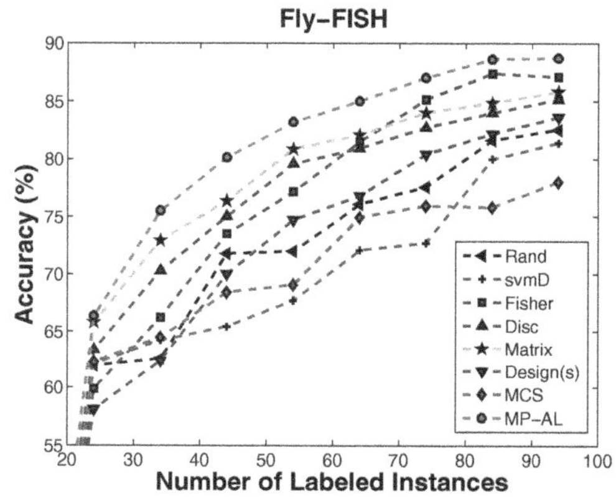

Figure 4: Comparative performance of different active learning methods on the Fly-FISH dataset.

Table 2: Average run time (in seconds).

Dataset	# instances x features	MP-AL	Matrix	Disc	Fisher
Vehicles	94 x 19	0.42	3.35	4.42	1.14
Iris	150 x 5	0.58	6.64	7.97	2.96
Wine	178 x 3	0.59	7.81	10.76	8.38
Sonar	208 x 60	0.76	8.68	12.78	10.04
Image Segmentation	210 x 19	0.76	12.47	22.43	16.51
Heart	270 x 13	1.21	26.14	26.93	18.88
Waveform	350 x 21	2.54	52.21	81.28	38.57
Musk	476 x 167	3.81	153.02	265.71	121.23
Fly-FISH	511 x 3850	6.5	360.70	3330.16	923.30

Efficiency Comparison. We compared the average time taken to select a batch of unlabeled points by the proposed *MP-AL* versus the nearest competitors *Matrix*, *Fisher* and *Disc*. All algorithms were implemented using MATLAB on a four-core Intel processor with 2.66 GHz CPU and 8 GB RAM. Table 2 presents the comparative run times on different UCI and Fly-FISH datasets. We note that *MP-AL* is much more efficient than the other three batch-mode active learning methods for all datasets. *Matrix* method involved solving a quadratic programming problem multiple times, per batch

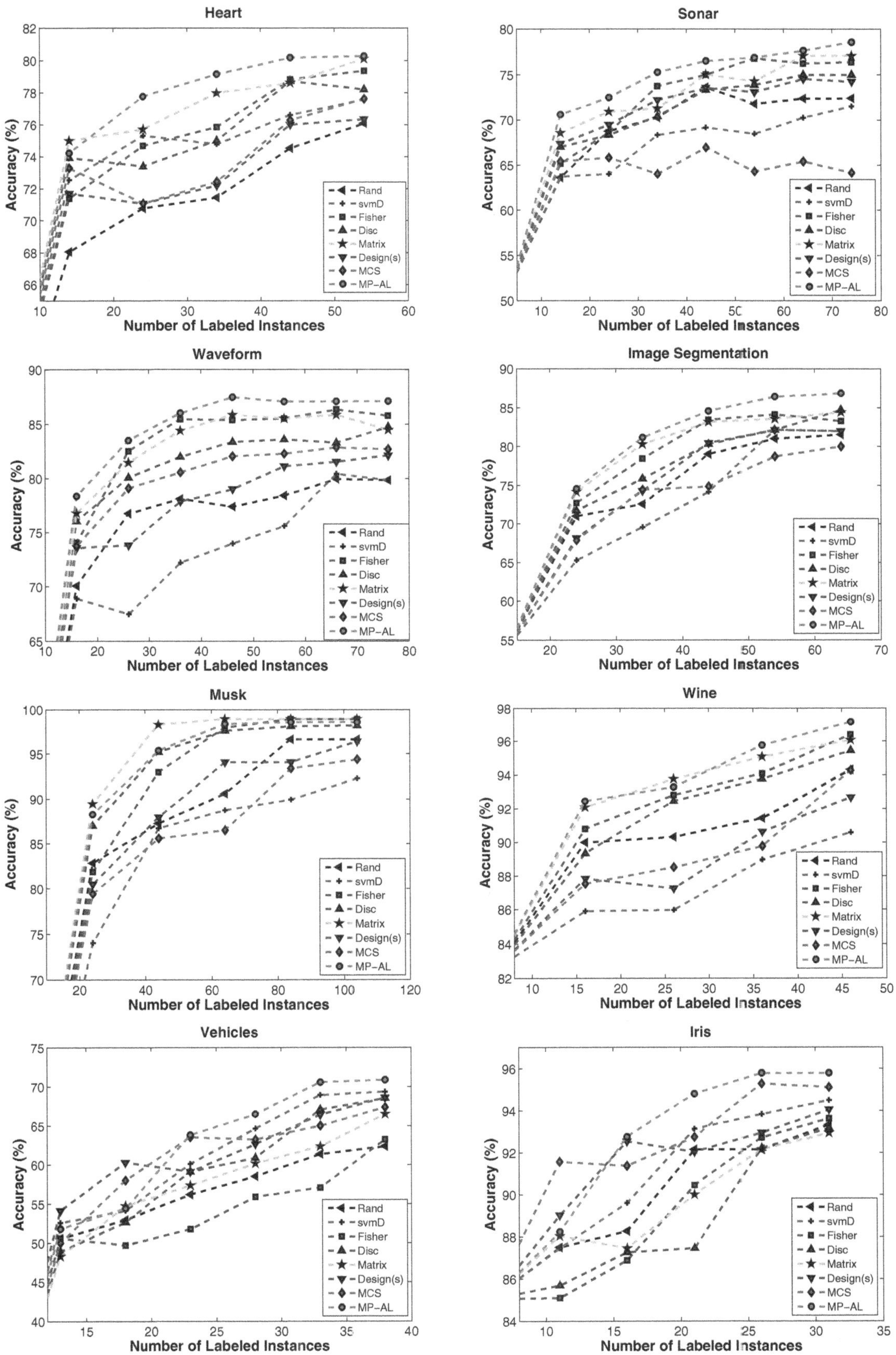

Figure 2: Comparative performance of different active learning methods on UCI datasets. Accuracy at the start point, which is same for all methods is not shown in the figures (figures best viewed in color). Results of 2-sided paired t-test at the level of $p < 0.05$ for *MP-AL* vs. *Matrix*, *Fisher* and *Disc* are presented in Table 1.

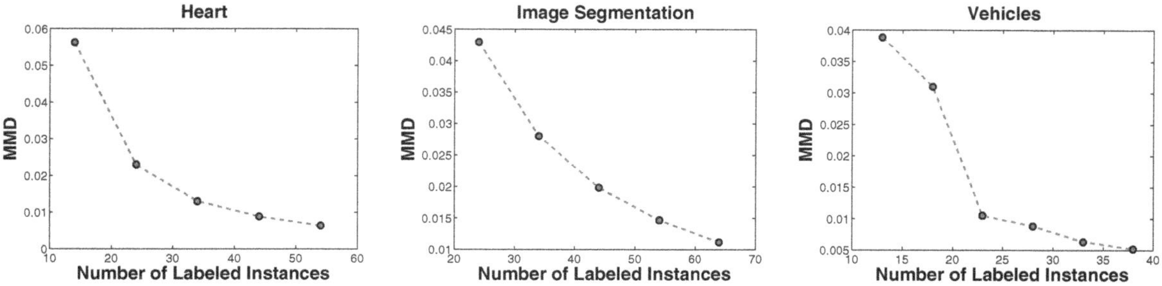

Figure 3: MMD value between the training and unlabeled data as more instances are selected by MP-AL.

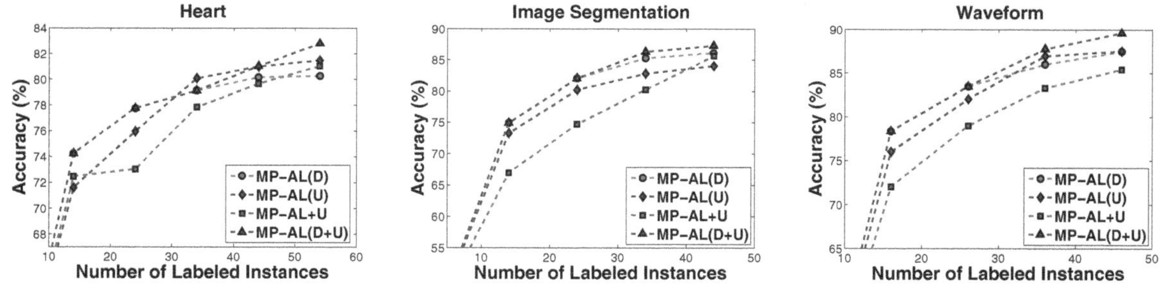

Figure 5: MP-AL with Uncertainty on UCI datasets.

of query points selection. *Fisher* involved training of a classifier multiple times per query batch selection. The *Disc* method involved training of a classifier followed by solving a quadratic programming problem multiple times per selection of a query batch and the *MP-AL* on the other hand, required solving a quadratic programming problem once per batch of query points selection.

5. EXTENSIONS OF MP-AL

5.1 Incorporating Uncertainty in MP-AL

The proposed *MP-AL* framework can be readily extended to incorporate uncertainty of prediction of unlabeled data in the query selection process. We experimented with the following three alternative algorithms: (1) At each iteration a classifier is learned on the available labeled data, and the unlabeled data is ranked based on uncertainty of predictions $M(x_i)$ measured for each unlabeled data x_i using entropy of predicted labels as in [12]. The *MP-AL* method is then applied only on the most uncertain set of unlabeled data (top 70%) instead of on the complete unlabeled data, referred to as *MP-AL*(U). (2) Query selection is based on *MP-AL* at initial iterations and during later iterations based on the *MP-AL*(U), referred to as *MP-AL*(D+U). (3) Add the prediction uncertainty vector M as a separate linear term ($-M^T\alpha$) in the formulation in Equation (11), referred to as *MP-AL+U*. The base *MP-AL* method is referred to as *MP-AL*(D). Figure 5 presents the comparative results obtained on some of the representative UCI datasets. Similar patterns were obtained on other datasets. We observe that for initial iterations *MP-AL*(D) and *MP-AL*(D+U) outperform *MP-AL*(U) and *MP-AL+U*. However the performance of these methods improve during later iterations, as the classifier becomes more reliable when learned on a larger number of labeled data. Indeed we can observe that *MP-AL*(D+U) performs best for most cases as it combines the strengths of both *MP-AL*(D) and *MP-AL*(U).

5.2 Transfer Learning in MP-AL

The problem of insufficient labeled data (in a target domain) is addressed in *Active learning* by querying labels of most informative instances. An alternative to address the same problem is by borrowing samples from an already labeled dataset belonging to a related domain (source domain), known as *Transfer Learning* [21]. Different transfer learning methodologies have been developed to address the distribution difference between a source and a target domain, so that the source domain data can be efficiently used to label the target domain data. Re-weighting source domain data to match the marginal probability distributions is a commonly used strategy [15, 3, 25] in transfer learning. In our experiments we used an existing re-weighting method [15], to re-weight the source domain data to match the distribution of the unlabeled set (target domain). We incorporate transfer learning in our MP-AL framework as follows: At each iteration, we combine the re-weighted source samples with the queried and labeled samples from the unlabeled set (in the target domain) and compute the classification accuracy on the other unseen fixed test set, similar to earlier experiments. We evaluated the proposed transfer learning extension of *MP-AL* on the 20 Newsgroups dataset for document categorization. We built three sets of source domain data vs. unlabeled data (target domain) as follows: (1) Sports: rec.sport.hockey vs. rec.sport.baseball; (2) Hardware: comp.sys.mac.hardware vs. comp.sys.ibm.pc.hardware and (3) Scientific: sci.med vs. sci.electronics. The positive class of each source and target domain data consists of 200 documents randomly sampled from the respective categories and the negative class consists of a random mixture of 200 samples from other categories as suggested in [8]. We represented each document as a binary vector consisting of the 200 most discriminating words determined by Weka's info-gain filter [29], after removing stop words and using a document frequency of 5. We start with no selected labeled instances and use a batch size of 10. The experiments were repeated 10 times and the average results are reported. Figure 6 shows the accuracies obtained by the extended method denoted as *MP-AL+TL* and by the base *MP-AL* method without using the source domain data, on the 20 Newsgroups dataset. We observe that during intial iterations *MP-AL* has poorer performance, due to insufficient labeled data. We observe that combining transfer learning with active learning (*MP-AL+TL*) improves the classification accuracy significantly during the initial iterations. However as the number of labeled data from the unlabeled set (target domain) increases, the performance of *MP-AL* improves and outperforms *MP-AL+TL* for Scientific and Hardware test cases. It has been shown

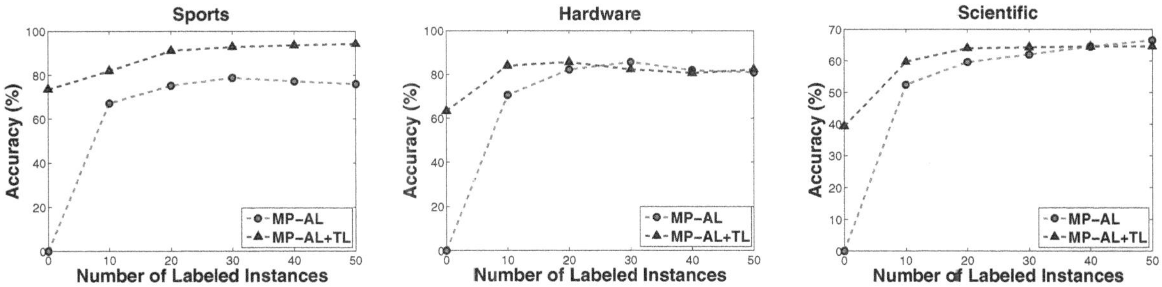

Figure 6: MP-AL with transfer learning on 20 Newsgroups dataset.

both theoretically and empirically in [2] that if there are enough data from the target domain then no source data are needed, and in fact using additional source data may degrade the performance. We also observe that improvement in classification accuracies due to incorporation of transfer learning is more for Sports and moderate for Scientific and Hardware. This can be attributed to the extent of difference in distribution between the source and target domains in each of these test cases; one way to measure the distribution difference is to compute the MMD value between the source and target domains. The MMD value is 0.0121, 0.0237 and 0.0239 for Sports, Hardware and Scientific respectively. This is consistent with our observation in Figure 6.

6. CONCLUSION AND FUTURE WORK

In this paper, we propose a novel batch-mode active learning method that selects a set of query samples from the unlabeled data so that the marginal probability distribution represented by the labeled data after annotation, is similar to the marginal probability distribution represented by the unlabeled data. The motivation behind this approach is to ensure that a classifier learned on labeled data with similar distribution has good generalization performance on the unlabeled data and also on the unseen data coming from the same distribution. The proposed method fully explores the available unlabeled and the already labeled data and demonstrates sensible data selection properties. It is formulated as an integer quadratic programming problem; besides, we also present an equivalent linear programming formulation. Our empirical studies show that the proposed approach achieves superior or comparable performance, besides being computationally highly efficient, compared to the existing batch-mode active learning methods. In addition, we present two extensions by incorporating uncertainty of the predicted labels of the unlabeled data and transfer learning in the proposed formulation. Our empirical studies on UCI and 20 Newsgroup datasets show that incorporating uncertainty information in the proposed formulation improves performance at later iterations and including transfer learning improves the performance of the classifier during initial iterations. In future work, we plan to study the theoretical properties of the proposed formulation. In addition, we plan to extend MP-AL to the multi-label setting.

7. ACKNOWLEDGMENTS

The authors are grateful to Prof. Arthur Gretton (Gatsby Computational Neuroscience Unit, UCL, London, UK) for providing valuable suggestions and feedback. This research is sponsored in part by NSF IIS-0953662, CCF-1025177, NIH LM010730, and ONR N00014-11-1-0108.

8. REFERENCES

[1] A.Gretton, K.M.Borgwardt, M.Rasch, B.Schölkopf, and A.J.Smola. A kernel method for the two-sample-problem. In *NIPS*, 2007.

[2] S. Ben-David, J. Blitzer, K. Crammer, A. Kulesza, F. Pereira, and J. Vaughan. A theory of learning from different domains. *JMLR*, 79:151–175, 2010.

[3] S. Bickel, M. Brückner, and T. Scheffer. Discriminative learning under covariate shift. *JMLR*, 10:2137–2155, 2009.

[4] K. Borgwardt, A. Gretton, M. Rasch, H. Kriegel, B.Schölkopf, and A. Smola. Integrating structured biological data by kernel maximum mean discrepancy. *Bioinformatics*, 22(14):49–57, 2006.

[5] K. Brinker. Incorporating diversity in active learning with support vector machines. In *ICML*, 2003.

[6] C. Campbell, N. Cristianini, and A. Smola. Query learning with large margin classifiers. In *ICML*, 2000.

[7] I. Dagan and S. Engelson. Committee-based sampling for training probabilistic classifiers. In *ICML*, 1995.

[8] E. Eaton and M. desJardins. Set-based boosting for instance-level transfer. In *ICDM*, 2009.

[9] Y. Freund, H. Seung, E. Shamir, and N Tishby. Selective sampling using query by committee algorithm. *Mach. Learn.* 28, 1997.

[10] M. Grant and S. Boyd. CVX: Matlab software for disciplined convex programming, version 1.21, 2007.

[11] Y. Guo. Active instance sampling via matrix partition. In *NIPS*, 2010.

[12] Y. Guo and D. Schuurmans. Discriminative batch mode active learning. In *NIPS*, 2007.

[13] S. Hoi, R. Jin, J. Zhu, and M. Lyu. Batch mode active learning and its application to medical image classification. In *ICML*, 2006.

[14] S. Hoi, R. Jin, J. Zhu, and M. Lyu. Semi-supervised svm batch mode active learning for image retrieval. In *CVPR*, 2008.

[15] J. Huang, A. Smola, A. Gretton, K. Borgwardt, and B. Scholkopf. Correcting sample selection bias by unlabeled data. In *NIPS*, 2007.

[16] F. Jing, M. Li, H. Zhang, and B. Zhang. Entropy based active learning with support vector machines for content based image retrieval. In *ICME*, 2004.

[17] A. Joshi, F. Porikli, and N. Papanikolopoulos. Multi-class active learning for image classification. In *CVPR*, 2009.

[18] E. Lecuyer, H. Yoshida, N. Parthasarathy, C. Alm, and T. Babak. Global analysis of mrna localization reveals a prominent role in organizing cellular architecture and function. *Cell*, 2011.

[19] C. Liu and H. Wechsler. Gabor feature based classification using the enhanced fisher linear discriminant model for face recognition. *IEEE Trans. Image Processing*, 11:467–476, 2002.

[20] S. Pan, I. Tsang, J. Kwok, and Q. Yang. Domain adaptation via transfer component analysis. In *IJCAI*, 2009.

[21] S. Pan and Q. Yang. A survey on transfer learning. *TKDE*, 2009.

[22] G. Schohn and D. Cohn. Less is more: Active learning with support vector machines. In *ICML*, 2000.

[23] B. Settles. Active learning literature survey. In *Computer Sciences Technical Report 1648*. University of Wisconsin-Madison, 2009.

[24] H. Seung, M. Opper, and H. Sompolinsky. Query by committee. In *ACM Workshop on Computational Learning Theory*, 1992.

[25] H. Shimodaira. Improving predictive inference under covariate shift by weighting the log-likelihood function. *JSPI*, 90:227–244, 2000.

[26] B. Sriperumbudur, A. Gretton, K. Fukumizu, B.Schölkopf, and G. Lanckriet. Hilbert space embeddings and metrics on probability measures. *JMLR*, 11:1517–1561, 2010.

[27] I. Steinwart. On the influence of the kernel on the consistency of support vector machines. *JMLR*, 2:67–93, 2002.

[28] S. Tong and D. Koller. Support vector machine active learning with applications to text classification. *JMLR*, 2:45–66, 2000.

[29] I. Witten and E. Frank. Data mining: Practical machine learning tools with java implementations. Morgan Kaufmann, 2000.

[30] Y. Wu, I. Kozintsev, J. Bouguet, and C Dulong. Sampling strategies for active learning in personal photo retrieval. In *ICME*, 2006.

[31] K. Yu, J. Bi, and V. Tresp. Active learning via transductive experimental design. In *ICML*, 2006.

[32] T. Zhang and F. Oles. A probability analysis on the value of unlabeled data for classification problems. In *ICML*, 2000.

SPG-GMKL: Generalized Multiple Kernel Learning with a Million Kernels

Ashesh Jain
IIT Delhi
asheshjain399@gmail.com

S. V. N. Vishwanathan
Purdue University
vishy@stats.purdue.edu

Manik Varma
Microsoft Research India
manik@microsoft.com

ABSTRACT

Multiple Kernel Learning (MKL) aims to learn the kernel in an SVM from training data. Many MKL formulations have been proposed and some have proved effective in certain applications. Nevertheless, as MKL is a nascent field, many more formulations need to be developed to generalize across domains and meet the challenges of real world applications. However, each MKL formulation typically necessitates the development of a specialized optimization algorithm. The lack of an efficient, general purpose optimizer capable of handling a wide range of formulations presents a significant challenge to those looking to take MKL out of the lab and into the real world.

This problem was somewhat alleviated by the development of the Generalized Multiple Kernel Learning (GMKL) formulation which admits fairly general kernel parameterizations and regularizers subject to mild constraints. However, the projected gradient descent GMKL optimizer is inefficient as the computation of the step size and a reasonably accurate objective function value or gradient direction are all expensive. We overcome these limitations by developing a Spectral Projected Gradient (SPG) descent optimizer which: a) takes into account second order information in selecting step sizes; b) employs a non-monotone step size selection criterion requiring fewer function evaluations; c) is robust to gradient noise, and d) can take quick steps when far away from the optimum.

We show that our proposed SPG-GMKL optimizer can be an order of magnitude faster than projected gradient descent on even small and medium sized datasets. In some cases, SPG-GMKL can even outperform state-of-the-art specialized optimization algorithms developed for a single MKL formulation. Furthermore, we demonstrate that SPG-GMKL can scale well beyond gradient descent to large problems involving a million kernels or half a million data points. Our code and implementation are available publically.

KDD'12, August 12–16, 2012, Beijing, China.

Categories and Subject Descriptors

I.2.6 [**Artificial Intelligence**]: Learning

General Terms

Algorithms, Performance, Experimentations

Keywords

Multiple Kernel Learning, Support Vector Machines, Spectral Projected Gradient Descent

1. INTRODUCTION

Support Vector Machines (SVMs) have become ubiquitous in diverse areas ranging from computer vision to natural language processing to bioinformatics. One of the reasons for their widespread adoption is the availability of general purpose, efficient optimizers capable of handling various SVM formulations as demanded by real world applications.

The success of non-linear SVMs also depends on the choice of a good kernel. Multiple Kernel Learning (MKL) techniques aim to learn such a kernel from training data often as a combination of given base kernels. MKL can be used for various tasks such as learning a similarity measure tailored to the given application, heterogeneous feature combination and learning models with sparse structures. For instance, MKL techniques have yielded state-of-the-art results on very challenging object recognition [22] and object detection [30] problems in computer vision. They have also yielded superior results as compared to many state-of-the-art filter and wrapper methods for feature selection [28]. However, MKL techniques have not proved to be as popular as the baseline SVMs upon which they hope to improve.

The primary reason for this is that MKL is still a nascent field and, while a few formulations have shown promising results in certain contexts, many more need to be developed that are robust to over fitting and generalize across domains. At the same time, existing formulations need to be tried out on many real world applications in order to determine regimes in which they perform well. Unfortunately, there does not exist an efficient, general purpose optimizer which gives practitioners the flexibility to quickly prototype novel MKL formulations or try out existing ones on large scale applications. As things stand, the practitioner faces the significant challenge of having to come up with a different optimization technique for every novel MKL formulation that she might wish to explore.

This problem was somewhat alleviated by the development of the Generalized Multiple Kernel Learning (GMKL)

formulation [28]. The formulation allows learning fairly general kernel parameterizations, including linear and non-linear kernel combinations, subject to general regularization. The only restriction that is placed on the kernel and regularizer is that their derivative with respect to the kernel parameters must exist and be jointly continuous with the SVM dual variables $\boldsymbol{\alpha}$. Most of the kernel learning formulations proposed in the literature satisfy these constraints.

However, the general purpose, projected gradient descent based GMKL optimizer is not efficient and doesn't scale well. In particular, it has two significant shortcomings. First, the gradient descent step size is calculated via the Armijo rule to guarantee convergence. This necessitates the solving of many expensive, single kernel SVMs on the entire data set in order to take a single step. Second, the objective function value and the gradient descent direction are also obtained by solving an SVM. To avoid noise in these estimates the SVM Quadratic program (QP) has to be solved to a very high precision. Unfortunately, high precision solvers don't scale beyond toy problems, while large scale specialized SVM QP solvers based on chunking and decomposition [6] typically produce low precision results. Optimizing GMKL via projected gradient descent can thus be significantly slower than solving a single SVM.

Our objective, in this paper, is to speed up GMKL optimization by an order of magnitude in many cases. We achieve this by carefully designing an alternative optimizer based on Spectral Projected Gradient (SPG) descent [5]. SPG is a well known technique in the optimization community. Our contribution is to adapt it for the GMKL problem. Towards this end, we use a non-monotone line search criterion which allows the objective function to increase once in a while rather than strictly decrease at each step. This allows us to accept initial step size proposals based on the spectral step length, in many cases even the first, whereas gradient descent would need to try out many step sizes before accepting one that satisfies the Armijo rule. SPG steps are thus much quicker as they require fewer objective function and SVM evaluations.

We also engineer SPG to be more robust to the objective function and gradient noise encountered in large scale GMKL problems. Gradient descent will often get stuck due to inaccurate gradient computation. Only miniscule step sizes will satisfy the Armijo rule since the gradient is pointing in the wrong direction and gradient descent will either time out or take many small steps before recovering. SPG, on the other hand, can recover much faster due to the non-monotone line search criterion. We further exploit this property by deliberately computing objective function values and gradients at low precision when we are far away from the optimum. This allows our initial steps to be much quicker than gradient descent's. As the optimum is approached, we automatically increase the precision of the objective function and gradient computation according to a schedule based on the duality gap and the projected gradient. In many cases, due to this effective scheduling, we need to solve SVMs with a precision of only 10^{-1} at the beginning and at most 10^{-3} towards the end. On the other hand, we found that projected gradient descent needed to solve SVMs with a precision of 10^{-6} from the very start in order to converge.

We carried out extensive experiments comparing the performance of our proposed SPG optimizer to projected gradient descent . We observed that SPG was much faster on even small data sets, optimizing GMKL in a matter of seconds, while gradient descent often struggled to converge. Furthermore, SPG scaled well to large data sets where gradient descent based optimization was infeasible. For instance, without using any parallelization, we were able to train on the Sonar data set with a million kernels and on Covertype with over half a million data points. Note that Covertype is one of the largest data sets on which a single kernel SVM can be trained without parallelization and that our training time was much the same as that of a single SVM with a kernel defined to be the uniformly weighted sum of the given base kernels. In contrast, sequential MKL techniques proposed in the literature have mostly reported results on thousands of kernels or data points (with the exception of SMO-MKL [31]). Finally, in some cases, SPG even outperformed state-of-the-art specialized optimizers designed for a specific MKL formulation. Thus, not only can SPG handle diverse MKL formulations it is also the most efficient optimizer for many of them.

We have implemented SPG in C and use LibSVM [6] as the inner SVM solver. Our implementation builds on top of the LibSVM code base. Our code is easy to modify and new kernel parameterizations and regularizers can readily be plugged in. We therefore expect the code to be useful for trying out new MKL formulations as well as optimizing existing ones. Our objective is to provide a flexible and efficient tool for kernel learning and the SPG-GMKL code can be downloaded from [17].

2. RELATED WORK

Research in Multiple Kernel Learning has focused on both developing new MKL formulations as well as their optimization. Different formulations are required to address the needs of different applications. Early work focused on learning the kernel as a linear combination of given base kernels subject to l_1 or l_2 regularization [12, 19]. This was later extended to handle any $l_{p>1}$ regularizer [18], mixed block regularizers [1] as well as radius-margin based regularization [14]. Non-linear kernel combinations [11, 28], such as products of kernels and mixtures of polynomials, have also been shown to be appropriate in certain domains. Other formulations include multi-class MKL [34], learning over exponentially large kernel combinations [2], learning a different kernel combination per data point [15,20] and MKL discriminant and subspace analysis [9, 32]. Many of these formulations can be easily cast in the GMKL framework.

As regards optimization, specialized algorithms have been developed for many of these formulations. For instance, linear MKL subject to l_1 regularization has been optimized via semi-definite programming [19], M.-Y. regularization [3], semi-infinite linear programming [26] and mirror descent [1]. Sparse MKL models have also been learnt by direct, greedy minimization of the l_0 norm [25]. Linear MKL with l_p regularization has been optimized using the SMO algorithm [31], stochastic gradient descent [21] and semi-infinite linear programming [18]. Stochastic gradient descent has also been used for optimizing multi-class MKL [21,22] and second order cone programming [27] for learning hyper-kernels.

Unfortunately, most of these specialized optimization techniques are limited to their own formulation and do not generalize well. Gradient descent, on the other hand, can be used to optimize many formulations. It has been used to train linear MKL with l_1 regularization [8,23,29], multi-class

MKL with shared parameters [23], for learning local kernel combinations per data point [15], for hierarchical kernel learning over exponentially large kernel combinations [2] and for learning non-linear kernel combinations [28]. All of these formulations, even if they are not covered under GMKL, can benefit by replacing their gradient descent based optimizer by our proposed SPG algorithm.

3. GMKL: GENERALIZED MULTIPLE KERNEL LEARNING

We review the GMKL formulation in this section and discuss how it can be optimized via gradient descent. We focus on the binary classification problem though other convex loss functions can be substituted as desired.

Our objective is to learn a function of the form $f(\mathbf{x}) = \mathbf{w}^t\boldsymbol{\phi}_\mathbf{d}(\mathbf{x})+b$ with the kernel $k_\mathbf{d}(\mathbf{x}_i,\mathbf{x}_j) = \boldsymbol{\phi}^t_\mathbf{d}(\mathbf{x}_i)\boldsymbol{\phi}_\mathbf{d}(\mathbf{x}_j)$ representing the dot product in feature space $\boldsymbol{\phi}$ parameterized by $\mathbf{d}$. The goal in training an SVM is to learn the globally optimal values of $\mathbf{w}$ and b from training data $\{(\mathbf{x}_i, y_i)\}$. In addition, MKL also estimates the kernel parameters $\mathbf{d}$. The primal formulation of GMKL is

$$\underset{\mathbf{d}}{\text{Min}} \quad T(\mathbf{d}) \quad \text{subject to} \quad \mathbf{d} \geq 0 \tag{1}$$

$$\textit{where} \quad T(\mathbf{d}) = \underset{\mathbf{w},b}{\text{Min}}\ \tfrac{1}{2}\mathbf{w}^t\mathbf{w} + \sum_i l(y_i, f(\mathbf{x}_i)) + r(\mathbf{d})$$

where both the regularizer r and the kernel can be any general differentiable functions of $\mathbf{d}$ with continuous derivative and l could be one of various loss functions such as $l = C\ \max(0, 1 - y_i f(\mathbf{x}_i))$ for classification. The constraint $\mathbf{d} \geq 0$ can be strengthened or relaxed depending on the cost of projecting back into the feasible set so as to ensure that the parameterized kernel remains positive definite. Allowing the regularizer, kernel and loss function to have such general forms permits GMKL the flexibility to directly model, or be easily extended to, most of the formulations discussed in Section 2. For instance, the kernel can be learnt to be a linear combination of given base kernels, product of kernels or mixture of polynomials, *etc.* Similarly, the regularizer can be set to the 1-norm, any $p >$ 1-norm, a mixed block norm, the log determinant of the learnt kernel matrix, *etc.*

The GMKL primal was deliberately formulated as a nested optimization. The key idea is that once the kernel parameters $\mathbf{d}$ are fixed, an efficient, single kernel SVM solver, such as LibSVM, can be used to solve the inner optimization in T while T itself can be optimized via gradient descent.

In order to optimize T using gradient descent, we need to prove that $\boldsymbol{\nabla}_\mathbf{d}T$ exists and calculate it efficiently. This is best achieved by looking at T's dual given by

$$W(\mathbf{d}) = \max_{\boldsymbol{\alpha}} \quad \mathbf{1}^t\boldsymbol{\alpha} - \tfrac{1}{2}\boldsymbol{\alpha}^t\mathbf{Y}\mathbf{K}_\mathbf{d}\mathbf{Y}\boldsymbol{\alpha} + r(\mathbf{d}) \tag{2}$$

$$\text{subject to} \quad \mathbf{1}^t\mathbf{Y}\boldsymbol{\alpha} = 0, \quad 0 \leq \boldsymbol{\alpha} \leq C \tag{3}$$

where $\mathbf{K}_\mathbf{d}$ is the kernel matrix for a given $\mathbf{d}$ and $\mathbf{Y}$ is a diagonal matrix with the labels on the diagonal.

Note that we can write $T = r + P$ and $W = r + D$ with strong duality holding between P and D. Therefore, $T(\mathbf{d}) = W(\mathbf{d})$ for any given value of $\mathbf{d}$, and it is sufficient for us to show that W is differentiable and calculate $\boldsymbol{\nabla}_\mathbf{d}W$. Proof of the differentiability of W comes from Danskin's Theorem [13]. Since the feasible set is compact, the gradient can be shown to exist if k, r, $\boldsymbol{\nabla}_\mathbf{d}k$ and $\boldsymbol{\nabla}_\mathbf{d}r$ are smoothly varying functions of $\mathbf{d}$ and if $\boldsymbol{\alpha}^*$, the value of $\boldsymbol{\alpha}$ that optimizes W, is unique. Furthermore, a straight forward extension of Lemma 2 in [8] can be used to show that W have derivatives given by

$$\frac{\partial T}{\partial d_k} = \frac{\partial W}{\partial d_k} = \frac{\partial r}{\partial d_k} - \tfrac{1}{2}\boldsymbol{\alpha}^{*t}\frac{\partial \mathbf{H}}{\partial d_k}\boldsymbol{\alpha}^* \tag{4}$$

where $\mathbf{H} = \mathbf{YKY}$. Thus, in order to take a gradient step, all we need to do is obtain $\boldsymbol{\alpha}^*$. Note that since W is equivalent to the single kernel SVM dual with kernel matrix $\mathbf{K}_\mathbf{d}$, $\boldsymbol{\alpha}^*$ can be obtained by any SVM optimization package. The projection operator in our case is $\mathbf{P}(\mathbf{d}) = \max(\mathbf{0}, \mathbf{d})$.

To guarantee convergence, the step size s^n is chosen according to the Armijo rule so as to satisfy

$$W(\mathbf{d} + s^n\mathbf{g}) \leq W(\mathbf{d}) + \gamma s^n \mathbf{g}^t\boldsymbol{\nabla}W(\mathbf{d}) \tag{5}$$

where $\mathbf{g}$ is the chosen direction of descent, the negative gradient $-\boldsymbol{\nabla}W(\mathbf{d})$ in our case, and γ is a tolerance parameter.

4. SPECTRAL PROJECTED GRADIENT DESCENT OPTIMIZATION FOR GMKL

Spectral gradient descent iteratively approximates the objective function with a quadratic model and then optimizes the model at each iteration. It is particularly well suited to large scale problems since it builds a coarse approximation very efficiently and without any memory overhead. Early work by Barzilai and Borwein [4] laid the foundation for choosing the step size as the spectral step length. Grippo's classic non-monotone line search criterion for Newton methods [16] was incorporated into the algorithm by Raydan in [24]. The technique was extended to handle constrained optimization problems in [5] who recommended descending according to the spectral projected gradient rather than the regular gradient so as to reduce the number of projection operations. We refer to this algorithm as Spectral Projected Gradient (SPG) descent and efficiently adapt it for optimizing GMKL based on gradient precision tuning. In addition, we replace the classic non-monotone line search criterion by the one proposed in [33] based on averaging. Proofs of convergence for each of the methods can be found in their respective publications. A few attempts have been made to use SPG for optimizing machine learning problems [10]. However, SPG appears not to be a widely used technique in machine learning or data mining.

Our SPG-GMKL pseudo code is given in Algorithm 1. The three main components are the spectral step length and the spectral projected gradient computation, the non-monotone line search and the SVM solver precision tuning.

Algorithm 1 SPG-GMKL

$n \leftarrow 0$
Initialize $\mathbf{d}^0$ randomly
repeat
  $\boldsymbol{\alpha}^* \leftarrow \text{SolveSVM}_\epsilon(\mathbf{K}(\mathbf{d}^n))$
  $\lambda \leftarrow$ SpectralStepLength
  $\mathbf{p}^n \leftarrow \mathbf{d}^n - \mathbf{P}(\mathbf{d}^n - \lambda\nabla\mathbf{W}(\mathbf{d}^n))$
  $s^n \leftarrow$ Non-Monotone
  $\epsilon \leftarrow$ TuneSVMPrecision
  $\mathbf{d}^{n+1} \leftarrow \mathbf{d}^n - s^n\mathbf{p}^n$
until converged

We discuss these components in detail and also mention our convergence criterion and kernel caching strategy.

Spectral step length and projected gradient.
We describe how to move from the current iterate $\mathbf{d}^n$ to the next iterate $\mathbf{d}^{n+1}$. The step size and the descent direction are chosen so as to reduce the number of SVM evaluations and projection operations as compared to regular projected gradient descent.

SPG-GMKL chooses it's step size based on second order information. At each iteration, it approximates the GMKL objective function $W(\mathbf{d})$ by a quadratic in $\mathbf{d}$. The step size is then based on the eigenvalues of the approximated Hessian. A particularly simple choice of the Hessian, $\lambda^{-1}\mathbf{I}$, is made so as to be able to efficiently scale to large problems. Imposing the constraint that the directional derivatives of the objective and the approximated functions match at the current point leads to the following choice for λ

$$\lambda^n = \frac{\langle \mathbf{d}^n - \mathbf{d}^{n-1}, \mathbf{d}^n - \mathbf{d}^{n-1} \rangle}{\langle \mathbf{d}^n - \mathbf{d}^{n-1}, \nabla W(\mathbf{d}^n) - \nabla W(\mathbf{d}^{n-1}) \rangle} \quad (6)$$

If λ^n is negative then it is set to λ_{Max}, else it is clipped between $\lambda_{\text{Min}} = 10^{-30}$ and $\lambda_{\text{Max}} = 10$ so as to ensure that the steps are always bounded.

Standard methods would have taken a projected gradient step of size λ^n. However, in SPG, we instead step in the direction of the negative spectral projected gradient. In particular, the next iterate is obtained as

$$\mathbf{d}^{n+1} = \mathbf{d}^n - s^n \mathbf{p}^n \quad (7)$$

$$\text{where } \mathbf{p}^n = \mathbf{d}^n - \mathbf{P}(d^n - \lambda^n \nabla W(\mathbf{d}^n)) \quad (8)$$

where s^n is selected from $\{1, 1/2, 1/4, \ldots\}$ according to the non-monotone line search criterion, $\mathbf{p}$ is the spectral projected gradient and $\mathbf{P}$ is the projection operator in our case $\mathbf{P}(\mathbf{d}) = \max(\mathbf{d}, \mathbf{0})$. This choice of descent direction ensures that the projection operator needs to be applied only once per iteration. While the cost of projection is negligible in our case it might become significant if the constraints $\mathbf{d} \geq 0$ are replaced by more complicated ones.

Non-monotone line search criterion.
We employ a non-monotone line search criterion so as to reduce the number of SVM evaluations and be robust to the objective function and gradient noise inherent in GMKL optimization. The classical SPG non-monotone line search criterion selects step sizes s^n that satisfy

$$W(\mathbf{d}^n - s^n \mathbf{p}^n) \leq \max_{0 \leq j \leq M} W(\mathbf{d}^{n-j}) - \gamma s^n \nabla^t W(\mathbf{d}^n) \mathbf{p}^n \quad (9)$$

So as to allow the objective function to increase once in a while. However, [33] observed that, for unconstrained quasi-Newton methods, maximizing over the previous function values could be unstable in some cases and that averaging could be a much better alternative. We therefore incorporate their criterion into SPG-GMKL by choosing s^n satisfying

$$W(\mathbf{d}^n - s^n \mathbf{p}^n) \leq C^n - \gamma s^n \nabla^t W(\mathbf{d}^n) \mathbf{p}^n \quad (10)$$

$$Q^{n+1} = \eta^n Q^n + 1 \quad (11)$$

$$C^{n+1} = (\eta^n Q^n C^n + \mathbf{W}(\mathbf{d}^{n+1}))/Q^{n+1} \quad (12)$$

where we set $C^0 = W(\mathbf{d}^0)$, $Q^0 = 1$ and $\gamma = 10^{-4}$. The parameter η influences the number of iterations over which W is averaged. Setting $\eta = 0$ reduces the criterion to the Armijo rule while setting $\eta = 1$ implies averaging W over all previous iterations. We follow the heuristic of [33] and vary η dynamically depending on the behavior of the objective function and the approximated quadratic. If the approximation is good (bad) then we increase (decrease) η by 0.025 making sure to clip it between $[0.1, 1]$ else leave it unchanged.

Tuning the tolerance of the SVM solver.
The SPG-GMKL optimizer is robust to imprecisions in calculating the objective function and the gradient. We exploit this by solving SVMs with a tolerance of only 10^{-1} in the initial iterations. This is automatically decreased as we move closer to the optimum or the step size becomes too small. The SVM solver's tolerance is set as

$$\epsilon = \begin{cases} \min(\epsilon, 10^{-1}) & \text{if } (1 \leq u) \text{ or } (5 \leq v) \\ \min(\epsilon, 10^{-2}) & \text{if } (0.1 \leq u < 1) \text{ or } (1 \leq v < 5) \\ \min(\epsilon, 10^{-3}) & \text{if } (u < 0.1) \text{ or } (v < 1) \\ \max(\epsilon/10, 10^{-5}) & \text{if } s^n < 10^{-8} \end{cases} \quad (13)$$

where u is the duality gap (whenever available) and v is the projected gradient norm.

Convergence Criterion and Kernel Caching.
We declare the SPG-GMKL algorithm to have converged whenever the duality gap reduces below 10^{-3} or, if the duality gap is unavailable, whenever the l_2 or l_∞ norm of the projected gradient reduces below 0.04. The reason the stopping criterion is so loose in terms of the projected gradient norm is because we do not assume that our inner SVM solver produces high quality solutions, and hence there is significant noise in the gradient estimates. In fact, the condition on the projected gradient seems stricter since, in many of the small data sets, the duality gap fell below 10^{-3} before the projected gradient norm reduced below 0.04. However, on some of the larger data sets, the projected gradient norm was found to become small even when the duality gap was large. We therefore use the duality gap as a stable stopping criterion whenever it is available (for sum of kernels in our experiments).

Kernel caching strategies can have a big impact on performance since kernel computations can dominate everything else in some cases. While a few different kernel caching techniques have been explored for SVMs, we stick to the standard one used in LibSVM [6]. A Least Recently Used (LRU) cache is implemented as a circular queue. Each element in the queue is a pointer to a recently accessed (common) row of each of the individual kernel matrices.

Advantages over projected gradient descent.
Our SPG-GMKL implementation has a number of advantages over regular projected gradient descent. First, we are able to efficiently bring second order information into play by choosing our step size according to the spectral step length. This was found to be very beneficial for many data sets. Second, we can significantly reduce the number of SVM evaluations by combining the spectral step length computation with a non-monotone line search criterion. While gradient descent might take ten or more SVM evaluations to find a step size satisfying the Armijo rule, SPG-GMKL will frequently take only a single SVM evaluation as the first step size proposal is accepted. The non-monotone line

search might also have beneficial side effects. Non-convex kernel parameterizations might benefit as such criteria have been shown to sometimes help escape poor local optima. Furthermore, non-monotonicity can also be helpful in cases when the objective function starts resembling a long, narrow valley where standard gradient descent techniques can get stuck. Third, our SPG-GMKL implementation is robust to noise in the calculation of the gradient and the objective function. Gradient descent can require hundreds of SVM evaluations in a line search when the gradient is not pointing in the right direction. SPG-GMKL is typically more robust and can recover much faster. Fourth, by starting with a low SVM precision and then dynamically increasing it as required, we can make the cost of evaluating each SVM much lower. This was found to give an order of magnitude improvement over gradient descent on some large data sets where the cost of evaluating an SVM is very high.

5. EXPERIMENTS

We carry out extensive experiments to test the performance of SPG-GMKL along various dimensions. We benchmark its performance on small, medium and large scale data sets. We show that SPG-GMKL consistently outperforms projected gradient descent by a wide margin and that SPG-GMKL can often be more than ten times faster. We also demonstrate that SPG-GMKL can scale well to large problems involving a million kernels on Sonar or over half a million data points on Covertype. This is particularly significant as Covertype is one of the largest data sets on which an RBF SVM can be trained without parallelization.

We also optimize four different MKL formulations to demonstrate the flexibility of SPG-GMKL. We learn two different types of kernel combinations – sum of kernels with $K = \sum_k d_k K_k$ and product of kernels with $K = \prod_k K_k(d_k) = \prod_k e^{-d_k D_k}$ corresponding to tuning the RBF bandwidth while combining distance functions D_k. We regularize these with the l_1 and $l_{p>1}$ norms. We focus on the linear MKL formulations in Subsections 5.1 and 5.2. Specialized optimizers have been developed for learning a sum of base kernels subject to l_1 regularization as it is one of the most popular formulations. We show that the performance of general purpose SPG-GMKL can be much better than state-of-the-art implementations of some of these specialized optimizers. We then use SPG-GMKL to learn products of kernels in Subsections 5.3 and 5.4 which cannot be optimized using any other solver (apart from projected gradient descent, of course). We show that SPG-GMKL scales well to many problems where projected gradient descent fails to converge.

Finally, in Subsection 5.5, we study the scaling properties of SPG-GMKL and the contribution of each of the individual components. On the data sets that we tried, SPG-GMKL exhibited a linear dependence on the number of kernels and a sub-quadratic dependence on the number of training points. We also show that each of the three major components of SPG-GMKL, namely the spectral step length, the non-monotone line search and the SVM solver precision tuning, are necessary and that removing any of them can lead to substantial degradations in performance.

We briefly describe the various implementations that we tested. We refer to our algorithm as SPG-GMKL and the projected gradient descent algorithm as PGD. The SPG-GMKL implementation is obtained by starting from the PGD codebase and adding spectral step length computation, the non-monotone line search criterion and SVM solver tolerance tuning. This ensures an absolutely fair comparison between the two implementations. Another projected gradient descent implementation is available in the form of SimpleMKL [23]. The code was downloaded from the authors' website. However, this implementation is meant only for linear MKL subject to l_1 regularization and hence we compare to it only in Subsection 5.2. For this formulation, a very efficient implementation of the SILP-MKL [26] optimizer is available in the Shogun toolbox. We downloaded the latest version of Shogun (v 0.9.3) and used the highly optimized CPLEX solver to solve their outer loop LP. Note that the linear MKL formulations can be made convex with a simple change of variables. As such, SPG-GMKL and PGD converge to the same solution. SimpleMKL and SILP-MKL can also be made to converge to the same solution with an appropriate choice of parameters. We therefore report only the training time in our experiments as the objective function value, number of kernels selected and prediction accuracy on the test set are similar for all the methods. SPG-GMKL and PGD might potentially converge to different solutions for the non-convex formulations involving products of kernels. We did not observe this behavior though, and both implementations returned very similar solutions. Table 1 summarizes the statistics of the data sets that were tried. For linear MKL, kernels were generated as recommended in [23] for the small data sets. We generated RBF kernels with ten bandwidths for each individual dimension of the feature vector as well as the full feature vector itself. Similarly, we also generated polynomial kernels of degrees 1, 2 and 3. Kernel matrices were pre-computed and normalized to have unit trace. A fixed number of kernels were computed on the fly for the medium and large data sets. All kernels were computed on the fly for products of kernels where we defined one RBF kernel per feature for the small data sets and a fixed number for the large data sets. We perform 5 fold cross validation on the small data sets. This gives both the mean training time and its variance so as to better judge

Table 1: Data set statistics

Data sets	# Train	# Dim	# Kernels Sum	# Kernels Product
Leukemia	38	7129		7129
Wpbc	194	34	455	34
Sonar	208	60	793	60
Liver	345	6	91	6
Ionosphere	351	34	455	34
Breast-Cancer	683	10	143	10
Australian	690	14	195	14
Diabetes	768	8	117	8
Letter	20000	16		16
RCV1	20242	47236		50
Adult-8	22696	123	50	42
Web-7	24692	300	50	43
Poker	25010	10		10
Adult-9	32561	123	50	42
Web-8	49749	300	50	43
KDDCup04-Physics	50000	71	50	
Cod-RNA	59535	8	50	8
Real-Sim	72309	20958	25	
Covertype	581012	54	5	

Table 2: $l_{p>1}$-SumMKL results on small data sets.

	$p = 1.1$		$p = 1.33$		$p = 2.0$	
Data sets	PGD (s)	SPG-GMKL (s)	PGD (s)	SPG-GMKL (s)	PGD (s)	SPG-GMKL (s)
Australian	39.4 ± 6.0	7.0 ± 1.6	248.3 ± 329.7	6.9 ± 1.2	23.5 ± 2.3	6.0 ± 0.2
Liver	282.2 ± 226.0	0.8 ± 0.1	3.3 ± 2.5	0.7 ± 0.1	0.7 ± 0.1	0.6 ± 0.1
Sonar	785.5 ± 471.1	9.0 ± 1.8	57.8 ± 39.8	4.2 ± 0.4	7.7 ± 1.1	3.1 ± 0.3
Breast-Cancer	237.2 ± 97.8	8.6 ± 2.2	11.2 ± 2.4	3.3 ± 0.1	6.6 ± 0.6	2.7 ± 0.1
Diabetes	73.6 ± 38.8	4.1 ± 0.5	11.5 ± 2.4	3.0 ± 0.1	3.6 ± 0.1	2.5 ± 0.1
Wpbc	44.4 ± 11.6	1.2 ± 0.4	5.3 ± 1.8	1.3 ± 0.5	1.7 ± 0.2	1.2 ± 0.1

Table 3: $l_{p=1.33}$-SumMKL results on large data sets

Data sets	PGD (hrs)	SPG-GMKL (hrs)
Adult-9	31.77	4.42
Cod-RNA	66.48	19.10
KDDCup04	-	42.20
Covertype	-	64.46
Sonar1M	-	105.62

Table 6: l_1-SumMKL results on large data sets

Data sets	PGD (hrs)	SPG-GMKL (hrs)
Adult-9	35.84	4.55
Cod-RNA	-	25.17
KDDCup04	-	40.10
Real-Sim	-	45.94

the significance of our results. The SVM parameter C was chosen by validation so as to maximize the prediction accuracy. All experiments were carried out on a single core of a 2.1 Ghz AMD 6172 processor with 48 Gb RAM. The results on Covertype were obtained on a similar machine with only 14 Gb RAM.

5.1 Sum of kernels with $l_{p>1}$ regularization

We learn a linear combination of base kernels subject to $l_{p>1}$ regularization. This formulation has yielded state-of-the-art results [22] for combining multiple, heterogeneous features for recognizing objects on the challenging Caltech image data sets. We focus on comparing SPG-GMKL to PGD in this Subsection. Table 2 summarizes the results on the small data sets. For small values of p, the optimization problem is hard, and SPG-GMKL can be two orders of magnitude faster than PGD. As the value of p increases, the optimization problem becomes much simpler, and the two techniques become more comparable though SPG-GMKL can still be twice as fast as PGD.

Results on the larger data sets are given in Table 3. PGD is again much slower and fails to converge on KDDCup04-Physics with fifty thousand points, Covertype with nearly six hundred thousand points and Sonar with a million kernels. SPG-GMKL, without any parallelization, converged on Covertype with 26 SVM evaluations in 64 hours which is reasonable given that solving just the first SVM, equivalent to solving a single kernel SVM obtained by linearly summing the five base kernels with uniform weights, took 44 hours. Note that we were caching only 0.19% of the support vectors and thus the training time can be considerably speeded up by utilizing a larger kernel cache. Similar trends were observed for Sonar with a million kernels.

Figure 1 plots the decrease in objective value versus time on a log-log scale. SPG-GMKL's initial steps are much quicker than PGD's due to the combination of the spectral step length, the non-monotone line search and the coarse SVM precision. SPG-GMKL therefore gets close, and converges, to the optimum much faster than PGD. The non-monotone behavior of SPG-GMKL is prominent on both the Web and Sonar20K datasets. Note that, on Web, the objective function seems to dip below the global minimum. This is due to noise in the objective function because of the coarse SVM precision. PGD would have gotten stuck here as it insists on a strict decrease in the objective function at each iteration. SPG-GMKL can recover due to its non-monotone criterion and SVM precision tuning. This demonstrates that SPG-GMKL is more robust to noise than PGD.

5.2 Sum of kernels with l_1 regularization

One of the most popular MKL formulations is to learn a sum of given base kernels subject to l_1 regularization on the combination coefficients. The joint winner of the highly competitive PASCAL VOC object detection challenge [30] employed such a formulation to learn a sparse combination of features for efficient object detection in images. A number of optimizers have been developed for this formulation. The state-of-the-art is defined by SILP-MKL and SimpleMKL. Table 4 shows that SPG-MKL can not only outperform PGD on this formulation, it is also much better than SILP-MKL and SimpleMKL. For instance, SPG-GMKL is always more than twice as fast as SILP-MKL and can sometimes be orders of magnitude faster as the number of kernels is increased. This demonstrates that our general purpose SPG-GMKL solver can be more efficient than state-of-the-art optimizers designed for a specific formulation. SPG-GMKL is also an order of magnitude faster than SimpleMKL and PGD which are two different implementations of the projected gradient descent algorithm. HessianMKL [7] provides a second order method for optimizing this formulation. While we found HessianMKL to be an improvement over SimpleMKL on small data sets, it's performance was still much worse than that of SPG-GMKL.

5.3 Product of kernels with $l_{p>1}$ regularization

We demonstrate the flexibility of SPG-GMKL by using it to learn products of kernels subject to $l_{p>1}$ regularization. Note that this formulation presents a challenging non-convex optimization problem. Tables 5 and 8 detail performance on small and large data sets respectively. PGD failed to converge in many cases and, when it did, it was often ten to a hundred times slower than SPG-GMKL. We found that the main reason for PGD not converging was that its step size was approaching zero due to inaccurate gradient computation coupled with the Armijo rule. As a result, PGD required many SVM evaluations to take a miniscule step and timed out after a considerable period. On the other hand,

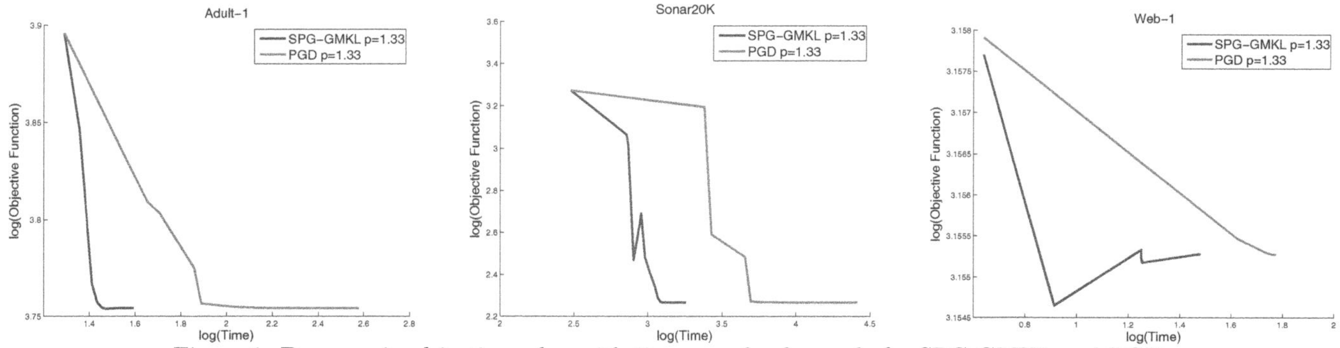

Figure 1: Decrease in objective value with time on a log-log scale for SPG-GMKL and PGD.

Table 4: l_1-SumMKL results on small data sets.

Data sets	SimpleMKL (s)	SILP-MKL (s)	PGD (s)	SPG-GMKL (s)
Wpbc	400.2 ± 128.4	15.5 ± 7.7	38.2 ± 17.6	6.2 ± 4.2
Breast-Cancer	676.1 ± 356.4	12.3 ± 1.2	57.9 ± 85.1	5.1 ± 0.6
Australian	383.2 ± 33.5	1094.9 ± 621.6	29.5 ± 7.1	10.1 ± 0.8
Ionosphere	1247.6 ± 680.0	107.8 ± 18.8	1392.4 ± 824.2	39.2 ± 6.8
Sonar	1468.2 ± 1252.7	935.1 ± 65.0	–	273.4 ± 64.0

Table 5: $l_{p>1}$-ProdMKL results on small data sets.

	$p = 1.1$		$p = 1.33$		$p = 2.0$	
Data sets	PGD (s)	SPG-GMKL (s)	PGD (s)	SPG-GMKL (s)	PGD (s)	SPG-GMKL (s)
Australian	–	22.0 ± 8.4	–	22.1 ± 6.7	–	21.6 ± 6.4
Liver	722.4 ± 880.0	1.0 ± 0.3	136.1 ± 167.9	0.6 ± 0.2	0.3 ± 0.1	0.4 ± 0.1
Sonar	–	7.4 ± 2.9	–	3.2 ± 0.5	293.8 ± 574.7	3.1 ± 0.5
Breast-Cancer	28.4 ± 42.5	4.0 ± 1.0	448.6 ± 691.5	3.3 ± 0.8	377.8 ± 712.0	3.2 ± 0.5
Diabetes	1232.5 ± 716.2	4.8 ± 2.4	364.4 ± 718.3	2.5 ± 0.5	2.1 ± 0.4	2.1 ± 0.1
Wpbc	1080.3 ± 90.9	4.4 ± 1.8	1064.7 ± 41.2	3.7 ± 1.4	209.3 ± 390.8	2.1 ± 0.4

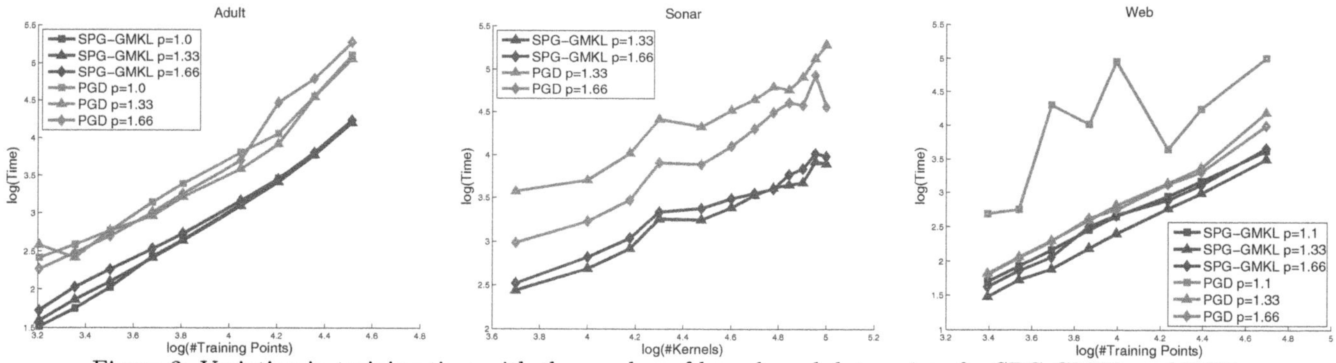

Figure 2: Variation in training time with the number of kernels and data points for SPG-GMKL and PGD.

Table 7: Effects of individual components on small data sets.

Data sets	PGD		PGD+N		PGD+S		PGD+N+S	
	Time (s)	# SVMs	Time (s)	# SVMs	Time (s)	# SVMs	Time (s)	# SVMs
Australian	39.4 ± 6.0	3230	32.7 ± 3.6	116	317.0 ± 49.1	5980	7.0 ± 1.6	621
Sonar	785.5 ± 471.1	209461	41.6 ± 17.1	3236	40.2 ± 24.6	3806	9.0 ± 1.8	2457
Breast-Cancer	237.2 ± 97.8	109599	42.2 ± 4.1	1187	14.9 ± 2.2	3537	8.6 ± 2.2	3006
Diabetes	73.6 ± 38.8	29347	26.3 ± 9.5	2966	10.5 ± 2.6	1239	4.1 ± 0.5	695
Wpbc	44.4 ± 11.6	14376	27.9 ± 13.6	9388	2.9 ± 0.8	340	1.2 ± 0.4	79
Adult-1	376	196	356	196	104	118	71	50
Adult-2	547	238	549	238	207	115	143	70

Table 8: $l_{p=1.33}$-ProdMKL results on large data sets.

Data sets	PGD (hrs)	SPG-GMKL (hrs)
Letter	18.89	0.66
Poker	2.29	0.96
Adult-8	-	3.42
Web-7	-	1.33
RCV1	-	15.93
Cod-RNA	-	8.99

SPG-GMKL generally required only a single SVM evaluation per iteration and converged quickly to the optimum.

5.4 Product of kernels with l_1 regularization

We finally use SPG-GMKL to learn products of kernels subject to l_1 regularization. This formulation was observed to be very good for feature selection [28] as it was significantly better than leading filter and wrapper methods. Tables 9 and 10 compare the performance of SPG-GMKL and PGD on small and large data sets respectively. The trends, and explanations, are much the same as for l_p regularized product of kernels but SPG-GMKL's gains over PGD are even bigger. For instance. On many of the small data sets, SPG-GMKL was a thousand times faster than PGD.

5.5 Scaling Properties and component contributions

We now investigate how SPG-GMKL scales with the number of kernels and data points. Figure 2 plots the results for linear MKL with various values of p on a log-log scale. The number of training points is varied on the Adult and Web data sets while the number of kernels is varied on Sonar. We estimate, from the plots, that SPG-GMKL, on average, scales linearly with the number of kernels on Sonar and as $n^{1.98}$ and $n^{1.52}$ with the number of training points on Adult and Web. The scaling factors are very similar for PGD though the constants involved are much bigger.

We also determine the contribution of each of the three major components of SPG-GMKL, namely the spectral step length, the non-monotone line search and the SVM precision tuning. In Table 7, we start with the PGD implementation as the baseline. We then turn on either the spectral step length computation (PGD+S), or the non-monotone line search (PGD+N), or both (PGD+N+S) and assess the impact on both training time and the number of SVM evaluations. As can be seen, adding either component in isolation does not lead to the best gains and, in fact, can sometimes degrade performance below the PGD baseline. It is only when both the components are combined that one consistently gets improvements in performance.

The full impact of tuning the SVM precision is best seen on larger data sets where the cost of evaluating an SVM is

Table 9: l_1-ProdMKL results on small data sets.

Data sets	PGD (s)	SPG-GMKL (s)
Australian	–	16.6 ± 7.2
Sonar	–	4.8 ± 1.7
Liver	1482.6 ± 635.7	2.6 ± 2.0
Breast-Cancer	1182.6 ± 662.4	4.4 ± 1.5
Diabetes	1525.7 ± 552.6	7.6 ± 6.6
Wpbc	1093.9 ± 187.5	2.7 ± 1.0
Leukemia	2961.5 ± 0.0	850.0 ± 0.0

Table 10: l_1-ProdMKL results on large data sets.

Data sets	PGD (hrs)	SPG-GMKL (hrs)
Letter	18.66	0.67
Poker	5.57	0.49
Adult-8	-	1.73
Web-7	-	0.88
RCV1	-	18.17
Cod-RNA	-	3.45

Table 11: Effects of individual components on large data sets

Data sets	PGD (hrs)	PGD+N+S (hrs)	SPG-GMKL (hrs)
Adult-9	31.77	8.33	4.43
Web-8	4.27	1.73	0.87
Sonar100K	53.91	3.35	2.19

significant. Table 11 shows that adding spectral step length computation and the non-monotone line search criterion to the PGD baseline cuts down its training time to at least half on Web and by more than fifteen times on Sonar. SPG-GMKL adds SVM precision tuning to the combination to further reduce the training time by a factor of two. Thus, each of the three major components that we proposed must be present in order for SPG-GMKL to be an efficient solver that scales well to large problems.

6. CONCLUSIONS

In this paper, we developed an efficient, spectral projected gradient descent based optimizer for the Generalized Multiple Kernel Learning framework. Starting from the projected gradient descent algorithm, we added three components based on the spectral step length, the non-monotone line search criterion and SVM precision tuning. We demonstrated that each of the components is necessary to the success of the SPG-GMKL optimizer.

We carried out extensive experiments benchmarking the performance of SPG-GMKL. We showed that SPG-GMKL routinely gives order of magnitude improvements over PGD and scales well to problems where PGD does not converge. For instance, SPG-GMKL was able to train on problems with a million kernels or half a million data points. This redefines the state-of-the-art in kernel learning optimization. Furthermore, SPG-GMKL, even though it is a general purpose solver, was able to outperform leading specialized solvers developed for a specific formulation. As such, SPG-GMKL is one of the most efficient techniques for kernel learning.

We tested the flexibility of SPG-GMKL by having it optimize four different MKL formulations. Our code is easy to modify and new formulations can readily be plugged in. Our objective is to provide an efficient tool for rapidly prototyping new MKL formulations and trying out existing ones on real world applications.

Acknowledgements

We are grateful to Kamal Gupta and to the Computer Services Center at IIT Delhi.

7. REFERENCES

[1] J. Aflalo, A. Ben-Tal, C. Bhattacharyya, J. S. Nath, and S. Raman. Variable sparsity kernel learning. *JMLR*, 12:565–592, 2011.

[2] F. R. Bach. Exploring large feature spaces with hierarchical multiple kernel learning. In *NIPS*, pages 105–112, 2008.

[3] F. R. Bach, G. R. G. Lanckriet, and M. I. Jordan. Multiple kernel learning, conic duality, and the SMO algorithm. In *ICML*, pages 6–13, 2004.

[4] J. Barzilai and J. Borwein. Two-point step size gradient methods. *IMA J. on Numerical Analysis*, 8:141–148, 1988.

[5] E. G. Birgin, J. M. Martinez, and M. Raydan. Nonmonotone spectral projected gradient methods on convex sets. *SIAM J. on Optimization*, 10(4):1196–1211, 2000.

[6] C.-C. Chang and C.-J. Lin. *LIBSVM: a library for support vector machines*, 2001. Software available at `http://www.csie.ntu.edu.tw/~cjlin/libsvm`.

[7] O. Chapelle and A. Rakotomamonjy. Second order optimization of kernel parameters. In *NIPS Workshop on Automatic Selection of Optimal Kernels*, 2008.

[8] O. Chapelle, V. Vapnik, O. Bousquet, and S. Mukherjee. Choosing multiple parameters for Support Vector Machines. *Machine Learning*, 46:131–159, 2002.

[9] J. Chen, S. Ji, B. Ceran, Q. Li, M. Wu, and J. Ye. Learning subspace kernels for classification. In *KDD*, pages 106–114, 2008.

[10] D. Cores, R. Escalante, M. Gonzalez-Lima, and O. Jimenez. On the use of the spectral projected gradient method for support vector machines. *Computational and Applied Mathematics*, 28(3):327–364, 2009.

[11] C. Cortes, M. Mohri, and A. Rostamizadeh. Learning non-linear combinations of kernels. In *NIPS*, pages 396–404, 2009.

[12] N. Cristianini, J. Shawe-Taylor, A. Elisseeff, and J. Kandola. On kernel-target alignment. In *NIPS*, pages 367–373, 2001.

[13] J. M. Danskin. *The Theorey of Max-Min and its Applications to Weapons Allocation Problems*. 1967.

[14] K. Gai, G. Chen, and C. Zhang. Learning kernels with radiuses of minimum enclosing balls. In *NIPS*, pages 649–657, 2010.

[15] M. Gonen and E. Alpaydin. Localized multiple kernel learning. In *ICML*, pages 352–359, 2008.

[16] L. Grippo, F. Lampariello, and S. Lucidi. A nonmonotone line search technique for newton's method. *SIAM J. on Numerical Analysis*, 23:707–716, 1986.

[17] A. Jain, S. V. N. Vishwanathan, and M. Varma, 2012. The SPG-GMKL code `http://research.microsoft.com/~manik/code/SPG-GMKL/download.html`.

[18] M. Kloft, U. Brefeld, S. Sonnenburg, P. Laskov, K.-R. Muller, and A. Zien. Efficient and accurate l_p-norm Multiple Kernel Learning. In *NIPS*, pages 997–1005, 2009.

[19] G. R. G. Lanckriet, N. Cristianini, P. Bartlett, L. El Ghaoui, and M. I. Jordan. Learning the kernel matrix with semidefinite programming. *JMLR*, 5:27–72, 2004.

[20] C. S. Ong, A. J. Smola, and R. C. Williamson. Learning the kernel with hyperkernels. *JMLR*, 6:1043–1071, 2005.

[21] F. Orabona and L. Jie. Ultra-fast optimization algorithm for sparse multi kernel learning. In *ICML*, pages 249–256, June 2011.

[22] F. Orabona, L. Jie, and B. Caputo. Online-batch strongly convex multi kernel learning. In *CVPR*, pages 787–794, San Francisco, California, June 2010.

[23] A. Rakotomamonjy, F. Bach, Y. Grandvalet, and S. Canu. SimpleMKL. *JMLR*, 9:2491–2521, 2008.

[24] M. Raydan. The barzilai and borwein gradient method for the large scale unconstrained minimization problem. *SIAM J. on Optimization*, 7(1):26–33, 1997.

[25] V. Sindhwani and A. C. Lozano. Non-parametric group orthogonal matching pursuit for sparse learning with multiple kernels. In *NIPS*, pages 2519–2527, 2011.

[26] S. Sonnenburg, G. Raetsch, C. Schaefer, and B. Schoelkopf. Large scale multiple kernel learning. *JMLR*, 7:1531–1565, 2006.

[27] I. W. Tsang and J. T. Kwok. Efficient hyperkernel learning using second-order cone programming. *IEEE Transactions on Neural Networks*, 17(1):48–58, 2006.

[28] M. Varma and B. R. Babu. More generality in efficient multiple kernel learning. In *ICML*, page 134, 2009.

[29] M. Varma and D. Ray. Learning the discriminative power-invariance trade-off. In *ICCV*, pages 1–8, 2007.

[30] A. Vedaldi, V. Gulshan, M. Varma, and A. Zisserman. Multiple kernels for object detection. In *ICCV*, pages 606–613, 2009.

[31] S. V. N. Vishwanathan, Z. Sun, N. Theera-Ampornpunt, and M. Varma. Multiple kernel learning and the SMO algorithm. In *NIPS*, pages 2361–2369, 2010.

[32] J. Ye, , S. Ji, and J. Chen. Multi-class discriminant kernel learning via convex programming. *JMLR*, 9:719–758, 2008.

[33] H. Zhang and W. W. Hager. A nonmonotone line search technique and its application to unconstrained optimization. *SIAM J. on Optimization*, 14(4):1043–1056, 2004.

[34] A. Zien and C. S. Ong. Multiclass multiple kernel learning. In *ICML*, pages 1191–1198, 2007.

Efficient Evaluation of Large Sequence Kernels

Pavel P. Kuksa
Machine Learning Department
NEC Laboratories America, Inc
Princeton, NJ 08540 USA
pkuksa@nec-labs.com

Vladimir Pavlovic
Department of Computer Science
Rutgers University
Piscataway, NJ 08854 USA
vladimir@cs.rutgers.edu

ABSTRACT

Classification of sequences drawn from a finite alphabet using a family of string kernels with inexact matching (e.g., spectrum or mismatch) has shown great success in machine learning. However, selection of optimal mismatch kernels for a particular task is severely limited by inability to compute such kernels for long substrings (k-mers) with potentially many mismatches (m). In this work we introduce a new method that allows us to exactly evaluate kernels for large k, m and arbitrary alphabet size. The task can be accomplished by first solving the more tractable problem for small alphabets, and then trivially generalizing to any alphabet using a small linear system of equations. This makes it possible to explore a larger set of kernels with a wide range of kernel parameters, opening a possibility to better model selection and improved performance of the string kernels. To investigate the utility of large (k,m) string kernels, we consider several sequence classification problems, including protein remote homology detection, fold prediction, and music classification. Our results show that increased k-mer lengths with larger substitutions can improve classification performance.

Categories and Subject Descriptors

I.2 [**Artificial Intelligence**]: Learning; I.5 [**Pattern Recognition**]: Applications; I.5.2. [**Pattern Recognition**]: Design Methodology

General Terms

Algorithms, Design, Measurement, Performance, Experimentation

Keywords

sequence classification, string kernels

1. INTRODUCTION

Analysis of large scale sequential data has become an important task in machine learning and data mining, inspired by applications such as biological sequence analysis, text and audio mining. Classification of string data, sequences of discrete symbols, has attracted particular interest and has led to a number of new algorithms [1, 7, 12, 19]. These algorithms often exhibit state-of-the-art performance on tasks such as protein superfamily and fold prediction, music genre classification and document topic elucidation. In particular, string kernel methods with inexact matching (e.g., mismatch) have been successful in solving challenging problems in bioinformatics, text mining, image categorization, music classification, etc (e.g. [15, 17, 16, 12, 7, 4]).

A family of state-of-the-art approaches to scoring similarity between pairs of sequences relies on fixed length, substring spectral representations and the notion of mismatch kernels, c.f. [7, 12]. There, a sequence is represented as the spectra (counts) of all short substrings (k-mers) contained within a sequence. The similarity score is established by exact or approximate matches of k-mers. Initial work, e.g., [12, 18], has demonstrated that this similarity can be computed using trie-based approaches in $O(k^{m+1}|\Sigma|^m(|X|+|Y|))$ time, for strings X and Y with symbols from alphabet Σ and up to m mismatches between k-mers (the $|\cdot|$ notation stands for the length of the sequence).

More recently,in [9] we introduced linear time algorithms with *alphabet-independent* complexity $O(c_{k,m}(|X|+|Y|))$ for a large class of existing string kernels. In particular, for mismatch kernels, their computation for strings X and Y is based on cumulative pairwise comparison of all substrings α and β contained in X and Y, with the level of similarity of each pair of substrings (α, β) taken as the number of identical substrings their mutational neighborhoods $N_{k,m}(\alpha)$ and $N_{k,m}(\beta)$ give rise to ($N_{k,m}(\alpha)$ is the set of all k-mers that differ from α by at most m mismatches). This result however requires that the number of identical substrings in (k, m)-mutational neighborhoods of k-mers a and b (the intersection size) be known in advance, for every possible pair of m and the Hamming distance d between k-mers (k and $|\Sigma|$ are free variables). Obtaining the closed form expression for the intersection size for arbitrary k, m is challenging, with no clear systematic way of enumerating the intersection of two mutational neighborhoods. Closed form solutions obtained in [9] were only provided for cases when m is small ($m \leq 3$).

In this work we introduce a systematic and efficient procedure for obtaining intersection sizes (Sec. 3) that can be used for large k and m and arbitrary alphabet size $|\Sigma|$. This will allow us to effectively explore a much larger class of (k, m) kernels in the process of model selection. We will investigate performance impact of using large (k,m) and il-

KDD'12, August 12–16, 2012, Beijing, China.

lustrate it on a number of sequence classification problems including detecting homology of remotely related proteins, multi-class fold prediction and classification of music samples (Sec. 4.1). We will show importance of kernel parameter selection in Sec. 4.2 and show that using large (k, m) kernels could further improve performance of the string kernel method.

2. BACKGROUND AND RELATED WORK

The key idea of basic string kernel methods is to apply a mapping $\Phi(\cdot)$ to map sequences of variable length into a fixed-dimensional vector space. In this space a standard kernel classifier, such as a support vector machine (SVM) [21], can then be applied. As SVMs require only inner products between examples in the feature space, rather than the feature vectors themselves, one can define a *string kernel* which computes the inner product in the feature space without explicitly computing the feature vectors:

$$K(X, Y) = \langle \Phi(X), \Phi(Y) \rangle, \tag{1}$$

where $X, Y \in D$, D is the set of all sequences composed of elements which take on a finite set of possible values from the alphabet Σ.

Sequence matching is frequently based on co-occurrence of exact sub-patterns (k-mers, features), as in spectrum kernels [11] or substring kernels [22]. Inexact comparison in this framework is typically achieved using different families of mismatch [12] or profile [7] kernels. Both spectrum-k and mismatch(k,m) kernel directly extract string features from the observed sequence, X. On the other hand, the profile kernel, proposed by Kuang *et al.* in [7], builds a profile [3] P_X and uses a similar $|\Sigma|^k$-dimensional representation, now derived from P_X. Constructing the profile for each sequence may not be practical in some application domains, since the size of the profile is dependent on the size of the alphabet set. While for bio-sequences $|\Sigma| = 4$ or 20, for music or text data $|\Sigma|$ can potentially be very large, on the order of tens of thousands of symbols.

Some of the most efficient available trie-based algorithms [12, 18] for mismatch kernels have a strong dependency on the size of alphabet set Σ and the number of allowed mismatches. Both need to be restricted in practice to control the complexity of matching algorithms. Under the trie-based framework, the list of k-mers extracted from given input strings is traversed in a depth-first search with branches corresponding to all possible $\sigma \in \Sigma$. Each leaf node at depth k corresponds to a particular k-mer feature (either exact or inexact instance of the observed exact string features) and contains a list of matching features from each string. The kernel matrix is updated at leaf nodes with corresponding matching feature counts. The complexity of the trie-based algorithm for mismatch kernel computation for two strings X and Y is $O(k^{m+1}|\Sigma|^m(|X|+|Y|))$ [12]. The algorithm complexity depends on the size of Σ, with possible substitutions explicitly drawn from Σ during the trie traversal. Consequently, to control the complexity of the algorithm we need to restrict the number of allowed mismatches (m), as well as the alphabet size ($|\Sigma|$). Typically, (k, m) are set to no more than $(5, 2)$ for alphabets of size $|\Sigma| = 20$.

Recent work in [9] introduced linear time algorithms with *alphabet-independent* complexity for Hamming-distance based matching. This enables efficient computation of a wide class of existing string kernels for datasets with large $|\Sigma|$. The authors show that it is possible to compute an inexact (k, m) kernel as

$$K(X, Y|m, k) = \sum_{a \in X} \sum_{b \in Y} \mathcal{I}(a, b) = \sum_{i=0}^{\min(2m,k)} M_i \mathcal{I}_i, \tag{2}$$

where a and b are k-mers contained in X and Y, $\mathcal{I}(a, b)$ is the number of common substrings in the intersection of the mutation neighborhoods of the k-mers a and b, $\mathcal{I}_i$ is the size of the intersection of k-mer mutational neighborhood for Hamming distance i, and M_i is the number of observed k-mer pairs in X and Y having Hamming distance i. The algorithms introduced in [9], however, require as an input the intersection sizes $\mathcal{I}_i$ (i.e. number of identical substrings in the mutational neighborhoods of k-mers a and b) for all possible Hamming distances between a and b. No systematic way of obtaining these intersection sizes has been proposed in [9]. Closed-form solutions have been suggested for cases of small m ($m \leq 3$). For larger values of m ($m > 3$), it becomes substantially more difficult to combinatorially enumerate the intersection of the neighborhoods as the neighborhoods grow exponentially with m. In the next section we address these issues and propose a systematic way of computing intersection sizes that can be used for larger k and m.

3. FINDING INTERSECTION SIZES FOR LARGE K AND M

For large values of k and m finding intersection sizes needed for kernel computation can be problematic. This is because while for smaller values of m combinatorial closed form solution can be found easily, for larger values of m finding it becomes more difficult due to an increase in the number of combinatorial possibilities as the mutational neighborhood increases (exponentially) in size. On the other hand, direct computation of the intersection by trie traversal algorithm is computationally difficult for large k and m as the complexity of traversal is $O(k^{m+1}|\Sigma|^m)$, i.e. it is exponential in both k and m. The above mentioned issues do not allow for efficient kernel evaluation for large k and m. We will further discuss in what follows approaches to computing intersection sizes and propose an efficient method that can effectively compute intersection sizes for large k and m and allows to explore more complex kernels (with large k and m) that as we will show in Section 4.2 can further improve performance of the string kernel method.

The number of k-mers at the Hamming distance of at most m from both k-mers a and b, $\mathcal{I}(a, b)$, can be found in a weighted form

$$\mathcal{I}(a, b) = \sum_{i=0}^{m} w_i (|\Sigma| - 1)^i. \tag{3}$$

Coefficients w_i depend only on the Hamming distance $d(a, b)$ between k-mers a and b for fixed k, m, and $|\Sigma|$ (intuitively, coefficients w_i are of combinatorial nature and do not depend on the alphabet size). The intersection size $\mathcal{I}$ and coefficients w_i can be precomputed for a given setting $(k, m, |\Sigma|)$ in a number of different ways. In the following, we discuss possible approaches for intersection size computation.

Brute-force. Directly computes intersection sizes for $0 \leq d \leq 2m$ by performing $2m$ trie traversals for k-mer pairs a and b over alphabet Σ at distances $d = 1 \ldots 2m$. This does not compute w_i explicitly. Brute-force trie traversal for computing intersection sizes is applicable only for moderate values of $|\Sigma|$, k, m.

Analytic (closed-form) solution. The set of coefficients w_i for every possible distance $d(a,b)$ and a fixed m can be found in a closed form with k and $|\Sigma|$ as variables (see [9]). For example, when $m=2$ the intersection sizes can be found in closed form as

$$\mathcal{I}(a,b) \atop (m=2) = \begin{cases} \sum_{i=0}^{m}\binom{k}{i}(|\Sigma|-1)^i, d(a,b)=0 \\ 1+k(|\Sigma|-1)+(k-1)(|\Sigma|-1)^2, d(a,b)=1 \\ 1+2(k-1)(|\Sigma|-1)+(|\Sigma|-1)^2, d(a,b)=2 \\ 6(|\Sigma|-1), d(a,b)=3 \\ \binom{4}{2}, d(a,b)=4 \end{cases}$$

Once the closed form solution is found for every (m,d) pair, the intersection sizes for given k, $|\Sigma|$ can be found in constant time. However, it is difficult to obtain closed form solution for larger k, m. Currently, analytic solutions are known for $m<4$, with no known solutions for $m \geq 4$.

Finding coefficients by solving linear systems of equations. It is possible to efficiently compute the intersection sizes by reducing $(k,m,|\Sigma|)$ intersection size problem to a set of less complex intersection size computations. We discuss this approach below.

3.1 Reduction-based computation of intersection size coefficients

Following Eq. 2, for every Hamming distance $0 \leq d(a,b) \leq 2m$, the corresponding set of coefficients $w_i, i=0,1,\dots,m$ satisfies the following linear system

$$Aw = \mathcal{I} \tag{4}$$

of $m+1$ equations with each equation corresponding to a particular alphabet size $|\Sigma| \in \{2,3,\dots,m+2\}$. The left-hand side matrix A is an $(m+1,m+1)$ matrix with elements $a_{ij}=(i+1)^{j-1}$, $i=1,\dots,m+1$, $j=1,\dots,m+1$.

$$A = \begin{pmatrix} 1^0 & 1^1 & 1^2 & \dots & 1^m \\ 2^0 & 2^1 & 2^2 & \dots & 2^m \\ & & & \dots & \\ (m+1)^0 & (m+1)^1 & (m+1)^2 & \dots & (m+1)^m \end{pmatrix}$$

The right-hand side $\mathcal{I}=(I_0,I_1,\dots,I_m)^T$ is a vector of intersection sizes for a particular setting of k, m, d, $|\Sigma| = 2,3,\dots,m+2$. Here, $I_i, i=0\dots m$ is the intersection size for a pair of k-mers over alphabet size $i+2$.

If $\mathcal{I}_i$ are known, the coefficients w_i in w can be fully determined by solving the system of equations 4, $w=A^{-1}\mathcal{I}$. Note that, in that case, $\mathcal{I}_i$ need only be computed for small alphabet sizes, up to $m+2$. Hence, this vector can feasibly be computed using a trie traversal for a pair of k-mers at Hamming distance d even for moderately large k as the size of the trie is only $(m+2)^k$ as opposed to $|\Sigma|^k$. This allows now to evaluate kernels for large k and m as the traversal is performed over much smaller tries, e.g., even in case of relatively small protein alphabet with $|\Sigma|=20$, for $m=6$ and $k=13$, the size of the trie is $20^{13}/(6+2)^{13}=149011$ times smaller. Coefficients w obtained by solving $Aw=\mathcal{I}$ do not depend on the alphabet size $|\Sigma|$. In other words, once found for a particular combination of values (k,m), these coefficients can be used to determine intersection sizes for any given finite alphabet $|\Sigma|$ using Eq. 3.

We summarize the intersection size computation in Algorithm 1. The algorithm receives as the input the problem parameters k, m, and $|\Sigma|$ and returns both the vector of $(\min(k,2m)+1)$ intersection sizes $\mathcal{I}_{k,m,|\Sigma|}$ (lookup table) for a given $(k,m,|\Sigma|)$-problem and the weight matrix $W_{k,m}$ that can be used to obtain intersection sizes for any alphabet size $|\Sigma|$. The overall complexity of the algorithm is $O((2m+1)k^{m+1}(m+2)^m)$. Compared to $O((2m+1)k^{m+1}|\Sigma|^m)$ complexity of computing intersection sizes directly using trie traversals, proposed algorithm has lower complexity by a factor of $\left(\frac{|\Sigma|}{m+2}\right)^m$ (as we show empirically in Sec. 4.3 this agrees with observed running time improvements). We also note that the running time of the proposed algorithm (Algorithm 1) is dominated by the trie traversals (lines 3-6 in Algorithm 1) used to obtain intersection sizes I (the right-hand side of the linear system $Aw=I$).

Algorithm 1: Intersection size computation

Input: kernel parameters k and m, alphabet size $|\Sigma|$
1: **for** $d=0$ to $\min(k,2m)$ **do**
2: {for each Hamming distance d}
3: **for** $i=2$ to $m+2$ **do**
4: {for each alphabet size $i=2\dots m+2$}
5: Create a pair of k-mers a and b with Hamming distance $h(a,b)=d$
6: Obtain intersection size I_i by computing (k,m)-mismatch kernel $K_{k,m}(a,b)$ using trie traversal over i^k tree.
7: **end for**
8: Set $(m+1)\times(m+1)$ matrix A with $a_{ij}=(i+1)^{(j-1)}$, $i=1,\dots,m+1$, $j=1,\dots,m+1$
9: Solve $Aw=I$ to obtain weight vector w
10: Set $(d+1)$th row of $W_{k,m}$ to w
11: **end for**
12: Compute vector of intersection sizes $\mathcal{I}_{k,m,|\Sigma|}=W_{k,m}((|\Sigma|-1)^0\dots(\Sigma-1)^m)^T$
Output: Weight matrix $W_{k,m}$ of size $(\min(k,2m)+1,m+1)$, vector of intersection sizes (lookup table) $\mathcal{I}_{k,m,|\Sigma|}$

Some examples of weight matrices $W_{k,m}$ for various settings of k and m are shown in the Appendix (the negative entries in the weight matrices seem to correspond to terms in Eq. 3 correcting for overcounting). Intersection sizes $\mathcal{I}$ can be obtained for a particular alphabet size $|\Sigma|$ by multiplying weight matrix $W_{k,m}$ by a vector of $(|\Sigma|-1)$ powers as in Eq. 3, i.e.

$$\mathcal{I}_{k,m,|\Sigma|} = W_{k,m}\left(\ |\Sigma|^0 \quad |\Sigma|^1 \quad \dots \quad |\Sigma|^{m-1} \ \right)^T.$$

We note that weight matrices $W_{k,m}$ (steps 1-11 of Algorithm 1) can be pre-computed, and then once computed used to solve (k,m)-mismatch problems for a given alphabet Σ (i.e. weight matrices $W_{k,m}$ are *alphabet-size independent*).

4. EXPERIMENTS

We evaluate the utility of large (k,m) computations as a proxy for model selection, by allowing a significantly wider range of kernel parameters to be investigated during the selection process. In these evaluations we follow the experimental settings considered in [10] and [9].

We use three standard benchmark datasets: the SCOP dataset (7329 sequences, 54 experiments) [23] for remote protein homology detection, the Ding-Dubchak dataset[1] (27 folds, 694 seqs) [2, 4] for multi-class protein fold recognition, and music genre data[2] (10 genres, 1000 seqs) [13] for multi-class genre prediction. For remote protein homology experiments, we follow standard experimental setup used in previous studies [23] and evaluate average classification performance on 54 remote homology experiments, each simulating the remote homology detection problem by training on a subset of families under the target superfamily and testing the superfamily classifier on the remaining (held out) families according to SCOP hierarchy (Figure 1). For music genre classification, we use vector quantization (VQ) to represent original sequences of 13-dim. MFCC vectors as strings over $|\Sigma| = 2048$ alphabet, and we use 5-fold cross-validation error to evaluate classification performance. For multi-class fold prediction, we use standard data splits as described in [2, 4]. Data and source code are available at the supplementary website [20].

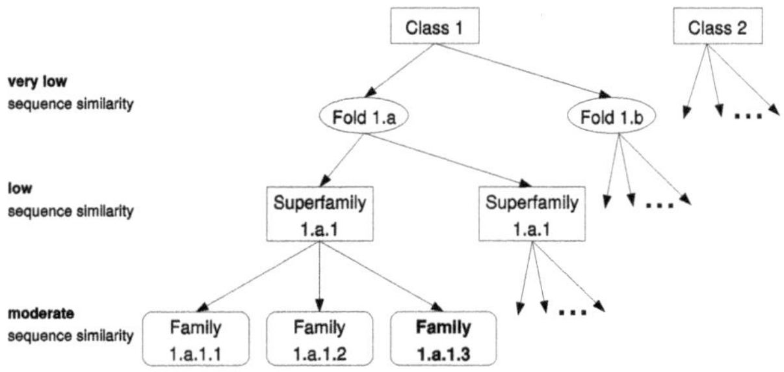

Figure 1: SCOP hierarchy. Protein domains organized into classes, folds, superfamilies, and families. Protein sequences from same superfamily but different families are considered remote homologs.

4.1 Large (k,m) performance evaluation

In this section, we investigate the impact of kernel parameters on the classification performance on the three sequence classification tasks. For each task, we evaluate classification performance over a large range of settings for k and m. Such large range evaluation is the first of its kind, made possible by our efficient kernel evaluation algorithm.

Evaluation measures. The methods are evaluated using 0-1 and top-q balanced error rates as well as F1 scores and precision and recall rates. Under the top-q error cost function, a classification is considered correct if the rank of the correct label, obtained by sorting all prediction confidences in non-increasing order, is at most q. On the other hand, under the balanced error cost function, the penalty of mis-classifying one sequence is inversely proportional to the number of sequences in the target class (i.e. mis-classifying a sequence from a class with a small number of examples results in a higher penalty compared to that of mis-classifying a sequence from a large, well represented class). We evaluate remote protein homology performance using standard Receiver Operating Characteristic (ROC) and ROC50 scores. The ROC50 score is the (normalized) area under the ROC curve computed for up to 50 false positives. With a small number of positive test sequences and a large number of negative test sequences, the ROC50 score is typically more indicative of the prediction accuracy of a homology detection method than the ROC score.

[1]`http://ranger.uta.edu/~chqding/bioinfo.html`

[2]`http://opihi.cs.uvic.ca/sound/genres`

Table 1: Remote homology. Classification performance (mean ROC50) of the mismatch kernel method in the supervised setting

Kernel	Mean ROC	Mean ROC50
mismatch(5,1)	87.75	41.92
mismatch(5,2)	90.67	49.09
mismatch(6,2)	90.74	49.66
mismatch(6,3)	90.98	49.36
mismatch(7,3)	91.31	52.00
mismatch(7,4)	90.84	49.29
mismatch(9,3)	90.27	47.00
mismatch(9,4)	91.45	53.51
mismatch(10,4)	91.02	50.49
mismatch(10,5)	**91.60**	**53.78**
mismatch(13,6)	90.98	50.11

Results of mismatch kernel classification for the remote homology detection problem are shown in Table 1. We observe that larger values of k and m perform better compared to typically used values of k=5-6, m=1-2. For instance, (k=10,m=5)-mismatch kernel achieves significantly higher average ROC50 score of 53.78 compared to ROC50 of 41.92 and 49.09 for the (k=5,m=1)- and (k=5,m=2)- mismatch kernels (with p-values 3.1e-6 and 1.8e-3, respectively). Table 2 shows for each of the (k, m) kernel methods p-values of the Wilcoxon signed-rank test on the ROC50 scores against other (k,m) kernels. The utility of such large mismatch kernels was not possible to investigate prior to this study. As can also be seen from comparison with other state-of-the-art methods (including PSI-BLAST, Smith-Waterman similarity-based SVM [14], subsequence [15] and recently proposed spatial sample kernels (SSSK) [8] and sequence learner (SEQL) [5] approaches) in Table 3, large (k, m) mismatch kernels display state-of-the-art performance.

Table 3: Remote homology prediction. Comparison with state-of-the-art methods

method	ROC	ROC50
PSI-BLAST [7]	74.29	29.25
SVM-Fisher [6, 7]	75.66	31.90
SVM-Pairwise (Smith-Waterman) [14]	89.30	43.40
Subsequence kernel [15]	87.23	40.37
SSSK [8]	91.48	51.18
SEQL [5]	**92.20**	52.37
Mismatch(k=10,m=5)	91.60	**53.78**

On the multi-class remote fold prediction problem (Table 4), larger values of k tend to increase precision and result in higher F1 scores. For instance, top-5 F1 score of 84.00 for the $(k = 11, m = 6)$-mismatch kernel is higher than that of $(k = 5, m = 1)$ or $(k = 5, m = 2)$ mismatch kernels with F1 scores of 81.68 and 80.88, respectively. For longer k increasing the maximum number of allowed mismatches m tends to increase recall rates, while keeping precision rates almost the same. For example, recall rates change from 36.16 to

Table 2: Statistical significance of the differences between (k,m) kernels (p-values according to signed rank test) and effect size. Kernels with large (k, m) perform better than the traditionally used (k, m) kernels

	(5,1)	(5,2)	(6,2)	(6,3)	(7,4)	(9,4)
(5,2)	3.4e-04/0.25					
(6,2)	3.7e-06/0.27	3.8e-01/0.02				
(6,3)	1.4e-03/0.26	7.2e-01/0.01	7.7e-01/-0.01			
(7,4)	2.2e-03/0.26	7.0e-01/0.01	9.8e-01/-0.01	8.7e-01/0.0		
(9,4)	1.6e-06/0.42	3.2e-03/0.16	7.3e-04/0.14	1.4e-02/0.15	2.9e-02/0.15	
(10,5)	3.1e-06/0.43	1.8e-03/0.17	1.5e-03/0.15	2.5e-03/0.16	9.4e-03/0.16	5.6e-01/0.01

Table 4: Multi-class remote fold prediction (Ding&Dubchak dataset). Classification performance of the mismatch kernel method in the supervised setting

Kernel	Error	Top-5 Error	Balanced Error	Top-5 Balanced Error	Recall	Top-5 Recall	Precision	Top-5 Precision	F1	Top-5 F1
mismatch(5,1)	51.17	22.19	53.22	28.65	46.78	71.35	90.52	95.50	61.69	81.68
mismatch(5,2)	**42.56**	19.32	**45.51**	22.60	**54.49**	77.40	67.18	84.68	60.17	80.88
mismatch(5,3)	47.78	23.24	49.69	24.94	50.31	75.06	57.81	77.09	53.80	76.06
mismatch(6,2)	46.74	19.06	50.85	24.55	49.15	75.45	89.64	95.24	63.49	**84.19**
mismatch(6,3)	43.34	19.84	46.74	**22.08**	53.26	**77.92**	65.40	83.77	58.71	80.74
mismatch(7,3)	43.86	18.80	47.21	22.68	52.79	77.32	86.46	93.85	**65.55**	**84.78**
mismatch(7,4)	43.60	20.37	47.15	22.68	52.85	77.32	63.92	81.98	57.86	79.58
mismatch(9,2)	63.71	34.46	63.65	43.94	36.35	56.06	**93.01**	96.88	52.27	71.02
mismatch(9,3)	57.96	30.29	61.51	40.76	38.49	59.24	91.51	96.01	54.19	73.27
mismatch(9,4)	54.57	21.15	57.42	29.00	42.58	71.00	91.56	96.44	58.13	81.79
mismatch(10,3)	63.97	32.64	63.84	43.05	36.16	56.95	**93.01**	**97.02**	52.07	71.77
mismatch(10,4)	57.96	28.72	61.53	39.21	38.47	60.79	91.36	96.00	54.14	74.44
mismatch(10,5)	51.70	19.58	55.65	26.90	44.35	73.10	91.76	96.55	59.80	83.20
mismatch(10,6)	**42.82**	19.06	47.28	**22.43**	52.72	**77.57**	76.32	89.43	62.36	83.08
mismatch(11,4)	62.92	30.81	64.08	42.36	35.92	57.64	92.28	96.90	51.72	72.28
mismatch(11,5)	57.70	27.68	61.37	38.53	38.63	61.47	91.32	96.01	54.29	74.95
mismatch(11,6)	48.56	**18.28**	53.33	25.28	46.67	74.72	90.80	95.91	61.65	**84.00**
mismatch(13,4)	65.80	34.20	65.40	44.97	34.60	55.03	**92.73**	96.91	50.40	70.19
mismatch(13,5)	64.75	32.11	64.68	44.05	35.32	55.95	**92.84**	**97.05**	51.18	70.98

52.72 for the $k = 10$ case as m changes from 3 to 6. We also note that using $m > k/2$ compared to $m \leq k/2$ can result in significant drops in precision rates, e.g. $(k = 10, m = 6)$-mismatch kernel has much lower precision rate of 76.32 compared to 91.76 of the $(k = 10, m = 5)$-mismatch kernel.

For the music genre classification task (Table 5), parameter combinations with moderately long k and larger values of m tend to perform better than kernels with small m. As can be seen from results, larger values of m are important for achieving good classification accuracy and outperform setting with small values of m. However, increasing (k,m) does not result in high performance gains, possibly because of significant reduction in recall for these large alphabet sequences.

Table 5: Multi-class music genre recognition. Classification performance of the mismatch method

Kernel	Error	Top-2 Error	F1	Top-2 F1
mismatch(5,1)	34.8±3.49	18.3	65.36	81.95
mismatch(5,2)	32.6±2.63	18.0	67.51	82.21
mismatch(6,3)	32.4±0.96	19.0	67.79	81.22
mismatch(7,4)	**31.1±2.07**	18.0	**68.96**	82.16
mismatch(9,3)	31.4±1.25	18.0	68.59	82.33
mismatch(9,4)	32.2±1.82	17.8	67.83	82.36
mismatch(10,3)	32.3±1.3	18.0	67.65	82.12
mismatch(10,4)	31.7±1.52	19.1	68.29	81.04

4.2 Class-specific kernel/parameter selection

In what follows, we discuss approaches for kernel parameter selection. In particular, we focus on the question of selecting mismatch kernel parameters k and m that would be appropriate for a task at hand. We note that reduced running time requirements of our algorithm open the possibility to consider various parameter selection strategies (validation, uniform, multiple kernel learning (MKL, e.g., [24])) with a larger set of (k,m) kernels. The results presented here demonstrate that such large (k,m) kernels could lead to significant performance improvements.

4.2.1 Parameter selection by validation

One approach to the parameter selection is to select k and m that perform best on average according to the validation set. We demonstrate this approach on remote protein homology detection task within SCOP hierarchy. In SCOP, a manually curated protein data set, sequences are grouped into a tree hierarchy containing classes, folds, superfamilies, and families, from root to leaf (Fig. 1). As validation data is not available on the standard benchmark dataset, we split the original training set into two disjoint subsets, a now smaller training subset and a validation subset. Validation subset is obtained by holding out a single family (positive validation examples) and 20% of the negative training sequences. After training on a now smaller training subset, the performance of a particular combination of values k and m is measured on a validation set. We then select the best performing combination (k, m) (according to the validation set) as kernel parameters for the mismatch kernel.

We show results in Table 6 for various choices of k and m (results are average ROC and ROC50 scores for 54 experiments). One can observe that according to performance on the validation set larger values of k and m are preferred. For instance, on the validation set, mismatch-(k=9, m=4) and (k=10,m=5) achieve top two ROC50 scores of 81.57 and 81.30 compared to 77.17 or 79.21 of traditionally used mismatch-(k=5,m=2) and (k=7,m=3). We also observe that best performing kernels according to the validation set also perform best on the test set. The top two kernels with (k=9,m=4) and (k=10,m=5) achieve highest average ROC50 scores of 52.59 and 52.96. Similar trends are observed with respect to ROC.

4.2.2 *Uniform multiple kernel combination*

Another approach for setting kernel parameters is to consider the kernel equivalent to a combination of multiple kernels, with each individual kernel corresponding to a particular choice of k and m. This approach does not select a particular value for k or m, it rather uses a set of (k, m) values in a uniform combination. This may be advantageous compared to selecting particular values for k and m as there might not be a single choice of parameter values which would work best in all cases, e.g., for all superfamilies. By not fixing the values of k and m, the classifier (e.g., SVM) can learn importance/usefulness of features corresponding to a range of k and m parameter values.

We present selection of results on remote homology detection in Table 7 using a uniform mixture of mismatch kernels with $k = 1...13$ and $m = 1...6$. As evident from the results, the performance of the uniform mixture (column 1) is very similar to the performance of the best single kernel as found by the validation (Sec. 4.2.1, Table 6).

4.2.3 *Multiple kernel learning*

Using a weighted combination of multiple kernels may potentially give better performance compared to a uniform kernel combination. Here we show results for using multiple kernel learning (MKL) [24] on remote homology detection. We again use the same large pool of mismatch kernels k=5...13, m=1...6 and learn a multiple kernel combination for each of the 54 remote homology problems.

The results for multiple kernel learning on remote homology detection are shown in Table 7 (only a selection of the tasks is shown). While the resulting average ROC50 (column 2 in Table 7) are slightly lower compared to uniform combination (column 1), the results are similar and seem to suggest that for different superfamilies, a different setting of parameters k and m may be needed. This is also clear from the best-case results for the selection of parameter values based on the test set performance (last column in Table 7). We observe that best performing k and m differ across different superfamilies, suggesting the need for a kernel combination.

4.2.4 *Comparison of kernel selection approaches*

According to the SCOP hierarchy, (1) a single kernel can be selected for the entire hierarchy, (2) kernels can be selected at a superfamily level, i.e. on a per-superfamily basis, (3) kernels can be selected at a family level, i.e. on a per-family basis. Selection itself can be based on train, validation, or test performance. In Table 8 we summarize performance of various kernel selection strategies including validation-based kernel selection, best-case (test-based) selection, uniform kernel combination and multiple kernel learning. While multiple kernel learning selects kernel mixture at a family level, uniform kernel combination is the same for all superfamilies/families, i.e. it is similar to selecting a single best kernel based on average performance across all superfamilies/families. For superfamily-level selection, a single kernel is selected for a given superfamily based on the average performance across families belonging to the superfamily.

Table 8: Remote homology. Comparison of kernel selection approaches.

Method	Mean ROC50
Validation-based selection (single kernel)	52.59
Validation-based selection (per family)	47.43
Validation-based selection (per superfamily)	49.89
Test-based selection (single kernel)	53.78
Test-based selection (per family)	60.32
Test-based selection (per superfamily)	56.16
Uniform multiple kernel combination	52.11
Multiple kernel learning (per family)	50.78

As we noted before, results for best-case selection (i.e. for selecting best kernel per superfamily/family based on test set performance) suggest the need for per-superfamily/per-family parameter selection to improve the classification performance. The reduced running time requirements of our algorithm allows to consider various parameter selection strategies (validation, uniform, MKL) with a larger set of (k,m) kernels. Our results show (Tables 7, 8) that per-class selection with large (k,m) could lead to significant improvements (average ROC50 53.78 $\rightarrow$ 60.32). However, for practical application (e.g., parameter selection using validation approach) more data is necessary.

4.3 Running time

We measure the running time for full mismatch kernel matrix computations for SCOP and music genre datasets (i.e. we compute 7329×7329 and 1000×1000 kernel matrices) with all of running time experiments performed on a single 3.0GHz CPU. As can be seen from the running times in Table 9 our method allows efficient evaluation for large k, m kernels (running times are given for protein (7329 seqs) and music (1000 seqs) datasets). We note that the running times include time required for intersection size computations (Algorithm 1).

In Table 10, we report running time improvements of our proposed method for intersection size computation (Algorithm 1) over brute-force (trie-based) computation of intersection sizes. As can be seen from the table, ratios of run-

Table 6: Remote homology. Classification performance (mean ROC and ROC50) of the mismatch kernel method in the supervised setting (with validation set)

Kernel	ROC (Test)	ROC50 (Test)	ROC (Validation)	ROC50 (Validation)
mismatch(5,1)	85.75	39.47	88.28	73.21
mismatch(5,2)	89.62	48.10	90.36	77.17
mismatch(6,2)	89.26	48.72	90.61	77.89
mismatch(6,3)	89.95	48.38	90.32	77.05
mismatch(7,3)	90.08	51.64	91.17	79.21
mismatch(7,4)	89.79	47.74	90.04	76.40
mismatch(9,3)	87.14	44.27	89.55	76.47
mismatch(9,4)	89.97	**52.59**	91.90	**81.57**
mismatch(10,4)	88.77	48.47	90.90	79.15
mismatch(10,5)	90.40	**52.96**	**92.34**	**81.30**
mismatch(11,5)	89.68	50.14	91.52	80.25
mismatch(11,6)	**90.58**	52.72	**92.38**	81.23
mismatch(13,5)	86.57	42.56	87.79	70.12

Table 7: Remote homology detection. Kernel selection. Note that best choice of parameter values (k,m) is class-specific (i.e. depends on protein superfamily/family). Kernels with larger values k,m achieve higher prediction accuracy compared to settings with smaller k,and m.

Experiment	Uniform kernel	MKL top (k,m)	Test ROC50	Best k, m (based on validation set)	Test ROC50	Best k, m (based on test set)	Test ROC50
2.56.1.2	13.75	(13,6)	**37.75**	11, 6)	17.35	(7, 3)	18.11
1.27.1.2	**58.57**	(13,6)	51.71	(11, 6)	51.02	(7, 3)	58.60
1.4.1.2	**67.20**	(7,3)	57.6	(5, 3)	62.04	(7, 3)	73.47
3.2.1.5	**57.71**	(13,6)	52.86	(11, 6)	52.48	(13, 4)	73.47
2.28.1.3	**30.40**	(13,6)	27.20	(6, 2)	26.12	(5, 3)	30.61
7.3.6.1	89.11	(5,2)	**97.56**	(5, 3)	80.95	(11, 6)	93.20
2.1.1.2	80.62	(7,3)	**90.50**	(11, 4)	81.76	(11, 5)	88.65
2.38.4.5	**46.25**	(13,6)	33.0	(9, 2)	0.00	(5, 3)	56.89
1.36.1.2	26.00	(7,3)	**36.33**	(5, 3)	1.36	(10, 5)	38.78
1.41.1.2	96.00	(7,3)	**97.67**	(5, 1)	73.47	(11, 6)	98.98
Mean ROC50:	51.47		50.78		47.43		60.32

Table 9: Running time for kernel computation on music and protein sequence data

$(k, m, \|\Sigma\|)$	Running time (s)
(9,2,2048)	235
(9,3,2048)	373
(9,4,2048)	416
(10,2,20)	82
(10,3,20)	196
(10,5,20)	610

ning times T_{trie}/T_{linear} as a function of kernel parameters k,m, and alphabet size $|\Sigma|$ are as expected from theoretical analysis. For example, the obtained speed-up for computing intersection sizes for k=10,m=5,$|\Sigma|$=20 is 208x, while the expected running time ratio $\left(\frac{|\Sigma|}{m+2}\right)^m$ is $(20/(5+2))^5$=190. We also note that because of high $O(k^{m+1}|\Sigma|^m)$ computational complexity of finding intersection sizes using explicit trie traversal, for $m > 3$ and large alphabet $|\Sigma|$ running time is excessively long (for these cases only expected running time ratios are shown in Table 10).

Table 10: Intersection size computation. Running time ratio T_{trie}/T_{linear} (speed-up) of the trie-based method and proposed algorithm as a function of kernel parameters k, m, and alphabet size $|\Sigma|$. Observed speed-ups are on the order of $\left(\frac{|\Sigma|}{m+2}\right)^m$ as expected from theoretical analysis

(k,m)	$\|\Sigma\| = 20$	$\|\Sigma\| = 100$
(5,2)	6	254
(5,3)	27	5931
(6,2)	9	393
(6,3)	45	10118
(7,2)	13	571
(7,3)	57	12848
(7,4)	120	n/a / $8 \times 10^{4\dagger}$
(9,4)	132	n/a / $8 \times 10^{4\dagger}$
(9,5)	197	n/a / $6 \times 10^{5\dagger}$
(10,5)	208	n/a / $6 \times 10^{5\dagger}$

† expected running time ratio only due to excessive running time for trie-based method

5. CONCLUSIONS

In this work we proposed a new systematic method that allows evaluation of inexact string family kernels for long substrings k with large number of mismatches m. The method finds the intersection set sizes by explicitly computing them for small alphabet size $|\Sigma|$ and then generalizing this to arbitrary large alphabets. We show that this enables one to explore a larger set of kernels corresponding to a wide range of kernel parameter values, which as we demonstrate experimentally can further improve performance of the string kernels. We illustrate impact of the kernel parameters on the classification performance on a number of sequence classification tasks and evaluate a number of kernel/parameter selection strategies. We demonstrate improved performance on protein remote homology detection, multi-class fold prediction, and classification of music samples.

6. REFERENCES

[1] J. Cheng and P. Baldi. A machine learning information retrieval approach to protein fold recognition. *Bioinformatics*, 22(12):1456–1463, June 2006.

[2] C. H. Ding and I. Dubchak. Multi-class protein fold recognition using support vector machines and neural networks. *Bioinformatics*, 17(4):349–358, 2001.

[3] M. Gribskov, A. McLachlan, and D. Eisenberg. Profile analysis: detection of distantly related proteins. *Proceedings of the National Academy of Sciences*, 84:4355–4358, 1987.

[4] E. Ie, J. Weston, W. S. Noble, and C. Leslie. Multi-class protein fold recognition using adaptive codes. In *ICML '05*, pages 329–336, New York, NY, USA, 2005. ACM.

[5] G. Ifrim and C. Wiuf. Bounded coordinate-descent for biological sequence classification in high dimensional predictor space. In *Proceedings of the 17th ACM SIGKDD international conference on Knowledge discovery and data mining*, KDD '11, pages 708–716, New York, NY, USA, 2011. ACM.

[6] T. Jaakkola, M. Diekhans, and D. Haussler. A discriminative framework for detecting remote protein homologies. *Journal of Computational Biology*, 7(1-2):95–114, 2000.

[7] R. Kuang, E. Ie, K. Wang, K. Wang, M. Siddiqi, Y. Freund, and C. S. Leslie. Profile-based string kernels for remote homology detection and motif extraction. In *CSB*, pages 152–160, 2004.

[8] P. Kuksa, P.-H. Huang, and V. Pavlovic. Fast protein homology and fold detection with sparse spatial sample kernels. In *ICPR 2008*, 2008.

[9] P. Kuksa, P.-H. Huang, and V. Pavlovic. Scalable algorithms for string kernels with inexact matching. In *NIPS*, 2008.

[10] P. P. Kuksa and V. Pavlovic. Spatial representation for efficient sequence classification. In *ICPR*, 2010.

[11] C. S. Leslie, E. Eskin, and W. S. Noble. The spectrum kernel: A string kernel for SVM protein classification. In *Pacific Symposium on Biocomputing*, pages 566–575, 2002.

[12] C. S. Leslie, E. Eskin, J. Weston, and W. S. Noble. Mismatch string kernels for SVM protein classification. In *NIPS*, pages 1417–1424, 2002.

[13] T. Li, M. Ogihara, and Q. Li. A comparative study on content-based music genre classification. In *SIGIR '03*, pages 282–289, New York, NY, USA, 2003. ACM.

[14] L. Liao and W. S. Noble. Combining pairwise sequence similarity and support vector machines for remote protein homology detection. In *RECOMB*, pages 225–232, 2002.

[15] H. Lodhi, C. Saunders, J. Shawe-Taylor, N. Cristianini, and C. Watkins. Text classification using string kernels. *J. Mach. Learn. Res.*, 2:419–444, 2002.

[16] Z. Lu and H. Ip. Image categorization with spatial mismatch kernels. In *Computer Vision and Pattern Recognition, 2009. CVPR 2009. IEEE Conference on*, pages 397 –404, june 2009.

[17] C. Saunders, D. R. Hardoon, J. Shawe-Taylor, and G. Widmer. Using string kernels to identify famous performers from their playing style. *Intell. Data Anal.*, 12:425–440, December 2008.

[18] J. Shawe-Taylor and N. Cristianini. *Kernel Methods for Pattern Analysis*. Cambridge University Press, New York, NY, USA, 2004.

[19] S. Sonnenburg, G. Rätsch, and B. Schölkopf. Large scale genomic sequence SVM classifiers. In *ICML '05*, pages 848–855, New York, NY, USA, 2005.

[20] Supplementary data and code. `http://seqam.rutgers.edu/projects/bioinfo/largekmkernels`.

[21] V. N. Vapnik. *Statistical Learning Theory*. Wiley-Interscience, September 1998.

[22] S. V. N. Vishwanathan and A. Smola. Fast kernels for string and tree matching. *Advances in Neural Information Processing Systems*, 15, 2002.

[23] J. Weston, C. Leslie, E. Ie, D. Zhou, A. Elisseeff, and W. S. Noble. Semi-supervised protein classification using cluster kernels. *Bioinformatics*, 21(15):3241–3247, 2005.

[24] Z. Xu, R. Jin, I. King, and M. R. Lyu. An extended level method for efficient multiple kernel learning. In *NIPS*, pages 1825–1832, 2008.

7. APPENDIX: EXAMPLES OF WEIGHT MATRICES

$$W_{6,3} = \begin{pmatrix} 1 & 6 & 15 & 20 \\ 1 & 6 & 15 & 10 \\ 1 & 6 & 21 & 4 \\ 1 & 3 & 21 & 1 \\ 2 & 12 & 12 & 0 \\ -10 & 30 & 0 & 0 \\ 20 & 0 & 0 & 0 \end{pmatrix}, \quad W_{7,3} = \begin{pmatrix} 1 & 7 & 21 & 35 \\ 1 & 7 & 21 & 15 \\ 1 & 7 & 31 & 5 \\ 1 & 3 & 27 & 1 \\ 2 & 18 & 12 & 0 \\ -10 & 30 & 0 & 0 \\ 20 & 0 & 0 & 0 \end{pmatrix},$$

$$W_{7,4} = \begin{pmatrix} 1 & 7 & 21 & 35 & 35 \\ 1 & 7 & 21 & 35 & 20 \\ 1 & 7 & 21 & 45 & 10 \\ 1 & 7 & 15 & 49 & 4 \\ 1 & 10 & 24 & 40 & 1 \\ 0 & -10 & 60 & 20 & 0 \\ 20 & -40 & 90 & 0 & 0 \\ -70 & 140 & 0 & 0 & 0 \end{pmatrix},$$

$$W_{9,4} = \begin{pmatrix} 1 & 9 & 36 & 84 & 126 \\ 1 & 9 & 36 & 84 & 56 \\ 1 & 9 & 36 & 119 & 21 \\ 1 & 9 & 21 & 109 & 6 \\ 1 & 14 & 66 & 64 & 1 \\ 0 & -30 & 120 & 20 & 0 \\ 20 & 0 & 90 & 0 & 0 \\ -70 & 140 & 0 & 0 & 0 \\ 70 & 0 & 0 & 0 & 0 \end{pmatrix},$$

$$W_{10,5} = \begin{pmatrix} 1 & 10 & 45 & 120 & 210 & 252 \\ 1 & 10 & 45 & 120 & 210 & 126 \\ 1 & 10 & 45 & 120 & 280 & 56 \\ 1 & 10 & 45 & 85 & 280 & 21 \\ 1 & 10 & 60 & 160 & 205 & 6 \\ 1 & 5 & -40 & 310 & 105 & 1 \\ 2 & 80 & -90 & 360 & 30 & 0 \\ -28 & -70 & 210 & 210 & 0 & 0 \\ 182 & -420 & 560 & 0 & 0 & 0 \\ -378 & 630 & 0 & 0 & 0 & 0 \\ 252 & 0 & 0 & 0 & 0 & 0 \end{pmatrix},$$

$$W_{11,6} = \begin{pmatrix} 1 & 11 & 55 & 165 & 330 & 462 & 462 \\ 1 & 11 & 55 & 165 & 330 & 462 & 252 \\ 1 & 11 & 55 & 165 & 330 & 588 & 126 \\ 1 & 11 & 55 & 165 & 260 & 616 & 56 \\ 1 & 11 & 55 & 200 & 365 & 511 & 21 \\ 1 & 11 & 40 & 20 & 665 & 331 & 6 \\ 1 & 16 & 215 & -230 & 915 & 156 & 1 \\ 0 & -98 & 140 & 70 & 840 & 42 & 0 \\ 42 & 322 & -910 & 1120 & 420 & 0 & 0 \\ -378 & 882 & -1260 & 1680 & 0 & 0 & 0 \\ 1302 & -3528 & 3150 & 0 & 0 & 0 & 0 \\ -1848 & 2772 & 0 & 0 & 0 & 0 & 0 \end{pmatrix}$$

Estimating Conversion Rate in Display Advertising from Past Performance Data

Kuang-chih Lee, Burkay Orten, Ali Dasdan, Wentong Li
Turn Inc., 835 Main Street, Redwood City, CA 94063
{klee, borten, adasdan, wli}@turn.com

ABSTRACT

In targeted display advertising, the goal is to identify the *best* opportunities to display a banner ad to an online user who is most likely to take a desired action such as purchasing a product or signing up for a newsletter. Finding the best ad impression, i.e., the opportunity to show an ad to a user, requires the ability to estimate the probability that the user who sees the ad on his or her browser will take an action, i.e., the user will *convert*. However, conversion probability estimation is a challenging task since there is extreme data sparsity across different data dimensions and the conversion event occurs rarely. In this paper, we present our approach to conversion rate estimation which relies on utilizing past performance observations along *user*, *publisher* and *advertiser* data hierarchies. More specifically, we model the conversion event at different *select* hierarchical levels with separate binomial distributions and estimate the distribution parameters individually. Then we demonstrate how we can combine these individual estimators using logistic regression to accurately identify conversion events. In our presentation, we also discuss main practical considerations such as data imbalance, missing data, and output probability calibration, which render this estimation problem more difficult but yet need solving for a real-world implementation of the approach. We provide results from real advertising campaigns to demonstrate the effectiveness of our proposed approach.

Categories and Subject Descriptors

H.3.5 [**Information Storage and Retrieval**]: Online Information Services; G.3 [**Probability and Statistics**]: Correlation and regression analysis; I.2.6 [**Artificial Intelligence**]: Learning

General Terms

Algorithms, Experimentation, Theory

Keywords

Action rate estimation, algorithmic advertising, computational advertising, logistic regression

1. INTRODUCTION

In online display advertising world, advertisers try to market their product to many users by embedding their graphical advertisement within the content in publisher web pages, e.g., the pages of news portals. The advertiser's main goal is to reach the most receptive online audience in the right context, which will then engage with their displayed ad and eventually take a desired action, identified by the type of the campaign, e.g., brand advertising or direct product marketing. The complexity of realizing this goal is so high that advertisers need specialized technology solutions called demand-side platforms (DSP).

DSPs help manage such display advertising campaigns for many different advertisers simultaneously across multiple direct buy markets or ad exchanges where ad impressions can be acquired through real-time auctions or bidding. In a direct buy market, the impression price is decided in advance according to the business negotiations between publishers and advertisers directly. On the other hand, in a real-time ad exchange, a bid has to be submitted for each impression (submitted via ad calls) by DSPs and the impression is sold to the highest bidder in a public auction. DSPs are the platforms where all the information about users, pages, ads, and campaign constraints come together to make the best decision for advertisers (see § 2.1 for an overview).

Advertisers seek the optimal price to bid for each ad call to maximize their campaign performance. The optimal bid price of an ad impression depends on the *value* of that impression to a given advertiser. This value is provided to DSPs as a campaign performance parameter in the form of cost-per-click (CPC) or cost-per-action (CPA) goals. If a CPC or CPA goal is set up, then the optimal bid price can be determined from the *expected cost-per-impression*, which is equal to the click-through-rate (CTR) for this impression multiplied by the CPC goal, or the conversion rate (CVR) multiplied by the CPA goal [8].

In this scenario, campaign performance directly depends on how well the CTR or CVR can be estimated and the performance optimization can be considered as the problem of accurately estimating CTR or CVR. If these quantities are overestimated, bid prices will always be higher than what they should be, the advertiser will waste campaign budget on useless impressions; on the other hand, if these quantities are underestimated, the advertiser will miss high-value impressions that may have led to actions and the campaign will under deliver.

The CTR and the CVR are directly related to the intention of the user interacting with the ad in a given context and they are fundamentally difficult to directly model and predict. In practice, CVR is even harder to estimate than CTR since conversion events are far rarer than click events. Also, the view-through conversions have longer delays in the logging process (sometimes up to a week), which makes the off-line modeling more difficult. Finally, the ad serving system needs to perform in real-time, requiring the CVR or CTR estimation, optimal bid price calculation, and bid submission to exchanges to be completed in a few milliseconds.

In this paper, we present a simple but effective approach to estimating CVR of ad impressions, to be used in a DSP. Our conversion rate estimation method models the conversion event at different *select* levels of the cross-product of *user*, *publisher* and *advertiser* data hierarchies with separate binomial distributions and estimate the distribution parameters individually. These individual estimators are than combined using logistic regression to obtain a final estimate that can more accurately predict the conversion outcome for each impression.

The rest of the paper is as follows. In § 2, we review the ad call flow, formulate our problem, and discuss previous related work in the literature. In § 3, we describe the CVR estimators using the past performance observations across data hierarchies and also describe the use of logistic regression as a means of combining these individual rate estimates for improved predictive performance. Various practical issues encountered during CVR modeling in a DSP and the proposed solutions are discussed in § 4. Thorough experimental results are presented in § 5, and § 6 lists some concluding remarks and possible future work.

2. BACKGROUND AND RELATED WORK

In this section, we first review the ad call flow. We then formulate the problem of estimating the conversion rate of an event given an ad impression. Finally, we explain the user, publisher and advertiser data hierarchies and also discuss some previous work in the literature related to the estimation of rare events.

2.1 Overview of Ad Call Flow

To put the proposed approach in perspective, let us use the simplified ad call flow in Fig. 1. Thinking of the rectangular bounding box around this figure, the right side is the supply or publisher side. The supply side provides the pages on which there are places that ads can go. The left side is the demand or advertiser side. The demand side provides the ads and constraints such as targeting and budget constraints.

Given a user with a profile, a page with some context, and campaigns from various advertisers (where a campaign include some constraints and ads), the goal (sometimes called the fundamental problem of computational advertising) is to find the best ad under constraints for the user and the page. The mechanics of how this is done is explained next with the help of numbered steps in Fig. 1.

The call is initiated when a user with id <uid> starts to open a web page at URL <url>. The call first reaches the ad exchange the publisher is integrated with. The ad exchange appends <uid> and <url> to a request that it sends to its demand side platform (DSP) partners to ask for an ad and a bid. The request usually contains other information such as geographical location for targeting purposes. The partner DSPs may or may not respond to the request; those that respond (bidding DSPs) need to use <uid> and <url> to gather more information about the user and the page, respectively. (Information about users and pages are usually provided via data management platforms.) The bidding DSPs also search through their respository of previously created campaigns to find a set of candidate ads that can be targeted to the user and the page. The contribution in this paper is at the hearth of the decision engine that selects the best ad from the candidate ads and computes the corresponding bid.

The bidding DSPs return back their proposed ad and bid pair back to the ad exchange. Once the ad exchange collects all the bids, it runs an auction (usually a second price auction) and determines the winning bid and the corresponding ad. It then passes the winning ad and the location of its creative back to the browser. The browser then collects the creative and finally returns the page to the user.

Note that this entire flow needs to happen within one-tenth of a second so that the user can see the page with ads as soon as she opens the page on her web browser. Moreover, the top DSPs can get such ad calls as many as 500,000 times per second as 100s of millions of users open pages on their browsers at any given instant. This latency and throughput constraints put extreme time constraints on each bidding DSP and their decision engines. The proposed approach works under such time constraints and performs well.

2.2 Problem Setup and Formulation

Per § 2.1, an ad call request is sent along with the user and publisher information. Let $\mathcal{U} = \{u_1, u_2, ..., u_l\}$, $\mathcal{P} = \{p_1, p_2, ..., p_m\}$ and $\mathcal{A} = \{a_1, a_2, ..., a_n\}$ represent all the users, publisher web pages and ads (with creatives) in a DSP, respectively. For simplicity, an ad call request to a DSP can be considered to arrive in the form $adrequest = \{user : u_i, page : p_j\}$. The goal is to find the ad among all n ads that has the highest probability of conversion. Mathematically, this can be written as:

$$ad^* = \arg\max_{k=1,\dots,n} p(conversion|user = u_i, page = p_j, ad = a_k) \quad (1)$$

where ad^* denotes the optimal ad, i.e., the ad with the highest CVR. Note that at a single user level, an event has only two possible outcomes: conversion or no conversion. Then we can see that a conversion event can be modeled as a *Bernoulli* random variable. Let $Y_{ijk} \in \{0, 1\}$ represent the random outcome of the event, when the user u_i is shown ad a_k on site p_j. Then, we can compactly write:

$$Y_{ijk} \sim Bernoulli(p_{ijk}),\ p_{ijk} = p(Y = 1|u_i, p_j, a_k). \quad (2)$$

and with this new representation, equation (1) becomes:

$$ad^* = \arg\max_{k=1,\dots,n} p(Y = 1|u_i, p_j, a_k) \quad (3)$$

One way of modeling the conversion event outcome is to represent the user, publisher and advertisement using a set of explicit features and build a classification model. Examples of this approach in the sponsored search advertising context can be found [10, 15]. Since low-level data features are poorly correlated with a user's direct intention of taking

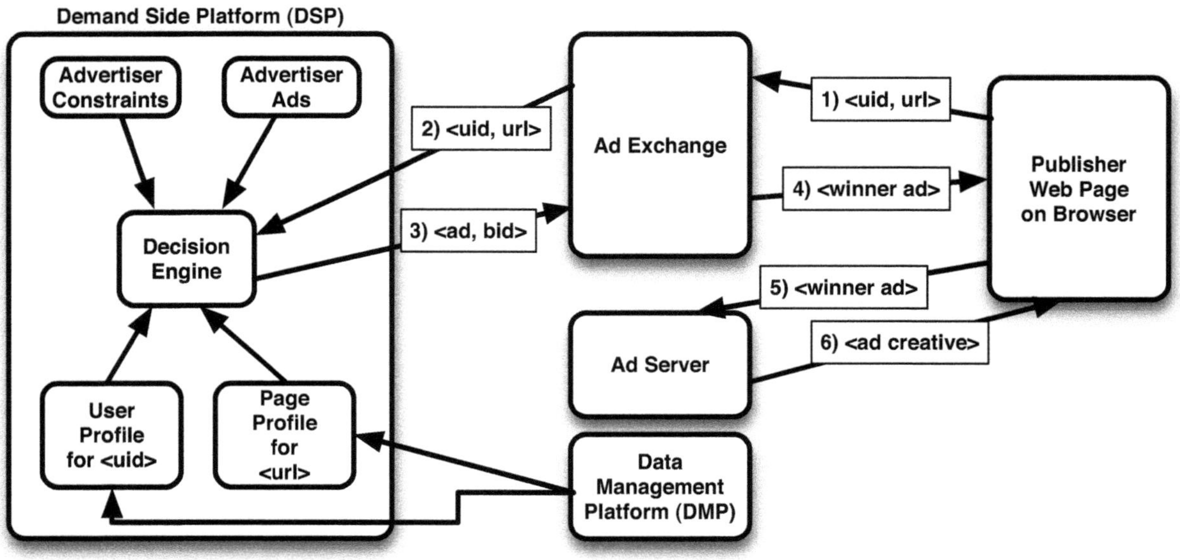

Figure 1: Ad call flow between a web browser and a demand side platform, the place where all information is collected to make the optimal decision. A data management platform aggregates user data. The ad exchange is used to run the auction to match the winning ad to the page and the price of the match.

an action on a display ad, models that are based on these features perform poorly in our context. An alternative idea is to compute the number of times this ad was displayed to "similar" users on this website and observe how many of these impressions result in a conversion. Then, the conversion rate for this user can simply be estimated as the total number of conversions among all similar users divided by the total number of impressions. Note that this is nothing but the *maximum likelihood estimate* (MLE) of the conversion rate and can be written as follows:

$$\begin{aligned} \tilde{Y}_{ijk} &\sim Binomial(T_{ijk}, \tilde{p}_{ijk}), \\ \tilde{p}_{ijk} &= p(Y = 1 | u \in UsrClust_i, p_j, a_k), \\ \tilde{p}_{ijk}^{\text{MLE}} &= \begin{cases} \frac{S_{ijk}}{T_{ijk}}, & \text{if } T_{ijk} \neq 0 \\ \text{unknown}, & \text{if } T_{ijk} = 0, \end{cases} \end{aligned} \tag{4}$$

where T_{ijk} denotes the number of trials (i.e., impressions) and S_{ijk} denotes the number of successes (i.e., conversions) when ad a_k was shown to users from $u \in UsrClust_i$ on website p_j. It is important to point out that in equation (4), i does not index the particular user whose conversion rate we are trying to estimate, but it indexes a cluster of users whose conversion rates are assumed to be similar to this user. Subsequently, $\tilde{Y}_{ijk}$ represents the conversion event of all the users in cluster $UsrClust_i$ (hence Binomial) whereas Y_{ijk} represents only the event of user i converting (i.e., Bernoulli event). This kind of user grouping can either be achieved by explicit clustering based on some similarity metric or it can be implicitly done by using data hierarchies as we will explain in the next section.

2.3 Data Hierarchies

In the display advertising context user, publisher and advertiser related data can be considered as adhering to some hierarchical structure. For example, every ad in the DSP can be considered as belonging to an advertising campaign which in turn belongs to an advertiser (e.g., Advertiser: 'Acme Cars' → Campaign: '2011 Year End Sales' → Ad: 'Incredible Year End Sales Event!'). Similarly, a website on which an ad will be displayed is under a top level domain (TLD) which is owned by a publisher and the publisher itself might belong to some category based on its main content (e.g., Publisher Type: 'News' → Publisher: 'Acme City Times' → Page: 'Auto News'). An example taxonomy demonstrating this hierarchical structure for the user, publisher and advertiser data is shown in Fig. 2.2. Note that this figure does not represent Turn Inc.'s data taxonomy and it is mainly provided for illustrative purposes and clarity of presentation.

The data hierarchies enable us to define explicit or implicit 'user clusters'. Explicit user clustering, as one might guess, is based on representing each user by a set of features (e.g., demographic information, geographic features, income level, type of websites they frequently visit, activity level etc.) and clustering them based on some similarity metric such as the Euclidean distance. On the other hand, implicit clustering is based on using data hierarchies rather than the user features. For example, the group of users who visit websites in a certain category, such as sports, can be considered as an implicit cluster. We can represent this grouping by the Cartesian product {Users × Publisher Type}. As another example, we can also consider all the users who were shown an ad from ad-campaign (such as 'Acme Cars Year End Sales') on a particular site (e.g., Acme Times Autos), which can be represented by the Cartesian product {Users × Publisher Type × Campaign}. If we assume that user, publisher and advertiser data have ℓ_u, ℓ_p and ℓ_a levels in their respective data hierarchies, there are $\ell_u \times \ell_p \times \ell_a$ such possible implicit user clusters. Then, given that $adrequest = \{user : u_i, page : p_j\}$, we can identify the suitable explicit and implicit user clusters from the data hierarchies and use past count data (i.e., number of impressions and number of conversions) of each level to get different estimates of

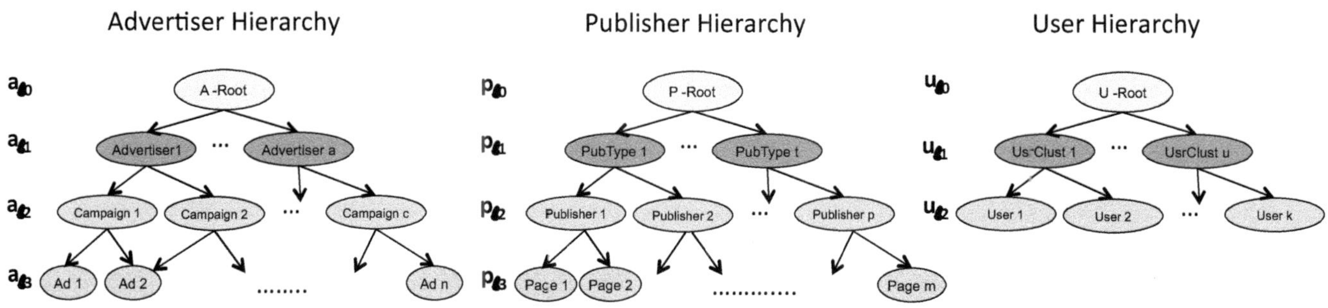

Figure 2: Sample user, publisher and advertiser taxonomy representing the hierarchical structure of the data. The subscript ℓ_i designates the i-th level in each component's data hierarchy.

$p_{ijk} = p(Y = 1|u_i, p_j, a_k)$. This is explained in more detail in § 3.1.

2.4 Related Work

Among the few attempts aiming to utilize the data hierarchies to estimate the CVR/CTR [2, 1, 19, 14], Agarwal et al. [1, 19] relax the dependency between user information and (advertiser, publisher) pairs in the following:

$$p(Y = 1|u_i, p_j, a_k) \propto p(Y = 1|u_i)p(Y = 1|p_j, a_k). \quad (5)$$

They propose to estimate $p(Y = 1|u_i)$ by regression methods on user features, such as demographic, geographic, and temporal (recency/frequency) information, and $p(Y = 1|p_j, a_k)$ by some probabilistic inference on pre-defined strict hierarchies of (publisher, advertiser) pairs. If the pair (publisher, advertiser) does not have enough number of successes, the CVR/CTR estimation will be based on its parent node. Menon et al. utilizes the same hierarchical constraints to estimate CVR/CTR by using collaborative filtering [14]. We argue that those approaches are hard to be carried out in our setting. First, the ordering of hierarchies is not straightforward in some cases. For example, it is hard to judge that tier (site quality) information or inventory source (exchanger id) should be the parent node given a publisher site. Furthermore, our proposed hierarchies contain user information and the structure becomes more complicated. As the level of hierarchies becomes deeper, the probabilistic inference proposed in [2, 1] will be hard to satisfy the real-time ad serving constraint.

On the contrary, there are also some studies that try to cluster users based on their behaviors and interests without considering data hierarchy. Cerrato et al. [7] propose a rule-based approach to learn a set of DNF rules that maximize the coverage of conversion users. Ahmed et al. [3] present an unsupervised user clustering framework based on Latent Dirichlet Allocation [5], where each user cluster captures some user interests directly. They demonstrate that this framework can be applied for audience selection in display advertising.

Richardson et al. [15] apply logistic regression to estimate CTR using relative term CTR, ad quality, and other features for search engine advertising. Our work bears some resemblance to their method in the sense that both methods combine a set of individual CVR/CTR estimators in different context using logistic regression to obtain a final estimate. However in this paper, we consider our individual estimators come from different levels of domains ($user, publisher, advertiser$) in data hierarchies, which capture versatile information compared to term CTR used in [15]. Furthermore, since conversion events are typically sparser than click events, our implementation needs to handle many practical issues, such as data skewness and missing features, and our proposed solutions are discussed in § 4.

3. CONVERSION RATE ESTIMATION

In this section, we provide details of our conversion rate (CVR) estimation method. We first revisit data hierarchies and explain how past observations from different levels in the hierarchies yield 'weak' estimators of the desired CVR for a given ad call. Afterwards, we discuss how we can combine these weak estimators using logistic regression to get a more accurate estimator.

3.1 Past Performance at Different Hierarchical Levels

Recall from equation (1) that given an ad request parameterized by $\{user : u_i, page : p_j\}$, we would like to find the ad, a_k, which has the highest CVR, p^*_{ijk}. As we explained in the last section, if we can identify a group of users whose CVR is similar to that of user u_i's, then we can make the following approximation:

$$p_{ijk} = p(Y = 1|u_i, p_j, a_k) \approx \tilde{p}_{ijk} = p(\tilde{Y} = 1|u \in \mathcal{C}_{u_i}, p_j, a_k) \quad (6)$$

where $\mathcal{C}_{u_i}$ denotes a cluster of users in which u_i belongs. Note that this approximation relies on an explicit user clustering and observes all the users in $\mathcal{C}_{u_i}$ who were shown ad a_k when they visited website p_j. Then, the simplest possible estimator for p_{ijk} is given by:

$$\hat{p}_{ijk} = \hat{\tilde{p}}^{\text{MLE}}_{ijk} = \begin{cases} \frac{S_{ijk}}{T_{ijk}}, & \text{if } T_{ijk} \neq 0 \\ \text{unknown}, & \text{if } T_{ijk} = 0, \end{cases} \quad (7)$$

this simple estimator has the advantage that if all the users in cluster $\mathcal{C}_{u_i}$ have the same CVR and if we have increasingly more observations T_{ijk}, $\hat{p}_{ijk}$ will converge to the true value p_{ijk} (i.e., estimator is consistent). The first challenge is to identify a group users who truly have the same or very similar CVRs. This is related to identifying the users' conversion/purchase intentions and inherently a difficult problem as we pointed out earlier. Even if we can find such clusters that are reasonably *homogeneous* in terms of users' behaviors (and hence their CVRs), the main challenge is to collect enough data at the granularity of ad a_k and website p_j. In other words, we generally will not have enough observations at (ad, website) level. Mathematically, this means that T_{ijk} will usually be slow. Also recall that conversion is a very rare event. Therefore, for a true conversion rate that is on the order of 10^{-5}, we need many impressions (on the order of millions, e.g., see the formulas in [4]) at the (ad, website) level before we can get a reliable maximum likelihood estimate. This data sparsity problem can be alleviated by going up in the user, publisher and advertiser data hierarchies since there will certainly be more observations at higher levels than there are at lower levels. We can then generalize equation (6) as follows:

$$p_{ijk} \approx \tilde{p}_{ijk} = p(\tilde{Y} = 1 | u \in \mathcal{C}_{u_i}, p \in \mathcal{C}_{p_j}, a \in \mathcal{C}_{a_k}). \quad (8)$$

In equation (8), $\mathcal{C}_{p_j}$ and $\mathcal{C}_{a_k}$ define grouping of the webpages and advertisers, respectively. These groupings are dictated by the respective data hierarchies as shown in Fig. 2.2. For example, at level $\ell_a = \ell_2$, we group together all ads that belong to the same campaign and at level $\ell_p = \ell_1$ we group together all webpages of all publishers that are of the same type (e.g., automotive related publishers). Then we can identify the groups at levels ℓ_u, ℓ_p and ℓ_a as $\mathcal{C}_{u_i} = \{\mathcal{C}_u : u_i \in \mathcal{C}_u^{\ell_u}\}$, $\mathcal{C}_{p_j} = \{\mathcal{C}_p : p_j \in \mathcal{C}_p^{\ell_p}\}$ and $\mathcal{C}_{a_k} = \{\mathcal{C}_a : a_k \in \mathcal{C}_a^{\ell_a}\}$, respectively. In this compact representation, $\mathcal{C}_u^{\ell_u}$ identifies all the user groups at the ℓ_u-th level in the user hierarchy. $\mathcal{C}_p^{\ell_p}$ and $\mathcal{C}_a^{\ell_a}$ similarly identify the webpage and ad groupings at the ℓ_p-th and ℓ_a-th levels.

As we identified in § 2.3, if the user, publisher and advertiser data have ℓ_u, ℓ_p and ℓ_a levels in their respective hierarchies, there are $\ell_u \times \ell_p \times \ell_a$ possible ways of combining count data from different levels. Let $\hat{\tilde{p}}_{ijk}^1, ..., \hat{\tilde{p}}_{ijk}^M$ denote maximum likelihood estimates of the CVRs at M different combinations of (user, publisher, advertiser) hierarchical levels. For example, $\tilde{p}_{ijk}^1$ can be $p(Y = 1 | u \in \mathcal{C}_{u_i}^{\ell_2}, p \in \mathcal{C}_{p_j}^{\ell_3}, a \in \mathcal{C}_{a_k}^{\ell_3},)$ and $\tilde{p}_{ijk}^M$ can be $p(Y = 1 | u \in \mathcal{C}_{u_i}^{\ell_1}, p \in \mathcal{C}_{p_j}^{\ell_1}, a \in \mathcal{C}_{a_k}^{\ell_1},)$

While going up along the data hierarchies solves the problem of data sparsity, it introduces bias in the CVR estimation. This is not really surprising since grouping together more distinct type of users at higher levels violates the assumption that the users in the same group have similar CVRs. Consequently, many of the M estimators are quite 'weak' in the sense that their CVR values, $\tilde{p}_{ijk}$, are poorly correlated with the true p_{ijk}. Therefore, many of these weak estimators are discarded and we use only a *select* few set of estimators that are highly correlated with the true CVR. In the next section, we discuss how we can combine these weak estimators to obtain a final estimator that has better predictive performance.

3.2 Combining Estimators using Logistic Regression

Following the notation of § 3.1, let $\hat{\tilde{p}}_{ijk}^1, ..., \hat{\tilde{p}}_{ijk}^M$ denote maximum likelihood estimates of the CVRs of events at M different levels. Recall that each of these levels correspond to a distinct combination of the user, publisher and advertiser hierarchies and, as such, it is not always clear which one will yield the best estimate of the true event CTR, p_{ijk}. Rather than trying to pick the best one among all M estimators, we seek to optimally combine these estimators. In other words, we would like to obtain:

$$p_{ijk} = f(\hat{\tilde{p}}_{ijk}^1, ..., \hat{\tilde{p}}_{ijk}^M; \boldsymbol{\beta}) \quad (9)$$

for some function $f(\cdot) : [0,1]^M \to [0,1]$ which has a set of parameters denoted by $\boldsymbol{\beta}$. Note that for every impression, the outcome of all M estimators can be computed and logged in a database. Additionally, in the 'ad-exploration' stage, we can serve impressions with different ads and observe whether the impression resulted in a conversion or not. Assume that for a running campaign we collect such training data for N different impressions. Let $y_s \in \{0,1\}$ encode the conversion outcome of the s-th impression and $\hat{\tilde{p}}^{s1}, ..., \hat{\tilde{p}}^{sM}$ denote the associated maximum value estimates of the CVR value for the same impression, where $s = 1, ..., N$. Note that for clarity of presentation we dropped the subscripts i, j and k and compactly represent the impression by the subscript s. However, it should be clear that every impression is served to a different user on a new website with a different ad and the dependence of the CVR p^s on these data components is always implied. The log-likelihood of this training data can be written as follows:

$$\begin{aligned}\mathcal{L}(\boldsymbol{\beta}) &= \sum_{s=1}^{N} y_s \log p^s(\boldsymbol{\beta}) + (1 - y_s) \log(1 - p^s(\boldsymbol{\beta})) \\ &= \sum_{s=1}^{N} y_s \log f(\hat{\tilde{p}}^{s1}, ..., \hat{\tilde{p}}^{sM}; \boldsymbol{\beta}) + \\ &\quad (1 - y_s) \log(1 - f(\hat{\tilde{p}}^{s1}, ..., \hat{\tilde{p}}^{sM}; \boldsymbol{\beta})) \end{aligned} \quad (10)$$

We can use log-likelihood as a goodness-of-fit measure and choose the set of parameters $\boldsymbol{\beta}$ such that they will maximize the $\mathcal{L}(\boldsymbol{\beta})$ over the training set. In our system we are using the sigmoid function $f(\mathbf{x}; \boldsymbol{\beta}) = \frac{1}{1+e^{-\boldsymbol{\beta}^T \mathbf{x}}}$ to combine different CVR estimates since it always produces estimates between 0 and 1 and the resulting model can be interpreted easily by comparing their linear combination coefficients. With this choice of $f(\cdot)$, the optimum set of parameters can be found by solving the following optimization problem:

$$\begin{aligned}\boldsymbol{\beta}^* &= \arg\max_{\boldsymbol{\beta}} \mathcal{L}(\boldsymbol{\beta}) \\ &= \arg\max_{\boldsymbol{\beta}} \sum_{s=1}^{N} y_s [\boldsymbol{\beta}^T \hat{\tilde{\mathbf{p}}}^s - \log(1 + \boldsymbol{\beta}^T \hat{\tilde{\mathbf{p}}}^s)] \end{aligned} \quad (11)$$

where $\hat{\tilde{\mathbf{p}}}^s = [\hat{\tilde{p}}^{s1} \ \hat{\tilde{p}}^{s2} \ ... \ \hat{\tilde{p}}^{sM}]^T$. Another way to interpret this formulation is to think of the M individual estimators as factors (or features) in a classification model and the optimization process as finding the optimal linear combination coefficients that will classify the training data (i.e., the conversion impressions and no conversion impressions) as accurately as possible. However, we should point out that since we are not actually interested in classifying an impression but rather in estimating its probability of conversion, we only need the probabilistic scores assigned by logistic regression and we never have to select a classification threshold.

In order to measure how well the estimated p^s values explain the training data, we can compute the data likelihood using the fitted $\boldsymbol{\beta}^*$ as shown in equation (10). We can also measure the performance by treating the logistic regression output as classification scores and computing the *area under the receiver operating characteristics curve.* We will refer to this as the AUC metric. This metric explains how well the logistic regression scores of the conversion and no conversion impressions separate.

4. PRACTICAL ISSUES IN CONVERSION RATE ESTIMATION

In this section, we discuss several practical issues encountered in implementing our proposed CVR estimation method in our DSP and present our current solutions.

4.1 Data Imbalance

When we consider the CVR estimation as a classification problem (see § 3.2), we ideally would like to have sufficient amount of training examples from both the conversion and no-conversion event classes. However, typical conversion rates in a display advertising campaign ranges anywhere from 10^{-3} to 10^{-6}. In other words, only 1 out of a million impressions may result in a conversion event on average. Hence, any training data we collect will be highly skewed towards the no-conversion class. In the learning context there are different scenarios that might result in skewed training data [16, 17], but in our problem the two main reasons for having data imbalance can be identified as follows:

1. The average conversion rate of an advertising campaign is inherently very low and we do not get to observe sufficient amount of conversion events.
2. The ratio of the number of no-conversion events to that of conversion events is very large, but we still have reasonable amount of data from the minority (i.e., conversion) class.

In the first scenario, we do not have enough number of representative examples from the minority class and we can not reliably train a CVR estimation model. Then, we simply use a different manually-crafted, rule-based model that combines the base estimators $\hat{\hat{p}}^{s1}, ..., \hat{\hat{p}}^{sM}$ and never train a logistic regression model.

In the second case we are able to train a logistic regression model using the skewed data. Performance of a model when trained on a highly skewed data set has to be carefully analyzed and as Visa et al. [16] and Weiss [17] suggested, we use AUC as a metric since it is more robust in imbalanced data scenarios. In our experiments, we observed that data imbalance does not necessarily effect the AUC performance of the logistic regression model as long as we have sufficient amount of examples from the minority class and this observation is also verified by Maloof [12]. While building a CVR estimation model for a specific campaign, we try to keep all examples from the minority class to ensure sufficient representation but only a subset of the majority class due to memory constraints.

4.2 Output Calibration

For training data collection, we use stratified sampling strategy and only retain a small subset of the examples from the no-conversion class. This strategy results in a training data set where the proportion of the examples from different classes does not match the true data proportions (i.e., the inherent conversion rate for the campaign). Subsequently, the output scores of the logistic regression model optimized on such training data do not represent the actual scale of the CVR values for this advertising campaign. Since the bidding process requires accurate estimates of the CVR values, we need to calibrate the logistic regression output scores to take into account the true proportions of the event classes. The goal of the calibration process can be simply expressed as finding the true CVR value for the s-th impression given the logistic regression score:

$$\hat{p}^s = p(Y^s = 1 | f(\hat{\hat{\mathbf{p}}}^s; \boldsymbol{\beta}^*)) \tag{12}$$

where $f(\hat{\hat{\mathbf{p}}}^s; \boldsymbol{\beta}^*)$ represent the logistic regression score given the M weak estimator values and $\hat{p}^s$ represent the *final* CVR estimate for this impression after the calibration. One way of obtaining this mapping from the logistic regression score to the calibrated output is to assume a parametric form for the density in equation (12) and compute its parameters using the training examples. However, this procedure requires some information or intuition about what the true density might look like. Instead, we follow an empirical approach and make the following approximation:

$$\hat{p}^s \approx p(Y^s = 1 | v_1 \leq f(\hat{\hat{\mathbf{p}}}^s; \boldsymbol{\beta}^*) < v_2) \tag{13}$$

for some score values within the range v_1 and v_2. Specifically, we group the logistic regression output scores into n equal sized bins, where $0 \leq v_1 < v_2 < \ldots, v_{n+1} \leq 1$ define the range of scores in each bin. Then we can approximate the calibration output $\hat{p}^s$ for the i-th bin using the maximum value estimation as follows:

$$\begin{aligned}\hat{p}(i) &\approx p(Y^s = 1 | v_i \leq f(\hat{\hat{\mathbf{p}}}^s; \boldsymbol{\beta}^*) < v_{i+1}) \\ &\approx \frac{\#\text{ Conversion examples with } f(\hat{\hat{\mathbf{p}}}^s; \boldsymbol{\beta}^*) \in [v_i, v_{i+1})}{\#\text{ All examples with } f(\hat{\hat{\mathbf{p}}}^s; \boldsymbol{\beta}^*) \in [v_i, v_{i+1})}\end{aligned} \tag{14}$$

In other words, calibration procedure becomes a simple conversion rate estimation in each score bin. As a result, we obtain the calibrated CVR for every bin $\hat{p}(1), ..., \hat{p}(n)$. At runtime, when we need to estimate the CVR for a new impression, we first compute the logistic regression score and convert it to the final estimate by:

$$\begin{aligned}\hat{p}^{Test} &\approx p(Y^{Test} = 1 | v_i \leq f(\hat{\hat{\mathbf{p}}}^{Test}; \boldsymbol{\beta}^*) < v_{i+1}) \\ &= \alpha \hat{p}(v_i) + (1 - \alpha)\hat{p}(v_{i+1})\end{aligned} \tag{15}$$

assuming the logistic regression score falls within $[v_i, v_{i+1})$, where $\alpha = \frac{v_{i+1} - f(\hat{\hat{\mathbf{p}}}^{Test}; \boldsymbol{\beta}^*)}{v_{i+1} - v_i}$. In practice, even the bin conversion rates, $\hat{p}(v_i)$, may be not accurately estimated in case there is only a small number of observations in a score bin. For this reason we employ some post-processing to smoothen the $\hat{p}(v_i)$ values. Specifically, we enforce that $\hat{p}(v_i)$'s are monotonically increasing by applying Pool Adjacent Violators Algorithm (PAVA) [9]. The whole conversion curve can be further smoothed by fitting an exponential function to it.

4.3 Missing Features

Even though we would like to combine all the weak estimator outputs $\hat{\hat{p}}^1, ..., \hat{\hat{p}}^M$ using logistic regression, some of these values may not be available for certain impressions. For example, if user IDs are not found in the user profile servers, or the publisher's webpage does not match any of the known categories in the publisher taxonomy, the estimators using these information sources simply can not be computed. Moreover, there may not be sufficient number of conversion events in one of the hierarchical levels to calculate a reliable estimator output using the past performance observations.

Little et al. [11] classify the nature of missing data into missing completely at random (MCAR), missing at random (MAR), and not missing at random (NMAR). For simplicity, we assume that our impression data follows the MAR pattern, meaning that whether some portion of the data is missing or not only depends on the data being observed. Under the MAR assumption, one simple but effective approach widely used in the data mining community to handle missing data is called *imputation*, which attempts to complete the missing attributes by filling them with specific values.

Here, we present a probabilistic framework for missing value imputation, which subsumes the strategy that we ended up using. Assume that the past performance estimators of a given impression s are partitioned into two groups $\hat{\hat{\mathbf{p}}}^{s} = [\hat{\hat{\mathbf{p}}}^{so_s}, \hat{\hat{\mathbf{p}}}^{sm_s}]^T$, where $\hat{\hat{\mathbf{p}}}^{so_s}$ and $\hat{\hat{\mathbf{p}}}^{sm_s}$ represent the sub-vectors for the observed and missing past performance estimators, respectively. Furthermore, assume that $\hat{\hat{\mathbf{p}}}^{so_s}$ and $\hat{\hat{\mathbf{p}}}^{sm_s}$ are jointly Gaussian, so that

$$\begin{aligned} \hat{\hat{\mathbf{p}}}^{s} &\sim \mathcal{N}(\boldsymbol{\mu}, \Sigma), \\ \hat{\hat{\mathbf{p}}}^{so_s} &\sim \mathcal{N}(\boldsymbol{\mu}_{o_s}, \Sigma_{o_s}), \\ \hat{\hat{\mathbf{p}}}^{sm_s} &\sim \mathcal{N}(\boldsymbol{\mu}_{m_s}, \Sigma_{m_s}) \end{aligned} \tag{16}$$

where $\boldsymbol{\mu} = [\boldsymbol{\mu}_{m_s}^T, \boldsymbol{\mu}_{o_s}^T]^T$, and $\Sigma = \begin{pmatrix} \Sigma_{m_s} & \Sigma_{m_s o_s} \\ \Sigma_{m_s o_s}^T & \Sigma_{o_s} \end{pmatrix}$.

One can show that $\hat{\hat{\mathbf{p}}}^{sm_s} | \hat{\hat{\mathbf{p}}}^{so_s}$ is also normally distributed:

$$\hat{\hat{\mathbf{p}}}^{sm_s} | \hat{\hat{\mathbf{p}}}^{so_s} \sim \mathcal{N}\Big(\boldsymbol{\mu}_{m_s} + \Sigma_{m_s o_s}(\Sigma_{o_s})^{-1}(\hat{\hat{\mathbf{p}}}^{so_s} - \boldsymbol{\mu}_{o_s}), \quad \Sigma_{m_s} - \Sigma_{m_s o_s}(\Sigma_{o_s})^{-1}\Sigma_{m_s o_s}^T\Big). \tag{17}$$

Then, it is easy to see that the optimal estimate of $\hat{\hat{\mathbf{p}}}^{sm_s}$ (in the least squares sense) is the mean of the conditional distribution in equation (17), which we refer to as the *Bayesian Least Squares Estimator* (BLSE). We can adopt this framework for missing value imputation by replacing the Gaussian parameters in equation (17) with their empirical estimates. Specifically, we can replace $\boldsymbol{\mu}$ by its sample mean estimate, and Σ by the sample covariance matrix, which is computed using the pair-wise complete observation scheme. Then, the BLSE-based imputation method estimates the missing attribute values using:

$$\hat{\hat{\mathbf{p}}}^{sm_s}_{BLSE} = \hat{\boldsymbol{\mu}}_{m_s} + \hat{\Sigma}_{m_s o_s}(\hat{\Sigma}_{o_s})^{-1}(\hat{\hat{\mathbf{p}}}^{so_s} - \hat{\boldsymbol{\mu}}_{o_s}) \tag{18}$$

Other common imputation strategies, such as unconditional mean (or median) imputation, and conditional mean (or median) imputation, can be treated as simple variations or special cases of this probabilistic framework. For example, mean (or median) imputation does not use the second term in equation (18) and simply estimates the missing attribute values using the columnwise means (or medians). There are other imputation methods in the literature that are worth mentioning, such as imputation by singular value decomposition (SVD) [6], Gaussian mixture modeling (GMM) [18] and Collaborative Filtering [13]. However, those approaches come with the cost of increased computational complexity with little or no effect on the final CVR estimation.

After experimenting with different strategies (see § 5.2), we decided to use unconditional median imputation, which simply fills in all the missing values for an attribute by the median of all the non-missing values for the same attribute among the training examples. Median imputation is an attractive choice since its computation time is very small (satisfying the runtime constraints) and its performance is on par with the other computationally expensive approaches.

4.4 Feature Selection

The final practical step we would like to mention is a simple 'feature selection step'. Considering the past performance estimators $\hat{\hat{p}}^1, ..., \hat{\hat{p}}^M$ as features for the logistic regression algorithm, we first analyze the data to observe its attribute statistics. If many of the training examples have a certain attribute missing, we do not want to impute that attribute from a very limited set of examples as it will result in a poor model fit with a poor predictive performance. In our modeling approach, we discard such attributes if more than %65 of the training examples have that particular attribute missing. Finally, we discard those attributes whose variance is below a certain threshold. We set that threshold to 10^{-8}. After these simple preprocessing steps, we impute the remaining attributes' missing values and use the resulting data for model fitting.

5. EXPERIMENTAL RESULTS AND DISCUSSION

The proposed framework has been implemented and deployed in Turn, a leading DSP in the online advertising industry. In this section, we present several results demonstrating the performance of our algorithms on 5 different campaigns, Camp1 to Camp5, that are on flight in our platform as of this writing. All of these campaigns serve large number of daily impressions (in millions), which makes model training more robust, and also each belongs a different advertising category, e.g., autos and gifts. In our experiments, we have used impression log data from January of 2012. We split the data into two parts according to the impression date and use the first week's observations for campaign specific model training, and the second week's observations for model testing.

We denote the imbalance ratio (IR) as the number of impressions without conversion events divided by the number of impressions with conversion events. The imbalance ratio among these campaigns ranges through multiple 100s, which shows that the actual (i.e., full) datasets are heavily imbalanced. As discussed in § 4.1, we try to retain all impressions resulting in conversions to ensure sufficient representation during model training, but only a subset of the impressions without conversions due to memory constraints. After splitting the conversion impressions among the train and test datasets, we subsampled the no-conversion impressions for each campaign to keep the imbalance ratio around $2-4$.

5.1 Data Imbalance and Score Calibration

In this part, we explore the influence of dataset imbalance on the model performance for each campaign. As we have already pointed out, we use the area under the ROC curve (AUC) as a performance metric. For each campaign we subsampled the training data before modeling to simulate the balanced, moderately skewed, and highly skewed data scenarios by choosing $IR = \{1, 3, 10\}$, respectively. Performance results on the test datasets are shown in Table 1.
We can see from these results that the data imbalance does not have any significant influence on model performance. Note that even with an IR of 10 there was sufficient amount of examples from the conversion class in the training data.

IR	Camp1	Camp2	Camp3	Camp4	Camp5
1	0.744	0.865	0.738	0.66	0.84
3	0.743	0.881	0.741	0.661	0.837
10	0.740	0.885	0.745	0.646	0.833

Table 1: Test AUCs for different imbalance ratios.

Even though there was no significant performance change due to data imbalance, the scale of the logistic regression output scores are quite different for different imbalance scenarios, as illustrated in Fig. 5.1. This plot shows the histogram of the logistic regression output scores for campaign 5 on the left hand side, for different values of IR (other campaign score distributions have similar patterns and are omitted). Since our goal is to accurately estimate the CVR for an impression, we need to calibrate the logistic regression output to obtain scores that represent the actual scale of the event probabilities. After the calibration (see § 4.2 for details), the scores of different data skew scenarios are much closer to each other and their scale coincides with the actual campaign conversion rates (the RHS of Fig. 5.1).

5.2 Missing Value Imputation

Missing data is another very common practical problem we encounter in our system and in this subsection we test the performance of the two imputation methods: median imputation and Bayesian least squares estimation-based (BLSE) imputation. For this experiment, we have imputed the missing attribute values (i.e., the missing base estimator values) and train logistic regression models for each campaign using the imputed data. The performance results on the test data are shown in Table 2.

Imp. Method	Camp1	Camp2	Camp3	Camp4	Camp5
median	0.741	0.876	0.742	0.663	0.836
BLSE	0.741	0.875	0.746	0.662	0.834

Table 2: Test AUCs for the two imputation methods.

These results indicate that there is no significant difference in the model's predictive performance among the two imputation method. Due to its simplicity and computational advantages, we use median imputation before model training in our platform.

5.3 Baseline Estimators vs Logistic Regression

Baseline estimators using past performance observations from distinct hierarchical levels have different CVR estimation performance. Here, we compare the CVR estimation performance of logistic regression to that of two different baseline estimators to demonstrate the performance lift we can achieve by using information from finer hierarchical levels and also the lift we observe by optimally combining these baseline estimators. The first baseline estimator uses a generic user cluster and campaign level count data to estimate the performance. That is, it estimates the CVR, p_{ijk}, of the user u_i (when served with the ad a_k on page p_j) as:

$$p_{ijk} \approx \hat{\hat{p}}^1 = p^{MLE}(Y = 1 | u_i \in \mathcal{C}^G_{u_i}, a_k \in Campaign_{a_k}) \quad (19)$$

where $\mathcal{C}^G_{u_i}$ represents the group of users similar to user u_i according to some generic (i.e., not campaign specific) features such as demographics, past browsing patterns, etc. The second baseline estimator we compare against utilizes past performance data in a finer user cluster, which was generated using campaign specific clustering/targeting criteria. Also, rather than using observations on all the ads in the campaign, it uses only observations for the ad a_k. This estimator can be written as:

$$p_{ijk} \approx \hat{\hat{p}}^2 = p^{MLE}(Y = 1 | u_i \in \mathcal{C}^A_{u_i}, a_k) \quad (20)$$

where $\mathcal{C}^A_{u_i}$ represents the users similar to u_i according to campaign specific features. Performance of all these estimators for each campaign on the test data is given in Table 3. The first thing to note in these results is the

Est.	Camp1	Camp2	Camp3	Camp4	Camp5
$\hat{\hat{p}}^1$	0.583	0.618	0.578	0.522	0.714
$\hat{\hat{p}}^2$	0.710	0.851	0.639	0.653	0.799
LR	0.741	0.876	0.742	0.663	0.836

Table 3: AUC of different conversion rate estimators.

relative performance increase by using $\hat{\hat{p}}^2$ over $\hat{\hat{p}}^1$, which uses ad (rather than campaign) level and campaign specific user cluster (rather than generic user cluster) level observations. This is somewhat expected since $\hat{\hat{p}}^2$ estimates the CVR among users which are more homogeneous from a campaign goal perspective. Logistic regression, which combines several baseline estimators, performs even better than $\hat{\hat{p}}^2$. The average performance lift achieved by logistic regression over the two baseline estimators are %28.2 and %5.92 respectively. Hence, using as many quality baseline estimators as possible and combining their outcomes optimally using logistic regression will yield a more accurate CVR estimate.

6. CONCLUSIONS

We have presented a flexible and principled approach to estimate conversion rates for serving display advertisements in real-time. We have shown that our algorithm provides consistent improvement in conversion rate estimation over some baseline estimators. The presented approach also provides simple but effective recipes for handling practical issues persistent in a real DSP, such as missing data and dataset imbalance. The offline training for the proposed approach over a large number of campaigns runs fast thanks to parallelization on a distributed computing cluster using R, Pig, and Java on Hadoop.

As future work, we also would like to incorporate more user and publisher information obtained from third party media providers into data hierarchies to improve model prediction.

Acknowledgments

We would like to thank Goutham Kurra, Santanu Kolay, and Andrey Svirsky for many insightful discussions and for their feedback.

7. REFERENCES

[1] D. Agarwal, R. Agrawal, and R. Khanna. Estimating rates of rare events with multiple hierarchies through scalable log-linear models. *ACM SIGKDD Conf. on Knowledge Discovery and Data Mining*, 2010.

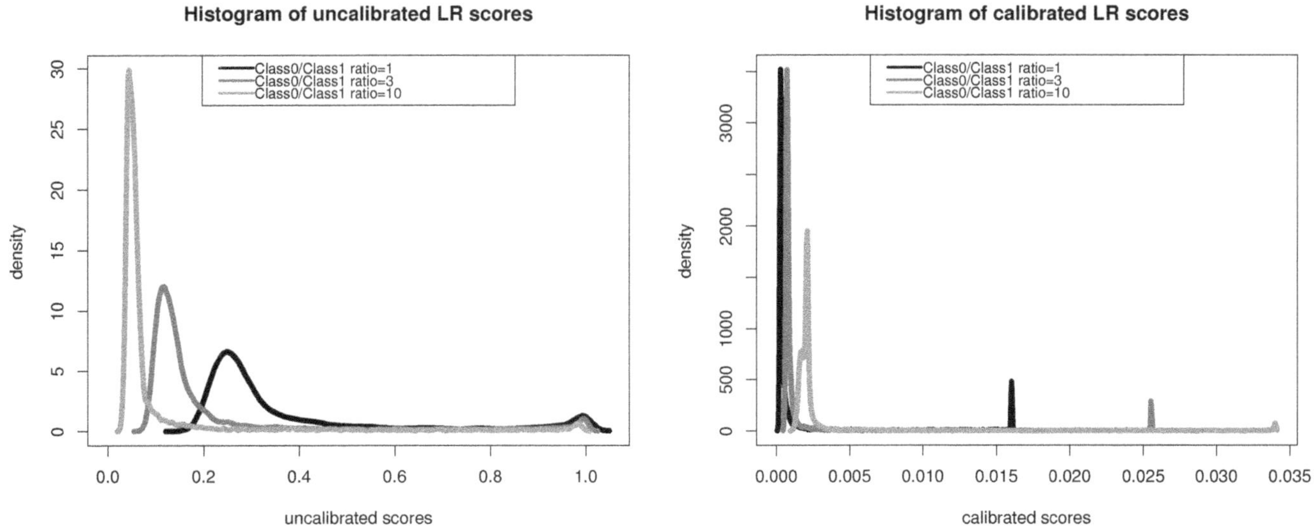

Figure 3: Score calibration.

[2] D. Agarwal, A. Broder, D. Chakrabarti, D. Diklic, V. Josifovski, and M. Sayyadian. Estimating rates of rare events at multiple resolutions. *ACM SIGKDD Conf. on Knowledge Discovery and Data Mining*, 2007.

[3] A. Ahmed, Y. Low, M. Aly, V. Josifovski, and A. J. Smola. Scalable distributed inference of dynamic user interests for behavioral targeting. *ACM SIGKDD Conf. on Knowledge Discovery and Data Mining*, 2011.

[4] E. Bax, A. Kuratti, P. Mcafee, and J. Romero. Comparing predicted prices in auctions for online advertising. *Int. J. of Industrial Organization*, 30:80–88, 2012.

[5] D. Blei, A. Ng, and M. Jordan. Latent dirichlet allocation. *J. of Machine Learning Research*, 3:993–1022, 2003.

[6] J.-F. Cai, E. J. Candes, and Z. Shen. A singular value thresholding algorithm for matrix completion. *SIAM J. on Optimization*, 20:1956–1982, 2008.

[7] D. Cerrato, R. Jones, and A. Gupta. Classification of proxy labeled examples for marketing segment generation. *ACM SIGKDD Conf. on Knowledge Discovery and Data Mining*, 2011.

[8] Y. Chen, P. Berkhin, B. Anderson, and N. R. Devanur. Real-time bidding algorithms for performance-based display ad allocation. *ACM SIGKDD Conf. on Knowledge Discovery and Data Mining*, 2011.

[9] J. de Leeuw, K. Hornik, and P. Mair. Isotone optimization in r: Pool-adjacent-violators algorithm (pava) and active set methods. *J. of Statistical Software*, 32(5):1–24, 2009.

[10] T. Graepel, J. Q. Candela, T. Borchert, and R. Herbrich. Web-scale bayesian click-through rate prediction for sponsored search advertising in microsoft's bing search engine. *International Conf. on Machine Learning*, 2010.

[11] R. J. A. Little and D. B. Rubin. *Statistical Analysis with Missing Data*. John Wiley and Sons, 1987.

[12] M. A. Maloof. Learning when data sets are imbalanced and when costs are unequal and unknown. *ICML Workshop on Learning from Imbalanced Datasets II*, 2003.

[13] B. M. Marlin and R. S. Zemel. Collaborative prediction and ranking with non-random missing data. *3rd ACM Conf. on Recommender Systems*, 2009.

[14] A. Menon, K. Chitrapura, S. Garg, D. Agarwal, and N. Kota. Response prediction using collaborative filtering with hierarchies and side-information. *ACM SIGKDD Conf. on Knowledge Discovery and Data Mining*, 2011.

[15] M. Richardson, E. Dominowska, and R. Ragno. Predicting clicks: estimating the click-through rate for new ads. *WWW*, pages 521–530, 2007.

[16] S. Visa and A. Ralescu. Issues in mining imbalanced data sets - a review paper. *Proc. of the 16th Midwest AI and Cognitive Science Conf.*, pages 67–73, 2005.

[17] G. M. Weiss. Mining with rarity: A unifying framework. *ACM SIGKDD Explorations*, 6:7–19, 2004.

[18] D. Williams, X. Liao, Y. Xue, L. Carin, and B. Krishnapuram. On classification with incomplete data. *IEEE Trans. On Pattern Analysis And Machine Intelligence*, 29, 2007.

[19] L. Zhang and D. Agarwal. Fast computation of posterior mode in multi-level hierarchical models. *Neural Information Processing Systems Foundation*, 2008.

Multimedia Features for Click Prediction of New Ads in Display Advertising

Haibin Cheng, Roelof van Zwol, Javad Azimi[+], Eren Manavoglu
Ruofei Zhang, Yang Zhou, Vidhya Navalpakkam
Yahoo! Labs, Santa Clara, CA
Oregon State University, Corvallis, OR[+]
{hcheng,roelof,erenm,rzhang,yangzhou,nvidhya}@yahoo-inc.com
azimi@eecs.oregonstate.edu[+]

ABSTRACT

Non-guaranteed display advertising (NGD) is a multi-billion dollar business that has been growing rapidly in recent years. Advertisers in NGD sell a large portion of their ad campaigns using performance dependent pricing models such as cost-per-click (**CPC**) and cost-per-action (**CPA**). An accurate prediction of the probability that users click on ads is a crucial task in NGD advertising because this value is required to compute the expected revenue. State-of-the-art prediction algorithms rely heavily on historical information collected for advertisers, users and publishers. Click prediction of new ads in the system is a challenging task due to the lack of such historical data. The objective of this paper is to mitigate this problem by integrating multimedia features extracted from display ads into the click prediction models. Multimedia features can help us capture the attractiveness of the ads with similar contents or aesthetics. In this paper we evaluate the use of numerous multimedia features (in addition to commonly used user, advertiser and publisher features) for the purposes of improving click prediction in ads with no history. We provide analytical results generated over billions of samples and demonstrate that adding multimedia features can significantly improve the accuracy of click prediction for new ads, compared to a state-of-the-art baseline model.

Categories and Subject Descriptors

H.4 [**Information Systems Applications**]: Miscellaneous; D.2.8 [**Software Engineering**]: Metrics—*complexity measures, performance measures*

Keywords

Multimedia Features, Image, Flash, Click Prediction, New Ads, Display Advertising, GMM

1. INTRODUCTION

Display advertising generates revenue by showing graphical ads on web pages. It is traditionally sold as a guaranteed delivery (GD) contract, which constitutes a deal between a publisher and an advertiser to deliver a pre-specified number of impressions over a certain period of time at a fixed price per impression (CPM). An alternative mechanism for delivery that has been growing in the recent years is spot markets, where the impressions are sold one at a time. Spot markets, such as Right Media Exchange (Yahoo), lets the advertisers bid differently for each impression, allowing them to use highly granular targeting methods. Most spot markets also provide advertisers with a wider range of pricing models. Similar to GD, advertisers can choose to pay per impression (CPM). However many advertisers would prefer to pay only if the ad attracted the user's attention. To address this concern, many NGD exchanges provide performance based pricing models such as pay-per click (CPC) and pay-per-conversion (CPA), which can be further categorized as post-view or post-click, depending on there being a click before the conversion event. In a marketplace where ads with different payment models are competing for the same opportunity, the auction mechanism needs to convert the bids to a common currency. This is often done by computing expected revenue (eCPM). For a CPM ad the expected revenue is obviously going to be the same as the bid. For a CPC ad, however, the expected revenue depends on the probability that the user will click on that ad. Similarly, the expected revenue of a post-view CPA ad depends on the probability of conversion after the user views the ad; and for post-click CPA the expected revenue calculation needs to take into account both the click and the conversion probability. As a result, accurate prediction of click probability plays an important role in NGD advertising.

A state-of-the-art NGD system typically relies on machine learning models to estimate the click probability of eligible CPC/CPA ads. These models are trained using data collected from live systems. The identity of the users, publishers and ads are typically used as features in such models, together with some high level category information. For ads that have been in the system for a long period of time, the estimation of click probability using identifier based features is generally reliable, however it becomes a challenging problem for new ads. Besides, identifier based features for advertisers fail to provide any information about the aesthetics or the content of the ads, which is the key factor that the user responds to.

This cold-start problem is often addressed by the use of content based features. However, most literature in this area focuses on textual representation of content. What makes this a unique problem for display advertising is the fact that the ads are not represented as text; display ads are graphical ads. In this paper we propose the use of multimedia features to represent the content (and aesthetics) of such ads. The contributions of our paper are as follows: We develop features that can be extracted from both static images as well as animated flash ads. We explore the use of global features to capture the visual characteristics of the entire image, local features to describe the sub sections in an image, and high level features to capture the user's perception. For flash ads, we develop an additional set of features that are extracted from the meta data. We also propose a clustering model based approach to capture the shared visual content of these images, and investigate the use of the group id as features. A feature selection algorithm is also developed to remove features with low click relevancy and high redundancy. Finally, we show experimental results on data sets collected from a commercial NGD exchange demonstrating multimedia features significantly improve the click prediction for new ads, compared to a state-of-the-art baseline model.

The paper is organized as follows. In Section 2, we describe the baseline NGD click prediction model. The multimedia features used in our work are introduced in Section 3 followed by the introduction of our feature selection method in Section 4. We present the feature analysis and modeling results in Section 5. Related work is discussed in Section 6.

2. NGD CLICK PREDICTION

In NGD advertising a spot auction is run for every ad slot on the publisher's page, in which all advertisers with matching target profiles participate. The ads are ranked based on their expected revenue and the winning ad is displayed. Estimating the expected revenue for pay-per click and post-click conversion payment models requires knowing the probability that the user will click on the candidate ad if shown in that ad slot on the publisher's page.

2.1 Model

The click prediction problem in NGD can be formulated as a classification problem, where each data point represents a publisher-ad pair presented to the user. Assume there is a set of n training samples, $\mathcal{D} = \{(\mathbf{f}(p_j, a_j, u_j), c_j)\}_{j=1}^{n}$, where $\mathbf{f}(p_j, a_j, u_j) \in \Re^d$ represents the d-dimensional feature space for publisher-ad-user tuple j and $c_j \in \{-1, +1\}$ is the corresponding class label ($+1$: click or -1 : no-click). Given a publisher p, ad a and user u, the problem is to calculate the probability of click $p(c|p, a, u)$. We use a maximum entropy algorithm for this supervised learning task because of its simplicity and strength in combining diverse features and large scale learning [3]. The maximum-entropy model, also known as logistic regression, has the following form:

$$p(c|p, a, u) = \frac{1}{1 + \exp(\sum_{i=1}^{d} w_i f_i(p, a, u))} \quad (1)$$

where $f_i(p, a, u)$ is the i-th feature derived from the publisher-ad-user tuple (p, a, u) and $w_i \in \mathbf{w}$ is the weight associated with it. Given the training set $\mathcal{D}$, the model learns the weight vector $\mathbf{w}$ by minimizing the total losses in the data formulated as:

$$LOSS(\mathbf{w}) = \sum_{i}^{n} L(\mathbf{w}; f_i(p_i, a_i, u_i), c_i) + \frac{\lambda}{2} \|\mathbf{w}\|^2 \quad (2)$$

where $L()$ is a logistic loss function used in this paper and λ controls the degree of $L2$ regularization to smooth the objective function. L-BFGS [5] is well suited to solve this kind of large scale convex optimization problem.

2.2 Features

Designing informative features is very important for supervised learning algorithms. Many features are derived from the publisher-ad-user tuple. On the user side, demographic information such as age and gender are common features used for click prediction. On the publisher and advertiser side there are hierarchies of entities. The entity identifiers are typically used as features in click models to capture the click behavior at different levels of abstraction. Publishers use site id to label their sites and section id to tag different parts of their pages. The *url* and *host* of the page are also informative features. An advertiser can set up multiple campaigns and creatives and the same creative can be used in multiple campaigns. And finally, publishers and advertisers connect to ad exchanges via networks, which constitute the root of the hierarchies.

The identifier features are all binary indicators that take the value 1 when present and 0 otherwise. Other ad features that are useful include the size of the ad, the topical category and the format (e.g. pop-up, floating or static banner ads).

Conjunctions are used to capture the interaction between different feature groups, such as user and publisher, publisher and ad, and user and ad conjunctions The number of features will grow exponentially after feature conjunction. Given a large set of identifiers, the final number of parameters in the model will be very large. Feature hashing [29] is a simple and effective dimension reduction technique to limit the feature space as well as maintaining the model performance by hashing the feature to a predefined number of bins.

3. MULTIMEDIA FEATURES

Display ads are mainly created in two formats, image and flash, from which we derive four sets of features. The first set is composed of features generated from images and image elements in flash ads. They are designed to capture the visual aspects of the images that may strongly affect users' response to the ads. The second set of features consists of meta information extracted from flash ads. In addition, we extract the latent mixture components from the images to capture their shared visual content as a separate set of features for click prediction. Finally, the image and flash features extracted from the ads are conjoined with user and publisher side features. For instance, the user age and ad color can be used as an additional feature to capture the variations in different age groups' responses to different colors.

3.1 Image Features

A digital image with resolution $X \times Y$ is typically treated as a grid of pixels with X rows and Y columns. The intensity of each pixel at location (x, y) can be represented in various color spaces including but not limited to RGB,

Grayscale, HSV, HSL and YUV. RGB stores individual values for red (R), green (G) and blue (B) for each pixel at (x, y). RGB can be easily converted to grayscale and consequently to binary, black or white, by setting a threshold value on grayscale value. HSV (hue, saturation, value) is another color space that takes human perception into account in the color encoding. In HSV, the brightness of a pure color is equal to the brightness of white. HSL (hue, saturation, lightness/luminance) is similar to HSV, except that the lightness of a pure color is equal to the lightness of a medium gray. The YUV model defines a color space in terms of one luma (Y) and two chrominance (UV) components. Different color spaces characterize an image from different perspective, based on which we can extract various features to describe the content of the image.

The features extracted from the image are divided into three categories, global features, local features and high level features. Global features are utilized to describe the content of the entire image using a small number of values while local features represent the characteristics of the local regions of the image. Both global and local features are computed directly from the image. The high-level features attempt to capture the human visual perception of the image. They involve more complex processing of the underlying image data, that typically requires applying a model trained on an additional image corpus. A subset of these high-level visual features has been used in the context of predicting a user's photo preferences in social media sharing sites [28].

3.1.1 Global Features

Global features capture the visual effect of the entire image as a whole and are generally easy to calculate. The global features used in our work are introduced as following:

- **Brightness** of an image can be derived directly from two color spaces, the YUV color space [23] where "Y" stands for the luma component (the brightness) and HSL color space [18] where "L" measures the lightness of the image. The average, standard deviation, maximum and minimum of the luminance and lightness values of all the pixels in the image are derived as brightness features.

- **Saturation** measures the vividness of an image, whose value can be established directly from the HSV or HSL color space. Similar to brightness, we calculate the average, standard deviation, maximum and minimum of the saturation of all the pixels in the image.

- **Colorfulness** of an image is a measure of its difference against gray, which is calculated in RGB [12] as:

$$\begin{aligned} CF &= \sqrt{\sigma_{rg}^2 + \sigma_{yb}^2} + 0.3\sqrt{\mu_{rg}^2 + \mu_{yb}^2} \quad (3) \\ rg &= R - G \\ yb &= \frac{R+G}{2} - B \end{aligned}$$

- **Naturalness** is the degree of correspondence between images and human perception of reality. Huang et al. [15] proposed an approach to obtain a quantitative description of Naturalness by grouping the pixels with $20 \leq L \leq 80$ and $S > 0.1$ in HSL color space according to their hue (H coordinate) value into three sets: Skin, Grass and Sky. The naturalness score $NS_{skin}, NS_{grass}, NS_{sky}$ as well as the proportion of pixels $NP_{skin}, NP_{grass}, NP_{sky}$ are derived from the image. The final naturalness score feature is calculated as:

$$NS = \sum_i NS_i \times NP_i, i \in \{\text{Skin, Grass, Sky}\} \quad (4)$$

- **Contrast** measures relative variation of luminance across the image in HSL color space. The simplest definition of contrast is the standard deviation of the luminance $L(x, y)$ of all image pixels. An extended version is to calculate the standard deviation of the normalized luminance $\frac{L(x,y)-L_{min}}{L_{max}-L_{min}}$ of all image pixels as the contrast.

- **Sharpness** measures the clarity level of detail of an image. Sharpness can be determined as a function of its Laplacian, normalized by the local average luminance in the surroundings of each pixel:

$$SH = \sum_{x,y} \frac{LP(x,y)}{\mu_{xy}}, LP(x,y) = \frac{\partial^2 L}{\partial x^2} + \frac{\partial^2 L}{\partial y^2} \quad (5)$$

where μ_{xy} denotes the average luminance around pixel (x,y).

- **Texture** features correspond to human visual perception by capturing the spatial arrangement of color or intensities in an image. One of the most widely used texture feature set is developed by Tamura et al. [27], which achieved correspondences with psychological measurements successfully. Three out of the six Tamura textual features are utilized in our work, which describe the coarseness, contrast and directionality of the image.

- **Grayscale simplicity** features are extracted to represent the properties of the gray level image. Three features are extracted from the gray level histogram of the image consisting of 255 bins [2]. The first one calculates the contrast of the image by measuring the width of the gray level histogram which consists of 95% of the pixels in the image. The second feature counts the number of gray bins which contains the significant number of pixels. This feature measures the simplicity of the image in grayscale. The third feature simply calculates the standard deviation of the gray level values of all the pixels in the image. Javad et.al in [2] show that the proposed gray level features are very effective in predicting the CTR of ads.

- **RGB simplicity** features can represent the simplicity of a color image [22]. Similar to [2], we quantize the RGB space into 512 bins by dividing each channel into 8 equal intervals. The number of RGB bins whose number of pixels are above a certain threshold is calculated as the simplicity feature in RGB space. We also take out the RGB bin with the maximum number of pixels as the dominant color and calculate its ratio with regard to the total number of pixels in the image as another features. Two similar features can also be calculated in the HSV color space.

- **Color harmony** property of an image is assumed to be correlated with the appeal of an image to a random user [8]. Two features are extracted from the image based on the 7 color harmonic distribution templates[16, 17] created from the hue value of HSV color space. From the HSV color space of an image, we calculate the average deviation from each color harmony template and the deviation from the best two fitted models are reported as two color harmony features [2].

- **Hue histogram** features are based on the hue value of all the pixels in image. Each Hue value in HSL or HSV color space represents a color by itself. Similar to [2], three features are extracted based on hue histogram of an image consisting of 20 bins. The first feature counts the number of bins including number of pixels more than a threshold value, indicated as number of significant hues. The second feature calculates the contrast of the hue histogram as the maximum arc length distance between any two significant bins. The third feature calculates the standard deviation of the hue arc length of all the pixels in the image, which shows the distribution of the hue color in the images.

3.1.2 Local Features

Users often pay more attention to certain regions in an image. Features that are generated from local regions can therefore be useful. To generate local features, we first divide the image into many segments using a connected component algorithm [25]. Let $S = S_1, S_2, ...S_g$ be the final g set of segments created from the image (note that segments smaller than 5% of the image are dropped). Some of the global features introduced in Section 3.1.1 can be extended to local features by calculating them in local segments similar to [2]. The local features used in our work are described as follows:

- **Basic segment statistics** features are extracted from the basic statistics of the segments. The first feature is simply the number of segments g in the image, which may indicate how busy an image is. Another feature is the contrast of segment sizes, which is calculated as the difference between the size of the largest and the smallest component. The third feature calculates the ratio of the largest connected color component to the whole image in terms of number of pixels. This feature will have a larger value for a smooth image. The fourth feature is defined as the rank of the hue bin, considering the bin size in descending order, associated with the largest connected component in the image. The last two features are calculated in the same way as the third and fourth feature except that they are based on the second largest connected component.

- **Segment hue histogram** is generated for each segment in the image. Similar to the global hue histogram features, six local hue features are extracted: 1) the number of significant hues in the image falling in the largest segment, 2) the number of significant hues in the largest segment, 3) the largest number of significant hues among all the segments, 4) the contrast of the number of significant hues among all segments, 5) the contrast of the hues in the largest segment, and 6) the standard deviation of all segment's hue contrasts.

- **Segment color harmony** features are similar to the global color harmony features except that they are computed on the largest segment. Two features are generated, the minimum deviation from the best fitted color harmony model and the average deviation of the best two fitted color harmony models.

- **Segment brightness** features are based on the lightness of each segment calculated in HSL color space. Three features are calculated, 1) the average lightness of all the pixels in the largest segment, 2)the standard deviation of average lightness among all the segments, and 3) the contrast of average lightness among all the segments.

3.1.3 High Level Features

Most of the global and local features introduced above describe the content of the image at low level of visual perception. In this section, we introduce a set of more advanced features that is able to capture high level interpretation of an image.

- **Interest points** are the pixels in the image that constitute the edges, e.g. high-contrast regions, of objects in an image. Lowe et al. [21] developed the SIFT algorithm (Scale-invariant feature transform) to identify the interesting points for object detection. We simply use the number of interesting points as a feature for our task, which may indicate the complexity of an image in terms of the number of objects it contains.

- **Saliency map** is a binary map detected from the image using saliency detection algorithms such as [14] to distinguish the objects from the background whose saliency value is less than a predefined threshold. Similar to [2], based on the saliency map, many features are extracted such as: 1) the ratio of background to the whole image, 2) the number of connected components of background, 3) the ratio of the largest connected component of background to the whole image, 4) the number of connect components in the saliency map, 5) the ratio of the largest connected saliency area to the whole image, 6) the average weight of the largest connected components of saliency map, 7) the distortion of the connected saliency areas calculated as the overall distance among all the components centroids, and 8) overall distance of all component centroids from the center of image.

- **Text** in an image can be extracted using standard OCR (Optical Character Recognition) algorithms [26]. Simple features such as the number of characters and number of words can be easily created afterward as two possible features. Note that these two features are independent from the content of the text and therefore do not need a very accurate OCR toolbox.

- **Human faces** in an image can be extracted by face detection algorithms [4]. For our ad click prediction task, we created four features using the recognized faces in the image: the number of profile faces, the proportion of profile faces in terms of pixels, the number of frontal faces, the proportion of frontal faces in terms of pixels.

3.2 Flash Features

Flash is commonly used in display advertising, because it enriches the user experience by supporting streamlining of video, audio, animation of text, drawings and images.

Compared with static image ads, flash ads are more attractive and therefore more likely to be clicked by users. Hence features extracted from flash ads can provide additional information to click models. In our work, a flash ad is decomposed into many elements including image, sound, font, text, button, shape, frame, and action. Obviously the image features introduced in Section 3.1 can be extracted from the image element of a flash ad. A list of flash specific features are introduced as following:

- **Basic flash** features are derived by counting the number of movie clips, shapes, fonts and frames in the flash.
- **Audio** feature is a binary feature indicating whether a flash ad contains audio. A flash ad with audio may be more attractive to users than ads with no sound.
- **Text** features such as number of characters, number of words and a number of pre-determined keywords (e.g., "click", "free") are derived from the text elements in the flash.

3.3 Mixture Component Features

When users look at a display ad they do not perceive it as a matrix of pixels, but rather they process the content of the ad. Images with similar content may receive similar responses from users. One way to capture this is to cluster images based on content similarity and use the cluster membership as a feature. We use a Gaussian Mixture Component (GMM) model for this purpose, instead of more advanced models such as Probabilistic Latent Semantic Analysis (PLSA) [13], because of its scalability. The weight of mixtures as well as the mean vectors and covariance matrices for each mixture are learned through a maximum likelihood process from the images in the training set, which are described as vectors of image features introduced in Section 3.1. For every image in the test data we estimate the probability of component membership from the learned model. The component id with the maximum posterior probability is then used as the mixture component feature in the click model.

3.4 User and Publisher Conjunction Features

The "attractiveness" of a rich media ad to different users will vary because users may have different interests and taste. For example, male and female users will certainly react differently when seeing an ad with a beautiful human face; young users may be more attracted to ads with cartoons than older users. The ad performance on different publishers also varies. As an example, ads with cars in the image are more likely to be clicked when shown on a automobile related site than when shown on a fashion site. These factors are not taken into account by the multimedia features introduced above since they are extracted from the ad content only. To solve this problem we use conjunction features, generated by taking the cross product of multimedia features with user features (such as age, genderetc.) or publisher features (such as publisher id, url, etc.).

4. FEATURE SELECTION

Some of the multimedia features introduced above may not be relevant to the click prediction task or can be redundant because of the intrinsic correlations with other features. Including all of them in the model may not only increase the model complexity but also degrade the model performance. In this paper, a clustering based feature selection algorithm is developed to remove irrelevant and redundant features. First, features are ranked based on their relevance to the target in the training data, measured using a standard mutual information method [32]. Irrelevant features are removed by thresholding the relevance score.

We use a spectral clustering method to group similar features together. A fully connected similarity graph is constructed, in which nodes represent features and edge weights are defined by the similarity (in terms of mutual information) of the two features they connect. A normalized cut method [9] is then applied to the graph to obtain clusters of features that are strongly correlated with each other. Finally features within each cluster are ranked using the relevance score and only the top k features in each cluster are selected to build the model. Clearly, there is a trade-off between relevance and redundancy that can be tuned by varying the k according to the size of the cluster.

Table 1: Feature set in baseline model for click prediction.

Feature Group	Feature Name
Publisher	publisher id, publisher network id, section id, url, host
User	age,gender
Ad ID	advertiser id, campaign id, creative id, advertiser network id
Ad Type	ad size, offer type id, pop type id

5. EXPERIMENTS

In this section, we first describe the features, data sets and models used in the experimental evaluations. Then we present a click-through rate (CTR) analysis of the image features. Finally, we compare the click prediction model with multimedia features to a baseline model on click prediction of new ads.

5.1 Experimental Setup

We conducted our experiments on data sampled from Yahoo's NGD advertising system, from a period of 5 weeks. Each sample is an impression of an ad and is labeled as "clicked" or "not clicked", as derived from the user click logs. The data from first 4 weeks is used as training set and the last week is treated as test set. There are approximately 2.3 billion samples in the training data. The data contains about 1.4 million unique display ads. 54% of the ads are images and the rest 46% are flash objects. The first image of the flash ad is extracted as its image representation. In order to evaluate the performance of multimedia features on new ads, we further create subsets of test data, which include only impressions with new ads that never appeared in the training period.

The baseline model used for comparison is trained based on numerous features extracted from users, publishers and advertisers. Table 1 summarizes all the basic features used in the baseline model. The baseline model also includes all the conjunction features conjoining every pair of feature groups in Table 1. A 24-bit hash function is used to hash all the features into 16 million bins. With 16 million features, the baseline model is considered strong. To evaluate the

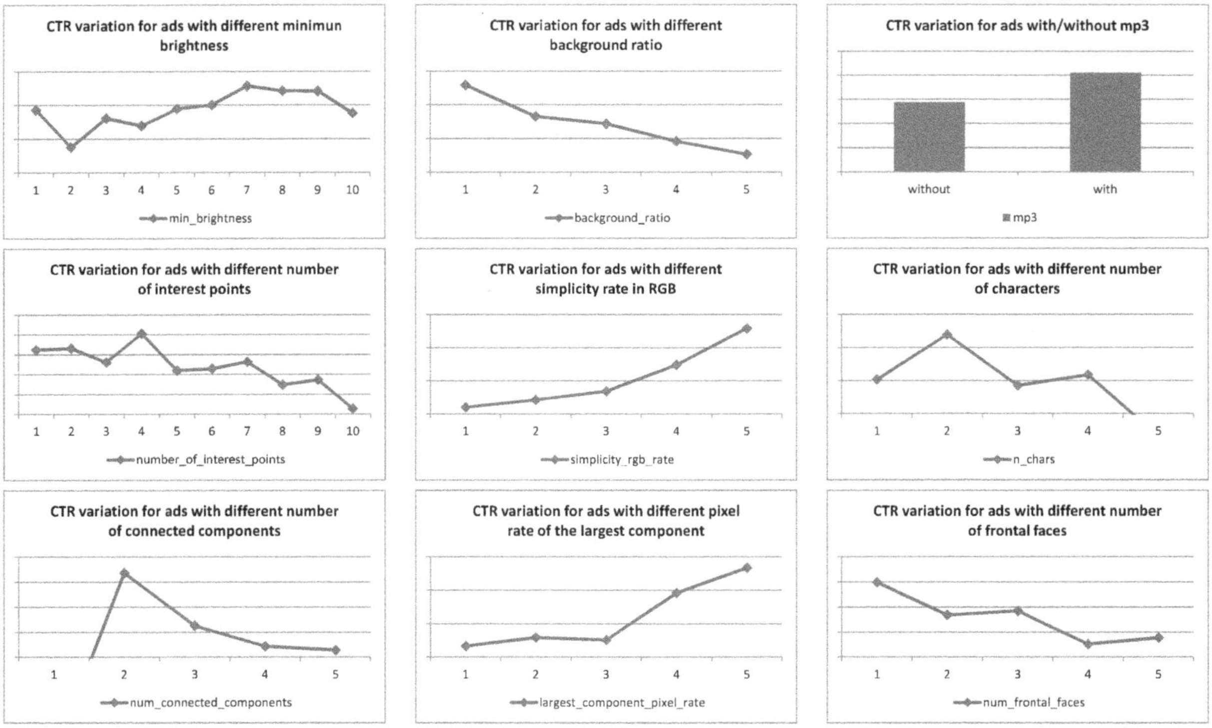

Figure 1: Variation of CTR with regard to different multimedia features

performance of multimedia features in click prediction, we retrain a model by adding multimedia features to each training sample as additional features. Events in the test set are ordered by the predicted clickability score. Precision-recall (**P-R**) curves as well as area under the ROC curve (**AUC**) are calculated to measure the accuracy of the models.

We evaluated three click prediction models with multimedia features. The first model uses all the multimedia features introduced in Section 3. The second model adds only the mixture component feature to the baseline model. We set the number of components to 150, largest we could use without increasing the cost of feature generation beyond our latency budget. The third model utilizes a subset of the multimedia features selected using the method presented in Section 4. Note that all the models use the same 24-bit hash function to hash all the features. As a result, adding multimedia features does not increase the model size.

5.2 Feature Analysis

Here we conduct an initial study on various multimedia features to obtain an intuitive understanding of their impact on user's ad click behavior. One week of test data is used for this analysis. We quantize each multimedia feature into multiple bins using a k-means clustering algorithm and the CTR for each bin is calculated. Figure 1 shows the CTR distribution for 9 representative multimedia features selected in our study. The Y-axis of each figure shows the CTR and the X-axis represents the bin index of features. The actual CTR values in the figures are omitted to protect proprietary information. Our observations from Figure 1 are listed as follows (note that images referred below include flash images):

- CTR increases nearly linearly with the minimum brightness of the ads.
- Large background image ads receive less clicks than small background image ads.
- Flash ads with audio generate more clicks than flash ads without audio.
- Ads with larger number of interest points have lower CTR than ads with a small number of interest points.
- When an image ad has more pixels of dominant color (simpler), it is likely to generate more clicks.
- There is a negative correlation between the CTR and the number of characters detected in the image.
- Image ads with a small number of connected components obtained from segmentation are generally preferred by users over image ads with a large number of connected components.
- Image ads whose largest connected component is big are likely to receive more clicks.
- There is a negative correlation between the CTR and the number of faces detected in the image.

It is clear that all these features are highly correlated with CTR and therefore have a great potential to improve the performance of click models. In fact, many of these observations are consistent with each other. For example, "simple" images often have a small number of interest points, a few connected components, or a high ratio of dominant color. These observations can also be used to guide the creative design process for the purpose of increasing their CTR.

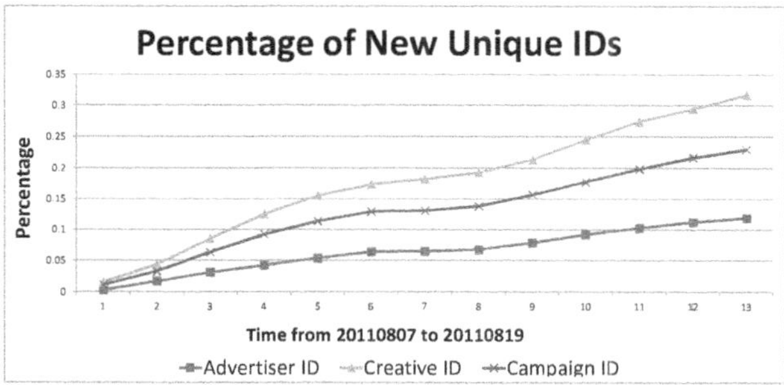

Figure 2: Percentage of new unique advertiser identifiers, creatives and campaigns emerging for each day in one month (relative to those existing in the training period).

5.3 Click Prediction for New Ads

Modeling multimedia features allows us to improve the click prediction for new ads by enabling the use of historical performance of pre-existing ads with similar content. In order to evaluate the scope of the problem we first measure the burst rate of new ads in the data. For this analysis we treat the first 4 weeks of data as the reference set, and calculate the ratio of new ads per day for the following 2 weeks. Advertiser campaigns often have an inherent structure: one advertiser can have multiple campaigns, and one campaign might have multiple creatives. In the case of Yahoo's exchange the same creative can actually appear in multiple campaigns. To understand the problem space better we measure the burst rate at each of these levels separately. As shown in Figure 2, it is clear that the burst rate is increasing steadily day by day for all three levels, however creative has the most significant change. 31.7% of unique ads are new creatives after a period of 13 days. The burst rate of campaigns is slower, with 23.0% of new unique ads after a period of 13 days. The advertiser is the most stable of the three levels, which still has 11.9% new unique ads. This underlines the impact of our work on the performance of the NGD advertising system.

Table 2: Performance improvement in terms of AUC of click prediction model with multimedia features on new ads with different level of newness.

Newness Level	AUC Gain
New Advertiser ID (newest)	6.50%
New Creative ID	2.15%
New Campaign ID	1.27%
New Campaign+Creative ID	3.31%

Next we evaluate the performance of the three click models with multimedia features as introduced in Section 5.1 on new ads. Specifically we create multiple slices of test data which contain new ads represented at four different levels: advertiser, creative, campaign and campaign×creative. The campaign×creative slice includes ads with either new campaigns or new creatives. The P-R curve and corresponding AUC for each slice of test data are shown in Figure 3. Looking at the test data with new advertiser id, we observe a significant improvement by adding the multimedia features. The model with all multimedia features gains 6.03% in terms of AUC. Using feature selection method introduced in Section 4 improves the performance even more, with a 6.50% gain over baseline. This is not surprising since a lot of features introduced in Section 3 seem strongly correlated with each other. It is also worth mentioning that the mixture component feature is so informative that adding it alone brings 1.5% gain over the baseline. We also observe notable improvements by adding multimedia features on the other new ad slices. The improvements are relatively smaller compared to the result on the new advertiser slice. This is expected because advertisers use the same advertiser identifier for new creatives and new campaigns thus providing some historical information even for new ads. Table 2 summarizes the AUC gains compared to the baseline for the model with selected multimedia features using the method introduced in Section 4. All the improvements are statistically significant ($p < 0.01$) based on a simple paired t−test on the prediction results generated by thresholding the prediction score of the compared models using the equal error point (EER). In summary, multimedia features play an important role on advertisers with limited historical information. Note that all these improvements are achieved without adding model complexity in terms of the total number of features due to the feature hashing strategy.

6. RELATED WORK

Click prediction in on-line advertising has received increasing attention from the research community in recent years. Most of the work in the literature can be categorized broadly as either new feature or new model development. In terms of feature development, Liu et al. [20] propose to use syntactic features for sponsored search to model the relevance between query and ad by treating the ad's text as a short document and building a language model as in classic information retrieval; Chakrabarti et al. [6] developed click feedback features [6] based on aggregated historical click data, which has proven to be very effective in click prediction; Cheng et al. [7] developed a personalized click model by including user specific features and demographic features which dramatically improve the performance of click prediction. In terms of model development, maximum entropy [7, 3] or decision trees [10] are common models used for click prediction in on-line advertising. Specifically for sponsored search we see the use of generative graphical models [30] that focus on identifying the factors that affect the user's response to ads on a search page; Graepel et al. [11] propose a Bayesian on-line learning algorithm used for CTR prediction in Bing's sponsored search product.

Most published work in the area of click prediction for new ads is focused on identifying new ads either by using categories [6] or identifying a set of similar ads by using the textual content of the ads [10], which cannot be applied to display advertising directly. In our case, some level of ad and page category was already being utilized by the baseline models. An alternative approach was proposed by Agarwal et al. [1] that utilizes the hierarchy in the advertisers campaigns to improve the prediction for new ads. While we did not use the exact same model, we did use features that capture part of this information in our baseline models. Therefore the improvements we present in this paper are complementary to their work.

Image features have been widely researched for the task of content based image retrieval (CBIR)[31, 24] including both global features and local features. Global features capture

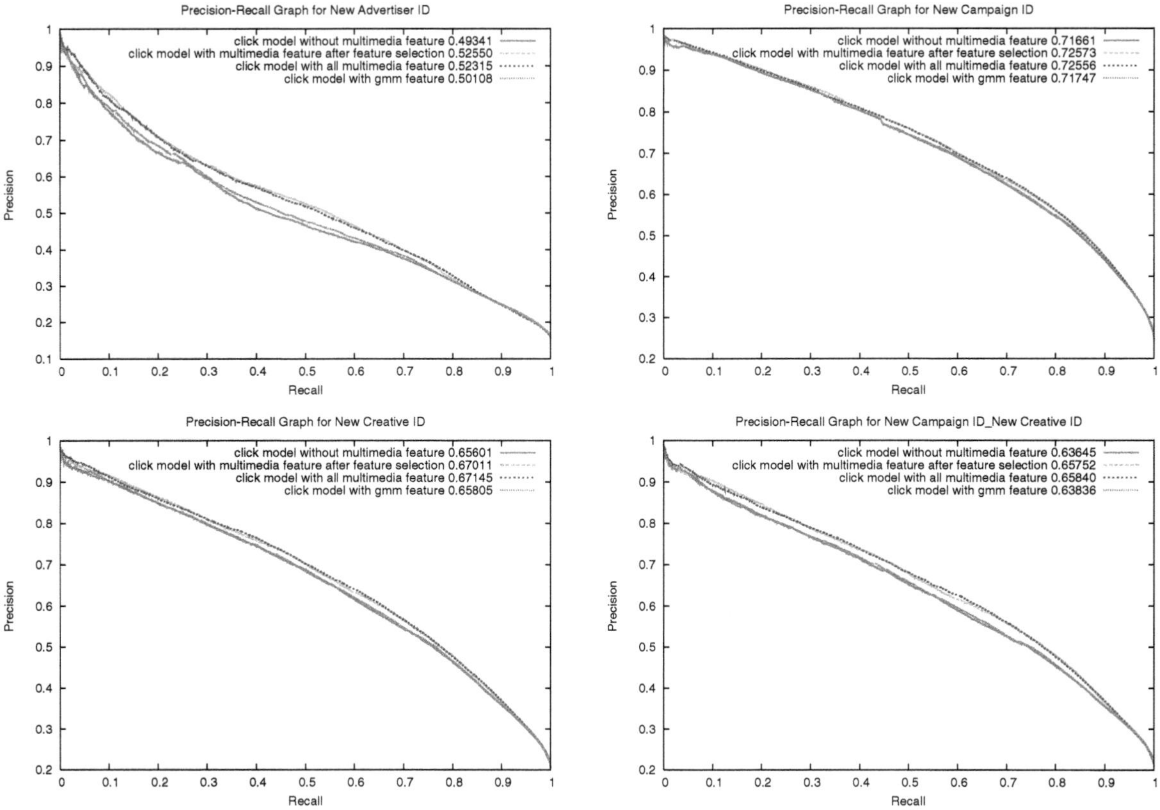

Figure 3: Variation of CTR with regard to different multimedia features

global characteristics of images such as color histogram, texture values, shape parameters. For example, Yoo et al. [31] developed a set of global visual features for the task of large scale image searching. Global features fail to work when the retrieval task is targeted to specific local objects, e.g. human face recognition. Local features are typically used in such tasks [24]. CBIR mainly focuses on finding similar images in a database, whereas our task requires measuring the "attractiveness" of the image particularly in terms of CTR. There is some work in literature developing features to estimate the beauty of an image using many features [33, 19], however little work is found on exploring their correlation with CTR. In addition to the features being studied in this paper, there are other derivatives from the computer vision domain that could have a strong impact on user's response to the ads, such as company logos. We would like to extend our analysis to include these features.

To the best of our knowledge Azimi et al.'s [2] proposal is the first use of multimedia features for the purposes of estimating click probability of display ads. Some of the image features described in Section 3.1 were introduced in their work. However their proposal was limited to static image ads in the absence of publisher and user information, and the experimental results provided in their work used a simple weighted sampling based CTR estimation as baseline on a small set of samples.

7. CONCLUSIONS

In this paper, we propose to use multimedia features to improve the accuracy of click prediction for new ads in a NGD advertising system. Specifically, we developed image and flash features that describe the visual perception of the content of display ads. We analyzed the click distributions for the different multimedia features and observed a strong correlation between the CTR and features defined. We further tested the models with multimedia features on large scale data collected from real traffic. Compared to a state-of-the-art baseline model without multimedia features, we observed significant improvement in terms of prediction accuracy on test data with new ads. We also developed a feature selection algorithm to remove the redundant and highly correlated features, which was shown to improve the accuracy of the final prediction task.

8. ACKNOWLEDGMENTS

We thank our colleagues Kannan Achan, Lihong Li, Olivier Chapelle and Rómer Rosales for their assistance with data collection and model discussions.

9. REFERENCES

[1] D. Agarwal, R. Agrawal, R. Khanna, and N. Kota. Estimating rates of rare events with multiple hierarchies through scalable log-linear models. In *Proceedings of the 16th ACM SIGKDD international conference on Knowledge discovery and data mining*, KDD '10, pages 213–222, New York, NY, USA, 2010. ACM.

[2] J. Azimi, R. Zhang, Y. Zhou, V. Navalpakkam, J. Mao, and X. Fern. The impact of visual appearance

on user response in online display advertising. In *WWW (Companion Volume)*, pages 457–458, 2012.

[3] A. L. Berger and V. J. D. Pietra. A maximum entropy approach to natural language processing. *Computational Linguistics*, 22:39–71, 1996.

[4] G. Bradski and A. Kaehler. *Learning OpenCV: Computer Vision with the OpenCV Library*. O'Reilly Media, 2008.

[5] R. H. Byrd, J. Nocedal, R. B. Schnabel, R. H. B. J. Nocedal, and R. B. Representations of quasi-newton matrices and their use in limited memory methods. *Mathematical Programming*, 63:129–156, 1994.

[6] D. Chakrabarti, D. Agarwal, and V. Josifovski. Contextual advertising by combining relevance with click feedback. In *Proceeding of the 17th international conference on World Wide Web*, pages 417–426, New York, NY, USA, 2008. ACM.

[7] H. Cheng and E. Cantú-Paz. Personalized click prediction in sponsored search. In *Proceedings of the third ACM international conference on Web search and data mining*, WSDM '10, pages 351–360, New York, NY, USA, 2010. ACM.

[8] D. Cohen-Or, O. Sorkine, R. Gal, T. Leyvand, and Y.-Q. Xu. Color harmonization. In *ACM Transactions on Graphics*, pages 624–630.

[9] T. Cour, F. Benezit, and J. Shi. Spectral segmentation with multiscale graph decomposition. In *IEEE International Conference on Computer Vision and Pattern Recognition*, pages 1124–1131, 2005.

[10] K. S. Dave and V. Varma. Learning the click-through rate for rare/new ads from similar ads. In *Proceedings of the 33rd international ACM SIGIR conference on Research and development in information retrieval*, SIGIR '10, pages 897–898, New York, NY, USA, 2010. ACM.

[11] T. Graepel, J. Q. Candel, T. Borchert, and R. Herbrich. Web-scale bayesian click-through rate prediction for sponsored search advertising in microsoft's bing search engine. In *Proceedings of the 27th International Conference on Machine Learning*, 2010.

[12] D. Hasler and S. E. Suesstrunk. Measuring colorfulness in natural images. *Human Vision and Electronic Imaging VIII, Proceedings of the SPIE*, 5007:87–95, 2003.

[13] E. Horster, R. Lienhart, and M. Slaney. Continuous visual vocabulary models for plsa-based scene recognition. In *ACM International Conference on Image and Video Retrieval*, pages 319–382, 2008.

[14] X. Hou and L. Zhang. Saliency detection: A spectral residual approach. In *In IEEE Conference on Computer Vision and Pattern Recognition*, pages 1–8, 2007.

[15] K.-Q. Huang, Q. Wang, and Z.-Y. Wu. Natural color image enhancement and evaluation algorithm based on human visual system. *Computer Vision and Image Understanding*, 103:52–63, 2006.

[16] J. Itten. The art of color. *New York: Van Nostrand Reinhold Company*, 1960.

[17] J. Itten. Color design. *Asakura Shoten*, 1995.

[18] G. H. Joblove and D. Greenberg. Color spaces for computer graphics. *Computer Graphics (SIGGRAPH '78 Proceedings)*, 12(3):20–25, Aug. 1978.

[19] N. Kalidindi, A. Le, J. Picone, H. Y. L. Zheng, and V. A. Rudis. Scenic beauty estimate of forestry images. In *Proceedings of the IEEE Southeastcon*, pages 337–339, 1997.

[20] C. Liu, H. Wang, S. Mcclean, J. Liu, and S. Wu. Syntactic information retrieval. In *Proceedings of the 2007 IEEE International Conference on Granular Computing*, page 703, Washington, DC, USA, 2007. IEEE Computer Society.

[21] D. G. Lowe. Object recognition from local scale-invariant features. *Proceedings of the International Conference on Computer Vision*, 2:1150–1157, 1999.

[22] Y. Luo and X. Tang. Photo and video quality evaluation: Focusing on the subject. *Proceedings of the 10th European Conference on Computer Vision: Part III*, pages 386–399, 2008.

[23] C. Poynton. Yuv and luminance considered harmful: A plea for precise terminology in video. *Engineering*, pages 1–4, 2008.

[24] Z. R. Srihari and A. Rao. Image background search: Combining object detection techniques with content based image retrieval(cbir) systems. In *Proceedings of the IEEE workshop on Content Based Access of Image and video Libraries*, pages 97–101, 1999.

[25] L. G. Shapiro and G. C. Stockman. *Computer Vision*. Prentice Hall, 2002.

[26] C. Y. Suen, M. Berthod, and S. Mori. Automatic recognition of handprinted characters — the state of the art. *Proceedings of the IEEE*, 68:469–487, 1980.

[27] H. Tamura, S. Mori, and T. Yamawaki. Textural features corresponding to visual perception. *IEEE Transactions on Systems, Man and Cybernetics*, 8:460–473, 1978.

[28] R. van Zwol, A. Rae, and L. G. Pueyo. Prediction of favourite photos using social, visual, and textual signals. In *ACM Multimedia*, pages 1015–1018, 2010.

[29] K. Weinberger, A. Dasgupta, J. Langford, A. Smola, and J. Attenberg. Feature hashing for large scale multitask learning. In *Proceedings of the 26th Annual International Conference on Machine Learning*, pages 1113–1120, 2007.

[30] W. Xu, E. Manavoglu, and E. Cantú-Paz. Temporal click model for sponsored search. SIGIR '10, pages 106–113, New York, NY, USA, 2010. ACM.

[31] H.-W. Yoo, D.-S. Jang, S.-H. Jung, J.-H. Park, and K.-S. Song. Visual information retrieval system via content-based approach. *Pattern Recognition*, 35(3):749–769, 2002.

[32] M. Zaffalon and M. Hutter. Robust feature selection by mutual information distributions. In *18th International Conference on Uncertainty in Artificial Intelligence*, pages 577–584, 2002.

[33] X. Zhang, V. Ramani, Z. Long, Y. Zeng, A. Ganapathiraju, , and J. Picone. Scenic beauty estimation using independent component analysis and support vector machines. In *Proceedings of IEEE Southeastcon*, pages 97–101, 1999.

Trustworthy Online Controlled Experiments: Five Puzzling Outcomes Explained

Ron Kohavi, Alex Deng, Brian Frasca, Roger Longbotham, Toby Walker, Ya Xu
Microsoft, One Microsoft Way, Redmond, WA 98052
{ronnyk, alexdeng, brianfra, rogerlon, towalker, yaxu}@microsoft.com

ABSTRACT
Online controlled experiments are often utilized to make data-driven decisions at Amazon, Microsoft, eBay, Facebook, Google, Yahoo, Zynga, and at many other companies. While the theory of a controlled experiment is simple, and dates back to Sir Ronald A. Fisher's experiments at the Rothamsted Agricultural Experimental Station in England in the 1920s, the deployment and mining of online controlled experiments at scale—thousands of experiments now—has taught us many lessons. These exemplify the proverb that the difference between theory and practice is greater in practice than in theory. We present our learnings as they happened: puzzling outcomes of controlled experiments that we analyzed deeply to understand and explain. Each of these took multiple-person weeks to months to properly analyze and get to the often surprising root cause. The root causes behind these puzzling results are not isolated incidents; these issues generalized to multiple experiments. The heightened awareness should help readers increase the trustworthiness of the results coming out of controlled experiments. At Microsoft's Bing, it is not uncommon to see experiments that impact annual revenue by millions of dollars, thus getting trustworthy results is critical and investing in understanding anomalies has tremendous payoff: reversing a single incorrect decision based on the results of an experiment can fund a whole team of analysts. The topics we cover include: the OEC (Overall Evaluation Criterion), click tracking, effect trends, experiment length and power, and carryover effects.

Categories and Subject Descriptors
G.3 Probability and Statistics/Experimental Design: controlled experiments, randomized experiments, A/B testing.

General Terms
Measurement, Design, Experimentation

Keywords
Controlled experiments, A/B testing, search, online experiments

1. INTRODUCTION
Online controlled experiments are often utilized to make data-driven decisions at Amazon, Microsoft, eBay, Facebook, Google, Yahoo, Zynga, and at many other companies [1; 2; 3; 4].

Deploying and mining online controlled experiments at large scale—thousands of experiments—at Microsoft has taught us many lessons. Most experiments are simple, but several caused us to step back and evaluate fundamental assumptions. Each of these examples entailed weeks to months of analysis, and the insights are surprising.

KDD'12, August 12–16, 2012, Beijing, China.

We begin with a motivating visual example of a controlled experiment that ran at Microsoft [2]. The team running the MSN Real Estate site (http://realestate.msn.com) wanted to test different designs for the "Find a home" widget. Visitors who click on this widget are sent to partner sites, and Microsoft receives a referral fee. Six different designs of this widget, including the incumbent, were proposed, and are shown in Figure 1.

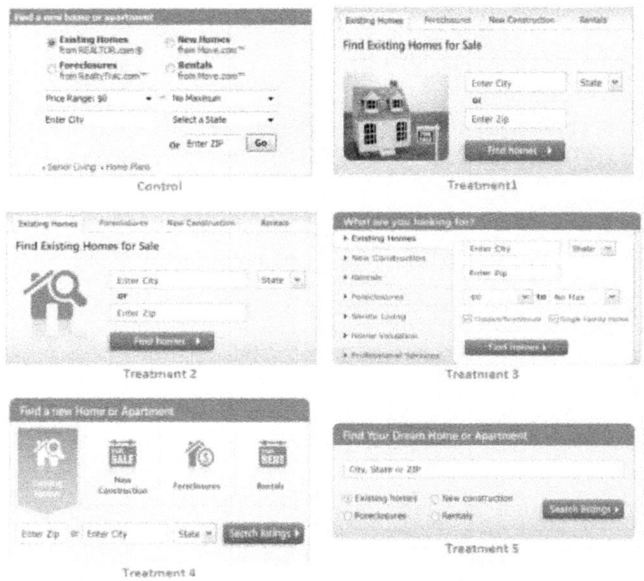

Figure 1: Widgets tested for MSN Real Estate

In a controlled experiment, users are randomly split between the variants (e.g., the six designs for the Real Estate widget) in a persistent manner (a user receives the same experience in multiple visits) during the experiment period. Their interactions are instrumented and key metrics computed. In this experiment, the Overall Evaluation Criterion (OEC) was simple: average revenue per user. The winner, Treatment 5, increased revenues by almost 10% (due to increased clickthrough). The Return-On-Investment (ROI) for MSN Real Estate was phenomenal, as this is their main source of revenue, which increased significantly through a simple change.

While the above example is visual, controlled experiments are used heavily not just for visual changes, but also for evaluating backend changes, such as relevance algorithms for Bing, Microsoft's search engine. For example, when a user queries a search engine for "Mahjong," one may ask whether an authoritative site like Wikipedia should show up first, or whether sites providing the game online be shown first. Provided there is agreement on the Overall Evaluation Criterion (OEC) for an experiment, which is usually tied to end-user behavior, ideas can be evaluated objectively with controlled experiments.

One interesting statistic about innovation is how poor we are at assessing the values of our ideas. Features are built because teams believe they are useful, yet we often joke that our job, as the team that builds the experimentation platform, is to tell our clients that their new baby is ugly, as the reality is that most ideas fail to move the metrics they were designed to improve. In the paper *Online Experimentation at Microsoft* [2], we shared the statistic that only one third of ideas tested at Microsoft improved the metric(s) they were designed to improve. For domains that are not well understood, the statistics are much worse. In the recently published book *Uncontrolled: The Surprising Payoff of Trial-and-Error for Business, Politics, and Society* [5], Jim Manzi wrote that "Google ran approximately 12,000 randomized experiments in 2009, with [only] about 10 percent of these leading to business changes." Avinash Kaushik, author of *Web Analytics: An Hour a Day*, wrote in his Experimentation and Testing primer [6] that "80% of the time you/we are wrong about what a customer wants." In Do It Wrong Quickly [7 p. 240], Mike Moran wrote that Netflix considers 90% of what they try to be wrong. Regis Hadiaris from Quicken Loans wrote that "in the five years I've been running tests, I'm only about as correct in guessing the results as a major league baseball player is in hitting the ball. That's right - I've been doing this for 5 years, and I can only "guess" the outcome of a test about 33% of the time!" [8].

With such statistics, it is critical that the results be trustworthy: incorrect results may cause bad ideas to be deployed or good ideas to be incorrectly ruled out.

To whet the reader's appetite, here is a summary of the five experiments we drill deeper into in this paper, motivated by the surprising findings.

1. Bing, Microsoft's search engine, had a bug in an experiment, which resulted in very poor search results being shown to users. Two key organizational metrics that Bing measures progress by are share and revenue, and both improved significantly: distinct queries per user went up over 10%, and revenue per user went up over 30%! How should Bing evaluate experiments? What is the Overall Evaluation Criterion?

2. A piece of code was added, such that when a user clicked on a search result, JavaScript was executed. This slowed down the user experience slightly, yet the experiment showed that users were clicking more! Why would that be?

3. When an experiment starts, it is followed closely by the feature owners. In many cases, the effect in the first few days seems to be trending up or down. For example, below is the effect from four days of an actual experiment on a key metric, where each point on the graph shows the cumulative effect (delta) up to that day, as tracked by the feature owner.

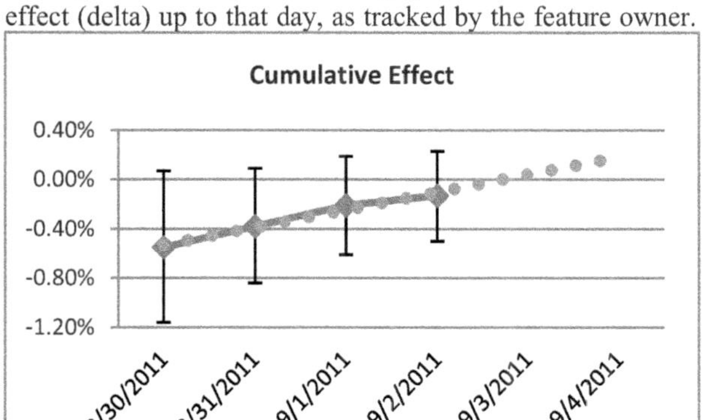

   The effect shows a strong positive trend over the first four days. The dotted line shows a linear extrapolation, which implies that on the next day, the effect will cross 0% and start to be positive by the sixth day. Are there delayed effects? Primacy effects? Users must be starting to like the feature more and more, right? Wrong! In many cases this is expected and we'll tell you why.

4. From basic statistics, as an experiment runs longer, and as additional users are being admitted into the experiment, the confidence interval (CI) of the mean of a metric and the CI of the effect (percent change in mean) should both be narrower. After all, these confidence intervals are proportional to $1/\sqrt{n}$ when n is the number of users, which is growing. This is usually the case, but for several of our key metrics, the confidence interval of the percent effect does not shrink over time. Running the experiment longer does not provide additional statistical power.

5. An experiment ran and the results were very surprising. This by itself is usually fine, as counterintuitive results help improve our understanding of novel ideas, but metrics unrelated to the change moved in unexpected directions and the effects were highly statistically significant. We reran the experiment, and many of the effects disappeared. This happened often enough that it was not a one-time anomaly and we decided to analyze the reasons more deeply.

Our contribution in this paper is to increase trustworthiness of online experiments by disseminating puzzling outcomes, explaining them, and sharing the insights and mitigations. At Bing, it is not uncommon to see experiments that impact annual revenue by millions of dollars, sometimes tens of millions of dollars. An incorrect decision, either deploying something that appears positive, but is really negative, or deciding not to pursue an idea that appears negative, but is really positive, is detrimental to the business. Anomalies are therefore analyzed deeply because understanding them could have tremendous payoff, especially when it leads to generalized insights for multiple future experiments. The root causes behind these puzzling results are not isolated incidents; these issues generalized to multiple experiments, allowing for quicker diagnosis, mitigation, and better decision-making. Online controlled experimentation is a relatively new discipline and best practices are still emerging. Others who deploy controlled experiments online should be aware of these issues, build the proper safeguards, and consider the root causes mentioned here to improve the quality and trustworthiness of their results and make better data-driven decisions.

The paper is organized as follows. Section 2 provides the background and terminology. Section 3 is the heart of the paper with five subsections, one for each of the puzzling outcomes. We explain the result and discuss insights and mitigations. Section 4 concludes with a summary.

2. BACKGROUND and TERMINOLOGY

In the simplest controlled experiment, often referred to as an A/B test, users are randomly exposed to one of two **variants**: Control (A), or Treatment (B) as shown in Figure 2 [9; 10; 11; 12; 3]. There are several primers on running controlled experiments on the web [13; 14; 15; 16]. In this paper, we follow the terminology in *Controlled experiments on the web: survey and practical guide* [17], where additional motivating examples and multiple references to the literature are provided.

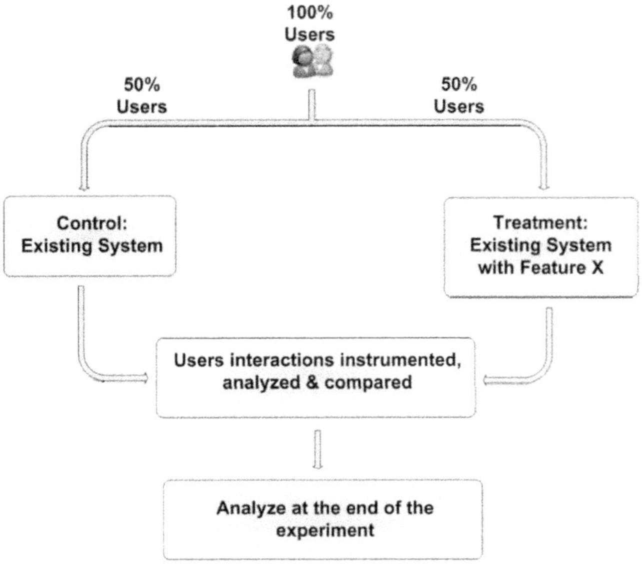

Figure 2: High-level flow for A/B test

The **Overall Evaluation Criterion** (OEC) [18] is a quantitative measure of the experiment's objective. In statistics this is often called the **Response** or **Dependent Variable** [9; 10]; other synonyms include **Endpoint**, **Outcome**, **Evaluation metric**, **Performance metric**, **Key Performance Indicator (KPI)**, or **Fitness Function** [19]. Experiments may have multiple objectives and a balanced scorecard approach might be taken [20], or selecting a single metric, possibly as a weighted combination of such objectives [18 p. 50].

The **Experimental Unit** is the entity randomly assigned to the control and treatment**.** The examples in this paper use the experimental unit as the analysis unit. For each entity**,** metrics are calculated per unit and averaged over all units in each experiment variant. The units are assumed to be independent. On the web, the user identifier is a common experimental unit, and this is the unit we use throughout our examples.

The **Null Hypothesis**, often referred to as $H_{0,}$ is the hypothesis that the OECs for the variants are not different and that any observed differences during the experiment are due to random fluctuations.

The **Confidence level** is the probability of failing to reject (i.e., retaining) the null hypothesis when it is true. A 95% confidence level is commonly used for evaluating one Treatment versus a Control.

The statistical **Power** is the probability of correctly rejecting the null hypothesis, H_0, when it is false. Power measures our ability to detect a difference when it indeed exists.

Standard Deviation (Std-Dev) is a measure of variability, typically denoted by .

The **Standard Error (Std-Err)** of a statistic is the standard deviation of the sampling distribution of the sample statistic [9]. For a mean of independent observations, it is ‾, where is the estimated standard deviation.

An experiment effect is **Statistically Significant** if the Overall Evaluation Criterion differs for user groups exposed to Treatment and Control variants according to a statistical test. If the test rejects the null hypothesis that the OECs are not different, then we accept a Treatment as being statistically significantly different from the Control. We will not review the details of statistical tests, as they are described very well in many statistical books [9; 10; 11]. Throughout this paper, statistically significant results are with respect to a 95% confidence interval.

An **A/A Test,** or a Null Test [13] is an experiment where instead of an A/B test, you exercise the experimentation system, assigning users to one of two groups, but expose them to exactly the same experience. An A/A test can be used to (i) collect data and assess its variability for power calculations, and (ii) test the experimentation system (the Null hypothesis should be rejected about 5% of the time when a 95% confidence level is used). The A/A test has been our most useful tool in identifying issues in practical systems. We strongly recommend that every practical system continuously run A/A tests.

3. PUZZLING OUTCOMES EXPLAINED

We now review the five puzzling outcomes. These follow the order of the examples in the Introduction. In each subsection, we provide background information, the puzzling outcome, explanations, insights, and ways to mitigate the issue or resolve it.

3.1 The OEC for a Search Engine

3.1.1 Background

Picking a good OEC, or Overall Evaluation Criterion, is critical to the overall business endeavor. This is the metric that drives the go/no-go decisions for ideas. In our prior work [12; 17], we emphasized the need to be long-term focused and suggested lifetime value as a guiding principle. Metrics like Daily Active Users (DAU) are now being used by some companies [21]. In *Seven Pitfalls to Avoid when Running Controlled Experiments on the Web* [22], the first pitfall is

> Picking an OEC for which it is easy to beat the control by doing something clearly "wrong" from a business perspective.

When we tried to derive an OEC for Bing, Microsoft's search engine, we looked at the business goals first. There are two top level long-term goals at the President and key executives' level (among other goals): query share and revenue per search. Indeed, many projects were incented to increase these, but this is a great example where short-term and long-term objectives diverge diametrically.

3.1.2 Puzzling Outcome

When Bing had a bug in an experiment, which resulted in very poor results being shown to users, two key organizational metrics improved significantly: distinct queries per user went up over 10%, and revenue per user went up over 30%! How should Bing evaluate experiments? What is the Overall Evaluation Criterion?

Clearly these long-term goals do not align with short-term measurements in experiments. If they did, we would intentionally degrade quality to raise query share and revenue!

3.1.3 Explanation

From a search engine perspective, degraded algorithmic results (the main search engine results shown to users, sometimes referred to as the 10 blue links) force people to issue more queries (increasing queries per user) and click more on ads (increasing revenues). However, these are clearly short-term improvements, similar to raising prices at a retail store: you can increase short-term revenues, but customers will prefer the competition over time, so the average customer lifetime value will decline.

To understand the problem, we decompose query share. Monthly **Query Share** is defined as distinct queries on Bing divided by distinct queries for all search engines over a month, as measured by comScore (distinct means that consecutive duplicate queries by the same user in under half-hour in the same search engine vertical, such as web or images, are counted as one). Since at Bing we can easily measure the numerator (our own distinct queries rather than the overall market), the goal is to increase that component. Distinct queries per month can be decomposed into the product of three terms:

$$\frac{Users}{Month} \times \frac{Sessions}{User} \times \frac{Distinct\ queries}{Session}, \qquad (1)$$

where the 2nd and 3rd terms in the product are computed over the month, and a session is defined as user activity that begins with a query and ends with 30 minutes of inactivity on the search engine.

If the goal of a search engine is to allow users to find their answer or complete their task quickly, then reducing the distinct queries per task is a clear goal, which conflicts with the business objective of increasing share. Since this metric correlates highly with distinct queries per session (more easily measurable than tasks), we recommend that distinct queries alone not be used as an OEC for search experiments.

Given the decomposition of distinct queries shown in Equation 1, let's look at the three terms

1. Users per month. In a controlled experiment, the number of unique users is going to be determined by the design. For example, in an equal A/B test, the number of users that fall into the two variants will be approximately the same. (If the ratio of users in the variants varies significantly from the design, it's a good indication of a bug.) For that reason, this term cannot be part of the OEC for controlled experiments.
2. Distinct queries per task should be minimized, but it is hard to measure. Distinct queries per session is a surrogate metric that can be used. This is a subtle metric, however, because increasing it may indicate that users have to issue more queries to complete the task, but decreasing it may indicate abandonment. This metric should be minimized subject to the task being successfully completed.
3. Sessions/user is the key metric to optimize (increase) in experiments, as satisfied users will come more. This is a key component of our OEC in Bing. If we had a good way to identify tasks, the decomposition in Equation 1 would be by task, and we would optimize Tasks/user.

Degrading algorithmic results shown on a search engine result page gives users an obviously worse search experience but causes users to click more on ads, whose relative relevance increases, which increases short-term revenue. Revenue per user should likewise not be used as an OEC for search and ad experiments without other constraints. When looking at revenue metrics, we want to increase them without negatively impacting engagements metrics like sessions/user.

3.1.4 Lessons Learned

The decomposition of query volume, the long-term goal for search, reveals conflicting components: some should be increased short term (sessions/user), others (queries/session) could be decreased short term subject to successful task completion. The assumption we make is that a better experience will increase users/month, the last component, which can't be measured in a control experiment.

This analysis is not just impacting search experiments, but also efforts like SEM (Search Engine Marketing). When deciding the bid amount for ads to a search engine, it is natural to try and optimize for the number of queries in the session that started with the ad click. However, long sessions may indicate user frustration (e.g., driving users to mediocre result pages).

Lifetime customer value should typically be the guiding principal for determining your organization's OEC. The choice of specific short-term metrics for controlled experiments needs to be done with a good understanding of the business, and it's critical to understand that long-term goals do not always align with short-term metrics, as shown above.

3.2 Click Tracking

3.2.1 Background

Tracking users' online clicks and form submits (e.g., searches) is critical for web analytics, controlled experiments, and business intelligence. Most sites use web beacons (1x1 pixel images requested from a server) to track user actions, but waiting for the beacon to return on clicks and submits slows the next action (e.g., showing search results or the destination page). One possibility is to use a short timeout and common wisdom is that the more time given to the tracking mechanism (suspending the user action), the lower the data loss. Research from Amazon, Google, and Microsoft showed that small delays of a few hundreds of milliseconds have dramatic negative impact on revenue and user experience [17 p. 173], yet we found that many websites allow long delays in order to collect click data reliably. For example, until March 2010, multiple Microsoft sites waited for click beacons to return with a 2-second timeout, introducing an average delay of about 400msec on user clicks. A white paper about the topic was recently published [23]. To the best of our knowledge, this issue is not well understood by most site owners, and implementations have significant click losses. For ads, where clicks are tied to payments, redirects are typically used to avoid click loss. This, however, introduces an additional delay for users and hence not commonly used for tracking clicks.

3.2.2 Puzzling Outcome

A piece of code was added, such that when a user clicked on a search result, additional JavaScript was executed. The reason that piece of JavaScript needed to be executed at that point was that a session-cookie was updated with the destination before the browser was allowed to proceed and open that destination.

This slowed down the user experience slightly, yet the experiment showed that users were clicking more! Why would that be?

3.2.3 Explanation

The "success" of getting users to click more was not real, but rather an instrumentation difference. Chrome, Firefox, and Safari are aggressive about terminating requests on navigation away from the current page and a non-negligible percentage of click-beacons never make it to the server [23]. This is especially true for the Safari browser, where losses are sometimes over 50%. Adding even a small delay gives the beacon more time, and hence more click request beacons reach the server. We have seen multiple experiments where added delays made an experiment look better artificially. Internet Explorer (IE) continues to execute image/beacon requests even after navigation, a decision that relates to backwards compatibility issues, which makes click tracking more reliable.

The above explanation generalizes a previous scenario that we reported [2]. In that scenario, the Hotmail link on the MSN home page was changed to open Hotmail in a separate tab/window. Although the naïve experiment results showed that users clicked more on the Hotmail link when it opened in a new window, the majority of the observed effect was artificial for non-IE browsers. The click was more likely to be logged since opening Hotmail in a separate tab/window did not navigate away from the current page and thus gave the web beacon a greater chance of reaching the server.

In a final example related to click tracking, a change was made in an experiment Treatment for Bing Search so that when a user clicked on a related search, the page would update rather than navigate to a new URL. While the transition looked smoother, we didn't expect such a significant increase to the feature usage as the experiment results showed. In reality, the click logging was simply more reliable and fewer beacon requests were lost. Indeed, the total number of searches (including the related searches) did not increase as much as the clicks had implied.

3.2.4 Mitigation

This problem, although severe, is easy to detect when looking at the experiment results, as Internet Explorer (IE) does not terminate image requests even when navigating away. Thus, if an experiment has an increase in clicks that is attributed to the non-IE browsers, it's likely to be related to the click beacons. This is a good example of a pattern that's easily observable once the underlying root cause is understood. More generally, differences in effects for different browsers are yellow flags for instrumentation issues or differences in HTML/JavaScript parsing.

Long-term, we believe that HTML should have explicit support for beacons.

3.3 Initial Effects Appear to Trend

3.3.1 Background

Given the high failure rate for ideas evaluated through controlled experiments as mentioned in the Introduction, it is very common for new ideas to be followed closely in the first few days of the controlled experiment to see if the new idea is a winner or if it should be terminated early.

In this context, it is useful to mention two effects that could occur when new features are introduced: **Primacy** and **Novelty** (or newness) effects [17]. These are opposite effects that sometimes impact experiments. Primacy effect occurs when you change the navigation on a web site, and experienced users may be less efficient until they get used to the new navigation, thus giving an inherent advantage to the Control. Conversely, when a new design or feature is introduced, some users will investigate the new feature, click everywhere, and thus introduce a "novelty" bias that dies quickly if the feature is not truly useful. This bias is sometimes associated with the Hawthorne Effect [24], i.e., a short-lived improvement. The experiment mentioned above, where the Hotmail link on the MSN home page was changed to open Hotmail in a separate tab/window [2] had a strong Novelty effect: users were probably surprised and tried it again several times. While Novelty effects die out after a short duration, and result in a smaller effect, the long-term impact could still be positive, insignificant, or negative. In this case, the long-term effect was positive and the feature is live on the MSN home page.

The existence of Primacy and Novelty effects can be assessed by generating the delta graph (between Control and Treatment) over time, and evaluating trends, visually or analytically. If we suspect such a trend, we can extend the experiment. To evaluate the true effect, an analysis can be done where the OEC is computed only for new users on the different variants, since they are not affected by Primacy and Novelty. Another option is to exclude the first week, as the delta usually stabilizes after a week. But this is where our surprising result comes in: most cases of suspected Primacy and Novelty effects are not real, but just a statistical artifact.

3.3.2 Puzzling Outcome

In many experiments, the effect in the first few days seems to be trending up or down. For example, **Figure 3** shows the effect from the first four days of an actual experiment on a key metric, where each point on the graph shows the cumulative effect (delta) up to that day, as tracked by the feature owner.

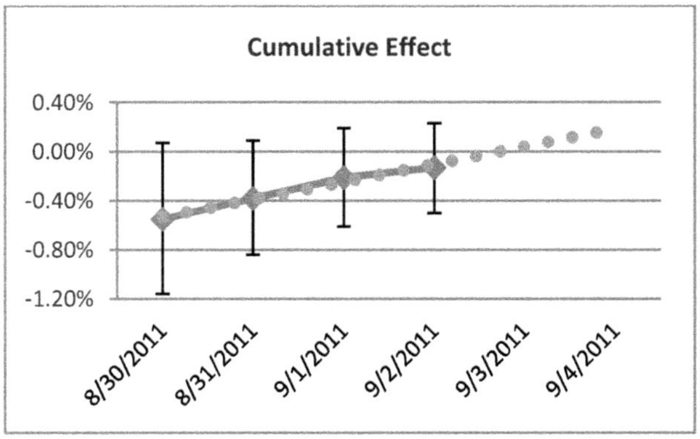

Figure 3: Effect appears to trend over time

The effect shows a strong positive trend over the first four days. The experimenter, which is hoping for a positive outcome, sees the initial negative delta, but extrapolates the trend linearly using the dotted line and thinks that on the next day, the effect will cross 0% and start to be positive by the sixth day. The thinking is usually: my feature is obviously great, but it just takes time for users to get used to it, i.e., these are just Primacy effects we're seeing in the first few days. Users must be starting to like the feature more and more, right? Wrong! In many cases this is expected.

3.3.3 Explanation

For many metrics, the standard deviation of the mean is proportional to $1 / \sqrt{n}$, where n is the number of users. For simplicity, assume no repeat users, i.e., each user visits once during the experiment (the results don't change much when using sub-linear growth that happens in practice), so that n is proportional to the number of days. The 95% confidence graph for the measured effect when the actual effect is 0 is shown in Figure 4.

The first few days are highly variable and therefore the effect in the initial days can be much higher or lower than the effect after two or three weeks. For example, the first day has a 67% chance of falling outside the 95% confidence bound at the end of the experiment; the second day has a 55% chance of falling outside this bound. Because the series is auto-correlated, there are two implications

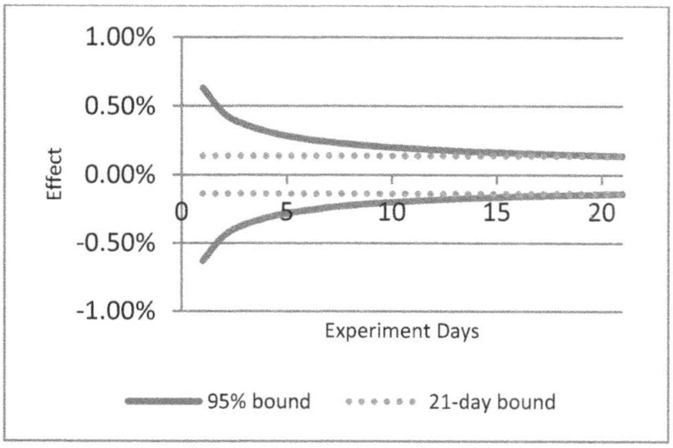

Figure 4: 95% Confidence Interval over time

1. The effects in the initial days usually seem overly positive or negative relative to final results published from prior experiments, which ran for much longer. Even if the experiment effect is zero, the initial days show relatively large effects and users typically think: wow, if this 0.8% effect stays, this is a huge win.
2. During the first few days, the cumulative results seem to trend. For example, assume an experiment with no effect on the metric of interest. The first day may be negative at -0.6%, but as more data is accumulated and the effect regresses to the true mean at zero following the 95% confidence cone. Feature owners incorrectly assume the effect is trending and will cross the zero line soon. Of course, this rarely happens.

The graph in Figure 3 actually is from an A/A test (no difference between the control and treatment) where we know the mean of the effect is zero. The first day had a negative delta (note that the wide confidence interval crossed zero) and as more days go by and the confidence interval shrinks, the results regress to the mean. Indeed, as Figure 5 shows, the graph stabilized around zero over time.

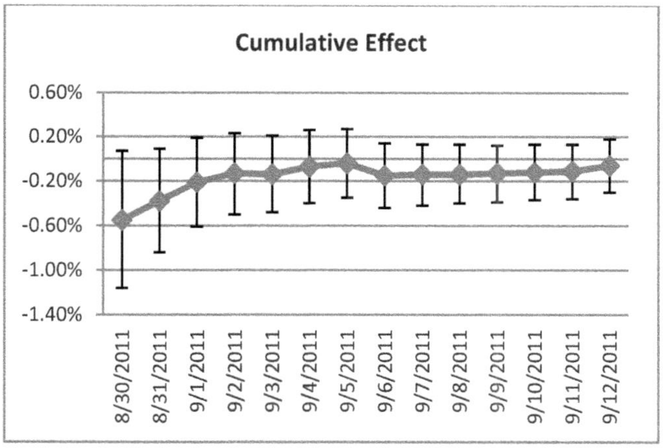

Figure 5: Effect stabilizes over time

3.3.4 Lessons Learned

The occurrence of "trends" shown is expected, so we view it as an educational and awareness issue, although we admit that hindsight is 20/20 and we were also fooled by initial trends multiple times. When you've been involved in the implementation of an idea and want it to succeed, the confirmation bias [25] is strong, and the initial negative results are often suppressed as you build a hypothesis that it's trending in the right direction.

Experiments we have run rarely have Primacy effects that reverse the initial effects, i.e., where the feature is initially negative until users learn it and get used to it, then it starts to be positive. We could not find a single experiment where a statistically significant result in one direction became statistically significant in the other direction due to these effects (e.g., a statistically significantly negative becoming statistically significantly positive).

Most experiments have a stable effect (constant mean), but the high variance means that we need to collect enough data to get better estimates; early results are often misleading. While there are true Novelty effects (initially positive effects that die down) or Primacy effects (effects that grows over time), it is more common for a statistically significant negative effect to be more negative over time, and for a statistically significant positive effect to be more positive over time. It is of little value to extend experiments that are statistically significantly negative after a couple of weeks. Failing fast and moving on to the next idea is better.

3.4 Experiment Length and Statistical Power

3.4.1 Background

Unlike most offline experiments, online experiments recruit users continuously instead of having a recruitment period before the experiment. As a result, sample size increases as the experiments run longer. One might therefore naturally expect that running an experiment longer provides a better estimate of the treatment effect, and also higher statistical power. Note that for some metrics, such as Sessions/User, the mean increases as the experiment runs longer. We therefore look at percent change relative to the mean in experiments, and likewise calculate power based on percent change.

3.4.2 Puzzling Outcome

For some of our key metrics, including Sessions/user, the confidence interval of the percent effect does not shrink over time. Running the experiment longer does **not** provide additional statistical power for these metrics.

3.4.3 Explanation

The width of the 95% confidence interval of the percentage change can be shown to be determined by two numbers: coefficient of variation and sample size. The coefficient of variation (CV) is the ratio of the standard deviation to the mean, which reflects the level of variation relative to the magnitude of the metric. Assuming Treatment and Control have the same size and same population variance, the width of the 95% confidence interval for percentage change is roughly proportional to:

$$\frac{\text{CV}}{\sqrt{\text{sample size}}}$$

In most statistical applications, samples are modeled as independent and identically distributed, so the CV is determined by the underlying distribution and a larger sample size from the same distribution does not change the CV. Therefore, one naturally expects the 95% confidence interval to shrink by the square root of the sample size as shown in Figure 4. However, empirical data shows that CV does change over time for many online metrics, including Sessions/User. Figure 6 shows the change in the mean, standard deviation and the growth of $\sqrt{\text{sample size}}$ over a 31 day period for a random sample of users. (Note that each series was standardized so they could be plotted on same axis.) The standard deviation is increasing faster than the mean, so CV increases over time.

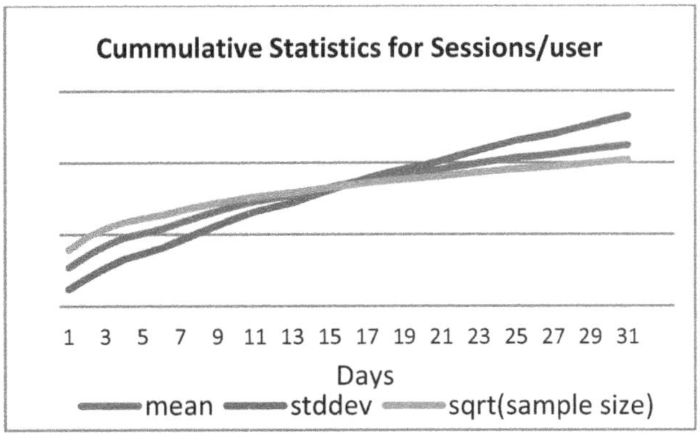

Figure 6: Change in Mean, Standard Deviation and Sqrt(sample size) for Sessions/user over 31 day period

In Figure 7, we see that the ratio, CV/√sample-size, is fairly constant (less than 10% change) over the 31 day period.

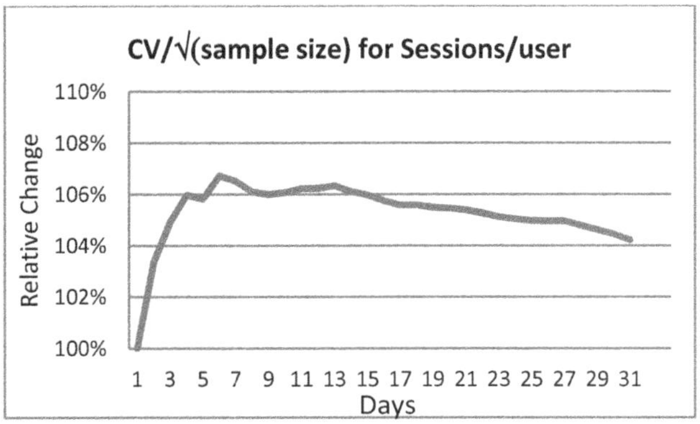

Figure 7: Change in CV/$\sqrt{\text{sample size}}$ for Sessions/User over 31 day period

The naïve approach is to use the Poisson distribution to model count metrics, such as Sessions/User, but this is clearly a poor model, given our data. The Poisson distribution has mean and variance equal to the parameter λ. As we run experiment longer, we expect Sessions/User to increase, i.e., the parameter λ for the mean is not stationary and increases over time. But even if λ were modeled as $\lambda(t)$, the CV of Poisson would be $1/\sqrt{\lambda(t)}$, which decreases as $\lambda(t)$ increases, contradicting our empirical data that CV increases over time. Rosset and Borodovsky recently showed that the Negative Binomial is a better way to model count metrics [26]. Moreover, for online user tracking, cookie churn and birth creates further variance for user based metrics. Since this ratio also determines the statistical power, the above result can be rephrased into the following: for metrics like Sessions/user, statistical power does not necessarily increase as an experiment runs longer.

3.4.4 Lessons Learned

For many metrics, especially bounded metrics like clickthrough, the confidence interval for the percent effect shrinks with the experiment duration; running an experiment longer increases statistical power. However, for some metrics like Sessions/user, the confidence interval width does not change much over time. When looking for effects on such metrics, we must run the experiments with more users per day in the Treatment and Control.

If running an experiment longer does not help reduce the width of the confidence interval or increase its statistical power, then why do we run an experiment more than a week? (We consider a week to be the minimum to look at day-of-week effects.) The key reason is that the treatment effect might be delayed due to Primacy and Novelty effects. As we previously noted, this is rare, but we are concerned about the risk.

3.5 Carryover Effects

3.5.1 Background

Some online experimentation platforms, including at Bing, Google, and Yahoo, rely on the "bucket system" to assign users to experiments [3]. The bucket system randomizes users into different buckets and then assigns buckets to experiments. It is a flexible system and allows easy reuse of users in subsequent experiments.

3.5.2 Puzzling Outcome

An experiment ran and the results were very surprising. This by itself is usually fine, as counterintuitive results help improve our understanding of novel ideas, but metrics unrelated to the change moved in unexpected directions and the effects were highly statistically significant. We reran the experiment on a larger sample to increase statistical power, and many of the effects disappeared.

3.5.3 Explanation

One big drawback with the "bucket system" is its vulnerability to carryover effects, where the same users who were impacted by the first experiment are being used for the follow-on experiment. This is known, and A/A tests can be run to check for carryover effects, but when they fail, we lose capacity until we re-randomize the bucket assignment. What was surprising to us is the duration of the carryover effect. We share two examples below.

In the first example, we ran the experiment in three stages where we had a 7-day A/A experiment on the user buckets before the A/B experiment was turned on for 47 days. After we finished the experiment, we turned it off and we continued to monitor the same user buckets for more than three weeks. Figure 8 shows the daily percent delta on the OEC (Sessions/User) between the treatment and the control. The gray bars indicate the division for the three stages.

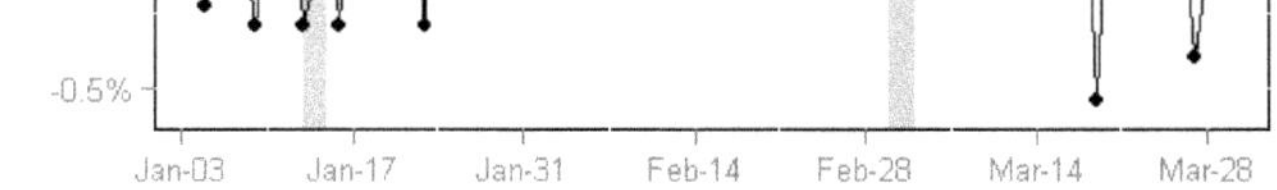

Figure 8: Carryover Effects Lasted Weeks

It is clear that there was a carryover effect on users after the experiment finished. The carryover effect seems to die out at about the third week after the experiment.

In another example, shown in Figure 9, a bug exposed users in the experiment to a really bad experience. The carryover effect lasted for much longer. Even after three months, the user buckets still had not fully recovered to their pre-experiment levels.

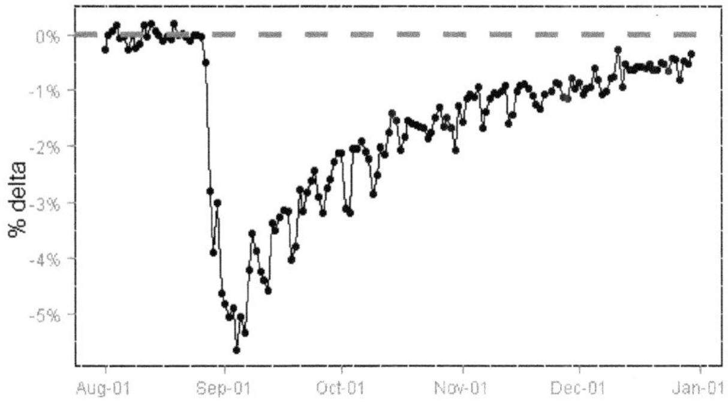

Figure 9: Long Lasting (3 Months) Carryover Effects

3.5.4 Mitigation

Even though understanding the carryover effect itself is important to experimenters, it's even more crucial for a quality experimentation platform to guard against it. In the bucket system, because user buckets are recycled from one experiment to another, any carryover impact can easily cause results to be biased for subsequent experiments.

One way to mitigate the issue is local randomization. The root cause of a carryover effect is the fact that the bucket system does not re-randomize for each experiment. The whole bucket system relies on an infrequent bucket re-assignment to randomize the population then the bucket assignment remains constant for a relatively long period. Re-randomizing users into the bucket system can be accomplished by changing the hashing function, but the bucket system couples all experiments in a "bucket line," or "layer" [3], such that we need to stop all running experiments in that bucket line to change the hashing function, hurting capacity and agility. An alternative is to use a two-level bucket system that can accommodate localized re-randomization; that is, re-randomizing only on a subset of buckets, but not affecting others.

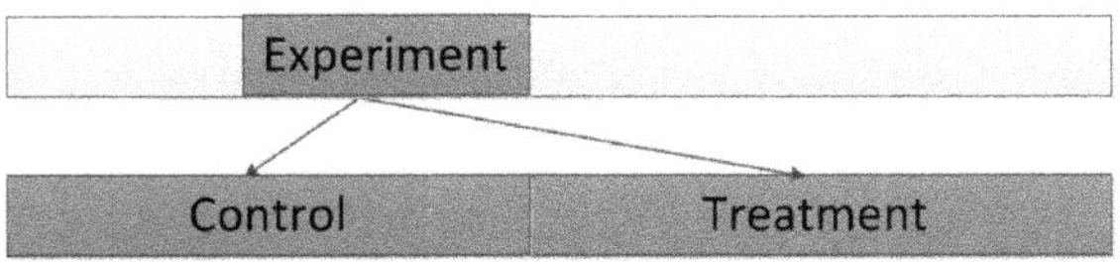

The above diagram illustrates how localized re-randomization can be achieved through two-level bucket system. The top level bucket system defines a set of experiment units included in the experiment and treatment assignment resides in the second level bucket system. For each experiment, the second level hashing uses a different hash seed. This guarantees a per-experiment randomization so that treatment assignment is independent of any historical events, including carryover effects from previous experiments. One disadvantage of the above is that one can't use a shared Control: each experiment needs its own Control so that any carryover from an experiment is "mixed" into the Control and Treatment(s).

One nice benefit of localized randomization is that we can run a "retrospective" A/A experiment without actually taking up calendar time. By changing the hashing function, we can re-evaluate the last few days the experiment ran as A/A experiment before starting the A/B experiment. By the independence property of localized re-randomization, if we retrospectively compare users that would have been assigned to control and treatment for any period before the experiment, this comparison will be an A/A. If the A/A shows an effect for key metrics, say p-value < 0.2 (due to an "unlucky" split), we change the hashing key and retry.

4. SUMMARY

Controlled experiments are the gold standard in science for proving causality. The FDA, for example, requires controlled experiments (randomized clinical trials) for approving drugs. In the software world, online controlled experiments are being used heavily to make data-driven decisions, especially in areas where the forefront of knowledge is being pushed: Search being a prime example. We are trying a lot of ideas, failing on most, but the successful ones are the ones that help us build a useful theory and apply it. Discovering what works and what doesn't is real Knowledge Discovery in our domain, and it's enabled by a lot of hypothesis generation from mining the data and by running controlled experiments to confirm (or reject) those hypotheses.

The statistical theory of controlled experiments is well understood, but the devil is in the details and the difference between theory and practice is greater in practice than in theory. We have shared five puzzling experiment outcomes, which we were able to analyze deeply and explain. What separates these from many other surprising results is that we found ourselves referring to them over and over. The insight and lessons from the analysis is general and useful not only to other experiments for us, but to many online experiments in other domains, and to many metrics computed for reporting and Business Intelligence reasons.

Generalizing from these puzzles, we see two themes. One is that instrumentation is not as precise as we would like it to be, interacting in subtle ways with experiments: we shared a prime examples where click tracking is brittle. Instrumentation issues are related to the concept of measure validity, i.e., the extent to which the metric used captures the concept we intended to measure [27]. A second theme is that lessons from offline experiments don't always map well online: we have to deal with carryover effects and confidence intervals that don't shrink as we extend the duration and increase the number of users in the experiment. But, fortunately, we get to experiment with very large populations of millions of users and detect small effects to improve our intuition and understanding of the domain.

Anyone can run online controlled experiments and generate numbers with six digits after the decimal point. It's easy to generate p-values and beautiful 3D graphs of trends over time. But the real challenge is in understanding when the results are invalid, not at the sixth decimal place, but before the decimal point, or even at the plus/minus for the percent effect; that's what these analyses did to the initial results. We hope we've managed to shed light on puzzling outcomes and we encourage others to drill deep and share other similar results. Generating numbers is easy; generating numbers you should trust is hard!

ACKNOWLEDGMENTS

We wish to thank Xin Fu, Sara Javanmardi, Greg Linden, David Messner, Saharon Rosset, Maria Stone, Harry Shum, Zijian Zheng, Jing Zhong, and the members of the Experimentation Platform and Bing Data Mining teams.

REFERENCES

1. Kohavi, Ron and Round, Matt. *Front Line Internet Analytics at Amazon.com.* [ed.] Jim Sterne. Santa Barbara, CA : s.n., 2004. http://ai.stanford.edu/~ronnyk/emetricsAmazon.pdf.

2. Kohavi, Ron, Crook, Thomas and Longbotham, Roger. Online Experimentation at Microsoft. *Third Workshop on Data Mining Case Studies and Practice Prize.* 2009. http://exp-platform.com/expMicrosoft.aspx.

3. Tang, Diane, et al. Overlapping Experiment Infrastructure: More, Better, Faster Experimentation. *Proceedings 16th Conference on Knowledge Discovery and Data Mining.* 2010, pp. 17-26.

4. Patil, DJ, et al. Competing on Analytics at the Highest Level. [Online] Apr 9, 2010. http://www.svforum.org/index.cfm?fuseaction=Page.ViewPage&PageID=997.

5. Manzi, Jim. *Uncontrolled: The Surprising Payoff of Trial-and-Error for Business, Politics, and Society.* s.l. : Basic Books, 2012. 978-0-465-02931-0.

6. Kaushik, Avinash. Experimentation and Testing: A Primer. *Occam's Razor.* [Online] May 22, 2006. http://www.kaushik.net/avinash/2006/05/experimentation-and-testing-a-primer.html.

7. Moran, Mike. *Do It Wrong Quickly: How the Web Changes the Old Marketing Rules* . s.l. : IBM Press, 2007. 0132255960.

8. —. Multivariate Testing in Action: Quicken Loan's Regis Hadiaris on multivariate testing. *Biznology Blog by Mike Moran.* [Online] December 23, 2008. http://www.biznology.com/2008/12/multivariate_testing_in_action/.

9. Mason, Robert L, Gunst, Richard F and Hess, James L. *Statistical Design and Analysis of Experiments With Applications to Engineering and Science.* s.l. : John Wiley & Sons, 1989. 047185364X .

10. Box, George E.P., Hunter, J Stuart and Hunter, William G. *Statistics for Experimenters: Design, Innovation, and Discovery.* 2nd. s.l. : John Wiley & Sons, Inc, 2005. 0471718130.

11. Keppel, Geoffrey, Saufley, William H and Tokunaga, Howard. *Introduction to Design and Analysis.* 2nd. s.l. : W.H. Freeman and Company, 1992.

12. Kohavi, Ron, Henne, Randal M and Sommerfield, Dan. Practical Guide to Controlled Experiments on the Web: Listen to Your Customers not to the HiPPO. *The Thirteenth ACM SIGKDD International Conference on Knowledge Discovery and Data Mining (KDD 2007).* August 2007, pp. 959-967. http://exp-platform.com/hippo.aspx.

13. Peterson, Eric T. *Web Analytics Demystified: A Marketer's Guide to Understanding How Your Web Site Affects Your Business.* s.l. : Celilo Group Media and CafePress, 2004. 0974358428.

14. Eisenberg, Bryan. How to Improve A/B Testing. *ClickZ Network.* [Online] April 29, 2005. http://www.clickz.com/showPage.html?page=3500811.

15. Chatham, Bob, Temkin, Bruce D and Amato, Michelle. *A Primer on A/B Testing.* s.l. : Forrester Research, 2004.

16. Miller, Scott. How to Design a Split Test. *Web Marketing Today, Conversion/Testing.* [Online] Jan 18, 2007. http://www.wilsonweb.com/conversion/.

17. Kohavi, Ron, et al. Controlled experiments on the web: survey and practical guide. *Data Mining and Knowledge Discovery.* February 2009, Vol. 18, 1, pp. 140-181. http://exp-platform.com/hippo_long.aspx.

18. Roy, Ranjit K. *Design of Experiments using the Taguchi Approach : 16 Steps to Product and Process Improvement.* s.l. : John Wiley & Sons, Inc, 2001. 0-471-36101-1.

19. Quarto-vonTivadar, John. AB Testing: Too Little, Too Soon. *Future Now.* [Online] 2006. http://www.futurenowinc.com/abtesting.pdf.

20. Kaplan, Robert S and Norton, David P. *The Balanced Scorecard: Translating Strategy into Action.* s.l. : Harvard Business School Press, 1996. 0875846513.

21. Cheshire, Tom. Test. Test. Test: How wooga turned the games business into a science. *Wired Magazine UK, http://www.wired.co.uk/magazine/archive/2012/01/features/test-test-test?page=all.* January 5, 2012.

22. Crook, Thomas, et al. Seven Pitfalls to Avoid when Running Controlled Experiments on the Web. [ed.] Peter Flach and Mohammed Zaki. *KDD '09: Proceedings of the 15th ACM SIGKDD international conference on Knowledge discovery and data mining.* 2009, pp. 1105-1114. http://exp-platform.com/ExPpitfalls.aspx.

23. Kohavi, Ron, et al. *Tracking Users' Clicks and Submits: Tradeoffs between User Experience and Data Loss.* Redmond, WA : s.n., 2010. Microsoft White pape, http://www.exp-platform.com/Pages/TrackingClicksSubmits.aspx.

24. Hawthorne effect. *Wikipedia.* [Online] 2007. http://en.wikipedia.org/wiki/Hawthorne_experiments.

25. Nickerson, Raymond S. Confirmation Bias: A Ubiquitous Phenomenon in Many Guises. *Review of General Psychology.* 1998, Vol. 2, 2, pp. 175-220.

26. Rosset, Saharon and Borodovsky, Slava. A/B Testing Using the Negative Binomial Distribution in an Internet Search Application, Submitted. [Online] 2012. http://www.tau.ac.il/~saharon/papers/AB%20testing%20with%20NB%20distribution%20-%20revision.pdf.

27. Weiss, Carol H. *Evaluation: Methods for Studying Programs and Policies.* 2nd. s.l. : Prentice Hall, 1997. 0-13-309725-0.

Position-Normalized Click Prediction in Search Advertising

Ye Chen
Microsoft Corporation
1065 La Avenida
Mountain View, CA 94043
yec@microsoft.com

Tak W. Yan
Microsoft Corporation
1065 La Avenida
Mountain View, CA 94043
takyan@microsoft.com

ABSTRACT

Click-through rate (CTR) prediction plays a central role in search advertising. One needs CTR estimates unbiased by positional effect in order for ad ranking, allocation, and pricing to be based upon ad relevance or quality in terms of click propensity. However, the observed click-through data has been confounded by positional bias, that is, users tend to click more on ads shown in higher positions than lower ones, regardless of the ad relevance. We describe a probabilistic factor model as a general principled approach to studying these exogenous and often overwhelming phenomena. The model is simple and linear in nature, while empirically justified by the advertising domain. Our experimental results with artificial and real-world sponsored search data show the soundness of the underlying model assumption, which in turn yields superior prediction accuracy.

Categories and Subject Descriptors

I.5.1 [**Pattern Recognition**]: Models—*Statistical*

General Terms

Algorithms, Theory, Experimentation

Keywords

Search advertising, factor models, exogeneity

1. INTRODUCTION

A click-through rate (CTR) prediction system for sponsored search advertising aims to estimate the CTR given a query-ad pair, typically along with other contextual knowledge such as about the user. The CTR prediction is pivotal for ad ranking, allocation, pricing, and the payoff of users and advertisers as well [7]. The estimated CTR serves as a measure of query-ad relevance, and hence should be made independent of other non-relevance factors. In practice, however, there are factors exogenous to the relevance-based click-through system, and often playing a dominant role in the observed click-through data. One classic example is the ad presentation position. A less cautious treatment of these exogenous factors may lead to a sub-optimal CTR prediction, and many real-world systems have been seen with these flaws.

We propose a probabilistic factor model as a general principled approach to studying these exogenous and often overwhelming phenomena. The model is simple and linear in nature, while empirically justified by the advertising domain. Extensive research has been undergone for correcting positional bias in algorithmic search, among which representative works are the examination model [12], the cascade model [5], and the dynamic Bayesian network (DBN) model [3], but less so for search advertising. Our approach adopts the same factorization assumption as in the examination model, that is, the probability of clicking on an item (result link for algorithmic search and ad for sponsored search) is the product of a positional prior probability and a relevance-based probability which is independent of position. Moreover, we specialize the concept of position into the ad domain, by incorporating other advertising specific yet important signals, e.g., the query-ad keyword match type and the total number of ads shown.

Other models originating from algorithmic search typically assume that the estimated CTR of an item is dependent on the relevance of items shown above on the search result page, as in the cascade and DBN models. These more sophisticated assumptions are appropriate for algorithmic search results where users have a high probability of clicking on one of the result links. For ads, however, the probability of clicking on ads generally is extremely low, usually a fraction of a percent. As a consequence, the effect of (not clicking) higher ads is a product of factors which are extremely close to one. In this case for example, the DBN positional prior reduces to a negative exponential function, which is a good fit to the empirical distribution derived from our factor model as described below.

2. THE FACTOR MODEL

Let i denote a query-ad pair, j be the ad position, c be the number of clicks, and v be the number of impressions. The observed CTR is an empirical conditional probability $p(\text{click}|i, j)$. We make the following simplifying yet classic assumptions in sponsored search advertising [2, 6, 11]:

1. Clicking an ad is independent of its position, given that it is physically examined.

KDD'12, August 12–16, 2012, Beijing, China.

2. Examining an ad is independent of its content or relevance, given its position.

Formally, the position-dependent CTR is factorized as

$$p(\text{click}|i, j) = p(\text{click}|\text{exam}, i)p(\text{exam}|j). \quad (1)$$

The first factor $p(\text{click}|\text{exam}, i)$, simply denoted as p_i, is a position-normalized CTR that represents the relevance of ad. The second factor $p(\text{exam}|j)$, simply denoted as q_j, reflects the positional bias. With this CTR factorization, we now proceed with two natural stochastic models of clicking behavior, and then arrive at the deployed model smoothed by a spike and slab prior [1,9].

3. THE BINOMIAL MODEL

It is natural to assume that the number of clicks follows a binomial distribution

$$c_{ij} \sim \text{Binomial}(v_{ij}, p_i q_j), \forall i, j. \quad (2)$$

Given a training data set $D = \{(c_{ij}, v_{ij})\}$, we wish to learn the model parameters $\theta = (p, q)$, where p is a vector of relevance CTR p_i's and q is a vector of positional priors q_j's. The likelihood of the training data is

$$p(D|\theta) = \prod_{i,j} \binom{v_{ij}}{c_{ij}} (p_i q_j)^{c_{ij}} (1 - p_i q_j)^{v_{ij} - c_{ij}}. \quad (3)$$

The log likelihood is

$$\begin{aligned} \ell(\theta) = \sum_{i,j} \Big(\log \binom{v_{ij}}{c_{ij}} &+ c_{ij} \log(p_i q_j) \\ &+ (v_{ij} - c_{ij}) \log(1 - p_i q_j) \Big). \end{aligned} \quad (4)$$

We regard one of model parameters as latent variable, e.g., q, and derive an EM algorithm to estimate the MLE of both $\theta = (p, q)$. Notice though the objective function is not necessarily concave, even w.r.t. one univariate p_i or q_j, hence we only seek local optimal. By taking the partial derivatives w.r.t. p_i and q_j, respectively, we have

$$\frac{\partial \ell}{\partial q_j} = \sum_i \left(\frac{c_{ij}}{q_j} - \frac{(v_{ij} - c_{ij}) p_i}{1 - p_i q_j} \right); \quad (5)$$

$$\frac{\partial \ell}{\partial p_i} = \sum_j \left(\frac{c_{ij}}{p_i} - \frac{(v_{ij} - c_{ij}) q_j}{1 - p_i q_j} \right). \quad (6)$$

Since the model parameters are non-negative, we apply the following multiplicative recurrence [4,10]

$$\text{E-step:} \quad q'_j \leftarrow \frac{\sum_i c_{ij}}{\sum_i (v_{ij} - c_{ij}) p_i / (1 - p_i q_j)}; \quad (7)$$

$$\text{M-step:} \quad p'_i \leftarrow \frac{\sum_j c_{ij}}{\sum_j (v_{ij} - c_{ij}) q_j / (1 - p_i q_j)}. \quad (8)$$

4. THE POISSON MODEL

If the number of trials n is sufficiently large and the success probability p is sufficiently small, $\text{Binomial}(n, p) \rightsquigarrow \text{Poisson}(np)$. Since ad is such a domain, we now derive the Poisson model which yields a similar yet more efficient update. The generative model is

$$c_{ij} \sim \text{Poisson}(v_{ij} p_i q_j), \forall i, j. \quad (9)$$

The data likelihood is

$$p(D|\theta) = \prod_{i,j} \frac{(v_{ij} p_i q_j)^{c_{ij}} \exp(-v_{ij} p_i q_j)}{c_{ij}!}. \quad (10)$$

The log likelihood is

$$\ell(\theta) = \sum_{i,j} (c_{ij} \log(v_{ij} p_i q_j) - v_{ij} p_i q_j - \log(c_{ij}!)). \quad (11)$$

By taking the partial derivatives w.r.t. p_i and q_j we have

$$\frac{\partial \ell}{\partial q_j} = \sum_i \left(\frac{c_{ij}}{q_j} - v_{ij} p_i \right); \quad (12)$$

$$\frac{\partial \ell}{\partial p_i} = \sum_j \left(\frac{c_{ij}}{p_i} - v_{ij} q_j \right). \quad (13)$$

We then derive the following multiplicative recurrence by leveraging the non-negativity of model parameters

$$\text{E-step:} \quad q'_j \leftarrow \frac{\sum_i c_{ij}}{\sum_i v_{ij} p_i}; \quad (14)$$

$$\text{M-step:} \quad p'_i \leftarrow \frac{\sum_j c_{ij}}{\sum_j v_{ij} q_j}. \quad (15)$$

It is clear, by comparing with the binomial recurrence, what the Poisson approximation implies for the EM recurrence. Moreover, it can be shown that the Poisson EM recurrence is globally convergent w.r.t. a univariate p_i or q_j, thus guaranteed to find a unique global maximum. When the E and M-steps are combined, however, the recurrence is still convergent but a global maximum is not guaranteed. Further, the E-step in Eq. (14) reveals the tempting "double-discounting" trap found in the naïve estimator as empirical positional CTR $q_j = \sum_i c_{ij} / \sum_i v_{ij}$.

5. THE GAMMA-POISSON MODEL

For both empirical and regularization purposes, we impose a gamma prior on the positional factor in the Poisson model

$$q_j \sim \text{Gamma}(\alpha, \beta), \forall j. \quad (16)$$

Empirically, the observed CTR is geometrically decreasing as the position lowers down [11], exhibiting a good fit to the gamma signature. In practice, inferior positions (e.g., bottom positions in side bar) might suffer from severe data sparsity, particularly clicks; thus regularizing or smoothing those noisy estimates will yield better generalization. The gamma distribution is a convenient choice, since it is a conjugate prior of Poisson.

The data likelihood (posterior for q) with a gamma prior is

$$\begin{aligned} p(D, q|p, \alpha, \beta) = &\prod_{i,j} \frac{(v_{ij} p_i q_j)^{c_{ij}} \exp(-v_{ij} p_i q_j)}{c_{ij}!} \\ &\times \prod_j \frac{q_j^{\alpha-1} \exp(-q_j/\beta)}{\beta^\alpha \Gamma(\alpha)}. \end{aligned} \quad (17)$$

The log likelihood is

$$\begin{aligned} \ell(\theta) = &\sum_{i,j} (c_{ij} \log(v_{ij} p_i q_j) - v_{ij} p_i q_j - \log(c_{ij}!)) \\ &+ \sum_j ((\alpha - 1) \log q_j - q_j/\beta - \alpha \log \beta - \log \Gamma(\alpha)). \end{aligned} \quad (18)$$

By taking the partial derivatives w.r.t. p_i and q_j we have

$$\frac{\partial \ell}{\partial q_j} = \sum_i \left(\frac{c_{ij}}{q_j} - v_{ij} p_i \right) + (\alpha - 1)/q_j - 1/\beta; \quad (19)$$

$$\frac{\partial \ell}{\partial p_i} = \sum_j \left(\frac{c_{ij}}{p_i} - v_{ij} q_j \right). \quad (20)$$

The EM multiplicative recurrence is

$$\text{E-step:} \quad q_j' \leftarrow \frac{\sum_i c_{ij} + (\alpha - 1)}{\sum_i v_{ij} p_i + 1/\beta}; \quad (21)$$

$$\text{M-step:} \quad p_i' \leftarrow \frac{\sum_j c_{ij}}{\sum_j v_{ij} q_j}. \quad (22)$$

The regularization is on q_j in E-step only and the interpretation of smoothing is obvious. When $\alpha = 1$ and $\beta \to \infty$, the gamma distribution approaches a uniform distribution, i.e., no prior.

6. THE CLICK MODEL

A click model or a CTR prediction model aims to estimate a positional-unbiased CTR for a given query-ad pair, i.e., the relevance CTR $p(\text{click}|\text{exam}, i)$ or p_i. The positional normalized click model described above does exactly this, as well as produces the positional priors $p(\text{exam}|j)$ or q_j. Another view of the factor model is a kNN model smoothed over ad positions; and when the feature space only contains query-ad pairs, $k = 1$. It is plausible that for query-ad pairs with sufficient historical clicks, the factor model might perform reasonably well. For a principled treatment of the cold-start problem, a trivial extension would be appending queries and ads unigram features into the feature space, and backing-off CTR estimates when new pairs are encountered in prediction time.

The positional normalized click model can also be applied independently of and in conjunction with other click models that estimate relevance-only CTR [1, 4]. More rigorously, we make the assumption that the positional factor is independent of other relevance factors. In model training, one shall normalize each ad impression by its positional prior $v_{ij} q_j$. In prediction, the CTR predictor learned from position-normalized training data produces exactly the relevance-only CTR, as we desire.

7. EXPERIMENTS

7.1 Simulation with synthetic data

We first simulated the Gamma-Poisson model on an artificial data set generated by a probabilistic model in the same spirit, i.e., given a sound model assumption. The synthetic data largely mimics the real-world search ad data, by carefully designed model parameters. Although the simulated data cannot fully reflect a real-world system, it has at least two advantages: (1) allowing for a quick study of the effects of a large number of parameters while abstracted from real-world noises; and (2) exposing the true distributions underlying the data to verify the learned model, which is impossible with real-world data.

The data was generated as follows:

1. $\forall$ position $j \in [1, \ldots, m]$, generate a $q_j \sim \text{Gamma}(\alpha, \beta)$, sort q in descending order, and scale q by $1/q_1$;
2. $\forall$ query-ad pair $i \in [1, \ldots, n]$, generate a $p_i \sim \text{Beta}(\gamma, \delta)$;
3. $\forall i$, generate a number of impressions $s_i \sim \text{Poisson}(\lambda)$;
4. $\forall i$, construct a multinomial distribution over positions $\phi_i \propto 1/\left(p_i/\mu(p_i)\right)^{j-1}$, to push good ads higher up;
5. $\forall i$, generate an impression allocation vector over positions $v_i \sim \text{Multinomial}(s_i\ \phi_i)$, to form an $n \times m$ matrix of impression V;
6. Derive an $n \times m$ matrix of CTRs $Z = pq^\top$;
7. Derive an $n \times m$ matrix of Poisson means $Y = V.Z$, where '.' is element-wise multiplication;
8. Generate an $n \times m$ matrix of clicks $C \sim \text{Poisson}(Y)$, and $C \leftarrow \min(C, V)$, element-wise.

The underlying distributions are $\theta = (p, q)$. We used the same true distributions to generate a training set $D^{trn} = \{C, V\}$ and a testing set $D^{tst} = \{C', V'\}$. The parameters of the generative model are summarized in Table 1.

Table 1: Parameters of the generative model

Parameter	Description	Value
n	num of query-ad pairs	100,000
m	num of positions	9
(α, β)	Gamma parameters	(1.2, 0.01)
(γ, δ)	Beta parameters	(1, 99)
λ	Poisson mean of row sum s_i	$m \times 100$

After generating the training data $D^{trn} = \{C, V\}$, we examined the empirical positional CTR $q_j^{emp} = \sum_i c_{ij} / \sum_i v_{ij}$ and the positional prior CTR $q_j^{pri} = \mu(p_i) q_j$. The latter will only realize were ads shown randomly. The coupling of positional bias with ad quality bias is evident from the empirical positional CTR curve (the dashed line) in Figure 1(a), in other words, higher-CTR ads tend to be shown in higher positions. A tempting trap is averaging CTR for each position as the positional prior, referred to as the COEC (clicks over expected clicks) model [8, 13]. This leads to the "double-discounting" problem, as revealed by the COEC learned positional priors (the dashed line) in Figure 1(b). The factor model decouples the positional and relevance factors in a principled way, hence perfectly recovers the true positional priors, as shown in Figure 1(b) (the solid and dotted lines).

Since we know the underlying true distributions $\theta = (p, q)$, we then compared the learned distributions $\hat{\theta} = (\hat{p}, \hat{q})$ with the true ones, as plotted in Figure 2. Both scatter plots for relevance CTR $p_i = p(\text{click}|\text{exam})$ and positional-biased CTR $p_{ij} = p(\text{click}|\text{position})$ show that the true and learned CTRs are well calibrated.

We then evaluated the trained factor model using the testing set $D^{tst} = \{C', V'\}$ generated from the same underlying distributions, with the only statistical fluctuations from Steps 3, 5, and 8, the Poisson and multinomial processes in the generative model. Figure 3(a) plots the true vs. learned relevance CTR $p_i = p(\text{click}|\text{exam})$ by both the factor and COEC models. In the higher CTR range ($p_i \geq \mu(p_i)$), both models calibrate well with the observed. In the lower CTR range ($p_i < \mu(p_i)$), however, both models tend to overestimate, in particular the COEC model performs worse. The first reason is legitimate and applies to both models, that

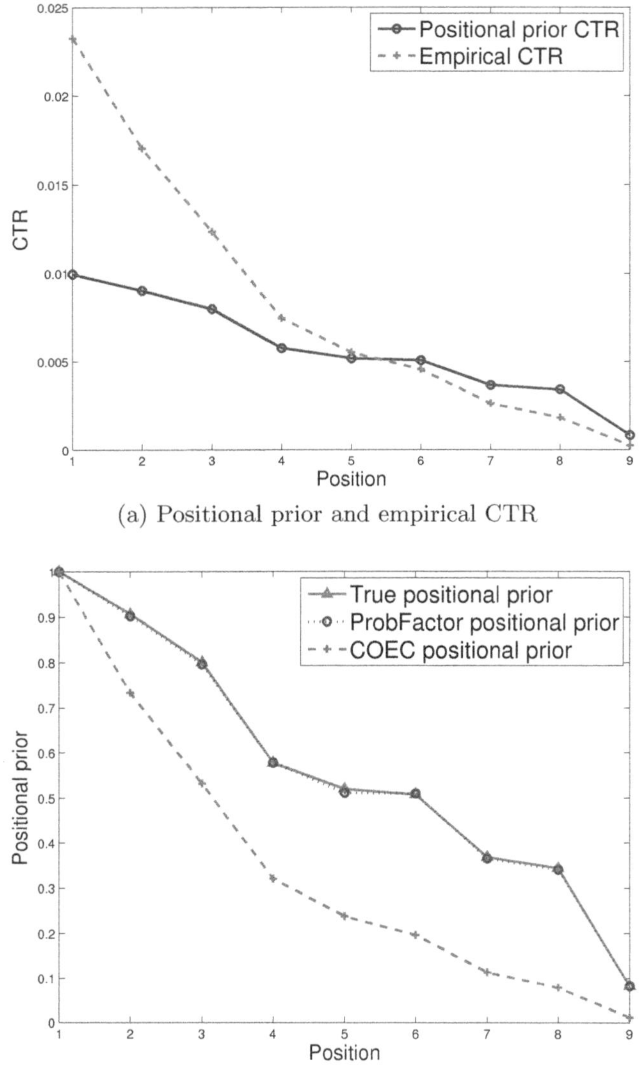

(a) Positional prior and empirical CTR

(b) True positional, Factor and COEC learned

Figure 1: Positional bias coupled with ad relevance bias in empirical data.

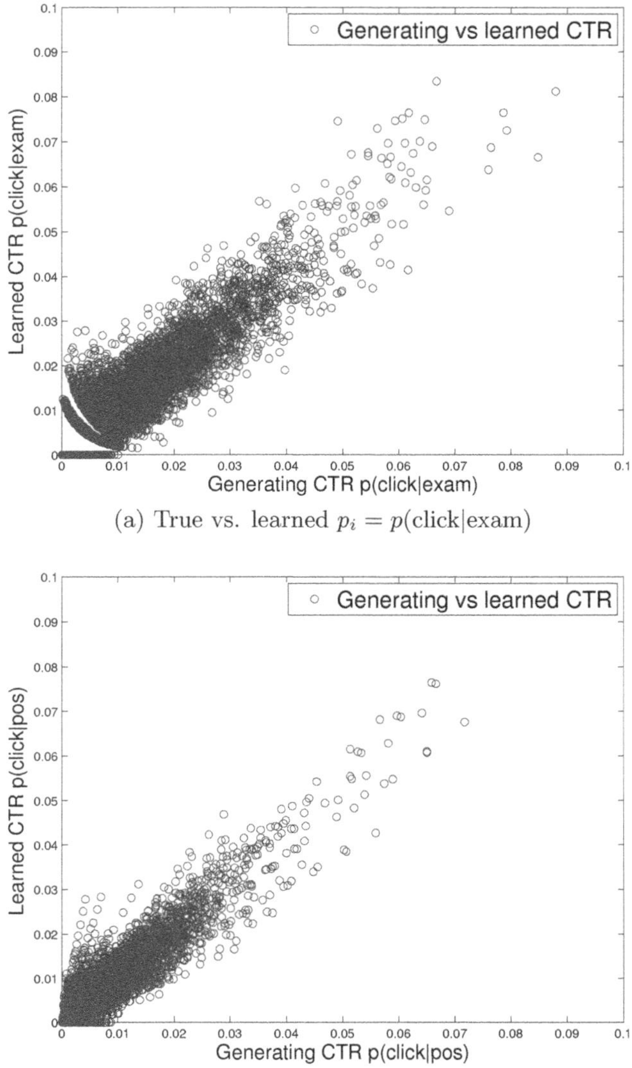

(a) True vs. learned $p_i = p(\text{click}|\text{exam})$

(b) True vs. learned $p_{ij} = p(\text{click}|\text{pos})$

Figure 2: True vs. learned CTR.

is, we impose a gamma prior on q_j and seek MAP estimate. The second reason exposes the flaw in the COEC model. Impressions with lower-than-average CTRs tend to be allocated to lower positions by the design of the generative process. The COEC model performs poorly because of the "double-discounted" positional effect, that is, q_j's for lower j's are over-penalized, and hence p_i's allocated to those lower j's (lower-CTR i's) are more widely overestimated. Figure 3(b) plots the observed vs. predicted positional biased CTR $p_{ij} = p(\text{click}|\text{position})$ for both the factor and COEC models. We observed a similar pattern as the relevance CTR calibration plots.

One primary objective of CTR prediction is to rank ads (RankScore = Bid × CTR)[1], hence we plot the ROC curves of click recall vs. view recall[2] in Figures 4 and 5. The ROC curves for the factor and COEC models across all positions are shown in Figure 4, and the area under the curve (AUC) results are summarized in the "AUC@all" column in Table 2. The factor model performs better than the COEC model by a small margin. The gain is small because ranking among different positions is relatively easy, given the strong positional effect.

We further compared the ranking performance between the two models at individual positions, mainline (ML) 1 and 4, and sidebar (SB) 8, as plotted in Figure 5 and numerically reported in Table 2. Mainline refers to the positions above the algorithmic results, and sidebar refers to the positions right to the algorithmic results. The factor model performs better than the COEC model for every individ-

[1]Real-world sponsored search systems may have other variants such as CTR exponent and relevance terms, but our discussion carries over.

[2]The CTR term in rank score is estimated to capture the ad relevance in terms of click feedback, hence for evaluating a CTR predictive model, it is sufficient to rank ads by CTR estimates alone.

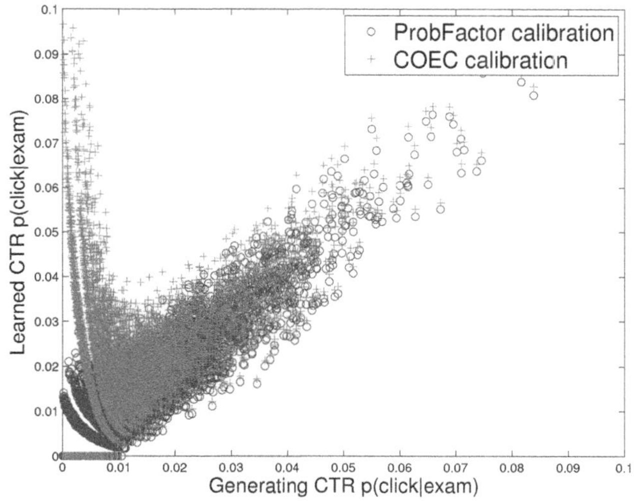

(a) True vs. learned $p_i = p(\text{click}|\text{exam})$

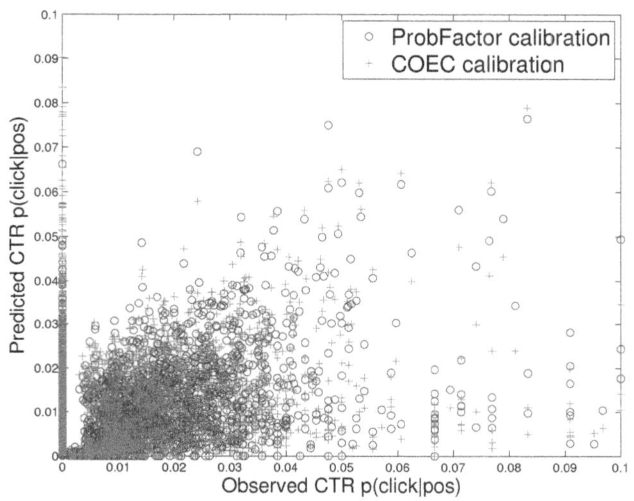

(b) Observed vs. predicted $p_{ij} = p(\text{click}|\text{pos})$

Figure 3: Calibratedness of Factor and COEC.

ual position, and the gain is widened as the position lowers down. The reason is actually revealed in Figure 1(b). Ranking ad position-dependent CTRs within a same position is essentially ranking their relevance-only CTRs, given a fixed positional prior. An over-penalized positional prior, as the COEC model estimates, will yield overestimated relevance CTRs, especially for those low-quality ads mostly pushed down. On the other hand, this error does not appear as a universal scaling for all ads, since some good-quality ads will be shown in higher positions sometimes. Consequently, the true relevance ranking would be more polluted in lower positions, in the presence of a poorly estimated positional prior.

Table 2: Simulation AUC of Factor and COEC

Model	AUC@all	AUC@ML1	AUC@ML4	AUC@SB8
Factor	0.8219	0.6130	0.5870	0.5899
COEC	0.8187	0.6045	0.5509	0.5467

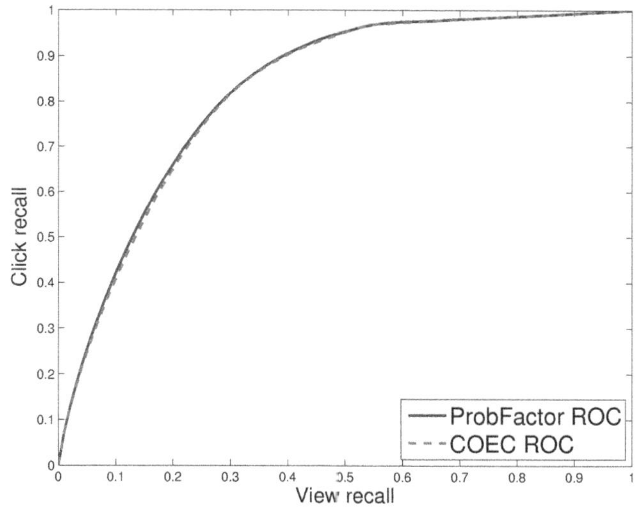

Figure 4: Simulation ROC curves for Factor and COEC.

7.2 Experiments with real-world data

We then evaluated the Gamma-Poisson model on a real-world search advertising data set from Microsoft adCenter. We collected one week (10/01/2011-10/07/2011) ad click and impression count data for training, and the following day (10/08/2011) for testing. Each training example is uniquely identified by the composite key (UserId, Query, AdId, OrderItemId, Position, MainlineAds, MatchTypeId), and the data contains approximately $50M$ examples per day (for all users having Windows Live Id). A query-ad pair is uniquely identified by (Query, AdId, OrderItemId). The Position value is the absolute order from the ad showed in the top position. The MainlineAds value is the number of ads showed in mainline (also jargoned as Dude State from Yahoo!). An absolute position and a mainline ad count (or simply noted as dude) jointly determine the relative position, e.g., position = 3 along with dude = 4 gives ML3, while position = 3 when dude = 2 gives SB1[3]. In addition, we leverage the match type by which an ad is retrieved for a given query, e.g., exact match or broad match.

We maintain the individual identities of features (i.e., query, ad id, and order item id) present in a number of examples above a threshold $c * d$, where d is the number of training days and c is a tuning factor; and group features below the threshold into a "minority" bin. By cross validation, we set $c = 100$ and the training data contains $1.2M$ query-ad pairs. The match type feature shall carry important information for predicting CTR, and intuitively can be leveraged in two ways: either as an additional feature to form the query-ad-matchtype triplet or as an additional dimension in the relative position. Empirically we found the second approach yielded better results. The training data contains 200 distinct position-dude-matchtype triplets, with 12 absolute positions $[1 \ldots 12]$, 5 dude states $[1 \ldots 5]$ (we encode zero ML ads as dude = 5 for convenience of illustration), and 4 match types $[1 \ldots 4]$. We used the same parameters for the gamma prior ($\alpha = 1.2, \beta = 0.01$). For the EM recurrence,

[3]We ignored bottom ads for simplicity and their negligible revenue impact.

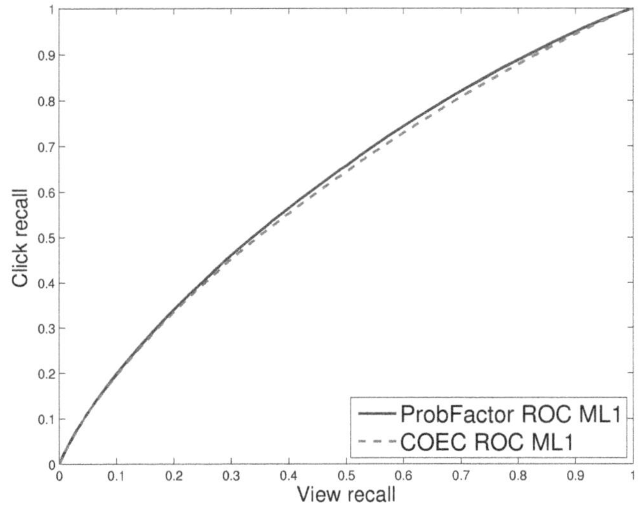

(a) ROC of Factor and COEC for ML1

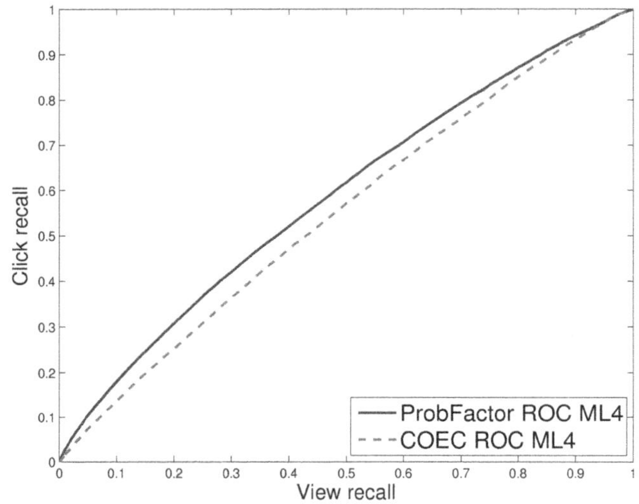

(b) ROC of Factor and COEC for ML4

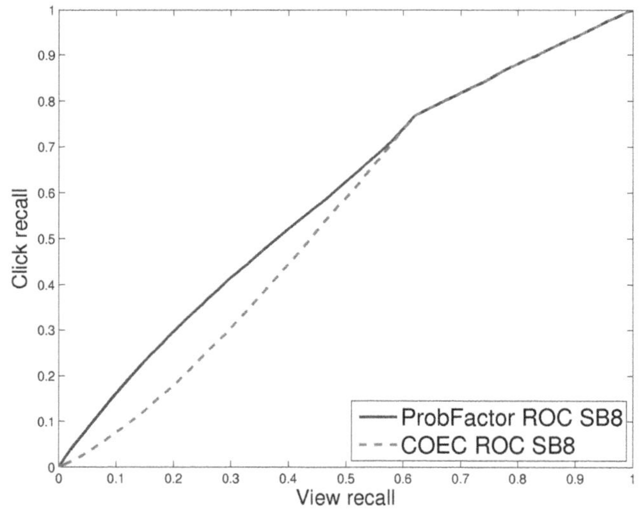

(c) ROC of Factor and COEC for SB8

Figure 5: Positional ROC curves Factor and COEC.

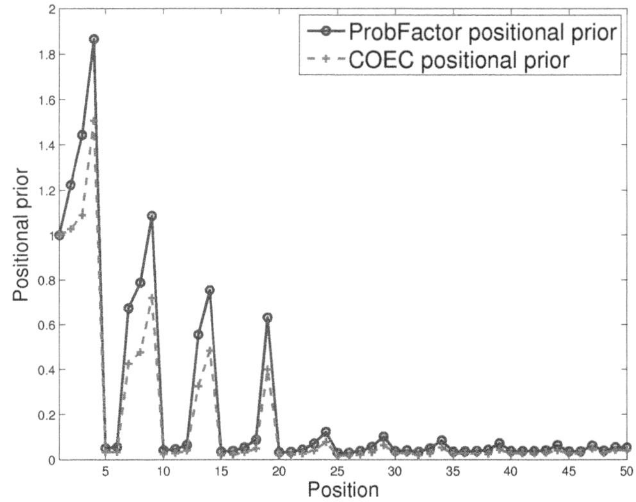

(a) Positional priors per (position-dude) pair by factor and COEC models

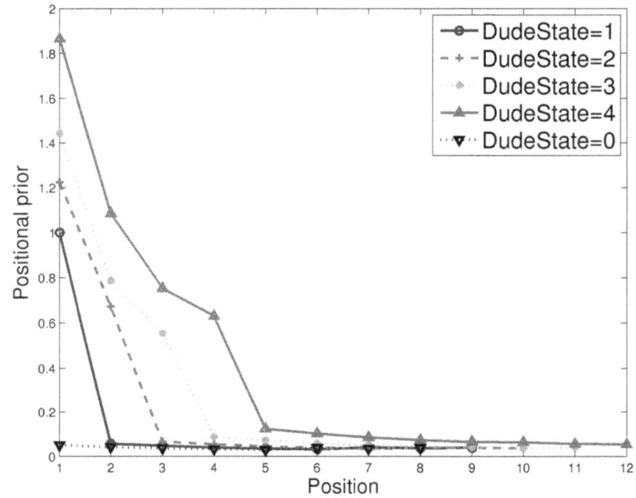

(b) Positional priors per absolute position by factor model for different dude states

Figure 6: Positional priors per (a) relative positions defined by (position-dude) for factor and COEC models, (b) absolute positions by factor model for different dude states.

we initialize the model parameters $\theta = (p, q)$ to be empirical expectation. This data-driven initialization leverages data sparsity well since, under the multiplicative recurrence as in Eq. (22), initial zero p_i's (due to no clicks) will remain zero.

The positional effect is a function of relative position. More precisely, the positional prior q_j depends on at least three factors: (1) the page section, e.g., ML or SB; (2) the relative position or the number of ads above in section, e.g., ML2; and (3) the number of ads below in section, e.g., ML2 with dude = 4 has two ads below in ML. The learned positional priors as shown in Figures 6 and 7 support the above observations.

Figure 6(a) plots the positional priors q_j where a position j is defined by an (absolute position, dude) pair. The x-axis indexes (absolute position, dude) pairs in ascending order,

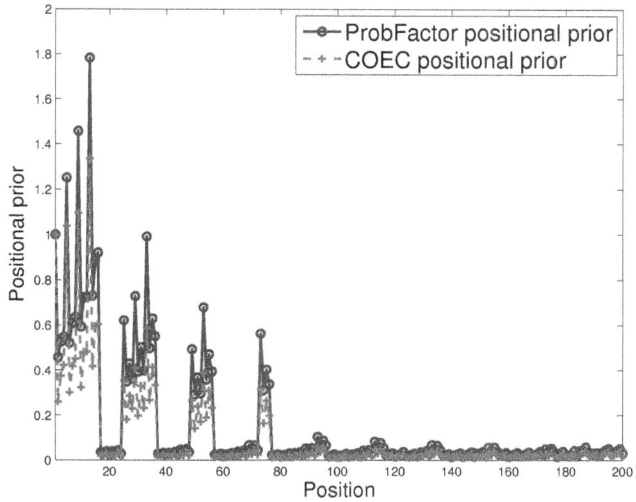

(a) Positional priors per (position-dude-matchtype) triplet by factor and COEC models

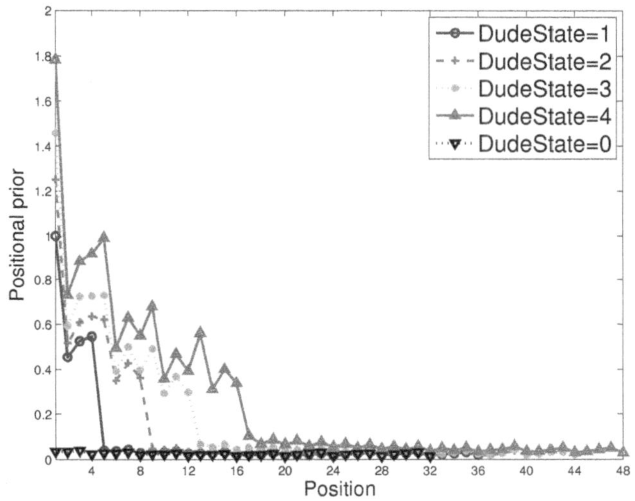

(b) Positional priors per (position-matchtype) pair by factor model for different dude states

Figure 7: Positional priors per (a) relative positions defined by (position-dude-match) for factor and COEC models, (b) relative positions defined by (position-match) by factor model for different dude states.

e.g., $x = 1$ for $(1, 1)$, $x = 2$ for $(1, 2)$, and so forth. The global descending trend (by examining local peaks $x = 4, 9, 14, \ldots$) reflects the positional bias. The discrepancy between the factor and COEC models confirms the "double-discounting" trap. The dude factor (the number of ads in ML) comes into play in two ways. Firstly and intuitively, when a dude value moves an ad to SB, the positional prior drops drastically (by examining the points at $x = 5, 6, 10, 11, 12, \ldots$). Secondly and more interestingly, when the number of ads below in section increases, the positional prior rises substantially. For example, the positional priors at $x = 1 \ldots 4$ are all for ML1 but with dude $= 1 \ldots 4$, and the increase is almost two folds from dude $= 1$ to 4. One plausible explanation is that more ML ads prevents a user from moving away from ads to algorithmic results. Another evidence for the effect of the number of ads below can be appreciated by comparing the positional priors at $x = 1$ (for ML1 with dude $= 1$) and $x = 9$ (for ML2 with dude $= 4$). In this case, ML2 has a higher positional prior than ML1. Figure 6(b) plots the positional priors q_j where a position j is defined by an absolute position, and one line per dude state. It is evident that, for each dude line, the positional prior drops most drastically at the dude value, that is, moving from ML to SB.

Figure 7(a), where a position is defined by an (absolute position, dude, match type) triplet, shows the effect of match type. For instance, the positional priors at $x = 1 \ldots 4$ are all for ML1 and dude $= 1$ but with matchtype $= 1 \ldots 4$. The difference between matchtype $= 1$ (exact match) and matchtype $= 2$ (broad match) is greater than two folds. Figure 7(b) separate one line per each dude state, by defining position as a (absolute position, match type) pair. The impact of match type given a same position can be appreciated by examining local variations for each position (the points at $x = 1 \ldots 4, 5 \ldots 8$, and so on.

We now evaluate the CTR prediction accuracy of the trained models. Besides the ranking metric AUC, we use the metric of relative information gain (RIG), defined as follows.

$$\text{RIG} = \frac{\sum_i \left(y_i \log p_i + (1 - y_i) \log (1 - p_i)\right)}{nH(p)} + 1, \quad (23)$$

where i indexes impressions in the testing data set, $y_i \in \{0, 1\}$ indicates click or not, p_i is the predicted CTR, n is the number of testing impressions, and $H(p)$ is the entropy of the empirical expected CTR, i.e., $\sum_i y_i/n$. RIG is a normalized average log likelihood under the binomial assumption, or a normalized negative cross entropy. RIG can be interpreted as the relative gain of a model $p_i, \forall i$ over a trivial yet foresighted one-parameter model by predicting every impression as the empirical expected CTR, that is, when $p_i = \sum_{i'} y_{i'}/n, \forall i$, RIG $= 0$.

We compare models with different definitions of relative position, factor or COEC positional handling, and treating match type as exogenous or endogenous variables, as summarized in Table 3. The results are shown in Table 4.

Table 3: Different modeling methods

Model	Position def.	Learning	Match
Factor(pos)	abs. position	factor	none
COEC(pos)	abs. position	COEC	none
Factor(pos-dud)	(position,dude)	factor	none
COEC(pos-dud)	(position,dude)	COEC	none
Factor(pos-dud-mat)	(position,dude,match)	factor	exog.
COEC(pos-dud-mat)	(position,dude,match)	COEC	exog.
Factor(admat-pos-dud)	(position,dude)	factor	endog.
COEC(admat-pos-dud)	(position,dude)	COEC	endog.

Table 4: Experimental results

Model	RIG	AUC@all	@ML1	@ML4
Factor(pos)	0.1126	0.8225	0.7725	0.6942
COEC(pos)	0.1126	0.8216	0.7723	0.6935
Factor(pos-dud)	0.1797	0.8716	0.8363	0.8207
COEC(pos-dud)	0.1797	0.8712	0.8357	0.8200
Factor(pos-dud-mat)	**0.1861**	**0.8750**	0.8435	0.8257
COEC(pos-dud-mat)	0.1861	0.8744	0.8424	0.8252
Factor(admat-pos-dud)	0.1430	0.8713	0.8419	0.8190
COEC(admat-pos-dud)	0.1430	0.8706	0.8414	0.8183

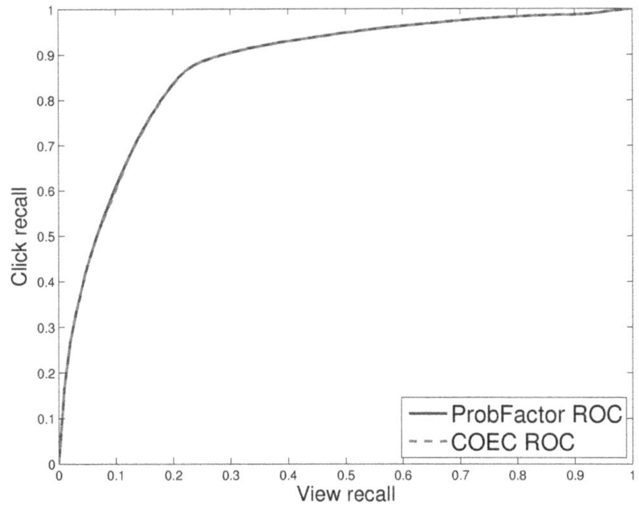

(a) ROC of Factor and COEC with (position-dude) prior

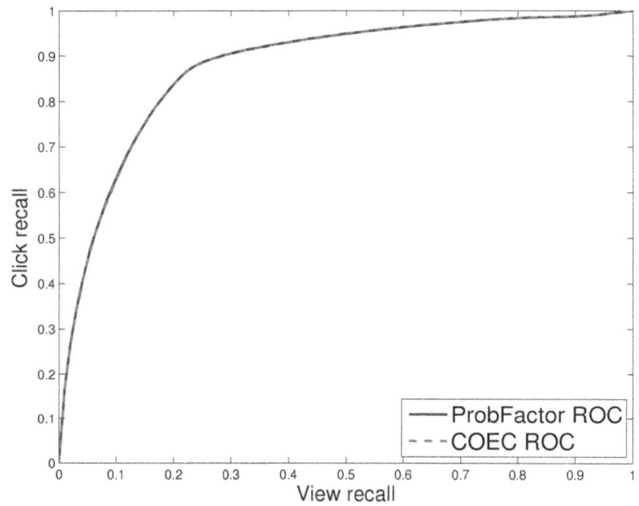

(b) ROC of Factor and COEC with (position-dude-matchtype) prior

Figure 8: Experimental ROC curves for Factor and COEC with (a) (position-dude) positional prior, and (b) (position-dude-matchtype) positional prior.

The best empirical results were obtained by the factor model using the (position, dude, match) positional prior, with a RIG 0.1861 and an AUC 0.8750. When only using absolute position to derive positional prior, the prediction accuracy is much worse, with a RIG 0.1126 and an AUC 0.8225. The factor model consistently outperforms the COEC model, yet by a small margin. Adding match type into feature vector does not gain incremental ranking performance (from an AUC of 0.8716 by Factor(pos-dud) to an AUC of 0.8713 by Factor(admat-pos-dud)), and even impairs the testing data log likelihood metric (from a RIG of 0.1797 by Factor(pos-dud) to a RIG of 0.1430 by Factor(admat-pos-dud)), likely due to overfitting as a consequence of increasing the number of model parameters by four folds. The ROC curves of the Factor(pos-dude) and Factor(pos-dud-match) models are shown in Figure 8.

To evaluate the impact of the size of training data on the prediction performance, we varied the number of training days from 1, 7, to 13 preceding a same testing day using the empirically best model (Factor(pos-dud-match)), and the results are shown in Table 5.

Table 5: The impact of training data size

Model	RIG	AUC@all
Factor(pos-dud-match) 1-day train	−0.1058	0.8519
Factor(pos-dud-match) 7-day train	0.1861	0.8750
Factor(pos-dud-mat) 13-day train	**0.2219**	**0.8809**

It is evident that more training data gives better model generality, under the position-smoothed kNN model we are experimenting with. In particular, up to 13-day training, both RIG and AUC metrics monotonically increase. With only one day of training data, although the ranking metric is reasonable ($AUC = 0.8519$), the model likely suffers from overfitting ($RIG = -0.1058$). Another tuning parameter influencing the trade-off between model capacity and generality is the feature selection threshold factor c, and its choice should be made empirically or by cross validation. For this evaluation, we intentionally used the data from a smaller non-US market (UK), and the comparison results are shown in Table 6.

Table 6: The impact of feature selection

Model	RIG	AUC@all
Factor(pos-dud) $c = 20$	−0.0912	0.8508
Factor(pos-dud-match) $c = 20$	−0.0887	0.8521
Factor(pos-dud) $c = 100$	0.1693	0.8612
Factor(pos-dud-mat) $c = 100$	**0.1755**	**0.8648**

8. CONCLUSIONS

We have presented a probabilistic factor model to estimate CTR for search advertising, particularly to normalize out the positional bias. Our approach is simple yet principled, and empirically justified by the advertising domain. Moreover, we have generalized the concept of position to other important factors specific to ads, including keyword match type and ad presentation layout. Hence our approach shall serve as a general framework to study changes exogenous to the relevance-based CTR model. Finally, we conducted extensive experiments with synthetic and real-world ad data, and established that removing those confounding factors is critical to achieve accurate CTR prediction.

9. REFERENCES

[1] D. Agarwal, R. Agrawal, R. Khanna, and N. Kota. Estimating rates of rare events with multiple hierarchies through scalable log-linear models. *Proceedings of the 16th ACM SIGKDD International Conference on Knowledge Discovery and Data Mining (KDD 2010)*, pages 213–222, 2010.

[2] S. Athey and D. Nekipelov. A structural model of sponsored search advertising auctions. *Proceedings of the 6th Ad Auctions Workshop*, 2010.

[3] O. Chapelle and Y. Zhang. A dynamic Bayesian network click model for web search ranking.

Proceedings of the 18th International Conference on World Wide Web (WWW 2009), pages 1–10, 2009.

[4] Y. Chen, M. Kapralov, D. Pavlov, and J. F. Canny. Factor modeling for advertisement targeting. *Advances in Neural Information Processing Systems (NIPS 2009)*, 22:324–332, 2009.

[5] N. Craswell, O. Zoeter, M. Taylor, and B. Ramsey. An experimental comparison of click position-bias models. *Proceedings of the First ACM International Conference on Web Search and Data Mining (WSDM 2008)*, pages 87–94, 2008.

[6] B. Edelman, M. Ostrovsky, and M. Schwarz. Internet advertising and the generalized second price auction: selling billions of dollars worth of keywords. *American Economic Review*, 97:242–259, 2005.

[7] T. Graepel, J. Q. Candela, T. Borchert, and R. Herbrich. Web-scale Bayesian click-through rate prediction for sponsored search advertising in Microsoft's Bing search engine. *Proceedings of the 27th International Conference on Machine Learning (ICML 2010)*, pages 13–20, 2010.

[8] D. Hillard, E. Manavoglu, H. Raghavan, C. Leggetter, E. Cantú-Paz, and R. Iyer. The sum of its parts: reducing sparsity in click estimation with query segments. *Information Retrieval*, 14:315–336, 2011.

[9] H. Ishwaran and J. Rao. Spike and slab variable selection: frequentist and Bayesian strategies. *Annals of Statistics*, 33(2):730–773, 2005.

[10] D. D. Lee and H. S. Seung. Algorithms for non-negative matrix factorization. *Advances in Neural Information Processing Systems (NIPS 2000)*, 13:556–562, 2000.

[11] F. Pin and P. Key. Stochastic variability in sponsored search auctions: observations and models. *Proceedings of the 12th ACM Conference on Electronic Commerce (EC 2011)*, pages 61–70, 2011.

[12] M. Richardson, E. Dominowska, and R. Ragno. Predicting clicks: estimating the click-through rate for new ads. *Proceedings of the 16th International Conference on World Wide Web (WWW 2007)*, pages 521–530, 2007.

[13] W. V. Zhang and R. Jones. Comparing click logs and editorial labels for training query rewriting. *WWW 2007 Workshop on Query Log Analysis: Social And Technological Challenges*, 2007.

Bid Optimizing and Inventory Scoring in Targeted Online Advertising

Claudia Perlich,Brian Dalessandro, Rod Hook,Ori Stitelman,Troy Raeder
Media6Degrees
37 East 18th Street
New York, NY, 10003
claudia,briand,rod,ori,troy@m6d.com

Foster Provost
NYU Stern School of Business
New York, NY, 10012
fprovost@stern.nyu.edu

ABSTRACT

Billions of online display advertising spots are purchased on a daily basis through real time bidding exchanges (RTBs). Advertising companies bid for these spots on behalf of a company or brand in order to purchase these spots to display banner advertisements. These bidding decisions must be made in fractions of a second after the potential purchaser is informed of what location (Internet site) has a spot available and who would see the advertisement. The entire transaction must be completed in near real-time to avoid delays loading the page and maintain a good users experience. This paper presents a bid-optimization approach that is implemented in production at Media6Degrees for bidding on these advertising opportunities at an appropriate price. The approach combines several supervised learning algorithms, as well as second price auction theory, to determine the correct price to ensure that the right message is delivered to the right person, at the right time.

Categories and Subject Descriptors

I.5.4 [**Computing Methodologies**]: Pattern Recognition-Applications

Keywords

Probability Estimation, Online Advertising, Causality, Bid Optimization, Logistic Regression

1. INTRODUCTION

In recent years online advertising has seen a major shift toward real time bidding (RTB) ad-exchanges [7]. As the term suggests, RTBs allow advertisers to bid on the opportunity to show an ad to a specific browser on a specific site with a display ad slot. Advertisers are integrated into the exchanges through APIs and collect different data to decide whether or not they want to bid and at what price. RTBs provide liquidity on both supply and demand and have created a complex economic ecosystem of publishers, advertisers, marketers, and data providers [12]. Media6Degreed (m6d) is one of the players in the online display targeting sector with a main focus on prospecting — finding new customers for a product or brand. We find and target browsers for over 100 marketers delivering millions of ads daily. Before we get into some of the inner workings of this ecosystem, lets have a short and intuitive clarification of the terminology of the players in the display advertising ecosystem:

- The **marketer, brand, or product** is the one who is interested in advertising. It could for instance be Nike that wants to promote a new running shoe.
- The **advertiser** is the entity charged with executing an advertising campaign. This includes finding the right people and showing them the ad and would for instance be m6d.
- The **publisher or inventory** is the place where the ad will be shown. In particular, the online version of the New York Times is a publisher, but so are blogs and many other places online that have room for ads. We use the term inventory whenever we are looking at a particular publisher site appearing in an online display auction.
- The **browser or cookie** is conceptually the person who is going to see the ad. While there typically is a real person on the other side somewhere (unless it is a bot), from the advertiser's perspective it is really the cookie that is currently associated with the auction. There is not necessarily a one-to-one mapping between a person and a cookie.
- **Data providers** are in the business of annotating the inventory, the browser or both and selling this data to advertisers to help them make better targeting decisions. There are for instance sets of people labeled "credit card shoppers" that can be purchased. This information is typically the result of some modeling and is a prediction rather than ground truth.
- **Ad exchanges** bring together advertisers, browsers, publishers and data providers by running auctions. The result of an auction is an **impression**: the showing of an ad by the advertiser with the highest bid on the publisher inventory to the browser. Advertisers are

KDD'12, August 12–16, 2012, Beijing, China.

typically connected to multiple exchanges. In particular, m6d currently works with more than 15 different RTBs.

Strategies for targeting and bidding vary greatly between different advertisers and are primarily a function of the data an advertiser is willing and capable of using. The ultimate goal from the marketer's perspective is the holy grail of advertising:

We want to address the **right browser** with the **right message** at the **right moment** and preferably at the **right price**.

Consider for instance search-based advertising: When a browser is entering "car insurance" as a search term, it is pretty straightforward to decide that this is a great opportunity for Geico or Allstate to show an ad for their insurance products. However, matching a search term to a product is typically not that simple. The 'right browser' is any browser who is currently searching for a keyword that is matched either manually or using machine learning [19] to the product or brand. The browser also defines the right time: the time of the search since he is obviously thinking about the product at that moment.

Contextual advertising has a similar flavor: if the browser is currently reading a review about used cars, right now might be a good opportunity to show him a car or car insurance ad. The challenge is again to associate the content of the page with the product or message. This works well only for a small set of well-understood content and very clearly-defined products.

Both of the above strategies suffer from high competition and limited scale. The number of total searches is finite and determined by the browsers. In cases where the match between the keyword and the product is obvious, the competition for showing the browser an ad is high and as a result the winning bid price in the auction is high as well. The same is true for very well defined content with clear product association. In addition, the latter scenario is typically managed through a direct agreement between a larger publisher and the relevant marketers. As a result, few such opportunities appear in the auctions. For the majority of products or things one might want to advertise, the association of content and product is highly non-trivial [19].

The m6d targeting strategy goes beyond this information. Through our data partners we collect historical information on browsers and use machine learning to build high-dimensional supervised ranking models to identify browsers with a high interest in the brand or high likelihood of buying the product. The actual targeting model is not the focus of this paper and is presented in more detail in [14, 15]. An important distinction between the above strategies and the m6d approach is that the latter targets browsers, not just singluar impression opportunities. In other words, even before the browser gets to the inventory, we already know some measure of fit between him and all our marketers. Using supervised machine learning on data that includes positively labeled browsers who already took some relevant brand action typically provides more relevant information (for conversion prediction) than the match between the content of the current inventory and an advertiser. At the point of the auction, we already have a good measure on the fit between browser and marketer, what we now want to do is adjust the bid price to reflect the last piece of the puzzle: is this the right place and time?

One important consideration in the discussion of the *value* of an advertising opportunity is the evaluation. We may have some high-level intuition about this, but in reality we have to focus on measurable outcomes to evaluate opportunities as well as advertising strategies. Primarily due to convenience, the industry has historically focused on clicks. This is rather unfortunate, as many studies have shown a rather loose if not inverse relationship between clicks and purchases for display advertising [1, 4]. Instead m6d measures *post-view* conversions that allow for a certain time period between the ad impression and some relevant action (e.g. visiting the marketer's website, downloading code, subscribing to some service, or purchasing a product). Keep in mind that both the advertiser and the marketer can trace the events of a browser through time using cookies (of course only as long as they do not get deleted).

Yet another layer to the optimization puzzle is attribution. My incentive as an advertiser is not just to increase the conversion rate or brand recognition of my customer, but to be fairly compensated for it. Attribution in the context of multi-touch and view through conversion is an entire research topic by itself [16, 5] and we will leave it for future work to tie our bid strategy to the attributed value. The biggest problem from our perspective is the complete lack of visibility. We do not know who else might have shown an ad to the browser and ultimately receives the credit for the conversion. Unfortunately, short-sighted attribution can have a strong impact on optimization strategies that are overall suboptimal for the marketer (and the industry in general). Last touch attribution leads for instance to a 'carpet bombing' strategy where some advertisers might try to buy huge volumes of cheap inventory that is not even seen by the browser. Even though attribution is not the focus of this paper, we are assuming a 'fair' attribution method where the advertiser has the incentive to evaluate opportunities with respect to the impact on a browser's conversion probability.

So to recast, we want to bid on the **right browser** with the **right message** at the **right inventory** at a price that reflects the true value of the opportunity to the marketer.

The rest of the paper is organized as follows: Section 2 will give a brief overview of the m6d targeting and bidding to clarify the constraints under which the bid optimization solution was developed. Section 3 initially presents consideration on *why* and *how* inventory affects the value of an opportunity and proposes a formal measure for opportunity value. Section 4 covers the estimation task and some modeling results. Finally, section 5 focuses on translating model predictions into bid strategies and measuring the actual performance impact on 15 advertising campaigns.

2. THE FLOW OF M6D TARGETING

In order to perform bid optimization one must first be able to determine the value of a particular inventory that is placed up for auction. However, determining the quality of a particular inventory is a challenging task because past decisions to show ads on a given inventory depend in part on the browser's propensity to convert. In other words, inventory quality is confounded by the many different decisions that m6d has made as a company that make it possible to operate our large scale targeting machine. As a result, the quality of browsers that we observe at a piece of inventory is not equal across all inventory. Understanding the different pieces of the m6d infrastructure and how the components of that infrastructure contribute the quality of browsers at a particular inventory is essential for valuing each piece of inventory. For the purpose of this paper we will take a browser centric view and visit the sequence of events that ultimately lead to an impression of a particular ad to a particular user at a particular inventory. By illuminating this process one can better understand what issues contribute to the differential quality of browsers across the different inventories on which m6d receives bid requests. We are deliberately skipping the core m6d targeting component that builds a conversion propensity model for every campaign. Details can be found in [15]. The following steps highlight the process of browsers through the m6d system:

1. **Initiate** - A browser is first observed by m6d either through data partners or the marketer. They typically place a pixel on their page allowing m6d to write a cookie on the browsers computer. This cookie will contain in our case a random identifier that is assigned to the browser and allows us to recognize him again.

2. **Monitor** - m6d anonymously tracks the browser's Internet surfing behavior.

3. **Score and Segment** - The browsing history is used to score the browser for hundreds of active advertising campaigns. For all those campaigns that the browser scores high enough, he is placed into a discrete 'segment'. Each campaign has multiple segments for different thresholds and different models. Typically only about 1% of browsers qualify for any segment of a given campaign. The notion of discrete segments rather than continuous scores is a remnant of traditional demographic and behavioral targeting. It is still useful to discretely limit the set of eligible browsers, for which the RTB forwards bid requests.

4. **Sync with Exchange** - Once a browser is placed into a relevant segment, we have to communicate to the exchange that we would like to receive bid requests for him from now on. This process is called syncing.

5. **Activate Segment** - Account managers determine what segments to activate for a particular campaign, what base price to assign to each segment, and in which exchanges to run them. The base bid price is determined by the account manager and reflects the specifics of the contract with the customer, as well as margin and performance considerations. These decisions are assisted by reports that notify the account manager of the predicted conversion rate for the browsers in the segment and the anticipated number of browsers in each segment.

6. **Receive Bid Request** - Subsequently, m6d begins receiving bid requests for the browser. At the time of the request we know the identity of the browser, the current inventory, as well as additional generic information about the user agent, etc.

7. **Bid** - m6d first determines internally the set of active segments of the browser and checks against campaign volume goals and individual browser frequency cap. The segment with the highest price is then chosen and a bid is submitted on that campaign's behalf (this is all done in milliseconds). Every segment has a base price that is set by the account manager. In the case of bid optimization the price is adjusted to reflect the quality of the inventory as described in the following sections.

8. **Show Impression** - If the m6d bid was the highest across all bids for this auction, we get to show the creative for the campaign and pay the price equal to the second highest bid.

9. **Track Conversion** - We observe the browser for some campaign-specific conversion period, recording if the browser converts.

10. **The Cycle** - The entire process repeates where more data is collected, the browser is re-scored and more bid requests are received and ads shown.

11. **Cookie Deletion** - The browser at some point deletes its cookie and is no longer seen by the system. If we observe him again, he will receive a new cookie with a new random identifier and we start over again.

3. INVENTORY AND AD EFFECTIVENESS

We typically observe browsers/users multiple times during the day browsing different sites. The goal of this work is to quantify the value of a specific opportunity O where an opportunity is given by a triplet $O = (U, A, I)$ of an ad A for a marketer to a user U at a particular inventory I. Given the value of this opportunity we want to adjust the bid price B accordingly. So what is the relationship between the inventory and the browser's probability of converting? Inventory relates to the probability of conversion in two distinct ways. The first is independent of the ad whereas the second reflects an interaction between the inventory and the ad experience.

Organic Propensity

In some cases, the mere fact that the person visits a particular inventory can change our best estimate of his conversion probability. Reasons for this are:

1. **Contextual Relevance:** There is a correlation between the content of the inventory and the product or the brand. A purely-contextual targeting approach would take only the current content of the inventory URL into account when making a targeting decision. In the m6d context it is just one more data point and can be seen as an incremental update of the previous m6d propensity score. The main difference between the last content and the earlier ones is the relative timeliness that makes it potentially more relevant.

2. **Current Intentions:** If the browser is already engaged in online shopping, the probability that he might purchase from our marketer (regardless of the impression) is notably higher than if he was currently involved in some activity completely unrelated to shopping.

3. **Life Expectation:** Presumably, there can be a correlation between the kind of inventory a user sees and his probability of deleting the cookie. While this relationship is unlikely to be significant for most inventories, it might be notable for some. As a result of an increased probability of cookie deletion, the probability of *observed* conversion is lower.

Causal Impact

The objective of advertising is of course to increase the browser's propensity to convert. The effects below capture interactions between the inventory and the causal effect of showing an ad.

1. **Perceptiveness:** Even beyond the current intentions, the inventory can be related to the probability that a browser perceives an ad. While looking for the correct syntax of a SQL query on a forum page, a user is much less likely to take note of the impression on the side than if he is browsing around in news stories. Psychological experiments (the 'gorilla in the room' [3]) show that perception of external stimuli decreases significantly when the mind is focused on a specific task.

2. **Impression Quality:** There has been recently a lot of concern about the actual time that an impression is 'in view'. According to a recent study [9] as few as 37% of all impressions are actually seen (defined as being in the visible part of the page and actually displayed for at least 2 seconds) by the browser. Potential reasons for lack of viewability are that it may take too long for the impression to load or that the impression is 'displayed' below the fold or in some other invisible part of the page.

While it might be possible to quantify and model all 5 different factors independently, the true reason why a piece of inventory is particularly good is not nearly as relevant as a reliable measurement of the *relative* value of one piece of inventory over another.

Optimization Objective

So far we have focused on the conversion probability. However, the value of an opportunity depends on the objectives of the marketer and the advertiser. In an auction-theoretic framework [18], the optimal bid price of a second-price auction is determined by the expected value of the outcome

$$P(c|u,a,i) * V(c) \tag{1}$$

where $V(c)$ is the value of a conversion. In reality, for online targeting, $V(c)$ ends up playing only a minor role in bid optimization. For all intents and purposes, $V(c)$ is typically unknown or simply assumed to be constant across all users. In that case, the value of the opportunity is proportional to the probability of conversion. This implies that the bid price should be proportional to the conversion probability as well.

In conclusion, we want to modify our bid proportionally to the effect of the inventory. If showing an ad on a particular piece of inventory doubles the probability of conversion over some random inventory, the bid price should be twice the average bid price as well.

$$\Phi^* = \frac{p(c|u,i,a)}{E_j[p(c|u,j,a)]}. \tag{2}$$

The formulation in Equation 2 has another advantage: it is independent of a campaign's base conversion rate and can be handled by our system the same way no matter what the base rate of the campaign is. In particular, we can easily integrate it with the base bid price B determined by the account management team as a multiplier:

$$B^* = B * \Phi^*. \tag{3}$$

One last observation on Equation 2 is its close relationship to the notion of relative impact in the context of causal analysis. Our definition of value compares the outcome of serving an ad at inventory i to the expectations over all counterfactual events of showing the ad at different inventories j. However, in order for a counterfactual analysis to produce unbiased estimates of a true causal effect (both in observational and experimental settings), several strict assumptions must be made about the data that we are not fully considering here [17].

4. ESTIMATION DETAILS AND MODELING RESULTS

Equation 2 states a well defined supervised modeling problem. We need to estimate $p(c|u,i,a)$ for all pieces of inventory i. We will estimate this quantity for each advertising campaign a independently leaving us with $p_a(c|u,i)$. The inventory i is originally provided in form of an URL. M6d parses the URL to a meaningful level. A subset of relatively common canonical URLs are assigned unique inventory IDs and the remaining long tail distribution of URLs is typically collected in an exchange-specific DEFAULT inventory. Note that the inventory is exchange-specific. This implies that the same hostname (e.g., `www.facebook.com`) can map into multiple inventories. In total we maintain about 5,000 unique inventories.

4.1 Reducing the User Information

What do we know about the user at the time of the auction? We know the identity of the browser and could in principle retrieve all relevant information from the cookie to estimate $p_a(c|u,i)$. But is a tall order for sophisticated targeting in real time. However, we already have a highly optimized and pre-calculated estimate of the user's propensity to convert $p_a(c|u)$ from the m6d targeting that has assigned the browser into a segment of only the good prospects for a given campaign. So given the time constraint of a real time auction — where one of the worst case scenarios is timing out and not being able to bid — the only really relevant browser information is his segment s. And since trafficking and base price are affected by segment, we have to control for it anyway. Consider if all the best prospects are targeted in exchange E_1 and the lower prospects in E_2. This would induce a major bias that makes the inventory in exchange E_1 look great unless we control during model estimation for all the variables that drive the trafficking decision.

4.2 Data Preparation

To estimate inventory values for a given campaign, we need a sample of impressions delivered across multiple inventories, along with the segment information of each targeted user. In addition, we track for each impression whether or not the user converted according to the rules of the campaign. For a campaign where the marketer insists on eval-

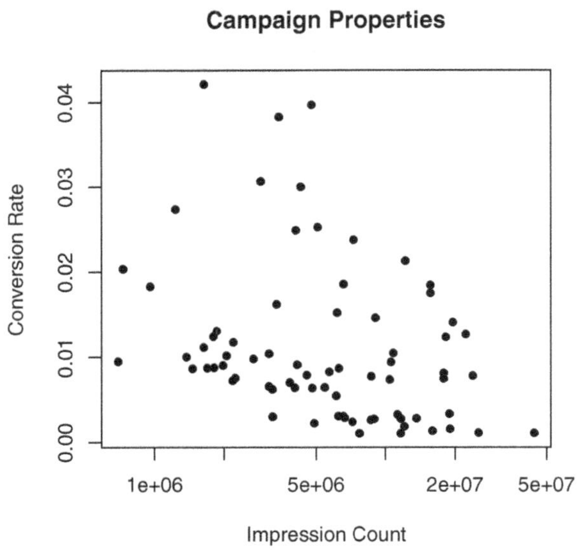

Figure 1: Number of impressions in a 3 week period and conversion rates for the 100 largest campaigns.

uating the click through rate, we can alternatively use only clicks as positives. Note that this leaves us with an interesting sparse representation where every example has exactly 2 binary non-zero features: one for the segment and one for the inventory.

Before we discuss the data for estimation, let us consider the dimensionality of the problem. We currently have 5,000 unique inventories across 20 exchanges, about 1,000 of which have notable volume. In addition, the average campaign uses between 10 and 50 different segments. The estimation task in its simplest form has an effective dimensionality of $\geq$1,000. If one was to consider interaction terms, the dimensionality grows easily by an order of magnitude.

Conversion rates on the other hand are typically low and range between 0.04 in the best case and below 0.001 for others. This implies that the desirable amount of data for estimation is rather large. As a result, we typically use three weeks of impression data. Figure 1 shows typical impression counts and conversion rates for several of our campaigns. On average we show 15 million impressions, observe 250,000 conversions (mostly site visits) at an average conversion rate of 1%.

Our models are by default built against post-view conversion for a 7 day conversion window. The m6d system automatically assigns conversions to the last impression prior to the conversion. At this point it can be debated whether the implicit 'last touch' attribution of this labeling is adequate. To make the estimation process efficient, we downsample the negative set from to a base conversion rate of 20% in the training set of each campaign. Note that this will affect the raw predictions and in turn the performance ratio, so we have to post-correct the model predictions [10].

Model Estimation and Feature Selection

We estimate $p(c|s,i)$ using L1-constrained logistic regression (with the default penalty weight) as implemented in the `bbr` software package [8]. Having an L1 penalty implicitly selects only the relevant features and provides a sparse solution. For many inventories, the parameter is set to zero and as a result the estimated impact factor is 1 and will not change the bid price (see the formal explanation below in Equation 4). Additionally, we applied an initial filter that included an inventory feature only if its volume was sufficient to yield *at least 5 conversions in expectation* given the base conversion rate of the campaign. Otherwise it was assigned to a default 'other' bucket. We need to include all observations to ensure the calibration of the model when we implicitly integrate over all inventories to calculate the expected value.

	AUC	Lift 10	Lift 20	Lift 50
Segment	0.729	1.802	1.744	1.461
Seg&Inventory	0.7636	2.121	1.952	1.524
Delta	0.0346	0.318	0.207	0.062
% Improved	97%	96%	95%	95%
% Delta	4.7%	17.6%	11.8%	4.3%
p-value	0	0	0	0

Table 1: Out of sample performance of the segment & inventory models is significantly better across different metrics (AUC and Lift at different percentage cutoffs) than the segment-only model. The p-value is for a paired t-test is always below 10^{-15}. Accounting for inventory almost never hurts targeting performance.

The careful reader might have noticed some built-in dependence at this point. In the current setting, the sign of the inventory effect is bound to be the same across all segments. In a linear model without interaction terms, the relative effect of the inventory will always point in the same direction (either greater or smaller than one) because the estimated parameter on the inventory indicator is either positive or negative. As a result, for a given campaign, the inventory score from Equation 2 can only differ in relative magnitude across segments, but this is purely a function of the different conversion rates of the segments. This effect is intuitively appealing if we consider the drivers of inventory impact from section 3. It is hard to imagine that there is a very strong non-monotonic interaction effect between the conversion rate $p(c|s)$ and the inventory i. Either the inventory is of high quality with the impression in view or not. Something similar can be said for the current intention of the browser and his state of mind. Nevertheless we also build the models allowing for interactions between the segment and the inventory. Note that this increases the parameter space significantly (about a factor of 10) and typically hurts model performance due to overfitting.

Estimating Φ_i^*

We do not need to explicitly integrate over all inventories to estimate $E_j[p(c|u,j,a)]$. Instead we use the empirical distribution of j in the data. All that is needed is to build the same models as before on the exact same dataset but using only the segment variables as features.

$$E_j[p(c|u,j,a)] \sim \hat{p_a}(c|s) \tag{4}$$

This is also a great baseline to evaluate whether there is indeed any predictive information in the inventory i that can be picked up by a model (see next paragraph). Only if

Inventory	Hotel $\hat{\Phi}_i^*$
Social Media Site	0.3
Travel Site	3.9
Dating Site	0.6
Movie Site	1.2
Video Site	1.4

Table 2: Example inventory scores $\hat{\Phi}_i^*$ for a hotel chain campaign.

inventory can provide additional explanatory power above and beyond the segment would we consider to use it for bid optimization.

At this point we have two models for each marketer a, one that can predict $\hat{p_a}(c|s,i)$ and one that predicts $\hat{p}_a(c|i)$. Both are miscalibrated due to the initial downsampling of negatives. We correct both probability estimates according to the sample rate [10] and arrive at:

$$\hat{\Phi}_a^*(i,s) = \frac{\hat{p}_a(c|s,i)}{\hat{p}_a(c|s)} \quad (5)$$

Model Performance
Before using this in production we would like to assess how much information the inventory can provide beyond ordinary m6d targeting. Table 1 compares the out-of-sample performance (using cross validation) of the estimates of $\hat{p}(c|s,i)$ and $\hat{p}(c|s)$. The results for both AUC and lift at different percentage cutoffs are very encouraging with significantly higher performance of the inventory model. The AUC increases on average by 0.03, which corresponds to a 5% increase in performance due to the additional information from inventory. Similarly, lift (more relevant to targeting) increases as well, obviously more so for higher cutoffs. Lift 20 calculates the lift of the top 20% of browsers who saw and ad compared to all browsers who were shown an ad. Note that the reported lift is only within the 1-3% browsers out of all browsers known to our system, that actually saw an ad for the specific campaign. Recall that the set of eligible browsers are identified by our main targeting model based on their browsing history and are selected because they have the highest conversion probabilities. So the reported lift is **not** the lift of our full targeting and bid optimization, but only the lift of inventory selection on top of the regular selection. As a results, this is a vast understatement of the true lift of our entire campaign where the baseline set of browsers contains the other 97-99% that we deliberately chose not to show ads to.

Example Predictions
Figure 2 shows the distribution of the estimates of $\hat{\Phi}_i^*$ across all inventories i for a particular hotel chain campaign. The scores are well-calibrated around 1 and show some promising signal for inventory that represents travel sites. Table 2 shows some example scores for the hotel chain campaign. Not surprisingly, travel sites have an extremely high score. They meet most of the influence criteria outlined in section 3 for the organic category. Dating and social media sites, on the other hand, do not seem very suitable for hotel advertisement. They probably score low across multiple dimensions of inventory impact (bad target, low on current intent and low on perceptiveness).

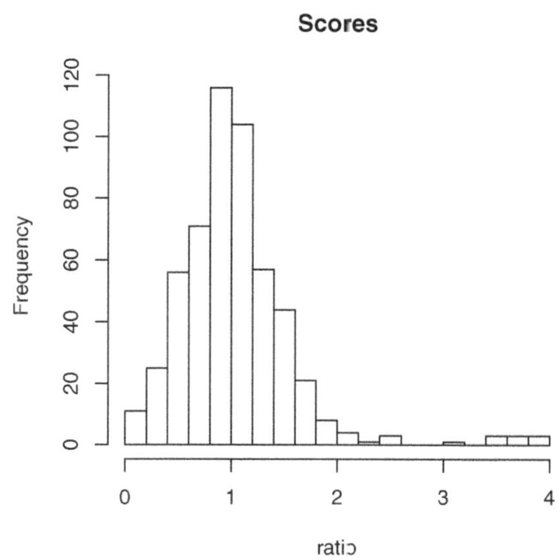

Figure 2: Distribution of the estimates of $\hat{\Phi}_i^*$ for a hotel chain campaign. The mean score was 1.03. The high-scoring inventories are all travel sites.

5. CAMPAIGN PERFORMANCE IMPACT

Satisfied by the above results we integrated the inventory scores into the m6d production system and studied the effectiveness of several inventory-based bid strategies on campaign performance. We present results on 15 campaigns come from a variety of industries including telecommunications, services, retail, travel, and others. The main selection criterion for choosing campaigns was a sufficient post-view site-visit rate to allow for significance in the results on approximately 2 weeks of data. We anticipated a performance increase of 5% lift. We back out the required number of impressions given the empirical conversion rate that we see for that campaign and include only campaigns that deliver a sufficient number of impressions such that a 5% increase should be significant under the assumption of a binomial distribution. Some subset of campaigns meeting this criterion were excluded since the account management team felt that they were unfit for experimentation. The characteristics of the the trial campaigns are very similar to those shown in Figure 1.

5.1 Bid Strategies

Using the inventory score in real time requires a very short response time. The technical implementation uses a lookup table by campaign, inventory, and segment that only keeps non-one scores to limit the size and increase the speed of the lookup. We have not observed a notable increase in response time or timeouts since we implemented the inventory-based bid strategies.

- **Strategy 0:** The old strategy will serve as baseline where we always bid the base price of the segment as determined by the account managers. Note that this corresponds to a constant score of 1 across all inventories and is consistent with an uninformative inventory model.

- **Strategy 1:** The first optimization strategy takes an auction-theoretic view. Given that it is a second price auction, all players have the incentive to bid what the opportunity is worth to them. So we multiply the base price by the score ratio of the particular inventory.
- **Strategy 2:** The second optimization strategy is more aggressive towards performance than the previous one. Instead of bidding what we think an opportunity is worth, we apply a step function to the model ratio to translate it into a factor applied to the price. Any ratio below 0.8 yields a bid price of 0 (so not bidding), ratios between 0.8 and 1.2 are set to 1 and ratios above 1.2 bid twice the base price.

M6d has a number of other bid strategies that are inventory independent and are not discussed further. However, the design of the bid optimization as a multiplicative modifier allows for any arbitrary combination of strategies provided they are all centered at 1 for neutrality.

During fall 2011, m6d implemented a flexible bidding platform that can test multiple bid strategies on the same campaign simultaneously. For this purpose, we assign each browser randomly to exactly one strategy even if they qualify for multiple segments of the same campaign.

5.2 Campaign Results

We evaluate the bid strategies with respect to:

1. **Conversion Rate (PVSVR):** Percentage of impressions leading to site visits within 7 days. Higher conversion rates are better.
2. **Cost per Acquisition (CPA):** This metric combines cost and conversion rate and looks at the total cost of impressions for a given strategy relative to the total number of conversion. Lower CPA is better.

Both measures are of practical relevance and related to the previous discussions. The majority of m6d's customer agreements specify a cost per mille (CPM) payment model where we are paid independently of the conversion rate. However, the conversion rate is considered by the customer as a performance metric to compare us against other vendors. CPA is directly relevant to our margin. For a given conversion performance we would like to minimize the CPA or alternatively for a given cost, we will try to deliver more conversions. Note that from the marketer's perspective on a CPM campaign there is a direct relationship between the PVSVR the CPA. In more general terms, CPA measures economic efficiency and should be closely related to strategy 1. Lets assume for the moment that the actual cost is equal or proportional to the bid price. Under strategy 1 we would expect that the tradeoff between CPA and PVSVR is better than the suboptimal strategy 0 – either CPA is lower for approximately the same conversion rate or higher conversion rate for similar CPA. Setting the bid price proportional to the conversion probability does not maximize PVSVR. As a matter of fact, the optimal strategy for maximizing the conversion rate is to neglect any cost calculation and simply bid the practical equivalent of infinity for every opportunity above a certain threshold that is determined by the total desired number of impressions.

However, this is clearly not in our best interest considering margins. Strategy 2 is closer to this extreme whereas strategy 1 is aimed at economic efficiency in terms of the cost of acquisition. We have a number of campaigns that are evaluated with respect to the cost per acquisition.

Campaign	Measure	Str 0	Str 1	Str 2
1	PVSVR	0.00274	0.00294	**0.00333**
2	PVSVR	0.00080	0.00087	**0.00097**
3	PVSVR	0.00031	0.00033	**0.00041**
4	PVSVR	0.00044	0.00047	**0.00053**
5	PVSVR	0.00183	0.00193	**0.00229**
6	PVSVR	0.00037	**0.00041**	0.00040
7	PVSVR	**0.00526**	0.00432	0.00441
8	PVSVR	0.00020	**0.00026**	0.00025
9	PVSVR	0.00185	NA	**0.00205**
10	PVSVR	0.00439	NA	**0.00600**
11	PVSVR	0.00104	NA	**0.00119**
12	PVSVR	0.00889	NA	**0.01088**
13	PVSVR	0.00387	NA	**0.00464**
14	PVSVR	0.00204	NA	**0.00299**
15	PVSVR	0.00292	NA	**0.00319**
1	CPA	**0.4434**	0.5048	0.5640
2	CPA	1.3406	**1.2799**	1.4807
3	CPA	**4.5124**	4.6714	5.2446
4	CPA	**2.3304**	2.5129	2.7400
5	CPA	0.4854	**0.4785**	0.5100
6	CPA	2.7487	**2.6566**	3.3143
7	CPA	**0.1201**	0.1382	0.192
8	CPA	6.1238	**5.6980**	7.9599
9	CPA	0.4764	NA	**0.4261**
10	CPA	**0.1966**	NA	0.2242
11	CPA	**1.1136**	NA	1.5764
12	CPA	**0.1804**	NA	0.2086
13	CPA	**0.3524**	NA	0.4354
14	CPA	0.6074	NA	**0.5497**
15	CPA	**0.4698**	NA	0.6207

Table 3: Bid optimization performance in terms of PVSVR and CPA for identifying new customers (Prospecting). Bold indicates better performance, while not necessarily significant.

Tables 3 and 4 show detailed results for the three bid strategies. A 'NA' indicates that this marketer did not use that particular strategy. Given the results m6d decided that overall strategy 2 held more promise and ran only strategy 2 during the second stage of our experiment. We have separated the results into two browser groups: those with very high conversion rate (retargeting) and those with lower conversion rates (prospecting). Recall that the model is estimated jointly over both populations.

In both populations we observe that the more aggressive strategy 2 outperforms strategies 0 and 1 in terms of the post-view site visit rate (PVSVR) by a large margin. This is very consistent with our expectations. The performance increase over the baseline is on average 24% for retargeting and 21% for prospecting. For comparison, a lift of 20% is considered quite substantial in marketing and this does not even include the core m6d targeting component. So the performance gains realized through strategy 2 are very impressive and as a result this strategy got rolled out to a larger number of campaigns than strategy 1.

In terms of CPA, we see that strategy 2 is on average 5%

Campaign	Measure	Str 0	Str 1	Str 2
1	PVSVR	0.0062	0.0065	**0.0126**
2	PVSVR	0.0025	0.0026	**0.0030**
3	PVSVR	0.0013	0.0014	**0.0018**
4	PVSVR	0.0055	0.0056	**0.0064**
5	PVSVR	0.0192	0.0193	**0.0236**
6	PVSVR	0.0016	0.0016	**0.0026**
7	PVSVR	0.0168	0.0183	**0.0218**
8	PVSVR	0.0026	0.0026	**0.0028**
9	PVSVR	0.0094	NA	**0.0118**
10	PVSVR	0.0092	NA	**0.0154**
11	PVSVR	0.0283	NA	**0.0338**
12	PVSVR	0.0126	NA	**0.0163**
13	PVSVR	0.0270	NA	**0.0316**
14	PVSVR	**0.0075**	NA	0.0074
15	PVSVR	0.0309	NA	**0.0404**
1	CPA	0.3407	0.3074	**0.1854**
2	CPA	0.9108	**0.8995**	0.9430
3	CPA	**1.3419**	1.3667	1.3526
4	CPA	0.4459	0.4285	**0.3928**
5	CPA	0.0677	0.0693	**0.0666**
6	CPA	**1.7629**	1.7813	1.1997
7	CPA	0.1785	0.1665	**0.1551**
8	CPA	**0.9503**	0.9619	1.0223
9	CPA	**0.2058**	NA	0.2109
10	CPA	0.1155	NA	**0.1000**
11	CPA	**0.0803**	NA	0.0837
12	CPA	0.1580	NA	**0.1478**
13	CPA	**0.0631**	NA	0.0708
14	CPA	**0.2141**	NA	0.2823
15	CPA	0.0444	NA	**0.0480**

Table 4: Bid optimization performance in terms of PVSVR and CPA for predicting the return of an existing customer (Retargeting). Bold indicates better performance, while not necessarily significant.

lower than strategy 0 in retargeting, beating the baseline in 7 of 15 cases, but 18% higher for prospecting and exceeds the baseline in all but one campaign. The decline in the CPA performance was expected for strategy 2. It is a positive surprise that strategy 2 is actually better both in terms of CPA and PVSVR for the retargeting group.

The reason for the CPA increase for prospecting is that the model estimates are affected more by the retargeting population due to the notably higher conversion rate and as a result, the model is more accurate for retargeting. But even in the prospecting case, the cost increase for strategy 2 reflects only a 10-20% reduction of our margin, which is acceptable when we need to drive conversions. This suggests that we may not implement this strategy across all campaigns but rather use it as a tool to manage performance more effectively when renewal or the size of a followup deal is under consideration.

Strategy 1 beats strategy 0 on 7 out of 8 campaigns in terms of PVSVR for both browser groups and realizes an average lift of 6% on prospecting and 3% on retargeting. However, it provides economic efficiency gains (CPA) over the the baseline in only 4 out of 8 cases - clearly not significant in either group. In summary we observe a higher conversion rate at equal CPA: an overall better economic position.

We would like to finish the discussion with an interesting observation. In most CPM campaigns where we are paid for a fixed number of impressions independently of the conversions, we are still subject to comparative evaluation against other advertisers in terms of the implied CPA. Note that our PVSVR translates directly into the marketer's measure of cost per acquisition. So while our direct incentive may not be to increase the conversion rate, in a repeated game where we have to win renewal or a larger budget in direct comparison to other advertisers, it is very much in our interest to trade short term margin for long term growth.

6. RELATED WORK

Ad exchanges and real time bidding are fairly new and have revolutionized the advertising industry only in the last 1-2 years. Most reports are short blogs or white papers with very limited technical and performance details. The majority of published related work is in the more established application area of search advertising [2, 11, 6, 13]. In search term bidding the auction is for a given search term and the bid price determines the relative position in the ranking of the returned offers. One major difference in this setting is the payout structure. In our case, we always pay if we have the winning bid whereas in most of search advertising the bidder only pays his exact bid price if the offer was clicked on by the browser. That puts a larger burden of analytical optimization on the search provider (Google, Yahoo, etc.) and gives them the incentive to develop more elaborate auction styles where the bid price may not be the sole decision criterion. In addition, the bid price is not really determined in real time and is not browser specific. The advertisers could typically submit and change their bid price for a given term at any time throughout the day. The predictive modeling component typically evolves around estimating the conditional click propensity and on the side of the advertiser the expected revenue given click.

7. CONCLUSION AND FUTURE WORK

Bid optimization has become one standard component of the production system of m6d targeting. We developed a predictive modeling approach that estimates reliably and efficiently the relative impact of inventory on the conversion probability. It is interesting to note the scale of the underlying models: We are estimating close to 1,000 parameters by downsampling from an average of 50 million impressions per campaign semi-automatically with a model refresh rate of about 2 weeks. The scores can be applied as factors to the base-prices previously set by the account management team. The empirical results suggest a clear improvement of the campaign performance in terms of conversion rate that can be used to tune the campaign to satisfy the performance expectations of the marketer. One factor that could currently limit our performance is the internal selection of the campaign with the highest (post-adjustment) bid price. Since we are picking the max of a distribution, this can lead to an over-inflation of the bid price and amplify overfitting (the highest scores in most models are not necessarily the most reliable). Understanding this effect is one of out immediate future work efforts and should lead to reliable cross-campaign optimization. In addition we are embarking on a deep dive into the modeling process with a stronger focus on the prospecting group. The main advantage of pooling the two groups is a favorable bias - variance tradeoff. However we think there is potentially a better solution that can improve the prospecting CPA further. Finally we see great potential in expanding the scope of bid optimization to bring together in real time additional information from the cookie, such as age and activity level, and combine the performance-centric optimization approach with other tuning parameters. One such parameter is the frequency of ad exposure for a given marketer. There is presumably a diminishing causal impact of each subsequent impression on browser conversion. Future bid optimization will consider the impression history for that browser in addition to inventory considerations.

8. REFERENCES

[1] L. Abraham. Is the click the right currency for display advertising effectiveness. ComScore, 2011. http://paidcontent.org/files/uploads/DLD_2011_Linda_Abraham.pdf.

[2] G. Aggarwal, A. Goel, and R. Motwani. Truthful auctions for pricing search keywords. In *Proceddings of ACM Electronic Commerce*, 2006.

[3] C. Chabris and D. Simons. *The Invisible Gorilla.* Broadway, 2011.

[4] B. Dalessandro, F. Provost, C. Perlich, and R. Hook. Surrogate training for online conversion modeling. In *EMPGENS2*, 2012.

[5] B. Dalessandro, O. Stitelman, C. Perlich, and F. Provost. Causally motivated attribution for online advertising. In *Proceedings of the Workshop on Data Mining and Audience Intelligence for Online Advertising at KDD*, 2012.

[6] B. Edelman and M. Ostrovsky. Strategic bidder behavior in sponsored search auctions. In *Proceedings of ACM Electronic Commerce*, 2005.

[7] B. Edelman, M. Ostrovsky, and M. Schwarz. Internet advertising and the generalized second-price auction: Selling billions of dollars worth of keywords. *American Economic Review*, 97(1):242–259, 2007.

[8] A. Genkin, D. D. Lewis, and D. Madigan. Large-scale bayesian logistic regression for text categorization. *Technometrics*, 49(3):291–304, 2007.

[9] M. Hughes. Taking issues with viewable impressions, 2012. http://www.adexchanger.com/data-driven-thinking/taking-issue/.

[10] G. King and L. Zeng. Logistic regression in rare events data. *Political Analysis*, 9(2):137–163, 2001.

[11] B. Kitts and B. LeBlanc. Optimal bidding on keyword auctions. *Electronic Markets*, 14(3):186–201, 2004.

[12] M. Muthukrishnan. Data mining problems in internet ad systems. In *Tutorial at ACM SIGKDD*, 2011.

[13] B. Edelman M. Ostrovsky and M. Schwartz. Internet advertising and the generalized second prize auction: Selling billions of dollars worth of keywords. *American Economic Review*, 2006.

[14] F. Provost, B. Dalessandro, R. Hook, X. Zhang, and A. Murray. Audience selection for on-line brand advertising: privacy-friendly social network targeting. In *Proceedings of the 15th ACM SIGKDD International Conference on Knowledge discovery and data mining*, 2009.

[15] T. Raeder, B. Dalessandro, O. Stitelman, C. Perlich, and F. Provost. Design principles of massive, robust prediction systems. In *Proceedings of the 18th ACM SIGKDD International Conference on Knowledge Discovery and Data Mining*, 2012.

[16] X. Shao and L. Li. Data-driven multi-touch attribution models. In *Proceedings of the 17th ACM SIGKDD International Conference on Knowledge Discovery and Data Mining*, pages 258–264, 2011.

[17] A.A. Tsiatis. *Semiparametric theory and missing data* Springer Verlag, 2006.

[18] W. Vickrey. Counterspeculation, auctions, and competitive sealed tenders. *Journal of Finance*, (16):8–27, 1961.

[19] C. Xiong, T. Wang, W. Ding, Y. Shen, and T.Y. Liu. Relational click prediction for sponsored search. In *Proceedings of WSDM*, 2012.

Algorithms for Mining Uncertain Graph Data

Jianzhong Li
Harbin Institute of Technology
China
lijzh@hit.edu.cn

Abstract

With the rapid development of advanced data acquisition techniques such as high-throughput biological experiments and wireless sensor networks, large amount of graph-structured data, graph data for short, have been collected in a wide range of applications. Discovering knowledge from graph data has witnessed a number of applications and received a lot of research attentions. Recently, it is observed that uncertainties are inherent in the structures of some graph data. For example, protein-protein interaction (PPI) data can be represented as a graph, where vertices represent proteins, and edges represent PPI's. Due to the limits of PPI detection methods, it is uncertain that a detected PPI exist in practice. Other examples of uncertain graph data include topologies of wireless sensor networks, social networks and so on. Managing and mining such large-scale uncertain graph data is of both theoretical and practical significance. Many solid works have been conducted on uncertain graph mining from the aspects of models, semantics, methodology and algorithms in last few years. A number of research papers on managing and mining uncertain graph data have been published in the database and data mining conferences such as VLDB, ICDE, KDD, CIKM and EDBT. This talk focuses on the data model, semantics, computational complexity and algorithms of uncertain graph mining. In the talk, some typical research work in the field of uncertain graph mining will also be introduced, including frequent subgraph pattern mining, dense subgraph detection, reliable subgraph discovery, and clustering on uncertain graph data.

Categories & Subject Descriptors: H. Information Systems: H.2 DATABASE MANAGEMENT: H.2.8 Database applications: Subjects: Data mining

Author Keywords: Graph Mining; Uncertain Data

Bio

Jianzhong Li is a professor and the chairman of the Department of Computer Science and Engineering at the Harbin Institute of Technology, China. He worked in the University of California at Berkeley as a visiting scholar in 1985. From 1986 to 1987 and from 1992 to 1993, he was a scientist in the Information Research Group in the Department of Computer Science at Lawrence Berkeley National Laboratory, USA. He was also a visiting professor at the University of Minnesota at Minneapolis, Minnesota, USA, from 1991 to 1992 and from 1998 to 1999. His current research interests include database systems, data intensive super-computing, and wireless sensor networks. He has published more than 200 papers in refereed journals and conference proceedings. He has been involved in the program committees of major computer science and technology conferences, including SIGMOD, VLDB, ICDE, INFOCOM, ICDCS, and WWW. He has also served on the editorial boards for distinguished journals, including Knowledge and Data Engineering, and refereed papers for varied journals and proceedings.

KDD'12, August 12-16, 2012, Beijing, China.
ACM 978-1-4503-1462-6 /12/08.

Experience with Discovering Knowledge by Acquiring it

Paul Compton
University of New South Wales
Australia
compton@cse.unsw.edu.au

Abstract

Machines and people have complementary skills in Knowledge Discovery. Automated techniques can process enormous amounts of data to find new relationships, but generally these are represented by fairly simple models. On the other hand people are endlessly inventive in creating models to explain data at hand, but have problems developing consistent overall models to explain all the data that might occur in a domain; and the larger the model, the more difficult it becomes to maintain consistency. Ripple-Down Rules is a technique that has been developed to allow people to make real-time updates to a model whenever they notice some data that the model does not yet explain, while at the same time maintaining consistency. This allows an entire knowledge base to be built while it is already in use by making updates. There are now 100s of Ripple-Down-Rule knowledge bases in use and this paper presents some observations from log files tracking how people build these systems, and also outlines some recent research on how such techniques can be used to add greater specificity to the simpler models developed by automated techniques.

Categories & Subject Descriptors: H. Information Systems: H.2 DATABASE MANAGEMENT: H.2.8 Database applications: Subjects: Data mining

Author Keywords: Knowledge Base; Rule-based Model

Bio

Paul Compton is an emeritus professor of Computer Science at the University of New South Wales, where he was head of the School of Computer Science and Engineering for 12 years. In the 1980s he was involved in the development of GARVAN-ES1, one of the first medical expert systems to go into routine clinical use. The maintenance problems with this, led to his interest in incremental knowledge acquisition and in particular the development of Ripple-Down Rules as a way of minimizing the maintenance effort. His research over the last 20 years has focused on extending this incremental approach to a range of different problems. Ripple-Down Rules have been commercialized by a number of companies with applications ranging from interpreting pathology reports (Pacific Knowledge Systems) to data cleansing for big data applications (IBM).

KDD'12, August 12-16, 2012, Beijing, China.
ACM 978-1-4503-1462-6 /12/08.

Bayesian Relational Data Analysis

Naonori Ueda
NTT Communication Lab
Japan
ueda.naonori@lab.ntt.co.jp

Abstract

Recently there have been many collections of relational data in diverse areas such as the internet, social networks, customer shopping records, bioinformatics, etc. The main goal of the relational data analysis is to discover latent structure from the data. The conventional data mining algorithms based on exhaustive enumeration have an inherent limitation for this purpose because of the combinatorial nature of the methods. In contrast, in machine learning a lot of statistical models have been proposed for the relational data analysis. In this talk, first I will review the statistical approach, especially Bayesian approach, for the relational data analysis with recent advancements in machine learning literature. Then, as a future research I will also talk about a statistical approach for combining multiple relational data.

Categories & Subject Descriptors: H. Information Systems: H.2 DATABASE MANAGEMENT: H.2.8 Database applications: Subjects: Data mining

Author Keywords: Relational Data; Bayesian Analysis

Bio

Naonori Ueda received the B.S., M.S., and Ph D degrees in Communication Engineering from Osaka University, Osaka, Japan, in 1982, 1984, and 1992, respectively. In 1984, he joined the Electrical Communication Laboratories, NTT, Japan, where he was engaged in research on image processing, pattern recognition, and computer vision. In 1991, he joined the NTT Communication Science Laboratories, where he has invented a significant learning principle for optimal vector quantizer design and has developed some novel learning algorithms including deterministic annealing EM (DAEM) algorithm, ensemble learning, the split and merge EM (SMEM) algorithm, semi-supervised learning, variational Bayesian model search algorithm for mixture models and its application to speech recognition, and probabilistic generative models for multi-labeled text in WWW. His current research interests include parametric and non-parametric Bayesian approach to machine learning, pattern recognition, data mining, signal processing, and cyber-physical systems. From 1993 to 1994, he was a visiting scholar at Purdue University, West Lafayette, USA. Currently, he is a director of NTT Communication Science Laboratories. He is an associate editor of Neurocomputing and Journal of Neural Networks, and is a member of the Institute of Electronics, Information, and Communication Engineers (IEICE), and IEEE.

KDD'12, August 12-16, 2012, Beijing, China.
ACM 978-1-4503-1462-6 /12/08.

Cross-Media Knowledge Discovery

Zhongzhi Shi
Chinese Academy of Sciences
China
shizz@ics.ict.ac.cn

Abstract

In this talk I introduce cloud computing based cross-media knowledge discovery. We propose a framework for cross-media semantic understanding which contains discriminative modeling, generative modeling and cognitive modeling. In cognitive modeling a new model entitled CAM is proposed which is suitable for cross-media semantic understanding. We develop an agent-aid model for load balance in cloud computing environment. For quality of service we present a utility function to evaluate the cloud performance. A Cross-Media Intelligent Retrieval System (CMIRS), which is managed by ontology-based knowledge system KMSphere, will be illustrated. Finally, the directions for further researches on cloud computing based cross-media knowledge discovery will be pointed out and discussed.

Categories & Subject Descriptors: H. Information Systems: H.2 DATABASE MANAGEMENT: H.2.8 Database applications: Subjects: Data mining

Author Keywords: Cloud Computing; Cross-media Knowledge Discovery

Bio

Zhongzhi Shi is a professor at the Institute of Computing Technology, Chinese Academy of Sciences, leading the Intelligence Science Laboratory. His research interests include intelligence science, image processing and cognitive computing, machine learning, multi-agent systems, semantic Web and service computing. Professor Shi has published 14 monographs, 15 books and more than 450 research papers in journals and conferences. He has won a 2nd-Grade National Award at Science and Technology Progress of China in 2002, two 2nd-Grade Awards at Science and Technology Progress of the Chinese Academy of Sciences in 1998 and 2001, respectively. He is a senior member of IEEE, member of AAAI and ACM, Chair for the WG 12.2 of IFIP. He serves as Chief Editor of Series on Intelligence Science. He has served as Vice President for Chinese Association of Artificial Intelligence.

KDD'12, August 12-16, 2012, Beijing, China.
ACM 978-1-4503-1462-6 /12/08.

Author Index

www.ingramcontent.com/pod-product-compliance
Ingram Content Group UK Ltd.
Pitfield, Milton Keynes, MK11 3LW, UK
UKHW051454290926
15471UKWH00008B/1204

9 781450 319461